Dictionary of Legal, Commercial and Political Terms

Wörterbuch für Recht, Wirtschaft und Politik

DICTIONARY OF LEGAL, COMMERCIAL AND POLITICAL TERMS

with illustrative examples, explanatory notes
and commentaries on comparative law

PART I
ENGLISH–GERMAN

incorporating American usage

by

Dr. jur. Clara-Erika Dietl
Göttingen

Dr. jur. Egon Lorenz
Professor at the University
of Mannheim

In Collaboration with Dr. jur. Wiebke Buxbaum, LL.M., LL.B.
Attorney-at-law, San Francisco/USA

Completely Revised and Expanded Fifth Edition

C.H.BECK'SCHE VERLAGSBUCHHANDLUNG
MÜNCHEN 1990

WÖRTERBUCH FÜR RECHT, WIRTSCHAFT UND POLITIK

mit erläuternden und rechtsvergleichenden Kommentaren

TEIL I
ENGLISCH–DEUTSCH

einschließlich der Besonderheiten des amerikanischen Sprachgebrauchs

von

Dr. jur. Clara-Erika Dietl
Göttingen

Dr. jur. Egon Lorenz
o. Professor an der Universität
Mannheim

unter Mitarbeit von Dr. jur. Wiebke Buxbaum, LL.M., LL.B.
Attorney-at-law, San Francisco/USA

Fünfte, völlig neu bearbeitete und erweiterte Auflage

C.H.BECK'SCHE VERLAGSBUCHHANDLUNG
MÜNCHEN 1990

CIP-Titelaufnahme der Deutschen Bibliothek

Wörterbuch für Recht, Wirtschaft und Politik : mit erläuternden und rechtsvergleichenden Kommentaren ; einschließlich der Besonderheiten des amerikanischen Sprachgebrauchs. – München : Beck.
Paralleltitel: Dictionary of legal, commercial and political terms. – Teilw. außerdem im Bender-Verl., New York
NE: PT

Teil 1. Englisch-Deutsch / von Clara-Erika Dietl ; Egon Lorenz. Unter Mitarb. von Wiebke Buxbaum. – 5., völlig neubearb. u. erw. Aufl. – 1990
ISBN 3 406 34166 7
NE: Dietl, Clara-Erika [Mitverf.]

ISBN 3 406 34166 7

Druck der C. H. Beck'schen Buchdruckerei Nördlingen
Printed in Germany

Vorwort zur 5. Auflage

In der 5. Auflage ist der Teil I des Wörterbuchs erneut völlig überarbeitet, auf den neuesten Stand gebracht und erweitert worden. Dankbar aufgenommen wurden wiederum die Anregungen in den vielen, durchweg freundlichen, sachkundigen und eindringlichen Besprechungen der Vorauflage und die sonstigen schriftlichen und mündlichen Hinweise in- und ausländischer Benutzer. Die konzeptionellen Grundlinien des Werkes wurden nicht verändert, weil sie allgemein Zustimmung gefunden haben. Wie bei jeder Neuauflage war häufig zu überlegen, inwieweit die Terminologie des deutschen Rechts bei der Übersetzung englischer und amerikanischer Begriffe verwendet werden kann, ohne Fehlvorstellungen hervorzurufen. Der gelegentlich vertretenen Ansicht, in kritischen Fällen einfach auf jede Übersetzung zu verzichten, folgt dieses Wörterbuch nicht. Um den Übersetzer ohne Fachbibliothek nicht im Stich zu lassen, bietet es vielmehr stets Übersetzungen an. Dabei begegnet es der Gefahr von Mißverständnissen so weit wie möglich durch Sätze aus Texten, in denen der Begriff vorkommt, durch Verweisungen auf andere Begriffe, durch kurze Kommentare oder durch sonstige Hinweise.

Teilweise geändert worden ist die lexikographische Gestaltung, um die Benutzerfreundlichkeit des Wörterbuchs noch zu erhöhen. Nach wie vor werden jedoch manche Begriffe mit einer jeweils vorangestellten arabischen Zahl wiederholt. Dadurch soll hervorgehoben werden, daß diese Begriffe ganz verschiedene und deshalb auch in der Textanordnung zu trennende Bedeutungen haben.

Das seit dem Erscheinen der Vorauflage angefallene Material ist gesichtet und nach den bisher maßgebenden Kriterien eingearbeitet worden. Wichtiges Material für die Aktualisierung lieferten insbesondere neue britische und amerikanische Gesetze, neue Abkommen mit europäischen und außereuropäischen Vertragsstaaten und neu entstandenen internationalen Organisationen. Die für notwendig gehaltenen Nachweise finden sich in den Fußnoten, die auch insoweit den neuesten Stand ausweisen.

Die beträchtlichen Erweiterungen der Neuauflage sind durch verschiedene wichtige Gründe veranlaßt worden. Zu nennen sind beispielsweise: die fortschreitende Internationalisierung der Wirtschaft, durch die immer neue Formen grenzüberschreitender Zusammenarbeit hervorgebracht werden; die zunehmende Bedeutung internationaler Finanz- und Devisenmärkte, die es notwendig gemacht hat, den bisherigen Bestand der Begriffe aus dem Geld-, Bank- und Börsenwesen stark zu vergrößern; und nicht zuletzt das ständig wachsende Recht der Europäischen Gemeinschaft, das den in dem EWG-Vertrag geschaffenen rechtlichen Rahmen des bevorstehenden europäischen Binnenmarkts ausfüllt. In dieser Hinsicht ist dem Wörterbuch auch die Aufgabe zugefallen, in seinem Arbeitsgebiet auf die sprachlichen Anforderungen des europäischen Binnenmarkts vorzubereiten und zu deren zukünftiger Bewältigung beizutragen.

Auch bei der Erarbeitung dieser Neuauflage haben uns wiederum viele sachkundig durch Rat und Hilfe unterstützt. Allen sei noch einmal herzlich gedankt, ganz besonders Herrn Donald B. Leaver, früher The Times, London, der das gesamte Werk durchgesehen hat; Frau Rechtsassessorin Angelika Baumgarte, M. A., Leiterin der Rechtsabteilung der Deutschen Industrie- und Handelskammer in London, die sich um die Aktualisierung und Erweiterung der britischen Rechtsbegriffe sehr verdient gemacht hat; Herrn Dr. Paul Katzenberger, Max Planck Institut für Ausländisches und Internationales Patent-, Urheber- und Wettbewerbsrecht in München, für seine Mitarbeit in diesen Fachgebieten; Herrn

Dipl.-Hdl. Jan P. Weber für seine Hilfe (als examinierte wissenschaftliche Hilfskraft am Institut für Betriebswirtschaftliche Geldwirtschaft der Universität Göttingen) bei der Übersetzung und Erläuterung neuer Finanzierungsinstrumente an den internationalen Finanzmärkten – insbesondere am Euromarkt – sowie neuer Technologien im Bankwesen; Frau Studienassessorin Marga Teichmann und Frau Dolmetscherin Monika Senger, die uns bei lexikographischen Arbeiten und bei den Korrekturen unermüdlich unterstützt haben.

Göttingen, Januar 1990 — Clara-Erika Dietl

Preface to the Fifth Edition

With this fifth edition Part I of the dictionary has again been fully revised, brought up to date and expanded. We have gratefully accepted suggestions made in the many, consistently friendly, expert and pithy reviews of the previous edition, and in other written and verbal comments from users in this country and abroad. The basic concept of the work has not been changed, since it has met with general approval. As with each edition, we had frequently to consider to what extent German legal terminology could be applied to the translation of English and American terms without creating false conceptions. Our dictionary does not adhere to the view occasionally adopted, that one should simply forgo any attempt at translation in debatable cases. In order not to leave in the lurch the interpreter without a specialist library, we prefer always to offer translations. At the same time we guard against the danger of misunderstandings by the use of sample sentences in which such terms occur, by references to other expressions, short commentaries and other pointers.

The lexicographical arrangement has been partly altered to make the dictionary still more "user friendly". As before, however, many terms have been given more than once, each entry being numbered. In this way it is intended to emphasize that these terms have quite different meanings which should be given separately in the layout of the text.

Material that has become available since publication of the previous edition has been sifted and incorporated in accordance with the criteria already followed. Important material for updating the dictionary has been provided especially by new British and American laws, new agreements with European and non-European contracting states, and newly emerged international organizations. Source references deemed to be necessary are given in the footnotes, which have also been brought up to date.

The considerable extensions in the new edition have been occasioned by a variety of important factors. To give examples: the progressive internationalization of trade and industry leading to ever new forms of cooperation across the frontiers; the growing significance of international financial and currency markets, necessitating the enlargement of the existing vocabulary of monetary, banking and stock exchange terms; and not least the growing body of law of the European Community, now filling the legal framework created by the EEC Treaty for the impending European internal market. In this respect also it falls to this dictionary to prepare in its field for the linguistic requirements of the European internal market and to contribute to their future satisfaction.

In the hard work of producing this new edition we have again been supported by much expert advice and help. Our sincere thanks are due to all concerned, more especially to Mr. Donald B. Leaver, formerly of The Times, London, who has checked the entire work; Frau Ass. Jur. Angelika Baumgarte M. A., head of the legal department of the German Chamber of Industry and Commerce in London; Dr. Paul Katzenberger, of the Max Planck Institut für Ausländisches und Internationales Patent-, Urheber- und Wettbewerbsrecht in Munich, for his collaboration in these fields; Dipl.-Hdl. Jan P. Weber for his help (as certificated scientific assistant at the Institut für Betriebswirtschaftliche Geldwirtschaft at Göttingen University) in the translation and explanation of new financing instruments in the international markets, especially the Euromarket, as well as new banking technology; and Frau Studienassessorin Marga Teichmann und Frau Dolmetscherin Monika Senger, who have tirelessly supported us with lexicographical work and proof corrections.

Göttingen, January 1990 Clara-Erika Dietl

Aus dem Vorwort der 1. Auflage

Die Schwierigkeit einer wörtlichen Übersetzung englischer und amerikanischer juristischer Texte in die deutsche Sprache und umgekehrt liegt in der historisch begründeten Verschiedenheit der einzelnen Rechtssysteme. Das anglo-amerikanische Recht, auf Common Law, Equity und Statute Law beruhend, ist dem kontinentalen, in Kodifikationen denkenden Juristen fremd. Hinzu kommt, daß im Vereinigten Königreich verschiedene Rechtssysteme für England, Wales, Nordirland und für Schottland bestehen. Das Recht vieler Länder des britischen Commonwealth beruht weitgehend auf der Grundlage des englischen Rechts und wurde durch eigene Gesetzgebung selbständig weiterentwickelt. In den Vereinigten Staaten von Amerika stehen bundes- und einzelstaatliche Gerichte sowie bundes- und einzelstaatliches Recht mit oft unterschiedlichen Terminologien nebeneinander.

Das vorliegende Wörterbuch, das in jahrelanger Arbeit unter Heranziehung eines umfassenden Quellenmaterials vielfältiger Art entstanden ist, versucht diesen Schwierigkeiten Rechnung zu tragen. Es hat sich dabei nicht auf abstrakte Begriffe beschränkt, sondern die Darstellung auf Wortgruppen ausgedehnt. Die im englischen und amerikanischen Sprachgebrauch voneinander abweichenden Begriffe sind mit *Br* und *Am* bezeichnet und, sofern es sich um nur für das jeweilige Land typische Institutionen handelt (z. B. barrister, attorney) oder um solche anglo-amerikanischen Termini, deren Bedeutung von dem entsprechenden deutschen Wort abweicht (z. B. mortgage – Hypothek), in kurzen Definitionen erläutert.

Auf wirtschaftlichem Gebiet sind besonders berücksichtigt: Handel und Industrie, Volks- und Betriebswirtschaft, Geld-, Bank- und Börsenwesen, Steuern, Versicherungswesen, Verkehr und Schiffahrt, Werbung und Meinungsforschung. Die wichtigsten Wirtschaftsorganisationen sowie die Großbritannien, die Vereinigten Staaten und die Bundesrepublik betreffenden bilateralen und multilateralen Wirtschaftsverträge sind durch einen Kurzkommentar erläutert.

Auf dem politischen Sektor ist der durch die politische Entwicklung bedingten Neubildung von Wörtern Rechnung getragen. Die amtliche Bezeichnung der wichtigsten Staaten und ihrer Staatsangehörigen sind in Englisch und Deutsch angeführt. Darüber hinaus sind die Großbritannien, die Vereinigten Staaten und die Bundesrepublik betreffenden bilateralen und multilateralen politischen Verträge sowie die wichtigsten europäischen und internationalen Organisationen in englischer und deutscher Sprache aufgeführt und mit einem Kurzkommentar versehen. ...

From the Introduction to the 1st Edition

The difficulty of a literal translation of British and American legal texts into the German language and vice versa lies in the differences between the legal systems, which for historical reasons have developed their distinct characteristics. The continental lawyer, used to codifications, finds the Anglo-American system, based on Common Law, Equity and Statute Law strange and unfamiliar. Moreover, within the United Kingdom there are different legal systems for England, Wales and Northern Ireland and for Scotland. The law of most of the Commonwealth countries is mainly based on English law and has been independently developed. In the United States the Federal courts and the State courts exist concurrently, applying different laws and often a different legal terminology.

We have as far as possible tried to overcome these difficulties in our dictionary, which has been compiled over a period of many years from the considerable material available to us. It does not only contain isolated words but also illustrates their use in idiomatic phrases and expressions. Where British and American terms vary, this has been indicated by *Br* and *Am*. There are short definitions of typical Anglo-American institutions (e. g. barrister, attorney) and explanatory notes on comparative law where the meaning of the Anglo-American term differs from the closest equivalent German word (e. g. mortgage – Hypothek).

Particular attention has been given to commerce and industry, banking, insurance, shipping, stock exchange practice, taxation, advertising and public opinion research.

The most important economic institutions as well as the bilateral and multilateral agreements in the economic and political field concerning Great Britain, the United States and the Federal Republic of Germany and the most important European and international organizations have been provided with a short commentary.

In the field of politics, new words and phrases based on recent developments have been included. The official designation of the most important countries and their nationals are given in English and in German. In addition, the bilateral and multilateral political agreements affecting Great Britain, the United States and the Federal Republic of Germany as well as the most important European and international organizations can be found in both languages, together with short commentaries. . . .

Hinweise für den Benutzer

Die Rechtschreibung des vorliegenden Wörterbuches richtet sich im Englischen nach „The Concise Oxford Dictionary of Current English" und im Amerikanischen nach „Webster's Third New International Dictionary".
Während die begrifflichen Unterschiede zwischen dem britischen und amerikanischen Englisch jeweils durch *Br* und *Am* gekennzeichnet sind, ist die unterschiedliche Schreibweise ohne besondere Kennzeichnung nach folgendem Schema gehandhabt:

Br	Am	In diesem Wörterbuch gebrauchte Schreibweise
honour	honor	hono(u)r
licence	license	licen|ce (~se)
centre	center	cent|re (~er)
catalogue	catalog(ue)	catalog(ue)
traveller	traveler	travel(l)er
co-ordination	coordination	co(-)ordination

Die britische Schreibweise steht also in der Regel an erster Stelle, die amerikanische folgt in Klammern. Ebenso ist ein im amerikanischen Englisch ausfallender Buchstabe (z. B. „u" in honour) oder ein im britischen Englisch verdoppelter Buchstabe (z. B. „l" in traveller) in Klammern gesetzt. Um bei der Verwendung des Bindestrichs Einheitlichkeit zu erzielen, ist der amerikanischen Tendenz, den Bindestrich fortzulassen, weitgehend gefolgt worden.

Advice to the User

For British and American spelling this dictionary relies respectively on "The Concise Oxford Dictionary of Current English", and Webster's "Third New International Dictionary".
Conceptual differences between British and American terms are indicated by the signs *Br* and *Am*. However no special signs are used to distinguish between British and American spellings, which are dealt with in the following manner:

Br	Am	Spelling employed in this Dictionary
honour	honor	hono(u)r
licence	license	licen|ce(~se)
centre	center	cent|re(~er)
catalogue	catalog(ue)	catalog(ue)
traveller	traveler	travel(l)er

Thus British spelling generally comes first, followed by the American in brackets. A letter omitted in American spelling is also placed in brackets, e. g. the "u" in honour, and so is a consonant doubled in the British form, e. g. the "l" in traveller.
In order to achieve uniformity the American tendency to omit the hyphen has largely been followed.

In diesem Wörterbuch verwandte Abkürzungen

Abbreviations used in this Dictionary

Abl. EGem	Amtsblatt der Europäischen Gemeinschaften
abbr	abbreviation
Abk.	Abkürzung
AG	Aktiengesellschaft
Am	American English (Vereinigte Staaten von Nordamerika)
bes.	besonders
betr.	betreffend
BGBl	Bundesgesetzblatt
Br	British English (Großbritannien und Nordirland außer Schottland)
cf.	compare
colloq.	colloquial
com	commercial term
DBA	Doppelbesteuerungsabkommen
dipl	diplomatic term
eccl	ecclesiastical term
EDV	elektronische Datenverarbeitung
EG	Europäische Gemeinschaften
etc	usw.
etw.	etwas
EuGH	Europäischer Gerichtshof
fig	figuratively
Fr	French
gegr.	gegründet
Ger	German
Ggs.	Gegensatz
GmbH	Gesellschaft mit beschränkter Haftung
hist	historical
IPR	Internationales Privatrecht
IWF	Internationaler Währungsfonds
mil	military term
MMF	Markt- und Meinungsforschung
obs.	obsolete
od.	oder
opp.	as opposed to
o. s.	oneself
p.	person
parl	parliamentary term
PatR	Patentrecht
pol	political term
ProzeßR	Prozeßrecht
RGBl	Reichsgesetzblatt
s.	see
sb.	somebody
Scot	Scottish
SeeversR	Seeversicherungsrecht
sl.	slang
s. th., sth.	something
SteuerR	Steuerrecht
StGB	Strafgesetzbuch
StPO	Strafprozeßordnung
StrafR	Strafrecht
th.	thing
UK	United Kingdom
UN	United Nations
univ	university
USA	United States of America
v	Verb
VersR	Versicherungsrecht
vgl.	vergleiche
VölkerR	Völkerrecht
WechselR	Wechselrecht
z. B.	zum Beispiel
e-e	eine
e-m	einem
e-n	einen
e-r	einer
e-s	eines
jd	jemand
jdm	jemandem
jdn	jemanden
jds	jemandes
s-e	seine
s-m	seinem
s-n	seinen
s-r	seiner
s-s	seines

Abbreviations-Abkürzungen

A

a.	acre(s); (*Shipping News*) arrived
AA	American Airlines; Advertising Association; Alcoholics Anonymous
A. A.	anti-aircraft; Automobile Association
a. a.	always afloat
AAA	American Automobile Association; American Accounting Association; American Arbitration Association
A. A. A.	Association for Average Adjusters
AAAA	American Association of Advertising Agencies
AAPOR	American Association for Public Opinion Research
AARP	American Association for Retired People
A. A. A. S.	American Academy of Arts and Sciences; American Association for the Advancement of Science
AAP	Australian Associated Press
a. a. r.	against all risks; all average recoverable
A. A. S.	Fellow of the American Academy (*Academiae Americanae Socius*)
AASMM	Associated African States, Madagascar and Mauritius
AASO	Association of American Shipowners
AATG	American Association of Teachers of German
A. A. U. P.	American Association of University Professors
A. A. U. W.	American Association of University Women
A. B.	able-bodied (seaman); air base; Bachelor of Arts (*Artium Bacchalaureus*)
ABA	American Bankers' Association; American Bar Association
ABAJ	American Bar Association Journal
A. B. C.	American Broadcasting Company; Argentina, Brazil and Chile; Australian Broadcasting Commission
A. B. C. C.	Association of British Chambers of Commerce
ab init.	from the beginning (*ab initio*)
ABM	anti-ballistic missiles
A-bomb	atom(ic) bomb
A. B. R.	American Bankruptcy Reports
A. B. S.	American Bureau of Shipping
abs. re.	the defendant being absent *(absente reo)*
A. C.	Appeal Cases (Law Reports); Appeal Court; Army Corps; Assistant Commissioner
A/C	account; assistant cashier
a. c.	of the present year *(anni currentis)*
a/c, A/c	account
A. C. A.	Adoption of Children Act; Associate of the Institute of Chartered Accountants in England and Wales
ACAS	Advisory, Conciliation and Arbitration Service
ACCA	Associate of the Chartered Association of Certified Accountants; Association of Certified and Corporate Accountants
accr. int.	accrued interest
A. C. C. S.	Associate of the Corporation of Certified Secretaries
acct. & aud.	accountant and auditor
A. C. G. B.	Arts Council of Great Britain
A. C. G. B. I.	Automobile Club of Great Britain and Ireland
A. Ch. S.	American Chemical Society
A. C. I. A.	Associate of the Corporation of Insurance Agents
A. C. I. B.	Associate of the Corporation of Insurance Brokers
A. C. I. S.	Associate of the Chartered Institute of Secretaries (Chartered Secretary)
ACMA	Associate of the Chartered Institute of Management Accountants
ACP	African, Caribbean and Pacific countries

ACPA	Associate of the Institution of Certified Public Accountants
acpt.	acceptance
ACR	American Criminal Reports
A.C.R.A.	Associate of the Corporation of Registered Accountants
ACRS	Accelerated Cost Recovery System; Advisory Committee on Reactor Safeguards
A.C.S.	→A.Ch.S.; American Cancer Society
ACSC	Association of Casualty and Surety Companies
A/cs Pay.	accounts payable
A/cs Rec.	accounts receivable
ACT	Advance Corporation Tax; Air Cargo Transport
A.C.T.U.	Australian Council of Trade Unions
act. wt.	actual weight
AD	American Decisions; Annual Digest and Reports of Public International Law Cases; Appellate Division
A.D.	in the year of our Lord *(Anno Domini)*
a.d.	active duty; after date
ADA	Assistant District Attorney; Atomic Development Authority
ADB	African Development Bank; Asian Development Bank
ADELA	Antlantic Development for Latin America
ADG	Assistant Director-General
ad int.	in the meantime *(ad interim)*
ad lib.	at one's pleasure *(ad libitum)*
ad loc.	at the place *(ad locum)*
ADM	atomic demolition munition
Adm. Ct.	Admiralty Court
ADP	automatic data processing
ADR	American Depositary Receipt
ads.	advertisements; at the suit *(ad sectam)*
a.d.s.	autograph document signed
a.d.t.	automatic debit transfer
adv.	advance(d); against *(adversus)*
ad val.	according to value *(ad valorem)*
adv. chgs.	advance charges
adv. frt.	advanced freight
Adv. Gen.	Advocate General
advt	advertisement
ADW	air defense warning
A.E.A.	Administration of Estates Act; Atomic Energy Authority
AEAA	Association of Export Advertising Agencies
AEC	Atomic Energy Commission
A.E.I.	Associated Electrical Industries; American Enterprise Institute
A.E. and P.	Ambassador Extraordinary and Plenipotentiary
A.E.R.	All England Reports
A.E.R.E.	Atomic Energy Research Establishment
AETR	European Agreement Concerning the Work of Crews of Vehicles Engaged in the International Road Transport
A.E.U.	Amalgamated Engineering Union
a/f	*(Shipping News)* also for:
AFA	Advertising Federation of America
a.f.b.	air freight bill
AFDC	Aid to Families with Dependant Children
afft	affidavit
AFGE	American Federation of Government Employees
AFIA	American Foreign Insurance Association
AFIDA	Agricultural Foreign Investment Disclosure Act
AFII	American Federation of International Institutes
AFL/CIO	American Federation of Labor/Congress of Industrial Organizations
aflt	afloat
AFRC	Agriculture and Food Research Council
A.F.S.	American Field Service *(international scholarships);* Auxiliary Fire Service

A. G.	Accountant General; Adjutant-General; Agent-General; Attorney(-) General
a. g. b.	any good brand
AGM	Annual General Meeting
AGR	European Agreement on Main International Traffic Arteries
Agt, agt	agent
A/H	Antwerp/Hamburg range
a. & h.	accident and health *(insurance)*
a. h. l.	at this place *(ad hunc locum)*
A. H. Q.	Army Headquarters
AHRGB	Association of Hotels and Restaurants of Great Britain
A. I. A.	American Institute of Accountants; American Institute of Aeronautics; American Institute of Architects; American Insurance Association
A. I. A. A.	Association of International Advertising Agencies
A. I. B.	American Institute of Banking; Association of International Bond Dealers
AICPA	American Institute of Certified Public Accountants
A. I. D.	Agency for International Development; Army Intelligence Department
A. I. D. A.	Association Internationale de Droit des Assurances (International Association for Insurance Law)
Aids	acquired immune deficiency syndrome
AIF	annual improvement factor
A. I. H.	artificial insemination by husband
A. I. I. A.	Associate of the Institute of Industrial Administration
AIMS	American Institute of Merchant Shipping
A. I. M. U.	American Institute of Marine Underwriters
A. I. P. O.	American Institute of Public Opinion
AISG	Accountants International Study Group
A. J.	Associate Justice
A. J. I. L.	American Journal of International Law
a. k. a.	also known as
Ala.	Alabama *(Staat der USA)*
ALALC	(Associactión Latinamericana de Libre Commercio) Latin American Free Trade Association (→LAFTA)
Alas.,	Alaska *(Staat der USA)*
ALCM	air launched cruise missile
ALCU	American Civil Liberties Union
aliter	otherwise
A. L. I.	American Law Institute
A. L. J.	Australian Law Journal
All E. R.	All England Law Reports *(seit 1936)*
A. L. R.	American Law Reports; Argus Law Reports
ALRA	Abortion Law Reform Association
a. l. s.	autograph letter signed
A. M.	Master of Arts *(Artium Magister)*; Associate Member
a. m.	before noon *(ante meridiem)*
a/m	above mentioned
A. M. A.	American Management Association; American Maritime Association; American Medical Association; American Marketing Association; Automobile Manufacturers Association
Am. Assn. Sci.	American Association for the Advancement of Science
AMC	American Maritime Cases; Army Medical Center *(Washington, D. C.)*
Am. Chem. Soc.	= A. Ch. S.
Am. Corp. Cas.	American Corporation Cases
am. cur.	a friend of the court *(amicus curiae)*
Am. Dec.	American Decisions
Amer.	America, American
Amer. Law Rev.	American Law Review
Amex	American Stock Exchange
Amexco	American Express Company Inc.
AMIA	American Mutual Insurance Association
Am. Ins. Rep.	American Insolvency Reports

Am. J. Comp. Law	American Journal of Comparative Law
Am. J. Int. Law.	American Journal of International Law
Am. Jour. Pol.	American Journal of Politics
Am. Law. J. (NS)	American Law Journal, New Series
Am. L. Rev.	American Law Review
A. M. M. I.	American Merchant Marine Institute
Am. Prob. Rep.	American Probate Reports
Am. Rep.	American Reports
Am. St. R.	American State Reports
AMUUS	Association of Marine Underwriters of the United States
AMVETS	American Veterans (of World War II)
An.	anonymous
a. n.	above-named
ANA	Arab News Agency *(Kairo)*
anal.	analogous; analogy
ANAM	American National Association of Manufacturers
ANC	African National Congress
Ann. Rep.	annual report
Ann. St.	Annotated Statutes
Anon.	anonymous
ANPA	American Newspaper Publishers Association
ANRPC	Association of Natural Rubber Producing Countries
ANS	American Nuclear Society
ANSI	American National Standards Institute
ant. frt.	anticipated freight
a. o.	amongst others
a/o	(to the) account of
A. O. A.	Affiliation Order Act
AOB	any other business
a./or	and/or
AP	Associated Press
A. P.	Act of Parliament; additional premium; American Patent; answer prepaid
A/P	account purchases; authority to purchase
APA	(Federal) Administrative Procedure Act
APB	Accounting Principles Board
APC	Auditing Practices Committee
A. Phys. S.	American Physical Society
APP	Associated Press of Pakistan *(Karatschi)*
App.	Appeals; Appellate (Court)
app.	apparent(ly); appendix
App. Cas.	Appeal Cases (Law Reports)
App. Ct.	Appellate Court
App. D. C.	District of Columbia Appeals
App. Div.	Appellate Division *(N. Y. Supreme Court)*
App. N. Z.	Appeal Reports, New Zealand
APR	annualized percentage rate
approx.	approximate(ly)
appurts	appurtenances
AQ	achievement quotient
AQL	acceptable quality level
apt(s).	apartment(s)
A. R.	advice of receipt; (against) all risks; American Reports; annual return; in the year of the reign *(anno regni)*; Arrival and Return; Atlantic Reporter
a/r	(against) all risks
A/R	accounts receivable
A. R. A.	American Railway Association; Associate of the Royal Academy *(London)*
A. R. A. A.	Alien Restriction (Amendment) Act
A. R. A. L.	Associate of the Royal Academy of Literature
ARB	Accounting Research Bulletin
A. R. C.	American Red Cross; Automobile Racing Club
Ariz.	Arizona *(Staat der USA)*

Ark.	Arkansas *(Staat der USA)*
ARP	Air Raid Precautions
A. R. R.	in the year of the King's (Queen's) reign *(Anno Regni Regis [Reginae])*
arr.	arranged; arrival
ARS	Accounting Research Study
A. R. S. A.	Associate of the Royal Scottish Academy; Associate of the Royal Society of Arts
A. R. U.	American Railway Union
AS., A. S.	Academy of Science
A/S	account sales
a/s	account sales; after sight; alongside
A. S. A.	American Statistical Association; Atomic Scientists' Association
A. S. A. A.	Associate of the Society of Incorporated Accountants and Auditors (Incorporated Accountant)
ASC	Accounting Standards Committee
ASCAP	American Society of Composers, Authors and Publishers
ASCE	American Society of Civil Engineers
A. S. E.	Amalgamated Society of Engineers; American Stock Exchange; Associate of the Society of Engineers
ASEAN	Association of South East Asian Nations
A. S. G.	Assistant Solicitor-General
ASH	Action on Smoking and Health
A. S. I. A.	Associate of Society of Incorporated Accountants
ASIL	American Society of International Law
ASLIB	Association of Special Libraries and Information Bureaux
ASME	American Society of Mechanical Engineers
ASNE	American Society of Newspaper Editors
ASP	accelerated surface post
ASPCA	American Society for Prevention of Cruelty to Animals
ASM	air-to-surface missile
ASR	Accounting Series Release of the SEC
Assn., assn.	association
Assoc., assoc.	associate; association
Asst, asst	assistant
asst'd	assorted
ASTM	American Society for Testing Materials
ASTMS	Association of Scientific Technical and Managerial Staffs
A. S. U.	American Students Union
A/T	American Terms *(Grain trade)*
ATA	admission temporaire, temporary admission (→Customs Convention on the ATA Carnet); American Teachers Association
A. T. C.	Annotated Tax Cases (Law Reports)
ATD	Automatic Teaching Device
Atl.	Atlantic; Atlantic Reporter
ATM	automated teller machine
ATP	Agreement on the →International Carriage of Perishable Foodstuffs
ATS	American Television Service; automatic transfer service
ats.	at the suit of
A. T. T.	American Telephone and Telegraph Company
Att.	Attaché; Attorney
att.	attached; attorney
ATTA	American Tin Trade Association
Att.-Gen.	Attorney-General
Atty, atty	attorney
Atty & C.	attorney and client
Atty Gen. Op.	Attorney General's Opinion
at. wt.	atomic weight
Aud.-Gen.	Auditor-General
AUEW	Amalgamated Union of Engineering Workers
AUP	Australian United Press *(Melbourne)*
A. U. S.	Ambassador of the United States; Army of the United States

Austr. L. J.	Australian Law Journal
A. U. T.	Association of University Teachers
Av.	Avenue
av.	avenue; average; avoirdupois
a. v., a/v	to the value of *(ad valorem)*
AVC	American Veterans' Committee
avdp.	avoirdupois
AVWW II	American Veterans of World War II
a. w.	atomic weight
a/w	actual weight
AWACS	Airborne Warning and Control System
a. w. b.	airway bill
A. W. O. L.	absent (absence) without leave
A. W. V. S.	American Women's Voluntary Services
A. Y. H.	American Youth Hostels
Az. Is.	Azores Islands

B

B	bag; bale; bonds
B–, b/	bag(s); bale(s)
b.	born; *(stock exchange)* buyers
BA	Bachelor of Arts; Banking Act; Bankruptcy Act; British Academy; British Airways; British Army
BAA	British Airports Authority
BAAS	British Association (for the Advancement of Science)
BACH	business accounts harmonized data bank
BACS	Bankers' Automated Clearing Services
BACIE	British Association for Commercial and Industrial Education
BAe	British Aerospace
B. A. E. A.	British Atomic Energy Authority
BAERE	British Atomic Energy Research Establishment
B. A. I. E.	British Association of Industrial Editors
Bal., bal.	balance
BALPA	British Airline Pilots' Association
Bank. and Ins. R.	Bankruptcy and Insolvency Reports
BAOR	British Army of the Rhine
bar.	barrel; barrister
barr.	barrister
Bart.	Baronet
B/B	both-to-blame
b. & b.	bed and breakfast
B. B. A.	Bachelor of Business Administration; British Bankers' Association
B. & Bar	Bench and Bar
BBB	British Bank Bills
b. b. b.	bed, breakfast and bath
B. B. C.	British Broadcasting Corporation
B. B. S.	Bachelor of Business Science
B. Bus. Ad.	Bachelor of Business Administration
B. C.	Bachelor of Commerce; Bankruptcy Cases; Bankruptcy Court; before Christ; Board of Control; Borough Council; Bristol Channel; British Columbia
BCC	British Coal Corporation
BCE	Board of Customs and Excise
B/Ch	Bristol Channel
B. C. L.	Bachelor of Civil Law; Business Corporation Law
B. C. M.	British Consular Mail
B. Com.	Bachelor of Commerce

B. Com. Sc.	Bachelor of Commercial Science
B. C. S.	Bachelor of Commercial Science
b. d.	bank debits; bank draft; bills discounted
bds	boards *(timber trade)*; bonds
B. E.	Bachelor of Education; Bachelor of Engineering; Bank of England; bill of entry
B/E, b. e.	bill of exchange
B/E	Bill of Entry
BEA	Bills of Exchange Act; Bureau of Economic Analysis
Beds.	Bedfordshire
B. E. F.	British Expeditionary Force
B. E. M.	British Empire Medal
Benelux	Belgium, Netherlands, and Luxembourg
Berks.	Berkshire
B. E. S. A.	British Engineering Standards Association
B. E. T. R. O.	British Export Trade Research Organization
b. f.	in good faith *(bona fide)*
b/fwd	brought forward
B. G.	bonded goods
B/G, b/g	bonded goods
bg(s)	bag(s)
BGS	British Gas Corporation
B. H.	bill of health; Brest/Hamburg inclusive
B/H	Bill of Health; Bordeaux/Hamburg range
B.I.A.	British Insurance Association
B. I. F.	British Industries Fair
BILA	British Insurance Law Association
BIM	British Institute of Management
B. & I. M. C., BIMCO	Baltic and International Maritime Conference
B. I. N. C.	British Industries National Council
B. I. R.	Board of Inland Revenue
B. I. S.	Bank for International Settlements; British Intelligence (or Information) Services
B.J.	Bachelor of Journalism
Bk, bk	bank
bk(r)pt	bankrupt
B. L.	Bachelor of Law; bill of lading; British Library
B/L, b. l.	bill of lading
bl.	bale; barrel
B. L. A., B. & L. Assn.	Building and Loan Association
B/L att.	bill of lading attached
BLL.	Bachelor of Laws *(Bacchalaureus Legum)*
bls	bales; barrels
b. m.	board measure *(timber)*
BMC	British Motor Corporation
BMEWS	Ballistic-Missiles Early Warning System
BMMA	British Match Makers Association
B. N. A.	British Nationality Act
BNP	Banque Nationale de Paris
B. O., b. o.	beneficial owner; branch office; buyer's option
b/o	brought over
B. o. D.	board of directors
BoE	Bank of England
B. O. P.	balance of payments
Bor., bor.	borough
BP	British Patent; British Petroleum; British Pharmacopoeia
B. P., b. p.	bill of parcels; bill(s) payable
B. Pay.	bill(s) payable
B. P. B., b. p. b.	bank post bill

B. P. C.	British Pharmaceutical Codex
B. P. S.	Burma Press Syndicate *(Rangun)*
BRB	British Railways Board
B. R. C. S.	British Red Cross Society
Brit.	Britain; British
Brit. Mus.	British Museum
Brit. Jb. Int. L.	British Year Book of International Law
brl(s)	barrel(s)
Bros.	Brothers
B. S.	Bachelor of Science; balance sheet; bill of sale; British Standard
B/S, b/s.	balance sheet; bill of sale; bill of stores
B/s	bags; bales
BSB	British Satellite Broadcasting
BSC	British Steel Corporation; Broadcasting Standards Council
B. Sc.	Bachelor of Science
B. S. C. and E.	Bachelor of Science in Commerce and Economics
B. S. Comm.	Bachelor of Science in Commerce
B. S. E.	Boston Stock Exchange
B. S. Econ.	Bachelor of Science in Economics
B. S. G.	British Standard Gauge
b. s. g. d. g.	patented without Government guarantee *(Fr breveté sans garantie du gouvernement)*
B. S. Home Econ.	Bachelor of Science in Home Economics
B. S. I.	British Standards Institution
B. S. Ind. Eng.	Bachelor of Science in Industrial Engineering
Bs/L, Bs/Ldg	bills of lading
B.S.S.	British Standard Specification
B. S. T.	British Summer Time; British Standard Time
BTA	British Tourist Authority
BTB	British Treasury Bills
bt. fwd.	brought forward
BTG	British Technology Group
BTN	Brussels Tariff Nomenclature
B. T. O.	Brussels Treaty Organization
Btu	British thermal unit
B. U.	Board of Underwriters *(New York)*
bu	bushel(s)
Bucks.	Buckinghamshire
Bus. Law.	Business Lawyer
b. v.	book value
B. W., b. w.	biological warfare; Board of Works; bonded warehouse
BWB	British Waterways Board
bxs	boxes
BYIL	British Yearbook of International Law

C

C.	Catholic; Centigrade; Chancellor; Chancery; Command (Paper) (1836–1869; 1870–1899); Conservative
©	copyright
c.	*(Shipping News)* called; cent(s); chapter; about *(circa)*
CA	Companies Act
C. A.	Central America; chartered accountant; chief accountant; consular agent; Court of Appeal(s); current account
ca.	about *(circa)*
CAA	Civil Aeronautics Administration; Civil Aviation Authority
C. A. B.	Citizens' Advice Bureau
CAC	Central Arbitration Committee

CACA	Central After-Care Association; Chartered Association of Certified Accountants
CACM	Central American Common Market
CAD	computer-aided design
c. a. d.	cash against documents
CAEF	Chemical and Allied Employers' Federation
CAL	computer-assisted learning
Cal.	California *(Staat der USA)*
Cal. Rptr.	California Reporter
Calif. L. Rev.	California Law Review
CALTEX	California-Texas Oil Corporation
CAM	computer-aided manufacturing
CAMA	Continental Advertising and Marketing Agencies
Camb.	Cambridge
Cambs.	Cambridgeshire
Can.	Canada; Canadian
canc.	cancel(l)ed
Cantab.	of Cambridge *(Cantabrigiensis)*
Cantuar.	of Canterbury *(Cantuariensis)*
CAP	Common Agricultural Policy; computer-aided planning
cap.	capital; chapter *(caput)*
CAPM	capital asset pricing model
Capt.	Captain
CAQ	computer-aided quality assurance
CAR	contractors' all risks insurance
C. A. R.	Civil Air Regulations; Criminal Appeal Reports
CARE	*(originally:)* Cooperative for American Remittances to Europe; *(now:)* Cooperative for American Relief Elsewhere
CARICOM	Caribbean Community and Common Market
CATA	Clayton (Anti-Trust) Act
Cath.	Catholic
CATs	Certificates of Accrual on Treasury Securities
Cau	Caucasian (white race)
C. a. v.	the Court desires to consider *(curia advisari vult)*
C. B.	cash book; Companion of the (Order of the) Bath; Confidential Book; confinement to barracks; County Borough
C. B. C.	Canadian Broadcasting Corporation
C. B. D., c. b. d.	cash before delivery
C. B. E.	Commander of the (Order of the) British Empire
C. B. & H.	Continent between Bordeaux and Hamburg
CBI	Confederation of British Industry
CBOE	Chicago Board Options Exchange
CBOT	Chicago Board of Trade
CBS	Columbia Broadcasting System
C. C.	Chamber of Commerce; Circuit Court; Civil Commotion(s); County Clerk; County Council(l)or; County Court; Crown Cases; Customs Code
c. c.	account current *(Fr compte courant);* continuation clause; cubic centimet|re (~er)
CCA	Circuit Court of Appeals; United States Circuit Court of Appeals Reports; County Courts Act 1959; Court of Criminal Appeal; current cost accounting
CCAB	Consultative Committee of Accountancy Bodies
C. C. C.	Central Criminal Court; Commodity Credit Corporation; Council for Cultural Cooperation *(im Europarat)*
C. C. E.	Commissioners of Customs and Excise
CCIO	Classification of Commodities by Industrial Origin
C. C. J.	Circuit Court Judge
CCJO	Consultative Council of Jewish Organizations
CCL	customs clearance
C. Cls.	Court of Claims
C. C. P.	Code of Civil Procedure; Court of Common Pleas

CCPA	U. S. Court of Customs and Patent Appeals
CCR	Cox's Criminal Law Reports; Crown Cases Reserved; County Court Rules 1981
C. Cr. P.	Code of Criminal Procedure
CCT	Common Customs Tariff
CD	corporate design
C. D.	Chancery Division; Civil Defen|ce (~se); Coast Defence; contagious diseases; Corps Diplomatique
C/D	Certificate of Deposit
C. & D., c. d.	collected and delivered
c. d.	cash discount; certificate of deposit; with dividend *(cum dividendo)*
C. D. A.	Contagious Diseases Act
CDB	Caribbean Development Bank
cd fwd	carried forward
c. div.	with dividend *(cum dividendo)*
c. d. v.	visiting card *(Fr carte de visite)*
CE	Council of Europe *(Fr Conseil de l'Europe)*
C. E.	Chief Engineer; Church of England; Civil Engineer
C/E	customs entry
CEB	Central Electricity Board
Cedel	Centrale de Livraison de Valeur Mobilières (international computerized clearing house for Eurobonds)
C. E. G. B.	Central Electricity Generating Board
C. E. M. A.	Council for the Encouragement of Music and Arts
Cems	Community of European Management Schools
CEMT	*Fr* Conférence Européenne des Ministres des Transports
cent.	hundred *(centum)*
C. Eng.	chartered engineer
CENTO	Central Treaty Organization
CEO	Chief Executive Officer
CERCLA	Comprehensive Environmental Response, Compensation, and Liability Act
CERN	European Organization for Nuclear Research *(Fr Conseil Européen pour la Recherche Nucléaire)*
cert., certif.	certificate, certified
Cert. AIB	Certificated Associate of the Institute of Bankers
cert. denied	certiorari denied
cert. inv.	certified invoice
CET	Central European Time; Common External Tariff
cet. par.	other things being equal *(ceteris paribus)*
C. F.	Corresponding Fellow; most illustrious woman *(clarissima femina)*
C. F., c. f.	cost and freight
C/F	carriage forward
cf.	compare *(confer; conferatur)*
c. f.	illustrated *(cum figurus)*
c/f	carried forward
C & F, c & f	cost and freight
C. F. I., c. f. i.	cost, freight and insurance
CFR	Code of Federal Regulations; Council on Foreign Relations
C. F. S.	Container Freight Station
c. ft.	cubic feet
CFTC	Commodity Futures Trading Commission
C. G.	Coast Guard; Commanding General; Consul-General
C. G. A., c. g. a.	cargo's proportion of general average
CGPDTM	Comptroller General of Patents, Designs and Trade Marks
C. G. S. A.	Carriage of Goods by Sea Act
CGT	Capital Gains Tax
Ch.	Chancery; Chancery Appeals; Chancery Cases; Chancery Division (Law Reports)
C. H.	clearing house; confirming house; customs house; Companion of Honour
ch.	chapter

Cha.Ca.	Cases in Chancery
Ch. Acct.	chief accountant
Chanc.	Chancellor; Chancery
Ch. App. Cas.	Chancery Appeal Cases
C.H.C.	Clerk to the House of Commons
Ch. D.	Chancery Division (Law Reports)
Ch. D(iv).	Chancery Division
Ches.	Cheshire
ch. fwd	charges forward
chg. acct	charge account
chgd	charged
chges ppd	charges prepaid
C. H. & H.	Continent between Havre and Hamburg
CHIPS	Clearing House Interbank Payment System
Ch. J.	Chief Justice
ch. pd	charges paid
ch. ppd	charges prepaid
CI	Corporate Identity
C. I.	Channel Islands; Consular Invoice
c/i	certificate of insurance
c & i	cost and insurance
CIA	Canadian Institute of International Affairs; Central Intelligence Agency
CIC	Counter Intelligence Corps
CICA	Canadian Institute of Chartered Accountants
CID	Criminal Investigation Department
C. I. E.	Captain's imperfect entry *(customs)*
Cie	company *(Fr compagnie)*
CIF, cif	cost, insurance and freight
cifci	cost, insurance, freight, commissio, and interest
CIM	International Convention Concerning the Transport of Goods by Rail *(Fr Convention International concernant le Transport des Marchandises par Chemins de Fer)*; computer-integrated manufacturing
CIMA	Chartered Institute of Management Accountants
C.-in-C.	Commander-in-Chief
CINCAF	Commander in Chief, Asiatic Fleet *(US Navy)*
CINCLANT	Commander in Chief, Atlantic Fleet *(US Navy)*
CINCPAC	Commander in Chief, Pacific Fleet *(US Navy)*
CINCPOA	Commander in Chief, Pacific Operations Area *(US Navy)*
C. I. O.	Congress of Industrial Organizations
CIPA	Chartered Institute of Patents Agents
CIPFA	Chartered Institute of Public Finance and Accountancy
Circ. J.	Circuit Judge
Cir. Ct.	Circuit Court
CIS	Chartered Institute of Secretaries; Counter-Intelligence Service
CIT	Court of International Trade
CITES	Convention on International Trade in Endangered Species of Wild Fauna and Flora
City Ct. R.	City Court Reports
City Ct. R. Supp.	City Court Reports, Supplement
City H. Rec.	City Hall Recorder
CIV	International Convention concerning the Transport of Passengers and Baggage by Rail *(Fr Convention Internationale concernant le Transport des Voyageurs et des Bagages par Chemins de Fer)*
Civ. Eng.	Civil Engineer
C. J.	Chief Judge; Chief Justice; Corpus Juris
C. J. S.	Corpus Juris Secundum
C. K. D.	completely knocked down
cks	casks
c. l.	carload
c. l. c.	commercial letter of credit
CLCB	Committee of London Clearing Bankers

cld	called; cleared *(customs)*
C. L. J.	Cambridge Law Journal
CLLA	Commercial Law League of America
CLR	Common Law Reports
C. M.	Corresponding Member; court-martial
c/m	call of more (stocks)
CMA	cash management account
Cmd.	Command Paper (1919–1956)
CMI	Comité Maritime International
C. M. L. Rev.	Common Market Law Review
CMO	collateralized mortgage obligation
CMR	Convention on the Contract for the → International Carriage of Goods by Road
CMS	Cash Management System; Church Missionary Society
C/N	circular note; consignment note; credit note
C. O.	Commanding Officer; Conscientious Objector
Co.	Company; county
C/O	cash order; certificate of origin
c/o	care of; carried over
COB	Commission des opérations de bourse (Stock Exchange Commission, France)
COBOL	common business-oriented language
COCOM	Coordinating Committee for Multilateral Export Controls
C. O. D., c. o. d.	cash on delivery; collect on delivery
Cod. Jur. Civ.	Justinian's Code *(Codex Juris Civilis)*
C. O. G. S. A.	Carriage of Goods by Sea Act
Co. Inst.	Coke's Institutes of the Laws of England
Col.	Colonel; Colorado; Columbia
col.	colonel; colonial; colony; colo(u)red; column
COLA	cost-of-living adjustment
Col. L. Rev.	Columbia Law Review
coll. tr.	collateral trust *(bonds)*
Colo.	Colorado *(Staat der USA)*
com.	commerce; commercial; commission; commissioned; commissioner; committee
Com. Cas.	Commercial Cases
COMECON	Council for Mutual Economic Assistance
COMEX	Commodity Exchange, New York
COMINFORM	Communist Information Bureau
Comintern	Communist International
Comp. Gen.	Comptroller General
Comp. Stat.	Compiled Statutes
Comr.	Commissioner
COMSAT	Communications Satellite
conf.	compare *(confer)*
Conn.	Connecticut *(Staat der USA)*
Cons.	Conservative; Consignees; Consols; Consul
cons., consd	consolidated
Cons.-Gen.	Consul-General
Consols	Consolidated Annuities *(British Government stock)*
Cont (A. H.)	Continent, Antwerp-Hamburg range
Cont (B. H.)	Continent, Bordeaux-Hamburg range
cont. bon. mor.	contrary to good manners *(contra bonos mores)*
Cont (H. H.)	Continent, Havre-Hamburg range
contwood	The Baltic and International Maritime Conference Wood Charter, 1937
Coop	Cooperative (Society)
Cor.	coroner
cor.	in the presence of *(coram)*
Corn.	Cornwall
Corp., corp.	corporation
Corr. Mem.	Corresponding Member

C.O.S.	cash on shipment; Chamber of Shipping; Chief of Staff; Charity Organization Society
COSPAR	Committee for Space Research
COST	European Cooperation on Scientific and Technical Research
COTIF	Convention relative aux transports internationaux ferroviaires
c.o.w.	cash with order
Cox C.C.	E. W. Cox's Criminal Law Cases
CP	Canadian Press *(Ottawa)*
C.P.	Charter Party; Clerk of the Peace; Code of Procedure; Common Pleas; Communist Party; Court of Probate
C/P	carriage paid; charter party; custom of the port *(grain trade)*
c.p.	carriage paid
c/p	custom of the port *(grain trade)*
CPA	Certified Public Accountant; Chartered Patent Agent
C.P.C.	Clerk of the Privy Council
C.P.D., c.p.d.	charterers pay dues
C.P.G.B.	Communist Party of Great Britain
CPH	certificate of public health
CPI	consumer price index
CPLR	Civil Practise Law and Rules
cp. off	coupon off *(bonds)*
cp. on	coupon on *(bonds)*
CPQ	Code of Civil Procedure *(Quebeck)*
C.P.R.	Canadian Pacific Railway
C.P.R.E.	Council for the Preservation of Rural England
CPS	Crown Prosecution Service; Keeper of the Privy Seal *(Custos Privati Sigilli)*
CPSC	Consumer Product Safety Commission
Cpt.	Captain
c.q.d., cqd	customary quick dispatch
cr	credit (in double entry bookkeeping)
Cr.App.	Criminal Appeal (Law Reports)
Cr.Ca.	Criminal Cases (Law Reports)
CRC	current replacement cost
Crim.App.R.	Criminal Appeal Reports
crim.con.	criminal conservation
Crim.L.Rep.	Criminal Law Reporter
Crim.L.R.	Criminal Law Review
C. Rob.	C. Robinson's Admiralty Reports
C.R.U.	Collective Reserve Unit
C.S.	chartered surveyor; Civil Service; Court of Session; Keeper of the Seal *(Custos Sigilli)*
c/s	cases
C.S.C.	Civil Service Commission; Conspicuous Service Cross; International Convention for Safe Containers
CSCE	Conference on Security and Cooperation in Europe
CSE	Certificate of Secondary Education
CT	cubic tonnage
C.T., c.t.	cable transfer; commercial travel(l)er; conference terms; Corporation Tax
ct	cent
c.t.a.	with the will annexed *(cum testamento annexo)*
Ct. App.	Court of Appeals
Ct. Cl.	Court of Claims
C.T.L., c.t.l.	constructive total loss
ctl.	central (100 lb. weight)
c.t.l.o.	constructive total loss only
cts.	cents
CTT	Capital Transfer Tax *(obs.)*
CTV	commercial television
Cty Ct	County Court
C.U.	Cambridge University
cub.	cubic

cu. ft	cubic foot (feet)
Cumb.	Cumberland
cum d., cum div.	with dividend *(cum dividendo)*
cum int.	with interest *(cum interest)*
cum. part. pref.	cumulative participating preference shares
cum. pref.	cumulative preference shares
cur. adv. vult	the court wishes to deliberate *(curia advisari vult)*
C.V.	contributing value (G. A.)
C.W.	Canada West; chemical warfare; commercial weight
c.w.	commercial weight
c.w.o.	cash with order
C.W.S.	Church World Service; Cooperative Wholesale Society
cwt	hundredweight (*Br* 112 pounds, *Am* 100 pounds)
CYMS	Catholic Young Men's Society of Great Britain
C.Y.O.	Catholic Youth Organization

D

d.	date; pence; *(former)* penny *(denarius)*
D.A.	Defense Act; Deposit Account; District Attorney
D/A	days after acceptance; deposit account; discharge afloat; documents against acceptance; documents attached
d/a	days after acceptance; documents against (or on) acceptance
D.A.A.	Deed of Arrangement Act
DAC	Development Assistance Committee (OECD)
DAF	delivered at frontier
Dak.	Dakota *(Staat der USA)*
D.A.V.	disabled American veterans
D.B., d.b.	day book; deals and battens *(timber trade)*
d.b.a., d/b/a	doing business as
D.B.B., d.b.b.	deals, battens and board *(timber trade)*
d.b.n.	of the goods not (yet administered) *(de bonis non)*
DC	Diners Club
D.C.	Deviation Clause; District of Columbia; District Court; Divisional Court
DCE	domestic credit expansion
D.C.L.	Doctor of Civil Law
D.C.M.	Distinguished Conduct Medal; District Court Martial
D.D.	damage done; Dishonorable Discharge
D/D	delivered at docks; demand draft; documentary draft
d.d.	days after date; days' date; direct debiting; gave as a gift *(dono dedit)*
D.D.A.	Dangerous Drugs Act
D-day	Debarkation Day *(Date of Allied Invasion of France; June 6, 1944)*; day on which decimal currency came into use *(Feb. 15, 1971)*
DDD	direct distance dial(l)ing
DDP	delivered duty paid
dds	delivered in sound condition
dd/s	delivered sound *(grain trade)*
deb.	debenture
dec., decd	deceased
Def., deft	defendant
Del.	Delaware *(Staat der USA)*
dely (and redely)	delivery (and redelivery)
Dem.	Democrat; Democratic
dep.	departure; deputy
Dep(t)	department
dev.	deviation
D.F.	Dean of Faculty
dft	defendant; draft
D.G.	Dangerous Goods; director-general

d.h.d.	dispatch half demurrage
d.h.d.a.t.s.	dispatch money half demurrage all time saved
d.h.d.w.s.	dispatch money half demurrage working time saved
dieb. alt.	every other day *(diebus alternis)*
DISC	Domestic International Sales Corporation
disc., disct	discount
dist.	distance; district
Dist. Atty	District Attorney
Dist. Ct.	District Court
Dist. J.	District Judge
distr.	distributed; distribution; distributor
Dist. Rep.	District Reports
Div., div.	dividend; division
DJAG	Deputy Judge Advocate-General
DJIA	Dow Jones Industrial Average
DKB	Dai-Ichi Kangyo Bank (biggest Japanese commercial bank)
D.L.	Doctor of Law
D.L.O.	Dead Letter Office
d.l.o.	dispatch loading only
dls/shr.	dollars per share
DM	D-Mark, deutschemark
DMU	decision-making unit
d/n	debit note
do	ditto (the same)
D.O.A.	dead on arrival *(e.g. at hospital)*
DOC	Department of Commerce
doc.	document
DOD	Department of Defense
DOE	Department of Employment; Department of the Environment
DOJ	Department of Justice
DOL	Department of Labor
dol.	dollar
dom.	domestic; domicile
Dom. Proc.	House of Lords *(Domus Procerum)*
doz.	dozen
D.P.	Displaced Person(s)
DPB, dpb	deposit pass book
DPMA	Data Processing Management Association
D.P.P.	Director of Public Prosecutions
dpt	department
D.R.	daily report; District Registry
D/R	deposit receipt
Dr	debtor; Doctor
dr	debit (in double entry bookkeeping)
D/S, d/s., d.s.	days after sight
D.S.B.	Drug Supervisory Body
D.S.C.	Distinguished Service Cross
D.S.M.	Distinguished Service Medal
D.S.O.	Distinguished Service Order; deck stowage only
d.s.p.	died without issue *(decessit sine parole)*
DSS	decision support system
DTI	Department of Trade and Industry
D/W	divident warrant; dock warrant
d.w., d/w	deadweight
d.w.c.	deadweight capacity
d.w.c.c.	deadweight cargo capacity
DWI	driving while intoxicated
dwt	pennyweight *(denarius weight)*
d.w.t.	deadweight tonnage
dz.	dozen(s)

E

E.A.	Education Act; Economic Adviser
EAAA	European Association of Advertising Agencies
E.A.E.C.	European Atomic Energy Community (Euratom)
EAES	European Atomic Energy Society
EAGGF	European Agricultural Guidance and Guarantee Fund
EAL	Eastern Air Lines *(New York)*
E.A.M.	electronic accounting machine
EAN	European article number
E. & O.E.	errors and omissions excepted
EARN	European Academic and Research Network
EAT	Employment Appeal Tribunal
E.B.	Encyclopaedia Britannica
E. & B.	Ellis and Blackburn's Queen's Bench Reports
EBIT	earnings before interest and tax
E.C.	East Central *(London postal district);* East Coast; Established Church
EC	European Communities
ECA	Economic Commission for Africa (of the United Nations); European Communities Act; Exchange Control Act
ECAFE	Economic Commission for Asia and the Far East (of the United Nations)
ECCS	emergency core-cooling system
ECE	Economic Commission for Europe (of the United Nations)
E.C.G.B.	East Coast of Great Britain
E.C.G.D.	Export Credits Guarantee Department
E.C.I.T.O.	European Central Inland Transport Organization
ECLA	Economic Commission for Latin America (of the United Nations)
E.C.M.	European Common Market
ECMA	European Computer Manufacturers Association
ECMT	European Conference of Ministers of Transport
ECNR	European Council for Nuclear Research (CERN)
ECO	European Coal Organization
Econ.	Economics
ECOSOC	Economic and Social Council (of the United Nations)
ECOWAS	Economic Community of West African States
ECP	eurocommercial paper
ECS	Echantillons Commerciaux (Commercial Samples)
ECSC	European Coal and Steel Community (Montanunion)
ECU, ecu	European currency unit
ed.	edited; edition; editor
Ed. in Ch.	Editor in Chief
EDF	European Development Fund
EDI	electronic data interchange
EDP(M)	electronic data processing (machine)
E.E., e.e.	errors excepted
E. & E.	Ellis and Ellis' Queen's Bench Reports
EEC	European Economic Community (EWG)
EEDB	European Energy Data Base
EEIG	European Economic Interest Grouping
E.E. & M.P.	Envoy Extraordinary and Minister Plenipotentiary
EEOC	Equal Employment Opportunity Commission
E.E.T.	Eastern European Time
EFF	extended fund facility
EFT	electronic funds transfer
EFTA	European Free Trade Association; Electronic Fund Transfer Act
EFTPOS	electronic funds transfer at point of sale
e.g.	for example *(exempli gratia);* of a like kind *(ejusdem generis)*
Ehlass	European home and leisure accident surveillance act
E/I	endorsement irregular
EIA	environmental impact assessment

EIB	European Investment Bank
ejusd.	of the same kind *(ejusdem)*
EMA	European Monetary Agreement
EMBC	European Molecular Biology Conference
EMBL	European Molecular Biology Laboratory
EMBO	European Molecular Biology Organization
EMCF	European Monetary Cooperation Fund
Emer.	Emeritus
EMF	European Metal Workers' Federation
EMS	European Monetary System
encl.	enclosure(s)
ENEA	European Nuclear Energy Agency
ENET	European Nuclear Energy Tribunal
Engl.	England; English
Engl.Rep.	English Reports
Ent. Sta.Hall	entered at Stationers' Hall
Env. Ext.	Envoy Extraordinary
e.o.d.	every other day
EOE	European Options Exchange
E. & O.E., E. & o.e.	errors and omissions excepted
e.o.h.p.	except otherwise herein provided
E.O.M.	end of month; every other month
EOQ	economic order quantity
EP	European Parliament
Ep.	Bishop *(episcopus)*
E. and P.	extraordinary and plenipotentiary
E.P.A.	European Productivity Agency; Environmental Protection Agency
E.P.D.	excess profits duty
Episc.	Episcopal
EPO	European Patent Office
EPPO	European Plant Protection Organization
EPS	earnings per share
EPT	excess profits tax
EPTA	Expanded Program(me) of Technical Assistance
Epus	Bishop *(Episcopus)*
Eq.	equity (cases)
Eq.Ca.Ab.	equity cases abridged
EQS	Environmental Quality Standards
E.R.	Queen Elizabeth *(Elizabeth Regina);* English Reports
ERDC	Energy Research and Development Committee
ERDF	European Regional Development Fund
ERISA	Employee Retirement Income Security Act
ERM	exchange rate mechanism
ERP	European Recovery Program(me)
ESA	European Space Agency
ESAF	enhanced structural adjustment facility
E.S.C.	Economic and Social Council (of United Nations); Engineering Standards Commission
ESCAP	Economic and Social Commission for Asia and the Pacific
ESF	European Social Fund
ESOMAR	European Society for Opinion and Marketing Research
ESOP, Esop	Employee Stock Ownership Plan
esp.	especially
Esprit	European Strategic Programme for Research and Development in Information Technology
Esq.	Esquire
ESRA	European Safety and Reliability Association
ESRC	Economic and Social Research Council
ESSA	environmental survey satellite
EST	Eastern Standard Time

ETA, eta	estimated time of arrival
eta.	expected to arrive
et al.	and elsewhere *(et alibi)*; and others *(et alii)*
etc.	and so forth *(et cetera)*
ETD, etd	estimated time of departure
ets.	expected to sail
et seq., et sq.	and the following *(et sequens)*
et seqq., et sqq.	and those following *(et sequentes)*
ETUC	European Trade Union Confederation
ETV	Educational Television
EUA	European Unit of Account
EUMETSAT	European Organization for the Exploitation of Metereological Satellites
Euratom	European Atomic Energy Community
Eureca	European Research Coordinating Agency
Eur.L.Rev.	European Law Review
Eurochemic	European Company for the Chemical Processing of Irradiated Nuclear Fuels
Eurocontrol	European Organization for the Safety of Air Navigation
Euromarket	European Common Market
Euronet	European data network
EUTELSAT	European Telecommunications Satellite Organization
EV	economic value
EVCA	European Venture Capital Association
EWADAT	Europ. Waste Data Bank
Ex.	Exchange; Exchequer Reports
Exch.	Exchange; Exchequer; Exchequer Reports
excl.	excluding; exclusive
ex cp.	not including right to coupon *(ex coupon)*
exd	examined; exchanged; excluded; executed
Ex. D.	Exchequer Division (Law Reports)
ex div.	without dividend *(ex dividendo)*
exec.	executed; executive; executor
ex gr.	for example *(exempli gratia)*
Eximbank	Export-Import Bank *(Washington)*
ex int.	not including interest *(ex interest)*
ex n.	excluding the right to new shares *(ex new [shares])*
Ex. O.	Executive Order
ex off.	by authority of his office *(ex officio)*
exp.	expected; expenses; export(ed)
ex p.	on the application of; of one side only *(ex parte)*
ex rel.	ex relatione (on the relation or information)
ex ss.	ex steamer
ex tm.	in accordance with the testament *(ex testamento)*
ex whf	ex wharf
ex whse	ex warehouse

F

F.	Fahrenheit; Federal Reporter; Fellow; franc(s); Fraser's Scottish Reports
f.	feet; folio; foot; franc(s)
F. 2d	Federal Reporter, 2nd Series
f.a.	free alongside
F.A.	Finance Act
f.a.a.	free from all average
FAAAS	Fellow of the American Association for the Advancement of Science; Fellow of the American Academy of Arts and Science
FAC	Federal Advisory Council
fac.	facsimile
f.a.c.	fast as can

FACCA	Fellow of the Association of Certified and Corporate Accountants
facs.	facilities; facsimile
F.A.O.	Food and Agriculture Organization (of the United Nations)
faq, f.a.q.	fair average quality; free at quay
faqs	fair average quality of season
FARA	Foreign Agents' Registration Act
fas	free alongside ship
FASB	Financial Accounting Standards Board
FAST	Forecasting and Assessment in Science and Technology
f.b.	freight bill
F.B.A.	Federal Bar Association; Fellow of the British Academy
FBAA	Fellow of the British Association of Accountants and Auditors
F.B.I.	Federal Bureau of Investigation
FBLA	Federal Bills of Lading Act
FBM	Fleet Ballistic Missiles
F.C.	Finance Company; Free Church (of Scotland)
F.C.A.	Farm Credit Administration; Federal Code Annotated; Fellow of the (Institute of) Chartered Accountants (Chartered Accountant)
FCAC	Federal Council of American Churches
FCC	Federal Communications Commission
FCDA	Federal Civil Defense Administration
FCI	Factors Chain International; Fellow of the Institute of Commerce
F.C.I.A.	Fellow of the Corporation of Insurance Agents; Foreign Credit Insurance Association
F.C.I.B.	Fellow of the Corporation of Insurance Brokers
FCIC	Foreign Credit Insurance Corporation; Federal Crop Insurance Corporation
FCII	Fellow of the Chartered Insurance Institute
F.C.I.S.	Fellow of the Chartered Institute of Secretaries (Chartered Secretary)
FCN Treaty	Treaty of Friendship, Commerce and Navigation
F.C.P.A.	Fellow of the Institute of Certified Public Accountants; Foreign Corrupt Practices Act
F.C.R.	forwarding agent's certificate of receipt
F.C.(&)S., f.c.s.	free of capture and seizure
fcsad	free of capture, seizure, arrest and detainment
F.C.S.R. & C.C. fcsrcc	free of capture, seizure, riots and civil commotions
f.d.	free discharge; free dispatch; free delivery; free docks
F.&D., f.&d.	freight and demurrage
FDA	Food and Drugs Administration
FDCA	Federal Food, Drug and Cosmetic Act
FDI	Foreign Direct Investment
FDIC	Federal Deposit Insurance Corporation
FEA	Federal Energy Administration
fec.	he (she) made it *(fecit)*
Fed.	Federal; Federal Reporter
fed.	federal
Fed. 2d	Federal Reporter, 2nd Series
Fed. Aud.	Federal Auditor
Fed.Bar.J.	Federal Bar Association Journal
Fed. Cas.	Federal Cases
Fed.R.Civ.P.	Federal Rules of Civil Procedure
Fed.Reg.	Federal Register
Fed.Supp.	Federal Supplement
F.E.P.C.	Fair Employment Practices Committee
FERA	Federal Emergency Relief Administration
FERC	Federal Energy Regulatory Commission
ff.	folios; following pages
FFI	Finance for Industry
FFMC	Federal Farm Mortgage Corporation
F.G.	Federal Government

FGA	Foreign General Agent
F.G.A., f.g.a.	foreign general average; free from general average
F.H.A.	Federal Housing Administration
FHLB	Federal Home Loan Banks
f.i.	for instance
F.I.A.	Factory Insurance Association; Fellow of the Institute of Actuaries
f.i.a.	full interest admitted
f.i.a.s.	free in and stowed
FIBOR	Frankfurt Interbank Offered Rate
f.i.c., fic	freight, insurance, carriage
FICA	Federal Insurance Contributions Act; Fellow of the Institute of Chartered Accountants
FICB	Federal Intermediate Credit Banks
FICS	Fellow of the Institute of Chartered Shipbrokers
fi.fa.	you may cause it to be done *(fieri facias)*
fifo	first-in-first-out
FII	franked investment income
FIJ	Fellow of the Institute of Journalists
FIO, fio	free in and out
FIRPTA	Foreign Investment in Real Property Tax Act of 1980
FIS	freight, insurance and shipping charges
F.I.T.	Federal Income Tax; *Fr* Fédération Internationale des Traducteurs; Fixed Investment Trust
FITA	Foreign Investors Tax Act
fl.	florin(s)
FLA	First Lord of the Admiralty
Fla.	Florida *(Staat der USA)*
FLB	Federal Land Bank
FLSA	Fair Labor Standards Act
F.M.C.	Federal Maritime Commission
FMCS	Federal Mediation and Conciliation Service
F.M.S.	Fellow of the Medical Society
FMV	fair market value
FNMA	Federal National Mortgage Association
F.O.	Federal Official; Foreign Office
Fo., fo.	folio
f.o.	firm offer; free out; full out terms *(grain trade)*
FOA	Faculty of Advocates; Foreign Operations Administration
f.o.b., fob	free on board
FOBS	Fractional Orbital Bombing System
FOC	flags of convenience
f.o.c.	free on car; free of charge
f.o.d.	free of damage
fol.	folio
foll.	following
FOMC	Federal Open Market Committee
F.O.P., f.o.p.	free on plane
foq	free on quay
FOR, for	free on rail
Foratom	European Atomic Forum
f.o.r.&c.c.	free of riots and civil commotions
FOT, fot	free of tax; free on truck
F.O.W., f.o.w.	first open water; free on wag(g)on
F.P.	fire policy; floating policy; foreign policy; French Patent
f.p.	fire policy; floating policy; foreign policy; fully paid *(premium)*
FPA	Family Planning Association; Federal Power Act; Foreign Press Association
F.P.A., f.p.a.	free from particular average
FPAD	freight payable at destination
F.P.C.	Federal Power Commission
f.pd.	fully paid

FPHC	Foreign Personal Holding Company
fpil	full premium if (vessel) lost
FPO	Federal Post Office
FR	Federal Register; Federal Reporter
fr.	franc(s)
FRA	forward rate agreement; future rate agreement
frat.	fraternity
FRB	Federal Reserve Bank (Board)
FR Bk	Federal Reserve Bank
FRC	free carrier
f.r.&c.c.	free of riots and civil commotions
FRCP	Federal Rules of Civil Procedure
FRD	Federal Rules Decisions
FR Dist	Federal Reserve District
F.R.Ec.S.	Fellow of the Royal Economic Society
F.R.G.	Federal Republic of Germany (West Germany)
FRN	floating rate note
Fr.P.	French Patent
FRS	Federal Reserve System
F.R.S.	Fellow of the Royal Society
frs	francs
frt	freight
frt pd	freight paid
frt ppd	freight prepaid
frt fwd	freight forward
F/S	financial statement
FSA	Federal Securities Act; Federal Security Agency; Financial Services Act 1986
FSAA	Fellow of the Society of Incorporated Accountants and Auditors (Incorporated Accountant)
FSIA	Foreign Sovereign Immunity Act
FSLA	Federal Savings and Loan Association
F.S.L.I.C.	Federal Savings and Loan Insurance Corporation
F.Supp.	Federal Supplement
ft	feet; foot
ft^2	square foot
F.T.	Financial Times (newspaper)
FTC	Federal Trade Commission
FTCA	Federal Trade Commission Act
FUA	Farm Underwriters Association
FUIA	Federal Unemployment Insurance Act
FWA	Federal Works Agency
F.W.A.	Factories and Workshops Act
fwd	forward
f.w.d.	fresh water damage
FWSAB	Federation of Women Shareholders in American Business
FWT	flexible working time
F.X., f.x.	foreign exchange
f.y.	fiscal year
f.y.i.	for your information
fy pd	fully paid

G

G 5 →	Group of Five
G 7 →	Group of Seven
G 10 →	Group of Ten
g.	gauge; gram(me)(s); guinea
Ga.	Georgia *(Staat der USA)*

G.A.	General Agent; General Assembly
G.A., g.a., G/A	general average
G.A.A.	general average agreement
GAAP	generally accepted accounting principles
GAAS	generally accepted auditing standards
GAB	General Arrangements to Borrow
G.A./con.	general average contribution
G.A./dep.	general average deposit
gall.	gallon(s)
G.A.O.	General Accounting Office
GAOR	Official Records of the General Assembly (of the United Nations)
G.A.Q.	general average quality
GATT	General Agreement on Tariffs and Trade
G.A.W.	guaranteed annual wage
gaz.	gazette(d); gazetter
G.B.	Great Britain
G.B.E.	Knight (or Dame) Grand Cross (of the Order) of the British Empire
G.B.&I.	Great Britain and Ireland
g.b.o.	goods in bad order
GCBS	General Council of British Shipping
G.C.E.	General Certificate of Education
G.C.M.	General Court-Martial
GCR	general cargo rates
G.C.S.E.	General Certificate of Secondary Education
g.d.	good delivery
GDP	Gross Domestic Product
GDR	German Democratic Republic (East Germany)
GEMM	gilt-edged market maker
GFR	German Federal Republic
Gen. Ass., Off. Rec.	General Assembly, Official Records
Gen.Aud.	General Auditor
gen.av.	general average
Gen.Man.	General Manager
Ger.Pat.	German Patent
g.f.a.	good fair average
g.gr., g.gross	great gross *(144 dozen)*
G.I.	Government Issue
Gib.	Gibraltar
Glos.	Gloucestershire
gloss.	glossary
G.M.	General Manager; General Motors; guided missile
GMB, g.m.b.	good merchantable brand
G.M.C.	General Medical Council
g.m.q.	good merchantable quality
G.M.T.	Greenwich Mean Time
G.N.	Government Notices
GNP	Gross National Product
gns	guineas
g.o.b.	good ordinary brand
Goffex	German Options and Financial Futures Exchange
GOP	Grand Old Party *(Republican Party USA)*
Gov.	Government; Governor
Gov.Gen.	Governor-General
Gov.Pr.Off.	Government Printing Office
Govt	Government
G.P.	Gallup poll; General Practitioner; German Patent; Grand Prix
G.P.O.	Government Printing Office
GPP	general purchasing power accounting
G.R.	King George *(Georgius Rex)*
gr.	gross; grain

Gr.Brit.	Great Britain
G.R.T., g.r.t.	gross register ton(s)
gr.wt	gross weight
GSP	Generalized System of Preferences
G.T.	Greenwich time; gross ton
g.t.	gross terms
Gt.Br.	Great Britain
G.T.C., g.t.c.	good till cancel(l)ed (or countermanded)
g.t.m.	good this month
g.t.w.	good this week
guar.	guarantee(d)
GUN	grantor underwritten note
G.V.	gross value; Fast Train *(Fr grande vitesse)*

H

h.	hour(s); husband
ha	hectare(s)
h.a.	in this year *(hoc anno)*
hab. corp.	habeas corpus
H.A. or D.	Havre, Antwerp or Dunkerque (Dunkirk)
Hals. Stat.	Halsbury's Statutes of England
h. & c.	hot and cold (water)
Harv. Int. L.J.	Harvard International Law Journal
Harv. L. Rev.	Harvard Law Review
H.B.	House Bill
H.B.M.	Her (His) Britannic Majesty
H-bomb	hydrogen bomb
H.C.	High Court; House of Commons
h.c.	held covered; home consumption; honoris causa
H.C.B.	House of Commons Bill
H.C.(J.)	High Court (of Justice)
h. c. l.	high cost of living
H.Com.	High Commissioner
H.Con.Res.	House Concurrent Resolution
H.C.R.	(UN-)High Commissioner for Refugees
HDTV	high-definition television
H.E.	His Eminence; His Excellency
Heref.	Herefordshire
Herts.	Hertfordshire
hf	half
hgt	height
H.G.V.	heavy goods vehicle
H.H.	Her (His) Highness; His Holiness (the Pope)
H/H	Havre/Hamburg range
hifo	highest-in-first-out
H.I.H.	Her (His) Imperial Highness
H.I.M.	Her (His) Imperial Majesty
H.J.Res.	House joint resolution
H.K.	House of Keys
H.L.	House of Lords; House of Lords Appeals
hl	hectolitre(s)
HLB	Home Loan Bank
HLBB	Home Loan Bank Board
H.L.Cas.	House of Lords Cases
H.L.R.	Harvard Law Review
H.L.Rep.	House of Lords Reports
H.M.	headmaster; Her (His) Majesty; Home Mission
H.&M.	hull and machinery

H.M.C.	Her (His) Majesty's Customs
H.M.F.	Her (His) Majesty's Forces
H.M.G.	Her (His) Majesty's Government
H.M.I.	Her Majesty's Inspector (of Schools)
HMO	health maintenance organization
H.M.S.	Her (His) Majesty's Service; Her (His) Majesty's Ship (or Steamer)
HMSO	Her (His) Majesty's Stationery Office
H.M.T.	Her (His) Majesty's Transport
H.N.C.	Higher National Certificate
H.N.D.	Higher National Diploma
H.O.	Head Office; Home Office
H. ofR.	House of Representatives
HOLC	Home Owners' Loan Corporation
Hon.	Honorary; Hono(u)rable
hon.sec.	honorary secretary
HP	hire purchase
h.p.	half-pay; horse-power
H.P.R.	Hungarian People's Republic
H.Q., Hq.	Headquarters
H.R.	Home Rule; House of Representatives
H.R.H.	Her (His) Royal Highness
hr(s)	hour(s)
HS	Harmonized System
H.S.E.	here is buried *(hic sepultus est)*
HST	highest spring tide
H.T.	hired transport; under this title *(hoc titulo)*
ht	height
HUD	housing and urban development
Hunts.	Huntingdonshire
h.v.	under this word *(hoc verbo)*
H.W., h.w.	high water
H/W	husband and wife
H.W.M.	high water mark
H.W.M.C.	House Ways and Means Committee

I

I.	Idaho *(Staat der USA)*
IA	first quality; Iraqui Airlines
I.A.	Incorporated Accountant; Industrial Assurance
Ia.	Iowa *(Staat der USA)*
i. a.	inter alia
IAA	Incorporated Accountants and Auditors; Insurance Accountants Association; International Advertising Association
IABA	Inter-American Bar Association; International Aircraft Brokers Association
IAC	Inter-American Conference
IACSU	International Association of Casualty and Surety Underwriters
IADB	Inter-American Development Bank
IAEA	International Atomic Energy Agency
IAES	International Association of Exchange Students
IAF	International Aeronautical Federation; International Automobile Federation
IANEC	Inter-American Nuclear Energy Commission
IAPIP	International Association for the Protection of Industrial Property
IASC	International Accounting Standards Committee
IATA	International Air Transport Association
IAU	International Association of Universities
IAUPL	International Association of University Professors and Lecturers

IAVG	International Association for Vocational Guidance
I.A.W.	International Alliance of Women
i.a.w.	in accordance with
I.B.	Invoice Book
ib., ibid.	in the same place *(ibidem)*
IBA	Independent Broadcasting Authority; International Bar Association
IBAA	Investment Bankers Association of America
IBF	International Banking Facility
I.B.I.	International Broadcast Institute
IBM	International Business Machines
I.B.M.	Intercontinental Ballistic Missile
IBRD	International Bank for Reconstruction and Development *(World Bank)*
IBSFC	International Baltic Sea Fishery Commission
i/c, i./c.	in charge (of)
ICA	International Commodity Agreement or Arrangement; International Cooperative Alliance; Interstate Commerce Act; Investment Company Act
ICAO	International Civil Aviation Organization
ICAEW	Institute of Chartered Accountants in England and Wales
ICB	International Commodity Body
ICBM	Intercontinental Ballistic Missile
ICC	International Chamber of Commerce; Interstate Commerce Commission
I.C.C.	Institute Cargo Clauses
I.C.&C.	invoice, cost and charges
I.C.E.	Institution of Civil Engineers
ICEF	(UN)International Children's Emergency Fund
ICES	International Council for the Exploration of the Sea
I.C.F.C.	Industrial and Commercial Finance Corporation
ICFTU	International Confederation of Free Trade Unions
I.C.I.	Imperial Chemical Industries
ICIE	International Council of Industrial Editors
ICJ	International Court of Justice
I.C.L.Q.	International and Comparative Law Quarterly
ICM	Intergovernmental Committee for Migration
ICNAF	International Convention for the Northwest Atlantic Fisheries
ICO	International Coffee Organization; International Commodity Organization
ICPO	International Criminal Police Organization (Interpol)
ICRC	International Committee of the Red Cross
ICRF	International Cancer Research Foundation
ICS	Institute of Chartered Shipbrokers; International Chamber of Shipping
ICSID	International Centre for the Settlement of Investment Disputes
ICSM	International Committee of Scientific Management
ICSU	International Council of Scientific Unions
ICTUS	Counselor at Law *(iurisconsultus)*
ICU	International Code Use
ICW	International Council of Women
I.D.	Intelligence Department
Id.	Idaho (Staat der USA)
id.	the same (idem)
IDA	International Development Association
I.D.B.	Inter-American Development Bank; International Development Association (of the United Nations); illicit diamond buying
IDD	international direct dial(l)ing
i.e.	that is to say *(id est)*
IEA	International Energy Agency *(OECD)*
IEFC	Insurance Export Finance Company
IET	Interest Equalization Tax
I/F	insufficient funds
IFA	International Fiscal Association
IFAD	International Fund for Agricultural Development

I.F.C.	International Finance Corporation
IFCTU	International Federation of Christian Trade Unions
IFJ	International Federation of Journalists
IFORS	International Federation of Operational Societies
I.F.R.	illness frequency rate; instrument flight rules
IFT	International Federation of Translators
IFUW	International Federation of University Women
IFWL	International Federation of Women Lawyers
IHA	International Hotel Association
IHF	International Hospitals Federation
I/I	indorsement irregular
IIA	Institute of Internal Auditors; Insurance Institute of America
IIRI	International Industrial Relations Institute
IISPS	International Institute of Social and Political Sciences
I.L.	Institute of Linguists
ILA	International Law Association
ILAAB	International Law Association, American Branch
ILC	International Law Commission; irrevocable letter of credit
Ill.	Illinois *(Staat der USA)*
Ill.L.Rev.	Illinois Law Review
ILO	International Labour Office; International Labour Organization
ILQ	International Law Quarterly
ILR	International Law Reports (Lauterpacht)
ILS	Incorporated Law Society
I.M.	Isle of Man
IMC	International Missionary Council
IMCS	International Movement of Catholic Students
IMF	International Marketing Federation; International Monetary Fund
I.M.M.	Institution of Mining and Metallurgy
IMO	International Maritime Organization; International Money Order
IMP	Integrated Mediterranean Programme
Imp.	Imperial
in.	inch(es)
in^2	square inch
INA	Immigration and Nationality Act; Indian National Airways; Irish News Agency *(Dublin)*
in b.	in the goods of *(in bonis)*
Inc.	Incorporated
incl.	including; inclusive
incorp.	incorporated
Incoterms	International Commercial Terms
Ind.	Indiana *(Staat der USA)*
ind.	independent; industrial
Inex	International News Exchange
INF	Intermediate-Range Nuclear Forces
inf.	below *(infra)*
Infoterm	International Information Centre for Terminology
in init.	in the beginning *(in initio)*
in liq., in liqn	in liquidation
in loc.	in the place of *(in loco)*
in loc. cit.	in the place cited *(in loco citato)*
INMARSAT	International Maritime Satellite Organization
in re	in the matter of
INS	Immigration and Naturalization Service
Ins., ins.	insurance
insce	insurance
INSEAD	European Institute of Business Administration *(in Fontainebleau)*
ins.int.	insurable interest
Ins.L.J.	Insurance Law Journal
Inst.	institute; institution
inst.	of the current month *(instant)*; instal(l)ment; institute

Inst. Act.	Institute of Actuaries
Inst. Bks	Institute of Bankers
Inst.J.	Institutes of Justinian
insur.	insurance
int.	interest
int.al.	among other things *(inter alia)*
Intelsat	International Telecommunications Satellite Organization
Int.Encycl.Comp.L.	International Encyclopedia of Comparative Law
internat.	international
Int.and Comp. L.Q., Int.Law Quarterly	International and Comparative Law Quarterly
Interpol	International Criminal Police Organization
in trans.	in transit *(in transitu)*
Int.Rev.	Internal Revenue
Io.	Iowa *(Staat der USA)*
IOA	Institute of Actuaries; Institute of Arbitrators
IOB	Institute of Bankers
IOC	International Olympic Committee
IOCA	International Organization for Civil Aviation
IOCU	International Office of Consumers' Unions
IOE	International Organization of Employers
IOLM	International Organization of Legal Metrology
I.o.M.	Isle of Man
I.o.W.	Isle of Wight
I.O.G.T.	International Order of Good Templars
IOJ	International Organization of Journalists; Institute of Journalists
IOP	Institute of Patentees
i.o.p.	irrespective of percentage
IOS	International Organization for Standardization; Investors' Overseas Services
IOU	I owe you
i.o.w.	in other words
I.P.	Imperial preference; inland post
I&P	indexed and paged *(of account books)*
IPA	Institute of Practitioners of Advertising; International Publishers' Association
i.p.a.	including particular average
IPC	International Patent Classification; Iraq Petroleum Company
IPD	interest, profits and dividends
IPI	International Press Institute
IPR	(British) Institute of Public Relations
IPU	Interparliamentary Union
I.Q.	intelligence quotient
i.q.	the same as *(idem quod)*
iqued	that which was to be proved *(id quod erat demonstrandum)*
I.R.	Inland Revenue; Internal Revenue; Irish Reports
IRA	Industrial Relations Act; Irish Republican Army
I.R.B.M.	intermediate-range ballistic missile
IRC	Inland Revenue Commissioners; Internal Revenue Code; International Red Cross
IRCA	Immigration Reform and Control Act
IRD	Internal Revenue Department
IREM	Institute of Real Estate Management
IRF	International Road Federation
IRI	Industrial Research Institute
Ir.L.T.	Irish Law Times
Ir.L.T.Rep.	Irish Law Times Reports
IRM	information research management
I.R.O.	Inland Revenue Office; Internal Revenue Office
IRP	Index of Retail Prices

Ir.R.	Irish Reports
IRR	internal rate of return
IRS	Internal Revenue Service
IRU	International Road Transport Union
Is.	Island(s); Isle(s)
I.&S.	Iron and Steel
ISALPA	Incorporated Society of Auctioneers and Landed Property Agents
ISBN	international standard book number
ISC	International Sugar Council
ISDA	International Swap Dealers Association
ISDN	Integrated Services Digital Network
ISF	International Shipping Federation
ISI	International Statistical Institute
ISM	Imperial Service Medal
I.S.M.A.	Incorporated Sales Managers' Association
ISO	Imperial Service Order; International Standardization Organization
Isro	International Securities Regulatory Organisation
ISS	International Student Service
IT	Information Technology
I.T.	Income tax; Inner Temple; investment trust
i.t.	in transit *(in transitu)*
ITA	International Trade Administration; Independent Television Authority; International Tourist Association
ITC	International Trade Commission; International Trade Center; International Tin Council
ITN	Independent Television News
ITTO	International Tropical Timber Organization
ITT	International Telephone and Telegraph Corporation
ITU	International Telecommunication Union
ITV	Independent Television
ITWF	International Transport Workers' Federation
IUA	International Union of Advertising
IUAI	International Union of Aviation Insurers
IUHR	International Union of Hotel, Restaurant and Bar Workers
IULA	International Union of Local Authorities
IULIA	International Union of Life Insurance Agents
IUMI	International Union of Marine Insurance
IUOTO	International Union of Official Travel Organizations
IUPN	International Union for the Protection of Nature
IUSY	International Union of Socialist Youth
i.v.	increased value; invoice value
I.W.A.	Institute of World Affairs; International Wheat Agreement
I.W.T.	inland water transport
IWTO	International Wool Textile Organization
IYHF	International Youth Hostel Federation

J

J.	Journal; Judge; Justice
J.A.	Judge Advocate; Justice of Appeal
J./A., j./a.	joint account
J.Adv.Gen. J.A.G.	Judge Advocate General
JB	Bachelor of Law *(Jurum Baccalaureus)*
JBL	Journal of Business Law
JC	jurisconsult *(jurisconsultus)*; Justice Clerk; Juvenile Court
JCB	Bachelor of Canon Law *(Juris Canonici Baccalaureus)*; Bachelor of Civil Law *(Juris Civilis Baccalaureus)*
J.C.D.	Doctor of Civil Law *(Juris Civilis Doctor)*

JCLIL	Journal of Comparative Legislation and International Law
J.C.P.C.	Judicial Committee of the Privy Council
J.E.	joint enterprise
JEIA	Joint Export Import Agency
JET	Joint European Torus
JETRO	Japan External Trade Organization
JIGE	Joint Intergovernmental Group of Experts on Maritime Liens and Mortgages and Related Subjects
Jnr	Junior
J.P.	Justice of the Peace
J.Prob.	Judge of Probate
J.Pub.L.	Journal of Public Law
J.Q.B.	Justice of the Queen's Bench
Jr, jr	Junior
JRC	Joint Research Centre
JSLB	Joint Stock Land Banks
J.U.D.	Doctor of both Laws (i.e. the Canon and the Civil Law) *(Juris utriusque Doctor)*
Jud.Com.P.C.	Judicial Committee of the Privy Council
jun.	junior
Jun(r).	Junior
Jur.D.	Doctor of Law *(Juris Doctor)*
jurisp.	jurisprudence
Jus.P.	Justice of the Peace
juv.	juvenile
J.&W.O., j.&w.o.	jettison and washing overboard

K

k	kilo
k.	knot
Kan., Kans.	Kansas *(Staat der USA)*
K.D., k.d.	knocked down
k.d.c.l.	knocked down, in carloads
Ken.	Kentucky *(Staat der USA)*
kg	kilogram(me)
K.L.M.	Royal Dutch Air Lines
km	kilomet|re (~er)
kn	knot(s)
Knt.	Knight
kos.	kilos
k.p.h.	kilomet|res (~ers) per hour
Ky	Kentucky *(Staat der USA)*

L

L.	learner-driver; Liberal
l.	left; lira; lire; litre(s); liter(s)
£	pound(s) sterling *(libra[e])*
£E	Egyptian pound
£s.d.	pounds, shillings, pence *(librae, soldi, denarii)*
£stg	pound sterling
La.	Louisiana *(Staat der USA)*
L.A.	Larceny Act; Law Agent; Legislative Assembly; Licensing Act; Los Angeles
L/A	Letter of Authority

La. Ann.	Louisiana Annual Reports
Lab.	Labour (Party)
lab	laboratory
Labor L.J.	Labor Law Journal
LAFTA	Latin-American Free Trade Association
LAIA	Latin American Integration Association
La. L. Rev.	Louisiana Law Review
Lancs.	Lancashire
L.A.S.	Lord Advocate of Scotland
lat.	latitude
L.A.U.A.	Lloyd's Aviation Underwriters' Association
Law & Contemp. Prob.	Law and Contemporary Problems
Law Q. Rev.	Law Quarterly Review
Law Rep.	Law Reports
Law Soc. J.	Law Society Journal
lb.	pound (in weight) *(libra)*
L.B.C.H.	London Bankers' Clearing House
L.B.H.	Length, Breadth, Height
LBO	leveraged buyout
lbs.	pounds
L.C.	Leading Cases; Library of Congress; London Clause *(shipping);* Lord Chamberlain; Lord Chancellor; Lower Canada
L/C, l/c	letter of credit
l.c.	leading cases; legal currency; in the place cited *(loco citato)*
L.C.A.	Land Charges Act; Licensed Company Auditor; letter of credit
L.C.C.	London Chamber of Commerce
LCE	London Commodity Exchange
L.Ch.A.	Land Charges Act
L.C.J.	Lord Chief Justice
L.C.L., l.c.l.	less than carload lot(s)
L.C.L.J.	Lower Canada Law Journal
L.C.R.	Lower Canada Reports
L.C.T.A.	London Corn Trade Association
L&D	loans and discounts; loss and damage
Ld	Lord
LDCs	Less Developed Countries
ldg	landing; loading
ldg & dely	landing and delivery
L.D.M.A.	London Discount Market Association
L.E.A.	Local Education Authority
Leb.	Lebanon
L. Ed.	Lawyers' Edition *(U. S. Supreme Court Reports)*
Leics.	Leicestershire
l.f.a.	local freight agent
L.G.	Life Guards; London Gazette
L.G.B.	Local Government Board
L.G.R.	Local Government Reports
lgth	length
lg tn	long ton
L.H.	Licensing Hours
L.H.A.	Local Health Authority
L.H.A.R.	London, Hull, Antwerp, or Rotterdam
L.H.C.	Lord High Chancellor
LIAMA	Life Insurance Agency Management
Lib.	Liberal; *colloq.* Liberation
LIBID	London Interbank Bid Rate
LIBOR	London Interbank Offered Rate
LIFFE	London International Financial Futures Exchange
lifo, LIFO	last-in-first-out (*or* last in, first out)
LIMEAN	London Interbank Mean

Lincs.	Lincolnshire
L.I.P.	Life Insurance Policy
liq.	liquid
L.J.	Law Journal; Lord Justice of Appeal
L.J.Ch.	Law Journal, Chancery Division
L.J.Ex.	Law Journal, Exchequer
L.J.H.L.	Law Journal, House of Lords
L.JJ.	Lords Justices of Appeal
L.J. (Q.B., P.C.)	Law Journal, Queen's Bench, Privy Council
L.J.M.C.	Law Journal, Magistrates' Cases
L.J.P.&M.	Law Journal, Probate and Matrimonial
L.J. Q.B.	Law Journal, Queen's Bench
L.J.R.	Law Journal Reports
L.J.Rep., N.S.	Law Journal Reports, New Series
L.J.U.C.	Law Journal, Upper Canada
L.L.	Law List; Lending Library
LL.B.	Bachelor of Laws *(legum baccalaureus)*
LL.D.	Doctor of Laws *(legum doctor)*
LLDC	least developed countries
L.Lib.J.	Law Library Journal
Lloyd's Rep.	Lloyd's Reports
Ll.L.R.	Lloyd's Law Reports *(1919–1950)*
LL.M.	Master of Laws *(legum magister)*
LNG	liquefied national gas
Lloyd's Rep.	Lloyd's List Report *(1951 bis heute)*
L.L.T.	London Landed Terms
L.M.	Lord Mayor
L.M.C.	Labour Management Committee
l.m.c.	low middling clause *(cotton trade)*
LME	London Metal Exchange
LMRA	Labor Management Relations Act
L.M.S.	London Medical Society
L.O.	Liaison Officer
L.O.A.	leave of absence
loc.cit.	at the place cited *(loco citato)*
L. of C.	Library of Congress
long.	longitude
Loran	long-range navigation
Lords Journals	Journals of the House of Lords
Lou.	Louisiana
L.P.	Labour Party; Liberal Party; Life Policy; London Port; Lord Provost
L.P.A.	Law of Property Act; Leather Producers' Association for England
L.P.S.	London Press Service; Lord Privy Seal
L.Q.R., L.Q.Rev.	Law Quarterly Review
L.R.	Land Registry; Law Report(s); Law Review; Lloyd's Register (of Shipping)
L.R.A.	Land Registration Act; Lawyers' Reports Annotated
L.R.C.A.	London Retail Credit Association
LRCS	League of Red Cross Societies
L.Rev.	Law Review
LRINF	longer-range INF
L.R.R.P.C.	Law Reports, Restricitive Practices Cases
L.R.S.	Land Registry Stamp; Lloyd's Register of Shipping
L.R.S.A.	Law Reports, South Australia
LRTAP	long-range transboundary air pollution
L.S., l.s.	place of the seal *(locus sigilli)*
L.S.A.	Louisiana Statutes Annotated
L.S.B.	London School Board
l.s.c.	in the place before cited *(loco supra citato)*
L.S.E.	London School of Economics; London Stock Exchange
L.S.G.	Law Society Gazette
L.S.S.	Life-saving-Service

L.S.T.	Local Standard Time
L.T.	Law Times; Law Times Reports; Letter Telegram
L/T	landlord and tenant; long ton
L.T.A.	London Teachers' Association
L.(T.C.)	Tax Cases Leaflets
L.T.C.A.	Law Times Reports, Court of Appeals
Ltd, ltd	Limited
LTFV	less than fair value
Lt.Gov.	Lieutenant Governor
L.T.J.	Law Times Journal
l.t.l.	less than truckload
L.T.R.	Law Times Reports
L.T.R.A.	Lands Tribunal Rating Appeals
Lt.V.	light vessel
L&U	loading and unloading *(railway)*
L.V.	Licensed Victualler; luncheon voucher
L.V.A.	Licensed Victuallers Association
L.V.App.Ct.	Lands Valuation Appeal Court *(Scotland)*
L.W.	low water
LWOP	leave without pay

M

M.	motorway
m.	male; married; metre(s); meter(s); mile(s); minute(s); month
M.A.	Marriage Act; Master of Arts *(magister artium);* Military Academy
M.A.F.F.	Ministry of Agriculture, Fisheries and Food
Mag.Ct	Magistrates' Court
M.Agr.	Master of Agriculture
Man.Dir.	Managing Director
M.A.N.S.	Member of the Academy of Natural Sciences
manuf.	manufacture; manufacturing
M.A.P.	maximum average price
MAPI	Machinery and Allied Products Institute
mar.	married
marg.	margin(al)
Mar.L.Cas.	Maritime Law Cases
Mass.	Massachusetts *(Staat der USA)*
Mass. L.Q.	Massachusetts Law Quarterly
Mass. L.R.	Massachusetts Law Reporter
M.A. (S.S.)	Master of Arts in Social Science
MAST	marine science and technology
M.B.	Bachelor of Medicine *(medicinae baccalaureus)*
M.B.A.	Master of Business Administration
M.B.C.	Municipal Borough Council
MBCA	Model Business Corporation Act
M.B.E.	Member (of the Order) of the British Empire
MBFR	Mutual and Balanced Reduction of Forces
MBI	management buyin
M.B.I.M.	Member of the British Institute of Management
M.B.M.	Master of Business Management
MBO	management by objectives; management buyout
M.C.	Magistrates' Cases; Magistrates' Court; Maritime Commission; marriage certificate; Member of Congress; Military Committee *(NATO);* Monopoly Commission
MCA	Matrimonial Causes Act; monetary compensatory amount
MCAUS	Manufacturing Chemists' Association of the U.S.
M.C.E.	Master of Civil Engineering

M.C.L.	Malaysian Common Market; Master of Civil Law; Master of Comparative Law
MCM	Manual for Courts Martial *(US Army)*
M.Com.	Master of Commerce
MCPS	Mechanical Copyright Protection Society
M.C.S.	Master of Commercial Science
M.C.W.	Maternity and Child Welfare
M.D.	Managing Director; Medical Department; Medicinae Doctor *(Doctor of Medicine);* Memorandum of Deposit; mentally deficient
Md.	Maryland *(Staat der USA)*
Md. L.Rev.	Maryland Law Review
m.d., m/d	months after date; months' date
Mddx.	Middlesex
MDS	measured daywork system
M.D.N.A.	Machinery Dealers' National Association
M.E.	Middle East(ern); Mining Engineer
Me.	Maine *(Staat der USA)*
M.Ec.	Master of Economics
M.Ed.	Master of Education
MEDICO	Medical International Cooperation
mem.	member; remember *(memento);* memorandum
M.E.M.A.	Motor and Equipment Manufacturers' Association
Memo.	Memorandum
MEP	Member of the European Parliament
M.E.P.C.	Metropolitan Estate and Property Corporation
MerchShA	Merchant Shipping Act
Messrs	Messieurs
M.E.T.	Mid European Time
M.E.W.A.	Motor and Equipment Wholesalers' Association
MFA	Multifibre Arrangement
MFN	most favo(u)red nation
M.H.	Medal of Honor
M.Hon.	Most Honourable
M.H.R.	Member of the House of Representatives
M.H.R.T.	Mental Health Review Tribunal
M.I.	Military Intelligence (M.I.5 security service; M.I.6 espionage department)
M.I.A.	Marine Insurance Act
M.I.C.E.	Member of the Institution of Civil Engineers
Mich.	Michigan *(Staat der USA)*
Mich. L.Rev.	Michigan Law Review
MIGA	Multilateral Investment Guarantee Agency
M.I.J.	Member of the Institute of Journalists
M.I.L.	Member of the Institute of Linguistos
Mil.Att.	Military Attaché
Mil.Gov.	Military Government
Min.	Minister; Ministry
min.	minimum; mining
Minn.	Minnesota *(Staat der USA)*
Minn.L.Rev.	Minnesota Law Review
Min.Plen.	Minister Plenipotentiary
M.I.P.	Marine Insurance Policy
MIRV	Multiple Independently Targetable Reentry Vehicles
Misc.	Miscellaneous Reports *(N.Y.)*
Miss.	Mississippi *(Staat der USA)*
Miss.L.J.	Mississippi Law Journal
M.I.T.	Management Investment Trust
MIT	Massachusetts Institute of Technology
MITI	Ministry of International Trade and Industry (of Japan)
Mk	Mark; marketing
Mkt	Market
m/l	more or less

M.L.A.	Member of Legislative Assembly; Modern Language Association (of America)
M.L.A.U.S.	Maritime Law Association of the United States
M.L.C.	Member of Legislative Council
M.L.R.	Modern Law Review; Minimum Lending Rate
M.M.	Mercantile Marine; Military Medal
MM	Messieurs
M.M.A.	Merchandise Marks Act
MMC	money market certificate; Monopolies and Mergers Commission
M.M.O.	Mercantile Marine Officer
M.N.	Merchant Navy
M.N.A.S.	Member of the National Academy of Sciences
MNC	multinational company (or corporation)
MNE	multinational enterprise
M.O.	Medical Officer; Money Order
MoD	Ministry of Defence
Mo.	Missouri *(Staat der USA);* Monday
Mo.App.	Missouri Court of Appeals Reports
mod.cons.	(with all) modern conveniences
Mod.L.Rev.	Modern Law Review
M.O.H.	Medical Officer of Health; Ministry of Health
MOL	Manned Orbiting Laboratory
Mo.L.Rev.	Missouri Law Review
Mont.	Montana *(Staat der USA)*
Month.L.Mag.	Monthly Law Magazine *(London)*
Month.L.Rev.	Monthly Law Review
Mont.L.Rev.	Montana Law Review
Montr.cond.Rep.	Montreal Condensed Reports
Montr.Leg.N.	Montreal Legal News
mortg.	mortgage
MoT	Ministry of Transport
MOU	memorandum of understanding
M.P.	Member of Parliament; Military Police(man)
M/P	memorandum of partnership
m.p.	manu propria
M.P.B. and W.	Ministry of Public Buildings and Works
MPC	Model Penal Code
mph	miles per hour
M.P.L.	Master of Patent Law
M.P.R.	Maritime Provinces Reports, Canada
M.R.	Master of the Rolls; Motivation Research
M/R, m/r	mate's receipt
M.R.A.S.	Member of the Royal Academy of Science
MRA	Moral Rearmament
M.R.B.M.	medium-range ballistic missile
M.R.C.	Medical Research Council
M.R.C.A.	multi-role combat aircraft
M.R.S.	Market Research Society
MRV	multiple re-entry vehicle
M.S.	Master of Science; Merchant Shipping; motor ship
MS.	manuscript
m.s., m/s	mail steamer; months after sight
ms., mss.	manuscript(s)
M.S.A.	Merchant Shipping Act; Mutual Security Agency
MSAC	most seriously affected countries
MSC	Manpower Services Commission
M.Sc.	Master of Science
Ms.D. (Patents)	Manuscript Decisions
M.S.J.	Master of Science in Journalism
MsMC	Monopolies and Merger Commission
MSS.	manuscripts

M.T.	metric ton
MTN	multilateral trade negotiations
Mt.Rev.	Most Reverend
M.T.T.A.	Machine Tools Trades' Association
M/U	making up price
mun.	municipal
Mun.Corp.Cas.	Municipal Corporation Cases
Mun.Ct.	Municipal Court
Mun.L.J.	Municipal Law Journal
M.V., m.v.	Motor Vessel
M.V.O.	Member of the (Royal) Victorian Order
M.W.P.A.	Married Women's Property Act
Mx	Middlesex

N

n.	born *(natus);* new; note
N.A.	it is not allowed *(non allocatur);* North America
n/a.	no account
N.A.A.	National Aeronautic Association; National Automobile Association
N.A.A.C.P.	National Association for the Advancement of Colored People
N.A.A.F.I.	Navy, Army and Air Force Institutes
NACA	National Advisory Committee for Aeronautics
NACRO	National Association for the Care and Resettlement of Offenders
NADPAS	National Association of Discharged Prisoners' Aid Societies
NAEA	National Association of Estate Agents
NAFFP	National Association of Frozen Food Producers
NAFO	Northwest Atlantic Fisheries Organization
NAIC	National Association of Insurance Commissioners
NAII	National Association of Independent Insurers
N.A.L.G.O.	National and Local Government Officers' Association
N.A.M.	National Association of Manufacturers
NAMH	National Association for Mental Health
NAMIC	National Association of Mutual Insurance Companies
N.A.N.A.	North American Newspaper Association
NAPAN	National Association for the Prevention of Addiction to Narcotics
NARF	Native American Rights Fund
N.A.S.	National Academy of Sciences; National Association of Schoolmasters; Noise Abatement Society
NASA	National Aeronautics and Space Administration
NASDAQ	National Association of Securities Dealers Automated Quotations System
NASD	National Association of Securities Dealers
NASDIM	National Association of Security Dealers and Investment Managers
NASDQ	National Association of Securities Dealers Automated Quotation
Nat.B.J.	National Bar Journal
Nat. Corp. Rep.	National Corporation Reporter
Nat.Inc. Tax Mag.	National Income Tax Magazine
Nat.Lawyers Guild Q.	National Lawyers Guild Quarterly
N.A.T.O.	North Atlantic Treaty Organization; National Association of Travel Organizations
naut.m.	nautical mile
N.A.V.	net annual value
N.B.	Scotland (North Britain); mark well *(nota bene)*
n.b.	new bonds; mark well *(nota bene);* no goods *(nulla bona)*
N.B.C.	National Broadcasting Corporation
NBNA	National Bank of North America
N.B.S.	National Bureau of Standards (USA)
N.C.	North Carolina *(Staat der USA)*

NCC	Nature Conservancy Council
NCCL	National Council for Civil Liberties
NCI	New Community (borrowing and lending) Instrument
N.C.L.Rev.	North Carolina Law Review
NCR	National Cash Register Company
N.D.	North Dakota *(Staat der USA)*
n.d.	no date; not dated
N.Dak.	North Dakota *(Staat der USA)*
N.D.L.Rev.	North Dakota Law Review
N.D.S.B.	Narcotic Drugs Supervisory Body
N.E.	North-Eastern; North Eastern Reporter
N.E.2d	North Eastern Reporter, 2d Series
N/E	no effects
n.e.	not exceeding
NEA	National Education Association; Nuclear Energy Agency *(OECD)*
NEAFC	North-East Atlantic Fisheries Commission
Neb(r).	Nebraska *(Staat der USA)*
Neb.L.Bull.	Nebraska Law Bulletin
NEC	National Executive Committee
NEDC, Neddy	National Economic Development Council
Neg.Ins.	Negotiable Instrument
nem.con.	nobody contradicting *(nemine contradicente)*
nem.diss.	nobody dissenting *(nemine dissentiente)*
NEPA	National Environmental Policy Act
N.E.R.C.	National Environment Research Council
NEST	Nuclear Energy Search Team
Nev.	Nevada *(Staat der USA)*
NF	National Front; Nouveau Franc
N/F.	no funds
NFA	National Futures Association
N.F.U.	National Farmers' Union
NGO	Non-governmental Organization
N.H.	New Hampshire *(Staat der USA)*
N.H.I.	National Health Insurance
NHS	National Health Service
NHTSA	National Highway Traffic Safety Commission
N.I.	National Insurance; Northern Ireland; Northern Ireland Law Reports
N.I.A.	National Insurance Act
NIBOR	New York Interbank Offered Rate
N.I.C.	National Investors' Corporation
N.I.C.B.	National Industrial Conference Board *(New York)*
NICs	newly industrialized countries
N.I.E.S.R.	National Institute of Economic and Social Research
NIF	note insurance facility
NIL	Negotiable Instruments Law
N.I.L.Q.	Northern Ireland Legal Quarterly
NIMEXE	Nomenclature of Goods for the External Trade Statistics of the Community and Statistics of Trade between Member States
ni.pri.	unless previously *(nisi prius)*
NIS	Norwegian International Ship Register
N.J.	New Jersey *(Staat der USA)*
N.J.L.J.	New Jersey Law Journal
N.J.L.Rev.	New Jersey Law Review
N.J.Super.	New Jersey Superior Courts Reports
N.L.	it is not clear *(non liquet)*
N.L.B.	National Labor Board
N.L.J.	New Law Journal
NLRA	National Labor Relations Act
NLRB	National Labor Relations Board
N.M.	New Mexico *(Staat der USA)*
n.m.	nautical mile

N.M.B.	National Maritime Board
N.Mex.	New Mexico *(Staat der USA)*
N.N.P.	Net National Product
N/O.	no orders
No., no.	number
n.o.h.p.	not otherwise herein provided
nol.pros.	to be unwilling to prosecute *(nolle prosequi)*
non cum.	non cumulative
non pros.	he does not prosecute *(non prosequitur)*
n.o.p.	not otherwise provided (for)
n.o.r.	not otherwise rated
Northants.	Northamptonshire
Northumb.	Northumberland
Nos., nos	numbers
Notts.	Nottinghamshire
NOW	negotiable order of withdrawal
N.P.	unless before *(nisi prius)*; no protest; Notary Public
n.p.	net proceeds; new paragraph
N.P.A.	Newspaper Publishers' Association
NPC	non-participating country
NPG	Nuclear Planning Group
NPT	Non-Proliferation Treaty
NPV	no par value; net present value
N/R, n.r.	no risk
NRA	nonresident alien
n.r.a.d.	no risk after discharge
NRC	Nuclear Regulatory Commission
NRPB	National Radiation Protection Board
NRT, n.r.t.	net register ton
N.S.	New Series; New Style; not sufficient (funds)
NSA	National Security Agency; National Shipping Authority
N.S.B.	National Savings Bank; National Bureau of Standards *(in Washington)*
NSC	National Security Council
N.S.F.	National Science Foundation
n.s.f.	not sufficient funds
N.S.G.T.	Non-Self-Governing Territories
N.S.P.C.C.	National Society for the Prevention of Cruelty to Children
N.S.W.	New South Wales
N.S.W.St.R.	New South Wales State Reports
NTB	non-tariff barriers
nt. wt.	net weight
N.U.J.	National Union of Journalists
NUM	National Union of Manufacturers; National Union of Mineworkers
N.U.R.	National Union of Railwaymen
N.U.S.	National Union of Students; National Union of Seamen
N.W.	North-West(ern); North Western Reporter
N.W. 2d	North Western Reporter, Second Series
N.Y.	New York *(Staat der USA)*
N.Y.C.	New York City
NYFE	New York Futures Exchange
N.Y.L.J.	New York Law Journal
N.Y.S.	New York State; New York Supplement
N.Y.S. 2d	New York Supplement, Second Series
NYSE	New York Stock Exchange
N.Y.Supp.	New York Supplement
N.Y.U.L.Q.Rev.	New York Universitiy Law Quarterly Review
N.Y.U.L.Rev.	New York University Law Review
N.Z.	New Zealand
N.Z.L.R.	New Zealand Law Reports
NZPA	New Zealand Press Association

O

O.	Ohio *(Staat der USA)*
OAP	Old Age Pensioner
OAPEC	Organization of Arab Petroleum Exporting Countries
OAS	on active service; Organization of American States
OASDI	Old Age, Survivors' and Disability Insurance
OAU	Organization of African Unity
O.B.	Ordinary Business
ob.	died *(obiit)*
O.B.E.	Officer of the Order of the British Empire
ob.s.p.	died without issue *(obiit sine prole)*
O.C.	Orphans' Court
o.c.	office copy; in the work cited *(opere citato)*
OCAS	Organization of Central American States
OCC	Office of the Comptroller of the Currency
O.C.D.	Office of Civil Defense
Ocis	Organized Crime Information System
OCL	Overseas Container Ltd.
OCT	Overseas Countries and Territories
O.E., o.e.	omissions excepted
OEA	Office of Export Administration
OECD	Organization for Economic Cooperation and Development
O.F.C.	Overseas Food Corporation
OFT	Office of Fair Trading
O.G. Pat.Off.	Official Gazette, United States Patent Office
O.G.O.	Orbiting Geophysical Observatory
Ohio Dec.	Ohio Decisions
Ohio S.L.J.	Ohio State Law Journal
Ohio St.	Ohio State Reports
O.H.M.S.	On Her (His) Majesty's Service
Okla.	Oklahoma *(Staat der USA)*
Okla.L.R.	Oklahoma Law Review
O.M.	Order of Merit
OMA	Orderly Market Arrangement
ONA	Overseas News Agency *(New York)*
O.N.C.	Ordinary National Certificate
O.N.D.	Ordinary National Diploma
ONS	Overseas News Service *(London)*
Ont.	Ontario
Ont.App.	Ontario Appeals
Ont. L.R.	Ontario Law Reports
O.P.	open policy; Out of Print
o.p.	out of print
op. cit	in the work quoted *(opere citato)*
OPEC	Organization of Petroleum Exporting Countries
OPIC	Overseas Private Investment Corporation
OPS	open price system
O.R.	Official Receiver; operational (operations) research; Other Ranks; owner's risk
o.r.	owner's risk
Ord.	Order
ord., ordy	ordinary; ordinary shares (or stock)
Ore(g).	Oregon *(Staat der USA)*
Ore. L.Rev.	Oregon Law Review
O.S.	Old Style; ordinary seaman; Ordnance Survey; outsize; out of stock
o/s.	on sale; out of stock
OSHA	Occupational Safety and Health Act
OSO	Orbiting Solar Observatory
O.T.	overtime

OTC	Overseas Trade Corporation; over-the-counter (market)
OtN	order to negotiate
o.t.o.r.	on truck or railway
o.w.h.	ordinary working hours
oz(s).	ounce(s)

P

P.	Pacific Reporter; (car) park; pedestrian *(crossing);* Probate Division *(Law Reports)*
p.	page; paid; (new) penny; person
P.A.	particular average; Patents Act; Personal Assistant; power of attorney; Press Attaché; Press Association; Public Accountant; public address
P/A.	power of attorney; private account
Pa.	Pennsylvania *(Staat der USA);* Pennsylvania State Reports
p.a.	yearly *(per annum)*
PAA	Pan-American World Airways
PABX	private automatic branch exchange
PAC	Pan-American Congress; perishable agricultural commodities
Pac.	Pacific Reporter; put and call
Pac. 2d	Pacific Reporter, Second Series
p.a.c.	put and call
Pan-Am.	Pan-American World Airways
P.&I.	protection and indemnity
P.&L.	profit and loss
P.&L. A/c.	profit and loss account
Panhonlib	Panama, Honduras, and Liberia
par.	paragraph; parish
Para.	Paraguay(an)
Parl.	Parliament(ary)
Parl.S.	Parliamentary Secretary
part.	participating
part.pref.	participating preference shares
Pa. Super	Pennsylvania Superior Court
patd	patented
Pat. Off.	Patent Office
P.A.U.	Pan American Union
P.A.X.	private automatic (telephone) exchange
PAYE	Pay-As-You-Earn (Income Tax, Schedule E)
payt, paymt	payment
P.B.	Prayer Book; British Pharmacopoeia *(Pharmacopoeia Britannica)*
PBGC	Pension Benefit Guaranty Corporation
PC	personal computer
P.C.	Parish Concil(lor); Patent Cases; petty cash; Police Constable; prices current; Privy Council(lor); Public Company
p.c., pc.	per cent
PCIJ	Permanent Court of International Justice
pcl	parcel
PCNB	Permanent Central Narcotics Board
PCOB	Permanent Central Opium Board
PCT	Patent Cooperation Treaty
P.D.	Police Department; Postal District; Probate Division *(Law Reports)*
p.d.	by the day *(per diem);* port dues
pd	paid
P.E., p.e.	probable error
P/E	price/earnings (ratio)
PEFCO	Private Export Funding Corporation
P.E.N., PEN	(International Association of) Poets, Playwrights, Editors, Essayists, and Novelists

Penn(a).	Pennsylvania *(Staat der USA)*
P.E.R.; P/E ratio	price-earnings ratio
per an.	yearly *(per annum)*
per cur.	by the court *(per curiam)*
perks	perquisites
per pro(c).	by proxy *(per procurationem)*
pers.	person(s)
PERT	Programme Evaluation and Review Technique
pet.	petitioner
pf (or pfd)	preferred (or preference) shares or stock
pf. (or pfd) ord.	preferred ordinary shares
P.G.	German Pharmacopoeia *(Pharmacopoeia Germanica);* Paying Guest
P.H.A.	Public Housing Administration
Ph.D.	Philosophiae Doctor *(Doctor of Philosophy)*
Ph.D., D.B.A.	Doctor of Philosophy in Business Administration
P.H.S.	Public Health Service
P & I	protection and indemnity
PIN	personal identification number
pk(g)	package
pkt	packet
P.L.	Public Law
P/L, P & L	profit and loss
P.L.A.	Port of London Authority
PLC, plc	public limited company
Plen.	Plenipotentiary
pltf.	Plaintiff
P.L.O.	Palestinian Liberation Organization
P.M.	Paymaster; Police Magistrate; Postmaster; Prime Minister; Provost Marshal
p.m.	afternoon *(post meridiem);* after death *(post mortem)*
PMD	Program for Management Development
P.M.G.	Paymaster-General; Postmaster-General; Provost Marshal General
p.m.h.	production per man-hour
PMLA	Publication of the Modern Language Association (of America)
PMTS	Predetermined Motion Time System
P/N., p.n.	promissory note
P.N.E.U.	Parents' National Educational Union
PNYA	Port of New York Authority
P.O.	Patent Office; Petty Officer; Pilot Officer; postal order; Post Office
P.O.B.	Post Office Box
p.o.c.	port of call
P.O.D.	pay on delivery; Post Office Department
Pol.Econ.	political economy
pol(it).	political; politics
P.O.O.	post office order
P.O.R.	payable on receipt
POS	point of sale system
P.O.S.B.	Post Office Savings Bank
POW	prisoner of war
P.P.	parcel post; Parish Priest
p.p.	parcel post; by proxy *(per procuration[em])*
PPBS	planning-programming-budgeting system
ppd	prepaid
P.P.R.	Polish People's Republic
P.P.S.	Parliamentary Private Secretary
P.Q.	Political Quarterly; Province of Quebec
P.Q.'s	Parliamentary Questions
P.R.	proportional representation; public relations; Puerto Rico
PR	Press Release; payroll
PrC	private company
Prec. Ch.	Precedents in Chancery

Pref.	Preface
pref., prefs	preferred (or preference) shares (or stock)
prefab.	prefabricated
Pres.	President
Press	press telegram
prev.	previous(ly)
prm	premium
P.R.O.	Public Record Office; Public Relations Officer
Pro.Am.Soc. Int.L.	Proceedings of American Society of International Law
Proc.	Proctor
proc.	proceedings; procuration
prop.	property
pro quer.	for the plaintiff *(pro querente)*
pro tem.	for the time being *(pro tempore)*
Prov.	Province; Provost
prox.	next month *(proximo)*
P.R.S.	Performing Right Society
P.R.S.A.	Public Relations Society of America
p.r.t.	pro rata temporis; petroleum revenue tax
Pru.	Prudential Assurance Company
P.S.	Parliamentary Secretary; Permanent Secretary; postscript(um); private secretary
PSBR	Public Sector Borrowing Requirement
P.S.C.	Public Service Commission
psd	*(Shipping News)* passed
P.SS.	postscripta
P.S.T.	Pacific Standard Time
P.S.V.	public service vehicle
P.T.	physical training; Public Trustee
PTIA	Protection of Trading Interests Act
ptly pd	partly paid
PTO	Patent and Trademark Office; please turn over
P.U.	Public Utilities
pub	public house
pub.	public; published; publisher; publishing
Pub.Adm.Rev.	Public Administration Review
Pub.Doc.	Public Documents
P.U.C.	Public Utilities Commission
P.U.D.	Public Utility District
PUF	prime underwriting facility
P.U.H.C.A.	Public Utility Holding Company Act
P.U.R.	Public Utility Reports
P.U.S.	Parliamentary Under-Secretary; Pharmacopoeia of the United States
P.W.	prisoner of war
P.W.A.	Public Works Administration
P.W.D.	Public Works Department
PWLB	Public Works Loan Board
pwt.	pennyweight
PX	Post Exchange

Q

Q.	Quebec; Queen('s); Question; Quotient
q.	quarter; query
Q.A.B.	Queen Anne's Bounty
Q.B.	Queen's Bench Division *(Law Reports)*
Q.B.D.	Queen's Bench Division
Q.C.	Queen's Counsel

q.c.f.	quare clausum fregit *(wherefore he broke the clause)*
q.d.	as if he should say *(quasi dicat)*
q.e.	which is *(quod est)*
Q.E.D.	which was to be proved *(quod erat demonstrandum)*
Q.J.P.R.	Queensland Justice of the Peace Reports
Q.L.R.	Queensland Law Reporter
Q.M.	Quartermaster
Q.M.G.	Quartermaster-General
Q.N.S.	Quantity not Sufficient
Q.R.	Quarterly Review
Q.R.S.C.	Quebec Reports, Superior Court
Q.S.	Quarter Sessions
Q.S.R.	Queensland State Reports
Quar.L.R.	Quarterly Law Review
q.v.	which see *(quod vide)*

R

R.	Queen *(Regina)*; Registered; King *(Rex)*; Royal; Rupee(s)
RA	resident alien
R.A.	Regular Army; Royal Academician; Royal Academy
R.A.A.	Royal Academy of Arts
R.A.C.	Royal Automobile Club
R.A.C.A.	Royal Automobile Club of Australia
RADAR	radio detection and ranging
RADWAR	radiological warfare
R.A.F.(V.R.)	Royal Air Force (Volunteer Reserve)
r.&c.c.	riots and civil commotions
R.&D.	research and development
R.A.S.	Royal Aeronautical Society; Royal Agricultural Society
R.B.N.	Registry of Business Names
R.C.	Red Cross; Research Centre; Roman Catholic; Royal College; Royal Commission
R.C.A.	Radio Corporation of America; Royal College of Art
r.c.c.&s.	riots, civil commotions and strike
R.C.L.	Ruling Case Law
RCRA	Resource Conservation and Recovery Act of 1980
R.C.S.	Royal College of Science
R/D	refer to drawer
Rd	road
R & D	Research and Development
R.D.C.	Research and Documentation Centre; running down clause
re	in the matter of
recd	received
ref.	refer; reference; referred; refused
Reg.	Queen *(Regina)*; Register; Registrar; Registry; Regulation
regd	registered
Reg.-Gen.	Registrar-General
Reg. T.M.	registered trade mark
reg. tn	register ton
REIF	revolving Euronote issuance facility
REIT	real estate investment trust
rel.	relating; relative(ly); religion
rep.	report(s); reporter
Rep.Att.Gen.	Reports of the Attorney General
repo	repurchase agreement
Rep. Pat. Cas.	Reports of Patent Cases
Repub.	Republic(an)
Resp.	respondent

resp.	respective(ly)
Rev.	Reverend
Rev.Ed.	Revised Edition
Rev.Rul.	Revenue Ruling
Rev.St(at).	Revised Statutes
rgd	registered
R.H.	Royal Highness
R.I.	Rhode Island *(Staat der USA);* Reinsurance; Rotary International; Royal Institute
R.I.B.A.	Royal Institute of British Architects
RIE	Recognized Investment Exchange
R.I.I.A.	Reports of International Arbitral Awards; Royal Institute of International Affairs
R.L.O.	Returned Letter Office
R.M.	Royal Mail; Royal Marines
RMBCA	Revised Model Business Corporation Act
R.M.S.	Royal Mail Steamer; Royal Medical Society
R.N.	registered nurse; Royal Navy
ROCE	return on capital employed
ROI, RoI	return(s) on investment
RoR	Rule of Reason; rate of return
Rospa	Royal Society for the Prevention of Accidents
R.O.T.C.	Reserve Officers' Training Corps
RP	repurchase agreement
R.P.	Regius Professor; reply paid *(telegram)*
R.P.C.	Reports of Patent (Design, Trademark, and other) Cases; Restrictive Practices Court
R.P.D.	Doctor of Political Science *(Rerum Politicarum Doctor)*
RPI	Retail Price Index
RPM	resale price maintencance
R.R.	Revised Reports; Right Reverend
R.R.C.	Reports of Rating Cases; (Lady of the) Royal Red Cross
R.S.	Revised Statutes; Royal Society
Rs	rupees
R.S.A.	Royal Scottish Academy; Royal Society of Arts
RSC	Rules of the Supreme Court (Revision) 1965; Revised Statutes of Canada
RSG	Rate Support Grant (to local authorities)
R.S.P.C.A.	Royal Society for the Prevention of Cruelty to Animals
R.S.S.	Fellow of the Royal Society *(Regiae Societatis Socius)*
R.S.V.P.	please reply *(répondez s'il vous plaît)*
R.T.	radio telegraphy; radio telephony; rye terms
R.T.A.	Road Traffic Act
R.T.A.A.	Reciprocal Trade Agreements Act
R & TD	research and technological development
Rt Hon.	Right Honourable
R.T.P.A.	Restrictive Trade Practices Act
R.T.R.A.	Radio and Television Retailers' Association
Rt Rev.	Right Reverend
RTT	radio teletyper
RUC	Royal Ulster Constabulary
RUF	revolving underwriting facility
R.V.	rat(e)able value
R.V.O.	Royal Victorian Order
R. & V.R.	Rating and Valuation Reports

S

S.	Seller; Senate (bill); South(ern); Southern Reporter
s.	section; see; shilling(s)

S.A.	Salvation Army; Securities Act; semi-annual; South Africa; South America; South Australia; Statutes Annotated; société anonyme (French, Belgian, Luxembourg or Swiss public company)
S.A.B.C.	South African Broadcasting Corporation
S.A.C.	Scottish Automobile Club
SACEUR	Supreme Allied Commander Europe
SACLANT	Supreme Allied Commander Atlantic
SAD	Single Administrative Document
S.A.E., s.a.e.	stamped addressed envelope
SAF	structural adjustment facility
S.A.L.J.	South African Law Journal
S.A.L.R.	South African Law Reports
SALT	Strategic Arms Limitation Talks
Salv.	Salvador
S.Am.	South-America(n)
Sam(s)	surface-to-air missile(s)
S.&F.A.	Shipping and Forwarding Agents
s.&h.c.	sundays and holidays excepted
SAPA	South African Press Association
SARs	stock appreciation rights
S.A.S.	Scandinavian Airlines System
S.A.S.R.	South Australian State Reports
S.Aus.	South Australia
SAYE	save as you earn
SB	Supplementary Benefit
S.B.	sales book; Savings Bank; Bachelor of Science *(Scientiae Baccalaureus)*
SBA	Small Business Administration
S.B.Comm.	Bachelor of Science in Commerce
SBIA	Small Business Investment Act
S.B.I.C.	Small Business Investment Companies
S.C.	Salvage Charges; same case; Session Cases; South Carolina *(Staat der USA)*; Supreme Court; Supreme Court Reporter
SC	Security Council *(UN)*
sc.	namely *(scilicet)*
SCAN	Stock Market Computer Answering Network
Sc.&T.	Science and Technology
SCAPA	Society for Checking the Abuses of Public Advertising
Sc.B.	Bachelor of Science *(→S.B.)*
Sc.D.	Doctor of Science *(scientiae doctor)*
S.C.(H.L.)	Session Cases (House of Lords)
sched.	schedule
S.C.L.Q.	South Carolina Law Quarterly
sci.fa.	please make known *(scire facias)*
scil.	namely *(scilicet)*
S.C.J.	Supreme Court of Judicature
S.C.(J.)	Session Cases (High Court of Judiciary)
S.Con.Res.	Senate concurrent resolution
Scot.	Scotland; Scotsman; Scottish
Scot.L.R.	Scottish Law Reports
Scot.L.Rev.	Scottish Law Review
S.Ct.	Supreme Court Reporter
S.D.	Doctor of Science *(Scientiae Doctor)*, South Dakota *(Staat der USA)*; State Department
S/D.	sea-damaged
s.d.	several dates; sight draft; without day *(sine die)*
S.Dak.	South Dakota *(Staat der USA)*
SDI	Strategic Defense Iniative; State Disability Insurance
S.D.N.Y.	Southern District New York
SDP	Social Democratic Party
SDR	Special Drawing Right
S.E.	South-Eastern; South Eastern Reporter; stock exchange

S.E.2d	South Eastern Reporter, Second Series
SEA	Securities Exchange Act
S.E.A.O.	save error and omission
SEAQ	Stock Exchange Automated Quotation System
SEATO	South East Asia Treaty Organization
SEC	Securities and Exchange Commission
sec., secs.	section, sections
Sec.C., Off.Rec.	Security Council, Official Records
SEMBs	Stock Exchange Money Brokers
Sen.	Senate; Senator; Senior
Senr.	Senior
seq.	the following *(sequens)*
seqq.	the following *(sequentes, sequentia)*
SERPS	State Earnings-Related Pension Scheme
Sess. cas.	Session cases
SFAS	statement of financial accounting standards
SFES	small firms employment subsidies
SFR	Swiss franc
S.G.	for the sake of safety *(salutis gratia);* Solicitor-General
SGA	Sale of Goods Act
sgd	signed
s.g.d.g.	without government guarantee *(sans garantie du gouvernement)*
SHAPE	Supreme Headquarters of the Allied Powers in Europe
shex	sundays and holidays excepted
shipt	shipment
S.I.	Statutory Instrument
SIA	Securities Industry Association
SIB	Securities and Investments Board
SIC	Standard Industrial Classification
SIF	stock-index futures
sig.miss.	signature missing
SIPC	Securities Investor Protection Corporation
SIT	State Income Tax
SITA	Students' International Travel Association
SITC	Standard International Trade Classification
S.I.U.	Seamen's International Union
S.J.	Solicitors' Journal
S.J.D.	Doctor of Juridical Science *(Scientiae Juridicae Doctor)*
S.J.Res.	Senate joint resolution
S & L	savings and loan association
S.L.A.D.E.	Society of Lithographic Artists, Designers, Engravers, and Process Workers
SLBM	Submarine Launched Ballistic Missile
S/L.C.	sue and labour clause
SLCM	sea-launched cruise missile
S.L.G.	Scottish Law Gazette
s.l.p.	without lawful issue *(sine legitima prole)*
S.L.R.	Scottish Land Reports
S.L.Rev.	Scottish Law Review
S.L.T.	Scots Law Times
S.L.T. (Land Ct.)	Scots Law Times Land Court Report
S.L.T. (Notes)	Scots Law Times Notes of Recent Decisions
S.M.	Master of Science *(Scientiae Magister);* Stipendiary Magistrate
SMEs	small and medium-sized enterprises
s.m.p.	without male issue *(sine mascula prole)*
S.N., S/N	shipping note
SNG	synthetic natural gas
S.N.P.	Scottish National Party
Soc., soc.	society
So. Calif.L.Rev.	Southern California Law Review
SOFFEX	Swiss Options and Financial Futures Exchange

Sol.	Solicitor
SOLAS	International Convention for the Safety of Life at Sea
Sol.-Gen.	Solicitor-General
S.P.	Shore Patrol; *(bills of exchange)* supra protest
s.p.	without issue *(sine prole)*
SPADATS	Space Detection and Tracking System
S.P.C.A.	Society for Prevention of Cruelty to Animals
sq.	square
sq.ft.	square foot (feet)
sq.in(s)	square inch(es)
sq.m.	square mile(s)
sq(q)	the following *(sequentes, sequentia)*
S.R.B.M.	Short Range Ballistic Missile
S.R.C.C.	strike, riots, and civil commotions
S.Res.	Senate Resolution
SRINF	shorter range INF
S.R. (N.S.W.)	State Reports, New South Wales
SRO	Self-Regulating Organization
S.R.&O.	Statutory Rules and Orders
S.R.S.	Fellow of the Royal Society *(Societatis Regiae Socius)*
S.S.	Social Security; Standard Size; steamship
ss.	sections; signum sigilli; steamship
SSA	Social Security Administration
SSAP	Statement of Standard Accounting Practice
s/s, s.s.	steamship
S.S.C.	Solicitor to the Supreme Court
SSI	Supplemental Security Income
S.S.M.	Surface to Surface Missile
S.S.S.	Selective Service System
S.T.	Standard Time; Summer Time
Stabex	System for the stabilization of ACP and OCT export earnings
Stan.L.Rev.	Stanford Law Review
STANY	Securities Traders Association of New York
STAR	Satellites for Telecommunications
START	Strategic Arms Reduction Talks
Stat.	Statute(s); Statute(s) at Large
Stat.Hall.	Stationers' Hall
St. Ex., St. Exch.	Stock Exchange
stg.	sterling
StIA	State Immunity Act
STOL	short take-off and landing (aircraft)
Str.	street
S.T.U.C.	Scottish Trades Union Congress
SUB	supplementary unemployment benefits
Suff.	Suffolk
SUI	State Unemployment Insurance
S.U.N.F.E.D.	Special United Nations Fund for Economic Development
sup.	above *(supra)*
Sup. Ct.	Supreme Court; Supreme Court Reporter
Super Ct.	Superior Court
supp., suppl.	supplement(ary)
supr.	supreme
Supt	Superintendent
Sur.	Surrey
Surr. Ct.	Surrogate's Court
Suss.	Sussex
S.W.	South Wales; South West(ern); South Western Reporter
S.W.2d	South Western Reporter, 2d series
Swapo	South West African People's Organization
SWIFT	Society for Worldwide Interbank Financial Telecommunication

S.W.L.J.	South Western Law Journal
Sx.	Sussex

T

t.	ton(s)
T.A.	telegraphic address; Translators' Association; Trustee Act
Ta	tare
TAA	Technical Assistance Administration; Transaustralia Air Lines
T.A.B.	Technical Assistance Board
TACs	total allowable catches
TAMRA	Technical and Miscellaneous Revenue Act
TAP	Transarabian Pipeline
Tax Cas.	Tax Cases
Tax L.Rev.	Tax Law Review
Tax Mag.	Tax Magazine
T.B.	Treasury Bill; Trial Balance
T.B., t.b.	trial balance
T.C.	Tax Cases; Tax Court; Town Council(lor); Trusteeship Council
T.D.	Treasury Decisions; Treasury Department
T.D.B.	total disability benefit
TDF	transborder data flow
TDO	Table of Denial Orders
tdw.	tons deadweight
T.E.A.	Trade Expansion Act; Trading with the Enemy Act
TEE	Trans-Europe Express
TEFRA	Tax Equity and Fiscal Responsibility Act
tel.	telegram; telegraph(ic); telephone
teleg.	telegram; telegraphy
Tel.No.	Telephone Number
Temple L.Q.	Temple Law Quarterly
Tenn.	Tennessee *(Staat der USA)*
Tenn.L.Rev.	Tennessee Law Review
Tex.	Texas *(Staat der USA)*
Tex.L.Rev.	Texas Law Review
T/F	technological forecasting
T.G.W.U.	Transport and General Workers' Union
Thro.B.L.	Through Bill of Lading
TIAS	Treaties and other International Acts Series
TICs	transferable loan certificates
TIGRs	Treasury Investment Growth Receipts
T.I.M.S., TIMS	The Institute of Management Sciences
TIR	international road transport *(Transport International Routier)*
T.L., t.l.	time loan; total loss
T.L.O., t.l.o.	total loss only
T.L.R.	Times Law Reports
TM	multiple (address) telegram *(télégramme [à adresses] multiples)*
TMA	Trade Marks Act 1938
T.M.O.	telegraph(ic) money order
TMVA	(National) Traffic and Motor Vehicle Safety Act 1966
tn	ton(s)
TNC	transntional corporation
TNE	transnational enterprise
tns	tons
T.O.	telegraph office; telegraphic order; transport officer; turn over
TOB	take-over bid
TOEFL	Test of English as a Foreign Language
TOFC	trailer-on-float-car transport
tonn.	tonnage

ToP	terms of payment
ToT	terms of trade
T.Q., t/q.	tale quale
T.R.	Taxation Reports; Term Reports; Trust Receipt
TR.	telegram to be called for *(télégramme adressé télégraphe restant)*
TRA	Tax Reform Act
Treas.	Treasurer; Treasury
Treas. Bds	Treasury Bonds
Treas.Reg.	Tresury Regulations
Trib.	Tribunal
TRO	temporary restraining order
TRT	Trademark Registration Treaty
T.S.	time-sharing; Treasury-Solicitor; Treaty Series
ts	tons
T.S.B.	Trustee Savings Bank
T.S.C.A.	Toxic Substances Control Act
TSUS	Tariff Schedules of the United States
T.T.	telegraphic transfer; teletypewriter
T.U.	Trade Union
T.U.A.C.	Trade Unions Advisory Committee (to O.E.C.D.)
TUC	Trades Union Congress
T.V.	television (set)
T.W.A.	Trans-World Airlines
T.W.I.	Training within Industry
T.W.U.(A).	Transport Workers' Union (of America)

U

U.	universal; University; Utah *(Staat der USA)*
UA, u. a.	Unit of Account
U.C.	University College; Upper Canada
UCC	Uniform Commercial Code
u. c. e.	unforeseen circumstances excluded
U.Chi.L.Rev.	University of Chicago Law Review
Ucits	undertakings for collective investment in transferable securities
UCP	Uniform Customs and Practice for Documentary Credits
UCSA	Uniform Conditional Sales Act
UDR	Ulster Defence Regiment
U.F.C.	United Free Church (of Scotland)
UFCA	Uniform Fraudulent Conveyance Act
UFCT	United Federation of College Teachers
UFI	Union of International Fairs *(Union des foires internationales)*
UFO	Unidentified Flying Object(s)
UGC	University Grants Committee
U.I.	Unemployment Insurance
u.i.	as below *(ut infra)*
U.I.C.	International Union of Railways *(Union internationale des chemins de fer)*
U.I.C.C.	International Union against Cancer *(Union internationale contre le cancer)*
U.J.D.	Doctor of Civil and Canon Law *(Utriusque Juris Doctor)*
U.K.	United Kingdom (of Great Britain and Northern Ireland)
U.K.A.E.A.	United Kingdom Atomic Energy Authority
U.K./C. U.K. or Cont.	United Kingdom or Continent of Europe
U.K.H.A.D.	United Kingdom, Havre, Antwerp, or Dunkirk
Ukr.	Ukraine
U.L.A.	Uniform Laws Annotated
ULCC	ultra large crude carrier
ULMS	undersea long-range missile system
ULPA	Uniform Limited Partnership Act

ult.	in the preceding month *(ultimo)*
u/m	undermentioned
U.Miami L.Rev.	University of Miami Law Review
UMS	Universal Maintenance Standards
U.M.T.	Universal Military Training
UN	United Nations
UNAEC	United Nations Atomic Energy Commission
UNCITRAL	United Nations Commission on International Trade Law
UNCLOS	UN Conference on the Law of the Sea
UNCTAD	United Nations Conference on Trade and Development
UNCTC	United Nations Centre on Transnational Corporations
UN Doc.	United Nations Documents; Documents issued by the United Nations
UN Doc.A.	United Nations Documents General Assembly
UN Doc. E.	United Nations Documents Economic and Social Council
UN Doc. S.	United Nations Documents Security Council
UN Doc. ST	United Nations Documents Secretariat
UN Doc. T.	United Nations Documents Trusteeship Council
UNDP	United Nations Development Programme
UNDRO	United Nations Disaster Relief Organization
UNEF	United Nations Emergency Force
UNEP	United Nations Environment Programme
UNESCO	United Nations Educational, Scientific, and Cultural Organization
UNFPA	United Nations Fund for Population Activities
UNGA	United Nations General Assembly
UNHCR	United Nations High Commissioner for Refugees
UNHQ	United Nations Headquarters
UNIC	United Nations Information Centre
UNICEF	United Nations International Children's Emergency Fund
UNIDO	United Nations Industrial Development Organization
UNIDROIT	International Institute for the Unification of Private Law *(Institut international pour l'unification du droit privé)*
UNIL	Uniform Negotiable Instruments Law
unm.	unmarried
UNO	United Nations Organization
UNRWA	United Nations Relief and Works Agency (for Palestine Refugees)
UNSC	United States Security Council
UNTA(A)	United Nations Technical Assistance (Administration)
UN-tag	United Nations Transition Assistance Group
U.N.T.C.	United Nations Trusteeship Council
U.N.T.S.	United Nations Treaty Series
UNYB	United Nations Yearbook
UOTAA	Universal Organization of Travel Agents Associations (in Montreal)
UPA	Uniform Partnership Act
U.Pa.L.Rev.	University of Pennsylvania Law Review
UPC	Universal Postal Convention; universal product code
UPI	United Press International
UPLA	Uniform Product Liability Act
UPU	Universal Postal Union
UR	under the rule
URESA	Uniform Reciprocal Enforcement of Support Act
Uru.	Uruguay
U.S.	United States; United States Supreme Court Reports
u.s.	as above *(up supra)*
USA	Uniform Sales Act; United States Army; United States (of America)
U.S.A.E.C.	United States Atomic Energy Commission
U.S.A.F.	United States Air Force
USAID	US Agency for International Development
USAREUR	United States Army, Europe
U.S.C.	United States Code; University of Southern California
U.S.C.A.	United States Code Annotated
U.S.C.C.	United States Circuit Court

U.S.C.C.A.	United States Circuit Court of Appeals
U.S.C.C.P.A.	United States Court of Customs and Patent Appeals
U.S.C.G.	United States Coast Guard
U.S.C.Supp.	United States Code Supplement
U.S.Ct.Cl.	United States Court of Claims Reports
USD	United States dollar
USES	United States Employment Service
U.S.F.	United States Forces
U.S.G.	United States Government
U.S.I.S.	United States Information Service
U.S.L.Ed.	United States Report (Lawyers Edition)
U.S.L.Rev.	United States Law Review
U.S.L.Week	United States Law Week
U.S.M.	United States Mail; United States Marines; Unlisted Securities Market
U.S.M.C.	United States Maritime Commission
U.S.N.	United States Navy
U.S.N.C.	United States National Guard
U.S.N.F.	United States Naval Reserve
USP	unique selling proposition
U.S.P(at).	United States Patent
U.S.P(har).	United States Pharmacopoeia
U.S.P.Q.	United States Patent Quarterly
U.S.S.	United States Senate; United States Ship (or Steamer)
U.S.S.C.	United States Supreme Court
USSR	Union of Soviet Socialist Republics
U.S.Supr.Ct.Dig.	Digest of United States Supreme Court Reports
USTR	US Trade Representative
Ut.	Utah *(Staat der USA)*
UT(M)	Unitary Taxation (Method)
UTO	Universal Tourism Organization
U.Toronto L.J.	University of Toronto Law Journal
u.u.r.	under (the) usual reserve
U/w	underwriter
UWRA	Uniform Warehouse Receipts Act

V

v.	against *(versus)*; see *(vide)*
V/A	voucher attached
Va.	Virginia *(Staat der USA)*
Va.L.Rev.	Virginia Law Review
VAT	value added tax
V.C.	Vice-Chairman; Vice-Chancellor; Vice-Consul; Victoria Cross
V.D.	Venereal Disease
VDU	visual display unit
V.E. day	Victory in Europe Day *(8. 5. 1945)*
Venez.	Venezuela
VER	voluntary export restraint
Vet. Admin.	Veterans' Administration
VFR	Visual Flight Rules
V.F.W.	Veterans of Foreign Wars
V.I.	Virgin Islands
vid.	see *(vide)*
V.I.P.	Very Important Person
Vis(c).	Viscount
viz.	namely *(videlicet)*
V.J.day	Victory in Japan day *(Br 15. 8. 1945; Am 2. 9. 1945)*
V.O.A.	Voice of America
vol.	volume

vols	volumes
V.P.	Vice-President
VRA	voluntary restraint agreement
V.S.	Veterinary Surgeon
v.s.	see above *(vide supra)*
vs.	against *(versus)*
V.S.O.	Voluntary Service Overseas
Vt.	Vermont *(Staat der USA)*
V.T.C.	voting trust certificate
VTOL	vertical take-off and landing (aircraft)
v.v.	conversely *(vice versa)*

W

W.A.	West Africa; Western Australia; Wills Act
w.a., W.A.	with average
W.A.L.R.	Western Australian Law Reports
WAPOR	World Association for Public Opinion Research
War(w).	Warwickshire
Wash.	Washington *(Staat der USA)*
Wash. L. Rep.	Washington Law Reporter
Wash. L. Rev.	Washington Law Review
Wash.U.L.Q.	Washington University Law Quarterly
WATA	World Association of Travel Agencies
W.B., W/B	waybill
w.b.s.	without benefit of salvage
W.C.A.	Workmen's Compensation Act
W.C.C.	World Council of Churches
W.C. & Ins.Rep.	Workmen's Compensation and Insurance Reports
WCL	World Confederation of Labour
W.C.O.T.P.	World Confederation of Organizations of the Teaching Profession
W.D.	War Department; Works Department; Western District
WDV	written-down value
Weekly L. Bull.	Weekly Law Bulletin
w.e.f.	with effect from
West. Weekly R.	Western Weekly Reports *(Canada)*
W.E.T.	Western European Time
W.E.U.	Western European Union
W.F.P.	World Food Program
W.F.P.A.	World Federation for the Protection of Animals
W.F.S.W.	World Federation of Scientific Workers
W.F.T.U.	World Federation of Trade Unions
w.g.	weight guaranteed
W.H.O.	World Health Organization
W.I.	West Indies
w.i.	when issued *(stocks)*
wing	warrants into negotiable Government securities
WIP	work in process
WIPO	World Intellectual Property Organization
Wis(c).	Wisconsin *(Staat der USA)*
Wis.L.Rev.	Wisconsin Law Review
W.J.C.	World Jewish Congress
WLR	Weekly Law Reports *(seit 1953)*
W.M.A.	World Medical Association
W.M.O.	World Meteorological Organization
W.N. (N.S.W.)	Weekly Notes, New South Wales
Women Law J.	Women Lawyers Journal
Worc.	Worcestershire
W.P., w.p.	weather permitting
w.p., w/p.	without prejudice

W.P.A., w.p.a.	with particular average
WPI	Wholesale Price Index
w.p.m.	words per minute
W.R.	Weekly Reporter
W/R	warehouse receipt
WRI	War Resisters' International
W.S.	writer to the signet
W.T., W/T	wireless telegraphy; wireless telephony
W.T.O.	Warsaw Treaty Organization; World Tourism Organization
W.Va.	West Virginia *(Staat der USA)*
W/W	warehouse warrant
ww	with warrants
W.W.D.	weather working day(s)
WWF	World Wildlife Fund
W.W.R.	Western Weekly Reports
Wy(o).	Wyoming *(Staat der USA)*
Wyo.L.J.	Wyoming Law Journal

X

x	ex(cluding) dividend
xd., xdiv.	not including right to dividend *(ex dividend)*
x.i., x.int.	not including right to next interest *(ex interest)*
x.mill	ex mill
x.n.	not including right to new shares *(ex new [shares])*
x.roads	cross roads
x.rts.	without rights *(→right 2.)*
x.ship	ex ship
xw	without warrants
x.whse	ex warehouse
x.wks	ex works

Y

Y	yen
Y/A.	York-Antwerp (Rules)
Yale L.J.	Yale Law Journal
Y.A.R., YAR	York-Antwerp Rules
Y.B.	Year Book
YBHR	Yearbook of Human Rights
YBILC	Yearbook of the International Law Commission
Y.C.W.	(International) Young Christian Workers
yd(s.)	yard(s)
Y.H.A.	Youth Hostels' Association
Y.M.C.A.	Young Men's Christian Association
Yorks.	Yorkshire
YTS	Youth Training Scheme
Y.W.C.A.	Young Women's Christian Association

Z

ZANU	Zimbabwe African National Union
ZAPO	Zimbabwe African People's Union
ZBB	zero base budgeting
Z.I.P.	Zoning Improvement Plan
Z.P.G.	zero population growth

A

A 1 (first class) erste Klasse, Ware erster Güte; ~ **at Lloyd's** *Br* höchste Klasse e-s im → Lloyd's Register eingetragenen Schiffes

A.B.A. (American Bankers' Association) **Number** *Am* Bankleitzahl

a fortiori (much more; with stronger reason) um so mehr, erst recht

a mensa et thora (from board and bed) *(Trennung)* von Tisch und Bett *(jetzt:* →judicial separation)

a priori (from the cause to the effect) von vornherein

A.R. (Anno Regni) im Jahre der Regierungszeit

a vinculo matrimonii (from the bond of matrimony) *(Trennung)* vom Band der Ehe (*jetzt:* → decree of nullity)

abandon *v (Recht, Plan)* aufgeben, fallenlassen; *(auf etw.)* verzichten; überlassen; verlassen, im Stich lassen; *(SeeversR)* abandonnieren; **to ~ an appeal** e-e Berufung (od. Beschwerde) zurücknehmen; **to ~ an application** *(PatR)* e-e Anmeldung fallen lassen (od. aufgeben); **to ~ an attempt** *(StrafR)* vom Versuch zurücktreten; **to ~ the defen|ce (~se)** die Vertretung des Beklagten niederlegen; **to ~ one's → domicile; to ~ an enterprise** ein Unternehmen aufgeben; **to ~ an invention** *(PatR)* e-e Erfindung fallen lassen; **to ~ an option** e-e Option aufgeben (od. nicht ausüben); **to ~ possession** den Besitz aufgeben; **to ~ a (damaged) ship to the underwriter** ein (beschädigtes) Schiff dem Versicherer überlassen *(gegen Empfang der Versicherungssumme)*

abandonee *(SeeversR)* Versicherer, dem das *(beschädigte)* Schiff überlassen ist

abandonment Abandon; (Rechts-)Aufgabe *(Aufgabe e-s Rechts zur Entlastung von e-r damit verbundenen Pflicht);* Preisgabe; Verzicht(leistung); Verlassen, Imstichlassen; *(StrafR)* Rücktritt; *(VölkerR)* Dereliktion (→*dereliction*); **notice of ~** Abandonerklärung; **~ of action** Klagerücknahme; **~ of (the) appeal** Zurücknahme der Berufung (od. Beschwerde); **~ of an attempt** *(StrafR)* Rücktritt vom Versuch; **~ of a business** Geschäftsaufgabe; **~ of a child (young person)** Aussetzung e-s Kindes (e-r jugendlichen Person); **~ clause** Abandonklausel; **~ of condemnation** *Am* Abbruch des Enteignungsverfahrens; **~ of domicile** Aufgabe des Wohnsitzes (→*domicile*); **~ of an invention** *(PatR)* Fallenlassen e-r Erfindung; **~ of the option** Aufgabe (od. Nichtausübung, Verfallenlassen) der Option; **~ of a trade mark**[1] Aufgabe e-s Warenzeichens

abate *v (Preise, Steuern)* herabsetzen, ermäßigen; sich mindern; abschaffen; beseitigen; streichen; niederschlagen; *(Gerichtsverfahren)* einstellen *(z.B. wegen Formfehlers); (Ansprüche, Vermächtnisse) (verhältnismäßig)* kürzen (od. streichen) *(bei nicht ausreichender Masse);* **to ~ a fee** e-e Gebühr niederschlagen; e-e Gebühr ermäßigen; **to ~ a nuisance** e-e Störung beseitigen (od. abstellen); **to ~ the purchase price** den Kaufpreis herabsetzen; mindern

abatement (Preis-, Steuer-)Nachlaß, Herabsetzung, Ermäßigung; Streichung; Niederschlagung; Rabatt *(bei Barzahlung);* Abschaffung, Beseitigung; **~ of action** Einstellung des Gerichtsverfahrens; **~ of a fee** Niederschlagung e-r Gebühr; Gebührenermäßigung; **~ of a legacy** *(verhältnismäßige)* Kürzung (od. Streichung) e-s Vermächtnisses *(bei nicht ausreichender Erbmasse);* **~ of nuisance** Beseitigung der Störung *(durch Klage od. Selbsthilfe);* **~ of purchase-money** Herabsetzung des Kaufpreises; Minderung

abatement, claim for ~ Beseitigungsanspruch; **plea in ~**[2] *(peremptorische)* prozessuale Einrede; **tax ~** Herabsetzung der Steuer; Steuernachlaß; **to allow** (or **make**) **an ~** e-n Nachlaß gewähren

ABC weapons ABC Waffen (*atomic, bacteriological and chemical weapons*)

abdicate *v* abdanken; **to ~ the throne** auf den Thron verzichten

abdication Abdankung; **~ of responsibility** Ablehnung der Verantwortung; **~ of the throne** Thronverzicht; **instrument of ~** Abdankungsurkunde

abduct *v* entführen

abduction Entführung; Menschenraub

abet *v (StrafR)* Beihilfe leisten; Vorschub leisten *(meist to aid and ~)*

abetment *(StrafR)* Beihilfe; Vorschub

abettor (*Am* auch **abetter**) *(StrafR)* Gehilfe; Mittäter *(bei Begehung der strafbaren Handlung zugegen; cf. accessory)*

abeyance Schwebezustand; **in ~** unentschieden, in der Schwebe; **to hold a decision in ~** (sich) e-e Entscheidung vorbehalten

abide *v* bleiben; abwarten, warten auf; wohnen *(with sb. bei jdm; at, in in);* **to ~ by** festhalten an, sich abfinden mit; **to ~ by an agreement** sich an e-n Vertrag halten, e-n Vertrag einhalten; **to ~ by an arbitral award** e-n Schiedsspruch befolgen; **to ~ by a decision** e-e Entscheidung befolgen; sich mit e-r Entscheidung abfinden; **I ~ by what I have said** ich bleibe bei meiner Aussage
abiding, law ~ die Gesetze befolgend; friedlich, ordnungsliebend

abilit|y Fähigkeit, Befähigung; **~ies** Fähigkeiten, geistige Anlagen; **~ to pay** Zahlungsfähigkeit, Solvenz; **~ to work** Arbeitsfähigkeit; **proof of ~** Befähigungsnachweis; **to the best of one's ~** nach bestem Können (od. Vermögen)

ab initio von Anfang an; **the contract is void ~** der Vertrag ist nichtig ex tunc

ab intestato *Am* von e-m ohne Testament Verstorbenen (erben) *(from a person who has died intestate);* **~ heir** Intestaterbe

abjure *v* abschwören; unter Eid versprechen, zu verzichten

able fähig; tüchtig; **~ to earn** erwerbsfähig; **~ to meet competition** konkurrenzfähig; **~ to pay** zahlungsfähig; **~ to work** arbeitsfähig
able-bodied diensttauglich; wehrfähig; **~ labo(u)r** voll einsatzfähige *(körperlich taugliche)* Arbeitskräfte; **~ seaman** (A. B.) Vollmatrose

ABM-Treaty Raketenabwehrvertrag *(→anti-ballistic missile)*

abode Wohnsitz; Aufenthalt(sort); **without fixed ~** ohne festen Wohnsitz; **habitual (place of) ~** gewöhnlicher Aufenthalt(sort); **permanent ~** ständiger Wohnsitz; **place of ~** Aufenthaltsort; Ort des gewöhnlichen Aufenthalts; **right of ~ in the United Kingdom** Recht des Wohnsitzes im Vereinigten Königreich; **temporary ~** vorübergehender Aufenthaltsort; **to take up one's ~** s-n Wohnsitz begründen, sich niederlassen

abolish *v* abschaffen, aufheben, beseitigen; **to ~ customs duties** Zölle abschaffen (od. aufheben); **to ~ imprisonment for debt** die Schuldhaft abschaffen; **to ~ restrictions** Beschränkungen aufheben *(z.B. nach einem Krieg)*

abolition Abschaffung, Aufhebung, Beseitigung; Niederschlagung *(e-s Strafverfahrens);* **~ of the death sentence** Abschaffung der Todesstrafe; **~ of duties** Abschaffung der Zölle; **~ of provisions** Aufhebung von Bestimmungen; **~ of slavery** Abschaffung der Sklaverei

aborigines Urbewohner, Ureinwohner

abortifacient Abtreibungsmittel

abortion Abtreibung; **justifiable ~** *Am*[3] gerechtfertigte Abtreibung; **unjustified ~** *Am*[4] ungerechtfertigte Abtreibung; **to perform an ~** die Schwangerschaft unterbrechen *(Arzt);* **to secure (an) ~** abtreiben

abortionist jd, der abtreibt; Abtreiber(in)

abortive verfehlt; ergebnislos; **the plans proved ~** die Pläne erwiesen sich als Fehlschlag

abound *v* Überfluß haben *(in an);* im Überfluß haben (od. vorhanden sein)
abounding in fish fischreich *(Gewässer)*

above oben; darüber; **~ (the) average** überdurchschnittlich; **~ the line item** →line 2.; **~ mentioned** (a/m) oben erwähnt; **~ named** oben genannt; **~ par** über pari; über dem Nennwert; **~ party** überparteilich
above, as stated ~ wie oben angeführt (wurde); **those ~ me** meine Vorgesetzten

abreast nebeneinander; **to keep ~** (of or with) *(mit der Wissenschaft etc)* Schritt halten; sich auf dem laufenden halten

abridge *v* (ab)kürzen; *(Recht)* beeinträchtigen, einschränken; **~d edition** gekürzte Ausgabe

abridg(e)ment Abkürzung; gekürzte Fassung, Zusammenfassung; Einschränkung; **~ of a right** Beeinträchtigung (od. Einschränkung) e-s Rechts; **~ of specification** Kurzfassung der Patentschrift

abroad im (ins) Ausland; **at home and ~** im In- und Ausland; **stay ~** Auslandsaufenthalt; **to go ~** ins Ausland gehen (od. fahren)

abrogate *v* abschaffen; abrogieren; *(Gesetz, völkerrechtl. Vertrag)* aufheben, außer Kraft setzen; **to be ~d** außer Kraft treten

abrogation Abschaffung; Abrogation, *(endgültige)* Aufhebung, Außerkraftsetzung *(e-s Gesetzes, e-s völkerrechtl. Vertrages; opp. derogation)*

abscond *v* flüchtig werden, sich entziehen; **to ~ from justice** sich der Festnahme entziehen; **the debtor is about to ~** der Schuldner will flüchten
absconding debtor flüchtiger Schuldner; sich seinen Gläubigern entziehender Schuldner

absence Abwesenheit *(opp. presence);* Fernbleiben, Nichterscheinen *(from in, zu);* Fehlen, Nichtvorhandensein; **~ beyond the seas** *Br* Abwesenheit vom Vereinigten Königreich; **(on) leave of ~** (auf) Urlaub; **~ of consideration** Fehlen der Gegenleistung; **~ from duty** (or **work**) Dienstabwesenheit; **~ without leave** (AWOL) *mil* unerlaubte Entfernung von der Truppe; eigenmächtige Abwesenheit;

~ **without valid excuse** unentschuldigtes Fernbleiben

absence, in the ~ of ohne; in Ermangelung von, mangels; **in the ~ of (an) agreement to the contrary** mangels gegenteiliger Vereinbarung; **in the ~ of evidence** mangels Beweises; **in the ~ of statute** beim Fehlen gesetzlicher Vorschriften; **trial in the ~ of the defendant** Versäumnisverfahren; **to be sentenced in one's ~** in Abwesenheit verurteilt werden

absent *v*, **to ~ oneself** sich *(unerlaubt)* entfernen *(from von)*; **to ~ oneself from work** von der Arbeit fernbleiben

absent abwesend, nicht zugegen *(opp. present)*; ~ **voting** Briefwahl; ~ **with leave** *mil* beurlaubt; ~ **without leave** (AWOL) unerlaubt entfernt; **to be ~ with leave** entschuldigt fehlen; **to be ~ without leave** unentschuldigt fehlen

absentee Abwesender; jd, der nicht zur Arbeit erscheint; ~ **ballot** Briefwahlzettel; ~ **landlord** (or **owner**) nicht auf Gut (od. Grundbesitz) lebender Gutsherr (od. Eigentümer); **~s' list** Abwesenheitsliste; ~ **voter** Briefwähler; ~ **voting** Briefwahl

absenteeism *(häufiges, meist unnötiges)* Fernbleiben *(vom Arbeitsplatz)*; Arbeitsversäumnis, Fehlschichten; ~ **rate** Abwesenheitsrate

absolute absolut, unbeschränkt; endgültig; rechtskräftig; ~ **advantage** *(Außenwirtschaft)* absoluter Kostenvorteil; ~ **bill of sale** *Br* Eigentumsübertragungsurkunde *(für Mobilien)*; ~ **liability** verschuldensunabhängige Haftung, Gefährdungshaftung; ~ **majority** absolute Mehrheit; ~ **→ownership**; ~ **proof** einwandfreier Beweis; ~ **right** absolutes Recht; uneingeschränktes Recht; ~ **title**[5] unbedingtes Eigentum, Volleigentum *(opp. qualified or conditional title)*; **→decree ~; to be ~ly liable** bedingungslos haften *(opp. contingently liable)*; **to become ~** rechtskräftig werden

absolve *v* lossprechen, freisprechen; **to be ~d from (all) liability** von (aller) Verantwortung befreit sein

absorb *v* (in sich) aufnehmen; absorbieren; gänzlich beanspruchen; **to ~ buying power** Kaufkraft abschöpfen; **to ~ losses** Verluste abfangen; **one (existing) company ~s another** e-e (bestehende) Gesellschaft nimmt die andere (in sich) auf *(→merger)*

absorbing, ~ capacity Aufnahmefähigkeit *(des Marktes)*; **capable of ~** aufnahmefähig *(Markt)*

absorption Aufnahme, Absorption; ~ **costing** Vollkostenrechnung; ~ **of buying power** Abschöpfung der Kaufkraft; ~ **of cost** Kostenübernahme; **freight ~** Übernahme der Frachtkosten *(seitens des Verkäufers)*

absorptive capacity of the market Aufnahmefähigkeit des Marktes

abstain *v*, **to ~ from voting** sich der Stimme enthalten

abstention Enthaltung; *(stillschweigender)* Verzicht *(e-s Erben)*; ~ **(from voting)** Stimmenthaltung; **10 votes for, five against and two ~s** 10 Stimmen dafür, 5 Stimmen dagegen und 2 Stimmenthaltungen; **~s shall not be considered as votes** Stimmenthaltung gilt nicht als Stimmabgabe

abstract Auszug, Abriß; *(Patentanmeldung)* Zusammenfassung; ~ **of account** Rechnungsauszug; Kontoauszug; ~ **of record** Aktenauszug; ~ **of title**[6] Eigentumsnachweis *(Urkunde, in der Eigentumsrecht an Grundbesitz beschrieben ist, Br von → unregistered land)*; **the ~ shall indicate the title of the invention** die Zusammenfassung muß die Bezeichnung der Erfindung enthalten; **to file the ~** die Zusammenfassung einreichen

abstract *v* Auszug machen (from aus); *colloq.* entwenden, stehlen; **to ~ an account** e-n Kontoauszug erstellen (od. machen)

abstraction Entwendung, Beiseiteschaffung; **fraudulent ~** *(PatR)* widerrechtliche Entnahme

abuse Mißbrauch; Beschimpfung; Mißhandlung; ~ **of authority** Amtsmißbrauch; ~ **of the dead** Leichenschändung; ~ **of discretion** (or **power**) Ermessensmißbrauch; ~ **of distress** widerrechtliche Benutzung e-r gepfändeten Sache (od. gepfändeten Viehs); ~ **of legal right** Rechtsmißbrauch; ~ **of office** Amtsmißbrauch; ~ **of patent** mißbräuchliche Patent(be)nutzung; ~ **of power** Machtmißbrauch; ~ **of process** Mißbrauch des Prozeßverfahrens *(bei schikanösen Klagen)*; ~ **of rights** Rechtsmißbrauch; **evident ~ in relation to the applicant** *(PatR)* offensichtlicher Mißbrauch zum Nachteil des Anmelders

abuse *v* mißbrauchen; unzulässig gebrauchen; beschimpfen; mißhandeln

abusive mißbräuchlich; schmähend; ~ **clause in a contract** mißbräuchliche Bestimmung in e-m Vertrag; ~ **language** Schimpfworte

abut *v*, **to ~ (up)on** grenzen an; **~ting owner** → abutter; **~ting property** angrenzender Grundbesitz

abuttals Grenzen *(e-s Grundstücks)*

abutter angrenzender Besitzer, Anrainer, Anlieger *(e-s Grundstücks)*

accede *v* *(Ansicht etc)* beistimmen; *(Vertrag, Verein)* beitreten; **to ~ to an international agreement** e-m internationalen Abkommen beitreten; **to ~ to an office** ein Amt antreten; **to ~ to terms** Bedingungen zustimmen; **to ~ to a treaty** *(VölkerR)* e-m Vertrag beitreten

acceding Beitritt; beitretend; **the ~ states** die beitretenden Staaten

accelerate *v* beschleunigen; *(Fälligkeitstermin)* vorverlegen; *(z.B. Wechsel)* vorzeitig fällig stellen

accelerated, A~ Cost Recovery System (ACRS) *Am* beschleunigte Abschreibung der Anschaffungs- od. Herstellungskosten; **~ depreciation** beschleunigte Abschreibung; **~ express goods** beschleunigtes Eilgut; **~ surface post** (ASP) *Br* eilige Drucksachen und Pakete; **an instrument is ~** ein (Handels-)Papier ist vorzeitig fällig gestellt

acceleration Beschleunigung, vorzeitige Fälligstellung *(z.B. e-s Wechsels od. e-s Ratenzahlungsvertrages)*; **~ clause** Fälligkeitsklausel, Klausel über Vorverlegung der Fälligkeit; **~ in growth** Wachstumsbeschleunigung; **~ principle** Akzelerationsprinzip

accept *v* annehmen, abnehmen; *(Wechsel)* annehmen, akzeptieren, mit Akzept versehen; *(etw.)* hinnehmen, akzeptieren; **to ~ in blank** blanko akzeptieren; **to ~ a proposal** e-n Vorschlag annehmen; **to ~ service** die Zustellung *(rechtswirksam)* annehmen; **to ~ the tender** den Zuschlag erteilen *(bei Ausschreibungen)*; **to ~ the terms** die Bedingungen annehmen

accepted angenommen; akzeptiert; mit Akzept versehen; allgemein anerkannt; **~ draft** mit e-m Akzept versehene Tratte; **~ fact** allgemein anerkannte Tatsache; **~ service** →service 3.

acceptable annehmbar *(Preis, Bedingungen, Vorschlag)*; **~ as collateral** beleihbar, lombardfähig; **~ quality level** (AQL) annehmbare Qualitätsgrenzlage

acceptability Annehmbarkeit; Brauchbarkeit

acceptance 1. Akzeptanz; Annahme; Abnahme; Vertragsannahme *(opp. offer)*; Billigung; **(up)on ~** bei Annahme; **~ date** Annahmedatum; **~ of a bid** Annahme e-s Angebots *(bei Auktionen)*; **~ of conditions** Annahme von Bedingungen; **~ of liability** Anerkennung der Haftung; **~ of an offer** Annahme e-s Angebots; **~ of service** Annahme der Zustellung; **~ of tender** Auftragsvergabe *(bei Ausschreibungen)*; **~ test** Abnahmeprüfung

acceptance, conditional ~ bedingte Annahme; Annahme unter Vorbehalt; **non-~** Nichtannahme; Annahmeverweigerung; **refusal of ~** Annahmeverweigerung; **voluntary ~ of risk** Handeln auf eigene Gefahr; **to be in default of ~** in Annahmeverzug sein

acceptance 2. *(WechselR)* Annahme, Akzept, Akzeptleistung; **~ bill** *(Außenhandelsgeschäft)* Dokumententratte; **~ in blank** Blankoakzept; **~ charge** Akzeptgebühr; **~ credit** Rembourskredit; **~ for hono(u)r** (or **by intervention**) Ehrenannahme, Ehrenakzept *(e-s notleidenden Wechsels)*; **~ house** *Br* Akzeptbank (→*accepting house*); **~ liability** Akzeptverbindlichkeit, Akzeptverpflichtung; **~ supra protest** Ehrenannahme, Ehrenakzept *(e-s notleidenden Wechsels)*; **accommodation ~** Gefälligkeitsakzept; **blank ~** Blankoakzept; **collateral ~** Avalakzept; **general ~** uneingeschränktes Akzept, bedingungslose Annahme; **returned for want of ~** mangels Annahme zurück; **term of ~** Akzeptfrist; **unconditional** (or **unqualified**) **~** uneingeschränktes Akzept, bedingungslose Annahme; **trade ~** Handelsakzept; Warenwechsel; **to hono(u)r** (or **meet**) **an ~** ein Akzept einlösen; **to obtain ~** Akzept einholen; **to present for ~** zum Akzept vorlegen; **to provide with ~** mit Akzept versehen, akzeptieren

acceptance 3. *(VölkerR)* Annahme; **instrument of ~** Annahmeurkunde; **to be open for ~** zur Annahme aufliegen; **to be subject to ~** der Annahme bedürfen

accepter, acceptor Annehmer, Akzeptant *(e-s Wechsels)*; **~ for hono(u)r** (or **by intervention, supra protest**) Ehrenakzeptant, Honorant

accepting house *Br* Akzeptbank

Bank, die Wechsel für Kunden gegen Bezahlung akzeptiert. Sie widmet sich heute auch dem Emissions- und anderen Finanzgeschäften

Access *Br* Kreditkarte von Lloyd's, Midland, National Westminster, and Williams & Glyn's Banks

access Zutritt, Zugang, Zufahrt (to zu); Zugänglichkeit; *(EDV)* Zugriff; (Möglichkeit der) Beiwohnung; *pol* freier Zugang; **~ (to children)** *(EheR)* Recht, die Kinder zu sehen; **~ to the courts** (Möglichkeit des) Zugang(s) zu den Gerichten; **~ to the data bank** *(EDV)* Zugriff zur Datenbank; **~ to the market** Zugang zum Markt; **~ to the sea** Zugang zum Meer

access, difficult of ~ schwer zugänglich; **unrestricted ~** freier Zugang (to zu); **right of ~** Zutrittsrecht, Zugangsrecht, Zufahrtsrecht; *(EheR)* Recht des persönlichen Verkehrs mit den Kindern

access, to deny ~ Zutritt verweigern; nicht zulassen; **to have ~ to the defendant** Zutritt zum Angeklagten haben; **to have ~ to the files** (Möglichkeit der) Einsicht in Akten haben

accessary *Am* →accessory 1.

accessible zugänglich (to für); erhältlich, erreichbar

accession 1. Zunahme, Zuwachs, Hinzukommen; Zuwachs *(e-r Neben- zu e-r Hauptsache)*; Verarbeitung *(e-r Sache zu e-r neuen)*; Anwachsung *(e-s Staatsgebiets);* ~**s** Zugänge, Neuanschaffungen; ~ **by confusion** Eigentumserwerb durch Vermischung; ~ **to an estate** Antritt e-r Erbschaft; ~ **to power** Machtübernahme; ~ **of property** Hinzukommen von Vermögen, Vermögenszuwachs; ~ **to the throne** Thronbesteigung; Regierungsantritt; **a list of** ~**s to a library** e-e Liste der Zugänge für e-e Bücherei

accession 2. *(VölkerR)* Beitritt *(e-s Staates zu e-m bestehenden Vertrag);* ~ **negotiations** *(EG)* Beitrittsverhandlungen; **Act of A**~ (Act Concerning the Conditions of A~ and the Adjustments to the Treaties) *(EG)* Beitrittsakte (Akte über die Beitrittsbedingungen und die Anpassungen der Verträge); **declaration of** ~ Beitrittserklärung; **instrument of** ~ Beitrittsurkunde; **Treaty of A**~ Beitrittsvertrag; ~ **shall be effected by** ... der Beitritt erfolgt durch ...; **the present protocol shall be open for** ~ **by** ... dieses Protokoll liegt für ... zum Beitritt auf

accessorial services zusätzliche Dienstleistungen *(des Spediteurs; sorting, packing, precooling etc)*

accessoriness (of a security interest) Akzessorität (e-s Sicherungsrechts)

accessory 1. *(StrafR)* Teilnehmer *(opp. principal);* Mittäter, Komplice, Mitschuldiger *(bei Begehung der strafbaren Handlung nicht zugegen; cf. abettor);* mitschuldig; ~ **after the fact** nach Begehung der Tat Beteiligter *(bes. Begünstiger, Hehler);* **acting as an** ~ **after the fact** Begünstigung; ~ **before the fact** vor Begehung der Tat Beteiligter *(bes. Anstifter, Gehilfe; jetzt meist als →principal behandelt);* **acting as an** ~ **before the fact** Beihilfe

accessory 2. Zubehör(teil); hinzukommend, zusätzlich; nebensächlich; Neben-; akzessorisch; ~ **charges** Nebengebühren; ~ **circumstance** Nebenumstand, Begleitumstand; ~ **claim** Anspruch auf Nebenleistung; ~ **contract** Nebenvertrag, Zusatzvertrag; Sicherungsgeschäft *(z.B. Bürgschaft-, Garantie-, Pfand- und Hypothekenbestellung, Sicherungsübereignung);* ~ **expenses** Nebenausgaben; ~ **obligation** zusätzliche Verpflichtung; akzessorische Verpflichtung; **property** ~ **to immovable property** Zubehör zum unbeweglichen Vermögen; **to be** ~ **to** beitragen zu

accident Unfall; Zufall; ~ **annuity** Unfallrente; ~ **benefit** Unfallentschädigung; Unfallrente; ~ **book** *Br (gesetzl. vorgeschriebenes)* Unfallbuch *(zur Registrierung von Betriebsunfällen);* ~ **claim** durch Unfall begründete Forderung; ~ **compensation** Schadensersatz für durch Unfall geschädigte Personen; ~ **damage** Unfallschaden; ~ **arising out of a p.'s employment** Betriebsunfall; ~ **(frequency) rate** Unfall(häufigkeits)ziffer; ~ **hazard** Unfallrisiko; ~ **insurance** Unfallversicherung; ~ **prevention** Unfallverhütung; ~ **ratio** Unfallquote; ~ **report** Unfallbericht; ~ **risk** Unfallrisiko; ~ **at work** Arbeitsunfall

accident, automobile ~ *Am* Kraftfahrzeugunfall, Autounfall; **by** ~ **or design** zufällig oder absichtlich; **cause of** ~ Unfallursache; **death by** ~ Tod infolge e-s Unfalles; **double** ~ *Br* **benefit** (*Am* **indemnity**) (*VersR*) doppelte Leistung bei Unfalltod; **failing to stop after an** ~ unerlaubtes Entfernen vom Unfallort; Fahrerflucht; **fatal** ~ tödlicher Unfall; **in an** ~ bei e-m Unfall; **industrial** ~ Betriebsunfall, Arbeitsunfall; **injured in an** ~ unfallverletzt; **investigation of** ~**s** Unfalluntersuchung; **major** ~ Großunfall; **motoring** ~ Autounfall; **nonoccupational** ~ Nichtbetriebsunfall; Nichtberufsunfall; **notice of** ~ Unfallanzeige; **the party at fault in an** ~ der Schuldige e-s Unfalls; **place of** ~ Unfallsort, Unfallstätte; **prevention of** ~**s** Unfallverhütung; **railway** *Br* (**railroad** *Am*) ~ Eisenbahnunglück; **road** (or **street**) ~ (Straßen-)Verkehrsunfall; **third party** ~ **insurance** Unfall-Haftpflichtversicherung; **to have** (or **meet with**) **an** ~ e-n Unfall haben, verunglücken; **an** ~ **occurred** ein Unfall ereignete sich (od. geschah); **to settle claims arising from** ~**s** Schadensfälle abwickeln

accidental zufällig; Unfall-; ~ **damage** Unfallschaden; unabsichtlich (od. durch Unfall) verursachter Schaden; ~ **death** tödlicher Unfall, Unfalltod

acclamation Akklamation, Zuruf; **voting by** ~ Abstimmung durch Akklamation; **elected by** ~ durch Akklamation gewählt

accommodate *v (jdm)* e-e Gefälligkeit erweisen, e-n Gefallen tun; *(jdn)* versorgen (with mit); *(jdn)* unterbringen, aufnehmen (können); anpassen, in Einklang bringen; *(Streit)* beilegen (od. schlichten); **to** ~ **sb. with a loan** jdm. Kredit gewähren; **person** ~**d** *(WechselR)* Gefälligkeitsbegünstigter

accommodating gefällig, entgegenkommend, kulant; **person** ~ *(WechselR)* Gefälligkeitsschuldner; **on** ~ **terms** unter annehmbaren Bedingungen

accommodation Gefälligkeit; geldliche Hilfe; *(ungesichertes)* Darlehen; Unterbringung(smöglichkeit); Unterkunft(smöglichkeit); *Am* Räumlichkeit; Anpassung; Beilegung *(e-s Streites);* ~ **acceptance** *(WechselR)* Gefälligkeitsakzept; ~ **acceptor** *(WechselR)* Gefälligkeitsakzeptant; ~ **address** Gefälligkeitsadresse, Deckadresse; ~ **allowance** Unterkunftsvergütung; ~ **bill** Gefälligkeitswechsel; ~ **of conflicting interests** Angleichung widerstreitender Interessen; ~ **credit** Überbrückungskredit; ~ **indorsement** *(WechselR)* Gefälligkeitsindossament; ~ **loan** Überbrückungskredit; ~ **maker** *Am* Aussteller e-s Gefälligkeitswechsels; ~ **note** *Br* →~ **bill;** ~ **paper** Gefälligkeitswechsel; ~ **party to a bill** *(WechselR)*[7] Gefälligkeitsbeteiligter, Gefälligkeitszeichner; ~ **registry** *Br* Wohnungsnachweis

accommodation, bank ~ Bankdarlehen; **hotel** ~ Unterbringung im Hotel

accommodation, to find ~ unterkommen; **to provide for** ~ für Unterkunft sorgen; **the instrument was accepted for his** ~ das Papier war aus Gefälligkeit für ihn akzeptiert

accompan|y *v* begleiten; ~**ied by** begleitet (od. in Begleitung) von; ~**ying documents** Begleitpapiere; ~**ying letter** Begleitbrief

accomplice *(StrafR)* Mittäter, Mitschuldiger; Helfershelfer *(principal or accessory)*

accomplish *v* ausführen; vollenden; begehen; **to** ~ **a task** e-e Aufgabe erfüllen; ~**ed fact** vollendete Tatsache

accomplishment Ausführung; Vollendung; Leistung; Können; ~**s** Fertigkeiten, Kenntnisse

accord Übereinkommen, Einverständnis; Vergleich *(zwischen Schuldner und einzelnem Gläubiger; cf. composition); (VölkerR)* Übereinkunft, Verständigung; **by common** ~ in gegenseitigem Einvernehmen; **in** ~ **with** in Einklang mit; **of one's own** ~ aus eigenem Antrieb, freiwillig; **with one** ~ einstimmig

accord and satisfaction[8] vergleichsweise Erfüllung *(e-r schuldrechtlichen Verpflichtung als rechtsvernichtende Einwendung) (Vertragsänderung)*

accordance, in ~ **with** in Übereinstimmung mit, gemäß; **in** ~ **with the accounts** (or **books**) rechnungsgemäß; **in** ~ **with your instructions** weisungsgemäß

according to laut, gemäß; nach Maßgabe; ~ **the articles** satzungsgemäß; ~ **circumstances** nach Lage der Dinge; den Umständen gemäß; ~ **(the) contract** vertragsgemäß; ~ **law** gesetzmäßig

account 1. Rechnung; Konto; Bericht(erstattung); *Am* Geschäftsforderung (→ *accounts*); ~ **agreed upon** →~ stated; ~ **balance** Kontostand; ~ **book** Kontobuch; Journal; ~ **books** Geschäftsbücher; ~ **classification** Kontenaufgliederung; ~ **closed** Konto abgeschlossen; ~ **credit** Anschreibekredit; ~ **current** (A/C) Kontokorrentkonto, laufendes Konto; ~ **customer** Kunde, der anschreiben läßt; Kreditkunde; ~ **executive** Sachbearbeiter für Kundenwerbung; Kundenberater; Kontaktmann *(e-r Werbeagentur zu Kunden); Am* Börsenauftragsnehmer; ~ **files** Kontounterlagen; ~ **for documentary credits** (A/c for doc. credits) Akkreditivkonto; ~ **for guarantees** (A/c for guarantees) Avalkonto; ~ **holder** Kontoinhaber; ~ **in arrears** Rechnungsrückstand; ~ **in foreign currency** Devisenkonto; (Fremd-)Währungskonto; ~ **management** (Abteilung für) Großkundenbetreuung; ~ **manager** Kundenberater(in); ~ **mandate** Kontovollmacht; ~ **number** Kontonummer; ~ **of charges** Spesenkonto; Unkostenkonto; Gebührenaufstellung; ~ **of disbursements** Auslagenaufstellung; ~ **of expenses** Spesenkonto, Unkostenkonto; ~ **of goods purchased** Einkaufsrechnung; Einkaufskonto; ~ **of proceedings** Verhandlungsbericht; **A**~ **Payee** (only) (A/c Payee only) *Br (gekreuzter Scheck)* nur für Rechnung des Schecknehmers *(Weisung an die Bank, die Schecksumme dem Konto des Zahlungsempfängers gutzuschreiben);* ~ **rendered** *(zur Prüfung und Bezahlung)* vorgelegte Rechnung; **(as) per** ~ **rendered** laut Abrechnung; laut *(früher)* ausgestellter Rechnung; ~ **sales** (A/S.) Verkaufsrechnung; Abrechnung des Verkaufskommissionärs; ~ **service** Kundenberatung; ~ **stated** anerkannter Rechnungsabschluß (od. Kontokorrentauszug); ~ **statement** *(Bank)* Kontoauszug; ~ **turnover** Kontoumsatz; ~ **with a bank** Bankkonto; ~ **with customers** Kundenkonto

account, abstract of ~ Kontoauszug; Rechnungsauszug; **acceptance** ~ Akzeptkonto; **active** ~ umsatzstarkes Konto *(opp. dead ~)*; **advance** ~ Vorschußkonto; **as per** ~ laut Rechnung; **(as) per** ~ **rendered** laut Abrechnung; **bank** ~ Bankkonto; **bill** ~ Wechselrechnung; **cash** ~ Kassenkonto; **charge** ~ Kundenkreditkonto; Abzahlungskonto *(bei Teilzahlungen);* **collection** ~ Inkassokonto; **collective** ~ Sammelkonto; **commission** ~ Provisionskonto; **contra** (or **counter**) ~ Gegenkonto; **cost** ~ Unkostenkonto; →**current** ~; **custodianship** ~ *Am* Effektendepot(konto); **dead** ~ unbewegtes Konto *(opp. active ~)*; **deposit** ~ Einlagekonto; *Br* Sparkonto; **deposit** ~**s** Depositeneinlagen; **detailed** ~ eingehender Bericht; spezifizierte Rechnung; **discretionary** ~ Konto, für das der Inhaber seiner Bank Verwaltungsvollmacht erteilt hat; **dormant** ~ **s. dead** →account; **earmarked** ~ zweckgebundenes Konto; **external** ~ Auslandskonto; **extract of** ~ Kontoauszug; Rechnungsauszug; **final** ~ Schlußbericht; Schlußabrechnung; **for** ~ **only** nur zur Verrechnung *(auf Schecks);* **for the** ~ **of another** für fremde Rechnung; **for the** ~ **and risk of** für Rechnung und Gefahr von; **for one's own** ~ für eigene Rechnung; **for** ~ **of whom it may concern** *(für Rechnung wen es angeht)* Gemeinschaftsrechnung; Gemeinschaftskonto; **foreign** ~ Auslandskonto; **guarantee** ~ (A/c for guarantees) Avalkonto; **giro** ~ *Br* Postgirokonto; **half-yearly** ~ Halbjahresrechnung; **holder of an** ~ Kontoinhaber; **impersonal** ~ Sachkonto (*opp. personal* ~); **intermediate** ~ Zwischenrechnung; **investment** ~ Anlagekonto; Einlagekonto; **item of** ~ Rechnungsposten; **itemized** ~ spezifizierte Rechnung

account, joint ~ (J/A) gemeinsames Konto; Partizipationskonto; Metakonto; gemeinsame Rechnung; **business on joint** ~ Partizipationsgeschäft; Konsortialgeschäft; Metageschäft *(Gemeinschaftsgeschäft von 2 Parteien [Metisten]);* **credit given on joint** ~ Metakredit; **for** (or **on**) **joint** ~ für (od. auf) gemeinsame Rechnung; a metà *(auf gemeinsame Rechnung zu zweit);* **transaction on joint** ~ s. business on joint →~

account, liability ~ Passivkonto; **loan** ~ Darlehenskonto; Vorschußkonto; **nominal** ~ *Br* Sachkonto

account, NOW ~ *Am* verzinstes Sparkonto, über das mit → negotiable orders of withdrawal verfügt werden kann; **super NOW** ~ *Am* verzinstes Sparkonto, über das unbegrenzt mit Schecks verfügt werden kann (gesetzl. begrenzter Inhaberkreis)

account, on ~ auf Rechnung; auf Abschlag; als Anzahlung; **amount paid on** ~ Anzahlung(sbetrag); **payment on** ~ Anzahlung; Abschlagszahlung; Akontozahlung; **payment on** ~ **of costs** Kostenvorschuß *(auf Anwaltsgebühren);* **to pay on** ~ anzahlen, Anzahlung leisten; auf Abschlag zahlen

account, only for ~ nur zur Verrechnung *(Vermerk auf Scheck);* **open** ~ offenstehende Rechnung; Konto in laufender Rechnung, Kontokorrentkonto; **opening of an** ~ Eröffnung e-s Kontos; **by order and for** ~ im Auftrag und für Rechnung; **other** ~**s** sonstige Konten

account, holding of securities for own ~ Nostroeffekten; **on own** ~ für eigene Rechnung; **on one's own** ~ für sich; **to be in business on one's own** ~ selbständig geschäftstätig sein, sein eigenes Geschäft haben

account, overdrawn ~ überzogenes Konto; **personal** ~ Personenkonto; Privatkonto, Kundenkonto (*opp. impersonal* ~); **postal check** ~ *Am* Postgirokonto; **public** ~ *Br* Konto für staatliche Gelder; **purchase** ~ Wareneingangskonto; Wareneingangsrechnung; **real** ~ Bestandskonto; Sachkonto; **realization** ~ Liquidationskonto *(e-r Gesellschaft);* **rendering an** ~ Rechenschaftslegung; **reserve** ~ Rücklagenkonto; **running** ~ laufende Rechnung; laufendes Konto; **salary** ~ Gehaltskonto; **sales** ~ Warenausgangsrechnung; Warenausgangskonto; **savings** ~ Sparkonto, Sparguthaben; **semi-annual** (or **sixmonthly**) ~ Halbjahresrechnung; halbjährlicher Kontoauszug; **settled** ~ bezahlte Rechnung; ausgeglichenes Konto; **settling** (or **settlement**) **of** ~**s** Bezahlung von Rechnungen; **special** ~ Sonderkonto; **special advance** ~ Kreditsonderkonto; **state of an** ~ Kontostand; **statement of** ~ →statement 2.; **subsidiary** ~ Hilfskonto; **sundry** ~ Konto „Verschiedenes"; **sweep** ~ *Am* Investitions-Girokonto-Kombination bei US-Brokerhäusern (→ *cash management account*); **target** ~ *Am* Zielkonto (→ *pooling* 2.); →**trading** ~; **unsettled** ~ offenstehende Rechnung; **yearly** ~ Jahres(ab)rechnung

account, to adjust ~**s** Konten bereinigen; **to appear in an** ~ auf e-r Rechnung stehen; **to audit an** ~ e-e Rechnung (od. ein Konto) prüfen; **to balance an** ~ ein Konto saldieren (od. ausgleichen); e-e Rechnung abschließen; **to call to** ~ zur Rechenschaft ziehen; **to close an** ~ ein Konto abschließen; ein Konto auflösen; **to credit an** ~ (with an amount) e-m Konto gutschreiben; ein Konto erkennen; **to debit an** ~ (with an amount) ein Konto belasten; **to draw up an** ~ e-e Rechnung aufstellen; **to draw on the** ~ vom Konto abheben; **to enter a sum to a p.'s** ~ jds Konto e-e Summe gutschreiben; **to give an** ~ **of** berichten (od. Bericht erstatten) über; **to give** ~ **of** Rechenschaft ablegen über; **to hold** (or **keep**) **an** ~ **with a bank** ein Konto bei e-r Bank haben; **to make out an** ~ e-e Rechnung ausstellen; **to make up an** ~ e-e Rechnung aufstellen; **to open an** ~ ein Konto eröffnen; **to operate an** ~ ein Konto unterhalten; **to overdraw an** ~ ein Konto überziehen; **to pass to the credit of an** ~ e-m Konto gutschreiben; **to pay into an** ~ auf ein Konto einzahlen; **to place** (or **put**) **to a p.'s** ~ jdm etw. berechnen (od. in Rechnung stellen); **to settle an** ~ e-e Rechnung bezahlen; ein Konto ausgleichen; **to take (due)** ~ **(of)** (gebührend) berücksichtigen; **to take into** ~ *(etw.)* in Betracht ziehen; *(e-r Sache)* Rechnung tragen; **to transfer money to an** ~ Geld auf ein Konto überweisen; **to withdraw from an** ~ von e-m Konto abheben

account 2. *Br (Börse) (14-tägige)* Abrechnung; ~ **day** Abrechnungstag; Liquidationstag; ~ **period** Abrechnungsperiode; **dealings for the** ~ Termingeschäfte; **endmonth** ~ Ultimoabrechnung; **midmonth** (or **fortnightly**) ~ Medioabrechnung; **to buy for the** ~ auf Termin kaufen

accounts Rechnungen; Konti; Bücher *(der Buchhaltung);* Abrechnung(en); (Jahres-)Abschluß; *Am* Geschäftsforderungen *(Zahlungsansprüche aus Kauf-, Miet- od. Pacht- sowie Dienstleistungsverträgen, die nicht durch Wertpapiere od. → chattel paper verkörpert sind);* ~ **department** Buchhaltung

accounts payable (A/cs Pay.) Verbindlichkeiten; Kreditoren *(aus Buchlieferantenschulden);* Verbindlichkeiten auf Grund von Warenlieferungen od. Leistungen; ~ **department** *Am* Kreditorenbuchhaltung

accounts receivable (A/cs Rec.) Forderungen,

Außenstände; Debitoren; Forderungen auf Grund von Warenlieferungen od. Leistungen; ~ **financing** *Am*[9] Finanzierung durch Vorausabtretung von Geschäftsforderungen; **assignment of** ~ Forderungsabtretung

accounts, annual ~ Jahresabschluß (→*annual*); **group** ~ Konzernabschluß

accounts, to keep the ~ die Bücher führen; **to make up one's** ~ seinen Jahresabschluß machen; seine Abrechnung machen; **to publish the** ~ den Jahresabschluß veröffentlichen; **to settle** ~ **with** abrechnen mit

account *v* **to** ~ **for** Rechenschaft (od. Rechnung) ablegen über; (sich) erklären, begründen; *(zahlenmäßig)* ausmachen

accountability Verantwortlichkeit (to gegenüber); Rechenschaftspflicht; **area of** ~ Verantwortungsbereich; ~ **for one's actions** Zurechnungsfähigkeit

accountable verantwortlich; rechenschaftspflichtig; abrechnungspflichtig

accountancy Buchführungswesen; Rechnungswesen; Steuerberatungswesen; Wirtschaftsprüfungswesen *(Beruf, Tätigkeit e-s →accountant)*; ~ **profession** Beruf des Steuerberaters, Wirtschaftsprüfers und Buchprüfers

accountant Buchhalter; Buchhaltungsfachmann; Buchprüfer, Abschlußprüfer, Wirtschaftsprüfer, Steuerberater[10]; ~**s** Buchprüfungs-, Wirtschaftsprüfungs- und Steuerberatungsfirma; ~**'s certificate** (Buch-)Prüfungsbescheinigung; ~**'s report** Prüfungsvermerk des Wirtschaftsprüfers

accountant, certified[11] (or **chartered**)[12] ~ *Br* konzessionierter Buchprüfer (od. Wirtschaftsprüfer und Steuerberater); **certified public** ~ (C. P. A.) *Am*[13] Wirtschaftsprüfer; **to call in an** ~ e-n Wirtschaftsprüfer (etc) hinzuziehen

accounting Buchführung, Buchhaltung; Buchungs-; Buchhaltungs-; Rechnungslegung, Abrechnung; Rechnungswesen; ~ **deficit** Rechnungsdefizit; ~ **department** Buchhaltungsabteilung; ~ **dollar** Verrechnungsdollar; ~ **frauds** Bilanzdelikte; ~ **machine** Buchungsmaschine; ~ **methods**[14] Buchführungsmethoden; ~ **operations** Buchungsvorgänge; ~ **period** Abrechnungszeitraum; Geschäftsjahr; *(im öffentl. Haushalt)* Rechnungsjahr; ~ **principles** (or **rules**) Bilanzierungsgrundsätze; Rechnungslegungsgrundsätze; **for** ~ **purposes** zu Buchführungszwecken; für Zwecke der Abrechnung; ~ **records** Buchungsunterlagen, Buchungsbelege; ~ **system** Buchungssystem; Buchführungssystem; ~ **transaction** Buchhaltungsvorgang; ~ **year** Geschäftsjahr; Wirtschaftsjahr

accounting, → **false** ~; **group** ~ Rechnungslegung von Konzernen; **industrial** ~ Betriebsbuchhaltung; **operational** ~ Betriebsabrechnung; **ordinary commercial** ~ **principles** Grundsätze ordnungsgemäßer kaufmännischer Buchhaltung; **personnel** ~ Lohn- und Gehaltsbuchhaltung; **property** ~ Anlagenbuchhaltung

accredit *v* 1. akkreditieren, ein Akkreditiv stellen; bevollmächtigen; bescheinigen, daß der erforderliche (od. gewünschte) Standard besteht

accredited agent, the parties may be represented by ~**s** die Parteien mögen durch bevollmächtigte Personen vertreten sein *(z.B. im Schiedsverfahren)*

accredited, ~ **broker** amtlich bestätigter Makler; ~ **party** *(beim Akkreditiv)* Akkreditierter, Begünstigter; ~ **representative** bevollmächtigter Vertreter

accredit *v* 2. *(VölkerR)* akkreditieren, *(dipl. Vertreter e-s Landes)* beglaubigen; **to be** ~**ed as head of a mission by the receiving State** als Missionschef bei dem Empfangsstaat beglaubigt werden *(cf. agrément)*

accretion (Wert-, Vermögens-)Zuwachs, Zunahme; Anwachsen *(e-s Erbteils beim Wegfall e-s Miterben od. Mitvermächtnisnehmers)*; *(VölkerR)* Akkretion, Anwachsung; ~ **of land** Landzuwachs *(Gebietserwerb durch Neubildung von Land; cf. alluvion, avulsion)*

accrual Anfall *(während e-r bestimmten Zeit)*; Auflaufen *(von Zinsen)*; (Zeitpunkt der) Entstehung *(e-s Anspruchs, Rechts)*; ~**s** *Am* antizipative Passiva (→*accrued charges*); ~ **accounting method** *Am (SteuerR)* Methode des Betriebsvermögensvergleichs; ~ **basis** Fälligkeitsbasis *(auf der Basis fällig werdender Forderungen)*; ~ **of the cause of action** Entstehung des Klaganspruchs; ~ **date** Fälligkeitstag; ~ **of a dividend** Anfall e-r Dividende; ~ **of an heritance** *Am* Anfall e-r Erbschaft; Erb(an)fall; ~ **of interest** Auflaufen von Zinsen; ~ **of a right** Anfall (od. Entstehung) e-s Rechts

accrue *v (jdm)* anfallen, zuwachsen; zufallen, zufließen *(z.B. Gewinn)*; auflaufen *(Zinsen)*; entstehen *(Recht, Anspruch)*; fällig werden; **costs** ~ Kosten entstehen; **a right** ~**s** ein Recht entsteht (od. wird erworben) *(bes. bei Eintritt e-s Zeitpunktes)*; **insurer's liability** ~**s** die Haftung des Versicherers tritt ein

accrued, ~ **assets** (or **income**) antizipative Aktiva; ~ **charges** (or *Am* **expense**) *(Bilanz)* antizipative Passiva *(Aufwendungen e-s Geschäftsjahres, die erst im folgenden zu Ausgaben führen)*; ~ **costs** aufgelaufene Kosten; angefallene Kosten; ~ **depreciation** → accumulated depreciation; ~ **income** antizipative Aktiva *(verdiente, aber noch nicht eingenommene Einnahmen)*; **net** ~ **income** Nettoeinkommenszuwachs; ~ **interest** (accr.int.) aufgelaufene *(aber noch nicht ge-*

zahlte od. zahlbare) Zinsen; Stückzinsen; ~ **liabilities** antizipative Passiva; Rückstellungen; ~ **pension right** Pensionsanwartschaftsrecht; ~ **taxes** *(Bilanz)* Rückstellungen für Steuern; **interest** ~ Stückzinsen

accruing *(später)* fällig werdend, entstehend *(opp. owing)*; ~ **amounts** anfallende Beträge; ~ **interest** *(später)* fällig werdende Zinsen; noch nicht fällige Zinsen; ~ **right** *(ohne besonderen Übertragungsakt)* zuwachsendes Recht

accumulate *v* (sich) anhäufen; (sich) ansammeln; kumulieren; (sich) stapeln; auflaufen *(Zinsen)*; horten; *(Gewinn)* thesaurieren; **to** ~ **capital** Kapital ansammeln

accumulated, ~ **debt** aufgelaufene Schuld; ~ **demand** Nachholbedarf; Nachfrageballung; ~ **depreciation** *Am* ansteigende Abschreibung *(die im Laufe der Jahre so lange wächst, bis sie den Wert des abzuschreibenden Objekts absorbiert)*; ~ **earnings** (or **profit**) *Am (Bilanz)* thesaurierter Gewinn; ~ **earnings credit** *Am (SteuerR)* Gewinnansammlungsfreigrenze; ~ **earnings tax** *Am* (Bundes-)Steuer auf nicht ausgeschüttete Gewinne; ~ **loss** *Am* Bilanzverlust; ~ **risk** *(VersR)* Kumulrisiko

accumulation Anhäufung, Ansammlung; Zusammenballung; Thesaurierung; ~ **of capital** Kapitalansammlung, Kapitalbildung; ~ **distribution** Ausschüttung der Ansammlung *(des vom Trust in früheren Jahren versteuerten Einkommens)*; ~ **of interest** Auflaufen von Zinsen; ~ **of reserve** Reservebildung; ~ **of risk** *(VersR)* Risikenhäufung; ~ **plan** *Am* Sparvertrag zum Erwerb von Investmentanteilen *(opp. contractual plan)*; ~ **schedule** Kapitalbildungsplan; **unreasonable** ~**s tax** *Am*[15] Steuer von angesammelten Einkommen; **rule against** ~ →rule 2.

accumulative (sich) anhäufend, kumulativ; ~ **dividend** kumulative Dividende; ~ **sentence** →cumulative sentence

accuracy Richtigkeit; Genauigkeit *(z.B. e-s Ergebnisses in der Marktforschung)*; ~ **of a statement** Richtigkeit e-r Aussage

accurate(ly) genau

accusation *(nicht formelle)* Anklage *(cf. indictment)*; Anschuldigung, Beschuldigung

accuse *v* anklagen; anschuldigen, beschuldigen (of a th. wegen; to bei); **to** ~ **sb. of having done** jdn anklagen, daß er getan hat; ~**d (person)** Angeklagter; Beschuldigter, Angeschuldigter *(cf. defendant, prisoner)*

accuser Ankläger

achievement Ausführung, Vollendung; Erlangung; Leistung; ~ **of objectives** Erreichung von Zielen; ~ **quotient** (AQ) Leistungsquotient; **intellectual** ~ *(UrhR)* geistige Errungenschaft; **outstanding** ~ überragende Leistung

acknowledge *v* anerkennen; *(Empfang)* bestätigen, quittieren; zugeben, eingestehen; *(Errichtung e- r Urkunde vor Urkundsperson)* förmlich anerkennen; *(etwa:)* notariell beglaubigen; **to** ~ **receipt of a letter** Empfang (od. Eingang) e-s Briefes bestätigen

acknowledg(e)ment Anerkennung; Anerkenntnis; (Empfangs-)Bestätigung; Zugeständnis; *(etwa:)* notarielle Beglaubigung; ~ **of a debt** *(schriftl.)* Schuldanerkenntnis; ~ **of indebtedness** Schuldschein, Schuldanerkenntnis; *Am* Schatzanweisung; ~ **of order** Auftragsbestätigung; ~ **of paternity** Vaterschaftsanerkennung; ~ **of receipt** Empfangsbestätigung; *(bei Einschreiben)* Rückschein; **(filing of an)** ~ **of service and notice of intention to defend** *Br* Bestätigung der Zustellung *(der Klageschrift)* und Anzeige der Einlassungsabsicht; **written** ~ schriftliches Anerkenntnis

ACP-countries → African, Caribbean and Pacific countries

acid test Verhältnis von flüssigen Mitteln zu kurzfristigen Verbindlichkeiten *(eine Art Liquiditätsmaß)*

acquaint *v* bekannt machen; **to** ~ **o.s. with regulations** sich mit Bestimmungen vertraut machen; **to be** ~**ed with sb.** jdn persönlich kennen; **to become** ~**ed with** sich einarbeiten in; *(jdn)* kennenlernen

acquiesce *v* sich fügen; sich zufriedengeben (in mit); sich beruhigen (in bei); *(stillschweigend)* einwilligen, dulden; **to** ~ **in a decision** sich mit e-r Entscheidung abfinden; auf ein Rechtsmittel verzichten; **to** ~ **an order** e-e Anordnung billigen; **to** ~ **in an amicable settlement** in e-n Vergleich einwilligen

acquiescence *(stillschweigende)* Einwilligung; Sichfügen; Duldung *(bes. e-r Rechtsverletzung; cf. laches)*

acquire *v* erwerben, erlangen; anschaffen; **to** ~ **a company** *Am* e-e Gesellschaft übernehmen; **to** ~ **customers** Kunden gewinnen; **to** ~ **property** Vermögen erwerben; **to** ~ **by purchase** käuflich erwerben; **to** ~ **real property** Grundeigentum erwerben

acquired, ~ **company** übernommene Gesellschaft; ~ **nationality** erworbene Staatsangehörigkeit; **duly** ~ **rights** wohlerworbene Rechte; ~ **rights and rights in course of acquisition** erworbene Rechte und Anwartschaftsrechte

acquiring company übernehmende Gesellschaft

acquisition Erwerb; Anschaffung; (Neu-)Erwerbung; Aufkauf, Übernahme *(e-s Unternehmens)*; ~ **agent** *(VersR)* Abschlußvermittler; ~ **agreement** *Am* Übernahmevertrag; ~ **commission** *(VersR)* Abschlußprovision; ~ **cost** Anschaffungskosten; *(VersR)* Abschlußkosten; ~ **of a company** (or **an enterprise**); *Am* Übernahme e-r Gesellschaft (od. e-s Unternehmens) *(durch ein anderes)*; ~ **of data** Erhebung von Daten; ~ **fee** *(VersR)* Abschlußgebühr; ~ **of gain** Gewinnerzielung; ~ **of property** Eigentumserwerb; Vermögenserwerb; ~ **of territory** Gebietserwerb; ~ **of title** Eigentumserwerb; ~ **value** Anschaffungswert

acquisition, cost of ~ Anschaffungskosten; **new ~s** Neuerwerbungen, Neuanschaffungen; →**pre-~**; →**post-~**

acquisitive prescription *Am* Ersitzung

acquit *v* freisprechen (of a charge von e-r Anklage) *(Br bei Verfahren vor höheren Gerichten; cf. dismiss)*; **to ~ a debt** e-e Schuld abtragen; **to ~ sb. from an obligation** jdn von e-r Verbindlichkeit befreien

acquittal Freispruch; **to pronounce an ~** Freispruch verkünden; freisprechen

acquittance Bescheinigung *(über Befreiung von Schuld od. Verpflichtung)*; Quittung; Entlastung

acre Flächenmaß *(1 ~ = 0,4047 ha = 1 Morgen)*

acreage Flächeninhalt (od. Umfang) nach acres; Anbaufläche, Weidenfläche

across the board (im) allgemein(en); global, umfassend

act 1. Gesetz *(cf. statute)*; **A~ (of Congress)** *Am* (Bundes-)Gesetz; **A~ (of Parliament)** *Br* Gesetz; **A~ of Settlement** *Br* Thronfolgegesetz *(1701; begründete Anwartschaft des Hauses Hannover)*; **A~s of Union** *Br* Unionsgesetze *(Vereinigung Englands mit Wales [1536], Schottland [1706, 1707] und Irland [1800] unter einer Krone und einem Parlament)*

act, commencement of an ~ Inkrafttreten e-s Gesetzes; **private ~s** Gesetze, die lokale Fragen od. Rechtsverhältnisse einzelner Personen regeln; **public ~s** Gesetze allgemeinen Inhalts.

In Großbritannien bezeichnet die übliche Zitierweise ein Gesetz nach dem Regierungsjahr des Souveräns unter Beifügung der Kapitalnummer (z. B. Town and Country Planning Act, 1954: 2 & 3 Eliz. 2, c. 72).

Die anglo-amerikanischen Gesetze sind in sections und subsections eingeteilt

act 2. Tat; Akt, Handlung, Rechtshandlung; ~ **of administrative authorities** Verwaltungsakt; ~ **of bankruptcy** Konkurshandlung; Konkursgrund; ~ **of God** höhere Gewalt *(durch Naturereignisse; cf. force majeure)*; ~ **of grace** Gnadenakt, Amnestie *(bes. bei Regierungsantritt des Souveräns)*; ~ **of hono(u)r** Ehreneintritt *(bei Wechselprotest)*; ~ **of law** rechtsgestaltender Gesetzesakt *(Begründung, Veränderung od. Vernichtung e-s Rechts durch gesetzl. Eingriff)*; **by ~ of law** kraft Gesetzes; ~ **of protest** *(WechselR)* Protest(aufnahme); Protesturkunde

Act of State staatlicher Hoheitsakt; *Br (politische)* Maßnahme der Krone *(z. B. Kriegserklärung)*; ~ **doctrine** *(IPR)* Act of State-Lehre

Eine die Rechtspraxis beherrschende Lehre, nach der ausländische Hoheitsakte (insbes. Enteignungen) anzuerkennen sind, wenn sich der ausländische Staat innerhalb der Grenzen seiner Macht gehalten hat. Insoweit ist die Vorbehaltsklausel (ordre public, *[cf. public policy, policy 1.]*) unanwendbar. Grenzen der Macht werden in den einzelnen Staaten unterschiedlich beurteilt

act, ~s of violence Gewalttaten; ~ **of war** Kriegshandlung; **final** ~ *(VölkerR)* Schlußakte; **general** ~ *(VölkerR)* Generalakte; **illegal** ~ gesetzwidrige Handlung; **official** ~ Amtshandlung; **overt** ~ offenkundige Handlung; **punishable** ~ strafbare Handlung

act, to be caught in the ~ (of doing sth.) auf frischer Tat betroffen werden

act *v* handeln; **to ~ as** tätig sein (od. fungieren) als; **to ~ as agent** *(jdn)* vertreten; in fremdem Namen handeln; **to ~ for sb.** jdn vertreten; **the solicitor ~s for his client** *Br* der Anwalt vertritt s-n Mandanten; **to ~ upon** sich richten nach; **to ~ upon sb.'s order** sich nach jds Anordnung richten

acting amtierend, diensttuend; stellvertretend; geschäftsführend; ~ **for** in Vertretung von; ~ **as agent for the EEC** im Auftrag der EWG; ~ **chairman** geschäftsführender Vorsitzender; ~ **chief** amtierender Leiter; ~ **manager** stellvertretender Leiter; geschäftsführender Leiter; ~ **minister** stellvertretender Minister; amtierender Minister; ~ **partner** geschäftsführender *(persönlich haftender)* Gesellschafter *(opp. sleeping, dormant, silent partner)*

action 1. Klage, Prozeß; ~ **at law** Klage nach →common law *(opp. suit in equity)*; ~ **for damages** Schadensersatzklage; ~ **ex contractu** Klage aus Vertrag; ~ **ex delicto** Klage aus unerlaubter Handlung; ~ **for declaration** Feststellungsklage; ~ **for failure to act** Untätigkeitsklage; ~ **for infringement (of a patent)** Patentverletzungsklage; ~ **for injunction** Unterlassungsklage; ~ **for libel** Beleidigungsklage, Verleumdungsklage; ~ **for money had and received** *(unspezifizierte)* Geldforderungsklage *(z. B. Klage auf Herausgabe der ungerechtfertigten Bereicherung)*; ~ **for the recovery of land** *Br* Räumungsklage; ~ **for the recovery of property** Herausgabeklage; ~ **for replevin** Klage auf Herausgabe e-r *(entzogenen)* beweglichen Sache *(→replevin)*; ~ **for specific performance** Klage auf Erfüllung des Vertrages *(→ performance)*; ~ **for unlawful detainer** *Am* Räumungsklage; ~ **in personam** obligatorische Klage; ~ **in rem** dingliche Klage; ~ **in tort** Klage aus unerlaubter Handlung; ~ **of eviction** *Am* Räumungsklage; ~ **on a debt** →debt; ~ **on a (foreign) judgment** Verfahren zur Anerkennung und Vollstreckung e-s ausländischen Urteils; ~ **quasi in rem** *Am* quasidingliche Klage *(→jurisdiction quasi in rem)*

action, bringing an ~ Erhebung e-r Klage, Klageerhebung; **cause of** ~ Klagegrund; **chose in** ~ Forderung(srecht), obligatorischer Anspruch; unkörperlicher Rechtsgegenstand; **civil** ~ Zivilprozeß, bürgerlicher Rechtsstreit; **commencement of an** ~ Klageerhebung; **criminal** ~ strafrechtliche Verfolgung; →**derivative** ~; **discontinuance of** ~ Klagerücknahme; **dismissal of** ~ Klageabweisung; **legal** ~ Prozeß; **limitation of** ~**s** (prozessuale) Klageverjährung (→limitation 2.); **local** ~ *Am* Anspruch, der nur an Ort und Stelle eingeklagt werden kann; **personal** ~ obligatorische Klage; **real** ~ dingliche Klage; **right of** ~ Klagebefugnis, Klagerecht; **by way of** ~ im Klageweg

action, to bring an ~ **against a p.** gegen jdn klagen (od. Klage erheben); jdn verklagen; **to discontinue an** ~ e-e Klage zurücknehmen; **to dismiss an** ~ e-e Klage abweisen; **an** ~ **lies** e-e Klage ist zulässig (od. begründet); **to withdraw an** ~ e-e Klage zurücknehmen

action 2. Handlung, Vorgehen; Maßnahme(n); *mil* Kampfhandlung; *dipl* Aktion; ~ **report** Tätigkeitsbericht; **administrative** ~ Verwaltungsmaßnahme(n); **common** ~ gemeinsames Vorgehen; **concerted** ~ konzertierte Aktion; einvernehmliches Vorgehen; **diplomatic** ~ diplomatischer Schritt; **field of** ~ Arbeitsgebiet; **for further** (or **appropriate**) ~ zur weiteren Veranlassung; **group of** ~**s** Gesamtheit von Maßnahmen; **joint** ~ gemeinsames Handeln (od. Vorgehen); **killed in** ~ *mil (im Einsatz)* gefallen; **sphere** (or **scope**) **of** ~ Tätigkeitsbereich; Wirkungskreis; **to take** ~ *(etw.)* veranlassen; Schritte unternehmen; Maßnahmen treffen

actionable (ein)klagbar, belangbar; ~ *Br* **on proof of damage** (*Am* **per quod**) (nur) klagbar mit Schadensnachweis; ~ **per se** (ein)klagbar ohne Schadensnachweis *(z. B. bei gewissen unerlaubten Handlungen)*; klagbar ohne besonderen Verletzungsnachweis *(bei Beleidigungen durch Veröffentlichungen)*

activate *v* aktivieren

active tätig, aktiv; lebhaft *(Handel)*; *mil* aktiv *(opp. reserve)*; ~ **account** umsatzstarkes Konto; ~ **bonds** Obligationen mit überdurchschnittlichen Umsätzen; ~ **debt** ausstehende Schuld (od. Forderung) *(opp. passive debt)*; ~ **demand** lebhafte Nachfrage; ~ **files** noch nicht erledigte Akten; ~ **list** *mil* Liste der im aktiven Dienst stehenden Offiziere; ~ **partner** tätiger (od. geschäftsführender) Gesellschafter; **on** ~ **service** *mil* im aktiven Dienst an der Front; im Krieg *(Navy, Army, Air Force)*; ~ **service allowance** *mil* Frontzulage; ~ **service pay** *mil* Wehrsold; ~ **stocks** lebhaft gehandelte Aktien; ~ **trust** Trust mit Pflichten des Treuhänders *(z. B. das trust property zu verkaufen und unter die Berechtigten zu verteilen; opp. passive trust)*

activist *pol* Aktivist

activit|y Tätigkeit, Betätigung; Lebhaftigkeit *(im Handel)*; ~ **abroad** Auslandstätigkeit; ~ **rate** *(Arbeitsmarkt)* Erwerbsquote; **course of** ~ Konjunkturverlauf; **field of** ~ Tätigkeitsgebiet, Arbeitsgebiet; **in full** ~ in vollem Gang (od. Betrieb); **low point of** ~ Konjunkturtief; **main seat of** ~ Hauptniederlassung; **managerial** ~**ies** leitende Tätigkeit; **political** ~ politische Betätigung; **sphere of** ~ Wirkungskreis; Aufgabengebiet; **subsidiary** ~ Nebentätigkeit; **world** ~ Weltkonjunktur; **to be engaged in an** ~ e-e Tätigkeit ausüben

actor (*StrafR*) Täter

actual wirklich, tatsächlich, effektiv; gegenwärtig; ~ **amount** Effektivbetrag; ~ **authority** Vertretungsmacht im Einzelfalle; ~ **cash value** Zeitwert; ~ **cost** tatsächlich entstandene Kosten, Istkosten; Selbstkosten; ~ **deaths** *(VersR)* eingetretene Todesfälle *(opp. expected deaths)*; ~ →**delivery**; ~ **expenses** Barauslagen; Nettoauslagen; ~ **hours** tatsächliche Arbeitsstunden; ~ **possession** unmittelbarer Besitz *(opp. constructive possession)*; ~ **premium** (*VersR*) Istprämie; ~ **price** Tagespreis; Marktpreis; ~ **receipt** effektive Abnahme *(z. B. von Wertpapieren)*; ~ **reserve** Istreserve; ~ **situation** Sachverhalt; ~ **strength** *mil* Iststärke; ~ **total loss** *(SeeVers)* wirklicher Totalverlust *(opp. constructive total loss)*; ~ **time** tatsächlich *(für e-e Arbeit)* aufgewandte Zeit; ~ **value** tatsächlicher (od. wirklicher) Wert, Effektivwert *(opp. nominal value)*

acutals sofort verfügbare Ware (*opp. futures*); Istzahlen

actuarial versicherungsmathematisch; versicherungstechnisch; ~ **department** Abteilung für Versicherungsmathematik; ~ **computation** (or **valuation**) Schätzung (od. Wertbestimmung) durch e-n Versicherungsmathematiker; ~ **science** (Lebens-)Versicherungstechnik; **to give** ~ **advice** versicherungsmathematisch beraten

actuary Versicherungsmathematiker, Aktuar; *(berufsmäßiger)* Schätzer

actuating Ingangsetzung (*e-s Betriebes*)

actus reus *Am (StrafR)* rechtswidrige Tatbestandsverwirklichung, Tat *(cf. mens rea)*

ad *colloq.* Anzeige, Inserat; ~ **agency** Werbeagentur; ~ **man** Werbe(fach)mann

adapt *v* anpassen; *(Text)* bearbeiten, umarbeiten; **to ~ o.s. to circumstances** sich den Verhältnissen anpassen

adaptable anpassungsfähig

adaptation Anpassung; (Text-)Bearbeitung; Herstellung von Bearbeitungen; ~ **clause** Anpassungsklausel; ~ **of contracts** Anpassung von Verträgen; Vertragsanpassung; **A~ Decision** *(EG)*[16] Anpassungsbeschluß; ~ **of prices** Anpassung der Preise; ~ **of principles** Anwendung von Grundsätzen (to auf); ~ **procedure** (*EG*) Anpassungsverfahren; **re-** ~ Wiederanpassung

add *v* hinzufügen; zuzahlen, nachschießen; beiladen; **to ~ to** vermehren; **to ~ to a list** in e-e Liste aufnehmen; **to ~ to the price** auf den Preis aufschlagen; **to ~ up** addieren, zusammenzählen; **to ~ up one's accounts** *Am* seine Abrechnung machen

added value Wertschöpfung, Mehrwert (→*value added tax*)

addendum Zusatz, Nachtrag

addict Süchtiger; **drug** ~ Rauschgiftsüchtiger; **opium** ~ Opiumsüchtiger

addicted süchtig; ~ **to alcohol** alkoholsüchtig; ~ **to drugs** rauschgiftsüchtig

addiction Süchtigkeit; **drug** ~ Rauschgiftsucht

adding machine Addiermaschine

ad diem am festgesetzten Tag

addition Hinzufügen, Zusatz; Nachtrag; Zugang, Zuwachs; Anbau (to an); *Am* (Land-)Zukauf; ~**s** *(Bilanz)* Zugänge *(e-s Anlagegutes)* *(opp. retirements)*; ~ **to the price** Preiszuschlag; **certificate of** ~ *(PatR)* Zusatzbescheinigung; **patent of** ~ Zusatzpatent; **without** ~ **(to) or alteration (of)** ohne Hinzufügung oder Änderung; **to pay in** ~ zuzahlen

additional zusätzlich; Zusatz-; Mehr-, Extra-; Neben-; ~ **agreement** Zusatzabkommen; Nebenabrede; ~ **allowance** Zuschuß; ~ **application** *(PatR)* Zusatzanmeldung; ~ **article** Zusatzartikel; ~ **charge** →charge 4; ~ **charges** (or **costs**) zusätzliche Kosten; Mehrkosten; Nebenkosten; ~ **claim** (or **demand**) Nachforderung, Mehrforderung; ~ **clause** Zusatzklausel; ~ **conditions** Zusatzbedingungen; ~ →**cover**; ~ **duty** Steuerzuschlag; Zollzuschlag; ~ **expenditure** Mehrausgaben; ~ **expenses** zusätzliche Kosten, Mehrkosten; ~ **fee** Zusatzgebühr; ~ **income** Nebeneinkommen; Zusatzeinkommen; ~ **insurance** Zusatzversicherung; ~ **invention** *(PatR)* Zusatzerfindung; ~ **order** Nachbestellung; ~ **payment** zusätzliche Zahlung; Nachzahlung; Nachschuß; ~ **premium** *(VersR)* Prämienzuschlag; Zusatzprämie; ~ **price** Mehrpreis; ~ **protocol** *(VölkerR)* Zusatzprotokoll; ~ **requirement** Mehrbedarf; ~ **respite** (or **time**) Nachfrist; ~ **tax** Zusatzsteuer

additives in feedingstuffs Zusatzstoffe in der Tierernährung

address 1. Adresse, Anschrift; ~ **in case of need** Notadresse *(beim Wechselregreß)*; ~ **commission** *(vom Reeder dem Befrachter vergütete)* Provision bei Frachtabschluß über ganze Schiffsladungen; ~ **for service** Zustellungsadresse

address, accommodation ~ Deckadresse; **business** ~ Geschäftsadresse; **cable** ~ Drahtanschrift; **in case of change of** ~ falls verzogen; **home** ~ Heimatanschrift; **mailing** ~ *Am* Postanschrift; **postal** ~ Postanschrift; **to change the** ~ umadressieren

address 2. Anrede; Ansprache; ~ **of welcome** Begrüßungsansprache; ~ **to the Court** Anrede des Gerichts; **closing** ~ Schlußansprache; **opening** ~ Eröffnungsansprache; to **deliver** (or **give**) **an** ~ e-e Ansprache halten

address *v* adressieren; anreden; sprechen zu, Ansprache halten; **to ~ an appeal** *pol* e-n Aufruf richten (to an); **to ~ a meeting** das Wort in e-r Versammlung ergreifen; **to ask to ~ the meeting** um das Wort bitten; **to ~ the House** *parl* das Wort ergreifen

addressed bill Domizilwechsel

addressee Empfänger, Adressat *(opp. sender)*

addressing machine (or **addressograph**) Adressiermaschine, Adremagerät

adduce *v*, **to ~ evidence** Beweis erbringen, Beweismaterial liefern; **to ~ reasons** Gründe anführen

ADELA (Atlantic Development for Latin America) private Beteiligungs- und Finanzgesellschaft, deren Aufgabe es ist, Kapitalinvestitionen in private Unternehmen Lateinamerikas zu fördern *(Hauptsitz Luxemburg)*

ademption of a legacy Wegfall e-s Vermächtnisses *(durch Untergang des vermachten Gegenstandes vor Erbfall, z.B. Erfüllung der vermachten Forderung an den Erblasser, Vernichtung e-r vermachten Sache)*

adequacy Adäquanz; Angemessenheit; ~ **of resources** Zulänglichkeit von Geldmitteln

adequate adäquat; angemessen (to für); ausreichend; ~ **recompense** angemessene Vergütung (od. Belohnung); **state of being** ~ Adäquanz

adhere *v* festhalten (to an); einhalten, befolgen; angehören, anhängen; *Scot (das Urteil e-s unteren Gerichts)* bestätigen; **to ~ to a convention** *(VölkerR)* e-m Abkommen beitreten; ein Abkommen einhalten; **to ~ to a political party** e-r politischen Partei treu bleiben; **to ~ to a program(me)** bei e-m Programm bleiben; ein Programm einhalten

adherence Festhalten (to an); Einhaltung, Befolgung; *(VölkerR)* Beitritt *(e-s Staates zu e-m bestehenden Vertrag)*; **~ to a convention** *(VölkerR)* Beitritt zu e-m Abkommen; Einhaltung e-s Abkommens; **instrument of ~** Beitrittsurkunde; **to be open for ~ (by)** *(jdm)* zum Beitritt offen stehen

adherent Anhänger *(e-r Bewegung, Religion)*

adhesion Festhalten (to an); *(VölkerR)* Beitritt; **~ to an opinion** Festhalten an e-r Meinung; **~ to a plan** Festhalten an e-m Plan

adhesive stamp aufklebbare Briefmarke *(opp. impressed stamp)*

ad hoc ad hoc; *(nur)* zu diesem Zweck *(opp. standing)*; **~ agency** *(VölkerR)* ad hoc-Stelle; **~ arrangement** ad hoc-Vereinbarung; **~ body** ad hoc-Organ; **~ committee** ad hoc-Ausschuß; von Fall zu Fall gebildeter Ausschuß; **~ working party** ad hoc-Arbeitsgruppe

ad interim vorläufig, Zwischen-

adjacent benachbart (to von); in der Nähe liegend *(nicht notwendigerweise angrenzend, cf. adjoining)*; **~ countries** benachbarte Länder; **~ land (or property)** Nachbargrundstück; **~ owner** Nachbareigentümer; **~ waters** Küstengewässer

adjective law Verfahrensrecht, formelles Recht *(opp. substantive law)*

adjoining benachbart, *(direkt)* angrenzend *(cf. adjacent)*; **~ owner** Nachbareigentümer; **~ property** Nachbargrundstück; **~ property assessments** Anliegerbeiträge; **~ table** nebenstehende Tabelle

adjourn *v* aufschieben; *(zeitl. od. örtl.)* verlegen; (sich) vertagen; sich *(an e-n anderen Ort)* begeben; **to ~ generally** (or **sine die**) (sich) auf unbestimmte Zeit vertagen; **to ~ to a fixed day** (sich) auf e-n bestimmten Tag vertagen; **to ~ a decision** e-e Entscheidung aussetzen; **to ~ the hearing** (or **proceedings**) die Verhandlung vertagen

adjourned aufgeschoben; verlegt; vertagt *(und zu e-m späteren Zeitpunkt fortgesetzt)*; **to declare the meeting ~** die Sitzung vertagen; **the meeting ~ to four o'clock** die Sitzung vertagte sich auf 4 Uhr; **the meeting was ~ for a week** die Sitzung wurde um eine Woche vertagt; **the meeting ~ to another room** die Versammlungsteilnehmer begaben sich in e-n anderen Raum; **to stand ~** sich vertagen

adjournment Aufschiebung; Verlegung *(auf e-e andere Zeit od. an e-n anderen Ort)*; Vertagung; **~ sine die** Vertagung auf unbestimmte Zeit; **~ to a fixed day** (or **date**) Vertagung auf e-e bestimmte Zeit; **~ of a petition (in bankruptcy)** Aufschub e-s Konkursantrags; **motion for ~** Antrag auf Vertagung; **to apply for an ~** Vertagung beantragen

adjudge *v (richterl.)* erkennen, entscheiden; *(gerichtl.)* zuerkennen (od. zusprechen); **to ~ a case** e-e Sache *(gerichtl.)* entscheiden; **to ~ the debtor (a) bankrupt** den Schuldner für zahlungsunfähig erklären; das Konkursverfahren (od. den Konkurs) über das Vermögen des Schuldners eröffnen; **to ~ a prize to sb.** jdm e-n Preis zuerkennen; **to ~ a sum as compensation** *(jdm)* Schadensersatz zusprechen

adjudicate *v (richterl.)* erkennen, entscheiden (on über), erklären; *(gerichtl.)* zuerkennen (od. zusprechen); *(bei Auktionen)* Zuschlag erteilen; **to ~ the debtor a bankrupt** →to adjudge the debtor a bankrupt; **to ~ (up)on a case** e-e Sache (gerichtlich) entscheiden; **to ~ a claim for damages** über e-n Schadensersatzanspruch (gerichtlich) entscheiden

adjudicated bankrupt Gemeinschuldner

adjudication *(richterl.)* Entscheidung, Urteil, Rechtsspruch; Zuerkennung, Zusprechung; *(bei Auktionen)* Zuschlag(serteilung); *Scot* Zwangsvollstreckung in das unbewegliche Vermögen; **~ (in bankruptcy)** Eröffnung des Konkursverfahrens, Konkurseröffnung; *(VölkerR)* Adjudikation *(Zuerkennung von Gebiet durch Entscheidung internationaler Gerichte, bes. durch Schiedsspruch)*; **final ~** rechtskräftige Entscheidung; **to obtain an ~ in bankruptcy** (on one's own petition) *Br* e-n Konkurseröffnungsbeschluß erwirken; **to submit to ~** *(VölkerR)* sich e-m *(internationalen)* Rechtsspruch unterwerfen

adjudication, ~ order (or **order of ~**) Konkurseröffnungsbeschluß; **annulment of ~ order** Aufhebung des Eröffnungsbeschlusses

adjust *v* berichtigen, richtigstellen; anpassen, angleichen (to an); ausgleichen; sich einordnen; bereinigen; *(VersR) (Schaden)* regulieren; *(Streit)* schlichten, beilegen; **to ~ accounts** Konten bereinigen; **to ~ the average** die Dispache aufmachen; **to ~ damages** *(VersR)* den Schadensersatzanspruch festsetzen; **to ~ a weight** ein Gewicht eichen

adjusted, ~ gross income *Am (Einkommensteuer)*[17] berichtigtes Bruttoeinkommen; **~ for price** preisbereinigt; **seasonally ~** saisonbereinigt *(beim Index)*

adjusting of fields Flurbereinigung

adjustable anpassungsfähig; ~ **currency** elastische Währung; ~ **insurance** offene Versicherung

adjuster *(VersR)* Regulierungsbeamter; Dispacheur, Schadenssachverständiger; **insurance** ~ *Am* Versicherungsangestellter, der zum Abschluß von Vergleichen befugt ist

adjustment Berichtigung, Richtigstellung; Anpassung, Angleichung; Ausgleichung; Bereinigung; Regulierung *(des Schadens);* Schlichtung, Beilegung *(e-s Streites);* ~ **of average** Dispache, Havarieberechnung; ~ **of capital** Kapitalberichtigung; ~ **of claims** *(VersR)* Schadensberechnung; ~ **of complaints** Regelung (od. Beilegung) von Beschwerden; ~ **of debts of an individual with regular income** *Am*[18] Vergleich für natürliche Personen mit geregeltem Einkommen *(nur für Schuldner mit ungesicherten Schulden unter $ 100.000 und gesicherten Schulden unter $ 350.000);* ~ **of a difference** Ausgleich e-r Differenz; **amicable** ~ **of differences** gütliche Beilegung von Streitigkeiten; ~ **of the interest rates** Zinsanpassung; ~ **of prices** Angleichung der Preise; Preisanpassung *(an bestimmte Umstände);* ~ **of sum insured** Anpassung der Versicherungssummen; ~ **of wages** Anpassung der Löhne; Lohnangleichung

adjustment, currency ~ Währungsangleichung; **economic** ~ wirtschaftliche Anpassung; **end of year** ~ *(AktienR)* Rechnungsabgrenzung; **financial** ~ Finanzausgleich; **global** ~ **of values** Sammelwertberichtigung; **gradual** ~ allmähliche Anpassung; **loss** ~ *(VersR)* Schadensregulierung; **period of vocational** ~ Einarbeitungszeit; **to make the appropriate** ~**s gradually** geeignete Anpassungen stufenweise durchführen

ad lib. (ad libitum) nach Belieben

adman *Am colloq.* Werbe(fach)mann

administer *v* verwalten; handhaben; als Nachlaßverwalter tätig sein; **to** ~ **an estate** e-n Nachlaß (od. ein Vermögen) verwalten; **to** ~ **justice** Recht sprechen; Gerechtigkeit üben; **to** ~ **the law** Recht sprechen; das Recht handhaben; **to** ~ **an oath** (to a p.) (jdm) e-n Eid abnehmen, (jdn) vereidigen, (jdn) beeidigen

administered interest rate administrierter Zinssatz

administered prices administrierte Preise *(vom Staat festgesetzte od. kontrollierte Preise, z. B. Postgebühren); (von e-m Unternehmen)* willkürlich festgesetzte Preise *(ohne Berücksichtigung der Kosten)*

administering authority[19] *(VölkerR)* Verwaltungsmacht *(cf. trusteeship authority)*

administration 1. Verwaltung; Handhabung; (Unternehmens-)Führung, Leitung; *Br (KonkursR)* Verwaltung (→*administrator*); **the A**~ *Am* Regierung; Amtsperiode *(des Präsidenten, e-s Gouverneurs od. Bürgermeisters);* ~ **bill** *Am* Gesetzesvorlage, Regierungsvorlage; ~ **board** Kuratorium, Verwaltungsrat; ~ **charge** Verwaltungskosten; ~ **costs** (or **expenses**) Verwaltungskosten; ~ **fine** Bußgeld; ~ **headquarters** Hauptverwaltungsstelle; ~ **in bankruptcy of the estate of a p. dying insolvent** *Br* Nachlaßkonkurs; ~ **of a business** Geschäftsführung; ~ **of discipline** Disziplinargewalt; ~ **of an estate** Vermögensverwaltung *(z. B. Verwaltung e-s trust estate);* ~ **of the estate of a person of unsound mind** (or *Br* **a patient**) Pflegschaft über das Vermögen e-s Geisteskranken; ~ **of an insolvent** (*Am* **decedent's**) **estate** Nachlaßkonkurs; ~ **of justice** Rechtspflege; Justizverwaltung; ~ **of the law** Rechtsprechung; ~ **of an oath** Eidesabnahme, Vereidigung; ~ **official** *Am* Regierungsbeamter; ~ **of property** Vermögensverwaltung; ~ **of restrictions** Handhabung von Beschränkungen; ~ **order** *Br* Vermögensverwaltungsanordnung *(des Gerichts für Verwaltung e-s trust);* ~ **practices** Verwaltungspraktiken

administration, change of the A~ *Am* Regierungswechsel; **central** ~ **office** Hauptverwaltung

Administration, to form an ~ *Am* e-e Regierung bilden

administration 2. *(vom Gericht bestimmte)* Erbschaftsverwaltung; *(etwa:)* Nachlaßverwaltung, Nachlaßpflegschaft (cf. *administrator, executor*); ~ **action** *Br* Klage auf ordnungsgemäße Erbschaftsverwaltung; ~ **ad colligenda bona** Erbschaftsverwaltung zur Verwertung verderblicher od. sonst gefährdeter Nachlaßgegenstände; ~ **bond** Sicherheitsleistung des Erbschaftsverwalters (administrator); ~ **de bonis non administratis** Erbschaftsverwaltung für Nachlaßgegenstände, deren Verwaltung ein früherer executor oder administrator nicht abgeschlossen hat; ~ **expenses** Kosten der Erbschaftsverwaltung; ~ **of estates** Erbschaftsverwaltung; *(ungenau:)* Nachlaßverwaltung; **A**~ **of Estates Act** *Br* Gesetz zur Regelung der gesetzlichen Erbfolge; ~ **of decedent's estates** *Am* Nachlaßabwicklung; ~ **order** Anordnung *(des Gerichts)* zur Bestellung e-s Verwalters (→*administrator 2.*); ~ **with the will annexed** gerichtlich angeordnete Erbschaftsverwaltung *(wenn Erblasser keinen executor benannt hat oder dieser aus irgendeinem Grunde ausfällt)*

administration, letters of ~ Erbschaftsverwalterzeugnis *(die dem administrator über seine Bestellung erteilte Urkunde);* **letters of** ~ **with will annexed** Bestellung e-s Erbschaftsverwalters *(wenn Erblasser ein Testament hinterlassen, aber keinen executor benannt hat oder dieser ausfällt);* **grant(ing) of letters of** ~ Bestellung zum

Erbschaftsverwalter; **to grant letters of** ~ *(jdn)* zum Erbschaftsverwalter bestellen; **to take out letters of** ~ sich zum Erbschaftsverwalter bestellen lassen

administration, order for ~ Verteilungsanordnung *(des Gerichts mit Rangbestimmung bei unzureichender Masse, z.B. bei Nachlaßverbindlichkeiten)*

administrative Verwaltungs-; verwaltungsmäßig; verwaltungstechnisch; ~ **action** Verwaltungsakt, Verwaltungsmaßnahme(n); ~ **agency** *Am*[20] *(und VölkerR)* Verwaltungsstelle; ~ **agreement** Verwaltungsvereinbarung; *(VölkerR) (wenn zweiseitig)* Verwaltungsabkommen; *(wenn mehrseitig)* Verwaltungsübereinkommen; ~ **apparatus** Verwaltungsapparat; ~ **arrangement** Verwaltungsvereinbarung; ~ **assistance** Amtshilfe; ~ **assistant** Sachbearbeiter für die Verwaltung; ~ **authorities** Verwaltungsbehörden; ~ **autonomy** Selbstverwaltung; ~ **bodies** Verwaltungsorgane; ~ **body** Verwaltungsgremium; **through** ~ **channels** auf dem Verwaltungswege; ~ **charge** Verwaltungsgebühr; ~ **coercion** Verwaltungszwang; ~ **committee** *(VölkerR)* Verwaltungsausschuß; ~ **cooperation** Zusammenarbeit der Verwaltungen; Amtshilfe; ~ **council** Verwaltungsrat; ~ **decision** Verwaltungsentscheidung; ~ **discretion** Verwaltungsermessen; ~ **enforcement** Verwaltungsvollstreckung; ~ **expense(s)** Verwaltungskosten; Verwaltungsgemeinkosten; ~ **fee** Verwaltungsgebühr; ~ **fine** Geldbuße; Bußgeld; ~ **functions** Verwaltungsaufgaben; ~ **grade** *Br* oberste Stufe des Beamtentums *(Civil Service und Local Government)*; ~ **instructions** Verwaltungsvorschriften; ~ **law** Verwaltungsrecht; *Am* das sich auf die Regelung einzelner Sachgebiete und auf die Normsetzung *(Erlaß von Rechtsverordnungen)* beschränkende Verwaltungsrecht; ~ **machinery** Verwaltungsapparat; ~ **matters** Verwaltungssachen; ~ **measure** Verwaltungsmaßnahme; **chief** ~ **office** Hauptverwaltung; ~ **officer** *(höherer)* Verwaltungsbeamter; **chief** ~ **officer** oberster Verwaltungsbeamter; ~ **organs** Verwaltungsorgane; ~ **post** Stelle in der Verwaltung; leitende Stellung; ~ **powers** verwaltungsmäßige Befugnisse; ~ **practices** Verwaltungsbrauch; **(Federal) A** ~ **Procedure Act** (APA) *Am*[21] (Bundes-)Verwaltungsverfahrensgesetz; **legal or** ~ **provisions** Rechts- od. Verwaltungsvorschriften; ~ **quasi-legislation** *Br* gesetzgebungsartige Verwaltungsanordnung

administrative receiver[21a] *Br* Zwangsverwalter; Verwalter über das ganze oder überwiegende Vermögen e-r Kapitalgesellschaft, der von den durch e-e →floating charge gesicherten Gläubigern bestellt wird

administrative, ~ **regulation** Verwaltungsvorschrift; ~ **representative** *Am* Regierungsvertreter; **A**~ **Rule Making** *Am* Erlaß verbindlicher Verwaltungsordnungen; ~ **supervision** Verwaltungsaufsicht; ~ **tribunals** *Br* Verwaltungsgerichte *(für bestimmte Sachgebiete)*

administratively, to review ~ auf dem Verwaltungswege überprüfen

administrator 1. Verwalter; Erbschaftsverwalter; *(etwa)* Nachlaßverwalter, Nachlaßpfleger; *(cf. personal representative)*; *Am* Registrierungsstelle

Der administrator wird bei Intestaterbfolge, ungültigem Testament oder Wegfall des executor durch das Nachlaßgericht bestellt

administrator, ~**'s bond** Sicherheitsleistung des Erbschaftsverwalters; ~ **ad colligenda bona** Erbschaftsverwalter für verderbliche oder sonst gefährdete Nachlaßgegenstände; ~ **at law** *Scot* (Vater als) gesetzlicher Vertreter *(für minderjährige Kinder)*; ~ **de bonis non administratis** Erbschaftsverwalter für bestimmte Nachlaßgegenstände (→*administration* 2.) ~ **of an estate** Erbschaftsverwalter; ~ **with the will annexed** (*Am* ~ **cum testamento annexo**) gerichtlich bestimmter Testamentsvollstrecker *(bei Ausfall des executor)*

administrator, ancillary ~ *Am* Nebenerbschaftsverwalter, Hilfserbschaftsverwalter (→ *ancillary administration*); **attorney** ~ *Br* stellvertretender Erbschaftsverwalter *(z.B. für e-n im Ausland lebenden administrator)*; **domiciliary** ~ *Am* Haupterbschaftsverwalter; **principal** ~ *(IPR)* der im Domizilstaat benannte Erbschaftsverwalter

administrator 2. *Br (KonkursR) (durch den →Insolvency Act 1985 eingeführter)* Verwalter

Das Gericht kann einen Verwalter zur Weiterführung bzw. zur Verwertung des vom Konkurs bedrohten Geschäftsbetriebes einer Kapitalgesellschaft benennen

administratrix Erbschaftsverwalterin

admiralty Admiralität; ~ **actions** seerechtliche Streitigkeiten; **A**~ **Court** *Br*[22] Gericht für seerechtliche Streitigkeiten; ~ **jurisdiction** Seegerichtsbarkeit; ~ **law** Seerecht; ~ **proceedings** Seeprozeß

admissible zulässig, erlaubt; ~ **evidence** zulässiges Beweismittel; **the appeal is** ~ die Beschwerde (etc) ist zulässig

admission Zulassung (to zu), Aufnahme (to in); Eintritt, Zutritt; *(Zivilprozeß)* Zugeben, Zugeständnis, Anerkenntnis, Nichtbestreiten *(e-r Tatsache)*; *(Strafprozeß)* Zugeständnis *(der zur Last gelegten Straftat)*; ~ **of aliens into a country** Aufnahme von Ausländern in ein Land; ~ **as attorney** *Am* Zulassung als (Rechts-)Anwalt; ~ **to the Bar** Zulassung als (Rechts-)Anwalt *(Br als barrister)*; **A** ~ **Bill** *Am* Gesetzesvorlage auf Zulassung als Bundesstaat; ~ **charge** (or **fee**) Aufnahmegebühr; Zulassungsgebühr; Eintrittspreis; ~ **of a fact** Zugeben (od. Eingeständnis) e-r Tatsache; ~ **free** Eintritt frei; ~ **of guilt** Schuldgeständnis; **(compulsory)** ~ **to a (mental) hospital**[23] Einweisung in e-e psychiatrische Klinik; ~ **of a partner** Aufnahme e-s Teilhabers; ~ **to membership** Aufnahme als Mitglied; ~ **of securities to the stock exchange** Börsenzulassung von Wertpapieren; ~ **as solicitor** *Br* Zulassung als (Rechts-)Anwalt; ~ **tax** *Am (einzelstaatl.)* (Kraftfahrzeug-)Zulassungssteuer; ~ **ticket** Eintrittskarte

admission, to be eligible for ~ die erforderliche Voraussetzung für die Zulassung (od. Aufnahme) erfüllen; **to seek** ~ um Zulassung nachsuchen

admit *v* zulassen, aufnehmen; zugeben, zugestehen, anerkennen; **to** ~ **of** zulassen, erlauben; **to** ~ **as attorney** *Am* als (Rechts-)Anwalt zulassen; **to** ~ **to bail** gegen Sicherheitsleistung aus der Haft entlassen; **to** ~ **to the Bar** als Anwalt *(Br als barrister)* zulassen; **to** ~ **in evidence** als Beweis(mittel) zulassen; **to** ~ **one's guilt** sich schuldig bekennen; s-e Schuld zugeben; **to** ~ **new members** neue Mitglieder aufnehmen (to in)

admitted, ~ **claim** *(VersR)* anerkannter (Schadensersatz-)Anspruch; ~ **fact** anerkannte Tatsache; **young persons** (or **children**) **under the age of** . . . **(are) not** ~ Jugendliche unter . . . Jahren haben keinen Zutritt; **to be** ~ **to citizenship (by naturalization)** *Am* eingebürgert werden; **to be** ~ **as solicitor** *Br* als (Rechts-) Anwalt (solicitor) zugelassen werden

admittedly zugegebenermaßen

admittance Eintritt, Zutritt; Zulassung; Anerkennung; **no** ~ Eintritt verboten; **no** ~ **except on business** Unbefugten ist der Zutritt verboten; **terms of** ~ Zulassungsbedingungen

admonish *v* ermahnen; (ver)warnen; Verweis erteilen; *(Geschworenen)* Rechtsbelehrung erteilen; **to** ~ **to tell the truth** zur Wahrheit ermahnen

admonition Ermahnung; Verwarnung; Verweis; Rechtsbelehrung *(der Geschworenen)*

admonitory letter Mahnbrief

adopt *v* adoptieren *(an Kindes Statt)* annehmen; sich aneignen, annehmen; aufnehmen; **to** ~ **the annual accounts** den Jahresabschluß feststellen; **to** ~ **the budget** den Haushaltsplan verabschieden; **to** ~ **a p. as a candidate** *Br parl* e-n Kandidaten aufstellen; **to** ~ **a resolution** e-e Entschließung annehmen; e-n Beschluß fassen

adopted, ~ **child** Adoptivkind, angenommenes Kind; **A**~ **Children Register** *Br (vom Registrar General geführtes)* Register für adoptierte Kinder; ~ **country** neues Vaterland, Wahlheimat; **the opinion was unanimously** ~ die Stellungnahme wurde einstimmig verabschiedet

adoptee Adoptierte(r), Adoptivkind

adopter (or **adopting parent**) Annehmender

adoption[24] 1. Adoption, Annahme als Kind; ~ **of a child** Adoption e-s Kindes; ~ **order** *(gerichtl.)* Adoptionsbeschluß; **revocation of the** ~ **order** Widerruf des Adoptionsbeschlusses; **brother by** ~ Adoptivbruder; **decree** (or **order**) **of** ~ *(gerichtl.)* Adoptionsbeschluß; **to apply for an** ~ e-e Adoption beantragen

adoption 2. Annahme *(e-s Planes etc)*; Aufnahme; ~ **of the budget** Verabschiedung des Haushaltsplans; ~ **of a contract** Annahme e-s Vertrages *(als bindend, unter Ausschluß seiner Anfechtung)*; ~ **of a foreign corporation** *Am* Aufnahme e-r ausländischen Gesellschaft; ~ **of a new policy** Annahme e-r neuen Politik; **country of his** ~ Wahlheimat

adoptive, ~ **parents** Adoptiveltern; ~ **son** Adoptivsohn

adrate *colloq.* Anzeigengebühr

ad referendum ad referendum; zur Berichterstattung

adult Erwachsener *(opp. infant)*; erwachsen; ~ **dependant** erwachsener Unterhaltsberechtigter; ~ **education** Erwachsenenbildung; **A**~ **Education Courses** *(etwa:)* Volkshochschule; ~ **person** Erwachsener

adulterate *v* verfälschen *(bes. Lebensmittel)*; **to** ~ **coins** (or **the coinage**) Münzen verfälschen; ~**d money** falsches Geld

adulterer Ehebrecher
adulteress Ehebrecherin

adulteration, ~ **of the coinage** Münzverfälschung; ~ **of food** Verfälschung von Nahrungsmitteln; Lebensmittelfälschung; **warranted free from** ~ Reinheit garantiert

adulterous ehebrecherisch; ~ **relations** (or **association**) ehebrecherische Beziehungen

adultery Ehebruch; **to commit** ~ Ehebruch begehen, die Ehe brechen

ad valorem (ad val.) dem Werte nach; *(prozentual)* vom Wert; ~ **duty** Wertzoll *(Zollbemessung nach dem Warenwert) (opp. specific duty)*; ~ **stamp duty** *Br*[25] Wertstempelsteuer; ~ **tariff** Werttarif; ~ **tax** *Am* Vermögensteuer

advance Fortschritt; Vorschuß, Vorschußzahlung; Vorauszahlung; Darlehen, Kredit; *Am* Anzahlung; Erhöhen, Steigen *(der Preise, Kurse)*; Beförderung; Aufrücken *(im Amt)*; *(ErbR)* Vorausempfang(enes); ~**s** *(kurzfristige)* Darlehen; ~ **in the art** *(PatR)* gewerblicher (od. technischer) Fortschritt; ~ **bill** Vorschußwechsel; ~ **booking** Vorbestellung *(Theater, Hotel etc)*; ~ **calculation** Vorausberechnung; ~ **commitment** Kreditzusage; ~ **for costs** *Am* Kostenvorschuß *(bei Gericht)*; ~ **corporation tax** (ACT) *Br* auf ausgeschüttete Gewinne vorausgezahlte Körperschaftsteuer; ~ **on current account** Kontokorrentkredit; ~ **financing** Vorfinanzierung; ~ **free of interest** zinsloses Darlehen; ~ **freight** vorausbezahlte Fracht; ~ **on freight** Frachtvorschuß; ~ **on goods** (or **merchandise**) Vorschüsse auf Waren, Warenlombard; ~ **money** *Am* Vorschuß, Anzahlung; ~ **note** *Br* Vorschußanweisung *(des Kapitäns an den Seemann)*; ~ **notice** Vorankündigung, Voranzeige; ~ **on an offer** Mehrgebot; ~ **order** Vorausbestellung; ~ **pay** *Am* Gehaltsvorschuß

advance payment Vorauszahlung; Vorschußzahlung; *Am* Anzahlung; ~ **of fees** *Am* Gebührenvorschuß; ~ **guarantee** Anzahlungsgarantie; ~ **on taxes** Steuervorauszahlung; **to ask for an** ~ um Vorschuß bitten; **to make an** ~ e-n Vorschuß leisten; *Am* e-e Anzahlung leisten; pränumerando zahlen; **to receive ~s of one's salary** Gehaltsvorschuß bekommen

advance, ~ in price(s) Preiserhöhung, Preissteigerung; Steigen (od. Anziehen) der Preise (od. Kurse); Kurssteigerung; ~ **against products** Warenbevorschussung; ~ **in profits** Gewinnsteigerung; ~ **quota** Vorgriffskontingent; ~ **rate** Lombardsatz; ~ **on the rent** Mietvorauszahlung

advance on salary Gehaltsvorschuß; **to receive an ~ on one's salary** Gehaltsvorschuß bekommen

advance against security Lombardkredit; **rate for** ~ Lombardsatz

advance, ~s on securities Effektenlombard; **~s on the succeeding budget** Haushaltsvorgriffe; ~ **by seniority** Beförderung nach dem Dienstalter; ~ **ticket sale** Kartenvorverkauf; ~ **for travel(l)ing expenses** Reisekostenvorschuß; ~ **on wages** Lohnvorschuß

advance, bank ~ Bankdarlehen, Bankkredit; **blank** ~ Blankovorschuß; Blankokredit; **cash** ~ Barvorschuß; **collateral** ~ Lombardvorschuß, Lombardkredit; **economic** ~ wirtschaftlicher Fortschritt; **grant of an** ~ Vorschußbewilligung

advance, in ~ im voraus; pränumerando; **amount paid in** ~ vorausbezahlter Betrag, Vorauszahlung; **money in** ~ Vorschuß; **payment in** ~ Vorauszahlung, Vorschußzahlung; **to pay in** ~ im voraus zahlen, vorausbezahlen; pränumerando zahlen; **to receive part of one's salary in** ~ Gehaltsvorschuß bekommen

advance, salary ~ Gehaltsvorschuß; **secured** ~ gesichertes Darlehen; Lombardkredit; **technical** ~ technischer Fortschritt

advance, to ask for an ~ um Vorschuß bitten; **to grant an** ~ bevorschussen; Vorschuß gewähren; **to make an** ~ (or ~**s**) Darlehen geben; Vorschuß zahlen; **science has made great ~s** die Wissenschaft hat große Fortschritte gemacht; **to reimburse the ~s plus interest** die (erhaltenen) Vorschüsse mit Zinsen zurückerstatten

advance *v* Fortschritte machen, fortschreiten; fördern; *(Geld)* vorschießen, auslegen, vorstrecken; Vorschuß leisten, bevorschussen; steigen, anziehen *(Preise, Kurse)*; *(Preis)* erhöhen, heraufsetzen; *(Meinung)* vorbringen; *(im Amt)* befördern; vorrücken, befördert werden; **to ~ an amount** e-n Betrag vorschießen (od. auslegen); **to ~ a child** *(ErbR)* e-m Kinde den Vorausempfang geben; **to ~ a claim** e-n Anspruch vorbringen (od. geltend machen); **to ~ the costs** die Kosten vorschießen; **to ~ funds** Mittel vorschießen; **to ~ a p.'s interests** jds Interesse fördern; **to ~ money** Geld vorstrecken (od. vorschießen); Vorschuß leisten (on auf); **to ~ money on securities** Wertpapiere beleihen (od. lombardieren); **to ~ a p. in office** jdn befördern; **to ~ the price** den Preis heraufsetzen; **to ~ in price** im Preis steigen; **to ~ a project** e-n Plan fördern; **to ~ a proposal** e-n Vorschlag vorbringen; **to ~ reasons** Gründe vorbringen; **prices ~ sharply** die Preise (od. Kurse) ziehen scharf an

advanced vorgeschritten, fortgeschritten; fortschrittlich, hochmodern; zukünftig, auf die Zukunft gerichtet; ~ **age** vorgerücktes Alter; ~ **course** Kursus für Fortgeschrittene; ~ **and developing countries** Industrienationen und Entwicklungsländer; ~ **freight** (a. f.) vorausbezahlte Fracht; ~ **member** *Br* Bausparer *(e-r Bauspargesellschaft)*, dessen Zuteilungsdarlehen ausgezahlt ist *(opp. unadvanced member)*; ~ **price** erhöhter (od. heraufgesetzter) Preis; ~ **training** Fortbildung; ~ **views** moderne (od. fortschrittliche) Ansichten; **prices ~ from ... to ...** die Kurse stiegen von ... auf ...; **to be** ~ befördert werden

advancement Beförderung *(im Amt)*; Förderung; Fortschritt; *(ErbR)* Vorempfang(enes); *Am* Vorschuß(zahlung); **social** ~ sozialer Aufstieg; soziale Förderung; **stage of social** ~ soziale Entwicklungsstufe; **opportunity for** ~ Aufstiegsmöglichkeit, Beförderungsmöglichkeit

advantage Vorteil, Nutzen; Gewinn; **commercial** ~ Handelsvorteil; **commercial ~ between states** Präferenzsystem zwischen Staaten; **economic** ~ wirtschaftlicher Vorteil; **with the intent to gain** ~ in gewinnsüchtiger Absicht; **little** ~ geringer Nutzen; **granting or promising ~s** Gewährung od. Versprechen von Vorteilen; **to derive ~ from** Nutzen ziehen aus; **to execute an order to the best** ~ e-n Auftrag bestens ausführen; **to gain a pecuniary** ~ e-n Vermögensvorteil erlangen; **to grant ~s** Vorteile gewähren; **to receive an** ~ e-n Vorteil erlangen; **to sell to (good)** ~ mit Gewinn verkaufen; gut verkaufen; **to take** ~ **(of)** Vorteil ziehen (aus), ausnützen, sich zugute machen, profitieren (von); **to take undue** ~ **(of)** ausnützen; **to turn sth. to** ~ sich etw. zunutze machen

advantageous vorteilhaft, günstig; ~ **position** günstige Stellung; **on** ~ **terms** zu günstigen Bedingungen

advent to power *pol* Machtantritt

adventitious zufällig; hinzukommend

adventure Abenteuer; *(gewagtes)* Unternehmen; Risiko, Risikogeschäft; Spekulation(sgeschäft); **gross** ~ Bodmerei; **joint** ~ gemeinsames Unternehmen; Gelegenheitsgesellschaft *(→joint venture)*; **maritime** ~ Seeunternehmen; **parties to the** ~ an dem Unternehmen Beteiligte

adventurer Abenteurer; Spekulant

adversary Gegner, gegnerische Partei; Prozeßgegner; ~ **system** Verhandlungsgrundsatz, Verhandlungsmaxime *(opp. inquisitorial system)*

adverse gegnerisch, feindlich; ungünstig, nachteilig; entgegenstehend, mit den eigenen Ansprüchen unvereinbar; ~ **balance** passive Bilanz; ~ **balance of payments** passive Zahlungsbilanz; ~ **balance of trade** passive Handelsbilanz; ~ **claim** entgegenstehender Anspruch; ~ **decision** nachteilige (od. ablehnende) Entscheidung; ~ **majority** Mehrheit gegen den Antrag; ~ **party** gegnerische Partei; Antragsgegner

adverse possession[26] Ersitzung *(von Land)*; **to acquire by** ~ ersitzen

adverse, ~ **solicitor** *Br* gegnerischer Anwalt; ~ **trade balance** passive Handelsbilanz *(opp. favourable trade balance)*; ~ **witness** feindlicher Zeuge

adversely, to affect ~ nachteilig beeinflussen; **to be** ~ **affected by the decision** durch die Entscheidung beschwert sein

advertise *v (öffentl.)* anzeigen (od. bekanntmachen); Anzeige (od. Inserat) aufgeben, annoncieren, inserieren; werben, Werbung treiben, Reklame machen für; **to** ~ **for** *(etw.)* durch Inserat suchen, annoncieren nach; **to** ~ **(for) bids** *Am* ausschreiben; to ~ **a reward** *(durch öffentl. Bekanntmachung)* e-e Belohnung aussetzen; **to** ~ **a vacancy** e-e (freie) Stelle ausschreiben

advertised position annoncierte Stelle

advertisement (advt, ad) *(öffentl.)* Anzeige, Ankündigung, Bekanntmachung; Inserat, Annonce; Werbung, Reklame; **~s** Inserate; Anzeigenteil; ~ **of appointment** Stellenanzeige; ~ **canvasser** Anzeigenakquisiteur; ~ **columns** Anzeigenteil *(e-r Zeitung)*; ~ **contractor** Werbeunternehmen; ~ **department** Anzeigenabteilung, Inseratenannahme *(e-r Zeitung)*; **~(s) for deposits** *Br* Einlagenwerbung; ~ **manager** Anzeigenleiter; ~ **material** Werbematerial, Reklamematerial; ~ **materials** Werbeschriften; ~ **for positions** Stellenanzeige *(e-r Zeitung)*; ~ **rates** Anzeigentarif; ~ **of a sale** Verkaufsanzeige; Ausverkaufsanzeige; ~ **of a vacancy** Ausschreibung e-r Stelle; Stellenanzeige

advertisement, by ~ durch Zeitungsanzeige; **classified** ~ Kleinanzeige; **display-type** ~ besonders gestaltete Anzeige (*opp. classified* ~); **full page** ~ ganzseitige Anzeige; **joint** ~ Gemeinschaftswerbung; **wanted** ~ Suchanzeige

advertisement, to answer an ~ auf e-e Anzeige antworten; **to insert** (or **put**) **an** ~ **in a newspaper** ein Inserat aufgeben, inserieren

advertiser (Zeitungs-)Inserent, Aufgeber e-r Anzeige; Werbung Betreibender; **industrial** ~ Anzeigenblatt der Wirtschaft

advertising Werbung; Reklame; Inserieren; Werbewesen; Anzeigenwesen; Ankündigung durch Werbung; ~ **activity** Werbetätigkeit, Reklametätigkeit; ~ **agency** Werbeagentur; Anzeigenannahme; ~ **agent** Werbeleiter; ~ **appropriations** *(bewilligte)* Werbemittel, Reklamemittel

Advertising Association (AA) *Br* Verband der gesamten Werbewirtschaft; **International** ~ (IAA) Internationaler Werbeverband

advertising, ~ **brochure** Werbeschrift; ~ **budget** Werbeetat; ~ **campaign** Werbefeldzug; ~ **charges** (or **costs**) Werbekosten; Reklamekosten; Kosten e-r Anzeige; ~ **columns** Anzeigenspalten, Anzeigenteil; ~ **consultant** Werbeberater; ~ **copy** Werbetext; Reklametext; ~ **costs** Reklamekosten; Werbekosten; ~ **department** Werbeabteilung; Reklameabteilung; *Am* Inseratenannahme *(e-r Zeitung)*; ~ **devices** Werbemittel; ~ **effectiveness** Wirksamkeit der Werbung; ~ **ethics** Werbeethik; ~ **expenditure** Werbeausgaben; Werbekosten; Werbeaufwand; ~ **expenses** Werbekosten; Reklamekosten; ~ **expert** (or **man**) Werbefachmann; ~ **gift** Werbegeschenk; ~ **industry** Werbewirtschaft; Werbebranche; ~ **manager** Werbeleiter; Reklameleiter; ~ **matter** Werbedrucksache; ~ **medium** Werbeträger; ~ **page** Anzeigenseite

advertising practices, International Council on A~ P~ Internationale Schiedsstelle *(der Internationalen Handelskammer)* für unlautere Werbung; **unfair** ~ unlautere Werbung

advertising, ~ **profession** Werbeberuf; **for** ~

purposes für Werbezwecke, für Reklamezwecke; ~ **rates** Anzeigentarif; ~ **space** Werbefläche; ~ **specialist** →~ expert; ~ **slogan** Werbeslogan, Werbeschlagwort; ~ **tactics** Werbetaktik, Werbestrategie

advertising, aerial ~ Luftreklame, Himmelsschrift; **billboard** ~ Plakatwerbung; **broadcast** ~ Rundfunkwerbung; **commercial** ~ Wirtschaftswerbung; **co(-)operative** ~ Gemeinschaftswerbung; **electric sign** ~ Lichtreklame, Leuchtreklame; **false** ~ unwahre Werbung; **foreign** ~ Auslandswerbung; **formal** ~ **for bids** *Am* Ausschreibung; **misleading** ~ irreführende Werbung; **national** ~ *Am* Werbung in den ganzen Vereinigten Staaten; **outdoor** ~ Außenwerbung; **pictorial** ~ Bildwerbung; **poster** ~ Plakatwerbung; **selective** ~ gezielte Werbung; **tourist** ~ Fremdenverkehrswerbung; **window** ~ Schaufensterreklame; **to launch an** ~ **campaign** e-n Reklamefeldzug starten

advice Rat(schläge); Nachricht, Benachrichtigung, Bescheid; *com* Avis, Avisierung, Anzeige, Mitteilung, Ankündigung; **as per** ~ laut Bericht (od. Anzeige, Avis); **on the** ~ **of** auf Anraten von; **for want of** ~ mangels Bericht *(auf Wechseln)*

advice note Ankunftsanzeige *(der Ware);* Gutschriftsanzeige *(der Bank)*

advice, ~ **of arrival** Ankunftsanzeige; Eingangsanzeige; ~ **of collection** Inkassoanzeige; ~ **and consent** *Am* Zustimmung; ~ **of credit** Gutschriftsanzeige; ~ **of deal** *Br (Börse)* Ausführungsanzeige; ~ **of debit** Lastschriftanzeige; ~ **of** →**delivery**; ~ **of dispatch** Versandanzeige; ~ **of drawing** Scheckavis; ~ **without engagement** unverbindliche Benachrichtigung; ~ **of execution** *(Börse)* Ausführungsanzeige; ~ **of fate** Scheckdeckungsanzeige; Bezahltmeldung (od. Nichtbezahltmeldung) *(beim Dokumenteninkasso);* ~ **of loss** Schadensanzeige; ~ **of negotiation** Begebungsaviso; ~ **note** Versandanzeige; ~ **of payment** Zahlungsanzeige *(amtl. Nachricht über Auszahlung e-r Postanweisung); (beim Inkasso)* Bezahltmeldung; ~ **of receipt** (A. R.) Empfangsanzeige; ~ **of shipment** Verschiffungsanzeige, Versandanzeige; **expert** ~ fachkundige Beratung; →**legal** ~; **letter of** ~ → letter 2.

advice, to act on sb.'s ~ jds Rat befolgen; **to ask for** ~ um Rat fragen; **to follow the** ~ den Rat befolgen; **to give** ~ **(to sb.)** (jdn) beraten, (jdm) Rat erteilen; **to seek** (or **take**) ~ Rat einholen, sich beraten lassen; **to take the** ~ den Rat annehmen

advise *v* (be)raten, anempfehlen; benachrichtigen, verständigen; *com* avisieren, anzeigen, mitteilen; **to** ~ **and assist** mit Rat und Tat unterstützen; **to** ~ **a client** e-n Mandanten beraten; **to** ~ **a credit** ein Akkreditiv avisieren; ~ **fate** Scheckdeckungsanfrage; **to** ~ **a government** e-e Regierung verständigen

advised benachrichtigt; avisiert; **as** ~ wie angekündigt; laut Bericht; **to be** ~ **by the court** vom Gericht belehrt werden

advising Avisierung; ~ **bank** avisierende Bank *(beim Akkreditiv)*

adviser Berater; ~ **to the Government** Berater der Regierung; ~ **on inventions** Erfinderberater; **foreign policy** ~ außenpolitischer Berater; **legal** ~ Rechtsberater, juristischer Berater; **technical** ~ technischer Berater; Fachberater

advisory beratend; gutachtlich; ~ **board** Beratungsstelle; Konsultativrat

advisory capacity, in an ~ in beratender Funktion; **to attend in an** ~ **only** nur beratende Stimme haben

Advisory, Conciliation and Arbitration Service (ACAS) *Br* Beratungs-, Schlichtungs- und Schiedsgerichtsdienst *(unabhängige Behörde zur Verbesserung der Beziehungen zwischen den Sozialpartnern)*

advisory committee beratender Ausschuß; Beratungsausschuß; Gutachterausschuß; **to establish an** ~ e-n Beratungsausschuß einsetzen

advisory council Beirat; **permanent** ~ ständiger Beirat

advisory opinion *Am (und International Court of Justice) (gerichtl.)* Gutachten, Rechtsgutachten; **request for an** ~ *(on legal questions)* Ersuchen um Erstattung e-s Rechtsgutachtens; **to give** (or **render**) **an** ~ ein Gutachten erstatten; **to request an** ~ ein Gutachten einholen

advisory procedure *(VölkerR)* Gutachterverfahren; Konsultativverfahren

advocacy Befürwortung, Eintreten (of für); Plädoyer

advocate *Scot* (Rechts-)Anwalt; *Am* Rechtsbeistand; Sprecher, Fürsprecher *(für Interessengruppen);* Befürworter, Verfechter; **A~-General** Generalanwalt *(am Gerichtshof der EG);* **Faculty of A~s** *Scot* Anwaltskammer; **Lord A~** *Scot* Kronanwalt *(entspricht dem →Attorney-General)*

advocate *v* befürworten, eintreten für; plädieren; **he ~d that** er plädierte dafür, daß; er trat dafür ein, daß

advowson *eccl* Recht, *e-e* Pfründe zu besetzen

aegis, under the ~ **of** unter der Schirmherrschaft von

aerial Luft-; *Br* Antenne; ~ **advertising** Luftwerbung, Luftreklame (Himmelsschrift); ~ **bombardment** Luftbombardement; ~ **combat** Luftkampf; ~ **defen**|**ce (-se)** Luftabwehr, Luftverteidigung; ~ **dominance** Luftherrschaft; ~ **incident** Luftzwischenfall; ~ **navi-**

gation Luftfahrt; ~ **photo** Luftaufnahme; ~ **railway** Schwebebahn; **prohibited** ~ **space** Luftsperrgebiet; ~ **war(fare)** Luftkrieg

aerodrome *Br* Flughafen, Flugplatz; *mil* Luftwaffenstützpunkt; **alternate** ~ Ausweichflughafen; **departure** ~ Abgangsflughafen; **destination** ~ Ankunftsflughafen

aerogramme Aerogramm, Luftpostbrief

aeronautical aeronautisch, Luftfahrt-; ~ **affairs** Luftfahrtwesen; ~ **agreement** Luftfahrtvereinbarung; ~ **authority** Luftfahrtbehörde; ~ **research** Luftfahrtforschung; ~ **technology** Luftfahrttechnologie

aeronautics Luft- und Raumfahrt; Flugwesen; **Civil A~ Board** *Am* Zivilluftfahrtamt *(oberste Behörde für Zivilluftfahrt);* **National A~ and Space Administration** (NASA) *Am* (Bundes-)Behörde für Luft- und Raumfahrt; **National A~ Council** *Am* Raumfahrt-Beratungsgremium *(des Präsidenten)*

aeroplane *Br* Flugzeug; ~ **hijacking** Flugzeugentführung

aerospace Luft- und Weltraum; ~ **industry** Luft- und Raumfahrtindustrie; ~ **medicine** Luft- und Raumfahrtmedizin

aesthetic creations *(PatR)* ästhetische Formschöpfungen

affair Angelegenheit, Sache; Geschäft; (Liebes-)Verhältnis; ~ **of hono(u)r** Duell; ~**s of state** Staatsgeschäfte; Staatsangelegenheiten; **family** ~**s** Familienangelegenheiten; **foreign** ~ auswärtige Angelegenheiten; Außenpolitik; **private** ~**s** Privatangelegenheiten; **public** ~**s** öffentliche Angelegenheiten; **state of** ~**s** →state 2.; **statement of** ~**s** → statement 2.

affect *v* einwirken auf, beeinflussen; angehen, betreffen; **to** ~ **the market** den Markt beeinflussen; **to** ~ **the rights** die Rechte berühren

affected, ~ **property** *(WiedergutmachungsR)* entzogene Vermögensgegenstände; **to be adversely** ~ **by a decision** durch e-e Entscheidung beschwert sein; **these provisions shall not be** ~ diese Vorschriften bleiben unberührt

affection value *(VersR)* Liebhaberwert

affiant *Am* Aussteller e-s →affidavit *(gebräuchlicher: deponent)*

affidavit Affidavit; *(schriftl.)* eidliche Erklärung; *(ungenau:)* eidesstattliche Versicherung; ~ **of documents** *Br* beeidigte Liste aller im Besitz e-r Partei befindlichen, den Prozeß betreffenden Urkunden; ~ **evidence** (or **evidence on** ~) Affidavit-Aussage[27] *(eidesstattl. schriftl. Zeugenaussage);* ~ **of increase** *Am (SteuerR)* eidesstattliche Erklärung über erhöhte Unkosten

affidavit of means *(etwa:)* Offenbarungsversicherung[28]; **to swear an** ~ e-e Offenbarungsversicherung abgeben

affidavit of merits *Br* beschworene Urkunde (affidavit), in welcher der durch ein in seiner Abwesenheit ergangenes Urteil verurteilte Beklagte Umstände darlegt, die seine Verteidigung gegen die Klage aussichtsreich erscheinen lassen

affidavit of plight and condition *Br* Versicherung, daß sich das Testament in dem bei der Auffindung vorhandenen Zustand befindet

affidavit of support *Am* Bürgschaftserklärung *(Übernahme der Haftung für den Unterhalt e-s Einwanderers);* **to secure an** ~ sich die Bürgschaftserklärung beschaffen

affidavit, to affirm an ~ e-e *(schriftl.)* eidesstattliche Versicherung abgeben *(no oath involved, cf. to swear an ~);* **to file an** ~ ein Affidavit *(bei Gericht)* einreichen; **to swear an** ~ e-e *(schriftl.)* eidliche Versicherung abgeben; **knowingly swearing a false** ~ →false swearing; **to take an** ~ e-e *(schriftl.)* eidliche Versicherung entgegennehmen; **verified by** ~ durch eidliche Erklärung bekräftigt

Das affidavit wird von dem →deponent vor einer für die Abnahme zuständigen Person (*Br* meist solicitor) abgegeben. Es findet nicht nur in gerichtlichen Verfahren Anwendung, sondern gilt ganz allgemein im Rechtsverkehr. Im Gegensatz zu der deutschen eidesstattlichen Versicherung steht das affidavit unter den Strafbestimmungen des Meineids.

In Amerika geht die Tendenz dahin, das affidavit durch eine formelle Bekräftigung zu ersetzen

affiliate Beteiligungsgesellschaft; Konzerngesellschaft, Schwestergesellschaft, Tochtergesellschaft[29]; *Am* Zweiggesellschaft, Zweigfirma, Filiale; Mitglied; ~**s and nonmembers** Mitglieder und Nichtmitglieder; **IDA is an** ~ **of the World Bank** die Internationale Entwicklungsorganisation ist der Weltbank angegliedert

affiliate *v* angliedern, sich anschließen (to, with an); *(als Mitglied)* aufnehmen; **to** ~ **with an association** sich e-m Verband anschließen; e-m Verband beitreten; **to** ~ **a child on a p.** jdm die Vaterschaft e-s *(nichtehelichen)* Kindes zuschreiben; jds Vaterschaft *(gerichtl.)* feststellen

affiliated angegliedert, angeschlossen; **non-**~ *parl* fraktionslos; ~ **company** nahestehende Gesellschaft; Konzerngesellschaft, Schwestergesellschaft; ~ **enterprises** verbundene Unternehmen; ~ **group (of corporations)** *Am* Konzern; ~ **institution** Zweiganstalt; ~ **member** →affiliate; **to be** ~ **to a party** e-r *(politischen)* Partei nahestehen *(bei Organisationen)*

affiliation 1. Angliederung; Mitgliedsaufnahme; Zugehörigkeit; geschäftliche Verbindung; ~ **fees** Mitgliedsbeiträge; ~ **privilege** *Am* Schachtelprivileg *(zur Vermeidung der Doppel-*

besteuerung von Gesellschaften, die in e-m Verhältnis von herrschender und abhängiger Gesellschaft zueinander stehen); ~ **relationship** *Am* Verhältnis zwischen Mutter- und Tochtergesellschaft; **application of** ~ Aufnahmeantrag; **party** ~ Zugehörigkeit zu e-r Partei

affiliation 2. *(gerichtl.)* Feststellung der *(außerehelichen)* Vaterschaft; ~ **order** Urteil im Vaterschaftsprozeß *(gerichtl. Feststellung der Vaterschaft);* Unterhaltsverfügung *(des Gerichts gegen den nichtehelichen Vater);* **application for an** ~ **order** *Br* Unterhaltsklage *(für ein nichteheliches Kind);* ~ **proceedings** Vaterschaftsprozeß *(Verfahren zur Feststellung der nichtehelichen Vaterschaft und Unterhaltspflicht)*

affinity Verwandtschaft *(durch Heirat);* Schwägerschaft *(cf. consanguinity);* **consanguinity or** ~ **within the prohibited degrees** Verwandtschaft oder Schwägerschaft innerhalb der verbotenen Verwandtschaftsgrade *(cf. impediment to marriage);* **degree of** ~ Verwandtschaftsgrad

affirm *v* bestätigen, bekräftigen *(opp. to deny);* an Eides Statt versichern *(cf. affirmation);* **to re**~ erneut bestätigen; **to** ~ **falsely** falsche eidesstattliche Erklärung abgeben; **to** ~ **a judgment** ein Urteil *(des unteren Gerichts)* bestätigen

affirming in Bekräftigung

affirmant Abgeber e-r →affirmation

affirmation[30] Bestätigung, Bekräftigung, Beteuerung *(opp. denial); (förml.)* eidesgleiche Bekräftigung; **to administer an** ~ e-e eidesgleiche Bekräftigung abnehmen; **to make an** ~ beteuern, e-e eidesgleiche Bekräftigung abgeben

Die (solemn) affirmation wird im Zivil- und Strafprozeß bei Ablehnung der Eidesleistung wegen religiöser Bedenken an Stelle des affidavit abgegeben und steht wie der Fall des § 155 I StGB unter den Strafbestimmungen des Meineids. Form einer affirmation: „I, A. B. solemnly and sincerely affirm and declare as follows."

affirmative bejahend *(opp. negative)*

affirmative action *Am* Maßnahmen zur Beseitigung und Verhütung von Diskriminierung und zur Behebung (Wiedergutmachung) der Folgen vergangener Diskriminierung *(bes. auf dem Arbeitsmarkt);* ~ **plan** *Am* Aktionsplan *(z. B. e-r Firma),* der auf die Anstellung von bisher diskriminierten Minoritäten abzielt

affirmative, ~ **defense** *Am (Zivilprozeß)* Einrede(n) des Beklagten *(e.g. contributory negligence, statute of limitations, estoppel); (Strafprozeß)* Behauptung(en), die der Angeklagte glaubhaft zu machen hat; ~ **judgment** *Am* obsiegendes Urteil; ~ **vote** Zustimmung; Ja-Stimme *(opp. negative vote);* **to answer in the** ~ bejahen; **to be** ~ **defense** *Am* vom Beklagten glaubhaft zu machen sein; **to hold the** ~ **burden of proof** *Am* beweispflichtig sein; **40 votes were in the** ~, **10 in the negative** es gab 40 Ja-Stimmen und 10 Nein-Stimmen

affix *v* anheften, aufkleben, *(Siegel, Stempel)* aufdrücken; **to** ~ **a seal to a document** e-e Urkunde mit e-m Siegel versehen, e-e Urkunde siegeln; **to** ~ **one's signature to an agreement** e-n Vertrag unterschreiben; ~**ed to land** mit dem Grundstück fest verbunden

affluence Reichtum, Überfluß

affluent wohlhabend, reich (in an); ~ **society** Wohlstandsgesellschaft

afflux of capital Kapitalzufluß

afforest *v* aufforsten

afforestation Aufforstung

affray *(öffentl.)* Schlägerei; Raufhandel *(als Störung der öffentl. Ordnung; cf. assault)*

affreight *v* befrachten; *(Frachtschiff)* chartern

affreightment Befrachtung *(e-s Schiffes);* **(contract of)** ~ (See-)Frachtvertrag *(cf. charter party, bill of lading, freighter)*

AFL/CIO[31] *Am* Spitzenverband der amerikanischen Gewerkschaften

Afghan Afghane; Afghanin; afghanisch

Afghanistan Afghanistan; **Republic of** ~ Republik Afghanistan

afloat schwimmend, flott; auf See; an Bord; *(von Gerüchten)* in Umlauf, zirkulierend; in Gang; **ashore or** ~ an Land oder auf See; **goods** ~ schwimmende (od. unterwegs befindliche) Waren

aforementioned (or **aforesaid**) vorher erwähnt, vorgenannt

aforethought vorbedacht, vorsätzlich; **malice** ~ *(StrafR)* vorbedachte böse Absicht (→*malice*)

African, Caribbean and Pacific countries (ACP countries) Staaten in Afrika, im Karibischen Raum und Pazifischen Ozean (AKP-Staaten)

African Development Bank[32] (ADB) Afrikanische Entwicklungsbank *(ihr gehören 50 regionale und 25 nicht-regionale Länder an. Die Bundesrepublik Deutschland ist seit 1982 Mitglied)*

African Development Fund[32a] Afrikanischer Entwicklungsfonds

African National Congress (ANC) afrikanischer Nationalkongress *(wendet sich gegen die Politik der →apartheid; verbotene schwarze Befreiungsbewegung)*

African, Associated ~ **States, Madagascar and Mauritius** (AASMM) Assoziierte Afrikanische Staaten, Madagaskar und Mauritius (AASMM)

African, Organization of ~ Unity (OAU) Organisation für die Einheit Afrikas (→*organization*)

after, ~-acquired property *Am* nach e-m bestimmten Datum erworbenes Vermögen *(bezüglich dessen bestimmte Rechte bestehen);* **~-born child** nach dem Tode des Erblassers geborenes Kind; ~ **care** Nachbehandlung *(z.B. von →drug addicts);* Entlassenenfürsorge *(für Strafgefangene);* ~ **costs** nachträgliche Kosten; ~ **date** (A/D, a/d) nach dato, nach heute; **~-date bill** Datowechsel; **~-date** *v* nachdatieren, mit späterem Datum versehen; ~ **hours** nach Büroschluß (od. Ladenschluß); nach der Polizeistunde; Nachbörse; nachbörslich *(opp. before hours);* ~ **sales service** Kundendienst; ~ **sight** (a/s.) nach Sicht; **~-tax profit** Gewinn nach Abzug von Steuern

against all risks (a. a. r.) *(VersR)* gegen alle Gefahren

age Alter; ~ **admitted** *(VersR)* anerkanntes Alter; ~ **allowance** *Br* (Steuer-)Freibetrag *(für Personen über 65 Jahre);* Altersfreibetrag; ~ **bracket** Altersgruppe; ~ **class** *mil* Jahrgang; ~ **at entry** *(VersR)* Eintrittsalter; ~ **at expiry** *(VersR)* Endalter; ~ **group** Altersklasse; Jahrgang

age limit Altersgrenze; **to retire under the** ~ infolge der Erreichung der Altersgrenze in den Ruhestand treten

age, ~ of retirement Pensionierungsalter; ~ **structure** Altersaufbau; ~ **at withdrawal** *(VersR)* Austrittsalter; →**full** ~

age, of ~ volljährig, mündig; **not being of** ~ minderjährig, unmündig; **to be of** ~ mündig sein; **to come of** ~[33] mündig (od. volljährig) werden

age, minimum ~ Mindestalter; **old** ~ (hohes) Alter (→*old*); **over** ~ zu alt *(über das vorgeschriebene Alter hinaus);* **pensionable** ~ pensionsfähiges Alter; **retirement** (or **retiring**) ~ Ruhestandsalter, Pensionierungsalter; **school- leaving** ~ Schulabgangsalter; **under** ~ minderjährig, unmündig

age *v*, **to ~ accounts** Konten nach ihrer Fälligkeit aufgliedern

agency 1. Vertretung, Stellvertretung; Handelsvertretung; Bevollmächtigung; Vollmacht; ~ **agreement** (or **contract**) Handelsvertretervertrag; Auftrag, Geschäftsbesorgungsvertrag *(Innenverhältnis);* Vollmacht *(Außenverhältnis);* ~ **by estoppel** durch schlüssiges Verhalten erteilte Vollmacht (→*estoppel*); ~ **by ratification** Vollmacht (od. Bevollmächtigung) durch nachträgliche Genehmigung; ~ **of necessity** Ermächtigung durch zwingende Gründe; Geschäftsführung ohne Auftrag; **sole and exclusive** ~ **rights** Alleinvertretung(srecht) *(des Handelsvertreters)*

agency, by (or **through**) **the** ~ **of** durch Vermittlung von, mit Hilfe von; **chief** ~ Generalvertretung; **commercial** ~ Handelsvertretung; **commercial ~ contract** Handelsvertretervertrag; **contract of** ~ Vertretungsvertrag; **contractual** ~ Vollmacht; **general** ~ Generalvertretung; Generalvollmacht; Generalhandlungsvollmacht; **implied** ~ stillschweigend erteilte Vollmacht; **joint** ~ gemeinsame Vertretung; →**mercantile** ~; **relation of** ~ Vertretungsverhältnis; **sole** ~ Alleinvertretung; **special** ~ Sondervollmacht; Einzelvollmacht; **statutory** ~ gesetzliche Vertretung; →**sub~**; **unauthorized** ~ Vertretung ohne Vertretungsmacht; **undisclosed** ~ verdeckte (od. mittelbare) Stellvertretung; **to resign an** ~ e-e Vertretung niederlegen; **to take up an** ~ e-e Vertretung übernehmen

agency 2. Agentur, Geschäftsstelle (*e-s →agent*); Geschäftsnebenstelle; Betriebsstätte; Niederlassung; Stelle, Verwaltung(sstelle); Vermittlungsstelle; *bes. Am (und VölkerR)* Amt, Dienststelle, Behörde, Einrichtung, Organ, Organisation; ~ **agreement** (or **contract**) Agenturvertrag; Vertrag zwischen e-r Werbeagentur und Auftraggeber; ~ **commission** Agenturprovision; ~ **fee** Vertretergebühr; Klarierungsgebühr *(des Schiffsmaklers)*

agency, ~ report *Am* Bericht e-r Kreditauskunftei; ~ **representative** Agenturvertreter; ~ **shop** *Br* gewerkschaftspflichtiger Betrieb *(alle im Betrieb Beschäftigten müssen Gewerkschaftsbeiträge bezahlen, auch wenn sie kein Mitglied sind);* ~ **work** Vertretertätigkeit

agency, administrative ~ Verwaltungsstelle; **advertising** ~ Werbeagentur; **commercial** ~ *Am* (Kredit-)Auskunftei; **employment** ~ *Br (private)* Arbeitsvermittlungsstelle; **forwarding** ~ Speditionsgeschäft; **general** ~ Generalvertretung; Hauptagentur; **government** ~ Regierungsstelle; Behörde; staatliche Stelle; **head of an** ~ *Am* Behördenleiter; **insurance** ~ Versicherungsagentur; **intergovernmental** ~ zwischenstaatliche Einrichtung; **international ~ies** internationale Behörden; →**mercantile** ~; **regional ~ies** *Am* regionale Einrichtungen; **special** ~ Agentur (od. Vertretung) für bestimmte Waren; **specialized ~ies** Sonderorganisationen *(der Vereinten Nationen; → United Nations);* → **sub~**

agenda Tagesordnung; zu erörternde Punkte *(auf e-r Versammlung etc);* **adoption of the** ~ Annahme der Tagesordnung; **inclusion in the** ~ Aufnahme in die Tagesordnung; **item on the** ~ Gegenstand (od. Punkt) der Tagesordnung; **item 5 is next on the** ~ wir kommen zu Punkt 5 der Tagesordnung; **to appear on the** ~ auf der Tagesordnung stehen; **the ~ calls for the discussion of** . . . auf der Tagesordnung steht . . .; **to draw up the** ~ die Tagesordnung aufstellen (od. festsetzen); **to include in the** ~ auf die Tagesordnung setzen; **to place** (or **put down**) **on the** ~ auf die Tagesordnung setzen; **to prepare the** ~ die Tagesordnung aufstellen; **to remove from the** ~ von der Tagesordnung absetzen

agent Vertreter, Stellvertreter; Beauftragter, Bevollmächtigter; Handelsvertreter (→*agency agreement*); Handlungsbevollmächtigter; Agent; *(Außenhandelsfinanzierung)* Korrespondenzbank; *Am* Korrespondent e-r Auskunftei; **principal and** ~ Auftraggeber und Beauftragter *(z. B. Vertreter);* Vollmachtgeber und Bevollmächtigter; Geschäftsherr und Vertreter

Der anglo-amerikanische Begriff des agent ist umfassender als der des deutschen (Stell-)Vertreters und umfaßt jede Person, die für einen anderen in dessen Auftrag und Interesse tätig ist, z. B. auch den Kommissionär, Makler und Spediteur.

Agent und servant werden von der Rechtsprechung häufig synonym gebraucht; agent *(im engeren Sinne:)* der, welcher den principal bei Rechtsgeschäften vertritt; *(im weiteren Sinne:)* jeder, der für einen anderen Dienste verrichtet (also auch der servant)

agent, ~'s authority Vertretungsmacht, Vertretungsbefugnis; ~ **for collection** Einzugsbeauftragter; Inkassobevollmächtigter; **~'s commission** Vertreterprovision; ~ **general** s. general →~; **A~ General** *Br* Vertreter bestimmter Commonwealth-Länder in London; ~ **of necessity** Geschäftsführer ohne Auftrag *(durch zwingende Gründe als ermächtigt anzusehender Vertreter);* ~ **provocateur** Lockspitzel; **~'s territory** Vertreterbezirk, Verkaufsgebiet e-s Vertreters

agent, advertising ~ Werbeleiter; **appointment of an** ~ Bestellung e-s Vertreters; **authorized** ~ bevollmächtigter Vertreter, Bevollmächtigter; **buying** ~ Einkaufsvertreter, Einkäufer; Einkaufskommissionär; **chief** ~ Generalvertreter; **commercial** ~ Handelsvertreter; **commission** ~ Kommissionär; **commission allowed to an** ~ Vertreterprovision; **consular** ~ Konsularagent, konsularischer Vertreter; **diplomatic** ~ diplomatischer Vertreter; **estate** ~ *Br* Grundstücksmakler; Wohnungsmakler; **exclusive** ~ Alleinvertreter; **forwarding** ~ Spediteur; **general** ~ allgemeiner (Handels-)Vertreter *(der im Rahmen seiner gewöhnlichen Geschäfte handelt; opp. special* ~); Generalbevollmächtigter; Handlungsbevollmächtigter; **head** ~ s. general →~; **house** ~ *Br* Immobilienmakler; **insurance** ~ Versicherungsagent; **land** ~ Immobilienmakler; Gütermakler; *Br* Gutsverwalter; **(law)** ~ *Scot* Anwalt *(solicitor);* **legal** ~ gesetzlicher Vertreter; **managing** ~ Geschäftsführer; **manufacturer's** ~ *Am* Werksvertreter, Fabrikvertreter, Generalvertreter; **mercantile** ~ Handelsvertreter; *(auch:)* Makler, Kommissionär; **patent** ~ Patentanwalt; **paying** ~ zahlende Stelle; **political** ~ politischer Agent; **power of an** ~ →~'s authority; **purchasing** ~ Einkaufsvertreter, Einkäufer; **real estate** ~ *Am* Grundstücksmakler; **sales** ~ Verkaufsvertreter; **secret** ~ Geheimagent; Spion; **selling** ~ Verkaufsvertreter; Verkaufskommissionär; **shipping** ~ Schiffsagent; Seehafenspediteur; **sole** ~ Alleinvertreter; **special** ~ Handelsvertreter für bestimmte Gruppen von Waren; handelsrechtlicher Vertreter (od. Bevollmächtigter) für besondere Rechtsgeschäfte; Sonderbevollmächtigter; **statutory** ~ gesetzlicher Vertreter; **sub~** Untervertreter; Unterbevollmächtigter; **transfer** ~ *Am* Transferagent (→ *transfer 4.*); **traveling buying** ~ *Am* für Importeure in fremden Märkten reisender Einkäufer; **unauthorized** ~ Vertreter ohne Vertretungsmacht; **universal** ~ Generalbevollmächtigter

agent, to act as ~ in fremdem Namen handeln; *(jdn)* vertreten; **to appoint an** ~ e-n Vertreter ernennen (od. bestellen); **to be** ~ **for sb.** jdn vertreten; **to be sole** ~ Alleinvertretung haben

agglomeration Ballung(sgebiet)

aggrandizement, territorial ~ territoriale Vergrößerung

aggravate *v* erschweren, verschärfen

aggravated, ~ →**assault**; ~ **risk** *(VersR)* erhöhtes Risiko

aggravating circumstances erschwerende *(strafverschärfende)* Umstände *(opp. mitigating circumstances)*

aggravation Erschwerung, Verschärfung; ~ **of the risk** *(VersR)* Gefahrerhöhung; ~ **of the political situation** Verschärfung der politischen Lage

aggregate Menge, Masse, Summe; gesamt, Gesamt-; **in the** ~ insgesamt, im ganzen; alles zusammengerechnet; →**corporation** ~

aggregate, ~ **amount** Gesamtbetrag, Gesamtsumme; ~ **demand** Gesamtnachfrage; ~ **fine** Gesamtgeldstrafe; ~ **foreign trade** Gesamtaußenhandel; ~ **income** Gesamteinkommen; ~ **number** Gesamtzahl; ~ **supply** Gesamtangebot; ~ **value** Gesamtwert *(z. B. e-s Geschäfts)*

aggregate *v* im ganzen betragen, sich belaufen (to auf); zusammenrechnen

aggregation Ansammlung; Kumulierung; Zusammenrechnung

aggression Aggression; Angriff; **act of** ~ Angriffshandlung; **conclusion of a non-~ pact** Abschluß e-s Nichtangriffspaktes; **war of** ~ Angriffskrieg

aggressive aggressiv, angriffslustig; ~ **portion** *Am* risikoreicherer Teil *(des Effektenportefeuille e-s investment trust; opp. defensive portion);* ~

war Angriffskrieg; ~ **weapons** Angriffswaffen

aggressor *(VölkerR)* Angreifer

aggrieve *v*, **to feel ~d** sich beschwert (od. ungerecht behandelt) fühlen; sich in s-m Recht verletzt fühlen

aging accounts receivable *Am* überfällige Außenstände

agio *(Effektenmarkt)* Agio, Aufgeld *(opp. disagio)*

agiotage Agiotage *(bestimmte Art der Kursspekulation)*

agistment Weidenlassen *(von Vieh)*

agitate *v* debattieren, verhandeln; *pol* agitieren, aufreizend werben, hetzen; **to ~ for higher wages** für höhere Löhne agitieren

agitation *pol* Agitation, Aufwiegelung, Hetze

agitator *pol* Agitator, Aufwiegler, Hetzredner

agnate Agnat, männlicher (Bluts-)Verwandter; agnatisch, väterlicherseits verwandt *(opp. cognate)*

agnation Agnation, (Bluts-)Verwandtschaft väterlicherseits *(opp. cognation)*

agrarian landwirtschaftlich, Agrar-; ~ **country** Agrarland; ~ **exports** Agrarexporte; ~ **legislation** Agrargesetzgebung; ~ **market** Agrarmarkt; ~ **policy** Agrarpolitik; ~ **reform** Bodenreform; ~ **state** Agrarstaat; ~ **structure** Agrarstruktur

agree *v* sich einig werden, sich einigen, sich verständigen (on/about über); vereinbaren, verabreden, abmachen; zustimmen (to zu), sich einverstanden erklären (to mit); einig sein, übereinstimmen (with mit); **to ~ tacitly** stillschweigend zustimmen; **to ~ accounts** (or **to make accounts ~**) Konten abstimmen; **to ~ (up)on a price** e-n Preis vereinbaren; **to ~ (up)on the terms** sich über die Bedingungen einigen

agreed, ~ abgemacht! einverstanden!; **as ~ (upon)** wie verabredet, wie vereinbart; **date ~ upon** vereinbarter Termin; ~ **declaration** *(VölkerR)* vereinbarte Erklärung; ~ **minutes** *(VölkerR)* vereinbarte Niederschrift; ~ **price** vereinbarter Preis; ~ **value** *(VersR)* vereinbarter Wert; ~ **wage rates** Tariflöhne

agreed, it was generally ~ man war sich allgemein darüber einig; **they were** ~ sie waren sich einig (on über); **the Governments have ~ as follows** die Regierungen haben folgendes vereinbart (od. sind wie folgt übereingekommen); **unless otherwise** ~ falls nichts anderes vereinbart wird; **unless otherwise ~ by the parties** vorbehaltlich abweichender Vereinbarungen

agreement 1. Übereinstimmung, Einvernehmen; Übereinkunft; Verständigung; Vereinbarung, Abmachung; Vertrag; Kartell; *(KartellR)* Vereinbarung, Absprache; **by ~ between themselves** in gegenseitigem Einvernehmen; **in ~ with** in Einvernehmen mit; **in the absence of ~ to the contrary** mangels gegenseitiger Vereinbarung; ~ **between the parties** Parteivereinbarung; ~ **between undertakings** *(KartellR)* Unternehmensabsprache; ~ **for sale and purchase of land** *Br* Grundstückskaufvertrag *(cf. completion)*; ~ **in principle** Grundsatzvereinbarung; ~ **in restraint of trade** wettbewerbsbeschränkende Absprache; ~ **in writing** schriftliche Vereinbarung; schriftlicher Vertrag; ~ **of consolidation** Fusionsvertrag; ~ **of interests** Interessenabstimmung; ~ **of purchase and sale** *Am* Kaufvertrag; ~ **of purchase and sale of real property** *Am* Grundstückskaufvertrag; ~ **subject to registration** *Br (KartellR)* der Meldepflicht unterliegende Absprache; ~ **to arbitrate** Schiedsvereinbarung; ~ **to disagree** *(VölkerR)* Einvernehmen, daß man sich nicht einigen kann; ~ **to sell** *Br* Kaufvertrag *(Eigentumsübergang kann vom Eintritt e-r Bedingung abhängig gemacht werden)*

agreement, according to ~ vertragsmäßig, vertraglich; laut Abmachung; **additional** ~ Nebenabrede, Zusatzvereinbarung; →**administrative** ~; **agency** ~ →agency 1. und 2.; **arbitration** ~ Schiedsvertrag, Schiedsvereinbarung (→*arbitration*); **articles of** ~ *(schriftl.)* Vertragsbestimmungen; Vertragspunkte; **basis of** ~ Vertragsgrundlage; **as per** ~ s. according to →~; **cartel** ~ Kartellabsprache; **collateral** ~ Nebenabmachung; Begleitvertrag; **collective** ~ Tarifvertrag; Gesamtarbeitsvertrag; **contrary to** ~ vertragswidrig; **covering** ~ Mantelvertrag; **credit** ~ Kreditvereinbarung; **draft** ~ Vertragsentwurf; **executed** ~ erfüllter Vertrag; **executory** ~ noch zu erfüllender Vertrag; **expiration of an** ~ Ablauf e-s Vertrages; **express** ~ ausdrückliche Abmachung; **extension of an** ~ Verlängerung e-s Vertrages; **failing special** ~ in Ermangelung besonderer Vereinbarung; **implicit** ~ stillschweigend getroffene Vereinbarung; **industrial** ~ Tarifabkommen; **invalid** ~ ungültiger Vertrag; **licensing** ~ gegenseitiger Lizenzvertrag; **marketing** ~ Marktabsprache; **monopoly** ~ Monopolabsprache; **mutual** ~ gegenseitige Vereinbarung; gegenseitiges Einvernehmen; **oral** ~ mündliche Vereinbarung; →**parol ~; party to an** ~ Vertragspartei; **previous** ~ frühere Abmachung; **private** ~ Privatabkommen; **prolongation of an** ~ Verlängerung e-s Vertrages; **reciprocal** ~ gegenseitiger Vertrag; **sales** ~ Kaufvertrag; Verkaufsvereinbarung; **skeleton** ~ Rahmenabkommen; **special** ~ besondere Vereinbarung; **sub-**

sidiary ~ Nebenabrede; **supplementary** ~ zusätzliche Vereinbarung; **tenancy** ~ Mietvertrag; Pachtvertrag; **terms of an** ~ Vertragsbestimmungen; **verbal** ~ mündliche Vereinbarung (od. Absprache); **wages** ~ Lohnvereinbarung; **written** ~ schriftliche Vereinbarung

agreement, to come to an ~ zu e-r Einigung kommen; e-e Verständigung erzielen; **to be in** ~ übereinstimmen; **to conclude** (or **enter into**) **an** ~ e-e Vereinbarung treffen; e-n Vertrag (etc) schließen (od. eingehen); übereinkommen; **to fail to adhere to an** ~ e-e Abmachung nicht einhalten; **to make an** ~ e-e Vereinbarung treffen; *(KartellR)* e-e Absprache treffen; **to reach an** ~ zu e-r Verständigung gelangen; e-e Einigung erzielen; sich einigen; **in the event of the parties failing to reach** ~ falls sich die Parteien nicht einigen; **to withdraw from an** ~ von e-m Vertrage zurücktreten; **there is** ~ es besteht Einvernehmen (by bei); **no** ~ **was reached** es wurde keine Einigung erzielt

agreement 2. *Am* Tarifvertrag (→ *collective agreement*); **association** ~ *Am* Tarifvertrag *(zwischen Unternehmerverband und Gewerkschaft);* **coverage of** ~ *Am* erfaßter Bereich des Tarifvertrages; **joint** ~ *Am* gemeinsames Übereinkommen *(verschiedener Gewerkschaften mit einem Unternehmer oder verschiedener Unternehmer mit einer Gewerkschaft);* **master** (or **standard**) ~ *Am* Mustertarifvertrag; **trade** ~ *Am* Tarifvertrag

agreement 3. *(VölkerR) (zweiseitige Übereinkunft:)* Abkommen, Vereinbarung; *(mehrseitige Übereinkunft:)* Übereinkommen; ~ **countries** Abkommensländer; Übereinkommensländer; **administrative** ~ Verwaltungsabkommen; Verwaltungsübereinkommen; **commercial** ~ Handelsabkommen; **currency** ~ Währungsabkommen; **monetary** ~ Währungsabkommen; **partial** ~ Teilabkommen; **payments** ~ Zahlungsabkommen; **preliminary** ~ Vorvereinbarung; **special** ~ Sonderabkommen, Sondervereinbarung; Sonderübereinkommen; **supplementary** (or **supplemental**) ~ Zusatzabkommen, Zusatzvereinbarung; Zusatzübereinkommen; **trade** ~ Handelsabkommen; **transfer** ~ Transferabkommen

agreement, ~**s have been negotiated** Abkommen wurden ausgehandelt; **to terminate an** ~ ein Abkommen (etc) außer Kraft setzen

agrément *Fr (VölkerR)* Agrément[34] *(Zustimmung des Empfangsstaates zur Entsendung des Missionschefs);* **to grant the** ~ *(dem Missionschef)* das Agrément erteilen; **to be granted one's** ~ das Agrément erhalten

agricultural landwirtschaftlich; Landwirtschafts-, Agrar-; ~ **bank** Landwirtschaftsbank; Agrarkreditinstitut; ~ **commodities** landwirtschaftliche Erzeugnisse; landwirtschaftliche Grundstoffe; ~ **cooperative** *(Br* **society**) landwirtschaftliche Absatzgenossenschaft; ~ **country** Agrarland, Agrarstaat; ~ **credit** Agrarkredit; ~ **enterprise** landwirtschaftlicher Betrieb; ~ **expenditure** Agrarausgaben; ~ **exports** Agrarexporte; ~ **fair** Landwirtschaftsmesse; ~ **fixture** dem landwirtschaftlichen Zweck dienendes Zubehör; **A~ Foreign Investment Disclosure Act,** 1978 (AFIDA) *Am* Gesetz über Offenlegungspflicht ausländischer Investitionen in landwirtschaftlichen Grundbesitz in den USA; ~ **holding** *Br* Pachtgut, Pachthof, Pachtland; ~ **implements** landwirtschaftliche Geräte; ~ **labo(u)rer** Landarbeiter; ~ **land** Ackerbauland; ~ **lands** landwirtschaftliche Grundstücke; ~ **loan** Agrarkredit; ~ **market** Agrarmarkt; ~ **market organization** *(EG)* Agrarmarktordnung; **A~ Mortgage Corporation** *Br* Agrarkreditinstitut *(gewährt der Landwirtschaft Hypotheken und langfristige Darlehen);* ~ **output** Gesamtproduktion der Landwirtschaft

agricultural policy, common ~ (C. A. P.) *(EG)* gemeinsame Agrarpolitik, gemeinsame Politik auf dem Gebiet der Landwirtschaft *(cf. common organization of the market);* **establishment of a common** ~ Gestaltung e-r gemeinsamen Argarpolitik; **to develop gradually the common** ~ schrittweise die gemeinsame Agrarpolitik entwickeln

agricultural, ~ **prices** Agrarpreise; ~ **produce** (or **products**) landwirtschaftliche Erzeugnisse; ~ **production** landwirtschaftliche Erzeugung; ~ **relief** *Am* Agrarhilfe; ~ **research** Agrarforschung; ~ **show** Landwirtschaftsausstellung; ~ **subsidies** Agrarsubventionen, Agrarhilfe; ~ **surplus** Agrarüberschuß; ~ **tariff** Agrarzoll; ~ **tenant** Pächter; ~ **undertaking** landwirtschaftlicher Betrieb; ~ **work** landwirtschaftliche Arbeit; ~ **worker** Arbeitnehmer in der Landwirtschaft, Landarbeiter

agriculture Landwirtschaft; **Department of A~** *Am* Landwirtschaftsministerium; **Secretary of A~** *Am* Landwirtschaftsminister; **Minister (Ministry) of A~, Fisheries and Food** *Br* Minister (Ministerium) für Landwirtschaft, Fischerei und Ernährung; **to be engaged in** ~ in der Landwirtschaft beschäftigt sein

aground am Grunde aufgelaufen, gestrandet; **the ship ran** ~ das Schiff ist auf Grund gelaufen; **the ship ran** ~ **the coast** das Schiff strandete an der Küste

ahead voraus, weiter vor; ~ **only** *Br* nur geradeaus fahren; **the years** ~ die kommenden Jahre; **to date** ~ vordatieren

aid Hilfe, Unterstützung; Beistand, Beihilfe; ~ **to developing countries** Entwicklungshilfe; **A~ to Families with Dependent Children**

(AFDC) *Am* Unterstützung bedürftiger Familien mit unterhaltsberechtigten Kindern; ~ **fund** Unterstützungsfonds; ~ **granted by the state** staatliche Unterstützung; ~ **scheme** Beihilferegelung
aid, civil a~ certificate *Br* Armenrechtsbescheinigung *(in Zivilsachen; cf. legal ~)*; **development** ~ Entwicklungshilfe; **emergency** ~ Soforthilfe; **financial** ~ finanzielle Hilfe; Beihilfe; **foreign** ~ Auslandshilfe; **→legal** ~; **military** ~ Militärhilfe; **state** ~ staatliche Unterstützung (od. Beihilfe)
aid, to call in the ~ of an *Am* **attorney** *(Br* **solicitor***)* e-n Anwalt befragen (od. zu Rate ziehen); **to grant** ~**(s)** Beihilfe(n) gewähren; **to give** (or **lend**) ~ (to sb.) (jdm) Hilfe leisten

aid *v* helfen; **to ~ and abet** *(StrafR)* Beihilfe leisten; **to ~ and comfort** *(dem Feinde)* Vorschub leisten
aided, government (or **state**) ~ staatlich unterstützt
aider and abettor *(StrafR)* Gehilfe
aiding, ~ and abetting Beihilfe *(bei e-r strafbaren Handlung)*; Mittäterschaft; ~ **and comforting the enemy** Feindbegünstigung

aide-mémoire *Fr dipl* Aide-mémoire
Schriftliche Fixierung einer mündlichen Besprechung, die auf diplomatischem Wege zugestellt wird

aids (acquired immune deficiency syndrome) Aids; **campaign against** ~ Aids-Bekämpfung

ailing company sich in Schwierigkeiten befindliches Unternehmen

aim Ziel; Zweck, Vorhaben

aim *v*, **to ~ at** (hin)zielen auf, gerichtet sein auf

air Luft; ~**-to-**~ Bord zu Bord; ~**-to-ground** Bord-Boden; ~**-to-surface missile** (ASM) Flugkörper zur Bekämpfung von See- und Erdzielen *(vom Flugzeug aus)*
air, ~ accident Flugzeugunglück; ~ **base** Luftwaffenstützpunkt; ~ **bill of lading** *Am* Luftfrachtbrief; ~ **bridge** Luftbrücke; ~ **cargo** (or **carriage**) Luftfracht; ~ **carrier** Luftfrachtführer; Lufttransportgesellschaft; Luftverkehrsgesellschaft; ~ **(chartering) broker** Luftfrachtmakler; ~ **conditioning** Klimaanlage; ~ **connection** Luftverbindung; ~ **consignment note** *Br* Luftfrachtbrief; ~ **conveyance** Lufttransport; ~ **corridor** Luftkorridor, Luftschneise
air, by ~ per Flugzeug, auf dem Luftwege; **connection by** ~ Flugverbindung; **passage by** ~ Flug; Luftreise; **rules of the** ~ Luftverkehrsregeln
air, to be on the ~ *(Radio und Fernsehen)* senden; *(im Radio und Fernsehen)* gesendet (od. gehört) werden; **to go** (or **travel**) **by** ~ per Flugzeug reisen; fliegen

air *v* an die Öffentlichkeit bringen

Airborne Warning and Control System (AWACS) *mil* fliegendes Frühwarn- und Kontrollsystem
aircraft Flugzeug(e); Luftfahrzeug(e); ~**s** *(Börse)* Luftfahrtwerte; ~ **accident** Flugzeugunfall (od. ~unglück); ~ **carrier** Flugzeugträger; ~ **factory** Flugzeugfabrik; ~ **industry** Flugzeugindustrie; ~ **hull insurance** Flugzeug-Kaskoversicherung; ~ **insurance** Luftfahrtversicherung; ~ **liability insurance** Lufthaftpflichtversicherung; ~ **mortgage** Pfandrecht an Luftfahrzeugen; ~ **noise** Fluglärm; ~ **passenger** Fluggast; ~ **register** Luftfahrzeugrolle; Verzeichnis der Luftfahrzeuge; ~ **traffic** Luftverkehr
aircraft, anti-~ (A. A.) Flugabwehr, Flak; **chartered** ~ Charterflugzeug; **commercial** ~**s** gewerbliche(s) Luftfahrzeug(e); Verkehrsflugzeug(e); **departure (landing) of an** ~ Abflug (Landung) e-s Flugzeugs; **large-capacity** ~ Großraumflugzeug(e); **register of** ~ s. ~ →register; **unlawful seizure of** ~[35] widerrechtliche Inbesitznahme von Luftfahrzeugen; **an** ~ **(has) crashed** ein Flugzeug ist verunglückt
air, ~ crash Flugzeugunglück; ~ **crew** Flugzeugbesatzung; fliegendes Personal; ~ **defen|ce (se)** Luftverteidigung; Luftabwehr; ~**-drome** *Am* Flughafen, Flugplatz; ~ **express** *Am* Lufteilgut *(beschleunigter Luftpäckchendienst)*; ~ **fares** Flugpreise; ~ **fee** Luftpostgebühr
airfield Flugplatz, Flughafen; **civil** ~ Zivilflugplatz; **military** ~ Militärflugplatz
Air Force Luftwaffe; ~**s** Luftstreitkräfte; **Royal** ~ (R. A. F.) *Br* Luftwaffe; **Department of the** ~ *Am* Luftfahrtministerium; **Secretary of the** ~ *Am* Luftfahrtminister
air freight Luftfracht *(Frachtgut und Frachtgebühr)*; ~ **bill** Luftfrachtbrief; ~ **charges** Luftfracht *(Gebühren)*
air, ~ freighter Frachtflugzeug; ~ **incident** *(VölkerR)* Luftzwischenfall; ~ **insurance company** Luftfahrtversicherungsgesellschaft; ~ **law** Luftrecht; ~ **legislation** Luftfahrtgesetzgebung; ~ **letter** Luftpostbrief; ~ **lift** Luftbrücke *(bes. in Krisenzeiten)*; Lufttransport
airline Luftverkehrslinie; Fluglinie (od. ~strekke); Fluggesellschaft, Luftverkehrsgesellschaft; ~**s** *(Börse)* Flugzeugwerte; **national** ~ inländische Fluggesellschaft; **regular** ~**s** Linienfluggesellschaft; ~ **company** (or *Am* **corporation**) Luftverkehrsgesellschaft; ~ **fare** Flugpreis; ~ **operations** Fluglinienverkehr; ~ **operator** Luftfahrtunternehmer; **to operate** ~ **companies** Luftverkehrsunternehmen betreiben
airliner Flugzeug im Linienverkehr; **commercial** ~ Linienflugzeug

airmail Luftpost; **by** ~ mit Luftpost; ~ **fee** Luftpostgebühr; ~ **letter** Luftpostbrief; ~ **receipt** Luftposteinlieferungsschein; ~ **service** Luftpostdienst; Luftpostverkehr; ~ **stamp** Luftpostmarke
airmail *v*, **to** ~ **a letter** e-n Luftpostbrief senden
air navigation Luftfahrt; ~ **(services)** Flugsicherung; ~ **(services) authority** (or **administration)** Flugsicherungsbehörde; ~ **(services) facilities** Flugsicherungseinrichtungen
air, ~**park** *Am* kleiner Flughafen; ~ **parcel** *Br* Luftpostpaket; ~ **passage** Flug; Luftreise; ~ **passenger** Fluggast; Luftreisender
airplane *Am* Flugzeug; **private** ~ *Am* Privatflugzeug
air pollutants luftverunreinigende Stoffe
air pollution, ~ **caused by motor vehicle exhaust** Luftverschmutzung durch Abgase von Kraftfahrzeugmotoren; **Convention on Long-Range Transboundary A**~ **P**~[36] Übereinkommen über weiträumige grenzüberschreitende Luftverunreinigung
airport Flugplatz; Flughafen; ~ **bus** Zubringerbus; ~ **of departure** Abgangsflughafen; ~ **of entry** Ankunftsflughafen; Zollflughafen
air power Luftmacht
air raid Fliegerangriff; Luftangriff; ~ **precautionary measures** Luftschutzmaßnahmen; ~ **precaution(s)** (A. R. P.) Luftschutz; ~ **protection** Luftschutz; ~ **shelter** Luftschutzraum; ~ **warden** Luftschutzwart; ~ **warning** Fliegeralarm
air, ~ **regulations** Luftverkehrsvorschriften; ~ **route** Luftverkehrslinie; Flugstrecke; ~ **safety** Flugsicherheit
air service[37] Luftverkehr; Fluglinienverkehr; ~ **schedule** Flugplan; **scheduled** ~ planmäßiger Fluglinienverkehr; **to establish** ~**s** Fluglinienverkehr aufnehmen; **to inaugurate the** ~**s** den Fluglinienverkehr eröffnen
air sovereignty Lufthoheit
air space Luftraum; **sovereignty over the** ~ Lufthoheit; **territorial** ~ Lufthoheitsgebiet
air, ~ **staff** Flugpersonal; ~ **superiority** *mil* Luftüberlegenheit; ~ **supremacy** *mil* Luftherrschaft; ~ **surcharge** Luftpostzuschlag; ~ **tariff** Flugtarif; ~ **terminal** Großflughafen; ~ **ticket** Flugkarte, Flugschein; ~ **tourism** Flugtourismus; ~ **traffic** Flugverkehr, Luftverkehr; ~ **traffic control** Flugverkehrskontrolle; ~ **traffic controller** Fluglotse, Flugverkehrsleiter; ~ **traffic regulations** Luftverkehrsbestimmungen
air transport Luftverkehr, Lufttransport, Beförderung auf dem Luftwege; ~ **convention** Luftverkehrsabkommen; ~ **services** Luftverkehrsdienste
air, ~ **travel** Flug, Luftreise; ~ **travel(l)er** Luftreisender; ~ **trip** Flug; ~ **war** Luftkrieg; ~ **warfare** Luftkriegsführung; ~**way** Luftverkehrslinie; Flugstrecke; ~**way bill** (a. w. b.) Luftfrachtbrief
airworthiness, certificate of ~[38] Lufttüchtigkeitszeugnis

Albania Albanien; **Socialist People's Republic of** ~ Sozialistische Volksrepublik Albanien
Albanian Albaner(in); albanisch

alcohol Alkohol; ~ **addict** Alkoholsüchtiger; ~ **blood test** Alkoholblutprobe; ~ **monopoly** Alkoholmonopol; Branntweinmonopol; ~ **smuggler** Alkoholschmuggler; ~ **smuggling** Alkoholschmuggel
alcohol, abuse of ~ Alkoholmißbrauch; **addicted to** ~ alkoholsüchtig; **affected by** ~ unter Alkohol stehend; **excessive consumption of** ~ Alkoholmißbrauch; **consumption of** ~ **by a driver** Alkoholgenuß e-s Fahrers; **lack of driving ability due to consumption of** ~ Fahruntüchtigkeit infolge Genusses von Alkohol
alcohol, illicit distilling of ~ unerlaubte Herstellung von Alkohol
alcohol, crimes committed under the influence of ~ Alkoholdelikte; **driver who is under the influence of** ~ Verkehrssünder am Steuer; **to be under the influence of** ~ unter Alkohol stehen; in angetrunkenem Zustand sein
alcohol, misuse of ~ Alkoholmißbrauch

alcoholic Alkoholiker(in); alkoholisch; ~ **beverages** alkoholische Getränke; **non-**~ **beverages** (or **drinks)** alkoholfreie Getränke; ~ **content** (or **strength)** Alkoholgehalt *(in Getränken)*; **transfer to an institution for** ~**s** Unterbringung in e-r Trinkerheilstätte

alderman *Br* Beigeordneter *(der Corporation of the City of London)*

aleatory contract aleatorischer Vertrag *(dessen Rechtswirkung von e-m ungewissen Ereignis abhängt; z.B. Spiel-, Wettvertrag)*

Algeria Algerien; **People's Democratic Republic of** ~ Demokratische Volksrepublik Algerien
Algerian Algerier(in); algerisch

alias sonst auch (genannt); ~**es** *(z.B. auf Fragebogen)* andere Namen *(unter denen man bekannt ist)*; Aliasnamen

alibi Alibi *(Aufenthalt an e-m anderen Ort als dem Tatort)*; **to produce an** ~ ein Alibi beibringen; **to prove one's** ~ sein Alibi nachweisen; den Alibinachweis erbringen; **to set up a false** ~ ein unwahres Alibi vorbringen

alien fremd, ausländisch *(einer anderen Person oder Sache zugehörend, einem anderen Staat zugehörend)*
alien[39] Ausländer *(der sich dauernd im fremden*

Lande aufhält); ~ **ami** (or **amy**) befreundeter Ausländer; ~ **corporation** *Am* ausländische (Kapital-)Gesellschaft; ~ **culture** wesensfremde Kultur; ~**s' department** (of a police force) Fremdenpolizei; ~ **employee** ausländischer Arbeitnehmer; ~ **enemy** feindlicher Ausländer *(→ ememy alien);* ~ **friend** befreundeter Ausländer; ~**'s identity card** Personalausweis für Ausländer; ~**'s labo(u)r permit** Arbeitserlaubnis für Ausländer; ~ **né** Ausländer von Geburt; **A~'s Order** *Br* Verordnung über Kontrollbestimmungen für in Großbritannien lebende Ausländer

alien property Ausländervermögen; Ausländereigentum; **A~ P~ Custodian** *Am* Verwalter feindlichen Vermögens *(während des 2. Weltkrieges)*

alien, ~'s registration *(polizeil.)* Registrierung von Ausländern; ~ **registration card** *Am* Ausländerregistrierungskarte; ~**s' registration requirement** Meldepflicht der Ausländer; ~**'s residence permit** Aufenthaltsgenehmigung für Ausländer; ~ **resident** *Am* ansässiger Ausländer; ~ **rule** Fremdherrschaft

alien, certificate in respect of the employment of ~s *Br*[40] Arbeitsbescheinigung für Ausländer

alien, enemy ~ feindlicher Ausländer

Jede Person, die ihren Wohnsitz oder Handelsbetrieb im feindlichen oder feindbesetzten Gebiet hat. Entscheidend ist nach anglo-amerikanischem Recht nicht die Nationalität der betreffenden Person, sondern der Ort, an dem sich ihr (freiwilliger) Wohnsitz oder der Sitz ihres Handelsbetriebes zur Zeit des Krieges befindet (Territorialitätsprinzip)

alien, entry and sojourn of ~s Einreise und Aufenthalt von Ausländern; **friendly ~** befreundeter Ausländer; **law concerning ~s** Ausländerrecht; Fremdenrecht; **law regulating the legal position of ~s** Ausländerstatut; **legal standing (or status) of ~s** Ausländerstatus, Rechtsstellung e-s Ausländers; **treatment of an ~** Ausländerbehandlung

alien, to deport an undesirable ~ e-n unerwünschten (od. lästigen) Ausländer abschieben

alienable veräußerlich; übertragbar

alienage Ausländereigenschaft

alienate *v* veräußern, übertragen *(meist Grundbesitz);* entfremden; **to ~ customers** Kunden ausspannen; **to ~ in mortmain** an die tote Hand veräußern

alienation Veräußerung, Übertragung *(bes. von Grundbesitz);* Entfremdung; ~ **of affection** Entfremdung ehelicher Zuneigung; Erlöschen ehelicher Zuneigung; **restraint on ~** Veräußerungsverbot

alienee Erwerber; neuer Eigentümer, Zessionar

alienor Veräußerer; Zedent

align *v* ausrichten; angleichen; **to ~ o. s. with** sich anschließen an; **non-~ed** politisch nicht gebunden; **non-~ed countries** *pol* blockfreie Länder

alignment Ausrichtung; *pol* Blockbildung, Gruppierung; **non-~** *pol* Bündnislosigkeit; Blockfreiheit

aliment *Scot* Unterhalt(sbetrag)

aliment *v Scot* Unterhalt zahlen

alimony Unterhalt(sbetrag) *(Br [jetzt:] →* maintenance; *Am [jetzt:]* →spousal support)

aliter (otherwise) sonst

all, ~ clear *(Luftschutz)* Entwarnung; ~ **freight ship** Mehrzweckfrachter; ~**-German** gesamtdeutsch; ~**-in insurance** *Br* Gesamtversicherung; ~**-loss insurance** *Am* Gesamtversicherung; ~ **participation clause** Allbeteiligungsklausel; ~ **rights reserved** alle Rechte vorbehalten *(cf. copyright);* ~ **risks** (A. R.) alle Gefahren *(Versicherung gegen alle Gefahren e-r Seereise ohne Franchise, soweit sie von außen her auf die Güter einwirken);* ~**-risks insurance** Gesamtversicherung; ~**-round inquiry** Rundfrage; ~**-round price** Pauschalpreis, Gesamtpreis; ~ **sales final** kein Umtausch; **all-savers certificate** *Am* steuerbegünstigtes, nicht übertragbares Sparzertifikat von US-Depositeninstitutionen; ~**-stage tax** Allphasensteuer; ~ **the year (round)** ganzjährig, das ganze Jahr (hindurch)

allegation Anführung; *(bes. unerwiesene)* Behauptung; Parteivorbringen; **to make ~s** Behauptungen aufstellen

allege *v* anführen; *(Unerwiesenes)* behaupten; *(bei Gericht)* vorbringen, geltend machen; ~**d part in the robbery** angebliche Teilnahme am Raubüberfall; ~**d thief** angeblicher Dieb

allegiance *(öffentl. rechtl.)* Treuepflicht; Staatstreue; Loyalität; **duty of ~** Treuepflicht *(des Staatsbürgers)* (to gegenüber)

allegiance, oath of ~ Treueeid *(z.B. bestimmter höherer Beamter od. bei Einbürgerung); mil* Fahneneid; **to administer the oath of ~ (to sb.)** (jdm) den Treueeid abnehmen, (jdn) vereidigen; **to swear** (or **take**) **the oath of ~** den Treueeid leisten

alliance Bund, Bündnis; Allianz; Verwandtschaft *(durch Heirat);* **defensive ~** Verteidigungsbündnis; **to accede to a military ~** e-m Militärbündnis beitreten; **to enter into** (or **form, make**) **an ~** ein Bündnis schließen; sich alliieren; **to join an ~** e-m Bündnis beitreten

allied alliiert verbündet; ~ **companies** verbundene Gesellschaften, Konzerngesellschaften

Allied and Associated Powers Alliierte und Assoziierte Mächte

Gegner Deutschlands im 1. und 2. Weltkrieg

allocable *(SteuerR)* zurechenbar

allocate *v* zuteilen, zuweisen; vergeben; zurechnen; aufteilen; umlegen (to auf); **to ~ duties** Pflichten zuweisen; **to ~ expense(s)** Gemeinkosten umlegen (oder aufteilen); Unkosten verteilen; **to ~ profits** *(SteuerR)* Gewinne zurechnen; **to ~ to reserves** den Rücklagen zuführen; **to ~ shares** Aktien zuteilen
allocated oil zugeteiltes Öl

allocation Zuteilung, Zuweisung; Bereitstellung; Zurechnung; Aufteilung; Kontingentierung; **~ of costs** Aufteilung der Kosten; **~ of duties** Zuweisung von Pflichten; Geschäftsverteilung; **~ of expense(s)** Unkostenverteilung; Aufteilung (od. Umlage) von Gemeinkosten; **~ of funds** Mittelvergabe, Mittelzuweisung; **~ of markets** Aufteilung der Märkte; **~ of profits** *(SteuerR)* Gewinnzurechnung; **~ to reserves** Zuführung an die Rücklagen; **~ of seats between the Member States** *(EG)* Verteilung der Sitze auf die Mitgliedstaaten; **~ of shares** Zuteilung von Aktien; **~ of surplus to policyholders** *(VersR)* Überschußzuweisung an Versicherungsnehmer
allocation, basis of ~ Schlüssel *(für Aufteilung von Gemeinkosten)*; **financial ~** finanzielle Zuwendung; **foreign exchange ~** Devisenzuteilung; **re~** Neuzuteilung

allocatur *Br* Kostenfestsetzungsbeschluß

allodial erbeigen *(opp. feudal)*

allonge Allonge, Ansatzstück *(an Wechseln)*

allot *v* *(anteilsmäßig)* zuweisen, zuteilen; *(durch Los)* verteilen, auslosen; **to ~ shares** (to an applicant) Aktien zuteilen

allotment 1. *(anteilsmäßige)* Zuweisung, Zuteilung; Verteilung (durch Los); **on ~** bei Zuteilung *(der Aktien)*; **~ letter** *Br* **(certificate of ~** *Am)* Interimsschein *(Mitteilung über Zuteilung von Aktien)*; **~ of seats** *parl* Sitzverteilung; **application for ~ of shares** Antrag auf Zuteilung von Aktien, Zeichnung von Aktien
allotment 2. *Br (an Arbeiter verpachtete od. verkaufte)* Parzelle; Schrebergarten; **~ holder** *Br* Schrebergärtner, Inhaber e-s Schrebergartens

allottee jd, dem etw. zugeteilt wird; Zuteilungsempfänger

allow *v* erlauben, gestatten; bewilligen, zuerkennen, zukommen lassen; anerkennen; in Abzug (oder Anrechnung) bringen, anrechnen, vergüten; *(SteuerR)* als absetzbar anerkennen; **to ~ for** in Betracht ziehen, berücksichtigen; **to ~ in full** voll vergüten; **to ~ 4 per cent** mit 4% verzinsen; **to ~ 4 per cent interest on deposits** Einlagen mit 4% verzinsen; **to ~ an appeal** e-r Berufung stattgeben; **to ~ a claim** e-n Anspruch anerkennen; **to ~ a credit** e-n Kredit geben (od. einräumen); **to ~ U. S. taxes as credit against Federal Republic taxes** *(DBA)* Steuern der Vereinigten Staaten auf Steuern der Bundesrepublik anrechnen; **to ~ a discount** Rabatt (od. Skonto) gewähren (on auf); **to ~ extenuating circumstances** *(StrafR)* mildernde Umstände zubilligen; **to ~ a reasonable time** e-e angemessene Frist zubilligen; **to ~ a p. a sum** jdm e-e Summe aussetzen

allowable gewährbar; zulässig, abziehbar; *(SteuerR)* absetzbar; **~ claim** zulässige Forderung; *(KonkursR)* anmeldbare Forderung; *(PatR)* gewährbarer Anspruch; **non-~ charges** nicht absetzbare Ausgaben
allowance Erlaubnis, Bewilligung; Zubilligung, Anerkennung; ausgesetzte Summe (Kostgeld, Taschengeld, Monatsgeld, Rente etc); Zuschuß, *(geldl.)* Zuwendung, (Sozial-)Beihilfe; Aufwandsentschädigung; Vergütung, Rabatt, Preisnachlaß *(bei mangelhaften Waren)*; *Br* (Steuer-)Freibetrag; Toleranz, zulässige Abweichung; **after ~ for** nach Abzug von; **without ~ (for)** ohne Berücksichtigung; **~ coal** Deputatkohle; **~ for bad debts** Wertberichtigung auf uneinbringliche Forderungen; **~ for depletion** *(SteuerR)* Absetzung für Substanzverringerung; **~ for doubtful accounts** Wertberichtigung auf zweifelhafte Forderungen; **~ for possible loan losses** *Am (Bilanzrecht)* allgemeine Bewertungsreserve; **~s in kind** Sachbezüge, Sachleistungen; Deputat; **~ of a claim** Anerkennung e-r Forderung; **~ of a credit** Einräumung e-s Kredits; **~ of discount** Gewährung von Rabatt; **~ of interest** Vergütung von Zinsen; **~ of a patent claim** *Am* Annahme e-r Patentanmeldung *(durch das Patentamt)*; **~ of US taxes as credit against German taxes** *(DBA)* Anrechnung von amerikanischen auf deutsche Steuern
allowance, →annual ~; →capital ~; child ~ Steuerfreibetrag für Kinder; **children ~** Kindergeld; **daily ~** Tagegeld(er); *parl* Diäten; **dependent relatives ~** *Br* Steuerfreibetrag für Unterstützung abhängiger Verwandter; **entertainment ~** Aufwandsentschädigung; **extra ~** Sondervergütung; Sonderbeihilfe; *(gerichtl. anerkannte)* erhöhte Kostenrechnung; **family ~** Familienbeihilfe; *Am* Familienzulage; **fixed ~** Fixum; **housekeeper ~** *Br (SteuerR)* Freibetrag für Wirtschafterin; **initial ~s** *Br (SteuerR)* Erstabschreibung (od. Sonderabschreibung) bei Neuanschaffungen; **investment ~** *(SteuerR)* Investitionsabschreibung; **married ~** *Br (SteuerR)* persönlicher Freibetrag für Eheleute; **mileage ~** Kilometergeld; **monthly ~** Monatszuschuß; Monatswechsel *(e-s Studenten)*; **overtime ~** Vergütung für Überstunden; **per diem ~** Tagessatz, Reisespesensatz; **personal ~** *Br* (persönl.) (Steuer-)Freibetrag; **rental ~** *Am* Woh-

nungsgeld(zuschuß); **representation** ~ Aufwandsentschädigung; **seniority** ~ *Am* Dienstalterzulage; **separation** ~ Trennungsentschädigung; **single** ~ *Br (SteuerR)* persönlicher Freibetrag; **supplementary** ~ Zusatzrente; zusätzliche Bewilligung; **tax** ~ *Br* (Steuer-)Freibetrag; **travel(l)ing** ~ Reisekostenvergütung

allowance, to make an ~ e-e Summe aussetzen; *(vom Preise)* nachlassen, Rabatt geben; **to make** ~ **for** berücksichtigen

alloy Legierung; ~ **of gold** Goldlegierung; **of base** ~ *(Gold, Silber)* von geringem Gehalt, geringhaltig

alluvion, alluvium Alluvium, angeschwemmtes Land *(cf. avulsion)*

ally Verbündeter; Alliierter; Bundesgenosse *(cf. allied)*

aloofness *pol* abwartende Haltung

alphabetical, ~ **index** alphabetisches Verzeichnis; ~ **order** alphabetische Reihenfolge; **arranged** ~**ly** alphabetisch geordnet

alpha stocks *(Börse) Br* die 60 am lebhaftesten gehandelten Aktien am Londoner Markt, jede mit mindestens 10 →market makers

alter *v* (ab-, ver)ändern; **to** ~ **a cheque** *(Am* **check)** e-n Scheck fälschen; **to** ~ **one's plans** s-e Pläne ändern

altered, materially ~ wesentlich geändert *(cf. alteration)*

altering a document with intent to defraud Verfälschung e-r (echten) Urkunde *(cf. forgery)*

alteration Änderung (to an), Veränderung, Abänderung; (Ver-)Fälschung *(e-r Urkunde);* ~ **to** (or **of) a contract** Vertragsänderung; **apparent** ~ augenscheinliche Änderung; **material** ~[41] wesentliche Änderung; **material** ~ **of an instrument** (rechts)erhebliche Änderung e-r Urkunde *(beeinflußt deren Rechtswirksamkeit und hat ihre Unwirksamkeit jedermann gegenüber zur Folge; cf. spoliation);* **prohibited** ~**s** *(UrheberR)* verbotene Änderungen; **subject to** ~**s** Änderungen vorbehalten; **to effect** (or **make)** ~**s** (Ab-)Änderungen vornehmen

alternat *(VölkerR)* Alternat, Unterschriftenfolge

alternate *Am* Stellvertreter, Vertreter; *Am* Ersatzmann; stellvertretendes Mitglied; stellvertretend, abwechselnd; ~ **director** stellvertretender Direktor *(bes. bei Abwesenheit im Ausland od. bei Krankheit);* ~ **heir** *Am* Ersatzerbe; ~ **member** stellvertretendes Mitglied; **to appoint (designate) an** ~ *Am* e-n Stellvertreter ernennen (bestimmen)

alternative Alternative; Ausweg (to für); alternativ, abwechselnd; einander ausschließend, anders möglich; ~ **claim** Hilfsanspruch; *(PatR)* Hilfsantrag; ~ **draft** Gegenentwurf; ~ **offer** Alternativangebot; ~ **proposal** Gegenvorschlag; ~ **sentence** Ersatzfreiheitsstrafe; **there is no** ~ **to my proposal** es gibt keine Alternative für meinen Vorschlag

amalgamate *v* verschmelzen; zusammenlegen, fusionieren; sich zusammenschließen

amalgamation[42] Verschmelzung, Zusammenschluß, Fusion *(2 od. mehrere Gesellschaften verschmelzen durch Zusammenschluß zu e-r neuen Gesellschaft; cf. merger);* ~ **agreement** Fusionsvertrag

amateur value Liebhaberwert

ambassador Botschafter; ~**-at-large** Sonderbotschafter; ~ **extraordinary and plenipotentiary** außerordentlicher und bevollmächtigter Botschafter *(förml. Bezeichnung, cf. diplomatic agents)*

ambassadorial level, on ~ auf Botschafterebene

ambassadorship Botschafterposten

amber *(Verkehrsampel)* Gelblicht

ambiguity, latent ~ versteckter Dissens; **patent** ~ offener Dissens

ambiguous zweideutig; unklar; ~ **instrument** *Br* unklar abgefaßter Wechsel; ~ **terms** mehrdeutige Begriffe

ambit Umfang, Grenzen *(z.B. e-r Vollmacht)*

ambulatory umherziehend, Wander-; ~ **will** widerrufliches Testament

ambush Hinterhalt; **to wait in** ~ **for sb.** jdm auflauern

ameliorate *v (bes. Ackerboden)* verbessern, meliorieren; sich bessern, besser werden

amelioration Verbesserung; ~ **of the soil** Melioration, Bodenverbesserung; ~ **of the condition of the wounded** *(VölkerR)* Verbesserung des Loses der Verwundeten (→*Geneva Convention)*

amenable zugänglich (to für), unterworfen; ~ **to jurisdiction** der Gerichtsbarkeit unterworfen

amend *v* (ab)ändern, ergänzen; verbessern; **power to** ~ (Ab-)Änderungsbefugnis; **to** ~ **a bill** e-n Gesetzesentwurf abändern; **to** ~ **a law** ein Gesetz novellieren; **to** ~ **the terms** die Bedingungen abändern

amended, ~ **claim** geänderter Patentanspruch; ~ **tax return** *Am* Ergänzungssteuererklärung; **the Act as** ~ **on** . . . das Gesetz in der Fassung vom . . .

amending, ~ **letter** Berichtigungsschreiben; ~ →**statute**

amendment (Ab-)Änderung, Ergänzung; Nachtrag; Berichtigung; *parl* Änderung(santrag), Ergänzung(santrag); (Gesetzes-)Novelle; **A ~s** *Am* Zusatzartikel zur Verfassung der USA von 1787 (→ *Bill of Rights)* und zu den Verfassungen der Einzelstaaten; **~ of** (or **to**) **an Act** (or **statute**) Gesetzesänderung; **A~ Bill** Entwurf e-s Änderungsgesetzes; **~ of claim** Anspruchsänderung; **~ of a law** Novellierung e-s Gesetzes; **~ of (the) pleadings** Berichtigung (od. Änderung) des Klagevorbringens (od. der Klagebeantwortung); Klageänderung; **~ of (statement of) claim** Klageänderung; **~ of terms** Änderung von Bedingungen; **power of ~** (Ab-)Änderungsbefugnis; **to move** (or **introduce, propose**) **an ~** e-n (Ab-)Änderungsantrag stellen (oder einbringen); **to pass** (or **adopt**) **an ~** e-n (Ab-)Änderungsantrag annehmen; **to take the Fifth** *Am* vom Aussageverweigerungsrecht Gebrauch machen (→*privilege against self-incrimination)*

amends Schadensersatz; Wiedergutmachung; (Geld-)Buße; **to make ~** Schadensersatz leisten (for für); wiedergutmachen; **to make ~ to sb. for** ... jdm wegen ... Schadensersatz (od. Buße) zahlen

amenities, ~ centre *Br* Freizeitzentrum; **public ~** Anlagen (oder Einrichtungen) zur Freizeitgestaltung *(Parks, Schwimmbäder, Kinderspielplätze, Bibliotheken etc)*

amercement *Am* Geldstrafe, Buße *(z.B. wegen Dienstvergehen)*

Americans amerikanische Aktien
American Association for the Advancement of Science (A.A.A.S.) Amerikanische Gesellschaft zur Förderung der Naturwissenschaften *(gegr. 1848)*
American Association of Advertising Agencies (AAAA) Amerikanische Vereinigung der Werbeagenturen
American Bankers Association (ABA) Amerikanische Banken- und Bankiervereinigung
American Bar Association (ABA) Amerikanischer Bundesverband der Anwaltschaft; *(etwa:)* Bundesanwaltskammer
American Bureau of Shipping (ABS) Amerikanische Klassifikationsgesellschaft
American Chemical Society (A.C.S.) Gesellschaft amerikanischer Chemiker
American Civil Liberties Union Amerikanische Bürgerrechtsvereinigung
American Depositary Receipts (ADR) *(von amerikanischen Banken für im Depot befindliche nichtamerikanische Aktien ausgestellte)* Aktienzertifikate; **owner of an ADR** ADR-Inhaber
American Federation of Labor and Congress of Industrial Organizations (AFL/CIO) US-Gewerkschaftsdachverband
American Institute of Aeronautics (A.I.A.) Amerikanisches Luftfahrt-Institut
American Institute of Certified Public Accountants (AICPA) Amerikanisches Institut der Wirtschaftsprüfer
American Insurance Association (AIA) Verband amerikanischer Versicherer
American Law Institute (ALI) Amerikanisches Rechtsinstitut
Private Organisation hervorragender amerikanischer Juristen zur Schaffung des → Restatement von Modellgesetzen und mit anderen Aufgaben der Rechtsreform
American Management Association (AMA) Amerikanischer Verband für Betriebsführung
American Medical Association (AMA) Amerikanischer Bundesverband der Ärzte; *(etwa:)* Amerikanische Bundesärztekammer
American Mutual Insurance Alliance (AMIA) Vereinigung amerikanischer Versicherungsvereine auf Gegenseitigkeit
American National Standards Institute (ANSJ) *Am* nationale Standardisierungsorganisation *(Nachfolgerin der American Standards Association)*
American Newspaper Publishers Association (ANPA) Amerikanischer Zeitungsverlegerverband
American Nuclear Society (ANS) Amerikanische Kerntechnische Gesellschaft
American Stock Exchange (A.S.E., AMEX) *(zweitgrößte von 13)* Wertpapierbörse*(n der USA)*
Zulassung zur Notierung ist leichter als an der → New York Stock Exchange

Amex → American Stock Exchange

ami →next friend

amiable compositeur *Fr (privater)* Schiedsrichter *(der auf Wunsch der Parteien nach billigem Ermessen endgültig entscheidet)*; **the arbitrator acts as ~** der Schiedsrichter entscheidet nach billigem Ermessen
amiable composition *Fr* Schiedsverfahren *(nach billigem Ermessen unter Beiseitelassung e-r strengen Rechtsanwendung)*

amica curiae →amicus curiae

amicable gütlich, freund(schaft)lich; **settlement of a dispute by ~ arrangement** Beilegung e-r Streitigkeit auf dem Vergleichsweg; **~ settlement** gütliche Beilegung; Vergleich; **in the course of arbitration, the parties sometimes reach an ~ settlement of the dispute** im Verlauf des Schiedsverfahrens kommen die Parteien manchmal zu e-r vergleichsweisen Beilegung des Streites
amicably, to settle the dispute ~ den Streitfall vergleichsweise beilegen

amicus curiae sachverständiger Beistand im Prozeß *(zur Erläuterung streitiger Tat- od. Rechtsfragen)*; ~ **brief** amicus-Schriftsatz *(Stellungnahme mit Begründung durch interessierte, aber an e-m Prozeß nicht beteiligte Personen)*

amity, treaty of ~ *(VölkerR)* Freundschaftsvertrag

amnesty Amnestie, allgemeiner Straferlaß *(bes. bei politischen Straftaten)*; **to be covered by an** ~ unter e-e Amnestie fallen; **to grant** ~ amnestieren

Amnesty International Amnesty International
Private internationale Organisation (mit 47 nationalen Sektionen), die sich für die Freilassung und humanitäre Behandlung von Personen einsetzt, die unter Verletzung der UNO-Menschenrechtserklärung von 1948 Freiheitsbeschränkungen unterworfen sind

amortizable amortisierbar, tilgbar; abschreibbar

amortization Amortisation, Amortisierung; *(ratenweise)* Tilgung *(by means of a sinking fund)*; *(ratenweise)* Rückzahlung; *(SteuerR)*[43] Abschreibung *(auf immaterielle Anlagegüter)*; ~ **fund** Amortisations-, Tilgungsfonds; ~ **loan** Tilgungsanleihe; ~ **of a loan** Tilgung e-r Anleihe; ~ **mortgage** Amortisations-, Tilgungshypothek; ~ **of a mortgage** Tilgung e-r Hypothek; ~ **quota** Amortisationsquote, Amortisationsrate; ~ **on replacement value** *Am* Abschreibung auf den Wiederbeschaffungswert; ~ **table** Tilgungsplan; **method of** ~ Tilgungsart; **terms of** ~ Tilgungsbedingungen

amortize *v* amortisieren; *(ratenweise)* tilgen; *(in Raten)* zurückzahlen; *(SteuerR)* abschreiben

amount Betrag; (Gesamt-)Summe; Bestand; Höhe; ~ **brought forward** Vortrag *(aus letzter Spalte od. Seite)*; ~ **carried forward** Übertrag *(auf nächste Spalte od. Seite)*; ~ **in cash** Kassenbestand; Barvorrat; ~ **in controversy** *Am* Streitwert; ~ **in dispute** Streitwert; ~ **due** geschuldeter Betrag; ~ **estimated** geschätzter Betrag; ~ **in figures** Betrag in Zahlen; ~ **insured** Versicherungssumme; ~ **of interest** Zinshöhe; ~ **of (an) invoice** Rechnungsbetrag; ~ **of loss** Schadenssumme, Schadenshöhe; ~ **of money** Geldbetrag; ~ **at risk** *(VersR)* Risikosumme *(Unterschied zwischen Versicherungssumme und Deckungskapital)*; ~ **sued for** eingeklagter Betrag; ~ **in words** Betrag in Worten; ~ **written off** Abschreibungsbetrag

amount, actual ~ Istbestand, Effektivbestand; **any** ~ beliebiger Betrag; **bond** ~ Anleihebetrag; **estimated** ~ veranschlagte Summe; **gross** ~ Bruttobetrag; **net** ~ Nettobetrag, Reinbetrag; **in one** ~ in einer Summe, auf einmal *(opp. by instalments)*; **partial** ~ Teilbetrag; **total** ~ Gesamtbetrag, Gesamtsumme; **(up) to the** ~ **of** bis zum Betrage von, bis zur Höhe von

amount *v* sich belaufen (od. beziffern) (to auf); hinauslaufen (to auf); betragen; **to** ~ **to an invention** (PatR) Erfindungshöhe erreichen; **the testimony** ~**s to very little** das Zeugnis war nicht sehr wichtig (od. bedeutete nicht viel); **the damage** ~**s to** der Schaden beläuft sich auf

amounting to in Höhe von; im Betrage von

ample reichlich; genügend; ~ **means** reichliche (od. genügende) Mittel; ~ **security** ausreichende Sicherheit

amply supplied with money reichlich mit Geld versehen

amusement tax Vergnügungssteuer

amy, prochain ~ → next friend

analogy, ~ **process** *(PatR)* Analogieverfahren; **by** ~ **(with)** (or **on the** ~ **of**) im Wege der Analogie; analog nach; **argument by** (or **from**) ~ Analogieschluß

analy|se *(Am* ~**ze**) *v* analysieren, aufgliedern, untersuchen; *(Unterlagen)* auswerten

analysis Analyse, Aufgliederung, Untersuchung; Auswertung; ~ **sheet** Bilanzanalyse, Bilanzaufgliederung(sbogen); **account** ~ Kontoanalyse; **market** ~ Marktanalyse

analyst (Markt-, Bilanz-) Analytiker; Marktberater

anarchism Anarchismus

anarchist Anarchist

ancestral die Vorfahren betreffend; ~ **estate** ererbter Grundbesitz

ancestry Ahnen, Vorfahren; ~ **research** Ahnenforschung

anchor *v* ankern, vor Anker gehen (od. liegen)

anchored ship Schiff vor Anker

anchorage Ankern, Vorankerliegen; Ankerplatz; Ankergebühr

ancient documents Urkunden, die wenigstens 20 Jahre alt sind *(und für deren Ausfertigung [execution] kein Beweis erbracht zu werden braucht)*

ancient lights *(durch mehr als 20jährige*[44] *Nutzung ersessenes)* Licht- und Fensterrecht

ancient writings →ancient documents

ancillary ergänzend, zusätzlich, untergeordnet; Hilfs-, **administration** Neben-, Hilfserbschaftsverwaltung *(Br für im Ausland belegene Erbschaftsgegenstände e-s am englischen Wohnsitz verstorbenen Engländers) (opp. Br principal administration, Am domiciliary administration)*; ~ **administrator** Neben-, Hilfserbschaftsverwalter *(für die Abwicklung des örtlichen Nachlasses e-s zuletzt im Ausland [od. Am in e-m Schwesternstaat] domizilierten Erben) (opp. Br principal administrator, Am domiciliary administrator)*; ~

clauses untergeordnete Nebenverpflichtungen *(e-s Vertrages);* ~ **executor** Neben-, Hilfstestamentsvollstrecker *(cf. ~ administrator);* ~ **industries** Zulieferbetriebe; ~ **letters of administration** *Am* Hilfserbschaftsverwalterzeugnis; ~ **letters testamentary** *Am* Hilfstestamentsvollstreckerzeugnis; ~ **object** Nebenzweck; ~ **orders** *Br* (zusätzliche) gerichtliche Zwangsmittel zur Erlangung von Beweisen *(z.B. →interrogatories, →Anton Piller order);* ~ **papers** Beiakten; ~ **plant** Nebenbetrieb, Hilfsbetrieb; ~ **receiver** Hilfs-, Nebenkonkursverwalter; Hilfs-, Nebenzwangsverwalter; ~ **relief** zusätzlicher *(durch die Klage verlangter)* Rechtsschutz; ~ **probate** *Am* gerichtl. Testamentsbestätigung für Nachlaßwerte außerhalb des Staates des Wohnsitzes; ~ **right** angrenzendes Recht *(z.B. copyright an Funksendungen);* ~ **services** Nebenleistungen; Hilfsdienste; ~ **work** Zulieferarbeiten

Andean Pact Andenpakt
Zu den Andenpaktstaaten gehören Bolivien, Ecuador, Kolumbien, Peru und Venezuela

Andorra, the Principality of ~ das Fürstentum Andorra
Andorran Andorraner(in); andorranisch

angary, right of ~ *(VölkerR)* Angarienrecht
Recht e-s kriegführenden Staates, bei Notstand im Transportwesen gegen Entschädigung neutrale Schiffe zu beschlagnahmen oder zu zerstören

Anglican *Br* Mitglied der Anglikanischen Kirche (Church of England)
Anglican Church *Br* Anglikanische Kirche *(protestantische Staatskirche) (cf. High Church, Low Church, Broad Church)*
Anglican Communion Anglikanischer Kirchenbund
Umfaßt the Church of England, the Church of Ireland, the Episcopal Church in Scotland, the Church in Wales, the Protestant Episcopal Church in the United Staates etc

Anglo-German Foundation for the Study of Industrial Society Deutsch-Britische Stiftung für das Studium der Industriegesellschaft

Angola Angola; **People's Republic of** ~ Volksrepublik Angola
Angolan Angolaner(in); angolanisch

Anglophil Englandfreund

animal Tier; ~ **breeds and plant varieties** Tier- und Pflanzenzüchtungen; ~ **husbandry** Viehzucht; **cruelty to ~s** Tierquälerei; **keeper of ~s** Tierhalter; **keeping a domestic** ~ Halten e-s Haustieres; **liability for ~s** Tierhalterhaftung; →**European Convention for the Protection of A~s during International Transport; Royal Society for the Prevention of Cruelty to A~s** (RSPCA) *Br* Tierschutzverein

annex, ~ **(to a document) Anlage, Anhang;** ~ **(to a hotel** etc) Anbau, Nebengebäude, Dépendance

annex *v (als untergeordneten Teil)* beifügen; *(VölkerR) (Gebiet)* annektieren
annexed to the land mit dem Grund und Boden fest verbunden

annexation Beifügung; *(VölkerR)* Annexion, Einverleibung *(e-s Gebietes durch Eroberung und Gewalt; cf. occupation, conquest)*

anniversary Jahrestag, Jahresfeier; Jubiläum; ~ **publication** Festschrift; **wedding** ~ Hochzeitstag

annotate *v* mit Anmerkungen versehen, kommentieren

annotation Anmerkung; Kommentar

announcement Bekanntgabe, Bekanntmachung, Ankündigung; *(Rundfunk, Fernsehen)* Ansage; ~ **of birth (of death, of marriage)** Geburts-, (Todes-, Heirats)anzeige *(in Zeitungen);* ~ **of execution** *(Börse)* Ausführungsanzeige; ~ **of a sale** Verkaufsanzeige; **personal** ~ Familienanzeige *(in Zeitungen)*

annual jährlich, Jahres-; Jahrbuch; ~ **account** Jahresrechnung; ~ **accounts** *Br* Jahresabschluß *(balance sheet and profit and loss account);* **to approve the** ~ **accounts** den Jahresabschluß genehmigen
annual, ~ **allowance** *Am* jährlicher Abschreibungsbetrag; ~ **audit** Jahresabschlußprüfung; ~ **balance sheet** Jahresbilanz, Jahresabschluß; ~ **estimate** Haushaltsplan; ~ **examination of financial statement** *Am* Jahresabschlußprüfung; ~ **exclusion** *Am (Schenkungsteuer)* jährlicher Freibetrag; ~ **fee** Jahresgebühr(en); Jahreshonorar; ~ **financial statement** *Am* Jahresabschluß; ~ **general meeting** (A.G.M.) *Br (ordentl.)* Hauptversammlung; ~ **grant** Jahreszuschuß; ~ **improvement factor** (AIF) produktionsgebundene Lohnsteigerungsklausel; ~ **income** Jahreseinkommen; ~ **meeting of stockholders** *Am* Jahreshauptversammlung; **the A~ Practice** →Practice; ~ **premium** Jahresprämie; ~ **rate** Jahressatz; ~ **report** Jahresbericht;~ **return** jährliche (Einkommen)-Steuererklärung; *Br*[45] Jahresbericht *(e-r Kapitalgesellschaft [ltd. od. plc.] an den Registrar of Companies);* ~ **statement** Jahresausweis; Jahresbericht; ~ **statement of accounts** Jahresabschluß; **A~ Statutes** *Br (in der Königl. Druckerei hergestellte)* offizielle Ausgabe der im Laufe e-s Jahres erlassenen Gesetze; ~ **summary** *Br* jährliche Aufstellung der Aktiven und Passiven *(e-r AG);* ~ **value** *Br* Jahres(ertrags)wert *(Miet- bzw. Pachtwert von Immobilien als Grundlage der Besteuerung von Einkünften aus Grundvermögen);* ~ **wages** Jahreslohn(summe)

annualized percentage rate (APR) Prozentsatz auf Jahresbasis umgerechnet

annuitant Rentner(in), Empfänger(in) e-r Rente; Rentenempfänger(in); **life** ~ Empfänger(in) e-r Lebensrente

annuit|y (jährl.) Rente; Jahresgeld; jährl. Zahlung, Annuität; Jahresgebühr; Rentenzahlung; Rentenbrief (→~ *bond*); ~**ies** Renten; Jahreszahlungen; ~ **basis** Rentenbasis; ~ **bond** Annuitätenanleihe *(Staatsanleihe, für die e-e Rückzahlung nicht vorgesehen ist)*; ~ **certain** Zeitrente *(Rente mit begrenzter Laufzeit)*; ~ **charge** Rentenschuld; ~ **contract** Rentenvertrag; ~ **insurance** (private) Rentenversicherung; ~ **payment** Rentenzahlung

annuit|y, complete ~ Rente, die bis zum Todestag des Rentners gezahlt wird; **contingent** ~ bedingte Annuität *(deren Zahlung von bestimmten Ereignissen abhängig ist)*; Rente mit unbestimmter Laufzeit; **deferred** ~ aufgeschobene Rente *(erst nach e-r bestimmten Zeit fällig werdende Rente)*; **government** ~ Staatsrente; **holder of an** ~ Rentenempfänger(in); Rentenberechtigte(r); **immediate** ~ sofort fällig werdende Rente; **irredeemable** ~ nicht ablösbare Rente; **life** ~ Leibrente; lebenslängliche Rente; **old age** ~ Altersrente; **payment of** ~**ies** *(PatR)* Zahlung der Jahresgebühren; **perpetual** ~ ewige (od. unkündbare) Rente; **redeemable** ~ ablösbare Rente; **reversionary** (or **survivorship**) ~ *(Lebensvers.)* Rente auf den Überlebensfall; **temporary** ~ Zeitrente; **terminable** ~ befristete (od. kündbare) Rente; **widow's** ~ Witwenrente

annuity, to hold (or **receive**) an ~ e-e Rente beziehen; **to settle an** ~ **on a p.** jdm e-e Rente (od. ein Jahresgeld) aussetzen

annul *v* für nichtig (od. ungültig) erklären, annulieren; *(Entscheidung)* aufheben; **to** ~ **an appointment** e-e Ernennung rückgängig machen; **to** ~ **a contract** e-n Vertrag für nichtig erklären; **to** ~ **a document** e-e Urkunde für ungültig erklären; **to** ~ **a marriage** e-e Ehe aufheben, für nichtig erklären

annulment Nichtig(keits)erklärung, Ungültigkeitserklärung, Annullierung; Aufhebung; Löschung; ~ **of marriage** Aufhebung, Nichtigkeitserklärung der Ehe *(die Gründe für ~ sind nach deutschen Recht teils Aufhebungs-, teils Nichtigkeitsgründe)*; **action for** ~ Nichtigkeitsklage; Aufhebungsklage

annum, per ~ jährlich

answer Antwort, Bescheid, Erwiderung (to auf); Klageerwiderung; ~ **prepaid** (A.P.) *(Telegramm)* Antwort bezahlt; ~ **to the charge** Erwiderung auf die Anklage(schrift); **in** ~ **to your letter** in Beantwortung Ihres Schreibens; **affirmative** ~ zustimmende Antwort; **negative** ~ ablehnende Antwort; **time for** ~ Erklärungsfrist; **an** ~ **is requested** um Antwort wird gebeten

answer *v* (be)antworten, erwidern (to auf); **to** ~ **for** haften für; bürgen (od. einstehen) für; **to** ~ **to** entsprechen; **to** ~ **a bill (of exchange)** e-n Wechsel einlösen (od. honorieren); **to** ~ **a charge** sich wegen e-r Anklage (od. Beschuldigung) verantworten; **to** ~ **in the affirmative (negative)** bejahend (verneinend) antworten; **to** ~ **a summons** e-r *(gerichtl.)* Vorladung Folge leisten; **to** ~ **to the description** der Beschreibung entsprechen; **to** ~ **to the purpose** dem Zweck entsprechen; **time to** ~ Klagebeantwortungsfrist

answering service *tel* Auftragsdienst

answerable verantwortlich, haftbar (for für); ~ **for damages** schadensersatzpflichtig; **to be** ~ **before the court** sich vor Gericht verantworten müssen

Antarctic agreement[46] Antarktis Vertrag

Antarctic Marine Living Resources, Convention on the Conservation of ~[47] Übereinkommen über die Erhaltung der lebenden Meeresschätze der Antarktis

Antarctic Seals, Convention for the Conservation of ~[48] Übereinkommen zur Erhaltung der antarktischen Robben

antecedent vorhergehend, früher (to als); ~ **claim** früherer Anspruch; ~ **debt** frühere Schuld *(opp. present debt)*; ~ **party** Vormann; ~ **transactions** Geschäfte *(des Schuldners)* vor Konkurseröffnung

antecedent das Vorhergehende; ~**s** Vorleben, Vorgeschichte; Vorfahren, Abstammung

antedate *v* rückdatieren *(ein früheres Datum einsetzen)*; *(zeitlich)* vorangehen *(opp. to postdate)*

antedating Rückdatierung; ~ **of an order** Vorziehen e-s Auftrags

ante meridiem (a.m.) vormittags

antenuptial, ~ **agreement** (or **contract**) vorehelicher Vertrag; ~ **debts** voreheliche Schulden; ~ **settlement** vorehelicher güterrechtlicher Vertrag; Ehevertrag (→*marriage settlement*)

anthem, national ~ Nationalhymne

anti-aircraft (defen|ce, ~se) (A.A.) Fliegerabwehr, Luftabwehr, Flak

anti-ballistic missile (ABM) Raketenabwehrrakete *(gegen einfliegende Feindraketen)*

anti-cartel kartellfeindlich, gegen Kartellbestrebungen gerichtet

anticipate *v* vorwegnehmen, vorausnehmen; *(PatR)* *(neuheitsschädlich)* vorwegnehmen;

(Geld, Einkommen etc) im voraus ausgeben; im voraus bezahlen; **to ~ a bill** e-n Wechsel vor Verfall einlösen; **to ~ a payment** im voraus (od. vor Fälligkeit) bezahlen; **to ~ one's salary** Gehaltsvorschuß nehmen

anticipated vorzeitig, vor Fälligkeit; **right of ~ arrest** *(VölkerR)* Recht auf vorbeugende Beschlagnahme *(e-s Schiffes im Falle e-r Seeblockade)*; **~ bonus** *(VersR) (in Form von Prämienermäßigung)* vorweggenommener Gewinnanteil; **~ invention** vorweggenommene Erfindung; **~ payment** Vorauszahlung; Vorschuß;**~ redemption** vorzeitiger Rückkauf *(e-r Schuldverschreibung)*; vorzeitige Tilgung

anticipation Vorwegnahme, Vorausnahme *(e-s erst später zu erwartenden Ereignisses)*; Vorauszahlung *(Zahlung vor Fälligkeitstermin)*; Vorgriff (of auf); Vorausschätzung; **~ of an invention** *(PatR) (neuheitsschädl.)* Vorwegnahme e-r Erfindung *(durch Veröffentlichung od. Vorbenutzung)*; neuheitsschädliches Material; **~ of life** vermutliche Lebensdauer; **~ of payment** Zahlung vor Fälligkeit, Vorauszahlung; **by** (or **in**) **~** im voraus, vorweg; **in ~ of** im Vorgriff auf

anticipatory vorwegnehmend; vorweggenommen; *(PatR)* neuheitsschädlich; **~ breach of contract** antizipierter *(vorzeitig angekündigter od. erkennbarer)* Vertragsbruch; vor Fälligkeit erklärte Erfüllungsverweigerung *(z.B. des Verkäufers)* oder Verhalten, das beabsichtigten Vertragsbruch andeutet; **~ credit** *Br* →packing credit; **~ drawing of a draft** Vorausziehung e-r Tratte; **~ seizure** *(dingl.)* Arrest; **order for ~ seizure** Entscheidung zum Zwecke e-r vorweggenommenen Zwangsvollstrekkung (Arrestbefehl)

anticompetitive wettbewerbsfeindlich; **~ agreement** wettbewerbsschädliche Absprache

anti-crisis plan Krisenplan

anticyclical antizyklisch; **for ~ reasons** aus konjunkturpolitischen Gründen

anti-deficiency legislation *Am* Gesetze zum Schutz des Schuldners e-s hypothekarisch gesicherten Darlehens für den Fall, daß der Gläubiger bei der Verwertung des Grundstücks ausfällt

antidumping Antidumping-, gegen das Dumping gerichtet; **~ duty** Antidumping-Zoll; **~ investigations** Antidumping-Untersuchungen; **~ legislation** Antidumping-Rechtsvorschriften

antifraud provisions *Am* Vorschriften zur Bekämpfung des Betruges

anti-freeze Frostschutzmittel

anti-inflationary policy antiinflationäre Politik; Inflationsbekämpfungspolitik

antimissile *mil* Abwehrflugkörper, Antirakete

antinomy Antinomie; Widerspruch *(zwischen zwei Rechtssätzen in e-m Gesetz)*

anti-nukes Atomkraftgegner

antipollution, ~ costs Kosten des Umweltschutzes; **~ devices** Umweltschutzeinrichtungen; **~ investments** Investitionen zum Schutz der Umwelt

antiquity, simulating objects of ~ *Am*[49] Nachmachen von Antiquitäten

anti-satellite weapon Satellitenabwehrwaffe

antisemitic antisemitisch
antisemitism Antisemitismus

antisocial asozial; gemeinschaftsfeindlich, gesellschaftsschädigend

antitrust, ~ action *Am* Kartellklage; **~ authorities** Antitrustbehörden, Kartellbehörden *(Am →Antitrust Division und →Federal Trade Commission)*
Antitrust Civil Process Act *Am* Antitrust-Zivilprozeßgesetz *(von 1962)*
Es räumt der Antitrustbehörde die Befugnis ein, in Zivilverfahren die Vorlage von schriftl. Beweismaterial von den beteiligten Unternehmen zu verlangen
antitrust, A~ Committee *Am* Kartellausschuß; **A~ Division** (of the Justice Department) *Am* Kartellabteilung (des Justizministeriums); **~ investigations** Kartelluntersuchungen; **~ provisions** *Am* Kartellvorschriften
antitrust law *Am* Antitrustgesetz; Antitrustrecht; Kartellrecht; Kartellgesetz
Das amerikanische Antitrustrecht geht zurück auf die im → Common Law entwickelte Lehre vom → restraint of trade und hat seine Grundlage in dem Sherman Act (1890), Federal Trade Commission Act (1914), Clayton Act (1914), Robinson Patman Act (1936) und Miller-Tydings Act (1937). Die Rechtsprechung zum Antitrustrecht wird im wesentlichen von zwei Prinzipien beherrscht, der →rule of reason-Doktrin und der violation per se-Doktrin *(s. per se)*
antitrust, ~ legislation *Am* Kartellgesetzgebung; **~ policy** Kartellpolitik

anti-union gewerkschaftsfeindlich
anti-unionist Gewerkschaftsgegner

Anton Piller order *Br (vorläufige)* gerichtl. Verfügung zwecks Eigentumssicherung *(Antragsteller darf Räume des Gegners durchsuchen und Gegenstände wegnehmen)*

anxious in dem Bemühen (od. Bestreben); bestrebt (for um); bedacht

A.O.B. (any other business) *(auf Tagesordnung)* Sonstiges

apanage Apanage

apart beiseite, abgesondert; getrennt; ~ **from** abgesehen von; **to live** ~ getrennt leben *(Eheleute)*; **he lives** ~ **from his wife** er lebt getrennt von seiner Frau; **to set** ~ beiseitetun, absondern

apartheid Apartheid, Rassentrennung(spolitik) *(in Südafrika)*; **abolition of** ~ Abschaffung der Apartheit; **anti-~ demonstrator** jd, der gegen die (Politik der) Rassentrennung demonstriert; **condemnation of the policy of** ~ Verurteilung der Apartheidpolitik

apartment (Etagen-)Wohnung; *Br* Zimmer; Apartment; ~ **house** *Am* Etagenwohnhaus; ~ **hotel** *Am* Apartmenthotel; **exchange of ~s** *Am* Wohnungstausch

apolog|y Entschuldigung; **letter of** ~ Entschuldigungsschreiben; **to offer one's ~ies** sich entschuldigen; **to publish an** ~ **for a libel** e-e Entschuldigung wegen e-r Beleidigung veröffentlichen

appanage Apanage

apparel Kleidung; ~ **industry** *Am* Bekleidungsindustrie; **articles of** ~ Bekleidung(sgegenstände); **necessary wearing and bedding** ~ *(KonkursR)* notwendige Kleidungs- und Bettstücke

apparent offensichtlich, offenbar; ~ **authority** *(nach den Umständen der agency zu entnehmende)* Anscheinsvollmacht *(die den principal bindet)*; ~ **defect** offensichtlicher Mangel *(opp. hidden defect)*; →**heir** ~

appeal 1. Rechtsmittel *(gegen richterl. Entscheidung)*; Berufung, Revision, Beschwerde, Einspruch (from gegen); Rechtsbehelf; *(PatR)* Beschwerde; **an** ~ **to a higher court from a decision** e-e Berufung (etc) an ein höheres Gericht gegen e-e Entscheidung; **the** ~ **from the judgment lies to** . . . die Berufung (etc) gegen das Urteil ist zulässig an . . .

Das anglo-amerikanische Recht kennt nicht den scharfen Unterschied zwischen Berufung und Revision und bezeichnet alle Rechtsmittel als appeal

appeal, ~ **bond** *Am* Kaution für die Kosten der Berufung; ~ **court** Rechtsmittelgericht (→ court of ~); ~ **fee** Rechtsmittelgebühr (Berufungsgebühr, Beschwerdegebühr etc); ~ **period** Beschwerdefrist; ~ **on a point of law** Revision; *(PatR)* Rechtsbeschwerde; ~ **procedure** Rechtsmittelverfahren (Berufungs-, Beschwerdeverfahren etc)

appeal, Board of A~ *(Europ. PatentR)* Beschwerdekammer, Beschwerdesenat; **exclusion of or objection to members of the Board of** ~ Ausschließung od. Ablehnung von Mitgliedern der Beschwerdekammer

appeal, cross-~ Anschlußberufung; **decision on** ~ Rechtsmittelentscheidung (Berufungsentscheidung etc); **the decision under** ~ die mit der Beschwerde (etc) angefochtene Entscheidung; → **grounds for** ~

appeal, notice of ~ Benachrichtigung von der Einlegung e-s Rechtsmittels (e-r Berufung etc); Berufungsschrift; *(PatR)* Beschwerdeschrift; **time to give notice of** ~ Rechtsmittelfrist (Berufungsfrist etc); **to give notice of** ~ ein Rechtsmittel (Berufung etc) einlegen

appeal, period (allowed) for ~ (or **period for lodging an** ~) Rechtsmittelfrist; *(PatR)* Beschwerdefrist; **person entitled to an** ~ *(PatR)* Beschwerdeberechtigter; **proceedings on** ~ Rechtsmittelverfahren (Berufungsverfahren etc); **right of** ~ Recht auf Einlegung e-s Rechtsmittels; **stages of** ~ Instanzenweg; **subject to** ~ der Berufung *(etc)* unterliegend; beschwerdefähig (etc)

appeal, time (allowed) for ~ Rechtsmittelfrist (Berufungsfrist etc); **the time for** ~ **has elapsed** die Rechtsmittelfrist ist abgelaufen; **to extend the time for** ~ die Rechtsmittelfrist verlängern

appeal, well-founded ~ begründete Berufung

appeal, to allow an ~ e-m Rechtsmittel (Berufung etc) stattgeben; e-r Beschwerde abhelfen; **the** ~ **is allowed** der Beschwerde wird abgeholfen; **to bring an** ~ **to a higher court** ein Rechtsmittel (Berufung etc) bei e-m höheren Gericht einlegen (from a judgment gegen ein Urteil); **to dismiss an** ~ ein Rechtsmittel (Berufung etc) verwerfen; **to enter an** ~ e-e Berufungserklärung *(bei der Gerichtskanzlei)* eintragen; **to file an** ~ ein Rechtsmittel (Berufung etc) einlegen; **to grant an** ~ →to allow an ~; **to hear an** ~ über ein Rechtsmittel (Berufung etc) verhandeln; **to institute proceedings by way of** ~ ein Rechtsmittel (Berufung etc) einlegen; **an** ~ **lies** ein Rechtsmittel (Berufung etc) ist zulässig (to, with bei); **to lodge an** ~ s. to file an →~; **to reject an** ~ ein Rechtsmittel (Berufung etc) zurückweisen; **to be subject to an** ~ e-m Rechtsmittel (e-r Berufung etc) unterliegen; **to reject the** ~ **as inadmissible** die Beschwerde als unzulässig verwerfen; **to withdraw an** ~ ein Rechtsmittel (Berufung etc) zurücknehmen

appeal 2. Appell, Aufruf; Spendenaufruf; dringende Bitte (for um); ~ **to the country** *Br* Auflösung des Parlaments; Ausschreibung von Neuwahlen; ~ **to the Court** Anrufung des Gerichts; ~ **for mercy** Gnadengesuch; **to issue an** ~ e-n Aufruf erlassen; **to make an** ~ e-n Appell (od. Aufruf) richten, appellieren (to an)

appeal 3. *com* Reiz, Anreiz, Anklang (to bei); ~ **to customers** Anziehungskraft auf Kunden; **the article had wide** ~ der Artikel ist *(beim Publikum)* gut angekommen

appeal *v* 1. ein Rechtsmittel (Berufung, Revision, Beschwerde, Einspruch) einlegen (against, from gegen; to bei); **person entitled to** ~ Beschwerdeberechtigter; **to** ~ **a case** (or **suit**) *Am* ein Rechtsmittel (Berufung etc) einlegen; **to** ~ **from a decision** gegen e-e Entscheidung ein Rechtsmittel (Berufung etc) einlegen; **to** ~ **in writing** schriftlich Beschwerde (etc) einlegen (from gegen)

appealed, ~ **case** *Am* Berufungssache; Beschwerdesache; **the judgment cannot be** ~ **against** gegen das Urteil kann kein Rechtsmittel (Berufung etc) eingelegt werden

appealing, party ~ (or ~ **party**) Berufungskläger; Beschwerdeführer; **time for** ~ Rechtsmittelfrist (Berufungsfrist etc)

appeal *v* 2. appellieren, sich wenden (to an); dringend ersuchen; *com* Anklang finden (to bei), gefallen, zusagen; **to** ~ **to the country** *Br* das Parlament auflösen; Neuwahlen ausschreiben; **to** ~ **to a court** ein Gericht anrufen; **to** ~ **urgently** dringenden Appell richten (to an)

appealable berufungsfähig; revisionsfähig; beschwerdefähig; **non**~ rechtskräftig

appear *v* 1. erscheinen, sich zeigen; scheinen, den Anschein haben; *(Buch)* herauskommen; *(als Künstler etc)* auftreten; **to** ~ **from** hervorgehen aus; **the book will soon** ~ das Buch wird bald erscheinen; **it** ~**s by** (or **from**) **the records** es geht aus den Akten hervor

appear *v* 2. *(Zivilprozeß) (vor Gericht)* erscheinen, auftreten; **to** ~ **in an action on behalf of the plaintiff** vor Gericht für den Beklagten auftreten *(Br als barrister)*; **to** ~ **against a p.** gegen jdn vor Gericht auftreten; **to** ~ **by one's attorney** *Am* sich anwaltlich vertreten lassen; **to** ~ **by counsel** sich durch e-n Anwalt *(Br barrister)* vertreten lassen; **to** ~ **in** (or **before**) **a court** vor Gericht erscheinen; **to** ~ **for the defendant (plaintiff)** den Beklagten (Kläger) *(als Anwalt)* vor Gericht vertreten; **to** ~ **in person** (or **personally**) in Person (od. persönlich) erscheinen; **a party** ~**s in person or by (his) counsel** e-e Partei erscheint persönlich oder wird durch ihren Anwalt vertreten; **(unexcused) failure to** ~ (unentschuldigtes) Nichterscheinen vor Gericht

appearing, the person ~ der (die) Erschienene; **counsel** ~ **for the defendant** der für den Beklagten erschienene Anwalt

appearance 1. Erscheinen; Vorkommen; Aussehen, äußerer Eindruck; *(öffentl.)* Auftreten; ~**s** äußerer Schein; **in** ~ dem Anschein nach; **public** ~ Auftreten in der Öffentlichkeit

appearance 2. *(Zivilprozeß)* Erscheinen (in court vor Gericht); *Am* (Klage-)Einlassung (*Br* →acknowledgment of service); ~ **in person** persönliches Erscheinen; **conditional** ~ Einlassung unter Vorbehalt *(der Bestreitung der Zuständigkeit des Gerichts od. der Ordnungsmäßigkeit des →writ of summons)*; **default of** ~ Versäumnis der Einlassung; **entering an** ~ Klageeinlassung; **failure to enter an** ~ Versäumnis der Einlassung; **general** ~ vorbehaltlose Einlassung; **non-**~ Nichterscheinen; **notice of** ~ Mitteilung erfolgter Einlassung; **time for (entering an)** ~ Einlassungsfrist; **the time for** ~ **is 8 days** die Einlassungsfrist beträgt 8 Tage; **to enter an** ~ sich auf e-e Klage einlassen; **no** ~ **has been entered** es ist keine Einlassung erfolgt; **to make default of** ~ die Einlassung versäumen; e-n Termin versäumen

appease *v pol (durch Konzessionen)* zu beschwichtigen versuchen

appeasement (policy) Beschwichtigung(spolitik) *(durch Konzessionen)*, Befriedigungspolitik

appeaser Beschwichtiger; konzessionsbereiter Befriedigungspolitiker

appellant (Berufungs-)Kläger(in); Beschwerdeführer(in); Revisionskläger(in) *(opp. appellee, respondent)*

appellate Rechtsmittel- (Berufungs- etc); ~ **court** Rechtsmittelgericht; Gericht zweiter Instanz; Berufungsgericht; Revisionsgericht; Beschwerdegericht; ~ **jurisdiction** Zuständigkeit in der Rechtsmittelinstanz (Berufungsinstanz etc) *(opp. original jurisdiction)*; ~ **procedure** Rechtsmittelverfahren (Berufungsverfahren etc); **to have** ~ **jurisdiction over** Rechtsmittelinstanz sein für; für die Berufung (etc) gegen ... zuständig sein

appellee *Am* (Berufungs-)Beklagte(r), Beschwerdegegner(in), Revisionsbeklagte(r) *(opp. appellant)*

append *v* anhängen, befestigen (to an); beifügen (to zu); **to** ~ **a seal to a document** e-e Urkunde mit e-m Siegel versehen; **to** ~ **one's signature** mit s-r Unterschrift versehen; ~**ed documents** beigefügte Unterlagen

appendant zugehörig; anhängend; beigefügt; verbunden (to mit)

appendi|x Anhang; Anlage; Zusatz; ~**ces** Zusätze

applicability Anwendbarkeit; Eignung (to für); Verwendbarkeit; **area of** (or **territorial)** ~ örtlicher (od. räumlicher) Geltungsbereich; **industrial** ~ *(PatR)* gewerbliche Verwendbarkeit

applicable anwendbar (to auf); verwendbar; **the law** ~ **to this case** das auf diesen Fall anwendbare Gesetz

applicant 1. Antragsteller(in); Bewerber(in); ~ **country** Bewerberland; ~ **for credit** Kreditantragsteller; ~ **for (documentary) credit** Akkreditiv-Auftraggeber; ~ **for a post** (or **position**) Bewerber um e-e Stellung, Stellensuchender; ~ **for shares** *Br* Aktienzeichner; **the** ~ **state** der antragstellende Staat

applicant 2. *(PatR)* Anmelder; ~ **in needy circumstances** bedürftiger Anmelder; **co-**~ (or **joint** ~) Mitanmelder; **joint** ~**s** gemeinsame Anmelder; **multiple** ~**s** mehrere Anmelder; **prior** ~ früherer Anmelder, Voranmelder; **single** ~ Einzelanmelder; **subsequent** ~ späterer Anmelder, Nachanmelder

application 1. Antrag (for auf, to an); Eingabe, Gesuch (for um); Bewerbung; Anmeldung *(z. B. zur Teilnahme an e-r Messe);* Verwendung, Anwendung *(z. B. e-s Gesetzes);* ~ **for (allotment of) shares** Antrag auf Zuteilung von Aktien, Aktienzeichnung; ~ **blank** →~ form; ~ **country** *(EG)* Bewerberland; ~ **for credit** Kreditantrag; ~ **for discharge** Rehabilitierungsantrag *(des Konkursschuldners);* ~ **form** Antragsformular, Anmeldeformular; Bewertungsformular; Zeichnungsschein; ~ **for funds** Beantragung von Mitteln; ~ **of funds** Mittelverwendung; ~ **list** Zeichnungsliste; ~ **for membership** Beitrittsgesuch; ~ **for a post** (or **position**) Stellenbewerbung; ~ **of profits** Gewinnverwendung; ~**s received so far** bisher vorliegende Anmeldungen (etc); ~ **for respite** Stundungsgesuch

application, area of ~ Anwendungsbereich *(z. B. e-s Gesetzes);* Geltungsbereich; **cancellation of** ~ Abmeldung; **continued** ~ **of provisions** Weitergeltung von Bestimmungen; **form of** ~ Anmeldeformular; **improper** ~ unsachgemäße Handhabung; **letter of** ~ Bewerbungsschreiben; *Br* Antrag auf Zuteilung von Wertpapieren; **range of** ~ Anwendungsbereich; **scope of** ~ s. area of →~; **territorial** ~ räumlicher Geltungsbereich; Anwendungsbereich; **time of** ~ Zeitpunkt der Anmeldung; **time for** ~ Anmeldefrist; Antragsfrist; **up(on)** ~ auf Antrag

application, to file an ~ (with) e-n Antrag einreichen (bei); ein Gesuch richten (an); ~ **may be filed by** ... antragsberechtigt ist ...; **to grant an** ~ e-n Antrag genehmigen; e-m Antrag stattgeben; **to make an** ~ e-n Antrag stellen, beantragen; ersuchen; ein Gesuch einreichen; sich bewerben (for a th. um etw.; to a p. bei jdm); **to refuse** (or **reject**) **an** ~ e-n Antrag ablehnen; **to withdraw an** ~ e-n Antrag zurückziehen; **to withdraw one's** ~ sich abmelden; von der Teilnahme *(z. B. an e-r Messe)* zurücktreten

application 2. *(PatR)* Patentanmeldung; ~ **date** Anmeldetag; ~ **documents** Anmeldeunterlagen; ~ **fee** Anmeldegebühr; ~ **form** Anmeldeschein; ~ **for a patent** (or *Br* ~ **for Letters Patent**) Patentanmeldung

application, additional ~ Zusatzanmeldung; **divisional** ~ ausgeschiedene Anmeldung, Ausscheidungsanmeldung; Teilanmeldung; **documents of the** ~ Anmeldungsunterlagen; **earlier** ~ frühere Anmeldung; **examination of** ~ Prüfung der Anmeldung; **first** (or **original**) ~ Erstanmeldung; →**international** ~; →**national** ~; **parent** ~ Hauptanmeldung; **patent** ~ Patentanmeldung (→ *patent)*

application, pending ~ anhängige Anmeldung; **co-pending** ~ Parallelanmeldung; **backlog of pending** ~**s** Anmeldungsstau

application, previous ~ ältere (od. frühere) Anmeldung; **prior** ~ frühere (od. vorausgegangene) Anmeldung; **published** ~ bekanntgemachte Anmeldung; **regular national** ~ *(Europ. PatentR)* vorschriftsmäßige nationale Anmeldung; **rejection of** ~ Zurückweisung der Anmeldung; **subject matter of the** ~ Anmeldungsgegenstand; **subsequent** ~ jüngere Anmeldung; **undisposed** ~ schwebende Anmeldung; **unsettled** ~ unerledigte Anmeldung

application, to abandon an ~ e-e Anmeldung fallen lassen; **to examine an** ~ e-e Anmeldung prüfen; **to file an** ~ e-e Anmeldung einreichen; **to refuse** (or **reject**) **an** ~ e-e Anmeldung zurückweisen; **to prosecute an** ~ e-e Anmeldung weiterverfolgen; **to withdraw an** ~ e-e Anmeldung zurückziehen

applied praktisch, angewandt; **patent** ~ **for** Patent angemeldet; **works of** ~ **art** *(UrhR)* Werke der angewandten Kunst

applied, ~ **art** Kunstgewerbe; ~ **economics** angewandte Wirtschaftswissenschaften

apply *v* beantragen (for a th. etw.); sich bewerben (for um); einkommen, nachsuchen (for wegen); sich wenden (to an); Anwendung finden, anwendbar sein; anwenden, verwenden; gelten (to für); ~ **to** ... wenden Sie sich an ...; **to** ~ **for consent** Genehmigung einholen; **to** ~ **to a court** ein Gericht anrufen; **to** ~ **for information** um Auskunft bitten (to bei); **to** ~ **for a patent** ein Patent anmelden; **to** ~ **a provision** e-e Bestimmung anwenden; **to** ~ **for shares** *Br* Aktien zeichnen; **to** ~ **for a situation** sich um e-e Stelle bewerben; **to** ~ **in writing** schriftlich nachsuchen; ein schriftliches Gesuch einreichen; **a law does not** ~ ein Gesetz ist nicht anwendbar

appoint *v* ernennen, *(in e-e Stelle)* einsetzen; bestellen, berufen; einstellen, anstellen; festsetzen, anberaumen; verabreden; **to** ~ **a day** e-n Tag festsetzen (for für); **to** ~ **a day for a hearing** (or **trial**) e-n Termin anberaumen; **to** ~ **a p. one's heir** *Am* jdn zu s-m Erben einsetzen; **to** ~ **a p. as proxy** jdn zum Bevollmächtigten ernennen; jdn zum Vertreter bestellen

appointed, ~ **by the articles** satzungsmäßig bestellt; ~ **day** festgesetzter Tag; Termin; **to be** ~ **judge** zum Richter ernannt werden

appointee der (die) Ernannte; der (die) Berufene; *Am* Amtsträger, Amtsinhaber; jd, zu dessen

Gunsten e-e →power of appointment ausgestellt ist

appointive office *Am* durch Ernennung zu besetzendes Amt

appointment Ernennung, Einsetzung, Bestellung, Berufung; Einstellung, Anstellung *(opp. dismissal);* Verabredung; Festsetzung, Anberaumung *(e-s Termins);* Stelle, Posten, Amt; ~**s** Ausstattung *(e-s Hotels);* **by** ~ laut Verabredung; ~ **book** Terminkalender; ~ **as a director** Stelle als Direktor; ~ **of a guardian** Bestellung e-s Vormunds; ~ **for a meeting** Anberaumung e-r Sitzung; ~ **and dismissal of staff** Anstellung und Entlassung von Personal; ~ **of an heir** *Am* Einsetzung e-s Erben, Erbeinsetzung; ~ **for life** Ernennung auf Lebenszeit; Lebensstellung
appointment, business ~ geschäftliche Verabredung; **certificate of** ~ Bestallungsurkunde; Ernennungsurkunde; **conditions of** ~ Anstellungsbedingungen; **fixed** (or **permanent**) ~ feste Anstellung; **letter of** ~ s. certificate of →~; **period of** ~ Amtsdauer; **power of** ~ Recht zur Bestimmung e-s Berechtigten od. Nacherben (→*power 1.*); **by special** ~ **to Her Majesty** *Br* Königlicher Hoflieferant; **termination of** ~ Entlassung
appointment, to hold an ~ e-e Stelle innehaben; **to fix** (or **make**) **an** ~ e-e Verabredung treffen, sich verabreden (with sb. mit jdm); **to keep an** ~ e-e Verabredung (ein)halten

apportion *v (verhältnismäßig)* verteilen, aufteilen, umlegen; zuteilen, zumessen; *(Börse)* repartieren; **to** ~ **the expense** (or **to** ~ **expenses**) die Kosten verteilen (od. umlegen) (among auf); **to** ~ **the loss** den Schaden aufteilen (among zwischen); **to** ~ **the profit** den Gewinn aufteilen (od. verteilen)

apportionable aufteilbar; ~ **costs** Gemeinkosten (Schlüsselkosten)

apportionment *(verhältnismäßige)* Verteilung, Aufteilung, Umlegung *(der Kosten);* Umlage; Zuteilung, Zumessung; *(Börse)* Repartierung; ~ **of contract** Sukzessivlieferungsvertrag; ~ **of costs** Verteilung der Kosten; Kostenumlage; ~ **of dividends** Zuteilung von Dividenden; **(legislative)** ~ *Am* Wahlkreiseinteilung *(Zuteilung von Abgeordnetensitzen an die Einzelstaaten nach Maßgabe der Bevölkerungsdichte)*

appraisal (Ab-)Schätzung, Bewertung; geschätzter Wert; Beurteilung; ~ **clause** *(VersR)* Abschätzungsklausel *(Klausel, wonach Versicherer od. Versicherter Schaden abschätzen darf);* ~ **of damage** Schadensabschätzung; ~ **of the situation** Beurteilung der Lage; ~ **right** *Am* Recht der Aktionäre, die e-r Fusion nicht zugestimmt haben, auf Barabfindung; **personnel** (or **staff**) ~ Personalbeurteilung, Leistungsbeurteilung; **to make an** ~ abschätzen, bewerten *(z. B. den Versicherungsschaden)*

appraise *v* (ab)schätzen, bewerten, taxieren; ~**d value** abgeschätzter Wert, Taxwert

appraisement (Ab-)Schätzung, Taxierung; geschätzter Wert, Taxwert; **to make an** ~ (ab-)schätzen, taxieren

appraiser *(amtl.)* Schätzer

appreciable spürbar, nennenswert

appreciate *v* schätzen, zu würdigen wissen; Wert (od. Preis) erhöhen; im Werte (od. Preise) steigen; *(Währung)* aufwerten *(opp. to depreciate);* **to** ~ **in value** an Wert zunehmen, e-e Wertsteigerung erfahren
appreciated, countries whose currency has ~ Aufwertungsländer; **transfer of** ~ **securities**[50] Übertragung von im Werte gestiegenen Wertpapieren

appreciation (Ein-)Schätzung, Würdigung, Verständnis (of für); Preiserhöhung; ~ (in value) Wertsteigerung, Werterhöhung, Wertzuwachs; ~ **of currency** Aufwertung der Währung *(opp. depreciation);* ~ **of fixed assets** *Am* Höherbewertung von Anlagegütern

apprehend *v (jdn)* festnehmen, verhaften; begreifen, erfassen; befürchten

apprehension Festnahme, Verhaftung; Begriff, Vorstellung; Befürchtung

apprehensive period *(VersR)* Periode erhöhter Gefahr

apprentice Lehrling, Auszubildender[51]; ~ **training** Lehrlingsausbildung, Ausbildung des Auszubildenden; **master-** ~ **relationship** Berufsausbildungsverhältnis

apprentice *v* in die Lehre (od. Ausbildung) geben
apprenticed in der Lehre (od. Ausbildung) befindlich; **to be** ~ **to** in der Lehre (od. Ausbildung) sein bei; **to be** ~ **in the building trade** das Bauhandwerk erlernen

apprenticeship Lehre, Lehrzeit; Ausbildung, Ausbildungszeit; **applicant for an** ~ Lehrstellenbewerber; **articles** (or **indenture**) **of** ~ (Berufs-)Ausbildungsvertrag; Lehrvertrag; **term of** ~ Ausbildungsdauer, -zeit; **to finish one's** ~ s-e Ausbildung (od. Lehrzeit) beenden; auslernen; **to serve one's** ~ s-e (Berufs-)Ausbildung erhalten, seine Lehrzeit durchmachen (with bei)

apprise *v (förmlich)* in Kenntnis setzen (of von)

approach Vorgehensweise, Vorgehen; Art u. Weise, an e-e Sache heranzugehen; Zutritt, Zugang, Auffahrt, Zufahrt; ~ **to a problem** Herangehen an ein Problem, Lösungsversuch e-s Problems; **better law** ~ *(IPR)* (Bestreben nach) Anwendung des (inhaltlich) besseren (od. günstigeren) Rechts; **right of** ~ *(VölkerR)* Recht auf Flaggenerkundung *(Recht der Annäherung zur Feststellung der Nationalität e-s Handelsschiffes)*

approach *v* herangehen (od. herantreten, sich wenden) (a p. an jdn); *(auch fig)* sich nähern, herankommen (to an); sich anbahnen; **to** ~ **in value** annähernd gleichwertig sein

approbate *v bes. Am (amtl. od. formell)* Genehmigung (od. Lizenz) erteilen *(bes. zur Berufsausübung)*; **to** ~ **and reprobate** *Scot* teils zugeben, teils bestreiten

approbation *(formelle)* Genehmigung

appropriate *(den Umständen)* angemessen, geeignet; zweckdienlich; zuständig; **for** ~ **action** zur weiteren Veranlassung *(mit der Bitte, das Nötige zu unternehmen)*; **in the** ~ **circumstances** gegebenenfalls; ~ **literature** einschlägige Literatur; **at the** ~ **time** zur gegebenen Zeit; **where** ~ wo es zweckmäßig erscheint; gegebenenfalls; **to take** ~ **steps** zweckdienliche Maßnahmen treffen

appropriate *v* sich aneignen, in Besitz nehmen; *(Geld für bestimmten Zweck)* bewilligen, bereitstellen, zuweisen; *(für bestimmten Zweck)* bestimmen, verwenden; **to** ~ **funds** Mittel bewilligen; **to** ~ **goods to the contract**[52] die Ware konkretisieren (od. spezifizieren) *(zur Erfüllung des Vertrages)*; **to** ~ **a payment to a debt** e-e Zahlung auf e-e Schuld anrechnen; **to** ~ **unlawfully** sich rechtswidrig aneignen

appropriated surplus →surplus 2.

appropriation 1. Aneignung, Inbesitznahme; *(zweckgebundene)* Bereitstellung, Zuweisung; *(für besondere Zwecke bereitgestellter)* (Geld-)Betrag; (Zweck-)Bestimmung, Verwendung; *Am (right of privacy)* Mißbrauch des Namens od. e-r Abbildung des Klägers zu des Beklagten Vorteil; Souveränität im Weltraum; ~ **account** *Br (Bilanz)* Gewinnverteilungskonto; ~ **to the contract**[52] Bestimmung für den Vertrag *(Konkretisierung der Ware zur Erfüllung des Vertrages)*; ~ **to a debt** Anrechnung *(e-r Zahlung)* auf e-e Schuld; ~ **of funds** Bereitstellung von Mitteln für bestimmten Zweck; ~ **by a personal representative** *Br*[53] Zuweisung *(durch den → personal representative)* e-s bestimmten Teiles des Nachlasses an e-n Erben oder Bestimmung des Teiles zu e-m besonderen Zweck *(z.B. Tilgung von Schulden)*; ~ **of (the) profit** Verwendung des Gewinns; ~ **to the reserve** Zuweisung zur Rücklage

appropriation, notice of ~ Mitteilung über Bestimmung e-r Ware *(cf. ~ to the contract)*

appropriation 2. *parl* Bewilligung (od. Bereitstellung, Zuweisung) von (Haushalts-)Mitteln; Mittelbereitstellung; bewilligter Betrag; ~**s (in the budget)** (im Haushaltsplan) *(bewilligte od. bereitgestellte)* Mittel; ~ **bill** *Br* Ausgabebudget *(enthält die Bewilligung der in den Ausgabevoranschlägen vorgesehenen Ausgaben)*; *Am* Haushaltsvorlage; ~ **of budget funds** Bewilligung von Haushaltsmitteln; **A~s Committee** *Am* Haushaltsausschuß, Bewilligungsausschuß; ~**s not yet committed** noch nicht gebundene Haushaltsmittel; ~ **for commitment** *(EG)* Verpflichtungsermächtigung; ~ **for payment** *(EG)* Zahlungsermächtigung

appropriation, allotted ~**s** zugewiesene Mittel; **budget(ary)** ~**s** Haushaltsbewilligung; Ansätze des Haushaltsplans; **continuing** ~ ständige Bewilligung; **deficiency** ~**s** *Am* Nachtragsbewilligungen; **estimate of** ~**s** Haushaltsvoranschlag; **lapsing** ~ *Am* Bewilligung, über die nur innerhalb der Budgetperiode verfügt werden darf

appropriation, within the limits of the ~ im Rahmen der (zugewiesenen) (Haushalts-)Mittel; **to exceed the limit of** ~**s** die (Haushalts-)Mittel überschreiten

appropriation, operational ~**s** Verwaltungsmittel; **permanent** ~ ständige Bewilligung; **request for** ~ Mittelanforderung; **supplementary** ~**s** Nachtragsbewilligungen; **transfer of** ~**s** Mittelübertragung

appropriation, to carry forward unexpended ~**s to the next** *Br* **financial** (*Am* **fiscal**) **year** nicht verbrauchte Mittel auf das nächste Haushaltsjahr übertragen; **to increase** ~**s** die Mittel erhöhen; **to reduce** ~**s** die Mittel kürzen; **to vote the** ~ *Am* Gelder bewilligen

appropriations (of surplus) 3. *Am (Bilanz)* Rücklagen; **contractual** (or **statutory**) ~ satzungsmäßige Rücklagen; **discretionary** ~ freie Rücklagen; **legal** ~ gesetzliche Rücklagen

approval (appro.) Billigung, Genehmigung, Zustimmung; Beifall; „gesehen"(-Vermerk)

approval, formal ~ **of sb.'s acts** jds Entlastung; **to grant** ~ **of sb.'s acts** jdm Entlastung erteilen

approval, on ~ (Lieferung) nach Billigung; zur Ansicht; auf Probe; **consignment on** ~ Ansichtssendung; **sale on** ~ Kauf auf Probe

approval, prior ~ Einwilligung, vorherige Zustimmung

approval, to be subject to sb.'s ~ jds Genehmigung bedürfen; **to give one's** ~ Genehmigung erteilen; **to give formal** ~ (to the action of) jdn entlasten; **to meet with sb.'s** ~ jds Zustimmung finden; **to receive** ~ Genehmigung erhalten; **to refuse** ~ Genehmigung versagen; **to require the** ~ **of** der Genehmigung seitens ... bedürfen

approve (of) *v* billigen, genehmigen, zustimmen; prüfen und für richtig befinden; **to** ~ **the**

minutes die Niederschrift (oder das Protokoll) genehmigen; **to ~ a proposal** e-m Vorschlag zustimmen
approved anerkannt; altbewährt; genehmigt; zugelassen; **~ bank** erstklassige Bank; **~ bill** *(als einwandfrei)* anerkannter Wechsel; **read and ~** gelesen und genehmigt

approver *Br* Kronzeuge *(who turns Queen's → evidence)*

approximat|e *v* angleichen, annähern; sich (an-)nähern, nahekommen; **to ~ policies** Politiken einander angleichen; **progressively ~ing the economic policies** *(EG)* schrittweise Annäherung der Wirtschaftspolitik
approximate(ly) (approx.) ungefähr, annähernd

approximation Angleichung, Annäherung; **progressive ~** schrittweise Annäherung; **~ of laws** Rechtsangleichung; **~ of the municipal laws** *(EG)* Angleichung der innerstaatlichen Rechtsvorschriften

appurtenances Zubehör, zugehöriges Recht *(bes. Realrecht, das dem Eigentum an der herrschenden Liegenschaft folgt, z.B. Wegerecht);* Schiffszubehör; **~ (to land)** Grundstückszubehör *(easements, esp. right of way)*
Appurtenances umfaßt also – anders als im deutschen Recht (§ 97 BGB) – auch Grunddienstbarkeiten; so ist Wegerecht Zubehör des herrschenden Grundstücks

appurtenant 1. *Br* →appurtenance
appurtenant 2. zugehörig, gehörig (to zu); **rights ~** *(dem jeweiligen Eigentümer e-s Grundstücks)* zustehende Rechte

aptitude test Eignungsprüfung

Arab League Arabische Liga

Arab Republic of Egypt Arabische Republik Ägypten
Arab, United ~ Emirates Vereinigte Arabische Emirate
Am 2. 12. 1971 unabhängig gewordener Zusammenschluß von Abu Dhabi, Adschman, Dubai, Fudschaira, Ras al Chaima, Schardscha und Umm al Kuwain.

arabic numerals arabische Zahlen

arable land anbaufähiges Land, Ackerland; Anbaufläche *(opp. barren land, waste land)*

arbiter *Scot* Schiedsrichter; Schiedsmann

arbitrable schiedsrichterlich beilegbar; schiedsgerichtsfähig

arbitrage *(Börse)* Arbitrage *(Ausnutzung der Kursunterschiede zwischen Börsenplätzen);* **~ in bullion** Goldarbitrage; **~ dealer** Arbitragehändler
arbitrage dealings Arbitragegeschäft; **interest-rate ~** Zinsarbitragegeschäft

arbitrage, ~ in exchange Wechselkursarbitrage, Devisenarbitrage; **~ in securities** (or **stocks**) Effektenarbitrage; **~ transactions** Arbitragegeschäfte; **compound ~** zusammengesetzte Arbitrage; **currency ~** Devisenarbitrage; **simple ~** einfache Arbitrage; **stock ~** Effektenarbitrage

arbitrager (or **arbitrageur, arbitragist**) *(Börse)* Arbitrageur, Arbitragehändler

arbitral schiedsrichterlich; **~ agreement** → arbitration agreement; **~ authority** Schiedsgericht; Schiedsinstanz; **~ case** Schiedssache; **~ tribunal** Schiedsgericht; **to appeal to an ~ authority** e-e Schiedsinstanz anrufen
arbitral award Schiedsspruch; **domestic ~** inländischer Schiedsspruch; **the ~ shall be final** der Schiedsspruch ist endgültig
arbitral award, foreign ~ ausländischer Schiedsspruch; **Convention on the Recognition and Enforcement of Foreign A~ A~s** Übereinkommen über die Anerkennung und Vollstreckung ausländischer Schiedssprüche *(von 1958)*[54]; **to apply for (refuse) recognition and enforcement of foreign ~s** (um) Anerkennung und Vollstreckung ausländischer Schiedssprüche nachsuchen (versagen)
arbitral, ~ body Schiedsinstanz, Schiedsstelle; **~ clause** →arbitration clause; **~ court** Schiedsgericht(shof); **~ decision** →~ award; **~ jurisdiction** Schiedsgerichtsbarkeit; **~ procedure** Schieds(gerichts)verfahren, Verfahren in Schiedssachen, schiedsrichterliches Verfahren; **~ settlement** schiedsgerichtliche Beilegung
arbitral tribunal Schiedsgericht(shof); **chairman of the ~** Vorsitzender des Schiedsgerichts

arbitrament Schiedsspruch; Entscheidung durch die Schiedsrichter

arbitrary in das Ermessen gestellt; nach eigenem Ermessen; willkürlich, eigenmächtig; **~ action** Willkürakt; **~ assessment** (Einkommen-)Steuerveranlagung auf Grund von Schätzung; **~ price** willkürlicher Preis; **~ punishment** Strafe nach freiem Ermessen; **~ rule** (or **government**) Willkürherrschaft

arbitrate *v* schiedsrichterlich entscheiden; *(durch Schiedsspruch)* schlichten; *com* Arbitragegeschäfte machen; **agreement to ~** Schiedsvereinbarung; **to ~ a case** über e-e Sache schiedsrichterlich verhandeln

arbitration 1. Schieds(gerichts)verfahren; Schiedsgerichtsbarkeit; Schiedswesen; schiedsrichterliche Entscheidung; Regelung durch ein Schiedsgericht *(cf. conciliation);* **A~ Act** *Br* Schiedsgerichtsgesetz (1975 und 1979)
arbitration agreement Schiedsvereinbarung; Schiedsabrede (relating to existing disputes); Schiedsklausel (relating to future disputes); **to**

sign an ~ e-e Schiedsvereinbarung treffen; **to recognise the validity of an** ~ die Gültigkeit e-r Schiedsvereinbarung anerkennen

The term "arbitration agreement" (within the meaning of the European Convention on Commercial Arbitration)[55] shall mean either an arbitral clause in a contract or an arbitration agreement, the contract or arbitration agreement being signed by the parties, or contained in an exchange of letters, telegrams, or in a communication by teleprinter and, in relations between States whose laws do not require that an arbitration agreement be made in writing, any arbitration agreement concluded in the form authorized by these laws.

„Schiedsvereinbarung" (im Sinne des Europäischen Übereinkommens über die Internationale Handelsschiedsgerichtsbarkeit)[55] ist eine Schiedsklausel in einem Vertrag oder eine Schiedsabrede, sofern der Vertrag oder die Schiedsabrede von den Parteien unterzeichnet oder in Briefen, Telegrammen oder Fernschreiben, die sie gewechselt haben, enthalten ist und im Verhältnis zwischen Staaten, die in ihrem Recht für Schiedsvereinbarungen nicht die Schriftform fordern, jede Vereinbarung, die in den nach diesen Rechtsordnungen zulässigen Formen geschlossen ist

arbitration, ~ **award** →arbitral award; ~ **board** Schiedsstelle, Schlichtungsstelle

arbitration clause Schiedsklausel; **absence of the** ~ Fehlen der Schiedsklausel; **existence or validity of the** ~ Bestand oder Gültigkeit der Schiedsklausel; **an** ~ **binding the parties exists** e-e für die Parteien bindende Schiedsklausel besteht

Arbitration Clause, Standard ICC[56]-~ Standard-Schiedsklausel der ICC; **the insertion of the following** ~ **in foreign contracts is recommended by the International Chamber of Commerce** die Einfügung der nachstehenden Schiedsklausel in Verträge mit dem Ausland wird von der Internationalen Handelskammer empfohlen[57]

"All disputes arising in connection with the present contract shall be finally settled under the Rules of Conciliation and Arbitration of the International Chamber of Commerce by one or more arbitrators appointed in accordance with the said Rules".

„Alle aus dem gegenwärtigen Vertrag sich ergebenden Streitigkeiten werden nach der Vergleichs- und Schiedsgerichtsordnung der Internationalen Handelskammer von einem oder mehreren gemäß dieser Ordnung ernannten Schiedsrichtern endgültig entschieden"

arbitration clause, recourse to the ICC-[56] ~ **is not restricted to members of the ICC** die Inanspruchnahme der ICC-Schiedsklausel ist nicht auf Mitglieder der IHK[58] beschränkt

arbitration commission (or **committee**) Schiedsausschuß; Schlichtungsausschuß

arbitration costs Schiedsgerichtskosten; Kosten des Schiedsverfahrens; **payment of the deposit in respect of** ~ Vorschuß für Schiedsgerichtskosten

arbitration proceedings Schieds(gerichts)verfahren; **country where** ~ **take place** Land, in dem das Verfahren vor dem Schiedsrichter stattfindet

Arbitration Rules, (ICC) ~ →Rules of Conciliation and Arbitration

arbitration tribunal Schiedsgericht(shof)

arbitration, board of ~ Schiedsstelle, Schiedskommission; **commercial** ~[59] Handelsschiedsgerichtsbarkeit; **compulsory** ~ *Am* Zwangsschlichtung(sverfahren); zwangsweise Schlichtung von Arbeitsstreitigkeiten durch Regierungsstellen *(in den vom Gesetz bestimmten Fällen)*; **contractual** ~ vertragliche Schiedsgerichtsbarkeit

arbitration, costs of ~ Kosten des Schiedsverfahrens; **decision regarding costs of** ~ Entscheidung über die Kosten des Schiedsverfahrens

arbitration, ICC-~ (arbitration of the International Chamber of Commerce) ICC-Schiedsgerichtsbarkeit (Schiedsgerichtsbarkeit der Internationalen Handelskammer); **to conduct ICC-**~ **in accordance with the →"Rules of Conciliation and A**~ **of the International Chamber of Commerce"** der Schiedsgerichtsbarkeit die „Vergleichs- und Schiedsordnung der Internationalen Handelskammer" zugrundelegen; **to decline** ~ **by the ICC** die Schiedsgerichtsbarkeit der ICC ablehnen; **to have recourse to** ~ **by the ICC** das Schiedsverfahren der ICC in Anspruch nehmen; **to submit a dispute to ICC-**~ die Schiedsgerichtsbarkeit der ICC in Anspruch nehmen; **the parties agree to submit their case to** ~ **by the ICC** die Parteien vereinbaren das Schiedsverfahren der ICC *(s. Standard ICC →A ~ Clause)*

arbitration, ICC Court of A~ (Court of A~ of the International Chamber of Commerce) ICC-Schiedsgerichtshof (Schiedsgerichtshof der Internationalen Handelskammer)

The Court of Arbitration does not itself settle disputes. Insofar as the parties shall not have provided otherwise, it appoints or confirms the appointments of arbitrators *(Art. 2 of the Rules of Arbitration of the ICC)*.

Der Schiedsgerichtshof entscheidet nicht selbst die Streitfälle. Soweit die Parteien nichts anderes bestimmt haben, ernennt oder bestätigt er die Schiedsrichter *(Art. 2 der Schiedsgerichtsordnung der IHK)*

arbitration, jurisdictional ~ gerichtliche Schiedsgerichtsbarkeit; →**maritime** ~

arbitration, Permanent Court of A~ *(noch heute bestehender)* Ständiger Schiedshof, Haager Schieds(gerichts)hof

Auf den Haager Friedenskonferenzen 1899/1907 geschaffenes internationales Gericht zur schiedsgerichtlichen Beilegung von Staatenstreitigkeiten. Bestellung des Richterkollegiums erfolgt durch die Streitteile. Durch Errichtung des →International Court of Justice hat der Haager Schiedshof an Bedeutung verloren

arbitration, place of ~ Schiedsort; Ort, an dem das schiedsrichterliche Verfahren durchgeführt wird; **to agree in advance (up)on the place of** ~ im voraus den Ort der Schiedsgerichtsbarkeit vereinbaren; **to fix the place of** ~ den Schiedsort bestimmen

arbitration, request for ~ Schiedsantrag; Schiedsklage; Antrag auf Einleitung des Schiedsverfahrens; **reply to the request for** ~ Klagebeantwortung (im Schiedsverfahren)

arbitration, Rules of A~ *Br* Schiedsordnung; **Rules of Conciliation and A~** (of the International Chamber of Commerce) Vergleichs- und Schiedsordnung (der Internationalen Handelskammer)

arbitration, settlement by ~ Regelung auf schiedsrichterlichem Wege; schiedsgerichtliche Beilegung; **subject matter capable of settlement by** ~ Gegenstand, der auf schiedsrichterlichem Wege geregelt werden kann; **recognition of contracts that provide for settlement by** ~ Anerkennung von Schiedsverträgen

arbitration, to go to ~ schiedsrichterliche Entscheidung einholen; ~ **is to be held in the USA** die Schiedsgerichtsbarkeit findet in den USA statt; **to refer a dispute to** ~ e-n Streitfall e-m Schiedsgericht unterbreiten; **to refer a dispute to** ~ **or bring an action at law** ein Schiedsverfahren beantragen oder sich an die zuständigen Gerichte wenden; **to submit to** ~ sich e-m Schiedsverfahren unterwerfen; **the** ~ **takes place** das Schiedsverfahren findet statt

arbitration 2. *(Börse)* Arbitrage(geschäft); **compound** ~ zusammengesetzte Arbitrage; Mehrfacharbitrage; ~ **of exchange** Devisenarbitrage

arbitrator Schiedsrichter; Schiedsmann; ~**'s award** Schiedsspruch; ~**'s fees** Honorar des Schiedsrichters; ~**'s →terms of reference**

arbitrator, alternate ~ Schiedsmann-Stellvertreter; **appointment of an** ~ Ernennung e-s Schiedsrichters; **challenging of an** ~ Ablehnung e-s Schiedsrichters; **choice of an** ~ Wahl e-s Schiedsrichters; **presiding** ~ Obmann des Schiedsgerichts; **sole** ~ Einzelschiedsrichter

arbitrator, to appoint an ~ e-n Schiedsrichter ernennen (od. bestellen)

archaeological, ~ **discoveries** archäologische Entdeckungen; **market in** ~ **finds** Handel mit archäologischen Fundstücken; ~ **heritage** archäologisches Kulturgut (→*European Convention on the Protection of A~ Heritage*); ~ **objects** archäologische Gegenstände

architect, ~**'s liability** Architektenhaftpflicht; **Royal Institute of British** ~**s** Dachorganisation der britischen Architekten

Architectural Heritage of Europe, Convention for the Protection of the ~[60] Übereinkommen zum Schutz des architektonischen Erbes Europas

architecture, author of works of ~[61] Urheber von Werken der Baukunst

archives Archiv; Registratur; **in the** ~ im Archiv

archivist Archivar

arcs of circles *(VölkerR)* Kreisbogen *(zur Festsetzung der Hoheitsgrenze bei Küstengewässern)*

area Bezirk; Gebiet; (Boden-)Fläche; *fig* Bereich; ~ **of activity** Tätigkeitsbereich; ~ **of applicability** räumlicher Geltungsbereich; ~ **of operations** Tätigkeitsgebiet; ~ **of operations of blockading naval force** *(VölkerR)* Aktionsbereich der Blockade führenden Seemächte; ~ **of use** *(PatR)* Anwendungsbereich; ~ **planning** Raumplanung; ~ **sample** Flächenstichprobe; ~ **under cultivation** Anbaufläche

area, agricultural ~ landwirtschaftliches Gebiet; **prohibited** ~ Sperrzone; **special** ~**s** *Br* Notstandsgebiete

Argentina Argentinien

Argentine Argentinier(in); argentinisch; ~ **Republic** Argentinische Republik

arguable diskutierbar; ~ **position** vertretbarer Standpunkt

argue *v* argumentieren; streiten (about, over über); begründen, Gründe vorbringen (for or against für od. gegen); *(Zivilprozeß)* vorbringen, vortragen; über etw. *(mündlich)* verhandeln; **the counsel** ~**d the case** der Anwalt trug die Sache vor; **to** ~ **a point of law** e-e Rechtsfrage erörtern; **to** ~ **with sb.** sich mit jdm auseinandersetzen; **the motion must be** ~**d** über den Antrag kann erst nach mündlicher Verhandlung entschieden werden

argument 1. Argument, Beweisgrund; *(Zivilprozeß)* Vorbringen, Ausführung(en), Vortrag; **(factual)** ~**s** Beweisausführungen; **(legal)** ~**s** Rechtsausführungen; ~ **on appeal** *Am* Verhandlung in der Berufung(sinstanz); ~ **of a motion** *Am* Verhandlung über e-n Antrag; ~**s of the parties** Parteivorbringen; **to advance** (or **offer, put forward) an** ~ ein Argument vorbringen; **a party concludes its** ~**s** e-e Partei stellt ihre Schlußanträge

argument 2. Meinungsverschiedenheit, Streit (about über); **there is** ~ **whether** man ist sich nicht einig darüber, ob; **that clinches the** ~ damit ist der Streit erledigt

argumentation Argumentation; Beweisführung

argumentum e contrario Umkehrschluß

Ariel *Br* Computersystem, das die Abwicklung

von Wertpapiergeschäften unter Umgehung der Londoner Börse ermöglicht

arise *v* entstehen, sich zeigen, auftreten; hervorgehen (from aus); **the difficulties which have ~n** die aufgetretenen Schwierigkeiten; **the question ~s** es entsteht die Frage

arithmetical average einfaches (od. arithmetisches) Mittel
Nach Art. 19 Abs. 1 des EWG-Vertrages[62] bestimmen sich die Sätze des gemeinsamen Zolltarifs aus dem arithmetischen Mittel der in den vier Zollgebieten der EWG angewandten Zollsätze

arm's length, ~ approach zu den Gewinnen, die e-e Gesellschaft ausgewiesen hat, sind diejenigen hinzuzurechnen, die die Firma ins Ausland übertragen hat; **~ dealing standards** Rechtsnormen, die verbundene Unternehmen als fiskalisch unabhängige Einheiten behandeln; **~ negotiations** unabhängige Verhandlungen, die nicht durch ein Abhängigkeitsverhältnis beeinträchtigt werden; **~ principle** *(intern. SteuerR)* Prinzip der wirtschaftlichen Selbständigkeit der Betriebsstätte; **to determine a permanent establishment's profits by application of the ~ rule** *(inter. SteuerR)*[63] den Betriebsstättengewinn nach dem ~-Prinzip bestimmen

arm's length, at ~ auf rein geschäftlicher Basis; **enterprise dealing at ~** unabhängig handelndes Unternhemen; **sale at ~** Verkauf zwischen voneinander unabhängigen Personen; **to deal at ~ with sb.** mit jdm auf rein geschäftlicher Basis verhandeln *(ohne vorhergehendes Vertrauensverhältnis)*; **the branch is treated as if it were a separate enterprise dealing at ~ with its home office** die Niederlassung wird so behandelt, als sei sie ein getrenntes Unternehmen, das dem Stammhaus wie e-m Dritten gegenübertritt

arms Waffen; **~ control** Rüstungskontrolle; **~ embargo** Waffenembargo, Waffenausfuhrverbot; **~ expenditure** Rüstungsausgaben; **~ race** Wettrüsten; **~ race in outer space** Weltraumwettrüsten; **~ reduction** Rüstungsminderung; **~ shipment** Waffenlieferung; **by force of ~** mit Waffengewalt; **illegal** (or **unlawful**) **possession of ~** unerlaubter Waffenbesitz; **Royal ~** *Br* Königliches Wappen; **store of ~** Waffenlager; **to lay down ~** die Waffen niederlegen

arm *v* bewaffnen

armed bewaffnet; **~ attack** *(VölkerR)* bewaffneter Angriff; **~ conflict** *(VölkerR)* kriegerischer Konflikt; bewaffnete (od. gewaltsame) Auseinandersetzung; **~ forces** Streitkräfte; Wehrmacht; **~ intervention** *(VölkerR)* gewaltsames Eingreifen; **~ neutrality** *(VölkerR)* bewaffnete Neutralität; **~ resistance** bewaffneter Widerstand; **~ robbery** bewaffneter Raubüberfall

armament(s) (Kriegs-)Rüstung; Rüstungsgüter; Aufrüstung; Ausrüstung *(e-s Schiffes)*; **~ control** Rüstungskontrolle; **~ factory** (or **works**) Rüstungsbetrieb; **~s industry** Rüstungsindustrie; **~ in excess of defence (~se) needs** Überrüstung; **~ limitation** Rüstungsbeschränkung; **~ order** Rüstungsauftrag; **~ race** Wettrüsten; **excessive ~s** Überrüstung; **level of ~s** Rüstungsstand; **limitation of ~s** Rüstungsbeschränkung; **reduction of ~** Rüstungsabbau

armchair politician Stammtischpolitiker, Salonpolitiker

armistice Waffenstillstand *(cf. truce)*; **~ terms** Waffenstillstandsbedingungen; **negotiations for (an) ~** Waffenstillstandsverhandlungen

army Heer; Armee; **~ command staff** Heeresleitung; **~ contractor** Heereslieferant; **A~ Emergency Reserve** *Br* Heeresnotreserve; **A~ List** *Br* Heeresrangliste; **~ manual** Heeresdienstvorschrift (H.D.V.); **A~ HQ Staff** Armee-Oberkommando; **A~ Register** *Am* Heerespersonalregister *(das auch den Rang enthält)*; **~ training ground** Truppenübungsplatz; **A~ War College** *Am* Kriegsakademie; **official ~ communiqué** Heeresbericht; **regular** (or **standing**) **~** stehendes (od. aktives) Heer; **Secretary of the A~** *Am* Heeresminister; **Territorial A~** *Br* Landwehr; **to enter** (or **join**) **the ~** in das Heer eintreten; Soldat werden; **to serve in the ~** beim Heer Dienst tun

arraign *v (Strafprozeß)* zur Anklage vernehmen; vor Gericht stellen

arraignment Aufruf *(des Angeklagten)* zum Zwecke der Antwort auf die Anklage

arrange *v* sich vergleichen, vergleichsweise festsetzen; (an)ordnen, regeln; vereinbaren, abmachen, Abmachungen treffen; vorbereiten, Vorkehrungen treffen; *(Streit)* schlichten; **to ~ for sth.** etw. veranlassen; **to ~ one's business affairs** s-e geschäftlichen Angelegenheiten regeln; **to ~ with one's creditors** mit s-n Gläubigern e-n Vergleich schließen (od. sich vergleichen); **to ~ with one's creditors** (either privately or in the Bankruptcy Court) **for discharge of one's liabilities by partial payment or composition** sich mit s-n Gläubigern (entweder privat od. vor dem Konkursgericht) über die Bezahlung seiner Verbindlichkeiten durch Teilzahlung oder Zahlung e-r Vergleichssumme einigen; **to ~ with a p.** mit jdm vereinbaren (od. Vereinbarungen treffen) (for für); **to ~ a matter amicably** e-e Angelegenheit gütlich regeln

arranged, the meeting ~ for today die für heute vereinbarte Sitzung; **at an ~ price** zu e-m vereinbarten Preis

arrangement gütliche Einigung, Vergleich (*Br* cf. deed of ~); Vereinbarung, Abmachung,

Absprache; Ordnen, Anordnung; ~**s** Vorkehrungen, Vorbereitungen; ~ **in bankruptcy** gerichtlicher Vergleich; Zwangsvergleich; ~ **out of bankruptcy** außergerichtlicher Vergleich; ~ **patent** Anordnungspatent; ~ **proceedings** Vergleichsverfahren

arrangement, as per ~ laut Vereinbarung; **binding** ~ bindende Abmachung; **compulsory** ~ Zwangsvergleich; →**deed of** ~; **financial** ~ Zahlungsvereinbarung; finanzielle Vereinbarung; **private** ~ private Abmachung; Absprache; außergerichtlicher Vergleich; **proposal for a (scheme of)** ~ Vergleichsvorschlag; **revised** ~ Neuregelung; **scheme of** ~ Vergleichsplan; **separate** ~ Sondervereinbarung

arrangement, to accept an ~ e-n Vergleich(svorschlag) annehmen; **to arrive at** (or **come to**) **an** ~ **with a p.** zu e-m Vergleich mit jdm kommen, sich mit jdm vergleichen; **to be a matter for** ~ besprochen (od. vereinbart) werden müssen; **to enter into** (or **make**) **an** ~ e-e Vereinbarung (od. Regelung) treffen, vereinbaren; e-n Vergleich schließen, sich vergleichen; **to make** ~**s** Vorkehrungen treffen

array *bes. Am* (Aufstellung der) Geschworenenliste; **to challenge the** ~ die Geschworenen ablehnen

array *v*, **to** ~ **(the) jurors on the panel** *bes. Am* die Geschworenenliste aufstellen; die Geschworenen aufrufen

arrears Rückstände; rückständige Summe; ~ **of interest** rückständige Zinsen, Zinsrückstände; ~ **on interest** Verzugszinsen; ~ **of rent** Mietrückstände, rückständige Miete; ~ **of payment** Zahlungsrückstände; **payment of** ~ **of salary** Gehaltsnachzahlung

arrears, in ~ im Rückstand, rückständig; **rent in** ~ rückständige Miete; **payment of salary in** ~ Gehaltsnachzahlung; **to be in** ~ im Rückstand (od. Verzuge) sein; **he got in** ~ **with the rent** er geriet in Mietrückstände; **to pay arrears (of)** nachzahlen

arrest Verhaftung, Festnahme; Arrest; (Sicherungs-)Beschlagnahme *(e-s Schiffes od. der Ladung); (VölkerR)* Anhalten *(e-s verdächtigen neutralen Handelsschiffes durch ein Kriegsschiff);* ~ **of judgment** *(Strafprozeß)* Vertagung des Urteils *(nach dem Schuldausspruch bei Rüge von Verfahrensmängeln);* Aussetzung des Verfahrens; ~ **of a ship**[64] Vollziehung des Arrestes in ein Schiff; ~ **of an offender** Festnahme e-s Täters; **ground of** ~ Grund der Festnahme; **personal** ~ *mil* Strafarrest; **preventive** ~ Schutzhaft; **wrongful** ~ ungesetzliche Haft *(cf. false imprisonment)*

arrest, under ~ in Haft; **to be under** ~ in Haft (od. inhaftiert) sein; **to be placed** (or **put**) **under** ~ in Haft genommen werden

arrest, warrant of ~ Haftbefehl; Beschlagnahmeverfügung *(für Schiffe) (→admiralty actions)*; **warrant of** ~ **for a fugitive offender** Steckbrief; **to issue a warrant of** ~ e-n Haftbefehl erlassen

arrest, to carry out (or **make**) **an** ~ e-e Verhaftung (od. Festnahme) durchführen; **to free from** ~ aus dem Arrest entlassen *(Schiff);* **the Police made several** ~**s** die Polizei nahm mehrere Verhaftungen vor; **to resist** ~ sich der Verhaftung widersetzen

arrest *v* verhaften, in Haft nehmen, festnehmen; **to** ~ **judgment** das Urteil *(wegen Verfahrensmängel)* vertagen; **to** ~ **a ship** ein Schiff mit Arrest belegen

arrested person Festgenommene(r); Verhaftete(r); (Untersuchungs-)Gefangene(r)

arrestment *Scot* Verhaftung *(cf. arrest);* Beschlagnahme des beweglichen Vermögens des Schuldners *(das sich in den Händen e-s Dritten befindet)*

arrival Ankunft; Eingang *(von Post, Waren);* Landung *(e-s Flugzeugs);* ~ **and departure** Ankunft und Abfahrt *(von Zügen);* ~ **of goods** Wareneingang; **on** ~ **of goods** bei Ankunft (od. Eintreffen) der Waren; ~ **and sailing** Ankunft und Abfahrt *(von Schiffen)*

arrival, book of ~**s** Eingangsbuch; **probable date of** ~ vermutlicher Ankunftstag

arrive *v* ankommen, eintreffen, eingehen; landen *(Flugzeug);* einlaufen *(Schiff);* **to** ~ **at an age** ein Alter erreichen; **to** ~ **at a decision** zu e-r Entscheidung kommen

arrogation of patents Patentberühmung

arson[65] *(vorsätzliche)* Brandstiftung

art 1. Kunst; **the** ~**s** die Geisteswissenschaften; **Faculty of A**~**s** *univ* philosophische Fakultät; **the fine** ~**s** die schönen Künste *(drawing, painting, sculpture, architecture etc);* **work of** ~ Kunstwerk, Kunstgegenstand; ~ **exhibition** Kunstausstellung; ~ **object**[66] Kunstgegenstand

art 2. *(PatR)* Fach, Fachgebiet; Fachkenntnis, Fertigkeit; **advance in the** ~ technischer Fortschritt; **background** ~ bisheriger Stand der Technik

art, prior ~ Stand der Technik; **claim met by the prior** ~ durch den Stand der Technik neuheitsschädlich getroffener Anspruch; **improvement upon the prior** ~ Fortschritt gegenüber dem Stand der Technik; **list of prior** ~ **documents** Liste der Vorveröffentlichungen; **relevant prior** ~ einschlägiger Stand der Technik; **statement of prior** ~ Angabe der Vorveröffentlichungen

art, (state of the) ~ (Stand der) Technik; **state of the** ~ **defen|ce (**~**se)** Einwand des Standes der Technik; **person skilled** (or **expert**) **in the** ~ Fachmann; **person ordinarily skilled in the** ~

Durchschnittsfachmann; **usual knowledge of the man skilled in the** ~ fachmännisches Können; **those skilled in the** ~ Fachleute, Fachwelt; **to be skilled in the** ~ auf dem Fachgebiet erfahren sein; fachkundig sein; **to form part of the state of the** ~ zum Stand der Technik gehören

arterial, ~ **highway** Fernverkehrsstraße; ~ **railway** (Eisenbahn-)Hauptstrecke; ~ **road** Hauptverkehrsstraße

artery of trade Haupthandelsweg

article 1. Artikel; Gegenstand, Ware(nposten); Abschnitt, Paragraph *(e-s Gesetzes, Vertrages);* (Zeitungs-)Artikel; ~ **of daily use** Gebrauchsgegenstand; ~ **of merchandise** (Handels-)Ware; ~**s of war** Kriegsartikel *(Militärstrafgesetzbuch)*

article, branded ~ Markenartikel; **export** ~ Exportartikel; **import** ~ Importartikel; **leading** ~ Leitartikel *(e-r Zeitung);* **newspaper** ~ Zeitungsartikel; **scarce** ~**s** Mangelware(n); **superior** ~**s** Qualitätsware(n); **the Thirty-Nine A~s** *Br* die 39 Glaubensartikel *(der Anglikanischen Kirche);* **to be out of an** ~ e-n Artikel nicht mehr führen; **to deal in** (or **keep**) **an** ~ e-n Artikel führen

articles 2. Vertragsbestimmungen *(e-r Urkunde);* Satzung; Ausbildungsvertrag, *(früher:)* Lehrvertrag; Musterrolle *(der Schiffsmannschaft);* ~ **of agreement** *(schriftl.)* Vertragsbestimmungen, Vertragspunkte

articles, ~ **(of apprenticeship)** Ausbildungsvertrag, *(früher)* Lehrvertrag; **to bind an apprentice by** ~ jdn *(durch formellen Vertrag)* in die Ausbildung (od. Lehre) aufnehmen; **to serve one's** ~ seine Ausbildungszeit (od. Lehrzeit) durchmachen; **to take into** ~ als →articled clerk (od. als →accountant) einstellen

articles of association *Br*[67] Gesellschaftsvertrag, Satzung *(e-r Kapitalgesellschaft; regeln u. a. das Verhältnis zwischen Gesellschaftern, Direktoren und der Gesellschaft) (→memorandum of association);* **according to the** ~ satzungsmäßig; **alteration of** ~ Satzungsänderung; **appointed by the** ~ satzungsgemäß bestellt; **contrary to the** ~ satzungswidrig; **filing of** ~ Einreichung der Satzung

articles, ~ **of clerkship** *Br* Vertrag, der den Vorbereitungsdienst e-s →articled clerk bei e-m →solicitor oder e-m→accountant regelt; ~ **of employment** Anstellungsvertrag; ~ **of incorporation** *Am* Gründungsurkunde; Satzung *(e-r Kapitalgesellschaft);* ~ **of organization** *Am* Gründungsurkunde *(z. B. in Massachusetts);* ~ **of partnership** Gesellschaftsvertrag *(e-r Personengesellschaft)*

articles, marriage ~ (Hauptpunkte e-s) Ehevertrag(es); **ship's** ~ Heuervertrag; **to sign the ship's** ~ sich anheuern lassen

article *v* in die Ausbildung (od. Lehre) geben (to bei); ~**d clerk** *Br (bei e-m → solicitor angestellter)* Anwärter für die Anwaltslaufbahn; *(bei e-m →accountant angestellter)* Anwärter für die Steuerberaterlaufbahn

articulated lorry Sattelschlepper

artificial künstlich; ~ **insemination** künstliche Befruchtung; ~ **person** juristische Person; ~**ly inseminated** künstlich befruchtet

artisan Handwerker; ~**'s lien** Zurückbehaltungsrecht des Handwerkers an Mobilien

artist Künstler; Graphiker; ~**'s name** *(UrhR)* Künstlerzeichen

artistic works *(UrhR)* Werke der bildenden Künste *(paintings, drawings, engravings, photographs etc.; cf. copyright)*

as, ~ **accords (of law)** *Scot* gesetzmäßig; ~ **and if required** falls und wie benötigt *(Vorbehaltsklausel);* ~ **the case may be** je nach Lage der Sache; je nachdem: beziehungsweise (bzw.); ~ **far** ~ **practicable** soweit durchführbar; ~ **from** mit Wirkung vom; ~ **from January 1** ab 1. Januar, vom 1. Januar ab; ~ **is** ohne Mängelgewähr; ~ **occasion may require** nach Bedarf

as of, member ~ **right** Mitglied kraft Amtes; **to meet** ~ **right** automatisch zusammentreten *(ohne Einberufung)*

as per laut, gemäß; ~ **account** laut Rechnung; ~ **advice** laut Avis (od. Bericht, Anzeige); ~ **agreement** laut Übereinkunft; ~ **January 1** nach dem Stande vom 1. Januar

as, ~ **requested** wunschgemäß; ~ **(and when) required** nach Bedarf; ~ **soon** ~ **possible** sobald wie möglich, baldmöglichst

ascendant Vorfahr *(opp. descendant)*

ascending line, related in the ~ in aufsteigender Linie verwandt

ascertain *v* feststellen, Feststellungen machen; sich vergewissern; ermitteln; **to** ~ **the damage** den Schaden feststellen; **to** ~ **the price** den Preis ermitteln (od. feststellen)

ascertained goods bestimmte (besonders ausgesuchte) Waren; **purchase of** ~ Spezieskauf

ascertainable feststellbar, nachweisbar

ascertainment Feststellung; Ermittlung; ~ **of damage** (or **loss**) Schadenfeststellung; ~ **of price** Preisermittlung; ~ **of profits** Gewinnfeststellung

ASEAN (Association of South East Asian Nations) Vereinigung südostasiatischer Nationen
Eine aus Indonesien, Thailand, Malaysia, den Philippinen, Singapur und Brunei bestehende Staatengruppe, deren Ziel eine wirtschaftliche Stabilisierung der Region und eine sicherheitspolitische Konsolidierung ist

asexualization Sterilisierung *(e-s Mannes)*

ashore an(s) Land; auf Grund geraten; ~ **or afloat** an Land oder auf See; **a ship has run** ~ ein Schiff ist gestrandet

Asian Development Bank[68] (ADB) Asiatische Entwicklungsbank (AEB) *(Sitz: Manila)*
Hauptaufgaben der Bank sind die Förderung öffentlicher und privater Kapitalinvestitionen für Entwicklungszwecke und die Finanzierung nationaler und regionaler Entwicklungsvorhaben

ask *v,* **to** ~ **(for)** fragen, bitten (um); (an)fordern; **to** ~ **a p.'s advice** jdn um Rat fragen; **to** ~ **a p.'s permission** jdn um Erlaubnis bitten; **to** ~ **the price** nach dem Preise fragen; sich nach dem Preise erkundigen; **to** ~ **to speak** sich zum Wort melden

asked *(Börse) (vom Verkäufer)* gefordert, Brief; ~ **and bid** *(Börse)* Brief (Angebot) und Geld (Nachfrage); ~ **price** geforderter Preis; *(Börse)* Briefkurs

asperse *v* verleumden; **to** ~ **sb.'s reputation** jdn in schlechten Ruf bringen

aspirant to an office Bewerber für ein Amt

asportation[69] *(widerrechtl.)* Fortschaffen *(von bewegl. Sachen)*

assassin Attentäter; Meuchelmörder; **hired** ~ gedungener Attentäter; **search for** ~**s** Fahndung nach Attentätern

assassinate *v (bes. aus politischen Gründen)* ermorden; durch Attentat (od. meuchlerisch) umbringen

assassination Attentat, *bes.* politischer Mord; Ermordung; Meuchelmord; ~ **attempt** Mordanschlag; Attentatsversuch; ~ **clause** *(VölkerR)* Attentatsklausel

assault (Versuch od. Bedrohung mit e-m) tätl. Angriff; *(versuchte)* Gewaltanwendung; tätliche Bedrohung; tätliche Beleidigung; *Am*[70] Körperverletzung; ~ **and battery** →assault; ~ **occasioning actual bodily harm** *Am* Anwendung von Gewalt, die e-e Körperverletzung zur Folge hat; vorsätzliche Körperverletzung; ~ **on privacy** *(EDV)* Angriff auf die Privatsphäre; ~ **with intent to do grievous bodily injury** vorsätzliche schwere Körperverletzung; **aggravated** ~ **(including** ~ **with a dangerous or deadly weapon)** *Am*[71] schwere Körperverletzung; *Br* gewalttätiger Angriff auf Frauen od. Kinder; **criminal** (or **indecent**) ~ unzüchtige Handlung *(unter Androhung od. Anwendung von Gewalt); (versuchte)* Vergewaltigung, Notzucht *(cf. rape);* **felonious** ~ *Am* (versuchte) Gewaltanwendung (od. Körperverletzung) mit e-r tödlichen Waffe; **sexual** ~ *Am*[72] geschlechtlicher Mißbrauch, Notzucht

assault *v* angreifen; tätlich bedrohen (od. beleidigen)

assemble *v* (sich) versammeln; *(Teile)* zusammensetzen, montieren; **Parliament** ~**d** das Parlament trat zusammen (on am)

assembly 1. Versammlung; **A**~ *Am (in einigen Staaten)* Unterhaus; *(EG)* Versammlung *(des Europäischen Parlaments);* ~ **man** *Am* Abgeordneter e-s Unterhauses; ~ **in the open air** Versammlung unter freiem Himmel; ~ **room** Versammlungsraum; Sitzungssaal

assembly, annual ~ Jahresversammlung; **consultative** ~ beratende Versammlung; **general** ~ Generalversammlung, Vollversammlung; **General A**~ *Am* Parlament *(einiger Einzelstaaten, bestehend aus Senate and A*~); *Scot* oberstes kirchliches Gericht *(oberste gesetzgebende und gerichtl. Instanz der schottischen presbyterischen Kirche);* **General A**~ **(of the United Nations)** (UNO-)Vollversammlung *(aus sämtlichen Mitgliedern bestehendes Organ der Vereinten Nationen; cf. organs of the →United Nations);* **House of A**~ gesetzgebende Körperschaft; Unterhaus; **Legislative A**~ gesetzgebende Versammlung; Parlament; **National** ~ Nationalversammlung (*Fr* Assemblée Nationale); **plenary** ~ Vollversammlung; **prohibition of** ~ Versammlungsverbot; **right of** ~ Versammlungsrecht; **unlawful** ~ Zusammenrottung; Auflauf

assembly, to convene an ~ e-e Versammlung abhalten; **the A**~ **shall meet as of right** die Versammlung tritt zusammen, ohne daß es e-r Einberufung bedarf

assembly 2. Zusammenstellung, Zusammensetzung, Montage; ~ **line** Montagebahn, Fließband; ~ **line production** Fließbandproduktion; ~ **shop** Montagehalle, -werkstatt

assent Zustimmung, Genehmigung; ~ **of executor** *Br*[73] schriftl. Zustimmung des → executor zum Eigentumsübergang des Vermächtnisses (legacy od. devise) an den Testamentserben od. Vermächtnisnehmer

assent, notice of ~ Bekanntgabe der Zustimmung(serklärung); **Royal A**~ *Br* Königl. Zustimmung *(die dem Gesetzesentwurf Gesetzeskraft verleiht);* **to declare one's** ~ seine Zustimmung erklären

assent *v* zustimmen, beipflichten, beistimmen (to a th. e-r Sache)

assert *v* geltend machen, vorbringen; behaupten; **to** ~ **o.s.** sich durchsetzen; **to** ~ **a claim** e-n Anspruch geltend machen; **to** ~ **one's rights** s-e Rechte geltend machen (against gegen); auf s-n Rechten bestehen

assertion Geltendmachung *(e-s Anspruches);* Vorbringen; Behauptung; **to make an** ~ e-e Behauptung aufstellen

assertory oath *Am* Beteuerung unter Eid

assess *v* (ab-, ein)schätzen, taxieren, bewerten; *(Schaden[sbetrag], Umlage, Abgabe)* festsetzen, berechnen; besteuern; *(zur Steuer)* veranlagen (at mit); umlegen (at auf); **to ~ a building** ein Gebäude (ab)schätzen; **to ~ the damage** den (Versicherungs-)Schaden festsetzen (od. aufnehmen); **to ~ the (amount of) damages** die Entschädigungssumme festsetzen (at auf); **to ~ opinions** Meinungen abschätzen (od. feststellen)

assessed, ~ person der/die zur Steuer Veranlagte, Besteuerte; **~ value** geschätzter Wert; *(für Steuerzwecke)* festgesetzter Wert, Einheitswert; **the club ~ each member 10 dollars** der Verein belegte jedes Mitglied mit 10 Dollar; der Verein setzte für jedes Mitglied e-e Umlage von 10 Dollar fest

assessable steuerpflichtig; abgabepflichtig; umlagepflichtig; festsetzbar, abschätzbar, taxierbar; **~ income** steuerpflichtiges Einkommen; **~ stock** *Am* nachschußpflichtige Aktien; **non-~** steuerfrei, abgabefrei; nachschußfrei

assessment Einschätzung, Abschätzung, Taxierung, Bewertung; Festsetzung, Berechnung *(e-s Betrages, z. B. Steuer, Geldstrafe)*; (Steuer-)Veranlagung; (Abgaben-)Umlage, Umlagebetrag; Feststellung der Zahlungsverpflichtung *(z. B. für Aktien od. Gemeindesteuern)*; **additional ~s** Nachschüsse; **on the ~ basis** auf der Basis des Umlageverfahrens; **~ of a claim** Bewertung e-s Anspruchs; **~ of contributions** Festsetzung der Beiträge; **~ of damage** (or **loss**) Schadensfeststellung *(der Höhe nach)*; Schadensabschätzung; **~ of damages** Festsetzung e-r Entschädigungssumme; **~ of duty** Zollfestsetzung; **~ on income** Veranlagung zur Einkommensteuer; **~ insurance** *Am* Versicherung mit Umlageverfahren; **~ notice** Steuerbescheid; **~ period** Veranlagungszeitraum *(für Steuer)*; **~ of personnel** Bewertung (od. Beurteilung) von Personal *(bei der Einstellung)*; **~ of profit** Gewinnberechnung, Gewinnermittlung; **~ of results** Ergebnisbeurteilung; **~ of taxes** Festsetzung der Steuer; Steuerveranlagung; **~ of value** Wertberechnung, Wertermittlung

assessment, amount of ~ Betrag der Umlage; **basis of ~** Steuerbemessungsgrundlage; **notice of ~** Steuerbescheid; **rate of ~** Steuersatz; Hebesatz; **→ special ~; stock ~** *Am* Aufforderung zu Nachschußzahlungen auf Aktien *(bei Kapitalverlust der Gesellschaft)*; Zahlungsaufforderung *(an Aktienzeichner)*; **tax ~** Steuerveranlagung; **year of ~** Steuerjahr; **to appeal against an ~ (to tax)** gegen e-e (Steuer-)Veranlagung Einspruch erheben; **to levy ~** *Am* zur Zahlung *(auf das gezeichnete Grundkapital)* auffordern; **to make an ~ to (income) tax** zur Einkommensteuer veranlagen

assessor Taxator; *Am* (Grund-)Steuerveranlagungsbeamter; *Br*[74] sachverständiger Beisitzer *(sachverständiger Gehilfe e-s Richters in technischen od. wissenschaftlichen Fragen; hat im Ggs. zum →referee kein eigenes Stimmrecht)*; *Scot* (Einkommen-)Steuerveranlagungsbeamter; **loss ~** *Br (VersR)* Regulierungsbeamter; **nautical ~** *Br* sachverständiger Beisitzer für Schiffahrtsfragen; **to call in (the aid of) an ~** e-n Schadensabschätzer (etc.) zuziehen

asset Vermögenswert; Vermögensgegenstand; Nachlaßgegenstand; Wirtschaftsgut; *(Bilanz)* Posten auf der Aktivseite, Aktivposten; *(wichtiger)* Faktor (for für); **~ account** Aktivkonto; Bestandskonto; **~ acquisition** *Am* Kauf der Wirtschaftsgüter *(bei Übernahme e-r Gesellschaft; opp. stock acquisition)*; **~ and liability statement** *Am* Bilanz; **~-equity swap** Schuldenswap (*→swap*)

asset formation Vermögensbildung; **personal ~ by workers** Vermögensbildung in Arbeitnehmerhand

asset, ~ management Vermögensverwaltung; **~ purchase** *Am* Kauf der Aktiva *(bei Firmenübernahme)*; **~ stripping** Aufkauf e-s Unternehmens mit anschließendem gewinnbringenden Verkauf einzelner Teile dieses Unternehmens

asset, economic ~ Wirtschaftswert; **fixed ~** Anlagegegenstand; **net ~ value** Substanzwert *(e-s Unternehmens)*; Nettovermögenswert; **real ~** unbeweglicher Vermögensgegenstand

assets Vermögen(swerte); Aktiven, Aktiva *(opp. liabilities)*; Aktivvermögen; Betriebsvermögen; (Kapital-)Anlagen; Guthaben; Wirtschaftsgüter; *(der zur Schuldendeckung und Befriedigung der im Testament Bedachten verfügbare)* Nachlaß; *(Bilanz)* Aktivseite *(Anlage- und Umlaufvermögen)*; **~ (held) abroad** ausländisches Vermögen, Vermögenswerte im Ausland; **~ brought in** (or **into a business**) Einlage; **~ of a business** Geschäftsvermögen, Betriebsvermögen; **~ of a company** Gesellschaftsvermögen; **~ on current account** Kontokorrentguthaben; **~ available for distribution** Teilungsmasse *(im Konkurs)*; **~ in foreign currency** Devisenguthaben; **~ in kind** Sachwerte; **~ in kind brought in** Sacheinlage; **~ and liabilities** Aktiva und Passiva; **~ of a partnership** Gesellschaftsvermögen; **~ receivable** Forderungen; Debitoren

assets side *(Bilanz)* Aktivseite; **to enter** (or **post**) **on the ~** aktivieren

assets under a will Nachlaß

assets, amount of ~ Vermögenshöhe; **(bankrupt's) ~** *(die zur Befriedigung der Gläubiger zur Verfügung stehenden Aktiven e-r)* Konkursmasse; **business ~** Betriebsvermögen, Geschäftsvermögen; **capital ~** Anlagevermögen; *(DBA)* Vermögenswerte (*opp. circulating or current ~*); **cash ~** Barvermögen; **company's** (or *Am* **corporate**) **~** Gesellschaftsvermögen; **circulating**

~ s. current →~; **concealed** ~ stille Reserven; **current** ~ Umlaufvermögen, sofort realisierbare Aktiven *(cash, stock and book debts; opp. capital or fixed ~)*; **external** ~ Vermögenswerte im Ausland, Auslandsvermögen; Auslandsanlagen; **financial** ~ Finanzanlagen; finanzielle Aktiva; **fixed** ~ feste (od. festliegende) Anlagen; Sachanlagen; Anlagevermögen *(buildings, plant and machinery; opp. circulating or current ~)*; **floating** ~ Umlaufvermögen; **foreign** ~ s. external →~; **free** ~ frei verfügbare Guthaben; **hidden** ~ stille Reserven; **immaterial** (or **intangible**) ~ immaterielle Werte *(e-s Unternehmens, z.B. goodwill oder Patente)*; **liquid** ~ flüssiges Vermögen; flüssige Mittel; **material** ~ →tangible ~; **net** ~ Reinvermögen; **nominal** ~ Buchwerte; **operating** ~ Betriebsvermögen; **original** ~ Anfangsvermögen, Anfangskapital; **other** ~ *(Bilanz)* sonstige Aktiva; **permanent** ~ s. capital →~; **personal** ~ Privatvermögen; *(der zur Bezahlung der Schulden des Erblassers verfügbare)* Nachlaß an beweglichem Vermögen; beweglicher Nachlaß; **quick** ~ leicht realisierbare Aktiva; *Am (Bilanz)* Umlaufvermögen; **real** ~ Immobiliarvermögen; Grundbesitz, Liegenschaften; *(der zur Bezahlung der Schulden des Erblassers verfügbare)* Immobiliarnachlaß; **remaining** ~ *(KonkursR)* Restmasse; **shortlife** ~ kurzlebige Wirtschaftsgüter; **→tangible ~; →wasting ~**

asseverate *v*, **to ~ one's innocence** s-e Unschuld beteuern

asseveration Beteuerung

assign →assignee

assign *(Rechte, Forderungen)* übertragen, abtreten, zedieren (to an); zuweisen, zuteilen, anweisen; festsetzen, bestimmen; benennen, bestellen *(für e-e Tätigkeit)*; **to ~ a case to a judge** e-m Richter e-e Sache zuweisen; **to ~ a counsel to the accused** dem Angeklagten e-n Anwalt *(als Offizialverteidiger)* beiordnen; **to ~ a claim** (or **debt**) e-e Forderung abtreten; **to ~ a day for trial** e-n (Verhandlungs-)Termin festsetzen; **to ~ a patent** ein Patent abtreten (to an); ein Patent übertragen (to auf); **to ~ a reason** e-n Grund angeben; **to ~ a task to a p.** (or **to ~ a p. to task**) jdm e-e Aufgabe zuweisen; jdn einsetzen für e-e Aufgabe

assigned claim abgetretene Forderung

assignability Übertragbarkeit, Abtretbarkeit; Begebbarkeit

assignable übertragbar, abtretbar; zuzuschreiben; zuweisbar; bestimmbar; **~ instrument** begebbares Papier

assignation *Scot* Übertragung e-s Rechts; **~ house** *Am* Bordell

assignee Rechtsnachfolger *(durch Abtretung)*; Erwerber; Zessionar

assignment Übertragung, Abtretung, Zession *(von Rechten, Forderungen)*; Zuweisung, Zuteilung, Anweisung; Festsetzung, Bestimmung; Aufgabe(ngebiet); nähere Angabe, Spezifizierung; *bes. Am* Stellung, Posten; ~ **abroad** Auslandseinsatz; **~s** (or ~ **of business** or **functions**) Geschäftsverteilung *(e-s Gerichts)*; ~ **for the benefit of creditors** außerkonkursrechtliche Geschäftsabwicklung durch privatgeschäftlich bestellten Vertreter *(Br cf. deed of ~ for the benefit of creditors)*; ~ **of a claim** (or **debt**, or **choses in action**) Forderungsabtretung; ~ **of contract** Vertragsabtretung *(schließt in der Regel e-e Schuldübernahme mit ein)*; ~ **of dower** *Am* Spezifizierung des Nießbrauchs des verwitweten Ehegatten am Grundbesitz des verstorbenen Ehegatten; ~ **of errors** *Am* Angabe des Berufungsgrundes; ~ **of interest** Anteilsübertragung; ~ **of land** Landzuweisung; ~ **by operation of law** Übergang *(von Rechten und Pflichten)* kraft Gesetzes; ~ **of a patent** Übertragung e-s Patents; ~ **of property** (to creditors) Vermögensübertragung (an Gläubiger); ~ **of a representative for a particular task** Bestellung e-s Vertreters für e-e bestimmte Aufgabe; ~ **by way of security** Abtretung sicherheitshalber; ~ **of tasks** Zuweisung von Aufgaben; ~ **of wages** (Voraus-)Abtretung des Lohns *(oft in Zusammenhang mit Abzahlungsgeschäften)*

assignment, contract of ~ Abtretungsvertrag; **declaration** (or **statement**) **of** ~ Abtretungserklärung; **deed of** ~ Abtretungsurkunde, Zessionsurkunde; **equitable** ~ Abtretung (od. Übertragung) nach Billigkeitsrecht *(Zessionar kann keine Rechte im eigenen Namen gegen den Schuldner geltend machen)*; **foreign** ~ im Ausland vorgenommene Übertragung

assignment, legal ~ gesetzliche (Voll-)Abtretung

Br Die gesetzliche Abtretung ist in sec. 136 Law of Property Act 1925 geregelt. Nichtige gesetzliche Abtretung kann als equitable assignment wirksam sein, berechtigt den Zessionar aber nicht, Rechte im eigenen Namen gegen den Schuldner geltend zu machen

assignment, prohibition of a ~ Abtretungsverbot; **to make an** ~ abtreten, zedieren, übertragen

assignor Abtretender, Zedent; Übertragender

assimilate *v* anpassen, angleichen; assimilieren

assimilation Anpassung, Angleichung; Assimilation

assist *v* beistehen, helfen, unterstützen; **to ~ each other** sich gegenseitig unterstützen; **the authorities ~ one another** die Behörden leisten sich gegenseitig (Amts-)Hilfe

assisted area *Br* Fördergebiet

assisted person *Br (Zivilprozeß)* Partei, der Prozeßkostenhilfe *(früher: Armenrecht)* oder Beratungshilfe gewährt worden ist; **to institute** (or **defend**) **proceedings as an** ~ *Br* e-n Prozeß unter Inanspruchnahme von Prozeßkostenhilfe *(früher: Armenrecht)* führen (→*legal aid*)

assistance Beistand, Hilfe; Unterstützung (in bei); Fürsorge(unterstützung), Sozialhilfe; ~ **in criminal matters**[75] Rechtshilfe in Strafsachen; ~ **to ships in distress** Hilfeleistung in Seenot; ~ **under Legal Advice Scheme** *Br* Beratungshilfe; **financial** ~ finanzielle Unterstützung; **government(al)** ~ staatliche Unterstützung

assistance, judicial ~ Rechtshilfe(verkehr); **mutual judicial** ~ **agreement** Rechtshilfeabkommen; **request for judicial** ~ Rechtshilfeersuchen; **to grant judicial** ~ Rechtshilfe gewähren *(cf. Br letters of request, Am letters rogatory)*

assistance, measures of ~ Hilfsmaßnahmen; **mutual** ~ gegenseitiger Beistand; →**national** ~; **in need of** ~ hilfsbedürftig; **official** ~ Amtshilfe; **public** ~ *Am* Sozialhilfe; **recipient of public** ~ *Am* Sozialhilfeempfänger; **to render** ~ Hilfe (od. Beistand) leisten

assistant Assistent(in), Gehilfe, Gehilfin; Mitarbeiter(in); Hilfs-; stellvertretend; ~ **cashier** (A/C) zweiter Kassierer; ~ **examiner** *(PatR)* Hilfsprüfer; ~ **judge** Hilfsrichter; ~ **manager** stellvertretender Leiter; ~ **professor** (without tenure) *Am* Privatdozent; ~ **secretary of state** *Am* Ministerialdirektor; **(shop)** ~ Ladenangestellte(r), Verkäufer(in)

assize(s), (court of assize) *Br* Assisen(gericht)
Der Courts Act, 1971, schaffte die courts of assize und quarter sessions ab und errichtete die Crown Courts. Die Zivilgerichtsbarkeit der assizes wurde auf den High Court übertragen

associate Mitarbeiter(in), Kollege, Kollegin; Teilhaber(in), Gesellschafter(in), Sozius; Partner; assoziiertes Mitglied; angeschlossen, assoziiert; ~**s** *Br* Justizbeamte des Supreme Court; ~ **(attorney)** *Am* in e-r Sozietät angestellter Anwalt; **A**~ **Justice** *Am* →justice; ~ **(member)** korrespondierendes (auswärtiges) Mitglied *(e-r wissenschaftl. Gesellschaft)*; ~ **professor** *Am univ* außerordentlicher Professor

associate *v.* 1. (sich) verbinden, zusammenschließen (with mit); in Zusammenhang bringen (with mit); **to** ~ **for the purpose of forming a company** sich mit jdm zu e-r Handelsgesellschaft verbinden

associated, ~ **company** *Br* →related company; ~ **enterprises** wirtschaftlich verbundene Unternehmen; **A**~ **Press** (AP) *Am* Nachrichtenagentur; ~ **(trade) marks** verbundene Warenzeichen *(ein od. mehrere Warenzeichen, die mit e-m für denselben Anmelder bereits eingetragenen und für dieselben Waren verwendeten Warenzeichen zum Verwechseln ähnlich sind)*; **to be** ~ **in business** geschäftlich verbunden sein (with mit)

associate *v* 2. *pol* assoziieren; **A**~**d African States, Madagascar and Mauritius** (AASMM) *(EG)* Assoziierte Afrikanische Staaten, Madagaskar und Mauritius

association 1. (Personen-)Vereinigung; Verband; Gesellschaft *(des bürgerl. Rechts)*; Bund; Verein *(meist ohne Rechtspersönlichkeit)*; ~ **agreement** *Am* →agreement 2.; **A**~ **of Certified Accountants** *Br* (ein) Verband der Wirtschaftsprüfer; ~ **of enterprises** Unternehmensvereinigung; **A**~ **of South-East Asian Nations** →ASEAN

association, industrial ~ *Am* Industrieverband; Wirtschaftsverband; →**memorandum of** ~; **professional** ~ Berufsverband; **non-profit (making)** ~ Gesellschaft, die keinen Erwerbszweck verfolgt; Idealverein; →**unincorporated** ~

association, to form (or **set up**) **an** ~ e-n Verband gründen; **to join an** ~ e-m Verband beitreten; **to withdraw from an** ~ aus e-m Verband austreten

association 2. *pol* Assoziierung, Assoziation; ~ **agreement** *(EG)* Assoziierungsabkommen; **A**~ **Committee** *(EG)* Assoziationsausschuß; **expiry of the** ~ **agreement** Ablauf des Assoziierungsabkommens; **purpose of the** ~[76] Ziel der Assoziierung

assort *v* sortieren, passend zusammenstellen; assortieren, nach Warenarten ordnen; **to** ~ **samples** Muster *(passend)* zusammenstellen

assortment Sortiment, (Waren-)Auswahl; Kollektion; ~ **of goods** Warensortiment; ~ **of patterns** Musterkollektion; ~ **for selection** Auswahlsendung

assume *v* annehmen, übernehmen, auf sich nehmen; *(als wahr)* annehmen, vermuten; voraussetzen; **to** ~ **a debt** Schuld *(e-s anderen)* übernehmen; **to** ~ **an obligation** e-e Verbindlichkeit eingehen; e-e Verpflichtung übernehmen; **to** ~ **an office** ein Amt übernehmen; **to** ~ **a risk** die Gefahr auf sich nehmen; ein Risiko übernehmen

assumed, ~ **infringer** vermeintlicher Patentverletzer; ~ **name** angenommener Name; Deckname; Pseudonym; **it may be initially** ~ es kann davon ausgegangen werden

assumpsit ("he has undertaken") formloses *(schriftl. od mündlich gegebenes)* Versprechen *(zur Übernahme e-r Leistungsverbindlichkeit)*

assumption Annahme, Übernahme *(von Rechten od. Pflichten)*; Annahme, Vermutung; Voraussetzung; **(unlawful)** ~ **of authority** Amtsan-

maßung; ~ **of debt** Schuldübernahme; ~ **of the executorship** Annahme des Amtes des Erbschaftsverwalters (→*executor*); ~ **of liability** Haftungsübernahme; ~ **of power** Machtübernahme; ~ **of risk** Risikoübernahme; Handeln auf eigene Gefahr (→*risk* 1.)
assumption, on the ~ that unter der Annahme (od. Voraussetzung) daß; **the ~s on which . . . are based** die Voraussetzungen, auf denen . . . beruht

assurable interest versicherbares Interesse

assurance 1. Versicherung, Zusicherung, Zusage; **(common)** ~[77] Übertragung *(von Grundbesitz);* Übertragungskunde; →**further** ~; **to give an** ~ e-e Zusicherung geben; **to obtain** (or **receive**) **an** ~ e-e Zusicherung erhalten
assurance 2. *bes. Br* (Lebens-)Versicherung *(cf. insurance);* ~ **benefit** Versicherungsleistung; ~ **company** *Br* Lebensversicherungsgesellschaft; **A~ Companies Acts** *Br*[78] Gesetze für Versicherungsgesellschaften *(von 1909 und 1946);* ~ **payable at death** Todesfallversicherung; **industrial** ~ *Br* Kleinlebensversicherung; **life** ~ Lebensversicherung; **ordinary life** ~ *Br* Großlebensversicherung; **term of the** ~ Laufzeit der Versicherung
assurance 3. *dipl* **accept, Excellency, the ~ of my highest consideration** *(Briefschluß)* genehmigen Sie, Exzellenz, die Versicherung meiner ausgezeichneten Hochachtung

assure *v (jdn e-r Sache)* versichern; *(jdm etw.)* zusichern; *bes. Br (Leben)* versichern; *(Grundbesitz)* übertragen; **to ~ one's life with a company** sein Leben bei e-r Gesellschaft versichern
assured gesichert, versichert; ~ **market** sicherer Absatzmarkt; ~ **(person)** Versicherungsnehmer, Versicherter; *Am* jd, zu dessen Gunsten e-e Versicherung abgeschlossen ist; **sum** ~ *Br* Versicherungssumme; **to have one's life** ~ sich versichern lassen

assurer *bes. Br* Versicherer

astray, to go ~ fehllaufen, verlorengehen

astronaut Astronaut, (Welt-)Raumfahrer *(→ outer space)*

astronautics Astronautik, (Wissenschaft von der) Raumfahrt

asylum 1. *(VölkerR)* Asyl(recht); **countries providing** ~ Aufnahmeländer; **diplomatic** ~ diplomatisches Asyl *(Asylgewährung im Gesandtschaftsgebäude);* **grant of** ~ Gewährung des Asyls; **neutral** ~ Asylgewährung durch ein neutrales Land; **person granted** ~ unter Asylschutz Stehender; **person seeking** ~ Asylsuchender, Asylant; **political** ~ politisches Asyl; **right of** ~ Asylrecht; **to ask for political** ~ um politisches Asyl bitten; **to grant** ~ Asyl gewähren; **to seek** ~ Asyl beantragen

asylum 2. *Am* (Pflege-)Heim

A.T.A. Convention A.T.A. Übereinkommen *(→Customs Convention on the A.T.A. Carnet)*

Atlantic Charter Atlantic-Charta
Erklärung der USA und Großbritanniens über ihre Kriegs- und Friedensziele von 1941
Atlantic Treaty →North Atlantic Treaty

atom(ic) bomb (A-bomb) Atombombe; ~ **tests** Atombombenversuche
atomic, ~ age Atomzeitalter; ~ **control** Atomkontrolle; ~ **demolition munition** (ADM) Atomminen, nukleare Minen
atomic energy Atomenergie; **A~ E~Authority** *Br* Atomenergiebehörde; ~ **law** Atomrecht; **A~ E~ Research Establishment** (AERE) *Br* Atomforschungszentrum; **application of ~ to peaceful pursuits** (or **peaceful use of** ~) friedliche Verwendung der Atomenergie; **European A~ E~ Community** (EAEC) Europäische Atomgemeinschaft (Euratom) (→*European*); **International A~ E~ Agency** (IAEA)[79] Internationale Atomenergie-Organisation (→*international*)
atomic, ~ explosion Atomexplosion; ~ **fallout** Atomstaub, Atomregen; radioaktiver Niederschlag
atomic, European A~ Forum (Foratom) Europäisches Atomforum (Foratom)
atomic information, to disseminate ~[80] Atominformationen verbreiten
atomic, ~ pile Atomreaktor; ~ **power** Atomkraft; **A~ Powers** Atommächte; ~ **research** Atomforschung; ~ **scientist** Atomwissenschaftler; ~ **warfare** Atomkrieg; atomare Kriegsführung; ~ **waste** Atomabfall
atomic weapons Atomwaffen; **prohibition of** ~ Verbot von Atomwaffen; **suspension of ~ tests** Einstellung von Atomwaffenversuchen
atomic, non-~ country Land, das nicht im Besitz der Atomwaffe ist

atone *v* wiedergutmachen, sühnen

atonement Wiedergutmachung, Sühne(maßnahme)

atrocity Greueltat; ~ **propaganda** Greuelpropaganda

ats (ad sectam) (at the suit of) in dem Rechtsstreit des/der

attach *v (Forderungen)* pfänden; in Beschlag nehmen, beschlagnahmen; beifügen, anheften, anbringen (to an); sich anschließen (to an); *(jdn)* festnehmen, verhaften *(für Zwecke des Zivilprozesses); (als Rechtsfolge)* eintreten; *mil* kommandieren (to zu); **to ~ an account** *Am* ein Konto pfänden; **to ~ a claim** (or **debt**) e-e Forderung pfänden; **to ~ conditions to** Bedingungen knüpfen an; **to ~ debts owing from a firm** Schulden e-r Firma pfänden; **to ~ a debt**

by **garnishee proceedings** e-e Forderung beim Drittschuldner pfänden; **to ~ importance** Bedeutung beimessen; **to ~ oneself to a political party** sich e-r politischen Partei anschließen; **the risk ~es** *(VersR)* das Risiko beginnt; **to ~ wages** Lohn pfänden

attached, ~ debtor gepfändeter Schuldner; **~ to** angeschlossen an *(Behörden etc)*; **rights ~ to a patent** mit e-m Patent verbundene Rechte; **~ to this letter** als Anlage zu diesem Brief; **non-~** *pol* fraktionslos; **to become ~** sich angliedern (to an)

attaching creditor Pfändungsgläubiger; Gläubiger, der e-n dinglichen Arrest erwirkt hat

attachable pfändbar; beschlagnahmefähig; beizulegen(d)

attaché *(VölkerR)* Attaché; **air ~** Luftattaché; **commercial ~** Handelsattaché; **cultural ~** Kulturattaché; **military ~** Militärattaché; **naval ~** Marineattaché: **press ~** Presseattaché

attachment Pfändung *(von Forderungen); (gerichtl.)* Beschlagnahme; *(dingl.)* Arrest; *Am* Begründung e-s Sicherheitsrechts zwischen den Parteien *(zu unterscheiden vom Zeitpunkt der →perfection)*; **(body) ~** persönlicher Arrest, Verhaftung *(wegen →contempt of court)*; Angliederung; **~ of an annuity** Pfändung e-r Rente; **~ bond** *Am* → bond 3.; **~ of a debt** Forderungspfändung; **~ of earnings** *Br*[81] Lohn- (od. Gehalts-)pfändung *(bei Unterhaltszahlungen)*; **~ execution** *Am* Forderungspfändung mit summarischer Drittschuldnerklage; **~ order** s. order of →~

attachment, foreign ~ *Am* vorläufige Pfändung des Vermögens e-s Ausländers; Beschlagnahme e-s Gegenstandes mit Drittverbot *(im Wege der einstweiligen Verfügung zwecks Sicherung der Zwangsvollstreckung* [*→garnishment*], *oft auch zur Begründung e-s Gerichtsstandes des Vermögens)*; **levy of ~** Pfändung *(aufgrund e-s Vollstreckungstitels)*; **order of ~** *Am* Pfändungsbeschluß; Beschlagnahmeverfügung; *Br* Anordnung des persönlichen Arrestes *(wegen contempt of court)*; **not subject to ~** unpfändbar; nicht der Beschlagnahme unterliegend; **→writ of ~; to be subject to ~** der Pfändung (od. Beschlagnahme) unterliegen

attain *v* erreichen, gelangen zu; **to ~ one's end** s-n Zweck erreichen, zum Ziel gelangen; **on ~ing the age of 18 years** nach Vollendung des 18. Lebensjahres

attainment Erreichung; das Erreichte, die Errungenschaft; **~s** Kenntnisse, Fertigkeiten; **legal ~s** juristische Kenntnisse

attempt 1. Versuch; **criminal ~** strafbarer Versuch; **~ at →conciliation; ~ at →reconciliation; ~ to escape** (or **escape ~**) Fluchtversuch; **~ to commit an offence (~se)** Versuch der Begehung e-r strafbaren Handlung; **~ at resistance** Widerstandsversuch; **abandonment of an ~** Rücktritt vom Versuch; **an ~ is punishable** ein Versuch ist strafbar

attempt 2., **~ (up)on** Angriff, Attentat auf; **to make an ~ on a p.'s life** ein Attentat auf jdn machen (od. begehen)

attempt *v* versuchen; **the prisoner ~ed to escape** der Gefangene versuchte zu entkommen, der Gefangene machte e-n Fluchtversuch; **~ed coup** Putschversuch

attend *v (Schule, Versammlung etc)* besuchen; anwesend (od. zugegen) sein (at bei); teilnehmen an; bedienen; *(als Arzt)* behandeln; *(dienstlich)* begleiten; **to ~ on a p.** jdn bedienen; jdn pflegen; **to ~ to** sich befassen mit; achtgeben auf; besorgen, sehen nach; **to ~ court** vor Gericht erscheinen; **to ~ to customers** Kunden bedienen (od. abfertigen); **to ~ to a p.'s interests** jds Interessen wahrnehmen; **to ~ a lecture** e-e Vorlesung besuchen (od. hören); **to ~ a matter promptly** e-e Sache schnell erledigen; **to ~ a meeting** e-e Versammlung besuchen; **to ~ to orders** Aufträge erledigen

attended, well ~ *(von Vorträgen, Versammlungen etc)* gut besucht; **poorly ~** schlecht besucht; **to be ~ with difficulties** mit Schwierigkeiten verbunden sein

attending country Teilnehmerland *(z.B. an e-r Konferenz)*

attendance Besuch, Anwesenheit (at bei); Teilnahme, Beteiligung; Zuhörerschaft, Besucherzahl; (Kunden-)Abfertigung; Bedienung; **~ allowance** *Br* Pflegegeld *(für Hilfe e-r körperlich od. geistig schwerbehinderten Person)*; **A~ Centre** *Br* (Ort für) Freizeitarrest *(für straffällige Jugendliche über 12 Jahren)*; **~ fee** Tagegeld; **~ figure** Besucherzahl

attendance list Anwesenheitsliste; Teilnehmerverzeichnis; **to circulate an ~** e-e Anwesenheitsliste herumgehen lassen; **to enter one's name on the ~** sich in die Anwesenheitsliste eintragen

attendance, ~ at a meeting Teilnahme an e-r Sitzung; **~ at school** (or **school ~**) Schulbesuch

attendance of witnesses Erscheinen von Zeugen; **to enforce the ~** das zwangsweise Erscheinen von Zeugen veranlassen

attendance, compulsory ~ zwangsweise Vorführung; **medical ~** ärztliche Behandlung; **record ~** Rekordbesuch

attendant 1. Begleiter; Diener; Aufseher *(z.B. im Museum)*; *Am* Sachbearbeiter *(z.B. bei e-r Bank)*; Krankenpfleger; **~s** Begleitung, Gefolge; **court ~** *Br* Gerichtsdiener

attendant 2. abhängig (to von); begleitend; folgend; **~ circumstances** Begleitumstände

attention Aufmerksamkeit, Beachtung; **(for the)** ~ **(of) Mr. X** zu Händen von (z. Hd. v.) Herrn X; **for immediate** ~ zur sofortigen Veranlassung; **prompt** ~ **to business** schnelle Erledigung der Geschäfte; **to bring to the** ~ **of a p.** jdn unterrichten (über); **to call** (or **direct, draw**) ~ **to** Aufmerksamkeit richten (od. aufmerksam machen) auf; **to come to the** ~ zur Kenntnis gelangen; **to give one's best** ~ **to orders** *(jds)* Aufträge bestens ausführen; **to give urgent** ~ **(to)** *(etw.)* vordringlich behandeln; **to pay** ~ **(to)** Aufmerksamkeit zuwenden, achtgeben (auf)

attest *v (als Zeuge)* bestätigen; *(bes. Unterschrift od. Errichtung e-r Urkunde)* bezeugen; *(als Zeuge)* unterschreiben; *(Abschrift, Unterschrift) (amtl.)* beglaubigen; beurkunden; verbriefen; *mil* vereidigen; **to** ~ **to a fact** e-e Tatsache bestätigen; **to** ~ **a signature** e-e Unterschrift beglaubigen; **to** ~ **to the truth of a statement** die Wahrheit e-r Aussage bestätigen

attested, ~ **by a notary public** öffentlich beglaubigt; ~ **copy** beglaubigte Abschrift; ~ **will** von Zeugen unterschriebenes Testament; **to get a document** ~ **by a notary** (or **to get a document notarially** ~) e-e Urkunde vom Notar beglaubigen lassen

attesting, ~ **notary** der beglaubigende (od. beurkundende) Notar; ~ **witness** Unterschriftszeuge; Zeuge der Errichtung e-r Urkunde *(cf. attestation clause)*

attestation Zeugenvermerk *(bei Errichtung e-r Urkunde, bes. e-s Testaments)*; Bestätigung; Beglaubigung; Beurkundung; *mil* Vereidigung; ~ **clause** Zeugenformel *(bes. bei Testamenten)*; ~ **of signature** Unterschriftsbeglaubigung *(amtl. od. durch Zeugen)*; **to obtain a notarial** ~ **to a document** e-e Urkunde vom Notar beglaubigen lassen

Gebräuchlichste Form einer attestation clause:
Signed by the above-named testator as his will in the presence of us present at the same time, who at his request in his presence and in the presence of each other have hereunto subscribed our names as witnesses.
Von dem obengenannten Erblasser als sein letzter Wille in unserer Gegenwart unterzeichnet; wir haben auf seinen Wunsch in seiner und unserer aller Gegenwart unseren Namen als Zeugen hierunter gesetzt

attire, official ~ Amtstracht

attitude Haltung, Verhalten, Einstellung (to zu, towards gegenüber); Stellung; **to adopt a negative** ~ **towards** e-e negative Haltung einnehmen zu

attitudinal research Verhaltensforschung

attorn *v* Pacht- (od. Miet-)verhältnis *(mit dem neuen Eigentümer)* fortsetzen

attorney (der/die) Bevollmächtigte; *Am* Rechtsanwalt, Rechtsanwältin (→ ~ at law); ~ **(in fact)** (Stell-)Vertreter(in); *(durch power of ~)* Beauftragte(r), Bevollmächtigte(r)

attorney (at law) *Am* Rechtsanwalt, Rechtsanwältin; **to consult an** ~ e-n Anwalt zuziehen

Ursprünglich der niedrigere Grad gegenüber dem counselor; jetzt ist dieser Unterschied in fast allen Staaten aufgegeben. Vor den amerikanischen Bundesgerichten besteht kein Anwaltszwang, in der Praxis bestellen die Parteien aber regelmäßig einen Anwalt (für die ausländische Partei wichtig wegen der Formstrenge des Prozeßverfahrens)

attorney, U.S. ~ *Am* Bundesanwalt *(Staatsanwalt in der Bundesanklagebehörde)*

attorney, ~**-client privilege** *Am* Aussageverweigerungsrecht des Anwalts; *(begründet)* Anwaltsgeheimnis; ~ **for the defendant** (or **defense**) *Am (Zivilprozeß)* Anwalt des Beklagten; *(Strafprozeß)* Verteidiger

attorney's fees *Am* Anwaltsgebühren

Die Anwaltsgebühren sind gesetzlich nicht geregelt; sie werden frei vereinbart, meist in Form eines → quota litis

Attorney-General 1. *Br* Kronanwalt *(cf. Solicitor-General)*

Berater der Regierung in Rechtsfragen (Mitglied der Regierung, mit der er wechselt). Tritt als Ankläger in besonders wichtigen Strafprozessen, insbes. in allen Verfahren wegen Hochverrats, auf

Attorney-General 2. *Am* Justizminister *(in Bundesverwaltung und in den Einzelstaaten)*; oberster Vertreter der Anklagebehörde

attorney, ~ **of record** *Am (durch Akten)* ausgewiesener Anwalt *(für e-n bestimmten Prozeß)*; prozeßbevollmächtigter Anwalt; ~**'s speech** *Am* Anwaltsplädoyer

attorney, appointment of an ~ Bestellung e-s Bevollmächtigten; **by** ~ im Auftrag, in Vertretung *(opp. in person)*; **circuit** (or **district**) ~ *Am* Staatsanwalt; **letter of** ~ *(schriftl.)* Vollmacht, Vollmachtsurkunde; *Am* Prozeßvollmacht; **patent** ~ *Am* Patentanwalt; **power of** ~ →power 1.; **representation by** ~ *Am* Vertretung durch e-n Anwalt; **represented by** ~ *Am* durch e-n Anwalt vertreten; **warrant of** ~ *(bes. Am) (schriftl.)* Vollmacht, Vollmachtsurkunde

attorneyship *Am* Anwaltschaft, anwaltschaftliche Tätigkeit

attornment Fortsetzung des Pacht- (od. Miet-)verhältnisses *(mit dem neuen Eigentümer)*; **to make** ~ →to attorn

attract *v (Kunden)* anlocken; *(Kapital)* heranziehen

attractive nuisance *Am* Gefahrenquelle, die Kinder anzieht

Nach der attractive nuisance theory, die in einigen Einzelstaaten abgelehnt wird, ist der Besitzer eines Grundstücks verpflichtet, zum Schutze jugendlicher Nichtberechtigter besondere Sorgfalt anzuwenden.

Bei Verletzung dieser Sorgfaltspflicht haftet er für Fahrlässigkeit

attributable zuzuschreiben; zurechenbar, zuzurechnend; **the profit is ~ to** der Gewinn ist zuzurechnen auf, der Gewinn entfällt auf

attribute *v* zuschreiben, zurechnen; zurückführen (to auf); **to ~ false motives to sb.** jdm falsche Beweggründe unterschieben

attrition Abnutzung, Verschleiß; *Am* der in bar ausgezahlte Teil e-r fälligen Emission; **war of ~** *mil* Zermürbungskrieg

atypical transactions atypische Geschäfte

aubaine *Fr* Ausländer (alien); **right of ~** *(VölkerR)* Heimfallrecht (jus albinatus)

auction *(öffentl.)* Versteigerung, Auktion; **~ buyer** Ersteigerer, Ersteher *(cf. person making the highest →bid)*; **~ day** Versteigerungstermin; **~ fees** Auktionsgebühren;**~ price** -Auktionspreis, Versteigerungspreis; **~ room** Auktionslokal; **~ sale** Auktion, Versteigerung

auction, compulsory ~ Zwangsversteigerung; **date fixed for the ~** Versteigerungstermin; → **Dutch ~; mock ~** Scheinauktion; **sale at ~** *Am* (**sale by ~** *Br*) Versteigerung

auction, to attend an ~ e-e Versteigerung besuchen; **to buy at ~** *Am* (**by ~** *Br*) ersteigern; **to conduct** (or **hold**) **an ~** e-e Versteigerung abhalten; **to purchase at ~** *Am* (**by ~** *Br*) ersteigern; **to put up for ~** *(etw.)* zur Versteigerung bringen, versteigern; **to sell at ~** *Am* (**by ~** *Br*) versteigern

auction (off) *v* versteigern; **to ~ to the highest bidder** meistbietend versteigern

auctioneer Auktionator, *(öffentl.)* Versteigerer; **~'s fees** Auktionsgebühren

audience 1. Audienz (of, with a p. bei jdm); Anhörung, Gehör; **leave-taking ~** Abschiedsaudienz; **private ~** Privataudienz; **right of ~** → right 1.; **to ask for an ~** um e-e Audienz bitten; **to give** (or **grant**) **a p. an ~** jdm e-e Audienz erteilen (od. gewähren); **to be received in ~** in Audienz empfangen werden

audience 2. Publikum, Hörer(schaft), Leser(-schaft); **his book has reached a wide ~** sein Buch hat e-n großen Leserkreis gefunden

audio, ~-typing Schreiben mit Diktiergerät; **~-typist** Phonotypistin *(die nach Diktiergerät schreibt)*

audio-visual, ~ media audiovisuelle Medien; **~ piracy** Bild- und Tonpiraterie; widerrechtliche Verwendung audiovisuellen Materials

audit Buchprüfung, Abschlußprüfung, Wirtschaftsprüfung; Revision; **~ adjustment** durch die Revision veranlaßte Berichtigungsbuchung; **~ book** Revisionsbuch; **~ certificate** Prüfungsbescheinigung; Bestätigungsvermerk des Abschlußprüfers; **~ committee** *Am* Prüfungsausschuß in e-m amerikanischen Unternehmen *(dient der Information und der Kontrolle der Geschäftsführung)*; **A~ Department** *Br*[82] Rechnungshof; **~ fees** (Buch-, Wirtschafts-)Prüfungsgebühren; **~ of personnel** *Am* Prüfung (od. Beurteilung) von Personal; **~ program(me)** Prüfungsplan; **~ report** Prüfungsbericht; Revisionsbericht

audit requirement, to be subject to a statutory ~ prüfungspflichtig sein *(Kapitalgesellschaft)*

audit, ~ test stichprobenweise Prüfung; **~ year** Prüfungsjahr, Revisionsjahr

audit, annual ~ Jahresabschlußprüfung; **annual ~ of the books** jährliche Überprüfung der Bücher; **cash ~** Kassenprüfung, Kassenrevision; **external ~** außerbetriebliche Revision; **general ~** allgemeine Buchprüfung, Jahresabschlußprüfung; **internal ~** betriebsinterne Revision; **to make** (or **undertake, perform**) **an ~** e-e (Buch-)Prüfung (od. Revision) vornehmen

audit *v (Bücher, Rechnungen)* prüfen; **to ~ the accounts of a company** die Bücher e-r Gesellschaft prüfen

audited, ~ balance (sheet) geprüfte Bilanz; **~ and found correct** geprüft und für richtig befunden

auditing (Buch-, Rechnungs-)Prüfung, Revision; Wirtschaftsprüfung; Prüfungswesen; **~ of accounts** Rechnungsprüfung; Buchprüfung; **~ company** Wirtschafts-Prüfungsgesellschaft; **~ department** Revisionsabteilung; **~ office** Rechnungsprüfungsamt; **~ procedure** Prüfungsverfahren, Revisionsverfahren; **~ standards** Prüfungsgrundsätze, Prüfungsrichtlinien; **external ~** außerbetriebliche Revision *(durch betriebsfremde Prüfer)*; **industrial ~** Wirtschaftprüfung; **internal ~** betriebsinterne Revision

auditor Buchprüfer, Abschlußprüfer; Wirtschaftsprüfer; *Am univ* Gasthörer; **~ of annual accounts** Abschlußprüfer; **~'s certificate** → audit certificate; **~'s report** Prüfungsbericht des Abschlußprüfers; →**Court of ~s**

Br Auditor ist im Verhältnis zum →accountant der engere Begriff. Obgleich es sich nicht um identische Begriffe handelt, werden die Bezeichnungen „auditor" und „accountant" heute in England oft gleichbedeutend gebraucht. Ein auditor muß Mitglied einer anerkannten Organisation der →accountants sein

augment *v* vermehren, vergrößern; zunehmen

augmentation Vermehrung, Vergrößerung; Zunahme

auspices, under the ~ of unter der Schirmherrschaft von

austerity *(selbstauferlegte)* strenge Einschränkung *(des Lebensstandards);* Konsumbeschränkung *(bes. als Kriegsfolge);* ~ **measure** Einschränkungsmaßnahme; ~ **program(me)** Einschränkungsprogramm

Australia Australien
Australian Australier(in); australisch

Austria Österreich; **Republic of** ~ Republik Österreich
Austrian Österreicher(in); österreichisch

autarchy 1. Autarkie *(cf. self-sufficiency);* 2. Autokratie *(Selbstherrschaft)*

autarky → autarchy 1.

authentic echt, authentisch *(ordnungsgemäß ausgefertigt od. beglaubigt);* glaubwürdig; maßgeblich, verbindlich; ~ **text** maßgebender Text; verbindlicher Wortlaut; authentische Fassung; **the English and German texts are equally** ~ der englische und deutsche Wortlaut sind gleichermaßen verbindlich

authenticate *v* authentifizieren, die Echtheit nachweisen; authentisieren; rechtsgültig machen; beglaubigen; beurkunden; **to** ~ **a signature** e-e Unterschrift beglaubigen
authenticated, ~ **copy** beglaubigte Abschrift; ~ **power of attorney** beglaubigte Vollmacht; ~ **by a public notary** durch e-n Notar beglaubigt (od. beurkundet); **to have a document** ~ e-e Urkunde beglaubigen (od. beurkunden) lassen

authentication Authentifizierung, Bescheinigung der Echtheit *(durch e-n dafür zuständigen Beamten);* Beglaubigung, Beurkundung; ~ **of a signature** Unterschriftsbeglaubigung

authenticity Authentizität, Echtheit; Glaubwürdigkeit; ~ **of a signature** Echtheit e-r Unterschrift; **the** ~ **is established** die Echtheit steht fest; **the** ~ **of the document was verified by a notary** die Echtheit der Urkunde wurde durch e-n Notar bescheinigt; **to test the** ~ die Echtheit prüfen

author Autor, Verfasser; Urheber; **~'s alterations** Autorenkorrektur; **~'s designation** Urheberbezeichnung; **~s of literary, scientific and artistic works** Urheber von Werken der Literatur, Wissenschaft und Kunst; **~'s right(s)** Autorenrecht(e); **~'s personal rights** Urheberpersönlichkeitsrechte; **joint ~(s)** Mitverfasser, Miturheber

authoritarian state autoritärer Staat

authoritative autoritativ, maßgebend; verbindlich; glaubwürdig, authentisch; ~ **report** authentischer Bericht; **both texts are equally** ~ beide Wortlaute sind gleichermaßen verbindlich

authorities 1. Behörden, Dienststellen; Obrigkeit; →**central, regional and local** ~; **competent** ~ zuständige Behörden; **military** ~ Militärbehörden; **public** ~ Behörden; öffentlich-rechtliche Körperschaften; **territorial** ~ Gebietskörperschaften
authorities 2. Rechtsquellen; **legal** ~ Präzedenzentscheidungen; **unbroken line of** ~ ständige Rechtsprechung; **to quote one's** ~ s-e Quellen angeben

authority 1. Amtsgewalt; Autorität; Behörde; ~ (for sth. or to do sth.) Befugnis, Genehmigung (etw. zu tun); Vollmacht; ~ **to act** Vertretungsbefugnis; ~ **to collect** Inkassovollmacht; ~ **to contract** Abschlußvollmacht; ~ **to dispose** Verfügungsmacht; ~ **by estoppel** → estoppel; ~ **coupled with an interest** Vollmacht mit eigenem Interesse des Bevollmächtigten; ~ **at a higher level** übergeordnete (od. vorgesetzte) Dienststelle; ~ **at a lower level** nachgeordnete Dienststelle; ~ **to negotiate** Verhandlungsvollmacht; ~ **to pay** Zahlungsermächtigung
authority to purchase *(Außenhandelsfinanzierung)* Ankaufsermächtigung *(hinsichtl. der vom Exporteur auf den Importeur gezogenen Tratten)*

Form des Negoziierungskredits. Die Bank des Exporteurs wird durch die Bank des Importeurs ermächtigt, vom Exporteur auf den Importeur gezogene Tratten bei gleichzeitiger Einreichung der dazugehörenden Dokumente anzukaufen

authority, ~ **to represent sb.** Vertretungsbefugnis; ~ **to sell** Verkaufsvollmacht; ~ **to sign** Zeichnungsberechtigung; Unterschriftsvollmacht; ~ **from the state** *Am* staatliche Ermächtigung
authority, actual ~ Vertretungsmacht im Einzelfalle; **agent's** ~ Vertretungsbefugnis; →**apparent** ~; **by** ~ **of** mit Erlaubnis von, ermächtigt durch; **by higher** ~ höheren Ortes; **competent** ~ zuständige Stelle (od. Behörde); **court of equal** ~ gleichgeordnetes Gericht; **delegation of** ~ Übertragung der Vollmacht; **exercise of** ~ Ausübung öffentlicher Gewalt; **express** ~ ausdrückliche (od. ausdrücklich erteilte) Vollmacht; **governmental** ~ Regierungsbehörde, Staatsbehörde; Staatsgewalt; **implied** ~ stillschweigende (od. stillschweigend erteilte) Vollmacht; **misuse of** ~ Mißbrauch der Amtsgewalt; **person invested with** ~ Bevollmächtigter; **post** (or **position**) **of** ~ einflußreiches Amt; verantwortliche Stelle; **public** ~ öffentliche Gewalt; Staatsgewalt; **revocation of an** ~ Widerruf e-r Vollmacht; **all State** ~ **emanates from the people** alle Staatsgewalt geht vom Volke aus; **superior** ~ vorgesetzte Behörde; **supervisory** ~ Aufsichtsbehörde; **by** (or **in**) **virtue of my** ~ auf Grund meiner Ermächtigung; **without** ~ unbefugt, unberechtigterweise; **to act within the scope**

of one's ~ im Rahmen seiner Befugnisse handeln; **to assume (exercise) supreme** ~ die oberste (Regierungs-)Gewalt übernehmen (ausüben); **to be under the** ~ **of a p.** jdm unterstehen; **to be vested with** ~ mit Vollmacht ausgestattet sein; **to confer** ~ **on a p.** jdn ermächtigen; jdn bevollmächtigen; **to exceed one's** ~ s-e Vollmacht überschreiten; **to give a p.** ~ (to do) jdm Vollmacht erteilen; **to have** ~ ermächtigt (od. befugt) sein (to zu); **to have** ~ **over a p.** jdm übergeordnet sein; **to withdraw the** ~ die Vollmacht widerrufen

authority 2. maßgebliche Gerichtsentscheidung *(die Bestandteil des →case law geworden ist);* Rechtsquelle *(in der geltendes Recht seinen Ausdruck findet);* Präjudiz; bindende Kraft *(e-r gerichtl. Vorentscheidung);* Quelle, Belegstelle; **the decision of a court of equal rank has only persuasive** ~ die Entscheidung e-s gleichrangigen Gerichts ist nicht bindend *(wird dennoch vom Gericht in Betracht gezogen);* **on good** ~ glaubwürdig; aus guter Quelle; **to cite** (or **quote**) **as** ~ als (Rechts-)Quelle angeben

authority 3. Autorität, *(auf bestimmtem Gebiete)* maßgebende Person, Fachgröße, Kapazität

authorization Ermächtigung, Bevollmächtigung; *(vorherige)* Genehmigung, Erlaubnis; *Br (Banking Act 1987)* Erlaubnis, Bankgeschäfte zu betreiben; **subject to** ~ genehmigungspflichtig; **under the** ~ **of** mit Ermächtigung von; **to have** ~ ermächtigt (od. befugt) sein

authorize *v* autorisieren; ermächtigen, bevollmächtigen; genehmigen, bewilligen

authorized autorisiert; ermächtigt, bevollmächtigt; befugt; ~ **agent** bevollmächtigter Vertreter; Bevollmächtigter; Disponent; ~ **capital**[83] autorisiertes *(zur Ausgabe genehmigtes)* Aktienkapital; **through** ~ **channels** auf dem Dienstwege; ~ **depository** *Br* autorisierte Hinterlegungsstelle für Devisenwerte *(solicitor od. Bank);* ~ **issue** *Am* →~ capital; ~ **person** Bevollmächtigter; ~ **recipient** Zustellungsbevollmächtigter; ~ **to sign** zeichnungsberechtigt, unterschriftsberechtigt; ~ **signatory** Unterschriftsberechtigter; ~ **shares** im Gründungszertifikat nach Nennbetrag und Anzahl festgelegte Kapitalanteile; ~ **stock** *Am* →~ capital; **duly** ~ gehörig befugt; **the undersigned, being duly** ~ *(VölkerR)* die hierzu gehörig befugten Unterzeichner

authorship *(UrhR)* Urheberschaft, Autorschaft; **joint** ~ Miturheberschaft; **original works of** ~ *Am (durch den Copyright Act geschützte)* originäre Geisteswerke; **presumption of** ~ Vermutung der Urheberschaft; **work of joint** ~ in Mitarbeit geschaffenes Werk

autocracy Autokratie *(unumschränkte Staatsgewalt)*

autograph Originalhandschrift *(bes. Unterschrift);* Autogramm; ~ **book** Unterschriftenverzeichnis *(e-r Bank);* **to ask for an** ~ um ein Autogramm bitten

autograph *v* eigenhändig signieren

automate *v* automatisieren; vollautomatisch machen (od. betreiben); ~**d data file** automatisierte Datei (od. Datensammlung); ~**d teller machine** (ATM) Geldautomat, Bankautomat

automatic automatisch; **semi-**~ halbautomatisch; ~ **currency** elastische Währung; ~ **debit transfer** Einzugsverfahren; ~ **processing of personal data** automatische Verarbeitung personenbezogener Daten; ~ **renewal** stillschweigende Verlängerung *(von Verträgen);* ~ **selling** Automatenverkauf, Verkauf durch Automaten; ~ **stay** *Am* Verfahrensstillstand *(nach Konkurseröffnung);* Konkurssperre; **A**~ **Teaching Device** (ATD) *univ* Lehrautomat; ~ **telephone system** Selbstanschluß

automatic transfer service *Am* Verrechnungsdienst zwischen Spar- und Girokonten *(Transfer verzinster Sparguthaben auf unverzinste Girokonten zur Deckung von Schecks);* ~ **account** (ATS account) *Am* quasi-verzinstes Girokonto

automatic vending machine Verkaufsautomat

automatically ohne weiteres, automatisch; **to extend** ~ automatisch verlängern

automation Automation; Automatisierung; Programmieren *(e-r Maschine)*

automati|sation (~zation) →automation

automi|se (~ze) *v* →automate *v*

automobile *bes. Am* Auto, Kraftwagen, Personenkraftwagen (PKW); ~ **accident** *Am* Autounfall; **A**~ **Association** (AA) *Br*[84] Kraftfahrerverband; ~ **insurance** *Am* Kraftfahrzeugversicherung; ~ **liability insurance** *Am (in einzelnen Staaten)* Autohaftpflichtversicherung; ~ **license fee** *Am* Kraftfahrzeugsteuer; ~ **plant** Autofabrik; ~ **registration** *Am* Zulassung von Kraftfahrzeugen; ~ **shares** *Am* Auto(mobil)aktien; ~ **show** Auto(mobil)ausstellung

automotive, ~ **industry** *Am* Auto(mobil)industrie; ~ **repair** *Am* Kraftfahrzeugreparatur

autonomous autonom, sich selbst regierend (od. verwaltend); ~ **tariff** autonomer Zoll

autonomy Autonomie; Selbstregierung; Selbstverwaltung; **collective bargaining** ~ Tarifautonomie; **to achieve** ~ autonom werden

autopsy Obduktion, Leichenöffnung; **to conduct an** ~ e-e Obduktion vornehmen (upon bei)

autre droit, in ~ (in another's right) im Namen Dritter

autrefois acquit (formerly acquitted) Einwendung des Freispruches aufgrund derselben Tat in e-m früheren Verfahren *(cf. in jeopardy)*

auxiliary, ~ body Hilfsorgan; **~ committee** Hilfsausschuß; **~ personnel** (or **staff**) Hilfspersonal

avail of a sale by auction *Am* Versteigerungserlös

avail *v* nützen, nützlich sein; **to ~ oneself of** Gebrauch machen von, Nutzen ziehen aus; **to ~ oneself of an arbitral award** sich auf e-n Schiedsspruch berufen; **he has ~ed himself of the right** er hat von dem Recht Gebrauch gemacht; er hat das Recht für sich in Anspruch genommen

availability Verfügbarkeit; Vorhandensein; Verwendbarkeit; *Am pol* Erfolgschance *(e-s Kandidaten)*; **~ of assets** (or **capital, funds**) Verfügbarkeit von Kapital; **period of ~** Gültigkeitsdauer *(z. B. e-s Fahrausweises)*; **subject to ~ of funds** unter dem Vorbehalt, daß Mittel vorhanden sind

available verfügbar; vorhanden; erhältlich; verwendbar; gültig; **~ candidate** *Am* aussichtsreicher Kandidat; **~ capital** verfügbares Kapital; **~ information** zur Verfügung stehende Information; **~ plea** *Am* gültige Einrede; **to be ~** zur Verfügung stehen; **to make ~** zur Verfügung stellen, bereitstellen; zugänglich machen

availment Inanspruchnahme *(z. B. e-s Kredits)*

average 1. Havarie, Haverei, Seeschaden *(an Schiff od. Ladung)*; **~ account** (or **bill**) Havarierechnung; **~ adjuster** Dispacheur *(Sachverständiger für die Feststellung des Seeschadens)*; **~ adjustment** →~ statement; **~ agent** Havarieagent; **~ bond** Havarie(verpflichtungs-)schein; **~ charges** (or **expenses**) Havariegelder, Havariekosten; **~ clause** Havarieklausel, Freizeichnungsklausel *(des Versicherers)*; **~ contribution** Havariebeitrag

average statement Dispache; (Aufmachung der) Schadensberechnung (und -verteilung auf die Beteiligten); **to make up the ~** die Dispache *(über den Seeschaden)* aufmachen

average, ~ stater (or **taker**) Dispacheur; **~ surveyor** Havariekommissar

average, adjustment of ~ (Aufmachung der) Dispache; **all ~ recoverable** (a. a. r.) jeder Schaden zu ersetzen; **case of ~** Havariefall; **free from ~** frei von Havarie *(nicht gegen Havarie versichert)*; **free from all ~** (F. A. A.) frei von jeder Havarie *(nicht gegen große und besondere Havarie versichert)*

average, general ~ (G. A.) große Havarie (od. Haverei); Havarie-Grosse *(cf. York-Antwerp Rules)*; **general ~ act** Havarie-Grosse-Maßnahme; **general ~ bond** Havarie-Grosse-Verpflichtungsschein; **general ~ statement** (or **adjustment of general ~**) Dispache der großen Havarie; **free from general ~** (F. G. A.) frei von großer Havarie *(nicht gegen große Havarie versichert)*; **to be admitted** (or **allowed**) **as general ~** als große Havarie vergütet werden; **to be entitled to receive general ~ contributions** Recht auf Vergütung in Havarie- Grosse haben; **to be liable to pay general ~ contributions** beitragspflichtig zu e-r Havarie-Grosse sein

average, gross ~ s. general →~

average, particular ~ (P. A.) besondere Havarie (od. Haverei), Partikularhavarie; **particular ~ adjustment** Dispache für besondere Havarie; **particular ~ loss** Schaden durch besondere Havarie; **free from particular ~** (F. P. A.) frei von besonderer Havarie *(nicht gegen Beschädigung versichert; Schadensersatzanspruch nur bei Verlust)* (unless the ship be stranded außer im Strandungsfalle); **goods covered against particular ~** gegen Teilhavarie versicherte Waren; **with particular ~** (W. P. A.) einschließlich besonderer Havarie

average, petty ~ kleine Havarie, Teilschaden *(cf. pilotage, harbo(u)r, [cost] light dues, towage)*

average, ship under ~ havariertes Schiff; **with ~** (W. A.) einschließlich Havarie; **to adjust** (or **make up**) **the ~** die Dispache aufmachen; **to recover ~** Ersatz für Havarie erhalten; **to settle** (or **state**) **the ~** s. to adjust the →~

average 2. Durchschnitt; durchschnittlich, Durchschnitts-; arithmetisches Mittel; *Am*[85] *(Börse)* Aktienindex; **~ citizen** Durchschnittsbürger; **~ costs** Durchschnittskosten; **~ duration of life** *(VersR)* durchschnittliche Lebensdauer; **~ earnings** durchschnittlicher Verdienst; **~ human being** Durchschnittsmensch; **of ~ kind and quality** von mittlerer Art und Güte; **~ mechanic skilled in the art** *(PatR)* Durchschnittsfachmann; **~ price** Durchschnittspreis; *(Börse)* Durchschnittskurs; **~ rate** Durchschnittssatz; **~ value** Durchschnittswert, Mittelwert

average, →arithmetical ~; fair ~ quality (f. a. q.) gute Durchschnittsqualität; gute Mittelqualität; Handelsgut mittlerer Art und Güte; **monthly ~** Monatsdurchschnitt; **on (an) ~** im Durchschnitt, durchschnittlich; **rough ~** annähernder Durchschnitt; **to strike** (or **take**) **an** (or **the**) **~** den Durchschnitt nehmen (od. ausrechnen)

average *v* durchschnittlich betragen (od. ausmachen); den Durchschnitt nehmen von; im Durchschnitt erzielen; **to ~ (down** or **up)** *(Börse)* Wertpapiere (od. Waren) zusätzlich kaufen od. verkaufen, um e-n günstigeren Durchschnittspreis zu erzielen; **to ~ more (less) than** im Durchschnitt über (unter) liegen; **to ~ up** den Durchschnitt ausrechnen

averaging den Durchschnitt bildend; →**income ~**

averment (Tatsachen-)Behauptung, Vorbringen *(im Prozeß)*; → **immaterial ~**

avert *v*, **to ~ bankruptcy proceedings** das Konkursverfahren abwenden

aviation Luftfahrt, Flugwesen; **~ authority** Luftfahrtbehörde; **~ company** Luftverkehrsgesellschaft; **~ insurance** Luft(fahrt)versicherung; Lufttransportversicherung; **~ security** Flugsicherheit; **civil ~** zivile Luftfahrt; Passagierflugverkehr; **International Civil A~ Organisation** →international; **commercial ~** Verkehrsluftfahrt

avoid *v* vermeiden, abwenden; umgehen; für ungültig (od. nichtig) erklären, aufheben; anfechten; **to ~ a contract** e-n Vertrag anfechten; e-n Vertrag aufheben (od. annullieren); **to ~ a patent** ein Patent (als ungültig) anfechten; **to ~ double taxation** Doppelbesteuerung vermeiden; **to ~ taxes** Steuern *(legal)* umgehen

avoided, to declare a contract ~ die Aufhebung e-s Vertrages erklären

avoidable vermeidbar; aufhebbar; anfechtbar; **~ danger** vermeidbare Gefahr; **without ~ delay** ohne unangemessene Verzögerung

avoidance Vermeidung, Umgehung; Ungültigerklärung, Aufhebung; Anfechtung; **~ clause** Anfechtungsklausel

avoidance of a contract Aufhebung (od. Anfechtung) e-s Vertrages; **to give notice of ~** e-n Vertrag aufheben (od. anfechten)

avoidance, ~ of sale Wandelung *(Rücktritt vom Kaufvertrag)*; **~ on the ground of mistake** Anfechtung wegen Irrtums; **~ of taxes** *(erlaubte)* Umgehung von Steuern; *(legale)* Steuervermeidung *(cf. tax evasion)*

avoidance, defence (-se) by confession and ~ Einrede *(ohne Leugnen des Klagevorbringens)*; **party opposing ~** Anfechtungsgegner; **right of ~** Anfechtungsrecht

avoirdupois (avdp.) Handelsgewicht (1 pound = 16 ounces = 453,59 g) *(cf. troy weight)*
In England für alle Waren außer Edelmetallen, Edelsteinen und Arzneien übliche Gewichtseinheit vor der Umstellung auf das metrische System (metrification)

avow *v* *(offen)* bekennen, eingestehen

avowal Bekenntnis, Geständnis

avulsion Abschwemmen *(von Land)* *(cf. alluvion)*

award 1. Zuerkennung, Zubilligung; Verleihung *(e-s Ordens, Preises)*; *(verliehene)* Auszeichnung, Preis, *(zuerkannte)* Belohnung, Prämie; **~ of the contract** Auftragsvergebung, Zuschlag *(bei Ausschreibungen)*; **~ of public works contracts** Vergabe öffentlicher Bauaufträge; **~ of damages** Zubilligung von Schadensersatz; **~ to inventors** Erfinderprämie; **~ of maintenance** *Br* Zuerkennung von Unterhalt

award 2. Schiedsspruch (→*arbitral ~*); **~ made by consent of the parties** Schiedsspruch durch Parteivereinbarung; Schiedsvergleich; **arbitration ~** Schiedsspruch; **deposit of the ~** Hinterlegung des Schiedsspruches; **domestic ~** inländischer Schiedsspruch; **drafting of the ~** Abfassung des Schiedsspruches; **foreign ~** ausländischer Schiedsspruch *(cf. foreign →arbitral ~)*; **pronouncement of the ~** Verkündung des Schiedsspruches

award, setting aside of the ~ Aufhebung des Schiedsspruches; **to make an application for the setting aside or suspension of the ~** e-n Antrag stellen, den Schiedsspruch aufzuheben oder in seinen Wirkungen einstweilen zu hemmen

award, subject matter of the ~ Gegenstand des Schiedsspruches; **time-limit of an ~** Frist, innerhalb welcher der Schiedsspruch ergehen muß

award, to annul an ~ e-n Schiedsspruch für nichtig erklären; **to claim enforcement of the ~** Vollstreckung des Schiedsspruches beantragen; **to contest the validity of an ~** die Gültigkeit e-s Schiedsspruches anfechten; **to execute an ~** e-n Schiedsspruch vollstrecken; **to invoke an ~ against a party** e-n Schiedsspruch gegen e-e Partei geltend machen; **to make** (or **render**) **an ~** e-n Schiedsspruch fällen; **the ~ was made** der Schiedsspruch ist ergangen; **the ~ is notified to each of the parties** der Schiedsspruch wird jeder der Parteien zugestellt; **to refuse recognition and enforcement of the ~** Anerkennung und Vollstreckung des Schiedsspruches versagen; **to rely upon the ~** den Schiedsspruch geltend machen; **country in which the ~ is sought to be relied upon** Land, in dem der Schiedsspruch geltend gemacht wird; **to set aside an ~** e-n Schiedsspruch aufheben; **to submit to an ~** sich e-m Schiedsspruch unterwerfen

award *v (durch Urteil od. Schiedsspruch)* zuerkennen, zusprechen, zubilligen; *(als Ergebnis e-r Entscheidung)* verleihen, vergeben; **to ~ a concession** e-e Konzession vergeben; **to ~ the contract** *(bei Ausschreibungen)* den Auftrag vergeben, Zuschlag erteilen; (→ *contract* 2.); →**costs were ~ed against him; the court ~ed costs to the plaintiff** das Gericht legte dem Beklagten die Kosten auf; **to ~ damages** auf

Schadensersatz erkennen; **to be ~ed damages** Schadensersatz zugesprochen bekommen; **to ~ a prize** e-n Preis verleihen (od. zuerkennen); prämiieren

awarding, ~ of costs Kostenauferlegung; **fee for the ~ of costs** *(PatR)* Kostenfestsetzungsgebühr; **~ of government contracts** Vergebung von Regierungsaufträgen; **party ~ a contract** den Zuschlag erteilende Partei

aware in Anbetracht; angesichts; in dem Bewußtsein; in Kenntnis; **to be ~ that** sich bewußt sein, daß

away-going crop vom Pächter gesäte Ernte *(die unter s-m Nachfolger reif wird);* Ernte auf dem Halm

axe *v Br colloq. (Kosten)* reduzieren; *(Dienststellen etc)* abbauen

axiom *(unbestreitbarer)* Grundsatz; **~ of law** Rechtsgrundsatz

Axis Powers Achsenmächte
Deutschland, Italien und ihre Verbündeten im zweiten Weltkrieg

Ayes *bes. parl* Ja-Stimmen *(opp. Noes);* **the ~ have it** die Mehrheit ist für den Antrag; der Antrag ist angenommen

B

baby, ~ bonds *Am* Kleinobligationen; klein gestückelte Schuldverschreibungen *(bis zu 100 Dollar);* **~ stock** *Am* kleine Aktien

bachelor 1. Junggeselle
bachelor 2. niedrigster akademischer Grad; **B~ of Arts** (B. A., A. B.) niedrigster akad. Grad der philosophischen Fakultät; **B~ of Laws** (LL. B., B. L.) niedrigster akademischer Grad der juristischen Fakultät; **B~ of Science** (B. Sc.) niedrigster akademischer Grad der naturwissenschaftlichen Fakultät

back Rückseite; Hinter-, Rück-; rückständig; zurück; **~-bencher** *parl* Hinterbänkler; *Br* Abgeordneter, der nicht Kabinettsmitglied ist *(opp. front bencher);* **~ benches** *Br* →bench 2.; **~ biting** Verleumdung; verleumderisch; **~ bond** Rückbürgschaft; →bond 2.; **~-to-~credit** Gegenakkreditiv, Unterakkreditiv; Gegenkredit; **~ freight** Rückfracht *(für Güter, die am Bestimmungshafen nicht ausgeladen werden konnten);* **~ interest** rückständige Zinsen; **~ number** alte Nummer *(e-r Zeitung);* **~ order** noch nicht erledigter Auftrag; **~ pay** rückständiger Lohn; **~ rent** rückständige Miete (od. Pacht); **~ tax** rückständige Steuer; **to pay ~** zurück(be)zahlen; **to take ~** *(Beleidigung etc)* zurücknehmen

back *v* auf der Rückseite beschreiben; *(bes. finanziell)* unterstützen; *(Währung)* stützen; **to ~ a bill** e-n Wechsel *(als dritte Person)* unterzeichnen *(gewöhnlich auf der Rückseite) (→ backing a bill);* **to ~ the currency** die Währung stützen; **to ~ a horse** auf ein Pferd wetten (od. setzen)

backdate *v* rückdatieren
backdating Rückdatierung

backer Hintermann *(der mit Rat od. Geld Unterstützung gibt);* **(financial) ~** Geldgeber

background Hintergrund; Werdegang; Vergangenheit; **~ art** *(PatR)* Stand der Technik; **educational ~** (Aus-)Bildungsgang

backing Unterstützung, Förderung; *(Börse)* Stützungskäufe *(um Kurse nicht absinken zu lassen);* **mass-~** *pol* Unterstützung durch die (Wähler-)Masse
backing a bill wechselrechtliche Verpflichtung e-s Dritten durch Unterschrift auf der Rückseite
Die dritte Person wird allen nachfolgenden Inhabern ebenso verpflichtet wie der Aussteller, nicht aber gegenüber früheren Wechselbeteiligten (die Institution der Wechselbürgschaft [Aval] im Sinne des kontinentalen Rechts kennt das anglo-amerikanische Recht nicht)

backlash starke Reaktion

backlog (Auftrags-, Arbeits-)Rückstand; **~ of pending applications** *(PatR)* Anmeldungsstau; **~ demand** Nachholbedarf; **~ depreciation** nachgeholte Abschreibung; **~ of (unfilled) orders** Auftragsrückstand, Auftragsüberhang; **to have a ~ of work** mit seiner Arbeit im Rückstand sein

backtracking Beibehaltung der langjährigen Arbeitnehmer im Falle von Entlassungen

back-up facility (or **line**) Deckungsfazilität, Deckungslinie

backward rückständig, zurückgeblieben; **the country is in a ~ state** das Land ist rückständig

backwardation (back.) *(Londoner Börse)* Deport, Kursabschlag *(opp. contango);* **~ (business)** Deportgeschäft; **~ rate** Deportsatz

backwardness Rückständigkeit

bacteriological, ~ warfare *(VölkerR)* bakteriologische Kriegsführung; **~ weapons** bakteriologische Waffen *(→toxic weapons)*

bad schlecht; **~ cheque (check)** ungedeckter Scheck; **~ debt** uneinbringliche Forderung; **~ debt allowance** Forderungsabschreibung; **in ~ → faith; ~ investment** Fehlinvestition;

~**lands** *Am* unfruchtbares Land; ~ **title** mangelhafter Rechtstitel

badge (Dienst-, Rang-)Abzeichen; *(bei Kongressen)* Namensschild; ~ **of rank** Rangabzeichen; **party** ~ Parteiabzeichen

bag Sack; Tasche; Behälter; ~ **cargo** Sackgut; **sealed** ~ versiegelter Behälter

baggage (Reise-)Gepäck; ~ **car** *Am* Gepäckwagen; ~ **check** *(Flugverkehr)* Gepäckschein; ~ **insurance** (Reise-)Gepäckversicherung; ~ **label** *Am* Gepäckanhänger; ~ **liability limitation** *(Flugverkehr)* Haftungsbeschränkung für Gepäck; ~ **room** *Am* Gepäckannahme, Gepäckaufbewahrung; **damage to** ~ Gepäckschaden, Beschädigung des Gepäcks; **to check the** ~ *Am* das Gepäck aufgeben

Bahamas, the ~ die Bahamas (pl.); **Commonwealth of the** ~ Bund der Bahamas
Bahamian Bahamaer(in); bahamaisch

Bahrain Bahrain; **State of** ~ Staat Bahrain
Bahraini Bahrainer(in); bahrainisch

bail[1] *(StrafR)* Kaution, Sicherheitsleistung *(zur Abwendung der Untersuchungshaft od. zur Freilassung aus der Haft);* Kautionssumme, Sicherheit; der die Sicherheit Leistende; Bürge; *(SeeR) Br* Sicherheitsleistung *(zur Freigabe e-s beschlagnahmten Schiffes);* ~ **bond** *(schriftl.)* Verpflichtungserklärung *(des Untersuchungsgefangenen, Angeschuldigten od. s-s Bürgen anstelle von Zahlung e-r Kautionssumme);* ~ **bondsman** *Am* professioneller Kautionsbürge; ~ **jumping** s. forfeiture of →~; **able to give** ~ kautionsfähig; **additional** ~ Nebenbürge; **forfeiture of** ~ Verfall der Sicherheitsleistung *(bei Nichterscheinen vor Gericht);* **granting** ~ Haftverschonung gegen Sicherheitsleistung; **on** ~ gegen Sicherheitsleistung (od. Kaution); **release** (or **remand**) **on** ~ Haftentlassung gegen Sicherheitsleistung; Freilassung gegen Kaution; **saving of** ~ Freiwerden der Sicherheitsleistung *(bei Erscheinen vor Gericht);* **to be admitted to** ~ gegen Sicherheitsleistung (od Kaution) aus der Haft entlassen werden; **to be out on** ~ sich gegen Sicherheitsleistung auf freiem Fuß befinden; **to find** ~ sich Bürgen verschaffen; **to forfeit one's** ~ der geleisteten Sicherheit verlustig gehen, die Kaution verlieren *(bes. bei Nichterscheinen vor Gericht);* **to furnish** (or **give**) ~ Sicherheit leisten, Kaution stellen; **to go** ~ **for sb.** s. to stand →~; **to grant** ~ Sicherheitsleistung (od. Kaution) zulassen; gegen Sicherheitsleistung aus der Haft entlassen; **to jump** ~ *Am*[1] *colloq.* die Sicherheitsleistung *(bei Nichterscheinen etc)* verfallen lassen; **to release** (or **remand**) **on** ~ gegen Sicherheitsleistung (od. Kaution) aus der Haft entlassen; **to stand** ~ **for sb.** für jdn Sicherheit leisten; für jdn Kaution stellen

bail *v* 1. *(zur treuhänderischen Verwahrung)* übergeben; hinterlegen *(cf. bailment);* **to** ~ **goods to a carrier** Waren e-m Frachtführer übergeben
bailed goods zur treuhänderischen Verwahrung (Hinterlegung, Verpfändung, Beförderung etc) übergebene Sachen
bail *v* 2. Sicherheit leisten, Kaution stellen; **to** ~ **a p. (out)** durch Sicherheitsleistung erwirken, daß jd freigelassen wird
bailed person jd, für den Sicherheit geleistet (od. Kaution gestellt) ist *(zur Freilassung aus der Haft)*

bailable gegen Sicherheitsleistung freizulassen(d); kautionsfähig

bailee Übernehmer *(e-r bewegl. Sache);* Gewahrsamsinhaber, Fremdbesitzer *(auf vertraglicher Grundlage);* Besitzer *(mit dinglichem Recht gegenüber Dritten),* Verwahrer, Depositar, Pfandgläubiger, Frachtführer, Spediteur *(etc);* ~ **clause** *(Institute Cargo clause)* Gewahrsamsklausel; ~**'s lien** Zurückbehaltungsrecht des berechtigten Fremdbesitzers an den ihm übergebenen Sachen *(zur Sicherung der Ansprüche gegen den Eigentümer aus dem Besitzmittlungsverhältnis)*

bailie *Scot*[2] Ratsherr, Stadtverordneter

bailiff *Br* Hilfsbeamter e-s →sheriff, Gerichtsvollzieher; *Am* Justizwachtmeister; Vollstreckungsbeamter; *Br* Gutsverwalter

bailment Übertragung des Besitzes an e-r beweglichen Sache *(vom bailor auf den bailee)* auf Zeit; Verwahrung; Hinterlegung; Verpfändung; anvertrautes Gut; hinterlegte Sache; ~ **for custody** Verwahrungsvertrag; ~ **lease** *Am* →hire purchase agreement; **constructive** (or **involuntary**) ~ auf Gesetz beruhender Verwahrungsvertrag; **contract of** ~ Verwahrungsvertrag

bailor Übergeber *(e-r bewegl. Sache) (jd, der den Besitz an e-r bewegl. Sache auf Zeit überträgt);* Hinterleger, Verpfänder *(etc.);* ~ **for a term** bailor mit Rückforderungsrecht nach Ablauf e-r bestimmten Frist; ~ **at will** bailor mit jederzeitigem Rückforderungsrecht

balance (bal., blce) 1. *(allgemein)* Bilanz; **adverse** ~ Unterbilanz; **favo(u)rable** ~ aktive Bilanz, Aktivbilanz; **rough** (or **trial**) ~ Rohbilanz, Probebilanz; **unfavo(u)rable** ~ passive Bilanz, Passivbilanz; **to strike a** ~ die Bilanz ziehen
balance sheet *(aufgestellte)* Bilanz; ~ **accounting** Bilanzbuchhaltung; ~ **analysis** Bilanzanalyse; ~ **audit** Bilanzprüfung; ~ **of a bank** Bankbilanz; ~ **book** Bilanzbuch; Inventarbuch; ~ **for fiscal year** *Am* Jahresbilanz; ~ **item** Bilanzposten; ~ **total** Bilanzsumme; Bilanzvolumen; ~ **value** Bilanzwert

balance sheet, annual ~ Jahresbilanz (as at per); Jahresabschluß; **presentation of the annual** ~ Vorlage des Jahresabschlusses

balance sheet, as appearing on the ~ bilanzmäßig; **approval of the** ~ Genehmigung der Bilanz; **closing** ~ Schlußbilanz; **commercial** ~ Handelsbilanz; **consolidated** ~ *(bei Konzerngesellschaften)* konsolidierte (od. gemeinsame) Bilanz; **date of** ~ Bilanzstichtag; **extract from** ~ Bilanzauszug; **faking of the** ~ Bilanzverschleierung; **group** ~ Konzernbilanz; **item of the** ~ Bilanzposten; **first** (or **opening**) ~ Eröffnungsbilanz; **to audit the** ~ die Bilanz prüfen; **to draw up** (or **make up, prepare**) **the** ~ die Bilanz aufstellen; den Rechnungsabschluß machen

balance 2. *(Volkswirtschaft)* Bilanz *(s. ~ of payments);* ~ **of capital transactions** Kapitalbilanz; ~ **on current account** (i. e. of goods and services) Leistungsbilanz

balance of payments (BOP) Zahlungsbilanz *(Gegenüberstellung sämtl. Soll- und Habenposten im zwischenstaatl. Zahlungsverkehr e-s Landes im Laufe e-s Jahres);* ~ **on current account** Leistungsbilanz; ~ **deficit** Zahlungsbilanzdefizit; Passivsaldo der Zahlungsbilanz; ~ **in disequilibrium** unausgeglichene Zahlungsbilanz; ~ **equilibrium** Zahlungsbilanzgleichgewicht; ~ **surplus** Zahlungsbilanzüberschuß; Aktivsaldo der Zahlungsbilanz; **to reduce the surplus in the** ~ den Zahlungsbilanzüberschuß abbauen; **gap in the** ~ Zahlungsbilanzlücke

balance, ~ **of invisible payments** Bilanz der unsichtbaren Leistungen; ~ **of service transaction** Dienstleistungsbilanz

balance of trade Handelsbilanz; **adverse** ~ passive Handelsbilanz; **favo(u)rable** ~ aktive Handelsbilanz; **surplus in the** ~ Aktivsaldo der Handelsbilanz; Handelsbilanzüberschuß

balance of transfer payments Bilanz der unentgeltlichen Leistungen

balance 3. (Rechnungs-)Abschluß; Saldo; Rest (-betrag); Guthaben; Gleichgewicht; Kontostand; ~ **account** Ausgleichskonto; ~ **of an account** Restbetrag e-r Rechnung; ~ **on an account** Kontenstand; ~ **on current account** Kontokorrentguthaben; **what is the** ~ **on my account?** wie ist mein Kontostand? ~ **brought forward** (B/F) **(from last account)** Vortrag aus letzter Rechnung, Saldovortrag; ~ **carried forward (to new account)** Vortrag auf neue Rechnung, Saldovortrag; ~ **in cash** Ausgleichssumme; Barguthaben; ~ **of commitment** Lieferpflichtsaldo; ~ **standing to my (your) credit** mein (Ihr) gegenwärtiges Guthaben; ~ **of debt** Restschuld; ~ **deficit** Verlustabschluß; ~ **due** Debetsaldo; geschuldeter Restbetrag; Restschuld; ~ **in your favo(u)r** Saldo zu Ihren Gunsten; ~ **in** (or **on**) **hand** Barbestand; Kassenbestand; Kassensaldo; ~ **order** *Br* Anordnung der Zahlungsaufforderung an Aktienzeichner *(im Falle der Liquidation der Gesellschaft);* ~ **of power** *pol* Gleichgewicht der Kräfte; politisches Gleichgewicht; Machtverhältnis; ~ **of profit** Restgewinn; ~ **of purchase price** Restkaufgeld; ~ **reconcilement** Saldenabstimmung; ~ **reparting** *Am* Darstellung von Kontoinformationen; elektronischer Kontoauszug e-s →cash management system

balance, actual ~ Istbestand, Effektivbestand *(an Wechseln, Wertpapieren etc);* **bank** ~ Bankguthaben; **clearing** ~ Verrechnungssaldo; **credit** ~ Habensaldo, Kreditsaldo; Guthaben; Gewinnabschluß; **debit** (or **due**) ~ Sollsaldo, Debetsaldo; Verlustabschluß; **on** ~ per Saldo; **outstanding** ~ ausstehender Restbetrag; **sufficient** ~ ausreichendes Guthaben; **to carry the** ~ **forward (to new account)** den Saldo (auf neue Rechnung) vortragen; **to have a** ~ **in one's favo(u)r** e-e Summe (od. e-n Betrag) guthaben; **to pay the** ~ den Restbetrag bezahlen; **a** ~ **of . . . is shown** als Saldo ergibt sich ein Betrag von . . .; **to restore the** ~ das Gleichgewicht wiederherstellen; **to strike a** ~ den Saldo ziehen

balance *v* saldieren; *(Saldo)* ausgleichen; *(Konten, Bücher)* abschließen; ausgeglichen sein; **to** ~ **an account** ein Konto ausgleichen (od. saldieren); e-e Rechnung abschließen; **to** ~ **accounts** abrechnen, die Abrechnung machen; **to** ~ **the books** die Bücher abschließen; die Bilanz aufstellen; **to** ~ **the budget** den (Staats-)Haushalt ausgleichen; **to** ~ **the cash** Kasse(nsturz) machen; **to** ~ **the ledger** das Hauptbuch saldieren; **the expenses** ~ **the receipts** die Ausgaben und Einnahmen decken sich; **the account** ~**s** die Rechnung stimmt

balanced ausgeglichen; ausgewogen; ~ **budget** ausgeglichener (Staats-)Haushalt; ~ **fund** gemischter (Investment-)Fonds *(je zur Hälfte aus Aktien und Schuldverschreibungen);* ~ **trade** ausgeglichener Handelsverkehr

balancing Saldieren, Saldierung; (Konten-, Bücher-)Abschluß; Ausgleich; ~ **amount** Ausgleichsbetrag; **annual** ~ **of the books** Jahresabschluß der Bücher; ~ **of the cash account** Kassenabschluß; ~ **of equities** Ausgleich zwischen verschiedenen Billigkeitsgesichtspunkten; ~ **of interests** Abwägung der Interessen; ~ **of portfolio** *(VersR)* Risikoausgleich; **in** ~ **our accounts** (or **books**) beim Abschluß unserer Bücher

bale Ballen; ~ **cargo** Ballenladung; ~ **of cotton** Ballen Baumwolle; ~ **goods** Güter in Ballen; Ballenware; **in** ~**s** ballenweise

ballast Ballastladung; **in** ~ (or **carrying** ~ **only**) nur mit Ballast geladen

ballasting Ballasteinnahme

ballistic missile Raketengeschoß, (Fernlenk-)-Rakete; **B~ M~s Early Warning System** (BMEWS) Frühwarnsystem; → **Intercontinental B~ M~**

balloon *v Am (Kurse)* in die Höhe treiben

ballot *(meist geheime)* Wahl (od. Abstimmung); Wahlzettel, Stimmzettel; Wahlgang; *(abgegebene)* Stimmen; ~ **box** Wahlurne; ~ **paper** Wahlzettel, Stimmzettel; Abstimmungskarte; **blank ~ paper** leerer Stimmzettel
ballot, additional ~ Stichwahl; **by** ~ durch Abstimmung; **defeat in the** ~ Wahlniederlage; **election by (secret)** ~ geheime Wahl; **the election is by (secret)** ~ die Wahl ist geheim; **the election of the president takes place by (secret)** ~ der Präsident wird in geheimer Abstimmung gewählt
ballot, final ~ Stichwahl; **at the first** ~ im ersten Wahlgang
ballot, second ~ zweiter Wahlgang; Stichwahl; **a second ~ is held** ein zweiter Wahlgang findet statt; **to hold a second** ~ zum zweiten Wahlgang schreiten
ballot, (secret) ~ geheime Abstimmung; **voting by (secret)** ~ geheime Abstimmung; **the vote shall be by (secret)** ~ die Abstimmung erfolgt in geheimer Wahl
ballot, to cast a ~e-n Stimmzettel abgeben; **to elect by secret** ~ in geheimer Abstimmung wählen; **to request a** ~ e-e Abstimmung beantragen; **to take a** ~ (or **to vote by** ~) in geheimer Wahl (od. durch Stimmzettel) abstimmen

ballot *v (geheim od. durch Stimmzettel)* abstimmen, wählen; **to ~ for a candidate** *Am* für e-n Kandidaten stimmen; e-n Kandidaten wählen
balloting geheime Abstimmung; Wahl durch Stimmzettel

Baltic (Mercantile and Shipping) Exchange Londoner See- und Flugfrachtenbörse und Kornbörse
Baltic and International Maritime Conference (BIMCO) Schiffahrtskonferenz der Trampschiffahrt (→*conference 2.*)
Baltic Sea Ostsee; **States of the ~ basin** Ostseeanliegerstaaten

ban *(bes. amtliches)* Verbot (on gegen); Sperre; ~ **on arms** Waffen(ausfuhr)verbot; ~ **on competition** Wettbewerbsverbot; ~ **on export** Verbot der Ausfuhr; ~ **on immigration** Einwanderungsverbot, Einwanderungssperre; ~ **on delivery (of)** Liefersperre; **import** ~ Einfuhrverbot; **to lift a** ~ ein Verbot aufheben; **to place a ~ on** ein Verbot (od. e-e Sperre) verhängen über

ban *v (amtl.)* verbieten; e-e Sperre verhängen über; **to ~ a play** ein Theaterstück verbieten

Bandung-Conference *pol* Bandung-Konferenz; **Countries of the** ~ Bandung-Staaten

In Bandung auf Java erklärten 1955 23 asiatische und 6 afrikanische Staaten unter Teilnahme Chinas ihren Willen zur Selbstbestimmung, verurteilten Kolonialismus und Rassendiskriminierung

Bangladesh Bangladesh; **People's Republic of** ~ Volksrepublik Bangladesh; **(of)** ~ Bangladescher(in), bangladeschisch
Bangladeshi Bangladescher(in), bangladeschisch

bank 1. Bank, Bankhaus; ~ **acceptance** Bankakzept *(von e-r Bank akzeptierter Wechsel)*
bank account Bankkonto; **to open a** ~ ein Bankkonto eröffnen (od. errichten)
bank, ~ **accountant** Bankbuchhalter; **B~ Act** *Br* Bankgesetz *(auf ihm beruht der Aufbau der B~ of England)*; ~ **annuities** *Br* Konsols, konsolidierte Staatsanleihen; ~ **auditing** Bankrevision; ~ **balance** Bankguthaben, Banksaldo; Kontostand bei e-r Bank; ~ **bill** Bankwechsel; *Am* Banknote; ~ **book** Bankbuch; Sparbuch *(auch für Postsparkasse)*; ~ **burglary insurance** Bankeinbruchsversicherung; ~ **card** *Am* „Bankkarte" *(Karte, um Geld am Geldautomaten abzuheben od. einzuzahlen)* ~ **charges** Bankkosten, Bankgebühren; ~ **charter** Konzessionsurkunde e-r Bank; ~ **check** *Am* Bankscheck *(von e-r Bank auf sich selbst oder bei besonderer Vereinbarung auf e-e andere Bank gezogener Scheck)*; ~ **of circulation** Notenbank; ~ **clerk** Bankangestellte(r); (~) →**code number;** ~ **credit** Bankkredit; ~ **credit card** *(von e-r Bank ausgegebene)* Kundenkreditkarte; ~ **crisis** Bankenkrise; ~ **customer** Bankkunde; ~ **deposit** Bankeinlage (→ *demand deposit,* →*time deposit*); ~ **of deposit** Depositenbank; ~ **discount** Bankdiskont; ~ **of discount** Diskontbank; ~ **draft** *Am* Bankwechsel, Banktratte *(von einer Bank auf ihr Konto bei einer anderen Bank gezogene Tratte)*
Bank of England Bank von England (Zentralnotenbank); ~ **Return** *(wöchentl.)* Ausweis der Bank of England
Gegründet 1694 als private Aktienbank, 1946 verstaatlicht und dem Schatzamt unterstellt *(cf. Banking Department, Issue Department)*
bank, ~ **failure** Bankkrach, Bankzusammenbruch; ~ **giro** Banküberweisung im bargeldlosen Zahlungsverkehr; ~ **guarantee (guaranty)** Bankgarantie, Bankbürgschaft
bank holidays Bankfeiertage
Br 1. Jan., Ostermontag, letzter Montag im Mai, letzter Montag im August, 25. und 26. Dezember. *Am* 1. Jan., 22. Febr., 30. Mai, 4. Juli, 1. Montag im Sept., 1. Dienstag im Nov., letzter Donnerstag im Nov., 25. Dez.
bank, ~ **identification number** *Am* Bankleitzahl; ~ **inquiry** Bankauskunft; ~ **interest** Bankzinsen
Bank for International Settlements (B. I. S.)[3] Bank für Internationalen Zahlungsausgleich (B. I. Z.)
1930 von den Zentralbanken Belgiens, Deutschlands,

Frankreichs, Großbritanniens, Italiens, Japans (hat 1951 auf sämtl. Rechte verzichtet) und der Schweiz eröffnete Aktienbank, zu der auch eine Gruppe von Banken in USA gehören. Im Ggs. zu → IMF und → IBRD eine im wesentl. europäische Einrichtung. Sitz: Basel.
Aufgabe: Förderung der internationalen Zusammenarbeit der Zentralbanken und des Internationalen Zahlungsausgleichs. Kreditgewährung im Rahmen des → EMA (Agent des → European Fund)

bank, ~ **of issue** Notenbank; Emissionsbank; ~ **liquidity** Bankenliquidität; ~ **loan** Bankkredit, Bankdarlehen; ~ **manager** Bankdirektor; ~ **money** Giralgeld, Buchgeld

bank note Banknote, Papiergeld; **counterfeiting** (or **forging**) **of** ~**s** Banknotenfälschung; ~ **printing** Banknotendruck

bank, ~ **official** Bankbeamter, -beamtin; Bankangestellte(r); ~ **paper** Bankpapier, Bankwechsel *(opp. trade paper);* ~ **pass book** Bankbuch, Sparbuch; ~ **place** Bankplatz; ~ **post bill** (BPB, b. p. b.) *Br* Bankpostwechsel *(Solawechsel der Bank von England);* ~ **premises** Bankgebäude und -grundstücke

bank rate Diskontsatz *(e-r Notenbank; Am → rediscount rate);* ~ **for loans** Lombardsatz; **increase in the** ~ s. raising of the →~; **lowering of the** ~ Diskontherabsetzung, Diskontsenkung; **raising of the** ~ Diskonterhöhung, Erhöhung des Diskontsatzes; **reduction in the** ~ s. lowering of the →~; **to lower** (or **reduce**) **the** ~ den Diskontsatz senken; **to increase** (or **raise**) **the** ~ den Diskontsatz erhöhen

bank, ~ **raid** Überfall auf e-e Bank, Banküberfall, Bankraub; ~ **receipt** Bankquittung; ~ **records** Bankbelege; ~ **reference** Bankauskunft; ~ **return** *Br* Bankausweis; ~ **robbery** Bankraub, Banküberfall; ~ **roll** Bündel Banknoten; ~**roll** *v Am* finanzieren; ~ **routing number** *Am* Bankleitzahl; ~ **secrecy** Bankgeheimnis; ~ **share** Bankaktie; ~ **statement** Bankauszug, Kontoauszug; *Am* Bankausweis; ~ **stock** Bankkapital, Aktienkapital e-r Bank; *Br bes.* Kapital der Bank of England; ~ **supervision** Bank(en)aufsicht; ~ **supervisory authority** Bank(en)aufsichtsbehörde; ~ **teller** Bankkassierer; ~ **transfer** Banküberweisung; ~ **underwriting syndicate** Bankübernahmekonsortium; ~ **vault** Banktresor; ~ **window** Bankschalter; ~ **withdrawal** Bankabhebung

bank, big ~ Großbank; **branch** ~ Filialbank, Bankfiliale; **cash at** ~ Bankguthaben; →**central** ~; **clearing** ~ →clearing 1.; **commercial** ~ Geschäftsbank *(betreibt im wesentlichen das Depositen- und Darlehensgeschäft);* **cooperative** ~ genossenschaftliches Kreditinstitut; **correspondent** ~ Korrespondenzbank; **country** ~ Provinzbank; **credit** ~ Kreditbank; **credit at the** ~ Bankkredit; **customer of a** ~ Bankkunde; **deposit** ~ Depositenbank; **deposit in a** ~ Einlage bei e-r Bank; Depositenguthaben; **discount** ~ Diskontbank; → **Federal Reserve B**~**s; group of** ~**s** Bankengruppe; →**Home B**~; →**International B**~ **for Reconstruction and Development; investment** ~ *Am* Investmentbank *(keine Bank im deutschen Sinne, sondern Wertpapierhändler; opp. commercial →~);* **joint stock** ~ *Br* Aktienbank; **loan** ~ *Br* Darlehnskasse, Kreditanstalt; **member** ~ *Am* Mitgliedsbank des → Federal Reserve System; **merchant** ~ *Br* Handelsbank; **multiple office** ~ Bank mit mehreren Geschäftsstellen; **National B**~**s** *Am* Nationalbanken *(unter Bundesaufsicht stehende Banken; opp. State B~s);* **private** ~ Privatbank; **rules and regulations of a** ~ allgemeine Geschäftsbedingungen e-r Bank; **run on a** ~ Ansturm auf e-e Bank; **savings** ~ Sparkasse; **savings** ~ **pass book** Bankssparbuch; **single office** ~ Bank mit nur einem Geschäftslokal; **State B**~**s** *Am* Staatsbanken *(unter Aufsicht der Einzelstaaten stehende Banken; opp. National B~s);* **unit** ~ *Am* filiallose Bank; Bank ohne Zweigstelle; **to have** (or **keep**) **money in** (or **at**) **a** ~ Geld auf e-r Bank (stehen) haben; **to direct** (or **instruct**) **a** ~ **to remit money** e-e Bank anweisen, Geld zu überweisen; **to open an account at a** ~ ein Bankkonto eröffnen; **to pay money into a** ~ Geld bei e-r Bank einzahlen; **to pay a p. through a** ~ jdm Geld durch e-e Bank anweisen; **to remit** (or **pay**) **money through a** ~ Geld durch e-e Bank überweisen

bank 2. (Spiel-)Bank; **blood** ~ Blutbank *(für Krankenhäuser);* **to break the** ~ die Bank sprengen

bank *v (Geld)* auf die Bank bringen, bei der Bank einzahlen; Bankkonto haben (with bei); Bankgeschäfte machen; mit e-r Bank arbeiten

bankable bankfähig; diskontierbar; ~ **securities** bankmäßige Sicherheiten

banker Bankier; ~**s** Bankleute; ~**'s acceptance** Bankakzept; bankgirierter Warenwechsel; →**eligible** ~**s' acceptance; B**~**s' Almanac and Year Book** *Br* Nachschlagewerk für alle wichtigen Banken der Welt; ~**'s bill** Bankwechsel; ~**'s cheque (check)** Bankscheck *(von e-r Bank auf e-e andere Bank gezogener Scheck);* ~**'s correspondent (abroad)** (ausländische) Bankverbindung; befreundetes Kreditinstitut *(im Ausland);* ~**'s deposit rate** Zinssatz für Depositengelder; ~**'s discount** Bankdiskont; ~**'s discretion** Bankgeheimnis; ~**'s draft** *Br* Bankscheck *(von Zweigstelle e-r Bank auf Hauptverwaltung od. andere Zweigstelle gezogene Zahlungsanweisung);* ~**'s duty of secrecy** Bankgeheimnis

banker's order *Br* Zahlungsauftrag *(e-s Kunden)* an e-e Bank; Dauerauftrag *(an Bank);* **to give a** ~ **to pay** die Bank anweisen, zu zahlen; **to pay by** ~ *(Geld)* durch die Bank überweisen

banker, ~'s reference Bankauskunft; **~'s rule** *Br* goldene Bankregel *(zur Aufrechterhaltung der Liquidität);* **~'s ticket** (on dishono[u]red bill) Rückrechnung *(beim Wechselregreß);* **~'s transfer** Banküberweisung

banking Bankwesen; Bankgeschäft(e); Bankverkehr
B~ Act 1979 *Br* Bankgesetz
Gesetzliche Regelung des britischen Bankwesens und der staatlichen Bankenaufsicht durch die →Bank of England
banking, ~ activity Banktätigkeit; **to be in ~** im Bankfach arbeiten
banking business Bankgeschäft(e); Bankwesen; Bankfach; **in ~** im Bankverkehr; **to do ~** Bankgeschäfte machen
banking, ~ circles Bankkreise; **~ commission** Bankprovision; **~ connection** Bankverbindung; **~ credit** Bankkredit; **~ custom** Bankusancen; **B~ Department** Abteilung für Bankgeschäfte *(der → Bank of England);* **~ doctrine** *Br* Auffassung, nach der nur ⅓ Dekkung durch Edelmetall für umlaufende Banknoten vorhanden sein muß *(opp. currency doctrine);* **~ establishment** →~ firm; **~ facilities** Bankfazilitäten; **~ failure** Bankzusammenbruch, Bankkrach; **~ firm** Bank(haus); **supplementary ~ functions** irreguläre Bankgeschäfte; **~ hours** Geschäftsstunden *(e-r Bank);* Schalterstunden; **~ house** Bank(-haus); **the ~ interests** die Bankkreise; **~ licence** *(EG)* Bankzulassung
banking line Bankfach; **to be in the ~** im Bankfach tätig sein
banking, ~ matters Bankangelegenheiten; **~ operation** *(das einzelne durchgeführte)* Bankgeschäft; **~ principle** (or **theory**) →~ doctrine; **~ secrecy** Bankgeheimnis; **~ services** Bank(dienst)leistungen; **~ statistics** Bankstatistik; bankstatistische Erhebungen; **~ supervision** Bankenaufsicht; **~ system** Banksystem; Bankwesen; **~ transaction** →~ operation
banking, branch ~ Filialbanksystem; **chain ~** *Am* Kettenbanksystem; Banken mit vielen Zweigstellen; **commercial ~**[4] Einlagen- und Kreditgeschäft der Banken *(opp. investment ~)*; **group ~** *Am* Bankengruppensystem; →**home ~**; **investment ~** Wertpapiergeschäft der Banken *(opp. commercial ~)*; **merchant ~** Großkundengeschäft der Banken; **public supervision of ~** Bank(en)aufsicht; **wholesale ~** Bankgeschäfte mit großen Unternehmen
banking, engaged in ~ im Bankgeschäft tätig

bankrupt Konkursschuldner, Gemeinschuldner; Bankrotteur; Zahlungsunfähiger; in Konkurs (befindlich); bankrott; zahlungsunfähig; **~'s →assets**
bankrupt's creditor Konkursgläubiger; **schedule of the ~s** Konkurstabelle
bankrupt's estate (or **property**) Konkursmasse; **administration of a ~** Konkursverwaltung, Masseverwaltung; **division** (or **distribution**) **of a ~** Ausschüttung e-r Konkursmasse; **trustee of a ~** →trustee in bankruptcy; **to divide** (or **distribute**) **a ~** e-e Konkursmasse ausschütten
bankrupt, creditor of a ~ Konkursgläubiger; **discharge of a ~** Entlastung e-s Gemeinschuldners *(von künftiger Haftung bezügl. der unbezahlt gebliebenen Schulden);* **undischarged ~** (noch) nicht entlasteter Gemeinschuldner; **to adjudicate** (or **adjudge**) **the debtor (a) ~** das Konkursverfahren über das Vermögen des Schuldners eröffnen; **to become (a)** (or *colloq.* **to go**) **~** in Konkurs geraten; Bankrott machen

bankruptcy Konkurs; Bankrott
Bankruptcy Act 1914 *Br* Konkursordnung
Bis zum Inkrafttreten des →Insolvency Act 1985 wurde das Konkursverfahren von natürlichen Personen, Einzelkaufleuten und Personengesellschaften durch den Bankruptcy Act geregelt
Bankruptcy Code of 1978, as amended *Am*[5] Konkursgesetz *(einschließlich →reorganization)*
Zusätzliche Bestimmungen finden sich in The Bankruptcy Act of 1978, in Bankruptcy Amendments and Federal Judgeship Act of 1984 und anderen Gesetzen. Diese zusätzlichen Bestimmungen betreffen Zuständigkeit der Konkursgerichte, Ernennung der Konkursrichter usw., also nicht das eigentliche materielle Konkursrecht.
Das Konkursrecht der Vereinigten Staaten gilt für juristische wie für natürliche Personen. Der Konkurs hat (mit gewissen Ausnahmen) Streichung aller Schulden zur Folge
bankruptcy, ~ bond Kaution des Konkursverwalters; **~ court** Konkursgericht; **~ creditor** Konkursgläubiger; **~ of a decedent's estate** *Am* Nachlaßkonkurs; **~ law** Konkursrecht; Konkursgesetz; **~ notice** *(gerichtl.)* Zahlungsaufforderung mit Konkursandrohung; Konkurserklärung; befristete Aufforderung des Gläubigers an den Gemeinschuldner, der Zahlungspflicht nachzukommen; **~ offence (~se)** Konkursdelikt; **~ petition** Konkursantrag (→ *petition in ~*)
bankruptcy proceedings Konkursverfahren; **commencement** (or **initiation, institution**) **of ~** Eröffnung des Konkursverfahrens, Konkurseröffnung; **maliciously taking proceedings in bankruptcy** böswillige Einleitung des Konkursverfahrens; **termination of ~** Konkursbeendigung (Aufhebung od. Einstellung des Konkursverfahrens); **to apply for ~** Antrag auf Eröffnung des Konkursverfahrens stellen; **to initiate** (or **institute**) **~** den Konkurs (od. das Konkursverfahren) eröffnen; **to terminate ~** den Konkurs aufheben (od. einstellen)

bankruptcy, act of ~ Konkurshandlung, Konkursgrund; **adjudication of ~** Konkurseröffnung(sbeschluß); Konkursanmeldung; Bankrotterklärung; **discharge in ~** s. discharge of a →bankrupt; **dividend in ~** Konkursquote; **fraudulent ~** betrügerischer Konkurs; **involuntary ~** *Am* unfreiwilliger Konkurs *(Anmeldung durch den Gläubiger)*; **law of ~** → ~ law; **matter of ~** Konkurssache; **national ~** Staatsbankrott; **petition in ~** → petition 2.

bankruptcy, proceedings in ~ →~ proceedings; **referee in ~** *Am* Konkursrichter *(Berichterstatter für das Konkursgericht)*; **trustee in ~** *(von Gläubigern ernannter)* Konkursverwalter (→ *trustee)*; **voluntary ~** *Am* freiwilliger Konkurs *(Anmeldung durch den Schuldner)*

bankruptcy, to commit an act of ~ e-n Konkursgrund liefern; **to serve a ~ notice on sb.** jdm e-e Konkurserklärung zustellen lassen

banner Transparent *(für Werbung, Demonstration)*

banns (of marriage) *(kirchl.)* Aufgebot *(vor der Eheschließung)*; **publication of the ~** Erlaß des Aufgebots; **to have one's ~ called** sich aufbieten lassen; **to forbid the ~** gegen die Eheschließung Einspruch erheben; **to publish the ~** *(Brautpaar)* aufbieten

baptism Taufe; **~ register** Taufregister; **certificate of ~** Taufschein

baptismal name Taufname

bar 1. Schranke *(im Gerichtssaal)*; das *(tagende)* Gericht; **the B~** die Anwaltschaft *(Br der barristers)*

Bar Association *Am* Anwaltsverein(igung)
Bundes- und einzelstaatliche Berufsvereinigung der Rechtsanwälte, zu der auch Industriesyndici, Universitätsprofessoren etc gehören

Bar Council (General Council of the Bar) *Br* Organ der Standesvertretung der →barristers
Überwacht Standes- und Ehrenfragen der barristers *(cf. Law Society)*

bar exam *Am* →bar examination

bar, ~ examination Anwaltsprüfung; **B~ of Scotland** →Faculty of Advocates; **admission to the B~** Zulassung zur (Rechts-)Anwaltschaft *(Br als barrister)*

bar, at the ~ vor Gericht; **case at ~** *Am* zur Verhandlung stehender Fall; **prisoner at the ~** Angeklagter; **trial at ~** Verhandlung vor dem Gericht in vollständiger Besetzung; **to plead at the ~** vor Gericht plädieren

Bar, the Bench and the ~ Richter und Anwälte *(Br barristers)*; **call(ing) to the ~** *Br* Zulassung zur (Rechts-)Anwaltschaft *(als barrister)*; **International ~ Association** (IBA) Internationale Anwaltsvereinigung; **Patent ~** Patentanwaltschaft

Bar, to be admitted to the ~ *Am* als (Rechts-)Anwalt zugelassen werden; **to call to the ~** *Br* als Anwalt *(barrister)* zulassen; **to go to the ~** *Br* Rechtsanwalt *(barrister)* werden; **to read for the ~** *Br* Jura studieren *(um barrister zu werden)*

bar 2. Hindernis; Ausschluß; **~ period** *Am* Ausschlußfrist; **~ to marriage** Ehehindernis; **~ to patentability** Patenthindernis; **~ to registration** Eintragungshindernis; **colo(u)r ~** Rassenschranke; **to constitute a ~ as to novelty** *(PatR)* neuheitsschädlich sein

bar 3. Barren *(Gold, Silber)*; Riegel, Querbalken; **~ gold** Barrengold; **~ of gold** Goldbarren; **~ to a medal** Ordensspange

bar *v* hemmen, hindern (from an); verbieten, untersagen, ausschließen; verriegeln; (ab)sperren; **to ~ a p. from** jdn ausschließen von; jdm den Zutritt versagen; **to ~ a right** ein Recht ausschließen

barred, ~ by limitation (or **under the Statutes of Limitation**) verjährt; →**statute-~**

Barbadian Barbadier(in); barbadisch

Barbados Barbados

Barclaycard *Br* Kreditkarte von Barclay's Bank

bare bloß; nackt; dürftig, arm; **~ majority of votes** einfache Stimmenmehrheit; **~ necessities of life** notwendiger Lebensbedarf

bareboat charter Chartern (od. Miete) e-s bloßen Schiffskörpers *(ohne Ausrüstung und Bemannung)*

bargain Handel, Geschäftsabschluß; Vereinbarung, Übereinkunft; *(vorteilhaftes)* Geschäft; Gelegenheitskauf, „Gelegenheit"; günstiges Kaufobjekt, preisgünstige Sache; billige Ware; *(Londoner Börse) (einzelner)* Abschluß; **~ for account** *Br (Börse)* Termingeschäft; **~ for cash** *(Börse)* (or **money**) Barabschluß; **~ counter** Ladentisch mit Sonderangeboten; **~s done** *(Börse)* vollzogene Abschlüsse (oder Umsätze); **~ penny** *Am* Draufgeld, Handgeld; **~ price** besonders günstiger Preis; Gelegenheitspreis; *Am* Ausverkaufspreis; **~ sale** Verkauf zu herabgesetzten Preisen; (Ramsch-)Ausverkauf; *Am* Sonderangebot; **~ sales advertising** *Am* Werbung für Sonderangebote; **~ and sale** *Am* Kaufvertrag *(bes. bei Grundstücksverkäufen)*; **bad ~** schlechtes Geschäft; **chance ~** Gelegenheitskauf; **conclusion of a ~** Geschäftsabschluß; **good ~** guter Kauf; vorteilhaftes Geschäft; **into the ~** als Zugabe (od. Beigabe); obendrein; **time ~** *Br (Börse)* Termingeschäft; **to make** (or **strike**) **a ~ with sb.** (over sth.) mit jdm e-n Handel (od. ein Geschäft) abschließen (über); mit jdm handelseinig werden

bargain *v* verhandeln, übereinkommen (for über), handeln; zur Bedingung machen (that daß); **to ~ for sth.** etw. aushandeln; um etw. feilschen; **to ~ away** *(bes. mit Verlust)* verkaufen; billig abgeben; **to ~ collectively** e-n Tarifvertrag aushandeln; über e-n Kollektivvertrag verhandeln; **right to ~ collectively** Recht zu Kollektivverhandlungen

bargaining Verhandeln; Handeln; Aushandeln, Feilschen; **~ agent** Verhandlungspartner *(bei Tarifverhandlungen)*; **strong ~ position** starke Verhandlungsposition; **~ power** Verhandlungsstärke; **exclusive ~ representatives** *Am* Arbeitnehmervertretung für Tarifverhandlungen; **~ right** *Am* Recht zu Kollektivverhandlungen; **~ unit** *Am* Verhandlungseinheit *(tariffähige Partei) (e-s Betriebes)* zur Aufnahme von Tarifverhandlungen mit Arbeitgeber(n); **collective ~** Tarifverhandlung(en) (→*collective*)

barge Schute; Leichter; **~ operator** Partikulier

bargainor Verkäufer *(Am cf. bargain and sale)*

Baronet (Bt.) *Br* Baronet

Nicht zur Oberhausmitgliedschaft berechtigtes Mitglied des niederen Adels. Baronets bilden mit den Knights die Klasse des Gentry *(cf. nobility)*. Anrede: Sir (Sir A. B., Bt.)

barrack Baracke; **~s** Kaserne; **confinement to ~s** (C.B.) Kasernenarrest; **to be confined to ~s** Kasernenarrest haben

barrack *v* in Kasernen (od. Baracken) unterbringen

barrage Talsperre; *mil* Sperrfeuer

barrator Querulant, Prozeßstifter; jd, der → barratry begeht

barratry 1. *(SeeversR)* Baratterie, betrügerische Handlungen e-s Schiffskapitäns *(zum Schaden des Reeders od. der Ladungsbeteiligten)*

barratry 2., **(common)** ~ *(gewohnheitsmäßiges)* schikanöses Prozessieren

barrel Faß, Tonne; Barrel *(Hohlmaß)*; **goods in ~s** Faßwaren; **1 ~ of oil** eine Tonne Öl (158,97 l)

barrelled in ein Faß gefüllt

barren unfruchtbar; unproduktiv, wertlos; **~ land** nicht anbaufähiges Land *(opp. arable land)*; **~ money** (or **capital**) totes Kapital

barrier Schranke; Hindernis; Schlagbaum; **~s blocking imports** Einfuhrhindernisse; **~s to trade** (or **trade ~s**) Handelshemmnisse; **to remove** (or **abolish**) **~s to trade** Handelshemmnisse beseitigen

barring abgesehen von, ausgenommen; **~ clause** Sperrfristklausel; **~ errors** Irrtümer vorbehalten

barrister *(voller Titel:* **~-at-law**) *Br* Barrister, *(plädierender)* Rechtsanwalt *(cf. counsel)* →**utter~; to call a ~ to the bar** e-n Barrister zulassen *(cf. Inns of Court)*

Die barristers (diejenigen, die vor der → Bar stehen) bilden in England den höheren Anwaltsstand gegenüber den solicitors. Der barrister hat das ausschließliche Recht, bei öffentlichen Verhandlungen vor höheren Gerichten aufzutreten (aber kein Anwaltszwang!). Er wird nicht durch den Mandanten, sondern durch den solicitor beauftragt.

Die Ausbildung und Zulassung erfolgt durch die → Inns of Court. Die wichtigsten Richterposten werden durch die barristers besetzt.

Die Gebühren der barristers sind gesetzlich nicht geregelt. Der General Council of the Bar hat gewisse Richtlinien erlassen

barter Tausch(handel); **~ deal** (or **transaction**) Tauschgeschäft; *(Außenhandel)* Bartergeschäft, Kompensationsgeschäft; **~ goods** Tauschwaren; **pure ~** zeitgleicher Tausch von Güter- und/oder Dienstleistungen zwischen zwei Parteien ohne Verwendung von Devisen; **trade by ~** Tauschhandel

barter *v* tauschen (for, against gegen); **to ~ sth. away** etw. im Tausch weggeben, etw. (ein-)tauschen

base 1. Basis, Grundlage; *mil* Stützpunkt; **~ company** Basisgesellschaft *(Finanzzentrale für den ihr unterstellten Kreis von Gesellschaften in anderen Ländern)*; **~ date** Basisdatum *(Startpunkt für e-e Indexberechnung)*; **~ fee** auflösend bedingtes Eigentumsrecht an Grundstücken; **~s pact** Stützpunktabkommen; **~ period** Grundzeitraum; **~ of supplies** *mil* Nachschubbasis; **~ services** *mil* (Luftwaffen-)Bodendienste; **~ stock** eiserner Bestand; **~ year** Basisjahr

base, (air) ~ Luftwaffenstützpunkt; **naval ~** Flottenstützpunkt

base 2. gemein, niederträchtig; falsch, unecht; **~ coin** *Br* falsche Münze, Falschgeld; *Am* Scheidemünze; **~ metals** Nichtedelmetalle; **acting from ~ motives** aus niedrigen Beweggründen handelnd

base *v* (sich) gründen (on auf); aufbauen (on auf); **to be ~d on** beruhen (od. basieren) auf

basic grundlegend, fundamental; **~ agreement** *(ArbeitsR)* Rahmenvertrag; *Am* Manteltarifvertrag, Rahmentarifvertrag; **~ commodities** Grundstoffe, Rohstoffe; **~ contract** Hauptvertrag; **~ documents** →~ instruments; **~ fact** grundlegende Tatsache; **~ freedoms** Grundfreiheiten; **~ industry** Grund(stoff)industrie, Schlüsselindustrie; **~ instruments of the organization** *(VölkerR)* die für die (Tätigkeit der) Organisation maßgebenden Urkunden; **~ materials** Grundstoffe; Ausgangsstoffe; **~ objective** Grundziel; **~ patent** Basispatent; **~ pay** Grundlohn, Ecklohn; **~ premium** *(VersR)* Grundprämie; **~ price** Grundpreis; Basispreis; **~ rate** Grundlohn; *(VersR)* Grundprämie(nsatz); **~ rate of interest** Eckzins; **~ research** Grundlagenforschung; **~ rights**

Grundrechte; ~ **salary** Grundgehalt; ~ **standards** Grundnormen

basic term *Am (beim Leasing)* Grundmietzeit; ~ **leasing** Leasing-Vertrag, der während des basic leasing nicht gekündigt werden kann

basic, ~ and advanced training (Grund-)Ausbildung und Weiterbildung; ~ **wage** Grundlohn, Ecklohn

basing point system *Am* Frachtbasisausgangspunktsystem *(Preisberechnungsverfahren von e-r einheitlichen Versandbasis aus)*

basis (*pl.* bases) Basis, Grundlage; ~ **of (an) agreement** Vertragsgrundlage; ~ **of assessment** *(Einkommensteuer)* Bemessungsgrundlage; ~ **of calculation** Berechnungsgrundlage; ~ **of comparison** Vergleichsbasis; ~ **of discussion** Diskussionsgrundlage; ~ **point** $^1/_{100}$ eines Prozentes *(Devisenkurs, Zinssatz etc)*; ~ **price** Grundpreis; ~ **rates** Grundtarif; ~ **of valuation** Bewertungsgrundlage

basis, on the assessment ~ auf der Basis des Umlageverfahrens; **common** ~ gemeinsame Basis; **negotiation** ~ Verhandlungsgrundlage; **on a sound** ~ auf gesunder Grundlage; **to form** (or **lay**) **the** ~ **of** den Grund legen für; **to take as** ~ zugrundelegen

basket, →**currency** ~

bastard (child) *bes. Am* uneheliches Kind; unehelich

bastardize *Am (gerichtlich)* für unehelich erklären

bastardy uneheliche Geburt; Unehelichkeit; ~ **order** *Am* →affiliation order; ~ **proceedings** *Am* →affiliation proceedings

batch Schub, Gruppe *(gleicher Personen od. Sachen)*; Serie; ~ **of letters** Stapel Briefe; ~ **patent** Bündelpatent; ~ **processing** *(EDV)* Stapelverarbeitung *(opp. real time processing)*; ~ **production** Serien(an)fertigung, Reihenfertigung

Bath, Order of the ~ *Br* Bathorden *(der vierthöchste Orden; cf. knighthood)*

battered, ~ **child** durch Mißhandlung schwer geschädigtes Kind; ~ **wives** *(von ihren Männern)* mißhandelte Ehefrauen; ~ **wives house** Frauenhaus

battery *(tatsächl.)* Gewaltanwendung; Tätlichkeit; tätliche Beleidigung; Körperverletzung *(cf. assault and ~)*

battle of the forms *Br* Kampf der Formulare *(umschreibt die Verwendung einander widersprechender Angebots- und Annahmebedingungen)*

bawdy house Bordell

Bayer injunction *Br* gerichtl. Anordnung, die dem Beklagten das Verlassen Englands verbietet, bis er im Rahmen einer →Mareva injunction oder einer →Anton Piller order Fragen über sein Vermögen beantwortet sowie Dokumente freigegeben hat

bear *(Börse)* Baissespekulant, Baissier *(opp. bull)*; ~**s** *Am* fallende Kurse; ~**s** (or ~ **account**) *Br* Baisseposition; ~ **campaign** Angriff der Baissepartei; ~ **covering** Deckungskauf der Baissepartei; ~ **hug** Vorverhandlungen mit den Aktionären e-s Unternehmens zwecks Übernahmeangebot; ~ **market** (Börsen-)Baisse; ~ **operation** Baissespekulation; ~ **position** Baisseposition; ~ **sale** Leerverkauf; ~ **seller** Leerverkäufer, Baissespekulant; ~ **speculation** Baissespekulation; ~ **transaction** →~ operation; **to sell a** ~ auf Baisse spekulieren, fixen *(opp. to buy a bull)*

bear *v* 1. tragen, bringen; überbringen; ertragen; **to ~ (up)on** Bezug haben (od. sich beziehen) auf; **to ~ the costs** die Kosten tragen; **to ~ a date** datiert sein; **to ~ interest** Zinsen tragen (od. bringen); **to ~ a loss** e-n Verlust (er)tragen; **to ~ a name** e-n Namen tragen (od. führen); **to ~ the responsibility** die Verantwortung tragen; **to ~ out a statement** e-e Aussage bestätigen (od. bekräftigen); **to ~ false witness** falsches Zeugnis ablegen

bearing tragend; Betragen, Verhalten; Beziehung, Bezug; Tragweite, Bedeutung (on für); ~ **3 per cent** dreiprozentig; ~ **the date of** mit Datum von (→*date*); ~ **no interest** unverzinslich; ~ **in mind** in dem Bewußtsein; wenn man bedenkt (daß)

bear *v* 2. *(Börse)* auf Baisse spekulieren, fixen *(opp. to bull)*; **to ~ the market** die Kurse zu drücken versuchen, fixen

bearer Inhaber *(e-s Wertpapiers)*; Überbringer; ~ **of a bill** Wechselinhaber; ~ **bond** (or **bond payable to** ~) Inhaberobligation, Inhaberschuldverschreibung; ~ **certificate** Inhaberpapier; ~ **cheque (check)** Inhaberscheck; ~ **of a cheque (check)** Scheckinhaber; ~ **clause** Überbringerklausel; ~ **debenture** Inhaberschuldverschreibung; ~ **instrument** (or **instrument payable to** ~) Inhaberpapier; ~ **of a letter** Überbringer e-s Schreibens; ~ **of risk** Risikoträger; ~ **scrip** Interimsschein *(für e-e auf den Inhaber lautende Schuldverschreibung)*; ~ **securities** Inhaberpapiere *(Br cf. share warrants)*; ~ **share** Inhaberaktie; ~ **stock** *Am* Inhaberaktien; **cheque (check) to** ~ Inhaberscheck; **payable to** ~ zahlbar an den Überbringer; auf den Inhaber lautend; **share warrant to** ~ *Br* Inhaberaktienschein; **to make out to** ~ auf den Inhaber ausstellen

bearish (Börse) fallend, baisse-tendenziös *(opp. bullish)*; ~ **demonstration** Baisseangriff; ~ **market** fallende Börse; ~ **operation** (or

speculation) Baissespekulation; ~ **tendency** Baissetendenz

beat *v*, **to ~ down prices** Preise drücken (od. herunterhandeln); **to ~ a record** e-n Rekord schlagen

bed, ~ and board → board 3; ~ **and breakfast deal** nachbörslicher Verkauf von Aktien und Rückkauf am nächsten Morgen mit Verlust *(um aus steuerlichen Gründen gegen Gewinn aufzurechnen)*; **~sitter** Einzimmerwohnung

bedroom community (or **suburb**) *Am* Wohnvorort, Schlafstadt

before, ~ hours Vorbörse; vorbörslich *(opp. after hours)*; ~ **long** bald; ~ **witnesses** vor Zeugen; **the week ~ last** vorletzte Woche

beforehand im voraus; **he is always ~ with his rent** er bezahlt seine Miete immer im voraus *(vor Fälligkeit)*

beg *v* bitten um; erbitten, ersuchen; betteln; **I ~ to inform you** ich erlaube mir, Ihnen mitzuteilen; **to ~ leave** um Erlaubnis bitten; **to ~ the question** die strittige Frage als bewiesen annehmen

beggar Bettler *(cf. idle and disorderly person)*; **~-my neighbo(u)r policy** Abschieben wirtschaftlicher Lasten auf den Handelspartner

behalf, in ~ of *Am* im Interesse von; **on ~ of** im Interesse von, für, zugunsten von; im Namen von; **on ~ of a third party** für e-n Dritten; **to act on one's own ~** im eigenen Namen handeln

behavio(u)r Benehmen, Verhalten, Betragen; ~ **circumstance elements** *Am (StrafR)* Tatbestand; Sachverhalt; ~ **observation** *(Marktforschung)* Verhaltensbeobachtung; **during good ~** bei guter Führung; *Am (entspricht etwa:)* auf Lebenszeit

behavio(u)ral sciences Verhaltenswissenschaften *(z.B. Soziologie, Anthropologie, Staatswissenschaften, moderne Geschichte, Literatur, Sprachenkunde, Statistik)*

behavio(u)rist Verhaltensforscher

behind, to be ~ with one's payments mit s-n Zahlungen im Verzug sein; **to be ~ with one's work** mit s-r Arbeit im Rückstand sein

behindhand verspätet; *(hinter anderen)* zurückgeblieben; im (in) Rückstand; **to be ~ with the rent** mit der Miete im Rückstand sein; **to get ~ in one's work** mit s-r Arbeit in Rückstand kommen

being, for the time ~ gegenwärtig; **in ~** bestehend, tatsächlich vorhanden; **it ~ the case that** in Anbetracht des Umstandes, daß

belated claim *(VersR)* Spätschaden

Belgian Belgier(in); belgisch

Belgium Belgien; **Kingdom of ~** Königreich Belgien; **~-Luxembourg Economic Union** Belgisch-Luxemburgische Wirtschaftsunion (BLWU)[6]

belief Glaube, Überzeugung; **(religious) ~** Glaube, Konfession; **to the best of one's knowledge and ~** nach jds bestem Wissen und Gewissen; **upon information and ~** *Am* nach meinem besten Wissen und Unterrichtung *(auf Grund von mir zugegangenen Mitteilungen, die ich für richtig halte) (opp. from personal knowledge)*; **reasonable ~** *(StrafR)* vernünftiger *(durch die Umstände gerechtfertigter)* Glaube *(zu dem der Täter weder leichtfertig noch fahrlässig gelangte)*

Belize Belize *(früher British Honduras)*

Belizean Belizer(in), belizisch

belligerency *(VölkerR)* Kriegszustand; Teilnahme am Krieg; **non-~** Nichtkriegführung *(Bezeichnung für wohlwollende neutrale Haltung einiger Staaten während des 2. Weltkrieges)*

belligerent *(VölkerR)* Kriegführender; kriegführend; **non-~** nicht am Krieg Teilnehmender *(Staat od. Person)*; nicht am Krieg teilnehmend; ~ **occupation** kriegerische Besetzung; ~ **rights** Rechte e-s kriegführenden Staates

belongings Habseligkeiten, Sachen; **personal ~** Gegenstände des persönlichen Gebrauchs

below unten; unter; nachstehend; ~ **the line item** →line 2.; ~ **par** unter pari; **court ~** untere Instanz, Vorinstanz *(opp. court above)*

bench 1. Richterstuhl, Richterbank; Gericht *(entweder Kollegialgericht od. Einzelrichter)*; Richterschaft *(Gesamtheit der Richter e-s Gerichts)*; **B~ and Bar** Richter und Anwälte *(Br barristers)*; ~ **trial** Gerichtsverhandlung ohne jury; ~ **warrant** Haftbefehl *(des vorsitzenden Richters während der Verhandlung)*

bench, Queen's B~ Division (Q.B.D.) *Br* Abteilung des High → Court of Justice

Die Queen's Bench Division ist zuständig für Obligations- und Deliktsrecht, für Handels- und Steuersachen (Commercial Court) sowie für Seesachen (Admiralty Court). Sie ist Rechtsmittelgericht als Divisional Court (→*court*). In Strafsachen ist sie oberste Instanz für → summary offences bei wichtigen Rechtsfragen. Sie wendet in erster Linie → Common Law an. Sie ist besetzt mit dem → Lord Chief Justice als Präsident und mindestens 17 Richtern (puisne judges)

bench, → Treasury ~; witness ~ Zeugenbank; **to be on the B~** Richter sein; **to raise a barrister to the B~** *Br* e-n barrister zum Richter ernennen

bench 2. *parl* Abgeordnetenbank; **back ~es** *Br* hintere Bänke auf der Regierungs- und Oppositionsseite *(für die weniger wichtigen Abgeordne-*

ten); **front ~es** *Br (für Minister und Oppositionsführer reservierte)* vordere Bänke *(im House of Commons);* **opposition ~es** *Br* Bänke der Opposition

benchers *Br* Vorstandsmitglieder e-r der vier → Inns of Court

benefice *eccl* Pfründe; **right of presenting to a ~** Vorschlagsrecht für die Besetzung e-s Kirchenamtes (→*patronage*); **a bishop collates** (or **admits) a clergyman to a ~** ein Bischof setzt e-n Geistlichen in e-e Pfründe ein

beneficed *eccl* im Genuß e-r Pfründe befindlich

beneficial nutznießend, den Vorteil genießend; nutzbringend, vorteilhaft, günstig; **~ association** (or **society**) →benefit society; **this has a ~ effect** dies hat e-e gute (nützliche) Wirkung

beneficial interest materieller Eigentumsanspruch; **the ~ is vested in Mr. X** Herr X ist der materielle Rechtsinhaber

Recht des materiellen Rechtsinhabers *(des beneficial owner od. beneficiary im Ggs. zum nominal owner od. bare legal owner, z.B. trustee)* an einem Vermögensgegenstand. Auch Recht aus einem Vertrag oder Rechtsgeschäft, bei dem der beneficiary nicht direkte Vertragspartei ist

beneficial, ~ owner (B.O.) wirtschaftlicher Eigentümer *(opp. trustee);* Nutzungsberechtigter; **~ ownership** Eigentum *(im eigenen Interesse, i. Ggs. zum formalen Eigentum des trustee in fremdem Interesse)*

beneficially, to be ~ interested der materielle Rechtsinhaber sein; faktisches Eigentumsrecht haben *(z.B. der Begünstigte im Treuhandverhältnis)*

beneficiary (der/die) Begünstigte, (Bezugs-, Empfangs-)Berechtigte, Empfangsberechtigte, (Leistungs-)Empfänger(in); *(VersR)* Anspruchsberechtigter, Begünstigter *(aus e-m Versicherungsvertrag); (ErbR) (durch Testament od. Vermächtnis)* Bedachter (od. Begünstigter), Erbberechtigter (→ *~ under a will*); Berechtigter *(in e-m Rechtsgeschäft, in dem er nicht direkte Vertragspartei ist, z.B. der durch e-n → executor Betreute od. derjenige, zu dessen Gunsten ein → trust errichtet ist);* Treuhandbegünstigter; Empfänger der Einkünfte und Endverteilung e-s trust;[7] Nutzungsberechtigter, Nutznießer; **~ country** *(Entwicklungshilfe)* Empfängerland *(opp. donor country);* **~ of a credit** Begünstigter e-s Akkreditivs; **~ state** Staat, der Kredite *(etc)* erhält; **~ under a will** Testamentserbe; Vermächtnisnehmer; **to be a ~ under a will** durch ein Testament begünstigt sein

beneficiary, authorized (or **rightful**) **~** Empfangsberechtigter; **nominated ~** *(VersR)* bezeichneter Anspruchsberechtigter; **third party ~** Begünstigter *(im Vertrag zugunsten Dritter);* begünstigter Dritter, Drittbegünstigter

benefit 1. Vorteil, Gewinn; Nutzen, Hilfe, Vergünstigung; Rechtswohltat; ~ (under a will) Erbschaft (durch Testament); **~ in cash** → cash ~; **~ clause** Begünstigungsklausel *(in e-r Lebensversicherung);* **~ of clergy** *(strafrechtl.)* Besserstellung der Geistlichkeit *(obs.);* **~ of division** Einrede von Mitbürgen, nur anteilig zu haften

benefit of the doubt *(StrafR)* günstige Auslegung zweifelhafter Umstände *(Rechtswohltat des Satzes „in dubio pro reo" zugunsten des Angeklagten);* **to give a p. the ~** im Zweifelsfalle zu jds Gunsten entscheiden

benefit, ~ fund Unterstützungsfonds; Versicherungsfonds auf Gegenseitigkeit; **~ of an invention** Erlös aus e-r Erfindung; **~ of inventory** Begrenzung der Schuldenhaftung e-s Erben auf den Wert des Nachlasses (→*inventory)*

benefit, financial ~ Vermögensvorteil

benefit, for the ~ of zugunsten von; **for the ~ of third parties** zugunsten Dritter; **for the public ~** im öffentlichen Interesse, zum allgemeinen Wohl

benefit, material ~ materieller Vorteil; **measurable ~ to the enterprise** *(PatR)* erfaßbarer betrieblicher Nutzen; **pecuniary ~** Vermögensvorteil; **personal ~** persönlicher Vorteil; **tax ~** Steuervergünstigung; **unjustified ~** ungerechtfertigte Bereicherung

benefit, to derive a~ e-n Vorteil (od. Nutzen) ziehen (from aus); **to give sb. the ~ of sth.** jdn in den Genuß e-r Sache kommen lassen

benefit 2. (Versicherungs-)Leistung; Rente; **~ check** *Am* Scheck über (monatl.) Rente; **~s in kind** Sachleistungen; **~ insurance system** Rentenversicherungen; **~s offered** *(VersR)* Leistungsangebot; **~ for orphans** Waisenrente; **~ society** *bes. Br* Versicherungsverein auf Gegenseitigkeit *(e-e Art → friendly society);* **~ for survivors** Hinterbliebenenrente; **accident ~** Unfallrente; **cash ~** *(VersR)* Geldleistung; **computation of a ~** Berechnung e-r Rente; → **contributory ~s; death ~s** Leistungen in Sterbefällen; **dependant's ~** *Br* →dependant; **disability insurance ~** *Am* Rente wegen Erwerbsunfähigkeit; Invaliditätsrente; **eligibility for a ~** Eintritt des Versicherungsfalles; **entitlement to ~s** Leistungsanspruch; **exclusion of ~s** Leistungsausschluß; **fringe ~s** →fringe; **immediate ~** sofortige Versicherungsleistung; sogleich beginnende Leistung; **industrial death ~** (for widows and other dependants) *Br* Hinterbliebenenrente; **injury ~** *Br* Krankengeld (→*injury*); **insurance ~** Versicherungsleistung; **→invalidity benefit; maternity ~** Mutterschaftsgeld; **maximum ~** Höchstleistung; **minimum ~** Mindestleistung; **mutual ~ society** *Am* Versicherungsverein auf Gegenseitigkeit; **old age insurance ~** *Am* Altersrente; **recipient of ~s** Empfänger von Leistungen; **right to ~(s)** Leistungsanspruch; **sickness** ~ Krankengeld; **social security** ~**s** Sozialrenten; Sozialleistungen; →**supplementary** ~**s** *Br*; **survivor's** ~ *Am* Hinterbliebenenrente; **unemployment** ~*Br* Arbeitslosengeld; **weekly** ~ Wochengeld *(für Zeit der Arbeitsunfähigkeit)*; →**widow's** ~

benefit, to draw a ~ e-e Rente beziehen; **to pay** ~**s** (to) Renten aus der Sozialversicherung zahlen; **the** ~**s have been suspended** die (Versicherungs-)Leistungen ruhen

benefit *v* begünstigen, fördern *(jdn., etw.)*; nützen, zugutekommen *(jdm., etw.)*; **to** ~ **by** (or **from**) Vorteil(e) haben durch, Nutzen ziehen aus; **to** ~ **the public interest** im öffentlichen Interesse liegen; **to** ~ **unjustly** sich ungerechtfertigt bereichern; **to** ~ **under a will** durch ein Testament begünstigt sein

Benelux Benelux *(Belgien, Niederlande, Luxemburg)*; ~ **countries** Benelux-Länder
Sammelname für die drei Länder, soweit diese wirtschaftlich, kulturell oder politisch zusammenwirken und nach außen als Einheit auftreten.
Im engeren Sinne die von den drei Ländern gebildete Wirtschaftsunion (Economic Union) von 1958, die mit dem 1944 abgeschlossenen Zollabkommen (Customs Convention) als Zollunion (Customs Union) ihren Anfang nahm und allmählich durch die EWG ersetzt wird

benevolent wohlwollend; Wohltätigkeits-, Unterstützungs-; ~ **association** Wohltätigkeitsverein; ~ **fund** Unterstützungsfonds, Unterstützungskasse; ~ **neutrality** wohlwollende Neutralität; ~ **society** *Br*[8] →friendly society

Benin Benin; **People's Republic of** ~Volksrepublik Benin

Beninese Beniner(in); beninisch

benzene, hazards of poisoning arising from ~[9] durch Benzol verursachte Vergiftungsgefahren

bequeath *v (testamentarisch)* vermachen, vererben, hinterlassen *(Br bes. bewegliche Sachen und Geld; cf. to devise)*

bequeather Erblasser, Testator

bequest Vermächtnis; letztwillige Zuwendung *(Br bes. von beweglichen Sachen od. Geld; cf. devise)*; ~ **encumbered with a charge** Vermächtnis unter Auflage; **amount of the** ~ Betrag (od. Höhe) des Vermächtnisses; **disclaimer of onerous** ~ *Br* Ausschlagung e-s beschwerten Vermächtnisses von Geld und sonstigen beweglichen Gegenständen; **to make** (or **leave**) **a** ~ **to sb.** jdm etw. vermachen (od. vererben); jdm ein Vermächtnis aussetzen

Bermuda Bermuda, die Bermudas; Bermuder(in); bermudisch

Berne Convention (Convention of the International Union for the Protection of Literary and Artistic Works) Berner (Verbands-)Übereinkunft (→ *Convention 1.*)

Berne Implementation Act of 1988 *Am* Gesetz, das den USA den Beitritt zur Revidierten Berner Übereinkunft *(Revised Berne →Convention)* ermöglichte

Berne Union Berner[10] Verband
Der durch die Berne Convention errichtete internationale Verband

berth Ankerplatz, Liegeplatz *(e-s Schiffes)*; Koje, Kajüttenbett; Schlafwagen; *Br colloq.* Stelle, Stellung; ~ **clause** Berth-Klausel *(Löschzeit beginnt nicht vor dem Erreichen des festgelegten Löschplatzes)*; ~ **freighting** s. loading on the →~; ~**-terms** (b. t). Platzbedingungen; **customs** ~ Zollandungsplatz; **discharging** ~ Löschplatz; **loading** ~ Ladeplatz; **loading on the** ~ Stückgutbefrachtung

berth *v* anlegen, vor Anker gehen

berthage Kaigebühren; Ankerplatz

Best's Key Rating Guide *Am* Best's Versicherungsjahrbuch

best, ~ **evidence** primärer Beweis *(opp. secondary evidence)*; **at** ~ **(price)** *(Börse)* bestens, bestmöglich; **to the** ~ **of sb.'s knowledge and belief** nach jds bestem Wissen und Gewissen

bestow, *v* zuwenden; **to** ~ **a title on sb.** jdm e-n Titel verleihen

bestowal Zuwendung

bet Wette *(bes. bei Sport und Spiel)*; ~ **reception** Wettannahme; **racing** ~ Rennwette; **to make a** ~ e-e Wette machen (od. eingehen); **to take up a** ~ e-e Wette annehmen

bet *v* wetten (a th. um etw.)

beta stocks (or **securities**) *Br (Börse)* nach den →alpha stocks die beliebtesten 500 Aktien an der Londoner Börse

betrayal Verrat; ~ **of confidence** (or **trust**) Vertrauensbruch

better law →**approach**

better *v* (sich) bessern; besser werden; verbessern; **to** ~ **oneself** sich (od. seine Lage) verbessern

betterment Verbesserung; Melioration; Wertsteigerung von Grundbesitz; ~ **tax** *Am* Steuer auf Wertsteigerung von Grundbesitz

betting Wetten; ~ **and gaming** →gaming; ~ **debt** Wettschuld; ~ **office** Wettannahme(stelle); ~ **shop** *Br* →~ office; ~ **slip** Wettschein; ~ **tax** Wettsteuer; ~ **transaction** *Br* Wette mit e-m Buchmacher

beverage Getränk; ~ **industries** Getränkeindustrie; ~ **tax** *Am* Getränkesteuer

beware Vorsicht, Achtung; ~ **of pickpockets** vor Taschendieben wird gewarnt!

Bhutan Bhutan; **Kingdom of** ~ Königreich Bhutan

Bhutanese Bhutaner(in); bhutanisch

bias Voreingenommenheit, Befangenheit, Parteilichkeit; **free from** ~ unvoreingenommen, unparteiisch; **to challenge a judge on the ground of** ~ →challenge *v; **to declare oneself disqualified on the ground of*** ~ *Am* sich für befangen erklären; **to withdraw (from a case) on the grounds of** ~ *Br* sich für befangen erklären

biassed befangen, voreingenommen

bicameral *parl* Zweikammer- *(opp. unicameral)*

bicentennial celebration Zweihundertjahrfeier

bicycle theft insurance Fahrraddiebstahlversicherung

bid 1. Gebot *(bei Auktionen); Am* Angebot *(bes. bei Ausschreibungen); (bei Auktionen)* Preisangebot, Lieferungsangebot, Kostenanschlag; ~ **bond** Bietungsgarantie; ~ **price** Angebotspreis, gebotener Preis; *(fondsgebundene Versicherung)* Rückkaufkurs; **advertising for** ~**s** *Am* Ausschreibung; **best** ~ Meistgebot

bid, first ~ Erstgebot; **to make the first** ~ das erste Gebot abgeben

bid, (formal) invitation for ~**s** *Am (öffentl.)* Ausschreibung; **higher** ~ höheres Gebot, Mehrgebot; **to make a higher** ~ höher (od. mehr) bieten; **highest** ~ Meistgebot; **person making the highest** ~ Meistbietender, Höchstbietender; **lowest** ~ niedrigstes Gebot, Mindestgebot; **solicitation for** ~**s** *Am* Ausschreibung; **takeover** ~ Übernahmeangebot; **to invite** ~**s** (or **to solicit** or **to advertise** ~**s**) *Am* Angebote einholen; ausschreiben; **to make a** ~ ein Gebot abgeben; **to make a** ~ **for** ein Angebot machen für, sich bewerben um; **to submit a** ~ *(bei Ausschreibung)* ein Angebot abgeben; **to withdraw a** ~ ein Gebot zurücknehmen

bid 2. *(Börse)* „Geld" *(Nachfrage);* ~ **and asked** Geld und Brief; ... ~, ... **offered** ... Geld, ... Brief; ~ **price** *(vom Käufer gebotener)* Geldkurs; ~ **rate** Ankaufs(zins)satz

bid *v (bei Auktionen)* bieten, ein Gebot abgeben (for für); steigern; *Am (bei Ausschreibungen)* (Preis-, Lieferungs-)Angebot machen (→ *contract 2.*); **to** ~ **against a p.** jdn überbieten; **to** ~ **in** *Am (im Interesse des Eigentümers)* überbieten; **to** ~ **on** *Am (bei Ausschreibungen)* ein Angebot machen für; **to** ~ **up** *(durch Bieten)* den Preis in die Höhe treiben

bidder Bietender, Steigerer; *Am (bei Ausschreibungen)* Submittent, Bewerber um e-n Auftrag; **highest** (or **best**) ~ Meistbietender, Höchstbietender; **knocking down to the highest** ~ Zuschlag an den Meistbietenden

bidding *(bei Auktionen)* Bieten, Steigern, Gebot, Abgabe von Geboten; *Am (bei Ausschreibungen)* Angebot, Abgabe von Angeboten; Anbietung (od. Ausschreibung) freier Arbeitsplätze *(z.B. am schwarzen Brett);* ~ **conditions** *Am* Ausschreibungsbedingungen; ~ **guarantee** Ausbietungsgarantie; ~ **period** *Am* Ausschreibungsfrist; **to start the** ~ das erste Gebot machen

biennial zweijährig, alle zwei Jahre

Big Bang *Br* „großer Knall"
(27. 10. 1986) Liberalisierung an der Londoner Börse, Einführung e-s elektronischen Handelssystems, Übergang von festen zu frei verhandelbaren Maklergebühren, Gleichstellung von →jobber und →broker (→dual capacity system), Einführung des →SEAQ-Systems

big, ~ **bank** Großbank; **B**~ **Board** *Am* → New York Stock Exchange

big business Großbetrieb(e), Großindustrie; Großunternehmen *(auch in negativem Sinne);* großbetriebliche Wirtschaftsform

big, ~ **finance** *Am* Hochfinanz; **"B~ Four"** *Br* die vier großen Londoner Großbanken *(Barclays, Lloyd's, the Midland, and the National Westminster);* ~ **ticket leasing** Leasing von Großobjekten *(z.B. Schiffe, Flugzeuge, Kraftwerke);* ~**wig** *sl.* Bonze

bigamist Bigamist

bigamous bigamisch; ~ **marriage** Doppelehe

bigamy[11] Bigamie, Doppelehe

bilateral bilateral, zweiseitig; ~ **agreement** zweiseitiges Abkommen *(opp. multilateral agreement);* ~ →**divorce**

bilker Zechpreller

bill 1. Schriftstück; förml. Urkunde; Schein, Zettel; Rechnung, Faktura; Liste, Verzeichnis; Plakat, Anschlag(szettel); *Am* Geldschein, Banknote; ~ **board** *Am* Anschlagbrett; Plakatwand; ~ **of charges** *Am* Kostenrechnung, Gebührenrechnung; Spesenrechnung; ~ **of costs** Kostenberechnung; *Br* Gebührenrechnung *(des → solicitor); Am* Prozeßkostenaufstellung *(des Gerichts); (der obsiegenden Partei zu erstattende)* (Gerichts-)Kosten; ~ **of entry** (B.E.) *Br* Zolleingangsschein *(für eingeführte Waren);* Einfuhrerklärung; ~ **of expenses** Spesenrechnung, Unkostenrechnung; ~ **forger** *Am* Banknotenfälscher; ~ **forgery** *Am* Banknotenfälschung; ~**head** Kopf e-r Rechnung; Rechnungsformular

bill of health (B.H.) Gesundheitspaß *(amtl. Bescheinigung für auslaufendes Schiff über Infektionskrankheiten im Schiff und im Hafen);* **clean** ~ Gesundheitspaß mit Vermerk: ohne Krankheit; **foul** ~ Gesundheitspaß mit Vermerk: ansteckende Krankheit

bill of lading[12] (B/L) Konnossement, Seefrachtbrief; *(Binnenschiffahrt)* Ladeschein; *Am (auch:)* Frachtbrief; ~ **to bearer** Inhaberkonnossement; ~ **clause** Konnossementsklausel; ~ **contract** *(Seefrachtgeschäft)* Stückgutvertrag; ~ **drawn in 2 copies** Konnossement in doppelter Ausfertigung; ~ **form** (See-)Frachtbrief-Formular; ~ **to order** Orderkonnossement; **air** ~ *Am* Luftfrachtbrief; **as per** ~ laut Konnossement; **on board** ~ Bordkonnossement; **clean** ~ reines Konnossement *(der Frachtführer hat keine Unregelmäßigkeit vermerkt; opp. foul ~);* **custody** ~ Lagerhalter-Konnossement; **foul** ~ unreines Konnossement *(mit Vorbehalten, z.B. Mängelvermerk);* **full set of bills of lading** voller Satz des Konnossements; **inland waterway** ~ Flußladeschein, Binnenkonnossement; **marine** (or **ocean**) ~ Seefrachtbrief; **order** ~ Orderkonnossement; **port** ~ Hafenkonnossement; **railroad** ~ *Am* Eisenbahnfrachtbrief; **received for shipment** ~ Übernahmekonnossement; **shipped** ~ Bordkonnossement; **straight** ~ *Am* Namenskonnossement; **through** ~ durchgehendes Konnossement, Durchkonnossement; **tran(s)shipment** ~ Umladekonnossement; **to make out a** ~ ein Konnossement ausstellen

bill, ~ **of materials** Stückliste; ~ **of parcels** (B/P) Faktura, (spezifizierte) Warenrechnung; ~ **of →quantities**

bill of sale (B/S) Verkaufsurkunde *(über bewegl. Sachen);* ~ **(by way of security)** *Br* Urkunde über Sicherungsübereignung *(dem Gläubiger werden einzelne Werte durch Übergabe e-r Urkunde verschrieben, die in ein öffentl. Register eingetragen werden muß);* **absolute** ~ *Br* Eigentumsübertragungsurkunde *(für Mobilien)*

bill, ~**(-)poster** →~ sticker; ~**(-)posting** →~ sticking; ~ **(-)sticker** Zettelankleber, Plakatankleber; ~ **(-)sticking** Zettelankleben, Plakatanschlag; ~ **of sufferance** *Br* Zollpassierschein *(Erlaubnis, bestimmte Waren zollfrei an bestimmten Häfen zu landen)*

bill, (bank) ~ *Am* Banknote; **receipted** ~ quittierte Rechnung; **to foot a** ~ e-e Rechnung begleichen; **to make out a** ~ e-e Rechnung ausstellen; **to pay a** ~ e-e Rechnung begleichen (od. bezahlen); **to post** ~**s** →to stick ~s; **to receipt a** ~ e-e Rechnung quittieren; **to settle a** ~ s. to pay a →~; **to stick** ~**s** Zettel ankleben; Plakate anschlagen; **stick no** ~**s** das Ankleben von Zetteln ist verboten

bill 2. *(ProzeßR),* ~ **(in equity)** *Am (förml.)* Antrag *(im equity-Prozeß);* ~ **of exceptions** *Am* →exception; ~ **of indictment** Anklageschrift; ~ **of particulars** *Am* ergänzender Schriftsatz *(Angabe von Einzelheiten bei allzu knapp gehaltenem Vorbringen);* **true** ~ *Am (von der grand jury)* für begründet erklärte Anklage *(Vermerk auf dem bill of indictment);* **to find a true** ~ *Am* die Anklage für begründet erklären

bill 3. *parl* Gesetzesentwurf, Gesetzesvorlage; *(feierliches)* Gesetz; **B~ of Rights** *Br* Freiheitsurkunde *(von 1689); Am* verfassungsmäßig garantierte Grundrechte, *(bes.)* die ersten zehn →amendments *(zur Verfassung von 1787);* **administration** ~ *Am* Regierungsvorlage; **government** ~ *Br* Regierungsvorlage; **hybrid** ~ gemischte Gesetzesvorlage *(teils private, teils public bill; → hybrid);* **navy** ~ Flottenvorlage; **private** ~ *Br (von e-m →promoter eingereichter)* Gesetzesantrag in privatem od. lokalem Interesse; **private member's** ~ *Br* Gesetzesvorlage e-s Abgeordneten *(opp. government bill);* **public** ~ *Br* von der Regierung *(e-m Minister)* eingebrachte Gesetzesvorlage *(die öffentliche Angelegenheiten betrifft);* **to adopt a** ~ e-n Gesetzesentwurf annehmen; **to amend a** ~ e-n Gesetzesentwurf abändern; **to bring in a** ~e-n Gesetzesentwurf einbringen; **the** ~ **was carried** der Gesetzesentwurf wurde angenommen; der Gesetzesentwurf ging durch; **to commit a** ~ **to a committee** e-n Gesetzesentwurf e-m Ausschuß überweisen; **to drop a** ~ e-n Gesetzesentwurf nicht weiterbehandeln; **to get a** ~ **through Parliament** e-n Gesetzesentwurf durchbringen; **to introduce a** ~ *(Br into Parliament, Am into Congress)* e-n Gesetzesentwurf einbringen; **to pass a** ~ ein Gesetz verabschieden; **the** ~ **was passed** der Gesetzesentwurf wurde angenommen (od. ging durch); **to pass** (or **refer**) **a** ~ **to a committee** e-n Gesetzesentwurf e-m Ausschuß überweisen; **the** ~ **was rejected** der Gesetzesentwurf wurde abgelehnt; **to shelve** *Br* (**to table** *Am*) **a** ~ e-e Gesetzesvorlage auf unbestimmte Zeit zurückstellen; **to vote on a** ~ über e-e Gesetzesvorlage abstimmen

bill 4. **(~ of exchange)** (B/E) *(gezogener)* Wechsel, Tratte *(cf. draft, promissory note)*

Während das deutsche Wechselgesetz (Wechselordnung von 1933) auf dem international vereinheitlichten, von einer Anzahl europäischer Staaten übernommenen Wechselrecht der Genfer Wechselrechtskonferenz von 1930[13] beruht, gelten für Großbritannien und Nordirland der Bills of Exchange Act von 1882, für die Vereinigten Staaten der Uniform Negotiable Instruments Law von 1896 sowie neuerdings der bisher in der Mehrzahl der Einzelstaaten angenommene Uniform Commercial Code von 1957 (Art. 3, Commercial Paper). Der Unterschied zwischen den beiden Systemen, der nicht so groß ist wie sonst zwischen dem Common Law and Civil Law, liegt vor allem in der geringeren Formstrenge des anglo-amerikanischen Wechselrechts

bill, ~**s account** Wechselrechnung; Wechselkonto; ~ **after date** Datowechsel; ~ **at short date** Wechsel auf kurze Sicht, kurzfristiger Wechsel; ~ **after sight** Nachsichtwechsel; ~ **at sight** Sichtwechsel; ~ **at usance** Usowechsel; ~ **book** Wechselbuch, Wechselkopierbuch; ~ **broker** Wechselmakler, Wechselhändler; ~ **brokers** *Br* Wechselmaklerfirmen *(discount houses)* des Londoner Geldmarktes *(die bes. →Treasury bills kaufen)*; ~ **brokerage** Wechselhandel; Wechselcourtage; ~ **business** Wechselgeschäft; ~ **case** Wechselportefeuille, Wechselbestand; ~ **charges** Wechselspesen; ~**s in circulation** in Umlauf befindliche Wechsel, laufende Wechsel; ~ **collection** Wechselinkasso; ~ **for collection** Inkassowechsel; ~ **creditor** Wechselgläubiger; ~ **debt** Wechselschuld; ~ **discount rate** Wechseldiskontsatz; ~ **discounter** Wechseldiskontierer; ~ **discounting** Wechseldiskontierung, Diskontierung von Wechseln; ~ **drawn on o. s.** eigener Wechsel; ~ **drawn on a non-existing person** Kellerwechsel; ~ **of exchange** (B/E, b.e.) *(gezogener)* Wechsel, Tratte; **B~s of Exchange Act** (BEA) *Br*[14] Wechselgesetz, Wechselordnung; ~ **forger** Wechselfälscher; ~ **forgery** Wechselfälschung; ~ **form** Wechselvordruck; ~ **holder** Wechselinhaber, Wechselgläubiger; ~ **holdings** Wechselbestand; Wechselportefeuille; ~ **in (foreign) currency** Wechsel in ausländischer Währung, Devisenwechsel; ~ **jobber** *Br* Wechselreiter, Wechselspekulant; ~ **jobbing** *Br* Wechselreiterei, Wechselspekulation; **within the ~'s maturity** innerhalb der Laufzeit des Wechsels; ~ **on demand** Sichtwechsel; ~ **on goods** Warenwechsel; ~**s payable** (B.P., b.p.) zu zahlende Wechsel, Schuldwechsel *(Wechselschulden)*; ~ **payable after date** Datowechsel; ~ **payable after sight** Nachsichtwechsel; ~ **payable at sight** Sichtwechsel; ~ **payable on demand** Wechsel zahlbar auf Anforderung; Sichtwechsel; ~ **protest** Wechselprotest; ~**s receivable** (B.R., b.r.) einzulösende Wechsel, Besitzwechsel *(Wechselforderungen)*; ~ **given as security** Kautionswechsel

bills in a set Wechsel in mehrfacher Ausfertigung; **to draw bills in sets of 2** Wechsel in 2 Ausfertigungen ausstellen

bill, ~ **stamp** Wechselsteuermarke; ~ **surety** Wechselbürge; Wechselbürgschaft; ~ **transactions** Wechselgeschäfte

bill, acceptance ~ *(Außenhandel)* Dokumententratte; **acceptance of a** ~ Wechselakzept; **action on** (or **arising out of**) **a** ~ Wechselklage; **addressed** ~ Domizilwechsel; **after date** ~ Datowechsel; **after sight** ~ Nachsichtwechsel; **amount of the** ~ Wechselsumme; **bank** ~ Bankwechsel; **bearer of a** ~ Wechselinhaber; **circulation of** ~**s** Wechselumlauf, Wechselverkehr; **claim arising from a** ~ Wechselforderung; **clean** ~ reiner *(nicht von Rechte übertragenden Dokumenten begleiteter)* Wechsel *(opp. documentary ~)*; **commercial** ~ Handelswechsel, Warenwechsel; **copy of a** ~ Wechselkopie; **date of maturity of a** ~ Fälligkeitstag e-s Wechsels; **debt on a** ~ Wechselschuld; **dishono(u)red** ~ nicht eingelöster (od. notleidender) Wechsel; **documentary** ~ *(Überseehandel)* Dokumententratte *(Wechsel mit angehefteten, Rechte übertragenden Dokumenten)*; **domestic** ~ *bes. Am* Inlandswechsel; **domiciled** (or **domiciliated**) ~ Domizilwechsel *(opp. local ~)*; **drawee of a** ~ Bezogener, Trassat; **drawer of a** ~ Wechselaussteller, Trassant; **drawing of a** ~ Wechselausstellung; **duplicate (of a)** ~ Wechselduplikat; **fictitious** ~ *Br* Kellerwechsel, Scheinwechsel; **finance** ~ Finanzwechsel *(opp. trade ~)*; **first** ~ **(of exchange)** Primawechsel; **foreign** ~ im Ausland zahlbarer Wechsel, Auslandswechsel *(opp. inland ~)*; **forger of a** ~ Wechselfälscher; **forging of a** ~ Wechselfälschung; **guarantee of a** ~ Wechselbürgschaft; **guarantor of a** ~ Wechselbürge; **holder of a** ~ Wechselinhaber, Wechselgläubiger; **inland** ~ Inlandswechsel *(opp. foreign ~)*; **issue of a** ~ Ausstellung e-s Wechsels; **jobbing in** ~**s** *Br* Wechselreiterei; **party liable on a** ~ Wechselverpflichteter; **local** ~ *Br* Platzwechsel *(opp. domiciled ~)*; **long-dated** ~ langfristiger Wechsel, Wechsel auf lange Sicht; **negotiation of a** ~ Begebung (od. Übertragung) e-s Wechsels; **non-negotiable** ~ *Br* →negotiable; **overdue** ~ abgelaufener Wechsel; **payee of a** ~ Wechselnehmer; **payment of a** ~ Zahlung (od. Einlösung) e-s Wechsels; **presentation of a** ~ Vorlegung e-s Wechsels; **prescription of a** ~ Wechselverjährung; **prolongation of a** ~ Prolongation (od. Verlängerung) e-s Wechsels; **protest of a** ~ Wechselprotest; **protesting of a** ~ Protestaufnahme; **renewal of a** ~ Prolongation (od. Verlängerung) e-s Wechsels; **second** ~ Sekundawechsel, zweite Wechselausfertigung; **sight** ~ Sichtwechsel; **short-dated** ~ kurzfristiger Wechsel; **sole** ~ Solawechsel *(der nur in e-r Ausfertigung vorhanden ist)*; **stamp duty payable on** ~**s** Wechselsteuer; **surety for (payment of) a** ~ Wechselbürgschaft; Wechselbürge; **taker of a** ~ Wechselnehmer; **term** ~ *Br* Wechsel mit bestimmter Frist; **time** (or **term**) **(allowed) for the payment of a** ~ Wechselfrist; **title to the** ~ Wechselanspruch; **town** ~ Platzwechsel; **trade** ~ Handelswechsel, Warenwechsel *(opp. finance ~)*; →**Treasury** ~; **validity of a** ~ **as regards requisites in form** Formgültigkeit e-s Wechsels

bill, to accept a ~ e-n Wechsel annehmen (od. akzeptieren); **to bring an action on a** ~ Zahlung e-s Wechsels einklagen; **to cancel a** ~ e-n Wechsel durchstreichen; **to cash a** ~ e-n Wechsel einlösen; **to collect a** ~ e-e Wechselforderung einziehen; **to discount a** ~ e-n

Wechsel diskontieren; **to get a ~ discounted** e-n Wechsel diskontieren lassen; **to draw a ~** e-n Wechsel ausstellen (od. ziehen) (on auf); **entitled to draw ~s** wechselfähig; **to furnish a ~ with a stamp** e-n Wechsel verstempeln; **to give a ~** e-n Wechsel ausstellen; **to give security for a ~** e-n Wechsel decken; **to guarantee a ~** Wechselbürgschaft leisten; **to hono(u)r a ~** e-n Wechsel einlösen (od. bezahlen); **to issue a ~** e-n Wechsel ausstellen; **to become liable on a ~** wechselverpflichtet werden; **to make out a ~** e-n Wechsel ausstellen; **the ~ matures on** der Wechsel wird fällig am; **to meet a ~** e-n Wechsel einlösen; **to negotiate a ~** e-n Wechsel begeben (od. übertragen); **to have a ~ noted** e-n Wechsel zu Protest gehen lassen; **to pay a ~** e-n Wechsel bezahlen (od. einlösen); **to pay by means of ~s** mit Wechseln bezahlen; **the ~ has become payable** der Wechsel ist abgelaufen; **to make a ~ payable at sight** e-n Wechsel auf Sicht ziehen; **to present a ~ for acceptance** (for **payment**) e-n Wechsel zur Annahme (zur Zahlung) vorlegen; **to protest a ~** (Wechsel-)Protest aufnehmen *(Notar);* zu Protest gehen lassen *(Inhaber e-s Wechsels);* **to have** (or **get**) **a ~ protested** e-n Wechsel zu Protest gehen lassen, Protest aufnehmen lassen; **to renew a ~** e-n Wechsel verlängern (od. prolongieren); **to retire a ~** e-n Wechsel zurückziehen; **to sue on a ~** Zahlung e-s Wechsels einklagen; **to take up a ~** e-n Wechsel einlösen (od. bezahlen); **to leave a ~ unpaid** e-n Wechsel nicht einlösen; **to return a ~ unpaid** e-n Wechsel unbezahlt zurückgehen lassen; **to withdraw a ~** e-n Wechsel zurückziehen

bill *v* in Rechnung stellen, fakturieren; e-e Rechnung (aus)schreiben; *(durch Anschlag)* ankündigen; in e-e Liste aufnehmen

billing Rechnungschreibung; Fakturierung; Inrechnungstellen; Zettelankleben; **~ date** *Am* Rechnungsdatum; **~ machine** Fakturiermaschine

billet *mil* Quartier; Quartierzettel; *colloq.* Stelle

billet *v mil* einquartieren (on bei)

billeting *mil* Einquartierung; (Privat-)Quartier; **~ officer** Quartiermacher; **~ paper** (or **order**) Quartierschein

billion (bil.) *Br* Billion; *Am* Milliarde

BIMCO (Baltic and International Maritime Conference)

Vereinigung von mit der Schiffahrt verbundenen Personen (Reeder, Partenreeder, Reederverbände und Makler [shipbrokers]). Erteilung von Informationen. Ausarbeitung und Vereinheitlichung von Charterverträgen und -dokumenten.
Sitz: Kopenhagen

bi-monthly alle 2 Monate

bind *v* binden, verpflichten; **to ~ oneself to do sth.** sich verpflichten (od. versprechen), etw. zu tun; **to ~ oneself under oath** sich eidlich verpflichten; **to ~ sb. over (to keep the peace)** *Br* jdn unter der Bedingung künftiger guter Führung freisprechen; *(etwa:)* jdm e-e Bewährungsfrist geben *(cf. bound over);* **to ~ sb. as an apprentice** jdn in die Lehre (od. Ausbildung) geben (to bei)

binding bindend, verpflichtend, verbindlich, zwingend (on für); **~ authority** (or **force**) bindende Kraft *(gerichtlicher Entscheidungen);* **~ law** zwingendes Recht; **~ receipt** (or **slip**) *Am (VersR)* vorläufige Versicherungspolice; **legally ~** rechtsverbindlich; **not ~** unverbindlich, freibleibend; **not ~ offer** freibleibendes Angebot; **to be ~ (up)on sb.** jdn binden; (rechts)verbindlich sein für jdn; **to remain ~** verbindlich bleiben

binder *Am (Grundstückskauf)* Vorverkaufsvertrag; *Am (VersR)* Deckungszusage, vorläufige Versicherungspolice; Aktendeckel

biological, ~ warfare biologischer Krieg, Bazillenkrieg; **~ weapons** biologische Waffen *(→toxic weapons)*

biomedical research[15] biomedizinische Forschung

biotechnology Biotechnologie

bipartisan *pol* aus Mitgliedern von zwei Parteien bestehend; Zweiparteien-

bipartite in doppelter Ausfertigung *(von Urkunden);* zweiteilig

bird sanctuaries Vogelschutzgebiete

birth Geburt; **~ certificate** Geburtsurkunde; **~day honours** *Br* Ehrenverleihungen anläßlich des Geburtstags der Königin; **~day ~ control** Geburtenregelung; Familienplanung; **~ place** Geburtsort

birth rate Geburtenziffer; **decline in** (or **falling of**) **the ~** Rückgang der Geburtenziffer; Geburtenrückgang; **increase** (or **rise**) **in the ~** Steigen der Geburtenziffer; Geburtenzunahme; **measures to reduce the ~** Geburtenbeschränkung; **the ~ is rising** die Geburtenziffer steigt

birth, announcement of ~ Geburtsanzeige *(in Zeitung);* **by ~** von Geburt; **certificate of ~** Geburtsurkunde; **date of ~** Geburtsdatum; **notification of ~** Anzeige der Geburt; **place of ~** Geburtsort; **registration of ~s** *(amtl.)* Registrierung der Geburten; **still ~** Totgeburt; **surplus of ~s over deaths** Geburtenüberschuß; **to give ~ to a child** ein Kind bekommen; von e-m Kind entbunden werden

biweekly alle 2 Wochen

bizonal Zweizonen-; bizonal

blackball *v (als Mitglied in e-m Klub etc)* nicht aufnehmen; **to ~ a p.** gegen jds Aufnahme stimmen

blackcoated worker →white collar worker

black economy Schattenwirtschaft

blacketeer *Am* →black marketeer

black labo(u)r Schwarzarbeit

blackleg *Br* Streikbrecher

black list schwarze Liste; **to put on the ~** auf die schwarze Liste setzen

blacklist *v (jdn)* auf die schwarze Liste setzen; **to be ~ed** auf der schwarzen Liste stehen

blackmail Erpressung *(durch Drohung);* erpreßtes Geld; **attempted ~(ing)** Erpressungsversuch; →**nuclear ~**

blackmail *v,* **to ~ a p.** jdn erpressen; von jdm Geld erpressen; **to be ~ed into doing** sich erpressen lassen, zu tun
blackmailing Erpressung

blackmailer Erpresser

Black Maria „Grüne Minna" *(Wagen für Gefangenentransporte)*

black market schwarzer Markt; Schwarzhandel; Schleichhandel; **~ dealer** Schwarzhändler; **~ dealings** (or **transactions**) Schwarzmarktgeschäfte; **~ price** Schwarzmarktpreis; **to deal on the ~** Schwarzhandel treiben

black market *v* Schwarzhandel treiben
black marketing →black marketeering

black marketeer Schwarzhändler; Schleichhändler
black marketeering Schwarzhandel; Schleichhandel

black(-)out *(Luftschutz)* Verdunkelung; (Strom-, Nachrichten-)Sperre; **news ~** Nachrichtensperre

black-out *v (Luftschutz)* verdunkeln; *(Nachrichten durch Zensur)* unterdrücken; *(Rundfunksendung)* stören

Black Power *pol (Sammelbegriff für)* radikale Negerorganisationen, schwarzer Radikalismus

blame Tadel; Schuld, Verantwortung; **to lay** (or **put**) **the ~ on sb. for sth.** jdm die Schuld geben für; jdn verantwortlich machen für; **the ~ lies with** die Schuld liegt bei

blame *v* tadeln; **to ~ sb. for sth.** jdm die Schuld an e-r Sache geben; jdm etw. vorwerfen; **to be to ~ for** schuld sein an; verantwortlich sein für; **both are equally to ~** beide *(Parteien)* sind zu gleichen Teilen schuld *(z. B. bei Verkehrsunfällen)*

blameworthiness *(StrafR)* Schuld

blank freie Stelle *(auf Schriftstück für nachträgliche Einfügungen); Am* nicht ausgefülltes Formular; Vordruck; unbeschrieben, leer; blanko; *(Lotterielos)* Niete; **~ acceptance** Blankoakzept, Blankoannahme; **~ bill** Blankowechsel; **~ cheque (check)** Blankoscheck; Scheckformular; **~ credit** Blankokredit; **~ endorsement** Blankoindossament; **~ (form)** Vordruck, unausgefülltes Formular; **~ policy** Generalpolice; **~ power of attorney** Blankovollmacht; **~ receipt** Blankoquittung; **~ signature** Blankounterschrift; **~ transfer** →transfer 4. **~ voting paper** (or **slip**) nicht ausgefüllter (od. leerer) Stimmzettel; **to leave ~** unausgefüllt lassen
blank, in ~ blanko; **to accept in ~** blanko akzeptieren; **made out in ~** in blanko *(z. B. unter Offenlassung des Betrages)* ausgestellt; **to endorse in ~** blanko indossieren; mit e-m Blankoindossament versehen

blanket alles umfassend; Gesamt-; generell; **~ clause** Generalklausel; **~ instructions** generelle Anweisungen; **~ coverage** Pauschaldeckung; **~ insurance policy** Generalpolice, Pauschalpolice; **~ mortgage** Gesamthypothek; **~ price** *Am* Pauschalpreis; alles einschließender Preis; **~ rate** *Am* Pauschalsatz

blasphemy Gotteslästerung

blend Mischung *(verschiedener Sorten);* Verschnitt *(Wein)*

blind blind; **the ~** die Blinden; **articles for the use of the ~** *(Post)* Blindenschriftsendungen; **home for the ~** Blindenanstalt
blind persons Blinde; **~ cared for in an institution or home** Blinde in Anstalts- oder Heimpflege; **~' workshop** Blindenwerkstätte; **merchandise made by ~** Blindenware(n)

bloc *pol* Block; **~ policy** Blockpolitik; **formation of ~s** Blockbildung

bloc-licence (~se) *(PatR)* En-bloc-Lizenz, Pauschallizenz *(Vergebung aller Lizenzen in e-m geschlossenen Block)*

block Block; Häuserblock; *Am* Straßenquadrat; Hindernis; **~ exemption** Gruppenfreistellung; **~ of flats** *Br* Mietshaus, Mehrfamilienhaus; Wohnblock
block letters, in ~ in Blockschrift, in großer Druckschrift; **to write one's name in ~** s-n Namen in Blockschrift schreiben
block, ~ of shares Aktienpaket; **~ trading** *(Börse)* Pakethandel; **~ vote** *Br* (trade unions) Sammelstimme; **road ~** Straßensperre; **traffic ~** Verkehrsstauung

block *v* (ab-, ver)sperren, blockieren; hemmen, hindern; **to ~ an account** ein Konto sperren;

to ~ a bill *Br parl* die Verabschiedung e-r Gesetzesvorlage *(durch Hinausziehen der Diskussion)* verhindern; **to ~ a credit** e-n Kredit sperren; **to ~ (up) a road** e-e Straße (ab)-sperren

blocked, ~ account gesperrtes Konto, Sperrkonto; **~ credit** eingefrorener Kredit; **~ (credit) balance** gesperrtes Guthaben, Sperrguthaben; **~ (foreign) currency** (or **exchange**) blockierte (od. nicht frei konvertierbare) Devisen; **~ property** gesperrtes Vermögen; **~ securities** Sperrstücke; **~ sterling account** *Br* blockiertes Sterlingkonto *(ausländisches Pfundkonto, auf welches der Erlös aus Verkäufen englischer Wertpapiere gutgeschrieben wird)*

blocking Sperre, Sperrung; Absperren; **~ of account** Kontensperre; **~ minority** Sperrminorität; **~ note** Sperrvermerk; **~ period** Sperrfrist; **~ of property** Vermögenssperre; **~ statute** Abwehrgesetz; **~ of a street** Straßensperrung; **note** (or **notice**) **of ~** Sperrvermerk

blockade *(VölkerR)* Blockade *(cf. Declaration of Paris; contraband, prize)*; **area of ~** Blokkadegebiet; **declaration of ~** Blockadeerklärung; **economic ~** Wirtschaftsblockade; **long distance ~** Fernblockade *(Bildung von Sperrzonen auf hoher See)*; **pacific ~** Friedensblockade *(Sperrung der Seeverbindungen e-s anderen Staates in Friedenszeiten als Repressalie)*; **paper ~** Papierblockade *(verhängte, aber unwirksam gebliebene Blockade)*; **to break the ~** die Blockade durchbrechen; **to impose a ~** e-e Blockade verhängen; **to lift** (or **raise**) **the ~** die Blockade aufheben; **to run the ~** die Blockade brechen; **to tighten the ~** die Blockade verschärfen

blood Blut; Abstammung; **~ alcohol limit** Promillegrenze; **~ group (test)** Blutgruppe(nuntersuchung)

Blood-grouping, European Agreement on the Exchanges of ~ Reagents[16] Europäisches Übereinkommen über den Austausch von Reagenzien zur Blutgruppenbestimmung

blood, ~ relation Blutsverwandte(r); **~ relationship** Blutsverwandtschaft

blood test Blutprobe; **taking of ~s** Entnahme von Blutproben

blood, brother of the full ~ leiblicher Bruder, Vollbruder; **brother of the half ~** Halbbruder; **brother(s) and sister(s) of the half ~** Halbgeschwister *(ein gemeinsamer Elternteil)*; **of mixed ~** gemischter Abstammung; Mischling; **related by ~** blutsverwandt; **of the whole ~** vollbürtig *(durch beide Eltern verwandt)*; **to examine the ~** Blutprobe machen

blotter Journal zur Eintragung von Tages-Geschäftsvorfällen

blue, ~ book *pol* Blaubuch; **~ chips** *(Börse)* Spitzenpapiere, Standardwerte; **~ chip rate** →prime rate; **~ chip undertaking** Spitzenunternehmen; **B~ Cross (Plans)** *Am* privates Krankenversicherungssystem (prepaid health insurance); **~ collar worker** *Am* Arbeiter *(opp. white collar worker)*; **~ laws** *Am* Sonntagsgesetze *(Gesetze betr. Heilighaltung von Sonn- und Feiertagen)*; **~ print** Lichtpause; *(politischer, militärischer od. sozialer)* Plan; Planung; Entwurf

blueprint *v* Plan ausarbeiten; planen, umreißen, festlegen

Blue Shield (Plans) *Am* →Blue Cross

Blue Sky Laws *Am* „Luftschloß-Gesetze"
Gesetze zum Schutze von Erwerbern gegen Unredlichkeiten im Wertpapierhandel *(cf. SEC)*

board 1. (Verwaltungs-)Stelle, Leitungsstab; Direktorium, Verwaltungsrat; Direktoren (→ *board of directors*); Behörde, Amt, Dienststelle; Gremium; *Br* Ministerium, Ministerialabteilung; **~ of arbitration** Schiedskommission, Schiedsstelle; **B~ of Appeal** →appeal 1.; **~ of brokers** Maklersyndikat; **~ (of a company** or *Am* **corporation)** →~ of directors; **~ of control** Kontrollamt, Kontrollstelle; **~ of creditors** Gläubigerausschuß *(im Konkurs)*; **B~ of Customs and Excise** *Br* Ministerialabteilung für Zölle und Verbrauchsteuern

board of directors (B.o.D.) board; (Gremium der) Direktoren
Von den Aktionären (shareholders/stockholders) gewählte höchste Aufsichts- und (originäre) Verwaltungsinstanz der anglo-amerikanischen Aktiengesellschaft. Statt Vorstand und Aufsichtsrat der deutschen Aktiengesellschaft gibt es den einheitlichen board of directors, der formell die Führungsspitze der Gesellschaft ist; er bestellt das →management, überwacht dessen Geschäftsführung und entscheidet über Grundsatzfragen. In der Praxis hat sich häufig die Zweiteilung in → inside board (versieht etwa die Aufgaben des *Vorstandes* der deutschen AG) und → outside board (hat etwa die Aufgaben des *Aufsichtsrats* der deutschen AG) durchgesetzt. Während nach deutschem Aktienrecht niemand gleichzeitig Mitglied des Aufsichtsrats und des Vorstandes sein kann, ist es zulässig, board-Mitglied und gleichzeitig leitender Angestellter (officer, executive) zu sein

board of directors, chairman of the ~ board-Vorsitzender; **committee of the ~** board-Ausschuß *(cf. executive committee, management committee)*; **member of the ~** board-Mitglied; **to be on the ~** board-Mitglied sein; **the ~ shall be composed of 10 directors and 10 alternate directors** der board of directors besteht aus 10 ordentlichen und 10 stellvertretenden Direktoren

board, ~ election board-Wahl; Wahl des Verwaltungsrates; **~ of examiners** Prüfungsausschuß

Board of Governors Gouverneursrat *(z.B. des International Monetary Fund)*; *Am* Börsenvorstand *(z.B. der NYSE)*; **~ (of the Federal Re-**

serve System) *Am* Rat der Gouverneure des Federal Reserve System, Bundesbankrat *(bestimmt die Politik des →FRS)*
Board of Inland Revenue *Br* oberste Steuerbehörde *(für direkte Steuern)*
board of management (or **managers**) Vorstand; Verwaltungsrat; **to be on the ~** Mitglied des Vorstandes sein
board, ~ of mediation *(VölkerR)* Vermittlungskommission; **~ meeting** board-Sitzung, Sitzung des Verwaltungsrats; **~ member** board-Mitglied, Mitglied des Verwaltungsrats; **~ of review** Überprüfungsausschuß; Berufungsausschuß; **~ room** Sitzungssaal *(des Verwaltungsrats);* **B~ of Trade** *Am* Handelskammer *(für bestimmte Industrien);* **~ of trustees** Treuhänderausschuß; Kuratorium
board, advisory ~ Beratungsstelle; Konsultativrat; **planning ~** Planungsamt, Planungsstelle; **to be on the ~** (or **to be a member of the ~**) im board (od. Verwaltungsrat) sitzen; dem board (of directors) angehören; **to call a meeting of the ~** den board einberufen
board 2. Bord; **on ~ a ship** (or **aircraft**) an Bord e-s Schiffes (od. Flugzeugs); **free on ~** frei an Bord *(des Schiffes im Abgangshafen) (cf. fob);* **over ~** über Bord; **to go on ~** an Bord gehen; **to take on ~** an Bord nehmen; **to ship on ~** an Bord verladen; **to throw over ~** über Bord werfen
board 3. Kost(geld); Beköstigung, Verpflegung; Pension; **~ and lodging** Unterkunft und Verpflegung; **allowance for ~** Verpflegungsgeld; **full ~** volle Pension
board, bed and ~ Tisch und Bett; **divorce from bed and ~** (a mensa et thoro) *bes. Am* Trennung von Tisch und Bett *(Br jetzt →judicial separation)*
board 4. *Am (Börse),* **Big B~** *sl.* →New York Stock Exchange
board 5. Brett; Anschlagtafel; Karton, Pappe; **~ measure** (b.m) Holzmaß; **bulletin ~** *Am* (**notice ~** *Br*) Anschlagtafel, schwarzes Brett; **to put on the notice ~** an das schwarze Brett anschlagen

board *v (Flugzeug, Zug etc)* besteigen; einsteigen in, an Bord gehen; in Pension haben, verpflegen; in Pension sein; *mil* entern; **to ~ an aircraft** (or **a plane**) ein Flugzeug besteigen; **to ~ a ship** an Bord e-s Schiffes gehen; *mil* ein Schiff entern; **to ~ a student** e-n Schüler in Pension haben
boarded-out child *Br* Pflegekind
boarding Anbordgehen; Einsteigen in; Beköstigung, Verpflegung; **~ house** Fremdenheim, Pension; **~ officer** Prisenoffizier; **~-out allowance** *Br* Vergütung für Pflegekind (→ foster child); **~ school** *Br* Internat

boarder Gast *(auf längere Zeit);* Pensionsgast; Internatsschüler

boat Boot, Wasserfahrzeug; **~ train** Zug mit Schiffsanschluß

bodily 1. körperlich, Körper-; **~ harm** (or **injury**) *(StrafR)* Körperverletzung; **~ injury** *(VersR)* Personenschaden; **~ or mental harm** körperlicher oder seelischer Schaden; **grievous ~ harm** *Br* schwere Körperverletzung *(ernsterer Art als → battery);* **serious ~ injury** schwere Körperverletzung; **~ search** körperliche Untersuchung; Leibesvisitation
bodily 2. als Ganzes; geschlossen; **the audience rose ~** die Zuhörerschaft erhob sich geschlossen

body Körper; Leiche; Körperschaft; Gesamtheit, Masse, Menge; Hauptteil; Organ, Stelle, Gremium; **as** (or **in**) **a ~** geschlossen, (alle) gemeinsam; **to resign as a ~** geschlossen zurücktreten
bod|y, ~ corporate juristische Person; Körperschaft; **~guard** Leibwächter; **~ of creditors** Gesamtheit der Gläubiger; **~ of deed** (or **instrument**) wesentlicher Teil (od. Text) e-r Urkunde (→ *operative part im Ggs. zu den → recitals);* **~ of laws** Gesetzessammlung; **~ of a letter** Text e-s Briefes; **~ politic** Staat(swesen); **~ search** Leibesvisitation; **~ snatching** Leichendiebstahl; **ad hoc ~** ad hoc-Organ; **administrative ~** Verwaltungsstelle; **corporate ~** Körperschaft, juristische Person; **deliberate ~** beratende Körperschaft; **diplomatic ~** diplomatisches Korps; **executive ~** ausführendes Organ; **governing ~** leitendes Organ, Leitung; Verwaltungsrat; Vorstand; **legislative ~** gesetzgebende Körperschaft; **parent ~** Stammorgan; **permanent ~** ständiges Organ; **subsidiary ~ies** Nebenorgane; **public ~** öffentlich-rechtliche Körperschaft; **public and private ~ies** öffentliche und private Stellen; **standing ~** ständiges Organ (od. Gremium); **technical ~ies** Fachgremien

bogged down *fig* festgefahren

bogus falsch, unecht; Schwindel-; **~ claim** erdichtete Forderung; **~ company** Schwindelgesellschaft; **~ firm** Schwindelfirma; Schwindelunternehmen; **~ transactions** Scheingeschäfte, Schwindelgeschäfte

Bolivia Bolivien; **Republic of ~** Republik Bolivien
Bolivian Bolivianer(in); bolivianisch

bolt *Am pol* sich lossagen *(von seiner Partei); (Entscheidungen der eigenen Partei)* nicht unterstützen

bomb Bombe; **~ attack** *(ausgeführtes)* Bombenattentat; **~ attempt** *(geplantes)* Bombenattentat (on sb.'s life auf jdn); **~ carpet** *mil* Bombenteppich; **~ damage** Bombenschaden; **~ damaged** bombengeschädigt; **~ disposal**

Bombenräumung; ~ **hoax** falsche Bombendrohung; ~ **shelter** Luftschutzraum; ~ **threat** Bombendrohung; **to defuse a** ~ e-e Bombe entschärfen; **to drop** ~**s** Bomben abwerfen; **to plant a** ~ e-e Bombe legen

bomb *v* Bomben legen; mit Bomben belegen; **to** ~ **out** ausbomben

bombed premises durch Bomben zerstörte Gebäude

bombing Bombenanschlag, -anschläge; ~ **attack** (or **raid**) *mil* Bombenangriff; ~ **of target areas** *(VölkerR)* Flächenbombardement; **carpet** ~ Bombenteppichwurf; **interdiction** ~ *Am* Luftangriff mit dem Ziel, dem Gegner den Zugang zu bestimmten Objekten unmöglich zu machen; **saturation** ~ *Am* Bombardierung e-s Zieles, bis es zerstört ist; **terror** ~ Terror-Bombenanschlag

bombardment by naval forces in time of war *(VölkerR)* Beschießung durch Seestreitkräfte in Kriegszeiten

bomber Bombenflugzeug; Bombenleger *(Terrorist)*

bona fide in gutem Glauben, gutgläubig, redlich *(opp. mala fide)*; ~ **creditor** gutgläubiger Forderungsinhaber; ~ **holder for value** gutgläubiger Inhaber *(e-s Wertpapiers)*; ~ **owner** gutgläubiger Eigentümer; ~ **purchaser** gutgläubiger Erwerber; ~ **purchaser for value** *Am* Erwerber, der rechtsgeschäftlich und entgeltlich erworben hat; ~ **resident** *Am* (DBA) Steuerpflichtiger mit echtem ausländischem Wohnsitz; ~ **rights of third parties** Rechte gutgläubiger Dritter; **to act** ~ in gutem Glauben handeln

bona fides guter Glaube

bona vacantia *Br* Heimfallsgut *(e.g. royal fish, shipwrecks, treasure trove)*; **the residuary estate of an intestate passes to the Crown** (or to the Duchy of Lancaster, or to the Duke of Cornwall, as the case may be) **as** ~ *Br* der → residuary estate e-s ohne Testament verstorbenen Erblassers geht als Heimfallsgut auf die Krone über; **to take as** ~ *Br* als Heimfallsgut einziehen

bond 1. *(allgemein)* gesiegelte Schuldurkunde; Schuldschein; Verpflichtungsschein; Kaution; ~ **of indebtedness** Schuldschein, Schuldanerkenntnis; →**safety** ~; **to enter into** (or **give, furnish**) **a** ~ *(durch Urkunde)* e-e Verpflichtung eingehen, e-n Verpflichtungsschein ausstellen

bond 2. *(festverzinsl.)* Wertpapier; (Industrie-, Kommunal-)Obligation, Schuldverschreibung; Pfandbrief; Anleihe; ~**s** Rentenwerte; Obligationen

Im amerikanischen Sprachgebrauch ist der Gegensatz zwischen bonds (festverzinsl. Papieren) und stocks (Dividendenpapieren) scharf. In England ist er weniger scharf, da die von der Regierung den früheren Eigentümern nationalisierter Betriebe als Entschädigung ausgehändigten Papiere vielfach als stocks bezeichnet werden

bond, ~ **capital** Anleihekapital; ~ **certificate** Anleiheschein; ~ **circular** Prospekt über die Ausgabe von Obligationen; ~ **coupon** Zinsschein; ~ **creditor** →~holder; ~ **cum warrants** *Am* Anleihe mit Optionsschein; ~ **debt** Anleiheschuld; ~ **debtor** Obligationsschuldner; Pfandbriefschuldner; ~ **ex warrants** *Am* Anleihe ohne Optionsschein; ~ **funds** *(Investmentfonds)* Rentenfonds; ~ **holder** Wertpapierinhaber; Obligationeninhaber; Pfandbriefgläubiger; ~**s in circulation** umlaufende Anleihestücke; ~**s in (foreign) currency** Fremdwährungsschuldverschreibungen; ~ **indebtedness** Obligationsschulden; ~ **interest** Obligationszinsen; ~ **interest accrued** Stückzinsen; ~ **investment (insurance) business** *Br* Sparversicherung

bond issue Emission von Obligationen; Obligationsausgabe; Anleiheemission; Pfandbriefausgabe; **public** ~ *Am* öffentliche Anleihe; **subscriber to a** ~ Zeichner e-r Obligationsausgabe; **to float a** ~ Obligationen (od. Anleihe) ausgeben (od. auflegen)

bond, ~ **market** Rentenmarkt, Markt der festverzinslichen (Wert-)Papiere; Obligationenmarkt; Pfandbriefmarkt; Anleihemarkt; ~**s payable** *(Bilanz)* ausgegebene Obligationen; ~**s (payable) to bearer** Schuldverschreibungen auf den Inhaber, Inhaberschuldverschreibungen *(opp. registered ~s)*; ~ **portfolio** Rentenportefeuille; ~ **premium** Obligationsagio; ~ **price** Rentenkurs; ~ **sinking fund** Obligationstilgungsfonds; Tilgungsfonds für Obligationen; ~ **subscription** Zeichnung e-r Anleihe; ~ **table** Tabelle zur Berechnung der effektiven Verzinsung der ~s; ~ **warrant** Optionsanleihe, Anleihe mit Optionsschein

bond, annuity ~ Rentenanleihe; **back** ~ Anleihe mit garantiertem Zins, die e-e Optionsanleihe ablöst; **bearer** ~ Inhaberschuldverschreibung *(opp. registered ~)*; **collateral trust** ~**s** *Am* durch treuhänderische Effektenhinterlegung gesicherte Obligationen; **convertible** ~**s** Wandelschuldverschreibungen; **corporation** (or **corporate**) ~**s** *Am* Industrieobligationen; **debenture** ~ Schuldverschreibung, Obligation *(Am meist ohne Sicherheit)*; **domestic** ~ inländische Anleihe; **Exchequer** ~**s** *Br* Schatzanweisungen; **external** (or **foreign**) ~**s** ausländische Wertpapiere; Auslandsschuldverschreibungen; Auslandsanleihen; **government** ~**s** Staatspapiere, Staatsschuldverschreibungen, Staatsanleihen; *Am* Bundesanleihen; **income** ~**s** Gewinnschuldverschreibungen; **industrial** ~**s** Industrieobligationen; **irredeemable** ~**s** nicht kündbare (od. rückzahlbare) Obligationen; →**junk** ~**s; lottery** ~ Lotterieanleihe,

Auslosungsanleihe; **mortgage** ~ (Hypotheken-)Pfandbrief; **municipal** ~**s** Kommunalobligationen; **participating** ~**s** *Am* Gewinnschuldverschreibungen; Obligationen mit Gewinnbeteiligung; **preference** ~**s** *Br* Prioritätsobligationen; **premium** ~ Prämienanleihe, Losanleihe; **private** ~**s** (Industrie-)Obligationen; **public** ~**s** Anleihen der öffentlichen Hand; **redeemable** ~**s** *(vor Fälligkeit)* kündbare Obligationen; **registered** ~**s** Namensschuldverschreibungen *(opp. bearer ~s)*; **secured** ~**s** *Am* gesicherte Obligationen *(cf. mortgage bonds, equipment trust bonds, collateral trust bonds; opp. debentures)*; **sinking fund** ~ Amortisationsobligation; Tilgungsanleihe; **State** ~ Staatspapier, Staatsanleihe; *Am* Anleihe e-s Einzelstaates; →**tap** ~**s**; **war** ~**s** Kriegsanleihen; →**Yankee** ~**s**

bond, to float a ~ **issue** Obligationen (od. Anleihen) ausgeben (od. auflegen); **to incur** ~ **indebtedness** Obligationsschulden aufnehmen; **to issue** ~**s** Obligationen ausgeben; **to redeem** ~**s** Obligationen einlösen (od. tilgen); **the** ~ **offers a yield of 7%** die Rendite der Anleihe beträgt 7%

bond 3. *(vertraglich bestimmtes)* Haftungsversprechen *(bes. in bezug auf Steuern od. Zollbeträge, aber auch in bezug auf Schadloshaltung, z. B. e-r Versicherung für Unterschlagung e-s Angestellten)*; Bürgschaft, Kaution; *(schriftl.)* Garantieerklärung, Garantieschein; ~ **forfeited** Kaution verfallen; ~ **premium** Prämie für e-e Vertrauensschadenversicherung *(Kautions-Versicherung für Pfleger von Vermögen e-s Geisteskranken, Erbschaftsverwalter etc)*; **administration** ~ →administration 2.; **appeal** ~ *Am* Sicherheitsleistung für Kosten der Berufung; **attachment** ~ *Am* Sicherheitsleistung für die Bewilligung e-r einstweiligen Verfügung etc; →**bail bond; bid** ~ *Am* Bietungsgarantie; **conditional** (or **double**) ~ (Zahlungs-)Versprechen, das bei Eintritt e-r auflösenden Bedingung *(z. B. geschuldeter Ausführung od. Unterlassung e-r Handlung)* hinfällig wird *(entspricht der Sache nach dem deutschen Vertragsstrafeversprechen § 339 BGB)*; →**fidelity** ~; **guarantee** ~ schriftl. Garantieerklärung, Garantieschein; **indemnity** ~ Schadloshaltungsverpflichtung, Ausfallbürgschaft; **official** ~ *Am* Sicherheitsleistung e-s Vormunds, Testamentsvollstreckers etc; →**surety** ~; **to enter into a** ~ Kaution stellen; **the** ~ **shall be forfeited** die Kaution verfällt; **to file** (or **lodge**) **a** ~ **in court** Sicherheit bei Gericht leisten; **to furnish** (or **give**) **a** ~ Kaution stellen; Sicherheit leisten; **to set a** ~ e-e Kaution festsetzen; **a** ~ **is required** e-e Kaution muß gestellt werden

bond 4. *bes. Br* (Zoll-)Verschluß; ~ **note** Zollversandschein; ~ **papers** Zollbegleitpapiere; ~ **warrant** →~ note

bond, in ~ unter Zollverschluß; unverzollt *(opp. duty paid)*; **goods in** ~ Waren unter Zollverschluß; Zollgut; **to place** (or **put**) **goods in** ~ Waren unter Zollverschluß nehmen; **to store in** ~ unter Zollverschluß einlagern

bond, out of ~ verzollt; vom unverzollten Lager; **goods out of** ~ verzollte Ware; **to take goods out of** ~ Waren aus dem Zollverschluß herausnehmen; Waren vom Zollamt abholen; Waren verzollen

bond *v* 1. mit Obligationsschuld (od. Anleiheschuld) (bonded debt) belasten; durch Obligation(en) sichern

bonded, ~ **claim** Forderung aus Schuldverschreibung; ~ **debt** Obligationsschuld, Anleiheschuld; ~ **indebtedness** Obligationsschulden(last); ~ **loan** Anleihe

bonding, ~ **company** *Am* Kautionsversicherungsgesellschaft (→ *bond 3.*); ~ **underwriters** Übernahmekonsortium für Obligationen (od. Pfandbriefe)

bond *v* 2. in Zollverschluß lagern

bonded, ~ **goods** (B.G.) Waren unter Zollverschluß; zollpflichtige Waren, Zollgut; ~ **store** *Br* →~ warehouse; ~ **value** unverzollter Wert *(opp. duty paid value)*; ~ **warehouse** Zoll(gut-)lager, Zollspeicher *(in dem Ware unverzollt eingelagert werden darf)*

bondsman *Am* Bürge; *Am* Person, die gewerblich Kaution stellt

bonis, in ~ **(defuncti)** (i.b.) ("among the goods") *Am* unter den Sachen *(des Erblassers)*; im Nachlaß

bonus 1. Bonus, Extrazahlung; *(AktienR)* Extradividende, Sondervergütung *(neben der Dividende)*; Prämie; Gratifikation; Tantieme; *(ArbeitsR) (über den Grundlohn hinaus gezahlte)* Sondervergütung; (Weihnachts-)Gratifikation; ~ **issue** *(bei e-r Kapitalerhöhung ausgegebene)* Gratisaktie; ~ **payments** freiwillige Leistungen *(des Arbeitgebers)*; ~ **scheme** *(z. B. EG)* Prämienregelung(splan); ~ **system** Prämiensystem *(für Arbeiter)*; ~ **shares** *Br* Gratisaktien *(die z. B. anstelle e-r Bardividende ausgegeben werden; kein Geschenk an Aktionäre, sondern Form der Selbstfinanzierung)*; Kapitalberichtigungsaktien; ~ **stock** *Am (als Geschenk od [Anreiz-]Prämie verteilte)* Gratisaktien *(→ watered stock)*; **cash** ~ Barbonus, Barvergütung; **Christmas** ~ Weihnachtsgratifikation; **cost of living** ~ Teuerungszulage; **incentive** ~ Leistungszulage; **local** ~ Ortszulage; **special** ~ Sonderzulage

bonus 2. *(VersR) bes. Br* Gewinnanteil, Dividende; ~ **in cash** Bardividende; ~ **reserve** Gewinnanteilrücklage; ~ **scheme** Gewinnplan; **allocation of** ~ Gewinnanteilzuweisung; **cash** ~ Bardividende; **compound** ~ zusammengesetzte Dividende; **no claims** ~ *Br (Kfz-Vers.)* Schadensfreiheitsrabatt; **reversionary** ~ Summenzuwachs; **simple** ~ einfache Dividende; **terminal** ~ Schlußdividende

bonus *v* e-n Bonus geben; e-e Extrazahlung gewähren

book Buch; ~**s** Geschäftsbücher; ~ **of accounts** Kontobuch; ~**s of account** Geschäftsbücher; ~ **claim** Buchforderung; buchmäßige Forderung; ~ **of commission** (Waren-)Bestellbuch; Orderbuch; ~ **debts** Buchschulden; buchmäßige Schulden; ~ **depreciation** bilanzmäßige Abschreibung; ~ **entry** Buchung; ~ **of entries** Eingangsbuch; ~ **of original entry** Grundbuch *(in der Buchführung);* ~ **fair** Buchmesse; ~ **of forms** Formularbuch, Formularsammlung; ~ **of invoices** Fakturenbuch; ~ **(-)keeper** Buchhalter

book(-)keeping Buchhaltung, Buchführung; ~ **department** Buchhaltung(sabteilung); **general** ~ **department** Hauptbuchhaltung; ~ **entry** Buchung; Buchungsposten; ~ **by double entry** doppelte Buchführung; ~ **by single entry** einfache Buchführung; ~ **method** Buchführungsverfahren; Buchhaltungstechnik; ~ **records** Buchungsunterlagen; ~ **voucher** Buchhaltungsbeleg, Buchungsbeleg; **mechanical** ~ Durchschreibebuchführung

book, ~ **loss** Buchverlust, buchmäßiger Verlust; ~**(-)maker** Buchmacher *(bei Pferderennen);* ~ **profit** Buchgewinn, buchmäßiger Gewinn *(opp. realized profit);* ~ **receivables** Buchforderungen; ~ **of reference** Nachschlagewerk; ~**s of reference** benutzte Literatur, Quellen; ~ **of remittances** Überweisungsbuch; ~ **review** Buchbesprechung; ~ **of sales** (Waren-)Ausgangsbuch; ~ **value** Buchwert, buchmäßiger Wert *(opp. market value)*

Book *pol,* **Blue** ~ Blaubuch; **White** ~ Weißbuch *(bes. BRD);* **Yellow** ~ Gelbbuch

book, closing (or **settlement**) **of** ~**s** Abschluß der Bücher; **in consulting our** ~**s** bei Durchsicht unserer Bücher; **order** ~ Bestellbuch; **postage** ~ Portobuch; **sales** ~ Warenausgangsbuch

book, to audit the ~**s** die Bücher prüfen; **to enter in the** ~**s** buchen; **to falsify the** ~**s** die Bücher fälschen; **to keep** ~**s** Bücher führen; **as shown in the** ~**s** buchmäßig; **to take one's name off the** ~**s** *(aus e-m Verein etc)* austreten; seine Mitgliedschaft aufgeben

book *v (in Buch od. Liste)* eintragen; aufschreiben *(auch von Polizei);* (ver)buchen; *(Platz, Zimmer)* (vor)bestellen, reservieren (lassen); **to** ~ **(in advance)** im voraus bestellen; *(Karten)* im Vorverkauf besorgen; **to** ~ **for** die *(vorher bestellte)* (Schiffs- od. Flug-)Karte lösen nach; **to** ~ **freight space** Frachtraum belegen; **to** ~ **an order** e-n Auftrag vormerken (od. annehmen); **to** ~ **one's passage** seine Schiffskarte (od. Flugkarte) bestellen

booked, to be (fully) ~ **up** besetzt (od. ausverkauft) sein; **to be** ~ **for exceeding the speed limit** *(von der Polizei)* wegen Überschreitung der Höchstgeschwindigkeit aufgeschrieben werden

booking Buchung; Eintragung; (Vor-)Bestellung; Reservierung, reservierter Platz; *(beim Stückgütervertrag)* Buchung *(Anmeldung der Güter zur Beförderung),* Belegung von Frachtraum; ~ **clerk** *Br* Fahrkartenverkäufer, Schalterbeamter; ~ **office** Fahrkartenschalter; Buchungsstelle; *Am* (Theater- etc) Kasse, Vorverkaufskasse; **advance** ~ (Karten-)Vorverkauf; Vorbestellung; **to cancel a** ~ Karten abbestellen; Platzbestellung rückgängig machen

booklet Broschüre, Prospekt, kleine Werbeschrift

boom Hochkonjunktur, wirtschaftlicher Aufschwung; *(Börse)* Hausse *(opp. recession, slump);* Wahlpropaganda; Stimmungsmache *(für e-n Kandidaten od. e-e Sache);* anwachsende Stimmung (für); ~ **market** Haussemarkt; ~ **mentality** Haussestimmung; ~ **period** Konjunkturperiode; ~ **profit** Konjunkturgewinn; ~ **years** Jahre der Hochkonjunktur; **overheated** ~ überhitzte Konjunktur; **stock market** ~ Aktienhausse; **to check** (or **curb**) **the** ~ die Hochkonjunktur bremsen

boom *v* rapide ansteigen, in die Höhe gehen *(Preise, Kurse);* in die Höhe treiben; e-n rapiden Aufschwung nehmen, sich schnell entwickeln; **to** ~ **the market** die Kurse in die Höhe treiben

booming florierend; im Aufschwung begriffen; ~ **prices** schnell (an)steigende Preise; **business is** ~ das Geschäft geht glänzend

boost *colloq.* Erhöhung *(der Preise, Löhne, Produktion etc);* Preistreiberei; Förderung *(Verbesserung der Lage, des Rufes etc);* Reklame; ~ **in pay** *Am sl.* Gehaltserhöhung

boost *v colloq. (Preise, Löhne, Produktion etc)* erhöhen (od. hinauftreiben); Reklame machen für, anpreisen; **to** ~ **the economy** die Wirtschaft ankurbeln

booth Bude; Marktstand; **polling** ~ Wahlzelle, -kabine; **telephone** ~ Telefonzelle

bootleg *v, Am sl. (bes. Alkohol)* schmuggeln; *(Alkohol)* unerlaubt herstellen (od. verkaufen); **to** ~ **aliens into a country** *Am sl.* Ausländer in ein Land einschmuggeln

bootlegging *Am* (Alkohol-)Schmuggel; illegale *(heimliche)* Tätigkeit

bootlegger *Am* (Alkohol-)Schmuggler; Schieber

booty of war Kriegsbeute *(zu Land) (opp. prize);* Beutegut

border Grenze *(e-s Landes);* **the B~** Grenze zwischen England und Schottland; ~ **area** Grenzgebiet; ~ **control** Grenzkontrolle; Grenzüberwachung; **(illegal)** ~ **crosser** Grenzgänger; ~ **check point** Grenzübergangsstelle; ~ **district** Grenzbezirk; ~ **incident** Grenzzwischenfall; ~ **line** Grenzlinie; ~**line case** Grenzfall; ~ **police** Grenzpolizei; ~ **state** Grenzstaat; ~ **town** Grenzstadt; ~ **traffic** Grenzverkehr; ~ **violation** Grenzverletzung; **on the** ~ an der Grenze; **regular services across the** ~ grenzüberschreitender Linienverkehr; **to cross the** ~ die Grenze überschreiten, über die Grenze gehen; **to escape over the** ~ über die Grenze entweichen

border *v* grenzen (on an); ~**ing** angrenzend, anliegend; ~**ing state** Anliegerstaat

bordereau Bordereau, Verzeichnis; *(VersR)* Annahmeschein

borderer Grenzbewohner

born geboren; **first-~** erstgeboren; **native-~ citizen** *Am* gebürtiger Amerikaner; **natural-~ British subject** von Geburt britischer Untertan

borough Stadt, Stadtbezirk; **B~ Council** *Br* Stadtrat, Gemeinderat (mayor and councillors); **B~ Councillor** *Br* Stadtrat, Ratsherr *(cf. B~ Council);* **B~ English** *Br* Vererbung auf den jüngsten Sohn *(obs.);* **the 5 B~s of New York** *Am* die 5 Stadtbezirke von New York; **the 32 London B~s** die 32 Stadtteile von Greater London (→ *London*); **municipal** ~ *Br* grafschaftsangehörige Stadt *(untersteht der Verwaltung e-s →county);* **parliamentary** ~ *Br* städtischer Wahlkreis, Wahlbezirk *(für Wahl von Parlamentsmitgliedern)*

borrow *v* borgen; (ent)leihen (from von); Darlehen aufnehmen *(opp. to lend);* **to ~ money** Geld (od. Darlehen, Kredit) aufnehmen; **to ~ on a policy** e-e Police beleihen; **to ~ on securities** Effekten lombardieren

borrowed capital Fremdkapital

borrowing Borgen; Entleihen; Darlehensaufnahme, Kreditaufnahme; ~ **authorization** Ermächtigung zur Kreditaufnahme; ~ **cost** Kreditkosten; ~ **country** kreditnehmendes Land, Schuldnerland *(opp. creditor country);* ~ **demand** Kreditbedarf; ~ **limit** Kreditgrenze; ~ **member** (of a building society) *Br* →advanced member; ~ **needs** Kreditbedarf; ~ **power** Kreditaufnahmefähigkeit; Ermächtigung zur Kreditaufnahme; ~ **rate** Kreditzinssatz; Darlehenszinssatz; ~ **requirement** Kreditbedarf; Finanzierungsbedarf

borrower Entleiher; Darlehensnehmer, Geldnehmer; Anleihenehmer; Kreditnehmer *(opp. lender);* ~ **(of capital)** Kapitalnehmer; ~**s' note** Schuldschein; ~**s' notes against ad rem security** dinglich gesicherte Schuldscheine; ~**s' notes loans** Schuldscheindarlehen; ~ **options for notes and underwritten standbys** (BONUS) Variante e-r →note issuance facility durch Begebung von Titeln am Euro- wie am US-commercial paper Markt zur Finanzmittelbeschaffung

Borstal, ~ **Institution** *Br*[17] *(erzieherisch gestaltete)* Jugendstrafanstalt *(für die Altersgruppe 15–21);* ~ **training** *Br* Strafvollzug in e-r ~ Institution

boss *colloq.* Chef, Vorgesetzter; Meister; Vorarbeiter; *Am pol* Führer e-r politischen Clique, (Partei-)Bonze *(Chef e-r → machine)*

both sides of industry Tarifpartner, Sozialpartner

both-to-blame collision clause *Br*[18] Klausel über Kollisionen *(von Schiffen)* bei beiderseitigem Verschulden

Botswana, Republic of ~ Republik Botsuana; **(of)** ~ Botsuaner(in); botsuanisch

bottle(-)neck Straßenverengung, Engstelle *(im Verkehr); fig* Engpaß *(z.B. in der Produktion durch Rohstoffmangel)*

bottom Boden *(e-s Fasses etc);* Grundlage, Basis; Schiffsboden; (Fracht-)Schiff; niedrigster Stand, Tiefstand *(Kurse, Preise);* unten *(Aufschrift auf Kisten; opp. top);* **at the** ~ ganz unten; ~ **price** niedrigster Preis (od. Kurs); ~ **quality** schlechteste Qualität; ~ **of the sea** Meeresboden; **prices have touched** ~ die Preise haben den tiefsten Stand erreicht

bottomry Bodmerei, Schiffsverpfändung; ~ **bond** Bodmereibrief *(sog. Seewechsel);* ~ **bondholder** Bodmereigläubiger; ~ **contract** Bodmereivertrag; ~ **lien** Bodmereipfandrecht; ~ **loan** Bodmereidarlehen; **borrower on** ~ Bodmereinehmer, Bodmereischuldner; **lender on** ~ Bodmereigeber, Bodmereigläubiger; **to borrow** (or **raise**) **money on** ~ verbodmen, Geld auf Bodmerei aufnehmen; **to give** (or **lend**) **money on** ~ Geld auf Bodmerei geben

bought verkauft; ~ **at auction** ersteigert; ~ **book** (or **journal**) Einkaufsbuch, Einkaufsjournal; ~ **deal** Anleiheemission, bei der das Emissionskonsortium bis zur Plazierung das Kursrisiko trägt *(opp. pricing);* ~ **note** *Br (Börse) (für den Kauf ausgestellter)* Schlußschein, Schlußnote *(des Maklers; opp. sold note)*

bouncer *colloq.* geplatzter Scheck

bound Grenze, Schranke; **out of ~s** außerhalb der erlaubten Grenzen (od. des erlaubten Gebietes) *(z.B. für Militärpersonen, Gefangene, Schulkinder)*

bound 1. gefunden, verpflichtet (→*to bind*); **to be ~ by contract** vertraglich verpflichtet sein; **to be ~ over for two years** (to keep the peace or to be of good behaviour) *Br (etwa:)* e-e Bewährungsfrist von 2 Jahren erhalten (in the sum of ... gegen Kaution von ...)
bound 2., **~ for** bestimmt (od. unterwegs) nach *(von Schiffen)*; **homeward ~** auf der Heimreise (od. Rückreise) (befindlich); **outward ~** auf der Hin- (od. Aus-)reise (befindlich)

boundar|y Grenze; Grenzlinie; Bannmeile; **~ies of state territory** Grenzen des Staatsgebietes; **~ convention** *(VölkerR)* Grenzvertrag; **~ crossing** Grenzüberschreitung; Grenzübergang; **~ dispute** Grenzstreit(igkeit)
boundary line Grenzlinie; **course of the ~** Verlauf der Grenzlinie
boundary sign Grenzzeichen; **to move a ~** ein Grenzzeichen verrücken
boundar|y, ~ stone Grenzstein; **~ treaty** *(VölkerR)* Grenzvertrag; **fixation of ~ies** Grenzbestimmung; Grenzziehung; **natural and artificial ~ies** natürliche und künstliche Grenzen; **rectification of ~ies** Grenzberichtigung; **to fix a ~** e-e Grenze bestimmen (od. ziehen, festlegen); **the ~ is no longer recognizable** der Grenzverlauf *(e-s Grundstücks)* ist unkenntlich geworden

bounty Spende *(bes. an Arme)*; Prämie, Subvention *(zur Förderung des Handels, der Produktion etc)*; *(als Belohnung ausgesetzte)* Prämie; **~ on exports** Ausfuhrprämie; **~-fed** durch staatliche Zuschüsse unterstützt; subventioniert

bourgeois *Fr* bürgerlich *(im verächtlichen Sinne)*

Bourse *(ausländische, bes. Pariser)* Börse

box Kasten, Kiste; **~es** (bxs) Kisten; **~ car** *Am (geschlossener)* Güterwagen
box number *Br (Inserat)* Chiffrenummer; **advertisement under ~** *Br* Anzeige unter Chiffre
box, ~ office Theaterkasse; Kasse; **~ waggon** *Br (geschlossener)* Güterwagen
box, ballot ~ Wahlurne; **cash ~** Geldkassette; **deed ~** Kassette für Urkunden und Wertpapiere; **money ~** Sparbüchse; **safe deposit ~** (Bank-)Schließfach, Safe; **telephone ~** Telefonzelle; **witness ~** Zeugenbank

boycott Boykott; *(KartellR)* Sperre; **primary ~** primärer (od. unmittelbarer) Boykott; **secondary ~** mittelbare(r) Boykott(maßnahme) *(gegenüber Kunden od. Lieferanten)*; **incitement** (or **stirring up**) **to ~** Boykotthetze; **to call off a ~** e-n Boykott aufheben; **to declare a ~** e-n Boykott verhängen

boycott *v* boykottieren; in Verruf erklären; sperren
boycotted party Boykottierter; Gesperrter; Verrufener

boycotter Boykottierer, Verrufer *(party inducing boycott)*; Sperrer *(party responding to a boycott request)*

boycotting Boykottierung; Boykott; Sperre

bracket Gruppe, Stufe, Klasse; **age ~** Altersgruppe; **income ~** Einkommensgruppe; **tax ~** Steuerklasse

brain Gehirn; **~ drain** Abwanderung von Fachkräften *(bes. nach USA)*; **~ power** Wissenschaftler *(als Sammelbegriff)*; wissenschaftliche Führungskräfte; **~storming** spontane Problembewältigung durch e-e Gruppe; **B~ Trust** *Am (politischer und wirtschaftl.)* Beraterstab *(von erstklassigen Fachleuten)*; *Br* Expertengruppe, die Rat erteilt oder Fragen beantwortet *(z. B. als Radioprogramm)*; **~ work** geistige Arbeit; **~ worker** Geistesarbeiter

brainwash *v pol* Gehirnwäsche vornehmen *(ideologisch beeinflussen)*; **~ed** der Gehirnwäsche unterzogen; **~ing** Gehirnwäsche

branch Zweigstelle, Filiale, Zweigniederlassung; Nebenstelle; (Geschäfts-)Zweig, Betriebsstätte, Branche, Sparte; **~ account** Filialkonto *(opp. head office account)*; **~ bank** Filialbank; **~ of a bank** Bankfiliale; **~ banking** Filialbanksystem; **~ business** Zweiggeschäft; **~ of (a) business** Geschäftszweig; **~ establishment** Zweigniederlassung, Zweigstelle, Zweiggeschäft, Filiale; **~ (of a family)** Linie, Seitenlinie; **~ firm** *Am* Filialbetrieb, Filialunternehmen; **~ house** Filiale *(opp. parent house)*; **~ of industry** Industriezweig; **~ of insurance** Versicherungszweig; **~ line** Zweigbahn, Nebenlinie; **~ manager** Filialleiter; **~ network** Filialnetz; **~ office** (B.O.) Zweigstelle, Zweigniederlassung, Zweigbüro *(opp. head office)*; **~ profits tax** *Am* Quellensteuer für US-Zweigniederlassungen; **~ of the service** *mil* Waffengattung, Truppengattung; **~ store** Zweiggeschäft, Filiale; **~ of trade** Wirtschaftszweig
branch, city ~ Stadtfiliale; **local ~** *(örtl.)* Zweigstelle, Filiale; **main ~** Hauptfiliale, Hauptstelle; **special ~** Sonderabteilung; **Special B~** *Br* Staatssicherheitspolizei; **to establish a ~ office** e-e Zweigstelle errichten; **to maintain ~es** Zweigstellen unterhalten; **to open a ~** e-e Filiale eröffnen

brand Handelsmarke, Warenzeichen, Fabrikmarke *(auf Kisten, Büchsen, Schachteln etc)*; Sorte; **~ advertising** Marken(artikel)werbung; **~ choice** Markenwahl; **~ competition** Marken(artikel)wettbewerb; **~ family** Markenfamilie; **~ manager** Vertriebsleiter für e-n bestimmten Markenartikel; **~ name goods** Markenartikel; **~ preference** Markenbevorzugung; **a good ~** e-e gute Sorte; **house ~** Eigenmarke; **national** ~ *Am* Herstellermarke, Schutzmarke *(e-s Artikels, der im ganzen Lande verkauft wird);* **private** (or **special**) ~ *Am* Händlermarke; **producer's** ~ Herstellermarke; **rival** ~ Konkurrenzmarke

brand *v* mit *(eingebranntem)* Zeichen versehen
branded articles (or **goods, merchandise**) Markenartikel, Markenware
branding, double ~ *Am* zweigleisiger Vertrieb von Markenwaren; Preisspaltung

brass-tacks, to get down to ~ *sl.* zur Sache kommen

brawl Schlägerei, Raufhandel; lärmender Streit; Auflauf; **to take part in a** ~ an e-r Schlägerei teilnehmen

brawler Lärmer; **common** ~ Raufbold

brawling *Br* Ruhestörung *(bes. in Kirchen und auf Friedhöfen);* **street** ~ Straßenauflauf

Brazil Brasilien; **Federative Republic of** ~ Föderative Republik Brasilien
Brazilian Brasilianer(in); brasilianisch

breach Bruch; Verstoß (of gegen); Verletzung; ~ **of agreement** →~ of contract; ~ **of close** widerrechtliches Betreten fremden Besitztums; ~ **of condition** Nichteinhaltung der Bedingung; ~ **of condition (of a contract)** *Br* Verletzung e-r wesentlichen Vertragsbestimmung *(opp. breach of warranty);* ~ **of confidence** Vertrauensbruch; Verletzung der Geheimhaltungspflicht
breach of contract Vertragsbruch; Vertragsverletzung; Nichterfüllung e-s Vertrages; **inducing a** ~ Verleitung zum Vertragsbruch; Verhinderung der Vertragserfüllung; **material** ~ erhebliche Vertragsverletzung; **minor** ~ geringfügige Vertragsverletzung; **to commit a** ~ vertragsbrüchig werden; e-n Vertrag nicht erfüllen (od. einhalten)
Breach of contract gibt – außer im Immobiliarrecht – im allgemeinen nur Anlaß zu einer Schadensersatzklage, nicht zu einer Klage auf Erfüllung (specific performance). Bei einer Vertragsverletzung wird grundsätzlich auch ohne Verschulden gehaftet (→ *contract 1.)*
breach, ~ **of covenant** Nichteinhaltung e-r *(ausdrücklich erklärten)* Vertragspflicht; ~ **of duty** (Amts-)Pflichtverletzung; ~ **of etiquette** Verstoß gegen die Etikette; ~ **of professional etiquette** standeswidriges Verhalten; ~ **of form** Formverletzung; ~ **of (the) law** Gesetzesverletzung, Rechtsbruch; ~ **of the peace** Störung der öffentlichen Sicherheit und Ordnung (→*peace 2.);* Bruch des Friedens[19]; ~ **of pound** Verstrickungsbruch *(hinsichtlich gepfändeten Viehs);* ~ **of prison** Ausbruch aus dem Gefängnis; ~ **of privilege** *Br* Verletzung der Rechte e-r privilegierten Körperschaft *(bes. des Parlaments);* ~ **of professional secrecy** Bruch des Berufsgeheimnisses; ~ **of promise** (of marriage)[20] Verlöbnisbruch; Bruch des Eheversprechens; ~ **of trust** Vertrauensbruch, Veruntreuung; Verletzung der Verpflichtung e-r Person in Vertrauensstellung *(bes. des trustee od. executor); Scot* Betrug *(cf. fraud);* ~ **of warranty** → warranty 1. und 2.

breadline Armutsgrenze

breadwinner Ernährer *(e-r Familie);* Haushaltsvorstand

break Bruch; Unterbrechung, Pause; Verletzung; ~**bulk cargo** Stückgut; ~ **(in prices)** Preissturz; Kurssturz; Kurseinbruch; ~ **of journey** Fahrtunterbrechung
breakaway group abgespaltene Gruppe
breakdown 1. Zusammenbruch, Scheitern; Betriebsstörung; Verkehrsstörung; Panne *(e-s Autos);* ~ **of a marriage** Scheitern e-r Ehe; **irretrievable** ~ **of marriage** *Br*[21] **(irremediable** ~ **of marriage** *Am***)** unheilbare Zerrüttung der Ehe; ~ **of negotiations** Scheitern der Verhandlungen; ~ **service** Pannendienst; ~ **vehicle** *Br* Abschleppwagen
breakdown 2. Aufgliederung, Untergliederung, Aufschlüsselung; ~ **of costs** Kostenaufgliederung; ~ **by occupation** berufliche Aufgliederung; Einteilung (od. Aufschlüsselung) nach Berufen
break-even *Am* Geschäftsabschluß ohne Gewinn und Verlust; ~ **point** Rentabilitätsgrenze *(e-s Betriebes);* Gewinnschwelle; Nutzschwelle
break in Einbruch (at the bank in die Bank)
breakthrough Durchbruch; bahnbrechende Erfindung (od. Leistung)
breakup Auflösung, Ende *(e-r Koalition, Ehe etc);* ~ **of a conglomerate** Entflechtung e-s Konzerns; ~ **of marriage** →breakdown of marriage; ~ **of a meeting** Abbruch e-r Sitzung; ~ **value** *Br* Liquidationswert *(opp. going concern);* Abbruchs-, Ausschlachtungswert

break *v* (auf-, er-, zer)brechen; *(Gesetz, Vertrag)* verletzen; unterbrechen; bankrott machen, zugrunde richten; **to** ~ **a bank** e-e (Spiel-)Bank sprengen; **to** ~ **one's budget** s-n Etat überziehen; **to** ~ **bulk** →bulk 2.; **to** ~ **a contract** e-n Vertrag nicht einhalten; vertragsbrüchig werden; **to** ~ **an engagement** e-e Abmachung nicht einhalten; **to** ~ **the law** das Gesetz verletzen; **to** ~ **one's oath** s-n Eid brechen, eidbrüchig werden; **to** ~ **the peace** die öffentliche Sicherheit und Ordnung stören; **to** ~ **one's promise** sein Versprechen nicht halten; **to** ~ **a strike** e-n Streik brechen
break down *v* zusammenbrechen, scheitern; *(Kosten etc)* aufgliedern, aufschlüsseln; e-e Panne haben; **the negotiations have broken down** die Verhandlungen sind gescheitert; **to** ~ **opposition** den Widerstand brechen

break and enter *v* einbrechen
break even *v* sich *(gerade)* noch finanziell rentieren; kostendeckend *(ohne Gewinn od. Verlust)* arbeiten; *(gerade)* genug verdienen, um Auslagen zu decken
break in *v* einbrechen, eindringen; **burglars have broken in** Diebe sind eingebrochen
break into *v*, **to ~ one's capital** sein Kapital angreifen; **to ~ a house** in ein Haus einbrechen
break off *v* abbrechen; **to ~ a conversation** e-e Unterredung abbrechen; **to ~ diplomatic relations** diplomatische Beziehungen abbrechen; **to ~ the engagement** die Verlobung auflösen
break out *v* ausbrechen *(Krieg, Feuer)*; **to ~ of prison** aus dem Gefängnis ausbrechen
break up *v* sich auflösen, auseinandergehen; aufteilen (among unter); aufspalten; **to ~ a house** ein Haus aufbrechen; **to ~ one's household** seinen Haushalt auflösen; **to ~ a meeting** e-e Versammlung *(durch die Polizei)* auflösen; e-e Sitzung abbrechen; **to ~ a ship** ein Schiff abwracken

breakable zerbrechlich

breakage Bruch(schaden); Entschädigung für Bruchschaden, Refaktie; **~ clause** Bruchklausel; **danger of ~** Bruchgefahr; **free from ~** *(VersR)* frei von Bruch; **owner's risk of ~** (o. r. b.) Bruchrisiko des Eigentümers; **allowance for ~** Refaktie; **to pay for ~** den Bruchschaden ersetzen

breaking Bruch; **~ bulk** Beginn der Entladung; Löschen der Ladung; Mengenumgruppierung *(zu kleineren Mengen)*; **~ the close** → breach of close; **~ and entering** Einbruch; **~ in** Eingewöhnung; *(StrafR)* Einbruch; **~ of an oath** Eidbruch; **~ off (of diplomatic) relations** Abbruch der (diplomatischen) Beziehungen

breathalyse *v* Atemprobe entnehmen

breathalyser Alkoholteströhrchen, Pusteröhrchen

brevet (rank) Titularrang (of als); **~ major** Hauptmann im Rang e-s Majors *(ohne entsprechendes Gehalt)*

brewery shares Brauereiaktien

bribable bestechlich

bribe Bestechung(sgeld); Schmiergeld; **~giver** *Am* Bestechender, jd, der bestechen will; **accepting** (or **taking**) **of ~s** passive Bestechung; **giving** (or **offering**) **of ~s** aktive Bestechung; **to accept** (or **take**) **a ~** sich bestechen lassen; **to give** (or **offer**) **a ~** bestechen (wollen)

bribe *v* bestechen
bribing Bestechung; **~ of a civil servant** Beamtenbestechung; **~ of witnesses** Zeugenbestechung

briber Bestechender

bribery[22] *(aktive und passive)* Bestechung *(Tätigkeit)*; **~ and corruption** *Br* Bestechungsunwesen; **~ of employees** Bestechung von Angestellten *(e-s Konkurrenten)*; Angestelltenbestechung; **attempt at** (or **attempted**) **~** Bestechungsversuch; **open to ~** bestechlich; **to practise ~** bestechen

bridge Brücke; **~head** *mil* Brückenkopf; **~ load carrying capacity** Brückentragfähigkeit

bridge *v fig* überbrücken
bridging, ~ loan Überbrückungskredit; **~ finance** Zwischenfinanzierung

brief *Br* schriftl. Beauftragung und Information *(des barrister durch den solicitor)* zur Vertretung vor Gericht; Schriftsatz; *Am* schriftl. Information des Gerichts *(durch den counsel)*; Anweisung(en); **~ on appeal** *Am* Berufungsbegründung *(des Anwalts)*; **(papal) ~** Breve (des Papstes) *(im Ggs. zu bull Erlaß von geringerer Bedeutung)*; **attorney on the ~** *Am* Anwalt, der den Schriftsatz gefertigt (od. an ihm mitgearbeitet) hat; **trial ~** *Am* Verhandlungsschriftsatz *(des Anwalts)*
brief, to hold a watching ~ for a p. jds Interesse *(bei Gericht)* als Beobachter vertreten
brief, to deliver (or **give, send**) **a ~ to a barrister** (or **counsel**) *Br* e-n barrister beauftragen; **to hold (a) ~ (for)** vor Gericht vertreten; als Anwalt auftreten (für); **to obtain a ~** *Br (als barrister)* e-e Rechtssache *(zur mündl. Verhandlung)* übertragen bekommen; **to take a ~** e-e Rechtssache übernehmen

brief kurz, bündig; **to invite the speaker to be ~** den Redner bitten, sich kurz zu fassen
briefly kurz; mit wenigen Worten

brief *v (letzte und präzise)* informierende Instruktionen erteilen; **to ~ sb. on** jdn informieren (od. unterrichten) über; jdn kurz einweisen in; **to ~ a counsel** *Br* e-n Anwalt (barrister) mit der Verhandlung *(vor Gericht)* beauftragen (→ briefing counsel)
briefing Information, *(kurze)* Zusammenfassung; Anweisung, Unterweisung; Einsatzbesprechung; *(Presse) (meist formloses)* Informationsgespräch *(zu dem ein Minister, ein Parlamentarier od. der Regierungssprecher ladet. Die Informationen sind manchmal vertraulich [off the record])*; **~ a counsel** *Br* Bestellung e-s vor Gericht auftretenden Anwalts (barrister) durch e-n solicitor; **~ meeting** Informationssitzung

briefless ohne Mandanten *(Br barrister)*

bring *v* (herbei-, ein-, er-, über)bringen; **to ~ about** zustandebringen, herbeiführen; **to ~ about a reconciliation** e-e Versöhnung herbeiführen; **to ~ down prices** die Preise herabsetzen; **to ~ forward** *(Beweise, Argumente)* vorbringen; *(Sitzung)* vorverlegen; *(Buchführung)* (b/f) übertragen, vortragen; **to ~ in** *(Geld, Gewinn)* einbringen; **to ~ in a bill** e-n Gesetzesentwurf einbringen; **the jury ~s in a verdict of guilty** die Geschworenen verkünden den Schuldspruch; **to ~ in(to) a business** in ein Geschäft einbringen; **to ~ out** *(Buch)* herausbringen, veröffentlichen; *(Ware)* auf den Markt bringen; **to ~ up** *(Kind)* erziehen; **to ~ sb. up for trial** jdn *(in e-r Strafsache)* vor Gericht bringen; **to ~ up to date** auf den gegenwärtigen (od. neuesten) Stand bringen

bring *v*, **to ~ to account** in Rechnung stellen; zur Rechenschaft ziehen; **to ~ an action against sb.** gegen jdn klagen; jdn verklagen; **to ~ to a close** zum Abschluß bringen; **to ~ sb. to justice** jdn gerichtlich belangen

bringing an action Erhebung e-r Klage, Klageerhebung

brinkmanship Politik am Rande des Abgrunds

brisk *(Börse, Handel)* lebhaft *(opp. dull)*; **~ state of trade** lebhafter Geschäftsgang

British Briten *(pl)* *(cf Briton)*; britisch; **~ Academy** Britische Akademie der (Geistes-)Wissenschaften; **~ Aerospace** (BAe) Britisches Luft- u. Raumfahrtunternehmen; **~ Airports Authority** (BAA) Britische Flughafenbehörde; **~ Airways** (B. A.) *(private)* Luftverkehrsgesellschaft; **~ Association for the Advancement of Science** Britische Vereinigung zur Förderung der (Natur-)Wissenschaften; **~ Bank Bills** (BBB) kurzfristige Geldmarktpapiere

Britisch Bankers' Association (BBA) Britischer Bankenverband; **~ terms** Richtlinien des BBA für standardisierte Kontrakte über Zinsswaps, Devisenoptionen und Zinsterminkontrakte

British, ~ Broadcasting Corporation (BBC) Britische Rundfunkgesellschaft; **~ citizenship** britische Staatsbürgerschaft *(→citizenship)*; **~ Coal** *(staatl.)* Britische Kohlebehörde; **~ Commonwealth of Nations** → Commonwealth; **~ Council** staatl. Organisation zur Sprach- u. Kulturpflege im Ausland; **~ Council of Churches** Zusammenschluß der anglikanischen Kirche mit den nichtkatholischen Glaubensgemeinschaften Englands

British Empire Britisches (Welt-)Reich *(jetzt: →* Commonwealth); **Order of the ~** Orden des Britischen Reiches *(Militär- und Zivilorden für Männer und Frauen)*

British, ~ funds → fund 1; **~ government stock** britische Staatspapiere; **~ Industries Fair** (B.I.F.) Britische Industriemesse; **~ Institute of Management** (B.I.M.) Britisches Betriebswirtschaftsinstitut; **~ Insurance Association** Verband Britischer Versicherer; **~ Isles** Britische Inseln *(Great Britain, Ireland, Channel Islands, and Isle of Man)*; **~ Museum** Britisches Museum *(Bibliothek und Museum in London)*; **~ protected persons**[23] britische Schutzangehörige *(Angehörige der Protektorate, Schutzstaaten, Mandats- od. Treuhandgebiete)*; **~ Rail** *(staatl.)* Britische Eisenbahngesellschaft; **~ Railways Board** *(staatl.)* Britische Eisenbahnverwaltung; **~ Steel Corporation** Dachgesellschaft der verstaatlichten britischen Stahlunternehmen

British subject britischer Staatsbürger; **natural-born ~** geborener britischer Staatsbürger; **naturalized ~** eingebürgerter britischer Staatsbürger; **to cease to be a ~** die britische Staatsangehörigkeit verlieren

British subject hat gemäß British Nationality Act, 1948, Part I, Art. 1 die gleiche Bedeutung wie Commonwealth Citizen

British, ~ Telecom ehemalige staatliche Gesellschaft für Fernmeldewesen *(jetzt privatisiert)*; **~ Tourist Authority** britischer Fremdenverkehrsverband; **~ Travel and Holiday Association** (B.T.H.A.) *Br* amtliche Zentralorganisation für den Fremdenverkehr; **~ Treasury Bills** (BTB) kurzfristige Geldmarktpapiere

Briton Brite, Britin *(cf British)*

broach *v*, **to ~ a question** e-e Frage anschneiden

broadcast Rundfunksendung, Fernsehsendung; Rundfunk- od. Fernsehansprache; **news ~** Nachrichtensendung; **right of communicating ~s** *(UrhR)* Recht der Wiedergabe von Rundfunk- (od. Fernseh-)Sendungen

broadcast *v (durch Rundfunk od. Fernsehen)* übertragen (od. senden); im Rundfunk od. Fernsehen sprechen

broadcasting Rundfunk und Fernsehen; **right of ~** *(UrhR)* Senderecht; **unauthorized ~ of radio or television signals** Funkpiraterie

broad claim weitgefaßter Anspruch

broaden *v* (sich) erweitern, ausweiten

broadening *(PatR)* Erweiterung

broader, in a ~ sense in weiterem Sinne

broadly weitgehend

Broadmoor, ~ Institution *Br*[24] staatliche Anstalt für geisteskranke Kriminelle; **~ patient** geisteskranker Krimineller

brochure *Fr* Broschüre, Prospekt

broker (Handels-)Makler, (Geschäfts-)Vermittler *(schließt im Ggs. zum →factor nicht im eigenen Namen ab)*; *(Börse)* *Br* *(vor dem →Big Bang)* Börsenhändler *(→dual capacity system)*; *Am* Börsenmakler; *(EDV)* Informationsvermittler; **~'s ~** *Am* Makler großen Stils *(der für kleinere Makler arbeitet)*; **~'s commission** (or **fee**) Maklergebühr, Maklerprovision; **~-dealer**

Am Kursmakler *(Firma im over-the-counter market, die sowohl als Makler wie als Händler auftritt);* ~ **firm** Maklerfirma; ~**'s loan** *Am* Maklerdarlehen; ~**'s note** Schlußschein, Schlußnote; ~**'s order** *Br* Verladungsanweisung; **bill** ~ Wechselmakler (→ *bill* 4.); **exchange** ~ Wechselmakler; →**floor** ~; **insurance** ~ Versicherungsmakler; **note** ~ *Am* Wechselmakler; **odd-lot** ~ *Am* Makler in kleinen Effektenabschnitten; **produce** ~ Warenmakler; **real estate** ~ *Am* Grundstücksmakler, Immobilienmakler; **ship**~ Schiffsmakler; **stock**~ *Am* Börsenmakler, Effektenmakler

brokerage Maklergebühr, Maklerprovision; Maklergeschäft, Vermittlungsgeschäft; ~ **agreement** (or **contract**) Maklervertrag; ~ **fee** Maklergebühr, Vergütung des Maklers; ~ **firm** *Am* Maklerfirma; ~ **house** Maklerfirma; **buying** ~ Einkaufsprovision; **exchange** ~ Wechselcourtage; **official** ~ amtliche Maklergebühr; **selling** ~ Verkaufsprovision

broking Maklergeschäft, Vermittlungsgeschäft

Bros. (= brothers), **Smith** ~ Gebrüder Smith *(Firmenbezeichnung)*

brothel Bordell

brother Bruder; ~ **of the full (half) blood** → blood

brothers and sisters Geschwister; ~ **of the half blood** Halbgeschwister *(ein gemeinsamer Elternteil)*

(brought) forward (b/f., bt fwd) Vortrag *(aus letzter Rechnung; opp. carried forward)*

brought-in capital *(in e-e Gesellschaft)* eingebrachtes Kapital, Kapitaleinlage; Geschäftseinlage

brownout *Am* →dim out

Brunei Darussalam Brunei Darussalam; **of** ~ Bruneier(in); bruneisch

Brussels Customs Cooperative Council[25] Brüsseler Zollrat (Rat für die Zusammenarbeit auf dem Gebiet des Zollwesens)

Brussels Tariff Nomenclature (BTN)[25a] Brüsseler Zollnomenklatur

bubble *Br* Schwindelunternehmen; ~ **company** Schwindelgesellschaft

bucket shop Winkelbank; nicht zur Börse zugelassene *(unreelle)* Maklerfirma *(die nicht börsenfähige Papiere zu verkaufen versucht); (auch)* Reisebüro, das billige Flugkarten anbietet; ~ **keeper** (or **operator**) Winkelbankier

buckete(e)r *Am* unreeller Börsenmakler; Winkelbankier

bucketing *Am (Börse)* Betreiben unreeller Maklergeschäfte

budget Etat, Haushaltsplan; (Staats-)Haushalt; Budget; Finanzplan *(e-s Unternehmens);* ~ **account** Kundenkreditkonto; ~ **allocation** Haushaltszuweisung

budget appropriations im Haushalt bereitgestellte Mittel; Haushaltsansätze; **cut of** ~ Haushaltsabstrich

budget, ~ **bill** *Am* Haushaltsvorlage; ~ **cuts** Haushaltsabstriche; Haushaltskürzungen; ~ **control** Haushaltskontrolle; ~ **debate** (or **discussion**) Haushaltsdebatte; Etatberatung; ~ **deductions** →~ cuts; ~ **deficit** Haushaltsdefizit; Defizit im (Staats-)Haushalt; ~ **economies** Haushaltseinsparungen; ~ **estimates** Haushaltsvoranschlag; Etatansätze; ~ **expenditure** (Staats-)Haushaltsausgaben; ~ **funds** Haushaltsmittel; ~ **grant** bewilligte Haushaltsmittel; ~ **issues** Haushaltsfragen; ~ **item** Etatposten; Titel des Haushaltsplans; ~ **means** Haushaltsmittel; ~ **plan system** Kundenkreditkauf *(der zu monatlichen Abschlagszahlungen verpflichtet);* ~ **policy measures** haushaltspolitische Maßnahmen; ~ **receipts** Haushaltseinnahmen; ~ **savings** Haushaltseinsparungen; **(unappropriated)** ~ **surplus** Haushaltsüberschuß; ~ **vote** Haushaltsabstimmung; ~ **year** Haushaltsjahr

budget, according to the ~ etatmäßig; **additional** ~ Nachtragshaushalt; **adoption of the** ~ Annahme des Haushaltsplans; **advances on the succeeding** ~ Haushaltsvorgriffe

budget, adverse ~ nicht ausgeglichener Haushalt; **to balance an adverse** ~ ein Haushaltsdefizit ausgleichen

budget, appropriations in the ~ im Haushaltsplan vorgesehene Mittel; Mittelansätze; **approval of the** ~ Genehmigung des Haushaltsplans; **cash** ~ *Am* Zahlungshaushalt; **corrective** ~ Berichtigungshaushalt; **Community** ~ *(EG)* Gemeinschaftshaushalt; **defen ce (~se)** ~ Verteidigungshaushalt; **deficit in the** ~ Haushaltsdefizit

budget, draft ~ Entwurf des Haushaltsplans; Haushaltsvoranschlag; **preliminary draft** ~ Vorentwurf des Haushaltsplans; **to establish the draft** ~ den Entwurf des Haushaltsplans aufstellen

budget, executive ~ *Am (vom Präsidenten dem Congress vorzulegender)* Haushaltsplan; **expenditure exceeding the** ~ Haushaltsüberschreitung; **extraordinary** ~ außerordentlicher Haushalt; **financial** ~ Finanzplan *(e-s Unternehmens);* **not included in the** ~ außeretatmäßig; **item of the** ~ Titel des Haushaltsplans; Etatposten; **legislative** ~ *Am* Haushaltsgesetz; **municipal** ~ Gemeindehaushalt; **ordinary** ~ ordentlicher Haushalt; **preparation of the** ~ Aufstellung des Haushaltsplans; **proposed** ~ Haushaltsvorlage; **(public)** ~ öffentlicher Haushalt; Staatshaushalt; **rectifying** ~ Berichtigungshaushalt; **regular** ~ ordentlicher Haushalt; **state** ~ Staatshaushalt(splan); **supplementary** ~ Nachtragshaushalt(splan); **unbalanced** ~ unausgeglichener Haushalt

budget, to adopt the ~ den Haushaltsplan verabschieden; **to approve the** ~ den Haushaltsplan genehmigen; **to balance the** ~ den Haushaltsplan ausgleichen; **to bring in the** ~ den Haushaltsplan vorlegen; **to draw up the** ~ den Haushaltsplan aufstellen; **to include in the** ~ in den Haushaltsplan aufnehmen; **to introduce the** ~ den Haushaltsplan vorlegen; **to live within one's** ~ s-n Etat nicht überziehen; **to make** (or **prepare**) **the** ~ den Haushaltsplan aufstellen; **to open the** ~ *Am* den Haushaltsplan vorlegen; **to pass the** ~ den Haushaltsplan verabschieden; **to present the** ~ den Haushaltsplan vorlegen; **to reduce the** ~ den Haushaltsplan kürzen; **to review the** ~ den Haushaltsplan prüfen; **to vote the** ~ den Haushaltsplan verabschieden

budget for *v* im Haushalt veranschlagen (od. vorsehen); etatisieren; **not ~ed for** im Etat nicht vorgesehen

budgetary haushaltsmäßig, etatmäßig; Haushalts-, Etat-; ~ **accounting** Finanzplanung; ~ **arrangements** Haushaltsvereinbarungen; ~ **authority** Haushaltsbefugnisse; ~ **bill** Haushaltsvorlage; ~ **committee** Haushaltsausschuß; ~ **control** Haushaltskontrolle; Finanzkontrolle; ~ **deficit** Haushaltsdefizit; ~ **difficulties** Haushaltsschwierigkeiten; ~ **economies** Haushaltseinsparungen; ~ **expenditure** Haushaltsausgaben; ~ **funds** Haushaltsmittel; ~ **imbalance** Unausgeglichenheit des Haushalts; ~ **issues** Haushaltsfragen

budgetary law Haushaltsrecht; **for reasons of** ~ aus haushaltsrechtlichen Gründen

budgetary, ~ **losses** Haushaltsausfälle; ~ **management** Haushaltsführung; ~ **means** Haushaltsmittel; ~ **overspending** Haushaltsüberschreitung; ~ **planning** Haushaltsplanung; Finanzplanung; ~ **policies** Haushaltspolitik; ~ **powers** Haushaltsbefugnisse; **for** ~ **reasons** aus haushaltsrechtlichen Gründen; ~ **regulations** Haushaltsvorschriften; ~ **receipts** Haushaltseinnahmen; ~ **resources** Haushaltsmittel; ~ **revenues** Haushaltseinnahmen; ~ **situation** Haushaltslage, Etatlage; ~ **year** Haushaltsjahr

budgeting Budgetierung, Aufstellung e-s Haushaltsplans; Haushaltsplanung; Finanzplanung; Etatisierung

buffer state Pufferstaat

buffer stock[26] Puffervorrat, Ausgleichsvorrat; Vorratslager; (Markt-)Ausgleichslager *(für Rohstoffe, z.B. Zinn, Kupfer, Erdöl);* ~ **facility** *IWF*[26a] Fazilität zur Finanzierung von Rohstoff-Ausgleichslagern *(Zinn, Kakao, Zucker, Kautschuk);* ~ **sales** Ausgleichslagerverkäufe; ~ **transaction** Ausgleichslagergeschäft

bug *colloq.* „Wanze" *(Abhörgerät); Am sl.* Alarmanlage; *Am sl.* Gewerkschaftsetikett *(an Waren)*

bug *v* abhören

bugging, ~ **installation** Abhöranlage; ~ **scandal** Abhörskandal

buggery *(StrafR)* Sodomie; widernatürliche Unzucht

builder Bauunternehmer; ~**'s estimate** Baukostenvoranschlag; ~**'s risk insurance** Bauhaftpflichtversicherung

building Bau, Gebäude; (Hoch-)Bauwesen; Bauen; ~ **activity** Bautätigkeit; ~ **ban** Bauverbot; ~ **by(e)-laws** *(örtl.)* Bauvorschriften; ~ **commission** Bauauftrag; ~ **under construction** im Bau befindliches Haus; ~ **contract** Bauvertrag; ~ **contractor** Bauunternehmer; ~ **contractors** Baufirma; ~ **costs** Baukosten; ~ **developer** Bauunternehmer; ~ **estimate** Baukostenvoranschlag; ~ **expenses** Baukosten; ~ **firm** Baufirma; ~ **funds** Baugelder; ~ **industry** Baugewerbe, Bauwirtschaft; ~ **investments** Bauinvestitionen; ~ **land** Bauland, Baugelände; ~ **lease** *Br*[27] *(erbbaurechtsähnl.)* Baupacht(vertrag) *(mit Bau- und Nutzungsrecht für den Pächter, öfters auf 999 od. 99 Jahre; cf. ground rent);* ~ **licen|ce (~se)** Bauerlaubnis, Baugenehmigung; baupolizeiliche Genehmigung; ~ **line** Fluchtlinie; ~ **loan** Baukredit; Baudarlehen; ~ **and loan association** *Am (genossenschaftl. organisierte)* Bausparkasse; ~ **lot** →~ site; ~ **market** Baumarkt; ~ **materials** Baumaterial(ien), Baustoffe; ~ **operations** Bauarbeiten; ~ **order** Bauauftrag; ~ **owner** Bauherr

building permit Baugenehmigung; **to grant a** ~ e-e Baugenehmigung erteilen

building, ~ **plot** Bauplatz, -grundstück; **(public)** ~ **project** (öffentl.) Bauvorhaben; ~ **quota** Baukontingent; ~ **regulations** Bauvorschriften; ~ **restrictions** baurechtliche Beschränkungen; ~ **scheme** Bebauungsplan; ~ **site** Bauplatz, Baustelle

building society *Br*[28] Bausparkasse; ~ **savings agreement** *Br* Bausparvertrag

building, ~ **standing empty** leerstehendes Gebäude; ~ **trade** Baugewerbe; ~ **worker** Bauarbeiter

building, additional ~ Anbau; **adjacent** ~ Nebengebäude; **alteration to a** ~ Umbau; **main** ~ Hauptgebäude; **occupied** ~ bewohntes Gebäude; **public** ~ öffentliches Gebäude; **rate in** ~ Bautempo; **side** ~ Anbau

buildup Anstieg, Zunahme; Entwicklung; Aufbauschung, übertriebene Propaganda; *mil* Aufmarsch, Truppenzusammenziehung; ~ **of traffic** Zunahme des Verkehrs

build up *v* ansteigen, zunehmen; *fig* aufbauen;

aufbauschen; **to ~ to** entwickeln zu; **to ~ a business** ein Geschäft aufbauen; **to ~ a case** (Beweis-)Material zusammenstellen; **to ~ a reputation** sich e-n Namen machen

built, ~-in eingebaut; Einbau-; **~-in obsolescence** geplantes Veralten; **~-on site** bebautes Gelände; **~-up area** bebautes Gebiet; *(Verkehr)* geschlossene Ortschaft

Bulgaria Bulgarien; **People's Republic of ~** Volksrepublik Bulgarien

Bulgarian Bulgare, Bulgarin; bulgarisch

bulge *(Börse)* plötzliches *(vorübergehendes)* Steigen der Kurse

bulk 1. Umfang, Größe; Masse, Menge; Hauptteil, größter Teil; (gekaufte) Gesamtheit; **~ of one's business** *colloq.* Hauptgeschäft; größter Teil e-s Geschäfts; **~ buying** Massenankauf; Mengeneinkauf; Großeinkauf; **~ cargo** Schüttladung; Massenfrachtgut; sperrige Ladung; **~ carrier** Massengutfrachter; **~ commodity** Massengut; **~ consignment** Massenlieferung, Engroslieferung; **~ consumer** Großverbraucher; **~ goods** lose (od. unverpackte) Waren, Schüttgut *(opp. packed goods)*; **~ load** Bulkladung; **~ mail** Postwurfsendung; **~ mortgage** *Am* Verpfändung ganzer Bestände; **~ posting** Postwurfsendung, Massensendung; **~ purchase** → **~** buying; **~ sale** (or **selling**) Massenabsatz; Verkauf in Bausch und Bogen *(ohne abzumessen, zu zählen od. zu wiegen)*; *Am* Gesamtverkauf, Veräußerung *(der beweglichen Sachwerte e-s Unternehmens)* als ganzes; **~ sampling** Stichprobenentnahme; **~ shipping** Massengutversand, Versand von Schüttgütern *(opp. general cargo shipping)*; **~ transfer** *Am*[29] Übertragung der beweglichen Sachwerte e-s Unternehmens als ganzes; Geschäftsübertragung; **by the ~** im ganzen, in Bausch und Bogen; **in ~** gesamt; lose, unverpackt; **in ~** s. by the →~; **production in ~** Massenherstellung; Massenproduktion; **sale by the ~** →~ sale; **to buy in ~** in großen Mengen kaufen

bulk 2. Schiffsladung; **to break ~** mit dem Entladen beginnen; die Ladung löschen; *(in kleinere Mengen)* umgruppieren

bulkhead deck Schottendeck *(e-s Schiffes)*

bulky sperrig; **~ goods** sperrige Güter, Sperrgut

bull *(Börse)* Haussier, Haussespekulant *(opp. bear)*; **~s** *Am* steigende Kurse; *eccl* (päpstliche) Bulle (cf. *[papal] brief*); **~ account** *Br* Haussеposition; **~-and-bear bond** Anleihe, deren Rückzahlungskurs an e-n Aktienindex gebunden ist; **~ buying** Haussekauf; **~ campaign** Kurstreiberei *(Angriffe der Haussepartei)*; **~ clique** Haussepartei; **~ market** (Börsen-)Hausse; **~ movement** Hausse(bewegung); **~ operation** (or **transaction**) Haussegeschäft, Haussespekulation; **~ speculation** Haussespekulation; **on ~ support** infolge von Stützungskäufen der Haussepartei; **to buy a ~** auf Hausse kaufen *(opp. to sell a bear)*; **the market is all ~s** es herrscht Haussestimmung an der Börse

bull *v (Börse)* auf Hausse spekulieren; *(Kurse)* in die Höhe treiben *(opp. to bear)*; **to ~ (the market)** auf Hausse spekulieren; im Hinblick auf e-e Hausse kaufen

bulldog bond *Br* in Sterling durch ausländische Regierungen oder Unternehmen emittierte Anleihe; **~ market** britischer Kapitalmarkt für Pfund Sterling Auslandsanleihen

bullet Anleihe, die am Ende der Laufzeit in e-r Gesamtsumme getilgt wird

bulletin Bulletin, amtliche Bekanntmachung, Tagesbericht *(bes. des Pressedienstes e-r Regierung)*; *Br* gekürzte Ausgabe der London Gazette; **~ board** *Am* Anschlagtafel, schwarzes Brett; **(daily) ~** (tägl.) Nachrichtenblatt; **Federal B~** *Ger* Bundesanzeiger; **to issue a ~** ein Bulletin herausgeben

bullion Goldbarren, Silberbarren; ungemünztes Gold od. Silber; Edelmetall; Goldkern; **~ broker** Makler im Edelmetallhandel; **~ dealer** Edelmetallhändler; **~ point** Goldpunkt; **~ reserve** Gold- und Silberbestand *(e-r Bank)*; **~ trade** Handel mit ungemünztem Gold oder Silber; **gold ~ standard** Goldkernwährung

bullish haussierend, steigend, in Hausse *(opp. bearish)*; **~ tendency** (or **trend**) Haussetendenz; **~ tendency in prices** Kursaufschwung; **~ tone** Haussestimmung

bump *v* e-n anderen Arbeitnehmer von dessen Arbeitsplatz verdrängen *(um die Entlassung e-s Arbeitnehmers mit langer Betriebszugehörigkeit [→seniority] zu vermeiden)*

bundle Bündel, Stoß; **~ of documents** Bündel des schriftlichen Beweismaterials *(originals and copies)*; **~ of papers** Aktenbündel; **~ of notes** Banknotenbündel

buoyancy steigende Tendenz *(der Kurse, Preise)*

buoyage Markierung durch Bojen, Betonnung; **~ and lighting** Betonnung und Befeuerung *(Fahrwasserbezeichnung, Seezeichen)*

buoyant steigend *(Preise, Kurse)*; **~ market** feste Börse

burden Last; Belastung; Auflage; *Am* Gemeinkosten; Tonnage *(e-s Schiffes)*; **~ of debt(s)** Schuldenlast

burden of expenditure, to face a steadily grow-

ing ~ sich e-r ständig wachsenden Ausgabenlast gegenübersehen

burden, ~ of proof Beweislast (→*proof 1.*); ~ **of taxation** Steuerlast; ~ **sharing** *pol* Anteil an den (Verteidigungs-)Lasten *(größerer Anteil der europäischen Verbündeten an den Verteidigungslasten der NATO);* **real** ~ *Scot* Grundstücksbelastung; →**tax** ~; →**testamentary** ~

burden, the ~ of establishing guilt is on X die Beweislast für die Schuld obliegt X

burden *v fig* belasten

bureau Schreibtisch; Büro(raum); Amt, Dienststelle; *bes. Am* Abteilung e-s Ministeriums (od. Amt, das e-m Ministerium untersteht[30]); **B~ of Public Roads** (BPR) *Am* Straßenverkehrsamt; **Census B~** *Am* Statistisches Bundesamt

bureaucratic bürokratisch

bureaucracy Bürokratie; (Berufs-)Beamtentum; Amtsschimmel

bureaucratism (Unwesen der) Bürokratie; bürokratische Einstellung

burgess Stadtrat, Ratsherr *(e-s borough council); Am (Pennsylvania)* Bürgermeister

burgh *Scot (städtische)* Gemeinde, Stadt; **small** ~ *Scot* Kleinstadt; **large** ~ *Scot* Großstadt

burgh entspricht einem →borough. Jeder burgh hat einen town council, bestehend aus provost, councillors und bailies

burglar Einbrecher; ~ **alarm** Einbruchsalarm; **~-proof** diebessicher; einbruchssicher; **gang of ~s** Einbrecherbande

burglarize *v Am* einbrechen (in)

burglary[31] Einbruch(sdiebstahl); Einbrecher; ~ **insurance** Einbruchs(diebstahl)versicherung; **attempted** ~ Einbruchsversuch; **to commit** ~ einbrechen

burgle *v Br* einbrechen (in); **the house has been ~d** in das Haus ist eingebrochen worden

burial Beerdigung, Beisetzung; **~s** Bestattungswesen; ~ **expenses** Beerdigungskosten; ~ **fund** Sterbekasse; **~-ground** Friedhof; ~ **insurance** Sterbeversicherung; ~ **service** Trauerfeier

Burkina Faso *(früher Upper Volta)* Burkina Faso; **(of)** ~ Burkiner(in); burkinisch

Burma Birma; **Union of** ~ Birmanische Union

Burmese Birmane, Birmanin; birmanisch

Burundi Burundi; **Republic of** ~ Republik Burundi

Burundi, (of) ~ Burundier(in); burundisch

bus (*pl* buses) Bus, Autobus, Omnibus; ~ **line** (or **route**) Omnibuslinie; ~ **ride** Omnibusfahrt; **regular services performed by ~es and coaches** Linienverkehr mit Kraftomnibussen

busing *Am pol* Bustransport farbiger Schüler in die Schulen der weißen Stadtteile und umgekehrt *(zur Förderung der Rassenintegration)*

bushel[32] (bu) Bushel, Scheffel

business Geschäft(e); (Geschäfts-)Betrieb; (Handels-)Unternehmen; Geschäft *(shop, store);* Gewerbe; Geschäfts-, Betriebs-, Unternehmens-; geschäftliche Tätigkeit; Angelegenheit, Sache; Beschäftigung

business ist ein weitgehenderer Begriff als trade und umfaßt alle gewerblichen Tätigkeiten

business, to attend to one's ~ seinen Geschäften nachgehen; **to be in** ~ im Geschäftsleben stehen, geschäftlich tätig sein; **to be away on** ~ (or **to be on a** ~ **trip**) geschäftlich unterwegs (od. verreist) sein; **to be engaged in** ~ geschäftlich zu tun haben; sich geschäftlich (od. gewerblich) betätigen; **to bring in(to) a** ~ in ein Geschäft einbringen; **to carry on** ~ Geschäfte betreiben, geschäftlich tätig sein; **to carry on a** ~ ein Geschäft führen (od. betreiben); ein Geschäft weiterführen; **to commence a** ~ ein Geschäft eröffnen; den Geschäftsbetrieb beginnen

business, to conduct a ~ ein Geschäft führen; **authority** (or **permission**) **to conduct (a)** ~ Geschäftserlaubnis

business, to do ~ with sb. mit jdm Geschäfte machen, mit jdm in Geschäftsverbindung stehen; mit jdm geschäftlich zu tun haben; **to do a large ~ in** gute Geschäfte machen mit; **to establish a** ~ ein Geschäft eröffnen (od. gründen); **to extend a** ~ ein Geschäft erweitern (od. ausbauen); **to get down to** ~ zur Sache kommen; **to give up one's** ~ sein Geschäft aufgeben; sich vom Geschäft zurückziehen; **to go into** ~ Kaufmann werden; **to go out of** ~ das Geschäft aufgeben; **to lose** ~ Kundschaft (od. Aufträge) verlieren; **to manage a** ~ ein Geschäft (od. e-n Betrieb) führen; **to manage a ~ of another** die Besorgung e-s Geschäftes für e-n anderen übernehmen; **to open a** ~ ein Geschäft eröffnen; **to proceed to the next** ~ zur Tagesordnung übergehen; **to retire from** ~ sich vom Geschäft (od. aus dem Geschäftsleben) zurückziehen; sich geschäftlich zur Ruhe setzen; **to run a** ~ *colloq.* ein Geschäft führen (od. betreiben); **to set up** (or **start**) **a** ~ ein Geschäft eröffnen; **to take over a** ~ ein Geschäft übernehmen; **to transact** ~ Geschäfte machen (od. tätigen); **to travel on** ~ Geschäftsreisen machen; **to withdraw from** ~ s. to retire from →~

business accounts harmonized data bank (BACH) *(EG)* Datenbank über die Rechnungslegung von Unternehmen (BACH)

business activit|y Geschäftstätigkeit; Geschäftsbetrieb; Konjunktur; ~**ies** Geschäftsverkehr; **depending on** ~ konjunkturbedingt; **decline in** ~ Konjunkturrückgang; **increase in** ~ Konjunkturaufschwung, -belebung; **to pep up** ~ die Wirtschaft ankurbeln

business, ~ **administration** Betriebswirtschaft(slehre); ~ **advertising** Wirtschaftswerbung; ~ **agent** Handelsvertreter; *Am* Gewerkschaftsfunktionär; ~ **assets** Geschäftsvermögen; Betriebsvermögen; ~ **association** Wirtschaftsverband; ~ **branch** Geschäftszweig; ~ **call** Geschäftsbesuch; *tel* geschäftlicher Anruf; ~ **capital** Betriebskapital, Geschäftskapital; ~ **centre** (*Am* **center**) Geschäftszentrum; Geschäftsviertel *(e-r Großstadt);* ~ **circles** Geschäftskreise; Wirtschaftskreise; ~ **combination** Geschäfts-, Firmen-, Unternehmenszusammenschluß; ~ **commitments** geschäftliche Verpflichtungen; ~ **concern** Geschäftsbetrieb; Handelsunternehmen; ~ **confidence** Vertrauen *(der Geschäftswelt)* in die Wirtschaftslage

business connection befreundete Firma; ~**s** Geschäftsverbindungen, -beziehungen; **breaking off** (or **discontinuance**) **of** ~**s** Abbruch von Geschäftsverbindungen; **entering into** ~**s** Eingehen von Geschäftsverbindungen; **to enter into** ~**s** in Geschäftsverbindung treten (to mit); **to establish** ~**s** Geschäftsverbindungen herstellen; **to have** ~**s** in Geschäftsverbindung stehen (with mit)

business, ~ **consultant** Betriebsberater; ~ **consultants** Unternehmensberatung(sfirma); ~ **contract** Geschäftsvertrag; ~ **cooperation** Unternehmenskooperation; ~ **corporation** *Am* Kapitalgesellschaft; ~ **corporation franchise tax** *Am* Besteuerung des Gewinns e-r im Staate New York errichteten Tochtergesellschaft; **B**~ **Corporation Act** *Am (einzelstaatl.)* Gesetz zur Regelung des Rechts der Kapitalgesellschaften *(→Model Business Corporation Act);* ~ **correspondence** Geschäftskorrespondenz; ~ **criminality** Wirtschaftskriminalität

business cycle Konjunkturzyklus, Konjunkturverlauf *(boom, recession, depression, recovery);* ~ **adjustment** Anpassung an den Konjunkturzyklus; ~ **policy** Konjunkturpolitik

business, ~ **data** Geschäftsunterlagen; ~ **day** Werktag, Geschäftstag; Börsentag; (~) **deal** Geschäftsabschluß, abgeschlossenes Geschäft; ~ **dealings** geschäftliche Transaktionen; Geschäftsverkehr, Wirtschaftsverkehr; ~ **debts** Geschäftsschulden; ~ **development** Geschäftsentwicklung; ~ **difficulties** geschäftliche Schwierigkeiten

business dispute geschäftliche Streitigkeit; **settlement of** ~**s of an international character by conciliation or arbitration**[33] Beilegung geschäftlicher Streitigkeiten internationalen Charakters im Wege des Vergleichs oder durch Schiedsspruch

business done (bd.) *(Börse) (tatsächlich getätigte)* Börsenabschlüsse; Umsatz(betrag); **no** ~ ohne Umsatz

business, ~ **economics** *Br* Betriebswirtschaft(slehre); ~ **economist** *Br* Betriebswirt; ~ **engineer** *Am* Betriebsberater *(zur Verbesserung der Betriebsorganisation);* ~ **enterprise** geschäftliches (od. gewerbliches) Unternehmen; Wirtschaftsunternehmen; Geschäftsbetrieb; Gewerbebetrieb (*→enterprise*)

business entertainment, cost of ~ Kosten der Unterhaltung und Bewirtung (od. Bewirtungsspesen) von Geschäftsfreunden; Repräsentationskosten

business, ~ **espionage** Wirtschaftsspionage; ~ **ethics** Geschäftsmoral; ~ **executive** leitender Angestellter *(e-s kaufmännischen Unternehmens);* betriebliche Führungskraft; ~ **expansion** Geschäftserweiterung; ~ **expenditure** (or **expenses**) Geschäftsausgaben, Geschäftsunkosten; Betriebsausgaben; ~ **experience** Geschäftserfahrung; ~ **extension** Geschäftserweiterung; ~ **failure** Geschäftszusammenbruch; Insolvenz; ~ **firm** Firma; ~ **forecasting** Konjunkturprognose; ~ **friend** Geschäftsfreund; ~ **in futures** *(Börse)* Termingeschäft(e); ~ **game** Unternehmensspiel; ~ **hazard** *(allgemeines)* Unternehmerwagnis

business hours Geschäftszeit; Geschäftsstunden; **after** ~ nach Geschäftsschluß

business, ~ **income** Geschäftseinkommen; gewerbliche Einkünfte; Unternehmensgewinn; ~ **interest** Geschäftsbeteiligung, Geschäftsanteil; Geschäftsinteresse; ~ **interests** Geschäftsinteressen, Geschäftswelt; ~ **interruption insurance** *Am* Betriebsunterbrechungsversicherung; ~ **inventory** Geschäftsinventar, Betriebsinventar; ~ **investments** betriebliche Investitionen

business judgment rule *Am* Grundsatz über die Haftung der Unternehmensleitung wegen Pflichtverletzung

Haftung beseht nicht für die Folgen ordnungsgemäßer (der Sorgfalt eines ordentlichen und gewissenhaften Geschäftsleiters entsprechenden) Geschäftsführung (vgl. § 93 AktG)

business, ~ **law** Handelsrecht; **B**~ **League** *Am* Vereinigung von Geschäftsleuten; ~ **liabilities** Geschäftsschulden, -verbindlichkeiten; ~ **life** Geschäftsleben, Wirtschaftsleben; ~**-like** geschäftsmäßig; ~ **line** Geschäftszweig; Geschäfts-Telefonanschluß; ~ **loss** Geschäftsausfall; geschäftlicher Verlust

businessman Geschäftsmann; Kaufmann; Gewerbetreibender; **to exercise the care of an ordinary** (or **a reasonable**) ~ die Sorgfalt e-s ordentlichen Kaufmanns anwenden

businessmen Geschäftsleute; die Geschäftswelt

business, ~ **management** Geschäftsführung, Betriebsführung; ~ **manager** leitender Angestellter *(e-r Firma);* kaufmännischer Direktor; Geschäftsführer; ~ **matter** geschäftliche Angelegenheit; ~ **methods** Geschäftsmethoden; ~ **morality** Geschäftsmoral; ~ **name** Firma; Firmenname; ~ **objective** Betriebszweck; ~ **obligations** Geschäftsverbindlichkeiten; ~ **operations** →~ dealings; ~ **outlook** Geschäftsaussichten; Konjunkturaussichten; Aussichten für die Wirtschaft

business organization Unternehmensverband; **form** (or **type**) **of** ~ Unternehmensform des Handelsrechts

business practices Geschäftspraktiken, geschäftliche Gepflogenheiten; Geschäftsgebaren; **customary** ~ übliche Geschäftspraktiken; **unfair** ~ unfaire Geschäftspraktiken

business, ~ **premises** Geschäftsräume; gewerbliche Räume; Geschäftsgrundstück; ~ **profit** Geschäftsgewinn; Gewinn aus Gewerbebetrieb; Unternehmensgewinn; ~ **property** Geschäftsgrundstück, Betriebsgrundstück; ~ **prospects** Geschäftsaussichten; ~ **quarter** Geschäftsviertel, -gegend; ~ **real estate** *Am* Geschäftsgrundstück; ~ **recession** Geschäftsrückgang, Rezession; ~ **records** Geschäftsunterlagen; ~ **reputation** geschäftliches Ansehen; ~ **research** Konjunkturforschung; ~ **revival** Geschäftsbelebung; Konjunkturbelebung; ~ **risk** Geschäftsrisiko, Unternehmensrisiko; Investitionsrisiko; ~ **savings** Ersparnisse e-s Unternehmens; betriebliche Einsparungen; nicht entnommener Gewinn; ~ **school** Handelsschule

business secret Geschäftsgeheimnis, Betriebsgeheimnis; **disclosure of** ~**s** Verrat von Geschäftsgeheimnissen; **protection of** ~**s** Wahrung von Geschäftsgeheimnissen; **to divulge** (or **disclose**) **a** ~ ein Geschäftsgeheimnis preisgeben (od. nicht wahren)

business, ~ **section** Handelsteil *(e-r Zeitung);* ~ **in securities** Effektenhandel; ~ **services** Dienstleistungen für Geschäftsbetriebe; ~ **setback** Konjunkturrückschlag; ~ **situation** Geschäftslage; Konjunktur(lage); Wirtschaftslage, wirtschaftliche Lage; ~ **spy** Wirtschaftsspion; ~ **standing** geschäftliches Ansehen; Ansehen (od. Ruf) e-s Geschäfts; ~ **statistics** Betriebsstatistik; ~ **strategy** Unternehmensstrategie; ~ **style** Geschäftsstil; ~ **training** Ausbildung als Kaufmann; ~ **to be transacted** Tagesordnung

business transaction *(abgeschlossenes)* Geschäft, Geschäftsvorfall; geschäftlicher Vorgang; ~**s** Geschäfte; Geschäftsverkehr; **to enter into a** ~ Geschäfte machen (od. tätigen)

business, ~ **trend** Konjunkturentwicklung; Wirtschaftsentwicklung; Geschäftsentwicklung; ~ **trip** Geschäftsreise; ~ **trust** *Am* → Massachusetts trust; ~ **tycoon** Großindustrieller; ~ **undertaking** Geschäftsunternehmen; (Wirtschafts-)Betrieb; ~ **usage** Handelsbrauch; ~**woman** Geschäftsfrau; ~ **world** Geschäftswelt

business year Geschäftsjahr *(für Inventar- und Bilanzaufstellung);* **current** ~ laufendes Geschäftsjahr; **incomplete** ~ Rumpfgeschäftsjahr; **last** (or **past**) ~ abgelaufenes (od. vergangenes) Geschäftsjahr

business, administration of a ~ Geschäftsführung; **any other** ~ → A.O.B.; **big** ~ Großindustrie; große Betriebe (od. Unternehmen) *(opp. small business);* **closing of a** ~ Geschäftsaufgabe; **commencement of a** ~ Inbetriebnahme e-s Geschäfts; Beginn e-s Geschäftsbetriebes; **conduct of** ~ Geschäftsführung; Geschäftsgebaren; →**course of** ~; **current** ~ laufende Geschäfte; **decline** (or **decrease**) **in** ~ Geschäftsrückgang; **direction of a** ~ Geschäftsführung; **doing** ~ →doing; **establishment of a** ~ Eröffnung (od. Gründung) e-s Geschäfts; Geschäftsgründung; Geschäftserrichtung; **extension of a** ~ Geschäftserweiterung; **general** ~ *(auf Tagesordnung)* Verschiedenes; *Br (VersR)* Schadensversicherung *(opp. long term* ~*);* **giving up of a** ~ Geschäftsaufgabe; **hours of** ~ Geschäftszeit, -stunden; **large** ~ gutes Geschäft; **line of** ~ Geschäftszweig, Branche; **long term** ~ *Br (VersR)* Personenversicherung (→*long term*); **losing** ~ verlustbringendes Geschäft; Verlustgeschäft; **no** ~ **(done)** *(Börse)* ohne Umsatz; **non-**~ **days** Nichtwerktage; **official** ~ →official 2.

business, on ~ geschäftlich, in geschäftlichen Angelegenheiten; **on a** ~ **trip** geschäftlich verreist

business, one-line ~ Spezialgeschäft; **opening of a** ~ Geschäftseröffnung; **order of** ~ *parl* Tagesordnung; **owner of a** ~ Geschäftsinhaber; **operation of a** ~ Betrieb e-s Geschäfts; **ordinary** ~ normaler Geschäftsgang; **paying** ~ rentables Geschäft; **place of** ~ Geschäftssitz, (Geschäfts-)Niederlassung (→*place*); **retail** ~ Einzelhandelsgeschäft; Kleinhandel; **routine** ~ laufende Geschäftsangelegenheiten; **scope of** ~ Umfang des Geschäfts, Geschäftsbereich; **sham** ~ Scheingeschäft; **small** ~ kleinere u. mittlere Unternehmen (KMU); Klein- und Mittelbetriebe (KMB); gewerblicher Mittelstand; **terms (and conditions) of** ~ Geschäftsbedingungen; **type of** ~ Art des Geschäfts; **wholesale** ~ Engrosgeschäft; Großhandel

buy gutes Geschäft; ~ **back** Form e-s →barter deal, bei dem Produktionsmittel gegen noch zu produzierende Güter getauscht werden; ~-**back-barter** besondere Art e-s Kompensationsgeschäftes *(ein ausländisches Unternehmen errichtet e-e Fabrikationsstätte in e-m sozialistischen Land und erhält hierfür e-n Teil der Produktion)*

buy-out, →**leveraged** ~; →**management** ~

buy *v* (an-, auf-, ein)kaufen (from von, at bei); beziehen; **to** ~ **and sell** Handel treiben; **to** ~

for the account *Br (Börse)* auf Termin kaufen; **to ~ by auction** ersteigern; auf e-r Auktion kaufen; **to ~ back** (zu)rückkaufen; **to ~ a borough** *Br* Wahlstimmen kaufen; **to ~ a bull** *Br (Börse)* auf Hausse kaufen *(opp. to sell a bear)*; **to ~ for cash** gegen bar kaufen; **to ~ cheap** billig kaufen; **to ~ on commission** auf Kommission kaufen; **to ~ on credit** auf Kredit kaufen; anschreiben lassen; **to ~ on a fall** *(Börse)* auf Baisse kaufen (od. spekulieren); **to ~ firm** fest kaufen; **to ~ forward** *(Börse)* auf Termin kaufen; **to ~ (at) first hand** aus erster Hand beziehen; **to ~ at a high price** teuer kaufen; **to ~ on hire purchase** *Br*[34] **(on the instal(l)ment system** *Am*) auf Abzahlung kaufen; **to ~ in** einkaufen, ankaufen; *(Börse)* sich eindecken mit; *(auf Auktion)* zurückkaufen, *(eigene Sachen)* selbst ersteigern; **to ~ long** auf Hausse kaufen (od. spekulieren); **to ~ off** sich *(durch e-e Zahlung z.B. an e-n Erpresser)* loskaufen; **to ~ out** *(jdn)* auskaufen, auszahlen *(z.B. durch den Erwerb seiner Geschäftsanteile)*; **to ~ out an execution** e-e Pfändung durch Geldzahlung verhindern; **to ~ out a partner** e-n Teilhaber abfinden (od. auszahlen); **to ~ over** *(jdn)* durch Bestechung für sich gewinnen; *(jdn)* kaufen; *(jdn)* bestechen; **to ~ for ready money** gegen bar kaufen; **to ~ for a rise** *(Börse)* auf Hausse kaufen (od. spekulieren); **to ~ for the settlement** *Br (Börse)* auf Termin kaufen; **to ~ spot** *(Börse)* per Kasse kaufen; **to ~ up** *(etw.)* aufkaufen

buy and lease back „kaufe und miete zurück" *(Kauf e-s Objekts, das man dem Leasing-Unternehmen gibt, von dem man es zurückmietet)*

buyer Käufer(in); Einkäufer(in); Abnehmer(in) *(opp. seller)*; **~s** *(Kurszettel)* Geld; **~s' combine** Einkaufskartell; **~ country** Abnehmerland; **~'s guide** Bezugsquellennachweis; **~s' market** Käufermarkt *(opp. sellers' market)*; **~'s monopoly** Käufermonopol; **at ~'s option** nach Käufers Wahl; **~'s option to double** *Br (Börse)* Nochgeschäft *(in Käufers Wahl)*; **~'s or seller's option** *Am (Börse)* Lieferung nach Wahl des Käufers oder Verkäufers; **~s over** *Br* (Börse) mehr Nachfrage als Angebot; mehr Geld als Brief; **~'s resistance** Käuferwiderstand; **at ~'s risk** auf Gefahr des Käufers; **~s' strike** Käuferstreik; **~-up** Aufkäufer

buying Kaufen; Kauf, Ankauf, Einkauf; Erwerb, Anschaffung, Beschaffung *(opp. selling)*; **~ back** Rückkauf; *(Börse) (of bear sellers)* Eindeckung; **~ hedge** Absicherung des Käufers; **~ in** Einkauf, Ankauf, Eindeckung; *(Börse) (zwangsweise)* Eindeckung *(von Effekten)*; **~-in price** Ankaufspreis; *(Börse)* Rückkaufskurs; **~ on margin** →margin bying; **~ out of a partner** Auszahlung e-s Teilhabers; **~-up** Aufkauf

buying, ~ activity Einkaufstätigkeit; **~ agent** Einkaufsvertreter, Einkäufer; Einkaufskommissionär; **~ combine** Einkaufsverband; **~ commission** Einkaufsprovision; **~ costs** *(vom Käufer zu tragende)* Bezugskosten; **~ department** Einkaufsabteilung *(opp. sales department)*; **~ habits** Kaufgewohnheiten; **~ incentive** Kaufanreiz; **~ interest** Kaufinteresse; **~ long** Haussespekulation, Haussekauf *(opp. selling short)*; **~ spree** plötzliche Kauflust

buying order Kaufauftrag, Kauforder; **to give a ~** Kaufauftrag erteilen; zum Kauf aufgeben

buying power Kaufkraft; **to absorb the excessive ~** die überschüssige Kaufkraft abschöpfen

buying, ~ price Kaufpreis; Ankaufspreis; **~ quota** Einkaufskontingent; **~ rate** *(Devisenmarkt)* Ankaufskurs, Geldkurs; **~ or selling rate** An- od. Verkaufskurs; **~ resource** Einkaufsquelle, Bezugsquelle; **~ on time** *Am* Abzahlungskauf; **~ of votes** Stimmenkauf; **~ wave** Ansturm der Käufer

by, ~ the hour stundenweise; **~ letter** brieflich; **~ next week** bis spätestens nächste Woche; **to stand ~ sb.** jdn unterstützen

by-bidder Scheinbieter *(zur Höhertreibung des Preises bei Auktionen)*

by-election *Br parl* Nachwahl, Ersatzwahl *(für eingetretene Vakanz)*

Byelorussian Soviet Socialist Republic Weissrussische Sozialistische Sowjetrepublik

Byelorussian SSR Weissrussische Sozialistische Sowjetrepublik

Byelorussian Weissrusse, ~russin; weissrussisch

by(e)-laws Satzung; Geschäftsordnung; *Br (local authorities)* Gemeindeverordnung, städtische Verordnung; Ortsstatuten; *Am (die insbes. das Innenverhältnis e-s Vereins od e-r Gesellschaft regelnde)* Nebensatzung *(AktienR: ergänzt die →corporate charter, deren Inhalt in den einzelnen Staaten genau vorgeschrieben ist)*; **according to the ~** satzungsgemäß; **adoption of ~** Annahme der Satzung; **amendment of ~** Satzungsänderung; **repeal of ~** Aufhebung der Satzung; **to adopt new ~** e-e neue Satzung annehmen; **to make ~** die Satzung erlassen

by(-)pass Umgehungsstraße; Umleitungsstraße

by-product Nebenprodukt, Nebenerzeugnis

bystander außenstehender Dritter; **innocent ~** *(bei Produzentenhaftung)* unbeteiligter Dritter

C

cab Taxi; ~ **driver** (or **man**) Taxifahrer; ~ **rank** (or **stand**) Taxistand; **to call a** ~ ein Taxi bestellen

cabinet *pol* Kabinett; *Br* engerer Kreis der wichtigsten Minister *(nicht Gesamtregierung; cf. government); Am* Sammelbezeichnung für die Leiter der Bundesministerien *(zur Beratung des Präsidenten);* **C~ Committee** *Br* Kabinettsausschuß; **C~ Meeting** Kabinettssitzung; **C~ Minister** *Br* (Kabinetts-)Minister; **C~ Office** *Br* Kabinettskanzlei; **C~ Officer** *Am* (Kabinetts-)Minister; **C~ rank** Kabinettsrang; **C~ reshuffle** Regierungsumbildung; **formation of the C~** Regierungsbildung; **member of the C~** Kabinettsmitglied; **shadow C~** *Br* Schattenkabinett *(führender Persönlichkeiten der Oppositionspartei);* **to leave** (or **resign from**) **the C~** aus dem Kabinett ausscheiden; **the C~ meets** das Kabinett tritt zusammen; **the C~ has resigned** die Regierung ist zurückgetreten; **to sit** (or **serve**) **in the** ~ dem Kabinett angehören

cable Kabel(telegramm), Kabelgramm, Überseetelegramm; ~ **advice** Drahtaviso; ~ **expenses** Telegrammspesen; **~gram** Kabelgramm, Überseetelegramm; ~ **order** Kabelauftrag; ~ **pound sterling** Kabelpfund; ~ **rate** Kabelkurs; ~ **report** Kabelbericht, Drahtbericht; ~ **transfer** (C. T.) telegrafische Auszahlung, telegrafische Überweisung *(bes. im überseeischen Devisenverkehr; cf. telegraphic transfer);* **by** ~ telegrafisch; **information sent by** ~ Kabelnachricht; **to send a** ~ **(message)** kabeln

cable *v* kabeln, telegrafieren, drahten

cablese *Am* Telegrammstil

cabotage Kabotage *(Darbietung und Erbringung von Beförderungsleistungen innerhalb der Landesgrenzen); (Recht e-s Staates zur)* Küstenschifffahrt; *Am* Verkehr zwischen Städten des gleichen Staates; *(Recht e-s Staates zum)* Binnenluftverkehr; Luftkabotage; *(Außenhandel)* Kosten des Versandes innerhalb der Landesgrenzen *(bes. vom Haupt- zum Nebenhafen)*

ca'canny *Scot* absichtliche Arbeitsverlangsamung *(zur Durchsetzung bestimmter Forderungen);* Bummelstreik *(cf. go-slow)*

cadastral Kataster-; Flurbuch-; ~ **survey** Katasterplan

calaboose *Am sl.* Gefängnis

calamity Unglück; **victim of a** ~ Opfer e-r Katastrophe

calculate *v* berechnen, errechnen, ausrechnen; kalkulieren; **to** ~ **the damage** den Schaden berechnen; **to** ~ **the interest** die Zinsen berechnen

calculated, to be ~ **to** bestimmt (od. berechnet) sein für

calculating Rechnen; ~ **and accounting** Rechnen und Buchen; ~ **machine** Rechenmaschine

calculation Berechnung, Errechnung, Ausrechnung; (Kosten-)Voranschlag; ~ **basis** Berechnungsgrundlage; ~ **of cost** (or **expenses**) Kostenberechnung; ~ **of interest** Zinsberechnung; ~ **of losses caused by operational deficiencies** Verlustquellenrechnung; ~ **of pensions** Pensionsberechnung, Rentenberechnung; ~ **of probabilities** Wahrscheinlichkeitsrechnung; ~ **of (prospective) profits** Rentabilitätsberechnung; Gewinnkalkulation; ~ **of requirements** Bedarfsrechnung

calculation, close ~ genaue (od. knappe) Berechnung; **basis of** ~ →~ basis; **faulty** ~ Fehlkalkulation; **at the lowest** ~ bei niedrigster Berechnung; **method of** ~ Berechnungsmethode; Rechnungsart; **mis~** Fehlkalkulation; **preliminary** ~ Voranschlag; Überschlag; **to be out in one's** ~ sich verrechnet haben; **to make a** ~ e-e Berechnung anstellen; **to make a close** ~ genau berechnen (od. kalkulieren)

calendar Kalender; Verzeichnis, Liste; ~ **call** *Am* Aufruf e-r Sache *(vor Gericht);* ~ **of causes** (or **court** ~) *Am (gerichtl.)* Terminkalender; ~ **of prisoners** *Br* Liste der Untersuchungsgefangenen; ~ **year** Kalenderjahr; **to place** (or **put**) **a case on the** ~ *Am* e-n Termin anberaumen

calibration Eichung

call 1. Ruf; Aufruf; Aufforderung; Einforderung (od. Abruf) *(z. B. von Geldern);* Einlösungsaufforderung *(auf Schuldverschreibungen);* Anforderung, Nachfrage (for nach); Einlaufen *(in e-n Hafen); univ* Ruf; ~ **to arms** Einberufung *(zum Militärdienst);* ~ **to the Bar** *Br* Zulassung als Anwalt *(barrister);* ~ **to a chair** *Am univ* Ruf auf e-n Lehrstuhl; ~ **to the colo(u)rs** →~ to arms; ~ **day** *Br* Zulassungstag für barristers; ~ **deposits** Sichteinlagen; ~ **for funds** Einforderung von Geldern; Aufforderung zur Zahlung von Geldern; ~ **loan** *Br* kurzfristiges Darlehen an Börsenmakler

call money tägliches Geld *(opp. time money);* ~ **market** Markt für tägliches Geld; ~ **rate** Satz für tägliches Geld

call, ~ **to order** *parl* Ordnungsruf; **~-over** Namensaufruf; ~ **for redemption** Aufforderung zur Einlösung; Kündigung; ~ **for tenders** Ausschreibung; **~up** *Br mil* Einberufung

call, at ~ auf Abruf *(bezieht sich auf geliehenes Geld und auf Warenlieferung)*; **delivery at** ~ Lieferung auf Abruf; **money at** ~ tägliches Geld *(täglich kündbares Geld; opp. time money)*
call, on ~ auf Abruf *(bezieht sich auch auf Personen)*; jederzeit kündbar *(Geld)*; **money on** ~ tägliches Geld; **to be on** ~ auf Abruf zur Verfügung stehen
call, to accept (or **follow**) **the** ~ *univ* den Ruf annehmen; **to make a** ~ e-n Hafen anlaufen
call 2. *(AktienR)* (Nach-)Zahlungsaufforderung *(an Aktienzeichner)*; **~s in arrears** eingeforderte ausstehende Einlagen; ~ **letter** schriftl. Aufforderung zur Einzahlung auf Aktien; ~ **receipt** Einzahlungsquittung; ~ **on shares** Aufforderung zur Einzahlung der Einlagen auf gezeichnete Aktien; **payment of ~s** Einzahlung der *(von der Gesellschaft geforderten)* Einlagen auf gezeichnete Aktien; **to make a ~ on shares** zur Einzahlung der Einlagen auf gezeichnete Aktien auffordern; **to pay a** ~ e-e Einzahlung auf Aktien leisten
call 3. *(kurzer)* Besuch; **~-back** Wiederholungsbesuch; ~ **on customers** Kundenbesuch; ~ **of a sales representative** Besuch e-s Vertreters; Vertreterbesuch; **courtesy** (or **duty**) ~ Höflichkeitsbesuch; **farewell** ~ Abschiedsbesuch; **first** ~ Antrittsbesuch; **to make** (or **pay**) **a** ~ e-n Besuch machen; **to return a** ~ e-n Besuch erwidern
call 4. *(Börse)* (Kauf-)Option; Vorprämie *(opp. put)*; ~ **of more** Nochgeschäft *(in Käufers Wahl)*; ~ **option** (or **premium**) Kaufoption, Vorprämie; ~ **price** Vorprämienkurs; **giver for a** ~ Käufer e-r Vorprämie; **put and ~ option** Stellagegeschäft (→*straddle*); **taker for a** ~ Verkäufer e-r Vorprämie; **trading in ~s** Vorprämiengeschäfte; **to buy a ~ option** e-e Vorprämie kaufen; **to give for the** ~ e-e Vorprämie kaufen; **to take for the** ~ e-e Vorprämie verkaufen
call 5. Telefongespräch, Anruf; **collect** ~ *Am* R-Gespräch; **international** ~ *Br* Auslandsgespräch; **local** ~ Ortsgespräch; **national** ~ *Br* Ferngespräch; **official** ~ Dienstgespräch; **transferred-charge call** R-Gespräch; **to make a** ~ anrufen; **to make a long-distance ~ to sb.** ein Ferngespräch mit jdm führen; **to make the ~ collect** *Am* ein R-Gespräch führen; **to take a** ~ e-n Anruf entgegennehmen

call *v* rufen, nennen; aufrufen; abrufen; *(Versammlung)* einberufen; *(Gelder)* einfordern; zur Einzahlung (od. Nachzahlung) auffordern; *(Börse)* kaufen, nehmen *(opp. to put)*; **to ~ to account** zur Rechenschaft ziehen; **to ~ to the Bar** *Br* als Anwalt *(barrister)* zulassen; **to ~ bonds for redemption** Obligationen zur Tilgung aufrufen; **to ~ a case** e-e Sache *(bei Gericht)* aufrufen; **to ~ to the colo(u)rs** zum Militärdienst einberufen; **to ~ an instalment of DM ... on shares** zur Einzahlung von DM ... auf Aktien auffordern; **to ~ the jury** die Geschworenen auslosen; **to ~ a meeting** e-e Versammlung einberufen (for 11 o'clock auf 11 Uhr); **to ~ a meeting of shareholders** die Hauptversammlung einberufen; **to ~ money** Gelder abrufen; **to ~ an option** ein Prämiengeschäft eingehen; **to ~ to order** *parl* zur Ordnung rufen; **to ~ at a port** e-n Hafen anlaufen, in e-n Hafen einlaufen; **to ~ the roll** die Namensliste verlesen; *(namentlich)* aufrufen; *mil* Appell abhalten; **to ~ the shareholders together** die Aktionäre zusammenrufen; **to ~ a witness** e-n Zeugen aufrufen; **to ~ sb. as a witness** jdn als Zeugen benennen
call away *v (jdn)* abrufen (from von)
call back *v* zurück(be)rufen; *tel colloq.* zurückrufen
call for *v (etw.)* verlangen, (er)fordern; *(Bericht etc)* anfordern; abholen; *(Waren)* abrufen; **to ~ the mail** die Post abholen; **to ~ payment** zur Zahlung auffordern; **to ~ production of documents** die Vorlage von Urkunden anfordern
call in *v (Schulden)* einfordern; *(Kredit, Hypothek)* kündigen; *(Forderungen etc)* einziehen; **to ~ bank bills** *Am* (**bank notes** *Br*) Banknoten einziehen; **to ~ an expert** e-n Sachverständigen beiziehen (od. zuziehen); **to ~ a loan** ein Darlehen kündigen; **to ~ records** Akten anfordern
call off *v (vom Posten)* abberufen; *(Warenlieferung)* abrufen; **to ~ boycott measures** Boykottmaßnahmen widerrufen; **to ~ a strike** e-n Streik abbrechen
call on *v*, **to ~ a p.** jdn *(kurz)* besuchen, jdn aufsuchen, bei jdm *(kurz)* vorsprechen; **to ~ on a p.** (to do sth.) jdn auffordern (etw. zu tun); **to ~ the capital market** sich des Kapitalmarktes bedienen
call out *v*, **to ~ on strike** zum Streik aufrufen
call over *v (Namen, Liste)* verlesen
call together *v* zusammenrufen; einberufen
call up *v* aufrufen; einfordern; *tel* anrufen; *mil* einberufen
call upon *v*, **to ~ a p.** jdn auffordern (zu tun), jdn ersuchen; sich wenden an jdn; **I ~ Mr. X to speak** ich erteile Herrn X das Wort
called genannt; zur Einzahlung aufgefordert; *(Börse)* (cld) abgerufen; ~ **up capital** *(von Aktionären)* eingefordertes Kapital; *(zur Zahlung)* aufgerufenes Aktienkapital; **to be (kept till) ~ for** postlagernd; **to be ~ for at the station office** bahn(post)lagernd; **to take such action as seems (to be) ~ for** die Maßnahmen ergreifen, die notwendig erscheinen
calling Beruf; Einberufung *(e-r Versammlung)*; Aufforderung *(an Aktionäre zur Einzahlung od. Nachzahlung)*; Aufruf *(von Zeugen)*; ~ **card** *Am* Visitenkarte; ~ **hours** *Am* Sprechstunden *(bei Behörden)*; ~ **the roll** Verlesen der Namensliste; **to exercise a** ~ e-n Beruf ausüben
calling in Einforderung (od. Kündigung) *(von*

Geldern); Einziehung *(von Forderungen);* Zuziehung *(e-s Sachverständigen);* Anforderung *(von Akten)*

callable abrufbar; kündbar *(Geld etc);* einziehbar; ~ **bonds** *(vorzeitig)* kündbare Schuldverschreibungen

caller Besucher; *tel* Anrufer; *Br* Auktionator *(cf. ring trading)*

calumniate *v* verleumden

calumniation Verleumdung *(nicht technisch; cf. defamation)*

calumnious report verleumderischer Bericht

calumn|y Verleumdung; **to utter ~ies** verleumden

Calvo Clause (Doctrine) *(VölkerR)* Calvo-Klausel (Doktrin)
Nach der in Lateinamerika verbreiteten Calvo-Doktrin ist es unzulässig, die Kreditverträge mit ausländischen Gläubigern ausländischem Recht zu unterstellen und die Zuständigkeit ausländischer Gerichte zu vereinbaren

cambist Geldwechsler; Devisenhändler

Cambodia Kambodscha
Cambodian Kambodschaner(in), kambodschanisch

camera, in ~ unter Ausschluß der Öffentlichkeit *(opp. in public);* **trial** (or **hearing**) **in ~** nichtöffentliche Hauptverhandlung, Verhandlung unter Ausschluß der Öffentlichkeit *(opp. in open court);* **to order a trial in ~** die Öffentlichkeit ausschließen; **to sit in ~** unter Ausschluß der Öffentlichkeit verhandeln

Cameroon Kamerun; **Republic of ~** Republik Kamerun
Cameroonian Kameruner(in); kamerunisch

camouflage Tarnung; ~ **measures** Verschleierungsmaßnahmen; **danger of ~** Verdunklungsgefahr

camouflage *v* tarnen

camp Lager; *fig* Lager *(Anhänger der gleichen, bes. politischen Richtung);* ~ **commander** Lagerkommandant; ~ **meeting** religiöse Versammlung im Freien; **concentration ~** Konzentrationslager; **internment ~** Internierungslager; **prisoner of war ~** Kriegsgefangenenlager; **transit ~** Durchgangslager; **to close down a ~** ein Lager auflösen; **to be released from a ~** aus e-m Lager entlassen werden

campaign (Presse-, Wahl-, Werbe-)Feldzug; Kampagne; Wahlkampf; Aktion; *mil* Feldzug; ~ **against pollution** Aktion gegen Umweltverschmutzung; ~ **expenses** Wahlkampfausgaben; ~ **for members** Mitgliederwerbung; ~ **funds** Wahlkampfgelder; ~ **to raise funds** Sammelaktion; ~ **issue** Hauptthema des Wahlkampfes; ~ **pledge** Wahlkampfversprechen

campaign, advertising ~ Reklamefeldzug; Werbeaktion; **election** (or **electoral**) ~ Wahlkampf, Wahlkampagne; **fund-raising ~** Sammelaktion; **press ~** Pressefeldzug; **publicity ~** Werbekampagne; **slander ~** Verleumdungskampagne; **to conduct a ~** e-n (Werbe- etc)-Feldzug führen; **to launch a ~** e-e (Wahl- etc)-Kampagne aufziehen (od. starten); **to run a ~** s. to conduct a →~; **to start a ~** s. to launch a →~; **to support a political ~** e-e politische Aktion unterstützen; **to take part in a ~** an e-r Kampagne teilnehmen

campaign *v* an e-r Kampagne *(e-m Werbefeldzug, Wahlkampf etc)* teilnehmen; Wahlfeldzug führen; Wahlpropaganda machen; **to ~ on behalf of sb.** während des Wahlkampfes für jdn eintreten

campaigning technique Technik der Wahlkampfführung

campaigner Wahlredner

campus Campus, Universitätsgelände *(Gesamtanlage e-r Universität od. e-s College)*

Canada Kanada
Canadian Kanadier; Kanadierin; kanadisch; ~ **Labor Congress** (CLC) Vereinigung kanadischer Gewerkschaften

canalize *v* kanalisieren; *fig* in bestimmte Bahnen leiten; **to ~ one's efforts into** seine Bemühungen richten auf

canard Zeitungsente, Falschmeldung, Lüge

cancel *v* für ungültig erklären, ungültig (od. rückgängig) machen; für kraftlos erklären; widerrufen; aufheben, annullieren; löschen; (durch-, aus)streichen; stornieren; *(Verabredung etc)* absagen; *(Brief-, Stempelmarken)* entwerten; *(IWF) (Sonderziehungsrechte)* aus dem Verkehr ziehen, einziehen (→*Special Drawing Rights*); **to ~ a booking** e-e Reservierung abbestellen; **to ~ a contract** e-n Vertrag aufheben, von e-m Vertrag zurücktreten; **to ~ an entry** e-e Eintragung löschen; e-e Buchung stornieren; **to ~ a licen|ce (-se)** e-e Lizenz widerrufen; **to ~ an order** e-n Auftrag streichen (od. stornieren); *(etw.)* abbestellen; e-e Verfügung aufheben; **to ~ a paper** e-e Zeitung abbestellen; **to ~ a patent** ein Patent löschen; **petition to ~ a registration** Löschungsantrag; **to ~ a premium** *(VersR)* e-e Prämie stornieren; **to ~ a vote** e-e Abstimmung für ungültig erklären; **to ~ a will** ein Testament für ungültig erklären

cancel(l)ed, ~ appropriations gestrichene (Haushalts-)Mittel; ~ **cheque** *(Am* **check)** annullierter Scheck; ~ **stamps** entwertete Brief-

(od. Stempel-)marken; **until** ~ bis auf Widerruf

cancel(l)ing Annullierung, Aufhebung *(etc.; → to cancel);* ~ **clause** Cancelling-Klausel *(gibt dem Charterer ein Kündigungs- od. Rücktrittsrecht aus bestimmten Gründen)*

cancellation Ungültigkeitserklärung, Ungültigmachung, Rückgängigmachung, Kraftloserklärung; Widerruf; Rücktrittserklärung; Kündigung; Aufhebung, Annullierung; Löschung; Streichung; Stornierung, Storno; Entwertung *(von Brief- od. Stempelmarken); (IWF)* Einziehung (→*Special Drawing Rights*); ~ **clause** Rücktrittsklausel; ~ **of a contract** Aufhebung e-s Vertrages, Rücktritt vom Vertrag *(hat Nichtigkeit ex nunc zur Folge; cf. avoidance);* ~ **of customs duties** Niederschlagung von Zollabgaben; ~ **of debts** Streichung von Schulden; ~ **of an entry** Löschung e-r Eintragung; Stornobuchung, Stornierung; ~ **of a licence (~se)** Widerruf e-r Lizenz; ~ **of a mortgage** *Am* Löschung e-r Hypothek; ~ **of an order** Annullierung (od. Stornierung) e-s Auftrags; Abbestellung; ~ **of a patent** Aufhebung e-s Patents; ~ **of premium** *(VersR)* Stornierung der Prämie; ~ **proceedings** *Am (Warenzeichen R)*[1] Löschungsverfahren; ~ **of the registration of a firm in the register of business names** Löschung e-r Firma im Handelsregister; ~ **of securities** Kraftloserklärung (od. Kraftloswerden) von *(abhandengekommenen)* Wertpapieren; ~ **of shares** (or *Am* **stocks**) Verfallserklärung (od. Kaduzierung) von Aktien; ~ **of a trade mark** Löschung e-s Warenzeichens; **petition for** ~ *(PatR)* Antrag auf Erklärung der Nichtigkeit; **request for** ~ **(of a registration)** Löschungsantrag; **right of** ~ Rücktrittsrecht; Aufhebungsrecht; Kündigungsrecht; **subject to** ~ kündbar

candidacy *Am* Kandidatur; Bewerbung; Anwartschaft

candidate Kandidat, Anwärter; (Amts-)Bewerber; Prüfungskandidat, Prüfling; ~ **for an office** (or **a post**) Bewerber um e-e Stellung; **list of (party)** ~**s** Kandidatenliste; **strong** ~ aussichtsreicher Kandidat; **to agree to be a** ~ die Kandidatur annehmen; **to be on the short list of** ~**s** als Kandidat in der engeren Wahl stehen; **to come forward as a** ~ *parl* als Kandidat auftreten; **to offer oneself as a** ~ kandidieren, **to put up** (or **nominate**) **a** ~ *parl* e-n Kandidaten aufstellen (od. vorschlagen, nominieren); **to stand as a** ~ **for** *parl* sich bewerben um; sich als Kandidaten aufstellen lassen für; kandidieren für

candidature *Br* Kandidatur; Bewerbung; **to maintain (withdraw) one's** ~seine Kandidatur aufrechterhalten (zurückziehen)

canon Regel, Richtschnur; *eccl* kirchliche Vorschrift; *(Verzeichnis der)* Ordensregeln; ~**s of construction** Auslegungsregeln; ~ **of descent**[2] Regeln der gesetzlichen Erbfolge; ~ **law** kanonisches Recht; Kirchenrecht; ~**s of professional ethics** Standesregeln *(der Anwälte, Ärzte etc)*

canonical kanonisch; kirchenrechtlich

canvass Kundenwerbung, persönliche Werbung *(durch Hausbesuch);* (Wahl-)Stimmenwerbung; *Am parl* Wahl(stimmen)prüfung

canvass *v (Kunden od. Wahlkreise)* besuchen; *(um Kunden od. Wahlstimmen)* werben; Wahlpropaganda machen; *(Gebiet)* bereisen, bearbeiten *(um Aufträge zu sammeln etc);* eingehend erörtern; *Am* Wahlstimmen überprüfen; *Am* von Haus zu Haus gehen, hausieren; als Kundenwerber tätig sein; **to** ~ **on behalf of a charity** für e-e wohltätige Organisation werben; **to** ~ **election returns** *Am* Wahlstimmen zählen (→*returning board*); **to** ~ **for a newspaper** *(Abonnenten)* für e-e Zeitung werben; **to** ~ **(for) orders** Aufträge hereinholen; **to** ~ **(a district) for votes** um Wahlstimmen werben

canvasser Kundenwerber; Werbevertreter; Anzeigenvertreter; Wahlstimmenwerber; Wahlpropagandist; *Am* Wahl(stimmen)prüfer; *Am* Hausierer; ~**s** *Br* freiwillige Propagandisten, die während des Wahlkampfes die Parteikomitees unterstützen; ~ **of subscriptions** Abonnentenwerber; **advertising** ~ Anzeigeneinholer; **insurance** ~ Versicherungsvertreter

canvassing Kundenwerbung, Anwerbung von *(neuen)* Kunden; Hereinholen von Aufträgen; Kundenfang; Wahl(stimmen)werbung; *Am* Wahlstimmenüberprüfung; ~ **campaign** Werbeaktion; ~ **department** Kundenwerbeabteilung

CAP Zinsbegrenzung nach oben *(→capping)*
cap rate (of interest) Maximalzinssatz

capability *(körperliche od. geistige)* Fähigkeit; Befähigung; Fähigkeit zur Durchführung e-r Arbeit

capable fähig, imstande (of zu); tauglich (of zu); befähigt, tüchtig; ~ **of entering into a contract** vertragsfähig, geschäftsfähig; ~ **of repetition** wiederholbar

capacity Fähigkeit; Kapazität *(e-s Betriebes);* Geschäftsfähigkeit; Rechtsfähigkeit; Leistungsfähigkeit; Eigenschaft, Funktion; Tragfähigkeit, Ladefähigkeit, Tonnengehalt *(e-s Schiffes);* ~ **audience** vollbesetztes Haus; ~ **bottleneck** Kapazitätsengpaß; ~ **limit** Kapazitätsgrenze; ~ **of production** Produktionskapazität; ~ **to conclude** (or **make**) **a contract** Vertragsfähigkeit, Geschäftsfähigkeit; ~ **to marry** Ehefähigkeit; ~ **to pay** Zahlungsfähigkeit; ~ **to sue** *Am* Prozeßfähigkeit; Aktivlegitimation; ~ **to be sued** *Am* Passivlegitimation; ~ **utilization** Kapazitätsauslastung; ~ **to work** Arbeitsfähigkeit

capacity, annual ~ Jahreskapazität; **carrying** ~ Tragfähigkeit, Ladefähigkeit; →**contractual ~; financial** ~ finanzielle Leistungsfähigkeit; **idle** ~ *Am* ungenützte Kapazität; **in the** ~ **of** in der Eigenschaft als; **industrial** ~ Industriekapazität

capacity, legal ~ Rechtsfähigkeit; Geschäftsfähigkeit; **of** (or **having**) **legal** ~ rechtsfähig; geschäftsfähig; **of full legal** ~ voll geschäftsfähig *(opp. of limited legal capacity, under legal disability);* **person deprived of legal** ~ Entmündigter; **to be without (full) legal** ~ geschäftsunfähig sein; **a person of unsound mind is without legal** ~ *Am* ein Geisteskranker ist geschäftsunfähig

capacity, in his ~ **as a civil servant** in seiner Beamteneigenschaft; **in a managerial** ~ in leitender Stelle; **in his ministerial** ~ in s-r Eigenschaft als Minister; **in an official** ~ in amtlicher Eigenschaft; **plant** ~ Betriebskapazität; **in a private** ~ privat, nicht amtlich; **production** ~ Produktionskapazität; **in a professional** ~ beruflich; **purchasing** ~ Kaufkraft; **spare** ~ *Br* ungenützte Kapazität; **taxable** ~ Steuerkraft; **testamentary** ~ Testierfähigkeit; **in an unofficial** ~ inoffiziell, nicht amtlich; **the meeting room was filled to** ~ der Versammlungsraum war voll besetzt

capias, writ of ~ →writ

capita, per ~ ("by heads") auf den Kopf (der Bevölkerung); pro Kopf; *(ErbR)* nach Köpfen *(opp. per stirpes);* **per** ~ **GDP** Bruttoinlandsprodukt pro Kopf der Bevölkerung; **per** ~ **wages** pro Kopf-Löhne

capital 1. Kapital; Vermögen

capital, to add interest to the ~ die Zinsen zum Kapital schlagen; **to attract** ~ Kapital heranziehen; **to convert into** ~ kapitalisieren; **to increase the** ~ *(AktienR)* das (Grund-)Kapital erhöhen; **to invest** ~ Kapital anlegen (od. hineinstecken); **to live on one's** ~ von seinem Kapital leben, sein Kapital verbrauchen; **to lock up** ~ Kapital fest anlegen; **to make** ~ **out of** *fig* Kapital schlagen aus; **to procure** ~ Kapital beschaffen; **to provide with** ~ mit Kapital versehen; **to raise** ~ Kapital aufnehmen (od. aufbringen); **to reduce** ~ *Br (AktienR)* das (Grund-)Kapital herabsetzen

capital, ~ **account** Kapitalkonto *(opp. private account);* ~ **accumulation** Kapitalbildung, Vermögensbildung; ~ **allowance** *Br (SteuerR)* Abschreibung *(von Anlagewerten);* ~ **appreciation** Vermögenszuwachs; ~ **appropriation** Investitionsbewilligung; ~ **asset** Kapitalanlagegegenstand; ~ **assets** Kapitalvermögen; *(Bilanz)* Anlagevermögen; *(DBA)* Vermögenswerte *(opp. circulating/current assets);* ~ **budgeting** Investitionsrechnung; ~ **charges** Kapitalkosten; ~ **of a company** *Br* (**corporation** *Am*) Grundkapital *(e-r AG);* ~ **consolidation** Kapitalkonsolidierung; ~ **contribution** (Kapital-)-Einlage *(in e-e Personengesellschaft);* Geschäftseinlage; ~ **decrease** *(AktienR)* Kapitalherabsetzung; ~ **deepening** Kapitalvertiefung; ~ **demand** Kapitalbedarf; ~ **distribution** Ausschüttung von Kapital; ~ **duty** *Br* Stempelsteuer auf Kapitalaufnahme durch Kapitalgesellschaften (limited companies) und Kommanditgesellschaften (limited partnerships); ~ **equipment** Kapitalausstattung

capital expenditure Investitionsaufwand, Investitionsausgaben *(für Anlagegüter zur Schaffung neuer Werte; opp. revenue expenditure);* Anlagekosten; *Am (SteuerR)*[3] vermögensbildende Aufwendungen; ~ **activity** Investitionstätigkeit; ~ **planning** Investitionsplanung; ~ **program(me)** Investitionsprogramm

capital, ~ **flight** Kapitalflucht; ~ **flow** Kapitalfluß; ~ **formation** Kapitalbildung

capital gain (Kapital-)Veräußerungsgewinn, Gewinn aus der Veräußerung von Vermögen; *(Investmentgesellschaft)* realisierter Kursgewinn; ~ **distribution** Ausschüttung realisierter Kursgewinne, Gewinnausschüttung; ~**s tax**[3a] Kapitalgewinnsteuer; **net long-term** ~ *Am* langfristiger Nettoveräußerungsgewinn *(cf. capital loss).*

capital goods Investitionsgüter *(opp. consumer goods);* ~ **industry** Investitionsgüterindustrie; ~ **orders** Anlageaufträge, Aufträge im Anlagegeschäft

capital, ~ **impairment** Verminderung des Grundkapitals *(durch Verluste od. Ausschüttungen);* Unterbilanz; *(bei völliger Aufzehrung des Kapitals)* Überschuldung; ~ **impairment rule** *Am* Regel, die die Ausschüttung von Dividenden aus dem Grundkapital verbietet; ~ **income** Kapitalertrag, -erträge; ~ **increase** *(AktienR)* Kapitalerhöhung; ~ **indemnification** Kapitalabfindung; ~ **inflow** (or **influx**) Kapitalzufluß; ~ **interest** Kapitalanteil

capital investments *(langfristige)* Kapitalanlage, Investitionen; Investitionsausgaben; ~ **on equipment** Ausrüstungsinvestitionen; ~ **plan** Investitionsplan

capital, ~ **issue** Effektenemission; ~ **job** Investitionsauftrag; **C~ and Labo(u)r** Kapital und Arbeit *(Unternehmer[tum] und Arbeiter[schaft]);* ~ **levy** Vermögensabgabe, Kapitalabgabe *(an den Staat);* ~ **liabilities** Kapitalverbindlichkeiten; ~ **link** Kapitalverflechtung; ~ **loan** Investitionskredit

capital loss Kapitalverlust; Kapitalveräußerungsverlust, Verlust aus der Veräußerung von Kapitalanlagegegenständen; **net short term** ~*Am*[4] kurzfristiger Nettoveräußerungsverlust; **to take a deduction of one half of the excess of net long term capital gains over net short term ~ es** *Am*[5] die Hälfte des Überschusses der langfristigen Nettoveräußerungsgewinne über die kurzfristigen Nettoveräußerungsverluste abziehen

capital market Kapitalmarkt *(für langfristige Kredite; opp. money market);* ~ **rates** Kapitalmarktsätze; ~ **situation** Kapitalmarktlage

capital, ~ money *Br (nach dem Settled Land Act)* dem trustee zu zahlende od. gezahlte Beträge; ~ **movements** Kapitalbewegungen; Kapitalverkehr; ~ **needs** Kapitalbedarf; ~ **outflow** Kapitalabfluß; ~ **output ratio** Kapitalkoeffizient; ~ **from outside sources** Fremdkapital; ~ **ownership** *Am (Bilanz)* Eigenkapital

capital projects Investitionsvorhaben; **misconceived** ~ Fehlinvestitionen

capital, ~ rating Kapitalbewertung; geschätzte finanzielle Stellung, Beurteilung *(e-s Unternehmens);* ~ **redemption reserve fund** *Br* Reservefonds zur Tilgung von Vorzugsaktien; Rückkaufsfonds; ~ **reduction** *(AktienR)* Kapitalherabsetzung; ~ **reequipment** Kapitalerhöhung; Kapitalaufstockung; ~ **requirement(s)** Kapitalbedarf; ~ **reserve** Kapitalreserve; *(AktienR)* Kapitalrücklage; ~ **seeking investment** anlagesuchendes Kapital; ~ **spending** Investitionsaufwendungen

capital stock *Am* Aktienkapital, Grundkapital *(e-r AG);* Stammkapital *(e-r GmbH);* **decrease of** ~ s. reduction of →~; **increase of** ~ Erhöhung des Grundkapitals; **issue of** ~ Aktienausgabe; **reduction of** ~ Herabsetzung des Grundkapitals; **share of** ~ Anteil des einzelnen Aktionärs am Grundkapital; **subscription of** ~ Aktienzeichnung; **to decrease** (or **reduce**) **the** ~ das Grundkapital herabsetzen; **to increase the** ~ das Grundkapital erhöhen

capital, ~ structure Kapitalstruktur; ~ **sum** Kapitalbetrag, Kapitalsumme; ~ **surplus** *Am (AktienR)* Rücklagen, die nicht aus Jahresüberschüssen stammen (→*surplus 2.*); ~ **tax** *(DBA)* Vermögensteuer; ~ **tie-up** Kapitalbindung; ~ **transactions** Kapitalverkehr; ~ **transfer** Kapitaltransferierung; ~ **transfer tax** (CTT) *Br*[6] Schenkung- und Erbschaftsteuer; ~ **turnover** Kapitalumschlag; ~ **widening** Kapitalausweitung; ~ **yield** Kapitalertrag; ~ **yields tax** *Br* Kapitalertragssteuer

capital, accumulation of ~ Kapitalansammlung, Kapitalbildung; **amount of** ~ Kapitalbetrag, Kapitalhöhe; **authorized** ~ *(AktienR)* zur Ausgabe genehmigtes (od. autorisiertes) Kapital *(opp. issued ~);* **borrowed** ~ Fremdkapital; **circulating** ~ s. floating →~; **circulation of** ~ Kapitalumlauf; **exodus of** ~ Kapitalabwanderung, Kapitalflucht; **fixed** ~ festliegendes Kapital, Anlagekapital *(Maschinen etc);* **floating** ~ Umlaufkapital, Betriebskapital *(Waren, Geld etc);* **holding of** ~ Kapitalbesitz; **idle** ~ totes (od. brachliegendes) Kapital; **increase of** ~ *(AktienR)* Kapitalerhöhung; **influx of** ~ Kapitalzufluß; **invested** ~ angelegtes Kapital, Anlagekapital; **investment of** ~ Kapitalanlage, Geldanlage; **issued** ~ *Br* (**issued ~ stock** *Am*) *(AktienR)* ausgegebenes Kapital; **lack of** ~ Kapitalmangel; **loss of** ~ Kapitalverlust

capital, nominal ~ Nominalkapital; Grundkapital *(e-r AG);* Gesellschaftskapital; Stammkapital *(e-r GmbH); Am* nominelles *(geringfügiges)* Kapital; **statement of nominal** ~ *Br* Erklärung über das Grundkapital *(Gründungserfordernis e-r AG)*

capital, original ~ *Am* Anfangskapital; Gründungskapital; **paid-up** ~ *(von den Aktionären)* voll eingezahltes Kapital; **partnership** ~ Gesellschaftskapital; **procurement of** ~ (or **procuring** ~) Kapitalbeschaffung; **well provided with** ~ kapitalkräftig; **raising of** ~ Kapitalaufnahme; **reduction of** ~ *(AktienR)* Kapitalherabsetzung; **reflux of** ~ Kapitalrückwanderung; **requisite** ~ nötiges (od. erforderliches) Kapital; **share** ~ →share 2.; **share in the** ~ Kapitalanteil; **subscribed** ~ *Am* →subscribe 3.; **supply of** ~ Kapitalversorgung; **taking up of** ~ Kapitalaufnahme; **tied-up** ~ festliegendes Kapital; **trading** ~ Betriebskapital; **turnover of** ~ Umschlag des Kapitals; **uncalled** ~ noch nicht aufgerufenes (od. eingefordertes) Kapital; **unpaid** ~ noch nicht eingezahltes Kapital *(cf. paid-up ~);* **unproductive** ~ totes Kapital; **working** ~ Betriebskapital; **working ~ fund** Betriebsmittelfonds

capital 2. Hauptstadt; Haupt-; hauptsächlich; ~ **city** Hauptstadt; ~ **error** grundlegender Irrtum; ~ **(letter)** großer Buchstabe; **to write one's name in ~s** seinen Namen in großen Buchstaben schreiben

capital 3. Todes-; ~ **crime** Kapitalverbrechen *(auf welchem die Todesstrafe steht);* ~ **or otherwise infamous crime** *Am* Kapital- oder sonstiges schweres Verbrechen; ~ **punishment** Todesstrafe; **retention of ~ punishment** Beibehaltung der Todesstrafe; **to abolish ~ punishment** die Todesstrafe abschaffen

capitalism Kapitalismus

capitalist Kapitalist; ~ **economy** kapitalistische Wirtschaft

capitalistic system kapitalistisches System, Kapitalismus

capitalizable kapitalisierbar

capitalization Kapitalisierung; Aktivierung; ~ **of interest** Übernahme der Zinsen zum Kapital; ~ **of profits** Aktivierung des Gewinns; ~ **of reserves** Umwandlung von Rücklagen in Aktienkapital

capitalize *v* kapitalisieren; in Kapital umwandeln; mit Kapital ausstatten; *(Bilanz)* aktivieren; mit großen (Anfangs-)Buchstaben schreiben; **to ~ on** Nutzen ziehen aus; ausnützen; sich konzentrieren auf; **to ~ an annuity** e-e Rente kapitalisieren; **to ~ the goodwill** den Goodwill aktivieren; **to ~ interest** die Zinsen zum Kapital nehmen

capitalized value kapitalisierter Wert

capitation tax Kopfsteuer

Capitol *Am* Kapitol *(Kongreßgebäude)*

capitulation *mil* Kapitulation(svertrag)

capitulate *v mil* kapitulieren, sich ergeben

capping Plafondierung des Zinssatzes e-r Anleihe mit variabler Verzinsung; **rate ~** →rate 1.

captain Kapitän; Führer; *Am* Wahlagent; *mil* Hauptmann; **~ of industry** Industrieführer; Großindustrieller; **~'s protest** Seeprotest, Verklarung

caption einleitende Formel, Kopf *(e-r Urkunde);* Überschrift; *(ProzeßR)* Rubrum *(Bezeichnung der Parteien und des Gerichts);* Untertitel *(bes. bei e-m Film);* Bildtext; *Scot* Verhaftung, Festnahme

caption *v* rubrizieren

captive Gefangener, gefangen; *com* für den Eigenbedarf *(nicht für den Markt);* **~ agent** *Am* Einfirmenvertreter; **~ insurance company** (or **~ insurer**) *Am* Versicherungstochtergesellschaft e-s Industrieunternehmens; **~ shop** *Am* zum Betrieb gehöriges Geschäft; **broad ~** *Am* Versicherungsmuttergesellschaft, die auch Fremdrisiken versichert *(neben den Risiken ihrer Tochtergesellschaft);* **matured** (or **senior**) **~** s. broad →~; **to hold a p. ~** jdn gefangen halten; **to take ~** gefangen nehmen

captivity Gefangenschaft; Kriegsgefangenschaft

captor jd, der ein Schiff aufbringt; Prisennehmer

capture Aufbringung *(e-s Schiffes);* Beschlagnahme, Prise; **~ of a criminal** Festnahme (od. Ergreifung) e-s Verbrechers; **~ of an enemy** Gefangennahme e-s Feindes; **~ of a thief** Ergreifung e-s Diebes; **free of ~ and seizure** (F. C. & S.) *(SeeversR)* frei von Aufbringung und Beschlagnahme *(Ausschluß von Kriegsrisiko);* **right of ~** *(VölkerR)* Prisenrecht, Beuterecht *(cf. contraband, blockade);* **to be liable to ~** der Beschlagnahme verfallen *(Prise)*

capture *v* gefangennehmen; festnehmen, ergreifen; *(Schiff)* aufbringen; *(VölkerR) (im Kriege)* erbeuten (property ~d on land →booty of war; property ~d at sea →prize 2.); **to be ~d during the war** während des Krieges in Gefangenschaft geraten

captured ship als Prise aufgebrachtes Schiff

Cape Verde Kap Verde; **Republic of ~** Republik Kap Verde

Cape Verdean Kapverdier(in); kapverdisch

car Auto; Kraftfahrzeug (Kfz.); Personenwagen; (Straßenbahn-)Wagen; *Am* Waggon, Eisenbahnwagen; **~ dealer** Autohändler; **~hire** *Br* Autovermietung; **~ licen|ce (~se)** Zulassungsschein für das Auto; **~ owner** Kraftwagenhalter, Halter e-s Kraftfahrzeugs; **~ park** *Br* Parkplatz; **~ plant** Autofabrik; **~ pool** Fahrgemeinschaft; *(auch:)* Fahrbereitschaft (Fahrdienst); **~ registration** *Br* Zulassung von Kraftfahrzeugen; **~ rental service** Autovermietung; **~ tax** *Br* Kraftfahrzeugsteuer *(bei Einfuhr u. Kauf zu zahlen);* **~ theft** Autodiebstahl; **~ trust** *Am* Finanzierungsgesellschaft für Eisenbahnbedarf; **by ~** mit dem Auto; **dining ~** Speisewagen; **freight ~** *Am* Güterwagen; **licen|ced (~sed) ~** zugelassenes Auto; **passenger ~** *Am (Eisenbahn)* (Personen-)Wagen; Personenkraftwagen (Pkw); **sleeping ~** Schlafwagen; **stealing a ~** Autodiebstahl

caravan Wohnwagen

carbon copy Durchschlag

carcinogenic substances krebserzeugende Stoffe

card Karte; **~s** Arbeitslosenversicherungs- und Krankenversicherungskarten; **~ carrying member** eingeschriebenes Mitglied *(e-r Partei, Gewerkschaft etc);* **~ catalog(ue)** Katalog

card index Kartei, Kartothek; **~ file** Kartei; **to compile a ~** e-e Kartei anlegen; **to enter on a ~** in e-e Kartei eintragen

card, admission ~ Eintrittskarte; **index ~** Karteikarte; **insurance ~** Versicherungskarte; **letter ~** Briefkarte; **on the ~s** möglich; **visiting ~** Visitenkarte; **to be given one's ~s** *colloq.* entlassen werden; **to play one's ~ well** geschickt verhandeln

care Sorge, Sorgfalt; Obhut, Aufsicht, Pflege, Betreuung; **~ of** (c/o) *(auf Briefen)* per Adresse, bei; **~ for sb.** Betreuung jds; **~ of the child** Sorge für die Person des Kindes; **~ and control of a child** Sorge für die Person e-s Kindes *(tägliche Betreuung des Kindes; cf. custody);* **~ order** *Br*[7] Anordnung des Jugendgerichts, durch die ein Kind oder Jugendlicher wegen Begehung e-r mit Strafe bedrohten Handlung oder aus Gründen der Schutz- oder Fürsorgebedürftigkeit der Ortsbehörde zur Obhut und Personenfürsorge überwiesen wird; **children in ~** *Br*[8] Kinder oder Jugendliche, die unter der Obhut und Personenfürsorge der Ortsbehörde (local authority) oder e-r wohltätigen Organisation (voluntary organization, voluntary home) stehen; **due ~** gebührende (od. angemessene, gehörige) Sorgfalt *(wie in eigenen*

Angelegenheiten); **duty to take** ~ Sorgfaltspflicht
care, ordinary ~ verkehrsübliche Sorgfalt; **failure to use ordinary** ~ Fehlen der verkehrsüblichen Sorgfalt; **to exercise ordinary** ~ die verkehrsübliche Sorgfalt anwenden
care, proper ~ nötige (od. erforderliche) Sorgfalt; **reasonable** ~ angemessene Sorgfalt; Sorgfalt e-s ordentlichen Kaufmanns
care, to be in a p.'s ~ unter jds Aufsicht (od. Obhut) stehen; **to be (placed) under the** ~ **of a guardian** unter Vormundschaft stehen; **to entrust to the** ~ **of a p.** jds Obhut anvertrauen; **to exercise** (or **take**) ~ Sorgfalt anwenden; **to have the** ~ **of a p.** die Aufsicht haben über jdn; **to take** ~ sich in acht nehmen; sorgen (of für)

care *v*, **to** ~ **for** sorgen für, sich kümmern um; **to** ~ **about** sich Sorgen machen über, sich sorgen um

career Laufbahn, Karriere; Berufsverlauf; ~ **adviser** Berufsberater; ~ **civil servant** *Am* Berufsbeamter; ~ **civil service** *Am* Berufsbeamtentum; ~ **consul** Berufskonsul; ~ **diplomat** (or **man**) *Am* Berufsdiplomat; ~ **officer** *Am* höherer Beamter, Berufsbeamter; ~ **woman** Karrierefrau; **legal** ~ juristische Laufbahn; **occupational** (or **professional**) ~ berufliche Laufbahn; **previous** ~ bisherige Tätigkeit; →**two-**~ **family; to enter upon a** ~ e-e Laufbahn einschlagen

careful sorgfältig, sorgsam; vorsichtig; **upon** ~ **consideration** nach reiflicher Überlegung; ~ **execution** sorgfältige Ausführung
carefulness Sorgfalt; Vorsicht

careless sorglos, nachlässig; fahrlässig; unbekümmert (about); ~ **and inconsiderate driving** *Br*[9] fahrlässiges Führen e-s Kraftfahrzeugs, unachtsames Fahren

carelessness Nachlässigkeit; Fahrlässigkeit

caretaker Hausverwalter; *Br* Hausmeister; Wärter *(z. B. in e-m Museum);* ~ **government** Übergangsregierung, Interimsregierung

Carey Street *Br colloq.* Konkurs *(Londoner Straße, in der früher viele Konkursanwälte ihre Kanzleien hatten)*

carfare *Am* Fahrpreis *(für Straßenbahn)*

cargo (Schiffs-, Flugzeug-)Ladung, Fracht(gut); ~ **aircraft** Frachtflugzeug; ~ **boat** Frachtschiff; ~ **book** Ladebuch; ~ **(carrying) capacity** Ladefähigkeit; ~ **coal** Bunkerkohle; ~ **handling facilities** Güterverladungsanlagen; ~ **insurance** Frachtversicherung, Güterversicherung; ~ **lien** Ladungspfandrecht; ~ **liner** Linienfrachtschiff; ~ **owner** Eigentümer der Ladung; ~ **passage** Seereise mit Fracht *(opp. ballast passage);* ~ **policy** Frachtversicherungspolice; ~ **ship** Frachtschiff; ~ **space** Laderaum; ~ **steamer** Frachtdampfer; ~ **vessel** Frachtschiff *(opp. passenger vessel);* ~ **underwriter** Frachtversicherer
cargo, air ~ Luftfracht; **closure for** ~ Verladeschluß; **damage to** ~ Schaden an Ladung; **fitness for special** ~ Ladetüchtigkeit; **general** ~ Stückgut(ladung), Stückgüter; **light** ~ Leichtgut; **loss of** ~ Verlust von Ladung; **mixed** ~ gemischte Ladung; Stückgutladung, Stückgüter; **outward** ~ Hinfracht; **part** ~ Teilfracht, Teilladung; **return** ~ Rückfracht; **undeclared** ~ nicht deklarierte Ladung
cargo, to carry ~ Fracht befördern; **to discharge a** ~ Ladung löschen; **to embark** (or **take in**) ~ Ladung *(auf das Schiff)* einnehmen, einladen; **to unload** ~ Ladung löschen, ausladen

Caribbean, ~ **Community** (CARICOM) Karibische Gemeinschaft; ~ **Development Bank** (CDB)[10] Karibische Entwicklungsbank

carload *Am* Wagenladung, Waggonladung *(a load that fills a car); Am* Mindestlademenge *(die für e-n ermäßigten Frachttarif notwendig ist);* ~ **freight** *Am* Waggonfracht(gut); **less-than-**~ **freight** *Am* Stückgut(fracht); ~ **lot** (C. L.) *Am* Waggonladung *(die e-e für den ermäßigten Frachttarif erforderliche Mindestlademenge hat);* **less-than-**~**lot** (L. C. L.) *Am* Stückgut; ~ **rate** (C. L.-rate) *Am* Waggonfrachtrate *(ermäßigter Frachttarif für große Frachtsendungen);* **less-than-**~ **rate** (L. C. L.-rate) *Am (nicht ermäßigte)* Stückgutfrachtrate; **mixed** ~ gemischte Ladung, Sammelladung; Stückgutladung, Stückgüter

carloading *Am* Waggonladung

carnal knowledge Geschlechtsverkehr

Carnet ATA →Customs Convention on the ATA Carnet for the temporary admission of goods
Carnet TIR[11] *Fr* Zollbegleitscheinheft *(für internationalen Straßengüterverkehr);* **holder of the** ~ Carnet TIR-Inhaber
Carnet de Passages (en Douane)[12] *Fr* Zollpassierscheinheft *(Zollbürgschaft für Kraftwagen bei Grenzübertritt für Reisen in verschiedene Länder, gültig für ein Jahr) (cf. triptych)*
Carnets, Customs Convention Regarding E. C. S. ~**s for commercial samples**[13] Zollabkommen über Carnets E. S. C. für Warenmuster

carpet bombing Bombenteppichwurf

carport Behelfsgarage

carriage *(bes.* Güter-, *auch* Personen-)Transport, Beförderung, Fracht; Transportkosten, Versandkosten, Frachtkosten; Fuhrgeld, Rollgeld; *Br* Eisenbahnwagen, Waggon; *Br* Paketporto;

~ **account** Frachtkonto; ~ **by air** Lufttransport, Beförderung auf dem Luftweg; ~ **by rail** Eisenbahntransport, Beförderung per Bahn; ~ **by sea** Seetransport, Beförderung auf dem Seeweg; Verfrachtung *(cf. bill of lading)*

carriage, ~ **charges** Transportkosten, Fracht (-kosten); ~ **and duty prepaid** franko Fracht und Zoll; ~ **forward** (C/F) *Br* Frachtkosten per Nachnahme; unfrei; ~ **free** frachtfrei, Fracht *(vom Absender)* bezahlt; ~ **paid** (C/P) →~ free

carriage of goods Beförderung von Waren, Gütertransport, Güterbeförderung; *(Seefrachtgeschäft)* Verladung von Gütern; ~ **by land** Binnengüterverkehr; ~ **by inland waterway** Binnenschiffsgüterverkehr; ~ **by rail** Eisenbahngüterverkehr; ~ **by road** Güterkraftverkehr; **international ~ by road**[14] internationaler Straßengüterverkehr *(→international);* →**European Agreement Concerning the International Carriage of Dangerous Goods by Road; C~ of G~ by Sea Act** (COGSA) Seefrachtrechtsgesetz

carriage, additional ~ Frachtaufschlag, Frachtzuschlag; **contract of** ~ (Stückgut-)Frachtvertrag; Beförderungsvertrag; Transportvertrag; **cost of** ~ Frachtkosten; Transportkosten; Beförderungskosten; **means of** ~ Transportmittel; **through** ~ *Br* Kurswagen

carriageable transportierbar; befahrbar *(Weg)*

carriageway Fahrbahn; **dual** ~ *Br* Straße mit zwei *(getrennten)* Fahrbahnen; **principal** ~ Hauptfahrbahn

carried forward (c/f., cd fwd) *(Buchführung)* Vortrag *(auf neue Rechnung)*

carried, to be ~ angenommen werden, durchgehen; **the motion was** ~ der Antrag wurde angenommen; der Antrag ging durch; **person ~ over** →to carry over; **unanimously** ~ einstimmig angenommen

carrier *(Person od. Gesellschaft, die gewerbsmäßig Personen od. Sachen befördern:)* Beförderer; Spediteur, Speditionsfirma; Verkehrsunternehmen, Verkehrsunternehmer; Fluggesellschaft, Luftverkehrsgesellschaft; *(Landfracht und Binnenschiffahrt)* Frachtführer; *(Seefracht)* Verfrachter; *(Luftfracht)* Luftfrachtführer; ~**s** Verkehrsunternehmen; Speditionsfirma; ~ **by land** Frachtführer; ~ **by sea** Verfrachter; ~**'s business** Speditionsgeschäft; ~**'s charges** Transportkosten; Speditionskosten; ~**'s liability** Haftpflicht des Frachtführers; Transporthaftung *(der carrier haftet für die ihm anvertrauten Güter bis zur [aber ausschließlich] höheren Gewalt, während sonst der bailee nur für ordinary →negligence haftet);* ~**'s lien** Pfandrecht des Frachtführers; ~**'s receipt** Ladeschein; Spediteurbescheinigung ~ **(of a risk)** *Am* Versicherer

carrier, common ~ *(öffentl.)* Frachtführer; *(bahnamtlicher)* Spediteur; Speditionsfirma; Transportunternehmen; *Am* öffentl. Verkehrsmittel; Verkehrsunternehmen *(z.B. Eisenbahn-, Schiffahrts-, Luftverkehrsgesellschaft); Am* Luftverkehrslinie; **common** ~ **by air** Luftfrachtspediteur

carrier, highway ~ *Am* Beförderungsgesellschaft; **private** ~ privater Frachtführer *(opp. common carrier);* Gelegenheitsspediteur *(der gelegentlich gegen Entgelt Transporte übernimmt)*

carry, ~ **back** *Am (SteuerR)* Verlustrücktrag, Verlustrückbeziehung *(steuerl. Verrechnung von Betriebsverlusten mit den Gewinnen der vorhergehenden 2 Jahre);* ~ **back and** ~ **forward of excess credits** *Am*[15] Rücktrag und Vortrag von (Steuer-)Anrechnungsbeträgen; ~ **forward** *(SteuerR)* Verlustvortrag *(auf die folgenden Jahre);* ~**over** *Br (Börse)* Prolongation, Report *(cf. contango, backwardation); Am (SteuerR)* Verlustvortrag *(steuerl. Verrechnung von Betriebsverlusten mit den Gewinnen der folgenden 5 Jahre);* ~**over rate** *Br* Reportsatz

carry *v* tragen; befördern, transportieren; *parl (Antrag)* durchbringen (od. annehmen); *Am (Ware)* führen; **to ~ a bill** ein Gesetz verabschieden; **to ~ conviction** überzeugend sein; **to ~ a customer** e-n Kunden in seinen Büchern *(als Schuldner)* führen; **to ~ an election** *parl* e-e Wahl gewinnen; **to ~ goods** Fracht befördern; *Am* Waren führen; **to ~ insurance** *Am* versichert sein; **to ~ interest at (the rate of) 5 per cent** sich mit 5% verzinsen; **to ~ a motion** e-n Antrag annehmen *(cf. the motion was → carried);* **to ~ a State** *Am (bei der Wahl)* e-n Einzelstaat für sich gewinnen; **to ~ stock** *(Waren)* führen, auf Lager haben

carry, to ~ back *Am (SteuerR)* (Betriebs-)Verluste mit den Gewinnen der letzten 2 Jahre verrechnen; **to ~ forward** vortragen; übertragen; **to ~ forward to new account** auf neue Rechnung vortragen; **to ~ forward one's losses** *(SteuerR)* die (Betriebs-)Verluste mit den Gewinnen späterer Jahre verrechnen; **to ~ into effect** ausführen; **to ~ it off well** es *(in e-r schwierigen Lage)* erfolgreich durchführen

carry on *v* weiterführen, fortsetzen; *(Geschäfte)* betreiben; *(Prozeß)* führen; **to ~ (a) business** ein Geschäft (weiter)betreiben; geschäftlich tätig sein; ein Geschäft fortführen; **to ~ a conversation** e-e Unterhaltung fortsetzen; **to ~ trade** Handel treiben; **to ~ with one's work** s-e Arbeit fortsetzen

carry out *v* ausführen, durchführen; **to ~ a project** e-n Plan ausführen (od. zur Ausführung bringen); **to ~ a reform** e-e Reform durchführen; **to ~ a threat** e-e Drohung wahrmachen

carr|y over *v* übertragen; vortragen; *Br (Börse)* prolongieren; **to ~ a balance** e-n Saldo vortragen; **person ~ied over** Reportgeber; **person ~ying over** Reportnehmer

carry through *v* durchführen, ausführen; *(jdn)* durchbringen; **to ~ a promise** ein *(gegebenes)* Versprechen ausführen

carrying Beförderung, Transport; ~ **agent** Spediteur; ~ **of a bill** Gesetzesannahme; ~ **capacity** Tragfähigkeit, Ladefähigkeit; ~ **charges** Transportkosten, Speditionsgebühren; *Am* Zinsen *(für Teilzahlungskredit)*; ~ **costs** *Am* Betriebskosten *(z.B. bis ein Grundstück verkauft werden kann, wie Versicherungsprämien etc)*; **judgment ~ costs** Urteil, das die Prozeßkosten der unterliegenden Partei auferlegt

carrying out Ausführung, Durchführung; ~ **of an order** Ausführung e-s Auftrags; ~ **of a process** *(PatR)* Ausführung e-s Verfahrens

carrying over Übertrag; Vortrag *(auf neue Rechnung)*; *Br (Börse)* Prolongation *(im Reportgeschäft)*; ~ **day** *Br* Reporttag; (Prämien-)Erklärungstag; ~ **price** (or **rate**) *Br* Prolongationsgebühr; Reportsatz; **person** ~ Reportnehmer

cart *v* anrollen; ~**ed goods** Rollgut

cartage Rollfuhr; Anfuhr; Rollgeld

carte blanche Blankovollmacht

cartel *com* Kartell; *(VölkerR)* Abkommen über den Austausch von Kriegsgefangenen; ~ **agreement** Kartellvertrag; Kartellabsprache; ~ **authority** Kartellbehörde; ~ **interests** Kartellanteile; ~ **member** Mitglied e-s Kartells; ~ **participant** Kartellmitglied; ~ **participation** Kartellbeteiligung; ~ **policy** Kartellpolitik; ~ **price** Kartellpreis, gebundener Preis; ~ **provisions** Kartellbestimmungen; ~ **termination** Kartellkündigung

cartel, compulsory ~ Zwangskartell; **domestic** ~ Binnenkartell; **export** ~ Exportkartell; **import** ~ Importkartell; **price** ~ Preiskartell; **sales** ~ Absatzkartell; **to break up a** ~ ein Kartell auflösen; **to join a** ~ e-m Kartell beitreten

case 1. Fall; (Rechts-)Sache, Rechtsstreit; Standpunkt *(e-r Partei in e-m Rechtsstreit)*; ~**s and controversies** *Am* Streitigkeiten; ~ **at bar** zur Verhandlung stehender Fall; ~ **at issue** →issue 1.; ~ **book** *Am* kommentierte Entscheidungssammlung *(für den juristischen Unterricht)*; ~ **for the defendant** *(zusammenfassende)* Klagebeantwortung *(Plädoyer)*; ~ **history** Personalgeschichte; Vorgeschichte; Krankheitsgeschichte *(Anamnese)*; ~ **in point** einschlägiges Beispiel *(das ein Argument veranschaulicht)*

case law *(durch Urteile gebildetes, nicht kodifiziertes)* Fallrecht, Präzedenzrecht, Rechtsprechungsrecht *(durch richterl. Entscheidung geschaffenes Recht; cf. precedents; opp. statute law)*; **prevailing** ~ herrschende Rechtsprechung

case, ~ **of conscience** Gewissensfrage; ~ **on appeal** Berufungssache

case records →records 1.

case stated *Br* Rechtssache, die dem High Court (→court) zur Entscheidung über e-e Rechtsfrage vorgelegt ist; **appeal by** ~ *Br (Strafprozeß)* Revisionsantrag

case, ~ **studies** *(Meinungsforschung)* Einzelfallstudien; ~ **work** *(Sozialhilfe)* Einzelfallhilfe, soziale Einzelarbeit; ~ **worker** Fürsorger(in), soziale(r) Sachbearbeiter(in) *(der/die die individuellen Fälle betreut)*

case, civil ~ Zivilsache, Zivilprozeß; **criminal** ~ Strafsache, Strafprozeß; **divorce** ~ Ehescheidungssache, Ehescheidungsprozeß; **exceptional** ~ Ausnahmefall; →**opening the** ~; **paternity** ~ Vaterschaftsprozeß; **petty** ~ Bagatellsache

case, in ~ **of** für den Fall, im Falle; **in** ~ **of emergency** im Notfall

case, in ~ **of need** nötigenfalls, im Notfalle; **in** ~ **of need with** notfalls bei *(Notadresse auf Wechseln)*; **referee in** ~ **of need** *(WechselR)* Notadressat; **in** ~ **of need apply to** nötigenfalls bei

case, as the ~ **may be** je nach Lage der Sache; je nachdem; beziehungsweise (bzw.); **it is a** ~ **of** es handelt sich um; **to close the** ~ den Klageantrag (od. die Klageerwiderung) beenden; **to come to** ~**s** zur Sache kommen; **to deal with a** ~ **upon its merits** über den Grund des Anspruchs verhandeln; zur Hauptsache verhandeln; **to have a good** ~ das Recht auf seiner Seite haben; e-n haltbaren Anspruch haben; gute Prozeßaussichten haben; **to hear a** ~ über e-e Sache verhandeln; **to lose one's** ~ s-n Prozeß verlieren, unterliegen; **to make out one's** ~ seine Sache als schlüssig vorbringen; **to make out a good** ~ **(for)** e-e Seite der Sache überzeugend darstellen; **to prepare a** ~ e-e Rechtssache vorbereiten; **to remit a** ~ e-e Rechtssache *(in der Rechtsmittelinstanz an das untere Gericht)* verweisen; **to reopen a** ~ ein Verfahren wieder aufnehmen; **to set down a** ~ **for hearing** e-n Termin zur mündlichen Verhandlung anberaumen; **to sit on a** ~ e-e Sache verhandeln; e-n Fall entscheiden; **to state one's** ~ s-n Fall unterbreiten; s-e Sache vortragen; s-n Standpunkt vertreten; **to state a** ~ **for the determination of the High Court** *Br* dem High Court (→court) die Sache zur Entscheidung e-r Rechtsfrage vorlegen; **to try a** ~ über e-e (Zivil- od. Straf-)Sache gerichtlich verhandeln; über e-e Sache mündlich verhandeln; **the** ~ **went against him** es wurde *(vom Gericht)* gegen ihn entschieden; **to win one's** ~ s-n Prozeß gewinnen; obsiegen

case 2. Kisten, Kasten, Behälter, Gehäuse; ~**s and casks** Rollgut; **brief**~ Aktentasche

cash Kasse; bares Geld, Bargeld, Barmittel; *(Bilanz)* flüssige Mittel *(einschließlich Bankguthaben)*; *Am (Börse)* per Kasse *(Lieferung am gleichen Tage; cf. regular way)*

cash, to balance the ~ Kasse(nsturz) machen; Kassenabschluß machen; **to be out of** ~ nicht bei Kasse sein; kein Geld haben; **to convert into** ~ zu Geld machen, versilbern; **to give** ~ **for a cheque (check)** e-n Scheck einlösen; **to keep the** ~ die Kasse führen; **to make up the** ~ die Kasse machen; **to pay in** ~ (or ~ **down**) bar zahlen; **to reckon up the** ~ Kasse machen

cash, ~ **account** Kassenkonto; Kontokorrentkonto; ~ **advance** Barkredit; Barvorschuß, Kassenvorschuß; ~ **against documents** (c. a. d.) *(Außenhandel)* Zahlung gegen Dokumente (Lieferung gegen Nachnahme) *(der Käufer muß bei Vorlage der Dokumente [Rechnung, Versicherungsschein, Ausfuhrbewilligung etc] Zahlung leisten)*

cash and carry Selbstabholung gegen Barzahlung

cash, ~ **assets** *(Bilanz)* Kassenbestand; ~ **audit (-ing)** Kassenprüfung, Kassenrevision

cash balance Kassenbestand; Kassensaldo; Barguthaben; **adverse** ~ Kassendefizit

cash, ~ **at** (or **in**) **bank** Bankguthaben; ~ **basis accounting** Buchführung auf Ein- und Ausgabenbasis; **on a** ~ **basis** gegen Barzahlung; ~ **before delivery** (c. b. d.) Kasse vor Lieferung; ~ **benefit** *(VersR)* Geldleistung; ~ **bonus** *(VersR)* Bardividende; ~ **book** Kassenbuch; Ausgabenbuch; ~ **budget** Zahlungsplan; Liquiditätsbudget; ~ **budgeting** Liquiditätsplanung; ~ **business** Kassageschäft, Bar(zahlungs)geschäft

cash, ~ **cheque** *Br* Barscheck; ~ **credit** Barkredit; ~ **deficit** Kassendefizit; Kassenmanko; ~ **deposit** Bareinlage; Bardepot; Hinterlegung in bar; ~ **desk** Kasse *(in Geschäften)*; Zahlstelle *(bei Behörden)*; ~ **disbursements** bare Auslagen; Kassenauszahlungen; ~ **discount** (Kassa-)Skonto, Barzahlungsrabatt; ~ **less 3 per cent discount** mit 3% Skonto; ~ **dispenser** Geldausgabeautomat; Bankomat; ~ **distribution** Barausschüttung; ~ **dividend** Bardividende

cash, ~ **dollar agreements** Sofortzahlungsgeschäfte auf Dollarbasis; ~ **down** gegen Barzahlung, in bar; ~ **drawings** Barentnahmen, Barabhebungen; ~ **earnings** Bareinnahmen; Barverdienst; ~ **entry** Kasseneintragung, Kassenbuchung; ~ **expenditure** (or **expenses**) Barausgaben, Barauslagen

cash flow „Kassenfluß", „Barmittelstrom"

Cash flow ist eine Meßzahl, die einmal den Reingewinn eines Unternehmens in einer bestimmten Rechnungsperiode offenlegt, zum anderen den für Investitionen und Rückzahlung von Verbindlichkeiten zur Verfügung stehenden Betrag anzeigt

cash flow, ~ **cycle** normale Geschäftsumschlagperiode *(Zeit, die benötigt wird, investiertes Geld wieder in cash umzuwandeln)*; ~**-underwriting** *(VersR)* Versicherungs- u. Prämienkalkulation unter voller (strikter) Berücksichtigung der Zinserträge

cash, ~ **forecasting** Liquiditätsplanung; ~ **funds** Barmittel; ~ **holding** Kassenbestand; ~ **income** Bareinnahmen; ~ **infusion** Geldspritze; ~ **in** (or **on**) **hand** Kassenbestand, Barbestand; ~ **indemnity** Mankogeld, Fehlgeldentschädigung; ~ **injection** Kapitalspritze; ~ **item** Kassenposten; ~ **keeper** *Am* Kassenführer; ~ **keeping** *Am* Kassenführung; ~ **limit** auf ein Haushaltsjahr begrenzte Mittel e-s Ministeriums

cash management *Am* Finanzmanagement *(Planung, Disposition und Kontrolle der Unternehmensliquidität)*; ~ **account** *Am* Investitions-Girokonto-Kombination bei US-Brokerhäusern; ~ **system** *Am* elektronische Informationsleistung von Banken zur Unterstützung der kurzfristigen Finanzwirtschaft von Unternehmen

cash, ~ **market** *(Börse)* Kassamarkt; ~ **messenger insurance** Botenberaubungsversicherung; ~ **note** Kassenanweisung; Auszahlungsanweisung

cash on delivery (c. o. d.) zahlbar bei Lieferung, Lieferung gegen Nachnahme; **C- on D~ Agreement** Postnachnahmeabkommen; ~ **items** *Br* Postnachnahmesendungen

cash, ~ **operations** *(Börse)* Kassageschäfte; ~ **order** (C/O) Zahlungsanweisung; Kassenanweisung; ~ **outlay** Barauslagen, bare Auslagen; ~ **over(s)** *Am* Kassenüberschuß *(durch Irrtum)*; ~ **paid and received** Einzahlungen und Abhebungen *(e-s Kunden bei e-r Bank)*; ~ **payment** Barzahlung, Zahlung in bar; ~ **payments** Kassenauszahlungen, Kassenausgänge; ~ **point** *Br* Bankautomat; ~ **position** Kassenstand; Barposition, Liquidität(slage); ~ **price** Barpreis, Preis bei Barzahlung; *(Börse)* Kassakurs, Kurs bei Barzahlung; ~ **purchase** Barkauf, Kauf gegen Kasse; *(Börse)* Kassakauf; Handkauf; ~ **quotation** *(Effektenbörse)* Kassakurs; ~ **receipt** Kasseneingang, Bareingang; ~ **receipts** Bareinnahmen, Bareingänge; Kasseneingänge; ~ **receipts and payments** Kassenein- und -ausgänge; ~ **register** Registrierkasse; ~ **remittance** Barüberweisung, Geldsendung; ~ **report** Kassenbericht; ~ **requirement** Geldbedarf; Kassen(mittel)bedarf; Baranforderung

cash reserve Kassenreserve; Barreserve; **operating** ~ Betriebsmittelrücklage

cash, ~ **sale** Barverkauf; *(Börse)* Kassageschäft; ~ **settlement** Barabfindung, Geldabfindung, Kapitalabfindung; ~ **short(s)** Kassendefizit, Kassenfehlbetrag; ~ **statement** Kassenbericht; ~ **subscription** Bareinlage *(bei Firmengründung)*; ~ **surplus** Kassenüberschuß; ~ **surrender value** *(VersR)* Rückkaufswert *(e-r Police)*; ~ **system** Barzahlungssystem; ~ **tender offer** →tender 2.

cash terms Zahlungsbedingungen bei Barzahlung; ~ **only** nur gegen Barzahlung; **business on** ~ Bar(zahlungs)geschäft; **trade on** ~ Bargeldverkehr

cash, ~ transaction Bargeschäft; *(Börse)* Kassageschäft; **~ transactions** Kassenumsatz, Kassenverkehr; Bareinzahlungen und -auszahlungen; **~ value** Barwert, Wert in bar; **~ voucher** Kassenbeleg; **~ with order** (c. w. o.) Barzahlung bei Bestellung (od. Auftragserteilung)

cash, for ~ gegen Barzahlung, gegen Kasse; *Am (Börse)* Lieferung am gleichen Tage *(cf. regular way)*; **for ~ only** nur gegen Barzahlung; **discount for ~** Barzahlungsrabatt; **3 per cent discount for ~** bei Barzahlung 3% Rabatt; **purchase for ~** Barkauf, Bareinkauf; **terms strictly for ~** nur gegen Barzahlung; **to buy** (or **purchase**) **for ~** gegen Barzahlung kaufen; **to sell for ~** gegen Barzahlung verkaufen

cash, in ~ bar, per Kasse; **amount in ~** Barbetrag; **payable in ~** in bar zahlbar; **payment in ~** Barzahlung, Zahlung in bar; **property in ~** bares Vermögen; **settlement in ~** Barabfindung, Kapitalabfindung; **to be in ~** bei Kasse sein

cash, loose ~ Münzgeld, Kleingeld; **making up the ~** Kassenabschluß; **net ~** bar ohne Abzug; **(for) prompt** (or **ready**) **~** (gegen) sofortige Bezahlung; **ready ~** bares Geld, Bargeld; **short of ~** knapp bei Kasse; **their terms are ~ only** sie verkaufen nur gegen bar

cash *v* zu Geld machen; (ein)kassieren; vereinnahmen; *(Wechsel, Scheck etc)* einlösen; **to ~ up** Kasse machen; **to ~ a bill** e-n Wechsel einlösen; e-n Wechsel zur Bezahlung vorlegen

cashed, to get a cheque (check) ~ at a bank e-n Scheck bei e-r Bank eingelöst bekommen

cashing Einkassieren; Einziehung, Inkasso; **~ of a cheque (check)** Einlösung e-s Schecks

cashier Kassenbeamter, Schalterbeamter, Kassenwart; höherer Bankbeamter; **~'s check** *Am* Bankscheck; **~'s desk** (or **office**) Kasse; Zahlstelle; **chief ~** Hauptkassier; **Chief C~** *Br* höchster Beamter der Bank of England; **paying ~** auszahlender Schalterbeamter; **to act as ~** die Kasse führen, Kassierer sein

cashier *v mil (unehrenhaft)* entlassen; *(Offizier)* aus der Wehrmacht ausstoßen

cashless unbar; bargeldlos; **~ payment** bargeldlose(r) Zahlung(sverkehr); **~ transfer** *Am* Banküberweisung

cask Faß; **~s and cases** Rollgut

casket Kästchen; *Am* Sarg

cassation Kassation, Ungültigkeitserklärung; **court of ~** Kassationshof, Revisionsgericht *(in Frankreich)*

cast Berechnung; Addition; Guß; Rollenbesetzung; Art, Typ

cast *v*, **to ~ a balance** den Saldo ziehen; **to ~ a ballot** e-n Stimmzettel abgeben; **to ~ lots** losen; **to ~ up** berechnen, zusammenrechnen, addieren; **to ~ one's vote** s-e Stimme abgeben

casting, ~ vote entscheidende (od. ausschlaggebende) Stimme; **~ of votes** Abgabe von Stimmen

casual zufällig; gelegentlich *(opp. regular)*; **~ criminal** Gelegenheitsverbrecher; **~ employment** gelegentliche Beschäftigung; **~ labo(u)r** Gelegenheitsarbeit; Gelegenheitsarbeiter *(pl.)*; **~ profits** *Br (Einkommensteuer)* gelegentliche Gewinne; **~ revenue** Nebeneinkommen; **~ sale** Gelegenheitsverkauf; **~ work** Gelegenheitsarbeit *(cf. decasualization)*; **~ worker** Gelegenheitsarbeiter, Aushilfskraft *(opp. permanent employee)*

casualt|y Unglücksfall; *(tödlicher)* (Verkehrs-)Unfall; *(bei e-m Unfall)* Verunglückte(r); Tote(r); **~ies** Verluste *(bes. im Krieg)*; Todesfälle; **~ department** Unfallstation *(e-s Krankenhauses)*; **~ insurance** Schadenversicherung *(opp. property insurance)*; *Am* Unfall-Haftpflichtversicherung; **~ list** (or **returns**) *mil* Verlustliste; Liste der Toten und Verwundeten; **civilian ~ies** Verluste der Zivilbevölkerung; **maritime ~** Seeunfall; **state affected by the maritime ~** durch den Seeunfall betroffener Staat; →**mutual ~ insurance company; oil pollution ~** Ölverschmutzungsunfall

casus belli *(VölkerR)* Kriegsfall, Kriegsgrund, kriegsauslösendes Ereignis

casus foederis *(VölkerR)* vertraglich vorgesehener Fall, bei dessen Eintritt bestimmte Verpflichtungen des Bündnispartners wirksam werden

cat, ~ burglar Fassadenkletterer; **~s and dogs** *Am* billige Spekulationspapiere; **~'s paw** *(willenloses)* Werkzeug; **to make a ~'s paw of a p.** jdn als Werkzeug benutzen

catalog(ue) Katalog, Verzeichnis, Liste; *Am univ* Vorlesungsverzeichnis; **~ number** Katalognummer; **~ price** Katalogpreis, Listenpreis; **~ of sale** Auktionsliste; **~ sales** Versandhausverkäufe, -umsatz; **author ~** Autorenkatalog; **fair ~** Messekatalog; **price ~** Preisliste; **subject ~** Sachkatalog; **title ~** Titelkatalog; **to list** (or **put**) **in a ~** in e-n Katalog aufnehmen, katalogisieren

catalog(ue) *v* katalogisieren, in den Katalog aufnehmen

catalyst Katalysator

catalytic converter (Auto-)Katalysator

catastrophe reserve *(VersR)* Katastrophenreserve, Katastrophenrücklage

catch *v* fangen, ergreifen; *(jdn)* einholen; *(Zug)*

erreichen; ertappen; **to ~ in the (very) act** auf frischer Tat ertappen; **to ~ the Speaker's eye** *Br parl* das Wort (vom →Speaker) erhalten; **to ~ up on** *(Rückstand)* aufholen; **to ~ up with** *fig (jdn od. e-n Vorsprung)* einholen; gleichen Schritt halten mit; den Anschluß bekommen an

catching bargain Rechtsgeschäft (bes. Darlehen) zu unfairen od. wucherischen Bedingungen *(unter Ausnutzung fremder Notlage)*; Ablistung des Erbanteils *(von unerfahrenen Erben)*

catchpenny article Schundware

catch quotas Fangquoten

categorical kategorisch

categorization Einreihung, Einstufung

categorize *v (nach Kategorien)* (ein)ordnen; kategorisieren

categor|y Kategorie, Art, Gruppe, Klasse; **in the ~ of basic materials** im Bereich der Grundstoffe; **~ of risks** *(VersR)* Gefahrenklasse; **by ~ies of trade** nach Branchengruppen; **higher ~ies of workers** gehobene Arbeiterschichten; **patent ~** Patentkategorie; **to come in** (or **under**) **a ~** zu e-r Kategorie gehören; **to fall within a ~** in e-e Kategorie fallen; **to place in a ~** *(in e-e Kategorie)* einstufen

cater *v* Lebensmittel (od. Fertigmahlzeiten) liefern; **to ~ for** *(Kantinen, Flughafen etc mit Fertiggerichten)* beliefern; sorgen für; sich bemühen um

catering Großverpflegung; Lieferung von Fertigmahlzeiten; Belieferung von Kantinen, Parties etc; **~ firm** Unternehmen, das Fertigmahlzeiten etc liefert; **~ trade** Hotel- und Gaststättengewerbe

caterer Lieferant von Fertigmahlzeiten; Lebensmittellieferant; Inhaber (od. Leiter) e-s Restaurants; **party ~** Party-Lieferant

Catholic Katholik; katholisch

CATS (Certificates of Accrual on Treasury Securities) *Am* →Zerobonds

cattle (Rind-)Vieh; **~ breeding** Viehzucht; **~ dealer** Viehhändler; **~ insurance** Viehversicherung; **~ lifter** *Br* Viehdieb; **~ lifting** *Br* Viehdiebstahl; **~ raising** Viehzucht; **~ rustler** *Am* Viehdieb; **~ show** Viehausstellung; **~ stealing** Viehdiebstahl; **~ thief** Viehdieb; **~ trade** Viehhandel; **~ trader** Viehhändler; **~ truck** (or **wagon**) Viehwagen

Caucasian race *Am* weiße *(indogermanische)* Rasse

caucus *pol* Fraktionsversammlung; Vorbesprechung e-s Parteigremiums *(Arbeitsgruppe e-r politischen Partei zur Festlegung der Fraktionspolitik und Aufstellung der Kandidaten)*

caucus *v Am* e-e Fraktionsversammlung abhalten; innerhalb e-r Partei beraten

causal connection (or **relationship**) Kausalzusammenhang

causality Ursächlichkeit, Kausalität

causation Verursachung; Kausalität; **chain of ~** Kausalzusammenhang; →**intervening ~**; **presumption of ~** Kausalitätsvermutung

cause Ursache, Grund; Rechtssache, Prozeßsache; gerechte (od. gute) Sache

cause of action Klagegrund; *(klagbarer)* Anspruch; Gegenstand der Klage; **contractual ~** Anspruch aus Vertrag; **tort ~** Anspruch aus unerlaubter Handlung; **the ~ accrues** der Klageanspruch erwächst; der Klagegrund entsteht

cause, ~ for complaint (or **to complain**) Beschwerdegrund; Klagegrund; **~ beyond control** höhere Gewalt; **~ of death** Todesursache; **~ of divorce** Scheidungsgrund; **~ list** *Br* Terminkalender; Verhandlungsliste der Gerichtsfälle; **~ of loss** Schadensursache; **~ of war** Kriegsursache, Kriegsgrund

cause, commercial ~s *(gerichtl.)* Handelssachen; **common ~** gemeinsame Sache; **direct ~** unmittelbare Ursache; **for ~** aus wichtigem Grund

cause, good ~ wichtiger (od. triftiger) Grund; **upon good ~ shown** bei Vorliegen von triftigen Gründen; bei nachgewiesener Begründetheit; **without good ~** ohne triftigen Grund; **to show good ~ (for)** wichtige Gründe darlegen (die ... rechtfertigen)

cause, matrimonial ~s Ehesachen (→*matrimonial*); **petty ~** *(StrafR)* Bagatellsache; **probable ~** vermutlicher Grund; hinreichender (Verdachts-)Grund; **proximate ~** unmittelbare Ursache; **reasonable ~** triftiger Grund; hinreichender Anlaß; **without a sufficient ~** ohne ausreichenden Grund, unbegründet

cause, to give ~ for complaint Grund zur Beschwerde geben; **to plead a ~** e-e Sache (vor Gericht) vertreten; **to show ~** seine Gründe vorbringen *(bes. gegen die beabsichtigte Entscheidung) (s. order to show ~, →order 2.)*; **to uphold a ~** e-e Sache vertreten

cause *v* verursachen, veranlassen, bewirken; **to ~ a p. to do** jdn veranlassen zu tun; bewirken, daß jd tut; **to ~ damage** Schaden verursachen

causing an insured loss deliberately *(VersR)* vorsätzliche Herbeiführung e-s Versicherungsfalles

cautio judicatum solvi Sicherheitsleistung für Prozeßkosten (→*security for costs*)

caution Vorsicht; Warnung; *Br (von der Polizei erteilte schriftl.)* Verwarnung; Eidesbelehrung; Rechtsmittelbelehrung; *Br* Antrag beim Grundbuch auf Benachrichtigung von Anträgen Dritter, die eigene Rechte des Antragstellers gefährden; *bes. Scot* Kaution, Bürgschaft; Bürge; ~ **mark** Vorsichtsmarkierung *(auf Verpackung);* ~ **money** *Br und Scot* Kaution, Bürgschaftssumme *(bes. für eventuell verursachte Schäden auf Universität);* ~ **over new investment** Zurückhaltung bei der Neuanlage *(von Vermögenswerten);* **to give a** ~ e-e Verwarnung erteilen; **to lodge a** ~ *(with the Land Registrar) Br* e-n Antrag beim Grundbuchamt auf Benachrichtigung von Anträgen Dritter stellen

caution *v* warnen; *(strafend)* verwarnen; belehren (about über); **to** ~ **the parties** die Parteien belehren

cautioning as to rights Rechtsmittelbelehrung

cautionary warnend; ~ **instruction** warnende Belehrung; ~ **signal** Warnsignal *(e-s Schiffes)*

cautioner *Scot* Bürge; *Br* Antragsteller (→caution); *Scot* Bürge

caveat *(vorbeugende)* Warnung; Einspruch; Vorbehalt *(Vermerk, daß bestimmte Maßnahmen erst nach Benachrichtigung des caveator getroffen werden dürfen); Br* Einspruch gegen die Erneuerung e-s Patents; *Am* Nachricht an das Patentamt von e-r möglichen Patentanmeldung; ~ **to a will** Vorbehalt gegen Testamentsbestätigung; **to put in** (or **enter, file**) **a** ~ *(vorbeugend)* warnen *(bestimmte Schritte nicht zu unternehmen);* Einspruch erheben (against gegen)

caveat emptor ("let the buyer beware") Ausschluß der Gewährleistung, Mängelausschluß (des Verkäufers: „Auge auf, Kauf ist Kauf")

Am der Uniform Sales Act begründet eine allgemeine Sachmängelhaftung des Verkäufers. Damit verliert der Grundsatz „caveat emptor" an Bedeutung *(cf. warranty of merchantability)*

caveator jd, der e-e Vorbeugungsmaßnahme trifft; *Br (PatR)* Einsprucherhebender

CCT (Common Customs Tariff) *(EG)* GZT (Gemeinsamer Zolltarif); **collection of** ~ **duties** Erhebung der Zölle des GZT; **current** ~ **duties for subheadings** derzeitige Zollsätze des GZT für Tarifstellen

cease and desist order *Am* Unterlassungsanordnung; Verfügung auf Unterlassung *(bes. durch die →Federal Trade Commission),* durch die ein unlauteres Geschäfts- od. Werbeverhalten untersagt wird (→*consent order*)

cease-fire *mil* Feuereinstellung, Waffenruhe

cease *v* aufhören, ablassen (from von); einstellen; **to** ~ **and desist** *Am* unlautere Geschäftspraktiken einstellen; **to** ~ **to exist** nicht mehr bestehen; erlöschen, eingehen *(Firma);* **to** ~ **farming** die landwirtschaftliche Tätigkeit einstellen; **to** ~ **fire** *mil* Feuer einstellen; **to** ~ **to have effect** außer Kraft treten; **to** ~ **to hold office** aus dem Amt ausscheiden; **to** ~ **payments** Zahlungen einstellen *(Bank);* **to** ~ **to work** (or **working**) Arbeit einstellen; **the newspaper will** ~ **publication** (or **to be published**) die Zeitung stellt ihr Erscheinen ein

cede *v (bes. Gebiet)* abtreten, zedieren; überlassen; abgeben

Cedel (Centrale de Livraison de Valeurs Mobilières) computergestütztes Clearinghaus für Eurobonds und andere internationale Wertpapiere *(mit Sitz in Luxemburg)*

cedent *Scot* Zedent, Abtretender

ceiling Decke; Plafond; *(amtl. festgesetzte)* Höchstgrenze; *Am* Zinshöchstgrenze für Bankeinlagen gemäß →Regulation Q; Höchst-, Stopp- *(opp. floor);* ~ **price** *(amtl.)* Höchstpreis; ~ **wages** *(amtl. festgesetzte)* Höchstlöhne; **financial** ~ Finanzierungsplafond; **price** ~ *(amtl.)* Höchstgrenze der Preise; **to exceed the** ~**s** das Plafond überschreiten

celebrate *v (festlich)* begehen; **to** ~ **a marriage** die Eheschließung (od. Trauung) vollziehen; **to** ~ **a wedding** e-e Hochzeit feiern

celebration Feier; ~ **of marriage** Eheschließung; ~ **parade** Festaufmarsch

cell 1. *(Gefängnis)* Zelle; Haftraum; **single** ~ Einzelzelle; **to be confined** (or **imprisoned, locked up**) **in a** ~ in e-r Zelle eingesperrt sein

cell 2. *pol* Zelle *(politische Arbeitsgruppe);* **Communist** ~ kommunistische Zelle; **to set up** ~**s in a factory** in e-r Fabrik Zellen bilden

Celler-Kefauver Act *Am* Anti-Trustgesetz (1950)

Abänderungsgesetz des Fusionsparagraphen (section 7) des →Clayton Act

censor *(amtl.)* Zensor; **deletion by the** ~ Streichung durch die Zensur; **bound to pass the** ~ zensurpflichtig; **suppressed by the** ~ durch die Zensur verboten

censor *v* zensieren, *(amtl.)* Zensur ausüben

censored, to be ~ zensiert werden; durch die Zensur gehen; von der Zensur verboten werden

censoring *(amtl.)* Zensur; **to do** ~ Zensur vornehmen, zensieren

censorship *(amtl.)* Zensur; ~ **of films** Filmzensur; ~ **of the press** Pressezensur; ~ **order** (or **regulation**) Zensurbestimmung; **evasion of** ~ Umgehung der Zensur; **subject to** ~ zensurpflichtig; **to apply** ~ (to) der Zensur unterwerfen; **no** ~ **shall be applied to the correspondence** die Korrespondenz unterliegt nicht der Zensur; **to be subject to** ~ der Zensur unterliegen; **to exercise** ~ **over letters** Briefe zensieren; **to lift the** ~ die Zensur aufheben;

to submit to a severe (or **strict, rigid**) ~ e-r strengen Zensur unterwerfen; **to tighten up the** ~ die Zensur verschärfen

censure Rüge, Verweis *(z. B. durch e-n Vorgesetzten);* Mißbilligung; **motion of** ~ →motion 1.; **subject to** ~ tadelnswert; **vote of** ~ *parl* Mißbilligungsvotum; **to pass a vote of** ~ (on sb. jdm) ein Mißbilligungsvotum aussprechen

censure *v,* **to** ~ **sb.** (for) jdm e-e Rüge erteilen, jdn tadeln

census Zählung; Volkszählung; *(statistische)* Erhebung; **C~ Bureau** *Am* Statistisches Bundesamt; ~ **data** (Betriebs-)Erhebungsangaben; ~ **of opinion** Meinungsbefragung; ~ **of population** Volkszählung; ~ **on a representative basis** Mikrozensus *(Repräsentativstatistik der Bevölkerung und des Erwerbslebens);* **industrial** ~ Betriebszählung; **to take a** ~ e-e (Volks-)-Zählung vornehmen

centenary Hundertjahrfeier

center *Am* →centre

central zentral, Mittel-; Haupt-; *Am* (Telefon-)-Zentrale; ~ **administration** Zentralverwaltung

Central African Republic Zentralafrikanische Republik; **of the** ~ Zentralafrikaner, ~in, zentralafrikanisch

central agency *Am* Zentralstelle

Central American Common Market (CACM) Gemeinsamer Markt der fünf mittelamerikanischen Länder (→*Central American Community*)

Central American Community[16] Zentralamerikanische Wirtschaftsgemeinschaft *(Gemeinsamer Markt Zentralamerikas)*

Die 5 Mitgliedstaaten sind El Salvador, Guatemala, Honduras, Nicaragua und Costa Rica. Innerhalb des Gemeinsamen Marktes sind die Zollschranken verschwunden. Drittländern gegenüber bilden die Vertragsstaaten eine Zollunion mit einheitlichem Zolltarif

central, C~ Arbitration Committee (CAC) *Br* Zentrale Schiedskommission; ~**, regional and local authorities** Gebietskörperschaften; ~ **bank** Zentralbank, Notenbank; **C~ Criminal Court** *Br* →court 2.; **C~ European Time** (C. E. T.) Mitteleuropäische Zeit (MEZ); ~ **file** Zentralkartei; **C~ Intelligence Agency** (CIA) *Am* Geheimdienst *(zentrale Organisation des Nachrichtendienstes [Spionageabwehr] im Ausland)*

central management and control *Br (SteuerR)* zentrale Geschäftsführung und Steuerung *(e-r Gesellschaft)*

Wichtige Kriterien für Regelung der Doppelansässigkeit einer company. Nur wenn central management and control innerhalb des United Kingdom ausgeübt sind, gilt eine Gesellschaft mit Sitz in Großbritannien als in Großbritannien ansässig

central management and control test Test *(der britischen Steuerverwaltung)* zur Feststellung der Ansässigkeit eines Unternehmens im U. K.

Der Test erfolgt anhand der Frage, wo zentrale Geschäftsführung und Steuerung des Unternehmens ausgeübt werden

central, ~ **market** Hauptabsatzgebiet; ~ **office** Zentrale; **C~ Office** *Br* Zentralkanzlei *(des Supreme Court);* ~ **rate** *(EG)* Leitkurs

centralism *pol* Zentralismus *(cf. federalism)*

centralization Zentralisierung

centralize *v* zentralisieren, in e-m (Mittel-)Punkt vereinigen

centre *Br (Am* **center***)* Zentrum, Mittelpunkt; Zentrale, Zentralstelle; *Am* (Telefon-)Zentrale; *pol* Parteien der Mitte; ~ **of commerce** Handelszentrum, Wirtschaftszentrum; ~ **of gravity** *(IPR)* rechtlicher Schwerpunkt, Schwerpunkt e-s Rechtsverhältnisses *(bei der Bestimmung des anzuwendenden Rechts);* ~ **of** →**vital interests; politician of the left** ~ Politiker der linken Mitte; **business** ~ Geschäftszentrum; **shopping** ~ Einkaufszentrum

cereal(s) Getreide; ~ **exports** Getreideausfuhren

ceremonial zeremoniell; förmlich, protokollarisch; ~ **marriage** *Am* formgerecht eingegangene Ehe *(opp. common law marriage);* ~ **occasion** förmlicher Anlaß; offizielle Festlichkeit; ~ **precedence** protokollarische Rangordnung; ~ **opening** festliche Eröffnung *(e-r Tagung)*

ceremony Feier(lichkeit); Förmlichkeit; **marriage** ~ Trauung(sfeier); Eheschließung(sakt) (→*marriage);* **state** ~ Staatsfeierlichkeit(en)

CERN →European Organization for Nuclear Research

certain sicher; bestimmt; **day** ~ bestimmter Tag; **to a** ~ **degree** bis zu e-m bestimmten Grade; **a sum** ~ **in money** e-e bestimmte Geldsumme; **to make** ~ **of a th.** sich etw. sichern, sich e-r Sache vergewissern

certainty Gewißheit, Sicherheit; Rechtssicherheit *(opp. uncertainty);* **with near** ~ mit an Sicherheit grenzender Wahrscheinlichkeit; **with reasonable** ~ mit hinreichender Sicherheit

certificate 1. Schein, Bescheinigung, Bestätigung, Zeugnis, Zertifikat; ~ **of addition** *(PatR)* Zusatzbescheinigung; ~ **of appointment** Bestallungs-, Ernennungsurkunde; ~ **of apprenticeship** Lehrbrief; ~ **of average** Havariezertifikat; ~ **of baptism** Taufschein; ~ **of birth** Geburtsurkunde; ~ **of citizenship** *Am* Staatsangehörigkeitsausweis; ~ **of competency** Befähigungsnachweis; ~ **of compliance**

Am[17] Unbedenklichkeitsbescheinigung *(z.B. Bescheinigung, daß Einkommensteuer bezahlt worden ist)*; ~ **of (good) conduct** Leumundszeugnis, Führungszeugnis; ~ **of correction** *(PatR)* Berichtigungsbescheinigung; ~ **of custody** *Am* Depotschein; ~ **of death** Sterbeurkunde; Totenschein

Certificate of Deposit (CD) Einlagezertifikat *(mit kurzer bis mittelfristiger Laufzeit, üblicherweise 1, 3, 6, 9 oder 12 Monate)*
Verbriefte Gläubigerrechte an kurz- und mittelfristigen Termineinlagen bei Kreditinstituten (können negotiable oder nonnegotiable sein). Negotiable certificates of deposit sind handelbar und spielen eine wichtige Rolle im amerikanischen Geldmarkt

certificate, ~ **of employment** *Am* Arbeitszeugnis; ~ **of exhibition** *(PatR)* Ausstellungsbescheinigung; ~ **of existence** Lebensbescheinigung, Lebensnachweis; ~ **of good delivery** *(Börse)* Lieferbarkeitsbescheinigung; ~ **of good standing** (of a corporation) *Am* amtl. Bescheinigung, daß Anmelde-, Eintragungs- und Gebührenpflichten erfüllt sind; ~ **of health** Gesundheitszeugnis; ~ **of identity** *Am* Personalausweis; ~ **of incorporation**[18] *(vom registrar ausgestellte)* Gründungsbescheinigung; Urkunde über die Eintragung *(e-r Kapitalgesellschaft)*; ~ **of indebtedness** Schuldschein; *Am* Schatzanweisung; ~ **of inspection** Beschaffenheitszeugnis *(bes. für verderbliche Waren, die auf Schiffen verfrachtet werden)*; ~ **of insurance** Versicherungszertifikat; ~ **of marriage** Trauschein, Heiratsurkunde; ~ **of measurement** Meßbrief *(Schiff)*; ~ **of misfortune** (gerichtl.) Bestätigung des Unglücks (als Konkursgrund) *(die den Gemeinschuldner rehabilitiert; →certificated bankrupt)*; ~ **of nationality** *Am* Staatsangehörigkeitsausweis; ~ **of naturalization** Einbürgerungsurkunde; ~ **of origin** Ursprungszeugnis, Herkunftsbescheinigung; ~ **of ownership** *Am (z.B. in Kalifornien)* Kraftfahrzeugbrief; ~ **of posting** Postversandbescheinigung; ~ **of poverty** Armutszeugnis; ~ **of priority** Dringlichkeitsbescheinigung; ~ **of protest** *(WechselR)* Protesturkunde; ~ **of public convenience and necessity** behördliche Erlaubnis zur Betreibung bestimmter, im öffentlichen Interesse liegender Gewerbe *(z.B. Routenzertifikat im Luft- und Omnibusverkehr)*; ~ **of qualification** Befähigungsnachweis; ~ **of redemption** Tilgungsbescheinigung; ~ **of registration** Registrierungsbescheinigung; ~ **of registry** Schiffsregisterbrief; Flaggenattest; ~ **of shares** *Br*[19] Aktienzertifikat; ~ **of shipment** Ladeschein, Verschiffungsbescheinigung; ~ **of stock** *Am* Aktienzertifikat; ~ **of survey** Besichtigungsschein *(der Hafenbehörde)*; ~ **of title** →title 2.

certificate, to issue (or **make out**) **a** ~ e-e Bescheinigung ausstellen (od. erteilen); **to present** (or **produce**) **a** ~ e-e Bescheinigung vorlegen; **to take out a** ~ sich e-e Bescheinigung ausstellen lassen

certificate 2. **(investment)** ~ Investmentzertifikat, Investmentanteil, Anteilschein *(→investment fund ~)*; ~ **buyer** Investmentkäufer; ~ **holder** (or **owner**) Anteilseigner *(e-s investment trust)*; Zertifikatsinhaber

certificate *v (etw.)* bescheinigen; *(jdm)* e-e Bescheinigung ausstellen über

certificated staatlich zugelassen (od. anerkannt); *Br* Diplom-; ~ **bankrupt** *Br* rehabilitierter Konkursschuldner; ~ **engineer** Diplom-Ingenieur (Dipl.Ing.)

certification Bescheinigung; Beglaubigung; *Am*[20] Bestätigung *(e-s Schecks durch e-e Bank)*; ~ **fees** Beglaubigungsgebühren; ~ **of the financial statement** *Am* Bestätigung des Jahresabschlusses *(durch den →certified public accountant)*; ~ **mark** *Am* Gütemarke, Gütezeichen; **C~ Officer** *Br*[21] (Leiter des) Registrierungsamt(s) für Gewerkschaften und Arbeitgeberverbände; ~ **of signature** Unterschriftsbeglaubigung; ~ **trade mark** *Br* Gütemarke, Gütezeichen

certified bescheinigt, bestätigt; beglaubigt; *Am* Diplom-; ~ **accountant** *Br (konzessionierter)* Buchprüfer (od. Wirtschaftsprüfer) und Steuerberater; ~ **cheque** *Br* (**check** *Am*) *(von der bezogenen Bank als gedeckt)* bestätigter Scheck; ~ **copy** *(amtlich)* beglaubigte Abschrift; ~ **copy of a judgment** *(vom Gericht)* beglaubigte Ausfertigung e-s Urteils; ~ **mail** *Am* Einschreibesendung; ~ **public accountant** (CPA) *Am (konzessionierter)* Wirtschaftsprüfer; ~ **transfer** *Br* Bescheinigung über die Eintragung von Effekten; ~ **true copy** beglaubigte Abschrift; beglaubigte Ausfertigung

certified 2. *Br (amtl.)* für geisteskrank erklärt, entmündigt; **he was** ~ **insane** *Br* er wurde *(amtl.)* für geisteskrank erklärt

certify *v* bescheinigen, bestätigen; beglaubigen; *(Scheck als gedeckt)* bestätigen; *univ* testieren; **this is to** ~ **that** hiermit wird bescheinigt, daß; **to** ~ **a person insane** *Br* jdn *(amtlich)* für geisteskrank erklären

certifying *Am* Bestätigung(svermerk) *(auf Schecks)*

certiorari ("to be more fully informed of"), ~ **denied** (cert. denied) *Am* Revisionsantrag *(vom Supreme Court)* abgelehnt; **order of** ~ *Br*[22] Certiorari-Verfügung *(Anweisung e-s höheren an ein niederes Gericht zur Übersendung der Prozeßakten zum Zwecke der Entscheidung über e-n Berufungs- bzw. Revisionsantrag. Dieses Verfahren ist besonders wichtig zur Überprüfung der Entscheidungen der administrative tribunals)*; ~ **proceedings** *Br* Antragsverfahren auf Erlaß e-r order of ~ bei Ablehnung der Prozeßkostenhilfe durch die → Law Society; →**petition of** ~; →**writ of** ~; **to grant** ~ *Am* die Revision zulassen *(im Ermessen des Gerichts)*

cessation Aufhören; Einstellung; Beendigung; ~ **of delivery** Einstellung der Lieferung; ~ **of hostilities** Einstellung der Feindseligkeiten; ~ **of membership** Erlöschen der Mitgliedschaft; ~ **of payment** Einstellung der Zahlung; Zahlungseinstellung

cesser Aufhören; Ablauf *(e-r Periode od. wiederkehrenden Zahlung);* ~ **clause** Cesser-Klausel *(nach der die Haftung des Befrachters mit Abladung der Güter endet)*

cession Abtretung, Zession; Überlassung (to an); ~ **of the administration** *(VölkerR)* Übertragung der Verwaltungshoheit; ~ **of property** Vermögensabtretung; ~ **of a territory** *(VölkerR)* Gebietsabtretung *(cf. annexion)*

cessionary Zessionar; Forderungsübernehmer; Rechtsnachfolger

cestui que trust[23] ("he for whom is the trust") Treuhandbegünstigter; Empfänger der Einkünfte od. Endverteilung e-s trust *(opp. trustee)*

Ceylon Ceylon (→*Sri Lanka)*

C. & F., c. & f. (cost and freight) ... (named port of destination) Kosten und Fracht ... (benannter Bestimmungshafen) *(Vertragsformel entsprechend den →Incoterms 1980)*

Chad Tschad; **Republic of** ~ Republik Tschad
Chad, (of) ~ Tschader(in); tschadisch

chain Kette; Zusammenschluß von Einzelhändlern; zusammenarbeitende Gruppe; Filialbetriebe; Folge, Reihe; ~ **banking** Kettenbanksystem *(Banken mit vielen Zweigstellen);* ~ **brand** *Am* Eigenmarke von Filialbetrieben; **complete** ~ **of evidence** lückenlose Beweiskette
chain of causation Kausalzusammenhang; **break of the** ~ Unterbrechung des Kausalzusammenhangs
chain, ~ **store** Filialgeschäft; *(serienweise errichteter)* Kettenladen *(in dem Massenartikel des tägl. Bedarfs verkauft werden);* ~ **of department stores** Warenhauskette; ~ **of title** Kette von Rechtstiteln

chair 1. Vorsitz, Präsidium *(in e-r Sitzung);* Vorsitzender; ~, ~ *Br parl* zur Ordnung! **with Mr. X in the** ~ unter dem Vorsitz von Herrn X; **to address the** ~ sich an den Vorsitzenden wenden; **to be in the** ~ den Vorsitz haben, vorsitzen; **to call a p. to the** ~ jdn zum Vorsitzenden ernennen; **to elect a p. to the** ~ jdn zum Vorsitzenden wählen; **to leave the** ~ die Sitzung aufheben; **to take the** ~ den Vorsitz übernehmen, vorsitzen

chair 2. *univ* Lehrstuhl; **call to a (vacant)** ~ Ruf auf e-n (unbesetzten) Lehrstuhl; **holder of a** ~ Lehrstuhlinhaber; **tenure of a** ~ Innehaben e-s Lehrstuhls; **to appoint** (or **call**) **a p. to a** ~ jdn auf e-n Lehrstuhl berufen; **to establish a** ~ e-n Lehrstuhl errichten; **to offer s.o. a** ~ jdn auf e-n Lehrstuhl berufen; **to be offered a** ~ **at a university** e-n Ruf an e-e Universität erhalten

chair *v,* **to** ~ **a meeting** den Vorsitz in e-r Versammlung haben, e-r Versammlung vorsitzen; ~**ed by** unter dem Vorsitz von

chairman Vorsitzender, Präsident; Obmann *(e-s Schiedsgerichts); parl* Vorsitzender *(e-s Ausschusses);* ~ **of the party** Parteivorsitzender; ~**'s report** *Br (der Hauptversammlung vorgelegter)* Jahresbericht des Vorsitzenden; ~ **by seniority** *parl* Alterspräsident; **deputy** ~ stellvertretender Vorsitzender; Vizepräsident; **honorary** ~ Ehrenvorsitzender; **vice** ~ stellvertretender Vorsitzender; **with Mr. X as** ~ unter dem Vorsitz von Herrn X; **to act as** ~ den Vorsitz *(in e-r Versammlung)* führen; **to elect a p.** ~ jdn zum Vorsitzenden wählen

chairmanship Vorsitz *(in e-r Sitzung);* **rotating** ~ turnusmäßig wechselnder Vorsitz; **vice-**~ stellvertretender Vorsitz; **under the** ~ **of** unter dem Vorsitz von; **he took over the** ~ er übernahm den Vorsitz

chairwoman Vorsitzende

challenge Herausforderung; *(zukünftige)* schwierige Aufgabe; Ablehnung *(von Richtern od. Geschworenen);* Anfechtung, Bestreitung; *Am* Einwendung gegen Echtheit od. Erheblichkeit e-s Beweismittels; ~ **to the array** Ablehnung der gesamten Geschworenen; ~ **for cause** Ablehnung *(von Geschworenen)* unter Angabe e-s bestimmten Grundes; ~ **without (showing) cause** Ablehnung *(von Geschworenen)* ohne Angabe der Gründe; ~ **of an examiner** *(PatR)* Ablehnung e-s Prüfers; ~ **for favo(u)r** Ablehnung *(von Geschworenen)* wegen Besorgnis der Befangenheit; ~ **to a fight** Forderung zum Duell; ~ **to the panel** → ~ to the array; ~ **to the polls** Ablehnung der einzelnen Geschworenen; ~ **to the validity of the award** Anfechtung der Gültigkeit des Schiedsspruches; **peremptory** ~ →~ without cause
challenge, to face the ~ sich der Aufgabe stellen, der Herausforderung begegnen; **to file** ~**s** *Am* Einwendungen gegen Echtheit oder Erheblichkeit e-s Beweismittels einreichen; **to present a** ~ *pol* e-e Herausforderung (od. Bedrohung) darstellen; **to respond to the** ~ →to face the ~

challenge *v* *(Richter od. Geschworene)* ablehnen; *(Testament etc)* anfechten; bestreiten, in Frage stellen; in Zweifel ziehen; *(jdn)* auffordern *(etw. zu tun); (Aufmerksamkeit)* abnötigen; **to ~ the accuracy of a statement** die Richtigkeit e-r Aussage bestreiten (od. anzweifeln); **to ~ the competence** die Zuständigkeit bestreiten; die Zuständigkeitsfrage aufwerfen; **to ~ an election** die Gültigkeit e-r Wahl anfechten; **to ~ a judge on grounds of bias** *Am* e-n Richter wegen Besorgnis der Befangenheit ablehnen; **to ~ a result** ein (Wahl-)Ergebnis anfechten; **to ~ a vote** die Gültigkeit e-r Abstimmung anfechten; **to ~ a witness** die Glaubwürdigkeit e-s Zeugen anzweifeln

challenged judge *(wegen Befangenheit)* abgelehnter Richter

challenging an arbitrator Ablehnung e-s Schiedsrichters

chamber 1. Kammer; *parl* Haus; **~ of commerce** Handelskammer; *Am* Unternehmerverband (→*commerce*); **~ of crafts** (or **trade**) Handwerkskammer; **Lower Ch~** *parl* Unterhaus *(Br House of Commons, Am House of Representatives);* **Upper Ch~** *parl* Oberhaus *(Br House of Lords, Am Senate)*

chamber(s) 2. *Br* Anwaltsbüro *(e-s barrister, bes. im Inns of Court);* **~s** *Br* Anwaltsbüro(gemeinschaft) *(e-s od. mehrerer barrister);* **~ counsel** *Br (nur)* beratender Anwalt *(barrister);* **~ practice** *Br* Beratungspraxis *(e-s barrister);* **~ work** *Br* Tätigkeit e-s barrister in seiner Kanzlei

chambers 3. Amtszimmer eines Richters *(für richterliche Geschäfte, die außerhalb der Gerichtssitzung erledigt werden können);* Bürogemeinschaft der barristers; **in ~** im Amtszimmer des Richters; in nicht öffentlicher Sitzung, unter Ausschluß der Öffentlichkeit; *(opp. in open court);* **judge in ~** *Br* der Richter *(nicht auch master und registrar)* in seiner Funktion im Chamber-Verfahren; **hearing in ~** *Br* Verhandlung unter Ausschluß der Öffentlichkeit; **to sit in ~** *Br* im Chamber-Verfahren tagen und entscheiden

Br Chamber-Verfahren ist das nicht öffentliche gerichtliche Verfahren (Vor-, Neben-, Nachverfahren) außerhalb der Hauptverhandlung (trial) in dem Amtszimmer eines Richters unterschiedlicher Stellung (judge, master, registrar).

Am Es kommt auch im amerikanischen Recht vor, hat dort aber nicht die gleiche prozeß-institutionelle Bedeutung

chamberlain *Scot* (Stadt-)Kämmerer *(Kämmerer e-s →burgh);* **Lord Ch~ (of the Household)** *Br* Lord-Haushofmeister (→*Lord*); **Lord Great Ch~** *Br* Lord-Großkämmerer (→*Lord*)

champertous contract between counsel and client *Am* Mandatsvereinbarung auf der Basis von Erfolgshonorar

champerty *Br* Unterstützung e-r Prozeßpartei *(gegen Zusicherung e-s Teils des Prozeßgewinns)*

champion Vorkämpfer (of für); Kämpfer, Verfechter

champion *v*, **to ~ a cause** für e-e *(gute)* Sache eintreten, sich für e-e *(gute)* Sache einsetzen

chance Zufall; Chance, Aussicht; gute Gelegenheit; **~ bargain** Gelegenheitskauf; **~ customer** Gelegenheitskunde, Laufkunde; **~ fluctuations** zufallsbedingte Schwankungen; **~ purchase** Gelegenheitskauf; **~s of success** Erfolgsaussichten; **game of ~** Glücksspiel; **last clear ~** *Am* letzte Rettungschance *(des unmittelbar von e-m Unfall Bedrohten. Schaden ist von dem zu tragen, der die letzte Möglichkeit zu seiner Abwendung hatte)*

chancellery Dienstgebäude e-s Kanzlers; Kanzlei *(e-r diplomatischen od. konsularischen Vertretung)*

chancellor Kanzler; *Am* Richter (od. Vorsitzender) e-s →chancery court; *Scot* Obmann e-r →jury; *Am univ* Rektor (od. Oberverwaltungsbeamter); **Ch~ of a Diocese** *Br* Rechtsberater e-s Bischofs; **Ch~ of the Exchequer** *Br* Schatzkanzler, Finanzminister; **Ch~ of England** →Lord Ch~; **Ch~ of the University of Oxford (Cambridge)** *Br (ehrenamtl.)* Rektor der Universität Oxford (Cambridge); **Federal Ch~** Bundeskanzler *(in Deutschland und Österreich);* **Lord Ch~** *Br* Lordkanzler *(Justizminister und Präsident des House of Lords);* **vice-~** Vizekanzler; *Br univ* geschäftsführender Rektor

chancery *Am* Rechtsprechung nach equity-Recht; *Br (ursprünglich Gericht für equity-Fälle; seit →Judicature Act in den →High Court of Justice übergegangen; jetzt: Ch~ Division);* **Ch~ Bar** *Br* barristers, die vor der →Chancery Division auftreten; **~ court** *Am* Gericht, das nach den Grundsätzen des →equity urteilt

Chancery Division *Br (erstinstanzl.)* Abteilung des High Court of Justice

Die Chancery Division ist zuständig bes. für Trust-, Grundstücks-, (streitige) Erbschaftssachen (contentious probate business), partnerships und Patentrechtsklagen. Sie wendet in erster Linie →equity an. Sie ist besetzt mit dem Lord Chancellor und 7 weiteren Richtern *(puisne judges)*

chancery master *Br (etwa:)* Rechtspfleger für gewisse Verhandlungen in der Chancery Division

change 1. Änderung, Veränderung, Wechsel; Abänderung; Wechselgeld, Kleingeld; **~ of abode** →**~** of residence; **~ in articles (of association)** Satzungsänderung; **~ in the book value of stocks** Änderung des Buchwerts e-s Warenlagers; **~ of domicile** Wohnsitzverlegung *(in ein anderes Land);* **~ of government** Regierungswechsel; **~ of name** Namensänderung

change-over Wechsel, Änderung, Umstellung (from ... to von ... auf); **~ to convertibility** Übergang zur Konvertierbarkeit

change, ~ in ownership Eigentumswechsel, Besitzwechsel; ~ **of position** Stellungswechsel; ~ **in prices** Preisänderung; ~ **of program(me)** Programmänderung; ~ **of residence** Wohnsitzverlegung; Wohnortwechsel; ~ **of shift** Schichtwechsel; ~ **in the staff** Personalwechsel; ~ **of venue** Änderung des Gerichtsstandes *(Verweisung [e-r Rechtssache] an ein anderes Gericht wegen örtl. Unzuständigkeit);* ~ **for the worse** Änderung zum Schlechteren, Verschlechterung

change, cyclical ~**s** konjunkturelle Änderungen; **fundamental** ~ grundlegende Änderung; **minor** ~ geringfügige Änderung; **suggestion for** ~ Änderungsvorschlag; **subject to** ~ **without notice** freibleibend; **to be subject to** ~ Änderungen unterliegen; **to undergo a** ~ e-e Änderung erfahren

change 2. Wechselgeld, Kleingeld; herausgegebenes Geld; **(small)** ~ Kleingeld; **to get** ~ (kleines) Geld herausbekommen; **to give** ~ (Wechsel-)Geld herausgeben (for auf); wechseln; **can you give me** ~ **for £10?** können Sie mir £10 wechseln?, können Sie mir auf £10 herausgeben?

Change 3. *Br* Börse

change *v* (ab-, ver)ändern; wechseln; tauschen; **to** ~ **the guard** die Wache ablösen; **to** ~ **hands** in andere Hände übergehen; den Besitzer wechseln; **to** ~ **hands at** *(Börse)* gehandelt werden zu; **the house has** ~**d hands several times** das Haus hat mehrere Male den Besitzer gewechselt; **to** ~ **(one's) lodgings** umziehen; **to** ~ **one's mind** seine Ansicht ändern; **to** ~ **money** Geld wechseln *(in Kleingeld);* **to** ~ **one's opinion** seine Meinung ändern; **to** ~ **owners** →to ~ hands; **to** ~ **over** *(Industrie etc)* umstellen; **to** ~ **position** die Stelle wechseln; **to** ~ **the subject** das Thema wechseln; **to** ~ **trains** umsteigen

channel Kanal; Fahrrinne; Weg *(e-r Mitteilung);* Geschäftsweg; ~**s of commerce** Handelswege; Handelsverbindungen; ~ **of communication** Nachrichtenweg; ~ **of distribution** Absatzweg; **C~ Islands** *Br* Kanalinseln *(die wichtigsten: Jersey, Guernsey, Alderney und Sark);* ~ **markings** Fahrwasserbezeichnung; ~**s of supply** Versorgungswege

channels of trade (or **trade channels**) Handelswege, Absatzwege; **opening of new** ~ Erschließung neuer Absatzgebiete

Channel Tunnel Ärmelkanaltunnel

channel, through diplomatic ~**s** auf diplomatischem Wege; **through official** ~**s** auf dem Dienstwege; **through the usual** ~**s** auf dem gewöhnlichen Weg *(Br parl durch die Parteiführung);* **to go through official** (or **the proper**) ~**s** den Dienstweg einhalten; **to ignore** (or **to circumvent**) **the official** ~**s** den Dienstweg nicht einhalten

channel *v fig* zuführen, vermitteln; in e-e *(bestimmte)* Richtung lenken, steuern; **to** ~ **through** durchleiten

chapel Kapelle; *Br* Gotteshaus *(der →dissenters)*

chaplain Kaplan; (Militär-, Gefängnis-, Anstalts-, Schiffs-)Geistlicher

chapter (cap., ch., c.) Kapitel; Abschnitt *(e-s Gesetzes); eccl* Domkapitel; *Br parl* Titel der einzelnen Parlamentsbeschlüsse einer Session; **C~ 11 Proceeding** *Am (KonkursR)* Reorganisationsverfahren *(bei Zahlungsunfähigkeit bleibt das Unternehmen unter Aufsicht des Gerichts weiterhin tätig);* **to give** ~ **and verse for a statement** e-e Behauptung eingehend begründen

character Charakter; Leumund, *(guter)* Ruf; Art, Eigenschaft; (Arbeits-, Dienst-)Zeugnis; (Schrift-)Zeichen; ~ **reference** Führungszeugnis; ~ **assassination** Rufmord; →**false** ~; **of good moral** ~ charakterlich einwandfrei; **evidence of good** ~ Beweis für den guten Leumund; **in his** ~ **as** in seiner Eigenschaft als; **to be of good** ~ in gutem Ruf stehen; **to give sb. a good** ~ *colloq.* jdm ein gutes Zeugnis ausstellen

characteristic *(charakteristisches)* Kennzeichen, Merkmal; charakteristisch, bezeichnend (of für); ~ **feature** charakteristisches Kennzeichen; ~ **(sign)** wesentliches Merkmal; **chief** ~ Hauptkennzeichen

characterization *(IPR)* Qualifikation

charge 1. Anklage(schrift); Anklagepunkt *(e-e → information od. →indictment kann mehrere ~s enthalten);* Beschuldigung *(bes. durch die Polizei);* Strafanzeige; ~ **(to a jury)** *bes. Am* Rechtsbelehrung der Geschworenen *(durch den Richter);* Belehrung *(der Geistlichen durch den Bischof),* Hirtenbrief; **on a** ~ **of theft** angeklagt wegen Diebstahls; ~ **not proven** *Scot* Freispruch mangels Beweises; ~ **sheet** polizeiliches Aktenblatt über Person des Beschuldigten und die ihm zur Last gelegte Tat *(in der Hand e-s Polizeibeamten, der die Anklage vor e-m →Magistrate Court vertritt)*

charge, bringing a ~ (against sb.) Erhebung e-r Anklage (gegen jdn); Vorbringung e-r Beschuldigung (gegen jdn); Erstattung e-r Strafanzeige (gegen jdn)

charge, to answer a ~ sich wegen e-r Anklage (od. Beschuldigung) verantworten; **to bring a** ~ **against sb.** gegen jdn e-e Anklage erheben; gegen jdn e-e Beschuldigung vorbringen; (Straf-)Anzeige gegen jdn erstatten; **to face a** ~ (of sth.) sich *(vor Gericht)* zu verantworten haben (wegen); **to lay sth. to sb.'s** ~ jdm etw. zur Last legen; **to make** ~**s against** Beschuldigungen erheben gegen; **to prefer a** ~ **against sb.** jdn anklagen; **the** ~ **cannot stand** die Anklage kann nicht aufrechterhalten werden

charge 2. (Vermögens-)Belastung; (Grundstücks-)Belastung; Sicherungsrecht *(das der Sicherungsgeber an seinem Vermögen bestellt); Br* Hypothek; Grundpfandrecht; Last; *(ErbR)* Auflage; ~ **by way of legal mortgage** *Br*[24] *(auf e-e deed begründete)* Hypothek *(Ggs. die weniger formelle equitable charge);* ~ **certificate** *(vom Grundbuchamt ausgestellte)* Eigentumsurkunde, die die hypothekarischen Belastungen des Grundstücks ausweist

charge on land Belastung von Grundbesitz, Grundstücksbelastung (→*land charge*); **creation of charges (on land)** Belastung e-s Grundstücks; **to create a** ~ ein Grundpfandrecht *(Hypothek, Grundschuld)* bestellen

charge, ~s and mortgages Belastungen und Hypotheken; **~s on property** (*Am* **on real estate**) Grundstückslasten

charge, creation of a ~ *Br* Bestellung e-r Hypothek; **encumbered with a** ~ belastet; mit e-r Auflage beschwert; **fiscal ~s** Steuerlasten; **fixed** ~ feste Belastung; Belastung, die sich auf e-n bestimmten Gegenstand bezieht; **floating** ~ fließende (od. schwebende) Belastung *(Belastung e-s im Betrieb befindlichen Unternehmens)* (→*floating* 2.); **mortgage** ~ *Br* hypothekarische Belastung; **property subject to a** ~ belasteter Grundbesitz; **to have a ~ on** ein Grundpfandrecht haben an

charge, public ~ öffentliche Last; jd, der unter Sozialfürsorge steht; **to be a public** ~ (or **to be a ~ on the public**) der Öffentlichkeit zur Last fallen

charge 3. Obhut, Sorge (of für); anvertraute Person; Mündel; anvertrautes Gut; Obliegenheit; Verantwortung, Aufsicht; ~ **hand** Vorarbeiter; **to be in the ~ of** in der Obhut sein von; *(etw.)* leiten; die Leitung haben von; die Verantwortung (od. Sorge) haben für; **to commit to the** ~ (of) *(jdm)* anvertrauen; **to give sth. in** ~ etw. zur Verwahrung geben; **to put sb. in ~ of sth.** jdm die Verantwortung für e-e Sache (od. die Leitung e-r Sache) übertragen; **to take ~ of sth.** etw. in seine Obhut (od. in Gewahrsam) nehmen; die Leitung von etw. übernehmen; **to take sb. in** ~ jdn festnehmen; **to take sth. in** ~ etw. übernehmen

charge 4. Gebühr; in Rechnung gestellter Betrag (od. Preis); **~s** Gebühren; *Br* Anwaltsgebühren; Kosten, Spesen, Unkosten; ~ **account** Kundenkreditkonto; Abzahlungskonto *(bei Teilzahlungen);* ~ **for admittance** Eintrittsgebühr; **no ~ for admittance** Eintritt frei; **~s (to be) collected** Nachnahmegebühren; **~s for conveyance** Versendungskosten; ~ **customer** Kreditkunde *(der anschreiben läßt);* **~s (to be) deducted** abzüglich der Spesen (od. Unkosten); **all ~s deducted** nach Abzug aller Kosten; ~ **for delivery** Zustellgebühr; **no ~ for delivery** frei Haus; **~s and expenses** Kosten und Auslagen; **~s forward** (ch. fwd) *Br* per Nachnahme; **~s for freight** Frachtkosten; **~s included** einschließlich der Kosten (od. Spesen); **all ~s included** sämtliche Spesen inbegriffen; **~s paid** gebührenfrei, spesenfrei; **~s paid in advance** Gebührenvorschuß

charge, additional ~ Zusatzgebühr; Zuschlag; **additional ~s** zusätzliche Kosten (od. Gebühren); **to involve additional ~s** mit weiteren Unkosten verbunden sein

charge, extra ~(s) Preisaufschlag; Sonderkosten, Sondergebühren; **free of** ~ gebührenfrei; ohne Unkosten, spesenfrei; kostenfrei, kostenlos; **including the ~s** einschließlich der Kosten (od. Spesen); **supplementary** ~ Zuschlag *(z.B. im Zug);* Gebührenzuschlag; **usual ~s** übliche (Un-)Kosten; **without** ~ gebührenfrei; spesenfrei, kostenlos

charge, to defray the ~s die Kosten tragen; **to levy ~s** Gebühren erheben; **a ~ is made** e-e Gebühr wird erhoben; **to repay ~s and expenses** Kosten und Auslagen erstatten; ~ **having an effect equivalent to customs duties** Abgabe gleicher Wirkung wie Einfuhrzoll

charge *v* 1. anklagen, unter Anklage stellen; anschuldigen, beschuldigen; bezichtigen, zur Last legen, vorwerfen; *(jdn)* verantwortlich machen (with für); beauftragen (with mit); **to ~ sb. with theft** jdn wegen Diebstahls anklagen; jdn des Diebstahls bezichtigen; **to ~ the defendant with knowledge** geltend machen, daß Beklagter gewußt hat; **to ~ the jury** den Geschworenen Rechtsbelehrung erteilen

charged, to be ~ beschuldigt sein; beauftragt sein (with mit); **to be ~ with doing** angeklagt werden, getan zu haben; **to be ~ with an offen|ce (~se)** wegen e-r strafbaren Handlung angeklagt sein

charge *v* 2. berechnen, in Rechnung stellen; anrechnen; belasten; anschreiben (lassen); **to ~ against** verrechnen; **to ~ an amount to sb.'s account** jds Konto mit e-m Betrag belasten; jdm e-n Betrag in Rechnung stellen; **to ~ commission** Provision berechnen; **to ~ per day** pro Tag berechnen (od. verlangen); **to ~ the expenses to sb.** jdm die Ausgaben in Rechnung stellen; **to ~ fees** Gebühren berechnen; Honorar liquidieren; **to ~ interest** Zinsen berechnen; **to ~ one's land** s-n Grundbesitz belasten; **to ~ a p. a price** jdm e-n Preis berechnen; von jdm e-n Preis fordern (od. verlangen)

charged in Rechnung gestellt; **he ~ me two dollars for it** er berechnete mir 2 Dollar dafür; **the expenses are to be ~ to ...** die Unkosten gehen zu Lasten von ...

chargeable anrechenbar, zu berechnen; zu verantworten (to von); ~ **accounting period** *Br (SteuerR)* Bemessungszeitraum; *(DBA)* steuerpflichtiges Wirtschaftsjahr; ~ **with duty** der Besteuerung (od. Verzollung) unterliegend; zu besteuern (od. verzollen); ~ **to tax** *Br* steuerpflichtig; ~ **weight** frachtpflichtiges Gewicht

chargeable, to be ~ to zu Lasten gehen von; anzurechnen sein auf; **to be ~ with theft** sich wegen Diebstahls zu verantworten haben; **the defendant is ~ with knowledge** dem Beklagten ist die Kenntnis zuzurechnen

chargee *Br* Hypothekengläubiger

chargé d'affaires *(VölkerR)*[25] Geschäftsträger

charging lien *(mit Besitz nicht verbundenes, pfandrechtsähnl.)* Sicherungsrecht *(opp. possessory lien)*; **attorney's** *Am* (**solicitor's** *Br*) ~ Pfandrecht des Anwalts an der Streitforderung *(sichert Ansprüche gegen den Klienten aus der Prozeßführung)*

charging order *Br* Beschlagnahmeverfügung *(gerichtl. Beschlagnahme von Vermögen, Gesellschaftsanteilen od. sonstigen Geldwerten zur Sicherstellung für die Dauer des Prozesses)*; *Br (gerichtl.)* Verfügung e-r Zwangshypothek

chargor *Br* Hypothekenschuldner

charitable wohltätig(en Zwecken dienend); karitativ, für karitative Zwecke; gemeinnützig(en Zwecken dienend); ~ **bequest** Vermächtnis zugunsten wohltätiger Anstalten (od. Einrichtungen); ~ **bequests and devises** Vermächtnisse oder sonstige letztwillige Verfügungen zugunsten wohltätiger Einrichtungen; ~ **contributions**[26] Beiträge (od. Zuwendungen) für gemeinnützige Zwecke; ~ **corporation** *Am* gemeinnützige Körperschaft

charitable deductions, to claim ~ *Am (SteuerR)* Abzüge wegen gemeinnütziger Aufwendungen geltend machen

charitable, ~ **endowment** Stiftung für gemeinnützige Zwecke; ~ **gifts** Geschenke (od Zuwendungen) gemeinnütziger Art; ~ **institution** gemeinnützige Einrichtung; wohltätigen Zwecken dienende Einrichtung; ~ **organization** wohltätigen (od. karitativen) Zwecken dienende Organisation; Hilfswerk; **for ~ purposes** für karitative (od. gemeinnützige) Zwecke; ~ **society** Wohltätigkeitsverein; ~ **trust** gemeinnütziger Trust; *(bes. testamentarische)* Stiftung für gemeinnützige (od. wohltätige) Zwecke

charities gemeinnützige Einrichtungen *(z.B. Unterrichtsanstalten, Forschungsinstitute, Krankenhäuser, Kirchen, Theater etc)*; **contributions to ~** Zuwendungen an gemeinnützige Einrichtungen

charity Wohltätigkeit(sorganisation); gemeinnützige Einrichtung; wohltätige Stiftung; karitative Organisation; ~ **bazaar** Wohltätigkeitsbazar; ~ **collection** Sammlung zu wohltätigen Zwecken; ~ **organization** Wohltätigkeitsorganisation

chart Schaubild, graphische Darstellung *(bes. der Kursentwicklung e-r Aktie)*; Übersichtstafel; Tabelle; Seekarte; ~ **of accounts** Kontenplan; **nautical** ~ Seekarte; **organization** ~ Organisationsplan

chart *v* graphisch darstellen

charter 1. Urkunde *(durch die ein Privileg od. die Eigenschaft e-r juristischen Person verliehen wird)*; Privileg; Konzession(surkunde); Verfassungsurkunde; Verleihungsurkunde, Gründungsurkunde *(e-r juristischen Person des öffentl. od. privaten Rechts)*; *(VölkerR)* Charta; ~ **of a borough** (**city** etc) Satzung (Verfassung) e-r Stadt; ~ **of a corporation** *Am* Gründungsurkunde e-r AG

Am Die charter e-r corporation (in einigen Staaten auch certificate of incorporation genannt) stellt mit den →bylaws die Satzung der AG dar. Sie regelt im wesentlichen das Außenverhältnis und wird durch die bylaws fortgesetzt und ergänzt

Charter of the United Nations[27] Satzung der Vereinten Nationen (SVN)

charter, bank ~ Bankkonzession; **Federal** ~ *Am* Bankkonzession durch Bundesregierung; **state** ~ *Am* Bankkonzession durch Regierung e-s Einzelstaates

Charter, Royal ~ *Br* Königl. Konzession *(durch die e-e rechtsfähige Körperschaft errichtet wird)*; **company incorporated by Royal** ~ Gesellschaft kraft Königl. Verleihung

charter, to be incorporated by ~ durch Charter gegründet sein; **to grant a** ~ e-e Konzession verleihen (od. erteilen)

charter 2. Chartern *(e-s Schiffes, Flugzeugs)*; ~ **aircraft** Charterflugzeug, -maschine; ~ **flight** Charterflug; ~ **money** Chartermiete; Schiffsmiete, Flugzeugmiete *(Vergütung)*

charterparty (C/P) Charterpartie, (Urkunde über) Chartervertrag; Raumfrachtvertrag; ~ **bill of lading** Charterpartykonnossement; **bareboat** ~ Chartervertrag über ein Schiff ohne Besatzung und Service; **time** ~ Zeitchartervertrag; **to be subject to a** ~ e-r Charterpartie unterworfen sein; **to conclude a** ~ e-n Chartervertrag abschließen

charter, ~ **price** Charterpreis; ~ **rates** Chartersätze, Befrachtungssätze; ~ **service** Charterdienst

charter, air(craft) ~ **agreement** Luftchartervertrag; →**bareboat** ~; →**demise** ~; **head** ~ Hauptfrachtvertrag; **sub-**~ Unterfrachtvertrag; **time** ~ Zeitcharter, Zeitfrachtvertrag; Schiffsmiete für bestimmte Zeit; **trip** (or **voyage**) ~ Reisecharter; Schiffsmiete für bestimmte Reise; **to let out on** ~ vermieten; **to take on** ~ chartern, mieten

charter *v (Privileg od. Konzession)* erteilen; *(Recht, Privileg)* verbriefen; *(durch →charter)* gründen (od. errichten); *(Schiff, Flugzeug)* chartern, mieten; verchartern, vermieten; befrachten; **to ~ by the lump** im ganzen befrachten

chartered privilegiert; konzessioniert; verbrieft; gechartert; befrachtet; **~ accountant** (C. A.) *Br (konzessionierter)* Wirtschaftsprüfer und Steuerberater; *(konzessionierter)* Buchprüfer; **Institute of Ch~ Accountants** *Br* Berufsorganisation der Wirtschaftsprüfer; **~ aircraft** Charterflugzeug, -maschine; **~ bank** konzessionierte Bank *(z. B. Bank of England und Handelsbank im British Commonwealth, bes. in Kanada);* **national ~ bank** *Am* bundesaufsichtsrechtlich kontrollierte Bank; **state ~ bank** *Am* einzelstaatlich zugelassene und kontrollierte Bank

chartered company *Br* durch Verleihung der Krone *(letters patent)* entstandene Gesellschaft

chartered, ~ corporation staatlich *(Br durch Royal Charter)* konzessionierte juristische Person *(Br z. B. the Bank of England);* **C~ Insurance Institute** *Br* konzessioniertes Versicherungsinstitut; **~ rights** verbriefte Rechte; **~ ship** gechartertes Schiff

chartering Chartern, Charterung; Mieten, Vermieten *(e-s Schiffes od. Flugzeugs);* Befrachtung; **~ broker** Befrachtungsmakler; **~ conditions** Charterbedingungen; **~ State** *Am* die Konzession erteilender (Einzel-)Staat

charterer Charterer, Schiffs- (od. Flugzeug-)Mieter; Befrachter; **~ by demise** Charterer e-s Schiffes, der Ausrüster ist (→*demise*); **~ pays dues** (c. p. d.) Charterer zahlt die Abgaben; **owner and ~** Verfrachter und Befrachter; **time ~** Zeitbefrachter

chartist *(Börse)* Chart-Analyst *(von Aktienkurstendenzen)*

chase Jagd; *fig* Verfolgung; **~ after the criminal** Jagd nach dem Verbrecher

chasm *(auch pol)* Kluft, Spalt

chattel bewegliche Sache, Fahrnis; **~s** bewegliches Vermögen *(umfaßt auch choses in action);* **~ interest** Recht an beweglichen Sachen

chattel mortgage Mobiliarhypothek, Pfandrecht an beweglichen Sachen; (→ *purchase money ~*); **~ with after-acquired property clause** *Am* Erstreckung der ~ auf Neuerwerb des Sicherungsgebers

Die chattel mortgage entspricht nach Struktur und Funktion der deutschen Sicherungsübereignung.

Am In mehreren Einzelstaaten gelten für Eintragung von chattel mortgage und Eigentumsvorbehalt dieselben Registervorschriften.

Chattel mortgages sind vom Uniform Commercial Code mit anderen dinglichen Sicherungsrechten an Fahrnis konsolidiert

chattel, ~ mortgagee Pfandgläubiger; Sicherungsnehmer; **~ mortgagor** Pfandgeber; Sicherungsgeber

chattel paper *Am*[28] Urkunde, die sowohl e-e Zahlungsverpflichtung wie ein Sicherheitsrecht bescheinigt

Hauptbeispiel: Ratenzahlungsverkauf oder Mietvertrag (leasing), wobei dem Gläubiger ein Sicherungsrecht an der verkauften oder vermieteten Sache eingeräumt ist (Art. 9 UCC)

chattels real Rechte an e-m Grundstück unterhalb des Eigentumsrechts *(z. B. Hypotheken, Grunddienstbarkeiten, Pachtrecht, Ernte auf dem Halm)*

chattel, action to recover a ~ Klage auf Herausgabe oder Wertersatz e-r beweglichen Sache

chattel, incorporeal ~s immaterielle Vermögenswerte (→*incorporeal*); **land and ~s** Grundeigentum und bewegliche Sachen; →**personal ~s**

cheap billig, preiswert; **~ flags** billige Flaggen (→*Panhonlib[co]);* **~ money** billiges Geld *(Kreditgewährung zu niedrigen Zinssätzen);* **~-price countries** Billigpreisländer; **~ quality** minderwertige Qualität; **to buy (sell) sth. ~** etw. billig kaufen (verkaufen)

cheapen *v* billiger werden, im Preise sinken; verbilligen, im Preise herabsetzen

cheapest route frachtgünstigster Weg

cheat Betrüger(in), Schwindler(in); Betrug, Betrügereien, Schwindel

cheat *v* betrügen, (be)schwindeln; übervorteilen; **to ~ sb. out of sth.** jdn. um etw. beschwindeln; **to ~ justice** sich der *(gerechten)* Strafe entziehen

cheater Betrüger(in), Schwindler(in)

cheating Betrug *(untechnisch; cf. fraud);* Schwindel, Betrügerei; Übervorteilen; **~ at cards** Betrügen beim Kartenspiel; Falschspielen

check 1. Scheck (for über) (→*cheque*); **~ account** Scheckkonto; **~ alteration and forgery insurance** Versicherung gegen Scheckfälschungen; **~ book** *Am* Scheckbuch; **~ book money** Giralgeld, Buchgeld; **~ clearing** Scheckverrechnung; **~ for collection (only)** Inkassoscheck; **~ embargo** Schecksperre; **~ for deposit (only)** Verrechnungsscheck; **~ form** Scheckformular; **cashier's ~** Bankscheck; **certified ~** *(von e-r Bank)* bestätigter Scheck; **counter ~** Kassenscheck *(Quittungsformular für Barabhebungen vom Bankkonto);* **marked ~** *(zur Verhütung von Fälschungen)* besonders gekennzeichneter Scheck; →**negotiable ~**; **pay ~** Gehaltsscheck, Lohnscheck; **rubber ~** ungedeckter Scheck; **stopped ~** gesperrter Scheck; **traveler's ~** Reisescheck

check 2. Hemmnis; Kontrolle, Überprüfung, Nachprüfung; *(neben überprüften Posten gesetzter)* Haken; *Am* Rechnung *(im Lokal); Am* Kontrollmarke, Garderobenmarke; *Am* Gepäckschein; ~ **account** *Am* Gegenrechnung; Kontrollkonto

checks and balances *Am (StaatsR)* gegenseitige Kontrolle; wechselseitige Hemmungen und Gleichgewicht der 3 Gewalten (Exekutive, Legislative und Bundesjustiz) *(zur Verhinderung der Ausübung unkontrollierbarer Machtbefugnisse e-s Regierungsorgans)*

check, ~ at frontier Grenzkontrolle; ~ **book** *Br* Kontrollbuch; ~ **counter** (Abfertigungs-)-Schalter *(am Flughafen)*; ~ **on (taking) delivery** Abnahmekontrolle; ~ **on the documents** Nachprüfung der Unterlagen; ~ **list** Kontrolliste; ~ **mark** Kontrollmarke, Kontrollzeichen; ~ **number** Kontrollnummer

checkoff Einbehaltung der Gewerkschaftsbeiträge durch den Betrieb durch Abzug vom Lohn; **compulsory** ~ Zwangsbeitragseinziehung

check, ~out Ausgangskasse *(in e-m Supermarkt, wo Ware vorgezeigt und bezahlt wird)*; ~ **over** Nachprüfung; ~ **point** (on the border) (Grenz)-Kontrollstelle; Grenzabfertigung; Grenzübergangsstelle; ~ **room** *Am* Gepäckaufbewahrung; Garderobenaufbewahrung

checkup Kontrolle, Nachprüfung; Vorsorgeuntersuchung; ~ **of cash** Kassenrevision

check, ~ weigher *Br* (~ **weighman** *Am*) Gewichtskontrolleur, Gewichtsprüfer *(Am bes. im Kohlenbergbau, soweit auf Gewichtsbasis entlohnt wird)*; ~ **weighing** Nachwiegen

check, to keep in ~ in Schach halten; **to keep a** ~ **on** unter Beobachtung halten; ständig kontrollieren; **to put a** ~ **on production** die Produktion drosseln

check *v* 1. hemmen, bremsen, aufhalten; **to** ~ **competition** der Konkurrenz Einhalt gebieten; **to** ~ **imports** die Einfuhr drosseln; **to** ~ **the rise in prices** den Preisauftrieb bremsen; **to** ~ **production** die Produktion drosseln; **investments were ~ed** Investitionen wurden gebremst

check *v* 2. *(Personen, Rechnungen etc)* kontrollieren, (nach)prüfen; abhaken; kollationieren, *(Abschrift mit Urschrift)* vergleichen; **to** ~ **against** vergleichend nachprüfen; **to** ~ **in** sich anmelden *(in e-m Hotel)*; *(bei Arbeitsanfang) (Karte)* stempeln; **to** ~ **off** *(Namen auf e-r Liste)* abhaken; **to** ~ **out** seine Rechnung bezahlen und ein Hotel *(etc)* verlassen; *(bei Arbeitsbeendigung) (Karte)* stempeln; **to** ~ **sth. up** (or **to** ~ **up on sth.**) etw. nachprüfen, kontrollieren

check *v*, **to** ~ **the baggage** das Gepäck kontrollieren; *Am* das Gepäck *(zur Beförderung)* aufgeben; **to** ~ **a bill** e-e Rechnung prüfen; **to** ~ **the copy with** (or **against**) **the original** die Abschrift mit der Urschrift vergleichen; **to** ~ **an entry** e-n Posten *(beim Kollationieren)* abhaken; **to** ~ **(upon) sb.'s statements** jds Angaben nachprüfen

checkable demand deposits *Am* Sichteinlagen, über die durch Scheck verfügt werden kann

checkable deposit →deposit 3.

checker Kontrolleur, Überprüfer

checking Kontrolle, Nachprüfung, Prüfen; Drosseln, Bremsen; ~ **account** *Am* Girokonto *(über das mit Scheck verfügt werden kann)*; ~ **of accounts** Rechnungsprüfung; ~ **of baggage** *Am* Gepäckaufgabe; ~ **calculation** Kontrollrechnung; ~ **of the cash account** Kassenrevision; ~ **device** Kontrollvorrichtung; ~ **of goods** Warenkontrolle; ~ **of investment activity** Dämpfung der Investitionen; ~ **privilege** *Am* Liquidation von Anteilen an →money market funds durch Zeichnung von Schecks; ~ **of quality** Qualitätsprüfung

chemical chemisch; ~**s** Chemikalien; *(Börse)* chemische Werte, Chemieaktien; ~ **engineering** Industriechemie; ~**s in the environment** Umweltchemikalien; ~ **shares** Chemieaktien, Chemiewerte; ~ **warfare** chemische Kriegsführung

chemical weapons, banning and destruction of ~ Verbot und Vernichtung der chemischen Waffen

chemical, manufacture of ~s and ~ products chemische Industrie

chemist's (shop) *Br* Drogerie; **dispensing** ~ *Br* Apotheke

cheque *Br* Scheck (for über, auf) *(→check)*

Während das deutsche Scheckgesetz von 1933 auf dem international vereinheitlichten Scheckrecht der Genfer Scheckrechtskonferenz von 1931 beruht, gelten für Großbritannien und Nordirland sections 73–82 des Bills of Exchange Act von 1882 und der Cheques Act von 1957, für die Vereinigten Staaten Art. 3 des Uniform Commercial Code (UCC). Das Genfer Scheckrecht, das von einer großen Anzahl europäischer Staaten übernommen worden ist, hat strengere Formerfordernisse als das anglo-amerikanische Scheckrecht

cheque, to block a lost ~ e-n abhanden gekommenen Scheck sperren; **to cash a** ~ e-n Scheck einlösen; **to certify a** ~ e-n Scheck bestätigen; **to collect a** ~ e-n Scheck einziehen; **to →cross a** ~; **to draw a** ~ e-n Scheck ausstellen (od. ziehen) (on a bank auf e-e Bank); **to draw a** ~ **in sb.'s favour** jdm e-n Scheck ausstellen; **the** ~ **has expired** der Scheck ist abgelaufen; **to make out a** ~ **in a p.'s name** e-n Scheck in jds Namen (od. für jdn) ausstellen (for über); **to pay by** ~ mit Scheck bezahlen; **to stop a lost** ~ e-n abhandengekommenen Scheck sperren; **the** ~ **is void** der Scheck ist abgelaufen

cheque, ~ account Scheckkonto; ~ **only for account** *Br* Verrechnungsscheck; ~ **alteration** Änderung (od Fälschung) e-s Schecks; ~ **and bill transactions** Scheck- und Wechselverkehr; ~ **blocking** Schecksperre; ~ **book** Scheckbuch; ~ **card** Scheckkarte; ~ **clearing** Scheckverrechnung; ~ **collection** Inkasso von Schecks; ~ **crossed not negotiable** s. non-→negotiable ~; ~ **for deposit only** Verrechnungsscheck;

~ **forger** Scheckfälscher; ~ **form** Scheckformular; ~ **guarantee card** Bankkundenkarte; ~**s in hand** Scheckbestand; ~ **number** Schecknummer; ~ **(payable) to order** Orderscheck; ~ **not to order** Rektascheck; ~ **rate** Sichtkurs; ~ **with receipt form attached** Scheck mit angehefteter Quittung; ~ **without sufficient funds** ungedeckter Scheck; ~ **transactions** Scheckverkehr

cheque, bad ~ ungedeckter Scheck; **bearer** ~ Inhaberscheck; **blank** ~ Blankoscheck; **cancelled** ~ entwerteter Scheck; **certified** ~ bankbestätigter Scheck; **collection** ~ Inkassoscheck

cheque, crossed ~ gekreuzter Scheck, Verrechnungsscheck

Das Institut des gekreuzten Schecks, geregelt in Art. 37, 38 SchG, ist in der Bundesrepublik noch nicht eingeführt – vgl. Art. 1 Abs. 1 EGSchG. Nach Art. 3 EGSchG sind im Ausland ausgestellte gekreuzte Schecks als Verrechnungsschecks, Art. 39 SchG, zu behandeln. Die Kreuzung erfolgt durch zwei parallele Striche auf der Vorderseite des Schecks.

Beim gekreuzten Scheck ist der Kreis der Empfangsberechtigten beschränkt

cheque, generally crossed ~ allgemein gekreuzter Scheck

Die Kreuzung ist allgemein, wenn zwischen den beiden Strichen keine Angabe oder die Bezeichnung „Bankier" oder ein gleichbedeutender Vermerk steht. Ein allgemein gekreuzter Scheck darf vom Bezogenen nur an einen Bankier oder an einen Kunden des Bezogenen gezahlt werden

cheque, specially crossed ~ besonders gekreuzter Scheck

Die Kreuzung ist eine besondere, wenn der Name eines Bankiers zwischen die beiden Striche gesetzt ist. Ein besonders gekreuzter Scheck darf von dem Bezogenen nur an den bezeichneten Bankier oder, wenn dieser selbst Bezogener ist, an dessen Kunden bezahlt werden

cheque, counter ~ Kassenscheck; **dishono(u)red** ~ nicht eingelöster Scheck; **foreign** ~ Auslandsscheck; **forged** ~ gefälschter Scheck; **giro** ~ *Br* Giroscheck (→ *giro*); **kite** ~ ungedeckter Scheck; **lost** ~ abhanden gekommener Scheck; **marked** ~ bestätigter Scheck; **non-negotiable** ~ →negotiable; **open** ~ Barscheck *(opp. crossed ~)*; **order** ~ Orderscheck; **stale** ~ abgelaufener Scheck; **stopped** ~ gesperrter Scheck; **traveller's** ~ Reisescheck; **uncrossed** ~ nicht gekreuzter Scheck, Barscheck

cheque, bearer of a ~ Scheckinhaber; **capacity to draw** ~**s** Scheckfähigkeit; **collection of** ~**s** Scheckinkasso; **drawee of a** ~ Scheckbezogener; **drawer of a** ~ Aussteller e-s Schecks; **drawing of a** ~ Ausstellung (od. Ziehung) e-s Schecks; **endorsement of a** ~ Scheckindossierung; **forgery of a** ~ Scheckfälschung; **holder of a** ~ Scheckinhaber; **issuing bad** ~**s** Scheckbetrug; **payment by** ~ Scheckzahlung

Chernobyl nuclear disaster Reaktorkatastrophe von Tschernobyl

Chicago Board of Trade (CBOT) Chigaoer Terminbörse *(größte Terminbörse der Welt)*

chief Chef, Leiter; Vorgesetzter; Haupt-; hauptsächlich; ~ **accountant** Hauptbuchhalter; erster Buchhalter; ~ **clerk** Bürovorsteher; erster Buchhalter; *Br* richterlicher Nebenbeamter; ~ **constable** *Br* Polizeipräsident *(e-s county od. e-s borough)*; ~ **of a department** Abteilungsleiter; ~ **editor** Chefredakteur; Hauptschriftleiter; ~ **examiner** *(PatR)* Oberprüfer; Hauptprüfer; **Ch**~ **Executive** *Am* oberste Verwaltungsspitze *(President, Vice-President, Governor, Mayor)*; ~ **executive** oberste Führungskraft

chief executive officer (CEO) (oberster) Unternehmensleiter; Generaldirektor

Der chief executive officer ist meist auch Präsident des Unternehmens. Seine Funktionen decken sich aber nicht voll mit denen eines Vorstandsvorsitzenden nach deutschem Recht

chief, Ch~ **Justice** →justice; ~ **land registrar** *Br* Leiter des Grundbuchamtes; ~ **magistrate** *Am* →magistrate 2.

chief officer höchster (od. leitender) Beamter; ~ **of an agency** *Am* Leiter e-r Dienststelle

Chief of Police *Am* Polizeipräsident

child Kind; ~ **abuse** Kindesmißhandlung; sexueller Mißbrauch von Kindern; ~ **allowance** (Steuer-)Freibetrag für Kinder; ~**'s special allowance** *Br* Kindergeld *(für Kind e-r Witwe, deren Ehe geschieden od. aufgehoben ist, sofern sie nicht wiedergeheiratet hat)*

childbed Wochenbett, Niederkunft; **woman in** ~ Wöchnerin

child, ~ **benefit** *Br* Kindergeld; ~**birth** Geburt, Niederkunft; ~ **born in wedlock** eheliches Kind; ~ **destruction** *(StrafR)* (Kindestötung durch) Abtreibung; ~ **under guardianship** Mündel; ~**'s insurance benefit** *Am (Sozialvers.)* (Zusatz- od. Waisen-)Rente für Kind des Hauptbezugsberechtigten; ~ **labo(u)r** Kinderarbeit; ~ **stealing** *(StrafR)* Kindesraub; ~ **support** *Am* Kindesunterhalt; ~ **support payment** Unterhaltszahlung für Kinder

child, abandoning (or **exposing**) **a** ~ *(StrafR)* Kindesaussetzung; **adopted** ~ angenommenes Kind, Adoptivkind; **care of the** ~ Sorge für die Person des Kindes; **illegitimate** (or **natural**) ~ nichteheliches Kind; **legitimate** ~ eheliches Kind; **substitution of a** ~ Kindesunterschiebung

child, to be with ~ ein Kind erwarten

childless, a ~ **couple** ein kinderloses Ehepaar

children Kinder; **Ch**~ **Act** Kinderschutzgesetz; ~ **allowance** Kindergeld; ~ **in** →**care;** ~ **exemption** *Am* (Steuer-)Freibetrag für Kinder;

ch~'s officer *Br* (Leiter des) Jugendamt(es); **Ch~'s Services** staatl. Kinderfürsorge

children, employment of ~ Kinderarbeit; **fatherless** (or **motherless**) ~ Halbwaisen; **foster** ~ Pflegekinder; **protected** ~ →protect *v;* **United Nations Ch~'s Fund** (UNICEF) Weltkinderhilfswerk der Vereinten Nationen (→*United Nations*)

Chile Chile; **Republic of** ~ Republik Chile

Chilean Chilene, Chilenin; chilenisch

chilled cargo Kühlgut; gekühlte Ladung

China China; **People's Republic of** ~ Volksrepublik China

Chinese Chinese, Chinesin; chinesisch

Chinese wall *Br*[29] „Chinesische Mauer" Auskunftsperre zwischen unterschiedlichen Teilen desselben Geschäftsunternehmens, um Mißbrauch bei konfliktierenden Interessen vorzubeugen

chip card Chip-Karte *(elektronische Zahlungskarte, die der Eigentümer mit e-r selbstbestimmten Geheimzahl benutzt)*

choice 1. Wahl; Auswahl; Sortiment; Auslese; **a wide** ~ **of candidates** viele Bewerber; **free** ~ **of the doctor** freie Arztwahl; ~ **of occupation** (or **employment, profession**) Berufswahl; ~ **of jurisdiction clause** Gerichtsstandsklausel; ~ **of law** *(IPR)* Rechtswahl; Bestimmung des anwendbaren Rechts; ~ **of law clause** *(IPR)* Rechtswahlklausel; Vertragsklausel, die das anwendbare Recht bestimmt; **general** ~ **of law rule** *(IPR)* allgemeine Rechtsanwendungsregel; **to have no (other)** ~ keine andere Wahl (od. Möglichkeit) haben; **to make** (or **take**) **one's** ~ seine Wahl treffen; wählen

choice 2. auserlesen, ausgesucht; ~ **articles** (or **goods**) ausgesuchte Ware(n); Qualitätsware(n); ~ **brand** vorzügliche Sorte *(z.B. Wein, Zigarren);* ~ **quality** ausgesuchte (od. erste) Qualität

choke off *v*, **to** ~ **access** *pol* Zugang (ab)drosseln

choreographic works *(UrhR)* choreographische Werke, Werke der Tanzkunst

chose in action *(einklagbares)* Forderungsrecht; obligatorischer Anspruch *(der Gegenstand e-r Klage sein kann);* unkörperlicher Rechtsgegenstand *(Wechsel, Sparguthaben, Patente, Urheberrecht, Versicherungspolice, Rente etc)*

chose in possession *(im Besitz e-r Person befindliche)* bewegliche Sache

Christian, ~ **faith** (or **belief**) christlicher Glaube; ~ **name** Vorname, Taufname

Christmas bonus Weihnachtsgratifikation

chronological, in ~ **order** in chronologischer Reihenfolge

church Kirche; **Ch~ Assembly** *Br* Kirchenparlament (→*National Assembly of the Ch~ of England);* ~ **affiliation** Zugehörigkeit zu e-r Kirche; ~ **authorities** Kirchenbehörden; ~ **council** Kirchenvorstand; **Ch~ of England** Englische Kirche *(protestantische Staatskirche);* **Ch~ Estate Commissioners** *Br* Gesamtverwaltung des Kirchenvermögens; ~ **institution** kirchliche Einrichtung; ~ **marriage** kirchliche Trauung; ~ **meeting** Gemeindeversammlung; **Ch~ Missionary Society** *Br (größte)* kirchliche Missionsgesellschaft; ~ **property** Kirchenvermögen; ~ **robbery** Kirchenraub; ~ **service** Gottesdienst; **Ch~ of Scotland** Schottische Kirche *(protestantische presbyterianische Staatskirche);* ~ **warden** *Br* Kirchenvorsteher; *Am* Vermögensverwalter e-r Kirche

church, breaking into a ~ Kirchen(einbruchs-)diebstahl; **disturbing** ~ **service** Störung des Gottesdienstes; **Established Ch~** Staatskirche *(z.B. Ch~ of England, Ch~ of Scotland);* **Free Ch~** Freikirche *(vom Staate unabhängige Kirche;* →*dissenter);* **separation of Ch~ and State** Trennung von Staat und Kirche; **secession from the** ~ Austritt aus der Kirche; →**World Council of Ch~es**

church, to belong to a ~ e-r Kirche angehören; **to enter the Ch~** Geistlicher werden; **to leave** (or **sever connection with**) **the** ~ aus der Kirche austreten

CID officer *Br* Kriminalbeamter

CIF, cif[30] (cost, insurance, freight) . . . (named port of destination) (Verlade-)Kosten, Versicherung, Fracht . . . (benannter Bestimmungshafen) *(Vertragsformel entsprechend den →Incoterms* 1980); ~ **delivery** cif-Lieferung; ~ **landed** Verkäufer übernimmt außer den Verpflichtungen der cif-Klausel auch die Abladekosten; ~ **price** cif-Preis; ~ **sound delivered** Verkäufer übernimmt außer den Verpflichtungen der cif-Klausel auch Qualitätsverschlechterung der Ware; ~ **value** cif-Wert

cifci (cost, insurance, freight, commission, interest) Kosten, Versicherung, Fracht, (Vertreter-)-Provision und Zinsen

cinema Kino, Lichtspieltheater; ~ **advertising** Kinowerbung; ~ **industry** Filmindustrie

cinematographic, ~ **adaptation of a work** *(UrhR)* Verfilmung e-s Werkes; ~ **works** *(UrhR)* Filmwerke

cipher Ziffer, Zahl; Chiffre, Geheimschrift; Schlüssel *(zur Geheimschrift);* ~ **code** Geheimcode, Code; ~ **key** Schlüssel zu Geheimschriften, Code(schlüssel), Telegrammschlüssel; ~ **telegram(me)** Chiffretelegramm; **in** ~ chiffriert; **not in** ~ unchiffriert

cipher *v* chiffrieren, in Geheimschrift abfassen; verschlüsseln

ciphering Chiffrieren, Verschlüsselung

circle Kreis; **in business** (or **commercial**) **~s** in Geschäftskreisen; **in government(al) ~s** in Regierungskreisen; **specialist ~s** Fachkreise, Fachwelt

circuit[31] Gerichtsbezirk *(in dem, oft an verschiedenen Orten, regelmäßig Gerichtstage abgehalten werden); Br* Rundreise e-s Richters; *Am* Bezirk e-s (Bundes-)Berufungsgerichts *(e-s Court of Appeals for the particular circuit);* **~ judge** *Br*[32] Strafrichter eines Crown Court (→*court*); *(in Zivilsachen)* Richter e-s County Court (→ *court*); **~ justice** *Am* Richter des Supreme Court für e-n bestimmten circuit; **County Court ~** *Br* Bezirk mehrerer county courts *(in dem ein County Court judge regelmäßig Gerichtstage abhält);* **Federal judicial ~** *Am* Gerichtsbezirk des Bundes *(es gibt im ganzen 11 judicial ~s);* **to go on ~** auf Rundreise gehen

circular *(vervielfältigtes)* Rundschreiben; **Court C~** *Br* Hofnachrichten *(in Zeitung);* **~ letter of credit** (c. l. c.) Reisekreditbrief; **~ note** Reisescheck; *dipl* Zirkularnote; **~ order** Umlauf; Runderlaß; **~ ticket** Rundreisebillet; **~ tour** (or **trip**) Rundreise

circularize *v* Rundschreiben *(bes. Prospekte)* senden an

circulate *v* umlaufen, in Umlauf sein, kursieren; in Umlauf setzen; **to ~ quickly (slowly)** schnell (langsam) umlaufen; hohe (niedrige) Umlaufgeschwindigkeit haben; **to ~ false news** falsche Nachrichten verbreiten

circulating umlaufend, in Umlauf (befindlich); **~ assets** Umlaufvermögen, flüssige Mittel; **~ bank notes** in Umlauf befindliche Banknoten; **~ capital** Umlaufkapital, Betriebskapital *(opp. fixed capital);* **~ library** Leihbücherei

circulation Umlauf *(z.B. von Geld, Wechseln);* Verbreitung *(z.B. von Gerüchten);* Auflage(nziffer) *(e-r Zeitung);* **~ analysis** Auflagenanalyse; **~ area** Verbreitungsgebiet; **~ of bank notes** (Bank-)Notenumlauf; **~ of bills** Wechselverkehr, Wechselumlauf; **~ of capital** Kapitalverkehr; **~ figure** Auflagenziffer; **~ of goods** Warenverkehr; Güterumlauf; **~ of money** Geldumlauf, Geldkreislauf; **~ of notes and coins** Bargeldumlauf; **~ rates** Auflagenziffer; **~ rate base** auf der Auflage beruhende Anzeigenpreisliste; **~ of securities** Wertpapierumlauf; **~ statement** *Am* Bericht *(des Schatzamtes)* über den Notenumlauf

circulation, in ~ in Umlauf (befindlich); umlaufend; **in free ~** im freien Verkehr; **bank notes in ~** Banknotenumlauf; **bills in ~** in Umlauf befindliche Wechsel; **loans in ~** in Umlauf befindliche Anleihen; **money in ~** Geldumlauf; **notes and coins in ~** Bargeldumlauf

circulation, with a large ~ auflagenstark; **low ~** niedrige Auflage; **mass ~ newspaper** Zeitung mit Massenauflage; Massenblatt; **means of ~** Umlaufmittel; **out of ~** außer Kurs (gesetzt); nicht mehr im Umlauf; **wide ~** hohe Auflage; **withdrawal from ~** Außerkurssetzung; Einziehung; **withdrawn from ~** aus dem Verkehr gezogen; außer Verkehr (gesetzt)

circulation, to be in ~ umlaufen, in Umlauf sein; kursieren; **to be out of ~** nicht mehr im Umlauf sein; **to bring** (or **put**) **into ~** in den Verkehr bringen; in Umlauf setzen; **to enter goods for free ~** Waren zum zollrechtlich freien Verkehr anmelden; **to withdraw from ~** aus dem Verkehr ziehen; *(Münzen, Banknoten etc)* einziehen; **these coins have been withdrawn from ~** diese Münzen sind aus dem Verkehr gezogen

circumlunar flight Mondumkreisung

circumstances 1. Umstände; Sachlage, Sachverhalt; **~ of a case** Umstände e-s Falles; **having regard to all the ~ of the case** unter Würdigung aller Umstände des Falles

circumstance, ~ beyond the lessor's control vom Vermieter nicht zu vertretender Umstand; **~s due to the →default of the party; ~s for which seller may not be held liable** vom Verkäufer nicht zu vertretende Umstände; **~s permitting** wenn es die Umstände erlauben; unter Umständen

circumstances, according to the ~ je nach den Umständen; nach Lage der Dinge; **all ~ considered** unter Berücksichtigung aller Umstände; **in** (or **under**) **the ~** unter diesen Umständen; bei dieser Sachlage; **in** (or **under**) **no ~** unter keinen Umständen; auf keinen Fall; **under the present ~** bei der gegenwärtigen Sachlage; unter den gegenwärtigen Umständen (od. Verhältnissen); **in the same ~** unter den gleichen Umständen

circumstances, aggravating ~ erschwerende (od. strafverschärfende) Umstände; **attendant** (or **collateral**) **~** Begleitumstände, Nebenumstände; **exceptional ~** außergewöhnliche Umstände; **extenuating** (or **mitigating**) **~** mildernde Umstände (→*mitigating*); **material ~** wesentliche Umstände; **particular ~** besondere Umstände; **political ~ of a country** politische Verhältnisse e-s Landes; **set of ~** Tatumstände, Tatbestand

circumstances, ~ arise Umstände treten ein; **as and when ~ permit** soweit und sobald die Verhältnisse gestatten; **to state the ~** die näheren Umstände angeben

circumstances 2. finanzielle Verhältnisse, Vermögensverhältnisse; **in easy (good) ~** in guten (Vermögens-)Verhältnissen; **pecuniary ~** Vermögensverhältnisse; **in reduced** (or **straitened**) **~** in beschränkten Verhältnissen

circumstantial eingehend, detailliert; sich aus

den Umständen ergebend; umständlich; ~ **evidence** Indizienbeweis; **to convict sb. on ~ evidence** jdn auf Grund von Indizien schuldig sprechen

circumstantiate *v* durch Indizien beweisen; umständlich darstellen

circumvent *v (Gesetz etc)* umgehen; *(jdn)* übervorteilen; *(jds Plan)* vereiteln

circumvention, ~ of the law Umgehung des Gesetzes; Rechtsbeugung; **~ of a patent** Umgehung e-s Patents

citation Zitat, Anführung *(e-r gerichtl. Vorentscheidung, ohne sie im vollen Wortlaut wiederzugeben); Am* lobende Erwähnung; Ladung, Vorladung *(Br nur noch in Nachlaßsachen); (PatR)* Entgegenhaltung; **issuance and service of a ~** *Am* Ausstellung und Zustellung e-r Ladung; **to serve a ~ upon a p.** jdm e-e Ladung zustellen

citatory, letters ~ *Am* schriftliche Ladung

cite *v* anführen, zitieren *(z. B. als gerichtliche Vorentscheidung);* (vor)laden; **to ~ (as) an authority** sich auf e-e *(maßgebl.)* Vorentscheidung berufen

cited, ~ documents angeführte Schriftstücke; **to be ~ to appear** vorgeladen werden

citizen Staatsangehöriger, Staatsbürger; staatsbürgerlich; **C~'s Advice Bureau** (CAB) *Br (gebührenfreie)* Beratungs- und Auskunftsstelle *(z. B. hinsichtlich welfare benefits, → amenities etc);* **~ of the U.S.** (or **American ~**) amerikanischer Staatsangehöriger; →**Commonwealth ~**; **fellow ~** Mitbürger; **native-born ~** *Am* gebürtiger Amerikaner; **naturalized ~** *Am* naturalisierter *(eingebürgerter)* Amerikaner; **to cease to be a ~** die Staatsangehörigkeit verlieren

citizenry *Am* Bürgerschaft; die Staatsbürger

citizenship Staatsbürgerschaft, Staatsangehörigkeit; **~ by birth (descent, incorporation of territory, legitimation, naturalization, registration)** *Br* Staatsangehörigkeit durch Geburt (Abstammung, Eingliederung fremden Staatsgebietes, Legitimation, Einbürgerung, Registrierung); **~ papers** *Am* Einbürgerungspapiere; **British ~**[33] britische Staatsangehörigkeit; **British Dependent Territories ~** britische Staatsangehörigkeit der Einwohner britischer Territorien *(außerhalb des U. K.);* **British overseas ~** britische Staatsangehörigkeit der Einwohner der überseeischen Gebiete; **dual ~** doppelte Staatsangehörigkeit; **federal ~** *Am* Bundesstaatsangehörigkeit; **state ~** *Am* Staatsangehörigkeit zu e-m Einzelstaat; **U. S. ~** amerikanische Staatsangehörigkeit

citizenship, certificate of ~ *Am* Staatsangehörigkeitsausweis; **deprivation of ~**[34] Aberkennung der Staatsangehörigkeit; **grant of ~** Verleihung der Staatsangehörigkeit; **renunciation of ~**[34] Verzichterklärung der Staatsangehörigkeit; **rights of ~** Staatsbürgerrechte

citizenship, to be admitted to ~ (by naturalization) *Am* eingebürgert werden; **to apply for ~** *Am* Staatsangehörigkeit beantragen; **to grant (refuse) an application for ~** *bes. Am* e-n Antrag auf Erwerb der Staatsangehörigkeit genehmigen (ablehnen); **to reclaim one's ~** seine Staatsangehörigkeit wieder beantragen; **to renounce one's ~** seine Staatsangehörigkeit aufgeben; **to retain one's ~** seine Staatsangehörigkeit beibehalten

city *(große)* Stadt, Großstadt; *Br* Ehrentitel für bestimmte Städte; *Am* Stadtgemeinde, Stadt mit Selbstverwaltung; großstädtisch; **the C~** *Br* Londoner Finanzwelt; Geschäftszentrum Londons; **~ arms** Stadtwappen; **C~ article** *Br* Börsenbericht *(e-r Zeitung);* **~ attorney** *Am* städtischer rechtskundiger Beamter; **~ authorities** Stadtverwaltung; **~ bonds** *Am* städtische Anleihen; **~ branch** Stadtfiliale; **~ building** *Am* Städtebau; **~ bylaw** städtische Satzung; **~ clerk** *Am* höherer städtischer Angestellter; **C~ Code** *Br* →Takeover Code; **~ council** Gemeinderat, Stadtrat; **~ councillor** Mitglied des Stadtrates; **~ editor** *Br* Schriftleiter des Handelsteils *(e-r Zeitung);* Wirtschaftsredakteur; *Am* Schriftleiter des Lokalteils *(e-r Zeitung);* Lokalredakteur; **~ employee** *Am* städtischer Angestellter; **~ government** *Am* Stadtrat, Stadtverwaltung; **C~ Guild** (Livery Company of the City of London) *Br* Gilde der Londoner City; **~ hall** *Am* Rathaus; **~ manager** *Am* (Ober-)Stadtdirektor; **~ news** Börsennachrichten, Handelsnachrichten *(e-r Zeitung);* **~ ordinance** *Am* Gemeindeordnung; **C~ Panel** *Br* Aufsichtsbehörde für →Takeover-Code; **~ planning** *Am* Stadtplanung; **~ property** *Am* städtischer Grundbesitz; *Br* Grundbesitz in der C~ of London; **~ solicitor** *Br* Rechtsanwalt mit Büro in der C~ of London; *Am* städtischer rechtskundiger Beamter; **~ traffic** großstädtischer Verkehr; Verkehr in der Innenstadt; **~ treasurer** Stadtkämmerer; **~ zone** *Am* Stadtgebiet; **to be in the ~** Geschäftsmann sein

civic bürgerlich; staatsbürgerlich, städtisch, Stadt-; **~s** Staatsbürgerkunde; **~ authorities** Stadtverwaltung; Gemeindeverwaltung; **~ cent|re (~er)** Behördenzentrum; **~ duties** Bürgerpflichten, staatsbürgerliche Pflichten; **~ education** staatsbürgerliche Erziehung; **~ group** Bürgergruppe *(meist mit ideellen Zielen);* **~ obligations** →**~** duties; **~ reception** *Br* Empfang durch die Stadtverwaltung; ~

rights (Staats-)Bürgerrechte; **to deprive a p. of his ~ rights** jdm die Bürgerrechte aberkennen (→*civil death*)

civil bürgerlich; zivilrechtlich *(opp. criminal);* zivil *(opp. military);* ~ **action** Zivilprozeß, bürgerlicher Rechtsstreit; ~ **administration** Zivilverwaltung; ~ **aid certificate** *Br* Prozeßkostenhilfebescheinigung *(in Zivilsachen);* ~ **authorities** Zivilbehörden; ~ **aviation** zivile Luftfahrt; **C~ Aviation Authority** *Br* Luftfahrtbehörde; ~ **bonds** *Am* Schuldverschreibungen der öffentlichen Hand *(opp. corporation bonds);* ~ **case** Zivilsache, Zivilprozeß; ~ **ceremony** standesamtliche Trauung; **C~ Code** *Ger* Bürgerliches Gesetzbuch (BGB); ~ **commotion** (C. C.) Aufruhr (od. Unruhen) im Land, Bürgerkrieg; ~ **conflict** Bürgerkrieg; ~ **corporation** →corporation; ~ **death** bürgerlicher Tod *(Verlust der Rechtsfähigkeit);* ~ **defen|ce (~se)** (C. D.) Zivilverteidigung, ziviler Luftschutz; ~ **disobedience** *pol (organisierter)* bürgerlicher Ungehorsam *(als politisches Kampfmittel);* passiver Widerstand

civil disorder Bürgerunruhen; **offenses against the laws relating to ~s** *Am* Landfriedensbruch

civil, ~ employment Zivilbeschäftigung; ~ **engineer** (C. E.) Bauingenieur; *(etwa:)* Diplomingenieur; ~ **engineering** Tiefbau; ~ **expenditure appropriations** Haushaltsansätze für die zivilen Ausgaben; ~ **government** *mil* Zivilverwaltung; **Civil Investigative Demand** (CID) *Am*[35] *(Verbraucherschutz)* Aufforderung zur Abgabe von Auskünften oder Herausgabe von Unterlagen *(bei Annahme von unlauteren Praktiken im Handel)*

Civil Jurisdiction and Judgments Act *Br* Gesetz über zivilrechtliche Zuständigkeit und Entscheidungen

Das Gesetz setzt das Europäische Gerichtsstands- und Vollstreckungsübereinkommen (EuGVÜ) in britisches Recht um

Civil Law römisches Recht *(Corpus Juris Civilis);* das auf dem römischen Recht beruhende Rechtssystem des europäischen Kontinents und Lateinamerikas *(opp. Common Law)*

civil law Zivilrecht *(opp. criminal law)*

civil, ~ league *Am* Bürgervereinigung; ~ **liability** zivilrechtliche Haftung; ~ **liberties** *Am (verfassungsmäßig garantierte)* Bürgerrechte, Grundrechte; **C~ List** *Br parl* Zivilliste, Krondotation; ~ **loan** Anleihe der öffentlichen Hand; ~ **marriage** *Br (ohne religiöse Zeremonie, aber rechtlich anerkannte)* zivile Eheschließung; standesamtliche Trauung; **C~ Practise Law and Rules** (CPLR) Zivilprozeßordnung des Staates New York; ~ **proceedings** Zivilprozeß

civil procedure Zivilprozeß; →**Hague Convention on C~ P~**

civil rights (Staats-)Bürgerrechte; politische Rechte; ~ **campaigner** (or **supporter**) Bürgerrechtler; ~ **legislation** *Am* Gesetzgebung über die Reform der Bürgerrechte

civil servant Staatsbeamter; öffentlich Bediensteter; Berufsbeamter *(der Unterschied zwischen Beamten und Angestellten des Civil Service ist nicht erheblich);* **~s** Beamtenschaft; ~ **~'s pension** Beamtenpension; **career** ~ *Am* Berufsbeamter; festangestellter (od. planmäßiger) Beamter; →**established ~; lower grade ~** *Br* unterer Beamter; **to become a ~** in den Staatsdienst eintreten (od. gehen); Staatsbeamter werden

Civil Service Staatsdienst, öffentlicher Dienst, Berufsbeamtentum; *Am* Zivildienst *(der Zivilbeamten im Ggs. zum Militärdienst);* **C~ S~ Commission** (CSC) *Am* zentrale Personalbehörde *(des Bundes);* **C~ S~ Commissioners** *Br* Kommission für Examen für den öffentlichen Dienst; ~ **employee** *Am* Angestellter im öffentl. Dienst; ~ **machinery** Beamtenapparat; ~ **pay** Beamtenbesoldung; ~ **relationship** Beamtenverhältnis; ~ **status** Beamteneigenschaft; ~ **system** Berufsbeamtentum *(auf der Basis von →competitive examinations)*

Civil Service, candidate for the ~ Beamtenanwärter; **classified** ~ *Am* Berufsbeamtentum *(nach dem →merit system);* **lower grades of the ~** *Br* der untere Beamtenstand; **National ~ ~ Act** *Am* Beamtengesetz

Civil Service, to be admitted to the ~ in den Staatsdienst aufgenommen werden; **to enter the ~** in den Staatsdienst eintreten; die Beamtenlaufbahn einschlagen; **to have ~ status** im Beamtenverhältnis stehen

civil, ~ status Personenstand; ~ **stock** Schuldverschreibungen der öffentlichen Hand; ~ **suit** Zivilprozeß; ~ **war** Bürgerkrieg; *Am* Sezessionskrieg *(1861–65);* ~ **wrong** unerlaubte Handlung *(opp. crime)*

civilian Zivilperson, Zivilist; Kenner des → Civil Law

civilian dress Zivilkleidung; **wearing of ~** Tragen von Zivilkleidung

civilian employment, persons in ~ zivile Erwerbstätige *(ohne Soldaten)*

civilian, ~ labo(u)r force zivile Erwerbspersonen; **in ~ life** im Zivilleben; ~ **population** Zivilbevölkerung

civ|y *Am* Zivilist; **in ~ies** (or **civvies**) in Zivil

claim 1. Anspruch, Rechtsanspruch (for or to auf); Forderung; Beanspruchung *(e-s Rechts etc);* Behauptung; Klagebegehren; Reklamation, Beanstandung, Beschwerde; Versicherungsanspruch, Schaden(sfall) (→*claim* 2.); Patentanspruch (→*claim* 3.); *(BergR)* Mutung; Antrag auf Verleihung des Gewinnungsrechts; *Am (Anspruch auf ein Stück)* Staatsland *(zum Siedeln);* beanspruchtes Gebiet; Anteil an e-r Goldgräberunternehmung; ~ **under an Act** Anspruch auf Grund e-s Gesetzes, gesetzlicher Anspruch; ~ **against a bankrupt's estate** Konkursforderung; ~ **barred by prescription** verjährte Forderung, verjährter Anspruch; ~ **based on a bill of exchange** Wechselforderung; ~ **based upon a property right** dinglicher Anspruch; ~ **under civil law** zivilrechtlicher Anspruch; ~ **for compensation** (Schadens-)Ersatzanspruch, Entschädigungsanspruch; ~ **under a contract** (or **based upon a contract**) obligatorischer Anspruch; Anspruch aus e-m Vertrag; ~ **for damages** Schadensersatzanspruch, Schadensersatzforderung; ~ **debtor** Anspruchsschuldner; ~**s for defects** Anspruch aus Mängeln; ~ **due** fälliger Anspruch; ~ **against the estate** Forderung gegen den Nachlaß; ~**s for expenses** Zurückforderung von Auslagen; ~ **for indemnification** (or **indemnity**) Anspruch auf Entschädigung, Ersatzanspruch; ~ **to inheritance** *Am* Erbschaftsanspruch; ~ **for interest** Zinsforderung; ~ **letter** Beschwerdebrief; ~ **for maintenance** Unterhaltsanspruch; ~ **for money** Geldforderung; ~ **of ownership** Eigentumsanspruch; ~ **for payment** Zahlungsanspruch; ~ **for possession** *Br* Räumungsanspruch; ~ **of recourse** Regreßanspruch; ~ **for refund** Erstattungsanspruch; ~ **in rem** dinglicher Anspruch; ~ **settlement** Befriedigung e-s Anspruchs; ~ **for support** *Am* Unterhaltsanspruch; ~ **sued on** eingeklagte Forderung; ~ **based upon a statute** gesetzlicher Anspruch; ~ **in tort** (or **based upon a tort**) (Schadens-)Ersatzanspruch aus unerlaubter Handlung; obligatorischer Anspruch

claim, allowance of ~s Anerkennung von Forderungen; **amount of the** ~ Höhe der Forderung; **assignment of a** ~ Forderungsabtretung; **collection of a** ~ Einziehung e-r Forderung; **enforcement of a** ~ Geltendmachung (od. Durchsetzung) e-s Anspruchs; **entitled to a** ~ anspruchsberechtigt; **any further ~s excluded** unter Ausschluß weiterer Ansprüche; **limitation of a** ~ Anspruchsverjährung; **period for making a** ~ Rügefrist; **proof of** ~ Forderungsnachweis; **ranking of ~s** Rangordnung der Forderungen; **rejection of a** ~ Bestreiten e-s Anspruchs; Zurückweisung e-r Reklamation; **satisfaction of a** ~ Befriedigung e-s Anspruchs

claim, statement of ~ Klageschrift; *(schriftl.)* Klagebegründung; Angabe der Ansprüche; **to deliver a statement of** ~ die Klage schriftlich begründen

claim, time limit for ~s Rügefrist

claim, accessory ~ Anspruch auf Nebenleistung; **adverse** ~ entgegenstehender Anspruch; **alternative** ~ wahlweiser Anspruch; **contractual** ~ vertraglicher Anspruch; **disputed** ~ strittige Forderung; **enforceable** ~ (ein)klagbare Forderung; **equitable** ~ auf →equity beruhender Anspruch; **false** ~ unberechtigter Anspruch; **forfeited** ~ verfallener Anspruch; **joint** ~ gemeinsame Forderung; **legal** ~ Rechtsanspruch, gesetzlicher Anspruch; auf →common law beruhender Anspruch *(opp. equitable ~);* **legitimate** ~ berechtigter (od. rechtmäßiger) Anspruch; **main** ~ Hauptanspruch; **matured** ~ fällige Forderung; **minimum** ~ Mindestforderung; **mortgage** ~ Hypothekenforderung; **pay** ~ Gehaltsanspruch; **plaintiff's** ~ Klagebegehren; **pecuniary** ~ Geldforderung; **pension** ~ Pensionsanspruch; Rentenanspruch; **preferential** (or **preferred**) ~ bevorrechtigte Forderung; **prior** ~ älterer Anspruch; **priority** ~ Prioritätsanspruch; **rightful** ~ berechtigter Anspruch; **subsequent** ~ späterer Anspruch; **substantiated** ~ begründeter Anspruch; **tort** ~ Anspruch aus unerlaubter Handlung; **total** ~ Gesamtforderung; **unenforceable** ~ nicht (ein)klagbare Forderung; **wage** ~ Lohnforderung

claim, to abandon a ~ auf e-n Anspruch verzichten; e-e Forderung aufgeben; **to admit** (or **allow**) **a** ~ e-e Forderung anerkennen; e-m Anspruch stattgeben; **to advance one's ~s** seine Ansprüche vorbringen; **a** ~ **arises** ein Anspruch entsteht; **to assert a** ~ e-e Forderung geltend machen; **to assign a** ~ e-e Forderung abtreten; **to bring a** ~ **against sb.** e-n Anspruch gegen jdn geltend machen; **to collect a** ~ e-e Forderung beitreiben; **to disallow a** ~ e-n Anspruch zurückweisen; e-e Forderung nicht anerkennen; **to enforce a** ~ e-e Forderung geltend machen (od. durchsetzen); **to enter a** ~ Anspruch erheben (for auf); e-n Anspruch anmelden; **to file a** ~ e-e (Konkurs-)Forderung anmelden; beanstanden, rügen, reklamieren; **to grant a** ~ e-r Beschwerde stattgeben; e-e Beanstandung anerkennen; **to jump a** ~ *colloq.* sich über e-n *(fremden)* Anspruch hinwegsetzen; Land (od. Abbaurecht [mining right]) e-s anderen in Besitz nehmen; **to lay** ~ Anspruch erheben (to auf); beanspruchen; **to lodge a** ~ e-n Anspruch erheben (od. geltend machen); e-e Beschwerde einreichen (about wegen); beanstanden, reklamieren; **to make a** ~ Anspruch erheben (for auf); **to make a** ~ **in respect of a defect** e-n Mangel rügen; Mängelrüge vorbringen; **to make a** ~ **against sb. for damage sustained** gegen jdn e-n Anspruch wegen e-s erlittenen Schadens vorbringen; **to meet a** ~ e-n Anspruch befriedigen; **to prefer** (or **put in**) **a** ~ Anspruch erheben (for auf); beanspruchen; **to raise a** ~ e-n Anspruch erheben; e-e Forderung geltend machen; **to raise a** ~ **under a guarantee** e-e Garantie in Anspruch nehmen; **to recognize a** ~ e-n Anspruch anerkennen; **to reduce a** ~ e-e

Forderung herabsetzen; **the ~ has been reduced to judgment** *Am* der Anspruch ist urteilsmäßig festgestellt; **to refuse a ~** e-n Anspruch zurückweisen (od. bestreiten); e-e Beanstandung zurückweisen; e-e Beschwerde ablehnen; **to reject a ~** e-n Anspruch zurückweisen (od. bestreiten); e-e Reklamation zurückweisen; **to reject a ~ as unfounded** e-n Anspruch als unbegründet zurückweisen; **to renounce a ~** auf e-n Anspruch verzichten; e-n Anspruch (od. e-e Forderung) aufgeben; **to satisfy a ~** e-n Anspruch (od. e-e Forderung) befriedigen; **to set up a ~** e-e Forderung geltend machen; **to settle a ~** e-n Anspruch befriedigen; **to submit a ~** e-e Forderung vorbringen; **to substantiate a ~** e-n Anspruch näher begründen (od. nachweisen); **to take up ~s** *(BergR)* muten; **to waive a ~** auf e-n Anspruch verzichten; **to withdraw a ~** e-n Anspruch zurückziehen

claim 2. *(VersR)* Schaden(sfall); Versicherungsanspruch; Versicherungssumme; **~ adjuster** (or **agent**) Schadensregulierer; **~s department** Schadensabteilung; **~ form** Antragsformular *(für geltend zu machende Schäden)*; **~-free period** *(Kraftfahrvers.)* schadenfreie Zeit; **~s inspector** Schadensregulierer; **~ paid** bezahlter Schaden; **~s percentage** Schadensquote; **~s reserve** Rückstellung für Schadensfälle; **~s settlement** Schadensregulierung; **~-settling agreement** *(Autovers.)* Vereinbarung über die Schadensregulierung; **~s staff** Schadensbearbeitungspersonal; **~s supervisor** *Br* Leiter der Schadensabteilung

claim, amount payable when the policy becomes a ~ bei Fälligkeit der Versicherung zahlbarer Betrag; **(due) date of ~** Fälligkeitstag der Versicherungssumme; **outstanding ~** noch nicht abgewickelter Schaden; schwebender Schaden; **outstanding ~s reserve** Schadensreserve; **provision for outstanding ~s** Rückstellung für noch nicht abgewickelte Schäden; **payable when the policy becomes a ~** zahlbar bei Fälligkeit der Versicherung; **to enter a ~** e-n Schaden(sfall) melden; **to establish the allowable ~ payment** die Schadensregulierung durchführen; **to settle a ~** e-n Schaden regulieren

claim 3. *(PatR)* Patentanspruch; **~s incurring fees** gebührenpflichtige Patentansprüche; **~ met by the art** durch den Stand der Technik neuheitsschädlich getroffener Anspruch; **alternative ~** Hilfsantrag; **amended ~** geänderter Patentanspruch; **amendment of ~** Anspruchsänderung; **broad ~** weitgefaßter Anspruch; **dependent ~** Unteranspruch; abhängiger Patentanspruch; **divisional ~** ausgeschiedener Anspruch; **independent ~** Nebenanspruch; **main ~** Hauptanspruch; **narrowing of ~s** Beschränkung der Ansprüche; **sub-~** Unteranspruch

claim *v* fordern, beanspruchen; behaupten; **to ~ sth.** Anspruch auf etw. erheben; **to ~ back** zurückfordern; **to ~ compensation in case of dismissal** im Falle der Entlassung Abfindung verlangen; **to ~ a mining concession** muten; **to ~ payment** Zahlung fordern; **to ~ priority** Priorität (od. Vorrang) beanspruchen; **to ~ a share in the profits** e-n Anteil am Gewinn beanspruchen; **to ~ to be the owner** behaupten, der Eigentümer zu sein

claimed, to find for the plaintiff as ~ dem Klagebegehren stattgeben

claiming priority *(PatR)* Beanspruchung der Priorität

claimable zu beanspruchen, zu fordern; beanspruchbar, einforderbar; reklamierbar

claimant Anspruchsteller; Beanspruchender; Antragsteller; Kläger, klagende Partei *(z. B. im Schiedsverfahren od. bei seerechtlichen Streitigkeiten); (PatR)* Anmelder; *(VersR)* Geschädigter; *com* Reklamant; *(BergR)* Muter; **(rightful) ~** Anspruchsberechtigter

claimer →claimant

clandestine geheim *(bes. unerlaubt)*; **~ meeting** geheime Zusammenkunft; **~ trade** Schleichhandel; **~ transmitting station** Geheimsender; **~ work** Schwarzarbeit

clarification Klarstellung, (Er-)Klärung; (Abwasser-)Klärung; **~ plant** Kläranlage

clash Kollision, Widerstreit; *fig* Zusammenstoß; Überschneidung *(von Veranstaltungen)*; **~ of arms** bewaffneter Zusammenstoß; **~ of interests** Interessenkollision; **~ of opinion** Meinungsverschiedenheit; **~es with the police** Zusammenstöße mit der Polizei; **~ of powers** Kompetenzstreitigkeit

clash *v* kollidieren, *(zeitlich)* zusammenfallen, sich überschneiden; in Widerstreit stehen (with mit); **to ~ with the police** mit der Polizei zusammenstoßen; **our plans ~ed** unsere Pläne kollidierten (od. überschnitten sich)

clashing interests kollidierende (od. widerstreitende) Interessen

class Klasse, Gruppe; Interessengruppe; Gattung, Kategorie; Güteklasse, Qualität; Schulklasse; Kursus *(Teilnehmer)*; Gesellschaftsklasse; *Am univ* Jahrgang; **~ action** Gruppenklage; von e-r Interessengruppe *(z. B. Aktionären)* angestrengte Klage; **~ conflict** Klassenkampf; **~ consciousness** Klassenbewußtsein; **~ fee** *(Pat)* Klassengebühr; **~ gifts** *Am* Zuwendungen an e-e Gruppe von Personen; **~ index of patents** Verzeichnis der Patentklassen; **~ list** *Br univ* Benotungsliste; **~ meeting of shareholders** Versammlung der Aktionäre der gleichen Aktiengattung; **~ of business** Geschäftssparte; **~ of consumers** Verbraucherschicht; **~ of con-**

tribution *(Soz. Vers.)* Beitragsklasse; **~es of goods** Warenklassen, Warensorten; **~ of income** Einkunftsart; **~ of insurance** Versicherungszweig; **~ of investment** Anlageart; **~es of persons** Personengruppen; **~ of risk** *(VersR)* Gefahrenklasse; **~ of shares** (or *Am* **stocks**) Aktiengattung; **~ plaintiff** Kläger bei e-r →~ action; **~ prejudice** Standesvorurteil; **~ price** Preis für höhere soziale Schichten; **~ rate** Gruppen(fracht)tarif *(opp. commodity rate)*; **~ struggle** (or **warfare**) Klassenkampf

class, definite ~ bestimmte Gruppe; **evening ~es** Abendkurse; **first ~** erste(r) Klasse; erstklassig; **first ~ carriage** *Br* (Eisenbahn-)Wagen erster Klasse; **first-~, second-~,** *Am* **third-~,** *Am* **fourth-~ mail** →mail; **high-~ goods** erstklassige Waren; **indefinite ~** unbestimmte Gruppe; **middle ~(es)** Mittelstand; **the working ~(es)** der Arbeiterstand

class, to attend ~es Kurse besuchen

class *v* in e-e Klasse (od. Gruppe) einordnen, klassifizieren; **to ~ with** gleichstellen mit

classless society klassenlose Gesellschaft

classification 1. Klassifikation, Klassifizierung, Einteilung, Einordnung, Einstufung *(in Klassen)*; (Ein-, Auf-)Gliederung; *(Zoll)* Tarifierung; *(IPR)* Qualifikation; *Am* Einstufung *(im Staatsdienst nach sachl. Anforderungen und Gehalt)*; *(PatR)* Auszeichnung; **~ certificate** Einstufungsbescheinigung; Klassifikationsattest *(für Schiffe)*

classification change, demotional ~ *Am* Einstufung in e-e niedrigere Gehalts- (od. Lohn-)stufe; **promotional ~** *Am* Einstufung in e-e höhere Gehalts- (od. Lohn-)stufe

classification code given to the European patent application Symbole der Klassifikation der europäischen Patentanmeldung

classification, ~ rating Tarifeinstufung; **~ register** (Schiffs-)Klassenregister; **~ society** *(SeeversR)* (Schiffs-)Klassifizierungsgesellschaft *(cf. Lloyd's)*

classification, C~ of Commodities by Industrial Origin (CCIO) *Am* Warenklassifikation nach dem industriellen Ursprung der Güter; **~ of costs** Kostenarten *(im Handel)*; Kostenaufgliederung; **~ of diplomatic agents** Rangordnung der diplomatischen Vertreter; **~ of expenses** Kostenaufgliederung

classification of goods Warenklasseneinteilung; **~ in customs tariffs** Einteilung von Waren in Zolltarife; Tarifierung von Waren *(cf. nomenclature)*; **Arrangement of Nice Concerning the International C~ of G~ and Services to which Trade Marks Apply** Nizzaer Klassifikationsabkommen (→*Nice*)

classification of goods, international ~ Internationale Warenklasseneinteilung (34 Klassen)

Für die international registrierten Marken wird die vom Berner (jetzt Genfer) Internationalen Büro[36] im Jahre 1935 veröffentlichte Warenklasseneinteilung benutzt, die in verschiedenen Ländern (Ägypten, Frankreich, Großbritannien, Irak, Iran, Irland, Israel, Marokko, Neuseeland, Pakistan, Portugal, Singapur, Tanger) eingeführt ist

classification of patents Patentklassifikation, Klassifizierung von Patenten (→*European Convention on the International C~ of Patents for Invention und →Strasbourg Agreement Concerning the International Patent Classification*)

classification, ~ of risks *(VersR)* Risikoeinstufung; **~ of ships** Schiffsklassifikation, Klassifizierung von Schiffen

classification 2. *bes. Am* Geheimhaltung(s-); **~ and declassification of restricted data** Geheimhaltung und Freigabe von Geheimdaten; **~ arrangement** Geheimhaltungsvorkehrungen; **~ of an invention** Geheimhaltung e-r Erfindung; **~ of defense-related inventions** Geheimhaltung verteidigungswichtiger Erfindungen; **~ policy** Geheimhaltungspolitik; **~ rules** Geheimhaltungsvorschriften

classification, extension of ~ Verlängerung des Geheimhaltungsschutzes; **security ~** Geheimhaltungseinstufung

classified klassifiziert, in Klassen eingeteilt, eingeordnet; geheim *(unter Geheimschutz stehend)*; **~ advertisement** (*colloq.* **~ ad**) Kleinanzeige *(in e-r bestimmten Rubrik)*; **~ bonds** in verschiedenen Serien ausgegebene Schuldverschreibungen; **~ civil service** *Am* regulärer öffentlicher Dienst; **~ directory** Branchenadreßbuch; **~ information** unter Geheimschutz gestellte Information; Verschlußsachen; **~ material** Geheimmaterial; **~ matter** Verschlußsache(n); **~ report** Geheimbericht; **~ stamp** *mil* Geheimhaltungsstempel; **~ by subjects** nach Sachgebieten (ein)geordnet

classifier *(PatR)* Auszeichner

classify *v* klassifizieren; *(in Klassen)* einteilen, einordnen, einstufen; ein-, aufgliedern; *(Zoll)* tarifieren

clause Klausel; Absatz, Abschnitt *(z.B. e-s Testaments)*; Vereinbarung, Bestimmung *(in e-r Urkunde)*; **~ of a contract** Vertragsklausel; Nebenbedingung in e-m Vertrag; Absatz e-s Vertrags; **~ reserving errors** Irrtumsvorbehaltsklausel; **~ restricting competition** Wettbewerbsklausel; **~ of a will** Testamentsbestimmung; Absatz (od. Paragraph) e-s Testamentes

clause, acceleration ~ Fälligkeitsklausel; **arbitration ~** Schiedsklausel; **average ~** Havarieklausel; Freizeichnungsklausel *(des Versicherers)*; **blanket ~** Generalklausel; **cancellation ~** Rücktrittsklausel; **collision ~** Kollisionsklausel; **contract ~** Vertragsklausel; **currency ~** Währungsklausel; **devaluation ~** Abwertungsklausel; **escalator** ~ (Preis-, Lohn-)Gleitklausel; Indexklausel; **escape** ~ Ausweichklausel (→*escape*); **exemption** ~ Freizeichnungsklausel; **gold** ~ Goldklausel; **hardship** ~ Härteklausel; **hedged in by** ~**s** verklausuliert; **interpretation** ~ Auslegungsklausel; **jurisdictional** ~ Zuständigkeitsklausel; *(VölkerR)* Gerichtsklausel; **most favo(u)red nation** ~ Meistbegünstigungsklausel; **non-liability** ~ Haftungsausschlußklausel; **onerous** ~ lästige Bedingung; **optional** ~ Fakultativklausel; **order** ~ Orderklausel; **penal(ty) clause** Strafklausel, Strafbestimmung *(in e-m Vertrag);* **protective** ~ Schutzklausel; **reciprocity** ~ Gegenseitigkeitsklausel; **restrictive** ~ einschränkende Bestimmung; **saving** ~ Vorbehaltsklausel; **testamentary** ~ testamentarische Bestimmung

clause, to insert a ~ **in the agreement** e-e Klausel in das Abkommen aufnehmen

clausula rebus sic stantibus clausula rebus sic stantibus
Abrede, wonach ein Vertrag nur so lange gelten soll, als die bei seinem Zustandekommen maßgebenden Umstände fortbestehen

clawback Rückforderung (bes. von durch das Finanzamt od. e-e andere Behörde gewährten finanziellen Vergünstigungen *[z.B. Steuervergünstigung]* durch den Fiskus)

Clayton (Anti-Trust) Act (CATA) *Am* Anti-Trust Gesetz (1914) *(cf. Anti-Trust Acts)*
Der Clayton Act formuliert einzelne Verbotstatbestände, die die Gerichte nicht ohne weiteres auf Grund des →Sherman Act erfassen konnten. Section 2 wurde 1936 durch den →Robinson-Patman Act abgeändert. Section 7 wurde 1950 durch den → Celler-Kefauver Act abgeändert. Weitere Änderung brachte 1976 der Hart-Scott-Rodino Act

clean rein; fehlerfrei; einwandfrei; ohne Einschränkung *(opp. foul);* nicht unter Einfluß von Drogen; ~ **acceptance** (of a bill of exchange) vorbehaltloses Akzept; **C~ Air Act** *Br* Gesetz zur Bekämpfung der Luftverschmutzung; ~ **bill (of exchange)** nicht dokumentärer Wechsel *(opp. documentary bill);* ~ **bill (of health)** reiner Gesundheitspaß (→*bill of health*); ~ **bill of lading** reines Konnossement *(opp. foul bill of lading);* ~ **copy** Reinschrift; ~ **credit** Blankokredit; nicht durch Dokumente gesichertes Akkreditiv; ~ **draft** Tratte ohne Dokumente; ~→**float; with** ~ **hands** mit reinen Händen *(wer e-n equity-Anspruch geltend macht, muß sich selbst einwandfrei verhalten haben);* ~ **payment** Zahlung gegen offene Rechnung; ~ **receipt** Quittung ohne Vorbehalt; ~ **record** einwandfreie Vergangenheit; **to be** ~ keine Vorbehalte aufweisen

clean *v* reinigen, säubern; **to** ~ **out a place** alles an e-m Ort stehlen; **to** ~ **out sb.** *sl.* jdn schröpfen (od. ausnehmen); **to** ~ **up** *(auch fig)* säubern, in Ordnung bringen; sanieren; *colloq.* viel Geld erzielen (od. einheimsen)

cleaning, ~ **action** *pol* Säuberungsaktion; ~ **woman** Raumpflegerin

clear klar, zweifelsfrei; frei, offen; unbelastet; lastenfrei; ohne Abzug; netto, Rein-; ~ **amount** Nettobetrag; ~ **annuity** steuerfreie Rente; ~ **of charges** spesenfrei, gebührenfrei; ~ **cut** klar umrissen; deutlich; ~ **days** volle Tage *(bei Fristberechnung);* ~ **of debt** schuldenfrei; ~ **evidence** eindeutiger Beweis; ~ **gain** Nettogewinn, Reingewinn; ~ **income** Nettoeinkommen; ~ **loss** Nettoverlust, reiner Verlust; ~ (or ~**ly defined**) **objective** scharf umrissenes Ziel; ~ **profit** Reingewinn; ~ **road** freie Straße; ~ **text** Klartext; ~ **title** unbestrittenes Recht

clear, "All C~" *(Luftschutz)* Entwarnung; **politically not** ~ politisch belastet

clear *v* (auf)klären; *(von e-m Verdacht)* freimachen, entlasten; räumen, freimachen; ausverkaufen; *(Schulden)* abtragen, bezahlen; *(im Clearing)* verrechnen, abrechnen (lassen); als Reingewinn erzielen; verzollen, zollamtlich abfertigen; *(Schiff)* (ein-, aus)klarieren; *(Briefkasten)* leeren; **to** ~ **oneself** sich rechtfertigen (od. entlasten); **to** ~ **an account** e-e Rechnung bezahlen; **to** ~ **a balance** e-n Saldo ausgleichen; **to** ~ **a bill** e-e Rechnung bezahlen; **to** ~ **a bill of exchange (a cheque, check)** e-n Wechsel (Scheck) *(im Clearing)* verrechnen; **to** ~ **(the customs)** verzollen; **to** ~ **the docket** *Am* anhängige Gerichtsfälle erledigen; **to** ~ **goods** Waren räumen, ausverkaufen; **to** ~ **goods through customs** Waren verzollen, Waren zollamtlich abfertigen (lassen); **to** ~ **10 per cent** *sl.* 10 Prozent Reingewinn erzielen; **to** ~ **a mortgage** e-e Hypothek tilgen; **to** ~ **a port** aus e-m Hafen auslaufen *(nach Zollabfertigung);* **to** ~ **a shop** ausverkaufen; **to** ~ **the stock** das Lager räumen

clear *v*, **to** ~ **in(wards)** *(Schiff)* einklarieren; **to** ~ **off a debt** sich von e-r Schuld befreien; e-e Schuld tilgen; **to** ~ **out** ausräumen, ausleeren; **to** ~ **out(wards)** *(Schiff)* ausklarieren; *(Schiff)* Erlaubnis erteilen, auszulaufen; **to** ~ **up** *(Fall, Sachlage)* klären; **to** ~ **up a matter** e-e Angelegenheit klarstellen

cleared (cld.) verzollt; ausverkauft; **not** ~ unverzollt; **the goods have** ~ **the customs** die Waren sind verzollt; **to get** (or **have**) **the hall** ~ den Saal räumen lassen; **to order the court to be** ~ den Gerichtssaal räumen lassen

clearance 1. (Auf-, Weg-)Räumung; volle Bezahlung, Tilgung; Verrechnung, Abrechnung *(im Clearing);* freier Raum, Zwischenraum; *Am* Billigung (→*merger* ~); ~ **area** *Br* Räumungsgebiet *(bei gesundheitspolizeiwidrigem Zustand von Gebäuden);* ~ **card** Zeugnis *(bei*

Beendigung des Dienstes); ~ **certificate** Unbedenklichkeitsbescheinigung; ~ **order** *Br* Räumungsverfügung *(durch die Ortsbehörde; cf.* ~ *area);* ~ **procedure** *Am (AntitrustR)* Negativattestverfahren (→ *negative* ~); ~ **price** Ausverkaufspreis; ~ **sale** (Räumungs-)Ausverkauf

clearance, merger ~ *Am (AntitrustR)* Billigung der Konzentration; **negative** ~ *Am und EWG* Negativattest; **slum** ~ Beseitigung von Elendsvierteln

clearance 2., **(ship's)** ~ Zollabfertigung, Verzollung; Klarierung; Auslaufgenehmigung *(e-s Schiffes);* ~ **certificate** Zoll(abfertigungs-)schein *(e-s Schiffes);* ~ **charges** Zollabfertigungsgebühren, Verzollungsgebühren; ~ **(through the customs)** Zollabfertigung, Verzollung; ~ **for entry** Einfuhrverzollung; ~ **for home use** (Zoll-)Abfertigung zum freien Verkehr; ~ **in(wards)** Einklarierung *(zollamtl. Abfertigung des einlaufenden Schiffes);* ~ **out(-wards)** Ausklarierung *(zollamtl. Abfertigung des auslaufenden Schiffes);* ~ **papers** Verzollungspapiere, Zollpapiere

clearance, bill of ~ Zoll(abfertigungs)schein; **charges for** ~ Klarierungsspesen; **customs** ~ Zollabfertigung, Verzollung; **to give** ~ **to** ausklarieren; **to hold up the** ~ die Zollabfertigung verzögern

clearing 1. Clearing, Clearingverkehr *(bargeldlose Aufrechnung von gegenseitigen Forderungen und Verbindlichkeiten der Clearingteilnehmer im inländischen und internationalen Zahlungsverkehr, so daß lediglich die Verrechnungssalden ausgezahlt werden);* Räumung; ~ **account** Clearingkonto, Verrechnungskonto; ~ **agreement** (or **arrangement**) Clearingabkommen, Verrechnungsabkommen; ~ **assets** Clearingguthaben; ~ **balance** Verrechnungssaldo; ~ **banks** *Br* Clearingbanken *(zu denen auch die →Big Four gehören);* ~ **claim** Clearingforderung; ~ **country** am Clearing Abkommen beteiligtes Land; ~ **currency** Verrechnungswährung; ~ **debt** Clearingschuld, Verrechnungsschuld

clearing(-)house Clearinghaus, Abrechnungsstelle; ~ **agent** Mitglied e-s Clearinghauses, das mit Nichtmitgliedern im Verrechnungsverkehr steht; ~ **association** Clearing(haus-)vereinigung *(Vereinigung von Banken, die sich zum Zwecke des Clearing zusammengeschlossen haben);* ~ **cheque (check)** Verrechnungsscheck *(im Clearing)*

clearing, ~ **item** Verrechnungsposten; ~ **office** Verrechnungsstelle; ~ **payment** Einzahlung im Clearing; ~ **of payments** Abrechnung des Zahlungsverkehrs *(im Clearing);* ~ **rate** Verrechnungskurs; ~ **sale** (Räumungs-)Ausverkauf; ~ **sheet** *(Börse)* Abrechnungsbogen

clearing system, cheque (check) ~ Scheckverrechnungssystem

clearing transactions Clearinggeschäfte

clearing, bilateral ~ bilaterales Clearing *(Aufrechnung von gegenseitigen Forderungen zweier Länder; cf. swing);* **international** ~ internationaler Verrechnungsverkehr; **multilateral** ~ multilaterales Clearing *(Verrechnungsverkehr zwischen e-r Mehrheit von Ländern);* **in-~ bill (cheque)** Debetwechsel (Debetscheck) *(im Clearing);* **out-~ bill (cheque)** Kreditwechsel (Kreditscheck) *(im Clearing)*

clearing 2., **(ship's)** ~ Verzollung *(e-r Schiffsladung);* (Schiffs-)Klarierung; ~ **certificate** Zollabfertigungsschein *(e-s Schiffes);* ~ **the goods for exportation** Zollabfertigung der Ware zur Ausfuhr; ~ **papers** Zollpapiere, Verzollungspapiere

clearing 3., ~ **of forests** Abholzung

clemency Gnade; ~ **cases** Gnadensachen; ~ **procedure** Gnadeverfahren; **petition** (or **plea**) **for** ~ Gnadengesuch; **to refuse a** ~ **plea** ein Gnadengesuch ablehnen

clergy Geistlichkeit *(opp. laity);* Klerus, Geistliche *(Br der →established church)*

clergyman *Am* Geistlicher; *Br (bes. anglikanischer)* Geistlicher; Pfarrer, Pastor

cleric Geistlicher

clerical Schreib-, Büro-; klerikal, geistlich; ~ **equipment** *Am* Bürobedarf; ~ **error** (or **mistake**) Schreibfehler; Flüchtigkeitsfehler; ~ **officer** *Br* Beamter des mittleren Dienstes; ~ **operations** Büroarbeiten; ~ **staff** Büropersonal; Schreibkräfte; ~ **work** *(untergeordnete)* Büroarbeit; ~ **worker** Büroangestellter

clerk Büroangestellter; kaufmännischer Angestellter; Buchhalter; Handlungsgehilfe; Schreibkraft, Sekretär; Protokollführer; Justizbeamter; *Am* Verkäufer(in); ~ **of the court** Leiter der Gerichtskanzlei; ~ **in holy orders** *Br (anglikanischer)* Geistlicher; **C~ of the House of Commons** *Br* Protokoll- und Urkundsbeamter des Unterhauses; ~ **to the justices** *Br* → justices' ~; **~'s office** *Am* Geschäftsstelle e-s Gerichts; **C~ of the Parliaments** *Br* Protokoll- und Urkundsbeamter des Oberhauses; ~ **typist** Schreibkraft

clerk, bank ~ Bankangestellter; →**chief** ~; → **city** ~; **counsel's** ~ *Br* Bürovorsteher *(e-s barrister);* **county** ~ *Am* Verwaltungsbeamter e-s county; **head** ~ Bürovorsteher; **senior** ~ Hauptbuchhalter; Bürovorsteher; **solicitor's** ~ *Br* Kanzleikraft *(e-s solicitor)*

clerk *v Am* als →clerk arbeiten; als Verkäufer(in) tätig sein

clerkship Posten e-s →clerk

client Kunde, Kundin; Klient(in); Mandant(in); ~ (of a factoring company) Anschlußkunde (e-r Factoring-Gesellschaft) **~s' ledger** *Br* Kontobuch *(des Anwalts für seine Mandanten)*

clientele (Stamm-)Kundschaft; Kundenkreis; Mandantschaft, Mandanten(stamm); **claim for compensation for loss of ~** Ausgleichsanspruch des Handelsvertreters für Verlust der Kundschaft *(nach Beendigung des Handelsvertretervertrages)*

climate Klima; ~ **of industrial relations** Betriebsklima; ~ **of confidence** Vertrauensklima; ~ **for investment** Anlageklima; **business** ~ Konjunkturklima; **political** ~ politisches Klima

clinic Klinik; *Am* Seminar, Symposium

clip *v (Zeitungsartikel)* ausschneiden; befestigen, anklammern; **to ~ an article out of a newspaper** e-n Zeitungsartikel ausschneiden; **to ~ a coin** ein Geldstück beschneiden (od. kippen)

clipping (Zeitungs-)Ausschnitt; ~ **bureau** Zeitungsausschnittsbüro; ~ **service** Zeitungsausschnittsdienst

cloak *v fig* verschleiern, bemänteln

cloak(-)room Garderobe, Kleiderablage; *Br* Gepäckaufbewahrung, Gepäckaufgabe *(auf der Bahn)*; ~ **ticket** Garderobenmarke; *Br* Gepäckschein

clock card Stechkarte; Anwesenheitskarte; ~ **rate** *Am* garantierter Stundenlohn; ~ **stamp** Eingangsstempel *(mit Datum und Uhrzeit)*

clock in (or **out**) *v* Arbeitszeit *(Arbeitsbeginn od. -ende)* registrieren

clock off *v (das Arbeitsende)* stempeln

close 1. Schluß, Abschluß; Ende; ~ **of business** Geschäftsschluß; ~ **of plaintiff's** (or **defendant's**) **case** Beendigung des Klagevortrages (od. der Klageerwiderung); ~ **of the Exchange** Börsenschluß; **~-out sale** *Am* Ausverkauf; ~ **of a session** Schluß e-r Tagung; ~ **of a semester** *Am* (or *Br* **term**) Semesterschluß; ~ **of a year** Jahresschluß; **to bring a matter to a ~** e-e Sache zum Abschluß bringen

close 2. eingefriedetes Grundstück; **breach of ~** widerrechtliches Betreten fremden Besitztums

close nahe, dicht, eng; abgegrenzt; knapp; ~ **association** enge Verbindung; ~ **blockade** strenge Blockade; ~ **combat** *mil* Nahkampf; ~ **company** (*Am* ~ **corporation**)[37] Kapitalgesellschaft mit wenigen *(Br nicht mehr als 5)* Gesellschaftern *(entspricht etwa der deutschen GmbH)*; ~ **confinement** strenge Haft

close contact enger Kontakt; **to be in ~ with sb.** mit jdm in enger Verbindung stehen

close, ~ **election** knappe Wahl *(mit fast gleicher Stimmenzahl)*; ~ **investigation** eingehende Untersuchung; ~ **port** *Br* an e-m Fluß gelegener Hafen, Binnenhafen *(opp. outport)*; ~ **price** scharf kalkulierter Preis; ~ **prisoner** streng bewachter Gefangener; ~ **reasoning** lückenlose Beweisführung; ~ **scholarship** nur auf bestimmte Personen beschränktes Stipendium; ~ **season** Schonzeit *(für Wild od. Fische; opp. open season)*; ~ **translation** wortgetreue Übersetzung; ~ **vote** knappes Abstimmungsergebnis

closely, to be ~ connected with sb. mit jdm in enger Verbindung stehen; ~ **contested election** hart umstrittene Wahl; ~ **held corporation** →close corporation; **to translate** ~ wortgetreu übersetzen

close *v* (ab-, ein-, zu)schließen; *(Geschäft)* abschließen; beenden; *(durch Verbot)* sperren; **to ~ down** *(Betrieb)* stillegen (od. einstellen); *(Geschäft)* schließen (od. aufgeben); *(Radio)* Sendung beenden; **to ~ off** absperren; **to ~ up** abschließen, zumachen; **to ~ with sb.** mit jdm handelseinig werden

close *v*, **to ~ an account** eine Rechnung (od. ein Konto) abschließen; ein Konto auflösen; **to ~ accounts with** abrechnen mit; **to ~ bankruptcy proceedings** das Konkursverfahren einstellen; **to ~ the books** die Bücher abschließen; **to ~ a border crossing** e-n Grenzübergang sperren; **to ~ the case** den Klageantrag (od. die Klageerwiderung) beenden; die Beweisaufnahme schließen; **to ~ the court to the public** die Öffentlichkeit ausschließen

close, to ~ a deal ein Geschäft abschließen; **I cannot ~ the deal at this price** zu diesem Preis kann ich nicht abschließen

close, to ~ the debate die Debatte schließen; **to ~ a meeting** e-e Sitzung (od. Versammlung) schließen; **to ~ the proceedings** das Verfahren einstellen; **to ~ a road** e-e Straße sperren; **the bank ~s its doors** die Bank schließt ihre Schalter *(stellt ihre Zahlungen ein)*

closed (ab)geschlossen; gesperrt (to für) *(opp. open)*; ~ **account** abgeschlossenes Konto; ~ **area** Sperrgebiet; ~ **corporation** →close corporation

closed doors, the trial is held behind ~ die Verhandlung findet unter Ausschluß der Öffentlichkeit statt; **to sit behind ~** e-e geheime Beratung abhalten

closed-end fund *Am* geschlossener (Investment-)Fonds *(mit beschränkter Zahl von umlaufenden Anteilscheinen ohne Rücknahmeverpflichtung; opp. open-end fund)*

closed-end investment company (or **trust**) *Am* Closed-end Investment-Gesellschaft

Investment-Gesellschaft mit konstantem Kapital. Die Zahl der Zertifikate und ihr Betrag steht von vornherein fest. Neuausgaben erfolgen nicht mehr *(opp. open-end investment company)*

closed-end, ~ **mortgage** →mortgage; ~ **order** Auftrag mit Preisbegrenzung

closed, ~ **issue** erledigte Frage; ~ **meeting** geschlossene Versammlung; ~ **sea** *(VölkerR)* geschlossenes Meer; zum Hoheitsgebiet e-s Staa-

tes gehöriges Gewässer *(mare clausum; opp. open sea)*; ~ **season** →close season
closed session nicht öffentliche Sitzung; **to hear a case in** ~ unter Ausschluß der Öffentlichkeit verhandeln
closed shop[38] gewerkschaftspflichtiger Betrieb *(in welchem nur union members beschäftigt werden; cf. open shop, union shop)*
closed union *Am (für weitere Mitglieder)* geschlossene Gewerkschaft
closed to vehicles *(Straße)* für Fahrzeuge gesperrt
closed, Wall Street index ~ **at** ... *(Börse)* der Wall Street Index schloß bei ...

closing Schluß; Abschluß, Beendigung; Schließung; Sperre, Absperrung
closing *Am* Zeitpunkt des Geschäftsabschlusses *(in dem die Parteien ihre jeweilige Leistung austauschen, z.B. Geld für ein Grundstück, Zeichnung e-r Schuldverschreibung gegen Auszahlung des Darlehens)*; **real estate** (or **real property**) ~ Zeitpunkt der Übereignung von Grundbesitz
closing, ~ **of an account** Rechnungsabschluß, Kontenabschluß; Kontoauflösung; Kontensperre; ~ **of bankruptcy proceedings** Einstellung des Konkursverfahrens; ~ **of books** Abschluß der Bücher *(zum Jahresende)*; ~ **of a business** →~ down of the business; ~ **for cargo** Verladeschluß; ~ **date** Schlußtag *(z.B. e-r Ausschreibung)*; letzter Termin; ~ **date** *Am* (Geschäfts-)Abschluß, Tag des (Geschäfts-)Abschlusses; ~ **date (for advertisement)** Anzeigenschluß
closing down, ~ **of the business** Geschäftsschließung, Geschäftsaufgabe; Betriebseinstellung; **owing to the** ~ **of my business** wegen Aufgabe meines Geschäfts; ~ **the plant** Betriebsstillegung; ~ **sale** (Total-)Ausverkauf (od. Räumungsverkauf) *(wegen Aufgabe des Geschäfts)*
closing, ~ **entry** Abschlußbuchung; Schlußeintrag; ~ **hours** Geschäftsschluß, Ladenschluß; Dienstschluß; Betriebsschluß(zeiten); Polizeistunde; ~ **of a port** Schließung e-s Hafens; ~ **price** *(Börse)* Schlußkurs *(opp. opening price)*; ~ **quotation** *(Börse)* Schlußnotierung; ~ **rate** *(Devisen)* Schlußkurs; ~ **of a road** Straßensperre; ~ **sitting** Schlußsitzung; ~ **speech** Schlußrede, Schlußansprache; ~ **statements** Schlußbemerkungen der Anwälte; ~ **stock** Schlußbestand *(opp. opening stock)*; ~ **of the Stock Exchange** Börsenschluß; ~ **of subscription** Zeichnungsschluß; Listenschluß; ~ **time** Geschäftsschluß; Dienstschluß; Polizeistunde; ~ **of title** *Am* Eigentumsübertragung an Grundbesitz *(in Erfüllung des Kaufvertrages)*

closure Schließung; *(endgültige)* Stillegung; Ende, Schluß *(e-r Sitzung, e-s Verfahrens)*; Abschluß; *parl* Schluß der Debatte *(auf Antrag)*; ~ **for cargo** Verladeschluß; ~ **of the frontier** Schließung (od. Abriegelung) der Grenze; ~ **of pits** Stillegung von Kohlenbergwerken; ~ **of ports** Schließung von Häfen; **affected by the** ~ von der Stillegung *(e-s Betriebes)* betroffen; **to move (for) the** ~ (of the debate) *parl* Antrag auf Schluß der Debatte stellen

closure *v*, **to** ~ **the debate** *parl* die Debatte *(auf Antrag)* schließen (od. zum Abschluß bringen)

clothing Bekleidung(sgegenstand); Kleidung; ~ **allowance** *mil* Kleidergeld; ~ **industry** Bekleidungsindustrie; ~ **store** *Am* (Herren-)Bekleidungsgeschäft

cloture *Am parl* →closure
cloture *v Am* →to closure

cloud on title *Am* mit Mängeln behaftetes Eigentumsrecht an Grundbesitz

club Klub, Verein; *(geschlossene)* Gesellschaft; ~ **deal** *Am* festes Konsortium aus Banken mit gleicher Quote bei e-m →rollover credit; ~ **member** Klubmitglied; Klubkamerad; Vereinsmitglied; ~ **rules** Vereinssatzung; **monthly** ~ **subscription** monatlicher Klubbeitrag

clue Anhaltspunkt (to für); **to give some** ~ **as to how** Aufschluß darüber geben, wie

coaccused Mitangeklagter

coach Omnibus, Bus *(für Fernverkehr)*; *Am (Eisenbahn)* (Personen-)Wagen; Repetitor, Privatlehrer; Sporttrainer; externer Berater zum Arbeits- und Sozialverhalten e-r Führungskraft; **railway** ~ **es** *Am* (Personen-)Wagen

coaching Privatunterricht; Methode der Verhaltensüberprüfung und -korrektur e-r Führungskraft

coal (Stein-)Kohle(n); ~ **and steel industry** Montanindustrie; ~ **consumption** Kohleverbrauch; ~ **deposit(s)** Kohlevorkommen; ~ **district** (or **field**) Kohlengebiet; ~ **merchant** Kohlenhändler
coal mine Kohlenbergwerk, Kohlenzeche; **share in a** ~ Kohlenkux
coal mining Kohlenbergbau; ~ **industry** Steinkohlenbau
coal, ~ **pit** Kohlengrube; ~ **production year** Kohlenwirtschaftsjahr; ~ **stores** Kohlenlager; ~ **supply** Kohlenvorrat; Kohlenversorgung; ~ **syndicate** Kohlesyndikat; ~ **technology** Kohletechnologie; ~ **tip** Kohlenabladeplatz; ~ **trade** Kohlenhandel
coal, amount of ~ Kohlenmenge, Kohlenbestand; →**British Coal; hard** ~ Steinkohle; **house** ~ Hausbrand
coal, output of ~ Kohlenförderung; **to increase the output of** ~ die Kohlenförderung steigern
coal, pit ~ Steinkohle; **shortage of** ~ Kohlenmangel; **the price of** ~ **has risen (fallen)** die Kohlen sind im Preise gestiegen (gefallen)

coalition Verbindung; *pol* Koalition; ~ **cabinet** (or **government**) Koalitionsregierung *(von mehreren Parteien gebildete Regierung)*
coalition level Koalitionsebene; **to carry on talks on a** ~ Gespräche auf Koalitionsebene führen
coalition, ~ **negotiation** Koalitionsverhandlung; ~ **partner** Koalitionspartner; ~ **party** Koalitionspartei; ~ **talks** Koalitionsgespräche
coalition, freedom of ~ Koalitionsfreiheit; **government** ~ Regierungskoalition; **left-wing** ~ Linkskoalition; **right-wing** ~ Rechtskoalition; **right of** ~ Koalitionsfreiheit
coalition, to break up the ~ die Koalition auflösen (od. aufgeben); **to enter into a** ~ e-e Koalition eingehen; **to form a** ~ e-e Koalition bilden; koalieren; **to join a** ~ sich e-r Koalition anschließen

co-applicant *(PatR)* Mitanmelder

coast Küste; ~ **guard** Küstenwache, Küstenpolizei *(Am des Bundes)*; ~**-to-**~ **radio speech** *Am* Radioansprache über alle Sender; ~ **trade** Küstenhandel

coast *v* Küstenschiffahrt betreiben
coasting Küsten(schiff)fahrt *(cf. cabotage)*; ~ **cargo** Küstenfracht *(opp. foreign cargo)*; ~ **(trade)** Küstenhandel; ~ **vessel** Küstenfahrzeug, Küstenschiff

coastal, ~ **aircraft** Küstenflugzeug; ~ **district** Küstengebiet; ~ **fishery** (or **fishing**) Küstenfischerei; ~ **protection** Küstenschutz; ~ **sea** Küstenmeer; ~ **shipping** Küstenschiffahrt; ~ **signal** Küstensignal; ~ **state** Küstenstaat; ~ **trade** Küstenhandel
coastal traffic Küstenhandel, Küstenverkehr; **inter-**~ *Am* großer Küstenverkehr
coastal, ~ **vessel** Küstenschiff; ~ **waters** Küstengewässer

coaster Küstenfahrer, Küstendampfer

coastwise Küsten-, an der Küste entlang *(opp. over seas, cross-channel)*; ~ **shipping** *Am* Küstenschiffahrt; ~ **trade** Küstenhandel; ~ **traffic** Küstenhandel, Küstenverkehr

coat of arms of a city Stadtwappen

co-author Mitautor, Mitverfasser

co-beneficiary Mitberechtigter, Mitbegünstigter

co-chairman Kopräsident

Cocoa, International ~ **Agreement,** 1986[38a] Internationales Kakao-Übereinkommen von 1986

COCOM (Coordinating Committee for Multilateral Export Controls) COCOM (Koordinierungsausschuß für multilaterale Exportkontrolle)
Aufgabe: Kontrolle des Exportes westlicher Investitionsgüter – einschließlich Computer – in den Ostblock.
Die dem COCOM angehörenden 16 Länder – alle NATO-Nationen außer Island, dafür aber Japan – sind verpflichtet, die auf sog. Embargo-Listen stehenden Waren nicht oder nur beschränkt in die Ostblockstaaten auszuführen.

co-creditor Mitgläubiger

C.O.D., c.o.d. *(Zahlungsklausel im internationalen Handelsverkehr)* Barzahlung bei Lieferung (Zahlung gegen Nachnahme) *(Br →cash on delivery, Am →collect on delivery)*; ~ **consignment** Nachnahmesendung; ~ **fee** Nachnahmegebühr; ~ **inpayment money order** Nachnahmezahlkarte; ~ **money order** Nachnahmepostanweisung; ~ **parcel** Nachnahmepaket; **to send** ~ per Nachnahme senden

code 1. Gesetzbuch
Code in der Bedeutung „Gesetzbuch" wird nur für das kontinentale Europa und (bes. hinsichtl. des Zivil- und Strafprozeßrechts und neuerdings des Handelsrechts *[cf. Uniform Commercial Code]*) einige Einzelstaaten Nordamerikas gebraucht, da das angloamerikanische Recht nur in einzelnen Rechtsgebieten kodifiziert ist *(cf. case law)*
Code, ~ **of Civil Procedure** (or **Practice**) Zivilprozeßordnung (ZPO); ~ **of Commercial Law** Handelsgesetzbuch (HGB);~ **of Criminal Procedure** Strafprozeßordnung (StPO); **C**~ **of Federal Regulations** (CFR) *Am* (Veröffentlichung von) Bundesverordnungen und Verwaltungsvorschriften; ~ **of practice** Verhaltensregeln; ~ **procedure** *Am* modernes Prozeßverfahren *(bes. hinsichtlich der pleadings)*; **Civil** ~ Zivilgesetzbuch; Bürgerliches Gesetzbuch (BGB); **Commercial** ~ Handelsgesetzbuch (HGB); **Uniform Commercial** ~ *Am* Modellkodifikation des Handelsrechts; **Criminal** ~ Strafgesetzbuch (StGB); *Am* Bundesstrafgesetzbuch; **Highway** ~ *Br* Straßenverkehrsordnung; **Judicial** ~ *Am* offizielle Sammlung von (Bundes-)Rechtsvorschriften in bezug auf die Gerichte; **Military** ~ Militärgesetzbuch; **Penal** ~ s. Criminal →~; **United States** ~ *Am* offizielle Sammlung von Bundesgesetzen
code 2. Code, (Anzeigen-)Kennwort; Chiffre; (Telegramm-, Signal-)Schlüssel; ~ **date** Datumsangabe *(z.B. bei Lebensmitteln)*; ~ **flag** Signalbuchflagge; ~ **number** *Br* Bankleitzahl; ~ **of signals** Flaggensignalsystem; ~ **telegram(me)** Chiffretelegramm; verschlüsseltes Telegramm; ~ **word** Kennwort; Chiffre; Schlüsselwort *(für e-n Code)*; **to break a** ~ e-n (Geheim-)Code entschlüsseln
code 3. (Ehren-)Kodex; ~ **of conduct** Verhaltenskodex; ~ **of ethics** Ehrenkodex; ~ **of hono(u)r** Ehrenkodex; ~ **of obligations** Kodex von Verhaltensregeln

code *v* chiffrieren, verschlüsseln *(cf. to decode)*
coded text verschlüsselter Text
coding Chiffrierung, Verschlüsselung; *(EDV)* Codierung, Verschlüsseln von Daten; ~ **and ciphering apparatus** Chiffriervorrichtung

co-debtor Mitschuldner

co-defendant *(Zivilprozeß)* Mitbeklagter; *(Strafprozeß)* Mitangeklagter

codetermination (of labo[u]r) Mitbestimmungsrecht *(der Arbeitnehmer)*; **equality in** ~ paritätische Mitbestimmung

codetermine (or **codeterminate**) *v* mitbestimmen

codicil Kodizill, Testamentsnachtrag; Nachtrag *(zu e-r Urkunde)*

codification Kodifikation, Kodifizierung; Vereinigung von Gesetzen in e-m Gesetzbuch (→ *code*)

codif|y *v* kodifizieren; ~**ied law** kodifiziertes Recht *(opp. case law)*

coemption Aufkauf *(der ganzen Menge e-r Ware zur Preiskontrolle etc)*

coequal gleichrangig, gleichgestellt

coerce *v* (er)zwingen, nötigen, **to** ~ **sb. into doing sth.** jdn zwingen, etw. zu tun

coercible erzwingbar

coercion Zwang, Nötigung; **criminal** ~ *Am*[39] strafbare Nötigung; **means of** ~ Zwangsmittel; **measure of** ~ Zwangsmaßnahme; **under** ~ unter Zwang

coercive, to use ~ **measures** Zwangsmaßnahmen ergreifen

co(-)executor Mit(testaments)vollstrecker

coexist *v* gleichzeitig bestehen, koexistieren

coexistence Koexistenz *(gleichzeitiges Bestehen politischer Systeme)*; **peaceful** ~ friedliche Koexistenz

coexistent gleichzeitig (od. nebeneinander) bestehend, koexistent

coffee Kaffee; ~ **stocks** Kaffeevorräte; **consumption of** ~ Kaffeeverbrauch; **green** ~ Rohkaffee

cofinancing gemeinsame Finanzierung

cofounder Mitbegründer

cogency zwingende (od. überzeugende) Kraft; Stichhaltigkeit; ~ **of an argument** überzeugende Kraft e-s Argumentes

cogent zwingend, überzeugend, triftig; ~ **argument** zwingendes Argument

cognate 1. *Scot* Verwandte(r) *(mütterlicherseits)*
cognate 2. *Scot* verwandt *(mütterlicherseits)*; *fig* (art)verwandt, mit gleichen Eigenschaften; ~ **inventions** *(PatR)* verwandte Erfindungen

cognation *Scot* Verwandtschaft *(bes. mütterlicherseits)*

cognition Erkenntnis, Wahrnehmung

cognizable gerichtlich verfolgbar; der Gerichtsbarkeit unterworfen; **to be exclusively** ~ der ausschließlichen Zuständigkeit unterliegen

cognizance *(richterl.)* Erkenntnis; Kenntnisnahme *(des Gerichts)*; *(richterl.)* Zuständigkeit *(im Einzelfall; Br* Anerkenntnis; *(richterl.)* Verhandlung *(e-r Sache)*; **judicial** ~ Gerichtskundigkeit; **to be beyond a p.'s** ~ außerhalb jds Zuständigkeit liegen; **to come under the** ~ **of** ... zur Zuständigkeit von ... gehören; **to fall within a p.'s** ~ innerhalb jds Zuständigkeit liegen, zu jds Zuständigkeit gehören; **to take** ~ **(of)** (etw.) *(offiziell)* zur Kenntnis nehmen

cognizant unterrichtet, wissend; zuständig (of für); **to be** ~ **of** Kenntnis haben von; zuständig sein für

cognovit, ~ **clause** *Am* Anerkenntnisklausel; Unterwerfungsklausel *(in e-m Wechsel)*; ~ **note** *Am* eigener Wechsel mit Unterwerfungsklausel

co-guarantor Mitbürge

co-guardian Gegenvormund; Mitvormund

co-guardianship Mitvormund

cohabit *v* *(als Eheleute)* zusammenleben; in wilder Ehe leben; beiwohnen

cohabitant Lebensgefährte, Lebensgefährtin

cohabitation Zusammenleben *(als Eheleute od. als „Lebensgefährten")*, **(marital)** ~ eheliche Lebensgemeinschaft; **(extra-marital)** ~ nichteheliche Lebensgemeinschaft; **to resume the** ~ die *(eheliche)* Lebensgemeinschaft wieder aufnehmen

cohabitee →cohabitant

coheir *Am* Miterbe *(cf. heir)*

coheiress *Am* Miterbin

coherent *(logisch)* zusammenhängend; einheitlich, klar; **to be** ~ **in one's speech** e-e klare Ausdrucksweise haben

cohesion Zusammenhang, Zusammenhalt *(z. B. innerhalb e-r Partei)*

coimperium *(VölkerR)* Mitherrschaft *(zweier od. mehrerer Staaten auf fremden Gebiet; cf. condominium)*

coin Münze, Geldstück; Metallgeld, Hartgeld; ~ **box telephone** *Am* Münzfernsprecher; ~-

operated machine Münzapparat; ~ **and paper money** Metall- und Papiergeld; **base** ~ *Br* falsche Münze, Falschgeld; *Am* Scheidemünze; **counterfeit** ~ falsche Münze, Falschgeld; **counterfeiting** ~**s** Falschmünzerei; **current** ~ gangbare Münze; gültiges Hartgeld; **divisional** (or **fractional**) ~ Scheidemünze; **gold** ~ Goldmünze, Goldstück; **home** ~ inländisches Metallgeld; **impairing** ~**s** Münzverringerung; **legal** ~ gesetzliches Zahlungsmittel; **small** ~ Kleingeld; Scheidemünze; **worn** ~ abgegriffene Münze

coin, to clip a ~ ein Geldstück beschneiden (od. kippen); **to counterfeit** ~**s** Münzen fälschen, Metallgeld nachmachen; **to** →**deface a** ~; **to mint** (or **strike**) ~**s** Münzen prägen (od. schlagen); **to put new** ~**s in circulation** neue Münzen in Umlauf setzen

coin *v (Münzen)* schlagen, (aus)prägen; *fig (Wort)* prägen, erfinden; **to** ~ **base** (or **false**) **money** falschmünzen

coined (aus)gemünzt; ~ **and arbitrary trademarks** *Am* Phantasiezeichen; ~ **money** gemünztes Geld, Hartgeld; ~ **word** erfundenes Wort, Phantasiewort *(z.B. für Markennamen)*

coining, ~ **of money** Geldprägung; ~ **of counterfeit money** Falschmünzerei; ~ **offen|ces (~ses)** →coinage offences; **charge for** ~ Münzgebühr

coinage[40] Prägen, Ausprägung *(von Münzen)*; gemünztes Geld, Münzgeld; Münzsystem; ~ **die** Münzstempel; ~ **gold** Münzgold; ~ **offen|ce(s) (~se [s])** Münzdelikt(e); Münzfälschung *(Falschmünzerei; Münzverfälschung)*; ~ **right** (or **right of** ~) Münzhoheit; Münzrecht *(Rechtsvorschriften)*; **right to strike** ~ Münzregal *(Recht, Münzen auszuprägen)*; **standard of** ~ Münzfuß

coincide *v (örtl. od. zeitl.)* zusammentreffen; übereinstimmen; zur gleichen Zeit vorhanden sein; **the judges did not** ~ **in opinion** die Richter stimmten in ihrer Ansicht nicht überein

coiner Münzer, Präger, *Br* Falschmünzer

co(-)inhabitant Mitbewohner

co(-)inheritance Miterbschaft, gemeinsame Erbschaft

coinsurance *Am* Versicherung mit Risikobeteiligung des Versicherten *(z.B. bei Feuerversicherung)*

co(-)inventor Miterfinder

cold call(ing) Werbemethode durch →unsolicited call *(unaufgeforderter Besuch e-s Vertreters)*

coldstore *v Am* im Kühlhaus lagern

co(-)legatee Mitvermächtnisnehmer (→*legatee*)

co(-)lessee Mitpächter; Mitmieter

collaborate *v* zusammenarbeiten, mitarbeiten; *pol (mit dem Feind)* zusammenarbeiten, kollaborieren

collaboration Zusammenarbeit, Mitarbeit; *pol* Kollaboration, Zusammenarbeit mit dem Feind; **close** ~ enge Zusammenarbeit; **to work in** ~ **with** zusammenarbeiten mit

collaborationist *pol* Kollaborateur

collaborator Mitarbeiter; *pol* Kollaborateur

collapse Zusammenbruch; Einsturz; Sturz; ~ **of a bank** Bankkrach; ~ **of a building** Einsturz e-s Gebäudes; ~ **of currency** Währungszusammenbruch; ~ **of an enterprise** Zusammenbruch e-s Unternehmens; ~ **of prices** *(starker)* Preissturz, Kurssturz

collapse *v* zusammenbrechen; einstürzen; stürzen *(Preise, Kurse)*; **the plan** ~**d** der Plan brach zusammen

collar, blue ~ **worker** *Am* Arbeiter; **white** ~ **worker** Angestellter

collate *v* kollationieren; *(Abschrift mit dem Original)* vergleichen; *eccl (in e-e Pfründe)* einsetzen

collateral 1. Verwandte(r) in der Seitenlinie; von der Seitenlinie abstammend *(opp. lineal)*; ~ **descendant** Nachkomme in der Seitenlinie; ~ **descent** Abstammung in der Seitenlinie; ~ **inheritance** Erbschaft von der Seitenlinie

collateral line Seitenlinie; **related in the** ~ in der Seitenlinie verwandt; **succession in the** ~ Erbfolge in der Seitenlinie

collateral relative Verwandte(r) in der Seitenlinie; Seitenverwandte(r)

collateral[41] 2. Sicherungsgegenstand *(Gegenstand od. Gesamtheit der Gegenstände, die verpfändet oder hypothekarisch belastet sind oder in anderer Weise als Sicherheit dienen)*; Sicherheit *(bes. für Kredit)*; zusätzliche Sicherheit, Nebensicherheit; Neben-; zusätzlich, subsidiär; akzessorisch; ~ **acceptance** Avalakzept; ~ **advance** Lombardkredit; ~ **agreement** Nebenabmachung; Begleitvertrag; ~ **bill** Sicherheitswechsel, Depotwechsel; ~ **circumstances** Nebenumstände; ~ **clause** Nebenbestimmung; ~ **contract** Nebenvertrag; ~ **credit** Lombardkredit; abgesicherter Kredit; ~ **damage** Nebenschaden; ~ **duties** Nebenpflichten; ~ **estoppel** *Am* →estoppel; ~ **evidence** unterstützendes Beweismaterial; ~ **facts** Nebenumstände; ~ **fund** Nebensicherheitsfonds; ~ **insurance** Nebenversicherung, zusätzliche Versicherung; ~ **issue** Nebenfrage, Nebenstreitpunkt; ~ **loan** Lombardkredit, Lombarddarlehen; Realkredit; ~ **mortgage bonds** durch Hypotheken gedeckte Schuldverschreibungen; Pfandbriefe; ~ **note** Bescheinigung über erfolgte Hinterlegung von Effekten *(zur Sicherung e-s Kredits); Am (durch stocks, bonds etc)* gesicherter Schuldschein; ~ **proceedings** Verfahren außerhalb der Streitverhandlung; Nebenverfahren; ~ **promise** Schuldmitübernahme; ~ **securities** beliehene (od. lombardierte) Wertpapiere; ~ **security** Sicherheit (od. Deckung) durch Hinterlegung von Effekten; akzessorische Sicherheit; Nebensicherheit; ~ **transaction** mit dem Vertrag zusammenhängendes Rechtsgeschäft; ~ **trust bonds** *Am (durch treuhänderische Effektenhinterlegung)* gesicherte Obligationen *(von Investmentgesellschaften);* ~ **trust certificates** *Am* Schuldverschreibungen *(von Investmentgesellschaften),* deren Gegenwert in verschiedenen anderen Wertpapieren angelegt ist; ~ **value** Beleihungswert, Lombardwert

collateral, acceptable (or **eligible**) **as** ~ beleihbar; lombardfähig, lombardierbar; **loan without** ~ Kredit ohne Sicherheit; **securities lodged as** ~ lombardierte Effekten

collateral, to accept as ~ *(Waren od. Wertpapiere)* lombardieren; **to furnish** (or **give**) ~ **(security)** *(zusätzliche)* Sicherheit leisten; **to give** (or **offer**) **securities as** ~ Effekten beleihen lassen; **to lend on** ~ **(security)** lombardieren; **to serve as** ~ als Deckung *(e-s Kredits)* dienen

collaterally zusätzlich, subsidiär; in der Seitenlinie *(opp. lineally)*

collateralized mortgage obligation (CMO) *Am* private Schuldverschreibung, deren Zinserträge von e-m Bündel hypothekarisch gesicherter Forderungen des Wertpapieremittenten stammen

collation Kollation, Vergleich (e-r Abschrift mit der Urschrift); *Br eccl* Einsetzung in e-e Pfründe; *Am* Ausgleich des Vorempfangs unter gesetzlichen Erben

collect *Am* Nachnahme-; ~ **call** *Am tel* R-Gespräch *(Empfänger zahlt die Gebühren);* **to make the call** ~ *Am* ein R-Gespräch führen; **a telegram sent** ~ *Am* ein Telegramm, das der Empfänger bezahlt

collect on delivery (c. o. d.) *Am* Barzahlung bei Lieferung; gegen Nachnahme; *(als Frachtvermerk)* Rechnungsbetrag und *(in der Regel)* Fracht sind nachzunehmen; ~ **items** *Am* Postnachnahmesendungen; **to send sth.** ~ *Am* etw. per Nachnahme senden

collect *v* (ab)holen; (ein)sammeln; *(Geld, Steuern etc)* beitreiben, einziehen; das Inkasso besorgen; *(feste Beträge, Miete, Rechnungen etc)* kassieren; sich ansammeln, sich versammeln; **to** ~ **a bill** den Betrag e-r Rechnung (ein)kassieren; e-e Wechselforderung einziehen; das Inkasso e-s Wechsels besorgen; **to** ~ **a cheque** (*Am* **check**) e-n Scheck einziehen; **to** ~ **contributions** Beiträge einsammeln

collect *v*, **to** ~ **debts** Forderungen einziehen; **authority to** ~ **debts** Ermächtigung, Schulden einzuziehen; Inkassovollmacht

collect *v*, **to** ~ **evidence** Beweismaterial sammeln; **to** ~ **information** Erkundigungen einziehen (on über); **to** ~ **money** Geld einsammeln; **to** ~ **money for charitable purposes** Geld für wohltätige Zwecke sammeln; **to** ~ **orders** Aufträge sammeln; **to** ~ **a parcel at the post office** ein Paket von der Post abholen; **to** ~ **stamps** Briefmarken sammeln; **to** ~ **taxes** Steuern einziehen

collected, ~ **and delivered** (c. & d.) eingezogen und ausgeliefert; ~ **works** gesammelte Werke; **amount to be** ~ **on delivery** Nachnahmebetrag

collecting Einzahlung, Beitreibung, Inkasso; Abholung; ~ **agency** Inkassostelle; Inkassobüro; ~ **agent** Inkassovertreter; Inkassobeauftragter; ~ **bank(er)** Inkassobank; einziehende Bank; ~ **business** Inkassogeschäft; ~ **charges** Inkassospesen, Inkassogebühren; Abholgebühren; ~ **commission** Inkassoprovision; ~ **of bills of exchange** Wechselinkasso; ~ **point** Sammelstelle; ~ **power** Inkassovollmacht

collectable, collectible einziehbar, beitreibbar; einzuziehen, beizutreiben

collection 1. Einziehung, Einzug, Inkasso, Beitreibung, Abholung; *eccl* Kollekte; (Briefkasten-)Leerung; ~ **account** Inkassokonto; ~ **agency** Inkassostelle, Inkassobüro; ~ **agent** Inkassovertreter; Inkassobeauftragter; ~ **against documents** Dokumenteninkasso; ~ **at source** Steuererhebung an der Quelle *(Bezahlung von Steuern im Wege des Einzugs vom Einkommen, z. B. vom Verdienst, durch den Arbeitgeber; cf. pay-as-you-earn);* ~ **authority** Inkassovollmacht; ~ **by the customer** Selbstabholung; ~ **business** Inkassogeschäft; ~ **charge** *(VersR)* Hebegebühr; ~ **charges** Inkassogebühren, -spesen; Einzugsgebühren; ~ **costs** Inkassokosten; ~ **department** Inkassoabteilung; ~ **expenses** Inkassospesen, Einziehungskosten; ~ **fee** Inkassogebühr; Abholgebühr; *Am* Nachnahmegebühr; ~ **letter** Mahnbrief, Mahnschreiben

collection of a bill Einziehung e-s Rechnungsbetrages; Inkasso e-s Wechsels, Wechselinkasso; Einziehung e-r Wechselforderung; **to undertake the** ~ das Inkasso e-s Wechsels übernehmen (od. besorgen)

Collection of Bills Agreement[41a] Postauftragsabkommen

collection, ~ **of a claim** Einziehung e-r Forderung; Forderungsbeitreibung; ~ **of data** *(EDV)* Erfassung von Daten; ~ **of debts** Einziehung der Forderungen; ~ **of dividends** Dividendenbezug; ~ **of fees** Einziehung der Gebühren; ~ **of a fine** Beitreibung e-r Geldstrafe;

~ **of luggage** Gepäckabholung; ~ **of mail** Postabholung; ~ **of news** Einholung von Nachrichten; ~ **of outstanding debts** Einziehung von Außenständen; ~ **of premiums** *(VersR)* Prämieneinziehung, Prämieninkasso; ~ **of refuse** Müllabfuhr; ~ **of statistics** statistische Erhebungen; ~ **of taxes** Einziehung (od. Beitreibung) von Steuern; ~ **on delivery** gegen Nachnahme (→*collect on delivery*); ~ **order** Inkassoauftrag; ~ **proceeds** Inkassoerlös; ~ **risk** Delkredererisiko *(Inkassorisiko)*; ~ **service** Inkassodienst; ~ **system** Einzugsverfahren

collection, bill for ~ Wechsel zum Inkasso, Inkassowechsel; **charges for** ~ Inkassogebühren; Einzugsgebühren; **conditions of** ~ Inkassobedingungen; **documents sent for** ~ Inkassopapiere; **expenses of** ~ Inkassospesen; **for** ~ zum Inkasso; zur Einziehung; **proceeds of a** ~ Erlös e-r Sammlung; **proceeds of** ~ Inkassoerlöse; **ready for** ~ zum Abholen bereit; **(ICC) Uniform Rules for** ~**s**[41b] Einheitliche Richtlinien für Inkassi

collection, to accept bills for ~ Wechsel zum Inkasso hereinnehmen; **to attend to the** ~ **of a bill** das Inkasso e-s Wechsels besorgen; **to effect the** ~ das Inkasso besorgen; **to entrust the operation of** ~ **to a bank** e-r Bank e-n Inkassoauftrag erteilen; **to present for** ~ zum Inkasso (od. zur Einlösung) vorlegen; **to undertake the** ~ das Inkasso übernehmen; **the** ~ **is still outstanding** das Inkasso ist noch unerledigt

collection 2. Kollektion, Zusammenstellung; ~ **of patterns** Musterkollektion *(bes. von Stoffen etc)*; ~ **of samples** Musterkollektion; **to prepare a sample** ~ e-e Musterkollektion zusammenstellen

collection 3. Sammlung; Sammeln; ~**s** *(UrhR)* Sammelwerke; ~ **for charitable purposes** Sammlung zu wohltätigen Zwecken; ~ **of coins** Münzensammlung; ~ **of statutes** Gesetzessammlung; **stamp** ~ Briefmarkensammlung; **street** ~ Straßensammlung; **to organize** (or **hold**) **a** ~ e-e Sammlung veranstalten (od. durchführen); **to raise a** ~ sammeln (for für)

collective kollektiv, gemeinsam, gemeinschaftlich; Gesamt-, Gemeinschafts-, Sammel-; ~ **account** Sammelkonto; ~ **advertising** Gemeinschaftswerbung

collective agreement Tarifvertrag; Kollektivvertrag; Gesamtarbeitsvertrag; ~ **and individual agreements** Tarif- und Einzelarbeitsverträge; ~ **negotiations** *Br* Tarifverhandlungen; ~ **provisions** Tarifvertragsbestimmungen; **conclusion of a** ~ Tarifabschluß; **disputes involving** ~ ~**s** tarifrechtliche Streitigkeiten; **parties to a** ~ Tarifpartner; **under** ~ ~**s** tarifvertraglich

collective bargaining Verhandlungen *(der Sozialpartner)* über Abschluß e-s Tarifvertrages *(wages, hours, working conditions)*; Tarifverhandlungen; ~ **agreement** →collective agreement; ~ **contract** *Am* →collective contract; **free** ~ Tariffreiheit; **relations between the** ~ **partners** Tarifpartnerbeziehungen; **to take part in** ~ an Tarifverhandlungen teilnehmen

collective, ~ **bill of lading** Sammelkonnossement; ~ **charge** Gesamtbelastung *(Belastung mehrerer Grundstücke)*; *Br* Gesamthypothek; ~ **consignment** Sammelladung

collective contract Kollektivvertrag *(opp. individual contract)*; Tarifvertrag; ~ **negotiations** *Am* Tarifverhandlungen; ~ **termination** *Am* Tarifkündigung

collective, ~ **culpability** →~ guilt; ~ **deed** Sammelurkunde; ~ **deposit (of securities)** Sammeldepot; ~ **farm** Kolchose; ~ **farming** kollektiv betriebene Landwirtschaft; ~ **fine** Kollektiv-, Gesamtgeldstrafe; ~ **guarantee** *(VölkerR)* Kollektivgarantie, gemeinsame Garantie; ~ **guilt** *(VölkerR)* Kollektivschuld; ~ **insurance** *(VersR)* Kollektivversicherung; Gruppenversicherung

collecitive investment, ~ **scheme** gemeinsames Kapitalanlageprojekt; **undertakings for** ~ **in transferable securities** (Ucits) Organismen für gemeinsame Anlagen in Wertpapieren

collective, ~ **labo(u)r agreement** *Am* e-n ganzen Industriezweig umfassendes Tarifabkommen; ~ **liability** Gesamtverpflichtung, -schuld; *(VölkerR)* Kollektivhaftung

collective measures, to take ~ Kollektivmaßnahmen ergreifen

collective, ~ **mortgage** Gesamthypothek; ~ **negotiation** →~ bargaining; ~ **note** *(VölkerR)* Kollektivnote; *(von mehreren Staaten unterzeichnete)* gemeinsame Note; ~ **ownership** Gemein(schafts)besitz; Kollektiveigentum; ~ **passport** Sammelpaß; ~ **refusal to deal** Gruppenboykott; **C~ Reserve Unit** (C.R.U.) *(intern. Währungspolitik)* kollektive Reserveeinheit; ~ **resignation** Gesamtrücktritt; ~ **responsibility** Kollektivverantwortung, Gesamtverantwortlichkeit; ~ **security** *(VölkerR)* kollektive Sicherheit; ~ **self-defence (~se)** *(VölkerR)* kollektive Selbstverteidigung; ~ **shipment** Sammelladung; ~ **ticket** Sammelfahrschein; ~ **trade mark** Verbandszeichen; ~ **transport** Sammeltransport; ~ **treaty** *(VölkerR)* Kollektivvertrag *(cf. multilateral treaty)*; ~ **(wage) agreement** Lohntarifvertrag; ~ **work** *(UrhR)* Sammelwerk *(z. B. Enzyklopädie, Anthologie)*

collectively insgesamt; als Gesamtheit; gemeinsam; ~ **agreed earnings** (or **rates**) Tarifverdienst; ~ **agreed wage increase** Tariflohnerhöhung; **to bargain** ~ über e-n Tarifvertrag verhandeln; Tarifverhandlungen führen

collector 1. (Geld-, Zoll-, Steuer-, Lotterie-)Einnehmer; Kassierer *(von Beiträgen etc)*; ~ **of**

customs Zolleinnehmer; ~ **of customs and excise** *Br* Zollamt; ~ **of taxes** Steuereinnehmer; **debt** ~ Inkassobeauftragter; **tax** ~ Steuereinnehmer; **to act as** ~ das Inkasso besorgen

collector 2. Sammler; ~ **of antiques** Antiquitätensammler; ~ **of coins** Münzensammler; ~**'s item** (or **piece**) Sammlerstück; ~**'s value** Liebhaberwert; **art** ~ Kunstsammler; **stamp** ~ Briefmarkensammler

collectivism Kollektivismus *(opp. individualism)*

collectivist Anhänger des Kollektivismus; kollektivistisch

collectivization Kollektivisierung; Kollektivierung; **compulsory** ~ Zwangskollektivisierung

collectivize *v* kollektivieren

college College, höhere Schule; Universität, Hochschule; *Am* Universitätsinstitut; *Br* Studienheim *(mit Selbstverwaltung; cf. master, fellows);* Akademie *(Fachhochschule);* Kollegium; ~ **of cardinals** Kardinalskollegium; ~ **degree** *Am* akademischer Grad; ~ **dues** *Am* (~ **fees** *Br*) Studiengebühren; ~ **education** *Am* akademische Bildung; **C~ of Agriculture** *Br* landwirtschaftliche Hochschule; ~ **of education** Pädagogische Hochschule (P.H.); **C~ of Justice** *Scot* formelle Bezeichnung des →Court of Session; **C~ of Technology** *Br* Technische Hochschule (T.H.); ~ **training** *Am* akademische Ausbildung; **commercial** ~ Handelshochschule; →**electoral** ~

collegialism Kollegialsystem *(in der Verwaltung)*

collegiate zu e-m Kollegium od. College gehörig; Kollegial-; Universitäts-; ~ **character** Kollegialcharakter; **one-man or** ~ *Am* direktorial oder kollegial

collide *v* kollidieren; zusammenstoßen (with mit) *(Züge, Schiffe, Kraftwagen etc);* in Widerspruch stehen (with zu); sich überschneiden

colliding interests widerstreitende (od. kollidierende) Interessen; Interessenkollision

collier Bergmann, Grubenarbeiter; Kumpel; Kohlenschiff

colliery Kohlenbergwerk; (Kohlen-)Zeche; Steinkohlenbergwerk; ~ **company** Bergwerksgesellschaft; ~ **worker** Arbeitnehmer des (Stein-)Kohlenbergbaus

collision Kollision; Zusammenstoß, Widerstreit; Überschneidung *(von Interessen etc)*

collision at sea Zusammenstoß auf See; Schiffszusammenstoß; **International Regulations for Preventing C~s at S~**[42] Internationale Regeln zur Verhütung von Zusammenstößen auf See; Seestraßenordnung

collision, ~ **clause** *(SeeversR)* Kollisionsklausel; ~ **insurance** (or **coverage**) *Am* Kaskoversicherung; ~ **of interests** Interessenkollision; ~ **of trains** (or **train** ~) Eisenbahnzusammenstoß; **head-on** ~ *(Auto)* Frontalzusammenstoß; **rearend** ~ *(Auto)* Auffahrunfall; **to come into** ~ **with** zusammenstoßen mit

collocation Anordnung; Reihenfolge *(in der Schulden bezahlt werden)*

collude *v* in heimlichem *(unerlaubtem)* Einverständnis stehen (od. handeln); kolludieren

collusion geheimes *(unerlaubtes)* Einverständnis; Absprache, heimliche Verständigung *(zum Nachteil Dritter od. zur Irreführung des Gerichts);* geheime *(betrügerische)* Verabredung; Kollusion; Prozeßbetrug *(durch Zusammenwirken von zwei oder mehr Personen);* ~ **of facts** Verdunkelung des Sachverhalts; **risk** (or **danger**) **of** ~ Verdunkelungsgefahr; **to act in** ~ **with** in geheimem Einverständnis handeln mit; **to be in** ~ **with** in geheimem Einverständnis stehen mit; **to enter into a** ~ **with** heimlich in Verbindung treten mit, sich heimlich verständigen mit

collusive verabredet, abgesprochen; heimlich; ~ **agreement** heimliche Absprache *(bes. zur Irreführung des Gerichts);* ~ **bidding** (or **tendering**) Ausschreibungsabsprache, Absprache bei der Vergabe öffentlicher Aufträge; **to enter into a** ~ **agreement** sich heimlich verständigen; heimlich in Verbindung treten (with mit)

Colombia Kolumbien; **the Republic of** ~ Republik Kolumbien

Colombian Kolumbianer(in); kolumbianisch

colonial Kolonial-, kolonial; ~ **possessions** Kolonialbesitz

colonialization Kolonalisation

colonize *v* kolonisieren

colony Kolonie; **the American C~** die amerikanische Kolonie *(z.B. in Paris);* **Crown C~** *Br* Kronkolonie *(z.B. Hongkong)*

colo(u)r Farbe; Vorwand, Anschein; ~**s** Fahne, (National-)Flagge; ~ **bar** Rassenschranke; **under** ~ **of law** mit dem Anschein des Rechts; ~ **line** *(soziale)* Trennungslinie zwischen Weißen und Farbigen *(bes. Negern)*

colour of office Handlung unter Amtsmißbrauch; Amtsanmaßung; **under** ~ unter dem Vorwand e-r Amtshandlung

colo(u)r, ~ **prejudice** Vorurteil gegen Farbige; Rassenvorurteil; ~ **problem** Rassenfrage; ~ **of title** Anschein e-s Rechts *(unzureichende od. mangelhafte schriftl. Unterlage zur Substantiierung des Eigentumsanspruchs im Liegenschaftsrecht);* **political** ~ politische Tendenz *(e-r Zei-*

tung); **Trooping the C~** Fahnenparade *(Br z.B. am offiziellen Geburtstag der Königin);* **service with the ~s** Militärdienst *(opp. in the reserve);* **serving with the ~s** *mil* aktiv; **to give** (or **lend**) **~ to a th.** e-r Sache den Anschein von Wahrscheinlichkeit geben; **to join the ~s** *mil* in die Armee eintreten; **to serve with the ~s** Militärdienst ableisten; **to show the ~s** die Flagge hissen; **to stick to one's ~s** *fig* sich weigern, s-e Ansicht (od. Partei) zu ändern; **to troop the ~s** Fahnenparade abnehmen

colo(u)r *v* „gefärbt" darstellen; beschönigen

colo(u)red farbig; gefärbt, beschönigt; **C~s** Farbige *(bes. in Afrika);* **~ labo(u)r** farbige Arbeiter (od. Arbeitskräfte); **~ man** Farbiger; **~ people** Farbige; **~ report** gefärbter Bericht; **~ woman** Farbige

colo(u)rable anscheinend echt (od. glaubwürdig); angeblich; unecht, vorgetäuscht; **~ imitation** täuschend ähnliche Nachahmung *(Fälschung e-s Warenzeichens); (UrhR)* sklavische Nachahmung; **~ transaction** Scheingeschäft

column Säule; Rubrik, Spalte; Kolonne; **~ of figures** Zahlenreihe, Zahlenkolonne; **advertising ~s** Anzeigenteil *(e-r Zeitung);* **commercial and financial ~s** Wirtschaftsteil *(e-r Zeitung);* **printed in double ~s** zweispaltig gedruckt; **Fifth C~** *pol* Fünfte Kolonne; **the article takes up 2 ~s** der Artikel nimmt 2 Spalten ein

columnist *Am* Kolumnist, Zeitungsartikelschreiber *(für e-e bestimmte Spalte)*

co(-)management Mitbestimmung(srecht) *(der Arbeitnehmer)*

combat Kampf; **~ allowance** *mil* Frontzulage; **~ area** Kampfgebiet; **~ zone** *(VölkerR)* Kampfzone

combat *v* **to ~ crime** Verbrechen bekämpfen

combating, ~ of crime Verbrechensbekämpfung; **~ a fire** Brandbekämpfung

combatant Kombattant, *(aktiver)* Kriegsteilnehmer; **non-~** Nichtkombattant

combination Kombination; Verbindung, Vereinigung, Interessengemeinschaft; (Unternehmens-)Zusammenschluß; *Am* Konzern; Kartell; Verband; *(PatR)* Kombination *(Vereinigung alter und neuer Elemente); Am (AntitrustR)* Zusammenwirken *(durch das e-e Beschränkung des Wettbewerbs bewirkt wird);* **~ in restraint of trade** Zusammenschluß zur Beschränkung des Wettbewerbs; **~ patent** Kombinationspatent; **~ policy** *(VersR)* kombinierte Police; Kartell *(im engeren Sinne);* **~ sale** Kopplungsverkauf; **close ~s** *Am* Zusammenschlüsse auf kapitalistischer Basis *(etwa den deutschen Konzernen entsprechend);* **loose** (or **contract**) **~s** *Am* lockere (od. vertragliche) Zusammenschlüsse *(etwa den deutschen Kartellen entsprechend);* **price ~** Preiskartell; **production ~** Produktionskartell; **to enter into ~ with** sich zusammenschließen mit

combine (Unternehmer-)Zusammenschluß; *Br* Kartell; Verband; Konzern; **C~s Investigation Act** *(Kanada)* Kartellgesetz; **~ price** Verbandspreis; **~ of producers** Erzeugerverband

combine *v* verbinden; *(in sich)* vereinigen; sich zusammenschließen; zusammenwirken

combined gemeinsam, gemeinschaftlich; **~ action** gemeinsames Vorgehen; **~ annual fee** pauschale Jahresgebühr; **~ arms** *mil* gemischte Verbände, Truppenverband; **~ buyers** Einkaufskartell; **~ endowment and whole life insurance** *(VersR)* gemischte Lebensversicherung *(auf den Erlebens- und Todesfall);* **~ financial statement** Konzernbilanz; **~ income** gemeinsames Einkommen *(der Eheleute);* **~ rail/road traffic** kombinierter Güterverkehr Schiene/Straße; Huckepackverkehr

combustibles feuergefährliche Güter

combustion, large ~ plant Großfeuerungsanlage

come *v* kommen; **to ~ of age** volljährig werden; **to ~ to an agreement** zu e-r Einigung kommen; e-e Verständigung erzielen; **to ~ forward as a candidate** *parl* als Kandidat auftreten; **to ~ under a contract** unter e-n Vertrag fallen; **to ~ before a court** vor ein Gericht kommen *(Sache, Fall);* **to ~ to an end** zu Ende gehen, auslaufen; **to ~ up to expectations** der Erwartung entsprechen; **to ~ into force** in Kraft treten; **to ~ into a fortune** ein Vermögen erben; **to ~ to hand** eingehen, einlaufen *(z.B. Aufträge);* **to ~ to a head** sich zuspitzen *(Lage, Situation);* **to ~ under a law** unter ein Gesetz fallen; **to ~ into money** *(plötzlich)* zu Geld kommen *(bes. durch Erbschaft);* **to ~ into operation** in Kraft treten; **to ~ into possession** in den Besitz gelangen; **to ~ into power** zur Macht kommen, an die Macht gelangen *(politische Partei);* **to ~ into property** *(unbewegl.)* Vermögen erben (od. erwerben); **to ~ within the scope of law** unter ein Gesetz fallen; **to ~ on stream** in Betrieb gehen; **to ~ out (on strike)** in Streik treten, streiken; **to ~ to terms** sich einigen, zu e-m Vergleich kommen, sich vergleichen; **to within the terms of a contract (law)** unter die Bestimmungen e-s Vertrages (Gesetzes) fallen

come *v*, **to ~ about** sich ereignen, zustande kommen; *(Sache, Fall);* **to ~ down** fallen *(im Preise);* heruntergehen (to auf); **to ~ from** kommen (od. stammen) aus; herrühren von; **to ~ in** *(als Partner)* eintreten; hereinkommen, eintreffen *(Ware);* eingehen *(Geld, Aufträge, Waren);* ankommen, einlaufen *(Zug);* **to ~**

into eintreten in; erben; **to ~ out** *(mit e-m Artikel od. Buch)* herauskommen, erscheinen, **to ~ to** sich belaufen auf, betragen; **to ~ to know sb.** jdn kennen lernen; **to ~ through** *tel* durchkommen; **to ~ under** fallen (od. stehen) unter; **to ~ up to** herankommen an, entsprechen; **to ~ up with sth.** mit etw. herauskommen; etw. auf den Markt bringen

coming 1., **~ of age** Mündigwerden; **on ~ of age** bei Erreichung der Volljährigkeit; **~ in** Eingang *(Geld, Aufträge, Waren)*; **(on) ~ into force** (bei) Inkrafttreten; **~ out of a book** Erscheinen e-s Buches

coming 2. künftig, kommend; **the ~ man** der kommende Mann; **in the ~ years** in den kommenden Jahren

COMECON (Council for Mutual Economic Assistance) (CMEA) Rat für gegenseitige Wirtschaftshilfe (RGW); **~ countries** RGW-Länder
Im Abkommen von 1949 vereinbarte wirtschaftliche Zusammenarbeit der Staaten des Ostblocks (UdSSR, Polen, Rumänien, Bulgarien, die Tschechoslowakai, Ungarn, die DDR), der Mongolischen Volksrepublik und Kuba, seit 1978 auch Vietnam. Jugoslawien ist seit 1964 assoziiertes Mitglied. *Sitz:* Moskau. *Ziel:* Gemeinsames Arbeitssystem zur Koordinierung der Wirtschaftspläne. Arbeitsteilung der Produktion. Technischer und wissenschaftlicher Erfahrungsaustausch. Reform des Zahlungs- und Währungssystems

Comex →Commodity Exchange *(New York)*

comfort Komfort, Bequemlichkeit; Trost, Erleichterung; **to give the enemy aid and ~** dem Feinde Vorschub leisten *(cf. treason)*

comfortable, in ~ circumstances in guten Verhältnissen; wohlhabend

comfortably, to be ~ off ein gutes Auskommen haben

comity of nations Comitas gentium, Courtoisie, Völkersitte; **international ~** internationales Entgegenkommen unter Staaten; **judicial ~** Anerkennung ausländischer Gerichtsentscheidungen
Konventionsregeln des entgegenkommenden Verhaltens der Staaten untereinander. Kein Völkerrecht *(im Ggs. zum →customary international law)*

command Befehl; Weisung; Verfügung (of über); *mil* (Ober-)Befehl, Kommando; **by ~ of Her Majesty** *Br* auf Anordnung Ihrer Majestät; **~ authority** *mil* Befehlsbefugnis; **~ of a language** Beherrschung e-r Sprache; **~ of the market** Beherrschung des Marktes; **right of ~** Weisungsbefugnis; **to have at one's ~** zu seiner Verfügung haben, verfügen über

Command Paper *Br parl (dem Parlament vorgelegter)* Kabinettsbeschluß
Abkürzung C., Cd., Cmd., Cmnd. mit anschließender Nummer; z. B. Cmd 4900 (vgl. Abkürzungsverzeichnis)

command *v* befehlen, anordnen, Weisung geben; verfügen über, zur Verfügung haben; *mil* kommandieren, das Kommando führen, befehligen; **to ~ the market** den Markt beherrschen; **to ~ a high price** hoch im Preise stehen; e-n hohen Preis erzielen

commander *mil* Befehlshaber; Kommandeur, Kommandant; **C~-in-Chief** (C.-in-C.) Oberbefehlshaber

commemoration, in ~ of zur Erinnerung (od. zum Gedächtnis) an; **(ceremony of) ~** Gedenkfeier, Gedächtnisfeier; **~ day** (or **festival**) Stiftungsfest

commence *v* anfangen, beginnen; *Br (an der Universität Cambridge)* e-n akademischen Grad erwerben; **to ~ an action** Klage erheben, klagen; **to ~ a business** ein Geschäft eröffnen; den Geschäftsbetrieb beginnen; **to ~ duty** den Dienst antreten; **to ~ (legal) proceedings** ein Gerichtsverfahren einleiten; **to ~ a suit** *Am* → to ~ an action

commencing, ~ salary Anfangsgehalt; **~ a suit** *Am* Klageerhebung

commencement Anfang, Beginn; *Am univ (Br Cambridge und Dublin)* feierliche Verleihung von akademischen Graden; **~ of an Act** (Tag des) Inkrafttreten(s) e-s Gesetzes; **~ of an action** Klageerhebung; Einleitung e-s Prozesses; **~ of business** Inbetriebnahme des Geschäfts; Geschäftsbeginn; Aufnahme der Geschäftstätigkeit; **~ of a policy** Versicherungsbeginn; **~ of the sentence** Strafantritt; **~ of service** Dienstantritt

commendatory letter Empfehlungsschreiben

comment Erklärung, Stellungnahme (on zu); Bemerkung, Kritik (on an); *(kritische)* Anmerkung; **fair ~** (on a matter of public interest) sachliche Kritik *(cf. fair)*; **press ~** Pressekommentar; **to make ~s on** sich äußern über, Stellung nehmen zu

commentary Kommentar, Erläuterung (on zu); Berichterstattung; **legal ~** juristischer Kommentar; **press ~** Pressekommentar; **running ~** *(Radio)* fortlaufender Kommentar
Kommentare zu Gesetzen haben im anglo-amerikanischen Recht nicht die Bedeutung wie im deutschen Recht und werden weniger beachtet als Urteile (precedents) und dicta

commentator Kommentator; Rundfunkkommentator

commerce[43] Handel *(bes. in großem Umfange und Außenhandel)*; Handelsverkehr; Wirtschaftsverkehr; **~ among the states** *Am* Wirtschaftsverkehr zwischen den Einzelstaaten (→*interstate commerce*); **~ and industry** Handel und Wirtschaft

Commerce Clause *Am* Handelsklausel
Bezeichnung für Art. I sec. 8 der Verfassung, der die ausschließliche Bundeszuständigkeit für den Außenhandel und den zwischenstaatlichen Handel (zwischen den Einzelstaaten) begründet

commerce, Chamber of C~ Handelskammer; **Association of British Chambers of C~** Spitzenorgan der britischen Handelskammer;[44] →**International Chamber of C~**

commerce, channels of ~ Handelswege, Handelsverbindungen; **Department of C~** *Am* Wirtschaftsministerium; **foreign and domestic** ~ *Am* Außen- und Binnenhandel; **free flow of** ~ *Am* freier Güterverkehr; **internal** ~ *Am* Binnenhandel; **international** ~ Welthandel; **regulations of** ~ Handelsvorschriften; **Secretary of C~** *Am* Wirtschaftsminister; **Treaty of Friendship, C~ and Navigation**→ friendship; **world(-wide)** ~ Welthandel

commercial Handels-, Wirtschafts-, Geschäfts-; kaufmännisch, geschäftlich, gewerblich; handelsüblich; wirtschaftlich; ~**s** Werbesendung *(im Radio od. Fernsehen)* ~ **activity** Handelstätigkeit; ~ **advertising** Wirtschaftswerbung

commercial agency[44a] Handelsvertretung; *Am* Kreditauskunftei; ~ **contract** Handelsvertretervertrag

commercial, ~ **agent** (Handels-)Vertreter; ~ **arbitration** Handelsschiedsgerichtsbarkeit; ~ **art** Werbegraphik; ~ **artist** Werbegraphiker; ~ **attaché** Handelsattaché; ~→**bank**; ~ →**banking**

commercial basis, on a ~ geschäftsmäßig

commercial, ~ **bill (of exchange)** gewerblicher Wechsel; Handelswechsel, Warenwechsel; ~ **blockade** Handelsblockade; ~ **broker** Handelsmakler; ~ **career** kaufmännische Berufslaufbahn; ~ **causes** *(gerichtl.)* Handelssachen *(Br cf. C~ Court)*; ~ **channel** Handelsweg; ~ **circles** Geschäftskreise; ~ **class** Handel(sstand); ~ **clerk** kaufmännische(r) Angestellte(r); **C~ Code** →code 1.; ~ **college** Handels(hoch)schule; Wirtschafts(ober)schule; ~ **column** Wirtschaftsteil *(e-r Zeitung)*; ~ **convention** Handelsabkommen; ~ **correspondence** Handelskorrespondenz, Geschäftskorrespondenz

Commercial Court Handelsgericht
Br Aus 5 Richtern bestehendes Gericht (Teil der Queen's Bench Division), von dem Handelssachen durch ein vereinfachtes Verfahren schnell erledigt werden können (→*points of claim*, → *points of defence*)

commercial credit *(kurzfristiger)* Handelskredit, Warenkredit; ~ **company** Kundenkreditbank; *Am* Finanzierungsunternehmen *(bes. für →factoring und Teilzahlungsfinanzierung)*

commercial, ~ **custom** Handelsbrauch; Geschäftsbrauch; Usance; ~ **designer** Werbegraphiker; ~ **development** wirtschaftliche Entwicklung;~ **directory** Branchenadreßbuch; ~ **discount** handelsüblicher Rabatt; ~ **disputes** Handelsstreitigkeiten; ~ **documents** Handelspapier;~ **enterprise** geschäftliches (od. gewerbliches) Unternehmen; Geschäftsunternehmen

commercial exception *(IPR) Am* Ausnahme vom Grundsatz der Staatenimmunität
Vorgesehen im →Foreign Sovereign Immunity Act (FISA). Sie greift ein, wenn sich der ausländische Staat handelsrechtlich (privatrechtlich) in den USA betätigt hat

commercial, ~ **executive** kaufmännischer Angestellter in leitender Stellung; ~ **firm** (or **house**) Handelsfirma; ~ **guarantee insurance** Vertrauensschadenversicherung, Veruntreuungsversicherung; ~ **instrument** Handelspapier; ~ **intercourse** Handelsverkehr, Geschäftsverkehr; ~ **invoice** Warenrechnung, Handelsrechnung

commercial law Handelsrecht; *(gerichtl. anerkanntes)* Handelsgewohnheitsrecht *(→law merchant)*
Grundlage des anglo-amerikanischen Handelsrechts ist das in den Gerichtsentscheidungen zum Ausdruck kommende Gewohnheitsrecht (common law), das jetzt teilweise in einzelnen Gesetzen kodifiziert ist (*Br* z. B. Bills of Exchange Act, Bankruptcy Act, Sale of Goods Act, Companies Acts, Partnership Act, Marine Insurance Act, Trade Marks Act, *Am* bundesgesetzlich z. B. Bankruptcy Reform Act, Patent Law, Shipping Act, Merchant Marine Act, Carriage of Goods by Sea Act und Copyright Act). Durch den in der Mehrzahl der amerikanischen Einzelstaaten angenommenen Uniform Commercial Code gibt es in neuester Zeit in den USA eine einheitliche, nach Materien gegliederte, umfassende Kodifikation des Handelsrechts.
Das anglo-amerikanische Handelsrecht ist schon seit dem Mittelalter stark durch das Handelsrecht anderer Länder beeinflußt, dem deutschen Recht deshalb näher als andere Zweige des Common Law

commercial, ~ **legislation** Handelsgesetzgebung; ~ **letter of credit** (CLC) Akkreditiv (→*letter of credit*); ~ **list** Liste für *(gerichtl.)* Handelssachen; ~ **loan** Warenkredit; ~ **marine** Handelsmarine; ~ **mark** Warenzeichen; Fabrikmarke; ~ **matters** Handelssachen; ~ **name** Handelsname; ~ **negotiations** Handelsbesprechungen; ~ **news** Handelsnachrichten *(e-r Zeitung)*; ~ **paper**[45, 46] Handelspapier *(kurzfristiges Geldmarktpapier privater Kreditnehmer; bes. Wechsel und Solawechsel)*; ~ **papers** *(Post)* Geschäftspapiere; ~ **paper house** *Am* bankähnliches Institut, das Wechseldiskontgeschäfte für eigene Rechnung betreibt; ~ **partnership** Handelsgesellschaft

commercial policy Handelspolitik, Wirtschaftspolitik; ~ **measures** handelspolitische Maßnahmen

commercial practice Handelsbrauch, Geschäftsbrauch, Geschäftspraxis; **usual** ~ üblicher Handelsbrauch, Verkehrssitte

commercial principles, in accordance with ~ nach kaufmännischen Grundsätzen

commercial, ~ **production** handelsmäßige Produktion; ~ **profits** gewerbliche Gewinne; ~ **property** gewerblich genutzter Grundbesitz; Geschäftsgrundstück; ~ **purposes** wirtschaftliche (od. gewerbliche) Zwecke; **non-~ quantities** nicht zum Handel geeignete Mengen; ~ **relations** Handelsbeziehungen; ~ **representative** Handelsvertreter; ~ **risk** wirtschaftliches Risiko; Unternehmerwagnis

commercial sample Warenmuster; **International Convention to facilitate the importation of ~s and advertising materials**[47] Internationales Abkommen zur Erleichterung der Einfuhr von Warenmustern und Werbematerial

commercial scale, on a ~ gewerbsmäßig; **working on a ~ scale** *Br (PatR)* Ausführung *(der Erfindung)* in gewerblichem Umfang

commercial, ~ **shipping** Handelsschiffahrt; ~ **size** marktgängige Größe *(z.B. bei der Fischerei);* ~ **statistics** Handelsstatistiken; ~ **style** Geschäftsstil; ~ **television** Werbefernsehen *(aus Werbeeinkünften finanziertes Fernsehprogramm);* ~ **transactions** geschäftliche Transaktionen; ~ **trainee** als Kaufmann Auszubildender; Handlungslehrling; ~ **travel(l)er** *(nicht selbständiger)* Vertreter, Handlungsreisender, Geschäftsreisender

commercial treaty Handelsvertrag; **to conclude a** ~ e-n Handelsvertrag abschließen

commercial undertaking gewerbliches Unternehmen; kaufmännischer Betrieb

commercial usage Handelsbrauch, Geschäftsbrauch; **in accordance with** ~ handelsüblich

commercial, ~ **user** gewerblicher Verbraucher; ~ **value** Handelswert, Marktwert; ~ **vehicle** Nutzfahrzeug *(vans, lorries etc);* ~ **weight** (c.w.) Handelsgewicht

commercialese Geschäftssprache; Kaufmannsstil

commercialism Geschäftsgeist; Geschäftstüchtigkeit

commercialize *v* geschäftlich (od. gewerblich) verwenden

commissary Kommissar; Beauftragter; *Scot* Richter e-s Grafschaftsgerichts; *Br* Universitätsrichter *(Cambridge); eccl* bischöflicher Kommissar

commission 1. Kommission; ~ **of inquiry** Untersuchungskommission; **government** ~ Regierungskommission; **joint** ~ gemischte Kommission; **member of the** ~ Kommissionsmitglied; **on the** ~ in der Kommission; zu der Kommission gehörig; →**Royal C~**; **standing** ~ ständige Kommission; **sub~** Unterkommission; **to be on the** ~ Mitglied der Kommission sein; **to establish a** ~ e-e Kommission einsetzen (od. bilden); **to form part of a** ~ e-r Kommission angehören; **to cease to form part of a** ~ aus e-r Kommission ausscheiden; **to set up a** ~s. to establish a →~; **to sit on a** ~ Mitglied e-r Kommission sein; **the** ~ **sits** (or **is in session**) die Kommission tagt

Commission (of the European Communities) Kommission (der Europäischen Gemeinschaften); EG-Kommission; ~ **draft** *(EG)* Kommissionsentwurf

Commission of the Churches on International Affairs (CCIA) Kommission der Kirchen für internationale Angelegenheiten *(in London)*

Commission of the Peace *Br* Beauftragung der Friedensrichter *(in e-m bestimmten Bezirk);* Gesamtheit der Friedensrichter

commission 2. Provision *(Vergütung für geleistete Dienste);* Kurtage *(des Börsenmaklers);* ~ **account** Provisionskonto; Provisionsrechnung; ~ **accounts** Provisionsabrechnung; ~ **agent** Provisionsvertreter; **on a** ~ **basis** auf Provisionsbasis; ~ **broker** *Am (Börse)* Makler auf Provisionsbasis *(führt Kundenaufträge im Namen e-r Firma [Commission House] an der Börse aus);* ~ **charge** Provision; Kurtage; ~ **for collection (of bills)** Inkassoprovision; ~ **on guarantee (guaranty)** Avalprovision *(beim Avalkredit);* ~ **income** Provisionsertrag; ~ **rate** Provisionssatz; Satz der Maklerprovision; ~ **on sale** Verkaufsprovision; Umsatzprovision; ~ **statement** Provisionsaufstellung, -berechnung; ~ **on turnover** Umsatzprovision

commission, accepting ~ Akzeptprovision; **agent's** ~ Vertreterprovision; **banker's** ~ Bankprovision; **buying** ~ Einkaufsprovision; **claim for** ~ Provisionsanspruch; **final** ~ Abschlußprovision; **free of** ~ provisionsfrei; **guarantee** ~ Bürgschaftsprovision; **liable to** ~ provisionspflichtig; **on** ~ gegen Provision; **rate of** ~ Provisionssatz; **sale on** ~ Verkauf gegen Provision; **sales** ~ Verkaufsprovision; **salesman** ~ Vertreterprovision; **selling** ~ Verkaufsprovision; **statement of** ~ Provisionsaufstellung, -berechnung; **subject to** ~ provisionspflichtig; **underwriting** ~ Provision für Übernahme e-r Effektenemission

commission, to be subject to a ~ e-r Provision unterliegen; **to charge a** ~ Provision berechnen; **to draw a** ~ Provision beziehen; **the** ~ **amounts to** ... die Provision beträgt ...; **we will pay you a** ~ **of 2 percent on the invoice amount** wir vergüten Ihnen als Provision 2% des Rechnungsbetrages; **to sell goods on** ~ Waren gegen Provision verkaufen

commission 3. *(StrafR)* Begehung, Verübung *(e-r strafbaren Handlung);* ~ **of an offence (~se)** (or **crime**) Begehung e-r Straftat; ~**s and omissions** Handlungen und Unterlassungen

commission 4. Kommission *(Ausführung e-s Geschäftes für Rechnung e-s anderen im eigenen Namen mit Dritten);* ~ **agency** Kommission(sgeschäft); ~ **agent** Kommissionär; ~ **business**

Kommissionsgeschäft, Kommissionshandel; ~ **buyer** Einkaufskommissionär; ~ **goods** Kommissionsware; ~ **house** *Am* Maklerfirma *(die das Börsengeschäft mit dem Publikum auf Kommissionsbasis betreibt);* ~ **merchant** Kommissionär; ~ **sale** Kommissionsverkauf; **buying** ~ Einkaufskommission; **by (way of)** ~ kommissionsweise

commission, on ~ in Kommission *(im eigenen Namen für fremde Rechnung);* kommissionsweise; **goods on** ~ Kommissionswaren; **purchase on** ~ Kommissionseinkauf; **sale on** ~ Kommissionsverkauf; **stock on** ~ Kommissionslager; **transaction on** ~ Kommissionsgeschäft; **to buy and sell on** ~ Kommissionsgeschäfte machen; **to take goods on** ~ Waren in Kommission nehmen

commission 5. *Am* kommissarische Stellung (od. Verwaltung); **to hold an office in** ~ *Am* ein Amt kommissarisch (od. vorübergehend) innehaben; **to put in(to)** ~ *Am* unter kommissarische Verwaltung stellen

commission 6. Ermächtigung zur Ausübung bestimmter Funktionen; Beauftragung; Auftrag; *Scot* Vollmacht; *mil* Offizierspatent; ~ **for examination of witnesses** (or ~ **to examine witnesses**) *Am* Beauftragung zur Vernehmung von Zeugen (beim Rechtshilfeersuchen); **candidate for a** ~ Offiziersanwärter; **Her Majesty's C**~ *Br* Königliches Offizierspatent; **in** ~ ermächtigt, beauftragt; in Dienst gestellt *(Schiff);* **to discharge a** ~ e-n Auftrag ausführen; **to entrust sb. with a** ~ jdm e-n Auftrag erteilen; **to give sth. in** ~ etw in Auftrag geben; **to hold a** ~ e-e Offiziersstelle innehaben; **to obtain a** ~ zum Offizier befördert werden; **to resign one's** ~ *mil* seinen Abschied nehmen; **he has secured a** ~ er hat e-n Auftrag erhalten

commission *v* beauftragen (for mit); ermächtigen, bevollmächtigen; in Auftrag geben, bestellen; *mil* das Offizierspatent verleihen; *(Schiff)* in Dienst stellen; *(Kraftwerk etc)* in Betrieb nehmen

commissioned beauftragt; bevollmächtigt; in Dienst gestellt *(Schiff); mil* durch Patent zum Offizier ernannt; ~ **invention** *(PatR)* Auftragserfindung; ~ **judge** beauftragter Richter; ~ **since** *mil* Patent vom; ~ **work** *(UrhR)* Auftragswerk; in Auftrag gegebene Arbeit; **non-~ officer** Unteroffizier

commissioning Indienststellung *(e-s Schiffes);* ~ **of experts** Beauftragung von Sachverständigen; ~ **of a reactor** Inbetriebnahme e-s Reaktors

commissioner (Comr.) *(amtl. od. gerichtl.)* Beauftragter, Bevollmächtigter; leitender Beamter *(dem ein Verwaltungszweig od. e-e Kommission untersteht);* leitender Beamter für Sonderaufgaben; Kommissar; *(Kanada)* Präsident der Kartellbehörde; *Am (von der deutschen Auslandsvertretung ersuchte)* Person zur Durchführung e-s Rechtshilfeersuchens in den USA *(falls die zu erscheinende Person nicht freiwillig erscheint);* **C**~ **of Customs** *Am* oberster Beamter für das Zollwesen; **C**~ **of Customs and Excise** (CCE) *Br* Mitglied des →Board of Customs and Excise

Commissioner of Deeds *Am (dem deutschen Notar ähnliche)* Urkundsperson

Er beurkundet insbes. Rechtsgeschäfte außerhalb des Einzelstaates zur Verwendung in dem Einzelstaat, für den er bestellt ist

Commissioner of the European Communities EG-Kommissar

Commissioners of Inland Revenue *Br* Ministerialabteilung für Steuer *(im Finanzministerium); (auch:)* Richter in Steuersachen (General Commissioners Laienrichter; Special Commissioners juristisch ausgebildete Richter); **all duties of inland revenue are collected by the** ~ *Br* alle inländischen Steuern und Abgaben werden von den ~ eingezogen

commissioner, ~ **of insurance** *Am* →insurance commissioner; **C**~ **of Internal Revenue** *Am* Bundesfinanzbehörde; **C**~ **of the Metropolitan Police** Polizeipräsident der Londoner Polizei

Commissioner for Oaths *Br (vom Lord Chancellor ernannte)* Urkundsperson

Alle Solicitors haben die Befugnisse e-s Commissioner for Oaths. Er ist berechtigt zur Abnahme von Eiden und eidesstattlichen Erklärungen *(cf. affidavit, affirmation, declaration)*

Commissioner of Patents and Trademarks *Am* Präsident des Patentamtes; **Assistant** ~ *Am* Stellvertreter des Präsidenten des Patentamtes; **First Assistant** ~ *Am* Vizepräsident des Patentamtes

commissioner, by a ~ kommissarisch

Commissioner, General ~ → Commissioners of Inland Revenue

commissioner, government ~ Regierungsbeauftragter

Commissioner, High ~ Hoher Kommissar, Hochkommissar

Oberster Verwaltungsbeamter eines Staates in einem von diesem verwalteten Gebiet. *Br* jetzt bes. Titel der offiziellen Vertreter der Commonwealth-Länder im Botschaftsrang

commissioner, insurance ~ *Am* →insurance; **special** ~ Sonderbeauftragter; **Special C**~**s** *Br* →Commissioners of Inland Revenue

commit *v* übergeben, anvertrauen; *(Straftat)* begehen, verüben; *(in das Gefängnis)* einliefern; *(in e-e Anstalt)* einweisen; **to** ~ **oneself** sich verpflichten, e-e Verpflichtung eingehen; sich festlegen (to auf); **to** ~ **oneself to pay the costs** sich zur Übernahme der Kosten verpflichten; **to** ~ **a bill** *parl* e-n Gesetzentwurf *(an e-n Ausschuß)* überweisen; **to** ~

to a p.'s charge jdm anvertrauen; **to ~ a patient to a mental →hospital**; **to ~ an offence (~se)** e-e strafbare Handlung begehen; **to ~ to prison** in das Gefängnis einliefern; **to ~ for trial** *(durch die →magistrates an das höhere Gericht)* zur Verhandlung und Aburteilung überweisen

committed engagiert; **to be ~** verpflichtet (od. festgelegt) sein (to auf); sich festgelegt haben; *(auch pol)* gebunden sein; **non-~** *(noch)* nicht gebunden, ungebunden

committing magistrate *Br* Untersuchungsrichter

commitment 1. Verpflichtung, Verbindlichkeit, Engagement; Zusage; Übergeben (to an); Einlieferung *(in das Gefängnis)*; Einweisung, Unterbringung *(in e-e[-r] Anstalt)*; Begehung *(e-r strafbaren Handlung)*; *parl* Überweisung *(e-s Gesetzentwurfs)* an e-n Ausschuß; Bindung (to an); Mittelbindung; Festlegung (to auf); **~ appropriations** *(EG)* Verpflichtungsermächtigungen; **~ commission** Bereitstellungsprovision *(für Kredite)*; **~ credit** Bereitstellungskredit; **~s arising from endorsements** Indossamentverbindlichkeiten; **~ fee** →~commission; **~ of funds** Mittelbindung; **~ to a mental hospital** (or *Am* **psychiatric clinic**) Einweisung in ein psychiatrisches Krankenhaus; **~ for observation** Einweisung *(in e-e Anstalt)* zur Beobachtung

commitment, contractual ~ vertragliche Verpflichtung; **European ~** europäisches Engagement; **financial ~** Finanzierungszusage; **order of ~ (to prison)** Einweisungsanordnung; *(etwa:)* Anordnung der Inhaftnahme, Haftbefehl; **political ~** politische Bindung; **re-~** *pol* Wiederverpflichtung, erneute Bindung (to an); **social ~** soziales Engagement; gesellschaftliche Verpflichtung; **without any ~** unverbindlich; **to enter into a ~** e-e Verpflichtung übernehmen (od. eingehen); **to fail to meet one's ~s** seinen Verpflichtungen nicht nachkommen; **to fulfil** (or **meet**) **~s** Verpflichtungen erfüllen (od. nachkommen); **to incur** (or **make, undertake**) **a ~** e-e Verpflichtung eingehen

commitment 2. *Am (Börse)* Engagement; **~s for future delivery** Terminengagements; **foreign exchange ~** Devisenengagement; **to make a ~** *Am* e-n Abschluß tätigen

committal Übergeben, Überweisen; Einlieferung *(in das Gefängnis)*; **~ for failure to pay a fine** *(etwa:)* Ersatzfreiheitsstrafe; **~ to hospital** →hospital; **~ order** *Br*[48] Einlieferungsverfügung in das Gefängnis; *(etwa:)* Anordnung der Inhaftnahme, Haftbefehl *(bes. wegen →contempt of court, aber auch um die Zahlung e-r Urteilsschuld aus e-m Unterhaltsurteil [maintenance order] oder von Steuern und ähnlichen Abgaben an den Staat*[49] *aus anderen Urteilen od. Entscheidungen zu erzwingen.)*; **~ proceedings** *Br (Strafprozeß)* Vorverfahren vor dem Magistrates' Court (→*preliminary examination*) **~ for sentence** Verweisung an ein höheres Gericht zur Festsetzung der Strafe *(nach Verurteilung)*; **~ for trial** *Br (Strafprozeß) (von den →examining magistrates getroffene)* Anordnung der Hauptverhandlung *(vor e-m Gericht mit Geschworenen)*; **non-~** unverbindlich; sich nicht festlegend

committee 1. Ausschuß; Komitee; **~ of control** Kontrollausschuß; **~ of experts** Sachverständigenausschuß, Fachausschuß; **~ of four** Viererausschuß; **~ of hono(u)r** Ehrenkomitee; **~ of inquiry** Untersuchungsausschuß

committee of inspection *Br* Gläubigerausschuß *(zur Überwachung der Verwaltung des schuldnerischen Vermögens durch den Konkursverwalter; → trustee in bankruptcy)*; **~ in a winding up** *Br* Überwachungsausschuß bei e-r Liquidation

committee, C~ of Investigation Untersuchungsausschuß; **~ on legal affairs** Rechtsausschuß; **C~ of London Clearing Bankers** (CLCB) Ausschuß der Präsidenten der sechs englischen Clearingbanken *(Barclays, the National Westminster, the Midland, Lloyd's, Williams & Clyn's and Coutts)*; **~ man** Mitglied e-s Ausschusses; **~ of management** Verwaltungsausschuß

committee meeting Ausschußsitzung; **to attend a ~** an e-r Ausschußsitzung teilnehmen

committee, ~ room Ausschußzimmer; **C~ for Space Research** (COSPAR) *Am* Komitee für Raumforschung; **C~ on Stock List** *Am* Zulassungsstelle an der New Yorker Börse; **C~ of (on) Ways and Means** →committee 2.

committee, ad hoc ~ Ad-hoc-Ausschuß; **advisory ~** beratender Ausschuß; **budget(ary) ~** Haushaltsausschuß; **consultative ~** beratender Ausschuß; **coordinating ~** Koordinierungsausschuß; **economic ~** Wirtschaftsausschuß; **editorial ~** Redaktionsausschuß; **election** (or **electoral**) **~** Wahlausschuß; **financial ~** Finanzausschuß; **government(al) ~** Regierungsausschuß; **→grievance ~**; **interim ~** Interimsausschuß; **legal ~** Rechtsausschuß; **managing ~** geschäftsführender Ausschuß; Verwaltungsausschuß; Vorstand; **mediation ~** Vermittlungsausschuß, Schlichtungsausschuß; **mixed ~** gemischter Ausschuß; **negotiating ~** Verhandlungsausschuß; **on the ~** im Ausschuß; **permanent ~** ständiger Ausschuß; **planning ~** Planungsausschuß; **preparatory ~** vorbereitender Ausschuß; **procedural ~** Verfahrensausschuß; **provisional ~** für vorübergehende Angelegenheit ernanntes Komitee; Ad-hoc-Ausschuß; **specialized ~** Fachausschuß; **standing ~** ständiger Ausschuß; **steering ~** Lenkungsausschuß; **sub-~**

Unterausschuß; **subsidiary** ~ Nebenausschuß, nachgeordneter Ausschuß; **technical** ~ Fachausschuß; **working** ~ Arbeitsausschuß

committee, to appoint a ~ e-n Ausschuß einsetzen; **to be on the** ~ dem Ausschuß angehören; Mitglied des Ausschusses sein; **to establish** (or **form**) **a** ~ s. to set up a →~; **to refer to a** ~ e-m Ausschuß überweisen; **to set up a** ~ e-n Ausschuß bilden; e-n Ausschuß einsetzen; **to sit on the** ~ s. to be on the →~; **the** ~ **is sitting** (or **in session**) der Ausschuß hält e-e Sitzung ab (od. tagt)

Committee 2. *parl* Ausschuß; ~ **on Foreign Relations** *Am* Ausschuß für auswärtige Angelegenheiten; ~ **of Privileges** *Br* Ausschuß, der Privilegienbrüche untersucht

committee stage, the bill is in the ~ der Gesetzesentwurf liegt dem Ausschuß vor

Committee, ~ **of Supply** *Br* Haushaltsausschuß; ~ **of Ways and Means** *Br* Bewilligungsausschuß *(des Unterhauses);* ~ **on Ways and Means** *Am* Ausschuß *(des Repräsentantenhauses)* für Haushaltsfragen; ~ **of the Whole House** *Br* Ausschuß des ganzen House of Commons; Plenarausschuß *(das als Ausschuß tagende Plenum);* **General**~ *(V.N.)* Präsidialausschuß; →**joint** ~; →**Parliamentary** ~; →**Select** ~; **Standing** ~ Ständiger Ausschuß; **to go into** ~ in Einzelberatungen eintreten; in (Fach-)Ausschüssen beraten; **the** ~ **is sitting** (or **in session**) der Ausschuß hält e-e Sitzung ab (od. tagt); **the House resolves itself into a** ~ *Br* das (Unter-)Haus verwandelt sich in einen Ausschuß; das Parlament tagt als (ein) Ausschuß

commodities Waren; Güter; Rohstoffe, Grundstoffe, Grunderzeugnisse; ~ **broker** *(Warenbörse)* Kursmakler; ~ **for export** Exportwaren; ~ **offered as security** als Sicherheit angebotene Waren

commodities, agricultural ~ landwirtschaftliche Grundstoffe; **basic** ~ Grundstoffe, Rohstoffe; **essential** ~ lebenswichtige Güter; **exchange of** ~ Güteraustausch; **import** ~ Einfuhrwaren; **inland** ~ einheimische Waren; **(primary)** ~ Rohstoffe, Grundstoffe; **staple** ~ Stapelwaren; Haupthandelsartikel *(e-s Landes)*

commodity Ware(n), (Handels-)Artikel, Gebrauchsgegenstand; Rohstoff, Grundstoff; ~ **agreement** Rohstoffabkommen, Grundstoffabkommen, Abkommen über Grunderzeugnisse; Warenabkommen; **C~ Classification for Foreign Trade Statistics** Warenverzeichnis für die Außenhandelsstatistik; ~ **credit** Warenkredit; **C~ Credit Corporation** (CCC) *Am* Gesellschaft für Stützung der Landwirtschaftspreise; ~**-dependent countries** rohstoffabhängige Länder; ~ **dividend** in Waren gezahlte Dividende; **C~ Exchange** (Comex) Warenbörse; **C~ Exchange Act** (CEA) *Am* Warenbörsengesetz; ~ **exports** Grundstoffausfuhren, Rohstoffexporte; ~ **forward dealings** (or **trading**) Warenterminhandel; ~ **futures** *(Börse)* Warentermingeschäft; ~ **index** Warenverzeichnis; **C~ Futures Exchange** Warenterminbörse; **C~ Futures Trading Commission** (CFTC) *Am* Aufsichtsbehörde für die US-Warenterminbörsen; ~ **group** Warensorte; ~ **market** Warenmarkt; Warenbörse; Rohstoffmarkt; ~ **marketing** Warenabsatz; ~ **papers** Warenpapiere *(Verschiffungsdokumente im Überseegeschäft);* ~ **prices** Rohstoffpreise; Grundstoffpreise; Warenpreise; Preise an der Warenbörse; ~ **rate** *Am* Einzel(fracht)-tarif *(opp. class rate);* Vorzugstarif *(im Luftfrachtverkehr bei namentlich aufgeführten Warengattungen);* ~ **sales** Warenverkauf; ~ **trade** Warenhandel; ~ **value** Warenwert; Sachwert

commodit|y, Common Fund for C~ies[49a] Gemeinsamer Fonds für Rohstoffe; **export** ~ Exportware; **import** ~ Importware; **intergovernmental** ~ **agreement** zwischenstaatliches Grundstoffabkommen; →**International C~ Agreement or Arrangement;** →**International C~ Body;** →**International C~ Organization**

commodity, international ~ **trade** internationaler Rohstoffhandel; **Commission for International C~ Trade** *(1954 vom Wirtschafts- und Sozialrat der V.N. gegründete)* Kommission für Internationalen Rohstoffhandel

common 1., ~ **(land)** Gemeindeland, Gemeindewiese; ~**(s)** *Am (öffentl.)* Park; **(right of)** ~ gemeinschaftliches Nutzungsrecht (→*of estovers,* →*of fishery,* →*of pasture,* →*of turbary*); ~ **of estovers** Holzgerechtigkeit; Recht, Holz zu entnehmen; ~ **of fishery** (or **piscary**) Fischereigerechtigkeit; Fischereiberechtigung *(in den Gewässern e-s anderen zusammen mit dem Eigentümer od. anderen Berechtigten; cf. common →fishery.);* ~ **of pasture** Weidegerechtigkeit, Weiderecht; ~ **of turbary** Torfgerechtigkeit; Recht, Torf abzustechen

common 2. gemeinschaftlich, gemeinsam, allgemein; **C~ Agricultural Policy** (CAP) *(EG)* gemeinsame Agrarpolitik; ~ **assurances** *Br* Beweisurkunde über e-e Grundstücksübereignung; ~ **business oriented language** (COBOL) Programmiersprache; ~ **carrier** → carrier; **C~ Council** *Am* Stadtrat, Gemeinderat; *Br* Rat der City of London; ~ **councilman** *Br* Mitglied des Rates der City of London; *Am* Mitglied des Stadtrates; **C~ Customs Tariff** *(EG)* Gemeinsamer Zolltarif (→*CCT*); ~ **debtor** *Scot* Gemeinschuldner; ~ **end** gemeinsames Ziel; **C~ Fisheries Policy** *(EG)* Gemeinsame Fischereipolitik; ~ **fishery** → fishery; ~ **fund** gemeinsamer Fonds, gemeinsame Kasse; ~ **fund costs** *Br* Prozeßkosten *(die höher sind als die → party and party costs);* **for the** ~

good im öffentlichen Interesse; ~ **ground** Gemeindeland; gemeinsame Basis; ~ **household** häusliche Gemeinschaft; Wohngemeinschaft; ~ →**informer;** ~ **interest** →interest 1.; **it is** ~ **knowledge** es ist allgemein bekannt

Common Law 1. *(ursprünglich auf Gewohnheitsrecht beruhendes)* durch richterliche Entscheidungen weiterentwickeltes *(ungeschriebenes)* Recht *(opp. statute law; cf. case law, law reports, precedents, stare decisis, ratio decidendi);* 2. das gesamte anglo-amerikanische Rechtssystem *(opp. Civil Law);* 3. das in den früheren Gerichten in England angewandte strengere Recht *(opp. equity);* 4. Rechtsregeln der allgemeinen Gerichte *(opp. special courts)*
Das Common Law erstreckt sich nicht über alle Rechtsgebiete, es befaßt sich hauptsächlich mit Sachenrecht, Erbrecht und Obligationsrecht, d. h. contracts, torts and quasi-contracts. Auch das Internationale Privatrecht ist – mit wenigen Ausnahmen – Common Law. *Am* Das Common Law ist kein einheitliches Bundesgesetz. Jeder Staat hat sein eigenes Common Law

common law, ~ **marriage** *Am (die durch einfachen Konsens der Brautleute ohne behördl. Mitwirkung geschlossene)* Ehe, Konsensehe *(in 15 Staaten anerkannt; opp. ceremonial marriage);* **C~ L~ states** Staaten, die dem anglo-amerikanischen Rechtskreis angehören; ~ **wife** in nichtehelicher Lebensgemeinschaft lebende Frau

Common Market Gemeinsamer Markt *(der Mitgliedstaaten der EG) (→ European Communities);* ~ **country** Mitgliedsland des Gemeinsamen Marktes; **entry into the** ~ Beitritt zum Gemeinsamen Markt; **internal** ~ gemeinsamer Binnenmarkt; **to join the** ~ dem Gemeinsamen Markt beitreten

common, ~ **memorandum** →memorandum; ~ **mistake** allgemein verbreiteter Irrtum; gemeinsamer Irrtum *(beider Vertragsparteien);* ~ **nuisance** öffentliches Ärgernis; Störung der Allgemeinheit; ~ **organization of the market** *(EG)* gemeinsame Marktordnung; **Book of C~ Prayer** *Br* anglikanische Liturgie, Gebetbuch der Anglikanischen Kirche; ~ **price** üblicher Preis; ~ **property** gemeinschaftliches Eigentum (od. Vermögen); Allgemeingut; ~ **purse** gemeinsame Kasse; ~ **repute** Ruf, Renommee; ~ **rule** gemeinsame Regel, Richtlinie; **the** ~ **run** das Gewöhnliche; Durchschnitt(sklasse); ~ **seal** übliches Siegel; ~ **shares** (or **stocks**) *Am* Stammaktien; ~ **stockholder** *Am* Stammaktionär; ~ **usage** weit verbreiteter Gebrauch; **in** ~ **use** in allgemeinem Gebrauch; ~ **wall** gemeinsame Mauer

common, in ~ 1. gemeinschaftlich, in ungeteilter Gemeinschaft; 2. nach Bruchteilen *(jeder kann über seinen Teil verfügen);* **tenancy in** ~ Miteigentum *(an Grundbesitz) (Bruchteilseigentum);* **tenants in** ~ Miteigentümer *(an Grundbesitz) (nach Bruchteilen)*

commonable, ~ **cattle** Vieh, das auf Gemeindeland weiden darf; ~ **land** Land, das dem (right of) →common unterliegt

commoner *Br* Bürgerlicher (Nichtadliger); **C~** Mitglied des Unterhauses; **the First C~** → Speaker

Commons, the ~ *Br* das Unterhaus *(opp. the Lords)*

Commonwealth *Br* Commonwealth *(bis 1947 British C~ of Nations) (Zusammenschluß der die Krone anerkennenden 49 Mitgliedsländer ohne eigene Völkerrechtssubjektivität); Am* (Einzel-)Staat *(z.B. Massachusetts, Pennsylvania, Virginia, Kentucky)*

Commonwealth citizen[50] Staatsangehöriger des Commonwealth *(hat die gleiche Bedeutung wie British subject)*

Commonwealth citizenship Commonwealth-Staatsangehörigkeit *(Staatsangehörigkeit des → British subject)*
Umfaßt alle Staatsangehörigen sämtlicher Commonwealth-Länder *(cf. patrials)*. Nur staatsrechtlicher Begriff, völkerrechtlich irrelevant

Commonwealth Conference Commonwealth-Konferenz
Jahreskonferenz der Ministerpräsidenten des Vereinigten Königreichs und der Commonwealth-Länder

Commonwealth, ~ **Country** *Br* Commonwealth-Land; ~**-Day** *Br* Commonwealth-Feiertag *(24. Mai, Geburtstag der Queen Victoria)*

commorientes Kommorienten *(Personen, die durch den gleichen Unfall sterben)*

commotion, civil ~**(s)** (C.C.) innere Unruhen

communal Gemeinde-, Kommunal-; Gemeinschafts- *(in gemeinsamer Benutzung)*

communalization Kommunalisierung

communalize *v* kommunalisieren, in Gemeindeeigentum überführen

Communauté *Fr* Französische Gemeinschaft (French Community)
Durch die neue Verfassung der V. Republik vom 4. 10. 1958 geschaffene Nachfolgeorganisation der Französischen Union (Zusammenschluß der Französischen Republik und ihrer ehemaligen Kolonien in Afrika)

communicate *v* übermitteln; **to** ~ **with sb.** sich mit jdm in Verbindung setzen, mit jdm in Verbindung stehen; sich an jdn wenden; **to** ~ **sth. to sb.** jdm etw. mitteilen; jdn von etw. benachrichtigen; **to** ~ **a disease** e-e Krankheit übertragen

communicating, right of ~ **broadcasts** *(UrhR)* Recht der Wiedergabe von Funksendungen; **right of** ~ **the work by means of sound or visual records** *(UrhR)* Recht der Wiedergabe durch Bild- oder Tonträger

communicatee *Am* Verbindungsmann

communication Kommunikation; Mitteilung (to an); Nachricht; Nachrichtenverbindung; Verkehr (between zwischen); Verkehrswege, Verkehrsverbindung; *(UrhR)* (öffentl.) Wiedergabe *(e-r Funk- od. Fernsehsendung)*; **~s** Verkehr(swege); Nachrichtenverkehr; Fernmeldewesen; *mil* Nachschublinien; **~ with the enemy** Verkehr mit dem Feinde; **~ facilities** Fernmeldeanlagen; Fernmeldeeinrichtungen; **~ of information** Nachrichtenübermittlung; **~ lines** Verkehrsverbindungen; **~ by rail** Eisenbahnverbindung; **~s satellite** Fernmeldesatellit, Nachrichtensatellit

communication, rail, sea, air, telegraphic, radio and other means of ~ Eisenbahn-, See-, Luft-, Draht-, Funk- und sonstige Verbindungen; **channel of ~** Nachrichtenweg; Fernmeldekanal; **confidential ~s** vertrauliche Mitteilungen; **Federal C~s Commission** →federal; **lines of ~** Verkehrsverbindungen; *mil* Etappe; **means of ~** Nachrichtenmittel; Verkehrsmittel; **official ~** offizielle Mitteilung; **official ~s** amtlicher Nachrichtenverkehr; **postal ~** Postverbindung; Postverkehr; **press ~s** Pressenachrichten; **privileged ~** →privileged; **public ~** *(UrhR)* öffentliche Wiedergabe; **repeated ~** *(UrhR)* wiederholbare Wiedergabe; **telephone ~** Telefonverbindung

communication, to be in ~ with sb. mit jdm in Verbindung stehen; **to break off all ~s** jeglichen Verkehr abbrechen; **to get into ~ with sb.** sich mit jdm in Verbindung setzen; mit jdm Verbindung aufnehmen

communiqué *pol* Kommuniqué; (regierungs-)amtliche Verlautbarung; Pressemitteilung; **final ~** Schlußkommuniqué; **to issue a ~** ein Kommuniqué herausgeben

Communism Kommunismus

Communist Kommunist; kommunistisch; **~ Party** Kommunistische Partei; **~ penetration** kommunistische Durchdringung (od. Infiltrierung, Unterwanderung)

community 1. Gemeinschaft, Gemeinwesen; Gemeinde; **the ~** die Allgemeinheit, die Öffentlichkeit; **the Anglo-Jewish C~** die englischen Juden; **~ by undivided shares** Gemeinschaft nach Bruchteilen; **~ charge** *Br*[50a] Gemeindesteuer, Kommunalsteuer; **~ chest** *Am* Wohltätigkeitsfonds *(aus privaten Zuwendungen)*; **~ council** *Am* Gemeinderat; **~ of goods** Gütergemeinschaft; **~ of heirs** Erbengemeinschaft; **~ of interest** Interessengemeinschaft; **~ of property** (between spouses) eheliche Gütergemeinschaft; **~ of property in joint ownership** Gemeinschaft zur gesamten Hand; **~ service** gemeinnützige Arbeit *(anstelle von Strafe)*; **~ service order** *Br* Anordnung, nach der ein Täter (offender) anstelle e-r Freiheitsstrafe im Dienst der Allgemeinheit *(z.B. für alte Menschen)* für bestimmte Stunden unbezahlte Arbeit verrichten muß; **~ trust** *Am* städtische Treuhandgesellschaft zur Verwaltung von öffentlichen Stiftungen

communit|y, European C~ies → community 3.; **the industrial ~** die Industrie(fachleute); **the scientific ~** die Wissenschaftler; **scientific ~ies** wissenschaftliche Gremien; **working ~** Arbeitsgemeinschaft

community 2., **~ property** *Am (EheR)* Gütergemeinschaft, *(meist)* Errungenschaftsgemeinschaft; *Am* Gesamtgut *(alles während bestehender Ehe erworbenes Vermögen, das nicht e-m Ehegatten geschenkt od. von ihm geerbt worden ist, bes. das Arbeitseinkommen)*; **~ property states** *Am*[51] community property-Staaten *(in denen die Gütergemeinschaft und nicht Gütertrennung als gesetzlicher Güterstand gilt; opp. common law states)*
Durch die Married Women's Acts bildet die Gütertrennung in den USA den gesetzlichen Güterstand mit Ausnahme der 8 community property-Staaten,[51] in denen das System der Errungenschaftsgemeinschaft besteht. Die Regelung ist staatenweise verschieden. Es gibt 3 Vermögensmassen: 1. das community property (Gesamtgut) (das, was der Mann od. die Frau während Bestehens der Ehe erwirbt); 2. und 3. the husband's separate property und the wife's separate property (Sondergut [entspricht etwa dem eingebrachten Gut der deutschen Errungenschaftsgemeinschaft]: das voreheliche Vermögen und Erwerb durch Schenkung [by gift] oder Erbschaft [by bequest or devise] während der Ehe). Im allgemeinen wird das community property während des Bestehens der Ehe vom Manne verwaltet, nach Auflösung der Ehe zur Hälfte geteilt. Über the wife's separate property hat die Ehefrau allein freie Verfügungsgewalt

Communit|y 3. *(EuropaR)* Gemeinschaft *(Europäische Wirtschaftsgemeinschaft [EWG])*; Europäische Gemeinschaft(en) *[EG])*; Gemeinschafts- *(opp. national)*; **~ budget** Gemeinschaftshaushalt; **~ citizen** Gemeinschaftsbürger; **~ customs territory** Zollgebiet der Gemeinschaft; **~ funds** Gemeinschaftsmittel; **~ institutions** Gemeinschaftsorgane, Organe der (drei) Europäischen Gemeinschaften *(→Commission, →Council, → European Parliament, →Court of Justice)*

Community law Gemeinschaftsrecht *(Recht der drei Europäischen Gemeinschaften; opp. national law)*; **derogations from ~** Abweichungen vom Gemeinschaftsrecht; **incompatible with ~** mit dem Gemeinschaftsrecht unvereinbar; **infringement of ~** Verstöße gegen das Gemeinschaftsrecht; **precedence of ~** Vorrang des Gemeinschaftsrechts

Community legislation, precedence of ~ over national legislation Vorrang der gemeinschaftlichen gegenüber den einzelstaatlichen Rechtsvorschriften

Community, at ~ level auf Gemeinschaftsebene; ~ **loan** Gemeinschaftsanleihe; Gemeinschaftsdarlehen; ~ **of Twelfe** *(EG)* Zwölfergemeinschaft; ~ **policy** Gemeinschaftspolitik; ~ **quota** Gemeinschaftskontingent; ~ **tariff quota** Gemeinschaftszollkontingent; ~ **trade mark** *(geplante)* Gemeinschaftsmarke; ~ **transit (procedure)** *(EG)* gemeinschaftliches Versandverfahren; ~ **waters** Gemeinschaftsgewässer

Community, membership of the ~ EG[52]-Mitgliedschaft; EWG[53]-Mitgliedschaft

commutable umwandelbar; *(durch Geld)* ablösbar

commutation Austausch; Umwandlung; Ablösung *(durch Geld);* ~ **of an annuity** Ablösung e-r Rente; ~ **debt** Ablösungsschuld; ~ **fare** *Am* Abonnementsfahrpreis; ~ **payment** Abfindung(szahlung); einmalige Zahlung; ~ **of a penalty** (or **sentence**) Strafumwandlung *(bes. e-r Todesstrafe in Freiheitsstrafe);* Strafmilderung; ~ **ticket** *Am* Abonnementsfahrkarte, Zeitkarte

commutation, cost of ~ from home to place of business *Am* Kosten der Fahrten zwischen Wohnung und Arbeitsstätte; **entitlement to** ~ Ablösungsberechtigung; **loan ~ debt** Anleiheablösungsschuld; **party entitled to** ~ Ablösungsberechtigter; **right to** ~ Recht auf Ablösung

commute *v* austauschen; *(Lasten, Verpflichtungen)* umwandeln; *(durch Geld)* ablösen; *(durch Ablösung)* abfinden; mit Abonnementsfahrkarte hin- und herfahren; *Am* pendeln (im täglichen Berufsverkehr) *(→commuter);* **to ~ an annuity into** (or **for**) **a lump sum** e-e Rente durch e-e Kapitalabfindung ablösen; **to ~ the death sentence to life imprisonment** die Todesstrafe in e-e lebenslängliche Freiheitsstrafe umwandeln; **to ~ a sentence to a fine** Freiheitsstrafe in Geldstrafe umwandeln

commuting between home and place of work Fahrt zwischen Wohnung und Arbeitsstätte

commuter Inhaber e-r Abonnementsfahrkarte, Zeitkarteninhaber; Pendler *(mit Zeitkarte),* Vorortzugbenutzer *(mit Zeitkarte); Am* Pendler *(auch Autofahrer)* im täglichen Berufsverkehr; ~ **flows** Pendlerströme; ~ **traffic** Berufsverkehr; ~ **train** Vorortzug; **frontier** ~ Grenzgänger *(Arbeiter, Schüler)*

Comorian Komorer, Komorin; komorisch

Comoros, the ~ die Komoren

compact Vertrag, Pakt; Übereinkunft; kurz, bündig; **to enter into** (or **make**) **a** ~ e-e Übereinkunft schließen

companion Gesellschafter, Begleiter; Handbuch; *Br* Inhaber e-r Ordensklasse; **C~ of the Bath** (C.B.) *Br* Ritter des Bath-Ordens

Companies Act (C.A.) *Br* Gesetz über die Kapitalgesellschaften (enthält das Aktienrecht)

Die in den Companies Acts 1948–1981 und im Companies (Beneficial Interests) Act 1983 kodifizierten Vorschriften über companies in Großbritannien wurden im Companies Act 1985 zusammengefaßt. Die Konsolidierung umfaßt auch die einschlägigen Bestimmungen des European Communities Act 1972. Ergänzend findet das common law Anwendung

company (Co., Coy or Compy) Gesellschaft; *Br* Kapitalgesellschaft *(etwa Aktiengesellschaft od. Gesellschaft mit beschränkter Haftung);* Unternehmen; *Br* Gilde *(der Londoner City); mil* Kompanie; **a ~ and its affiliates** *Amt* e-e Gesellschaft und ihre Zweiggesellschaften

Br Handelsgesellschaft mit meist durch charter, besonderes Parlamentsgesetz oder Registrierung verliehener Rechtspersönlichkeit, bes. Kapitalgesellschaft (AG und GmbH) *(entsprechend der amerikanischen → corporation). Am* Alle juristischen Formen von Handelsgesellschaften *(sole proprietorship, partnership or corporation)*

company, ~ acquisition Unternehmenskauf; ~ **agreement** Gesellschaftsvertrag; ~ **branches** Zweigniederlassungen von Kapitalgesellschaften; ~ **concentration** Unternehmenszusammenschluß; ~ **debts** Gesellschaftsschulden; ~ **group** Unternehmensgruppe; ~ **law** Gesellschaftsrecht; *Br* Recht der Kapitalgesellschaften; Aktienrecht; ~ **history** Firmengeschichte; **at ~ level** auf Unternehmensebene

company limited by guarantee *Br* Gesellschaft mit beschränkter Nachschußpflicht

Die Gesellschafter haften nur bis zu Höhe einer im Falle der Liquidation übernommenen Garantiesumme. Die ~ kommt namentlich für Unternehmen in Betracht, die nicht auf Gewinnerzielung ausgerichtet sind, z. B. für karitative Vereine[54]

company limited by shares *Br* Kapitalgesellschaft *(entweder public company [limited by shares] = public [limited] company oder private company [limited by shares] = private [limited] company)*

company, ~ man Angestellter e-r Gesellschaft; ~ **meeting** *(AG)* Hauptversammlung; *(GmbH)* Gesellschafterversammlung; ~ **merger** Unternehmenszusammenschluß; ~ **name** Firmenname; ~ **objective** Unternehmensziel; ~ **pension scheme** betriebliche Altersversorgung; ~ **plant** Werksanlage; ~ **profit** Gesellschaftsgewinn; ~ **purchase and sale** Unternehmenskauf und -verkauf

Companies Registration Office *Br*[55] Gesellschaftsregister

Anschrift: Companies Registration Office, Companies House, Crown Way, Maindy, Cardiff CF4 3UZ (zuständig für England und Wales); Companies Registration Office for Scotland, 102 George Street, Edinburgh EH2 3DJ; Companies Registration Office, IDB House, 64 Chichester Street, Belfast BT1 (zuständig für Nordirland)

company residence *Br* Sitz e-r (Kapital-)Gesellschaft

Wenn →central management and control außerhalb des Vereinigten Königreichs ausgeübt werden, gelten britische Gesellschaften als nicht in Großbritannien ansässig

company, ~'s risk (C.R.) auf Gefahr der Gesellschaft; ~ **secretary** *Br* oberster Verwaltungsbeamter e-r company; ~ **securities** Unternehmenspapiere; ~ **seniority** (Dauer der) Betriebszugehörigkeit; ~ **store** Firmenladen; betriebseigenes Geschäft; ~ **town** *Am* Firmensiedlung; ~ **union** *Am* Betriebsgewerkschaft

company, →affilated ~; →associated ~; → chartered ~; →City C~; →close ~; →incorporated ~

company, joint stock ~ *Br* Aktiengesellschaft (AG); *Am* Handelsgesellschaft ohne eigene Rechtspersönlichkeit mit auf den Anteil beschränkbarer Haftung und frei veräußerlichen Anteilen (shares) am Grundkapital *(enthält Elemente der Kapitalgesellschaft [corporation] und der Personalgesellschaft (partnership))*

company, limited (liability) ~ *Br* Kapitalgesellschaft, Aktiengesellschaft *(company limited by shares oder company limited by guarantee; opp. unlimited company)*

company, one-man ~ Einmanngesellschaft; → **oversea(s) ~; parent ~** Muttergesellschaft, Obergesellschaft

company, private (limited) ~ (PrC) *Br (etwa)* Gesellschaft mit beschränkter Haftung (GmbH)

Die private company ist die Gesellschaft für mittlere und kleinere Unternehmen. Sie muß in ihre Firma den Zusatz "limited" aufnehmen

company, public (limited) ~ (plc) *Br*[56] Aktiengesellschaft (AG)

Die public company, deren Aktien im Ggs. zur private company öffentlich zur Zeichnung aufgelegt werden und die sehr strengen Formvorschriften unterworfen ist, ist die Gesellschaftsform des Großkapitals. Zur Gründung sind mindestens 2 Personen erforderlich. Sie muß ein Nominalkapital von mindestens £ 50.000 haben. Die Aktien einer public (limited) company sind – mit wenigen Ausnahmen – Namensaktien, und der Eigentümer ist im →Register of members eingetragen

company, registered ~ eingetragene Gesellschaft *(Br unlimited company, company limited by guarantee, company limited by shares)*

compan|y, related ~ies verbundene Gesellschaften; **ship's ~** Schiffsbesatzung; **shipping ~** Schiffahrtsgesellschaft; Reederei; **stock ~** *Am* Aktiengesellschaft, **subsidiary ~** Tochtergesellschaft; **→target ~; trading ~** Handelsgesellschaft; **trust ~** *Am* Treuhandgesellschaft, Treuhandbank *(→trust 1.)*

company, unlimited ~ *Br* Gesellschaft mit unbeschränkter Haftung

Sie ist eine Kapitlgesellschaft. Abgesehen von der unbeschränkten Haftung der Gesllschafter und der Befreiung von der Pflicht, einen Jahresabschluß zu veröffentlichen, gelten für sie alle Bestimmungen des Companies Act 1985, die für die private limited company gelten

company, to dissolve a ~ e-e Gesellschaft auflösen; **to form** (or **float, set up**) **a ~** e-e Gesellschaft gründen; **to register a ~** e-e Gesellschaft in das Register eintragen; **to wind up a ~** die Liquidation e-r Gesellschaft durchführen

comparable vergleichbar (with mit); ~ **period** Vergleichszeitraum

comparative vergleichend; relativ, verhältnismäßig; **~ly** vergleichsweise; ~ **advantage** vergleichender (wirtschaftlicher) Vorteil; ~ **balance sheet** Vergleichsbilanz; ~ **figure** Vergleichszahl; ~ **jurisprudence** vergleichende Rechtswissenschaft; ~ **law** Rechtsvergleichung; ~ **negligence** *Am* →negligence; ~ **price analysis** Preisgegenüberstellung; ~ **rectitude** *Am (EhescheidungsR)* Abwägen der beiderseitigen Schuld; **Society of C~ Legislation** Gesellschaft für Rechtsvergleichung

compare *v* vergleichen; vergleichend gegenüberstellen; *(Abschrift mit Urschrift)* kollationieren; **to ~ notes with** Feststellungen (od. Meinungen) austauschen mit

compared, as ~ with im Vergleich mit (od. zu)

comparison Vergleich, Nebeneinanderstellung; ~ **of handwritings** Schriftenvergleich; ~ **of texts** Textvergleich; **basis for ~** Vergleichsbasis; **in ~ with** in Vergleich mit (od. zu); **to draw** (or **make**) **a ~** e-n Vergleich ziehen

compassionate, ~ allowance *(aus menschl. Erwägungen und nicht auf gesetzl. Grundlage gewährtes)* Gnadengehalt; freiwillige Rente an Angehörige; ~ **leave** *mil* Sonderurlaub *(aus familiären Gründen)*

compatible vereinbar, im Einklang stehend (with mit); *pol* verträglich

compatriot Landsmann; **~s** Landsleute

compear *v Scot* vor Gericht erscheinen

compel *v (jdn)* zwingen; *(etw.)* erzwingen; **~ling reasons** zwingende Gründe

compellability of witness Erzwingbarkeit von Zeugenaussagen

compellable erzwingbar; **non-~ witness** zur Verweigerung der Aussage berechtigter Zeuge

compensable ausgleichbar, ersetzbar; ~ **injury** *Am (nach den Workmen's Compensation Acts)* zu Schadensersatz berechtigende (Betriebs-)Unfallverletzung

compensate *v* entschädigen, (Schadens-)Ersatz leisten (for für); ausgleichen, ersetzen; *(jdm etw.)* vergüten; *(jdn)* abfinden; *(Ansprüche etc)* aufrechnen; **to ~ sb. for a loss** jdn für e-n Verlust entschädigen; jdm für e-n Verlust Ersatz leisten; **to ~ oneself** sich schadlos halten; **differences which ~ each other** Verschiedenheiten, die sich gegenseitig aufheben

compensating entschädigend, Kompensations-; ausgleichend; Ausgleichs-; sich gegenseitig aufhebend

compensating financial facility e-e Fazilität des Internationalen Währungsfonds zur Bekämpfung der Zahlungsbilanzprobleme von Entwicklungsländern bei vorübergehenden Rohstoff-Preisstürzen

compensation Entschädigung(~sleistung) *(auch für enteigneten Grundbesitz; Br cf. compulsory purchase; Am cf. eminent domain);* Schadensersatz, Ersatzleistung; Vergütung; Ausgleich(-ung); Abfindung; Abstandsgeld; *Scot* Aufrechnung; *Am* Gehalt; *Am* (Betriebs-)Unfallentschädigung, Geldrente für durch Unfall erlittene Verletzung; **~ account** Ausgleichskonto; **~ for damage** Schadensersatz; **~ for unfair dismissal** *Br*[57] Abfindung bei ungerechtfertigter Entlassung; **~ for expropriation** Enteignungsentschädigung; **~ fund** Ausgleichsfonds; *Br (Börse)* Kompensationsfonds *(zum Schutz der Anleger);* **~ for improvements** Ersatz für werterhöhende Aufwendungen *(des Pächters bei Beendigung der Pacht);* **~ insurance** *Am* (Arbeiter-)-Unfallversicherung; **~ for loss of office** Abfindung bei Entlassung; **~ for pain and suffering** Schmerzensgeld; **~ payment** Entschädigungsleistung; Abfindungszahlung; **~ period** Entschädigungszeitraum; **~ transactions** Kompensationsgeschäfte; **~ for use** Nutzungsentschädigung

compensation, adequate ~ angemessene Entschädigung; **(amount of) ~** Entschädigungssumme; Abfindungsbetrag; **as** (or **by way of**) **~** als Entschädigung; als Abfindung; zum Ausgleich (for für); **claim for ~** Entschädigungsanspruch; (Schadens-)Ersatzanspruch; **determination of a ~** Festsetzung e-r Entschädigung; **fair** (or **reasonable**) **~** angemessene Entschädigung (od. Vergütung); **giving** (or **making**) **of ~** Leistung der Entschädigung; **money** (or **pecuniary**) **~** Entschädigung in Geld; **rate of ~** Entschädigungssatz; **workmen's ~** *Am* (Betriebs-)Unfallentschädigung

compensation, to assess (or **determine**) **(the) ~** die Entschädigung festsetzen; **to be entitled to ~** Anspruch auf Entschädigung haben; **to give** (or **make**) **~** Ersatz leisten, ersetzen; Schaden vergüten; abfinden; **to receive ~** Entschädigung erhalten; **to set the ~** *Am* das Gehalt festsetzen; **to settle the amount of ~** e-e Abfindung vereinbaren

compensative →compensatory

compensatory ausgleichend, Entschädigungs-; **~ adjustment** ausgleichende Regelung; **monetary ~ amount** *(EG)* Währungsausgleichsbetrag; **~ →damages; ~ measures** Ausgleichsmaßnahmen

compete *v* im Wettbewerb stehen, konkurrieren (with mit); sich mitbewerben (for um); **to ~ with** (or **against**) **a p.** jdm Konkurrenz machen; **to ~ with one another** sich gegenseitig Konkurrenz machen; miteinander konkurrieren; **to ~ for a prize** an e-m Preisausschreiben teilnehmen; **able to ~** konkurrenzfähig

competing konkurrierend; **not ~** außer Konkurrenz; **~ business** Konkurrenzgeschäft; **~ industry** Konkurrenzindustrie; **~ offer** Konkurrenzangebot; **to be ~ on the market** auf dem Markt miteinander in Wettbewerb stehen

competence *(sachl.)* Zuständigkeit, Kompetenz; Befugnis(se); Fähigkeit, Befähigung, Tauglichkeit; Geschäftsfähigkeit; Sachkunde, Autorität *(auf e-m Fachgebiet); (finanzielles)* Auskommen; **~ of a court** Zuständigkeit e-s Gerichts; **~ in a matter** sachliche Zuständigkeit; **~ of a witness** Fähigkeit, Zeuge zu sein

competence, certificate of (professional) ~ Befähigungsnachweis; **legal ~** Geschäftsfähigkeit; **person having legal ~** Geschäftsfähiger; **matters within the ~ of a p.** Angelegenheiten, für die jd zuständig ist; **technical ~** fachliches Können; **transfer of ~** Kompetenzübertragung

competence, to be within the ~ of a court zu der Zuständigkeit e-s Gerichts gehören; **to challenge the ~** die Zuständigkeit bestreiten; **to come within the ~ of a p.** unter jds Zuständigkeit fallen; **to exceed one's ~** s-e Befugnisse überschreiten; **to have ~** zuständig sein

competency →competence

competent kompetent, zuständig, befugt; fähig, befähigt, qualifiziert; sachkundig, sachverständig; *Am* geschäftsfähig; zurechnungsfähig; **~ authority** zuständige Behörde (od. Stelle); **~ court** (or **court of ~ jurisdiction**) zuständiges Gericht; **~ judge** zuständiger Richter; **~ as testator** testierfähig; **~ to contract** geschäftsfähig; zum Vertragsabschluß befugt; **~ to dispose by will** testierfähig; **~ to make decisions** beschlußfähig; **~ to give evidence** *(rechtl.)* fähig, Zeuge zu sein; **~ to stand trial** *Am* prozeßfähig; **~ as testator** testierfähig; **~ witness** *(rechtl.)* zulässiger Zeuge *(der nicht Beteiligter ist);* **to be ~** zuständig sein, Zuständigkeit haben; *Am* geschäftsfähig sein; **to declare oneself to be ~** sich für zuständig erklären

competition Wettbewerb (with sb. for sth. mit jdm um etw.); Konkurrenz; **~ in armaments** Wettrüsten; **~ condition** Wettbewerbsbedingung; **~ contest** Preisausschreiben

competition law Wettbewerbsrecht

Br Fair Trading Act 1973, Resale Prices Act 1976,

Restrictive Trade Practises Act 1976, Competition Act 1980

competition, ~ policy Wettbewerbspolitik; **~ position** Wettbewerbsposition; **~ rules** Wettbewerbsregeln; **~ in weapons** Rüstungswettlauf

competition, able to meet ~ konkurrenzfähig; **agreements restricting ~** wettbewerbsbeschränkende Absprachen; **clause restricting ~** Wettbewerbsklausel; **conditions of ~** Wettbewerbsverhältnisse, -bedingungen; **cut-throat ~** mörderischer Wettbewerb; Schmutzkonkurrenz; **fair ~** lauterer (od. redlicher) Wettbewerb; **free ~** freier Wettbewerb; **imperfect ~** unvollkommener Wettbewerb; **keen ~** scharfer Wettbewerb; scharfe Konkurrenz; **maintaining ~** Aufrechterhaltung des Wettbewerbs; **non ~ clause** Konkurrenzklausel *(Wettbewerbsausschluß)*; **open ~** freier Wettbewerb; **perfect ~** vollkommener Wettbewerb; **(prize) ~** Preisausschreiben; **prohibition of ~** Wettbewerbsverbot; **restraint** (or **restriction**) **of ~** Wettbewerbsschränkung; **rule against ~** *Br* Regel, nach der ein Gesellschafter, der zugleich Gläubiger ist, im Falle des Konkurses der Gesellschaft nicht neben den anderen Gläubigern Anspruch auf das Gesellschaftsvermögen (Konkursmasse) hat; **rules on ~** Wettbewerbsregeln; **severe ~** scharfe Konkurrenz, scharfer Wettbewerb

competition, unfair ~ unlauterer Wettbewerb; **unfair methods of ~** unlautere Wettbewerbsmethoden; **to engage in unfair ~** unlauteren Wettbewerb betreiben

Das englische Wettbewerbsrecht beruht auf dem Monopolies and Restrictive Trade Practices Act (1948), dem Restrictive Trade Practices Act (1956) und dem Fair Trading Act (1975). Bestimmte Formen des unlauteren Wettbewerbs werden als →tort angesehen (bes. passing off, injurious falsehood).

In den USA ist eine Möglichkeit der Bekämpfung des unlauteren Wettbewerbs durch den Lanham Act von 1946 und den Federal Trade Commission Act geschaffen. – Die torts, die wie in England unlautere Wettbewerbshandlungen erfassen, sind bes. passing off und disparagement, daneben auch Verstöße gegen die Antitrust-Gesetzgebung

competition, unreasonable ~ unvernünftige Konkurrenz; **without ~** konkurrenzlos; **workable ~** *Am* funktionsfähiger Wettbewerb; wirksame Konkurrenz

competition, to advertise a ~ e-n Wettbewerb ausschreiben; **to be in ~ with sb.** mit jdm in Konkurrenz stehen; **to beat the ~** die Konkurrenz schlagen; **to eliminate the ~** die Konkurrenz ausschalten; **to enter into ~ with sb.** mit jdm in Konkurrenz treten; anfangen, jdm Konkurrenz zu machen; **to be exposed to severe ~** scharfer Konkurrenz ausgesetzt sein; **to lessen ~** den Wettbewerb mindern; **to meet ~** es mit e-r Konkurrenz zu tun haben; der Konkurrenz standhalten; **to restrain ~** den Wettbewerb beschränken; **to take part in a ~** sich an e-m Wettbewerb beteiligen; **to win a ~** ein Preisausschreiben gewinnen

competitive wettbewerbsfähig; konkurrenzfähig; auf Wettbewerb eingestellt; im Wettbewerb stehend; **~ advantage** wettbewerblicher Vorteil; **~ article** Konkurrenzartikel; **on a ~ basis** auf Wettbewerbsgrundlage; **~ bid** *Br (im sog. Tenderverfahren, →tender 2.)* Mitabgabe von Geboten *(durch Banken und Makler)*; **~ capacity** Wettbewerbsfähigkeit; Konkurrenzfähigkeit; **~ copy** aggressiver *(den Konkurrenten angreifender)* Werbetext; **~ economy** Wettbewerbswirtschaft; **~ (entrance) examination** Ausleseprüfung; schriftl. Eignungsprüfung im Wettbewerb mit anderen *(bes. für [Berufs-]Beamte zwecks Aufnahme in den Staatsdienst; Am opp. spoils system)*; **C~ Equality Banking Act** (of 1987) *Am* Gesetz zur wettbewerblichen Gleichstellung von Banken; **~ firm** Konkurrenzfirma; **~ inequality** Wettbewerbsungleichheit; **non- ~ clause** Konkurrenzklausel; **~ performance** Wettbewerbsleistung; **~ position** Wettbewerbslage; **~ policy** Wettbewerbspolitik; **unfair ~ practices** unlauterer Wettbewerb; **~ price** Konkurrenzpreis; konkurrenzfähiger (od. wettbewerbsfähiger) Preis; **~ strength** Wettbewerbsfähigkeit; **~ tendering** *(bei Ausschreibungen)* Mitabgabe von Angeboten

competitive, to become ~ konkurrenzfähig werden

competitiveness Konkurrenzfähigkeit; Wettbewerbsfähigkeit; **to increase ~** die Wettbewerbsfähigkeit erhöhen

competitor Konkurrent; Wettbewerber; Mitbewerber; Konkurrenzfirma; **~ firm** Konkurrenzfirma; **without ~s** konkurrenzlos; **the firm has big ~s** die Firma hat starke Konkurrenz; **to beat a ~** e-n Konkurrenten schlagen; **to undercut a ~ in trade** e-n Konkurrenten im Handel unterbieten

compilation Kompilation, Zusammenstellung; Sammlung *(z.B. von gesetzl. Vorschriften)*; Sammelwerk

compile *v* sammeln, zusammenstellen (from aus); **to ~ a dictionary** ein Wörterbuch zusammenstellen; **to ~ a list** e-e Liste aufstellen

complain *v* sich beschweren, Beschwerde führen (about, of über; to bei); *com* beanstanden, reklamieren

complainant Kläger(in); Beschwerdeführer(in); *Am* Erstatter e-r Strafanzeige *(in Verkehrssachen)*

complainer *Scot* →complainant

complaint Beschwerde(schrift); *(Zivilprozeß)*

Klageschrift *(Br im Verfahren vor dem →justice of the peace); Am (Strafprozeß)* Anklageschrift; *Am* Klageerhebung *(des Staates bei der Antitrustabteilung); com* Reklamation, Beanstandung; Mängelrüge; *(VersR)* Schadensanzeige; *(VölkerR)* Beschwerde; ~**s, if any** eventuelle Beschwerden; ~**cases** *Am* formlose Erledigung von Fällen unlauteren Wettbewerbs durch die →FTC ohne hearing *(beginnend mit e-r complaint);* ~ **of defects** Mängelrüge; ~**s panel** Beschwerdeausschuß; ~**s procedure** Beschwerdeverfahren; ~ **regarding the quality** Qualitätsrüge; ~ **regarding the quantity** Mängelrüge wegen Mengenfehler

complaint, amendment of the ~ Klageänderung; **answer to a** ~ *Am* Klagebeantwortung; **cause** (or **ground**) **of** ~ Klagegrund; Beschwerdegrund; **country making a** ~ beschwerdeführendes Land; →**criminal** ~; **on** ~ **by** auf die Beschwerde von; **person making a** ~ Beschwerdeführer; **third party** ~ *Am* Streitverkündung

complaint, to adjust a ~ e-r Beschwerde abhelfen; **to consider** ~**s** Mängelrügen berücksichtigen; **to file a** ~ **with** e-e Klage einreichen bei (for wegen); **to file a** ~ **with the Commission** *(EG)* eine Beschwerde an die Kommission richten; **to lodge** (or **make) a** ~ Beschwerde einlegen (od. führen) (with bei); sich beschweren (about, of über); beanstanden; e-e Mängelrüge erheben; *Am* Anzeige erstatten; Klage(-schrift) einreichen; **there is a general** ~ es wird allgemein darüber geklagt

complementary Komplementär-; ergänzend; ~ **agreement** Ergänzungsabkommen; ~ **goods** Komplementärgüter; ~ **rules** Ergänzungsvorschriften

complete vollständig, komplett; lückenlos; ~ **knowledge** umfassende Kenntnis(se); ~ **patent** endgültiges Patent *(opp. provisional patent);* ~ **specification** *(PatR)* endgültige Beschreibung *(opp. provisional specification);* **a** ~ **chain of evidence** e-e lückenlose Beweiskette

complete *v* beenden, abschließen; vervollständigen, ergänzen, fertigstellen; erledigen; ausfüllen; **to** ~ **a contract** e-n Vertrag erfüllen; **to** ~ **a form** ein Formular ausfüllen; **to** ~ **one's sentence** seine Strafe verbüßen; **to** ~ **one's work** seine Arbeit beenden

completed, an offen|ce (~**se) is** ~ e-e Straftat ist vollendet

completion Beendigung, Abschluß; Ablauf; Vervollständigung, Fertigstellung; Ergänzung; Erledigung; Ausfüllung *(e-s Formulars);* ~ **(of sale)** *Br* Erfüllung des Grundstückskaufvertrages durch Zahlung des Kaufpreises und Übergabe der Übertragungs- und Eigentumsurkunde; ~ **of attempt** *(StrafR)* Vollendung des Versuchs; **after** ~ **of the business year** nach Ablauf des Geschäftsjahres; ~ **of the contract** Erfüllung des Vertrages; ~ **date** Datum der Fertigstellung e-s Auftrags; *Br* Datum der Erfüllung des Kaufvertrages; ~ **of the internal market** *(EG)* Vollendung des Binnenmarktes *(planned for 1992);* ~ **of sentence** Beendigung der Strafverbüßung (od. Strafzeit); Strafende; ~ **of service** Ablauf der Dienstzeit; **(up)on** ~ **of** nach Vollendung (od. Ablauf) von; **to bring to** ~ zum Abschluß bringen

compliance (with) Einhaltung, Befolgung, Erfüllung; Einwilligung; ~ **with a condition** Erfüllung e-r Bedingung; ~ **with a law** Beachtung e-s Gesetzes; ~ **with the terms** Einhaltung der Bedingungen

compliance, →certificate of ~**; declaration of** ~ *Br* Erklärung, daß die Gründungsvorschriften beachtet worden sind; **defective** ~ mangelhafte Erfüllung; **in** ~ **with** gemäß; in Befolgung von; entsprechend; **in case of non-**~ bei Nichteinhaltung (od. Nichtbefolgung); **to act in** ~ **with** weisungsgemäß handeln

complicated verwirklicht *(z.B. Vorschriften)*

complication Komplikation; **if no** ~**s arise** wenn keine Komplikationen eintreten

complicity *(StrafR)* Mittäterschaft (in bei); Tatbeteiligung

compliment Kompliment; ~**s** Empfehlungen, Grüße; ~**s slip** Kurzbrief, Kurzantwort, Übersendungszettel (mit Anlage); **with** ~**s of the author** mit Empfehlungen des Verfassers; **to present one's** ~**s to sb.** sich jdm empfehlen lassen

compliment *v* **to** ~ **sb.** jdm ein Kompliment machen; jdm gratulieren, jdn beglückwünschen (on zu)

complimentary, ~ **copy** *(vom Verfasser gewidmetes)* Freiexemplar; Werbenummer *(Zeitschrift);* ~ **ticket** Freikarte; Ehrenkarte

comply (with) *v* entsprechen, nachkommen; einhalten, befolgen; **to** ~ **with the conditions** die Bedingungen erfüllen; **to** ~ **with instructions** sich an die Weisungen halten; **to** ~ **with obligations** Verpflichtungen einhalten; **to** ~ **with regulations** Vorschriften befolgen; **to** ~ **with a request** e-m Gesuch stattgeben; **to** ~ **with a summons** e-r Ladung Folge leisten; **to** ~ **with a time limit** e-e Frist einhalten

comply *v***, failure to** ~ **(with)** Nichteinhaltung, Nichtbefolgung, Nichterfüllung

complying with your desire wunschgemäß

component *(wesentl.)* Bestandteil; Bauteil; ~ **parts** Einzelteile

compos mentis geistig gesund; zurechnungsfähig; **non** ~ unzurechungsfähig; **person non** ~ Unzurechnungsfähiger

compose *v* zusammensetzen; *(Streit)* beilegen, schlichten; *(Schriftstück)* abfassen; *(Gesuch etc)* aufsetzen; komponieren; **to ~ differences** Differenzen beheben, Streitigkeiten beilegen

composed, to be ~ of sich zusammensetzen aus

composer of musical works Urheber von Werken der Tonkunst

composite zusammengesetzt, gemischt (of aus); **~ depreciation** Gruppenabschreibung, Pauschalabschreibung; **~ entry** Sammelbuchung; **~ insurance company** (or **office**) *Am* Universalversicherer; **~ rate** *Br (SteuerR)* Pauschsatz *(für Zinsen aus Bausparkasseneinzahlungen);* **~ work** *(UrhR)* Sammelwerk; **~ works** verbundene Werke

composition Zusammensetzung; Vergleich *(zwischen Schuldner und mehreren Gläubigern, zur Abwendung des Konkurses; cf. accord);* Vergleichssumme, Pauschalsumme; Pauschalierung; Abfassung *(e-s Schriftstücks); (PatR)* Stoffgemisch; **~ in bankruptcy** Zwangsvergleich im Konkursverfahren; **~ of a court** Zusammensetzung e-s Gerichts; **~ deed** *(schriftl.)* Vergleichsvereinbarung *(→deed);* **~ by deed of arrangement** *Br (außergerichtl.)* Vergleich *(demzufolge der Schuldner sich gegenüber seinen Gläubigern verpflichtet, e-n Teil s-r Schulden zu tilgen);* **~ of a matter** *(PatR)* (chemische) Zusammensetzung; Stoffverbindung; **~ offered** Vergleichsvorschlag; **~ payment** Abfindungszahlung; Pauschalzahlung; **~ proceedings** Vergleichsverfahren; **~ for stamp duty** Stempelsteuerpauschalierung

composition, bankruptcy ~ →~ in bankruptcy; **by way of ~** durch Vergleich; vergleichsweise; **compulsory ~** Zwangsvergleich; **deed of ~** →~ deed; **proposal for a ~** Vergleichsvorschlag; **terms of ~** Vergleichsbedingungen

composition, to accept a ~ e-n Vergleich annehmen; **to make** (or **effect**) a ~ e-n Vergleich schließen; **to execute a ~** e-n Vergleich ausführen; **to institute a ~ with one's creditors** ein Vergleichsverfahren einleiten; **to reject a ~** e-n Vergleich ablehnen; **to set aside a ~** e-n Vergleich aufheben

compound Zusammensetzung; Mischung; chemische Verbindung; bebautes Grundstück *(z.B. e-e Anzahl von Häusern);* **(chemical) ~ patent** Stoffpatent

compound zusammengesetzt, Verbund-; **~ arbitration** Mehrfach-Arbitrage; **~ duty** Mischzoll; **~ interest** Zinseszinsen; Staffelzinsen; **~ larceny** *Am* schwerer Diebstahl; **~ settlement** *Br* e-e aus verschiedenen Urkunden bestehende Verfügung über Grundbesitz; **~ tariff** gemischter (od. kombinierter) Zolltarif *(→tariff 1.)*

compound *v* sich *(mit Gläubigern)* vergleichen; durch Vergleich erledigen, sich einigen; **to ~ with one's creditors** mit seinen Gläubigern e-n Vergleich schließen (od. sich vergleichen); **to ~ for a debt** Zahlung e-r Schuld vergleichsweise erledigen; **to ~ a felony** *Am* gegen Annahme von Geld von der Anzeige wegen e-r →felony absehen

compounding, ~ of claims vergleichsweise Forderungsbefriedigung; **~ of felony** *Am*[58] *(StrafR)* entgeltliche Vereinbarung, von Strafanzeige wegen begangener →felony abzusehen

comprehensive umfassend; **~ balance sheet** Gesamtbilanz; **~ (coverage)** *Am* Fahrzeugversicherung; *(etwa:)* Teilkasko; **~ description** umfassende Beschreibung; **~ education** *Br* Ausbildung in e-r Gesamtschule; **~ →household insurance; ~ motor car insurance** *Br* Kraftfahrzeug-Kaskoversicherung; **~ plus collision** *Am (Auto)* Haftpflicht- und Kaskoversicherung; **~ report** umfassender (od. eingehender) Bericht; **~ school** *Br* Gesamtschule *(für alle Kinder über 11 Jahre)*

compromise Kompromiß; *(bes. außergerichtl.)* Vergleich; **~ proposal** Vergleichsvorschlag; Kompromißvorschlag; **~ and settlement** Vergleich; **~ solution** Kompromißlösung

compromise, by way of ~ auf dem Vergleichswege, durch Vergleich; **conclusion of a ~** Vergleichsabschluß; **offer of** (or **proposal for**) **a ~** Vergleichsvorschlag; Kompromißvorschlag; **readiness to reach a ~** Kompromißbereitschaft; **to arrive at** (or **effect, make**) **a ~** zu e-m Vergleich (od. Kompromiß) kommen; e-n Vergleich (od. Kompromiß) schließen; sich vergleichen; **a ~ was made** ein Vergleich ist zustande gekommen; **to settle by ~** durch Vergleich erledigen, auf dem Vergleichswege beilegen

compromise *v* sich vergleichen; e-n Vergleich (od. Kompromiß) schließen; durch Vergleich (od. Kompromiß) erledigen; kompromittieren; *(Ruf, Stellung etc)* gefährden; **to ~ onself** (or **one's reputation**) sich kompromittieren; **willing to ~** kompromißbereit

comptroller staatlicher Rechnungsprüfer *(im Ggs. zum →auditor höherer Beamter); Br* höherer Verwaltungsbeamter *(bes. in Verbindung mit dem königl. Haushalt); Am (mit der Finanzverwaltung betrauter)* leitender Angestellter *(e-s Industrieunternehmens);* **C~ and Auditor-General** *Br* Präsident des Rechnungshofes *(oberster Beamter des →Exchequer and Audit Department)*

Comptroller of the Currency *Am* Kontrolleur der Umlaufmittel

Beamter beim Schatzamt, der die →National Banks überwacht und die →Federal Reserve Notes ausgibt

comptroller, C~ General *Am* Präsident des Rechnungshofes; *Br* Präsident des Patentamtes (*genau:* C~-General of Patents, Designs and Trade Marks)

compulsion Zwang; **under** (or **upon)** ~ unter Zwang, gezwungen

compulsorily zwangsweise; **he was ~ retired** er wurde zwangsweise pensioniert (od. in den Ruhestand versetzt)

compulsory zwingend, Zwangs-; obligatorisch, verbindlich *(opp. optional, voluntary)*; ~ **administration** Zwangsverwaltung; ~ **arbitral procedure** obligatorisches Schiedsgerichtsverfahren; ~ **attendance** Präsenzpflicht; ~ **attendance of witness** Zwangsvorführung von Zeugen; ~ **cartel** Zwangskartell; ~ **education** allgemeine Schulpflicht; ~ **evacuation** Zwangsräumung; ~ **expenditure** *(EG)* obligatorische Ausgaben (OA)

compulsory insurance Pflichtversicherung, Zwangsversicherung; ~ **against third party risks** Unfallhaftpflichtversicherung; **exempt from** ~ nicht versicherungspflichtig

compulsory, ~ joinder *Am* notwendige Streitgenossenschaft; ~ **levy** Zwangsabgabe; ~ **licen|ce (~se)** →licence (~se) 3.; ~ **liquidation** Zwangsliquidation; ~ **loan** Zwangsanleihe; ~ **measure** Zwangsmaßnahme; ~ **membership** Pflichtmitgliedschaft; Zwangsbeitritt, Beitrittszwang; ~ **military service** Militärdienstpflicht; allgemeine Wehrpflicht; ~ **pilotage** Lotsenzwang; ~ **purchase** *Br*[59] Enteignung *(von Grundbesitz; cf. compensation)*; ~ **retirement** Zwangspensionierung; ~ **sale** *Am* Zwangsverkauf, Zwangsversteigerung

compulsory school age Schulpflichtalter; **child of** ~ schulpflichtiges Kind

compulsory, ~ surrender *Scot* Enteignung; ~ **winding up** (of a company) →winding up by the court

computable berechenbar; zu berechnen(d)

computation Errechnung, Berechnung; Kalkulation, Überschlag, Schätzung; ~ **of cost** Kostenberechnung, Kostenanschlag; ~ **of exchange** Devisen(be)rechnung; ~ **of interest** Zinsberechnung; ~ **of taxable profit** *(SteuerR)* Gewinnermittlung; ~ **of time** Zeitberechnung, Fristberechnung

computation, basis of ~ Berechnungsgrundlage; **lowest** ~ äußerste (niedrigste) Berechnung; **period of** ~ Berechnungszeitraum; **at a rough** ~ bei vorläufiger Schätzung; **tax** ~ Selbstveranlagung des Steuerpflichtigen; **to make a ~ of sth.** etw. berechnen, etw. errechnen

compute *v* errechnen, berechnen, ausrechnen; kalkulieren, überschlagen, schätzen; **to ~ a period** (or **time-limit**) e-e Frist berechnen; **to ~ the profit** den Gewinn errechnen; **he ~d his losses at £ 100** er schätzte seine Verluste auf £ 100

computer Computer, Datenverarbeitungsanlage; **~-aided banking** computergestütztes Bankgeschäft; **~-aided design** (CAD) computergestütztes Konstruieren; **~-aided manufacturing** (CAM) computergestützte Überwachung und Steuerung der Fertigung; **~-aided planning** (CAP) computergestützte Arbeitsplanung; **~-aided quality assurance** (CAQ) computergestützte Qualitätssicherung; **~-assisted learning** (CAL) computergestützter Unterricht; **~-based** auf Computerbasis; ~ **breakdown** (or **outage**) Computerausfall; ~ **cent|re (~er)** Rechenzentrum; ~ **department** Datenverarbeitungsabteilung; ~ **forecast** (or **projection**) Hochrechnung; ~ **installation** Datenverarbeitungsanlage; **~-integrated manufacturing** (CIM) rechnergestützte (od. computerintegrierte) Fertigung; ~ **mail** elektronische Post; ~ **science** Informatik; ~ **screen** Computerbildschirm; **large scale ~ system** Großrechenanlage; ~ **trading** Verwendung von Computerprogrammen

computerize *v* computerisieren; mit Hilfe e-s Computers errechnen; auf Computer umstellen

con *v colloq.* betrügen

con (contra) gegen; **to weigh the pros and ~s** die Gründe für und wider abwägen

conceal *v* verbergen (from vor); verheimlichen, verschweigen; *(Bilanzen etc)* verschleiern; **to ~ sb.** jdm Unterschlupf gewähren, jdn verbergen; **to ~ evidence** Beweismaterial unterdrükken; **to ~ a fact** e-e Tatsache verheimlichen (od. unterdrücken); **to ~ an invention** e-e Erfindung verborgen halten; **to ~ property** Vermögenswerte verheimlichen *(z.B. im Konkursverfahren)*

concealed assets verheimlichte (od. verschleierte) Vermögenswerte *(z.B. im Konkursverfahren)*; *(Buchführung)* unsichtbare Aktiva *(z.B. goodwill)*

concealment Verbergen; Versteck; Verheimlichung, Verschweigen *(von Tatsachen)*; Verschleierung; ~ **of assets** *(KonkursR)* Verheimlichung von Vermögenswerten; ~ **of birth** *Br* Verschweigen der Geburt e-s *(vor, bei od. nach Geburt gestorbenen)* Kindes (Unterlassen der Geburtsanmeldung); ~ **of a criminal** Gewährung von Unterschlupf an e-n Verbrecher; ~ **of documents** Urkundenunterdrückung; ~ **of facts** Verschweigen (od. Unterdrücken) von Tatsachen; ~ **of pregnancy** *Scot* →~ of birth; ~ **of property** *(KonkursR)* Verbergen von Vermögensgegenständen; **fraudulent** ~ betrügerisches (od. arglistiges) Verschweigen; **material** ~ *(VersR)* Verschweigen e-s wesentlichen (od. rechtserheblichen) Umstandes; **place of** ~ Versteck

concede *v* einräumen, gewähren; zugestehen; *Am pol (in e-m Wahlkampf)* Niederlage zugeben; **to ~ a point** in e-m Punkt nachgeben; **to ~ a privilege** ein Vorrecht einräumen

concededly zugestandenermaßen

concentrate *v (sich)* konzentrieren; **to ~ troops** Truppen zusammenziehen

concentration Konzentration; Zusammenballung, Anhäufung; Ballung; (Unternehmens-) Zusammenschluß; **~ camp** Konzentrationslager; **~ of capital** Kapitalkonzentration; **~ of economic power** Konzentration wirtschaftlicher Macht *(Unternehmenszusammenschlüsse);* **~ of vehicles** Ansammlung von Fahrzeugen

concept Begriff, Grundgedanke; **~ of English law** Begriff des englischen Rechts; **~ of invention** Begriff der Erfindung

conception 1. Vorstellung, Auffassung (of von); gedankliche Erfassung; **inventive ~** Erfindungsgedanke; **legal ~** Rechtsauffassung

conception 2. Empfängnis *(e-s Kindes);* **(statutory) period of ~** *(gesetzliche)* Empfängniszeit

conceptual difference *(PatR)* verschiedene Erfindungsgedanken

concern 1. Angelegenheit, Sache; Sorge, Besorgnis (at, about, for wegen); Wichtigkeit, Belang; Interesse, Anteil; **matters of common ~** gemeinsame Belange; **matter of domestic ~** innerstaatliche Angelegenheit; **matter of official ~** Dienstsache; **of the utmost ~** *(Sache)* von äußerster Wichtigkeit; **private ~** Privatangelegenheit; **questions of common ~** Fragen von allgemeinem Interesse; **to be a matter of ~** Anlaß zur Beunruhigung geben; **it is a matter of minor ~ to us** es ist unwichtig für uns; **to have no ~ with** nichts zu tun haben mit

concern 2. Unternehmen, Betrieb, Firma; **big ~** großes Unternehmen, Großbetrieb; **business ~** Handelsunternehmen, Geschäftsbetrieb; **→going ~; industrial ~** Industrieunternehmen, Wirtschaftsunternehmen; **large ~** s. big **→~; medium-sized ~** mittleres Unternehmen, Mittelbetrieb; **paying ~** rentables Unternehmen

concern *v* betreffen, angehen; von Wichtigkeit sein für; interessieren, beschäftigen; beunruhigen; **to ~ oneself** sich beschäftigen (with mit); sich kümmern (about um); **to whom it may ~** an alle, die es angeht; an die betreffenden Sachbearbeiter *(bei Anschreiben);* **as ~s** was anbetrifft

concerned beteiligt (in an od. bei); interessiert (in an); besorgt (od. beunruhigt) (about über); verwickelt (in in); **as far as ... is ~** was ... angeht (od. betrifft); **the goods ~** die betreffenden Waren; **the parties** (or **those**) **~** die Beteiligten; die Interessierten; **authorities ~ with implementation of a law** die mit der Durchführung e-s Gesetzes befaßten Behörden; **to be ~ in a plot** in e-e Verschwörung verwickelt sein; **to be ~ with** sich beschäftigen (od. befassen) mit; mit e-r Sache beschäftigt sein

concerning betreffend; bezüglich; hinsichtlich; **the records ~ this case** die diesen Fall betreffenden Akten

concert Einverständnis, Einvernehmen; *dipl* Abkommen über gemeinsames Handeln; **~ party** *Br*[60a] Konsortium; Gruppe von Investoren, von denen jeder einzeln zum gemeinsamen Ankauf e-s Unternehmens kleine Anteile kauft; **to act in ~ with** gemeinsam (in Einklang) handeln (od. vorgehen) mit

concerted gemeinsam geplant (od. ausgeführt); abgestimmt; **~ action** konzertierte Aktion; abgestimmtes Vorgehen; *(AntitrustR)* aufeinander abgestimmtes Verhalten, Absprache; **~ action liability** Haftung für gemeinsam begangene planvolle unerlaubte Handlung; **~ policy** abgestimmte Politik

concerted practices *(AntitrustR)*[60] aufeinander abgestimmte Verhaltensweisen; Absprachen; verabredete Praktiken

concession Konzession, Zugeständnis; Zollzugeständnis *(cf. GATT);* Konzession, *(staatl.)* Verleihung *(e-s Sonderrechts); (behördl.)* Zulassung, Genehmigung *(zur Ausübung e-s Gewerbes); (VölkerR)* Konzession, Niederlassung *(in fremdem Staat mit eigenem Hoheitsrecht, z.B. früher in China);* **~ of land** Landverleihung; Überlassung von Grund und Boden

concession, application for a ~ Konzessionsgesuch; *(BergR)* Mutung; **awarding of ~s** Vergebung (od. Erteilung) von Konzessionen; **commercial ~s** Handelszugeständnisse; **grant (-ing) of a ~** Konzessionserteilung; **holder of a ~** Konzessionsinhaber; **mining ~** Bergwerkskonzession; **oil ~** Erdölkonzession; **price ~** Preiszugeständnis; **railway ~** Konzession zum Betrieb e-r Eisenbahn; **renewal of a ~** Verlängerung e-r Konzession; **Schedules of C~s** Zollzugeständnislisten *(e-s →GATT-Mitgliedstaates für den Warenverkehr mit den übrigen Mitgliedstaaten; cf. escape clause);* **withdrawal of a ~** Konzessionsentziehung

concession, to apply for a ~ um e-e Konzession nachsuchen; **to grant a ~** e-e Konzession vergeben (od. erteilen); **to make ~s** Zugeständnisse machen; **to obtain a ~** e-e Konzession erhalten; **to withdraw a ~** e-e Konzession entziehen; ein Zugeständnis zurücknehmen

concessionaire Konzessionsinhaber; Konzessionierter

concessional transaction Vorzugsgeschäft

concessionary Konzessionsinhaber; **on ~ terms** zu sehr günstigen Bedingungen; **~ fares** ermäßigte Fahrpreise; **~ funds** *(gewährte)* Mittel zu sehr günstigen Bedingungen; **~ interest rate** Vorzugszinssatz

concessive Zugeständnisse machend, einräumend

conciliate *v* aussöhnen, versöhnen; schlichten; in Einklang bringen; **attempt to ~** Schlichtungsversuch

conciliation Versöhnung, Aussöhnung; Schlichtung *(bes. von Arbeits- und Staatenstreitigkeiten); (VölkerR) (organisierte)* Vermittlung *(cf. mediation)*

conciliation and arbitration costs, schedule of ~ *(of the →ICC)*[61] Kostentabelle für Schlichtungs- und Schiedsverfahren *(der Internationalen Handelskammer)*

conciliation, ~ efforts Schlichtungsversuch; **~ hearing** Güteverhandlung; **~ officer** *Br* Schlichter *(hauptberuflich Angestellter von →ACAS)*

conciliation process[62] Schlichtungsverfahren; **initiation and conduct of the ~** Einleitung und Durchführung des Schlichtungsverfahrens

conciliation, ~ rules →Rules of C~ and Arbitration

conciliation, attempt at ~ Schlichtungsversuch; **Federal Mediation and C~ Service** *Am* Bundesschlichtungsamt; **international mandatory ~**[62a] internationale Zwangsschlichtung

conciliation, optional ~ freiwillige Schlichtung; **Rules of Optional C~** (of the ICC)[63] Vergleichsordnung; Verfahrensordnung für freiwillige Schlichtungsverfahren

conciliation, request for ~ Schlichtungsantrag

conciliation, to recourse to ~ ein Schlichtungsverfahren in Anspruch nehmen; **to settle differences by ~** Meinungsverschiedenheiten gütlich beilegen

conciliator Schlichter; Vermittler; **the ~s shall decide ex aequo et bono** die Schlichter entscheiden nach billigem Ermessen

conciliatory proposal Vermittlungsvorschlag; Vergleichsvorschlag

concise kurz, bündig; prägnant; **~ style** prägnanter Stil

conclave geheime Versammlung; *eccl* Konklave *(Versammlung der Kardinäle zur Papstwahl)*

conclude *v (Vertrag, Geschäft etc)* (ab)schließen; beenden, schließen; folgern (from aus); *(Zivilprozeß) (von der Bestreitung)* ausschließen *(cf. to estop); Am* entscheiden; **to ~ an agreement** e-e Abmachung treffen; **to ~ the negotiations** die Verhandlungen abschließen; **to ~ peace** Frieden schließen *(Staaten untereinander);* **to ~ a sale** e-n Verkauf abschließen; **to ~ a speech** e-e Rede beenden; **to ~ a treaty** *(VölkerR)* e-n Vertrag schließen; **the meeting ~d at 8 o'clock** die Sitzung schloß um 8 Uhr

concluding remark abschließende Bemerkung; Schlußwort

conclusion Abschluß *(e-s Vertrags, Geschäfts etc);* Schluß, Ende, Beendigung; Schlußfolgerung; Beschluß, Entscheidung; *(Zivilprozeß)* Unzulässigkeit der Erhebung e-r prozeßhindernden Einrede *(cf. estoppel);* Schlußplädoyer, Schlußausführung *(der Parteivertreter in der mündlichen Verhandlung);* **~ of an agreement** Vertrags(ab)schluß; **~ of business** Beendigung der Besprechung (od. Verhandlung, Sitzung etc); **~ of a contract** Vertrags(ab)schluß; **~ of a deal** Geschäftsabschluß; **~ of law** Rechtsfolgerung *(durch das Gericht);* **successful ~ of negotiations** erfolgreicher Abschluß der Verhandlungen; **~ of peace** Friedensschluß; **~ of a treaty** *(VölkerR)* Abschluß e-s Vertrages

conclusion, after the ~ of the investigation nach Abschluß der Untersuchung; **at the ~ of his speech** am Ende seiner Rede; **in ~** abschließend; **on ~ of the contract** bei Vertragsabschluß

conclusion, to bring a matter to a ~ e-e Sache zum Abschluß bringen; **to draw ~s** Schlußfolgerungen ziehen; **to come to** (or **reach**) **a ~** zu e-r Entscheidung kommen (on über)

conclusive entscheidend, endgültig, überzeugend, schlüssig; **~ evidence** schlüssiger Beweis; **~ presumption** unwiderlegbare (Rechts)-Vermutung; **the petition disclosed a ~ cause of action** der Antrag war schlüssig begründet

conclusively, to argue ~ schlüssig argumentieren

conclusiveness Endgültigkeit; Schlüssigkeit; *(zwingende)* Beweiskraft

concoct *v (Entschuldigung etc)* erfinden, ersinnen; **to ~ a conspiracy** ein Komplott aushecken

concomitant begleitend; **~s** (or **~ circumstances**) Begleitumstände; **~ measures** flankierende Maßnahmen

concordance, in ~ with in Übereinstimmung mit

concordat *eccl* Konkordat, Vertrag zwischen Staat und dem Vatikan

concourse Zusammenkommen, Zusammentreffen, Versammlung, Menge; **unforeseen ~ of circumstances** unvorhergesehenes Zusammentreffen von Umständen

concrete konkret, gegenständlich, wirklich *(opp. abstract);* Beton; **~ building** (or **construction**) Betonbau; **~ evidence** (or **proof**) konkreter Beweis

concur *v (von Ereignissen)* zusammentreffen, zusammenfallen; konkurrieren; *(von Personen)* übereinstimmen (with mit); zustimmen; **to ~ in sb.'s opinion** sich jds Ansicht anschließen

concurring konkurrierend *(Ansprüche etc)*; **~ opinion** *Am* zustimmendes Votum (→*opinion 1.)*

concurrence Zusammentreffen; *(zeitliches)* Zusammenwirken; Übereinstimmung; Zustimmung; **~ (between)** Zug-um-Zug(-Leistung); **~ between delivery of the goods and payment of the price** Zug-um-Zug-Erfüllung der Lieferung der Sache und der Zahlung des Kaufpreises; **~ of opinion** einstimmige Meinung; **to act in ~ with** gemeinschaftlich vorgehen

concurrent übereinstimmend (with mit); nebeneinander bestehend; gleichzeitig; konkurrierend; zusammenwirkend; **~ condition** Zug um Zug zu erfüllende Bedingung; **~ fire insurance** gleichzeitige Feuerversicherung bei mehreren Gesellschaften; **~ jurisdiction** konkurrierende Zuständigkeit *(mehrerer Gerichte)*; **~ registration** *Am* gleiche Markeneintragung mehrerer Anmelder; **~ resolution** →resolution 4.; **~ sentence** *(durch Urteil angeordnete)* gleichzeitige Verbüßung zweier Freiheitsstrafen *(opp. consecutive sentence)*; **~ use** *(WarenzeichenR)* gleichrangiger Gebrauch; **~ writs** → writs in doppelter Ausfertigung; **in cases where the right to exercise jurisdiction is ~** in Fällen konkurrierender Zuständigkeit

concurrently with zusammen (od. gleichzeitig) mit; Zug um Zug *(opp. successively)*

condemn *v* verurteilen; mißbilligen; tadeln (for wegen); *(Ware)* für unbrauchbar erklären; *(Gebäude)* als unbewohnbar erklären; *(Schmuggelware etc)* als verfallen erklären, beschlagnahmen; *(Schiff)* für seeuntüchtig erklären, ausrangieren; *(VölkerR) (Schiff)* kondemnieren, prisengerichtlich einziehen; *Am (zur öffentl. Benutzung)* enteignen *(cf. right of public domain)*; **to ~ to death** zum Tode verurteilen; **to ~ the plaintiff (defendant) in costs** den Kläger (Beklagten) zur Zahlung der Prozeßkosten verurteilen; **to ~ a (captured) vessel and her cargo** ein (aufgebrachtes) Schiff und seine Ladung prisengerichtlich einziehen; **to ~ as a lawful prize** als gute Prise erklären

condemnation Verurteilung; Mißbilligung, Tadel; Unbrauchbarerklärung; Bestimmung zum Abbruch *(e-s Gebäudes)*; *Am* Enteignung; *(SeeR)* Kondemnation, gerichtl. Unbrauchbarerklärung e-s Schiffes *(z.B. wegen Reparaturunfähigkeit)*; *(VölkerR)* Kondemnation, prisengerichtliche Einziehung *(e-s Schiffes; cf. capture, prize)*; Beschlagnahme; **~ (money)** Entschädigungsbetrag; **~ as prize** Entscheidung des Prisengerichts über die Rechtmäßigkeit der Aufbringung als Prise; **~ award** *Am* Enteignungsentschädigung; **~ order** *Am* Enteignungsbeschluß; **~ proceedings** *Am* Enteignungsverfahren

condensed report zusammenfassender Bericht

condition 1. Bedingung; *Br* wesentliche Vertragsbestimmung; *Br (ausdrückl. od. stillschweigende)* Zusicherung der Eigenschaften e-r Ware; **~ of title** *Br* Gewährübernahme durch den Verkäufer für die Verschaffung des Eigentums *(als wesentliche Vertragsbedingung)*; Gewährleistung wegen Rechtsmängel

Br Eine condition ist eine grundlegende Vertragsklausel, deren Verletzung dem Käufer das Recht gewährt, vom Vertrag zurückzutreten und Schadensersatz zu verlangen (warranties sind dagegen Vertragsklauseln von geringerer Bedeutung, deren Verletzung nur Schadensersatzansprüche auslöst; → warranty).

Die historisch bedingte Unterscheidung zwischen conditions und warranties, die das amerikanische Recht aufgegeben hat, kann zu Abgrenzungsschwierigkeiten führen, da die Feststellung, ob einer Vertragsklausel grundlegende Bedeutung zukommt, nicht immer leicht zu treffen ist

condition 2. Bedingung, Voraussetzung (of für); Auflage; Lage, Zustand, Beschaffenheit; Vermögenslage; Stand, Personenstand, Familienstand; **~s** Verhältnisse, Gegebenheiten; **~s binding on sb.** jdn bindende Auflagen; **~ in deed** s. express **→~**; **~ in law** s. implied **→~**; **~(s) of business** Geschäftslage; **(terms and) ~s of business** Geschäftsbedingungen; **~s of carriage** Beförderungsbedingungen; **~s of competition** Wettbewerbsbedingungen; **~s of a contract** Vertragsbedingungen; **~s of delivery** Lieferungsbedingungen; **~s of labo(u)r** Arbeitsbedingungen; **~**; **~s of payment** Zahlungsbedingungen; **~s of sale** Verkaufsbedingungen; **~s of transport** Transportbedingungen; **~s of work** Arbeitsbedingungen; **~ precedent** Vorbedingung, Voraussetzung; aufschiebende Bedingung; **~ subsequent** auflösende Bedingung

condition (1. und 2.), **breach of ~** Nichteinhaltung der Bedingung(en); **breach of ~** (of a contract) *Br* Verletzung e-r wesentlichen Vertragsbestimmung; **under existing ~s** unter diesen Umständen; unter normalen Bedingungen; **express ~** ausdrückliche Bedingung (od. Vertragsbestimmung); **financial ~** Finanzlage, Vermögenslage; **upon the happening of the ~** beim Eintritt der Bedingung; **implied ~** stillschweigend mit eingeschlossene Bedingung; *Br* stillschweigende wesentliche Vertragsbestimmung *(Bruch e-r implied ~ berechtigt den Käufer zu Annullierung [repudiation] des Vertrages; cf. implied warranty)*; **local ~s** örtliche Verhältnisse (od. Gegebenheiten); Platzbedingungen; **main ~** Hauptbedingung, Grundbedingung; **mutual ~** gegenseitige Bedingung; **occurrence of a** ~ Eintritt e-r Bedingung; **on no** ~ unter keiner Bedingung; **on** ~ **that** unter (od. mit) der Bedingung, daß; vorausgesetzt, daß; **standard** ~**s** normale (Vertrags-)Bedingungen *(die in e-r bestimmten Art von Verträgen üblichen Bedingungen);* **working** ~**s** Arbeitsverhältnisse

condition, to comply with a ~ e-e Bedingung einhalten (od. erfüllen); **the** ~**s have been complied with** (or **fulfil[l]ed**) die Voraussetzungen sind gegeben (od. liegen vor); die Bedingungen sind erfüllt; ~ **which must be complied with** Auflage; **to create favo(u)rable** ~**s** günstige Bedingungen (od. Voraussetzungen) schaffen; **to determine** ~**s** Bedingungen festsetzen; **to impose** ~**s** Bedingungen auferlegen; Auflagen machen; **to make it a** ~ sich ausbedingen; es zur Bedingung (od. Auflage) machen; **to make sth. subject to a** ~ etw. an e-e Bedingung knüpfen; **to meet a** ~ e-e Bedingung erfüllen; **to observe a** ~ e-e Bedingung erfüllen; e-e Auflage beachten; **to set a** ~ e-e Bedingung stellen; **to stipulate** ~**s** Bedingungen festsetzen (od. machen); **a** ~ **fails** e-e Bedingung tritt nicht ein; **a** ~ **happens** (or **occurs**) e-e Bedingung tritt ein

condition *v* zur Bedingung machen; in den gewünschten Zustand bringen; *(Textilien)* konditionieren, *Am (auf Beschaffenheit)* prüfen; *Am univ* Nachprüfung auferlegen

conditioned bedingt, abhängig; *(Textilien)* konditioniert; beschaffen, geartet; **ill-**~ in schlechtem Zustand; in schlechter Verfassung; **well-**~ in gutem Zustand; **to be** ~ **by** abhängen von

conditional bedingt (upon durch); abhängig (upon von); ~ **acceptance** bedingte Annahme; Annahme unter e-r Bedingung; ~ **agreement** an Bedingungen geknüpfte Vereinbarung; ~ **appearance** →appearance 2.; ~ **bond** → bond 3.; ~ **discharge** →discharge 2.; ~ **offer** bedingtes Angebot; ~ **sale** Verkauf unter Eigentumsvorbehalt; Vorbehaltskauf; ~ **sale agreement** Kaufvertrag unter Eigentumsvorbehalt; *(Br*[64] *bezieht sich auf Sachen und Grundstücke);* ~ **title** von e-r Bedingung abhängiges Eigentum; **to be** ~ **on** bedingt sein durch; abhängig sein von

conditionally (up)on the payment of unter der Bedingung der Zahlung von

condolence, letter of ~ Beileidsschreiben; **to offer sb. one's** ~ jdm sein Beileid aussprechen

condominium *(VölkerR)* Kondominium *(gemeinsame Herrschaft mehrerer Staaten über eignes Gebiet) (cf. coimperium); Am* Eigentumswohnung, Wohnungseigentum *(Stockwerkseigentum) (cf. cooperative);* ~ **association** *Am* Gemeinschaft der Wohnungseigentümer

condonation Verzeihung *(bes. bei Ehescheidungen)*[65]

condone *v* verzeihen, vergeben *(bes. ehel. Untreue und Grausamkeit)*

conduce *v*, **to** ~ **to(wards)** beitragen zu, förderlich sein

conducive dienlich, förderlich (to für)

conduct 1. Verhalten, Betragen, Führung; *Am (StrafR)* Handlung od. Unterlassung *(einschließl. des ihr zugrundeliegenden state of mind);* ~ **money** Zeugenspesen; dem Zeugen zu zahlende Aufwendungen; ~ **unbecoming an officer and a gentleman** standes- und ehrenwidriges Betragen; ~ **unbefitting a solicitor** *Br* standeswidriges Verhalten e-s Anwalts; **bad** ~ schlechtes Betragen (od. Benehmen); **certificate of (good)** ~ Leumundszeugnis; Führungszeugnis; **code of** ~ →code 3.; **criminal** ~ strafbares Verhalten; **disorderly** ~ ordnungswidriges Verhalten; **general** ~ Allgemeinverhalten; **good** ~ gute Führung; gutes Benehmen; **improper** ~ ungehöriges Verhalten; **professional** ~ standesgemäßes Verhalten; **professional mis**~ standeswidriges Verhalten; **standards of** ~ Verhaltensnormen; **unbecoming** ~ ungebührliches Verhalten; **unreasonable** ~ unzumutbares Benehmen *(ground for → divorce)*

conduct 2. Führung, Leitung; ~ **of one's own affairs** Besorgung (od. Erledigung) der eigenen Angelegenheiten; ~ **of business** Führung der Geschäfte, Geschäftsführung; ~ **of a case** Führung e-s Prozesses *(als Anwalt);* ~ **of litigation** Prozeßführung; ~ **of a meeting** Leitung e-r Sitzung; ~ **of negotiations** Führung von Verhandlungen; Verhandlungsführung; ~ **of war** Kriegsführung; **safe** ~ sicheres (od. freies) Geleit

conduct *v* führen, leiten; **to** ~ **onself** sich benehmen (od. führen, betragen); **to** ~ **one's affairs** seine Angelegenheiten besorgen; **to** ~ **a business** ein Geschäft führen *(→business);* **to** ~ **one's own case** seinen Fall *(vor Gericht)* selbst vertreten; **to** ~ **an investigation** e-e Untersuchung durchführen; **to** ~ **a lawsuit** e-n Prozeß *(für e-n Klienten)* führen; **to** ~ **negotiations** Verhandlungen führen

conduit, *Am* Durchleitstelle *(für steuerliche Behandlung e-s trust);* **American** ~**s**[66] transparente amerikanische Fonds; **non-**~ **fund** nicht transparenter Fonds

confederacy Bund; Staatenbund; *(StrafR)* Komplott, Verschwörung; **the (Southern) C**~ → Confederate States of America

confederate Verbündeter, Bundesgenosse; verbündet; Komplice *(bei e-m Attentat etc);* **C**~ *Am* Konföderierter, Südstaatler *(im Sezessions-*

krieg); **C~ States of America** Konföderierte Staaten von Amerika *(Zusammenschluß der 11 Südstaaten im Sezessionskrieg 1861–1865)*

confederate *v* sich verbünden (with mit); **~d states** Staatenbund

confederation Bund, Bündnis; **~ (of states)** Staatenbund; **C~ of British Industry** (CBI)[67] Spitzenverband britischer Unternehmer und Unternehmerverbände; Arbeitgeberverband; **Swiss C~** Schweizerische Eidgenossenschaft

confer *v* übertragen, *(Ehren, Titel etc)* verleihen (on a p. jdm); konferieren, sich beraten, e-e Unterredung haben, Rücksprache nehmen, (sich) besprechen (with mit); **to ~ authority on a p.** jdn ermächtigen; jdn bevollmächtigen; **to ~ with one's counsel** sich mit s-m Anwalt besprechen (od. beraten); **to ~ a degree on a p.** jdm e-n akademischen Grad verleihen; **to ~ jurisdiction on a court** die Zuständigkeit e-s Gerichtes begründen; **to ~ a right** ein Recht übertragen; **to ~ a title on sb.** jdm e-n Titel verleihen

conferee jd, dem etw. übertragen wird; *Am* Konferenzteilnehmer, Besprechungsteilnehmer

conference 1. Konferenz, Tagung; Besprechung, Beratung, Verhandlung; Parteiversammlung; **~ committee** *Am* Vermittlungsausschuß *(Sitzung der Ausschüsse der beiden Häuser des Kongresses bei Meinungsverschiedenheiten);* **~ decision** Konferenzbeschluß; **~ of delegates** *Br* Parteitag, Parteikongreß *(Parteivertreterversammlung);* **C~ of European Ministers for Cultural Affairs** *(EG)* Konferenz der Europäischen Kultusminister; **C~ on Confidence- and Security-building Measures and Disarmament in Europe** Konferenz über vertrauens- und sicherheitsbildende Maßnahmen und Abrüstung in Europa (KVAE); **C~ on International Economic Cooperation** (CIEC) ("North-South Dialogue") Konferenz über die internationale wirtschaftliche Zusammenarbeit (KIWZ) („Nord/Süd Dialog"); **(UN) C~ on the Law of the Sea** (UNCLOS) Seerechtskonferenz (der Vereinten Nationen); **~ paper** Tagungsbericht; **C~ on Security and Cooperation in Europe** (CSCE) Konferenz über Sicherheit und Zusammenarbeit in Europa (KSZE) *(Helsinki-Konferenz von 1975; Mitglieder: 35 Staaten);* **UN C~ on Trade and Development** →UNCTAD; **~ participant** Tagungsteilnehmer

conference, Annual C~ *Br* jährlicher Parteikongreß *(der Labour Party);* **business ~** geschäftliche Besprechung; **commercial ~** Handelsbesprechung; **foreign ministers' ~** Außenministerkonferenz; **party ~** Parteitag; **press ~** Pressekonferenz; **summit ~** Gipfelkonferenz; **three power ~** Dreimächtekonferenz; **top level ~** Konferenz auf höchster Ebene; **tripartite ~** Dreierkonferenz

conference, to attend a ~ an e-r Konferenz teilnehmen; **to convene** (or **call, convoke**) **a ~** e-e Konferenz einberufen; **to hold a ~** e-e Konferenz (od. Beratung) abhalten; sich besprechen; **a ~ is held** e-e Konferenz findet statt; **to sit in ~** tagen; **to submit a case for ~** *Am* e-e Sache zur Verhandlung bringen; **to take part in a ~** an e-r Konferenz teilnehmen

conference 2. Konferenz *(Kartell der internationalen Schiffahrtslinien);* **~ agreement** Konferenzvertrag; **~ rates** Konferenzfrachtraten; **~ steamer** Schiff e-r Konferenzreederei; **~ tariff** Konferenztarif; **~ terms** (C. T.) Konferenzbedingungen; **Ocean Freight C~ System** *Am* Seefrachtkonferenzsystem; **Shipping C~** Schiffahrtskonferenz *(kartellartiger Zusammenschluß verschiedener Linienreedereien)*

conferment Verleihung (upon an); **~ of authority** Bevollmächtigung

confess *v* gestehen; *(Strafprozeß) (Schuld, Verbrechen etc)* (ein)gestehen, ein Geständnis ablegen *(opp. to deny); (Zivilprozeß) (förmlich)* anerkennen; *eccl* beichten; Beichte abnehmen; **to ~ one's guilt** s-e Schuld gestehen

confessed eingestanden; **~ly** eingestandenermaßen; **the murderer has ~** der Mörder ist geständig

confessing one's guilt geständig

confession Bekennen, Bekenntnis; *(Strafprozeß)* (Schuld-)Geständnis; *(Zivilprozeß) (förml.)* Anerkenntnis; *eccl* Beichte; **~ and avoidance** Gegenvorbringen ohne Bestreitung des Klageanspruchs; **~ of faith** Glaubensbekenntnis, Konfession; **~ of guilt** Schuldgeständnis; **~ of judgment** *Am (prozeßrechtl. sowie materiellrechtl. schriftliches)* Anerkenntnis e-r Urteilsschuld *(vergleichbar § 307 ZPO);* **~ of judgment clause** *Am* Unterwerfungsklausel *(in e-m Wechsel)*

confession, by (or **on**) **his own ~** nach s-m eigenen Geständnis; **dying ~** Bekenntnis auf dem Sterbebett; **full ~** umfassendes Geständnis; **judgment by ~** *Am* Anerkenntnisurteil; **seal of ~** Beichtgeheimnis

confession, to extort a ~ ein Geständnis erpressen; **to make a ~** ein Geständnis ablegen; geständig sein; **to refuse to make a ~** nicht geständig sein; **to retract a ~** ein Geständnis widerrufen

confessor Beichtvater

confide *v* vertrauen (in auf); *(etw.)* anvertrauen (to a p. jdm); **to ~ sth. to a p.** jdm e-e vertrauliche Mitteilung machen

confidence Vertrauen (in zu, auf); vertrauliche Mitteilung; **~ game** *Am* →**~ trick**; **~ man**

gewerbsmäßiger Schwindler; ~ **trick** Schwindlertrick; Erschleichung des Vertrauens, Hochstapelei; ~ **trickster** gewerbsmäßiger Schwindler, Hochstapler

confidence, abuse of ~ Vertrauensmißbrauch; **breach of** ~ Vertrauensbruch; Verletzung der Geheimhaltungspflicht

confidence, question of ~ Vertrauensfrage; **to put the question of** ~ die Vertrauensfrage stellen

confidence, in (strict) ~ streng vertraulich; im Vertrauen; **all replies treated in** ~ die Antwort wird vertraulich behandelt

confidence, vote of ~ *parl* Vertrauensvotum; **vote of no** ~ *parl* Mißtrauensvotum; **to ask for a vote of** ~ die Vertrauensfrage stellen; **to present a motion of no-**~ e-n Mißtrauensantrag einbringen

confidence, to be in a p.'s ~ (or **to enjoy a p.'s** ~) jds Vertrauen genießen; **to express one's** ~ **in the government** der Regierung sein Vertrauen aussprechen; **to place (one's)** ~ **in sb.** in jdn sein Vertrauen setzen; **to withdraw one's** ~ **from sb.** jdm sein Vertrauen entziehen

confidential vertraulich; **strictly** ~ streng vertraulich; ~ **agent** Vertrauensmann; ~ **books** (C. B.) Geheimsachen; ~ **clerk** Privatsekretär (-in); ~ **communications** vertrauliche Mitteilungen; Berufsgeheimnis (→*privileged communications);* ~ **data** vertrauliche Angaben; ~ **information** vertrauliche Mitteilung; ~ **matter** Vertrauenssache; ~ **post** Vertrauensstellung, -posten; ~ **relationship** Vertrauensverhältnis; ~ **report** vertraulicher Bericht *(z. B. Personalbeurteilung zu den Akten);* ~ **secretary** Privatsekretär(in); **inquiries are treated ~ly on request** Anfragen werden auf Wunsch vertraulich behandelt

confidentiality Vertraulichkeit; vertrauliche Behandlung; **professional** ~ Berufsgeheimnis

configuration *(MusterR)* Form(gebung); ~ **of goods**[68] äußere Gestaltung e-r Ware

confine(s) Grenze(n)

confine *v* beschränken, begrenzen; *(jdn)* inhaftieren, einsperren, gefangen halten; **to** ~ **oneself to** sich beschränken auf; **to be ~d to barracks** Kasernenarrest haben; **to be ~d as a patient** *Br* in e-r psychiatrischen Klinik untergebracht sein

confinement Begrenzung, Beschränkung; Haft, Inhaftierung, Unterbringung *(in e-r Anstalt);* Entbindung, Niederkunft; *mil* Arrest; Einsperrung; ~ **to barracks** (C. B.) Kasernenarrest; ~ **expenses** Entbindungskosten; ~ **in a mental hospital** Unterbringung in e-r psychiatrischen Klinik

confinement, close ~ strenge Haft; **false** ~ ungesetzliche Haft; **solitary** ~ Einzelhaft

confinement, to place sb. in ~ jdn in Haft nehmen (od. einsperren); jdn in e-r Anstalt unterbringen

confirm *v* bestätigen; bekräftigen, erhärten; genehmigen; *eccl* konfirmieren *(protestantische Kirche);* firmen *(katholische Kirche);* **to** ~ **an appointment** e-e Ernennung bestätigen; **to** ~ **by charter** *(Recht, Privileg etc)* verbriefen; **to** ~ **a credit** ein Akkreditiv bestätigen; **to** ~ **sth. under** (or **by**) **oath** etw. eidlich erhärten; **to** ~ **sb. in office** jdn in s-m Amt bestätigen; **to** ~ **an order** e-n Auftrag bestätigen; **to** ~ **a statement** e-e Aussage bestätigen (od. bekräftigen); **that ~ed my suspicion** das bestätigte meinen Verdacht; **to** ~ **in writing** schriftlich bestätigen

confirmed, ~ **drunkard** chronischer Trinker, Gewohnheitstrinker; **a** ~ **invalid** ein ständig (od. chronisch) Kranker; ~ **irrevocable (letter of) credit** bestätigtes unwiderrufliches Akkreditiv; **to be** ~ sich bestätigen

confirming house (C. H.) *Br* Kommissionär od. Eigenhändler, der Exportgeschäfte abwickelt od. finanziert

confirmation Bestätigung; Bekräftigung, Erhärtung; Genehmigung, nachträgliche Zustimmung; *eccl (protestantisch)* Konfirmation, *(katholisch)* Firmung; *Scot* Bestätigung der Bestellung zum →executor; ~ **of balance** (Bank-)-Saldenbestätigung; ~ **by oath** eidliche Bekräftigung; ~ **of order** Auftragsbestätigung; ~ **of signature** Unterschriftsbeglaubigung; **in** ~ **of this statement** zur Bekräftigung dieser Behauptung

confirmation, contract ~ Vertragsbestätigung; **letter of** ~ Bestätigungsschreiben; **note of** ~ Bestätigungsvermerk

confirmatory bestätigend, bekräftigend; ~ **letter** Bestätigungsschreiben; ~ **note** *Am* Auftragsbestätigung *(Übernahmebescheinigung des Spediteurs)*

confiscable einziehbar, beschlagnahmbar

confiscate *v* konfiszieren; *(Privateigentum) (entschädigungslos)* einziehen, beschlagnahmen; **to** ~ **falsely entered goods** *(beim Zoll)* falsch deklarierte Waren einziehen

confiscation Konfiskation, Konfiszierung; *(entschädigungslose)* Einziehung, Beschlagnahme *(von Privateigentum); (VölkerR)* Einziehung *(von Konterbande);* ~ **order** (or **order for** ~) Einziehungsverfügung, Beschlagnahmeanordnung; **smuggled goods are liable to** ~ Schmuggelwaren unterliegen der Einziehung

conflagration *(ausgedehnter)* Brand; ~ **area** *(Feuervers.)* Großbrandbereich; **cause of** ~ Brandursache

conflict Konflikt, Streit; *fig* Widerstreit, Widerspruch, Kollision; ~ **of evidence** Beweiskonflikt (→*conflicting evidence);* ~ **of interests** Interessenkollision, Interessenkonflikt; ~ **of jurisdiction** Zuständigkeitsstreit, Kompetenzstreit; ~ **law** Kollisionsrecht

conflict of laws Gesetzeskollision, Kollision von Gesetzen *(mehrerer Staaten in bezug auf eine Person);* Internationales Privatrecht *(IPR);* **conflict of laws rules** Kollisionsnormen; **law of** ~ *Am* Internationales Privatrecht

conflict, armed ~ kriegerischer Konflikt; bewaffnete Auseinandersetzung; **labo(u)r** ~ arbeitsrechtliche Streitigkeit; **settlement of ~s** Schlichtung von Streitigkeiten; **the decisions are in** ~ die Entscheidungen widersprechen sich; **to be in** ~ in Widerspruch stehen, kollidieren (with mit)

conflict *v* im Widerspruch stehen (with zu); sich widersprechen, nicht übereinstimmen; kollidieren (with mit)

conflicting (sich) widersprechend, entgegengesetzt; ~ **claim** *(PatR)* entgegengesetzter (kollidierender) Anspruch; ~ **evidence** sich widersprechende Beweise (od. Zeugenaussagen); ~ **interests** widerstreitende (od. kollidierende) Interessen; ~ **jurisdiction** →conflict of jurisdiction; ~ **laws** einander widersprechende Gesetze; ~ **registered trade marks** Kollision e-s angemeldeten mit e-m früher angemeldeten Warenzeichen; ~ **statements** sich widersprechende Angaben (od. Aussagen)

conform *v* übereinstimmen (with mit); **to** ~ **to** sich anpassen an, sich richten nach, entsprechen; *Br* der Staatskirche anhängen; **to** ~ **to sb.'s plans** sich nach jds Plänen richten; **to** ~ **to the provisions** in Übereinstimmung mit den Bestimmungen handeln; sich an die Bestimmungen halten

conformed copy *Am* gleichlautende Abschrift

conforming to entsprechend

conformable übereinstimmend (to mit); entsprechend; vereinbar (to mit); gleichlautend; ~ **to duty** pflichtgemäß; **to be** ~ **to** entsprechen

conformist Konformist *(Br Anhänger der engl. Staatskirche; opp. dissenter)*

conformity Übereinstimmung (with mit); Anpassung (to gegenüber); Vereinbarkeit (to mit); **in** ~ **with** gemäß; übereinstimmend (od. gleichlautend) mit; ~ **with the contract** Vertragsgemäßheit; **lack of** ~ **with the contract** Vertragswidrigkeit; **not in** ~ **with the contract** vertragswidrig; **in** ~ **with the market** marktgerecht; **in** ~ **with your order** Ihrem Auftrag gemäß; **to be in** ~ **with the contract** vertragsgemäß sein

confrère (Fach-)Kollege

confront *v* gegenüberstellen, konfrontieren; **to** ~ **two witnesses** zwei Zeugen gegenüberstellen

confronted, to be ~ **with difficulties** Schwierigkeiten gegenüberstehen

confrontation Gegenüberstellung, Konfrontierung; Konfrontation

confusable trademarks verwechselbare Warenzeichen

confuse *v* (miteinander) verwechseln; verwirren; vertauschen; vermischen, vermengen

confused, trade marks which are easily ~ verwechslungsfähige Warenzeichen

confusion Verwechslung; Verwirrung; ~ **(of goods)** Vermischung, Vermengung *(bewegl. Sachen verschiedener Eigentümer als Eigentumserwerbsgrund);* ~ **of boundaries** Grenzverwirrung; ~ **of names** Namensverwechslung; ~ **of rights** *Am* Vereinigung von Gläubiger und Schuldner in e-r Person; Konfusion; ~ **of source** *Am*[69] *(WarenzeichenR)* Verkehrsverwirrung; ~ **between trademarks** Verwechslung zwischen Warenzeichen

confusion, accession by ~ *Am* Eigentumserwerb durch Vermischung; **danger** (or **possibility**) **of** ~ Verwechslungsgefahr; **likelihood to** ~ *(WarenzeichenR)* Verwechslungsgefahr; **to cause** ~ Verwechslungen hervorrufen

confutable assertion widerlegbare Behauptung

confutation Widerlegung

confute *v* widerlegen

congenital defect Geburtsfehler

congest *v* überfüllen; sich ansammeln; **to** ~ **the market** den Markt überschwemmen

congested, ~ **area** (or **district**) dichtbesiedeltes (od. überfülltes) Gebiet; Ballungsgebiet; ~ **state of the goods traffic** Stockung im Güterverkehr

congestion Ansammlung; Stauung; Überfüllung; Verkehrsstauung; ~ **charge** (or **surcharge**) Frachtzuschlag, Hafenverstopfungszuschlag *(in Häfen, in denen sich Löschung aus technischen Gründen verzögert);* ~ **of population** Übervölkerung; Bevölkerungsballung; **traffic** ~ Verkehrsstauung, Verkehrsstockung

conglomerate (merger) Konglomerat, Mischkonzern *(Fusion branchenfremder Firmen)*

Congo, the ~ Kongo; **People's Republic of the** ~ Volksrepublik Kongo

Congolese Kongolese, Kongolesin; kongolesisch

congratulatory letter Glückwunschschreiben

congregate *v* (sich) versammeln

congregation Versammlung; *eccl.* Gemeinde

congregationalist *eccl* Kongregationalist
Angehöriger e-r Sekte (früher Independents), die das Staatskirchentum ablehnt und die Unabhängigkeit der Einzelgemeinde (congregation) betont

Congress 1. *Am* Kongreß
Gesetzgebende Körperschaft, bestehend aus Senate und House of Representatives. Daneben hat der Congress nichtgesetzgebende Befugnisse (constituent, electoral, executive, directory and supervisory, investigating and judicial powers)[70]

Congress, Member of ~ (MC) *Am* Kongreßabgeordneter; **c~man** *Am* Kongreßabgeordneter *(Mitglied des House of Representatives; opp. Senator);* **to introduce in** ~ im Kongreß einbringen

congress 2. Kongreß, Tagung; ~ **member** Kongreßteilnehmer

congress, at the ~ auf dem Kongreß; **international** ~ internationaler Kongreß; **medical** ~ medizinischer Kongreß, Ärztekongreß; **to attend a** ~ an e-m Kongreß teilnehmen

congressional, ~ **committee** *Am* Kongreßausschuß; ~ **district** *Am* Wahlbezirk für die Abgeordneten des House of Representatives; ~ **election** *Am* Wahl zum House of Representatives; **C~ Medal of (Honor)** *Am* höchste Tapferkeitsauszeichnung; **C~ Record** *(tägl.)* Sitzungsbericht des Kongresses

conjoint(ly) gemeinsam; gesamtschuldnerisch

conjugal ehelich, Ehe-; ~ **community** *Am* eheliche Lebensgemeinschaft; ~ **fidelity** eheliche Treue; ~ **rights** eheliche Rechte; **extra-~** außerehelich

conjunct gemeinsam; ~ **and several** *Scot* gesamtschuldnerisch

conjuncture Zusammentreffen von Umständen

connate angeboren

connect *v* verbinden; in Verbindung (od. Zusammenhang) bringen; Anschluß haben *(von Zügen);* anschließen

connected verbunden; ~ **by marriage** verschwägert; **to be** ~ **with** in Verbindung (od. in Zusammenhang) stehen mit; **to be effectively** ~ **with a US trade or business** *Am* sich aktiv im amerikanischen Geschäft betätigen; **to be well** ~ gute Beziehungen haben; aus guter Familie stammen; **to become** ~ **with** in Verbindung treten mit; in verwandtschaftliche Beziehungen treten zu

connecting, ~ **factor** *(IPR)* Anknüpfungspunkt; ~ **train** Anschlußzug

connection Verbindung; Verkehrsverbindung; telefonische Verbindung; Beziehung (with zu); Zusammenhang; Anschluß *(Zug, Flugzeug);* Verwandtschaft; Kundschaft; *(IPR)* Anknüpfung; ~**s** Beziehungen, Verbindungen; Kundenkreis; ~ **by air** Flugverbindung; ~ **by marriage** Schwägerschaft; ~ **by sea** Schiffsverbindung

connection, business ~**s** Geschäftsbeziehungen, -verbindungen *(→business);* **causal** ~ Kausalzusammenhang; **foreign** ~**s** Auslandsbeziehungen; **in this** ~ in dieser Beziehung, in diesem Zusammenhang; **in** ~ **with** im Zusammenhang mit; **rail(way)** ~ (Eisen-)Bahnverbindung, Eisenbahnanschluß; **telephone** ~ Fernsprechverbindung; **train** ~ Zugverbindung; **wide** ~ ausgedehnte (od. große) Kundschaft

connection, to be in ~ **with** in Verbindung stehen mit; **to break off a** ~ e-e Verbindung abbrechen; **to make new** ~**s** neue Verbindungen anknüpfen; **to run in** ~ **with** Anschluß haben an; **to sever one's** ~**s with** sich trennen von

connivance *(strafbares)* geheimes Einverständnis *(mit e-r gesetzwidrigen Handlung); (stillschweigende)* Zustimmung *(bes. e-s Ehegatten zum Ehebruch des anderen; Einrede gegen Scheidungsklage)*

connive *v (etw. Unerlaubtes)* stillschweigend dulden; *(e-r gesetzwidrigen Handlung)* zustimmen; **to** ~ **at an escape from prison** jds Flucht aus dem Gefängnis stillschweigend dulden

connubial ehelich, Ehe-

conquest *(VölkerR)* Eroberung; gewaltsamer Erwerb *(von fremdem Staatsgebiet)*

consanguineous blutsverwandt

consanguinity (Bluts-)Verwandtschaft *(cf. affinity);* **collateral** ~ (Bluts-)Verwandtschaft in der Seitenlinie; **degree of** ~ Grad der (Bluts-)-Verwandtschaft; **lineal** ~ (Bluts-)Verwandtschaft in der geraden Linie

conscience Gewissen; ~ **clause** Gewissensklausel; ~ **money** *Br* anonyme Steuernachzahlung; **case of** ~ Gewissensfrage; **for reasons of** ~ aus Gewissensgründen

conscientious gewissenhaft; ~ **objection** Wehrdienstverweigerung; ~ **objector** (C. O.) *(sl.* conchy) Wehrdienstverweigerer *(aus Gewissensgründen)*

conscionability test *Am* gerichtliche Billigkeitsüberprüfung ehegüter- und unterhaltsrechtlicher Scheidungsvereinbarungen

conscious bewußt; ~ **ly** wissentlich; ~ **(of)** in dem Bewußtsein, eingedenk; **he was** ~ **of his guilt** er war sich s-r Schuld bewußt

conscious parallelism of action *Am* bewußtes Parallelverhalten *(häufigster Fall: gleichförmiges Preisverhalten; →parallelism)*

consciousness Bewußtsein; ~ **of guilt** Schuldbewußtsein

conscript *mil* Einberufener; Wehrpflichtiger

conscript *v mil (Wehrpflichtige)* einberufen

conscriptee *Am* →conscript

conscription Einberufung; *(allgemeine)* Wehrpflicht

consecutive aufeinanderfolgend, zusammenhängend; **on five ~ days** fünf Tage hintereinander; **~ number** laufende Nummer; **~ sentence** *(durch Urteil angeordnete)* nacheinander erfolgende Verbüßung zweier Freiheitsstrafen; **to number ~ ly** fortlaufend numerieren

consensus Konsens; Übereinstimmung; **~ of opinion** übereinstimmende Meinung

consent Einwilligung (to in); Zustimmung, Genehmigung (to zu); Einverständnis; **~ decree** *Am* →~ order; **~ to marriage** Einwilligung zur Ehe; Heiratserlaubnis; **~ obtained by fraud** durch Betrug erlangte Einwilligung; **~ order** *Am* Verfügung der F. T. C., die mit Zustimmung der Betroffenen im Vergleichswege ergeht; **C~ Statutes** *Am (einzelstaatl.)* Gesetze, die Schadensersatzanspruch gegen Kfz-Eigentümer begründen *(vorausgesetzt daß dieser dem Kfz-Führer die Zustimmung zum Gebrauch des Kfz erteilt)*

consent, age of ~ Einwilligungsalter *(zur Ehe od. zum außerehelichen Geschlechtsverkehr)*; **by common** ~ einstimmig; **decree by** ~ →~ decree; **express** ~ ausdrückliche Einwilligung; **implicit** (or **implied)** ~ stillschweigende Zustimmung; **by mutual** ~ in gegenseitigem Einvernehmen; einverständlich; **silence gives** ~ Schweigen gilt als Zustimmung

consent, to declare one's ~ sein Einverständnis erklären; **to give one's** ~ s-e Zustimmung erteilen; *(in etw.)* einwilligen; **to obtain the** ~ die Zustimmung erhalten; **to refuse** (or **withhold) one's** ~ seine Einwilligung verweigern; **to withdraw one's** ~ seine Einwilligung widerrufen; **sth. meets with general** ~ etw. findet allgemeine Zustimmung

consent *v* zustimmen, einwilligen; sich einverstanden erklären (to mit); **to ~ to an order** e-e Anordnung billigen

consequence Folge, Konsequenz; Bedeutung, Wichtigkeit; **~s of war** Kriegsfolgen; **in ~ of** als Folge (od. infolge) von; **legal ~** Rechtsfolge; **of little ~** von geringer Bedeutung (to für); **of no ~** ohne Bedeutung, unwichtig; **person of ~** einflußreiche Person; **serious ~s** ernste Folgen; **to take the ~s** die Folgen tragen

consequent, to be ~ on die Folge sein von

consequential folgend (on, upon auf); folgerichtig; kausal bedingt; mittelbar; **~ costs** Schadensfolgekosten; **~ damage** (or **loss)** mittelbarer Schaden, Folgeschaden; **~ damages** Ersatz für Folgeschaden

consequential, to be ~ on folgen auf; sich ergeben aus

conservancy *Br* Kontrollbehörde *(für Flüsse, Häfen, Forsten etc)*; **Thames C~** Kontrollbehörde für die Themse

conservation (Bestands-)Erhaltung; Schutz *(der Wälder etc)*, Naturschutz; Umweltschutz; **~ of the assets** Erhaltung der Vermögenswerte; **~ of energy** Energieeinsparung; **~ of evidence** Beweissicherung; **~ of fish stocks** Erhaltung der Fischbestände; **measures of ~** Schutzmaßnahmen; **nature ~** Naturschutz

conservationist Naturschützer, Umweltschützer

conservative 1. *Br* Konservativer *(Mitglied der Konservativen Partei)*; konservativ; **C~ Party** *Br* Konservative Partei; **C~ policy** *Br* Politik der Konservativen

conservative 2. vorsichtig; **~ estimate** vorsichtige Schätzung

conservator *(amtl.)* Konservator; Aufsichtsbeamter *(e-s Forstes etc)*; *Am* Pfleger, Vermögensverwalter *(für entmündigte od. geistesschwache Personen)*; **~s of rivers** *Br* Flußkontrollbehörde *(→conservancy)*

consider *v* erwägen, in Betracht ziehen, prüfen, überlegen; berücksichtigen, beachten; finden, halten für; **to ~ a p. to be** jdn halten für; **to ~ doing a th.** erwägen, etwas zu tun; **to ~ sth. well** etw. gut (od. reiflich) überlegen; **to ~ sth. necessary** etw. für notwendig erachten; **to ~ in mitigation** strafmildernd berücksichtigen

consider *v*, **to ~ a case** e-n Fall prüfen; **to ~ a fact** e-e Tatsache in Erwägung ziehen; **to ~ a proposal** e-n Vorschlag in Erwägung ziehen; **to ~ a p.'s youth** jds Jugend berücksichtigen; **the court ~s** das Gericht ist der Meinung

considered wohlüberlegt *(z.B. Meinung)*; **all things ~** wenn man alles in Erwägung zieht; **the proposal is being ~** der Vorschlag wird geprüft; **he ~ whether** er erwog, ob

considering in der Erwägung; **~ that** in Anbetracht (dessen), daß; mit Rücksicht darauf, daß; **~ all circumstances** in Anbetracht aller Umstände

considerable beträchtlich, erheblich; bedeutend, wichtig; *colloq.* sehr viel, eine Menge; **bought at a ~ expense** mit erheblichen Kosten gekauft

consideration 1. Gegenleistung, Entgelt *(als Wirksamkeitsvoraussetzung e-s formlosen schuldrechtl. Vertrages)*; Preis, Kaufpreis

Das aus dem Common Law stammende Rechtsinstitut ist eine Besonderheit des englischen Vertragsrechts. Danach ist ein Vertrag, wenn er formlos abgeschlossen ist, nur klagbar, wenn sich der Kläger zu einer consideration verpflichtet hat (executory ~) oder die consideration gegeben hat (executed ~), die allerdings nicht angemessen zu sein braucht.

Eine consideration ist für die Klagbarkeit nicht erforderlich, wenn über den Vertrag eine gesiegelte Urkunde (deed) vorliegt.
Die Lehre von der consideration hat in der neueren Rechtspraxis allerdings einige Abschwächungen erfahren.
Das schottische Vertragsrecht kennt das Prinzip der consideration nicht

consideration, adequate ~ angemessene Gegenleistung; **executed** ~ erbrachte Gegenleistung; **executory** ~ zukünftige *(noch zu erbringende)* Gegenleistung; **failure of** ~ Mangel der Gegenleistung; **fair** ~ angemessene Gegenleistung; **for a** ~ entgeltlich; gegen Zahlung; **good** ~ *(in e-r Schenkungsurkunde erwähnte, auf "natural love and affection" oder Verwandtschaft beruhende)* Gegenleistung *(opp. valuable ~)*; **in ~ of** als Gegenleistung (od. Entgelt) für; gegen Vergütung von; **in ~ of £... (the receipt whereof is hereby acknowledged)** gegen Zahlung von £... (dessen Empfang hiermit bestätigt wird); **money** ~ Gegenleistung in Geld; geldeswerte Gegenleistung; **nominal** ~ geringe, unbedeutende Gegenleistung *(die e-n rechtswirksamen Vertrag begründen kann)*; geringer Preis; **past** ~ in der Vergangenheit liegende *(und daher für die Wirksamkeit des nunmehrigen Vertrages nichtausreichende)* Gegenleistung *(des Vertragspartners)*; **pecuniary** ~ s. money →~; **valuable** ~ entgeltliche (od. geldwerte) Gegenleistung; **for valuable** ~ gegen Entgelt, entgeltlich; **for want of** ~ mangels Gegenleistung; **without** ~ unentgeltlich

consideration, to give ~ for sth. für etw. zahlen (od. Gegenleistung geben)

consideration 2. Erwägung, Überlegung; Prüfung; Berücksichtigung; Rücksicht(nahme); Bedeutung, Wichtigkeit; ~ **of a bill** Gesetzesberatung; ~ **of evidence** Beweiswürdigung; **case under** ~ vorliegender Fall; **time for** ~ Bedenkzeit, Bedenkfrist; **want of** ~ Rücksichtslosigkeit

consideration, after careful (or **due**) ~ nach reiflicher Überlegung; **for further** ~ zur weiteren Prüfung; **on further** ~ bei weiterer Überlegung; **in ~ of the special circumstances** unter Berücksichtigung der besonderen Umstände; **out of ~ for sb.** aus Rücksicht auf jdn; **taking into** ~ Berücksichtigung; **without ~ for** ohne Rücksicht auf

consideration, to be under ~ erwogen (od. geprüft) werden; **to give ~ to sth.** etw. prüfen (od. in Erwägung ziehen); **to give due** ~ gebührend Rücksicht nehmen (to auf); **to give favo(u)rable** (or **sympathetic**) ~ wohlwollend prüfen (od. berücksichtigen, erwägen); **to give urgent** ~ dringlich behandeln; **to leave sth. out of** ~ etw unberücksichtigt lassen; **to show ~ for** Rücksicht nehmen auf; **to submit for ~ and approval** zur Prüfung und Genehmigung vorlegen; **to take into** ~ in Betracht ziehen, berücksichtigen; Rücksicht nehmen auf

consideration, money is of no ~ der Preis spielt keine Rolle; **the proposal is under** ~ der Vorschlag wird geprüft

consign *v (Waren)* versenden, übersenden, zusenden, liefern; *(Überseehandel)* konsignieren, in Kommission (od. Konsignation) geben; übergeben, anvertrauen; *Scot (Geld)* hinterlegen; **to ~ goods for sale** Waren in Kommission geben

consigned goods *(Überseehandel)* Konsignationswaren, Kommissionswaren

consignation *Scot* Hinterlegung

consignee Empfänger, Adressat *(von Waren, Fracht)*; *(Überseehandel)* Konsignatar, Verkaufskommissionär; **duty for ~'s account** Zoll geht zu Lasten des Empfängers

consigner →consignor

consignment (consgt) Versendung, Übersendung, Zusendung *(von Waren)*; (Waren-)Sendung; Konsignationsware(n); Konsignation *(im Überseehandel vorkommende Art des Kommissionsgeschäftes)*; ~ **account** Konsignationskonto; ~ **by mail** *Am* Postsendung; ~ **contract** Konsignationsvertrag; ~ **for approval** Ansichtssendung; ~ **goods** Konsignationswaren; ~ **invoice** Konsignationsfaktura; ~ **of goods** Warensendung; Warenversand; Güterabfertigung

consignment note Frachtbrief; *(Flußladegeschäft)* Ladeschein; ~ **form** Frachtbriefformular; **duplicate (of the)** ~ Frachtbriefduplikat; **to make out a** ~ e-n Frachtbrief ausstellen

consignment, ~ **of replacement** Ersatzlieferung; ~ **sale** Konsignationsverkauf; ~ **stock** Konsignationslager

consignment, collective (or **mixed**) ~ Sammelladung; **contract of** ~ Konsignationsvertrag

consignment, on ~ auf dem Konsignationswege, in Kommission; **goods on** ~ Konsignationswaren; **sale on** ~ Konsignationsverkauf; **to give goods on** ~ Waren in Kommission (od. Konsignation) geben

consignment, small ~ Stückgut(sendung); Kleinsendung

consignor (Waren-)Absender, Versender; Verkäufer *(beim Versendungskauf)*; *(Überseehandel)* Konsignant; *Scot* Hinterleger

consistency Folgerichtigkeit; Widerspruchslosigkeit, Übereinstimmung; Beständigkeit, Stetigkeit

consistent folgerichtig; ohne Widerspruch, übereinstimmend; stetig; ~ **with** vereinbar (od. in Übereinstimmung) mit; **not ~ with** unvereinbar mit; ~ **practice (of a court)** ständige Rechtsprechung

consistently with para 2 gemäß Absatz 2

consistory *eccl* Konsistorium; Kardinalsversammlung *(unter Vorsitz des Papstes)*

consolidate *v* (be)festigen; vereinigen, zusammenlegen, verschmelzen; konsolidieren *(kurzfristige Staatsschulden in Anleihen umwandeln; mehrere Anleihen zu einer neuen zusammenfassen)*; **to ~ actions** Klagen miteinander verbinden; **to ~ debts** Schulden konsolidieren *(schwebende Schulden in fundierte umwandeln)*; **to ~ one's position** seine Stellung befestigen; **to ~ shares** Aktien *(zu größeren Stücken)* zusammenlegen; **to ~ shipments** *Am* Sammelladungen zusammenstellen; **to ~ statutes** Gesetze zusammenfassen

consolidated konsolidiert; **~ accounts** *Br* Konzernabschluß; konsolidierter Abschluß; **~ annuities** *Br* →Consols; **~ balance sheet** konsolidierte Bilanz, Gesamtbilanz; Konzernbilanz; **~ bond** konsolidierte Anleihe; **~ cargo** *Am* Sammelladung; **~ debt** konsolidierte (od. fundierte) Schuld *(opp. floating debt)*; **~ (financial) statements** *Am* Konzernabschluß

Consolidated Fund (of the United Kingdom) *Br* Konsolidierter Staatsfonds (des Vereinigten Königreichs); **~ (Appropriation) Act** *Br* Ausgabegesetz; Ausgabebudget; **~ Charges** *Br* Dauerbelastungen *(Zivilliste, Beamtengehälter etc)*

In den Consolidated Fund werden die Steuern eingezahlt, aus ihm werden die Staatsausgaben finanziert

consolidated, ~ group Konzern; **~ loan** konsolidierte Anleihe; **~ mortgage** *Am* Gesamthypothek *(Vereinigung mehrerer Hypotheken eines Gläubigers od. der Hypotheken mehrerer Gläubiger)*; **~ mortage bonds** *Am* durch e-e Gesamthypothek gesicherte Obligationen; **~ net worth** *Am* Vermögenslage des Konzerns; **~ profit and loss account** konsolidierte Gewinn- und Verlustrechnung; **~ report** zusammengefaßter Bericht; **~ results of operations** *Am* Ertragslage des Konzerns; **~ return** *Am*[71] Konzernbilanz; **~ statement of earnings** Konzerngewinn- und -verlustrechnung; **~ stocks** *Br* →Consols; **~ tax return** *Am* gemeinsame Steuererklärung *(von verbundenen Kapitalgesellschaften)*; **to file a ~ tax return** *Am*[72] e-e konsolidierte Steuererklärung einreichen

consolidating statute Zusammenfassungsgesetz *(zur Modernisierung einzelner Gesetzgebungsmaterien)*

consolidation (Be-)Festigung; Vereinigung, Zusammenlegung; Konsolidierung, Konsolidation *(Umwandlung schwebender Schulden in fundierte Schulden; Zusammenfassung mehrerer Anleihen zu e-r neuen Anleihe)*; Fusion, Verschmelzung *(durch Neugründung) (e-e od. mehrere Gesellschaften gehen in e-e neue Gesellschaft auf; z. B. die Gesellschaft A und die Gesellschaft B gehen in die neue Gesellschaft C auf; cf. merger)*; **C~ Act** Gesetz, das das in Einzelgesetzen vertretene Recht zusammenfaßt; **~ of actions** Klagenverbindung, Klagenhäufung; **~ of arable land** Flurbereinigung; **~ of banks** Bankenfusion; **~ of companies** (or *Am* **corporations**) Zusammenlegung (od. Fusion) von (Kapital)-Gesellschaften; Unternehmenszusammenschluß; **~ of democracy** Festigung der Demokratie; **~ of the market** Befestigung des Marktes; **~ of mortgages** Zusammenschreibung von Hypotheken *(zu e-r Gesamthypothek)*; **right of ~ of mortgages** Anspruch *(des mortgagee)* auf gleichzeitige Befriedigung aus mehreren Hypotheken an mehreren Grundstücken; **~ of shares** Zusammenlegung von Aktien; **~ of statutes** Zusammenfassung von Gesetzen; **~ profit** Fusionsgewinn

consolidation, agreement of ~ Fusionsvertrag; **corporate ~** *Am* Unternehmenszusammenschluß; **political ~** politische Konsolidierung

consolidator Sammelladungsspediteur

Consols (Cons.) *Br* Konsols; konsolidierte (od. fundierte) Staatsanleihen (od. Staatspapiere, Staatsrenten) *(festverzinsliche Schuldverschreibungen, für die kein fester Rückzahlungstermin besteht)*; **~ certificate** *Br* Staatsanleiheschein

consort Gemahl(in); im Geleitzug fahrendes Schiff; **the Prince C~** Prinzgemahl; **the Queen C~** Gemahlin des regierenden Königs

consortium 1. (Recht der) eheliche(n) Lebensgemeinschaft; → **loss of ~**

consortium 2. Konsortium; **~ bank** *Br* Konsortialbank; **~ of banks** Bankenkonsortium; **~ credit** Konsortialkredit

conspicuous auffallend, auffällig; gut sichtbar; *fig* hervorragend; **~ consumption** Geltungskonsum; **to post in a ~ place** *(etw.)* an gut sichtbarer Stelle postieren (od. aufstellen)

conspicuously an sichtbarer Stelle; *fig* in hervorragender Weise

conspiracy 1. Verschwörung, Komplott; **~ to commit an offence (~se)** *(strafbare)* Verabredung zur Begehung e-r Straftat; **to become involved in a ~** in e-e Verschwörung verwikkelt werden; **to discover** (or **unmask**) **a ~** e-e Verschwörung aufdecken; **to form** (or **hatch**) **a ~** e-e Verschwörung anzetteln

conspiracy 2. geheime Absprache (od. Verabredung); *Am (AntitrustR)*[73] *(wettbewerbsbeschränkendes)* Zusammenwirken mehrerer Personen; abgestimmtes Verhalten; **~ in restraint of trade** *Am* wettbewerbsbeschränkende Absprache; **implied ~** *Am* vermutetes abgestimmtes Verhalten *(der Wettbewerber) (cf. conscious →parallelism of action)*; **intra-enterprise ~** Absprache zwischen Leitern verschiedener Konzernunternehmen

conspirator Verschwörer

conspiratorial auf geheimem Einverständnis beruhend; Verschwörungs-

conspire *v* sich verschwören, konspirieren (against gegen); sich *(heimlich)* verabreden *(e-e strafbare Handlung zu begehen); Am (AntitrustR)* sich zusammenschließen *(um in illegaler Weise den Markt an sich zu ziehen);* dazu beitragen *(von Ereignissen)*

constable *bes. Br* Polizist; ~ **(on the beat)** Polizist auf Streife; **Chief C~** *Br* Polizeipräsident *(e-s County);* **special** ~ Hilfspolizist

constabulary Polizei

constant konstant, gleichbleibend; ~ **costs** konstante Kosten; ~ **risk** gleichbleibendes Risiko

constituency *parl* Wählerschaft; Wahlbezirk, Wahlkreis; ~ **association** *Br (die Wähler e-s Wahlkreises zusammenfassende)* Wahlvereinigung *(e-r Partei);* ~ **man** Parlamentarier, der sich auf die Belange s-s Wahlbezirks konzentriert; **borough (county)** ~ *Br* die Wählerschaft e-s →borough (county) *(für das House of Commons);* **to stand for a** ~ in e-m Wahlkreis kandidieren, sich als Kandidat aufstellen lassen

constituent 1. Wähler; Vollmachtgeber, Auftraggeber *(gebräuchlicher: principal);* ~ **(part)** Bestandteil

constituent 2. konstituierend, verfassungsgebend; e-n Teil bildend; Bestandteil; ~ **assembly** verfassunggebende Versammlung; ~ **body** Wählerschaft; ~ **fact** Tatbestandsmerkmal; ~ **(part)** Bestandteil; ~ **states** einzelne Staaten (od. Länder) *(e-s Bundesstaates);* Gliedstaaten; ~ **territories** zugehörige Gebiete; **Federation and its** ~ **units** Bund und seine Gliedstaaten

constitute *v* errichten, (be)gründen; *(in ein Amt etc)* einsetzen, ernennen; darstellen, ausmachen; **to** ~ **a committee** e-n Ausschuß einsetzen; **to** ~ **a p. one's heir** *Am* jdn zum Erben einsetzen; **to** ~ **an offen|ce (~se)** e-e strafbare Handlung darstellen; die Tatbestandsmerkmale e-r strafbaren Handlung erfüllen; **this ~s a precedent** dies stellt e-n Präzedenzfall dar; **to** ~ **a quorum** beschlußfähig sein; **to** ~ **a right** ein Recht begründen; **to** ~ **a tribunal** e-n Gerichtshof bilden (od. einsetzen)

constituted, the ~ **authorities** die verfassungsmäßigen Behörden; **they** ~ **themselves a party** sie bildeten e-e Partei; **to be** ~ errichtet (od. gegründet, gebildet) werden

constitution (Staats-)Verfassung; Grundgesetz; Satzung *(e-s Verbandes, Vereins);* Errichtung, Bildung, Gründung; Beschaffenheit; *Am* Börsenordnung *(z.B. der →NYSE);* ~ **of a committee** Einsetzung e-s Ausschusses; ~ **of a company** Gründung e-r Gesellschaft; ~ **of a court** Zusammensetzung e-s Gerichts; ~ **of a right** Begründung e-s Rechts

constitution, amendment to the ~ Verfassungsänderung; Satzungsänderung; **breach of the** ~ Verfassungsbruch; **charter of the** ~ Verfassungsurkunde; **Convention of the C~** *Br* →convention 3.; **draft** ~ Verfassungsentwurf; **Federal C~** *Am* Bundesverfassung; **law amending the** ~ verfassungsänderndes Gesetz; **infringement of the** ~ Verfassungsbruch; **State C~** *Am* Verfassung e-s Einzelstaates; **unwritten** ~ ungeschriebene Verfassung

constitution, to abrogate the ~ die Verfassung aufheben; **to amend the** ~ die Verfassung ändern; **to draw up the** ~ die Satzung *(e-s Vereins etc)* abfassen

Br Es gibt keine Verfassungsurkunde. Die Verfassung beruht auf Gewohnheitsrecht und einer Anzahl von Gesetzen (Magna Charta [Libertatum], Petition of Rights, Habeas Corpus Act, Bill of Rights, Act of Settlement etc)

Am Die amerikanische (Bundes-)Verfassung beruht auf der Federal Constitution von 1787 und den → Amendments. Jeder der 50 Einzelstaaten hat eine eigene Verfassung. Daneben besteht ein ungeschriebenes Verfassungsrecht, das auf Verfassungsübung und der Rechtsprechung des Supreme Court beruht

constitutional konstitutionell, verfassungsmäßig; verfassungsrechtlich; ~ **amendment** Verfassungsänderung; Zusatz zur Verfassung; ~ **charter** Verfassungsurkunde; ~ **complaint** Verfassungsbeschwerde; ~ **conventions** *Br* Konventionalregeln *(pragmatische Regeln für die politischen Verhaltensweisen bestimmter Staatsorgane);* ~ **court** *Am* →court 2.; ~ **crisis** Verfassungskrise; ~ **duties** verfassungsmäßige Pflichten; ~ **history** Verfassungsgeschichte; ~ **law** Verfassungsrecht; ~ **lawyer** *Am* Jurist für Verfassungsfragen; ~ **limitation** verfassungsrechtliche Beschränkungen; ~ **monarchy** konstitutionelle Monarchie; ~ **reform** Verfassungsreform; ~ **right** *Am* verfassungsmäßig garantiertes Recht; Grundrecht; ~ **state** Rechtsstaat

constitutionality Verfassungsmäßigkeit

constitutive konstituierend; konstitutiv, (rechts-)begründend *(opp. declaratory)*

constraint Zwang; *Scot* Nötigung *(cf. duress);* **administrative** ~ behördlicher Zwang; **position of** ~ Zwangslage; **to act under** ~ unter Zwang handeln; **to be under** ~ unter Zwang (od. Druck) stehen

construct *v* bauen, errichten; **to** ~ **a factory** e-e Fabrik bauen

construction 1. Auslegung, (Sinn-)Deutung; ~ **clause** Auslegungsklausel; ~ **of contracts** Auslegung von Verträgen, Vertragsauslegung; **lib-**

eral ~ weite Auslegung; **strict** ~ enge Auslegung; **to put a** ~ **upon** (etw.) auslegen

construction 2. Bau, (Er-)Bauen, Errichtung; Bau(werk), Gebäude; Bauweise, Bauausführung, Konstruktion; ~ **costs** Baukosten; ~ **engineering** Hochbau; ~ **financing** *Am* Baufinanzierung; ~ **industry** Bauwirtschaft; Baugewerbe; ~ **laws** Baugesetze; ~ **loan** Baudarlehen; ~ **period** Baufrist, Bauzeit; ~ **prices** Baupreise; ~ **regulation** Bauvorschrift; ~ **of a road** Bau e-r Straße; ~ **site** Baustelle; ~ **works** Bauarbeiten; ~ **worker** Bauarbeiter

construction, commencement of ~ Baubeginn; **in course of** ~ im Bau befindlich; **housing** ~ Wohnungsbau; **new** ~ Neubau; **type of** ~ Bauart; **under** ~ im Bau befindlich

constructional Bau-, Konstruktions-; ~ **defect** Baufehler; Konstruktionsfehler; ~ **engineering** Maschinenbau

constructive 1. präsumptiv, gefolgert, kraft gesetzlicher Auslegung, auszulegen als; fingiert; ~ **condition** unterstellte Bedingung; *(aus Gründen der Billigkeit)* vom Gericht ergänzte Vertragsbedingung; ~ **conversion** Umdeutung von beweglichem in unbewegliches Vermögen (und umgekehrt) *(aus der Interessenlage heraus, bes. bei Auslegung e-s Testaments)*; ~ → **delivery;** ~ **dismissal** fingierte Entlassung; ~ **dividends** *(SteuerR)* verdeckte Gewinnausschüttungen; ~ **fraud** Betrug kraft gesetzlicher Vermutung; ~ **notice** zurechenbare Kenntnis *(der Rechte Dritter)*; schuldhafte Nichtkenntnis (Kennenmüssen) *(→ notice 2.)*; ~ **possession** mittelbarer Besitz *(z. B. des Verpächters bei unmittelbarem Besitz des Pächters)*; *(auch)* rechtlicher (fingierter) Besitz *(z. B. des Besitzers e-s Hauses an allen Sachen in dem Haus; des →executor an den Nachlaßgegenständen)*; ~ **revocation** Widerruf kraft Gesetzes *(unabhängig vom Willen der Parteien)*; ~ **total loss** *(SeeversR)* fingierter Totalverlust *(als Totalschaden angenommener Teilschaden, wenn Wiederbeschaffung zu kostspielig sein würde; opp. actual total loss)*; ~ **trust** (auf Grund e-r construction of equity) fingiertes Treuhandverhältnis *(Rechtsfolgen: Haftung aus Geschäftsführung ohne Auftrag od. ungerechtfertigter Bereicherung; →trust 1.)*

constructive 2. konstruktiv, aufbauend; positiv; Bau-; ~ **counter-proposal** konstruktiver Gegenvorschlag; ~ **criticism** positive Kritik

constructual and civil engineering Hoch- und Tiefbau

construe *v (Gesetz etc)* auslegen; **to** ~ **extensively** weit auslegen; **to** ~ **restrictively** (or **strictly**) eng auslegen

consuetudinary law *Am* Gewohnheitsrecht

consul Konsul; ~**-general** Generalkonsul; **career** ~ *Am* Berufskonsul; **honorary** ~ Wahlkonsul; **professional** ~ Berufskonsul; **vice-**~ Vizekonsul

consulage *Am* Konsulatsgebühren

consular, ~ **agency** Konsularagentur; konsularische Vertretung; ~ **agent** Konsularagent; ~ **agreement** Konsularabkommen; ~ **archives** Konsulatsarchiv; ~ **authority** Konsularbehörde; ~ **certificate** konsularische Bescheinigung; ~ **convention**[74] Konsularvertrag, Konsularabkommen; ~ **court** Konsulargericht; ~ **district** Konsularbezirk, Amtsbezirk e-s Konsuls; ~ **employee** Konsulatsangehöriger; ~ **fees** Konsulargebühren; ~ **functions** konsularische Aufgaben; ~ **immunities** konsularische Immunitäten; ~ **invoice** Konsulatsfaktura; ~ **jurisdiction** Konsulargerichtsbarkeit

consular officer Konsul; Konsularbeamter; konsularischer Vertreter; **career** ~ Berufskonsul; **honorary** ~ Wahlkonsul

consular, ~ **protection** konsularischer Schutz; ~ **receipts** Konsulareinnahmen; ~ **relations**[75] konsularische Beziehungen; ~ **representation** konsularische Vertretung; ~ **representative** konsularischer Vertreter; ~ **revenues** Konsulatseinnahmen; ~ **service** Konsulatsdienst, konsularischer Dienst; ~ **tribunal** Konsulargericht; ~ **transaction** konsularische Amtshandlungen; ~ **visa** Konsulatssichtvermerk

consulate Konsulat *(Amt und Gebäude)*; ~**-general** Generalkonsulat; **closure of a** ~ Schließung e-s Konsulats

consulship Amt e-s Konsuls, Konsulat

consult *v*, **to** ~ **sb.** jdn um Rat fragen, jdn zu Rate ziehen; jdn befragen; jdn konsultieren; **to** ~ **sb. about sth.** mit jdm Rücksprache nehmen über etw.; **to** ~ **with sb.** sich mit jdm beraten; sich mit jdm ins Benehmen setzen; **to** ~ **counsel** e-n Anwalt *(Br barrister)* befragen (od. zuziehen); **to** ~ **a dictionary** in e-m Wörterbuch nachschlagen; **to** ~ **the doctor** den Arzt konsultieren; **to** ~ **an expert** e-n Fachmann zu Rate ziehen (od. befragen); **to** ~ **records** Akten herbeiziehen (od. einsehen)

consulting beratend; ~ **days** Sprechtage; ~ **engineers** technische Beratungsfirma; ~ **fee** Beratungshonorar; **on** ~ **our records** bei Durchsicht unserer Akten

consultancy Beratungstätigkeit, ~ **agreement** (Unternehmens-)Beratungsvertrag; ~ **fee** Beratungshonorar

consultant (Betriebs-, Industrie- etc) Berater; ~ **member** beratendes Mitglied *(ohne Stimmrecht)*; **business** (or **management**) ~ Betriebsberater; **political** ~ politischer Berater; **tax** ~ Steuerberater; **technical** ~ technischer Berater

consultation Beratung, Rücksprache (on über);

Befragung; Konsultation; ~ **of documents** Herbeiziehung von (od. Einsichtnahme in) Urkunden; **political** ~ politische Konsultation; ~ **fee** Beratungsgebühr; ~ **hours** Sprechstunden; **after** ~ **with** nach Beratung (od. Rücksprache) mit; **to enter into** ~**s** in Konsultationen eintreten; **to hold a** ~ e-e Beratung abhalten; **the court retired for** ~ das Gericht zog sich zur Beratung zurück

consultative beratend; konsultativ; ~ **assembly** beratende Versammlung; **in a** ~ **capacity** in beratender Eigenschaft; ~ **committee** beratender Ausschuß; ~ **member** beratendes Mitglied *(ohne Stimmrecht);* ~ **pact** *(VölkerR)* Konsultativpakt; ~ **papers** *Br* ergänzende Vorschriften zum Banking Act 1987

consumable goods Verbrauchsgüter

consume *v* verbrauchen, aufbrauchen; vergeuden, verschwenden; vernichten, zerstören

consuming, ~ **country** Verbraucherland *(opp. producing country);* **the** ~ **public** die Verbraucherschaft; ~ **states** Verbraucherstaaten

consumer Verbraucher, Konsument *(opp. producer);* ~**'s ability to buy** Konsumentenkaufkraft; ~ **advertising** Verbraucherwerbung; ~ **behavio(u)r** Verbraucherverhalten; ~ **banking** *Am* Einzelkundengeschäft der Banken; ~**s' cooperation** Genossenschaftswesen; ~**s' cooperative** *(Br* **society**) (co-op) Verbrauchergenossenschaft, Konsumverein; ~ **country** Verbraucherland *(opp. producer country);* ~ **credit** Konsumentenkredit, Konsum(tiv)kredit; ~ **credit agreement** *Br (den Bestimmungen des Consumer Credit Act, 1974, s. 8 unterliegender)* Kreditvertrag *(bis zu e-r gewissen Summe);* **C~ Credit Protection Act** *Am* Gesetz über den Konsumentenkredit; ~ **demand** Verbrauchernachfrage; ~ **durables** Gebrauchsgüter, langlebige Konsumgüter; ~ **economics** Verbraucherwirtschaft; ~ **electronics** Unterhaltungselektronik; Konsumelektronik; ~ **expenditure** Konsumausgaben; ~**s' expenditure deflator** *Br* Index der Verbraucherpreise; ~ **finance company** *Am* Teilzahlungsbank

consumer goods Konsumgüter, Verbrauchsgüter *(opp. producer goods, capital goods);* ~ **industry** Konsumgüterindustrie; **durable** ~ Gebrauchsgüter, langlebige Konsumgüter; **industrial** ~ gewerbliche Konsumgüter; **boom** (or **trend**) **in** ~ Verbrauchsgüterkonjunktur

consumer, ~ **group** Verbrauchergruppe; ~ **hire agreement** *Br (den Bestimmungen des Consumer Credit Act, 1974, s. 15 unterliegender)* Mietvertrag über bewegl. Sachen *(bis zu e-r bestimmten Summe);* ~ **hedging** Absicherung des Verbrauchers; ~ **inquiry** Verbraucherbefragung; ~ **loan company** *Am* Finanzierungsgesellschaft für Kleinkredite; ~ **market** Verbrauchermarkt; ~ **of electricity** Stromabnehmer

consumer price Verbraucherpreis, Konsumentenpreis; ~ **index** (CPI) *Am* Preisindex für die Lebenshaltung; Index der Verbraucherpreise; **rise in** ~**s** Anstieg der Verbraucherpreise; **to curb upward movement in** ~**s** den Anstieg der Verbraucherpreise bremsen

consumer, C~ Product Safety Commission *Am* Behörde für die Sicherheit von Verbrauchsgütern

Consumer Protection Act 1987 *Br* Verbraucherschutzgesetz

Es beinhaltet die Umsetzung der EG-Produkthaftungsrichtlinie (European Directive on Product Liability) in britisches Recht, ferner allgemeine Sicherheitsvorschriften für Konsumgüter und Regeln über irreführende Preisangaben

consumer, ~ **research** Verbraucherbefragung, -forschung; ~ **society** Konsumgsellschaft; ~**spending** Verbraucherausgaben; Gesamtausgaben der Verbraucher; ~**'s surplus** Konsumentenrente; ~ **survey** Verbraucherumfrage

consumer, average ~ Durchschnittsverbraucher; **bulk** ~ Großverbraucher; **final** ~ Endverbraucher; **large scale** ~ Großverbraucher; **last** ~ Letztverbraucher; **ultimate** ~ Endverbraucher

consumerism Konsumerismus

consummate vollendet, vollkommen, perfekt

consummate *v* vollenden; **to** ~ **the marriage** den Eheakt vollziehen; **the offen|ce (~se) is** ~**d** die Straftat ist vollendet

consummation of marriage Vollziehung des Eheaktes

consumption Verbrauch, Konsum *(opp. production);* ~ **area** Verbrauchsgebiet; ~ **capacity** Konsumkraft, Kaufkraft *(e-r Verbraucherschicht);* ~ **control** Verbraucherlenkung; ~ **economy** Verbrauchswirtschaft; ~ **goods** Konsumgüter, Verbrauchsgüter (→*consumer goods);* ~ **level** Verbrauchsstand; ~ **of materials** Materialverbrauch; ~ **ratio** Konsumquote

consumption, annual ~ Jahresverbrauch; **decrease of** (or **decreased**) ~ Verbrauchsrückgang; **domestic** (or **home, internal**) ~ Inlandsverbrauch; **increase of** (or **increased**) ~ Verbrauchssteigerung, Konsumsteigerung; **increasing** ~ steigender Verbrauch; **intended for human** ~ für den menschlichen Verzehr bestimmt; **power** ~ Stromverbrauch; **personal** (or **private**) ~ Eigenverbrauch, Selbstverbrauch; **producing for** ~ verbrauchsorientiert *(Industrie);* **rate of** ~ Verbrauchsrate; **rate of final** ~ Endverbrauchsrate; **seasonal** ~ Saisonbedarf; **unfit for human** ~ für die menschliche Ernährung ungeeignet; **for use and** ~ zum Gebrauch und Verbrauch

consumption, to cut ~ den Verbrauch reduzieren; **to enter goods for** ~ Waren zum freien Verkehr einführen; **to increase** ~ den Verbrauch (od. Konsum) steigern; **to reduce** ~ den Verbrauch einschränken

contact Verbindung, Kontakt, Fühlungnahme; Kontaktperson, Kontakter; ~ **with foreign law** *(IPR)* Auslandsberührung; ~ **man** Kontaktmann, Verbindungsmann, Kontakter; **in close** ~ in engem Kontakt; **establishment of** ~**s** Herstellung von Kontakten

contact, to be in ~ **with sb.** mit jdm in Verbindung stehen; **to break off all** ~**s with sb.** alle Verbindungen mit jdm abbrechen; **to enter into** ~ (or **to make** ~) **with sb.** mit jdm Verbindung (od. Kontakt) aufnehmen; **to take up direct** ~ **with** sich unmittelbar in Verbindung setzen mit

contact *v*, **to** ~ **a p.** mit jdm in Verbindung treten; sich mit jdm in Verbindung setzen

contagious disease ansteckende Krankheit, Seuche

contain *v* enthalten; fassen, Raum haben für; *pol* eindämmen

contained, self-~ in sich geschlossen; **self-**~ **flat** *Br* abgeschlossene Wohnung; **self-**~ **house** *Br* Einfamilienhaus

container Container, (Groß-)Behälter; ~ **construction** Containerbau; ~ **facilities** Anlagen für den Containerverkehr; ~ **ship** Containerschiff; ~ **shipment** Versand in Containern; ~ **transport** Containerverkehr, Behälterverkehr; **approval of individual** ~**s** Einzelzulassung von Containern; →**International Convention for Safe C**~**s; to construct** ~**s to standards** Container nach Normen herstellen; **to handle** ~**s** Container verladen

containerization Containerisierung, Umstellung auf Container

containment (policy) Eindämmungspolitik *(Politik der Eindämmung gegen e-n mögl. Feind, in der Hoffnung der Verständigung mit ihm; bes. Ingrenzenhalten des Kommunismus)*

contaminate *v* verunreinigen, verschmutzen; *(bes. radioaktiv)* verseuchen; ~**d food** verseuchte Nahrungsmittel

contamination Kontamination; Verschmutzung *(der See)*; Verunreinigung *(der Luft)*; *(radioaktive)* Verseuchung; ~ **of the sea by dumping of radioactive waste** Verseuchung des Meeres durch Versenken radioaktiver Abfälle; **environmental** ~ Umweltverschmutzung; **radioactive** ~ **of foodstuffs** radioaktive Verseuchung von Lebensmitteln

contango *(Londoner Börse)* Report, Kursaufschlag *(opp. backwardation)*; ~ **(business)** Reportgeschäft; ~ **day** Reporttag, Prolongationstag; ~ **rate** Prolongationssatz, Reportsatz

contemnor jd, der →contempt of court begeht

contemplate *v* erwägen, vorhaben, beabsichtigen; voraussehen, rechnen mit

contemplation Absicht, Vorhaben; **in** ~ **of death** im Hinblick auf den Tod; **to have in** ~ vorhaben, beabsichtigen

contemporaneous gleichzeitig (with mit); ~ **performance** Erfüllung Zug um Zug

contempt Mißachtung, Geringschätzung; Ungebühr *(bes. vor Gericht)*; **to have a p. in** ~ jdn verachten (od. mit Verachtung strafen)

contempt of court Mißachtung des Gerichts; Ungebühr vor Gericht; **to have a p. up for** ~ jdn wegen Ungebühr vor Gericht zur Verantwortung ziehen

Contempt of court ist z. B. ungebührliches Verhalten im Gerichtssaal, vorsätzliches Nichterscheinen, unberechtigte Aussageverweigerung als Zeuge; es ist aber auch außerhalb des Gerichts möglich, z. B. wenn ein Richter in einer Zeitung angegriffen wird oder wenn eine Zeitung einen Fall bespricht, bevor dieser vor Gericht verhandelt worden ist

contempt of Parliament Beleidigung des Parlaments

contemptuous →**damages**

contend *v* behaupten, vorbringen, geltend machen (that daß); **to** ~ **for sth.** um etw. streiten (od. wetteifern); sich für etw. einsetzen; **to** ~ **for a prize** um e-n Preis kämpfen; **to** ~ **with difficulties** mit Schwierigkeiten zu kämpfen haben

contending, ~ **claims** widerstreitende Ansprüche; ~ **parties** streitende Parteien, Prozeßparteien

content 1. Fassungsvermögen, Rauminhalt; (der) Gehalt; **alcohol** ~ Alkoholgehalt; **average** ~ Durchschnittsgehalt

contents Inhalt; Hausrat; ~ **of a bottle** Inhalt e-r Flasche; ~ **of a letter** Inhalt e-s Briefes; **declaration** (or **list**) of ~ Inhaltserklärung *(e-r Warensendung)*; **index of** ~ s. table of →~; **insurance on** ~ Hausratsversicherung; **table of** ~ Inhaltsverzeichnis *(e-s Buches)*

Content 2. *Br (House of Lords)* dafür (Ja-Stimme); **Not** ~ dagegen (Nein-Stimme)

contention (Wort-, Meinungs-)Streit; Streitigkeit; Behauptung, Vorbringen; **point of** ~ Streitpunkt; **my** ~ **is that ...** ich behaupte, daß ...

contentious streitig, strittig; ~ **business** *Br* streitige Zivilsache *(fast nur in Verbindung mit Nachlaßsachen)*; ~ **jurisdiction** streitige Gerichtsbarkeit *(Am bes. in Zusammenhang mit der Gerichtsbarkeit der Kirchengerichte)*; ~ **procedure**

(VölkerR) Verfahren zur Regelung e-s Streitfalles; **non-~ business**[76] Zivilsache der freiwilligen Gerichtsbarkeit; **non-~ jurisdiction** freiwillige Gerichtsbarkeit

contest Streit, Kontroverse, Auseinandersetzung; Wettstreit, Wettbewerb (for um); **to compete in a ~** sich an e-m Wettbewerb beteiligen

contest *v* streiten um; debattieren über; abstreiten, bestreiten, anfechten; sich bewerben um, an e-m Wettbewerb teilnehmen; kandidieren für; **to ~ a borough** *Br parl* in e-m *(städtischen)* Wahlkreis als Kandidat auftreten; für e-n Wahlkreis kandidieren; **to ~ a claim** e-n Anspruch bestreiten; **to ~ an election** die Gültigkeit e-r Wahl anfechten; sich als Kandidat aufstellen lassen; *(bei e-r Wahl)* als Kandidat auftreten; **to ~ sb.'s right** jds Recht abstreiten (od. streitig machen); **to ~ a seat** *parl* kandidieren; **to ~ the validity** die Gültigkeit anfechten; **to ~ a will** ein Testament anfechten

contested, ~ case Streitfall; **~ election** angefochtene Wahl; **(closely) ~ election** (hart) umstrittene Wahl *(bei der die Mehrheit sehr klein ist)*; **~ point** strittiger Punkt, Streitfrage

contestable bestreitbar; anfechtbar

contestant jd, der *(e-e Entscheidung, Wahlergebnis etc)* anficht; **~ for a prize** (Mit-)Bewerber um e-n Preis

contestation Streit; Bestreitung; Anfechtung; **~ of (a child's) legitimacy** Ehelichkeitsanfechtung

context Zusammenhang; zusammenhängender Text; **according to ~** (or **as the ~ requires**) je nach Zusammenhang; **unless the ~ otherwise requires** wenn sich aus dem Zusammenhang nichts anderes ergibt

contiguity *(VölkerR)* Kontiguität; Angrenzen (to an)

contiguous angrenzend (to an); benachbart; **~ to the coast** an die Küste angrenzend; **~ waters** Küstengewässer; **~ zone** *(VölkerR)* Kontiguitätszone, *(an die Küstengewässer)* angrenzende Zone *(außerhalb der [Dreimeilen- etc] Zone, in der der Uferstaat begrenzte Hoheitsrechte hat)*; **to be ~ to** grenzen an

continent Kontinent, Erdteil; **the C~** *Br* das europäische Festland

continental kontinental; *Br* Bewohner des europäischen Festlandes; *Br* zum *(europäischen)* Kontinent gehörend; **~ bills** *Br* Wechsel auf Plätze des europäischen Kontinents; **~ call** *Br* Auslandsgespräch *(mit dem europäischen Kontinent)*; **~ orders** *Br* Aufträge vom Festland; **~ shelf** *(VölkerR)* Kontinentalschelf, Festlandssockel; **~ trade** *Br* Europahandel *(ohne Großbritannien)*; **~ waters** Gewässer des Festlandes, Binnengewässer

contingencies unvorhergesehene Ereignisse; unvorhergesehene Ausgaben; Eventualverbindlichkeiten; *(VersR)* Schadensmöglichkeiten; **~ fund** →contingency fund; **~ reserve** →contingency reserve

contingency unvorhergesehenes *(von e-m Zufall od. e-r Bedingung abhängiges)* Ereignis; möglicher Fall, Eventualität, Eventualfall, *(aufschiebende)* Bedingung; **~ budget** Eventualhaushalt; **~ fee** *Am* Erfolgshonorar; **~ fund** Fonds für unvorhergesehene Ausgaben; Delkrederefonds; **~ insurance** Versicherung gegen besondere Risiken; **~ insured against** das versicherte Risiko; **~ reserve** Reserve für unvorhergesehene Ausgaben; Rückstellung für Eventualverbindlichkeiten; Delkredereserve, Delkredererückstellung; **~ risks insurance** Versicherung gegen außergewöhnliche Risiken; **a ~ comes to pass** e-e Bedingung tritt ein

contingent 1. (Beteiligungs-)Quote, Anteil; Kontingent, *(bes.)* Truppenkontingent; **to apportion as a ~** (or **to fix a ~**) kontingentieren

contingent 2. *(unter Umständen)* möglich, eventuell, Eventual-; abhängig (upon von); bedingt (upon durch); **~ →annuity; ~ beneficiary** *(bes. VersR)* bedingt Begünstigter *(dessen Recht vom Eintritt e-r Bedingung abhängt)*; **~ bequest** von e-r im Testament genannten Bedingung od. e-m Ereignis abhängiges Vermächtnis; bedingtes Vermächtnis; **~ claim** Eventualforderung; bedingter Anspruch; **~ estate** Anwartschaft auf ein Grundstücksrecht; **~ fee** *Am* Erfolgshonorar; **~ gain →~ profit; ~ gift →~ legacy; ~ interest** bedingtes Recht; Anwartschaft; **~ legacy** bedingtes Vermächtnis *(dessen Anfall vom Eintritt e-r Bedingung abhängt)*; **~ liabilities** *(Bilanz)* Eventualverbindlichkeiten; **~ liability** Eventualhaftung, Eventualverbindlichkeit; Ausfallhaftung; **~ order** gekoppelter Auftrag; **~ profit** eventueller *(noch nicht realisierbarer)* Gewinn; **~ remainder** →remainder 2.; **~ reserve** →contingency reserve; **~ right** Anwartschaftsrecht *(bedingte od. ungewisse Anwartschaft)*; **~ trust** bedingtes Treuhandverhältnis; **to be ~ (up)on sth.** von etw. abhängen; durch etw. bedingt sein; **to make sth. ~ (up)on** etw. abhängig machen von

contingently, to be ~ liable bedingt haften *(opp. to be absolutely liable)*

continuance Dauer, Fortdauer, Fortbestehen; *Am* Vertagung; **~ of a firm** Fortbestehen e-r Firma; **~ of a prior marriage** Fortbestehen e-r früheren Ehe *(cf. impediment to marriage)*; **~ in force** Weitergeltung; **~ in office** Verbleiben im Amt; **~ of proceedings** *Am* Vertagung des Verfahrens; **during the ~ of the war** während der Dauer des Krieges

continuation Fortsetzung, Fortbestand; Weiterführung; *Br (Börse)* Prolongation; ~ **bill** *Br* Prolongationswechsel; ~ **business** Prolongationsgeschäft; ~ **class(es)** →~ school; ~ **clause** *Br (SeeversR)* Verlängerungsklausel *(falls Schiff sich bei Ablauf der Police noch auf See befindet);* ~ **day** *Br (Börse)* Reporttag *(Tag für die Prolongation);* **~-in-part** *(PatR)* Teilweiterbehandlung; **~-in-part application** *Am (PatR)* Änderungsanmeldung; ~ **of a business** Weiterführung e-s Geschäftes; ~ **of use** *(PatR)* Weiterbenutzung; ~ **order** Anschlußauftrag; ~ **rate** *Br* Prolongationssatz, Reportsatz; ~ **school** Fortbildungsschule, -kurse; ~ **training** berufliche Fortbildung

continue *v* fortsetzen, fortfahren mit; fortdauern, weiterbestehen; *Am* vertagen; *Br (Börse)* prolongieren, in Prolongation (od. Report) nehmen; **to ~ a business** ein Geschäft fortführen; **to ~ in demand** weiter gefragt sein; **to ~ in effect** (or **in force**) in Kraft bleiben; **to ~ negotiations** Verhandlungen fortsetzen; **to ~ in office** im Amt verbleiben; **to ~ a p. in his post** jdn auf s-m Posten belassen; **to ~ proceedings** *Am* das Verfahren vertagen

continued, ~ bonds *Am* prolongierte Obligationen; ~ **contract** Dauerschuldvertrag; ~ **existence** Fortbestand; ~ **performance of functions** Fortführung von Aufgaben; ~ **use** *(PatentR)* Weiterbenutzung; ~ **validity** Fortdauer der Gültigkeit; **to be ~** Fortsetzung folgt

continuing, ~ account Kontokorrentkonto; ~ **boom** anhaltende Konjunktur; ~ **education** ständige Weiterbildung, Fortbildung

continuity Kontinuität, Stetigkeit; ununterbrochener Zusammenhang; *(Film)* Drehbuch; *(Rundfunk)* Manuskript; ~ **of life** unbegrenzte Lebensdauer; ~ **of rights** Fortbestehen von Rechten; ~ **of states** *(VölkerR)* Kontinuität (od. Fortdauer) von Staaten *(trotz innerer od. äußerer Wandlungen)*

continuous fortdauernd, ununterbrochen; kontinuierlich; ~ **employment** fortdauernde Beschäftigung; ~ **production** Fließfertigung; ~ **voyage** *(VölkerR)* einheitliche (od. fortgesetzte) Reise *(s. right of →capture)*

contra *v* rückbuchen, stornieren

contra gegen; ~ **account** Gegenrechnung; Gegenkonto; ~ **entry** Gegenbuchung, Storno (-buchung); ~ **bonos mores** gegen die guten Sitten; unsittlich

contraband *(VölkerR)* Konterbande, Bannware; Schmuggelware; Schleichhandel, Schmuggel; ~ **by analogy** ein der Konterbande gleichgesetzter Transport; ~ **articles** (or **goods**) Konterbande(waren), Bannware; Schmuggelware; ~ **of war** Kriegskonterbande *(für e-e kriegführende Macht transportierte Güter; s. right of →capture);* ~ **trade** Schmuggelhandel; **absolute ~** absolute Konterbande- *(Güter, die ausschließl. für Kriegszwecke verwendbar sind);* **relative ~** relative Konterbande *(Güter, die für Kriegs- und Friedenszwecke verwendbar sind);* **list of ~ (articles)** Konterbandeliste; **quasi-~** Quasi-Konterbande *(neutralitätswidrige Unterstützung);* **to be seized as ~** als Konterbande beschlagnahmt werden; **to run ~** Schleichhandel (od. Schmuggel) betreiben

contrabandist Schmuggler, Schleichhändler

contract 1. Vertrag; Vertragsurkunde

contract, to abide by a ~ sich an e-n Vertrag halten; **to accede to a ~** e-m Vertrag beitreten; **to annul** (or **avoid**) **a ~** e-n Vertrag annullieren (od. für nichtig erklären); **rights arising under a ~** Rechte aus e-m Vertrag; vertragliche Rechte; **to be bound by ~** (or **to be under a ~**) vertraglich verpflichtet sein; **to break a ~** e-n Vertrag brechen, vertragsbrüchig werden; **to cancel a ~** e-n Vertrag aufheben; von e-m Vertrag zurücktreten; **to come under a ~** unter e-n Vertrag fallen; **to complete a ~** e-n Vertrag erfüllen; **to conclude a ~** e-n Vertrag (ab)schließen; **to draw up a ~** e-n Vertrag aufsetzen; **to enter into a ~** e-n Vertrag (ab)schließen (od. eingehen); **to execute a ~** e-n Vertrag *(rechtsgültig)* ausfertigen; e-n Vertrag erfüllen; **a ~ expires** ein Vertrag läuft ab (od. erlischt); **to fall under a ~** unter e-n Vertrag fallen; **to fulfil a ~** e-n Vertrag erfüllen; **to infringe a ~** e-n Vertrag verletzen; **to make a ~** e-n Vertrag (ab)schließen; **to perform a ~** e-n Vertrag erfüllen; **to prepare a ~** e-n Vertrag aufsetzen; **to prolong a ~** e-n Vertrag verlängern; **to repudiate the ~** die Vertragserfüllung ablehnen; **to rescind a ~** e-n Vertrag aufheben, von e-m Vertrag zurücktreten; **to sign a ~** e-n Vertrag unterschreiben; **to sue on a ~** aus e-m Vertrag klagen; **to terminate a ~** e-n Vertrag kündigen; **to violate a ~** e-n Vertrag verletzen; **to withdraw from a ~** von e-m Vertrag zurücktreten

contract, ~ by specialty Vertrag unter Siegel (→*specialty 2.*); ~ **claim** vertraglicher Anspruch, Anspruch aus Vertrag; ~ **combination** *Am* vertraglicher (Unternehmens-)Zusammenschluß; Kartell

contract clause *Am*[77] *(StaatsR)* Vertragsschutzklausel

Gegen die Einzelstaaten gerichtetes Verbot, Staatsgesetze, die die bindende Kraft von Verträgen beeinträchtigen würden, zu erlassen

contract date vertraglich vorgesehenes Datum; Datum des Vertragsabschlusses

contract debt Vertragsschuld; vertraglich geschuldete Leistung; **recovery of the ~** Eintreibung von Vertragsschulden

contract description, goods of the ~ vertragsgemäße Waren; **the goods are of ~** die Waren entsprechen den vertraglich vereinbarten Bedingungen

contract, ~ for delivery Liefervertrag; **~ for a lease** Miet(vor)vertrag; Pacht(vor)vertrag; **~ for (the) sale of goods**[78] Vertrag über den Verkauf von Waren; Kaufvertrag über bewegl. Sachen; **~ for sale of land** Vertrag über den Verkauf von Grundbesitz; *(obligatorischer)* Grundstückskaufvertrag *(cf. completion [of sale])*; **~ for services** →service 1.; **~ for work and labo(u)r** Werkvertrag; **~ for work and materials** Werklieferungsvertrag; **~ freight** vertraglich vereinbarte *(ermäßigte)* Fracht

contract guarantees Vertragsgarantien; **(ICC) Uniform Rules for C~ G~**[78a] (ICC) Einheitliche Richtlinien für Vertragsgarantien (von 1979) *(→tender bond, →performance guarantee, →repayment guarantee)*

contract, ~ → implied in fact; ~ → implied in law; ~ in favo(u)r of a third party Vertrag zugunsten Dritter; **~ in restraint of trade** Vertrag wettbewerbsbeschränkenden Inhalts; **~ in writing** schriftlicher Vertrag; **~ interest** vertraglich vereinbarte Zinsen; **~ labo(u)r** Arbeitskräfte auf Zeit; **~ lien** Vertragspfandrecht; **~ negotiations** *Am* Tarifverhandlungen; **~ note** *Br (Börse) (von e-m Makler ausgestellter)* Schlußschein *(bought note or sold note)*; **~ of affreightment** Seefrachtvertrag; **~ of agency** Vertretungsvertrag; **~ of carriage** Frachtvertrag; Beförderungsvertrag; **~ of carriage by sea** Seetransportvertrag; **~ of chartering** Chartervertrag; **~ of combined transport** kombinierter Transportvertrag; **~ of → employment; ~ of guarantee (guaranty)** Garantievertrag; Bürgschaftsvertrag; **~ of hire** Mietvertrag über bewegliche Sachen; **~ of loan** Darlehensvertrag; **~ of loan for use** Leihvertrag; **~ of marine insurance** Seeversicherungsvertrag; **~ of record** durch das Gericht bewirkter Vertrag *(z.B. recognizance)*

contract of sale Kaufvertrag *(entweder sale = sofortige Eigentumsübertragung oder agreement to sell = zukünftige od. bedingte Eigentumsübertragung)*; **conformity of the goods stipulated in the ~** Übereinstimmung der Ware mit dem Kaufvertrag

contract, ~ of service Arbeitsvertrag (→service 1.); **~ penalty** Vertragsstrafe, Konventionalstrafe; **~ price** Vertragspreis, vertraglich vereinbarter Preis; **~ processing** Lohnveredelung

contract rights *Am*[79] Geschäftsforderungen

Zahlungsansprüche aus Kaufverträgen, Miet- oder Pachtverträgen oder Dienstleistungsverträgen, die nicht durch Wertpapiere oder →chattel paper verkörpert werden

Contract Sanctity Clause *Am* Klausel der Unantastbarkeit der Verträge

contract, ~ sheet Abrechnung des Börsenmaklers; **~ termination** *Am* Tarifkündigung; **~ terms** Vertragsbedingungen; **~ to sell** (personal property) *Am* Vertrag über den Verkauf beweglicher Sachen; Kaufvertrag; **~ under hand** *Br* einfacher Vertrag *(opp. ~ under seal)*

contract under seal gesiegelter Vertrag

Im anglo-amerikanischen Recht unterscheidet man zwei Hauptarten von Verträgen: unter Siegel abgeschlossene Verträge (contracts under seal, specialty contracts, deeds) und einfache Verträge (contracts under hand, simple contracts). Ein contract under seal ist ein beurkundeter Vertrag, der in zweifacher Hinsicht privilegiert ist: Er ist ohne →consideration gültig und Ansprüche aus ihm verjähren erst in 12 Jahren (normale Verjährungsfrist 6 Jahre). Für bestimmte Rechtsgeschäfte (z.B. Immobiliarübertragungen) ist der contract under seal zwingend vorgeschrieben

contract, ~ violation Vertragsverletzung; **~ wages** vertraglich vereinbarter Lohn; **~ work** *(im Werkvertrag)* übergebene (od. übernommene) Arbeit; nach Stück bezahlte Heimarbeit; **~ year** Vertragsjahr, Abschlußjahr

contract, accessory ~ Nebenvertrag, Zusatzvertrag; **according to the ~** vertragsgemäß; **action under a ~** Klage aus Vertrag; **alteration to a ~** Vertragsänderung; **annulment of ~** Annullierung des Vertrages; **article of a ~** Vertragspunkt; **as per ~** laut Vertrag; **basis of a ~** Vertragsgrundlage; **beginning of a ~** Vertragsbeginn; **bound by ~** vertraglich verpflichtet; **→breach of ~; by ~** vertraglich, vertragsgemäß *(vgl. auch contract 2. und 3.)*; **building ~** Bauvertrag; **cancellation of the ~** Aufhebung des Vertrages; **capable of entering into a ~** vertragsfähig; **collateral ~** Nebenvertrag; **commencement of the ~** Beginn des Vertrages; **conclusion of a ~** Vertragsabschluß; **conditional ~** bedingter Vertrag; **conditions of ~** Vertragsbedingungen; **contrary to a ~** vertragswidrig; **copy of a ~** Ausfertigung e-s Vertrages; **costs of the ~** Kosten des Vertragsabschlusses; Vertragskosten

contract, covered by ~ vertraglich gedeckt; **agreements relating to matters covered by this ~** Vereinbarungen, die Gegenstand dieses Vertrages sind

contract, currency of a ~ Laufzeit e-s Vertrages; **debt under a ~** vertraglich geschuldete Leistung; **discharge of a ~** Vertragserfüllung; **draft ~** Vertragsentwurf; **duty under a ~** Vertragspflicht; **upon entering into the ~** bei Vertragsabschluß; **→exchange of ~s; executed ~** erfüllter Vertrag; **executory ~** noch zu erfüllender Vertrag; **expiration of a ~** Ablauf e-s Vertrages; **fictitious ~** Scheinvertrag; fingierter Vertrag; **formal ~** förmlicher Vertrag, formbedürftiger Vertrag (*→formal*); **→formation of a ~; freedom of ~** Vertragsfreiheit; **→frustration of ~; fulfilment of a ~** Vertragserfüllung; **illegal ~** rechtswidriger Vertrag; **implied ~** sich aus den Umständen ergebender Vertrag; **informal** ~ formfreier Vertrag; **infringement of a** ~ Verletzung e-s Vertrages; **insurance** ~ Versicherungsvertrag; **law of** ~ Vertragsrecht, Recht der Schuldverhältnisse; **liable under a** ~ vertraglich verpflichtet; **liability under a** ~ Verpflichtung aus e-m Vertrag; Vertragspflicht; **life of a** ~ Vertragsdauer; **object of a** ~ Vertragsgegenstand; **offer of a** ~ Vertragsangebot; **party to a** ~ Vertragspartei; **parol** ~ mündlicher Vertrag; **performance of a** ~ Erfüllung e-s Vertrages, Vertragserfüllung; **place of the** ~ Ort des Vertragsabschlusses; **preliminary** ~ Vorvertrag (→*preliminary*)

contract, by private ~ unter der Hand; freihändig

contract, provisions of a ~ Vertragsbestimmungen; **to alter, modify or waive the provisions of the** ~ die Vertragsbestimmungen abändern od. aufheben

contract, quasi-~ Quasikontrakt; vertragsähnliches Schuldverhältnis; **real** ~ *Am* Vertrag über Liegenschaften; **reciprocal** ~ gegenseitiger Vertrag; **renewal of a** ~ Erneuerung e-s Vertrages; → **repudiation of a** ~; →**rescission of a** ~; **rights (and liabilities) under a** ~ Rechte (und Pflichten) aus e-m Vertrag; **sealed** ~ gesiegelter Vertrag *(opp. simple ~)*; **sham** ~ Scheinvertrag, fingierter Vertrag; **signing of the** ~ Unterzeichnung des Vertrages

contract, simple ~ formloser, einfacher *(mündl. od. schriftl., aber nicht unter Siegel abgeschlossener)* Vertrag *(opp. contract under seal)*

Br Ansprüche aus e-m simple contract sind nach 6 Jahren nicht mehr einklagbar, während Ansprüche aus e-m gesiegelten Vertrag erst in 12 Jahren verjähren

contract, specialty ~ gesiegelter Vertrag (→*specialty 2.)*; **stipulated by** ~ vertraglich vereinbart; **stipulations of a** ~ Vertragsbestimmungen; **subject matter of the** ~ Gegenstand des Vertrages; Vertragsinhalt; **suit under a** ~ Klage aus Vertrag

contract, term of a ~ Vertragsdauer; Wortlaut des Vertrags; **terms of a** ~ Vertragsbestimmungen; Vertragsbedingungen; **in accordance with the terms of the** ~ vertragsgemäß; **contrary to the terms of the** ~ vertragswidrig; **general terms of** ~ allgemeine Vertragsbedingungen; **to observe the terms of a** ~ die Vertragsbestimmungen einhalten

contract, at the time of making (or **entering into**) **the** ~ zur Zeit des Vertragsabschlusses; **third party beneficiary** ~ *Am* Vertrag zugunsten e-s Dritten; **under** ~ vertraglich verpflichtet; **verbal** ~ mündlicher Vertrag; **violation of a** ~ Vertragsverletzung; **void** ~ nichtiger Vertrag *(aus dem keinerlei Rechte entstehen)*; **voidable** ~ anfechtbarer Vertrag *(unter Umständen bedeutsam für das darauf beruhende Rechtsverhältnis e-s Dritten mit e-m Vertragspartner)*; **work on** ~ vertraglich übernommene (od. vergebene) Arbeit; **written** ~ schriftlicher Vertrag

contract 2. Submission, Ausschreibung; Auftrag *(bei Ausschreibungen)*; ~ **awarder** Auftraggeber; ~ **awarding company** ausschreibendes Unternehmen; Auftraggeber; ~ **by tender** Ausschreibung, Submission, Verdingung; ~ **placing authority** auftraggebende Behörde, öffentlicher Auftraggeber; ~ **for public works** Ausschreibung öffentlicher Arbeiten; **award of the** ~ Auftragsvergebung, Auftragserteilung *(bei Ausschreibungen)*; **by** ~ durch Ausschreibung; **conditions of** ~ Submissionsbedingungen; Auftragsbedingungen; **government** ~ Regierungsauftrag; **placing of** ~**s** Auftragsvergebung, Auftragserteilung; **public** ~**s** öffentliches Auftragswesen; **public supply** ~**s** öffentliche Lieferaufträge; **terms of** ~ →conditions of ~; **to award the** ~ den Zuschlag erteilen; den Auftrag vergeben; **to bid for a** ~ *Am* sich um e-n *(ausgeschriebenen)* Auftrag bewerben; **to give out work by** ~ Arbeit ausschreiben; Arbeitsauftrag *(im Submissionsweg)* vergeben; **to obtain the** ~ den *(ausgeschriebenen)* Auftrag erhalten; **to place the** ~ den Zuschlag erteilen; den Auftrag vergeben; **to receive the** ~ den Zuschlag erhalten; **to tender for a** ~ *Br* sich um e-n *(ausgeschriebenen)* Auftrag bewerben

contract 3. *Am (ArbeitsR)* Akkord; ~ **shop** *Am* Akkordbetrieb; ~ **system** Akkordsystem; System der Vergebung von Arbeiten im Akkord; ~ **work** Akkordarbeit; *(nach Stück bezahlte)* Heimarbeit; **by** ~ im Akkord; **to give out work by** ~ Arbeit im Akkord vergeben

contract *v* e-n Vertrag (ab)schließen (od. eingehen); kontrahieren; sich vertraglich verpflichten (to do sth. etw. zu tun); **to** ~ **for** *(etw.)* vertraglich übernehmen; **to** ~ **for work** Arbeit *(im Werkvertrag)* übernehmen (od. vergeben); **to** ~ **in** *Br* sich *(schriftl.)* zur Bezahlung des Parteibeitrages für die Labour Party verpflichten; **to** ~ **out** *(sich* od. *etw.)* vertraglich ausschließen; **to** ~ **out of an agreement** e-e Vereinbarung vertraglich ausschließen; **to** ~ **out work** Arbeit(en) vergeben

contract *v*, **to** ~ **debts** Schulden machen; ~ **liabilities** Verpflichtungen eingehen; **to** ~ **a loan** e-e Anleihe aufnehmen; **to** ~ **a marriage** die Ehe schließen

contracted, as ~ wie vertraglich vereinbart

contracting vertragschließend; ~ **government** Vertragsregierung, vertragschließende Regierung

contracting-out certificate *Br* Befreiungsbescheinigung *(für Verzicht auf e-n Teil der staatlichen Rentenversicherung)*

contracting-out clause *(VölkerR)* Freizeichnungsklausel

Klausel, die Beschlüsse vertraglich geschaffener internationaler Organisationen für bindend für jene Vertragsstaaten erklärt, die nicht binnen bestimmter Frist widersprochen haben

contracting, ~ party vertragschließende Partei; Vertragspartei, Kontrahent; **~ state** Vertragsstaat; **~ for work** Vergebung (od. Übernahme) von Arbeit *(im Werkvertrag)*

contracting, capable of ~ vertragsfähig; geschäftsfähig; **joint ~ party** Mitkontrahent; → **sub~**

contractant →contracting party

contraction Kontraktion, Verringerung, Schrumpfung; *(Konjunktur)* Kontraktion, Depression *(opp. expansion)*; *Am* Einschränkung des Notenumlaufs; **~ of credit** Einschränkung des Kredits, Kreditschrumpfung

contractive tendencies Abschwächungstendenzen

contractor Vertragschließender, Kontrahent; (Groß-)Lieferant; (Privat-)Unternehmer; Auftragnehmer, Submittent *(von Arbeits- od. Lieferaufträgen im Submissionswege)*; Unternehmer *(im Werkvertrag)*; **~s' all risk insurance** (CAR) Bauleistungsversicherung; **~ to the Crown** *Br* Staatslieferant; **~'s estimate** Baukostenvoranschlag; **~'s guarantee insurance** Baugarantieversicherung *(des Bauunternehmers)*; **~ loan** Unternehmerkredit

contractor, army ~ Heereslieferant; **building ~** (or **builder and ~**) Bauunternehmer; **government ~** Staatslieferant; **independent ~** *(Werkvertrag)* selbständiger Unternehmer *(der keinem Kontroll- und Weisungsrecht des Bestellers unterworfen ist)*; → **sub~**

contractual vertraglich, vertragsgemäß, auf Vertrag begründet; **~ agreement** (or **arrangement**) vertragliche Vereinbarung

contractual capacity Vertragsfähigkeit; Geschäftsfähigkeit; **to have ~** vertragsfähig sein; geschäftsfähig sein

contractual, ~ cause of action (or **~ claim**) Anspruch aus Vertrag; obligatorischer Anspruch; **to assert a ~ claim** e-n Anspruch aus e-m Vertrag geltend machen

contractual, ~ clause Vertragsklausel; **~ commitment** vertragliche Verpflichtung (od. Bindung); **~ date** im Vertrag vorgesehenes Datum; **~ due date** vereinbarter Zahlungstermin; **~ fidelity** Vertragstreue; **~ forum** Gerichtsstand des Vertrages; **~ liability** vertragliche Verpflichtung (od. Haftung); Vertragshaftung; **~ lien** Vertragspfandrecht

contractual obligation vertragliche Verpflichtung; **~ and non- ~s** vertragliche und außervertragliche Verpflichtungen; →**Convention on the Law Applicable to C~ O~s; fulfilment of** (or **performing**) **~s** Erfüllung vertraglicher Verpflichtungen

contractual, ~ penalty Vertragsstrafe; **~ period** Vertragszeit; **~ plan** *Am (bei Investmentgesellschaften)* Sparplan, bei dem der Anleger regelmäßige monatl. od. vierteljährl. Einzahlungen leisten muß; **~ power** Vollmacht zum Abschluß e-s Vertrages; **~ regime** *Am* vertragsmäßiges Güterrecht *(opp. statutory regime)*

contractual relations vertragliche Beziehungen; **regulation of ~** Anpassung von Verträgen; **Standby Committee for the C~ R~ of the ICC** Ständiger Ausschuß für die Anpassung von Verträgen der Internationalen Handelskammer

contractual, ~ relationship Vertragsverhältnis; **quasi-~ relationship** vertragsähnliches Rechtsverhältnis; **~ right** Vertragsrecht, obligatorisches Recht; vertraglich festgelegtes Recht; **~ tariff** Vertragszoll; **~ territory** Vertragsgebiet; Vertreterbezirk*(e-s Handelsvertreters)*; **~ treaty** *(VölkerR)* rechtsgeschäftlicher Vertrag *(opp. law-making treaty)*; **~ undertaking** vertragliches Versprechen; **~ wages** vertragsmäßiger Lohn, Tariflohn; Akkordlohn

contractually vertraglich; durch Vertrag

contradict *v* widersprechen; in Widerspruch stehen zu; **to ~ oneself** sich widersprechen; **to ~ a statement** e-r Behauptung widersprechen; **the facts ~ his statement** die Tatsachen widersprechen s-r Behauptung; **the statements ~ each other** die Aussagen widersprechen sich

contradiction Widerspruch; **~ in terms** innerer Widerspruch; **to become entangled in ~s** sich in Widersprüchen befinden

contradictory kontradiktorisch, (sich) widersprechend; **~ statements** sich widersprechende Aussagen

contrariety Widerspruch, Gegensatz (to zu)

contrary 1. Gegenteil; gegenteilig; **on the ~** im Gegenteil; **to the ~** gegenteilig, dagegen; **in the absence of any agreement to the ~** sofern nichts Gegenteiliges vereinbart ist; mangels gegenteiliger Abmachung; **evidence** (or **proof**) **to the ~** Gegenbeweis; Beweis des Gegenteils; **until proof of the ~** bis zum Beweis des Gegenteils; **unless ~ instructions are given** falls nicht gegenteilige Anweisungen vorliegen; **to be of the ~ opinion** entgegengesetzter Meinung sein; **to maintain the ~** das Gegenteil behaupten; **to prove the ~** das Gegenteil beweisen, den Gegenbeweis antreten

contrary 2. entgegengesetzt; zuwider; **~ to contract** (or **agreement**) vertragswidrig; **~ to one's duty** pflichtwidrig; **~ to all expectations** allen Erwartungen zuwider; **~ to one's knowledge** wider besseres Wissen; **~ to law** rechtswidrig, gesetzwidrig; **~ to public policy** → policy 1.; **~ to regulations** vorschriftswidrig; **~ to truth** wahrheitswidrig; **to act ~**

to instructions den Anweisungen zuwiderhandeln

contravene *v* zuwiderhandeln, verstoßen gegen; bestreiten, widersprechen; in Widerspruch stehen zu; **to ~ a law** gegen ein Gesetz verstoßen; ein Gesetz verletzen; **to ~ a statement** e-r Behauptung widersprechen

contravention Zuwiderhandlung; Zuwiderhandeln (of gegen); Übertretung; **in ~ of the law** unter Verletzung e-s Gesetzes; **to act in ~ of the law** dem Gesetz zuwiderhandeln; das Gesetz verletzen

contribute *v* beitragen, Beitrag leisten, beisteuern (to, towards zu); *(Geld, Gewinn)* einbringen; *(Kapital in e-e Firma)* einbringen; mitwirken (to an); spenden; *(Geld)* nachschießen *(bei Liquidation e-r Gesellschaft)*; **to ~ an article to a periodical** e-n Beitrag in e-r Zeitschrift veröffentlichen; e-n Artikel zu e-r Zeitschrift beitragen; **to ~ capital** Kapital einbringen; **to ~ cash** e-e Bareinlage leisten; **to ~ to a collection** e-n Beitrag zu e-r Sammlung leisten; sich an e-r Sammlung beteiligen; **to ~ to** (or **towards**) **the expenses** sich an den Unkosten beteiligen; Unkostenbeitrag leisten; **to ~ to a newspaper** für e-e Zeitung schreiben; **to ~ sth. to the Red Cross** etw. für das Rote Kreuz spenden

contribute *v*, **liable to ~** beitragspflichtig; *Br (bei Liquidation e-r Gesellschaft)* nachschußpflichtig *(to the assets of the company zum Vermögen der Gesellschaft)*; **interests liable to ~** *(zur Havarie)* beitragspflichtige Vermögenswerte

contributed, ~ capital eingebrachtes Kapital; **money ~ by a partner** (in the firm) Geldeinlage e-s Gesellschafters

contributing, ~ countries and developing countries Geberländer und Entwicklungsländer; **~ (interests and) values** *(zur Havarie)* beitragspflichtige Vermögenswerte

contribution Beitrag, Beitragsleistung; Mitgliedsbeitrag; *(wissenschaftlicher)* Beitrag; (Kapital-)Einlage *(in e-e Firma)*; Nachschuß; Mitwirkung (to an); Spende, Geldspende; *mil* Kontribution *(Zwangsauflage in Geld)*; **~s in arrears** Beitragsrückstände; **~ costing** Dekkungsbeitragsrechnung; **~ in cash** Bareinlage; **~ in kind** Sacheinlage; **~s in cash and kind** Geld- und Sachspenden; **~ income** Beitragsaufkommen; **~ of capital** Kapitaleinlage *(e-s Gesellschafters)*; Kapitaleinbringung, **period** Beitragszeit; **~ plan** *(VersR)* Gewinnverteilungsplan; **~ rate** Beitragssatz; **~ refund** Beitrags(rück)erstattung

contribution, ~ towards (or **to**) **the expenses** Unkostenbeitrag, Kostenbeitrag; **~ to general average** Havariebeitrag; **~ to a newspaper** Beitrag für e-e Zeitung; **~ to science** wissenschaftlicher Beitrag

contribution, additional ~ Nachschußleistung; **annual ~** Jahresbeitrag; **charitable ~** Beitrag für wohltätige Zwecke; **compulsory ~** Pflichtbeitrag; Beitragspflicht; **defen|ce(~se) ~** Wehrbeitrag; **employee's ~** Arbeitnehmeranteil *(zur Sozialversicherung)*; **employer's ~** Arbeitgeberanteil *(zur Sozialversicherung)*; **financial ~** Finanzbeitrag; finanzieller Beitrag; **initial ~** Stammeinlage; **liable to ~** beitragspflichtig; nachschußpflichtig; **loss in ~** Beitragsausfall; **payment of ~** Beitragsleistung; **period of ~** Beitragszeit; **periodical ~** laufender Beitrag; **pro rata ~** anteilsmäßiger Beitrag; **rate of ~** Beitragssatz, Beitragshöhe; **return of ~** Beitragsrückzahlung; **social security ~s** Sozialversicherungsbeiträge; **voluntary ~** freiwilliger Beitrag; Spende

contribution, to assess the ~ den Beitrag festsetzen; **to be in arrears with the payment of one's ~** mit s-r Beitragsleistung im Rückstand sein; **to collect ~s** Beiträge einsammeln; **to make a ~ (to)** e-n Beitrag leisten (zu); **to make ~s towards** beitragen zu; **to pay one's ~** s-n Beitrag zahlen

contributor Beitragleistender; Spender; Geldgeber, Mäzen; Mitarbeiter *(e-r Zeitung)*; **~ of capital** Kapitaleinleger

contributor|y Beitragspflichtiger; beitragspflichtiges Mitglied; *Br* Nachschußpflichtiger *(im Falle der Liquidation e-r Gesellschaft; bes. Aktionär von nicht voll eingezahlten Aktien)*; mitwirkend, beitragend (to zu); auf Beiträgen beruhend; beitragspflichtig; nachschußpflichtig; **~ benefits** *Br (Sozialvers.)* beitragsbezogene (od. auf Beiträgen beruhende) Leistungen; **~ causes** mitverursachende Umstände; **~ fund** Beitragsfonds; **~ infringement of patent** *(PatR)* mittelbare Patentverletzung *(mitwirkendes Verschulden des Patentinhabers)*; **~ mortgage** für mehrere Gläubiger bestellte Hypothek; **~ negligence** mitwirkendes (od. konkurrierendes) Verschulden *(auf Seiten des Verletzten; →negligence)*; **~ pension** beitragspflichtige Pension; **~ value** beitragspflichtiger Wert *(für die Festsetzung des Havariebeitrages)*; **→non-~**

contrivance Vorrichtung, Einrichtung; Kniff, Kunstgriff; Erfindung; **full of ~s** erfinderisch

contrive *v* erfinden, ersinnen; fertigbringen, zustandebringen; gut wirtschaften; **he ~d means for his escape** er fand Mittel und Wege zu s-r Flucht

control Kontrolle, Aufsicht (of über); Macht zur Ausübung e-s beherrschenden Einflusses, Beherrschung; Nachprüfung, Überwachung; Steuerung, Lenkung, Regelung; Bewirtschaftung *(von Preisen, Devisen etc)*

control, ~ contract Beherrschungsvertrag; **~ of exports** Exportkontrolle, Exportüberwachung; **~ by foreign capital** Überfremdung; **~ of foreign exchange** s. exchange →control; ~

of imports Einfuhrkontrolle, Einfuhrregelung; ~ **list** *Am* Liste der Exportkontrollen unterliegenden Waren; ~ **of the market** Marktbeherrschung; ~ **of mergers** Fusionskontrolle; ~ **of operations** Betriebsüberwachung; **under the ~ of the police** unter Polizeiaufsicht; ~ **of prices** Preiskontrolle, Preisüberwachung; *(staatl.)* Preisbindung

control, actual ~ tatsächliche Gewalt (of a th. über e-e Sache); **area of** ~ Kontrollgebiet; **birth** ~ Geburtenregelung; **circumstances beyond one's** ~ nicht zu vertretende Umstände; **economic** ~ Wirtschaftslenkung; (Zwangs-)Bewirtschaftung; **(foreign) exchange** ~ Devisenkontrolle, Devisenbewirtschaftung; **government** ~ staatliche Aufsicht (od. Lenkung); **measure of** ~ Kontrollmaßnahme; **power of** ~ Kontrollbefugnis; **price** ~ Preiskontrolle, Preisüberwachung; *(staatl.)* Preisbindung; **rent** ~ Überwachung der Mietpreise; **state** ~ staatliche Aufsicht (od. Lenkung); **subject to** ~ kontrollpflichtig; **traffic** ~ Verkehrsüberwachung, Verkehrsregelung; **wartime** ~ Kriegsbewirtschaftung; **without** ~ unbeaufsichtigt; frei, uneingeschränkt

control, to be in ~ of die Aufsicht führen über; die Leitung haben von; **to be subject to** ~ der Kontrolle unterliegen; **to be under** ~ unter Kontrolle (od. Aufsicht) stehen; **to exercise** ~ Kontrolle ausüben (over über); die Leitung führen; **to get out of** ~ außer Kontrolle geraten *(z.B. Auto, Feuer)*; **to increase ~s** die Kontrollen verschärfen; **to lose ~ of** die Kontrolle (od. Herrschaft) verlieren über; **to place under sb.'s** ~ unter jds Aufsicht stellen

control *v* kontrollieren, (nach)prüfen; beaufsichtigen, überwachen; leiten, beherrschen; ausschlaggebenden Einfluß haben; lenken, regeln, bewirtschaften; **to ~ expenditure** die Ausgaben niedrig halten; **to ~ the market** den Markt beherrschen; **to ~ traffic** den Verkehr regeln; **authority** (or **power**) **to** ~ Kontrollbefugnis

controlled, ~ **area** Kontrollgebiet; ~ **company** beherrschte Gesellschaft; abhängige Gesellschaft; Tochtergesellschaft; ~ **distribution** Absatzlenkung; ~ **economy** gelenkte Wirtschaft; ~ **foreign corporation** (CFC) *Am* beherrschte ausländische Gesellschaft *(deren Aktien mit Stimmrecht zu mehr als 50% amerikanischen Aktionären gehören)*; ~ **price** gebundener Preis; amtlich festgesetzter (Stopp-)Preis; ~ **sampling** Stichprobenauswahl nach statistischen Gesichtspunkten

controlled, government (or **state**) ~ staatlich kontrolliert, unter staatlicher Aufsicht; **to be ~ by** unterstehen, unterliegen

Controller Controller *(Mitglied der obersten Unternehmensführung, der Aufgaben des →Controlling wahrnimmt)*

controller of the file *(Datenschutzrecht)*[79a] Verantwortlicher für die Datei (Datensammlung); speichernde Stelle

Controlling Controlling; *(ergebnisorientierte)* Steuerung durch Planung und Kontrolle

controlling Aufsichts-; maßgebend; ~ **account** Gegenrechnung *(als Kontrollrechnung)*; ~ **agreement** *Am* Beherrschungsvertrag; ~ **authority** (or **body**) Aufsichtsbehörde; ~ **company** beherrschende Gesellschaft *(die die Mehrheit der Aktien hat)*; Holdinggesellschaft; ~ **interest** maßgebliche Beteiligung, Mehrheitsbeteiligung *(50%ige od. höhere Beteiligung an e-r Kapitalgesellschaft)*; ~ **shareholder** maßgeblicher Aktionär, Mehrheitsaktionär

controversial streitig, strittig, umstritten; streitsüchtig; ~ **opinion** umstrittene Ansicht; ~ **question** strittige Frage, Streitfrage; ~ **person** streitsüchtige Person; **to be** ~ umstritten sein

controvers|y Kontroverse, Streit, Streitigkeit; Polemik; **amount in** ~ *Am* Höhe des Streitwertes; **in** ~ streitig; **labor** ~ *Am* Arbeitsstreitigkeit; **matter in** ~ Streitgegenstand, Streitfall; **press** ~Pressepolemik; **without** (or **beyond**) ~ unbestritten, unstreitig; **to hear and determine ~ies** Streitfälle anhören und entscheiden

controvert *v* bestreiten; *(Meinungen etc)* bekämpfen; **to ~ a p.** jdm widersprechen

contumacious aufsässig, ungehorsam *(gegen das Gericht)*; *(trotz Ladung)* nicht erschienen

contumacy Kontumaz; Ungehorsam, Ungebühr *(Br bes. gegenüber dem kirchl. Gericht)*; *(vorsätzliche)* Nichtbeachtung der Ladung (od. Verfügung) e-s Gerichts

conurbation *(städtischer)* Ballungsraum, Ballungsgebiet; **large ~s** Ballungszentren

convene *v* *(Versammlung)* einberufen; *(vor Gericht)* laden, vorladen; sich versammeln, zusammentreten

convened, duly ~ meeting ordnungsgemäß einberufene Versammlung

convening, ~ **of the general meeting** Einberufung der Hauptversammlung; ~ **notice** Einberufungsbekanntmachung

convener Einberufer

convenience Angemessenheit; Belieben; Annehmlichkeit, Bequemlichkeit, Komfort; ~ **food** Fertiggerichte; ~ **goods** *Am* Waren des täglichen Bedarfs *(bequeme Bedarfsdeckung des Verbrauchers nahe der Wohnung)*; Verbrauchsgüter *(die spontan gekauft werden, wenn Bedarf vorliegt; opp. shopping goods)*; ~ **store** Nachbarschaftsladen *(Einzelhandelsgeschäft in Wohnungsnähe)*

convenience, at one's ~ nach Belieben; wenn es

gerade paßt; **at your early** (or **earliest**) ~ sobald wie möglich; **certificate of ~ and necessity** *Am* staatliche Konzession zur Errichtung e-r →public utility *(Bescheinigung der Angemessenheit und Notwendigkeit);* **flags of** ~ (FOC) billige Flaggen *(→flag);* **marriage of** ~ Vernunftehe; **as a matter of** ~ aus Zweckmäßigkeitsgründen; **with all modern ~s** mit allem Komfort; **public** ~ Bedürfnisanstalt; **whenever it suits your** ~ zu jeder Zeit, die Ihnen paßt; **to make a ~ of sb.** jdn ausnutzen

convenient geeignet, passend, genehm; bequem; ~ **to** in der Nähe von, nahe bei; **on ~ terms** mit bequemen Zahlungsbedingungen; **it is not ~ for me** es paßt mir schlecht; **when will it be ~ for you?** wann wird es Ihnen passen?

convention 1. *(VölkerR)* Konvention; Übereinkunft; *(wenn mehrseitig:)* Übereinkommen; *(wenn zweiseitig:)* Abkommen; →**International C~**

convention, Berne C~ (C~ of the International Union for the Protection of Literary and Artistic Works) Berner (Verbands)-Übereinkunft (BÜ) (Übereinkunft zum Schutze von Werken der Literatur und Kunst; Berner Union); **Revised Berne C~** Revidierte Berner Übereinkunft (RBÜ)

Die Berner Übereinkunft von 1886, zuletzt revidiert in Paris,[80] ist das erste multilaterale Abkommen für das Urheberrecht. Sie baut auf dem Grundsatz der Inländerbehandlung auf (Gleichstellung des ausländischen mit dem inländischen Urheber für alle Verbandsländer). Verbandsländer sind u. a. Großbritannien, die BRD[80a] und seit 1988 die USA (→Berne Implementation Act). Der Beitritt ist für die USA am 1. 3. 1989 wirksam geworden

convention, country adhering to the C~ →C~ country: **duration of a** ~ Laufzeit eines Abkommens; **member country of the C~** →C~ country

convention, Paris C~ (or **Union C~**) **(C~ for the Protection of Industrial Property)** Pariser (Verbands-)Übereinkunft (Pariser Verbandsübereinkunft zum Schutze des gewerblichen Eigentums; Patent-Konvention) (PVÜ, ParÜb., Unionsvertrag)

Die Pariser Verbandsübereinkunft von 1883, zuletzt revidiert in Stockholm 1967[80b], ist das führende multilaterale Abkommen für den gewerblichen Rechtsschutz. Sie gewährt den Angehörigen der Verbandsländer rechtliche Gleichstellung mit den Inländern hinsichtlich der Erfindungspatente, Gebrauchsmuster, gewerblichen Muster und Modelle, Warenzeichen, Handelsnamen, Herkunftszeichen sowie der Unterdrückung des unlauteren Wettbewerbs. Dem Unionsvertrag sind 47 Staaten beigetreten, darunter Großbritannien, die BRD und (anders als bei der RBÜ) die Vereinigten Staaten. Alle Staaten des Gemeinsamen Marktes sind Mitglieder der Pariser Verbandsübereinkunft.

Das Internationale Amt der Pariser Union ist mit dem Internationalen Amt der Berner Union unter einheitlicher Leitung zusammengefaßt (Sitz seit 1958 in Genf: Bureaux Internationaux Réunis pour la Protection de la Propriété Industrielle, Littéraire et Artistique)

convention, scope of a ~ Geltungsbereich (od. Anwendungsgebiet) e-s Abkommens; **States parties to a** ~ Vertragsstaaten e-s Abkommens; **tax** ~ Steuerabkommen; **universal** ~ Weltabkommen (→Universal Copyright C~, →Universal Postal C~)

Convention application Verbandsanmeldung, Anmeldung in e-m Verbandsland

Convention Concerning International Carriage by Rail[81] (COTIF[82]) Übereinkommen über den internationalen Eisenbahnverkehr

Convention, ~ country Verbandsland *(ein der Pariser od. Berner Übereinkunft angeschlossenes Land);* ~ **date** Datum der Verbandspriorität

Convention Establishing the →Multilateral Investment Guaranty Agency

Convention for the Establishment of a European Organization for the Exploitation of Meteorological Satellites[82a] Übereinkommen zur Gründung e-r europäischen Organisation für die Nutzung von meteorologischen Satelliten (EUMETSAT)

Convention for the Protection of the →Architectural Heritage of Europe

Convention for the Protection of Cultural Property in the Event of Armed Conflict[82b] Konvention zum Schutz von Kulturgut bei bewaffneten Konflikten

Convention for the Protection of Individuals with Regard to Automatic Processing of Personal Data[82c] Übereinkommen zum Schutz des Menschen bei der automatischen Verarbeitung personenbezogener Daten

Convention for the Protection of the World Cultural and Natural Heritage[82d] Übereinkommen zum Schutz des Kultur- und Naturerbes der Welt

Convention on Facilitation of International Marine Traffic[82e] Übereinkommen zur Erleichterung des internationalen Seeverkehrs

Convention on International Trade in Endangered Species of →Wild Fauna and Flora (CITES)

Convention on the Law Applicable to Contracutal Obligations[82f] Übereinkommen über das auf vertragliche Schuldverhältnisse anzuwendende Recht

Convention on the Law Applicable to Maintenance Obligations[82g] Übereinkommen über das auf Unterhaltspflichten anzuwendende Recht

(UN) Convention on the Law of the Sea Seerechtsübereinkommen der Vereinten Nationen (von 1982)

Convention on Long-Range Transboundary

Air Pollution[82h] Übereinkommen über weiträumige grenzüberschreitende Luftverunreinigung
Convention on the Prohibition of Military or any other Hostile Use of →Environmental Modification Techniques
Convention on the Recognition and Enforcement of Decisions Relating to Maintenance Obligations[82i] Übereinkommen über die Anerkennung und Vollstreckung von Unterhaltsentscheidungen
Convention on the Recognition and Enforcement of Foreign →Arbitral Awards
Convention on the Settlement of →Investment Disputes
Convention, ~ priority Verbandspriorität; Unionspriorität
convention, the present ~ does not apply to dieses Abkommen erstreckt sich nicht auf; **to accede** (or **adhere**) **to a** ~ e-m Abkommen beitreten; **to conclude a** ~ ein Abkommen schließen; **to denounce a** ~ ein Abkommen kündigen; **to join a** ~ e-m Abkommen beitreten
convention 2. Versammlung, Tagung; *(wissenschaftlicher)* Kongreß; Parteitag; *Am* Parteitag, Parteiversammlung *(bes. zur Aufstellung des Präsidentschaftskandidaten)*; **annual** ~ Jahresversammlung
convention 3., ~**(s)** Herkommen, Brauch; feste Regel, **C~ of the Constitution** *Br* ungeschriebene Regel des Verfassungsrechts *(→constitutional conventions)*

conventional herkömmlich, üblich, konventionell; vertraglich, vertragsmäßig *(opp. legal)*; ~ **design** übliches Muster; ~ **forces** *mil* konventionelle Streitkräfte; ~ **heir** *Am* Vertragserbe; ~ **lien** Vertragspfandrecht; ~ **penalty** Konventionalstrafe, Vertragsstrafe; ~ **rate of interest** üblicher Zinssatz; ~ **weapons** konventionelle (od. herkömmliche) Waffen *(opp. nuclear weapons)*

conventioner *Am* Versammlungsteilnehmer

conversation Unterhaltung, Unterredung, Besprechung; Gespräch; **subject of** ~ Gesprächsthema; **telephone** ~ Telefongespräch; **to carry on** (or **conduct, hold**) **a** ~ ein Gespräch (od. e-e Besprechung etc) führen; **to get into** (or **engage in**) ~ **with sb.** mit jdm ins Gespräch kommen

conversely umgekehrt

conversion 1. Umwandlung; Konversion, Konvertierung *(Abänderung der Zins- bzw. Tilgungsbedingungen e-r Anleihe)*; Umstellung *(e-s Unternehmens, der Produktion etc)*; *(Devisengeschäft)* Umrechnung, Umwechselung *(in e-e andere Währung)*; Umtausch *(e-r Kategorie Wertpapiere gegen e-e andere)*; Wandlung *(von Obligationen in Aktien; →convertible bonds)*; Umbau (of von, into in); *pol* Meinungswechsel; ~ **account** Umstellungsrechnung; ~ **balance** Konversionsguthaben; ~**fee** *(PatR)* Umwandlungsgebühr; ~ **loan** Konversionsanleihe, Wandelanleihe; *(EG)* Umstellungsdarlehen; ~ **into a national patent application** *(europ. PatR)* Umwandlung in e-e nationale Patentanmeldung; ~ **of a composition proceeding into a bankruptcy proceeding** *Am* Anschlußkonkurs; ~ **of one currency into another** Umrechnung e-r Währung in e-e andere; ~ **of debts** Schuldumwandlung; Umschuldung; ~ **of living accommodation to (rooms for) office use** Umwandlung (od. Umbau) von Wohn- in Büroräume; Zweckentfremdung e-r Wohnung; ~ **of a loan** Umwandlung e-r Anleihe *(in e-e Konversionsanleihe)*; ~ **of merchant ships into warships** *(VölkerR)* Umwandlung von Handelsschiffen (od. Kauffahrteischiffen) in Kriegsschiffe; ~ **of policy** *(VersR)* Umwandlung (od. Umtausch) e-r Versicherung *(in e-e andere Versicherungsform)*; ~ **of realty into personalty** (and vice versa) *(equity-Recht)* Umwandlung (od. Umdeutung) von unbeweglichem in bewegliches Vermögen (und umgekehrt) *(aus der Interessenlage heraus, bes. bei der Auslegung e-s Testaments)*; ~ **of shares into stocks** Umwandlung von Einzelaktien in Gesamtheit von Aktien; ~ **offer** Konversionsangebot, Konvertierungsangebot; ~ **period** Umtauschfrist; ~ **premium** Agio auf den Marktpreis von Wandelanleihen, aus dem sich der Tauschpreis in Aktien ergibt *(→convertible bonds)*; ~ **price** Wandlungskurs; ~ **rate** *(Devisenmarkt)* Umrechnungskurs; ~ **ratio** Umtauschverhältnis; ~ **right** Umtauschrecht *(Recht zur Umwandlung in Aktien)*; ~ **sheet** Umstellungsrechnung; ~ **table** Umrechnungstabelle
conversion, compulsory ~ Zwangskonversion; **constructive** (or **equitable**) ~ →~ of realty into personalty; **currency** ~ Währungskonvertierung; →**debt** ~; **industrial** ~ industrielle Umstellung; **involuntary** ~ *Am*[83] zwangsweise Umwandlung; **possibility of** ~ Konversionsmöglichkeit; **rate of** ~ Umrechnungskurs; **request for** ~ *(PatR)* Umwandlungsantrag
conversion 2. *(tort)* unrechtmäßiger Eigengebrauch fremden Eigentums *(rechtswidriges Ansichnehmen von beweglichen Sachen e-s anderen, das den Berechtigten um den Besitz od. Gebrauch bringt)*; ~ **of instrument** *Am* Entziehung des Papiers; ~ **to one's own use** unrechtmäßige Verwendung für sich selbst; Unterschlagung; ~ **to one's own use of found property** Fundunterschlagung; **action of** ~ Schadensersatzklage wegen rechtswidrigen Ansichnehmens von fremden Sachen; **fraudulent** ~ betrügerische Entziehung *(von Sachen)*; Untreue;

wrongful ~ **of public funds** Veruntreuung öffentlicher Mittel

convert *v* konvertieren, umwandeln; *(Fabrikbetrieb etc)* umstellen; *(in e-e andere Währung)* umrechnen, umwechseln; *(e-e Kategorie Wertpapiere in e-e andere)* umtauschen; *(fremdes bewegl. Vermögen)* entziehen (od. unrechtmäßig verwenden); *eccl* konvertieren; **to** ~ **into capital** in Kapital umwandeln; kapitalisieren; **to** ~ **into cash** zu Geld machen, realisieren, flüssig machen; **to** ~ **a debt** e-e Schuld umwandeln; **to** ~ **a house** ein Haus in kleine Wohnungen umbauen; **to** ~ **living accommodation to (rooms for) office use** Wohnräume in Büroräume umbauen (od. zweckentfremden); **to** ~ **a loan** e-e Anleihe umwandeln; **to** ~ **into money** →to ~ into cash; **to** ~ **a partnership into a company** (or *Am* **corporation**) e-e Personal- in e-e Kapitalgesellschaft umwandeln; **to** ~ **realty into personalty** unbewegliches in bewegliches Vermögen umwandeln (od. umdeuten); **to** ~ **to one's own use** *(etw.)* unrechtmäßig für sich verwenden

convertibility (Um-)Wandelbarkeit; Konvertibilität, Konvertierbarkeit *(Möglichkeit des Umtausches inländischer in fremde Währung);* ~ **into cash** Liquidierbarkeit

convertible (um)wandelbar; konvertierbar; austauschbar; umrechenbar; realisierbar; **non-**~ nicht konvertierbar (od. austauschbar); ~ **assets** konvertierbare Vermögenswerte; ~ **assurance** *Br* Umtauschversicherung; ~ **bonds** Wandelanleihen, Wandelschuldverschreibungen *(die in Aktien umgewandelt werden können);* **freely** ~ **currency** frei konvertierbare (od. austauschbare) Währung; ~ **debentures** →~ bonds; ~ **preferred stock** *Am* Vorzugsaktien mit Umtauschrecht

convey *v (Güter od. Personen)* befördern, transportieren; *(bes. Grundeigentum)* übertragen, übereignen; übermitteln, mitteilen; **to** ~ **one's congratulations to sb.** jdm seine Glückwünsche übermitteln; **to** ~ **by water** verschiffen

conveying Beförderung, Transport; Übermittlung; Förder-; ~ **capacity** Förderleistung; ~ **facilities** Fördereinrichtungen

conveyable transportierbar; übertragbar

conveyance 1. Übertragung *(von Eigentum, bes. Grundeigentum durch Urkunde);* Grundstücksübertragungsurkunde; ~ **of copyright** Übertragung des Urheberrechts; ~ **of (a piece of) land** *Br* Grundstücksübertragung *(hinsichtlich →unregistered land);* ~ **of property** Übertragung von Vermögen; Eigentumsübertragung; **deed of** ~ Übertragungsurkunde *(bei Grundbesitz);* →**fraudulent** ~; →**voluntary** ~

conveyance 2. Beförderung, Transport; Beförderungsmittel, Transportmittel; ~ **by aircraft** Lufttransport; ~ **of goods** Gütertransport, Güterbeförderung; ~ **by land** Landtransport; ~ **by rail** Bahntransport; ~ **by sea** Beförderung auf dem Seewege

conveyance, charges for ~ Speditionskosten, Transportkosten; **compulsory** ~ Beförderungszwang; **means of** ~ Transportmittel, Beförderungsmittel; **mode of** ~ Beförderungsart; **public (means of)** ~ öffentliche(s) Verkehrsmittel; **risk of** ~ Transportgefahr

conveyancer Spezialanwalt, der Eigentums- (bes. Grundstücks-)übertragungen vorbereitet

conveyancing Abfassung der Eigentumsübertragungsurkunden *(bes. bei Grundstücksübertragungen);* Eigentumsübertragungsrecht; ~ **costs** Kosten der Grundstücksübertragung; ~ **counsel of the court** *Br* Anwalt, der zur Unterstützung des Gerichts in grundstücksrechtlichen Angelegenheiten zugezogen wird; ~ **by deed** *Am* Verfügung über Grundbesitz durch gesiegelte Urkunde *(opp. registration of title to land);* **private** ~ *Am* (**unregistered** ~ *Br*) nicht registrierte Vornahme von Verfügungen über Grundstücksrechte; private Auflassung

conveyer Übertragender; Transporteur; Fördergerät, Fördermittel; Transport-, Förder-; ~ **belt** Transportband, Fließband; ~ **belt production** Fließbandfertigung

conveyor →conveyer

convict Strafgefangener *(an dem e-e Freiheitsstrafe vollzogen wird);* Sträfling; ~**'s clothing** *Am* Sträflingskleidung; ~ **labor** *Am* Gefangenenarbeit; ~**-made merchandise** *Am* von (Straf-)Gefangenen angefertigte Waren; ~ **settlement** Strafkolonie

convict *v* für schuldig befinden (of wegen); verurteilen (of wegen)

convicted, person ~ **of an offen|ce(~se)** (or ~ **person**) Verurteilter; **previously** ~ vorbestraft; ~ **felon** verurteilter Verbrecher; **to be** ~ **of doing** *(rechtskräftig)* verurteilt sein, getan zu haben; **he was** ~ **of fraud** er wurde wegen Betrugs verurteilt

conviction 1. Überführung *(e-r Straftat);* Schuldigsprechung, Schuldspruch *(bes. der Geschworenen); (strafgerichtl.)* Verurteilung (for wegen); **on** ~ nach (od. im Falle der) Überführung

conviction on indictment Verurteilung im Strafverfahren mit jury-Beteiligung *(sofern der Angeklagte nicht auf dieses Verfahren verzichtet [waiver] und Aburteilung durch e-n Einzelrichter vorzieht; opp. summary conviction)*

conviction, previous (or **prior**) ~ Vorstrafe *(Br cf. preventive detention, persistent offender; opp. first offender);* **record of prior** ~**s** *Am* (**statement of previous** ~**s** *Br*) Aufstellung der Vorstrafen des Angeklagten *(für Strafzumessung);* **register of (previous) ~(s)** Strafregister; **to have a previous ~** vorbestraft sein (for wegen); **to have no previous ~(s)** nicht vorbestraft sein

conviction, summary ~ Verurteilung im summarischen Verfahren *(auf Grund e-r →information; Br durch einen od. mehrere →justices of the peace od. andere →magistrates, in Großstädten durch →stipendiaries; opp. ~ on indictment)*

conviction, to quash (or **set aside**) **a ~** e-n Schuldspruch aufheben; **to uphold a ~** e-n Schuldspruch bestätigen

conviction 2. Überzeugung; **political ~** politische Überzeugung; **to carry ~** überzeugend sein; **to be open to ~** sich überzeugen lassen

convincing proof überzeugender Beweis

convocation Einberufung *(e-r Versammlung);* **C~** (Kirchen-)Synode; *Br* Provinzialsynode; *Br* gesetzgebende Versammlung *(einiger Universitäten);* **letter of ~** Einberufungsschreiben

convoke *v* einberufen, zusammenrufen; **to ~ Parliament** das Parlament einberufen

convoy *(VölkerR)* Konvoi, Geleitzug, Geleit *(von Handelsschiffen durch Kriegsschiffe im Krieg); mil* (Lkw-)Kolonne; **~ ship** Geleitschiff; **to sail under ~** im Geleit(zug) fahren; **to block** (or **stop**) **a ~** e-n Konvoi festhalten

cook *v sl. (Bilanz, Rechnung, Bücher)* verschleiern, frisieren; **to ~ a report** e-n Bericht frisieren (od. fälschen)

cooking of a balance sheet Bilanzverschleierung

cooling off Abkühlung; **~ contract** *(ArbeitsR)* Abkühlungsvertrag; **~ of the economy** Konjunkturabkühlung; **~ period** Überdenkungsperiode *(z.B. vor Vertragsabschluß); Am* Abkühlungszeit, Wartezeit *(während der Arbeitnehmer nicht streiken und Arbeitgeber nicht aussperren [lock out] dürfen; cf. Taft-Hartley Act);* **~ treaty** *(VölkerR)* Abkühlungsvertrag

cooperate *v* zusammenarbeiten (with mit); mitarbeiten, mitwirken (in bei); beitragen (to zu); **to ~ with a p. in an enterprise** mit jdm in e-m Unternehmen zusammenarbeiten

cooperation Kooperation; *(polit., wirtschaftl., wissenschaftl.)* Zusammenarbeit; *(gemeinsames)* Zusammenwirken; Mitwirkung; *(genossenschaftl.)* Zusammenschluß; *Br* Zusammenarbeit *(zwischen Betriebsführung und Belegschaft);* **~ agreement** Kooperationsabkommen; **C~ Treaty** *(Europ. PatR)* Zusammenarbeitsvertrag *(Vertrag über die internationale Zusammenarbeit auf dem Gebiete des Patentwesens)*

cooperation, administrative ~ Zusammenarbeit der Verwaltungen; verwaltungsmäßige Zusammenarbeit; Amtshilfe; **business ~** Unternehmenskooperation; **close and lasting ~** enge und dauernde Zusammenarbeit; **fiscal ~** Zusammenarbeit (od. gegenseitiger Beistand) in Steuersachen; **international ~** internationale Zusammenarbeit; **union-management ~** Zusammenarbeit zwischen Gewerkschaften und Unternehmern

cooperative *(Br*[84] *meist* **~ society**) Genossenschaft; Konsumgenossenschaft; Konsumverein; Konsumgeschäft; genossenschaftlich; kooperativ; zusammenarbeitend; *Am* Eigentumswohnung *(bes. im Staat New York);* **~ action programme** *(UNESCO)* Partnerschaftsprogramm; **~ apartment house** *Am* genossenschaftlich errichtetes Wohnhaus; **~ apartment ownership** *Am* Wohnungseigentum *(Beteiligung an e-r Genossenschaft, verbunden mit e-m Mietverhältnis);* **~ association** *Am* Genossenschaft; **~ bank** Genossenschaftsbank, genossenschaftliches Kreditinstitut; **~ building society** *Br* Bau(spar)genossenschaft; **~ buying association** Einkaufsgenossenschaft; **~ corporation** *Am* Genossenschaft; **~ credit union** Kreditgenossenschaft; **~ marketing association** Absatzgenossenschaft; **~ movement** Genossenschaftsbewegung; **C~ Productive Federation** *Br* Zusammenschluß der Produktivgenossenschaften

cooperative societ|y *Br* Genossenschaft; Konsumverein; Verbrauchergenossenschaft; **member of a ~** Genosse; **register of ~ies** Genossenschaftsregister; **share in a ~** Genossenschaftsanteil

cooperative, ~ store Konsumvereinsladen; **~ system** Genossenschaftswesen; **C~ Wholesale Society** *Br* (Groß-)Einkaufsgenossenschaft

cooperative, agricultural ~ (*Br* **society**) landwirtschaftliche Absatzgenossenschaft; **consumer ~** (*Br* **society**) Konsumgenossenschaft

cooperative, credit ~ (*Br* **society**) Kreditgenossenschaft; **agricultural credit ~** (*Br* **society**) ländliche Kreditgenossenschaft; **industrial credit ~** (*Br* **society**) gewerbliche Kreditgenossenschaft

cooperative, farmer's ~ landwirtschaftliche Genossenschaft; **marketing ~** Absatzgenossenschaft; **member of a ~** Genosse; **multi- purpose ~** Universalgenossenschaft; **producers' ~** Produktionsgenossenschaft; Produktivgenossenschaft

cooperator Mitarbeiter

coopt *v* hinzuwählen; **~ed member** zugewähltes (od. nachgewähltes) Mitglied

cooptation Kooptation, Hinzuwahl, Ergänzungswahl *(neuer Mitglieder durch die e-r Körperschaft angehörenden Mitglieder)*

coordinate koordiniert, gleichgestellt, gleichrangig *(opp. subordinate);* **~ court** gleichgeordnetes Gericht

coordinate *v* koordinieren, aufeinander abstimmen, aneinander angleichen; in Übereinstimmung bringen (with mit); gleichschalten, gleichordnen

coordinated policy aufeinander abgestimmte *(einheitliche)* Politik

coordination Koordinierung, *(gegenseitige)* Abstimmung (between zwischen); Angleichung; Gleichschaltung, Gleichordnung *(opp. subordination)*; ~ **allowance** *Am (sich über mehrere Monate erstreckende)* Ausgleichszahlung *(bei Entlassung)*; **C~ Committee**[85] Koordinierungsausschuß; ~ **of a policy** Koordinierung e-r Politik

co-owner Miteigentümer *(zur gesamten Hand od. nach Bruchteilen)*; Mitinhaber; ~ **(of a ship)** Miteigentümer an e-m Schiff, Mitreeder, Partenreeder

co-ownership Miteigentum; ~ **of ships** Partenreederei
co-ownership umfaßt tenancy in common, joint tenancy, tenancy in partnership, community property und tenancy by the entirety

cop, (traffic) ~ *sl.* (Verkehrs-)Polizist

coparcenary *hist.* gemeinsame Erbschaft

coparcener *hist.* Miterbe, Miteigentümer *(von ererbtem Grundbesitz*

copartner Teilhaber; Beteiligter *(Br am Gewinn der Gesellschaft)*

copartnership *Am (älteres Wort für)* →partnership; Teilhaberschaft; Beteiligung; *Br* Partnerschaft *(zwischen Unternehmensleitung und Arbeitnehmer; cf. profit-sharing scheme)*; **articles of** ~ *Am* Gesellschaftsvertrag; **labour** ~ *Br* Gewinnbeteiligung der Arbeitnehmer

copartnery →copartnership

cope *v* **to** ~ **with a situation** mit e-r Situation fertig werden, e-r Situation gewachsen sein

copending application *(PatR)* gleichzeitig anhängige Patentanmeldung; Parallelanmeldung

co-perpetrator *(StrafR)* Mittäter

co-perpetration *(StrafR)* Mittäterschaft

co-plaintiff Mitkläger *(aktiver Streitgenosse)*

copper Kupfer; Kupfermünze; ~**s** Kupfermünzen; *(Börse)* Kupferwerte; Kupferaktien; ~ **market** Markt für Kupferwerte; ~ **shares** → coppers

cop|y Abschrift, Durchschlag, Kopie *(opp. original)*; Exemplar *(e-s Buches)*; Nummer *(e-r Zeitung)*; Ausfertigung; Zeitungsstoff; ~ **accounts** Abschriften (od. Durchschlag) von Rechnungen; ~ **of a bill (of exchange)** Wechselkopie; ~ **certified correct** für die Richtigkeit der Abschrift *(als richtig bestätigte Abschrift)*; ~ **invoice** Rechnungsdurchschlag; ~**ies of the work** *(UrhR)* Werkstücke

cop|y, carbon ~ Durchschlag; **certified** ~ beglaubigte Abschrift; **clean** (or **fair**) ~ Reinschrift; **conformed** ~ *Am* s. true →~; **exemplified** ~ *Am* beglaubigte Abschrift; **first** ~ Original; **in two original** ~**ies** in zwei Urschriften *(bes. bei Staatsverträgen)*; **photostat(ic)** ~ (or **photo**~) Fotokopie; **rough** ~ Entwurf, Konzept; **in a single** ~ in einer Urschrift *(bes. bei Staatsverträgen)*; **top** ~ Original; **in two top** ~**ies** in zwei Urschriften; **true** ~ gleichlautende Abschrift

cop|y, to deliver (or **furnish**) **a** ~ e-e Abschrift (od. Ausfertigung) erteilen; **to retain one** ~ e-e Abschrift (für sich) behalten; **to make** (or **take**) ~**ies** Abschriften machen (od. anfertigen)

copy 2. Text, Werbetext, Anzeigentext; ~ **chief** Cheftexter; ~ **date** (or **deadline**) Anzeigenschluß; ~ **point** Werbeargument im Text; ~ **supervisor** Cheftexter; ~**-writer** Werbetexter, Anzeigentexter; ~**-writing** Abfassung von Werbetexten

copy *v* abschreiben, Abschrift machen

copying, ~ **fees** (Ab-)Schreibgebühren; ~ **machine** Kopiergerät

copyhold *Br* Lehensbesitz, Lehensgut
Bauerngut, das zu e-r Gutsherrschaft (manor) gehörte *(abgeschafft durch den Law of Property Act, 1922; jetzt: → freehold od. in gewissen Fällen → leasehold)*

copyholder *Br* Lehensgutpächter *(jetzt: → freeholder)*

copyist Abschreiber; Plagiator

copyright 1. Urheberrecht
Für das Urheberrecht sind die führenden multilateralen Abkommen die Revidierte Berner Übereinkunft (Revised Berne → Convention) und das Welturheberrechtsabkommen (Universal C~ Convention). Die Bundesrepublik Deutschland, Großbritannien und die USA sind Verbandsländer der Revidierten Berner Übereinkunft und Vertragsstaaten des Welturheberrechtsabkommens.
In Großbritannien ist das Urheberrecht durch den Copyright Act 1956 gesetzlich geregelt, der es Großbritannien ermöglicht hat, dem Welturheberrechtsabkommen vom 6. 9. 1952 beizutreten. Durch den neuen Copyright, Designs and Patents Act 1988, der eine Gesamtneuregelung des Britischen Urheberrechts enthält, wird das Gesetz von 1956 insgesamt außer Kraft gesetzt.
Schutz des Urheberrechts an Werken der Literatur und Kunst endet 50 Jahre nach Ablauf des Kalenderjahres, in dem der Autor verstorben ist.
In den Vereinigten Staaten ist das Urheberrecht bundesgesetzlich geregelt durch den Copyright Act von 1976. Dieser ist in wichtiger Hinsicht abgeändert durch den Computer Software Copyright Act von 1980. Die neue Schutzfrist nach dem Copyright Act

von 1976 ist 50 Jahre nach dem Tod des Urhebers. Inzwischen sind die USA der Revidierten Berner Übereinkunft beigetreten (→Berne Implementation Act of 1988). Seitdem bedarf es zur Begründung des Copyright-Schutzes in den USA nicht mehr eines Copyright-Vermerks. Gewisse prozessuale Vorzüge lassen es aber ratsam erscheinen, den Vermerk weiter anzubringen

copyright, ~ case Klage wegen Verletzung des Urheberrechts; Urheberrechtsstreitsache; **~ collecting societies** Verwertungsgesellschaften; **~ contract law** Urhebervertragsrecht; **~ in designs** *Br* Urheberrecht an Mustern; Musterschutz (→*design 2.*); **~ holder** Inhaber des Urheberrechts, Berechtigter; **~ in original works** *Br* Urheberrecht an ursprünglichen Werken (*opp. ancillary right*); **~ law** Urheberrechtsgesetz; **~ licen|ce (~se)** Urheberrechtslizenz; **~ licensing agreement** Urheberrechtslizenzvertrag; **~ litigation** Urheberrechtsstreitigkeit; **~ notice** *Am* Copyright-Vermerk; **~ of literary, artistic or scientific works** Urheberrecht an literarischen, künstlerischen od. wissenschaftlichen Werken

Copyright Office *Am* Urheberrechtsamt; **Register of ~** *Am* Leiter des Urheberrechtsamts

copyright, ~ period Schutzfrist; **~ proprietor** → **~ holder; ~ protection** Urheberrechtsschutz; **~ registration** Eintragung des Urheberrechts; **~ royalties** Lizenzgebühren für Urheberrechte; **C~ Royalty Tribunal** *Am* Schiedsstelle für Urheberrechtsvergütungen

copyright, acquisition and enjoyment of ~ Erwerb und Ausübung des Urheberrechts; **artistic ~** Urheberrecht an Werken der bildenden Künste (→*artistic works*); **condition of ~** Voraussetzung für den Urheberrechtsschutz; **conveyance of ~** Übertragung des Urheberrechts; **exclusive ~** Alleinurheberrecht; **film ~** Urheberrecht an Filmen

copyright, infringement of a ~ Verletzung e-s Urheberrechts (→*piracy*); **action** *Br* (**suit** *Am*) **for infringement of a ~** Klage wegen Urheberrechtsverletzung; **to constitute an infringement of ~** e-e Urheberrechtsverletzung darstellen

copyright, literary ~ Urheberrecht an literarischen Werken; **musical ~** Urheberrecht an Werken der Tonkunst (→*composer*); **out of ~** urheberrechtlich nicht mehr geschützt; **owner of a ~** Inhaber e-s Urheberrechts; **period of ~** Schutzfrist; **presumption of ~** Urheberrechtsvermutung; **protected by ~** urheberrechtlich geschützt; **protection of ~** Urheberrechtsschutz; **renewal of a ~** Verlängerung e-s Urheberrechts; **Universal C~ Convention**[86] Welturheberrechtsabkommen, (→universal); **to acquire a ~** ein Urheberrecht erwerben (in an); **the ~ expires** das Urheberrecht erlischt; **to infringe a ~** ein Urheberrecht verletzen; **to obtain a ~** ein Urheberrecht erlangen; **a ~ subsists** ein Urheberrecht besteht

copyright 2. urheberrechtlich geschützt (Nachdruck verboten, alle Rechte vorbehalten); **~ edition** urheberrechtlich geschützte Ausgabe; **to be ~** urheberrechtlichem Schutz unterliegen

copyright *v* urheberrechtlich schützen; sich das Urheberrecht sichern (für)

copyrighted urheberrechtlich geschützt

copyrighted works, unlawful exploitation of ~ unerlaubte Verwertung urheberrechtlich geschützter Werke

copyrightability Urheberrechtsschutzfähigkeit

coram, ~ nobis *Br* vor der Königin (= in Queen's Bench Division); **~ judice** vor e-m ordnungsgemäß besetzten Gericht

cordon off *v* absperren (*durch Polizei*)

coresponsibility level (*EG*) Mitverantwortungsabgabe

corn Getreide, Korn; *Am* Mais; *Br bes.* Weizen; *Scot* Hafer; **~ broker** Getreidemakler; **C~ Exchange** *Br* Getreidebörse; **~ trade clauses** (C.T.C.) Klauseln des Getreidehandels

corner (*Börsentermingeschäft*) Schwänze; (*spekulative*) Aufkäufergruppe; Aufkaufen; **~ man** *Br* Aufkäufer; **cotton ~** Baumwollring; **to make a ~** (auf)schwänzen, e-e Schwänze herbeiführen

corner *v* (*Börse*) (*bestimmte Effekten od. Waren*) aufkaufen, aufschwänzen (*damit die Baissepartei am Erfüllungstage alle Preisforderungen akzeptieren muß*); **to ~ the market in cotton** die Baumwollvorräte aufkaufen

cornerer *Br* Aufkäufer

corollary Folge(erscheinung), Ergebnis; **as a ~** als logische Folge

coronation Krönung; **~ ceremony** Krönungsfeierlichkeit; **~ oath** Krönungseid

coroner richterl. Beamter zur Untersuchung der Todesursache (*in Fällen gewaltsamen od. unnatürlichen Todes*); **~'s inquest** gerichtl. Verfahren zur Untersuchung der Todesursache (*mit Zeugenvernehmung*)

corporal punishment körperliche Züchtigung, Prügelstrafe

corporate körperschaftlich; korporativ; gemeinsam; *bes. Am* Gesellschafts-, Firmen-; Unternehmens-; **~ acquisition** *Am* Aufkauf von Gesellschaften

corporate action, to take ~ gemeinsam handeln

corporate, ~ account *Am* Gesellschaftskonto; **~ affairs** Angelegenheiten der Gesellschaft (od. Körperschaft); **~ agent** *Am* Vertreter der

Gesellschaft; ~ **America** *Am* Geschäftswelt; (Privat-)Wirtschaft; ~ **articles** *Am* Satzung e-r (Aktien-)Gesellschaft; ~ **assets** Vermögen e-r juristischen Person; *Am* Vermögenswerte e-r (Aktien-)Gesellschaft; Gesellschaftsvermögen; ~ **behavio(u)r** Verhalten e-s Unternehmens nach außen und nach innen; ~ **body** Körperschaft, juristische Person; ~ **bonds** *Am* Obligationen e-r (Aktien-)Gesellschaft; Industrieobligationen; ~ **books** *Am* (Geschäfts)-Bücher der (Aktien-)Gesellschaft

corporate business *Am* Geschäfte der Gesellschaft; **management of the** ~ Führung der Geschäfte der Gesellschaft

corporate, ~ **charter** *Am* Gründungsurkunde *(e-r Aktiengesellschaft);* ~ **consolidation** *Am* Unternehmenszusammenschluß; ~ **counsel** *Am* →corporation counsel; ~ **debts** *Am* Gesellschaftsschulden; ~ **design** (CD) formale Gestaltungskonstanten e-s Unternehmens *(z.B. Firmenzeichen);* ~ **dividend** *Am* Aktiendividende; ~ **duration** Dauer der Gesellschaft(od. juristischen Person); ~ **employee** *Am* Angestellter e-r Gesellschaft; ~ **equity** *Am* Firmenvermögen nach Abzug der Belastungen; ~ **executive** *Am* Direktor (od. leitender Angestellter) e-r AG; ~ **existence** Bestehen (od. Dauer) der Gesellschaft (od. juristischen Person); ~ **financial policy** *Am* Finanzpolitik der Unternehmen; ~ **franchise tax** *Am* Gesellschaftssteuer *(→franchise tax)*

corporate identity (CI) Corporate Identity, Unternehmensidentität *(das visuelle Erscheinungsbild e-s Unternehmens)*

Der sichtbar gemachte Charakter e-s Unternehmens, das nicht nur an der Qualität seiner Produkte und Dienstleistungen sondern auch an der Qualität seiner Verhaltensweisen gegenüber der Umwelt gemessen wird

corporate, ~ **image** →~ identity; ~ **income tax** *Am* Körperschaftssteuer; ~ **integration** *Am* gesellschaftliche Verflechtung; ~ **investment** *Am* Investition(stätigkeit) der Unternehmen; ~ **law** *Am* Aktienrecht; ~ **liability** *Am* Haftung e-r (Aktien-)Gesellschaft; Gesellschaftshaftung; ~ **liquidity** *Am* Unternehmensliquidität; ~ **losses** *Am* Verluste der Gesellschaft; Unternehmensverlust; ~ **meeting** *Am* Gesellschafterversammlung; ~ **member** Vollmitglied e-r Gesellschaft (od. juristischen Person) *(opp. associate or honorary member);* ~ **merger** *Am* Fusion von Gesellschaften; Unternehmenszusammenschluß; ~ **mortgage** *Am* Hypothek auf dem Gesellschaftsvermögen; ~ **name** *Am* Firmenname *(e-r AG); Br* Name e-r juristischen Person; ~ **officer** *Am (etwa:)* Vorstandsmitglied

corporate opportunity *Am* Geschäftschance *(des Direktors [e-s board of directors] als Interessenkonflikt);* ~ **doctrine** *Am* Lehre, die es den directors und officers verbietet, geschäftliche Möglichkeiten, die sich der Gesellschaft bieten, zu ihrem eigenen Vorteil auszunutzen

corporate, ~ **ownership** *Am* Eigentum der Gesellschaft; ~ **penalty tax** *Am* Zuschlag auf die Körperschaftssteuer; ~ **planning** Unternehmensplanung; ~ **powers** *Am* Gesellschaftsbefugnisse; Befugnisse e-r juristischen Person; ~ **profit** *Am* Gesellschaftsgewinn; Unternehmensgewinn; ~ **property** *Am* Gesellschaftsvermögen; Vermögen der Gesellschaft; *Br* Gemeindevermögen; ~ **purpose** *Am* Gesellschaftszweck; ~→**raider;** ~ **real property** *Am* unbewegliches Gesellschaftsvermögen; unbewegliches Vermögen e-r juristischen Person; ~ **responsibility** gemeinsame Verantwortung; ~ **rights** *Am* Gesellschaftsrechte; Rechte e-r juristischen Person; ~ **seal** *Am* Firmensiegel; *Br* Siegel e-r juristischen Person; ~ **signature** *Am* Firmenzeichnung; ~ **share** *Am* Anteil an e-r Gesellschaft; Gesellschaftsanteil; Aktie; ~ **shell** Firmenmantel; ~ **statement** *Am* Bilanz e-r Aktiengesellschaft; ~ **stock** *Am* Aktien *(e-r AG);* ~ **strategy** *Am* Unternehmensstrategie; ~ **structure** Gesellschaftsstruktur; ~ **tax** *Am* Körperschaftssteuer; ~ **trust** für e-e corporation bestellter →trust; ~ **underwriting** *Am* Übernahme von Industrieschuldverschreibungen; ~ **value** *Am* Unternehmenswert; ~→**veil**

corporately als Körperschaft, korporativ; gemeinsam

corporation Körperschaft, juristische Person; *bes. Am* (Kapital-)Gesellschaft *(etwa entsprechend der deutschen)* Aktiengesellschaft (AG); Gesellschaft mit beschränkter Haftung (GmbH); *Br* öffentlich-rechtliche Körperschaft, *(z.B.)* Stadtbehörde, Stadtverwaltung, Gemeindeverwaltung *(municipal ~);* (rechtsfähiger) Verein; *Br* Gilde, Innung; ~**s** *Br* →~ stock

Am Der Begriff "corporation" umfaßt auch den eingetragenen Verein, die Stiftung, Genossenschaft etc. Steuerrechtlich[87] umfaßt er auch associations, joint stock companies und insurance companies. Alle Erscheinungsformen treten hinter dem Begriff der Aktiengesellschaft zurück. Die corporation ist aber in den USA nicht nur die Organisationsform der Großunternehmen sondern auch von mittleren und kleineren Unternehmen (die in der Bundesrepublik in Form e-r GmbH betrieben würden)

Corporation Act, Business (or **General**) ~ *Am (einzelstaatl.)* Aktiengesetz

corporation, ~ **aggregate** juristische Person, die aus e-r Vereinigung mehrerer natürlicher Personen besteht *(z.B. Aktiengesellschaft, Kirchengemeinde etc., opp.* ~ *sole);* ~ **bonds** *Am* Obligationen e-r (Aktien-)Gesellschaft; Industrieobligationen; ~ **charter** *Am (vom Staat genehmigte)* Gründungsurkunde *(e-r AG);* ~ **counsel** *Am* Syndikus, Justitiar *(Rechtsanwalt e-r Handelsgesellschaft [Angestellter od. selbständi-*

ger Anwalt]); ~ **debts** *Am* Gesellschaftsschulden; ~ **executive** *Am* leitender Angestellter e-r Gesellschaft; ~ **income tax** *Am* Körperschaftssteuer

corporation law *Am* Aktienrecht; Aktiengesetz

Es gibt kein Bundesaktiengesetz; bundesgesetzlich ist nur die Überwachung geregelt. Die verschiedenen "corporation laws" der Einzelstaaten der USA sind im allgemeinen als "General Corporations Act" oder "Business Corporation Act" bezeichnet

corporation, ~ **loan** *Br* städtische Anleihe, Kommunalanleihe; ~ **meeting** *Am* Hauptversammlung; Gesellschafterversammlung; **C~ of London** *Br* autonome Verwaltung der City of London; ~ **of merchants** *Br* Handelsinnung; ~ **property** *Am* Gesellschaftsvermögen; *Br* Gemeindevermögen; ~ **under private law** Körperschaft des privaten Rechts, privatrechtliche Körperschaft; ~ **under public law** Körperschaft des öffentlichen Rechts, öffentlichrechtliche Körperschaft; ~ **sole** einzelne Person mit Rechtspersönlichkeit *(Br King, Bishop etc.);* Einmanngesellschaft; ~ **stock** *Br* Schuldverschreibungen der städtischen Behörden; Kommunalobligationen; Anleihen öffentlichrechtl. Körperschaften; ~ **tax** (C.T.) Körperschaftsteuer (→*tax*)

corporation, alien ~ *Am (außerhalb der Vereinigten Staaten errichtete)* ausländische (Kapital-)Gesellschaft *(cf. foreign ~);* **banking** ~ *Am* Bankgesellschaft; Aktienbank; **business** ~ *Am* Kapitalgesellschaft (AG, GmbH); **charitable** ~ *Am* gemeinnützige Körperschaft (od. juristische Person); →**chartered** ~; **civil** ~ *Br* eigennützige juristische Person *(Kommunalverbände, Handelsgesellschaften; opp. eleemosinary ~); Am* privatrechtliche Körperschaft *(bürgerlich-rechtliche od. handelsrechtliche juristische Person);* **close** ~ *Am* Gesellschaft mit geschlossener Mitgliederzahl *(etwa GmbH, Familien-AG; → close);* **cooperative** ~ *Am* Genossenschaft; **creation of a** ~ Gründung e-r Körperschaft (od. Gesellschaft); →**de facto** ~; →**de jure** ~; **domestic** ~ einzelstaatliche Kapitalgesellschaft *(opp. foreign ~);* **eleemosinary** ~ gemeinnützige juristische Person *(Krankenhäuser, Colleges etc);* **financial** ~**s** *Am* Banken und Versicherungen; →**foreign** ~; **formation of a** ~ s. creation of a →~; **local** ~ Gebietskörperschaft; Gemeinde; **special manufacturing** ~ *Am* besondere Fabrikationsgeschäfte betreibende Gesellschaft; **mayor and** ~ *Br* Bürgermeister und Stadtverwaltung; **membership** ~ *Am (eingetragener)* Verein; **mining** ~ *Am* Bergwerksgesellschaft; **moneyed** ~ *Am* Bank, Versicherungsgesellschaft; → **municipal** ~; **non-profit-making** ~ juristische Person ohne Erwerbscharakter; **nonstock** ~ *Am* Gesellschaft auf persönlicher Basis, die keine aktienähnlichen Anteile ausgibt *(z.B. rechtsfähiger Verein);* **nontrading** ~ *Am* nicht handeltreibende Körperschaft *(z.B. Universität);* **private** ~ *Am* privatrechtliche Körperschaft *(bürgerl.-rechtliche od. handelsrechtliche Körperschaft; opp. public ~);* **privately held** ~ *Am* s. close →~; **public** ~ öffentlich-rechtliche Körperschaft, juristische Person des öffentlichen Rechts *(opp. private ~); Br* wirtschaftliche Unternehmung der öffentlichen Hand *(z.B. British Broadcasting Corporation, British Airways); Am* Aktiengesellschaft mit breiterer Streuung des Aktienbesitzes *(deren Wertpapiere an der Börse zugelassen sind);* Publikumsgesellschaft; **public service** (or **public utility**) ~*Am* öffentl. Versorgungsunternehmen; →**quasipublic** ~; **railroad** ~ *Am* Eisenbahngesellschaft; **stock** ~ *Am* Kapitalgesellschaft (*bes.* AG); **trading** ~ *Am* Handelsgesellschaft (Kapitalgesellschaft); **transformation of a** ~ **into a partnership** *Am* Umwandlung e-r Kapitalin e-e Personengesellschaft; **to form a** ~ *Am* e-e (Kapital-)Gesellschaft gründen

corporative körperschaftlich, korporativ; ~ **investor** *Am* investierende Kapitalgesellschaft

corporator *Br* Mitglied der Stadtverwaltung

corporeal körperlich *(opp. immaterial);* ~ **hereditaments** → hereditament; ~ **things** bewegliche Sachen

Corps Diplomatique (C.D.) *Fr* diplomatisches Korps *(alle in e-m Lande akkreditierten ausländischen Diplomaten)*

corpse Leichnam *(cf. burial, cremation)*

corpus (Gesetzes-)Sammlung; Stamm des Vermögens; Kapital *(e-s trust);* ~ **delicti** *(StrafR) (ein veralteter, der römischen Rechtssprache entnommener und auch im gemeinen deutschen Recht gebrauchter Ausdruck für)* →actus reus; **C~ Juris Civilis** Sammlung des römischen Rechts Kaiser Justinians; **C~ Juris Secundum** *Am* Enzyklopädie der Rechtswissenschaft (Fortsetzung)

correct *v* verbessern, berichtigen; zurechtweisen, tadeln; **to** ~ **a defect** e-n Mangel beheben; **to** ~ **an error** e-n Fehler berichtigen (od. richtigstellen)

correcting entry Berichtigungsbuchung; Berichtigungseintragung

correction Verbesserung, Korrektur; *Am* Besserungsmaßnahmen; **Department of C~** *Am* Zentralverwaltung der Besserungsanstalten; **house of** ~ *Am* (Jugend-)Gefängnis, Arbeitshaus; **subject to** (or **under**) ~ ohne Gewähr; Berichtigung vorbehalten

correctional, ~ **institution** *Am*[88] Straf(vollzugs)anstalt, Gefängnis *(der Einzelstaaten und des Bundes für Freiheitsstrafen über ein Jahr);* ~ **treatment** *Am* Behandlung zwecks Besserung

corrective action (or **measure**) Abhilfemaßnahme

correctness of the accounts Richtigkeit der Abrechnungen

correlate *v*, **to ~ the dates** die Termine aufeinander abstimmen; **to ~ with** in Übereinstimmung bringen mit

correlative aufeinander abgestimmt; wechselseitig bedingt; entsprechend

correspond *v*, **to ~ to** entsprechen; **to ~ with** übereinstimmen mit; korrespondieren (od. in Briefwechsel stehen) mit; **to ~ with one's friends** mit s-n Freunden korrespondieren; **the report does not ~ to the facts** der Bericht entspricht nicht den Tatsachen; **to ~ to sample** dem Muster entsprechen

corresponding entsprechend; **~ attorney** *Am* Korrespondenzanwalt; **~ member** (C.M.) korrespondierendes *(auswärtiges)* Mitglied *(e-r wissenschaftlichen Gesellschaft)*

correspondence Übereinstimmung; Korrespondenz, Briefwechsel, Schriftverkehr; Briefe; Geschäftsverbindung *(bes. im Ausland)*; **~ classes** (or **course**) Fernunterricht; **~ clerk** Korrespondent; **~ course student** Fernstudent

correspondence, commercial ~ Handelskorrespondenz; **foreign ~** Auslandskorrespondenz

correspondence, to attend to (or **deal with**) **the ~** die Korrespondenz erledigen; **to be in (enter into) ~** in Briefwechsel stehen (treten) (with mit); **to carry on (a) ~** Briefwechsel führen (with mit); **to go through one's ~** die *(eingegangene)* Post durchsehen

correspondent Korrespondent, Berichterstatter *(e-r Zeitung)*; *(auswärtiger)* Geschäftsfreund *(Person, Firma, Bank)*; **~ bank** Korrespondenzbank; **~ banking** Geschäfte mit e-r Korrespondenzbank

correspondent, domestic (or **inland**) **~** Inlandskorrespondent; **foreign ~** Auslandskorrespondent *(e-r Zeitung)*; Korrespondenzbank; **special ~** Sonderberichterstatter; **war ~** Kriegsberichterstatter

corridor Korridor, Gang; *pol* Korridor *(Landstreifen durch fremdes Gebiet)*; **~ train** D-Zug

corrigend|um zu verbessernder Fehler *(bes. Druckfehler)*; Berichtigung; **~a** Druckfehlerverzeichnis

corroborate *v* bekräftigen, bestätigen, erhärten; **to ~ a p.'s evidence** jds Zeugenaussage bestätigen

corroborating (or **corroborative**) **evidence** (or **testimony**) bestätigende Zeugenaussage

corroboration Bestätigung, Bekräftigung *(bes. e-r Zeugenaussage)*; **in ~ of** zur Bestätigung von

corrupt korrupt, bestechlich; verdorben; entstellt *(Text)*; **~ administration** korrupte Verwaltung; **~ judge** bestechlicher Richter; **~ practices** korrupte Praktiken, Bestechungen, Bestechlichkeit, Korruption; *(bei Wahlen)* Bestechungsmanöver; **~ and illegal practices** Wahlfälschungen und rechtswidrige Wahlpraktiken; **C~ Practices Act** *Am* Bundesgesetz zur Regulierung des Parteifinanzwesens

corrupt *v* korrumpieren, bestechen, kaufen; *(Text)* entstellen, verfälschen; verderben

corruptibility Bestechlichkeit; Käuflichkeit

corruptible bestechlich; käuflich

corruption Korruption, *(aktive od. passive)* Bestechung; Entstellung *(e-s Textes)*; **~ of morals** Sittenverderbnis, Sittenverfall; **~ of witnesses** Zeugenbestechung; **bribery and ~** *Br* Bestechungsunwesen; **electoral ~** Wahlbestechung; **judicial ~** Richterbestechung

cortege, funeral ~ Leichenzug

Cortes Cortes *(gesetzgebende Versammlung in Spanien und Portugal)*

co(-)signatory Mitunterzeichner(in); mitunterzeichnend

cosmonaut Kosmonaut, (Welt-)Raumfahrer

cosmonautics Kosmonautik, Raumfahrt

COST *(EG)* →European Cooperation on Scientific and Technical Research (COST)

cost Kosten, Kostenbetrag; Selbstkosten; Aufwand

cost, to calculate the ~ die Kosten berechnen; **to share in the ~** sich an den Kosten beteiligen; **he built his house without regard to the ~** er baute sein Haus ohne Rücksicht auf die Kosten

cost, ~ account Kostenkonto *(der Betriebsbuchhaltung)*; **~ accountant** Kostenrechner; Betriebskalkulator; **~ accounting** Kostenrechnung; Betriebskalkulation; **~ accounting department** Kalkulationsabteilung; **~ allocation** Kostenumlage, Kostenverteilung; **~ and freight** →C. & F.; **~ basis** Bewertungsgrundlage; **~-benefit analysis** Kosten-Nutzen Analyse

cost(-)book Kalkulationsbuch; *Br* Kuxbuch; **~ (mining) company** *Br (bergrechtl.)* Gewerkschaft *(Teilhaberschaft)*; **member of a ~ company** Gewerke

cost, ~ budget Kostenplan; **~ cent|re (~er)** Kostenstelle; **~ chart** Kostentabelle; **~ control** Kostenlenkung; **~-covering** kostendeckend; **~ cutting** Kostensenkung; **~ data** Kostenunterlagen; **~ department** Kalkulationsabteilung; **~ distribution** Kostenverteilung; **~ effectiveness analysis** Kosten-Wirksamkeitsanalyse *(Wirtschaftlichkeitsrechnung);* ~ **estimate** Kosten(vor)anschlag; ~ **exemption** Kostenbefreiung; ~ **factor** Kostenfaktor; ~ **finding** Kostenerfassung; ~ **fixing** Kostenfestsetzung; ~ **free** kostenfrei, kostenlos; ~ **groups** Kostenarten; ~, **insurance and freight** →cif; ~, **insurance, freight, commission, interest** →cifci; ~ **incurred** entstandene Kosten; ~ **item** Kostenposten; ~ **of acquisition** Anschaffungskosten; ~ **of carriage** Fracht-, Transport-, Beförderungskosten; ~ **of collection** Einziehungskosten; ~ **of construction** Baukosten; ~ **of credit** Kreditkosten; ~ **of delivery** Lieferkosten, Versandkosten; ~ **of distribution** Vertriebskosten, Absatzkosten; ~ **of financing** Finanzierungskosten; ~ **of labo(u)r** Lohnkosten *(Löhne und Gehälter);* ~ **of litigation** Prozeßkosten

cost of living Lebenshaltungskosten; ~ **adjustment** Lohnangleichung an die Lebenshaltungskosten; ~ **allowance** (or **bonus**) Teuerungszulage *(Zulage für Anstieg der Lebenshaltungskosten);* ~ **index** Preisindex für die Lebenshaltung; **increased** ~ erhöhte Lebenshaltungskosten; **increase in the** ~ Anstieg der Lebenshaltungskosten; ~ **is rising** die Lebenshaltungskosten steigen

cost, ~ **of maintenance** Unterhaltskosten; Instandhaltungskosten; ~ **of management** Verwaltungskosten; ~ **of materials** Materialkosten; ~ **of operation** Betriebskosten; ~ **of production** Produktionskosten, Herstellungskosten, Gestehungskosten; ~ **of promotion** Gründungskosten; ~ **of repair(s)** Reparaturkosten; ~ **of sales** Absatzkosten, Vertriebskosten; ~ **of storage** Lagerkosten; ~ **of transfer** Übertragungskosten *(bei Aktienverkäufen);* ~ **per item** Stückkosten; ~ **plus** *Am* Herstellungskosten plus *(Prozentsatz der Kosten als)* Unternehmergewinn

cost price Selbstkostenpreis; (Netto-)Einkaufspreis, Einstandspreis; Gestehungskosten; **at** ~ zum Selbstkostenpreis (od. Einkaufspreis); *(bei Wertpapieren)* zum Ankaufskurs; *(bei Beteiligungen)* zum Erwerbswert; **to sell below** ~ unter Selbstkostenpreis verkaufen

cost, ~ **push inflation** Kostendruckinflation; ~ **recording** Kostenerfassung; ~ **recovery** Verrechnung von Aufwendungen; ~ **reduction** Kostensenkung; ~ **saving** Kosteneinsparung; kosten(er)sparend; ~ **sharing** Kostenteilung; Kostenbeteiligung; ~ **sheet** Kostenbogen, Kostenabrechnung; ~ **unit** Kostenträger; ~ **value** Anschaffungswert

cost, actual ~ tatsächlich entstandene Kosten, Istkosten; Selbstkosten; **additional** ~ zusätzliche Kosten, Mehrkosten; **advance on** ~ Kostenvorschuß; **allocation of the** ~ Aufteilung der Kosten; Kostenverteilung; **apportionment of the** ~ Umlegung der Kosten; **at** ~ zu(m) Selbstkosten(preis); zum Ankaufskurs *(bei Wertpapieren);* zum Erwerbswert *(bei Beteiligungen);* **at a** ~ **of** mit e-m Kostenaufwand von; **below** ~ unter Selbstkosten; unter Einkaufspreis; **calculation of** ~ Kostenberechnung; **estimate of** ~ Kostenüberschlag; Kosten(vor)anschlag; **excess** ~ Mehrkosten; **factory** ~ Herstellungskosten; **first** ~ →prime ~; **free of** ~ kostenfrei, kostenlos; **general** (or **indirect**) ~ Gemeinkosten; **initial** ~ Anschaffungskosten; **invoice** ~ (Brutto-)Einkaufspreis, Einkaufsrechnungspreis *(cf. cost price);* **marginal** ~ Grenzkosten; →**original** ~; **packing** ~ Verpackungskosten; →**prime** ~; **refund of the** ~ Kostenerstattung; **replacement** ~ Wiederbeschaffungskosten; **specific** ~ Einzelkosten, direkte Kosten *(opp. general ~)*

costs Kosten, Unkosten *(→cost); Br* Prozeßkosten *(einschließlich Anwaltsgebühren); Am (von der unterliegenden Partei zu erstattende, vom Wert des Streitgegenstandes unabhängige)* Gerichtskosten

In England fallen die Kosten im Zivilprozeß in zwei Klassen: party and party costs und common fund costs. Die unterliegende Partei wird fast immer (außer wenn ihr Legal Aid gewährt war) zur Zahlung der party and party costs verurteilt. Im amerikanischen Recht werden im Ggs. zum deutschen Recht die Anwaltsgebühren der obsiegenden Partei, wenn überhaupt, nur in beschränktem Umfange erstattet

costs, ~ **accrue** Kosten entstehen; **to allocate** (or **apportion**) **the** ~ die Kosten umlegen; die Kosten quoteln; **the plaintiff was awarded** ~ (against the defendant) dem Kläger wurden die Kosten auferlegt; ~ **were awarded against him** er wurde zur Zahlung der Kosten verurteilt; **to bear the** ~ die Kosten tragen; **the** ~ **shall be borne by the lessee** die Kosten gehen zu Lasten des Mieters; **to condemn a party in** ~ e-e Partei zur Zahlung der Prozeßkosten (od. zu den Kosten) verurteilen; **to dismiss with** ~ *(Klage)* kostenpflichtig abweisen; **to keep down the** ~ die Kosten *(möglichst)* niedrig halten; **to be liable to pay the** ~ zur Tragung der Kosten verpflichtet sein; **to order to pay the** ~ die (Gerichts-)Kosten auferlegen, zur Zahlung der Kosten verurteilen; **to tax the** ~ → tax *v* 2; **the** ~ **follow the event** die Kostenentscheidung richtet sich nach dem Ausgang des Prozesses

costs, ~ **of an action** Prozeßkosten; ~ **in the cause** Kosten der Hauptsache; ~ **of the contract** Vertragskosten, Kosten des Vertragsabschlusses; ~ **of the defence (~se)** Verteidigungskosten; ~ **and expenses** Kosten und Auslagen; ~ **incurred** entstandene (od. angefallene) Kosten; ~ **incurred by a party** die e-r Partei erwachsenen Kosten; ~ **of proceedings** Kosten des Verfahrens, Verfahrenskosten; ~ **per unit** Stückkosten

costs, advance on (court) ~ *Am* Gerichtskostenvorschuß; **advertising** ~ Reklamekosten,

Werbekosten; **agreed** ~ vereinbarte Kosten; **amount of the** ~ Höhe der Gerichtskosten; Unkostenbetrag; **bill of** ~ →bill 1.; **→common fund** ~; **court** ~ Gerichtskosten; **diminution of** ~ Kostenabbau; **judgment for the payment of** ~ Verurteilung in die Prozeßkosten; **legal** ~ *Br* Rechtskosten *(→legal)*; **money paid on account of** ~ *Br* (Gerichts-)Kostenvorschuß; **order for** ~ Kostenentscheidung; **party and party** ~ *Br (notwendig entstandene)* Prozeßkosten *(die von der unterliegenden Partei eingezogen werden können)*; **payment on account of** ~ *Br (e-m Solicitor zu zahlender)* Kostenvorschuß; **person liable for** ~ Kostenschuldner; **reduction of** ~ Kostensenkung; **reimbursement of** ~ Kostenerstattung; **rise in** ~ Kostensteigerung; **running** ~ laufende Kosten; **schedule of** ~ Kostenstelle

costs, security for ~ Sicherheitsleistung für Prozeßkosten

Die Befreiung von der Verpflichtung zur Sicherheitsleistung für die Prozeßkosten ist im Verhältnis Großbritannien zur Bundesrepublik durch Art. 14 des Deutsch-britischen Abkommens über den Rechtsverkehr vom 20. März 1928[89] geregelt. Danach ist Gegenseitigkeit nur verbürgt, wenn die beiderseitigen Staatsangehörigen ihren Wohnsitz in dem Staat haben, dessen Gericht sie angerufen haben (temporary residence genügt nicht).

Die Gegenseitigkeit bei der Befreiung von der Verpflichtung zur Sicherheitsleistung für Prozeßkosten ist im Verhältnis der Vereinigten Staaten zur Bundesrepublik durch Art. VI Abs. 1 des Freundschafts-, Handels- und Schiffahrtsvertrages vom 29. 10. 1954[90] in Verb. mit Nr. 6 des Protokolls vom 19. Oktober 1954[91] vertraglich geregelt. Auch das amerikanische Recht geht im Ggs. zum deutschen Recht (§ 110 ZPO knüpft an Staatsangehörigkeit an) grundsätzlich von der residence aus. Ein →nonresident ist also zur Sicherheitsleistung verpflichtet. Die Verbürgung der Gegenseitigkeit bezieht sich nicht nur auf Staatsangehörigkeit beider Vertragsteile, sondern darüber hinaus auch auf Gesellschaften. Sie erstreckt sich auch auf Prozesse vor den Gerichten der amerikanischen Einzelstaaten

costs, solicitor's ~ *Br* Anwaltsgebühren; **taxation of** ~ →taxation 2; **trend of** ~ Kostenentwicklung; **with** ~ (to plaintiff, defendant etc) kostenpflichtig; unter Auferlegung der Kosten *(mit dem Recht, die Kosten von der Gegenseite erstattet zu bekommen)*

cost *v* kosten, zu stehen kommen; Kosten ermitteln, kalkulieren; **it ~s too much** es kostet zuviel; **that will ~ me a great deal of money** *colloq.* das wird mich teuer zu stehen kommen

costed at mit e-m Kostenanschlag von

costing Kostenrechnung, Kalkulation; ~ **items** Kalkulationskosten; ~ **procedure** Kalkulationsverfahren; **marginal** ~ *Br* Grenzkostenrechnung; **standard** ~ Plankostenrechnung

Costa Rica Costa Rica; **Republic of** ~ Republik Costa Rica

Costa Rican Costaricaner(in); costaricanisch

costermonger *Br* Straßenhändler *(bes. mit Obst und Gemüse)*; Höker *(mit Marktwaren)*; **~s' trade** Hökerhandel

costly kostspielig; teuer

co(-)surety Mitbürgschaft; Mitbürge

Côte d'Ivoire, Republic ~ Republik Côte d'Ivoire *(→Ivorian)*

co(-)tenant Mitpächter, Mitmieter

cottage kleines Haus *(bes. auf dem Lande)*; ~ **industry** Heimindustrie; Heimgewerbe

cottar, cotter *bes. Scot* Pachthäusler, Kleinbauer

cotton Baumwolle; **C~ Belt** *Am* Baumwollbezirk; ~ **exchange** Baumwollbörse; ~ **futures** Baumwolltermingeschäft; ~ **goods** Baumwollwaren; ~ **textiles** Baumwollspinnstoffe; ~ **trade** Baumwollhandel

co(-)trustee Mittreuhänder

council Rat, Ratsversammlung; *colloq.* Ortsbehörde; *eccl* Konzil; **C~** (of the European Communities) Rat (der Europäischen Gemeinschaften); EG-Rat; **C~ of Economic Advisers** *Am* Wirtschaftsbeirat; **C~ of Europe** Europarat *(→Europe)*; **C~ of the Law Society** *Br* Vorstand der →Law Society; **C~ of Legal Education** *Br* Ausbildungs- und Prüfungskommission für Rechtskandidaten *(zur →Bar)*; **C~ of Ministers** *(EG)* Ministerrat; **C~ for Mutual Economic Assistance** (CMEA) Rat für Gegenseitige Wirtschaftshilfe (RGW) (→ *COMECON)*; **C~ of State** Staatsrat; **C~ of States** *(Schweiz)* Ständerat; **C~ of the Stock Exchange** *Br* Börsenrat *(Börsenvorstand)*

council, ~ **board** Ratsversammlung; Ratstisch, Sitzungstisch; ~ **chamber** →~ room; ~ **committee** Ratsausschuß; ~ **elections** Ratswahlen; ~ **estate** *Br (soziale)* Wohnsiedlung *(der Gemeinden)*; ~ **flat** (or **house**) *Br* gemeindeeigenes Wohnhaus; *(in e-m ~ estate mit niedrigen Mieten etwa:)* Sozialwohnung; ~ **meeting** Ratssitzung; **C~ Regulation** *(EG)* Ratsverordnung; ~ **room** Ratssaal, Sitzungssaal; ~ **tenant** *(etwa:)* Sozialmieter; Mieter e-r Sozialwohnung; ~ **vacancy** freigewordener Ratssitz

council, borough ~ *Br* Stadtrat *(→borough)*, **city** ~ Stadtrat, Gemeinderat; **Common C~** *Am* Stadtrat, Gemeinderat; *Br* Rat der City of London; **county** ~ *Br* Grafschaftsrat *(→county)*; **district** ~ *Br* Stadtrat; Gemeinderat; **local** ~ Stadtrat, Gemeinderat; **Order in C~, Order of C~** *Br* → order 2.; **Privy C~** *Br* Geheimer Staatsrat, Kronrat *(→privy)*; **session of the** ~ Ratssitzung; **works** ~ Betriebsrat

council, to call a ~ e-e Ratssitzung anberaumen;

to meet in ~ e-e Ratssitzung abhalten; **to summon a** ~ die Ratsmitglieder einberufen

councillor Ratsmitglied; Ratsherr; Stadtrat; **county** ~ Grafschaftsratsmitglied (→*county*); **town** ~ Ratsmitglied, Ratsherr, Stadtverordneter

councilman *Am* Ratsmitglied, Ratsherr, Stadtverordneter; **board of councilmen** *Am* (Stadt-)Rat, Stadtverordnetenversammlung

councilor *Am* →councillor

counsel 1. (Rechts-)Anwalt; *Br (vor Gericht plädierender)* Anwalt (barrister); Rechtsberater, Rechtsbeistand; *Am* die juristischen Berater im Prozeß; **of** ~ *Am* Prozeßspezialist, verhandlungsführender Anwalt; Berater für e-e Anwaltsfirma

Bei den englischen Gerichten besteht kein Anwaltszwang. In größeren Sachen sind meist zwei barristers tätig, ein Queen's Counsel und ein junior counsel

counsel, ~ **appointed for an indigent party** *Am* beigeordneter Anwalt; ~**'s brief** *Br* Beauftragung *(e-s barrister)* zur Vertretung vor Gericht; ~**'s clerk** *Br* Bürovorsteher e-s barrister; ~**'s fess** Anwaltsgebühren *(Br des barrister)*; ~ **for the Crown** *Br* öffentlicher Ankläger; ~ **for the defen|ce (~se)** *(Zivilprozeß)* Anwalt (od. Prozeßbevollmächtigter) des Beklagten; *(Strafprozeß)* Verteidiger; ~ **for the plaintiff** Anwalt (od. Prozeßbevollmächtigter) des Klägers; klägerischer Anwalt; ~ **for the prosecution** Anklagevertreter; ~**'s opinion** Rechtsgutachten *(Br e-s barrister)*; ~**'s speech** *Br* Anwaltsplädoyer *(des barrister)*

counsel, chamber ~ *Br (nur)* beratender Anwalt *(barrister)*; **corporation** ~ *Am* Syndikus (→ *corporation*); **defending** ~ →~ for the defen|ce (~se); **employment of (a)** ~ *Br* Zuziehung e-s *(zweiten)* Anwalts *(e-s barrister durch e-n solicitor)*; **general** ~ *Am* Hauptanwalt; **in-house** ~ *Am* Betriebs-Syndikus; **King's C~** (K. C.) s. Queen's →C~; **legal** ~ *Am* Rechtsberater; **opposing** ~ Gegenanwalt, gegnerischer Anwalt; **plaintiff's** ~ →~ for the plaintiff; **Queen's C~** (Q.C.) *Br* Anwalt der Krone *(höchste Stellung e-s barrister)*; **special** ~ *Am* Sonderanwalt

counsel, to act as ~ *(jdn)* als Anwalt vertreten; *(für jdn)* als Anwalt auftreten; **to brief** (or **employ, retain**) **(a)** ~ e-n Anwalt nehmen; *Br* e-n *(zweiten)* Anwalt *(barrister)* zuziehen; **to be represented by** ~ durch e-n Anwalt (*Br* barrister) vertreten sein; **to take** ~**'s opinion** ein Rechtsgutachten einholen

counsel 2. Beratung; Rat(schlag); **to take** ~ sich beraten; **to take** ~ **together** sich miteinander (od. gemeinsam) beraten; **to take** ~ **with sb.** sich Rat holen bei jdm; sich von jdm beraten lassen

counsel *v*, **to** ~ **sb.** jdn. beraten; jdm (an)raten (od. Rat erteilen) *(etw. zu tun)*; **to** ~ **and procure** *(StrafR)* Beihilfe leisten *(cf. accessory before the fact)*

counsel(l)ing Beratung; **investment** ~ Wertpapieranlageberatung

counsel(l)or *Am* juristischer Berater; *Am (und Irland)* Rechtsanwalt; Rechtsberater *(e-r diplomatischen Vertretung)*; **attorney and** ~ **at-law** *Am* Rechtsanwalt; ~ **(of embassy)** Botschaftsrat 1. Klasse; ~**(of legation)** Vortragender Legationsrat 1. Klasse; **C~ of State** *Br* Mitglied des →Privy Council; Mitglied der königlichen Familie als Stellvertreter

count Zählen; (Ab-, Auf-, Aus-)Zählung; *(Wahl)* Stimmenauszählung; (Be-)Rechnung; *(ermittelte)* Zahl, Endzahl; *(Zivilprozeß)* Punkt der Klagebegründung (od. Klagebeantwortung); **by this** ~ nach dieser Berechnung; ~ **of an indictment** *(Strafprozeß)* Anklagepunkt; ~**-out** *Br parl* Vertagung *(wegen Beschlußunfähigkeit)*; **action of** ~ **and reckoning** *Scot* Klage auf Rechnungslegung und Zahlung der Restschuld gegen e-n Beauftragten (agent); **to leave out of** ~ unberücksichtigt lassen; **to lose** ~ sich verzählen

count *v* zählen, (be)rechnen; **to** ~ **on** sich verlassen auf, rechnen mit; **to** ~ **out** *Br parl* vertagen *(wenn weniger als 40 Abgeordnete im House of Commons anwesend sind)*; **to** ~ **over** durchzählen; nachzählen; **to** ~ **towards** anrechnen auf; **to** ~ **up money** *colloq.* Geld zählen; **to** ~ **upon** →to ~ on; **to** ~ **wrong** sich verzählen, sich verrechnen

counting Zählen, Rechnen; ~ **of votes** Stimmenzählung

counter (Bank-, Post-, Kassen-)Schalter; Ladentisch; ~ **cash** Tageskasse; Geld für den täglichen Kassenbedarf; ~ **clerk** Schalterbeamter; ~ **service** Schalterdienst; →**over the** ~; **the** ~**s of the bank are closed** die Bank hat ihre Schalter geschlossen; **to hand in a parcel at the** ~ ein Paket am Schalter aufgeben

counter *v*, **to** ~ **sb.** jdm entgegentreten, jdm widersprechen; **to** ~ **sth.** e-r Sache zuwiderhandeln, etw. durchkreuzen; **to** ~ **an argument** e-m Argument widersprechen

counter to entgegen, zuwider; **to act** ~ **one's convictions** gegen s-e Überzeugung handeln; **to run** ~ **a plan** e-n Plan durchkreuzen

counter Gegen-, entgegen-; ~**act** *v* entgegenwirken, bekämpfen; vereiteln; durchkreuzen; *(Wirkung)* aufheben; ~**argument** Gegenargument; ~**balance** *fig* Gegengewicht; Gegensaldo; ~**balance** *v fig* ein Gegengewicht bilden zu; ausgleichen; aufheben; ~**bidding** Gegenbieten, Überbieten; ~**bond** Rückbürgschaft; ~**charge** Gegenbeschuldigung

counterclaim Gegenanspruch, Gegenforderung; Widerklage; **reply to a ~** Entgegnung *(des Klägers)* auf e-e Widerklage; **to make** (or **plead**) **a ~** e-n Gegenanspruch geltend machen; e-e Widerklage erheben

counterclaim *v* e-n Gegenanspruch geltend machen; e-e Widerklage erheben; **to ~ for sth.** etw. als Gegenforderung verlangen

counterclaimant Widerkläger

counterclaiming defendant Widerklage erhebender Beklagter

counter-cyclical antizyklisch

counter-declaration Gegenerklärung

counter(-)espionage Gegenspionage, (Spionage-)Abwehr; **~ office** Abwehrstelle

counter(-)evidence Gegenbeweis; **to put in** (or **produce**) **~** Gegenbeweis erbringen

counterfeit Fälschung, Nachahmung; Falschgeld; gefälscht, falsch, nachgemacht; **this ten-dollar note is a ~** dieser 10-Dollar-Geldschein ist eine Fälschung; **~ bank notes** gefälschte Banknoten

counterfeit coin falsche Münze, Falschgeld; **~ goods** nachgeahmte Waren; **maker of ~** Falschmünzer; **making of ~** Falschmünzerei

counterfeit money Falschgeld, nachgemachtes Geld; **coining of ~** Falschmünzerei

counterfeit *v* nachmachen, fälschen; **to ~ coins** Münzen fälschen, falschmünzen; Metallgeld nachmachen; **to ~ bank notes** Banknoten fälschen; **to ~ a signature** e-e Unterschrift fälschen

counterfeiting Fälschung; Nachahmung; **~ coins** Falschmünzerei *(Nachahmen echten [Metall- od. Papier-]Geldes)*; **~ of a document** Urkundenfälschung; **~ gang** Falschmünzerbande; **International Convention for the Suppression of C~ Currency**[92] Internationales Abkommen zur Bekämpfung der Falschmünzerei

counterfeiter (Banknoten-)Fälscher; Falschmünzer

counterfoil (Kontroll-)Abschnitt; Kupon, *(festverzinsl. Wertpapieren od. Aktien beigefügter)* Zins- od. Dividendenschein; Talon *(Erneuerungsschein)*; **~ book** Talonbuch; Abreißblock; **~ of receipt** Quittungsabschnitt

counter(-)intelligence Spionageabwehr; **C~I~Corps** (CIC) *Am* (Spionage-)Abwehrdienst *(militärische Abwehrorganisation)*; **C~I~Service** (CIS) *Am* Abwehrdienst

countermand Aufhebung *(e-r Anordnung)*; Widerruf; Abbestellung; Annullierung (od. Stornierung) *(e-s Auftrags)*; **~ of payment** Schecksperre

countermand *v (Anordnung)* aufheben; widerrufen; rückgängig machen, abbestellen; **to ~ an order** etw. abbestellen; Auftrag zurückziehen (od. annullieren, stornieren); **to ~ an order for goods** e-e Warenbestellung widerrufen; **to ~ by wire** abtelegrafieren

countermanded, payment ~ Zahlung gesperrt *(Anweisung an die Bank, e-n Scheck nicht zu honorieren)*; **unless ~** mangels gegenteiliger Nachricht; **until ~** bis auf Widerruf

counter, ~mark Gegenzeichen; **~(-)measure** Gegenmaßnahme; **~(-)motion** *parl* Gegenantrag; **~(-)offer** Gegenangebot; **~-opinion** Gegengutachten; **~(-)order** Abbestellung, Stornierung; Gegenorder

counterpart Duplikat, Doppel; zweite Ausfertigung *(e-r Urkunde)*; **~ account** Gegenwertkonto; **~ funds** Gegenwertmittel

counterplea *Am* Gegeneinwand, Replik *(Erwiderung des Klägers auf Klagebeantwortung des Beklagten)*

counterpurchase (Art von) Kompensationsgeschäft *(Verkäufer verpflichtet sich zum Erwerb von Waren oder Dienstleistungen des Käufers)*

counter(-)revolution Gegenrevolution

counter(-)security Rückbürgschaft; Rückbürge; Gegenbürge

countersign *mil* Kennwort, Parole

countersign *v* gegenzeichnen, mitunterzeichnen

counter(-)signature Gegenzeichnung, Mitunterschrift

counterstatement in opposition proceedings *(PatR)* Einspruchserwiderung

counter-surety *Br* →counter-security

countertrade Kompensationsgeschäft, Gegenlieferungsgeschäft, Tauschgeschäft *(bes. im Außenhandel)*

countertrading →countertrade

countervail *v* ausgleichen

countervailing, ~ credit Gegenakkreditiv; **~ duty** Ausgleichszoll; Ausgleichsabgabe; **~ power** ausgleichende Gegenkraft; *Am* gegengewichtige Marktmacht; Abwehrkartell

countervalue Gegenwert

counterweight *fig* Gegengewicht (to gegen)

country Land, Heimatland, Staat *(Am im Ggs. zu den Einzelstaaten)*; Land *(Ggs. Stadt)*; **~ of adoption** Wahlheimat; **~ of departure** *(Flug)* Abgangsland; **~ of destination** *(Post)* Bestimmungsland; **~ of origin** Herkunftsland, Ursprungsland; Reiseantrittsland; **~ of provenance** Herkunftsland; **~ of residence** Wohnsitzstaat

country, ~ bank *Br* Provinzbank; **~ branch** *Br* Provinzfiliale; **~ -by~-comparison** Vergleich der einzelnen Staaten untereinander; **~ gentleman** Gutsbesitzer; **~ house** Landhaus; **~ man** Landmann; Landsmann; **~ seat** Landsitz; Landgut; **C~side Commission** *Br* Kommission für Landschaftspflege; **~ solicitor** *Br* Rechtsanwalt aus der Provinz; **~ woman** Landfrau; Landsmännin

country, agricultural ~ Agrarstaat; **creditor ~** Gläubigerland; **debtor ~** Schuldnerland; **entering and leaving the ~** Ein- und Ausreise; **exporting ~** Ausfuhrland; **importing ~** Ein-

fuhrland; in the ~ auf dem Land; **industrial** ~ Industriestaat; **member** ~ Mitgliedstaat; **native** ~ Heimatstaat; **transit** ~ Durchfuhrland; **Union** ~ Verbandsland (→*Union 1.*); **within the** ~ im Inland

country, to appeal (or **go**) **to the** ~ *Br* das Parlament auflösen und Neuwahlen ausschreiben; **to leave a** ~ auswandern; aus e-m Land ausreisen; **to live in the** ~ auf dem Lande leben

county *Br* Grafschaft (= *shire*); Verwaltungsbezirk; *Am* (Land-)Kreis, Bezirk *(Verwaltungsbezirk der Einzelstaaten, mit Ausnahme von Louisiana; cf. parish)*

England und Wales (ausschließlich Greater London) sind für die Zwecke der örtlichen Selbstverwaltung in counties eingeteilt. Organe: chairman, councillors. Die counties sind unterteilt in county districts

county, ~ **administrator** *Am* →~ manager; ~ **attorney** *Am* Staatsanwalt; ~ **bond** *Am* Schuldverschreibung e-s county; ~ **clerk** *Am* Verwaltungsbeamter e-s county; ~ **commissioner** *Am (gewählter)* Verwaltungsbeamter *(in e-m Kreis)*

county council *Br (auf 3 Jahre gewählter)* Grafschaftsrat; **clerk to the** ~ oberster Verwaltungsbeamter e-s county; **officer of the** ~ Grafschaftsbeamter

count|y, ~ **councillor** *Br* Mitglied e-s Grafschaftsrats; Stadtrat; ~ **court** →court 2.; ~ **district** *Br*[93] Unterabteilung der ~**ies** *(bestehend aus →metropolitan districts or non-metropolitan districts)*; ~ **jail** *Am* Gemeindegefängnis; ~ **manager** *Am* oberster Verwaltungsbeamter e-s ~; ~ **officers** *Am* Kommunalbeamte; Kreisbeamte; Kreisbedienstete; **C**~ **Palatine** *Br* die *(früheren)* C~ies Chester, Durham and Lancaster; ~ **police** *Br* Grafschaftspolizei; ~ **seat** *Am* Kreis(haupt)stadt; ~ **stocks** *Br* Kommunalobligationen; ~ **town** *Br* Kreis(haupt)-stadt

count|y, →home ~ **ies**

coup (d'état) *Br pol* Staatsstreich; Putsch; **attempted** ~ Putschversuch; →**military** ~

couple Paar; **(married)** ~ Ehepaar

coupon Kupon, Coupon, *(der e-m festverzinsl. Wertpapier beigefügte)* Zinsschein (od. Dividendenschein); Gutschein, Bon; *Br (Postsparkasse)* Sparmarke; Abschnitt; ~ **bond** *Am* Inhaberschuldverschreibung mit Zinsschein; ~ **book** *Br (Postsparkasse)* Sparbuch; ~ **collection department** Kuponabteilung; ~ **holder** Kuponinhaber; ~ **rate** Zinssatz für festverzinsliche Wertpapiere; ~ **sheet** Kuponbogen

coupon, cum ~ mit Kupon; **ex** ~ ohne (od. ausschließlich) Kupon; **free gift** ~ Gutschein; **interest** ~ Zinsschein, Zinskupon; **international reply** ~ internationaler (Rück-)Antwortschein; **ration** ~ Lebensmittelkartenabschnitt; **sheet of** ~**s** Kuponbogen; **to detach a** ~ e-n Kupon abtrennen

courier *dipl* Kurier; ~ **luggage** Kuriergepäck; ~ **mail** Kurierpost; **special** ~ Sonderkurier

course 1. Lauf, Verlauf; Gang; Richtung *(e-r Straße, e-s Flusses etc)*; Flußlauf; Kurs *(Fahrtrichtung)*

course of business Geschäftsgang; **in the ordinary** ~ im gewöhnlichen (od. normalen) Geschäftsverkehr; **in the** ~ **or furtherance of any business** gewerbsmäßig

course, ~ **of commerce** Handelsverkehr; ~ **of dealing** regelmäßige Verhaltensweise *(bestimmter Personen im Gegensatz zum allgemeinen Handelsbrauch)*; ~ **of the economy** Wirtschaftsverlauf; ~ **of events** Gang der Ereignisse

course of justice Lauf der Gerechtigkeit; **to impede the** ~ in den Gang der Rechtspflege eingreifen

course, ~ **of law** Rechtsgang, Rechtsweg; ~ **of (one's) life** Lebenslauf; ~ **of procedure** Verfahrensgang

course, in the ~ **of** im Verlauf; **in the** ~ **of construction** im Bau befindlich; **in the** ~ **of conversation** im Laufe (od. Verlauf) des Gesprächs; **in** ~ **of time** im Laufe der Zeit, **in the** ~ **of proceedings** im Lauf des Verfahrens; **in the** ~ **of this week** im Laufe dieser Woche; **in the** ~ **of a year** binnen Jahresfrist

course, in →due ~; →**water** ~

course, to run (or **take**) **its** ~ seinen Gang (od. Verlauf) nehmen; **the ship is on her right** ~ das Schiff hält den Kurs ein

course 2. Kursus, Lehrgang; ~ **of instruction** Lehrgang; ~ **of lectures** Vortragsreihe; *univ* Vorlesung(sreihe); Lehrgang; ~ **of study** Lehrgang; **advanced** ~ Fortgeschrittenenkursus; **beginners'** ~ Anfängerkursus; **first-aid** ~ Lehrgang für Erste Hilfe; **to attend a** ~ an e-m Kursus teilnehmen; **to attend a** ~ **of lectures** e-e Vorlesung besuchen; **to enrol(l) for a** ~ e-n Kursus belegen; **to deliver** (or **give**) **a** ~ **of lectures** an e-e Vortragsreihe abhalten; **to hold a** ~ e-e Vorlesung abhalten; **to take a** ~ an e-m Kursus teilnehmen

Court 1. Hof; **c**~ **circular** Hofnachrichten *(für die Presse)*; **c**~ **etiquette** Hofzeremoniell; ~ **mourning** Hoftrauer; ~ **of St. James** britischer (Königs-)Hof *(bei dem ausländische Diplomaten beglaubigt werden)*; **at** ~ bei Hofe

court 2. Gericht, Gerichtshof

court, to appear in (or **before**) ~ vor Gericht erscheinen; **to come within the jurisdiction of a** ~ unter die Zuständigkeit e-s Gerichtes fallen; **to go before a** ~ vor Gericht gehen, klagen; **a** ~ **is held** e-e Gerichtssitzung wird abgehalten; **to order the** ~ **to be cleared** den

Gerichtssaal räumen lassen; **the ~ sits** (or **is sitting, holds a session, is in session**) das Gericht tagt; **to take a case to ~** e-e Sache vor Gericht bringen

court, ~ above oberes Gericht, höhere Instanz; **~ action** gerichtliches Vorgehen; Prozeß; **~ below** unteres Gericht, Vorinstanz; **~ clerk** *Br* Justizangestellte(r); **~ costs** Gerichtskosten; **~ expert** gerichtlicher Sachverständiger; **~ fees** Gerichtskosten; **~ fee stamp** Gerichtskostenmarke; **~ for Crown Cases Reserved** *Br* →C~ of Criminal Appeal; **~ interpreter** Gerichtsdolmetscher(in); **~ judgment** Gerichtsurteil

court-martial Kriegsgericht, Standgericht; **trial by ~** Verhandlung vor e-m Kriegsgericht; **to place before** (or **to subject to trial by) a ~** *(jdn)* vor ein Kriegsgericht stellen; **to be shot by sentence of ~** standrechtlich erschossen werden

Ein court-martial urteilt über Militärpersonen nach →military law

court-martial *v (jdn)* vor ein Kriegsgericht stellen; *(jdn)* standgerichtlich verurteilen

court of appeal Berufungsgericht, Berufungsinstanz; Revisionsgericht, Revisionsinstanz; Rechtsmittelgericht *(cf. reversal, overruling)*

Court of Appeal *Br* Berufungsgericht *(gegenüber Entscheidungen des →High Court [of Justice] und der County Courts)* (→court)

Der Court of Appeal ist die zweite große Abteilung des Supreme →Court of Judicature. Er ist Rechtsmittelgericht gegenüber Entscheidungen der County Courts und der 3 Divisions des High Court und entspricht etwa dem deutschen Oberlandesgericht. Seit 1966 ist er mit dem Court of Criminal Appeal – ohne Namensänderung – verschmolzen und auch für Strafsachen tätig. Gegen das Urteil des Court of Appeal kann (mit Genehmigung) Rechtsmittel beim House of Lords eingelegt werden, was sehr teuer und daher selten ist

Court of Appeals *Am* 1. (Bundes-)Berufungsgericht *(genaue Bezeichnung:* Court of Appeals for the particular circuit); 2. (einzelstaatl.) Berufungsgericht *(z.B. in Kentucky, Maryland, District of Columbia und New York)*

Zu 1.: Es gibt in den 11 judicial circuits, in die die Vereinigten Staaten eingeteilt sind, 11 Courts of Appeals. Jedes dieser Gerichte hat 3–9 →circuit judges. Die Courts of Appeals sind Berufungsgerichte gegenüber Entscheidungen der District →Courts. Sie sind ferner zuständig für richterliche Nachprüfung von Verwaltungsakten

court of arbitration Schiedsgericht(shof); **ICC C~ of A~** (Court of Arbitration of the International Chamber of Commerce) →arbitration; **Permanent C~ of A~** →arbitration

court, C~ of Arches *Br* Berufungsgericht des Erzbischofs von Canterbury; **~ of assize(s)** *Br*[96] *(früheres)* Assizengericht; **C~ of Auditors** *(EG)* Rechnungshof; **~ of bankruptcy** *Am* Konkursgericht

Court of Chancery Gericht, das nach den Grundsätzen des →equity urteilt *(Br cf. Chancery Division)*

Am In einigen Einzelstaaten werden (court of) chancery und (court of) equity synonym gebraucht

Court of Claims *Am*[94] 1. (Bundes-)Gericht für Entschädigungsansprüche gegen den Bund (*Sitz:* Washington); 2. (einzelstaatl.) Gericht für Ansprüche gegen ein →county

Court of Common Pleas *Br* e-s der drei früheren höheren Gerichte, in denen nach →common law geurteilt wurde. *Am (einzelstaatl.)* (erstinstanzl.) Gericht für Zivil- und Strafsachen

Court of County Commissioners *Am* (einzelstaatl.) *(ordentl.)* Gericht e-s →county

court of criminal appeal Berufungsgericht (od. Revisionsgericht) für Strafsachen; Berufungsstrafkammer; Strafsenat

Court of Criminal Appeal *Br (früheres)* Berufungs- oder Revisionsgericht in Strafsachen *(→Court of Appeal)*

Court of Customs and Patent Appeals *Am*[95] (Bundes-)Berufungsgericht in Zoll- und Patentsachen

Court of Faculties *Br* Amt des Erzbischofs von Canterbury *(zuständig z.B. für Ernennung und Abberufung der →notaries public)*

court of first instance Gericht erster Instanz *(opp. court of appeal)*

court of general jurisdiction Gericht allgemeiner Zuständigkeit *(→jurisdiction)*

Court of General Sessions *Am (einzelstaatl.)* erstinstanzliches Gericht für Strafsachen

court, ~ of hono(u)r Ehrengericht; **~ of inquiry** *Br* Untersuchungsausschuß *(bei schwerwiegenden Arbeitsstreitigkeiten); Br* Seeunfalluntersuchungsbehörde; *mil* Untersuchungsausschuß *(cases of indiscipline etc)*

Court of International Trade *Am* Gericht für Außenhandel

court of justice Gerichtshof

Court of Justice (of the European Communities) Gerichtshof (der Europäischen Gemeinschaften) (EuGH); **the Commission brought an action before the ~** *(EG)* die Kommission hat beim Gerichtshof e-e Klage erhoben

1958 errichteter gemeinsamer supranationaler Gerichtshof der EWG (→EEC), Euratom (→EAEC) und Montanunion (→ECSC). *Sitz:* Luxemburg.

Der Gerichtshof besteht aus 13 Richtern; er wird von 6 Generalanwälten unterstützt. Seine Aufgabe ist es, über Streitigkeiten zu unterscheiden, die aus der Anwendung der Verträge über die Errichtung der Gemeinschaften entstehen. Er erfüllt insbesondere die Funktionen eines Verfassungs-, Verwaltungs- und Arbeitsgerichts. Aufgabe der Generalanwälte ist es, in voller Unabhängigkeit am Schluß der mündlichen Verhandlung ein Gutachten („Schlußanträge") über den Rechtsstreit abzugeben.

Die Zuständigkeit des Gerichtshofes erstreckt sich vor allem auf Streitigkeiten zwischen der Gemeinschaft und den Mitgliedstaaten sowie privaten Wirtschaftsträgern (insbes. Unternehmen); Vorabentscheidungen über Fragen der Vertragsauslegung oder der Gültigkeit von Handlungen der Gemeinschaftsorgane; Streitigkeiten zwischen diesen Organen; Streitigkeiten zwischen Mitgliedstaaten; Schadensersatzklagen gegen die Gemeinschaft; Klagen der Gemeinschaftsbediensteten gegen ihren Arbeitgeber; Streitigkeiten aus Verträgen, die von einer Gemeinschaft oder für deren Rechnung abgeschlossen wurden und eine entsprechende Schiedsklausel enthalten

court, ~ of last resort Gericht letzter Instanz, letztinstanzliches Gericht; ~ **of law** s. law →court; ~ **of limited jurisdiction** Gericht beschränkter Zuständigkeit *(→jurisdiction);* **C~ of Ordinary** *Am (einzelstaatl.)* Nachlaßgericht *(z.B. in Georgia);* ~ **of ordinary jurisdiction** ordentliches Gericht *(opp. ~ of summary jurisdiction);* **C~ of Petty Sessions** *Br* s. Magistrates' →C~

Court of Protection *Br (Abteilung des High Court)* Vormundschaftsgericht zur Überwachung des Vermögens von Geisteskranken und Geistesschwachen; **to be made subject to an order of the ~** *Br* wegen Geisteskrankheit entmündigt werden

Court of Quarter Sessions *Br (früheres)*[96] Gericht für Strafsachen

courts of record ordentliche Gerichte

Gerichte vollen Rechts, einschließlich der Strafbefugnis, deren Entscheidungen zum dauernden Verbleib aufgezeichnet werden, wobei ein Gegenbeweis gegen die Richtigkeit der Beurkundung ausgeschlossen ist

courts not of record Spezialgerichte

Gerichte, deren Protokolle nicht unbedingte Beweiskraft haben (z.B. Gerichte der justices of the peace od. spezielle Verwaltungsgerichte)

court of review Berufungsgericht

Court of Session *Scot* Oberstes Gericht für Zivilsachen

Das Inner House, aus 2 Divisions bestehend, ist bes. für Berufungen gegenüber Entscheidungen der Sheriff →Courts zuständig. Das Outer House urteilt als erstinstanzliches Gericht (Lords Ordinary als Einzelrichter) bes. in Ehesachen

Court of (General or Special) Sessions *Am (einzelstaatl.)* Gericht für Strafsachen

court of summary jurisdiction Gericht niederer Ordnung, das im summarischen Verfahren Recht spricht *(Br Magistrates' Court) (opp. court of ordinary jurisdiction)*

court, ~ order gerichtliche Verfügung; ~ **practice** Praxis der Gerichte; ~ **proceedings** (or **procedure**) Gerichtsverfahren; ~ **records** (or **rolls**) Gerichtsakten; Prozeßakten; **~(-)room** Gerichtssaal, Sitzungszimmer; ~ **rules** Verfahrensvorschriften; ~ **ruling** Gerichtsentscheidung; ~ **trust** *Am* auf Grund e-r gerichtlichen Entscheidung verwaltetes Treuhandgut

court, Central Criminal C~ *Br* Gericht für Strafsachen von größerer Bedeutung für London und Umgebung *(alter Name: Old Bailey)*

court, city ~ *Am* Stadtgericht; **civil ~** Gericht für Zivilsachen; →**Commercial C~; constitutional ~s** *Am (in der Verfassung vorgesehene)* ordentliche Bundesgerichte *(cf. Federal Courts)*

court, County C~ *Br* Grafschaftsgericht; **County C~ registrar** *Br (etwa)* Rechtspfleger

Jeweils für ein district zuständiges erstinstanzliches Zivilgericht für weniger wichtige Sachen, praktisch alle Zivilsachen eines deutschen Amtsgerichts. Gegen die Urteile der County Courts kann Berufung an den Court of Appeal eingelegt werden

court, County C~ *Am* (einzelstaatl.) Kreisgericht

(Erstinstanzl.) Gericht für Strafsachen und für Zivilsachen geringerer Bedeutung; Berufungsinstanz gegenüber Entscheidungen der →justices of the peace und der municipal →courts, etwa dem deutschen Landgericht entsprechend

court, criminal ~ Gericht für Strafsachen; Strafkammer

Court, Crown C~ *Br*[97] Gericht für Strafsachen höherer Ordnung und einiger Zivilsachen

Der Crown Court hat ausschließliche Zuständigkeit für schwere Strafsachen (proceedings on indictment). Er ist auch Berufungsinstanz für die Magistrates' Courts und zuständig für Straf- und einige Zivilsachen der früheren Quarter Sessions (die Zivilgerichtsbarkeit der assizes ist vom High Court übernommen worden)

court, Customs C~[98] *Am* (Bundes-)Zollgericht

court, District C~[99] *Am* (Bundes-)Bezirksgericht *(genaue Bezeichnung:* United States District Court)

Erstinstanzliches Gericht für Strafsachen.[100] Erstinstanzliches Gericht für Zivilsachen, a) soweit der Streitwert ‰3000 übersteigt für Streitigkeiten zwischen Angehörigen von →diverse citizenship,[101] sowie für alle Streitsachen, in denen es sich um Anwendung od. Auslegung der Verfassung, Gesetze oder Verträge der Vereinigten Staaten handelt;[102] b) unabhängig von der Höhe des Streitwertes für bestimmte, in 28 U.S.C.A. §§ 1333–1356 aufgeführte Streitsachen (z.B. auf dem Gebiete des Seerechts, Konkursrechts, Kartell- und Antitrustrechts, Patent-, Urheber- und Warenzeichenrechts). In den meisten Fällen besteht konkurrierende Gerichtsbarkeit im Verhältnis zu den Gerichten der Einzelstaaten. Die wichtigsten Fälle der ausschließlichen Zuständigkeit der District Courts sind: Seerechtssachen,[103] Konkurssachen,[104] Patent- und Urheberrechtssachen,[105] Schadensersatzansprüche gegen den Bund,[106] Zivilklagen gegen ausländische Konsuln.[107] In jedem Einzelstaat gibt es wenigstens einen, insgesamt 87 District Courts. Gegen die Urteile der District Courts gibt es den appeal an die U.S. Courts of Appeals oder den direct appeal an den Supreme Court

court, Divisional C~ *Br* Abteilungsgericht

Spruchkörper verschiedener Abteilungen des High

Court; wird jeweils temporär gebildet und fungiert nur als Rechtsmittelgericht

Court, Divorce County ~s County Courts, die besonders für Ehestreitigkeiten zuständig sind

Court, European C~ of Human Rights[108] Europäischer Gerichtshof für Menschenrechte *(Sitz: Straßburg)*

Durch Abschnitt II und IV der Europäischen Menschenrechts-Konvention (Convention for the Protection of →Human Rights and Fundamental Freedoms) geschaffene zweite Instanz zur Entscheidung über Beschwerden wegen Verletzung der Menschenrechte, die dem (aus einer der Mitgliederzahl des Europarates entsprechenden Anzahl von Richtern bestehenden) Gerichtshof von den Vertragsstaaten oder der Kommission (→European Commission of Human Rights) unterbreitet werden

Court, Federal ~s *Am* Bundesgerichte *(opp. State Courts)*

Supreme Court (of the United States), U.S. Courts of Appeals, U.S. District Courts, Court of Claims, Court of Customs and Patent Appeals, Customs Court

court, full ~ Plenum; **in full ~** in pleno; (Verhandlung) vor dem vollbesetzten Gericht

Court, General ~ *Am* Gesetzgebende Körperschaft *(in Massachusetts und New Hampshire)*

Court, High ~ of Justice *Br* Oberstes *(erstinstanzliches)* (Zivil-)Gericht *(für England und Wales)*

Abteilung des Supreme →Court of Judicature, bestehend aus →Chancery Division, Queen's → Bench Division (including the Admiralty Court and the Commercial Court) und Family Division. Der High Court entspricht etwa dem deutschen Landgericht. Er ist als erstinstanzliches Gericht zuständig für alle Zivilsachen in ganz England, unabhängig von der Höhe des Streitwertes. Da die Prozeßkosten sehr hoch sind, kommen nur Rechtssachen von hohem Streitwert oder solche, die eine prinzipielle Entscheidung erfordern, vor den High Court.

Als Berufungsinstanz ist er zuständig für Entscheidungen der unteren Gerichte, z. B. der Magistrates' Court bei Rechtsfragen in Strafsachen (→case stated)

Court, High ~ of Judiciary *Scot* Oberstes Gericht für Strafsachen

Court, High C~ of Parliament *Br* Parlament *(bei offiziellen Anlässen)*

court, in ~ im Gericht; vor Gericht; in der Sitzung; **in and out of ~** gerichtlich und außergerichtlich

court, inferior ~ unteres Gericht, Gericht niederer Ordnung *(opp. superior ~)*; **International C~ of Justice** Internationaler Gerichtshof *(→international)*; **justice ~** *Am (einzelstaatl.)* Stadtgericht; **juvenile ~** Jugendgericht; **law ~** Gericht(shof) *(Gericht für Zivilsachen, das nach den Grundsätzen des →common law Recht spricht im Ggs. zu equity)*; **lower ~** Vorinstanz, untere (vorhergehende) Instanz

Court, Magistrates' ~ *Br* **(Magistrate's ~** *Am)*

Br erstinstanzliches Gericht für Strafsachen niederer Ordnung (einschließlich Jugendsachen), meist → summary offences, die im Schnellverfahren abgeurteilt od. im Untersuchungsverfahren e-m höheren Gericht überwiesen werden.

Zivilgericht mit Zuständigkeit für Unterhalts- und Ehetrennungs- (nicht Scheidungs-)Sachen, sowie Schankkonzession (licensing). In London auch Police Court genannt.

Gegen die Entscheidungen der Magistrates' Courts ist der appeal an den Crown Court zulässig, od. eine Prozeßpartei kann beantragen, daß die Sache dem High →Court zur Entscheidung einer Rechtsfrage vorgelegt wird (case stated).

Am (einzelstaatl.) erstinstanzliches Gericht für Straf- und manchmal Zivilsachen

court, municipal ~ *Am* Stadtgericht

Erstinstanzliches Gericht für Zivil- und Strafsachen minderer Bedeutung. Berufungsgericht gegenüber den Entscheidungen der →magistrates

court, open ~ öffentliche Gerichtsverhandlung; **in open ~** in öffentlicher Verhandlung *(opp. in chambers)*

court, ordinary ~ ordentliches Gericht

court, out of ~ außergerichtlich; **settlement out of ~** außergerichtlicher Vergleich; **to settle a case out of ~** e-e Sache außergerichtlich (od. auf gütlichem Wege) beilegen

Court, Permanent ~ of Arbitration →arbitration

Court, Petty Sessional ~ *Br* s. Magistrates' →~

court, police ~ Polizeigericht

Br Jetzt Magistrates' Court *(außer in London)*

Am (einzelstaatl.) Gericht mit Zuständigkeit für leichtere Strafsachen. In einigen Staaten beschränkte Zuständigkeit auch in Zivilsachen

court, probate ~ *Am (einzelstaatl.)* Nachlaßgericht; **Restrictive Practices C ~** *Br* Kartellgericht *(→Restrictive Practices)*; **sheriff ~** *Scot (niederes)* Gericht mit Zuständigkeit für Strafsachen *(Höchststrafe 2 Jahre)* und Zivilsachen *(von unbegrenztem Streitwert)*; **special ~** Sondergericht; **State C~s** *Am* einzelstaatliche Gerichte *(Superior C~s, C~s of Appeals und Supreme C~s; opp. Federal C~)*

court, superior ~ *Br* höheres Gericht *(House of Lords, Court of Appeal und High Court of Justice, deren Entscheidungen für die unteren Gerichte [inferior courts] bindend sind)*

Court, Superior ~ *Am (einzelstaatl.)* erstinstanzliches Gericht *(e-s county, etwa dem deutschen Landgericht entsprechend)*

Court, Supreme ~ (of the United States) (S.C.) *Am*[109] Oberstes Bundesgericht *(in Washington)*

Besetzt mit 9 Bundesrichtern (Associate Justices) unter dem Chief →Justice.

Höchstes Rechtsmittelgericht gegenüber Entscheidungen der Bundesgerichte und (in bestimmten Fällen) der einzelstaatlichen Gerichte. Der Supreme Court erfüllt Funktionen, die in der Bundesrepublik dem Bundesgerichtshof (und den anderen oberen Bundesgerichten) zufallen.

Erstinstanzliches Gericht:[110] a) ausschließliche Zuständigkeit in Streitsachen zwischen 2 od. mehr Einzelstaaten sowie in Rechtsstreitigkeiten gegen ausländische Botschafter od. Gesandte; b) (mit den Einzelstaaten) konkurrierende Zuständigkeit für Klagen ausländischer Botschafter od. Gesandter; ferner für Streitsachen zwischen den Vereinigten Staaten und einem Einzelstaat und für solche eines Einzelstaates gegen Angehörige eines anderen Einzelstaates od. gegen Ausländer

Court, Supreme ~ Reporter (S.Ct.) *Am (privat herausgegebene)* Sammlung der Entscheidungen des Supreme Court; **Lawyers' Edition of United States Supreme ~ Reports** (L. Ed.) *Am (privat herausgegebene)* Sammlung der Entscheidungen des Supreme Court

court, Supreme C~ *Am (einzelstaatl.)* höheres (Berufungs-)Gericht; *(in New York)* Gericht mit allgemeiner *(erstinstanzl.)* Zuständigkeit für sämtliche Streitsachen und Berufungsgerichtsbarkeit

court, Supreme C~ of Judicature *Br*[111] Oberster Gerichtshof für England und Wales (zusammenfassende Bezeichnung des obersten Zentralgerichts für England und Wales)

Zusammenfassung des Court of Appeal, des High Court of Justice und (neuerdings[112]) des Crown Court zu einem Gericht im staatsrechtlichen Sinne mit einer Gesamtgeschäftsstelle, dem Central Office, in London. Diese Zusammenfassung ist für den Instanzenzug ohne Bedeutung. Die Gerichte judizieren jedoch nach einer einheitlichen Verfahrensordnung, den →Rules of the Supreme Court, abgesehen vom Crown Court, der seine eigene Verfahrensordnung, die Crown Court Rules, hat. Der Bezeichnung zum Trotz ist das oberste Gericht das House of Lords und (für einige Commonwealth-Länder) Privy Council

court, surrogate's ~ *Am (einzelstaatl.)* Gericht für Nachlaß- und *(oft)* Pflegesachen

courtes|y Höflichkeit, Entgegenkommen; ~ **call** (or **visit**) Höflichkeitsbesuch; ~ **of the port** *Am* Recht *(e-s von e-m ausländischen Hafen kommenden Reisenden)* auf sofortige Zollabfertigung; ~ **of title** *Br* aus Entgegenkommen *(nicht auf Grund e-s Rechts)* verliehener Adelstitel; **by ~ of** mit freundlicher Genehmigung von; **exchange of international ~ies** Austausch von internationalen Höflichkeiten; **to exchange ~ies** Höflichkeiten austauschen

cousin Cousin, Vetter; Cousine; ~ **german** → german; **first ~s** Geschwisterkinder; Vettern 1. Grades; **second ~s** Kinder der Geschwisterkinder; Vettern 2. Grades

covenant *(in e-r Urkunde niedergelegte)* Vertragsabrede (od. vertragliches Versprechen); (vertragl.) Zusicherung *(bes. bei Grundstücksgeschäften)*; Verpflichtung; ~ **breaking** vertragsbrüchig; ~ **for freedom from encumbrances** Versicherung des Veräußerers, das Grundstück sei frei von Belastungen; ~ **for quiet enjoyment** Versicherung des Veräußerers, der Erwerber erlange ungestörten Rechtsgenuß; ~ **for right to convey** Versicherung des Veräußerers e-s Grundstücks, er sei zur Veräußerung befugt; **~s for title** →title 2.; ~ **in restraint of trade** Konkurrenzklausel *(cf. negative ~)*; ~ **not to compete** Vereinbarung von nachvertraglichen Wettbewerbsverboten; **~s running with the land** Vertragsbestimmungen dinglicher Natur, die mit dem Eigentum od. Pachtrecht an e-m Grundstück verbunden sind *(entspricht etwa der deutschen Grunddienstbarkeit)*

covenant, full ~ deed *Am* Grundstücksübertragungsurkunde *(mit bestimmten Zusicherungen)*; **→lien ~; negative ~** (vertragl.) Unterlassungsversprechen; **particular ~** (vertragl.) besondere Vereinbarung; **payment under a deed of ~** Zahlung auf Grund e-s vertraglichen Versprechens; **restrictive ~** vertragsmäßige Beschränkung; vertragl. Vereinbarung über Unterlassungspflichten in Verträgen *(z. B. ein verkauftes Grundstück darf nicht bebaut werden)*; **state party to the present ~** *(VölkerR)* Vertragsstaat; **to enter into a ~** sich vertraglich verpflichten; **he gives a ~ that he will pay a donation to a charity** *(bes. SteuerR)* er gibt ein bindendes Versprechen ab, an e-e gemeinnützige Einrichtung *(für e-e bestimmte Zeit)* e-e Zuwendung zu machen

covenant *v* (vertragl.) vereinbaren; (vertragl.) zusichern; sich (vertragl.) verpflichten; bindend versprechen

covenantee der *(aus e-r vertragl. Zusicherung)* Berechtigte; (Dritt-)Begünstigter

covenantor der *(aus e-r vertragl. Zusicherung)* Verpflichtete

cover Deckung; Versicherungsschutz; Verhältnis des Reingewinns e-r Gesellschaft zu ihren Dividendenzahlungen; Briefumschlag, Bucheinband; ~ **address** Deckadresse; ~ **of assurance** *Br (VersR)* Deckungskapital *(aus dem Prämienaufkommen angesammeltes Kapital bei Lebensversicherungsgesellschaften)*; ~ **funds** Deckungsmittel; ~ **note** *Br* Deckungszusage; Zwischenbescheinigung über abgeschlossene Versicherung; ~ **ratio** Deckungsverhältnis *(zwischen Banknoten und den zu ihrer Deckung bestimmten Gold- und Devisenbeständen)*

cover, additional ~ weitere Deckung, Nachschuß(zahlung); **liability to put up additional ~** Nachschußpflicht; **to make a call for additional ~** Nachschuß einfordern

cover, cash ~ Bardeckung, Barsicherheit; **confirmation of ~** Deckungszusage; **gold ~** Golddeckung; **limit of ~** Deckungsgrenze; **open ~** Deckung durch offene Police, laufende Police; **period of ~** Deckungsdauer; **provisional ~** vorläufiger Versicherungsschutz

cover, under ~ of unter dem Vorwand von; **letter under ~** an e-e Deckadresse geschriebener Brief; **under same ~** beigeschlossen, anliegend; **under separate** ~ in besonderem Umschlag; als besonderes Paket; **for want of** ~ mangels Deckung

cover, to furnish a p. with ~ jdm Deckung anschaffen; **to make provision of** ~ **for a bill of exchange** für e-n Wechsel Deckung anschaffen; **to provide** ~ **for a loan** e-n Kredit abdekken; **to provide the necessary** ~ den notwendigen Versicherungsschutz bieten; **to serve as** ~ als Deckung dienen; **the necessary** ~ **is available** die nötige Deckung ist vorhanden

cover *v* decken; *(finanziell)* sichern; *(Börse)* sich eindecken; *fig* umfassen, einschließen; sich erstrecken über; genügen für; *(Zeitung)* berichten über; **to** ~ **oneself** sich Deckung verschaffen; **to** ~ **up** *fig* verbergen, bemänteln; verschleiern; **to** ~ **a bill** Deckung für e-n Wechsel anschaffen; **to** ~ **a debt** e-e Schuld abdecken; **to** ~ **the elections** über die Wahlen berichten; **to** ~ **the expenses** die Ausgaben bestreiten; **to** ~ **all losses** *(VersR)* alle Schäden decken; **to** ~ **one's tracks** seine Spuren verdecken

covered, ~ **against fire** gegen Feuer versichert; ~ **by a mortgage** mit e-r Hypothek belastet; ~ **by comprehensive motor car insurance** *Br (etwa:)* vollkaskoversichert; ~ **by contract** vertraglich abgesichert; ~ **job** *Am (Sozialversicherung)* pflichtversicherte Tätigkeit; ~ **market** Markthalle, überdachter Markt *(opp. open-air market)*; ~ **truck** *Br* (or **wagon**) gedeckter Güterwagen *(opp. open truck or wagon)*; **period** ~ Berichtszeit; **to be** ~ Deckung in Händen halten; **to be** ~ **by the amount insured** voll durch die Versicherung gedeckt sein; **to be held** ~ **against** versichert sein gegen; **the case is** ~ **by the statute** der Fall fällt unter das Gesetz

covering Deckung; *(Börse)* Deckungskauf; ~ **agreement** Mantelvertrag; ~ **claim** Dekkungsforderung; ~ **funds** Deckungsmittel; ~ **letter** Begleitbrief, Begleitschreiben; ~ **note** →cover note; ~ **purchase** Deckungskauf; ~ **resources** Deckungsmittel; ~ **transactions** *(Börse)* Deckungsgeschäfte

covering, insurance policy ~ **a risk** Versicherungspolice gegen ein Risiko

coverable risk versicherbares Risiko

coverage *bes. Am* Deckung; Versicherungsschutz; Deckung von Tilgungs-, Zins- oder Dividendenzahlungen durch Erträge; Erfassung, erfaßter Bereich; *(Presse, Fernsehen etc)* Berichterstattung (of über); Reichweite, Verbreitungsgebiet *(z.B. von Zeitungen)*; ~ **of agreement** *Am (ArbeitsR)* erfaßter Bereich des Tarifvertrages *(Erfassung aller Arbeitnehmer, die gemäß den Bedingungen des Tarifvertrages arbeiten, ob sie Gewerkschaftsmitglieder sind oder nicht)*; **comprehensive** ~ *Am (etwa:)* Teilkasko; **domestic** ~ innenpolitische Berichte; **foreign** ~ Auslandsberichte; **year of** ~ Versicherungsjahr

covert, feme ~ verheiratete Frau

coverture Ehe, Ehestand der Frau; **during** ~ während der Ehe

covin geheimes Einverständnis *(zum Nachteil e-s anderen)*; Kollusion

craft 1. (gelerntes) Handwerk; ~**s** handwerkliche Berufe; ~ **(guild)** Handwerkerinnung; ~ **union** Fachgewerkschaft *(opp. industrial union)*; **small** ~ **undertaking** Handwerksbetrieb

craft 2. Fahrzeug(e); Boot, Kahn, Schiff(e); ~ **etc clause** Leichter- etc Klausel *(Institute Cargo Clause)*; **customs** ~ Zollboot; **(water)** ~ Wasserfahrzeug

craftsman *(gelernter)* Handwerker; Gewerbetreibender *(umfaßt mechanic und artisan)*; **master** ~ Handwerksmeister

crafty politician gerissener Politiker

cranage (or **crane charge**) Krangeld, Krangebühren

crash Zusammenstoß *(von Fahrzeugen)*; Absturz *(e-s Flugzeugs)*; (Börsen-)Krach, Zusammenbruch; ~ **course** Schnell-, Intensivkurs; ~ **program(me)** Sofortprogramm

crate Lattenkiste, Lattenverschlag

crawling peg, system of ~ *Am* System der gleitenden Parität, System der schrittweisen Paritätsanpassung; System der (Wechselkurs-)Stufenflexibilität

Danach wird der Wechselkurs eines Landes in gewissen Zeitabständen und in kleinen Schritten neu festgesetzt, wenn sich das Gleichgewicht auf den Devisenmärkten verschoben hat

create *v* schaffen, hervorbringen, verursachen; gründen, begründen; **to** ~ **a corporation** *Am* e-e Gesellschaft gründen; **to** ~ **jobs** Arbeitsplätze schaffen; **to** ~ **liability** Haftung begründen; **to** ~ **a mortgage** e-e Hypothek bestellen; **to** ~ **an obligation** ein Schuldverhältnis (od. e-e Verpflichtung) begründen; **to** ~ **money** Geld schöpfen; **to** ~ **a trust** ein Treuhandverhältnis begründen; **he was** ~**d a life peer** *Br* er wurde in den lebenslänglichen Adelsstand erhoben

creation Schaffung, Hervorbringung, Begründung, Gründung; (Kunst- etc) Schöpfung; ~ **of a company** Gründung e-r Gesellschaft; ~ **of credit** Kreditschöpfung; ~ **of jobs** Schaffung von Arbeitsplätzen; ~ **of money** Geldschöpfung; ~ **of a mortgage** Bestellung e-r Hypothek; ~ **of an obligation** Begründung e-s Schuldverhältnisses; ~ **of ownership** Eigentumsbildung (in der Hand der Arbeitnehmer); ~ **of a party** Gründung e-r Partei; ~ **of reser-**

ves Reservenbildung; ~ **of new resources** Erschließung neuer Hilfsquellen; ~ **of social unrest** Hervorrufen sozialer Unruhen; ~ **of a trust** Errichtung e-s Trust

creation, aesthetic ~s ästhetische Formschöpfung; →**job ~; personal intellectual ~s** *(UrhR)* persönliche geistige Schöpfungen

creative schöpferisch, gestaltend, kreativ; ~ **work** schöpferische Arbeit

credence Glaube; **letters of** ~ *(VölkerR)* Beglaubigungsschreiben *(des Missionschefs);* **to give** ~ (to) Glauben schenken

credentials 1. Empfehlungsschreiben, Referenzen; Ausweis(papiere); ~ **committee** Vollmachtprüfungsausschuß

credentials 2. *(VölkerR)* Beglaubigungsschreiben *(des Missionschefs);* **presentation of** ~ Überreichung des Beglaubigungsschreibens; **to present one's** ~ sein Beglaubigungsschreiben überreichen

credibility Glaubwürdigkeit; ~ **gap** Glaubwürdigkeitslücke; **to establish the** ~ **of sth.** etw. glaubhaft machen

credible glaubwürdig; glaubhaft; ~ **witness** glaubwürdiger Zeuge

credit 1. Kredit; Guthaben; Gutschrift; Ziel *(Zahlungsfrist);* Haben(seite) *(rechte Seite des Kontos; opp. debit)*

credit, to allow a ~ e-n Kredit bewilligen (od. geben, einräumen); **to be in** ~ **at the bank** Bankkredit haben; **to call in a** ~ e-n Kredit kündigen; **to cancel a** ~ e-n Kredit widerrufen; **to enjoy** ~ **facilities** Kredit(möglichkeiten) haben; **to enter an amount to a p.'s** ~ jdm e-n Betrag gutschreiben; **to establish a** ~ e-n Kredit eröffnen (with bei); **to exceed a** ~ e-n Kredit überschreiten; **to extend a** ~ e-n Kredit verlängern (up to bis); Kreditverlängerung gewähren; **to furnish with** ~ Kredit verschaffen; **to give a p.** ~ **for £100** jdm Kredit geben in Höhe von 100 Pfund; **to give on** ~ auf Kredit geben; **to grant a** ~ e-n Kredit bewilligen (od. einräumen); **to have** ~ **with a banker** Bankkredit haben; **to increase a** ~ e-n Kredit erhöhen; **to obtain** ~ Kredit bekommen; **to open a** ~ **in favo(u)r of a p.** für jdn e-n Kredit eröffnen (with a bank bei e-r Bank); **to overdraw a** ~ e-n Kredit überziehen; **to place an amount to sb. 's** ~ jdm e-n Betrag gutschreiben; **to raise** ~ Kredit aufnehmen; **to receive on** ~ auf Kredit erhalten; **to repay the** ~ den Kredit zurückzahlen (od. tilgen); **to use a** ~ e-n Kredit in Anspruch nehmen; **to withdraw a** ~ e-n Kredit zurückziehen (od. kündigen)

credit, ~ **accommodation** Zurverfügungstellung von Kredit; ~ **account** Konto mit Kreditsaldo; *Br* Kundenkreditkonto, Abzahlungskonto *(bei Teilzahlungen);* **for the** ~ **of your account** zur Gutschrift auf Ihr Konto; ~ **advice** Gutschriftsanzeige *(opp. debit advice)*

credit, ~ **agreement** Kreditvereinbarung, Kreditabkommen; ~ **and finance company** *Br* Kundenkreditgesellschaft; ~ **applicant** Kreditantragsteller; ~ **approval** Kreditzusage

credit balance Guthaben; Aktivsaldo; ~ **at the bank** Bankguthaben; **your** ~ Saldo zu Ihren Gunsten

credit, ~ **bank** Kreditbank, Kreditanstalt; ~ **with a bank** Bankguthaben; Bankkredit; ~ **broker** Finanzmakler; ~ **bureau** *Am* Kreditauskunftei; ~ **buying** Kreditkauf; ~ **capacity** Kreditfähigkeit

credit card Kreditkarte; ~ **holder** Kreditkarteninhaber

credit, ~ **charges** Kreditkosten, -gebühren; ~ **conditions** Kreditbedingungen; ~ **cooperative (society)** Kreditgenossenschaft (→*cooperative*); ~ **cost** Kreditkosten; ~ **demand** Kreditbedarf; ~ **entry** Gutschrift *(opp. debit entry);* ~ **expansion** Kreditausweitung; Kreditexpansion; ~ **facilities** Kreditfazilitäten, Kreditmöglichkeiten; ~ **form** *Am* Kreditvordruck; ~ **freeze** Kreditsperre; ~ **grantor** Kreditgeber; ~ **guarantee** Kreditbürgschaft; ~ **by way of guarantee** Avalkredit; ~ **in current account** Kontokorrentkredit; ~ **information** Kreditauskunft; Auskunft über Kreditfähigkeit; ~ **inquiry** Anfrage wegen Kreditwürdigkeit; ~ **inquiry agency** Auskunftei *(betr. jds. Kreditwürdigkeit);* ~ **institution** Kreditinstitut, Kreditanstalt; ~ **insurance** Kreditversicherung; ~ **interest** Habenzinsen *(e-r Bank);* ~ **investigation** Untersuchung der Kreditfähigkeit; ~ **item** Habenposten; Gutschriftposten; ~ **line** Kreditlinie, Kreditgrenze *(Höchstkredit);* ~ **loss** Kreditausfall, Kreditverlust; ~ **man** *Am (gewerbsmäßiger)* Kreditgeber; ~ **margin** Kreditmarge, Kreditgrenze

credit market, to draw heavily on the ~s die Kreditmärkte stark in Anspruch nehmen

credit, ~ **memo(randum)** *Am* Gutschriftsanzeige, Gutschein; ~ **note** (C/N) Gutschriftsanzeige, Gutschein *(opp. debit note);* ~ **on goods** Warenkredit; ~ **on joint account** Metakredit; ~ **on landed property** Immobiliarkredit, Realkredit; ~ **on real estate** Immobiliarkredit, Realkredit; ~ **operations** Kreditgeschäfte; ~ **order** Kreditauftrag; ~ **period** Laufzeit e-s Kredits; Zahlungsziel; ~ **policy** Kreditpolitik; ~ **purchase** Kreditkauf, Teilzahlungskauf *(opp. cash purchase);* ~ **rating** Einschätzung der Kreditfähigkeit, Bonitätseinschätzung; ~ **reference agency** *Br* Auskunftei *(betr. jds Kreditwürdigkeit);* ~ **report** Kreditauskunft; ~ **reporting agency** *Am* Auskunftei; ~ **resources** Kreditquellen, Kreditmöglichkeiten; ~ **restriction** Krediteinschränkung, Kreditrestriktion; ~ **risk** Kreditrisiko

credit sale Kredit(ver)kauf, Abzahlungskauf *(opp. cash sale)*; ~ **agreement** *Br*[113] Teilzahlungsvertrag *(Käufer erhält sofort Eigentum; opp. hire-purchase agreement)*

credit side Kreditseite, Habenseite; **entry on the** ~ Kreditposten

credit, ~ **situation** Kreditlage; ~ **slip** *Br* Einzahlungsbeleg, Einzahlungsschein; Gutschriftszettel; ~ **society** *Br* Kreditverein; ~ **squeeze** *Br* Kreditrestriktion *(durch Erhöhung des Diskontsatzes [bank rate] seitens der Regierung)*; Kreditdrosselung *(zur Eindämmung e-r Inflationsgefahr)*; ~ **standards** Kreditrichtlinien; ~ **standing** (or **status**) Kreditwürdigkeit; Bonität; ~ **status inquiry agency** (or **bureau**) Kreditauskunftei; ~ **stringency** Kreditknappheit; ~ **granted by supplier** Lieferantenkredit; ~ **supply** Kreditbeschaffung; Kreditangebot; ~ **system** Kreditwesen

credit terms Kreditbedingungen; **sale on** ~ Verkauf auf Kredit; Kreditkauf

credit, ~ **token** *Br* Kreditkarte *(die ein Kreditgeber an Private ausgibt)*; ~ **transactions** Kreditgeschäfte, Kreditverkehr

credit transfer Banküberweisung *(vom Konto) (im bargeldlosen Zahlungsverkehr)*; ~ **form** Überweisungsformular

credit, ~ **union** *Am* Kreditgenossenschaft; ~ **voucher** Einzahlungsbeleg; ~**worthiness** Kreditwürdigkeit, Bonität; ~**worthy** kreditwürdig

credit, acceptance ~ Rembourskredit; **allowance of a** ~ Einräumung e-s Kredits; **amount of the** ~ Höhe des Kredits; **applicant for** ~ Kreditsuchender; **application for a** ~ Kreditantrag; **availability of** ~ Verfügbarkeit von Kredit; **availment of** ~ Inanspruchnahme von Kredit; **bank** ~ Bankkredit; **blank** ~ Blankokredit; **book** ~ Buchkredit; **bulk** ~ Gesamtkredit; **cash** ~ Barkredit; **charges for** ~ Kreditkosten, -gebühren; **commercial** ~ Warenkredit; **consumer** ~ Verbraucherkredit; **cost of** ~ Kreditkosten; **creation of** ~ Kreditschöpfung; **thirty days'** ~ 30 Tage Ziel; **debit and** ~ Soll und Haben; **demand for** ~ Kreditnachfrage, Kreditbedarf; **easing of** ~ Kreditlockerung; **excess of** ~ Kreditüberschreitung; **exchange** ~ Fremdwährungskredit; **extended** ~ prolongierter Kredit; **extension of** ~ Kreditverlängerung; **extent of** ~ Höhe des Kredits; **farm** ~ Agrarkredit; **fresh** ~ neuer Kredit; **global** ~ Rahmenkredit; **granting of** ~ Kreditgewährung, Kreditbewilligung; **government** ~ Staatskredit; **industrial** ~ Industriekredit; **instalment** ~ Teilzahlungskredit; **interim** (or **intermediate**) ~ Zwischenkredit; **joint** ~ Konsortialkredit; **land** ~ Bodenkredit; **limit of** ~ Kreditgrenze; **limited** ~ Kredit in begrenzter Höhe; **long-term** ~ langfristiger Kredit; **loss of** ~ Kreditverlust; **low-interest** ~ Kredit zu niedrigem Zinssatz; →**mixed** ~**s**; **at one month's** ~ auf einen Monat Ziel

credit, obtaining ~ **by fraud** (or **by false pretences**) Kreditbetrug

credit, on ~ auf Kredit (od. Ziel); **purchase on** ~ Kreditkauf, Kauf auf Ziel; **sale on** ~ Kreditverkauf; **to buy (sell) sth. on** ~ etw. auf Kredit (od. Ziel) kaufen (verkaufen); **to supply on** ~ gegen Ziel liefern

credit, open ~ offener Kredit, Kontokorrentkredit; **opening of a** ~ Krediteröffnung; **overdraft of** ~ Kreditüberziehung; **personal** ~ Personalkredit; →**pre-authorized** ~; **raising of** ~ Kreditaufnahme; **repayment of a** ~ Rückzahlung e-s Kredits; **revolving** ~ revolvierender (sich automatisch erneuernder) Kredit; **secured** ~ gesicherter Kredit; Realkredit; **short term** ~ kurzfristiger Kredit; **stand-by** ~ Beistandskredit (→*stand- by*); **standing** ~ laufender Kredit; **starting** ~ Anlaufkredit; **supply of** ~ Kreditangebot; Kreditbeschaffung; **tax** ~ Steuergutschrift (→ *credit 3.*); **temporary** ~ Zwischenkredit; **terms of** ~ Kreditbedingungen; **unlimited** ~ unbeschränkter Kredit; **unused** ~ nicht in Anspruch genommener Kredit; **unsecured** ~ ungesicherter Kredit; **upon** ~ s. on →~; **used** ~ in Anspruch genommener Kredit; **volume of** ~ Kreditvolumen

credit 2. Akkreditiv *(s. letter of* ~*)*; ~ **accounts** Akkreditivkonten; ~ **instruction** Akkreditivauftrag; ~ **terms** Akkreditivbedingungen

credit, amount of the ~ Akkreditivbetrag; **applicant for the** ~ Akkreditiv-Auftraggeber; **conditions of a** ~ Akkreditivbedingungen; **documentary** ~ Dokumentar-Akkreditiv (→ *documentary*); **form and notification of** ~**s** Form und Anzeige der Akkreditive; **irrevocable** ~ unwiderrufliches Akkreditiv; **issuance of a** ~ Eröffnung e-s Akkreditivs; **revocable** ~ widerrufliches Akkreditiv; **terms of a** ~ Akkreditivbedingungen

credit, to advise a ~ ein Akkreditiv avisieren (od. anzeigen); **to cancel a** ~ ein Akkreditiv annullieren; **to confirm a** ~ ein Akkreditiv bestätigen; **to establish** (or **open**) **a** ~ ein Akkreditiv erstellen; **the** ~ **expires** das Akkreditiv läuft ab; **the** ~ **is valid until** . . . das Akkreditiv ist gültig bis . . .

credit 3. Anrechnung; Anrechnungsbetrag; *Am (von der Steuer)* abzugsfähiger Betrag, (Steuer-)-Gutschrift; ~ **against tax** Steueranrechnung; ~ **for dependants** *Am* Steuergutschrift für Familienangehörige; ~ **for foreign taxes** s. foreign tax →~; ~ **for time of detention prior to sentence** *Am* Anrechnung e-r vor der Straffestsetzung liegenden Haftzeit

credit system *Am (intern. SteuerR)* Anrechnungssystem, System der Steueranrechnung *(opp. exemption system)*

Die Besteuerungskompetenzen zwischen den Vertragsstaaten werden nicht aufgeteilt. Der Wohnsitzstaat behält sein volles Besteuerungsrecht auch hinsichtlich der Steuern, die vom Quellenstaat erhoben werden. Er hat aber die vom Quellenstaat erhobenen Steuern auf seine eigenen verhältnismäßig anzurechnen

credit, allowance of US taxes as ~ against German taxes *(DBA)* Anrechnung von amerikanischen auf deutsche Steuern; **foreign tax** ~[114] Anrechnung ausländischer Steuern; **retirement income** ~ *Am* Abzug bei Ruhestandseinkünften; →**tax~; taxes eligible for** ~ anrechenbare (ausländische) Steuern; **unified** ~ *Am* pauschale Steuergutschrift; **no ~ is available for foreign taxes** *Am* ausländische Steuern werden nicht angerechnet; **to give ~ for the foreign tax against the British tax** die ausländische Steuer auf die britische anrechnen

credit, to allow United States taxes as a ~ against Federal Republic taxes *(DBA)* Steuern der Vereinigten Staaten auf Steuern der Bundesrepublik anrechnen; **to make ~ to** *Am* anrechnen auf; **to take the** ~ *Am* die Anrechnung beanspruchen

credit 4. Glaubwürdigkeit; *(guter)* Ruf; Ehre; (das) Verdienst; Anerkennung; **(un)worthy of** ~ (un)glaubwürdig *(z. B. Zeuge)*; **to be to sb.'s** ~ jdm als Verdienst anzurechnen sein; **to deserve** ~ Anerkennung verdienen; **to enjoy (the) ~ for an achievement** die Anerkennung (od. Ehre) für e-e Leistung (od. e-n Erfolg) genießen; **to give ~ to sb.** jdm glauben; **to give sb. (the) ~ for sth.** jdm etw. als Verdienst anrechnen (od. zuschreiben); **to give ~ where it is due** gebührende Anerkennung nicht versagen; **to take (the) ~ for sth.** (sich od. jdm) etw. als Verdienst anrechnen

credit *v (Summe)* kreditieren, gutschreiben; erkennen *(auf der Habenseite des Kontos verbuchen; opp. to debit)*; **to ~ against** anrechnen auf; **to ~ an account** *(Buchhaltung)* ein Konto erkennen; **to ~ an amount to a p.** (or **to ~ a p. with an amount)** jdm e-n Betrag gutschreiben; **to ~ the foreign tax against the British tax** die ausländische auf die britische Steuer anrechnen

credited, ~ party Kreditnehmer; jd, dem ein Betrag gutgeschrieben ist; **he was ~ for his years of service** seine Dienstjahre wurden ihm angerechnet

crediting Kreditierung; Gutschrift; Anrechnung; ~ **of interest** Gutschrift der Zinsen; ~ **of the foreign tax against the German tax** Anrechnung der ausländischen auf die deutsche Steuer

creditable, ~ foreign tax anrechenbare ausländische Steuer; ~ **insurance years** anrechenbare Versicherungsjahre

creditor Gläubiger *(opp. debtor)*; *(Buchführung)* (Cr.) Kreditseite, Haben; **~s** *Br (Bilanz)* Kreditoren, Verbindlichkeiten; ~ **account** Kreditorenkonto; **~(s) of a bankrupt** Konkursgläubiger; ~ **of bankrupt's estate** Massegläubiger; **~s' committee** Gläubigerausschuß; ~ **country** Gläubigerland *(opp. borrowing country)*; ~ **by endorsement** Girogläubiger; ~ **of the estate** Nachlaßgläubiger; **~s' ledger** Kreditorenbuch

creditor interest rate Habenzinssatz; **agreement on** ~ Habenzinsabkommen

creditor, ~s' meeting *(KonkursR)* Gläubigerversammlung; ~ **on mortgage** Hypothekengläubiger; **~s' petition** Konkurseröffnungsantrag der Gläubiger; ~ **position** Gläubigerstellung; ~ **having priority** bevorrechtigter (Konkurs-)- Gläubiger; ~ **ranking equally** gleichrangiger Gläubiger; ~ **side** Kreditseite, Habenseite; ~ **state** Gläubigerstaat

creditor, arrangement with one's ~s Vergleich; **bill** ~ Wechselgläubiger; **board** (or **committee**) **of ~s** Gläubigerausschuß *(im Konkurs)*; **execution** ~ Vollstreckungsgläubiger; **general** ~ gewöhnlicher Gläubiger; nicht bevorrechtigter Gläubiger; **joint** ~ Gesamtgläubiger; **judgment** ~ Vollstreckungsgläubiger; →**lien ~; list of ~s of a bankrupt** Konkurstabelle; **meeting of ~s** Gläubigerversammlung *(im Konkurs)*; **mortgage** ~ Hypothekengläubiger; **ordinary** ~ gewöhnlicher (Konkurs-)-Gläubiger *(opp. preferential ~)*; **preferential** (or **preferred**) ~ bevorrechtigter (Konkurs-)-Gläubiger; **principal** ~ Hauptgläubiger; **privileged** ~ bevorrechtigter (Konkurs-)-Gläubiger; **non-privileged ~ of a bankrupt** Massegläubiger; **secured** ~ *(durch Hypothek etc)* gesicherter Gläubiger; **sundry ~s** verschiedene Gläubiger; **trade ~s** Lieferantenverbindlichkeiten; Warengläubiger; **unsecured** ~ nicht gesicherter Gläubiger

creditor, to arrange (or **compound**) **with one's ~s** mit s-n Gläubigern e-n Vergleich schließen (od. sich vergleichen); **to pay off** (or **satisfy**) **~s** Gläubiger befriedigen; **to secure a** ~ e-n Gläubiger sicherstellen; e-m Gläubiger Sicherheit geben; **to settle with one's ~s** sich mit s-n Gläubigern einigen

cremate *v*, **he wants to be ~d, not buried** er möchte eingeäschert, nicht beerdigt werden

cremation Einäscherung, Feuerbestattung; ~ **expenses insurance** Feuerbestattungsversicherung

crew Besatzung *(e-s Flugzeugs, Schiffes)*; Mannschaft *(e-s Schiffes)*; Fahrpersonal, Fahrzeugbesatzung; Arbeitsgruppe; **~'s accommodation** Mannschaftsraum; ~ **list** Mannschaftsliste, Musterrolle; ~ **member** Besatzungsmitglied; Mitglied des Fahrpersonals; **~'s wages** Mannschaftsheuer; **to engage a** ~ e-e Mannschaft heuern; **to pay off the** ~ die Mannschaft abmustern

crime Straftat, strafbare Handlung; Verbrechen, Vergehen
Nicht im Sinne der Zweiteilung der Straftaten des deutschen Strafgesetzbuches.
Crime umfaßt *Am*[115] felonies, misdemeanors und petty misdemeanors. *Br* Die Einteilung von Verbrechen in felonies und misdemeanours wurde durch den Criminal Justice Act, 1967, abgeschafft *(cf. felony, misdemeanour)*

crime, ~ against humanity Verbrechen gegen die Menschlichkeit; ~ **against nature** Sodomie; ~ **against peace** Verbrechen gegen den Frieden; ~ **prevention** Verbrechensverhütung; ~ **rate** Kriminalität(sziffer); Verbrechensquote *(Zahl der begangenen Straftaten im Verhältnis zur Bevölkerung);* ~ **sheet** *mil* Vorstrafenregister; **~s triable on indictment** → indictable offen|ces (~ses); **~s not triable on indictment** →summary offen|ces (~ses)

crime, capital ~ Kapitalverbrechen; **combatting** (or **fighting)** ~ Bekämpfung von Verbrechen; **commission of a** ~ Begehung e-r Straftat; **decrease in** ~ Abnahme der Kriminalität; **increase in** ~ Ansteigen der Kriminalität; **location** (or **place**) **of the** ~ s. scene of the →~; **major** ~ schweres Verbrechen, Kapitalverbrechen; **minor** ~ Vergehen; **perpetration of a** ~ s. commission of a →~; **prevention of** ~ Verhütung von Verbrechen; **scene of the** ~ Ort des Verbrechens; Tatort; **suppression of** ~ Verbrechensbekämpfung; **victim of a** ~ Opfer e-s Verbrechens

crime, to commit a ~ e-e Straftat begehen; **to detect** (or **discover**) a ~ e-e Straftat aufdecken; **to perpetrate a** ~e-e Straftat begehen

criminal 1. verbrecherisch, kriminell; strafbar; strafrechtlich *(opp. civil);* ~ **act** strafbare Handlung, Straftat; ~ **action** strafrechtliche Verfolgung; ~ **appeal** Berufung (od. Revision) in Strafsachen; ~ **assault** Sittlichkeitsverbrechen; *(versuchte)* Vergewaltigung; ~ **case** Strafsache; Strafprozeß; ~ **charge** Anklage wegen e-s Verbrechens; ~ **code** Strafgesetzbuch; *Am* Bundesstrafgesetzbuch; Strafprozeßordnung; ~ **complaint** Strafantrag; ~ **conduct** strafbares Verhalten; ~ **conversation** (crim. con.) *Am* Ehebruch *(als Schadensersatzgrund);* ~ →**court**; ~ →**damage**; ~ **discretion** Strafmündigkeit; ~ **disposition** kriminelle Veranlagung; ~ **evidence** Beweismittel im Strafverfahren; **C~ Injuries Compensation Board** *Br (1964 eingesetzte)* Entschädigungsstelle für Opfer von Gewaltverbrechen (od. deren Erben); ~ **intent** verbrecherische Absicht; **C~ Investigation Commission** (of IRS) *Am* Steuerfahndung; **C~ Investigation Department** (C. I. D.) *Br* Oberste Kriminalpolizeibehörde; Kripo; ~ **jurisdiction** Zuständigkeit in Strafsachen; Strafgerichtsbarkeit; ~ **justice** Strafgerichtsbarkeit; Strafrechtspflege; ~ **law** Strafrecht; Strafgesetz

criminal liability strafrechtliche Verantwortlichkeit; **limited** ~ beschränkte strafrechtliche Verantwortlichkeit; bedingte Strafmündigkeit; **to incur** ~ sich strafbar machen

criminal, ~ matter Strafsache; **~mischief** → mischief; ~ **negligence** *(strafbare)* Fahrlässigkeit; **~offen|ce (~se)** strafbare Handlung, strafrechtliches Delikt

criminal proceedings Strafverfahren, Strafprozeß; **to carry on** ~ ein Strafverfahren durchführen; **to institute** (or **take**) ~ ein Strafverfahren einleiten (against gegen); **to render oneself liable to** ~ sich strafrechtlicher Verfolgung aussetzen

criminal prosecution strafrechtliche Verfolgung; strafrechtliches Verfahren

criminal procedure Strafverfahren; **code of** ~ *Ger* Strafprozeßordnung

criminal record Strafregister; Vorstrafe(nverzeichnis); **no** ~ nicht vorbestraft; **to have a** ~ vorbestraft sein

criminal responsibility strafrechtliche Verantwortlichkeit; Zurechnungsfähigkeit; **age of** ~ Strafmündigkeit

criminal, ~ sanctions *Am* strafrechtliche Maßnahmen *(Gefängnis oder Geldstrafe);* ~ **suit** *Am (selten)* Strafprozeß; ~ **syndicalism** *Am* ungesetzliche Zusammenschlüsse *(zur Herbeiführung sozialer Umwälzungen durch Gewalt od. Terror);* ~ **trial** Strafverfahren

criminal 2. Verbrecher, Täter; **dangerous** ~ gemeingefährlicher Verbrecher; **gang of ~s** Verbrecherbande; **habitual** ~ Gewohnheitsverbrecher; **professional** ~ Berufsverbrecher

criminality Kriminalität, Verbrechertum

criminate *v (e-s Verbrechens)* beschuldigen

crimino-biological kriminalbiologisch

criminology Kriminologie *(wissenschaftl. Erforschung der Kriminalität)*

crisis Krise; ~ **area** Krisengebiet; ~ **management** Krisenmanagement *(Marketing-Strategie, wenn der Ruf e-s Unternehmens durch e-e Krise oder Katastrophe gefährdet ist);* ~ **management group** Krisenstab; ~ **manager** Krisenmanager; **~-proof** krisenfest; krisensicher; ~ **spot** Krisenherd

crisis, economic ~ Wirtschaftskrise; **in the event of a** ~ im Krisenfall; **financial** ~ Finanzkrise; **to bring to a** ~ der Entscheidung entgegenführen; **to get over** (or **overcome**) **a** ~ e-e Krise überwinden; **the car industry went through** (or **underwent**) **a major** ~ die Autoindustrie steckte in e-r schweren Krise

criterion Kriterium, (Unterscheidungs-)Kennzeichen, Merkmal; Tatbestandsmerkmal; ~ **for distinguishing** (between) Unterscheidungsmerkmal; ~ **for the valuation of shares** Maßstäbe für die Bewertung von Aktien; **to define ~s** (or **criteria**) Richtlinien aufstellen; **to be the** ~ maßgebend sein

critical kritisch (of a th. gegen etw.); entscheidend; bedenklich, gefährlich; ~ **circumstances** kritische Umstände; Fälle besonderer Dringlichkeit; ~ **date** entscheidender Zeitpunkt; Stichtag; *(VölkerR)* Feststellungsdatum *(bei Beweisaufnahme)*; **in case of ~ need** im Falle dringender Not; bei Versorgungskrisen; ~ **note** kritischer Vermerk; ~ **situation** kritische (od. gefährliche) Lage; ~ **supplies** Mangelgüter

criticism Kritik; **adverse** ~ abfällige (od. schlechte, ungünstige) Kritik; **fair** ~ anständige Kritik; **favo(u)rable** ~ gute (od. günstige) Kritik

crofter *bes. Scot* Kleinbauer

crofting *bes. Scot* Bewirtschaftung e-s kleinen Pachtgutes

crop Ernte, Ernteertrag; ~ **damage** Ernteschaden; ~ **failure** Mißernte; ~ **insurance** Ernteausfallversicherung; ~ **prospects** Ernteaussichten; ~ **shortfall** Ernteausfall; ~ **year** Erntejahr

crop, in ~ angebaut; **growing** (or **standing**) ~ Früchte auf dem Felde; Ernte auf dem Halm; **heavy** ~ reiche Ernte; **poor** ~ schlechte Ernte; **under** ~ angebaut; **to gather the ~s** die Ernte einbringen

cross sich kreuzend, quer, Quer-; entgegengesetzt, im Widerspruch zu; gegenseitig; **~-acceptance** Wechselreiterei

cross-action Widerklage; **to bring a** ~ e-e Widerklage erheben

cross, ~-appeal Anschlußberufung; **~-appeal** *v* Anschlußberufung einlegen; **~-benches** *Br parl* Bänke der Parteilosen *(die nicht regelmäßig für Regierung oder Opposition stimmen)*; **~-bencher** *Br parl* Neutraler; **~-bill** Rückwechsel; **~-border** grenzüberschreitend; **~-border leasing** →leasing 2.; ~ **checking** Gegenprüfung; **~-charge** Gegenbeschuldigung; **~-claim** (or **~-complaint**) *Am* Klage (od. Widerklage) gegen e-n anderen als den unmittelbaren Prozeßgegner in demselben Verfahren; **~-complainant** *Am* Widerkläger; **~-demand** Gegenforderung

cross-elasticity of demand and supply Kreuzelastizität (Wechselwirkung) von Angebot und Nachfrage

cross-entry Gegeneintragung; Gegenbuchung; **to make a** ~ e-e Gegenbuchung vornehmen

cross, ~-examination Kreuzverhör *(Befragung e-s Zeugen durch den Anwalt der Gegenpartei)*; **~-examine** *v (jdn)* ins Kreuzverhör nehmen; *(jdn)* e-m Kreuzverhör unterziehen

cross, ~ **frontier trade** *(EG)* grenzüberschreitender Handel; **~-liability** beiderseitige Haftpflicht *(bei beiderseitigem Verschulden)*

cross-licen|ce (~se) *(PatR)* wechselseitige Lizenz

cross-licensing agreement Lizenzaustauschvertrag; gegenseitiger Lizenzvertrag

cross-motion Gegenantrag; **~s** Antrag und Gegenantrag

cross-petition Gegenantrag; Widerklage *(bes. bei Ehescheidung)*; **to file a** ~ e-n Gegenantrag stellen; e-e Widerklage erheben

cross-petition *v* Gegenantrag stellen; Widerklage erheben *(bes. bei Ehescheidung)*

cross-purposes entgegengesetzte (od. gegensätzliche) Ziele; **to be at** ~ *(unabsichtlich)* entgegenhandeln, sich mißverstehen

cross, ~-question Kreuzfrage *(bei e-m Kreuzverhör)*; **~-question** *v* →~ examine *v*

cross-rates Kreuzkurse, Querkurse *(Kreuznotierungen zweier fremder Währungen gegeneinander)*

cross-refer *v (durch e-n Querverweis)* verweisen

cross-reference (Kreuz-)Verweisung *(in e-m Buch)*; **to make a** ~ *(von e-r Stelle auf e-e andere)* verweisen

cross, ~-suit *Am* Widerklage; **~-trade** (Schiffs-)Verkehr zwischen fremden Häfen *(bes. der Handelsflotten der Comecon-Länder)*

cross *v* kreuzen; *(Plan etc)* durchkreuzen, vereiteln; sich kreuzen *(z.B. Briefe)*; **to ~ out** ausstreichen, durchstreichen; ~ **out what does not apply** Nichtzutreffendes ist zu streichen; **to ~-subsidize** quersubventionieren; **to ~-sue** *Am* Widerklage erheben; **to ~-vote** panaschieren

cross *v*, **to ~ the border** (or **frontier**) die Grenze überschreiten; über die Grenze gehen; **to ~ a cheque** *Br* e-n Scheck *(durch 2 parallele Striche)* kreuzen *(d.h. mit Verrechnungsvermerk versehen)*; **to ~ the floor** (of the House) *Br pol* zur anderen Seite (zur Opposition) übergehen

crossed gekreuzt; **(generally, specially)** ~ **cheque** *Br* →cheque; **our letters have** ~ unsere Briefe haben sich gekreuzt

crossing 1. *Br* Kreuzen, Kreuzvermerk *(auf e-m Scheck) (Ziehen von 2 parallel laufenden Linien quer über die Vorderseite)*; **general** ~ allgemeine Kreuzung *(zwischen den Strichen ist keine bestimmte Bank angegeben; der Bezogene kann an jede Bank zahlen)*; **special** ~ besondere Kreuzung *(zwischen den Strichen steht der Name e-r bestimmten Bank; der Bezogene darf nur an diese zahlen)*

crossing 2. Übergang; Überfahrt; Überquerung *(der Straße)*; ~ **(of) the frontier** (or **border**) Grenzüberschreitung; Grenzübergang; **when ~ the frontier** beim Überschreiten der Grenze; ~ **the floor** *Br parl* Wechseln e-r Partei *(durch e-n →M. P.)*; ~ **point** (or **point of ~ the frontier**) Übergangsstelle an der Grenze

crossing, frontier ~ Grenzüberschreitung; Grenzübergang; **level** ~ schienengleicher Bahnübergang; **pedestrian** ~ Straßenübergang *(für Fußgänger)*

crowd (Menschen-)Menge, Gedränge; **~s (of people)** große Menschenmassen; ~ **behavio(u)r** Massenverhalten

crowded gedrängt, übervoll; ~ **city** dichtbevölkerte Stadt; ~ **profession** überfüllter Beruf; ~ **street** verkehrsreiche Straße; ~ **state** Überfüllung

crown Krone; **the C~** *Br* die Krone; Königin, König; Staat, Fiskus; **C~ Court** *Br* →court; **C~ debts** *Br* Forderungen der Krone; ~ **employee** *Br* Arbeitnehmer der Krone; **C~ estates** *Br* Krongüter, Staatsdomänen; **C~ Estate Commissioners** *Br* Domänenverwaltung; ~ **jewel defense** *Am* Veräußerung besonders wertvoller Betriebsteile *(um den Plan e-s an der [Unternehmens-]Übernahme Interessierten zu verderben)*; **C~ land** *Br* staatlicher Grundbesitz; **C~ lands** →C~ estates; **C~ law** *Br* Strafrecht; ~ **prince** Kronprinz; ~ **princess** Kronprinzessin; **C~ privilege** *Br* Recht der Krone, die Vorlage von Urkunden zu verweigern *(wegen Gefährdung des öffentlichen Interesses)*; **C~ proceedings** *Br* Zivilklage der Krone (oder gegen die Krone); **C~ property** *Br* fiskalisches Eigentum; **C~ →Prosecution Service; C~ Prosecutor** *Br* Staatsanwalt; ~ **servants** *Br* Kronbeamte, Bedienstete der Krone; ~ **side** *Br* Strafgerichtsbarkeit der Queen's Bench Division *(opp. plea side)*; ~ **solicitor** *Br* Generalstaatsanwalt (*→Director of Public Prosecutions)*; ~ **user** *Br* Benutzung durch den Staat; ~ **witness** *Br* →witness 1.

crown, officer of the C~ *Br* Staatsbeamter; **minister of the C~** *Br* Staatsminister

Crown, the estate passes to the ~ *Br* der Nachlaß fällt an den Staat

crucial entscheidend, kritisch (to für); ~ **date** Stichtag; ~ **issue** entscheidende (Streit-)Frage; ~ **point** kritischer (od. springender) Punkt; ~ **question** Kernfrage; ~ **vote** Kampfabstimmung

crude roh, unbearbeitet; ~ **materials** Rohstoffe; ~ **oil** Rohöl; ~ **ore** Roherz; ~ **steel** Rohstahl

cruel act Grausamkeit

cruelty Grausamkeit; ~ **to animals** Tierquälerei; ~ **to children** Mißhandlung von Kindern; **mental** ~ *Am* seelische Grausamkeit *(als Ehescheidungsgrund)*; **Royal Society for the Prevention of C~ to Animals** *Br* Tierschutzverein

cruise missile (C. M.) *mil* Marschflugkörper *(unbemanntes Flugzeug mit Düsenantrieb, das sein Ziel im Tiefstflug präzisionsgelenkt anfliegt)*

crumble (away) *v (Börse)* abbröckeln, Kursrückgang erleiden

crumbling of prices Abbröckeln der Kurse

cryptanalysis Entzifferung von Geheimschrift

crypto-communist getarnter Kommunist

cryptogram Geheimtext

cryptophonie Sprachverschlüsselung

crystallize *v*, **the floating charge ~s** *Br* die schwebende Belastung wird zu e-r festen Belastung *(→fixed charge)*

CSCE Follow-up Meeting KSZE-Folgetreffen

cub (reporter) *Br* junger *(unerfahrener)* (Zeitungs-)Reporter

Cuba Kuba; **the Republic of** ~ Republik Kuba

Cuban Kubaner(in); kubanisch

cubic, ~ **capacity** Rauminhalt; *(Auto)* Hubraum; ~ **content** Rauminhalt; ~ **metre** *(Am* **meter***)* **of solid timber** Festmeter

culpability *(StrafR)* Schuld; **ground of precluding** ~ Schuldausschließungsgrund

culpable strafbar; schuldhaft; ~ **homicide** *Scot* Totschlag *(entspricht →homicide)*; ~ **negligence** schuldhafte Fahrlässigkeit

culprit Angeklagte(r); Angeschuldigte(r); Täter; **main** ~ Hauptschuldiger

cult, personality ~ Persönlichkeitskult

cultivate *v (Land)* bearbeiten, bestellen; anbauen; kultivieren

cultivated area Anbaufläche

cultivation Bearbeitung, Bestellung *(von Land)*; Urbarmachung; Anbau; Kultivierung; ~ **of cereals** Getreideanbau; **area under** ~ Anbaufläche

cultural kulturell; Kultur-; ~ **assets** Kulturgüter; ~ **attaché** Kulturattaché; ~ **award** Kulturpreis; ~ **centre (~er)** Kulturzentrum

cultural convention Kulturabkommen; **→European C~** Europäisches Kulturabkommen

cultural, ~ **exchange** Kulturaustausch; ~ **heritage** kulturelles Erbe, Kulturgut, ~ **institutions** kulturelle Einrichtungen; ~ **→lag**

cultural level Kulturstufe; **difference in** ~ Kulturgefälle; **on a high** ~ kulturell hochstehend

cultural, ~ **life** kulturelles Leben; ~ **policy** Kulturpolitik

cultural property Kulturgut, Kulturgüter; **Convention for the Protection of C~ P~ in the Event of Armed Conflict**[116] Konvention zum Schutze von Kulturgut bei bewaffneten Kon-

flikten; International Centre for the Study of the Preservation and Restoration of C~ P~[117] Internationale Studienzentrale für die Erhaltung und Restaurierung von Kulturgut

cultural, for ~ purposes für kulturelle Zwecke; **~ relations** kulturelle Beziehungen; **~ workers** Kulturschaffende

culturally kulturell, in kultureller Hinsicht

culture Kultur; Zivilisation; Bebauung, Anbau; Zucht; **~ area** Kulturraum; **co(-)operation in the field of ~** kulturelle Zusammenarbeit

cum mit, einschließlich; **~ coupon** mit Coupon *(opp. ex coupon)*; **~ dividend** mit Dividende *(opp. ex dividend)*; **~ interest** →interest 4.; **~ new** mit Bezugsrecht *(auf neue Aktien) (opp. ex new)*; **~ rights** mit Bezugsrecht *(auf neue Aktien) (opp. ex rights)*; **~ testamento annexo** →administration with the will annexed

cumbersome procedure schwerfälliges Verfahren

cumulate *v* (an)häufen; kumulieren; **to ~ reserves** Reserven ansammeln

cumulation Kumulierung

cumulative kumulativ, (sich) anhäufend; hinzukommend, zusätzlich; **~ dividend** kumulative (zur Nachzahlung berechtigende) Dividende *(auf Vorzugsaktien, wenn für ein od. mehrere vorhergehende Jahre keine Dividende ausgeschüttet worden war)*; **~ evidence** verstärkender Beweis; **~ legacy** zusätzliches Vermächtnis; **~ preference shares** *Br* kumulative Vorzugsaktien*(die den Inhaber berechtigen, Dividendenausfälle in ertragreichen Jahren nachzuholen)*; **~ preferred stock** *Am* kumulative Vorzugsaktien; **~ sentence** *Am* zusätzliche Strafzumessung; **~ voting** *Am* kumulative Stimmenabgabe (od. Abstimmung) *(als Mittel für die Minderheitenvertretung im →board of directors)*

curable defect heilbarer Mangel *(opp. incurable defect)*

curator Verwalter; Pfleger; *Am* Nachlaßpfleger *(bis zur Bestellung e-s administrator od. executor)*; Museumsdirektor; Konservator; **~ for an absent person** (or **~ absentis**) *Am* Abwesenheitspfleger; **~ ad litem** *Am* Prozeßpfleger; **~ appointed for a mentally or physically incapacitated person** Gebrechlichkeitspfleger; **~ bonis** *Scot* Pfleger *(des Vermögens e-s Minderjährigen od. Geisteskranken)*; **~ of an estate** *Am* und *Scot* Nachlaßpfleger

curatorship *Am* Pflegschaft

curb 1. *Am hist.* Freiverkehr(sbörse); **C~ Exchange** *Am* früherer Name der →American Stock Exchange

curb 2. Beschränkung, Drosselung *(z. B. des Imports)*

curb *v* drosseln, dämpfen, bremsen; **to ~ the boom** die (Hoch-)Konjunktur eindämmen (od. bremsen); **to ~ production** die Produktion drosseln; **to ~ spending** Ausgaben bremsen; **to ~ wages** Löhne beschränken (od. drosseln)

cure *v* heilen; **to ~ a default** e-n Verzug wiedergutmachen; **to ~ a defect** e-n (Rechts-)Mangel heilen; e-m Mangel abhelfen

curing of defects Heilung von Mängeln

curfew Sperrstunde, Ausgehverbot; **circulating during ~** Aufenthalt im Freien während der Sperrstunde; **to lift the ~** das Ausgehverbot aufheben; **to observe the ~** die Sperrstunde einhalten

currency 1. Währung; *(in Umlauf befindliches)* Geld; **(foreign) ~** Devisen *(Zahlungsmittel in ausländischer Währung)*; Valuta *(fremde Währung; → foreign ~)*; **~ account** Währungskonto; Devisenkonto; **~ agreement** Währungsabkommen; **~ area** Währungsgebiet; **~ arbitrage** Devisenarbitrage; **~ assets** Devisenguthaben

currency basket Währungskorb

Eine Rechnungseinheit vom Typ „Währungskorb" besteht aus e-m Sortiment verschiedener Landeswährungen (→ECU)

currency, ~ bill *Br* Wechsel in ausländischer Währung; Devisenwechsel; **~ bonds** Fremdwährungsschuldverschreibungen; Obligationen in ausländischer Währung; **~ clause** Fremdwährungsklausel, Valutaklausel; **~ component** (or **element**) *(internationale Währungspolitik)* Devisenkomponente; **~ control** Devisenkontrolle, Devisenbewirtschaftung

currency conversion Währungskonvertierung; **~ table** Währungstabelle

currency, ~crisis Währungskrise; **~ depreciation** (or **devaluation**) Währungsabwertung; niedrigere Bewertung e-r Währung; Geldentwertung; **~ doctrine** *Br* Auffassung, nach der volle Deckung durch Edelmetalle vorhanden sein muß *(opp. banking doctrine)*; **~ exchange business** Geldwechselgeschäft; **~ exchange facilities** Devisenumtauscherleichterungen; **~ futures** *(Börse)* Devisenterminkontrakte; **~ futures trading** Devisentermingeschäfte; **~ gain** Währungsgewinn; **~ holdings** Devisenbestände; **~ in circulation** Bargeldumlauf; **~ losses** Währungsverluste; **~ manipulation** Währungsmanipulation; **~ market rates** Devisenmarktkurse; **~ notes** *Br (1914 vom Schatzamt als Ersatz für Goldmünzen ausgegebene)* Schatzanweisungen; **~ offence (~se)** Devisenvergehen; **~ parity** Währungsparität; **~ policy** Währungspolitik; **~ position** Währungslage; **~ principle** →~ doctrine; **~ receipts** Deviseneinnahmen; **~ reform** Währungsreform; **~ regulations** Devisenbestimmungen; ~ **reserve** Devisenreserve; Währungsreserve; ~ **smuggling** Devisenschmuggel; ~ **snake** *(EG)* Währungsschlange; ~**speculator** Währungsspekulant; ~ **stability** Währungsstabilität; ~ **stabilization** Währungsstabilisierung; ~ **swap** Währungsswap *(→swap)*; ~ **system** Währungssystem; ~ **trade** Devisenhandel

currency transactions, international ~ internationaler Währungsverkehr *(z. B. im Rahmen des Internationalen Währungsfonds)*

currency, ~ **trafficker** Devisenschmuggler; ~ **transfer** Devisentransfer; ~ **unit** Währungseinheit; ~ **unrest** Währungsunruhe

currency, adjustable ~ elastische Währung; **appreciation of** ~ Höherbewertung der Währung; **clearing** ~ Verrechnungswährung; **depreciation** (or **devaluation**) **of** ~ Währungsabwertung; **domestic** ~ Binnenwährung; Inlandswährung; **double** ~ Doppelwährung; **emergency** ~ Notgeld; **floating** ~ Währung, deren Wechselkurs freigegeben ist; **fluctuations of** ~ Währungsschwankungen

currency, (foreign) ~ →foreign

currency, in German ~ in deutscher Währung; **gold** ~ Goldmünze; Goldwährung; **hard** ~ harte Währung (→*strong* ~); **home** ~ inländische Währung *(opp. foreign ~)*; **local** ~ Landeswährung; **managed** ~ manipulierte Währung; **metallic** ~ Metallwährung; Metallgeld *(opp. paper ~)*; **national** ~ Landeswährung; **paper** ~ Papiergeld; Papier(geld)währung *(opp. metallic ~)*; **safeguarding of the** ~ Sicherung der Währung

currency, soft ~ weiche Währung; **soft** ~ **country** währungsschwaches Land

currency, stability of ~ Währungsstabilität; **stabilization of** ~ Währungsstabilisierung

currency, strong ~ starke Währung; **strong** ~ **country** währungsstarkes Land

currency, weak ~ schwache Währung (→*soft* ~)

currency 2. (Geld-)Umlauf; Laufzeit, Gültigkeitsdauer; ~ **of bank notes** Banknotenumlauf; ~ **of a bill** Laufzeit e-s Wechsels; ~ **in circulation** Bargeldumlauf; ~**of a contract** Laufzeit e-s Vertrages; ~ **of an insurance** Laufzeit e-r Versicherung; ~ **of a lease** Laufzeit e-s Miet-(od. Pacht-)vertrages

current Strom; Strömung *(im Fluß)*; *fig* Tendenz, Richtung; ~ **consumption** Stromverbrauch; ~ **demand** Strombedarf; ~**s of trade** (or **trade** ~**s**) Handelsströme

current (cur.) laufend *(Monat, Jahr, Konto)*; umlaufend, kursierend *(Geld, Meinung etc)*; üblich, (markt)gängig; gegenwärtig, augenblicklich; allgemein üblich (od. verbreitet)

current account laufendes Konto, Kontokorrentkonto, Girokonto; laufende Rechnung; *(Börse)* laufende Abrechnung; *(Zahlungsbilanz)* Leistungsbilanz; ~ **adjustment** Leistungsbilanzanpassung; ~ **balance** Kontokorrentguthaben; Leistungsbilanzsaldo; ~ **credit** Kontokorrentkredit; ~ **deficit** Leistungsbilanzdefizit; ~ **imbalances** Leistungsbilanzungleichgewichte; ~ **loan** Kontokorrentkredit; ~ **money** *Am* Giralgeld; ~ **surplus** Leistungsbilanzüberschuß; **advance on** ~ Kontokorrentkredit; **deposits on** ~ Kontokorrenteinlagen; Sichteinlagen

current, ~ **affairs** Tagesereignisse, Tagespolitik; ~ **articles** gängige Ware; ~ **assets** Umlaufvermögen; sofort realisierbare Aktiva *(opp. fixed assets)*

current business, to attend to ~ die laufenden Geschäfte führen

current, ~ **capital** Betriebskapital, Umlaufkapital; ~ **coin** gängige Münze; ~ **or replacement cost** laufende oder Wiederbeschaffungskosten; ~ **cost accounting** *Br* Gegenwartsbewertung *(Anlagewerte dürfen zum Gegenwartswert eingesetzt und abgeschrieben werden)*; ~ **demand** laufende Nachfrage; ~ **deposits** Kontokorrenteinlagen; ~ **events** Tagesereignisse; ~ **on (the) Exchange** börsengängig; an der Börse eingeführt; ~ **expenses** (or **expenditure**) laufende Ausgaben (od. Unkosten); ~ **interest** laufende Zinsen; **of** ~ **interest** aktuell; ~ **liabilities** laufende (bes. kurzfristige) Verbindlichkeiten *(opp. long term liabilities)*; ~ **market price** gegenwärtiger Marktpreis; ~ **market value** gegenwärtiger Marktwert *(e-s Wirtschaftsgutes)*; *(Börse)* gegenwärtiger Börsenwert, Tageskurs; ~ **money** umlaufendes Geld; ~ **month** laufender Monat; ~ **operating expenses** laufende Betriebskosten; ~ **opinion** allgemeine (od. öffentliche) Meinung; ~ **payments** laufende Zahlungen; ~ **price** Marktpreis, Tagespreis; gegenwärtiger Preis; *(Börse)* Tageskurs; **at the** ~ **price** zum Tagespreis; zum Tageskurs; ~ **rate (of exchange)** Tageskurs; ~ **ratio** *Am* Liquiditätskennzahl *(Verhältnis der flüssigen Aktiven zu den laufenden Verbindlichkeiten: current assets divided by liabilities)*; ~ **receivables** innerhalb e-s Jahres fällig werdende Forderungen; *Am (Bilanz)* Umlaufvermögen; ~ **revenue** laufende Einnahmen; ~ **transactions** laufende Geschäfte; ~ **value** derzeitiger Wert; Tageswert; Zeitwert; ~ **year** laufendes Jahr; ~ **yield** laufende Rendite

curriculum Lehrplan; Ausbildungsplan; Studienplan; ~ **vitae** (c. v.) Lebenslauf *(für Bewerbungen etc)*

curtail *v* (ab-, ver)kürzen; beschränken, einschränken, verringern; **to** ~ **one's expenses** s-e Ausgaben einschränken (od. verringern); **to** ~ **production** die Produktion beschränken (od. drosseln); **to** ~ **a speech** e-e Rede kürzen

curtailed expectation of life abgekürzte Lebenserwartung

curtailment Abkürzung, Verkürzung, Kürzung; Beschränkung, Einschränkung, Verringerung; ~ **of expenses** Einschränkung der Ausgaben; ~ **of production** Produktionsbeschränkung, Produktionsdrosselung

curtain, iron ~ *pol* eiserner Vorhang

curtesy *Am (in wenigen Einzelstaaten)* Nießbrauch (life estate) des Witwers am Grundbesitz der verstorbenen Ehefrau*(Br obs.)*

custodial Aufsichts-; *Am* vormundschaftlich; Vormundschafts-; ~ **care** Obhut; Verantwortung als Verwahrer; ~ **parent** Elternteil, der das Sorgerecht hat; ~ **sentence** Freiheitsstrafe; **non-~ penalties** Nichtfreiheitsstrafen (→*fine*)

custodian Verwahrer; Vermögensverwalter; *Br* Hausmeister; *Am* Vormund; *Am* Sorgeberechtigter, -beauftragter; *Am* Hinterlegungsstelle *(z.B. für die Anlagewerte e-s →mutual fund)*; ~ **account** *Am* Depot(konto); ~ **bank** *Am* Depotbank; **C~ of Enemy Property** *Br* (**Alien Property C~** *Am*) Verwalter feindlichen Vermögens *(während des 2. Weltkrieges)*; ~ **trustee** →trustee

custodian, appointment of a ~ Bestellung (od. Einsetzung) e-s Verwahrers;**gratuitous** ~ unentgeltlicher Verwahrer; **legal** ~ amtliche Verwahrungsstelle (od. Hinterlegungsstelle); **to be the legal ~ (of)** (etw.) in amtlicher Verwahrung haben

custodianship Verwaltung; *Am* Effektenverwaltung *(durch die Banken)*; *Am* Sorge für die Person des Kindes, Vormundschaft; ~ **account** *Am* Effektendepot(konto); ~ **fee** *Am* Depotgebühr; ~ **receipt** *Am* Depotschein; **service of** ~ *Am* Depotverwaltung

custody 1. Sorgerecht der Eltern; ~ **order** *Br* gerichtl. Regelung der elterlichen Sorge für Kinder unter 16 Jahren; ~ **proceedings** Verfahren zur Feststellung des Sorgeberechtigten; **entitled to the ~ of the child** sorgeberechtigt; **joint** ~ gemeinsames (od. geteiltes) Sorgerecht *(der Eltern)*; **to apply for** ~ das Sorgerecht beantragen; **to award** ~ das Sorgerecht zusprechen; **he was granted** ~ er erhielt das Sorgerecht

custody 2. Verwahrung, Aufbewahrung; Gewahrsam, Obhut; *Am* Depot *(ohne Verwaltung)*; ~ **agreement** Verwahrungsvertrag; ~ **bill of lading** Lagerhaltungs-Konnossement

custody of a bank, the securities are in the ~ *Am* die Wertpapiere sind im Depot e-r Bank

custody of goods Aufbewahrung (od. Verwahrung) von Waren; **to take** ~ Güter aufbewahren (od. verwahren)

custody of sb.'s property Verwahrung jds Vermögen

custody, contract (or **bailment**) **for** ~ Verwahrungsvertrag; **in** ~ *Am* im Depot; **official** ~ amtliche Verwahrung; **place of** ~ Aufbewahrungsort

custody, safe ~ sichere Aufbewahrung; *Br* Verwahrung, Aufbewahrung *(von Wertpapieren und Wertgegenständen)*; Depot; **in safe** ~ *Br* im Depot; **safe ~ account** *Br* Depot(konto) *(bei Banken)*; **safe ~ department** *Br* Depotabteilung; **safe ~ charge** *Br* Depotgebühr; **safe ~ deposit** *Br* Streifbanddepot; **safe ~ receipt** *Br* Depotschein; **safe ~ of securities** *Br* Effektenverwahrung; **contract for safe** ~ *Br* Depotvertrag; **to keep in safe** ~ sicher aufbewahren; **to place** (or **deposit**) **securities in safe** ~ *Br* Wertpapiere in Depot geben; **to keep in safe** ~ sicher aufbewahren

custody, taking into ~ Gewahrsamnahme

custody, to be in sb.'s ~ sich in jds Verwahrung befinden; **to give into** ~ in Verwahrung geben; zur Verwahrung übergeben; **to hold** (or **keep**) **in** ~ verwahren; in Verwahrung (od. Aufbewahrung) haben; **to take into** ~ in Verwahrung nehmen

custody 3. Haft; Untersuchungshaft; **discharge from** ~ Haftentlassung; **in** ~ in Haft

custody, period of ~ Haftzeit; **to make allowance for the period of** ~ die Untersuchungshaft anrechnen

custody, person held in ~ pending trial Untersuchungsgefangener; →**police** ~; →**youth** ~; **preventive** ~ Sicherungsverwahrung; **protective** ~ Schutzhaft; **to detain in** ~ in (Untersuchungs-)Haft halten; **to give sb. into the ~ of the →police; to be (held) in** ~ sich in (Untersuchungs-)Haft befinden; **to hold in** ~ in (Untersuchungs-)Haft halten; **to release from** ~ aus der Haft entlassen; **to be remanded in** ~ *Br* (**into** ~ *Am*) in die Haft zurückgesandt werden (→*remand v*); **to take in** ~ verhaften; in Haft nehmen, festnehmen

custom 1. Brauch, Orts(ge)brauch, Handels(ge)brauch; Gewohnheit, Gepflogenheit, Usance *(Verkehrssitte unter Kaufleuten)*; Gewohnheitsrecht; Handelsgewohnheitsrecht; ~ **of merchants** Handelsgewohnheitsrecht *(gerichtlich anerkanntes kaufmännisches Gewohnheitsrecht)*; ~ **of the port** (c. o. p., c/p) Hafenusance, Hafenbrauch; **~s of the Realm** *Br* Landesbrauch; Gewohnheitsrecht; ~ **of the sea** See(manns-)brauch

custom of (the) trade Handels(ge)brauch, Usance; **established** ~ bestehender Handelsbrauch; **recognized** ~ anerkannter Handelsbrauch; **it is the custom of a particular trade** es ist in e-r Branche üblich

custom and usage Sitte

custom, in accordance with ~ (or **according to** ~) usancemäßig; **banking** ~ Bankusance; **by** ~ kraft Gewohnheit; **established ~s** Sitten und Gebräuche; **international** ~ internationa-

les Gewohnheitsrecht; **legal** ~ *Am* Gewohnheitsrecht
custom, local ~ Orts(ge)brauch, Platzgebrauch; partikuläres Gewohnheitsrecht; **in accordance with local ~s** ortsüblich
custom, manners and ~s of a country Sitten und Gebräuche e-s Landes; **maritime** ~ See(manns)brauch; **mercantile** ~ Handelsbrauch; **national** ~ Landesbrauch; **stock exchange** ~ Börsenusance
custom, trade ~ Handelsbrauch, Usance; **according to trade** ~ handelsüblich; **to comply with trade** ~ sich nach Handelsbrauch richten
custom, to be →sanctioned by ~
custom 2. Zoll (→customs)
custom(-)house Zollamt, Zollbehörde; ~ **broker** Schiffszollmakler; Zollagent; ~ **entry** Verzollung; ~ **officer** *Br* Zollbeamter; ~ **receipt** Zollquittung
custom 3. Kundschaft; Kundenkreis; **~-made** nach Maß (od. Bestellung) angefertigt; **large** ~ große Kundschaft; **little** ~ wenig Kundschaft; **loss of** ~ Verlieren von Kunden

customs Zoll, Zölle; **the C~** die Zollbehörde
customs, to clear goods through the ~ Waren verzollen; **to declare sth. at the** ~ etw. beim Zoll angeben; **to get one's luggage** *Br* (**baggage** *Am*) **through the** ~ sein Gepäck zollamtlich abfertigen lassen; **to pass through the** ~ durch den Zoll gehen, den Zoll passieren
customs, ~ **abandonment** Verzicht auf das Zollgut; ~ **account** Zollrechnung; ~ **administration** Zollverwaltung; ~ **agent** Zollagent; ~ **airport** Zollflughafen
customs and excise, ~ **bond** Kaution für Zölle und Verbrauchsteuern; ~ **duties** *Br* Zölle und Abgaben; **Board of C~ and E~** *Br* Ministerialabteilung für Zölle und Verbrauchsteuern
customs, ~ **authorities** Zollbehörde, Zollverwaltung; ~ **barrier** Zollschranke; ~ **berth** Zollandungsplatz; ~ **bond** Kaution des Importeurs *(für Schaden der durch Nichtbefolgung von Zollbestimmungen entsteht);* ~ **broker** *Br* Spediteur, der die Zollabfertigung übernimmt; *Am* Zollmakler *(der die gesamte Einfuhrabwicklung übernimmt);* ~ **charges** Zollgebühren; ~ **check** Zollkontrolle; ~ **classification** Zolltarifierung
customs clearance Zollabfertigung; Verzollung; **to enter goods for** ~ Waren zur Verzollung anmelden
customs, ~ **cleared** verzollt; zollabgefertigt; ~ **code** (C. C.) Zollgesetz; ~ **convention** Zollabkommen, Zollübereinkommen
Customs Convention on the A. T. A. Carnet for the temporary admission of goods (A. T. A.[118] Convention)[119] Zollübereinkommen über das Carnet A. T. A. für die vorübergehende Einfuhr von Waren (A. T. A. Übereinkommen)
Customs Convention Regarding E. C. S.[120] **Carnets for Commercial Samples**[121] Zollabkommen über Carnets E. C. S. für Warenmuster
Customs Convention Concerning Facilities for the Importation of Goods for Display or Use at Exhibitions, Fairs, Meetings or Similar Events[122] Zollübereinkommen über Erleichterungen für die Einfuhr von Waren, die auf Ausstellungen, Messen, Kongressen od. ähnlichen Veranstaltungen ausgestellt od. verwendet werden sollen
Customs Convention on the International Transit of Goods Zollübereinkommen über die grenzüberschreitende Warendurchfuhr
Customs Convention on the International Transport of Goods under Cover of TIR Carnets (TIR Convention)[123] Zollübereinkommen über den internationalen Warentransport mit Carnets TIR (TIR Übereinkommen)
Customs Convention on the Temporary Importation of Commercial Road Vehicles[124] Zollabkommen über die vorübergehende Einfuhr gewerblicher Straßenfahrzeuge
Customs Convention on the Temporary Importation of Pedagogic Material[124a] Zollübereinkommen über die vorübergehende Einfuhr von Lehrmaterial
Customs Convention on the Temporary Importation of Private Road Vehicles[125] Zollabkommen über die vorübergehende Einfuhr privater Straßenfahrzeuge *(cf. Diptych)*
Customs Convention on the Temporary Importation for Private Use of Aircraft and Pleasure Boats[126] Zollabkommen über die vorübergehende Einfuhr von Wasserfahrzeugen und Luftfahrzeugen zum eigenen Gebrauch
Customs Convention on the Temporary Importation of Professional Equipment[126a] Zollübereinkommen über die vorübergehende Einfuhr von Berufsausrüstung
Customs Convention on the Temporary Importation of Scientific Equipment[127] Zollübereinkommen über die vorübergehende Einfuhr von wissenschaftlichem Gerät
Customs Cooperation Council (CCC) Rat für die Zusammenarbeit auf dem Gebiete des Zollwesens (RZZ)[128] (Brüsseler Zollrat)
customs, ~ **debt** Zollschuld; ~ **declarant** Zolldeklarant; ~ **declaration** Zollerklärung, Zollanmeldung; *Br* Einfuhrerklärung; *(Post)* Zollinhaltserklärung; ~ **differential** Zollgefälle; ~ **district** Zollbezirk, Zollgebiet; ~ **documentation** (or **documents**) Zollpapiere; (~) **drawback** Zollrückvergütung *(bei Wiederausfuhr);* Rückzoll; ~ **dues** →~ duties
customs duties Zölle, Zollgebühren, Zollabgaben; ~ **and charges of any kind** Zölle und Belastungen aller Art; ~ **of a fiscal nature** Finanzzölle

customs duties, elimination of ~ Abschaffung der Zölle; **evasion of** ~ Zollhinterziehung; **free of** ~ zollfrei; **increase of** ~ Zollerhöhung; **liability to pay** ~ Zollpflicht; **liable to pay** ~ zollpflichtig; **lowering** (or **reduction**) **of** ~ Zollermäßigung, Zollsenkung; **payment of** ~ Zollentrichtung; **rates of** ~ Zollsätze; **increase of rates of** ~ Erhöhung der Zollsätze; **to abolish** ~ Zölle abschaffen; **to be exempt from** ~ vom Zoll befreit sein; **to collect** ~ Zoll einziehen; **to evade** ~ Zollhinterziehung begehen; **to lower** (or **reduce**) **the** ~ die Zollsätze herabsetzen; **to pay** ~ **on** Zoll bezahlen für

(customs) duty Zoll (→*duty 2.*); **assessment of** ~ Zollfestsetzung

customs enclave Zollanschlußgebiet

customs entry Zollanmeldung, Zollerklärung; *Br* Einfuhrerklärung; ~ **for home use** (or **home consumption**) *Br* Anmeldung von *(zollpflichtigen)* Waren für den Inlandsverbrauch; **to file a** ~ zur Verzollung anmelden

customs examination Zollrevision, Zollbeschau; ~ **of baggage** *Br* Gepäckkontrolle *(durch Zollbeamte)*; **record of the** ~ Zollbefund

customs exemption Zollfreiheit

customs facilities Zollerleichterungen; **Convention concerning C~ F~ for Touring**[129] Abkommen über die Zollerleichterung im Touristenverkehr

customs fine Zollstrafe

customs formalities Zollformalitäten; **completion of the** ~ Erledigung der Zollformalitäten; **to attend to** ~ Zollformalitäten erledigen

customs, ~ **fraud** Zollhinterziehung; **~-free zone** Zollausschlußgebiet; ~ **guard** *Am* Zollbeamter; ~ **inspection** →~ examination; ~ **investigation (service)** Zollfahndung(sdienst); ~ **invoice** Zollfaktura; ~ **inwards** Einfuhrzoll; ~ **jurisdiction** Zollhoheit

customs law Zollgesetz; **~s and regulations** Zollvorschriften; **infringement of the ~s** Verstoß gegen die Zollgesetze

customs, ~ **lock** Zollverschluß; **to be ~-locked** unter Zollverschluß stehen; ~ **manifest** Zollladungsverzeichnis; ~ **maritime zone** Seezollzone; ~ **nomenclature** Zollnomenklatur; ~ **offence (~se)** Zollvergehen

customs office Zollamt; Zollstelle; **inland** ~ Binnenzollamt; **operations at** ~ Zollabfertigung; ~ **of departure** Abgangszollstelle; ~ **of destination** Bestimmungszollstelle; ~ **en route** Durchgangszollstelle

customs, ~ **officer** (or **official**) Zollbeamter; ~ **officers** Zollbedienstete; ~ **outwards** Ausfuhrzoll; ~ **penalty** Zollstrafe; ~ **permit** Zollabfertigungsschein; ~ **policy** Zollpolitik

customs, ~ **procedure** Zollverfahren; **for** ~ **purposes** für Zollzwecke; ~ **rebate** *Am* Zollrückvergütung; ~ **receipt** Zollquittung; ~ **receipts** Zolleinnahmen; ~ **regulations** Zollvorschriften, Zollbestimmungen; ~ **report** Zollerklärung, Zolldeklaration; ~ **revenue** Zolleinnahmen, Zollaufkommen

customs seal Zollplombe; Zollverschluß; **under** ~ unter Zollverschluß; **affixed** ~ angelegter Zollverschluß; **breaking of** ~ Aufbrechen des Zollverschlusses; **recognized** ~ anerkannter Zollverschluß

customs, ~ **service** Zolldienst; **C~ Service** *Am* Zollverwaltung; ~ **shed** Zollschuppen; ~ **sovereignty** Zollhoheit; ~ **specification** Verzeichnis aller zu verzollender Waren; ~ **supervision** Zollaufsicht; ~ **surveillance zone** Zollgrenzbezirk

customs tariff Zolltarif; ~ **modification** Zolltarifänderung; ~ **rate** Zollsatz

customs territory Zollgebiet; **domestic** ~ Zollinland; **foreign** ~ Zollausland

customs transit Zollgutversand; **goods in** ~ Zollversandgut

customs, ~ **treatment** zollrechtliche Behandlung; ~ **treaty** Zollvertrag

customs union Zollunion; **establishment** (or **institution**) **of a** ~ Bildung e-r Zollunion; **to enter into a** ~ e-r Zollunion beitreten

customs value Zollwert; **average values for determining the** ~ **of** Mittelwerte für die Ermittlung des Zollwertes von

customs, ~ **violation** Zollzuwiderhandlungen; ~ **warehouse** Zollager; staatl. Zollniederlage; ~ **warehousing procedure** Zollagerverfahren, Zollgutlagerung; ~ **waters** Seezollgebiet

customable zollpflichtig

customary gebräuchlich, üblich; handelsüblich; ~ **clause** übliche Klausel; **to the** ~ **extent** in handelsüblichem Umfang; ~ **gifts** übliche Geschenke; ~ **in a country** landesüblich; ~ **in a certain place** ortsüblich; ~ **in the trade** handelsüblich; ~ **international law** völkerrechtliches Gewohnheitsrecht; ~ **law** Gewohnheitsrecht; ~ **rate of interest** landesüblicher Zins

customary rates, to charge at ~ seine üblichen Gebühren berechnen *(Anwalt, Architekt etc)*

customary risks handelsübliche Risiken

customer Kunde, Kundin; Abnehmer, Käufer; Nachfrager *(opp. supplier)*; *(beim Werkvertrag)* Besteller, Auftraggeber; Kontoinhaber; **~s** Kundschaft, Kundenkreis; ~ **allowance** Kundenrabatt; **~'s bill** Kundenwechsel; **~'s broker** (or **man**) *Am* Angestellter e-s broker, der Kunden berät; **~'s check** *Am* Barscheck; ~ **complaint** Kundenbeschwerde, Reklamation; ~ **country** Abnehmerland; ~ **credit card** *(vom Einzelhändler ausgegebene)* Kundenkreditkarte; ~ **deposits** Kundenanzahlungen; **~'s ledger** Kontokorrentbuch; ~ **list** Kundenkartei; **~'s loan** Kundenkredit, Kundendarlehen *(durch ein Kreditinstitut)*; ~ **needs** Bedarf der Kunden; **~'s order** Kundenauftrag; ~ **ownership** *Am* Aktienbesitz der Kundschaft von Versorgungsbetrieben *(public utilities)*; ~ **restraints** *Am* Kundenbindungen *(→vertical restraint guidelines)*; ~**'s security department** Depotabteilung; ~ **service** Kundendienst; ~**'s statement** Kontoauszug

customer, account ~ Kunde, der anschreiben läßt; **big** ~ Großkunde; **defaulting** ~ (or ~ **in default**) säumiger Kunde; **list of** ~**s** Kundenliste; **prospective** ~ voraussichtlicher Kunde; Kaufanwärter; **regular** ~ Stammkunde; fester Kunde, ständiger Abnehmer; Stammgast *(e-s Restaurants etc)*; **service to the** ~ Kundendienst; **street** ~ Laufkunde

customer, to acquire ~**s** neue Kunden erwerben (od. gewinnen); **to draw** (or **entice**) **away** ~**s** Kunden abspenstig machen; **to lose** ~**s** Kunden verlieren; **to serve** ~**s** Kunden bedienen; **to solicit new** ~**s** neue Kunden werben

cut (Ab-, Ein-, Aus-)Schnitt; Kürzung, Herabsetzung, Verringerung; (Zins-)Kupon *(an Wertpapieren)*; *Am colloq.* Gewinnanteil; ~**s in a (newspaper) article** Streichungen in e-m (Zeitungs-)Artikel; ~ **in the budget** Etatkürzung; ~ **in the expenses** Verringerung der Ausgaben; ~ **in income** Einkommensminderung; ~ **in price(s)** Preissenkung, Preisherabsetzung; ~ **in rates** Tarifabbau; Gebührensenkung; ~ **in salary** Gehaltskürzung; Herabsetzung des Gehalts; ~ **in tariffs** Zollsenkung; ~ **in wage(s)** Lohnsenkung, Lohnherabsetzung

cutback Kürzung *(z.B. im Etat)*; plötzliche Einschränkung *(der Produktion etc)*; Abstrich; Rückgang; ~ **in expenditure** Ausgabeneinschränkung; ~ **in investments** Einschränkung der Investitionstätigkeit; ~ **on manpower** (or **staff**) Abbau von Arbeitskräften; Personaleinschränkung; ~ **in production** Produktionseinschränkung, Produktionsdrosselung

cut-off date Stichtag

cut price, at ~**s** zu herabgesetzten (od. ermäßigten) Preisen

cut-throat halsabschneiderisch, ruinös; ~ **competition** existenzgefährdende Konkurrenz; ~ **price** Kampfpreis; Schleuderpreis, Werbepreis

cut, manpower ~ Abbau (od. Entlassung) von Arbeitskräften; **power** ~ Stromsperre; **price** ~ Preissenkung, Preisherabsetzung; **salary** ~ Gehaltskürzung; **tax** ~ Steuersenkung; Steuerermäßigung; **wages** ~ Lohnherabsetzung, Senkung der Löhne

cut, to make ~**s in the budget** Abstriche am Etat machen

cut *v* schneiden; *(Gehalt etc)* kürzen; *(Preise etc)* herabsetzen (to auf); ermäßigen, reduzieren; senken (by um); **to** ~ **by half** um die Hälfte herabsetzen; **to** ~ **one's claim** s-n Anspruch herabsetzen (od. reduzieren); **to** ~ **the discount rate** den Diskontsatz herabsetzen; **to** ~ **one's expenses** seine Ausgaben reduzieren; **to** ~ **an inventory** ein Lager abbauen; **to** ~ **one's losses** s-e Verluste vermindern

cut *v*, **to** ~ **sth. short** etw. kürzen; etw. kurz unterbrechen; **to** ~ **a speech short** e-e Rede kürzen; e-e Rede abbrechen; **to** ~ **sb. short** jdm das Wort abschneiden

cut *v*, **to** ~ **a melon** *Am* e-e größere Dividende ausschütten; Dividende in Form von Gratisaktien verteilen; **to** ~ **the price** den Preis herabsetzen (od ermäßigen); **to** ~ **rates** Gebühren senken; **to** ~ **speed** Geschwindigkeit verringern; **to** ~ **taxes** Steuern senken; **to** ~ **wages** Löhne kürzen

cut back *v* einschränken, kürzen; **to** ~ **production** die Produktion einschränken (od. drosseln)

cut down *v* herabsetzen, kürzen, verringern, reduzieren; **to** ~ **on** einschränken, geringer (od. kleiner) machen; **to** ~ **the housekeeping allowance** das Wirtschaftsgeld kürzen; **to** ~ **expenses** Ausgaben einschränken; Unkosten verringern; **to** ~ **a speech** e-e Rede kürzen (od. zusammenstreichen); **to** ~ **a text** e-n Text kürzen (od. beschneiden)

cut off *v* abschneiden, (ab)trennen; **to cut sb. off** *tel* jdn trennen; *colloq.* jdn enterben; **to be** ~ **from** abgeschnitten sein von; **to** ~ **the connection during a conversation** die Telefonverbindung während e-s Gesprächs unterbrechen; **we were** ~ *tel* wir wurden getrennt; **to** ~ **a coupon** e-n Kupon abtrennen; **to** ~ **the electricity (supply)** den elektrischen Strom abschneiden (od. abstellen) *(z.B. wegen Nichtbezahlung der Strom-Rechnung)*; **to** ~ **an entail** *Am* die Beschränkung der Erbfolge aufheben; **to** ~ **food supplies** die Lebensmittelzufuhr abschneiden; **towns** ~ *(von der Außenwelt)* abgeschnittene Städte

cut out *v* ausschneiden; auslassen; **to cut a competitor out** e-n Konkurrenten vom Markt drängen

cutting Schneiden; Ausschneiden, (Zeitungs-)Ausschnitt; Herabsetzung, Kürzung; **press** ~ Zeitungsausschnitt; ~ **costs** Verringerung der Kosten; ~ **off** Absperrung; ~ **of prices** Herabsetzung der Preise, Preisherabsetzung; ~ **a melon** *Am* Verteilung e-r Dividende in Form von Gratisaktien; ~ **of wages** Herabsetzung der Löhne; Lohnkürzung

cybernetics Kybernetik

cycle Zyklus, Kreislauf; Folge, Reihe, Serie *(Schriften)*; *colloq.* Fahrrad; **business** (or **economic**) ~ Konjunkturzyklus

cyclical zyklisch, konjunkturrhythmisch, konjunkturell; konjunkturpolitisch; konjunkturabhängig; ~ **budgeting** Ausdehnung der Haushaltsperiode über e-n Konjunkturzyklus;

zyklischer Budgetausgleich; ~ **climate** konjunkturelles Klima; ~ **considerations** konjunkturbedingte Gesichtspunkte; konjunkturpolitische Erwägungen; ~ **course** Konjunkturverlauf; ~ **development** Konjunkturentwicklung; ~ **downswing** Konjunkturabschwung

cyclical fluctuations Konjunkturschwankungen; **sensitive to** ~ konjunkturempfindlich

cyclical movement Konjunkturbewegung; **control of** ~**s** Konjunkturlenkung

cyclical, ~ **policy** Konjunkturpolitik; ~ **prospects** Konjunkturaussichten; ~ **recovery** Konjunkturanstieg; ~ **research** Konjunkturforschung; ~ **situation** konjunkturpolitische Lage; ~ **stocks** *Am* von der Konjunktur abhängige Aktien; ~ **strains** konjunkturelle Spannungen; ~ **trend** konjunkturelle Entwicklung, Konjunkturverlauf; ~ **unemployment** konjunkturbedingte Arbeitslosigkeit; ~ **upswing** Konjunkturaufschwung, -anstieg

cypher, Royal C~ *Br* Königliche Initialen *(ER II)*

cy-près, rule of ~ Auslegungsregel, nach der unter gewissen Umständen bei e-r nicht durchführbaren letztwilligen Verfügung (od. e-m gemeinnützigen Trust) den Absichten des Erblassers stattzugeben ist (od. dem Trustzweck so nahe wie möglich zu kommen ist) *(Br bes. bei Vermächtnissen an wohltätige Einrichtungen)*

Cypriot Zyprer, Zyprerin; zyprisch

Cyprus, Republic of ~ Republik Zypern

Czechoslovak Tschechoslowake, Tschechoslowakin; tschechoslowakisch; ~ **Socialist Republic** Tschechoslowakische Sozialistische Republik

Czechoslovakia Tschechoslowakei

D

D-Day Tag X *(bes. für ein militärisches Unternehmen)*

dabble *v* sich *(als Hobby, nicht berufsmäßig)* beschäftigen mit; **to** ~ **on the stock exchange** sich mit kleinen Börsenspekulationen befassen; **to** ~ **in politics** sich *(nebenbei)* mit Politik befassen

dabbler kleiner Börsenspekulant

dactylogram Fingerabdruck

Dail Eireann *parl* Abgeordnetenhaus der Irischen Republik *(Eire) (cf. Oireachtas)*

dailies Tagespresse; **leading** ~ führende Tageszeitungen

daily täglich; Tageszeitung; ~ **allowance** Tagegeld(er); *parl* Diäten; ~ **average** Tagesdurchschnitt; ~ **cause list** *Br* tägliche Verhandlungsliste der Gerichtsfälle; tägliches Terminverzeichnis; ~ **earnings** Tagesverdienst; ~ **expense allowance** *Br (House of Lords)* Diäten; ~ **interest** Tageszinsen; ~ **loan(s)** *(Geldmarkt)* tägliches Geld, Tagesgeld; ~ **money** →~ loan; ~ **output** *(Bergbau)* Tagesförderung; Tagesleistung *(e-s Unternehmens, e-r Maschine)*; ~ **(paper)** Tageszeitung; ~ **pay** Tageslohn; ~ **quotation** *(Börse)* Tagesnotierung, Tageskurs; ~ **rate** Tagessatz; ~ **receipts** (or **takings**) Tageseinnahmen; ~ **sheet**[1] Tageskontrollblatt; Kontrollbuch *(des Fahrpersonals)*; ~ **turnover** Tagesumsatz; ~ **wages** Tageslohn; ~ **wage rate** Tageslohnsatz; **the paper appears** ~ die Zeitung erscheint täglich

dairy Milchwirtschaft; Molkerei; ~ **farm** Meierei, Molkerei; ~ **farming** Milchwirtschaft

damage Schaden *(als Tatbestand; cf. damages)*; Beschädigung; Verlust, Einbuße (to an); ~ **to baggage** (or *Br* **luggage**) Gepäckschaden; ~ **by sea** Seeschaden, Havarie; ~ **to a car** Autobeschädigung; ~ **to cargo** Beschädigung der Ladung; ~ **flowing** (or **arising**) **from breach of contract** Vertragsschaden; ~ **resulting from a late delivery** Schaden wegen verspäteter Lieferung; Verzugsschaden; ~ **done** zugefügter Schaden; ~ **(caused) by fire** Brandschaden; ~ **done by game** Wildschaden; ~ **in law** s. general →~; ~ **to property** Sachschaden; Sachbeschädigung; ~ **report** Havariegutachten; ~ **to reputation** Schädigung des Rufes; Rufschaden; ~ **suffered** erlittener Schaden; ~ **survey** Schadensuntersuchung, Schadensbesichtigung; Havarieuntersuchung; ~ **in transit** Beschädigung auf dem Transport; Transportschaden; ~ **through loss of use** Nutzungsschaden; ~ **(caused) by water** Wasserschaden

damage, actual ~ tatsächlicher Schaden; **case of** ~ Schadensfall; **cause of** ~ Schadensursache; **certificate of** ~ Schadensbescheinigung; Havariezertifikat; **compensation for** ~ Schadensersatz; **compensation for** ~ **in kind** Naturalrestitution; **consequential** ~ Folgeschaden; **criminal** ~*Br*[1a] strafbare Sachbeschädigung; **direct** ~ unmittelbarer Schaden; **extent of the** ~ Höhe (od. Umfang) des Schadens; Schadenshöhe; **financial** ~ Vermögensschaden; **general** ~ allgemeiner Schaden *(der als natürli-*

che und notwendige Folge des zu Ersatz verpflichtenden Umstandes erscheint; opp. special ~); **malicious ~ to property** vorsätzliche Sachbeschädigung; **material ~** Sachschaden; Materialschaden; **minor ~** geringfügiger Schaden; **nominal ~** *(lediglich)* nomineller Schaden *(ohne meßbaren Wert)*; **pecuniary ~** Vermögensschaden; **proof of ~** Schadensnachweis; **property ~** →damage to property; **special ~** besonderer (od. konkreter) Schaden *(der im Verfahren ausdrücklich vorgebracht und bewiesen werden muß; z.B. die über den general ~ hinausgehende Einbuße des Käufers)*; **statement of ~** Schadensaufstellung; **substantiated ~** nachgewiesener Schaden; **war ~** Kriegsschaden

damage, to ascertain the ~ den Schaden feststellen; **to be liable for ~** für e-n Schaden haftbar sein; **to bear the ~** den Schaden tragen; **to cause ~** den Schaden verursachen; **to do** (or **inflict**) ~ Schaden zufügen; **to →mitigate the ~**; **to repair the ~** den Schaden beheben; **to suffer** (or **sustain**) ~ e-n Schaden erleiden; Havarie erleiden; **place where the ~ has occurred** Ort, an dem sich der Schaden ereignet hat

damage *v (Sachen)* beschädigen; Schaden zufügen, schaden

damaged beschädigt; schadhaft, defekt; **in a ~ condition** in beschädigtem (od. defektem) Zustand; ~ **forests** geschädigte Wälder; ~ **value** *(VersR)* Wert in beschädigtem Zustand *(opp. sound value)*; **badly (partially, totally) ~** schwer (teilweise, vollständig) beschädigt; **sea ~** havariert; **severely ~** schwer beschädigt; **slightly ~** leicht beschädigt

damaging action schädigende Handlung

damages Schadensersatz; Entschädigung(ssumme)

Im Gegensatz zum deutschen Recht (§ 249 BGB) geht nach anglo-amerikanischem Recht der Schadensersatzanspruch im allgemeinen nicht auf Naturalherstellung, sondern auf Entschädigung in Geld

damages, ~ for breach of contract Entschädigung für Vertragsbruch; ~ **for pain and suffering** Schmerzensgeld; ~ **for unfair dismissal** *Br* Schadensersatz für unfaire Entlassung

damages, action for ~ (or **action to recover ~**) Schadensersatzklage; **to bring an action for ~** auf Schadensersatz klagen

damages, claim for ~ Schadensersatzanspruch; **to make** (or **file**) **a claim for ~** auf Schadensersatz klagen

damages, compensatory ~ *Am* kompensatorischer (od. entschädigender) Schadensersatz *(Ersatz des tatsächlichen Schadens; opp. punitive ~)*; **contemptuous ~** *Br* nur symbolischer Schadensersatz *(wenn die Entstehung des Schadens zwar bewiesen ist, das Gericht den Fall aber abschätzig beurteilt)*; **determination of ~** Festsetzung des Schadensersatzes; **duty to mitigate ~** Pflicht *(des Geschädigten)*, den Schaden so niedrig wie möglich zu halten; **exemplary ~** verschärfter Schadensersatz *(über den Betrag des tatsächl. Schadens hinausgehende Entschädigung mit Strafzweck; z.B. bei libel, slander, breach of promise)*; **liability for ~** Schadensersatzpflicht; **liable for ~** schadensersatzpflichtig

damages, liquidated ~ im voraus der Höhe nach bestimmter Schadensersatz *(der im Falle e-s Vertragsbruchs [z.B. Lieferungsverzug] anstelle des tatsächlich geldwerten Schadens fällig werden soll)*; Vertragsstrafe; **to agree upon liquidated ~** e-e Vertragsstrafe vereinbaren

damages, measure of ~ Höhe des Schadensersatzes; **nominal ~** nomineller *(nur symbolischer)* Schadensersatz *(opp. substantial ~)*; **prospective ~** Ersatz für zukünftigen Schaden; **punitive ~** *Am* →exemplary ~; **quantum of ~** Betrag des Schadensersatzes; **→unliquidated ~**

damages, to assess the ~ den Schadensersatz festsetzen; **to award the ~** auf Schadensersatz erkennen, den Schadensersatz zubilligen; **to be awarded** (or **to obtain**) ~ Schadensersatz erhalten, entschädigt werden; **to be liable for ~** schadensersatzpflichtig sein; **to claim ~** Schadensersatz beanspruchen; Schadensersatzansprüche geltend machen; ~ **were claimed against him** er wurde auf Schadensersatz in Anspruch genommen

damages, to pay ~ Schadensersatz leisten; **liable to pay ~** schadensersatzpflichtig; **to order to pay ~** zur Schadensersatzleistung verurteilen

damages, to recover ~ Schadensersatz erhalten, entschädigt werden; **to sue for ~** auf Schadensersatz klagen

damnification Beeinträchtigung, Schädigung

dampening of the uptrend in costs Dämpfung des Kostenauftriebs

Dane Däne, Dänin

Danish dänisch *(cf. Denmark)*

danger Gefahr (to für); Bedrohung, Risiko; ~ **area** Gefahrenzone; ~ **of absconding** Fluchtgefahr; ~ **of breakage** Bruchgefahr; ~ **of fire** Feuergefahr; ~ **of inflation** Inflationsgefahr; ~ **to life** Lebensgefahr; ~ **money** Gefahrenzulage; Angstgeld; ~ **zone** Gefahrenzone; **imminent ~** unmittelbar bevorstehende (od. drohende) Gefahr; **in case** (or **in the event**) **of ~** im Schadensfalle; **in case of imminent ~** bei Gefahr im Verzug; **there is a ~ that** es besteht Gefahr, daß; **to escape ~** der Gefahr entkommen; **to get into ~** in Gefahr geraten

dangerous gefährlich, gefahrvoll (to für); ~ **drugs** Rauschgifte; **carriage of ~ goods** Transport gefährlicher Güter (→*European Agreement Concerning the International Carriage of D~ Goods by Road*); ~ **substances** gefährliche Stoffe

data 1. Angaben, Daten, Unterlagen; **business** ~ Geschäftsunterlagen; **personal** ~ Personalangaben, Personalien; **statistical** ~ statistische Unterlagen; **sufficient ~ are available** es gibt genügend Unterlagen; **to furnish** ~ Angaben machen

data 2. *(EDV)* Daten, Informationen; ~ **abuse** Datenmißbrauch; ~ **bank** (or **base**) Datenbank; ~ **carrier** Datenträger; ~ **codification** Datenverschlüsselung

data collection Datenerfassung; **magnetic tape** ~ Datenerfassung auf Magnetband

data, ~ **communication** Datenübermittlung; ~ **decoding** Datenentschlüsselung; ~ **evaluation** Datenauswertung; ~ **exchange** Datenaustausch; ~ **files** Datenspeicher; ~ **gathering** Datenerfassung; ~ **input** Dateneingabe; ~ **liability** Datenverantwortlichkeit; Datenhaftung; ~ **medium** Datenträger; ~ **output** Datenausgabe; ~ **preparation** Datenaufbereitung

data processing Datenverarbeitung; Informatik; ~ **facilities** Datenverarbeitungsanlagen; **D~ P~ Management Association** (DPMA) *Am* Verband datenverarbeitender Unternehmen

data, ~ **protection** Datenschutz; **D~ Protection Act 1984** *Br* Datenschutzgesetz; ~ **recording** Datenaufzeichnung; ~ **register** Datenregister, Datenkartei; ~ **security** Datensicherung; ~ **sheet** statistische Tabelle; ~ **(storage) medium** Datenträger; ~ **subject**[1b] *(Datenschutzrecht)* Betroffener; ~ **telecommunication** Datenfernverbindung; ~ **theft** Informationsdiebstahl; ~ **transmission** Datenübertragung; **remote ~ transmission** Datenfernübertragung; ~ **user** Datenbenutzer

data, automated ~ file automatisierte Datei

Data, Convention for the Protection of Individuals with Regard to Automatic Processing of Personal ~[1b] Übereinkommen zum Schutz des Menschen bei der automatischen Verarbeitung personenbezogener Daten

data, encoding of ~ Datenverschlüsselung; **erasure of** ~ Löschung von Daten; **modification of** ~ Datenveränderung; **personal** ~ personenbezogene Daten; **personal ~ files**[1b] Dateien mit personenbezogenen Daten; **storage of** ~ Datenspeicherung; **stored** ~ gespeicherte Daten; →**transborder d~ flow**

data, to block ~ Daten sperren; **to collect** ~ Daten erfassen; **to process** ~ Daten verarbeiten; **to recall** ~ Daten abrufen; **to store** ~ Daten speichern

date Datum; Zeit(angabe, -punkt); Termin, Frist; Datumsangabe; ~ **of acceptance** Annahmetag; **(due) ~ of a bill** Fälligkeitstag e-s Wechsels; ~ **of birth** Geburtsdatum; ~ **of claim** Fälligkeitstag der Versicherungssumme; ~ **of delivery** Liefertermin; ~ **of dispatch** Versanddatum; Absendetag; ~ **draft** Dato-Wechsel; ~ **of expiry** Verfallstag; Zeitpunkt des Ablaufs *(z. B. e-s Abkommens)*; ~ **of filing** *(PatR)* Anmeldetag; ~ **of forwarding** Versanddatum; ~ **of interest due** Zinsfälligkeitstermin; ~ **of invoice** Rechnungsdatum; ~ **of issue** Emissionstag; Ausstellungsdatum; ~ **line** (internationale) Datumsgrenze *(180. Grad östl. von Greenwich)*

date of maturity Fälligkeitsdatum; Fälligkeitstag; Verfalltag; ~ **of a bill** (or **draft**) Fälligkeit(stag) e-s Wechsels

date, ~ **of payment** Zahlungstermin; ~ **as per postmark** Datum des Poststempels; ~ **of receipt** Eingangsdatum; Empfangsdatum; ~ **of shipment** Versandtermin; ~ **stamp** Tagesstempel, Datumsstempel; ~ **of trial** Verhandlungstermin

date, after ~ nach dato *(bestimmte Zeit nach Ausstellung e-s Wechsels; opp. on demand, after sight)*; **bill (payable) after** ~ Datowechsel

date, agreed ~ vereinbarter Termin; **as per** ~ bis zum heutigen Tag

date, bearing ~ datiert (vom); **bearing ~ 20th May** mit Datum vom 20. Mai; **bearing no** ~ undatiert

date, by this ~ bis zu diesem Termin; **by the set** ~ fristgemäß; **contract** ~ Tag des Vertragsabschlusses; **contract(ual)** ~ im Vertrag vorgesehenes Datum; **critical** ~ Stichtag (→*critical*); **due** ~ Fälligkeitsdatum, -termin, -tag; **at an earlier** ~ zu e-m früheren Termin; **at the earliest practicable** ~ sobald wie möglich; **at an early** ~ bald, in nächster Zeit; **effective** ~ Tag (od. Zeitpunkt) des Inkrafttretens *(e-s Gesetzes)*; **of even** ~ vom gleichen Tag, gleichen Datums; **final** ~ letzter Termin; **fixed** ~ (fester) Termin; **key** ~ Stichtag; **at a later** ~ zu e-m späteren Zeitpunkt; **at a long** ~ auf lange Sicht

date, out of ~ veraltet; überholt; unmodern; **the edition was out of** ~ die Ausgabe war veraltet; **to become out of** ~ veralten

date, of the same ~ vom gleichen Tag; gleichen Datums; **set** ~ Termin; **of this** ~ vom heutigen Datum; **interest to** ~ Zinsen bis heute

date, up to ~ bis heute; bis in die Gegenwart reichend; auf dem laufenden; zeitgemäß, modern; aktuell; **to be up to** ~ auf dem laufenden sein; **to bring up to** ~ auf den heutigen (od. neuesten) Stand bringen; **to keep up to** ~auf dem laufenden halten

date, without ~ undatiert, ohne Zeitangabe

date, to bear a ~ datiert sein; **to fix** (or **set**) **a** ~ e-e(n) Zeit(punkt) (od. Termin) festsetzen; **to insert the** ~ das Datum einsetzen; **to put a** ~ (to) befristen

date *v* datieren; datiert sein (von); veralten; **to ~ in advance** im voraus datieren; **to** →**ante~**; **to ~ back** zurückdatieren; zurückgehen (to auf), zurückreichen (to bis); **to mis~** falsch datieren; **to post~** →post 4.

dated datiert; mit Datum versehen; überholt, veraltet; **un**~ ohne Datum, nicht datiert; ~ **January 1** vom 1. Januar; **the letter is** ~ **March 1** der Brief ist vom 1. März datiert

dating Datierung; ~ **back** Rückdatierung; **ante**~ Vordatierung; Zurückdatierung; **post**~ Nachdatierung

dater *Am* Datumsstempel, Tagesstempel

dative, executor- ~ *Scot* vom Gericht ernannter →executor

datum gegebene Tatsache (od. Größe); Grundlage; ~ **quantity** Referenzmenge; **to establish** ~ **quantities** Referenzmengen festsetzen

daughter Tochter; ~**-in law** Schwiegertochter; **grand**~ Enkelin

dawn raid *Br* Übernahmetaktik (takeover tactic), mit der man Aktien e-s Unternehmens kauft *(der höchste Ankauf, ehe ein Übernahmeangebot obligatorisch wird)*

day Tag; Termin; ~ **of account** Abrechnungstag; ~**s after acceptance** (d/a) Tage nach Akzeptierung; ~**s after sight** →~s' sight; **the** ~ **before** der (od. am) Vortag; **the** ~ **before yesterday** vorgestern; ~ **bill** Tag(es)wechsel, Datumswechsel *(opp. bill after date)*; ~ **of birth** Tag der Geburt, Geburtstag; ~ **book** (d. b.) Journal *(der Buchführung)*, Grundbuch; ~ **in court** *Am* rechtliches Gehör; **a p.'s** ~ **in court** *Am* jds Erscheinen vor Gericht *(nach ordnungsgemäßer Ladung)*; ~**s' date** (or ~**s after date**) (d. d.) Tage nach dato; ~ **of death** Todestag; Sterbetag; ~ **of delivery** Liefertag; Ablieferungstermin; ~ **of entry** Einklarierungstag; ~**s of grace** *(WechselR)* Respekttage *(Br und Am [in einzelnen Staaten] 3 Respekttage)*; *(VersR)* Nachfrist; ~ **of hearing** Gerichtstag, Termin; ~ **of issue** Ausgabetag; Erscheinungstermin *(Wertpapiere)*; ~ **labo(u)rer** Arbeiter im Tageslohn

daylight, ~ **overdraft** *Am* Kontoüberziehung „tagsüber" *(sie muß am Ende desselben Arbeitstages gedeckt sein)*; ~ **saving time** Sommerzeit *(vorverlegte Stundenzählung)*; ~ **trading** *Am* An- und Verkauf von Wertpapieren am selben Tag; Leerverkauf, der am selben Tag gedeckt wird

day, ~ **loan** *Am* →morning loan; ~ **off** dienstfreier Tag; ~ **order** *Am (Börse)* Tagesauftrag; Auftrag, der nur einen Tag Gültigkeit hat; ~ **of payment** Zahlungstermin, Zahltag; ~**'s rate** Tagessatz; Tageslohn; *(Börse)* Tageskurs; ~**'s receipts** Tageseinnahmen; ~ **release** bezahlter Arbeitstag zur berufl. Fortbildung; ~**s of respite** *(bes. WechselR)* Respekttage; ~ **shift** Tagesschicht; ~**s' sight** (d. s.) Tage nach Sicht

day-to-day, ~ **business matters** laufende Geschäftsangelegenheiten; ~ **loan** (or **money**) *(Geldmarkt)* Tagesgeld

Day Wireless Bulletin (DWB) *Am* Presseagentur

daywork *Am* Tagesarbeit, Tagesschicht *(Arbeit, die nach festen Tages- od. Stundensätzen entlohnt wird; Ggs. Akkordlohn)*

day, on the appointed ~ fristgerecht; **calendar** ~**s** Kalendertage; **clear** ~**s** volle Tage *(bei Fristberechnung)*; **eight-hour** ~ Achtstundentag; **fixed** ~ festgesetzter Tag; Termin; **on a given** ~ an e-m bestimmten Tag; **pay** ~ Zahltag; *Br (Terminbörse)* Abrechnungstag; **settling** ~ *Br (Terminbörse)* Liquidationstag, Abrechnungstag; **this** ~ am heutigen Tage; heute; **this** ~ **fortnight** heute in 14 Tagen; **this** ~ **week** heute in 1 Woche; **(up) to this** ~ bis heute; **in these** ~**s** heutzutage; **work(ing)** ~ Werktag, Arbeitstag

day, to appoint (or **fix**) **a** ~ e-n Termin anberaumen; **to appoint a** ~ **for hearing** e-n Gerichtstermin anberaumen; **to take a** ~ **off** sich e-n Tag freinehmen; **to work by the** ~ gegen Tagelohn arbeiten

de bonis non (administratis) von nicht verwalteten Nachlaßgegenständen

de bonis propriis aus eigenem Vermögen; aus eigener Tasche

DC-Card Diners (Club) Card *(Kreditkarte)*

de facto tatsächlich (bestehend); de facto *(durch Tatsachen begründeter, noch nicht zu Recht bestehender Zustand, opp. de jure)*; ~ **corporation** *Am* Gesellschaft, die trotz des Bestehens von Mängeln im Gründungstatbestand als →corporation behandelt wird; faktische Gesellschaft; ~ **government** Defacto-Regierung; ~ **recognition** *(VölkerR)* De-facto-Anerkennung, vorläufige Anerkennung

de jure de jure, rechtlich (betrachtet) *(opp. de facto)*; ~ **corporation** *Am* ordnungsgemäß gegründete corporation *(opp. de facto corporation)*; ~ **recognition** *(VölkerR)* De-jure- (od. endgültige) Anerkennung

de lege ferenda vom Standpunkt einer zukünftigen Gesetzgebung aus

de lege lata vom Standpunkt des geltenden Rechts

dead tot, gestorben, verstorben; *com* still, flau; unproduktiv, unergiebig; ~ **account** umsatzloses (od. unbewegtes) Konto; ~ **assets** unproduktive (Kapital-)Anlagen; ~ **bargain** spottbilliger Preis; spottbillige Ware; ~ **body** Leiche; ~**(-)born** totgeboren; ~**(-)born child** Totgeburt; ~ **capital** totes (ungenutztes) Kapital; ~**-end** nicht weiterführend; Sackgasse; ~**-end job** Endstellung *(ohne weitere Beförderungsmöglichkeit)*; ~ **files** abgelegte Akten; ~ **freight** (d. f.) Leerfracht, Fehlfracht, Fautfracht *(an den Verfrachter zu zahlender Schadensersatz für unbenutzten Schiffsraum)*; ~**head** frei beförderte Person (od. Sache); Freikarteninhaber, blinder Passagier; *Am sl.* leerer Zug, leeres Taxi *(z. B. auf der Rückfahrt)*; **~head** *v Am sl.* auf ein totes Gleis abschieben; in der Beförderung *(wegen mangelnder Qualifikation)* übergehen

dead letter toter Buchstabe *(noch bestehendes, aber nicht angewandtes Gesetz)*; nicht zustellbarer Brief; ~ **office** Postabteilung für unzustellbare Briefe

deadline *(letzter)* Termin; *(äußerste)* Frist; Stichtag; Anzeigenschluß; Redaktionsschluß; ~ **for application** Anmeldeschluß; ~ **for denouncing an agreement** *(VölkerR)* Kündigungsfrist für e-n Vertrag; ~ **for loading** Verladeschluß; **the work has a** ~ die Arbeit ist an e-n Termin gebunden; **to exceed the** ~ den Termin überschreiten; **to meet a** ~ e-n Termin (od. e-e Frist) einhalten; **to meet the delivery** ~ den Liefertermin einhalten; **to let a** ~ **pass** e-e Frist verstreichen lassen

dead load Eigengewicht, Leergewicht

deadlock *(völliger)* Stillstand; Stockung; völliges Erliegen; ausweglose Situation; Sackgasse; **at a** ~ auf dem toten Punkt; festgefahren; **to break the** ~ den toten Punkt überwinden; **to find a way out of the** ~ e-n Ausweg aus der Sackgasse finden; **the negotiations came to** (or **reached**) **a** ~ die Verhandlungen hatten sich festgefahren (od. waren auf dem toten Punkt angelangt)

deadlock *v* zum Stillstand (od. völligen Erliegen) kommen; **negotiations ~ed** die Verhandlungen sind festgefahren

dead, ~ **loss** Totalverlust; ~ **money** totes Kapital; ~ **rent** *Br (BergR)* Mindestpacht, fester Pachtzins *(unabhängig vom Schürferfolg; cf. royalty rent)*; ~ **season** tote Saison, geschäftslose Zeit; ~ **stock** unverkäufliche Ware(nbestände); totes Inventar; ~ **time** *(betrieblich bedingte)* Verlustzeit; Wartezeit *(z. B. wegen Maschinenschadens, für die der Arbeiter in der Regel s-n Lohn erhält)*

deadweight (d. w.) *(Bezeichnung für)* Schwergutlade- od. Tragfähigkeit *(e-s Seeschiffes nach Abzug von Bunkermaterial, Proviant etc)*; Leergewicht, Eigengewicht; ~ **capacity** (d. w. c.) Tragfähigkeit, Ladefähigkeit *(e-s Schiffes)*; ~ **cargo** Schwergut *(opp. measurement goods)*; ~ **carrying capacity** (Schwergut-)Tragfähigkeit *(e-s Schiffes in Gewichtstonnen)*; Bruttoladefähigkeit; ~ **loading capacity** (Schwergut-)Lademöglichkeit *(e-s Schiffes in Gewichtstonnen)*; Nettoladefähigkeit; ~ **tonnage** →~ capacity

dead, to declare a p. (legally) ~ jdn (amtl.) für tot erklären *(→declaration of death)*

deadly weapon tödliche Waffe

deal *(abgeschlossenes)* Geschäft; (Geschäfts-)Abschluß; Abmachung; *colloq.* Handlungsweise, Verfahren; *Am sl.* unsauberes Geschäft, unsaubere Abmachung *(an der beide Parteien profitieren)*; ~ **on joint account** Metageschäft; **cash** ~ Bargeschäft; **fair** ~[2] anständige (od. faire) Handlungsweise; **foreign currency ~s** Devisengeschäfte; **a great** ~ *colloq.* sehr viel; **new** ~[3] Neubeginn *(Änderung zum Besseren)*; neuer Anfang *(zu fairem sozialen Verhalten)*; neuer Plan *(wirtschaftl. od. soziale Maßnahmen zur Verbesserung der Lage e-r Bevölkerungsschicht)*; **to effect exchange ~s in London** Abschlüsse auf Devisen in London tätigen; **to have** (or **to be given**) **a** ~ fair behandelt werden; **to make a** ~ *sl.* ein Geschäft abschließen; e-e Abmachung treffen

deal *v* 1., **to** ~ **with sth.** sich mit etw. befassen; etw. übernehmen (od. bearbeiten, erledigen); mit etw. fertig werden; von etw. handeln *(Buch etc)*; **to** ~ **with sb.** sich mit jdm befassen; sich jdm gegenüber verhalten; **to** ~ **with an application** ein Gesuch bearbeiten; **to** ~ **at arm's length with sb.** →arm 2.; **to** ~ **with a case** mit e-r Sache befaßt sein; **to** ~ **with difficulties** mit Schwierigkeiten fertig werden; **to** ~ **in politics** sich mit Politik befassen; **to** ~ **with a problem** sich mit e-m Problem auseinandersetzen

deal *v* 2. handeln, Handel treiben; **to** ~ **in sth.** mit etw. handeln; **to** ~ **in textiles** Textilien führen; **to** ~ **with sb.** mit jdm Geschäfte machen (od. in Geschäftsverbindung stehen); bei jdm kaufen; **to** ~ **on the stock exchange** Börsengeschäfte betreiben

dealt in, to be ~ gehandelt werden; **securities** ~ **on the stock exchange** an der Börse gehandelte Papiere

deal out *v* austeilen, verteilen

dealer Händler; *(Börse)* Wertpapierhändler, Eigenhändler; *(auch)* Drogenhändler; **~'s brand** Händlermarke; **~'s buyer** Wiederverkäufer; **~'s discount** Händlerrabatt; **~'s margin** Handelsspanne; ~ **organization** Händlerorganisation; Organisation von Handelsbetrieben; **~'s price** Wiederverkaufspreis; ~ **rebate** Händlerrabatt; ~ **in securities** Effektenhändler, Wertpapierhändler; ~ **in stocks** *Am* Effektenhändler; ~ **survey** *(Marktforschung)* Händlerbefragung

dealer, antique ~ Antiquitätenhändler; **authorized** ~ Vertragshändler; **cattle** ~ Viehhändler; **foreign exchange** ~ Devisenhändler; →**licensed** ~; **money** ~ Geldwechsler; Devisenhändler; **retail** ~ Einzelhändler; **second-hand** ~ Altwarenhändler; **wholesale** ~ Großhändler, Grossist

dealership contract *Am* Vertragshändlervereinbarung

dealing Verhalten(sweise) (with gegenüber); Geschäftsgebaren; Geschäftsverkehr; *Br* Effektenhandel; Handel (in mit); Geschäft; Abschluß; ~**s** Geschäfte; Transaktionen; Umsätze; Beziehungen; Verbindungen; Umgang; Geschäftsbeziehungen, -verbindungen; ~ **at** →**arm's length;** ~**s for the account** *Br (Börse)* Termingeschäfte; ~**s for cash** *(Börse)* Bargeschäfte, Kassageschäfte; ~ **for a fall** *(Börse)* Baissespekulation; ~ **for future delivery** *(Börse)* Termingeschäft, Fixgeschäft; ~**s for money** →~s for cash; ~ **for a rise** *(Börse)* Haussespekulation; ~**s for the settlement** → ~s for the account; ~**s in foreign exchange** Devisenhandel; ~**s in option** Prämiengeschäfte; ~**s in real estate** *bes. Am* Immobilienhandel; ~ **in securities** Wertpapierhandel; ~ **in shares** (*Am* **stocks**) Aktienhandel; ~ **out** Austeilen; Verteilung; **his** ~**s with subordinates** sein Umgang mit Untergebenen

dealing, business ~**s** Geschäftsverkehr; geschäftliche Transaktionen; **commercial** ~**s with** Geschäftsbeziehungen zu; **exclusive** ~ **contract** *Am* Ausschließlichkeitsvertrag *(Bezugsbindung von Käufern);* **fair** ~ redliches Verhalten; anständiges Geschäftsgebaren; Kulanz; Fairness; **few** ~**s** *(Börse)* wenig Umsätze; **foreign exchange** ~**s** Devisengeschäfte; **stock exchange** ~**s** Börsengeschäfte; **unofficial** ~**s** *(Börse)* Freiverkehr; ~**s are conducted at arm's length** die Geschäfte werden zwischen voneinander unabhängigen Personen geführt; **to have** ~**s with sb.** mit jdm in (Geschäfts-)Verbindung stehen; mit jdm etw. zu tun haben

dean *univ* Dekan; *eccl* Dechant; Superintendent; *Am dipl* Doyen; *Br* Hauptgeistlicher e-r Kathedrale; *Br univ* →fellow mit bestimmten Aufgaben; *Am univ* Vorsteher(in); **D~ of Arches** *Br* Laienrichter des →Court of Arches; **D~ of the Diplomatic Corps** Doyen des diplomatischen Corps; **D~ of Faculty** *Scot* Präsident der →Faculty of Advocates; **D~ of Guild** *Scot* Richter in bestimmten →burghs

deanery *eccl* Dekanat; **rural** ~ Landdekanat

dear teuer; hoch *(Preis);* ~ **money** teures Geld; **to be** ~ teuer sein, viel Geld kosten; ~**ly** teuer

dearer, to get ~ teurer werden, im Preise steigen

dearness hoher Preis; Kostspieligkeit

death Tod; Todesfall; Ableben; ~**s** Sterbefälle; ~ **by accident** Unfalltod; ~ **by** (or **from**) **drowning** Tod durch Ertrinken; ~ **by hanging** Tod durch den Strang

death bed declaration (confession), to make a ~ e-e Erklärung (ein Geständnis) auf dem Sterbebett machen

death benefit bei Todesfall fällige Versicherungsleistung; Sterbegeld *(Br cf. industrial death benefit for widows and other dependants);* ~**s fund** Sterbekasse; ~ **insurance** Sterbegeldversicherung

death, ~ **cell** Todeszelle; ~ **certificate** Sterbeurkunde, Totenschein; ~ **grant** *Br* Sterbegeld; ~ **notice** Todesanzeige; ~ **penalty**[4] Todesstrafe; ~ **rate** Sterblichkeitsziffer; ~ **risk** *(VersR)* Sterberisiko; ~ **roll** Verlustliste *(Krieg, Erdbeben etc)*

death sentence Todesurteil *(cf. death penalty);* **execution of the** ~ Vollstreckung des Todesurteils, Hinrichtung; **to carry out** (or **execute**) **a** ~ ein Todesurteil vollstrecken; **to impose** (or **pass**) **a** ~ **on sb.** gegen jdn auf Todesstrafe erkennen; jdn zum Tode verurteilen; **to reprieve sb. from the** ~ den zum Tode Verurteilten begnadigen

death statutes, wrongful ~ *Am* Gesetze, die Schadensersatzansprüche wegen schuldhaft verursachten Todes *(vorsätzlich od. fahrlässig)* e-s Menschen gewähren

death tax *Am* Erbschaftssteuer, Nachlaßsteuer

death warrant richterliche Anordnung der Vollstreckung e-s Todesurteils; Hinrichtungsbefehl

death, anniversary of sb.'s ~ jds Todestag *(Jahrestag);* **at sb.'s** ~ bei jds Tode; **cause of** ~ Todesursache; **certificate of** ~ Totenschein; Sterbeurkunde; **civil** ~ *Am (in einigen Staaten)* bürgerlicher Tod *(Verlust der Rechtsfähigkeit*[5]*);* **clinical** ~ klinischer Tod; **in contemplation of** ~ angesichts (od. in Erwartung) des Todes; **in danger of** ~ in Todesgefahr; **day of** ~ Todestag

death, declaration of ~ Todeserklärung *(durch das Gericht);* **Convention on the Declaration of D~ of Missing Persons** Konvention über die Todeserklärung Verschollener[6]

Großbritannien und die Vereinigten Staaten kennen weder eine Todes- noch eine Verschollenheitserklärung, nur eine Todesvermutung

death, in contemplation of ~ angesichts (od. in Erwartung) des Todes; **disposition in contemplation of** ~ Verfügung von Todes wegen

death, in the event of ~ im Todesfalle; **hour of** ~ Todesstunde; **impending** ~ bevorstehender Tod; **manner of** ~ Todesart; **natural** ~ natürlicher Tod *(opp. violent ~)*

death, on ~ beim Tode, im Todesfalle; **property passing on** ~ Vermögensübergang im Todesfalle; **on penalty of** ~ bei Todesstrafe

death, presumption of ~ Todesvermutung; **proof of** ~ Nachweis des Todes; **sentence of** ~ Todesurteil

death, sum payable at ~ Sterbegeld; **upon** ~ beim Tode, im Todesfalle; **violent** ~ gewaltsamer Tod *(opp. natural ~);* **wrongful** →~ **statutes**

death, to be burnt to ~ verbrennen; **to be sentenced to** ~ zum Tode verurteilt sein; **to die a natural** ~ e-s natürlichen Todes sterben; **to freeze to** ~ erfrieren; **to notify a** ~ e-n Todesfall (an)melden; **to starve to** ~ Hungers sterben; verhungern; **to starve sb. to ~** jdn verhungern lassen

debar *v* ausschließen (from von); hindern (from an); **to ~ from appearing before a court** *(e-m Anwalt)* das Auftreten vor Gericht versagen
debarred from succession von der Erbschaft ausgeschlossen

debase *v* entwerten, im Wert herabsetzen; *(Münzen)* verschlechtern

debasement of coinage Münzverschlechterung

debatable diskutierbar; fraglich, umstritten; **this is a ~ point** diese Frage ist umstritten

debate *(auch parl)* Debatte, Verhandlung, Aussprache, Diskussion, Beratung (on über); **the D~s** *parl* gedruckter Bericht; **D~ on the budget** *parl* Haushaltsdebatte; **~ on foreign policy** *parl* außenpolitische Debatte; **~ on social affairs** *parl* Sozialdebatte; **closure of the ~** Schluß der Debatte; **full dress ~** *Br* →full dress; **question in** (or **under**) **~** zur Diskussion stehende Frage
debate, to close the ~ die Debatte schließen; **to intervene in a ~** in e-e Debatte eingreifen; **to open the ~** die Debatte eröffnen; **to participate** (or **take part**) **in the ~** an der Debatte teilnehmen

debate *v* debattieren; beraten über; **to ~ with sb. on sth.** mit jdm über etw. debattieren; **to ~ a Bill on third reading** e-e Gesetzesvorlage in dritter Lesung beraten
debated, to be ~ zur Debatte stehen
debating society Debattierklub

debater Debattenredner, Diskussionsredner

debellation *(VölkerR)* Debellation *(völlige Besiegung)*

debenture (deb.) 1. Obligation, Schuldverschreibung *(e-r Handelsgesellschaft od. Br e-r öffentl. rechtl. Körperschaft); Br* Pfandbrief; Schuldschein, Schuldanerkenntnis
Br Der Begriff debenture bezeichnet eine ganze Kategorie von Schuldanerkenntnissen, wie Schuldschein, Obligation, die durch Pfandbestellung gesicherte Forderung und auch den Gesamtbetrag einer Anleihe *(vgl. Companies Act 1985 s. 744)*
debenture, ~ bond (or **certificate**) *Br* Schuldverschreibung, Obligation; **~ bonds** *Am (ungesicherte)* Obligationen; **~ capital** in Schuldverschreibungen angelegtes Kapital; Erlös aus dem Verkauf von Schuldverschreibungen; Anleihekapital; **~ debt** Obligationsschuld; *Br* Pfandbriefschuld; **~ holder** Inhaber e-r Schuldverschreibung, Obligationär; *Br* Pfandbriefinhaber; **~ issue** Emission von Schuldverschreibungen; Obligationsausgabe; **~ stock** *Br* Anleihekapital *(e-r juristischen Person od. Handelsgesellschaft) (Gesamtfonds des Anleihekapitals, an dem dem einzelnen Obligationär [holder] ein Bruchteil zusteht); (auch:)* (die einzelne) Schuldverschreibung (od. Obligation); *Am* Aktien mit Vorrang vor den Vorzugsaktien; **~ stock certificate** *Br* über e-e Anzahl von Schuldverschreibungen ausgestelltes Zertifikat; **~ trust deed** Treuhandurkunde über Schuldverschreibungen
debenture, bearer ~ Inhaberobligation, Inhaberschuldverschreibung; **fractional ~** Teilschuldverschreibung; **holder of a ~** →~ holder; **mortgage ~** *Br* (Hypotheken-)Pfandbrief; **naked ~** *Br* ungesicherte Schuldverschreibung; **participating ~** Gewinnschuldverschreibung; **railway ~** *Br* Eisenbahnobligation; **registered ~** *Br* auf den Namen lautende Schuldverschreibung; **to issue ~s** Schuldverschreibungen ausgeben
debenture 2. Rückzollschein *(cf. drawback);* **~ goods** Rückzollgüter

debentured goods Rückzollgüter

debit Debet, Soll; Sollseite *(linke Seite des Kontos; opp. credit);* Debetposten; Lastschrift; Belastung *(e-s Kontos);* → **pre-authorized ~; to the ~ of** zu Lasten von; **~ account** Debetkonto, Debitorenkonto; **~ advice** Belastungsanzeige, Lastschriftanzeige
debit balance Sollsaldo, Debetsaldo; *(Bilanz)* Verlustabschluß; **interest on ~s** Debetzinsen; **your ~** Saldo zu Ihren Lasten; **to show a ~** ein Debetsaldo aufweisen; passiv abschließen
debit, ~ card plastische Karte, die jds. Konto automatisch belastet bei Benutzung von Geldautomaten und automatisierten Kassensystemen (→ *point of sale terminal*); **~ entry** Debetbuchung, Sollbuchung; **~ interest** Sollzinsen *(e-r Bank);* **~ item** Debetposten, Passivposten; Lastschrift(posten); **~ memo(randum)** *Am* Belastungsanzeige; **~ note** (D/N) Belastungsanzeige, Lastschriftanzeige; **~ rate** Sollzinssatz
debit side Passivseite *(e-s Kontos);* **entry on the ~** Debetposten; **to be on the ~** im Debet stehen
debit, ~ to an account Belastung e-s Kontos; **~ transfer** Überweisung im Einzugsauftrag *(cf. direct debiting, automatic ~ transfer);* **~ voucher** Lastschriftbeleg
debit, to enter (or **place**) **an amount to the ~ of a p.'s account** jds Konto mit e-m Betrag belasten; **to pass** (or **put**) **an amount to a p.'s ~** (or **to the ~ of a p.**) jdn mit e-m Betrag belasten; jdm e-n Betrag in Rechnung stellen; e-n Betrag für jdn anschreiben

debit *v* belasten; *(Buchhaltung)* im Soll buchen *(opp. to credit);* **to ~ an account** ein Konto belasten; **to ~ directly** *(im Lastschriftverfahren)* abbuchen; **to ~ a p. with an amount** (or **to ~ an amount to a p.**) jdm e-n Betrag in Rechnung stellen; e-n Betrag für jdn anschreiben; jdn mit e-m Betrag belasten

debiting Belastung; Lastschrift; **direct** ~ Kontenbelastung durch Einzugsauftrag; Abbuchung auf Grund e-r Einzugsermächtigung

debt Schuld *(geschuldeter Betrag);* Forderung; ~ **adjustment** Umschuldung; ~ **balance** Debetsaldo; ~ **buy-backs** *(IMF)* Schuldenrückkäufe; ~ **capital** Fremdkapital; ~-**claim** e-r Schuld zugrundeliegende Forderung; ~ **collecting agency** Inkassobüro; ~ **collection** Einziehung von Forderungen; ~ **collector** Inkassobeauftragter; ~ **conversion** Schuldenumwandlung, Umschuldung; ~ **due** (from sb.) fällige Forderung; ~ **due to X** dem X geschuldeter Betrag; ~ **enforcement proceedings** Mahnverfahren; ~-**equity ratio** Verhältnis von Fremd- zu Eigenkapital; Verschuldungsgrad; ~-**equity swap** Transformation von Bankkrediten in Beteiligungskapital *(Schuldenproblem der Dritten Welt);* ~ **founded on bills** Wechselschuld; ~**s in foreign countries** Auslandsschulden; Auslandsverschuldung; ~ **limit** Verschuldungsgrenze; ~ **management** Handhabung von Schulden; Staatsschuldenpolitik; Maßnahmen der Schuldenstrukturpolitik; ~**s of a business enterprise** Geschäftsschulden; ~**s of the estate** Nachlaßschulden, Masseschulden *(im Konkurs);* ~**s of a firm** Geschäftsschulden; ~ **of hono(u)r** Ehrenschuld; ~ **of record** gerichtlich festgestellte Forderung; ~ **on mortgage** hypothekarische Schuld; ~ **owed by A. to B.** Forderung des B. an A.; ~**s owing and accruing** gegenwärtige und künftige Forderungen; ~**s provable in bankruptcy** im Konkurs anmeldbare Forderungen; anmeldbare Konkursforderungen; ~ **ratio** →~-equity ratio; ~**s receivable** Außenstände; ~ **recovery** Einziehung von Forderungen; ~ **redemption** Schuldentilgung; ~ **relief** Entschuldung; ~ **rescheduling** (or **restructuring**) Umschuldung; ~ **secured by a document** verbriefte Forderung, Briefschuld; ~ **secured by mortgage** hypothekarisch gesicherte Forderung; ~ **service** Schuldendienst; ~ **servicing difficulties** Schwierigkeiten *(e-s Landes)* bei der Schuldenrückzahlung; ~ **stocks** Schuldenbestand *(e-s Landes);* ~ **swap** Schuldentausch

debt, acknowledgement of ~ Schuldanerkenntnis

debt, action on a ~ Einklagung e-r Forderung; **to bring an action on a** ~ e-e Forderung einklagen

debt, active ~ zinstragende Schuld *(opp. passive ~);* **active** ~**s** ausstehende Forderungen, Außenstände; **amount of the** ~ geschuldeter Betrag; **assignment of a** ~ Forderungsabtretung; **assumption of** ~ Schuldübernahme; **attachment of a** ~ Forderungspfändung; **bad** ~**s** nicht beitreibbare Forderungen; **barred** ~ verjährte Forderung; **book** ~ Buchschuld, buchmäßige Schuld; **cancellation of a** ~ Streichung e-r Schuld; **civil** ~ privatrechtliche Schuld; **collection of** ~**s** Einziehung von Forderungen; Inkasso; **commercial** ~**s** Geschäftsschulden, Warenschulden; **company** ~**s** Gesellschaftsschulden; **consolidated** ~ konsolidierte (od. fundierte) Schuld *(opp. floating ~);* **conversion of a** ~ Umwandlung e-r Schuld; Umschuldung; **corporation** ~**s** *Am* Gesellschaftsschulden; **cost of** ~ Fremdkapitalkosten; **deferred** ~ *(im Rang)* nachgehende Konkursforderung; **discharge of a** ~ Tilgung e-r Schuld; Schuldentilgung; **doubtful** ~ zweifelhafte Forderung; **doubtful** ~**s** Dubiosen; **due** ~ fällige Forderung

debt, external ~**s** Auslandsschulden; Auslandsverschuldung; **Agreement on German External D**~**s** Abkommen über deutsche Auslandsschulden (Londoner Schuldenabkommen von 1953)[7]

debt, floating ~ schwebende Schuld; **foreign** ~ →external ~; **free from** ~ schuldenfrei; **frozen** ~**s** eingefrorene Forderungen; Stillhalteschulden; **funded** ~ fundierte Schuld; Anleiheschuld *(opp. unfunded ~);* **in** ~ verschuldet; **internal** ~**s** Inlandsschulden; **involved in** ~**s** verschuldet; **judgment** ~ →judgment; **liability for** ~**s** Schuldenhaftung; **liquidation of** ~**s** Schuldentilgung; **long-term** ~ langfristige Schuld; **money** ~ Geldschuld; **national** ~ Staatsschuld (→*national*); **outstanding** ~**s** Außenstände; **partnership** ~**s** Gesellschaftsschulden; Firmenschulden; **passive** ~ nicht zinstragende Schuld *(opp. active ~);* **payment of** ~**s** Bezahlung von Schulden; Schuldenbegleichung; **in payment of a** ~ zur Begleichung e-r Schuld; **preferential** (or **privileged**) ~ bevorrechtigte Forderung *(Recht auf vorzugsweise Befriedigung, bes. im Konkurs);* **proof of** ~ Anmeldung e-r Konkursforderung; Nachweis e-r Forderung (→*proof 2.*); **provable** ~ *(im Konkurs)* anmeldbare Forderung; **public** ~ *Am* öffentliche Schuld, Staatsschuld; **recoverable** ~ beitreibbare Forderung; **recovery of a** ~ Eintreibung e-r Forderung; **remission of a** ~ Schulderlaß; **retainer of** ~**s** →retainer 2.; **running into** ~ Verschuldung; **secured** ~ gesicherte Forderung; **settlement of** ~**s** Schuldenregelung; Bezahlung von Schulden; **short term** ~ kurzfristige Schuld; →**simple contract** ~**s**; **specialty** ~**s** →specialty 2.; **statute-barred** ~ verjährte Forderung; **suit for a** ~ *Am* Einklagung e-r Forderung; **total** ~ Gesamtschuld; **unfunded** ~ *Br* unfundierte (od. schwebende) *(öffentliche)* Schuld *(opp. funded ~);* **unsecured** ~ nicht gesicherte Forderung; **war** ~**s** Kriegsschulden; **without** ~**s** schuldenfrei

debt, to accept responsibility for the ~**s incur-**

red by one's wife für die Schulden seiner Frau einstehen; **to acknowledge a** ~ e-e Forderung anerkennen; **to assign a** ~ e-e Forderung abtreten; **to attach a** ~ e-e Forderung pfänden; **to be in** ~ verschuldet sein, Schulden haben; **to be in** ~ **to sb.** jdm etw. schulden; **to be out of** ~ schuldenfrei sein; keine Schulden (mehr) haben; **to collect a** ~ e-e Forderung einziehen (od. beitreiben); **to contract** ~**s** Schulden machen; **to get in** ~**s** in Schulden geraten; **to get out of** ~**s** seine Schulden loswerden; sich schuldenfrei machen; **to incur** ~**s** s. to contract →~s; **to liquidate a** ~ e-e Schuld tilgen; **to make over a** ~ e-e Forderung abtreten; **to pay one's** ~**s** seine Schulden bezahlen; **to prove a** ~ e-e Forderung nachweisen (od. belegen); **to prove a** ~ **(in bankruptcy)** e-e Forderung im Konkurs anmelden; **to recover a** ~ e-e Forderung beitreiben (od. einziehen) *(Br cf. default summons)*; **to settle a** ~ e-e Schuld begleichen; **to run up** ~**s** Schulden anwachsen lassen; **to sue for (the recovery of) a** ~ e-e Forderung einklagen

debtor Schuldner(in) *(opp. creditor)*; Darlehnsnehmer, Kreditnehmer; *(Buchführung)* (Dr.) Debet(seite), Soll; ~**s** *(Bilanz)* Debitoren, Forderungen; ~ **account** Debetkonto; ~ **for the balance (of an account)** Schuldner e-s Restbetrages; ~ **country** Schuldnerland; ~**'s default** Schuldnerverzug; ~ **in default** in Verzug befindlicher Schuldner; ~ **by endorsement** Giroschuldner; ~ **executor** zum Erbschaftsverwalter (→*executor*) bestellter Schuldner des Erblassers; ~**'s ledger** Debitorenbuch; ~ **on mortgage** Hypothekenschuldner; ~ **nation** Schuldnerland; ~**'s petition** Antrag auf Konkurseröffnung durch den Schuldner; ~**'s property** Schuldnervermögen; ~ **relief** Entschuldung

debtor side Sollseite, Debetseite; **to be on the** ~ im Soll stehen

debtor, bill ~ Wechselschuldner; **bond** ~ Obligationsschuldner; Pfandbriefschuldner; **default of the** ~ Schuldnerverzug; **defaulting** ~ säumiger Schuldner; **execution** ~ Vollstreckungsschuldner; **joint** ~ gemeinsamer Schuldner, Mitschuldner (→*joint*); **judgment** ~ Urteilsschuldner; Vollstreckungsschuldner; **primary** ~ Erstschuldner; **secondary** ~ Zweitschuldner; **sundry** ~**s** *(Bilanz)* verschiedene Debitoren (od. Forderungen)

decade Dekade; Jahrzehnt; Zeitraum von 10 Jahren

decartelization Entkartellisierung; (Konzern-)Entflechtung

decartelize *v* entkartellisieren, entflechten

decasualization Überführung von Gelegenheitsarbeit in Dauerarbeit; Umstellung auf Dauerbeschäftigung *(von →casual labo[u]r)*

decay, the house is in ~ das Haus ist verfallen

decease *(jds)* Tod, Ableben

deceased (decd.) verstorben; **the** ~ **(person)** der/die Verstorbene; Erblasser(in); **X** ~ der verstorbene X; ~**'s estate** (or **estate of a** ~ **[person]**) Nachlaß

decedent *Am* der/die Verstorbene; *(mit od. ohne Testament verstorbene[r])* Erblasser(in); ~**'s estate** Nachlaß; ~ **estate law** *Am (New York)* Erbrecht

deceit Täuschung; Irreführung; Betrug; arglistige Täuschung

deceitful betrügerisch

deceive *v* täuschen; irreführen; betrügen; **intention to** ~ betrügerische Absicht

deceleration lane Verzögerungsstreifen

decentralization Dezentralisierung, Dezentralisation

decentralize *v* dezentralisieren

decenc|y Anstand, Schicklichkeit; ~**ies** Anstandsformen

deception Täuschung; Irreführung; Betrug

deceptive täuschend, irreführend; ~ **advertising** täuschende Reklame; ~ **trade mark** irreführendes Warenzeichen; ~ **practices** betrügerische (Geschäfts-)Praktiken

decide *v* entscheiden; sich entscheiden, sich entschließen, beschließen (on über); erkennen; *(VölkerR) (Empfehlungen)* beschließen; *(rechtsverbindliche)* Beschlüsse fassen; **the judge** ~**d for** (or **in favo[u]r of**) **the plaintiff** der Richter entschied für den Kläger; **the judge** ~**d against the plaintiff** der Richter entschied gegen den Kläger; **to** ~ **a case** e-n Fall entscheiden; in e-r (Rechts-)Sache entscheiden; **to** ~ **a point of law** e-e Rechtsfrage entscheiden; **to** ~ **on the record** nach Aktenlage entscheiden; **to** ~ **provisionally** vorläufig beschließen; **to** ~ **unanimously** einstimmig beschließen

decided entschieden, bestimmt; entschlossen; ~ **opinion** entschiedene Meinung; **having** ~ entschlossen, in dem Entschluß

decimal, ~ **coinage** (or **currency**) Dezimalwährung; ~ **pound** *Br* Dezimalpfund; ~ **system** Dezimalsystem

decimalization *Br*[8] Umstellung auf das Dezimalsystem

decimalize *v* dezimalisieren

decipher *v* entziffern; *(Geheimschrift)* dechiffrieren

decipherable entzifferbar

decision Entscheidung; Beschluß; Entschluß; Bescheid; *(Zivilprozeß)* Urteil; ~ **appealed from** (or **complained of**) die angefochtene Entscheidung; ~**-maker** jd, der Entscheidungen trifft; Entscheidungsträger

decision-making Entscheidungs-; beschließend; Fällen von Entscheidungen; Entscheidungsfindung; Beschlußfassung; ~ **power** Entscheidungsbefugnis; ~ **unit** (DMU) Entscheidungsinstanz; **share in** ~ Mitspracherecht

decision, ~ of the court gerichtliche Entscheidung; Urteil; ~ **of the court below** (angefochtene) Entscheidung der unteren Instanz; ~ **of the majority** Mehrheitsbeschluß; ~ **on appeal** →appeal 1.; ~ **on costs** Entscheidung über die Kosten; ~ **on the merits** Sachentscheidung; ~ **set aside** Entscheidung *(durch Rechtsmittelinstanz)* aufgehoben; ~ **subject to appeal** *(PatR)* beschwerdefähige Entscheidung; ~ **support system** (DSS) Entscheidungsunterstützungssystem *(computergestütztes Planungs- und Informationssystem)*; ~ **supported by reasons** mit Gründen versehene Entscheidung; ~**-taker** Entscheidungsträger; ~**-taking bodies** Entscheidungsgremien; ~ **to invest** Investitionsentscheidung

decision, court ~ gerichtliche Entscheidung, Urteil; **discretionary** ~ Ermessensentscheidung; **final** ~ endgültige Entscheidung; Endurteil; **grounds of the** ~ Entscheidungsgründe; **judicial** ~ gerichtliche Entscheidung, Urteil; **leading** ~ grundsätzliche *(gerichtl.)* Entscheidung *(über e-e Rechtsfrage)*; **power of** ~ Entscheidungsgewalt; Entscheidungsbefugnis; **preliminary** ~ Vor(ab)entscheidung, vorläufige Entscheidung; **provisional** ~ vorläufige Entscheidung; vorläufiger Bescheid; **reasoned** ~ mit Gründen versehene Entscheidung; **taking of** ~**s** Beschlußfassung

decision, to appeal from a ~ gegen e-e Entscheidung ein Rechtsmittel *(Berufung etc)* einlegen; **to arrive at**(or **come to**) **a** ~ zu e-r Entscheidung kommen, sich entscheiden; **to cancel a** ~ e-n Beschluß aufheben; **to give a** ~ **on a case** e-e Sache entscheiden; **to make a** ~ s. to reach a →~; **to pass a** ~ e-e Entscheidung fällen; *(gerichtlich)* entscheiden (on über); **to postpone a** ~ e-e Entscheidung *(etc)* vertagen; to reach a ~ e-e Entscheidung treffen; entscheiden; e-n Entschluß fassen; beschließen; **to refer for** ~ zur Entscheidung vorlegen; **to rescind a** ~ e-e Entscheidung aufheben; e-n Beschluß für nichtig erklären; **to reverse the** ~ **of a lower court** die Entscheidung der unteren Instanz aufheben; **to reserve one's** ~ sich die Entscheidung vorbehalten; **to submit for** ~ zur Entscheidung vorlegen; **to submit to a** ~ sich mit e-r Entscheidung abfinden; **to take a** ~ s. to reach a →~; **to uphold the** ~ die Entscheidung aufrechterhalten (od. bestätigen)

decisive entscheidend, ausschlaggebend (for für); ~ **date** (or **day**) Stichtag; ~ **vote** ausschlaggebende Stimme

declarant der/die Erklärende; jd, der e-e Erklärung *(Br bes. statutory →declaration)* abgibt; *Am* Anwärter auf die Staatsbürgerschaft (→ *declaration of intention)*; **customs** ~ Zolldeklarant, Zollanmelder

declaration 1. *(förml.)* Erklärung; *Am* Klageschrift *(im common law-Prozeß)*; *Am (feierliche)* Zeugenaussage an Stelle des Eides *(auf die die Strafbestimmungen von →perjury Anwendung finden)*; Versicherung an Eides Statt *(Br →statutory ~)*; *Am* Einkommensteuererklärung *(betr. das mutmaßliche Einkommen des kommenden Jahres)*; *(VersR)* Angabe *(des Wertes)*; *(VölkerR)* Deklaration; ~ **above the value** zu hohe Wertangabe; ~ **against interest** *(als indirekter Beweis zugelassene)* Erklärung (die jd. gegen seine eigenen Interessen gemacht hat); ~ **in lieu of oath** *Br* s. statutory →~; ~ **of accession** *(VölkerR)* Beitrittserklärung *(zum bestehenden Vertrag)*; ~ **of assignment** Abtretungserklärung; ~ **of bankruptcy** Konkurserklärung, Konkurseröffnung; ~ **of consent** Zustimmungserklärung; ~ **of death** *(gerichtl.)* Todeserklärung (→*death*); ~ **of defaulters** *Br* Erklärung des Börsenvorstandes *(gegen ein Börsenmitglied, das seinen Verpflichtungen nicht nachgekommen ist)*; ~ **of a dividend** Dividendenerklärung, Festsetzung e-r Dividende; ~ **of inability to pay debts** Erklärung der Zahlungseinstellung *(als Konkursgrund)*; ~ **of income** Einkommensteuererklärung *(Br für den Inspector of Taxes)*; **D**~ **of Independence** *Am* Unabhängigkeitserklärung *(4. 7. 1776)*; ~ **of intent(-ion)** Willenserklärung; Absichtserklärung; *Am*[9] Erklärung des Einwanderers, daß er amerikanischer Staatsbürger werden will; ~ **of legitimacy** Ehelichkeitserklärung (→*legitimacy*); ~ **of majority** Volljährigkeitserklärung; ~ **of membership** Beitrittserklärung; ~ **of option** (to buy or sell securities) *(Börse)* Prämienerklärung; **D**~ **of Paris** Pariser Seerechtsdeklaration *(von 1856)*; ~ **of policy** Absichtserklärung; ~ **of principle** Grundsatzerklärung; ~ **of property** Vermögensanmeldung; ~ **of reciprocity** Gegenseitigkeitserklärung; ~ **of solvency** *Br* Liquidationserklärung *(bei Gesellschaftsauflösung)*; ~ **of suretyship** Bürgschaftserklärung; ~ **of trust** *(schriftl.)* Begründung e-s Treuhandverhältnisses; ~ **of value** Angabe des Wertes, Wertangabe; ~ **of war** Kriegserklärung; ~ **policy** *(Seevers.)* Pauschalpolice, offene Police; Abschreibepolice; ~ **under the value** zu niedrige Wertangabe; **to make a** ~ e-e Erklärung abgeben; *Am* e-e (Zeugen-)Aussage machen

declaration, statutory ~ *Br*[10] schriftliche eidesstattliche Versicherung; Versicherung an Eides Statt; **making a false statutory** ~ Abgabe e-r falschen eidesstattlichen Versicherung

Die vor einem justice of the peace od. einem Com-

missioner for Oaths abzugebende statutory declaration dient der Vermeidung des häufigen Gebrauches des Eides in außergerichtlichen Verfahren. Im Gegensatz zum deutschen Recht (§ 156 StGB) steht sie unter den Strafbestimmungen des Meineides *(cf. affirmation)*.
Form der statutory declaration: "I, A. B., do solemnly and sincerely declare that . . . and I make this solemn declaration conscientiously believing the same to be true and by virtue of the Statutory Declarations Act, 1835"

declaration 2., **(customs)** ~ Zolldeklaration, Zollerklärung; Zollanmeldung; ~ **of contents** Inhaltsangabe, Inhaltserklärung; ~ **inwards** *Br* (Zoll-)Einfuhrdeklaration; ~ **outwards** *Br* (Zoll-)Ausfuhrdeklaration; **to make a** ~ e-e Zollerklärung abgeben

declarator, action of ~ *Scot* Feststellungsklage

declaratory deklaratorisch *(opp. constitutive)*; (rechts)erklärend, feststellend; ~ **judgment** (or **decree**) Feststellungsurteil; ~ **part of a judgment** rechtliche Begründung e-s Urteils; **action for** ~ **judgment** Feststellungsklage; ~ **statute** Ausführungsgesetz *(das den bisherigen Rechtszustand nicht ändern, sondern nur klarstellen will)*

declare *v* erklären, e-e Erklärung abgeben; *(über etw.)* aussagen; *Br* an Eides Statt versichern; *(Wert)* angeben; zur Verzollung anmelden, verzollen; **to** ~ **oneself a bankrupt** seinen Konkurs anmelden; **to** ~ **sth. at the customs** etw. beim Zoll anmelden; **to** ~ **a person (legally) dead** jdn für tot erklären; **to** ~ **oneself disqualified on the ground of bias** sich für befangen erklären; **to** ~ **a dividend** e-e Dividende festsetzen (od. beschließen); **to** ~ **due** für fällig erklären; **to** ~ **one's income** *Br* sein Einkommen *(für Steuerzwecke)* angeben; **to** ~ **one's insolvency** sich für zahlungsunfähig erklären; **to** ~ **one's interest** →interest 1.; **to** ~ **the meeting closed** die Sitzung für geschlossen erklären; die Sitzung schließen; **to** ~ **the result of the election** das Wahlergebnis bekanntgeben; **to** ~ **a right** durch Feststellungsurteil feststellen; **to** ~ **a strike** e-n Streik ausrufen; **to** ~ **a state of emergency** den Ausnahmezustand verhängen; **to** ~ **oneself (to be) the successor** sich zum Nachfolger erklären; **to** ~ **a trust** ein Treuhandverhältnis begründen; **to** ~ **the value** den Wert angeben (od. deklarieren) (at the customs house beim Zollamt); **to** ~ **war (up)on a country** e-m Land den Krieg erklären; **to** ~ **one's willingness** s-e Bereitwilligkeit erklären; sich bereit erklären

declared offen erklärt (od. angegeben); zollamtlich erklärt, deklariert; ~ **abstention** angegebene Stimmenenthaltung; ~ **capital** festgesetztes Kapital; ~ **value** angegebener Wert, Wertangabe

declassification Freigabe aus der Geheimhaltung *(opp. classification 2.)*

declassify *v* Geheimmaterial freigeben; von der Geheimhaltungsliste streichen

declinature *Scot* Ablehnung *(e-s Richters wegen Befangenheit)*

decline Abnahme, Rückgang, Niedergang, Verfall; ~ **in the birth rate** Geburtenrückgang

decline of (or **in**) **business** Rückgang des Geschäfts, Geschäftsrückgang; **general** ~ allgemeiner Geschäftsrückgang (→*recession*)

decline, ~ **in demand** Nachfragerückgang; ~ **in economic activity** Konjunkturabschwächung; ~ **in exports (imports)** Rückgang der Ausfuhr (Einfuhr); ~ **in investment** Investitionsrückgang; ~ **in prices** Rückgang der Preise; Kursrückgang; ~ **in production** Produktionsrückgang; ~ **in sales** Rückgang des Absatzes (od. Umsatzes); ~ **in social position** sozialer Abstieg; ~ **in stock prices** Aktienkursverfall; ~ **in value** Wertminderung; ~ **of democracy** Niedergang der Demokratie; ~ **of the dollar** Rückgang des Dollar; ~ **list** *(VersR)* Verzeichnis der abzulehnenden Risiken; ~ **of an offer** Ablehnung e-s Angebots

decline, to be on the ~ zurückgehen; fallen *(Preise, Kurse)*; im Rückgang (od. Abnehmen) begriffen sein; **to experience** (or **suffer**) **a** ~ e-n Rückgang erfahren

decline *v* abnehmen, zurückgehen; rückläufig sein; fallen, sinken *(Preise, Kurse)*; *(Angebot etc)* ablehnen; *(Börse)* nachgeben; verfallen, in Verfall geraten; **to** ~ **an invitation** e-e Einladung absagen; **to** ~ **an offer** ein Angebot ablehnen; **to** ~ **responsibility** die Verantwortung (od. Haftung) ablehnen

declined, the deficit ~ das Defizit ging zurück; **stock prices** ~ die Aktienkurse gingen zurück (od. fielen)

declining zurückgehend, rückläufig; *(Börse)* nachgebend *(geringe Neigung zu Kurssenkungen)*

declining balance, ~ **depreciation** *(Am)* degressive Abschreibung, Buchwertabschreibung; ~ **method** degressives Abschreibungsverfahren *(Abschreibung in fallenden Jahresbeträgen; opp. straight-line method)*; **double rate** ~ *Am*[11] degressive Doppelsatzabschreibung

declining, ~ **economic activity** abklingende Konjunktur; ~ **industrial regions** im Niedergang befindliche Industriegebiete; ~ **market** fallende (Aktien-)Kurse; ~ **sales** Absatzrückgang

decode *v* dechiffrieren, entschlüsseln

decoding Dechiffrierung, Entschlüsselung

decolonialization Entkolonialisierung

decolonize *v* entkolonialisieren

decommission *v (Kernkraftwerk)* außer Betrieb setzen

decommissioning of nuclear power plants Stilllegung von Kernkraftwerken

deconcentrate *v Am* dekonzentrieren, dezentralisieren; entflechten

deconcentration *Am* Dekonzentration, Dezentralisierung; Entflechtung

decontaminate *v* entgiften, entseuchen, entgasen *(cf. to contaminate)*

decontamination Dekontaminierung; Entgiftung, Entseuchung, Entgasung *(cf. contamination)*

decontrol Aufhebung der *(staatl.)* Kontrolle; Beendigung der Zwangswirtschaft; Freigabe *(der Ware)*; ~ **of imports** Liberalisierung der Einfuhr

decontrol *v (staatl.)* Kontrolle (od. Zwangswirtschaft) *(bes. in Kriegszeiten)* aufheben; aus der Bewirtschaftung (od. Zwangswirtschaft) herausnehmen; *(Ware, Mieten etc)* freigeben

decontrolled nicht mehr bewirtschaftet, frei; liberalisiert

decorate *v* dekorieren; *(mit Orden etc)* auszeichnen

decoration Dekorierung; Orden, Ehrenzeichen; **D~ Day** *Am* →Memorial Day; **(repairs for) interior** ~ Schönheitsreparaturen; **to award a** ~ e-e Auszeichnung (od. e-n Orden) verleihen

decoy Köder; Spitzel; *mil* Scheinanlage; ~ **(ship)** U-Boot-Falle

decoy *v* ködern, (ver)locken; **to ~ sb. across the frontier** jdn über die Grenze locken

decrease Abnahme, Verminderung, Verringerung, Rückgang (in an) *(opp. increase)*; ~ **in capital** *(GesellschaftsR)* Kapitalherabsetzung; ~ **in consumption** Verbrauchsrückgang; ~ **in crime** Rückgang der Kriminalität; ~ **in demand** Nachfragerückgang, -abnahme; ~ **in output** Leistungsrückgang; Produktionsrückgang; ~ **in population** Bevölkerungsrückgang, -abnahme; ~ **in prices** (or **in the price of**) Preisrückgang, Rückgang im Preise; ~ **in the receipts** Rückgang der Einnahmen; Mindereinnahmen; ~ **in risk(s)** *(VersR)* Gefahrverminderung; ~ **in speed** Geschwindigkeitsverminderung; ~ **in turnover** Umsatzrückgang; ~ **in** (or **of**) **value** Wertminderung; **on the** ~ in der Abnahme begriffen, im Abnehmen

decrease *v* abnehmen, sich verringern; zurückgehen, abflauen; reduzieren, herabsetzen

decreased, the population has ~ by die Bevölkerung hat abgenommen um

decreasing, ~ **returns to scale** →diseconomies of scale; **to be** ~ im Rückgang (od. Abnehmen) begriffen sein

decree Urteil *(Am in equity, admiralty, probate and divorce-Sachen)*; *(richterl.)* Verfügung; *(amtl.)* Verordnung; Erlaß; *Scot (Zivilprozeß)* Urteil; ~ **in absence** *Scot* Versäumnisurteil; ~ **absolute** (of dissolution of marriage or of divorce) *Br*[12] rechtskräftiges Scheidungsurteil; ~ **arbitral** *Scot* Schiedsspruch; ~ **in bankruptcy** Konkurseröffnungsbeschluß; ~ **conform** *Scot* Urteilsbestätigung *(durch den →Court of Sessions)*; ~ **of constitution** *Scot* Feststellungsurteil; ~ **dative** *Scot* Ernennung e-s Testamentsvollstreckers (→*executor*) durch das Gericht; ~ **nisi** (of dissolution of marriage or of divorce) vorläufiges *(noch nicht rechtskräftiges)* Scheidungsurteil *(Br das erst mit Ablauf von 6 Wochen auf Antrag e-r Partei durch gerichtl. Verfügung „absolute" wird, es sei denn, daß das Gericht e-e kürzere Frist festsetzt)*; ~ **nisi for foreclosure** gerichtl. Verfügung, nach der alle Rechte des Schuldners *(auch die Rechte e-s späteren Gläubigers)* am verpfändeten Grundstück auf den Gläubiger übergehen, wenn Schuldner oder späterer Gläubiger die Hypothek nicht innerhalb e-r bestimmten Frist ablöst; ~ **of nullity** Ehenichtigkeitsurteil; ~ **of restitution of conjugal rights**[13] Urteil auf Wiederherstellung der ehelichen Lebensgemeinschaft

decree, to issue a ~ e-e Verfügung erlassen; e-n Erlaß herausgeben; **to make** (or **pronounce**) **a** ~ ein (Scheidungs-)Urteil erlassen; **to order by** ~ durch Gerichtsbeschluß verfügen

decree *v* richterlich verfügen (od. anordnen); *(amtlich)* verfügen

decrement Verringerung, Abnahme, Abgang; **table of ~s** *(VersR)* Ausscheidetafel *(deaths, surrender etc)*

decretal *eccl* Dekretale *(päpstliche Entscheidung)*; ~ **epistle** Dekretalbrief

decrypt *v Am* entschlüsseln

decryptment *Am* Entschlüsselung

dedicate *v* widmen; *(Kirche etc)* einweihen; zur öffentlichen Benutzung übergeben; *Am (feierlich)* eröffnen; **to ~ a highway** e-e Straße dem öffentlichen Verkehr übergeben; **to ~ to the public** *Am (auf Patente etc)* zugunsten der Allgemeinheit verzichten

dedication Widmung; Einweihung *(z.B. e-r Kirche)*; *Am (feierl.)* Eröffnung; Übergabe *(z.B. e-s privaten Weges)* zur öffentlichen Benutzung

deduce *v* herleiten (from von); folgern, schließen (from aus)

deduct *v (etw.)* abziehen, in Abzug (od. Abrechnung) bringen, abrechnen; *(Betrag)* einbehalten; *(von der Steuer)* absetzen; folgern; **to ~ as depreciation** *(SteuerR) (wegen Abnutzung etc)* absetzen; **to ~ one's expenses** seine Unkosten abziehen (od. abrechnen); **to ~ an item** e-n (Rechnungs-)Posten abziehen (od. in Abzug bringen); e-n (Buchungs-)Posten abbuchen; **to ~ from the wages** vom Lohn einbehalten (od. abziehen); **to be able to ~ sth. from one's taxable income** etw. steuerlich absetzen können

deducted abzüglich; **all expenses ~** abzüglich (od. nach Abzug) aller Unkosten; **tax ~** nach Abzug der Steuern; **tax ~ at the source** Quellensteuer

deducting, after ~ nach Abzug von; **~ expenses** abzüglich der (Un-)Kosten

deductible abzugsfähig; *(von der Steuer)* absetzbar; **~ (franchise)** *Am (Kraftfahrversicherung)* Abzugsfranchise *(Teil des Schadens, den Versicherter selbst zahlen muß)*; Selbstbehalt; **~ expenditures** *Am* (**expenses** *Br*) *(SteuerR)* abzugsfähige Ausgaben

deduction 1. Abzug (from von); abgezogener Betrag; Einbehaltung; Nachlaß, Rabatt; **~ in advance** Vorwegabzug; **~ from the price** Preisnachlaß; **~ from salary** Gehaltsabzug; Einbehaltung vom Gehalt; **~ of £100 from (the) salary** Abzug von £ 100 vom Gehalt; **~ of →union dues from wages**; **payroll ~s** *Am* →payroll; **to make ~ of interest** Zinsen in Abzug bringen; **to retain ~s** Abzüge *(vom Lohn)* einbehalten

deduction 2. *(SteuerR)* Abzug; Absetzung *(von der Steuer)*; **~s** *(zulässige)* Steuerabzüge, Abzugsbeträge; abzugsfähige Aufwendungen *(z.B. Werbungskosten, Betriebsausgaben)*; *Am* Freibeträge; **~ for depletion** Absetzung für Substanzverringerung; **~ for depreciation** *(e.g. loss of value due to age)* Absetzung für Abnutzung (AfA) *(z.B. Wertverfall durch Altern)*; **~ for exemption** *Am (zulässiger)* (Steuer-)Abzug; **~ for expenses** *Br* Abzug für Geschäftsauslagen *(Büromiete, Gehälter etc)*; **~ of input tax** *Br (VAT)* Vorsteuerabzug; **~ of tax at source** Steuerabzug an der Quelle, Quellenbesteuerung *(die Quellensteuer wird von der Stelle, bei der das Einkommen des Steuerpflichtigen entsteht, einbehalten und direkt an das Finanzamt abgeführt)*

deduction, admitted as ~ *(von der Steuer)* abzugsfähig; **itemized ~** *Am* Einzelabzug; **→marital ~; standard ~** *Am (abzugsfähiger)* Pauschalbetrag (→*standard* 1.); **statutory ~s** gesetzliche Steuerabzüge; **~s are allowed for** abzugsfähig ist/sind

deduction 3. Schlußfolgerung, Deduktion *(opp. induction)*; **to draw ~s** Schlußfolgerungen ziehen

deed gesiegelte *(dem Vertragsgegner zu übergebende)* Urkunde *(durch die ein Recht od. Vermögen übertragen od. e-e Verpflichtung begründet wird)*; gesiegelter (od. förmlicher) Vertrag *(cf. consideration)*; *Am* (Grundstücks-)Übertragungsurkunde; Tat, Handlung; **~s and simple contracts** förmliche und einfache Verträge; **~ of accession** Zustimmung des Konkursgläubigers zu e-m außergerichtlichen Vergleich; **~ of arrangement** *Br* schriftl. Vergleichsvereinbarung; **D~ of Arrangement Act** (D.A.A.) *Br* Gesetz über Vergleichsverfahren *(zur Vermeidung des Konkurses)*; **~ of assignment** Abtretungsurkunde; **~ of composition** s. composition →~; **~ of conveyance** Übertragungsurkunde *(bei Grundeigentum)*; **~ of covenant** Versprechensurkunde; **~ of donation** Schenkungsurkunde; **~ of gift** Schenkungsurkunde; **~ of partnership** Gesellschaftsvertrag; **~ of protest** *(WechselR)* Protesturkunde; **~ poll** einseitige *(gesiegelte)* Erklärung *(e-r Vertragspartei) (opp. indenture)*; **~s registration** *Am*[14] Registrierung von Urkunden über Übereignung und Belastungen von Grundbesitz; **~ of title** *Am* Urkunde über Übertragung von Grundeigentum; Grundstücksübertragungsurkunde; **~ of transfer** (Eigentums-) Übertragungsurkunde; Aktienübertragungsurkunde (→*transfer 4.*); **~ of trust** Urkunde über die Errichtung e-s Treuhandverhältnisses, Treuhandvertrag; *Am* Urkunde über die Bestellung e-s Sicherungsrechtes *(an Sachen od. Rechten)*; *Am* Urkunde, die e-m Dritten als Treuhänder zur Sicherung der Finanzierung des Grundstückserwerbs übergeben wird

deed, composition ~ *Br (schriftl.)* Vergleich *(zwischen Schuldner und Gläubigern)*
Schuldner behält sein Vermögen. Es wird ihm ein Teil der Schulden erlassen od. Stundung gewährt *(cf. deed of arrangement)*

deed, delivery of a ~ *(förmliche)* Aushändigung e-r Urkunde; **execution of a ~** Ausfertigung e-r Urkunde; **liable under a ~** vertraglich verpflichtet; **title ~** Eigentumsurkunde (→*title 2.*); **warranty ~** *Am* Grundstücksübereignungsurkunde *(mit bestimmten Zusicherungen)*

deed, to draw up a ~ e-e Urkunde aufsetzen; **to execute a ~** e-e Urkunde *(rechtsgültig)* ausfertigen; **to make a ~** e-n förmlichen Vertrag schließen

deem *v* halten für, betrachten als

deemed, to be ~ (to be) angesehen werden als, gelten als

deep discount, ~ bond fest verzinsliche Anleihe mit niedrigem Nominalzins und hohem Disagio; **~ securities** stark abgezinste Wertpapiere

deep-sea Tiefsee-; Hochsee-

Deep Seabed Areas, Agreement on the Confidentiality of Data Concerning ~[14a] Übereinkommen über die Wahrung der Vertraulichkeit von Daten betreffend Tiefseebodenfelder

deep-sea, ~ **fishing** Hochseefischerei; ~ **mining** Tiefseebergbau; ~ **research** Tiefseeforschung

de-escalation Deeskalation, Abbau der Eskalation (→*escalation*)

deface *v* verunstalten; unkenntlich (od. unleserlich) machen; *(Briefmarken etc)* entwerten; **to ~ a coin** Wert e-r Münze *(rechtswidrig)* mindern (→*defacement*); **to ~ a monument** ein Denkmal beschädigen

defaced shares verunstaltete Aktien

defacement Entstellung, Unkenntlichmachung; Entwertung *(von Briefmarken etc)*; ~ **of coins** Münzverringerung; *(rechtswidrige)* Wertminderung von Metallgeldstücken *(durch Beschneiden, Abfeilen etc [Kippen und Wippen])*

de facto →de

defalcate *v* unterschlagen; veruntreuen, Untreue begehen

defalcation Unterschlagung, Veruntreuung *(von Geldern)*; veruntreutes Geld; Untreue *(im Sinne von § 266 StGB)*

defamation[15] Ehrverletzung; *(Oberbegriff für)* Beleidigung; Verleumdung (→*libel*); üble Nachrede (→*slander*); verleumderische Behauptung; Diffamierung; ~ **action** Beleidigungsklage, Verleumdungsklage; ~ **case** Beleidigungsprozeß; ~ **of a competitor's reputation** Anschwärzung; **unintentional** ~[16] unbeabsichtigte Beleidigung

defamatory beleidigend, verleumderisch; diffamierend; Schmäh-; ~ **statement** diffamierende Bemerkung; beleidigende Äußerung; üble Nachrede; ~ **upon its face** offenkundig beleidigend

defame *v* beleidigen, verleumden; schmähen; **to ~ a competitor's reputation** e-n Konkurrenten anschwärzen

default Nichterfüllung *(e-r Verpflichtung, bes. rechtl. od. finanzieller Art)*; Unterlassung; Säumnis *(Versäumung e-s Termins zur mündl. Verhandlung)*; Nichterscheinen *(vor Gericht)*, Ausbleiben *(im Termin)*; Leistungsstörung; Verzug, Zahlungsverzug, Nichtzahlung; Mangel *(Fehlen der geschuldeten Leistung)*; Verfehlung; ~ **action** *Br* Klage auf feststehenden Geldbetrag *(Schnellverfahren im County Court)*; Klage im Mahnverfahren; ~ **clause** *(Euromarkt)* Default-Klausel *(Kündigungsmöglichkeit für den Kreditgeber [meist e-e Bank] im Falle des Zahlungsverzugs des Schuldners)*; ~ **in delivery** Lieferverzug; ~ **in payment** Nichtzahlung; Zahlungsverzug; ~ **in taking delivery** Annahmeverzug; ~ **interest** Verzugszinsen; ~ **judgment** Versäumnisurteil (→*judgment by* ~); ~ **of acceptance** Annahmeverzug; ~ **of appearance** *(Zivilprozeß)* Versäumnis der Einlassung; ~ **of the debtor** Schuldnerverzug; ~ **of defence** (~**se**) Unterlassung rechtzeitiger Klagebeantwortung; ~ **of interest** Zinsverzug

default of the party, circumstances due to the ~ auf dem Versäumnis der Partei beruhende Umstände

default, ~ **(of pleading)** Unterlassen der fristgerechten Einreichung des Schriftsatzes; ~ **procedure** *Br* Versäumnisverfahren *(cf. judgment by ~)*; ~ **rate** Ausfallquote *(im Kreditgeschäft e-r Bank)*; ~ **risk** Ausfallrisiko; ~→**summons** 1.

default, in ~ säumig; in Verzug befindlich; **in ~ of** mangels; in Ermangelung von; **in ~ of acceptance** in Annahmeverzug; **in ~ of agreement** (between the parties) mangels Übereinkunft; **in case** (or **in the event**) **of** ~ bei Unterlassung; bei Säumnis; im Verzugsfalle; bei nicht erfolgter Einlassung; bei Nichterscheinen; **in case of ~ of the debtor** im Falle des Verzuges des Schuldners; **in ~ of defence** → defence 1; **in case of ~ the plaintiff may be nonsuited** *Am* erscheint der Kläger nicht, kann er mit der Klage abgewiesen werden

default, interest for ~ Verzugszinsen; **judgment by** ~ Versäumnisurteil (→*judgment*); **party in** ~ *(zum Termin)* nicht erschienene Partei, säumige Partei; in Verzug befindliche Partei; **upon** ~ bei Nichtzahlung; bei Verzug

default, to be in ~ im Verzug sein, sich im Verzug befinden; **the party is in ~ in complying with an order of the court** die Partei hat es unterlassen, e-e Anordnung des Gerichts zu befolgen; **to cure a** ~ e-n Verzug wiedergutmachen; **to declare the party in** ~ gegen die Partei ein Versäumnisurteil erlassen; **to make** ~ e-r Verpflichtung nicht nachkommen; in Verzug geraten; im Verzug sein; vor Gericht nicht erscheinen; **to make ~ of appearance** *(Zivilprozeß)* den Termin versäumen; die Einlassung versäumen; **to make ~ in payment** nicht bezahlen; in Zahlungsverzug geraten; **to make ~ in the payment of interest** (or **in interest payments**) mit der Zinszahlung im Verzug sein; **to put in** ~ in Verzug setzen

default *v* seinen Verpflichtungen nicht nachkommen; *(vor Gericht)* nicht erscheinen, Termin versäumen; Frist versäumen; wegen Nichterscheinens verurteilen; in (Zahlungs-)Verzug geraten; nicht bezahlen (können); **to ~ on a debt** e-e Schuld nicht bezahlen; **to ~ on the payment of the rent** mit der Mietzahlung in Verzug (geraten) sein

defaulted, ~ **bonds** *Am* notleidende Obligationen; ~ **mortgage** in Verzug befindliche Hypothek; **the account has** ~ die (Geschäfts-) Forderung ist uneinbringlich geworden

defaulting säumig; in Verzug; nicht erschienen;

Br (Börse) zahlungsunfähig; ~ **debtor** säumiger Schuldner; in Zahlungsverzug geratener Schuldner; ~ **witness** ausbleibender Zeuge

defaulter jd, der s-r Verpflichtung nicht nachgekommen ist; säumiger Zahler; vor Gericht Ausbleibender, zum Termin nicht Erschienener; *Br (Börse)* Insolvent *(cf. to hammer); Br* Angeklagter *(in e-m Militärgerichtsverfahren);* **declaration of** ~**s** *Br (gegen ein Börsenmitglied, das seinen Verpflichtungen nicht nachgekommen ist, erlassene)* Erklärung des Börsenvorstandes

defeasance Aufhebung, Annullierung; ~ **clause** Aufhebungsklausel, Verwirkungsklausel

defeasible *(durch auflösende Bedingung)* annullierbar; auflösend bedingt

defeat Niederlage, Unterliegen; Vereitelung *(e-s Plans);* Aufhebung, Ungültigkeitserklärung; ~ **at an election** (or **at the polls,** or **election** ~) Wahlniederlage; **to meet with** (or **suffer**) **a** ~ e-e Niederlage erleiden; **to suffer a** ~ e-e Niederlage erleiden; **to suffer** ~ **in an action** (or **a law-suit**) im Prozeß unterliegen

defeat *v* besiegen, schlagen; *(Plan, Zweck)* vereiteln; *(Antrag etc)* zu Fall bringen; aufheben, rückgängig machen; **to** ~ **a Bill** e-n Gesetzesentwurf zu Fall bringen; **to** ~ **the opposing candidate** den Gegenkandidaten besiegen; **to** ~ **one's creditors** den Gläubigeranspruch vereiteln; s-e Gläubiger benachteiligen *(als Konkursgrund);* **to** ~ **a motion by 10 votes against 5** *parl* e-n Antrag mit 10 gegen 5 Stimmen zu Fall bringen; **to** ~ **sb. at the polls** über jdn e-n Wahlsieg erringen; **to** ~ **a right** ein Recht zunichtemachen, ein Recht entziehen; **to** ~ **by vote** niederstimmen

defeated, ~ **Governor** *Am pol* der besiegte Gouverneur; ~ **party** *Am (im Prozeß)* unterliegende Partei; **to be** ~ unterliegen; *parl* überstimmt werden; **to be** ~ **at the polls** e-e Wahlniederlage erleiden; **the motion was** ~ **by an overwhelming (narrow) majority** der Antrag wurde mit e-r überwältigenden (knappen) Mehrheit zu Fall gebracht (od. überstimmt)

defeating of a creditor Vereitelung e-s Gläubigeranspruchs; Gläubigerbenachteiligung *(als Konkursgrund)*

defeatism *pol* Defätismus

defeatist *pol* Defätist

defect Fehler; Mangel; ~ **of form** Formmangel, Formfehler; (→*form*); ~**s in the product** Fehler im Fabrikat (→*product liability*); ~ **of quality** Sachmangel; ~ **of proceedings** Verfahrensmangel; ~ **in title** Rechtsmangel; Mangel im (Eigentums-)Recht *(bei Grundbesitz) (cf. title insurance, title 2.);* ~ **in workmanship** Arbeitsfehler, Bearbeitungsmangel

defect, apparent ~ offener (od. sichtbarer) Mangel *(beim Kauf);* **claim based on** ~**s** Mängelanspruch; **congenital** ~ Geburtsfehler; **discovery of a** ~ Entdeckung e-s Mangels; **formal** ~ Formfehler; **hidden** ~ verborgener Mangel *(beim Kauf; cf. caveat emptor);* **free from** ~**(s)** mangelfrei, fehlerfrei; **latent** ~ versteckter (od. verborgener) Mangel *(beim Kauf);* **legal** ~ →~ in title; **liability for** ~**s** Mängelhaftung; **manufacturing** ~ Fabrikationsfehler; **mental** ~ Geistesschwäche; Geistesstörung (→*mental*); **notice of** ~ Mängelrüge, Mängelanzeige; **obvious** ~ offensichtlicher Mangel; **patent** ~ offener (od. sichtbarer) Mangel; **redhibitory** ~ *Am* Gewährsmangel; **remedy of** ~**s** Beseitigung von Mängeln *(z.B. der Patentanmeldung)*

defect, to ascertain ~**s** Mängel feststellen; **to be liable for** ~**s** für Mängel haften; **to conceal a** ~ e-n Mangel verschweigen; **to cure a** ~ **of form** e-n Formmangel heilen; **to remedy** ~**s** Mängel beheben (od. beseitigen)

defection Abfall, Abtrünnigwerden (from a party von e-r Partei)

defective, (mental) ~ *Br*[17] Geistesgestörter, Geistesschwacher

defective mangelhaft, fehlerhaft, schadhaft; **mentally** ~ geistesgestört, geistesschwach; ~ **company** (*Am* **corporation**) mangelhaft errichtete Gesellschaft; ~ **condition** (or **state**) mangelhafter (od. schadhafter) Zustand; Schadhaftigkeit; ~ **contract** fehlerhafter Vertrag; ~ **packing** mangelhafte Verpackung; ~ **products** fehlerhafte Produkte; ~ **title** fehlerhafter Rechtstitel; mit Mängeln behaftetes Recht

defectiveness Mangelhaftigkeit, Fehlerhaftigkeit

defen|ce (~se) 1. (Rechts-)Verteidigung; *(Zivilprozeß)* Klagebeantwortung; Verteidigungsvorbringen; Einrede, Einwendung, Einwand, (to gegen); *(Strafprozeß)* Verteidigung *(des Angeklagten); (das dem Angeklagten günstige Vorbringen:)* Einlassung; Leugnung; Rechtfertigung; ~**s** Verteidigungsvorbringen; Klagebeantwortung; ~ **attorney** *Am (Zivilprozeß)* Anwalt des Beklagten; *(Strafprozeß)* Verteidiger; ~ **counsel** *(Strafprozeß)* Verteidiger; ~ **of fraud** Einrede der Arglist; ~ **of privilege** Vorbringen e-s Rechtfertigungsgrundes *(Einwendung gegenüber Beleidigungsklagen, z.B. Berufung auf Wahrnehmung berechtigter Interessen; cf. absolute, qualified privilege,* →*privilege);* ~ **of set-off** Einwendung der Aufrechnung; ~ **of truth** *Am* Vorbringen des Wahrheitsbeweises *(bei Beleidigungsklagen; cf. justification)*

defense *Am,* →**affirmative** ~; →**attorney for the** ~

defen|ce (~se), costs of the ~ Kosten der Verteidigung; **counsel for the** ~ →counsel 1.; **in default of** ~ bei fehlender Klagebeantwortung; **equitable** ~ auf →equity-Recht begründete

Einrede (od. Einwendung); **inadmissible ~** unzulässiges Verteidigungsvorbringen

defen|ce (~se), good ~ begründete Einrede; berechtigtes Verteidigungsvorbringen; **it shall be a good ~ for the accused to prove** zur Entlastung des Angeklagten genügt der Nachweis

defence, points of ~ *Br (in Handelssachen)* formlose *(kurze)* Klagebeantwortung *(anstelle von defence)*

defen|ce (~se), self-~ *(StrafR)* Notwehr *(cf. ~ 2.)*; **statement of ~** *Br* Klagebeantwortung; **time for (service of) ~** Frist zur Klagebeantwortung; →**witness for the ~**

defen|ce (~se), by way of ~ im Wege der Einrede

defen|ce (~se), to abandon the ~ die Vertretung des Beklagten (od. die Verteidigung des Angeklagten) niederlegen; **to conduct the ~ (of)** *(den Angeklagten)* verteidigen; **to conduct one's own ~** sich selbst *(vor Gericht)* verteidigen; **to deliver the ~** die Klagebeantwortung einreichen; **to put forward** (or **set up**) **a ~** e-e Einrede vorbringen (od. geltend machen); e-e Einwendung entgegensetzen

defen|ce (~se) 2. *(VölkerR)*, **self-~** Selbstverteidigung; **individual or collective self-~** individuelle oder kollektive Selbstverteidigung; **right of self-~** Selbsterhaltungsrecht *(Notstand und Selbstschutz)*

defen|ce (~se) 3. *mil* Verteidigung; Wehr-, Rüstungs-; **~s** Verteidigungsanlagen; **~ bonds** *Br*[18] Kriegsanleihe(n); **~ contract** Rüstungsauftrag; **~ contribution** Verteidigungsbeitrag, Wehrbeitrag; **~ contractor** Rüstungslieferant; **~ cuts** Kürzung der Verteidigungsausgaben; **~ economy** Wehrwirtschaft; **~ estimates** Voranschläge der Verteidigungsausgaben; **~ expenditure** Verteidigungsausgaben; **~-induced costs** Verteidigungsfolgekosten; **D~ Intelligence Agency** *Am* militärischer Geheimdienst; **~ order** Rüstungsauftrag; **~ plant** Rüstungsbetrieb; **~ purchases** Rüstungskäufe; **for ~ purposes** für Verteidigungszwecke; **~ spending** Verteidigungsausgaben, Rüstungsausgaben

defen|ce (~se), Department of D~ *Am* Verteidigungsministerium; **Minister (Ministry) of ~** *Br* Verteidigungsminister (-ministerium); **national ~** Landesverteidigung; **Secretary of D~** *Am* Verteidigungsminister; **state of ~** Verteidigungszustand; **weapons of ~** Verteidigungswaffen *(opp. weapons of offen|ce [~se])*

defend *v* verteidigen; schützen, bewahren (from vor); **to ~ oneself** sich verteidigen; **to ~ the defendant** *(Strafprozeß)* den Angeklagten verteidigen; **to ~ one's point of view** seinen Standpunkt verteidigen; **to ~ the suit** *bes. Am* den Klageanspruch bestreiten

defending counsel Verteidiger

defendant *(Zivilprozeß)* Beklagte(r); beklagte Partei *(z.B. vor dem Schiedsgerichtshof; opp. claimant)*; *(Strafprozeß)* Angeklagte(r); **~'s answer** Klagebeantwortung; **~ company** (*Am* **corporation**) verklagte Gesellschaft; **~ in error** Revisionsbeklagte(r) *(Br obs.)*; **co-~** Mitbeklagte(r); Mitangeklagte(r); **plaintiff and ~** *(Zivilprozeß)* Kläger(in) und Beklagte(r)

defender Verteidiger; *Scot* Beklagte(r); **public ~** *Am* Pflichtverteidiger

defense *Am* →defence

defensible verteidigungsfähig; zu rechtfertigen(d), vertretbar *(Meinung)*

defensive Verteidigung, Defensive; Defensiv-, Schutz- *(opp. offensive)*; **~ alliance** Verteidigungsbündnis; **~ measures** Verteidigungsmaßnahmen; **~ portion** *Am* risikoärmerer Teil *(des Effektenportefeuilles e-s investment trust)*; **~ registration** *Am (WarenzeichenR)* defensive Eintragung *(der im zwischenstaatl. Handel benutzten Marke)*; **~ strike** Abwehrstreik; **~ war** Verteidigungskrieg; **~ warfare** Defensivkrieg; **~ weapons** Defensivwaffen *(opp. offensive weapons)*; **to be on the ~** sich in der Defensive befinden

defer *v* aufschieben, hinausschieben; stunden; zurückstellen *(auch vom Wehrdienst)*; sich unterordnen, sich fügen; **to ~ judgment** die Urteilsverkündung aussetzen; **to ~ payment** die Zahlung hinausschieben (od. aufschieben); **to ~ payment of taxes** *Am* die Steuern stunden; **to ~ a sentence** die Urteilsverkündung aussetzen; **to ~ until further notice** bis auf weiteres verschieben

deferred aufgeschoben, hinausgeschoben; gestundet; *(auch mil)* zurückgestellt; **~ annuity** hinausgeschobene Rente *(die erst nach e-r bestimmten Zeit fällig wird)*; **~ benefit** spätere Versicherungsleistung *(opp. immediate benefit)*; **~ bonds** *Am* Obligationen mit aufgeschobener Zinszahlung; **~ charges** *Am (Bilanz)* transitorische Aktiva; Bilanzposten der Rechnungsabgrenzung; **~ compensation** *Am (Betriebs-Altersversorgung)* später fällig werdende Vergütungen für Arbeitsleistungen *(wenn die Steuerbelastung geringer sein wird)*; **~ debt** *(im Rang)* nachgehende (Konkurs-)Forderung; **~ dividend** Dividende mit aufgeschobener Fälligkeit; **~ expense** *Am (Bilanz)* transitorische Aktiva; **~ income** *Am (Bilanz)* transitorische Passiva; **~ income tax** gestundete Einkommensteuer; **~ items** *Am (Bilanz)* Posten der Rechnungsabgrenzung; transitorische Posten; **~ liabilities** langfristige Verbindlichkeiten; **~ life annuity** hinausgeschobene lebenslängliche Rente

deferred payment hinausgeschobene Zahlung; *Am* Ratenzahlung, Abzahlung; **~ agreement**

Am Kaufvertrag, bei dem der Kaufpreis gestundet wird; ~ **bond** Euroanleihe, die erst nach Zeichnungsschluß eingezahlt wird; ~ **sale** *Am* Ratenkauf, Verkauf auf Abzahlung; ~ **of taxes** *Am* Steuerstundung; **to buy on a ~ basis** *Am* auf Teilzahlung kaufen

deferred, ~ rebate zurückgestellter Rabatt; ~ **revenue** *Am (Bilanz)* transitorische Passiva; ~ **shares** Nachzugsaktien *(Dividenden können im Ggs. zu den ordinary shares erst nach allen anderen Aktien beansprucht werden);* ~ **stock** *Br* Obligationen mit aufgeschobener Zinszahlung; ~ **taxes** latente Steuern

deferred terms, payment on ~ Ratenzahlung, Teilzahlung; **to buy on ~** *Am* auf Abzahlung kaufen

deferred, to allow payment to be ~ die Zahlung stunden

deference Nachgiebigkeit, Unterordnung; Ehrerbietung (to für); **with all (due) ~** bei aller Hochachtung (to vor) *(Höflichkeitsformel bei Meinungsverschiedenheiten);* ~ **of the federal court of state legislation** *Am* Unterordnung des Bundesgerichts unter die einzelstaatliche Gesetzgebung

deferment Aufschub; Verschiebung; Zurückstellung *(vom Militärdienst);* ~ **of a date** Verlängerung e-r Frist; ~ **of a deadline** Verschiebung e-s Termins; ~ **of payment** Zahlungsaufschub; **to grant** (or **allow**) **a ~** Zahlung stunden

deferral *Am* →deferment; **request for a ~** *Am* Stundungsgesuch; **to grant a ~** *Am* Aufschub gewähren

deficiency Mangel, Fehlen, Unvollständigkeit; Fehlbetrag, Minderbetrag, Defizit; Ausfallbetrag; *Am* Steuernachforderung; ~ **account** Verlustkonto; ~ **advances** *Br* Vorschüsse der Bank von England *(an das britische Schatzamt);* ~ **appropriation** *Am parl* Nachtragsbewilligung; ~ **of assets** *(KonkursR)* Fehlen von Vermögenswerten; ~ **bill** Gesetz zur Bewilligung des Nachtragsetat *(zur Deckung e-s Defizits);* ~ **bills** *Br* kurzfristige Anleihen der britischen Regierung bei der Bank von England; ~ **of food** Mangel an Nahrungsmitteln; ~ **guarantee** Ausfallbürgschaft; ~ **judgment** *Am* Ausfallurteil; Zahlungsurteil für den Hypothekengläubiger in Höhe seines Ausfalls bei der Zwangsversteigerung; ~ **note** Fehlmengenmitteilung; ~ **in the proceeds** Minderertrag; ~ **in receipts** Mindereinnahme; ~ **reserve** Rückstellung für Mindereinnahmen; ~ **in taxes** *Am* zu geringe Steuerzahlung; ~ **in title** Rechtsmangel; ~ **in weight** Fehlgewicht, Gewichtsmanko; Mindergewicht

deficienc|y, formal ~ies formelle Mängel; **mental ~** Störung der Geistestätigkeit, Geistesschwäche; **notice of ~** *Am (SteuerR)* Nachforderungsbescheid (→*notice 1.*); **obvious ~ies** offensichtliche Mängel; **examination for obvious ~ies** *(PatR)* Offensichtlichkeitsprüfung

deficienc|y, to disclose ~ies Mängel aufdecken; **to correct ~ies** Mängel beseitigen; **to make good** (or **make up, meet**) **a ~** ein Defizit decken; **to supply the ~** das Fehlende ergänzen; das Defizit ausgleichen

deficient 1. mangelhaft, ungenügend, arm (in an); fehlend; ~ **amount** Fehlbetrag; ~ **delivery** fehlerhafte Lieferung; **to be ~ in weight** kein volles Gewicht haben, nicht vollwichtig sein; **to make up the ~ amount** den Fehlbetrag ergänzen

deficient 2., **mentally ~** geistesgestört, geistesschwach; **mentally ~ person** Geistesgestörter, Geistesschwacher

deficit Defizit, Fehlbetrag; Minderbetrag *(opp. surplus);* Ausfall; Passivsaldo; ~ **account** Verlustkonto; ~ **in the balance of payments** Zahlungsbilanzdefizit, Passivsaldo der Zahlungsbilanz; ~ **in the trade balance** Handelsbilanzdefizit; Passivsaldo der Handelsbilanz; ~ **financing** Finanzierung durch Staatsverschuldung; ~ **on foreign trade** Außenhandelsdefizit; ~ **margin** Verlustspanne; ~ **spending** Defizitfinanzierung *(Finanzierung öffentl. Investitionen durch Vorgriff auf künftige Haushaltsmittel, also Überschuß der Ausgaben über die Einnahmen [→fiscal policy]);* ~ **in taxes** Steuerausfall; Minderaufkommen an Steuern

deficit, annual ~ Jahresfehlbetrag; **budgetary ~** Haushaltsdefizit; **cash ~** Kassendefizit; **countries running heavy ~s** defizitäre Länder; **fiscal ~** Fehlbetrag im Staatshaushalt; **foreign trade ~** Außenhandelsdefizit; **trade ~** Handelsbilanzdefizit

deficit, the financial year closes with a ~ das Rechnungsjahr schließt mit e-m Defizit ab; **to meet a ~** ein Defizit decken; **to reduce a ~** ein Defizit abbauen; **to run a ~** ein Defizit haben; **to settle a ~** ein Defizit ausgleichen; **to show a ~** ein Defizit (od. e-n Passivsaldo) aufweisen

define *v* definieren, (genau) erklären, festlegen; formulieren; abgrenzen; vorschreiben; **to ~ a common policy** e-e gemeinsame Politik festlegen; **to ~ one's position** seinen Standpunkt darlegen; Stellung nehmen (to zu); **to ~ sb.'s powers** jds Vollmachten abgrenzen

defined, as ~ in the Act im Sinne des Gesetzes

definite bestimmt, *(genau)* festgesetzt; klar, deutlich; endgültig, abschließend; ~ **answer** klare (od. präzise) Antwort; ~ **order** fester Auftrag; **for a ~ period** für e-e bestimmte Zeit

definition Definition, Begriffsbestimmung; **legal** (or **statutory**) ~ Legaldefinition

definitional element *(StrafR)* Tatbestandsmerkmal

definitive endgültig, definitiv; klar umrissen, genau festgelegt; ~ **answer** endgültige Antwort

deflation Deflation; ~ **of credit** Kreditrestriktion; ~ **of the currency** (or **monetary** ~) Beschränkung (od. Verringerung) der Geldmenge; **policy of** ~ Deflationspolitik

deflationary deflationistisch, deflatorisch; ~ **gap** deflatorische Lücke; ~ **policy** Deflationspolitik

deflationist Deflationsanhänger

deflator Deflator

deflection of trade Verkehrsverlagerung, Handelsverlagerung

deforcement *Scot* Widerstand gegen Vollstreckungsbeamte

deforestation Entwaldung, Abholzung

defraud *v* betrügen; *(Steuern, Zölle)* hinterziehen; **with intent to** ~ in betrügerischer Absicht; **with intent to** ~ **creditors** *(KonkursR)* zum Zwecke der Benachteiligung der Gläubiger; **to** ~ **the customs** Zoll hinterziehen
defrauding the Revenue Steuerhinterziehung

defraudation, ~ **of the customs** Zollhinterziehung; ~ **of the Revenue** Steuerhinterziehung

defray *v (Kosten)* bestreiten (od. bezahlen, tragen); aufkommen für; **to** ~ **sb.'s expenses** jds Auslagen bestreiten; jdn freihalten; **liable to** ~ **the charges** (or **costs**) kostenpflichtig

defunct verstorben; erloschen; ~ **company** nicht mehr bestehende (od. erloschene) Gesellschaft

defuse *v*, **to** ~ **a bomb** e-e Bombe entschärfen

defy *v*, **to** ~ **the law** das Gesetz mißachten

deglomeration Deglomeration *(opp. agglomeration)*

degree 1. Grad; Rang; Stufe; Verwandtschaftsgrad; Grad der Strafbarkeit; ~ **of accuracy** Genauigkeitsgrad; ~ **of classification** Geheimhaltungsstufe; ~ **of consanguinity** (or **relationship**) Verwandtschaftsgrad; ~ **of development** Entwicklungsstufe; ~ **of fame** Bekanntheitsgrad
degree, of high ~ von hohem Rang; **murder in the first (second)** ~ *Am* →murder; **principal of the first (second)** ~ →principal; **prohibited** ~ (of relationship) *(für die Heirat)* verbotener Verwandtschaftsgrad; **relation in the second** ~ Verwandte(r) zweiten Grades; **third** ~ *(unzulässige)* Polizeimaßnahme *(zur Erzwingung e-s Geständnisses)*
degree 2. *univ* akademischer Grad; Diplom; **doctor's** ~ Doktorwürde (→*doctor*); **honorary** ~ ehrenhalber verliehener akademischer Grad; **to confer a** ~ **on sb.** jdm e-n akademischen Grad verleihen; **to confer an honorary** ~ **on sb.** jdm die Würde e-s Ehrendoktors verleihen; **to receive the honorary** ~ **of doctor of law** den Ehrendoktor (Dr. jur. h. c.) verliehen bekommen; **to take one's** ~ e-n akademischen Grad erlangen; promovieren

degression Degression, degressive Abnahme; Absteigen *(z. B. der Steuer)*

degressive, ~ **depreciation** degressive Abschreibung *(Abschreibung mit fallenden Quoten)*; ~ **tax** degressive Steuer

dehiring process Auslaufen des Anstellungsverhältnisses *(Entlassung bes. e-r Führungskraft)*

de jure → de

delate *v Scot* anzeigen, denunzieren; beschuldigen

delation *Scot* Anzeige, Denunziation; Beschuldigung

delator *Scot* Denunziant

delay Aufschub, Aufschiebung, Verzögerung; Verschleppung; Verzug; Verspätung *(Zug, Flugzeug etc.)*; ~ **in accepting delivery** (or **performance**) Annahmeverzug; ~ **in claiming** Anspruchsverzögerung; Verspätung bei Erhebung e-s Anspruchs; ~ **of the creditor** Gläubigerverzug *(Annahmeverzug)*; ~ **of the debtor** Schuldnerverzug; ~ **in delivery** Lieferverzögerung; Lieferverzug; ~ **in loading** Ladeverzögerung; ~ **in payment** Zahlungsverzug; Zahlungsaufschub; ~ **in (the) proceedings** Prozeßverschleppung; ~ **time** betrieblich bedingte Verlustzeit
delay, creditor's ~ Gläubigerverzug; **damage caused by** ~ Verzugsschaden; **debtor's** ~ Schuldnerverzug; **excusable** ~ entschuldbare Verzögerung; **request for** ~ **(of payment)** Stundungsgesuch; **without** ~ unverzüglich, umgehend; **without undue** ~ ohne schuldhafte (ungehörige) Verzögerung
delay, this matter allows no ~ diese Angelegenheit duldet keinen Aufschub; **to be in** ~ in Verzug sein; **the buyer is in** ~ **in taking delivery of the goods** der Käufer nimmt die Ware nicht rechtzeitig ab; der Käufer ist in Annahmeverzug; **to prevent** ~**s** Verzögerungen vermeiden

delay *v* aufschieben, hinausschieben, verzögern; verschleppen; **to** ~ **one's creditors** seine Gläubiger hinhalten *(Konkursgrund)*; **to** ~ **a payment** (or **to** ~ **payment of a debt**) mit e-r Zahlung in Verzug sein; in Zahlungsverzug sein; **to** ~ **the proceedings** den Prozeß verschleppen
delayed aufgeschoben, verzögert; verspätet; ~ **delivery** verspätete Lieferung; ~ **effects of ionizing radiation** Spätwirkungen ionisieren-

der Strahlen; ~ **payment** verspätete Zahlung; ~ **taking** Annahmeverzug

delaying, ~ **effect** aufschiebende Wirkung; ~ **tactics** Verzögerungstaktik

del credere Delkredere *(Garantie für die Leistungsfähigkeit e-s Dritten, bes. für den Eingang e-r Forderung);* ~ **account** Delkrederekonto; ~ **agent** Delkrederevertreter; ~ **commission** Delkredereprovision *(z. B. des Kommissionärs);* **to assume** (or **undertake**) **the** ~ das Delkredere übernehmen

delegate Delegierter, Abgeordneter; *Am* Kongreßabgeordneter *(e-s Einzelstaates);* ~ **(to a meeting)** Sitzungsteilnehmer, Konferenzteilnehmer; **employers'** ~ Vertreter der Arbeitgeber; **list of** ~**s** Delegiertenliste; **permanent** ~ ständiger Delegierter; **workers'** ~ Vertreter der Arbeitnehmer; **to appoint as** ~ als Delegierten bestimmen; **to send a** ~ **to a conference** jdn zu e-r Konferenz delegieren

delegate *v (jdn)* delegieren, abordnen; *(Amtsgewalt, Vollmacht etc)* delegieren, (weiter)übertragen; **to** ~ **one's authority** (or **power[s]**) **to sb.** seine Befugnisse auf jdn delegieren; jdm Vollmacht (weiter)übertragen; jdn unterbevollmächtigen

delegated legislation delegierte Gesetzgebung; Normen *(Gesetze, Verordnungen etc)* auf Grund delegierter Gesetzgebungsgewalt *(Br bes. Orders in Council, Statutory Instruments)*

delegation Delegierung, Abordnung; Delegation; (Weiter-)Übertragung; Schuldübernahme; ~ **of authority** (or **powers**) Delegierung von Befugnissen; Übertragung der Vollmacht; Unterbevollmächtigung; ~ **of (legislative) power** Delegierung der Gesetzgebungsgewalt *(an die Exekutive; z. B. zum Erlaß von Verordnungen);* **head** (or **leader**) **of a** ~ Delegationsleiter; **trade** ~ Handelsdelegation; **to head a** ~ e-e Delegation führen

delete *v* (aus)löschen, (aus)streichen; **to** ~ **from the agenda** von der Tagesordnung streichen (od. absetzen); **to** ~ **an entry** e-e Eintragung löschen

deleterious (gesundheits)schädlich, ungesund

deletion (Aus-)Streichung, Löschung; ~ **(made) by the censor** Streichung durch die Zensur

deliberate (wohl)überlegt; vorsätzlich; absichtlich; bewußt; ~ **action** mit Vorsatz begangene Handlung; ~ **policy** gezielte Politik

deliberate *v* überlegen; beraten (on a judgment über ein Urteil); **to retire to** ~ sich zur Beratung zurückziehen

deliberateness *bes. Am* Absicht; Bedachtsamkeit; *Am (AntitrustR)* Monopolisierungsabsicht

deliberation Überlegung, Beratung (on über); ~ **on a bill** Gesetzesberatung; **after careful** (or **due**) ~ nach sorgfältiger Beratung; nach reiflicher Überlegung; **final** ~ Schlußberatung; **time for** ~ Bedenkzeit; **to enter into a** ~ in e-e Beratung eintreten; **the** ~**s of the court take place in private** die Beratungen des Gerichts sind geheim

deliberative beratend; ~ **assembly** beratende Versammlung; ~ **function** beratende Funktion

delict Delikt; unerlaubte Handlung

delicta juris gentium *(von Einzelpersonen begangene)* Delikte wider das Völkerrecht

delimit(ate) *v* abgrenzen, die Grenzen festlegen

delimitation Abgrenzung, Begrenzung; ~ **of a frontier** Grenzziehung, Grenzabsteckung

delinquency Pflichtverletzung; (Ver-)Säumnis; Vergehen; Kriminalität; **debt** ~ Zahlungsverzug, Nichtzahlung; **juvenile** ~ Jugendkriminalität; →**tax** ~

delinquent Delinquent, Täter; säumig; straffällig; **juvenile** ~ jugendlicher Täter; ~ **return** *Am* rückständige Steuererklärung; ~ **tax** *Am* rückständige Steuer; ~ **taxpayer** *Am* säumiger Steuerzahler; **the customer is 30 days** ~ der Kunde ist 30 Tage in Zahlungsverzug

deliver *v* aushändigen, überbringen; (ein-, ab-, aus)liefern; andienen; *(Briefe, Telegramme)* zustellen; **to** ~ **over** übergeben, überreichen; **to** ~ **up** herausgeben; *(Besitz)* aufgeben; **to** ~ **oneself up to the police** sich der Polizei stellen; **to** ~ **up possession of premises** die Wohnung *(an den Vermieter)* übergeben, die Wohnung räumen

deliver *v,* **to** ~ **a copy** e-e Abschrift (od. Ausfertigung) erteilen; **to** ~ **a deed** e-e Urkunde aushändigen; **to** ~ **goods** Waren (aus)liefern; **to** ~ **a judgment** ein Urteil erlassen (od. fällen, verkünden); **to** ~ **a lecture** e-n Vortrag halten; **to** ~ **letters** Briefe zustellen (od. austragen); **to** ~ **an opinion** ein Gutachten abgeben; Stellung nehmen (on zu); **to** ~ **a speech** e-e Rede halten (to vor); **to** ~ **subsequently** nachliefern; **to** ~ **a telegram** ein Telegramm zustellen; **to** ~ **a telegram by telephone** Telegramm telefonisch durchsagen; **to** ~ **within the time stipulated** fristgerecht liefern; die Lieferfrist einhalten

delivered (aus)geliefert; ~ **at docks** (D/D) im Dock abgeliefert; ~ **at frontier ...** (named place of delivery at frontier) (DAF) geliefert Grenze ... (benannter Lieferort an der Grenze) *(Incoterms 1980);* ~ **duty paid ...** (named place of destination in the country of importation) (DDP) geliefert verzollt ... (benannter Bestimmungsort im Einfuhrland) *(In-*

coterms 1980); ~ **free house** (or **domicile**) Lieferung frei Haus; ~ **free London** franko London; ~ **free at station** Lieferung franko (od. frei) Bahnhof; ~ **price** Lieferpreis; Frankopreis; ~ **weight** ausgeliefertes Gewicht; **when** ~ nach *(erfolgter)* Lieferung; **to be** ~ **in 6 days** in 6 Tagen lieferbar; mit 6tägiger Lieferfrist; **to be** ~ **at London** Erfüllungsort London

delivered 2., **to be** ~ **of a child** von e-m Kind entbunden werden

deliverable lieferbar, zu liefern(d)

deliverance *Scot* gerichtl. Entscheidung; Befreiung, Errettung (from aus)

deliverer Befreier; Lieferer; Überbringer; *(Post)* Zusteller

delivering (Ab-, Aus-)Lieferung; Überbringung; Zustellung; ~ **area** Lieferbezirk; *(Post)* Zustellungsbezirk; ~ **office** Zustellpostamt; ~ **station** Bestimmungsbahnhof

delivery (dely) Übergabe, Aushändigung, Überbringung; Lieferung, Einlieferung, Ablieferung, Auslieferung (to an); Andienung; *(Post)* Zustellung, Austragung; Entbindung

delivery, to be bad (good) ~ *(Börse)* nicht (gut) lieferbar sein; **to be late in taking** ~ die Ware verspätet abnehmen; **to adhere to** (or **meet**) **the** ~ **date** den Liefertermin einhalten; **to keep to the** ~ **promise** das Lieferversprechen einhalten; **to refuse** ~ die (Aus-) Lieferung verweigern; **to refuse to take** ~ die Annahme verweigern; **to take** ~ **of sth.** etwas abnehmen (od. entgegennehmen)

delivery, ~ **and redelivery** *(Zeitcharter)* Auslieferung und Rücklieferung; ~ **area** Lieferbezirk; *(Post)* Zustellbezirk; ~ **book** Lieferbuch; ~ **by hand** unmittelbare Übergabe

delivery by instal(l)ments Lieferung in Raten; Teillieferung; Sukzessivlieferung; **contract for** ~ Sukzessivlieferungsvertrag

delivery, ~ **charge** Zustellungsgebühr; ~ **charges** Lieferkosten

delivery clause (d/c) Lieferklausel

Klausel in zwischenstaatlichen Kaufverträgen, mit der Wareneigentümer dem Gewahrsamsinhaber (Frachtführer etc) Anweisungen über Aushändigung der Ware erteilt

delivery, ~ **contract** Liefervertrag; ~ **date** Liefertermin; ~ **day** *(Börse)* Liefer(ungs)tag; ~ **deadline** *(letzter)* Liefertermin; ~ **expenses** Lieferkosten; ~ **man** (Liefer-)Bote; Austräger; Lieferant; ~ **note** Lieferschein; ~ **of the decision** Erlaß (od. Verkündung) der Entscheidung; ~ **of a deed** *(förml.)* Aushändigung e-r Urkunde; ~ **of the documents** Auslieferung der Dokumente

delivery of goods Warenlieferung; Warenzustellung; Übergabe von Waren *(beim Kauf)*; **to refuse to take** ~ die Annahme der Ware verweigern

delivery, ~ **of a judgment** Erlaß (od. Verkündung) e-s Urteils; ~ **of the mail** Postzustellung; ~ **of a message** Übermittlung e-r Nachricht; ~ **of possession** Besitzübergabe, Besitzübertragung; ~ **of a prisoner** Einlieferung e-s Gefangenen; ~ **of a →verdict;** ~ **order** (D/O, d/o) Auslieferungsanweisung; Konnossementsteilschein; ~ **period** Lieferzeit; ~ **place** Lieferort, Erfüllungsort; ~ **promise** Lieferversprechen; ~ **receipt** Lieferschein; Warenempfangsschein; ~ **van** *Br* Lieferwagen

delivery schedule Lieferplan; **to adhere to the** ~ **as indicated** die angegebene Lieferzeit einhalten

delivery, ~ **service** Zustelldienst; ~ **of telegrams** Telegrammzustellung; ~ **terms** Lieferbedingungen; ~ **ticket** *(Börse)* Schlußzettel; ~ **times** Lieferfristen, Lieferzeiten; ~ **truck** *Am* Lieferwagen; ~ **verification** Wareneingangsbescheinigung; ~ **warehouse** Auslieferungslager

delivery, accomplished ~ vollzogene Lieferung; Erfüllung; **actual** ~ tatsächliche Übergabe; direkte Besitzübertragung *(opp. constructive ~)*; *(Börse)* effektive Lieferung; **advice of** ~ Avis der Lieferung; *(Post)* Rückschein; **bill of** ~ Lieferschein; **cash on** ~ *Br* (**collect on** ~ *Am*) gegen Nachnahme; zahlbar bei Lieferung (→*C.O.D.*); **conditions for** ~ Lieferbedingungen; **general conditions of supply and** ~ allgemeine Lieferbedingungen; **constructive** ~ symbolische (fingierte) Übergabe *(z.B. Übergabe e-s Schlüssels)*; **contract for** ~ Liefervertrag; **cost of** ~ Versandkosten, Lieferkosten; **date of** ~ Liefertermin, Lieferzeitpunkt; **day of** (or **fixed for**) ~ Liefertag; **delayed** ~ verspätete Lieferung; **express** ~ *Br* Eilzustellung, Zustellung durch Eilboten (→ *express)*; **forward** ~ *(Börse)* Terminlieferung; **free** ~ Lieferung (od. Zustellung) frei Haus; **future** ~ *(Börse)* Terminlieferung; **general** ~ *Br* gewöhnliche Zustellung *(opp. express ~)*; **general** ~ **(mail)** *Am* postlagernd(e Post); **house** ~ Lieferung frei Haus; **immediate** ~ sofortige Lieferung; **late** ~ verspätete Lieferung

delivery, non- ~ Nichtlieferung; Nichtzustellung, **in case of non-**~ falls die Lieferung unterbleibt; *(Post)* im Falle der Unzustellbarkeit

delivery, on ~ bei Lieferung; nach Ablieferung; gegen Aushändigung (of von); **amount to be collected on** ~ Nachnahmebetrag; **cash** *Br* (**collect** *Am*) **on** ~ (Zahlung) gegen Nachnahme; **charges collected on** ~ unter Nachnahme der Kosten; **to collect money** (or **charge**) **on** ~ durch Nachnahme erheben; **payable on** ~ zahlbar bei Lieferung; gegen Nachnahme; **to pay on** ~ bei Lieferung zahlen

delivery, parcel ~ Paketzustellung; **partial** ~ Teillieferung; **place of** ~ Lieferort, Erfüllungsort; Ort der Zustellung; **postal** ~ Zustellung durch die Post; **prompt** ~ sofortige Lieferung; **ready for** ~ lieferbereit; auf Abruf; **recorded** ~ *Br*[19] Sendung *(von Post)* gegen Empfangsbestätigung; **rural** ~ Landpostzustellung; **special** ~ *Am* Eilzustellung; Zustellung durch Eilboten *(→special)*; **subsequent** ~ Nachlieferung; **taking** ~ (of the goods) Abnahme (der Ware); **term of** ~ Lieferfrist *(→term 2.)*; **terms of** ~ Liefer(ungs)bedingungen

delivery, time of ~ Lieferzeit; Lieferfrist; Zeit der Zustellung; **non-compliance with the time of** ~ Nichteinhaltung der Lieferfrist; **to adhere to the time of** ~ die Lieferfrist einhalten

delivery, upon ~ s. on →~; →**writ of** ~

demogogic demagogisch

demagogy Demagogie

demand 1. Forderung, Verlangen; Ersuchen, Aufforderung; Anforderung; Erfordernis; ~ **for** Nachfrage nach; Bedarf an; ~ **account** *Am* laufendes Konto, Kontokorrentkonto; ~ **curve** Nachfragekurve; ~ **for advances** Kreditbedarf; ~ **for capital** Kapitalbedarf; ~ **for credit** Kreditbedarf; Kreditnachfrage; ~ **for extradition** Auslieferungsersuchen; ~ **for labo(u)r** Nachfrage nach Arbeitskräften; ~ **for money** Geldnachfrage; ~ **for payment** Zahlungsaufforderung, Mahnung; ~ **for return** Rückforderung; ~ **loan** täglich kündbares Darlehen; ~ **management** Nachfragesteuerung; ~ **note** *Br* Steuerbescheid *(für städtische Grundsteuer)*; **excessive** ~ **pressure** überhöhter Nachfragedruck; ~ **price** geforderter Preis; *(Börse)* Geldkurs; **~-pull inflation** nachfrageinduzierte Inflation; **~-shift inflation** Nachfrageverschiebungsinflation

demand, aggregate ~ Gesamtnachfrage; **brisk** ~ lebhafte Nachfrage; **cross** ~ Gegenforderung; **decline in (the)** ~ Rückgang der Nachfrage; **decreasing** ~ abnehmende Nachfrage; **domestic** ~ Inlandsnachfrage; Inlandsbedarf; **foreign** ~ Auslandsnachfrage; Auslandsbedarf; **great** ~ starke (od. große) Nachfrage; **home** ~ Inlandsnachfrage; inländischer Bedarf

demand, in ~ begehrt, gefragt, gesucht; **not in** ~ ohne Nachfrage; **to be in great** ~ sehr gefragt sein; **to continue in** ~ weiter gefragt sein

demand, increased ~ gesteigerter Bedarf; Bedarfszunahme; **increasing** ~ steigende Nachfrage; **inelastic** ~ starrer Bedarf; unelastische Nachfrage; **little** ~ wenig (od. geringe) Nachfrage; **market** ~**s** Marktbedürfnisse; **on** ~ auf Anforderung (od. Verlangen); **pent up** ~ *Am* Nachholbedarf; **supply and** ~ Angebot und Nachfrage; **upon** ~ s. on →~; **upturn in** ~ Nachfragesteigerung; **world** ~ Weltbedarf

demand, to be in ~ gefragt (od. begehrt) sein; **to be in great (little)** ~ stark (wenig) gefragt sein; **to check the** ~ die Nachfrage drosseln; **the** ~ **exceeds the supply** die Nachfrage übersteigt das Angebot; **to make high** (or **heavy**) ~**s on sb.** hohe Anforderungen an jdn stellen; **a** ~ **for payment has been made** e-e Zahlungsaufforderung ist ergangen; **to meet** (or **satisfy**) **the** ~ die Nachfrage befriedigen; den Bedarf decken; die Forderung erfüllen; **to meet the** ~**s** den Anforderungen entsprechen

demand 2. Sicht-; **on** ~ bei Sicht, bei Vorlage; ~ **balances** *Am* Sichtguthaben; ~ **bill** *Am* Sichtwechsel; ~ **deposits** *Am* Sichteinlagen; kurzfristige Einlagen; ~ **deposit account** Sichteinlagenkonto; ~ **draft** *Am* Sichtwechsel, Sichttratte; ~ **instrument** *Am* Sichtpapier, Sichtwechsel; ~ **liabilities** *Am* Sichtverbindlichkeiten; ~ **note** Sichtwechsel; ~ **price** *(Börse)* Sichtkurs; ~ **rate** *(Devisenmarkt)* Sichtkurs

demand *v* fordern, verlangen; fragen nach *(z.B. dem Namen)*; beanspruchen; **to** ~ **back** zurückfordern, zurückverlangen; **to** ~ **payment** (from sb.) (jdn) zur Zahlung auffordern; die Zahlung anmahnen

demanding state ersuchender Staat

demarcate *v (Grundstück etc)* abgrenzen; **to** ~ **a frontier** e-e Grenze festsetzen (od. ziehen)

demarcation Abgrenzung; Grenzziehung; ~ **dispute** *(ArbeitsR)* Streit über Tätigkeitsabgrenzung; **line of** ~ *(VölkerR)* Demarkationslinie

démarche *Fr dipl* Demarche, *dipl* Schritt *(meist e-r Gesandtschaft od. Botschaft bei der Regierung des anderen Staates); (im engeren Sinne)* formeller Protest

demarketing Anti-Marketing *(z.B. Nichtraucherkampagne)*

demented geistesgestört

demeano(u)r Betragen, Benehmen, Verhalten

démenti *Fr* Dementi; Richtigstellung, Widerruf *(durch offizielle Erklärung)*

demesne Landbesitz; (Land-)Gut *(bes. der nicht verpachtete Teil e-s Gutes, z.B. Park)*; ~ **(lands) of the Crown** *Br* Krongüter, Staatsdomänen *(opp. private estates of the sovereign)*; **Royal** ~ *Br* Krongüter, Staatsdomänen

demilitarization Entmilitarisierung, Demilitarisierung

demilitarize *v* entmilitarisieren, demilitarisieren; ~**d zone** entmilitarisierte Zone

demisable übertragbar; verpachtbar

demise Übertragung *(von Grundbesitz durch Testament od. Pachtvertrag);* Verpachtung; Vermietung; Ableben, Tod *(bes. des Souveräns);* Übertragung *(e-s Schiffes an Charterer);* ~ **charter** Mietvertrag *(betr. Schiff ohne Besatzung; Charterer haftet wie ein Eigentümer; cf. bareboat charter);* ~ **charterer** Ausrüster; ~ **of the Crown** *Br* Übergang der Krone *(durch Tod od. Abdankung)*

demise *v (Grundbesitz testamentarisch od. auf Zeit)* übertragen; verpachten; vermieten; sterben *(bes. vom Souverän); (durch Testament od. Erbfolge auf jdn)* übergehen; ~**d premises** vermietete (od. verpachtete) Grundstücke (od. Räumlichkeiten)

demission Demission *(freiwilliger od. erzwungener Rücktritt)*

demobilize *v* demobilisieren; aus dem Wehrdienst entlassen

democracy Demokratie; **parliamentary** ~ parlamentarische Demokratie; **consolidation of** ~ Festigung der Demokratie; **restoration of** ~ Wiederherstellung der Demokratie; **to restore** ~ die Demokratie wieder einführen

democrat Demokrat; *Am* Mitglied der Demokratischen Partei

Democratic Party *Am* Demokratische Partei *(cf. Republican Party)*

democratic principles, to stand by ~ zu den demokratischen Grundsätzen stehen

democratization Demokratisierung

democratize *v* demokratisieren

demographer Demograph

demographic Bevölkerungs-; demographisch; ~ **decline** Bevölkerungsrückgang; ~ **increase** Bevölkerungszunahme; ~ **policy** Bevölkerungspolitik; ~ **situation** Bevölkerungslage; ~ **statistics** Bevölkerungsstatistik

demography Demographie, Bevölkerungswissenschaft

demolish *v* zerstören, abreißen; **to** ~ **an argument** ein Argument zunichte machen (od. widerlegen); **to** ~ **a building** ein Gebäude abreißen

demolition Zerstörung; Abbruch; ~ **contractors** Abbruchfirma, Abbruchunternehmen; ~ **cost** Abbruchkosten; ~ **detail** *mil* Sprengkommando; ~ **order** *Br*[20] Abbruchverfügung *(behördl. Verfügung, ein nicht mehr reparaturfähiges Gebäude abzureißen);* ~ **works** Abbrucharbeiten

demonetization Demonetisierung; Außerkurssetzung *(von Metallgeld)*

demonetize *v* demonetisieren; *(Münzen)* außer Kurs setzen

demonstrate *v* darlegen; beweisen; *com (Gerät, Auto etc)* vorführen; demonstrieren; an e-r Kundgebung teilnehmen; e-e Kundgebung veranstalten; **right to** ~ *pol* Demonstrationsrecht

demonstration Darlegung; Beweis(führung); *com* Demonstration, Vorführung; *pol* Demonstration, *(öffentl.)* Kundgebung; **counter-**~ Gegendemonstration; ~ **project** *com* Demonstrationsvorhaben; **protest** ~ Protestkundgebung; **to disperse a** ~ e-e Demonstration zerstreuen; **to organize a** ~ e-e Demonstration veranstalten; **to take part in a** ~ an e-r Demonstration teilnehmen

demonstrative beweisend, überzeugend; ~ **force** Beweiskraft; ~ →**legacy; to be** ~ **of** der überzeugende Beweis sein für

demonstrator *pol* Demonstrant; Teilnehmer an e-r Demonstration; *com* Vorführer, Demonstrator; **to take** ~**s into custody** *pol* Demonstranten festnehmen

demoralization of the armed forces *(etwa)* Wehrkraftzersetzung

demote *v* degradieren, im Rang herabsetzen *(opp. promote v);* niedriger einstufen

demotion Degradierung; niedrigere Einstufung, Zurückstufung *(in e-e niedrigere Gehaltsgruppe als Disziplinarmaßnahme)*

demotional →**classification change**

demur, without ~ ohne Einwand

demur *v Am (unter Zugeständnis der Tatsachen) (rechtl.)* Einwände geltend machen; einwenden, Einwendungen machen (at, to gegen); beanstanden

demurrage Überliegezeit *(von Schiffen od. Bahnfrachten);* ~ **(charge[s])** Liegegeld *(bei Überschreitung der Ladezeit); (Bahn)* Wagenstandgeld; ~ **days** (or **days of** ~) Überliegetage, Überliegezeit; ~ **rate** Liegegeldsatz; **to be on** ~ Ladezeit (od. Löschzeit) überschritten haben

demurrer *Am* Rechtseinwand (to gegen); Abweisungsbegehren *(aus Rechtsgründen bei Zugeständnis des gegnerischen Tatsachenvorbringens);* mangelnde Schlüssigkeit; ~ **to action** *Am* prozeßhindernde Einrede; ~ **to evidence** *Am* Einrede des unzureichenden Beweises; **to interpose a** ~ *Am* →to demur

denationalization Beraubung des Status als Nation; Zurückführung *(der verstaatlichten Industrie)* in Privatwirtschaft, Reprivatisierung

denationalize *v (Völker)* des Status als Nation berauben; *(verstaatlichte Industrie)* in Privatwirtschaft zurückführen, reprivatisieren

denaturalization Entziehung der Staatsangehörigkeit, Ausbürgerung

denaturalize *v* Staatsangehörigkeit entziehen, ausbürgern; **to become ~d** die Staatsangehörigkeit verlieren

denazification *Ger pol* Entnazifizierung

denazify *v Ger pol* entnazifizieren

denature *v* denaturieren, ungenießbar machen

denial 1. *(Zivilprozeß)* Bestreiten *(des Klagevorbringens);* **general ~** Bestreiten des gesamten Klagevorbringens; **specific ~** Bestreiten einzelner Klagebehauptungen; **~ (up)on oath** Bestreiten unter Eid

denial 2. Leugnen, Ableugnung, Dementi; Verneinung; Ablehnung; Versagung; abschlägiger Bescheid, Absage; **~ of export privileges** *Am* Entzug des Exportprivilegs *(zur Durchsetzung des →Export Administration Act);* **~ of justice** Rechtsversagung; Verweigerung von Rechtsschutz; **~ of patentability** Nichtanerkennung der Patentfähigkeit; **~ of responsibility** Ablehnung der Verantwortung; **~ of sexual intercourse** Verweigerung des ehelichen (Geschlechts-)Verkehrs

denial 3., (**official** or **formal**) ~ Dementi; **to give a ~** dementieren (to sth. etw.); **to issue a ~** ein Dementi herausgeben; **to publish a ~** ein Dementi veröffentlichen

denied on the law als rechtlich unbegründet abgewiesen

Denmark Dänemark; **Kingdom of ~** Königreich Dänemark *(cf. Dane)*

denominate *v* (be)nennen, bezeichnen; *(Wertpapiere)* stückeln

denominated, bonds ~ in dollars auf Dollar lautende Schuldverschreibungen; **~ quantity** bezeichnete Menge

denomination Benennung, Bezeichnung; Klasse, Kategorie; Nennwert; Stückelung *(von Banknoten, Anleihen od. Aktien); eccl* Sekte, Glaubensgemeinschaft; Konfession; **~s** Stükke, Abschnitte *(Teilbeträge e-s Wertpapiers);* **~ of goods** Warenbenennung

denomination, in any ~s in allen Abschnitten; **in the ~ of** in der Stückelung von; **in ~s of** in Stücken (od. Abschnitten) zu; **big ~s** (of shares) große Abschnitte; **share** (*Am* **stock**) ~ Aktienstückelung; **small ~s** (of banknotes) kleine Werte

denominational konfessionell; **~ organization** konfessionell gebundene Organisation; **~ school** Konfessionsschule

denounce *v (jdn)* denunzieren; *(gegen jdn)* Strafanzeige erstatten, *(jdn)* anzeigen; *(jdn)* öffentl. rügen, anprangern; *(VölkerR) (Vertrag, Abkommen etc)* kündigen; **duty to ~ a crime** Anzeigepflicht e-s Verbrechens; **to ~ a treaty with 3 months' notice** e-n (Staats-)Vertrag mit 3monatiger Frist kündigen

denouncing, obligation of ~ a crime Anzeigepflicht e-s Verbrechens

denouncer Denunziant; jd, der e-e Anzeige erstattet

denouncement Denunziation, Anzeige; öffentliche Rüge

densely populated dicht bevölkert

density Dichte; **~ of population** Bevölkerungsdichte; **~ of traffic** Verkehrsdichte

denuclearized zone atomfreie Zone

denunciate *v* denunzieren, anzeigen

denunciation Denunziation, Denunzierung; Anzeige; *(VölkerR)* Kündigung *(e-s Vertrages od. Abkommens);* **clause of ~** Kündigungsklausel; **instrument of ~** *(VölkerR)* Kündigungsurkunde; **subject to ~** kündbar; **to exercise the right of ~** von dem Kündigungsrecht Gebrauch machen; **the ~ takes effect on ...** die Kündigung wird wirksam am ...

denunciator Denunziant

deny *v* (ab)leugnen, abstreiten, bestreiten; in Abrede stellen, verneinen, *(Antrag etc)* ablehnen, abschlagen, verweigern, dementieren; **to ~ an assertion** e-e Behauptung bestreiten; **to ~ liability** die Haftpflicht bestreiten; **to ~ a motion** e-n Antrag ablehnen; **to ~ (up)on oath** unter Eid bestreiten; eidlich ableugnen; **to ~** (**formally** or **officially**) dementieren; **to ~ paternity** die Vaterschaft ableugnen; **to ~ all responsibility** jede Verantwortung ablehnen; **to ~ sb. a right** jdm ein Recht absprechen; **to ~ one's signature** seine Unterschrift nicht anerkennen

depart *v* abreisen, abfahren, abfliegen (for nach); *(pleading)* vom früheren Parteivorbringen abweichen; **to ~ from the course** vom *(vorgeschriebenen)* Kurs abweichen; **to ~ from a custom** von e-m Brauch abgehen; **to ~ from one's plan** seinen Plan aufgeben

department Abteilung; Dienststelle, Regierungsstelle; Ministerium *(Br meist government ~);* Dezernat; Ressort; Fach *(Arbeitsgebiet); Am* die drei Funktionen der Staatsgewalt *(im Sinne der Gewaltenteilung; legislative, executive and judicial);* *(univ)* Seminar; **~ head** *(bei Behörden)* Abteilungsleiter; Dezernent; **D~ of Agriculture** *Am* Landwirtschaftsministerium; **D~ of the Air Force** *Am* Luftfahrtministerium; **D~ of the Army** *Am* Heeresministerium; **D~ of Commerce** *Am* Wirtschaftsministerium; **D~ of Correction** *Am* →correction;

D~ of Defense *Am* Verteidigungsministerium; **D~ of Education and Science** *Br* Ministerium für Erziehung und (Natur-)Wissenschaft; **D~ of Employment** *Br* Arbeitsministerium; **D~ of Energy** *Am* Energieministerium; **D ~ of the Environment** *Br* Ministerium für Umweltfragen; **D~ of Health** *Br* Gesundheitsministerium; **D~ of Health and Welfare** *Am (einzelstaatl.)* Gesundheitsministerium;**D~of Insurance** *Am (einzelstaatl.)* Amt für das Versicherungswesen; **D~ of the Interior** *Am*[21] Innenministerium; **D~ of Justice** *Am* Justizministerium; **D~ of Labor** *Am* Arbeitsministerium; **D~ of the Navy** *Am* Marineministerium; **D~ of Social Security** *Br* Sozialversicherungsministerium; **D~ of State** *Am* s. State →~; **D~ of Trade and Industry** *Br* Ministerium für Handel und Industrie; Wirtschaftsministerium; **D~ of** *Br* Transport (*Am* Transportation) Verkehrsministerium; **D~ of the Treasury** *Am* Finanzministerium

department store Warenhaus, Kaufhaus; **~ combine** (or **group**) Warenhauskonzern; **chain of ~s** Warenhauskette

department trial *Am* Disziplinarverfahren gegen e-n Beamten

department, accounting ~ Buchhaltung; **government ~** *Br* Ministerium; **head of a ~** Abteilungsleiter; Dezernent; **legal ~** Rechtsabteilung; **personnel ~** Personalabteilung; **Post Office D~** *Am* Postministerium; **State D~** *Am* Außenministerium, Auswärtiges Amt; **Treasury D~** *Am* (Bundes-)Finanzministerium

departmental Abteilungs-; Ministerial-, ministeriell; Regierungs-; **~ charges** direkte Kosten, Einzelkosten *(opp. fixed, indirect or overhead charges)*; **~ head** Abteilungsleiter; **~ manager** Abteilungsleiter; Disponent; **~ officials** *Am* Ministerialbeamte; **~ order** *Am* Ministerialerlaß; **~ store** Warenhaus; **~ trial** *Am* Disziplinarverfahren gegen e-n (Ministerial-) Beamten

departmentalization Gliederung nach Abteilungen

departure Abreise, Abfahrt, Abgang; Abflug; Auslaufen *(e-s Schiffes)*; Schiffsabfahrt; Ausreise (from aus) *(opp. entry into)*; Abweichen *(von e-r Regel)*; Klageänderung *(Abweichung vom ersten Parteivorbringen)*; **~ from the law** Rechtsbeugung; **to complete the ~ proceedings** *(Luftverkehr)* sich abfertigen lassen; **~ station** Abgangsbahnhof; Versandbahnhof; **~ from the truth** Abgehen von der Wahrheit

departure, new ~ neuer Anfang, Neuorientierung; **place of ~** Abfahrtsort, Abgangsort, Abflugsort; **(point of) ~** Abfahrtsort; **port of ~** Abgangshafen; **time of ~** Abfahrtszeit; Abflugszeit

depend *v* abhängen, abhängig sein (on, upon von); bedingt sein (on durch); sich verlassen (on, upon auf); **to ~ on sb.'s permission** von jds Erlaubnis abhängen; **to ~ on foreign supplies** von ausländischen Lieferungen abhängig sein; **prices ~ on supply and demand** die Preise richten sich nach Angebot und Nachfrage; **it ~s on him** es hängt von ihm ab; **he ~s on him** er ist von ihm abhängig; er verläßt sich auf ihn

dependant der/die *(abhängige oder unterhaltsbedürftige)* (Familien-)Angehörige; **~s** (of deceased person) Hinterbliebene; →**adult ~**; **~'s benefit** *Br*[22] Invalidenrente für Angehörige*(z.B. Kinderzuschuß)*; **industrial death benefit for widows and other ~s** *Br*[22] Hinterbliebenenrente für Witwen und andere Angehörige

dependence Abhängigkeit (on, upon von); Vertrauen, Verlaß (on auf); **~ on imports** Einfuhrabhängigkeit

dependency Abhängigkeit (on, upon von); *(VölkerR)* abhängiges (od. schutzherrliches) Gebiet; Protektorat; **~ allowance** *Am* Kinderbeihilfe; **~ benefits** *Am* Familienbeihilfe

dependent 1. →dependant

dependent 2. abhängig (on, upon von); unterhaltsberechtigt; unterhaltsbedürftig; **in a ~ capacity** unselbständig; **~ claim** *(PatR)* abhängiger Anspruch, Unteranspruch; **~ child** unterhaltsberechtigtes Kind; **~ contract** bedingter *(von der Erfüllung e-r Bedingung abhängiger)* Vertrag; **~ personal services** unselbständige Arbeit; **~ relatives allowance** *Br* (Steuer-)Freibetrag für Unterstützung *(bestimmter)* abhängiger Verwandter

depersonalization Entpersönlichung, Vermassung

deplane *v* (Flugzeug) entladen, ausladen; (aus dem Flugzeug) aussteigen

deplete *v* erschöpfen; verarmen *(von Lagerstätten)*; abschreiben

depleted stocks erschöpfte Bestände

depletion Erschöpfung, Substanzverringerung; **~ allowance** *(SteuerR)* Absetzung für Substanzverringerung *(Betrag, der aufgrund der Substanzverringerung z.B. e-s Bergwerks od. Ölvorkommens steuerabzugsfähig ist)*; **~ of capital** Kapitalentblößung; **~ of resources** Erschöpfung der natürlichen Hilfsquellen

deploy *v mil* aufmarschieren, sich im Gelände verteilen; *(Raketenwaffen)* aufstellen, stationieren; **to ~ forces** Truppen einsetzen; **to ~ missiles** Raketen stationieren

deployment, ~ of labo(u)r Einsatz der Arbeitskräfte; **~ of missiles** Aufstellung (od. Stationierung) von Raketen, Raketenstationierung

deponent unter Eid aussagender Zeuge *(dessen Aussage protokolliert wird);* Aussteller e-s → affidavit

depopulate *v* entvölkern; **a country ~d by war** ein durch Krieg entvölkertes Land

deport *v (lästigen Ausländer)* abschieben; ausweisen; deportieren

deported person Ausgewiesener, Deportierter; (Zwangs-)Umsiedler

deportation Landesverweisung, Ausweisung; Deportation, Verschleppung, Zwangsverschickung; ~ **of an undesirable alien** Abschiebung e-s lästigen Ausländers; ~ **order** Ausweisungsbefehl; **mass** ~ Massendeportation

deportee →deported person

depose *v* schriftliche eidliche Erklärung abgeben; eidliche Aussage zu Protokoll geben; *(jdn)* absetzen, des Amtes entheben

deposit 1. Verwahrung(svertrag); Aufbewahrung; Hinterlegung; hinterlegter Gegenstand; hinterlegter Betrag; hinterlegte Sicherheit, Kaution(szahlung); Depot *(bei e-r Bank zur Verwahrung gegebene Gegenstände);* ~ **of assets** *Am (VersR)* Hinterlegung von Vermögenswerten *(Kautionszahlung e-r Versicherungsgesellschaft als Sicherheit für die Versicherungsnehmer);* ~ **book** Depotbuch *(Verwahrungsbuch der Depotabteilung); Br* Spar(kassen)buch; ~ **certificate** Hinterlegungsschein; Depotbescheinigung *(der Bank über in Verwahrung genommene Wertpapiere);* ~ **of documents in court** Hinterlegung von Dokumenten bei Gericht; ~ **fee** Depotgebühr; ~ **of industrial designs and models** Hinterlegung gewerblicher Muster und Modelle (→*design 2.);* ~ **insurance** Depotversicherung; ~ **receipt** Depotschein; Aufbewahrungsschein; ~ **records** Depotunterlagen; ~ **of a security** Hinterlegung e-r Sicherheit; ~ **of securities** *Am* Effektendepot, Wertpapierdepot; ~ **scheme** *(EG)* Kautionsregelung; ~ **slip** *Am* Depotschein; ~ **of title deeds** *Br*[23] Hinterlegung von Eigentumsurkunden *(meist bei einer Bank; häufige und einfache Art e-r Hypothekenbestellung);* ~ **warrant** Hinterlegungsschein

deposit, alternate ~ Gemeinschaftsdepot, gemeinsames Depot *(jeder einzelne ist verfügungsberechtigt; opp. joint* ~); **certificate of** ~ →~ certificate; **collective** ~ Sammeldepot; **contract of** ~ Hinterlegungsvertrag; Verwahrungsvertrag; **general** ~ Sammeldepot; Sammelverwahrung; **gratuitous** ~ unentgeltliche Verwahrung; **(guarantee)** ~ hinterlegte Sicherheit, Kaution; **joint** ~ gemeinsames Depot, Gemeinschaftsdepot; **kept on** ~ depotverwahrt; **misapplication** (or **misappropriation**) **of** ~ Depotunterschlagung; **on** ~ im Depot; deponiert (with bei); in (od. zur) Verwahrung; **place of** ~ Hinterlegungsort; **property capable of** (or **suitable for**) **official** ~ hinterlegungsfähige Sachen; **safe** ~ **box** (Bank-) Schließfach; Safe; **safe** ~ **vault** *Am* Stahlkammer; **security** ~ →security 1.; **statement of** ~ Depotauszug; **sum on** ~ hinterlegter Betrag; Hinterlegungssumme

deposit, to leave a ~ e-n Betrag hinterlegen (→ *deposit 2.*); **to make** (or **pay**) **a** ~ e-e Kaution hinterlegen; **to put securities into a** ~ Wertpapiere in ein Depot geben

deposit 2. Anzahlung; Draufgabe, Angeld *(bes. bei Abschluß e-s Grundstückskaufvertrages; Br meist 10% des Kaufpreises);* ~ **laid down for the expenses incurred** Kostenvorschuß *(z.B. beim Vergleichsverfahren der Intern. Handelskammer);* ~ **of costs** Vorschuß für Verfahrenskosten; **amount of the** ~ Kostenvorschuß; **payment of the** ~ **in respect of arbitration** Vorschuß für die Schiedsgerichtskosten; **initial** ~ Anzahlung; **return of the** ~[24] Rückgabe der Draufgabe; **to forfeit one's** ~ seine Draufgabe einbüßen; seiner Draufgabe verlustig gehen; **to leave a** ~ e-e Zahlung machen, anzahlen; **to make a** ~ e-n Vorschuß leisten; *Am* anzahlen *(bes. bei Ratenzahlungsverträgen);* **to pay a** ~ anzahlen; Draufgeld bezahlen

deposit 3. (Geld-)Einlage, Guthaben *(bei e-r Bank),* Bankeinlage; *Br* Spareinlage; Einzahlung, eingezahltes Geld; ~**s** Depositen, Depositengelder *(Geldeinlagen);* ~ **account** (with a bank) Depositenkonto für befristete Einlagen *(opp. current account); Br* Sparkonto; ~ **accounts** (Depositenkonten für) Termineinlagen; ~**s and withdrawings** Einzahlungen und Abhebungen; ~**s at call** Sichteinlagen, Sichtdepositen; ~ **at long notice** langfristige Einlage; ~**s at notice** Einlagen mit Kündigungsfrist; Kündigungsgelder; ~ **at post office** Postscheckguthaben; ~ **at short notice** kurzfristige Einlage; ~ **by customers** fremde Gelder *(e-s Kreditinstituts);* ~ **banking** Depositengeschäft *(e-r Bank);* ~ **book** Depositenbuch *(Einlagenbuch);* ~ **currency** *Am* Giralgeld, Buchgeld; ~ **department** Depositenabteilung; ~ **insurance** Einlagenversicherung; ~ **interest** Einlagezinsen; ~ **interest rates** *Br* Zinssätze auf Spareinlagen; ~ **money** *Br* Giralgeld, Buchgeld; ~ **on current account** Kontokorrenteinlage; ~ **passbook** (DPB) Depositenbuch; **D~ Protection Board** *Br* Einlagensicherungsausschuß *(der Bank of England);* **D~ Protection Fund** Einlagensicherungsfonds *(der britischen Banken);* ~ **rate** Zinssatz für Depositengelder; ~ **receipt** (or **slip**) Einzahlungsbeleg *(über Einzahlungen auf Depositenkonto);* ~**s with fixed period** befristete (Depositen-)Gelder

deposit, advertisement for ~**s** Einlagenwerbung; **amount of the** ~ Höhe der Einlage; **bank**~ Bankeinlage; **cash** ~ Bareinlage; **cer-**

tificate of ~ Depositenschein; **checkable** ~**s** *Am* quasi-verzinsliche Sichteinlagen bei US-Banken (→*automatic transfer service accounts und Now* →*accounts); **demand** ~**s** *Am* Sichteinlagen, Sichtdepositen; **fixed** ~**s** feste Gelder, Termingelder; **other** ~**s** Privatdepositen *(opp. public ~s)*; **public** ~**s** *Br* Staatsdepositen, öffentliche Gelder *(Einlagen der Regierung od. anderer Behörden bei Kreditinstituten in England)*; **savings bank** ~ Spareinlage; **sight** ~**s** Sichteinlagen; **special** ~**s** *Br*[25] *(1960 eingeführte Form von)* Mindestreserven; **term** ~**s** *Br* Termineinlagen, befristete Einlagen; **time** ~**s** *Am* Termineinlagen, befristete Einlagen *(Festgelder und Spareinlagen mit e-r Kündigungsfrist von mindestens 30 Tagen)*; **total** ~**s** Gesamteinlagen

deposit, to allow 4% on ~**s** Einlagen mit 4% verzinsen; **to make a** ~ *Am* e-e Einlage machen; **to withdraw a** ~ e-e Einlage abheben

deposit 4. Lager(stätten); Vorkommen; **exploitation of** ~**s of tin** Abbau von Zinnerzlagern; **main** ~ **of oil** Hauptvorkommen von Öl

deposit *v* hinterlegen, deponieren, aufbewahren (with bei); in Depot geben; in Verwahrung (od. zur Aufbewahrung) geben; *(Geld auf das eigene Konto)* einzahlen; e-e Einlage machen; anzahlen, Anzahlung machen; **to** ~ **in court** bei Gericht hinterlegen; **to** ~ **securities** Wertpapiere hinterlegen; **to** ~ **as security** als Sicherheit hinterlegen; **to** ~ **one's will** sein Testament hinterlegen (with bei)

deposited assets, certificate of ~ Depotbescheinigung

deposited chattel, withdrawal of the ~ Rücknahme der hinterlegten Sache

deposited securities in Depot gegebene Wertpapiere; **statement of** ~ Depotauszug

depositing Hinterlegung; Einzahlung *(bei der Bank)*; ~ **business** Depotgeschäft; ~ **of money or securities** Hinterlegung von Geld od. Wertpapieren; ~ **as security** Hinterlegung als Sicherheitsleistung

depositary Verwahrer; *(Bank)* Depositar; ~**(bank)** *Am* Depotbank (für ADRs); ~ **government** Verwahrerregierung; Depositarregierung; ~ **state** Verwahrerstaat; **the credit institution acting as initial** ~ das erstverwahrende Kreditinstitut

depositation *Scot* Verwahrung(svertrag)

deposition eidliche mündliche Zeugenaussage *(vor einem bes. beauftragten Richter, z.B. auf Grund von Rechtshilfeersuchen)*; Beweisaufnahmeprotokoll *(bes. von Zeugenaussagen durch e-n besonders beauftragten Richter)*; Amtsenthebung, Absetzung; Hinterlegung, Verwahrung; **evidence by** ~ *(zu Protokoll genommene)* eidliche Zeugenaussage *(die vor der Verhandlung vor e-m vom Gericht ernannten examiner oder e-r ausländischen Behörde [foreign judicial authority] entgegengenommen ist)*; **to file a** ~ e-e *(zu Protokoll genommene)* eidliche Zeugenaussage zu den Gerichtsakten einreichen *(for use at trial)*; **to make a** ~ e-e eidliche Erklärung abgeben; **to place a** ~ **on the court records** eidliche Zeugenaussage zu Protokoll nehmen; **to take** ~**s** eidliche Aussagen entgegennehmen

depositor Hinterleger, Deponent; Einzahler *(in e-e Bank)*, Einleger; ~**'s book** Einlagenbuch

depository Hinterlegungsstelle; Verwahrungsstelle; Verwahrer; Aufbewahrungsort; Lager(-haus), Speicher; *Am* Bank für öffentliche Gelder; **D**~ **Institutions Deregulation and Monetary Control Act of 1980** *Am* Gesetz zur Deregulierung der Finanzmarktregulationen des Federal Reserve Board (→*Regulations*); ~ **of record** Registratur, Archiv; →**authorized** ~

depot Depot, Lager(haus), Magazin; *mil* Lager, Depot; *Am* Bahnhof; **goods** ~ *Am* Güterbahnhof; **supply** ~ *mil* Nachschublager

depreciable abschreibbar, abschreibungsfähig; absetzbar; abnutzbar; ~ **amount** Abschreibungsbetrag

depreciate *v (Wert, Preis)* herabsetzen; niedriger bewerten, abwerten; *(im Werte)* sinken (od. fallen); *(Wertminderung)* abschreiben; **to** ~ **a currency** e-e Währung abwerten

depreciated, ~ **currency** niedriger bewertete (od. abgewertete) Währung *(opp. appreciated currency)*; ~ **money** entwertetes Geld; ~ **value** Abschreibungsrestwert; **countries whose currencies have** ~ Abwertungsländer; **the price has** ~ der Kurs ist gefallen

depreciation Wertminderung, Wertherabsetzung; Entwertung, niedrigere Bewertung, Abwertung; Kursverlust; Abschreibung *(für Wertminderung)*; ~ **account** Abschreibungskonto; ~ **allowance** Absetzung für Abnutzung (AfA); Wertberichtigung; ~ **amount** Abschreibungsbetrag; ~ **on buildings** Abschreibung auf Gebäude; ~ **of capital** Kapitalentwertung; ~ **charge** Abschreibung(sbetrag); ~ **of currency** Währungsabwertung; ~ **fund** Abschreibungsfonds; Rückstellung für Wertminderung; ~ **of the lira** Abwertung der Lira; ~ **of money** Geldentwertung; ~ **period** Abschreibungsdauer; ~ **procedure** Abschreibungsverfahren; ~ **rate** Abschreibungssatz; ~ **on replacement value** Absetzung vom Wiederbeschaffungswert; ~ **reserve** Rückstellung für Wertminderung; ~ **for tax purposes** steuerliche Abschreibung; ~ **for wear and tear** Absetzung für Abnutzung

depreciation, accelerated ~ beschleunigte Abschreibung; **accrued** ~ *Am* Wertberichtigung für Abnutzung; **actual** ~ wirkliche Wertminderung; **annual** ~ jährliche Absetzung für Abnutzung; →**declining balance** ~; **deduction for** ~ →deduction 2.; **extraordinary** ~ außerordentliche (od. außerplanmäßige) Abschreibung; **ordinary** ~ ordentliche Abschreibung, planmäßige Abschreibung; **regular** ~ regelmäßige Abschreibung; →**straight line** ~

depreciation, to allow for ~ die Wertminderung berücksichtigen; **to deduct as** ~ abschreiben; **to make a** ~ e-e Abschreibung vornehmen; ~ **is computed on a straight line, declining balance or sum of the years digit basis** *Am* die Absetzungen für Abnutzung werden nach der linearen, der degressiven oder der digitalen Methode berechnet; **to use high rates of** ~ hohe Abschreibungen machen

depredation Plünderung, Raub; *Scot* gewaltsames Abtreiben von Vieh

depress *v*, **to** ~ **the market** die Kurse drücken; **to** ~ **the prices** die Preise drücken

depressed *(Handel, Börse)* flau; gedrückt; von der Krise betroffen; ~ **area** Notstandsgebiet; **industry is** ~ die Industrie liegt darnieder

depression Depression, *(tiefe)* Wirtschaftskrise, Konjunkturtief(stand) *(opp. boom)*; ~ **period** Depressionszeit; ~ **year** Krisenjahr, schlechtes Geschäftsjahr

depression, (economic) ~ Wirtschaftskrise; Konjunkturrückgang; **trade** ~ Darniederliegen des Handels

deprivation Beraubung; Entziehung; Verlust; **unlawful** ~ *(PatR)* widerrechtliche Entnahme; ~ **(of benefice)** Amtsenthebung e-s Geistlichen; ~ **of citizenship**[26] Aberkennung der Staatsangehörigkeit; Ausbürgerung; ~ **of civil rights** Aberkennung der bürgerlichen Ehrenrechte; ~ **of enjoyment** Entziehung des Genusses; ~ **of liberty** Freiheitsentziehung, Freiheitsberaubung; ~ **of pension** Aberkennung des Ruhegehalts; ~ **of possession** Besitzentziehung

deprive *v*, **to** ~ **sb. of sth.** jdn e-r Sache berauben; jdm etw. entziehen; **to** ~ **sb. of his citizenship** jdm die Staatsangehörigkeit aberkennen; jdn ausbürgern; **to** ~ **a clergyman** *Br* e-n Geistlichen s-s Amtes entheben

deputation Deputation, Abordnung

depute *v (jdn)* abordnen, bevollmächtigen; *(Aufgabe, Vollmacht etc)* übertragen

deputize *v*, **to** ~ **(for sb.)** jdn vertreten, als jds Vertreter fungieren; *Am (jdn)* abordnen, *(jdn)* zum Stellvertreter ernennen

deputy *parl* Deputierter, Abgeordneter; Stellvertreter, Vertreter; *Br* Hilfsrichter beim County Court *(bei Verhinderung des ordentlichen Richters)*; Vize-; stellvertretend; ~ **chairman** stellvertretender Vorsitzender; Vizepräsident; ~ **chief executive** *Am* stellvertretender Generaldirektor; ~ **editor** stellvertretender Redakteur; ~ **leader** *Br* stellvertretender Parteiführer; **at** ~ **level** auf Stellvertreterebene; ~ **lieutenant** *Br* Vertreter des →Lord Lieutenant; ~ **manager** stellvertretender Geschäftsführer (od. Leiter); ~ **sheriff** Sheriff-Stellvertreter; **acting as** ~ in Vertretung; **appointment of a** ~ Ernennung e-s Stellvertreters; **to act as sb.'s** ~ (or **to act as** ~ **for sb.**) jdn. vertreten; **to appoint a** ~ e-n Vertreter ernennen (od. bestellen)

deranged, (mentally) ~ geistesgestört, geistesschwach

derangement, (mental) ~ Geistesstörung, Geistesschwäche

deregistration Löschung im Register

deregulate *v* deregulieren; einschränkende Bestimmungen aufheben

deregulation Deregulation, Deregulierung; Aufhebung einschränkender Bestimmungen; Verringerung normativer Beschränkungen des Geld- und Kapitalverkehrs

derelict herrenlose Sache; aufgegebenes Schiff; treibendes Wrack, Wrackgut; verlassen, aufgegeben, herrenlos; *Am* pflichtvergessen; ~ **(farm)land** zum Ödland gewordenes Gebiet; ~ **(property)** herrenlose Sache; ~ **vessel** *(auf hoher See)* aufgegebenes Schiff; ~ **village** *(von der Bevölkerung)* verlassenes Dorf

dereliction Dereliktion, Eigentumsaufgabe; *(VölkerR)* Dereliktion *(Aufgabe e-s Gebietes durch einseitigen Verzicht)*; Austrocknen des Flußbettes *(und dadurch Landgewinn)*; Pflichtverletzung; ~ **of duty** Amtspflichtverletzung

derequisition *v (beschlagnahmtes Vermögen etc)* freigeben; Beschlagnahme aufheben

derequisitioning Freigabe; Aufhebung der Beschlagnahme

derestrict *v* Einschränkungsmaßnahme lockern; **to** ~ **a road** die Geschwindigkeitsbeschränkung aufheben

derivation Ableitung, Herleitung; ~ **of a claim** Herleitung e-s Anspruchs

derivative derivativ, nicht originär; ~ **action** (or *Am* **suit**) Aktionärsklage; abgeleitete Klage *(mit der ein Aktionär in Prozeßstandschaft Recht der Gesellschaft einklagt)*; ~ **claim** Anspruch e-s mittelbar Geschädigten; ~ **title** derivativ erworbenes Eigentum; ~ **work** *(ArbR)* Bearbeitung

derive *v* ableiten, herleiten (from von); **to** ~ **a profit** Nutzen ziehen (from aus); **to** ~ **revenue** (or **income**) Einkünfte beziehen; **to** ~ **title** Recht herleiten (from aus)

derived demand abgeleitete Nachfrage

derogate *v* derogieren, *(Gesetz etc)* teilweise aufheben; Abbruch tun, mindern, beeinträchtigen (from sth. etw.); *(nachteilig)* abweichen (from von); **to ~ from a p.'s rights** jds Rechte beeinträchtigen, jdn in s-n Rechten schmälern

derogation Derogation, Teilaufhebung, teilweise Außerkraftsetzung; Abbruch, Minderung, Beeinträchtigung (from a th. e-r Sache); **~s from Community Law** *(EG)* Abweichungen vom Gemeinschaftsrecht; **in ~ of** abweichend von; **statutes in ~ of the Common Law** Gesetze in Abänderung des Common Law

derogatory nachteilig, abträglich (to für); **~ clause** Abänderungsklausel *(Verfügung in e-r Urkunde, daß Abänderungen nur in bestimmter Form gültig sein sollen);* **to be ~ (to)** schaden, beeinträchtigen

descend *v* abstammen (from von); *(im Wege der gesetzlichen Erbfolge)* übergehen (to auf)

descended, Dutch ~ holländischer Abstammung; **lineally ~ from** in gerade Linie abstammend von; **to be ~ from** abstammen von, Nachkomme sein von

descending, in the ~ line in absteigender Linie

descendable vererbbar

descendant Nachkomme, Abkömmling *(opp. ancestor, ascendant);* **~s** Nachkommen(schaft)

descent 1. Abstammung, Herkunft; *(gesetzl.)* Erbfolge *(in unbewegl. Vermögen);* Übergang *(von Grundbesitz auf Grund von gesetzl. Erbfolge); fig* Niedergang, Verfall; **by ~** im Erbwege; **~ in direct line** s. lineal →~; **collateral ~** Abstammung in der Seitenlinie; **illegitimate ~** nichteheliche Abstammung; **legitimate ~** eheliche Abstammung; **lineal ~** Abstammung in gerader Linie; **title by ~** Rechtstitel auf Grund gesetzlicher Erbfolge; **to succeed to land by ~** *Am* Grundbesitz *(auf Grund gesetzl. Erbfolge)* erben; **to trace one's ~** Abstammung (od. Familie) zurückverfolgen

descent 2., **~ upon the enemy** *(VölkerR)* feindlicher Einfall, Invasion

description Beschreibung, Darstellung; Bezeichnung, Personenbeschreibung; *colloq.* Gattung, Art, Sorte; **~ of contents** Inhaltsbezeichnung, Inhaltsangabe; **~ of goods** Beschreibung der Ware; Warenbezeichnung; **~ of the invention** Beschreibung der Erfindung; **~ of land** Grundstücksbeschreibung; **~ (of a person)** Personenbeschreibung; **~ of securities** Effektengattung

description, by ~ nach Beschreibung (od. Angabe); **goods by ~** Ware(n) nach Beschreibung *(z.B. e-s Katalogs);* Gattungsware(n); **sale by ~**[27] Verkauf nach (Waren-)Beschreibung *(z.B. e-s Katalogs);* Gattungskauf; **goods of the contract ~** vertragsgemäße Waren; **goods of the same ~** *(WarenzeichenR)* gleichartige Waren; **name, address and ~ of a p.** jds Namen, Anschrift und Beruf *(od. Familienstand bei e-r Frau);* **patent ~** Patentbeschreibung

description, printed ~ Patentschrift; **prior public printed ~** *(PatR)* Vorveröffentlichung; **publication of the printed ~** Herausgabe der Patentschrift

description, to answer to the ~ der Beschreibung entsprechen

descriptive beschreibend; darstellend; **~ words** lediglich bezeichnende Worte *(die nicht als Warenzeichen geschützt werden können)*

desegregate *v* Rassentrennung aufheben

desegregated nicht mehr nach Rassen getrennt

desegregation *Am* Aufhebung der Rassentrennung *(bes. an Schulen)*

deselection Abwahl

desert *v (Familie, Ehepartner) (böswillig)* verlassen; abfallen von; *mil* desertieren, fahnenflüchtig werden, zum Feind überlaufen; **to induce to ~** zur Fahnenflucht verleiten; **to ~ the forces** (or **one's colo[u]rs**) fahnenflüchtig werden; **to ~ a party** e-r Partei untreu werden, von s-r Partei abfallen

deserted verlassen; unbelebt; unbewohnt

deserter *mil* Fahnenflüchtiger, Deserteur, Überläufer; bordflüchtiger Seemann

desertification Wüstenbildung, Verödung

desertion Verlassen *(des Ehepartners; cf. divorce);* Abfall *(von e-r Partei); mil* Desertion, Fahnenflucht; **assisting in ~** Beihilfe zur Fahnenflucht

design 1. Absicht, Vorhaben; Entwurf, Plan (-ung), Zeichnung, Konstruktion; **~s** *(geheime)* Absichten; **~ defect(s)** Konstruktionsfehler; **by ~** absichtlich, beabsichtigt; **faulty ~** Konstruktionsfehler; **latest ~** letztes Modell; **unity of ~** planvolles Zusammenwirken

design 2. Muster *(geschmacklicher od. technischer Art); (industrielle)* Formgebung

In Großbritannien beruht das Musterrecht auf dem Registered Design Act 1949, zuletzt geändert durch den Copyright, Designs and Patents Act 1988. Die Muster werden in dem beim Patentamt geführten Musterregister eingetragen und genießen einen Schutz von 5–15 Jahren.

In den Vereinigten Staaten kann auf Grund des Patentgesetzes von 1952 nach einer Vorprüfung ein Musterpatent (design patent) erteilt werden.

Grundlage des internationalen Musterrechts ist die Pariser Verbandsübereinkunft zum Schutze des gewerblichen Eigentums (Londoner Fassung) *(s. Paris →Convention).* Die Angehörigen der Verbandsländer genießen in den anderen Verbandsländern den Schutz der dort geltenden Mustergesetze.

Weitergehende Vereinbarungen über den internationalen Musterschutz sind in dem Haager Muster-Abkommen getroffen *(cf.* →*Hague Agreement Concerning the International Deposit of Industrial Designs or Models)*

design, ~ data Musterangaben, Beschreibung des Musters; ~ **patent** *Am* geschütztes Geschmacksmuster *(eigenartiges und ornamentales Muster e-s Fabrikationsgegenstandes)*; ~ **requirements** *(erforderliche)* charakteristische Eigenschaften des Musters; ~ **pooling agreement** (Geschmacks-, Gebrauchs-)Musterkartell

design, conventional ~ übliches (od. gängiges) Muster; **copyright in ~s** *Br*[28] Urheberrecht an Mustern; Musterschutz

design, industrial ~ gewerbliches Muster; industrielle Formgebung *(zum Zwecke e-r das Publikum ansprechenden formschönen Gestaltung technischer Geräte)*; **international deposit of industrial ~s** internationale Hinterlegung gewerblicher Muster *(cf.* →*Hague Agreement Concerning the International Deposit of Industrial D~s or Models)*

design, ornamental ~ Geschmacksmuster; **ownership of ~s or models** Eigentum an Mustern oder Modellen; **patent for ~s**→~ patent; **proprietor of a** ~ Inhaber e-s Musters; **Register of ~s** *Br* Musterregister

design, registered ~ *Br*[29] eingetragenes (Gebrauchs-)Muster; **protection of registered ~s** *Br* (Gebrauchs-)Musterschutz

Gebrauchsmusterschutz für eingetragene Muster wird auf 5 Jahre erteilt (kann auf Antrag verlängert werden). Zuständig für Erteilung und Verlängerung ist das Patent Office.

Der Copyright, Designs and Patents Act 1988 hat zusätzlich zum Schutz von registered designs einen weiteren Designschutz von kürzerer Schutzdauer eingeführt

design, registration of a ~ Eintragung e-s Musters; **representation of a** ~ *(bildliche)* Darstellung e-s Musters

design *v* planen, beabsichtigen; bestimmen (for für); zeichnen, entwerfen, konstruieren

designate *v* bezeichnen, kennzeichnen; benennen, ernennen, bestimmen, ausersehen (for zu); **to ~ the boundaries of a country** die Grenzen e-s Landes bestimmen (od. kennzeichnen); **to ~ an heir** *Am* e-n Erben bestimmen; **to ~ a successor** e-n Nachfolger bestimmen

designated, ~ office *(Europ. PatR)* Bestimmungsamt; ~ **time** bestimmte (od. vorgesehene) Zeit; **transaction ~ as corrupt** als unredlich bezeichnete Transaktion

designate designiert, vorgesehen, ernannt *(aber noch nicht im Amt bestätigt)*

designation Bezeichnung, Kennzeichnung; Name; Benennung, Bestimmung *(für ein Amt etc.)*; ~ **fee** *(Europ. PatR)* Benennungsgebühr; ~ **of the inventor** *(PatR)* Erfinder(be-)nennung; **country of** ~ *(Europ. PatR)* Bestimmungsland; **technical** ~ *(PatR)* technische Bezeichnung der Erfindung

designee für ein Amt Ernannter *(aber noch nicht Tätiger)*

designer, industrial ~ Formgestalter, Formgeber *(industrieller Erzeugnisse)*

desirous in dem Bestreben (od. Wunsch); von dem Wunsch geleitet; **the parties are** ~ (to do) die Parteien beabsichtigen

desist *v* ablassen (from von); aufhören; **to →cease and ~**; →**cease and ~ order** *Am*

desk Schreibtisch; Schalter; *(Hotel)* Empfang(sschalter); *Am* Redaktion; Referat *(e-s Ministeriums)*; ~ **clerk** Portier *(an der Rezeption)*; ~**man** *Am* Redaktionsmitglied; ~ **research** *(Marktforschung)* Sekundärforschung, Schreibtischforschung *(opp. field research)*; ~ **work** Schreibtischarbeit, Büroarbeit; **pay** ~ Kassenschalter, Kasse; **please pay at the** ~ zahlen Sie bitte an der Kasse

desmesne of the Crown *Br* Domäne

despatch *v* →dispatch *v*

despoliation Plünderung, Beraubung; ~ **of the landscape by development** Zersiedlung der Landschaft

despotism *pol* Despotismus, Despotie, Gewaltherrschaft

destabilization, policy of ~ Destabilisierungspolitik

destabilize *v* destabilisieren

destination Bestimmung, Bestimmungsort; Reiseziel; *Scot* Erbeinsetzung; ~ **country** Bestimmungsland; **hostile** ~ *(VölkerR)* feindliche Bestimmung *(cf. contraband)*; **place of** ~ Bestimmungsort; **port of** ~ Bestimmungshafen; **station of** ~ Bestimmungsbahnhof

destined for exportation zur Ausfuhr bestimmt

destitute mittellos, verarmt; **the** ~ die Notleidenden; **the claim is ~ of merit** der Anspruch entbehrt jeder Grundlage

destruction Zerstörung, Vernichtung; ~ **of documents** Vernichtung von Urkunden; **risk of ~ or loss of the goods** Gefahr für Untergang oder Beschädigung der Sachen

destructive zerstörend, destruktiv; ~ **criticism** vernichtende Kritik

desuetude Außergebrauchkommen; **to fall into** ~ außer Gebrauch kommen

detach *v* abtrennen, abschneiden, ablösen (from von); absondern; *mil* abkommandieren

detached abgetrennt; alleinstehend *(Haus)*; uninteressiert, gleichgültig (about gegen); **semi-~ house** Hälfte e-s Doppelhauses

detaching of coupons Abtrennung von Coupons

detachable abtrennbar

detachment Abtrennung, Loslösung (from von); Absonderung; Gleichgültigkeit (from gegen); *mil* Kommando; ~ **of police** Polizeiaufgebot, Polizeiabteilung

detail Einzelheit; *mil* (Sonder-)Kommando; ~**s** Einzelheiten, nähere Angaben, das Nähere; **in** ~ ausführlich, im einzelnen; ~**s can be obtained from** Näheres ist zu erfahren bei; **to give full** ~**s** nähere Einzelheiten anführen; **to go into** ~**s** ins einzelne gehen

detail *v* ins einzelne gehen; einzeln aufführen, im einzelnen beschreiben; *mil* abkommandieren; **to** ~ **a claim** e-n Anspruch zergliedern

detailed eingehend, ausführlich; ~ **account** spezifizierte Rechnung; eingehender Bericht; ~ **negotiation** ins einzelne gehende Verhandlung; ~ **statement** detaillierte Darlegung; Einzelaufstellung; ~ **for special work** (or **on special service**) zur besonderen Verfügung (z. b. V.)

detain *v* 1. in Haft nehmen (od. halten); festnehmen, inhaftieren; internieren; *(Geisteskranke, straffällige Jugendliche etc)* in e-r Anstalt unterbringen; **to** ~ **in custody** in (Untersuchungs-) Haft halten

detained in (Untersuchungs-)Haft, inhaftiert; **person summarily** ~ ohne Gerichtsverfahren inhaftierte Person; ~ **by the police** von der Polizei festgenommen; **to be** ~ **during Her Majesty's pleasure** *Br*[30] auf unbestimmte Zeit in Haft gehalten werden

detaining power Gewahrsamsstaat *(in dem sich der auszuliefernde Gefangene befindet)*

detain *v* 2. *(jdn)* aufhalten, zurückhalten; *(etw.)* zurückhalten, vorenthalten; **to** ~ **goods** Waren anhalten (od. zurückhalten); **to be** ~**ed in a port** in e-m Hafen aufgehalten werden

detainee Inhaftierter; *(politischer)* Häftling; Internierter; **civilian** ~ Zivilinternierter

detainer, wrongful (or **forcible**) ~ rechtswidrige Vorenthaltung *(von Grundbesitz)*; **forcible entry and** ~ gewaltsame und unerlaubte Inbesitzhaltung *(von Grundbesitz)*; **unlawful** ~ **action** *Am* Räumungsklage

detainment →detention

detect *v* entdecken; **to** ~ **a crime** ein Verbrechen aufdecken

detection Entdeckung, Aufdeckung; Ermittlung; *Am* Feststellung *(der Kernwaffen-Erschütterung in e-m anderen Land; cf. location)*; ~ **of a fraud** Aufdeckung e-s Betruges

detective Geheimpolizist; (Privat-)Detektiv; **private** ~ Privatdetektiv; ~ **agency** Detektei, Detektivbüro; ~ **officer** Kriminalbeamter; **to be watched by a** ~ von e-m Detektiv überwacht werden

détente *pol* Entspannung(spolitik); **policy of** ~ Entspannungspolitik

detention 1. (Untersuchungs-)Haft; Inhaftierung; Festnahme; Gefangenhaltung; Internierung; *mil* Einschließung; ~ **barracks** *Br* Militärgefängnis; ~ **centre** *Br* Jugendarrestanstalt, Jugendgefängnis; ~ **home** *Am* Jugend(untersuchungs)- gefängnis; ~ **by police** Polizeihaft; ~ **awaiting** (or **pending**) **trial** Untersuchungshaft

detention, compulsory ~ zwangsweise Unterbringung *(e-s Geisteskranken etc)*; **leave from** ~ Hafturlaub; **preventive** ~ *Br*[31] Sicherungsverwahrung; **temporary** ~ vorläufige Inhaftierung; **unlawful** ~ ungesetzliche Haft; Freiheitsberaubung

detention 2. Zurückhaltung, Vorenthaltung; Aufhaltung; ~ **of a ship** Zurückhaltung e-s Schiffes *(unfreiwilliger Aufenthalt)*; **damages for** ~ Aufenthaltsentschädigung *(des Verfrachters)*; **right of** ~ Zurückbehaltungsrecht

deter *v* abschrecken, abhalten (from von); ~**ring effect** abschreckende Wirkung *(e-r Strafe)*

detergents Detergentien (→*European Agreement on the Restriction of the Use of Certain D~s . . .)*

deteriorate *v* (sich) verschlechtern; im Wert sinken; im Wert mindern; verderben; **the financial situation** ~**d considerably** die finanzielle Lage hat sich wesentlich verschlechtert; **the goods** ~**d during storage** die Waren verdarben während der Lagerung

deteriorating, ~ **economic situation** Verschlechterung der Wirtschaftslage; ~ **urban areas** an Wert verlierende städtische Gegenden

deterioration Verschlechterung; Wertminderung; Verderb; Verschleiß; ~ **in the quality** Qualitätsverminderung; ~ **of the financial situation** Verschlechterung der Vermögensverhältnisse; ~ **of the value of money** Geldverschlechterung; **intrinsic** ~ innerer Verderb

determent Abschreckung(smittel)

determinable feststellbar, bestimmbar; befristet, beendbar, kündbar, ~ **contract** kündbarer (od. aufhebbarer) Vertrag; ~ **interest** auflösend bedingtes Recht an Grundbesitz

determinate bestimmt; entschieden; endgültig

determination 1. Bestimmung, Festsetzung; Entscheidung; Entschlossenheit, Entschluß (to do sth.); ~ **of conditions** Festsetzung von Bedingungen; ~ **of a court** gerichtliche Entscheidung; ~ **of the measure of a penalty**

Strafzumessung; ~ **of prices** Preisbestimmung; ~ **of profits for tax purposes** steuerliche Gewinnermittlung
determination, co-~ of labo(u)r Mitbestimmung(srecht) der Arbeitnehmer; **(right of) self-~ (of peoples)** Selbstbestimmungsrecht (der Völker)
determination 2. Ablauf, Ende; ~ **of an agreement** *(bes. KartellR)* Aufhebung e-r Absprache; ~ **of a lease** Pachtablauf; Ende des Pacht- (od. Miet-)Verhältnisses; ~ **of the suit** Ende des Prozesses

determine *v (Preis, Strafe etc)* bestimmen, festsetzen; festlegen; entscheiden; beschließen; e-n Entschluß fassen; *(etw.)* bestimmen (bestimmend beeinflussen); ablaufen, zu Ende gehen; beendigen, auflösen; **to ~ a cause** e-e Sache *(gerichtl.)* entscheiden; **to ~ the damages** den Schadensersatz festsetzen; **to ~ a price** e-n Preis bestimmen; **to hear and ~** richterlich entscheiden
determined entschlossen; in dem Entschluß; in dem (festen) Willen; **to be ~ by** sich richten (od. bestimmen) nach; bestimmt sein von
determining entscheidend; ~ **factor** entscheidender (od. ausschlaggebender) Faktor; **in ~ profits** bei der Gewinnermittlung

deterrence *bes. mil* Abschreckung; **graduated ~** abgestufte Abschreckung

deterrent abschreckend; *bes. mil* Abschreckungsmittel; Abschreckungswaffe; ~ **effect of a sentence** abschreckende Wirkung e-r Strafe; ~ **(force)** Abschreckungsstreitmacht; **to serve as a ~** als Abschreckungsmittel dienen

detinue *(widerrechtl.)* Vorenthaltung *(des Besitzes an e-r bewegl. Sache)*

detract *v*, **to ~ from** *(etw.)* beeinträchtigen, wegnehmen von; **to ~ from the firm's reputation** das Ansehen der Firma beeinträchtigen

detraction Beeinträchtigung, Schmälerung

detriment Nachteil, Schaden; Beeinträchtigung; **to the ~ of** zum Nachteil von; **legal ~** Rechtsnachteil; **without ~ to the interests** ohne Beeinträchtigung der Belange; **nothing is known to his ~** es ist nichts Nachteiliges über ihn bekannt

detrimental schädlich, nachteilig; ~ **as to novelty** *(PatR)* neuheitsschädlich; **to be ~ to** nachteilig (od. abträglich) sein für; schaden, beeinträchtigen

devaluation Devalvation, Abwertung *(e-r Währung)*; ~ **measures** Abwertungsmaßnahmen; ~ **of money** Geldentwertung

devalue (or **devaluate**) *v (Währung)* abwerten
devaluing country Abwertungsland

devastation *(VölkerR)* Verwüstung, Devastation; ~**s of the war** Kriegsverwüstungen; **general ~** allgemeine Zerstörung *(Praxis der versengten Erde durch den abziehenden Feind)*

devastavit ("he has wasted") *Br* Verschleuderungen von Vermögenswerten der Erbmasse durch den Erbschaftsverwalter (→*personal representative)*

develop *v* entwickeln; weiterbilden, ausbauen, fördern; *(Bauland, Naturschätze)* erschließen, nutzbar machen; sich entwickeln (from aus; into zu); zutage treten, sich zeigen; **to ~ one's business** sein Geschäft ausbauen (od. erweitern); **to ~ land** Bauland erschließen; **to ~ trade between two countries** Handelsbeziehungen zwischen zwei Ländern ausbauen; **application for permission to ~** *Br* Antrag auf behördliche Baubewilligung
developed *(hoch)* entwickelt; erschlossen, baureif; ~ **country** Industrieland *(im Ggs. zur dritten Welt)*; ~ **and developing countries** Industrieländer und Entwicklungsländer; ~ **land** erschlossenes Land; *Br (Bilanz)* bebauter Grund und Boden; ~ **and undeveloped land** *Br (Bilanz)* bebaute und unbebaute Grundstücke; →**least ~ countries;** →**less ~ countries**
developing countries Entwicklungsländer *(opp. industrialized countries)*; **aid to ~** Entwicklungshilfe

development Entwicklung; Weiterbildung; *(weiterer)* Ausbau; Förderung *(z. B. von Unternehmen)*; Erschließung *(z. B. von Bauland)*; ~ **aid** Entwicklungshilfe; ~ **area** *Br* Notstandsgebiet, Förderungsgebiet *(in dem die Regierung Ansiedlung von Industrien unterstützt zur Bekämpfung der Arbeitslosigkeit)*
development, ~ aid volunteer Entwicklungshelfer; **D~ Assistance Committee** (DAC) Entwicklungshilfeausschuß der OECD; ~ **banks**[32] Entwicklungsbanken *(staatl. Spezialinstitute oder überstaatliche Banken für die Finanzierung öffentlicher Entwicklungsprojekte im internationalen Bereich)*; ~ **company** Gesellschaft zur Erschließung von Baugelände; ~ **cost** Entwicklungskosten; ~ **of energy resources** Erschließung von Energiequellen; ~ **expense** Entwicklungskosten; Erschließungskosten; ~ **group** *Am* Baugesellschaft; ~ **land** *Br*[33] für bestimmte Erschließungen innerhalb der nächsten 10 Jahre benötigtes Land (od. Grundbesitz); ~ **land →tax;** ~ **of land for building** Erschließung von Bauland; ~ **plan** *Br*[34] Erschließungsplan *(der Ortsbehörden)*; *(etwa)* Flächennutzungsplan;[35] Sanierungsplan; **final ~ plan** *Br* endgültiger Bebauungsplan; ~ **policy** Entwicklungspolitik; →**United Nations D~ Programme** (UNDP)
development risk Entwicklungsrisiko; ~ **de-**

fence Einwand des Entwicklungsrisikos *(vorgesehen in Art. 7 der →European Directive on Product Liability und in s. 4 (1) (e) des →Consumer Protection Act 1987)*

development scheme Ausbauplan

development, economic ~ wirtschaftliche Entwicklung; **further** ~ *(bes. PatR)* Weiterentwicklung; **housing** ~ Wohnsiedlung; →**industrial** ~; **level of** ~ Entwicklungsstand; **progressive** ~ schrittweise (od. allmähliche) Entwicklung, Weiterentwicklung *(z. B. des Rechts)*; **ready** (or **ripe**) **for** ~ baureif

development, to authorize ~ *Br* Baubewilligung erteilen; **to provide** ~ **aid** Entwicklungshilfe leisten

developmental entwicklungsmäßig, Entwicklungs-; ~ **requirements** Entwicklungsbedürfnisse

devest *v* →divest *v*

deviate *v* abweichen, abgehen (from von); **to** ~ **from one's course** vom Kurs abweichen; **to** ~ **from instructions** von Anweisungen abweichen; **to** ~ **from justice** das Recht beugen; **to** ~ **from the main subject** vom eigentlichen Thema abkommen

deviation Abweichung; *(SeeversR)* Deviation, Abweichung *(von der ursprüngl. Schiffsroute)*; **reasonable** ~ gerechtfertigte Abweichung; ~ **clause** (D/C) *(SeeversR)* (Weg-)Abweichungsklausel; *com* Abweichungsklausel, Toleranzklausel *(Klausel in zwischenstaatlichen Kaufverträgen, nach der gewisse Abweichungen von den vereinbarten Waren erlaubt sind)*; ~ **from conditions set out in a contract** (or **from the terms of a contract**) Abweichung von Vertragsbedingungen; ~ **from the course** Abweichung (od. Abgehen) vom Kurs; ~ **from the party line** Abweichung von der Parteilinie; ~ **from quality** Qualitätsabweichung; ~ **from voyage** Abweichung von der Reiseroute *(befreit den Versicherer von der Haftung)*

deviationism *pol* Abweichlertum; Abweichen von der Parteilinie; Mangel an Linientreue

deviationist *pol* von der Parteilinie Abweichender; Abtrünniger

device Plan, Vorhaben; Trick; Erfindung; Vorrichtung; Gerät; Sinnbild; Wappen; ~ **patent** Vorrichtungspatent, **national** Hoheitsabzeichen; **procedural** ~ Verfahrenstrick

devil *Br* Anwaltsassessor *(bei e-m barrister)*

devil *v*, **to** ~ **for a barrister** *Br* als Anwaltsvertreter (barrister) für e-n anderen barrister tätig sein; ~**ling** *Br* Tätigkeit e-s →devil

devisable vererbbar *(Grundbesitz)*

devise letztwillige Verfügung (od. Vermächtnis) *(über Grundbesitz) (cf. legacy)*; **contingent** ~ bedingte letztwillige Verfügung über Grundbesitz *(z. B. Nacherbeneinsetzung)*; **executory** ~ bestimmte Art noch zu erfüllender letztwilliger Verfügung *(über Grundbesitz)*; **lapsed** ~ *(durch den Tod des Bedachten)* hinfällig gewordene letztwillige Verfügung *(über Grundbesitz)*; **residuary** ~ letztwillige Zuwendung des unbeweglichen Restnachlasses; **specific** ~ letztwillige Verfügung über bestimmten Grundbesitz

devise, to take lands by ~ Grundbesitz *(auf Grund letztwilliger Verfügung)* erben

devise *v* 1. *(über Grundbesitz)* letztwillig verfügen; *(Grundbesitz)* vermachen; **to** ~ **and bequeath real and personal property** unbewegliches und bewegliches Vermögen vermachen

devising, will ~ **realty** Testament über Liegenschaften

devise *v* 2. ausdenken, planen; **to** ~ **a plot** e-e Verschwörung anzetteln

devisee testamentarischer Erbe (od. Vermächtnisnehmer) *(von Grundbesitz)*; **residuary** ~ (Testaments-)Erbe (od. Vermächtnisnehmer) des unbeweglichen Restnachlasses

devisor Erblasser, Testator *(von Grundbesitz)*

devolution Übergang *(e-s Rechts od. Besitzes auf e-n anderen kraft Gesetzes)*; Anfall *(von Grundbesitz im Wege der gesetzl. Erbfolge)*; Übertragung; *Br bes. parl* Überweisung *(an e-n Ausschuß oder e-e Kommission)*; *Br pol* Devolution, Dezentralisierung mit dem Ziel der Teilautonomie; Übergang zur Selbstverwaltung; ~ **of authority** Delegierung von Amtsgewalt *(Dezentralisierung der Verwaltung)*; ~ **of the Crown** Thronfolge; ~ **(up)on death** (Eigentums-)Übergang von Todes wegen *(auf den →personal representative)*; ~ **of estate** Vermögensübergang *(von Todes wegen od. bei Konkurs od. Zahlungsunfähigkeit auf den →personal representative oder →official receiver od. →trustee)*; ~ **of ownership** (or **property**) Eigentumsübergang; ~ **of real property upon intestacy or under a will** Erbfolge bei Grundvermögen – entweder aufgrund gesetzlicher Erbfolge oder aufgrund eines Testaments; ~ **of title** Rechtsübergang, Eigentumsübergang

devolution, clause of ~ *Scot* Klausel, die ein Amt od. e-e (Dienst-)Pflicht überträgt *(auf A. im Falle e-r Versäumnis des B.)*

devolve *v* übergehen (on, upon auf); *(im Wege der gesetzl. Erbfolge)* anfallen, zufallen, fallen an; *(Eigentum, Funktionen etc)* übertragen (on, upon auf); **the property** ~**s on the heir** das Eigentum geht auf den Erben über; **rights** ~**d by law** kraft Gesetzes übergegangene Rechte

diagram Diagramm, grafische Darstellung, Schaubild

dialectic materialism *pol* dialektischer Materialismus

dial(l)ing *tel* Wählen der Nummer; ~ **code** *Br* Vorwählnummer; Ortsnetzkennzahl; **automatic ~ system** Selbstwählverkehr; **direct ~** Durchwahl; **direct ~ of national calls** (or **national ~**) *Br* Selbstwählfernverkehr; **direct distance ~** (DDD) *Am* Selbstwählfernverkehr; **international direct ~ (IDD)** *Br* Selbstwählfernverkehr *(für Ausland);* **toll-line ~** *Am* Selbstwählfernverkehr

dialogue, North-South D~[36] Nord-Süd-Dialog (→*Conference on International Economic Cooperation)*

diary Tagebuch; Journal; Terminkalender

dichotomous question *(MMF)* Alternativfrage, Ja-Nein-Frage

dicta Bestandteile der Urteilsgründe, welche zwar die Entscheidung nicht tragen, die bei der Gesamtauslegung des Urteils für die Rechtsentwicklung jedoch von Bedeutung sein können (*s. obiter →dictum)*

dictaphone Diktaphon, Diktiergerät

dictatorship Diktatur; **to establish** (or **set up**) **a military ~** e-e Militärdiktatur errichten

dictum *(richterl.)* Ausspruch; **obiter ~** ("a saying by the way") gelegentliche Äußerung, beiläufige Bemerkung *(e-r Rechtsansicht in den Entscheidungsgründen, auf der die Entscheidung selbst nicht beruht. Im Ggs. zu →ratio decidendi nicht bindend)*

die *v* sterben (of an); **to ~ intestate** ohne Hinterlassung e-s Testaments sterben; **to ~ a natural (violent) death** e-s natürlichen (gewaltsamen) Todes sterben

die-hard *Br* extrem konservativer Politiker

diem, per ~ pro Tag (→*per)*

dies, ~ a quo Anfangstermin; **~ ad quem** Endtermin

diet, the D~ *(nicht Br od. Am)* das Parlament; Landtag, Bundestag, Reichstag; *Scot* Gerichtstermin; **Federal D~** *Ger* Bundestag

dietetics Ökotrophologie (Ernährungskunde)

differ *v* sich unterscheiden, verschieden sein (from von); anderer Meinung sein (from als); nicht übereinstimmen (from mit); **to ~ in opinion** verschiedener Meinung sein; **to ~ in price** im Preis verschieden sein; **to agree to ~** sich auf verschiedene Standpunkte einigen; **the witnesses ~** die Zeugenaussagen widersprechen sich; **I beg to ~** ich bin leider anderer Ansicht

differring terms sich widersprechende Bedingungen

difference 1. Unterschied, Verschiedenheit; (Gewichts-, Preis-, Kurs-)Differenz; **~ of** (or **on**) **exchange** Kursdifferenz; **~ of opinion** Meinungsverschiedenheit; **~ in price(s)** Preisunterschied, Preisdifferenz; Kursunterschied, Kursdifferenz; **~ in rates** (*Devisenkurs*) Kursunterschied, Kursdifferenz; **to make a ~ between** e-n Unterschied machen zwischen

difference 2. Streit(igkeit), Meinungsverschiedenheit; **settlement of ~s** Beilegung von Streitigkeiten; **~s have arisen** Streitigkeiten sind entstanden

differential Unterscheidungs-; unterschiedlich; Differential-, gestaffelt; (Lohn-, Tarif- etc) Unterschied; **~s** s. wage →~s; **~ duties** Differentialzölle *(auf Waren e-r Gattung verschiedener Herkunftsgebiete);* **~ freight rate** Differentialfracht; **~ piece rate system** Differentialstücklohnsystem; **~ price** gestaffelter Preis; **~ rates** unterschiedliche (Transport-)Tarifsätze; Ausnahmesätze; **~ tariff** *(Zoll)* Staffeltarif, Differentialtarif; **~ tariff items** Staffeltarifposten; **~ wage** Staffellohn

differential, (freight) ~s Frachtunterschiede; **price ~** Preisunterschied, Preisgefälle; **(wage) ~s** Lohnunterschiede, Lohngefälle *(zwischen Arbeitnehmern verschiedener Industrien oder zwischen Facharbeitern und ungelernten Arbeitern)*

differentiate *v*, **to ~ between** unterscheiden zwischen

difficult to dispose of schwer verkäuflich

difficult|y Schwierigkeit; **~ies which may arise** etwa entstehende Schwierigkeiten; **~ies in selling** Absatzschwierigkeiten; **~ of interpretation** Auslegungsschwierigkeit; **financial** (or **pecuniary**) **~ies** finanzielle Schwierigkeiten; **to alleviate ~ies** Schwierigkeiten erleichtern (od. mindern); **to be** (or **find oneself**) **in ~ies** sich in Schwierigkeiten befinden, Schwierigkeiten haben; **to be in financial ~ies** finanzielle Schwierigkeiten (od. Geldnöte) haben; **to overcome ~ies** Schwierigkeiten überwinden

digest Auszug, (kurze) Übersicht; **~s** Auszüge *(aus Gerichtsentscheidungen);* **the D~** *(römisches Recht)* die Digesten (od. Pandekten)
Die digests bringen in systematischer Ordnung Auszüge aus Gerichtsentscheidungen mit Quellenangaben. Sie sind eine Ergänzung zu den →text books

digit Zahl unter 10 *(0 bis 9);* Ziffer; Zeichen

digital, ~ computer Ziffernrechner, Digitalrechenmaschine; **~ data** Digitaldaten, Ziffernmaterial

dignatory *(bes. kirchlicher)* Würdenträger

digress *v* vom Thema abkommen

digression Abschweifung

dike Deich; ~ **breach** Deich(ein)bruch; ~ **law** Deichrecht; ~ **office** Deichamt

dilapidation Baufälligkeit; Verfall(enlassen) *(von Gebäuden);* **schedule** (or **list**) **of ~s** *Br* Liste notwendiger Reparaturen *(deren Ausführung dem Mieter gemäß Mietvertrag obliegt)*

dilapidated abbruchreif

dilatory dilatorisch, aufschiebend, hinhaltend; ~ **defen|ce (~se)** (or *Am* **plea**) dilatorische (od. prozeßhindernde) Einrede *(opp. peremptory plea);* ~ **payment** langsame (od. hinhaltende) Zahlung; ~ **methods** Verschleppungsmethoden; ~ **policy** Verzögerungstaktik

diligence Fleiß; Sorgfalt *(opp. negligence; cf. care); Scot* (Zwangs-)Vollstreckung; **due** ~ gebührende Sorgfalt; *(etwa)* verkehrsübliche Sorgfalt (diligentia boni patris familiae); **great** ~ (or **high degree of** ~) große Sorgfalt; **necessary** ~ erforderliche Sorgfalt; **ordinary** ~ gewöhnliche (od. übliche) Sorgfalt *(wie in eigenen Angelegenheiten)* (diligentia quam in suis rebus); **in exercising reasonable** ~ bei Anwendung genügender (od. angemessener) Sorgfalt; **want of due** ~ Fehlen der verkehrsüblichen Sorgfalt

dilute *v,* **to** ~ **(skilled) labo(u)r** ungelernte Arbeiter als Facharbeiter einsetzen

dilutee *(als Facharbeiter eingesetzter)* ungelernter Arbeiter; Anlernling

dilution Verwässerung, Verdünnung; Verringerung; **equity** ~ Verwässerung des Aktienkapitals

dime *Am* Zehncentstück; ~ **store** *Am* billiges Warenhaus, Einheitspreisgeschäft

diminish *v* vermindern, verringern; sich vermindern, sich verringern, abnehmen *(opp. to augment, to increase);* **to** ~ **in value** an Wert geringer werden (od. verlieren)

diminished responsibility verminderte Zurechnungsfähigkeit (→*responsibility*)

diminishing, ~ **receipts** abnehmende Einnahmen; ~ **the receipts** Verringerung der Einnahmen

diminishing returns abnehmende Skalenerträge *(cf. economies of scale)*

diminution Abnahme, Verminderung, Verringerung; ~ **of expenses** Kostenverringerung; ~ **of profits** Gewinnschrumpfung; ~ **in value** Wertminderung

dimissory Entlassungs-; ~ **letter** *eccl* Dimissoriale

dimout *(Luftschutz)* teilweise Verdunklung

dinar Dinar

Währungseinheit in Jugoslawien, im Irak, in Jordanien und Tunesien

diocesan *eccl* (Diözesan-)Bischof

diocese *eccl* Diözese *(Amtsbezirk e-s regierenden Bischofs)*

dip *v (Flagge)* dippen; *(Scheinwerfer)* abblenden

diploma Diplom; **high school** ~ *Am (etwa)* Abitur; →**European Convention on the Equivalence of D~s Leading to Admission to Universities; mutual recognition of ~s** gegenseitige Anerkennung der Diplome; **to award a** ~ ein Diplom erteilen; **to be awarded** (or **to obtain**) **a** ~ ein Diplom erhalten

diplomacy Diplomatie; **secret** ~ Geheimdiplomatie

diplomatic diplomatisch; ~ **achievement** diplomatische Leistung, diplomatischer Erfolg; ~ **action** diplomatischer Schritt; ~ **agencies abroad** diplomatische Vertretungen im Ausland

diplomatic agent diplomatischer Vertreter, Diplomat; **rank of ~s** diplomatische Rangordnung[37]; **status of ~s** besondere Stellung der Diplomaten; **to appoint a** ~ e-n diplomatischen Vertreter ernennen (od. bestellen); **to recall a** ~ e-n diplomatischen Vertreter abberufen

diplomatic, ~ **asylum** *(VölkerR)* diplomatisches Asyl; ~ **bag** Kuriergepäck; ~ **body** diplomatisches Corps

diplomatic career Diplomatenlaufbahn; **to take up a** ~ die diplomatische Laufbahn einschlagen

diplomatic, through (ordinary) ~ **channels** auf dem (üblichen) diplomatischen Wege; **in** ~ **circles** in diplomatischen Kreisen; **D** ~ **Corps** (D. C.) Diplomatisches Corps; ~ **courier** (diplomatischer) Kurier; ~ **envoy** →~ agent; ~ **exchange** Auseinandersetzung *(zwischen Staaten)* auf diplomatischer Ebene *(protest, answer to a protest etc)*

diplomatic immunit|y diplomatische Immunität *(cf. exterritoriality);* **abuse of** ~ Mißbrauch der diplomatischen Immunität; **to enjoy ~ies** diplomatische Immunität genießen

diplomatic, ~ **intercourse** diplomatischer Verkehr; ~ **intervention** diplomatische Intervention; **at** ~ **level** auf diplomatischer Ebene; ~ **luggage** Diplomatengepäck

diplomatic mission diplomatische Vertretung; **head of a** ~ Missionschef; **staff of a** ~ Personal e-r diplomatischen Vertretung

diplomatic note diplomatische Note; **exchange of ~s** diplomatischer Notenaustausch

diplomatic, ~ **officer** diplomatischer Vertreter; Angehöriger des diplomatischen Dienstes; ~ **pouch** Kuriergepäck; ~ **privileges and immunities** diplomatische Vorrechte und Immunitäten; ~ **protection** diplomatischer Schutz; ~ **quarter** Diplomatenviertel

diplomatic relations[38] diplomatische Beziehungen; **breaking off of** ~ Abbruch der dipl. Beziehungen; **establishment of** ~ Aufnahme der dipl. Beziehungen; **resumption of** ~ Wiederaufnahme der dipl. Beziehungen; **rupture** (or **severance**) **of** ~ Abbruch der dipl. Beziehungen; **suspension of** ~ Unterbrechung der dipl. Beziehungen; **to break off** ~ dipl. Beziehungen abbrechen; **to enter into** (or **establish**) ~ dipl. Beziehungen aufnehmen; **to entertain** (or **maintain**) ~ dipl. Beziehungen unterhalten; **to re-establish** (or **restore**) ~ dipl. Beziehungen wiederherstellen; **to resume** ~ dipl. Beziehungen wiederaufnehmen; **to sever** ~ dipl. Beziehungen abbrechen; **to suspend** ~ dipl. Beziehungen unterbrechen

diplomatic, ~ representation diplomatische Vertretung *(e-s Staates im Ausland)*; ~ **representation abroad** Auslandsvertretung; ~ **representative** diplomatischer Vertreter

diplomatic service diplomatischer Dienst; **to enter the** ~ in den diplomatischen Dienst eintreten

diplomatic staff, members of the ~ Mitglieder des diplomatischen Personals

diptyc[39] Diptyk *(Zollpapier für die vorübergehende Einfuhr e-s Kraftfahrzeugs)*; **to issue a** ~ ein Diptyk ausgeben.

direct direkt, unmittelbar; ~ **action** direkte Aktion *(pol. z.B. Demonstration, Streik)*; ~ **advertising** Direktwerbung

direct beneficiary, to be the ~ **under the policy** *(VersR)* nach dem Vertrag unmittelbar begünstigt sein

direct, ~ **buying** → ~ purchase; ~ **cost** Einzelkosten *(opp. indirect cost)*; ~ **costing** Grenz(plan-)rechnung; ~ **damage** unmittelbarer Schaden

direct debit, ~**(ing)** Einzug(sverfahren); ~ **authorization** Einzugsermächtigung; ~ **order** Einzugsauftrag

direct, ~ **election of the European Parliament** Direktwahl des Europäischen Parlaments; ~ **evidence** unmittelbarer Beweis, Beweis aus eigener Wahrnehmung *(opp. circumstantial evidence)*; ~ **examination** *Am* erste Befragung e-s Zeugen durch die den Zeugen stellende Partei; ~ **exchange** *(Devisenkurs)* Mengenkurs, Mengennotierung *(opp. indirect exchange)*; ~ **insurer** Erstversicherer *(opp. reinsurer)*; ~ **leasing** →leasing 2.; **(in the)** ~ **line** (in) gerade(r) Linie *(opp. collateral line)*; ~ **loss (by fire)** unmittelbarer (durch das Feuer entstandener) Schaden *(opp. remote loss)*; ~ **mail advertising** Werbung durch Postwurfsendungen; ~ **material** Einzelmaterial; ~ **offering** freihändiger Verkauf *(e-r Emission)*; ~ **port** direkter (vorher bestimmter) Hafen; ~ **purchase** (from producer or wholesaler) Direktkauf, Beziehungskauf *(unter Umgehung des Groß- oder Einzelhandels)*; ~ **result** unmittelbare Folge; ~ **sale to the public** *(Börse)* freihändiger Verkauf; ~ **selling** Direktverkauf *(unter Umgehung des Groß- od. Einzelhandels)*; ~ **taxes** direkte Steuern *(opp. indirect taxes)*; ~ **train** durchgehender Zug; ~ **universal suffrage** *(EG)* Direktwahl; ~ **voting** direkte Wahl; ~ **wages** direkte Löhne, Einzellöhne

direct *v* anordnen, anweisen, verfügen; *(im Testament od. e-m settlement)* bestimmen; *(Betrieb)* leiten; den Weg zeigen; *(Brief)* adressieren, richten (to an); **the judge** ~**s the jury** (in point of law) *Br* der Richter erteilt den Geschworenen Rechtsbelehrung; **to** ~ **labo(u)r** Arbeitskräfte lenken (od. einsetzen); **to** ~ **a person to a room** jdm ein Zimmer anweisen; **to** ~ **the traffic** den Verkehr lenken

directed, as ~ wie angewiesen; laut Verfügung; nach Vorschrift

direction Anordnung, Anweisung; Leitung, Führung; Geschäftsleitung; Lenkung; Richtung; *Br* Rechtsbelehrung *(der Geschworenen durch den Richter)*; ~**s** Adresse, Aufschrift *(Paket, Brief etc.)*

directions *Br* prozeßleitende Verfügungen *(durch den →master)*; **summons for** ~ Gesuch *(des Klägers an den master)*, prozeßleitende Verfügungen zu treffen *(zur Vorbereitung der mündlichen Verhandlung)*

direction, ~ **of capital** Kapitallenkung; ~ **of a company (corporation)** Leitung e-r Gesellschaft; ~ **of consumption** Verbrauchslenkung; ~ **to a jury** *Br* Rechtsbelehrung der Geschworenen; ~ **of labo(u)r** Lenkung (od. Einsatz) der Arbeitskräfte *(z.B. von e-m Bezirk in e-n anderen)*; ~**(s) for use** Gebrauchsanweisung

direction, according to ~**s** weisungsgemäß; **by** ~ **of** auf Anordnung von; **under the** ~ **of** unter der Leitung von

direction, to give ~**s** Weisungen erteilen

directive Direktive, Richtlinie, Weisung; Anordnung; ~ **of authorities** behördliche Anordnung; **proposal for a** ~ Richtlinienvorschlag

director Direktor; leitender Angestellter; *(AktienR)* board-Mitglied, Mitglied e-s →board of directors

Am Der Titel „director" ist vorwiegend den inaktiven Mitgliedern des board of directors vorbehalten, während die Inhaber wichtiger Positionen in der Geschäftsleitung als officers bezeichnet werden

director, ~**s' and officers' liability insurance** *Am* Haftpflichtversicherung für Führungskräfte; ~**'s fees** Vergütung (od. Bezüge) e-s board-Mitglieds; ~**-general** Generaldirektor; ~**s' meeting** Sitzung des board of directors; ~ **of insurance** *Am* → insurance commissioner; **D**~ **of Public Prosecutions** (DPP) *Br (der Dienstaufsicht des Attorney-General unterstehender)* Strafverfolger; Anklagebehörde *(für schwere Straffälle; →prosecution)*

directors' report[39a] Geschäftsbericht *(des Verwaltungsrats e-r AG)*; Lagebericht; **acceptance of** ~ Entlastung der Direktoren (od. board-Mitglieder)

director, alternate ~ *Am* stellvertretender Direktor; **board of ~s** ~ →board 1.; →**executive** ~; **independent** ~ →outside ~; →**inside** ~; **managing** ~ geschäftsführender Direktor; Generaldirektor; **ordinary** ~ gewöhnlicher Direktor *(hat im Zweifel keine Einzelvertretungsmacht)*; →**outside** ~

directorate Stelle e-s Direktors; Direktorium; Direktion; Verwaltungsrat (→*board of directors*); **~-general** Generaldirektion

directorship Direktorenstelle

directory 1. Adreßbuch; Fernsprechbuch; (Namens-)Verzeichnis; **D~ Enquiries** *Br tel* Auskunft; **classified** (or **trade**) ~ Branchenadreßbuch; **telephone** ~ Fernsprechbuch, Telefonbuch; **to look up an address in a** ~ e-e Anschrift im Adreßbuch nachschlagen

directory 2. anweisend, beratend, richtunggebend *(opp. mandatory)*; ~ **provision** Sollvorschrift; ~ **trust** Treuhandverwaltung nach Anweisung *(ohne Ermessen)*

dirigisme Dirigismus (gelenkte Wirtschaft)

dirty →**float**

disabilit|y Unfähigkeit, Unvermögen; Geschäftsunfähigkeit *(bes. Minderjähriger und Geisteskranker)*; Prozeßunfähigkeit; Arbeitsunfähigkeit, Erwerbsunfähigkeit, Dienstunfähigkeit, Invalidität; *(körperliche od. geistige)* Behinderung; **~ies** Hemmungsgründe *(z.B. der Minderjährigkeit, Geisteskrankheit)*; Ehehindernisse; ~ **benefit** Erwerbsunfähigkeitsrente; ~ **clause** *(VersR)* Erwerbsunfähigkeitsklausel *(Klausel in e-r Lebensversicherung, auf Grund derer bei Erwerbsunfähigkeit des Versicherten Anspruch auf prämienfreie Rente besteht)*; ~ **degree** Grad der Minderung der Erwerbsfähigkeit (od. Invalidität); ~ **insurance** Invaliditätsversicherung;[40] ~ **insurance benefit** *Am (Sozialvers.)* Rente wegen Erwerbsunfähigkeit, Invaliditätsrente; ~ **pension** Pension (od. Rente) bei Dienstunfähigkeit; Invaliditätsrente; (Kriegs-)Beschädigtenrente; ~ **pensioner** Bezieher von Pension (od. Rente) bei Dienstunfähigkeit; ~ **for service** Arbeitsunfähigkeit, Dienstunfähigkeit; ~ **to sue** Prozeßunfähigkeit

disabilit|y, certificate of removal of ~ies gerichtliche Bescheinigung, daß Konkurs auf unverschuldetes Unglück zurückzuführen ist *(beseitigt die öffentl.-rechtlichen Rechtsfolgen des Konkurses)*; **legal** ~ Geschäftsunfähigkeit; *Am* Prozeßunfähigkeit; **partial** ~ teilweise Arbeitsunfähigkeit; **permanent** ~ dauernde Arbeitsunfähigkeit; **person under** ~ Geschäftsunfähiger; Prozeßunfähiger; **temporary** ~ vorübergehende Arbeitsunfähigkeit; **total** ~ vollständige Arbeitsunfähigkeit; Vollinvalidität; **infants and persons of unsound mind are under** ~ Minderjährige und Geisteskranke sind nicht geschäftsfähig; **to be under a** ~ geschäftsunfähig sein; **to be under a (legal)** ~ *Am* prozeßunfähig sein; **to cease to be under a** ~ geschäftsfähig werden.

disable *v* für unfähig erklären; unfähig (od. untauglich) machen.

disabled 1., **the** ~ die (Körper-)Behinderten; die Versehrten; **the seriously** ~ die Schwerbehinderten; **the seriously** ~ **ex-servicemen** die Schwerkriegsbeschädigten; **special facilities for the** ~ besondere Einrichtungen für die Behinderten

disabled 2. geschäftsunfähig; dienstunfähig, erwerbsunfähig, berufsunfähig, arbeitsunfähig; *(körperlich oder geistig)* behindert; (kriegs-)versehrt; ~ **ex-serviceman** Kriegsbeschädigter, Versehrter; **physically or mentally** ~ körperlich od. geistig behindert; **seriously** ~ schwerbehindert

disabled person[41] Arbeitsunfähiger, Dienstunfähiger, Erwerbsunfähiger; (Körper-)Behinderter; Versehrter; **seriously** ~ Schwerbehinderter

disabled, to become ~ arbeitsunfähig *(etc)* werden

disablement Arbeitsunfähigkeit, Dienstunfähigkeit, Erwerbsunfähigkeit; Invalidität, Behinderung; ~ **benefit** *Br (nach Aufhören von* → *injury benefit zu zahlende)* Erwerbsunfähigkeitsrente, Invaliditätsrente; ~ **gratuity** *Br (Sozialvers.) (bei Arbeitsunfall od. Berufsunfähigkeit zu zahlende)* einmalige Abfindung; ~ **insurance** Invaliditätsversicherung, Invalidenversicherung[40]; ~ **pension** *Br (Sozialvers.)* Arbeitsunfallrente *(wenn die Beeinträchtigung 20% od. mehr ausmacht)*

disablement, degree of ~ Grad der Minderung der Erwerbsfähigkeit (od. Behinderung); **partial (permanent, temporary, total)** ~ s. partial, permanent, temporary, total →disability; **war** ~ Kriegsbeschädigung

disadvantage Nachteil; Schaden; ungünstige Lage; **to the** ~ **of** zum Nachteil von; **to be at a** ~ im Nachteil sein; **to bring ~s to** Nachteile bringen für; **to put sb. at a** ~ jdn benachteiligen; jds Chancen beeinträchtigen; **to sell at a** ~ mit Verlust verkaufen

disadvantaged benachteiligt

disaffected to the government unzufrieden mit der Regierung

disaffection *(bes. politische)* Unzufriedenheit; →**incitement to** ~; **public** ~ **towards the government** Staatsverdrossenheit

disaffirm *v* nicht bestätigen *(opp. to affirm)*; *(Gerichtsentscheidung)* aufheben; *(Aussage)* zurücknehmen; *(vom Vertrag)* zurücktreten, *(Vertrag)* annullieren

disafforest *v* abforsten, entwalden; *Br (Wald)* den gesetzlichen Charakter e-s Forstes nehmen; **~ed** *Br* nicht mehr dem Forstrecht unterstehend

disafforestation (or **disafforestment**) Abforstung, Entwaldung; Freigabe von Wald für andere Benutzung des Bodens *(und Herausnahme aus dem Forstrecht)*

disagio Disagio, Abschlag *(opp. agio)*

disagree *v* verschiedener Meinung sein, nicht übereinstimmen (od. zustimmen), sich nicht einigen (on über); im Widerspruch miteinander stehen, sich widersprechen; **the witnesses ~** die Zeugen widersprechen einander

disagreement Meinungsverschiedenheit; Widerspruch (between zwischen); mangelnde Übereinstimmung; **a ~ has arisen** e-e Meinungsverschiedenheit ist entstanden

disallow *v* nicht erlauben; nicht anerkennen, nicht gelten lassen; **to ~ a claim** e-n Anspruch zurückweisen; e-e Forderung nicht anerkennen; **to ~ registration** *(WarenzeichenR)* die Anmeldung zurückweisen
disallowed deductions *Am (SteuerR)* nicht absetzbare Ausgaben

disallowable *(SteuerR)* nicht absetzbar *(opp. allowable)*

disallowance Nichtanerkennung; Zurückweisung

disapproval Mißbilligung, Ablehnung

disapprove *v* mißbilligen, ablehnen (of a th. etw.)

disarm *v* abrüsten; entwaffnen; *(Sprengkörper)* entschärfen

disarmament Abrüstung; Entwaffnung; **~ commission** Abrüstungskommission; **in the ~ field** auf dem Gebiete der Abrüstung; **~ talks** Abrüstungsgespräche

disarmer Befürworter der Abrüstung

disaster Katastrophe; *(plötzliches)* Unglück; **~ area** Katastrophengebiet; **~ relief** Katastrophenhilfe; **~ at sea** Seeunfall, Unglücksfall zur See; **aid for ~ victims** Katastrophenhilfe; **air ~** Flugzeugunglück; **railway ~** Eisenbahnunglück; **victim of a ~** Opfer e-r Katastrophe

disavow *v* nicht anerkennen; ableugnen, nicht wahr haben wollen

disavowal Nichtanerkennung; Ableugnen; Dementi

disband *v (Truppen etc)* auflösen, entlassen; sich auflösen, auseinandergehen

disbandment Auflösung; Entlassung *(von Truppen)*

disbar *v (Anwalt, Br barrister)* aus der Anwaltschaft ausschließen *(Br durch →benchers od. auf eigenen Antrag)*; von der Anwaltsliste streichen
disbarring Streichung von der Anwaltsliste *(Br der barrister; cf. striking off the roll)*

disbarment Ausschluß *(Br e-s barrister)* aus der Anwaltschaft; **~ order** *Am* Verbot der Ausübung der Anwaltspraxis

disbench *v Br (jdm)* die Mitgliedschaft e-s der → Inns of Court entziehen

disburse *v* auszahlen, ausgeben; *(Geld)* auslegen, verauslagen

disbursement Auszahlung; Auslage, verauslagter Betrag; **~s** (Bar-)Auslagen; **~ voucher** Auslagenbeleg; **cash ~s** Kassenauszahlungen; bare Auslagen; **specification of ~s** Auslagenaufstellung; **to recover one's ~s** seine Auslagen vergütet bekommen

discharge 1. Entlassung; Abberufung *(von e-m Posten); mil* Abschied *(von Offizieren);* Entlassung *(aus dem Wehrdienst);* Befreiung *(von Verpflichtungen);* Entlastung; Erfüllung *(von Verpflichtungen);* Tilgung, Bezahlung, Begleichung*(e-r Schuld); (KonkursR)* Forderungsuntergang *(nach Abschluß des Konkursverfahrens);* Schulderlaß *(hinsichtlich der nicht befriedigten Forderungen);* **in ~ of** zur Begleichung von; **to our ~** zu unserer Entlastung; **~ of attachment order** Aufhebung des Pfändungsbeschlusses; **~ of a bankrupt** Entlastung e-s Gemeinschuldners; **~ of a bill** Einlösung e-s Wechsels; Erlöschen e-s Wechsels; **~ certificate** *mil* Entlassungsschein; **~ of a contract** Vertragserfüllung; **~ of a debt** Tilgung e-r Schuld, Schuldtilgung
discharge of duty Pflichterfüllung; Ausübung des Dienstes; **in the ~ of one's ~ies** bei der Wahrnehmung seiner Aufgaben (od. Obliegenheiten); in Ausübung seiner (Amts-)-Pflichten
discharge, ~ (of a patient) **from a hospital** Entlassung aus e-m Krankenhaus (od. *Br* aus e-m psychiatrischen Krankenhaus); **~ of liabilities** Erfüllung von Verpflichtungen; Tilgung von Schulden; **~ of a mortgage** Löschung e-r Hypothek; **~ from office** Amtsenthebung; **~ of seamen** Abmusterung von Seeleuten; **~ of a trustee** Entlastung e-s Treuhänders
discharge, cause for ~ Entlassungsgrund; **certificate of ~** *(Zoll)* Erledigungsbescheinigung; **dishono(u)rable ~** *mil* unehrenhafte Entlassung; **formal ~** (from responsibility) Entlastung; **hono(u)rable ~** *mil* ehrenvoller Abschied; **order of ~** *(KonkursR) Br* Entlastungsbeschluß des Gerichts *(Anordnung über die Befreiung des Konkursschuldners von seinen restlichen Schulden);* **receipt in full ~** endgültige Quittung

discharge, to give a ~ from the army aus dem Heer entlassen; **to give a ~** (or **to give effectual ~**) *(rechtswirksame)* Entlastung erteilen; **to receive one's ~** entlastet werden

discharge 2. *(StrafR)* Freilassung, Entlassung *(von Gefangenen)*; **~ from custody** Entlassung aus der Haft; **~ from prison** Entlassung aus dem Gefängnis; Freilassung; **absolute ~** unbeschränkte Entlassung *(trotz strafgerichtl. Verurteilung)*; **conditional ~** Strafaussetzung zur Bewährung, bedingte Entlassung *(Br Angeklagter wird unter der Bedingung entlassen, daß er innerhalb von 12 Monaten nicht straffällig wird)*; **unconditional ~** bedingungslose Entlassung

discharge 3. Entladen, Ausladen; *(See- und Flußfrachtgeschäft)* Löschen, Löschung; *(Umweltschutz)* Ableitung; **~ of cargo** Löschung der Ladung; **~ of oil from ships** Ablassen von Öl aus Schiffen; **~ of waste at sea** Ableitung von Abfällen ins Meer; **~ overside** Ausladung über Schiffsseite; **port of ~** Entladehafen, Löschhafen *(opp. port of lading)*

discharge *v (aus dem Arbeitsverhältnis)* entlassen; *(von e-m Posten)* abberufen; verabschieden; *mil* entlassen; *(aus dem Gefängnis)* entlassen, freilassen; *(von Verpflichtungen)* befreien; entlasten; erledigen; *(Schuld)* tilgen, bezahlen, begleichen; *(Ladung)* abladen, ausladen; *(Schiffsladung)* löschen; **to ~ the accused** den Angeklagten außer Verfolgung setzen; **to ~ a bankrupt** e-n Gemeinschuldner entlasten; **to ~ a bill** e-n Wechsel einlösen; **to ~ cargo** Ladung löschen, entladen; **to ~ a contract** e-n Vertrag erledigen *(z. B. durch Erfüllung)*; **to ~ a debt** e-e Schuld tilgen; **to ~ the directors from their responsibilities** die Direktoren entlasten; **to ~ one's duties** seine (Amts-)Pflichten ausüben; seine Aufgaben wahrnehmen; **to ~ one's liabilities** seinen Verpflichtungen nachkommen; seine Schulden bezahlen; **to ~ a mortgage** e-e Hypothek löschen; **to ~ oil from ships** Öl aus Schiffen ablassen; **to ~ an order** e-e Verfügung aufheben; **to ~ from prison** aus der Haft entlassen; **to ~ seamen** Seeleute abmustern; **to ~ a surety** e-n Bürgen entlasten; **to ~ a task** e-e Aufgabe erfüllen; **to ~ a writ** e-e gerichtl. Verfügung aufheben

discharged, ~ bankrupt entlasteter Gemeinschuldner; **~ bill** eingelöster Wechsel; **~ prisoners' aid** Entlassenenfürsorge; **to be ~ from liability** von der Haftung befreit sein; **to order the defendant to be ~** die Entlassung des Angeklagten anordnen

discharging Ausladen, Löschen; **~ cargo** Löschen von (Schiffs-)Ladung; **~ expenses** Löschkosten; Entladekosten; **~ place** Löschplatz; Entladestelle; **costs of ~** →**~** expenses

disciplinary disziplinarisch; dienststrafrechtlich; **~ action** Disziplinarmaßnahmen, Disziplinarverfahren; **to take ~ action** disziplinarisch vorgehen (against gegen)

disciplinary, ~ authority Disziplinargewalt; **~ board** Disziplinarkammer, Dienststrafkammer; **~ case** Disziplinarfall; **D~ Committee** *Br (vom Master of the Rolls ernanntes)* Ehrengericht *(der solicitors)*; **~ court** Disziplinargericht

disciplinary fine Diziplinarstrafe *(Geldstrafe)*; **to impose a ~** e-e Disziplinarstrafe verhängen (upon gegen)

disciplinary measures Disziplinarmaßnahmen; **to take ~** Disziplinarmaßnahmen treffen, disziplinarisch vorgehen (against gegen)

disciplinary offence (~se) Disziplinarvergehen, Dienstvergehen

disciplinary penalty Disziplinarstrafe; **award of a ~** Verhängung e-r Disziplinarstrafe; **to award** (or **impose**) **a ~** e-e Disziplinarstrafe verhängen; disziplinarisch bestrafen

disciplinary power(s) Disziplinargewalt

disciplinary proceedings Disziplinarverfahren, Dienststrafverfahren; **by way of ~** auf dem Disziplinarwege

disciplinary punishment →disciplinary penalty

disciplinary reasons, transfer for ~ Strafversetzung; **to transfer for ~** strafversetzen

disciplinary regulations Disziplinarbestimmungen, Dienststrafbestimmungen

discipline Disziplin; **administration of ~** Disziplinargewalt; **breach of ~** Verstoß gegen die Disziplin; Dienstpflichtverletzung; **party ~** Parteidisziplin; Fraktionsdisziplin; **power of ~** Disziplinarbefugnis; **to maintain ~** Disziplin aufrechterhalten

disclaim *v* verzichten auf, den Anspruch aufgeben auf; nicht anerkennen; ablehnen; dementieren; **to ~ sth.** etw. bestreiten; etw. dementieren; bestreiten, der Eigentümer von etw. zu sein; **to ~ (one's share in) an estate** (or *Am* **inheritance**) e-e Erbschaft ausschlagen; **to ~ liability** die Haftung ablehnen; **to ~ responsibility** die Verantwortung ablehnen; **to ~ a right** auf ein Recht verzichten; **to ~ any trade mark of the word** ... ausdrücklich erklären, daß kein markenrechtlicher Schutz des Wortes ... in Anspruch genommen wird

disclaimer Verzicht(leistung), Verzichterklärung; Rechtsverzicht; Aufgabe e-s Anspruchs; Ablehnung; Widerruf, Dementi; Verzichtleistender; **~ by trustee** Nichtannahme des Treuhandamtes; **~ of an estate** (or *Am* **inheritance**) Ausschlagung e-r Erbschaft; **~ of jurisdiction** Bestreiten der Zuständigkeit; **~ of liability** Ablehnung der Haftung; **~ of onerous bequest** Ausschlagung e-s beschwerten Vermächtnisses von Geld und sonstigen beweglichen Gegenständen; **~ of onerous devise** Ausschlagung e-s beschwerten Grundstücksvermächtnisses; **~ of onorous property** *(KonkursR)* Ausschlagung e-s Vermögens mit Belastungen; **~ of a right** Rechtsverzicht; **official ~ of a statement** amtliches Dementi e-r Behauptung; ~ **of testamentary gift** Ausschlagung e-s Vermächtnisses

disclose *v* offenbaren, offenlegen, bekanntgeben, aufdecken; preisgeben; **to ~ a confidence** e-e vertrauliche Mitteilung preisgeben (od. weitergeben); **to ~ a fraud** e-n Betrug aufdekken; **to ~ the invention in a matter sufficiently clear and complete** *(PatR)* die Erfindung deutlich und vollständig offenbaren; **duty** (or **obligation**) **to ~** Offenlegungspflicht; Anzeigepflicht *(Benachrichtigung); (VersR)* Auskunftspflicht; **to swear that all papers relevant to the proceedings have been ~d** schwören, daß alle für das Verfahren erheblichen Papiere vorgelegt sind *(Br →affidavit of documents)*

disclosed, ~ principal Vertretener, dessen Identität der (Handels-)Vertreter nicht offenbart hat *(opp. undisclosed principal)*; **~ reserves** *(Bilanz)* offene Rücklagen *(opp. hidden reserves)*

disclosure Offenbarung, Offenlegung; Aufdekkung; Publizität; öffentliche Darlegung; Bekanntgabe; Preisgabe*(von Informationen)*; **~ of assets** Offenlegung von Vermögenswerten; **~ of business secrets** Preisgabe von Geschäftsgeheimnissen; **~ of deficiencies** Aufdeckung von Mängeln; **~ of information** Offenlegung von Information; Weitergabe (od. Preisgabe) von Informationen; **~ of an invention** *(PatR)* Offenbarung (od. Darstellung) e-r Erfindung; **~ of property** Auskunft *(des Schuldners)* über sein Vermögen; **~ requirement** Publizitätserfordernis; Offenlegungspflicht *(für Jahresabschluß)*; **duty of ~** *(VersR)* Auskunftspflicht; **non-prejudicial ~** *(PatR)* unschädliche Offenbarung *(e-r Erfindung)*; **public ~** öffentliche Bekanntmachung; *Am* Veröffentlichung unangenehmer Tatsachen privater Natur *(über den Kläger)*; **to be privileged from ~** nicht offenlegungspflichtig sein

discontinuance Unterbrechung, Einstellung; Aufhören; **~ (of action)** Klagerücknahme; **~ of (a) business** Geschäftsaufgabe; Betriebseinstellung; **~ of execution** Einstellung der Zwangsvollstreckung; **~ of criminal proceedings** Einstellung des Strafverfahrens; **~ of propaganda** Einstellung der Propaganda; **~ of subscription** Abbestellung *(z.B. e-r Zeitung)*

discontinue *v* unterbrechen, einstellen; aufhören; **to ~ an action** e-e Klage zurücknehmen; **to ~ a business** ein Geschäft aufgeben; den Geschäftsbetrieb einstellen; **to ~ a licence (~se)** e-e Lizenz nicht verlängern; **to ~ the manufacture of** die Herstellung von . . . einstellen; **to ~ membership** als Mitglied austreten; **to ~ a newspaper** das Erscheinen e-r Zeitung einstellen; **to ~ a practice** ein Geschäftsgebaren (od. Verfahren) einstellen; e-e (Anwalts-)Praxis aufgeben; **to ~ the proceedings** das Verfahren einstellen; **to ~ one's subscription to a (news-)paper** e-e Zeitung abbestellen; **to ~ a suit** *Am* e-e Klage zurücknehmen; **to direct the speaker to ~ his speech** dem Redner das Wort entziehen

discount 1. Diskont *(Zinsabzug bei noch nicht fälligen Forderungen, bes. beim Ankauf von Wechseln)*; **~s** Diskonten *(inländische Wechsel)*, Diskontwechsel; **~ bank** Diskontbank; **~ bill** Diskontwechsel; **~ of a bill** Wechseldiskont; **~ broker** Wechselmakler; **~ charges** Diskontspesen; **~ credit** Diskontkredit; **~ department** Wechselabteilung; **~ earned** Diskonterlös; **~ expenses** Wechselspesen; **~ holdings** Bestand an Diskonten (od. Diskontwechseln); **~ house** *Br* Diskontbank *(Spezialbank für Wechseldiskontierung); Am →*commercial credit company; **~ loan** Diskontkredit; **~ market** *Br (aus den 12 Londoner Diskontbanken bestehender)* Diskontmarkt; **~ period** Diskontierungszeitraum; **~ policy** Diskontpolitik; **~ promise** Diskontzusage

discount rate Diskontsatz; **fluctuation of the ~** Diskontbewegung; **increase in the ~** Erhöhung des Diskontsatzes, Diskonterhöhung; **lowering of the ~** Senkung des Diskontsatzes, Diskontsenkung, Diskontherabsetzung; **raising of the ~** s. increase in the →~; **reduction in** (or **of**) **the ~** s. lowering of the →~; **rise in** (or **of**) **the ~** s. increase in the →~; **to lower** (or **reduce**) **the ~** den Diskont senken (od. herabsetzen); **to increase** (or **raise**) **the ~** den Diskont heraufsetzen (od. erhöhen)

discount, ~ terms Diskontbedingungen; **~ transactions** Diskontgeschäfte, Wechselgeschäfte; **~ window** *Am* Rediskontierungsstelle e-r Federal Reserve Bank, bei der Banken kurzfristige Anleihen mit Diskontsatz bekommen können

discount, to give a bill on ~ e-n Wechsel diskontieren lassen; **to increase the ~** den Diskont erhöhen; **to lower the ~** den Diskont senken; **to raise the ~** s. to increase the →~; **to reduce the ~** s. to lower the →~; **to take a bill on ~** e-n Wechsel diskontieren

discount 2. Rabatt, *(vorausgewährter)* Preisnachlaß; Skonto; *(VersR)* Prämienrabatt, Beitragsermäßigung; **~ allowed** Skontogewährung; **~ houses** Discountgeschäfte, Rabatthandelshäuser *(Einzelhandelsgeschäfte, die infolge niedriger Vertriebskosten Waren, bes. preisgebundene Markenartikel, mit Rabatt verkaufen)*; **~ percentage** Skontosatz; **~ period** Skontofrist; **~ sale** Verkauf mit Preisnachlaß; **~ store** *Am* Diskountgeschäft; **~ ticket** Rabattmarke

discount, cash ~ Barzahlungsrabatt, Skonto; **deducting ~** abzüglich Skonto; **distributor ~** s. trade →~; **extra ~** Sonderrabatt; **functional ~** Funktionsrabatt *(→functional)*; **less ~** abzüglich Skonto; **3 per cent ~ for cash** bei Barzahlung 3% Rabatt; **quantity ~** Mengenrabatt; **special ~** Sonderrabatt; **trade ~** Rabatt für Wiederverkäufer, Handelsrabatt

discount, to allow (or **give, offer**) ~ Rabatt (od. Skonto) gewähren (on auf); rabattieren; skontieren; **to deduct ~** (in the case of cash payment) *(bei Barzahlung)* Skonto abziehen, skontieren; **to give 3 per cent ~ for cash** bei Barzahlung 3% Skonto geben; **to take a ~** Skonto in Anspruch nehmen; **this price is subject to (a) ~** von diesem Preis geht ein Rabatt ab

discount (dis., disc. disct) 3. *(Börse)*Disagio, Abschlag *(opp. premium)*; **at a ~** unter pari; **issue at a ~** Unterpariemission; **to be** (or **stand**) **at ~** unter pari stehen; **to sell at a ~** mit Disagio (od. Verlust) verkaufen

discount 4. Deport; **~ rate** Deportsatz

discount *v* diskontieren; abzinsen; von vornherein in Rechnung stellen, einkalkulieren; abziehen, nicht mitrechnen; nicht ganz glauben; **to ~ a bill** e-n Wechsel diskontieren

discounted, ~ bills Diskonten, Diskontwechsel; **to have** (or **get**) **a bill ~** e-n Wechsel diskontieren lassen

discounting Diskontierung; Abzinsung; Einkalkulieren; abzüglich, nicht mitrechnend, nicht mitzählend; **~ any period** (during which) *Br* die Zeit nicht mitrechnend *(Hemmung der Verjährung)*; **~ of bills** Diskontierung von Wechseln; **~ charges** Diskontspesen; **~ rate** Abzinsungssatz

discountable diskontfähig, diskontierbar

discounter Diskontgeber, Diskontierer; Discounter, Inhaber e-s Discount-Geschäftes

discover *v* entdecken; ausfindig machen; feststellen; offen legen, Auskunft geben; **to ~ a plot** e-e Verschwörung aufdecken

discovery Entdeckung; Offenlegung, Bekanntgabe, Auskunftserteilung; *(VersR)* Anzeige; *(Zivilprozeß)* Erforschung, Ausforschung; erzwingbare Bekanntgabe von für den Rechtsstreit bedeutsamen Tatsachen und Urkunden *(an die Gegenpartei vor Beginn des Prozesses)*; *(BergR)* Fund; **~ of debtor's property** Offenlegung des schuldnerischen Vermögens; **~ of documents** Urkundenvorlegung; Offenlegung *(prozeßwichtiger)* Urkunden vor dem Prozeß durch Mitteilung an den Prozeßgegner; **~ by list** *Br* Offenlegung *(prozeßwichtiger)* Urkunden vor dem Prozeß durch Übersendung e-r Liste der Urkunden *(ohne affidavit, cf. ~ upon oath)*; **~ upon oath** *Br* Offenlegung *(prozeßwichtiger)* Urkunden vor dem Prozeß durch Übersendung e-s → affidavit of documents an den Prozeßgegner; **~ proceedings** *Am (etwa:)* Offenbarungseid, *(jetzt)* eidesstattliche Versicherung

discovery, bill of ~ *Am* Anordnung der Auskunftserteilung (od. Offenlegung); **duty of ~** Auskunftspflicht; Vorlagepflicht; **liable to ~** auskunftspflichtig; vorlagepflichtig; **pretrial ~** verhandlungsvorbereitende Offenlegung *(z.B. Urkundenvorlage; →pretrial)*; **privilege against ~** Recht, die Offenlegung zu verweigern; **right of ~** Recht *(e-r Prozeßpartei)*, Urkunden *(die im Besitz der Gegenpartei sind)* einzusehen und Abschrift davon zu nehmen

discover|y, scientific ~ies wissenschaftliche Entdeckungen; **protection of scientific ~ies**[42] Schutz wissenschaftlicher Entdeckungen

discovery, to make ~ *(dem Prozeßgegner)* Tatsachen mitteilen (od. Urkunden vorlegen); **to be privileged against** (or **from**) **~** nicht vorlegungspflichtig (od. offenlegungspflichtig) sein

discredit Mißkredit; schlechter Ruf; Unglaubwürdigkeit; **to bring into ~** in Mißkredit bringen

discredit *v* in Mißkredit (od. Verruf) bringen; anzweifeln, nicht glauben; **to ~ the evidence of a witness** die Aussage e-s Zeugen anzweifeln; **to ~ a witness** die Glaubwürdigkeit e-s Zeugen erschüttern *(z.B. durch Hinweis darauf, daß er sich widersprochen hat)*

discrepanc|y Widerspruch, Unstimmigkeit, Abweichung; **~ in a deposition of a witness** Widerspruch in e-r Zeugenaussage; **if ~ies arise** (or **in the event of ~ies**) bei Widersprüchen (od. Abweichungen)

discretion Ermessen, Belieben, Gutdünken; Diskretion, Verschwiegenheit; Klugheit, Besonnenheit; **absolute ~** freies Ermessen; **abuse of ~** Ermessensmißbrauch; **administrative ~** Ermessen der Verwaltungsbehörde; **at one's own ~** nach eigenem Ermessen; **banker's ~** Bankgeheimnis; **criminal ~** Strafmündigkeit; **duty of ~** Schweigepflicht; **exercise of the ~** Ausübung des Ermessens; **judicial ~** richterliches Ermessen; **margin of ~** Ermessensspielraum; **matter of ~** Ermessensfrage; **power of ~** Ermessensfreiheit; **professional ~** berufliche Schweigepflicht; Berufsgeheimnis

discretion, to be within the ~ of the court im Ermessen des Gerichtes liegen; **to leave to sb.'s ~** in jds Ermessen stellen, jds Ermessen überlassen; **to use one's ~** nach eigenem Ermessen handeln

discretionary im Ermessen stehend, dem Ermessen überlassen; Ermessens-; beliebig, willkürlich; **~ →account; ~ clause** Kannvorschrift; **~ income** frei verfügbares Einkommen; **~ jurisdiction** Befugnis, Ermessensentscheidungen vorzunehmen

discretionary power Ermessen(sfreiheit); unbeschränkte Vollmacht; **to exceed one's ~** Ermessensmißbrauch üben; willkürlich handeln

discretionary trust →trust 1.

discriminate *v* diskriminieren, unterschiedlich behandeln; unterscheiden (between zwischen); **to ~ against sb.** jdn benachteiligen (od. nachteilig behandeln); **to ~ in favo(u)r of sb.** jdn bevorzugen (od. bevorzugt behandeln)

discriminating duty Differentialzoll

discrimination Diskriminierung, unterschiedliche Behandlung; **~ against sb.** jds Benachteiligung (od. Schlechterstellung); **~ in favo(u)r of sb.** jds Bevorzugung; **~ in respect of employment and occupation**[43] Diskriminierung in Beschäftigung und Beruf

Discrimination, Convention on the Elimination of all Forms of ~ against Women[43a] Übereinkommen über die Beseitigung jeder Form der Diskriminierung der Frau

discrimination based on nationality,[44] **prohibition of ~** Verbot der Diskriminierung aus Gründen der Staatsangehörigkeit

discrimination, job *~Am* Benachteiligung *(bestimmter Personen)* im Arbeitsleben; **on a basis of non-~** auf der Grundlage der Gleichbehandlung (od. Gleichberechtigung); **positive ~** bessere Behandlung *(bes. wegen Rasse)* für benachteiligte Schichten der Bevölkerung; **rule of non-~** Regel der Nichtdiskriminierung; **racial ~** Rassendiskriminierung *(bes. der Neger)*; **to eliminate ~s** Diskriminierungen beseitigen (od. ausschalten)

discriminative unterscheidend; e-n Unterschied machend; **~ features** Unterscheidungsmerkmale; **~ treatment** unterschiedliche (bes. benachteiligende) Behandlung

discriminatory →discriminative; **~ action** diskriminierende Handlungsweise; **~ legislation** Ausnahmegesetzgebung; **~ taxation** unterschiedliche Besteuerung; **on a non-~ basis** auf der Grundlage der Gleichbehandlung; unter Vermeidung unterschiedlicher Behandlung

discuss *v* diskutieren, beraten über; erörtern, besprechen; *Scot* Einrede der Vorausklage erheben; **to ~ the situation** die Lage besprechen

discussion Diskussion, Besprechung, Erörterung; Aussprache; Debatte; Meinungsaustausch; **basis of ~** Diskussionsgrundlage; **matter for ~** Diskussionsgegenstand; **preliminary ~** Vorbesprechung; **subject for ~** Diskussionsthema; **under ~** zur Diskussion (od. Debatte) stehend; **to be still under ~** noch besprochen (od. beraten) werden; **to be beyond the scope of a ~** über den Rahmen e-r Aussprache hinausgehen; **to bring the question up for ~** die Frage zur Diskussion stellen; **to come up for ~** zur Diskussion gestellt werden; **to hold ~s** verhandeln; **to participate in a ~** an e-r Diskussion teilnehmen

disease Krankheit; **contagious** (or **infectious**) **~** ansteckende Krankheit; **epidemic ~** epidemische Krankheit; **hereditary ~** Erbkrankheit; **industrial ~** Berufskrankheit; **mental ~** Geisteskrankheit; **occupational** (or **vocational**) **~** Berufskrankheit; **to contract a ~** sich e-e Krankheit zuziehen

diseconomies of scale Ertragsverringerung pro Produktionseinheit bei steigender Betriebs-/ Unternehmensgröße aufgrund Kostenprogression *(wenn z.B. die Unternehmensgröße ein Optimum überschreitet und Verwaltungsaufwendungen überproportional wachsen)*[45]

disencumber *v* freimachen (from von), entschulden; **to ~ the property** die auf dem Grundstück lastende Hypothek löschen

disengage *v* (sich) freimachen, (sich) lösen (from von); *mil* sich absetzen

disengagement Freimachung *(von Verpflichtungen)*; *pol* Disengagement *(Auseinanderrücken von Machtblöcken)*; **~ of troops** Truppenentflechtung, Auseinanderrücken der Truppen

disentail *v* Erbfolge *(für Grundbesitz)* aufheben *(cf. to entail)*

disentailment Aufhebung der Erbfolge *(für Grundbesitz)*

disentomb *v* exhumieren;*(Leichen od. archäologische Funde)* ausgraben

disequilibrium gestörtes Gleichgewicht, Ungleichgewicht; **~ in the balance of payments** Ungleichgewicht der Zahlungsbilanz; **economic ~** wirtschaftliches (od. konjunkturelles) Ungleichgewicht

disestablish *v (Kirche)* vom Staat trennen

disestablishment of the Church Trennung von Staat und Kirche

disfranchise *v (jdm)* das Wahlrecht entziehen; *(jdm)* e-e Konzession entziehen

disfranchisement Entziehung des Wahlrechts

disgrace Schande (to für); Schandfleck; **to bring ~ to a person** jdm zur Unehre gereichen

disguise Verkleidung, Verstellung

disguise *v* verschleiern, verbergen

disherison Enterbung

dishonest unehrlich, unredlich; unreell; **~ profits** unredliche Gewinne

dishono(u)r Nichthonorieren *(e-s Wechsels od. Schecks)*; Notleiden *(e-s Wechsels)*; **~ (by non-acceptance)** Annahmeverweigerung *(e-s Wechsels)*; **~ (by non-payment)** Nichtzahlung *(e-s Wechsels)*; Zahlungsverweigerung; **in case of ~** bei Nichtannahme (od. Nichtzahlung) *(e-s Wechsels);* bei Nichteinlösung *(e-s Schecks);* **notice of** ~ Mitteilung der Annahmeverweigerung (od. Nichtzahlung); Notanzeige (→*notice* 1.); **to make a protest (of a bill of exchange) in case of** ~ bei Annahmeverweigerung oder Nichtzahlung *(e-s Wechsels)* Protest erheben

dishono(u)r *v* nicht erfüllen, zurückweisen; *(Wechsel, Scheck)* nicht honorieren; *(e-n Wechsel)* Not leiden lassen; **to** ~ **a bill (by non-acceptance)** Annahme e-s Wechsels verweigern; e-n Wechsel nicht akzeptieren; **to** ~ **a bill (by non-payment)** e-n Wechsel nicht bezahlen (od. einlösen); **to** ~ **a contract** e-n Vertrag nicht einhalten
dishono(u)red bill nicht honorierter (nicht akzeptierter, nicht bezahlter) Wechsel; notleidender Wechsel; ~ **cheque (check)** nicht eingelöster Scheck

dishono(u)rable unehrenhaft, ehrlos; ~ **discharge** *mil* unehrenhafte Entlassung

disincentive Abschreckungsmittel; lähmender (z. B. arbeitshemmender) Faktor *(opp. incentive)*
disinflation Desinflation*(Rückgang der inflationären Entwicklung)*

disinflationary desinflationistisch
disinherit *v* enterben

disinheritance *Am* Enterbung

disintegration Desintegration; Auflösung *(e-s Ganzen in seine Teile);* Zerfall; **signs of** ~ Auflösungserscheinungen

disinter *v* exhumieren

disinterested desinteressiert; uneigennützig; unparteiisch, unbefangen

disintermediation abnehmender Einfluß der Banken als Mittler im Finanzierungskreislauf zwischen Geldgebern und Geldnehmern (→*securitization*)

disinvestment Desinvestition; Zurückziehung von Anlagekapital; Reduzierung der Gesamtheit der Investitionsgüter

disjunctive einander ausschließend

dislocate *v* verlagern; *(Verkehr, Geschäft etc)* in Unordnung bringen, stören; **to** ~ **workers** Arbeitskräfte umplacieren

dislocation Verlagerung; Störung, Verwirrung; ~ **of traffic** Verkehrsdurcheinander

disloyal illoyal, nicht loyal (to gegenüber)

dismantle *v* demontieren, *(bes. Fabrikanlagen)* abbauen, abmontieren, abbrechen; *(Fabrikeinrichtung)* ausbauen; *(Schiff)* abtakeln, *(Wrack)* abwracken

dismantling Demontage, Abbau, Abbruch; Ausbau; Abwracken; ~ **cost** Demontagekosten; Abbruchkosten; ~ **list** Demontageliste; ~ **of customs duties** Abbau der Zölle; ~ **of missiles** Raketenabbau

dismember *v* zerreißen, zergliedern; *(Gebiet)* aufteilen, zerstückeln

dismemberment Zerreißung, Zergliederung; Zerstückelung *(von Land)*

dismiss *v* 1. *(aus dem Dienst od. Amt)* entlassen; *(von e-m Posten)* abberufen; **to** ~ **an employee** e-n Angestellten entlassen; **to** ~ **sb. from office** jdn aus dem Dienst entlassen; jdn seines Amtes entheben; **to** ~ **summarily** (or **without notice**) fristlos entlassen; **to be** ~**ed from the service** aus dem Militärdienst entlassen werden
dismiss *v.* 2. abweisen, zurückweisen; **to** ~ **an action** e-e Klage *(als unzulässig od. unbegründet)* abweisen (with costs kostenpflichtig); **to** ~ **the appeal** die Berufung verwerfen; **to** ~ **the case as being unfounded** die Klage als unbegründet abweisen; **to** ~ **the charge** *(Strafprozeß)* die Eröffnung des Hauptverfahrens ablehnen; das Verfahren einstellen; **to** ~ **a complaint on the merits** e-e Klage als unbegründet abweisen; **to** ~ **an indictment** →to ~ the charge; **to** ~ **a petition** e-n Antrag ablehnen (od. abschlägig bescheiden)
dismissed, case ~ Verfahren eingestellt

dismissal 1. (Dienst-)Entlassung; Amtsenthebung; Abberufung *(von e-m Posten) (opp. appointment);*~ **of workers** Entlassung von Arbeitern; ~ **pay** Entlassungsabfindung; ~ **without notice** fristlose Entlassung; **cause of** (or **ground for**) ~ Entlassungsgrund; **collective** ~**s** Massenentlassungen; **instant** ~ sofortige Entlassung; **protection against** ~Kündigungsschutz; **settlement on** ~ Abfindung bei Entlassung; **summary** ~ fristlose Entlassung; →**unfair**~; **to claim compensation in case of** ~ bei Entlassung Abfindung verlangen
dismissal 2. Abweisung, Zurückweisung; ~ **(of action)** Klageabweisung; ~ **of appeal** Verwerfung (od. Zurückweisung) der Berufung; ~ **of a criminal case** Einstellung e-s Strafverfahrens; ~ **on the merits** Klageabweisung auf Grund e-r Sachentscheidung *(z. B. über e-n point of law);* ~ **for want of prosecution or default** Klageabweisung wegen Unterlassung e-s erforderlichen Schrittes in der Prozeßführung

disobedience Ungehorsam (to gegen) *(z. B. gegenüber gerichtl. Anordnungen)*

disobey *v (Gesetz, Befehl etc)* nicht befolgen; **to** ~ **a court order** e-e gerichtl. Verfügung nicht befolgen

disorder Unordnung; Störung; *pol* Unruhen; **civil ~s** innere Unruhen; **mental ~** Geistesstörung (→*mental*)

disordered, mentally ~ person Geistesgestörter *(→mental disorder)*

disorderly unordentlich; aufrührerisch; öffentl. Ärgernis erregend, ordnungswidrig; **~ conduct** ordnungswidriges Verhalten, Ärgernis erregendes Benehmen; **~ crowds** aufrührerische Menge; **~ house** Bordell; **~ person** Ruhestörer; gegen die öffentliche Ordnung und Sicherheit verstoßende Person; Erreger öffentlichen Ärgernisses

disown *v* ableugnen, verleugnen; nichts zu tun haben wollen mit; *(Kind)* verstoßen; **to ~ one's signature** seine Unterschrift nicht anerkennen

disparage *v* verunglimpfen, in Verruf bringen; *(Waren des Mitbewerbers)* herabsetzen; anschwärzen

disparaging statement herabsetzende Behauptung

disparagement Verunglimpfung; Verächtlichmachung; Herabsetzung *(der Ware des Mitbewerbers);* Anschwärzung *(des Konkurrenten und seiner Ware)*

disparit|y Disparität, Ungleichheit, Verschiedenheit; **~ in age** Altersunterschied; **~ies in income** Einkommensunterschiede; **structural** (or **natural**) **~ies** strukturelle (naturbedingte) Unterschiede; **elimination of social ~ies** Abbau der sozialen Unterschiede; **to remove legal ~ies** Rechtsunterschiede beseitigen

dispark *v* die Öffentlichkeit von e-m Park ausschließen; Parkland für andere Zwecke verwenden

dispatch Absendung, Versendung, Versand; Beförderung; Abfertigung; schnelle Erledigung, Eile; schnelles Laden (od. Löschen) *(gesparte Tage; opp. demurrage);*(Presse-)Nachricht; **~ box** *dipl* Kuriergepäck; **~ by post** Versendung mit der Post; **~ by rail** Bahnversand; **~ goods** *Am* Eilgut; **~ instructions** Versandvorschriften

dispatch money Eilgeld, Beschleunigungsgebühr *(Vergütung für Einsparung von Lade- od. Löschzeit e-s Schiffes; opp. demurrage);* **~ half demurrage all time saved** (d. h. d. a. t. s.) Eilgeld in Höhe des halben Liegegeldes für die gesamte gesparte Zeit; **~ half demurrage working time saved** (d. h. d. w. s.) Eilgeld in Höhe des halben Liegegeldes für die gesparte Arbeitszeit

dispatch, ~ note Versandanzeige; Paketkarte *(für Auslandspakete);* **~ of business** Erledigung von Geschäften; **~ of goods** Warenversand; Güterabfertigung; **~ of goods by train** Versendung von Waren per Bahn; **~ of luggage** Gepäckabfertigung; **~ of mail** Postabfertigung; **~ of petition** schnelle Erledigung e-s Gesuchs; **~ of a telegram** Aufgabe e-s Telegramms; **~ of troops** Entsendung von Truppen; **~ regulations** Versandvorschriften; **~ rider** *mil* Meldefahrer; **~ tube** *(Rohrpost)* Beförderungsrohr

dispatch, advice of ~ Versandanzeige; **bearer of ~es** *dipl* Kurier; **country of ~** Versandland; **mode of ~** Versendungsart; **ready for ~** versandbereit; **with ~** sofort, mit Beschleunigung

dispatch *v* absenden, versenden, abfertigen; *(Geschäfte)* schnell ausführen (od. erledigen); töten; **to ~ goods** Waren versenden (od. befördern); **to ~ a telegram** ein Telegramm aufgeben

dispatching, ~ the goods Warenversand; Güterbeförderung; **~ office** Absendepostamt

dispatcher Absender, Versender, Expedient; *Am* Betriebs-(od. Abteilungs-)leiter für Planung und Kontrolle des Produktionsprozesses

dispauper *Am* das Armenrecht entziehen *(cf. to sue in forma pauperis);* **to be ~ed** das Armenrecht verlieren

dispensation Befreiung *(von e-r Verpflichtung); eccl* Dispens; Verteilung

dispense *v* befreien, dispensieren (from von); ausgeben, verteilen; **to ~ with** auskommen ohne, verzichten auf; absehen von; überflüssig machen; abschaffen; **to ~ charity** Almosen verteilen, wohltätig sein; **to ~ justice** Recht sprechen; **to ~ with the calling of a witness** auf den Aufruf e-s Zeugen verzichten

dispensing chemist Apotheker

dispersal →dispersion

disperse *v* zerstreuen; verbreiten; sich zerstreuen, auseinandergehen *(cf. riot);* auflockern; **the Jews are ~d among all nations** die Juden sind unter allen Nationen verstreut

dispersion Streuung; Zerstreuung, Verteilung, Verbreitung; Auflockerung; *eccl* Diaspora; **~ of assets** Vermögensaufspaltung; Anlagenstreuung; **~ of industry** Verteilung der Industrie *(industrielle Auflockerung);* **~ of ownership** Eigentumsstreuung

displace *v* verlagern; verschleppen; umsiedeln; an *(jds)* Stelle treten, *(jdn)* ersetzen; an die Stelle setzen von

displaced, ~ persons (D. P.) verschleppte Personen *(die im 2. Weltkrieg aus ihrer Heimat weggeführten Ausländer, bes. Zwangsarbeiter);* Zwangsumsiedler; **~ population** umgesiedelte Bevölkerung

displacement Verlagerung, Verschiebung; Verschleppung; *(zwangsweise)* Umsiedlung; Ersatz (by durch); Wasserverdrängung, Tonnage, Tonnengehalt; ~ **of funds** anderweitige Kapitalverwendung; ~ **of wealth** Verlagerung des Wohlstandes; **light** ~ Leertonnage; **load** ~ Ladetonnage

display Display, (Form der) Warenauslage; Entfaltung; hervorgehobene Textstelle; Großanzeige; ~ **advertising** Schlagzeilenwerbung; ~ **case** Schaukasten, Vitrine; ~ **of power** Machtentfaltung; ~ **of prices** Preisauszeichnung; ~ **screen** *(EDV)* Bildschirm; ~ **in shop window** (or **window** ~) Schaufensterauslage; ~**-type advertisement** besonders gestaltete Anzeige *(opp. classified advertisement)*; ~ **work** Auslagengestaltung

display *v* *(Waren)* auslegen, ausstellen; zur Schau stellen, zeigen; *(Macht etc)* entfalten; **to** ~ **a flag** flaggen; **to** ~ **a notice** e-n Anschlag aushängen

dispone *v Scot (Grundbesitz)* übertragen

disposable verfügbar; wegwerfbar; ~ **goods** sofort verfügbare (od. lieferbare) Waren; ~ **income** *Br* verfügbares Einkommen *(der das Armenrecht beantragenden Partei)*; *Am* verfügbares *(persönl.)* Einkommen *(nach Abzug der Steuern und Sozialversicherungsabgaben)*

disposal Verfügung(srecht) *(e-r Privatperson)* (of über); Erledigung; Beseitigung, Wegschaffen; Veräußerung, Verkauf; **for** ~ zum Verkauf; zu verkaufen; **(power of)** ~ Verfügungsgewalt; Verfügungsrecht; **right of** ~ Verfügungsrecht; ~ **of property** Verfügung über Vermögen; ~ **of waste** Beseitigung von Abfällen; ~ **of** →**radioactive waste**

disposal, restraint on ~ Verfügungsbeschränkung; **to be at sb.'s** ~ jdm zur Verfügung stehen; **to have the** ~ die Verfügung(sgewalt) haben (of über); **to have at one's** ~ zu seiner Verfügung haben; verfügen über; **to place at sb.'s** ~ jdm zur Verfügung stellen

dispose *v* verfügen (of über); erledigen; beseitigen; veräußern, verkaufen; anordnen, einrichten; **to** ~ **of one's business** sein Geschäft verkaufen; **to** ~ **of a case** e-n Rechtsfall entscheiden; **to** ~ **of goods** Waren verkaufen; **to** ~ **of an issue** e-e Anleihe begeben; **to** ~ **of one's mail** seine Post erledigen; **to** ~ **of a p.** jdn beseitigen; **to** ~ **(of sth.) by will** (über etw.) letztwillig verfügen; (etw.) vermachen; **right to** ~ **of** Verfügungsrecht

disposed geneigt, gewillt, bereit; **easily** ~ **of** leicht verkäuflich; leicht zu beseitigen (wegwerfbar); **this difficulty can be easily** ~ **of** diese Schwierigkeit kann leicht beseitigt werden

disposing, ~ **capacity** *Am* Testierfähigkeit; **capable of** ~ verfügungsfähig; testierfähig; **power of** ~ Verfügungsbefugnis; **right of** ~ Verfügungsrecht; **to be of sound and** ~ **mind** *Am* testierfähig sein *(die Fähigkeit haben, ein Testament zu errichten)*

disposition Verfügung(sgewalt) (of über); Anordnung, Einteilung; (Charakter-)Anlage; Neigung; Bestimmung, Verwendung; *Scot* Übertragungsurkunde; ~**s** Anordnungen, Vorkehrungen; ~ **of funds** Mittelverwendung; ~ **of profits** Gewinnverwendung; ~ **of immovable property** Verfügung über unbewegliches Vermögen; ~ **of rooms in a building** Zimmeraufteilung in e-m Gebäude; ~ **of troops** Truppeneinsatz

disposition, criminal ~ verbrecherische Veranlagung; **money at sb.'s** ~ zu jds Verfügung stehendes Geld; **power of** ~ Verfügungsgewalt; **testamentary** ~ letztwillige Verfügung; Testament

disposition, to make ~**s** Verfügungen (od. Anordnungen) treffen

dispositive, ~ **clause** *Scot* Klausel in e-r Urkunde, durch die Vermögen übertragen wird; ~ **law** dispositives Recht; ~ **restraint** Verfügungsbeschränkung

dispossess *v (widerrechtl.)* den (Immobiliar-)Besitz entziehen *(der rechtmäßig od. rechtswidrig erworben war)*; *(den gegenwärtigen Besitzer, bes. im Grundstücksrecht)* aus dem Besitz setzen; *(Mieter, Pächter)* zur Räumung zwingen *(cf. eject v)*

dispossession *(widerrechtl.)* Entziehung des (Immobiliar-)Besitzes; zwangsweise Entfernung *(des Mieters, Pächters)*; Räumung

disproof Widerlegung, Gegenbeweis; **to offer evidence in** ~ den Gegenbeweis bringen

disprovable widerlegbar

disprove *v (Behauptung)* widerlegen; *(etw.)* als falsch nachweisen

dispute Streit(igkeit); Streitfall; **beyond** ~ unstreitig; **existing** ~**s** bereits bestehende Streitigkeiten; **frontier** ~ Grenzstreitigkeit; **future** ~**s** künftige Streitigkeiten

dispute, in ~ streitig, strittig, bestritten; **matter in** ~ streitige Sache, Streitgegenstand

dispute, industrial ~ s. labo(u)r →~; **international** ~ internationaler Streitfall; **settlement of international** ~**s** Beilegung (od. Regelung) internationaler Streitfälle; →**jurisdictional** ~; **labo(u)r** ~ arbeitsrechtliche Streitigkeit; **parties to a** ~ Parteien e-s Streitfalles; **settling** ~**s** Beilegung (od. Schlichtung) von Streitigkeiten, Streitbeilegung *(cf. conciliation, arbitration, mediation)*; **trade** ~ Arbeitsstreitigkeit; **wage** ~ Lohnstreitigkeit; ~ **settlement** Streitbeilegung

dispute, a ~ **arises** ein Streit entsteht (as to whether darüber, ob); **to be in** ~ strittig sein; **to settle a** ~ **by negotiation** e-n Streit(fall) auf dem Verhandlungswege beilegen (od. schlichten); **to submit a ~ to a court** (or **tribunal**) e-n Streitfall vor ein Gericht bringen

dispute *v* streiten; bestreiten, in Zweifel ziehen, bezweifeln; erörtern, diskutieren; **to ~ an assertion** e-e Behauptung bestreiten; **to ~ an election** die Gültigkeit e-r Wahl (od. ein Wahlergebnis) anfechten; **to ~ the validity of a document** die Gültigkeit e-r Urkunde bestreiten; **to ~ a will** ein Testament anfechten; die (Rechts-)Gültigkeit e-s Testamentes bestreiten

disputed streitig, bestritten; **~ claim** strittige Forderung; **~ election** *Br* angefochtene Wahl; **~ title** bestrittenes Eigentum(srecht)

disputing, ~ an election *Br* Anfechtung e-r Wahl; **the ~ parties** die streitenden Parteien

disqualification Unfähigkeit, Untauglichkeit; Aberkennung der Fähigkeit, Erklärung der Unfähigkeit; Disqualifizierung, Feststellung der Nichteignung (from zu); Ausschluß, Ausschließung; **~ of a bankrupt** Rechtsverluste des Konkursschuldners; **~ on the ground of bias** Ausschluß *(e-s Richters)* wegen Befangenheit; **~ for public office** Unfähigkeit zur Bekleidung e-s öffentlichen Amtes; **~ from being a witness** Unfähigkeit, Zeuge zu sein

disqualif|y *v* unfähig (od. untauglich) machen; für unfähig (od. nicht geeignet) erklären; ausschließen, disqualifizieren; **to ~ from driving** *Br* die Fahrerlaubnis (od. den Führerschein) entziehen; **the judge ~ies himself** der Richter erklärt sich für befangen

disqualified unfähig, untauglich; nicht berechtigt; ausgeschlossen (from von); disqualifiziert; **to be ~ from driving** (or **from holding** or **obtaining a licence**) *Br* die Fahrerlaubnis verlieren; **to be ~ for an office** unfähig zur Bekleidung e-s Amtes sein; **to declare oneself ~** sich für befangen erklären

disregard *v* nicht beachten, außer acht lassen; mißachten; ignorieren

disrepair Baufälligkeit, schlechter baulicher Zustand; Reparaturbedürftigkeit; **to be in ~** in schlechtem baulichen Zustand (od. reparaturbedürftig) sein; **to fall into ~** verfallen, baufällig (od. reparaturbedürftig) werden

disreputable von schlechtem Ruf, anrüchig; **to lead a ~ life** e-n anrüchigen Lebenswandel führen

disrupt *v* zerbrechen, *(gewaltsam)* unterbrechen; **to ~ a coalition** e-e Koalition sprengen

disrupting of meetings and processions Sprengung von Versammlungen und Umzügen

disruption Bruch, Riß, Spaltung; *(gewaltsame)* Unterbrechung; **the D~** Spaltung der Kirche von Schottland *(1843)*

disruptive activities zersetzende Tätigkeiten

dissect *v*, **to ~ an account** ein Konto aufgliedern

dissection Zergliederung; Aufgliederung *(z. B. von Konten); med* Sektion

dissei|se, ~ze *v (widerrechtl.)* den (Immobiliar-)-Besitz *(freehold)* entziehen

dissei|sin, ~zin *(widerrechtl.)* Entziehung des (Immobiliar-)Besitzes *(freehold)*

disseminate *v* verbreiten, ausstreuen; **~d works** *(UrhR)* veröffentlichte Werke

dissemination Verbreitung; Weitergabe; **~ of rumo(u)rs** Verbreitung von Gerüchten; **right of ~** *(UrhR)* Veröffentlichungsrecht

dissension Meinungsverschiedenheit, Uneinigkeit (between zwischen)

dissent Dissens, Meinungsverschiedenheit; abweichende Meinung (from von); Meinung der Minderheit; *Br* Abweichung von der anglikanischen Kirche; **agreed ~** vereinbarte Abweichung

dissent *v* anderer Meinung sein (from als); nicht übereinstimmen (od. zustimmen) *(opp. to assent)*

dissenting nicht zustimmend, abweichend; **~ minister** *Br* Geistlicher, der nicht der engl. Staatskirche angehört; Sektengeistlicher; **~ minority** widersprechende Minderheit; **~ opinion** abweichende Meinung *(der überstimmten Richter bei e-r Kollegialentscheidung);* abweichendes Votum, Minderheitsvotum; **~ shareholders** *Br* nicht dem →take-over bid zustimmende Aktionäre; **~ vote** abweichende Stimme, Gegenstimme; **to cast a ~ vote** e-e abweichende Stimme abgeben

dissenter Dissenter, Andersdenkender, Abweichler; *eccl* Dissident *(zu keiner staatl. anerkannten Kirchengemeinschaft gehörende Person); Br* Dissenter, Nonkonformist *(Mitglied e-r der anglikanischen Kirche nicht angehörenden Sekte [denomination])*

dissentient Andersdenkender; andersdenkend *(als die Mehrheit),* abweichend

dissident *bes. pol.* Dissident, Abweichler; andersdenkend; abweichend (from von)

dissociate *v auch pol* sich lossagen (od. abrükken) (from von); unterscheiden (from von)

dissolution Auflösung, Aufhebung; *Am (AntitrustR)* Entflechtung; **~ of an assembly** Auflösung (od. Aufhebung) e-r Versammlung; **~ of an association** Auflösung e-r Gesellschaft; **~ of a company**[46] (or *Am* **corporation**) Auflösung e-r (Handels-)Gesellschaft; **~ of marriage** Auflösung der Ehe *(durch Scheidungsur-*

teil); Ehescheidung; ~ **of Parliament** *Br* Auflösung des Parlaments

dissolve *v* auflösen, aufheben; *Am (AntitrustR)* entflechten; **to ~ a company** e-e (Handels-)Gesellschaft auflösen; **to ~ an injunction** e-e einstweilige Verfügung aufheben; **to ~ a marriage** e-e Ehe scheiden *(durch den Richter);* **to ~ Parliament** *Br* das Parlament auflösen

distance Entfernung; Strecke; Abstand; ~ **freight** Distanzfracht; Mehrfracht *(bei Ausladung in e-m sicheren Ersatzhafen);* **little ~** geringer Abstand; **long-~ call** *tel* Ferngespräch; **long-~ goods traffic** *Br* Güterfernverkehr; **long-~ hauling** *Am* Güterfernverkehr; **short-~ goods traffic** *Br* Güternahverkehr; **to drive at an adequate ~** (from the preceding vehicle) e-n ausreichenden Abstand (zum vorausfahrenden Fahrzeug) halten

distantly related entfernt (od. weitläufig) verwandt

distinction Unterscheidung; Unterschied, unterscheidendes Merkmal; Auszeichnung; **class ~** Klassenunterschied; ~ **of rank** Rangunterschied; **without ~ of person** ohne Ansehen der Person; **without ~ of race** ohne Unterschied der Rasse; **to confer a ~ upon sb.** jdm e-e Auszeichnung verleihen; **to make a ~ between** e-n Unterschied machen zwischen; **to receive a ~** e-e Auszeichnung erhalten; **he has won ~ in public life** er hat sich im öffentlichen Leben ausgezeichnet

distinctive charakteristisch, kennzeichnend (of für); sich unterscheidend

distinctive character Unterscheidungskraft; **trade marks which have no ~** Marken, die keine Unterscheidungskraft haben; **to acquire a ~** Unterscheidungskraft erlangen

distinctive, ~ feature Kennzeichen, Unterscheidungsmerkmal; ~ **flag** *(VölkerR)* Schutzflagge; ~ **mark** *(WarenzeichenR)* unterscheidungskräftiges Zeichen; **non-~ trade mark** Warenzeichen ohne Unterscheidungskraft

distinctiveness *(WarenzeichenR)* Unterscheidungskraft; **lack of ~** mangelnde Unterscheidungskraft

distinguish *v* unterscheiden, auseinanderhalten; **to ~ o.s.** sich auszeichnen

distinguished hervorragend, ausgezeichnet; berühmt, bedeutend; ~ **by** kenntlich an; bemerkenswert durch; **my ~ colleague** mein verehrter Kollege; **D~ Conduct Medal** (D. C. M.) *Br* Kriegsverdienstmedaille *(für Unteroffiziere und Soldaten);* **D~ Service Cross** (D. S. C.) Kriegsverdienstkreuz; **D~ Service Order** (D. S. O.) *Br* Kriegsverdienstorden *(für Offiziere)*

distinguishing unterscheidend; charakteristisch; ~ **characteristics** Unterscheidungsmerkmale; ~ **mark** Kennzeichen; ~ **sign of motor vehicles in international traffic**[46a] Unterscheidungszeichen der Kraftfahrzeuge im internationalen Verkehr; **capable of ~** *(Warenzeichen R)* unterscheidungsfähig

distort *v* verzerren; verdrehen, entstellen; **to ~ the conditions of competition** die Wettbewerbsbedingungen verzerren

distortion Verzerrung; Verdrehung, Entstellung; ~ **of competition** Wettbewerbsverzerrung; ~ **of facts** Verdrehung von Tatsachen; **~s to trade** Handelsverzerrungen; ~ **of the work** *(UrhR)* Entstellung des Werkes

distrain *v (bewegl. Sachen als Sicherheit für die Bezahlung e-r Schuld ohne Inanspruchnahme des Gerichts berechtigt)* in Besitz nehmen; *(im Wege der Selbsthilfe)* mit Beschlag belegen *(vgl. im deutschen Recht § 561 BGB);*[47] **to ~ for rent** *(bewegl. Sachen des Mieters)* wegen rückständiger Miete in Besitz nehmen; **to ~ on goods** Waren mit Beschlag belegen

distrained, cattle ~ (up)on mit Beschlag belegtes Vieh

distrainable mit Beschlag belegbar

distrainee jd, dessen bewegl. Sachen in Beschlag genommen werden

distrainer, ~or jd, der bewegl. Sachen *(als Sicherheit für Ansprüche)* in Beschlag nimmt

distraint Inbesitznahme, Beschlagnahme[47]

distress 1. Inbesitznahme, Beschlagnahme[47] *(bes. zur Sicherung von Miet-, Pacht- oder Steuerforderungen od. des durch Vieh entstandenen Schadens);* in Beschlag genommene Sachen; ~ **damage-feasant** *Br* Beschlagnahme von Vieh, das auf dem Land des Grundbesitzes Schaden angerichtet hat *(bis zur Bezahlung von Schadensersatz);* ~ **for rent** Inbesitznahme *(der bewegl. Sachen des Mieters od. Pächters)* wegen rückständiger Miete od. Pacht; ~ **sale** Verkauf der in Beschlag genommenen Gegenstände des Schuldners *(zur Begleichung seiner Schuld);* ~ **warrant** →warrant of ~ *(warrant 1.)*

distress, landlord's right of ~ *(ungenau)* Vermieterpfandrecht, Pächterpfandrecht *(gesetzl. Pfandrecht des Vermieters od. Verpächters für die Forderung aus dem Miet- od. Pachtvertrag);* →**warrant of ~**

distress, to be subject to ~ der Beschlagnahme unterliegen; **to levy a ~ (on)** →to distrain; **the ~ is levied** die Beschlagnahme wird vorgenommen

distress 2. (große) Not(lage), Bedürftigkeit; Kummer; ~ **at sea** Seenot; ~ **call** Notsignal e-s Schiffes (SOS); ~ **flag** Notflagge; ~ **signal** Notsignal; **port of ~** Nothafen; **ship in ~**

Schiff in Seenot; **to relieve the common** ~ die allgemeine Not lindern

distress *v* →to distrain
distressed in Not, notleidend, bedrängt; ~ **area** Notstandsgebiet; Elendsbezirk; ~ **condition** Notlage; ~ **mortgage** in Verzug befindliche Hypothek; **to take advantage of sb.s** ~ **condition** jds Notlage ausnutzen

distributable verteilbar, austeilbar, ausschüttbar, ausschüttungsfähig; ~ **profit** ausschüttbarer (od. zur Verteilung kommender) Gewinn

distribute *v* verteilen (among unter; to an); zuteilen, austeilen; *(Dividende)* ausschütten; *(Gewinne)* auskehren; *(Ware)* verteilen, absetzen; **to** ~ **equally** gleichmäßig aufteilen; **to** ~ **the assets** (among the partners) sich auseinandersetzen *(unter Gesellschaftern)*; **to** ~ **by lot** durch Los verteilen; **to** ~ **profits** Gewinne auskehren
distribute *v*, **right to** ~ Vertriebsrecht
distributed profit ausgeschütteter (od. verteilter) Gewinn
distributing, ~ **agent** (Groß-)Handelsvertreter; ~ **company** Vertriebsgesellschaft *(für Investmentanteile)*; ~ **network** (or **system**) Verteilungsnetz

distributee jd, dem etw. zugeteilt wird; *Am* Erbe

distribution Verteilung, Zuteilung, Austeilung; Ausschüttung *(z.B. e-r Dividende od. der Gewinne bei Anteilen e-s Investmentfonds)*; Streuung; *com* Verteilung, Vertrieb, Absatz; Distribution; ~ **agency** Vertriebsagentur; Verteilungsstelle; ~ **agreement** *(KartellR)* Vertriebsabsprache; ~ **cartel** Absatzkartell, Vertriebskartell; ~ **code** Verteilerschlüssel; ~ **cost** → ~ expense; ~ **expense(s)** Absatzkosten, Vertriebskosten;~ **made on investment fund shares** Ausschüttung auf Investmentanteile; ~ **manager** Vertriebsleiter; ~ **network** Vertriebsnetz; ~ **of bankrupt's estate** Ausschüttung (od. Verteilung) der Konkursmasse; ~ **of business** Geschäftsverteilung *(e-s Gerichts)*; ~ **of the dividend** Ausschüttung (od. Verteilung) der Dividende; ~ **of films** Filmverleih; ~ **of income** Einkommensverteilung; Einkommensstreuung; ~ **of prizes** Preisverteilung; ~ **of profits** Gewinnverteilung, Gewinnausschüttung; ~ **of property** Vermögensverteilung; ~ **of risk** Risikoverteilung; ~ **of seats** *parl* Sitzverteilung; ~ **of surplus** Überschußverteilung; ~ **policy** Distributionspolitik
distribution, channels of ~ Vertriebswege, Absatzwege; **cost** ~ Kostenverteilung; **cost of** ~ Vertriebskosten, Absatzkosten; **plan of** ~ Verteilungsplan; **right of** ~ *(UrhR)* Verbreitungsrecht; **statutory order of** ~ gesetzliche Erbfolgeordnung; **to be available for** ~ **among the creditors** zur Verteilung unter die Gläubiger verfügbar sein

distributive verteilend; ~ **share** *Am* Anteil; (gesetzlicher) Erbteil; **national income by** ~ **shares** *Am* Volkseinkommen nach Einkommensarten; ~ **trades** Handel (und Verteilung) *(alle Absatzstufen)*

distributor Verteiler; Vertriebsstelle; Eigenhändler; Großhändler, Grossist; Generalvertreter *(für e-n bestimmten Bezirk)*; (Film-)Verleiher; **sole** ~Alleinvertriebshändler; **wholesale and retail** ~ Groß- und Einzelhändler; **to be sole** ~ den alleinigen Vertrieb haben (for für)

district Distrikt, (Verwaltungs-)Bezirk *(Br nächstkleinere Verwaltungseinheit nach e-m → county)*; ~ **attorney** *Am* (Bezirks-)Staatsanwalt
District of Columbia (D. C.) *Am* Bundesdistrikt Columbia
Vom Kongreß unmittelbar verwalteter Bundesdistrikt mit der Bundeshauptstadt Washington
district, ~ **committee** Bezirksausschuß; ~ **council** *Br* Stadtrat, Gemeinderat; **D**~ **Court** *Am* (Bundes-)Bezirksgericht (→*court)*; ~ **judge** *Am* Richter e-s D~ Court; **D**~ **Line** *Br* Linie der Londoner Untergrundbahn; ~ **manager** Bezirksdirektor; Gebietsverkaufsleiter; ~ **nurse** Gemeindeschwester; ~ **registrar** *Br* Leiter e-r →~ registry; ~ **registry** *Br* Zweiggeschäftsstelle des High Court of Justice *(in den größeren Städten)*; ~ **surveyor** Bauaufseher
district, election (or **electoral**) ~ Wahlbezirk; **judicial** ~ *Am* Gerichtsbezirk; **residential** ~ Wohngegend

disturb *v* stören, beeinträchtigen; beunruhigen; **to** ~ **the market** den Markt stören; **to** ~**sb.'s plans** jds Pläne durchkreuzen; **to** ~ **the traffic** den Verkehr behindern
disturbing the peace →disturbance of the peace

disturbance Störung, Ruhestörung; Behinderung *(im Genuß e-s Rechtes)*; ~**s** Unruhen; ~ **of the peace** Störung der öffentlichen Sicherheit und Ordnung; ~ **of possession** Besitzstörung; ~ **of public** (or **religious**) **worship** Störung des Gottesdienstes
disturbance, economic ~**s** wirtschaftliche Störungen; **political** ~**s** politische Unruhen; **public** ~**s** Unruhen *(cf. affray, unlawful assembly, brawling, riot)*; **to cause** ~**s** Unruhen verursachen

disunion Trennung; Spaltung; ~**ism** *pol* Lostrennungsbewegung

disuse Nichtgebrauch, Nichtverwendung; **to fall into** ~ außer Gebrauch kommen, nicht mehr verwendet werden

diverge *v* divergieren, abweichen (from von)
diverging, agreements ~ from the contract vom Vertrag abweichende Vereinbarungen

divergence Divergenz, Abweichung; **~ of judicial decisions** Abweichung gerichtlicher Entscheidungen voneinander; **~ of opinions** Meinungsverschiedenheit

divergent testimonies von einander abweichende (od. sich widersprechende) Zeugenaussagen

diverse citizenship *Am* verschiedene Staatsangehörigkeit *(cf. diversity of citizenship)*

diversification Diversifikation, Diversifizierung; Verschiedenartigkeit, Vielseitigkeit; Anlagenstreuung; Risikoverteilung; Auswahl der Effekten *(e-s investment trust)*; **~ merger** *Am* Mischkonzern, Konglomerat; **~ of investments** Anlagestreuung; **~ of products** Vielseitigkeit im Produktionsprogramm *(zur Krisenfestigkeit gegenüber Konjunkturschwankungen)*; **~ (of risk)** Risikoverteilung, Verteilung des Risikos

diversify *v* diversifizieren; verschieden(artig) gestalten; auffächern; *(Sortiment)* ausweiten; **to ~ shares** Aktien verschiedenartig anlegen
diversified, ~ company Gesellschaft mit breitem Produktionsprogramm; **~ fund** Investmentfonds mit breiter Anlagestreuung; **non-~ investment company** Investmentgesellschaft, die auf Risikomischung verzichtet; **~ portfolio** gut sortiertes Portefeuille; **~ risk** verteiltes Risiko
diversifying Diversifizierung

diversion Ablenkung; Ablenkungsmanöver; Umleitung; *(StrafR)* Diversion *(Bremsen krimineller Neigungen jugendlicher Täter durch Ablenkung)*; **~ order** *(VölkerR)* Kursanweisung; Befehl *(e-s Kriegsschiffes an ein Handelsschiff)* zum Anlaufen e-s bestimmten Punktes zwecks Durchsuchung *(cf. right of visit and search, →visit 2.)*; **(traffic) ~** *Br* Umleitung des Verkehrs

diversity Verschiedenheit; **~ of citizenship** *Am* Verschiedenheit der *(einzelstaatl.)* Staatsangehörigkeit *(bes. bei Kläger und Beklagtem; wichtig für Begründung der Zuständigkeit des bundesgerichtl. District Court)*; **~ jurisdiction**[47a] *Am* Zuständigkeit der Bundesrichter bei Streitigkeiten zwischen Parteien verschiedener Einzelstaaten und zwischen amerikanischen Staatsangehörigen und Ausländern; **~ of opinion** Meinungsverschiedenheit

divert *v* ablenken; *(Straßenverkehr)* umleiten; *(Geld)* abzweigen, anders verwenden; **to ~ the law** das Recht beugen
diverted funds anderweitig verwendete Mittel

divest *v*, **to ~ sb. of sth.** jdm etw. (ab)nehmen, jdm etw. entziehen; **to ~ oneself of** sich trennen von, verzichten auf; **to ~ oneself of a right** auf ein Recht verzichten; **to be ~ed of an estate** (or **interest**) ein Eigentumsrecht verlieren

divestiture *Am (AntitrustR)* Entflechtung; Auflösung *(e-r Fusion)*

divide *v* teilen, aufteilen; einteilen (into in); verteilen (among, between unter), trennen; sich teilen, sich trennen; *parl* durch Hammelsprung abstimmen (lassen); *pol (Land)* teilen, spalten; **to ~ the Ayes from the Noes** *Br parl* die Ja- von den Nein-Stimmen trennen; **to ~ the House** *Br parl (durch Hammelsprung)* abstimmen lassen; **to ~ markets** Märkte aufteilen; **to ~ profits** Gewinne aufteilen (between, among unter); Gewinne teilen; **to ~ up the work** die Arbeit aufteilen
divided geteilt; getrennt; *pol* gespalten; **the court is ~** das Gericht ist verschiedener Meinung (on über); **the judges are equally ~** die Zahl der Richter für und gegen e-e Entscheidung ist gleich; **the House ~** *Br parl* das Haus stimmte ab
dividing, drawing the ~ line Abgrenzung (between zwischen)

dividend (div.) Dividende; Quote *(e-r Konkursmasse)*; *(VersR) bes. Am* Bonus, Gewinnanteil *(Überschußzuweisungen an die Versicherungsnehmer)*; **~ account** Dividendenkonto; **~ on account** s. interim →~; **~ arrears** Dividendenrückstände; **~ in arrears** rückständige Dividende; **~ in bankruptcy** Konkursquote; **~ claim** Dividendenanspruch; **~ coupon** Dividendenschein, Gewinnanteilschein; **~ cover** Gewinn/Dividende Verhältnis; **~ distribution** Dividendenausschüttung; **~ due** fällige Dividende; **~ guarantee** Dividendengarantie; **~ off** *Am* s. ex →~; **~ on** *Am* s. cum →~; **~ payable in kind** Sachdividende; **~ paying company** Dividende zahlende Gesellschaft *(opp. company paying no ~)*; **~ payment** Dividendenzahlung; **~ payout** Dividendenausschüttung; **~ policy** Dividendenpolitik; Ausschüttungspolitik; **~ rate** Dividendensatz; **~s receivable** Dividendenforderungen; **~s received deduction** *Am (SteuerR)*[47b] Abzug für bezogene Dividenden; **~ reserve fund** Dividendenreserve, Dividendenrücklage; **~ rights** Dividendenrechte; **~share** Gewinnanteil; **~ warrant** Dividendenschein, Anrechtsschein auf Dividende; **~ yield** Dividendenertrag
dividend, accumulated ~ aufgelaufene Dividende; **annual ~** Jahresdividende; **bond ~** Dividende in Form von Obligationen; **cash ~** Bardividende; **collected ~** abgehobene Dividende; **cum ~** (c.d., cum div.) *Br* einschließlich Dividende *(die nächste Dividende erhält der*

Käufer); **cumulative** ~ kumulative Dividende (→*cumulative);* **declaration of** ~ Dividendenerklärung, Festsetzung der Dividende; **distribution of a** ~ Verteilung (od Ausschüttung) e-r Dividende; **ex** ~ (ex div.) ausschließlich Dividende; **extra** ~ außerordentliche Dividende; Bonus; **final** ~ Schlußdividende; *(im Konkursverfahren)* Schlußquote; **guarantee as to** ~**s** Dividendengarantie; **increase of** ~**s** Dividendenerhöhung; **interim** ~ Interimsdividende, Abschlagsdividende; **notification of** ~ Dividendenankündigung; **optional** ~ *(nach Wahl des Aktionärs)* in bar oder (Gratis-)Aktie zahlbare Dividende; →**ordinary** ~; **passing of the** ~ Dividendenausfall; **payment of the** ~ Dividendenzahlung; **preference** (or **preferred**) ~ Vorzugsdividende; **reduction of** ~**s** Dividendenherabsetzung; **reversionary** ~ *Am (VersR)* Summenzuwachs; **scrip** ~ Dividende in Form von Interimsscheinen; **sham** ~ Scheindividende; **share** ~ s. stock →~; **statutory** ~ satzungsmäßige Dividende; **stock** ~ *Am* (Dividende in Form von) Gratisaktie(n); **unclaimed** ~ nicht abgehobene Dividende

dividend, to declare a ~ e-e Dividende erklären (od. beschließen); **to distribute a** ~ e-e Dividende verteilen (od ausschütten); **to pass a** ~ e-e Dividende ausfallen lassen; keine Dividende zahlen; **to rank for** ~**s** *Br* dividendenberechtigt sein

divisible, ~ **contract** teilbarer Vertrag *(opp. entire contract);* ~ **performance** teilbare Leistung; ~ **surplus** aufteilbarer Überschuß

division 1. Teilung; Einteilung (into in); Verteilung, Aufteilung; Abteilung *(e-s Ministeriums);* Betriebsabteilung; Kammer, Senat *(e-s Gerichts);* Grenze; Uneinigkeit, Spaltung; *pol* Teilung, Spaltung *(e-s Landes);* ~ **of an estate** (among the persons entitled) Teilung e-r Erbschaft, Erbteilung; ~ **of Germany** Teilung Deutschlands (→*Germany);* ~ **of labo(u)r** Arbeitsteilung; ~ **of markets** Marktaufteilung; Aufteilung von Märkten; ~ **(of opinion)** Meinungsverschiedenheit; Uneinigkeit, Spaltung; ~ **of powers** *pol* Gewaltenteilung, Gewaltentrennung *(cf. executive, legislative and judicial powers); Am* Teilung der obersten Gewalt zwischen Bund und Einzelstaaten; ~ **of profits** Gewinnverteilung

division, action of ~ *Scot* Teilungsklage; **head of a** ~ Abteilungsleiter; **legal** ~ Rechtsabteilung; **political sub-** ~ *Am* Gebietskörperschaft

division 2. *parl* Abstimmung (od. Abstimmenlassen) *(durch Hammelsprung)*[48]; **upon a** ~ nach Abstimmung; **in case of equal** ~ bei Stimmengleichheit; **tie** ~ unentschiedene Abstimmung (→*tie);* **to go into** (or **take**) **a** ~ zur Abstimmung schreiten; **the** ~ **results in a majority of 10 votes (cast)** die Abstimmung ergibt e-e Mehrheit von 10 Stimmen; **a** ~ **is taken** e-e Abstimmung wird vorgenommen (od. durchgeführt)

Br Normalerweise wird im Unterhaus durch Zuruf ("Aye" or "No") oder durch Aufstehen abgestimmt. Bei division verlassen alle Abgeordneten den Saal, den sie durch einen der beiden an der Seite des Saales angebauten Abstimmungsräume – je ein Raum für Ja-Stimmen und Nein-Stimmen – nach 6 Minuten wieder betreten. In den Räumen werden die Abstimmenden von den →tellers gezählt und ihre Namen in den Listen abgehakt. Wer sich der Stimme enthalten will, bleibt der Abstimmung fern

divisional Abteilungs-; Teilungs-; ~ **application** *(PatR)* Ausscheidungsanmeldung, Teilanmeldung; ~ **claim** *(PatR)* ausgeschiedener Anspruch; **D**~ **Court** *Br* →court; ~ **head** (or **manager**) Abteilungsleiter

divorce (Ehe-)Scheidung; *fig* Trennung; ~ **case** (Ehe-)Scheidungssache, -prozeß; ~ **by consent** *Br* Scheidung in beiderseitigem Einverständnis; ~ **court** (Ehe-)Scheidungsgericht; ~ **decree** Scheidungsurteil

divorce petition Scheidungsantrag; **to dismiss a** ~ e-n Scheidungsantrag abweisen; **to file** (or **present**) **a** ~ e-n Scheidungsantrag einreichen

divorce proceedings (Ehe-)Scheidungsverfahren; **to take** (or **start**) ~ das Scheidungsverfahren einleiten; die Scheidung beantragen

divorce suit (Ehe-)Scheidungsprozeß

divorce, bilateral ~ *Am* Scheidung, bei der das Gericht auch für den Antragsgegner zuständig ist

divorce, decree of ~ Scheidungsurteil *(cf. decree absolute, decree nisi);* **to pronounce a decree of** ~ ein Scheidungsurteil verkünden

divorce, divisible ~ **doctrine** *Am* Lehre, nach der bei der Anerkennung ausländischer Scheidungsurteile zwischen Scheidung und Scheidungsfolgen zu differenzieren ist

divorce, ex parte ~ Scheidung, bei der das Gericht nur für den Antragsteller zuständig ist

divorce, ground for ~ Scheidungsgrund

Under the Matrimonial Causes Act 1973, s. 1 there is only one ground for divorce: irretrievable breakdown of marriage. This can be proved only by satisfying the court of one of the 5 following facts:

1. adultery
2. unreasonable conduct
3. 2 years' desertion
4. 2 years' separation and consent
5. 5 years' separation

Nach dem Matrimonial Causes Act 1973, s. 1 gibt es nur einen Scheidungsgrund: unheilbare Zerrüttung der Ehe, die durch eine der folgenden 5 Tatsachen nachgewiesen werden muß:

1. Ehebruch
2. unzumutbares Benehmen des Antragsgegners
3. böswilliges Verlassen für mindestens 2 Jahre
4. 2jährige Trennung und Einwilligung des Antragsgegners

5. 5jährige Trennung (auch ohne Einwilligung des Antragsgegners)

divorce, limited ~ *Am* gestattetes Getrenntleben *(entspricht →judicial separation)*

divorce, to grant a ~ auf Scheidung erkennen; **to get** (or **obtain**) **a** ~ geschieden werden; **to petition for** (or **seek, sue for a**) ~ die Scheidung beantragen; **to oppose the granting of a** ~ sich der Scheidung widersetzen

divorce *v* sich scheiden lassen (one's husband von seinem Ehemann); *fig* trennen

divorced geschieden; ~ **parties** geschiedene Ehegatten; **he** ~ **his wife** er ließ sich von seiner Frau scheiden; **they have been** ~ sie haben sich scheiden lassen

divorcee Geschiedene(r)

divorcement *Am* →divorce; *Am (AntitrustR)* Entflechtung *(e-s Unternehmens auf Grund e-s Gerichtsurteils)*

divorcer *Am* Scheidungsgrund *(der die Ehescheidung veranlassende Teil)*

divulge *v* preisgeben, enthüllen; **to** ~ **information** e-e *(geheime)* Information weitergeben

Djibouti Dschibuti; **Republic of** ~ Republik Dschibuti

Djiboutian (or **of Djibouti**) Dschibutier(in); dschibutisch

D-Ns (→notice 1.)

do *v*, **to** ~ **away with** abschaffen; **to** ~ **business** Geschäfte machen (od. betreiben); **to** ~ **business with sb.** mit jdm in Geschäftsverbindung stehen; **to be admitted to** ~ **business** *Am* die Geschäftserlaubnis haben; **to** ~ **well** gute Geschäfte machen; erfolgreich sein; **to** ~ **time** *sl.* e-e Freiheitsstrafe verbüßen

doing business *Am* Ausübung des Geschäftsbetriebes; Geschäftstätigkeit; ~ **as** *Am* Firmenname; **company** ~ **in the jurisdiction of a state** *Am* im Zuständigkeitsbereich e-s Staates tätige Gesellschaft

done geschehen, ausgefertigt; *(Börse)* gehandelt; abgemacht; ~ **in duplicate** in zweifacher Ausfertigung; *dipl* geschehen in 2 Urschriften; ~ **in three original texts** *dipl* geschehen in 3 Urschriften; ~ **at ... this .. th day of ..., 19..** *dipl* geschehen zu ... am ..., 19..

dock 1. Dock; *Am* Kai; *Am (Eisenbahn)* Laderampe; ~**s** Hafenanlagen; ~ **charges** (or **dues**) Dockgebühren; *Am* Kaigebühren; ~ **receipt** *Am* Kaiempfangsschein, Übernahmeschein *(über Anlieferung von Gütern zur Verschiffung)*; ~ **warrant** *Br* Docklagerschein; ~ **work** Hafenarbeit; ~ **worker** Dockarbeiter, Hafenarbeiter; ~**-yard** (Schiffs-)Werft

dock, dry ~ Trockendock; **floating** ~ Schwimmdock

dock 2. Anklagebank; ~ **brief** *Br* Beauftragung e-s im Gericht anwesenden barrister mit der Verteidigung *(durch den Angeklagten, gegen e-e sehr niedrige Gebühr)*; **to be in the** ~ auf der Anklagebank sitzen

dock *v (Schiff)* docken; ins Dock bringen, ins Dock gehen; *(im Weltraum)* ankoppeln; *(Löhne etc)* kürzen; **to** ~ **the entail** *Am* die Erbfolge aufheben

docked, to have one's salary ~ e-e Gehaltskürzung erfahren

dockage Dockgebühren; Docken *(von Schiffen)*; *Am* Kürzung

docker Hafenarbeiter, Dockarbeiter, Schauermann

docket Register mit Inhaltsangabe *(an Akten od. Urkunden)*; Aktenschwanz; Auszug *(aus Urteil etc)*; Liste *(mit kurzen Angaben)*; Etikett *(mit Inhaltsangabe)*; *Am* Tagesordnung; *Br* Lieferschein; *Br* Zollquittung; **trial** ~ *Am* Liste der anhängigen Prozesse; Terminkalender; **to be on the** ~ *Am* auf der Tagesordnung stehen; **to clear the** ~ *Am* anhängige Gerichtsfälle erledigen

docket *v* mit Inhaltsangabe (od. Etikett) versehen, in ein Register eintragen; **to** ~ **a case** *Am* in e-r Sache Termin ansetzen (od. anberaumen); **to** ~ **goods** Waren etikettieren

doctor Doktor (Dr.); Arzt; ~**'s bill** Arztrechnung; ~**'s certificate** (ärztliches) Attest

doctor's degree Doktorgrad; **candidate for a** ~ Doktorand(in); **to confer an honorary** ~ den Ehrendoktor verleihen; **to take one's** ~ seinen Doktor machen; den Doktortitel erwerben

doctor's fees Arztgebühren, Arzthonorar

doctor, honorary ~ Ehrendoktor

doctor *v colloq. (Kranken)* verarzten; *(Nahrungsmittel)* verfälschen; *(Abrechnungen)* zurechtmachen, manipulieren; *(Bilanz)* verschleiern (od. frisieren); **to** ~ **election results** Wahlergebnisse fälschen

doctrine Lehre, Doktrin; Lehrmeinung

document Dokument, Urkunde; Schriftstück, Beleg; Akte(nstück); ~**s** Papiere; Unterlagen; *(im Außenhandelsgeschäft)* Dokumente *(Urkunden über Warensendungen[49])*; ~**s accompanying the goods** Begleitpapiere; ~**s against acceptance** (d/a) Dokumente gegen Akzept *(Aushändigung der Dokumente gegen Akzeptierung der Tratte durch den Importeur)*; ~**s against payment** (d/p) s. cash against →~s

document, ~**s in support** Beleg(stücke), Unterlagen; ~**s of the application** *(PatR)* Anmeldungsunterlagen *(cf. European patent application)*; ~ **request** Ersuchen um Vorlage von Urkunden; ~ **under hand** nicht gesiegelte Urkunde *(opp.* ~ *under seal)*; ~ **under seal** gesiegelte Urkunde

document of title Urkunde über e-n Rechtsanspruch *(bes. über [Grund-]Eigentum);* ~ (**to goods**) Traditionspapier; Dispositionspapier; ~ **to land** Eigentumsnachweis für Grundbesitz

document, affidavit of ~s *Br* →affidavit; **altering a ~ with intent to defraud** Urkundenfälschung; Verfälschung e-r *(echten)* Urkunde; → **ancient ~s**; **authentic ~** echte Urkunde; →**bundle of ~s**; **cash against ~s** (C.A.D.) Kasse (od. Zahlung) gegen Dokumente; →**discovery of ~s**; **falsification** (or **forgery**) **of ~s** Urkundenfälschung; **individual ~** Einzelurkunde; **inspection of ~s** Einsicht in Urkunden; **list of ~s** Verzeichnis (od. Liste) des schriftlichen Beweismaterials e-r Prozeßpartei; **official ~** öffentliche Urkunde; **on the ~s** auf Grund der Akten; **private ~** private Urkunde; **production of ~s** Vorlage von Urkunden; **public ~** öffentliche Urkunde

document, relevant ~s wichtige Urkunden; Unterlagen; **to decide a case on the relevant ~s** e-n Fall aufgrund der Aktenlage entscheiden

document, →shipping ~s; suppression of ~s Urkundenunterdrückung

document, to get a ~ attested by a notary (or **notarially attested**) e-e Urkunde durch e-n Notar beglaubigen lassen; **to draw up a ~** e-e Urkunde aufsetzen (od. abfassen, erstellen); **to execute a ~** e-e Urkunde *(rechtsgültig)* errichten; e-e Urkunde unterzeichnen (und, falls nötig, siegeln); **to furnish ~s** Unterlagen beibringen; **to make out a ~** e-e Urkunde ausstellen; **to present** (or **produce**) **a ~** e-e Urkunde vorlegen; **to prove** (or **support**) **by ~s** urkundlich belegen; **to tender ~s** Urkunden vorlegen; Dokumente andienen

document *v* mit Dokumenten (od. Unterlagen) versehen; urkundlich (od. dokumentarisch) belegen; *Am* ein Schiffszertifikat *(über Eigentum und Nationalität)* ausstellen*(→certificate of registry);* **to ~ one's claim** seinen Anspruch durch Urkunden belegen

documentary urkundlich, dokumentarisch; aktenmäßig; ~ **acceptance credit** Rembourskredit; ~ **bill** (or **draft**) *(Überseehandel)* Dokumententratte *(Wechsel mit angehefteten, Rechte übertragenden Dokumenten)*

documentary credit Dokumenten-Akkreditiv; ~ **applicant** Akkreditiv-Auftraggeber; ~ **application** Akkreditiveröffnungsauftrag; ~ **issuance** Akkreditiveröffnung; ~ **operations** Dokumenten-Akkreditiv-Geschäfte; **Uniform Customs and Practice for D~ C~s** (UCP)[50] Einheitliche Richtlinien und Gebräuche für Dokumenten-Akkreditive (ERA) *(Revision von 1983)*

documentary evidence Beweis durch Urkunden; Urkundenbeweis, urkundlicher Beleg; **primary ~** Beweis durch Vorlegung des Originals der Urkunde; **secondary ~** Beweis durch Vorlegung der beglaubigten Abschrift der Urkunde; **to furnish** (or **give**) ~ **(of)** *(etw.)* urkundlich belegen; Urkundenbeweis erbringen; **to support by ~** durch Urkunden belegen

documentary, ~ remittance[51] dokumentäre Rimesse; ~ **stamp tax** *Am* Urkundenstempelsteuer *(z.B. auf Wechseln, Testamenten)*

documentation Dokumentation; urkundliche Belegung, urkundlicher Nachweis; Heranziehung (od. Benutzung) von Dokumenten; ~ **centre** Dokumentationszentrum; **patent ~** Patentdokumentation; **to compile** (or **collect**) **the ~ for a meeting** die Unterlagen für e-e Sitzung zusammenstellen

dodger, insurance ~ *colloq.* pflichtwidrig nicht versicherter Fahrer; **tax ~** Steuerhinterzieher

Doe, John ~ fiktiver Name in e-m Prozeß *(zur Bezeichnung einer unbekannten oder fingierten Partei; cf. Richard →Roe)*

dog licence *Br (behördl.)* Genehmigung, e-n Hund zu halten (Hundesteuer)

doing (business) →do *v*

dole *Br* Arbeitslosenunterstützung; Almosen, milde Gabe, Spende; **to be** (or **go**) **on the ~** *Br* Arbeitslosenunterstützung beziehen, stempeln gehen

dollar Dollar (‰) *(Währungseinheit in den USA, Kanada, Australien und anderen Ländern);* ~ **amount** Dollarbetrag; ~ **area** Dollar(zahlungs)raum; ~ **balance** Dollarguthaben

dollar bonds Dollarbonds, Dollaranleihen; **validation of German ~** Bereinigung deutscher Dollarbonds[52]

dollar, ~ draft auf Dollar ausgestellter Wechsel; ~ **drain** Dollarabfluß; ~ **drive** Maßnahmen zur Exportförderung in den Dollarraum; ~ **exchange** in US-Dollar zahlbarer Wechsel; ~ **gap** Dollarlücke *(Fehlbetrag in der Dollarbilanz e-s Staates);* ~ **holdings** Dollarbestände; ~ **inflows** Dollarzuflüsse; ~ **loan** Dollaranleihe; ~ **rate** Dollarkurs

dolose *(StrafR)* dolos, mit böser Absicht

domain Grundbesitz, Gebiet, Bereich; **economic ~** Wirtschaftsgebiet; **eminent ~** *Am und VölkerR* (Zwangs-)Enteignungsrecht (→ *eminent);* **public ~** öffentliches Eigentum, Gemeingut; *Am* Staatsländereien, staatlicher Grundbesitz *(einschließl. Indian reservations und national parks);* **to be in the public ~** *(PatR, UrhR)* nicht mehr geschützt sein, den Schutz verloren haben; allgemein zugänglich sein

Domesday Book *Br* ältestes Reichsgrundbuch *(von 1086)*

domestic inländisch, einheimisch; innerstaatlich, innenpolitisch, Landes- *(opp. foreign, international);* Familien-; Haushalts-; Hausangestellte(r); ~ **affairs** innenpolitische Angelegenheiten; häusliche Angelegenheiten; ~ **and external** Inlands- und Auslands-; ~ **and foreign policy** Innen- und Außenpolitik; ~ **and foreign trade and payments** Binnen- und Außenwirtschaft; ~ **bill** (of exchange) Inlandswechsel; ~ **bond** Inlandsanleihe; ~ **business** Binnengeschäft, Inlandsgeschäft; ~ **carriers** *Am* Luftverkehrsgesellschaft *(des binnenamerikanischen Luftverkehrs);* ~ **commerce** *Am* Binnenhandel; **matter of** ~ **concern** innerstaatliche Angelegenheit; ~ **consumption** inländischer Verbrauch; Eigenverbrauch; ~ **corporation** *Am* inländische *(in e-m Einzelstaat errichtete)* (Kapital-)Gesellschaft; ~ **court** innerstaatliches Gericht; ~ **credit expansion** (DCE) inländische Kreditausweitung; ~ **demand** Inlandsnachfrage, Binnennachfrage; Inlandsbedarf; ~ **economic activity** Binnenkonjunktur; ~ **economy** einheimische Wirtschaft; Haushaltswirtschaft

Domestic Equity Market *Br* britischer Wertpapiermarkt

Dieser Markt deckt drei Bereiche ab:
1. den notierten Markt *(für etablierte Unternehmen)* (listed market); 2. den Markt mit nichtnotierten Papieren (Unlisted Securities Market) *(1980 eingeführt, um die Bedürfnisse von zwar etablierten, aber kleineren, wenig entwickelten Unternehmen zu erfüllen);* 3. den dritten Markt (Third Market) *(1987 eingeführt, um jungen, noch im Wachstum begriffenen britischen Unternehmen zu helfen, auf einfache und kosteneffektive Weise Kapital zu beschaffen)*

domestic, in the ~ **field** innenpolitisch; ~ **freight traffic** *Am* →freight; ~ **goods** einheimische Waren; ~ **help** Haushaltshilfe; ~ **industry** einheimische Industrie

Domestic International Sales Corporation (DISC) *Am* für den Export bestimmte einheimische Vertriebsgesellschaft *(Exportgewinne brauchen nur teilweise versteuert zu werden)*

domestic, ~ **investment** inländische Investitionen; ~ **issue** Inlandsemission; innenpolitisches Problem; **on** ~ **issues** in innerpolitischen Fragen

domestic jurisdiction *(VölkerR)* innerstaatliche Zuständigkeit *(den Staaten vorbehaltene Zuständigkeit);* **to be within the** ~ **of a state** zur ausschließlichen Zuständigkeit e-s Staates gehören

domestic, ~ **law** inländisches Recht, innerstaatliches Recht; Heimatrecht; ~ **life** Familienleben; ~ **loan** Inlandsanleihe *(opp. foreign loan);* ~ **market** Inlandsmarkt, inländischer Markt, Binnenmarkt; ~ **needs** Inlandsbedarf; Haushaltsbedarf; ~ **news** Inlandsnachrichten *(opp. foreign news);* ~ **order** Inlandsauftrag, Binnenauftrag *(opp. foreign or export order);* ~ **policies** Innenpolitik; ~ **postage** *Am* Inlandsporto; ~ **price** Inlandspreis; ~ **producer** inländischer Erzeuger; ~ **products** Inlandsprodukte; einheimische Erzeugnisse; ~ **production** Inlandsproduktion; ~ **public bond issue** *Am* inländische öffentliche Anleihe

domestic relations *Am* Familiensachen; ~ **court** *Am* Familiengericht; **law of** ~ *Am* Familienrecht

domestic, ~ **remedies** *(VölkerR)* innerstaatliche Rechtsbehelfe; ~ **representative** einheimischer Vertreter; *(Europ. PatR)* Zustellungsbevollmächtigter; ~ **safety** innere Sicherheit; ~ **sales** Inlandabsatz; ~ **services** hauswirtschaftliche Dienste; ~ **science college** Haushaltungsschule; ~ **staff** (Haushalts-)Personal; Haushaltsangestellte; ~ **struggles** innerpolitische Kämpfe; ~ **subsidies** heimische Subventionen; **in** ~ **terms** was die Innenpolitik anbetrifft; ~ **trade** Binnenhandel *(opp. foreign trade);* ~ **trade and payments** Binnenwirtschaft; ~ **tribunal** *Br (etwa)* Ehrengericht; ~ **work** Haus(halts)arbeit; ~ **workers** inländische Arbeitnehmer

domestication of a foreign corporation *Am* Verleihung des Charakters e-r inländischen an e-e ausländische Gesellschaft; Ansässigwerden e-r ausländischen Gesellschaft

domicil(e) Domizil; *(etwa)* Wohnsitz; Zahlungsort *(e-s Wechsels);* Zahlstelle; Sitz e-r Firma

Domicil(e) bezieht sich aber nicht auf einzelnen Ort, sondern auf Rechtsgebiet (also z. B. nicht in San Francisco, sondern in Kalifornien). Domicile ist weitergehend als der deutsche Wohnsitzbegriff und erheblich weitergehend als →residence; eine Person kann mehrere residences, aber nur ein domicile haben.

Der Domizilbegriff ist im englischen und amerikanischen Recht nicht gleich.

a) In England gibt es zunächst das domicile of origin, das ersetzt werden kann durch das domicile of choice, aber wieder auflebt, wenn das maßgebliche domicile of choice aufgegeben und ein neues nicht begründet wird. Die Anforderungen an ein domicile of choice sind in England aber so hochgeschraubt, daß es im allgemeinen bei dem domicile of origin verbleibt und ein Engländer im Ausland fast immer nur sein →residence hat. Das ist sehr bedeutsam für das internationale Privatrecht, wo das domicile als Anknüpfungsbegriff verwendet wird.

b) Die Rechtsprechung der USA ist bei dem konservativen englischen Domizilbegriff nicht stehengeblieben. Das amerikanische domicile ist dem deutschen Wohnsitz weitgehend vergleichbar.

An Stelle des domicile of origin kann das domicile of choice begründet werden. Voraussetzungen hierfür sind 1. physische Anwesenheit an dem Ort und 2. die feste Absicht, den Ort zu einem „home" zu machen. Das (neu erworbene) domicile of choice bleibt solange bestehen, bis ein neues domicile of choice begründet oder das domicile of origin zurückerworben wird. Bloße Abwesenheit von dem gerade maßgeblichen domicile führt solange nicht zu dessen Verlust und zur Begründung eines neuen domicile, wie der Rückkehrwille (animus revertendi) erhalten bleibt

domicil(e), ~ of choice Wahldomizil, Domizil eigener Wahl *(wird erworben durch den Aufenthalt in e-m Lande mit der Absicht, dort ständig zu bleiben)*; ~ **of dependence** *Br (vom Wohnsitz e-r anderen Person)* abhängiges Domizil *(erwerben Kinder und wegen Geisteskrankheit Entmündigte)*; ~ **by operation of law** gesetzliches Domizil *(Br cf. ~ of dependence)*; ~ **of origin** Ursprungsdomizil *(wird mit der Geburt erworben)*

domicil(e), change of ~ Wechsel des Domizil; **fiscal** ~ *(DBA)* steuerlicher Wohnsitz; **legal** ~ gesetzliches Domizil; **legal ~ of a company** Sitz e-r (Handels-)Gesellschaft; **natural** ~ Geburtsdomizil; **right of** ~ Recht zur Wohnsitzbegründung; Niederlassungsrecht

domicil(e), to abandon one's ~ sein Domizil aufgeben; **to establish a** ~ ein Domizil begründen; **to be governed by the law of** ~ nach dem Recht des Domizils beurteilt werden; **to take up one's** ~ sich niederlassen

domicile *v* ansässig (od. wohnhaft) sein (od. machen); domizilieren, auf bestimmten Ort ausstellen; **to ~ a bill** e-n Wechsel domizilieren (od zahlbar stellen) (at a bank bei e-r Bank)

domiciled ansässig, wohnhaft; domiziliert; ~ **bill** Domizilwechsel; **to be ~ abroad** im Ausland ansässig sein

domiciling, commission for ~ Domizilprovision

domiciliary den Wohnort betreffend; Heimats-, Haus-; ~ **administration** *Am* Haupterbschaftsverwaltung am Wohnort des Erblassers; ~ **administrator** *Am* Haupterbschaftsverwalter *(der am Domizil des Erblassers ernannt ist; opp. ancillary administrator)*

domiciliate *v (Wechsel)* domizilieren, an besondere Stelle zahlbar stellen

domiciliated, ~ bill Domizilwechsel; **to be** ~ ansässig sein

domiciliation Domizilierung, Zahlbarstellung *(e-s Wechsels)*; Domizilvermerk

dominan|ce, ~cy Vorherrschaft, Übergewicht

dominant (vor)herrschend; ~ **enterprise** beherrschendes Unternehmen; ~ **estate** →~ tenement; ~ **feature** vorherrschende Eigenschaft; ~ **firm** marktbeherrschendes Unternehmen; Marktführer; ~ **market power** Marktbeherrschung; ~ **position in the market** überragende Marktstellung; ~ **tenement** *(bei Grunddienstbarkeit)* herrschendes Grundstück *(opp. servient tenement)*; **to abuse one's ~ position** seine beherrschende Stellung mißbräuchlich ausnutzen

dominate *v*, **to ~ the market** den Markt beherrschen

domination Herrschaft; Beherrschung; **under Soviet** ~ unter Sowjetherrschaft

Dominica Dominica; **Commonwealth of** ~ Dominicanischer Bund; **(of)** ~ Dominicaner(in); dominicanisch

Dominican Dominikaner(in); dominikanisch; ~ **Republic** Dominikanische Republik

dominion Herrschaft(sbefugnis) (over über); Hoheitsgebiet; Eigentum(srecht) *(nicht technisch, cf. ownership)*; *Br* Dominion *(ehemalige Bezeichnung für die souveränen Staaten des → British Empire; seit 1949 offizielle Bezeichnung: Commonwealth country)*

donate *v* schenken, Schenkung machen; spenden; stiften

donated fund Fonds aus freiwilligen Spenden

donatio, ~ inter vivos Schenkung unter Lebenden; ~ **mortis causa** *Br* Schenkung in Erwartung des Todes

donation Schenkung, *(unentgeltl.)* Zuwendung; Spende, Geldspende, Stiftung; ~ **in kind** Sachspende; ~**s to political parties** Parteienspende; ~ **to the Red Cross** Spende an das Rote Kreuz

donation, charitable ~ wohltätige Stiftung; **deed of** ~ Schenkungsurkunde, Schenkungsbrief; **promise to make a** ~ Schenkungsversprechen; **revocation of a** ~ Widerruf e-r Schenkung; **to make a ~ of sth.** e-e Schenkung (od. Spende) machen; **to solicit ~s** um Spenden bitten

done →do *v*

donee Beschenkter, Schenkungsempfänger; der/ die in e-r (Schenkungs-)Urkunde Begünstigte; ~ **(of a power of appointment)** Bevollmächtigte(r) (→*power* 1.)

donor Schenkungsgeber; Spender; Treugeber, Stifter *(e-s Treuhandverhältnisses)*; Aussteller e-r (Schenkungs-)Urkunde; ~ **(of a power of appointment)** Erteiler e-r Befugnis, den Berechtigten (od. Rechtsnachfolger) e-s Gegenstandes zu bestimmen (→*power* 1.); ~ **country** *(Entwicklungshilfe)* Geberland *(opp. receiving country)*; **blood** ~ Blutspender

door (Haus-)Tür; ~ **delivery** Zustellung frei Haus

door-to-door container service Haus-zu-Haus Behälterverkehr *(→freight liner)*

Door-to-Door and Similar Dealings, Law Regarding Revocation of ~[52a] Gesetz über den Widerruf von Haustürgeschäften und ähnlichen Geschäften

door-to-door, ~ salesman Hausierer; ~ **selling**

Verkauf an der Haustür; ~ **transport** Haus-zu-Haus Transport

door, the bank closes its ~s die Bank schließt ihre Schalter *(stellt ihre Zahlungen ein)*

dope *sl.* Rauschgift *(bes. Opium); sl. (vertraul.)* Information; ~ **dealer** (~ **pusher** *Am*) *sl.* Rauschgifthändler; ~ **smuggler** *sl.* Rauschgiftschmuggler

dope *v* künstlich stimulieren

dormant ungebraucht, ungenutzt; still, untätig; ~ **account** umsatzloses Konto; ~ **capital** totes Kapital; ~ **claim** ruhender, noch nicht geltend gemachter Anspruch; ~ **funds** →fund 1.; ~ →**partner;** ~ **title** ruhender Rechtstitel; **to lie** ~ unverzinslich sein

dormitory suburb Wohnvorort

dossier Akten(stück); *(urkundl.)* Unterlagen; **personal** ~ Personalakten

dot Mitgift, Aussteuer

dotage Altersschwäche, Senilität

dotation Dotation; Dotierung

dotted line punktierte Linie; **to sign on the** ~ ohne eigene Kritik unterschreiben (od. tun)

double doppelt, zweifach; ~ **accident benefit** *Br* (**indemnity** *Am*) *(VersR)* doppelte Leistung bei Unfalltod; ~ **the amount** doppelter Betrag; ~ **assessment** Doppelveranlagung; ~ **bond** →bond 3.; ~ **earnings** Doppelverdienst; ~ **eagle** *Am* 20-Dollar-Stück *(Goldmünze);* ~-**entry bookkeeping** doppelte Buchführung; ~ **indemnity** *(VersR)* doppelte Entschädigung *(bei Unfalltod);* ~ **insurance** Doppelversicherung; ~ →**jeopardy**; ~ **option** *Br (Börse)* Doppelprämie(ngeschäft), Stellage; ~ **patenting** Doppelpatentierung; ~ **standard** Doppelwährung

double taxation Doppelbesteuerung; ~ **relief** Befreiung von der Doppelbesteuerung *(→ relief 3.);* **Convention for the Avoidance of D~ T~** Doppelbesteuerungsabkommen (DBA)[53]; **taxes eligible for** ~ **relief** *Br (nach dem DBA)* anrechenbare ausländische Steuer

double, ~ **the value** der doppelte Wert; ~ **wage earner** Doppelverdiener; ~ **zero option** doppelte Nullösung *(Verzicht auf nukleare Mittelstreckensysteme kürzerer und größerer Reichweite);* **to pay** ~ **the sum** das Doppelte bezahlen

doubling Verdoppelung

doubt Zweifel, Bedenken; **benefit of the** ~ günstige Auslegung zweifelhafter Umstände (→ *benefit 1.*); **beyond** ~ ohne Zweifel, unzweifelhaft

doubt, reasonable ~ berechtigter Zweifel; **certificate of reasonable** ~ *Am* gerichtliche Entscheidung über begründete Zweifel an der Richtigkeit e-r Entscheidung *(als Grundlage für die Einlegung e-s Rechtsmittels in bestimmten Fällen);* **proof of guilt beyond reasonable** ~ *(Strafprozeß) (für den Schuldspruch erforderlicher)* Schuldbeweis, der jeden Zweifel ausschließt

doubt, ~s have arisen Zweifel sind entstanden; **to have no** ~ **that** nicht bezweifeln, daß; **to remove ~s** Zweifel beseitigen

doubt *v* zweifeln, bezweifeln; **to** ~ **the truth of a statement** die Wahrheit e-r Aussage bezweifeln

doubtful zweifelhaft; bedenklich; ~ **accounts (receivable)** *Am* (~ **debts** *Br*) zweifelhafte Forderungen, Dubiosen; ~ **title** zweifelhafter Rechtstitel

Dow Jones Industrial Average (DJIA) Aktienindex der New Yorker Börse *(der den Durchschnittskurs e-r Auswahl von 30 Aktien wiedergibt)*

dowager *Br* Witwe vom Stande; **D~ Duchess** Herzoginwitwe; **D~ Lady X** die verwitwete Lady X; ~ **Queen** Königinwitwe

dower *Am (in einigen Staaten)* lebenslängliches Nießbrauchsrecht (→*life estate*) des verwitweten Ehegatten[54] an ⅓ des Grundbesitzes des verstorbenen Ehegatten; →**assignment of** ~

down *v*, **to** ~ **tools** *bes. Br* die Arbeit niederlegen

down, cash ~ gegen bar; **to be** ~ gefallen sein *(Preise);* billiger geworden sein *(Ware);* **to go** ~ fallen, sinken; **to pay** ~ anzahlen, Anzahlung leisten

downfall Sturz, Fall; Niedergang; **to bring about a minister's** ~ den Sturz e-s Ministers herbeiführen

downgrade *v* niedriger einstufen *(opp. to upgrade)*

downgrading niedrigere Einstufung, Herabstufung

down payment Anzahlung *(z.B. bei Ratenzahlung);* **minimum** ~ Mindestanzahlung; **to make a** ~ e-e Anzahlung leisten

down periods *Am* (kurze) Betriebsschließungen *(z.B. für Reinigung, Renovierung)*

downstream stromabwärts

downswing Abschwung; **cyclical** ~ Konjunkturabschwung

downtime (Betriebs-)Stillstandszeit *(z.B. wegen Maschinenschadens),* Ausfallzeit

downtown *Am* (in der) Innenstadt, (im) Stadtzentrum (od. Geschäftszentrum) (gelegen)

downtrend Abwärtsbewegung *(opp. uptrend);* ~ **of share prices** Abwärtsbewegung der Aktienkurse

downturn (Konjunktur-)Abschwung; Geschäftsrückgang, Rezession

downward, ~ **movement** Abwärtsbewegung, rückläufige Bewegung; ~ **tendency** (or **trend**)

fallende (od. rückläufige) Tendenz; **prices with a ~ tendency** Preise mit fallender Tendenz
downway *(VölkerR)* Talweg *(tiefste Schiffahrtsrinne)*

dowry Mitgift, Aussteuer

doyen *dipl* Doyen *(dienstältester Diplomat des diplomatischen Corps)*

draft *1. (gezogener)* Wechsel, Tratte (on auf) *(Am*[55] *bes. Inlandswechsel, Br bes. Bankwechsel);* ~ **collection** Wechselinkasso; ~ **credit** Trassierungskredit; ~ **(payable) at sight** Sichttratte, Sichtwechsel
draft, advice of ~ Trattenavis; **amount of** ~ Trattenbetrag; **bank** ~ *Br* Banktratte, Bankwechsel; →**banker's** ~; **documentary** ~ Dokumententratte; **sight** ~ Sichttratte, Sichtwechsel; **time** ~ Zeitwechsel
draft, to draw (or **make out**) **a** ~ **on sb.** e-e Tratte (od. e-n Wechsel) auf jdn ziehen; **to negotiate a** ~ *(Außenhandel)* e-e Tratte ankaufen; **the** ~ **will be duly hono(u)red by the drawee** die Tratte wird durch den Bezogenen ordnungsmäßig bezahlt
draft 2. Entwurf, Konzept; Skizze; ~ **agreement** Vertragsentwurf; Abkommensentwurf; ~ **bill** Entwurf e-r Gesetzesvorlage; ~ **bill (of costs)** Entwurf e-r (Anwalts-)Rechnung; ~ **for a Parliamentary Bill** *Br* Gesetzesentwurf; ~ →**budget**; ~ **contract** Vertragsentwurf; ~ **convention** Entwurf e-s Abkommens (→*convention 1.*); ~ **(for a) letter** Entwurf e-s Briefes
draft resolution, to submit a ~ e-n Entschließungsentwurf vorlegen
draft, ~ **statement** *pol* Entwurf e-r Erklärung; ~ **text** Textentwurf
draft, alternative ~ Gegenentwurf; **amended** ~ abgeänderter Entwurf; **preliminary** ~ Vorentwurf; **to make a** ~ **of sth.** etw. entwerfen; **to work out a** ~ e-n Entwurf ausarbeiten
draft 3. *Am* starke Inanspruchnahme, Belastung (on für)
draft 4. *Am mil* Einberufung; ~ **bracket** *Am* wehrpflichtiger Jahrgang; ~ **call** *Am* Einberufung; ~ **card** *Am* Einberufungsbescheid; ~-**exempt** *Am* vom Militärdienst befreit; ~ **order** *Am* Einberufungsbefehl, Gestellungsbefehl; ~ **resister** *Am* Wehrdienstverweigerer; **to refuse the** ~ *Am* den Wehrdienst verweigern

draft *v (Schriftstück)* entwerfen (od. aufsetzen); redaktionell fassen; *Am mil* einberufen; **to** ~ **the budget** den Haushaltsplan aufstellen
drafting Entwurf, Aufsetzung *(z.B. e-s Vertrags);* ~ **amendments** redaktionelle Änderungen; ~ **committee** Redaktionsausschuß; ~ **of claims** *(PatR)* Formulierung der Ansprüche; ~ **of contracts** Abfassung von Verträgen

draftee *Am mil* Einberufener

drafter →draftsman; Wechselaussteller

draftsman Entwerfer; jd, der Rechtsurkunden aufsetzt; *Br* jd, der Gesetzesentwürfe formuliert; Konstruktionszeichner

drag Hemmnis, Hindernis, Belastung (on für); *fig* Bremse

dragnet clause *Am* Vereinbarung, wonach sich die hypothekarische Haftung des Grundstücks auch auf weitere (bes. erst künftig entstehende) Forderungen erstreckt

drain (Geld-)Abfluß; *(starke)* Inanspruchnahme, Belastung; Abwasserrohr *(unter der Erde);* ~**s** Abzüge *(vom Geldmarkt);* ~ **of capital** Kapitalabfluß; ~ **of gold** Goldabfluß; **a strong** ~ **on the dollar holdings** ein starker Sog auf die Dollarbestände; ~ **on the resources** Inanspruchnahme der Hilfsquellen; **capital** ~ Abfluß von Kapital *(ins Ausland);* Kapitalwanderung; **foreign** ~ (Geld-)Abfluß nach dem Ausland

drain *v* abfließen lassen; *(Boden)* drainieren; **the country was** ~**ed of its wealth** der Wohlstand des Landes war erschöpft

drainage Drainage; Kanalisation; ~ **basis** Flußeinzugsgebiet

dram engl. Gewichtsmaß (1 d = 1,773 g)

dramatic works *(UrhR)* dramatische Werke

draught Tiefgang *(e-s Schiffes)*

draughtsman Entwerfer; Zeichner

draw *v (Vergleiche, Schlüsse, Lose)* ziehen; *(Wechsel, Scheck)* ausstellen (on auf); *(Waren, Gehalt, Pension)* beziehen; *(Muster etc)* entwerfen; *(Geld)* entnehmen, abheben; **to** ~ **a bill of exchange** e-n Wechsel ausstellen (od. trassieren, ziehen) (on auf); **to** ~ **bonds for redemption** Obligationen auslosen; **to** ~ **a cheque (check)** e-n Scheck ausstellen; **to** ~ **a commission** e-e Provision beziehen; **to** ~ **conclusions** Schlüsse ziehen; **to** ~ **the consequences** Folgerungen ziehen (from aus); **to** ~ **heavily on the credit market** den Kreditmarkt stark in Anspruch nehmen; **to** ~ **the frontier** die Grenze ziehen; **to** ~ **lots** losen (for um); **to** ~ **lots for sth.** etw. auslosen; **to** ~ **money from an account** Geld von e-m Konto abheben; **to** ~ **a moral from** e-e Lehre ziehen aus; **to** ~ **one's salary** sein Gehalt beziehen; **to** ~ **a ticket** ein Los ziehen
draw *v* **to** ~ **on an account** vom Konto abheben; **to** ~ **on a loan** e-n Kredit in Anspruch nehmen; **to** ~ **on the reserves** die Reserven angreifen; **to** ~ **on one's savings** seine Ersparnisse angreifen; **the bank drawn upon** die bezogene Bank
draw *v*, **to** ~ **out** *fig* in die Länge ziehen

draw up *v (Urkunde)* aufsetzen, abfassen, erstellen; *(Liste, Plan)* aufstellen; **to ~ an account** e-e Rechnung aufstellen; e-e Abrechnung machen; **to ~ a balance sheet** e-e Bilanz aufstellen; **to ~ a budget** e-n Etat aufstellen; **to ~ a contract** e-n Vertrag abschließen; **to ~ an estimate** e-n Kostenanschlag machen; **to ~ the →judgment; to ~ a letter** e-n Brief aufsetzen; **to ~ the minutes** Protokoll aufnehmen, protokollieren; **to ~ a petition** e-e Bittschrift aufsetzen (od. abfassen); **to ~ the program(me)** das Programm aufstellen; **to ~ a report** e-n Bericht abfassen (od. erstellen); **to ~ a statement of account** e-n Kontoauszug machen; **to ~ up a will** ein Testament errichten (od. aufsetzen)

drawback Nachteil (to für); **customs ~** Zollrückvergütung *(bei Wiederausfuhr)*

drawee Bezogener, Trassat *(e-s Wechsels)*; bezogene Firma; **~ bank** bezogene Bank

drawer Aussteller *(e-s Wechsels, Schecks)*; Trassant *(e-s Wechsels)*; **~'s domicile** Ausstellungsort

drawing Ausstellung *(e-s Wechsels, Schecks)*; Entnahme *(von Geld, Proben)*; (Geld-)Abhebung; Ziehung; Auslosung *(bei Tilgung von Schuldverschreibungen)*; Zeichnung; Abbildung; **~s** (Geld-)Abhebung; Entnahmen *(von Geld)*; entnommenes Geld; **~ account** Girokonto; Konten für Privatentnahmen *(e-s Gesellschafters; opp. capital account)*; Spesen- od. Vorschußkonto *(für e-n Gesellschafter od. Angestellten)*; **~ authorization** *(im Überseegeschäft)* Ermächtigung, Wechsel zu ziehen *(Auftrag e-r ausländischen Bank an Bank des inländischen Exporteurs, dessen Dokumententratten anzukaufen)*; Negoziierungskredit *(Abart des Dokumentenakkreditivs)*; **~ certificate** Auslosungsschein; **~ credit** Trassierungskredit; **~s on current account** Kontokorrentabhebungen; **~ day** *(Lotterie)* Ziehungstag; **~ (of lots)** Auslosung; **~ and redrawing** Wechselreiterei; **~ rights** Ziehungsrechte *(e-s Mitglieds des IWF)*; **~ up** Abfassung, Erstellung *(e-r Urkunde)*; Aufstellung *(e-r Rechnung, e-r Bilanz, e-s Programms)*; **~ up of contracts** Abschluß von Verträgen

drawing, annual ~s jährliche Auslosungen; **date of ~** Ausstellungstag *(e-s Wechsels, Schecks)*; **list of ~s** Auslosungsliste; **personal ~s** Privatentnahmen; **place of ~** Ausstellungsort; **private ~s** Privatentnahmen; **redeemable by ~s** durch Auslosung rückzahlbar *(Obligationen)*; **scientific** (or **technical**) **~s** *(UrhR)* Abbildungen wissenschaftlicher od. technischer Art

drawing, to apply to the IMF for the ~ of . . . million dollars beim IWF die Ziehung von . . . Millionen Dollar beantragen; **to redeem a loan by ~** e-e Anleihe durch Auslosung tilgen

dress *v (Rohstoffe)* aufbereiten; **to ~ a (shop) window** ein Schaufenster dekorieren; **to ~ up** *colloq. (Rechnungen, Bericht, Bilanz etc)* „frisieren"

dressing Aufbereiten *(von Rohstoffen)*; **~ up** Vorspiegelung falscher Tatsachen; **→ window-~**

drift, ~ (of labo[u]r) from the land Landflucht *(Abwanderung vom Land in die Stadt)*; **~ of scientists abroad** Abwanderung von Wissenschaftlern ins Ausland; **policy of ~** Politik der Untätigkeit *(des Sichtreibenlassens)*

drill *v (Öl)* bohren

drilling rig (or **platform**) Bohrinsel, Erdölinsel

drink driving →drunken driving

drive Aktion, Vorstoß; (Werbe-)Feldzug; *Am (Börse)* Baisseangriff *(seitens der Verkäufer)*; *Br* Garageneinfahrt; Auffahrt, Zufahrt *(zu e-r Villa etc)*; Fahrt *(im Auto etc)*; **export ~** (Aktion zur) Exportförderung; **membership ~** Aktion zur Mitgliederwerbung; **~ to raise money for** große Sammelaktion zugunsten von; **to launch** (or **start**) **a ~** e-e Aktion starten

drive-in, ~ bank Bank mit Autoschalter; **~ cinema** *bes. Am* Autokino; **~ store** *Am* Ladengeschäft mit besonderem Bedienungsfenster, von dem aus der Kunde im Auto bedient wird

drive *v (Kraftwagen)* fahren, lenken, steuern; **permission to ~** Fahrerlaubnis; **to ~ a hard bargain** in e-er Geschäftsverhandlung nicht leicht nachgeben, hart verhandeln; **to ~ up the price** den Preis in die Höhe treiben

driven unterground *pol* in den Untergrund getrieben

driver Fahrer *(e-s Kraftwagens)*

driver's license *Am* Führerschein; **withdrawal of the ~** *Am* Entziehung des Führerscheins (od. der Fahrerlaubnis); **to grant the ~** *Am* die Fahrerlaubnis erteilen; **to suspend the ~** *Am* die Fahrerlaubnis vorläufig entziehen

driver, ~'s test *Am* Fahrprüfung; **hit-and-run ~** flüchtiger Fahrer *(nach Unfall)*; **learner ~** Fahrschüler

driveway *Am (für Lastkraftwagen verbotene)* Fahrstraße; *Am (private)* Auffahrt, Garageneinfahrt

driving Fahren *(e-s Kraftwagens)*; **~ ban** Entzug des Führerscheins (od. der Fahrerlaubnis); **~ conviction** Verurteilung wegen Verkehrsvergehen; **~ instructor** Fahrlehrer; **~ lessons** Fahrstunden

driving licence *Br* Führerschein; Erlaubnis zum Führen von Kraftfahrzeugen; **checking of the ~** *Br* Kontrolle des Führerscheins; **revocation of the ~** *Br* Entzug des Führerscheins (od. der Fahrerlaubnis); **to appeal against the revocation of the ~** die Entziehung der Fahrerlaubnis anfechten; **to be disqualified from hold-**

ing a ~ den Führerschein entzogen bekommen
driving offen|ce (~se) Verkehrsdelikt; **conviction for a** ~ Verurteilung wegen Verkehrsvergehens
driving period[55a] Lenkzeit *(e-s Fahrers)*; **continuous** ~ ununterbrochene Lenkzeit; **daily** ~ tägliche Lenkzeit
driving test *Br* Fahrprüfung; **to pass the** ~ die Fahrprüfung bestehen; **to take the** ~ die Fahrprüfung machen
driving, ~ **while disqualified** Fahren trotz eingezogenen Führerscheins; ~ **while under the influence of drink** *Br* **(alcohol** *Am***)** Fahren unter Einfluß von Alkohol; ~ **while intoxicated** (DWI) *Am* Fahren in betrunkenem Zustand
driving, dangerous ~ gefährliches Fahren; **drunk** ~ Trunkenheit am Steuer; **hit-and-run** ~ Fahrerflucht; **reckless** ~ rücksichtsloses Fahren

droit de suite *(UrhR)* Folgerecht

droop *v* fallen *(Preise)*; nachgeben *(Kurse)*

drop Fallen, Sinken *(von Preisen)*; Rückgang; *(Börse)* Baisse; ~ **in earnings from exports** Rückgang der Einnahmen aus der Ausfuhr; ~ **in the pound** *Br* Rückgang des Pfundes; ~ **in prices** Preisrückgang; Sinken der Preise; Fallen der Kurse; ~ **in production** Produktionsrückgang; ~ **lock floater** →floater 2.; ~ **shipment** Streckengeschäft *(Direktlieferung an den Kunden)*; ~ **shipment wholesaler** Großhändler mit Streckengeschäft

drop *v* fallen, sinken *(von Preisen, Kursen)*; *fig* zurückgehen; einstellen, fallen lassen; *(Passagiere)* absetzen; *(Bomben)* abwerfen; *(z. B. beim Glücksspiel Geld)* verlieren; **to** ~ **the action** die Klage zurücknehmen; **to** ~ **a bill** e-n Gesetzesentwurf nicht weiterbehandeln; **to** ~ **the charge** die Anklage fallen lassen; die Strafverfolgung einstellen; **to** ~ **the correspondence** die Korrespondenz einstellen; **to** ~ **the prosecution** s. to →~ the charge; **to** ~ **in quality** in der Qualität zurückgehen; **to** ~ **the subject** das Thema fallen lassen
drop *v*, **to** ~ **in** einlaufen *(Aufträge)*; **to** ~ **in on sb.** *colloq.* jdn ohne vorherige Verabredung besuchen
dropped, not to be ~ *(Vorsichtsmarkierung)* nicht stürzen!; **prices have** ~ die Preise (od. Kurse) sind gefallen
dropping, prices stopped ~ die Kurse hörten auf zu fallen

drought Trockenheit, Dürreperiode; **countries affected by** ~ von der Trockenheit betroffene Länder

drown *v*, **to be** ~**ed** (or **to** ~) ertrinken; **death by** ~**ing** Tod durch Ertrinken

drug Droge; Arznei; Rauschgift; ~**s** Suchtstoffe; Betäubungsmittel; ~ **abuse** Drogenmißbrauch; ~ **addict** Rauschgiftsüchtige(r); ~ **addiction** Drogensucht; ~ **dealing** Rauschgifthandel; **D**~ **Enforcement Administration** (DEA) *Am* Behörde mit Zuständigkeit für die Beschaffung von Nachrichten über den internationalen Rauschgifthandel; ~ **on the market** Ladenhüter *(unverkäufliche Ware)*; ~**-producing countries** drogenerzeugende Länder; ~ **racketeer** Drogenhändler; ~ **requirement** Suchtstoffbedarf; ~ **store** *Am* Drogerie *(in der auch pharmazeutische Artikel, alkoholfreie Getränke, Tabakwaren, Zeitschriften etc verkauft werden)* mit Schnellgaststätte; ~ **traffic** (or **trafficking**) Rauschgifthandel; Drogenhandel; ~ **pedlar** (or *colloq.* **pusher**) Rauschgifthändler; ~ **vendor** Rauschgiftverkäufer; ~ **withdrawal** Rauschgiftentziehung
drug, confiscation of ~**s** Einziehung von Suchtstoffen; **dangerous** ~**s** Rauschgifte *(Opium etc)*; **narcotic** ~**s** Suchtstoffe, Rauschgifte (→*narcotic*); **seizure of** ~**s** Beschlagnahme von Suchtstoffen; **to deliver** ~**s** Rauschgifte ausliefern

(drumhead) court-martial Standgericht

drum *v* Kunden werben; **to** ~ **up business** *colloq.* die Werbetrommel rühren, **to** ~ **up customers** Kunden werben

drummer *Am* Handlungsreisender, Vertreter

drunk *colloq.* Betrunkener; Trunkenbold; betrunken; **charged (by the police) with being** ~ **and disorderly** (durch die Polizei) beschuldigt, betrunken zu sein; ~ **driving** →drunken driving

drunkard Trinker; Betrunkener

drunken betrunken; ~ **driver** betrunkener Fahrer
drunken driving Trunkenheit am Steuer; Fahren im Zustand der Trunkenheit
Br[56] drunk(en) driving umfaßt "Being in charge of motor vehicle when unfit through drink or drugs" und "Being in charge of motor vehicle with alcohol above prescribed limit"
drunken person Betrunkener

drunkenness Betrunkenheit, Rausch; ~ **at the wheel** *Am* Trunkenheit am Steuer; **public** ~ *Am* Trunkenheit in der Öffentlichkeit

dry trocken; *Am* unter Alkoholverbot; *Am* Anhänger der Prohibition; ~ **dock** Trockendock; ~ **goods** *Am* Textilwaren, Kurzwaren *(opp. groceries, jewelry etc)*; ~ **law** *Am* Prohibitionsgesetz
dry-dock *v* *(Schiff)* auf Trockendock legen; ins Trockendock gehen

dual zweifach, doppelt; ~ **banking system** *Am*

duales Bankensystem *(s. national →chartered bank und state →chartered bank)*

dual capacity system *Br* Doppelfunktionssystem

Regelung der Londoner Börse, wonach Börsenmitglieder seit 1986 sowohl Eigen- als auch Kundengeschäfte tätigen dürfen (→*Big Bang*)

dual, ~ citizenship doppelte Staatsangehörigkeit; ~ **distribution** *Am* zweigleisiger Vertrieb *(über Händler od. eigene Vertriebsfilialen);* ~ **foreign exchange market** gespaltener Devisenmarkt; ~ **gold price** gespaltener Goldpreis; ~ **membership** Doppelmitgliedschaft; ~ **national** Doppelstaater; ~ **nationality** Doppelstaatsangehörigkeit; ~ **pricing** Doppelpreissystem; ~**-purpose** Doppelzweck-; ~**-purpose expenses** *(SteuerR)* gemischte Aufwendungen

dubious dubios, zweifelhaft; ~ **debt** zweifelhafte Forderung; ~ **transactions** zweifelhafte Geschäfte

dud cheque (check) ungedeckter Scheck

due das Geschuldete (od. Zustehende); schuldig, geschuldet; zustehend; fällig, zahlbar; ordnungsmäßig, gebührend; ~ **to** infolge von, wegen

due, ~ from banks *(Bilanz) (ausstehende)* Bankforderungen, Nostroguthaben; ~ **to banks** *(Bilanz)* Bankschulden, Nostroverpflichtungen; ~ **bill** fällige Rechnung; *Am (nicht indossierbares)* schriftliches Zahlungsversprechen; ~ **bonds** fällige Schuldverschreibungen; ~ **at call** täglich fällig; ~ **care** gehörige Sorgfalt; ~ **care and attention** gehörige Sorgfalt *(im Straßenverkehr);* **after ~ consideration** nach reiflicher Überlegung; ~ **course of law** →~ process of law

due course, in ~ zur angemessenen (od. richtigen, gehörigen) Zeit; rechtzeitig; im ordentlichen Geschäftsverlauf; ordnungsgemäß; **holder in ~** redlicher Inhaber; *(kraft guten Glaubens)* legitimierter Inhaber *(e-s Wechsels, Schecks) (→holder);* **payment in ~** ordnungsgemäße Zahlung; **payment is made in ~** die Zahlung ist ordnungsgemäß erfolgt

due, ~ date Fälligkeitsdatum, -termin, -tag; ~ **debt** fällige Forderung; ~ **diligence** gebührende Sorgfalt; *(etwa)* im Verkehr erforderliche Sorgfalt; **in ~ form** formgerecht, in gehöriger Form (*→form 1.);* ~ **notice** ordnungsgemäße Benachrichtigung; fristgerechte Kündigung; ~**-on-encumbrance (sale) clause** *Am* Vereinbarung, wonach ein hypothekarisch gesichertes Darlehen fällig wird, sobald das belastete Grundstück zusätzlich belastet (veräußert) wird; ~ **payment** fristgerechte Zahlung; ~ **process of law**[57] ordnungsgemäßes Verfahren; ordentliches (Gerichts-)Verfahren *(Rechtsstaatsprinzip);* ~ **reward** gebührender Lohn, angemessene Belohnung; **in ~ time** fristgerecht, rechtzeitig

due, amount ~ geschuldeter Betrag; **balance ~** Debetsaldo; geschuldeter Restbetrag; Restschuld; →**debt ~**; **rent ~** fällige Miete; **when ~** bei Fälligkeit, bei Verfall

due, to be ~ fällig sein; geschuldet werden; zurückzuführen sein (to auf); **to be ~ to sb.** jdm zustehen (od. gebühren); **to be ~ for retirement** reif zur Pensionierung sein; die Altersgrenze erreicht haben; **to become** (or **fall**) ~ fällig werden; **the amount is ~** der Betrag ist fällig; **the amount is ~ to me** der Betrag wird mir geschuldet; **the date on which a loan falls ~** der Fälligkeitstermin e-s Darlehens

dues Gebühren, Abgaben; (Mitglieds-)Beitrag; ~ **checkoff** *Am* Einbehaltung der Gewerkschaftsbeiträge durch Abzug vom Lohn; ~**-payer** beitragzahlendes Mitglied; Gebührenzahler; **harbo(u)r ~** Hafengebühren, Hafengeld; **market ~** Marktgebühren, Standgebühren; **membership ~** Mitgliedsbeitrag; **public ~** öffentliche Abgaben; **union ~** Gewerkschaftsbeiträge; **to levy ~** Gebühren erheben

duel Zweikampf, Duell; **student's ~** *Ger* Mensur

duke Herzog *(Br höchster Adelstitel)*

dull flau, still, lustlos *(Handel, Börse);* geschäftslos *(opp. brisk);* ~ **goods** wenig gefragte Waren; ~ **season** tote Saison

dullness Flaute, Stille *(im Handel); (Börse)* Lustlosigkeit

duly gebührend, gehörig, ordnungsgemäß; zur rechten Zeit, rechtzeitig; ~ **appointed** ordnungsgemäß ernannt; ~ **authorized** ordnungsgemäß bevollmächtigt; gehörig befugt; ~ **completed** ordnungsgemäß erledigt; ~ **received** richtig erhalten

dummy Strohmann, Werkzeug *(vorgeschobene Person);* fingiert, Schein-; ~ **company** →~ corporation; ~ **concern** Scheinunternehmen; ~ **corporation** *Am* Scheingesellschaft, vorgeschobene Gesellschaft; ~ **(pack)** Schaupakkung, Attrappe; ~ **transaction** Scheingeschäft

dump Abfallplatz, Schuttabladeplatz, Halde *(für Abfälle)*

dump *v (Waren)* zu Schleuderpreisen auf den ausländischen Markt bringen (od. ausführen) *(um den ausländischen Markt zu erobern);* Dumping betreiben; verschleudern, unterbieten; *(Schüttgut od. Abfallstoffe)* abladen, versenken

dumping 1. Dumping; Ausfuhr zu Schleuderpreisen *(unter dem normalen Wert der Ware);*

Unterbietung der Exportpreise; ~ **practices** Dumping-Praktiken; **anti-~** Antidumping-, gegen das Dumping gerichtet; **hidden** ~ verschleiertes Dumping; **margin of** ~ Dumpingspanne; **price** ~ Preisdumping

dumping 2. Abladen, Entladen *(von Schüttgut oder Abfallstoffen);* ~ **ground** Schuttabladeplatz; Haldengelände; **pollution of the sea from the** ~ **of radio-active waste** Verseuchung des Meeres durch das Versenken radioaktiver Abfälle; ~ **of large quantities of acids and alkalis** Einbringen großer Mengen von Säuren und Laugen; ~ **of waste at sea** Verklappung von Abfällen; ~ **of waste from ships** Einbringen von Abfallstoffen durch Schiffe (→*marine pollution*); ~ **site** Einbringungsort *(→marine pollution);* →**ocean** ~

dun drängender *(lästiger)* Gläubiger; drängende Mahnung (od. Zahlungsaufforderung)

dun *v (fortsetzen zu)* mahnen; **to** ~ **for payment** *(dringend)* zur Zahlung auffordern

dunning letter dringende *(schriftl.)* Zahlungsaufforderung; *(energischer)* Mahnbrief

duopoly Duopol, Marktkontrolle durch zwei Verkäufer

duopsony Duopson *(Industrie, die mehrere Hersteller, aber nur 2 Käufer hat)*

duplex (house) *Am* Zweifamilienhaus

duplicate Duplikat, Zweitschrift, Doppel-; zweite Ausfertigung *(e-r Urkunde);* zweifach, Doppel-; ~ **bill** Wechselduplikat; ~ **bookkeeping system** Durchschreibebuchführung

duplicate (of the) consignment note Frachtbriefduplikat; **to provide a** ~ e-n Duplikatfrachtbrief andienen

duplicate, ~ **(of a) document** zweite Ausfertigung e-r Urkunde; ~ **of exchange** Wechselduplikat; ~ **invoice** Duplikatfaktura, Rechnungsdoppel; ~ **receipt** Duplikatquittung, Quittungsduplikat; ~ **waybill** →~ consignment note; ~ **will** Testament in zwei Urschriften; Zweitschrift e-s Testaments

duplicate, in ~ in doppelter Ausfertigung; **done in** ~ in zweifacher Ausfertigung; *dipl* geschehen in 2 Urschriften; **a will executed in** ~ ein Testament in zwei Urschriften; **to make out in** ~ doppelt ausfertigen

duplicate *v* e-e *(genaue)* Abschrift anfertigen; vervielfältigen; **to** ~ **work** Arbeit *(unnötigerweise)* doppelt tun

duplicating machine →duplicator

duplicator Vervielfältigungsgerät, Hektograph

duplicity *(im pleading) (unzulässige)* Häufung mehrerer Klagegründe in einer Klageschrift

durability Haltbarkeit

durable haltbar, dauerhaft; ~**s** (or ~ **consumer goods, consumer** ~**s**) langlebige Konsumgüter, Gebrauchsgüter *(größere Anschaffungen, die nicht in jedem Jahr wiederholt werden);* **non-~s** (or **non-~ consumer goods**) kurzlebige Konsumgüter, Verbrauchsgüter

duration Dauer; Laufzeit; ~ **of an agreement** Laufzeit e-s Vertrages (od. Abkommens); ~ **of a bill** Laufzeit e-s Wechsels; ~ **of the contract** Vertragsdauer, Geltungsdauer des Vertrages; ~ **of copyright** Laufzeit des Urheberrechts; Schutzfrist; ~ **of cover** *(VersR)* Garantiezeit; ~ **of a lease** Miet-, Pachtzeit; Miet-, Pachtdauer; ~ **of life** Lebensdauer; ~ **of a loan** Laufzeit e-s Darlehens (od. e-r Anleihe); ~ **of the prohibition** Verbotsdauer; ~ **of a time-limit** Dauer e-r Frist; ~ **of validity** Gültigkeitsdauer; ~ **of the war** Kriegsdauer

duration, the agreement will be of indefinite ~ das Abkommen hat e-e unbegrenzte Geltungsdauer; **contract of limited** ~ befristeter Vertrag; **an agreement of unlimited** ~ auf e-e unbestimmte Zeit geschlossenes Abkommen

duress Zwang, Nötigung *(im Sinne von § 52 alte Fassung, nicht von § 240 StGB);* **marriage induced by** ~[58] erzwungene Eheschließung; **mental** ~ psychischer Zwang; **physical** ~ physischer Zwang; **under** ~ unter Zwang; gezwungen; durch Nötigung

Dutch Holländer *(pl);* holländisch; ~**man** Holländer; ~**woman** Holländerin *(cf Netherlands)*

Dutch auction niederländische Auktion *(Versteigerung unter allmählicher Ermäßigung des – zunächst über dem Werte liegenden – Ausbietungspreises, bis sich ein Käufer findet)*

dutiable abgabenpflichtig; zollpflichtig; ~ **goods** Zollgut; zollpflichtige Waren *(opp. [duty-]free goods)*

dutiable value Zollwert; **assessment of** ~ Festsetzung des Zollwerts

duties on buyer's account Zoll zu Lasten des Käufers

duty 1. Pflicht, Obliegenheit, Aufgabe; Dienst;~ **call** Höflichkeitsbesuch; ~ **of care** Sorgfaltspflicht; ~ **of disclosure** Auskunftspflicht, Anzeigepflicht; ~ **of discretion** Schweigepflicht; ~ **of maintenance** (or ~ **to maintain**) Unterhaltspflicht; ~ **roster** *mil* Dienstplan; ~ **solicitors** *Br*[59] *(staatlich bezahlte)* Anwälte, die im Magistrates' Court nötigenfalls Angeklagte beraten und vertreten; ~ **to denounce a crime** Anzeigepflicht *(Strafanzeige);* ~ **to inform the police** Anzeigepflicht *(Strafanzeige);* ~ **to notify** (or **to give notice [of]**) Anzeigepflicht *(Benachrichtigung);* ~ **to report an offence** (~**se**) (or **crime**) Anzeigepflicht *(Strafanzeige);* ~ **to take due care** Sorgfaltspflicht

dut|y, (gross) breach of ~ (grobe) Pflichtverletzung; **conformable to (one's)** ~ pflichtgemäß; **in the course of** ~ in Ausübung des Dienstes, dienstlich; **discharge of** ~ Pflichterfüllung; Ausübung des Dienstes (→ *discharge*); **entering upon one's ~ies** Amtsantritt; **execution of a** ~ Erfüllung e-r Verpflichtung; **an officer acting in the execution of his** ~ ein Beamter bei Ausübung seines Dienstes; **off** ~ dienstfrei; **on** ~ im Dienst, diensthabend; **performance of ~ies** Erfüllung von Pflichten; **scope of ~ies** Aufgabenkreis; **special** ~ Sonderaufgabe; **sphere of ~ies** Aufgabenbereich

dut|y, to be off ~ keinen Dienst haben, dienstfrei sein; **to be on** ~ Dienst haben, im Dienst sein; **to come off** ~ aus dem Dienst kommen; **to discharge one's ~ies** seine Aufgaben erfüllen, seinen Pflichten nachkommen; **to enter upon one's ~ies** seine Tätigkeit aufnehmen, seinen Dienst antreten; **to go on** ~ in den Dienst gehen; **to report for** ~ sich zum Dienst melden; **to take up one's ~ies** s. to enter upon one's →~ies

dut|y 2. *(öffentl.)* Abgabe; Zoll(gebühr); ~ **per article** Stückzoll; ~ **on entry** Einfuhrzoll; ~ **on exports** Ausfuhrzoll, Ausfuhrabgabe; **~ies chargeable on goods** auf Waren zu erhebende Zölle; **~ies, imposts and excises** *Am* Zölle und Abgaben

duty-free zollfrei; abgabenfrei; gebührenfrei; ~ **entry** zollfreie (od. abgabenfreie) Einfuhr; ~ **entry certificate** Bescheinigung über abgabenfreies Verbringen in das Zollgebiet; ~ **goods** zollfreie Waren; abgabenfreie Waren; ~ **return** zollfreie Wiedereinfuhr; **the goods enter the country** ~ die Waren werden zollfrei eingeführt

duty paid verzollt; ~ **goods** verzollte Waren; ~ **price** Preis einschließlich Zoll; ~ **sale** Verkauf nach erfolgter Verzollung

duty, ~ **receipt** Zollquittung; ~ **relief** Zollbefreiung; ~ **unpaid** unverzollt

dut|y, additional ~ Zollaufschlag; **ad valorem** ~ Wertzoll; **agricultural** ~ Agrarzoll; **assessment of** ~ Zollfestsetzung; **basic** ~ Ausgangszollsatz; **conventional** ~ Vertragszollsatz; **(customs)** ~ Zoll (→*customs*); **exempt from** ~ zollfrei; abgabenfrei; **export** ~ Ausfuhrzoll; **external ~ies** Außenzölle; **free of** ~ →~-free; **import** ~ Einfuhrzoll; **increase of ~ies** Zollerhöhung; **method of levying ~ies** Erhebungsverfahren für Zölle; **liable to** ~ zollpflichtig; abgabenpflichtig; gebührenpflichtig; **mixed** ~ gemischter Zoll; **payment of** ~ Verzollung; **port ~ies** Hafengebühren; **preferential** ~ Vorzugszoll; **prohibitive** (or **protective**) ~ Schutzzoll; **rate of** ~ Zollsatz; Abgabensatz; **retaliatory** ~ Retorsionszoll, Kampfzoll; →**specific** ~; **stamp** ~ Stempelgebühr; **subject to** ~ s. liable to →~; **transit** ~ Durchgangszoll; **uniform** ~ Einheitszoll; **valuation for** ~ **purposes** Zollwertermittlung

dut|y, to be subject to ~ zollpflichtig sein; **to impose ~ies** (on) mit Steuern (od. Abgaben) belegen, besteuern; **to charge** (or **levy**) **~ies** Zölle erheben; **to pay ~ies** (on) verzollen, Zoll bezahlen für

dweller Bewohner(in); **town** ~ Stadtbewohner(in)

dwelling Wohnung; **~s** Wohnhäuser, -gebäude; ~ **house** Wohnhaus; ~ **place** Wohnort; **exchange of ~s** Wohnungstausch; **multiple family** ~ Mehrfamilienhaus; **private** (or **privately owned**) ~ Privatwohnung; **to let a private** ~ e-e Wohnung vermieten

dwindle *v* an Wert abnehmen

dwindling of assets Kapitalschwund

dying, ~ **declaration** *(BeweisR)* Erklärung auf dem Sterbebett; ~ **off of forests** Waldsterben

E

eagle *Am* 10-Dollar-Stück *(Goldmünze)*

EAN (European article number) europäische Artikelnummer *(zur Identifikation der Artikel [Nahrungsmittel] e-s Herstellers)*; ~ **coding** europäische Artikelnummerkodierung

earl *Br* Graf

Dritthöchster Adelstitel zwischen → marquis und → viscount mit erblichem Sitz im House of Lords. In amtlichen Urkunden wird er von dem Souverän "trusty and well-beloved cousin" genannt. Ehefrau des earl ist die countess

Earl Marshal *Br* Oberzeremonienmeister *(bei Staatsfeierlichkeiten)*

earlier application *(PatR)* frühere Anmeldung

earliest, at the ~ **on** frühestens am; **at your** ~ **convenience** sobald wie möglich; **at the** ~ **possible date** zum frühest möglichen Zeitpunkt

early früh(zeitig); vorzeitig; Früh-; **in** ~ **May** in der ersten Hälfte vom Mai; ~ **answer** baldige Antwort; ~ **closing (day)** früher Ladenschluß; nachmittags geschlossen; ~ **payment** vorzeitige Zahlung *(Zahlung e-r noch nicht fälligen Schuld)*; ~ **retirement** vorzeitige Pensionierung; ~ **warning system** *mil* Frühwarnsystem

earmark Kennzeichen; Eigentumszeichen *(am Ohr e-s Haustiers)*

earmark *v* kennzeichnen; *(für besonderen Zweck)* beiseitelegen (od. bereitstellen); **to ~ a fund** (or **a sum of money**) **for research** e-n Fonds (od. e-n Geldbetrag) für Forschungszwecke bestimmen (od. bereitstellen)

earmarked, ~ asset zweckgebundener Vermögenswert; **~ balances at foreign banks** zweckgebundene Guthaben bei ausländischen Banken; **~ gold** für fremde Rechnung verwahrtes Gold *(das, um die Transportkosten zu sparen, nicht versandt wird)*; **funds ~ for special purposes** zweckgebundene Mittel; **to hold gold ~ for foreign account** Gold für ausländische Rechnung im Depot halten *(um die Transportkosten zu sparen)*

earmarking *(zweckgebundene)* Bereitstellung; **~ of expenditure** Zweckbindung von Ausgaben; **~ of funds** Bereitstellung von Mitteln *(für e-n bestimmten Zweck)*; **~ of gold** Übertragung von Gold von e-m Eigentümer auf den anderen *(ohne Ortsveränderung und ohne Besitzwechsel)*

earn *v (Geld)* verdienen, als Lohn erhalten; erwerben; *(Zinsen)* (ein)bringen; **to ~ one's living** seinen Lebensunterhalt verdienen; **to ~ a good salary (to ~ good wages)** gut verdienen

earned, ~ income Arbeitseinkommen, Einkommen aus selbständiger und nicht selbständiger Tätigkeit, Erwerbseinkommen *(opp. unearned income)*; **~ income exclusion** *Am*[1] Steuerbefreiung für Arbeitseinkünfte; **~ premium** verdiente (od. eingezahlte) Prämie; **~ surplus** unverteilter Reingewinn, Gewinnrücklage (→*surplus 2.*); **~ tax credit** *Am (SteuerR)* Gutschrift für Arbeitseinkommen; **~ value** *Am* Gewinne, die außerhalb e-s Einzelstaates entstanden sind

earner Verdiener; **double ~** Doppelverdiener; **salary ~** Gehaltsempfänger; **wage ~** Lohnempfänger

earnest money Draufgabe, Draufgeld, Handgeld *(als Zeichen des Vertragsabschlusses)*

earning Gewinn, Ertrag; ertragbringend, Ertrags-

earning capacity Erwerbsfähigkeit,, Ertragsfähigkeit; **loss of ~** Verlust der Erwerbsfähigkeit; **reduction in ~** Minderung der Erwerbsfähigkeit; **to impair the ~** die Erwerbsfähigkeit mindern

earning, ~ power Ertragskraft; **~ value** Ertragswert

earnings Einkommen, Einkünfte, Einnahmen; *(erarbeiteter)* Gewinn; Ertrag, Erträge; **~ →lag; ~ of management** Unternehmergewinn; **~ from the practice of a profession** Einkünfte aus freien Berufen; **~-related contributions** *Br (Sozialvers.)* einkommensbezogene Beiträge; **~-related pension** *Br*[2] gehaltsbezogene Pension; lohnbezogene Rente *(die vom früheren Verdienst abhängt)*; **~-related supplement** *Br (Sozialvers.)* lohnbezogener Zuschlag *(zum Arbeitslosen-, Mutterschafts- od. Unfallgeld)*; **~ report** *Am* Gewinn- und Verlustrechnung; **~ reserve** Gewinnrücklage; **~ retention** →retention of earnings; **~ yield** *(Aktienkurswert)* Gewinnrendite

earnings, company (*Am* **corporation**) **~** Gesellschaftsgewinn; **decline in ~** Ertragsminderung; **gross ~** Bruttoeinkommen; Bruttoverdienst; Bruttogewinn; **individual ~** pro-Kopf-Einkommen; **loss of ~** Verdienstausfall; Gewinneinbuße; **net ~** Nettoeinkommen; Nettoverdienst; Nettogewinn; **operating ~** Betriebsertrag; **personal ~** Einkünfte aus eigener Arbeit; **professional ~** Einkünfte aus freien Berufen; **retained ~** *Am (Bilanz)* thesaurierter Gewinn; **to suffer loss of ~** Verdienstausfall haben

earthquake Erdbeben; **~ relief** Erdbebenhilfe; **~ victim** Erdbebenopfer; **hit by the ~** vom Erdbeben getroffen

earwitness Ohrenzeuge

ease *v* erleichtern; auflockern; nachlassen; **to ~ (off)** nachlassen, sich vermindern; *(Börse)* abbröckeln, fallen; **to ~ off tension** *pol* entspannen, Spannungen verringern; **the situation has ~d (off)** *pol* die Lage hat sich entspannt; **prices have ~d off** die Kurse haben nachgegeben

easing, ~ of the capital market Auflockerung des Kapitalmarktes; **~ of money market rates** Entspannung am Geldmarkt; **~ of (share) prices** Abbröckeln der Kurse; **~ of tension** (between two countries) *pol* Entspannung

easement Grunddienstbarkeit *(bes. Wegerecht, Lichtrecht, Wasserrecht, Abstützungsrecht, Zaunrecht; cf. dominant and servient tenement)*; **~ of access** Wegerecht; **~ appurtenant** Grunddienstbarkeit; **~ in gross** *Am* beschränkt persönliche Dienstbarkeit; **affirmative** (or **positive**) **~** Grunddienstbarkeit, bei der der Eigentümer des herrschenden Grundstücks befugt ist, das dienende Grundstück in bestimmter Hinsicht zu benutzen oder bestimmte Handlungen auf ihm vorzunehmen; **negative ~** Grunddienstbarkeit, bei der der Eigentümer des belasteten Grundstücks bestimmte Handlungen nicht vornehmen darf oder bestimmte Handlungen des Eigentümers des herrschenden Grundstücks dulden muß; **to grant an ~** e-e Grunddienstbarkeit bestellen

easiness on the money market Flüssigkeit auf dem Geldmarkt

East, ~ bloc →Eastern Bloc; ~ **Germany** →German Democratic Republic

Eastern Bloc Ostblock *(cf. Warsaw Pact)*; ~ **countries** Ostblockländer; **state of the** ~ Ostblockstaat; **trade with the** ~ Osthandel

Eastern, ~ Europe Osteuropa; ~ **European Time** (E. E. T.) osteuropäische Zeit

easy leicht, mühelos; *com* ruhig, flau; ~ **care** pflegeleicht; ~ **market** Markt mit großem Geld-(Waren-)angebot und niedrigen Zinsen (Preisen) *(opp. tight market)*; ~ **money** billiges Geld; leicht verdientes Geld; ~ **of access** leicht zugänglich (od. erreichbar); ~ **terms (of payment)** günstige Zahlungsbedingungen; Zahlungserleichterungen; **on** ~ **terms** unter günstigen (Zahlungs-)Bedingungen; auf Abzahlung; ~ **to dispose of** leicht verkäuflich

eavesdrop *v* abhören

eavesdropping Lauschen, Horchen, Abhören *(→wire tapping)*

ecclesiastical kirchlich, geistlich; ~ **court** Kirchengericht *(Br die wichtigsten sind die beiden Provinzialgerichte von Canterbury und York und die Gerichte e-r Diözese)*; ~ **law** Kirchenrecht; ~ **office** kirchliches Amt; ~ **property** Kirchenvermögen

ecocidal umweltzerstörend

ecocide Umweltzerstörung

ecological ökologisch; **disturbing the** ~ **balance** Landschaftszerstörung; ~ **conservation** Erhaltung des ökologischen Gleichgewichts; ~ **hazard** Gefahr für die Umwelt; ~ **pressure** Belastung des Naturhaushalts

ecologically, ~ beneficial umweltfreundlich; ~ **harmful** umweltfeindlich

ecologist Umweltschützer

ecology Ökologie *(Wissenschaft von den Beziehungen der Lebewesen zu ihrer Umwelt)*

econometrics Ökonometrie

economic wirtschaftlich; volkswirtschaftlich; ökonomisch; wirtschaftswissenschaftlich; Wirtschafts-

economic, to establish close ~ relations enge Wirtschaftsbeziehungen herstellen; **to intensify** ~ **cooperation** die wirtschaftliche Zusammenarbeit vertiefen

economic activity wirtschaftliche Betätigung, Konjunktur; **decline in** ~ Konjunkturrückgang; **fluctuations in** ~ Konjunkturschwankungen; **increase in** ~ Konjunkturanstieg; **slowdown of** ~ Abschwächung der Wirtschaftstätigkeit; **to pep up the** ~ die Wirtschaft ankurbeln

economic, ~ adjustment wirtschaftliche Anpassung; ~ **adviser** Wirtschaftsberater; ~ **agreement** Wirtschaftsabkommen, Handelsabkommen; ~ **aid** →~ assistance; ~ **analysis** Wirtschaftsanalyse

Economic and Social Commission for Asia and the Pacific (ESCAP) UN-Wirtschaftskommission für Asien und den Pazifik

Economic and Social Committee *(EG)* Wirtschafts- und Sozialausschuß

Aus Vertretern verschiedener Berufsgruppen bestehendes beratendes Organ der Europäischen Gemeinschaften

economic, E~ and Social Council (ECOSOC) Wirtschafts- und Sozialrat *(cf. organs of the → United Nations)*; ~ **and social science(s)** Wirtschafts- und Sozialwissenschaften

economic assistance Wirtschaftshilfe; **to furnish** (or **give, grant**) ~ Wirtschaftshilfe leisten

economic, ~ bloc Wirtschaftsblock; ~ **blockade** Wirtschaftsblockade; ~ **commission** Wirtschaftskommission; **E~ Commission for Africa** (ECA) Wirtschaftskommission *(der UNO)* für Afrika *(Sitz: Addis Abbeba)*; **E~ Commission for Asia and the Far East** (ECAFE) Wirtschaftskommission *(der UNO)* für Asien und den Fernen Osten *(Sitz: Bangkok)*; **E~ Commission for Europe** (ECE) Wirtschaftskommission *(der UNO)* für Europa *(Sitz:* Genf); **E~ Commission for Latin America** (ECLA) Wirtschaftskommission *(der UNO)* für Lateinamerika *(Sitz:* Santiago); **E~ Community of West African States** (ECOWAS) Wirtschaftsgemeinschaft der westafrikanischen Staaten

economic condition(s) Wirtschaftslage, Konjunktur; **improvement in the** ~ Konjunkturbelebung; **sound ~s** gesunde wirtschaftliche Verhältnisse; **(general) world** ~ (allgemeine) Weltwirtschaftslage

economic, ~ cooperation wirtschaftliche Zusammenarbeit; ~ **crisis** Wirtschaftskrise; ~ **cycle** Konjunkturzyklus, Konjunkturablauf *(cf. boom, recession* [or *downswing*], *depression, recovery* [or *upswing*]); ~ **decline** wirtschaftlicher Niedergang

economic development Entwicklung der Wirtschaft, wirtschaftliche Entwicklung; **measures for** ~ wirtschaftsfördernde Maßnahmen; **short term** ~ Konjunkturverlauf

economic, ~ depression Wirtschaftsdepression, wirtschaftlicher Tiefstand; ~ **disequilibrium** Störung des wirtschaftlichen Gleichgewichts; ~ **distress** wirtschaftliche Not(lage); ~ **domination over other countries** wirtschaftliche Vorherrschaft über andere Länder; ~ **efficiency** Wirtschaftlichkeit; ~ **equilibrium** wirtschaftliches Gleichgewicht; **in the** ~ **field** auf wirtschaftlichem Gebiete; ~ **fluctuations** Konjunkturschwankungen; ~ **forces** wirtschaftliche Kräfte; ~ **geography** Wirtschaftsgeographie; ~ **growth** Wirtschaftswachstum; ~ **instability** mangelnde wirtschaftliche Stabilität; ~ **law** Wirtschaftsrecht; ~ **liberalism** Wirtschaftsliberalismus; ~ **life** wirtschaftliche Nutzungsdauer; ~ **management** Wirtschaftsführung; **in** ~ **matters** in wirtschaftlichen Angelegenheiten; ~ **miracle** Wirtschaftswunder; ~ **negotiations** Wirtschaftsverhandlungen; ~ **order** (or **organization**) Wirtschaftsordnung; ~ **outlook** Konjunkturaussichten; ~ **period** Wirtschaftsperiode; Konjunkturperiode; ~ **planning** Wirtschaftsplanung; ~ **policy** (or **policies**) Wirtschaftspolitik; Konjunkturpolitik; ~ **potential** Wirtschaftspotential; ~ **power** Wirtschaftskraft, Wirtschaftsmacht(stellung); ~ **preeminence** wirtschaftliche Vorrangstellung; ~ **problems** Wirtschaftsprobleme; ~ **progress** wirtschaftlicher Fortschritt; ~ **prospects** Konjunkturaussichten; ~ **recovery** wirtschaftlicher (Wieder-)Aufstieg; Wiederbelebung der Konjunktur; **E~ Recovery Tax Act,** 1981 (ERTA) *Am* Steuergesetz (Änderungsgesetz zum Internal Revenue Code); **E~ Regulation Administration** *Am* Wirtschaftsaufsichtsbehörde; ~ **relations** Wirtschaftsbeziehungen; ~ **sabotage** Wirtschaftssabotage; ~ **sanctions** Wirtschaftssanktionen; ~ **scheme** Wirtschaftsordnung; ~ **science** Volkswirtschaftslehre; Wirtschaftswissenschaften; ~ **sector** Wirtschaftssektor; ~ **situation** Wirtschaftslage, wirtschaftliche Lage; Konjunktur(lage); ~ **stability** Wirtschaftsstabilität; ~ **struggle** Wirtschaftskampf; ~ **summit** Wirtschaftsgipfel; ~ **superiority** wirtschaftliche Überlegenheit; ~ **system** Wirtschaftssystem, Wirtschaftsform; ~ **talks** Wirtschaftsgespräche

economic trend Konjunkturentwicklung, konjunkturelle Entwicklung; Wirtschaftsentwicklung; **determined** (or **influenced**) **by the** ~ konjunkturbedingt; **policy relating to ~s** Konjunkturpolitik; **world** ~ Weltkonjunktur (-entwicklung)

economic, ~ **union** *pol* Wirtschaftsunion; ~ **value** wirtschaftlicher Wert; ~ **warfare** Wirtschaftskrieg, Handelskrieg

economical sparsam (of mit); wirtschaftlich, ökonomisch; haushälterisch; ~ **car** wirtschaftlicher *(Kosten, Benzin etc sparender)* Wagen; ~ **working method** rationelle Arbeitsweise; **politico-~** wirtschaftspolitisch

economically active population erwerbstätige Bevölkerung

economics Volkswirtschaft(slehre); Wirtschaftswissenschaften; ~ **of sea transport**[3] Seeverkehrswirtschaft; **applied** ~ angewandte (Volks-)Wirtschaftstheorie; **business** ~ Betriebswirtschaftslehre; **international** ~ Weltwirtschaft; **pure** ~ Wirtschaftstheorie; **social** ~ Sozialwissenschaft; **world** ~ Weltwirtschaft

economies Einsparungen; Sparmaßnahmen; Abstriche; ~ **of scale** Größenvorteile; Größeneffekt; Kostenersparnisse durch Vergrößerung des Betriebes bis zum optimalen Umfang; ~ **of scope** Umfangsvorteile; Diversifikationsvorteile

economist Wirtschaftler; Wirtschaftsfachmann; Wirtschaftswissenschaftler; Volkswirt; **Administration** ~ *Am* Wirtschaftsberater der Regierung; **business** ~ Betriebswirt; **(political)** ~ Volkswirt(schaftler), Nationalökonom

economize *v* sparsam wirtschaften; haushalten; (ein)sparen; rationalisieren; **to** ~ **on expenses** Kosten sparen

economizing Einsparung; ~ **measures** Sparmaßnahmen

economization Rationalisierung

economy Wirtschaft; Wirtschaftlichkeit, Sparsamkeit; Volkswirtschaft(slehre); ~ **measure** Sparmaßnahme; ~ **as a whole** gesamte Wirtschaft; **controlled** ~ gelenkte Wirtschaft; Dirigismus; **domestic** ~ Binnenwirtschaft; **free enterprise** ~ freie Marktwirtschaft; **(national)** ~ Volkswirtschaft(slehre); Nationalökonomie; **peacetime** ~ Friedenswirtschaft; **planned** ~ Planwirtschaft; **(political)** ~ Volkswirtschaft(slehre), Nationalökonomie; **private** ~ Privatwirtschaft; **for reasons of** ~ aus Gründen der Sparsamkeit; **uncontrolled** ~ freie Wirtschaft; **war-time** ~ Kriegswirtschaft; **world(-wide)** ~ Weltwirtschaft

ECSC-Treaty EGKS-Vertrag, Montanvertrag (→*European Coal and Steel Community*)

ECU ECU (→*European Currency Unit*); ~ **central rate** ECU-Leitkurs
Der ECU ist ein Währungskorb. Er setzt sich aus festgelegten Bruchteilen der Währungen von 12 Mitgliedstaaten der Europäischen Gemeinschaft zusammen, deren jeweiliger Prozentanteil sich mit der täglichen Kursentwicklung verändert

Ecuador Ecuador; **Republic of** ~ Republik Ecuador

Ecuadorian Ecuadorianer(in); ecuadorianisch

ecumenical →oecumenical

Edge Act Corporation *Am*[4] Tochterbank e-r inländischen od. ausländischen Bank, deren Zweck auf internationale oder ausländische Bank- und Finanzgeschäfte beschränkt ist

edict Edikt, Erlaß

edition Ausgabe, Herausgabe *(e-s Buches etc)*; Auflage *(e-s Werkes)*; **abridged** ~ gekürzte Auflage; **new** ~ Neuauflage; **pirated** ~ Raubdruck; **pocket** ~ Taschenausgabe; **revised** ~ neu bearbeitete Auflage; **Sunday** ~ Sonntagsausgabe; **the book has gone through ten ~s**

das Buch hat zehn Auflagen erlebt; **the newspaper will run a special** ~ die Zeitung will e-e Sonderausgabe herausgeben

editor Herausgeber; Schriftleiter, (Chef-)Redakteur *(e-r Zeitung);* ~ **in chief** (or **chief** ~) Hauptherausgeber; Hauptschriftleiter; Chefredakteur; **city** (or **financial**) ~ Schriftleiter des Handels- od. Wirtschaftsteiles; Wirtschaftsredakteur; **deputy** ~ stellvertretender Redakteur; **letter to the** ~ „Eingesandt"

editorial Leitartikel; redaktionell, Redaktions-; ~ **committee** Redaktionsausschuß; ~ **office** Redaktion *(Büro);* ~ **staff** Redaktion *(Personal);* Redaktionsstab; **head of** ~ **staff** Redaktionsleiter

education Erziehung(swesen); Bildung(swesen); Schulwesen, Unterrichtswesen; (Schul-)Ausbildung

education, ~ **expenses** Ausbildungskosten; ~ **policy** Bildungspolitik; **adult** ~ Erwachsenenbildung; **Board of E**~ *Am* städtische Schulbehörde; **compulsory** ~ (allgemeine) Schulpflicht; **Department of E**~ *Am (einzelstaatl.)* oberste Schulbehörde; **Department of E**~ **and Science** *Br* Erziehungs- und Wissenschaftsministerium; **further** ~ Weiterbildung, Fortbildung; *Br* Fortbildungsunterricht *(cf. evening classes);* **further** ~ **award** *Br (univ.)* Stipendium; **higher** ~ Collegeausbildung; Hochschulausbildung; Hochschulwesen; **lack of** ~ Bildungsmangel; **occupational** ~ berufliche Ausbildung, Berufsausbildung; **Office of E**~ *Am* (bundes)staatliche Schulbehörde; **primary** ~ Primarausbildung; Primarschulwesen; **public** ~ öffentliches Erziehungswesen; öffentliches Schulwesen; **re-**~ Umschulung; **secondary** ~ Sekundarausbildung; Sekundarschulwesen; weiterführende Bildung; **university** ~ akademische Bildung; **vocational** ~ s. occupational →~

educational Erziehungs-, Bildungs-; ~ **background** (Aus-)Bildungsgang *(schulmäßige Vorbildung);* ~ **endowment insurance** Schulgeldversicherung für teure Privatschulen *(Br bes. public schools);* Ausbildungsversicherung; Studiengeldversicherung; ~ **establishment** Lehranstalt, Bildungsanstalt; ~ **facilities** Bildungsmöglichkeiten; ~ **institution** →~ establishment; ~ **journey** Studienreise; ~ **leave** Bildungsurlaub

educational opportunit|y Bildungsmöglichkeit; **equal** ~ gleiche Bildungschance; **inequality of** ~**ies** Ungleichheit der Bildungschancen; **lack of** ~**ies** Bildungsnotstand

educational, ~ **system** Ausbildungssystem; Erziehungswesen, Schulwesen; ~ **tariff** Erziehungszoll *(Schutzzoll)*

effect Wirkung (on auf); Ergebnis, Folge; Kraft, Gültigkeit; Sinn, Inhalt; **binding** ~ bindende Wirkung; **legal** ~ Rechtswirkung; **with retroactive** ~ mit rückwirkender Kraft; rückwirkend; **to the** ~ **that** des Inhalts (mit dem Ergebnis), daß; **with** ~ **from** mit Wirkung vom; **of no** ~ (or **without** ~) ohne Wirkung, wirkungslos; **to bring** (or **carry**) **into** ~ ausführen; **to cease to have** ~ unwirksam werden; **to come into** ~ in Kraft treten; **to deprive of** ~ außer Kraft setzen; **to give** ~ **to** durchführen, in Kraft setzen; rechtswirksam werden lassen; **to have (an)** ~ **on the market** den Markt beeinflussen; **to remain in** ~ in Kraft bleiben, wirksam bleiben; **to take** ~ in Kraft treten, wirksam werden; **this law shall take** ~ **on** dieses Gesetz tritt am . . . in Kraft

effects Vermögen(swerte), Sachbesitz; persönliche Habe; Effekten; Auswirkungen; ~ **of the atomic weapons tests** Auswirkungen der Atomwaffenversuche; **"no** ~**"** (N/E) keine Deckung *(Scheckvermerk);* **personal** ~ persönliche Sachen, Gegenstände des persönlichen Gebrauchs

effect *v* bewirken, zur Folge haben; zustande bringen, ausführen, tätigen; **to** ~ **a compromise** zu e-m Vergleich kommen, sich vergleichen; **to** ~ **exchange deals in London** Abschlüsse *(in Devisen)* auf London tätigen; **to** ~ **an insurance policy** e-e Versicherung abschließen; sich versichern lassen; **to** ~ **a reconciliation** e-e Versöhnung zustande bringen; **to** ~ **a sale** e-n Verkauf abschließen (od. tätigen); **to** ~ **a settlement** e-n Vergleich zustande bringen, sich vergleichen

effected, to be ~ ausgeführt werden, zustande kommen; **acceptance shall be** ~ . . . die Annahme erfolgt . . .

effective effektiv, tatsächlich, wirklich (vorhanden); eindrucksvoll; wirksam, erfolgreich; (rechts)wirksam, gültig; ~ **(as from) April 1** mit Wirkung vom 1. April; ~ **connection between income and trade or business** *Am (SteuerR)*[5] tatsächlicher Zusammenhang zwischen Einkünften und der gewerblichen Tätigkeit; ~ **connection of the shareholding to the permanent establishment**[6] tatsächliche Zugehörigkeit der Kapitalbeteiligung zur Betriebsstätte; ~ **conversion** echte Konversion; ~ **date** Tag (od. Zeitpunkt) des Inkrafttretens *(e-s Gesetzes);* ~ **interest yield** Effektivverzinsung, **management** tatsächliche Geschäftsführung; ~ **money** Bargeld; ~ **strength** *mil* Iststärke; ~ **value** Effektivwert; **immediately** ~ mit sofortiger Wirkung; **legally** ~ rechtswirksam; **to be** ~ in Kraft sein, gelten; **to become** ~ in Kraft treten, wirksam werden; **after the law becomes** ~ nach Inkrafttreten des Gesetzes; **to cease to be** ~ außer Kraft treten, unwirksam werden; **to remain** ~ wirksam bleiben

effectively connected with, income which is ~ the conduct of a trade or business within the U.S. Einkünfte, die mit e-r Geschäftstätigkeit in den USA tatsächlich zusammenhängen

effectiveness Wirksamkeit; Leistungsfähigkeit

effectual wirksam; rechtswirksam, gültig; **~ punishment** wirksame Strafe; **to be ~** wirken

efficiency Effizienz, Wirksamkeit; Leistungsfähigkeit, Tüchtigkeit; Ergiebigkeit; Leistung(sstand); **~ bonus** Leistungszulage; **~ expert** *Am* Rationalisierungsfachmann; **~-oriented** leistungsorientiert; **~ rating** Leistungsbewertung *(für Beförderung e-s Beamten)*; **~ report** Personalbeurteilung; **(commercial) ~** Wirtschaftlichkeit; **economic ~** Wirtschaftlichkeit; **increased ~** Mehrleistung; **principle of ~** Leistungsprinzip; **highest standard of ~** Höchstmaß an Leistung(sfähigkeit)

efficient wirksam; leistungsfähig, tüchtig; ergiebig; wirtschaftlich, rationell; gut funktionierend; **~ enterprise** leistungsfähiges Unternehmen

efflux (Geld-)Abfluß; **~ of foreign exchange** Devisenabfluß, Devisenabflüsse; **~ of funds** Mittelabflüsse *(bei Kreditinstituten)*; **~ of gold** Goldabfluß; **~ of liquidity** Liquiditätsabfluß

effluxion of time Zeitablauf

effort Bemühung, Anstrengung; mühevolle Arbeit(en); **combined** (or **common, joint**) **~** gemeinsame Anstrengung; **scientific ~** wissenschaftliche Arbeit(en); **to make every ~** alle Anstrengungen machen; **to slacken one's ~s** in seinen Anstrengungen nachlassen; **to use one's best ~s** (to do) nach besten Kräften bemüht sein

EFTA →European Free Trade Association; **~ countries** EFTA-Staaten, Länder der Europäischen Freihandelsassoziation
Nach dem Ausscheiden von Großbritannien und Dänemark aus der EFTA (1973) sind die sog. Rest-EFTA-Staaten noch Österreich, Norwegen, Schweden, die Schweiz, Island, Finnland und Liechtenstein. Ab 1. 7. 1977 wurden zwischen den EG-Mitgliedsländern und den EFTA-Staaten im wesentlichen keine Binnenzölle mehr erhoben (außer für gewisse empfindliche Waren). Damit ist in Westeuropa eine Freihandelszone (ohne Zollschranken) mit rund 300 Millionen Einwohnern entstanden

Egypt Ägypten; **Arab Republic of ~** Arabische Republik Ägypten
Egyptian Ägypter(in); ägyptisch

eight-hour-day Achtstundentag

Eire →Ireland; **status of citizens of ~**[7] Rechtsstellung von Staatsangehörigen der Republik Irland

eject *v* heraussetzen (lassen), entfernen; *(Mieter, Pächter)* zur Räumung zwingen *(→to evict)*; **to ~ an agitator from a meeting** e-n Agitator aus e-r Versammlung heraussetzen (lassen)

ejection *(zwangsweise)* Entfernung; Vertreibung

ejectment *Am* Entziehung des Immobiliarbesitzes *(bezieht sich auf Grundbesitz, nicht auf Mietwohnungen)*; Besitzentziehung *(Grundstück)*; **~ order** *Am* Räumungsbefehl; **action of ~** *Am* Räumungsklage *(des Eigentümers gegen den nichtberechtigten Besitzer)*; Herausgabeklage *(gegen den nichtberechtigten Besitzer e-s Grundstücks)*; **writ of ~** *Am* →writ; **to recover possession in an ~ action** *Am* mit seiner Räumungsklage durchdringen; **the court makes an order for ~** *Am* das Gericht erkennt auf Räumung; **to take legal proceedings for ~** *Am* Räumungsklage erheben, auf Räumung klagen

ejusdem generis ("of the same kind") derselben Art *(Ähnlichkeitserfordernis)*

elaborate *v* *(sorgsam)* ausarbeiten; genauere Einzelheiten angeben

elaborate ausführlich; *(sorgfältig)* ausgearbeitet

elapse *v* verstreichen, vergehen; **6 months have ~d** 6 Monate sind vergangen; **the time for . . . has ~d** die Frist für . . . ist verstrichen

elastic currency elastische Währung

elasticity, ~ of demand Nachfrageelastizität; **~ of supply** Angebotselastizität; **cross-~** Kreuzelastizität; **price ~** Preiselastizität

elder, ~ statesman erfahrener Staatsmann *(meist im Ruhestand, dessen inoffizieller Rat gesucht wird)*; **~ title** älterer Anspruch

elect gewählt; designiert; **President-~** *Am* der gewählte Präsident *(vor Amtsantritt)*

elect *v* wählen, **to ~ freely by secret ballot** in freier und geheimer Wahl wählen; **to ~ sb. unanimously** jdn einstimmig wählen
elected gewählt; **newly ~** neu gewählt; **re-~** wieder gewählt; **right to vote or to be ~** aktives oder passives Wahlrecht; **to be ~ into Parliament** ins Parlament gewählt werden; **to be ~ president** zum Präsidenten gewählt werden; **to be ~ for a term of four years** auf vier Jahre gewählt werden

election *bes. pol* Wahl; **~ address** Wahlaufruf; Wahlrede; **~ agent** Wahlagent, Wahlvertreter; **~** (of Parliament) **by direct universal suffrage** allgemeine, unmittelbare Wahl; **~ campaign** Wahlkampf; **~ campaign financing** Wahlfinanzierung; **~ commissioner** *Br* Wahlprüfer *(Mitglied des Wahlprüfungsausschusses)*; **~ battle** Wahlkampf; **~ college** *Am* Wahlmännerkollegium; **~ committee** Wahlausschuß; Wahlvorstand; ~ **day** Wahltag; ~ **defeat** Wahlniederlage; ~ **district** *Am* Wahlbezirk, Wahlkreis; ~ **expenses** Wahlkosten; ~ **manifesto** Wahlprogramm; ~ **meeting** Wahlversammlung; ~ **offen|ces (~ses)** Wahldelikte; ~ **petition** *Br* Wahlprotest; ~ **platform** Wahlprogramm; ~ **pledge(s)** (or **promise[s]**) Wahlversprechen; ~ **poster** Wahlplakat; ~ **practices** Wahlpraktiken; ~ **program(me)** Wahlprogramm; ~ **propaganda** Wahlpropaganda; ~ **protest** Wahleinspruch; ~ **rally** Wahlversammlung; ~ **regulations** Wahlordnung; ~ **result** Wahlergebnis; ~ **return** Wahlbericht; ~ **returns** Wahlergebnisse; ~ **speech** Wahlrede; ~ **tactics** Wahltaktik; ~ **victory** Wahlsieg; ~ **votes** *Am* Stimmen der Wahlmänner *(opp. popular votes);* **~-weary** wahlmüde

election, by-~ *Br parl* Ersatzwahl *(e-s Abgeordneten);* **chances in the ~** Wahlaussichten; **closely contested ~** hart umstrittene Wahl *(bei der die Mehrheit sehr klein ist);* **conduct of an ~** Durchführung e-r Wahl; **direct ~** direkte Wahl; **disputed ~** angefochtene Wahl; **eligible for ~** wählbar; **free ~** freie Wahl; **general ~s** *Br* allgemeine Wahlen; Parlamentswahlen; →**local government ~**; **mode of ~** Wahlmodus, Wahlverfahren; →**municipal ~**; **outcome of the ~** Wahlausgang; **qualified for ~** wählbar; **result of ~** Wahlergebnis; **right of ~** Wahlrecht; *Br* Wahl zwischen zwei Rechten *(jd, dem durch e-e Urkunde etwas zugewendet worden ist, darf diese Zuwendung nur fordern, wenn er gleichzeitig andere in der Urkunde getroffene [seine Rechte verletzende] Verfügungen genehmigt);* **turnout at the ~** Wahlbeteiligung; **uncontested ~** Wahl ohne Gegenkandidaten; **victory at the ~s** Wahlsieg

election, to accept one's ~ die Wahl annehmen; **to be up for ~** auf der Wahlliste stehen; **to contest** (or **challenge, dispute**) **an ~** die Gültigkeit e-r Wahl anfechten; **to be defeated in an ~** in e-m Wahlkampf unterliegen; **to hold an ~** e-e Wahl abhalten (od. durchführen); **to order ~s** Wahlen ausschreiben; **to put up for ~** zur Wahl vorschlagen; **to run as a candidate in an ~** bei e-r Wahl kandidieren; **to stand for ~** sich als Kandidat aufstellen lassen, kandidieren; **to win an ~** e-e Wahl gewinnen

electioneer Wahlredner

electioneer *v* Wahlpropaganda machen; um Wahlstimmen werben

electioneering Wahlpropaganda, Wahlagitation; ~ **practices** Wahlumtriebe

elective Wahl-; ~ **body** *Am* Wahlorgan; ~ **chances** *Am* Wahlaussichten; ~ **franchise** *Am* Wahlrecht, Wahlberechtigung; ~ **subject** Wahlfach

elector *(stimmberechtigter)* Wähler; *Am* Wahlmann *(bei der Präsidentenwahl);* **list of ~s** *Am* Wahlliste, Wählerliste

electoral Wähler; Wahl-; ~ **address** Wahlrede; ~ **alliance** Wahlbündnis; ~ **area** Wahlbezirk; ~ **arrangements** Wahlabmachungen; ~ **assistant** Wahlhelfer; ~ **chances** *Am* Wahlaussichten; ~ **college** *Am* Wahlmänner-Gremium *(Gremium der Wähler der Einzelstaaten zur Präsidentenwahl);* ~ **campaign** Wahlfeldzug; ~ **coalition** Wahlbündnis; ~ **corruption** Wahlbestechung; ~ **count** *Am* Stimme der Wahlmänner; ~ **defeat** Wahlniederlage; ~ **district** *Am* Wahlbezirk; ~ **franchise** *Br* Wahlrecht; Stimmrecht; Wahlberechtigung; ~ **fraud** Wahlfälschung; Wahlbetrug; ~ **law** Wahlrecht; Wahlgesetz; ~ **prospects** Wahlaussichten; ~ **rally** Wahlversammlung; ~ **ratio** Wahlquotient; ~ **reform** Wahlreform; ~ **register** Wahlliste; Wählerliste; ~ **slogan** Wahlparole; ~ **system** Wahlsystem; ~ **victory** Wahlsieg; ~ **vote** *Am* Stimme (od. Stimmabgabe) der Wahlmänner; Wahl durch Wahlmänner *(opp. popular vote);* ~ **ward** Wahlkreis

electorate die (gesamte) Wählerschaft, Wahlberechtigte; (wahlberechtigte) Bürger(schaft); **pledge given to the ~** Wahlversprechen

electric elektrisch; ~ **chair** *Am* elektrischer Stuhl *(für Hinrichtungen);* ~ **equipment producing industry** elektrotechnische Industrie; ~ **meter** Stromzähler; ~ **power consumption** Stromverbrauch; ~ **power station** Elektrizitätswerk, E-Werk

electrical elektrisch; ~ **engineering** Elektrotechnik; ~ **shares** (or **stocks**) Elektrowerte

electricity Elektrizität; ~ **bill** Stromrechnung; ~ **consumption** Stromverbrauch; ~ **cut** Stromsperre; ~ **industry** Elektroindustrie; ~ **supply industry** Elektrizitätswirtschaft; ~ **tariff** Stromtarif; **consumer of ~** Stromverbraucher; **the ~ was cut (off)** der Strom fiel aus

electrocute *v* durch den elektrischen Stuhl hinrichten; durch elektrischen Schock töten

electrocution Vollziehung der Todesstrafe durch elektrischen Stuhl; Tod durch elektrischen Schock

electronic elektronisch; ~ **banking** elektronisches Bankgeschäft; ~ **banking services** elektronische Bankdienstleistungen; ~ **brain** Elektronenhirn; ~ **calculating machine** elektronische Rechenmaschine; ~ **computer** elektronische Rechenanlage; ~ **conferencing** Computerkonferenz; ~ **data interchange** (EDI) elektronischer Datenaustausch; ~ **data processing** (EDP) elektronische Datenverarbeitung (EDV); ~ **data processing machine** (EDPM) Elektronenrechenmaschine *(elektronische datenverarbeitende Rechenmaschine)*

electronic debit, customers pay for their supermarket purchases via ~ to their bank ac-

counts *Am* Kunden begleichen ihre Supermarkt-Einkäufe durch elektronisches Abbuchen der Summe von ihrem Bankkonto

electronic, ~ embezzlement elektronische Manipulationen; **E~ Fund Transfer Act** *Am* Bundesgesetz über den elektronischen Zahlungsverkehr

electronic fund(s) transfer (EFT) elektronischer Zahlungsverkehr (EZV) *(der über Terminal, Telefon, Computer oder Magnetband ausgelöst wird);* **~ at point of sale** (EFTPOS) elektronischer Zahlungsverkehr an der Verkaufsstelle (→*preauthorized ~*)

electronic, ~ market price information system elektronisches Kursinformationssystem (→*SEAQ*); **~ terminal** elektronisches Eingabegerät

electronical voting elektronische Abstimmung

eleemosynary wohltätig, karitativ; **~ corporation** gemeinnützige juristische Person *(Krankenhäuser, Colleges etc);* **~ institution** karitative Einrichtung

element Element, Bestandteil; Faktor; **the ~s** die Grundlagen *(e-r Wissenschaft);* **~s of the invention** Merkmale der Erfindung; **essential ~s of the invention** erfindungswesentliche Merkmale; **~s of national wealth** Bestandteile des Volksvermögens; **~ of an offen|ce (~se)** *(StrafR)* Tatbestand(smerkmal)

eligibility Wählbarkeit; Eignung, Qualifikation; Vorzüglichkeit; **~ for a benefit** Infragekommen für e-e Rente *(Eintritt des Versicherungsfalles);* **~ (to stand) for election** Wählbarkeit; passives Wahlrecht; **~ for appointment** Qualifikation zur Anstellung; **~ for naturalization**[8] Einbürgerungsfähigkeit; **~ for office** Qualifikation für ein Amt; **~ for (annual) leave** *Br* (**for vacation** *Am*) Urlaubsanspruch

eligible wählbar, passiv wahlfähig; geeignet, qualifiziert (for für); vorzüglich; in Frage (od. Betracht) kommend *(opp. ineligible);* **~ for admission** die *(erforderliche)* Voraussetzung für die Zulassung (od. Aufnahme) erfüllend; **~ bank** *Br* anerkannte Bank; **~ banker's acceptance** *Am* diskontfähiger, von e-r Bank akzeptierter Warenwechsel; diskontfähiges Bankakzept; **~ bill** rediskontfähiger Wechsel; **bill ~ for (re)discount** (re)diskontfähiger Wechsel; **~ charities** *Am* steuerbegünstigte gemeinnützige Einrichtungen; **~ (to serve) as collateral** lombardfähig, beleihbar *(Wertpapiere);* **~ dependant(s)** unterhaltsberechtigte(r) Angehörige(r); **~ for election** wählbar; **~ investment** *Am* besonders sichere *(mündelsichere)* Anlage; **~ for membership** als Mitglied in Frage kommend; **~ for the office (of)** qualifiziert für das Amt; **~ for a pension** pensionsberechtigt

eligible for re-election wiederwählbar; **the members are ~** die Wiederwahl der Mitglieder ist zulässig

eligible, ~ securities mündelsichere Wertpapiere; **~ taxpayer** *Am* für Steuerbefreiung in Frage kommender Steuerzahler; **~ for tax relief** steuerbegünstigt; **~ vote** wahlberechtigte Stimme; **~ to vote** wahlberechtigt; **to be ~ for** in Frage (od. Betracht) kommen für; qualifiziert sein für; die Voraussetzungen erfüllen für

eliminate *v* beseitigen; ausschalten; **to ~ difficulties** Schwierigkeiten beseitigen; **to ~ wholesalers** den Großhandel ausschalten

elimination Beseitigung; Ausschaltung; **~ of competition** Ausschaltung der Konkurrenz

elope *v (aus dem Elternhaus)* entlaufen; durchgehen

elopement Entlaufen, Durchbrennen

El Salvador El Salvador; **Republic of ~** Republik El Salvador (→*Salvadorian*)

elucidation Aufklärung; Erklärung, Erläuterung

elude *v*, **to ~ a law** ein Gesetz umgehen

elusion of a law Gesetzesumgehung

elusive, ~ answer ausweichende Antwort; **~ criminal** schwer faßbarer Verbrecher

emanate *v* herkommen, herstammen (from von); **the request ~d from** das Ersuchen ging aus von

emancipate *v* emanzipieren, befreien; *Am* für volljährig erklären (→*emancipation*)

emancipation Emanzipation, Befreiung *(aus e-m Zustand der Abhängigkeit od. Beschränkung); Am* Entlassung aus der elterlichen Gewalt *(mit der Wirkung, daß das minderjährige Kind sein Arbeitseinkommen [earnings] nach eigenem Ermessen verwenden kann);* **E~ Proclamation** *Am* Erklärung, die den Sklaven der Südstaaten die Freiheit verlieh *(1862)*

embargo Embargo; Sperre; Handelssperre, Hafensperre, Liefersperre; Verbot der Ausfuhr od. Einfuhr bestimmter Waren; *(vorübergehende)* Beschlagnahme; **~ on exports** Ausfuhrverbot, Ausfuhrsperre, Exportembargo; **~ on foreign exchange** Devisensperre; **~ on gold** Goldembargo; **~ on imports** Einfuhrverbot, Einfuhrsperre, Importembargo; **arms ~** Waffenembargo, Waffenausfuhrverbot; **civil ~** Embargo gegen die eigenen Staatsangehörigen; **hostile ~** Embargo gegen fremde Schiffe *(bei Kriegsausbruch od. drohender Kriegsgefahr);* **imposition of an ~** Verhängung e-s Embargo; **to be subject to an ~** e-m Embargo unterliegen; **to impose an ~** ein Embargo verhängen; e-e Sperre auferlegen; **to lay** (or **place**)

sth. under (an) ~ (or **to put an** ~ **on sth.**) ein Embargo legen auf etw.; etw. mit Beschlag belegen; **to lift** (or **raise**) **the** ~ das Embargo (od. die Beschlagnahme) aufheben

embargo *v (Schiff, Waren)* e-m Embargo unterwerfen; beschlagnahmen; *(Hafen, Ausfuhr, Einfuhr)* sperren

embark *v* an Bord gehen, sich einschiffen (for nach); *(Personen, Fracht)* an Bord nehmen; sich einlassen (on auf); **to** ~ **(up)on sth.** etw. beginnen (od. in Angriff nehmen); **to** ~ **on a venture** sich auf ein (gewagtes) Unternehmen einlassen
embarked an Bord gegangen

embarkation Einschiffung, Verladung *(opp. disembarkation)*; **port of** ~ Einschiffungshafen

embarassment, (financial or **pecuniary)** ~ Geldverlegenheit; Zahlungsschwierigkeit

embassy Botschaft; Botschaftsgebäude; ~ **official** Botschaftsangehöriger; ~ **staff** Botschaftspersonal

embezzle *v* veruntreuen, Untreue begehen; unterschlagen

embezzlement Veruntreuung, Untreue, Unterschlagung

embezzler Veruntreuer

emblem Emblem, Sinnbild; Kennzeichen; Hoheitszeichen; **national** ~ Hoheitszeichen

emblements Ernte(ertrag) *(Früchte, die durch Bodenkultur gewonnen sind)*; Früchte auf dem Halm *(die Pächter bei Beendigung der Pacht mitnehmen darf)*

embodiment Verkörperung, Ausgestaltung; **particular** ~ *(PatR)* besondere Ausführungsart *(e-r Erfindung)*

embody *v* verkörpern; aufnehmen; **to** ~ **terms in an agreement** Bestimmungen in e-n Vertrag aufnehmen
embodied, to be ~ **in a law** in e-m Gesetz enthalten sein

emboss *v (Metall)* prägen
embossed stamp Prägestempel, Trockenstempel

embrace *v (Geschworene)* bestechen; umfassen, einschließen; **to** ~ **an offer** ein Angebot annehmen

embracery *(aktive od. passive)* Bestechung *(von Geschworenen)*

emergency dringende Not, Notlage, Not(zu)stand; Notfall; ~ **action** Sofortmaßnahme, Notstandsmaßnahme(n); ~ **aid** Soforthilfe; ~ **budget** Notetat, Nothaushalt; ~ **call** *tel* Notruf; ~ **(case)** dringender Fall; ~ **clause** Notklausel; ~ **conditions** Notstand *(nicht im strafrechtl. Sinne)*; ~ **core-cooling system** (ECCS) Reaktorkernnotkühlung; ~ **currency** Notgeld
emergency decree Notverordnung; **to issue an** ~ e-e Notverordnung erlassen
emergency, ~ **facilities (for defense)** *Am* Notstandsanlagen für die Landesverteidigung; **UN E**~ **Fund** Sicherheitsfonds der VN; ~ **labo(u)r** Aushilfskräfte; ~ **law** Notstandsgesetz; ~ **legislation** Notstandsgesetzgebung; Ausnahmegesetzgebung; ~ **measures** *pol* Notstandsmaßnahmen, außerordentliche Maßnahmen; ~ **money** Notgeld; ~ **number** Notruf; ~ **plan** Notstandsplan; ~ **port** Nothafen
emergency powers Ermächtigung *(Am des Kongresses, Br der Krone)* zur Anwendung außerordentlicher Maßnahmen *(im Falle e-s Staatsnotstandes)*; **E**~ **P**~ **Act** *Br* Notstandsgesetz
emergency, ~ **provisions** Notstandsbestimmungen; ~ **reserves** Notstandsreserven; ~ **reserve commitment**[9] Pflicht-Notstandsreserven; ~ **self-sufficiency** Selbstversorgung in Notständen *(z. B. mit Öl)*; ~ **service** Notdienst; Bereitschaftsdienst; ~ **stocks** Sicherheitsbestände
emergenc|y, in case of (or **in an**) ~ im Notfall; **national** ~ nationaler Notstand, Staatsnotstand; **period of** ~ Notzeit; **port of** ~ Nothafen; **public** ~ öffentlicher Notstand; **state of** ~ *pol* Notstand; *(staatlicher)* Ausnahmezustand; **wartime** ~ kriegsbedingter Notstand; **to declare** (or **proclaim**) **a state of** ~ den Ausnahmezustand erklären; **to lift the state of** ~ den Ausnahmezustand aufheben; **to provide for** ~**ies** gegen Notfälle Vorsorge treffen

emergent aufsteigend, emporkommend; ~ **continent** aufstrebender Kontinent; ~ **countries of Africa** aufstrebende Länder Afrikas

emeritus *univ* emeritiert

emigrant *bes. pol* Emigrant, Auswanderer

emigrate *v* emigrieren; auswandern

emigration Emigration *(bes. aus politischen Gründen)*; Auswanderung; ~ **of a company** Sitzverlegung e-r Gesellschaft ins Ausland; **country of** ~ Auswanderungsland; **flow** (or **stream**) **of** ~ Auswanderungsstrom

eminence hohe Stellung; Berühmtheit; **His (Your) E**~ Seine (Eure) Eminenz *(Titel des Kardinals)*

eminent hervorragend, bedeutend

eminent domain *Am und VölkerR* (Zwangs-)Enteignungsrecht *(Obereigentum des Staates am Grundbesitz mit dem Recht der Enteignung [gegen Entschädigung])*; **right** (or **power**) **of** ~ *Am* Enteignungsrecht *(des Staates)*; **taking by (the power of)** ~ *Am* Enteignung; **to take land by (the power of)** ~ *Am* enteignen

eminent, ~ scientists hervorragende Wissenschaftler; **to render ~ services** hervorragende Dienste leisten

emissary Emissär, Abgesandter *(mit geheimem Auftrag)*

emission Emission; Ausgabe *(von Banknoten, Wertpapieren);* Ausströmen, Ausfluß; **~s of pollutants** Schadstoffemissionen; **to meet the Federal ~ standards** *Am* die bundesbehördlichen Emissionsnormen *(zur Vermeidung schädlicher Abgase etc)* einhalten

emit *v (Banknoten, Aktien)* ausgeben; ausströmen, ausfließen lassen

emoluments Einkünfte (und Vorteile) *(aus e-m Amt);* (Dienst-)Bezüge; **(casual) ~** Nebeneinkünfte, Nebeneinnahmen *(cf. perquisites);* **foreign ~** *Br* Einkünfte aus e-m Dienstverhältnis bei e-m im Ausland ansässigen Unternehmer; **official ~** Dienstbezüge; **salaries and other ~** Gehalt und andere Bezüge

emotional emotional; **~ act** Affekthandlung; **~ disturbance** emotionale (psychische) Störung

empanel *v* →impanel *v*

empire Reich, Imperium, Weltreich; **E~ City** *Am* die Stadt New York; **E~ preferences** →Commonwealth preferences; **E~ State** *Am* der Staat New York

emplacement of nuclear missiles Aufstellung von Atomraketen

emplane *v* in ein Flugzeug verladen; in ein Flugzeug steigen

employ, in the ~ of angestellt (od. beschäftigt) bei

employ *v* beschäftigen (in mit); anstellen, einstellen; *(Anwalt)* nehmen; gebrauchen, benutzen, verwenden

employed beschäftigt; angestellt; unselbständig tätig; gebraucht, verwendet; **~ inventor** *(PatR)* angestellter Erfinder; Arbeitnehmererfinder; **~ person** Beschäftigte(r); Arbeitnehmer(in); unselbständig Erwerbstätige(r); **~ on full time** ganztägig (od. voll)beschäftigt; **~ on probation** auf Probe angestellt; **(~) worker** Arbeitnehmer(in); **gainfully ~** erwerbstätig; **non-~ person** *Br* Nichtbeschäftigte(r), nicht beruflich Tätige(r) *(andere[r] als ~ and self-~ person);* **permanently ~** dauernd beschäftigt; fest angestellt; →**self-~(person)**

employee Arbeitnehmer(in); Betriebsangehörige(r); Angestellte(r); Bedienstete(r); **~s** Beschäftigte; Belegschaft; Arbeitnehmer(schaft)
Der Begriff des employee geht weiter als der deutsche Begriff des Angestellten, umfaßt auch Arbeiter eines Betriebes. Der Begriff des official bzw. officer umfaßt auch den employee, also nicht die scharfe Unterscheidung zwischen Beamten und Angestellten wie im deutschen Recht

employee, ~s' amenities soziale Einrichtungen *(e-s Betriebes);* **~ appraisal** Beurteilung e-s Arbeitnehmers; **~s' association** Arbeitnehmerverband; **~ benefit plans** *Am* Arbeitnehmervergünstigungspläne *(nach denen Arbeitern und Angestellten bestimmte Leistungen [Ruhegeld, Hinterbliebenenunterstützung, Krankengelder etc] gezahlt werden);* **~'s contribution** Arbeitnehmeranteil *(zur Sozialversicherung);* **~s' council** Betriebsrat; **~ discount** Angestelltenrabatt; **~s' insurance** Angestelltenversicherung; **~'s invention** Arbeitnehmererfindung; **~ participation** Mitbestimmung der Arbeitnehmer; **~s' profit sharing** Gewinnbeteiligung der Arbeitnehmer; **~ rating** →~ appraisal; **E~ Retirement Income Security Act** (ERISA) *Am* Betriebsrentengesetz; **~s' shares** (or **stocks**) Arbeitnehmeranteile

employee share scheme *Br* Belegschaftsaktienplan *(um Beteiligungen an e-m Unternehmen von früheren und derzeitigen Arbeitnehmern zu fördern)*

employee stock ownership Beteiligung der Angestellten am Aktienkapital der Firma; **~ plan** (E. S. O. P.) *Am* Aktienerwerbsplan für Arbeitnehmer
Das Unternehmen bildet einen Treuhandfonds (Trust), der keine Gewinne erzielen und daher Finanzmittel steuerfrei empfangen darf. Der Trust nimmt dann Geld bei einer Bank auf und kauft damit Aktien des betreffenden Unternehmens, die den Arbeitnehmern buchungsmäßig überschrieben werden

employee, executive ~ leitende(r) Angestellte(r); **full-time ~** ganztägig (od. voll) beschäftigte(r) Angestellte(r); →**government ~**; →**managerial ~; number of ~s** Personalbestand; →**part-time ~**; →**professional ~; public ~** Angestellte(r) des öffentlichen Dienstes; **salaried ~** *bes. Br* Angestellte(r); Gehaltsempfänger(in); **supervisory ~** *Am* →supervisor; **to to be a permanent ~** in festem Dienstverhältnis stehen; fest angestellt sein

employer Arbeitgeber; Unternehmer; **~s** Arbeitgeber(schaft); Unternehmer(tum); **~s and employees** (or **employed**) Arbeitgeber und Arbeitnehmer; **~s' association** Arbeitgeberverband; **workers' and ~s' associations** (or **organizations**) Sozialpartner; **~'s contribution** Arbeitgeberanteil *(zur Sozialversicherung);* **~s' federation** Arbeitgeberverband; **~-employee relations** Beziehungen zwischen Arbeitgebern und Arbeitnehmern; **~-employee relationship** Arbeitgeber-Arbeitnehmerverhältnis; Dienstverhältnis

employer's liability Unternehmerhaftpflicht *(Haftpflicht der Arbeitgeber bei Betriebsunfällen);* **E~ L~ Act** *Am* Gesetz betr. Arbeitgeberhaftpflicht; **~ insurance** Arbeitgeberhaftpflichtversicherung *(Versicherung für Arbeitgeber gegen*

Schadensersatzansprüche von Betriebsangehörigen wegen betriebsbedingter Verletzungen und Erkrankungen; ergänzt Am →workmen's compensation insurance, die obligatorisch ist)

employer, ~'s representative Arbeitgebervertreter; **~'s share** *Am* →~'s contribution; **~s' union** Arbeitgeberverband; **a person in the service of an ~** ein unselbständig Erwerbstätiger

employment Beschäftigung; Anstellung, Einstellung; *(nicht selbständige)* Arbeit, Tätigkeit, Stelle; Arbeits-, Beschäftigungs-, Angestellten-, Dienstverhältnis; Gebrauch, Verwendung; **E~ Act 1980** *Br* Arbeitsgesetz; **~ agency** *(private)* Arbeits-, Stellenvermittlung; **~ agent** Stellenvermittler; **~ agreement** *Am* →~ contract

Employment Appeal Tribunal (EAT) *Br* Rechtsmittelinstanz in Arbeitssachen

Rechtsmittelinstanz gegenüber Entscheidungen der →Industrial Tribunals und des →Certification Officer. Revisionsinstanz gegenüber seinen Entscheidungen ist der →Court of Appeal

employment, ~ bureau →~ agency; **~ entailing compulsory contributions to a pension scheme** rentenversicherungspflichtige Beschäftigung; **~ contract** s. contract of →~; **~ exchange** Arbeitsamt; **~ history** beruflicher Werdegang; **E~ Incentive Scheme** Beihilferegelung zur Schaffung von Arbeitsplätzen; **~ law** Arbeitsrecht; **~ market** Stellenmarkt, Arbeitsmarkt; **~ of capital** Verwendung von Kapital; **~ of a counsel** *Br* Zuziehung e-s zweiten Anwalts *(e-s barrister durch e-n solicitor)*; **~ of a fund** Verwendung e-s Fonds; **~ of money** Verwendung von Geld; Geldanlage; **(government) ~ office** *Am* Arbeitsamt; **~ opportunities** Beschäftigungsmöglichkeiten; **~ period** Anstellungszeit; **~ procedure** Einstellungsverfahren; **~ prospects** Beschäftigungsaussichten; **~ protection**[10] Arbeitsschutz; **~ records** *Am* Arbeitspapiere; **~ services** *Br* behördliche Arbeitsvermittlung und Rehabilitation

employment situation Beschäftigungslage, Arbeitsmarktlage; **improvement of the ~** Verbesserung der Beschäftigungslage

employment, ~ status Beschäftigungsstand; **~ tax** *Am* Beschäftigungssteuer

employment, applicant for ~ Stellensuchender; **application for ~** Stellengesuch; Einstellungsgesuch; **persons in civilian ~** zivile Erwerbstätige *(Ggs. Militär)*; **change of ~** Stellenwechsel; **conditions of ~** Anstellungsbedingungen; Beschäftigungs-, Arbeitsbedingungen

employment, contract of ~ Arbeitsvertrag, Dienstvertrag; Anstellungsvertrag; **to terminate the ~** den Dienstvertrag (od. das Angestelltenverhältnis) kündigen

employment, covered ~ *Am* versicherte Tätigkeit; **decline in ~** Beschäftigungsrückgang; **fitness for ~** Arbeitstauglichkeit; →**full ~**; →**full-time ~**; **gainful ~** Erwerbstätigkeit; **incapacity for ~** Erwerbsunfähigkeit; **injury contracted in the course of ~** Arbeitsunfall; Betriebsunfall; **(high) level of ~** (hoher) Beschäftigungsstand; **maximum ~** Beschäftigungsoptimum; **notice of termination of ~** Kündigung des Dienstverhältnisses (→*notice 3.)*; **offer of ~** Angebot auf dem Stellenmarkt; **out of ~** stellenlos, arbeitslos; **over~** Überbeschäftigung *(opp. under~)*; →**part-time ~**; **permanent ~** feste Anstellung; Dauerstellung, Dauerbeschäftigung *(opp. temporary ~)*; **place of ~** Arbeitsplatz, Arbeitsstätte; Beschäftigungsort; **probationary ~** Probebeschäftigung, Probearbeitsverhältnis; **provision for ~** → provision 2.; **public ~** Beschäftigung (od. Anstellung) im öffentlichen Dienst (od. Staatsdienst); →**self-~**; **sideline ~** Nebenbeschäftigung; **suitable ~** passende Beschäftigung (od. Stelle); **temporary ~** vorübergehende Beschäftigung *(opp. permanent ~)*; **temporary ~ business** gewerbsmäßige Arbeitnehmerüberlassung; **terms of ~** s. conditions of →~; **under~** Unterbeschäftigung *(opp. over~)*

employment, to be in ~ beschäftigt (od. angestellt) sein; **to find ~** unterkommen, Beschäftigung (od. e-e Stelle) finden; **to find ~ for sb.** jdm e-e Stelle verschaffen; jdn unterbringen; für jdn Arbeit vermitteln; **to obtain ~** Arbeit erhalten; **to procure ~ for sb.** jdm e-e Anstellung verschaffen (as als); **to secure ~** e-e Stelle finden; Arbeitsplätze sichern; **to seek ~** Beschäftigung (od. Arbeit) suchen; **to take ~** Arbeit (od. Beschäftigung) annehmen; **to terminate sb.'s ~** jdm kündigen; jds Beschäftigungsverhältnis beenden

emporium Handelszentrum; Markt; Warenhaus

empower *v (jdn)* berechtigen, ermächtigen (to do zu tun)

emptor Käufer, Erwerber

empties Leergut; leere Fässer; gebrauchte Verpackung; **~ returned** Leergut zurück; **return of ~** Rücksendung von (leeren) Verpackungen; Leergutrücksendungen

empty leer; leerstehend, unbewohnt; **~ flat** *Br* leerstehende Wohnung; **building standing ~** leerstehendes Gebäude; **returned ~** leer zurück

emulsifiers (or **emulsifying agents**) Emulgatoren *(cf. food additives)*

en autre droit ("in the right of another") in fremdem Recht

en ventre sa mère ("in the womb of its mother") im Mutterleib; noch nicht geboren

enable *v (jdn)* berechtigen, ermächtigen; *(jdn)* befähigen, in den Stand setzen

Enabling Act (or **Statute**) Ermächtigungsgesetz

enact *v* gesetzlich verordnen (od. bestimmen);

Gesetzeskraft verleihen, zum Gesetz erklären; *(Gesetz)* erlassen
enacted, ~ law Gesetzesrecht; **as by law ~** wie es gesetzlich bestimmt ist; **be it ~ as follows** *parl* es wird folgendes Gesetz beschlossen; **to be ~** Gesetzeskraft erlangen
enacting clause *parl* Inkrafttretungsklausel *(e-s Gesetzes) ("be it enacted ...")*

enactment Erhebung zum Gesetz; Erlaß e-s Gesetzes; Gesetz, gesetzliche Bestimmung, Rechtsvorschrift; **by legislative ~** durch e-n Akt der Gesetzgebung

encash *v* einkassieren, einziehen; einlösen; **to ~ a cheque** *Br* e-n Scheck einlösen

encashment Einkassierung, Inkasso; Einlösung; **~ charges** Inkassospesen; **to effect ~** das Inkasso besorgen

encipher *v* verschlüsseln, chiffrieren

encirclement *pol* Einkreisung, *mil* Einkesselung; **policy of ~** Einkreisungspolitik

enclave *(VölkerR)* Enklave *(Gebietsteil e-s Staates innerhalb e-s anderen Staates)*

enclose *v (Brief etc)* einlegen, beifügen; *(Land)* einfried(ig)en
enclosed, ~ (herewith) in der Anlage, anliegend; **~ sea** Binnenmeer
enclosing unter Beifügung von

enclosure Anlage, Beilage, Einlage *(e-s Briefes etc)*; Einfried(ig)ung, abgezäuntes Grundstück, Umzäunung

encode *v (nach e-m Code)* verschlüsseln, kodieren
encoding Verschlüsselung; **~ machine** Codiergerät

encounter *(plötzliches od. unerwartetes)* Zusammentreffen (with mit); Begegnung; Zusammenstoß

encourage *v* ermutigen; fördern, unterstützen; **to ~ imports** die Einfuhr fördern

encouragement Ermutigung; Förderung, Unterstützung; **~ of investments** Förderung von Investitionen

encroach *v (unberechtigt)* übergreifen (upon auf); eingreifen (upon in); **to ~ upon adjoining land** über die Grenzen bauen; überbauen; in angrenzenden Grundbesitz eindringen; **to ~ upon the functions of another department** in die Befugnisse e-r anderen Dienststelle eingreifen; **to ~ upon sb.'s rights** in jds Rechte eingreifen

encroachment Übergriff, Eingriff *(in fremde Rechte)*; Beeinträchtigung; **~ upon adjoining land** Überbau

encumber *v* beschweren; *(mit e-r Hypothek od. mit Schulden)* belasten; **to ~ an estate with mortgages** ein Grundstück mit Hypotheken belasten
encumbered, ~ with debts mit Schulden belastet; **~ with mortgage(s)** hypothekarisch belastet

encumbrance Last (to für); Schuldenlast *(auf Grundstücken etc)*; Belastung (on land e-s Grundstücks); **~s** Hypothekenschulden; **free from ~s** lastenfrei, schuldenfrei; hypothekenfrei; **without ~(s)** ohne Belastungen; ohne Kinder

encumbrancer Hypothekengläubiger; Berechtigter aus e-m Grundpfandrecht

encyclical *eccl* Enzyklika; päpstliches Rundschreiben

encyclop(a)edia Enzyklopädie

end Ende, Schluß; Ziel; Absicht, Zweck; **~ in itself** Selbstzweck; **~-items** Fertigwaren; **~ next (account)** *Br (Börse)* Ende des nächsten Monats; **~ this account** *Br (Börse)* Ende des laufenden Monats
end of month (E. O. M.) Monatsende, Ultimo; **~ figures** Monatsendstände; **~ requirements** Bedarf zu Monatsende; **~ settlement loan** Ultimogeld; **~ terms** Ultimobedingungen; **bill maturing at the ~** Ultimowechsel; **settlement at the ~** Ultimoregulierung; **for settlement at the ~** per ultimo
end, ~ of the mid-year Halbjahresultimo; **~ of season sale** Saisonschlußverkauf; **at the ~ of his speech** am Ende seiner Rede; **~ of the year** Jahresultimo; **~ of year adjustment** *(AktienR)* Rechnungsabgrenzung; **at the ~ of the year** am Ende des Jahres; **attainment of common ~s** Erreichung gemeinsamer Ziele; **private ~s** Privatzwecke; **year-~** Jahresultimo; **to be at the ~ of one's resources** mit seinen Mitteln am Ende sein; **the meeting came to an ~** die Sitzung ging zu Ende; **to gain one's ~(s)** seinen Zweck (od. sein Ziel) erreichen; **to make both ~s meet** mit seinen Einkünften gerade auskommen; **to serve one's ~(s)** den eigenen Zwecken dienen

endanger *v* gefährden, in Gefahr bringen; **to ~ a country** die Sicherheit e-s Landes gefährden;
endangered gefährdet, in Gefahr; **~ species of →wild fauna and flora**

endeavo(u)r Bemühung, Bestreben (to do etw. zu tun); **to use one's best ~s** sich nach besten Kräften bemühen; sich voll einsetzen

endorsable indossabel, durch Indossament übertragbar

endorse *v (auf der Rückseite e-r Urkunde)* vermerken; *(Wechsel, Scheck)* indossieren, girieren, mit Indossament (od. Giro) versehen; zustimmen, billigen, bestätigen; **capacity to ~** Indossierungsfähigkeit; **to ~ back** durch Indossament rückübertragen; **to ~ blank** blanko indossieren; **to ~ a licence (~se)** e-e Strafe auf dem Führerschein vermerken; **to ~ over** durch Indossament übertragen; **to ~ specially** voll indossieren (*s. special →endorsement); **to ~ a notice** e-n Vermerk setzen auf; **to ~ an opinion** e-r Ansicht zustimmen; **to ~ sb.'s view** sich jds Ansicht anschließen

endorsed, ~ in blank blanko indossiert; **specially ~ writ** *Br* Ladung, auf der der geltend gemachte Anspruch *(bes. im Falle e-s →liquidated demand)* im einzelnen bezeichnet ist *(erster Schritt in e-m Schnellverfahren)*

endorsee Indossat(ar), Girat(ar)

endorsement Vermerk *(auf der Rückseite e-r Urkunde);* Indossament, Giro; Zustimmung, Billigung, Bestätigung; *(VersR)* Nachtrag *(zu e-r Versicherungspolice),* Versicherungsnachtrag; *Am pol* Wahlempfehlung; **~ book** *(VersR)* Nachtragsregister; **~ in blank** Blankoindossament, Blankogiro; **~ in full** s. special →~; **~ irregular** (E/I) Indossament nicht in Ordnung *(auf Wechsel od. Scheck);* **~ of claim** *Br* Vermerk über die Forderung auf dem →writ of summons; **~ of service of writ** *Br* Vermerk, ob ein writ zugestellt ist; **~ of a writ** (by the court) gerichtliche Verfügung; **~ of a writ for an account** *Br (auf der Rückseite e-r Ladung befindlicher)* Vermerk, der die Forderung des Klägers auf Rechnungslegung enthält; **~ on the policy** *(VersR)* Policenvermerk, Nachtrag zu e-r Police; **~ required** Indossament fehlt; **~ supra protest** Indossament nach Protest; **~ without recourse** Indossament ohne Regreß; **accommodation ~** Gefälligkeitsindossament; **blank ~** Blankoindossament, Blankogiro; **conditional ~** bedingtes Indossament; **continuous chain of ~s** ununterbrochene Reihe von Indossamenten; **creditor by ~** Girogläubiger; **debtor by ~** Giroschuldner; **general ~** Blankoindossament; **partial ~** Teilindossament; **qualified ~** eingeschränktes Indossament, Indossament ohne Obligo; **restrictive ~** einschränkendes Indossament (→*restrictive*); **special ~** Vollindossament, Vollgiro *(opp. ~ in blank);* **to place an ~ (on)** indossieren, girieren; **to transfer by ~** durch Indossament (od. Giro) übertragen

endorser Indossant, Girant; **~'s liabilities** Indossamentsverbindlichkeiten; **preceding ~** Vormann *(beim Giro von Wechseln oder Schecks);* **subsequent ~** nachfolgender Indossant, Nachmann *(beim Giro von Wechseln oder Schecks)*

endow *v* ausstatten; dotieren; *(Stiftung od. Anstalt)* mit Vermögenswerten ausstatten; stiften; **to ~ an institution with £ 1000** e-e Anstalt mit £ 1,000 dotieren

endowed ausgestattet, dotiert; **~ institution** Stiftung; **~ with ample financial means** mit reichlichen finanziellen Mitteln ausgestattet

endowment Ausstattung; Dotation; Ausstattung *(von Stiftungen od. Anstalten)* mit Vermögenswerten; Stiftung; (Widmung von) Stiftungskapital; **~s** Stiftungsgelder; **~ fund** Stiftungsfonds; **~ (life) insurance** (*Br* **assurance**) Lebensversicherung (und zwar sowohl auf den Todes- als auch auf den Erlebensfall); gemischte Lebensversicherung; **~ loan** →~ mortgage; **~ mortgage** Hypothekendarlehn mit Tilgungssicherung durch Lebensversicherungsvertrag (→~ insurance, *Br* assurance) *(Darlehnsschuldner zahlt nur Zinsen für Darlehn und Prämie für Versicherungsvertrag, dessen Versicherungssumme zu einem bestimmten Zeitpunkt oder bei vorzeitigem Tode der Gefahrperson fällig wird und das Darlehn tilgt);* **~ policy** Versicherungspolice, Versicherungsschein der →~ insurance (*Br* assurance); **children's ~ assurance** *Br* Kinderlebensversicherung; **educational ~ insurance** Ausbildungsversicherung

enemy Feind; **public ~** *Am* Nation (od. Angehöriger dieser Nation), mit der ein Staat im Kriegszustand ist; Volksfeind; **~ action** Feindeinwirkung, Kriegseinwirkung; **~ aircraft** feindliches Flugzeug; **~ alien** feindlicher Ausländer (→*alien*); **~ flag** feindliche Flagge; **~ forces** feindliche Streitkräfte; **~-occupied** vom Feinde besetzt; **~ property** Feindvermögen, feindliches Eigentum; **~ ship** feindliches Schiff; **~ state**[10a] Feindstaat; **~ state clause** Feindstaatenklausel; **~ territory** feindliches Gebiet

energy Energie; **~ consumption** Energieverbrauch; **~ crisis** Energiekrise; **~ demand** Energiebedarf; Energienachfrage; **~ dependence** Energieabhängigkeit; **~ economy** Energieeinsparung; **~ gap** Energielücke; **~ policy** Energiepolitik

energy price, increased ~ Energiepreisanstieg

energy program, international ~[11] internationales Energieprogramm

energy sources Energiequellen; Energieträger; **to develop ~** Energiequellen erschließen

energy supply Energieversorgung; Energieangebot; **~ supply crisis** Versorgungskrise im Energiebereich

energy, demand for ~ Energiebedarf; **Federal E~ Administration** (FEA) *Am* Bundesenergieamt; **nuclear ~** Kernenergie (→*nuclear*); **solar ~** Sonnenenergie; **utilization of ~** Energienutzung; **to produce ~** Energie erzeugen

enface *v* auf die Vorderseite *(e-s Wechsels etc)* schreiben; mit Aufdruck versehen

enfacement Aufdruck

enforce *v (zwangsweise)* durchführen, durchsetzen, erzwingen; beitreiben; Geltung verschaffen; *(gerichtl.)* geltend machen; vollstrecken; **to ~ a claim** e-n Anspruch geltend machen (od. durchsetzen); **to ~ a claim by court action** e-e Forderung auf gerichtlichem Wege eintreiben; e-e Forderung einklagen; **to ~ conditions** Bedingungen durchsetzen; **to ~ a contract** Rechte aus e-m Vertrag geltend machen; aus e-m Vertrag klagen; **to ~ a course of action upon sb.** jdn zu Schritten (od. Maßnahmen) zwingen; **to ~ a judgment** aus e-m Urteil vollstrecken; die Vollstreckung aus e-m Urteil betreiben; **to ~ a judgement by execution** aus e-m Urteil zwangsvollstrecken; **to ~ legally** rechtlich erzwingen; **to ~ a lien** ein Pfandrecht geltend machen; ein Pfand verwerten; **to ~ an order** aus e-r gerichtlichen Entscheidung vollstrecken; **to ~ the payment of debts** Schulden *(gerichtl.)* beitreiben; Zahlung der Schulden erzwingen (od. beitreiben); **to ~ one's rights** seine Rechte durchsetzen (od. einklagen)

enforced liquidation Zwangsliquidation

enforceability Vollstreckbarkeit; Einklagbarkeit

enforceable erzwingbar; beitreibbar; vollstreckbar; einklagbar; **~ by action** (ein)klagbar; **~ by legal proceedings** im Rechtsweg durchsetzbar; **legally ~** rechtlich erzwingbar; **provisionally ~** vorläufig vollstreckbar; **a contract is ~** aus e-m Vertrag kann geklagt werden; **the judgment is ~** das Urteil ist vollstreckbar; **to be ~** vollstreckbar sein; **to render ~** vollstreckbar machen

enforcement *(zwangsweise)* Durchführung, Durchsetzung; Erzwingung; *(gerichtl.)* Geltendmachung; Beitreibung; Vollstreckung

enforcement action *(VölkerR)* Zwangsaktion, Zwangsmaßnahme; **to take preventive or ~** Vorbeugungs- oder Zwangsmaßnahmen ergreifen

enforcement measures, application of ~ Anwendung von Zwangsmaßnahmen

enforcement, ~ notice Vollstreckungsbenachrichtigung; **~ of a claim** Geltendmachung (od. Durchsetzung) e-s Anspruchs

enforcement, ~ of a judgment Vollstreckung e-s Urteils (given against ergangen gegen); **~ of foreign judgments** →judgment; **court haring jurisdiction over ~ (of a judgment)** Vollstreckungsgericht; **reciprocal recognition and ~ of judgments**[12] gegenseitige Anerkennung und Vollstreckung von gerichtlichen Entscheidungen; **to make application for the ~ of a judgment** die Vollstreckbarerklärung e-r Entscheidung beantragen

enforcement of a lien Verwertung (od. Geltendmachung) e-s Pfandes; Pfandverwertung; **~ of an order** (by means of a writ of execution) Vollstreckung e-r gerichtlichen Verfügung; **~ of payment of a fine** Beitreibung e-r Geldstrafe; **~ on account of money due** Vollstreckung wegen Geldforderungen; **~ order** Vollzugsanordnung, Vollstreckungsauftrag; **~ proceedings** Verfahren der Vollstreckbarerklärung *(ausländischer Urteile od. Schiedssprüche; cf. action on a [foreign] judgment)*

enforcement, to refuse recognition and ~ of the award Anerkennung und Vollstreckung des Schiedsspruchs versagen

enfranchise *v* Wahlrecht (od. Bürgerrecht) verleihen; befreien; **to be ~d** das Wahlrecht erhalten

enfranchisement Verleihung des Wahlrechts; Befreiung; Übertragung des Stimmrechts *(z. B. auf vorher nicht stimmberechtigte Aktien);* **→leasehold ~**

engage *v (jdn)* einstellen, anstellen, engagieren; anheuern; versprechen, garantieren (for für); (sich) verpflichten; **to ~ a secretary** e-e Sekretärin einstellen; **to ~ seamen** Seeleute anmustern (od. anheuern); **to ~ in** sich einlassen auf, teilnehmen an; **to ~ in an activity** e-e Tätigkeit ausüben; e-e Tätigkeit aufnehmen; **to ~ in business** geschäftlich tätig sein; **to ~ in unfair competition** unlauteren Wettbewerb treiben; **to ~ in politics** sich mit Politik befassen

engaged eingestellt, angestellt; beschäftigt, nicht abkömmlich; verlobt; *Br (Platz)* belegt, besetzt; *tel* besetzt; **~ couple** Brautpaar; **~ in trade or business in the United States** in den USA am Handel od. Geschäft beteiligt; in den USA gewerblich tätig; **to be ~** beschäftigt sein (in doing sth. mit etw.); **to be ~** (to be married) verlobt sein; **to be ~ in business** geschäftlich tätig sein; sich geschäftlich betätigen; **to be ~ in politics** sich mit Politik befassen; **to become** (or **get**) **~** sich verloben (to mit)

engaging Einstellung, Engagements; verbindlich, anziehend

engagement *(formelles)* Versprechen, Verpflichtung, Verbindlichkeit (to sb. jdm gegenüber); Verlöbnis, Verlobung (to mit); Stelle, Posten; Einstellung; *(Theater)* Engagement; Abmachung, Verabredung; *mil* Kampf(handlung), Gefecht; **~s** *(Börse)* Engagements, Höhe der Verpflichtungen aus Börsentermingeschäften; Verbindlichkeiten, (Zahlungs-)Verpflichtungen; **~ of office staff** Einstellung von Büropersonal; **~ (to marry)** Verlobung, Verlöbnis

engagement, announcement of an ~ Verlobungsanzeige; **bear ~s** *(Börse)* Engagements der Baissepartei; **bull ~s** *(Börse)* Engagements der Haussepartei; **current ~s** laufende Verpflichtungen; **fresh ~** Neueinstellung; **social ~s** gesellschaftliche Verpflichtungen; **without ~** *Am* freibleibend, ohne Gewähr, unverbindlich; **to be under an ~ to sb.** jdm gegenüber verpflichtet sein; **to break an** ~ e-e Abmachung nicht einhalten; **to break off the** ~ die Verlobung auflösen, sich entloben; **to carry out one's** ~**s** seinen Verpflichtungen nachkommen; **to enter into an** ~ e-e Verpflichtung eingehen (od. übernehmen); **to meet one's** ~**s** seinen Verpflichtungen nachkommen; seine Verpflichtungen einhalten

engineer Ingenieur, Techniker; *mil* Pionier; **business** ~ *Am* Betriebsberater *(zur Verbesserung der Betriebsorganisation);* **civil** ~ Bauingenieur; *(etwa)* Diplomingenieur; **electrical** ~ Elektroingenieur; **manufacturing** ~ Betriebsingenieur; **mechanical** ~ Maschinenbautechniker; **mining** ~Bergingenieur; **operating** ~ Betriebsingenieur

engineering Technik *(bes.* Konstruktion*);* Maschinenbau; technisch; ~ **education** Ingenieurs-Ausbildung; ~ **fair** technische Messe; ~ **improvement** technische Verbesserung; ~ **industry** Maschinenbau(industrie); ~ **manager** technischer Direktor; ~ **process** technisches Verfahren; ~ **progress** *(PatR)* technischer Fortschritt; **E**~ **Standards Committee** (E. S. C.) *Br* (Industrie-)Normenausschuß

engineering, civil ~ Hoch- und Tiefbau; **electrical** ~ Elektrotechnik; **income** ~ *Am* Budgetaufstellung; **mechanical** ~ Maschinenbau; **production** ~ Fertigungstechnik

English reports *Br* Neudruck der gerichtlichen Entscheidungen von 1220–1865

engraving *(UrhR)* (Kupfer-, Stahl-)Stich

engross *v (von Urkunde)* Reinschrift anfertigen; *(Urkunde)* ausfertigen; große Mengen von Waren aufkaufen *(zur Beherrschung des Marktes)*

engrossing Anfertigung e-r Reinschrift; Ausfertigung; Aufkauf großer Mengen von Waren *(zur Beherrschung des Marktes);* ~ **hand** Kanzleischrift

engrossment (Anfertigung e-r) Reinschrift; (Ausfertigung e-r) Urkunde; **two** ~**s of this contract have been prepared** dieser Vertrag ist in zwei Urkunden ausgefertigt

enhance *v (Wert, Preis)* erhöhen, steigern; **to** ~ **the value** den Wert erhöhen

enhanced structural adjustment facility (ESAF) erweiterte Strukturanpassungsfazilität
1987 geschaffene spezielle Fazilität des IWF für die ärmsten Entwicklungsländer zu „weichen" Konditionen mit langen Laufzeiten

enhancement Erhöhung, Steigerung; ~ **in** (or **of**) **value** Wertsteigerung

enjoin *v* auferlegen, vorschreiben (on sb. jdm); *Am* untersagen, verbieten (from doing zu tun); **to** ~ **sb. to do** or **refrain from doing sth.** *Am* jdm *(gerichtlich)* aufgeben, etw. zu tun oder zu unterlassen; **to** ~ **the defendant from entering** *Am* dem Beklagten *(gerichtlich)* das Betreten verbieten; **to** ~ **a strike** *Am*[13] e-n Streik verbieten

enjoy *v* genießen; sich *(e-s Besitzes)* erfreuen; *(etw.)* haben, besitzen; **to** ~ **credit** Kredit haben (od. genießen); **to** ~ **the privilege** (of doing) das Vorrecht haben (zu tun); **to** ~ **a right** ein Recht haben, berechtigt sein

enjoyment Genuß; ~ **of a right** Ausübung e-s Rechts, Rechtsausübung; **quiet** ~ **of possession** ungestörter Besitz; **(right of)** ~ Benutzungsrecht

enlarge *v* erweitern, vergrößern; *(Frist)* verlängern; **to** ~ **one's business** seinen Betrieb vergrößern

enlarged, ~ **Community** *(EG)* erweiterte Gemeinschaft; ~ **edition** erweiterte Ausgabe

enlargement Erweiterung, Vergrößerung; ~ **of a business** Geschäftsvergrößerung

enlighten *v* aufklären, Aufklärung geben (on über)

enlist *v (in e-e Liste)* eintragen; *mil* sich *(freiwillig)* melden; Soldat werden; *(in das Heer, die Marine, Luftwaffe)* eintreten; *mil* sich verpflichten; *mil* einstellen; gewinnen, in Anspruch nehmen; **to** ~ **in the Air Force** sich *(freiwillig)* zur Luftwaffe melden; **to** ~ **sb.'s help in a charitable cause** jds Hilfe für e-e karitative Sache gewinnen; **to** ~ **members** Mitglieder werben; **to** ~ **sb.'s services** jds Dienste in Anspruch nehmen

enlisted, ~ **men** (E. M.) Soldaten; Mannschaften; **E**~ **Reserve Corps** *Am mil* Reservisten

enlistment Gewinnung *(zur Mitarbeit etc); mil* Einstellung; *mil* Eintritt *(in Heer, Marine etc); Am* (Dauer der) Militärdienstzeit

ennoble *v* in den Adelsstand erheben

enquire *v* →inquire *v*

enquiry →inquiry

enrich *v,* **to** ~ **oneself** sich bereichern

enrichment Bereicherung; Anreicherung *(z. B. bei Uran);* **unjust** ~ ungerechtfertigte Bereicherung

enrol(l) *v (in e-e Liste od. ein Register)* eintragen; sich eintragen lassen; sich anmelden; *(amtl.)* aufzeichnen; *Am (von Urkunde)* Reinschrift herstellen; *mil* einstellen; **to** ~ **sb. in a society** jdn *(als Mitglied)* in e-e Gesellschaft aufnehmen; **to** ~ **for a course** e-n Kursus belegen; **to** ~ **at a university** sich an e-r Universität immatrikulieren lassen; **to** ~ **workers** Arbeiter einstellen

enrol(l)ed member of a party *pol* eingetragenes Parteimitglied

enrollee *Am* Kursteilnehmer; Antragsteller

enrol(l)ment Eintragung, Einschreibung *(als Mitglied, Teilnehmer etc);* Aufnahme; Beitrittserklärung; Einstellung *(von Arbeitern); mil* Einstellung; *univ* Immatrikulation; Zahl der *(als Mitglied etc)* Eingetragenen (Hörerzahl, Schülerzahl etc)

ensign (Rang-)Abzeichen; (National-)Flagge *(Br Union Jack, Am Stars and Stripes);* Fahne *(als Hoheitszeichen);* Schiffsflagge; *Am* Leutnant zur See; **Blue E~** *Br* Flagge der Marinereserve; **Red E~** *Br* Flagge der Handelsmarine; **White E~** *Br* Flagge der Kriegsmarine

ensue *v* (darauf) folgen; **to ~ from** sich ergeben aus

ensuing (nach)folgend

ensure *v* gewährleisten, garantieren; sichern, sicherstellen (against gegen)

entail (Vererbung als od. Umwandlung in ein) Erbgut (→*estate in [fee] tail*); festgelegte Erbfolge für Grundbesitz; **to bar** (or **cut off**) **the ~** die Erbfolge aufheben *(durch disentailing deed)*

entail *v* in ein Erbgut umwandeln; als Erbgut vererben; die Erbfolge *(für ein Gut)* bestimmen; zur Folge haben, nach sich ziehen; **to ~ harmful consequences for** sich nachteilig auswirken auf

entailed erbrechtlich beschränkt; **~ estate** *(erbrechtlich gebundenes)* Erb-, Familiengut *(vergleichbar dem früheren deutschen Fideikommiß);* **~ interest** *Br (equity-Recht)* beschränktes Eigentumsrecht

entailment (Vererbung als od. Umwandlung in ein) Erbgut

entanglement, external ~s außenpolitische Verwicklungen

entente *(VölkerR)* Entente, Bündnis

enter *v* eintreten, betreten; einreisen; (jdn od. sich) einschreiben; *(beim Zollamt)* deklarieren; **to ~ in** eintragen, registrieren, (ver)buchen; **to ~ an action** →to join an action; **to ~ an appeal** die Berufungserklärung *(bei der Gerichtskanzlei)* eintragen; **to ~ an amount to sb.'s credit** jdm e-n Betrag gutschreiben; **to ~ an amount as expenditure (receipts)** e-n Betrag als Ausgabe (Einnahme) verbuchen; **to ~ an appearance** →appearance 2.; **to ~ the Army** in das Heer eintreten; Soldat werden; **to ~ in the books** buchen; **to ~ the Church** in den geistlichen Stand treten; **to ~ a country** in ein Land einreisen *(opp. to leave a country); mil* in ein Land einmarschieren; **to ~ the country illegally** illegal einreisen; **to ~ to sb.'s credit** jdm gutschreiben; **to ~ to sb.'s debit** jdm in Rechnung stellen; **to ~ the employ of** Dienst antreten (od. Beschäftigung aufnehmen) bei; **to ~ for an examination** sich zum Examen melden; **to ~ goods for home consumption** Waren zum inländischen Verbrauch (zur Verzollung) deklarieren; **to ~ goods at the customs** Waren zollamtlich deklarieren; **to ~ the harbo(u)r** in den Hafen einlaufen; **to ~ inwards** zum Einfuhrzoll deklarieren; **to ~ (a) judgment** ein Urteil eintragen (→*judgment*); **to ~ one's name** sich eintragen (od. einschreiben); **to ~ politics** in das politische Leben eintreten; **to ~ the port** in den Hafen einlaufen; **to ~ a protest** Verwahrung einlegen; Protest erheben; **to ~ on the record** in das Protokoll aufnehmen; im Protokoll vermerken; **to ~ a society** in e-e Gesellschaft eintreten; Mitglied e-r Gesellschaft werden; **to ~ a suit** *Am* →to join a suit; **to ~ the territory** das Hoheitsgebiet betreten *(opp. to leave the territory);* **to ~ the territory (by air)** in das Hoheitsgebiet einfliegen; **to ~ a university** e-e Universität beziehen; **to ~ the war** in den Krieg eintreten

enter *v*, **to ~ into** (sth.) teilnehmen an; eintreten in; eingehen, abschließen; **to ~ into a bond** e-e Verpflichtung eingehen; **to ~ into business** in das Geschäftsleben eintreten; **to ~ into competition with sb.** mit jdm in Konkurrenz treten; anfangen, jdm Konkurrenz zu machen; **to ~ into consultations with sb.** mit jdm in Beratungen eintreten; mit jdm Verhandlungen aufnehmen; **to ~ into a contract** e-n Vertrag (ab-) schließen (od. eingehen); **to ~ into correspondence with** in Korrespondenz treten mit; **to ~ into an engagement** e-e Verpflichtung eingehen (od. übernehmen); **to ~ into negotiations with sb.** mit jdm in Verhandlungen eintreten; **to ~ into obligations** Verpflichtungen eingehen (od. übernehmen); **to ~ into a partnership with sb.** sich mit jdm assoziieren, sich mit jdm geschäftlich verbinden; mit jdm e-e Teilhaberschaft eingehen; **to ~ into possession** in Besitz nehmen; **to ~ into a recognizance** e-e Anerkennung *(vor Gericht)* abgeben; e-e Verpflichtung eingehen; **to ~ into talks** Gespräche aufnehmen; **to ~ into a treaty** *(VölkerR)* e-n Vertrag schließen

enter *v*, **to ~ (up)on** *(Amt)* antreten, beginnen; eintreten in; **to ~ upon a career** e-e Laufbahn einschlagen; **to ~ upon one's duties** seinen Dienst antreten; **to ~ upon one's inheritance** seine Erbschaft antreten

entered, agreement ~ into between ... zwischen ... abgeschlossener Vertrag

entering Eintreten, Eintritt; Einreise *(opp. leaving);* Buchung, Eintragung, Registrierung; Übernahme *(von Verpflichtungen);* **~ into a contract** Vertragsabschluß; **when ~ the country** bei der Einreise; **when ~ upon one's**

duties (or **service**) bei Dienstantritt; ~ **and leaving the country** Ein- und Ausreise; **when ~ into office** bei Amtsantritt; ~ **into talks** Aufnahme von Gesprächen

enterprise Unternehmen, Betrieb; Unternehmen *(Vorhaben);* Unternehmungsgeist; ~ **affiliation** Unternehmensverflechtung; ~ **allowance** *Br* staatl. Zuschuß für Unternehmensgründung; ~ **liability** Unternehmenshaftung; ~ **profit** Unternehmensgewinn; ~ **representative** Betriebs(vertrauens)obmann; ~ **value** Unternehmenswert

enterprise, association of ~s Unternehmensvereinigung; **business ~** geschäftliches Unternehmen, Geschäftsunternehmen; Gewerbebetrieb; Wirtschaftsunternehmen; Handelsunternehmen; **proprietary interest in a business ~** Geschäftsanteil

enterprise, commercial ~ s. business →~; **chief executive of an ~** Unternehmensleiter; **domestic ~** inländisches Unternehmen; **family-owned ~** Familienunternehmen; **foreign ~** ausländisches Unternehmen; **form of ~** Unternehmensform; **free ~ (system)** freies Unternehmertum; **government ~** staatliches Unternehmen; **head of the ~** Unternehmensführer; **joint ~** Gemeinschaftsunternehmen; Gelegenheitsgesellschaft; **large-scale ~** Großunternehmen; Großbetrieb; →**mixed ~s**; **non-profit (making) ~** gemeinnütziges Unternehmen; **private ~** Privatunternehmen, Privatbetrieb; **private ~ (system)** Privatwirtschaft; privates Unternehmertum; **privately owned ~** Privatbetrieb, privates Unternehmen; **public(ly owned) ~** staatliches Unternehmen, Staatsbetrieb; Unternehmen der öffentlichen Hand; **small and medium-sized ~s** (SMEs) Klein- und Mittelbetriebe (KMB); **type of ~** Unternehmensform; **to carry on an ~** ein Unternehmen betreiben; **to establish an ~** ein Unternehmen errichten

entertain *v (Gäste)* empfangen, unterhalten, bewirten; *(Geschäftsbeziehungen)* unterhalten; *(Vorschlag, Gesuch)* in Erwägung ziehen, eingehen auf; *(Meinung, Verdacht)* hegen; **the court will not ~ an action based on** ... (a fraud etc) das Gericht erklärt sich nicht für zuständig für e-e Klage wegen ... (Betrugs etc); **to ~ an offer** ein Angebot in Erwägung ziehen; e-m Angebot näher treten; **to ~ a proposal** auf e-n Vorschlag eingehen; **to ~ a risk** ein Risiko eingehen *(Versicherung)*

entertainment *(gastl.)* Aufnahme, Bewirtung; Vergnügung; Unterhaltung; Aufführung, Darbietung; ~ **allowance** Aufwandsentschädigung; **~s duty** Vergnügungssteuer *(auf Filme und Fernsehen);* ~ **electronics** Unterhaltungselektronik; ~ **tax** Vergnügungssteuer; **business ~** Bewirtung von Geschäftsfreunden; **cost** (or **expenses**) **of ~** Bewirtungskosten, Repräsentationsspesen

entice *v* anlocken; abwerben; **to ~ away** weglocken, abspenstig machen; **to ~ away sb.'s customers** jds Kunden abspenstig machen (od. anlocken); **to ~ workmen** Arbeitskräfte abwerben

enticement Anlockung; Abwerbung; ~ **action** *Br* Klage wegen Abspenstigmachen des Ehegatten; ~ **of employees** Abwerbung von Arbeitskräften

entire ganz, gesamt, ungeteilt, voll; uneingeschränkt; ~ **amount** voller Betrag; ~ **contract** ungeteilter Vertrag *(opp. divisible contract)*

entirety Gesamtheit, Ungeteiltheit; **the contract in its ~** der gesamte Vertrag

entitle *v* betiteln, nennen; berechtigen (to zu)

entitled berechtigt (to zu); ~ **to a claim** anspruchsberechtigt; ~ **to damages** zum Schadensersatz berechtigt; ~ **to dispose (of)** verfügungsberechtigt; ~ **to inherit** *Am* erbberechtigt; ~ **to maintenance** unterhaltsberechtigt; ~ **party** berechtigte Partei; ~ **to receive a payment** zahlungsempfangsberechtigt; ~ **to a pension** pensionsberechtigt; ~ **to succeed to a deceased's estate** *Br* erbberechtigt; ~ **to sue** aktiv legitimiert; ~ **to vote** stimmberechtigt, wahlberechtigt

entitled, to be ~ to Anspruch haben auf; berechtigt sein zu; **to be ~ to possession** ein Recht zum Besitz haben

entitlement Berechtigung; ~ **to commutation** (or **redemption**) Ablösungsberechtigung

entity Einheit; Rechtssubjekt; Organisation; **(business) ~** Unternehmen, Firma; **legal ~** rechtliche Einheit; **separate legal ~ doctrine** Doktrin der eigenen Rechtspersönlichkeit von Tochtergesellschaften *(im Ausland);* **the purchased company remains an independent legal ~** die erworbene Gesellschaft bleibt als rechtliche Einheit selbständig

entrance Eintritt, Einfahrt, Eintreten; Eingang; Einlaß, Zutritt; ~ **(by air)** Einflug (into in); ~ **into an association** Eintritt in e-n Verband; ~ **upon one's duties** Dienstantritt; ~ **examination** Aufnahmeprüfung; ~ **fee** Eintrittsgebühr (→*fee* 2.); ~ **to harbo(u)r** (or **port**) Hafeneinfahrt; ~ **into** (or **upon**) **an office** Dienstantritt, Amtsantritt; ~ **of a ship into a port** Einlaufen e-s Schiffes in e-n Hafen; **no ~** Eintritt verboten; **no ~ except on business** Unbefugten ist der Eintritt verboten

entrant *(als Mitglied)* Beitretende(r); neues Mitglied; ~ (into a profession) Berufsanfänger; **new ~** neu in das Parlament Eintretender

entrench *v* verschanzen; **~ed** fest verankert; **~ed**

provisions Bestimmungen *(e-r Verfassung)*, die nur in e-m besonderen Verfahren geändert werden können

entrepôt (Waren-, Zoll-)Niederlage; Lagerplatz, Stapelplatz

entrepreneur Unternehmer(in)

entrepreneurial unternehmerisch; ~ **capability** unternehmerische Fähigkeit; ~ **income** Einkommen aus Unternehmertätigkeit; ~ **risk** unternehmerisches Risiko

entrepreneurship Unternehmertum

entrust *v (jdm etw.)* anvertrauen; *(jdn)* betrauen (with mit); **I have ~ed my money to him** ich habe ihm mein Geld anvertraut; **to be ~ed with the selling of the house** mit dem Verkauf des Hauses betraut sein

entruster *Am (beim trust receipt)* Sicherungsnehmer *(Gläubiger, der Sicherungsrecht erhält; opp. trustee)*

entry Eintritt, Zutritt; Beitritt; Eintreten, Betreten; Eindringen; Eingang (to zu); Einreise *(opp. departure); (feierlicher)* Einzug; Inbesitznahme (upon von); Eintrag, Eintragung; Buchung, *(gebuchter)* Posten; Einfuhr; Zollanmeldung, Zolldeklaration; ~ **(by air)** Einflug; ~ **of aliens** Einreise von Ausländern; ~ **of appearance** Einlassungserklärung *(zu Beginn des Prozesses)*; ~ **into an association** Eintritt in e-n Verband; **(illegal)** ~ **into a country** (ungesetzmäßige) Einreise (od. Einwanderung) in ein Land; ~ **and departure of a vessel** Einlaufen und Auslaufen e-s Schiffes; ~ **for duty-free goods** Zolldeklaration für zollfreie Waren; ~ **into force** Inkrafttreten; ~ **of goods** Einfuhr von Waren; ~ **for home use** Einfuhrdeklaration für Verbrauch im Inland; ~ **inwards** Einfuhranmeldung, Importdeklaration; ~ **of judgment** Eintragung des Urteils *(in das Register; → judgment)*; ~ **into the labour market** Eintritt in den Arbeitsmarkt; ~ **in the minutes** Protokollaufnahme; ~ **negotiations** (EG) Beitrittsverhandlungen; ~ **into office** Amtsantritt; ~ **outwards** Ausfuhrdeklaration; ~ **permit** Einreiseerlaubnis; ~ **procedure** *(Zoll)* Abfertigungsverfahren; ~ **of a ship into port** Einlaufen e-s Schiffes in e-n Hafen; ~ **in a register** Registereintragung; ~ **of satisfaction of mortgage** *Am* (Eintragung der) Hypothekenlöschung; ~ **into service** Dienstantritt; ~ **visa** Einreisevisum; ~ **into war** Kriegseintritt; ~ **for warehousing** Zolldeklaration zur Anmeldung unter Zollverschluß

entry, age at ~ *(VersR)* Beitrittsalter; **as per** ~ laut Eintrag; **bill of** ~ →bill 1.; **book-keeping by single (double)** ~ einfache (doppelte) Buchführung; **credit** ~ Kreditbuchung, Gutschrift; **customs** ~ Zollanmeldung *(Antrag auf Verzollung)*; **debit** ~ Debetbuchung, Lastschrift; **forcible** ~ gewaltsames Eindringen; Hausfriedensbruch; **measures restricting** ~ Einreisebeschränkungen; **point of** ~ Grenzübergangsstelle; **port of** ~ Zollhafen; **post(-)** ~ nachträgliche Eintragung (od. Buchung); nachträgliche Zollerklärung; **powers of** ~ Durchsuchungsrecht (→ *power 1.*); **right of** ~ Recht der Inbesitznahme *(von Grundbesitz)*; **supplementary** ~ Nachtragsbuchung; **upon** ~ **in the register** nach Eintragung in das Register

entry, to delete an ~ e-e Eintragung löschen; **to force an** ~ **into a building** in ein Gebäude eindringen; **to make an** ~ **of sth.** etw. eintragen, (ver)buchen; etw. beim Zoll anmelden; **to make a false** ~ falsch eintragen (od. buchen); **to post an** ~ e-n Posten eintragen (od. buchen)

enumerate *v (einzeln)* aufzählen

enumerated powers *Am (in der Verfassung)* aufgezählte Befugnisse des Congress; Bundesgesetzgebungskompetenz

enumeration Aufzählung; Liste, Verzeichnis

enumerator Zähler *(bei Volkszählungen)*

envelope (Brief-)Umschlag; **pay** ~ Lohntüte; **stamped addressed** ~ Freiumschlag

envelopment *mil* Umfassung, Umklammerung

environment Umwelt; Umgebung; Umfeld; Milieu; ~ **engineering** Umwelttechnik; ~ **pollution** Umweltbelastung; ~ **protection policy** Umweltschutzpolitik; →**Department of the E**~; **destroying the balance of the** ~ Zerstörung des ökologischen Gleichgewichts; **endangering the** ~ Umweltgefährdung; **enhancing the quality of the** ~ Verbesserung der Umweltqualität; **favo(u)rable to the** ~ umweltfreundlich; **harmful to the** ~ umweltfeindlich; **hazardous to the** ~ umweltgefährdend; **improvement of the** ~ Umweltverbesserung; **industries detrimental to their** ~ umweltbelastende Industrien; **obligation imposed on a company to protect the** ~ Umweltauflage e-s Unternehmens; **preservation** (or **protection**) **of the** ~ Umweltschutz; **social** ~ soziale Umwelt; **to reduce the harmful effects on the** ~ umweltschädliche Auswirkungen eindämmen

environmental Umwelt-; umweltbedingt; Umgebungs-; milieubedingt; ~ **action** Umweltschutzmaßnahme(n); ~ **chemicals** Umweltchemikalien; ~ **conditions** Umweltbedingungen; ~ **conscious** umweltbewußt; ~ **contamination** Umweltverschmutzung; ~ **disaster** Umweltkatastrophe; ~ **engineering** Verfahren zur Prüfung von Umwelteinflüssen

environmental factors Umweltfaktoren; **due to** ~ umweltbedingt

environmental impact assessment (EIA)Umweltverträglichkeitsprüfung

environmental influences Umwelteinflüsse; **impaired by** ~ umweltgeschädigt
environmental modification techniques, Convention on the Prohibition of Military or any other Hostile Use of E~ M~ T~[13a] Übereinkommen über das Verbot der militärischen oder einer sonstigen feindseligen Nutzung umweltverändernder Techniken (Umweltkriegsübereinkommen)
environmental, ~ **monitoring** Umweltüberwachung; ~ **planning** Umweltplanung; ~ **policy** Umweltpolitik; ~ **pollution** Umweltverschmutzung; ~ **problems** Umweltprobleme; ökologische Probleme
environmental protection Umweltschutz; **E~ P~Act** *Am* Umweltschutzgesetz; **E~ P~ Agency** (EPA) *Am* Umweltschutzbehörde; ~ **legislation** Umweltschutzgesetzgebung; ~ **programme** Umweltschutzprogramm
environmental quality Umweltbeschaffenheit; **E~ Q~ Standards** (EQS) Umweltqualitätsnormen; **assessment of the** ~ Beurteilung der Umweltqualität
environmental, ~ **requirements** Umwelterfordernisse; ~ **services** *Br* Dienstleistungen für gesunde Lebensbedingungen *(street cleaning, smoke control, planting trees, measures to prevent pollution etc);* ~ **standards** Umweltschutzvorschriften, -normen; ~ **survey satellite** (ESSA) Umweltbeobachtungssatellit

environmentalist Umweltschützer; Fachmann für Umweltfragen, Umweltexperte

envisage *v* betrachten, sich vorstellen

envoy diplomatischer Vertreter; Gesandter *(in weiterem Sinne; cf. diplomatic agent);* **special** ~ Sondergesandter

epidemics, danger of ~ Seuchengefahr

episcopal *eccl* Bischofs-, bischöflich; **E~ Church** Episkopalkirche *(nichtkatholische Kirche mit bischöflicher Verfassung; Br Church of England; Am Protestant E~ Church; Scot E~ Church of Scotland)*
episcopally ordained vom Bischof zum Priester ordiniert, bischöflich eingesetzt

Episcopalian *eccl* Episkopalist, Mitglied der Episkopalkirche; *Scot* Anglikaner

episcopate *eccl* Episkopat, Bischofswürde; Gesamtheit der Bischöfe

epizootic disease, International Office for E~ D~s Internationales Tierseuchenamt

equal gleich, gleich groß, gleichwertig; gleichberechtigt; paritätisch; ~ **to** angemessen, entsprechend, gemäß; **court of** ~ **authority** gleichgeordnetes Gericht; ~ **claims** gleichgestellte Ansprüche; ~ **educational opportunities** gleiche Bildungschancen

Equal Employment Opportunity, ~ **Act** *Am* Gesetz für gleiche Arbeitschancen; ~ **Commission** (EEOC) *Am* Behörde für die Gleichberechtigung am Arbeitsplatz
equal, ~ **opportunity** Chancengleichheit; ~ **partners** Gesellschafter zu gleichen Teilen; **in** ~ **parts** zu gleichen Teilen; ~ **pay for** ~ **work** gleiches Entgelt bei gleicher Arbeit *(für Männer und Frauen);* ~ **protection of the laws** *Am* Gleichheit vor dem Gesetz; **of** ~ **rank** gleichrangig; **court of** ~ **rank** gleichgeordnetes Gericht; **with** ~ **representation** paritätisch besetzt; ~ **right before the law** Gleichheit vor dem Gesetz; ~ **right of men and women** Gleichberechtigung von Mann und Frau; **E~ Rights Amendment** *Am* Verfassungs-Zusatzartikel zur Gleichberechtigung; **persons treated as having** ~ **status to these ...** diesen ... gleichgestellte Personen; **on** ~ **terms** zu gleichen Bedingungen; ~ **treatment** (for men and women) gleiche Behandlung (von Männern und Frauen) *(opp. discrimination);* **work of** ~ **value** gleichwertige Arbeit; ~ **voting** Stimmengleichheit; **of** ~ **worth** gleichwertig; **to be** ~ **to** gleichen; **to be** ~ **to sth.** e-r Sache gewachsen sein; e-r Sache entsprechen, gleichkommen; **to have** ~ **rights** gleichberechtigt sein
equally in gleicher Weise; zu gleichen Teilen; ~ **authentic** gleichermaßen maßgeblich; ~ **entitled** gleichberechtigt; ~ **ranking creditors** gleichrangige Gläubiger; **to rank** ~ **with** gleichen Rang haben wie, gleichrangig sein

equality Gleichheit, Gleichberechtigung; Parität; ~ **before the law** Gleichheit *(aller)* vor dem Gesetz; ~ **in co-determination** paritätische Mitbestimmung; ~ **in fact** tatsächliche Gleichheit; ~ **of educational opportunities** gleiche Bildungschance; ~ **of foreigners before the law** rechtliche Gleichstellung der Ausländer; ~ **(of rank) between creditors** Ranggleichheit zwischen Gläubigern; ~ **of rights** Gleichberechtigung; ~ **of status** politische Gleichberechtigung; gleicher staatsrechtlicher und diplomatischer Rang; Ranggleichheit; **(in the event of)** ~ **of votes** (bei) Stimmengleichheit
equality, on a basis (or **footing**) **of** ~ auf der Grundlage der Gleichberechtigung; paritätisch; **political** ~ politische Gleichberechtigung

equalization Ausgleich; Gleichmachung; ~ **benefit** Ausgleichsleistung; ~ **claim** Ausgleichsforderung; ~ **of dividends** Ausgleich von Dividenden; ~ **fund** Ausgleichsfonds; *(VersR)* Schwankungsrückstellung; ~ **payment** Ausgleichszahlung; ~ **reserve** Ausgleichsrücklage; **financial** ~ Finanzausgleich

equalize *v* ausgleichen, e-n Ausgleich schaffen

zu; gleichstellen; **to ~ accounts** Konten ausgleichen

equate with *v* gleichsetzen (od. gleichstellen) mit

equated, ~ account Staffelrechnung; **~ interest** Staffelzinsen; **~ calculation of interest** Staffelzinsrechnung

equation Ausgleich(ung), Gleichmachen; *(Mathematik)* Gleichung; **~ of payments** Zahlungsausgleich; **~ of prices** Preisausgleich; **~ of supply and demand** Ausgleich (od. Gleichgewicht) von Angebot und Nachfrage

Equatorial Guinea Äquatorialguinea; Äquatorialguineer(in); äquatorialguineisch; **Republic of ~** Republik Äquatorialguinea

equilibrated balance of payment ausgeglichene Zahlungsbilanz

equilibrium Gleichgewicht; **~ of balance of payment** Zahlungsbilanzgleichgewicht; **political ~** politisches Gleichgewicht; **to maintain (restore) the ~** das Gleichgewicht aufrechterhalten (wiederherstellen)

equip *v* ausrüsten, ausstatten, versehen (with mit); **to ~ a hospital** ein Krankenhaus einrichten; **to ~ a ship** ein Schiff ausrüsten (od. ausreeden)

equipment (Betriebs-, Geschäfts-)Einrichtung, Ausstattung; Ausrüstung(sgegenstände); Gerät(schaften); Anlage; *(Eisenbahn)* rollendes Material; *(Bilanz)* Betriebs- und Geschäftsausstattung; *(Leasing)* Mietsache; **~ account** Konto für Einrichtungsgegenstände; **~ and fittings** *Am* Betriebs- und Geschäftsausstattung; **~ bonds** *Br* Obligationen zum Ankauf von Ausrüstungsgegenständen; *Am* durch bewegl. Vermögensteile, meist rollendes Eisenbahnmaterial, gesicherte Obligationen; **~ investments** Ausrüstungsinvestitionen; **~ of a ship** Schiffsausrüstung; **~ leasing** →leasing 2.; **~ notes** *Am* →~ bonds; **~ trust** *Am* Finanzierungseinrichtung für Eisenbahn-, Flugzeugmaterial etc; **~ trust certificates** (or **bonds**) *Am (von e-m trustee ausgegebene)* Zertifikate zum Ankauf von Ausrüstungsgegenständen *(bes. für Eisenbahn- oder Flugzeugbedarf; die Ausrüstungsgegenstände werden an die Gesellschaft vermietet, die Miete wird an die Zertifikationsinhaber verteilt)*

equipment, capital ~ Kapitalausstattung; **office ~** Büroausstattung

equitable billig, billigerweise; gerecht; auf dem →equity-Recht beruhend *(opp. legal)*; **~ action** Klage nach equity-Recht; **~ →assignment**; **~ charge** *Br* s. ~ →mortgage; **~ claim** auf equity beruhender Anspruch *(opp. legal claim)*; **~ conversion** →conversion 1.; **~ defence (~se)** auf equity-Recht begründete Einrede (od. Einwendung); **~ distribution** *Am* billige (angemessene) Verteilung von Vermögensgeldern *(bei Scheidung)*; **~ estate** *Am*[14] durch equity geschütztes dingliches Recht an Immobilien; **~ →estoppel; ~ execution** Vollstreckung nach equity-Recht

equitable interest durch equity geschütztes Recht

Es entsteht z. B. bei Treuhandverhältnissen oder wenn Form für Bestellung oder Übertragung e-s legal →estate nicht eingehalten wurde. Steht dem legal estate im Range nach (obwohl equity meist dem Common Law vorgeht). Die Übertragung von ~ ist grundsätzlich formfrei

equitable, ~ →lien; ~ →mortgage; ~ →owner; ~ →ownership; ~ price angemessener (od. fairer) Preis

equitable relief, claim of ~ *Br* Verfahren, bei dem ein Steuerpflichtiger den Erlaß fälliger Steuern beantragen kann

equitable, ~ remedies →remedy 1.; **~ right** auf equity beruhendes Recht *(z.B. des beneficiary aus e-m trust; opp. legal right)*; **~ title** Eigentumsrecht nach equity-Recht *(cf. ~ ownership; opp. legal title)*; **to be ~** der Billigkeit entsprechen

equities Berechtigungen, die sich aus dem equity-Recht ergeben *(im Ggs. zum common law)*; Sachwerte; (Stamm-)Aktien, Dividendenwerte (→*equity* 2.); **the ~ of a case** die besonderen Merkmale e-s Tatbestandes, die an das Billigkeitsgefühl appellieren *(→equity 1.)*; **~ market** Aktienmarkt; **balancing of ~** Ausgleich zwischen verschiedenen Billigkeitsgesichtspunkten; **domestic ~** inländische Aktien; **foreign ~** ausländische Aktien

equity 1. Billigkeit; equity-Recht

Der anglo-amerikanische Begriff des equity ist nur historisch zu verstehen. Ursprünglich war equity das in den englischen Chancery-Gerichten zum Ausgleich von Härten, zunächst auf die Individualität des Einzelfalles gerichtete, dann aus der Praxis der verbindlichen →precedents zu einem festen Rechtssystem entwickelte, nicht kodifizierte Billigkeitsrecht, zur Ergänzung des älteren, verhältnismäßig primitiven →common law, vielfach mit Vorrang vor diesem. Zwar ist in England[15] und der Mehrzahl der Einzelstaaten der USA[16] das Prozeßrecht der common law- und equity-Gerichte weitgehend vereinheitlicht; der Gegensatz zwischen common law und dem weniger formalistischen equity durchzieht aber auch heute noch das anglo-amerikanische Rechtssystem (trusts, mortgage etc); der Unterschied von legal und equitable rights, der besonders das law of property durchzieht, besteht nach wie vor.

„Das equity-Recht hat im anglo-amerikanischen Rechtssystem die gleiche Funktion wie im deutschen Recht das an Hand der ‚Billigkeitsklausel' des § 242 BGB entwickelte Prinzipienbündel, das zur Durchbrechung des positiven Rechts dient. Billigkeit und Treu und Glauben entsprechen sich im Prinzip".[17]

Fast ausschließlich Gegenstand des equity-Rechts geworden ist u. a. das Zeichen- und Wettbewerbsrecht. Die besonderen Rechtsbehelfe (equitable remedies) enthalten vor allem die gesamten einstweiligen Verfügungen (injunctions und specific performance)

equity follows the law

Ein Leitgrundsatz des equity-Rechts, der besagt: Das equity-Recht setzt das Common Law nicht außer Kraft, sondern es ergänzt es durch (analoge) Anwendung und Fortbildung seiner Rechtsregeln zu besonderen Rechten und Rechtsbehelfen *(cf. equitable remedies)*

equity jurisdiction Rechtsprechung (od. Zuständigkeit) nach equity-Recht

equity of redemption 1. Auslösungsrecht *(auf equity beruhendes Recht des Hypothekenschuldners, e-e Hypothek [mit Kosten und Zinsen] auch nach Ablauf der Frist noch auszulösen, d.h. die Zwangsvollstreckung zu verhindern);* 2. Wert e-s Grundstücksanteils nach Abzug aller Belastungen (→*equity* 2.)

equity, in ~ im equity-Recht *(opp. at law);* **bill in** ~ *Am* Klage im equity-Recht; **claim in** ~ Anspruch nach equity-Recht; **fiscal** ~ Steuergerechtigkeit; **for reasons of** ~ aus Billigkeitsgründen

equity 2. Eigenkapital *(e-r Gesellschaft);* Rechte der Anteilseigner an Vermögenswerten *(e-s Unternehmens); (nicht festverzinsl.)* Anteils- od. Aktienkapital; *Am* Wert *(e-s Grundstücks- od. Gesellschaftsanteils)* nach Abzug aller Belastungen; *Br* Recht *(am Grundstücks- od. Gesellschaftsanteil)* nach Abzug der Belastungen; **I have an ~ of ‰ 5000 in this house** *Am* (**the ~ [in this property] is worth ‰ 5000** *Br*) nach Abzug der Hypotheken stellt das Haus e-n Vermögenswert von ‰ 5000 dar (*cf. equity of redemption,* →*equity 1.*)

equity, ~ **annuity** *Am* (aktien)fondsgebundene Rentenversicherung; ~ **capital** Eigenkapital *(e-s Unternehmens);* Anteilskapital; Beteiligungskapital; ~ **financing** Eigenfinanzierung *(e-s Unternehmens);* Beteiligungsfinanzierung; ~ **fund** Aktienfonds *(e-r Investmentgesellschaft;* →*fund 2.);* ~ **holder** Anteilseigner, Aktionär; ~ **holding** Kapitalbeteiligung *(e-s Anteileigners);* Aktienbeteiligung; ~ **interest** Kapitalbeteiligung; Aktienbeteiligung; Anteilsrecht; ~ **investment** Investitionen in *(nicht festverzinslichen)* Anteilspapieren; Anlage in Aktien; Kapitalbeteiligung; ~ **issue** Emission von Stammaktien; ~**-linked policy** *(VersR)* aktiengebundene Police, ~ **market** Aktienmarkt; ~ **ownership** Kapitalbeteiligung *(e-s Anteileigners);* ~ **participation in a business** (Aktien-)Beteiligung an e-m Unternehmen; ~ **position** Eigenkapitaldecke; ~ **price** Aktienkurs; ~ **ratio** Verhältnis der Aktiva zum Eigenkapital; ~ **return** Eigenkapitalrendite; ~ **securities** Stammaktien; Dividendenpapiere; ~ **shares** Aktien, Stammaktien; Anteilsrechte; ~ **share capital** Stammaktienkapital; ~ **shares of industrial companies** Unternehmensaktien; ~ **supplier** Eigenkapitalgeber; ~ **trading** Aktienhandel

equity, buying of the ~ Kauf der Anteilsrechte (Stammanteile) e-s anderen Unternehmens

equivalence Gleichwertigkeit; ~ **of degrees and diplomas** Gleichwertigkeit der Grade und Diplome

equivalent gleicher Wert, Gegenwert; gleichwertig, gleichbedeutend (to mit); **customs duties and charges having ~ effect** *(EG)* Zölle und Abgaben gleicher Wirkung; ~ **amount** (or **sum**) Gegenwert

era, to inaugurate a new ~ e-e neue Ära einleiten

erasure ausradierte Stelle; Löschung; ~ **of data**[18] *(EDV)* Löschen von Daten

erection Aufstellung, Montage, Errichtung; Bau(-werk); ~ **insurance** Montageversicherung

ergonomical ergonomisch

ergonomics Ergonomie, Arbeitswissenschaft *(z.B. [psychologische] Arbeitsplatzgestaltung)*

errand Botengang, Besorgung; ~ **boy** Botenjunge; Laufbursche; **to run ~s** Botengänge machen

errata Druckfehler(verzeichnis)

erroneous irrig, irrtümlich, falsch; fehlerhaft; ~ **entry** irrige (od. fehlerhafte) Eintragung; ~ **in point of law** rechtsfehlerhaft; ~ **judgment** Fehlurteil *(gerichtl. Entscheidung unter Verletzung des geltenden Rechts)*

erroneously irrtümlicherweise; unrichtigerweise

error Irrtum, Fehler, Versehen; **in** ~ irrtümlich, versehentlich; **~s excepted** (E E.) Irrtümer vorbehalten; **~s and omissions excepted** (E. & O. E.) Irrtümer und Auslassungen vorbehalten; ~ **in communicating a declaration** Übermittlungsfehler; ~ **in fact** Tatsachenirrtum; ~ **in** → **form**; ~ **in judgment** falsche Beurteilung; Schreibfehler in e-m Urteil; ~ **in law** Rechtsirrtum; ~ **of conversion** Umrechnungsfehler; **amount paid in** ~ irrtümlich gezahlter Betrag; **clause reserving ~s** Irrtumsvorbehalt; **clerical** ~ Schreibfehler; Flüchtigkeitsfehler; **reversible** die Anfechtbarkeit *(e-s Urteils)* begründender Fehler; **to commit** (or **make**) **an** ~ e-n Irrtum begehen; e-n Fehler machen; **to correct an** ~ e-n Fehler berichtigen; **to induce an** ~ e-n Irrtum verursachen; **an ~ has occurred** ein Fehler ist unterlaufen; **to rectify an** ~ e-n Irrtum richtigstellen

escalate *v* eskalieren, stufenweise steigern

escalation Eskalation, stufenweise Steigerung;

Am Anpassung der Preise (Löhne) an gestiegene (Lebenshaltungs-)Kosten; *Am (stufenweises)* Heraufschrauben der eingesetzten militärischen Mittel und damit des Konflikts; Konfliktsausweitung; ~ **clause** →escalator clause; **de**~ *mil* De-Eskalation; stufenweiser Abbau der militärischen Operationen; →**price ~ clause**

escalator Rolltreppe; Indexlohn; ~ **clause** (Preis-, Lohn-)Gleitklausel, Indexklausel; Wertsicherungsklausel

escapable cost vermeidbare Kosten

escape Flucht; Entweichen, Entweichenlassen; Ausströmen *(von Gas etc)*; ~ **agent** *pol* Fluchthelfer; ~ **attempt** Fluchtversuch

escape clause Vorbehaltsklausel, Rücktrittsklausel, Schutzklausel

Sie erlaubt es, sich unter bestimmten Bedingungen von e-r Verpflichtung zu befreien, z. B. Rückgängigmachen von Zollzugeständnissen, wenn einheimische Erzeugung durch Höhe der Einfuhr gefährdet ist (z. B. Art. XIX des →GATT).

Am ss. 201 ff of the Trade Act of 1974, neugefaßt durch section 1401 des →Omnibus Trade and Competitiveness Act of 1988. Sie schreibt die Praktiken der International Trade Commission (ITC) zur Feststellung eines ernsthaften Schadens der heimischen Industrie vor. Nach section 1401 können Unternehmen, Gewerkschaften etc. bei der ITC Anträge stellen, die darauf gerichtet sind, eine Anpassung an den internationalen Wettbewerb zu ermöglichen

escape,~ **plan** Fluchtplan; ~ **from prison** Entweichen (od. Flucht) aus dem Gefängnis; ~ **route** Fluchtweg; ~ **warrant** Haftbefehl für e-n entwichenen Strafgefangenen; **aiding the ~ of a prisoner** (or **assisting ~ from prison**) Beihilfe zur Flucht e-s Gefangenen; **attempted** ~ Fluchtversuch; **danger** (or **risk**) **of** ~ Fluchtgefahr; **negligent** ~ fahrlässiges Entweichenlassen *(e-s Gefangenen)*; **to have a narrow** ~ gerade noch einmal davonkommen; **to make one's** ~ entweichen; **to permit the ~ of a prisoner** e-n Gefangenen entweichen lassen

escape *v* flüchten, entweichen, entkommen; ausströmen *(Gas etc)*; um etw. herum kommen; vermeiden; **to ~ abroad** ins Ausland flüchten; **to ~ from prison** aus dem Gefängnis entkommen; **suspected of attempting to** ~ fluchtverdächtig; **to make an attempt** (or **to try**) **to** ~ e-n Fluchtversuch unternehmen

escaped prisoner, to recapture (or **retake**) **an** ~ e-n entwichenen Gefangenen wieder festnehmen

escapee entwichener (od. entkommener) Gefangener

escheat Anfall des Nachlasses an den Staat; *Am* Heimfall herrenlosen Vermögens an den Staat

escheat *v (dem Staat)* anheimfallen; *(als Heimfallsgut)* einziehen; ~**ed estate** (or **property**) *Am* Heimfallsgut; ~**ed inheritance** *Am* dem Staat anheimgefallene Erbschaft

escheatage Heimfallsrecht

escort Eskorte, (Ehren-)Geleit, Begleitung; Geleitschutz; Geleitfahrzeug; ~ **vessel** Geleitschiff; **police** ~ Polizeieskorte, polizeiliche Bedeckung

escrow bei e-m Dritten *(als Treuhänder)* hinterlegte Vertragsurkunde, die erst bei Erfüllung e-r Bedingung in Kraft tritt; ~ **account** (or **deposit**) Treuhandkonto; ~ **bond** *Am* bei e-m Dritten *(als Treuhänder)* hinterlegte Obligation; ~ **grantee** Dritter; ~ **holder** Mittelsmann, Treuhänder *(dem z. B. die Auflassungsurkunde übergeben wird mit der Bestimmung, sie beim Tod des Übertragenden an e-n bestimmten Dritten weiterzugeben)*; **delivery in** ~ Hinterlegung von Urkunden zu treuen Händen *(bis zur Erfüllung e-r Bedingung)*; **to give in** ~ bei e-m Dritten *(als Treuhänder)* hinterlegen *(bis zur Erfüllung e-r Vertragsbedingung)*; **to hold in** ~ treuhänderisch verwalten

espionage Spionage; ~ **case** Spionagefall; ~ **trial** Spionageprozeß; **business** ~ Wirtschaftsspionage; **counter-**~ Gegenspionage, Spionageabwehr; **industrial** ~ Werkspionage, Wirtschaftspionage, Betriebsspionage; **suspected of** ~ spionageverdächtig; **to commit** ~ (or **to engage in** ~) Spionage begehen

Esprit *(EG)* →European Strategic Programme for Research and Development in Information Technology

Esq. (Esquire) Höflichkeitszusatz auf Briefen hinter dem Namen *(Br für Herren im allgemeinen, Am für bestimmte Beamte und Anwälte)*

essence das Wesentliche; **(in)**~ (im) wesentlich(en); ~ **of the case** Kernpunkt des Rechtsstreites; ~ **of a contract** wesentliche Vertragserfordernisse; **time is of (the) ~ of the contract** die fristgemäße Erfüllung durch e-e Vertragspartei ist Voraussetzung für das Verlangen der Erfüllung durch die andere Partei

essential 1. ~**s** die wesentlichen Punkte, das Wichtigste, Notwendigste; lebenswichtige Güter *(Nahrungsmittel, Rohstoffe etc)*; ~**s of a contract** wesentliche Vertragserfordernisse; ~**s of life** das Lebensnotwendige

essential 2. unbedingt erforderlich (od. notwendig) (to für); wesentlich; lebenswichtig; ~ **goods** lebenswichtige Güter *(→essentials)*; ~ **requirements** wesentliche Erfordernisse; **E~ Trade Routes** *Am* Liniendienste von besonderem volkswirtschaftlichen Wert; ~ **to the war effort** kriegswichtig; **to be an ~ component of sth.** e-n wesentlichen Bestandteil von etw. bilden

establish *v* gründen, errichten, einrichten, eröffnen; Begründung für etw. geben, nachweisen; Begründung für etw. sein, darstellen; *(jdn)* einsetzen (as als); **to ~ oneself** sich niederlassen, sich selbständig machen; **to ~ an agency** e-e Vertretung einrichten; **to ~ a business** ein Geschäft gründen (od. eröffnen); **to ~ a chair** *univ* e-n Lehrstuhl errichten; **to ~ a church** zur Staatskirche machen; **to ~ a claim** e-n Anspruch nachweisen (od. glaubhaft machen); **to ~ a claim to the title** Eigentumsnachweis erbringen; **to ~ a company** e-e Gesellschaft gründen; **to ~ a credit** e-n Kredit (od. ein Akkreditiv) eröffnen; **to ~ a domicile** ein Domizil begründen; **to ~ one's identity** seine Identität nachweisen; **to ~ one's interest in** sein Anrecht auf ... nachweisen; **to ~ a prima facie case** *(dem Gericht)* glaubhaft machen; **to ~ relations** Verbindungen herstellen; **to ~ a legal relationship** ein Rechtsverhältnis begründen; **to ~ a reputation as a lawyer** sich e-n Ruf (od. Namen) als Anwalt schaffen; **to ~ a rule** e-e Regel aufstellen; **to ~ to the satisfaction (of)** zufriedenstellenden Nachweis erbringen; glaubhaft machen; **before the court will consider the detailed provisions of the contract, the plaintiff must ~ his right of action** ehe das Gericht sich mit den einzelnen Vertragsbestimmungen befaßt, muß der Kläger sein Klagerecht begründen

established feststehend, bestehend, ständig *(opp. temporary)*; planmäßig *(Beamter)*; **well-~ business** gut eingeführte Firma; **~ church** Staatskirche *(Br Church of England, Scot Church of Scotland)*

established civil servant *Br* festangestellter (od. planmäßiger) Beamter; **to be appointed an ~** *Br* zum Beamten auf Lebenszeit ernannt werden

established, ~ customs seit langem bestehende Bräuche; **~ facts** feststehende Tatsachen; Tatbestand; **well-~ interpretation** feste Auslegung; **~ law** bestehendes (od. geltendes) Recht; **~ place of a company** *Br* Sitz e-r Gesellschaft; **~ practice** bestehender Brauch; ständige Rechtsprechung; **~ principles of law** bestehende Rechtsgrundsätze; **~ product** im Markt gut eingeführtes Produkt; **~ shares (stocks)** Standardaktien; **~ trader** etablierter (od. gut eingeführter) Kaufmann; **to be ~** feststehen *(Bräuche, Tatsachen etc)*, begründet sein; *(seit längerer Zeit)* bestehen; ansässig sein; **to be resident or ~** seinen Wohnsitz oder Geschäftssitz haben

establishing, the burden of ~ guilt is on the prosecution die Beweislast für die Schuld obliegt der Anklagevertretung

establishment Gründung, Errichtung, Eröffnung, Einrichtung; Unternehmen, Geschäft, Betrieb; Anstalt, Institut; *(großer)* Haushalt; Feststellung; Personalbestand, Planstellen; **the E~** das Establishment; **~ of an agency** *Am* Errichtung e-r Behörde; **~ (in a budget)** Stellenplan; **~ charges** direkte Kosten *(opp. overhead, oncost, indirect charges)*; **~ of a company** Errichtung e-r Gesellschaft; **~ of contact** Verbindungsaufnahme; **~ of credit** Krediteröffnung; **~ of damage** (or **loss**) Schadensnachweis; **~ of diplomatic relations** Aufnahme diplomatischer Beziehungen; **~ of education** Bildungsanstalt; **~ of a fact** Feststellung e-r Tatsache; **~ of a government** Bildung e-r Regierung; **~ of paternity** Vaterschaftsnachweis; **~ of a partnership** Begründung e-s Gesellschaftsverhältnisses; **~ plan** Stellenplan; **~ of a solicitor's practice** *Br* Eröffnung e-r Anwaltspraxis; Niederlassung als Anwalt; **~ of residence** Wohnsitzbegründung

establishment, branch ~ Zweigniederlassung; **business** (or **commercial**) **~** Geschäftsbetrieb; geschäftliche (od. gewerbliche) Niederlassung; **educational ~** Bildungsanstalt, Erziehungsanstalt; **freedom of ~** Niederlassungsfreiheit (→ *freedom*); **industrial ~** Industrieunternehmen; **large ~** Großbetrieb; Großunternehmen; **main ~** Hauptniederlassung; **manufacturing ~** Fabrikanlage; Fabrikationsbetrieb; **mediumsized ~** Mittelbetrieb; **military ~** stehendes Heer; Kriegsmacht; *Am* militärische Führungsschicht; **new ~** Geschäftsneugründung; **employees in non-agricultural ~s** in nichtlandwirtschaftlichen Betrieben beschäftigte Personen; **peace ~** *mil* Friedensstärke

establishment, permanent ~ Betriebsstätte; **permanent ~ profit** Betriebsstättengewinn; **state of the permanent ~** *(internationales SteuerR)* Betriebsstättenstaat; **to be effectively connected with the permanent ~** tatsächlich zur Betriebsstätte gehören

establishment, place within the ~ Planstelle; **research ~** Forschungsanstalt; **right of ~** Niederlassungsrecht; **separate ~** getrennter Haushalt; getrenntes Geschäft; **small ~** Kleinbetrieb; **war ~** Kriegsstärke; **to be on the ~** Planstelle haben; fest angestellt sein; **to keep (up) a large ~** ein großes Haus führen

estate Vermögen(smasse), *(gesetzl. od. testamentarischer)* Nachlaß, Erbmasse; Konkursmasse; Vermögen e-s wegen Geisteskrankheit Entmündigten (*für den ein receiver* [→*receiver 2.*] *bestellt ist*); Grundeigentum, Grundbesitz, Grundstück, Besitzung, (Land-)Gut; Eigentumsrecht, Besitzrecht *(bes. an unbeweglichem Vermögen)*; Rang, Stand, Klasse; **~ accounting** Nachlaßrechnungslegung; **~ agency** *Br* Grundstücksvermittlung, Immobilienbüro; ~

agent *Br* Grundstücksmakler; ~ **(of a deceased person)** Nachlaß; ~ **at sufferance** *Am* geduldeter Besitz *(nach Pachtablauf stillschweigend weitergewährtes Besitzrecht)*; ~ **at will** →tenancy at will; ~ **contract** *Br* Vertrag zur Begründung (od. Übertragung) e-s Eigentumsrechts an Immobilien *(e-s legal →~)*; Grundstückskaufvertrag; ~ **duty** *Br*[19] *(frühere)* Erbschaftssteuer; ~ **for life** →life ~; ~ **for a term of years** *Am* auf bestimmte Zeit festgelegtes Besitzrecht *(an Immobilien)*; ~ **in expectancy** *(bestehendes)* Recht auf den zukünftigen Erwerb von Rechten an Liegenschaften (insbes. Eigentum) *(das z. B. in e-m settlement [→settlement 3.] enthalten ist)*; dingliches Anwartschaftsrecht auf Liegenschaften; ~ **(in) fee simple** unbeschränkt vererbliches (od. veräußerliches) Grundeigentum; Volleigentum; ~ **in fee simple absolute in possession** höchstmögliches Grundeigentum; ~ **(in) fee tail** erbrechtlich gebundenes Grundeigentum *(auf Lebenszeit des Berechtigten und bestimmter Nachkommen; vergleichbar dem früheren deutschen Fideikommiß)*; ~ **in possession** Recht an Grundstücken, die man in Besitz hat; ~ **(in) tail** →~ in fee tail; ~ **in tail male (female)** nur an die männlichen (weiblichen) Erben vererblicher Grundbesitz; ~ **inventory** Nachlaßverzeichnis; ~ **less than freehold** zeitlich befristetes Besitzrecht *(z. B. einjährige Miete)*; ~ **management** Grundstücksverwaltung; Gutsbewirtschaftung; ~ **of inheritance** *Am* Nachlaß; **E~s of the Realm** *Br* die Reichsstände *(Lords Spiritual, Lords Temporal and Commons)*; ~ **owner** Inhaber e-s Rechts an Grundbesitz *(Eigentümer, Pächter oder Mieter)*; ~ **planning** Planung der Nachlaßabwicklung *(unter Berücksichtigung der erb- und familienrechtlichen sowie der steuerrechtlichen Folgen von letztwilligen Vermögensverfügungen)*; ~ **tax** *Am* Erbschaftsteuer, Nachlaßsteuer

estate, administration of an ~ →administration 1. und 2.; **assets of an** ~ Nachlaßgegenstände; **bankrupt's** ~ Konkursmasse; **claim against the** ~ Nachlaßforderung; Konkursforderung; **country** ~ Landgut; **creditor of the** ~ Nachlaßgläubiger; **curator of the** ~ *Am und Scot* Nachlaßpfleger; **debts of the** ~ Nachlaßverbindlichkeiten; Masseschulden *(im Konkurs)*; **deceased's** (or *Am* **decedent's**) ~ Nachlaß; **distribution of the** ~ Aufteilung des (Intestat-)-Nachlasses; Erbauseinandersetzung; →**equitable ~; family** ~ Familiengut, Familienbesitz; **fourth** ~ Presse; **general** ~ allgemeiner Nachlaß *(opp. trust property)*; **gross** ~ Bruttonachlaß; **housing** ~ (Wohn-)- Siedlung; **inventory of an** ~ Nachlaßverzeichnis; **landed** ~ Grundbesitz, Grundeigentum; **large** ~ großes Landgut; großer Nachlaß; großes Vermögen *(e-s Konkursschuldners od. Geisteskranken, für den ein →receiver ernannt worden ist)*; →**leasehold** ~

estate, legal ~ dingliches Recht an Immobilien

Bestellung und Übertragung erfolgt durch gesiegelten und von den Parteien unterzeichneten Vertrag. Formlose Bestellung oder Übertragung eines dinglichen Rechts an einem Grundstück läßt nur schwächeres →equitable interest (estate) entstehen.

Br Seit dem Law of Property Act 1925 gibt es nur noch zwei legal estates (in land): a) an →estate in fee simple absolute in possession, b) a →term of years absolute. Alle anderen estates sind nur →equitable interests

estate, →life ~; in the matter of the ~ (of) in der Nachlaßsache; **monetary proceeds of assets of the** ~ *Am* Summenlegat; **owner of an** ~ Inhaber e-s Rechts an Grundbesitz (→~ owner); Gutsbesitzer; **owner of large ~s** Großgrundbesitzer; **particular** ~ minderes Recht an Grundbesitz, an dem e-r dritten Person ein →remainder oder →reversion eingeräumt ist; **personal** ~ bewegliches Vermögen, Mobilien, Mobiliarvermögen; beweglicher Nachlaß; **private** ~ Siedlung mit Eigentumswohnungen; →**privity of** ~; →**real** ~; →**residuary** ~; **Royal** ~ *Br* Staatsdomäne; **separate** ~[20] Sondervermögen; Privatvermögen *(des Gesellschafters)*; *Am* Vorbehaltsgut *(der Ehefrau)*; **share in an** ~ Anteil an e-m Nachlaß; Erbteil; **(suburban) housing** ~ Stadtrandsiedlung; →**taxable** ~; **the Three E~s** *Br* →E~s of the Realm

estate, to be entitled to (a share in) an ~ erbberechtigt sein

estimate Schätzung, Überschlag, Voranschlag, Kosten(vor)anschlag; Abschätzung, Bewertung; Schätzwert; **the E~s** *Br parl (veranschlagter)* Etat; Haushaltsvoranschlag; ~ **of cost** Kostenvoranschlag; ~ **of damage** Schadenberechnung; ~ **of expenditure** Voranschlag der Ausgaben; Kostenvoranschlag; Ausgabenschätzung; ~ **of profits** Ertragsschätzung; **in accordance with the E~s** *Br* etatmäßig; **approximate** ~ annähernde Schätzung; **building** ~ Baukosten(vor)anschlag; **civil E~s** *Br parl* Voranschläge der Zivilausgaben; **conservative** ~ vorsichtige Schätzung; **defen|ce (~se) E~s** *Br parl* Voranschläge der Verteidigungsausgaben; **detailed ~s** ins einzelne gehende Voranschläge; **official** ~ amtliche Schätzung; **preliminary** ~ Kostenvoranschlag; **rough** ~ Überschlag, ungefährer Voranschlag; **at a rough** ~ nach ungefährer Schätzung, grob überschlagen; **supplementary E~s** *Br parl* Nachtragsetat; **to draw up the E~s** *Br* den Etat aufstellen; **to form an ~ of sth.** sich e-e Meinung von etw. bilden; **to give** (or **make**) **an** ~ e-n Voranschlag machen; veranschlagen; **to make a cost** ~ e-n Kostenvoranschlag machen

estimate *v* (ab)schätzen (at auf); veranschlagen (at auf); überschlagen; Kostenvoranschlag machen; **to ~ the cost of a new house at ...** die Kosten e-s neuen Hauses veranschlagen auf ...; **to ~ a loss** e-n Verlust abschätzen; **to ~ the**

value of land den Grundstückswert abschätzen

estimated (ab)geschätzt; voraussichtlich; ~ **amount** geschätzter (od. veranschlagter) Betrag; ~ **charges** Kostenvoranschlag; Spesenvoranschlag; ~ **cost(s)** geschätzte (od. voraussichtliche) Kosten; Vorgabekosten, Sollkosten; ~ **income** geschätztes Einkommen; ~ **time of arrival** (ETA) *(Luftverkehr)* voraussichtliche Ankunftszeit; ~ **time of departure** (ETD) *(Luftverkehr)* voraussichtliche Abflugszeit; *(Schiff)* voraussichtliche Auslaufzeit; ~ **value** geschätzter Wert, Schätzwert; Taxwert

estimation Schätzung; ~ **of cost** Vorkalkulation

estop *v* Rechtsverwirkung geltend machen; rechtshemmenden Einwand erheben *(dem Gegner sein früheres Verhalten [„venire contra factum proprium"] entgegenhalten)*

estopped, to be ~ *(durch früheres Verhalten)* gehindert sein *(e-e Tatsache zu behaupten oder zu verneinen od. ein Recht geltend zu machen)*; **to be** ~ **by deed** durch e-e urkundlich gegebene Erklärung an der Geltendmachung seines Rechts gehindert sein

estoppel Hinderung(sgrund); Rechtsverwirkung; rechtshemmender Einwand

Der anglo-amerikanische Begriff des estoppel bedeutet die Verwirkung des Rechts, einen Tatbestand oder eine Rechtslage geltend zu machen, da mit „Treu und Glauben" unvereinbar, z. B. weil in Widerspruch zu früherem Verhalten („venire contra factum proprium")

estoppel, ~ **by conduct** Verwirkung des Rechts, e-n zu früherem tatsächlichen Verhalten im Widerspruch stehenden Tatbestand (od. Rechtslage) geltend zu machen; ~ **by deed** Verwirkung des Einwands gegen den Inhalt e-r gesiegelten Urkunde; ~ **by judgment** Ausschluß der nochmaligen Prozeßführung über denselben Streitgegenstand *(Rechtskraftwirkung)*; ~ **in pais** *Am* estoppel, das sich im Grundstücksrecht auf nicht eingetragene Tatsachen bezieht *(opp. ~ by deed)*; *Br* →~ by conduct; ~ **by record** Verwirkung des Einwands auf Grund entgegenstehender Urteile, Protokolle oder Urkunden über den gleichen Sachverhalt; ~ **by representation** →representation 3.; ~ **by treaty** *(VölkerR)* Verwirkung des Rechts, e-e Tatsache zu behaupten, da in Widerspruch zu früher abgeschlossenem Vertrag; **agency** (or **authority**) **by** ~ durch schlüssiges Verhalten erteilte Vollmacht; Verwirkung des Einwands, daß e-e Vollmacht nicht bestehe; **collateral** ~ Aussschluß von Tatsachenbehauptungen und Einwendungen einer Partei, soweit sie den Feststellungen e-s früheren rechtskräftigen Urteils widersprechen *(Präklusionswirkung aufgrund materieller Rechtskraft e-s früheren Urteils; cf. ~ by judgment)*; **corporation by** ~ *Am* durch schlüssiges Verhalten entstandene Gesellschaft; Verwirkung des Einwands, daß e-e Gesellschaft nicht bestehe; **direct** ~ *Am* →res judicata; **equitable** ~ auf equity beruhendes estoppel *(~ in pais, ~ by conduct and promissory ~)*; **partnership by** ~ *Br* Gesellschaft kraft Rechtsscheins; **promissory** ~ Verwirkung des Rechts, e-e zu e-m früheren *(ohne consideration gegebenen)* Versprechen in Widerspruch stehende Forderung durch Klage geltend zu machen

estovers gesetzlich zugestandener Bedarf *(bes. Holzbedarf des Pächters)*; *Am* Unterhaltsanspruch der geschiedenen Frau; **common of** ~ Holzgerechtigkeit (→*common 1.)*

estray herrenloses (od. entlaufenes) Tier

estreat *Br* beglaubigte Abschrift aus e-m Gerichtsprotokoll *(bes. im Zusammenhang mit Geldstrafen)*

estrepe *Am* Wertminderung *(von Grundbesitz während der Pachtzeit)*

et al. (et alii) und andere (u. a.)

et seq. (et sequentes) und folgende (ff.)

ethical (berufs)ethisch; dem Berufsethos entsprechend; ~ **code** Berufsethos

ethics *(auf Moral begründete)* Verhaltensregeln; **legal** ~ Standespflichten der Juristen; **professional** ~ Standespflichten *(z. B. e-s Anwalts, Arztes)*; Berufsethos; **breach of professional** ~ standeswidriges Verhalten; **high standard of** ~ hohes sittliches Niveau

Ethiopia, the People's Democratic Republic of ~ die Demokratische Volksrepublik Äthiopien

Ethiopian Äthiopier(in); äthiopisch

ethnic ethnisch, völkisch; ~ **German** Volksdeutscher; ~ **group** Volksgruppe; ~ **heritage** völkisches Erbgut; **person of German** ~ **origin** Person deutscher Volkszugehörigkeit

etiquette Etikette; ~ **of the profession** (or **professional** ~) Regeln des standesüblichen Verhaltens *(bes. von Ärzten und Anwälten)*; **breach of** ~ Verstoß gegen die Etikette; **breach of professional** ~ standeswidriges Verhalten; **demands of** ~ Erfordernisse der Etikette

EUMETSAT →Convention for the Establishment of a European Organization for the Exploitation of Meteorological Satellites

Eurasian Eurasier(in); eurasisch

Euratom →European Atomic Energy Community; ~ **Supply Agency** Euratom-Versorgungsagentur; ~ **Treaty** Euratom-Vertrag

Eureka →European Research Coordination Agency

Eurobond Euroanleihe, Eurobond *(am Euro-Kapitalmarkt gehandelte Anleihe);* ~ **market** Euroanleihemarkt

Eurocapital market Eurokapitalmarkt (Euroanleihemarkt, Eurobondmarkt); ~ **issue** (or **borrowing**) Kapitalmarktanleihe

Markt für internationale Anleihen, die außerhalb des Landes, auf dessen Währung sie lauten, begeben werden

Eurocard Kreditkarte für bargeldlose Zahlungen bei allem dem System angeschlossenen Unternehmen *(Hotels, Restaurants, Geschäfte)*

Eurochemic →European Company for the Chemical Processing of Irradiated Nuclear Fuels

Euro-commercial-paper (ECP) *(neues Finanzierungsinstrument am Euromarkt)* kurzfristiges *(nicht börsengängiges)* Geldmarktpapier erstklassiger Emittenten, das am Euromarkt *(ohne Übernahmegarantie e-r Bank)* emittiert wird; ~ **facility** →Euronote facility

Eurocontrol →European Organization for the Safety of Air Navigation

Eurocrat *(leitender)* Beamter der Europäischen Gemeinschaften (EG)

Eurocredit market Euro-Kreditmarkt; **borrowing in the** ~ Eurokreditaufnahme

Eurocurrencies Eurodevisen

Eurocurrency Eurowährung *(Guthaben gehalten außerhalb des Währungslandes, z.B. DM in London);* ~ **funds** Eurodevisen; ~ **loan** Euroanleihe, Eurowährungskredit

Eurocurrency market Euro(geld)markt *(Markt für Bankguthaben der wichtigsten konvertierbaren Währungen der Welt);* **to have access to the** ~ Zugang zum Euro(geld)markt haben; **supply of funds on the** ~ Angebot am Euro(geld)markt

Eurodollar Eurodollar *(gehalten von Banken, Firmen od. Personen außerhalb der USA);* ~**bond** Eurodollarobligation; ~ **deposits** Eurodollar-Einlagen; ~ **loan** Eurodollar-Anleihe; ~ **market** Eurodollarmarkt, ~ **rate of interest** Eurodollar-Zinssatz; ~ **term lending** Eurodollar-Darlehen mit befristeter Laufzeit

Euro facilities Eurofazilitäten

Fazilitäten zur Absicherung des revolvierenden Absatzes von kurzfristigen Papieren im Euromarkt, z.B. →NIF, →RUF od. →Euronote facility

Eurofima[21] Eurofima (European Company for the Financing of Railway Rolling Stock) Europäische Gesellschaft für die Finanzierung von Eisenbahnmaterial

Euro issue (of bonds) Euroemission

Euromarket *(→Eurocurrency market und →Eurocapital market)* Euromarkt; ~ **interest rates** Euro(zins)sätze

Der Euromarkt umfaßt alle Geld- und Kreditgeschäfte in einer Währung, die nicht Landeswährung eines der beteiligten Geschäftspartners ist.

Wichtigste Euromarktzentren sind London, Luxemburg, Zürich und Paris.

Auf Grund der Dominanz des US-Dollars am Euromarktgeschehen wird der Euromarkt häufig als Eurodollarmarkt bezeichnet

Euromoney market Eurogeldmarkt

Euronote *(neues Finanzierungsinstrument am Euromarkt)* kurzfristiges Geldmarktpapier (Laufzeit 3–6 Monate) e-s erstklassigen Emittenten, das im Rahmen e-r →Euronote facility oder e-r →Eurocommercial-paper facility begeben wird

Euronote (standby) facility mittel- bis langfristige Kreditrahmenzusage e-s Bankenkonsortiums für die revolvierende Emission kurzfristiger Geldmarktpapiere am Euromarkt

In der Regel kann der Schuldner 5–10 Jahre lang flexibel wiederholt Euronotes mit 1–6 Monaten Laufzeit begeben. Bei Nichtplazierung am Markt übernimmt das Bankenkonsortium diese Papiere oder gewährt entsprechend Kredit

Europe Europa; **building of** ~ Aufbau Europas

Europe, Council of ~ (CE) Europarat *(Sitz:* Straßburg); **General Agreement on Privileges and Immunities of the Council of** ~[22] Allgemeines Abkommen über die Vorrechte und Befreiungen des Europarats

Europe, Economic Commission for ~ (ECE) Wirtschaftskommission (der UNO) in Europa *(Sitz:* Genf)

Europe, a people's ~ *(EG)* Europa der Bürger

European Act, →**Single** ~

European Agreement Concerning the International Carriage of Dangerous Goods by Road[23] (ADR) Europäisches Übereinkommen über die internationale Beförderung gefährlicher Güter über die Straße

European Agreement Concerning the Provision of Medical Care to Persons during Temporary Residence[23a] Europäisches Übereinkommen über die Gewährung ärztlicher Betreuung an Personen bei vorübergehendem Aufenthalt

European Agreement Concerning the Work of Crews of Vehicles Engaged in International Road Transport[23b] (AETR) Europäisches Übereinkommen über die Arbeit des im Internationalen Straßenverkehr beschäftigten Fahrpersonals (AETR)

European Agreement of Continued Payment of Scholarships to Students Studying Abroad[24] Europäisches Übereinkommen über die Fortzahlung von Stipendien an Studierende im Ausland

European Agreement on the Instruction and Training of Nurses[24a] Europäisches Übereinkommen über die theoretische und praktische Ausbildung von Krankenschwestern und Krankenpflegern

European Agreement on Main International Railway Lines (AGC)[24b] Europäisches Übereinkommen über die Hauptlinien des internationalen Eisenbahnverkehrs (AGC)

European Agreement on Main International Traffic Arteries (AGR)[24c] Europäisches Übereinkommen über die Hauptstraßen des internationalen Verkehrs (AGR)

European Agreement for the Prevention of Broadcasts Transmitted from Stations outside National Territories[25] Europäisches Übereinkommen zur Verhütung von Rundfunksendungen, die von Sendestellen außerhalb der staatlichen Hoheitsgebiete gesendet werden

European Agreement on the Protection of Television Broadcasts[26] Europäisches Abkommen zum Schutz von Fernsehsendungen

European Agreement Relating to Persons Participating in Proceedings of the European Commission and Court of Human Rights[26a] Europäisches Übereinkommen über die am Verfahren vor der Europäischen Kommission und dem Europäischen Gerichtshof für Menschenrechte teilnehmenden Personen

European Agreement on the Restriction of the Use of Certain Detergents in Washing and Cleaning Products[27] Europäisches Übereinkommen über die Beschränkung bestimmter Detergentien in Wasch- und Reinigungsmitteln

European Agreement on Road Markings[27a] Europäisches Übereinkommen über Straßenmarkierungen

European Agreement(s) on Social Security[27b] Europäische(s) Abkommen über Soziale Sicherheit

European Agreement Supplementing the Convention on Road Traffic[27c] Europäisches Zusatzübereinkommen über den Straßenverkehr

European Agricultural Guidance and Guarantee Fund (EAGGF) *(EG)* Europäischer Ausrichtungs- und Garantiefonds für die Landwirtschaft (EAGFL)

European article number (→EAN) Europäische Artikelnummer (EAN)

European Atomic Energy Community (EAEC)[28] Europäische Atomgemeinschaft (EAG) (Euratom) (*Sitz:* Brüssel) (→*European Communities*)

European Atomic Energy Society (EAES) Europäische Atomenergie-Gesellschaft

European Atomic Forum (FORATOM) Europäisches Atomforum (FORATOM)

European Broadcasting Agreement Europäisches Rundfunkabkommen

European carnet *(EG) (Zoll)* Warenverkehrscarnet

European Centre for Medium-Range Weather Forecasts[28a] Europäisches Zentrum für mittelfristige Wettervorhersage

European Charter of Local Self-Government[28b] Europäsiche Charta der kommunalen Selbstverwaltung

European Coal and Steel Community (ECSC)[29] Europäische Gemeinschaft für Kohle und Stahl (EGKS) (Montanunion) (*Sitz:* Luxemburg) (→*European Communities*)

European Code of Social Security[30] Europäische Ordnung der Sozialen Sicherheit

European Commission for the Control of Foot-and-Mouth Disease[30a] Europäische Kommission zur Bekämpfung der Maul- und Klauenseuche

European Commission on Human Rights[30b] Europäische Kommission für Menschenrechte (→*human rights*)

European Committee for Standardization (CEN) Europäisches Komitee für Normung (CEN)

European Communities (EC) (EEC, ECSC, EAEC) Europäische Gemeinschaften (EG), (EWG, EGKS, EAG); ~ **Act,** 1972 *Br* Gesetz über die Angleichung des englischen Rechts an das EG-Recht *(bindet die englischen Gerichte grundsätzlich an die Entscheidungen des EuGH);* **Institutions of the** ~ Organe der EG *(Commission, Council [of Ministers]), European Parliament, Court of Justice);* **law of the** ~ Europarecht
Die Europäische Gemeinschaft (EG) ist eine supranationale Organisation, zu der sich 12 Staaten zusammengeschlossen haben (Belgien, Bundesrepublik Deutschland, Dänemark, Frankreich, Griechenland, Großbritannien und Nordirland, Irland, Italien, Luxemburg, Niederlande, Portugal und Spanien), bestehend aus der →European Economic Community, →European Coal and Steel Community und →European Atomic Energy Commission

European Company *(geplante)* europäische Aktiengesellschaft (Societas Europea)

European Company for the Chemical Processing of Irradiated Nuclear Fuels (Eurochemic)[31] Europäische Gesellschaft für die chemische Wiederaufbereitung bestrahlter Kernstoffe (*Sitz:* Mol/Belgien)

European Computer Manufacturers Association (ECMA) Vereinigung europäischer Computerhersteller (in Genf)

European Confederation of Trade Unions Europäischer Gewerkschaftsbund (EGB) *(1973 gegründet. Umfaßt 17 Gewerkschaftsorganisationen aus 14 europäischen Ländern)*

European Conference of Ministers of Transport (CEMT)[31a] Europäische Konferenz der Verkehrsminister (EKVM)

European Convention on the Abolition of Legalisation of Documents Executed by Diplomatic Agents or Consular Officers[32] Europäisches Übereinkommen zur Befreiung der von diplomatischen und konsularischen Vertretern errichteten Urkunden von der Legalisation

European Convention on the Academic Recognition of University Qualifications[32a] Europäisches Übereinkommen über die Anerkennung von akademischen Graden und Hochschulzeugnissen

European Convention on the Adoption of Children[32b] Europäisches Übereinkommen über die Adoption von Kindern

European Convention on Compulsory Insurance against Civil Liability in Respect of Motor Vehicles[33] Europäisches Übereinkommen über die obligatorische Haftpflichtversicherung für Kraftfahrzeuge

European Convention on the Control of the Acquisition and Possession of Firearms by Individuals[33a] Europäisches Übereinkommen über die Kontrolle des Erwerbs und des Besitzes von Schußwaffen durch Einzelpersonen

European Convention on Customs Treatment of Pallets Used in International Transport[33b] Europäisches Übereinkommen über die Zollbehandlung von Paletten, die im internationalen Verkehr verwendet werden

European Convention on the Equivalence of Diplomas Leading to Admission to Universities[34] Europäische Konvention über die Gleichwertigkeit der Reifezeugnisse

European Convention on the Equivalence of Period of University Study[34a] Europäisches Übereinkommen über die Gleichwertigkeit der Studienzeit an den Universitäten

European Convention on Establishment[35] Europäisches Niederlassungsabkommen

European Convention on Extradition[36] Europäisches Auslieferungsübereinkommen

European Convention on Information on Foreign Law[37] Europäisches Übereinkommen betr. Auskünfte über ausländisches Recht

European Convention on the International Classification of Patents for Invention[38] Europäische Übereinkunft über die Internationale Patentklassifikation

European Convention on International Commercial Arbitration[39] Europäisches Übereinkommen über die Internationale Handelsschiedsgerichtsbarkeit

European Convention on Jurisdiction and Enforcement of Judgment in Civil and Commercial Matters[39a] Europäisches Gerichtsstands- und Vollstreckungsübereinkommen in Zivil- und Handelssachen

European Convention on Mutual Assistance in Criminal Matters[39b] Europäisches Übereinkommen über die Rechtshilfe in Strafsachen

European Convention on the Obtaining Abroad of Information and Evidence in Administrative Matters[39c] Europäisches Übereinkommen über die Erlangung von Auskünften und Beweisen in Verwaltungssachen im Ausland

European Convention for the Peaceful Settlement of Disputes[40] Europäisches Übereinkommen zur friedlichen Beilegung von Streitigkeiten

European Convention for the Protection of Animals during International Transport[41] Europäisches Übereinkommen über den Schutz von Tieren beim internationalen Transport

European Convention for the Protection of Animals Kept for Farming Purposes[41a] Europäisches Übereinkommen zum Schutz von Tieren in landwirtschaftlichen Tierhaltungen

European Convention for the Protection of Animals for Slaughter[41b] Europäisches Übereinkommen über den Schutz von Schlachttieren

European Convention on the Protection of Archaeological Heritage[41c] Europäisches Übereinkommen zum Schutze archäologischen Kulturgutes

European Convention on the Service Abroad of Documents Relating to Administrative Matters[41d] Europäisches Übereinkommen über die Zustellung von Schriftstücken in Verwaltungssachen im Ausland

European Convention on Social and Medical Assistance[42] Europäisches Fürsorgeabkommen

European Convention on the Suppression of Terrorism[42a] Europäisches Übereinkommen zur Bekämpfung des Terrorismus

European Cooperation on Scientific and Technical Research (COST) Europäische Zusammenarbeit auf dem Gebiet der wissenschaftlichen und technischen Forschung (COST)

European Council Europäischer Rat *(Staats- und Regierungschefs der Mitgliedstaaten der EG)*

European Court →Court of Justice of the European Communities

European Court of Human Rights[42b] Europäischer Gerichtshof für Menschenrechte *(→court)*

European Cultural Convention[43] Europäisches Kulturabkommen

European Cultural Foundation Europäische Kulturstiftung

European Currency Unit (ECU) Europäische Währungseinheit (EWE) *(→ECU)*
Kernstück des Europäischen Währungssystems. Sie stellt einen Währungskorb dar, in dem die EWS-Währungen rechnerisch zusammengefaßt sind

European Development Fund (EDF)[43a] *(EG)* Europäischer Entwicklungsfonds (EEF)
Der EDF ist das wichtigste Instrument der EG, um ihre Politik der Finanzierung wirtschaftlicher und sozialer Investitionsprojekte und technische Hilfe für die AASMM sowie einige überseeische Länder und Gebiete zu verwirklichen. Die Mittel des EDF werden zum größten Teil in Form nichtrückzahlbarer Zuschüsse gewährt

European Directive on Product Liability *(EG)* Europäische Produkthaftpflichtrichtlinie

European Economic Community[44] (EEC) Europäische Wirtschaftsgemeinschaft (EWG) *(Sitz:* Brüssel) *(→European Communities)*

European Economic Interest Grouping (EEIG)[44a] Europäische Wirtschaftliche Interessenvereinigung (EWIV)
European election(s) Europawahl(en)
European emergency health card *(EG)* europäische Notfall-Gesundheitskarte
European Energy Data Base (EEDB) Europäische Energiedatenbank (EEDB)
European Environmental Bureau Europäisches Umweltbüro
European, ~ flag *(EG)* Europaflagge; **~ Foundation** Europäische Stiftung
European Free Trade Association (EFTA) Europäische Freihandelsassoziation *(→EFTA)*
European Goods Train Timetable Conference Europäische Güterzug-Fahrplankonferenz
European Investment Bank (EIB)[45] Europäische Investitionsbank (EIB)
(*Sitz:* Luxemburg) *(Mitglieder:* die 12 Mitgliedstaaten der EG*)*
Hauptaufgabe der EIB ist es, durch Gewährung von Darlehen und Bürgschaften die Finanzierung von Investitionsvorhaben in den Bereichen Industrie, Energieversorgung und Infrastruktur zu erleichtern
European Metalworkers' Federation (EMF) Europäischer Metallarbeiterverband (EMV)
European Molecular Biology, ~ Conference (EMBC) Europäische Molekularbiologiekonferenz; **~ Laboratory** (EMBL) Europäisches Laboratorium für Molekularbiologie; **~ Organization**[46] (EMBO) Europäische Molekularbiologieorganisation
European Monetary Cooperation Fund (EMCF) Europäischer Fonds für währungspolitische Zusammenarbeit (EFWZ)
European Monetary System (EMS) Europäisches Währungssystem (EWS)
Kern dieses Systems ist die Einführung der ECU und darauf bezogene Leitkurse für alle EG-Währungen
European Nuclear Energy Agency (ENEA) Europäische Kernenergie-Agentur (EKA) (Organ der →OECD) (*Sitz:* Paris)
European Nuclear Energy Tribunal[47] (ENET) Europäischer Kernenergie-Gerichtshof
European Nuclear Research Centre Europäisches Atomforschungszentrum
European Options Exchange (EOE) Europäische Optionsbörse (*Sitz:* Amsterdam)
European Organization for the Exploitation of Meteorological Satellites (EUMETSAT)[47a] Europäische Organisation für die Nutzung von meteorologischen Satelliten (EUMETSAT)
European Organization for Nuclear Research[48] (CERN) Europäische Organisation für Kernphysikalische Forschung (*Sitz:* Genf)
European Organization for the Safety of Air Navigation[49] (Eurocontrol) Europäische Organisation zur Sicherung der Luftfahrt (*Sitz:* Brüssel)
European Organization of the World Confederation of Labour Europäische Organisation des Weltverbandes der Arbeitnehmer (WVA)
European Outline Convention on Transfrontier Co-operation between Territorial Communities or Authorities[50] Europäisches Rahmenübereinkommen über die grenzüberschreitende Zusammenarbeit zwischen Gebietskörperschaften
European Parliament Europäisches Parlament (EP) *(Versammlung der Europäischen Gemeinschaften; →European Communities)*; **direct election to the ~** Direktwahl des Europäischen Parlaments
European patent[51] europäisches Patent
European patent application europäische Patentanmeldung; **description, claims or drawings of the ~** Beschreibung, Patentansprüche oder Zeichnungen der e. P.; **documents making up the ~** Unterlagen der e. P. *(request, description, claims, drawings and abstract Antrag, Beschreibung, Patentansprüche, Zeichnungen und Zusammenfassung)*; **filing of the ~** Einreichung der e. P.; **date of filing of the ~** Datum der e. P.; **refusal of the ~** Zurückweisung der e. P.; **renewal fees for the ~** Jahresgebühren für die e. P.; **subject matter of the ~** Gegenstand der e. P.; **text of the ~** Wortlaut der e. P.; **to refuse the ~** die e. P. zurückweisen; **the ~ has been finally refused** die e. P. ist rechtskräftig zurückgewiesen worden; **to withdraw the ~** die e. P. zurücknehmen
European Patent, ~ Bulletin Europäisches Patentblatt; **~ Convention** (Convention on the Grant of the European Patents)[52] Europäisches Patentübereinkommen (Übereinkommen über die Erteilung europäischer Patente)
European Patent Office (EPO)[53] Europäisches Patentamt (EPA); **Official Journal of the ~** Amtsblatt des Europäischen Patentamts; **premises of the ~** Dienstgebäude des Europäischen Patentamtes
European Patent Organisation[54] Europäische Patentorganisation
Organe: das Europäische Patentamt (European Patent Office), der Verwaltungsrat (Administrative Council). Die Organisation hat die Aufgabe, die europäischen Patente zu erteilen. Diese Aufgabe wird vom Europäischen Patentamt durchgeführt, dessen Tätigkeit vom Verwaltungsrat überwacht wird
European patent specification europäische Patentschrift
European patent, certificate for a ~ Urkunde über das europäische Patent
European patent, grant of the ~ Erteilung des europäischen Patents; **Convention on the Grant of ~s** Übereinkommen über die Erteilung europäischer Patente (→European Patent Convention); **fee for grant of the ~** Erteilungsgebühr; **request for the grant of a ~** Antrag auf Erteilung e-s europäischen Patents

European patent, maintenance of the ~ Aufrechterhaltung des e. P.; **opposing the ~** Einspruch gegen das e. P.; **person entitled to apply for and obtain an ~** zur Erreichung und Erlangung des Europäischen Patents berechtigte Person; **Register of ~s** Europäisches Patentregister *(→register)*; **revocation of the ~** Widerruf des e. P.; **specification of the ~** europäische Patentschrift

European patent, term of the ~ Laufzeit des e. P.; **the term of the ~ shall be 20 years as from the date of filing of the application** die Laufzeit des e. P. beträgt 20 Jahre vom Anmeldetag an; **transfer of the ~** Rechtsübergang des europäischen Patents

European patent, to grant the ~ das e. P. erteilen; **to give notice to ... of opposition to the ~ granted** gegen das erteilte europäische Patent Einspruch einlegen bei ...; **the ~ has been revoked in opposition proceedings** das e. P. ist im Einspruchsverfahren widerrufen worden

European Pharmacopoeia Commission[54a] Europäische Arzneibuchkommission

European Plant Protection Organization[54b] (EPPO) Europäische Pflanzenschutzorganisation

European Productivity Agency (EPA) Europäische Produktivitätszentrale (EPZ) *(Organ der OECD)*

European qualifying examination Europäische Eignungsprüfung *(als Vertreter vor dem Europ. Patentamt)*

European Regional Development Fund (ERDF) Europäischer Regionalfonds, Europäischer Fonds für regionale Entwicklung (EFRE)

European Research Coordination Agency (Eureka) Europäsiche Behörde für Koordinierung in der Forschung (Eureka) *(Europäische Technologiegemeinschaft. Dritte Computer-Großmacht neben Amerika und Japan)*

European Research and Development Committee (ERDC) *(EG)* Europäischer Ausschuß für Forschung und Entwicklung (EAFE)

European schools[54c] Europäische Schulen; **setting up of ~** Gründung europäischer Schulen; **Statute for ~ Establishing Regulations for the European Baccalaureate** Satzung der Europäischen Schulen über die Prüfungsordnung der Europäischen Reifeprüfung

European Science Foundation Europäische Wissenschaftsstiftung *(45 wissenschaftliche Einrichtungen aus 15 europäischen Ländern) (Sitz:* Straßburg)

European search report *(PatR)* europäischer Recherchenbericht; **drawing up of the ~** Erstellung des europäischen Recherchenberichts

European Social Budget *(EG)* Europäisches Sozialbudget *(wichtiges Informationsmittel für die Sozialpolitik der Gemeinschaft)*

European Social Charter[55] Europäische Sozialcharta

European Social Fund (ESF)[56] Europäischer Sozialfonds (ESF); **to receive assistance from the ~** Zuschüsse aus dem Europäischen Sozialfonds erhalten

European Society for Opinion and Marketing Research (ESOMAR) Europäische Gesellschaft für Meinungs- und Marktforschung

European Society for Radiation Protection Europäische Strahlenschutzgesellschaft

European Space Agency[57] (ESA) Europäische Weltraumorganisation (EWO); **Convention for the Establishment of a ~**[57a] Übereinkommen zur Gründung einer Europäischen Weltraumorganisation

European Strategic Programme for Research and Development in Information Technology (Esprit) Europäsches Strategieprogramm für Forschung und Entwicklung auf dem Gebiet der Informationstechnologie

European system for the grant of patents europäisches Patenterteilungsverfahren

European System of Integrated Economic Accounts (ESA) Europäisches System der volkswirtschaftlichen Gesamtrechnungen (ESVG)

Eureopean Telecommunications Satellite Organization (EUTELSAT)[57b] Europäische Fernmeldesatelliten-Organisation (EUTELSAT)

Ihr gehören 16 europäische Länder, darunter die 12 Mitgliedstaaten der EG an

European Trade Union Confederation (ETUC) Europäischer Gewerkschaftsbund (EGB)

European Travel Operators (ETO) gemeinsames Dienstleistungsnetz von 14 europäischen Reisebüros

European unit of account (EUA) *(EG)* Europäische Rechnungseinheit (ERE) *(ersetzt durch →ECU am 1. 1. 1981)*

European University Institute[57c] Europäisches Hochschulinstitut *(in Florenz)*

European Venture Capital Associaton (EVCA) Europäische Vereinigung für Risikokapital (EVCA)

Gegründet 1988. Sie fördert Gründung und Expansion von Firmen, die e-e europäische Dimension anstreben

European Wagon Community (EUROP) Europäische Güterwagengemeinschaft

European Waste Data Bank (EWADAT) Europäische Datenbank für Abfallwirtschaft

europeanize *v* europäisieren

Eurosterling Eurosterling, Europfund *(gehalten außerhalb Englands)*

EUTELSAT →European Telecommunications Satellite Organization; ~ **Space Segment**[57d] EUTELSAT-Weltraumsegment

euthanasia Euthanasie, Sterbehilfe

evacuate *v (Bevölkerung)* evakuieren; aussiedeln; *(Gebiet)* räumen; *(Betrieb)* verlagern

evacuation Evakuierung *(der Bevölkerung);* Aussiedlung; Räumung *(e-s Gebietes);* (Betriebs-)Verlagerung

evacuee Evakuierter; Aussiedler

evade *v* ausweichen; sich entziehen; vermeiden, umgehen (doing sth. etw. zu tun); **to ~ one's creditors** sich seinen Gläubigern entziehen; **to ~ customs duties** Zoll hinterziehen, Zollhinterziehung begehen; **to ~ a decision** e-r Entscheidung ausweichen; **to ~ military service** den Militärdienst umgehen; **to ~ payment** Zahlung umgehen; sich e-r Zahlungspflicht entziehen; **to ~ punishment** sich der Bestrafung entziehen; **to ~ regulations** Bestimmungen umgehen; **to ~ taxes** Steuern hinterziehen

evaluate *v* bewerten, (ab)schätzen; auswerten; würdigen, beurteilen; **to ~ evidence** Beweis würdigen

evaluation Bewertung, Wertung, (Ab-)Schätzung; Wertberechnung, Wertbestimmung; *(MMF)* Auswertung *(des Erhebungsmaterials);* **~ basis** Bewertungsgrundlage, Bemessungsgrundlage; **~ of evidence** Beweiswürdigung; **output ~** Leistungsbewertung

Evangelics *Br* Mitglieder der →Low Church

evasion Ausweichen; Sichentziehen; Umgehung, Vermeiden; Ausflucht; **~ of customs duties** Zollhinterziehung; **~ of a law** Umgehung e-s Gesetzes; **~ of taxes** *(unerlaubte)* Steuervermeidung (→*tax*); **draft ~** *Am* Umgehung des Militärdienstes; **fiscal ~**[58] *(unerlaubte)* Steuervermeidung; Steuerhinterziehung, Steuerverkürzung; **to use ~s** Ausflüchte machen

evasive ausweichend; **~ action** Ausweichmanöver

even *v* (ein)ebnen; gleichmachen; **to ~ up** ausgleichen, zu e-m Ausgleich kommen; *(Börse)* glattstellen

evening up *(Börse)* Glattstellung

even gleich; *(Zahl)* gerade *(opp. odd); (Zahlen-, Maßangabe)* genau; *colloq.* quitt; **(at) ~** *Br (Börse)* ohne Berechnung von Report- und Deportspesen; glatt; **of ~ date** gleichen Datums; **~-handed** unparteiisch; **~ lot** *Am* Aktienpaket mit durch 100 teilbarem Nennwert *(opp. round lot);* **~ running** *(Qualität)* gleichlaufend, gleichmäßig; **to get ~ with sb.** *fig* mit jdm abrechnen

evening courses Abendkurse *(→further education)*

event Ereignis, Fall; Ausgang, Ergebnis; **in the ~ of his death** im Falle seines Todes; **~ insured** Versicherungsfall; **in the ~ of war** im Falle e-s Krieges; **current ~s** Tagesereignisse, politische Ereignisse; **inevitable ~** unabwendbares Ereignis; **social ~s** Veranstaltungen; **table of ~s** Festprogramm, Veranstaltungsprogramm

eventuality Eventualität, Eventualfall; mögliches Ereignis

evict *v (Mieter, Pächter) (im Wege der Zwangsvollstreckung)* zur Räumung zwingen, heraussetzen; *(auf Grund e-s Titels)* Zwangsräumung betreiben

eviction Zwangsräumung; Heraussetzung *(e-s Pächters, Mieters);* **~ order** *Am* Räumungsurteil; **~ proceedings** Räumungsverfahren; **actual ~** tatsächliche Heraussetzung; **action of ~** *Am* Räumungsklage; **protection from** (or **against**) **~** Kündigungsschutz; **to sue for ~** *Am* auf Räumung klagen; **the court made an order for ~** *Am* das Gericht erkannte auf Räumung

evidence *(gerichtl. od. außergerichtl.)* Beweis(e); Beweismittel, Beweismaterial; Nachweis; *(beeidigte)* Zeugenaussage, Zeugnis

evidence, to admit in ~ e-m Beweisantrag stattgeben; als Beweis zulassen *(opp. to reject ~);* **to be ~ (of)** *(etw.)* beweisen; Beweismittel sein (für); **to be in ~** zutage treten, sichtbar werden; **to be used in ~** als Beweis verwendet werden; **to bear ~** Zeugnis ablegen; den Nachweis erbringen; **to collect fresh ~** neues Beweismaterial sammeln; **to evaluate ~** Beweis würdigen; **to furnish ~ (of)** Beweis erbringen (od. liefern) (für); beweisen; den Nachweis erbringen; **to give ~ of sth.** etw. unter Beweis stellen; über etw. *(als Zeuge)* aussagen; **to give ~ against (for) sb.** gegen (für) jdn aussagen; **to give ~ as a witness** als Zeuge aussagen; **to give ~ (up)on oath** eidlich aussagen; **to refuse to give ~** die Aussage verweigern; **right to refuse to give ~** Zeugnisverweigerungsrecht; **refusal to give ~** Aussageverweigerung; **to hear ~** Beweis aufnehmen; Beweisaufnahme vornehmen; Aussage hören (s. *hearing of* →~); **to introduce ~** Beweis antreten; **to offer in ~** als Beweis(-stück) vorlegen; **to produce** (or **present**) **~** Beweis antreten (od. erbringen); Nachweis erbringen; **to put in ~** als Beweis vorbringen; **to receive in ~** als beweiskräftig anerkennen; **to record ~** Beweis(aufnahme) protokollieren; **to submit ~** Beweis(e) antreten (od. erbringen); **he submitted ~ to establish the truth of his allegation** er trat Beweis für die Wahrheit seiner Behauptung an; **the document was submitted in ~** die Urkunde wurde zum Beweis vorgelegt; **to sum up ~** das Ergebnis der Beweisaufnahme zusammenfassen (→*summing up*); **supported by** ~ durch Beweismaterial belegt; **to take** ~ Beweis aufnehmen (od. erheben); Zeugenaussagen hören; **to take sb.'s** ~ jdn als Zeugen vernehmen; **facts in respect of which** ~ **is to be taken** Tatsachen, über die Beweis erhoben werden soll; **to order** ~ **to be taken** die Beweisaufnahme anordnen; **to tender** ~ s. to submit →~; **to weigh (the)** ~ Beweis würdigen

evidence, ~ **(given) by affidavit** schriftlich beeidete Zeugenaussage *(opp. parol ~)*; ~ **by →deposition;** ~ **by expert opinion** Beweis durch Sachverständige(n); ~ **for the defence (~se)** Entlastungsbeweis; ~ **for the prosecution** *(Strafprozeß)* belastendes Beweismaterial; ~ **of debt** Beweismittel für die Schuld *(e.g. IOU)*; ~ **of health** Gesundheitsnachweis; ~ **of ownership** Eigentumsnachweis; ~ **of service** Zustellungsnachweis; ~ **of title** Beweisurkunde über Eigentumsrechte *(im Grundstücksrecht)*; ~ **to the contrary** Gegenbeweis

evidence, admissible ~ zulässiger Beweis; **as** ~ **that** als Beweis (od. Nachweis) dafür, daß; **best** ~ primärer Beweis *(opp. secondary ~)*; **circumstantial** ~ Indizienbeweis; **conclusive** ~ schlüssiger Beweis; **conflicting** (or **contradicting**) ~ sich widersprechende Beweise (od. Zeugenaussagen); **corroborating** (or **corroborative**) ~ bestätigende Zeugenaussage; **criminal** ~ Beweismittel im Strafverfahren; **cumulative** ~ verstärkender Beweis; **direct** ~ unmittelbarer Beweis *(aus eigener Wahrnehmung)*; **documentary** ~ Urkundenbeweis, Beweis durch Urkunden; **expert** ~ Sachverständigenbeweis; **external** ~ s. extrinsic →~; **extrinsic** ~ Ergänzungs- od. Gegenbeweis zu e-m Urkundenbeweis *(gerichtet auf Klarstellung, Änderung oder Widerlegung des Gedankeninhalts der vorgelegten Beweisurkunde)*; **false** ~ falsche Zeugenaussage; **fresh** ~ neues Beweismaterial; **hearsay** ~ Beweis vom Hörensagen, mittelbarer Beweis; **inadmissible** ~ unzulässiger Beweis; **incriminating** ~ belastendes Beweismaterial; **indirect** ~ mittelbarer Beweis; **intrinsic** ~ reiner Urkundenbeweis *(ohne jede Ergänzung von außerhalb der Urkunde; cf. extrinsic ~)*; **King's** ~ s. Queen's →~; **oral** (or **parol**) ~ mündlicher Beweis; Beweis durch Zeugenaussagen *(opp. ~ by affidavit)*; **presumptive** ~ Indizienbeweis; **prima facie** ~ *(widerlegbarer)* Beweis des ersten Anscheins; **primary** ~ primäres Beweismittel, Beweismittel erster Ordnung *(opp. secondary ~, hearsay ~)*; **primary (documentary)** ~ Urkundenbeweis *(durch Vorlage der Originalurkunde)*

evidence, Queen's ~ *Br* (Aussage des) Kronzeuge(n), Belastungszeuge(n) *(der gegen Zusicherung der Straffreiheit gegen seine Mitschuldigen aussagt)*; **to turn Queen's** ~ als Kronzeuge auftreten, gegen seine Mitschuldigen aussagen

evidence, real ~ (Beweis durch) Augenscheineinnahme

evidence, rebuttal ~ *Am* (**rebutting** ~ *Br*) Gegenbeweis; **to produce rebuttal** ~ den Gegenbeweis führen

evidence, satisfactory ~ ausreichender Beweis; **second-hand** ~ Beweis aus zweiter Hand; **secondary** ~ sekundäres Beweismittel *(opp. primary ~)*; **secondary (documentary)** ~ indirekter Urkundenbeweis *(der Inhalt der Urkunde wird anders als durch die Urkunde selbst bewiesen)*

evidence, skilled ~ Sachverständigenbeweis; **State's** ~ *(Strafprozeß) Am* (Aussage des) Staatszeuge(n), Belastungszeuge(n) *(der gegen Zusicherung der Straffreiheit gegen seine Mitschuldigen aussagt)*; **substantial** ~ hinreichender Beweis; **sufficient** ~ hinreichender (od. ausreichender) Beweis; **sworn** ~ eidliche Zeugenaussage; **written** ~ schriftlicher Beweis (→*affidavit oder →deposition*)

evidence, in the absence of ~ mangels Beweises; **admissibility of** ~ Zulässigkeit von Beweismitteln; **on the basis of the** ~ auf Grund des Beweismaterials; **at the conclusion of the** ~ nach Abschluß der Beweisaufnahme; **consideration of** ~ Beweiswürdigung; **in default of** ~ mangels Beweises; **evaluation of** ~ Beweiswürdigung; **giving of** ~ Beweisantritt; Zeugenaussage

evidence, hearing of ~ Zeugenvernehmung; Beweisaufnahme; **record of the hearing of** ~ Beweisprotokoll

Besonderheit gegenüber dem deutschen Prozeß im anglo-amerikanischen Zivilprozeß: Die Zeugen werden nicht vom Richter, sondern von den Anwälten der Parteien vernommen (examination or cross-examination); der Richter stellt keine Fragen (he hears the evidence)

evidence, inadmissibility of ~ Unzulässigkeit von Beweismitteln; **for lack of** ~ mangels Beweises

evidence, law of ~ Beweisrecht

Das law of evidence, ein System der Regeln über die Zulässigkeit und Unzulässigkeit bestimmter Beweismittel, hat sich im anglo-amerikanischen Recht zu einem eigenen komplizierten Rechtsgebiet entwikkelt

evidence, motion for the admission of ~ Beweisantrag; **to grant (deny) a motion for the admission of** ~ e-n Beweisantrag zulassen (ablehnen)

evidence, offer to produce ~ Beweisantritt; **order to take** ~ Beweisbeschluß; **party giving** ~ beweisführende Partei; Beweisführer; **piece of** ~ Beweisstück; Beleg; **preservation of** ~ Beweissicherung; **production of** ~ Beibringung von Beweisen; Beweisantritt; **(fixed) rules of** ~ Beweisregeln, Vorschriften des Beweisrechts (*cf. law of* →~); **summary of** ~ *(Zivilprozeß)* Ergebnis der Beweisaufnahme; *(Strafprozeß)* Ergebnis der Ermittlungen

evidence, taking of ~ Beweisaufnahme, Beweiserhebung; →**Hague Convention on the Taking of E ~ Abroad in Civil or Commercial Matters; record of the taking of** ~ Beweisprotokoll

evidence, for want of ~ mangels Beweises; **to acquit the accused for want of** ~ den Angeklagten mangels Beweises freisprechen

evidence *v* beweisen; nachweisen; **to be ~d by** bewiesen sein durch

evident augenscheinlich, offenkundig; **to make** ~ beweisen, klarstellen

evidentiary beweismäßig; ~ **effect** Beweiskraft; ~ **fact** Indiztatsache, Hilfstatsache *(als Gegenstand des Indizienbeweises);* Tatumstände; ~ **force** (or **value**) Beweiskraft

evocation Ansichziehen e-r noch nicht erledigten Rechtssache *(durch das übergeordnete Gericht; cf. certiorari)*

evocandi, jus ~ *(VölkerR)* Recht *(e-s Staates),* seine Angehörigen aus dem Ausland zurückzuberufen

evoke *v*, **to** ~ **a case** e-e *(noch nicht erledigte)* Rechtssache an sich ziehen

ex ab *(Werk etc);* ohne, ausschließlich; früher, ehemalig; ~ **aequo et bono** nach billigem Ermessen; ~ **all** ausschließlich aller Rechte (Dividenden etc); ~ **cathedra** von maßgeblicher Seite; ~ **coupon** (ex cp.) ohne (od. ausschließlich) Coupon; ~ **dividend** (ex div.) ohne (od. ausschließlich) Dividende *(opp. cum dividend);* ~ **dock** *Am* ab Kai; ~ **factory** ab Fabrik

ex gratia *("as a favo[u]r")* freiwillig *(ohne Anerkennung e-r Rechtspflicht; opp. as of right);* ~ **payment** freiwillige Zahlung; Kulanzzahlung

ex, ~ **interest** (ex int.) ohne (od. ausschließlich) Zinsen *(opp. cum interest);* ~ **mero motu** *("from his mere motion")* aus eigenem Antrieb; von Amts wegen; ~ **new** (ex n., x-n.) *Br* ohne Bezugsrecht *(auf neue Aktien);* ~ **nunc** für die Zukunft; ~ **officio** von Amts wegen; ~ **officio member** Mitglied kraft Amtes

ex parte (ex p.) 1. einseitig, auf Antrag *(nur einer Partei);* 2. seitens einer Partei *(z.B. e-s am Rechtsstreit interessierten Dritten);* ~ **application** Antrag einer Partei *(ohne Anhörung der Gegenpartei);* **case** einseitiges *(ohne Vorladung der Gegenpartei durchgeführtes)* Verfahren *([ZivR] z.B. Verfahren des vorläufigen Rechtsschutzes; [StrafR] z.B. Beschlagnahme- od. Durchsuchungsverfahren);* ~ →**divorce**; ~ **proceedings** *(PatR)* Verfahren bis zur Bekanntmachung

ex, ~ **post facto law** (Straf-)Gesetz mit rückwirkender Kraft; ~ **proprio motu** *("of his own accord")* aus eigenem Antrieb

ex quay (duty paid) ... (named port) Ab Kai (verzollt) ... (benannter Hafen) (→*Incoterms 1980)*

ex quay (duties on buyer's account) ... (named port) Ab Kai (unverzollt) ... (benannter Hafen) (→*Incoterms 1980)*

ex rights ohne Bezugsrecht *(auf neue Aktien)*

ex ship ... (named port of destination) Ab Schiff ... (benannter Bestimmungshafen) (→*Incoterms 1980)*

ex warehouse (ex whse) ab Lagerhaus

ex works (ex factory, ex mill, ex plantation, ex warehouse etc) Ab Werk, ab Fabrik, ab Mühle, ab Pflanzung, ab Lagerhaus etc (→*Incoterms 1980)*

exact genau, exakt; pünktlich, gewissenhaft; ~ **account** genauer Bericht; ~ **copy** *(mit dem Original)* genau übereinstimmende Abschrift; ~ **formulation** präzise Formulierung; ~ **interest** *Am* Zinsen auf der Basis von 365 Tagen *(opp. ordinary interest);* ~ **payment** pünktliche Zahlung; ~ **reproduction** genaue Wiedergabe; **to be** ~ **in one's payments** pünktlich zahlen; pünktlicher Zahler sein

exact *v (ungesetzlich od. unstatthaft) (Gebühren etc)* erheben; *(Zahlung)* eintreiben, einfordern; **to** ~ **payment** Zahlung einfordern, auf e-r Zahlung bestehen

exaction *(ungesetzl. od. unstatthafte)* (Gebühren-)-Erhebung; (Zahlungs-)Eintreibung; (Forderungs-)Beitreibung; erzwungene Zahlung; hohe Anforderung

exaggerate *v* übertreiben; **to** ~ **the amount of the damage** den Schadensbetrag zu hoch ansetzen; **to** ~ **one's claims** übertrieben hohe Forderungen stellen

exaggerated price übertrieben hoher (od. übersetzter) Preis

exaggeration Übertreibung; ~ **of value** Überbewertung

examination 1. *(Zivilprozeß) (meist eidliche)* Zeugenvernehmung; *(Strafprozeß)* Verhör; ~ **before trial** *Am* Zeugenvernehmung einer Partei *(durch den gegnerischen Anwalt)* vor der Verhandlung; ~ **in chief** erste Zeugenvernehmung *(durch den Anwalt der Partei, die den Zeugen benannt hat; cf. cross-~, re~);* ~ **of parties** Vernehmung der Parteien; ~ **of scene of crime** *(Strafprozeß)* Augenscheinseinnahme am Tatort; ~ **of witnesses** Zeugenvernehmung; **cross-** ~ Kreuzverhör *(Befragung e-s Zeugen durch den Anwalt der Gegenpartei; cf. ~ in chief, re~);* **oral** ~ mündliche Vernehmung; **preliminary** ~ Voruntersuchung (→*preliminary*); **pretrial** ~ *Am* →~ before trial; **public** ~ *Br (KonkursR)* öffentliche Vernehmung; **re**~ erneute Zeugenvernehmung (→*reexamination*); **viva voce** ~ mündliche

Vernehmung; **to conduct the ~ of a witness** die Zeugenvernehmung durchführen; **to undergo an ~** vernommen (od. verhört) werden

examination 2. *(PatR)* Prüfung; **~ of appeal** Prüfung der Beschwerde; **~ on filing** Eingangsprüfung; **~ department** Prüfungsstelle; **~ as to novelty** Prüfung auf Neuheit; **~ of opposition** Prüfung des Einspruchs; **~ of the European patent application** Prüfung der europäischen Patentanmeldung; **rules for ~** Prüfungsrichtlinien; **to file the request for ~** den Prüfungsantrag stellen

examination 3. Prüfung, Revision, Untersuchung, Besichtigung, Durchsicht; **~ of the books** Prüfung (od. Revision) der Bücher; **~ of the goods** Besichtigung (od. Prüfung) der Waren; **~ of proposal** *(VersR)* Antragsprüfung; **medical ~** ärztliche Untersuchung; **physical ~** körperliche Durchsuchung; **post mortem ~** Leichenschau; **random ~** Stichprobe; **to make an ~** (of) *(etw.)* besichtigen; **to undergo an ~** sich e-r *(ärztlichen)* Untersuchung unterziehen

examination 4. Examen, Prüfung; **~ board** Prüfungskommission; **~ candidate** Prüfungskandidat; **~ result** Prüfungsergebnis; **~ standards** Prüfungsanforderungen; **~ of title** Prüfung der Eigentumsverhältnisse; **Bar ~** Anwaltsprüfung *(Br für Zulassung als barrister)*; **entrance ~** Aufnahmeprüfung; **final ~** Abschlußprüfung; **final ~ of the Law Society** *Br* Anwaltsprüfung *(für Zulassung als solicitor)*; **intermediate ~** Zwischenprüfung; **leaving ~** Abschlußprüfung; **oral ~** mündliche Prüfung; **qualifying ~** Eignungsprüfung; **viva voce ~** mündliche Prüfung; **written ~** schriftliche Prüfung, schriftliches Examen; **to admit to an ~** zum Examen zulassen; **to apply for admission to an ~** sich zum Examen melden; **to be under an ~** geprüft werden; **to fail in an ~** e-e Prüfung nicht bestehen; in e-r Prüfung durchfallen; **to go in for an ~** ein Examen machen; **to hold an ~** e-e Prüfung abhalten; **to pass an ~** ein Examen bestehen; **to sit for** (or **take**) **an ~** ein Examen machen; e-e Prüfung ablegen

examination 5. (Zoll)Beschau; Zollrevision; **~ of the baggage (luggage)** Gepäckrevision; **customs ~ of hand luggage** Zollrevision des Handgepäcks; **integral ~** *(Zoll)* Gesamtbeschau; **partial ~** *(Zoll)* Teilbeschau; **result of the customs ~** Zollbefund

examine *v (Zivilprozeß) (meist eidlich)* vernehmen; *(Strafprozeß)* verhören; prüfen, revidieren, untersuchen, besichtigen; **to ~ the books** die Bücher durchsehen (od. prüfen); **to ~ the goods** die Waren besichtigen (od. prüfen); **to ~ a student** e-n Studenten prüfen; **to ~ a witness** Zeugen eidlich vernehmen; **to ~ sympathetically** wohlwollend prüfen

examining board Prüfungsausschuß; **to be on the ~** dem Prüfungsausschuß angehören

examining, ~ countries *(PatR)* Prüfungsländer; **~ division** *(PatR)* Prüfungsabteilung; **~ magistrate** Untersuchungsrichter; **~ section** *(PatR)* Prüfungsstelle

examinee Prüfungskandidat

examiner Prüfer, Prüfungsbeamter; Revisor; *bes. Br (mit Beweisaufnahme beauftragter)* Richtergehilfe *(außerhalb der Hauptverhandlung)*; *(PatR)* Prüfer; Vorprüfer; **~ in chief** *Am (PatR)* Hauptprüfer; **legally qualified ~** *(PatR)* rechtskundiger Prüfer; **primary ~** *Am (PatR)* Vorprüfer; **reporting ~** *(PatR)* Berichterstatter *(im Erteilungsverfahren)*; **technical ~** *(PatR)* technisch vorgebildeter Prüfer

excavation *(Archäologie)* Ausgrabung; Vertiefung *(e-s Grundstücks)*; **illicit** (or **clandestine**) **~s** unzulässige Ausgrabungen; **official ~s** amtliche Ausgrabungen; **uncontrolled ~s** unüberwachte Ausgrabungen

exceed *v* überschreiten, übersteigen; *(an Größe, Bedeutung etc)* übertreffen; **to ~ one's authority** seine Vollmacht überschreiten; **to ~ one's credit** seinen Kredit überschreiten; **to ~ a limit** ein Limit überschreiten; **to ~ one's powers** seine Befugnisse überschreiten; **to ~ the time-limit** die Frist (od. den Termin) überschreiten; **to ~ in value** im Wert übersteigen; wertmäßig übertreffen; **demand ~s supply** die Nachfrage übersteigt (od. ist höher als) das Angebot

exceeding übersteigend, mehr als; **an amount ~ £100** ein Betrag von mehr als £100; **an amount not ~ £100** höchstens £100; **a fine not ~ £100** e-e Geldstrafe bis zu £100; **imprisonment not ~ three months** Gefängnis bis zu drei Monaten; **~ the speed limit** Überschreitung der zulässigen Höchstgeschwindigkeit

Excellency, His ~ Seine Exzellenz *(Titel von ambassadors, governors etc)*

except ausgenommen, außer; es sei denn (daß); **~ for** abgesehen von, bis auf; **~ as otherwise provided** vorbehaltlich anderslautender Bestimmung; **~ as otherwise herein provided** nur insoweit in diesem Vertrag nichts Entgegenstehendes vereinbart ist; **~ as provided in Art. 1** vorbehaltlich der Bestimmungen des Art. 1

except *v* ausnehmen, ausschließen (from von); vorbehalten; Einwendungen machen (to gegen); *Am (ProzeßR)* rügen, sich beschweren *(→exception)*

excepted perils clause Freizeichnungsklausel *(bei →charterparties and →bills of lading)*

excepting außer, ausgenommen; **~ (and reserving)** vorbehaltlich

exception Ausnahme (to von); Vorbehalt(sklausel); *Am und Scot* Einrede, Einwand, Einwendung (to gegen); Beanstandung; *Am* Beschwerde *(gegen Entscheidung e-s Prozeßgerichts als Vorbehalt der späteren Einlegung e-s Rechtsmittels); (VersR)* Risikoausschluß; ~ **to bail** *Am* Einwendung gegen die (zu geringe) Höhe der Kaution; ~ **to the rule** Ausnahme von der Regel; **bill of ~s** *Am* schriftlich eingelegte Beschwerde gegen das Verfahren des Richters der ersten Instanz; **by way of (an)** ~ ausnahmsweise; →**commercial** ~; **the ~s stipulated in a contract** die in e-m Vertrag genannten Ausnahmen; die Vorbehaltsklausel e-s Vertrages; **to take ~ to** Einwand erheben gegen; Einwendungen vorbringen gegen; *(an etw.)* Anstoß nehmen; beanstanden

exceptional ausnahmsweise; ungewöhnlich (for für); ~ **case** Ausnahmefall; ~ **circumstances** außergewöhnliche Umstände; ~ **income** außerordentliche Erträge; ~ **position** Ausnahmestellung, Sonderstellung; ~ **provision** Ausnahmebestimmung; ~ **price** Ausnahmepreis, Sonderpreis

excerpt Auszug (from aus); **by way of** ~ auszugsweise

excerpt *v* e-n Auszug machen (from aus)

excess Übermaß (of an); Überschuß; Mehr-; *Br (VersR)* Selbstbehalt *(Teil des Schadens, den Versicherter selbst tragen muß)*; Überschreitung; ~**es** *bes. pol* Ausschreitungen; ~ **(deductible)** *(VersR)* Abzugsfranchise; **in ~ of** mehr als; **an act in ~ of one's authority** Vollmachtsüberschreitung; **an amount in ~ of $ 500** über $ 500; **a claim in ~ of the limits of a policy** ein nicht durch die Versicherung gedeckter Anspruch

excess amount zuviel gezahlter Betrag; Mehrbetrag; Überschuß; **return of ~s** Rückerstattung zuviel gezahlter Beträge

excess application (for shares) Überzeichnung

excess baggage Übergewicht beim Gepäck *(im Luftverkehr)*; ~ **charge** (or **rate**) Gebühr für Übergewicht

excess, ~ **capacity** Überkapazität; ~ **charge** Kostenzuschlag; Gebührenzuschlag; ~ **consumption** Mehrverbrauch; ~ **expenditure** Mehrausgaben; ~ **exports** Ausfuhrüberschuß; ~ **fare** (Fahrpreis-)Zuschlag; ~ **freight** Frachtzuschlag; Überfracht; ~ **loan** über den gesetzlich zugelassenen Höchstbetrag hinausgehender Bankkredit; ~ **luggage** →~ baggage; ~ **money** Geldüberhang; ~ **mortality** *(VersR)* Übersterblichkeit

excess, ~ **of births over deaths** Geburtenüberschuß; ~ **(of) cash** Kassenüberschuß; ~ **of granted powers** Überschreitung verliehener Befugnisse (→*ultra vires action*); ~ **of imports over exports** Einfuhrüberschuß; ~ **of liabilities over assets** Überschuldung

excess of loss *(VersR)* Schadenexzedent; ~ **reinsurance** Schadensexzedentenrückversicherung

excess, ~ **offer** Überangebot; ~ **of receipts over expenditure** Einnahmeüberschuß; ~ **payment of tax** Steuerüberzahlung; ~ **postage** Nachgebühr, Strafporto; ~ **price** Überpreis; ~ **production** Überproduktion; Produktionsüberschuß

excess profit Mehrgewinn, Übergewinn; ~**s duty** (EPD) *(Br* ~**s tax** EPT*) Am* Steuer auf übermäßige Gewinne *(z.B. Kriegsgewinnsteuer)*

excess, ~ **purchasing power** Kaufkraftüberschuß;~ **reserves** Überschußreserven *(→reserve 1.)*; ~ **supply of labo(u)r** Überangebot an Arbeitskräften; ~ **vote** *parl* Nachbewilligung *(bei Etatüberschreitung)*; ~ **weight** Mehrgewicht, Übergewicht

excessive übermäßig, übertrieben; ~ **arms build-up** Überrüstung; ~ **bail** unangemessen hohe Kaution; ~ **boom** überhitzte Konjunktur; ~ **charge** übertrieben hohe Gebühr; ~ **demand** Übernachfrage; ~ **indebtedness** Überschuldung; ~ **price** Überpreis; ~ **stress** übermäßige Beanspruchung; ~ **supply** Überangebot; ~ **valuation** Überbewertung

exchange 1. Tausch, Austausch, Umtausch; ~ **advertisement** Tauschanzeige; ~ **of apartments** *Am* Wohnungstausch; ~ **of civilities** Austausch von Höflichkeiten; ~ **of commodities** Güteraustausch, Warenverkehr; ~ **of contracts** *Br* Abschluß des Kaufvertrages bei Grundstückskauf *(durch Austausch von 2 unterschriebenen Ausfertigungen)*; ~ **deal** Tauschgeschäft; ~ **of experience** Erfahrungsaustausch; ~ **of flats** *Br* Wohnungstausch; ~ **of goods and services** Waren- und Dienstleistungsverkehr; ~ **of information** Informationsaustausch; Austausch von Nachrichten (od. Auskünften); ~ **of instruments of ratification** *(VölkerR)* Austausch der Ratifikationsurkunden; ~ **of letters** Briefwechsel; ~ **of notes** *dipl* Notenwechsel; ~ **of population** *(VölkerR)* Bevölkerungsaustausch; ~ **of patents** Austausch von Patenten; ~ **of prisoners** Gefangenenaustausch; ~ **program participant** Teilnehmer an Austauschprogrammen; ~ **student** Austauschstudent; ~ **(tender) offer** Angebot des Aktientausches; ~ **of territory** *(VölkerR)* Gebietsaustausch; ~ **transaction** Tauschgeschäft; ~ **value** Tauschwert; ~ **of views** Meinungsaustausch; **cultural** ~ Kulturaustausch; →**diplomatic** ~; **in ~ for** (im Tausch) gegen; **labo(u)r** ~ Arbeitsamt, Arbeitsvermittlung; **period for** ~ Umtauschfrist; **student** ~ Studentenaustausch; **to give in ~ (for)** in Tausch geben (für), eintauschen (gegen); umtauschen; **to make an** ~ e-n Tausch machen, tauschen; **to obtain** (or **receive**) **in ~ for sth.** im Tausch gegen etw. erhalten; **to take in ~ (for)** in Tausch nehmen;

eintauschen (für od. gegen); **to take in part ~** in Zahlung nehmen

exchange 2. Devisen, *(fremde)* Währung (→*foreign exchange*); **~ allowance** Devisenzuteilung; **~ arbitrage** Devisenarbitrage; **~ assets** Devisenguthaben; **~ authorization** Devisengenehmigung; **~ balance** Devisenbilanz, Devisenguthaben; **~ broker** Devisenmakler; **~ calculation** (Wechsel-)Kursberechnung; **~ clause** (Wechsel-)Kursklausel

exchange control Devisenkontrolle, Devisenbewirtschaftung; **~ authority** (or **office**) Devisenbehörde; Devisenstelle; **~ regulations** Devisenbestimmungen, -vorschriften

exchange, ~ credit Fremdwährungskredit; **~ of the day** Tageskurs; **~ dealer** *Br* Devisenhändler; **~ depreciation** Währungsabwertung; **~ difference** Kursdifferenz, Kursspanne; **~ difficulties** Devisenschwierigkeiten; **~ embargo** Devisensperre; **E~ Equalization Account** *Br*[59] Währungsausgleichsfonds *(der alle Gold- und Devisenreserven Großbritanniens umfaßt oder enthält)*; **~ equilibrium** Zahlungsausgleich *(zwischen zwei Währungen)*; **~ facilities** Devisenerleichterungen; **~ fees** Gebühren bei Devisengeschäften; **~ fluctuations** (Wechsel-)Kursschwankungen; **~ for forward** (or **future**) **delivery** Termindevisen; **~ for spot delivery** Kassadevisen; **~ guarantee** (*Am* **guaranty**) Wechselkurssicherung; **~ inflows** Devisenzuflüsse; **~ list** (Devisen-)Kurszettel; **~ loss** (Wechsel-)Kursverlust

exchange market Devisenmarkt; **official dealings on ~s** amtliche Devisennotierungen

exchange, ~ office Wechselstube; **~ operation** Devisengeschäft; **~ outflow** Devisenabfluß *(ins Ausland)*; **~ parity** Kursparität *(Parität der Devisenkurse)*; **~ policy** Devisenpolitik; Devisenlage; Währungslage; **~ profit** (Wechsel-)Kursgewinn

exchange rate Wechselkurs; Devisenkurs; Umrechnungskurs; **~ adjustment** Wechselkursanpassung; **~ changes** Wechselkursänderungen; **~ differentials** Kursgefälle; **~ guarantee** (Wechsel-)Kursgarantie; **~ margin** Wechselkursmarge; Bandbreite der Wechselkurse; **~ mechanism** (ERM) Wechselkursmechanismus **(of the →European Monetary System)**; **fixed ~** fester Wechselkurs; **flexible ~** flexibler Wechselkurs; **floating ~** floatender (od. freier) Wechselkurs; **free(ly fluctuating) ~** freier (od. frei schwankender) Wechselkurs; **multiple ~** multipler Wechselkurs; **pegged ~** festgelegter Wechselkurs

exchange regulations Devisenbestimmungen; **in accordance with ~** devisenrechtlich

exchange restrictions Devisenverkehrsbeschränkungen

exchange risk (Wechsel-)Kursrisiko; **covering the ~** Kurssicherung; **to cover the ~** das Kursrisiko decken

exchange, ~ speculation Devisenspekulation; **~ stability** Stabilität der Wechselkurse; **~ stringency** Devisenknappheit; **~ transactions** Devisengeschäfte, **~ yielding** devisenbringend

exchange, bill of ~ →bill 4.; **calculation of the ~** (Wechsel-)Kursberechnung; **cross-~** *Br* Wechselarbitrage über mehrere Plätze; **in dollar ~** in Dollardevisen; **favo(u)rable ~** günstiger (Wechsel-)Kurs; **first of ~** Primawechsel; **foreign ~** Devisen (→*foreign*); **forward ~ transactions** Devisentermingeschäfte *(opp. spot exchange dealings)*; **par of ~** Kursparität; Währungsparität; **premium on ~** *(Devisenhandel)* Agio, Aufgeld *(Differenz zwischen Kassakurs und höchstem Terminkurs)*

exchange, rate of ~ Wechselkurs; Devisenkurs; Umrechnungskurs (→*exchange rate*)

exchange, second of ~ Sekundawechsel *(zweite Wechselausfertigung)*; **third of ~** Tertiawechsel; **unfavo(u)rable ~** ungünstiger (Wechsel-)Kurs

exchange 3. Börse; **~ advice** Börsenbericht; **~ broker** Börsenmakler; **~ arbitration tribunal** Börsenschiedsgericht; **~ building** Börsengebäude, Börse; **~ business** Börsengeschäft, Börsenhandel; **~ customs** Börsenusancen; **~ dealings** Börsengeschäfte; **~ hours** Börsenstunden; **~ operations** Börsengeschäfte; **~ order** Börsenauftrag, Order; **~ quotation** Börsennotierung; **~ regulations** Börsenbestimmungen; **~ report** Börsenbericht; **~ speculation** Börsenspekulation; **at the ~** auf der Börse *(im Gebäude)*; **attendance on the ~** Börsenbesuch; **close of ~** Börsenschluß; **coal ~** Kohlenbörse; **commodities ~** Warenbörse, Produktenbörse; **corn ~** Getreidebörse; **cotton ~** Baumwollbörse; **current on the ~** börsengängig; **on the ~** auf der Börse; **produce ~** Warenbörse; Produktenbörse; **quoted on the ~** börsengängig; **rules of the ~** Börsenordnung; **shipping ~** Schiffahrtsbörse, Frachtbörse; **stock ~** (Effekten-, Wertpapier-)Börse (→*stock 1.*)

exchange 4., **(telephone ~)** Fernsprechamt; Zentrale; Vermittlung; **~ line** *tel* Hauptanschluß

exchange *v* (aus-, ein, um)tauschen (for gegen); **right to ~** Umtauschrecht; **to ~ sth. for sth.** etw. eintauschen (od. umtauschen) gegen etw.; **to ~ contracts** *Br* e-n Vertrag *(über Grundstückskauf)* abschließen; **to ~ letters with sb.** mit jdm korrespondieren; **to ~ prisoners** Gefangene austauschen

exchanged, no goods ~ Umtausch nicht gestattet

exchangeable austauschbar, umtauschbar; auswechselbar *(z. B. Maschinenteile)*

exchequer, the E~ *Br (vom →Treasury kontrol-*

lierte) Staatskasse, Fiskus; *Br* Geldmittel, Finanzen *(e-r Firma);* **E~ Account** *Br* Exchequer-Konto *(bei der Bank of England für alle Regierungseinnahmen; der so gebildete Fonds ist der →Consolidated Fund);* **E~ and Audit Department** *Br* Oberrechnungshof; **E~ bill** *Br (kurzfristiger, verzinslicher)* Schatzwechsel *(ersetzt durch →Treasury bill);* **E~ bond** *Br (langfristige)* Schatzanweisung; **E~ Court of Canada** Oberstes Verwaltungsgericht; **~ grants** Staatszuschüsse an Selbstverwaltungskörper; **~ supplements** Staatszuschüsse; **Chancellor of the E~** *Br* Finanzminister

excisable verbrauchsteuerpflichtig

excise *(indirekte)* Steuer; Verbrauchsteuer *(auf inländische Waren);* **~ duties** *Br* Verbrauchsteuern *(auf im Inland erstellte Waren und Dienstleistungen);* **~ duty rates** Verbrauchsteuersätze; **~ licence** *Br* Lizenz zur Herstellung od. zum Verkauf gewisser Waren gegen Bezahlung e-r besonderen Steuer; Schankkonzession; **~ man** (or **officer**) Steuereinnehmer; **~ office** *Br* Steueramt für Verbrauchsteuern; **~ sales tax** *Am* Umsatzsteuer; **~ tax** *Am* indirekte Seuer, die auf e-e Lizenz oder ein Privileg erhoben wird *(z.B. das Recht, gewisse Waren zu importieren od. exportieren, oder e-e Schankkonzession);* Sonderumsatzsteuer des Bundes *(auf einige Waren, Transportleistungen, Telefongespräche etc); (auch)* Gewerbesteuer; →**Commissioners of Customs and E~**; **manufacturer's ~** *Am* (Bundes-)Umsatzsteuer auf der Herstellstufe; **retailer's ~** *Am* (Bundes-)Umsatzsteuer auf der Einzelhandelsstufe

excite *v* anregen, (an)reizen (to zu); **to ~ a riot** e-n Aufruhr hervorrufen

exclave *pol* Exklave

exclude *v (jdn)* ausschließen (from von); *(etw.)* ausschließen; zurückweisen; **to ~ sb. from membership of a society** jdn von der Mitgliedschaft in e-r Gesellschaft ausschließen; jdn als Mitglied in e-e Gesellschaft nicht zulassen; **to ~ evidence** *(ProzeßR)* ein Beweismittel nicht zulassen; **to ~ the (general) public** die Öffentlichkeit ausschließen

excluded ausgeschlossen; nicht zugelassen; **any further claims ~** unter Ausschluß weiterer Ansprüche; **to be ~ from gift tax** *Am* von der Schenkungssteuer freigestellt sein

excluding ausschließlich, ohne; ausgeschlossen, nicht mit einbezogen; unter Ausschluß von

exclusion Ausschließung, Ausschluß; Zurückweisung; *Am* Steuerbefreiung, Freibetrag; **~ agreement** Ausschlußvereinbarung *(Ausschluß der gerichtlichen Kontrolle bei Schiedsverfahren);* **~ of benefits** *(Sozialvers)* Leistungsausschluß; **~ clause** Freizeichnungsklausel; **~ of foreigners** Nichtzulassung von Ausländern *(in ein Land);* **~ of income earned abroad** *Am* Steuerbefreiung für ausländische Arbeitseinkünfte; **~ laws** *Am* Bundesgesetze, die bestimmte Ausländer von der Einwanderung ausschließen; **~ of the public** Ausschluß der Öffentlichkeit; **~ of liability** Ausschluß der Haftung; **period** (or **term**) **of ~** Ausschlußfrist; **to the ~ of** unter Ausschluß von

exclusive (excl.) ausschließlich; Allein-; alleinig; exklusiv *(auf e-n bestimmten Personenkreis beschränkt);* **~ (story)** Exklusivbericht *(e-r Zeitung);* **~ of** nicht mit eingerechnet, ausschließlich, ohne; **rent ~ of heating** Miete ohne Heizungskosten; **~ agency** Alleinvertretung; **~ agent** Alleinvertreter; **~ dealer** Alleinvertriebshändler; **~ dealing** *Am* Ausschließlichkeitsbindungen *(→requirement contract);* **~ dealing agreement** (or **contract**) *Am* Alleinbezugsvertrag *(Groß- od. Einzelhändler verpflichtet sich, keine Ware von der Konkurrenz des Fabrikanten zu handeln);* **~ distribution** Alleinvertrieb; **~ distributor** Alleinvertriebsberechtigter; **~ franchise** *Am* Alleinverkaufsrecht; Ausschließlichkeitsverpflichtung *(des Herstellers od. Lieferanten);* **~ jurisdiction** ausschließliche Zuständigkeit; **~ licen|ce (~se)** ausschließliche Lizenz; Alleinlizenz; *(UrhR)* ausschließliches Nutzungsrecht; **~ licensing agreement** *(Lizenzvertrag)* Ausschließlichkeitsvertrag; **~ listing** *Am* alleinige Beauftragung e-s Maklers, Grundbesitz zu verkaufen; Alleinauftrag (→*listing 4*); **~ patent** Ausschließlichkeitspatent; **~ possession** Alleinbesitz; ausschließlicher Besitz; **~ purchasing agreement** Alleinbezugsvereinbarung; **~ representation** *com* Alleinvertretung; **~ right** ausschließliches Recht; Alleinberechtigung; **~ (right of) sale** Alleinverkauf(srecht); **~ sales agreement** Alleinverkaufsvertrag; **~ use** *(PatR)* ausschließliche Benutzung; **to be ~ of sth.** etw. ausschließen

exclusionary rule *Am* Ausschließungsregel *(der Bundesgerichte, wonach in gesetzwidriger Weise erlangte Beweismittel vom Ankläger nicht im Strafverfahren benutzt werden dürfen)*

exclusory clause *Am (VersR)* Ausschlußbestimmung

exculpation Entschuldigung, Rechtfertigung

exculpatory, ~ clause Freizeichnungsklausel *(durch welche Haftung ausgeschlossen od. beschränkt wird)*

excusable entschuldbar; **~ →homicide**

excuse Entschuldigung, Entschuldigungsgrund; Befreiung; Ausrede, Ausflucht; **without ~** unentschuldigt; **absence without valid ~** unentschuldigtes Fernbleiben (od. Fehlen); **lawful ~** Rechtfertigungsgrund; **reasonable ~**

ausreichende Entschuldigung; **to make ~s** Ausflüchte machen; **to make** (or **offer**) **an ~** e-e Entschuldigung vorbringen; **he had no ~ to offer** er konnte keine Entschuldigung vorbringen; **there is no ~ for his conduct** sein Verhalten läßt sich nicht entschuldigen

excuse *v* entschuldigen (for wegen); befreien (from von); **to ~ oneself** sich entschuldigen; **please ~ my coming late** verzeihen Sie, daß ich zu spät komme; **to be ~d (from) attendance** vom Erscheinen befreit sein; **he was ~d the fee** ihm wurde die Gebühr erlassen

execute *v* ausführen, durchführen; erledigen; *(rechtsgültig)* ausfertigen *(durch Unterschrift und, falls nötig, Siegelung);* vollziehen; *(Urteil)* vollstrecken; *(Verbrecher)* hinrichten; **to ~ a contract** e-n Vertrag *(rechtsgültig)* ausfertigen; e-n Vertrag erfüllen; **to ~ a deed** (or **instrument**) e-e Urkunde *(rechtsgültig)* ausfertigen *(by signing, sealing and delivering it);* **to ~ a judgment** ein Urteil vollstrecken; **to ~ a mortgage** e-e Hypothek *(rechtsgültig)* ausfertigen *(durch Unterschrift etc);* **to ~ an office** ein Amt ausüben; **to ~ an order (promptly)** e-n Auftrag (schnell) ausführen; **to ~ a power of attorney** e-e Vollmacht ausstellen; **to ~ a will** ein Testament *(rechtsgültig)* ausfertigen *(by signing it in the presence of two witnesses)*

executed ausgeführt *(opp. executory);* **~ consideration** erbrachte Gegenleistung; **~ contract** erfüllter Vertrag; **~ copy** Ausfertigung; **~ in 3 copies** in 3facher Ausfertigung; **~ trust** genau festgelegtes Treuhandverhältnis; ausgeführtes Treuhandverhältnis; **~ writ** vollzogene gerichtliche Anweisung

executing, ~ creditor Vollstreckung betreibender Gläubiger; **self-~ treaty** unmittelbar *(ohne ausdrücklichen gesetzgeberischen Akt, innerstaatlich)* anwendbarer Vertrag *(Am Art. VI § 2 der Verfassung; EWG-Vertrag Art. 173 Abs. 2);* **non-self-~ treaty** Vertrag, der nicht ohne ausdrücklichen gesetzgeberischen Akt innerstaatlich angewendet werden kann

execution Ausführung, Durchführung, Erledigung; *(rechtsgültige)* Ausfertigung *(e-r Urkunde [by signing, sealing and delivering]);* Pfändung, Zwangsvollstreckung; Vollstreckung; Vollziehung; Hinrichtung

execution, to be exempt from ~ nicht der Zwangsvollstreckung unterliegen; unpfändbar sein; **to be liable** (or **subject**) **to ~** der Zwangsvollstreckung unterliegen; pfändbar sein; **a judgment is capable of ~** ein Urteil ist vollstreckbar; **to carry into ~** ausführen, durchführen; **to carry out the ~** die Zwangsvollstreckung durchführen; *(jdn)* hinrichten; **to issue** (or **levy**) **~ against the goods of the debtor** die Zwangsvollstreckung in Gegenstände des Schuldners betreiben; **~ levied (up)on the property of the judgment debtor** Zwangsvollstreckung in das Vermögen des Vollstreckungsschuldners; **to oppose ~** Widerspruch gegen die Zwangsvollstreckung geltend machen; **to stay ~** →stay *v;* **to suspend ~** die Zwangsvollstreckung aussetzen; **the ~ has been unsuccessful** die Vollstrekkung ist fruchtlos (od. erfolglos) geblieben; **to take sth. in ~** etw. pfänden; **to take out an ~ against sb.** jdn pfänden lassen

execution, ~ against a company (*Am* **corporation**) Zwangsvollstreckung in das Vermögen e-r Gesellschaft; **~ by (writ of) fi. fa.** Zwangsvollstreckung durch Pfändung und Wegnahme; **~ by (writ of) sequestration** Zwangsvollstreckung im Wege der Zwangsverwaltung; **~ creditor** Vollstreckungsgläubiger; **~ debtor** Vollstreckungsschuldner; **~ levied upon the property** Zwangsvollstrekkung in das Vermögen; **~ of an agreement** Durchführung e-s Abkommens; **~ of foreign awards** Vollstreckung ausländischer Schiedssprüche *(cf. arbitral award);* **~ of a contract** *(rechtsgültige)* Ausfertigung e-s Vertrages; **~ of a criminal** Hinrichtung e-s Verbrechers; **~ of the death sentence** Vollstreckung des Todesurteils; Hinrichtung; **~ of a deed** *(rechtsgültige)* Ausfertigung e-r Urkunde *(by signing, sealing and delivering);* **~ of hostages** Geiselerschießung; **~ of a judgement** Vollstreckung aus e-m Urteil; Urteilsvollstreckung; **~ of the letters of request** *Br* (**letters rogatory** *Am*) Erledigung des Rechtshilfeersuchens; **~ officer** Vollstreckungsbeamter; **~ of an order** Ausführung (od. Erledigung) e-s Auftrags; **~ of a policy** Ausstellung e-r Police; **~ of a trust** Auslaufen (od. Beendigung) e-s Treuhandverhältnisses; **~ of a will** *(rechtsgültige)* Ausfertigung e-s Testaments *(cf. to execute a will);* **~ proceedings** Vollstreckungsverfahren; **~ returned nulla bona** *Am* Unpfändbarkeitszeugnis; **~ sale** *Am* Zwangsversteigerung; **abortive ~** fruchtlose Pfändung (od. Vollstrekkung); **due ~ of a will** Errichtung *(od. Ausfertigung)* e-s Testamentes in gehöriger Form; **cancellation of ~** Aufhebung der Zwangsvollstreckung; **equitable ~** Vollstreckung nach equity-Recht; **exempt from ~** nicht der Zwangsvollstreckung unterliegend; unpfändbar; **goods taken in ~ by a sheriff** vom Sheriff *(als Gerichtsvollzieher)* zur Vollstreckung beschlagnahmte Sachen; **levy of ~** Betreibung der Zwangsvollstreckung; **measures of ~** Vollstreckungsmaßnahmen; **protection from ~** Vollstreckungsschutz; **sale of goods seized** (or **taken**) **in ~** Zwangsversteigerung; **sale under ~** Zwangsversteigerung; →**stay of ~**; **suspension of ~** Aussetzung der Zwangsvollstreckung; **unsatisfied ~** fruchtlose Zwangsvollstreckung; **writ of ~** *(an den →sheriff gerichteter)* Vollstreckungsbefehl (→*writ*)

executive 1., **the E~** die Exekutive, vollziehende Gewalt *(im Sinne der Gewaltenteilung; cf. legislative, judiciary); Am* der Präsident *(Chief E~);* ausübend, vollziehend; ~ **agreement** *Am (vom Präsidenten ohne Zustimmung des Senats abgeschlossener)* (Staats-)Vertrag; *(VölkerR)* Verwaltungsabkommen; ~ **authority** vollziehende Gewalt; ~ **bill** *Am* Regierungsvorlage; ~ **body** Exekutivorgan, Verwaltungsrat; ~ **branch** Exekutive; **E~ clemency** *Am* Straferlaß durch Fürsprache des Präsidenten; **National E~ Committee** *Br* Parteizentrale der Labour Party; **E~ Department** *Am* Exekutive; Kabinett; Ministerium; **E~ Mansion** *Am* Amtssitz des Präsidenten; das Weiße Haus; Amtssitz e-s Gouverneurs; **E~ Office** *Am* Kabinettskanzlei; ~ **officer** *Br* Beamter *(zweithöchste Stufe des Civil Service; cf. administrative →officer);* ~ **order** *Am* Exekutivorder, Verfügung *(des Präsidenten ohne parlamentarische Zustimmung);* ~ **power** vollziehende Gewalt, Exekutive; ~ **privileges** *Am* Vorrechte des Präsidenten *(z. B. dem Congress gewisse Informationen vorzuenthalten);*~ **session** *Am parl* Geheimsitzung *(des Senats);* ~ **treaty** *Am* →~ agreement; **Chief E~** *Am* oberster Regierungsbeamter *(im Bund:* President; *im Einzelstaat:* Governor; *in e-r Stadt:* Mayor); **legal** ~ *Br* Bürovorsteher *(e-s solicitor)*

executive 2. leitender Angestellter, Führungskraft; (Firmen-, Betriebs-, Unternehmens-)Leiter; verwaltend, leitend; ~ **ability** Eignung als Führungskraft; Fähigkeit, e-n leitenden Posten auszufüllen; ~ **board** Exekutivdirektorium; Geschäftsführung; ~ **committee** Exekutivausschuß; geschäftsführender Ausschuß; *Am* Führungsgremium *(Geschäftsführungsspitze e-s →board of directors);* ~ **council** Exekutivrat; ~ **director** *(hauptamtlicher)* Direktor; *(IMF)* Exekutivdirektor; **board of ~ directors** *(IMF)* Exekutivdirektorium; ~ **expenses** Geschäftsführungskosten; ~ **head** Leiter; **at ~ level** auf Führungsebene; ~ **management** *Am* Unternehmensleitung; ~ **office** *Am* Ort der Geschäftsleitung; ~ **officers** *Am* Geschäftsleitung; Unternehmensleitung; Angestellte *(e-s Unternehmens)* der obersten Führungsebene; ~ **personnel** leitende Angestellte; ~ **position** leitende Stellung; ~ **salaries** *Am* Gehalt der leitenden Angestellten; ~ **secretary** *Am* Geschäftsführer *(e-s Vereins, e-r Gesellschaft);* ~ **staff** leitende Angestellte; ~ **trainee** Nachwuchsführungskraft; ~ **vice-president** *Am* stellvertretender Generaldirektor *(e-r AG); (oft nur)* Abteilungsleiter

executive, →chief ~; →chief ~ officer; non-~s (or **non-~ directors**) *Br (den deutschen Aufsichtsräten vergleichbare)* nebenberufliche Direktoren; **young** ~ Nachwuchsführungskraft

executor *(durch Testament eingesetzter)* Erbschaftsverwalter (→*personal representative*); *(ungenau)* Testamentsvollstrecker; **~'s bond** Kaution des Erbschaftsverwalters; **~-dative** *Scot* vom Gericht ernannter Erbschaftsverwalter; **~-nominate** *Scot* vom Erblasser ernannter Erbschaftsverwalter; ~ **de son tort** unrechtmäßiger Erbschaftsverwalter *(cf. devastavit);* **→ancillary** ~; **acting** (or **proving**) **~s** *(von mehreren ernannten Erbschaftsverwaltern)* Erbschaftsverwalter, die das Testament anerkennen und bestätigen lassen *(prove the will);* **to appoint a p. (the) ~ of one's will** jdn als Testamentsvollstrecker einsetzen

Der executor des anglo-amerikanischen Rechts ist wesensverschieden von dem Testamentsvollstrecker des deutschen Rechts *(cf. personal representative).* Er wird wie ein →trustee Eigentümer des beweglichen (*Br* auch unbeweglichen) Nachlasses, an ihn halten sich die Nachlaßgläubiger, und nur er treibt die Nachlaßforderungen ein.

Der executor erhält vom Gericht die grant of probate

executorship Amt des Erbschaftsverwalters *(ungenau:* Testamentsvollstreckers); **assumption of the ~** Annahme des Amtes des Erbschaftsverwalters

executory (noch) auszuführen(d) (od. zu erfüllen[d]) *(opp. executed);* ~ **bequest** →~ devise; ~ **consideration** zukünftige (noch zu erbringende) Gegenleistung; ~ **contract** noch zu erfüllender Vertrag; ~ **devise** bestimmte Art e-r noch zu erfüllenden letztwilligen Verfügung; ~ **interest** aufschiebend bedingtes Grundstücksrecht; ~ **remainder** bedingtes Anwartschaftsrecht (→*remainder 2.*); ~ **trust** später noch festzulegendes Treuhandverhältnis

executrix *(testamentarisch ernannte)* Erbschaftsverwalterin *(cf. executor)*

executry *Scot* beweglicher Nachlaß

exemplary vorbildlich; abschreckend, exemplarisch; **~→damages**; ~ **punishment** exemplarische Bestrafung

exemplification Erläuterung durch Beispiele; beglaubigte Abschrift

exemplify *v* durch Beispiele erläutern; *Am* e-e Abschrift beglaubigen; **to ~ a deed** *Am* beglaubigte Abschrift e-r Urkunde anfertigen

exemplified copy *Am* beglaubigte Abschrift

exempt befreit, ausgenommen (from von); **→tax ~**; ~ **amount** *Am* (Steuer-)Freibetrag; ~ **from duties and charges** von Zöllen und Abgaben befreit; ~ **from duty** abgabenfrei; zollfrei; ~ **from execution** unpfändbar; ~ **from liability** von der Haftung befreit; ~ **from military service** vom Militärdienst befreit; ~ **from stamp duty** stempelfrei; ~ **from taxes** steuerfrei; ~ **property** unpfändbare (od. von der Pfändung ausgenommene) Sachen

exempt supplies *Br*[59a] *(UmsatzsteuerR)* steuerbefreite Leistungen
Bei den exempt supplies ist der Abzug der Vorsteuer im Gegensatz zu den →zero-rated supplies nicht möglich *(entspricht in etwa Steuerbefreiung ohne Vorsteuerabzugsberechtigung – § 4 i. V. m. § 15 Abs. 2 UStG)*

exempt, partially ~ *Br*[59b] *(UmsatzsteuerR)* teilweise steuerbefreit
Nur zum teilweisen Vorsteuerabzug berechtigte Gewerbetreibende, die sowohl steuerpflichtige als auch steuerbefreite Leistungen erbringen, dürfen grundsätzlich nur den Teil ihrer →input tax abziehen, der ihren steuerpflichtigen Leistungen entspricht

exempt *v (von Steuern, Verpflichtungen etc)* befreien; freistellen; **to ~ sb. from liability** jds Haftung ausschließen; **to ~ sb. from military service** jdn vom Militärdienst freistellen; **to ~ from taxes** von Steuern befreien; **to ~ a vehicle from the obligation to be registered** ein Fahrzeug von der Zulassungspflicht befreien

exempted, ~ **amount** (Steuer-)Freibetrag; ~ **business** Punkte außerhalb der Tagesordnung; ~ **from execution** von der Pfändung ausgenommen; unpfändbar; ~ **from →VAT; to be ~ by an order** unter e-e Ausnahmeregelung fallen

exemption Befreiung *(von Steuern, Lasten, Gerichtsbarkeit etc);* Freistellung; *Am* (Steuer-)Freibetrag; pfändungsfreier Gegenstand; Gegenstand, der nicht dem Konkurs unterworfen ist; Ausnahme(regelung); **~s** pfändungsfreie Gegenstände; ~ **from charges** Gebührenfreiheit; Abgabenbefreiung; ~ **of particular classes of goods** *Br*[60] Freistellung bestimmter Warenarten *(von der Preisbindung)*

exemption clause Freistellungsklausel, Haftungsausschlußklausel
Br Klausel, die die Haftung des Warenlieferers od. Unternehmers beschränkt oder ausschließt

exemption, ~ **from (customs) duty** Zollbefreiung; ~ **from execution** Unpfändbarkeit; ~ **from fees** Gebührenfreiheit; ~ **from income tax** Befreiung von der Einkommensteuer; ~ **from civil and criminal jurisdiction** Befreiung von der Zivil- und Strafgerichtsbarkeit *(cf. exterritoriality);* ~ **from liability** Haftungsausschluß; ~ **limit** *Am* (Steuer-)Freigrenze; ~ **from military service** Freistellung vom Militärdienst; ~ **from payment of premiums** *(VersR)* Prämienbefreiung; ~ **from seizure** Unpfändbarkeit; ~ **system** *(internationales SteuerR)* Methode der Steuerquellenzuteilung *(die einzelnen Steuerquellen werden dem einen od. dem anderen Vertragsstaat zur ausschließlichen Besteuerung überlassen; opp. tax credit system);* ~ **from taxation** Steuerbefreiung, Steuerfreiheit

exemption, dependency ~ *Am* Steuerfreibetrag für Familienangehörige; **old age** ~ *Am (SteuerR)* Altersfreibetrag; **personal** ~ *Am* persönlicher (Steuer-)Freibetrag; **spouse's** ~ *Am* Freibetrag für den Ehegatten; **→tax** ~; **→withholding** ~; **to apply for ~s** Ausnahmen beantragen; **to claim ‰ 1,000** ~ *Am* e-n Freibetrag von ‰ 1000 geltend machen; **to grant** ~ Befreiung gewähren; *Am* Steuerfreiheit gewähren

exequatur *(VölkerR)* Exequatur *(amtl. Anerkennung e-s ausländischen Konsuls durch den Empfangsstaat);* **withdrawal of** ~ Zurückziehung des Exequatur; **to grant** (or **issue**) **the** ~ das Exequatur erteilen

exercise Ausübung *(e-s Rechts, der Macht etc);* Geltendmachung; **~s** *Am (öffentliche)* Feierlichkeiten; **opening ~s** *Am* Eröffnungsfeierlichkeiten; ~ **of discretion** Ausübung des Ermessens; **in the ~ of one's duties** in Ausübung seiner (Dienst-)Pflichten; ~ **of functions** Wahrnehmung von Aufgaben; ~ **of influence** Geltendmachung des Einflusses; ~ **of jurisdiction** Ausübung der Gerichtsbarkeit; ~ **of power** Ausübung der Macht, Machtausübung; ~ **of a profession** Berufsausübung; ~ **of remedies** Gebrauch von Rechtsmitteln; ~ **of a right** Ausübung e-s Rechts, Rechtsausübung

exercise *v* ausüben; geltend machen; üben, anwenden, gebrauchen; **to ~ due care** gehörige Sorgfalt anwenden; **to ~ functions** Aufgaben wahrnehmen; *(amtl.)* Tätigkeit ausüben; **to ~ one's influence** seinen Einfluß geltend machen; **to ~→jurisdiction; to ~ an option** ein Optionsrecht ausüben; **to ~ power** Macht ausüben; **to ~ a privilege** ein Vorrecht geltend machen; **to ~ a remedy** von e-m Rechtsmittel Gebrauch machen; **to ~ a right** ein Recht ausüben (od. geltend machen); von e-m Recht Gebrauch machen

exert *v* anwenden, ausüben; **to ~ one's influence** seinen Einfluß geltend machen; **to ~ pressure** Druck ausüben

exhaust Auspuff(abgase); ~ **emissions from motor vehicles** Schadstoffemissionen von Kraftfahrzeugen

exhaust *v* erschöpfen, verbrauchen, aufbrauchen; **to ~ one's claims to insurance benefits** *(VersR)* ausgesteuert werden; **to ~ a quota** ein Kontingent voll verbrauchen; **to ~ the remedies** die Rechtsmittel erschöpfen; **to ~ the soil** Raubbau (be)treiben

exhausted, ~ **edition** vergriffene Auflage; ~ **reserves** erschöpfte Reserven; **remedies have been** ~ die Rechtsmittel sind erschöpft; **the stock is** ~ der Vorrat ist erschöpft

exhaustion Erschöpfung; Verzehr; ~ **of administrative remedies** Erschöpfung der verwaltungsinternen Rechtsmittel *(Kläger muß* *den Verwaltungsrechtsweg erschöpfen, bevor er ein ordentliches Gericht anrufen kann);* ~ **of local remedies** *(VölkerR)* Erschöpfung der innerstaatlichen Rechtsmittel; ~ **of quotas** Ausschöpfung der Quoten; ~ **of the reserves** Erschöpfung der Reserven; ~ **of sb.'s right to (sickness or unemployment) benefits** Aussteuerung; ~ **of the soil** Raubbau; **the property is subject to** ~ **of substance** die Vermögenswerte unterliegen der Erschöpfung *(z.B. Öl, Waldbestände)*

exhaustive erschöpfend; vollständig; ~ **cultivation** Raubbau

exheredate *v Am* enterben

exheredation *Am* Enterbung

exhibit Beweisstück; als Beweis vorgelegte Urkunde; Urkunde, auf die in e-m affidavit Bezug genommen wird; Ausstellungsstück; ~**s** Beweisstücke; Ausstellungsgüter; ausgestellte Waren; **to offer** (or **produce**) **an** ~ ein Beweisstück vorlegen

exhibit *v (zum Verkauf od. auf Ausstellung)* ausstellen; *(Urkunde)* vorlegen, vorzeigen; darlegen; **to** ~ **evidence** Beweis beibringen; **to** ~ **goods at a fair** Güter auf e-r Messe ausstellen

exhibited, ~ **articles** Ausstellungsgüter; ~ **object** Ausstellungsstück, -gegenstand; **goods** ~ **at a fair** Messegut

exhibition Ausstellung; Vorlage *(e-r Urkunde etc); Br* Stipendium; ~ **building** Ausstellungsgebäude; ~ **of documents** Vorlage von Urkunden; ~ **goods** Ausstellungsgüter; ~ **grounds** Ausstellungsgelände; ~ **hall** Ausstellungshalle; ~ **of household appliances** Haushaltswarenausstellung; ~ **room** Ausstellungsraum; ~ **stand** Ausstellungsstand; ~ **space** Ausstellungsfläche; ~ **of works of art** Kunstausstellung

exhibition, art ~ Kunstausstellung; **certificate of** ~ Ausstellungsbescheinigung; **export** ~ Exportausstellung; **industrial** ~ Industrieausstellung; **international** ~ Weltausstellung; **right of** ~ *(UrhR)* Ausstellungsrecht; **special** ~ Sonderausstellung; **touring** ~ Wanderausstellung; **universal** (or **world**) ~ Weltausstellung; **to open an** ~ e-e Ausstellung eröffnen; **to put on an** ~ e-e Ausstellung veranstalten

exhibitioner *Br* Stipendiat; Inhaber e-s Stipendiums

exhibitor Aussteller; Messeteilnehmer; **foreign** ~**s** ausländische Aussteller; Auslandsbeteiligung *(an e-r Ausstellung od. Messe);* **individual** ~ Einzelaussteller; **list of** ~**s** Ausstellerverzeichnis

exhumation Exhumierung, Ausgrabung von Leichen

exhume *v* exhumieren

exigence (~**cy**) Notlage, schwierige Lage; Dringlichkeit, dringendes Bedürfnis

exigible eintreibbar, einzutreiben(d)

exile Exil, Verbannung; Verbannte(r); **government-in-**~ Exilregierung; **to go into** ~ ins Exil gehen; **to send sb. into** ~ jdn verbannen

exile *v (jdn)* verbannen

Eximbank →Export-Import Bank

exist *v* bestehen, vorliegen; existieren; **able to** ~ existenzfähig

existing, under the ~ **circumstances** unter den gegenwärtigen Umständen; ~ **law** bestehendes (od. geltendes) Recht; ~ **practice** Gepflogenheit; ~ **right** bestehendes Recht

existence Existenz; Vorhandensein; ~ **of a right** Bestehen e-s Rechts; **conditions of** ~ Existenzbedingungen; **continued** ~ Fortbestand; **perpetual** ~ unbeschränkte Zeitdauer; **to be in** ~ bestehen; **to establish the** ~ **of a fact** das Bestehen e-r Tatsache beweisen; **to remain in** ~ weiterbestehen, fortbestehen

exit Ausreise; Ausgang (from aus); *(Lebensvers.)* Abgang; ~ **documents** Ausreisedokumente; ~ **permit** Ausreisegenehmigung; **place of** ~ Austrittsort *(im Durchfuhrverkehr)*

exitus Exitus, Tod

exodus Abwanderung; ~ **of capital** (or **capital** ~) Kapitalabwanderung *(nach dem Ausland);* **rural** ~ Landflucht; **urban** ~ Stadtflucht

exoner *v Scot* von der Haftung befreien

exonerate *v (jdn)* entlasten; *(von e-r Verpflichtung)* entbinden, befreien; **to** ~ **the bail** die Haftkaution freigeben; **to** ~ **sb. from liability** jdn von der Haftung befreien

exoneration Entlastung; Entbindung, Befreiung *(z.B. von der Bürgschaft);* ~ **clause** Freizeichnungsklausel

exor →executor

exorbitant übertrieben, übermäßig; ~ **interest** überhöhte Zinsen, Wucherzinsen; **to charge an** ~ **price** e-n zu hohen Preis (od. Wucherpreis) berechnen

exorcism Exorzismus, Teufelsaustreibung

expand *v* ausdehnen, (sich) erweitern

Expanded Program of Technical Assistance (EPTA) Plan über technische Hilfe für Entwicklungsländer *(im Rahmen der UNO)*

expansion Expansion, Ausdehnung, Erweiterung, Ausweitung *(opp. contraction); pol* Expansion, Ausdehnung, Gebietserweiterung; ~ **of business** Geschäftserweiterung; ~ **of credit**

Kreditausweitung; ~ **of exports** Ausfuhrexpansion, Ausweitung des Exports; ~ **of liquidity** Liquiditätsausweitung; ~ **of notes in circulation** Zunahme des Banknotenumlaufs;~ **of production** Ausweitung der Produktion; ~ **of trade** Ausweitung des Handels; **economic** ~ Wirtschaftsausweitung, Wirtschaftsexpansion; **industrial** ~ Industrieausweitung, industrielle Ausweitung; **policy of** ~ Expansionspolitik; **policy to check economic** ~ expansionsdämpfende Politik

expansionism Expansionspolitik

ex parte →ex

expatriate jd, der seine Staatsangehörigkeit aufgegeben hat; im Ausland lebende Person; ~**assignment** Auslandseinsatz; ~ **taxation** *Am* Besteuerung ehemaliger amerikanischer Staatsangehöriger

expatriate *v (jdn)* ausbürgern; **to ~ (oneself)** seine Staatsangehörigkeit aufgeben; **to be ~d** seine Staatsangehörigkeit verlieren

expatriation Ausbürgerung, Entziehung der Staatsangehörigkeit; Aufgabe der Staatsangehörigkeit;[61] ~ **allowance** *(EG)* Auslandszulage

expect *v (jdn, etw.)* erwarten

expected erwartet; voraussichtlich; ~ **deaths** *(VersR)* angenommene Todesfälle *(opp. actual deaths)*; ~ **time of arrival** (eta) voraussichtliche Ankunftszeit; ~ **time of sailing** (ets) voraussichtliche Abgangszeit; ~ **useful life** voraussichtliche Nutzungsdauer; **as may be reasonably** ~ aller Voraussicht nach

expecting that in der Erwartung, daß

expectancy Anwartschaft (on auf); ~ **of an estate** →estate in ~; ~ **of an inheritance** *Am* Erbanwartschaft; ~ **of life** (or **life** ~) *(VersR) (tabellenmäßige)* Lebenswahrscheinlichkeit, (mutmaßliche) Lebensdauer; (vermutete) Nutzungsdauer; **release of** ~ *Am* Erbverzicht

expectant erwartend; Anwärter (of auf); ~ **heir** Anwärter auf e-e Erbschaft, Erbanwärter *(im Ggs. zum Inhaber e-s aufschiebend bedingten Erbanrechts)*; ~ **mother** werdende Mutter; ~ **right** Anwartschaftsrecht

expectation Erwartung; Aussicht (of auf); ~**s** Erbaussichten (from bei); ~ **of life** Lebenserwartung; ~ **of (a) pension** Aussicht auf e-e Rente (od. Pension); **average ~ of life** mittlere Lebensdauer; **to fall short of sb.'s ~s** jds. Erwartungen nicht entsprechen

expedien|ce (~**cy**) Zweckmäßigkeit

expedient geeignetes Mittel, Notbehelf, Ausweg; zweckmäßig, zweckdienlich, sachdienlich; **by way of** ~ behelfsmäßig; **to consider sth.** ~ etw. für sachdienlich halten

expedite *v* beschleunigen; *bes. Am* befördern, absenden; **to ~ a matter** e-e Angelegenheit beschleunigen

expedited freight *Am* Eilfracht

expedition Beschleunigung; Expedition, Forschungsreise; **with the utmost** ~ mit größtmöglicher Beschleunigung

expel *v* ausschließen (from von); vertreiben, ausweisen, des Landes verweisen; *univ* relegieren; **to ~ a member from a club** ein Mitglied aus e-m Verein ausschließen; **to ~ from the hall** aus dem Saal verweisen; **to ~ sb. from a party** jdn aus e-r Partei ausstoßen

expellee *Am* (Heimat-)Vertriebener; *univ* Relegierter

expend *v (Geld)* ausgeben; *(Zeit, Sorgfalt etc)* aufwenden; **money received and ~ed** vereinnahmtes und verausgabtes Geld

expenditure Ausgabe(n); Aufwand, Aufwendung(en); Auslagen; Kosten; Unkosten; ~**(s)** Staatsausgaben *(opp. revenue)*; ~ **of a business** Geschäftsausgaben, Geschäftskosten; ~ **on capital goods** Ausgaben für Investitionsgüter; ~ **increase** Ausgabenerhöhung; ~ **incurred** entstandene Kosten; **actual** ~ Istausgaben; **additional** ~ Mehrausgaben; **capital** ~ Investitionsaufwendungen; **cash ~(s)** Barausgaben, Barauslagen; **current** ~ laufende Ausgaben; laufender Aufwand; **drop in** ~ Ausgabensenkung; **estimate of ~s** Kostenanschlag; **excess** ~ Mehrausgaben; **government** ~ Staatsausgaben; **growing** ~ wachsende Ausgaben; **heavy** ~ große Ausgaben; **item of** ~ Ausgabenposten; **national** ~ Staatsausgaben; **non-recurring** ~ einmalige Ausgabe(n); **office** ~ Bürokosten; **permanent** ~ laufende Ausgaben; **professional** ~ *(SteuerR)* Werbungskosten; **public** ~ öffentliche Ausgaben, Staatsausgaben; **routine** ~ tägliche Ausgaben; **social** ~ soziale Aufwendungen; Sozialausgaben; **special** ~ Sonderausgaben; **specification of ~s** Unkostenaufstellung; **to cut** ~ Ausgaben verringern (od. senken); **to incur** ~ Ausgaben machen; **to adjust ~ to income** die Ausgaben den Einnahmen anpassen; **the ~ exceeds the receipts** die Ausgaben übersteigen die Einnahmen

expense (Geld-)Ausgabe; Kosten; Aufwand; ~**s** Ausgaben; Kosten; Unkosten, Spesen; Aufwendungen; *Br (von der Einkommensteuer absetzbare)* Geschäftsausgaben; *Scot* Prozeßkosten

expense, to allocate ~ Gemeinkosten umlegen; Kosten verteilen; **to allow sb. his ~s** jdm seine Auslagen (od. Spesen) ersetzen; **to apportion the ~s** die Ausgaben (od. Kosten) verteilen (among auf); **to be a great ~ to sb.** jdm große Kosten verursachen; **to bear the ~s** die Kosten tragen; **to cover the ~s** die Kosten decken; **to**

cover one's ~s auf seine Kosten kommen; **to cut down one's ~s** seine Unkostenverringern; seine Ausgaben einschränken; **to defray the ~s** die Auslagen bestreiten; **to go to the ~ of** die Auslage (od. Ausgabe) auf sich nehmen für; **to go to great ~** es sich viel kosten lassen; **to incur ~s** sich in Unkosten stürzen; Kosten auf sich nehmen; Aufwendungen machen; Unkosten haben; **he has incurred ~s** ihm sind Kosten (od. Aufwendungen) entstanden; **~s were incurred** Unkosten sind entstanden; **to meet the ~s** für die Kosten aufkommen; die Kosten bestreiten; die Auslagen decken; **to put oneself to ~** sich in Unkosten stürzen; **to put sb. to the ~** jdn mit Auslagen belasten; **to put sb. to great ~s** jdm große Kosten verursachen; **to refund the ~s** die Kosten vergüten; die Auslagen zurückerstatten; **to save ~s** Kosten sparen; **to share (in) the ~s** sich an den Kosten beteiligen; **to state one's ~s** über Spesen (etc) abrechnen

expense, ~ account Spesenkonto, Konto für Geschäftsausgaben; **~s allowance** Aufwandsentschädigung; **daily ~ allowance** *Br (House of Lords)* Diäten; **~ of building** Baukosten; **~s of carrying on the business** laufende Geschäftskosten; **~s covered** Kosten gedeckt, kostenfrei; **~s deducted** nach Abzug der Kosten; **~ in employment** *Am* Werbungskosten; **~ fund** Unkostenfonds, Spesenfonds; **~ incurred** (by) entstandene Kosten; **the ~s involved** die damit verbundenen Kosten; **~s of issue** Emissionskosten; **~ item** Ausgabenposten; **~ ledger** Unkostenhauptbuch; **~ of maintenance** Unterhaltungskosten; **~ of management** Verwaltungskosten; **~s paid in advance** transitorische Aktiva; **~s of production** Herstellungskosten; **~ reimbursement** Kosten(rück)erstattung; Spesenvergütung; **~ report** Spesenabrechnung; **~s of selling** Vertriebskosten; Vertriebsgemeinkosten; **~sheet** Spesen(ab)rechnung *(des →travel(l)ing salesman)*; **~ voucher** Ausgabenbeleg; **~ of war** Kriegskosten

expense, administration ~ Kosten der Erbschaftsverwaltung *(durch den →administrator)*; **administrative ~s** Verwaltungskosten, Verwaltungsgemeinkosten; **advertising ~s** Werbekosten, Reklamekosten; **allocation of ~** Umlage von Gemeinkosten; Kostenverteilung; **at the ~ of** auf Kosten (od. zu Lasten) von; **at my ~** auf meine Kosten; **business** (or **commercial**) **~** Geschäftskosten; **current ~s** laufende Ausgaben; **after deducting ~s** nach Abzug der Kosten; **deduction for ~s** *Br (Einkommensteuer)* Abzug für Geschäftskosten; **diminution of the ~s** Kostenverringerung; **direct ~s** direkte Kosten, Einzelkosten; **entailing great ~** mit großen Kosten verbunden; **factory ~** Fertigungsgemeinkosten; **financial ~s** Finanzaufwendungen; **at the firm's ~** auf Kosten der Firma; auf Geschäftskosten; **free of ~** kostenfrei; ohne Kosten (od. Spesen)

expense, general ~(s) allgemeine Kosten; Gemeinkosten; **to allocate general ~(s)** Gemeinkosten umlegen

expense, at great ~ mit großen Kosten; sehr teuer; **incidental ~s** Nebenausgaben; **increase in ~** Ausgabenerhöhung; Kostenerhöhung; **"incur no ~s"** ohne Kosten *(auf Wechseln)*; **indirect ~** indirekte Kosten; Gemeinkosten; **at joint ~** auf gemeinsame Kosten; **note of ~s** Spesenrechnung; **office ~s** Bürokosten; **operating ~s** Betriebskosten; **organization ~s** *Am (Bilanz)* Gründungs- und Organisationskosten *(e-r AG)*; **out-of-pocket ~s** Barauslagen *(für Unkosten etc)*; **petty ~s** kleine Ausgaben (od. Spesen); **preliminary ~s** *Br (Bilanz)* Gründungs- und Organisationskosten

expense, at public ~ auf Staatskosten; **a person ist maintained at public ~** jds Unterhalt wird aus öffentlichen Mitteln bestritten

expense, receipts and ~s Einnahmen und Ausgaben; **running ~s** laufende Ausgaben (od. Kosten); *Br* Betriebskosten; **saving of ~** Kostenersparnis; Einsparung von Ausgaben; **selling ~s** Verkaufsspesen; Vertriebs(gemein)-kosten; **statement of ~s** Spesenaufstellung, Ausgabenaufstellung; **trade or business ~s** *Am*[62] Betriebsausgaben und Werbungskosten; **travel(l)ing ~s** Reisekosten, Reisespesen

expensive kostspielig, teuer, aufwendig; **to come ~** *colloq.* teuer zu stehen kommen

experience Erfahrung(en); Sachkunde; **~ abroad** Auslandserfahrung; **business ~** Geschäftserfahrung; **driving ~** Fahrpraxis; **exchange of ~** Erfahrungsaustausch; **professional ~** Berufserfahrung; **wide ~** große Erfahrung; **to lack ~** keine Erfahrung haben, unerfahren sein

experience *v*, **to ~ a decline (in prices)** e-n Kursrückgang erleiden; **to ~ difficulties** auf Schwierigkeiten stoßen

experienced erfahren; sachkundig; **~ in business** geschäftserfahren, geschäftskundig

experimental Versuchs-; **~ gaming** *Br* Planspiele; **~ method** Testmethode; **for ~ purposes** zu Versuchszwecken

expert Sachverständiger; sachverständiger Zeuge (→~ *witness*); Experte, Fachmann; Gutachter; sachverständig, sachkundig, fachmännisch; **~s** Fachleute; **among ~s** in der Fachwelt; **~ advice** sachkundiger (od. fachmännischer) Rat; fachkundige Beratung; **~ evidence** Sachverständigenbeweis; Beweis durch Sachverständige; **~s' fees** Sachverständigengebühren; **~ knowledge** Sachkenntnis, Fachkenntnis

expert opinion Begutachtung durch Sachverständigen; Sachverständigengutachten *(mündlich vor Gericht oder schriftliches Gutachten)*; **opposing** ~ Gegengutachten; **to give an** ~ ein Sachverständigengutachten erstatten; begutachten; **to obtain an** ~ ein Sachverständigengutachten einholen

expert testimony Aussage des sachverständigen Zeugen

expert witness sachverständiger Zeuge *(der vor Gericht über technische Fragen aussagt)*

Dem anglo-amerikanischen Recht sind unparteiische Gutachten von Sachverständigen nicht bekannt. Der Sachverständige wird nicht vom Gericht bestellt, sondern von einer Partei als Zeuge benannt und erstattet das Gutachten in Form einer Zeugenaussage

expert, body of ~s Expertengremium; **court** ~ *(auf Antrag e-r Partei bestellter)* Sachverständiger des Gerichts; **handwriting** ~ Schriftsachverständiger; **to call for a report by an** ~ ein Sachverständigengutachten anfordern; **to call in** (or **consult**) **an** ~ e-n Sachverständigen zu Rate ziehen; **to object to an** ~ e- n Sachverständigen ablehnen

expertise Expertise, Gutachten (od. Begutachtung) durch Sachverständigen; Sachkenntnis; **financial** ~ Sachkenntnis in Finanzfragen; **technical** ~ technisches Gutachten *(s. ICC International Centre for →Technical E~s)*

expiate *v* sühnen, (ab)büßen

expiration *bes. Am* Ablauf, Erlöschen; Verfall *(durch Zeit)*; Ende; **at the** ~ **of** bei Ablauf von; ~ **of an agreement** Ablauf e-s Vertrages; ~ **date of a patent** Zeitpunkt des Erlöschens e-s Patents; ~ **of an insurance** Erlöschen e-r Versicherung; ~ **of the patent term** *(PatR)* Ablauf der Schutzfrist; ~ **of period** Zeitablauf, Fristablauf; ~ **of the period of notice** Ablauf der Kündigungsfrist; ~ **of policy** Ablauf der Versicherung(spolice); ~ **of protection** Schutzablauf; ~ **of the term fixed** Ablauf der festgesetzten Zeit; Fristablauf; ~ **of the term of office** Ablauf der Amtszeit; ~ **of (the) time for service of the defence** Ablauf der Klagebeantwortungsfrist; ~ **of a truce** Ablauf (od. Ende) e-s Waffenstillstandes

expire *v* ablaufen, erlöschen; verfallen, außer Kraft treten; **the bill ~s** der Wechsel verfällt; **the insurance ~s** die Versicherung erlischt; **the period ~s** die Frist läuft ab

expired, ~ **insurance policy** abgelaufene Versicherungspolice; ~ **licen|ce (~se)** erloschene Konzession; ~ **patent** abgelaufenes (od. erloschenes) Patent; ~ **period** (or **time**) abgelaufene Frist; **the agreement has** ~ das Abkommen ist abgelaufen (on am); **the claim has** ~ die Forderung ist erloschen; **the ticket has** ~ die Karte ist abgelaufen (od. verfallen)

expiring, ~ **contract** ablaufender Vertrag; ~ **date** Verfalldatum, Verfalltag; **E~ Laws Continuance Act** *Br (jährlich erlassenes)* Gesetz über Verlängerung von Gesetzen *(die sonst erloschen wären)*

expiry *bes. Br* Ablauf, Erlöschen; Verfall *(durch Zeit)*; Ende; ~ **date** Verfalltag; ~ **date of an agreement** *(VölkerR)* Zeitpunkt des Auslaufens e-s Abkommens; ~ **of a term** (or **time limit**) Fristablauf; ~ **of truce** Ablauf (od. Ende) des Waffenstillstandes; **after the** ~ **of 2 years** nach Ablauf von zwei Jahren; **before the** ~ **of the time limit** vor Ablauf der Frist; **date of** ~ Verfalltag; **from the date of** ~ **of the period fixed** vom Ablauf der vereinbarten Frist an; **on the** ~ **of the time specified in section 1** mit Ablauf der in § 1 bezeichneten Frist

explain *v* erklären, erläutern; e-n Grund angeben für; **to** ~ **one's conduct** sein Verhalten rechtfertigen

explanation Erklärung (of für), Erläuterung (of zu); Begründung; **to give the parties opportunity for** ~ den Parteien rechtliches Gehör geben

explanatory erklärend, erläuternd; ~ **commentaries** erläuternde Bemerkungen; ~ **statement** Erklärung, Erläuterung

explicit klar, eindeutig, ausdrücklich *(opp. implicit)*; ~ **consent** ausdrückliche Einwilligung

exploit *v* ausnutzen, verwerten; *(Patente, Erfindungen etc)* auswerten; *(BergR)* ausbeuten, abbauen, gewinnen; ausnutzen, ausbeuten; **to** ~ **fish stocks** Fischbestände ausbeuten; **to** ~ **an invention** e-e Erfindung auswerten; **to** ~ **the work** *(UrhR)* das Werk verwerten

exploited, to be ~ **by sb.** von jdm ausgenutzt (od. ausgewertet) werden

exploitation Ausnutzung; Ausbeutung; Auswertung; Nutzung *(des Bodens)*; *(BergR)* Ausbeutung, Abbau, Gewinnung;~ **contract** Verwertungsvertrag; ~ **of fish stocks** Ausbeutung von Fischbeständen; ~ **of an invention** Verwertung e-r Erfindung; **improper** ~ **of a dominant position** mißbräuchliche Ausnutzung e-r beherrschenden Stellung; ~ **of industrial property rights** Verwertung von gewerblichen Schutzrechten; ~ **of a patent** Patentverwertung; ~ **of workers** Ausbeutung von Arbeitern; **capable of** ~ **in industry** *(PatR)* gewerblich anwendbar; **wasteful** ~ Raubbau

exploiter Verwerter; Ausbeuter

exploration Erforschung; Untersuchung; Schürfung; Auffinden *(von Lagerstätten)*; ~ **expenditures** *Am (SteuerR)* Aufwand zur Feststellung von Mineralvorkommen; ~ **of the sea** Meeresforschung

exploratory Entdeckungs-, Forschungs-; ~ **talks** Erkundungs-, Sondierungs-, Orientierungsgespräche

explosive Sprengstoff; **illegal possession of firearms and ~s** illegaler Waffen- und Sprengstoffbesitz

export Export, (Waren-)Ausfuhr; ~**s** Exportartikel, Ausfuhrgüter, Ausfuhrwaren; Gesamtausfuhr

export, to be engaged in the ~ trade im Export(handel) tätig sein; **to go for ~** *colloq.* für den Export bestimmt sein; **the ~s exceed the imports** die Exporte sind höher als die Importe; ~**s are falling** die Exporte gehen zurück; die Ausfuhr fällt; **to increase** (or **raise**) ~**s** die Ausfuhr steigern; **to promote the ~ trade** den Ausfuhrhandel fördern; **to subsidize ~s** die Ausfuhr *(staatlich)* fördern; ~**s increased** die Ausfuhr ist gestiegen (by um); ~**s are rising** die Ausfuhr steigt

export, E~ Administration Act (EAA) *Am*[62a] Export-Kontrollgesetz (→*Foreign Policy Controls*, →*National Security Controls*); **E~ Administration Office** *Am* → Office of E~ Administration; ~ **advertising** Exportwerbung; ~ **agent** Exportagent; Ausfuhragent; ~ **agreements** *Br*[63] *(KartellR)* Ausfuhrabsprachen; ~ **article** Exportartikel, Ausfuhrartikel; **E~ Association** *Am* Exportgemeinschaft *(Zusammenschluß verschiedener Firmen für Exportzwecke)*; ~ **authorization** Ausfuhrgenehmigung; ~ **ban** Ausfuhrverbot; ~ **bar** Goldbarren *(beim internationalen Goldexport)*; ~ **bonus** Exportbonus; ~ **bounty** Exportprämie, Ausfuhrprämie; ~ **bullion point** Goldausfuhrpunkt; ~ **business** Exportgeschäft; ~ **clearance** Ausfuhrabfertigung; ~ **commodities** Exportgüter, Exportwaren; ~ **company** Exportgesellschaft, Exportfirma; ~ **contract** Exportvertrag

export control Ausfuhrüberwachung; Ausfuhrlenkung; **internationally agreed ~ rules** international vereinbarte Regeln über Exportkontrolle (→*COCOM*)

export credit Exportkredit, Ausfuhrkredit; ~**s guarantee** (*Am* **guaranty**) Garantie für Exportkredite; Ausfuhrkreditbürgschaft; **E~ C~s Guarantee Department** (ECGD) *Br (staatl.)* Exportkreditabteilung *(gewährt dem Exporteur volle Deckung des wirtschaftl. und politischen Risikos)*, ~ **insurance** Exportkreditversicherung, **supporting of ~s** Stützung von Exportkrediten

export, ~ dealer Exporthändler; ~ **deficit** Außenhandelsdefizit; ~ **department** Exportabteilung; **E~ Development Corporation** staatliches Exportfinanzierungsinstitut

export duty Ausfuhrabgabe; Ausfuhrzoll; Ausgangszoll; **goods liable to ~** ausfuhrzollpflichtige Waren; **free of ~** ausfuhrzollfrei

export, ~ earnings Exporterlöse, Ausfuhrerlöse (→*Stabex system*); ~ **financing** Exportfinanzierung; ~ **firm** Exportfirma, Exporthaus; ~ **gold point** Goldausfuhrpunkt; ~ **goods** Exportwaren, Ausfuhrgüter; ~ **of goods** Warenausfuhr; ~ **guarantee** Exportbürgschaft; ~ **house** Exporthaus, Exportfirma

Export-Import Bank (Eximbank) *Am* Export-Importbank

Gegr. 1934. *Sitz:* Washington. Staatliches amerikanisches Exportfinanzierungs-Institut. Staatliche Risikodeckung (Exportkreditgarantien) bei Finanzierung amerikanischer Exporte für amerikanische und ausländische Banken. – Versicherung der Leasing-Einnahmen aus dem Ausland

Export-Import Bank of Japan staatliches japanisches Exportfinanzierungsinstitut

export, ~s in excess of imports Ausfuhrüberschuß; ~ **increase** Ausfuhrsteigerung; ~ **levy** *(EG)* Exportabschöpfung; Abschöpfung bei der Ausfuhr

export licen|ce (~se) Exportlizenz; Ausfuhrgenehmigung; **issue of an ~** Erteilung e-r Ausfuhrgenehmigung; **to issue an ~** e-e Ausfuhrgenehmigung erteilen

export, ~ loan Exportkredit; ~ **loss** Ausfuhrausfall; ~ **merchant** Exportkaufmann, Exporthändler; ~ **order** Exportauftrag *(opp. home or domestic order)*; ~ **orders received by industry** Auftragseingänge bei der Industrie aus dem Ausland; ~ **permit** Ausfuhrgenehmigung, Ausfuhrbewilligung; ~ **premium** Ausfuhrprämie; ~ **prohibition** Ausfuhrverbot; ~ **promotion** Ausfuhrförderung; ~ **publicity** Ausfuhrwerbung, Exportwerbung

export quota Exportquote, Ausfuhrkontingent; **initial ~** Exportausgangsquote, Ausfuhrausgangskontingent; **to exceed the ~** das Ausfuhrkontingent überschreiten

export, ~ refunds *(EG)* Exporterstattungen; ~ **regulations** Ausfuhrbestimmungen; ~ **requirements** Exportbedarf; ~ **restitutions** *(EG)* Exporterstattungen; ~ **restrictions** Exportrestriktionen; ~ **revenue** Exporteinnahmen, Exporterlöse; ~ **sales** Export(verkäufe); Auslandsabsatz; ~ **sample store** Exportmusterlager; ~ **shipment** Exportsendung; ~ **specie point** Goldausfuhrpunkt; ~ **specification** *Br (Zoll)* Ausfuhrerklärung; ~ **statistics** Ausfuhrstatistik; ~ **subsidy** Exportsubvention; ~ **surety** Exportbürgschaft; ~ **surplus** Ausfuhrüberschuß; ~ **tariff** Ausfuhrzolltarif; ~ **tonnage** Ausfuhrtonnage

export trade Exporthandel, Ausfuhrhandel; **E~ T~ Act** *Am* Exporthandelsgesetz; **(~) trade surplus** Außenhandelsüberschuß; **to promote the ~** den Ausfuhrhandel fördern

export, ~ transaction Exportgeschäft; ~ **volume** Exportvolumen, Ausfuhrmenge

export, bounty on ~s Ausfuhrprämie; **capital ~** Kapitalausfuhr; **cent|er (~re) for the ~ (of)** Exportzentrum; **chief ~s** (of a country) Hauptausfuhrgüter (e-s Landes); **claim arising from** ~ Ausfuhrforderung; **commodities for** ~ Exportwaren; **commodity ~s** Grundstoffausfuhren, Rohstoffexporte; **decline in ~s** Ausfuhrrückgang; →**duty on~s**; **embargo on ~s** Ausfuhrverbot; Ausfuhrsperre; **intended for** ~ für den Export bestimmt; **invisible ~s** unsichtbare Ausfuhren *(aktive Dienstleistungen)*; **lending for ~s** Exportkredit; **licen|ce (~se) for ~s** →~ licen|ce (~se); **proceeds of** (or **revenue from**) **~s** Ausfuhrerlöse; **rise in ~s** Ausfuhrsteigerung; **slackening of ~s** Abflauen (od. Nachlassen) des Exports; **total ~s** Gesamtausfuhr; **visible ~s** sichtbare Ausfuhr, Warenausfuhr

export *v* exportieren, ausführen

exported, ~ article Exportartikel; ~ **goods** Exportgüter, Ausfuhrgüter

exporting, ~ area Exportgebiet, Ausfuhrgebiet; ~ **country** Exportland, Ausfuhrland; ~ **firm** Exportfirma

exportable zur Ausfuhr geeignet, exportfähig

exportation Export, Ausfuhr; ~ **of goods** Warenausfuhr; **bounty on** ~ Ausfuhrprämie; **port of** ~ Ausfuhrhafen; **re-**~ Wiederausfuhr; **restriction of** ~ Ausfuhrbeschränkung

exporter Exporteur, Exporthändler; Ausführer; **~'s credit** Exportkredit; **E~ Credit Line** *Am* Kreditlinie der →Eximbank

expose *v (e-r Einwirkung)* aussetzen; *(zum Verkauf)* ausstellen, auslegen; aufdecken, enthüllen; *Scot* zur Versteigerung bringen, versteigern; **to ~ oneself** sich *(e-r Gefahr, Kritik etc)* aussetzen; sich bloßstellen; sich exhibitionieren, sich unsittlich der Öffentlichkeit zeigen; **to ~ an abuse** e-n Mißbrauch aufdecken (od. enthüllen); **to ~ goods for sale** Waren zum Verkauf ausstellen; **to ~ a newborn child** *Br* ein neugeborenes Kind aussetzen; **to ~ a plot** e-e Verschwörung aufdecken

exposed exponiert, preisgegeben, gefährdet; ~ **child** *Br* ausgesetztes Kind; ~ **for sale** zum Verkauf ausgestellt; ~ **to radiation** strahlenbelastet; **persons occupationally ~** beruflich exponierte *(z.B. strahlenexponierte)* Personen; **to be ~ (to)** ausgesetzt sein

exposing, ~ a child *Br* Kindesaussetzung; ~ **goods in a shop-window** Ausstellung von Waren im Schaufenster

expository statute *Am* Erläuterungsgesetz *(authentische Interpretation durch den Gesetzgeber)*

ex post facto law →ex

exposure Aussetzung, Ausgesetztsein; Ausstellung *(von Waren)*; *Am* Ausstellung; Bloßstellung; Aufdeckung, Enthüllung; ~ **(to rays)** *(AtomR)* Bestrahlung; ~ **hazard** *(Feuervers.)* Nachbarschaftsrisiko *(feuergefährdete Lage e-s Grundstücks)*; *(AtomR)* Bestrahlungsrisiko; ~ **of goods for sale** Ausstellung von Waren zum Verkauf; ~ **of person** s. indecent →~; ~ **of a plot** Aufdeckung e-r Verschwörung; **death by** ~ Tod durch Ausgesetztsein der Witterung *(z.B. durch Erfrieren)*; **indecent** ~ *(StrafR)* unsittliches Entblößen; Erregung öffentlichen Ärgernisses; **unnecessary** ~ *(Unfallvers.)* unnötiges Sichaussetzen e-r Gefahr

express 1. ausdrücklich, bestimmt; ~ **agreement** ausdrückliche Abmachung; ~ **authority** ausdrückliche (od. ausdrücklich erteilte) Vollmacht; ~ **condition** ausdrücklich festgelegte Bedingung; ~ **malice** ausdrücklich böse Absicht; ~ **trust** ausdrücklich *(durch Vertrag, letztwillige Verfügung etc)* geschaffenes Treuhandverhältnis; ~ →**warranty**

expressly, ~ or impliedly (or **by implication**) ausdrücklich oder stillschweigend; **unless ~ provided otherwise** soweit nicht ausdrücklich etwas anderes bestimmt ist

express 2. Eil-, Schnell- Express-; ~ **air cargo** Eilluftfracht; ~ **company** *Am* (Schnell-)-Transportfirma, Paketbeförderungsgesellschaft

express delivery *Br* Eilzustellung *(von Briefen und Paketen)*; Zustellung durch Eilboten; ~ **fee** Eilzustellgebühr; ~ **service** Eilzustelldienst

express, ~ fee Eilgebühr; ~ **highway** *Am* Schnellstraße, Autobahn; ~ **letter** *Br* Eilbrief; ~ **liner** *Am* Schnelldampfer; ~ **messenger** *Br* Eilbote; ~ **paid** Eilgebühr (od. Eilbote) bezahlt; ~ **parcel** Eilpaket; ~ **parcels** Schnellsendungen; ~ **road** Schnellstraße; ~ **service** Schnelldienst; ~ **train** Schnellzug, D-Zug; ~ **way** *Am* Autobahn

express, by (or **per**) ~ durch Eilboten *(zu bestellen)*; als Eilgut; **goods sent** ~ Eilfracht, Eilgut; **to send goods** ~ Waren als Eilfracht senden; **to send a letter** ~ e-n Eilbrief senden; **to send a parcel** ~ ein Eilpaket senden

express *v* ausdrücken, zum Ausdruck bringen; durch Eilboten (od. als Eilgut) senden; **to ~ one's astonishment** sein Befremden äußern; **they ~ed concern** sie gaben ihrer Besorgnis Ausdruck; **to ~ doubts** Zweifel (od. Bedenken) äußern; **to ~ one's regret** sein Bedauern ausdrücken; **to ~ one's thanks** seinen Dank aussprechen

expressed in dollars auf Dollar lautend

expressage *Am* Beförderung (von Waren, Briefen, Geld, Paketen) durch Eildienst; Beförderungsgebühr

expression Ausdruck; Redewendung; **freedom of** ~ Freiheit der Meinungsäußerung; **technical** ~ technischer Fachausdruck; **to give ~ to** zum Ausdruck bringen

expropriate *v* enteignen; **to ~ sb.'s property** jds

vermögenswertes Gut *(Grundstück, bewegliche Sache)* enteignen; **to ~ the owner of his land** jds Grundstück (od. Grundbesitz) enteignen; **to ~ property for public use** Privatbesitz zum Wohle der Allgemeinheit enteignen *(→public use)*

expropriation Enteignung; **~ upon payment of compensation** Enteignung gegen Entschädigung(sleistung); Enteignung gegen Zahlung e-r Entschädigungssumme

expulsion *(VölkerR)* Vertreibung; Ausweisung, Landesverweisung *(bes. e-s Ausländers; cf. undesirable alien)*; Ausschluß, Ausschließung *(e-s Mitglieds)*; **violent ~** gewaltsame Vertreibung; **~ damage** (or **loss**) Vertreibungsschaden; **~ decision** Ausweisungsbeschluß; **~ of a member from a club** Ausschluß e-s Mitglieds aus e-m Verein; **~ order** Ausweisungsbefehl; **~ of a partner** Ausschließung e-s Gesellschafters; **~ of a stateless person**[64] Ausweisung e-s Staatenlosen; **to make an ~ order** e-n Ausweisungsbefehl erlassen

expulsory proceedings Ausschlußverfahren *(Mitglied)*

expunge *v* ausstreichen; *(Eintragung)* löschen; **to ~ a p.'s name from the list** jds Namen von der Liste streichen

Extelcard verkürzter Prospekt im Rahmen des öffentlichen Angebots e-r Inhaberschuldverschreibung am Euromarkt

extend *v* verlängern; prolongieren; ausdehnen, erweitern, vergrößern; ausbauen; extensiv auslegen; *Am* den Wert *(von Grundbesitz des Vollstreckungsschuldners)* abschätzen; **to ~ the benefit** die (Versicherungs-)Leistung erweitern; **to ~ one's business** sein Geschäft vergrößern (od. ausbauen); **to ~ a bill** e-n Wechsel prolongieren; **to ~ a credit** e-n Kredit gewähren; e-n Kredit (od. ein Akkreditiv) verlängern; **to ~ hospitality to sb.** jdm Gastfreundschaft gewähren; **to ~ a lease** e-n Miet- (od. Pacht)vertrag verlängern; **to have one's passport ~ed** seinen Paß verlängern lassen; **to ~ a patent** ein Patent verlängern; **to ~ a period** e-e Frist verlängern; **to ~ one's premises** seinen Grundbesitz vergrößern; **to ~ a statutory provision** e-e Gesetzesbestimmung extensiv auslegen; **to ~ the term of office** die Amtszeit verlängern; **to ~ the time for payment** die Zahlungsfrist verlängern; **to ~ the validity** die Gültigkeitsdauer verlängern

extended, ~ clause erweiterter Eigentumsvorbehalt; **~ coverage insurance** Versicherung mit erhöhten Deckungsbeträgen; **~ family** Großfamilie

extended fund facility (EFF) *(IMF)* erweiterte Fondsfazilität

Mittelfristiges Programm zur Belebung strukturbedingter Ungleichgewichte in der Zahlungsbianz

extended →reservation of title

extended term, ~ insurance *(durch Verwendung des Rückkaufwertes [surrender value])* fortgesetzte Lebensversicherung *(ohne weitere Prämienzahlung)*; **~ of imprisonment** →term 2.

extendable, the agreement shall be ~ by mutual consent die Vereinbarung kann in gegenseitigem Einvernehmen verlängert werden

extension Verlängerung; Prolongation; Ausdehnung, Erweiterung, Vergrößerung; Ausweitung; Ausbau; Anbau; extensive Auslegung; *tel* Nebenanschluß; (Haus-)Apparat; **harbo(u)r ~** Ausbau e-s Hafens; **~ course** weiterführender Kurs; **~ (line)** *tel* Nebenanschluß; **~ of an agreement** Verlängerung e-s Vertrages; **~ of a business** Geschäftserweiterung; **~ of capacity** Kapazitätserweiterung; **~ of a conflict** Ausweitung e-s Konflikts; **~ of a credit** Kreditbereitstellung; Kreditverlängerung; Verlängerung e-s Akkreditivs; **~ to a house** Anbau e-s Hauses; **~ of influence** Ausdehnung des Einflusses (to auf); **~ of →judgments; ~ of jurisdiction** Zuständigkeitserweiterung; **~ of leave (of absence)** Urlaubsverlängerung; Nachurlaub; **~ plan** Ausbauvorhaben; **~ of the power of attorney** Verlängerung der Vollmacht; **~ of (the term of) a contract** Verlängerung e-s Vertrages, Vertragsverlängerung; **~ of (the term of) a patent** Verlängerung der Schutzdauer e-s Patents; Patentverlängerung; **~ of (the term of) payment** Zahlungsaufschub; Stundung

extension (of time) Verlängerung der Frist, Fristverlängerung; Nachfrist; **~ for payment** Verlängerung der Zahlungsfrist; Stundung; **application for ~** Fristgesuch; **request for ~** Antrag auf Fristverlängerung; **to get an ~** Fristverlängerung bekommen; **to grant an ~** Fristverlängerung gewähren; **to refuse an ~** Fristverlängerung verweigern; **to request an ~** um Fristverlängerung nachsuchen; Fristverlängerung beantragen

extension, ~ of time for appeal Verlängerung der Rechtsmittelfrist; **~ of validity** Verlängerung der Gültigkeitsdauer; **~ of works** Betriebserweiterung; **University E~** Volkshochschule; **to build an ~ to a hospital** e-n Anbau zu e-m Krankenhaus errichten

extensive extensiv; ausgedehnt, umfassend; **~ agriculture** extensive Wirtschaft *(opp. intensive)*; **~ interpretation** extensive Auslegung *(opp. restrictive)*; **~ knowledge** umfassende Kenntnisse

extent Ausdehnung, Länge, Höhe; Umfang, Ausmaß, Grad; **~ of a credit** Höhe e-s Kredits; **~ of damage (or loss)** Höhe (od. Umfang) des Schadens; Schadenshöhe; **~ of liability** Umfang der Haftung; **~ of a right** Umfang e-s Rechts; **to the ~ of** bis zur Höhe (od. bis zum Betrage) von; **to any ~** in beliebiger Höhe; **to a large ~** weitgehend; **to be liable to the ~ of**

one's property mit seinem ganzen Vermögen haften

extenuating circumstances, to allow ~ mildernde Umstände zubilligen

extenuation, in ~ of zur Milderung (od. Beschönigung) von

external auswärtig, Auslands-; äußere(r, -s); außerbetrieblich *(opp. internal);* außenwirtschaftlich; **~ account** *Br* Auslandskonto; **~ affairs** auswärtige Angelegenheiten *(e-s Landes);* außerbetriebliche Angelegenheiten *(e-r Firma);* **~ assets** Auslandsaktiva; Auslandsgelder; Vermögenswerte im Ausland; **~ assets and liabilities of domestic enterprises** Forderungen und Verbindlichkeiten inländischer Unternehmen gegenüber dem Ausland; **~ audit(ing)** außerbetriebliche Revision; **~ bill** Auslandswechsel; **~ bond** Auslandsschuldverschreibung, Auslandsanleihe; **~ claims** Auslandsforderungen; **E~ Contingency Facility** *(IMF)* (neue) Kreditfazilität *(für unvorhergesehene wirtschaftliche Notlagen der Schuldnerländer)*

external debt Auslandsschuld; **~ burden of a country** Auslandsverschuldung e-s Landes; **Agreement on German E~ D~s** →debt

external, ~ deficit Passivsaldo der Zahlungsbilanz *(opp. ~ surplus);* **~ disequilibrium** außenwirtschaftliches Ungleichgewicht; **~ duties** Außenzölle; **~ economic policy** Außenwirtschaftspolitik; **~ evidence** →extrinsic evidence; **~ factors** äußere Umstände; außenwirtschaftliche Umstände; **~ financing** Außenfinanzierung, Fremdfinanzierung

external frontiers, Community's ~ *(EG)* Außengrenzen der Gemeinschaft

external, ~ indebtedness Auslandsverschuldung; **~ liabilities** Auslandsverbindlichkeiten; **~ loan** Auslandsanleihe *(opp. domestic or internal loan);* **~ relations** Außenbeziehungen; auswärtige Beziehungen; außenwirtschaftliche Beziehungen; **~ relationship** Außenverhältnis; **~ research** außerbetriebliche Forschung; **~ surplus** Aktivsaldo der Zahlungsbilanz *(opp. ~ deficit);* **~ tariff** Außenzoll; **~ trade** Außenhandel; Transithandel; **~ transfer payments** *(Zahlungsbilanz)* Übertragungen *(unentgeltlicher Leistungen)* an das bzw. vom Ausland

exterritorial *(VölkerR)* exterritorial; **to possess ~ status** Exterritorialität genießen

exterritoriality *(VölkerR)* Exterritorialität *(cf. immunity)*

extinct erloschen; **~ firm** nicht mehr bestehende Firma; **to become ~** erlöschen; **the claim became ~** der Anspruch war erloschen; **a right is ~** ein Recht ist erloschen (od. untergegangen)

extinction Erlöschen, Untergang; **~ of a debt** Erlöschen e-r Schuld; **~ of the duty to pay the purchase price** Erlöschen der Zahlungsverpflichtung *(bei Sachmangel);* **~ of a right to damages** Erlöschen des Schadensersatzanspruches; **~ of a state** Untergang e-s Staates

extinctive prescription Verjährung; **period of ~** Verjährungsfrist

extinguish *v* tilgen; löschen; zum Erlöschen bringen; **to ~ a debt** e-e Schuld tilgen; **the mortgage has been ~ed** die Hypothek ist erloschen; **the obligations have been ~ed** die Verbindlichkeiten sind erloschen

extinguishment Tilgung; Löschung; Erlöschen; **~ of easements** Erlöschen von Grunddienstbarkeiten; **~ of the pledgor's lien** Erlöschen des Pfandrechts; **~ of a right** Erlöschen (od. Untergang) e-s Rechts

extort *v* erpressen; **to ~ a confession** ein Geständnis erpressen; **to ~ fees** unstatthafte Gebühren fordern; **threats with intent to ~ money or other things** Erpressung; erpresserisches Unternehmen *(schließt den Versuch des § 253 StGB ein)*

extortion Erpressung; unstatthafte Gebührenforderung; **~ of fees** Gebührenüberhebung; **~ by a public officer** Erpressung im Amt *(cf. colo[u]r of office)*

extortionist Erpresser

extra Extra-, Neben-, Sonder-; extra *(besonders);* fallweise eingestellte Arbeitskraft; **~s** Extrakosten, Extras; Nebenausgaben; Nebeneinnahmen; **~-budgetary** außeretatmäßig; **~ charge** Nebenkosten; Preisaufschlag; Zuschlag; **~ costs** Extrakosten; **~ duty** Zollaufschlag; **~-European** außereuropäisch; **~ fare** Zuschlag; **~ fee** Sonderhonorar; Zusatzgebühr; **~-hazardous employment** *(VersR) (für körperl. Sicherheit)* besonders gefährliche Beschäftigung; **~-hazardous risks** Sonderrisiken; **~ income** Nebeneinkommen; **~(-)judicial** außergerichtlich; **~marital cohabition** Ehe ohne Trauschein; **~marital relations** außereheliche Beziehungen; **~marital sexual intercourse** außerehelicher Geschlechtsverkehr; **~matrimonial** außerehelich

extramural außerhalb der Mauern *(e-r Stadt od. Universität);* **~ classes** (or **courses**) Hochschulkurse außerhalb der Universität; **~ student** Gasthörer

extraordinary außerordentlich, außergewöhnlich; außerplanmäßig; **~ depreciation** →depreciation; **~ expenses** außerordentliche Aufwendungen; **~ income** außerordentliche Erträge; **~ general meeting** *Br* außerordentliche Hauptversammlung *(e-r AG);* **~ powers** außerordentliche Vollmachten; **~ remedies** außerordentliche Rechtsbehelfe *(→Habeas Cor-*

pus, →certiorari etc); ~ **resolution** *Br (auf Hauptversammlung)* mit ¾ Mehrheit gefaßter Beschluß

extra, ~ **(-)parochial** außerhalb der (Pfarr-)Gemeinde; ~ **parliamentary** außerparlamentarisch; ~ **pay** Zulage *(zum Gehalt od. Lohn)*; Lohnzuschlag; ~ **premium** *(VersR)* erhöhte Prämie, Prämienzuschlag *(für bes. Risiken)*; ~**(-)-territorial** *(VölkerR)* exterritorial; außerhalb des Hoheitsgebietes; ~ **(-) territoriality** *(VölkerR)* Exterritorialität; ~ **vires** →ultra vires; ~ **work** Extraarbeit

extract Auszug; ~ **of account** Kontoauszug; Rechnungsauszug; **to make ~s from the records** Auszüge aus den Akten machen

extract *v* Auszug machen (from aus); *fig* etw. herausholen, entlocken; *(Bergbau)* fördern, gewinnen

extraction Abkunft, Herkunft; *(Bergbau)* Förderung, Gewinnung

extractive industry rohstofferzeugende Industrie *(mining, agriculture etc)*; Grundstoffindustrie

extraditable offen|ce (~se) auslieferungsfähige strafbare Handlung

extradite *v (VölkerR) (e-n flüchtigen Verbrecher zum Zwecke der Strafverfolgung)* ausliefern; **obligation to** ~ Auslieferungsverpflichtung; **person who has been ~d** der/die Ausgelieferte

extradition[65] *(VölkerR)* Auslieferung *(e-s flüchtigen Verbrechers)*; **European Convention of E~**[66] Europäisches Auslieferungsübereinkommen; **request for** ~ Auslieferungsersuchen; **treaty of** ~ Auslieferungsvertrag; **to grant (refuse)** ~ die Auslieferung gewähren (ablehnen); **to obtain the** ~ **of a fugitive criminal** die Auslieferung e-s flüchtigen Verbrechers erlangen

extraneous nicht gehörig (to zu); von außen (kommend); außerhalb der Sache liegend; fremd(ländisch); ~ **perils** *(VersR)* Sondergefahren

extreme äußerst; extrem, radikal; das Äußerste; Extrem; ~ **danger** höchste Gefahr; ~ **left** *pol* äußerste Linke; ~ **measure** drastische Maßnahme; ~ **opinions** →~ views; ~ **penalty** Todesstrafe; ~ **right** *pol* äußerste Rechte; **to hold** ~ **views** extreme (od. radikale) Ansichten vertreten

extremist *pol* Extremist, extrem Gesinnter, Radikaler; **left-wing** ~ **group** linksextremistischer (od. äußerster linker) Flügel

extremit|y höchster Grad; äußerste Not(lage); äußerstes Ende, Spitze; **~ies** äußerste Maßnahmen; **to proceed to ~ies** äußerste Maßnahmen ergreifen

extrinsic äußerlich, nicht zur Sache gehörend; nicht Bestandteil e-r Urkunde; unwesentlich *(opp. intrinsic)*; ~ **evidence** Beweis, der nicht aus der Urkunde selbst hervorgeht

eyecatcher Blickfang

eye(-)witness Augenzeuge; ~ **account of a crime** Augenzeugenbericht e-s Verbrechens

eye(-)witness *v Am* Augenzeuge sein

F

fabric Gefüge, Struktur; Bau, Bauerhaltung *(bes. von Kirchen)*; Gewebe, Stoff; **social** ~ soziales Gefüge

fabricate *v fig* erfinden, erdichten; fälschen; *(selten:)* fabrizieren, herstellen

fabricated, ~ **document** gefälschte Urkunde; ~ **evidence** *(nachträglich)* konstruierte Beweismittel

fabrication *fig* Erfindung, Erdichtung; Fälschung; *(selten:)* Fabrikation, Herstellung; ~ **of evidence** Herstellung falschen Beweismaterials

face Vorderseite *(opp. back)*; **on the** ~ der äußeren Aufmachung nach; **on the** ~ **of it** nach dem Äußeren, von außen gesehen; allem Anschein nach; **on the** ~ **of the bill** auf der Vorderseite des Wechsels; **on the** ~ **of a contract** im Text (od. Wortlaut) e-s Vertrages

face amount Nennwert, Nominalwert; ~ **certificates** *Am* Nennwert-Zertifikate; **F~ A~ Certificate Companies** *Am* (Investment-)Gesellschaften, die ~ certificates ausgeben

face, ~ **of the instrument** Wortlaut der Urkunde; ~ **of the judgment** Wortlaut des Urteils; ~ **value** Nennwert, Nominalwert; ~ **value swap** Forderungstausch zum Nominalwert

face *v (e-r Sache)* gegenüberstehen; gegenüberliegen; *(e-r Gefahr)* ins Auge sehen, hinnehmen; **to** ~ **competition** der Konkurrenz begegnen; **to** ~ **a charge** (of sth.) sich *(vor Gericht)* zu verantworten haben (wegen); **a country is ~d with economic difficulties** ein Land steht vor wirtschaftlichen Schwierigkeiten

facere *(VölkerR)* Tun *(Pflicht)*; **non** ~ Unterlassen, Nichteingreifen *(Enthaltungspflicht)*

facia Ladenschild

facilitate *v* erleichtern, fördern

facilities (facs) Möglichkeiten; Anlagen, Einrichtungen; ~ **for payment** Zahlungsmöglichkeiten; ~ **for loading** Ladeeinrichtungen; ~ **of production** Produktionsmittel; ~ **for the purpose of storage** Einrichtungen zur Lagerung; ~ **for travel** Reisemöglichkeiten *(Zug, Flugzeug etc)*; **credit** ~ Kreditfazilitäten; **port** ~ Hafenanlagen; **telephone** ~ Fernsprechanlage; **transport** ~ Transportmöglichkeiten

facility Fazilität *(Kreditrahmen von Banken; Kreditfazilität des Internationalen Währungsfonds)*

facsimile Faksimile; genaue Nachbildung; ~ **broadcasting** Bildfunk; ~ **signature** Faksimileunterschrift; ~ **stamp** Faksimilestempel, Namensstempel

facsimile *v* (*colloq.* fax) telekopieren

fact Tat; Tatsache, Umstand; ~**s of the case** Sachverhalt, Tatbestand; ~ **of common knowledge** allgemein bekannte Tatsache; **the ~s are as follows** (or **these are the ~s**) folgendes ist der Sachverhalt (od. Tatbestand)

fact-finding Tatsachenfeststellung; zur Feststellung des Sachverhalts (dienend); ~ **commission** Untersuchungskommission; ~ **tour** Informationsreise

facts in issue strittige (od. bestrittene) Tatsachen; zu beweisende Tatsachen *(facta probanda; opp. evidentiary facts)*

fact, accomplished ~ vollendete Tatsache; **admission of a** ~ Zugeben (od. Eingeständnis) e-r Tatsache; **ascertainment of ~s** Feststellung von Tatsachen, Tatsachenfeststellung; **constituent** ~ Tatbestandsmerkmal; **error in** ~ Tatsachenirrtum; **established** ~ feststehende Tatsache; **findings of ~(s)** Tatsachenfeststellung; **immaterial** ~ unwesentliche Tatsache

fact, in ~ tatsächlich; **in ~ and in law** in tatsächlicher und in rechtlicher Hinsicht

fact, issue of ~ Tat(sachen)frage; **matter of** ~ Tatsache; Tatbestand; *bes. Am (strittige)* Tatfrage *(die von der →jury zu entscheiden ist)*; **as a matter of** ~ tatsächlich

fact, mistake of ~ Tatsachenirrtum; **possession in** ~ tatsächlicher Besitz; **presumption of** ~ Tatsachenvermutung; **question of** ~ Tatfrage; **statement of ~s** Sachverhalt; Tatbestand; Darstellung des Tatbestandes

fact, to ascertain ~s Tatsachen feststellen; **to be in accordance with the ~s** den Tatsachen entsprechen; **to be founded on ~s** auf Tatsachen beruhen

faction *parl* Faktion; *(oft unzufriedener)* Flügel *(e-r Partei)*; **the party has split into ~s** die Partei hat sich in Splittergruppen (od. rivalisierende Gruppen) gespalten

factionalism *parl* Flügelbildung

factionalize *v*, **to be ~d** in Flügel zersplittert sein

factor 1. Faktor, Umstand; mitbestimmende Ursache; ~ **cost** Faktorkosten; ~ **of production** Produktionsfaktor; **determining** ~ entscheidender Faktor; **external (internal) ~s** äußere (innere) Umstände; **the human** ~ **in business** der Mensch im Betrieb **safety** ~ Sicherheitsfaktor; **success ~s** Erfolgsfaktoren

factor 2. Kommissionär *(der die Ware, die er verkauft, im Besitz hat und im Ggs. zum Makler [broker] im eigenen Namen handelt)*; *Scot* Gutsverwalter; **~'s lien** Kommissionärspfandrecht *(Zurückbehaltungs- und Befriedigungsrecht des Kommissionärs an Gegenständen des Kommittenten)*

factor 3. Factor *(Factoring-Bank oder -Gesellschaft, die Forderungen aufkaufen; →factoring)*

Factors Chain International (FCI) führender internationaler Factoring-Verband *(Sitz: Amsterdam. 66 Mitglieder in 27 Ländern)*

factor, ~'s lien *(gesetzl.)* Sicherungsrecht des Factor am gesamten Lager in seinem jeweiligen Bestand

factorage Provision des Kommissionärs *(factor 2.)*; Entgelt des Factor *(factor 3.)*

factoring Factoring(-geschäft); ~ **client** Factoring-Kunde, Anschlußkunde *(e-s Factoring-Instituts)*

Factoring ist eine Absatzfinanzierungsmethode, bei der eine Herstellerfirma ihre Außenstände an den Factor *(factor 3.)* verkauft, der die gesamte buchhalterische Arbeit, wie Fakturieren, Inkasso, Mahnen und Beitreiben der Forderungen (sowie das Kreditrisiko) übernimmt.

Im Ggs. zu den USA besteht in der Bundesrepublik Deutschland das den wirtschaftlichen Fortschritt behindernde Abtretungsverbot des § 399 BGB

factorize *v Am (z.B. in Connecticut, Vermont)* Drittschuldner pfänden

factorizing *Am* Pfändung e-s Drittschuldners

factor|y Fabrik, Fabrikgebäude; Fabrikationsstätte; Betrieb(sanlage); *Scot (auch)* Vollmacht; **(commercial)** ~ Faktorei, Handelsniederlassung *(in Übersee)*; **F~ies Acts** *Br* Arbeiterschutzgesetze *(safety regulations, working conditions etc)*; ~ **committee** Betriebsrat; ~ **cost** Herstellungskosten; ~ **expense** Fertigungsgemeinkosten; ~ **extension** Betriebserweiterung; ~ **hand** Fabrikarbeiter(in); ~ **inspection** *Br* Besichtigung von Fabriken *(zur Kontrolle, ob die F~ies Acts befolgt sind)*; **F~ Inspectors** (or **Inspectorate)** *Br* Gewerbepolizei; ~ **legislation** Arbeiterschutzgesetzgebung; **~-made** fabrikmäßig hergestellt; **~- made goods** Fabrikware(n); ~ **management** Fabrikleitung, Betriebsleitung; ~ **manager** Fabrikleiter, Betriebsleiter; ~ **overhead** Fertigungsgemeinkosten; ~ **owner** Fabrikbesitzer; ~ **plant** Fabrikanlage; ~ **price** Preis ab Fabrik; Fabrikpreis; ~ **regulations** Betriebsordnung; ~ **town** Fabrikstadt; ~ **vessel** Fischverarbeitungsschiff; ~ **worker** Fabrikarbeiter(in)

factory, ex~ ab Fabrik *(Käufer übernimmt Transportkosten und -gefahr ab Fabrik);* **to manage a ~** e-e Fabrik leiten; **to run a ~** e-e Fabrik betreiben; **to set up a ~** e-e Fabrik errichten

factual tatsächlich; auf Tatsachen beruhend; ~ **account** (or **report**) Tatsachenbericht; ~ **data** (or **material**) Tatsachenmaterial; ~ **issue** Beweisthema; ~ **and legal position** Sach- und Rechtslage

facultative fakultativ, freigestellt, dem Ermessen überlassen *(opp. obligatory);* ~ **compensation** Ermessensentschädigung; ~ **disposition** Kannvorschrift; ~ **reinsurance** fakultative Rückversicherung

facult|y Fähigkeit, Vermögen; *Br eccl* Dispens; *univ* Fakultät; *Am* Lehrkörper *(e-r Universität od. Schule);* **F~ of Actuaries** *Scot* Verein der Versicherungsmathematiker; **F~ of Advocates** *Scot* Anwaltsvereinigung; **F~ of Law** juristische Fakultät; →**Court of F~ies**

fail *v* keinen Erfolg haben, scheitern; *(im Prozeß)* unterliegen; *(im Examen)* durchfallen; nicht tun, unterlassen, versäumen; versagen; Bankrott machen, Zahlungen einstellen, in Konkurs geraten; **the attempt ~ed** der Versuch schlug fehl; **the condition ~s** die Bedingung entfällt; **the examiner ~ed the candidate** der Prüfer ließ den Kandidaten durchfallen; **the negotiations ~ed** die Verhandlungen scheiterten; **the supplies ~ed** die Vorräte gingen aus; **to ~ to appear** *(in e-m Termin)* nicht erscheinen, ausbleiben; **to ~ in one's duties** seine Pflichten vernachlässigen; **to ~ (in) an examination** e-e Prüfung nicht bestehen; **to ~ to inform** nicht anzeigen, Anzeige unterlassen; **to ~ to pay one's debts** seine Schulden nicht bezahlen; **to ~ in a suit** e-n Prozeß verlieren; **to ~ to settle a quarrel** keinen Erfolg haben, e-n Streit zu schlichten

failed marriage zerrüttete Ehe

failing Fehlschlagen, Scheitern; in Ermangelung (von), mangels; ~ **him** falls er ausfällt; ~ **this** andernfalls, wenn nicht; ~ **which** widrigenfalls; ~ **an answer** falls keine Antwort eingeht; **his ~ to appear in court** sein Nichterscheinen vor Gericht; ~ **company** sich in Schwierigkeiten befindende Gesellschaft

failing company defense *Am (bei Beurteilung der Kartellrechtswidrigkeit e-r Fusion)* Berufung darauf, daß e-s der fusionierenden Unternehmen ohne den Zusammenschluß insolviert würde

failing, ~ your consent in Ermangelung Ihrer Zustimmung; ~ **payment** mangels Zahlung; ~ **proof** mangels Beweises (od. des Nachweises); ~ **special agreement** in Ermangelung besonderer Vereinbarung

failure Mißerfolg, Scheitern; Unterlassung, Versäumnis, Versagen; Zusammenbruch *(e-s Unternehmens),* Bankrott, Zahlungseinstellung, Insolvenz; ~ **of a conference** Scheitern e-r Konferenz; ~ **of consideration** Mangel der Gegenleistung; ~ **of crop(s)** Mißernte; ~ **of an instal(l)ment** Ausbleiben e-r Rate; ~ **of issue** (Sterben) ohne Abkömmlinge; ~ **of justice** Versagen der Justiz; ~ **of marriage** Scheitern der Ehe; ~ **of a plan** Scheitern e-s Plans; ~ **of record** Nichtvorlage e-r Beweisurkunde *(durch den Beklagten);* ~ **of performance** Nichterfüllung; ~ **of proof** Mißlingen des Beweises; ~ **to answer questions** Nichtbeantwortung von Fragen; ~ **to appeal within the prescribed period** Versäumnis der Rechtsmittelfrist (Berufungsfrist etc); ~ **to appear in court** Nichterscheinen vor Gericht; ~ **to comply (with)** Nichteinhaltung, Nichtbefolgung, Nichterfüllung; Nichtbeachtung; ~ **to comply with a summons** Nichterscheinen, Ausbleiben *(vor Gericht);* ~ **to comply with the time-limit** Fristversäumnis, Fristüberschreitung; ~ **to deliver** Nichtlieferung; Liefer(ungs)verzug; ~ **to effect delivery** Nichtbewirkung der Lieferung; ~ **to enter an appearance** Versäumnis der Einlassung; ~ **to file a return** Nichteinreichung e-r (Einkommen-)Steuererklärung (od. *Br* des Berichts e-r Handelsgesellschaft); ~ **to fulfil** Nichterfüllung; ~ **to obey an order** Nichtbefolgung e-r Anordnung; ~ **to observe the law** Nichtbeachtung des Gesetzes; ~ **to observe the time limit** Fristversäumnis, Fristüberschreitung; ~ **to pay** Nichtzahlung; Zahlungsversäumnis; ~ **to pay on due date** Zahlungsverzug; ~ **to perform a contract** Nichterfüllung e-s Vertrags; ~ **to render a report** Nichterstattung e-r Meldung

failure, action for ~ to act →action; **banking ~** Bankkrach, Bankzusammenbruch; →**business ~**; **crop ~** Mißernte; **technical ~** technisches Versagen; **to bring about the ~ of sth.** etw. zum Scheitern bringen; **to be doomed to ~** zum Scheitern verurteilt sein

fair Messe; Ausstellung; Jahrmarkt; ~ **authorities** Messeleitung, Ausstellungsleitung; ~ **building** Messegebäude; Ausstellungsgebäude; ~ **catalog(ue)** (or **directory**) Messekatalog; Ausstellungsverzeichnis; ~ **ground(s)** (or **site**) Messegelände; Ausstellungsgelände; ~ **stand** Messestand; **agricultural ~** Landwirtschaftsausstellung; **British Industries F~** britische Industriemesse; **industrial** (or **industries**) ~ (Industrie-)Messe; Industrieausstellung; **management of a ~** Messeleitung; **samples ~** Mustermesse; **special** (or **specialized**) ~ Fachmesse; **textile goods ~** Textilmesse; **trade ~** Fachmesse; **Union of Industrial F~s** Internationaler Messeverband; **visitor to a ~** Messebesucher; **world ~** Weltausstellung; **to attend a ~** e-e Messe (od. Ausstellung) besuchen; **to display**

(or **exhibit**) **goods at a** ~ auf e-r Messe ausstellen; **to hold a** ~ e-e Messe abhalten; **to organize a** ~ e-e Messe veranstalten; **to register for a** ~ sich zu e-r Messe anmelden; **to visit a** ~ e-e Messe besuchen

fair gerecht, billig; fair, anständig; leidlich, einigermaßen gut, mittelmäßig; aussichtsreich, vielversprechend; angemessen, annehmbar *(Wert, Preis, Bedingungen, Lohn)*; ~ **and accurate report** sachlicher und wahrheitsgetreuer Bericht; ~ **and equitable** (ge)recht und billig; ~ **and reasonable compensation** angemessene Entschädigung; ~ **average quality** *(faq)* gute Durchschnittsqualität; Handelsgut mittlerer Art und Güte

fair comment[1] (on a matter of public interest) *(BeleidigungsR)* sachliche Kritik

Beklagter kann gegen eine Klage wegen libel oder slander einwenden, seine Äußerung stelle ein fair comment an einem Gegenstand des öffentlichen Interesses dar

fair, ~ **competition** redlicher Wettbewerb; ~ **copy** Reinschrift; druckfertiges Manuskript; **F~ Credit Reporting Act** *Am* Gesetz, das die faire Auskunft über persönliche Verhältnisse von Kreditnehmern sichern soll; ~ **damages** angemessene Entschädigung; ~→**deal;** ~ **dealing** redliches Verhalten; anständiges Geschäftsgebaren; Kulanz; ~ **dismissal** gerechtfertigte Entlassung

fair employment practices *Am* faire Beschäftigungsmethoden *(Nichtdiskriminierung bei Einstellung und Beschäftigung von Angestellten und Arbeitern)*; **F~ E~ P~ Committee** (FEPC) *Am* Kommission zur Überwachung der ~

fair, ~ **game** jagdbares Wild; ~ **hearing** rechtliches Gehör; **F~ Labor Standards Act** (FLSA) *Am*[1a] Gesetz für angemessene Arbeitsbedingungen; ~ **market value** (FMV) Marktwert, Verkehrswert; **F~ Plan** *Am (VersR)* „Fairer Plan" *(der den Grundstückseigentümern Schutz bieten soll, deren Grundbesitz sich in gefährdeten oder an Wert abnehmenden Gegenden befindet)*; ~ **play** ehrliches Spiel, redliches Verfahren; ~ **practices** anständiges Geschäftsgebaren; **F~ Practices Rules** *Am* →rule 1.; ~ **price** angemessener Preis; ~ **profit(s)** angemessener Gewinn; ~ **promise(s)** schöne Versprechungen *(z.B. e-s Politikers vor der Wahl)*; ~ **return method** Methode der Besteuerung auf Grundlage des angemessenen Gewinns; ~ **share** gerechter Anteil

fair trade *Am (vertikale)* Preisbindung; **F~ T~ Acts** *Am* Gesetze zur Legalisierung der Preisbindung der zweiten Hand von Markenartikeln *(in einigen Einzelstaaten für verfassungswidrig erklärt)*; ~ **agreement** *Br* Vereinbarung von →resale price maintenance

fair trading lauterer Handel; *Am colloq.* vertikale Preisbindung; **F~ T~ Act,** 1973 *Br* Verbraucherschutz- und Wettbewerbsgesetz; Kartellgesetz; ~ **firm** *Am* preisbindendes Unternehmen; **Director-General of F~ T~** *Br* Präsident des Office of Fair Trading *(ihm obliegen wichtige Aufgaben im Hinblick auf Handelspraktiken [unlauterer Wettbewerb] und den Verbraucherschutz), (→Office of F~ T~)*

fair, ~ **treatment** gerechte Behandlung; ~ **trial** unparteiisches (Beweis-)Verfahren; ~ **use** *(UrhR)* freie Benutzung; ~ **value** angemessener Wert

fairway Fahrrinne

fait accompli *Fr dipl (durch die Außenpolitik e-s Staates geschaffene)* vollendete Tatsache

faith Vertrauen, Glaube; Treue; Glaubensbekenntnis, Religion; **bad** ~ böser Glaube; *(etwa:)* Unredlichkeit; **in bad** ~ bösgläubig; unredlich; wider Treu und Glauben; **breach of** ~ Treubruch, Wortbruch; Vertrauensbruch; **Christian** ~ christlicher Glaube; christliche Religion; **freedom of** ~ Glaubensfreiheit, Religionsfreiheit

faith, full ~ **and credit** *Am* volle Anerkennung; **full** ~ **and credit clause** *Am* Bestimmung der Bundesverfassung *(Art. IV, section 1)*, wonach öffentliche Akten, Register und gerichtl. Verfahren e-s Einzelstaates im ganzen Bundesgebiet der USA anzuerkennen sind

faith, good ~ guter Glaube; Treu und Glauben; **in good** ~ in gutem Glauben, gutgläubig; nach Treu und Glauben; **protection of third parties acting in good** ~ Schutz gutgläubiger Dritter; **purchaser in good** ~ gutgläubiger Käufer; **to demonstrate good** ~ guten Glauben bezeugen

faithful treu; genau, gewissenhaft; ~ **translation** wortgetreue Übersetzung; **yours** ~**ly** *Br* hochachtungsvoll *(als Briefschluß)*

fake Fälschung, Nachahmung; gefälscht; ~ **oil-painting** gefälschtes Ölgemälde

fake *v* fälschen, nachahmen; *(Bilanz)* verschleiern

faking of a balance sheet Bilanzverschleierung

fall Fall, Sturz; Fallen, Sinken, Rückgang; *(Börse)* Kurssturz, Baisse *(opp. rise)*; *Am* Herbst

fall-back, ~ **payment** Mindestlohn für Akkordarbeiter *(→pieceworkers' guarantee clause)*; ~ **price** Mindestpreis

fall, ~ **in the birth rate** Geburtenrückgang; ~ **in demand** Rückgang der Nachfrage; ~ **in the interest rate** Zinsrückgang; ~ **in prices** Preisrückgang, Preissturz; *(Börse)* Kurssturz, Kurseinbruch; Baisse; ~ **of the government** *Br* Sturz der Regierung; ~ **of the hammer** Zuschlag *(bei Auktionen)*; ~ **of stocks and shares** Fallen der Aktien; **dealing for a** ~ *(Börse)* Baissespekulation; **to go** (or **speculate**) **for a** ~ auf Baisse spekulieren

fall(-)off in production Rückgang der Produktion

fall(-)out *(mit dem Hauptprodukt anfallendes)* Nebenprodukt; zusätzliches Ergebnis *(e-r Forschung);* Atomstaub

fall *v* fallen, heruntergehen, sinken *(Preise, Kurse);* **to ~ within an Act** unter ein Gesetz fallen; **to ~ within an agreement** unter e-n Vertrag fallen; **he fell into arrears with the rent** er geriet in Rückstand mit der Miete; **to ~ into** (or **within**) **a category** unter e-e Kategorie fallen; **to ~ in price** im Preise (od. Kurs) fallen; **to ~ to sb.'s share** auf jdn fallen, jdm zufallen; **to ~ within the terms of the convention** unter die Bestimmungen des Abkommens fallen; **to ~ in value** im Werte sinken, an Wert verlieren

fall *v,* **to ~ back** zurückfallen, zurückgehen (from von, to auf); **to ~ back (up)on** zurückgreifen auf; **to ~ behind** zurückfallen (hinter), im Rückstand sein; **to ~ below** unterschreiten; **to ~ down** einstürzen; **to ~ due** fällig werden; **the bill will ~ due on** der Wechsel wird fällig am; **to ~ in** einfallen, einstürzen; **the lease ~s in** die Pacht läuft ab; **to ~ in with** eingehen auf *(e-n Vorschlag* etc); übereinstimmen mit *(e-m Plan etc);* **to ~ off** abfallen, abtrünnig werden; absinken, zurückgehen, sich vermindern; **to ~ (up)on** zu Lasten gehen von; entfallen auf; *(jdm)* obliegen; **the loss ~s upon X** den Schaden trägt X

fallen, the ~ die *(im Krieg)* Gefallenen

fallen, the bill has ~ due der Wechsel ist fällig geworden

falling Fallen, Sinken, Rückgang; fallend, sinkend, abnehmend; **~ away** Abfall *(von e-r Partei);* **~ of the birth rate** Rückgang der Geburtenziffer, Geburtenrückgang; **~ demand** Nachfragerückgang; **~ of prices** Sinken der Preise; **~ off of orders** Rückgang der Aufträge; Auftragsrückgang; **~ off in the proceeds** Rückgang der Einnahmen, Einnahmerückgang; **~ shares** fallende Aktien; **~ value of the currency** Währungsverfall; **to be ~** *(im Preis, Kurs)* sinken (od. fallen)

false falsch, unrichtig, unwahr; unecht, nachgemacht, gefälscht; **~ accounting**[2] Erstellung falscher Abrechnungen; **~ accusation** falsche Anschuldigung; **~ alarm** blinder Alarm; **~ arrest** unberechtigte Festnahme; **~ character**[3] gefälschtes (od. fingiertes) Arbeits- (od. Dienst-)Zeugnis; **~ claim** vorgespiegelte Forderung; in Bereicherungsabsicht vorgespiegelte Forderung; **~ coin** Falschgeld; gefälschte Münze; **~ coining** Falschmünzerei; **~ coiner** Falschmünzer; **~ colo(u)rs** falsche Flagge; falsche Aufmachung; **~ data** falsche Angaben; **~ entry** falsche Eintragung (od. Buchung); gefälschte Eintragung (od. Buchung)

false evidence falsche (Zeugen-)Aussage; **to give ~** falsch aussagen

false, ~ imprisonment ungesetzliche Haft; Freiheitsberaubung *(cf. Habeas Corpus);* **~ information** *(absichtlich)* falsche Auskunft; **~ instrument** gefälschte Urkunde; **~ judgment** Fehlurteil; **~ lights** falsche Lichtsignale *(die ein Schiff irreführen);* **~ oath** Falscheid, Meineid *(→false swearing);* **~ personation** Sichausgeben für e-n anderen

false pretences falsche Darstellung, falsche Behauptung; **under ~** unter Vorspiegelung falscher Tatsachen; **obtaining credit by ~** Kreditbetrug; **obtaining** (goods, money etc) **by ~** *Br* Betrug

false, ~ report Falschmeldung; **~ representation** falsche Darstellung; unrichtige Angabe(n); Vorspiegelung falscher Tatsachen; **~ return** falscher Bericht; unrichtige Steuererklärung; falsch beurkundetes Protokoll e-s Gerichtsvollziehers (od. Vollstreckungs- od. Vollzugsbeamten) über die von ihm ausgeführte Amtshandlung

false statement falsche Angabe (od. Erklärung); falsche Aufstellung; Falschaussage; **~s of origin of merchandise** falsche Herkunftsangaben auf Waren *(cf. Madrid Arrangement);* **to make a ~ in court** vor Gericht falsch aussagen; **to make ~s in writing** falsche schriftliche Angaben machen

false swearing *Br*[4] *(außergerichtliches) (bewußtes)* Falschschwören *(wird wie perjury bestraft, aber nicht so benannt)*

Der fahrlässige Falscheid ist dem anglo-amerikanischen Recht unbekannt

false, ~ trade description falsche Warenbezeichnung; **~ verdict** Fehlurteil

false witness falsches Zeugnis; **to bear ~** falsche Zeugenaussage(n) machen

falsely, ~ accused falsch beschuldigt; **to suspect sb. ~** jdn falsch verdächtigen

falsehood Unwahrheit, Lüge; **~, fraud, and wilful imposition** *Scot* Betrug; **injurious ~** *Br* Anschwärzung *(umfaßt alle Fälle, in denen durch falsche Behauptungen e-m anderen maliciously Schaden zugefügt wird; cf. slander of title, slander of goods)*

falsification Fälschung, Verfälschung; Falschbekundung; **~ of accounts** Fälschung von Büchern (od. Abrechnungen); **~ of documents** Urkundenfälschung; **~ of a signature** Unterschriftsfälschung

falsifier Fälscher

falsify *v* fälschen, verfälschen; fälschlich anfertigen; als falsch nachweisen; **to ~ accounts** Abrechnungen fälschen; **to ~ an item in an account** *(vor Gericht)* beweisen, daß ein Rechnungsbetrag falsch ist

falsity Falschheit, Unrichtigkeit; Unwahrheit; ~ **of a statement** Unwahrheit e-r Behauptung

fame *(guter)* Ruf; **ill-~** schlechter Ruf

familiarize *v,* **to ~ oneself with sth.** sich mit etw. vertraut machen; sich in etw. einarbeiten

family Familie; ~ →**allowance;** ~ **arrangement** Familienübereinkunft *(betreffend das Familienvermögen);* **deed of ~ arrangement** zwischen Familienmitgliedern abgeschlossener Vertrag über Familienvermögen; ~ **benefits** Familienleistungen, Familienbeihilfen; ~ **bond** Familiensparbrief *(e-s Kleinversicherungsvereins);* ~ **business** Familienbetrieb; ~ **circumstances** Familienverhältnisse; ~ **claim** *(in Bereicherungsabsicht)* vorgetäuschter Anspruch; ~ **(- owned) company** Familiengesellschaft; ~ **council** Familienrat; ~ **coat of arms** Familienwappen; ~ **credit** *Br* Zuschuß zum Familieneinkommen (Sozialhilfe)

Family Division *Br*[5] Abteilung des High Court of Justice für Ehesachen, Mündelsachen, Adoptionen und nicht streitige Nachlaßsachen. Berufungsinstanz für Mündelsachen, Unterhaltssachen, Vaterschaftssachen (affiliation proceedings) und Adoptionen

family dwelling, single or duplex ~ *Am* Ein- oder Zweifamilienhaus

family, ~ **estate** Familiengut; ~ **expenses** *Am* Aufwendungen für den Unterhalt der Familie; ~ **expense statutes** *Am* Gesetze, nach denen die Ehefrau neben dem Ehemann für bestimmte Haushaltsausgaben *(necessaries)* haftet; ~ **helps** mitarbeitende Familienangehörige; ~ **holding** *(landwirtschaftl.)* Familienbetrieb; ~**-income policy** das Familieneinkommen sichernde Risikolebensversicherung; ~ **law** Familienrecht

Family Law Reform Act *Br* Reformgesetz zum Familienrecht *(von 1969)*

Das Gesetz stellt u. a. die gesetzliche Erbfolge auch zwischen Eltern und ihren nichtehelichen Kindern her (→intestacy)

family, ~ **matters** Familienangelegenheiten; ~ **member** Familienangehörige(r); ~ **name** Familienname; ~**-owned enterprise** Familienbetrieb; ~ **partnership** Familien-Personengesellschaft; ~ **planning** Familienplanung; ~ **provision** Versorgung für Familienangehörige *(aus dem Nachlaß zu zahlender Unterhalt);* ~ **-purpose doctrine** *Am* Kraftfahrzeughalter-Haftung für Familienangehörige; ~ **reunion** Familienzusammenführung *(e-r Flüchtlingsfamilie);* ~ **settlement** *Br* Erbregelungs- und Abfindungsvertrag *(Vorsorge für die Zukunft e-r schon bestehenden Familie; cf. marriage settlement);* ~ **shareholder** Familienaktionär; ~**-size package** Großpackung; ~ **tree** Stammbaum; Ahnentafel; ~ **trust** Familienstiftung; ~ **undertaking** Familienbetrieb; ~ **vault** Familiengruft

family, head of the ~ Familienvorstand, -oberhaupt; **large** ~ kinderreiche Familie

famine, countries threatened with ~ von Hungersnot bedrohte Länder; ~ **relief** Linderung der Hungersnot

fancy, ~ **articles** (or **goods)** Luxuswaren; Modeartikel; ~ **fair** Wohltätigkeitsbasar; ~ **name** Phantasiename, -bezeichnung; ~ **price** *colloq.* Phantasiepreis; ~ **stocks** *Am* unsichere Spekulationspapiere

Fannie Mae *Am* Börsenausdruck für die →Federal National Mortgage Association

fare Fahrgeld, Fahrpreis; Schiffspassage; Flugpreis; Fahrgast; Kost, Essen; ~ **increase** Fahrpreiserhöhung, Flugpreiserhöhung; ~ **stage** Teilstrecke; Tarifgrenze; **(air)** ~ Flugpreis; **bill of** ~ Speisekarte; **excess** ~ Zuschlag; **half** ~ **ticket** Fahrkarte zu halbem Preise; **full** ~ **ticket** Fahrkarte zu vollem Preise; **railway** *Br* **(railroad** *Am)* **(passenger)** ~**s** Eisenbahntarif *(für Personen);* **at (a) reduced** ~ zu ermäßigtem Fahrpreis; **return** ~ *(Am* **round trip** ~) Fahrpreis für Hin- und Rückfahrt; **single** ~ einfacher Fahrpreis; **train** ~**s** s. railway →~**s**; **to pay full** ~ den vollen Fahrpreis bezahlen

farewell, ~ **audience** Abschiedsaudienz; ~ **reception** Abschiedsempfang; ~ **speech** Abschiedsrede; ~ **visit** Abschiedsbesuch

farm Bauernhof, Pachthof; landwirtschaftlicher Betrieb, Agrarbetrieb; (Land-)Gut; Farm; *Am (einzelstaatl.)* Gefängnis *(bes. für misdemeanants);* ~ **bailiff** *Br* Gutsverwalter, Inspektor; ~ **bloc** *Am* „Grüne Front"; ~ **credit** Agrarkredit, Kredit an landwirtschaftliche Betriebe

Farm Credit Administration (FCA) *Am* oberste Aufsichtsbehörde des Agrarkreditwesens

Abteilung des →Department of Agriculture, beaufsichtigt →Federal Land Banks, →Federal Intermediate Credit Banks etc

farm, ~**hand** *bes. Am* Landarbeiter; ~ **income** landwirtschaftliche Einkünfte, Einkünfte aus Landwirtschaft; ~ **labo(u)rer** Landarbeiter; ~ **land** landwirtschaftliches Land, landwirtschaftliche Betriebsfläche; ~ **lease** *(landwirtschaftl.)* Pachtvertrag; ~ **let to a tenant** verpachteter Hof; ~ **loan** *Am* Darlehen an landwirtschaftliche Betriebe; Agrarkredit; **F**~ **Loan Bank** *Am* →Federal Land Bank; ~ **loan bonds** *Am (von den →Federal Land Banks)* gegen Sicherung durch Hypotheken auf landwirtschaftliche Grundstücke ausgegebene Obligationen; ~ **management** landwirtschaftliche Betriebsführung; Gutsbewirtschaftung; ~ **manager** *(landwirtschaftl.)* Verwalter; Gutsverwalter; ~ **mortgage** Hypothek an e-m landwirtschaftlich genutzten Grundstück; ~ **mutuals** *Am* landwirtschaftliche VVaGs *(Versicherungsvereine auf Gegenseitigkeit);* ~ **prices** Preise für landwirtschaftliche Produkte, Agrarpreise; **(ex)** ~ **price** Preis ab Hof

farm products landwirtschaftliche Erzeugnisse; **prices of** ~ Agrarpreise

farm, ~ **rent** Pacht(zins); ~**stead** Gehöft; Bauernhof; ~ **stock** landwirtschaftliches Inventar; Viehbestand; ~ **tenancy** Pacht e-s Hofes; ~ **worker** Landarbeiter, Arbeitnehmer in der Landwirtschaft; ~ **yard** Gehöft

farm, experimental ~ Versuchsgut; **home** (or **owner-operated**) ~ selbst bewirtschaftetes Gut; **model** ~ landwirtschaftlicher Musterbetrieb; **to let a** ~ **to a tenant** e-n Hof verpachten; **to rent a** ~ (or **to take a** ~ **on lease**) e-n Hof pachten

farm *v* *(Hof)* bewirtschaften; *(Land)* bebauen; *(Land od. andere Unternehmen)* gegen Pachtzins übernehmen, zur Bewirtschaftung übernehmen; **to** ~ **out** *(Arbeit etc)* zur Erledigung weitergeben; *(Hof)* verpachten; *(Kind)* in bezahlte Pflege geben

farmer Bauer, Landwirt; Farmer; Pächter; ~**s' cooperative** landwirtschaftliche Genossenschaft; **F**~**s' Home Administration** *Am* bundeseigene Agrarkrediteinrichtung; **cattle** ~ Viehzüchter; **tenant** ~ Pächter

farming Landwirtschaft; landwirtschaftliche Tätigkeit; Agrarwirtschaft, Ackerbau; ~ **and breeding** Ackerbau und Viehzucht; ~ **lease** Pachtvertrag *(über landwirtschaftliche Grundstücke etc);* ~ **occupation** Tätigkeit in der Landwirtschaft; **collective** ~ kollektiv betriebene Landwirtschaft; **large scale** ~ in großem Rahmen betriebene Landwirtschaft; **stock** ~ Viehwirtschaft; Viehzucht; **to** →**cease** ~; **to be engaged in** ~ Landwirtschaft betreiben; **to give up** ~ die landwirtschaftliche Tätigkeit einstellen

FAS, fas (free alongside ship) . . . (named port of shipment) Frei Längsseite Seeschiff . . . (benannter Verschiffungshafen) *(→Incoterms 1980)*

Fascism Faschismus

Fascist Faschist; faschistisch

FAST →Forecasting and Assessment in Science and Technology

fast schnell; **as** ~ **as you can** (fastcan) (f.a.c.) so schnell wie möglich *(so schnell das Schiff einnehmen bzw. ausliefern kann);* ~ **breeder reactor** Schneller Brutreaktor, Schneller Brüter; ~ **food restaurant** Schnellgaststätte; ~ **freight** *Am* Eilfracht; ~ **train** Eilzug; **goods sent by** ~ **train** *Am* Eilfracht

fatal accident tödlicher Unfall; **F**~ **A**~**s Act** *Br* Gesetz über tödliche Unfälle *(von 1959)*
Durch dieses Gesetz wird der Kreis der Familienangehörigen erweitert, die im Falle e-s durch Verschulden e-s Dritten verursachten tödlichen Unfalls Schadensersatz verlangen können

fatal, person reponsible for a ~ **road accident** Verursacher e-s tödlichen Verkehrsunfalls

fatality Unfalltod; Unglück(sfall); verhängnisvolle Wirkung

fate, to wire ~ telegrafische Nachricht über das Schicksal e-s Wechsels od. Schecks geben

father Vater; ~**-in-law** Schwiegervater; ~**hood** Vaterschaft; ~**land** Vaterland; ~**less** vaterlos; **related on one's** ~**'s side** väterlicherseits verwandt

father *v* Vater sein von; ins Leben rufen; zeugen

fatigue Ermüdung; ~ **accident** auf Ermüdung zurückzuführender Unfall

fault Schuld, Verschulden; Fehler, (Sach-)Mangel; ~ **attributable to sb.** jds Verschulden; ~ **of construction** Konstruktions-, Baufehler; **gross** ~ grobes Verschulden; **latent** ~ heimlicher Mangel, versteckter Mangel; **liability based on** ~ vom Verschulden abhängige Haftung; **the party at** ~ **in an accident** der Schuldige e-s Unfalls; **party not at** ~ nichtschuldige Partei; **serious** ~ grobes Verschulden; **through one's own** ~ durch eigenes Verschulden; **with all** ~**s** mit allen Mängeln; ohne Mängelgewähr; **to attribute the** ~ **to sb.** jdm die Schuld beimessen; **to be at** ~ Schuld haben, schuldig sein; schuldhaft handeln; **the accident was nobody's** ~ an dem Unfall hatte niemand Schuld; **the seller is at** ~ (or **the** ~ **is on the side of the seller**) den Verkäufer trifft ein Verschulden; **the buyer can be proved to be at** ~ dem Käufer kann ein Verschulden nachgewiesen werden; **to find** ~ **with sb.** an jdm etw. auszusetzen haben; jdn kritisieren; **to find** ~ **with sth.** etw. bemängeln, etw. beanstanden; **the** ~ **lies with him** er trägt die Schuld

faultiness Fehlerhaftigkeit, Mangelhaftigkeit

faulty fehlerhaft, mangelhaft; ~ **drafting** fehlerhafte Abfassung; ~ **execution** mangelhafte Ausführung; ~ **goods** fehlerhafte Waren; ~ **possession** fehlerhafter Besitz

favo(u)r Gunst, Gewogenheit, Wohlwollen; Gefallen; **balance in your** ~ Saldo zu Ihren Gunsten; **by** ~ **of** *(auf Briefumschlag)* durch Vermittlung von; **for past** ~**s** für erwiesene Gefallen; **to ask a** ~ **of sb.** jdn um e-n Gefallen bitten; **to be in** ~ **of a proposal** mit dem Vorschlag einverstanden sein; **to be in (great)** ~ *com* sehr gesucht (od. gefragt) sein; **to do sb. a**

~ jdm e-n Gefallen tun; **to speak in sb.'s** ~ für jdn eintreten; **the case went in his** ~ es wurde *(vom Gericht)* für ihn entschieden

favo(u)r *v* begünstigen; bevorzugen; *(jdn)* beehren (with mit)

favo(u)red, most-~ nation clause Meistbegünstigungsklausel; **most-~ nation treatment** Meistbegünstigung; **trusting to be ~ with your orders** indem wir hoffen, mit Ihren Aufträgen beehrt zu werden

favo(u)rable günstig, vorteilhaft; bejahend, zustimmend; ~ **balance of trade** aktive Handelsbilanz; **on ~ conditions** zu günstigen Bedingungen; ~ **exchange rate** günstiger (Wechsel-)Kurs; ~ **opinion** befürwortende Stellungnahme; ~ **opportunity** günstige Gelegenheit; **on ~ terms** zu günstigen Bedingungen; **to give the proposal a ~ reception** den Vorschlag günstig aufnehmen; den Vorschlag befürworten

favo(u)ritism Günstlingswesen, Vetternwirtschaft; Bevorzugung; ~ **in promotion** Protektionswirtschaft bei Beförderungen

fax terminal (or **machine**) Fernkopierer *(→facsimile)*

fax *v colloq.* telekopieren

feasance *Am* Erfüllung

feasibility Durchführbarkeit, Ausführbarkeit; Möglichkeit; ~ **study** Projektstudie; Planungsstudie

feasible durchführbar, ausführbar; tunlich

featherbedding[6] *(gewerkschaftl. geforderte, aber sachlich unberechtigte)* Überbesetzung mit Arbeitskräften *(zur Verhinderung von Arbeitslosigkeit)*; ~ **practices** gewerkschaftliche Arbeitereinstellungspraktiken

feature *(charakteristisches)* Kennzeichen, Merkmal, *(spezielle, charakteristische)* Eigenschaft, Eigenheit; Wesentliches; Haupt-; aktueller (Zeitungs-)Artikel; besondere Spalte *(e-r Zeitung)*; Kurzfilm; Hörfolge; ~ **program(me)** *(Radio, Fernsehen, Film)* (Haupt-)Programm; **distinctive** (or **distinguishing**) ~ Unterscheidungsmerkmal; **special** ~ Besonderheit; **special ~s** *pol* wichtige Ereignisse; **technical ~s of the invention** technische Merkmale der Erfindung; **to make a special ~ of sth.** sich auf etw. spezialisieren

feature *v* groß aufmachen; *(e-r Sache)* den Vorrang einräumen

federacy Föderation, Staatenverbindung

federal Bundes- *(Am opp. state)*; bundesstaatlich, föderalistisch; **F~ Accounting Office** *Am* Bundesrechnungshof; **F~ Advisory Council** (FAC) dem →Board of Governors zugeordnetes Beratungsorgan *(bestehend aus je einem Vertreter der 12 Federal Reserve districts)*; ~ **agency** *Am* Bundesbehörde; ~ **aid** *Am* Bundeshilfe *(finanzieller Beitrag des Bundes an die Einzelstaaten)*; ~ **allowance** *Am* Bundeszuschuß; ~ **authority** Bundesgewalt; **F~ Aviation Administration** *Am* Bundesluftfahrtbehörde; **F~ Bureau of Investigation** (FBI) *Am* Staatssicherheitsbehörde und Zentrale der Bundeskriminalpolizei *(deren Kompetenzen zum Teil denen des deutschen Bundeskriminalamtes und des Verfassungsschutzes ähneln)*; **F~ Chancellor** Bundeskanzler *(bes. in der Bundesrepublik und Österreich)*; ~ **citizenship** *Am* Bundesstaatsangehörigkeit *(opp. state citizenship)*; ~ **city** Bundeshauptstadt *(Am Washington, Ger Bonn)*; **F~ Civil Defense Administration** (FCDA) *Am* Bundesverwaltung für Zivilverteidigung; ~ **clause** *(VölkerR)* Bundesstaatklausel; **F~ Communications Commission** (F.C.C.) *Am* Bundesbehörde für das Fernmeldewesen *(Telegraf, Telefon, Radio, Fernsehen)*; **F~ Constitution** *Am* Bundesverfassung; **F~ Council** Bundesrat *(z.B. Bundesrepublik, Österreich, Schweiz)*; ~ **courts** *Am* Bundesgerichte *(→court)*; **F~ Credit Insurance Association** *Am* Bundeskreditversicherungsgesellschaft; ~ **crime** *Am* Straftat nach Bundesrecht

Federal Deposit Insurance Corporation (F.D.I.C.) *Am* Bundesanstalt zur Versicherung von Einlagen bei Kreditinstituten

Pflichtversicherung für alle Mitgliedstaaten des Federal Reserve System, freiwillige Versicherung für Nichtmitgliedbanken

federal, F~ Diet *Ger* Bundestag; **F~ District** *Am* Sitz der Regierung *(→District of Columbia)*; ~ **employees** Bundesangestellte; **F~ Estate Tax** *Am* Bundeserbschaftsteuer *(daneben wird vielfach von den Einzelstaaten e-e Erbschaftsteuer erhoben, unter Anrechnung auf die Bundessteuer)*; ~ **expenditure** Bundes(haushalts)ausgaben; **F~ Farm Loan Board** *Am* Bundesamt für landwirtschaftliches Kreditwesen; **F~ Food and Drug Administration** (FDA) *Am* Bundesverwaltung für Nahrungs- und Arzneimittel; **F~ Food, Drug and Cosmetic Act** *Am*[6a] Gesetz für Lebens-, Arzneimittel und Kosmetik *(wichtig für Prdodukthaftungsschaden)*; ~ **funds** *Am* Guthaben bei den →F~ Reserve Banks; ~ **funds rate** *Am* Tagesgeldsatz zwischen U.S. Banken aus ihren Überschußreserven; **F~ Gift Tax** *Am* Bundesschenkungsteuer

federal government Bundesregierung; *Am* Bund

Gewöhnlich mit Beschränkung auf die Exekutive *(z.B. in Bundesrepublik)*, gelegentlich aber *(z.B. Am)* alle drei Zweige der Bundesgewalt umfassend

federal, ~ grant *Am* Bundeszuschuß; **F~ Home Loan Banks** (FHLB) *Am* (11) Bundes-Wohnungsbaukredit-Banken; **F~ Housing Administration** (FHA) *Am* Bundesstelle für Wohnungsbau *(versichert langfristige Hypothekendarlehen gegen Zahlungsunfähigkeit des Hypothekenschuldners);* **F~ Income Tax** (F.I.T.) *Am* Bundeseinkommensteuer *(umfaßt die Einkommensteuer der natürlichen Personen, der Körperschaften [corporations], Trusts und Nachlässe [estates]);* **F~ Insurance Administration** *Am* Bundesversicherungs- Verwaltung; **F~ Insurance Contribution Act** (F.I.C.A.) *Am* Gesetz über die Sozialversicherungsabgaben; **F~ Intermediate Credit Banks** (FICB) *Am (12)* Bundesbanken für Zwischenkredite an die Landwirtschaft; ~ **judge** Bundesrichter *(Am opp. state judge);* ~ **jurisdiction** *Am* Bundesgerichtsbarkeit; Zuständigkeit der Bundesgerichte *(opp. state jurisdiction);* **F~ Land Banks** (FLB) *Am (12)* Bundeslandwirtschaftsbanken *(zur Gewährung von Hypothekarkrediten an Landwirtschaft);* **F~ Land Bank Bonds** *Am* →farm loan bonds; **under ~ law** nach Bundesrecht; ~ **legislation** Bundesgesetzgebung; **F~ Maritime Commission** (FMC) *Am* Bundesschiffahrtsbehörde; **F~ Mediation and Conciliation Service** (FMCS) *Am* Bundesschlichtungsamt *(für arbeitsrechtliche Streitigkeiten);* **F~ National Mortgage Association** (FNMA) *(colloq.* Fannie Mae) *Am* Bundes-Hypotheken-Vereinigung *(die Hypotheken von Banken und anderen Geldgebern aufkauft);* ~ **offense** *Am* Straftat nach Bundesrecht; **F~ Parliament** Bundestag; Parlament des Australischen Bundes; ~ **power** Bundesgewalt; **F~ Power Commission** (FPC) *Am* Bundesbehörde für die Energiewirtschaft; ~ **question** *Am (für die konkurrierende Zuständigkeit der →District Courts und der einzelstaatlichen Gerichte wichtige)* Frage der Verfassung, der Bundesgesetze oder der Verträge der Vereinigten Staaten; **F~ Register** (FR) *Am* Bundesanzeiger *(für Rechtsverordnungen);* **F~ Reporter** (Fed.) *Am* Sammlung der Entscheidungen der Bundesberufungsgerichte *(→reporter);* **F~ Republic of Germany** (FRG) Bundesrepublik Deutschland (BRD)

Federal Reserve, ~ **Act** *Am* Bundesgesetz *(von 1913),* das das ~ System begründete; ~ **Banks** (FRB) *Am (12)* Bundeszentralbanken, *(etwa)* Landeszentralbanken *(Notenbanken der USA und Zentralinstitute für Liquiditätsreserven der dem →FRS angehörenden Banken)*

Federal Reserve Board *Am* (= Board of Governors of the Federal Reserve System) Zentralbankrat *(in Washington)*

Er bildet zusammen mit den 12 regionalen →Federal Reserve Banks die amerikanische Zentralbank (Central Bank)

Federal (Reserve) Open Market Committee *Am (aus 7 Mitgliedern des Board of Governors und 5 Mitgliedern der Federal Banks bestehender)* Ausschuß für open market transactions *(open market 2.)* der Federal Reserve Banks

Federal Reserve System (FRS) *Am* Zentralbanksystem

Durch den Federal Reserve Act von 1941 geschaffenes Banksystem. Dem FRS müssen alle →National Banks als Mitglieder angehören; →State Banks können freiwillige Mitglieder sein

federal, ~ **rule** *Am* bundesrechtliche (od. bundesgerichtliche) Rechtsregel; **F~ Rules of Civil Procedure** (FRCP) *Am* Bundeszivilprozeßordnung; ~ **savings and loan associations** (FSLA) *Am* Bundes-Bauspar- und Darlehenskassen; **F~ Savings and Loan Insurance Corporation** (FSLIC) *Am* Bundesversicherungsanstalt für Bauspareinlagen *(versichert die Konten der Bausparer bis $ 10000 gegen Zahlungsunfähigkeit ihrer Banken)*

Federal Securities Acts (FSA) *Am* Bundeswertpapiergesetze

Genaue Bezeichnung der beiden Gesetze: Securities Act (1933) *(reguliert die öffentliche Emission von Wertpapieren),*
Securities Exchange Act (1934) *(reguliert den Verkehr in Wertpapieren)*

federal, F~ Security Agency (FSA) *Am* Bundesversicherungsanstalt *(zur Durchführung des Social Security Act und des Federal Unemployment Insurance Act);* ~ **specialities** *Am* Fälle der ausschließlichen Zuständigkeit der →district courts; ~ **spending** *Am* Bundesausgaben; **F~ Supplement** *Am* inoffizielle Sammlung von Entscheidungen der District Courts *(→court);* ~ **state** Bundesstaat; ~ **tax** *Am* Bundessteuer; ~ **taxation** Besteuerung durch den Bund

Federal Trade Commission (FTC) *Am* Bundesbehörde zur Bekämpfung des unlauteren Wettbewerbs und zur Durchführung der Kartellgesetze *(etwa vergleichbar mit dem deutschen Bundeskartellamt);*~ **Act** (FTCA) *Am* Kartellgesetz

Die FTC kann nur vorläufige Entscheidungen fällen. Der Betroffene kann eine gerichtliche Entscheidung herbeiführen. Die FTC hat gleichzeitig rechtsschöpferische Aufgaben (Aufstellung von Trade Practise Rules) *(a quasi-judicial agency)*

federalese *Am sl.* Amtssprache *(Sprache der Bundesbehörden)*

federalism *pol* Föderalismus *(opp. unitarianism)*

federalist Föderalist, Anhänger e-r Föderation; föderalistisch

federalize *v* föderalisieren; die Form e-r → federation geben

federate *v* sich *(in e-m Verband etc)* zusammenschließen; e-n Staatenbund bilden

federation Föderation, Staatenbund; Verband; ~ **and its constituent states** Bund und seine Gliedstaaten; ~ **of employers** Arbeitgeberverband; ~ **of trade unions** Gewerkschaftsverband; **economic** ~ Wirtschaftsverband

federative föderativ

Fedwire *Am* automatisiertes Clearing- und Kommunikationssytem des →Federal Reserve System

fee 1. Eigentumsrecht an Grund und Boden; Grundeigentum *(ursprünglich der lehensrechtliche Grundbesitz)*; ~ **farm rent** →rent-charge

fee simple *(meist unbeschränktes)* Eigentumsrecht *(an Grundbesitz)*; **estate in** ~ *(unbeschränkt vererbliches od. veräußerliches)* Grundeigentum; **owner in** ~ Grundeigentümer; ~ **absolute in possession** *Br* höchstmögliches Grundeigentum *(cf. legal → estate)*; ~ **ownership** *Am* absolutes, alleiniges Eigentum an Grundbesitz; **to hold in** ~ als Grundeigentümer besitzen

fee tail erbrechtlich gebundenes Grundeigentum; **estate (in)** ~ beschränkt vererbliches Grundeigentum *(vergleichbar dem früheren deutschen Fideikommiß)*

fee 2. Gebühr(en); Honorar *(für Arzt, Anwalt etc)*; Vergütung; Schulgeld; Trinkgeld; ~**s agreement** Honorarvereinbarung; ~**-charging** entgeltlich; ~**-charging employment agency** entgeltliche Arbeitsvermittlungsstelle; ~ **contract** Honorarvertrag; ~ **for appeal** Rechtsmittelgebühr; *(europ. PatR)* Beschwerdegebühr; ~ **for the awarding of costs** Kostenfestsetzungsgebühr; ~ **for consultation** Beratungsgebühr; ~ **for custodianship** *Am* Depotgebühr; ~ **for the grant (of a patent)** Erteilungsgebühr; ~ **for insurance** *(Post)* Versicherungsgebühr; ~**s for printing** *(PatR)* Druckkostengebühr; ~**s paid in advance** Honorarvorschuß; ~**-sheet** *Br* Gebührenrechnung *(des barrister)*

fee, administration ~ Verwaltungsgebühr; **agreement as to** ~**s** Honorarvereinbarung; **annual** ~ Jahresgebühr; **application** ~ *(PatR)* Anmeldegebühr; **appropriate** ~ angemessene Gebühr; **attorney's** ~**s** *Am* Anwaltshonorar; **barrister's** ~**s** *Br* Anwaltshonorar; **basic** ~ Grundgebühr; **booking** ~ Gebühr für Reservierung; **broker's** ~ Maklergebühr; **claims incurring** ~**s** gebührenpflichtige Patentansprüche *(claim 3.)*; **club** ~ Klubbeitrag, Vereinsbeitrag; **collection** ~ Inkassogebühr; **collection of** ~**s** Einziehung der Gebühren; **counsel's** ~**s** Anwaltshonorar *(Br des barrister)*; **court** ~**s** Gerichtsgebühren; Gerichtskosten; **director's** ~**s** Vergütung (od. Tantieme) der →board-Mitglieder; Aufsichtsrats- und Verwaltungsratsvergütung; **doctor's** ~ Arzthonorar; **entrance** ~ Eintrittsgebühr; Aufnahmegebühr *(für Verein etc)*; Zulassungsgebühr *(für Examen)*; **examination** ~**s** Prüfungsgebühren; **exempt from** ~**s** gebührenfrei; **expert's** ~ Sachverständigengebühr; **filing** ~ Anmeldegebühr *(z.B. für Patentanmeldung)*; **flat** ~ Pauschalgebühr, Pauschalhonorar; **improper** ~**s** unstatthafte Gebühren; **increase of** ~**s** Gebührenerhöhung; **legal** ~**s** Anwaltsgebühren; **liable to a** ~ gebührenpflichtig; **licence (~se)** ~**s** Lizenzgebühren; **opposition** ~ *(PatR)* Einspruchsgebühr; **against payment of a** ~ gegen Bezahlung (od. Entrichtung) e-r Gebühr; **professional** ~**(s)** Honorar; **reduction of** ~**s** Gebührenermäßigung; **refund of** ~**s** Gebührenerstattung; →**registration** ~; **remission of a** ~ Gebührenerlaß; **renewal** ~**s** *(PatR)* Jahresgebühren; **rules relating to** ~**s** Gebührenordnung; **safe deposit** ~ Aufbewahrungsgebühr; **scale of** ~**s** Gebührentabelle; **schedule of** ~**s** Gebührenordnung *(z.B. für Anwälte)*; **school** ~**(s)** Schulgeld; **solicitor's** ~**s** *Br* Anwaltsgebühren, Anwaltshonorar; **statutory** ~ gesetzliche Gebühr; **tariff of** ~**s** Gebührentarif; **witness** ~**s** Zeugengebühren; **to be subject to a** ~ gebührenpflichtig sein; **to charge** ~**s** Gebühren berechnen; Honorar liquidieren; **to fix** ~**s** Gebühren festsetzen; **to grant a respite for payment of** ~**s** Gebühren stunden; **to levy** ~**s** Gebühren erheben; **to pay** ~**s** Gebühren bezahlen (od. entrichten); **to remit** (or **waive**) ~**s** Gebühren erlassen

fee *v* **to** ~ **sb.** jdm e-e Gebühr (od. ein Honorar) bezahlen; an jdn e-e Gebühr entrichten

feeble-minded geistesschwach; ~ **person** Geistesschwacher *(Br im engeren Sinne)*

feeble-mindedness Geistesschwäche

feed *v*, **to** ~ **a fund** e-n Fonds speisen

feedback Rückkoppelung; Informationsrückfluß

feeder Zubringer; ~ **aircraft** Zubringerflugzeug; ~ **line** Zubringerlinie; ~ **road** Zubringerstraße; ~ **vessel** Zubringerschiff *(im Containertransport)*

feel *v*, **to** ~ **aggrieved** sich beschwert (od. benachteiligt) fühlen

feign *v* heucheln; simulieren; **to** ~ **illness** Krankheit vortäuschen

feigned vorgetäuscht, fingiert; ~ **action** Scheinprozeß; ~ **contract** fingierter Vertrag, Scheinvertrag

fellow Kamerad, Genosse; *univ* Stipendiat; *Br univ* Dozent e-s →college; Mitglied e-r wissenschaftlichen Gesellschaft; **F~ of the British Academy** (F.B.A.) *Br* Mitglied der →British Academy; ~ **citizen** Mitbürger; ~ **countryman** Landsmann; ~ **countrymen** Landsleute; ~ **employee** Mitarbeiter, Arbeitskollege; ~ **heir** *Am* Miterbe; ~ **lodger** Mitbewohner; ~ **passenger** Mitfahrender, Mitreisender; ~ **prisoner** Mitgefangener; **F~ of the Royal Society** (F.R.S.) *Br* Mitglied der →Royal Society; ~ **student** Kommilitone; ~ **travel(l)er** Mitreisender; *pol (bes. kommunistischer)* Mitläufer; ~ **unionist** *Am* Mitglied derselben Gewerkschaft; ~ **worker** Mitarbeiter, Kollege

fellowship Kameradschaft; Gemeinschaft; Gruppe, Gesellschaft; *Am univ* Stipendium *(für graduate students); Br univ* Stelle (od. Einkommen) e-s →fellow

felo de se Selbstmörder

felon Täter, Verbrecher *(der e-e →felony begangen hat);* **convicted** ~ verurteilter Verbrecher

felonious verbrecherisch; ~**ly** (or **with** ~ **intent**) in verbrecherischer Absicht; ~ →**homicide** *Am*

felon|y Verbrechen; **degrees of** ~**ies** *Am* nach Graden abgestufte Verbrechen (murder [Mord] ist z. B. ~ of the first degree, manslaughter [Totschlag] ~ of the second degree, negligent homicide [fahrlässige Tötung] ~ of the third degree)

Br Bezeichnung für eine nur historisch erklärbare Gruppe bestimmter, meist schwerer Verbrechen, ursprünglich Verfall des Vermögens nach sich ziehend. Die Einteilung in felony und misdemeanour ist durch den Criminal Law Act, 1967, beseitigt. Die strafbaren Handlungen werden jetzt in →indictable und non-indictable (or summary) offences eingeteilt. *Am* Allgemeine Bezeichnung für Verbrechen. Die Einteilung in felony und misdemeanor ist beibehalten. Der neue Model Penal Code z. B. unterscheidet zwischen felonies, misdemeanors und petty misdemeanors

female weibliche Person, weiblich *(opp. male);* ~ **child** Mädchen; ~ **labo(u)r** weibliche Arbeitskräfte; Frauenarbeit; ~ **suffrage** Frauenwahlrecht

feme Frau; ~ **covert** verheiratete Frau, Ehefrau; ~ **sole** nicht verheiratete Frau; *(bes.)* geschiedene Frau; ledige Frau; verwitwete Frau

feminist Frauenrechtlerin; ~ **movement** →women's liberation movement

fence Zaun; Umzäunung; *sl.* Hehler; ~ **month** (or **season, time**) *(Jagd)* Schonzeit; **to sit on the** ~ *colloq.* das Ergebnis abwarten; neutral bleiben

ferrous, non-~ Nichteisen- (NE-); **non-**~ **metals** NE-Metalle

ferry Fähre; Fährschiff; Fährrecht; ~ **(-)boat** Fähre; ~ **fare** Fährgeld; ~ **service** Fährbetrieb; **(right of)** ~ Fährrecht; **train-**~ Trajekt, Eisenbahnfähre

fertilizer Düngemittel, Kunstdünger

fetch *v* holen; abholen; *(Gewinn)* erzielen, einbringen; **to** ~ **a high price** e-n hohen Preis erzielen

fiancé Verlobter

fiancée Verlobte, Braut

fiat ("let it be done") Ermächtigung, Zulassung; *Br* richterliche Verfügung; **administrative** ~ *Am* Verwaltungsermächtigung; ~ **money** Papiergeld ohne Deckung

FIBOR (Frankfurt Interbank Offered Rate) Referenzzinsatz für in Frankfurt international tätige Banken *(in Anlehnung an →LIBOR)*

fiction Fiktion; Roman(literatur); gefälschte Unterschrift; **legal** ~ Rechtsfiktion

fictitious fingiert, fiktiv; vorgetäuscht; Schein-; ~ **bargain** Scheingeschäft; ~ **bill** *Br* Kellerwechsel; ~ **boom** Scheinblüte; ~ **business** vorgetäuschte Geschäftstätigkeit; ~ **claim** *(VersR)* vorgetäuschter (od. unechter) (Ersatz-)Anspruch; ~ **contract** Scheinvertrag; ~ **foundation of a company** Scheingründung; Gründungsschwindel; ~ **independence of the permanent establishment** fiktive Selbständigkeit der Betriebsstätte; ~ **marriage** Scheinehe; ~ **name** angenommener Name, Deckname, Pseudonym; ~ **payee** fingierter Zahlungsempfänger *(e-s Wechsels od. Schecks);* ~ **profit** Scheingewinn; ~ **sale** Scheinverkauf

fiddle *colloq.* Schwindelei, kleiner Betrug

fiddle *v colloq.* schwindeln, beschwindeln; **to** ~ **an income tax return** e-e Einkommensteuererklärung „frisieren"

fide, →**bona** ~; **bona** ~**s** guter Glauben; → **mala** ~

fidelity Treue; Genauigkeit; ~ **bond** Kaution(sverpflichtung) *(e-s Versicherers im Falle von Veruntreuung);* ~ **guarantee** Kaution; ~ **insurance** Personengarantieversicherung; Vertrauensschadenversicherung; Kautionsversicherung; **conjugal** ~ eheliche Treue; **contractual** ~ Vertragstreue; **to enter into a** ~ **bond** e-e Kaution stellen; **to translate sth. with** ~ etw. wortgetreu übersetzen

fiduciary Treuhänder *(z.B. trustee, executor, administrator);* Vermögensverwalter *(verwaltender Treuhänder);* treuhänderisch, fiduziarisch; ~ **agent** Treuhänder; ~ **assignment** fiduziarische Abtretung; ~ **bond** Kautionsverpflichtung; ~ **capacity** Treuhändereigenschaft; **in a** ~ **capacity** in treuhänderischer Eigenschaft, als Treuhänder; ~ **circulation** (or **currency**) *Br* ungedeckter Notenumlauf; ~ **duties** Pflichten des Treuhänders; Treuepflichten; ~ **duty of a bank** Verpflichtung e-r Bank, den Kunden treuhänderisch zu beraten; ~ **(note) issue** *Br* ungedeckte Notenausgabe *(der Bank of England);* ~ **loan** ungedeckter Kredit; ~ **management** Treuhandverwaltung; ~ **position** Vertrauensstellung; ~ **relation(ship)**

treuhänderisches (Rechts-)Verhältnis; Treueverhältnis; **to stand in a ~ relationship to sb.** zu jdm in Vertrauensverhältnis stehen *(z. B. principal and agent, solicitor and client, trustee and beneficiary)*

field Feld; (Arbeits-, Sach-)Gebiet, Bereich; Absatzgebiet; Außendienst *(außerhalb der Zentralstelle)*; **in the ~** im Außendienst; *mil* im Felde; **~ assignment** Außeneinsätze *(Personal)*; **~ audit** Außenprüfung; **~ boundary** Feldmark; **~ damage** Flurschaden; **~ executive** leitender Angestellter e-r Außenstelle *(bes. e-s Verkaufsbüros)*; **~ hospital** Feldlazarett; **~ interviewer** Befrager; **~ inventories** Außenlager; **~ investigation** Nachforschung an Ort und Stelle *(auch für Verwaltungszwecke)*; *(MMF)* →~ research; **~ investigator** Interviewer, Befrager; **~ of activity** Tätigkeitsbereich; Arbeitsgebiet; **~ of duty** Aufgabenbereich; **~ of law** Rechtsgebiet; **~ office** Außenstelle; **~ of operations** Tätigkeitsbereich, Arbeitsgebiet; **~ of politics** politisches Gebiet; **~ research** *(MMF)* Feldforschung, Primärerhebung *(an Ort und Stelle, bes. durch persönliche Befragung; opp. desk research)*; **~ sales manager** Außenstellenleiter; **~ service** Außendienst; **~ staff** im Außendienst tätige(r) Mitarbeiter(stab); **~ survey** → ~ research; **~→warehousing; ~ work** Feldarbeit; Außenarbeit, Außeneinsatz; *(MMF)* Primärerhebung *(persönliche Befragung)*; **~ worker** Außendienstmitarbeiter; *(MMF)* Befrager, Interviewer

field, agent in the ~ Vertreter im Außendienst; **coal ~** Kohlenfeld; **in the economic ~** auf wirtschaftlichem Gebiet, im Bereich der Wirtschaft

fieri facias (fi. fa.) ("you may cause it to be done") Pfändungsanordnung, Vollstreckungsbefehl *(an den →sheriff gerichteter Auftrag, das Urteil durch Pfändung zu vollstrecken)*

fieri feci ("I have caused to be done") Pfändungsprotokoll *(Bericht des →sheriff über vollzogene Pfändung)*

fi. fa., execution by (writ of) ~ Zwangsvollstreckung durch Pfändung und Wegnahme

fifo, FIFO →first-in-first-out *(Methode der Bewertung des Vorratsvermögens; cf. hifo, lifo)*

fifth column *pol* fünfte Kolonne *(Untergrundorganisation)*

fifth columnist *pol* Angehöriger e-r fünften Kolonne *(cf. subversive activities)*

fight Kampf (for um); Schlägerei; **~ for existence** Existenzkampf; **to make a ~ for sth.** um etw. kämpfen; **to show ~** sich zur Wehr setzen, Widerstand leisten

fight *v* kämpfen; **to ~ an action** (or **a lawsuit**) e-n Prozeß durchkämpfen; **to ~ sth. down** etw. niederkämpfen; **to ~ for the market** um den Markt kämpfen

fighting Kampf(-); **~ capacity** *mil* Schlagkraft; **~ chance** Erfolgschance *(wenn große Anstrengungen gemacht werden)*; **~ forces** *mil* Kampfkräfte, Fronttruppen; **~ zone** Kampfzone; **street ~** Straßenkampf

figurative trade mark Bildzeichen

figure Zahl, Ziffer; Figur; Persönlichkeit; *(WettbewerbsR)* Bildzeichen; *(PatR)* Abbildung; **~-head** Repräsentationsfigur; **in ~s and words** in Ziffern und Worten; **at a high ~** teuer; **at a low ~** billig; **to express in ~s** *(Betrag)* in Ziffern angeben; **it runs into three ~s** es geht in die Hunderte; **the same sheet of drawings may contain several ~s** *(PatR)* ein Zeichnungsblatt kann mehrere Abbildungen enthalten

figure *v* in Erscheinung treten, erscheinen; **to ~ on sth.** *Am* auf etw. rechnen; **to ~ out** ausrechnen, berechnen; veranschlagt werden (at auf); **to ~ in the papers** von der Presse erwähnt werden; in der Zeitung erscheinen

Fiji Fidschi; **the Republic of ~** die Republik Fidschi, **(of) ~** Fidschianer(in); fidschianisch

file (Brief-, Akten-)Ordner; Sammelmappe; Aktenbündel; *(EDV)* Datei; **for your ~s** für die dortigen Akten; **on ~** bei den Akten; abgelegt *(Akten)*; **~ card** Karteikarte; **~ copy** Ablagestück; Durchschlag für die Akten; **~ cover** Aktendeckel; **~ index** Aktenverzeichnis; **~ number** (or **reference)** Aktenzeichen

file, case ~s Prozeßakten; **dead ~s** abgelegte (od. erledigte) Akten; **on examining the ~s** bei Durchsicht der Akten; **keeping of ~s** Aufbewahrung von Akten; **letter ~** Ablage *(für Briefe)*; Briefordner; Schnellhefter; **master ~** Zentralkartei, Stammkartei; *(EDV)* Stammdatei; **personal ~s** Personalakten; **supplementary ~s** Beiakten; **to be on** (or **in**) **the ~** bei den Akten sein; **to inspect ~s** Akten einsehen; **to keep ~s** Akten führen; Akten aufbewahren; **to maintain ~s** Akten führen; **to open ~s** Akten anlegen; **to place** (or **put**) **on ~** zu den Akten nehmen; **to preserve ~s** Akten aufbewahren

file *v* einreichen (with bei); (ein)ordnen, (ein)heften; zu den Akten nehmen; *(Schriftgut)* ablegen; **to ~ (away)** ablegen; **to ~ an action** e-e Klage einreichen (od. erheben); **to ~ an appeal** ein Rechtsmittel *(Berufung etc)* einlegen; **to ~ an application** e-n Antrag einreichen (with bei); **to ~ an application for a patent** e-e Patentanmeldung einreichen, ein Patent anmelden; **to ~ a bankruptcy petition** den Konkurs anmelden; Antrag auf Konkurseröffnung stellen; **to ~ a claim** e-e Forderung anmelden; **to ~ one's claim** seine (Konkurs-)Forderung anmelden; **to ~ a →complaint; to ~ a →judgment; to ~ letters in order of date** Briefe nach dem Datum ablegen; **to ~ a protest** Einspruch einlegen; **to ~ a return at the registry** e-n *(gesetzl. vorgeschriebenen)* Bericht bei der Behörde einreichen *(Br* *bes. den Bericht mit Angaben über e-e Gesellschaft beim Registrar of Companies);* **to ~ a suit** *Am* Klage erheben; **to ~ under subjects** nach Sachgebieten einordnen

filed, document which has to be ~ within a time limit fristgebundenes Schriftstück; **to be ~** zu den Akten (z. d. A.)

filing Einreichung; Einordnung; Ablegen, Ablage *(von Akten, Schriftstücken etc);* **~ of the application** Antragstellung; *(PatR)* Einreichung der Anmeldung; **~ of the articles (or certificate) of incorporation** (with the Secretary of State) *Am* Anmeldung der Eintragung *(e-r Firma)* als Aktiengesellschaft; **~ cabinet** Aktenschrank; **~ card** Karteikarte; **~ clerk** Registrator

filing date Datum der Einreichung; *(PatR)* Zeitpunkt der Anmeldung, Anmeldedatum; **actual ~** *Am* tatsächliche Einreichung der Anmeldung *(beim Patentamt);* **priority of ~** *(PatR)* Anmeldepriorität

filing fee *(PatR)* Anmeldegebühr; **time limit for paying the ~** Frist zur Zahlung der Anmeldegebühr; **to pay the ~ in due time** die Anmeldegebühr rechtzeitig entrichten

filing, ~ period *(PatR)* Anmeldefrist; **~ of opposition** *(PatR)* Einlegung des Einspruchs *(gegen die Erteilung des Patents);* **~ of a petition** Einreichung e-s Antrags; **~ a petition for divorce** Einreichung e-s Scheidungsantrags; **~ one's petition** Konkursantrag (→*petition 2.);* **~ system** Ablagesystem; Registratursystem

filing, →date of ~; for ~ zu den Akten *(z. d. A.);* **formal ~ requirements** *(PatR)* Formvorschriften für die Anmeldung; **upon ~** *(PatR)* bei der Anmeldung

filer, delinquent ~ *Am* jd, der die Steuererklärung zu spät eingereicht hat

filiate *v Am* und *Scot* die außereheliche Vaterschaft feststellen

filiation Kindschaft(sverhältnis), Abstammung; *Am* und *Scot* gerichtliche Feststellung der außerehelichen Vaterschaft; **~ order** *Am* und *Scot* → affiliation order; **~ proceedings** *Am* und *Scot* Vaterschaftsprozeß

filibuster *parl* Obstruktion *(Verschleppungstaktik zur Verhinderung e-r Abstimmung);* Obstruktionspolitiker *(Abgeordneter, der durch Dauerreden Abstimmung verzögert od. verhindert)*

filibuster *v parl* Filibustertaktik anwenden, Obstruktion betreiben

filing →file *v*

Filipino Philippiner(in)

filius nullius ("son of nobody") *Am* nichteheliches Kind

fill *v* (sich) füllen; *(Amt, Stelle)* bekleiden, innehaben, einnehmen, besetzen; **to ~ the bill** *colloq.* den Anforderungen genügen; **to ~ an order** e-n Auftrag ausführen; **to ~ a vacancy** e-e *(freie)* Stelle besetzen; **to ~ in** eintragen, einsetzen; *(Formular, Scheck)* ausfüllen; **to ~ out** *Am (Formular etc)* ausfüllen; **to ~ up** ausfüllen; auffüllen

filled to capacity bis auf den letzten Platz besetzt

filling station Tankstelle

film Film; **~s** Filmindustrie; **~ adaptation** Filmbearbeitung; **~ censorship** Filmzensur; **~ distributor** Filmverleiher; **~ producer** Filmproduzent; **~ rights** Filmrechte, Verfilmungsrechte; **~ show** Filmvorführung; **distribution of ~s** Verleihung von Filmen; **documentary ~** Kulturfilm; **exhibition of ~s** Vorführung von Filmen; **production of ~s** Herstellung von Filmen; **to dub a ~** e-n Film synchronisieren; **to exhibit** (or **show**) **a ~** e-n Film vorführen

filmlet Kurzwerbefilm

fin(e)able e-r Geldstrafe unterliegend

final(s) (Ab-)Schlußprüfung; **to take one's ~** seine Abschlußprüfung machen

final End-, Schluß-; endgültig, abschließend; rechtskräftig; **~ account** Schluß(ab)rechnung; Schlußbericht; **~ act** *dipl* Schlußakte; **~ address** Schlußansprache; **~ age** *(VersR)* Schlußalter; **~ clause** Schlußklausel, Schlußbestimmung *(e-s Vertrages, Testaments etc);* **~ commission** Abschlußprovision; **~ consumer** Endverbraucher; **~ date** Endtermin; letzter (od. äußerster) Termin

final decision endgültige (od. abschließende) Entscheidung; rechtskräftige Entscheidung; **pending a ~** bis zur rechtskräftigen Entscheidung

final, ~ distribution Schlußverteilung; **~ dividend** Schlußdividende, Restdividende; *(KonkursR)* Schlußquote; **~ examination** Abschlußprüfung (→*examination 4.);* **~ information (given)** Endbescheid; **~ inspection** Schlußbesichtigung; **~ invoice** endgültige Rechnung *(opp. provisional invoice);* **~ judgment** Endurteil *(opp. interlocutory judgment);* rechtskräftiges Urteil *(not subject to appeal);* **~ meeting** Schlußsitzung; **~ order** Endverfügung; **~ payment** Abschlußzahlung; **~ protocol** *dipl* Schlußprotokoll; **~ provision** Schlußbestimmung; **~ quotation** *(Börse)* Schlußnotierung; Schlußkurs; **~ report** Abschlußbericht; endgültiger Bericht; **~ respite** letzte Frist; **~ result** Schlußergebnis; **~ salary** Endgehalt; **~ settlement** Schlußabrechnung; **~ →storage of radioactive waste; ~ vote** Schlußabstimmung

final, to become ~ rechtskräftig werden, Rechtskraft erlangen; **within a period of 3**

months after the decision has become ~ innerhalb von 3 Monaten nach Eintritt der Rechtskraft der Entscheidung; **to give a ~ ruling** endgültig entscheiden

finally, to decide sth. ~ etw. endgültig entscheiden; ~ **refused** rechtskräftig zurückgewiesen

finality Endgültigkeit

finalize *v* endgültig fertigstellen; endgültige Form geben

finance Finanzwesen; Finanzwissenschaft; Finanzwelt; ~**s** Finanzen; Staatsfinanzen; **F~Act** *Br* Finanzgesetz *(jährl. verabschiedetes Gesetz als Grundlage für die Besteuerung in Großbritannien);* **F~ Bill** *parl* Finanzvorlage; ~ **bill** Finanzwechsel *(opp. trade bill);* ~ **committee** Finanzausschuß

finance company Finanzierungsgesellschaft; *Br* →finance house; **personal** ~ *Am* Kundenkreditanstalt

Finance for Industry (F.F.I.) *Br (staatl.)* Finanzierungsinstitut für die Industrie
Gewährt langfristige Darlehen von £ 200,000 aufwärts zur Rationalisierung bestehender und Schaffung neuer Unternehmen *(cf. Industrial and Commercial Finance Corporation)*

finance, ~ house *Br* Kreditinstitut für die Kundenfinanzierung; Kundenkreditbank (→*hire-purchase company);* ~ **leasing** →leasing 2.; ~ **management** Finanzwesen *(e-s Unternehmens)*

finance, administration of the ~s Verwaltung der Finanzen; **high** ~ Hochfinanz; **home** ~ *Br* öffentliche Finanzen; **minister of** ~ Finanzminister *(Br Chancellor of the Exchequer; Am Secretary of the Treasury);* **Ministry of** ~ Finanzministerium *(Br the Treasury, Am Treasury Department);* **national ~s** Staatsfinanzen

finance, public ~ öffentliche Finanzen, Staatsfinanzen; öffentliches Finanzwesen; **from the point of view of public** ~ finanzpolitisch

finance, sound ~ gesunde Finanzen; **(world of)** ~ Finanzwelt; **to grant** ~ (to) *(Projekt od. Unternehmen)* finanzieren; *(jdm)* Geldmittel zur Verfügung stellen; **to occupy a big position in** ~ e-e große Stellung in der Finanzwelt innehaben; **his ~s are low** seine Finanzen stehen schlecht

finance *v (Unternehmen, Projekt etc)* finanzieren, mit Geldmitteln versehen; **project ~d** finanziertes Vorhaben; **state-~d** vom Staat *(Am Einzelstaat)* finanziert

financial finanziell, geldlich, pekuniär; Finanz-, Geld-; ~ **accountant** Finanzbuchhalter; ~ **accounting** Finanzbuchhaltung, Geschäftsbuchhaltung; **F~ Accounting Standards Board** (FASB) *Am* Behörde, die die Regeln für die Rechnungslegung amerikanischer Unternehmen festlegt; ~ **affairs** finanzielle Angelegenheiten, Geldangelegenheiten; ~ **agent** Finanzbeauftragter *(e-s Unternehmens);* ~ **agreement** Finanzabkommen; ~ **aid** finanzielle Hilfe (od. Unterstützung); ~ **analysis** Finanzanalyse; ~ **arrangement** finanzielle Abmachung, Finanzvereinbarung; ~ **assets** Finanzanlagen; ~ **assistance** →~ aid; ~ **backer** Geldgeber; ~ **backing** finanzielle Unterstützung; ~ **benefit** finanzieller Vorteil; ~ **bill** Finanzwechsel; ~ **books** Geschäftsbücher; ~ **budget** Finanzierungsplan *(e-s Unternehmens);* ~ **burden** finanzielle Belastung; ~ **capacity** finanzielle Leistungsfähigkeit; Finanzkraft; ~ **circles** Finanzkreise; ~ **circumstances** Vermögensverhältnisse; ~ **column** Handelsteil, Wirtschaftsteil *(e-r Zeitung);* ~ **commission** (or **committee**) Finanzausschuß

financial commitment finanzielle Verpflichtung; Finanzierungszusage; **to enter into** (or **incur, undertake**) **a** ~ e-e Zahlungsverpflichtung eingehen

financial compensation Finanzausgleich

financial condition finanzielle Lage, Vermögenslage; **unsound** ~ ungünstige (od. schlechte) Vermögenslage

financial, ~ contribution finanzieller Beitrag; Beitragsleistung; ~ **corporations** *Am* Banken und Versicherungen; ~ **counsel(l)ing** Beratung in Finanzfragen; ~ **control** *(staatl.)* Finanzkontrolle; ~ **crisis** Finanzkrise

financial difficulties, (temporary) ~ (vorübergehende) geldliche Schwierigkeiten, Zahlungsschwierigkeiten; **to get into** ~ in finanzielle Schwierigkeiten geraten

financial, ~ drain finanzielle Inanspruchnahme; ~ **duty** Finanzzoll *(opp. protective duty);* ~ **editor** Wirtschaftsredakteur, Schriftleiter des Wirtschaftsteils *(e-r Zeitung);* ~ **embarrassment** Geldverlegenheit; ~ **emergency** finanzielle Notlage; ~ **establishment** Kreditinstitut; ~ **failure** finanzieller Zusammenbruch; ~ **expenses** Finanzaufwendungen; ~ **forecast(ing)** Finanzvorschau; Vorausschau über die finanzielle Lage *(e-s Unternehmens)*

financial futures Finanzterminkontrakte (FTK) *(börsengängige Terminkontrakte über Kauf oder Verkauf standardisierter Finanztitel) (→currency futures, →precious metal futures, →stock index futures);* ~ **market** Finanzterminbörse

financial gap Finanzierungslücke

financial holding, to have a ~ in finanziell beteiligt sein an

financial, ~ innovation Finanzinnovation (→*secularization*); ~ **institution** Finanzinstitut, Geldinstitut; ~ **institutions insurance** *Am* Einlagenversicherung *(Versicherung privater Guthaben bei Kreditinstituten);* ~ **instrument** Finanzierungsinstrument, Kreditinstrument; ~ **interest** finanzielle Beteiligung (→*interest 2.*); finanzielles Interesse; ~ **interrelation** Kapitalverflechtung; ~ **leasing** →leasing 2.; ~ **legislation** Finanzgesetzgebung; ~ **magnate**

Finanzmagnat; ~ **management** Finanzmanagement *(e-s Unternehmens; Finanzentscheidungen und Investitionsentscheidungen)*; ~ **manager** Finanzdirektor; ~ **matters** Finanzangelegenheiten; ~ **means** Geldmittel; finanzielle Mittel; ~ **news** Börsennachrichten, Börsenbericht; ~ **newspaper** Börsenblatt, Handelsblatt

financial obligations finanzielle Verpflichtungen (to gegenüber); **to fulfil** (or **meet**) **one's** ~ seinen finanziellen Verpflichtungen nachkommen

financial ~ **operations** Finanzgeschäfte, Finanztransaktionen; ~ **paper** Börsenblatt, Finanzzeitung;~ **part** Handelsteil *(e-r Zeitung)*; ~ **plan** Finanzierungsplan; ~ **policy** Finanzpolitik, Finanzgebarung

financial position finanzielle Lage, Finanzlage; **bad** ~ schlechte Finanzlage; **sound** ~ gesunde Finanzlage; **statement of changes in the** ~ Bewegungsbilanz; Kapitalflußrechnung; **to be in a bad** ~ finanziell schlecht gestellt sein

financial, ~ **power** Finanzkraft; ~ **predicament** finanzielle Notlage: ~ **program(me)** Finanz(-ierungs)plan; ~ **proposal** Finanzvorlage

financial provision, ~ **for children of the family** *Br* Kindesunterhalt; ~ **for spouse** *Br* Ehegattenunterhalt *(bei Scheidung)*

finanical, ~ **quarters** Finanzkreise; ~ **records** Finanzunterlagen; ~ **reform** Finanzreform; ~ **regulations** Finanzvorschriften; *(EG)* Haushaltsordnung; ~ **requirements** Finanzbedarf

financial resources finanzielle Mittel *(e-s Unternehmens)*; **making available of** ~ Bereitstellung von finanziellen Mitteln; **with ample** ~ finanzkräftig

Financial Responsibility Law *Am (VersR) (einzelstaatl.)* Verantwortlichkeitsgesetz

Zweck ist die Sicherung der Forderung des Geschädigten. Der Kraftfahrer muß, wenn er wegen eines Verkehrsunfalls zu einer Geldstrafe verurteilt ist, seine finanzielle Leistungsfähigkeit nachweisen, widrigenfalls ihm die Fahrerlaubnis gesperrt wird

financial services Finanzdienstleistungen; **F~ S~ Act** 1986 *Br* Gesetz über Dienstleistungen im Finanz- und Investitionsbereich *(Neuregulierung der Überwachung im Wertpapiergeschäft zum besseren Schutz der Investoren)*

Das Gesetz unterwirft Anlageberater und Effektenhändler e-r Genehmigungspflicht und Überwachung

financial, ~ **settlement** finanzielle Abfindung, Abfindung in Geld; ~ **situation** finanzielle Lage, Finanzlage; ~ **sources** Finanzquellen; ~ **sovereignty** Finanzhoheit; ~ **standing** finanzielle Situation (od. Lage), Kreditfähigkeit

financial statement *Am* Jahresabschluß; Handelsbilanz; **certification** (or **approval**) **of the** ~ *Am* Bestätigung des Jahresabschlusses *(durch den Wirtschaftsprüfer)*; **consolidated** ~**s** konsolidierter Jahresabschluß; Konzernabschluß; **preparation and auditing of** ~**s** Aufstellung und Prüfung von Jahresabschlüssen

financial, ~ **statistics** Finanzstatistik; ~ **status** Finanzstatus; Finanzlage, finanzielle Lage; ~ **strength** Finanzkraft; ~ **supermarket** Finanz-Supermarkt *(vielseitiges finanzielles Konglomerat)*; ~ **support** finanzielle Unterstützung; ~ **swap** Finanzswap *(Austausch von Zahlungsströmen zwischen zwei oder mehr Vertragsparteien für e-e bestimmte Zeit)*; ~ **syndicate** Finanzkonsortium

Financial Times (FT), ~ **Actuaries Share Indices** e-e Reihe von 54 britischen Aktienindizes *(herausgegeben von der ~ in Verbindung mit den Actuary Institutes von London und Edinburg)*; ~ **Industrial Ordinary Share Index** (FT Index) Aktien-Index von 30 →blue chip Unternehmen *(von der ~, London, herausgegeben)*

financial, ~ **transactions** Finanztransaktionen, Finanzgeschäfte; finanzielle Vorgänge; ~ →**update**; ~ **world** Finanzwelt; ~ **year** *Br* Geschäftsjahr; Haushaltsjahr, Rechnungsjahr *(der öffentl. Haushalte) (1. April bis 31. März)*

financially finanziell, in finanzieller Hinsicht; ~ **independent** finanziell selbständig; ~ **sound** finanziell gesund; ~ **strong** kapitalstark; ~ **weak** kapitalschwach; **to be** ~ **secure** finanziell gesichert sein; **to be** ~ **supported** finanziell unterstützt werden

financier Finanzier, Geldmann; Finanz(fach)-mann

financing Finanzierung, Kapitalbeschaffung; ~ **by raising capital** Fremdfinanzierung; ~ **charges** Finanzierungskosten; ~ **deficiency** Finanzierungslücke; ~ **company** Finanzierungsgesellschaft; ~ **expenses** Finanzierungskosten; ~ **funds** Finanzierungsmittel; ~ **instrument** Finanzierungsinstrument; ~ **of capital expenditure** Investitionsfinanzierung; ~ **of housing** Wohnungsbaufinanzierung; ~ **of industry** Industriefinanzierung; ~ **of political parties** Parteienfinanzierung; ~ **plan** (or **program[me]**) Finanzierungsprogramm; ~ **promise** Finanzierungszusage; ~ **requirements** Finanzbedarf; ~ **statement** *Am* Finanzierungserklärung *(zur Eintragung e-s →security interest)*; von dem Schuldner unterzeichnete Erklärung über die Begründung e-s Sicherungsrechts; **conditions of** ~ Finanzierungsbedingungen; **cost of** ~ Finanzierungskosten; **debt** ~ Fremdfinanzierung; **direct** ~ Barfinanzierung; →**first stage** ~; **government** ~ Staatsfinanzierung; **interim** ~Zwischenfinanzierung; **own** ~ Eigenfinanzierung; **self-**~ Selbstfinanzierung, Eigenfinanzierung; **supplementary** ~ Nachfinanzierung; **terms of** ~ Finanzierungsbedingungen; **to secure** ~ die Finanzierung sicherstellen

find Fund *(Objekt)*; **small** ~ Kleinfund; **to take the** ~ **to the lost property office** *Br* den Fund zum Fundbüro bringen

find *v* finden; entdecken; *(vom Gericht)* befinden für, feststellen, erkennen; sich verschaffen, sich beschaffen; liefern, zur Verfügung stellen; **to ~ out** herausfinden, ermitteln; **to ~ bail** sich Bürgen beschaffen; **to ~→employment; to ~ against the defendant** *(Zivilprozeß)* den Beklagten verurteilen; e-r Klage stattgeben; *(Strafprozeß)* den Angeklagten verurteilen; **to ~ for sb.** zu jds Gunsten entscheiden; **to ~ for the defendant** *(Zivilprozeß)* die Klage abweisen; *(Strafprozeß)* den Angeklagten freisprechen; **to ~ for the plaintiff** e-r Klage stattgeben; **to ~ for the plaintiff as claimed** dem Klagebegehren stattgeben; **to ~ sb. guilty** jdn für schuldig erklären (od. befinden); **to ~ money** (or **capital**) **for sb.** jdm das (nötige od. erforderliche) Kapital beschaffen; **to ~ a post for sb.** jdm e-e Stelle beschaffen; **to ~ refuge** Zuflucht finden; **to ~ a true bill (of indictment)** *Am* e-e Klage für begründet erklären *(s. not →found)*

finder (of lost property) Finder; **~'s reward** Finderlohn; **~ will be rewarded** der Finder wird Belohnung bekommen

finding 1. Fund *(Finden)*; **~ of lost property** Fund; **~ and keeping of lost property** Fundunterschlagung

finding 2. (Tatsachen-)Feststellung *(des Gerichts od. der jury)*; Befund, Feststellung; Gerichtsentscheidung; Wahrspruch *(der jury)*; Beschaffung; **~s** Untersuchungsergebnis; **~ of capital** Kapitalbeschaffung **~s of the court** *(tatsächliche)* Feststellungen des Gerichts; **~ of facts** Tatsachenfeststellungen; **to make ~s** Feststellungen treffen

fine Geldstrafe; Geldbuße; Bußgeld; **administrative ~** Ordnungsstrafe, Bußgeld; **in default of payment of a ~** im Falle der Nichtbezahlung e-r Geldstrafe; im Nichtbeitreibungsfalle; **heavy ~** hohe Geldstrafe; **liable to a ~** e-r Geldstrafe unterliegend; **low ~** niedrige Geldstrafe; **punishable by a ~** mit Geldstrafe zu bestrafen; **recovery of ~s** Beitreibung von Geldstrafen; **remission of a ~** Erlaß e-r Geldstrafe; **to assess a ~** e-e Geldstrafe festsetzen; **to be liable to a ~ not exceeding** ... e-r Geldstrafe bis zu ... unterliegen; **to collect a ~** e-e Geldstrafe beitreiben; **to convert a sentence of imprisonment to a ~** e-e Freiheitsstrafe in Geldstrafe umwandeln; **to enforce payment of a ~** e-e Geldstrafe beitreiben; **to impose a ~ on sb.** jdn mit e-r Geldstrafe belegen; jdm e-e Geldstrafe auferlegen; **to remit a ~** e-e Geldstrafe erlassen

fine *v*, **to ~ sb.** jdn zu e-r Geldstrafe verurteilen; auf Geldstrafe erkennen; mit e-r Geldstrafe belegen; e-e Geldstrafe auferlegen; **to be ~d or imprisoned** zu Geld- od. Gefängnisstrafe verurteilt werden; **to be ~d £10** mit e-r Geldstrafe von £10 bestraft werden

fine fein, gut; *(Metall)* Fein-; **~ arts** schöne Künste; **~ bank bill** erstklassiger Bankwechsel; **~ trade bill** erstklassiger Handelswechsel

fine gold Feingold; **weight of ~** Feingoldgehalt

fineness Feinheit; Feingehalt *(von Gold etc)*; **degree of ~** Feinheitsgrad; **legal ~** gesetzlicher Feingehalt

fingerprint Fingerabdruck; **to take ~s** Fingerabdrücke nehmen

finish Ende, Schluß; Vollendung, letzte Feinheiten; **at the ~** am Ende (od. Schluß)

finish *v* (be)enden; fertig machen, fertig bearbeiten, vollenden; *(Produkt)* veredeln; **to ~ one's apprenticeship** auslernen

finished beendet; vollendet, vollkommen; **~ goods** (or **products**) Fertigware(n), Fertigfabrikate, Fertigerzeugnisse; **semi-~ goods** (or **products**) Halbware(n), Halbfabrikate, Halberzeugnisse

finishing Schluß; Fertigbearbeitung; Veredelung; **~ industry** Veredelungsindustrie; **~ process** Veredelungsverfahren; **~ time** Arbeitsschluß *(opp. starting time)*; **textile ~** Textilveredelung

Finland Finnland; **Republic of ~** Republik Finnland

Finn Finne, Finnin

Finnish finnisch

fio clause fio-Klausel *(cf. free in and out)*

Durch die fio-Klausel wird bei der Frachtcharter Ladung und Entlöschung vom Charterer oder Empfänger übernommen

fips bond (foreign interest payment security) inverse Doppelwährungsanleihe *(ewige Anleihe mit Zinszahlungen in anderer Währung als der Emissionswährung)*

fire Feuer, Brand; **~ alarm system** Feuermeldeanlage

firearms Schußwaffen; **~ certificate** Waffenschein; **unlawful possession of ~** unerlaubter Waffenbesitz

fire brigade (F.B.) *Br* Feuerwehr; **to call** (or **summon**) **the ~** die Feuerwehr alarmieren

fire, ~ damage Feuerschaden; **~ department** *Am* Feuerwehr; *Br* Abteilung *(e-r Versicherungsgesellschaft)* für Feuerversicherung; **~ engine** Feuerwehr(wagen); **~ escape** Rettungsleiter; Nottreppe; **~ exit** Notausgang; **~ fighting** Brandbekämpfung; **~ hazard** Feuergefahr; **~ house** *Am* Feuerwache, Feuermeldestelle

fire insurance Feuerversicherung; **~ company** Feuerversicherungsgesellschaft; **~ fund** Brandkasse, Feuerkasse; **~ mutual** Feuerversicherungsgesellschaft auf Gegenseitigkeit; **~ policy** Feuerversicherungspolice

fire, ~-man Feuerwehrmann; Heizer; **~ office** *Br* →**~** insurance company; **~ policy** (f.p.) *Br*

Feuerversicherungspolice; ~ **prevention** Brandverhütung; ~**-proof** feuersicher; ~ **protection** Brandschutz; ~ **raiser** *Br* Brandstifter; ~ **raising** *Br* Brandstiftung; ~ **risk** Feuergefahr; **F~ Service** *Br* Feuerwehr; ~**- station** *Br* Feuerwache, Feuermeldestelle; ~ **underwriter** Feuerversicherungsgesellschaft; **damage (caused) by** ~ Brandschaden; **danger of** ~ Feuergefahr; **liable to catch** ~ feuergefährlich; **prevention of** ~ Feuerverhütung; **scene of** ~ Brandstelle; **to cease** ~ *mil* das Feuer einstellen; **to extinguish the** ~ das Feuer löschen; **to open** ~ *mil* das Feuer eröffnen; **to set on** ~ in Brand setzen; **a** ~ **arose** (or **occurred**) ein Feuer entstand; **a** ~ **breaks out** ein Feuer bricht aus; **the house was on** ~ das Haus brannte

fire *v Am (Br sl.) (fristlos)* entlassen, hinauswerfen; **to** ~ **a shot** e-n Schuß abgeben; **to hire and** ~ *Am (Br sl.)* anstellen und entlassen

firm Firma, Betrieb, Unternehmen *(meist für offene Handelsgesellschaften [partnership] gebraucht);* ~**'s brand** Firmenzeichen; ~ **name** Firmenname; (Bezeichnung der) Firma; **change of the** ~ **name** Firmenänderung

firm, assets of a ~ Aktiva e-r Firma; Firmenvermögen; **amalgamation of** ~**s** Firmenzusammenschluß; **commercial** ~ Handelsfirma; **defunct** ~ nicht mehr bestehende (od. erloschene) Firma; **establishment** (or **foundation**) **of a** ~ Errichtung (od. Gründung) e-r Firma; **location of a** ~ Sitz e-r Firma; Firmensitz; **member of a** ~ Teilhaber; **old-established** ~ alteingesessene Firma; **owner of a** ~ Firmeninhaber; **partner in a** ~ Teilhaber; Gesellschafter; **property of the** ~ Firmenvermögen; **registration of a** ~ Eintragung e-r Firma; **setting up of a** ~ Errichtung e-r Firma; **to establish** (or **found**) **a** ~ e-e Firma gründen; **to sign for the** ~ für die Firma zeichnen; **an action may be brought by or against a** ~ (in the name of the ~) e-e Firma kann klagen oder verklagt werden

firm fest; entschlossen, bestimmt; ~ **appointment** feste Anstellung; ~ **bargain** (or **deal**) fester Abschluß; Festgeschäft, Fixgeschäft *(opp. option bargain; →option 2.);* ~ **offer** festes (bindendes) Angebot *(opp. conditional offer);* ~ **price** fester Preis, stabiler Preis; fester Kurs; ~ **stand** *pol* feste Stellungnahme, entschlossene Haltung; ~ **stock** *Br (Börse)* feste Werte *(opp. option stock; →option 2.);* **to buy (sell)** ~ fest kaufen (verkaufen); **to become** ~ sich festigen; **to make a** ~ **bargain** (or **deal**) fest abschließen

firm *v* fest werden, sich festigen; **the shares** ~**ed (up)** die Aktien zogen an

firming (up) of prices Befestigung der Preise (od. Kurse)

firmness Festigkeit, Beständigkeit; feste Haltung; ~ **of the market** Festigkeit der Börse; ~ **of prices** Preisstabilität

first erste(r, -s); zuerst, an erster Stelle, vorzüglich; ~**s** Waren erster Qualität; ~ **aid** erste Hilfe; ~ **aid post** (or **station**) Unfallstation; ~ **bid** Erstgebot; ~**-born** erstgeboren; ~ **claim** Vorhand

first class erstklassig; erstrangig; ~ **(university) degree** *Br (etwa)* mit summa cum laude erworbener erster akademischer Grad; ~ **hotel** Hotel erster Klasse; ~ **mail** Briefpost; ~ **securities** erstklassige Wertpapiere; ~ **ticket** Fahrkarte erster Klasse; **to travel** ~ erster Klasse reisen

first, ~ **cost** Selbstkosten(preis); Gestehungskosten, Anschaffungskosten; ~ **degree** →**murder; at** ~ **hand** aus erster Hand; direkt (bezogen); ~**-hand information** Nachricht aus erster Hand; **"~-in, ~-out"** „zuerst eingekauft – zuerst verbraucht" (→fifo); ~ **impression** erstmaliger Rechtsfall *(ohne Präzedenzfall)*

first instance, court of ~ Gericht erster Instanz, erstinstanzliches Gericht *(opp. appellate court)*

first, ~ **lien** erstrangiges Pfandrecht; ~**-line competition** *Am* Wettbewerb unter Verkäufern *(opp. secondary-line competition);* **F~ Lord of the Admiralty** *Br* Marineminister; **F~ Lord of the →Treasury;** ~**-loss insurance** Erstrisikoversicherung; Versicherung auf erstes Risiko

first mortgage erste Hypothek (→*mortgage);* ~ **bonds** *Am* durch erste Hypothek gesicherte Pfandbriefe

first, ~ **name** Vorname, Rufname; ~ **of exchange** Erstausfertigung e-s Wechsels; Primawechsel; ~ **offender** (noch) nicht Vorbestrafter; Ersttäter; **to be a** ~ **offender** nicht vorbestraft sein; ~ **open water** (F.O.W., f.o.w.) Verschiffung erst bei eisfreiem Hafen; ~ **option** Vorhand *(beim Kauf);* ~ **order goods** *Am* Konsumgüter; ~ **papers** *Am* vorläufige Einbürgerungspapiere *(cf. declaration of intention);* ~ **premium** Erstprämie *(opp. renewal premium);* ~ **purchaser** Ersterwerber

first-rate ersten Ranges, erstklassig, prima; **of** ~ **importance** von größter Wichtigkeit; ~ **powers** *pol* Großmächte

first refusal, right of ~ *Am* Vorkaufsrecht (→ *refusal)*

first right of purchase, to secure the ~ (of sth.) sich das Vorkaufsrecht sichern

first, ~**-stage financing** Finanzierung der Markteinführung von neuen Produkten; ~ **strike** *mil* Erstschlag; ~**-time voter** Erstwähler

first-to-file system *(PatR)* Anmeldeprinzip

first-to-invent system *(PatR)* Erfinderprinzip

fisc *bes. Scot* Fiskus

fiscal fiskalisch; Finanz- Steuer-; ~ **administration** Finanzverwaltung; ~ **agency** *Am* Finanzbehörde; ~ **agent** *Am* Finanzierungsberater; Kreditvermittler; ~ **authorities** Finanzbehörden, Steuerbehörden; ~ **burden** Steuerlast; **the state in its ~ capacity** der Staat als Fiskus; ~ **charges** steuerliche Lasten; Steueraufwendungen; ~ **concession** steuerliche Begünstigung; ~ **cooperation** Zusammenarbeit (od. gegenseitiger Beistand) in Steuersachen; ~ **court** Finanzgericht; ~ **deficit** Fehlbetrag im Staatshaushalt; ~ **domicil(e)** *(DBA)* steuerlicher Wohnsitz; ~ **duties** Finanzzölle; ~ **equity** fiskalische Gleichheit *(z.B. zwischen Gebietskörperschaften)*

fiscal evasion Steuerhinterziehung, Steuerverkürzung; **prevention of** ~[7] Verhinderung der Steuerverkürzung

fiscal, ~ **fraud** Steuerhinterziehung; ~ **immunity** Steuerfreiheit; ~ **jurisdiction** Steuerhoheit; ~ **law** Steuerrecht; Steuergesetz; ~ **matters** fiskalische Angelegenheiten; ~ **monopoly** Finanzmonopol *(Monopolisierung von Herstellung und Verkauf durch den Staat von Streichhölzern, Tabak etc);* ~ **neutrality** Steuerneutralität; ~ **offen|ces (~ses)** fiskalische strafbare Handlungen; Zoll- und Steuervergehen; ~ **officer** *Am* Finanzbeamter; ~ **policy** Fiskalpolitik *(finanzpolitische Maßnahmen des Staates, bes. hinsichtlich der Beschäftigungspolitik und der Konjunkturpolitik);* ~ **provisions** steuerrechtliche Vorschriften; ~ **report** Finanzbericht, Geschäftsbericht; ~ **system** Finanzsystem, Steuersystem; ~ **taxes** Finanzzölle; ~ **year** *Am* Geschäftsjahr *(12-Monats-Periode, die nicht mit 1. Januar zu beginnen braucht);* Haushaltsjahr, Rechnungsjahr *(1. Juli bis 30. Juni); Br* Steuerjahr *(6. April bis 5. April)*

fiscus → fisc

fish Fisch(e); ~ **products** Fischwaren; ~ **processing industry** fischverarbeitende Industrie; ~**monger(s)** *Br* Fischhändler; Fischhandlung; ~ **stocks** Fischbestände; ~ **trade** Fischhandel; **catching (of)** ~ Fischfang; **royal** ~ *Br* der Krone gehörende Fische *(in der Nähe der Küste gefangene Wale und Störe)*

fishery Fischerei *(Gewerbe);* Fischfang; Fischereigebiet; Fischgründe, Fischteiche; Fischereirecht; **F~ Limits Act** *Br* Gesetz *(von 1964),* das die Hoheitsgewässer (territorial waters) des Vereinigten Königreichs auf 12 Meilen ausdehnte

fishery resources, conservation of the ~ Erhaltung der Fischbestände; **exploitation of** ~ Nutzung der Fischbestände

fishery, coastal ~ Küstenfischerei; **common** ~ freier Fischfang, Freianglerrecht *(Befugnis der Allgemeinheit zur Ausübung des Fischfangs in öffentlichen Gewässern); Am* Fischgründe für die Allgemeinheit; **common of** ~ Fischereigerechtigkeit; Fischereiberechtigung *(in den Gewässern e-s anderen zusammen mit dem Eigentümer od. anderen Berechtigten);* **deep sea** ~ Hochseefischerei; **free** ~ *Br* vererbtes Regalfischereirecht (Fischereiprivileg) des einzelnen an öffentlichen Gewässern; **freshwater** (or **river**) ~ Binnenfischerei; **public** ~ s. common →~; **right of** ~ Fischereirecht; **Royal** ~ *Br* Fischereiregal der Krone an öffentlichen Gewässern; **sea** ~ Seefischerei; →**sedentary** ~; **several** ~ Eigentümerfischereirecht; Fischereiausübungsrecht *(ausschließliches Fischereirecht des Gewässergrundstückseigentümers oder des von ihm Ausübungsberechtigten, z.B. des Fischereipächters)*

fisheries, ~ **act** Fischereigesetz; ~ **agreement** Fischereiabkommen; **F~ Convention** (for defining a régime of ~ of a permanent character)[8] Fischereiübereinkommen (zur Festlegung e-r dauerhaften Regelung für die Fischerei); ~ **policy** Fischereipolitik; **jurisdiction over** ~ Fischereihoheit; **North East Atlantic F~**[9] Fischerei im Nordostatlantik; **North Sea F~**[10] Fischerei in der Nordsee; **North West Atlantic F~**[11] Fischerei im Nordwestatlantik

fishermen's articles of agreement Heuervertrag der Fischer

fishing Fischerei; Fischfang; ~ **area** Fanggebiet; ~ **boat** Fischereifahrzeug, Fischerboot; ~ **expedition** *Am (Zivilprozeß) (unerlaubter)* „Beweisfischzug" (Ausforschung); ~ **fleet** Fischereiflotte; ~ **grounds** Fischgründe, Fanggründe; ~ **industry** Fischerei(industrie); Fischwirtschaft; ~ **licen|ce (~se)** *(EG)* Fischereilizenz; ~ **limit** Fischereigrenze; **extension of ~ limits to 200 miles** *(EG)* Ausdehnung der Fischereigrenzen auf 200 Meilen; ~ **operations** Fischereitätigkeiten; **conduct of ~ operations** Verhalten beim Fischfang; ~ **periods** Fangzeiten; ~ **permit** *Am* Fischereischein; ~ **resources** Fischbestände; ~ **right** Fischereirecht; ~ **zone** Fischereizone

fisk → fisc

fission Kernspaltung

fissionable materials *(AtomR)* spaltbares Material

fit geeignet (for für); tauglich, fähig; ~ **for duty** dienstfähig; ~ **for habitation** bewohnbar; ~ **person** geeignete Person; ~ **for the purpose** dem Zweck entsprechend; ~ **for service** dienstfähig; ~ **for work** arbeitsfähig; ~ **to plead** verhandlungsfähig *(vor Gericht);* **to be** ~ gesund sein; **to be ~ for** sich eignen für

fit *v* ausstatten, versehen (with mit); *(Geschäft*

etc) einrichten; aufstellen, montieren; geeignet sein; geeignet machen; angemessen sein; *(jdm)* passen; **this ~s the purpose** dies ist für den Zweck angemessen; **he will ~ the vacancy** er wird für die Stelle geeignet sein; **he needs a training that will ~ him for the job** er braucht e-e Ausbildung, die ihn für die Stelle geeignet macht

fit *v*, **to ~ in with** passen zu; **to ~ out** ausrüsten, ausstatten; **to ~ up** einrichten, ausstatten

fitments Einrichtungsgegenstände; Einbauten; **kitchen ~** Kücheneinrichtung

fitness Tauglichkeit; Eignung, Qualifikation; gute körperliche Verfassung; **~ to drive** Fahrtüchtigkeit; **~ of goods for a particular purpose** *Br*[12] Eignung von Waren für e-n besonderen Zweck *(zugesicherte Eigenschaft)*; **~ for military service** Wehrtauglichkeit; **~ for work** Arbeitsfähigkeit; **certificate of ~** Gesundheitstest; **warranty of ~ for a particular purpose** *Am* Gewährleistung der Eignung für e-n bestimmten Zweck (→*warranty*)

fitting Einrichtung *(e-s Geschäfts od. Büros)*; Zubehör; **~s** Einrichtungsgegenstände; **~ (up)** Aufstellen *(e-r Maschine)*, Montage; **~ shop** Montagewerkstatt; **business ~s** Geschäftseinrichtung; **shop ~(s)** Ladeneinrichtung(sgegenstände); **fixtures and ~s** bewegliche und unbewegliche Einrichtungsgegenstände *(e-s Betriebes od. Wohnhauses)*; Betriebs- und Geschäftseinrichtung; *Br* Einbauten, Zubehör *(zu e-m Gebäude, z. B. elektrische Installationen)*

five fünf; **~s** *Am* fünfprozentige (Wert-)Papiere; **in ~ copies** in fünffacher Ausfertigung; **~-day week** Fünftagewoche; **~fold** fünffach; **~ per cent** (or **at ~ per cent**) fünfprozentig; **~-power agreement** *(VölkerR)* Fünfmächteabkommen, Fünferabkommen; **~-year plan** Fünfjahresplan; **to introduce the ~-day week** die Fünftagewoche einführen

fix *v* festsetzen, festlegen; bestimmen, anberaumen; **to ~ (up)on** sich entschließen für; *Am (jdm etw.)* zuschreiben; **the crime was ~ed on him** *Am* ihm wurde das Verbrechen zugeschrieben; **to ~ the amount of damages** den Schadensersatz feststellen; **to ~ a date for a meeting** e-e Sitzung ansetzen; **to ~ a day** e-n Termin anberaumen; **to ~ a (day for the) hearing** e-n (Gerichts-)Termin anberaumen; **to ~ a juror** *sl.* e-n Geschworenen bestechen; **to ~ a limit** ein Limit (fest)setzen; **to ~ a penalty** e-e Strafe festsetzen; das Strafmaß bestimmen; **to ~ the price** den Preis festsetzen (od. bestimmen); e-n Kurs festsetzen; **to ~ a quota** ein Kontingent festsetzen; **to ~ the rent** die Miete festsetzen; **to ~ a time limit** e-e Frist festsetzen; **to ~ the time limit for a debate** e-e Debatte befristen

fixed bestimmt, fest; festgelegt; *Br (auf Wechsel neben dem Fälligkeitsdatum)* ohne Respekttage; **~ abode** fester Wohnsitz; **~ allowance** Fixum; **~ asset** Anlagegegenstand; **~ asset account** Sachanlagenkonto *(opp. investment account)*

fixed assets feste (od. festliegende) Anlagen; Sachanlagen; Anlagevermögen *(opp. current assets)*; **addition to ~** *(Bilanz)* Anlagenzugänge; **disposal** (*Am* **retirement**) **of ~** Anlagenabgänge

fixed, ~ base *(DBA)* feste Einrichtung; **~ belief** →**~** opinion; **~ capital** festliegendes Kapital, Anlagekapital *(Maschinen etc)*; **~ charge** feststehende Belastung *(die sich auf e-n bestimmten Gegenstand bezieht; opp. floating charge)*; **~ charges** feste Kosten; fixe Kosten; Gemeinkosten *(opp. direct expenses)*; **~ construction** *(Patentklassifikation)* Bauwesen; **~ contract price** vertraglich festgesetzter Preis; **~ cost** feste Kosten, Fixkosten *(opp. variable cost)*; **~-coupon bonds** →straight bonds

fixed date fester Termin; **to sell sth. on a ~** etw. auf Ziel verkaufen

fixed, ~ debt →funded debt; **~ deposits** feste Gelder, Festgeld, Termineinlagen *(opp. demand deposits)*; **~ delivery date** festes Liefer(-ungs)datum; **~ exchange** *(Devisenkurs)* direkte Notierung, Mengennotierung; **~ exchange rate** fester Wechselkurs *(opp. floating exchange rate)*; **~ fund** *Am* Investmentfonds, dessen Wertpapierbestand unveränderlich ist *(opp. flexible, managed fund)*; **~ income** feste Einkünfte; **~ income securities** Rentenwerte; **~-interest securities** festverzinsliche Wertpapiere; **~ investment** feste (langfristige) Kapitalanlage; Anlageinvestition; **~ investment trust** →**~** trust; **~ liability** feste *(langfristige)* Verbindlichkeit; **~ opinion** vorgefaßte Meinung *(bes. als Grund für Ablehnung e-s Geschworenen)*

fixed place of business, maintenance of a ~ Unterhalten e-r festen Geschäftseinrichtung

fixed price Festpreis; festgesetzter Preis; gebundener Preis; **~ contract** Festpreisvereinbarung *(opp. escalation clause)*; **~s for resale** Preisbindung der zweiten Hand

fixed, ~ purchase fester Kauf; **~ rate of exchange** fester Wechselkurs *(opp. floating rate of exchange)*; **~ salary** festes Gehalt; **~ sum** bestimmte Summe; Fixum; **~ sum excess** *(VersR)* Abzugsfranchise; **~ tangible assets** Sachanlagen; **~ term** bestimmte Dauer *(z. B. e-s Vertrages, bes. e-s Miet- od. Pachtvertrages)*; **~ term deposits** Festgeldeinlagen; **at a ~ time** an e-m festgesetzten Zeitpunkt; **~ trust** trust, der dem trustee keine Ermessensfreiheit läßt *(opp. discretionary trust)*; Investmenttrust mit nach festen Regeln angelegtem Effektenbestand *(opp. flexible trust, management trust)*; **~ value** Festwert; **~-yield securities** festverzinsliche Wertpapiere

fixing Festsetzung, Bestimmung; Fixing (des Londoner Goldpreises); ~ **the boundary** Festlegung der Grenze; Grenzbestimmung; ~ **of costs** Kostenfestsetzung; ~ **a date** Festsetzung e-s Termins, Terminbestimmung; ~ **of quotas** Festsetzung der Quoten; Kontingentierung; **price** ~ Preisfestsetzung; Preisabsprache *(unter Wettbewerbern; →price 1.)*

fixation Festsetzung; *(psychischer)* Komplex; ~ **of boundaries** Festlegung der Grenzen; ~ **of a period** Festsetzung e-r Zeit, Fristbestimmung; ~ **of the premium for a given contract** *(VersR)* Festlegung der Prämie für e-n bestimmten Vertrag

fixture (wesentlicher) Bestandteil eines Grundstücks *([im Sinne des § 94 BGB]; umfaßt aber auch Scheinbestandteile [§ 95 BGB] und Zubehör [§ 97 BGB] eines Grundstücks [das z.B. der Pächter jederzeit entfernen kann])*

fixture, ~**s** eingebaute Anlagen, Einbauten, Grundstückszubehör; ~**s and equipment** *Am* Geschäfts- und Betriebseinrichtung; ~**s and fittings** →fittings; **agricultural** ~ dem landwirtschaftlichen Zweck dienendes Zubehör; **furniture and** ~**s** Geschäfts- und Betriebseinrichtung; **ornamental** ~ bewegliche Sachen, die zum Zwecke der Verschönerung mit dem Haus verbunden sind; **tenant's** ~**s** Zubehör, Einbauten *(etc)*, die ein Mieter oder Pächter für die Dauer seiner Besitzzeit anbringt; **trade** ~**s** Betriebsausstattung, Betriebsvorrichtung *(dem gewerblichen Zweck dienendes ~; z.B. eingebaute Maschinenanlage)*

flag Flagge, Fahne; ~**s of convenience** (FOC) billige Flaggen (→*Panholibco States); ~***-day** *Br* Straßensammeltag für wohltätige Zwecke; ~ **discrimination** Flaggendiskriminierung; ~ **of distress** Notflagge; ~ **misuse** Flaggenmißbrauch; ~ **salute** Flaggengruß, Schiffsgruß; ~ **state** Flaggenstaat

flag of truce Parlamentärsfahne, weiße Fahne; **bearer of the** ~ Parlamentär

flag, American ~ amerikanische Flagge *(Stars and Stripes);* **British** ~ britische Flagge *(Union Jack);* **false** ~ falsche Flagge; **law of the** ~ *(VölkerR)* Recht des Heimathafens; **maritime** ~ Seeflagge *(Br blue, red and white → ensign);* **merchant** ~ Handelsflagge; **national** ~ Landesflagge; **right to fly a** ~ Recht der Flaggenführung; **trade follows the** ~ der Handel folgt der Flagge; **transfer to (another)** ~ *(VölkerR)* Wechsel des Flaggenstaates (od. der Staatsangehörigkeit von Schiffen); **verification of the** ~ *(VölkerR)* Prüfung e-r Flagge *(durch ein Kriegsschiff);* **vessels flying the** ~ **of the United States** Schiffe unter US-Flagge; **white** ~ →~ of truce; **wrong** ~ falsche Flagge; **yellow** ~ Quarantänefahne; **to dip the** ~ Flagge dippen; **to fly a** ~ e-e Flagge führen; **to fly the** ~ **of** . . . unter der Flagge von . . . fahren; **to fly the British** ~ unter britischer Flagge fahren; **to fly the** ~ **at half-mast** halbmast flaggen; **to hoist the** ~ die Flagge hissen; **to lower the** ~ die Flagge einholen; **to show the** ~ flaggen

flag *v* beflaggen; signalisieren; nachlassen, abflauen; **to** ~ **(down)** *(Zug, Auto etc durch Zeichen)* anhalten

flagging tendency Abschwächungstendenz

flagrante delicto auf frischer Tat (ertappt), in flagranti

flat *bes. Br* (Etagen-, Miet-)Wohnung; Appartement; ~ **dweller(s)** Inhaber e-r Wohnung; ~**-hunting** *colloq.* Wohnungssuche; ~ **let at a high rent** Wohnung mit hoher Miete; ~ **with all modern conveniences** (mod. cons.) Wohnung mit allem Komfort; **block of** ~**s** Miethaus, Wohnblock; **exchange of** ~**s** Wohnungstausch; **furnished** ~ möblierte Wohnung; **the landlord lets the** ~ der Hauswirt vermietet die Wohnung; **the tenant takes the** ~ der Mieter mietet die Wohnung

flat einheitlich, gleichmäßig, pauschal; flau, lustlos; *Am* ohne (Berechnung aufgelaufener) Zinsen; glatt, offen, kategorisch; ~ **charge** Pauschale; ~ **cost** Selbstkosten(preis); Gestehungspreis; ~ **exemption** *Am* (steuerl.) Freibetrag; ~ **fee** Pauschalgebühr; Pauschalhonorar; ~ **market** ruhiger (od. flauer) Markt; lustlose Börse; ~ **price** Einheitspreis; ~ **quotation** *Am* Kursnotierung ohne Zinsberücksichtigung

flat rate Pauschalsatz; einheitlicher Satz; Grundgebühr; Einheits-; ~ **amount** Pauschbetrag; ~ **benefits** *Br (Sozialvers.)* Grundleistungen; ~ **contribution** *Br (Sozialvers.)* Grundbeitrag; einheitlicher Beitrag; **the motor vehicle licence duty is charged at a** ~ **of £ . . . p.a.** *Br* die Kraftfahrzeugsteuer wird zu e-m Einheitssatz von £ . . . pro Jahr erhoben

flat, ~ **refusal** glatte Absage; ~ **sum** Pauschalbetrag; ~ **tariff** Einheitstarif

flatness Faulheit, Lustlosigkeit

flaw Fehler, Unvollkommenheit, Mangel; (Fabrikations-)Fehler; ~ **in a title** Rechtsmangel; **hidden** ~ versteckter Fehler

fledged, fully-~ **member of the Communities** *(EG) (colloq.)* vollberechtigtes Mitglied der Gemeinschaften

flee *v* fliehen, flüchten; **to** ~ **the country** aus dem Lande flüchten; **to** ~ **from justice** sich der Strafverfolgung entziehen

fleet Flotte *(meist Kriegsflotte);* **F**~ **Ballistic Missiles** (FBM) *Am (mit ballistischen Großraketen bestückte)* atomgetriebene Unterseeboote; ~ **of cabs** Taxipark *(e-s Unternehmers);* ~ **of cars**

(e-m Eigentümer gehörende) Gruppe von Wagen; Fahrzeugpark; ~ **consumption** *Am* Flottenverbrauch; ~ →**leasing;** ~ **policy** *(VersR)* Kraftfahrzeugsammelpolice; Pauschalpolice *(für den Eigentümer mehrerer Kraftfahrzeuge);* ~ **of taxis** →~ of cabs; **air** ~ Luftflotte; **merchant** ~ Handelsflotte; **motor-vehicle** ~ Kraftfahrzeugpark

flexibility Flexibilität; Anpassungsfähigkeit; ~ **of working hours** Arbeitszeitflexibilität

flexible flexibel, elastisch, nachgiebig; anpassungsfähig; ~ **exchange rate** flexibler Wechselkurs; ~ **fund** *Am* Investmentfonds, dessen Wertpapierbestand sich ständig ändern kann *(opp. fixed fund);* ~ **law** nachgiebiges Recht; ~ **provision** nachgiebige Bestimmung; ~ **rate** flexibler (Wechsel-)Kurs; ~ **response** *Am mil* flexible Erwiderung, angemessene Entgegnung; ~ **schedule** *Am* flexible (od. gleitende) Arbeitszeit; ~ **time** →flexitime; ~ **(investment) trust** *Am* Investmentgesellschaft mit wechselndem Effektenbestand *(die in ihrer Anlagetätigkeit beweglich ist; opp. fixed trust);* **semi-** ~ **(investment) trust** „halbflexible" Investmentgesellschaft *(Zusammensetzung des Wertpapierbestandes ist in etwa festgelegt, es verbleibt aber noch ein gewisser Dispositionsrahmen);* ~ **working time** gleitende Arbeitszeit

flex time (or **flexitime**) gleitende Arbeitszeit; **to work** ~ in gleitender Arbeitszeit arbeiten

flight 1. Flucht; ~ **capital** Fluchtkapital; ~ **of capital** Kapitalflucht; ~ **from the land** Landflucht; **to take (to)** ~ fliehen, flüchten

flight 2. *(bestimmter)* Flug; ~ **allowance** Flugzulage; ~ **monitoring** Flugüberwachung; ~ **over a territory** Überfliegen e-s Gebietes; ~ **personnel** Flugpersonal; ~ **reservation** Reservierung von Flugplätzen; **duration of** ~ Flugdauer; **free** ~ Freiflug; **intelligence** ~ Spionageflug; **night** ~ Nachtflug; **route of** ~ Flugstrecke; **scheduled** ~ fahrplanmäßiger Flug; **space** ~ Raumflug; **transit** ~ Durchflug im internationalen Fluglinienverkehr; **trial** ~ Probeflug

flight deliver *v Am* mit dem Flugzeug transportieren

flip-flop floater →floater 2.

float Float; *(Bankwesen)* Wertstellungsdifferenz zwischen Belastung und Gutschrift e-r bargeldlosen Kontobewegung; schwebende Einzugswerte *(bes. Summe des im Einzug befindlichen Schecks); Br* kleine Kasse; *(Währung)* Freigabe des Wechselkurses (→ *floating);* **clean** ~ sauberes Floaten; freigegebener Wechselkurs ohne Intervention der Zentralbank; **dirty** ~ schmutziges Floaten; freigegebener Wechselkurs, wobei die Zentralbank den Wechselkurs durch Devisenkäufe und -verkäufe in e-m von ihr gewählten Rahmen (Bandbreite) hält; **downward** ~ **of the pound** Kursverfall des Pfundes

float *v* floaten; frei schwanken; in Umlauf sein, umlaufen; in Umlauf bringen; in Gang bringen; *(Schiff)* flott machen; **to** ~ **a company** e-e (Handels-)Gesellschaft gründen; **to** ~ **the dollar** den Wechselkurs des Dollars freigeben (→ *floating);* **to** ~ **the exchange rate** den Wechselkurs freigeben; **to** ~ **a loan** e-e Anleihe ausgeben (od. auflegen); **to permit the dollar to** ~ den Dollar frei schwanken lassen (→*floating*)

floatation Gründung *(e-s Unternehmens);* Ausgabe (od. Auflegen) *(e-r Anleihe);* Ingangbringen

floater 1. Gründer *(e-r Handelsgesellschaft); Br* erstklassiges Wertpapier; Pauschalversicherung (→*floating policy*); *Am* parteiloser (bes. käuflicher) Wähler; *Am* jd, der illegal in verschiedenen Wahlbezirken wählt; *Am colloq.* Arbeiter, der Arbeitsplatz häufig wechselt; **office** ~ *Am* Versicherung der Büroeinrichtung

floater 2. Kurzname für e-e zinsvariable Anleihe (→*floating rate note*); **collared** ~ s. mini-max →floater; **drop lock** ~ floater mit put option *(der Investor kann die Rückzahlung der Anleihe zum Nennwert verlangen, wenn der Emittent die Anleihebedingungen ändert);* **flip-flop** ~ floater mit dem Recht des Inhabers, nach einigen Jahren in e-e Anleihe mit kürzerer Laufzeit und auch wieder zurück zu wechseln; **mini-max** ~ floater mit variabler Verzinsung innerhalb e-s Mindest- und Höchstzinssatzes; **mismatch** ~ floater mit inkongruenter Bindungsfrist von Anleihezins und Refinanzierungszins

floating 1. Floaten *(Schwanken durch Freigabe des Wechselkurses);* Auflegung *(e-r Anleihe);* floatend

Das marktkonformste Instrument, mit dem unerwünschte Devisenzuflüsse gestoppt werden können, ist die Freigabe der Wechselkurse, das Floaten. Die Notenbanken sind nicht mehr gezwungen, Devisen anderer Länder zu den unteren Interventionspunkten zu kaufen oder zu den oberen zu verkaufen. Die Devisenkurse können völlig frei schwanken und sich nach Angebot und Nachfrage am Markt bilden

floating, ~ **exchange rate** floatender Wechselkurs *(opp. fixed exchange rate);* ~ **the exchange rate** Freigabe des Wechselkurses; ~ **pound** *Br* frei schwankendes Pfund; freigegebenes Pfund; ~ **rate** frei schwankender Wechselkurs; **country with freely** ~ **exchange rates** Land mit frei schwankenden Wechselkursen; **currencies which are** ~ Währungen, deren Wechselkurs freigegeben ist

floating 2. schwimmend, schwebend; in Umlauf befindlich; ~ **assets** Umlaufvermögen; flüssige Anlagen (od. Aktiva); ~ **capital** Betriebskapital; Umlaufvermögen *(inventory, receivables etc);* ~ **cargo** schwimmende (unterwegs befindliche) Fracht

floating charge[13] *Br (GesellschaftsR)* schwebendes Sicherungsrecht (am Gesamt- bzw. Teilvermögen e-r Gesellschaft) *(opp. fixed charge)*
Die Bestellung e-r "floating charge" erfolgt i. d. R. zur Sicherung von Bankdarlehen. Um gegenüber dem Liquidator bzw. anderen Gläubigern der Gesellschaft wirksam zu sein, muß sie innerhalb von 21 Tagen beim →Registrar of Companies angemeldet werden. Dieser veranlaßt die Eintragung in ein öffentliches Register (→*Register of Charges*). Der Bestand der mit der floating charge belasteten Gegenstände kann wechseln

floating, ~ debt schwebende (nicht fundierte) Schuld; kurzfristige Staatsschuld *(opp. consolidated or funded debt)*; ~ **dock** Schwimmdock; ~ **liabilities** kurzfristige Verbindlichkeiten; ~ **lien** *Am* Sicherungsrecht an e-m Vermögensgegenstand mit wechselndem Bestand; ~ **policy** (F. P.) laufende Police; Abschreibepolice

floating rate, ~ CD Einlagenzertifikat (certificate of deposit) mit variabler Verzinsung; ~-**drop-lock** s. drop lock →floater 2.

floating rate note (FRN) mittel- bis langfristige Schuldverschreibung mit variabler Verzinsung, die i. d. R. alle 3 od. 6 Monate auf der Basis e-s Referenzzinssatzes neu bestimmt wird; **convertible** ~ FRN, die durch Option des Inhabers in e-e festverzinsliche Anlage umgewandelt werden kann; **perpetual** ~ FRN ohne Endfälligkeit mit eigenkapitalähnlichem Charakter

flaoting rate of interest schwankender Zins

floating, ~ security *Br* →~ charge; **the ~ vote** die *(vor der Wahl)* nicht feststehenden Stimmen; ~ **voters** nicht parteigebundene Wähler *(schwankende Parteilose)*, Wechselwähler

flood Flut; Hochwasser, Überschwemmung; ~ **control** Hochwasserschutz; ~ **coverage** *Am* Versicherungsschutz gegen Überschwemmungsschäden; ~ **damage** Hochwasserschaden; ~ **disaster** Hochwasserkatastrophe; ~ **insurance** Überschwemmungsversicherung

flood *v* **to ~ the market** den Markt überschwemmen

floor Boden; Stockwerk; Mindestpreis; Börsensaal, Parkett; *parl* Sitzungssaal; ~ **broker** *Am* Börsenhändler *(Makler, der Aufträge für andere Makler ausführt)*; ~ **leader** *Am parl* Fraktionsführer; ~ **member** Börsenmitglied; ~ **of the House** *parl* Sitzungssaal, Plenarsaal; ~ **of the sea** Meeresboden; ~ **partner** *Am* Teilhaber e-r Maklerfirma; ~ **plan** Grundriß; Raumverteilungsplan *(z. B. bei e-r Ausstellung, Messe)*; ~ **price** Mindestpreis *(opp. ceiling price)*; ~ **rate of interest** Mindestzinssatz; ~ **space** Bodenfläche; Hallenfläche *(z. B. bei e-r Messe)*; Ausstellungsfläche; ~ **trader** *Am* Wertpapierhändler, der für eigene Rechnung handelt; ~ **walker** *Am* Ladenaufsicht *(in e-m Warenhaus)*; **second ~** *Br* erstes *(Am* zweites) Stockwerk; **to ask for** (or **claim**) **the ~** *Am* um das Wort bitten; **to cross the ~ of the House** *Br* zur Opposition übergehen; **to get** (or **be given**) **the ~** *Am* das Wort erhalten; **to have the ~** *Am* das Wort haben; **to hold the ~** *Am parl* e-e Rede halten; **to take the ~** das Wort ergreifen

flop (over) *v Am pol (zum Gegner)* übergehen

flotation →floatation

flotsam Treibgut, *(treibendes)* Wrackgut; seetriftige Güter; ~ **and jetsam** treibendes Wrack- und Strandgut

flourish *v* florieren, blühen; ~**ing business** florierendes Geschäft

flow Strom; (Zu-, Ab-)Fluß; Strömen, Fließen; ~ **chart** Arbeitsablaufdiagramm *(graphische Darstellung des Ablaufs e-s Fabrikationsprozesses im Rahmen des →forecasting program)*; ~ **diagram** →~chart; ~ **of capital** Kapitalwanderung *(von e-r Industrie in e-e andere)*; ~ **of commerce** *Am* Handelsverkehr; ~ **of credit** Kreditstrom; ~ **of funds** Geldstrom; ~ **of goods** Güterstrom; ~ **of money** Geldstrom; ~ **of traffic** Verkehrsstrom; ~ **of work** Arbeitsablauf; ~ **production** Fließbandfertigung; Fließarbeit; ~ **sheet** →~chart

fluctuate *v* schwanken, steigen und fallen, fluktuieren; **the income ~s between ... and ...** die Einkünfte schwanken zwischen ... und ...; **the profit ~s** der Gewinn schwankt

fluctuating prices schwankende Preise (od. Kurse)

fluctuation Fluktuation, Schwankung, Schwanken; ~ **in economic activity** Konjunkturschwankung; ~ **in the rate of exchange** Wechselkursschwankung; ~**s of interest rates** Zinsschwankungen; ~**s of the market** Marktschwankungen; Börsenschwankungen; **cyclical ~s** Konjunkturschwankungen; **margin of ~s** →margin 2.; **price ~s** Preisschwankungen; Kursschwankungen; **seasonal ~s** Saisonschwankungen; **to be subject to price ~s** Preis- (od. Kurs-)Schwankungen unterliegen

flush, to be ~ bei Kasse sein

fly *v* fliegen; (ent)fliehen *(Zeit etc)*; **to ~ an aircraft** ein Flugzeug fliegen (od. führen); **to ~ across the Atlantic** über den Atlantik fliegen; **to ~ across the territory** das Hoheitsgebiet überfliegen; **to ~ a flag** e-e Fahne hissen; *(Schiff)* unter e-r Flagge fahren; **to ~ a →kite; to ~ over a territory** ein Gebiet überfliegen

flying Flug; Fliegen; Fliegerei; ~ **officer** *Br* Oberleutnant *(der R. A. F.)*; ~ **speed** Fluggeschwindigkeit; ~ **squad** *Br* Überfallkommando; ~ **test** Flugprüfung; **ban on ~** Flugverbot

fly-by-night company *Am* kurzlebige (auf Betrug angelegte) Gesellschaft

flyer *Am* Flugblatt, Handzettel

fob (free on board) ... (named port of shipment) Frei an Bord ... (benannter Verschiffungshafen) *(→Incoterms 1980)*

fob airport (FOA) ... (named airport of departure) fob Flughafen ... (benannter Abgangsflughafen) *(→Incoterms 1980)*

focus Brennpunkt; ~ **of attention** Brennpunkt des Interesses; ~ **of conflict** Konfliktherd; **to bring into** ~ in den Brennpunkt rücken; *(etw.)* klar herausstellen

focus *v*, **to** ~ **(up)on** sich konzentrieren auf

fodder Futter(mittel) *(für Vieh)*

foetal death Totgeburt

foeticide Abtreibung

foetus Fötus, Leibesfrucht

fold up *v* zusammenlegen; zusammenbrechen; **the business** ~**ed up** das Geschäft brach zusammen *(z.B. es geriet in Konkurs)*

folder *(gefaltete)* Broschüre, (Falt-)Prospekt; Aktendeckel, Mappe, Schnellhefter

foliate *v (Buch)* mit Seitenzahlen versehen

folio (f., Fo., fo., Fol., fol.) (Folio-)Blatt, Folioformat; Seitenzahl; Kontobuchseite; Längeneinheitsmaß e-r Urkunde *(Br 72 Wörter [Urkunde], 90 Wörter [Testament]; Am 100 Wörter)*; ~ **size** Folioformat

folio *v* paginieren, mit Seitenzahlen versehen
folioing Paginierung; Seitennumerierung

follow *v* folgen; verfolgen; folgen auf, nachfolgen; sich ergeben (from aus); **to** ~ **sb.'s advice** jds Rat befolgen; **costs** ~ **the event** die Kostenentscheidung richtet sich nach dem Ausgang des Prozesses; **to** ~ **the party line** →party 3.; **to** ~ **a trade** ein Gewerbe ausüben; **to** ~ **up invoices** Zahlungseingang überwachen; **to** ~ **up a matter** e-r Sache weiter nachgehen; e-e Sache weiter verfolgen; **letter to** ~ Brief folgt

follow-up, ~ **conference** Nachfolgekonferenz; ~ **file** Wiedervorlagemappe; ~ **letter** Nachfaßbrief, Erinnerungsschreiben; ~ **order** Anschlußauftrag; ~ **system** Wiedervorlageverfahren

follower Anhänger; *pol* Mitläufer

food Nahrung; Nahrungsmittel, Lebensmittel; ~ **additives** Zusatzstoffe für Lebensmittel; ~ **adulteration** Lebensmittelfälschung; ~ **aid** Nahrungsmittelhilfe; **F~ Aid Convention** 1986[14] Nahrungsmittelhilfe-Übereinkommen von 1986

Food and Agricultural Organization (F.A.O.)[15] Organisation für Ernährung und Landwirtschaft (Welternährungsrat)
Sonderorganisation der Vereinten Nationen. *Sitz:* Rom

Food and Drugs, ~ **Act** *Br* Lebensmittel- und Arzneimittelgesetz; ~ **Administration** (FDA) *Am* Nahrungsmittel- und Medikamentenbehörde

Food and Nutrition Service *Am* Schulspeisung

food, ~ **chain (store)** Lebensmittelkettenfirma; ~ **contamination** Lebensmittelverseuchung; ~ **cuts** Lebensmittelkürzungen; ~ **deficit area** Nahrungsmittelzuschußgebiet; ~, **drink and tobacco industry** Nahrungs- und Genußmittelindustrie; ~ **imports** Lebensmitteleinfuhr; ~ **(manufacturing) industry** Nahrungsmittelindustrie; ~ **prices** Lebensmittelpreise; ~ **processing industry** Nahrungsmittelindustrie; ~ **ration card** Lebensmittelkarte; ~ **rationing** Lebensmittelrationierung, -bewirtschaftung; ~ **shares** Lebensmittelaktien; ~ **shortage** Lebensmittelverknappung, -knappheit; ~ **situation** Ernährungslage; ~ **stock** *Am* →~ shares; ~ **stocks** Lebensmittelvorräte

foodstuffs Nahrungsmittel, Lebensmittel; Ernährungsgüter; **perishable** ~ verderbliche Lebensmittel; **Agreement on the International Carriage of Perishable F~ and on the Special Equipment to be Used for such Carriage**[16] Übereinkommen über internationale Beförderung leicht verderblicher Lebensmittel und über die besonderen Beförderungsmittel, die für diese Beförderung zu verwenden sind; **manufacture of** ~**s** Lebensmittelherstellung; **prepared** ~ Waren der Lebensmittelindustrie

food, ~ **supplies** Nahrungsmittelvorräte; ~ **supply** Nahrungsmittelversorgung, Nahrungsmittelzufuhr; ~ **surplus** Nahrungsmittelüberschuß

food, adulteration of ~ Lebensmittelfälschung; **patent** ~**s** Markennahrungsmittel; **prepackaged** (or **prepacked**) ~**s** abgepackte Lebensmittel; **processed** ~**s** verarbeitete (od. veredelte) Lebensmittel; **refusal of** ~ Nahrungsverweigerung; **to relieve a critical shortage of** ~ kritischen Mangel an Lebensmitteln beheben; **to take** ~ Nahrung zu sich nehmen

foolscap *Br* Schreib- od. Druckpapierformat *(17 × 13½ inches)*

foot (pl. **feet**) Fuß *(als Längenmaß 12 inches = 0,3048 m)*; ~ **mark** Fußspur; ~ **note** Fußnote; ~ **and mouth disease** Maul- und Klauenseuche; ~ **of a page** Ende e-r Seite *(opp. head of a page)*; ~ **prints** Fußspuren, Fußabdrücke; **at** ~ **of page** untenstehend; **to set negotiations on** ~ Verhandlungen in die Wege leiten (od. in Gang bringen)

foot *v*, **to** ~ **(up)** zusammenrechnen, addieren;

to ~ up to sich belaufen auf; **to ~ a bill** *colloq.* e-e Rechnung begleichen

footing Grundlage, Basis; Einstand(sgeld); Endsumme, Gesamtsumme; Stellung *(in der Gesellschaft);* Beziehungen; ~ **(up)** Addition; **on an equal** ~ auf gleicher Grundlage; gleichgestellt; gleichberechtigt, paritätisch; **placing on an equal** ~ Gleichstellung; **on a peace** ~ im Frieden(szustand); **on a war** ~ im Krieg(szustand); **to be on friendly** ~ **with sb.** mit jdm auf freundschaftlichem Fuß stehen; **to pay one's** ~ seinen Einstand bezahlen; **to place on a** ~ **with sb.** jdm gleichstellen

Footsie *Br* Spitzname für FT-SE 100 stock
Computerisierter Aktienindex von 100 großen britischen Unternehmen. Am 1. 1. 1984 eingeführt von der Financial Times und der Londoner Börse

for für; in Vertretung (i. V.); im Auftrag (i. A.); ~ **and against** für und wider *(Meinungen etc);* ~ **and on behalf of** für und im Auftrage von; **to know** ~ **certain** sicher wissen; ~ **life** lebenslänglich; ~ **long** auf lang(e Zeit); ~ **sale** zum Verkauf; ~ **some days** einige Tage lang; ~ **some time past** seit längerer Zeit; **to take sb.** ~ jdn *(irrtümlich)* halten für

FOR/FOT, for/fot (free on rail/free on truck) ... (named departure point) Frei (franko) Waggon (od. offener Güterwagen) ... (benannter Abgangsort) *(→Incoterms 1980)*

forbear *v* sich enthalten (sth. e-r Sache); unterlassen, **to** ~ **suit** *Am* Klageerhebung unterlassen

forbearance Nachsicht; Stundung; *(bes. zivilrechtl.)* Unterlassung *(cf. omission);* ~ **to sue** Klageunterlassung

forbears Vorfahren, Ahnen

forbid *v* verbieten, untersagen

force 1. Gewalt; Kraft; Gültigkeit; ~ **of an argument** Überzeugungskraft e-s Arguments; **(by)** ~ **of arms** (mit) Waffengewalt; ~ **of law** Gesetzeskraft; ~ **majeure** höhere Gewalt *(weitergehend als →Act of God, umfaßt auch Krieg, Streik etc)*

force, binding ~ bindende Kraft; **by** ~ mit Gewalt, zwangsweise; **(pending the) coming into** ~ (bis zum) Inkrafttreten; **as from the date of the coming into** ~ vom Tag des Inkrafttretens an; **deadly** ~ *Am* tödliche Gewalt; **employment** (or **exercise**) **of** ~ Anwendung von Gewalt, Gewaltanwendung; **in** ~ in Kraft, gültig, geltend; **legal** ~ Rechtskraft, Rechtsgültigkeit, Gesetzeskraft (*→legal*); **probative** ~ Beweiskraft; **renunciation of** ~ *pol* Gewaltverzicht; **unlawful** ~ rechtswidrige Gewalt; **use of** ~ Anwendung von Gewalt, Gewaltanwendung

force, to be in ~ in Kraft sein, gelten; **to bring into** ~ in Kraft setzen; **to come** (or **enter**) **into** ~ in Kraft treten; **to have legal** ~ Rechtskraft haben, rechtskräftig sein; **to remain in** ~ in Kraft bleiben; **to remain in full** ~ **and effect** verbindlich bleiben; **to take by** ~ mit Gewalt nehmen; **to use** ~ Gewalt anwenden

force 2. Belegschaft; **labo(u)r** ~ Arbeitskräfte, Belegschaft; **police** ~ Polizei; **strong** ~ **of police** starkes Polizeiaufgebot; **sales** ~ Verkaufspersonal; **working** ~ Belegschaft

force 3. *mil* Truppe, Verband; ~**s** Truppen, Streitkräfte; ~**s reduction** Truppenreduzierung, -verminderung; **armed** ~**s** (of a country) Streitkräfte (e-s Landes); **air** ~ Luftwaffe; **Royal Air F**~ Britische Luftwaffe; **foreign** ~**s** ausländische Streitkräfte; **ground** ~**s** Bodenstreitkräfte; **land** ~**s** Landstreitkräfte; **naval** ~**s** Seestreitkräfte; **occupational** ~**s** Besatzungstruppen; **strength of the** ~ Truppenstärke

force *v* zwingen, erzwingen; *(Tür, Schloß)* aufbrechen, erbrechen; **to** ~ **sth. (up)on sb.** jdm etw. aufzwingen; **to** ~ **down prices** Preise drücken; **to** ~ **up prices** Preise (od. Kurse) in die Höhe treiben; **to** ~ **a confession from sb.** jds Geständnis erzwingen; **to** ~ **an entry** (into a building) sich den Eintritt erzwingen; sich gewaltsam Eintritt verschaffen; **the war had been** ~**d upon them** der Krieg war ihnen aufgezwungen worden

forced gezwungen, erzwungen; ~ **agreement** Zwangsvergleich; ~ **call** Anlaufen e-s Nothafens; ~ **currency** Zwangswährung; ~ **entry** gewaltsames Eindringen; ~ **heir** *Am* pflichtteilsberechtigter Erbe

forced heirship *Am* Pflichtteilsrecht
Pflichtteilsrecht gibt es, außer in Louisiana, nicht für Verwandte, sondern nur für den überlebenden Ehegatten

forced labo(u)r Zwangsarbeit; Zwangsarbeiter; **abolition of** ~Abschaffung der Zwangsarbeit

forced, ~ **landing** Notlandung; ~**loan** Zwangsanleihe; ~ **sale** Zwangsversteigerung, Vollstreckungsversteigerung, Vollstreckungsverkauf *(als Maßregeln der Zwangsvollstreckung);* ~ **savings** Zwangssparen; **statutory** ~ **share** *Am (ErbR)* Pflichtteil

forcible gewaltsam, Zwangs-; zwingend, überzeugend; ~ **abduction** Entführung unter Anwendung von Gewalt; ~ **argument** zwingendes Argument; ~ **detainer** rechtswidrige Vorenthaltung *(von Grundbesitz);* ~ **entry** (into a building) gewaltsames Eindringen; Hausfriedensbruch; ~ **entry and detainer** gewaltsame und unerlaubte Inbesitzhaltung *(von Grundbesitz);* ~ **feeding** Zwangsernährung

forcibly zwangsweise, gewaltsam, gezwungenermaßen; ~ **displaced** zwangsverschickt; zwangsweise umgesiedelt

Ford Foundation *Am* Ford-Stiftung
1936 von Henry Ford gegründete Organisation zur Förderung wissenschaftlicher, pädagogischer und karitativer Vorhaben

forebears *Am* Vorfahren, Ahnen

forecast Vorhersage, Voraussage; Vorausschätzung; Prognose; Voranschlag; **financial** ~ Finanzvorhersage, Finanzprognose; **population** ~ Bevölkerungsvorausschätzung; **sales** ~ Verkaufsprognose; **weather** ~ Wetterbericht, Wettervorhersage

forecast *v* vorhersagen, voraussagen; vorausberechnen, vorausplanen; Prognose stellen

forecasting Vorhersage, Vorausschau; Prognose; **F~ and Assessment in Science and Technology** (FAST) *(EG)* Vorausschau und Bewertung in Wissenschaft und Technologie; ~ **the economic activity** Konjunkturprognose; ~ **programme** Programm über den Einsatz von Elektronenrechnern in der Industrieplanung; ~ **techniques** Prognoseverfahren

forecaster wissenschaftlicher Zukunftsrechner

foreclose *v* ausschließen (from von); präkludieren; **to ~ a mortgage** e-e Hypothekenforderung geltend machen *(unter Ausschluß des →equity of redemption, nachdem der Schuldner seinen Zahlungsverpflichtungen nicht nachgekommen ist);* e-e Hypothek (od. ein Pfandrecht) gerichtlich für verfallen erklären; *Am* aus e-r Hypothek die Zwangsvollstreckung betreiben

foreclosure Ausschließung *(des Grundstückseigentümers od. Pfandgläubigers vom →equity of redemption);* gerichtliche Verfallerklärung e-r Hypothek *(wegen Verzugs des Hypothekenschuldners); Am* Zwangsvollstreckung *(in ein Grundstück); (WettbewerbsR)* Marktverstopfung; ~ **action** (or **suit**) Klage des Hypothekengläubigers auf Geltendmachung seiner Forderung; Ausschlußklage; Klage auf Ausschluß des Hypothekenschuldners von seinem Rücknahmerecht (*→equity of redemption*); Klage auf Ausschluß des Rücknahmerechts des Pfandgebers; *Am* Klage auf Befriedigung aus dem Pfand; *Am* Zwangsvollstreckungsklage *(des Hypothekengläubigers);* ~ **proceedings** Verfahren der Verfallerklärung *(e-r Hypothek od. e-s Pfandrechts); Am* Zwangsvollstreckungsverfahren; ~ **sale** *Am* Zwangsversteigerung; Pfandverkauf

foreclosure, judgment of ~ *Am* Urteil auf Zwangsvollstreckung in das Grundstück; **order for ~ nisi** *Br* vorläufige gerichtliche Verfallerklärung; **order for ~ absolute** *Br* rechtskräftige gerichtliche Verfallerklärung *(nachdem innerhalb e-r bestimmten Frist, meistens 6 Monaten, die Hypothekenschuld und Zinsen und Gerichtskosten nicht gezahlt sind)*

foregift *Br* Aufgeld *(des Pächters)*

foregoing Vorangehendes, Vorstehendes; obig, oben erwähnt; **the ~ provisions** die vorstehenden Bestimmungen

foregone conclusion von vornherein feststehendes Ende; ausgemachte Sache; Selbstverständlichkeit

forehand rent *Scot* im voraus zahlbare Miete (od. Pacht)

foreign ausländisch, auswärtig *(Am [auch] hinsichtlich e-s anderen Einzelstaates);* fremd(artig); Auslands- *(opp. domestic);* ~ **account** Auslandskonto; ~ **advertising** Auslandswerbung

foreign affairs auswärtige Angelegenheiten; Außenpolitik *(opp. home affairs);* **F~ A~ Committee** *Am (Repräsentantenhaus)* Außenpolitischer Ausschuß

foreign, ~ **agency** Auslandsvertretung; ~ **agent** Auslandsvertreter; ~ **aid** Auslandshilfe *(bes. Wirtschaftshilfe);* ~ **arbitral award** ausländischer Schiedsspruch (*→arbitral);* ~ **assets** Auslandsaktiva; ~ **assistance** *Am* Auslandshilfe *(wirtschaftl. und militärische Unterstützung an ausländische Länder);* ~ **→attachment;** ~ **availability** *Am* Verfügbarkeit (von Waren od. Technologie) im Ausland *(die Exportkontrollen erübrigen);* ~ **award** ausländischer Schiedsspruch; ~ **balance** Auslandsguthaben; ~ **bill (of exchange)** Auslandswechsel, im Ausland zahlbarer Wechsel *(opp. inland bill);* ~ **bonds** Auslandsanleihen; ausländische Obligationen; **~-born** im Ausland geboren; ~ **branch** Auslandsfiliale; ~ **business** Auslandsgeschäft; ~ **call** *Am* Auslandsgespräch; ~ **capital** Auslandskapital; ~ **coins and notes** ausländische Münzen und Banknoten; Sorten; ~ **commerce** *Am* Außenhandel; ~ **control** Auslandskontrolle; Überfremdung; **~-controlled** überfremdet; ~ **conviction** im Ausland erfolgte Verurteilung; ~ **corporation** *Am* ausländische (Kapital-)Gesellschaft *(die in e-m anderen Staat als ihrem Gründungsstaat [im Ausland od. in e-m Einzelstaat] ihre Geschäftstätigkeit ausübt);* ~ **correspondence clerk** Auslandskorrespondent(in) *(e-r Firma);* ~ **correspondent** Auslandskorrespondent(in) *(e-r Zeitung);* **F~ Corrupt Practices Act** of 1977 (FCPA) *Am* Gesetz zur Verhinderung der Bestechung ausländischer Regierungen durch Firmen od. Personen, die dem amerikanischen Gesetz unterstehen; ~ **countries** Ausland; **F~ Country Money Judgments Act** *Am* Gesetz betr. die Vollstreckung auf Zahlung lautender ausländischer Gerichtsurteile

Foreign Credit Insurance Association (FCIA) *Am* Auslandskreditversicherungs-Gesellschaft
Vereinigung privater Versicherer. Das politische Risiko kann versichert werden, ohne daß gleichzeitig das kommerzielle Risiko versichert wird

foreign currency Devisen, ausländisches Geld; Fremdwährung, ausländische Währung *(opp. home currency)*; ~ **acceptance** Valuta-Akzept *(auf ausländische Währung lautender Wechsel)*; ~ **account** Fremdwährungskonto, Valutakonto, Devisenkonto; ~ **bill** Fremdwährungswechsel, Devisenwechsel; ~ **bonds** Valutaanleihen, Valutabonds; Fremdwährungsschuldverschreibungen; ~ **borrowing** Kreditaufnahme in ausländischer Währung; ~ **clause** Valutaklausel; Devisenklausel; ~ **credit** Valutakredit, Fremdwährungskredit; ~ **debt** Valutaschuld, Fremdwährungsschuld; ~ **insurance** Valutaversicherung, Fremdwährungsversicherung; ~ **loan** Valutaanleihe, Fremdwährungsanleihe; Valutakredit, Fremdwährungskredit; ~ **market** Devisenmarkt; ~ **receipts** Deviseneinnahmen; ~ **reserves** Devisenreserven; ~ **securities** Valutapapiere; ~ **transactions** Transaktionen in Fremdwährung

foreign currency, account in ~ →~ account, **balances in** ~ Guthaben in fremder Währung; Devisenguthaben; **bill in** ~ →~ bill; **bonds in** ~ →~ bonds; **sales of** ~ Devisenverkäufe; **trade in** ~ Devisenhandel

foreign, ~ **debts** Auslandsschulden, Schulden im Ausland; ~ **demand** Auslandsnachfrage; ~ **department** Auslandsabteilung; ~ **deposits** Guthaben von Ausländern; **F~ Direct Investment** (FDI) ausländische Direktinvestition *(Aufbau od. Erwerb e-r eigenen Tochtergesellschaft im Gastland)*; ~ **domination** Fremdherrschaft; ~ **element** *(IPR)* Auslandsberührung

foreign equities *Br* ausländische Wertpapiere *(die nicht in London sondern an anderen Börsen im Ausland notiert sind)*; ~ **market** *Br* Markt für ausländische Wertpapiere (→*SEAQ System*)

foreign exchange Devisen *(Zahlungsmittel in ausländischer Währung)*; ~ **accruals** Devisenzugänge, Devisenzuflüsse; ~ **allotment** *Br* (or **allowance**) Devisenzuteilung; ~ **assets** Devisenwerte; Devisenguthaben; ~ **authorization** Devisengenehmigung; ~ **balance** Devisenguthaben; Devisenbilanz *(Teil der Zahlungsbilanz)*; ~ **branch** Auslandsfiliale *(e-r Bank)*; ~ **broker** Devisenmakler; ~ **commitments** Devisenengagements; ~ **control** Devisenbewirtschaftung (→ *exchange control*); ~ **dealer** Devisenhändler; ~ **dealings** Devisenhandel; Devisengeschäfte; ~ **department** Devisenabteilung; ~ **equalization fund** Devisenausgleichsfonds; ~ **expenditure** Devisenausgaben; ~ **facilities** Devisenerleichterungen; ~ **fees** Gebühren bei Devisengeschäften; ~ **for travel(l)ing** Reisedevisen; ~ **futures** *Am* Devisentermingeschäfte; ~ **guarantee** Kurssicherung; ~ **holdings** Devisenbestände; ~ **licence (~se)** Devisengenehmigung; ~ **list** (Devisen-)Kurszettel; ~ **market** Devisenmarkt; ~ **notes** Banknoten in fremder Währung; ~ **permit** Devisengenehmigung; ~ **position** Devisenlage; ~ **proceeds** Devisenerlöse; ~ **quota** Devisenkontingent; ~ **quotation** Devisennotierung; ~ **rate** Devisenkurs; ~ **rationing** Devisenkontingentierung; ~ **receipts** Deviseneinnahmen

foreign exchange regulations Devisenbestimmungen; devisenrechtliche Bestimmungen; **violation of the** ~ Devisenvergehen

foreign exchange, ~ **requirements** Devisenanforderungen; ~ **reserves** Devisenreserven; ~ **restrictions** devisenrechtliche Beschränkungen, Devisenrestriktionen; ~ **return** Devisenrückfluß *(ins Inland)*; ~ **risk** Kursrisiko; ~ **settlement** Devisenabrechnung; ~ **situation** Devisenlage; ~ **spending** Devisenausgaben; ~ **stabilization fund** Devisenausgleichsfonds; ~ **statement** Devisenabrechnung; ~ **stringency** Devisenknappheit; ~ **transactions** Devisenhandel; Devisengeschäfte

foreign exchange, arbitration in ~ Devisenarbitrage; **calculation** (or **computation**) **of** ~ Devisenberechnung; **certificate of** ~ Devisenbescheinigung; **embargo on** ~ Devisensperre; **forward** ~ **transaction** Devisentermingeschäft; **holdings of** ~ Bestände an Devisen; **(increased) need of** ~ (gesteigerter) Devisenbedarf; **purchase of** ~ Devisenkauf; **quotation of** ~ Devisennotierung; **countries short of** ~ devisenschwache Länder; **shortage of** ~ Devisenknappheit, Devisenmangel; **spot business in** ~ Devisenkassahandel; **transactions in** ~ Devisengeschäfte; Devisenhandel

foreign, ~ **general average** (FGA) ausländische Havariegrosse; ~**-going ship** Schiff auf Auslandsfahrt *(opp. homeward-bound ship)*; ~**-held** in ausländischem Besitz (befindlich); ~ **income** Auslandseinkommen; ~ **indebtedness** Auslandsverschuldung; ~ **interests** ausländische Beteiligungen

foreign investment Auslandsinvestitionen; **F~ I~ in Real Property Tax Act** (FIRPTA) *Am* Gesetz über ausländische Investitionen in Grundvermögen *(Besteuerung des Gewinns ausländischer Investoren bei der Veräußerung von amerikanischem Grundbesitz)*

foreign, F~Investors Tax Act (FITA) *Am* Steuergesetz für ausländische Kapitalanleger; ~ **issue** Auslandsemission; **F~ Issuer Integration Disclosure System** *Am* integriertes Publizitätssystem für ausländische Emittenten; ~ **→judgment**

foreign, ~ **jurisdiction** ausländische Gerichtsbarkeit; Gerichtsbarkeit e-s Staates *(internationale Zuständigkeit seiner Gerichte)* über Staatsangehörige, die im Ausland wohnen oder dort Handlungen vorgenommen haben; ~ **labo(u)r** ausländische Arbeitskräfte; Fremdarbeiter; ~ **language** Fremdsprache

foreign law ausländisches Recht; ausländisches

Gesetz; →**European Convention on Information on F~L~; judicial notice may not be taken of** ~ das Gericht hat ausländisches Recht nicht von sich aus zu ermitteln *(vgl. dazu aus dem deutschen Recht § 293 ZPO)*

foreign, F~ Legion Fremdenlegion; ~ **liabilities** Auslandsverbindlichkeiten; ~ **literature** Auslandsschrifttum; Literatur des Auslandes; ~ **loan** Auslandsanleihe; Auslandskredit; ~ **market value** ausländischer Marktwert *(der Ware)*

Foreign Marriage Act *Br* Gesetz über Eheschließungen im Ausland

Der Foreign Marriage Act von 1892 regelt die Eheschließung im Ausland vor einem →marriage officer (einer der Brautleute muß die britische Staatsangehörigkeit besitzen).

Der Foreign Marriage Act von 1947 regelt die Eheschließung von im Auslandseinsatz befindlichen britischen Soldaten.

Der Marriage with Foreigners Act von 1906 regelt die Eheschließung eines englischen Staatsangehörigen mit einem Ausländer im Ausland oder in England

foreign, ~ minister Außenminister; ~ **money** ausländische Zahlungsmittel; ~ **national** ausländischer Staatsangehöriger; Angehöriger e-s fremden Staates; ~ **notes and coin** ausländische Banknoten und Münzen; Sorten; **F~ Office** (F. O.) *Br* Auswärtiges Amt; ~ **order** Exportauftrag; ~ **oriented** auslandsorientiert; **~-owned** in ausländischem Besitz (od. Eigentum); ~ **parts** *Br* Ausland; ~ **plea** *Am* Einrede der Unzuständigkeit des Gerichts; ~ **policy** Außenpolitik; **domestic and ~ press** in- und ausländische Presse; **F~ Policy Controls** *Am*[17] Beschränkungen der Ausfuhr durch den Präsidenten *(soweit dies erforderlich ist, um die außenpolitischen Ziele der USA zu fördern od. internationale Verpflichtungen zu erfüllen)*; ~ **produce** (or **products**) Auslandserzeugnisse, ausländische Erzeugnisse *(opp. home produce)*; ~ **property** ausländisches Vermögen, Auslandsvermögen; ~ **relations** Beziehungen zum Ausland; Auslandsbeziehungen; **F~ Relations Committee** *Am* Außenpolitischer Ausschuß *(des Senats)*; ~ **resident** im Inland lebender (nicht ansässiger) Ausländer; ~ **rule** Fremdherrschaft; ~ **sales** Auslandsverkäufe; Auslandsabsatz; ~ **sales contract** Außenhandelsvertrag; **F~ Secretary** *Br* Außenminister; ~ **securities** ausländische Wertpapiere, Auslandswerte

Foreign Service auswärtiger (od. diplomatischer) Dienst; **F~S~ list** *Am (vom Department of State vierteljährlich herausgegebene)* Liste der Angehörigen des diplomatischen Dienstes

foreign source income, taxpayers deriving ~ Steuerpflichtige mit Einkommen aus ausländischen Quellen

foreign, ~ sovereign →immunity; ~ stocks Auslandswerte; ~ **subject** Ausländer; ~ **subsidiaries and branches of German banks** Auslandstöchter und -filialen deutscher Banken; ~ **tax** im Ausland gezahlte Steuer; ~ **tax credit** *Am* Anrechnung ausländischer Steuern; Steuergutschrift (→*credit 3.*)

foreign trade Außenhandel *(opp. domestic trade, home trade)*; ~ **agency** Außenhandelsstelle; ~ **and payments** Außenwirtschaft(sverkehr); ~ **and service transactions** Waren- und Dienstleistungsverkehr mit dem Ausland; ~ **balance** Außenhandelsbilanz; Außenhandelsgleichgewicht; ~ **deficit** Außenhandelsdefizit; ~ **policy** Außenhandelspolitik; ~ **zone** Freihandelszone *(Zollausschlußgebiet)*

foreign trade, aggregate ~ Gesamtaußenhandel; **combined ~** gemeinsamer Außenhandel; **total ~** Gesamtaußenhandel; ~ **has increased** der Außenhandel hat zugenommen

foreign, ~ trading station Faktorei *(Handelsniederlassung von europäischen Kaufleuten in Übersee)*; ~ **transactions** Außenhandelstransaktionen; ~ **travel** Auslandsreisen; Reisen im (od. ins) Ausland; ~ **worker** Fremdarbeiter, Gastarbeiter

foreigner Ausländer(in); Fremde(r); **~s** *(Börse)* ausländische Werte, Auslandswerte; **~s' deposits** Auslandseinlagen; **treatment of ~s** Ausländerbehandlung

forejudge *v* im voraus entscheiden

foreman Obmann *(e-r jury)*; Vorarbeiter, Meister; **shop ~** Werkmeister

forename Vorname

forensic gerichtlich, Gerichts-; **(~) handwriting expert** Schriftsachverständiger vor Gericht; ~ **medicine** Gerichtsmedizin; ~ **term** juristischer Fachausdruck

foreseeable vorhersehbar; **in the ~ future** in absehbarer Zeit

forest Wald, Forst; **dying-off of ~s** Waldsterben; **state** (or **national**) ~ Staatsforst; ~ **administration** Forstverwaltung; ~ **die-back** Waldsterben; ~ **enterprise** Forstbetrieb; ~ **exploitation** Forstnutzung; ~ **fire** Waldbrand; ~ **insurance** Waldversicherung

forest law Forstgesetz; Forstrecht; **offence (~se) against the ~s** Forstfrevel; Forstvergehen

forest, ~ officer Forstbeamter; ~ **service** Forstdienst; ~ **worker** Forstarbeiter

forestall *v* zuvorkommen; im voraus aufkaufen

forestalling Voraufkauf; Aufkauf von Waren, ehe sie den Markt erreichen

forfait *v* einfügen; forfaitieren (→*forfaiting*); **~ed debt** forfaitierte Forderung *(meist große Exportforderung mit langer Laufzeit)*

forfaiting Forfaitierung *(Ankauf von Wechseln od.*

Forderungen aus Exportgeschäften ohne Rückgriff auf den Exporteur [bei Vorliegen guter Sicherheiten]); ~ **house** Forfaiteur

forfaiter Forfaiteur

forfeit 1. Verwirkung; Verlust; verwirktes Pfand; ~ **(money)** Reugeld *(bei Vertragsrücktritt);* verwirkte Geldstrafe *(fine or penalty);* ~ **of civil rights** *Am* Verlust der Bürgerrechte; **to pay the** ~ das Reugeld bezahlen

forfeit 2. verwirkt, verfallen; **to declare** ~ für verwirkt (od. verfallen) erklären

forfeit *v (Eigentum, Recht)* verwirken, verlustig gehen, einbüßen; *(Aktien)* kaduzieren; **to** ~ **one's bail** die Kaution verlieren; der geleisteten Sicherheit verlustig gehen; **to** ~ **the right to a pension** den Ruhegehaltsanspruch verlieren; **to** ~ **a security** e-e Kaution einbüßen; **to** ~ **one's voting right** sein Stimmrecht verwirken

forfeited verwirkt, verfallen; ~ **pledge** verfallenes Pfand; ~ **shares** kaduzierte Aktien; **bond** ~ Kaution verfallen; **to become** ~ verfallen; **to declare** ~ für verwirkt (od. verfallen) erklären; kaduzieren

fortfeitable verfallbar

forfeiture Verwirkung, Verlust *(von Eigentum od. Rechten als Folge e-s Tuns od. Unterlassens);* Einziehung, Beschlagnahme; Verfall; Reugeld *(bei Vertragsrücktritt);* Vertragsstrafe; *(VersR)* Anspruchsverwirkung; ~ **of bond** Verfall der Kaution; ~ **clause** Verfallklausel; Verwirkungsklausel; ~ **of goods improperly imported** Beschlagnahme unvorschriftsmäßig eingeführter Waren; ~ **of lease** *(vorzeitige)* Beendigung e-s Miet-(od. Pacht-)verhältnisses wegen Vertragsbruchs des Mieters (od. Pächters) aufgrund entsprechender Verwirkungsklausel (forfeiture clause) im Miet- (od. Pacht-)Vertrag; ~ **of a pension** Verwirkung (od. Verfall) e-s Pensionsanspruchs; ~ **of public office** Verlust e-s Amtes; ~ **of seniority of rank** Rangverlust *(als Disziplinarstrafe);* ~ **of shares** Kaduzierung von Aktien

forfeiture, relief against ~[18] *(gerichtlicher)* Schutz des Mieters (od. Pächters) gegen *(vorzeitige)* Beendigung des Miet- (od. Pacht-)-Verhältnisses aufgrund seiner Vertragsverletzung *(cf. forfeiture of lease)*

forge *v* fälschen, verfälschen; **to** ~ **a cheque (check)** e-n Scheck fälschen; **to** ~ **coins** falschmünzen; Münzen verfälschen; **to** ~ **a document** e-e *(echte)* Urkunde verfälschen; e-e Urkunde fälschlich anfertigen; **to** ~ **a signature** e-e Unterschrift fälschen; **to** ~ **a will** ein Testament fälschen

forged gefälscht, verfälscht; **bringing** ~ **banknotes in circulation** Inverkehrbringen falschen Geldes; ~ **instrument** gefälschte Urkunde; ~ **trademark** nachgemachte Handelsmarke; ~ **share transfer**[19] betrügerische Aktienübertragung

forging Fälschung; ~ **of a document** Urkundenfälschung

forger Fälscher; Urkundenfälscher; ~ **of bank notes** Banknotenfälscher; ~ **of a bill (of exchange)** Wechselfälscher; ~ **of coin** Falschmünzer; ~ **(of documents)** Urkundenfälscher

forgery Fälschung, Verfälschung, Urkundenfälschung; ~ **of bills** s. bill →~; ~ **of a cheque (check)** Scheckfälschung; ~ **of a document** Urkundenfälschung; ~ **of a passport** Paßfälschung; **~-proof identity card** fälschungssicherer Personalausweis; **attempted** ~ (or **attempt at** ~) Fälschungsversuch; **bill** ~ Wechselfälschung; *Am* Banknotenfälschung; **to commit a** ~ e-e Fälschung begehen; **to pass off the** ~ **as the original** die Fälschung als das Original ausgeben

forgive *v* vergeben; **to** ~ **sb. a debt** jdm e-e Schuld erlassen

forgiveness of a debt Erlaß e-r Schuld

forint Forint *(seit 1946 Währungseinheit in Ungarn)*

forjudge *v (jdm durch Urteil etw.)* aberkennen

form 1. Form; Art (und Weise); Formalität; Förmlichkeit; ~ **of enterprise** Unternehmensform; ~ **of government** Regierungsform; Regierungssystem; ~ **of oath** Eidesformel *(cf. I swear by Almighty God ...);* ~ **of payment** Zahlungsweise; ~ **required by law** gesetzlich vorgeschriebene Form

form requirement, violation of substantial ~s Verletzung wesentlicher Formvorschriften

form, bad ~ schlechte *(gesellschaftliche)* Form; **breach of** ~ Formverletzung

form, defect of ~ Formmangel, Formfehler; **→invalidity of a transaction due to defect of ~; to cure a defect of** ~ e-n Formmangel heilen

form, error in ~ Formfehler; **substantial errors in** ~ Verletzung wesentlicher Formvorschriften

form, in ~ **and in substance** formell und materiell; **in due** ~ formgerecht; in gehöriger Form; **in due** ~ **and time** form- und fristgerecht; **the full powers found in good and due** ~ *dipl* die als gut und gehörig befundenen Vollmachten

form, legal ~ gesetzliche Form, gesetzlich vorgeschriebene Form; Rechtsform; **(mere) matter of** ~ (bloße) Formsache; **provision relating to** ~ Formvorschrift; **provisions as to** ~ **have been violated** die Formvorschriften sind verletzt

form, requirement of ~ Formvorschrift; Formerfordernis; **there is no requirement as to** ~ es besteht Formfreiheit

form, requisites in ~ Formerfordernisse; **validity as regards requisites in** ~ Formgültigkeit *(z.B. e-s Wechsels)*

form, not to be subject to any requirement as to ~ keinen Formvorschriften unterliegen

form 2. Formular; Vordruck; Formblatt; ~ **of application** Antragsformular; *(AktienR)* Zeichnungsschein; ~ **of bill of exchange** Wechselformular; ~ **of income tax return** Steuererklärungsformular; ~ **of proxy** Vollmachtsformular; ~ **of receipt** Quittungsformular; ~ **of transfer** *Br* Formular zur Übertragung e-s Wertpapiers; **application** ~ →~ of application; **bill** ~ Wechselvordruck, -formular; **cheque (check)** ~ Scheckformular; **completion of a** ~ Ausfüllung e-s Formulars; **order** ~ Auftragsformular; Bestellschein; **proposal** ~ *(VersR)* Antragsformular; **proxy** ~ Vollmachtsformular; **receipt** ~ Quittungsformular; **telegram** ~ Telegrammformular; **to fill in** (or *Am* **fill out,** *Br* **fill up**) **a (printed)** ~ ein Formular ausfüllen

form *v* bilden, gründen; **to** ~ **a company** e-e (Handels-)Gesellschaft gründen; **to** ~ **a government** e-e Regierung bilden; **to** ~ **an opinion** sich e-e Meinung bilden; **to** ~ **part of sth.** e-n Teil von etw. bilden

formed, newly ~ **company** neu gegründete Gesellschaft

forma pauperis ("in the character of a pauper"), **to sue in** ~ *Am* im Armenrecht klagen; **to withdraw the right to litigate in** ~ *Am* jdm das Armenrecht (die Prozeßkostenhilfe) entziehen

formal formal, formell, förmlich, offiziell; ~ **call** offizieller Besuch; Höflichkeitsbesuch; ~ **close of a meeting** förmlicher Schluß e-r Tagung ("I hereby declare the meeting closed"); ~ **contract** förmlicher Vertrag

Das anglo-amerikanische Recht ist im allgemeinen von dem Grundsatz der Formfreiheit beherrscht. Dieser Grundsatz wird durch das Statute of →Frauds und einige andere Gesetze (*Br* Law of Property Act, Hire-Purchase Act, Bills of Exchange Act etc) durchbrochen. Nach diesen Gesetzen bedürfen Verträge entweder der Schriftform oder sind nur klagbar, wenn schriftliches Beweismaterial vorliegt

formal defect Formmangel, Formfehler; ~ **in a will** Formfehler e-s Testaments

formal, ~ **denial** Dementi; ~ **error** Formfehler

formal requirements Formerfordernisse, Formvorschriften; **formal filing requirements** *(PatR)* Formvorschriften für die Anmeldung; **not in accordance with** ~ formwidrig; **examination as to** ~ *(PatR)* Formalprüfung

formal statements, to issue ~ *dipl* offizielle Erklärungen herausgeben

formalism Formalismus

formalistic formalistisch

formalit|y Förmlichkeit, Formalität; Formvorschrift; **completion of** ~**ies at the border** Erledigung von Formalitäten an der Grenze; ~**ies required for patent applications** Formerfordernisse bei Patentanmeldungen; **customs** ~**ies** Zollformalitäten; **legal** ~**ies** gesetzliche Formvorschriften; **necessary** ~**ies** erforderliche Formalitäten; **passport** ~**ies** Paßförmlichkeiten; **to comply with** (or **fulfil**) **the** ~**ies** die Formalitäten (od. Formvorschriften) erfüllen (od. einhalten)

formation Bildung, Gründung; ~ **expenses** Gründungskosten, Gründungsaufwand; ~ **of assets** Vermögensbildung; ~ **of tangible assets** Sachvermögensbildung; ~ **of blocs** *pol* Blockbildung; ~ **of a company** *Br* (**corporation** *Am*) Gründung e-r (Kapital-)Gesellschaft, Gesellschaftsgründung; ~ **of a contract** Vertragsabschluß, Zustandekommen e-s Vertrages; ~ **expenses** Gründungskosten; ~ **of a fund** (Investment-)Fondsgründung; ~ **of monetary wealth** Geldvermögensbildung; ~ **of prices** Preisbildung; ~ **of wealth** Vermögensbildung

formation, deed of ~ Gründungsvertrag

former ehemalig, früher

formula Formel; ~**s of courtesy** Höflichkeitsformeln; **secret** ~ geheime Formel

formulary *Am* Sammlung von (Gerichts-)Formularen

formulate *v* formulieren, abfassen, ausarbeiten; **to** ~ **a program(me)** ein Programm aufstellen; **to** ~ **proposals** Vorschläge ausarbeiten

formulation Formulierung; ~ **of a plan** Ausarbeitung e-s Plans

fornication außerehelicher Geschlechtsverkehr; Unzucht

forprise *(alter Begriff in Rechtsurkunden)* außer ("except"); Vorbehalt ("reserve")

forsake *v,* **to** ~ **one's wife** seine Frau verlassen

forstall *v* →forestall

forswear *v* verzichten auf, *(eidlich)* entsagen; **to** ~ **(oneself)** eidlich ableugnen; Meineid leisten

forthcoming bevorstehend; demnächst erscheinend *(Buch);* ~ **negotiations** bevorstehende Verhandlungen

forthwith sofort, unverzüglich (immediately); *(auch)* innerhalb e-r angemessenen Frist (within a reasonable time); ohne weiteres

fortnight, a ~ **ago** vor 14 Tagen; **in a** ~**'s time** in 14 Tagen

fortnightly vierzehntäglich, alle vierzehn Tage; halbmonatlich; Medio-; ~ **settlement** *Br (Börse)* Medioabrechnung; ~ **settlement loan** Mediogeld

Fortune 500 Verzeichnis der 500 größten US-Kapitalgesellschaften

fortune Vermögen; Glück; Schicksal; ~**-hunter** Mitgiftjäger; ~**-telling** Wahrsagen; **the whole of one's** ~ sein ganzes Vermögen; **to come into a** ~ ein Vermögen erben; **to make a** ~ (sich) ein Vermögen erwerben; **to tell sb.'s** ~ **from the cards** jdm die Karten legen

forum Forum; Gremium; *Am* öffentliche Diskussionsveranstaltung; *(IPR)* Gerichtsstand, örtliche Zuständigkeit *(cf. lex fori)*; ~ **contractus** *(IPR)* Gerichtsstand des Vertragsortes; ~ **for discussion** Diskussionsforum; ~ **domicilii** *(IPR)* Gerichtsstand des Wohnsitzes (→*domicile)*; ~ **law** →lex fori; ~ **non conveniens** *(IPR)* Lehre des ungeeigneten Gerichtsstandes; Lehre, daß ein für e-n ausländischen Rechtsstreit zuständiges Gericht sich für nicht zuständig erklären kann *(wenn die Durchführung des Verfahrens im Interesse der Sache nicht zweckmäßig erscheint)*; ~ **rei gestae** Gerichtsstand des Handlungsortes *(z. B. des Abschlußortes bei Verträgen, des Errichtungsortes bei Testamenten)*; Gerichtsstand des Tatortes; ~ **rei sitae** *(IPR)* Gerichtsstand der belegenen Sache; dinglicher Gerichtsstand; ~ **selection** Wahl des Gerichtsstandes

forum shopping *(IPR)* Zuständigkeitserschleichung; Suche nach e-m günstigeren Gerichtsstand

Die vom Kläger unter mehreren internationalen Gerichtsständen berechnend vorgenommene Wahl eines bestimmten Ortes der Prozeßführung in der Absicht, das für ihn günstige materielle Recht eines Staates zur Anwendung zu bringen

forum, contractual ~ Gerichtsstand des Vertrags; **international** ~**s** internationale Gremien; **law of the** ~ Recht des Gerichtsorts (das am Gerichtsort geltende Recht)

forward vorn (befindlich); fortschrittlich; kommend, künftig; auf Ziel (od. Zeit); *(Börse)* Termin- *(opp. spot)*; *(Buchhaltung)* Übertrag *(brought* ~); Vortrag *(carried* ~); ~ **business** Termingeschäft; ~ **buying** Terminkauf, Kauf auf *(künftige)* Lieferung; ~ **commodities** Terminwaren; ~ **contract** Terminkontrakt; ~ **cover** Kurssicherung durch Devisentermingeschäft; ~ **deal** Termingeschäft; ~ **delivery** Terminlieferung; ~ **dollar** Termindollar

forward exchange Termindevisen *(zu e-m späteren Zeitpunkt zahlbare Devisen)*; ~ **dealings** (or **operations, transactions**) Devisentermingeschäfte, Devisenterminhandel *(opp. spot exchange dealings)*; ~ **market** Devisenterminmarkt; ~ **rate** Devisenterminkurs; ~ **trading** Devisentermgeschäft

forward, ~ **market** *(Börse)* Terminmarkt *(opp. spot market)*; ~ **operation** →~ transaction; ~ **planning** Vorausplanung; ~ **price** Preis (od. Kurs) für Termingeschäfte; Terminkurs *(opp. spot price)*; ~ **quotation** Terminnotierung; ~ **rate** Devisenterminkurs; ~ **rate agreement** (FRA) nicht standardisierte od. börsenmäßig gehandelte Termingeschäfte *(zur Absicherung von Zinsschwankungen) (cf. financial futures)*; ~ **sale** Terminverkauf *(opp. spot sale)*; **costs of** ~ **rate cover** Kurssicherungskosten; ~ **securities** Terminwerte, Terminpapiere; ~ **strategy** *mil* Verteidigung an der vordersten Linie; ~ **transaction** Termingeschäft

forward, to bring ~ *(Buchhaltung)* übertragen (from von); **to buy** ~ auf Termin kaufen; **to carry** ~ vortragen (to auf); **to sell** ~ auf Termin verkaufen

forward *v* befördern, versenden, übersenden; nachsenden, weiterbefördern, weiterleiten; **to** ~ **a case to another attorney** *Am* e-e Sache an e-n *(auswärtigen)* Anwalt weitergeben; **to** ~ **goods by rail** Waren mit der Bahn befördern; **to** ~ **a letter to sb.** jdm e-n Brief nachsenden; **please** ~ bitte nachsenden

forwarded, application to have one's mail ~ Nachsendeantrag; **to be** ~ bitte nachsenden

forwarding Beförderung, Versendung, Übersendung; Spedition; Nachsendung; ~ **advice** Versendungsanzeige; ~ **agency** Speditionsfirma

forwarding agent Spediteur; ~**'s certificate of receipt** (FCR) Speditionsübernahmebescheinigung *(internationales Spediteurdokument)*

forwarding, ~ **business** Speditionsgeschäft; ~ **charges** Versendungskosten, Versandkosten; Speditionsgebühren; ~ **clerk** Expedient; ~ **country** Versandland; ~ **department** Versandabteilung, Expeditionsabteilung; ~ **of goods** Versendung von Gütern, Güterbeförderung; ~ **instructions** Versandvorschriften *(betreffend den Transportweg etc)*; ~ **merchant** *Am* Spediteur; ~ **note** Frachtbrief; ~ **by rail** Bahnversand; ~ **station** Versandbahnhof; ~ **trade** Speditionsgewerbe

forwarder Spediteur; ~**s** Speditionsfirma; ~**'s receipt** →forwarding agent's certificate of receipt

foster *v* pflegen, fördern; *(Kind)* aufziehen; ~**ing** Vermittlung von Pflegeplätzen

foster, ~**-child** Pflegekind; ~**-father** Pflegevater; ~**-mother** Pflegemutter; ~**-parents** Pflegeeltern

Br Nach dem Foster Children Act, 1980 sind Pflegekinder Kinder, die von einer Pflegeperson versorgt werden, die weder in Verwandtschafts- noch in Vormundschaftsverhältnis zu dem Kinde steht (cf. protected children)

foul unsauber; unredlich; ~ **bill of health** Gesundheitspaß mit Vermerk: ansteckende Krankheit *(opp. clean bill of health)*; ~ **bill of lading** →bill 1.; ~ **play** unfaires Spiel; Verbrechen *(z.B. murder)*; **to fall ~ of a ship** mit e-m Schiff zusammenstoßen

foul *v* verschmutzen; stoßen an, zusammenstoßen mit *(Schiffe)*

found *Am* (**all** ~ *Br*) Unterkunft und Verpflegung, freie Station; **‰50 a month and** ~ *Am* ‰50 monatlich und freie Station

found *v* 1. gründen, errichten; stiften; **to ~ sth. on sth.** etw. mit etw. begründen; **to ~ a firm** e-e Firma gründen; **to ~ a party** e-e Partei gründen; **to ~ one's suspicion on** seinen Verdacht gründen auf; **to ~ a university** e-e Universität gründen

founded, well-~ complaint begründete Beschwerde; ~ **on facts** auf Tatsachen beruhend; stichhaltig; **well-~ suspicion** begründeter Verdacht; **to be ~ (up)on** beruhen auf; **the appeal is well** ~ die Beschwerde (etc) ist begründet; **this action is ~ on tort** diese Klage beruht auf unerlaubter Handlung

found 2. gefunden, befunden (→*find v*); **the facts as ~ by the court** die vom Gericht festgestellten Tatsachen; **object** (or **property**) ~ Fundsache; **to be ~ guilty** für schuldig befunden werden; **not** ~ *Am* nicht für begründet erklärt(e Anklage) *(cf. to find an →indictment)*

foundation Gründung, Errichtung; *(gemeinnützige)* Stiftung *(z.B. Rockefeller F~)*; Fundament; *fig* Grundlage; ~ **charter** Gründungsurkunde; Stiftungsurkunde; ~ **of a firm** Gründung e-r Firma; ~ **fund** Gründungsfonds; ~ **syndicate** Gründungskonsortium

foundation stone Grundstein; **laying of the** ~ Grundsteinlegung

foundation, assets of a ~ Stiftungsvermögen; **charitable** ~ Stiftung mit gemeinnützigem Zweck; **company** ~ Gesellschaftsgründung; **deed of** ~ Stiftungsurkunde; **year of** ~ Gründungsjahr; **to be without any** ~ jeder Grundlage entbehren; **to lay the ~ of** den Grundstein legen für; die Grundlage schaffen zu

founder Gründer, Stifter; **~s** *Br* →~s' shares; ~ **member** Gründungsmitglied; Mitbegründer; **~s' preference rights** Gründerrechte; **~s' shares** *Br* Gründeraktien, Gründeranteile (→*management shares*); **~s' stock** *Am* Gründeraktien

foundering of a ship Untergang e-s Schiffes

foundling Findling, Findelkind

four copies, in ~ in vierfacher Ausfertigung

four corners, within the ~ of a document nur in der Urkunde selbst enthalten *(ohne Berücksichtigung der Umstände, unter denen sie errichtet wurde)*

Four Day Order *Br (in der →Chancery Division)* e-e Fristbestimmung enthaltende ergänzende Nachtragsverfügung des Gerichts zu e-r die Vornahme e-r Handlung *(oft die Beibringung von Rechnungsunterlagen oder die Beantwortung gerichtlicher Anfragen)* anordnenden gerichtlichen Entscheidung

four, ~-lane highway *Am* vierspurige Autobahn; ~ **(months)** *Br (Warenbörse)* 4 Monate *(Januar–April)*; **every ~ months** viermonatlich; **~-power agreement** Viermächteabkommen, Viererabkommen; **~-power conference** Viermächtekonferenz, Viererkonferenz; **within the ~ seas** *Br* innerhalb des Vereinigten Königreichs; **~-year plan** Vierjahresplan

fourth, ~ class mail *Am* Paketpost *(cf. mail)*; **F~ Directive** Vierte EG-Richtlinie *(Rechnungslegungsvorschriften für Unternehmen)*; ~ **estate** Presse

fraction Bruch; Bruchteil *(z.B. e-r Aktie)*; ~ **of a share** Teilaktie

fractional unbedeutend, geringfügig; Teil-; ~ **amount** Teilbetrag; ~ **apportionment** *(intern. SteuerR)* indirekte Gewinnermittlungsmethode *(opp. separate accountings)*; ~ **certificate** *Br* Teilschein *(Zertifikat über den Bruchteil e-r Aktie)*; ~ **coin** Scheidemünze (→~ *money)*; ~ **currency** Scheidemünze; ~ **debenture** Teilschuldverschreibung; ~ **lot** *(New Yorker Börse)* Paket von weniger als 100 Aktien; ~ **money** Scheidemünze *(Br 10p, 5p; Am half-dollar, quarter, dime, nickel)*; ~ **number** Bruchzahl; ~ **part** Bruchteil; ~ **shares** *(Börse)* Spitzen; ~ **unemployment** Fluktuationsarbeitslosigkeit

frame Rahmen; Form, Fassung; ~ **guarantee** Mantelgarantie

frame *v (Bericht etc)* abfassen, formulieren; sich anlassen, sich entwickeln; *sl.* jdn lügnerisch bezichtigen

framework Gefüge, Struktur, Rahmen; ~ **agreement** Rahmenabkommen; ~ **collective agreement** Manteltarifvertrag; ~ **legislation** Rahmengesetzgebung; ~ **treaty** Rahmenvertrag; **legal** ~ Gesetzesrahmen; **beyond (within) the ~ of this organization** außerhalb des Rahmens (im Rahmen) dieser Organisation

franc(s) (fr.) Frank(en) *(Währungseinheit bes. in Frankreich, Belgien, Luxemburg, Schweiz, Monaco und Liechtenstein)*

franc-tireur Franktireur, Freischärler

France Frankreich *(cf. French Republic)*

franchise Privileg; *Am* behördlich verliehenes Recht; Konzession(serteilung); *(aktives)* Wahlrecht; Abstimmungsbefugnis; *(VersR)* Franchise *(unter dem vereinbarten Prozentsatz liegen-*

der [Klein-]Schaden wird vom Versicherer nicht ersetzt; cf. deductible, excess); **(exclusive)** ~ *Am (AntitrustR)* Alleinvertriebsrecht; Ausschließlichkeitsverpflichtung *(Verpflichtung des Herstellers od. Lieferanten, e-m Groß- od. Einzelhändler für ein bestimmtes Gebiet ein Alleinvertriebsrecht zu gewähren, d.h. keinen anderen Händler in diesem Gebiet zu beliefern; cf. territorial restriction);* ~ **candidate** Franchisebewerber; ~ **clause** *(VersR)* Franchise-Klausel, Selbstbehalt-Klausel *(die auf verschiedene Weise eine Selbstbeteiligung des Versicherungsnehmers vorsehen kann, z.B. er trägt Schäden bis zu einer bestimmten Höhe stets selbst [→excess, →deductible], oder Versicherer trägt Schäden bis zu einer bestimmten Höhe nicht, diese Höhe übersteigende Schäden aber voll);* ~ **de l'hôtel** *(VölkerR)* Unverletzlichkeit des Gesandtschaftsgebäudes und der Amtswohnung des diplomatischen Vertreters;~ **of a corporation** *Am* Konzession zur Gründung e-r (Kapital-)Gesellschaft; Rechtspersönlichkeitsverleihung;~ **tax** *Am (dem privilegierten Unternehmen für die Erteilung der ~ auferlegte)* jährliche Konzessionsabgabe *(Sondersteuer e-r corporation);* **electoral** ~ Wahlrecht, Stimmrecht; **Equal F~ Act** *Br* Gesetz über die gleiche Wahlberechtigung von Männern und Frauen *(von 1928);* **local government** ~ *Br* Wahlrecht für Kommunalwahlen; **parliamentary** ~ *Br* Wahlrecht für Parlamentswahlen; **to give** (or **grant**) **a** ~ *Am* e-e Konzession erteilen; **to have the** ~ *Br* das Wahlrecht haben

franchised, ~ **dealer** konzessionierter Händler; ~ **firm** franchisiertes Unternehmen; ~**distributor** *Am* Generalvertreter *(mit e-r Konzession für ein bestimmtes Verkaufsgebiet)*

franchisee Franchise-Nehmer (→*franchising)*

franchising Franchising *(neues Vertriebssystem im Einzelhandel);* ~ **agreement** Franchisevereinbarung

Der Franchise-Geber gewährt dem Franchise-Nehmer das Recht (die Lizenz), bestimmte Waren auf e-m bestimmten Markt im eigenen Betrieb zu verkaufen oder Dienstleistungen anzubieten. Der Franchise-Nehmer ist ein selbständiger Kaufmann, der auf eigene Rechnung arbeitet und sich gegen Zahlung einer Lizenzgebühr des eingeführten Namens od. e-r Handelsmarke, der Verkaufstechnik und Unternehmenskonzeption des Franchise-Gebers bedient

franchisor Franchise-Geber (→*franchising)*

Franco, ~**-American** französisch-amerikanisch; ~**-German** französisch-deutsch; ~**phil(e)** frankophil, franzosenfreundlich

frank *v (mit Frankiermaschine)* frankieren

franked investment income *Br* Dividendenertrag e-s Unternehmens von e-m anderen Unternehmen nach Steuerabzug

franking, ~ **machine** Frankiermaschine; ~ **privilege** *Am* Freiportoprivileg *(z.B. der Parlamentarier)*

frank-fee →freehold

frank-tenement →freehold estate

Frankfurt Interbank Offered Rate (FIBOR) Frankfurter Interbanken-Angebotssatz

fraternal association (or **society**) *Am* Verein zur Förderung gemeinsamer Interessen

fraternity *Am* Studentenverbindung

fraternization *pol* Fraternisierung, Verbrüderung

fraternize *v pol* fraternisieren, sich verbrüdern *(bes. mit der feindl. Zivilbevölkerung)*

fraud *(StrafR)* Betrug (on gegenüber); *(Sammelbegriff für einzelne Tatbestände betrügerischen und veruntreuenden Charakters, z.B. false accounting, suppression of documents);* betrügerisches Verhalten; Veruntreuung; *(ZivilR)* arglistige Täuschung, Irreführung;~ **on the minority** Benachteiligung der Minderheit; ~ **on a power** *Br* betrügerische Ausübung e-r power of appointment (→*power 1.);* ~ **order** *Am (vom Postmaster General gegen e-e Einzelperson verfügte)* Postsperre wegen Betrugsverdacht; ~→**squad; attempt at** ~ (or **attempted** ~) Betrugsversuch; **consent obtained by** ~ durch Betrug erlangte Einwilligung; **constructive** ~ Betrug kraft gesetzlicher Vermutung; **conveyance made in** ~ **of creditors** →fraudulent conveyance; **fiscal** ~ Steuerhinterziehung; **obtaining credit by** ~ Kreditbetrug

fraud, Statute of F~s Gesetz, das die Schriftform anordnet; gesetzliche Vorschriften über die Schriftform *(zur Vermeidung von Arglist und Betrug)*

Der Statute of Frauds and Perjuries wurde 1677 in England zur Verhütung von Betrug und Meineid erlassen. Das Gesetz schrieb für die Klagbarkeit bestimmter Verträge, z. B. Kaufverträge über einen bestimmten Wert, die Schriftform vor.

Br Die meisten Bestimmungen des Gesetzes sind aufgehoben oder durch andere Gesetze ersetzt. Bedeutsam für das geltende Recht ist s. 4. Danach sind Garantie- und Bürgschaftsverträge nur klagbar, wenn die Garantie- oder Bürgschaftserklärung schriftlich vorliegt. Schriftform des gesamten Vertrages ist nicht erforderlich.

Der Statute of Frauds hat, im Gegensatz zu Nordirland, niemals Anwendung in Schottland gefunden.

Am Die Bestimmungen des Statute of Frauds sind in mehr oder minder abgeänderter Form von fast allen amerikanischen Einzelstaaten übernommen. S. 4 des Uniform Sales Act schreibt Schriftform für Mieten von mehr als 3jähriger Dauer vor (viele Einzelstaaten haben die Frist auf 1 Jahr herabgesetzt).

Nach dem Statute of Frauds bedürfen der Schriftform insbesondere Garantie- und Bürgschaftsversprechen, Kaufverträge über unbewegliche Sachen,

Kaufverträge über bewegliche Sachen im Werte von mehr als einem bestimmten Betrag (nach dem Uniform Sales Act ‰ 500)

fraud, to commit a ~ e-n Betrug begehen, betrügen, irreführen; **to obtain by** ~ sich durch Betrug verschaffen; erschleichen; **to perpetrate a** ~ **on the court** das Gericht irreführen; ~ **vitiates a contract** Betrug macht e-n Vertrag ungültig

fraudulent betrügerisch, arglistig; ~ **bankruptcy** betrügerischer Bankrott; ~ **business practices** betrügerische Geschäftspraktiken; ~ **concealment** (of a fact) arglistiges Verschweigen; ~ **conversion** betrügerische Entziehung; Unterschlagung; Veruntreuung

fraudulent conveyance *(KonkursR)* (Vermögensveräußerung mit der Absicht der) Gläubigerbenachteiligung; **to make a** ~ e-e betrügerische Vermögensübertragung vornehmen; Konkursgläubiger benachteiligen

fraudulent, ~ **intent** betrügerische Absicht, Täuschungsabsicht; ~ **means** betrügerische Mittel; ~ →**misrepresentation**; ~ **preference** *(KonkursR)* Gläubigerbegünstigung;~ **trading** *Br (KonkursR)* betrügerische Betriebsfortführung; ~ **transfers** →transfer 1.

fraudulently in betrügerischer Weise; durch Betrug; ~ **obtained** betrügerisch erlangt

Freddie Mac *Am* Börsenausdruck für die Federal Home Loan Mortgage Corporation

free *v* befreien; freimachen; liberalisieren; **to** ~ **the exchange rate** den Wechselkurs freigeben; **to** ~ **oneself from an obligation** sich von e-r Verpflichtung befreien

freeing of the DM rate of exchange Freigabe des DM-Wechselkurses

free frei; ~ **admission** freier Eintritt; ~ **allowance (of luggage)** Freigepäck *(opp. excess luggage)*; ~ **alongside ship** →fas; ~ **assets** frei verfügbare Guthaben; ~ **balance** zinsfreies Guthaben; ~ **carrier** (FRC) **...** (named point) frei Frachtführer ... (benannter Ort) (→*Incoterms 1980)*; **F**~ **Church** Freikirche *(vom Staate unabhängige Kirche; Br dissenters, non-conformists; Scot F~ Church of Scotland)*; ~ **city** *Ger* freie Stadt *(cf. Hanseatic towns)*; ~ **competition** freier Wettbewerb; ~ **copy** Freiexemplar; ~ **currency** frei konvertierbare Währung; ~ **delivery** Zustellung frei Haus; ~ **discharge** (f.d.) freies Löschen; ~ **dispatch** (f.d.) frei von Vergütung für gesparte Lade- od. Löschzeit (Eilgeld); ~ **enterprise** freies Unternehmertum; ~ **enterprise economy** freie Marktwirtschaft; ~ **entry** zollfreie Einfuhr; ~ **expression of opinion** freie Meinungsäußerung; ~ →**fishery**; ~ **flight** Freiflug; ~ **from all average** →average 1.; ~ **from general (particular) average** →average 1.; ~ **from breakage** frei von Bruch; ~ **from debt** schuldenfrei; ~ **from defect(s)** mangelfrei, fehlerfrei; ~ **from encumbrance** lastenfrei; ~ **gift** Zugabe; ~ **gift coupon** Gutschein; ~ **imports** zollfreie Einfuhr; ~ **items** spesenfreie Inkassi; ~ **labo(u)r** gewerkschaftlich nicht organisierte Arbeiterschaft; ~**-lance** *colloq.* freier Mitarbeiter; ~**-lance** *v* als freier Mitarbeiter tätig sein; ~ **list** Verzeichnis zollfreier Waren

free market freier Markt; *(Börse)* Freiverkehr; ~ **economy** freie Marktwirtschaft; ~ **price** *(Börse)* Freiverkehrskurs; **dealing in the** ~ *(Börse)* Freiverkehr

free membership beitragsfreie Mitgliedschaft

free movement freier Verkehr; ~ **of goods** freier Warenverkehr; ~ **of individuals** Freizügigkeit; ~ **of labo(u)r** Freizügigkeit der Arbeitskräfte; ~ **of persons** freier Personenverkehr; Freizügigkeit

free, ~ **of capture and seizure** (F.C.S.) *(SeeversR)* frei von Aufbringung und Beschlagnahme *(Ausschluß des Kriegsrisikos)*; ~ **of charge** gebührenfrei, kostenfrei, spesenfrei; ~ **of cost** kostenlos; ~ **of damage** frei von Beschädigung *(Beschädigung nicht zu unseren Lasten)*; ~ **of duty** zollfrei; abgabenfrei; ~ **of expense** kostenfrei, spesenfrei; ~ **of ice** eisfrei; ~ **of income tax** einkommensteuerfrei; ~ **of interest** zinsfrei; ~ **of rent** mietfrei; ~ **of riots and civil commotions** (f.r.c.c.) frei von Aufruhr und Bürgerkrieg; ~ **of postage** portofrei; ~ **of premium** prämienfrei; ~ **of tax** steuerfrei; ~ **on aircraft** (f.o.a.) frei an Bord des Flugzeugs; ~ **on board** frei an Bord (→*fob)*; ~ **on board clause** Fobklausel; ~ **on quay** (foq) frei auf den Kai ... (Hafen) *(heute meist →fas)*; **F**~ **on Rail/F**~ **on Truck** →FOR/FOT; ~ **on steamer** (fos) frei Schiff; ~ **on truck** (fot) *Br* frei Waggon; *Am* frei Lkw; ~ **pass** Freikarte, Freifahrtschein; ~ **policy** prämienfreie Versicherung

free port Freihafen; ~ **area** Freihafengebiet; ~ **store** Freihafenlager

free, ~ **ride** *(verbotenes)* kurzfristiges Spekulationsgeschäft mit neuen Anleihen und Aktien durch Weiterveräußerung vor Bezahlung; *colloq.* Freifahrt; ~ **rider** Spekulant *(cf.* ~ *ride)*; Trittbrettfahrer; ~ **speech** freie Meinungsäußerung; ~ **state** Freistaat; ~ **station** frei Bahnhof; ~ **time** Freizeit; Zeit zwischen der Anzeige der Ladebereitschaft und dem Beginn der Ladezeit

free trade Freihandel; ~ **agreement** Freihandelsabkommen; ~ **area** Freihandelsgebiet, Freihandelszone; ~ **policy** Freihandelspolitik; **creating a** ~ **area** Schaffung e-r Freihandelszone

free, ~ **trader** Anhänger des Freihandels; ~ **translation** freie Übersetzung; ~ **trial** kostenlose Warenprobe; ~ **vote** *parl* Abstimmung ohne Fraktionszwang; ~ **zone** Freizone, Freihafen(zone); Zollfreigebiet

free, to get sth. ~ *colloq.* etw. gratis bekommen;

to give sb. a ~ hand jdm freie Hand lassen; **to have sth. at one's ~ disposal** etw. zur freien Verfügung haben; **to set a prisoner ~** e-n Gefangenen freigeben

free(ly) fluctuating exchange rate freier Wechselkurs

freedom Freiheit; **~ from fear** Furchtlosigkeit *(cf. the Four F~s)*; **~ from taxation** Steuerfreiheit; **~ from want** Freiheit von Not *(cf. the Four F~s)*; **~ of action** Handlungsfreiheit; **~ of the air** Freiheit des Luftraumes; **~ of association** Vereinigungsfreiheit; Koalitionsfreiheit; **~ of belief** Glaubensfreiheit

freedom of a city (or **town**) Ehrenbürgerrecht; **to confer the ~ on sb.** (or **to give sb. the ~**) jdm das Ehrenbürgerrecht verleihen

freedom, ~ of a company *Br* Meisterrecht; **~ of competition** Wettbewerbsfreiheit; **~ of contract** Vertragsfreiheit

freedom of establishment *(EG)* Niederlassungsfreiheit; **restriction on ~** Niederlassungsbeschränkung

freedom of expression, right to ~ Recht der freien Meinungsäußerung

freedom, F~ of Information Act *Am* Gesetz zur Wahrung des Rechts auf Auskunft; **~ of movement** Bewegungsfreiheit; Freizügigkeit; **~ of opinion** Meinungsfreiheit; **~ of the person** persönliche Freiheit; **~ of the press** Pressefreiheit; **~ of religion** Religionsfreiheit; **~ of the (high) seas** *(VölkerR)* Freiheit der Meere; **~ of speech** Redefreiheit; Recht der freien Meinungsäußerung; **~ to provide** (or **supply**) **services** *(EG)* freier Dienstleistungsverkehr; Dienstleistungsfreiheit; **~ of trade** Gewerbefreiheit; **~ of transit** Durchfuhrfreiheit; **the Four F~s** die vier *(von Roosevelt 1941 verkündeten)* (Grund-)Freiheiten *(~ of speech, ~ of worship, ~ from fear, ~ from want)*

freefone *Br* R-Gespräch

freehold *(zeitlich unbeschränktes)* Eigentumsrecht (an Grundbesitz); Grundeigentum
Eigentumsrecht an einem Grundstück, das nicht an einem bestimmten Zeitpunkt abläuft, sondern entweder dem Eigentümer und dessen Erben für immer zusteht (fee simple) oder zu einem unbestimmten Zeitpunkt erlischt (z. B. wenn ein Eigentumsrecht auf Lebenszeit [estate for life] gewährt ist)

freehold, ~ estate *(nicht durch Zeitbegrenzung festgelegtes)* Eigentumsrecht an Grundbesitz; **~ flat** *Br* Eigentumswohnung; **~ land and buildings** *Br (Bilanz)* bebaute und unbebaute Grundstücke; **~ property** eigener *(zeitlich nicht begrenzter)* Grundbesitz, Grundeigentum *(opp. leasehold property)*; **owner of ~ property** →freeholder; **~ tenancy** *Am (mindestens lebenslängliches)* Eigentumsrecht an e-m Grundstück; ~ →**tenure**

freeholder Grundeigentümer, Grundbesitzer *(opp. leaseholder)*

freelance Freischaffender *(z. B. freier Schriftsteller od. Journalist)*; freiberuflich; **to work as a ~** freiberuflich tätig sein *(z. B. als Journalist)*; **~ translator** freiberuflicher Übersetzer

freeman Bürger; Ehrenbürger; Angehöriger e-r Gilde *(cf. liveryman)*; **(honorary) ~ of a city** *Br* Ehrenbürger; **to be admitted ~ of a city** zum Ehrenbürger ernannt werden

freemason Freimaurer; **~s' lodge** Freimaurerloge

freemasonry Freimaurerei

freeway *Am* Fernverkehrsstraße, Autobahn; **six-lane ~** Autobahn mit 6 Fahrspuren

freeze *v* einfrieren (lassen) *(bes. von ausländischen Guthaben, Konten)*; *(Guthaben, Kredite)* blockieren, sperren; **to ~ sb. out** jdn kaltstellen; **to ~ prices** Preisstopp durchführen; **to ~ wages** Lohnstopp durchführen

freezing, ~ of funds Sperrung der Mittel; **~ of prices** Einfrieren der Preise; **~ orders** *Br* gerichtliche Anordnungen, die Vermögen e-s Beklagten „einfrieren" (die Verschiebung verhindern)

freight (frt) Fracht; *bes. Br (auch)* Seefracht; Ladung, Frachtgut; *Br* Schiffsladung; Frachtkosten; **~ absorption** Übernahme der Frachtkosten *(durch den Verkäufer)*; **~ and carriage** *Br* See- und Landfracht; **~ and charges prepaid** fracht- und spesenfrei; **~ and demurrage** (F&D) Fracht- und Liegegeld; **~ bill** (f. b.) *Am* Frachtbrief; **~ booking** *Br* Belegung von Frachtraum; **~ broker** Frachtmakler; **~ brokerage** Frachtmaklergebühr; **~ broking** Frachtmaklergeschäft; **~ capacity** Frachtraum; **~ car** *Am* Güterwagen; **~/carriage and insurance paid** (CIP) **to ...** (named point of destination) frachtfrei versichert ... (benannter Bestimmungsort) (→*Incoterms 1980)*; **~ carrier** (or **~ carrying aircraft**) Frachtflugzeug; **~ charges** Frachtkosten, Frachtgebühren; **~ collect** *Am* Fracht gegen Nachnahme; unfrei; **F~ Conference System** *Am* Seefrachtkonferenzsystem (→*shipping conference)*; **~ contract** (See-)Frachtvertrag; **~ contracting** Befrachtung; **~ declaration** *(Zoll)* Anmeldung der Ladung; **~ deferment** Frachtstundung; **~ depot** Güterbahnhof; **~ at destination** *Br* Fracht zahlbar im Bestimmungshafen; **~ equalization** *Am* Frachtgleichstellung *(cf. basing point system)*; **~ forward** (frt fwd) *Br* Fracht gegen Nachnahme; Fracht unfrei *(opp. ~ prepaid)*; **~ forwarder** Spediteur; **~ forwarding** *Am* Spedition; **~ handling facilities** Güterverladeanlagen; **~ haulage** Güterkraftverkehr; **~ home(ward)** Rückfracht; **~ insurance** Frachtversicherung; Gütertransportversicherung; **~liner** *Br* Güterexpresszug *(zwischen Industriezentren und Seehäfen)*; **~ note** *Br* Frachtrechnung; **~ out (-ward)** Hinfracht; **~ out and home** Hin- und

Rückfracht; ~ **paid** Fracht bezahlt; ~ **payable at destination** (FPAD) Fracht zahlbar am Bestimmungsort; ~ **prepaid** (or **paid in advance**) Fracht im voraus bezahlt; frachtfrei *(opp. ~ forward)*; ~ **to be prepaid** Fracht im voraus zu zahlen; ~ **prepayable** (or ~ **payable in advance**) Fracht vorauszahlbar; ~ **pro rata** Distanzfracht; ~ **quotation** *(Börse)* Frachtnotierung; ~ **rate** Frachtrate, Frachtsatz; ~ **rates** *(Bahn)* Gütertarif, Frachttarif; ~ **rebate** Frachtnachlaß; Frachtrabatt; ~ **receipt** Frachtempfangsbescheinigung; ~ **reduction** Frachtermäßigung; **(road and rail)** ~ **services** Frachtdienst; ~ **shed** *Am* Güterschuppen; ~ **space** Frachtraum; ~ **station** Güterbahnhof; ~ **steamer** Frachtdampfer, Frachter; ~ **tariff** Gütertarif, Frachttarif; ~ **ton** Gewichtstonne; ~ **tonnage** Frachtraum; ~ **traffic** Frachtverkehr, Güterverkehr; ~ **train** Güterzug; **by** ~ **train** als Frachtgut; ~ **truck** *Am* Fernlaster; ~ **yard** Güterbahnhof

freight, additional ~ Frachtzuschlag; **advance on** ~ Frachtvorschuß; **advanced** ~ vorausbezahlte Fracht; **dead** ~ Leerfracht, Fautfracht (→*dead*); **domestic** ~ **traffic by major carriers** *Am* Fracht-Inlandsverkehr mit den wichtigsten Verkehrsunternehmen; **fast** ~ *Am* Eilgut, Eilfracht; **homeward** ~ *Br* Rückfracht, Rückladung *(opp. outward ~)*; **increase in** ~ Frachtzuschlag; **loss of** ~ Frachtverlust; **lump sum** ~ Pauschalfracht; **overcharge of** ~ zuviel berechnete Fracht; **outward** ~ *Br* Hinfracht, abgehende Fracht (od. Ladung) *(opp. homeward or return ~)*; **rail(road)** ~ *Am* Bahnfracht (→*railroad)*; **return** ~ *Br* Rückfracht, Rückladung; **terms of** ~ Frachtbedingungen; **time** ~ Zeitfracht *(opp. lump sum ~)*; **through** ~ Durchgangsfracht; **voyage** ~ Reisefracht

freight, to book ~ Frachtraum belegen; **to charge** ~ Fracht berechnen; **to send by** ~ per Fracht (od. als Frachtgut) senden; **to take in** ~ Ladung einnehmen; *(Güter)* verladen

freight *v (Schiff)* befrachten, beladen; *(Güter)* verfrachten, befördern; *(Schiff)* chartern od. verchartern

freighting Befrachtung; Beladung; Beförderung *(von Gütern)*; Chartern; ~ **by the piece** Stückgutbefrachtung; ~ **by contract** Pauschalfracht; ~ **on measurement** Maßfracht; ~ **ad valorem** Befrachtung nach dem Wert; ~ **on weight** Befrachtung nach dem Gewicht

freightage Frachtbeförderung, Transport; Fracht, Ladung; *Am* Frachtkosten

freighter Frachtschiff; Frachtflugzeug; *(Seefahrtgeschäft)* Verfrachter

French französisch; **the** ~ die Franzosen; ~ **Republic** Französische Republik *(cf. France)*; ~**man** Franzose; ~ **overseas departments** französische Überseedepartments; ~**woman** Französin

frequency *(bes. Statistik)* Häufigkeit; ~ **of accidents** Unfallhäufigkeit; ~ **of change** Änderungshäufigkeit; ~ **of crimes** Häufigkeit von Verbrechen

fresh frisch, neu; ~ **contract** neuer Vertrag; ~ **evidence** neue Beweise, neues Beweismaterial; ~ **issue** Neuemission; ~**man** Student im ersten Jahr *(Am auch College)*; ~ **pursuit** (or **suit**) sofortige Verfolgung; ~ **trial** neues Strafverfahren

freshwater Frischwasser; Süßwasser *(opp. sea water)*; ~ **fish** Süßwasserfische; **protection of international** ~ **courses** Schutz der internationalen Wasserläufe *(Übereinkommen von Straßburg)*

friction *fig* Reibung; Meinungsverschiedenheiten; Streit

friend Freund; **my** ~ *Br* mein verehrter Kollege *(Bezeichnung des Gegenanwalts – solicitor – vor Gericht)*; **my honourable** ~ *Br parl* mein Herr Vorredner *(übliche Anrede bei Mitgliedern des House of Commons)*; **my learned** ~ *Br* mein verehrter Kollege *(Bezeichnung des Gegenanwalts – junior counsel – vor Gericht)*; **my very learned** ~ *Br* mein verehrter Kollege *(Bezeichnung des Gegenanwalts – Queen's or leading counsel – vor Gericht)*; **next** ~ Prozeßpfleger (→*next*); **Society of F~s** Quäker

friendly freundschaftlich; freundlich; befreundet; ~ **arbitrator** Vermittler, Schlichter; ~ **nation** befreundete Nation; ~ **neutrality** wohlwollende Neutralität; ~ **power** befreundete Macht; ~ **relations** freundschaftliche Beziehungen; ~ **society** *Br*[20] (Sonderform des) Versicherungsverein(s) auf Gegenseitigkeit; Unterstützungskasse; Sterbekasse; **collecting** ~ **societies** Inkasso-Sterbekassen; ~ **suit** in gegenseitigem Einvernehmen der Parteien erhobene Klage (od. angestrengter Prozeß); ~ →**takeover**; **to be on** ~ **terms with sb.** zu jdm freundschaftliche Beziehungen haben

friendship, Treaty of F~, Commerce and Navigation between the Federal Republic of Germany and the United States of America Freundschafts-, Handels- und Schiffahrtsvertrag zwischen der Bundesrepublik Deutschland und den Vereinigten Staaten von Amerika *(von 1954)*[21]

Der Vertrag ist an die Stelle des Freundschafts-, Handels- und Konsularvertrages von 1923 getreten. Aus dem alten Vertrag sind aber die Art. XVII bis XXVIII, die das Konsularwesen betreffen, vorläufig noch in Kraft geblieben

F. R. G. →Federal Republic of Germany

fringe Rand-; Randbezirk; ~**s**→~ benefits; ~ **area** (Stadt-)Randgebiet; ~ **benefits** Gehaltsnebenleistungen *(z. B. Firmenwagen mit Chauffeur)*; freiwillige *(übertarifliche)* Lohnnebenleistungen (od. Sozialleistungen); ~ **groups** Randgruppen

frisk *v sl.* jdn *(nach verborgenen Waffen)* abtasten, durchsuchen

frivolous leichtfertig; unbedeutend, geringfügig; ~ **plea** *(Zivilprozeß)* schikanöser Einwand

FRN →floating rate note

from von ... an; ~ **... to August** *Br* (~**...through to August** *Am)* vom ... bis einschließlich August; ~ **the date of** nach; seit; ~ **today onwards** von heute an; **as** ~ **January 1** vom 1. Januar ab

front Vorderseite, vorderer Teil; *mil* Front; ~ **bench** *Br* →bench 2.; ~**man** Strohmann; ~ **page** (of a newspaper) erste Seite (e-r Zeitung); ~**-runner** *Am* Spitzenkandidat *(mit den besten Aussichten)*; **united** ~ Einheitsfront

front-end, ~ **fee** Konsortialgebühr für die Abwicklung e-r Finanzierungsfazilität; ~ **load** *Am (Investment)* Vorausbelastung von Ankaufsgebühren

frontage Vorderfront, Straßenfront, Frontseite; ~ **road** *Am* parallel zu e-r Autobahn verlaufende Straße *(mit Wohnhäusern, Geschäften, Tankstellen etc)*; **house with** ~**s on two streets** Haus mit zwei Straßenfronten

frontager Anlieger *(dessen Grundbesitz an Straße od. See angrenzt)*; Vorderhausbewohner

frontier *(politische)* Grenze; *Am* die westliche Siedlungsgrenze; der *(zuletzt besiedelte)* Westen der USA; *fig* äußerste Grenze; ~ **area** Grenzgebiet; ~ **check** Grenzkontrolle; ~ **commuter** Grenzgänger *(Arbeiter, Schüler)*

frontier control Grenzkontrolle, Grenzüberwachung; →**International Convention on the Harmonization of F**~ **C**~**s of Goods;** ~ **point** Zollgrenzstelle

frontier, illegal ~ **crosser** illegaler Grenzgänger; ~ **crossing** Grenzübergang; Grenzüberschreitung; Grenzüberflug; ~ **crossing point** Grenzübergangsstelle; ~ **dispute** Grenzstreitigkeit; ~ **district** Grenzbezirk, Grenzgebiet; ~ **guard** Grenzwache; ~ **incident** Grenzzwischenfall; ~ **pass** Grenzausweis, Grenzbescheinigung; ~ **passage** Grenzübertritt; ~ **patrol** Grenzstreife; ~ **police** Grenzpolizei; ~ **population** Grenzbevölkerung; ~ **post** Grenzpfahl; ~ **problem** Grenzproblem; ~ **protection** Grenzschutz; ~ **question** Grenzfrage; ~ **rectification** (or **revision**) Grenzberichtigung; ~**s of a state** Staatsgrenzen; ~ **station** Grenzstation, Grenzbahnhof; ~ **town** Grenzstadt; *Am* neu gegründete Stadt an Siedlungsgrenze; ~ **traffic** Grenzverkehr; ~ **treaty** *(VölkerR)* Grenzvertrag; ~ **violation** Grenzverletzung; ~ **worker** Grenzarbeitnehmer; Grenzgänger *(Arbeiter)*; ~ **zone** Grenzzone, Grenzgebiet

frontier, artificial ~ künstliche Grenze; **at the** ~ an der Grenze; **closing (of) the** ~ Schließung der Grenze; Grenzsperre; **course of the** ~ Grenzverlauf; **natural** ~ natürliche Grenze; **new** ~ *fig* neues Gebiet, Neuland; **on the** ~ an der Grenze; **supervision of the** ~ Grenzbewachung; **to close the** ~ die Grenze schließen; **to cross the** ~ die Grenze überschreiten; **to draw the** ~ die Grenze ziehen; **to rectify the** ~ die Grenze berichtigen

frontierman Grenzbewohner; Siedler, Pionier

frozen eingefroren, blockiert; Gefrier-; ~ **assets** eingefrorene Guthaben; ~ **capital** festliegendes Kapital; ~ **cargo** Gefrierladung; ~ **credit** eingefrorener Kredit; ~ **debts** eingefrorene Forderungen, Stillhalteschulden; ~ **food** Tiefkühlkost; ~ **goods** tiefgekühle Ware(n); Gefriergut

fructus naturales Bodenfrüchte

fruit Frucht, Früchte; Obst; ~ **processing industry** obstverarbeitende Industrie; **to grow** ~ Obst anbauen

frustrate *v (Pläne, Absichten)* vereiteln, durchkreuzen; **to** ~ **sb. in his plans** jdn an der Durchführung seiner Pläne hindern; **to** ~ **sb.'s plans** jds Pläne durchkreuzen

frustrated, Law Reform (F~ **Contracts) Act** (1943) *Br* Gesetz über Leistungshindernisse bei der Erfüllung e-s Vertrages
An die doctrine of →frustration of contract anknüpfend, regelt das Gesetz die Rechtsfolgen der →frustration of contract mit dem Ziel eines Interessenausgleichs zwischen den Vertragspartnern, indem es insbesondere einen Anspruch auf Rückzahlung geleisteter Zahlungen und auf Wertersatz für bereits erbrachte Erfüllungsleistungen gewährt

frustrated, ~ **contract** Vertrag, dessen Erfüllung durch von den Parteien unvorhergesehene Umstände unmöglich geworden ist; **a contract has become** (or **is**) ~ die Vertragserfüllung ist unmöglich geworden; *(etwa)* die Geschäftsgrundlage für e-n Vertrag ist weggefallen *(cf. doctrine of frustration of contract)*

frustration Vereitelung, Durchkreuzung *(von Plänen, Absichten)*; Verhinderung; objektive Unmöglichkeit *(der Leistung)*; Leistungshindernis; ~ **of a contract** objektive Unmöglichkeit der Vertragsleistung; *(etwa)* Wegfall der Geschäftsgrundlage *(völlige Veränderung der e-m Vertrag zugrundeliegenden Verhältnisse)*; ~ **of purpose** Vereitelung des *(vereinbarten)* Zweckes *(bei Vertragserfüllung)*

frustration, doctrine of ~ **of contract** Common-Law-Lehre von befreienden Leistungshindernissen bei der Erfüllung e-s Vertrages
Danach gibt der Vertragsschuldner sein Leistungsversprechen unter der stillschweigenden Bedingung ab, daß sich der zugesagten Leistung nicht nachträglich unüberwindliche Hindernisse entgegenstellen,

die bei Vertragsschluß nicht vorhergesehen werden konnten. Sie entspricht etwa den deutschen Lehren von dem Wegfall der Geschäftsgrundlage und von der wirtschaftlichen Unmöglichkeit der Leistung (der sog. „Opfergrenze")

frustration, existing (or **initial, original**) ~ anfängliche Unmöglichkeit *(der Leistung)*; **subsequent** (or **supervening**) ~ nachträgliche Unmöglichkeit *(der Leistung)*

F.T. Financial Times *(newspaper)*; ~ **100-Share Index** (→*Footsie*) Aktienindex von 100 großen britischen Unternehmen

FTC complaint *Am* Beschwerdeschrift der Federal Trade Commission

FT-SE 100 stock →Footsie

fuel Brennstoff, Treibstoff, Kraftstoff; Heiz-, Brennmaterial; Benzin; ~ **consumption** Brennstoffverbrauch; Benzinverbrauch; ~ **gas** Heizgas; ~ **oil** Heizöl; ~ **price** Benzinpreis; ~ **requirements** Brennstoffbedarf; ~ **supply** Brennstoffversorgung; ~ **taxes** *Am* Treibstoffsteuern; **increased cost of** ~ Heizöl-(etc)-Verteuerung; **saving in** ~ Brennstoffeinsparung; **to have run out of** ~ keinen Brennstoff mehr haben

fuel *v* Brennstoff einnehmen, tanken

fugitive Flüchtling; flüchtig; ~ **from justice** flüchtiger Rechtsbrecher; **search for a** ~ Fahndung; **warrant for arrest of a** ~ Steckbrief; **to be believed to be (a)** ~ **from justice** fluchtverdächtig sein

fulfil (*Am auch* **fulfill**) *v* erfüllen, ausführen; **to** ~ **a condition** e-e Bedingung erfüllen; **to** ~ **a contract** e-n Vertrag erfüllen; **to** ~ **one's obligations** seine Verpflichtungen erfüllen (od. einhalten); **to** ~ **an order** e-e Anordnung ausführen; **to** ~ **a promise** ein Versprechen erfüllen (od. halten); **to** ~ **the requirements** den Anforderungen entsprechen; die Voraussetzungen erfüllen

fulfil(l)ment Erfüllung, Ausführung; ~ **of a condition** Erfüllung e-r Bedingung; **non-**~ **of a contract** Nichterfüllung e-s Vertrages; **in the** ~ **of his duties** in Ausübung seines Amtes; **in the** ~ **of one's obligations** bei der Erfüllung seiner Verpflichtungen; **place of** ~ Erfüllungsort

full voll, ganz; vollständig; voll belegt *(Hotel)*; ausführlich, detailliert

full, in ~ völlig, voll(ständig); im ganzen; nicht abgekürzt; **in** ~ **and final payment** als endgültige Abfindung; **capital paid in** ~ voll eingezahltes Kapital; **receipt in** ~ Generalquittung; **to pay in** ~ **or by instal(l)ments** im ganzen oder in Raten bezahlen; **to write in** ~ ausschreiben

full age Mündigkeit, Volljährigkeit; **of** ~ mündig, volljährig; **person of** ~ **and capacity** volljährige und geschäftsfähige Person; **upon attaining** (or **on coming of**) ~ bei Erreichung der Volljährigkeit; **to attain** ~ mündig werden *(Br*[22] *mit dem 18. Lebensjahr)*

full, ~ **amount** voller (od. ganzer) Betrag; ~ **authority** unbeschränkte Vollmacht; ~ **cargo** volle Ladung; ~ **costs** Vollkosten

full court Plenum; **in** ~ in pleno; (Verhandlung) vor dem vollbesetzten Gericht

full, ~ **covenant deed** *Am* Grundstücksübertragungsurkunde mit bestimmten Zusicherungen; ~ **coverage** voller Versicherungsschutz, volle Schadensdeckung *(opp. franchise)*; ~ **description** ausführliche Beschreibung; ~ **details** genaue Einzelheiten; ~ **dress debate** *Br parl* vorbereitete Debatte über wichtige Frage

full employment Vollbeschäftigung; **restoration of** ~ Wiederherstellung der Vollbeschäftigung

full, ~ **faith and credit clause** →faith; ~ **fare** voller Fahrpreis; ~ **fare ticket** Fahrkarte zum vollen Preise; ~ **information** ausführliche Auskunft; ~ **interest admitted** (f. i. a.) volle Beteiligung zugesagt; ~ **liability** volle Haftung; ~ **line forcing** *Am* →line 7.; ~ **load** ganze Ladung; ~ **lot** *Am (Börse)* →round lot; ~ **membership** Vollmitgliedschaft; ~ **page advertisement** ganzseitige Anzeige; ~ **paid stock** *Am* voll eingezahlte Aktien; ~ **particulars** genaue Einzelheiten; Näheres

full pay voller Lohn, volles Gehalt; **to restore to** ~ *mil (Offizier)* reaktivieren; **to be retired on** ~ mit vollem Gehalt pensioniert werden

full payment volle Bezahlung; **in full and final payment** als endgültige Abfindung

full power(s) Vollmacht; Generalvollmacht; **to invest sb. with** ~ jdn mit Vollmacht versehen, jdn bevollmächtigen; **to have** ~ Vollmacht haben; bevollmächtigt sein

full, ~ **price** voller Preis; ~ **professor** *Am univ* ordentlicher Professor; Ordinarius; ~ **rates** volle Gebühren; ~ **rates (of customs duties)** allgemeiner (Zoll-)Tarif *(opp. preferential rates)*; ~ **reasons** eingehende Begründung; ~ **session** Plenarsitzung; ~ **set** voller Satz; alle Ausfertigungen; ~ **set of bills of lading** voller Satz des Konnossements; **in** ~ **settlement** zur endgültigen Abrechnung; ~ **statement** vollständige Darstellung; umfassende Erklärung; ~ **stock** *Am* Aktie mit Nennwert von $ 100; ~ **terms** volle Bedingungen; ~ **text** voller (ungekürzter) Text

full-time ganztägig, Ganztags-; Vollzeit-; hauptberuflich, hauptamtlich *(opp. part-time)*; ~ **employee** ganztägig beschäftigter Arbeitnehmer; ~ **employment** ganztägige Beschäftigung, Ganztagsbeschäftigung; ~ **work** ganztägige Arbeit; Ganzzeitarbeit; ~ **workers** Vollzeitarbeitskräfte; **to work** ~ (or **on a** ~

basis) ganztägig arbeiten; hauptamtlich (od. hauptberuflich) tätig sein
full(-)timer ganztägig Arbeitender
full-truck lot vollständige Lkw-Ladung (→*truck 2.)*
fully, ~ automatic voll automatisch; ~ **entitled** voll berechtigt; ~ **negotiable promissory note** umlauffähiger Solawechsel; ~ **paid (up) capital** voll eingezahltes Kapital; ~**-paid shares** *Br* voll (ein)gezahlte Aktien (od. Anteile); ~ **responsible** voll verantwortlich; ~ **secured creditor** voll gesicherter Gläubiger *(opp. partly secured creditor);* ~ **valid** voll gültig

fumes Abgase

function Funktion, Tätigkeit; Amtstätigkeit; Aufgabe; *(öffentliche)* Veranstaltung, Feier; ~**s of a judge** Funktionen (od. Tätigkeit) e-s Richters; ~**s of an organization** Aufgaben e-r Organisation; **in the exercise of his** ~**s** bei der Durchführung seiner Aufgaben; in der Ausübung seines Amtes; **judicial** ~**s** richterliche Funktionen
function, official ~ Amtshandlung; Amtsverrichtung; **outside one's official** ~**s** außerdienstlich; **to carry out official** ~**s** dienstliche Aufgaben wahrnehmen
function, performance of ~**s** Durchführung (od. Wahrnehmung) von Aufgaben; **continued performance of** ~**s** Fortführung von Aufgaben
function, scope of ~**s** Aufgabenkreis; Amtsbereich; **within the scope of one's** ~**s** im Rahmen seiner *(amtlichen)* Aufgaben; **to be beyond sb.'s** ~**s** außerhalb jds Aufgabenkreis liegen
function, state ~ offizielle Feier, Staatsempfang
function, to discharge ~**s** Aufgaben erfüllen; **in the exercise of one's** ~**s** in der Ausübung seines Amtes; **to perform** ~**s** Aufgaben wahrnehmen; **on the termination of their** ~**s** bei Beendigung ihres Dienstes

function *v* funktionieren; tätig sein
functioning *(ordnungsmäßiges)* Arbeiten, Funktionieren; **smooth** ~ reibungsloses Funktionieren; **to be** ~ funktionieren

functional funktional, funktionell; auf die Funktion bezüglich; wirksam; ~ **building** Zweckbau; ~ **commission** Fachkommission; ~ **discount** Funktionsrabatt *(der an bestimmte Käufergattungen, z. B. Groß-, Zwischen-, Kleinhändler gegeben wird);* ~ **manager** fachliche Führungskraft; ~ **protection** *(VölkerR)* Schutz der internationalen Beziehungen; ~ **specialists** Fachbeamte

functionary Beamter; Funktionär *(oft in verächtlichem Sinne)*

functus officio ("having discharged his duty") Erlöschen e-r Vollmacht oder sonstigen Befugnis zum Handeln durch Zweckerreichung

Fund →International Monetary Fund; **resources of the** ~ Mittel des IWF

fund 1. Fonds *(zweckgebundene Vermögensmasse);* ~**s** Gelder, (Geld-)Mittel; **The F**~**s** britische Staatspapiere, Staatsanleihen; *Am* Effekten (Schuldverschreibungen); *(VersR)* Rücklagen
fund, to be in ~**s** bei Kasse sein; **to be out of** ~**s** nicht bei Kasse sein, zahlungsunfähig sein; **to create a** ~ e-n Fonds bilden; **to establish a** ~ e-n Fonds errichten; **to furnish with** ~**s** mit Geld versehen; Deckung zur Verfügung stellen; **to invest money in** ~**s** *Br* Geld in Staatsanleihen anlegen; **to make** ~**s available** Mittel verfügbar machen; **to pass on the** ~**s to** die Mittel weiterleiten an; **to be placed in a** ~ e-m Fonds zufließen; **to be short of** ~**s** knapp mit Geld sein; **to raise** ~**s** Geldmittel aufbringen; **to vote** ~**s** *parl* Gelder *(durch Abstimmung)* bewilligen
fund, ~**s** →**earmarked for special purposes;** ~ **holder** *Br* Inhaber von Staatspapieren; ~**s in court** bei Gericht hinterlegte Gelder (od. Wertpapiere); ~**s of a company** Gesellschaftskapital; ~ **of donated contributions** Fonds aus freiwilligen Spenden; ~**s of a society** Vereinskasse; ~**s raised** aufgenommene (od. beschaffte) Gelder; ~ **raising** Geldbeschaffung für wohltätige Zwecke; *(auch)* organisiertes Auftreiben von Spenden; ~ **resources** Fondsmittel; ~**s statement** Kapitalflußrechnung
fund, allocation of ~**s** Zuweisung von Mitteln; Mittelvergabe; **appropriation of** ~**s** Bewilligung (od. Zweckbestimmung) von Geldern; Mittelzuweisung; **available** ~**s** verfügbare Geldmittel; **British F**~**s** britische Staatspapiere; **Consolidated F**~ *Br* konsolidierter Staatsfonds; **contingency** ~ Fonds für unvorhergesehene Ausgaben; Reservefonds; **cumulative** ~ thesaurierender Fonds; **depreciation** ~ Rückstellung für Wertminderung; Abschreibungsrücklage; **dissolving of a** ~ Auflösung e-s Fonds; **donated** ~ Fonds aus freiwilligen Spenden; **dormant** ~**s (in court)** bei Gericht hinterlegte, bereits 15 Jahre und mehr unberührt ruhende (unverzinsliche) Gelder oder Wertpapiere; →**electronic** ~**(s) transfer; employment of** ~**s** Verwendung von Mitteln; **establishment of a** ~ Errichtung e-s Fonds; **guarantee** ~ Garantiefonds; **in** ~**s** bei Kasse; **insufficient** ~**s** (I/F) ungenügende Deckung *(Vermerk auf Wechseln oder Schecks);* **insurance** ~ Versicherungsfonds; **investment** ~→fund 2.; **for lack of** ~**s** aus Mangel an Mitteln; **liquidation of a** ~ Auflösung e-s Fonds; **loan** ~**s** Fremdmittel; **management of a** ~ Fondsverwaltung; **no** ~**s** (N/F) *(ScheckR)* keine Deckung; **out of** ~**s** nicht bei Kasse; mittellos; **outside** ~**s** Fremdkapital
fund, pension ~ Pensionsfonds, Pensionskasse; **employees' pension** ~ Pensionsfonds für Arbeitnehmer

fund, provident ~ Unterstützungsfonds, Hilfskasse; **public** ~**s** öffentliche Mittel (od. Gelder); Staatsgelder; **redemption** ~ Tilgungsfonds; **relief** ~ Hilfsfonds, Unterstützungsfonds; **reserve** ~ Rücklage (→*reserve 1.*); **renewal** ~ Erneuerungsfonds; **revolving** ~ Umlauffonds; **secret** ~ Geheimfonds; **separate** (or **special**) ~ Sonderfonds; **sick** ~ Krankenkasse; **sinking** ~ (Schulden-)Tilgungsfonds; Amortisationsfonds; **strike** ~ Streikfonds, Streikkasse; **sufficient** ~**s** genügende Deckung; **cheque without sufficient** ~**s** ungedeckter Scheck; →**trust** ~**(s)**; **use of a** ~ Inanspruchnahme e-s Fonds; **want of** ~**s** Kapitalmangel; **for want of** ~**s** mangels Deckung; **returned for want of** ~**s** *(ScheckR)* mangels Deckung zurück; **welfare** ~ Unterstützungsfonds; **working** ~**s** Betriebsmittel

fund 2. **(investment)** ~ (Investment-)Fonds; ~ **assets** Fondsvermögen; **composition of** ~ **assets** Zusammensetzung des Fondsvermögens; ~ **holder** Fondsbesitzer; ~ **holdings** Fondsbestände; ~ **management** Fondsverwaltung; ~ **of funds** Dachfonds; ~ **sponsoring organization** Gründungsgesellschaft für Investmentfonds

fund, balanced ~ *Am* s. mixed →~; **bond** ~ Rentenfonds; **closed-end** ~ geschlossener Fonds (→*closed end*); **equity** ~ Aktienfonds; →**fixed** ~; →**flexible** ~; **go-go** ~ *Am* Wachstumsfonds *(der maximales Kapitalwachstum anstrebt)*; **growth** ~ Wachstumsfonds (→*growth*); **income** ~ Einkommensfonds *(opp. growth* ~*)*; →**leverage** ~; **managed** ~ Investmentfonds, dessen Effektenbestand jederzeit auswechselbar ist; **mixed** ~ gemischter Fonds *(Aktien und Rentenwerte)*; **mutual** ~ *Am* offener (Investment-)Fonds *(opp. closed-end fund)*; **open-end** ~ offener Fonds (→*open-end)*; **securities** ~ Wertpapierfonds; **share** ~ Aktiensfonds; **domestic and foreign share** ~ in- und ausländischer Aktienfonds *(e-r Investmentgesellschaft)*; **specialized** ~ *Am* Branchenfonds; **to promote the growth of the** ~ das Wachstum des Fonds fördern

fund *v* finanzieren; *Br (Geld)* in Staatspapieren anlegen; *(Schuld)* fundieren (od. konsolidieren); schwebende *(kurzfristige) (Br* Staats-)-Schulden in fundierte *(langfristige) (Br* Staats-)-Schulden (bes. Anleihen) umwandeln; *(schwebende Schuld)* kapitalisieren; **to** ~ **the public debt** die Staatsschuld konsolidieren

funded, ~ **debt** fundierte Schuld, Anleiheschuld *(Am bes. bonded debt)*; *Br* Staatspapiere, Staatsanleihen *(Consols, savings bonds, conversion loans)*; ~ **property** *Br* Besitz an Staatspapieren; ~ **reserve** in fest verzinslichen Wertpapieren angelegte Rücklage

funding Fundierung, Konsolidierung, Umwandlung kurzfristiger in langfristige (fundierte) Schulden; Finanzierung; ~ **loan** (or **bond**) Fundierungsanleihe, Konsolidierungsanleihe

fundamentals Grundlagen

fundamental grundlegend, fundamental; wesentlich (to für); grundsätzlich; ~ **breach of the contract** wesentliche Vertragsverletzung; ~ **facts** grundlegende Tatsachen; ~ **freedoms** Grundfreiheiten *(cf. Convention for the Protection of →Human Rights and F~ Freedoms)*; ~ **issue** Grundproblem; grundlegende Frage; ~ **order** Grundordnung e-s Staates; ~ **rights** Grundrechte

funeral Beerdigung, Begräbnis, Beisetzung; ~ **allowance** (or **benefit**) Sterbegeld; ~ **expenses** Begräbniskosten; ~ **expenses insurance** Begräbniskostenversicherung; Sterbegeldversicherung; ~ **service** Trauergottesdienst; **national** ~ *Am* (or **state** ~ *Br*) Staatsbegräbnis; **to attend a** ~ an e-m Begräbnis teilnehmen

fungibility Fungibilität, Vertretbarkeit *(von Sachen)*

fungible fungibel, vertretbar; ~**s** (or ~ **goods**) fungible (od. vertretbare) Sachen, Gattungssachen

furlough Urlaub *(bes. für Soldaten od. Staatsbedienstete)*; ~ **certificate** Urlaubsschein; **on** ~ beurlaubt; **to grant** ~ Urlaub erteilen; **to take** ~ Urlaub nehmen

furnish *v* versehen, ausstatten (with mit); liefern, beschaffen; **to** ~ **capital** Kapital beschaffen; **to** ~ **documents** Urkunden (od. Unterlagen) beibringen; **to** ~ **evidence** Beweis liefern (od. erbringen); **to** ~ **a guarantee** Garantie geben (od. leisten); **to** ~ **one's home** sich einrichten; **to** ~ **sb. with information** jdn mit Informationen versehen; **to** ~ **an office** ein Büro einrichten (od. möblieren); **to** ~ **sb. with full power(s)** jdn mit Vollmacht versehen, jdn bevollmächtigen; **to** ~ **proof** Nachweis erbringen (od. führen) (of für); **to** ~ **references** Referenzen beibringen

furnished room möbliertes Zimmer; **to live in a** ~ (or **flat**) möbliert wohnen

furniture Möbel; Wohnungseinrichtung; Mobiliar; ~ **exhibition** Möbelausstattung; ~ **and fixtures** *Am* Einrichtungsgegenstände; Geschäftsausstattung; ~ **industry** Möbelindustrie; ~ **mover** *Am* Möbelspediteur; ~ **of a ship** Ausrüstung e-s Schiffes; ~ **remover** (or **removal firm**) *Br* Möbelspediteur; ~ **van** *Br* Möbelwagen; **household** ~ Hausrat; **office** ~ Büroeinrichtung

further weiter; ~ **assurance**[23] Zusicherung, auf Wunsch und Kosten des Käufers alles weitere zu tun, um das Grundstück frei von Rechtsmängeln zu übertragen; ~ **cover** Nachschuß (-zahlung)

further education Weiterbildung, Fortbildung; ~ **award** *Br univ.* Stipendium; ~ **grant** *Br* Beihilfe zur Fortbildung

further, ~ **margin** Nachschuß(zahlung); **until** ~ **notice** bis auf weiteres; ~ **particulars** weitere Einzelheiten; **for** ~ **particulars apply to** Näheres bei; ~ **processing of a patent application** Weiterbehandlung e-r Patentanmeldung; ~ **remand (in custody)** Haftfortdauer; ~ **to our letter of** im Anschluß an unser Schreiben vom

further, to ask for a ~ **credit** um weiteren Kredit bitten; **to go** ~ **into a question** auf e-e Frage näher eingehen

further *v* fördern, unterstützen; **to** ~ **the cause of peace** der Sache des Friedens förderlich sein; **to** ~ **sales** den Verkauf fördern

furtherance Förderung, Unterstützung; **in** ~ **of sb.'s interests** zur Förderung jds Interessen

fuse *v* fusionieren, (sich) verschmelzen

fusion Fusion, Verschmelzung, Vereinigung *(von wirtschaftlichen Unternehmungen od. politischen Parteien);* Unternehmenszusammenschluß; *parl* Koalition; ~ **candidate** *Am* gemeinsamer Kandidat *(von zwei Parteien)*

futile attempt vergeblicher Versuch

future 1. Zukunft; (zu)künftig; ~ **advances** zukünftige Forderungen; ~ **advance clause** *Am* Klausel in e-r Sicherungsvereinbarung, wonach das Sicherungsgut auch zukünftige Forderungen sichern soll; ~ **estate** zukünftiges Recht an Grundbesitz *(z.B. contingent remainder, executory interest);* ~ **interest** künftiges Recht; *(etwa)* Nacherbfolge, Nachvermächtnis; ~ **right** zukünftiges Recht; Anwartschaft; ~ **supplies** zukünftige Lieferungen; **prospects for the** ~ Zukunftsaussichten

future 2. ~**s** *(Börse)* Termingeschäfte, Terminwaren *(Korn, Baumwolle, Wolle etc);* **F~ Commission Merchants** US-Banken und Brokerhäuser mit der Erlaubnis zur Abwicklung von Terminkontrakten; ~**s contract** Terminvertrag

future delivery spätere Lieferung, Terminlieferung *(opp. spot delivery);* **purchase for** ~ Terminkauf; **to sell for** ~ auf Termin verkaufen

future, ~**s exchange** Terminbörse; ~**s market** Terminmarkt; ~**s operation** (or **transaction**) Termingeschäft *(opp. spot transaction);* ~**s price** Preis (od. Kurs) für Termingeschäfte, Terminkurs *(opp. spot price);* ~**s purchase** *Am* Terminkauf, Kauf auf spätere Lieferung; ~**s rate** *(Devisen)* Terminkurs; ~ **rate agreement** (FRA) Zinsterminkontrakt; ~**s sale** *Am* Terminverkauf, Verkauf auf spätere Lieferung; ~**s trading** Terminhandel; **dealing** (or **operation, trading, transaction**) **in** ~**s** Termingeschäft; **precious metal** ~**s** *(Börse)* Edelmetallterminkontrakte; **to trade in** ~**s** Termingeschäfte betreiben

futurology Futurologie, Zukunftsforschung

G

G 5 →Group of Five
G 7 →Group of Seven
G 10 →Group of Ten

Gabon Gabun
Gabonese Republic Gabunische Republik
Gabonese Gabuner(in); gabunisch

gag Knebel; *parl* Debattenschluß

gag *v* knebeln; *pol (Presse etc)* mundtot machen, zum Schweigen bringen

gage *Am* →gauge

gain Gewinn *(opp. loss);* Steigerung, Zunahme; ~**s** *Am* Verdienst *(aus Geschäften); (Börse)* (Kurs-) Gewinn; ~**s from the sale of personal property** *Am (SteuerR)* Gewinne aus der Veräußerung beweglichen Vermögens; ~**s from the sale of realty** (or **realty** ~**s**) *Am (SteuerR)* Gewinne aus der Veräußerung unbeweglichen Vermögens; ~**-sharing** *Am* Gewinnbeteiligung *(der Arbeitnehmer);* →**capital** ~**s (tax)**; **clear** ~ Reingewinn; **net** ~ Reingewinn; **for personal** ~ aus Eigennutz; **with the object of** ~ in gewinnsüchtiger Absicht; **to show a** ~ e-n Gewinn aufweisen

gain *v* gewinnen *(opp. to lose);* erwerben, erlangen; **with the intent to** ~ **advantage** in gewinnsüchtiger Absicht; **to** ~ **sb. over** jdn für seine Sache gewinnen; **to** ~ **ground** Boden gewinnen; sich durchsetzen; **to** ~ **(an) influence over sb.** Einfluß über jdn gewinnen; **to** ~ **one's living** (or **livelihood**) seinen Lebensunterhalt verdienen; **to** ~ **a suit at law** *Am* e-n Prozeß gewinnen; **the pound sterling** ~**ed strongly** das Pfund Sterling zog scharf an; **to** ~ **time** Zeit gewinnen

gainful einträglich, gewinnbringend; ~ **employment** (or **occupation**) Erwerbstätigkeit; **pursuit of a** ~ **activity** Ausübung e-r Erwerbstätigkeit; **to be engaged in a** ~ **occupation** e-e Erwerbstätigkeit ausüben

gainfully employed (or **occupied**) **person** Erwerbstätige(r)

gainings Gewinne; Einkünfte

gala Fest(lichkeit); ~ **performance** Galavorstellung, Festvorstellung

gale *Br* periodische Pachtzahlung; ~**-day** Pachtzahlungstag

gallery Galerie; Tribüne; *(Theater)* oberster Rang; **art** ~ Kunstgalerie; **distinguished strangers'** ~ Diplomatentribüne; **press** ~ Pressetribüne; **public** ~ Publikumstribüne

Gallup poll Gallup-Meinungsumfrage
Erforschung der öffentlichen Meinung nach einem in den USA durch Gallup entwickelten Stichprobenverfahren (in Deutschland vertreten durch die EMNID-Institute)

Gambia, the ~ Gambia; **Republic of the** ~ Republik Gambia
Gambian Gambier(in); gambisch

gamble *v* um Geld spielen; Glücksspiel machen; etw. wagen *(für e-e Gewinnchance); (wagehalsig)* spekulieren; **to** ~ **away a fortune** ein Vermögen verspielen; durch Spielen ein Vermögen verlieren; **to** ~ **on the stock exchange** an der Börse spekulieren
gambling Spielen *(um Geld);* Glücksspiel; *(Börse) (wagehalsiges)* Spekulieren; ~ **casino** (Spiel-)-Kasino; ~ **contract** →wagering contract; ~ **debt** Spielschuld; ~ **in futures** *(Börsentermingeschäft)* Differenzgeschäft; ~ **house** Spielbank; ~ **machine** Spielautomat; ~ **policy** →wagering policy; ~ **on the stock exchange** Börsenspekulation; ~ **winnings** Spielgewinn; **losses incurred in** ~ Spielverluste; *(Börse)* Spekulationsverluste; **he lost all his money** ~ er hat sein ganzes Geld beim (Glücks-)Spiel verloren; **to carry on** ~ Glücksspiel betreiben

gambler (Glücks-)Spieler; (Börsen-)Spekulant

game 1. (Jagd-)Wild; ~**keeper** Wildhüter; Forstaufseher; ~ **law** Jagdgesetz; Jagdrecht; ~ **lessee** Jagdpächter
game licence *Br* Jagdschein; **to take out a** ~ sich e-n Jagdschein beschaffen
game, ~ **preserve** Jagdgehege; Wildpark; ~ **tenant** Jagdpächter; ~ **warden** Jagdaufseher
game, big ~ Großwild; **damage done by** ~ Wildschaden; **to kill** ~ Wild erlegen
game 2. Spiel *(bes. nach festen Regeln);* ~ **at cards** Kartenspiel; ~ **of chance** Glücksspiel
game(s) theory (O. R.) Spieltheorie
Mathematische Methode der Analyisierung von geschäftl. Problemen, z. B. Wettbewerb zwischen zwei Firmen in der Auffassung e-r Spielsituation
game, Olympic G~s Olympische Spiele; **to play a losing** ~ keine Aussichten haben

gaming Spielen *(um Geld);* Glücksspiel; ~ **casino** (Spiel-)Kasino; ~ **debt** Spielschuld; ~ **house** Spielbank; **commercial** ~[1] gewerbliches Glücksspiel; **betting and** ~[2] Wetten und Spiel

gang 1. (Arbeiter-)Kolonne; Trupp, Rotte *(von Arbeitern);* Schicht *(Belegschaft);* ~ **boss** *Am sl.* Vorarbeiter; ~ **leader** Kolonnenführer; ~ **man** Vorarbeiter
gang 2. *(meist kriminelle)* Bande; ~ **of burglars** Einbrecherbande; ~ **of forgers** Fälscherbande; ~ **leader** Bandenführer; Rädelsführer; ~ **robbery** Bandendiebstahl; ~ **of youths** Bande Jugendlicher

gang up *v* sich zusammenrotten (against gegen)

gangster Gangster, Mitglied e-r Verbrecherbande

gangway *(beweglicher)* Laufgang; Gang *(zwischen Sitzreihen); Br parl* Quergang *(im House of Commons);* **members above (below) the** ~ Mitglieder *(des House of Commons),* die mit der offiziellen Politik ihrer Partei einverstanden (nicht einverstanden) sind

gaol *bes. Br* Gefängnis (→*prison*); ~**-bird** *colloq.* alter Sträfling; Gewohnheitsverbrecher

gap Lücke; ~ **in education** Bildungslücke; ~ **between the views of two statesmen** Auseinandergehen der Meinungen von zwei Staatsmännern; ~ **in interest rates** Zinsgefälle *(Unterschied des Zinsniveaus an verschiedenen Orten);* **investment** ~ Investitionslücke; ~ **in the law** Lücke im Gesetz; Gesetzeslücke; **to fill** (or **stop**) **a** ~ e-e Lücke füllen (od. schließen)

garage Garage; Autowerkstatt; Tankstelle *(an der Landstraße); Am* kleiner Börsensaal; **parking** ~ *Am* Park(hoch)haus

garaging Unterbringung in e-r Garage

garbage (Küchen-)Abfälle; *bes. Am* Müll(abfälle); ~ **disposal** (or **collection**) *Am* Müllabfuhr; ~ **dump** *Am* Müllhalde, Schuttabladeplatz

garden Garten; ~ **city** (or **suburb**) Gartenstadt; ~ **party** Gartenfest; ~ **plot** Gartengrundstück; **to lay out a** ~ e-n Garten anlegen

garnish *v (dem Drittschuldner)* ein Zahlungsverbot zustellen; *(Forderung beim Drittschuldner)* pfänden; **to** ~ **an account** ein Konto pfänden

garnishee Drittschuldner *(Schuldner des Pfändungsschuldners bei Forderungspfändungen);* ~ **order** (Forderungs-)Pfändungsbeschluß; Zahlungsverbot an den Drittschuldner; **to serve a** ~ **order (on)** *Br (dem Drittschuldner)* ein Zahlungsverbot zustellen; ~ **proceedings** Verfahren für Forderungspfändungen; **to institute** ~ **proceedings** e-e Forderung beim Drittschuldner pfänden lassen

garnishee *v*, **to** ~ **wages** *Am* Lohn pfänden

garnisher *Am* (Pfändungs-)Pfandgläubiger; Partei, die e-e Forderungspfändung bewirkt hat

garnishment *bes. Am* Pfändung e-r (Geld-)-Forderung, Forderungspfändung; Verbot *(an Drittschuldner),* dem Schuldner Zahlung zu leisten; *Br* (jede Art von) Nachricht an den Prozeßgegner; ~ **order** *Am* Zahlungsverbot an den Drittschuldner; ~ **proceedings** *Am* Forderungspfändungsverfahren; ~ **of wages** *Am* Lohnpfändung; **pre-judgment** ~ *Am* vorsorglicher Arrest in Lohnforderungen; **to cause a** ~ **to be levied on the garnishee** (or **to institute** ~ **proceedings**) *Am* e-e Forderung beim Drittschuldner pfänden lassen

garnishor *Br* →garnisher

garrison *mil* Garnison, Standort; ~ **town** Garnisonstadt

gar(r)otting Hinrichtung durch Erdrosselung; Erdrosselung, um ein Verbrechen begehen zu können

Garter, Order of the ~ *Br* Hosenbandorden

gas Gas; *Am* Benzin (→*gasoline*); ~ **bill** Gasrechnung; ~ **consumption** Gasverbrauch; **G~-Cooled Reactors** (GCR) gasgekühlte Reaktoren; **~-Cooled Fast Breeder Reactor** (GCFBR) gasgekühlter Schneller Brutreaktor; ~ **deposits** Erdgasvorkommen; ~ **engineering** Gastechnik; ~ **grid** (Fern-)Gasnetz; ~ **grid system** Gasversorgungsnetz; ~ **law** Gasgesetz; ~ **main** (Haupt-)Gasleitung; ~ **pipeline** Gasleitung; ~ **poisoning** Gasvergiftung; ~ **resources** Erdgasvorkommen; ~ **station** *Am* Tankstelle; **~, electricity and water supply** Gas-, Elektrizitäts- und Wasserversorgung; ~ **supply industry** Gaswirtschaft; ~ **warfare** Gaskrieg; ~ **works** Gaswerk

gas, natural ~ Erdgas; **natural** ~ **field** Erdgasvorkommen; **natural** ~ **pipelines** Erdgasleitungen; **North Sea** ~ Erdgas der Nordsee

gasateria *Am* Selbstbedienungstankstelle

gasoline *Am* Benzin; Treibstoff; ~ **consumption** *Am* Benzinverbrauch; ~ **price** *Am* Benzinpreis; ~ **station** *Am* Tankstelle; ~ **tax** *Am* Benzin-, Kraftstoffsteuer; **lack** (or **shortage**) **of** ~ *Am* Benzinmangel; **leaded** ~ *Am* bleihaltiges (od. verbleites) Benzin; **lead-free** (or **unleaded**) ~ *Am* bleifreies (od. unverbleites) Benzin

gate Tor, Pforte; Sperre; *Am (Sport)* Besucherzahl; ~ **receipts** (at a sporting event) *Am* Geldeinnahme; ~ **way** *(KartellR)* Rechtfertigungsgrund; **to give sb. the** ~ *Am sl.* jdn entlassen

gather *v* (sich) versammeln; sammeln; **to** ~ (from) folgern, schließen, entnehmen (aus); **to** ~ **information** Erkundigungen einziehen, Auskünfte einholen (upon über)

gathering Versammlung; (Menschen-)Ansammlung; **at a public** ~ auf e-r öffentlichen Versammlung; **political** ~ politische Versammlung; **to attend a** ~ an e-r Versammlung teilnehmen; **to hold a** ~ e-e Versammlung abhalten

GATT (General Agreement on Tariffs and Trade) Allgemeines Zoll- und Handelsabkommen
Das Allgemeine Abkommen trat 1948 in Kraft. *Sitz* (des ständigen Sekretariats): Genf. *Mitglieder: (etwa)* 90 Staaten.
Aufgabe: Abbau der Handelsbeschränkungen zwischen den Mitgliedern durch gegenseitige Herabsetzung der Zölle und Beseitigung mengenmäßiger Beschränkung der Ein- und Ausfuhr. Prüfung und Beilegung von Handelsstreitigkeiten zwischen den Unterzeichnerstaaten. Schaffung eines GATT-Handelskodex, der den Entwicklungsländern zu höheren Exportquoten verhelfen soll

gauge Eichmaß; *(Eisenbahn)* Spurweite; Meßwerkzeug, -gerät; Pegel; *fig* Maßstab; **standard** ~ Normalspur; Normalmaß; **water** ~ Wasserstandsanzeiger

gauge *v* eichen; (aus)messen
gauged in terms of *fig* gemessen an

gauger Eichmeister; **~'s certificate** Eichschein; **~'s fee** Eichgebühr

gavel Hammer *(des Versammlungsleiters od. Auktionators, Am auch des Richters)*

gazette Zeitung; *Br* Amtsblatt, Staatsanzeiger *(in dem Rechtsverordnungen, Ernennungen, Beförderungen, Konkursverfahren etc veröffentlicht werden; London G~, Edinburgh G~, Belfast G~);* **Federal G~** *Ger* Bundesanzeiger; **official** ~ Amtsblatt; **to advertise a notice in the** ~ e-e Nachricht in der G~ veröffentlichen

gazette *v Br (Beförderung etc)* im Amtsblatt bekanntgegeben; **he has been ~d major** *Br* seine Beförderung zum Major ist im Staatsanzeiger veröffentlicht

gazump *v Br* in der Zeit zwischen der unverbindlichen Einigung über den Kaufpreis und dem Abschluß des Kaufvertrages *(bes. betreffend Grundbesitz)* den Kaufpreis erhöhen

gazumper *Br* Verkäufer, der zwischen der unverbindlichen Einigung über den Kaufpreis und dem Abschluß des Kaufvertrages den Kaufpreis erhöht

GDP (gross domestic product), **per capita** ~ Bruttoinlandsprodukt pro Kopf der Bevölkerung

gear *v* ineinandergreifen; **to** ~ **to** abstellen auf; **industry is ~ed to consumer needs** die Industrie paßt sich dem Bedarf der Verbraucher an
gearing Hebelwirkung; *Br* Verhältnis zwischen Eigenkapital *(equity)* und Obligationen und Vorzugsaktien; **high** ~ Fremdkapitalerhöhung (der Hauptteil des Gesellschaftskapitals besteht aus Fremdkapital und Vorzugsaktien); **low** ~ Herabsetzung des Fremdkapitalanteils (die vorrangigen Belastungen des Unternehmens [→*prior charges*] sind niedrig)

genealogic(al) genealogisch; ~ **research** Ahnenforschung; ~ **tree** Stammbaum

genealogy Genealogie, Ahnenforschung

general allgemein; generell; General-; *mil* General; ~ **acceptance** →acceptance 2.; ~ **account** Hauptkonto; **G~ Account of the IMF** Generalkonto des IWF; **G~ Accounting Office** (G. A. O.) *Am* Rechnungshof; ~ **agency** →agency 1. und 2.; ~ **agent** →agent

General Agreement on Tariffs and Trade →GATT

general, ~ **appearance** *(Zivilprozeß)* vorbehaltlose Einlassung; **G~ Arrangements to Borrow** (GAB) *(IMF)* Allgemeine Kreditvereinbarungen (AKV); ~ **assembly (G~ Assembly)** →assembly; ~ **audit** Buchprüfung; ~ **average (act, bond, statement)** →average 1.; **to the** ~ **benefit** zum allgemeinen Nutzen (od. Wohl); ~ **bill of lading** Sammelkonnossement; *Am (auch)* Sammelfrachtbrief; ~ **business** *(auf Tagesordnung)* Verschiedenes

general cargo Stückgut(ladung), Stückgüter; ~ **rates** (GCR) Frachtraten für Stückgut; ~ **ship** *(normales)* Frachtschiff; ~ **shipping** Stückgutversand

General Certificate of Secondary Education (GCSE) *Br* Prüfungsbescheinigung für Abschluß in der Mittelstufe (seit 1988) *(s. A-→level)*

general, ~ **choice of law rule** *(IPR)* allgemeine Kollisionsnorm; ~ **clause** Generalklausel; **G~ Commissioners of Income Tax** *Br* Laienrichter in Steuersachen *(die über Einspruch gegen Veranlagungsbescheid entscheiden)*; ~ **cost** Gemeinkosten; **G~ Council of the Bar** Organ der Standesvertretung der barristers *(→Bar Council)*; ~ **court** *Am* →court 2.; ~ **creditor** nicht bevorrechtigter (Konkurs-)Gläubiger; ~ **crossing** →crossing 1.; ~ **damage** →damage 1.; ~ **delivery** *Am* postlagernd; ~ **denial** Bestreiten des gesamten Klagevorbringens; ~ **deposit** Sammeldepot; Sammelverwahrung; ~ **education** Allgemeinbildung; ~ **election** allgemeine Wahlen; Parlamentswahlen; ~ **endorsement** Blankoindossament; ~ **expenses** Gemeinkosten; allgemeine Kosten; ~ **goods** Stückgut; ~ **guarantee** unbeschränkte Garantie; **G~ Headquarters** (G. H. Q.) *mil* Großes Hauptquartier; ~ **issue** →issue 1.; **court of** ~ **jurisdiction** Gericht allgemeiner Zuständigkeit; ~ **knowledge** Allgemeinbildung; ~ **ledger** Hauptbuch; ~→**legacy**; ~ →**licence (~se)**; ~ **lien** allgemeines Pfandrecht *(→lien)*; ~- **line jobber** *Am* Großhändler mit breitem Sortiment; ~ **listing** *Am* Beauftragung mehrerer Makler zur gleichen Zeit *(→listing 4.)*; ~ **management trust** *Am* → flexible trust; ~ **manager** leitender Angestellter, leitender Direktor, Hauptgeschäftsführer; *Am* Generaldirektor; **G~ Medical Council** *Br* Ärztekammer; ~ **meeting** Mitgliederversammlung *(e-s Vereins)*; Hauptversammlung *(e-r AG)*; ~ **mortgage** Gesamthypothek; Pfandrecht am gesamten Vermögen

general pardon Amnestie; **to issue a** ~ e-e Amnestie erlassen

general, ~ **partner** unbeschränkt *(persönlich)* haftender Gesellschafter, Komplementär; ~ →**partnership;** ~ **policy** Generalpolice, offene Police; ~ **policy conditions** allgemeine Versicherungsbedingungen

general power (of appointment) Bestimmungsbefugnis; Recht zur Bestimmung e-s oder mehrerer (beliebigen) Berechtigten oder Nacherben *(opp. special power)*

general power (of attorney) Generalvollmacht *(opp. special power)*

general, ~ **practice** übliches Verfahren; allgemeine Praxis *(opp. specialized practice)*; **G~ Practice Act** *Am* Zivilprozeßordnung (ZPO); ~ **practitioner** (G. P.) praktischer Arzt; Allgemeinmediziner *(opp. specialist)*; ~ **property tax** *Am* Vermögensteuer *(oft nur vom Grundbesitz erhoben)*; ~ **public** breite Öffentlichkeit; ~ **purpose** Mehrzweck; ~ **purpose computer** Computer für allgemeine Zwecke; ~ **receipt** Gesamtquittung; ~ **rule** allgemeine Regel, Norm, Grundregel; **as a** ~ **rule** in der Regel, meistens; ~ **sales agency** Generalvertriebsagentur; ~ **sales representative** *Am* Vertreter für Produkte mehrerer Firmen; ~ **situation** Gesamtlage; ~ **staff** *mil* Generalstab; ~ **strike** Generalstreik; ~ **terms and conditions** allgemeine Geschäftsbedingungen

generally im allgemeinen, allgemein; ~ **accepted accounting principles** (GAAP) Grundsätze ordnungsmäßiger Buchführung; **generally accepted auditing standards** (GAAS) *Am* allgemein anerkannte Prüfungsgrundsätze; ~ **accepted principles** allgemein anerkannte Grundsätze; ~ **accepted principles of international law** allgemein anerkannte Völkerrechtsgrundsätze; ~ **binding** allgemein verbindlich; ~ **speaking** allgemein gesprochen; ~ **and specially** im allgemeinen und besonderen; **it is** ~ **agreed** es ist die herrschende Meinung

generality Allgemeingültigkeit; **the** ~ **(of)** die Mehrzahl; der größte Teil

generalization Verallgemeinerung

generalize *v* verallgemeinern; der Allgemeinheit zugänglich machen; **G~d System of Preferences** (GSP) *Am* System der Vorzugszölle *(bestimmte Erzeugnisse aus bestimmten Entwicklungsländern können zollfrei eingeführt werden)*

generation 1. Generation

generation skipping, G~ S~ Tax *Am* Ersatzsteuer *(wenn z. B. ein Trust Begünstigte aus 2 verschiedenen Generationen hat, die beide der*

Generation des Gründers nachgeordnet sind); ~ **transfers** *Am* (Einführung e-r Steuerpflicht für) Generationen überspringende Vermögensübertragungen

generation 2. Erzeugung; ~ **of electricity** Stromerzeugung; ~ **of energy** Erzeugung von Energie

generic, ~ **claim** *(PatR)* mehrere Gattungen umfassender Anspruch; ~ **name** *Am (WarenzeichenR)* Gattungsbezeichnung; ~ **term** *Am (WarenzeichenR)* Gattungsbezeichnung; freier Warenname

genetic, ~ **engineering** (or **technology**) Gentechnologie; ~ **heritage** Erbanlagen

Geneva Conferences on the Law of the Sea Genfer Seerechtskonferenzen

Geneva Convention(s) Genfer Konvention(en) (od. [Rotkreuz-]Abkommen [von 1949]); 1. ~ **for the Amelioration of the Condition of the Wounded and Sick in Armed Forces in the Field** ~ zur Verbesserung des Loses der Verwundeten und Kranken der Streitkräfte im Felde; 2. ~ **for the Amelioration of the Condition of Wounded, Sick and Shipwrecked Members of Armed Forces at Sea** ~ zur Verbesserung des Loses der Verwundeten, Kranken und Schiffbrüchigen der Streitkräfte zur See; 3. ~ **relative to the Treatment of Prisoners of War** ~ hinsichtlich der Behandlung der Kriegsgefangenen; 4. ~ **relative to the Protection of Civilian Persons in Time of War** ~ zum Schutze von Zivilpersonen in Kriegszeiten (Zivilkonvention ZK)

Geneva Convention on the Execution of Foreign Arbitral Awards Genfer Abkommen zur Vollstreckung ausländischer Schiedssprüche *(von 1927)*

Geneva Protocol on Arbitration Clauses Genfer Protokoll über die Schiedsklauseln *(von 1924)*

genitor Erzeuger

genocide Genozid, Völkermord; **Convention on the Prevention and Punishment of the Crime of G~**[3] Konvention über die Verhütung und Bestrafung des Völkermordes

gentlemen's agreement Gentlemen's agreement *(auf gegenseitigem Vertrauen beruhende, nicht rechtsverbindliche Vereinbarung); (KartellR)* lose Absprache

gentry *Br* niedriger Adel *(baronets and knights);* gesamte Oberschicht *(außer Hochadel);* **landed** ~ Landadel; **nobility and** ~ hoher und niederer Adel

genuine echt, unverfälscht; ~ **link** *(VölkerR)*[4] echte Verbindung *(zwischen Schiff und Flaggenstaat);* ~ **coin** echte Münze; ~ **signature** echte Unterschrift

genuineness Echtheit; ~ **of a document** Echtheit e-r Urkunde; **warranty of** ~ vertragliche Zusicherung der Echtheit

geo-economic raumwirtschaftlich

geopolitical geopolitisch

geopolitics Geopolitik

germ warfare Kriegsführung mit Bakterien

german, cousin ~ Vetter (od. Cousine) ersten Grades

German deutsch; ~ **Democratic Republic** (GDR) Deutsche Demokratische Republik (DDR); ~ **Federal Republic** →Federal Republic of Germany; ~ **living abroad** Auslandsdeutscher; ~ **mark** Deutsche Mark (DM); ~ **national** deutscher Staatsangehöriger

German Options and Financial Future Exchange (Goffex) Deutsche Terminbörse (DTB)

Bundesweit operierende Computerbörse. Die DTB ist e-e vollelektronische Börse. Aufträge und Angebote der Börsenteilnehmer werden automatisch zusammengeführt und die Abschlüsse an e-e Clearing-Stelle weitergeleitet

German, intra ~ innerdeutsch

germane passend, gehörig (to zu); im Zusammenhang stehend (to mit); **a question** ~ **to the issue** zur Sache gehörige Frage; **to be not** ~ nicht zur Sache gehören

Germanophil Deutschenfreund; deutschfreundlich

Germanophobe Deutschenhasser; deutschfeindlich

Germany Deutschland; **Federal Republic of** ~ (FRG) Bundesrepublik Deutschland (West Germany) *(cf. German Democratic Republic)*; **reunification of** ~ Wiedervereinigung Deutschlands

gerrymander willkürliche Einteilung der Wahlkreise *(bes. zur Sicherung e-r Mehrheit);* Manipulierung

gerrymander *v* Wahlbezirke willkürlich einteilen; *(zur Erlangung e-s unlauteren Vorteils)* manipulieren

gerrymandering willkürliche Wahlkreisänderung; Manipulation von Wahlbezirksgrenzen

gestation Schwangerschaft; **period of** ~ Dauer der Schwangerschaft

get(-)up Ausstattung; Aufmachung; *Am* Unternehmungsgeist, Initiative; ~ **of a trademark** Ausstattung e-s Warenzeichens

get *v* bekommen, erhalten; verdienen, erwerben; *(Waren)* beziehen; (sich) beschaffen; veranlassen, bewegen; **to** ~ **an advance (of money)** e-n Vorschuß bekommen; **to** ~ **into arrears** in Rückstand kommen; **to** ~ **a bill passed** (or through) e-e Gesetzesvorlage durchbringen; **to ~ down to business** zur Sache kommen; **to ~ into debt** in Schulden geraten; **to ~ drunk** sich betrinken; **to ~ an extension of time** e-e Frist verlängert bekommen; **to ~ to know** erfahren; kennenlernen; **to ~ knowledge (of)** erfahren; **to ~ one's living** seinen Lebensunterhalt erwerben; **to ~ married** (sich ver)heiraten; **to ~ money** sich Geld beschaffen; **to ~ one's money's worth** *colloq.* vollen Wert für sein Geld bekommen; **to ~ an opportunity** e-e Gelegenheit bekommen; **to ~ orders** Aufträge erhalten; **to ~ rich** reich werden; **to ~ a situation for sb.** jdm e-e Stellung verschaffen; **to ~ one's way** sich durchsetzen; **he got two years (months)** er hat zwei Jahre (Monate) (Gefängnis) bekommen

get *v,* **to ~ about** umlaufen, bekannt werden *(Nachrichten);* **to ~ ahead of sb.** jdn überholen, übertreffen; **to ~ at a witness** *colloq.* e-n Zeugen bestechen; **the prisoner got away** der Gefangene entkam; **the ~ away car** das von Verbrechern benutzte Fluchtfahrzeug; **to ~ back** zurückbekommen; zurückkommen *(z. B. politische Partei nach Wahl);* **to ~ down to brass tacks** *colloq.* zur Sache kommen; **to ~ in** *(Zug)* ankommen, einlaufen; einsteigen; *parl* gewählt werden (for in); *(Ernte)* einbringen; **to ~ in orders** Aufträge hereinholen; **to ~ off** *colloq. (Brief, Paket)* absenden; *Am (Waren)* loswerden, absetzen; *(vor Strafe)* retten; davonkommen (with mit); **he got off with a fine** er kam mit e-r Geldstrafe davon; **to ~ on** vorwärts kommen, Fortschritte machen; **to ~ on to sb.** *colloq.* mit jdm Verbindung aufnehmen; **to ~ on with the work** die Arbeit fortführen; **to ~ out** aussteigen; herauskommen; *(Geheimnis)* herausbekommen; **to ~ out of business** *colloq.* sein Geschäft aufgeben; **to ~ out of doing sth.** umgehen, etw. zu tun; **to ~ through** *(im Examen)* durchkommen; *tel* durchkommen, Verbindung bekommen; **to ~ sb. through an examination** jdn im Examen durchbringen; **to ~ a Bill through Parliament** e-n Gesetzesentwurf im Parlament durchbringen; **to ~ to work** zur Arbeit kommen; mit der Arbeit beginnen; **to ~ to the point** zum wesentlichen Punkt kommen; **to ~ sth. under control** etw. unter Kontrolle bekommen

Ghana Ghana; **Republic of ~** Republik Ghana
Ghanaian Ghanaer(in); ghanaisch

giant riesig, sehr groß; **~ corporation** *Am* Mammutgesellschaft; **~ combine** Riesenkonzern; **~ retailing** Großbetriebsform des Einzelhandels; **~ tanker** Großtanker

gift Schenkung, *(unentgeltliche)* Zuwendung *(cf. donor, donee);* Geschenk; Begabung, Talent; *com* Zugabe; **~ and inheritance tax** *Am* Schenkung- und Erbschaftsteuer; **~ (by will)** letztwillige Schenkung, Vermächtnis *(bequest or devise);* **~ inter vivos** Schenkung unter Lebenden; **~ mortis causa** Schenkung in Erwartung des Todes; **~ giving** *Am* Zugabewesen; **~ parcel** Geschenkpaket; **~ tax** *Am* Schenkungsteuer; **~ tokens** *Br (zu Geschenkzwecken von der Postsparkasse ausgestellte)* Guthabenanerkenntnisse; **by way of ~** schenkungsweise, im Wege der Schenkung; **class ~s** Zuwendungen an e-e Gruppe von Personen; **free ~** Zugabe; **onerous ~** Schenkung unter Auflage *(die die Schenkung lästig oder wertlos macht);* **deed of ~** Schenkungsbrief, Schenkungsurkunde; **residuary ~** Vermächtnis des Vermögensrestes; Restvermächtnis; **substitutional ~** Ersatzvermächtnis; **to make a ~ of sth. to sb.** jdm etw. schenken (od. vermachen); **~s to charitable institutions may be restricted by mortmain statutes** *Am* Geschenke an wohltätigen Zwekken dienende Einrichtungen können begrenzt werden durch die →mortmain statutes; **to revoke a ~** e-e Schenkung widerrufen

gilt-edged goldgerändert; **~ market** *Br* Markt mit Staatspapieren; **~ market makers** (GEMMS) *Br* Wertpapierhändler für Staatspapiere; **~ securities** (or **stocks**) *Br* mündelsichere Staatspapiere

gilts →gilt-edged securities

Ginnie Mae *Am* Börsenausdruck für Government National Mortgage Association
Ein Unternehmen des öffentlichen Rechts (corporate instrument of the U. S.), das von der Bundesregierung garantierte Wertpapiere emittiert, die auf ein Pool von qualifizierten Hypotheken von Sparkassen gestützt sind *(cf. Fannie Mae und Freddie Mac)*

giro account Girokonto; *Br* Postgirokonto; **~ holder** *Br* Postgiroteilnehmer; **balance on ~** *Br* Postgiroguthaben

Giro, ~ Agreement Postgiroabkommen; **g~ cheque transfer** *Br* Postgiroüberweisung; **~ service** *Br* Postgirodienst, Postgiroverkehr; **~ standing order** *Br* Postgirodauerauftrag; **~ transfer** Giroüberweisung

Giro, →National ~; postal g~ Postgiro

gist Hauptpunkt, Kern; wesentlicher Inhalt

give and take gegenseitiges Entgegenkommen; Kompromiß(bereitschaft)

give *v* geben; überlassen; **to ~ account of** Rechenschaft ablegen über, berichten über; **to ~ and bequeath** *(jdm etw.)* vermachen, hinterlassen; **to ~ bail** Kaution stellen; Sicherheit leisten; **to ~ birth to a child** ein Kind zur Welt bringen; **to ~ credit** Kredit gewähren; **to ~ credit to a report** e-m Bericht Glauben schenken; **to ~ a decision on a case** e-e Sache entscheiden; **to ~ effect (to)** in Kraft treten lassen; **to ~ evidence of sth.** über etw. als Zeuge aussagen; **to ~ for the call** *Br (Börse)* Vorprämie kaufen; **to ~ for the put** *Br (Börse)* Rückprämie verkaufen; **to ~ grace** e-e Nachfrist gewähren; **to ~ information** Auskunft geben (od. erteilen) (about über); **to ~ judgment** ein Urteil abgeben (od. fällen); **to ~ a lecture** e-e Vorlesung (od. e-n Vortrag) halten (on über); **to ~ notice** Kenntnis geben (of von); benachrichtigen; kündigen; **to ~ offen|ce (~se)** Anstoß erregen; beleidigen; **to ~ in payment** in Zahlung geben; **to ~ an order** (for goods) e-n Auftrag erteilen (od. vergeben); bestellen; **to ~ prizes** Preise verteilen; **to ~ a reason** e-n Grund angeben; **to ~ a receipt** e-e Quittung geben (od. aushändigen); **to ~ rise to** Anlaß geben zu; bewirken; **to ~ on stock** *Br (Börse)* in Report geben, hineingeben; **to ~ time** stunden; **to ~ way** nachgeben; *Br* Vorfahrt gewähren; **to ~ way to sb.** jdm den Vorrang lassen

give *v*, **to ~ away** weggeben, verschenken; **to ~ away prizes** Preise verteilen; **to ~ sth. back to sb.** jdm etw. zurückgeben; **to ~ sth. in** etw. einreichen; **to ~ in one's name** sich eintragen lassen; **to ~ sb. into the custody of the police** jdn der Polizei übergeben; jdn verhaften lassen; **to ~ on to** hinausgehen auf *(Fenster)*; **to ~ out** ausgeben, verteilen; zu Ende gehen; **to ~ out by contract** →contract 2.; **to ~ sb. out to be** jdn ausgeben als; **to ~ over** übergeben, überlassen; **to ~ sb. over to the police** jdn der Polizei übergeben; **to ~ up** aufgeben; **to ~ up business** sein Geschäft aufgeben; **to ~ up a newspaper** e-e Zeitung abbestellen; **to ~ the thief up to the police** den Dieb der Polizei übergeben

given *(auf Dokumenten)* gegeben, ausgefertigt; bestimmt, festgesetzt; **~ under my hand** von mir unterschrieben; **under the ~ conditions** unter den gegebenen Bedingungen; **~ name** Vorname; **at a ~ price** zum festgesetzten Preis; **~ sum** bestimmte Summe; **within a ~ time** innerhalb e-r bestimmten Zeit, fristgemäß

giving up one's business Geschäftsaufgabe

giver Geber; Schenker; *Br (Börse)* Reportgeber, Hereingeber *(opp. taker)*; **~ for a call** *Br (Börse)* Käufer e-r Vorprämie; **~ of an option** *Br (Börse)* Prämienkäufer, Optionsgeber; **~ for a put** *Br (Börse)* Verkäufer e-r Rückprämie

glamo(u)r shares im Augenblick hoch im Kurs stehende Aktien

glass, with care Vorsicht, Glas!

Glass-Steagall Act of 1933 *Am* Vorschrift über das Trennbankensystem in den USA
Seitdem ist commercial →banking den commercial →banks und den →thrift institutions vorbehalten. Das →investment banking ist auf investment →banks und brokers und dealers beschränkt

global global, umfassend, Gesamt-; weltumfassend, Welt-; **~ design** Gesamtkonzept; **~ economy** Weltwirtschaft; **~ information** weltweite Information; **~ insurance** Pauschalversicherung; **~ loan** Globaldarlehen; **~ note** Schuldverschreibung, die es dem Finanzmittel suchenden Unternehmen ermöglicht, Geld sowohl an den Euro- als auch an den US-Märkten aufzunehmen; **~ quota** Globalkontingent; **~ responsibility** Verantwortlichkeit der Welt gegenüber; **~ satellite system** weltweites Satellitensystem

globalization Globalisierung

glossary Glossar; Wörterverzeichnis *(mit Erklärungen)*

glut Überfüllung, Überangebot (of sth. an etw.); Schwemme; **~ in the market** Überangebot auf dem Markt; Marktschwemme; **~ in the money market** Schwemme am Geldmarkt

glut *v*, **to ~ the market** den Markt überschwemmen

go, to have a ~ at sth. *colloq.* etw. versuchen

go-ahead *fig* freie Bahn ("green light"); unternehmend; fortschrittlich; **~ spirit** Unternehmungsgeist

go-between Vermittler; **to act as a ~** vermitteln

go-go fund →fund 2.

go-go shares Wuchsaktien mit stark spekulativem Charakter

go-slow *Br* planmäßiges Langsamarbeiten, Bummelstreik

go *v* gehen, reisen, fahren; verkauft (od. abgesetzt) werden; **to ~ abroad** ins Ausland gehen (od. fahren); **to ~ all out for** sich mit allen Mitteln einsetzen für; **to ~ bail for sb.** *colloq.* →to stand bail for sb.; **to ~ better** sich verbessern *(opp. to ~ worse)*; **to ~ a bear (a bull)** *Br (Börse)* auf Baisse (Hausse) spekulieren; **to ~ cheap** *sl.* billig verkauft werden; **to ~ free** straffrei ausgehen; **to ~ further into a question** tiefer in e-e Frage eindringen; **to ~ halves** (or **shares**) **in sth. with sb.** sich mit jdm in die Hälfte teilen; **to ~ sick** *mil* sich krank melden; **to ~ slow** *Br* in Bummelstreik treten; **to ~ surety for sb.** für jdn bürgen (od. Sicherheit leisten); **to ~ unpunished** straffrei ausgehen; **to ~ worse** sich verschlechtern *(Geschäft, Wirtschaftslage; opp. to ~ better)*

go *v*, **to ~ about** gehen an, sich befassen mit; um(her)gehen *(Gerüchte)*; **to ~ about one's business** seine eigenen Angelegenheiten verrichten; seinen Geschäften nachgehen; **the case went against him** es wurde *(vom Gericht)* gegen ihn entschieden; **to ~ ahead** Fortschritte machen; *(erfolgreich)* vorankommen; **to ~ beyond one's instructions** über seine Weisungen hinausgehen; **to ~ down** *(Preise, Kurse)* fallen, sinken; *(Schiff)* sinken, untergehen; **to**

~ **for** gehalten werden für, gelten als; **to ~ for a fall** *(Börse)* auf Baisse spekulieren; **to ~ in for law** Jura studieren; **to ~ into** untersuchen; *(in ein Unternehmen)* einsteigen; **to ~ into details** ins einzelne gehen; **to ~ into Parliament** *Br* Abgeordneter werden; **to ~ into partnership with** sich assoziieren mit; **to ~ off quickly** *sl.* guten Absatz finden, gut gehen, leicht verkäuflich sein; *(von Nahrungsmitteln)* schnell schlecht werden; **to ~ off rapidly (readily)** *sl.* reißenden (schnellen) Absatz finden; **to ~ off slowly** *sl.* schlechten Absatz finden; schlecht gehen; schwer verkäuflich sein; **to ~ out (of office)** *pol* zurücktreten; **to ~ out to** auswandern nach; **to ~ over** durchgehen, durchsehen; **to ~ over to** übergehen (od. übertreten) zu; **to ~ over an account** e-e Rechnung nachprüfen; **to ~ over to sb.** an jdn gehen (od. fallen); jdm zufallen *(z.B. Erbschaft)*; **to ~ over to the Conservatives** *Br* zu den Konservativen übergehen; die Konservativen wählen; **to ~ through** durchgehen, durchsehen; *parl* durchgehen, angenommen werden; **to ~ through with sth.** etw. zu Ende führen; **to ~ through one's correspondence** die eingegangene Post durchsehen; **to ~ to sb.** an jdn gehen (od. fallen); jdm zufallen *(z.B. Erbschaft)*; **to ~ to the country** *Br* das Parlament auflösen und Neuwahlen ausschreiben; **to ~ to court** (or **law**) vor Gericht gehen; **to ~ to expense** sich in Unkosten stürzen; **to ~ under** (or **by**) **the name of...** unter dem Namen ... gehen (od. bekannt sein); den Namen ... führen; **to ~ up** steigen, anziehen *(Preise, Kurse)*; *Br* Universität beziehen; **to have nothing to ~ upon** keine Unterlagen haben

going im Gange; funktionierend; gängig; ~ **concern** Unternehmen in vollem Betriebe; laufender Betrieb; arbeitendes *(nicht stillgelegtes)* Unternehmen; ~ **concern principle** Unternehmensfortführungsprinzip; **value of a ~ concern** Unternehmenswert; Gesamtwert e-s Unternehmens; **to sell an enterprise as a ~ concern** ein Unternehmen als ganzes verkaufen

going, ~, gone *(bei Versteigerungen)* zum ersten, zum zweiten, zum dritten!; ~ **market price** gängiger Marktpreis; **~-out-of-business sale** *Am* Totalausverkauf

goal Zweck, Ziel; Teilziel *(e-s Unternehmens)*; **to pursue a ~** ein Ziel verfolgen

God, Act of ~ höhere Gewalt *(durch Naturereignisse; cf. force majeure)*

god, ~child (~daughter, ~son) Patenkind; **~father (~parent)** Pate; Patenonkel; **~mother** Patin, Patentante

gold Gold; ~ **bar** Goldbarren; ~ **bonds** Goldobligationen; ~ **bullion** Gold in Barren; ~ **bullion standard** Goldkernwährung; ~ **buying price** Goldankaufspreis; ~ **certificate** *Am (gegen das eingelieferte Gold ausgegebenes)* Goldzertifikat; ~ **clause** Goldklausel; ~ **coin** Goldmünze, Goldstück; ~ **coin and bullion** Münz- und Barrengold; Goldbestand; ~ **coin standard** Goldmünzwährung; ~ **content** Goldgehalt *(e-r Münze)*; ~ **cover** Golddeckung; ~ **currency** Goldwährung; Goldumlauf; ~ **dealer** Goldhändler; ~ **embargo** Goldembargo, Goldausfuhrverbot; ~ **equities** Goldaktien; ~ **exchange standard** Golddevisenwährung; ~ **exporting point** Goldausfuhrpunkt, oberer Goldpunkt; ~ **fixing** Goldfixing, Festsetzung des Goldpreises; ~ **hoarding** Goldhortung; ~ **holdings** Goldbestand; ~ **importing point** Goldeinfuhrpunkt, unterer Goldpunkt; ~ **inflow** Goldzufluß; ~ **loan** Goldanleihe; ~ **mine** Goldgrube, Goldbergwerk; ~ **outflow** Goldabfluß; ~ **parity** Goldparität

gold point Goldpunkt; **export** (or **outgoing**) ~ Goldexportpunkt, oberer Goldpunkt; **import** (or **incoming**) ~ Goldimportpunkt, unterer Goldpunkt; **to reach the ~** den Goldpunkt erreichen

gold, ~ pool Goldpool; ~ **premium** Goldagio; ~ **price** Goldpreis; ~ **rate** Goldkurs; ~ **reserve** Goldbestand, Goldreserve; ~ **settlement fund** *Am* Goldausgleichsfonds *(der 12 →Federal Reserve Banks)*; ~ **shares** *Br* Aktien von Goldbergwerken; ~ **specie** gemünztes Gold; ~ **specie standard** Goldumlaufswährung

gold standard Goldwährung, Goldstandard; **to depart from the ~** den Goldstandard aufgeben

gold, ~ stock Goldbestand, Goldvorräte; ~ **tranche rights** *(IMF)* Goldtranchen-Ziehungsrechte *(IMF)*

gold value Goldwert; ~ **clause** Goldwertklausel

gold, alloy of ~ Goldlegierung; **bar ~** Barrengold; **coined ~** gemünztes Gold; **drain** (or **efflux**) **of ~** Goldabfluß; **fine ~** Feingold; **fineness of ~** Goldgehalt; **influx of ~** Goldzufluß; **ingot ~** Barrengold; **ingot of ~** Goldbarren; **movement of ~** Goldbewegung; **outflow of ~** Goldabfluß; **percentage of ~** Goldgehalt

golden, ~ handcuffs Bindung e-r Führungskraft an e-e Gesellschaft durch Zusage von Vergünstigungen, die von ihrem Verbleiben bei der Gesellschaft für e-e bestimmte Zeit abhängen; ~ **handshake** hohe Abfindung bei Entlassung; ~ **parachute** großzügiges Abfindungsversprechen an Vorstandsmitglieder, falls sie bei (Unternehmens-)Übernahme ausscheiden; ~ **share** *Br* von der Regierung zurückbehaltener Anteil an e-m privatisierten Unternehmen, um e-n Einfluß *(durch Veto etc)* auf die künftige Entwicklung des Unternehmens zu behalten

gondola car offener Güterwagen

good gut; (rechts)gültig; kreditfähig, zahlungsfähig; *(mit Unterschrift e-s Bankiers quer über den Scheck geschrieben)* Bestätigung *(e-s Schecks)*; **on ~ authority** aus guter Quelle; **~ behavio(u)r** gute Führung, gutes Benehmen; **during ~ behavio(u)r** bei guter Führung; *(entspricht etwa)* auf Lebenszeit; **~ cause** wichtiger (od. triftiger) Grund (→*cause*); **~ conduct** →conduct 1.; **~ debt** sichere Forderung *(opp. bad debt)*; **~ defen|ce (~se)** →defence 1.; **~ delivery** (G. D.) *(Börse)* gut lieferbar; **(in) ~ →faith**

good for *(auf Wechsel)* über den Betrag von; **to be ~ an amount** gut sein für e-e Summe

good, ~ in law rechtlich begründet; **~ merchantable quality** handelsübliche Qualität; **~ neighbo(u)r policy** (VölkerR) Politik der guten Nachbarschaft; **~ neighbo(u)rliness** gute Nachbarschaft; gutnachbarliche Beziehungen

good offices *(bes. VölkerR)* gute Dienste, Vermittlungsdienste *(e-s dritten Staates zur Beilegung e-s Streitfalles)*; **tender of ~** Angebot der guten Dienste; **to lend one's ~** gute Dienste leisten; **to make available one's ~** seine guten Dienste zur Verfügung stellen; **to use one's ~** seine guten Dienste einsetzen

good, ~ opportunity gute Gelegenheit; **in ~ order and condition** in gutem Zustand; **~ until cancel(l)ed** (or **recalled**) bis auf Widerruf gültig; **~ until cancel(l)ed order** *(Börse)* bis auf Widerruf gültiger Auftrag; **in ~ time** fristgemäß; **~ title** →title 2.

goodwill Goodwill; *(ideeller)* Firmenwert *(Lage, Ruf, Kundenkreis)*; *dipl* guter Wille, Verständigungsbereitschaft, Versöhnlichkeit; **~ mission** Goodwill-Mission

good, to hold ~ (noch) gelten

good, to make ~ ersetzen, vergüten; *(Versprechen)* halten; bestätigen, als berechtigt nachweisen; **to make ~ a claim** e-n Anspruch begründen; **to make ~ a defect** e-n Schaden beheben; **to make ~ a loss** e-n Schaden ersetzen; **liability to make ~ a loss** Schadensersatzpflicht

goods Ware(n) *(Einzahl:* commodity, merchandise*)*; Güter; *bes. Br.* (Eisenbahn-)Güter, Fracht; bewegliche Habe; **~ account** Warenkonto; Warenrechnung; **~ and capital movement** Waren- und Kapitalverkehr; **~ and chattels** bewegliche Sachen; Hab und Gut; Mobiliargut; **~ and services transactions** Waren- und Dienstleistungsverkehr; **~ delivery** Warenlieferung; **~ department** *Br* Güterabfertigung, Güterannahme; **~ for dispatch** Versandgut; **~ for home use** *Br (Zoll)* Waren für den Inlandsverbrauch; **~ in process** Halbfabrikate, Halberzeugnisse; **~ in short supply** Mangelware; **~ in stock** Lagerbestand, Warenbestand

goods in transit Transitgüter, Durchfuhrgut; **~ insurance** Gütertransportversicherung

goods, ~ office *Br* Frachtannahmestelle, Güterabfertigung; **~ of the contract description** vertragsgemäße Waren; **~ on commission** Kommissionswaren; **~ on consignment** Konsignationswaren; **~ on hand** Lagerbestand; Warenlager; **~ on sale or return** Kommissionswaren; **~ quota** Warenkontingent; **~ received** Wareneingänge; **~ receiving department** Warenannahme, Warenempfang; **~ returned** Retouren, zurückgesandte Waren; **~ service** *Br* →freight service

goods sold and delivered, action for ~ *Am* Klage *(des Verkäufers)* auf Zahlung des Kaufpreises

goods, ~ station *Br* →freight station; **~ to declare** *(beim Zoll)* anmeldepflichtige Waren; **~ traffic** Güterverkehr; **~ train** *Br* Güterzug; **~ transport** Warentransport; *Br* Güterverkehr; Güterbeförderung; **~ transport by inland waterway** Binnenschiffsgüterverkehr; **~ truck** *Br (offener)* Güterwagen; **~ van** *Br (gedeckter)* Güterwagen; **~ vehicles** Lastfahrzeuge; **~ wag(g)on** *Br* Güterwagen; **~ yard** *Br* Güterbahnhof

goods, ascertained ~ bestimmte *(besonders ausgesuchte)* Waren; **bill on ~** Warenwechsel; **bonded ~** Waren unter Zollverschluß; **capital ~** Investitionsgüter *(opp. consumer goods)*; **carriage of ~** Güterbeförderung, Gütertransport; **carted ~** Rollgut; **classification of ~** Warenklasseneinteilung (→*classification*); **complementary ~** Komplementärgüter; **consignee of ~** Warenempfänger; **consignment of ~** Warensendung; Warenversand; **consumer(s')** (or **consumption**) **~** Verbrauchsgüter, Konsumgüter *(opp. capital goods)*; **→convenience ~**; **durable consumer ~** langlebige Konsumgüter, Gebrauchsgüter; **exchange of ~** Warenaustausch, Güteraustausch; **fashion ~** Modeartikel; **finished ~** Fertigware(n); **fungible ~** vertretbare Sachen; **heavy ~** Schwergut; **home-made ~** inländische Waren; **incoming ~** eingehende Waren, Wareneingänge; **job ~** Ausschußware(n); **kind of ~** Warengattung; **light ~** Leichtgut; **list of ~** Warenverzeichnis, Warenkatalog; **lot of ~** Warenposten; **marketable ~** gut verkäufliche Waren; **order for ~** Warenbestellung; **outgoing ~** ausgehende Waren, Warenausgang; **perishable ~** (leicht) verderbliche Ware(n); **producer ~** Produktionsgüter *(opp. consumer ~)*; **requirement in ~** Warenbedarf; **sale of ~** Warenabsatz, Warenverkauf; **sample of ~** Warenprobe; **scarce ~** Mangelware(n); **semi- finished ~** Halbware(n); **specific ~** bestimmte Sachen *(beim Spezieskauf)*; **stock of ~** Warenbestand; **trade in ~** Warenhandel; **transit ~** Transitgüter; Durchfuhrgut; **unascertained ~** Gattungssachen

goods, to buy (or **get, obtain, procure**) **~** Waren beziehen (from von); **to consign** (or **dispatch, forward**) **~** Waren versenden; **to keep ~** Waren führen; **to order ~** Waren bestellen; **to lay**

(or **take**) ~ **in stock** Waren auf Lager nehmen; **to pass** ~ **in transit** Waren durch ein Land führen

G.O.P. (Grand Old Party) *Am colloq.* Republikanische Partei

govern *v* regieren, herrschen; lenken, leiten; bestimmen; bestimmend sein, den Ausschlag geben

governed, to be ~ **by** geleitet werden von *(z.B. e-r Gesellschaft)*; bestimmt werden durch; geregelt werden durch; *(e-r Gesetzesbestimmung etc)* unterliegen; **to be** ~ **by a law** unter ein Gesetz fallen; **to be** ~ **by foreign law** dem ausländischen Recht unterliegen

governing, ~ **body** Leitung, Direktion, Vorstand; (Selbst-)Verwaltungsorgan; ~ **classes** herrschende Klassen *(e-s Landes)*; ~ **council** Gouverneursrat; ~ **idea** Leitgedanke; ~ **law** maßgebendes Recht; ~ **party** an der Macht befindliche Partei

governing, non-self-~ **territories** *(VölkerR)*[5] Gebiete ohne Selbstregierung, nicht autonome Gebiete *(die von den Mitgliedern der Vereinten Nationen verwaltet werden)*

governance Regierungs-, Verwaltungs-, Herrschaftsstruktur; **corporate** ~ *Am* Verwaltungs- od. Herrschaftsstruktur e-s Unternehmens

government Regierung *(Br in weiterem Sinne, bestehend aus dem Cabinet, den Senior Ministers und Junior Ministers)*; Staat (Staatswesen); gesamter Staatsapparat; Herrschaft; ~ **agency** Regierungsstelle, Behörde; ~ **agent** *Am* Regierungsvertreter; ~ **aid** staatliche Unterstützung; ~ **bill** *Br parl* Regierungsvorlage; ~ **bond** *Br* staatliche Kaution (od. Sicherheitsleistung); ~ **bonds** Staatspapiere; *Am* Bundesanleihen; ~ **broker** *Br* Börsenmakler im Auftrag der Bank of England; **in** ~ **circles** in Regierungskreisen; ~ **commission** Regierungskommission; ~ **contract** Regierungsauftrag, Staatsauftrag *(→contract 2.)*; ~ **control** staatliche Kontrolle (od. Lenkung); ~**-controlled** unter staatlicher Aufsicht; ~ **declaration** Regierungserklärung; **G**~**-Department** *Br* Regierungsstelle, Behörde; Ministerium; ~ **depository** *Am* Bank für Staatsgelder; ~ **deposits** *Am* Bankguthaben des Staates; ~ **employee** Angestellter des öffentlichen Dienstes, Staatsbediensteter; Beamter des mittleren Dienstes; ~ **employment** staatliche Anstellung; ~ **expenditure** Staatsausgaben; ~ **funds** *Br* staatliche Mittel; Staatspapiere; ~ **grant** staatlicher Zuschuß, staatliche Beihilfe; ~ **guarantee** Staatsgarantie; **G**~ **House** *Br* Regierungsgebäude; ~**→indemnity**; ~**-in-exile** Exilregierung; ~ **instrumentalities** Regierungseinrichtungen; ~ **intervention** Eingreifen der Regierung; **G**~ **Issue** Staatslieferung *(von Ausrüstung und Kleidung)* für Soldaten; von der Regierung gestellt, Militär- (→G. I.); ~ **liability** Amtshaftung; ~ **life annuities** *Br* Staatsrenten; ~ **loan** Staatsanleihe, öffentliche Anleihe; ~ **monopoly** Staatsmonopol; **G**~ **National Mortgage Association** *Am* →Ginnie Mae; **G**~ **Notices** (G. N.) *Br* Regierungserlasse; ~ **obligations** *Am* Staatsanleihen; ~ **office** *Am* Regierungsbehörde; ~ **official** Staatsbeamter; ~ **order** Staatsauftrag; ~**-owned** im Staatseigentum stehend, staatseigen; ~ **ownership** Staatseigentum; ~ **papers** →~ securities; **G**~ **party** *Br* Regierungspartei; **G**~ **party to a convention** *(VölkerR)* Vertragsregierung; Hohe Vertragspartei; ~ **permission** *Br* staatliche Erlaubnis; **G**~ **Printing Office** (GPO) *Am* Staatsdruckerei *(druckt sämtliche Regierungsdokumente)*; ~ **procurement** staatliches Beschaffungswesen; ~ **property** Staatseigentum, Staatsbesitz; fiskalisches Eigentum; ~ **purchases** Regierungskäufe; ~ **representative** Regierungsvertreter; ~ **revenue** *Br* Staatseinnahmen; ~ **securities** *Br* Staatspapiere, Staatsanleihen; *Am* Bundesanleihen; **in** ~ **service** im Staatsdienst; ~ **spending** Staatsausgaben; ~ **spokesman** Regierungssprecher; ~**-sponsored** staatlich gefördert; ~ **stocks** *Br (festverzinsliche)* Staatspapiere (*→stock 1.*); ~ **subsidy** staatliche Unterstützung, Subvention; ~ **training centres** *Br* staatliche Ausbildungszentren; ~ **use** *(PatR)* staatliche Inanspruchnahme; ~ **(welfare) benefits** *Am* Sozialhilfe

government, arbitrary ~ Willkürherrschaft; **caretaker** ~ Übergangsregierung, Interimsregierung; **central** ~ *Br* Zentralregierung *(opp. local ~)*; **change of** ~ *Br* Regierungswechsel; **coalition** ~ *Br* Koalitionsregierung; **constitutional** ~ *Br* verfassungsmäßige Regierung; **the contracting** ~**s** die vertragsschließenden Regierungen; **democratic** ~ demokratische Staatsform, Demokratie; **depositary** ~ Verwahrregierung; **federal** ~ Bundesregierung; *Am* Bund (*→federal*); **foreign** ~ auswärtige Macht; **form of** ~ Regierungsform, Regierungssystem; **head of** ~ Regierungschef; **local** ~ Kommunalverwaltung; örtliche Selbstverwaltung (*→local*); **member** ~ Mitgliedsregierung, Regierung e-s Mitgliedstaates; **member of the G**~ *Br* Mitglied der Regierung; **military** ~ Militärregierung; **municipal** ~ *Am* Stadtverwaltung; **provisional** ~ provisorische Regierung; **puppet** ~ Marionettenregierung; **representative of a** ~ Regierungsvertreter; **self-**~ Selbstverwaltung; **signatory** ~ Unterzeichnerregierung

government, to form a G~ e-e Regierung bilden; **to be called upon to form a G**~ mit der Regierungsbildung beauftragt werden; **to overthrow a G**~ e-e Regierung stürzen; **the G**~ **has resigned** die Regierung ist zurückgetreten

governmental Regierungs-, Staats-; staatlich; ~ **action** Regierungsmaßnahme; ~ **agency** *Am* Regierungsstelle, Behörde; ~ **assistance** staatliche Unterstützung; ~ **forces** Regierungstruppen; ~ **grant** staatliche Beihilfe; ~ **interest test** *Am (IPR)* Methode zur Bestimmung des anzuwendenden Rechts, nach der das materielle Recht des Staates anzuwenden ist, der das größte Interesse an der Streitentscheidung hat; ~ **lethargy** Staatsverdrossenheit; ~ **machinery** Staatsapparat; ~ **measures** staatliche Maßnahmen; **non-~ organization** (NGO) Nichtregierungsorganisation (NRO); ~ **purchase of supplies** Beschaffungskäufe der Regierung; ~ **system** Regierungssystem, Staatsform

governmentalize *v (von Seiten der Regierung)* reglementieren

governor Gouverneur, oberster Verwaltungsbeamter; *Am (für 4 bzw. in einigen Staaten 2 Jahre gewählter)* Gouverneur *(oberster Verwaltungsbeamter e-s Einzelstaates, vergleichbar dem deutschen Ministerpräsidenten);* Direktor, Leiter *(z.B. e-r Schule, e-s Krankenhauses); Br* Gefängnisdirektor; **G~ of the Bank of England** *Br* Präsident der Bank of England; **G~ of a Federal Reserve Bank** *Am* Präsident e-r Bundeszentralbank; **G~-General** Generalgouverneur; *Br* Vertreter der Krone in einigen Commonwealth-Ländern; **Board of G~s** →board 1.; **deputy** ~ stellvertretender Gouverneur; **military** ~ Militärgouverneur

gown Robe, Talar; **town and** ~ Stadt und Universität; Bürgerschaft und Studenten

grace Gnade, Gunst(bezeigung); Gnadenfrist, Nachfrist; **Your G~** *Br* Euer Gnaden *(als Titel für duke, duchess, archbishop);* ~ **period** Gnadenfrist, Nachfrist; rückzahlungsfreie Zeit; *Am (PatR)* Neuheitsschonfrist; ~ **years** tilgungsfreie Jahre; **act of** ~ Gnadenakt; **days of** ~[6] Gnadenfrist, Nachfrist; Respekttage *(nach Fälligkeit e-s Wechsels eingeräumte Nachfrist);* **period of** ~ →~ period; **to give sb. a week's** ~ jdm e-e Gnadenfrist (od. Nachfrist) von einer Woche gewähren; **the European Investment Bank granted a loan for a term of 30 years including an 8- year period of** ~ das Darlehen der Europäischen Investitionsbank wurde für 30 Jahre, davon 8 tilgungsfrei gewährt

gradation Stufen(gang), Abstufung; Staffelung; **interest** ~ Zinsstaffelung

grade Grad, Stufe; Besoldungsgruppe; (Waren-)Klasse; Sorte, Qualität; *Am* Schulklasse; *Am (Schule)* Zensur; *Am mil* Dienstgrad; ~ **A** Waren erster Qualität; erste Klasse; ~ **label(l)ing** Güteklassenbezeichnung; ~ **school** *Am* Grundschule; ~ **teacher** *Am* Grundschullehrer; **commercial ~s** Handelssorten; **first** (or **high**)-~ erstklassig, prima, hochwertig; **a high ~ of civilization** ein hoher Grad der Kultur; **low-~** minderwertig, von minderer Qualität; **to reduce to a lower** ~ *Am mil* degradieren

grade *v* einstufen, sortieren; abstufen, staffeln; **to ~ goods** Waren nach Güteklassen einstufen; **to ~ salaries** Gehälter staffeln

graded tax *Am* gestaffelte Steuer *(höhere Steuer auf →unimproved land)*

grading Einstufung, Sortierung; Staffelung; ~ **of commodities** Einstufung von Waren nach Güteklassen; ~ **of premiums** *(VersR)* Beitragsstaffelung; ~ **test** Test zur Einstufung

graduate Graduierter, Akademiker *(jd, der e-n Universitätsgrad erworben hat; cf. undergraduate); Am (auch)* Absolvent e-r Schule od. e-s Lehrgangs *(jd, der e-e Ausbildung abgeschlossen hat, z.B. high school~, college~); Am* staatlich geprüft *(z.B. ~ nurse);* ~ **student** *Am* (**post-~ student** *Br)* Graduierter, Akademiker *(der z.B. den B.A. erworben hat und auf e-n höheren Grad hin studiert);* **to be a ~ of a school** *Am* e-e Schule absolviert haben

graduate *v* 1. e-n akademischen Grad erlangen; promovieren; *Am* e-n akademischen Grad verleihen; ein Abschlußzeugnis erteilen; *Am* e-e Abschlußprüfung machen; **to ~ from high school** *Am* die high school absolvieren; **to ~ in law** e-n juristischen akademischen Grad erlangen

graduate *v* 2. in Grade einteilen; abstufen, staffeln

graduated, ~ **interest** gestaffelte Zinsen; ~ **price** gestaffelter Preis; ~ **tax** gestaffelte Steuer

graduation 1. Erlangung (od. Verleihung) e-s akademischen Grades; Promotion; *Am* Abschlußprüfung; *Am* Absolvierung *(e-r Schule od. e-s Lehrgangs)*

graduation 2. Gradeinteilung; Abstufung, Staffelung; ~ **of prices** Preisstaffelung

graft *bes. Am* Schiebung, Korruption; Bestechungsgeld; Schmiergeld; durch Amtsmißbrauch erworbener Vorteil *(bes. in Verbindung mit Politik);* **to practise** ~ Schiebungen machen

graft *v* Schiebungen machen; Amtsmißbrauch treiben

grafter Schieber; korrupter Beamter

grain Getreide *(aller Art);* Gran *(Gewichtseinheit);* ~ **bill** gegen Getreidelieferungen gezogener Wechsel; ~ **broker** Getreidemakler; ~ **cargo** Getreideladung; ~ **exchange** Getreidebörse; ~ **export(ation)** Getreideausfuhr; ~ **futures** *(Börse)* Getreidetermingeschäfte; ~ **market** Getreidemarkt; ~ **trade** Getreidehandel

grand, ~ fathering *Am* Besitzstandregelung im Effekten- und Emissionsbereich; **~ jury** *Am* Anklagejury (→*jury*); **~ larceny** *Am* schwerer Diebstahl *(opp. petty larceny);* **~ total** Endsumme; Gesamtsumme

granny bonds indexgebundene Sparzertifikate

grant Bewilligung, Gewährung, Erteilung; Verleihung (to an); *(urkundl.)* Übertragung, Übereignung *(bes. von Grundbesitz);* schriftl. Schenkung; übertragene od. bewilligte Sache; *(staatl.)* Zuschuß; *(nicht rückzahlbare)* Finanzhilfe; (Studien-, Ausbildungs-)Beihilfe, Stipendium; **~s** Zuschüsse, Subventionen; bewilligte (od. zugewiesene) Gelder; **~ of an advance** Bewilligung e-s Vorschusses; **~-aided** staatlich unterstützt, subventioniert; **~-in-aid** *Br* Regierungszuschuß an Kommunalbehörden *(für bestimmte Zwecke); Am* Bundeszuschuß an Einzelstaaten *(bes. mit der Auflage, daß bestimmte Richtlinien beachtet werden);* **~ of a charter** (or **concession**) Verleihung (od. Erteilung) e-r Konzession; **~ of credit** Kreditgewährung; **~ of land** Landzuweisung; **~ of letters of administration** Bestellung zum Nachlaßverwalter; **~ of letters testamentary** *Am* →~ of probate; **~ of a patent** Patenterteilung; **~ of a pension** Bewilligung e-r Pension; **~ of probate** Testamentsvollstreckerzeugnis *(Bestätigungsurkunde für den →executor);* **~ procedure** *(PatR)* Erteilungsverfahren

grant, decision of ~ *(PatR)* Erteilungsbeschluß; **deed of ~** Übertragungsurkunde; **governmental ~** staatlicher Zuschuß (od. Beihilfe); **maintenance ~** Unterhaltsbeihilfe, Unterhaltszuschuß; **monetary ~** (Geld-)Beihilfe; **person in receipt of a ~** Beihilfeempfänger; **request for ~** *(PatR)* Erteilungsantrag; **study ~** Studienbeihilfe; **training ~** Ausbildungsbeihilfe; **to make a ~** e-n Zuschuß geben; e-e Beihilfe gewähren; *(etw.)* übertragen (od. bewilligen)

grant *v* bewilligen, gewähren, erteilen; verleihen (to an); einräumen, zugeben; *(Grundbesitz) (urkundlich)* übertragen, übereignen; **to ~ an advance** e-n Vorschuß gewähren, bevorschussen; **to ~ an application** e-m Antrag stattgeben; **to ~ a charter** e-e Konzession vergeben (od. erteilen); **to ~ compensation** Schadensersatz zubilligen; **to ~ credit** Kredit bewilligen (od. einräumen); **to ~ a discharge** Entlastung erteilen; **to ~ a divorce** auf Scheidung erkennen; **to ~ an extension of time** Fristverlängerung gewähren, stunden; **to ~ an injunction** e-e (einstweilige) Verfügung erlassen; **to ~ leave** Erlaubnis erteilen; für zulässig erklären; **to ~ leave of absence to sb.** jdn beurlauben; **to ~ leave to appeal** die Berufung *(formell)* zulassen; **to ~ a licen|ce (~se)** e-e Konzession (od. Lizenz) erteilen; **to ~ a loan** ein Darlehen geben (od. gewähren); **to ~ the motion** dem Antrag stattgeben; **to ~ a pardon to sb.** jdn begnadigen; **to ~ a patent** ein Patent erteilen; **to ~ a pension** e-e Pension bewilligen; **to ~ permission** Erlaubnis erteilen; **to ~ a request** e-m Gesuch stattgeben; **to ~ a respite** Vollstreckung e-s Urteils aussetzen; *Br* e-e Frist einräumen; stunden

granted *(PatR)* erteilt; **~ that** angenommen, daß

granting Bewilligung, Gewährung, Verleihung; **~ of a licen|ce (~se)** Lizenzerteilung; Konzessionserteilung; *(UrhR)* Einräumung e-s Nutzungsrechtes; **~ of a motion** Annahme e-s Antrages; **~ of a patent** Patenterteilung; **~ of a power of attorney** Erteilung e-r Vollmacht; **~ procedure** *(PatR)* Erteilungsverfahren; **~ of a respite** Fristgewährung

grantee jd, dem etw. bewilligt (od. urkundlich übertragen od. verliehen) ist; Rechtsnachfolger; Käufer, Erwerber *(bes. von Grundbesitz);* **~ of an annuity** Empfänger e-r Rente; **~ of a licen|ce (~se)** Konzessionsinhaber; Lizenznehmer; *(UrhR)* Erwerber e-s Nutzungsrechtes; **~ (of a patent)** Patentinhaber; **~ of real estate** Käufer (od. Erwerber) von Grundbesitz

grantor jd, der etw. bewilligt (od. urkundlich überträgt, od. verleiht); Rechtsvorgänger; Aussteller e-r Übereignungsurkunde; Veräußerer *(bes. von Grundbesitz);* **~ of a licen|ce (~se)** Verleiher e-r Konzession; Lizenzgeber; *(UrhR)* Verleiher e-s Nutzungsrechtes; **~ of a power of attorney** Vollmachtsgeber; **~ of real estate** Grundstücksverkäufer; **~ of a trust** *Am* Stifter (od. Besteller) e-s Treuhandverhältnisses, Begründer e-s Trust; **~ trust** *Am* Trust, bei dem der Errichter sich weitgehende Kontrollrechte vorbehält

graph graphische Darstellung, Schaubild

graph *v* graphisch darstellen

graphologist Graphologe, Handschriftendeuter

gratis gratis, unentgeltlich, kostenlos; **~ dictum** (mere assertion) bloße Behauptung

gratuitous unentgeltlich, kostenlos; unaufgefordert, unverlangt; grundlos; **~ information** unaufgeforderte Auskunft; **~ licensee** *Am* nur Befugter *(zwar befugt, aber nicht im Interesse des Besitzers handelnd);* **~ suspicion** grundloser Verdacht

gratuity *(kleines)* Geldgeschenk; Trinkgeld; Sondervergütung, Gratifikation; Abfindungssumme *(für Angestellte);* **he left the service with a ~** er ist mit e-r Sondervergütung ausgeschieden

grava|men (*pl* **~mina**) Beschwerde(grund)

gravity Schwere, Ernst; Bedeutung; **~ of the political situation** Ernst der politischen Lage;

increasing ~ **of the situation** *pol* Zuspitzung der Lage

gray market *Am* grauer Markt

Gray's Inn *Br* Barristerinnung *(cf. Inns of Court)*

great groß; **G~ Britain** Großbritannien *(England, Wales und Schottland);* **~-grandfather** Urgroßvater; **~-grandparents** Urgroßeltern; **~-grandson** Urenkel; **~landowner** Großgrundbesitzer; **G~ Powers** Großmächte; **G~ Seal** Großsiegel *(Br Staatssiegel für öffentliche Urkunden von besonderer Bedeutung)*

Greater London Groß-London

Greece Griechenland (→*Hellenic Republic*)
Greek Grieche, Griechin; griechisch

green, ~ **backs** *Am* Banknoten; ~ **belt** Grüngürtel *(e-r Stadt);* ~ **card** grüne Versicherungskarte *(für Autofahrer im Ausland);* ~ **house effect** Treibhauseffekt
greenmail(ing) *Am* Ankauf von Aktien über die Börse in der Absicht, sie an die Gesellschaft zu höherem Preis zurückzuverkaufen *(im U.S. Gesellschaftsrecht können corporations ihre eigenen Aktien erwerben)*
Quasi-Erpressung, die ein →predatory investor dadurch ausübt, daß er auf Grund eines Teil-Aktienbesitzes die Übernahme eines Zielunternehmens und die Ablösung des Managements androht, um den Rückkauf seiner Aktien zu einem weit höheren Preis zu verlangen[7]
green paper staatliche Veröffentlichung; Diskussionspapier
Greenpeace Umweltschutzorganisation, die durch aktive Aktionen die Umweltzerstörung zu verhindern sucht
green rates *(EG)* grüne Kurse *(Gegenwert der für Agrarpreise festgesetzten ECU in Landeswährungen)*

Greenwich (mean) time (GMT) Greenwicher (mittlere Sonnen-)Zeit, Weltzeit

greetings Gruß, Begrüßung; *Am* (Anfang des amtl.) Einberufungsbefehl(s); ~ **telegram** Glückwunschtelegramm

greffier Registrator; Gerichtsschreiber; Notar

Grenada Grenada
Grenadian Grenader(in); grenadisch

Gretna Green marriage *Br* Heirat in Gretna Green (Grenzdorf in Südschottland, wo englische Liebespaare rechtsgültig getraut wurden)

grey market *Br* grauer Markt

grievance Beschwerde(grund); (Grund zur) Klage; Mißstand; Arbeitsstreitigkeit(en); ~ **committee** *Am* Schlichtungsausschuß *(bei Arbeitsstreitigkeiten); Am* Disziplinarausschuß *(der Anwaltskammer);* ~ **procedure** Beschwerdeverfahren, Schlichtungsverfahren *(zur Beilegung individueller Arbeitsstreitigkeiten);* **to redress a** ~ e-m Mißstand (od. e-r Beschwerde) abhelfen; **to state one's** ~**s** Beschwerde führen

grievous bodily harm *(StrafR)* schwere Körperverletzung

groceries Lebensmittel; **to buy** ~ Lebensmittel einkaufen

gross 1. Brutto-, Roh- *(opp. net);* Gesamt-; ~ **amount** Bruttobetrag; Gesamtbetrag; ~ **assets** Bruttovermögen; ~ **average** Havarie-grosse (→*average 1.);* ~ **domestic investments** Bruttoinlandsinvestionen; ~ **domestic product** (GDP) Bruttoinlandsprodukt (BIP); ~ **earnings** Bruttoeinnahmen, Bruttoverdienst; ~ **estate** Bruttonachlaß; ~ **freight** Bruttofracht; ~ **income** Bruttoeinkommen (→*income);* ~ **interest** Bruttozinsen; ~ **leasing** Dienstleistungs-Leasing; ~ **investment in fixed assets** Bruttoanlageinvestitionen; ~ **margin** Bruttogewinnspanne; ~ **national income** Bruttovolkseinkommen
gross national product (GNP) Bruttosozialprodukt (BSP); **real value increase in the** ~ reale Zunahme des Bruttosozialprodukts
gross, ~ **pay** Bruttolohn; ~ **premium** *(VersR)* Bruttoprämie; ~ **price** Bruttopreis, Rohpreis; ~ **proceeds** Bruttoertrag, Rohertrag; ~ **profit(s)** Bruttogewinn, Rohgewinn; ~ **receipts** Bruttoeinnahmen, Roheinnahmen; ~ **register ton** (GRT) Bruttoregistertonne (BRT); ~ **return** Bruttorendite; Bruttoertrag; ~ **revenue** Bruttoeinnahmen, Bruttoertrag; ~ **terms** (g.t.) Bedingung, wonach Laden und Löschen für Rechnung des Schiffes gehen; ~ **tonnage** Bruttotonnengehalt, Bruttoraumgehalt; ~ **turnover** Bruttoumsatz; ~ **value** (G.V.) Brutto(anschaffungs)wert; ~ **weight** (gr.wt.) Bruttogewicht; **total** ~ **weight** Gesamtbruttogewicht
gross, in (the) ~ im ganzen, in Bausch und Bogen; **in** ~ unabhängig; an der Person haftend *(opp. attached to land; e.g. an advowson in ~)*
gross 2. grob; ~ **breach of duty** schwere Pflichtverletzung; ~ **insult** grobe (od. schwere) Beleidigung; ~ **miscarriage of justice** grobes Fehlurteil; ~ **misrepresentation** grobe Entstellung; ~ **negligence** grobe Fahrlässigkeit
grossly negligent grob fahrlässig

gross *v* e-n Bruttogewinn von . . . erzielen

ground 1. Grund und Boden; (Erd-)Boden; Meeresboden; Grundbesitz; Gebiet; Gelände; ~**s** *(ein Gebäude umgebende)* Park-, Gartenanlagen; Ländereien; ~**-controlled approach** vom Boden kontrollierter Radaranflug; ~ **crew** Bodenpersonal *(opp. air crew);* ~ **landlord** Grundstückseigentümer bei Verpachtung gegen Zahlung von →ground rent; ~ **lease** →building lease; ~ **rent** *Br* das beim →building lease von dem Pächter periodisch zu zahlende *(erbbauzinsähnliche)* Nutzungsentgelt; *Am (in Pennsylvania und Maryland) (veräußerl. und vererbl., auf Vertrag beruhendes)* dingliches Recht auf periodische Zahlung e-s Nutzungsentgelts für ein auf Dauer zu Eigentum (fee simple) überlassenes Grundstück; *(auch)* das Nutzungsentgelt selbst*(ähnlich dem deutschen Erbbauzins)*; ~ **staff** Bodenpersonal; ~**-to-air missile** Boden-Luft-Rakete

ground, above ~ *(BergR)* übertage; **below** ~ *(BergR)* untertage; **fishing** ~**s** Fischgründe; Fanggründe; **on German** ~ auf deutschem Gebiet; **hunting** ~ Jagdgebiet; **to break new** ~ *fig* neues Gebiet erschließen; **to gain** ~ (an) Boden gewinnen, vorwärtskommen; **to hold one's** ~ sich behaupten; **to lose** ~ (an) Boden verlieren; weichen; **to stand one's** ~ sich behaupten

ground 2. (Beweg-)Grund, Ursache, Veranlassung; ~**(s)** Begründung; **on the** ~ **of** wegen; **on the** ~**(s) that** mit der Begründung, daß; ~**s for appeal** Rechtsmittelbegründung (Berufungsbegründung etc); ~**s for a decision** Entscheidungsgründe; ~ **for discharge** (or **dismissal**) Entlassungsgrund; ~ **for divorce** (Ehe-)Scheidungsgrund (→*divorce*); ~ **for giving notice** Kündigungsgrund; ~**s for opposition** *(PatR)* Einspruchsgründe; ~ **for suspicion** Anhalt für den Verdacht; ~ **of nullity** Nichtigkeitsgrund; **cogent** ~ wichtiger Grund; **legal** ~ rechtlicher Grund; **on personal** ~**s** aus persönlichen Gründen; **on political** ~**s** aus politischen Gründen; **reasonable** ~ stichhaltiger Grund; **the appeal is dismissed for want of sufficient** ~**s** die Beschwerde wird als unbegründet zurückgewiesen; **to establish** (or **set forth**) ~**s (for)** Gründe vorbringen (für); begründen

ground *v* auf Grund laufen *(Schiff)*; *(Flugzeug)* am Starten hindern; **to** ~ **sb. in sth.** jdn einweisen in; jdm Vorkenntnisse geben in

groundage *Br* Ankergeld

group 1. Gruppe; ~ **banking** *Am* →chain banking; ~ **buying** Sammeleinkauf; ~ **collection** Sammelinkasso; ~ **exemption** Gruppenfreistellung; ~ **financing** Gemeinschaftsfinanzierung; ~ **floating** Gruppenfloating; ~ **insurance** Gruppenversicherung, Kollektivversicherung; ~ **life insurance** Gruppenlebensversicherung; ~ **of actions** Gesamtheit von Maßnahmen; ~ **piecework** Gruppenakkord; ~ **policy** Sammelpolice; ~ **practice** Gemeinschaftspraxis *(mehrerer Ärzte)*; ~ **travel** Gesellschaftsreisen; ~ **work** *Am* Gruppenpflege, soziale Arbeit an Gruppen *(opp. case work)*; **advisory** ~ Beratungsgruppe; **age** ~ Altersgruppe; Altersklasse; **occupational** ~ Berufsgruppe, Berufsverband; **rate charged for a** ~ Sammeltarif; **social** ~ gesellschaftliche Gruppe

group 2. Konzern; Unternehmensgruppe; ~→**accounting**; ~ **accounts** Konzernabschluß; ~ **auditor** Konzernabschlußprüfer; ~ **balance sheet** Konzernbilanz; ~ **consolidated balance sheet** konsolidierte Konzernbilanz; ~ **company** Konzerngesellschaft; ~ **(of companies)** Konzern; **law on** ~ **of companies** Konzernrecht; ~ **member** Konzernmitglied; ~ **member company** Konzerngesellschaft; ~ **profit** Konzerngewinn; ~ **results** Ertragslage des Konzerns; **international** ~ internationaler Konzern; **management of the** ~ Konzernleitung; **multi-stage** ~ mehrstufiger Konzern; **outside the** ~ konzernfremd; **sub-**~ Teilkonzern; **within the** ~ konzernintern

group 3., **(parliamentary)** ~ Fraktion; ~ **spokesman** Fraktionssprecher; **chairman of the** ~ Fraktionsvorsitzender; **inter-**~ interfraktionell; **leader of the** ~ Fraktionsführer; **member of the** ~ Fraktionsmitglied; **he had withdrawn his** ~**'s motion** er hatte den Antrag seiner Fraktion zurückgezogen

Group 4. informeller Zusammenschluß folgender Industrienationen:

Group of Five (G5) Fünfergruppe

USA, Japan, Bundesrepublik Deutschland, Großbritannien u. Frankreich

Group of Seven (G7) Siebenergruppe

Außer den G5-Ländern noch Kanada und Italien (wichtigste 7 Industriestaaten). Jährliches Zusammentreffen der Staats- u. Regierungschefs auf dem Weltwirtschaftsgipfel

Group of Ten (G10) Zehnergruppe

1962 gegründeter Zusammenschluß von 10 Industrienationen, die dem IMF im Rahmen der GAB Finanzmittel zur Verfügung stellen. Zur Zehnergruppe gehören Belgien, die Bundesrepublik Deutschland, Frankreich, Großbritannien, Italien, Japan, Kanada, die Niederlande, Schweden und die USA. 1984 kam die Schweiz als elftes Mitglied hinzu

groupage Sammelladung

grouping (Ein-)Gruppierung

grow *v* wachsen; (an)bauen, züchten; **to** ~ **better** sich bessern; **to** ~ **worse** sich verschlimmern

growing crop Früchte auf dem Halm; stehende Ernte; ~ **insurance** Ernteversicherung

growing, ~ **demand** wachsende Nachfrage; ~ **profit** steigender Gewinn

growth Wachstum; Zuwachs, Vergrößerung; Anbau; ~ **area** Entwicklungsgebiet *(e-s Landes)*; ~ **companies** Wachstumsgesellschaften; ~ **fund** *(Investmentfonds)* Wachstumsfonds; ~ **industry** Wachstumsindustrie; ~ **of capital** Anwachsen des Kapitals, Kapitalzuwachs; ~ **of employment** Beschäftigungswachstum; ~ **of exports** Exportwachstum;~ **of income** Einkommenszunahme; Einkommenszuwachs;~ **of industry** Wachstum der Industrie; ~ **of population** Anwachsen der Bevölkerung; ~ **of power** Zunahme der Macht; Machtzuwachs; ~**-oriented** wachstumsorientiert; ~ **policy** Wachstumspolitik; ~ **prospects** Wachstumsaussichten; ~ **rate** Wachstumsrate, Zuwachsrate; ~ **stocks** Wachstumsaktien *(die ein überdurchschnittliches Gewinnpotential erwarten lassen);* ~ **target** Wachstumsziel; ~ **of trade** Ansteigen des Handels

growth, decline in ~ Wachstumsrückgang; **economic** ~ Wirtschaftswachstum; **apples of foreign** ~ ausländische Äpfel; **lasting and regular** ~ dauerhaftes und regelmäßiges Wachstum; **sustained** ~ dauerhaftes Wachstum; **year-to-year-~ ratio** jährliche Zuwachsrate; →**zero** ~; **the economic** ~ **slowed down** das Wirtschaftswachstum verlangsamte sich

guarantee *Br* Garantie, Gewähr(leistung); Bürgschaft; Kaution; Empfänger e-r Garantie; Bürgschaftsnehmer, Kautionsnehmer; *(auch)* Bürge, Garant (→*guarantor*); ~ **agreement** →~ contract; ~ **(of a bill of exchange)** Wechselbürgschaft, Aval; ~ **bond** *(schriftl.)* Garantieerklärung, Garantieschein; ~ **certificate** Garantieschein; ~ **commission** Bürgschaftsprovision; ~ **contract** Garantievertrag;~ **deposit** Sicherheitshinterlegung; Kaution; ~ **document** Garantieurkunde; ~ **fund** *Br (Börse)* Garantiefonds *(für durch Versäumnisse von Börsenmitgliedern entstandene Verluste);* ~ **indebtedness** Bürgschaftsschuld; ~ **insurance** *Br* Kautionsversicherung

guarantee obligation Garantieverpflichtung; **performance of a** ~ Erfüllung e-r Garantiepflicht

guarantee, ~ **of delivery** Lieferungsgarantie; ~ **of tender** Bietungsgarantie; ~ **period** Garantiefrist; ~ **society** *Br* Kautionsversicherungsgesellschaft;~ **threshold** Garantieschwelle

guarantee, absolute ~ selbstschuldnerische Bürgschaft; **amount of the** ~ Garantiesumme; **bank(er's)** ~ Bankgarantie; Bankaval; **beneficiary under a** ~ Garantiebegünstigter; Bürgschaftsnehmer; **certificate of** ~ Garantieschein; **claim under a** ~ Garantieanspruch; **collective** ~ *(VölkerR)* kollektive (od. gemeinsame) Garantie; **commission on** ~ Avalprovision *(beim Avalkredit);* **company limited by** ~ *Br* Gesellschaft mit beschränkter Nachschußpflicht (→*company*); **constitutional** ~ verfassungsmäßige Garantie; **continuing** ~ Dauergarantie; unbefristete Bürgschaft; **contract** ~ Vertragsgarantie; **contract of** ~ Garantievertrag; Bürgschaftsvertrag; **credit** ~ Kreditbürgschaft; **credit by way of** ~ Avalkredit *(Kreditgewährung durch Bürgschaftsübernahme seitens e-r Bank);* **deficiency** ~ Ausfallbürgschaft; **frame** ~ Mantelgarantie; **government** ~ Staatsgarantie; **giving a** ~ Garantiegewährung; Bürgschaftsleistung; **person giving a** ~ Bürge; **individual** ~ *(VölkerR)* Einzelgarantie; **isolated** ~ Einzelbürgschaft; **joint** ~ Mitbürgschaft; Mitbürge; **line of** ~ Avallinie; **payment** ~ Zahlungsgarantie; **performance** ~ →performance bond; **tender** ~ *Br* Bietungsgarantie; **term** (or **validity**) **of a** ~ Gültigkeitsdauer e-r Garantie; **terms (and conditions) of a** ~ Gewährleistungsbedingungen; Garantiebedingungen; **treaty of** ~ *(VölkerR)* Garantievertrag; **with** ~ **for 2 years** mit zweijähriger Garantie; **without** ~ ohne Gewähr, ohne Garantie; ungesichert

guarantee, to be ~ **for** haften (od. einstehen, bürgen) für; **to cancel a** ~ e-e Garantie annullieren; **to discharge from a** ~ aus e-r Garantieverpflichtung entlassen; **a** ~ **expires** e-e Garantie läuft ab; **the** ~ **extinguishes** die Garantie erlischt; **to furnish** (or **give**) a ~ Garantie geben (od. leisten); Bürgschaft leisten, bürgen; e-e Kaution geben; **to →implement a** ~; **to issue a** ~ e-e Garantie ausstellen; **to make a claim under a** ~ e-n Anpsruch aus e-r Garantie stellen; **to offer a** ~ Garantie bieten; **to raise claims under a** ~ e-e Garantie in Anspruch nehmen; **to withdraw a** ~ e-e Garantie zurückziehen

guarantee *v* garantieren, Garantie leisten, gewährleisten; zusichern; Bürgschaft leisten; einstehen für; **to** ~ **a bill of exchange** Wechselbürgschaft leisten; **to** ~ **sb.'s debts** für jds Schulden bürgen; **to** ~ **a loan** für ein Darlehen bürgen; Bürgschaft für ein Darlehen übernehmen

guaranteed garantiert; mit Garantie; avaliert; ~ **annual wage** (G.A.W.) garantierter Jahreslohn; ~ **bill (of exchange)** avalierter Wechsel; ~ **bonds** *(durch e-e andere Firma, z.B. parent company von subsidiaries)* garantierte Obligationen *(Kapital- od. Zinsgarantie);*~ **debt** Bürgschaftsschuld; ~ **dividend** garantierte Dividende; ~ **minimum wage for all trades** garantierter absoluter Mindestlohn; ~ **mortgage** *Am* Hypothek mit Zins- und Tilgungszahlungsgarantie; ~ **prices** garantierte Preise; ~ **shares** (or **stocks**) (guard., gtd) gesicherte Werte; Aktien mit Divendengarantie; ~ **for 2 weeks** mit 2wöchiger Garantie

guaranteeing Garantieleistung; Bürgschaftsleistung *(bes. für Wechsel)*

guarantor, Garantiegeber, Garant; Bürge; Gewährsmann; ~ **(of a bill of exchange)** Wechselbürge, Avalist; **G~ Power** *pol* Garantiemacht; **~'s undertaking** Bürgschaftserklärung; **absolute** ~ (or ~ **with primary liability**) *Am* selbstschuldnerischer Bürge; **to act as** ~ **for sb.** für jdn bürgen; **to be sb.'s** ~ für jdn bürgen, jds Bürge sein

guaranty *Am* Garantie, Gewähr(leistung); Bürgschaft; Kaution; *Am* Bürge *(auch ohne Einrede der Vorausklage)*; **absolute** ~ selbstschuldnerische Bürgschaft; ~ **agreement** (or **contract of** ~) Garantievertrag; ~ **insurance** Kautionsversicherung; ~ **(of a bill of exchange)** Wechselbürgschaft, Aval; ~ **of collection** *Am* Ausfallbürgschaft; *Am* Bürgschaft od. Garantie unter Vereinbarung der Vorausklage gegen den Hauptschuldner; ~ **of payment** (or **absolute** ~) *Am* selbstschuldnerische Bürgschaft *(ohne Einrede der Vorausklage)*; ~ **of title insurance** *Am* Versicherung von Rechtsansprüchen auf Grundbesitz; ~ **threshold** Garantieschwelle

guard Wache, Wachmannschaft; Wachposten; Gefangenenaufseher, Gefängniswärter; *Br* (Zug-)Schaffner; ~ **duty** Wachdienst; ~ **of hono(u)r** Ehrenwache; **body** ~ Leibwache; **coast** ~ Küstenwache; **to be on** ~ auf Wache sein; **to keep** ~ Wache halten; **to relieve the** ~ die Wache ablösen; **to inspect the** ~ **of hono(u)r** die Ehrenkompanie abschreiten

guard *v*, **to** ~ **against** sich absichern gegen

guardian Vormund *(cf. ward)*; Pfleger; *(im weitesten Sinn:)* (überlebender) Elternteil; ~ **ad litem** *(vom Gericht für beklagten Minderjährigen od. beklagten nicht entmündigten Geisteskranken bestellter)* Prozeßpfleger *(cf. next friend)*; ~**'s allowance** *Br* Vormundschaftsgeld *(für Kinder, deren Eltern tot sind oder deren einer Elternteil tot, der andere verschollen oder in Haft ist)*; ~ **by election** von Minderjährigen gewählter Vormund; ~ **of a minor's person and estate** Vormund über die Person und das Vermögen e-s Minderjährigen

guardian, appointment of a ~ Bestellung e-s Vormunds; **controlling** ~ Gegenvormund; **statutory** ~ Vormund kraft Gesetzes *(der überlebende Elternteil als Vormund)*; **testamentary** ~ testamentarisch bestellter Vormund; **to appoint a p. (to be)** ~ jdn zum Vormund bestellen; **to appoint a** ~ **for a patient** *Br* e-n Geisteskranken entmündigen; **to be under the care of a** ~ unter Vormundschaft stehen; **persons suffering from mental disorder may be placed under the care of a** ~ Geistesgestörte können unter Vormundschaft gestellt werden

guardianship Vormundschaft; Pflegschaft; **letters of** ~ *Am* Urkunde über die Bestellung e-s Vormunds; **order placing a p. under** ~ Entmündigungsbeschluß; **person subject to** ~ **by reason of mental illness** wegen Geisteskrankheit unter Vormundschaft stehende Person; **testamentary** ~ Vormundschaft auf Grund letztwilliger Verfügung e-s Elternteils; **to be under** ~ unter Vormundschaft stehen; **to place under** ~ unter Vormundschaft stellen

Guatemala Guatemala; **Republic of** ~ Republik Guatemala

Guatemalan Guatemalteke, Guatemaltekin; guatemaltekisch

gubernatorial *Am* Gouverneurs-; ~ **bid** *Am* Bewerbung um das Gouverneursamt

guer(r)illa Partisan; ~ **forces** Partisanen; ~ **strike** wilder Streik, Teilaktionen; ~ **war** Partisanenkrieg; **urban** ~**s** Stadt-Guerillas

guesswork vage Schätzung

guest Gast; *Am (nicht zahlender)* Fahrgast, dessen Mitnahme an keine ausreichende Gegenleistung gebunden ist *(opp. passenger)*; ~ **lecturer** (or **professor**) Gastdozent; **G**~ **Statutes** *Am (einzelstaatl.)* Gesetze, die die Haftung des gefälligen Fahrers auf bestimmte Formen des schweren Verschuldens beschränken *(intoxication, gross negligence etc)*

guidance Führung, Leitung; Richtlinie; **for your** ~ zu Ihrer Orientierung; ~ **counsel(l)or** Psychologe zur Beratung Jugendlicher; **vocational** ~ Berufsberatung; **to serve as** ~ als Richtlinie dienen

guide Führer; Ratgeber; Reiseführer; Leitfaden; Anhaltspunkt; ~ **price** *(EG)* Orientierungspreis

guidelines Richtlinien; **policy** ~ Richtlinien für die Politik; **wage** ~ Lohnleitlinien; **to establish** ~ Orientierungslinien aufstellen

guide *v* führen, lenken; belehren

guided, ~ **missile** ferngelenktes Geschoß; **to be** ~ **by** sich richten nach

guiding figures Richtzahlen

guild Gilde, Zunft, Innung; **G**~**hall** *Br* Rathaus *(in der City of London)*; ~ **system** Innungswesen

guillotine Guillotine; *Br parl* Methode der Debattenkürzung durch Festsetzung bestimmter Zeiten für die Beratung e-s Gesetzesentwurfs *(nach Ablauf der Zeit wird ohne Fortsetzung der Debatte zur Abstimmung geschritten)*

guillotine *v Br parl* die Debatten kürzen

guilt *(StrafR)* Schuld
Der Begriff umfaßt:
1. die Tatsache, daß der Angeklagte die ihm zur Last gelegte Tat begangen hat *(im Sinne der deutschen Schuldfrage)*,
2. die auf der inneren Einstellung des Täters *(intent, recklessness, criminal negligence)* beruhende Vorwerfbarkeit *(guilty mind)*

guilt, admitting (or **confessing**) **one's** ~ geständig; **confession of** ~ Schuldbekenntnis; **collective** ~ *(VölkerR)* Kollektivschuld; **finding of** ~ Schuldspruch *(Br bei Jugendlichen an Stelle von conviction)*; **proof of** ~ Schuldbeweis; **war** ~ *(VölkerR)* Kriegsschuld; **to confess one's** ~ die Schuld zugeben; **to deny one's** ~ die Schuld leugnen

guiltless schuldlos, unschuldig

guilty schuldig; ~ **intention** *Scot* Vorsatz; ~ **mind** Schuldbewußtsein (→*guilt 2.); ~* **party** schuldiger Teil; Schuldige(r); **not** ~ unschuldig; **person found** ~ für schuldig Erklärter
guilty, plea of ~ Schuldbekenntnis, Schuldgeständnis; **plea of not** ~ Bestreiten (od. Leugnen) der Schuld; **verdict of** ~ Schuldigerklärung, Schuldspruch *(der jury);* **verdict of not** ~ Verneinung der Schuldfrage, Freispruch; **to enter a plea of** ~ →to plead ~; **to enter a plea of not** ~ →to plead not ~; **to find a p.** ~ jdn für schuldig befinden (od. erklären); jdn schuldig sprechen; **to find a p. not** ~ jdn für nicht schuldig befinden (od. erklären); jdn freisprechen; **to plead** ~ sich schuldig bekennen; **to plead not** ~ sich nicht schuldig bekennen; Schuld leugnen; Freispruch beantragen

Guinea Guinea; **Republic of** ~ Republik Guinea
Guinean Guineer(in); guineisch

Guinea-Bissau Guinea-Bissau; **Republic of** ~ Republik Guinea-Bissau

Guinea-Bissau, (of) ~ Guineer(in), guineisch

guise, under the ~ **(of)** unter dem Vorwand (od. Deckmantel)

Gulf, countries of the ~ Golfstaaten

gumshoe (man) *Am sl.* Detektiv; Polizist

GUN (grantor underwritten note) Variante der →note issuance facility
GUN verschafft weniger bekannten Kreditnehmern Zugang zum →Euronote-market durch ein Rückgriffsrecht des Euronote-Käufers auf die Garantiebank

gun Schußwaffe, Gewehr; Kanone; *Am colloq.* Revolver, Pistole; *Am sl.* Dieb; ~ **licence** *Br* Waffenschein; ~**man** bewaffneter Verbrecher, Gangster; ~**-running** unerlaubter Waffenhandel; Waffenschmuggel; ~**shot** Schuß (-weite)

gutter press Skandalpresse

Guyana Guyana; **the Co-operative Republic of** ~ die kooperative Republik Guyana
Guyanese Guyaner(in); guyanisch

H

H-bomb →hydrogen bomb

Habeas Corpus ("that you have the body"), **(writ of)** ~ gerichtliche Anordnung eines Haftprüfungstermins *(in dem Richter entweder Haftbefehl erläßt [falls nicht vorher geschehen], oder Fortdauer der Haft oder Freilassung anordnet)*
Geht zurück auf das *Br* durch die Habeascorpusakte von 1679, *Am* durch Art. I sec. 9 der Constitution of the United States niedergelegte Recht eines jeden Staatsbürgers, der seiner Freiheit beraubt worden ist, auf Einschaltung eines Richters innerhalb einer bestimmten Frist (Haftbefehl, Haftprüfung) *(im deutschen Recht vergleichbar §§ 112, 114, 128 StPO und Grundgesetz Art. 104).*
Im modernen Recht Ausweitung auch auf Auslieferung, Einlieferung in eine Heilstätte etc

habendum die Klausel e-r Übertragungsurkunde, die das erworbene Eigentumsrecht des Käufers definiert *(cf. parcel 2.)*

habit Gewohnheit, Gepflogenheit; Verhaltensweise; *sl.* Süchtigkeit *(Rauschgift);* ~ **survey** *(Marktforschung)* Untersuchung von Verbrauchergewohnheiten; **danger of** ~ **formation** Suchtgefahr *(Drogen etc);* **social** ~**s** gesellschaftliche Umgangsformen

habitat Habitat, Lebensraum, Vorkommen *(von Pflanzen, Tieren)*

habitual gewohnheitsmäßig; ~ **drunkard** Gewohnheitstrinker; ~ **offender** *Am* Gewohnheitsverbrecher; ~ **residence** gewöhnlicher Aufenthaltsort
habitually resident gewöhnlich ansässig

hack Lohnschreiber; *Am* Taxi, Droschke; ~ **license** *Am* Taxikonzession

hacker Computerbenutzer, der durch Anzapfung e-r Telefonleitung in fremde Computersysteme eindringt

hacking unerlaubtes Eindringen in Datenfernübertragungsnetze

Hague Agreement Concerning the International Deposit of Industrial Designs or Models[1] Haager Muster-Abkommen (HMA) (Haager Abkommen über die internationale Hinterlegung gewerblicher Muster oder Modelle)
Das Haager Muster-Abkommen (HMA) vom 6. Nov. 1925, revidiert in London 1934 und im Haag 1960, ergänzt durch die Vereinbarung von Monaco von 1961 und die Vereinbarung von Stockholm von 1967, ist ein im Rahmen der Pariser Übereinkunft *(cf. Paris →Convention)* geschlossenes Nebenabkommen. Jeder Angehörige eines der Vertragsstaaten (zu den Signatarstaaten des Abkommens in der Fassung von 1960 gehören neben der Bundesrepublik Deutschland auch Großbritannien und die USA) erlangt Musterschutz durch Hinterlegung eines Musters oder Modells bei dem Internationalen Büro in Genf. Die Dauer des Schutzes beträgt 15 Jahre vom Zeitpunkt der Hinterlegung an

Hague Conference on Private International Law[1a] Haager Konferenz für Internationales Privatrecht

Hague Conventions *(VölkerR)* Haager Konventionen, Haager Abkommen, Haager Übereinkommen

Hague Convention Concerning the Jurisdiction of Authorithies and the Law Applicable in Respect of the Protection of Minors[2] Haager Minderjährigenschutzabkommen (MSA) (Haager Übereinkommen über die Zuständigkeit der Behörden und das anzuwendende Recht auf dem Gebiet des Schutzes von Minderjährigen)

Hague Convention for the Pacific Settlement of International Disputes Haager Abkommen zur friedlichen Regelung internationaler Streitfälle *(1899 und 1907)*

Hague Convention on Civil Procedure Haager Abkommen über den Zivilprozeß, Haager Zivilprozeßabkommen (HZPr Abk.)

Zwischen einem Teil der Vertragsstaaten des HZPr Abk. von 1905 (für die Bundesrepublik Deutschland seit 1960) gilt jetzt das Haager Übereinkommen über den Zivilprozeß von 1954[3] (HZPr Übk.).

Weder Großbritannien und Nordirland noch die Vereinigten Staaten sind Mitgliedstaaten des HZPr Abk. oder des HZPr Übk.

Im Rechtsverkehr zwischen der Bundesrepublik Deutschland und Großbritannien mit Nordirland gilt das Deutsch-Britische Abkommen über den Rechtsverkehr vom 20. 3. 1928[4] nebst Ausführungsverordnung von 1929[5].

Im Rechtsverkehr zwischen der Bundesrepublik Deutschland und den USA gilt der Deutsch-Amerikanische Freundschafts-, Handels- und Schiffahrtsvertrag vom 29. 10. 1954[6]

Hague Convention on the Laws and Customs of War on Land Haager Landkriegsordnung (HLKO) *(1907)*

Hague Convention on the Service Abroad of Judicial and Extrajudicial Documents in Civil and Commercial Matters[7] Haager Übereinkommen über die Zustellung gerichtlicher und außergerichtlicher Schriftstücke im Ausland in Zivil- oder Handelssachen (Haager Zustellungsabkommen)

Hague Convention on the Taking of Evidence Abroad in Civil or Commercial Matters[8] Haager Beweisaufnahmeübereinkommen (Haager Übereinkommen über die Beweisaufnahme im Ausland in Zivil- und Handelssachen)

Hague Convention Relating to a Uniform Law of the Interational Sale of Goods[9] (1964 Hague Sales Convention) Haager Übereinkommen zur Einführung e-s Einheitlichen Gesetzes über den internationalen Kauf beweglicher Sachen (Haager Kaufrechtsübereinkommen von 1964)

Hague Convention Relating to a Uniform Law on the Formation of Contracts for the International Sale of Goods[9] (1964 Hague Formation Convention) Haager Übereinkommen zur Einführung e-s Einheitlichen Gesetzes über den Abschluß von Internationalen Kaufverträgen über bewegliche Sachen (Haager Abschlußübereinkommen von 1964)

Beide Übereinkommen über den Kauf beweglicher Sachen sind 1964 im Haag beschlossen worden. Zur Umsetzung durch die Vertragsstaaten Großbritannien und Bundesrepublik Deutschland, die nicht die alleinigen Vertragsstaaten sind, vgl. United Nations Convention on Contracts for the International Sale of Goods

Hague Rules Haager Regeln

Gemeint sind die Regeln der →International Convention for the Unification of Certain Rules of Law Relating to Bills of Lading

hail, ~ (storm) insurance (or **crop ~ insurance**) Hagelversicherung; **damage by ~ to property** Sachschaden durch Hagel

Haiti Haiti; **the Republic of ~** Republik Haiti

Haitian Haitianer(in); haitianisch

half Hälfte; halb; ~ **as much as** halb soviel wie; ~ **blood** →blood; **~-blooded** (or **~-bred**) halbbürtig, Halbblut-; **~-breed** Mischling; **~-brother** Halbbruder, Stiefbruder; **~-caste** Mischling *(bes. Anglo-Inder, Eurasier)*; ~ **commission** *(Börse)* halbe Provision *(e-s ~ commission man)*; ~ **commission man** *(Börse)* Vermittlungsagent e-s Effektenmaklers; **~-day employment** Halbtagsbeschäftigung; ~ **dollar** *Am* halber Dollar (50 cents); ~ **eagle** *Am* Fünfdollarstück *(Goldmünze)*; **~fare ticket** Fahrkarte zum halben Preis; **~-holiday** halber Tag frei, freier Nachmittag

half-interest Beteiligung zur Hälfte; **to have a ~ in a firm** an e-r Firma zur Hälfte beteiligt sein

half-mast halbmast; **flying flags at ~** Trauerbeflaggung; **to fly the flag at ~** halbmast flaggen

half-monthly halbmonatlich; zweimal monatlich

half pay halbes Gehalt, Wartegeld; ~ **major** (or **major on ~**) Major a. D. (außer Dienst); **to be placed on ~** auf Wartegeld gesetzt werden

half, one ~ penny (or **half a new penny**) (½ new penny) *Br* halber neuer Penny

half, at ~-price zum halben Preis

half quarter, ~ (day) Mitte des Quartals, Quartalsmedio; **~'s rent** halbe Vierteljahresmiete

half, ~-sister Halbschwester, Stiefschwester; ~ **stock** *Am* Aktie mit Nennwert von $ 50; **~-time** halbe Arbeitszeit; Kurzarbeitszeit; **time work** Kurzarbeit; **timer** Halbtagsarbeiter; in Kurzarbeit Tätiger; **~-weekly** halbwöchentlich; zweimal wöchentlich

half-yearly halbjährlich; zweimal jährlich; ~ **payment** Halbjahreszahlung; **in the course of the ~ period** im Laufe des Halbjahres

half, by ~ um die Hälfte; **division in ~** Halbierung; **prices have increased by ~** die Preise sind um die Hälfte gestiegen; **to work ~-day** (or **~-time**) halbtags arbeiten

hall Saal, Halle; *Br* Gutshaus, Herrenhaus; *Br* großer Speisesaal *(e-s college);* Versammlungsraum; Flur; **~mark** Feingehaltsstempel *(bei Edelmetallen);* **~ of residence** *Br* Studentenwohnheim

hall, city ~ Rathaus; **conference ~** Konferenzsaal; **town ~** *Br* Rathaus

hallmark Feingehaltstempel

hallmark *v* mit e-m Feingehaltstempel versehen

halves, to go ~ with sb. sich mit jdm (zu zweit) in die Kosten teilen

hamlet kleines Dorf *(ohne Kirche);* Weiler, Flecken

hammer Hammer; **~ and sickle** Hammer und Sichel *(in Verbindung mit dem Stern Abzeichen der Sowjetunion);* **to come under the ~** unter den Hammer kommen, versteigert werden

hammer *v,* **to ~ sb.** *Br (Börse)* (durch 3 Hammerschläge) erklären, daß Makler seinen finanziellen Verpflichtungen nicht nachgekommen ist; **to ~ (the market)** *(Börse)* durch Leerverkäufe die Kurse drücken

hand Hand; Arbeiter(in); Handschrift; Unterschrift; Handbreit *(4 Zoll, 10,16 cm);* **~bag snatching** Handtaschenraub; **~ bill** Handzettel; Flugblatt, Prospekt; **~cuffs** Handschellen; **~-made** mit der Hand gearbeitet, handgearbeitet; **~s-off policy** Nichteinmischungspolitik; **~out** *(zur Veröffentlichung freigegebene)* Mitteilung, Erklärung *(für die Presse);* Almosen, Gabe *(für Bettler)*

hand and seal Unterschrift und Siegel; **given under my ~** von mir eigenhändig unterschrieben und gesiegelt

handsale Verkauf *(beweglicher Sachen)* durch Handschlag

handwriting Handschrift; **(forensic) ~ expert** Schriftsachverständiger; **in a p.'s (own) ~** in eigener Handschrift, eigenhändig geschrieben; **~ sample** (or **specimen of ~**) Schriftprobe; **to make out a ~** e-e Handschrift entziffern

handwritten mit der Hand geschrieben; handschriftlich

hand, by ~ mit der Hand; durch Boten; **delivery by ~** unmittelbare Übergabe; **collection by ~** Inkasso durch Boten; Selbstabholung

hand, with clean ~s mit reinen Händen
Man kann im equity-Recht einen Anspruch nur dann geltend machen, wenn man sich selbst untadelig verhalten hat

hand, factory ~ Fabrikarbeiter(in); **farm ~** Landarbeiter(in); **at first ~** aus erster Hand; direkt (bezogen); **to buy sth. first-~** etw. aus erster Hand kaufen

hand, in ~ zur Verfügung, vorrätig; in Bearbeitung, unter Kontrolle; **cash in ~** Barbestand, Kassenbestand; **the letter in ~** der vorliegende Brief; **orders in ~** vorliegende Aufträge; **work in ~** in Bearbeitung befindliche Sachen; **to have sth. in ~** e-e Sache unter den Händen (od. in Arbeit) haben

hand, on ~ verfügbar, vorhanden, vorrätig; **on one's ~s** zur Last, „auf dem Halse"; **goods on ~** Warenbestand, Warenlager; **we have surplus stock on our ~s** unser Warenbestand ist zu groß

hand, second-~ aus zweiter Hand, gebraucht, antiquarisch (→*second*)

hand, under the ~ of unterzeichnet von; **under one's ~ and seal** eigenhändig unterschrieben und gesiegelt; **contract under ~** einfacher (nicht gesiegelter) Vertrag *(opp. contract under seal);* **document under ~** nicht gesiegelte Urkunde *(opp. document under seal)*

hand, vote by show of ~s Abstimmung durch Handaufheben; **as witness his ~(s)** laut eigener Unterschrift

hand, to be at ~ zur Hand sein; **to be short of ~s** zu wenig Arbeitskräfte haben; **to change ~s** in andere Hände übergehen; den Besitzer wechseln; **to come to ~** in jds Hände gelangen, eintreffen, eingehen *(Briefe, Aufträge);* **to have a ~ in** beteiligt sein an; **to have a matter in ~** e-e Sache in Arbeit haben; **to pass into private ~s** in Privatbesitz übergehen; **to pass through many ~s** durch viele Hände gehen; **to set one's ~ to** seine Unterschrift setzen unter; **to sign in one's own ~** eigenhändig unterschreiben

hand *v* aushändigen, überreichen, übergeben; **to ~ down to posterity** der Nachwelt überliefern; **to ~ in** *(Gesuch etc)* einreichen; *(etw.)* abgeben; **to ~ in one's resignation** sein Entlassungsgesuch einreichen; **to ~ on** weitergeben, weiterreichen; **to ~ over** übergeben; überlassen; aushändigen; **to ~ over to the police** *(jdn)* der Polizei übergeben; **to ~ over for trial** *(jdn)* zur Aburteilung übergeben

handed, heavy-~ plump, ungeschickt, undiplomatisch; drückend; **empty-~** mit leeren Händen; **open-~** freigiebig; **to be short-~** Mangel an Arbeitskräften haben

handing over of documents Übergabe von Dokumenten

handicapped behindert; **~ (persons)** Behinderte; **congenitally ~** mit e-r angeborenen Behinderung; **mentally ~** geistig behindert; **physically ~** Körperbehinderte; körperlich behindert

handicraft (Kunst-)Handwerk; **~ products** handgefertigte Erzeugnisse; **to exercise a ~** ein Handwerk ausüben

handle *v* handhaben, hantieren mit; behandeln, sich befassen mit; bearbeiten; *(Geschäfte, Angelegenheiten)* führen; handeln (in od. mit); *(Waren)* führen; *(Güter)* umschlagen; **~ with care, glass!** Vorsicht Glas! **to ~ the business of another** die Besorgung e-s Geschäfts für e-n anderen übernehmen; **to ~ a matter** e-e Angelegenheit besorgen; **to ~ large orders** große Aufträge bearbeiten; **to ~ a problem** ein Problem behandeln; **to ~ a ship** ein Schiff manövrieren

handling Handhabung; Behandlung; Manipulation; Bearbeitung; Umschlag; **~ charges** Bearbeitungsgebühr; Umschlagspesen; **~ fee** Bearbeitungsgebühr; **~ of business** Geschäftsbesorgung; **~ of cargo** Güterumschlag; **~ of complaints** Behandlung (od. Bearbeitung) von Beschwerden; **~ of goods** Umschlag der Güter; **~ of money** Umgehen mit Geld; Verwalten von Geld(ern); **~ stolen goods** *Br*[10] Hehlerei; **claims ~** Schadensabwicklung; **negligent ~** nachlässige Behandlung; **proper ~** richtige (od. sachgemäße) Behandlung; **much depends on the proper ~ of the situation** viel hängt davon ab, daß die Situation richtig erfaßt wird *(daß die richtigen Schritte unternommen werden)*

handsel Handgeld, Draufgeld

handwriting →hand

hang *v* aufhängen; *(an den Galgen)* hängen

hanging, execution by ~ Hinrichtung durch den Strang; **to sentence to death by ~** zum Tode durch den Strang verurteilen

hangar Flugzeughalle; Fahrzeugschuppen

hangman Henker, Scharfrichter

Hansard *Br* amtliches Parlamentsprotokoll *(nach dem Drucker Hansard benannt)*

hansardize *v Br (e-m M. P.)* seine frühere *(im Hansard protokollierte)* Aussage entgegenhalten

Hanseatic towns *Ger* Hansestädte (Hamburg, Bremen, Lübeck)

happen *v* geschehen, sich ereignen; **a condition ~s** e-e Bedingung tritt ein

happening Ereignis, Vorfall; **~ of the accident** Unfallereignis; **upon the ~ of the condition** bei Eintritt der Bedingung; **~ of the event insured** Eintritt des Versicherungsfalles

harass *v* belästigen

harassment Belästigung; **~ of tenants** Mieterbelästigung

harbo(u)r Hafen; *fig* Zufluchtsort; **~ authority** Hafenbehörde; **~ barrage** Hafensperre; **~ board** Hafenamt; **~ docks** Hafenanlagen; **~ dues** Hafengebühren, Hafengelder; **~ entrance** Hafeneinfahrt; **~ master** Hafenmeister; **~ police** Hafenpolizei; **~ of refuge** Nothafen, Zufluchtshafen; **~ regulations** Hafenordnung; **~ services** Hafenleistungen; **~ tug** Hafenschlepper; **to call at a ~** e-n Hafen anlaufen; **to enter a ~** in e-n Hafen einlaufen; **to leave a ~** aus e-m Hafen auslaufen

harbo(u)r *v* im Hafen anlegen (od. ankern); *(Schiff)* im Hafen Zuflucht gewähren; **to ~ an escaped criminal** e-m entwichenen Verbrecher Unterschlupf gewähren, e-n entwichenen Verbrecher verbergen

harbo(u)rage Zuflucht(sort)

hard hart *(opp. soft)*; schwierig *(opp. easy)*; fest, starr, unnachgiebig; **~ and fast rule** starre Rechtsnorm; bindende Regel *(die keine Abänderung zuläßt)*; **~ cash** Hartgeld; **~ copy** Original; **~ core** *fig* harter Kern *(z. B. e-r Untergrundbewegung)*; **~- core unemployed** längerfristig Arbeitsloser; **~ currency** harte Währung; **~-currency country** Hartwährungsland, währungsstarkes Land; **~ labor** *Am* Zwangsarbeit (→*labor 1.)*; **~-line posture** unnachgiebige Haltung; **~-liner** *pol* Befürworter e-s harten Kurses; **~ liquor** scharfe Getränke *(z. B. Whisky)*; **~ money** Hartgeld, Metallgeld *(opp. paper money)*; harte Währung; **~ selling** agressive Verkaufsmethode

hardship Härte; Unzumutbarkeit; **~ allowance** (or **grant**) Härtebeihilfe; **~ clause** Härteklausel; **settlement of ~ cases** Regelung von Härtefällen, Härteregelung; **to lead to undue ~** zu unbilligen Härten führen; **to relieve ~** Härten mildern

hardware Eisenwaren; Hardware *(technische Teile e-r EDV-Anlage; opp. software)*

hard, ~ wear starker Verschleiß; **~ work** schwere Arbeit

hard, to be ~ to sell sich schwer verkaufen lassen, schwer verkäuflich sein; **to be ~ up** nicht bei Kasse sein, mittellos sein; in Geldverlegenheit sein; **to drive a ~ bargain** aufs äußerste feilschen; *(auch fig)* e-n sehr hohen Preis verlangen; **to work ~** hart (od. fleißig, schwer) arbeiten

harden *v* fester werden; sich versteifen; steigen, anziehen *(Kurse, Preise)*

hardened criminal unverbesserlicher Verbrecher

hardening, prices are ~ die Preise festigen sich; die Kurse ziehen an; **~ of the market** Versteifung des Marktes

harm Schaden, Nachteil; **bodily ~** *(StrafR)* Körperverletzung; **grievous bodily ~** schwere Körperverletzung; **bodily or mental ~** körperlicher oder seelischer Schaden; **to do sb. ~** jdm Schaden zufügen; **to cause serious ~** ernstlich schädigen

harmful schädlich, nachteilig; **~ substance** Schadstoff; **to be ~ to the interests** die Interessen schädigen

harmless unschädlich, harmlos; **~ error** unerheblicher Verfahrensfehler *(ohne Einfluß auf das Urteil)*

harmonization Harmonisierung, Abstimmung *(z.B. von Tarifen);* Ausgleichung; →**International Convention on the H~ of Frontier Controls of Goods; ~ of legislation** *(EG)* Angleichung der Rechtsvorschriften; Rechtsangleichung; **~ of taxes** (or **tax ~**) Steuerharmonisierung

harmonize *v* harmonisieren; (miteinander) abstimmen; in Übereinstimmung bringen; *(EG) (Rechtsvorschriften)* angleichen; **to ~ policies** *(EG)* Politiken aufeinander abstimmen

Harmonized Commodity Description and Coding System →International Convention on the ~

harmony Harmonie, Einklang, Übereinstimmung; **~ in international affairs** Einklang in internationalen Angelegenheiten

harsh hart, streng; **~ judgment** hartes Urteil; **~ punishment** strenge Bestrafung

Harter Act *Am*[11] Seefrachtrechts-Gesetz *(von 1893)*

Der Harter Act, der die vertragliche Freizeichnung des Reeders für Gehilfenhaftung beschränkt und die gesetzliche Verfrachterhaftung einführt, findet auf amerikanische wie auf fremde Schiffe Anwendung, die aus amerikanischen Häfen auslaufen oder dort ankommen

harvest Ernte; **~ prospects** Ernteaussichten; **standing ~** Ernte auf dem Halm; **to bring in** (or **gather**) **the ~** die Ernte einbringen

hatch *v,* **to ~ a conspiracy** e-e Verschwörung anzetteln

haul Transport; Transportweg; (Fisch-)Zug; **long ~** Güterfernverkehr; **long ~ on the railway** *Br* (**railroad** *Am*) lange Transportwege auf der Eisenbahn; **short ~s** Güternahverkehr; **the thief made a good ~** der Dieb machte e-e gute Beute

haul *v* ziehen; *(Güter)* transportieren, befördern; *(Bergbau)* fördern; **to ~ down the flag** die Fahne niederholen, streichen *(opp. to hoist the flag)*

hauling Transport, Beförderung; **long distance ~** *Am* Güterfernverkehr

haulage Transport *(von Gütern);* Transportkosten; *(Bergbau)* Förderung; **~ contractor** Transportunternehmer; Güterkraftverkehrsunternehmer; Rollfuhrunternehmer; **road (freight) ~** Güterkraftverkehr *(Beförderung von Gütern mit Kraftfahrzeugen);* **long distance road ~** *Br* Güterfernverkehr; Fernlastverkehr; **road ~ firm** Güterkraftverkehrsunternehmen

hauler (or **haulier**), **road (freight) ~** Güterkraftverkehrsunternehmer

have *v,* **to ~ and to hold** *Am* innehaben, besitzen *(Klausel bei Eigentumsübertragung von Grundbesitz)*

have, the ~s and the ~-nots die Besitzenden und die Besitzlosen *(reiche und arme Länder)*

haver *Scot (in e-m Prozeß)* vorzeigepflichtiger Inhaber e-r Urkunde

hawk *pol* Falke

hawker Hausierer, Straßenhändler; Reisegewerbetreibender *(Br unterscheidet sich vom →pedlar durch Benutzung e-s Transportmittels);* **~'s licence (~se)** Reisegewerbekarte

hawking Hausieren; Hausierhandel, Straßenhandel; Reisegewerbe

hazard Gefahr, Risiko; Wagnis; Gefahrenquelle; *(VersR) (versicherbares)* Risiko; Hasardspiel *(Art Würfelspiel);* **~ not covered** *(VersR)* ausgeschlossenes Risiko; **~ to road safety** Gefahr für die Verkehrssicherheit; **~s of the sea** Seegefahr; **accident ~** Unfallrisiko; **fire ~s** Feuergefahr; **moral ~** *(VersR)* subjektives Risiko; Risiko falscher Angaben des Versicherten; **physical ~** *(VersR)* objektives Risiko

hazard *v* wagen, aufs Spiel setzen

hazardous gewagt, gefährlich, riskant; **~ contract** *Am* von e-m ungewissen Ereignis abhängiger Vertrag; Risikovertrag (→*aleatory contract);* **~ enterprise** Risikogeschäft; **~ goods** *(VersR)* gefährliche Güter; **~ speculation** gewagte Spekulation; **~ waste** gefährliche Abfälle

head Kopf; Leiter, Vorsteher, Chef, Führer; Einzelperson; Stück *(Vieh);* Überschrift; Hauptpunkt; **~ clerk** Bürovorsteher; **~ hunter** Personalberater für die Suche nach Führungskräften

headline Schlagzeile; **~s (news)** (or **~s of the news**) Rundfunknachrichten in Schlagzeilen; **~ catcher** Politiker, der Schlagzeilen macht; **to hit the ~s** in die Schlagzeilen geraten

head, ~master (~mistress) Direktor(in) e-r Schule; Schulleiter(in); **~money** Kopfgeld *(auf jds Ergreifung ausgesetzte Belohnung);* **~-notes** Leitsatz *(e-s Urteils) (in welchem in der Regel das der Entscheidung zugrundeliegende Rechtsprinzip formuliert wird)*

head, ~ of an agency *Am* Behördenleiter; **~s of (an) agreement** Hauptpunkte e-s Vertrages; **~ of cattle** Stück Vieh; **~s of the charge** Punkte der Anklage; **~ of a delegation** Delegationsleiter; **~ of a department** Abteilungsleiter; Dezernent; *Am* Minister; **~ of the family** Familienvorstand; **~ of the government** Regierungschef; **~ of household** Haushaltsvorstand, Familienvorstand; **~ of a letter** Briefkopf; **at the ~ of the list** an erster Stelle der Liste; **~ of a mission** *dipl* Missionschef (→*mission*); **~s of a speech** (Haupt-)Punkte e-r Rede;

~ **of state** Staatsoberhaupt; ~**s of state or government** Staats- oder Regierungschefs

head, to be at the ~ of an der Spitze stehen von; vorstehen; **to be at the ~ of affairs** an der Spitze stehen; **to be at the ~ of the →poll** *(1.)*

head, ~ office Hauptverwaltung, Hauptsitz, Zentrale, Direktion *(opp. branch office)*; ~**-on** *(Auto)* vorn aufgefahren; frontal *(cf. ~-on →collision)*

headquarters (H. Q., Hq.) *mil* Hauptquartier; *com* Hauptgeschäftsstelle, Hauptbüro, Zentrale; Sitz *(e-s Unternehmens)*; ~ **of an agency** *Am* (Haupt-)Sitz e-r Behörde; ~ **agreement** Abkommen über den Sitz e-r *(internationalen)* Organisation

headquarter *v Am* das Hauptbüro eröffnen; **to be ~ed** seinen Hauptsitz haben

headway Fortschritt; **to make some ~** einige Fortschritte erzielen

head *v* an der Spitze stehen; führen, leiten; mit e-r Überschrift versehen; **to ~ a delegation** e-e Delegation führen; **to ~ the list** an erster Stelle der Liste stehen; ~ **a revolt** an der Spitze e-r Revolte stehen, e-e Revolte anführen

headed by geführt sein von; unterstehen

heading Überschrift, Titel, Rubrik; *com* Posten, Position; ~ **of a bill** Kopf e-r Rechnung; ~ **of the customs tariff** Position des Zolltarifs; **letter ~** Briefkopf; **sub~** Untertitel; **this comes under a separate ~** dies fällt (od. gehört) in e-e besondere Rubrik

health Gesundheit; **H~ and Safety Commission** *Br*[12] Kommission für Gesundheit und Sicherheit der Arbeitnehmer; ~ **authorities** Gesundheitsbehörden; ~ **care** Gesundheitsvorsorge; ~ **centre** *Br* Poliklinik; ~ **certificate** Gesundheitszeugnis; **H~ Department** *Am* Gesundheitsministerium; ~ **economies** Gesundheitsökonomik; ~ **examination** Gesundheitsprüfung; ~ **food shop** *Br* (**store** *Am*) Reformhaus

health insurance Krankenversicherung; ~ **fund** Krankenkasse; **to belong to a (private) ~ scheme** *Br* Mitglied e-r Krankenkasse sein; **to be a member of a ~ plan** *Am* Mitglied e-r Krankenkasse sein; **to subscribe** (or **belong**) **to a ~ scheme** e-r Krankenversicherung angehören

health maintenance organization (HMO) *Am* private Krankenversicherungsorganisation *(gesetzlich anerkanntes Konzept, u. a. der vorbeugenden Medizin gewidmet, →prepaid medicine)*

health, ~ measures Maßnahmen für den Gesundheitsschutz; ~ **officer** *Am* Beamter des Gesundheitsamtes; Hafenarzt, Quarantänearzt; ~ **protection standards** Gesundheitsschutznormen; **for ~ reasons** aus gesundheitlichen Gründen; ~ **screening** Vorsorgeuntersuchung; **H~ Service Commissioner** Beschwerdebeauftragter für das Gesundheitswesen

health, bill of ~ Gesundheitspaß *(→bill 1.)*; **Board of H~** *Am (einzelstaatl.)* Gesundheitsamt; **Department of H~** *Am* Gesundheitsministerium; **Department of H~ and Social Security** *Br* →Department; **International H~ Regulations** Internationale Gesundheitsvorschriften *(der Weltgesundheitsorganisation; →World Health Organization)*; **mental ~** geistige Gesundheit; **National H~ Service** *Br* Staatlicher Gesundheitsdienst *(→National)*; **physical ~** physische Gesundheit; **public ~** Gesundheitswesen; Volksgesundheit; **→World H~ Organization; to injure sb.'s ~** jds Gesundheit schädigen

hear *v* hören; verhandeln (über); **to ~ a case** in e-r Sache verhandeln (the judge ~s the case); **to ~ and determine** richterlich entscheiden; **to ~ evidence** Beweis aufnehmen (od. erheben); die Beweisaufnahme vornehmen; Aussage hören; **to ~ the parties** die Parteien anhören; den Parteien rechtliches Gehör gewähren; **to ~ a motion** über e-n Antrag verhandeln

heard, after having ~ the parties nach Anhörung der Parteien; **to be ~ as a witness** als Zeuge gehört werden

hearing (Gerichts-)Verhandlung, mündliche Verhandlung, (Gerichts-)Sitzung; Termin; Anhörung, rechtliches Gehör; gerichtsähnliches Verfahren in Verwaltungssachen *(Verhandlung und Beweisaufnahme)*; *Am parl* Hearing, öffentl. Anhörung(sverfahren) *(Anhörung und Vernehmung vorgeladener Personen vor e-m Ausschuß des Kongresses)*; ~ **date** Verhandlungstermin; ~ **examiner** *Am* mit richterlicher Funktion ausgestatteter Beamter der →Federal Trade Commission; ~ **in camera** (*Br* **in chambers**) Verhandlung unter Ausschluß der Öffentlichkeit; ~ **of an appeal** Berufungsverhandlung; ~ **of evidence** Zeugenvernehmung; Beweisaufnahme *(→evidence)*; ~ **of witnesses** Zeugenvernehmung; ~ **officer** *Am* erstinstanzlicher Richter in e-m Verwaltungsverfahren

hearing, adjournment of a ~ Vertagung e-r Verhandlung; **at the ~ on** . . . im (Verhandlungs-)Termin vom . . .; **date** (or **day**) **of the ~** Verhandlungstermin; **(oral) ~** *(PatR)* Anhörung; **preliminary ~** Voruntersuchung; **public ~** öffentliche Verhandlung; **to adjourn a ~** e-e Verhandlung vertagen; **to be down** (or **to come up**) **for ~** zur Verhandlung anstehen; **to fix a (day for a) ~** e-n Termin anberaumen; **to get a fair ~** rechtliches Gehör bekommen; **to set a case down for a ~** in e-r Sache Termin ansetzen; **to suspend the ~** die Verhandlung aussetzen; **the ~ took place on** . . . die Verhandlung fand statt am . . .

hearsay Hörensagen, Gerücht; ~ **evidence** Beweis vom Hörensagen; Wiedergabe von Behauptungen Dritter *(vor Gericht)* *(opp. direct* *evidence of the witness himself);* ~ **rule** den ~ evidence verbietende Beweisregel *(Br*[13] *gilt nur noch für Strafverfahren)*

heating expense Heizungskosten

heavy schwer; ~ **buyer** Großabnehmer; guter Käufer; ~ **consumer** Großverbraucher; ~ **fall of prices** Kurssturz; ~ **fine** hohe Geldstrafe; ~ **freight** (or **goods**) Schwergut *(opp. light freight or goods);* ~ **goods vehicles** schwere Lastkraftwagen; ~ **indebtedness** hohe Verschuldung; ~ **industry** Schwerindustrie; ~ **industry shares** Aktien der Schwerindustrie; ~ **loss** schwerer Verlust; *(VersR)* Großschaden; ~ **market** gedrückter (oder lustloser) Markt *(in dem die Preise und Kurse fallen);* ~ **orders** große Aufträge; ~ **penalty** schwere (od. hohe) Strafe; ~ **sales** Massenverkäufe; ~ **traffic** starker Verkehr; ~ **weight** *bes. Am* Prominenter; ~ **work** Schwerarbeit; ~ **worker** Schwerarbeiter

heavily, ~ **fined** mit e-r hohen Geldstrafe bestraft; **to be** ~ **indebted** hoch verschuldet sein; *(jdm)* sehr zu Dank verpflichtet sein

hebdomadal wöchentlich

heckle *v pol (in e-r Versammlung)* störende Fragen stellen; *(während e-r Rede)* dazwischenrufen

heckler *pol* störender Fragesteller

hectograph Hektograph, Vervielfältigungsgerät

hedge Hecke; *com* Hedge, Sicherungsgeschäft, Deckungsgeschäft, Geschäft mit Gegendeckung *(Verbindung e-s Kaufs oder Verkaufs mit e-m Termingeschäft zur Verminderung der durch Preis- od. Kursschwankungen bedingten Verlustrisiken im börsenmäßigen Waren-, Devisen- oder Wertpapierverkehr);* ~ **clause** Schutzklausel; **inflation** ~ Absicherung gegen Inflation; **long** ~ Terminkaufshedge, Sicherungskauf auf Termin; **short** ~ Terminverkaufshedge, Sicherungsverkauf auf Termin

hedge *v* sich absichern, das Risiko eingrenzen; *(durch Abschluß e-s Warentermingeschäfts od. e-s Devisentermingeschäfts)* sich gegen Verluste sichern; Deckungsgeschäft abschließen; **the investor** ~**s against inflation** *(e.g. by purchasing equities)* der Anleger sichert sich gegen die Inflation

hedged in by clauses verklausuliert

hedging Hedging; Absicherung, Risikoeingrenzung; Abschluß e-s Deckungsgeschäfts *(cf. hedge); (im Wertpapierhandel)* Abschluß e-s Sicherungsgeschäfts *(bei dem e-e Position durch e-n Leerverkauf in e-m anderen Papier abgesichert wird);* ~ **a rate** Kurssicherung

hegemony Hegemonie, Vormachtstellung *(e-s Staates gegenüber e-m anderen)*

height Höhe; (Körper-)Größe

heir Erbe (to or of sb. jds)

Ursprünglich bedeutete heir der gesetzliche Erbe von unbeweglichem Vermögen.

Br Seit dem Administration of Estates Act, 1925, gilt bei Fehlen eines Testaments gleiches Erbfolgerecht in Mobilien und Immobilien. Der Begriff „heir" existiert im modernen englischen Erbrecht nicht mehr.

Am Der Begriff heir wird gelegentlich auf alle Personen ausgedehnt, auf die das Vermögen des Erblassers übergeht, und umfaßt auch →distributees. Die gesetzliche Erbfolge in den USA ist jetzt gewöhnlich ohne Rücksicht auf die Natur des Erbgegenstandes geregelt.

Im Ggs. zum deutschen Recht geht die Erbschaft nicht auf den Erben über, sondern auf einen Zwischenberechtigten (personal representative) und zwar *Br* hinsichtlich des beweglichen und unbeweglichen, *Am* des beweglichen Nachlasses

heir, ~ **apparent** *Br* gesetzlicher (od. rechtmäßiger) Erbe *(e-s noch Lebenden; bezieht sich nur auf titles of nobility);* Thronfolger; ~ **at law** gesetzlicher Erbe *(Am von Grundbesitz) (opp. ~ by devise);* ~ **by devise** *Am* testamentarischer Erbe *(von Grundbesitz);* ~ **collateral** aus der Seitenlinie stammender Erbe; ~ **general** *Am* →~ at law; ~ **in mobilibus** *Scot* Mobiliarerbe; ~ **presumptive** mutmaßlicher Erbe *(sofern kein näherer Verwandter mehr geboren wird);* ~ **to the throne** Thronerbe, Thronfolger

heir, alternate ~ *Am* Ersatzerbe; **appointment of an** ~ Einsetzung e-s Erben, Erbeinsetzung; **co-**~ Miterbe; **expectant** ~ Erbschaftsanwärter; **in default of male** ~**s** bei Nichtvorhandensein von männlichen Erben; **failing** ~**s** bei Nichtvorhandensein von Erben; **forced** ~ *Am* pflichtteilsberechtigter Erbe; **joint** ~ Miterbe; **lawful** ~ rechtmäßiger Erbe; **legal** ~ gesetzlicher Erbe; **presumptive** ~ →~ presumptive; **property to be divided among** ~**s** Erbmasse; **rightful** ~ rechtmäßiger Erbe; **sole** ~ Alleinerbe; Universalerbe; **statutory** ~ *Am* gesetzlicher Erbe, Intestaterbe; **substituted** ~ *Am* Ersatzerbe; **testamentary** ~ *Am* Testamentserbe, testamentarischer Erbe; **to appoint sb. one's** ~ jdn als Erben einsetzen; **to become** ~ **to an estate** e-e Erbschaft machen, erben; **to make sb. one's** ~ jdn zu seinem Erben einsetzen; **the property passes to the** ~**s** das Vermögen fällt an die Erben

heiress Erbin *(cf. heir)*

heirless ohne Erben

heirloom *(altes)* (Familien-)Erbstück *(das direkt an den Erben und nicht an den →executor fällt)*

heirship *Am und Scot* Erbeneigenschaft; Erbberechtigung; **forced** ~ *Am* Pflichtteil

held *(vom Gericht)* entschieden; **the court** ~ das

Gericht hat für Recht erkannt; **a court is** ~ e-e Gerichtssitzung wird abgehalten; ~ **by** im Besitz von; **to be (~) covered** *(VersR)* versichert sein

Hellenic Republic Griechische Republik *(cf. Greece)*

helm *fig* Ruder; **a political party is at the** ~ e-e politische Partei ist am Ruder

Helsinki, ~ **Agreement** Abkommen von Helsinki; ~ **Conference** Konferenz von Helsinki (→*Conference on Security and Cooperation in Europe);* **invoking the** ~ **Agreement** unter Hinweis auf das Abkommen von Helsinki

henchman *pol* Gefolgsmann, Anhänger

herbage *Br* Weiderecht

hereditable (ver)erblich, vererbbar *(Krankheit)*

hereditament *Br* bebautes oder unbebautes Grundstück *(als Bemessungsgrundlage für die Kommunalabgaben; Am* vererblicher Vermögensgegenstand *(kann zum bewegl. od. unbewegl. Vermögen gehören und e-e Sache od. anderer Rechtsgegenstand sein);* **corporeal ~s** *Br* Grundbesitz (freehold); *Am* vererbliche Gegenstände; **incorporeal ~s** *(mit dem Grund und Boden verbundene) (Am* vererbliche) Rechte *(z.B. easements)*

Br hereditament wird heute nur noch als Einheit für Steuerzwecke benutzt

hereditary erblich, vererblich; erbbedingt; ~ **aristocracy** Erbadel; ~ **defect** Erbfehler; ~ **disease** Erbkrankheit; ~ **monarchy** Erbmonarchie; ~ **peerage** *Br* Erbadel; ~ **succession** *Am* gesetzliche Erbfolge; ~ **taint** erbliche Belastung; ~ **tenancy** Erbpacht

heredity Erblichkeit, Vererbung *(im biologischen Sinne)*

here, ~**inabove** vorstehend, im vorstehenden; ~**inafter** nachstehend; im nachstehenden, im folgenden; ~**inbefore** vorstehend, im vorstehenden; ~**tofore** bisherig, bis jetzt, vorher; ~**under** untenstehend, weiter unten

herewith hiermit, anbei; **enclosed** ~ anliegend, beifolgend

heritable vererbbar; erbfähig; *Scot* dinglich; ~ **bonds** *Scot* Pfandbriefe; ~ **property** *Scot* Grundbesitz; ~ **rights** *Scot* Rechte an Grundbesitz; ~ **securities** *Scot* Pfandbriefe

heritage *(kulturelles)* Erbe, Erbgut; *Scot* Grundbesitz; **archaeological** ~ archäologisches Kulturgut; **Convention for the Protection of the World Cultural and Natural H~**[14] Übereinkommen zum Schutz des Kultur- und Naturerbes der Welt

heritor *Scot* Grundeigentümer

hiatus in relations between Stillstand in den Beziehungen zwischen

hidden geheim, verborgen; ~ **defects** versteckte Mängel *(opp. apparent defects);* ~ **dividends** versteckte Gewinnausschüttungen; ~ **economy** Untergrundwirtschaft, Schattenwirtschaft; ~ **reserves** stille Reserven *(opp. visible reserves);* ~ **offer** verstecktes Angebot *(in e-r Zeitung);* ~ **threat** versteckte Drohung; ~ **unemployment** verborgene Arbeitslosigkeit

hiding, to be in ~ sich verborgen halten

hierarchy Hierarchie, Rangordnung; ~ **of diplomatic agents** diplomatische Rangordnung

hifo →highest-in-first-out

high hoch; hochstehend; *sl.* angeheitert, *(durch Suchtstoffe)* berauscht

High Church *Br* Hochkirche

Hochkirchliche Richtung der →Anglican Church, in Lehre und Ritus der katholischen Kirche ähnlich (Anglokatholiken)

high, ~**-class goods** erstklassige Ware; ~ **command** *mil* Oberkommando; ~ **Commission** Hochkommission (*Vertretung eines Commonwealth-Staates in London*); **H~ →Commissioner; H~ Contracting Parties** Hohe Vertragsparteien; **H~ Court of Justice** *Br* Oberstes *(erstinstanzliches)* Zivilgericht (→*court);* **H~ Court of Judiciary** *Scot* Oberstes Gericht für Strafsachen; **H~ Court of Parliament** *Br* (das gesamte) Parlament; ~**-definition television** (HDTV) hochauflösendes Fernsehen (HDTV); ~ **finance** Hochfinanz; *Am colloq. (unredliche)* Spekulationsgeschäfte

high-grade hochwertig, erstklassig; ~ **investments** erstklassige Kapitalanlagen; ~ **securities** erstklassige Wertpapiere

high interest hohe Zinsen; **yielding** ~ hochverzinslich

high, ~ **official** hoher Beamter; ~ **pressure salesmanship** zielbewußte Verkaufsmethode; ~ **price** hoher Preis; ~**-priced** teuer *(Ware);* hoch im Kurs *(Wertpapiere);* **(of)** ~ **quality** hochwertig; ~**-quality goods** hochwertige Ware; Güter des gehobenen Bedarfs; **of** ~ **rank** hochgestellt; ~**ranking official** hoher Beamter

high rate hoher Satz (od. Preis, Kurs); **at a** ~ **(of interest)** zu hohen Zinsen

high, of ~ **repute** hoch angesehen, von gutem Ruf; ~**-rise flat** *Br* Wohnung im Hochhaus; ~ **school** höhere Schule; *Am* (Art) Mittelschule *(die Schüler zwischen 12 und 18 Jahren für das College vorbereitet)*

high sea(s) offenes Meer; hohe See *(außerhalb der Hoheitsgrenze; cf. territorial waters);* **Convention on the H~ S~**[15] Übereinkommen über die Hohe See; **at the ~s** auf hoher See

high, of ~ **standing** hoch angesehen; **H~ Tech(nology)** Hochtechnologie, Spitzentechnologie; ~ **treason** Hochverrat; Landesverrat; ~-**water mark** Flutmarke, Flutlinie; Hochwasserstand

high, orders are running ~ es kommen sehr viele Aufträge herein

higher höher; ~ **authority** übergeordnete Stelle, vorgesetzte Behörde

higher bid höheres Gebot, Mehrgebot; **to make a** ~ *(bei Versteigerungen)* höher bieten, überbieten

higher education Hochschul(aus)bildung; ~ **diploma** Hochschuldiplom; ~ **institutions** Hochschulen

higher, ~**-grade official** höherer Beamter; **the** ~ **grades of the civil service** der höhere Staatsdienst; ~ **price** höherer Preis (od. Kurs)

higher rate, inflation runs at a ~ **in England than in ...** die Inflationsrate ist in England höher als in ...; **Queen's Counsel charges (at) a** ~ **than junior counsel** Queen's Counsel berechnet höhere Gebühren als der junior counsel

higher, to bid ~ s. to make a →~ bid

highest höchst, oberst; ~ **amount** Höchstbetrag; ~ **authority** höchste Instanz; ~ **award** höchste Auszeichnung; ~ **bid** Höchstgebot *(bei Versteigerungen)*

highest bidder Meistbietender *(bei Versteigerungen)*; **to sell to the** ~ meistbietend verkaufen

highest-in-first-out (hifo) „am teuersten eingekauft – zuerst verbraucht" *(Methode der Bewertung des Vorratsvermögens; cf. fifo, lifo)*

highest, ~ **level** Höchststand *(von Preisen oder Kursen)*; ~ **price** Höchstpreis; Höchstkurs; ~ **and lowest prices** *(Börse)* höchste und niedrigste Kurse

highness, Her (His) Royal (Imperial) H~ Ihre (Seine) Königliche (Kaiserliche) Hoheit

highups *colloq.* prominente Personen

highway Straße, Hauptstraße, Landstraße; *bes. Am* Fern(verkehrs)straße, Autobahn; ~ **accident** *Am* Verkehrsunfall, Autounfall; **H**~ **Code** *Br* Straßenverkehrsordnung; ~ **(common) carrier** *Am* Beförderungsgesellschaft; Fernspediteur; ~**man** Straßenräuber; ~ **robbery** Straßenraub; ~ **transportation** Güterkraftverkehr; Güterverkehr mit Lastkraftwagen; ~ **use tax** *Am (z. B. im Staat New York)* Autobahnbenutzungsgebühr

highway, express ~ *Am* Schnellverkehrsstraße; Autobahn; **four-lane** ~ *Am* Autobahn mit vier Fahrbahnen; **maintenance of** ~**s** Instandhaltung von Landstraßen (od. *Am* Autobahnen); **rendering** ~**s dangerous** Gefährdung des Straßenverkehrs; **to keep** ~**s in repair** Landstraßen (etc) instandhalten

hijack *v (Flugzeug während des Fluges)* entführen; *(Güter)* stehlen von *(z. B. e-m zwangsweise gestoppten Lkw)*; *(Fahrzeug)* (anhalten und) berauben

hijacked plane entführte Maschine

hijacking[16] (Flugzeug-)Entführung *(während des Fluges)*; Luftpiraterie

hijacker Flugzeugentführer, Luftpirat

Hil. (**Hilary term** or **Hilary sittings**) *Br* Gerichtstermine in der Zeit vom 11. Januar bis Mittwoch vor Ostern

hill or mountain areas Berggebiete *(für Landwirtschaft)*

hint Hinweis; Wink; Anspielung (at auf)

hire Miete, Mieten *(nur von beweglichen Sachen)*; Mietpreis, Mietzins; Einstellen *(von Arbeitskräften)*; (Arbeits-)Lohn; ~ **car** *Br* Mietwagen; ~ **charges** Mietgebühren; ~ **contract** s. contract of →~; ~ **of labo(u)r** Einstellung von Arbeitskräften; ~ **of a motor car** Mieten e-s Kraftwagens; ~ **of a temporary worker** Entleihung e-s Leiharbeitnehmers

hire-purchase (H. P.) *Br* Teilzahlungskauf, Abzahlungskauf, Ratenkauf *(unter Eigentumsvorbehalt des Verkäufers bis zur vollständigen Zahlung des Kaufpreises; cf. credit sale agreement)*; ~ **agreement** *Br*[17] Teilzahlungsvertrag; Ratenkaufvertrag; ~ **company** *Br* Teilzahlungsinstitut, Kundenkreditbank; ~ **price** *Br* Abzahlungspreis; Preis bei Ratenzahlung; ~ **system** Abzahlungssystem; ~ **terms** *Br* Teilzahlungsbedingungen; ~ **transactions** *Br* Abzahlungsgeschäfte; **to buy a car on** ~ *Br* ein Auto auf Abzahlung kaufen; **to enter into a** ~ **agreement** e-n Abzahlungsvertrag abschließen

hire of services, contract for the ~ Dienstvertrag

hire, contract of ~ Mietvertrag; **to enter into a contract of** ~ e-n Mietvertrag abschließen

hire, for ~ zu vermieten; *(Taxi)* frei; **bicycles for** ~ Fahrräder zu vermieten; **carriage for** ~ entgeltliche Beförderung; **to be for** ~ zu vermieten sein

hire, on ~ zu vermieten; mietweise; **person letting on** ~ Vermieter *(beweglicher Sachen)*; **person taking on** ~ Mieter *(beweglicher Sachen)*; **to let (out) on** ~ vermieten; **to take on** ~ mieten

hire *v (bewegl. Sachen)* mieten; *(Arbeitskräfte)* anstellen, einstellen, in Dienst nehmen; **to** ~ **(out)** *(bewegl. Sachen)* vermieten; ausleihen; **to** ~ **out temporary workers** Leiharbeitnehmer *(an Entleiher)* überlassen; **to sub-**~ untervermieten; **to** ~ **a car** *Br* ein Auto mieten; **to** ~ **and fire** *Am* einstellen und entlassen; **to** ~ **an attorney** *Am* e-n Anwalt nehmen; **to** ~ **a murderer** e-n Mörder dingen; **to** ~ **a sailor** e-n Seemann anheuern

hired labo(u)r Leiharbeitskräfte

hiring Mieten; *Am* Einstellen, Anstellen; ~ **(out)** Vermieten *(beweglicher Sachen)*; ~ **age** *Am* Einstellungsalter; ~ **agreement** Mietvertrag *(über bewegl. Sachen)*; *Am* Dienstvertrag; ~ **charge** Miete, Mietgebühr *(für bewegl. Sachen)*; ~ **of goods** Mieten (od. Vermietung) *(von bewegl. Sachen)*; ~ **of labo(u)r** Einstellung von Arbeitskräften

hiring out, ~ **temporary workers** Arbeitnehmerüberlassung; **firm** ~ **temporary workers** Verleihunternehmen

hirer Mieter *(e-r bewegl. Sache)*; Vermieter *(e-r bewegl. Sache)*; *Br* Käufer *(bei e-m Mietkauf)*; ~ **and** ~**-out** Entleiher und Verleiher *(bei Arbeitnehmerüberlassung)*; ~ **of a safe** Mieter e-s Safes

historical building Baudenkmal; **preservation** (or **upkeep**) **of a** ~ Erhaltung e-s Baudenkmals

historical cost ursprüngliche Anschaffungskosten; ~ **accounting** Istkostenrechnung

history Geschichte; ~ **of law** Rechtsgeschichte

hit Zusammenstoß; (Erfolgs-)Treffer; treffende Bemerkung; Schlager; ~**-and-run** fahrerflüchtig; ~**-and-run driver** *(nach Unfall)* flüchtiger Fahrer; ~**-and-run driving** Fahrerflucht

hive off *v Br* Teile e-r Industrie (od. e-s Geschäftes) absondern; Teile e-r verstaatlichten Industrie reprivatisieren

hoard *v* ansammeln, Vorrat anlegen; horten; hamstern

hoarding Ansammlung; Horten; Hamsterei; *Br* Bretterzaun, Reklametafel; Plakatwand; Litfaßsäule, Anschlagbrett *(für Plakate od. Reklame)*; ~ **of money** Geldhortung *(Anspeichern von Zahlungsmitteln ohne nutzbringende Anlage)*; ~ **purchase** Hortungskauf

hobby income Einkünfte aus e-m Hobby

hoist *v* hochziehen, hochwinden; *(Flagge)* hissen *(opp. to haul down)*

hold Macht, *(starker)* Einfluß (on auf); Griff, (Fest-)Halten; **(ship's)** ~ Schiffsraum, Laderaum; **in the** ~ im Laderaum; **to get a** ~ **on sb.** jdn unter seinen Einfluß bekommen

holdback pay *Am (vom Arbeitgeber vorläufig)* zurückgehaltener Lohn

holdover das (od. der) Übriggebliebene; *Am (nach Ablauf der Amtszeit)* im Amt Verbliebener; ~ **appropriation** *Am parl* Bewilligung von Geldern, die bis zu ihrem Verbrauch für den Zweck, für den sie bewilligt wurden, verfügbar bleiben

hold(-)up Störung; Stockung; *(bewaffneter)* Überfall; **bank** ~ Überfall auf e-e Bank; **traffic** ~ Verkehrsstockung

hold *v* halten, festhalten; der Meinung sein, halten für; *(richterlich)* entscheiden; für Recht erkennen; innehaben, besitzen; *(Wahl etc)* abhalten; *(Waren für Kunden)* zurücklegen; **the court →held; a court is →held; to →have and to** ~

hold *v*, **to** ~ **back** zurückhalten; **the police held back the crowd** die Polizei hielt die Menge zurück; **to** ~ **back with a purchase** sich mit e-m Kauf zurückhalten; **to** ~ **covered** *(vorläufig)* versichern (od. durch Versicherung dekken); **to** ~ **prices down** die Preise niedrighalten; **to** ~ **on** durchhalten; sich behaupten; *(schwierige Lage)* durchsetzen; **to** ~ **on to one's shares** den Besitz seiner Aktien nicht aufgeben; **to** ~ **out** sich behaupten (against gegen); sich halten, fest sein; aushalten; (an)dauern; **to** ~ **out for** bestehen auf; **to** ~ **oneself out as a partner** sich als Gesellschafter ausgeben (→*holding o. s. out as a partner*); **to** ~ **over** verschieben, aufschieben; über die festgesetzte Zeit hinaus behalten; *(Wechsel, Schecks wegen Formfehler)* am Einlieferungstag nicht einlösen; *(nach Ablauf der Mietzeit)* Räumung verzögern; *(nach Ablauf der Pachtzeit)* in Besitz halten; *Am (über die Amtsdauer)* im Amt bleiben; **to** ~ **together** zusammenhalten; **to** ~ **up** in die Höhe halten; zeigen; aufhalten; überfallen (und ausrauben); **to** ~ **up the traffic** den Verkehr aufhalten; **to** ~ **sb. up for →contempt of court**

hold *v*, **to** ~ **a brief** vor Gericht vertreten; als Anwalt auftreten (for für); **to** ~ **counsel** sich beraten; **to** ~ **court** Gericht abhalten; **to** ~ **an election** e-e Wahl abhalten; **to** ~ **good** *(noch)* gelten, zutreffen; **to** ~ **harmless** schadlos halten; **to** ~ **on** (or **under**) **a lease** zur Miete haben; in Pacht haben; **to** ~ **the line** *tel* am Apparat bleiben; **to** ~ **a meeting** e-e Versammlung abhalten; **to** ~ **sb. for murder** jdn unter Mordverdacht in Haft halten; **to** ~ **an office** ein Amt innehaben; **to** ~ **office** an der Macht sein *(z. B. e-e Partei)*; **to** ~ **sb. a prisoner** jdn gefangen halten; **to** ~ **the purse** die Kasse führen; **to** ~ **sb. responsible for sth.** jdn für etw. verantwortlich machen; **to** ~ **shares** (or **stock**) Aktien besitzen; **to** ~ **on trust** *(etw.)* als Treuhänder verwalten; **to** ~ **a view** e-e Ansicht vertreten

holder Inhaber, Besitzer; ~ **of an account** Kontoinhaber; ~ **of an annuity** Rentenempfänger, Rentenberechtigter; ~ **of a bill (of exchange)** Wechselinhaber; ~ **of a cheque (check)** Scheckinhaber

holder in due course[18] *(kraft guten Glaubens)* legitimierter Inhaber *(e-s Wechsels, Schecks)*; gutgläubiger Erwerber *(e-s Wertpapiers)*

Jemand, der gutgläubig einen mit (nicht offensichtlichen, aus der Urkunde erkennbaren) Mängeln behafteten Wechsel oder Scheck gegen geldwerte Leistung erworben hat und der von jedem wechsel- oder scheckmäßig Haftenden Zahlung verlangen kann

holder, ~ in good faith gutgläubiger Inhaber (od. Besitzer); **~ of a licen|ce (~se)** Inhaber e-r Lizenz (od. Konzession); **~ of a pension** Pensionsempfänger, Pensionsberechtigter; **~ of a pledge** Pfandnehmer, Pfandgläubiger; **~ of a power of attorney** Inhaber e-r Vollmacht; **~ of record** *Am (im Aktienbuch der Gesellschaft)* eingetragener Aktionär; **~ of a right** Inhaber e-s Rechts; **~ of a share** Aktieninhaber, Aktionär; **~ for value**[19] entgeltlicher Inhaber *(e-s Wechsels, Schecks) (der das Papier gestützt auf e-e Gegenleistung besitzt)*

holder, actual ~ gegenwärtiger (od. tatsächlicher) Inhaber (od. Besitzer); **bona fide ~** gutgläubiger Inhaber (od. Besitzer); **lawful ~** rechtmäßiger Inhaber (od. Besitzer); **patent ~** Patentinhaber; **policy ~** Policeinhaber, Versicherungsnehmer; **previous ~** Vorbesitzer, früherer Inhaber *(z.B. e-s Wechsels)*; **small~** *Br* Kleinbauer; →**subsequent ~; to be made out in the name of the ~** auf den Inhaber lauten (od. ausgestellt sein)

holding Besitz, Bestand *(bes. an Effekten)*; Grundbesitz; *Am* Gerichtsentscheidung; **~(s)** Beteiligung(en) *(bes. durch Aktienbesitz)*; Anteil(e); *Am* tragende Entscheidungsgründe *(opp. dicta)*

holding company Holdinggesellschaft, Dachgesellschaft, Muttergesellschaft; **personal ~** *Am* personenbezogene Holdinggesellschaft

Kapitalgesellschaft, die Kapitalanteile (Aktien) anderer Gesellschaften, die rechtlich selbständig bleiben, erwirbt und verwaltet (heute die wichtigste Organisationsform im amerikanischen Konzernwesen)

holding, ~s in a business enterprise Geschäftsanteile, Gesellschaftsanteile; **~ in the capital of an undertaking** Beteiligung am Kapital e-s Unternehmens; **~s of land** Landbesitz, Grundbesitz; **~ of a meeting** Abhaltung e-r Versammlung; **~ of securities** Wertpapierbestand; **~ of shares** (or *Am* **stock**) Aktienbesitz; **~ oneself out as a partner** Sichausgeben als Gesellschafter *(Haftung des Nichtgesellschafters; Anwendung des →estoppel-Prinzips)*; **~ over** Inbesitzhalten *(nach Ablauf des Miet- od. Pachtvertrages)*; **~ period** *(SteuerR)* Besitzdauer, Eigentumsdauer

holding, agricultural ~ landwirtschaftlicher Grundbesitz (od. Betrieb); *Br*[20] Pachthof, Pachtland; **bill ~s** Wechselbestand; **the company's ~s** Effektenbestand der Gesellschaft; **foreign ~s** Auslandsbesitz; **gold ~s** Goldbestand; **majority ~** Mehrheitsbeteiligung; **minority ~** Minderheitsbeteiligung; **paper ~s** Effektenbesitz; **share ~** Aktienbesitz; **small- ~** landwirtschaftlicher Kleinbetrieb

holding, to have a ~ in a company an e-r Gesellschaft beteiligt sein

holiday (arbeits)freier Tag; *(religiöser od. gesetzl.)* Feiertag; **~(s)** Ferien, Urlaub; **~ address** *Br* Urlaubsanschrift; **~ camp** Ferienlager; **~ pay** Urlaubsgeld; *Am* besondere Zulage für die Arbeit an gesetzlichen Feiertagen; **~s with pay** *Br* bezahlter Urlaub; **annual ~s** Jahresurlaub; **bank ~** Bankfeiertage *(→bank)*; **half-~** halber Tag frei, freier Nachmittag; **legal ~** *Am* gesetzlicher (od. öffentlicher) Feiertag; **official ~** gesetzlicher Feiertag; **on ~** *Br* in den Ferien; auf Urlaub; **request for a ~** *Br* Urlaubsgesuch; **to ask for a fortnight's ~** *Br* um e-n 14tägigen Urlaub bitten; **to be on ~** *Br* in Urlaub sein; Ferien haben; **to take a ~** *Br* Urlaub nehmen

Holland Holland *(cf Netherlands, Dutch)*

holocaust Massenvernichtung *(bes. der Juden im 2. Weltkrieg)*

holograph(ic) eigenhändig geschrieben *(Urkunde oder Testament)*

Holy Father, the ~ der Heilige Vater *(der Papst)*

holy orders geistlicher Stand; Priesterweihe; **to be in ~** dem geistlichen Stand angehören; Geistlicher sein; **to take ~** die Priesterweihe erhalten; Geistlicher werden

Holy See, the ~ der Heilige Stuhl *(cf. Vatican City)*

home Heim, Wohnung; Heimat(land); (Pflege-) Heim, Anstalt; inländisch, einheimisch; Binnen-; **at ~** zu Hause; in der Heimat; **at ~ (day)** Empfangstag; **at ~ and abroad** im In- und Ausland; **~ address** Heimatanschrift; **~ affairs** *Br* innere Angelegenheiten; Innenpolitik; **~ banking** Abwicklung von Bankgeschäften von zu Hause aus durch Fernsehgerät, Computerterminal und Telefon; **H~ Banks** *Br* britische Banken *(opp. ausländische Banken, Commonwealth Banken)*; **~born** eingeboren, einheimisch; **~ computer** Heimcomputer; **~ consumption** (h. c.) Inlandsverbrauch; **~croft** *Am (kleines)* Arbeitersiedlungshaus *(in Stadtnähe)*; **~ counties** *Br* Grafschaften, die London unmittelbar umgeben *(Middlesex, Surrey, Kent, Essex und gelegentlich Hertford und Sussex)*; **~ currency** inländische Währung *(opp. foreign currency)*; **~ demand** inländischer Bedarf; Inlandsnachfrage; **~ economics** Hauswirtschaftslehre; **~-farm** Landwirtschaft für eigenen Betrieb *(opp. rented out farmland)*; **~ fleet** Flotte in Heimatgewässern; **~ for old people** Altersheim; **~ for the blind** Blindenheim; **~ forces** im Heimatlande stationierte Streitkräfte; **~-foreign insurance** *Br* Korrespondenzversicherung *(e-s Risikos im Ausland)*; **~ freight** *Br* →homeward freight; **~- grown** selbstangebaut; **~ industry** einheimische Industrie; Heimindustrie; **~land** Heimat(land); Siedlungsgebiet für Schwarze in der Rep. Südafrika; **~less** heimatlos; obdachlos; **~ loan(s)** Wohnungsbaudarlehen; Hypothek(en) für Eigenheim; →**Federal H~ Loan Bank**

home-made im Inland hergestellt, einheimisch, inländisch; selbstgemacht *(opp. bread, cakes etc. bought in shops)*; ~ **goods** inländische (od. einheimische) Waren

home, ~ **manufacture** einheimisches Erzeugnis; inländischer Markt, Binnenmarkt; ~ **market** Inlandsmarkt, Binnenmarkt; ~ **market price** Preis am Heimatmarkt *(Verkaufspreis im Ausfuhrland)*; **H~ Mission** Innere Mission; ~ **office** *Am* Hauptsitz, Zentrale *(opp. branch offices)*; **H~ Office** *Br* Ministerium des Innern, Innenministerium; ~ **order** Inlandsauftrag, Binnenauftrag *(opp. export, foreign order)*; ~**owners insurance** *Am* Hauseigentümerversicherung; ~ **policy** Innenpolitik; ~**port** Heimathafen *(opp. foreign port)*; ~**-produced goods** im Inland hergestellte Waren; ~ **produce** (or **product**) inländisches (od. einheimisches) Erzeugnis; ~ **requirement** Inlandsbedarf, eigener Bedarf *(e-s Landes)*; **H~ Rule** (H. R.) *Br* Selbstregierung, Selbstverwaltung; ~ **sales** Inlandsverkäufe, Inlandsabsatz; **H~ Secretary** (= Secretary of State for H~ Affairs) *Br* Innenminister, Minister des Innern; ~ **securities** *Br* inländische Wertpapiere, Inlandswerte *(opp. foreign securities or stocks)*; ~ **service** Inlandsdienst

homestead Heimstätte; *Am* Familienheim; ~ **aid benefit association** *Am* Bausparkasse; ~ **(exemption) laws** *Am* Gesetze zur Förderung und zum Schutz von Familienheimen *(die ~ ist dem Zugriff der meisten Gläubiger in der Zwangsvollstreckung entzogen)*

homesteader *Am* Heimstättenbesitzer, Heimstättenerwerber

home, ~ **stocks** *Br* →~ securities; ~ **study courses** Fernunterricht; ~ **supply** Inlandsbelieferung; ~ **town** Heimatstadt; ~ **trade** inländischer Handel, Binnenhandel *(opp. foreign trade)*; *Br* Küstenhandel; ~ **use** *Br* Inlandsverbrauch; ~ **use entry** *Br* Zolladung für Inlandsverbrauch

homeward Heim-, Rück- *(opp. outward)*; auf der Heim- (od. Rück-)Reise (befindlich); auf dem Rückflug; ~ **freight** *Br* Rückfracht, Rückladung *(opp. outward freight)*; ~ **journey** (or **passage, voyage**) *Br* Heimreise, Rückfahrt

home, ~ **waters** Heimatgewässer; ~ **work** Heimarbeit; Hausgewerbe; ~ **worker** Heimarbeiter(in), Hausgewerbetreibende(r); **to set up a** ~ e-n Hausstand gründen

homicide Tötung *(e-s Menschen)*; Totschlag (→*manslaughter*); Mord (→*murder*); ~ **by misadventure** Tötung als Folge e-s Unglücksfalls; Unglücksfall mit tödlichem Ausgang *(cf. excusable ~)*; ~ **with malice aforethought** Mord; **criminal** ~ *Am* Straftaten gegen das Leben *(murder, manslaughter or negligent homicide)*; **excusable** ~ entschuldbare Tötung *(Br als Folge von Unglücksfall [misadventure] oder in Notwehr [in self-defence])*; **felonious** ~ *Am* Tötung als Verbrechen *(umfaßt manslaughter, murder und infanticide)*; **justifiable** ~ rechtmäßige (zu rechtfertigende) Tötung *(z. B. im Strafvollzug)*; **negligent** ~ *Am* fahrlässige Tötung

homogeneous homogen, gleichartig, einheitlich *(opp. heterogeneous)*; ~ **products** gleichartige Erzeugnisse

homologate *v Scot* e-n *(anfechtbaren)* Vertrag bestätigen

homologation *Scot (ausdrücklich od. stillschweigende)* Bestätigung *(e-s anfechtbaren Vertrages)*

homosexual acts between adults in private are not an offence (provided that the parties consent thereto) *Br*[21] nicht öffentliche homosexuelle Handlungen zwischen Erwachsenen sind nicht strafbar

Honduras Honduras; **Republic of** ~ Republik Honduras

Honduran Honduraner(in); honduranisch

honorarium *(freiwillig gezahltes)* Honorar *(e-s Anwalts, Arztes etc)*

honorary (Hon.) ehrenamtlich, Ehren-; **in an** ~ **capacity** ehrenamtlich; ~ **debt** Ehrenschuld; ~ **degree** ehrenhalber verliehener akademischer Grad (→*degree 2.*); ~ **doctor** Ehrendoktor, Doktor h. c.; **(~) freeman of a city** *Br* Ehrenbürger e-r Stadt; ~ **member** Ehrenmitglied; ~ **membership** Ehrenmitgliedschaft; ~ **office** (or **post, position**) Ehrenamt, ehrenamtliche Stellung; ~ **president** ehrenamtlicher Präsident; ~ **title** ehrenhalber verliehener Titel; **to confer** ~ **membership on sb.** jdm die Ehrenmitgliedschaft verleihen; **to hold an** ~ **position** ein Ehrenamt bekleiden

hono(u)r Ehre; Auszeichnung; ~**s** Ehrenverleihungen; ~**s list** *Br* Liste für die Verteilung von Titeln und Orden; ~**s of war** Kriegsauszeichnungen; **acceptance for** ~ *(WechselR)* Ehrenannahme, Ehrenakzept; **affair of** ~ Ehrenhandel; Duell; **birthday** ~**s** *Br* Ehrenverleihungen am Geburtstag der Königin; **code of** ~ Ehrenkodex; **court of** ~ Ehrengericht; **debt of** ~ Ehrenschuld; **duty of** ~ Ehrenpflicht; **guard of** ~ Ehrenwache; **military** ~**s** militärische Ehren; **payer for** ~ *(WechselR)* Ehrenzahler, Honorant; **payment for** ~ Ehrenzahlung für e-n notleidenden Wechsel; **point of** ~ Ehrensache; **professional** ~ Berufsehre, Standesehre; **word of** ~ Ehrenwort; **I have the** ~ **to inform you** ich beehre mich, Ihnen mitzuteilen; **to render the last** ~**s to sb.** jdm. die letzte Ehre erweisen

hono(u)r *v* beehren (with mit); *(Wechsel, Scheck)*

honorieren, einlösen, (anerkennen und) bezahlen; **to ~ one's commitments** *pol* seinen Verpflichtungen nachkommen; **to ~ a contract** e-n Vertrag einhalten; **to ~ a debt** e-e Schuld begleichen; **to ~ one's obligations** seine Verpflichtungen *(bei Fälligkeit)* erfüllen

hono(u)red, person ~ *(WechselR)* Honorat *(jd, für den ein [notleidender] Wechsel bezahlt wird)*

hono(u)rable (Hon.) ehrenvoll; Ehrenwert *(Titel für Abgeordnete, höhere Richter und Beamte; Br für gewisse Mitglieder des Adels)*; **Most H~** *Br* Höchst Ehrenwert *(Titel für Marquis)*; **Right H~** *Br* Sehr Ehrenwert *(Titel für Adlige unter dem Marquis, Privy Councillor u.a.)*; **~ discharge** *mil* ehrenvoller Abschied; **my ~ friend** *parl* der Herr Vorredner; **the ~ member** *Br parl* der Abgeordnete (for für); **~ mention** ehrenvolle Erwähnung; **~ understanding** formlose Abreden über Wettbewerbsbeschränkungen; **to conclude an ~ peace** e-n ehrenvollen Frieden schließen

hooked *Am sl.* rauschgiftsüchtig

hooligan Rowdy *(bes. auf Straßen)*

hope, to express the ~ der Hoffnung Ausdruck geben

horizon(s) *fig* Grenzen; **to open up new ~s** *fig* neue Gebiete eröffnen, neue Grenzen setzen

horizontal, ~ amalgamation (or **combination**) horizontaler Zusammenschluß *(von Unternehmen)*; **~ group** einstufiger Konzern *(opp. multi-stage group)*; **~ integration** horizontale Integration *(Zusammenschluß mehrerer Unternehmen derselben Produktionsstufe; opp. vertical integration)*; **~ merger** →merger 2.; **~ →restraint**

hormone, ban on ~s Hormonverbot

horticultural products Erzeugnisse des Gartenbaus

hospital Krankenhaus; *Br* (*auch*) psychiatrische Klinik; **mental ~** *Am* psychiatrische Klinik; **~ charges** (or **costs**) Krankenhauskosten; **~ insurance** *Am* Krankenhausversicherung *(der Rentner) (→Medicare)*; **~ order** *Br* Unterbringungsbefehl *(Anordnung der Unterbringung einer e-r Straftat überführten Person in e-r psychiatrischen Klinik)*; **~ ship** Lazarettschiff; **~ train** Lazarettzug; **~ treatment** Krankenhausbehandlung

hospital, admission to ~ Aufnahme im Krankenhaus; (*Br auch* in e-m psychiatrischen Krankenhaus); **compulsory admission to ~** *Br* zwangsweise Unterbringung in e-r psychiatrischen Klinik; **committal to ~** (of an offender of unsound mind) *Br* Unterbringung in e-r psychiatrischen Klinik *(in Verbindung mit Strafsachen)*; **stay in a ~** Krankenhausaufenthalt; **to arrange for sb. to be admitted to ~** jdn in ein Krankenhaus legen; **to commit a patient to a** (*Am* **mental**) **~** e-n Geisteskranken in ein psychiatrisches Krankenhaus einweisen; **to order the admission of an offender to a ~** *Br* die Unterbringung eines (Straf-)Täters in e-r psychiatrischen Klinik anordnen; **to be remanded to a mental ~** *Am* in e-e psychiatrische Klinik eingewiesen werden; **to take sb. to ~** jdn in das Krankenhaus einliefern

hospitalization Einlieferung ins Krankenhaus; Aufnahme (od. Unterbringung) im Krankenhaus; Krankenhausaufenthalt; Krankenhausbehandlung; **~ benefits** *Br (durch die Versicherung gezahlte)* Krankenhauskosten; **cost of ~** Krankenhauskosten; **~ insurance** *Am (private)* Krankenhauskostenversicherung

hospitalize *v* in ein Krankenhaus einliefern (od. einweisen); im Krankenhaus aufnehmen (od. behandeln)

host Gastgeber; Gastwirt, Hotelier; *Am* gefälliger Fahrer *(der e-n Fahrgast aus Gefälligkeit mitnimmt; cf. guest)*; **a ~ of** sehr viel(e); **~ bond** Optionsanleihe mit Bezugsrecht für e-e weitere Anleihe mit garantiertem Zins *(→back bond)*; **~ country** Gastland; Aufnahmestaat; **~ government** Gastregierung

5hostage Geisel; **~ taking** Geiselnahme; **execution** (or **shooting**) **of ~s** Hinrichtung (od. Erschießung) von Geiseln; **liberation of ~s** Befreiung von Geiseln; **release of ~s** Freilassung von Geiseln; **to give ~s** Geiseln stellen; **to keep as ~** als Geisel behalten; **to release ~s** Geiseln freilassen; **to take ~s** Geiseln nehmen

hostel Herberge; *Br* Obdachlosenasyl; **students ~** *bes. Br* Studentenwohnheim; **youth ~** Jugendherberge

hostess Gastgeberin; Gastwirtin; Empfangsdame, Hosteß

hostile feindlich; feindselig (to gegen); **~ act** feindliche Handlung; **~ assistance** *(VölkerR)* Beistandsleistung *(e-s neutralen Schiffes für kriegführende Macht)*; **~ →takeover**; **~ territory** Feindgebiet, Feindesland; **~ witness** feindselig eingestellter Zeuge *(eigener Zeuge, der sich unerwartet als feindlich erweist)*

hostilit|y Feindschaft, Feindseligkeit; **~ies** Kriegshandlungen, Kampfhandlungen; **cessation of ~ies** Einstellung (od. Beendigung) der Feindseligkeiten; **opening of ~ies** Eröffnung der Feindseligkeiten; **outbreak of ~ies** Ausbruch der Feindseligkeiten; **to suspend ~** die Feindseligkeit einstellen

hot heiß; **~ cargo clause** *Am (unzulässige)* Vereinbarung, daß Arbeitgeber bestreiktes Unternehmen nicht beliefern darf; **~ goods** heiße

Ware *(Diebesgut, Schmuggelgut etc)*; ~ **issues** heiße Aktien *(neu ausgegebene Aktien von Gesellschaften, die noch nicht lange existieren)*; ~ **line** *pol* heißer Draht; ~ **money** heißes Geld *(fluktuierende Gelder, die aus Angst vor Geldentwertung von Land zu Land ziehen)*; ~ **news** sensationelle Nachrichten; ~ **pursuit** (of a ship) *(VölkerR)* Nacheile (nach e-m Schiff), Verfolgungsrecht *(Recht, ein Schiff fremder Staatsangehörigkeit wegen e-s begangenen Unrechts bis auf hohe See zu verfolgen und aufzubringen)*; ~ **war** heißer Krieg, Schießkrieg; ~ **wire** *pol* heißer Draht; **to be ~ on the trail of sb.** jdm dicht auf der Spur sein

hotchpot[22] Verteilungsverfahren bei Nachlässen unter Berücksichtigung der Vorausempfänge; **obligation to bring into ~** Ausgleichspflicht; **to bring one's advancement into ~** den Vorausempfang zur Ausgleichung bringen

hotel Hotel; ~ **accommodation** Hotelunterbringung; ~ **and catering** Hotel und Gaststättengewerbe; ~ **booking** *Br* Hotelzimmerbestellung; ~ **business** Hotelfach; ~ **and restaurant business** Gaststättengewerbe; ~ **industry** Hotelgewerbe; ~ **keeper** Hotelbesitzer; Hotelier; ~ **keeper's liability** Gastwirtshaftung; ~ **proprietor** Inhaber e-s Hotels; ~ **staff** Hotelpersonal; ~ **tariff** *Br* Zimmerpreise in e-m Hotel; **to book a room in a ~** *Br* ein Hotelzimmer bestellen; **to run a ~** ein Hotel leiten

hour Stunde; **~s of attendance** Anwesenheitszeit; Sprechstunden; **~s of business** Geschäftszeit, Geschäftsstunden; **~s of delivery** *(Post)* Zustellungszeit; **~s worked** *(geleistete)* Arbeitsstunden; **~s of work** →working ~s

hour, after ~s nachbörslich; **before ~s** vorbörslich; **business ~s** Geschäftszeit, Dienststunden; **by the ~** stundenweise; **pay by the ~** Stundenlohn; **payment by the ~** stundenweise Bezahlung; **consultation ~s** Sprechstunden *(e-s Arztes)*; **at the eleventh ~** *pol* im letzten Moment; **man-~** Arbeitsstunde; **office ~s** Dienststunden, Bürostunden; Sprechstunden; **stock exchange ~s** Börsenstunden; **working ~s** Dienststunden, Arbeitszeit; **to introduce the 35-~ week** die 35-Stundenwoche einführen

hourly stündlich; Stunden-; ~ **rate** Stundensatz; ~ **rate of pay** Stundenlohnsatz; ~ **wage(s)** Stundenlohn

house 1. Haus; Wohnhaus; (Handels-)Haus, Firma; Haushalt; **the H~** *Br colloq.* die (Londoner) Börse; ~ **agent** *Br* Grundstücksmakler; ~ **arrest** Hausarrest; ~ **bill** auf die eigene Geschäftsstelle gezogener Wechsel; ~ **brand** Eigenmarke, Hausmarke; **~breaker** Einbrecher; *Br* Abbruchunternehmer; **~breaking** Einbruch(diebstahl) *(cf. burglary)*; ~ **building** Hausbau; ~ **coal** Hausbrand, Kohle; ~ **of correction** *Am* (Jugend-)Gefängnis; ~ **detective** Hausdetektiv *(Kaufhaus, Hotel)*

household *(privater)* Haushalt; **the Royal H~** *Br* die Hofhaltung; ~ **appliances** Haushaltsgeräte; ~ **articles** Haushaltsgegenstände; ~ **equipment** (or **effects**) Hausrat; ~ **expenses** Haushaltungskosten; ~ **furniture** Hausrat

household insurance (verbundene) Hausratversicherung; **comprehensive ~** kombinierte Hausrat- und Gebäudeversicherung

household troops *Br* Leibgarde *(des Souveräns)*

household, common ~ häusliche Gemeinschaft; **head of ~** Haushalt(ung)svorstand; **to break up** (or **dissolve**) **a ~** e-n Haushalt auflösen

householder Haushalt(ung)svorstand

house, ~ of ill fame Bordell; ~ **insurance** Gebäudeversicherung; **~keeper** Wirtschafterin; Hausdame; **~keeping** Haushaltsführung; **~keeping allowance** (or **money**) Haushalt(ung)sgeld; ~ **man** (or ~ **officer**) Assistenzarzt; ~ **owner** Hauseigentümer, Hausbesitzer; ~ **owner's (comprehensive) policy** kombinierte Versicherung für Hauseigentümer; ~ **ownership** Hauseigentum, Hausbesitz; **H~ price** *Br* Börsenkurs; ~ **property** Hausbesitz; ~ **purchase** Hauskauf; ~ **search** Haussuchung

house-to-house, ~ collection Haussammlung; ~ **distribution** Postwurfsendung; ~ **search** (by the police) Durchsuchung von Häusern *(e-r Straße, z.B. nach Terroristen)*; ~ **selling** Direktverkauf an der Haustür, Türverkauf

house, apartment ~ Mietshaus; **boarding ~** Pension; **in-~** betriebseigen; **on the ~** auf Kosten der Firma; **occupied ~** bewohntes Haus; **public ~** (pub) *Br* Gastwirtschaft, Kneipe; **rules of the ~** Hausordnung; **unoccupied ~** unbewohntes (od. leerstehendes) Haus

house, to be under ~ arrest unter Hausarrest stehen; **to keep ~** e-n Haushalt führen; **to let a ~** ein Haus vermieten; **to rent a ~** ein Haus **mieten** (od. vermieten); **to take a ~ on lease** ein Haus mieten

House 2. *parl Br* Unterhaus; *Am bes.* Repräsentantenhaus; ~ **of Assembly** Unterhaus *(z.B. in Südafrika)*; ~ **Bill** *Am* Gesetzesvorlage des ~ of Representatives *(opp. Senate Bill)*; ~ **Judiciary Committee** *Am* Rechtsausschuß des Repräsentantenhauses; ~ **of Commons** *Br* Unterhaus; ~ **of Delegates** *Am (einzelstaatl.)* Abgeordnetenhaus *(Maryland, Virginia, West Virginia)*; ~ **of Keys** *Br* Unterhaus der Insel Man

House of Lords (H. L.) *Br* Oberhaus

Das House of Lords, bestehend aus den →Lords Spiritual und den →Lords Temporal, ist oberstes Rechtsmittelgericht für England, Schottland und Nordirland.

Die Mitglieder des Oberhauses können Gesetze nur verzögern, nicht verhindern. Über die Finanzgesetze entscheiden die Commons allein

House, ~ of Parliament *Br* Parlament(sgebäude); **~ of Representatives** (H. R.) *Am* Repräsentantenhaus *(cf. Congress)*

House, Lower ~ Unterhaus; **No ~** das Haus ist nicht beschlußfähig; **Upper ~** Oberhaus; **to constitute a ~** s. to make a →~; **to enter the ~** *Br* Mitglied des Parlaments werden; **to make a ~** *Br (im ~ of Commons)* e-e beschlußfähige Anzahl *(40 Abgeordnete)* aufweisen; beschlußfähig sein; **the President may convene both ~s or either of them** der Präsident kann beide Häuser des Kongresses oder nur eines einberufen

housing Unterbringung, Unterkunft; Wohnungen; Wohnungswesen; Wohnungsbeschaffung; (Ein-)Lagerung *(von Waren)*; **~ accommodation** Wohnraum; **H~ Act** Wohnungsbaugesetz; **~ allowance** Wohnungsgeldzuschuß, Wohngeld; **~ and urban development** (HUD) *Am* Wohnungs- und Städtebauentwicklung; **~ area** Wohngebiet; **~ association** *Br* Wohnungsgenossenschaft; **~ census** *(Statistik)* Haushaltszählung; **~ conditions** Wohnverhältnisse; Wohnbedingungen; **~ (construction)** Wohnungsbau; **~ costs** Kosten der Wohnungsbeschaffung *(z.B. für Einwanderer)*; **~ development plan** (or **scheme**) *Br* Wohnungsbauprojekt; **~ differential** *Am* unterschiedliche Zinsstruktur der Bankengruppen gemäß →Regulation Q; **~ estate** *(für Vermietung od. Verkauf durch Kommunalbehörden oder deren Organisationen gebaute)* (Wohn-)Siedlung; **(suburban) ~ estate** Stadtrandsiedlung; **~ famine** Wohnungsnot; **~ industry** Wohnungswirtschaft; **~ loan** Wohnungsbaudarlehen; **~ market** Wohnungsmarkt; **~ policy** Wohnungs(bau)politik; **~ problem** Wohnungsproblem; **~ shortage** Wohnungsmangel

housing, financing of ~ Wohnungsbaufinanzierung; **low-cost ~** billige Wohnungen; *(etwa)* Sozialwohnungen; **poor ~** schlechte Wohnungen; **→provision of ~**; **subsidized ~** staatlich subventionierte Wohnungen; Sozialwohnungen; **to provide ~** Wohnungen zur Verfügung stellen, Wohnungen (zum Vermieten) haben; mit Wohnung(en) versorgen

hovercraft Luftkissenfahrzeug

hull Schiffsrumpf; Flugzeugrumpf; **~ insurance** (Schiffs-, Flugzeug-)Kaskoversicherung; **~ policy** Kaskopolice; **~ and machinery** (H. & M.) Kasko und Maschine; **~ underwriter** Kaskoversicherer; **insurance on ~ and appurtenances** Kaskoversicherung

human menschlich; **~ capital** Humankapital (Arbeitsvermögen); **~ engineering** Ergonomie; Untersuchung der Voraussetzungen bei der Gestaltung der Arbeitsplätze und der Arbeitsabläufe; **the ~ factor in business** der Mensch im Betrieb; **~ relations** zwischenmenschliche Beziehungen; innerbetriebliche Mitarbeiterbeziehungen; **working conditions and ~ relations** *(etwa)* Betriebsklima; **~ resources** Humanvermögen *(menschliches Potential, z.B. Arbeitsleistung, Berufserfahrung)*; **~ resource accounting** Humanvermögensrechnung

human rights Menschenrechte; **Commission on H~ R~** Kommission für Menschenrechte
1946 vom Wirtschafts- und Sozialrat der Vereinten Nationen *(cf. United Nations)* eingesetzte Kommission, die eine Deklaration über den Schutz der Menschenrechte ausgearbeitet hat, die als Universal Declaration of Human Rights (UNO-Menschenrechtsdeklaration) von der Generalversammlung der Vereinten Nationen 1948 beschlossen wurde. Diese Deklaration bildet aber nur eine an die Staaten gerichtete Empfehlung

human rights, Convention for the Protection of H~ R~ and Fundamental Freedoms[23] Konvention zum Schutze der Menschenrechte und Grundfreiheiten (Europäische Menschenrechts-Konvention)
Vom Europarat (Council of →Europe) abgeschlossene Konvention *(cf. European Commission of →Human Rights, European →Court of Human Rights)*

human rights, European Commission of H~ R~ Europäische Kommission für Menschenrechte
Durch Abschnitt II und III der Europäischen Menschenrechts-Konvention (Convention for the Protection of →Human Rights and Fundamental Freedoms) geschaffene erste Instanz zur Entscheidung über Beschwerden wegen Verletzung der Menschenrechte *(cf. European →Court of Human Rights)*. Die Kommission kann nach Art. 25 der Konvention unter bestimmten Voraussetzungen auch von natürlichen Personen oder Personenvereinigungen angerufen werden

human rights, Inter-American Commission on H~ R~ (CIDH) Interamerikanische Menschenrechtskommission; **suppression of ~** Unterdrückung der Menschenrechte

humanitarian, ~ concerns humanitäre Belange; **to grant aid for ~ purposes** humanitäre Hilfe gewähren

humanities Geisteswissenschaften

humanity Menschlichkeit, Humanität; **crime against ~** Humanitätsverbrechen; Verbrechen gegen die Menschlichkeit

humanization Vermenschlichung, Humanisierung; **job ~** Humanisierung der Arbeit

hundredweight (cwt) *(etwa)* Zentner *(Br* 112 Pfund = 50,80 kg, *Am* 100 Pfund = 45,36 kg)

Hungarian Ungar(in); ungarisch; *(seit Okt. 1989)* **~ Republic** Republik Ungarn

Hungary Ungarn

hunger, ~ **strike** Hungerstreik; ~ **strikers** in Hungerstreik befindliche Häftlinge

hunt Jagd; ~ **for the criminal** Jagd (od. Suche) nach dem Verbrecher

hunt *v* jagen; **licen|ced (~sed) to** ~ jagdberechtigt

huntable jagdbar

hunting Jagen; Jagd-; ~ **accident** Jagdunfall; ~ **ground** Jagdrevier; Jagdgebiet; ~ **laws** Jagdgesetze; ~ **licen|ce (~se)** (or *Am* **permit**) Jagdschein; ~ **liability insurance** Jagdhaftpflichtversicherung; ~ **season** Jagdzeit; **to lease a** ~ **ground** e-e Jagd verpachten

husband Ehemann, Ehegatte; ~ **and wife** Eheleute; ~**'s insurance benefits** *Am (Sozialvers.)* Zusatzrente für Ehemann der Hauptberechtigten; **a** ~**'s liability for his wife's debts** Haftung des Ehemanns für die Schulden seiner Frau; ~**-wife privilege** *Am* Aussageverweigerungsrecht zwischen Eheleuten; **ship's** ~ Korrespondentreeder

husband *v* sparen, sparsam umgehen mit

husbandry Wirtschaftsführung; (Ausübung der) Landwirtschaft; Ackerbau; **animal** ~ Viehzucht

hush, ~ **money** Schweigegeld; ~ **project** Geheimprojekt

hybrid bill *Br* gemischte Gesetzesvorlage *(als public bill von der Regierung eingebrachte, aber bestimmte Person im öffentlichen Interesse angehende bill)*

hydrocarbons Kohlenwasserstoffe

hydroelectric power station Wasserkraftwerk

hydrogen bomb Wasserstoffbombe

hydrographic, International H~ Organization[24] Internationale Hydrographische Organisation

hygiene Hygiene; Gesundheitswesen, Gesundheitspflege; **industrial** ~ Betriebshygiene, Gesundheitsschutz bei der Arbeit

hygienic facilities sanitäre Anlagen (od. Einrichtungen)

hyperinflation Superinflation, galoppierende Inflation

hype übertriebene Werbung

hypothec *Scot* Hypothek; gesetzliches Pfandrecht; **maritime** ~ *Am* und *Scot (gesetzl.)* Schiffsgläubigerrecht

hypothecary hypothekarisch, pfandrechtlich; ~ **claim** Hypothekenforderung, Pfandforderung; ~ **debt** Hypothekenschuld; Pfandschuld; ~ **security** hypothekarische Sicherheit; Pfandsicherheit; ~ **value** Beleihungswert, Lombardwert

hypothecate *v* verpfänden; *(Schiff)* verbodmen; *(Wertpapiere)* lombardieren, beleihen

hypothecation Bestellung e-s *(besitzlosen, aber e-e Verwendungsmöglichkeit gebenden)* Pfandrechts; Pfandbestellung; Verbodmung, Bodmerei *(cf. bottomry, respondentia);* Lombardierung, Beleihung *(von Wertpapieren);* ~ **certificate** (or **letter of** ~) Verpfändungserklärung; Pfandbrief; ~ **as security for advances** Verpfändung als Sicherheit für ein Darlehen

hypothecator Verpfänder

I

IATA-agents →International Air Transport Association

ibels (interest-bearing eligible liabilities) verzinsliche mindestreservepflichtige Verbindlichkeiten

Ibero-America Ibero-Amerika *(das durch Sprache und Kultur mit der Iberischen Halbinsel [Spanien und Portugal] verbundene Lateinamerika)*

ibid(em) ("in the same place") am selben Ort, ebenda

ICA-Convention Abkommen über Internationale Zivilluftfahrt (→*International Civil Aviation*)

ICC IHK, ICC (→International Chamber of Commerce); ~ **arbitration** IHK-Schiedsgerichtsbarkeit *(→arbitration)*

ICC Arbitration Clause s. (Standard) ICC →Arbitration Clause

ICC arbitration proceedings ICC Schiedsverfahren

ICC Arbitration Rules (amended)[1] (geänderte) Schiedsgerichtsordnung

ICC Banking Commission ICC Bankenkommission

ICC-CMI[1a] **Arbitral Organization**[1c] ICC/CMI Schiedsgerichtsordnung

ICC-CMI[1a] **Rules**[1b] ICC-CMI Verfahrensordnung

ICC Commercial Practice Commission ICC Kommission für internationale Handelspraxis

ICC Conciliation Rules[1] ICC Vergleichsordnung

ICC Court of →**Arbitration**

ICC International Centre for →Technical Experts
ICC National Committee Landesgruppe der Internationalen Handelskammer (IHK)
ICC Uniform Rules for →Collections
ICC Uniform Rules for →Contract
ICC Rules of Conciliation and Arbitration →rule 3.
ICC, to agree upon the ~ conciliation procedure sich dem IHK-Vergleichsverfahren unterwerfen; **to secure the offices of the ~** die Dienste der IHK in Anspruch nehmen

ice Eis; **~-bound** zugefroren; **~-free** *(Hafen)* eisfrei

Iceland Island; **Republic of ~** Republik Island
Icelander Isländer(in)
Icelandic isländisch

idea Idee, Gedanke, Vorstellung; **association of ~s** Gedankenassoziation; **to have an ~ of** e-e Vorstellung haben von

idem (id.) derselbe, dieselbe, dasselbe; desgleichen
idem sonans ("sounding alike") gleichlautend *(das Gericht beachtet falsche Buchstabierung e-s Namens nicht, wenn das Klangbild ähnlich ist; z.B. Laurence statt Lawrence)*

identical identisch, gleichbedeutend, übereinstimmend; **under ~ circumstances** unter gleichen Umständen

identifiable identifizierbar, erkennbar; feststellbar; **~ property** feststellbare Vermögensgegenstände

identification Identifizierung; Feststellung der Identität (od. Persönlichkeit); Legitimation *(Ausweis über die Person); (Zoll)* Nämlichkeit; **~ card** Kennkarte; Personalausweis; **~ disk** *Am mil* Erkennungsmarke
identification evidence, to be convicted on ~ durch Zeugenaussagen verurteilt werden, auf Grund derer man identifiziert worden ist
identification, ~ mark Erkennungszeichen; Nämlichkeitszeichen
identification number, personal ~ (PIN) persönliche Identifikationsnummer
identification, ~ paper Ausweispapier; Personalausweis; **~ parade** Gegenüberstellung *(e-s Verdächtigen mit e-m Zeugen)* zum Zwecke der Identifizierung; **~ tag** *mil* Erkennungsmarke; **~ words**[1d] *tel* Buchstabierwörter; **certificate of ~** Nämlichkeitsbescheinigung

identify *v* identifizieren; *(jds)* Identität feststellen; wiedererkennen; kennzeichnen; **to ~ with** gleichsetzen mit; **to ~ oneself** sich ausweisen; **to ~ oneself with** *colloq.* sich eng verbunden fühlen (od. sich solidarisch erklären) mit *(e-r Partei, Politik etc)*; **to ~ stolen property** gestohlene Gegenstände wiedererkennen

identity Identität, Gleichheit; *(Zoll)* Nämlichkeit; Persönlichkeit; *(PatR)* Wesensgleichheit *(von 2 Erfindungen)*; **~ card** Personalausweis; **~ disk** *mil* Erkennungsmarke; **~ papers** Ausweispapiere; **of known ~** von Person bekannt; **mistaken ~** Personenverwechslung; **proof of ~** Nachweis der Identität; Personalausweis; **to establish sb.'s ~** jds Identität feststellen; **to establish the ~ of stolen goods** die Gleichheit mit den gestohlenen Gegenständen feststellen; **to prove one's ~** sich ausweisen (od. legitimieren)

ideological weltanschaulich; **on ~ grounds** aus ideologischen Gründen

idiocy Idiotie *(schwerste Form der Geistesschwäche; Br jetzt →mental disorder)*

idiot Idiot, Geistesschwacher *(Br[2] jetzt →patient)*

idle müßig, untätig; arbeitslos; faul, arbeitsscheu; stillstehend, nicht in Betrieb; unproduktiv, tot *(Kapital)*; **~ capacity** ungenutzte Kapazität; **~ capital** totes (od. nicht angelegtes) Kapital; **~ and disorderly person** *Br* arbeitsscheue und liederliche Person *(cf. vagrant)*; **~ funds** →~ capital; **~ period** (of a ship) Liegezeit; **~ plant** stilliegende Anlage; **~ shifts** Feierschichten; **~ threats** leere Drohungen; **to be ~** stillstehen *(Betrieb, Maschinen)*; **to lie ~** brachliegen *(Land)*; nicht arbeiten *(Geld)*

if, ~ any gegebenenfalls; **even ~** wenn auch, selbst wenn

ignorance Unwissenheit, Unkenntnis; **~ of the law excuses no one** ("ignorantia legis neminem excusat") Unkenntnis des Gesetzes entschuldigt nicht (od. schützt nicht vor Strafe); **voluntary ~** *Am* schuldhaftes Nichtwissen; **~ was due to negligence** die Unkenntnis beruhte auf Fahrlässigkeit; die Unkenntnis war schuldhaft; **to plead ~** sich auf Unkenntnis berufen

ignorant nicht wissend (od. kennend); **to be ~ of a fact** in Unkenntnis e-r Tatsache sein, e-e Tatsache nicht kennen

ignore *v* ignorieren, nicht beachten, außer acht lassen; nicht wissen (od. kennen); **to ~ a bill of indictment** *Am* e-e Anklage verwerfen *(cf. grand jury)*

ill krank; schlecht; **~-advised** schlecht beraten; unbesonnen; **~-conditioned goods** Waren in schlechtem Zustand; **~-founded** unbegründet; **~-reputed** schlecht beleumundet; **~-treatment** schlechte Behandlung, Mißhandlung; **gross ~-treatment** grobe Mißhandlung; **mentally ~** geisteskrank

illegal illegal, unrechtmäßig; gesetzwidrig, rechtswidrig *(opp. legal)*; **~ act** gesetzwidrige Handlung; **~ contracts** rechtswidrige Verträge; ~ **interest** ungesetzliche Zinsen; Wucherzinsen; ~ **practices** *Br* rechtswidrige (Wahl-)-Praktiken; ~ **production of goods and services** Schwarzarbeit; ~ **purpose** ungesetzlicher Zweck

illegality Illegalität, Unrechtmäßigkeit; Gesetzwidrigkeit, Rechtswidrigkeit *(opp. legality)*

illegitimacy Nichtehelichkeit, Unehelichkeit; Gesetzwidrigkeit, Unrechtmäßigkeit *(opp. legitimacy)*

illegitimate nichtehelich, unehelich; gesetzwidrig, unrechtmäßig *(opp. legitimate)*; ~ **child** nichteheliches Kind

illicit unerlaubt, *(gesetzlich)* verboten; ~ **trade** (or **trading**) Schwarzhandel, Schleichhandel; ~ **traffic** unerlaubter Handel *(z.B. mit Suchtstoffen)*; ~ **work** Schwarzarbeit

illiquid illiquide, nicht flüssig; *Am* und *Scot* unbestimmt *(Recht od. Anspruch)*

illiquidity Illiquidität, Mangel an flüssigen Mitteln

illiteracy Analphabetentum

illiterate (person) Analphabet

illness Krankheit; ~ **frequency rate** (I. F. R.) Krankheitshäufigkeitsziffer; **absence due to** ~ krankheitsbedingtes Fehlen

illuminate *v* beleuchten; erläutern, verständlich machen

illuminated advertising Leuchtreklame, Lichtwerbung

illustrate *v (durch Beispiele, Bilder etc)* erläutern; *(Text)* illustrieren, mit Abbildungen (od. Bildmotiven) versehen

illustrated, ~ **matter** Abbildung; ~ **(news-) paper** (or **magazine**) Illustrierte

illustration Erklärung, Erläuterung; Illustration, Abbildung; *(PatR)* bildliche Darstellung; ~**s of a scientific nature** *(UrhR)* Darstellungen wissenschaftlicher Art

image Bild; Image; Vorstellungsbild *(von e-r Person od. e-m Unternehmen)*; Leitbild; **by word and** ~ durch Wort und Bild; **corporate** ~ *Am* Vorstellungsbild e-s Unternehmens in der Öffentlichkeit

imaginary profit imaginärer Gewinn

imbalance Ungleichgewicht, mangelndes Gleichgewicht; Unausgeglichenheit *(z.B. zwischen Angebot und Nachfrage)*; ~ **in competition** Ungleichgewicht im Wettbewerb; ~ **in payments** Zahlungsungleichgewicht; unausgeglichene Zahlungsbilanz; ~ **of trade** Handelsbilanzungleichgewicht; **cyclical** ~ konjunkturelles Ungleichgewicht; **monetary** ~ Währungsungleichgewicht; **to remedy the** ~ das Ungleichgewicht beheben

imbecile[3] Geistesschwacher; geistesschwach

IMF IWF (→*International Monetary Fund)*; **granting of the** ~ **credit** Gewährung des IWF-Kredits; ~ **Board of Governors** Gouverneursrat des IWF

imitation Imitation; Nachahmung, Nachbildung; ~ **leather** Kunstleder; ~ **of trademarks** Nachahmung von Warenzeichen; ~ **products** Nachahmungserzeugnisse; **beware of** ~**s** vor Nachahmungen wird gewarnt; **colo(u)rable** ~ täuschend ähnliche Nachahmung; **prohibited** ~ verbotene Nachbildung; **slavish** ~ *(UrhR)* sklavische Nachahmung

immaterial immateriell, unkörperlich; unerheblich, unwichtig; ~ **averment** unerhebliches Vorbringen *(im Prozeß)*; ~ **damage** ideeller Schaden; ~ **variance** geringfügige Abweichung

immaturity Mangel an Reife

immediate unmittelbar, direkt; unverzüglich, sofort; ~ **action** Sofortmaßnahme; ~ **aid** Soforthilfe; ~ **annuity** sofort fällige Rente; ~ **benefit** sofort beginnende Versicherungsleistung; ~ **cause** unmittelbare Ursache *(opp. remote cause)*; ~ **cover** sofortiger Versicherungsschutz; ~ **danger** unmittelbare Gefahr; ~ **delivery** umgehende Lieferung; **for** ~ **employment** zur sofortigen Einstellung; ~ **heir** *Am* nächster Erbe; ~ **neighbo(u)r** unmittelbarer Nachbar; ~ **order** *(Börse)* nur für einen Tag gültiger Auftrag; ~ **payment** sofortige Zahlung; **house for sale with** ~ **possession** sofort beziehbares Haus zu verkaufen; ~ **reply** umgehende Antwort

immediately unverzüglich; ~ **effective** sofort gültig; mit sofortiger Wirkung; ~ **payable** sofort zahlbar; **to become** ~ **effective** sofort in Kraft treten

immigrant Immigrant, Einwanderer *(opp. emigrant)*; ~ **remittances** Überweisungen von Einwanderern an Angehörige ihres früheren Heimatlandes; →**non-**~; **to admit** ~**s** Einwanderer zulassen

immigration Einwanderung *(opp. emigration)*; **I**~ **and Nationality Act** (INA) *Am* Einwanderungs- und Staatsangehörigkeitsgesetz *(regelt Einreisebedingungen für Ausländer, die in die USA einwandern wollen)*; **I**~ **and Naturalization Service** (INS) *Am* Einwanderungs- und Einbürgerungsbehörde; ~ **authorities** Einwanderungsbehörden; ~ **country** Einwanderungsland; ~ **quota** (or **rate**) Einwanderungsquote

Immigration Reform and Control Act of 1986 (IRCA)

Am Die darin enthaltenen Neuregelungen sind insbes. für Arbeitgeber von Bedeutung. Das neue Gesetz findet auf alle nach dem 6. 11. 1986 begründeten Arbeitsverhältnisse Anwendung

immigration, ~ restrictions Einwanderungsbeschränkungen; **ban on ~** Einwanderungssperre, Einwanderungsverbot; **illegal ~** illegale Einwanderung; **to bar certain persons from ~ into the United States** gewissen Personen die Einwanderung in die Vereinigten Staaten verbieten

imminence Bevorstehen; **~ of danger** (unmittelbar) bevorstehende Gefahr; Gefahr im Verzug

imminent danger unmittelbar bevorstehende (od. drohende) Gefahr *(Voraussetzung der Notwehr);* **in case of ~** bei Gefahr im Verzug; **to avert an ~** e-e drohende Gefahr abwenden; **there is ~** es besteht Gefahr im Verzug

immobilization, ~ of capital Festlegung von Kapital *(opp. mobilization);* **~ of coins** Einziehung von Metallgeld; **~ of liquid funds** Liquiditätsbindung

immobilize *v (Geld)* festlegen; *(Metallgeld)* aus dem Verkehr ziehen

immobilized, money ~ in a bill of exchange in e-m Wechsel festgelegtes Geld

immoral unmoralisch, unsittlich; gegen die guten Sitten verstoßend; **~ conduct** sittenwidriges Verhalten; **~ contract** sittenwidriger Vertrag; Vertrag gegen die guten Sitten

immorality Sittenwidrigkeit; **life of ~** unsittlicher Lebenswandel

immovable property *(bes. IPR)* unbewegliches Vermögen, Immobilien; *Am* unbeweglicher Nachlaß

immovables Immobilien, Liegenschaften *(opp. movables)*

Immovables ist vor allem ein Begriff des Konfliktrechts. Das anglo-amerikanische Rechtssystem basiert auf dem Unterschied zwischen real and personal property

immune unverletzlich; befreit (from von); **to be ~ from legal process** hinsichtlich der Gerichtsbarkeit Immunität genießen; nicht der Gerichtsbarkeit unterworfen sein

immunities Befreiungen *(z.B. von Haftung, Steuern);* gewährte Privilegien; Haftungsprivilegien; **privileges and ~** *Am* Vorrechte und Befreiungen (→*privilege*)

Am Verkehrsopfer bleiben unter bestimmten Voraussetzungen selbst dann, wenn sich ein Verschulden des Schädigers nachweisen läßt, ohne Anspruch, falls der Schädiger sich auf gewisse immunities berufen kann (z. B. zugunsten von →charities, Familienangehörigen od. gefälligen Fahrern [→hosts])

immunity Befreiung; Privileg, Sonderrecht; *(VölkerR und parl)* Immunität; **~ from arrest or detention** Immunität von Festnahme oder Haft; **~ from civil jurisdiction** zivilrechtliche Immunität; **~ from criminal jurisdiction** strafrechtliche Immunität; **~ from prosecution** (of a witness) Schutz vor Strafverfolgung (e-s Zeugen); **~ from tax(es) of a corporation** *Am* Steuerfreiheit e-r AG; **diplomatic ~** diplomatische Immunität *(cf. exterritoriality)*

immunity, foreign sovereign ~ Immunität e-s fremden Staatsoberhauptes; **Foreign Sovereign I~ Act** of 1976 (FSIA) *Am* Gesetz über die Staatenimmunität

Danach unterliegen ausländische Staaten nicht der Gerichtsbarkeit der USA. Ausnahme: →commercial exception

immunity, legal ~ rechtliche Nichtverantwortlichkeit; **parliamentary ~** Immunität der Abgeordneten; **privilege of ~** Immunitätsrecht; **State ~**[4] Staatenimmunität; **withdrawal of sb.'s ~** Aufhebung jds Immunität; **to dispense with ~** die Immunität aufheben; **to enjoy ~** Immunität genießen; **to grant ~** Immunität gewähren; **to maintain ~** die Immunität aufrechterhalten; **to withdraw ~** die Immunität aufheben

impact Stoßkraft; Einwirkung (on auf); **~ of an advertisement** Werbewirkung e-r Anzeige; **~ of inflation** Auswirkungen der Inflation; **~ of a tax** erster Steueranfall *(vor Übertragung der Steuerlast);* **~ of a treaty** Auswirkung e-s Vertrages

impair *v* beeinträchtigen, vermindern, verschlechtern; *(Münzen)* verringern; **to ~ sb.'s interests** jds Interessen schädigen; **to ~ the earning capacity** die Erwerbsfähigkeit mindern

impaired capital *(z.B. durch Verluste)* vermindertes Kapital

impairing coins Münzverringerung

impairment Beeinträchtigung, Verminderung, Verschlechterung; **mental or physical ~** geistige od. körperliche Behinderung; **~ of capital** Verminderung des Kapitals; **~ of health** Beeinträchtigung der Gesundheit

impanel *v* die Namen der Geschworenen in e-e Liste eintragen; **to ~ a jury** *Am* die Geschworenenliste aufstellen

imparlance Besprechung zwischen Kläger und Beklagtem zur Beilegung des Rechtsstreites

impartial unparteiisch; unbefangen; **~ chairman** *Am* unparteiischer Vorsitzender *(zur Aushandlung und Anwendung von Tarifverträgen)*

impeach *v* anklagen, beschuldigen; *bes. Am* unter Amtsanklage stellen (→*impeachment*); *(Gültigkeit e-s Schriftstücks etc)* anfechten, in Zweifel ziehen, bestreiten; **to ~ a witness** *Am* die

Glaubwürdigkeit e-s Zeugen anzweifeln (od. erschüttern)

impeachment Anklage, Beschuldigung; *Am* Anklage gegen e-n höheren Beamten, bes. den US-Präsidenten, zum Zwecke der Amtsenthebung; Anfechtung, Bestreitung, Anzweiflung; ~ **of waste** Haftung *(des →limited owner)* für Wertminderung des Pachtlandes *(die Recht auf Schadensersatz oder auf e-e einstweilige Verfügung bewirken kann);* ~ **of witness** *Am* Anzweiflung der Glaubwürdigkeit eines Zeugen

Nach Art. II Abs. 4 der amerikanischen Verfassung können der Präsident, der Vizepräsident, Minister und hohe Staatsbeamte vom Kongreß „wegen Hochverrats, Bestechung oder anderer schwerer Verbrechen und Vergehen" angeklagt werden und im Falle der Verurteilung des Amtes enthoben werden.

Br Impeachment ist praktisch obsolet, der letzte Fall war 1805

impede *v* verhindern, behindern, hemmen; **to ~ the course of justice** in den Gang der Rechtspflege eingreifen

impediment Behinderung; *(rechtl.)* Hindernis; Hinderungsgrund; ~ **(to marriage)** Ehehindernis; ~ **to performance** Erfüllungshindernis; ~**s to trade** Handelshindernisse

impend *v* bevorstehen; ~**ing death** nahe bevorstehender Tod, naher Tod

imperative zwingend; absolut erforderlich *(opp. discretionary)*

imperfect unvollkommen, mangelhaft, nicht durchsetzbar, nicht einklagbar; ~ **competition** *Am* unvollkommener Wettbewerb; ~ **obligations** nicht einklagbare *(moralische od. soziale)* Verpflichtungen *(charity, gratitude etc);* Naturalobligationen; ~ **title** fehlerhafter Eigentumstitel; ~ **trust** ungenau festgelegtes Treuhandverhältnis

imperial kaiserlich, Reichs-; *Br* gesetzlich *(Maße und Gewichte);* **I~ Defence College** *Br* Kriegsakademie; **His I~ Majesty** Seine Kaiserliche Majestät; **I~ Service Order** (I. S. O.) *Br* Orden für Auszeichnung im Staatsdienst; ~ **taxes** *Br* Staatssteuern *(Ggs. Steuern der Ortsbehörden);* ~ **weights and measures** *Br* gesetzliche Maße und Gewichte *(opp. metric weights and measures)*

imperialism Imperialismus

imperialist Imperialist

imperilling life lebensgefährlich

impersonal unpersönlich; ~ **accounts** Sachkonten *(opp. personal accounts);* ~ **taxes** Sachsteuern

impersonate *v* personifizieren; sich *(fälschlich)* ausgeben für e-n anderen

impersonating a public servant *Am* Amtsanmaßung

impersonation Personifizierung; Sichausgeben für e-n anderen

impertinence Ungehörigkeit; *Am* Unerheblichkeit, Unsachlichkeit *(e-s Parteivorbringens)*

impertinent ungehörig; unerheblich, nicht zur Sache gehörig; ~ **allegation** unerhebliche Behauptung; ~ **remark** ungehörige Bemerkung

impignoration *Scot* Verpfändung

implead *v Am* (ver)klagen; *Am* e-e dritte Person in den Prozeß hineinbringen; *(ungenau)* den Streit verkünden

impleader *Am* Hineinbringen e-r dritten Person in den Prozeß; *(ungenau)* Streitverkündung

implement Werkzeug, Gerät; Zubehör; *Scot* Vertragserfüllung; ~**s of trade** Handwerksgeräte; Betriebsinventar; **agricultural ~s** landwirtschaftliche Geräte

implement *v* ausführen, durchführen; *Scot (Vertrag etc)* erfüllen; **to ~ an agreement** *(VölkerR)* ein Abkommen durchführen; **to ~ a guarantee** e-r Garantiepflicht nachkommen; e-e Garantie in Anspruch nehmen; **to ~ the provisions of a convention** die Bestimmungen e-s Abkommens in Kraft setzen; **to ~ the terms of an agreement** e-n Vertrag erfüllen

implementing, ~ **agency** ausführende Dienststelle; ~ **convention** Durchführungsabkommen; ~ **regulation** Durchführungs-, Ausführungsverordnung

implementation Ausführung, Durchführung; Erfüllung; ~ **of a contract** Erfüllung e-s Vertrages; ~ **of a convention** *(VölkerR)* Durchführung e-s Abkommens; ~ **of a guarantee** Erfüllung e-r Garantiepflicht; ~ **of a project** Durchführung e-s Plans (od. Vorhabens); ~ **of a promise** Erfüllung e-s Versprechens; **regulations for** ~ Ausführungsbestimmungen

implicate *v* verwickeln, hineinziehen, mitbelasten; mit einbegreifen; **to ~ sb. in a crime** jdn in ein Verbrechen verwickeln

implication Verwicklung; innewohnende Bedeutung; *(stillschweigende)* Folgerung; ~**s** Auswirkungen; **by** ~ stillschweigend; durch sinngemäße Auslegung *(e-r gesetzlichen Bestimmung);* **economic ~s** wirtschaftliche Auswirkungen; **to carry an** ~ Konsequenzen in sich bergen; Tragweite haben; **the contract was renewed by** ~ der Vertrag wurde stillschweigend verlängert

implicit stillschweigend; *(stillschweigend)* mit einbegriffen *(opp. explicit);* ~ **agreement** stillschweigend getroffene Vereinbarung; **with the ~ understanding that ...** unter der stillschweigenden Voraussetzung, daß ...

implicitly, ~ included stillschweigend mit einbegriffen; **the contract was ~ renewed** der Vertrag wurde stillschweigend verlängert

implied *(ohne ausdrückliche Vereinbarung od. Begründung, also etwa kraft Gesetzes oder auf Grund richterlicher Würdigung nach den objektiven Umständen, dem Verhalten oder der sonstigen Lage der Beteiligten)* eingeschlossen, einbegriffen, mitenthalten, als mitbegründet (od. mitvereinbart) geltend *(ohne Rücksicht auf den nicht geäußerten Willen der Beteiligten) (opp. express);* ~ **agency** als eingeschlossen (od. bestehend) geltende Vertretungsmacht e-s →agent *(vgl. § 56 HGB);* ~ **agreement** stillschweigende(r) Vereinbarung (od. Vertrag); ~ **authority** als eingeschlossen (od. bestehend, od. [stillschweigend] mitvereinbart) geltende Vertretungsmacht in Einzelfällen; ~ **condition** →condition 2.; ~ **consent** als eingeschlossen (od. [stillschweigend] miterteilt) geltende Einwilligung; ~ **conspiracy** *Am* vermutetes abgestimmtes Verhalten *(der Mitbewerber)* (→*conspiracy 2.*); ~ **contract** als abgeschlossen (od. bestehend) geltender Vertrag; als stillschweigend (mit)vereinbart geltende Verpflichtung *(vgl. z.B. Lohnzahlungspflicht ohne ausdrückliche Vereinbarung, § 612 BGB);* ~ **guarantee** als eingeschlossen (od. [stillschweigend] mitvereinbart) geltende Garantie (Gewährleistungspflicht); ~ **in fact** nach den Umständen als bestehend geltend; **contract ~ in fact** nach den Umständen als abgeschlossen (od. bestehend) geltender Vertrag; ~ **in law** kraft rechtlicher Fiktion, kraft Gesetzes (od. Rechts) *(entgegengesetzter Wille ist unerheblich);* **contract ~ in law** gesetzlich fingierter (konstruierter) Vertrag *(ohne Rücksicht auf den tatsächlichen Parteiwillen);* ~ **intent** *(nach den Umständen od. dem Verhalten einer Person)* als gegeben geltende (anzunehmende) Absicht; ~ **licen|ce (~se)** *(nach den Umständen etc)* als gewährt geltende Lizenz; Lizenz, die ohne ausdrückliche Vereinbarung als gewährt gilt; ~ **lien** kraft Gesetzes bestehendes (durch Gesetz begründetes) Pfandrecht, gesetzliches Pfandrecht; ~ **malice** vermutete böse Absicht *(z.B. bei Tötungen, die unbeabsichtigt, aber mit dem Bewußtsein des tödlichen Ausgangs begangen sind);* ~ **power** *(nach den Umständen etc)* als gegeben od. stillschweigend (mit)vereinbart geltende Vollmacht

implied powers *Am (die in den ausdrücklich aufgeführten Zuständigkeiten der Verfassung)* eingeschlossenen Hoheitsbefugnisse *(Zuständigkeitsabgrenzung zwischen Bund und Einzelstaaten)*

Dem Kongreß wird die Befugnis zugesprochen, zusätzlich zu den in Art. I section 8 aufgeführten Zuständigkeiten auch solche Hoheitsbefugnisse auszuüben, die in den ausdrücklich aufgeführten Zuständigkeiten eingeschlossen (implied) sind

implied terms[5] *(in e-m Vertrag nicht ausdrücklich aufgenommene, aber durch Parteiwillen, Gesetz oder Gewohnheit)* stillschweigend mit eingeschlossene Vertragsbedingungen; ~ **may be excluded by an express clause** stillschweigend mit eingeschlossene Bedingungen können durch eine Klausel ausdrücklich ausgeschlossen werden

implied, ~ trust *(nach den Umständen etc)* als bestehend (od. als vereinbart) geltendes Treuhandverhältnis (→*trust 1.);* ~ **warranty** →warranty; **to be ~ from** sich ergeben aus

imply *v (stillschweigend)* mit einbegreifen, einschließen, enthalten; bedeuten, zu verstehen geben; unterstellen

import 1. Einfuhr, Import *(opp. export);* ~**s** Einfuhr(waren); Import(artikel); ~ **agent** Einfuhrvertreter; ~ **application** Einfuhrantrag; ~ **arrangements** Einfuhrregelungen; ~ **authorization** Einfuhrbewilligung; ~ **ban** Einfuhrverbot, Einfuhrstopp; ~ **bullion point** Goldeinfuhrpunkt; ~ **certificate** Einfuhrlizenz; ~ **credit** Importkredit; ~ **dealer** Einfuhrhändler, Importeur; ~ **deposit** *Br*[6] Import-Bardepot

import duty Einfuhrabgabe, Eingangsabgabe; Einfuhrzoll; **maximum ~** Höchstzoll bei der Einfuhr

import, ~ entry Einfuhrdeklaration; ~ **control** Einfuhrkontrolle; ~ **firm** Importfirma; ~ **gold point** Goldeinfuhrpunkt; ~ **goods** Einfuhrwaren; ~ **house** Importhaus, -firma; ~**s in excess of exports** Einfuhrüberschuß; ~ **letter of credit** Importakkreditiv, Importkreditbrief

import licen|ce (~se) Einfuhrlizenz, Einfuhrgenehmigung; **granting** (or **issue**) **of ~s** Erteilung von Einfuhrlizenzen; **to grant an ~** e-e Einfuhrlizenz erteilen

import, ~ list Einfuhrliste; ~ **mark(-)up** Aufschlag auf den Einfuhrpreis; ~ **merchant** Einfuhrhändler; Importkaufmann, Importeur; ~ **of commodities** Wareneinfuhr

import permit Einfuhrbewilligung, Einfuhrgenehmigung; **application for ~** Importantrag

import prohibition Einfuhrverbot

import quota Einfuhrquote, Einfuhrkontingent; **introduction of ~s** Kontingentierung der Einfuhr; **publication of ~s** Einfuhrausschreibungen

import, ~ reduction Einfuhrrückgang; ~ **regulations** Einfuhrbestimmungen; ~ **requirements** Importbedarf; **(quantitive) ~ restrictions** (mengenmäßige) Einfuhrbeschränkungen, Importrestriktionen; ~ **specie point** Goldeinfuhrpunkt; ~ **subsidies** Importsubventionen; ~ **surplus** Einfuhrüberschuß; ~ **tariff** Einfuhrzoll(tarif); ~ **trade** Einfuhrhandel, Importhandel; ~ **transaction** Einfuhrgeschäft, Importgeschäft; ~ **value** Einfuhrwert; **I~ VAT** *Br* Einfuhrumsatzsteuer: ~ **volume** Einfuhrmenge

import, ban on ~s Einfuhrverbot, Einfuhrstopp; **bounty on ~s** Einfuhrprämie; **charge on ~s** Einfuhrabgabe; **consumer ~s** eingeführte Verbrauchsgüter; **embargo on ~** Einfuhrverbot, Einfuhrsperre; **food ~** Lebensmitteleinfuhr; **increase of ~s** Einfuhrsteigerung; **limitation of** (or **on**) **~s** Einfuhrbeschränkung; **list of ~s** Einfuhrliste; **merchandise ~s** *Am* Warenimporte; **non-quota ~s** nichtkontingentierte Einfuhrwaren; **quantity of ~s** Einfuhrmenge; **restriction on ~s** Einfuhrbeschränkung, Importrestriktion; **scale of ~s** Umfang der Einfuhr; **surplus of ~s** Einfuhrüberschuß; **token ~s** symbolische Einfuhr; **total ~s** Gesamteinfuhr

import, to increase ~s die Einfuhr erhöhen; **~s have increased** die Einfuhr ist gestiegen (by um); **to issue an ~ authorization** e-e Einfuhrgenehmigung erteilen; **to make ~s subject to a quota** Importe kontingentieren; **to reduce** (or **restrict**) **~s** die Einfuhr beschränken (od. drosseln)

import 2. Bedeutung, Wichtigkeit; **of general ~** von allgemeiner Bedeutung; **matter of great ~** Angelegenheit von großer Wichtigkeit

import *v* importieren, einführen (into a country in ein Land); bedeuten, Bedeutung haben; **to ~ a disease** e-e Krankheit einschleppen; **permission to ~** Einfuhrerlaubnis; **to ~ freely** unbehindert einführen

imported, ~ article Importartikel, Einfuhrartikel; **~ commodities** (or **goods,** *bes. Am* **merchandise**) Importware(n); **~ energy** Einfuhrenergie

importing, ~ country Importland, Einfuhrland; **~ firm** (or **house**) Importfirma

importance Wichtigkeit, Bedeutung; **of great (little, minor) ~** von großer (geringer, untergeordneter) Bedeutung; **to attach ~ to a matter** e-r Sache Bedeutung beimessen

importation Einfuhr, Import *(opp. exportation)*; **~ of goods in minimum commercial quantities** Einfuhr von Waren in handelsüblichen Mindestmengen; **articles of ~** Einfuhrwaren; **bounty on ~** Einfuhrprämie; **temporary ~** vorübergehende Einfuhr

importer Importeur; **firm of ~s** Importfirma

impose *v* auferlegen, verhängen; **to ~ charges** Abgaben erheben (on auf); **to ~ conditions** Bedingungen auferlegen; **to ~ an embargo** ein Embargo verhängen; e-e Sperre auferlegen; **to ~ a fine on sb.** jdn mit e-r Geldstrafe belegen; jdm e-e Geldstrafe auferlegen; **to ~ an obligation on sb.** jdm e-e Verpflichtung auferlegen; **to ~ a penalty on sb.** jdn mit e-r Strafe belegen; gegen jdn e-e Strafe verhängen; **to ~ restrictions** Einschränkungen auferlegen; **to ~ a tax on** mit e-r Steuer belegen; besteuern

imposed, an obligation ~ by a contract e-e Verpflichtung aus e-m Vertrag

imposition Auferlegung, Verhängung; *(öffentl.)* Abgabe, Steuer; Täuschung, Betrug; **~ of conditions** Auferlegung von Bedingungen; **~ of a penalty** Verhängung e-r Strafe; **~ of taxes** Besteuerung

impossibility of performance[7] *(befreiende)* Unmöglichkeit der Erfüllung (od. Leistung); **subsequent ~** nachträgliche Unmöglichkeit der Erfüllung; **~ of a contract ab initio renders the contract void** ein von Anfang an auf e-e unmögliche Leistung gerichteter Vertrag ist nichtig *(vgl. § 306 BGB)*

impost *(öffentl.)* Abgabe, Steuer; Einfuhrzoll

impostor Betrüger, Schwindler, Hochstapler

imposture Betrug, Schwindel; Hochstapelei

impound *v* in gerichtliche (od. behördliche) Verwahrung nehmen (od. geben); beschlagnahmen; sicherstellen; *(entwichene Tiere)* einsperren

impracticable unausführbar, undurchführbar; praktisch unmöglich; *(von Straßen)* ungangbar, unbenutzbar; **~ scheme** undurchführbarer Plan

imprescriptible nicht ersitzbar

impress Abdruck, Stempel

impress *v (Siegel etc)* aufdrücken; Eindruck machen

impressed, ~ seal Prägestempel; **~ stamp** eingedruckter Stempel, Prägestempel; eingedrucktes (Post-)Wertzeichen *(opp. adhesive stamp)*

impression Abdruck, Stempel; *(bes. unveränderte)* Auflage *(e-s Buches)*; Eindruck; **first ~ of 5000 copies** Erstauflage von 5000 Stück; **new ~** Neudruck, neue Auflage

imprest *Br* Vorschuß aus öffentlichen Mitteln; **~ account** Spesenbuch *(e-r Firma für kleinere Auslagen, z. B. Porti)*

imprimatur ("let it be printed") Druckerlaubnis

imprint Impressum, Druckvermerk

imprison *v* ins Gefängnis setzen, einsperren, inhaftieren

imprisoned, to be ~ inhaftiert sein; im Gefängnis sitzen

imprisonment Freiheitsstrafe, Gefängnis(strafe),[8] Haft; Inhaftierung; **~ for debt** Gefängnis wegen Nichtzahlung bestimmter Schulden *(Br bei Nichtbeachtung von Unterhaltsurteilen so-*

wie Nichtzahlung von Steuern und gewissen anderen öffentlichen Auflagen); ~ **for 3 months** 3 Monate Gefängnis; ~ **not exceeding 3 months** Freiheitsstrafe bis zu 3 Monaten; ~ **for failure to pay a fine** Ersatzfreiheitsstrafe; ~ **for life** lebenslängliche Freiheitsstrafe; ~ **with hard labor** *Am* Zuchthausstrafe

imprisonment, false ~ Freiheitsberaubung; ungesetzliche Haft; **life** ~ lebenslängliche Freiheitsstrafe; **under pain of** ~ bei Gefängnisstrafe;[8] **sentence of** ~ Freiheitsstrafe, Gefängnisstrafe;[8] **carrying out a sentence of** ~ Vollstreckung e-r Freiheitsstrafe; **term of** ~ (Dauer der) Freiheitsstrafe (od. Gefängnisstrafe[8]); Strafzeit (→*term 2.)*

imprisonment, to be liable to ~ **for a term not exceeding 3 months** mit e-r Freiheitsstrafe bis zu 3 Monaten zu bestrafen sein; **to be sentenced to one month's** ~ zu einem Monat Gefängnis verurteilt werden; **to commute a death penalty into life imprisonment** e-e Todesstrafe in lebenslängliche Freiheitsstrafe umwandeln; **to convert a sentence of imprisonment to a fine** e-e Freiheitsstrafe in Geldstrafe umwandeln; **to impose** ~ s. to pass a sentence of →~; **to impose a sentence of** ~ **for an extended term** auf e-e verlängerte Freiheitsstrafe erkennen; **to pass** (or **pronounce**) a sentence of ~ e-e Freiheitsstrafe verhängen; auf Gefängnis erkennen; **to sentence to a term of** ~ zu e-r Freiheitsstrafe verurteilen; mit Gefängnis bestrafen; **to serve one's sentence of** ~ seine Freiheitsstrafe verbüßen

improbable result unwahrscheinliches Ergebnis

improper unpassend, ungehörig; unrichtig, unvorschriftsmäßig; ~ **conduct** ungehöriges Verhalten; ~ **use** ungehörige Verwendung; **to make** ~ **use** mißbrauchen; **the court was** ~**ly constituted** das Gericht war unvorschriftsmäßig besetzt; **the venue is** ~ das Gericht ist (örtlich) nicht zuständig

improve *v* (sich) (ver)bessern; vervollkommnen, weiterbilden; *com* veredeln; *(Gehalt)* aufbessern; *(Land)* meliorieren, verbessern; *Am* Wert *(von Land)* erhöhen *(durch Bebauung, bauliche Verbesserungen etc);* steigen, anziehen *(Preise, Kurse);* **to** ~ **land** *Am* Bauland erschließen; **to** ~ **(up)on** übertreffen, überbieten; **to** ~ **on sb.'s offer** jds Angebot überbieten

improved, ~ **health** gebesserte Gesundheit; ~ **land** melioriertes Land; *Am* erschlossenes (bebautes) Land; ~ **and unimproved real property** *Am* bebaute und unbebaute Grundstücke

improvement Besserung, Verbesserung; Aufbesserung *(des Gehalts);* Fortschritt; Melioration, Bodenverbesserung; *(werterhöhende)* bauliche Verbesserung *(Bebauung, Ausbau, Reparatur); Am* Erschließung, Bebauung *(von Grundbesitz); Am* Grundstücksbestandteil; Anziehen, Steigen *(der Preise, Kurse); (PatR)* Verbesserung *(e-r bereits patentierten Sache);* ~**s** Grundstücksverbesserungen *(durch Bebauung usw.)*; ~ **bonds** *Am* der Verbesserung öffentlicher Einrichtungen dienende Kommunalanleihen; ~ **industry** Veredelungsindustrie; ~ **levies** *Am* Abgaben zur Erhaltung gewisser öffentlicher Einrichtungen; ~ **patent** Verbesserungspatent (Zusatzpatent); ~ **of** (or **in**) **prices** Kursbesserung; Kurserholung; ~ **in shares** Anziehen der Aktien; ~ **trade** Veredelungsverkehr; **land and** ~**s** *Am* Grundstück und Grundstücksbestandteile *(z.B. ein Haus);* **to constitute a technical** ~ e-n technischen Fortschritt darstellen; **to show an** ~ Besserung zeigen *(z.B. Preise, Kurse)*

impugn *v* anfechten; bestreiten; **to** ~ **a decision** e-e Entscheidung anfechten

impugnable anfechtbar; bestreitbar

impulse goods *Am* Waren, die spontan *(auf Grund des Aussehens)* gekauft werden

impunity Straflosigkeit, Straffreiheit; **with** ~ ungestraft, straflos

imputable zurechenbar

imputation Beschuldigung, Bezichtigung; Zuschreibung, Zurechnung; **to be under an** ~ bezichtigt werden

impute *v (jdm etw.)* zurechnen, zuschreiben, zur Last legen; **to** ~ **an accident to the driver's carelessness** den Unfall der Fahrlässigkeit des Fahrers zuschreiben

imputed, ~ **cost** kalkulatorische Kosten; ~ **income** *(SteuerR)* zurechenbares Einkommen; ~ **negligence** *Am* zurechenbare Fahrlässigkeit *(Haftung für fremdes Verschulden);* ~ **notice** zurechenbare Kenntnis; ~ **rent** veranschlagte Miete

in, ~**-and-out** *Am* Kauf und Verkauf e-s Wertpapiers innerhalb e-r sehr engen Zeitspanne; ~ **autre droit** ("in another's right") im Namen Dritter; ~ **bond** unter Zollverschluß, unverzollt (→*bond 4.*); ~ **bonis** *(i.b.) Am* in Sachen *(bei Nachlaßsachen);* ~ **camera** (or **chambers**) unter Ausschluß der Öffentlichkeit; ~ **commendam** ("in trust") zu treuen Händen; ~ **common** →common 2.; ~ **consimili casu** ("in a like case") in e-m gleichen Falle; ~ **curia** ("in open court") bei öffentlicher Gerichtsverhandlung; ~ **custody legis** ("in the custody of the law") in gerichtlichem Gewahrsam; ~ **esse** ("in being") tatsächlich vorhanden; ~ **flagrante delicto** ("in the act of doing the wrong") in flagranti, auf frischer Tat; ~ **futuro** ("in the future") in Zukunft; ~ **invitum** ("against a reluctant person") gegen e-e widerstrebende Person; ~ **lieu of** ("instead of") an Stelle von; ~ **loco parentis** ("in the place of a parent") an Stelle eines Elternteils; ~ **nomine** ("in the name of") im Namen von; ~ **pais** ("in the country") außergerichtlich (→*pais*); ~ **pari delicto, potior est conditio possidentis** ("where both parties are equally in fault, the condition of the possessor is the best") wenn beide Parteien in gleicher Weise schuldig sind, hat der Besitzer die günstigste Rechtslage; ~ **pari materia** ("in an analogous case") in einem analogen Falle; ~ **person** persönlich, in eigener Person *(ohne Hilfe e-s Anwalts)* (→*person*); ~ **personam** ("against a person") gegen e-e Person; schuldrechtlich *(opp. in rem)*; ~**-plant** *Am* innerbetrieblich; ~ **pleno** ("in full") im Plenum, Plenar-; ~ **posse** möglicherweise existent; ~ **praesenti** ("at the present time") gegenwärtig *(opp. in futuro)*; ~ **propria persona** ("in his own proper person") in eigener Person, persönlich; ~ **re** ("in the matter of") in Sachen; ~ **rem** dinglich *(opp. ~ personam)*; **action** ~ **rem** dingliche Klage; ~**-service training** *Am* betriebliche Berufsausbildung; ~ **situ** ("in its original situation") an Ort und Stelle (→*situs*); ~ **specie** ("in its own form and essence") in natura; in Metallgeld; ~ **status quo ante** ("in the former position") im vorigen Zustand; ~**-store computer** *Am* Laden-Computer; ~**-stream investments** Investitionen in branchenverwandten Unternehmen; ~ **terrorem** ("as a threat") als Abschreckung *(Klausel in e-m Testament, nach der ein Vermächtnis nichtig ist, wenn der Vermächtnisnehmer bestimmte Bedingung nicht erfüllt)*; ~ **transitu** ("in course of transit") unterwegs (→*stoppage in transitu*); ~ **trust** zu treuen Händen

inability Unfähigkeit, Unvermögen; ~ **to pay** Zahlungsunfähigkeit; ~ **to perform the duties of the office** Amtsunfähigkeit; ~ **to practice one's profession** Berufsunfähigkeit

inaccuracy Unrichtigkeit, Ungenauigkeit *(z.B. e-r Übersetzung)*

inaccurate unrichtig, ungenau; ~ **statement** ungenaue Angabe

inactive inaktiv, untätig; *com* flau, lustlos, geschäftslos; ~ **account** umsatzloses Konto; ~ **capital** brachliegendes Kapital; ~ **market** lustloser Markt

inactivity Untätigkeit; *com* Lustlosigkeit, Flaute

inadequate unangemessen; unzulänglich; unzureichend; ~ **means** nicht ausreichende Mittel; ~ **sentence** unzureichende Strafe; ~ **statement** unzulängliche Erklärung

inadmissibility Unzulässigkeit; ~ **of evidence** Unzulässigkeit von Beweismitteln

inadmissible unzulässig, nicht zulässig; ~ **assets** *Am (VersR)* nicht zulassungsfähige Vermögenswerte *(zur Sicherung der Leistungsfähigkeit von Versicherungsunternehmen; →inadmitted assets)*; ~ **evidence** unzulässige Beweismittel

inadmitted assets *Am (VersR)* nicht zugelassene Vermögenswerte *(zur Erfüllung gesetzlicher Anforderungen an die Vermögensausrüstung und Vermögensanlagenbildung von Versicherungsunternehmen)*

inalienability Unveräußerlichkeit; Unübertragbarkeit

inalienable unabdingbar; ~ **right** unveräußerliches (od. nicht übertragbares) Recht

inaugural Antritts-, Einführungs-, Einweihungs-; ~ **address** Antrittsrede; Eröffnungsansprache; *Am* Ansprache des Präsidenten bei Amtsübernahme; ~ **ceremony** Eröffnungsfeier; ~ **lecture** *univ* Antrittsvorlesung; ~ **meeting** erste Versammlung; Eröffnungssitzung; ~ **speech** →~ address; **to deliver the** ~ **address** die Antrittsrede halten

inaugurate *v (jdn feierlich)* in ein Amt einführen *(Am den Präsidenten, Gouverneur)*; einweihen; *(feierlich)* eröffnen; beginnen, einleiten; **to** ~ **an air service** e-n Fluglinienverkehr eröffnen; **to** ~ **a new era** e-e neue Ära einleiten

inauguration *(feierl.)* Amtseinführung; *Am (feierl.)* Vereidigung des Präsidenten der USA; Einweihung, Eröffnung, Beginn, Einleitung; ~ **address** →inaugural address; **I~ Day** *Am* Tag der Amtseinführung des Präsidenten der USA; ~ **of a new policy** Einleitung e-r neuen Politik

inbound auf der Heimfahrt befindlich *(Schiff) (opp. outbound)*

Inc. *Am* (als) AG (eingetragen) (→*incorporated*)

incapable unfähig, ungeeignet; nicht in der Lage (of doing zu tun); ~ **of holding public office** unfähig zur Bekleidung e-s öffentlichen Amtes; ~ **of making a will** testierunfähig; ~ **of managing one's own affairs** unfähig, seine eigenen Angelegenheiten zu besorgen; geschäftsunfähig; ~ **of working** arbeitsunfähig; **legally** ~ *Am* geschäftsunfähig

incapacitate *v* unfähig machen (for or from doing zu tun); für unfähig erklären; *(jdn)* disqualifizieren

incapacitated arbeitsunfähig, erwerbsunfähig; körperlich (od. geistig) behindert; **(legally)** ~ geschäftsunfähig; rechtsunfähig; ~ **for work** arbeitsunfähig *(wegen Krankheit od. Unfall)*; ~ **worker** Arbeitsunfähiger; **partly** ~ **person** Person mit verminderter Arbeitsfähigkeit; **physically** ~ körperlich behindert

incapacity Unfähigkeit; ~ **(for work)** Arbeitsunfähigkeit; ~ **to earn one's living** Erwerbsunfähigkeit; ~ **to sue** *Am* mangelnde Prozeßfähigkeit; ~ **to vote** Unfähigkeit zu wählen *(Fehlen des aktiven Wahlrechts)*; **permanent** ~ dauernde Erwerbsunfähigkeit

incendiarism Brandstiftung; Aufwiegelung

incendiary Brandstifter; durch Brandstiftung verursacht; Agitator; aufrührerisch; ~ **bomb** Brandbombe; ~ **letter** *Scot* Drohbrief; ~ **speech** Hetzrede

incentive Anreiz, Ansporn; anspornend; ~**s** Anreizeffekte *(opp. disincentives)*; ~ **bonus** Anspornprämie; Leistungszulage; ~ **bonus system** Prämiensystem zur Leistungssteigerung; ~ **calculation** *Am* Akkordberechnung; ~ **earnings** Leistungsverdienst; ~ **pay** höherer Lohn für höhere Leistung; Leistungslohn *(cf. piecework)*; ~ **plan** *Am* leistungsbezogenes Lohnsystem; ~ **wage** →~pay; ~**s for saving** Anreiz zum Sparen; **buying** ~ Kaufanreiz; **investment** ~**s** Investitionsanreize *(z.B. steuerliche Vergünstigungen)*; **wage** ~ **system** Anreizsystem zwecks Erreichung e-s höheren Lohns; **to provide** ~**s** Anreize schaffen

inception Anfang, Beginn; **at the** ~ **of the proceedings the plaintiff was a minor** am Anfang des Prozesses war der Kläger minderjährig; ~ **of insurance cover** Versicherungsbeginn

inch Zoll (2,54 cm)

incest Inzest, Blutschande

incestuous blutschänderisch

Inchmaree clause *(SeeversR)* Inchmaree-Klausel *(durch die ein ganzer Katalog von Gefahren zusätzlich mit unter die Gefahrtragung des Versicherers gestellt wird)*

inchoate angefangen *(aber noch nicht beendet)*; in der Entwicklung (od. Entstehung) begriffen; teilweise begründet (od. bestehend); ~ **agreement** Vertrag, der noch nicht von allen Parteien unterzeichnet ist; ~ **cheque (check)** noch nicht vollständig ausgefüllter Scheck; ~ **crimes** *Am* einleitende Straftaten *(z.B. attempt, solicitation, conspiracy)*; ~ **instrument** *Br* unvollständige Urkunde; unvollständiger Wechsel *(z.B. Blankoakzept)*; ~ **offences** *Br (bestimmte)* einleitende Straftaten *(z.B. conspiracy, incitement to commit an indictable offence; attempt to commit an indictable offence)*; ~ **right** (or **title**) noch in der Entstehung begriffenes Recht *(z.B. Am →dower zu Lebzeiten des Ehegatten)*

incidence Inzidenz, Vorkommen; Häufigkeit, Umfang; Auswirkung; Störfall; ~ **of divorces** Häufigkeit der Scheidungen; ~ **of loss** *(VersR)* Schadenhäufigkeit; ~ **(of a tax)** *(letzter)* Steueranfall; **the** ~ **of a tax is on the person who actually pays it** die Steuerinzidenz trifft die Person, die sie tatsächlich bezahlt *(cf. impact)*

incident 1. Vorfall, Zwischenfall, Ereignis; Nebenumstand; **border** (or **frontier**) ~ *pol* Grenzzwischenfall; **nuclear** ~ *(AtomR)* nuklearer Schadensfall

incident 2. verbunden (to mit); gehörend (to zu)

incidental zufällig; beiläufig, gelegentlich; Neben-; sekundär; ~**s** Nebenausgaben, Nebenkosten; sonstige Kosten; ~ **damages** *Am* Ersatz des beiläufig entstandenen Schadens; ~ **expenses** Nebenausgaben; Nebenkosten; ~ **income** Nebeneinkünfte; ~ **powers** Befugnisse, die sich aus der Natur der Sache ergeben; *Am (in die Bundeskompetenz fallende)* Befugnisse, die sich aus der Verfassung ergeben *(→implied powers)*

incidental to gehörig zu; verbunden mit; **expenses** ~ die bei . . . entstehenden Kosten; **to be** ~ gehören zu; verbunden sein mit

incineration Einäscherung, Verbrennung; ~ **of wastes at sea**[9] Verbrennung von Abfällen auf See

incite *v* verleiten, aufhetzen, aufwiegeln; *(StrafR)* anstiften

incitement Verleitung, Aufhetzung, Aufwiegelung; *(StrafR)* Anstiftung; ~ **to commit a crime** Anstiftung zum Verbrechen; ~ **to disaffection** *Br mil* Aufwiegelung zur Auflehnung; Wehrkraftzersetzung

incivism Mangel an staatsbürgerlicher Gesinnung

inclination, ~ **to buy** Kauflust; ~ **to invest** Neigung zu investieren

inclose *v* →enclose *v*

inclosure →enclosure; *Br* Übereignung von Gemeindeland (→*common 1.*) an Privatpersonen

include *v* einschließen, einbeziehen, (mit) einrechnen; **to** ~ **in the agenda** auf die Tagesordnung setzen; **to** ~ **in a bill** auf e-e Rechnung setzen; in e-e Rechnung aufnehmen; **to** ~ **in a report** in e-n Bericht aufnehmen; **to** ~ **sb. in a will** jdn im Testament bedenken

included einbegriffen, enthalten, eingeschlossen; inklusiv; **drinks** ~ inklusive Getränke; **not** ~ **in the budget** außeretatmäßig; **not** ~ **in the price** im Preis nicht mit inbegriffen

including (incl.) einschließlich *(opp. excluding)*; ~ **postage** einschließlich Porto; **up to and** ~ **July 31** bis einschließlich 31. Juli

inclusion Einschließung, Einbeziehung, Einrechnung; ~ **in the agenda** Aufnahme in die Tagesordnung; ~ **of conditions** Aufnahme von Bedingungen; ~ **in the contract** Einbeziehung in den Vertrag

inclusive (incl.) einschließlich *(opp. exclusive);* ~ **of costs** einschließlich der Kosten; ~ **of service** einschließlich Bedienung; ~ **terms** alles inbegriffen; *(im Hotel)* Preise einschließlich Bedienung; **from January 1 to January 31** ~ vom 1. bis 31. Januar einschließlich

income Einkommen; Einnahmen; Einkünfte; Ertrag, Erträge; *Am* (Geschäfts-)Gewinn; ~ **account** Ertragskonto; ~ **arisen in a country** in e-m Lande entstandene Einkünfte; ~ **arising from any office or employment of profit** Einkünfte aus unselbständiger Arbeit; ~ **arising out of the ownership of land** *Br* Einkünfte aus Grundbesitz; ~ **arising from participation in the capital and profits of a company** Einkünfte aus Kapital- und Gewinnanteilen an e-r Gesellschaft; ~ **averaging** *Am* Durchschnittsbesteuerung *(durchschnittliche Verteilung des Einkommens über die drei Jahre vor dem Steuerjahr zur Verringerung der Einkommensteuer in Jahren mit Spitzeneinkommen);* ~ **bonds** *Am* Gewinnschuldverschreibungen; Schuldverschreibungen mit vom Gewinn abhängiger Verzinsung; ~ **bracket** Einkommensstufe; **lower** ~ **brackets** untere Einkommensschichten; ~ **effectively connected with a United States trade or business**[10] *Am* Einkommen aus amerikanischer Geschäftstätigkeit; ~ **elasticity of demand** Einkommenselastizität der Nachfrage; ~ **exempt from taxes** steuerfreies Einkommen; ~ **for life** lebenslängliche Einkünfte; ~ **from capital** Einkünfte aus Kapitalvermögen; ~ **from employment** Einkünfte aus nichtselbständiger Arbeit; Arbeitseinkommen; ~ **from self-employment** Einkünfte aus selbständiger Tätigkeit; ~ **from investments** Einkünfte aus Anlagevermögen; Erträge aus Beteiligungen; ~ **from rents** Einkünfte aus Vermietungen und Verpachtungen; ~ **fund** *Am (Investmentfonds)* Einkommensfonds

income group Einkommensgruppe; **higher (lower, middle)** ~**s** obere (untere, mittlere) Einkommensgruppen

income, ~ **in kind** Naturaleinkommen; ~ **level** Einkommenshöhe, Einkommensstand; ~ **loss** Einkommensverlust; ~ **policy** Einkommenspolitik; ~ **producing property** *Am* ertragbringendes Vermögen

income schedules *Br* Einkunftstabellen *(die Einkommensarten werden nach 6 verschiedenen schedules besteuert)*

income statement *Am* Gewinn- und Verlustrechnung; Erfolgsrechnung; ~ **support** *Br* Sozialhilfe (Geldleistungen); ~ **support for farmers** Einkommensbeihilfen für Landwirte

(income) tax Einkommensteuer; ~ **(on wages)** *Br* Lohnsteuer; ~ **allowance** *Br* Einkommensteuervergünstigung *(z.B. für Zahlung auf Pensionskasse [superannuation]);* ~ **assessment** Einkommensteuerbescheid, -veranlagung; ~ **declaration** *Br* →tax return

income tax, ~ **on corporations** *Am* Körperschaftsteuer, Einkommenssteuer für Körperschaften (od. Kapitalgesellschaften); ~ **on individuals** *Am* Einkommensteuer für natürliche Personen; ~ **rate** Einkommensteuersatz; ~ **relief** *Br* Freibetrag, Steuerabzug (→*relief 3.*); ~ **upon return on investments** *Am* Kapitalertragsteuer

income tax return Einkommensteuererklärung; (**to fail**) **to file one's** ~ seine Einkommensteuererklärung (nicht) abgeben

income tax, corporate ~ *Am* Körperschaftsteuer; **deferred** ~ gestundete Einkommensteuer; **free of** ~ einkommensteuerfrei; **individual** ~ *Am* Einkommensteuer der natürlichen Personen; **standard** (or **basic**) **rate of** ~ *Br* Einheitssteuersatz; **state and municipal** ~ *Am* Einkommensteuer der Einzelstaaten und der Gemeinden; **to be subject to** ~ der Einkommensteuer unterliegen; **to incur** ~ **obligation** *Am* der Einkommensteuerpflicht unterworfen sein

income, accrued ~ antizipative Aktiva (→*accrued*); **additional** ~ Nebeneinkommen, Nebeneinnahmen; **amount of** ~ Einkommensbetrag; Höhe des Einkommens; **annual** ~ Jahreseinkommen; **assessable** ~ steuerpflichtiges (od. zu versteuerndes) Einkommen; **average** ~ Durchschnittseinkommen; **deferred** ~ *Am* transitorische Passiva; **determinable** ~ *(der Höhe nach)* bestimmbare Einkünfte; **disposable** ~ verfügbares Einkommen; →**earned** ~; **extra** ~ s. additional →~; **fixed** ~ festes Einkommen; **foreign** ~ Auslandseinkommen; **gross** ~ Bruttoeinkommen, Roheinkommen *(Gesamtbetrag aller Einnahmen);* **adjusted gross** ~ *Am* berichtigtes Roheinkommen *(nach Absetzung der zulässigen Abzüge);* **high** ~ hohes Einkommen; →**investment** ~; **low** ~ niedriges Einkommen; **national** ~ Volkseinkommen; **net** ~ Nettoeinkommen; Reinertrag; **nominal** ~ Nominaleinkommen; **personal** ~ Privateinkommen; **real** ~ Realeinkommen; effektives Einkommen; **regular** ~ festes Einkommen; **retirement** ~ Einkommen aus Altersrente (od. Pension); **settled** ~ festes Einkommen; **small** ~ geringes Einkommen; **source of** ~ Einkommensquelle; **statement of** ~ Einkommensaufstellung; **taxable** ~ steuerpflichtiges Einkommen; **tax exempt** ~ steuerfreies Einkommen; →**unearned** ~

income, the ~ **is effectively connected with trade or business** *Am (SteuerR)* die Einkünfte hängen tatsächlich mit e-r Gewerbetätigkeit zusammen; **to declare one's** ~ seine Steuererklärung abgeben; **to draw an** ~ (from) ein Einkommen beziehen; **to live on one's** ~ von seinen Einkünften leben; **to live within one's**

~ mit seinen Einkünften auskommen; **to live beyond one's** ~ über seine Verhältnisse leben

incomer Neueintretender; (Rechts-)Nachfolger *(Mieter, Pächter);* Eindringling

incoming neu eintretend; hereinkommend, einlaufend *(opp. outgoing);* ~**s** (Geld-)Eingänge, Einnahmen *(opp. outgoings);* ~ **goods** Wareneingang; **the** ~ **Government** die neue Regierung; ~ **mail** eingehende Post, Posteingang; ~ **order(s)** Auftragseingang; ~ **partner** eintretender Partner; ~ **payments** Zahlungseingänge; ~ **premium** *(VersR)* eingenommene Prämie; ~ **stocks** Wareneingang; ~ **tenant** neuer Mieter (od. Pächter)

incommunicado, the prisoner was kept ~ der Gefangene wurde ohne Möglichkeit der Verbindung mit der Außenwelt gelassen

incompatibility Unvereinbarkeit; ~ **between husband and wife** *Am (EheR)* unüberwindliche Abneigung *(in mehreren Staaten Scheidungsgrund)*

incompatible unvereinbar, nicht vereinbar (with mit); ~ **with Community law** mit dem Gemeinschaftsrecht unvereinbar

incompeten|ce (~cy) Unfähigkeit; Nichtzuständigkeit; *Am* Unzurechnungsfähigkeit, Geschäftsunfähigkeit; ~ **of evidence** *Am* Unzulässigkeit von Beweismitteln; ~ **to testify** (or **to act as witness** or **juror**) Unfähigkeit, Zeuge od. Geschworener zu sein

incompetent unfähig; unzuständig, nicht zuständig; *Am* unzurechnungsfähig, geschäftsunfähig; ~ **(person)** *Am* Geschäftsunfähiger; ~ **witness** unzulässiger Zeuge *(z.B. Partei, Beteiligter, Geisteskranker);* **to be adjudicated** ~ *Am (New York)* für geschäftsunfähig erklärt werden, entmündigt werden; **to be declared** ~ **due to physical or mental incapacity** *Am* infolge körperlicher oder geistiger Gebrechen für unzurechnungsfähig od. geschäftsunfähig erklärt werden

inconclusive nicht überzeugend; nicht schlüssig; ~ **vote** ergebnislose Abstimmung

inconclusiveness Mangel an Beweiskraft; Mangel an Schlüssigkeit

inconsistency Unvereinbarkeit; Widerspruch (with zu)

inconsistent unvereinbar, in Widerspruch stehend (with zu); ~ **statements** einander widersprechende Aussagen

incontestability Unanfechtbarkeit

incontestable unbestreitbar, unanfechtbar, endgültig *(z.B. Versicherungspolice)*

inconvenience *v,* **to be** ~**d** gestört (od. aufgehalten, belästigt) werden

inconvenient unbequem, lästig; nicht passend; **at a most** ~ **time** zu sehr ungelegener Zeit

inconvertibility Nichtkonvertierbarkeit, Nichteinlösbarkeit *(opp. convertibility)*

inconvertible nicht konvertierbar, nicht einlösbar *(opp. convertible)*

incorporate *v* Rechtspersönlichkeit verleihen; e-e juristische Person gründen; *Am* Kapitalgesellschaft gründen (od. errichten); als juristische Person (*Am* AG) eintragen (lassen) *(s. certificate of →incorporation); Br* Status e-r Gemeinde verleihen, eingemeinden; eingliedern (into in); aufnehmen (in in); **to** ~ **a clause into a contract** e-e Klausel e-m Vertrag einfügen; **to** ~ **a company** *Am* e-e Gesellschaft gründen; **to** ~ **in the law** in das Gesetz aufnehmen

incorporated (Inc.) *Am* als Kapitalgesellschaft *(amtlich)* eingetragen *(Inc. ist als Zusatz zum Namen e-r Aktiengesellschaft in vielen Einzelstaaten zwingend);* **not** ~ *Am* keine Haftungsbeschränkung *(da keine Kapitalgesellschaft);* ~ **accountant** *Br* Wirtschaftsprüfer; ~ **bank** *Am* Bank, die in der Form e-r Aktiengesellschaft betrieben wird; Aktienbank; ~ **city** Stadtgemeinde; ~ **company** *Am* Aktiengesellschaft; *Br* rechtsfähige (Handels-)Gesellschaft; ~ **insurance broker** *Br* Versicherungsmakler; ~ **society** eingetragener Verein; ~ **town** *Am* Stadtgemeinde; ~ **in the United Kingdom** *Br* mit Sitz im Vereinigten Königreich; **to be** ~ **in the contract** Vertragsbestandteil sein; **to be** ~ **in the records** zu den Akten genommen werden

Incorporating Act *Am* Gründungsgesetz *(für Investmentgesellschaften)*

incorporation Verleihung der Rechtspersönlichkeit; Gründung (od. Errichtung) e-r juristischen Person; *Am* Gründung e-r Kapitalgesellschaft; *Br* Eingemeindung; Eingliederung, Einfügung; Aufnahme (into in); ~ **of a document in a will** Einbeziehung e-r Urkunde in ein Testament; ~ **of a mutual (insurance) company** Gründung e-s Versicherungsvereins auf Gegenseitigkeit (VVaG); ~ **of foreign territory** Eingliederung fremden Staatsgebiets

incorporation by reference *Am* Bezugnahme in e-r Urkunde auf e-e zweite Urkunde, die dadurch Bestandteil der ersten wird

Bezieht sich z.B. ein ordnungsgemäß errichtetes Testament auf einen Brief, gilt dieser als Teil der letztwilligen Verfügung, sofern er zur Zeit der Errichtung des Testaments bereits existierte

incorporation, articles of ~ *Am* Gründungsurkunde; Satzung *(e-r Kapitalgesellschaft);* **cer-**

tificate of ~ Gründungsbescheinigung *(→certificate)*; **filing of the articles** (or **certificate**) **of** ~ *Am* Anmeldung der Eintragung e-r Firma als AG; **state of** ~ *Am (Doppelbesteuerungsabkommen)* Staat der Errichtung (od. Gründungsstaat) der (Kapital-)Gesellschaft

incorporator *Am* Gründungsmitglied *(e-r Kapitalgesellschaft)*, Gesellschaftsgründer

incorporeal nicht körperlich, immateriell; ~ **chattels** immaterielle Vermögenswerte *(z. B. Gesellschaftsanteile, Patente, copyrights)*; ~→**hereditaments;** ~ **right** Immaterialgüterrecht *(Patentrecht, Urheberrecht etc)*

incorrect unrichtig, ungenau; **supplying** ~ **information** Erteilung unrichtiger Auskünfte

Incoterms[11] (International Commercial Terms) Internationale Regeln für die Auslegung von Handelsklauseln

Die Internationale Handelskammer hat 1936 in deutscher, englischer und französischer Sprache, unabhängig von den nationalen Handelsbräuchen, Regeln für die Auslegung der im internationalen Handel üblichen Vertragsformeln veröffentlicht, die 1953, 1974, 1976 und 1980 neu gefaßt worden sind. Die Incoterms gelten nur, wenn die Parteien eines innerstaatlichen oder internationalen Kaufvertrages auf sie Bezug genommen haben (z. B. durch die Formel „Incoterms 1980 CIF")

increase Zunahme, Erhöhung, Vermehrung, Steigen, Steigerung, Verstärkung *(opp. decrease)*; ~ **of appropriations** Erhöhung des Diskontsatzes, Diskonterhöhung; ~ **of capital** *(Am* **capital stock***) (AktienR)* Kapitalerhöhung *(opp. reduction of capital)*; ~ **in charges** Gebührenerhöhung; ~ **in costs** Kostenzunahme, Kostensteigerung; ~ **in crime** Zunahme der Kriminalität; ~ **in demand** Nachfragesteigerung; wachsende Nachfrage (for nach); ~ **of duties** Zollerhöhung; ~ **in earnings** Zunahme des Verdienstes; ~ **in exports** Exportsteigerung; ~ **of fees** Gebührenerhöhung; ~ **in interest rates** Zinserhöhung; ~ **of penalty** Straferhöhung, Strafverschärfung; ~ **of performance** Leistungssteigerung; ~ **in (the) population** Bevölkerungszunahme; ~ **of premium** *(VersR)* Prämienerhöhung; ~ **in price(s)** Preissteigerung; Preiserhöhung; ~ **in production** Produktionssteigerung; ~ **in productivity** Produktivitätssteigerung; ~ **of profits** Gewinnerhöhung; ~ **of receipts** Mehreinnahme(n); ~ **of** (or **in**) **rent** Mieterhöhung; ~ **of risk** *(VersR)* Gefahrerhöhung; ~ **of** (or **in**) **salary** Gehaltserhöhung, Gehaltsaufbesserung, Gehaltszulage; ~ **in taxation** Steuererhöhung; ~ **in trade** Aufschwung des Handels; ~ **in value** Wertsteigerung, Werterhöhung; Wertzuwachs; ~ **of wages** Lohnerhöhung, Steigen der Löhne

increase, affidavit of ~ *Am (SteuerR)* →affidavit; **on the** ~ im Zunehmen, im Steigen; **price** ~ Preissteigerung, Preiserhöhung; **rate of** ~ Wachstumsrate, Zuwachsrate; **salary** ~ Gehaltserhöhung; **to be on the** ~ im Zunehmen begriffen sein; **to show an** ~ e-e Erhöhung zeigen, e-e Steigerung verzeichnen

increase *v* zunehmen, (sich) erhöhen (to auf), steigen, (an)steigen, anwachsen; steigern; **to** ~ **appropriations** die (Haushalts-)Mittel erhöhen; **to** ~ **the capital of a company** *Br* das Grundkapital erhöhen; **to** ~ **the capital stock of a corporation** *Am* das Grundkapital erhöhen; **to** ~ **a credit** e-n Kredit erhöhen; **to** ~ **exports** die Ausfuhr steigern; **to** ~ **the prices** die Preise erhöhen (od. heraufsetzen); **to** ~ **in price** im Preise steigen; teurer werden; **to** ~ **the salary** das Gehalt erhöhen (od. aufbessern); **to** ~ **the sales** den Absatz steigern; **to** ~ **a sentence** e-e Strafe erhöhen (od. verschärfen); **to** ~ **in value** an Wert zunehmen; **to** ~ **wages** die Löhne erhöhen

increased cost of living erhöhte Lebenshaltungskosten; ~ **bonus** Teuerungszulage

increased, ~ **demand** erhöhter Bedarf, Mehrbedarf; ~ **expectation of life** erhöhte Lebenserwartung; ~ **exports** gesteigerte Ausfuhr, Ausfuhrsteigerung; ~ **stability** größere Stabilität; **the population has** ~ die Bevölkerung hat zugenommen (by um)

increasing zunehmend, steigend; ~ **costs** steigende Kosten; Kostensteigerung; ~ **costs of production** steigende Produktionskosten; ~ **premium** *(VersR)* steigende Prämie; **at an** ~ **rate** in zunehmendem Maße

increment Zunahme, Zuwachs (in an); Wertzuwachs; Erhöhung, Steigerung; Gewinn; ~ **of net worth** Vermögenszuwachs; **pension** ~ Pensionserhöhung; Rentenerhöhung; **(salary)** ~ Gehaltssteigerung; Gehaltserhöhung; → **unearned** ~

incremental cost *Am* Grenzkosten

incriminate *v (jdn)* belasten, beschuldigen; **to** ~ **oneself** sich selbst bezichtigen; **to** ~ **another person falsely** gegen jdn falsche Anschuldigungen erheben

incriminating belastend; ~ **evidence** Belastungsmaterial, belastendes Material; ~ **document** *(StrafR)* Urkunde, deren Inhalt den Inhaber belasten könnte

incrimination →self-~

incubation period[12] Inkubationszeit

inculpate *v* beschuldigen; anklagen

inculpatory beschuldigend, belastend

incumbency Obliegenheit; *eccl* Pfründe(nbesitz); Innehaben e-s Amtes

incumbent 1. *Am* Amtsinhaber; *eccl* Pfründeinhaber (rector or vicar)

incumbent 2. obliegend; lastend (on auf); **functions ~ on sb.** jdm obliegende Aufgaben; **to be ~ on sb.** jdm obliegen

incumbrance →encumbrance
incumbrancer →encumbrancer

incur *v* sich zuziehen; auf sich laden, eingehen, übernehmen; sich *(e-r Gefahr etc)* aussetzen; **to ~ a danger** (or **risk**) sich e-r Gefahr aussetzen; **to ~ debts** Schulden machen (od. eingehen); **to ~ considerable expenditure** beträchtliche Aufwendungen machen (od. Ausgaben haben) (on für); **to ~ expenses** sich in Unkosten stürzen; Aufwendungen machen; **"~ no expense"** ohne Kosten *(auf Wechseln);* **to ~ a fine** sich e-e Geldstrafe zuziehen; e-e Geldstrafe verwirken; **to ~ a liability** e-e Verpflichtung eingehen; haften; **to ~ criminal liability** sich strafbar machen; **to ~ large losses** große Verluste erleiden; **to ~ an obligation** e-e Verpflichtung übernehmen; **to ~ a penalty** (or **punishment**) sich strafbar machen; e-e Strafe verwirken; **to ~ a risk** ein Risiko eingehen; sich e-r Gefahr aussetzen

incurred, costs (or **expenses**) **~ by him** ihm entstandene Kosten; **customs penalty ~** verwirkte Zollstrafe; **damage ~** entstandener Schaden; erlittener Verlust; **expenses ~ on my behalf** für mich gemachte Ausgaben (od. Auslagen); **heavy costs can be ~** hohe Kosten können entstehen; **loss ~** → s. damage →~

incurable defect unheilbarer Mangel *(opp. curable defect)*

incursion feindlicher Einfall (od. Einflug); Streifzug; *fig* Einbruch; **to make ~s into (the) capital** das Kapital angreifen

indebted verschuldet; schuldig; (zu Dank) verpflichtet; **heavily ~** schwer verschuldet; überschuldet; **to become ~** sich verschulden; **I am greatly ~ to you for ...** ich bin Ihnen zu großem Dank verpflichtet für ...

indebtedness Verschuldung, Schuld, Schulden (-last); Verpflichtung, Dankesschuld; **acknowledgment of ~** Schuldanerkenntnis; **amount of ~** Schuldbetrag; **bank ~** Bankverschuldung; Bankschulden; **discharge of ~** Tilgung von Schulden; **excessive ~** Überschuldung; **instrument of ~** Schuldurkunde

indecency Unanständigkeit; Unzucht; **~ies** unzüchtige Handlungen; **~ with children** Unzucht mit Kindern;[13] **gross ~** schwere Unzucht; **public ~** Erregung öffentlichen Ärgernisses

indecent unanständig; unzüchtig; ~ →**assault;** ~ →**exposure**

indefeasible unantastbar, unentziehbar; **~ right** unangreifbares Recht; **~ share** *Am* unangreifbarer Anteil am Nachlaß *(nicht auflösend bedingter Anteil);* **~ title** unbestreitbares Eigentum; **a right is ~** ein Recht kann nicht zerstört werden

indefinite unbegrenzt; unbestimmt; **contracts for an ~ period** Verträge mit unbestimmter Dauer; **the Convention shall remain in force ~ly** das Abkommen bleibt auf unbegrenzte Zeit in Kraft

indemnifiable ersatzpflichtig

indemnification Schadloshaltung, Sicherstellung; Entschädigung, Ersatzleistung, Wiedergutmachung, Abfindung; **~ clause** Haftungsfreistellungsklausel *(in Unternehmenssatzungen zugunsten des board of directors);* **~ of expropriated persons** Entschädigung enteigneter Personen

indemnify *v* schadlos halten; **to ~ sb. against** (or **from**) jdm Schadloshaltung zusagen gegen; jdn sicherstellen gegen *(zukünftigen Schaden);* jdn freistellen *(von der Haftung);* **to ~ sb. for sth.** jdm Schadensersatz leisten, jdn entschädigen für *(eingetretenen Schaden);* **to ~ the insured against loss** den Versicherten gegen Schaden sicherstellen; **to ~ the insured for a loss** dem Versicherten für e-n Schaden Ersatz leisten

indemnified, person ~ entschädigte Person; *(AtomR) (von der Haftung)* freigestellte Person

indemnifier zur Schadloshaltung Verpflichteter

indemnitee *Am* zur Schadloshaltung Berechtigter; Entschädigungsberechtigter

indemnitor *Am* zur Schadloshaltung Verpflichteter; Entschädigungsverpflichteter

indemnity (Versprechen der) Schadloshaltung *(durch Dritten),* Sicherstellung *(gegen künftigen Schaden);* Freistellung *(von der Haftung);* Entschädigung(sbetrag), Ersatzleistung *(für eingetretenen Schaden);* Abfindung(ssumme); *parl* Indemnität; *(Börse)* Prämiengeschäft *(bes. im Getreidetermingeschäft);* **~ against liability** Haftungsfreistellung; **~ agreement** Entschädigungsvereinbarung; **~ bond** Schadloshaltungsverpflichtung; Ausfallbürgschaft; **~ contract** Vertrag über Schadloshaltung; **~ insurance** Schadensversicherung; **professional ~ insurance** Berufshaftpflichtversicherung; **~ period** *(VersR)* Haftungszeitraum, versicherter Zeitraum; **bond of ~** →~ bond; **cash ~** Mankogeld, Fehlgeldentschädigung; **double ~** (in case of death by accident) *(VersR)* doppelte Entschädigung (od. Versicherungssumme) (bei Unfalltod); **government ~** *Br (von der Regierung gewährte)* Verpflichtung des Staates zur Freistellung von Schäden (od. Ausfällen), Staatsbürgschaft; staatl. Haftungsgarantie *(z. B. für gemeinnützige Institutionen zur Bewahrung nationalen Kulturgutes);* **letters of ~**

→letter 2.; →**limit of** ~; **right of** ~ Haftungsfreistellungsanspruch, Entschädigungsanspruch für Aufwendungen *(z. B. des personal representative hinsichtl. des Nachlasses od. des trustee hinsichtl. des Treuhandgutes);* **state** ~ *Am* s. government →~; **third party** ~ Haftpflicht; →**trustee's** ~; **war** ~ Kriegsentschädigung

indent (Auslands-)Auftrag; Warenbestellung *(aus Übersee); Br mil* Requisition von Vorräten
Das Indentgeschäft war ursprünglich ein zwischen Europäern oder Amerikanern und Asiaten übliches Geschäft, bei dem nur der asiatische Auftraggeber streng an den Vertrag gebunden war

indent *v* (Auslands-)Auftrag erteilen; *(Waren)* bestellen *(bes. aus Übersee)*

indenture *(in zwei Ausfertigungen vorliegender)* Vertrag; ~**s** (of apprenticeship) Berufsausbildungsvertrag, Lehrvertrag; ~ **deed** *(von zwei od. mehr Vertragspartnern ausgefertigte)* Vertragsurkunde *(opp. deed poll);* **trust** ~ *Am* Treuhandvertrag (→*trust 1.);* **to bind by** ~**s** in die Lehre nehmen; **to be bound by** ~**s** in e-m Berufsausbildungsverhältnis stehen; in der Lehre sein

indenture *v Br (jdn)* durch Berufsausbildungsvertrag (od. Lehrvertrag) verpflichten

independence Unabhängigkeit; Selbständigkeit; **I~ Day** *Am* Unabhängigkeitstag *(4. Juli);* **aspiration for** ~ Streben nach Unabhängigkeit; **Declaration of I~** *Am* Unabhängigkeitserklärung (4. 7. 1776); **judicial** ~ (or ~ **of the judiciary)** richterliche Unabhängigkeit; **to gain** (or **reach**) ~ *pol* Unabhängigkeit erlangen

independent 1. *pol* Unabhängiger, Parteiloser; **I~s** *eccl* Independenten *(Br cf. Congregationalist); Am* unabhängige Gewerkschaften *(die keinem Gewerkschaftsverband angehören)*

independent 2. unabhängig, selbständig; finanziell unabhängig; *pol* parteilos; **I~ (Regulatory) Agency** *Am* unabhängige Bundesverwaltungsbehörde *(für Sondergebiete; z. B. ICC, NASA);* ~ **agent** *Am* freier (Versicherungs-)Vertreter; **in an** ~ **capacity** selbständig; ~ **claim** *(PatentR)* Nebenanspruch; ~ →**contractor;** ~ **income** eigenes Vermögen, Privatvermögen; ~ **inventor** freier Erfinder; **of** ~ **means** finanziell unabhängig, **patent** selbständiges Patent; ~ **personal services** *(DBA)* selbständige Arbeit; ~ **retailer** selbständiger Einzelhändler; **I~ Television** (ITV) Unabhängiges Fernsehen *(Br von privaten Gesellschaften betriebenes und aus Werbeeinkünften finanziertes Fernsehprogramm);* ~ **union** *Am (von der AFL/CIO)* unabhängige Gewerkschaft; ~ **witness** unabhängiger *(nicht beeinflußter)* Zeuge

independently, ~ **owned** in Eigenbesitz befindlich; ~ **of the provisions of article 2** ungeachtet der Bestimmungen des Artikels 2; **two persons have made an invention** ~ **of each other** zwei Personen haben e-e Erfindung unabhängig voneinander gemacht

indeterminate unbestimmt; unsicher; ungenau; ~ **damages** der Höhe nach (noch) unbestimmter Schadensersatz; ~ **sentence** Strafe von unbestimmter Dauer *(im Rahmen e-r bestimmten Höchststrafe)*

index Index; (Inhalts-, Namens-, Sach-)Verzeichnis, Register; *eccl* Index *(Verzeichnis der verbotenen Bücher);* ~ **catalog** (or *Br* **catalogue**) Indexkatalog; ~**-card** Karteikarte; ~ **clause** Indexklausel *(Wertsicherungsklausel)*

index-linked indexgebunden, Index-; ~ **loan** Indexanleihe; ~ **National Savings Certificates** *Br* indexgebundene öffentliche Sparzertifikate
Der Wert der Zertifikate ist dem Lebenshaltungspreisindex (→ *Index of Retail Prices, RPI)* angepaßt und gegen Inflationsverluste abgesichert. Bei Einlösung der Zertifikate wird die Änderung des RPI zwischen den Monaten des Kaufs und der Einlösung berechnet. Ist z. B. der RPI seit dem Kauf der Zertifikate um 20% gestiegen, erhält der Zertifikatsinhaber bei Einlösung den Kaufbetrag + 20%.
Werden die Zertifikate bis zum Ende der Laufzeit (5 Jahre) gehalten, erhält der Inhaber eine Prämie (bonus) in Höhe von 4% des Nominalwertes (Konzeption des bonus kommt dem deutschen Prämiensparsystem nahe).
Die Einkünfte aus den Zertifikaten unterliegen weder der Einkommensteuer noch der Kapitalertragsteuer

index-linked, ~ **insurance** Indexversicherung; ~ **pension** indexgebundene *(und dadurch inflationsgesicherte)* Pension; ~ **wage** Indexlohn

index, ~ **linking** Indexbindung, Indexierung; ~ **number** *(Statistik)* Indexziffer; Nummer im Verzeichnis, Katalognummer

index, ~ **of cost of living** Lebenshaltungskostenindex; ~ **of employment** Beschäftigungsindex; ~ **of members** *Br* Aktionärsverzeichnis *(ist neben dem Aktionärsregister zu führen, wenn die Gesellschaft mehr als 50 Aktionäre hat);* ~ **of names** Namensverzeichnis; ~ **of patents** *Am* Patentindex

Index of Retail Prices (RPI) *Br* Preisindex für die Lebenshaltung
Der RPI ist ein jeden Monat neu errechneter Index zum Vergleich der Durchschnittspreise für Güter und Leistungen des täglichen Lebensbedarfs (food, clothing, rents, transport, drink, tobacco, coal, gas, electricity etc) mit dem des vergangenen Monats

index-tied indexgebunden, Index-; ~ **wages** Indexlohn

index, price ~ Preisindex; →**consumer price** ~; **retail price** ~ Einzelhandelspreisindex; **wholesale price** ~ Großhandelspreisindex

index, (adjusted) production ~ (bereinigter)

Produktionsindex; **share** ~ Aktienindex; **subject** ~ Sachverzeichnis; **tied to the** ~ an den Index gebunden; indexgebunden
index, to put on the ~ *eccl* auf den Index setzen; **the** ~ **stands at 400** der Index ist 400

index *v* indexieren; mit Register versehen; in ein Verzeichnis aufnehmen
indexed Index-; mit Register versehen; **card-**~ in e-r Kartei angelegt; ~ **bond** Indexanleihe; ~ **mortgage rate** indexgebundener Hypothekenzinssatz; ~ **new value insurance** gleitende Neuwertversicherung
indexing Indexbindung

indexation Indexbindung, Indexierung

India Indien; **Republic of** ~ Republik Indien
Indian Inder, Inderin; indisch; *Am* Indianer(in); indianisch; ~ **reservation** *Am* Indianer-Reservat

indicate *v* angeben; hinweisen auf; zum Ausdruck bringen; **to** ~ **reasons** Gründe angeben, begründen; **to** ~ **references** Referenzen angeben
indicated, amount ~ angegebener Betrag; **to be** ~ erforderlich sein

indication Angabe, Hinweis; Andeutung; Anzeichen (of für); Indiz; ~ **of origin** Ursprungsbezeichnung; **false** ~ **of origin on goods** falsche Herkunftsangabe auf Waren *(cf. the Arrangement of →Madrid for the Prevention of False I~s of Origin on Goods);* ~ **of price** Preisangabe; **letter of** ~ *(dem Reisekreditbrief von der Bank beigegebene)* Korrespondentenliste mit Unterschriftsprobe

indicative bezeichnend (of für); ~ **figure** Meßziffer, Kennzahl; **to be** ~ **of** hinweisen auf

indices *(cf. index),* **safeguarded by** ~ indexgesichert

indict *v (öffentlich)* anklagen; **to** ~ **for murder** wegen Mordes anklagen

indictable strafrechtlich verfolgbar; ~ **offen|ce (~se)** *Br* Straftat (Verbrechen, schweres Vergehen), die auf Grund e-s →indictment unter Mitwirkung von Geschworenen abgeurteilt werden kann *(die meisten ~ offences werden heute mit Einwilligung des Angeklagten im summarischen Verfahren, d.h. ohne Geschworene, von den unteren Gerichten, den Magistrates' courts, abgeurteilt; cf. information); Am* Straftat (Verbrechen, schweres Vergehen), die in der Regel auf Grund e-s →indictment von Geschworenen abgeurteilt wird *(es kann aber auf die Mitwirkung von Geschworenen im summarischen Verfahren verzichtet werden);* **non-**~ **offen|ce (~se)** summarisch verfolgbare (leichtere) Straftat *(Vergehen, bes. Verkehrsdelikte, auch Fälle von Körperverletzung und Sachbeschädigung; cf. summary offen|ce [~se])*

indictment formelle Anklageschrift *(Am der →grand jury auf Grund des bill of ~); (etwa)* Eröffnungsbeschluß; **bill of** ~ *(Br den zuständigen →officers of the court, Am der grand jury, vorgelegte)* Anklageschrift; **counts of an** ~ Anklagepunkte; **to bring an** ~ e-e Anklage erheben (against gegen); **to demand an** ~ e-n Strafantrag stellen; **to find an** ~ *Am* e-e Anklage für begründet erklären; *(etwa)* das Hauptverfahren eröffnen *(cf. true bill);* **to dismiss** (or **quash**) **the** ~ die Anklage für nicht begründet erklären; *(etwa)* den Angeschuldigten außer Verfolgung setzen; das Verfahren einstellen *(Am cf. not found, → found 2.);* **to prefer** (or **present**) **a bill of** ~ *(Br dem Gericht, Am der grand jury)* die Anklageschrift *(hinsichtlich e-s indictable offence)* vorlegen
Br In vielen, auch schweren Straftaten *(Am* bei →misdemeanors) genügt eine →information

indictor Ankläger

indigence Mittellosigkeit, Bedürftigkeit, Armut

indigent bedürftiger Armer

indigent mittellos, bedürftig, arm

indigenous eingeboren; einheimisch; ~ **inhabitants** Ureinwohner, Urbewohner, **production of energy from** ~ **sources** Energieerzeugung aus einheimischen Quellen

indignation Entrüstung; ~ **meeting** Protestversammlung

indignit|y unwürdige Behandlung; **~ies** *Am (EhescheidungsR)* unwürdige Kränkungen

indirect indirekt, mittelbar *(opp. direct);* ~ **arbitrage** indirekte Devisenarbitrage, Mehrfacharbitrage; ~ **cost** Gemeinkosten; ~ **damage** mittelbarer Schaden; ~ **elections** indirekte (od. mittelbare) Wahlen; ~ **evidence** mittelbarer Beweis; ~ **exchange** →~arbitrage; ~ **expenses** Gemeinkosten; ~ **labo(u)r** Fertigungsgemeinkosten; ~ **liability** Eventualverbindlichkeit; ~ **loss** Folgeschaden; ~ **material** Materialgemeinkosten; ~ **possession** mittelbarer Besitz; ~ **selling** indirekter Vertrieb; ~ **taxes** indirekte Steuern *(z.B. customs duties);* **to be in** ~ **possession** mittelbarer Besitzer sein

indisputable unbestreitbar, unstreitig

individual Einzelperson, Individuum; Privatperson; natürliche Person; einzeln, Einzel-; ~ **applicant** *(PatR)* Einzelanmelder; ~ **application** *(Art. 25 der Menschenrechtskonvention)* Individualbeschwerde; ~ **assets** Privatvermögen *(e-s Gesellschafters);* ~ **banker** *Am* Privatbankier; ~ **bargaining** Einzel(tarif)verhandlung *(zwischen Arbeitgeber und Arbeitnehmer; opp. collective bargaining);* ~ **consumer** Einzelverbraucher; ~ **control book** persönliches Kontrollbuch; ~ **credit** Personalkredit; ~ **earnings**

pro-Kopf-Einkommen; ~ **guarantee** *(VölkerR)* Einzelgarantie; ~ **income** Individualeinkommen; ~ **income tax** *Am* Einkommensteuer der natürlichen Personen; ~ **insurance** Individualversicherung, Einzelversicherung *(opp. group or collective insurance)*; ~ **insurer** Einzelversicherer; ~ **inventor** *(PatR)* Einzelerfinder; ~ **licen|ce (~se)** Einzelgenehmigung; ~ **proprietor** *Am* Einzelunternehmer; ~ **proprietorship** *Am* Einzelfirma; ~ **resident of the United States** *Am* natürliche Person mit Wohnsitz in den Vereinigten Staaten

individually einzeln, persönlich, in eigenem Namen; ~ **and collectively** einzeln und insgesamt; **to be liable** ~ einzeln (od. persönlich) haften

individualism Individualismus *(opp. collectivism); (im engeren Sinne:)* →laissez faire

individualizing method Methode der Einzelfallentscheidung

indivisible performance unteilbare Leistung

Indo-China Indochina *(zerfiel 1954 in Vietnam, Laos und Kambodscha)*

Indonesia Indonesien; **Republic of** ~ Republik Indonesien

Indonesian Indonesier(in); indonesisch

indoctrination Indoktrination

indoor Innen-, Haus-; ~ **patient** stationär behandelter Patient; ~ **staff** Hauspersonal; im Innendienst tätiges Personal *(opp. outdoor staff)*

indorsable →endorsable

indorse *v* →endorse *v*

indorsed →endorsed

indorsee →endorsee

indorsement →endorsement

indorser →endorser

indubitable →**proof** (or **evidence**)

induce *v* induzieren, bewirken; veranlassen, überreden; abwerben

inducement Veranlassung, Überredung; Abwerbung; Herbeiführung; *com* Anreiz; ~ **of breach of contract** Verleitung zum Vertragsbruch *(Verhinderung der Vertragserfüllung)*; **matters of** ~ einleitende Angaben im Plädoyer

induct *v (förmlich od. feierlich)* in ein Amt einführen; *Br eccl* einsetzen; *Am mil* einberufen

inductee *Am mil* Einberufener, Rekrut

induction Induktion; Einführung (in ein Amt); *Br* Einsetzung in ein Kirchenamt; *Am mil* Einberufung; ~ **into office** Amtseinführung; ~ **order** *Am* Gestellungsbefehl, Einberufungsbefehl

indulge *v* Nachsicht üben; *Am* (Zahlungs-)Frist gewähren

indulgence Nachsicht, Milde; *Am* Stundung

indulgent judge milder Richter

industrial 1. Industrieller; Gewerbetreibender; ~**s** Industriepapiere, Industriewerte; **heavy** ~**s** Aktien der Schwerindustrie

industrial 2. industriell, Industrie-; gewerblich, Gewerbe-; ~ **accident** Betriebsunfall, Arbeitsunfall; ~ **accounting** industrielles Rechnungswesen; Betriebsbuchhaltung; ~ **acquisitions** Erwerb von Industriebeteiligungen

industrial action Arbeitskampf, Arbeitskampfmaßnahmen *(Streik, Boykott, Aussperrung)*; **secondary** ~ mittelbare Arbeitskampfmaßnahmen; **unfair** ~ *Br* unfaires Verhalten im Arbeitskampf *(z. B. wilder Streik)*

industrial, ~ **administration** Betriebswirtschaft; ~ **advertising** Industriewerbung; Werbung für Industriegüter; ~ **adviser** *Am* Betriebsberater; ~ **affairs** gewerbliche Wirtschaft; ~ **agreement** Tarifabkommen

Industrial and Commercial Finance Corporation Ltd. (I. C. F. C.) *Br (staatl.)* Finanzinstitut für Industrie und Wirtschaft

Gewährung langfristiger Darlehen von £5,000 bis £200,000 an kleinere und mittlere Unternehmen *(cf. Finance Corporation for Industry)*

Industrial and Provident Societies *Br* (Erwerbs- und Wirtschafts-)Genossenschaften *(die Geschäfte aller Art, auch Bankgeschäfte betreiben)*

Fast alle britischen Genossenschaften (→co-operative societies) werden gemäß den Industrial and Provident Societies Acts, 1965 to 1975, registriert

industrial applicability *(PatR)* gewerbliche Verwertbarkeit

industrial application, ~ **of an invention** *(PatR)* gewerbliche Anwendung e-r Erfindung; **susceptible of** ~ gewerblich anwendbar

industrial, ~ **area** Industriegebiet, Industriegelände; ~ **art** Werbegraphik; ~ **artist** Werbegraphiker; ~ **association** Industrieverband, Wirtschaftsverband; ~ **bank** *Br* Teilzahlungsbank, Kundenkreditbank *(providing credit by hire-purchase)*; *Am* kleinere Geschäftsbank; ~ **bonds** Industriepapiere, Industrieobligationen; ~ **business** (I. B.) *Br* Kleinlebensversicherungsgeschäft; ~ **cent|re (~er)** Industriezentrum; ~ **code** Gewerbeordnung; ~ **collateral** *Am* Sicherheit durch Hinterlegung von Industrieaktien; ~ **concern** Industrieunternehmen, Wirtschaftsunternehmen; ~ **cooperation** Industriekooperation; industrielle Zusammenarbeit; ~ **cooperative** gewerbliche Genossenschaft; ~ **country** Industrieland; ~ **credit** Industriekredit; ~ **death benefit (for widows and other dependants)** *Br* Hinterbliebenenrente (für Witwen und andere Angehörige); ~ **design** gewerbliches Muster; industrielle Formgebung

(→*design 2.); (Kanada)* Geschmacksmuster; ~ **designer** Formgestalter *(industrieller Erzeugnisse);* ~ **development** industrielle Entwicklung *(cf. United Nationsl I~ Development Organization);* ~ **development bond** *Am* →revenue bond; ~ **development certificate** (I. D. C.) *Br (vom Board of Trade erteilte)* Erlaubnis zum Bau von Fabriken *(die dem Staat die Möglichkeit der Beeinflussung der Standortwahl überläßt);* **(~) disablement benefit** (for persons disabled through injury at work) *Br* (Sozialversicherungs-)Rente (als Folge von Arbeitsunfall); ~ **disease** Berufskrankheit; ~ **dispute** Arbeitsstreitigkeit; ~ **economics** Industrieökonomik; ~ **engineering** *Am* Betriebstechnik; Arbeitsgestaltung; Planung und Organisation der Fertigung; ~ **enterprise** Industrieunternehmen; Gewerbebetrieb; ~ **equities** Industrieaktien; ~ **espionage** Industriespionage, Werkspionage; ~ **estate** *Br* Industrie(an)siedlung; ~ **exhibition** Industrieausstellung; Gewerbeausstellung; ~ **expansion** Industrieausweitung; industrielle Expansion; ~ **firm** Industriefirma, Industrieunternehmen; ~ **goods** Industrieprodukte, Produktionsgüter, Investitionsgüter; ~ **hygiene** Betriebshygiene; Gesundheitsschutz bei der Arbeit

industrial injury Betriebsunfall, Arbeitsunfall; **to sustain an** ~ e-n Betriebsunfall erleiden

industrial insurance →~ life insurance; *Am (auch)* Berufsschadenversicherung; Unfallversicherung der Arbeiter (→*Workmen's Compensation Insurance);* ~ **injury benefits** *Br* Leistungen der Arbeitsunfallversicherung; ~ **company** *Br* Kleinlebensversicherungsgesellschaft

industrial, ~ **law** *Br* Arbeitsrecht; ~ **life** Arbeitsleben; ~ **life insurance** Kleinlebensversicherung; ~ **loan** Industriedarlehen, Industriekredit; ~ **magnate** Industriemagnat; Großindustrieller

industrial management Betriebsführung; **science of** ~ Betriebswirtschaftslehre

industrial, ~ **market** Absatzmarkt für industrielle Erzeugnisse; Investitionsgütermarkt; ~ **mobility** Freizügigkeit der Arbeitskräfte; ~ **nation** Industriestaat; ~ **organization** Betriebsorganisation; ~ **output** Industrieproduktion; ~ **park** *Am* Industriepark; ~ **partnership** Gewinnbeteiligung der Arbeitnehmer; ~ **peace** Arbeitsfrieden; ~ **plant** Industrieanlage, Werk(sanlage); ~ **policy** Industriepolitik; ~ **products** gewerbliche Erzeugnisse; industriell gefertigte Erzeugnisse; ~ **production** Industrieproduktion

industrial property gewerbliches Eigentum *(Patente, Gebrauchsmuster, Geschmackmuster und Warenzeichen);* ~ **rights** gewerbliche Eigentumsrechte, gewerbliche Schutzrechte; **legislation on** ~ **rights** Rechtsvorschriften über den gewerblichen Rechtsschutz; ~ **of a proprietary nature** rechtlich geschütztes gewerbliches Eigentum; **central** ~ **office (of a Contracting State)** Zentralbehörde für den gewerblichen Rechtsschutz *(e-s Vertragsstaates);* **protection of** ~ gewerblicher Rechtsschutz; **Paris Convention for the Protection of I~ P~** →Convention 1.

industrial, ~ **relations** betriebliche und kollektive Arbeitsbeziehungen; Arbeitgeber-/Arbeitnehmerbeziehungen; Beziehung zwischen Betriebsführung und Gewerkschaften *(den Sozialpartnern);* ~ **revenue bonds** *Am (meist steuerfreie)* Kommunalanleihen zur Finanzierung industrieller Neuansiedlungen;~ **revolution** industrielle Revolution (od. Umwälzung); ~ **safety** Betriebssicherheit; ~ **school** *Br* Gewerbeschule; *Am (einzelstaatl.)* Jugendgefängnis; ~ **securities** Industriepapiere; ~ **shares** (*Am* **stocks**) Industrieaktien, Industriewerte, Industriepapiere; ~ **society** Industriegesellschaft; ~ **sociology** Industriesoziologie, Betriebssoziologie; ~ **spying** *Am* Werkspionage; ~ **state** Industriestaat; ~ **targeting** staatliche Strukturpolitik zugunsten vermeintlicher Zukunftsbranchen; ~ **town** Industriestadt, Fabrikstadt; **I~ Training Act** *Br* Berufsausbildungsgesetz

Industrial Tribunal *Br*[14] Arbeitsgericht; **to present a complaint to the** ~ e-e Klage beim Arbeitsgericht einreichen

Sondergericht für arbeitsrechtliche Streitigkeiten (z. B. →unfair dismissals, →redundancy payments, →employment protection, health and safety at work). Rechtsmittelinstanz ist das →Employment Appeal Tribunal

industrial, ~ **trust** *Am* Finanzierungsgesellschaft für Industriebedarf; ~ **undertaking** Industrieunternehmen; ~ **union** Industriegewerkschaft *(opp. craft union);* ~ **use** industrielle Verwendung; ~ **wages** Industriearbeiterlöhne; ~ **waste** Industriemüll; ~ **widow's pension** *Br* Hinterbliebenenrente *(für Witwe e-s als Folge e-s Betriebsunfalls od. e-r Berufskrankheit Verstorbenen);* **to contract an** ~ **disease** sich e-e Berufskrankheit zuziehen; ~ **growth slackened** das Wachstum der Industrieproduktion verlangsamte sich

industrialist Industrieller; Unternehmer; **big** ~ Großindustrieller

industrialization Industrialisierung

industrialize *v* industrialisieren; zu e-m Industriestaat machen

industrialized countries Industriestaaten *(opp. developing countries);* **newly** ~ (NICs) Schwellenländer

industries Industriezweige, Wirtschaftszweige; **big** ~ Großindustrie; **British I~ Fair** (B. I. F.) Britische Industriemesse; **the cotton** ~ die Baumwollindustrie; **craft** ~ Handwerk

industry Industrie; gewerbliche Wirtschaft; Gewerbe; Industriezweig, Wirtschaftszweig; ~ **affecting commerce** *Am* industriebezogener Handel;~ **and commerce** Industrie und Handel; ~ **captive** „industrieeigenes“ Versicherungsunternehmen *(das die sie beherrschenden Industrieunternehmen versichert);*~ **division** Wirtschaftsbereich, Wirtschaftssektor; ~ **management** führende Wirtschaftskreise; ~ **sales** Industrieabsatz; ~ **standard** Industrienorm; ~**-wide** in der ganzen Industrie geltend

industry, aircraft ~ Luftfahrtindustrie; **armament** ~ Rüstungsindustrie; **automobile** (or *Am* **automotive**) ~ Kraftfahrzeugindustrie; **basic** ~ Grund(stoff)industrie; **building** ~ Bauindustrie; **capital goods** ~ Investitionsgüterindustrie; **consumer goods** ~ Verbrauchsgüterindustrie; **domestic** ~ einheimische Industrie; **electricity** ~ Elektroindustrie; **finishing** ~ Veredelungsindustrie; **food (processing)** ~ Nahrungsmittelindustrie; **heavy** ~ Schwerindustrie; **home** ~ einheimische Industrie; **infant** ~ junge Industrie *(im ersten Entwicklungsstadium);* **iron** ~ Eisenindustrie; **large-scale** ~ Großindustrie; **light** ~ Leichtindustrie; **metal** ~ Metallindustrie; **mining** ~ Montanindustrie; Bergbau; **motor car** ~ *Br* Kraftfahrzeugindustrie; **oil** ~ Erdölindustrie; **plastics** ~ Kunststoffindustrie; **private** ~ Privatindustrie; **processing** ~ Verarbeitungsindustrie; Veredelungsindustrie; **sector of** ~ Industriezweig; **both** (or **the two**) **sides of** ~ (trade unions and employers' associations) Sozialpartner; **small-scale** ~ Kleinindustrie; **steel** ~ (Eisen- und) Stahlindustrie; **textile** ~ Textilindustrie; **tourist** ~ Fremdenverkehrsgewerbe; **war** ~ Kriegsindustrie; **worker (employed) in** ~ Industriearbeiter

inebriate Betrunkener; Trinker; betrunken; **asylum for** ~**s** *Am* Trinkerheilanstalt

ineffective unwirksam, wirkungslos; **to become** ~ unwirksam werden, außer Kraft treten

inefficiency Ineffizienz; Unwirksamkeit; Unfähigkeit, mangelnde Leistungsfähigkeit; Unwirtschaftlichkeit *(opp. efficiency)*

inelastic, ~ **demand** unelastische Nachfrage; ~ **supply** unelastisches Angebot

ineligibility Nichtwählbarkeit; Unfähigkeit, für ein Amt gewählt zu werden; Ungeeignetheit *(opp. eligibility);* ~ **for naturalization**[15] Einbürgerungsunfähigkeit

ineligible nicht wählbar; nicht qualifiziert, ungeeignet; nicht in Frage kommend *(opp. eligible);* ~ **paper** *Am* nicht diskontfähiger Wechsel (bill or note); **to be** ~ **for election** für die Wahl nicht in Betracht kommen

inequality Ungleichheit; **elimination of social** ~**ies** Beseitigung der sozialen Ungleichheiten; **to suffer** ~ **of status** nicht gleichberechtigt sein

inequitable unbillig, ungerecht; ~ **division of the profits** ungerechte Teilung des Gewinns

inequity Unbilligkeit, Ungerechtigkeit *(bes. hinsichtl. Löhne, Arbeitsbedingungen etc)*

inescapable unvermeidbar; ~ **conclusion** zwingender Schluß

inevitable unvermeidbar; ~ **accident** Unfall, der durch normale Vorsichtsmaßnahmen nicht zu verhindern war *(Einrede bei Schadensersatzforderungen) (defendant will escape liability if accident occurred despite exercise of reasonable care)*

inexcusable delay(s) unentschuldbare Verzögerung(en)

INF (intermediate-range nuclear forces) nukleare Mittelstreckensysteme; ~ **modernization** Nachrüstung *(im Sinne des NATO-Doppelbeschlusses);* ~ **Treaty** INF-Vertrag *(über atomare Mittelstreckenwaffen)*

infamous ehrlos, schändlich, infam, niederträchtig; ~ **crime** niederträchtiges Verbrechen (*Am*[16] *das mit Gefängnis oder Zuchthaus zu bestrafen ist; Am (einzelstaatl.) das den Verlust der bürgerlichen Ehrenrechte nach sich zieht);* ~ **crime against nature** *Am* widernatürliche Unzucht, Sodomie

infamy Ehrlosigkeit; *Am* Verlust der bürgerlichen Ehrenrechte *(als Folge der Verurteilung wegen →infamous crime)*

infancy Minderjährigkeit (*→minority);* Kindheit; *fig* Anfang(sstadium); ~ **proceedings** *Am* Verfahren in Mündelsachen

infant Minderjährige(r) *(Br unter 18 Jahren);* (Klein-)Kind; Säugling; minderjährig; ~ **industry** junge Industrie *(im ersten Entwicklungsstadium);* ~ **mortality** Säuglingssterblichkeit; ~ **school** *Br* Grundschule *(für 5–7jährige Kinder);* ~ **welfare** Säuglingsfürsorge; **incapacity of an** ~ **to make a contract** fehlende (Vertrags-)Geschäftsfähigkeit e-s Minderjährigen

infanticide Kindestötung; Kindesmörder(in)

infect *v* anstecken; ~**ed district** verseuchtes Gebiet

infectious *Am* der Beschlagnahme ausgesetzt *(z. B. Schmuggelware)*

infectious disease, spreading of ~**s** Ausbreitung ansteckender Krankheiten

infectious goods Schmuggelware, die „infectious“ genannt wird, weil sie die ganze Ladung des Eigentümers infiziert

infer *v* folgern, schließen (from aus); darauf hindeuten, erkennen lassen; ~**(r)ed** gefolgert

inference Folgerung, Schlußfolgerung; Schluß, Rückschluß; **to draw** (or **make**) ~**s from ... to** Schlüsse ziehen von ... auf

inferential auf bloße Schlußfolgerung gegründet; ~ **evidence** Indizienbeweis

inferior 1. Untergebener *(opp. superior)*
inferior 2. *(im Rang)* niedriger, untergeordnet; *(an Qualität)* geringwertig, minderwertig; *(im Wert)* geringer, weniger wert (to als); ~ **court** unteres Gericht; ~ **material** schlechtes Material; ~ **officer** untergeordneter Beamter; **(of)** ~ **quality** (von) schlechte(r) Qualität; minderwertig; ~ **quality goods** minderwertige Waren; **goods** ~ **to sample** Waren, die gegenüber dem Muster abfallen; **goods of** ~ **workmanship** schlecht hergestellte (od. bearbeitete) Waren

infidelity, conjugal (or **marital**) ~ eheliche Untreue; „Seitensprünge" (→*irretrievable breakdown of marriage)*

infiltrate *v* infiltieren, eindringen; einschleusen; *pol* unterwandern

infiltration Infiltration, *(getarntes)* Eindringen *(feindlicher Agenten)*; Einschleusen; *pol* Unterwanderung; ~ **of spies** Einschleusung von Spionen; **Communist** ~ kommunistische Infiltration

infirm schwach; gebrechlich; ~ **of purpose** unentschlossen

infirmit|y (körperliches) Gebrechen; *Am* Mangel in e-r Urkunde; ~**ies of old age** Altersgebrechen

inflammable brennbar, feuergefährlich; ~ **cargo** feuergefährliche Ladung

inflammatory aufreizend, Hetz-; ~ **campaign** Hetzfeldzug; ~ **speech** aufreizende Rede, Hetzrede

inflate *v (Geldumlauf)* übermäßig steigern; *(Geld)* über die Deckung hinaus in Umlauf setzen
inflated prices überhöhte Preise

inflation Inflation; ~ **accounting** inflationsbereinigte Rechnungslegung; ~ **adjustment** Inflationsbereinigung; ~ **hedge** Absicherung gegenüber der Inflation; ~**-induced** inflatorisch bedingt; ~ **of credit** Kreditinflation; ~ **of currency** (Papier-)Geldinflation; **acceleration of** ~ Beschleunigung der Inflation; **continuous** ~ andauernde Inflation; **cost-push** ~ Kosten(druck)inflation; **countering** ~ Inflationsbekämpfung; **credit** ~ Kreditinflation; **creeping** ~ schleichende Inflation; **danger of** ~ Inflationsgefahr; **demand-pull** ~ Nachfragesoginflation; **galloping** ~ galoppierende Inflation; **monetary** ~ Geldinflation; **open** ~ offene Inflation, Preisinflation; **pent-up** ~ zurückgestaute Inflation; **period of** ~ Inflationszeit; **policy of** ~ Inflationspolitik; **profit arising from** ~ Inflationsgewinn; **rate of** ~ Inflationsrate; **run-away** ~ galoppierende Inflation; **struggle against** ~ Inflationsbekämpfung; **suppressed** ~ gestoppte Inflation; **to curb** ~ die Inflation eindämmen; **to feed** ~ die Inflation anheizen; **to fight** ~ die Inflation bekämpfen; **to reduce the rate of** ~ die Inflationsrate senken; **to support** ~ die Inflation fördern

inflationary inflationär, inflatorisch; inflationistisch; ~ **boom** inflatorischer Boom, inflationistische Konjunktur; ~ **compensation** Inflationsausgleich; ~ **danger** Inflationsgefahr; ~ **gain** Inflationsgewinn; ~ **gap** inflatorische Lücke; ~ **hedge** Absicherung gegenüber der Inflation; ~ **policy** Inflationspolitik; ~ **rate** Inflationsrate; ~ **situation** inflationäre Lage; ~ **spiral** Inflationsspirale; ~ **strains** inflationäre Spannungen; ~ **tendencies** (or **trends**) inflationäre Tendenzen; ~ **tendencies are easing off** die Inflationstendenzen beruhigen sich

inflationism Inflationismus; Inflationspolitik

inflationist Inflationist, Befürworter e-r Inflationspolitik

inflict *v* zufügen, auferlegen (on sb. jdm); **to** ~ **damage** (or **injury**) Schaden zufügen; **to** ~ **a penalty** (or **punishment**) e-e Strafe verhängen (on gegen); *(jdn)* bestrafen

infliction Zufügung, Auferlegung, Verhängung *(e-r Strafe)*; ~ **of damage** Schadenszufügung

inflow Zufluß, Zustrom *(opp. outflow)*; ~ **of capital** Kapitalzufluß *(aus dem Ausland)*; ~ **of foreign exchange** Devisenzufluß; ~ **of liquidity from abroad** Liquiditätszuflüsse aus dem Ausland; ~ **of refugees** Zustrom von Flüchtlingen

influence Einfluß ([up]on auf); Beeinflussung ([up]on sb. jds); Einwirkung; **under the** ~ **of alcohol** unter Alkoholeinfluß (od. Alkoholeinwirkung) (stehend); **sphere of** ~ Einflußsphäre, Einflußgebiet; *pol* Interessensphäre; **undue** ~ ungebührliche Beeinflussung *(z.B. bei Errichtung e-s Testaments od. bei Wahlen)*; **undue** ~ **of the voters** unzulässige (od. übermäßige) Beeinflussung der Wähler; **zone of** ~ *pol* Einflußzone, Einflußbereich; **to exercise** (or **exert**) **an** ~ **on sb.** auf jdn e-n Einfluß ausüben, jdn beeinflussen; **to use one's** ~ **on sb.'s behalf** seinen Einfluß zu jds Gunsten geltend machen, sich für jdn einsetzen

influence *v (jdn)* beeinflussen; *(auf jdn)* Einfluß ausüben

influential einflußreich; ~ **circles** maßgebende Kreise; ~ **politician** maßgeblicher Politiker

influx Zufluß, Zustrom *(opp. efflux)*; ~ **of capital** Kapitalzufluß; ~ **of funds** Mittelzuflüsse *(bei Kreditinstituten);* ~ **of gold** Goldzufluß; ~ **of visitors** Besucherstrom

inform *v* 1., **to ~ sb. of** (or **about**) **sth.** jdn benachrichtigen, in Kenntnis setzen, informieren über; jdm Nachricht geben von; jdm Auskunft geben über; **to ~ the police** die Polizei benachrichtigen (od. verständigen); **to ~ the public** die Öffentlichkeit unterrichten; **I beg to ~ you** ich erlaube mir, Ihnen mitzuteilen

informed, in well ~ circles in gut unterrichteten Kreisen; **to keep currently ~** fortlaufend unterrichten (od. auf dem laufenden halten)

inform *v* 2., **to ~ against sb.** jdn *(bei der Polizei)* anzeigen; gegen jdn (Straf-)Anzeige erstatten; **to ~ against** (or **on**) **sb.** jdn denunzieren; **duty to ~ (the police)** Anzeigepflicht

informal formlos, formfrei; informell, zwanglos; ~ **contract** formloser Vertrag; ~ **conversation** informelles Gespräch *(z.B. zwischen Staatsmännern);* ~ **investigation** *(MMF)* informelle Ermittlung

informality Formlosigkeit; Formmangel

informant Gewährsmann; Auskunftsgeber; Erstatter e-r Anzeige

informatics Informatik

information 1. Benachrichtigung, Nachricht, Mitteilung, Unterrichtung, Information(en), Auskunft (about, on über); *tel* „Auskunft"; **upon ~ and belief** *Am* nach bestem Wissen und Gewissen *(opp. from personal knowledge);* ~ **bureau** (or *Am* **center**) Auskunftstelle; ~ **desk** Auskunftschalter; ~ **disdosure** Weitergabe von Informationen; ~ **drive** Aufklärungsaktion; ~ **flow** Informationsfluß; ~ **lead** Informationsvorsprung;~ **office** Auskunftsbüro, Auskunftstelle; ~ **on foreign law** →European Convention on I~ on Foreign Law; ~ **research management** Informationsresourcenmanagement; ~ **returns** *Am* Fragebogen *(zur Überprüfung von Steuerangaben);* ~ **seeker** Informationssucher; ~ **services** *(EG)* Informationsdienste; ~ **stand** Auskunftsstand *(auf e-r Messe);* ~ **on stored data** Auskunft über gespeicherte Daten; ~ **technology** (IT) Informationstechnologie; ~ **window** Auskunftsschalter

information, Central Office of I~ *Br* Informationsbehörde; **credit ~** Kreditauskunft; **disclosure of confidential ~** Preisgabe (od. Weitergabe) vertraulicher Mitteilungen; **duty** (or **liability**) **to furnish ~** Auskunftspflicht; **exchange of ~** Informationsaustausch; **false ~** *(absichtlich)* falsche Auskunft (od. Nachricht); **for your ~** zu Ihrer Kenntnis (od. Orientierung); **furnishing of ~** Erteilung von Auskünften, Auskunfterteilung; **obtaining ~ under false pretences** →pretence; **person entitled to receive ~** Auskunftsberechtigter; **precise ~** genaue Auskunft; **presentation of ~** *(PatR)* Wiedergabe von Informationen; **request for ~** Auskunftersuchen; **right to (obtain) ~** Auskunftsrecht; Recht auf Auskunfterteilung; **source of ~** Informationsquelle; **supply of false ~** Erteilung unrichtiger Auskünfte; **wrong ~** *(auch unabsichtlich)* falsche Auskunft (od. Information)

information, to ask for ~ sich erkundigen (about nach); **to apply to sb. for ~ regarding** . . . sich an jdn wegen Auskunft über . . . wenden; **to collect ~** Erkundigungen einziehen (on, about über); Informationen beschaffen; **to furnish ~** Auskunft geben (od. erteilen) (about über); **to gather ~** Erkundigungen einziehen; Auskunft einholen (about über); **to get ~** Auskunft bekommen (od. erhalten); **to give ~** Auskunft geben (od. erteilen); **to lay ~ (against sb.)** Strafanzeige erstatten (gegen jdn); **to obtain** (or **receive**) ~ Auskunft erhalten; **to put out ~ to the public** die Öffentlichkeit informieren; **to render ~** Auskunft geben (od. erteilen); **to request ~** um Auskunft bitten; **to secure ~** sich Informationen beschaffen; **to submit** (or **supply**) ~ Auskunft geben (od. erteilen); Informationen liefern

information 2. (Straf-)Anzeige (with the police bei der Polizei); *(formelle)* Anklage *(Am ohne grand jury);* **dismissal of ~** Einstellung e-s Strafverfahrens; **upon an ~ being laid before a Justice of the Peace** *Br* bei Strafanzeige bei e-m Justice of the Peace; **to file an ~** *Am* Anklage erheben; **to give ~** (against sb.) *Am* Anzeige erstatten (gegen jdn); **to lay** (or **lodge**) **an ~** Anzeige erstatten

information 3. *(EDV)* Daten; ~ **retrieval** Datenabruf; ~ **sciences** Informatik; ~ **storage** Datenspeicherung; ~ **stored** gespeicherte Daten; **abuse or misuse of ~** mißbräuchliche oder zweckfremde Nutzung der Daten; **access to ~** Zugang zu Daten; **inaccurate ~** unrichtige Daten; **obsolete ~** veraltete Daten; **personal ~** persönliche (od. personenbezogene) Daten; **processing of ~** Verarbeitung von Daten; **to erase obsolete ~** veraltete Daten löschen; **to store personal ~ in electronic data banks** persönliche Daten in elektronischen Datenbanken speichern; ~ **is used for statistical purposes** Daten werden zu statistischen Zwecken verwendet

informative informativ, belehrend, aufschlußreich; ~ **advertising** informative Werbung; ~ **label(l)ing** erklärende Etikettierung *(Gewicht, Herstellungsland, Lagerfähigkeit etc der Ware)*

informer jd, der e-e Anzeige erstattet; Denunziant; Spitzel; ~ **system** Spitzelwesen; **common ~** *Am* jd, der e-n Teil des Betrages e-r Geldstrafe für sich beanspruchen darf, zu der der auf Grund seiner Anzeige Angeklagte verurteilt ist; **police ~** Polizeispitzel

infra ("below"), **see** ~ siehe (weiter) unten *(im Buch etc)*

infraction Verletzung, Verstoß; ~ **of the law** Gesetzesverletzung; ~ **of a treaty** *(VölkerR)* Vertragsverletzung

infrastructure Infrastruktur *(notwendige Grundlagen e-r hochentwickelten Wirtschaft) (z.B. Verkehrswege);* ~ **investments** Infrastrukturinvestitionen; ~ **projects** Infrastrukturvorhaben; **basis** ~ Basisinfrastruktur; **transport** ~ Verkehrsinfrastruktur

infringe *v (Recht)* verletzen; verstoßen gegen; übertreten; **to** ~ **upon sb. 's right** in jds Rechte eingreifen; **to** ~ **a copyright (patent, trademark)** ein Urheberrecht (Patent, Warenzeichen) verletzen; **to** ~ **a law** ein Gesetz verletzen; **to** ~ **an oath** e-n Eid verletzen; **to** ~ **the provisions** gegen die Bestimmungen verstoßen

infringing, ~ **party** *(PatR)* Verletzer; ~ **work** Werk, das gegen ein bestehendes Urheberrecht verstößt

infringement (Rechts-)Verletzung; Verstoß (of gegen); Zuwiderhandlung; Übertretung; ~ **upon sb.'s rights** Eingriff in jds Rechte; ~ **action** Verletzungsklage; Klage wegen Patentverletzung (od. Urheberrechtsverletzung); ~ **of the Constitution** Verstoß gegen die Verfassung; ~ **of a contract** Vertragsverletzung, Vertragsbruch; ~ **of a copyright** →copyright 1.; ~ **of a law** Verletzung e-s Gesetzes

infringement of a patent Patentverletzung; **action for** ~ Patentverletzungsklage; **contributory** ~ mittelbare (od. indirekte) Patentverletzung *(mitwirkendes Verschulden des Patentinhabers);* **intentional** ~ vorsätzliche Patentverletzung

Gegen rechtswidrige Verletzung ist das Patent durch Unterlassungsansprüche (injunction to restrain future infringement) und Schadensersatzansprüche (recovery of the damage caused or profit made by the past infringement) geschützt

infringement, ~ **proceedings** *(EG)* Verstoßverfahren; **(patent)** ~ **proceedings** Patentverletzungsverfahren; ~ **procedure** *(EG)* Verstoßverfahren *(z.B. gemäß Art. 169 des EWG-Vertrages);* ~ **of a right** Rechtsverletzung; ~ **of a trademark** Verletzung e-s Warenzeichens

infringement, action for ~ →~ action; **to bring an action** (or **to sue**) **for** ~ **of a patent** wegen Patentverletzung klagen; **to constitute an** ~ **of Art 85 of the EEC Treaty** e-n Verstoß gegen Art. 85 EWG-Vertrag darstellen

infringer Rechtsverletzer; Verletzer e-s Patents; **assumed** ~ vermeintlicher Patentverletzer

ingather *v Scot* einziehen, beitreiben *(executors, trustees etc)*

ingoing *(ein Amt)* antretend; ~ **mail** einlaufende Post; ~ **tenant** neuer Mieter (od. Pächter)

ingot Barren *(bes. aus Gold od. Silber);* ~ **(bar) gold** (or **gold in** ~**s**) Barrengold; ~ **of gold** Goldbarren

ingredient Ingredienz, Bestandteil; **chief** ~**s** Hauptbestandteile

ingress, egress, and regress *Am* ("entering on", "going out" and "coming back") freies Zugangsrecht *(des Pächters nach Ablauf der Pacht)*

ingrossing →engrossing

inherent anhaftend, angeboren, eigen, innewohnend; ~ **in the concept (of)** mit dem Begriff von ... zusammenhängend; ~ **defect** →~ vice; ~ **powers** *Am* aus der Rechtsnatur sich ergebende Befugnisse; ~ **right** naturgegebenes Recht; ~ **vice** innerer Fehler; inhärenter (od. innewohnender) Mangel

inherit *v* erben; **to** ~ **sth. from sb.** etw. von jdm erben; jdn beerben; **to** ~ **sb.'s property** jds Vermögen erben; jdn beerben

inherited portion *Am* Erbanteil

inheritable vererblich, vererbbar; erbfähig, erbberechtigt

inheritance Erbschaft; (das) Erbe *(Br bes. an Grundbesitz)*

Br Seit dem Administration of Estates Act, 1926, ist inheritance als juristischer Begriff veraltet *(cf. heir, estate)*

inheritance of copyright Vererbung des Urheberrechts

Inheritance (Provision for Family and Dependants) Act, 1975 *Br* Erbschaftsgesetz

Dieses Gesetz gewährt Angehörigen und anderen Personen, die der Erblasser zu Lebzeiten unterstützt hat, nach seinem Tode das Recht auf angemessenen Unterhalt aus dem Nachlaß, wenn sie nicht Erben sind oder der ihnen zugefallene Erbteil ihre Versorgung nicht ausreichend sicherstellt.

Das Gesetz widerruft weitgehend die frühere Family Provision-Gesetzgebung und erweitert den Kreis der Anspruchsberechtigten. Es schließt jetzt auch nicht verwandte Personen ein, die der Erblasser zu Lebzeiten unterstützt hat, z. B. Freundinnen (mistresses). Die notwendigen Anordnungen trifft das Gericht nach freiem Ermessen

inheritance tax Erbschaftsteuer; **crediting of the foreign against the German** ~ *(DBA)* Anrechnung der ausländischen auf die deutsche Erbschaftsteuer; **subject to** ~ erbschaftsteuerpflichtig

inheritance, agreement of ~ Erbvertrag; **claim to an** ~ Erb(schafts)anspruch; **disclaimer of an** ~ Erbschaftsausschlagung, Ausschlagung e-r Erbschaft; **entrance upon an** ~ Antritt e-r Erbschaft; **expectance of an** ~ *Am* Erbanwartschaft; **renunciation of an** ~ Erbverzicht; **right of** ~ *Am* Erbrecht, Erbberechtigung;

share in an ~ *Am* Erbteil; **succession by** ~ *Am* Erbfolge; **to acquire by** ~ durch Erbschaft erwerben; **to come into an** ~ e-e Erbschaft machen, erben; **to disclaim an** ~ e-e Erbschaft ausschlagen; **to enter upon an** ~ e-e Erbschaft antreten; **to receive sth. by** ~ etw. durch Erbschaft erhalten; **to renounce an** ~ *Am* auf e-e Erbschaft verzichten; **to take sth. by** ~ etw. erben

inhibit *v* verbieten, untersagen

inhibition Verbot, Untersagung; *Br*[17] Vormerkung *(welche zeitweilig jede weitere Verfügung über den Grundbesitz hindert)*

inhibitory verbietend

in-house betriebsintern; ~ **counsel** Betriebssyndikus

inhuman treatment unmenschliche Behandlung

initial 1. Initiale, großer Anfangsbuchstabe *(e-s Namens);* Paraphe, *(abgekürzter)* Namenszug; **to put one's ~s (to)** *(mit Anfangsbuchstaben e-s Namens)* unterzeichnen; paraphieren

initial 2. Anfangs-, anfänglich; ~ **allowance** *Br* Sonderabschreibung *(für Neuanschaffungen);* ~ **campaign** Einführungsaktion; ~ **capital** Anfangskapital, Einlagekapital, Gründungskapital; ~ **capital expenditure** Einrichtungskosten; Anlagekosten; ~ **cost** Anschaffungskosten; **(~) deposit** Anzahlung *(beim Abzahlungsvertrag); (Börse)* Einschuß; **credit institute acting as** ~ **depositary** erstverwahrendes Kreditinstitut; ~ **expenses** Anfangskosten; Einrichtungskosten; *(VersR)* Abschlußkosten; ~ **export quota** Exportausgangsquote; ~ **guarantee deposit** *(VersR)* Anfangskaution; ~ **offering price** *(Börse)* Ausgabekurs; ~ **placing of securities** Erstplazierung von Wertpapieren; ~ **policy debate** Orientierungsdebatte; ~ **premium** Anfangsprämie; ~ **price** Anfangspreis, Einführungspreis; *(bei Wertpapieren)* Anfangskurs; ~ **public offering** Erstemission *(von Wertpapieren);* ~ **salary** Anfangsgehalt; **in the** ~ **stage** im Anfangsstadium; ~ **subscription** Erstzeichnung; ~ **value** Anschaffungswert

initially zunächst; anfänglich; **it may be** ~ **assumed** es kann davon ausgegangen werden

initial *v (mit Anfangsbuchstaben e-s Namens)* unterzeichnen, abzeichnen; paraphieren; **to** ~ **a treaty** *(VölkerR)* e-n Vertrag paraphieren

initiate *v* beginnen, in Gang setzen, in Angriff nehmen; einführen; eröffnen; *(in das Parlament)* einbringen; **to** ~ **sb. into** jdn *(feierlich)* aufnehmen in *(e-e Gesellschaft etc);* jdn einführen in *(e-e Tätigkeit);* **to** ~ **legal action** (or **proceedings**) e-n Prozeß anstrengen (od. anhängig machen); klagen; **to** ~ **legislation** Gesetze einbringen; **to** ~ **negotiations** Verhandlungen einleiten

initiation Beginn; Inangriffnahme; *(feierliche)* Aufnahme; Einführung; ~ **fee** Aufnahmegebühr; *Am* Eintrittsgebühr *(in Gewerkschaft);* ~ **into an office** Einführung in ein Amt; ~ **of proceedings before the Court of Justice** *(EG)* Einleitung des Verfahrens vor dem Gerichtshof (der Europäischen Gemeinschaften)

initiative Initiative, Entschlußkraft, Unternehmungsgeist; einleitend, einführend; **(legislative)** ~ Gesetzesinitiative; Volksbegehren; **on one's own** ~ aus eigener Initiative; **to be lacking** ~ keine Initiative haben; **to take the** ~ die Initiative ergreifen

initiatory steps einleitende Schritte

injection, ~ **of capital** Kapitalspritze; ~ **of money** Geldeinschuß, Geldspritze

injunction einstweilige Verfügung, gerichtliche Anordnung *(Rechtsbehelf zur Erzwingung der Unterlassung oder Vornahme von Handlungen; cf. equitable remedy →remedy 1.);* **action** (or **application) for an** ~ Antrag auf Erlaß e-r einstweiligen Verfügung; **compulsive** ~ *Br* s. mandatory →~; **infringement of an** ~ Verstoß gegen e-e einstweilige Verfügung; **interim** ~ **s. interlocutory** →~; **interlocutory** ~ einstweilige Verfügung

Die interlocutory injunction entspricht der einstweiligen Verfügung des deutschen Rechts. Sie wird zur vorläufigen Regelung vor der eigentlichen Verhandlung erlassen und hat nur bis zur späteren Entscheidung Gültigkeit

injunction, mandatory ~ einstweilige Verfügung zur Vornahme e-r Handlung *(der Beseitigung des durch den Beklagten geschaffenen rechtswidrigen Zustandes);* **permanent** ~ *Am* s. perpetual →~; **action for permanent** ~ *Am* Unterlassungsklage; **perpetual** ~ endgültige gerichtl. Verfügung *(zur Unterlassung) (durch die die Rechtsbeziehungen der Parteien endgültig geregelt werden);* **preliminary** ~ *Am* einstweilige Verfügung *(zur Unterlassung e-r Handlung);* **preventive** ~ *Br* einstweilige Verfügung *(zur Unterlassung);* gerichtliches Verbot; **prohibitory** ~ einstweilige Verfügung *(zur Unterlassung);* **provisional** ~ einstweilige Verfügung; **restrictive** ~ *Br* s. preventive →~; **temporary** ~ *Am* einstweilige Verfügung; **motion for temporary** ~ *Am* Antrag auf Erlaß e-r einstweiligen Verfügung; **to apply for an** ~ Antrag auf Erlaß e-r einstweiligen Verfügung stellen; auf Unterlassung klagen; **to discharge** (or **lift**) **an** ~ e-e einstweilige Verfügung aufheben; **to grant an** ~ e-e einstweilige Verfügung erlassen; **to sue for an** ~ s. to apply for an →~

injunctive relief Unterlassungsanspruch *(z. B. des durch Patent- od. Urheberrechtsverletzung Geschädigten)*

injure *v* verletzen; schädigen, beeinträchtigen,

benachteiligen; **to ~ sb.'s interests** jds Interessen verletzen (od. schädigen); **to ~ a person** jdn verletzen, jdm e-e (Körper-)Verletzung zufügen; **to ~ sb.'s rights** jds Rechte verletzen (od. beeinträchtigen)

injured, ~ (party or **person)** der/die Verletzte, Geschädigte, Benachteiligte; **the Member State ~** der geschädigte Mitgliedstaat; **fatally ~** tödlich verletzt

injurious schädlich, nachteilig (to für); beleidigend; **~ falsehood** *Br* Anschwärzung (→*falsehood)*; **~ to health** gesundheitsschädlich; **to be ~ to sb.'s reputation** jds Ruf schaden (→ *reputation)*

injury Verletzung; Körperverletzung; Schaden, Schädigung, Beeinträchtigung, Benachteiligung; **~ caused by an accident** Unfallverletzung; Körperverletzung durch Unfall; **~ contracted in the course of employment** Arbeitsunfall; Betriebsunfall; **~ test** Prüfung der Schädigung;**~ to person** Personenschaden; **~ to property** Sachschaden; Sachbeschädigung; **~ to the public interest** Verletzung des öffentlichen Interesses; **~ to sb.'s reputation** Beeinträchtigung jds Rufes; **accidental ~** Unfallverletzung; Körperverletzung durch Unfall; **bodily ~** Körperverletzung; **civil ~** zivilrechtliches Delikt, zivilrechtlich verfolgbare Schädigung (→*tort)*; **disabling ~** zu Arbeitsunfähigkeit führende Verletzung; →**industrial ~**; **material ~** erheblicher Schaden; **minor ~** leichte Verletzung; **pecuniary ~** finanzieller Schaden; **personal ~** Körperverletzung; Personenschaden; **serious ~** schwere Verletzung; ernsthafter Schaden; **serious bodily ~** schwere Körperverletzung; **to inflict ~ upon sb.** jdm Schaden zufügen; **to suffer** (or **sustain**) **~** Schaden erleiden; beeinträchtigt (od. benachteiligt) werden.

inland Inland, Binnenland; Inlands-; Binnen-; inländisch; einheimisch; **~ account** im Inland geführtes Konto; **~ air traffic** Inlandsluftverkehr; **~ bill (of exchange)** Inlandswechsel *(opp. foreign bill)*; **~ commodities** einheimische Waren; **~ duties** Inlandsabgaben; **~ marine insurance** Binnentransportversicherung; Flußtransportversicherung; **~ mail** Inlandspost; **~ marine insurance** Binnentransportversicherung; **~ market** Binnenmarkt; **~ navigation** Binnenschiffahrt; Flußschiffahrt; **~ port** Binnenhafen; **~ postal** (or **postage**) **rates** Inlandspostgebühren; **~ produce** (or **products**) inländische Erzeugnisse, Landeserzeugnisse; **~ producer** inländischer Erzeuger

Inland Revenue (I. R.) *Br* Finanzverwaltung; *(etwa)* Finanzamt; **~ Commissioners** →Commissioners of ~; **~ officer** *Br* Finanzbeamter; **Board of ~** *Br* Oberste Steuerbehörde

inland revenue *Br* Steuereinnahmen; Staatseinkünfte *(aus inländischen direkten Steuern und Abgaben)*; **~ receipts** *Br* Steuereinnahmen; **~ stamp** *Br* Stempelsteuermarke; **~ warrants** *Br* Zahlungsanweisungen inländischer Steuerbehörden

inland, ~ state Binnenstaat; **~ town** Binnenstadt; **~ trade** Binnenhandel, inländischer Handel; **~ traffic** Binnenverkehr, Inlandsverkehr; **~ transport** Binnentransport; Binnenverkehr; **~ transportation insurance** Binnentransportversicherung; **~ waters** Binnengewässer, Eigengewässer; **~ water transport** (IWT) (Beförderung im) Binnenschiffahrtsverkehr

inland waterway Binnenwasserstraße; **~ B/L** Flußladeschein, Binnenkonnossement; **~ carrier** Binnenschiffahrtsunternehmen; **~ insurance** Binnentransportversicherung; **~ transport** Binnenschiffsverkehr

in-laws *colloq.* angeheiratete Verwandte *(Schwager, Schwiegereltern etc)*

Inmarsat →International Maritime Satellite Organization

inmate Bewohner, Insasse *(e-r Anstalt)*; **camp ~** Lagerinsasse; **prison ~** Häftling, Sträfling

inn Gaststätte, Gasthof; **to keep an ~** e-e Gaststätte führen

inner, I~ House *Scot* die beiden Appellate Divisions des →Court of Session; **I~ Temple** *Br* (Gebäude e-r) Barristerinnung (→*Inns of Court)*; **~ reserve** stille Reserve *(opp. visible reserve)*

innkeeper Gastwirt; **~'s liability** (for the loss or damage of guests' property)[18] Haftung des Gastwirts (für Verlust oder Beschädigung eingebrachter Sachen); **~'s →lien** *(pfandähnliches)* Zurückbehaltungsrecht des Gastwirts *(an den eingebrachten Sachen des Gastes) (entspricht dem deutschen Pfandrecht des Gastwirts, § 704 BGB)*

innocence Unschuld; **→presumption of ~**; **to establish one's ~** seine Unschuld nachweisen; **to protest one's ~** seine Unschuld beteuern

innocent unschuldig, nicht schuldig, schuldlos; **~ conveyance** *Am* erlaubte Übertragung e-s Landpächters, die nicht zur Verwirkung der Pacht führt; **~ →misrepresentation**; **~ party** nichtschuldiger Teil *(bei Ehescheidung)*; **~ third party** gutgläubiger Dritter; **~ passage** *(VölkerR)* friedliche Durchfahrt *(für Handelsschiffe)*; **~ purchaser** gutgläubiger Erwerber

innocently ohne Verschulden

innominate term *Br* unbestimmte Vertragsklausel *(die nicht ohne weiteres als →condition oder →warranty eingeordnet werden kann)*

innovate *v*, **readiness to ~** Innovationsbereitschaft

innovation Innovation, *(technisch-wissenschaftli-*

che) Neuerung *(Verbesserung der Produkte und des Produktionsverfahrens); Scot* Novation, Schuldumschaffung; **industrial** ~ industrielle Innovation; **to introduce ~s** Neuerungen einführen

innovative foreign policy neue Wege einschlagende Außenpolitik

Inns of Court *Br* (Gebäude der vier alten) Innungen der Barristers in London
Berufsorganisation der Barristers (bestehend aus Inner Temple, Middle Temple, Lincoln's Inn und Gray's Inn), die für Ausbildung und Zulassung der Barristers zuständig ist *(für Solicitors cf. Law Society)*. Aus den Innungen geht der höhere Richterstand hervor

innuendo *("by hinting or insinuating")* versteckte (od. geheime) Andeutung (od. Anspielung) *(bes. in Beleidigungsklagen)*
Mit Hilfe des innuendo kann ein Kläger den Nachweis erbringen, daß eine Äußerung, die prima facie nicht als defamatory erscheint, geeignet ist, seinen Ruf zu beeinträchtigen

inofficial nicht amtlich; inoffiziell; ~ **market** *(Börse)* Freiverkehr(smarkt)

inofficious pflichtwidrig; ~ **testament** (or **will**) *Am* gegen die natürlichen Pflichten *(bes. hinsichtl. der nächsten Angehörigen)* des Testators verstoßendes Testament

inoperative unwirksam, ungültig; ~ **account** *Br* umsatzloses Konto; **to become** ~ ungültig werden, außer Kraft treten

inops consilii ("without advice") ohne (Rechts-)Beratung

inordinatus Erblasser, der kein Testament hinterlassen hat

inpayment Einzahlung *(auf ein Konto)*

in-plant *Am* innerbetrieblich

input (Energie-)Einsatz; *pol* Einsatz; Produktionsfaktor; *(EDV)* Eingabe *(von Daten)*; **~-output analysis** Input- Output-Analyse *(Methode der produktionsmäßigen Beziehungen zwischen den einzelnen Wirtschaftszweigen)*; ~ **tax** *Br (Umsatzsteuer) (von e-r steuerpflichtigen Person für den Erhalt von Waren oder sonstigen Leistungen für gewerbliche Zwecke)* zu zahlende Umsatzsteuer od. Einfuhrumsatzsteuer; Vorsteuer *(opp. output tax)*; **deduction of ~ tax** *Br* Vorsteuerabzug; **work** ~ Arbeitseinsatz

inquest *(gerichtl.)* Untersuchung *(bes. durch Geschworene)*; Beweisaufnahme; amtliche Untersuchung verdächtiger Todesfälle; **coroner's** ~ amtliche Leichenschau *(bei ungeklärten Todesursachen)*

inquire *v* fragen, nachfragen, sich erkundigen (of sb., after or about sth. bei jdm nach etw.); **to ~ about the price** den Preis erfragen, sich nach dem Preis erkundigen; **to ~ about a train** sich nach e-m Zug erkundigen; **to ~ into sth.** etw. untersuchen, prüfen; **to ~ into a matter** e-e Angelegenheit untersuchen; **to ~ in writing** schriftlich anfragen; ~ **within** Näheres hier *(im Hause)*

inquir|y Untersuchung; Erkundigung, Anfrage, Nachfrage (for nach); Ermittlung, Nachforschung; *(MMF)* Erhebung, Befragung, Umfrage; ~ **agency** Auskunftei; ~ **agent** *Br* Privatdetektiv; ~ **charge** *Post)* Nachforschungsgebühr; ~ **office** Auskunft(sbüro) *(z.B. auf der Bahn)*; Auskunftstelle; Auskunftei; ~ **about price** Preisanfrage; **board** (or **commission**) **of** ~ Untersuchungsausschuß, Untersuchungskommission; **Board of Special I~** *Am* Ausschuß, der über die Zulassung von Einwanderern entscheidet; **Court of I~** →court; **credit** ~ Bitte um Kreditauskunft; **judicial** ~ gerichtliche Untersuchung; **official** ~ amtliche Untersuchung (od. Erhebung); **(up)on** ~ auf Anfrage; nach Erkundigung (of bei); **parliamentary** ~ parlamentarische Untersuchung; **preliminary** ~ Voruntersuchung *(z.B. e-s Seeunfalls)*; **statistical** ~ statistische Erhebung; **to hold** (or **conduct**) **an** ~ e-e Untersuchung durchführen; **to constitute** (or **set up**) **a board** (or **commission**) **of** ~ e-n Untersuchungsausschuß bilden (einsetzen); **an ~ (into ...) is ordered to be taken** e-e Untersuchung ist angeordnet; **to institute an** ~ e-e Untersuchung einleiten; **to make ~ies** Erkundigungen einziehen, Ermittlungen (od. Nachforschungen) anstellen (about über; of sb. bei jdm); **to make an** ~ anfragen

inquisition eindringliche Befragung; schriftl. Untersuchungsergebnis

inquisitor Untersuchungsbeamter, Untersuchungsrichter *(bes. coroner, sheriff)*

inquisitorial system Untersuchungsgrundsatz (od. -maxime) *(opp. adversary system)*

inroad *(feindlicher)* Überfall, Einfall (into a country in ein Land); Übergriff (on auf); *fig* Eingriff (on in); **~s of Japanese imports** Eindringen japanischer Importe; **to make ~s upon sb.'s savings** Einbrüche in jds. Ersparnisse machen

insane geisteskrank; ~ **person** *Am* Geisteskranke(r); **incurably** ~ unheilbar geisteskrank; **to certify a p.** ~ *Br* jdn *(amtlich)* für geisteskrank erklären

insanity Geisteskrankheit; Geistesgestörtheit, krankhafte Störung der Geistestätigkeit; **congenital** ~ angeborene Geisteskrankheit; **habitual** ~ chronische Geisteskrankheit; **plea of** ~ Einrede der Unzurechnungsfähigkeit;

temporary ~ vorübergehende Störung der Geistestätigkeit; **the accused is not guilty by reason of** ~ der Angeklagte ist wegen Geisteskrankheit nicht schuldig *(cf. diminished responsibility)*

inscribe *v (Namen)* einschreiben, eintragen; *(Buch)* widmen

inscribed stock *Br* Schuldbuchforderungen *(über die keine Zertifikate ausgestellt werden, sondern deren Inhaber in e-m Register der Emissionsstelle, z.B. der Bank of England, eingetragen sind)*

inscription Einschreibung, Eintragung; Aufschrift, Inschrift; **~s** *Br* registrierte Akten

insecure unsicher; *(Kredit)* ungedeckt

inseminated, artificially ~ künstlich befruchtet

insemination, artificial ~ künstliche Befruchtung

insensitive to the movement of interest rates zinsunempfindlich

insert (Zeitungs-, Zeitschriften-)Beilage; Einlage *(in e-m Brief etc)*

insert *v* einfügen, einsetzen; einschalten; aufnehmen; *(Münze)* einwerfen; **to ~ an advertisement in a newspaper** ein Inserat in e-e Zeitung setzen; inserieren; **to ~ conditions in a contract** in e-n Vertrag Bedingungen aufnehmen

insertion Einfügung; Einschaltung; Aufnahme; Einwurf *(Münze)*; **~ of an advertisement in a newspaper** Aufnahme e-r Anzeige in e-e Zeitung; **~ of date** Einfügung des Datums; **to file for ~ to the files** zu den Akten einreichen

inshore fishing (or **fishery**) Küstenfischerei

inside inner, Innen-; *Br sl.* im Gefängnis; **~ board (of directors)** *Am* board, dessen Mitglieder sich aus den leitenden Angestellten (officers) zusammensetzen *(Führungsgremium[19], das etwa die Funktionen des deutschen Vorstandes e-r AG versieht; →board 1)*; **~ director** *Am* vollzeitlich angestellte Spitzenführungskraft e-r corporation *(dem deutschen Vorstandsmitglied ähnlich) (opp. outside director)*; **~ information** interne Geschäftsinformationen; **~ job** *Br sl.* Diebstahl mit Hilfe von im Hause beschäftigten Personen; **~ staff** Personal vom Innendienst

insider Eingeweihter; Mitglied des →inside board; **~s** eingeweihte Kreise; Personen, die Kenntnisse über ein Unternehmen durch Zugehörigkeit zu diesem haben *(opp. outsiders)*; **~ dealing** (or **~ trading**) Insider-Geschäft, illegaler Aktienhandel auf Grund innerbetrieblicher Informationen

insignia Insignien; Ehrenzeichen; **~ of rank** *mil* Rangabzeichen; **national ~** Hoheitsabzeichen

insignificance Bedeutungslosigkeit; **to discontinue criminal proceedings on the ground of ~** das Strafverfahren wegen Geringfügigkeit einstellen

insinuation Anspielung, *(versteckte)* Andeutung; *Am* Eintragung in ein Register; **~ of a will** *Am* Vorlage e-s Testaments *(zum →probate)*

insist *v*, **to ~ on** bestehen auf, dringen auf; betonen, geltend machen; **to ~ on one's innocence** seine Unschuld beteuern

insolvency Insolvenz, Überschuldung, Zahlungsunfähigkeit; Zahlungseinstellung; Unfähigkeit des Kaufmanns, die laufenden Geschäftsverbindlichkeiten zu begleichen

Insolvency Act(s) 1985 and 1986 *Br* Insolvenzgesetz(e)

Die Gesetze finden sowohl auf den Konkurs natürlicher Personen (der auch heute noch bankruptcy heißt) als auch auf den Konkurs von Kapitalgesellschaften (liquidation, winding up) Anwendung. Der Insolvency Act 1985 führte das Amt des →administrator 2. ein

insolvency of an estate Überschuldung e-s Nachlasses

insolvency practitioner *Br* Insolvenzexperte

Nach dem Insovlency Act 1986 zugelassener Abwickler von Insolvenzen bei Privatpersonen und Kapitalgesellschaften *(→administrator, →liquidator, →receiver 2.)*

insolvency proceedings Insolvenzverfahren (Konkurs- bzw. Vergleichsverfahren); **~ rule** *Am* Vorschrift, die die Ausschüttung von Dividenden bei e-r →insolvency verbietet; **~ statutes** (or **laws**) *Am (einzelstaatl.)* Insolvenzgesetze; **involuntary ~** *Am* von den Gläubigern eingeleitetes Insolvenzverfahren (Konkurs- bzw. Vergleichsverfahren); **national ~** Staatsbankrott; **open ~** *Am* völlige Unpfändbarkeit (Vermögenslosigkeit) als Voraussetzung der Inanspruchnahme e-s Dritten *(z.B. e-s Bürgen)*; **total ~** Überschuldung; **voluntary ~** *Am* von dem Gemeinschuldner beantragtes Insolvenzverfahren (Konkurs- bzw. Vergleichsverfahren) *(um – anders als es nach deutschem Recht möglich wäre – vollständiges Erlöschen seiner Verbindlichkeit [Schulden] zu erreichen)*; **to declare one's ~** sich für zahlungsunfähig erklären; seine Zahlungen einstellen

insolvent insolvent, zahlungsunfähig, überschuldet, in Zahlungsschwierigkeiten befindlich; zahlungsunfähiger Schuldner; **~ estate** überschuldeter Nachlaß; **administration of an ~ estate** Nachlaßkonkurs; **to become ~** zahlungsunfähig werden; **to declare oneself ~** sich für zahlungsunfähig erklären; seine Zahlungen einstellen

inspect *v* besichtigen, einsehen, Einsicht nehmen in; Augenschein einnehmen; kontrollieren, prüfen, revidieren; **to ~ a car** Inspektion bei e-m Auto durchführen; **to ~ the scene of crime** den Tatort besichtigen; **to ~ documents** Urkunden einsehen; **to ~ the goods** die Waren prüfen (od. kontrollieren); **to ~ records** Akten einsehen

inspecting Besichtigung, Einsicht (of in); Einnahme des Augenscheins; (Über-)Prüfung, Kontrolle, Revision; ~ **by the judge** richterliche Augenscheinseinnahme; ~ **laws** *Am* Gesetze, die die amtliche Kontrolle von Waren *(bes. Lebensmittel)* regeln; ~ **of the books and accounts** Einsichtnahme in die (Geschäfts-)Bücher; ~ **of deeds** Akteneinsicht; ~ **of documents** Einsichtnahme in Urkunden *(des Prozeßgegners)*; ~ **of the files** (or **records**) Akteneinsicht *(bei Gericht od. Behörden)*; ~ **of goods** Kontrolle der Ware(n); ~ **order** Anordnung e-r (Zoll-)Revision; ~ **of property** Augenscheinseinnahme von Grundbesitz

inspection, certificate of ~ Beschaffenheitszeugnis *(bes. bei verderblichen Waren vor der Verladung)*; **committee of** ~ Gläubigerausschuß *(im Konkurs)*; **consignment for** ~ Ansichtssendung; **customs** ~ Zollrevision; **for** ~ zur Ansicht; zur Einsichtnahme; **free** ~ **invited** kein Kaufzwang; **local** ~ Augenscheinseinnahme; Ortsbesichtigung; Ortstermin; **passport** ~ Paßkontrolle; **Protocol on I~** Inspektionsprotokoll *(zum →INF-Vertrag)*; **purchase subject to** ~ Kauf zur Ansicht; **register available for** ~ Register, das eingesehen werden kann; **result of the** ~ Ergebnis des Augenscheins (etc); **right of** ~ Recht der Einsichtnahme; **tour of** ~ Besichtigungsreise; **trade** ~ Gewerbeaufsicht; **to be subject to** ~ der Prüfung (od. Kontrolle) unterliegen; **to carry out an** ~ e-e Kontrolle (od. Augenscheinseinnahme) durchführen; **to be open to** ~ zur Einsicht ausliegen; **the Register shall be open to public** ~ jedermann kann in das (Patent- etc) Register Einsicht nehmen; **to lay files open to** ~ Akteneinsicht gewähren; **to lay open to public** ~ öffentlich auslegen; **to grant** ~ Einsicht gewähren; **to obtain** ~ **of a file** Akteneinsicht erhalten

inspector Inspektor, Aufsichtsbeamter; Revisor; *(staatl.)* Prüfer; *mil* Inspekteur; *Br* Polizeikommissar; **I~ General** *mil* Generalinspektor; ~ **of factories** *Br* Gewerbeaufsichtsbeamter

Inspector of Taxes *Br* Finanzamtsleiter *(der auf Grund der Steuererklärung die Steuer veranlagt, die von dem Collector of Taxes eingezogen wird)*; **Chief** ~ *Br* höchster Steuerbeamter; **office of the** ~ *Br* Finanzamt

inspector, ~ **of weights and measures** Eichmeister; ~ **of works** Bauaufseher

inspectorate Aufsichtsbehörde; Amt (Stellung, Arbeit od. Bezirk) e-s Inspektors

inspectorship Inspektoramt; Aufsicht (of über)

instability mangelnde Stabilität, Unbeständigkeit; ~ **of prices** Schwanken der Preise

install *v* (*Am auch* **instal** *v*) *(in ein Amt)* einsetzen, einführen; installieren, *(technische Anlagen)* einrichten, einbauen; *(Maschine etc)* aufstellen, errichten; **to ~ oneself** sich einrichten

installation Einsetzung, Einführung *(in ein Amt)*; *(technische)* Anlage; Installation, Einrichtung, Einbau; Aufstellung, Montage; ~ **of a stand at a fair** Aufstellung e-s Messestandes; **heating** ~ Heizungsanlage; **military ~s** militärische Anlagen

instalment *(Am auch* **installment**) Rate; Tranche; Ratenzahlung, Teilzahlung, Abschlagszahlung; Teillieferung; Fortsetzung *(e-r Veröffentlichung)*; ~ **bonds** *Am* in Teilbeträgen rückzahlbare Obligationen; ~ **business** Teilzahlungs-, Ratenzahlungsgeschäft; ~ **buying** *Am* Teilzahlungs-, Ratenkauf; ~ **contract** Ratenkaufvertrag; Vertrag über aufeinanderfolgende Lieferungen; ~ **credit** Teilzahlungskredit; ~ **debt** in Raten rückzahlbare Schuld; ~ **due on December 1** am 1. Dezember fällige Rate; ~ **equipment loan** *Am (durch Eigentumsvorbehalt gesicherter)* Teilzahlungskredit zum Erwerb von Ausrüstungen; ~ **financing** Teilzahlungsfinanzierung; ~ **in arrears** Ratenrückstände; ~ **land contract** *Am* Grundstücksratenkauf unter Eigentumsvorbehalt; ~ **loan** Teilzahlungskredit; ~ **mortgage** *Am* Tilgungs-, Amortisationshypothek; ~ **of composition** *Br* Vergleichsquote; ~ **of the rent** Mietrate; ~ **order** *Br* Anordnung der Ratenzahlung durch das Gericht; ~ **payment** Teilzahlung, Abschlagszahlung, Ratenzahlung; ~ **plan** →~ system; ~ **purchase** *Am* →~ buying; ~ **purchase agreement** *Am* Ratenkaufvertrag; ~ **sale** *(meist drittfinanziertes)* Teilzahlungsgeschäft *(Br gewöhnlich in Form des →hire-purchase, Am des →conditional sale)*; **~s spread over 5 years** auf 5 Jahre verteilte Raten

instal(l)ment system Teilzahlungssystem, Ratenzahlungssystem; **business on the** ~ Ratenzahlungsgeschäft; **to buy (sell) on the** ~ auf Ratenzahlung kaufen (verkaufen)

instal(l)ment, ~ **transaction** *(einzelnes)* Ratenzahlungsgeschäft; ~ **trust** *Am* Trust, der Effekten gegen Anzahlung und Teilzahlung liefert

instal(l)ment, in (*Br auch* **by**) **~s** in Raten, ratenweise; **delivery in** (*Br auch* **by**) **~s** Teillieferung; **payment in** (*Br auch* **by**) **~s** Teilzahlung, Ratenzahlung; **repayable in** (*Br auch* **by**) **~s** in Raten rückzahlbar

instal(l)ment, annual ~ Jahresrate; **failure to keep up the** ~**s** Nichteinhaltung der Ratenzahlungen; **final** ~ letzte Rate, Schlußrate; **first** ~ erste Rate; **monthly** ~ Monatsrate; **in several** ~**s** in mehreren Fortsetzungen *(Zeitungsartikel etc)*; **tax** ~ *Am* Einkommensteuervorauszahlung; **yearly** ~ Jahresrate; **to be in arrears with an** ~ mit e-r Rate im Rückstand sein; **to make default in payment of an** ~ mit e-r Rate in Verzug geraten; **to meet the** ~**s** die Ratenzahlungen einhalten; **to pay an** ~ e-e Rate zahlen, Ratenzahlung leisten; **to pay in** (*Br auch* **by**) ~**s** in Raten (be)zahlen

instance Instanz; Beispiel; Fall; Drängen, Betreiben; **at the** ~ **of** auf Veranlassung (od. Betreiben) von; **court of first** ~ Gericht erster Instanz *(opp. appellate court)*; **for** ~ (e. g.) zum Beispiel (z. B.); **in a given** ~ in e-m Einzelfall; **higher** ~ höhere Instanz; **lower** ~ untere Instanz, Vorinstanz; **second** ~ zweite Instanz, Berufungsinstanz; Beschwerdeinstanz; **to quote an** ~ ein Beispiel anführen

instant gegenwärtig, laufend; sofortig; dringend; **the** ~ **case** der vorliegende Fall; ~ **dismissal** sofortige (od. fristlose) Entlassung; **on the 20th inst.** am 20. dieses Monats *(cf. proximo, ultimo)*

instigate *v (StrafR)*; anstiften; aufhetzen, antreiben (to zu); **to** ~ **a mutiny** zu e-r Meuterei anstiften

instigation *(StrafR)* Anstiftung; Aufhetzung, Antreibung (to zu); **at the** ~ **of** auf Betreiben von

instigator *(StrafR)* Anstifter; Aufhetzer

institute Institut; Anstalt; Einrichtung; **I~ Cargo Clauses**[20] (ICC) *(SeeversR)* offizielle Klauseln für Abschluß von Versicherungsverträgen über Ladungen; **I~ of Chartered Accountants** *Br* Institut der Wirtschaftsprüfer; **Chartered I~ of Patent Agents** *Br* Patentanwaltskammer; **I~ of Practitioners in Advertising** *Br* Organisation der Werbeagenturen; **research** ~ Forschungsinstitut

institutes Institutionen, (Rechts-)Kommentar; **I~ of Justinian** (or **Justinian I~**) (Just. Inst., Inst. J.) Institutionen Justinians *(1. Buch des Corpus Juris Civilis, "The I~ or Elements of Roman Law")*; **(Sir Edward) Coke's I~** (or **Coke's I~ of the Laws of England**) (Co. Inst.) Coke's Institutionen *(Zusammenfassung rechtslexikographischen Charakters des →Common Law von 1628)*

institute *v* einleiten; einführen, festsetzen; einsetzen; errichten, gründen; *eccl (in e-e Pfründe)* einsetzen; **to** ~ **an action at law** Klage erheben; **to** ~ **bankruptcy proceedings** das Konkursverfahren eröffnen; **to** ~ **into a benefice** *eccl* in e-e Pfründe einsetzen; **to** ~ **criminal proceedings** ein Strafverfahren einleiten; **to** ~ **a custom** e-n Brauch einführen; **to** ~ **sb. as heir** *Am* jdn als Erben einsetzen; **to** ~ **an inquiry** e-e Untersuchung einleiten; **to** ~ **inquiries** Nachforschungen anstellen; **to** ~ **investigations** Untersuchungen (od. Ermittlungen) einleiten; **to** ~ **(legal) proceedings against sb.** gerichtlich vorgehen gegen jdn; gerichtliches Verfahren einleiten gegen jdn; **to** ~ **proceedings by way of appeal** ein Rechtsmittel einlegen; **to** ~ **a suit** *Am* Klage einreichen, gerichtlich vorgehen

institution Institut, Anstalt; Institution; *(feststehende)* Einrichtung; Einleitung, Einführung, Festsetzung; Errichtung, Gründung; *eccl* Einsetzung; ~ **for alcoholics** *Am* Trinkerheilanstalt; ~**s of the European Communities** Organe der Europäischen Gemeinschaften; ~ **of an heir** *Am* Einsetzung e-s Erben; ~ **of an inquiry** Einleitung e-r Untersuchung; ~ **of legal proceedings** Einleitung e-s Gerichtsverfahrens; ~ **of restrictions** Einführung von Beschränkungen; ~ **under public law** Anstalt des öffentlichen Rechts; **charitable** ~ karitative Einrichtung; **educational** ~ Lehranstalt, Bildungsanstalt; **financial** ~ Geldinstitut, Kreditinstitut; **government** ~**s** Regierungseinrichtungen; **head of an** ~ Anstaltsleiter; →**mental** ~; **penal** ~ Straf(vollzugs-)anstalt; **permanent** ~ ständige Einrichtung; **public** ~ öffentliche Anstalt; **relations between the** ~**s** interinstitutionelle Beziehungen; **to put sb. in an** ~ jdn in e-r Anstalt unterbringen

institutional Instituts-, Anstalts-; institutionell; ~ **advertising** institutionelle Werbung, Goodwill-Werbung *(Firmenwerbung, die nicht unmittelbar auf den Verkauf von Produkten, sondern auf die Aufklärung über die technische und wirtschaftl. Bedeutung e-s Unternehmens abzielt)*; ~ **buying** Käufe durch institutionelle Anleger; ~ **care** Anstaltspflege; ~ **investors** institutionelle Anleger; Kapitalsammelstellen *(Banken, Versicherungen, Investmentgesellschaften etc)*

institutionalization Institutionalisierung; Anstaltsunterbringung

institutionalize *v* institutionalisieren; in e-r Anstalt unterbringen

instruct *v* unterrichten, belehren; informieren; Weisung geben, anweisen, einweisen, unterweisen; **the client** ~**s the solicitor** *Br* der Mandant versieht den solicitor mit Informationen; **the judge** ~**s the jury** der Richter erteilt den Geschworenen Rechtsbelehrung; **the principal** ~**s the agent** der Geschäftsherr erteilt dem Vertreter Weisungen; **the solicitor** ~**s a counsel** (or **a barrister**) *Br* der solicitor zieht e-n barrister hinzu

instructed, as ~ weisungsgemäß

instruction Anweisung, Weisung, Belehrung; Unterricht; **~s** Instruktionen, Vorschriften; Anweisungen, Informationen *(des Anwalts durch seinen Mandanten)*; **~s to counsel** Anweisungen an e-n Anwalt *(Br des solicitor an den barrister)*; **~s to the jury** *Am* Rechtsbelehrung der Geschworenen *(durch den Richter)*; ~ **sheet** *(MMF)* Intervieweranweisung; **~s for use** Gebrauchsanweisung; laut Vorschrift; **contrary to ~s** entgegen der Weisung; **course of** ~ Lehrgang; **official ~s** Dienstvorschriften; **shipping ~s** Versandvorschriften; **written ~s** schriftliche Weisungen; **to ask for ~s** Weisungen einholen; Anweisungen erbitten; **to carry out ~s** Weisungen ausführen; **to give ~s** Anweisungen erteilen; Instruktionen geben; **to give ~s to a jury** den Geschworenen Rechtsbelehrung erteilen; **to receive ~s** Weisungen entgegennehmen (od. erhalten); **to request ~s** s. to ask for →~s; **please, let us have your ~s** wir bitten Sie, uns Ihre Weisungen zu erteilen

instructional Unterrichts-, Lehr-, Erziehungs-; ~ **film** Kulturfilm; Lehrfilm; ~ **trip** Informationsreise

instructor Lehrer; Ausbilder; **chief** ~ Ausbildungsleiter; **training of ~s** Ausbildung von Ausbildern

instrument *(rechtl. bedeutsame)* Urkunde *(z.B. deed of conveyance)*; *Am* Handelspapier (→*negotiable* ~); *(VölkerR)* Übereinkunft *(als zusammenfassender Begriff für Vertrag, Übereinkommen etc)*; Gerät, Instrument; Werkzeug *(Person)*; ~ **of abdication** Abdankungsurkunde; ~ **of acceptance** *(VölkerR)* Annahmeurkunde; ~ **of accession** (or **adherence**) *(VölkerR)* Beitrittsurkunde; ~ **of assignment** Zessionsurkunde; ~ **of debt** Schuldurkunde; ~ **flight rules** (IFR) Instrumentenflugregeln *(opp. visual flight rules)*; ~ **(payable) to bearer** Inhaberpapier; ~ **(payable) to order** Orderpapier *(durch Indossament übertragbar)*; ~ **of payment** Zahlungsmittel; ~ **of ratification** *(VölkerR)* Ratifikationsurkunde; ~ **of sasine** *Scot* Auflassungsurkunde; ~ **of title** Besitzurkunde, Eigentumsurkunde; Urkunde, die e-n →title 2. verkörpert; ~ **of transfer** Übertragungsurkunde; Urkunde betr. die Übertragung von Eigentum an Grundbesitz; **authentic** ~ echte Urkunde; **commercial** ~ Handelspapier; **international ~s** internationale Vertragswerke; **measuring** ~ Meßgerät; **negotiable** ~ *(begebbares od. übertragbares)* Wertpapier (→*negotiable*); **statutory** ~ *Br* Rechts-, Ausführungs-, Durchführungsverordnung (→*statutory*); **trust** ~ Treuhandurkunde (→*trust 1.*); **written** ~ Urkunde; **to execute an** ~ e-e Urkunde *(rechtsgültig)* ausfertigen *(by signing, sealing and delivering it)*; **to sign the** ~ **of abdication** die Abdankungsurkunde unterzeichnen

instrumental behilflich, förderlich, mitwirkend; ~ **goods** *(all goods that aid labour in production)* Produktionsgüter; **to be** ~ **in** beitragen zu, mitwirken bei

instrumentality Mitwirkung Vermittlung; *Am* Institution, Einrichtung, Stelle; **through the** ~ **of** durch Vermittlung von

insubordinate ungehorsam, widersetzlich, aufsässig *(bes. gegen Vorgesetzte)*; ~ **conduct** Widersetzlichkeit

insubordination Insubordination; Ungehorsam *(gegen Vorgesetzte)*; *mil* Gehorsamsverweigerung

insufficiency Unzulänglichkeit; Mangel der Form *(e-r eidesstattl. Erklärung)*; ~ **of evidence** Unzulänglichkeit des Beweismaterials

insufficient unzulänglich, ungenügend; den Formvorschriften nicht genügend; *(Zivilprozeß)* nicht schlüssig; ~ **funds** (I/F) ungenügende Deckung *(Vermerk auf Wechseln od. Schecks)*; ~ **packing** ungenügende Verpackung; **the evidence is** ~ das Beweismaterial ist unzulänglich (od. reicht nicht aus)

insufficiently prepaid ungenügend frankiert

insularity Insellage; insulare Lage; ~ **of outlook** Engstirnigkeit

insulated hold Kühlraum

insult Beleidigung; Beschimpfung

insult *v* beleidigen; beschimpfen; **~ing behavio(u)r** beleidigendes Verhalten

insurability Versicherbarkeit; **examination as to** ~ Versicherbarkeitsuntersuchung

insurable versicherbar, versicherungsfähig; ~ **interest** versicherbares Interesse (od. Risiko); ~ **value** versicherbarer Wert; **measure of** ~ **value** Höhe des versicherbaren Wertes

insurance (ins., insce, insur.) Versicherung; **~s** Versicherungsaktien

insurance, to be engaged in (or **carry on**) ~ **business** Versicherungsgeschäfte betreiben; im Versicherungswesen tätig sein; **to carry** ~ *Am* versichert sein; **to conclude** (or **enter into**) **an** ~ **contract** e-n Versicherungsvertrag (od. e-e Versicherung) abschließen; **to effect an** ~ e-e Versicherung abschließen; sich versichern lassen; **an** ~ **expires** e-e Versicherung läuft ab (od. erlischt); **to have no further claims on an** ~ keine weiteren Versicherungsansprüche mehr haben; ausgesteuert sein; **to have** ~ **cover against** (or **for**) **sickness** gegen Krankheit versichert sein; **to negotiate an** ~ **contract** e-n Versicherungsvertrag aushandeln; **to provide** ~ **cover** Versicherungsschutz gewähren; **to reinstate an** ~ e-e Versicherung wieder in Kraft setzen; **the** ~ **runs** die Versicherung läuft; **to**

take out an ~ (policy) e-e Versicherung abschließen; sich versichern (lassen); **to transact the ~ business** das Versicherungsgeschäft betreiben

insurance, ~→adjuster; ~ against breakage Bruchschadenversicherung; **~ against damage by hail** Hagelversicherung; **~ against loss on exchange** Kursverlustversicherung; **~ against risk of transport** Transportversicherung; **~ against robbery** Beraubungsversicherung; **~ agency** Versicherungsagentur; **~ agent** Versicherungsagent, -vertreter; **~ benefit** Versicherungsleistung; **~ branch** Versicherungszweig; **~ broker** Versicherungsmakler; **~ business** Versicherungsgeschäft; **~ canvasser** Versicherungsvertreter; **~ carrier** Versicherungsträger; **~ certificate** Versicherungszertifikat; **~ charges** Versicherungskosten; **~ claim** Versicherungsanspruch; **~ (claim) adjuster** Schadensregulierer; **~ clause** Versicherungsklausel; **~ commissioner** Leiter e-r Versicherungsaufsichtsbehörde

insurance compan|y[21] Versicherungsgesellschaft; **~ies' operations** Geschäftsbetrieb der Versicherungsgesellschaften; **~ share** Versicherungsaktie; **alien ~** *Am* Versicherungsunternehmen mit Hauptsitz außerhalb der Vereinigten Staaten von Amerika; **→captive ~; domestic ~** *Am* Versicherungsunternehmen mit Hauptsitz im jeweiligen Einzelstaat; **foreign ~** *Am* Versicherungsunternehmen mit Hauptsitz in einem anderen Einzelstaat; **joint stock life ~** Lebensversicherungs-Aktiengesellschaft; **life ~** Lebensversicherungsgesellschaft; **mutual ~** Versicherungsgesellschaft (od. Versicherungsverein) auf Gegenseitigkeit (VVaG) *(→mutual);* **out of state ~** *Am* Versicherungsunternehmen mit Hauptsitz außerhalb des jeweiligen Einzelstaates; **property and casualty ~** Sach- und Schadensversicherungsgesellschaft

insurance, ~ conditions Versicherungsbedingungen; **~ contingency** Eintritt des Versicherungsfalles

insurance contract Versicherungsvertrag; **conclusion of** (or **effecting**) **an ~** Abschluß e-s Versicherungsvertrages; Versicherungsabschluß; **term of the ~** Laufzeit des Versicherungsvertrages; **restitution of an ~ that had been cancelled for non-payment of the premium** Wiederherstellung e-s Versicherungsvertrages, der wegen Nichtbezahlung der Prämie aufgehoben worden war

insurance, ~ corporation *Am* Versicherungsgesellschaft; **~ costs** Versicherungskosten; **~ cover(age)** Versicherungsschutz; Versicherungsdeckung; **I~ Department** *Am (einzelstaatliches)* Amt für Versicherungswesen; **~ dodger** *colloq.* pflichtwidrig nicht versicherter Fahrer; **~ en route** Transportversicherung; **~ exchange** Versicherungsbörse; **~ expense** Versicherungskosten; **~ fee** *(Post)* Versicherungsgebühr; **~ fraud** Versicherungsbetrug; **~ fund** Versicherungsfonds; **~ holder** Versicherungsnehmer; **~ in (foreign) currency** Fremdwährungsversicherung; **~ in force** bestehende (od. laufende) Versicherung; **~industry** Versicherungswirtschaft; **~ institution** Versicherungsträger; **I~ Law** *Am* Versicherungsaufsichtsgesetz; **~ note** vorläufiger Versicherungsschein; **~ of crops** Ernteversicherung; **~ of** (or **on**) **freight** Frachtversicherung; **~ of** (or **on**) **goods** Güterversicherung; **~ (of goods) in international trade** Versicherung im internationalen Warenverkehr; **~ of growing timber** Waldversicherung; **~ of persons** Personenverischerung; **~ of valuables** Wertsachenversicherung; **~ office** *Br* Versicherungsanstalt, -gesellschaft *(→office 3.);* **~→ officers; ~ on buildings** Gebäudeversicherung; **~ on cargo** Frachtversicherung; **~ on contents** Hausratversicherung; **~ on hull and appurtenances** (Schiffs-)Kaskoversicherung; **~ on** (or **of**) **merchandise** Warenversicherung; **~ on a premium basis** Versicherung gegen Prämie; **~ operations** Versicherungsgeschäfte; **~ payment** Versicherungszahlung, -leistung; **~ period** Versicherungszeit, -dauer

insurance policy Versicherungsschein, Police; **~ number** Nummer des Versicherungsscheines, Policennummer; **buyer of an ~** Versicherungsnehmer; **life ~** (L. I. P.) Lebensversicherungspolice; **to take out an ~** e-e Versicherung abschließen

insurance, ~ portfolio Versicherungsbestand; **~ premium** Versicherungsprämie; **~ proposal** Versicherungsantrag; **~ rate** Versicherungs(prämien)satz; **~ rating** Versicherungs-Tarifierung; **~ regulation** *Am* Versicherungsaufsicht; **~ regulations** Versicherungsvorschriften; **~ relationship** Versicherungsverhältnis; **~ salesman** Versicherungsvertreter; **~ shares** Versicherungsaktien; **~ superintendent** *Am* s. commissioner of →~; **~ swindling** Versicherungsbetrug; **~ syndicate** Versicherungskonsortium; **~ terms and conditions** Versicherungsbedingungen; **~ transaction** *(das einzelne)* Versicherungsgeschäft; **~ trust** *Am* Treuhandverwaltung für aus e-r Lebensversicherung herrührende Gelder; **~ with index clause** Indexversicherung *(→index clause);* **~ with limited premium** Versicherung mit abgekürzter Prämienzahlung; **~ with option** Versicherung mit der Möglichkeit der Wahl (Kapital- od. Rentenzahlung); **~ with (without) participation in profits** Versicherung mit (ohne) Gewinnbeteiligung

insurance, accident ~ Unfallversicherung; **accidental death ~** Unfalltodversicherung; **additional ~** Zusatzversicherung; Nachversicherung; **aircraft hull ~** Flugzeugkaskoversicherung; **aircraft passenger ~** Fluggastversicherung; **all-in** ~ Gesamtversicherung; **all-risk** ~ Versicherung gegen alle Gefahren, Gesamtversicherung; **American I~ Association** (AIA) Verband amerikanischer Versicherungen; **automobile** ~ *Am* Kraftfahrzeugversicherung; **aviation** ~ Luftfahrtversicherung; **baggage** ~ (Reise-)Gepäckversicherung; **bank burglary** ~ Bankeinbruchversicherung; **British I~ Association** Verband britischer Versicherungen; **burglary** ~ Einbruch(diebstahl)-versicherung; **business interruption** ~ Betriebsunterbrechungsversicherung; **cargo** ~ Frachtversicherung; Güterversicherung; **casualty** ~ *Am* Schadenversicherung; Unfall-Haftpflichtversicherung; **cattle** ~ Viehversicherung; **certificate of** ~ Versicherungszertifikat; **civil commotion** ~ Aufruhrversicherung; **co~** Mitversicherung; gemeinsame Versicherung; **collective** ~ Kollektivversicherung; Gruppenversicherung; **coming into force** (or **commencement**) **of** ~ Versicherungsbeginn; **commissioner of** ~ *Am* Versicherungskommissar *(für Durchführung der Versicherungsgesetzgebung verantwortlicher Staatsbeamter);* **comprehensive** ~ kombinierte Versicherung; **comprehensive motor car** ~ *Br* Gesamtkraftfahrzeugversicherung; **comprehensive plus collision** ~ *Am* Vollkaskoversicherung

insurance, compulsory ~ Pflichtversicherung, Zwangsversicherung; **exempt from compulsory** ~ nicht versicherungspflichtig; **subject to compulsory** ~ pflichtversichert

insurance, contract of ~ Versicherungsvertrag; **credit** ~ Kreditversicherung; **crop-hail** ~ Erntehagelversicherung; **Department of I~** *Am (einzelstaatl.)* Amt für das Versicherungswesen; **direct** ~ Direktversicherung; Erstversicherung; **disability** (or **disablement**) ~ Invaliditätsversicherung (→*disability*); **double** ~ Doppelversicherung; **earthquake** ~ Erdbebenversicherung; →**employer's liability** ~; →**endowment** ~; **exempt from** ~ versicherungsfrei; **Federal I~ Administration** *Am* Bundesversicherungsverwaltung; **fidelity** ~ Veruntreuungsversicherung, Vertrauensschadenversicherung; Kautionsversicherung; **fire** ~ Feuerversicherung, Brandversicherung; **first loss** ~ Erstrisikoversicherung; **flood** ~ Überschwemmungsversicherung; **freight** ~ Frachtversicherung; **frost** ~ Frostversicherung; **funeral expenses** ~ Begräbniskostenversicherung; **general (~) business** *Br* Sachversicherung(sgeschäft); **group** ~ Gruppenversicherung, Kollektivversicherung; **guarantee** (or **guaranty**) ~ Kautionsversicherung; **hail (-storm)** ~ Hagelversicherung; **health** ~ Krankenversicherung; →**household** ~; **hull** ~ (Schiffs-, Flugzeug-)Kaskoversicherung; **indemnity** ~ Schadensersatzversicherung; **individual** ~ Einzelversicherung *(opp. group or collective~);* →**industrial** ~; **industrial life** ~ Kleinlebensversicherung; **leasehold** ~ Pachtausfallversicherung; **legal expenses** ~ Rechtsschutzversicherung; **liability** ~ Haftpflichtversicherung; **life** ~ Lebensversicherung; **live stock** ~ Viehversicherung; **luggage** ~ *Br* (Reise-)Gepäckversicherung; → **malpractice ~; marine** (or **maritime**) ~ See(transport)versicherung (→*marine*); **motor** ~ *Br* Kraftfahrzeugversicherung; **mutual** ~ Versicherung auf Gegenseitigkeit, Gegenseitigkeitsversicherung; **mutual ~ company** Versicherungsverein auf Gegenseitigkeit (VVaG) (→*mutual*); **obligatory** ~ Pflichtversicherung; **old age** ~ Altersversicherung; **over~** Überversicherung; **own** ~ Selbstversicherung; **parcel post** ~ *Am* Paketversicherung; **partnership** ~ Teilhaberversicherung; **period of** ~ Versicherungsdauer; **personal** ~ Personenversicherung *(life, accident, health ~);* **personal liability** ~ Privathaftpflichtversicherung; **private** ~ Privatversicherung; **property** ~ Sachversicherung; →**public liability** ~; **rail transportation** ~ *Am* Bahntransportversicherung; **re~** Rückversicherung; **reciprocal** ~ *Am* Versicherung auf Gegenseitigkeit (→*reciprocal*); **registered mail** ~ *Am* Versicherung für eingeschriebene Postsendungen; **rent** ~ Mietverlustversicherung; **riot, strike and civil commotion** ~ Versicherung gegen Aufruhr, Streik und Bürgerkrieg; **residence burglary** ~ Wohnungseinbruchversicherung; **robbery** ~ Raubüberfallversicherung; **sickness** ~ Krankenversicherung; **subsequent** ~ Nachversicherung; **supplementary** ~ Zusatzversicherung; **surgical fees** ~ *Am* Operationskostenversicherung; **survivors'** ~ Hinterbliebenenversicherung; **term** ~ →term 2.; **term of the** ~ Versicherungsdauer; **third party (liability)** ~ Haftpflichtversicherung; Fremdversicherung; **at the time of effecting the** ~ zur Zeit des Versicherungsabschlusses; **title** ~ *Am* →title 2.; **(goods in) transit** ~ (Güter-)Transportversicherung; **under~** Unterversicherung; **unemployment** ~ Arbeitslosenversicherung; **use and occupancy** ~ *Am* Betriebsunterbrechungsversicherung (→*use 1.);* **voluntary** ~ freiwillige Versicherung; **voluntarily continued** ~ freiwillige Weiterversicherung; **whole life** ~ Lebensversicherung auf den Todesfall; **workmen's compensation** ~ *Am* Betriebsunfallversicherung

insurant Versicherter, Versicherungsnehmer

insure *v (jdn)* versichern (against gegen; for £... mit £...; with bei); sich versichern (lassen); **to ~ against theft** sich gegen Diebstahl versichern (lassen); **to ~ one's life for £...** sich (od. sein Leben) mit £... versichern (lassen); **to ~ a house against (the risk of) fire** ein Haus gegen Feuer versichern; **to ~ a letter** *Br* e-n Brief als Wertbrief senden; **to ~ against**

third party risks (sich) gegen Haftpflicht versichern

insured 1. (der/die) Versicherte; Versicherungsnehmer(in); ~ **and insurer** Versicherter und Versicherer; **to require the ~ to retain part of the risk uninsured** für e-n Versicherten Selbstbehalt vorschreiben

insured 2. versichert; ~ **item** Versicherungsgegenstand; ~**letter** *Br* Wertbrief; **in case of an ~ loss** im Falle des Eintritts des Versicherungsfalles; ~ **parcel** *Br* Wertpaket; **amount** ~ Versicherungssumme; **contingency ~ against** Risiko, gegen das man sich versichert hat; **(occurrence of the) event** ~ (Eintritt des) Versicherungsfall(es); **object** ~ versicherte Sache; **period** ~ Versicherungszeit; **subject matter (to be)** ~ Versicherungsobjekt; **sum** ~ Versicherungssumme; **value** ~ Versicherungswert; **to get oneself ~ against a risk** sich gegen ein Risiko versichern lassen; **to have one's life** ~ sich (od. sein Leben) versichern lassen

insurer Versicherer; Versicherungsträger; ~ **and insured** (or **assured**) Versicherer und Versicherter; **co-**~ Mitversicherer; **first** ~ Erstversicherer *(opp. re~)*; **individual** ~ Einzelversicherer; **private** ~ Privatversicherer; **National Association of Independent I~s** (NAII) *Am* Nationale Vereinigung unabhängiger Versicherer

insurgency Aufstand, Rebellion, Revolte; **counter-**~ Aufstandsbekämpfung

insurgent Aufständischer, Rebell; aufständisch; ~ **government** von Aufständischen gebildete Regierung

insurrection Aufstand, Rebellion, Revolte; **to put down an** ~ e-n Aufstand niederschlagen

insurrectional, insurrectionary aufständisch, rebellierend

insurrectionist Insurgent, Aufständischer, Rebell

intact seal unverletztes Siegel; unverletzter Zollverschluß

intactness of the work *(UrhR)* Unversehrtheit des Werkes

intake Aufnahme, Zahl der während e-r bestimmten Zeit aufgenommenen (od. eingetretenen) Personengruppe

intangible nicht greifbar, nicht körperlich; ~**s** →~ assets; ~ **assets** immaterielle Vermögenswerte (od. Wirtschaftsgüter) *(e-s Unternehmens) (Patente, Goodwill etc) (opp. tangible assets)*; ~ **fixed assets** *Am (Bilanz)* immaterielle Werte des Anlagevermögens; ~ **property** *Am* immaterielles Vermögen *(Wertpapiere, Hypotheken etc)*

integral ganz, vollständig; wesentlich; ~ **examination** *(Zoll)* Gesamtbeschau *(opp. part examination)*; ~ **part** *(wesentlicher)* Bestandteil; **to form an ~ part of an agreement** Bestandteil e-s Abkommens sein

integrate *v* integrieren, sich *(zu e-m Ganzen)* zusammenschließen; *(in ein Ganzes)* einbeziehen, eingliedern; die Rassenschranken aufheben zwischen; **to** ~ **into** aufnehmen in, vereinigen mit

integrated integriert; zusammenhängend, umfassend; verflochten *(Gesellschaften)*; ~ **economy** Verbundwirtschaft; **I~ Mediterranean Programme** (IMP) *(EG)* Integriertes Mittelmeerprogramm; ~ **school** *Am* Schule ohne Rassentrennung; **I~ Services Digital Network** (ISDN) dienstintegriertes digitales Fernmeldenetz; ~ **store** *Am* Kettenladen, Filiale; **to be economically** ~ wirtschaftlich eng verflochten sein; in Verbundwirtschaft arbeiten

integration Integration; Zusammenschluß *(z. B. von mehreren nationalen Industrien zu e-m übernationalen Markt)*; Zusammenfassung *(zu e-m Ganzen)*; Verflechtung; Einbeziehung, Eingliederung; *Am* System der rassisch gemischten Schulen; ~ **in(to) the labo(u)r market of foreign workers** Eingliederung von Fremdarbeitern in den Arbeitsmarkt; ~ **of markets** Marktverflechtung; ~ **of US and European business** Verflechtung der amerikanischen und europäischen Wirtschaft; **economic** ~ wirtschaftliche Integration; **economy in process of** ~ sich integrierende Wirtschaft; **military** ~ militärische Integration; **progressive** ~ progressive Integration; schrittweise Eingliederung; **racial** ~ Rassenintegration

integrity Integrität, Ehrlichkeit, Lauterkeit; Unversehrtheit; **territorial** ~ *(VölkerR)* territoriale Unversehrtheit

intellectual intellektuell; geistig; ~ **activity of a country** geistiges Leben e-s Landes; **personal ~ creations** *(UrhR)* persönliche geistige Schöpfungen; ~ **property** geistiges Eigentum (→*World I~ Property Organization*, →*International Bureau of I~ Property*); ~ **pursuits** geistige Beschäftigung *(hobbies)*; ~ **work** geistige Arbeit

intelligence Intelligenz; Nachrichten; *(außenpolitisch wichtige)* Informationen; *Am* Auskunft; *(geheimer)* Nachrichtendienst; ~ **agent** Geheimagent; **I~ Board** *Am* Nachrichtendienst, Geheimdienst; ~ **activities** Agententätigkeit; ~ **bureau** *Am* →~ department; **I~ Department** (I. D.) *mil (geheimer)* Nachrichtendienst; ~ **net(work)** *mil* Nachrichtennetz; ~ **office** *Am* Auskunftsbüro; ~ **officer** Nachrichtenoffizier; ~ **operations** Agententätigkeit; ~ **service** *mil (geheimer)* Nachrichtendienst; ~ **with the enemy** Verbindung mit dem Feind; **counter-~** Spionageabwehr (→*counter)*; →**Military I~**

Intelsat Intelsat *(weltweites kommerzielles Fernmelde-Satellitensystem; →International Telecommunications Satellite Organization)*; ~ **space segment** Intelsat-Weltraumsegment

intending purchaser Kaufreflektant, Kaufinteressent

intendment wahre Bedeutung; Auslegung; ~ **of the law** Rechtsvermutung

intensification of relations *pol* Vertiefung der Beziehungen

intensify *v* intensivieren, vertiefen, verstärken; **to ~ the relations** die Beziehungen vertiefen; **to ~ restrictions** Beschränkungen verschärfen

intensive intensiv *(opp. extensive)*; ~ **agriculture** intensive Wirtschaft; **capital-~** kapitalintensiv; **labo(u)r-~** arbeitsintensiv

intent Vorsatz *(dolus)*; Zweck, Absicht; Ziel; **to all ~s and purposes** in jeder Hinsicht; im Endeffekt, praktisch (genommen); **criminal ~** strafrechtlicher Vorsatz; **declaration of ~** →declaration 1.; **fraudulent ~** betrügerische Absicht, Täuschungsabsicht; **legislative ~** Absicht des Gesetzgebers; **letter of ~** →letter 2.; **specific ~** konkreter Vorsatz; **with ~** absichtlich, vorsätzlich; **with ~ to defraud** in betrügerischer Absicht; **to presume ~** Vorsatz vermuten (od. unterstellen)

intention Absicht; Wille, Willenserklärung; *(StrafR)* Vorsatz *(bewußte Herbeiführung rechtswidrigen Geschehens; cf. negligence, recklessness)*; ~ **to deceive** Täuschungsabsicht; ~ **of the legislator** Absicht des Gesetzgebers; ~ **of the parties** (or **party**) Parteiwille; ~ **of the testator** der wirkliche Wille des Erblassers; **bona fide ~ to use** *(WarenzeichenR)* ernsthafte Benutzungsabsicht; **declaration of ~** →declaration 1.; **guilty ~** *Scot* Vorsatz; **wrongful ~** widerrechtlicher Vorsatz; **to state the ~** die Absicht darlegen

intentional absichtlich; vorsätzlich; ~ **commission of a crime** vorsätzliche Begehung e-s Verbrechens

inter(-)agency Vermittlung; *Am* zwei oder mehr Regierungsstellen betreffend; ~ **agreement** *(VölkerR)* zwischen den Vereinten Nationen (od. zwischen den Sonderorganisationen untereinander) abgeschlossener Vertrag; ~ **organization** *Am* aus verschiedenen Behörden gebildete Organisation

inter(-)agent Vermittler

inter-allied interalliiert; mehrere Alliierten gemeinsam betreffend

Inter-American Development Bank (IDB)[21a] Interamerikanische Entwicklungsbank
Die IDB wurde 1959 von 19 lateinamerikanischen Staaten und den USA gegründet zur Finanzierung von Entwicklungsvorhaben, nach dem Muster der Weltbank. Ihr Tätigkeitsgebiet ist auf Lateinamerika beschränkt. Durch die Ausweitung der Mitgliedschaft auf außerregionale Industrieländer konnte die IDB ihre Kapitalbasis stärken. (1976 traten auch Großbritannien und die Bundesrepublik der IDB bei)

Inter-American Investment Corporation, Agreement Establishing the ~[21b] Übereinkommen zur Errichtung der Interamerikanischen Investitionsgesellschaft

interbank zwischen Kreditinstituten; ~ **balances** Guthaben einer Bank bei anderen Kreditinstituten; ~ **dealings** Interbankenhandel; **in ~ dealings** im Bankverkehr; ~ **money market** *(Eurogeldmarkt)* Interbankengeldmarkt; ~ **money rate** Interbankrate *(Zinssatz, zu dem am Eurogeldmarkt Geldgeschäfte unter Banken abgeschlossen werden)*

interbourse securities *Am* international gehandelte Wertpapiere

interbrand competition Wettbewerb zwischen verschiedenen Produkten (→intrabrand competition)

interceder Fürsprecher, Vermittler

intercept *v (Postsachen, Funkspruch etc)* abfangen; *(jdm)* den Weg abschneiden; **to ~ telephone calls** Telefongespräche abhören; **to ~ trade** den Handel behindern

interception Abfangen *(von Postsachen, Funksprüchen etc)*; Abhören *(von Telefongesprächen)*; Behinderung; ~ **by the censor** Anhalten von Post durch die Zensur; ~ **service** Abhördienst

interceptor Abfangender; Abhörender; Abfangflugzeug

intercession Vermittlung, Fürsprache; *(VölkerR)* Interzession *(zulässige Beeinflussung auf Wunsch des betroffenen Staates; cf. intervention)*

intercessor Vermittler, Fürsprecher (with bei)

interchange Austausch; Anschlußstelle *(Intern. E-Straßennetz)*; ~ **of civilities** Austausch von Höflichkeiten; ~ **of ideas** Gedankenaustausch; **holiday ~** Ferienaustausch

interchange *v (gegenseitig)* austauschen, auswechseln

interchangeability Austauschbarkeit

interchangeable austauschbar, auswechselbar; ~ **bonds** *Am* in Inhaberobligationen auswechselbare Namensschuldverschreibungen

intercitizenship *Am* gleichzeitige (od. doppelte) Staatsangehörigkeit *(bes. hinsichtlich verschiedener Einzelstaaten)*

intercoastal trade Küstenhandel

intercom(munication system) Haussprechanlage

intercommunicate *v* miteinander in Verbindung stehen (od. treten)

intercompany zwischenbetrieblich; zwischen Unternehmen *(z. B. parent-subsidiary company)*; konzernintern; ~ **accounts** *Am (Bilanz)* Forderungen an konzernabhängige Unternehmen; ~ **debts** (or **liabilities**) Konzernverbindlichkeiten; ~ **holdings** Beteiligungen zwischen Konzernunternehmen; ~ **loss** konzerninterner Verlust; ~ **sales** Verkäufe zwischen Konzerngesellschaften; ~ **transactions** Transaktionen (Lieferungen und Leistungen) innerhalb des Konzerns

interconnection of data banks Vernetzung von Datenbanken

intercontinental interkontinental; von Kontinent zu Kontinent; **I~ Ballistic Missile** (I. C. B. M.) *mil* Interkontinentalrakete, Fernrakete

intercorporate, ~ **privilege** *Am* Schachtelprivileg; ~ **stockholding** *Am*[22] Schachtelbeteiligung, Aktienbeteiligung verschiedener Gesellschafter untereinander

intercourse 1. Verkehr, Umgang; **commercial** ~ Geschäftsverkehr, Handelsverkehr; **diplomatic** ~ diplomatischer Verkehr; **economic** ~ Wirtschaftsverkehr; **social** ~ gesellschaftlicher Verkehr; **to have official** ~ **with** in amtlicher Eigenschaft verkehren mit

intercourse 2. (Geschlechts-)Verkehr; **conjugal** ~ ehelicher Verkehr; **extramarital** ~ außerehelicher Verkehr; **marital** ~ ehelicher Verkehr; **premarital** ~ vorehelicher Verkehr; **sexual** ~ Geschlechtsverkehr

interdepartmental zwischen Abteilungen (od. *Am* Ministerien); interministeriell; Ressort-; ~ **agreement** *(VölkerR)* Ressortübereinkommen, Ressortabkommen *(von einzelnen Ministern abgeschlossener Vertrag; cf. intergovernmental agreement)*; ~ **conference** Ressortbesprechung

interdependence Interdependenz, gegenseitige Abhängigkeit; Wechselbeziehung; ~ **of prices** Interdependenz der Preise

interdependent gegenseitig abhängig

interdict *(amtl.)* Verbot; *Scot* einstweilige Verfügung; gerichtliches Verbot; *eccl* Interdikt *(Verbot aller kirchlichen Amtshandlungen)*

interdict *v (amtl.)* verbieten, untersagen

interdiction *(amtl.)* Verbot; ~ **of commerce** Handelsverbot

inter-enterprise conspiracy Konzernabsprache; Absprache zwischen Leitern verschiedener Konzernunternehmen

interest 1. Interesse, Belang; Bedeutung, Wichtigkeit; ~**s** Interessen, Belange; Interessengruppen; ~ **group** Interessengruppe; ~ **of the general public** Gemeininteresse; ~ **of the publisher** *(bei Beleidigungsklagen)* berechtigtes Interesse des Mitteilenden; ~ **of the State** Staatsinteresse; ~ **suit** *Br* Prätendentenstreit um das Amt des Erbschaftsverwalters

interest, banking ~**s** Bankkreise; **business** ~ Geschäftsinteresse; **business** ~**s** Geschäftswelt; **clash of** ~**s** Interessenkollision; **common** ~ gemeinsames, wechselseitiges (berechtigtes) Interesse; *(bei Beleidigungsklagen)* berechtigtes Interesse des Mitteilenden (Beklagten) und der Person, der die Mitteilung gemacht wurde; **community of** ~**s** Interessengemeinschaft; **conflict of** ~**s** Interessenkollision; **conflicting** ~**s** widerstreitende Interessen; **declaration of one's** ~ Bekanntgabe seines Interesses (→*to declare one's* ~); **direct** ~ **in the subject matter of legal proceedings** unmittelbares Interesse am Prozeßgegenstand; **economic** ~**s** wirtschaftliche Belange; **general** ~ Gesamtinteresse *(opp. particular* ~*)*; **in the general** ~ im allgemeinen Interesse; **a matter of great** ~ e-e Angelegenheit von großer Bedeutung; **in sb.'s** ~ in jds Interesse; **landed** ~**s** Großgrundbesitz; Großgrundbesitzer *(als Interessengruppe)*; **legal** ~ rechtlich anerkanntes Interesse; **legitimate** ~ legitimes (od. berechtigtes) Interesse; **local** ~ Lokalinteresse; **moneyed** ~**s** Finanzwelt; **national** ~ nationales Interesse; **national** ~**s** nationale Belange; **particular** ~ Einzelinteresse *(opp. general* ~*)*; **pecuniary** ~ finanzielles Interesse, Vermögensinteresse; **professional** ~ berufliches Interesse; **protection of** ~**s** Wahrnehmung der Interessen; **public** ~ öffentliches Interesse; **injury to the public** ~ Verletzung des öffentlichen Interesses; **real party in** ~ →party 1.; **representation of** ~**s** Interessenvertretung; **sphere of** ~ *(VölkerR)* Interessengebiet; **vital** ~**s** *pol* lebenswichtige Interessen

interest, to affect the ~**s** die Interessen berühren; **to attend to sb.'s** ~**s** jds Interessen wahrnehmen (od. vertreten); **to be in sb.'s** ~ in jds Interesse liegen; **to be in** (or **to benefit**) **the public** ~ im öffentlichen Interesse liegen; **to be contrary to the public** ~ gegen das öffentliche Interesse verstoßen; **to be of** ~ **to** von Interesse sein für; **to declare one's** ~ (in the subject matter of a debate) sein Interesse an e-r Sache (über die diskutiert wird) bekanntgeben *(und sich für befangen erklären);* **to harm one's ~s** den eigenen Interessen entgegenstehen; **to have an ~ in** interessiert sein an; **to impair** (or **interfere with**) **sb.'s ~s** jds Interesse beeinträchtigen; **to look after sb.'s ~s** jds Interessen wahrnehmen; **to prejudice seriously sb.'s ~s** jds Interessen ernstlich schädigen; **to protect** (or **safeguard, see to**) **sb.'s ~s** jds Interessen wahren; **to represent the ~s of a country** die Interessen (od. Belange) e-s Landes vertreten; **to take an ~ in** sich interessieren für; **to take no ~ in politics** sich nicht für Politik interessieren

interest 2. Recht, Anrecht (in auf); *(finanzielle)* Beteiligung, Anteil(e) (in an); Nutzen, Nutznießung; **~ for life** →life ~; **~ in a business** *(finanzielle)* Beteiligung an e-m Geschäft; Geschäftsanteil; **~ in a firm** Kapitalanteil e-s (Firmen-)Teilhabers; Geschäftsanteil; **~ in land** Recht (od. Anteil) an Grundbesitz; **~ in the profits** Gewinnbeteiligung; Gewinnanteil; **~ in property** dingliches Recht, Sachenrecht; **~ in tail** auf Nachkommen beschränktes Recht; **~s of a permanent nature** Rechte (od. Anteile) mit Dauerrechtscharakter

interest, beneficial ~ materieller Eigentumsanspruch (→*beneficial);* **capital ~** Kapitalanteil; **contingent ~** bedingtes Recht; Erbanwartschaft; **controlling ~** ausschlaggebender Kapitalanteil; Mehrheitsbeteiligung; **determinable ~** auflösend bedingtes Eigentumsrecht an Grundbesitz; →**equitable ~**; **financial ~** finanzielle Beteiligung; **future ~s in property** zukünftige dingliche Rechte an unbeweglichen Sachen (→*reversion,* →*remainder etc);* **government ~s** staatliche Beteiligungen; **industrial ~s** Industriebeteiligungen; **legal ~** dingliches Recht an Immobilien *(s. legal →estate);* **legitimate ~** berechtigtes Interesse; →**life ~**; →**overriding ~s**; **partnership ~** Gesellschaftsanteil; Beteiligung an e-r Personengesellschaft; →**vested ~**

interest, to acquire an ~ in a company e-e Beteiligung an e-r Gesellschaft (od. e-n Gesellschaftsanteil) erwerben; **to acquire an ~ in land** Grundeigentum erwerben; **to have an ~ in** *(an e-r Firma, am Gewinn)* beteiligt sein; Anteil haben an; ein *(dingliches)* Recht haben an; ein Anrecht haben auf; **to hold a 10% ~ in a business** zu 10% an e-m Geschäft beteiligt sein; **to safeguard sb.'s ~s** jds Interessen wahren (od. wahrnehmen); **to secure** [illegible] Beteiligung erwerben

interest 3. (versichertes bzw. zu versicherndes) Interesse; **~-cap** Minimalversicherung e-r →floating rate note; Sicherungsmittel des Schuldners gegen extreme Zinssteigerungen *(opp. floor);* **~s liable to contribute** *(zur Havarie)* beitragspflichtige Vermögenswerte; **"~ or no ~"** Verzicht auf Nachweis e-s versicherbaren Interesses *(cf. policy proof of ~, →policy 2.);* **declaration of ~** Angabe des Wertes des versicherten Interesses; **insurable ~** versicherbares Interesse (od. Risiko)

interest 4. (int.) Zins, Zinsen

interest, to add the ~ to the capital Zinsen zum Kapital schlagen; **to allow ~** Zinsen vergüten (od. bewilligen); **to bear** (or **carry**) **~** Zinsen bringen; sich verzinsen; verzinslich sein; **to bear** (or **carry**) **~ at (the rate of) 3%** sich mit 3% verzinsen; **to borrow at high ~** zu hohen Zinsen Darlehen aufnehmen; **to calculate the ~** die Zinsen berechnen (od. ausrechnen); **to charge ~** Zinsen berechnen (od. in Rechnung stellen) (on für); **to collect ~** Zinsen ansammeln; **to compute the ~** die Zinsen berechnen; **to invest money at ~** Geld verzinslich anlegen; **to lend (out) money at** (or **on**) **~** Geld gegen Zinsen (aus)leihen; **to pay ~ (on)** Zinsen zahlen; verzinsen; **to pay 3% ~ on a sum** e-e Summe mit 3% verzinsen; **to put out at ~** zinstragend anlegen; **to raise the ~** die Zinsen erhöhen; **to reduce the ~** die Zinsen herabsetzen; **to take ~ into account** Zinsen in Rechnung stellen; **to yield ~ at 3%** sich mit 3% verzinsen; 3% Zinsen bringen; **~ is due** (or **payable**) **from January 1** die Zinsen laufen ab 1. Januar

interest, ~ account Zinsenkonto; **~ amount** Zinsbetrag; **~ arrears** Zinsrückstände; **~ at the rate of 3%** Zinsen zu 3%; **~ balance** Zinssaldo *(der täglichen Zinsberechnung zugrundeliegender Kontosaldo)*

interest-bearing verzinslich, zinstragend; **fixed ~ securities** festverzinsliche Wertpapiere; **non-~** keine Zinsen tragend; zinslos, unverzinslich

interest, ~ bonds *Am* an Stelle von Zinsen ausgegebene Obligationen; **~ calculation** Zinsberechnung; **~ charge** Zinsbelastung; **~ clause** Zinsklausel; **~ computation** Zinsberechnung; **~ coupon** Zinsschein, -bogen, -kupon; **~ credited** Zins(en)gutschrift; **~ differential** Zinsgefälle; **~ due** fällige Zinsen; **~ earned** Zinserträge; **I~ Equalization Tax** (IET) *Am* Zinsausgleichssteuer *(auf Käufe ausländischer Wertpapiere durch amerikanische Bürger);* **~ expenditure** (or **expense**) Zinsaufwand; **~ for default** (or **delay**) Verzugszinsen; **~-free** zinsfrei; ohne Berechnung von Zinsen; zinslos; unverzinslich; **~ in arrears** rückständige Zinsen; **~ instal(l)ment** Zinsrate; **~ level** Zinsniveau; **~ loss** Zinsverlust; **~ margin** Zinsmarge, Zinsspanne; **~ on bank loans** Bankzinsen; **~ on bonds** Obligationenzinsen; **~ on capital** Kapitalzinsen; **~ on credit balances** Habenzinsen; **~ on debit balances** Sollzinsen; **~ on debts** Schuldzinsen; **~ on deposits** Zinsen auf (Bank-)Einlagen; **~ on loan** Darlehenszinsen; **~ paid** Zinsaufwand; **~ payable** Zinsverbindlichkeiten; fällige Zinsen; Habenzinsen, Passivzinsen *(die die Bank zu zahlen* *hat);* ~ **(payable) on arrears** Verzugszinsen; ~ **payment** Zinszahlung, Zinsleistung; Verzinsung; ~ **policy** Zinspolitik

interest rate, ~ **adjustment** Zinsanpassung; ~ **advantage** Zinsvorteil; ~ **arbitrage** Zinsarbitrage; ~ **differential** Zinsgefälle; ~ **futures** *(Börse)* Zinsterminkontrakte; ~ **increase** Zinserhöhung, Zinssteigerung; ~ **on borrowings** Fremdkapitalzinssatz; ~ **policy** Zinspolitik; ~ **structure** Zinsstruktur, Zinsgefüge; ~→**swap; long-term** ~ Zinssatz für langfristige Kredite; Kapitalmarktzinsen; **mortgage** ~ Hypothekenzinssatz; **rise in** ~**s** Zinsanstieg; **short-term** ~ Zinssätze für kurzfristige Kredite; Geldmarktzinsen; **to increase** (or **raise**) **the** ~ den Zinssatz erhöhen; **to reduce the** ~ den Zinssatz senken; **to pay a high** ~ hohe Zinsen zahlen

interest, ~ **rebates** Zinsvergütungen; ~ **receipts** Zinseingänge; ~ **receivable** Sollzinsen, Aktivzinsen *(die Bank vom Kunden erhält); (Bilanz)* Zinsforderungen; ~ **revenue** Zinsertrag, Zinseinnahmen; ~ **sheet** Zinsbogen; ~ **statement** Zinsenaufstellung; Zinsabrechnung; ~ **subsidies** Zinsvergütungen, Zinssubventionen; ~ **table** Zinstabelle; ~ **upon defaults in payment** Verzugszinsen; ~ **voucher** (or **warrant**) Zinsschein; ~ **yield** Zinsertrag, Verzinsung

interest, accrued(or **accumulated**) ~ aufgelaufene Zinsen; fällige Zinsen; Stückzinsen; **accruing** ~ *(später)* fällig werdende Zinsen; **annual** ~ jährliche Zinsen, Jahreszins; **arrears of** ~ rückständige Zinsen, Zinsrückstände; **as** ~ zinsweise; **at** ~ gegen Zinsen; **at 4%** ~ zu 4% Zinsen; **back** ~ rückständige Zinsen; **bearing** ~ **(at the rate of)** verzinslich (mit); **bearing no** ~ unverzinslich; **bearing 3%** ~ mit 3% verzinslich; **calculation of** ~ Zinsberechnung; **equated** (or **graduated**) **calculation of** ~ Staffelzinsrechnung; **compound** ~ Zinseszins(en); **computation of** ~ Zinsberechnung; **contract** ~ *(vertraglich)* vereinbarte Zinsen; **credit** ~ Habenzinsen, Passivzinsen *(die die Bank zu zahlen hat);* **crediting of** ~ Gutschrift der Zinsen; **cum** ~ *(Käufer übernimmt Wertpapiere)* mit Zinsen *(opp. ex* ~); **current** ~ laufende Zinsen; **debit** ~ Sollzinsen, Aktivzinsen *(die die Bank von den Kunden erhält);* **equated** ~ Staffelzinsen, gestaffelte Zinsen; **ex** ~ ohne (od. ausschließlich) Zinsen *(opp. cum* ~); **exact** ~ *Am* Zinsen auf der Basis von 365 Tagen *(opp. ordinary* ~); **excessive** ~ überhöhte Zinsen, Wucherzinsen; **fixed** ~**- bearing** festverzinslich; **free of** ~ zinsfrei, ohne Berechnung von Zinsen; zinslos; unverzinslich; **graduated** ~ gestaffelte Zinsen; **high** ~ hohe Zinsen; **interim** ~ Zwischenzinsen; **lawful** ~ rechtmäßiger (Höchst-)Zins; **legal** ~ gesetzliche Zinsen; **less** ~ abzüglich der Zinsen; **loan on** ~ verzinsliche Darlehen; **loss of** ~ Zinsverlust; Zinsausfall; **low** ~ niedrige Zinsen; **marine** (or **maritime**) ~ Bodmereizinsen; **mesne** ~ Zwischenzinsen; **mortgage** ~ Hypothekenzinsen; **nominal** ~ Nominalzins *(opp. real* ~); →**ordinary** ~; **outstanding** ~ ausstehende (od. rückständige) Zinsen; **payment of** ~ Zinszahlung, Verzinsung; **principal and** ~ Kapital und Zinsen; **rate of** ~ Zinssatz, Zinsfuß *(s. interest rate und rate 2.);* **real** ~ Realzins *(opp. nominal* ~); **reduction of** ~ Zinssenkung, Zinsherabsetzung; **semi-annual** ~ halbjährliche Zinsen; **simple** ~ einfache Zinsen, Kapitalzinsen *(opp. compound* ~); **statutory** ~ gesetzliche Zinsen; **stipulated** ~ vertraglich vereinbarte Zinsen; **table of** ~ Zinstabelle; **terms of** ~ Zinsbedingungen; **usurious** ~ Wucherzinsen; **with** ~ mit Zinsen (s. *cum* →~); **without** ~ ohne Zinsen; **yielding** ~ verzinslich

interest *v (jdn)* interessieren (in für); beteiligen (in an), zum Teilhaber machen; *(jdn)* angehen, betreffen

interested interessiert (in für); beteiligt (in an); ~ **motives** eigennützige Beweggründe; ~ **party** Interessent; Beteiligter; ~ **witness** parteiischer Zeuge; **to be** ~ interessiert sein; beteiligt sein (in a business an e-m Geschäft); **to be legitimately** ~ ein berechtigtes Interesse haben

interface Wechselbeziehung, Wechselwirkung; wechselseitige Abhängigkeit; Zusammenspiel

interface *v* in Beziehung stehen zu; sich aufeinander beziehen; rückwirken

interfactory, ~ **comparative studies** (or ~ **comparisons**) Betriebsvergleiche

interfere *v* zusammenstoßen; dazwischenkommen; *Am (PatR)* das Prioritätsrecht geltend machen *(→interference proceedings);* **to** ~ **in** intervenieren, sich einmischen in; eingreifen in; **to** ~ **with** stören, beeinträchtigen; störend einwirken auf; sich kreuzen mit, kollidieren mit; **to** ~ **with an application** *(PatR)* mit e-r Anmeldung kollidieren; **to** ~ **with British interests in** ... britische Interessen in ... beeinträchtigen; **to** ~ **with sb.'s plans** jds Pläne durchkreuzen; **to** ~ **with sb.'s possession** jdn im Besitz stören; **to** ~ **with sb.'s rights** jds Rechte verletzen

interfering, ~ **claim** *(PatR)* kollidierender Anspruch; ~ **patent** kollidierendes Patent

interference Einmischung (with, in in); Störung, Beeinträchtigung, Eingriff; *Am* Kollision *(e-s Patentanspruchs mit e-m anderen Patentanspruch oder zwischen eingetragenen Warenzeichen); Am (PatR und MarkenR)* Geltendmachung des Prioritätsrechts; *(VölkerR)* Intervention, Einmischung; ~ **with advantageous relations** *Am* Geschäftsstörung; ~ **with contracts** Verleitung zum Vertragsbruch; ~ **with**

contractual relations Eingriff in vertragliche Beziehungen; ~ **with sb.'s possessions** Besitzstörung; ~ **proceedings** *Am* Prioritätsstreitverfahren; Verfahren zur Ermittlung des wahren Erfinders *(wenn mehrere Anmeldungen miteinander kollidieren);* Verfahren zur Feststellung der Erstbenutzung e-r Marke; ~ **with witnesses** Beeinflussung oder Belästigung von Zeugen (→*contempt of court*); **action to restrain** ~ Klage auf Unterlassung der Störung; **action for wrongful ~ with goods** *Br*[23] Klage auf Herausgabe (od. Schadensersatz) wegen Nichtherausgabe von Sachen; **unlawful** ~ (with the possession of another) Besitzstörung; verbotene Eigenmacht

interfirm zwischen Firmen, zwischenbetrieblich; ~ **comparative studies** (or ~ **comparisons**) Betriebsvergleiche; ~ **coordination** Zusammenarbeit zwischen Firmen

intergovernmental zwischen zwei (od. mehreren) Regierungen; Regierungs-; zwischenstaatlich; ~ **agreement** Regierungsübereinkommen, Regierungsabkommen *(zwischen Regierungen abgeschlossener Vertrag; cf. interdepartmental agreement);* ~ **arrangement** *(VölkerR) (formlose)* Regierungsvereinbarung; ~ **authority** zwischenstaatliche Behörde; ~ **bodies** zwischenstaatliche Gremien (od. Organisationen); ~ **committee** Ausschuß von Regierungsvertretern

Intergovernmental Committee for Migration (ICM) Zwischenstaatliches Komitee für Auswanderung

Gegr. 1952. *Sitz:* Genf. 32 europäische und außereuropäische Mitgliedstaaten

intergovernmental, ~ **conference** Regierungskonferenz; ~ **consultations** zwischenstaatliche Besprechungen; ~ **convention** Regierungsübereinkommen

interim vorläufig; Interims-, Zwischen-; ~ **account** Zwischenkonto, Interimskonto; ~ **agreement** *(VölkerR)* Interimsabkommen, Zwischenabkommen; vorläufige Vereinbarung; ~ **aid** Überbrückungshilfe; ~ **balance sheet** Zwischenbilanz; ~ **cabinet** *pol* Interimskabinett; ~ **certificate** Zwischenschein; ~ **commission** Interimskommission; ~ **committee** Interimsausschuß; ~ **credit** Zwischenkredit; ~ **decision** Zwischenentscheidung; ~ **development** zwischenzeitliche Entwicklung, vorläufige Erschließung *(von Bauland);* ~ **dividend** Abschlagsdividende; Zwischendividende *(cf. final dividend);* ~ **financing** Zwischenfinanzierung; ~ **injunction** einstweilige Verfügung; vorläufiges Verbot; ~ **interdict** *Scot* einstweilige Verfügung *(auf Antrag einer Partei);* ~ **interest** Zwischenzinsen; ~ **loan** Zwischenkredit; **(as an)** ~ **measure** (als) Zwischenmaßnahme (od. Zwischenlösung); ~ **order** einstweilige Anordnung; Zwischenverfügung; ~ **period** Zwischenzeit; ~ **question** Zwischenfrage; ~ **receipt** vorläufige Quittung; ~ **receiver** *Br (gerichtlich bestellter)* vorläufiger Konkursverwalter; ~ **report** Zwischenbericht; ~ **share** Aktienpromesse, Zwischenschein; ~ **trustee** *Am*[23a] vorläufiger Konkursverwalter

interinsurance *Am* Versicherung auf Gegenseitigkeit

interior inner(er, -e, -es); Innen- *(opp. exterior);* binnenländisch, Binnen-; Inlands- *(opp. foreign);* ~ **designer** (or **decorator**) Innenarchitekt; ~ **decoration** Innenausstattung *(e-r Wohnung);* ~ **decorative repairs** Schönheitsreparaturen; ~ **fittings** Innenausstattung *(e-s Autos);* **Department of the I~** *Am* Innenministerium; **Secretary of the I~** *Am* Innenminister

interlacing of capital Kapitalverflechtung

interlinked economy Verbundwirtschaft

interlinking, ~ **of business enterprises** Unternehmensverflechtung; ~ **of financial markets** Verflechtung der Finanzmärkte

interlock *v* ineinandergreifen

interlocked verschachtelt; verflochten

interlocking ineinandergreifend, sich verschachtelnd; ~ **capital arrangement** Kapitalverflechtung; ~ **combine** Konzernverflechtung; ~ **directorate** personelle Verflechtung von Unternehmen; Überkreuzverflechtung der Direktoren; *(Tätigkeit derselben Personen in der Verwaltung [board of directors] mehrerer Konzerngesellschaften);* ~ **interest** wechselseitige Beteiligung; ~ **stock ownership** *Am* Verschachtelung des Aktienbesitzes; Konzernverflechtung

interlocution Unterredung

interlocutor Gesprächspartner; *Scot* gerichtliche (Zwischen-)Entscheidung, Urteil

interlocutory Zwischen-; einstweilen, vorläufig; ~ **application** Zwischenantrag; ~ **decision** *(EG)* Vorabentscheidung; ~ **decree** *Am* Zwischenurteil; ~ **injunction** einstweilige Verfügung (→*injunction*)

interlocutory judgment Zwischenurteil *(das z.B. den Grund des Anspruchs bejaht, aber die Höhe noch offen läßt);* Zwischenentscheidung; ~ **of divorce** *Am* Scheidungsurteil, das erst nach e-r Übergangszeit die Ehe auflöst; **motion** (or **petition**) **for an** ~ Zwischenfeststellungsklage

interlocutory, ~ **order** Zwischenentscheidung, Zwischenurteil; ~ **proceedings** *(Zivilprozeß) Br (in den Händen von richterlichen Beamten – masters od. registrars – liegendes)* Vorverfahren; *(EG)* Vorabentscheidungsverfahren; ~ **revision** *(europ. PatR)* Abhilfe *(e-r Beschwerde);* **in the event of ~ revision** wenn der Beschwerde abgeholfen wird; ~ **relief** vorläufiger Rechtsbehelf (→*relief 1.*)

interloper Eindringling; Schleichhändler

intermarriage Heirat *(innerhalb der Familie, mit Ausländern, Andersgläubigen etc);* Wechselheirat; Mischheirat

intermarry *v* untereinander heiraten; *(nahe Verwandte)* sich heiraten; *(mit Andersgläubigen, Ausländern etc)* gemischte Ehe schließen

intermediary Vermittler, Mittelsperson; Makler; ~ **bank** *Am* eingeschaltete Bank; Zwischenbank; **through the ~ of** durch Vermittlung von; **to act as ~** vermitteln

intermediate dazwischen liegend; Zwischen-; ~ **account** Zwischenabrechnung; ~ **agent** Vermittler; ~ **airport** Zwischenflughafen; ~ **buyer** Zwischenkäufer; ~ **credit** Zwischenkredit; **I~ Credit Bank** *Am* →Federal I~ Credit Bank; ~ **invoice** Zwischenrechnung; ~ **product** Zwischenprodukt; **~-range ballistic missiles** Mittelstreckenraketen; **~-range nuclear forces** (INF) nukleare Mittelstreckensysteme;~ **seller** Zwischenverkäufer; ~ **size** Zwischengröße; ~ **trade** Zwischenhandel

intermediate *v* vermitteln, als Vermittler auftreten

interministerial interministeriell

intermission Pause, Unterbrechung; **to work without ~** ohne Unterbrechung arbeiten

intermittent intermittierend, zeitweilig aussetzend; nicht ständig; ~ **unemployment** zeitweilige Arbeitslosigkeit

intern(e) *Am* Assistenzarzt

intern *v* internieren

internal inländisch, Inlands-, Innen-, Binnen- *(opp. foreign);* intern; innere(r, -s); innerbetrieblich *(opp. external);* ~ **affairs** innere (od. innerstaatliche) Angelegenheiten *(e-s Landes);* innere (od. innerbetriebliche) Angelegenheiten *(e-r Firma);* ~ **air traffic** Inlandsluftverkehr; ~ **arrangements** interne Abmachungen; ~ **audit(ing)** betriebsinterne Revision; Innenrevision; ~ **charges** inländische Abgaben; ~ **commerce** *Am* Binnenhandel; ~ **Common Market** *(EG)* gemeinsamer Binnenmarkt; ~ **concerns** innenpolitische Belange; ~ **consumption** Inlandsverbrauch; ~ **control** innerbetriebliche Kontrolle; ~ **(national) debt** Inlandsschuld; innere (Staats-)Schuld; ~ **demand** Inlandsnachfrage; ~ **disorders** *pol* innere Unruhen; ~ **economic trend** Binnenkonjunktur; ~ **financing** Selbstfinanzierung *(e-s Unternehmens);* ~ **frontier** Binnengrenze; ~ **funds** eigene Mittel, Eigenmittel; ~ **injuries** (in an accident) innere Verletzungen (bei e-m Unfall); ~ **issue** Inlandsemission; ~ **law** innerstaatliches Recht; ~ **liabilities** Inlandsverbindlichkeiten; ~ **loan** Inlandsanleihe

internal market inländischer Markt; *(EG)* Binnenmarkt; **completion of the ~** Vollendung des Binnenmarktes *(geplant für 1992)*

On the planned realization of the common internal market by 1992, the member states of the European Community will consider other member states to be part of the domestic market.

Mit der geplanten Verwirklichung des gemeinsamen *Binnenmarktes* bis 1992 werden die Mitgliedsstaaten der Europäischen Gemeinschaft andere Mitgliedsstaaten als Teil des Binnenmarktes betrachten

internal medicine innere Medizin; **specialist for ~** Internist

internal, ~ policy Innenpolitik; ~ **pricing** innerbetriebliche Preisfestsetzung; ~ **rate of return** interner Zinsfluß *(e-r Investition)*

internal revenue *Am* Staatseinkünfte *(aus inländischen Steuern und Abgaben außer Zöllen);* Steuereinnahmen; ~ **authorities** *Am* Steuerbehörden; **I~ R~ Code** of 1986 (IRC) *Am* (Bundes-)Steuergesetz *(einschließlich Einkommensteuer);***I~ R~ Service** (IRS) *Am* Bundessteuerbehörde*(Abteilung des →Treasury Department)*

internal, ~ rules Geschäftsordnung; ~ **strains** innerpolitische Spannungen; ~ **tariff** Binnenzoll; ~ **taxes** innerstaatliche Steuern; ~ **trade** Binnenhandel; ~ **troubles** innere Unruhen; ~ **waters** Binnengewässer, Eigengewässer *(cf. territorial waters)*

International 1., **Socialist ~** Sozialistische Internationale (S. I.)

Zusammenschluß von etwa 40 sozialdemokratischen und sozialistischen Parteien vor allem Westeuropas

international 2. international, zwischenstaatlich; Welt-

International Advertising Association (IAA) Internationaler Werbeverband

International Agreement on Jute and Jute Products[23b] Internationales Übereinkommen *(von 1982)* über Jute und Jute-Erzeugnisse

International Agreement on Narcotizing Drugs[23c] Internationales Opiumabkommen

International Agreement on Railway Freight Traffic Internationales Übereinkommen über den Eisenbahnfrachtverkehr (CIM)[24]

International Agreement on Railway, Passenger and Luggage Traffic Internationales Übereinkommen über den Eisenbahn-, Personen- und Gepäckverkehr (CIV)[25]

International Aircraft Brokers' Association (IABA) Internationale Vereinigung von Luftfrachtmaklern

Interessenverband der im Luftverkehrs-Chartergeschäft tätigen europäischen Makler. Sitz: London

International Air Services Transit Agreement[26] Vereinbarung über den Durchflug im Internationalen Fluglinienverkehr

International Air Transport Association (IATA) Internationaler Luftverkehrsverband
Internationaler Verband der Linienfluggesellschaften. *Sitz:* Montreal.
Aufgabe: Regelung von Fragen des zwischenstaatlichen Luftverkehrs, z. B. Absprachen über Flugsicherheitsbestimmungen und Beförderungsbedingungen, Koordinierung der Flugpläne. Die Preisbestimmungen der IATA sind nicht mehr für ihre Mitglieder verbindlich. – Die Frachtabschlüsse mit den Luftverkehrsgesellschaften werden durch IATA-Spediteure, die als deren Agenten lizenziert sind (IATA-agents), getätigt

international, ~ application *(europ. PatentR)*[26a] *(nach dem →Patent Cooperation Treaty eingereichte)* internationale Anmeldung; ~ **arbitration** internationale Schiedsgerichtsbarkeit *(s. ICC Court of →Arbitration, →UNCITRAL Arbitration Rules);* **I~ Association for the Protection of Industrial Property** (IAPIP) Internationale Vereinigung zum Schutz des gewerblichen Eigentums (*Sitz:* Zürich); **I~ Association of Universities** (IAU) Internationaler Hochschulverband (*Sitz:* Paris); **I~ Association of University Professors and Lecturers** (IAUPL) Internationaler Verband der Hochschulprofessoren und Hochschullehrer (*Sitz:* London); **I~ Association for Vocational Guidance** (IAVG) Internationaler Verband für Berufsberatung (*Sitz:* Brüssel)

International Atomic Energy Agency (IAEA)[27] Internationale Atomenergie-Organisation (IAEO)
Gegr. 1957. *Sitz:* Wien; *Mitglieder:* ca. 110 Staaten
Organe: Generalkonferenz (General Conference), Gouverneursrat (Board of Governors), Generaldirektor (Director General)
Aufgabe: Förderung der Entwicklung der Atomenergie ausschließlich für friedliche Zwecke. Forschung und Schulung von Fachleuten für Atomkraftwerke. Technische Hilfeleistung für Entwicklungsländer. Kontrolltätigkeit im Rahmen des Atomsperrvertrages

International Baltic Sea Fishery Commission (IBSFC) Internationale Kommission für die Fischerei in der Ostsee

International Bank for Reconstruction and Development (IBRD) (World Bank)[28] Internationale Bank für Wiederaufbau und Entwicklung (Weltbank)
Gegr. 1946. *Sitz:* Washington. *Mitglieder:* 130 Staaten. *Organe:* Gouverneursrat (Board of Governors), Direktoren (Executive Directors) und Präsident (President).
Größtes Finanzierungsinstitut für Wirtschaftsprojekte in den Entwicklungsländern. Gewährung von mittel- und langfristigen Krediten für Projekte öffentlichen Interesses zur wirtschaftlichen Weiterentwicklung der Mitgliedstaaten (loan agreement). Soweit die Bank die Darlehen nicht direkt an einen Staat od. ein staatl. Unternehmen gibt, verlangt sie die Bürgschaft od. Garantie des Staates, in dem sich das Darlehnsobjekt befindet (guarantee agreement)

International Banking Facility (IBF) *Am* Internationale Bankeinrichtung
Unter Bankrecht genehmigte, bei einer inländischen Zweigstelle eingerichtete Buchungsstelle (mit getrennter Buchführung) für Eurowährungs- und andere Auslandsgeschäfte, die von Reservepflicht und für andere inländische Banken geltenden Beschränkungen befreit sind

International Bar Association (IBA) Internationale Anwaltsvereinigung
Zusammenschluß nationaler Anwaltsorganisationen aus ca. 40 Ländern. *Sitz:* New York

International, ~ Broadcast Institute (I. B. I.) Internationales Rundfunkinstitut; ~ **Bureau of Fiscal Documentation** Internationales Steuerdokumentationsbüro *(in Amsterdam);* ~ **Bureau of Intellectual Property**[29] Internationales Büro für geistiges Eigentum *(Sekretariat der Weltorganisation für geistiges Eigentum in Genf);* **i~ call** Auslandsgespräch

international carriage by air Beförderung im internationalen Luftverkehr (→ *Warsaw Convention*)

international carriage of dangerous goods by road internationale Beförderung gefährlicher Güter auf der Straße (→ *European Agreement concerning the ~*)

international carriage of goods by road, Convention on the Contract for the I~ C~ of G~ by R~ (CMR)[29a] Übereinkommen über den Beförderungsvertrag im internationalen Straßengüterverkehr

international carriage of perishable foodstuffs and the special equipment to be used for such carriage[29b] internationale Beförderung leicht verderblicher Lebensmittel und die besonderen Beförderungsmittel, die für diese Beförderung zu verwenden sind

International, ~ Centre for Settlement of Investment Disputes (ICSID)[29c] Internationales Zentrum zur Beilegung von Investitionsstreitigkeiten; Weltbankschiedszentrum; ~ **Centre for the Study of the Preservation and Restoration of Cultural Property (Rome Centre)**[29d] Internationale Studienzentrale für die Erhaltung und Restaurierung von Kulturgut; **(ICC) I~ Centre for →Technical Expertise**

International Chamber of Commerce (ICC) Internationale Handelskammer (IHK)
Sitz: Paris.
Organe: Kongreß (Congress), Rat (Council), in dem alle Landesgruppen (National Committees) vertreten sind (in der Bundesrepublik ist die IHK durch die Deutsche Gruppe in Köln vertreten); Vollzugsausschuß (Executive Committee); Präsident (President); Generalsekretär (Secretary General)
Aufgabe: Stellungnahme zu den grundlegenden Fragen der internationalen Wirtschaftspolitik: Erzeugung, Absatz- und Werbewesen; Transport und

Verkehr; Rechtsfragen und Handelspraxis. Die IHK hat wichtige Publikationen erarbeitet (z. B. →Incoterms,[30] Einheitliche Richtlinien und Gebräuche für Dokumentenakkreditive[31]). Sie unterhält einen eigenen Schiedsgerichtshof *(s. ICC Court of →Arbitration)*

International Chamber of Shipping (ICS) Internationale Schiffahrtskammer
Vereinigung nationaler Reederverbände. *Sitz:* London

international civil aviation internationale zivile Luftfahrt; **I~ C~ A~ Organization** (ICAO) Internationale Zivilluftfahrt-Organisation (IZLO); **Convention on I~ C~ A~**[32] Abkommen über die Internationale Zivilluftfahrt
Sitz: Montreal. 134 Mitglieder
Aufgabe: Förderung der Sicherheit und des technischen Fortschritts der internationalen Zivilluftfahrt. Aufstellung internationaler Normen (Richtlinien [standards] und Empfehlungen [recommended practices]) für die Zivilluftfahrt. Abwehr von Flugzeugentführungen

international, ~ claim völkerrechtlicher Anspruch; **~ classification of goods** internationale Warenklasseneinteilung (*→classification*); **~ classification of patents** →European Convention on the I~ Classification of Patents; **I~ Cocoa Council**[32a] Internationaler Kakaorat; **I~ Cocoa Organization** Internationale Kakaoorganisation; **I~ Code (of Signals)** Internationales Signalbuch; **I~ Coffee Agreement** Internationales Kaffeeübereinkommen; **I~ Coffee Organisation** Internationale Kaffee-Organisation; **~ comity** →comity of nations; **~ commerce** internationaler Handel, Welthandel; **~ commercial arbitration** internationale Handelsschiedsgerichtsbarkeit (*→European Convention on ~*); **I~ Commercial Terms** →Incoterms; **I~ Commission for the Protection of the Rhine against Pollution** Internationale Kommission zum Schutz des Rheins gegen Verunreinigung; **I~ Commission for the South-East Atlantic Fisheries** Internationale Kommission für die Fischerei im Südostatlantik; **I~ Commission of Jurists** Internationale Juristen- Kommission (IJK); **I~ Commission on Radiological Protection** (ICRP) Internationale Strahlenschutzkommission; **I~ Committee of the Red Cross** (ICRC) Internationales Komitee des Roten Kreuzes (IKRK) (*Sitz:* Genf); **I~ Committee of Scientific Managements** (ICSM) Internationales Komitee für wissenschaftliche Betriebsführung (*Sitz:* Genf)

International Commodity, ~ Agreement or Arrangement[32b] Internationale Rohstoffübereinkunft (Intern. Rohstoffübereinkommen od. Intern. Rohstoffvereinbarung); **~ Body**[32b] Internationales Rohstoffgremium; **~ Organization** (ICO[32b]) Internationale Rohstofforganisation

international community Völkergemeinschaft

International Confederation of Free Trade Unions (ICFTU) *(antikommunistischer)* Internationaler Bund Freier Gewerkschaften (IBFG) (*Sitz:* Brüssel)

international convention internationales Übereinkommen *(Berne Convention, Hague Convention, Paris Convention)*

International Convention against the Taking of Hostages[32c] Internationales Übereinkommen gegen Geiselnahme

International Convention for the Prevention of →Pollution from Ships

International Convention for the Prevention of →Pollution of the Sea by Oil

International Convention for the Prevention of New Varieties of Plants[33] Internationales Übereinkommen zum Schutz von Pflanzenzüchtungen

International Convention for the Protection of Performers, Producers of Phonograms and Broadcasting Organizations[34] Internationales Abkommen über den Schutz der ausübenden Künstler, der Hersteller von Tonträgern und der Sendeunternehmen

International Convention for Safe Containers (C. S. C.)[34a] Internationales Übereinkommen über sichere Container

International Convention for the Safety of Life at Sea (SOLAS)[35] Internationales Übereinkommen zum Schutz des menschlichen Lebens auf See

International Convention for the Unification of Certain Rules for Law Relating to Bills of Lading[36] Internationales Abkommen zur Vereinheitlichung bestimmter Regeln des Rechts der Konnossemente

International Convention on Certain Rules Concerning Civil Jurisdiction in Matters of Collision[36a] Internationales Übereinkommen zur Vereinheitlichung von Regeln über die zivilrechtliche Zuständigkeit bei Schiffszusammenstößen

International Convention on Civil Liability for Oil →Pollution Damage

International Convention on Load Lines[36b] Internationales Freibordübereinkommen

International Convention on the Elimination of All Forms of Racial Discrimination[36c] Internationales Übereinkommen zur Beseitigung von jeder Form der Rassendiskriminierung

International Convention on the Establishment of an International Fund for Compensation for Oil →Pollution Damage

International Convention on the Harmonization of Frontier Controls of Goods[36d] *(EG)* Internationales Übereinkommen zur Harmonisierung der Warenkontrollen an den Grenzen

International Convention on the Harmonized

Commodity Description and Coding System[36e] Internationales Übereinkommen über das harmonisierte System zur Bezeichnung und Codierung der Waren *(seit 1. 1. 88 für Zollfestsetzung eingeführt)*

International Convention on the Harmonized System (H. S.) Internationales Übereinkommen über das Harmonisierte System zur Bezeichnung und Codierung der Waren (HS)

International Convention Relating to Cooperation for the Safety of Air Navigation (→European Organization for the Safety of Air Navigation)[36f] Internationales Übereinkommen über Zusammenarbeit zur Sicherung der Luftfahrt (Eurocontrol)

International Convention Relating to the Arrest of Seagoing Ships[36g] Internationales Übereinkommen zur Vereinheitlichung von Regeln über den Arrest in Seeschiffe

International Convention Relating to Intervention on the High Seas in Cases of Oil →Pollution

International Convention Relating to the Limitation of the Liability of Owners of Sea-Going Ships[36h] Internationales Übereinkommen über die Beschränkung der Haftung der Eigentümer von Seeschiffen

International Convention to Faciliate the Importation of Commercial Samples and Advertising Materials[36i] Internationales Abkommen zur Erleichterung der Einfuhr von Warenmustern und Werbematerial

International Cooperation Administration (ICA) *Am* Institution zur Verwaltung der Mittel der amerikanischen Auslandshilfe

International Cooperative Alliance (ICA) Internationaler Genossenschaftsbund (IGB) (*Sitz:* London/Paris)

international copyright internationales Urheberrecht (cf. *Berne Convention, →convention 1.; →Universal Copyright Convention)*

International Cotton Advisory Committee (ICAC) Internationaler beratender Baumwollausschuß

International Council for the Exploration of the Sea (ICES) Internationaler Rat für Meeresforschung

International Council for Monuments and Sites (ICOS-MOS) Internationaler Rat für Denkmalspflege

International Council of Scientific Unions (ICSU) Internationaler Rat Wissenschaftlicher Vereinigungen

Dachorganisation von nationalen Forschungsorganisationen. Die Bundesrepublik Deutschland ist im ~ seit 1952 durch die Deutsche Forschungsgemeinschaft vertreten

International Court of Justice (ICJ)[37] Internationaler Gerichtshof (IGH)

Gegr. 1946. *Sitz:* Den Haag.

Bestellung der 15 für 9 Jahre gewählten Richter erfolgt nach regionalen Gesichtspunkten durch UNO-Generalversammlung und Sicherheitsrat. Nach Art. 31 müssen aber auch sog. Ad-hoc-Richter mitwirken, wenn die Parteien es verlangen. Die Zuständigkeit umfaßt alle dem IGH von den Parteien (Staaten) unterbreiteten Angelegenheiten, sowie die in der Satzung der Vereinten Nationen oder den geltenden Verträgen und Abkommen besonders bezeichneten Fälle (Art. 36 Ziffer 1 des Statuts).

Als juristisches Hauptorgan der Vereinten Nationen (principal juridic organ) erstattet der IGH auch Rechtsgutachten (advisory opinions)

International Covenant, ~ on Civil and Political Rights[37a] Internationaler Pakt über bürgerliche und politische Rechte; **~ on Economic, Social and Cultural Rights**[37b] Internationaler Pakt über wirtschaftliche, soziale und kulturelle Rechte

International Criminal Police Commission Internationale Kriminalpolizei-Kommission (Interpol)

Internationale Behörde zur gegenseitigen Unterstützung bei der Verfolgung von Verbrechen, die den nationalen Rahmen übersteigen. Internationale Koordinierung von Ermittlungsarbeiten. Amtshilfe in Form von Gutachten.

Sitz: Paris. Das Bundeskriminalamt in Wiesbaden arbeitet als deutsches Nationalbüro von Interpol

international custom internationales Gewohnheitsrecht

international data transmission services (datel services) Internationale Datenübertragungsdienste *(z. B. über das Fernsprech- od. Fernschreibesystem)*

International Democratic Union Internationale Demokratische Union (IDU)

international deposit of industrial designs and models internationale Hinterlegung gewerblicher Muster und Modelle *(→Hague Agreement Concerning the ~)*

International Development Association (IDA)[38] Internationale Entwicklungsorganisation

Tochterunternehmen der Weltbank (→IBRD), das den Entwicklungsländern Kredite zu günstigeren und längerfristigen Bedingungen als die Weltbank gewähren kann.

Sitz: Washington, D. C.

Organe: Gouverneursrat (Board of Governors), Direktoren (Executive Directors), Präsident (President)

international E-road network[38a] internationales E-Straßennetz

international economic cooperation internationale wirtschaftliche Zusammenarbeit; **Conference on I~ E~ C~** Konferenz über Internationale Wirtschaftliche Zusammenarbeit (KIWZ) (→*North-South Dialogue)*

International Energy Agency (IEA) Internationale Energie-Agentur (IEA) *(der →OECD)*

international energy program[38b] internationales Energieprogramm

International, ~ Federation of Journalists (IFJ)

Internationaler Journalistenverband *(Sitz:* Brüssel); ~ **Federation of Operational Research Societies** (IFORS) Internationaler Verband von Gesellschaften für Unternehmensforschung; ~ **Federation of University Women** (IFUW) Internationaler Verband der Akademikerinnen *(Sitz:* London); ~ **Federation of Women Lawyers** (IFWL) Internationale Vereinigung der Juristinnen; ~ **Film Festivals** Internationale Filmfestspiele

International Finance Corporation (IFC) Internationale Finanz-Corporation[38]
Ein zur Weltbankgruppe gehörendes internationales Finanzinstitut, das die private Unternehmerinitiative in den Entwicklungsländern anregen will.
Sitz: Washington, D. C.
Organe: Gouverneursrat (Board of Governors), Direktoren (Executive Directors), Präsident (President)

International, ~ Fiscal Association (IFA) Internationale Vereinigung für Steuerrecht; ~ **Fund for Agricultural Development** (IFAD) Internationaler Fonds für Agrarentwicklung; ~ **Fund for Compensation for Oil Pollution Damage**[38c] Internationaler Fonds zur Entschädigung für Ölverschmutzungsschäden; ~ **Health Regulations**[39] Internationale Gesundheitsvorschriften *(der Weltgesundheitsorganisation);* ~ **Hotel Association** (IHA) Internationaler Hotelverband (IHV) *(Sitz: Paris);* ~ **Hydrographic Association**[39a] Internationale Hydrographische Organisation; ~ **Import Certificate** Internationale Einfuhrbescheinigung; ~ **Institute of Refrigeration**[39b] Internationales Kälteinstitut; ~ **Institute for the Unification of Private Law** Internationales Institut für die Vereinheitlichung des Privatrechts; **i~ instruments** internationale Vertragswerke; **i~ jurisdiction** internationale Zuständigkeit

International, ~ Jute Council[39c] Internationaler Juterat; ~ **Jute Organization**[39c] Internationale Jute-Organisation

International Labour Office (ILO) Internationales Arbeitsamt (IAA) (*Sitz:* Genf)
Ständiges Sekretariat der →International Labour Organization

International Labour Organization (ILO)[40] Internationale Arbeitsorganisation (IAO)
Sitz: Genf. *Mitglieder:* über 100 Staaten.
Organe: Internationale Arbeitskonferenz (International Labour Conference), Verwaltungsrat (Governing Body) und Internationales Arbeitsamt (International Labour Office).
Aufgabe: Schaffung von Normen zum Schutze der Arbeitnehmer in Form von Übereinkommen (Conventions) und Empfehlungen (Recommendations), die der Ratifikation durch die Mitgliedstaaten bedürfen. Sammlung und Weiterleitung von Material über Fragen des Arbeitsrechts und der Sozialpolitik

international law internationales Recht, zwischenstaatliches Recht; Völkerrecht *(cf. private ~, public ~);* **binding under** ~ völkerrechtlich verbindlich; **declaration binding under** ~ völkerrechtlich bindende Erklärung; **breach of** ~ Völkerrechtsverletzung; **contrary to** ~ völkerrechtswidrig; **customary** ~ Völkergewohnheitsrecht; **offen|ce (~se) against** ~ völkerrechtliches Delikt; **relating to** ~ völkerrechtlich; **specialist in** ~ Völkerrechtler; **subject of** ~ Völkerrechtssubjekt

International Law Association (ILA) Vereinigung für Internationales Recht
1873 gegründet als privates Diskussionsforum zur Klarstellung und Fortbildung des internationalen Rechts. (Deutsche Landesgruppe ist die Deutsche Vereinigung für Internationales Recht in Heidelberg.)
Ständiges Büro in London.[41]
Alle zwei Jahre findet eine Vollversammlung der Mitglieder statt, über die Berichte (reports) veröffentlicht werden

International Law Commission (ILC) Internationale (Völker-)Rechtskommission (IRK)
Unterorgan des Wirtschafts- und Sozialrats der Vereinten Nationen.
Aufgabe: Vorbereitung einer Kodifikation des Völkerrechts

international law, private ~ internationales Privatrecht (IPR) (→*conflict of laws*)
Das britische internationale Privatrecht beruht im wesentlichen auf →precedents. Nur ausnahmsweise haben Kollisionsregeln gesetzliche Grundlagen (statute law; zu nennen ist hier z. B. der →Foreign Marriage Act). Etwas Besonderes gilt für diejenigen Teile des Commonwealth, deren Rechtsordnungen auf dem französischen Recht beruhen. Hier gelten die international-privatrechtlichen Bestimmungen des Code Civil, die jedoch teilweise durch örtliche Gesetze aufgehoben und ersetzt wurden (z. B. in Mauritius), oder insgesamt einer selbständigen Bearbeitung der französischen Prinzipien weichen mußten (so in dem Zivilgesetzbuch von Nieder-Kanada [Quebec]).
Auch das internationale Privatrecht der Vereinigten Staaten von Amerika ist überwiegend kein →statute law, sondern →common law. Es gibt lediglich vereinzelte weitgehend übereinstimmende gesetzliche international-privatrechtliche Bestimmungen in den Einzelstaaten. In der Bundesgesetzgebung betrifft z. B. das IPR section 1172 Code of Laws of the USA, title 22, betreffend die Eheschließung vor einem Konsul.
Die Rechtsprechung beruft sich fast immer auf →precedents. Sehr selten werden anwendbare gesetzliche Bestimmungen angeführt und noch seltener wird das →Restatement of the Law of Conflict of Laws als Rechtsquelle herangezogen

international law, public ~ Völkerrecht; **public ~ of the sea** Seevölkerrecht; Meeresvölkerrecht; **violation of public** ~ Völkerrechtsverletzung

international legal relations zwischenstaatlicher Rechtsverkehr

International Load Line Certificate Internationales Freibord-Zeugnis

international maritime, ~ arbitration internationale Seeschiedsgerichtsbarkeit; **I~ M~ Arbitration Organization**[41a] Internationale Organisation für Seeschiedgerichtsbarkeit *(→ICC-CMI Rules);* **I~ M~ Organization**[42] (IMO) Internationale Seeschiffahrtsorganisation; **I~ M~ Satellite Organization** (INMARSAT)[42a] Internationale Seefunksatelliten-Organisation

international maritime traffic internationaler Seeverkehr; **Convention on Facilitation of I~ M~ T~**[42b] Übereinkommen zur Erleichterung des internationalen Seeverkehrs

international, ~ market Weltmarkt; **I~ Marketing Federation** (IMF) Dachverband nationaler Marketing-Vereinigungen; **I~ Missionary Council** (IMC) Internationaler Missionsrat (IMR) *(Zusammenfassung der nichtkatholischen Missionen)*

International Monetary Fund (IMF) (FUND)[43] Internationaler Währungsfonds (IWF) (Weltwährungsfonds); **to draw on the ~** auf den IWF ziehen

Sitz: Washington. 151 Mitgliedsländer.
Organe: Gouverneursrat (Board of Governors), Exekutivdirektorium (Executive Directors), geschäftsführender Direktor (Managing Director).
Aufgaben: Erleichterung der währungspolitischen Zusammenarbeit. Förderung des Welthandels. Bereitstellung von Zahlungsbilanz-Krediten bei Zahlungsbilanzschwierigkeiten der Mitgliedstaaten, die aus einer gemeinsamen Kasse, in die jedes Land Beiträge (Quoten) einzahlt, gegeben werden *(cf. special drawing rights)*.
Daneben werden auch Kreditzusagen (standby arrangements) gewährt

international, ~ monetary system Weltwährungssysteme; **~ money order** (IMO) Auslandspostanweisung; **I~ Movement of Catholic Students** (IMCS) Internationale Katholische Studentenbewegung (Pax Romana); **I~ Narcotics Control Board** Internationales Suchtstoff-Kontrollamt (Suchtstoffamt); **I~ Natural Rubber Agreement**[43a] Internationales Naturkautschuk-Übereinkommen; **I~ Office for →Epozootic Diseases; I~ Oil Pollution Damage Compensation Fund** →International Fund for Compensation for Oil Pollution Damage; **I~ Olive Oil Agreement**[43b] Internationales Olivenöl-Übereinkommen; **I~ Olympic Committee** (IOC) Internationales Olympisches Komitee (IOK); **I~ Organization of Employers** (IOE) Internationale Organisation der Arbeitgeber *(Sitz:* Brüssel); **I~ Organization of Legal Metrology**[43c] Internationale Organisation für das gesetzliche Meßwesen; **I~ Patent Classification** (IPC)[43d] Internationale Patentklassifikation;**~ payments** (or **payment transactions**) internationaler Zahlungsverkehr; **~ personality** Völkerrechtssubjekt; **I~ Plant Protection Convention**[44] Internationales Pflanzenschutzabkommen; **~ practices** internationale Gepflogenheiten; **~ preliminary examination** *(PatR)* internationale vorläufige Prüfung

International Press Institute (IPI) Internationales Presseinstitut (*Sitz:* Zürich)

Wichtigste Aufgabe: Verteidigung der Pressefreiheit auf internationaler Ebene

international, I~ Publishers' Association (IPA) Weltbund der Verleger; **I~ Regime of Maritime Ports**[44a] Internationale Rechtsordnung der Seehäfen; **I~ Regulations for Preventing Collisions at Sea**[44b] Internationale Regeln zur Verhütung von Zusammenstößen auf See

international relations, to foster ~ internationale Beziehungen fördern

international, ~ reply coupon internationaler (Rück-)Antwortschein; **I~ Resources Bank** Internationale Rohstoffbank; **I~ Road Federation** (IRF) Internationaler Straßenverband (*Sitz:* Washington); **~ road signs** internationale Verkehrszeichen; **~ road traffic** internationaler Straßenverkehr; **~ sale of goods** internationaler Warenkauf (*→United Nations Convention on Contracts for the International Sale of Goods); ~* **sanitary conventions** internationale Abkommen auf dem Gebiete des Gesundheitswesens; **I~ Sanitary Regulations**[44c] Internationale Gesundheitsvorschriften; **I~ Savings Agreement** Postsparkassenabkommen; **~ search report** *(PatR)* internationaler Recherchenbericht; **I~ Searching Authority** *(PatR)*[44d] Internationale Recherchenbehörde; **~ securities** international gehandelte Wertpapiere

international settlement, Bank for I~ S~s Bank für Internationalen Zahlungsausgleich (→Bank)

International Shipping Federation (ISF) Internationaler Reederverein

Sitz: London. *Aufgabe:* Behandlung sozialer Probleme in der Seeschiffahrt

international standards internationale Richtlinien; völkerrechtliche Verhaltensnormen

International Standardization Organization (ISO) Internationaler Normenausschuß

Organisation zur Schaffung internationaler Normen. *Sitz:* Genf

international, I~ Statistical Institute (I. S. I.) Internationales Statistisches Institut

International Stock Exchange (of the United Kingdom and the Republic of Ireland) Ltd *Br* (Londoner) Internationale Wertpapierbörse (*→domestic equities, →gilt-edged securities, →options, →foreign equities*)

Sie ist als Überwachungsorganisation des Wertpapiermarktes eine →Recognized Investment Exchange (RIE) *(cf. Securities Association Ltd)*

International, ~ Student Service (ISS) Weltstudentenwerk; **~ Sugar Agreement** Internationales Zuckerabkommen; **~ Sugar Council** Internationaler Zuckerrat

International Swap Dealers Association (ISDA) Internationale Vereinigung der →Swap-Händler
Von 10 in New York ansässigen Banken gegründete selbständige Vereinigung, die jetzt weit über 50 Mitglieder aus aller Welt umfaßt

International Telecommunication Convention[45] Internationaler Fernmeldevertrag
1959 in Genf von 102 Staaten unterzeichnet mit folgenden 3 Ausschüssen: International Frequency Registration Board (I. F. R. B.) Internationaler Ausschuß zur Frequenzregistrierung; International Telegraph and Telephone Consultative Committee (C. C. I. T. T.) Internationaler Beratender Ausschuß für den Telegrafen- und Fernsprechdienst; International Radio Consultative Committee (C. C. I. R.) Internationaler Beratender Ausschuß für den Funkdienst

International Telecommunications Satellite Organization[46] Internationale Fernmeldesatellitenorganisation (→*Intelsat*)

International Telecommunication Union (ITU) Internationale Organisation für das Fernmeldewesen *(heute Sonderorganisation der Vereinten Nationen)*
Sitz: Genf. *Gesetzliche Grundlage:* →International Telecommunication Convention.
Aufgabe: Festsetzung internationaler Vorschriften für die Regelung des Fernmeldewesens; Entwicklung der Fernmeldetechnik; Verteilung der Rundfunkwellen

international, I~ Tin Agreement[46a] Internationales Zinnübereinkommen; **I~ Tin Council** Internationaler Zinnrat; **I~ Tourist Association** (I. T. A.) Internationale Touristenvereinigung; **I~ Tracing Service** Internationaler Suchdienst

international trade internationaler Handel; Welthandel; **I~ T~ Administration** (ITA) *Am* Internationale Handelsverwaltung (Abteilung des Department of Commerce); **I~ T~ Center** (ITC) Internationales Handelszentrum *(gemeinsames Sonderorgan des →GATT und der →UNCTAD; Sitz in Genf)*; **I~ T~ Commission** (ITC) *Am* Bundesbehörde für den Außenhandel; ~ **in textiles** internationaler Handel mit Textilien (→Multifibre Arrangement); ~ **law** internationales Handelsrecht (→*United Nations Commission on I~ T~ Law [UNCITRAL]*); ~ **unionism** internationales Gewerkschaftswesen (→trade unionism); **Convention on I~ T~ in Endangered Species of →Wild Fauna and Flora**; **→Standard I~ T~ Classification**

international, I~ Transport Workers' Federation (ITWF) Internationaler Transportarbeiterverband (*Sitz:* London); **I~ Tribunal for the Law of the Sea** (geplanter) Seegerichtshof; **I~ Tropical Timber Agreement**[46b] Internationales Tropenholz-Übereinkommen; **I~ Tropical Timber Organization** (ITTO) Internationale Tropenholzorganisation; ~ **understanding** internationale Verständigung; ~ **union** internationaler Verband, Weltverband; *Am* Gewerkschaft mit Mitgliedern in anderen Ländern, bes. in Kanada; **I~ Union for the Conservation of Nature and Natural Resources** (IUCN) Internationale Union zur Erhaltung der Natur und der natürlichen Hilfsquellen; **I~ Union of Local Authorities** (IULA) Internationaler Gemeindeverband (*Sitz:* Den Haag); **I~ Union of Railways** (UIC)[47] Internationaler Eisenbahnverband; ~ **usage** internationaler Brauch; ~ **waters** internationale Gewässer; **I~ →Whaling Commission; I~ Wheat Agreement**[47a] Internationale Weizenübereinkunft 1986; **I~ Wheat Council** Internationaler Weizenrat; **I~ Wine Office** Internationales Weinamt; **I~ Wool Textile Organization** (IWTO) Internationale Organisation für Wollstoffe; **I~ Youth Hostel Federation** (IYHF) Internationaler Jugendherbergsverband (*Sitz:* Kopenhagen)

internationally in internationaler Hinsicht; auf internationalem Wege; ~ **protected person** völkerrechtlich geschützte Person; **Convention on the Prevention and Punishment of Crimes against ~ Protected Persons, including Diplomatic Agents**[48] Übereinkommen über die Verhütung, Verfolgung und Bestrafung von Straftaten gegen völkerrechtlich geschützte Personen einschließlich Diplomaten (Diplomatenschutzkonvention)

internationalization Internationalisierung

internationalize *v* für international erklären, internationalisieren

internecine war gegenseitiger Vernichtungskrieg

internee Internierte(r)

internment Internierung; **to be released from an ~ camp** aus e-m Internierungslager entlassen werden

internuncio *(VölkerR)* Internuntius *(dem Gesandten gleichgestellter diplomatischer Vertreter des Vatikans in kleineren Staaten)*

inter-office trading (Wertpapier-)Handel im Telefonverkehr

Interparliamentary Union (IPU) Interparlamentarische Union
Sitz: Genf. *Mitglieder:* Abgeordnete der Parlamente verschiedener Staaten

interpellate *v (im ausländischen, bes. französischen Parlament)* interpellieren, e-e Anfrage richten an

interpellation *parl* Interpellation, *(große)* Anfrage; *Br* Vorladung

interpenetration gegenseitige Durchdringung; ~ **of capital markets** Verflechtung der Kapitalmärkte

interperiod tax allocation *Am* Zuordnung des Steueraufwands zur Steuerschuld verschiedener Perioden

interplanetary interplanetarisch; ~ **travel** Raumfahrt

interplead *v (im Wege des Beanspruchersstreits)* gerichtlich untereinander austragen, wer der wahre berechtigte Gläubiger ist *(cf. interpleader)*

interpleader[49] prozessuale Verfahrensmöglichkeit der Herbeiführung e-s Beanspruchersstreits *(zwischen rivalisierenden, gleichzeitig dasselbe beanspruchenden Gläubigern zur gerichtl. Feststellung des wahren Berechtigten);* ~ **relief** gerichtlicher Rechtsschutz im Wege der Herbeiführung e-s Beanspruchersstreits; **sheriff's** ~ interpleader des Gerichtsvollziehers, der die Zwangsvollstreckung in e-e vermeintlich dem Vollstreckungsschuldner gehörige Sache durchzuführen beabsichtigt, die ein Dritter für sich selbst in Anspruch nimmt; **stakeholder's** ~ *(dem Gläubigerstreit des § 75 ZPO vergleichbares)* interpleader des klagbedrohten od. bereits beklagten Schuldners *(der seine Schuld als solche nicht bestreitet)*

Interpol →International Criminal Police Commission

interpolate *v* einschalten; *(Worte in e-e Urkunde)* einsetzen, einfügen; *(Text)* durch Einschaltung ändern, fälschen

interpolation Interpolation; Einschaltung, Einschiebung; eingefügte Stelle; Textfälschung

interpose *v* vorbringen, einlegen; vermitteln (between zwischen); **to** ~ **in an action** e-m Verfahren beitreten (→*intervener*); **to** ~ **an objection** e-n Einwand vorbringen; e-n Einspruch einlegen; **to** ~ **a veto** ein Veto vorbringen

interpret *v* auslegen, interpretieren; (ver)dolmetschen; **to** ~ **data** *(EDV)* Daten deuten (od. auswerten); **to** ~ **broadly** weit auslegen; **to** ~ **closely** eng auslegen; **to** ~ **extensively** erweiternd (od. extensiv) auslegen; **to** ~ **liberally** großzügig (od. weit) auslegen; **to** ~ **restrictively** einschränkend (od. restriktiv) auslegen; **to** ~ **strictly** eng auslegen

interpreting Dolmetschen; Auslegung; **simultaneous** ~ Simultandolmetschen

interpretation Auslegung, Interpretation; Dolmetschen; Deutung (od. Auswertung) *(von Daten);* ~ **clause** Interpretationsklausel, Auslegungsbestimmung; ~ **of a contract** Vertragsauslegung; **authentic** ~ authentische Interpretation *(durch den Gesetzgeber);* **broad** ~ weite Auslegung; **close** ~ enge Auslegung; **extensive** ~ extensive (od. erweiternde) Auslegung; **grammatical** ~ grammatikalische Auslegung; **legal** ~ Legalinterpretation; **liberal** ~ großzügige (od. weite) Auslegung; **restrictive** ~ restriktive (od. einschränkende) Auslegung; **strict** ~ enge Auslegung; **simultaneous** ~ Simultandolmetschen

interpreter Dolmetscher(in); ~ **examination** Dolmetscherprüfung; ~**s' fees** Dolmetschergebühren; ~**s' school** Dolmetscherschule, -institut; **allowance paid to** ~**s** Dolmetschergebühren; **chief** ~ Chefdolmetscher; **court** ~ Gerichtsdolmetscher; **to act as** ~ als Dolmetscher tätig sein; **to call in an** ~ e-n Dolmetscher zuziehen; **to secure the services** (or **assistance**) **of** ~**s** Dolmetscher zuziehen; **to supply an** ~ e-n Dolmetscher stellen

interracial strife (or **conflict**) Rassenkonflikt

interregional interregional, zwischengebietlich; ~ **air services** interregionaler Luftverkehr

interregnum Interregnum, Zwischenherrschaft

interrelated, ~ **problems** zusammenhängende Probleme; **to be closely** ~ in enger Wechselbeziehung stehen

interrelation wechselseitige Beziehung; gegenseitige Abhängigkeit; **capital** ~ Kapitalverflechtung

interrogation Befragung; Vernehmung, Verhör; ~ **of the parties** Parteivernehmung; **police** ~ polizeiliche Vernehmung; **record of** ~ Vernehmungsprotokoll

interrogator Fragender; Vernehmungsbeamter, Vernehmender

interrogatories formelle Parteibefragung; schriftliche Beweisfragen *(an e-e Prozeßpartei vor der Verhandlung, die diese schriftlich unter Eid beantworten muß);* **to serve** ~ **on the other party** der anderen Partei schriftl. Beweisfragen zur Beantwortung zustellen

interrupt *v* unterbrechen; **the period shall be** ~**ed** die Frist wird unterbrochen

interruption Unterbrechung; ~ **of business** Geschäftsunterbrechung; ~ **of the (running of the) period of limitation** (or **prescriptive period**) Unterbrechung der Verjährung; ~ **of proceedings** Unterbrechung des Verfahrens; ~ **of traffic** Verkehrsstockung

intersection Schnittpunkt; (Straßen-)Kreuzung; **stop at** ~ *(Verkehr)* Halt vor der Kreuzung

intersessional committee Intersessionsausschuß

interstate zwischenstaatlich; *Am* zwischen den Einzelstaaten *(cf. intrastate);* ~ **commerce** *Am* Wirtschaftsverkehr zwischen den Einzelstaaten (→*Commerce Clause;* →*intrastate commerce);* **I**~ **Commerce Clause** *Am* →Commerce

Clause; **in ~ commerce** *Am* im Geschäftsverkehr über die Grenzen e-s Einzelstaates hinaus; **to be engaged in ~ commerce** *Am* über die Grenzen e-s Einzelstaates hinaus geschäftlich tätig sein

Interstate Commerce Commission (ICC) *Am* Bundesverkehrsbehörde
Bundesbehörde zur Beaufsichtigung des gesamten Transportwesens zwischen den Einzelstaaten (Eisenbahn-, Omnibus- und gewerblicher Lastkraftwagenverkehr)

interstate, ~ compact *Am* Vertrag zwischen zwei od. mehreren Einzelstaaten *(über gemeinsame Probleme)*; **~ conflict of laws** *Am* interlokales Privatrecht; **~ highway** *Am* Bundesautobahn; **~ rendition** *Am* Auslieferung *(e-r verdächtigen Person od. e-s Strafgefangenen)* zwischen den Einzelstaaten; **~ theft** *Am* Diebstahl, der über die Grenzen mehrerer Einzelstaaten hinweg verfolgt wird; **~ trade** *Am* zwischenstaatlicher Handel

interstellar, ~ aviation Raumfahrt; (~) **space** Weltraum

inter-union zwischengewerkschaftlich

interurban zwischen Städten (verkehrend); **~ traffic** Überlandverkehr

intervene *v* eingreifen, einschreiten; intervenieren, vermitteln, sich einmischen; dazwischentreten, -liegen; sich *(in der Zwischenzeit)* ereignen, eintreten *(Ereignis)*; *(e-m Verfahren)* beitreten; **to ~ in arbitral proceedings** dem Schiedsverfahren beitreten; **to ~ in case of need** *(WechselR)* als Notadressat *(für den Wechselverpflichteten)* eintreten; **to ~ in a dispute** in e-m Streit vermitteln; **to ~ on the foreign exchange market** in den Devisenmarkt eingreifen *(with the aim of influencing the rate of exchange; →intervention point)*; **to ~ in the opposition proceedings** *(PatR)* dem Einspruchsverfahren beitreten; **to ~ in a suit for divorce** e-m Ehescheidungsprozeß beitreten *(z.B. die des Ehebruchs bezichtigte Person)*

intervening, ~ causation überholende Kausalität; **~ cause** den Kausalzusammenhang unterbrechende Ursache; **~ party** *(dem Verfahren)* beitretende Partei; Nebenintervenient (→*intervener*); **~ rights** *(PatR)* Zwischenbenutzungsrechte; **~ years** dazwischenliegende Jahre

intervener *(Zivilprozeß)* Nebenintervenient, Streithelfer *(jd, der e-m Rechtsstreit zur Wahrung eigener od. öffentlicher Interessen beitritt)*; **to appear as ~** als Nebenintervenient auftreten

intervention Eingriff, Eingreifen, Einschreiten; Intervention, Einmischung *(staatl. Eingriff in Wirtschaftsleben)*; *(VölkerR)* Intervention *(unzulässige Einmischung e-s Staates in Verhältnisse e-s anderen Staates, cf. intercession)*; *(WechselR)* Intervention *(Ehreneintritt e-s Dritten bei Nichtannahme od. Nichtzahlung e-s Wechsels)*; *(Zivilprozeß)* Nebenintervention, Beitritt zu e-m Prozeß *(cf. intervener)*; *(EG)* Intervention, Eingriff; *(Devisenhandel)* Intervention, Eingriff *(der Zentralbanken, cf. ~ point)*; *(Börse)* Intervention, Eingreifen *(z.B. der Effektenbanken bei starken Kursveränderungen einzelner Wertpapiere)*; **~ agency** *(EG)* Interventionsstelle; **~ for hono(u)r** *(WechselR)* Ehreneintritt, Ehrenannahme; **~ point** *(Devisenhandel)* Interventionspunkt *(lower unterer, upper oberer; cf. floating 1.)*; **~ power** Eingriffsbefugnis; **~ price** *(EG)* Interventionspreis; *(Börse)* Interventionskurs; **~ stocks** *(EG)* Interventionsbestände; **acceptance by ~** *(WechselR)* Ehrenannahme *(e-s notleidenden Wechsels)*; **armed ~** bewaffnete Intervention; **government ~** Eingreifen der Regierung; **non-~** Nichteinmischung; **notice of ~ in opposition proceedings** *(PatR)* Antrag auf Beitritt zum Einspruchsverfahren; **police ~** Einschreiten der Polizei; **policy of ~** Interventionspolitik; **policy of non-~** Nichteinmischungspolitik; **state ~** Eingreifen des Staates; **third party ~** Einschreiten e-s Dritten; **the dollar rate has reached the lower point of ~** der Dollarkurs hat den unteren Interventionspunkt erreicht

interview Interview, Befragung; Vorstellung(sgespräch) *(bei Bewerbungen)*; **~ bias** *(Meinungsforschung)* Beeinflussung des Ergebnisses der Befragung *(z.B. durch falsches Verhalten des Befragers)*; **to give an ~** ein Interview geben

interview *v (jdn)* interviewen; *(jdn in e-m Interview)* befragen; *(mit jdm)* ein Vorstellungsgespräch durchführen

interviewee *(im Interview)* Befragter

interviewer Interviewer, Befrager

inter vivos unter Lebenden; **~ trust** Trust unter Lebenden; **gift ~** Schenkung zu Lebzeiten *(opp. testamentary gift)*

interzonal Interzonen-; interzonal

intestacy Sterben ohne Hinterlassung e-s Testaments; **distribution on ~** Nachlaßteilung bei gesetzlicher Erbfolge; **share (in an estate) under an ~** gesetzlicher Erbteil; **succession on ~** gesetzliche Erbfolge; **the property goes by ~** der Nachlaß fällt an die gesetzlichen Erben; **to succeed to the estate of a deceased person on ~ or under a will** jdn auf Grund gesetzlicher oder gewillkürter Erbfolge (Testament) beerben; **to succeed to** (or **inherit**) **land on ~** Grundbesitz als gesetzlicher Erbe erben; **an illegitimate child has the right to succeed on the ~ of either parent** *Br*[50] ein nichteheliches Kind ist gesetzlicher Erbe e-s Elternteils; **parents have the right to succeed on the ~ of an illegitimate child** *Br*[50] Eltern sind gesetzliche Erben e-s nichtehelichen Kindes; **to have the**

right to succeed on the ~ of gesetzlicher Erbe sein von

intestate ohne Testament (verstorben); Erblasser, der kein Testament hinterlassen hat; Intestats-; ~ **decedent** *Am* Intestaterblasser, Erblasser ohne Testament; **~'s estate**[51] Intestatnachlaß, Nachlaß e-s ohne Testament Verstorbenen; ~ **share** *Am* gesetzliches Erbteil; **share in an ~'s estate** gesetzliches Erbteil; **to succeed to an ~'s estate** als gesetzl. Erbe erben

intestate succession[51] Intestaterbfolge, gesetzliche Erbfolge; **estate passing by will or by ~** Nachlaß, der durch Testament oder kraft gesetzlicher Erbfolge auf den Erben übergeht; **by testate or ~** durch testamentarische oder gesetzliche Erbfolge

intestate successor *Am* Intestaterbe

intestate, person entitled to (a share in) an ~'s estate Intestaterbe, gesetzlicher Erbe *(e-s Erblassers, der kein Testament hinterlassen hat);* **right to succeed to the estate of an ~** gesetzliches Erbrecht; **to die ~** ohne Hinterlassung e-s Testamentes sterben; **to succeed to an ~'s estate** als gesetzlicher Erbe erben

intestine disorders *Am pol* innere Unruhen

intimacy Intimität; intime Beziehung; ehewidrige Beziehung

intimidate *v* einschüchtern; **to ~ a witness** e-n Zeugen *(durch Drohungen)* einschüchtern

intimidation of witnesses Einschüchterung von Zeugen, Zeugennötigung

intoxicant berauschendes Mittel; Rauschgift

intoxicate *v* betrunken machen; berauschen

intoxicated betrunken; **driving while ~** (DWI) *Am* Fahren in betrunkenem Zustand

intoxicating liquors alkoholische Getränke (*Br* spirits, beer, cider, wine and sweets); **smuggling of ~** Alkoholschmuggel

intoxication Betrunkenheit; Alkoholvergiftung; Rausch; **in a state of ~** in betrunkenem Zustand

intra-brand competition Wettbewerb unter verschiedenen Händlern ein und desselben Produktes *(→interbrand competition)*

intra-Community, ~ frontiers *(EG)* innergemeinschaftliche Grenzen; ~ **trade** *(EG)* innergemeinschaftlicher Handel *(opp. trade with third countries)*

intra-company innerhalb e-r Gesellschaft; innerbetrieblich *(cf. intercompany)*

intra-departmental innerbetrieblich

intra-enterprise conspiracy →conspiracy 2.

intra-European trade innereuropäischer Handel

intra-German, ~ relations innerdeutsche Beziehungen; ~ **trade** innerdeutscher Handel *(Waren-, Dienstleistungs- und Verrechnungsverkehr zwischen der BRD und der DDR; →German Federal Republic and →German Democratic Republic)*

intra-group konzernintern; ~ **holdings** Beteiligungen zwischen Konzernunternehmen; ~ **sales and purchases** konzerninterne Umsätze

intra-industrial studies Betriebsvergleiche

intramural innerhalb der Mauern *(e-r Stadt od. Universität; opp. extramural)*

intrastate *Am* innerstaatlich, innerhalb e-s Einzelstaates *(cf. interstate);* ~ **commerce** *Am* Wirtschaftsverkehr innerhalb e-s Einzelstaates; ~ **use** *Am* Benutzung *(e-s Warenzeichens)* innerhalb e-s Einzelstaates

intra vires ("within the powers") innerhalb der rechtlichen Befugnisse *(e-r juristischen Person; opp. ultra vires)*

intransigence *bes. pol* mangelnde Kompromißbereitschaft, Unnachgiebigkeit

intransigent *bes. pol* kompromißlos, radikal; Radikaler

intrigue Intrige; geheimer Plan; **~s** Machenschaften

intrigue *v* intrigieren (against sb. gegen jdn)

intriguer Intrigant

intrinsic innerlich; wirklich, eigentlich *(opp. extrinsic);* ~ **defect** innerer Mangel; ~ **evidence** reiner Urkundenbeweis *(ohne jede Ergänzung von außerhalb der Urkunde);* ~ **value** wirklicher (innerer) Wert; Substanzwert *(e-s Unternehmens);* **articles of ~ or sentimental value** Gegenstände von materiellem oder ideellem Wert

introduce *v (Personen, Maßnahmen, neue Ware, neue Ideen etc)* einführen; *(Thema)* anschneiden, zur Sprache bringen; **to ~ a person to sb.** jdn jdm vorstellen; jdn mit jdm bekanntmachen; **to ~ oneself** sich vorstellen; sich einführen; **to ~ a Bill** e-n Gesetzesentwurf einbringen *(Br into Parliament, Am into Congress);* **to ~ customs duties** Zölle einführen; **to ~ evidence** Beweis antreten; **to ~ goods into a country** Waren in ein Land *(neu)* einführen; Waren in ein Land bringen; **to ~ goods into** (or **on**) **the market** Waren auf den Markt bringen; Waren in den Markt *(neu)* einführen; **to ~ a new line** e-e neue Ware(nart) einführen *(in e-m Geschäft);* **to ~ a new method** e-e neue Methode einführen; **to ~ sb. into office** jdn in sein Amt einführen; **to ~ on the stock exchange** (or **market**) *(Wertpapiere)* an der Börse einführen; **may I ~ to you Mr. X** darf ich Ihnen Herrn X vorstellen

introduction Einführung; Vorstellung, Bekanntmachung; Einführung, Einleitung *(e-s Buches etc); parl* Einbringung *(e-s Gesetzesent-*

wurfs); ~ **into the market** Markteinführung; ~ **of a motion of censure** *parl* Einbringung e-s Mißtrauensantrages; ~ **offer** Einführungsangebot; ~ **of securities to official quotation on the stock exchange** *Br* Einführung von Wertpapieren zur amtlichen Notierung an der Börse; **letter of** ~ Einführungsschreiben

introductory Einführungs-; einführend; ~ **offer** Einführungsangebot; ~ **price** Einführungspreis; Einführungskurs; ~ **steps** einleitende Schritte; ~ **words** einleitende Worte

intrude *v* eindringen (on in); sich eindrängen (into in); sich aufdrängen (on, upon); *(Besitz)* stören

intruder Eindringling; Besitzstörer

intrusion Eindringen (into in); Aufdrängen (upon); Besitzstörung; rechtswidrige Inbesitznahme; ~ **upon sb.'s privacy** Eindringen in jds Intimsphäre

intrust *v Am* →entrust *v*

in trust zu treuen Händen (→*trust 2.*)

inure *v bes. Am* in Kraft treten, wirksam werden, sich auswirken; **to** ~ **oneself (sb.) to** sich (jdn) gewöhnen an; **to** ~ **to the benefit of sb.** jdm zugute kommen

invade *v* einfallen, eindringen in; **to** ~ **a country** in ein Land einfallen; **to** ~ **the principal** *Am* das Kapital angreifen; **to** ~ **sb.'s rights** in jds Rechte eingreifen, jds Rechte verletzen

invader Eindringling; Invasor

invalid 1. *bes. Br* Invalide; Arbeits-, Dienst-, Erwerbsunfähiger *(durch Krankheit od. Verletzung);* arbeits-, dienst-, erwerbsunfähig; kriegsbeschädigt

invalid 2. (rechts)ungültig, unwirksam, kraftlos; ~ **argument** unverfechtbares Argument; ~ **claim** nicht einklagbare Forderung; ~ **will** ungültiges Testament; **a patent declared** ~ ein Patent, das für nichtig erklärt worden ist; **to become** ~ ungültig werden

invalidate *v* ungültig machen; für ungültig (od. nichtig) erklären; **to** ~ **an agreement** (or **contract**) e-n Vertrag für nichtig erklären; **to** ~ **a will** ein Testament ungültig machen

invalidation Ungültigmachen; Ungültigkeitserklärung, Nichtigerklärung; Kraftloserklärung; ~ **of a patent** Nichtigerklärung e-s Patents; ~ **of securities** Kraftloserklärung von Wertpapieren

invalidity (Rechts-)Ungültigkeit, Nichtigkeit; Invalidität, Arbeits-, Erwerbs-, Berufsunfähigkeit; ~ **benefit** *(Sozialvers.)* Leistung bei Invalidität;~ **care allowance** *Br* Pflegegeld *(für Pflege Schwerbehinderter);* ~ **of a contract** Nichtigkeit e-s Vertrages; ~ **pension**[52] Invaliditätsrente; Rente wegen Berufs- od. Erwerbsunfähigkeit; ~ **of a legal transaction due to a defect of form** Nichtigkeit e-s Rechtsgeschäfts wegen Formmangels; **declaration of** ~ Ungültigkeitserklärung, Nichtigkeitserklärung

invariable unveränderlich, ständig; ~ **practice of a court** ständige Rechtsprechung

invasion Invasion; Eingriff (of in); ~ **of a country** Eindringen *(feindlicher Truppen)* in ein Land; ~ **of privacy** Eingriff in die Intimsphäre

invent *v* erfinden; **to** ~ **an excuse** e-e Entschuldigung ersinnen

invention *(PatR)* Erfindung; ~ **described in the patent specification** in der Patentschrift beschriebene Erfindung; ~ **made under contract** Auftragserfindung; ~ **of an employee** (or ~ **made by an employee**) Erfindung e-s Arbeitnehmers; Arbeitnehmererfindung; ~ **priority** Erfindungspriorität

invention, according to the ~ erfindungsgemäß; **commissioned** ~ Auftragserfindung; **disclosure of an** ~ Offenbarung e-r Erfindung; **exercise of an** ~ Ausübung e-r Erfindung; **exploitation of an** ~ Verwertung e-r Erfindung; **joint** ~ gemeinsame Erfindung; **level of** ~ Erfindungshöhe; **novelty of the** ~ Neuheit der Erfindung; **patent for** ~ Erfindungspatent; **priority of** ~ Erfindungspriorität; **reduction to practice of the** ~ praktische Verwertung der Erfindung; **right in an** ~ Recht an e-r Erfindung; **secrecy of** ~**s** Geheimhaltung von Erfindungen; **standard of** ~ Erfindungshöhe; **subject matter of an** ~ Gegenstand e-r Erfindung; Erfindungsgegenstand; **title of the** ~ Bezeichnung der Erfindung; **unexploited** ~ nicht verwertete Erfindung; **use of the** ~ Benutzung der Erfindung; **works** ~ Betriebserfindung

invention, to amount to an ~ Erfindungshöhe haben; **to carry the** ~ **into effect** die Erfindung ausführen; **to conceal an** ~ e-e Erfindung verborgen halten; **to determine priority of the** ~ die Priorität der Erfindung bestimmen (→*interference proceedings*); **to exploit an** ~ e-e Erfindung auswerten; **to have an** ~ **patented** e-e Erfindung patentieren lassen; **to reduce an** ~ **to practice** e-e Erfindung praktisch verwerten; **this** ~ **relates to** diese Erfindung betrifft; **to use the** ~ die Erfindung nutzen; **to utilize the** ~ **commercially** die Erfindung gewerbsmäßig verwerten

inventive *(PatR)* erfinderisch; ~ **concept(ion)** *(PatR)* Erfindungsgedanke; ~ **level** Erfindungshöhe; ~ **merit** erfinderische Leistung

inventive step erfinderische Tätigkeit; Erfindungshöhe; **lack of** ~ mangelnde Erfindungshöhe; **to deny the ~** die Erfindungshöhe verneinen; **to involve an ~** auf e-r erfinderischen Tätigkeit beruhen

inventiveness Erfindungsgabe; *(PatR)* Erfindungshöhe; **lack of ~** mangelnde Erfindungshöhe

inventor *(PatR)* Erfinder; **~'s certificate** Erfinderschein; **award to ~s** Erfindervergütung; **designation of the ~** Erfindernennung; **employee ~** angestellter Erfinder; **joint ~(s)** Miterfinder; **mention of the ~** Erfindernennung; **protection of ~s** Erfinderschutz; **right of the ~ to be mentioned** Recht auf Erfindernennung; **sole ~** Einzelerfinder

inventorship Erfindereigenschaft; **joint ~** Miterfinderschaft

inventories (Waren-)Vorräte, Bestände; Lagerbestände; **provision for replacement of ~** *Am (Bilanz)* Rückstellung für die Auffüllung des Lagerbestandes; **reduction of ~** Lagerabbau; **to reduce ~** Lager abbauen

inventory Warenvorrat, Warenbestand; Lager; *(HandelsR)* Inventar, *(zum Betrieb gehörige)* Einrichtungsgegenstände; Verzeichnis *(aller Vermögensgegenstände und Schulden);* Inventur *(Aufnahme des Inventars);* Bestandsaufnahme; *(ErbR)* Inventar, Nachlaßverzeichnis;[53] **~ audit** Inventurprüfung; **~ book** Inventarbuch; **~ changes** Lagerbestandsveränderungen; **~ clearance** Räumung des Lagers; **~ control** Lager(bestands)kontrolle; **~ depreciation** *(SteuerR)* Abschreibung auf Lagervorräte; **~ investment** Lagerinvestition; **~ item** Inventarposten, Inventarstück; **~ liquidation** *Am* Lagerabbau; **~ listings** Bestandsverzeichnis; **~ loan** Lagerfinanzierung durch Kredite; **~ period** *(ErbR)* Inventarfrist; **~ price decline** *Am (Bilanz)* Wertminderung der Bestände; **~ of property** Vermögensverzeichnis; **~ reserve** *(Bilanz)* Rückstellungen für Lagerabwertungen; **~ sale** Inventur(aus)verkauf; **~ sheet** Inventarverzeichnis; **~-taking** Aufstellung des Inventars; Bestandsaufnahme; Inentur; **~ turnover** Lagerumschlag; **~ valuation** Lagerbestandsbewertung; Bewertung des Vorratsvermögens; **~ value** Inventarwert

inventory, annual ~ jährliche Bestandsaufnahme, jährliche Inventur; **book ~** *Am* Buchwert der Lagerbestände; Buchinventur; **business ~** Geschäftsinventar; **closing ~** End(waren)bestand; Abschlußinventur; **filing of the ~** *(ErbR)* Inventarerrichtung *(Einreichung des Nachlaßverzeichnisses beim Gericht);* **opening ~** Anfangs(waren)bestand; Eröffnungsinventur; **perpetual ~** *Am* permanente Inventur; **physical ~** körperliche Bestandsaufnahme (od. Inventur); **~ power** Untersuchungsbefugnis; **taking of an ~** →~-taking

inventory, to draw up (or **make, take**) **an ~** ein Inventar (od. Bestandsverzeichnis) aufstellen; inventarisieren; Inventur machen; **to exhibit an ~ and account** *Br (ErbR)* ein Inventar errichten und Rechenschaft ablegen; **to file an ~ with the Court** *Am (ErbR)* ein Inventar bei Gericht einreichen; **to include in an ~** in ein Bestandsverzeichnis aufnehmen

inventory *v* Inventar (od. Bestand) aufnehmen; inventarisieren

invest *v (Geld)* anlegen, investieren, hineinstekken (in in); **incentives to ~** Investitionsanreize; **to ~ sb. with** jdn versehen (od. ausstatten) mit; **to ~ sb. with full authority** (or **powers**) jdn mit Vollmacht versehen, jdn bevollmächtigen; **to ~ capital in a business** Kapital in e-m Geschäft anlegen; Kapital in ein Geschäft stekken; **to ~ (one's money) in (real and leasehold) property** *Br* (**real estate** *Am*) sein Geld in Grundbesitz anlegen; **to ~ money at short notice** Geld kurzfristig anlegen; **to ~ the money permanently** das Geld fest anlegen; **to ~ one's money well** sein Geld gut anlegen; **to ~ sb. with an office** jdn *(feierlich)* in ein Amt einsetzen; **to ~ time in** Zeit investieren in

invested, ~ capital angelegtes Kapital; Anlagekapital; Kapitaleinlage *(e-s Gesellschafters);* **yield on ~ capital** Kapitalertrag; **amount of money ~** Höhe der Geldanlage

investing, ~ member (of a building society) *Br* Bausparer, dessen Zuteilungsdarlehen noch nicht ausgezahlt ist; **~ public** Anlagepublikum

investigate *v* untersuchen; erforschen, ermitteln; nachforschen; **to ~ the causes of unemployment** die Gründe der Arbeitslosigkeit erforschen (od. untersuchen); **to ~ a crime** ein Verbrechen untersuchen; wegen e-s Verbrechens Ermittlungen anstellen; **to ~ sth. statistically** statistische Erhebungen anstellen

investigating, ~ authority Untersuchungs-, Ermittlungsbehörde; **~ committee** Untersuchungsausschuß; **~ magistrate** Untersuchungsrichter

investigation Untersuchung; Erforschung, Ermittlung; Nachforschung; **~ of an accident** Unfalluntersuchung; **~ of a crime** Untersuchung e-s Verbrechens; **~s by the police** polizeiliche Ermittlungen; **~ service** (Zoll-)Fahndungsdienst; **~ of title** Prüfung der Eigentums- und Belastungsverhältnisse von Grundbesitz (→*title 2.);* **criminal ~** Ermittlungen *(durch Staatsanwalt oder Polizei);* **Criminal I~ Department** (C. I. D.) *Br*[54] Kriminalpolizei *(Oberste Kriminalpolizeibehörde);* **judicial ~** gerichtliche Untersuchung; **preliminary ~** Voruntersuchung; **result of the ~** Untersuchungsergebnis; **statistical ~s** statistische Erhebungen; **the matter is under ~** die Sache wird untersucht; **to carry out ~s** Untersuchungen (od. Ermittlungen) durchführen; **to cause ~s to be made** Nachforschungen anstellen lassen; **to complete ~s** Ermittlungen abschließen; **to conduct ~s** Untersuchungen (od. Nachforschungen, Ermittlungen) anstellen (od. durchführen); **to discontinue** (or **drop**) **~s** Ermittlungen einstellen; **to institute ~s** Untersuchungen (od. Ermittlungen) einleiten; **to make an ~** e-e Prüfung vornehmen; e-e Untersuchung durchführen; **to make ~s** Nachforschungen (od. Erhebungen) anstellen

investigator mit e-r Untersuchung betrauter Beamter, Untersuchungsbeamter; Ermittlungsbeamter; *(PatR)* Prüfer; *(MMF)* Befrager, Interviewer

investigatory, ~ material Ermittlungsmaterial; **~ powers** *Am* Untersuchungsbefugnisse

investiture Investitur; *(feierl.)* Amtseinsetzung

investment Investition, (Geld-, Kapital-)Anlage; Beteiligung (in a company an e-r Gesellschaft); Einlage *(e-s Gesellschafters)*; **~s** *(Bilanz)* Wertpapiere

investment, ~s were checked die Investitionen wurden gebremst; **to effect ~s** Investitionen vornehmen; **to go in for long-term (short-term) ~s** langfristig (kurzfristig) anlegen; **to hold an ~** im Besitz e-r Geldanlage sein, Aktien besitzen; **to issue ~ certificates in small units** Investmentzertifikate in kleinen Stücken ausgeben; **to issue ~ shares to the general public** Investmentanteile an die breite Öffentlichkeit ausgeben; **to make a good ~** Geld gut investieren (od. anlegen); **to promote ~** die Investition fördern

investment, ~s abroad Kapitalanlagen im Ausland; ausländische Investitionen; **~ account** (Finanz-)Anlagenkonto

investment activity Investitionstätigkeit; **brisk ~** rege Investitionstätigkeit; **checking of ~** Dämpfung der Investitionstätigkeit

investment, ~ adviser Anlageberater; **~ aid** Investitionshilfe; **~ allowance** *(SteuerR)* Investitionsabschreibung; **~ appraisal** (or **analysis**) Investitionsrechnung

investment bank *Am* Investmentbank, Emissionsbank (→*bank*); →**European I~ B~**

investment, ~ banker Bankier im Anlagegeschäft; **~ banking** Effektenbankgeschäft, Emissionsgeschäft *(opp. commercial banking)*; **~ bonds** festverzinsliche Anlagepapiere; **~ broker** Makler für Anlagewerte; **~ business** Anlagegeschäft *(e-r Kapitalanlagegesellschaft)*; **~ buying** Anlagekauf, Kauf zu Anlagezwecken; **~ capital** Anlagekapital, Investitionskapital; **~ of capital** Anlage von Kapital, Kapitalanlage; **(~) certificate** Investmentzertifikat, Anteilschein (→*certificate 2.*); **~ club** *Am* lose Vereinigung von Privatleuten, die an Kapitalanlage interessiert sind

investment compan|y[55] Investmentgesellschaft, Kapitalanlagegesellschaft; **diversified ~** Investmentgesellschaft mit Grundsatz der Risikomischung; **property ~** Immobilien-Investmentgesellschaft; **regulated ~** *Am* steuerbegünstigte Investmentgesellschaft; **security ~** Wertpapier-Investmentgesellschaft; **saving through ~ies** Investmentsparen

investment, ~ cost Investitionskosten; **~ counsel(l)ing** Anlageberatung; **~ counsel(l)or** Anlageberater; **~ credit** Investitionskredit; *Am (SteuerR)* Investitionsabschreibung; **~ dealers** *Am* Investitionshäuser; **~ decision** Investitionsentscheidung

investment disputes, Convention on the Settlement of I~ D~ between States and Nationals of Other States[56] Übereinkommen zur Beilegung von Investitionsstreitigkeiten zwischen Staaten und Angehörigen anderer Staaten (Weltbankübereinkommen)

investment, ~ expenditure Investitionsaufwand, -ausgabe; **~ failure** Fehlinvestition; **~ financing** Investitionsfinanzierung

investment fund Investmentfonds, Anlagefonds *(mit den Mitteln der Anleger erworbene Wertpapiere;* →*fund 2.)*; **~s** Investitionsmittel; **~ certificates** (or *Br* **units**) Investmentanteile

investment, ~ grant Investitionsbeihilfe *(des Staates)*; **~ incentives** Investitionsanreize *(steuerliche Vergünstigungen)*; **~ income** Erträge aus Beteiligungen; Kapitalerträge; **~ income surcharge** *Br* Steuerzuschlag auf Kapitalerträge; **~ in fixed assets** Anlageinvestiton; **~ in freehold and leasehold property** *Br* Kapitalanlage in Grundbesitz; **~ in inventory of goods** Lagerinvestition; **~s in plant and equipment** Ausrüstungsinvestitionen; **~ in securities** Wertpapieranlage; **~s in subsidiaries and associated companies** *Am (Bilanz)* Beteiligungen; **~ loan** Investitionsanleihe; Investitionskredit; **~ management** Verwaltung von Kapitalanlagen; Effektenverwaltung; Depotgeschäft; **~ management service** Kundendienst *(e-r Bank)* für Kapitalanlagen; **~ manager** Anlagenverwalter; **~ objective** Anlageziel; **~ opportunity** Investierungs-, Anlagemöglichkeit; **~ plan** Anlageplan; **~ planning** Investitionsplanung

investment policy Anlagepolitik; **business ~** betriebliche Investitionspolitik

investment, ~ portfolio Effektenportefeuille, Wertpapierbestand; **~ program(me)** Investitionsprogramm; **~ project** Investitionsvorhaben

investment purposes Anlagezwecke; **demand for ~** Anlagebedarf

investment, ~ quota Investitionsquote; **~ rating** *Am* Anlagebewertung; Schätzung des Wertes von Anlagepapieren; **~s (undertaken) for rationalization purposes** Rationalisierungsinvestitionen; **~ restrictions** Investitionsbeschränkungen *(e-r Investmentgesellschaft);* ~ **securities** Anlagepapiere, Anlagewerte *(Am Namens- und Inhaberaktien, Inhaberschuldverschreibungen; opp. speculative securities)*

investment share Investmentanteil; **distribution of foreign** ~**s** Vertrieb ausländischer Investmentanteile

investment, ~ **shares** (or **stocks**) Anlagewerte, Anlagepapiere; ~ **in shares** (or **stock**) Anlage in Aktien; ~ **spending** Investitionsaufwendungen; ~ **spread** Anlagestreuung; ~ **tax credit** *Am* Steuergutschrift für Neuinvestitionen; ~ **trends** Investitionsentwicklung; Investitionstendenzen

investment trust (I. T.) Investment Trust, Kapitalanlagegesellschaft (→**trust** 1.); ~ **certificate** Investmentzertifikat, Anteilschein; ~ **securities** Effekten e-s Investment Trust; →**closed-end** ~; **fixed** ~ (F. I. T.) Kapitalanlagegesellschaft mit festgelegtem Effektenbestand; →**flexible** ~; **management** ~ (M. I. T.) Kapitalanlagegesellschaft, die das eingezahlte Kapital nach eigenem Ermessen anlegt; →**open-end** ~; **property** ~ *Br* Grundstücks-Investmenttrust; **real estate** ~ (REIT) *Am* Grundstücks-Investment-Trust; Immobilien-Investmentgesellschaft; **unit** ~ *Br* →unit trust

investment, ~ **underwriters** *Am* Emissionshäuser; ~ **value** Anlagewert *(e-s Wertpapiers)*

investment, aids to promote ~**s** Investitionsbeihilfen *(→Multilateral Investment Guarantee Agency);* **business** ~**s** betriebliche Investitionen; **capital** ~ *(langfristige)* Kapitalanlage; **class of** ~ Anlageart; **direct** ~**s** Direktinvestitionen; **domestic** ~**s** Inlandsinvestitionen; **encouragement of** ~**s** Förderung der Investitionen; **equipment** ~**s** Ausrüstungsinvestitionen; **excess of** ~**s** Überhang von Investitionen; **fixed** ~**s** Anlageinvestitionen; **foreign** ~**s** Auslandsinvestitionen; **a good** ~ e-e gute Kapitalanlage; **government** ~**s** staatliche Investitionen; **gross** ~ Bruttoinvestition; **gross private domestic** ~**s** Brutto-Inlandsinvestitionen; **inventory** ~ Lagerinvestition; **legal** ~ *Am* mündelsichere Kapitalanlage; **long-term** ~**s** langfristige Anlagen; *Am (Bilanz)* Wertpapiere des Anlagevermögens; **mistaken** ~**s** Fehlinvestitionen; **net** ~ Nettoinvestition; **new** ~**s** Neuinvestitionen; **other** ~**s** *(Bilanz)* sonstige Anlagepapiere; **permanent** ~ Daueranlage; langfristige Kapitalanlage; **poor** ~ schlechte Geldanlage; **private** ~**s** private Investitionen; **promotion of** ~**s** Förderung von Investitionen; **property** ~ *Br* Kapitalanlage in Grundbesitz; **public** ~**s** Investitionen der öffentlichen Hand; **public** ~ **expenditure** öffentliche Investitionsausgaben; **rate of** ~ Investitionsrate, -quote; **real estate** ~ *bes. Am* Kapitalanlage in Grundbesitz; **returns on** ~ Ertrag aus Investitionen; **safe** ~ sichere Kapitalanlage; **share** ~ Geldanlage in Aktien; **short-term** ~ kurzfristige Kapitalanlage; **temporary** ~**s** vorübergehende Kapitalanlagen; *(Bilanz)* Wertpapiere des Umlaufvermögens; **terms of** ~ Anlagebedingungen; **trust** ~ *Am* mündelsichere Kapitalanlage; **trustee** ~ *Br* mündelsichere Kapitalanlage; **type of** ~ Anlageart

investor Investor, Investierer; Kapitalanleger, Anleger; ~**s** Anlagepublikum; ~ **protection** Schutz des Kapitalanlegers; ~ **relations** Pflege der guten Beziehungen e-r AG zu den Aktionären (od. e-r Investmentgesellschaft zu den Investmentsparern); ~ **with a building society** *Br* Anleger bei e-r Bausparkasse; **institutional** ~**s** institutionelle Anleger; Kapitalsammelstellen

invigorate *v* stärken, beleben; **to** ~ **the economy** die Wirtschaft ankurbeln

invisible unsichtbar; ~**s** *(Zahlungsbilanz)* unsichtbare Ausfuhren und Einfuhren *(Dienstleistungstransaktionen zwischen In- und Ausland, z.B. im Reiseverkehr);* ~ **exports** unsichtbare Ausfuhren *(aktive Dienstleistungen);* ~ **imports** unsichtbare Einfuhren *(passive Dienstleistungen);* ~ **items** (of foreign trade) unsichtbare Posten (→*invisibles)*

invitation Einladung; Aufforderung; **(formal)** ~ **to bid** (or **for bids**) *Am* Ausschreibung, Submission; Stellenausschreibung; ~ **to subscribe to a loan** Aufforderung zur Zeichnung e-r Anleihe; ~ **telex** *(Börse)* Fernschreiben an alle Mitlgieder e-s Emissionskonsortiums (od. Kreditkonsortiums) mit den Details e-r geplanten Finanzierungstransaktion

invitation to tender Ausschreibung, Submission; ~ **with discretionary award of contracts** freihändige Ausschreibung; **closed** (or **restricted**) ~ beschränkte Ausschreibung; **standing** ~ Dauerausschreibung

invitation, ~ **to treat** *Br* Aufforderung zur Abgabe e-s Angebots; **to accept an** ~ e-e Einladung annehmen; **to decline an** ~ e-e Einladung absagen; **to send out** ~**s** Einladungen herausgeben lassen; **to send out an** ~ **to tender** ausschreiben

invite *v* einladen; auffordern; ermutigen zu; **to** ~ **applications for a position** e-e Stelle ausschreiben; **to** ~ **criticism** zur Kritik ermutigen; **to** ~ **offers** zu Angeboten auffordern; **to** ~ **to subscribe for** *(Br auch* **to**) **shares** Aktien zur Zeichnung auslegen; **to** ~ **tenders (for)** *(bei Ausschreibungen)* zur Abgabe von Angeboten auffordern; Ausschreibung vornehmen, *(etw.)* ausschreiben

inviting country einladendes Land

invitee geschäftlicher Besucher; jd, der ein Grundstück od. e-e Räumlichkeit im Interesse od. mit Genehmigung des Besitzers betritt *(z.B. Kunde, Theaterbesucher)*

Br Haftpflicht bei Unfällen ist geregelt durch Occupiers' Liability Act 1957.
Am Die Haftpflicht richtet sich danach, ob der Verletzte ein invitee oder ein →licensee ist

invocation Anrufung; ~ **of papers** *Am* Aktenanforderung *(von e-m anderen Gericht)*

invoice (Waren-)Rechnung, Faktura; ~ **amount** Rechnungsbetrag, Betrag der Faktura; ~ **book** (I. B.) Rechnungsbuch, Fakturenbuch; Einkaufsjournal; ~ **checking** Rechnungsprüfung; ~ **clerk** Fakturist; ~ **copy** Rechnungsdurchschlag; ~ **cost** (Brutto-) Einkaufspreis, Einkaufsrechnungspreis; ~ **date** Rechnungsdatum; ~ **discounting** Bevorschussung von Rechnungen *(Br z. B. durch e-e Finance Company);* ~ **item** Rechnungsposten; ~ **number** Rechnungsnummer; ~ **of sundries** Rechnung über verschiedene Waren; ~ **price** Rechnungspreis, Fakturapreis; ~ **value** Fakturenwert

invoice, amount of ~ Rechnungsbetrag; **as per** ~ laut Rechnung, laut Faktura; **consular** ~ Konsulatsfaktura; **customs** ~ Zollfaktura; **pro forma** ~ Proformarechnung; **provisional** ~ vorläufige Rechnung; **purchase** ~ Eingangsrechnung; **sales** ~ Ausgangsrechnung; **shipping** ~ Versandrechnung

invoice, to enter on the ~ auf die Rechnung setzen; **to make out an** ~ e-e Rechnung ausstellen (of über); **to receipt an** ~ e-e Rechnung quittieren

invoice *v* Rechnung *(über e-e Ware)* ausstellen od. schreiben; fakturieren; *(Waren)* berechnen, in Rechnung stellen

invoiced, ~ **price** Rechnungspreis; **amount** ~ Rechnungsbetrag; **as** ~ laut Faktura

invoicing Inrechnungstellung, Fakturierung; Rechnungschreibung; ~ **machine** Fakturiermaschine

invoke *v (Hilfe etc)* anrufen; sich berufen auf; **to** ~ **the arbitration clause** sich auf die Schiedsklausel berufen; **to** ~ **an award against a party** →award 2.; **to** ~ **the provisions of a statute** sich auf die Gesetzesbestimmung berufen

involuntary unfreiwillig, erzwungen; unabsichtlich *(opp. voluntary);* ~ **bankruptcy** *Am* zwangsweiser Konkurs *(Anmeldung durch den Gläubiger);* ~ **manslaughter** fahrlässige Tötung *(dolus indirectus);* ~ **petition** *Am* →petition 2.; ~ **servitude** *Am* Zwangsarbeit; ~ **transfer** Übertragung kraft Gesetzes

involve *v (jdn)* verwickeln, hineinziehen (in in); nach sich ziehen, zur Folge haben; mit etw. verbunden sein; einschließen, betreffen; **to** ~ **oneself in a cause** sich mit e-r guten Sache befassen, sich für e-e gute Sache einsetzen *(z. B. Abschaffung der Rassenunterschiede);* **to** ~ **additional charges** mit weiteren Kosten verbunden sein; **to** ~ **sb. in a crime** jdn in ein Verbrechen hineinziehen (od. verwickeln); **to** ~ **expenses** Kosten zur Folge haben, mit Kosten verbunden sein; **to** ~ **the forfeiture of property** die Einziehung von Vermögen zur Folge haben; **the contract** ~**s** der Vertrag hat zum Gegenstand (od. betrifft)

involved verwickelt (in in); einbegriffen; kompliziert; ~ **in debts** verschuldet; ~ **in policies** mit der Politik verbunden; in die Politik verwickelt; **the costs** ~ die damit verbundenen Kosten; **the person** ~ der/die Betroffene; **to be** ~ auf dem Spiel stehen; in Frage kommen; **to be** ~ **in a th.** in e-e Sache verwickelt sein; **could you please tell me what is** ~ **here** könnten Sie mir bitte sagen, um was es sich hier handelt (od. um was es hier geht); **it** ~ **many difficulties** es war mit vielen Schwierigkeiten verbunden; **there are some** ~ **provisions in this law** dieses Gesetz hat einige komplizierte Bestimmungen; **to get** ~ **with** sich befassen mit; **to get** ~ **in a crime** in ein Verbrechen verwickelt werden

involving, cases ~ Rechtsstreitigkeiten, die ... zum Gegenstand haben

involvement Verwicklung; Hineingezogenwerden; Engagement; **social** ~ soziales Engagement

inward inner(er, -e, -es); nach innen (gehend); ~ **bill of lading** Importkonnossement *(opp. outward bill of lading);* ~ **bound vessel** *Br* auf der Heimfahrt befindliches Schiff *(opp. outward bound vessel);* ~ **manifest** Zolleinfuhrerklärung; ~ **processing** aktive(r) Veredelung(sverkehr)

ionize *v* ionisieren

ionizing, delayed effects of ~ **radiation** Spätwirkungen ionisierender Strahlen

IOU (I owe you) Schuldschein *(schriftl. Schuldanerkenntnis ohne Zahlungstermin)*

ipso facto ("by the fact itself") grade dadurch

ipso jure ("by the law itself") von Rechts wegen, ohne weiteres

Iran, the Islamic Republic of ~ die Islamische Republik Iran

Iranian Iraner(in); iranisch

Iraq Irak; **Republic of** ~ Republik Irak

Iraqi Iraker(in); irakisch

Ireland, Northern ~ Nordirland; **Republic of** ~ (Eire) Republik Irland

Irish irisch; **the** ~ die Iren; ~**man** Ire; ~ **Republican Army** (IRA) militante Untergrund-Organisation, die den Anschluß Nordirlands an die irische Republik anstrebt; ~**woman** Irin

iron Eisen; ~**clad** *Am colloq.* streng *(regulation, agreement etc);* ~, **coal and steel shares**

Montanaktien; ~ **curtain** *pol* eiserner Vorhang; ~ **ore mining** Eisenerzbergbau; ~ **and steel products** Stahlerzeugnisse; ~**ware** Eisenwaren; ~**works** Eisenhütte, Eisenwerk

irradiated nuclear fuels bestrahlte Kernbrennstoffe

irradiation Bestrahlung *(von Lebensmitteln)*; ~ **injury** *(AtomR)* Strahlenschädigung; **risk of** ~ Bestrahlungsrisiko

irrebuttable unwiderlegbar, unumstößlich; ~ **presumption** unwiderlegbare Rechtsvermutung (presumptio juris et de jure)

irreconcilable unvereinbar (with mit); unversöhnlich; ~ **differences** *Am* unheilbare Zerrüttung der Ehe

irrecoverable, ~ **debt** nicht beitreibbare Forderung; ~ **loss** unersetzlicher Verlust

irrecusable unablehnbar

irredeemable nicht rückzahlbar, nicht einlösbar; untilgbar; unkündbar; unwiederbringlich; ~ **annuity** nicht ablösbare Rente; ~ **bonds** (or ~ **debentures**) nicht rückzahlbare (od. tilgbare) Schuldverschreibungen; ~ **paper money** nicht *(in Gold)* einlösbares Papiergeld; ~ **preference shares** (*Am* **preferred stock**) nicht rückkaufbare Vorzugsaktien

irrefragable unwiderlegbar

irrefutable unwiderlegbar; ~ **evidence** nicht widerlegbare Zeugenaussage; unwiderlegbarer Beweis; ~ **fact** unbestreitbare Tatsache

irregular unvorschriftsmäßig, regelwidrig; nicht ordnungsmäßig, unordentlich; unregelmäßig, nicht einheitlich *(Preise, Kurse)*; *mil* irregulär; ~ **conduct** ordnungswidriges Verhalten; ~ **payments** unregelmäßige Zahlungen; ~ **proceedings** unter Formfehlern leidendes Verfahren; ~ **troops** irreguläre Truppen; Freischärler; **the trend of the share market was** ~ die Tendenz auf dem Aktienmarkt war uneinheitlich

irregularit|y Unregelmäßigkeit; Regelwidrigkeit; Uneinheitlichkeit; Ungehörigkeit; Fehler, Verstoß; ~ **in form** Formfehler; ~ **in the procedure** (or **proceedings**) Verfahrensfehler; **to commit** ~**ies** sich Unregelmäßigkeiten zuschulden kommen lassen; **to uncover** ~**ies** Unregelmäßigkeiten (od. Fehler) aufdecken

irrelevant irrelevant, unerheblich, belanglos; nicht zur Sache gehörig; ~ **evidence** *(für die Entscheidung)* unerheblicher Beweis; ~ **in law** rechtlich unerheblich

irremediable breakdown of marriage *Am* unheilbare Zerrüttung der Ehe

irremovability Unabsetzbarkeit *(z.B. der Richter)*

irremovable unabsetzbar

irreparable irreparabel; ~ **damage** nicht wiedergutzumachender Schaden; ~ **loss** unersetzlicher Verlust

irreplaceable records unersetzliche Unterlagen

irrepleviable nicht herausgebbar; nicht der Herausgabeklage (action for replevin) unterliegend

irresistible impulse unwiderstehlicher Trieb *(z.B. Kleptomanie)*

irrespective of ohne Rücksicht auf, unabhängig von; ~ **of percentage** (i.o.p.) *(VersR)* ohne Franchise

irresponsibility Unverantwortlichkeit; Verantwortungslosigkeit; *(StrafR)* Unzurechnungsfähigkeit

irretrievable nicht wiedergutzumachen(d); ~ **breakdown of marriage** unheilbare Zerrüttung der Ehe (→*divorce*); ~ **debt** uneinbringliche Forderung

irretrievably broken marriage *Am* unheilbar zerrüttete Ehe

irreversible decision unwiderrufliche Entscheidung

irrevocability Unwiderruflichkeit

irrevocable unwiderruflich; ~ **letter of credit** unwiderrufliches Akkreditiv; ~ **trust** unwiderruflicher Trust (→*trust 1.*)

irrigation Bewässerung, Berieselung; ~ **plant** Bewässerungsanlage; ~ **scheme** Bewässerungsvorhaben

irritancy *Scot* Beendigung e-s Vertrages; ~ **clause** *Scot* Beendigungsklausel; **conventional** ~ *Scot* Beendigung e-s Vertrages auf Grund e-r vertraglichen Bestimmung; **legal** ~ *Scot* Beendigung e-s Vertrages auf Grund e-r gesetzlichen Bestimmung *(z.B. e-s Pachtvertrages nach 2 Jahren Pachtrückständen)*

Islamic Republic of →**Iran**

island Insel; **I**~ **Company** *Br* Gesellschaft, die auf den →Channel Islands oder der Isle of Man errichtet worden ist; **traffic** ~ Verkehrsinsel

isle Insel; **the British I**~**s** die britischen Inseln

isolate *v* isolieren, absondern; abtrennen

isolated isoliert; **in** ~ **cases** in Einzelfällen; ~ **guarantee** Einzelbürgschaft

isolation Isolierung; Abtrennung; ~ **ward** Isolierstation

isolationism *pol* Isolationismus, isolationistische Politik

isolationist *pol* Isolationist; isolationistisch

Israel Israel; **State of ~** Staat Israel
Israeli Israeli, Israelin; israelisch

issuable auszugeben(d), emittierbar

issuance *bes. Am* Ausgabe; Ausstellung; Erteilung; ~ **of a credit** Eröffnugn e-s Akkreditivs; ~ **of a law** *Am* Erlaß e-s Gesetzes; ~ **of a license** *Am* Erteilung e-r Lizenz; ~ **of material** *Am* Materialausgabe; ~ **of an order** *Am* Erlaß e-s Befehls

issue 1. Streitfrage, strittiger Punkt; *bes. pol* Kernfrage, Problem; ~**s** wesentliche Streitpunkte, streitige Fragen *(im e-m Prozeß)*; **the ~ at stake** der springende Punkt; ~ **in dispute** strittige Frage; ~ **of fact** strittige Tatfrage; ~ **of law** strittige Rechtsfrage; ~ **preclusion** *Am* s. collateral →estoppel; ~ **question** *bes. pol* Frage von entscheidender Bedeutung; umstrittene Frage
issue, at ~ strittig, im Streit befangen; zur Diskussion; **the case at ~** der zur Entscheidung stehende Fall; der vorliegende Fall; **point at ~** Streitpunkt, strittiger Punkt; zu entscheidende Frage, zu entscheidender Punkt; **the point at ~ is** zur Entscheidung steht die Frage; **question at ~** Streitfrage; die zur Entscheidung stehende Frage; Kernfrage
issue, burning ~s of the day brennende Tagesfragen; **determination of an ~** gerichtliche Entscheidung über e-e Streitfrage *(vor der Verhandlung)*; **general ~** *(Strafprozeß)* Nichtschuldigerklärung (plea of not guilty); →**joinder of ~**; **legal ~** strittige Rechtsfrage; **matters** (or **points**) **at** (or **in**) ~ Streitgegenstand, Streitpunkte; zur Entscheidung stehende Punkte; **statement of the ~s (to be decided)** Aufstellung der Streitfragen
issue, to argue political ~s über politische Fragen diskutieren; **the parties are at ~** die Parteien haben sich *(nach Wechsel der Schriftsätze)* auf bestimmte *(im Prozeß zu entscheidende)* Fragen festgelegt; **to define the ~s** die wesentlichen Punkte festlegen; **to join ~** Tatsachenbehauptungen des letzten gegnerischen Schriftsatzes bestreiten *(ohne Vorbringen neuer Tatsachen)*; strittige *(zu entscheidende)* Fragen festlegen *(cf. joinder of ~)*; **to join ~ upon the defence (~se)** die Klagebeantwortung bestreiten; **to join ~ with sb.** gegenteilige Behauptung *(über e-n bestimmten Punkt)* vorbringen; **to raise an ~** e-e Frage aufwerfen; ein Problem anschneiden; ein Thema zur Debatte stellen; **the pleadings raise an ~** die Schriftsätze ergeben e-e formulierte Beweisfrage; **the question raises the whole ~** die Frage schneidet den ganzen Sachverhalt an; **to settle an ~** sich *(mit der Gegenpartei)* über die zu entscheidende wesentliche Frage einigen; **to take ~** *Br* mit jdm über e-n Punkt uneinig sein
issue 2. Nachkommen(schaft), Kind(er), Abkömmling(e) (→*lineal descendants)*; ~ **in tail male** *(GrundstücksR)* Nachkommen in der männlichen Linie *(als Erben von erbrechtlich gebundenem Grundbesitz)*; ~ **risk** *(VersR)* Risiko des Auftretens neuer Erben; **failure of ~** Kinderlosigkeit; **without ~** ohne Nachkommen(schaft); **without male ~** ohne männliche Nachkommen; **to die without ~** kinderlos sterben; **to leave ~** Nachkommen hinterlassen; **the ~ of the marriage are three children** aus der Ehe sind drei Kinder hervorgegangen
issue 3. Emission *(von Wertpapieren)*; Wertpapiere *(der gleichen Emission)*, Serie; Nummer *(e-r Zeitung od. Zeitschrift)*; Ausstellung *(e-s Ausweises, Reisepasses etc)*; ~ **above par** Emission über pari, Überpariemission; ~ **at a discount** →~below par; ~ **at par** Emission zum Nennwert, Pariemission; ~ **at a premium** →~above par; ~ **ban** Emissionssperre; ~ **below par** Emisson unter pari, Unterpariemission; ~ **by prospectus** *Br* Emission durch Prospekt *(Auflegung zur Zeichnung von neuen Wertpapieren durch [Zeichnungs-]Prospekt)*; ~ **by tender** Emission durch Zuteilung an den Meistbietenden *(→ tender 2.)*; **I~ Department** *Br* Abteilung für Banknotenausgabe; Emissionsabteilung *(der Bank of England)*; ~ **fee** *(PatR)* Erteilungsgebühr; ~ **market** Emissionsmarkt; ~ **of bank notes** Banknotenausgabe; ~ **of a bill (of exchange)** Ausstellung e-s Wechsels; ~ **of bonds** Ausgabe von Obligationen; ~ **of a cheque (check)** Ausstellung e-s Schecks; ~ **of a letter of credit** Ausstellung e-s Akkreditivs; ~ **of a loan** Begebung (od. Auflegung) e-r Anleihe; ~ **of an order** Erlaß e-s Befehls; ~ **of a patent** Erteilung e-s Patents (→*patent 2.)*; ~ **of a policy** *(VersR)* Ausstellung e-r Police; ~ ~ **of a prospectus** Herausgabe e-s Prospektes; ~ **of securities** Ausgabe von Wertpapieren, Effektenemission; ~ **of shares (stocks)** Aktienausgabe; ~ **premium** Emissionsagio; ~ **price** Ausgabekurs, Emissionskurs; ~ **syndicate** Emissionskonsortium; ~**through the tap** →tap issue; ~**s traded** Aktien gehandelt
issue, auction ~ Emissionsform am Euromarkt; **bank of ~** Notenbank; **bond ~** Anleiheemission; Anleihe; Emission von Obligationen; **country of ~** Emissionsland; **current ~** letzte Nummer *(e-r Zeitschrift)*; **date of ~** Emissionstag, Ausgabetag; Ausstellungstag, Datum der Ausstellung *(z.B. e-s Passes)*; **domestic ~** Inlandsemission; **dual currency ~** Doppelwährungsanleihe, bei der Zahlung des Emissionspreises und der Zinsen in anderer Währung erfolgt als die Rückzahlung der Anleihe bei Fälligkeit; **first ~** erste Serie; **foreign ~** Auslandsemission; **internal ~** Inlandsemission; **loan ~** Anleiheemission
issue, new ~s (Neu-)Emissionen; **borrowing through placing new ~s** Emissionskredit;

bringing out new ~**s** Auflegung neuer Emissionen; **market of new** ~**s** Emissionsmarkt

issue, over~ Überemission; **place of** ~ Ausgabeort, Ausstellungsort; **pre-underwritten** ~ Festübernahme e-r Emission durch ein Bankenkonsortium (→*bought deal);* **price of** ~ →~ price; **principal** ~ US-Regierungsanleihe; Anleihemantel ohne Zinsbogen; **public** ~ öffentliche Emission; **second** ~ zweite Serie; **straight** ~ →straight bonds;

issue, to float (or launch) an ~ e-e Emission auflegen (od. begeben); **the loan is offered to the public at an** ~ **price of 98%** die Anleihe hat e-n Ausgabekurs von 98%; **bond** ~ **maturing over 12 years** Anleihenserie mit e-r Laufzeit von 12 Jahren

issue 4. Ergebnis, Resultat; Ertrag, Einkünfte *(bes. aus Land);* Herausströmen; **unfavo(u)rable** ~ **of a lawsuit** ungünstiger Ausgang e-s Prozesses; **to await the** ~ das Ergebnis abwarten; **to force an** ~ e-e Entscheidung erzwingen

issue *v* herausgeben, erlassen, ergehen lassen; *(behördlich)* ausstellen; *(Wertpapiere)* emittieren, ausgeben, in Umlauf setzen; enden, zum Ergebnis haben; (her)stammen (from von); **to** ~ **sb. with sth.** *bes. mil* jdm etw. ausgeben, jdn mit etw. versehen; **to** ~ **bank notes** Banknoten ausgeben; **to** ~ **a bill (of exchange)** e-n Wechsel ausstellen; **to** ~ **bonds** Obligationen ausgeben; **to** ~ **a certificate** e-e Bescheinigung ausstellen; **to** ~ **a credit** ein Akkreditiv eröffnen; **to** ~ **a decree** e-e Verfügung erlassen; e-n Erlaß herausgeben; **to** ~ **execution against** Zwangsvollstreckung betreiben gegen; **to** ~ **a letter of credit** ein Akkreditiv eröffnen; **to** ~ **a loan** e-e Anleihe begeben (od. auflegen); **to** ~ **an order** e-e Anordnung erlassen; **to** ~ **a passport** e-n Paß ausstellen; ~ **a patent** ein Patent erteilen; **to** ~ **a prospectus** e-n Prospekt herausgeben (od. veröffentlichen); **to** ~ **shares** (*Am* **stocks**) Aktien ausgeben; **to** ~ **a warrant of arrest** e-n Haftbefehl erlassen; **a writ** ~**s** e-e richterliche Verfügung ergeht

issued, (~ **and) outstanding shares** begebene Aktien; **when** ~ *(Börse)* wenn ausgegeben, per Erscheinen

issuing Emission; Ausgabe; Ausstellung; ausstellend, emittierend; ~ **bank** Emissionsbank; die das Akkreditiv eröffnende Bank; ~ **company** emittierende Gesellschaft; ~ **date** Ausgabedatum; Ausstellungsdatum; ~ **house** *Br* Emissionsbank *(Institution des Kapitalmarktes, bes. für Unterbringung inländischer Emissionen);* ~ **office** Ausgabestelle *(z. B. für money orders; opp. paying office);* ~ **place** Ausgabeort; Ausstellungsort; ~ **prospectus** Emissionsprospekt; ~ **syndicate** Emissionskonsortium; ~ **transaction(s)** Emissionsgeschäft(e); **rents** ~ **from land** Pachteinnahmen aus Grundbesitz; **to be engaged in** ~ **transactions** sich mit Emissionsgeschäften befassen

issueless *Am* ohne Nachkommen, kinderlos

issuer Emittent; Aussteller

Italian Italiener(in); italienisch; ~ **Republic** Italienische Republik

Italy Italien

italics, in ~ kursiv

item 1. (Bilanz-, Rechnungs-, Buchungs-)Posten; *(einzelner)* Punkt; *(einzelner)* Gegenstand; Position, Einzelposten *(z. B. des Haushaltsplans); (bei Aufzählungen)* Nummer (Nr.); Tarifnummer (→*GATT*); Ziffer *(in e-m Vertrag);* Zeitungsnotiz, *(kurzer)* (Zeitungs-)Artikel; (Waren-)Artikel; ~ **in an account** Rechnungsposten; ~ **on the agenda** Gegenstand (od. Punkt) der Tagesordnung; ~ **in a bill** Rechnungsposten; ~ **of the budget** Etatposten, Titel des Haushaltsplanes; ~ **costing** Stückkostenkalkulation; ~ **of expense** Ausgabekosten; ~ **of property** Vermögensgegenstand; **budget(ary)** ~ →~ of the budget; **cash** ~ Kassenposten; **costs per** ~ Stückkosten; **credit** ~ Kreditposten, Gutschriftposten; **debit** ~ Debetposten, Lastschriftposten; **news** ~ *(kurzer)* Artikel, Zeitungsnotiz; **sub-**~ Unterposition, Nummer

item 2. (Post-)Sendung; ~**s liable to surcharge** zuschlagspflichtige Sendungen; **combined** ~**s** Sammelsendungen; **forces** ~**s** Militärpostsendungen; **registered** ~**s** eingeschriebene Sendungen

itemization *bes. Am* Einzelaufzählung, Spezifikation; Aufgliederung

itemize *v* näher angeben; *(Punkt für Punkt)* aufführen, spezifizieren; aufgliedern; **to** ~ **an account** e-e Rechnung spezifizieren; **to** ~ **costs** Kosten aufgliedern

itemized statement Aufstellung

itinerant reisend; umherziehend; ambulant; ~ **judge** *hist* Reiserichter; ~ **merchant** Reisegewerbetreibender; Hausierer; ~ **trade** Reisegewerbe; Hausierhandel; ~ **vendor** ambulanter Händler (→~ *merchant*)

itinerary Reiseroute; Reiseplan; Reisebericht

Ivorian Ivorer(in) *(→Côte d'Ivoir)*

J

jackroller *Am sl.* Dieb, der betrunkene od. schlafende Personen bestiehlt

jactitation falsche Behauptung; ~ **of marriage** Vorspiegelung des Bestehens e-r Ehe

jail Gefängnis; *bes. Am* (Stadt-, Kreis-)Gefängnis *(für kürzere Freiheitsstrafe und Untersuchungshaft; cf. prison);* ~**bird** *sl.* alter Sträfling; ~**breaker** Ausbrecher *(aus dem Gefängnis);* ~**breaking** Ausbruch aus dem Gefängnis; ~ **sentence** *Am* Gefängnisstrafe; **commitment to** ~ Einlieferung ins Gefängnis; **to be given a year and a half in** ~ 1½ Jahre Gefängnis bekommen; **to go to** ~ ins Gefängnis gehen; eingesperrt werden

jail *v* einsperren

jailer *Am* Gefängniswärter; Gefangenenaufseher

jam Gedränge; *sl.* schwierige Lage, „Klemme"; **traffic** ~ Verkehrsstockung

jam *v* verstopfen, blockieren, versperren; *(Radiosendung)* stören; eingeklemmt sein; **to** ~ **a bill through a legislature** *Am* e-e Gesetzesvorlage im Parlament durchdrücken; **a ship** ~**med in the ice** ein im Eis festsitzendes Schiff

jamming, ~ **of foreign broadcasts** Störung ausländischer Rundfunkübertragungen; ~ **station** Störsender

Jamaica Jamaika

Jamaican Jamaikaner(in); jamaikanisch

janitor Pförtner; Hausmeister

Japan Japan

Japanese Japaner(in); japanisch

Jason clause *bes. Am (Seevers.)* Versicherungsklausel gegen verborgene Mängel

jaywalker *colloq.* unachtsamer (und verkehrswidriger) Fußgänger

jaywalking *colloq.* unachtsames (und verkehrswidriges) Überqueren der Straße

jeopardize *v* gefährden; *(etw.)* der Gefahr *(des Verlustes etc)* aussetzen; **he** ~**d the success of the scheme by failure to obtain adequate financial backing** er gefährdete den Erfolg des Planes, weil er nicht die genügende finanzielle Unterstützung erhielt

jeopardy Gefahr; Gefährdung; Risiko; ~ **assessment** *Am* sofortige Steuerveranlagung und gleichzeitige Beschlagnahme des Eigentums des Veranlagten durch den Staat *(zur Befriedigung der Steuerforderung, z. B. weil Steuerzahler das Land verläßt);* **double** ~ *Am*[1] (Verbot der) doppelte(n) Strafverfolgung e-s Täters wegen derselben Tat *(etwa dem Grundsatz „ne bis in idem" entsprechend)*

jeopardy, in ~ der Gefahr e-r Verurteilung ausgesetzt *(cf. autrefois acquit)*

jerque *v Br (Schiffspapiere)* zollamtlich prüfen *(nach nicht deklarierter Ladung forschen)*

jerquer *Br* Zollbeamter *(der Schiffe prüft)*

jerry-built nicht solide gebaut *(schlechtes Material, keine Haltbarkeit)*

JET →Joint European Torus

jet, ~ **aircraft** (or **airliner**) Düsen(verkehrs)flugzeug; ~ **fighter** Düsenjäger; ~ **freighter** Düsenfrachtflugzeug; **large-capacity** ~ **liner** Großraumdüsen(verkehrs)flugzeug

jetsam Seewurf *(in Seenot über Bord geworfene Ladung); (geworfenes)* Strandgut; **flotsam and** ~ treibendes Wrack- und Strandgut

jettison Überbordwerfen *(von Gütern);* Seewurf *(als Tätigkeit; cf. jetsam);* ~ **of cargo** Ladungswurf; ~ **and washing overboard** (J. & W. O.) Überbordwerfen und -spülen

jettison *v* über Bord *(e-s Schiffes od. Flugzeugs)* werfen

Jew Jude; **Consultative Council of** ~**ish Organizations** (CCJO) Konsultativ-Rat der jüdischen Organisationen *(New York)*

jewel(le)ry, ~ **insurance** Schmucksachenversicherung; **theft of** ~ Juwelendienbstahl

job Arbeit; *(meist vorübergehende)* Tätigkeit, Beschäftigung; *(ausgeübter)* Beruf; Arbeitsplatz; (Stück) Arbeit; Akkordarbeit; *(zu bearbeitender)* Auftrag; (Profit-)Geschäft, Schiebung; *sl.* Straftat (bes. Diebstahl); ~ **accounting** *(EDV)* Auftragsabrechnung; ~ **analysis** Arbeitsplatzanalyse; ~ **application** Bewerbung um e-e Stelle; ~**s available** offene (od. freie) Arbeitsplätze; ~**centre** *Br* Arbeitsamt; ~ **change** Arbeitsplatzwechsel; ~ **classification** *Am* Berufsklassifizierung; Einteilung von Tätigkeiten in Klassen *(nach den zu ihrer Durchführung notwendigen Erfordernissen);* ~ **conditions** Arbeitsbedingungen *(Umwelteinflüsse);* ~ **content** *Am* Arbeitsinhalt, Inhalt der Arbeit; ~ **costing** Auftragskostenrechnung; ~ **counsellor** *Am* Berufsberater; ~ **creating measures** Arbeitsbeschaffungsmaßnahmen (ABM); ~ **creation** Arbeits(platz)beschaffung; Beschaffung von Arbeitsplätzen; ~ **description** Tätigkeitsbeschreibung, Arbeits(platz)beschreibung; ~ **discrimination** Benachteiligung im Arbeitsleben *(z. B. wegen Rasse, Religion, Parteizugehörigkeit);* ~ **enlargement** Arbeitserweiterung, Aufgabenvergrößerung; ~ **enrichment** Arbeitsbereicherung *(Änderung der Arbeit, damit sie mehr Befriedigung gibt);* ~ **evaluation** Arbeits(platz)bewertung *(zum Zwecke der Grundlohnbestimmung);* ~ **goods** Ramschwaren, Ausschußwaren; ~**holder** *Am* Stelleninhaber; **public** ~**holder** *Am* Staatsbediensteter, Beamter; ~ **hopping** häufiger Stellenwechsel; ~ **hunter** Stellenjäger, Stellungssuchender; ~ **hunting** *colloq.* Arbeitssuche, Stellensuche; Stellenjägerei; ~ **interview** Einstellungsgespräch

job, ~ **loss** Arbeitsplatzverlust; ~ **lot** Partieware(n), Ramschware(n); ~ **market** *Am* Stellenmarkt, Arbeitsmarkt; ~ **opportunities** Arbeitsmöglichkeiten; ~ **order** Arbeitsauftrag; Fabrikationsauftrag; *Am* Vermittlungsauftrag; ~ **placement** *Am* Stellenvermittlung; ~ **processing** Lohnveredelung; ~ **process card** Laufkarte *(für Arbeitsvorbereitung);* ~ **production** Einzelfertigung; ~ **rate** Akkordrichtsatz; ~ **rating** *Am* →~ evaluation; ~ **retraining** Umschulung; ~ **rotation** Arbeitsplatz(ring)tausch *(System, Mitarbeiter für Führungsaufgaben zu schulen);* ~ **satisfaction** Arbeitszufriedenheit, Befriedigung an der Arbeit; ~ **search** Arbeitsuche; ~ **security** Sicherheit des Arbeitsplatzes; ~ **seeker** Arbeitsuchender, Stellensucher; ~ **seniority** *Am* Dienstalter; ~ **sharing** Arbeitsplatzteilung; *(Besetzung e-s Vollzeitarbeitsplatzes durch ein Team aus Teilzeitarbeitskräften);* ~ **specification** Arbeits(platz)beschreibung; Tätigkeitsbeschreibung; ~ **splitting** Aufteilung e-s Arbeitsplatzes auf zwei Mitarbeiter; ~ **ticket** Arbeitsauftrag, Arbeitslaufzettel; Akkordzettel; ~ **title** Bezeichnung der Tätigkeit

job training Berufsausbildung; **off the** ~ Weiterbildung von betrieblichen Mitarbeitern in besonderen Kursen; **on the** ~ Ausbildung am Arbeitsplatz; innerbetriebliche Ausbildung

job, ~ **wage** Akkordlohn, Stücklohn; ~ **work** →piece work; ~ **worker** →piece worker

job, by the ~ im Akkord; stückweise; **to give out work by the** ~ Arbeit im Akkord vergeben; **to work by the** ~ im Akkord arbeiten

job, lack of ~**s** Mangel an Arbeitsplätzen; **maintenance of** ~**s** Erhaltung von Arbeitsplätzen

job, odd ~**s** gelegentliche *(kleine)* Arbeiten (od. Geschäfte); gelegentliche Tätigkeit; **odd** ~ **man** Gelegenheitsarbeiter; **to do odd** ~**s** gelegentliche Arbeiten verrichten

job, on the ~ am Arbeitsplatz; *Br colloq.* bei der Arbeit; **out of a** ~ arbeitslos; stellungslos, ohne Stelle; **permanent** ~ Dauerarbeitsplatz; **put-up** ~ *sl.* abgekartete Sache, Schiebung; **seasonal** ~ Saisonarbeitsplatz; **terminal** ~ *Am* Endstellung *(ohne weitere Aufstiegsmöglichkeit);* **to create new** ~**s** neue Arbeitsplätze schaffen; **to find a** ~ Arbeit finden; **to get a** ~ e-e Stelle bekommen; **to have a** ~ **in hand** *colloq.* mit e-r Arbeit (od. e-m Auftrag) beschäftigt sein; **to look for a** ~ Arbeit suchen; e-e Stelle suchen; **to lose one's** ~ seine Stelle verlieren; **to preserve** ~**s** Arbeitsplätze erhalten; **to provide** ~**s** Arbeitsplätze schaffen; **the** ~**s are directly at risk** die Arbeitsplätze sind unmittelbar bedroht; **to take a** ~ **as** e-e Stelle annehmen als

job *v* gelegentliche kleine Arbeiten verrichten; im Akkord arbeiten; *(Arbeit)* im Akkord vergeben; *Br (Börse)* als Makler (dealer) tätig sein; *(Börse)* spekulieren; Zwischenhandel treiben, Vermittler- od. Zwischenhandelsgeschäfte machen; *Am* Großhandel treiben; e-e Vertrauensstellung mißbrauchen; Schiebungen machen; **to** ~ **a contract** *Am* die Arbeit (od. den Auftrag) weitervergeben

jobber Gelegenheitsarbeiter; Akkordarbeiter; *Br (Börse)* Wertpapierhändler[1a] *(vor dem →Big Bang auf eigene Rechnung handelnder Börsenmakler; seine Tätigkeit wird jetzt von e-m →market maker durchgeführt); Am* Großhändler, Verteiler; Schieber; jd, der e-e Vertrauensstellung (od. amtliche Stellung) mißbraucht; ~ **in bills** *Br* Wechselreiter; ~**'s turn** *Br (Börse)* Kursgewinn des Effektenhändlers; →**rack** ~; **wagon** ~ *Am* Großhändler ohne eigenes Warenlager

jobbery Korruption, Schiebung; Vertrauensmißbrauch, Amtsmißbrauch; Börsenspekulation *(im verächtlichen Sinn)*

jobbing Gelegenheitsarbeit; Akkordarbeit; *Am* Großhandel; Zwischenhandel; Schiebung; ~ **in bills** Wechselreiterei; ~ **in contangoes** *Br (Börse)* Reportgeschäfte; **stock** ~ Börsenhandel, Effektenhandel; Börsenspekulation

jobless arbeitslos; ohne Stellung; ~ **benefit** Arbeitslosengeld; ~ **rate** Zahl der Arbeitslosen; Arbeitslosenquote

John Doe fiktiver Name *(in Rechtsstreitigkeiten; →Richard Roe)*

join *v* sich verbinden (od. vereinigen) (with mit); verbinden, vereinigen; beitreten, eintreten in; **to** ~ **in** sich beteiligen an; **to** ~ **an action** e-r Prozeßpartei *(zum Zwecke ihrer Unterstützung)* beitreten; **to** ~ **the army** in das Heer eintreten; Soldat werden; **to** ~ **in one action several causes of action** in einer Klage mehrere Ansprüche geltend machen; **to** ~ **a church** in e-e Kirche eintreten; **to** ~ **a class** an e-m Kursus teilnehmen; **to** ~ **a club** in e-n Klub eintreten; Mitglied e-s Klubs werden; **to** ~ **the colo(u)rs** in die Armee eintreten; **to** ~ **a firm as (a) partner** in e-e Firma als Teilhaber eintreten; **to** ~ **hands** sich vereinigen; anfangen, zusammenzuarbeiten; **to** ~ **X as a party (to the action)** dem Rechtsstreit des X beitreten; **to** ~ **issue** →issue 1.; **to** ~ **a lawsuit** *Am* e-m Prozeß beitreten; **to** ~ **the**

majority sich der Mehrheit anschließen; **to ~ in marriage** (jdn) trauen; **to ~ an organization** e-r Organisation beitreten; **to ~ a party** *pol* e-r Partei beitreten; Mitglied e-r Partei werden; **to ~ as plaintiff** als Streitgenosse klagen; **to ~ in a project** sich an e-m Plan beteiligen; **to ~ a suit** *Am* →to ~ an action; **to ~ a treaty** *(VölkerR)* e-m Vertrag beitreten; **to ~ up** *colloq.* Soldat werden

joined cases verbundene Rechtssachen

joining, ~ together Zusammenschluß; **date of ~** Eintrittsdatum

joinder Verbindung, Vereinigung *(bes. von Prozessen);* Beitritt; **~ of causes of action** Klageverbindung; Prozeßverbindung; objektive Klagenhäufung; **~ of issue** Festlegung der zu entscheidenden strittigen Fragen *(ausdrücklich [express] durch Bestreiten der Tatsachenbehauptung des letzten gegnerischen Schriftsatzes oder stillschweigend [implied] durch Nichtbeantworten des letzten gegnerischen Schriftsatzes);* **~ of parties** *(Vereinigung mehrerer Personen als Kläger od. Beklagte zu e-r)* Streitgenossenschaft; subjektive Klagenhäufung; **compulsory ~** notwendige Streitgenossenschaft; **non~** Nichtausdehnung e-r Klage auf notwendigen Streitgenossen

joint gemeinschaftlich, gemeinsam, zur gesamten Hand; Mit-, kollektiv; **~ account** →account 1.

joint action gemeinsames Vorgehen; gemeinsame Maßnahme(n); **to take ~** gemeinsam vorgehen; zusammenwirken

joint, ~ adventure →joint venture; **~ agent** gemeinsamer Vertreter; **~ agreement** *Am* →agreement 2.

joint and several gesamtschuldnerisch; gemeinsam, solidarisch; **~ creditor** Gesamtgläubiger *(kann z. B. gegen die Firma und gegen jeden Gesellschafter vorgehen);* **~ debt** Gesamtschuld; Gemeinschafts- und *(zugleich)* Einzelschuld

joint and several debtor Gesamtschuldner

Jeder der mehreren Schuldner haftet für die ganze Leistung *(entspricht im deutschen Recht § 421 BGB)*

joint and several, ~ liability gemeinsame *(gesamtschuldnerische)* Haftung; Gesamt- und *(zugleich)* Einzelhaftung; Verpflichtung als Gesamtschuldner; **~ note** *Am* gesamtschuldnerisches Schuldversprechen *(z. B. von mehreren Personen ausgestellter Scheck od. Schuldschein);* **~ →obligation**; **~ promisee** →~ creditor; **~ promisor** →~ debtor

joint, ~ annuity *Br* (**~ and survivor annuity** *Am*) Überlebensrente; **~ applicants** *(PatR)* gemeinsame Anmelder; Mitanmelder; **~ attorney** Mitbevollmächtigter; **~ authors** Miturheber, Mitautoren; **~ (bank) deposit** gemeinsame Einlage

joint business venture Metageschäft; **parties to a ~** Metisten

joint, ~ capital (of a company) Gesellschaftskapital; **~ cargo** Sammelladung; **~ committee** gemeinsamer (od. gemischter) Ausschuß; paritätischer Ausschuß

joint consultation *Br* gemeinsame Beratung *(zwischen Betriebsleitung und Arbeitnehmer);* **to settle a trade dispute by ~** e-e Arbeitsstreitigkeit durch gemeinsame Beratung regeln

joint creditor Mitgläubiger, gemeinsamer Gläubiger *(im deutschen Recht etwa vergleichbar dem Gesamthandsgläubiger)*

Mehrere joint creditors können eine Leistung nur gemeinsam fordern. Stirbt ein joint creditor, geht sein Forderungsrecht auf die Mitgläubiger und schließlich auf den Rechtsnachfolger des letzten überlebenden Gläubigers über

joint custody gemeinsames Sorgerecht

joint debt gemeinschaftliche Schuld, gemeinsame Verbindlichkeit *(im deutschen Recht etwa vergleichbar der Gesamthandsschuld)*

Verpflichtung mehrerer Personen, die nur gemeinsam belangt werden können. Verpflichtungen einer Gesellschaft sind regelmäßig joint debts der Gesellschafter

joint debtor Mitschuldner, gemeinsamer Schuldner; gemeinschaftlich Verpflichteter *(im deutschen Recht etwa vergleichbar dem Gesamthandsschuldner)*

Jeder haftet für die ganze Schuld, aber alle Schuldner können nur gemeinsam belangt werden. Stirbt ein joint debtor, geht die Verbindlichkeit auf die übrigen Mitschuldner über, bis schließlich eine vererbliche Einzelverbindlichkeit vorliegt. Von dieser Regel besteht eine Ausnahme, wenn die Mitschuldner Teilhaber (partners) der gleichen Firma sind

joint, ~ defendant Mitbeklagte(r); **~ demand** gemeinsame Forderung; **~ deposit** gemeinsames Depot, Gemeinschaftsdepot; gemeinsame Einlage; **~ editor** Mitherausgeber; **~ efforts** gemeinsame Anstregungen (od. Bemühungen); **~ enterprise** Zusammenschluß von Personen für e-n *(sachlich und zeitlich)* gemeinschaftlichen *(im Ggs zur →~ venture oft nicht wirtschaftlichen)* Zweck; **~ estate** →~ tenancy

Joint European Torus (JET) Gemeinsame Europäische Kernforschungsanstalt

Forschungsanstalt für die mögliche Nutzung der Kernfusion als langfristige Energiequelle. *Sitz:* Culham/England

joint, ~ guarantee (or **guaranty**) gemeinsame Garantie; Mitbürgschaft; Mitbürge; **~ guilt** Mitschuld; *(VölkerR)* Kollektivschuld; **~ heir** *bes. Am* Miterbe; **~ holder** Mitinhaber (of a share e-r Aktie); **~ household** gemeinsamer *(ehelicher)* Haushalt; **J~ Industrial Council** (JIC) *Br (ständiges)* Gremium von Arbeitgebern und Arbeitnehmern *(zur Beilegung von Arbeitsstreitigkeiten)*

Joint Intergovernmental Group of Experts on Maritime Liens and Mortgages and Related Subjects (JIGE) Gemeinsame Regierungssachverständigengruppe für Schiffsgläubiger-

rechte und Schiffshypotheken und verwandte Gebiete
Eingesetzt von der →International Maritime Organization (IMO) und der →UNCTAD

joint, ~ **invention** gemeinsame Erfindung; ~ **inventor** Miterfinder *(opp. sole inventor);* ~ **inventorship** Miterfinderschaft; ~ **legatee** Mitvermächtnisnehmer; ~ **letting** Vermietung *(e-s Raumes, Hauses etc)* an mehr als einen Mieter; ~ **liability** gemeinsame Verbindlichkeit, gemeinsame Haftung *(cf. ~ debt);* ~ **life assurance (insurance)** →~lives assurance; ~ **life policy** verbundene Lebensversicherung

joint lives verbundene Leben; ~ **assurance (insurance)** Lebensversicherung auf verbundene Leben; wechselseitige Überlebensversicherung; **for their** ~ solange sie beide (od. alle) leben

joint, ~ **management** gemeinsame Leitung; Mitleitung; ~ **manager** Mitdirektor; ~ **nominee** gemeinsamer (gemeinsam vorgeschlagener) Kandidat; ~ **obligation** gemeinsame Verpflichtung, gemeinsame Verbindlichkeit *(cf. ~ debt);* ~ **offender** Mittäter

joint owner Miteigentümer *(zur gesamten Hand);* Mitinhaber, Mitbesitzer (→*owner);* ~**s** gemeinsame Eigentümer; ~ **of a ship** Mitreeder, Partenreeder; **to be** ~**s** gemeinsam besitzen

joint ownership Miteigentum *(zur gesamten Hand);* gemeinsames Eigentum; Mitinhaberschaft *(an Rechten);* ~ **of a ship** Mitreederei, Partenreederei

joint, ~ **pension** *Br* Überlebensrente; ~ **plaintiff** Mitkläger; ~ **possession** Mitbesitz, gemeinsamer Besitz; ~ **power of attorney** Gesamtvollmacht; ~ **product** Kuppelprodukt, Verbundprodukt; ~ **promise** Gesamthandsverpflichtung; ~ **promisee** →~ creditor; ~ **promisor** →~ debtor; ~ **property** Miteigentum *(zur gesamten Hand);* gemeinsames Vermögen *(z. B. das im Gesamthandseigentum der Gesellschafter stehende Vermögen);* ~ **proprietors** Miteigentümer, Teilhaber, Mitinhaber; *Br* gemeinsame Markeninhaber; ~ **proprietors of a patent** gemeinsame Patentinhaber; ~ **purse** gemeinsame Kasse; **J~ Research Centre** (JRC) *(EG)* Gemeinsame Forschungsstelle (GFS); ~ **resolution** gemeinsame Entschließung; *Am parl* →resolution 4.; ~ **responsibility** gemeinsame Verantwortung; Solidarhaftung; ~ **(tax) return** gemeinsame Steuererklärung *(von Ehegatten);* ~ **security** →~ surety; ~ **statement** *pol* gemeinsame Erklärung

joint stock Gesellschaftskapital; Aktienkapital; ~ **association** *Am* Gesellschaft *(ohne eigene Rechtspersönlichkeit),* deren Kapital in Aktien oder Anteile zerlegt ist; für die Gesellschaftsschulden haften grundsätzlich die Mitglieder persönlich; *(etwa)* Kommanditgesellschaft auf Aktien; ~ **bank** *Br* Aktienbank; ~ **company** →company; ~ **life insurance company** Lebensversicherungs-Aktiengesellschaft

joint surety Mitbürge

joint tenancy gemeinsames Eigentum, Miteigentum *(zur gesamten Hand),* Gesamthandseigentum *(z. B. an Grundstücken, Bankkonten, Aktien; opp. tenancy in common);* Mitbesitz; Mitpacht, Mitmiete
Besonders charakteristisch für joint tenancy ist das Anwachsungsrecht (jus accrescendi). Nach dem Tode eines Beteiligten wächst sein Recht dem anderen Beteiligten an (by survivorship), also keine Vererbung des Anteils. Eine Ausnahme besteht bei der →partnership, wo der überlebende Partner als trustee für die Erben des Verstorbenen gilt (der Anteil des verstorbenen Gesellschafters ist an seine Rechtsnachfolger vererbbar)

joint tenant *(gesamthänderisch gebundener)* Miteigentümer *(opp. tenant in common);* Mitbesitzer; Mitmieter, Mitpächter; ~**s with right of survivorship** Miteigentümer mit Anwachsungsrecht

joint tortfeasors mehrere an der unerlaubten Handlung Beteiligte; gemeinsame Täter, Mittäter

joint undertaking gemeinsames Unternehmen, Gemeinschaftsunternehmen
Hierunter fallen z. B. die Unternehmen, die nach Art. 45 Euratomvertrag[2] eine privilegierte Stellung innehaben oder die im Rahmen der →OECD betriebenen Unternehmen und Forschungsanstalten, die der Sicherheitskontrollkonvention[3] unterliegen (z. B. Eurochemie)

joint use Mitbenutzung, gemeinsame Benutzung; **right for** ~ Mitbenutzungsrecht

joint venture gemeinsames Unternehmen, Gemeinschaftsunternehmen; Gelegenheitsgesellschaft
Rechtliche Verbindung von Personen, die ein Geschäft oder Unternehmen gemeinsam mit Gewinnabsicht betreiben wollen. Wird grundsätzlich wie eine →partnership behandelt, ist in der Organisation aber lockerer als diese

joint venture company *Am* von zwei od. mehreren Partnern begründete Kapitalgesellschaft

joint will gemeinschaftliches Testament (→*will 2.)*

jointly acquired property gemeinsam erworbenes Vermögen; *Am* Errungenschaftsgemeinschaft *(der Ehegatten)*

jointly and severally, to be ~ liable gesamtschuldnerisch (od. als Gesamtschuldner) haften; **to guarantee** ~ gesamtschuldnerisch bürgen;**we promise** ~ wir versprechen (od. verpflichten uns) gemeinsam *(als Gesamtschuldner)*

jointly, ~ **financed** gemeinsam finanziert; ~ **held** (or **owned**) **assets** Gesamthandsvermögen; ~ **held property** Miteigentum zur gesamten Hand, Gesamthandseigentum; ~ **interested party** Mitbeteiligter; ~ **liable** gemeinsam *(als Gesamthandsschuldner)* haftbar; ~ **owned** in gemeinsamen Eigentum befindlich; **to inherit** ~ gemeinsam erben; **to be ~ liable** gemeinsam *(als Gesamthandsschuldner)* haften; **to own a property ~ with others** ein Vermögen mit anderen gemeinsam besitzen; **we promise** ~ wir versprechen (od. verpflichten uns) gemeinsam (zur gesamten Hand)

jointress *Br* Frau, die Anspruch auf→jointure hat

jointure *(vom Ehemann verfügte)* Vermögenszuwendung für Ehefrau *(für die Zeit nach seinem Tode; meist lebenslänglicher Nießbrauch an Grundbesitz)*; **to settle a ~ upon one's wife** seiner Frau ein →jointure aussetzen

Jordan Jordanien; **Hashemite Kingdom of ~** Haschemitisches Königreich Jordanien
Jordanian Jordanier(in); jordanisch

journal Zeitschrift, (Tages-)Zeitung; Journal, Grundbuch *(der Buchführung)*; Logbuch; **J~s of Parliament** *Br* Parlamentsprotokolle; ~ **entry** Eintragung im Journal; Journalbuchung; **cash** ~ Kassenbuch; **official** ~ Amtsblatt; **professional** ~ Fachzeitschrift; **purchases** ~ Einkaufswarenbuch; **sales** ~ Verkaufswarenbuch; **to keep a** ~ ein Journal führen

journalese Zeitungsstil *(z.B. Zeitungsdeutsch, Zeitungsenglisch)*

journalism Journalismus; Pressewesen; **general** ~ allgemeine Publizistik

journalist Journalist; **J~'s Law** *Am* Pressegesetz

journalize *v* ein Journal führen; Eintragung im Journal machen; als Journalist tätig sein

journey Reise *(bes. zu Land; cf. voyage)*; Flugreise; ~ **abroad** Auslandsreise; ~ **log book** *(Flugzeug)* Bordbuch; ~ **there and back** Hin- und Rückfahrt; **to go on a** ~ auf Reisen gehen, verreisen

journeyman Geselle; ~ **locksmith** Schlossergeselle

joy riding Schwarzfahrt; unbefugter Gebrauch von Fahrzeugen; Gebrauchsanmaßung

judge Richter *(Br im Rang über Friedens- und Polizeirichter; Am jeder Richter)*; Schiedsrichter, Preisrichter; **the ~s** die Richterschaft, das Richterkollegium
Br In Großbritannien werden im Ggs. zur Bundesrepublik die judges nicht als solche ausgebildet, sondern aus den Reihen der Anwälte ernannt. Die höheren Richterposten können nur von barristers, die niedrigeren (seit 1971)[4] auch von solicitors besetzt werden. Wegen des starken Rückgriffs auf Laien in der Rechtsprechung kommt England mit verhältnismäßig wenigen Berufsrichtern aus. Ihr soziales Ansehen ist sehr hoch.
Am Im Bundessystem *(cf. federal →courts)* werden die Richter vom Präsidenten mit Zustimmung des Senats ernannt. In den meisten Fällen überläßt der Präsident die Auswahl dem Senat oder den hinter diesem stehenden Politikern. In den Einzelstaaten werden die Richter entweder vom Governor ernannt, oder die Bewerber um Richterposten werden an bestimmten Wahltagen von der Bevölkerung gewählt. Fast alle Richter haben vor ihrer Wahl oder Ernennung als Anwälte praktiziert

judge, ~ advocate (J.A.) Kriegsgerichtsrat; **J~ Advocate General** Chef der Militärjustiz; **~'s associate** Justizbeamter als Gehilfe des Richters; ~ **delegate** beauftragter Richter; ~ **in chambers** →chamber 3.; **~-made law** Richterrecht *(opp. statute law)*; ~ **of first instance** Richter der ersten Instanz; **J~ Ordinary** *Br* Präsident der →Family Division; *Am und Scot* ordentlicher Richter *(opp. ~ delegate)*; **J~s' Rules** *Br* Verhörrichtlinien für die Polizei; **alternate** ~ stellvertretender Richter; **assistant** ~ Hilfsrichter; **body of ~s** Richterkollegium; **chief** ~ *Am* den Vorsitz führender Richter, Vorsitzender; **deputy** ~ *Br* Richterstellvertreter *(z.B. Deputy High Court Judge, Deputy Circuit Judge)*; **lay** ~ *Am* Laienrichter; **ordinary** ~ *Br* einfacher Oberrichter *(opp. presiding ~)*; **part-time** ~ *Br* Richter auf Zeit *(→recorder)*; **presiding** ~ den Vorsitz führender Richter, Vorsitzender *(Br opp. ordinary ~)*; **senior** ~ dienstältester Richter; **to be appointed** ~ zum Richter ernannt werden; **to challenge a** ~ e-n Richter ablehnen

judge *v* richten, urteilen; *(richterlich)* entscheiden; *(als Preisrichter, Sachkenner etc)* entscheiden über, beurteilen; halten für; schließen (from aus)

judg(e)ment (Zivil- od. Straf-)Urteil; gerichtliche Entscheidung; Urteilsspruch; Beurteilung, Ansicht; Urteilskraft

judgment, to annul a ~ ein Urteil aufheben; **to appeal against a** ~ ein Rechtsmittel (Berufung etc) gegen ein Urteil einlegen; **to confirm a** ~ ein Urteil bestätigen; **to deliver a** ~ ein Urteil erlassen (od. verkünden); **to draw up the** ~ das *(mündliche)* Urteil des Gerichts schriftlich formulieren; **to enforce** (or **execute**) **a** ~ aus e-m Urteil vollstrecken; die Vollstreckung aus e-m Urteil betreiben; **to enter a** ~ ein Urteil *(durch die Geschäftsstelle des Gerichts auf Grund der Entscheidung des Richters)* eintragen *(cf. entry of ~)*; ~ **was entered against the defendant** ein Urteil gegen den Beklagten ist ergangen; der Beklagte wurde verurteilt; **to file a** ~ ein Urteil *(zwecks Vollstreckung)* einreichen (od. eintragen lassen); **to form a** ~ sich ein Urteil bilden; **to give** ~ ein Urteil fällen; e-e Entscheidung erlassen, entscheiden; ~ **has been given** ein Urteil ist ergangen; **to obtain a** ~ ein Urteil erwirken; **to pass** ~ ein Urteil fällen; urteilen; **to pass a ~ by default** ein Versäumnisurteil ergehen lassen; **to pass ~ on a prisoner** e-n Angeklagten verurteilen; **to quash a ~** ein Urteil aufheben; **to render ~** *Am* ein Urteil fällen (od. verkünden); **to reverse a ~** (on appeal) ein Urteil (in der Berufungsinstanz) aufheben; **to set aside a ~** ein Urteil aufheben; **to sit in ~ on sb.** über jdn zu Gericht sitzen; **to uphold a ~** ein Urteil bestätigen (od. aufrechterhalten); **to vacate a ~** *Am* ein Urteil aufheben

judgement, ~ bond *Am* Sicherheitsleistung des Berufungsklägers *(für Zahlung der Kosten des Rechtsstreits des unteren Gerichts, wenn die Berufung zurückgewiesen wird)*; **~ by confession** *Am* Anerkenntnisurteil; **~ by** (or **in**) **default** Versäumnisurteil; **~ carrying costs** Urteil, das die Prozeßkosten der unterliegenden Partei auferlegt; **~ creditor** Vollstreckungsgläubiger; Gläubiger, der ein vollstreckbares Urteil erwirkt hat; **~ debt** durch Urteil zuerkannte Forderung; vollstreckbare Forderung; **~ debtor** Urteilsschuldner; Schuldner, gegen den ein vollstreckbares Urteil ergangen ist; **~ docket** *Am* Urteilsregister; **~ for the payment of costs** Verurteilung in die Prozeßkosten; Kostenentscheidung; **~ given against** Urteil (ergangen) gegen; **~ in personam** Urteil betreffend obligatorische Ansprüche; **~ in rem** Urteil betreffend dingliche Ansprüche; ~→**lien**; **~ note** *Am* Schuldanerkenntnisschein; Wechsel, der e-e Unterwerfungsklausel enthält *(confession of judgement clause, cognovit clause)*; **~ obtained by fraud** arglistig erschlichenes Urteil; **~ on the merits** Sachurteil; Urteil auf Grund des materiell- rechtlichen Tatbestandes; **~ over** *Am* Regreßurteil; **~ proof** *Am* nicht eintreibbar, nicht pfändbar; **~ roll** *Am* Gerichtsprotokoll *(enthält Schriftsätze und Urteil)*

judgment summons *Br* gerichtliche Vorladung wegen Nichtzahlung der Urteilsschuld *(Richter entscheidet, in welchen Raten zu tilgen ist und – bei Steuern und Rückständen von Unterhaltszahlungen – ob der Schuldner e-e Gefängnisstrafe zu verbüßen hat)*;[5] **order on ~** auf Grund e-s judgment summons erlassene gerichtliche Verfügung

judgment, ~ with costs kostenpflichtige Entscheidung; **confession of ~ (clause)** *Am* →confession; **declaratory ~** Feststellungsurteil; **deficiency ~** *Am* →deficiency; **domestic ~** Urteil e-s inländischen Gerichts; *Am* in e-m Einzelstaat ergangenes Urteil; **provisionally enforceable ~** vorläufig vollstreckbares Urteil; **enforcement of a ~** Vollstreckung e-s Urteils *(cf. foreign judgment)*

judgment, entry of ~ Eintragung des Urteils, Urteilseintragung

Das Urteil des Gerichts wird von der obsiegenden Partei schriftlich aufgesetzt und auf ihr Ersuchen von der Geschäftsstelle in das Register eingetragen. Sie erhält dann ein Zertifikat, das etwa der deutschen vollstreckbaren Ausfertigung entspricht

judgment, executory ~ Leistungsurteil

judgment, extension of ~s *Br* gegenseitige Vollstreckung ausländischer Urteile; gegenseitige Vollstreckung der Urteile englischer, nordirischer und schottischer Gerichte

judgment, favo(u)rable ~ obsiegendes Urteil; **final ~** Endurteil *(opp. interlocutory ~)*

judgment, foreign ~ Urteil e-s ausländischen Gerichts; **reciprocal recognition and enforcement of foreign ~s** gegenseitige Anerkennung und Vollstreckung ausländischer (Zivil-) Urteile

Das grundlegende britische Gesetz ist Foreign Judgments (Reciprocal Enforcement) Act 1933.

Die gegenseitige Anerkennung und Vollstreckung von gerichtlichen Entscheidungen ist im Verhältnis von Großbritannien und Nordirland und der Bundesrepublik Deutschland durch das Abkommen über die gegenseitige Anerkennung und Vollstreckung von gerichtlichen Entscheidungen in Zivil- und Handelssachen von 1960[6] geregelt.

Im amerikanischen Recht ist die Anerkennung und Vollstreckung ausländischer gerichtlicher Entscheidungen dem materiellen Recht der Einzelstaaten zugeordnet. 12 Staaten haben das →Uniform Foreign Money-Judgments Recognition Act angenommen, welches den Gegenseitigkeitsgrundsatz fallen läßt. Die Anerkennung von Urteilen e-s Schwesterstaates der USA (die ebenfalls als „foreign judgments" bezeichnet werden) ist durch die Bundesverfassung geboten. Ihre Vollstreckung ist in 24 Staaten durch das →Uniform Enforcement of Foreign Judgments Act geregelt

judgment, in my ~ meines Erachtens; **interim ~** Zwischenurteil; **interlocutory ~** Zwischenurteil (→*interlocutory*); **money ~** Urteil auf Zahlung e-r bestimmten Geldsumme; **money of ~** Urteilswährung; **motion for ~**→motion 2,; **previous ~** früheres Urteil, Vorentscheidung; **publication of a ~** Urteilsbekanntmachung; **reasons on which the ~ is based** Gründe, auf denen die Entscheidung beruht; **rendition of ~** *Am* Urteilsfällung, Urteilsverkündung; **reversal of a ~** Aufhebung e-s Urteils *(durch das Rechtsmittelgericht)*; **summary ~** →summary 2.

judgeship Richteramt, Richterwürde

judicature Rechtspflege; Rechtsprechung; Justizverwaltung; Richter(schaft); Richterkollegium; Richterstand; **J~ Act** *Br*[7] Gerichtsverfassungsgesetz; **Supreme Court of J~** *Br* →court 2.

judicial gerichtlich, richterlich; Gerichts-; **~ act** richterliche Handlung; **~ admission** Zugeben (od. Nichtbestreiten) *(e-r Partei)* vor Gericht; **~ and extrajudicial** gerichtlich und außergerichtlich; **~ assistance** Rechtshilfe(verkehr) (→ *assistance*); **~ authorities** Gerichtsbehörden, Justizbehörden; **~ authority** richterliche (od. rechtsprechende) Gewalt; **the ~ bench** die Richter; **in his ~ capacity** in seiner Eigenschaft als Richter; ~ **circuit** *Am* Gerichtsbezirk *(cf. Court of Appeals)*; **J~ Code** *Am*[7a] Bundesgesetz *(regelt Zuständigkeitsvoraussetzungen der Bundesgerichte)*;~ **cognizance** Gerichtskundigkeit

Judicial Committee of the Privy Council (J. C. P. C) *Br* Rechtsausschuß des Kronrats

Revisionsinstanz für Rechtsstreitigkeiten und Strafsachen bestimmter Commonwealth-Länder. Höchstes oberstes Berufungsgericht für die geistlichen Gerichte (→ecclesiastical courts) und Prisengerichte (→prize courts)

judicial, ~ **confession** Geständnis vor Gericht; ~ **decision** gerichtliche (od. richterliche) Entscheidung; ~ **discretion** richterliches Ermessen; ~ **district** Gerichtsbezirk; ~ **error** Fehler des Gerichts; Justizirrtum; ~ **excecution** Zwangsvollstreckung; ~ **factor** *Scot* gerichtl. bestellter Vermögenspfleger *(z.B. bei Minderjährigkeit, Auslandsaufenthalt)*; ~ **function** richterliche Funktion; ~ **inquiry** gerichtliche Untersuchung; ~ **inspection** richterliche(r) Augenschein(seinnahme); ~ **investigation** gerichtliche Untersuchung; ~ **mortgage** *Am* durch Urteil begründete Hypothek am Grundbesitz des Schuldners; Zwangshypothek; ~ **murder** Justizmord

judicial notice Gerichtskenntnis *(Anerkenntnis e-r Tatsache als offenkundig, so daß es keines Beweises durch die Partei bedarf)*; **within** ~gerichtskundig, gerichtsnotorisch; **the court takes ~ of the fact** das Gericht anerkennt die Tatsache als offenkundig; ~ **may not be taken of foreign law** das Gericht hat ausländisches Recht nicht von sich aus zu ermitteln

judicial, ~ **oath** Richtereid, Amtseid; Eid vor Gericht; ~ **office** Richteramt, richterliches Amt; ~ **officer** Richter; Justizbeamter *(der Begriff umfaßt alle Organe der Rechtspflege, auch Anwälte und Wachtmeister)*; ~ **order** gerichtliche Anordnung (od. Verfügung); ~ **power** richterliche (od. rechtsprechende) Gewalt *(cf. executive, legislative power)*; (~) **precedent** (gerichtl.) Vorentscheidung, Präzedenzfall; ~ **procedure** Gerichtsverfahren, gerichtliches Verfahren; ~ **proceeding(s)** Gerichtsverhandlung; ~ **process** gerichtliches Verfahren; ~ **reference** *Scot* Überweisung e-r Sache an ein Schiedsgericht; ~ **reform** Justizreform; ~ **remedies** gerichtliche Rechtsbehelfe (od. Rechtsmittel); ~ **repossession** Einweisung des Sicherungsnehmers in den Besitz des Sicherungsguts durch ein Gericht zur Durchführung der Verwertung *(opp. self-help repossession)*; ~ **review** gerichtliche Überprüfung *(der Entscheidung e-r Vorinstanz od. von Verwaltungsakten)*; *Am* Normenkontrolle *(Befugnis der amerikanischen Gerichte, Gesetzgebungs- und Verwaltungsakte des Bundes od. der Einzelstaaten e-r Normenkontrolle zu unterziehen und sie gegebenenfalls für verfassungswidrig zu erklären)*; ~ **sale** gerichtliche Versteigerung, Zwangsversteigerung *(z.B. to →foreclose a mortgage)*; ~ **separation** gerichtliche Trennung e-r Ehe *(gerichtliche Regelung des Getrenntlebens)*; ~ **supremacy** Oberhoheit der Gerichte (→ *rule of law)*; ~ **system** Gerichtswesen, ~ **trustee** gerichtlich bestellter Treuhänder; ~ **writ** gerichtliche Verfügung

judicial, to discharge ~ functions richterliche Funktionen ausüben; **to grant ~ separation** *(EheR)* das Getrenntleben gestatten; **to hold ~ office** ein Richteramt innehaben (od. bekleiden)

judicially gerichtlich; in richterlicher Eigenschaft; unparteiisch; ~ **and extra-** ~ gerichtlich und außergerichtlich

judiciary Richter(stand); Gerichtswesen, Justiz; *Am* rechtsprechende Gewalt *(cf. legislature, executive)*; richterlich; **J~ Committee** *Am parl* Rechtsausschuß; ~ **function** richterliche (od. rechtsprechende) Funktion; ~ **law** Richterrecht *(→case law)*; **High Court of J~** *Scot* Oberster Gerichtshof für Strafsachen; **independence of the** ~ Unabhängigkeit der Richter

juggle *v (betrügerisch)* manipulieren; *(Bilanz etc)* „frisieren"

jumble sale *Br* Ramschverkauf; Wohltätigkeitsbasar

jumbo jet Großraumdüsenflugzeug

jump plötzliches Ansteigen, sprunghaftes Anwachsen; *Am sl.* Vorsprung; ~ **in prices** Preissprung; *(plötzlicher)* Kurssprung; ~ **in production** Produktionsanstieg

jump *v* springen; hinwegspringen über; *(Preise)* in die Höhe schnellen (lassen); **to ~ bail** *(e.g.* by non-appearance in court) *colloq.* (durch Nichterscheinen etc) die Sicherheitsleistung (Kaution) verfallen lassen; **to ~ channels** *colloq.* den Dienstweg nicht einhalten; **to ~ a claim** →claim 1.; **to ~ to conclusions** voreilige Schlußfolgerungen ziehen; **to ~ the rails** (or *Am* **track**) entgleisen; **the prices ~ed** die Preise sprangen in die Höhe; **the shares ~ed from . . . to . . .** die Aktien sprangen von . . . auf . . .

junction Verbindung, Berührungspunkt; **(railway)** ~ Eisenbahnknotenpunkt; **grade-separated** ~ höhenfreie Kreuzung *(Intern. E-Straßennetz)*; **(road)** ~ Abzweigung *(e-r Straße)*; Einmündung *(e-r Straße)*; Straßenkreuzung; **traffic** ~ Verkehrsknotenpunkt

juncture *(kritischer)* Augenblick; Lage (od. Stand) der Dinge; **at this** ~ in der augenblicklichen Lage, in diesem Augenblick

junior 1., **J~** (Jun., Jnr., Jr) *(nach e-m Namen)*

junior; der Jüngere; Sohn; ~ **manager** Juniorchef; ~ **partner** Juniorpartner

junior 2. jünger *(opp. senior); (im Amt)* untergeordnet, nachrangig; ~ **barrister** (or **counsel**) *Br* Anwalt (barrister), der kein →Queen's Counsel ist; ~ **clerk** untere(r) Büroangestellte(r); ~ **creditor** nachrangiger Gläubiger; ~ **doctor** Assistenzarzt; ~ **issue** Ausgabe *(von Obligationen)* geringeren Ranges; ~ **lien** *Am* nachrangiges Pfandrecht; ~ **management** unteres Management *(opp. middle management, top management);* ~ **mortgage** *Am* im Rang nachstehende (od. nachrangige) Hypothek *(opp. senior mortgage);* ~ **right** später entstandenes Recht; Erbfolge an den jüngsten Sohn (→*ultimogeniture);* ~ **school** *Br* Grundschule für 8–11 jährige; ~ **security** nachrangige Sicherheit; ~ **shares (stocks)** junge Aktien; ~ **staff** Nachwuchs(kräfte) *(e-s Unternehmens)*

junk Altmaterial; Altwaren; Schrott; ~ **bond** „Schundanleihe", hochverzinsliche Anleihe geringer Bonität; ~ **dealer** Altwarenhändler, Trödler; ~ **mail** *(Post)* (unerwünschte) Reklamesendung, Werbeprospekt; ~**shop** Altwarenladen, Trödelladen; ~ **value** Schrottwert; ~ **yard** *Am* Schuttabladeplatz; Autofriedhof

junkie *sl* Rauschgiftsüchtiger; Rauschgifthändler

junta *pol* Junta; **military** ~ Militärjunta

jurat Eidesformel in e-m →affidavit; *Br* Beamter der Insel Jersey; *Br (in Kent und Sussex)* Ratsherr (alderman)

juridical gerichtlich, juristisch, Rechts-; ~ **comparison** Rechtsvergleichung; ~ **days** *Am* Gerichtstage, Verhandlungstage *(des Gerichts);* ~ **person (under public law)** juristische Person (des öffentlichen Rechts)

juris et de jure ("of law and from law"), **presumption** ~ unwiderlegbare Vermutung

jurisconsult Rechtsgelehrter *(auf dem Gebiete des römischen Rechts od. Völkerrechts)*

jurisdiction, Gerichtsbarkeit; Gerichtshoheit, Entscheidungsbefugnis; Hoheitsgewalt; Zuständigkeit; Gerichtsstand; Gerichtsbezirk

Der Begriff „jurisdiction" umfaßt sowohl die Gerichtsbarkeit als auch die Zuständigkeit, die im deutschen Schrifttum überwiegend unterschieden werden

jurisdiction, to be subject to the ~ **(of)** der Gerichtsbarkeit unterstehen; **in the event of the** ~ **of the court being challenged** falls die Zuständigkeit des Gerichts nicht anerkannt wird (oder angefochten wird); **to come under the** ~ **of** unter die Zuständigkeit fallen von; **to decline** ~ sich für unzuständig erklären; **to establish** ~ die Zuständigkeit begründen; **to exercise** ~ Gerichtsbarkeit ausüben; *(VölkerR)* Hoheitsrechte ausüben; **to have exclusive** ~ ausschließlich zuständig sein; **to have original** ~ in erster Instanz zuständig sein; **the court has** ~ **of the person** *Am* das Gericht ist zuständig für e-e Klage gegen e-e Person; **the court has** ~ **in rem** *Am* das Gericht ist zuständig bezüglich e-s bestimmten Gegenstandes; **the court had no** ~ (or **lacked** ~) das Gericht war nicht zuständig; **the court lacked** ~ **over the defendant and the subject matter** das Gericht war örtlich und sachlich nicht zuständig; **to plead want of** ~ die Unzuständigkeit des Gerichts geltend machen; **to review the** ~ die Zuständigkeit nachprüfen

jurisdiction, ~ **agreement** Gerichtsstandsvereinbarung; ~ **clause** Zuständigkeitsklausel; Gerichtsstandsklausel; ~ **in personam** →personal ~; →**in rem** ~; ~ **of** (or **over**) **the person** →personal ~; ~ **over fisheries** Fischereihoheit; ~ **over the parties** Entscheidungsbefugnis über die Parteien *(bes. den Beklagten);* ~ **over the subject matter** sachliche Zuständigkeit

jurisdiction quasi in rem *Am* fingierte in rem-Zuständigkeit

Bestimmte obligatorische Klagen (→actions quasi in rem) werden als dingliche Klagen klassifiziert, indem man Vermögen des Beklagten zum Zwecke der Begründung der Zuständigkeit zwischen den Einzelstaaten (oder [selten] der internationalen Zuständigkeit) innerhalb der jurisdiction als res betrachtet

jurisdiction, administrative ~ Verwaltungsgerichtsbarkeit; **appellate** ~ Zuständigkeit als Rechtsmittelgericht (Berufungsinstanz etc) *(opp. original* ~); **choice of** ~ **clause** Gerichtsstandsklausel; **civil** ~ Zivilgerichtsbarkeit; Zuständigkeit in Zivilsachen *(opp. criminal* ~); **concurrent** ~ konkurrierende (od. nebeneinanderbestehende) Zuständigkeit *(mehrerer Gerichte);* nicht ausschließliche Zuständigkeit *(opp. exclusive* ~*);* **conflict of** ~ Zuständigkeitsstreit, Kompetenzstreit; **contentious** ~ streitige Gerichtsbarkeit; **court having** ~ zuständiges Gericht; **court lacking** ~ nicht zuständiges Gericht; **court of competent** ~ zuständiges Gericht

jurisdiction, court of general ~ Gericht allgemeiner Zuständigkeit *(opp. court of limited* ~*)*

Anders als im deutschen Zivilprozeß gibt es im anglo-amerikanischen Recht Gerichte mit Zuständigkeit für sämtliche Streitsachen, unabhängig von der Höhe des Streitwertes *(Br z. B. High Court of Justice)*

jurisdiction, court of limited ~ Gericht beschränkter Zuständigkeit *(bes. hinsichtlich der Höhe bei Geldforderungen; opp. court of general* ~*);* **court of ordinary** ~ ordentliches Gericht *(opp. court of summary* ~*)*

jurisdiction, criminal ~ Strafgerichtsbarkeit; Zuständigkeit in Strafsachen *(opp. civil* ~*);* **discretionary** ~ Befugnis, Ermessensentscheidungen vorzunehmen; **domestic** ~ innerstaatliche Zuständigkeit (→*domestic);* **ex-**

cess of ~ Unzuständigkeit; **exclusive** ~ ausschließliche Zuständigkeit *(opp. concurrent ~)*; **exemption from** ~ Befreiung von der Gerichtsbarkeit; **exercise of** ~ Ausübung der Gerichtsbarkeit; **federal** ~ *Am* Bundesgerichtsbarkeit; Zuständigkeit der Bundesgerichte; **fiscal** ~ Steuerhoheit

jurisdiction, foreign ~ ausländische Gerichtsbarkeit; Gerichtsbarkeit e-s Staates *(internationale Zuständigkeit seiner Gerichte)* über Staatsangehörige, die im Ausland wohnen oder dort Handlungen vorgenommen haben; **foreign ~ clause** Klausel *(in e-m Vertrag)*, die im Falle e-s Rechtsstreits die Zuständigkeit e-s ausländischen Gerichts vorsieht

jurisdiction, general ~ allgemeine Zuständigkeit (→*court of general ~*); **in personam** ~ *Am* s. personal →~; **in rem** ~ gerichtl. Zuständigkeit betreffend e-n bestimmten Gegenstand; Zuständigkeit, die auf der Lage e-s Vermögensgegenstandes im Zuständigkeitsbereich des Gerichts begründet ist; **international** ~ internationale Zuständigkeit; **lack of** ~ fehlende Zuständigkeit; Unzuständigkeit; **limitation of** ~Beschränkung der Zuständigkeit; **limited** ~ beschränkte Zuständigkeit (→*court of limited ~)*; **local** ~ örtliche Zuständigkeit; **matrimonial** ~ Zuständigkeit in Ehesachen; **non-contentious** ~ freiwillige Gerichtsbarkeit; **ordinary** ~ ordentliche Gerichtsbarkeit; **original** ~ Zuständigkeit in erster Instanz *(opp. appellate ~)*

jurisdiction, out of the ~ außerhalb der Gerichtshoheit (im Ausland); **service out of the** ~ Zustellung im Ausland

jurisdiction, penal ~ Strafgerichtsbarkeit; **personal** ~ Gerichtshoheit über e-e Person; gerichtliche Zuständigkeit für e-e Klage gegen e-e Person; **(place of)** ~ Gerichtsstand; **plea of no** ~ *Am* Einrede der Unzuständigkeit des Gerichts; **restriction on** ~ Beschränkung der Zuständigkeit

jurisdiction, separate ~ getrennte Gerichtsbarkeit; **there are in the United Kingdom three separate ~s** es gibt im Vereinigten Königreich drei getrennte Gerichtsbarkeiten *(cf. Scottish law)*

jurisdiction, specific ~ besondere Zuständigkeit; besonderer Gerichtsstand; **subject matter** ~ sachliche Zuständigkeit; **summary** ~ summarische Gerichtsbarkeit (→*summary 2.)*; →**territorial** ~; **unlimited** ~ unbeschränkte Gerichtsbarkeit; **voluntary** ~ freiwillige Gerichtsbarkeit; **want of** ~ Unzuständigkeit; Fehlen der Entscheidungsbefugnis

jurisdictional Gerichtsbarkeit-; Zuständigkeits-; ~ **arbitration,** Schiedsgerichtsbarkeit; ~ **amount** *Am* (Mindest-)Streitwert *(zur Begründung der Zuständigkeit e-s bestimmten Gerichts)*; ~ **clause** *(VölkerR)* Gerichtsklausel *(Ggs. Schiedsklausel)*; ~ **dispute** *Am* Zuständigkeitsstreit; *Am* Streit zwischen Gewerkschaften um die Mitgliedschaft von Arbeitern in bestimmten Gebieten od. Industrien; ~ **immunity** *(VölkerR)* Befreiung *(der Diplomaten)* von der Gerichtsbarkeit; ~ **waters** *(VölkerR)* Hoheitsgewässer; **the amount is** ~ *Am* der Streitwert bestimmt die Zuständigkeit

jurisprudence Jurisprudenz, Rechtswissenschaft, Rechtslehre; Rechtsphilosophie; **comparative** ~ vergleichende Rechtswissenschaft; **medical** ~ gerichtliche Medizin, Gerichtsmedizin

jurist *(bedeutender od. angesehener)* Jurist; Rechtsgelehrter *(bes. auf dem Gebiete des römischen Rechts od. Völkerrechts)*

juristic juristisch, rechtlich; ~ **act** Rechtsgeschäft; ~ **person** *Am* juristische Person; ~ **personality** *Am* Rechtspersönlichkeit

juror Geschworener; Schöffe;[8] Preisrichter; **~'s book** *Am* Geschworenenliste; **to challenge a** ~ e-n Geschworenen ablehnen; **to serve as** ~ Geschworener sein

jury[9] Geschworene; Schöffen;[8] Schwurgericht *(für Straf- und Zivilsachen)*; Jury

Erstinstanzliche Strafprozesse von größerer Bedeutung (indictable offences [~ses]) kommen zur Verhandlung vor ein Schwurgericht. Im Schwurgericht bildet ein einziger Richter den Gerichtshof, ihm zur Seite stehen die (meist 12) Geschworenen, die nur über Tatfragen zu entscheiden haben. Nach dem →summing up des Richters erklären sie in ihrem →verdict den Angeklagten eines bestimmten Delikts für schuldig oder für nicht schuldig. Gegen ein Urteil des Schwurgerichts kann ein auf Nachprüfung der Rechtsfrage beschränktes Rechtsmittel eingelegt werden.

Auch der →coroner sitzt mit einer jury.

Im Gegensatz zum deutschen Recht, wo Schöffen nur bei schweren Straftaten im Strafprozeß neben den ständigen Berufsrichtern mitwirken, kann auch in Zivilsachen vor der Jury verhandelt werden. In England ist die Jury für Zivilsachen so gut wie abgeschafft (außer bei Beleidigungsklagen).

In den Vereinigten Staaten ist in Zivilsachen die Hinzuziehung einer jury (bestehend aus 12 Geschworenen, wenn die Parteien sich nicht auf eine geringere Zahl einigen) unter bestimmten Voraussetzungen verfassungsmäßig gewährleistet[10]. Jede Partei kann in einer Sache, die auf das →common law gestützt ist und deren Streitwert £ 20 übersteigt, die Mitwirkung einer jury verlangen, was aber immer seltener geschieht

jury, ~ **action** Zivilprozeß mit Geschworenen; ~ **box** Geschworenenbank (Schöffenbank); ~ **list** Geschworenenliste (Schöffenliste); ~ **man** der Geschworene (Schöffe); ~ **panel** Geschworenenliste (Schöffenliste); ~ **process** *Am* Ladung der Geschworenen (Schöffen); ~ **selection** Auswahl der Geschworenen (Schöffen); ~ **trial** s. trial by →~; ~ **woman** die Geschworene (Schöffin); **coroner's** ~ Geschworene zur Untersuchung der Todesursache; **court sitting with a** ~ Schwurgericht; **discharge of a** ~ Entlassung der Geschworenen; **eligibility for** ~ **service** Fähigkeit zum Geschworenenamt (Schöffenamt); **grand** ~ *Am* Anklagejury *(Untersuchungsgremium von auf Zeit ernannten Bürgern, die die öffentliche Anklage [indictment] ablehnen oder für recht befinden)*; **petty** (or **petit**) ~ *Am* Urteilsjury (→*trial* ~); **special** ~ *(aus sozial und wirtschaftlich höheren Berufsklassen)* besonders zusammengesetzte Geschworene *(Br nur noch in der City of London für handelsrechtliche Fälle)*; **trial** ~ Geschworene (Schöffen) in e-m Prozeß; Urteilsjury *(entscheidet in Strafsachen über Schuld des Angeklagten, in Zivilsachen über den Klagegrund)*; **trial by** ~ Schwurgerichtsverfahren; Verhandlung vor e-m Gericht mit Geschworenen (Schöffen); **verdict of the** ~ Urteilsspruch der Geschworenen (Schöffen); **to be summoned to serve on a** ~ e-e Ladung bekommen, als Geschworener (Schöffe) mitzuwirken; **the** ~ **disagrees** die Geschworenen (Schöffen) einigen sich nicht; **to discharge the** ~ die Geschworenen (Schöffen) entlassen; **to draw the** ~ die Geschworenen (Schöffen) auslosen; **to empanel** (or **impanel**) **the** ~ die Geschworenen (Schöffen) aufstellen; **the judge instructs the** ~ der Richter erteilt den Geschworenen (Schöffen) Rechtsbelehrung; **to serve** (or **sit**) **on a** ~ Geschworener (Schöffe) sein; **to waive trial by** ~ auf Verhandlung vor dem Schwurgericht verzichten

jus Recht; ~ **accrescendi** *(the right of accrual)* Anwachsungsrecht *(cf. joint tenancy)*; ~ **disponendi** *(right of disposing)* Verfügungsrecht; ~ **evocandi** Recht e-s Staates, seine Angehörigen aus dem Ausland zurückzurufen; ~ **gentium** *(law of nations)* Völkerrecht; ~ **sanguinis** *(the legal principle that the nationality of a person is the same as his parents') (IPR)* Abstammungsprinzip; ~ **soli** *(the legal principle that nationality is determined by the place of birth) (IPR)* Bodenprinzip; Territorialitätsprinzip; ~ **tertii** das Recht einer dritten Person *(als Einrede)*

just gerecht (to sb. jdm gegenüber); berechtigt, rechtmäßig; redlich; ~ **and equitable** recht und billig; **without** ~ **cause** ohne ausreichenden Grund; unbegründet; ~ **compensation** angemessene Entschädigung *(Am bei Enteignung)*; ~ **reward** gerechter (od. wohlverdienter) Lohn; ~ **title** rechtmäßiger (Rechts-)Anspruch

justly mit (od. zu) Recht

justice Gerechtigkeit; Justiz, Rechtspflege; Richter *(Bezeichnung für die höchsten Richter [Br des High Court, Am des Supreme Court und hoher einzelstaatlicher Gerichte] oder für die niedrigsten Richter [justices of the peace])*; **J~s' Clerk** *Br* juristisch qualifizierter Beamter e-s Magistrates' Court *(juristischer Berater der justices of the peace, Führer des Strafregisters etc)*; **~s' licence** *Br* Konzession zum Verkauf von alkoholischen Getränken

justice of the peace (J. P.) Friedensrichter; **to be taken before a** ~ vor e-n Friedensrichter gebracht werden

Der Friedensrichter ist ein ehrenamtlicher (meist Laien-)Richter mit Zuständigkeit für Strafsachen und bestimmte Zivilsachen niederer Ordnung *(Br* z. B. Unterhaltsklagen auf familienrechtl. Grundlage); *Br* auch für Lizenzerteilung und für richterliche Funktionen in dem Crown Court

justice in respect of taxation Steuergerechtigkeit

justice's warrant *Br* Haftbefehl e-s niederen Richters *(z. B. e-s justice of the peace; opp. bench warrant)*

justice, administration of ~ Justizverwaltung; Rechtspflege; Rechtsprechung; **Associate J~** *Am* Bundesrichter *(einer der 8 Richter am Supreme Court of the U. S)*; *Am* beisitzender Richter der obersten einzelstaatlichen Gerichte *(opp. Chief J~)*; **Chief J~** (C. J.) *Am* Vorsitzender e-s hohen Gerichts; **Chief J~ (of the United States)** *Am* Präsident des Obersten Bundesgerichtshof (Supreme Court of the U. S.); **Court of J~** Gerichtshof *(der EG; →court)*; **denial of** ~ Rechtsverweigerung; **Department of J~** *Am* Justizministerium *(Justizminister: Attorney General)*; **examining** ~ *Br* Untersuchungsrichter; **fugitive from** ~ flüchtiger Rechtsbrecher; **High Court of J~** *Br* Oberstes *(erstinstanzliches)* (Zivil-)Gericht (→ *court)*; **International Court of J~** Internationaler Gerichtshof (→*international)*; **Lord Chief J~** *Br* Lordoberrichter (→*Lord)*; **miscarriage of** ~ Fehlurteil; Justizirrtum; **perversion of** ~ Rechtsbeugung; **sense of** ~ Gerechtigkeitsgefühl, Rechtsempfinden;

justice, to administer ~ Recht sprechen; Gerechtigkeit üben; **to bring to** ~ vor Gericht (od. den Richter) bringen; **to do sb.** ~ jdm Gerechtigkeit widerfahren lassen; **to obtain** (or **receive**) ~ Gerechtigkeit erfahren; **to pervert the course of** ~ das Recht beugen

justiceship Richteramt

justiciable justitiabel; e-r gerichtlichen Entscheidung unterworfen

justiciary, High Court of J *Scot* Oberstes Gericht für Strafsachen

justifiable zu rechtfertigen(d), vertretbar; ~ **abortion** *Am* →abortion; ~ **defence (~se)** Notwehr; ~→**homicide**; **legally** ~ rechtlich vertretbar; ~ **reasons** wichtige Gründe *(z. B. zur Kündigung)*

justification Rechtfertigung; *(bei Beleidigungsklage)* Verteidigungsvorbringen, Rechtfertigungsgrund; **plea of** ~ *(bei Beleidigungsklage)* Geltendmachung, daß die behauptete Tatsache wahr ist; **to plead** ~ *(bei Beleidigungsklagen)* geltend machen, daß die behauptete Tatsache wahr ist; **to prove (the defence of)** ~ den Wahrheitsbeweis antreten

justify *v* (sich) rechtfertigen; *(gegen e-e Beschuldigung)* Gründe anführen; **to** ~ **bail** seine Zahlungsfähigkeit nachweisen *(bei Stellung e-r Kaution)*

justifying documents Belege

jute Jute; →**International J~ Council;** →**International J~ Organization**

justness Gerechtigkeit, Billigkeit

juvenile Jugendlicher; jugendlich; ~ **cases** Jugendsachen; ~ **court** Jugendgericht; ~ **criminal cases** Jugendstrafsachen; ~ **delinquency** Jugendkriminalität; ~ **offen|ce (~se)** Straftat e-s Jugendlichen; ~ **offender** jugendlicher Täter *(Br zwischen 14 und 17 Jahren)*

juxtaposition Nebeneinanderstellung

K

Kaffirs südafrikanische Goldaktien

kangaroo *Br parl (House of Commons)* Befugnis *(des Chairman of a Committee),* die Wahl der Abänderungsanträge zu bestimmen; ~ **closure** Schluß der Debatte durch „Überspringen" (jumping over) von Anträgen (amendments)

keel, to remain on an even ~ ausgewogen (od. gleichmäßig) steuern *(z. B. die Wirtschaft)*

keelage *Br* Hafengebühren

keen scharf *(Kritik, Verhör etc);* ~ **competition** scharfer Wettbewerb; ~ **demand** lebhafte (od. starke) Nachfrage

keep (Lebens-)Unterhalt; Unterhaltskosten *(Verpflegung und Wohnung);* **to earn one's** ~ seinen Lebensunterhalt verdienen; für seinen Unterhalt arbeiten; **to work in return for one's** ~ gegen freie Station arbeiten

keep *v* halten, behalten; unterhalten, versorgen; verwahren, aufbewahren; einhalten, befolgen; sich halten (frisch bleiben); **to** ~ **an account** ein Konto haben (od. unterhalten) (with bei); **to** ~ **accounts** Bücher führen; **to** ~ **an article** e-n Artikel führen (od. auf Lager haben); **to** ~ **books (properly)** Bücher (ordnungsgemäß) führen; **to** ~ **books by double (single) entry** doppelte (einfache) Buchführung haben; **to** ~ **the cash** die Kasse führen; **to** ~ **a copy of a letter** e-n Durchschlag von e-m Brief behalten; **to** ~ **one's engagements** seine Verpflichtungen einhalten; seinen Verpflichtungen nachkommen; **to** ~ **files** Akten aufbewahren; Akten führen; **to** ~ **firm** fest bleiben; nicht sinken *(von Preisen);* **to** ~ **sth. going** etw. in Gang (od. in Betrieb) halten; **to** ~ **goods** Waren führen; **to** ~ **house for sb.** jdm den Haushalt führen; **to** ~ **house** *Br (KonkursR)* zu Hause bleiben; sich vor seinen Gläubigern verbergen; **to** ~ **sb. informed** jdn auf dem laufenden halten; **to** ~ **an inn** e-e Gaststätte führen; ~ **(to the) left!** links halten!; **to** ~ **within a limit** ein Limit einhalten; **to** ~ **a list** e-e Liste (od. ein Verzeichnis) führen; **to** ~ **the minutes** das Protokoll führen; **to** ~ **money with a bank** Geld bei e-r Bank haben; **to** ~ **the peace** die öffentliche Sicherheit und Ordnung bewahren; **to** ~ **sb. a prisoner** jdn gefangenhalten; **to** ~ **a promise** ein Versprechen halten; **to** ~ **records** →records 1.; **to** ~ **in repair** instandhalten; **to** ~ **in safe custody** sicher aufbewahren; **to** ~ **for sale** feilhalten; **to** ~ **a secret** ein Geheimnis bewahren; **to** ~ **secret** geheimhalten; **to** ~ **separate** getrennt halten; **to** ~ **sb. short of money** jdn knapp (mit Geld) halten

keep *v,* **to** ~ **back (from)** einbehalten, zurückbehalten (von); **to** ~ **(back) goods** Waren *(für Kunden)* zurücklegen; **to** ~ **down costs (prices)** Kosten (Preise) niedrighalten; **to** ~ **down a revolt** e-e Revolte unterdrücken; **to** ~ **down a rumour** ein Gerücht unterdrücken; **to** ~ **out (of)** sich heraushalten (aus); **to** ~ **to an agreement** an e-m Abkommen festhalten; **to** ~ **sb. under observation** jdn ständig beobachten; **to** ~ **up appearances** den Schein wahren; **to** ~ **up a custom** e-n Brauch beibehalten; **to** ~ **up (with) one's payments** seine Zahlungsverpflichtungen einhalten; **to** ~ **up prices** Preise beibehalten; **to** ~ **up to date** auf dem neuesten Stand halten

keeping, ~ **(of) accounts** (or **books**) Führung von Büchern; ~ **house** Haushaltsführung; *Br (KonkursR)* Sichverbergen vor seinen Gläubigern; ~ **... in good repair** Instandhaltung des ...; ~ **of a delivery promise** Einhaltung e-s Lieferversprechens; ~ **of files** Aufbewahrung (od. Führung) von Akten; ~ **of a motor vehicle** Halten e-s Kraftfahrzeugs; **for safe** ~ zur sicheren Aufbewahrung; **to be in** ~ **with** übereinstimmen mit

keeper Inhaber, Besitzer; Wärter, Aufseher *(z. B. in e-m Museum);* Verwahrer; ~ **of an animal** Tierhalter; ~ **of the archives** Archivar; ~ **of a car** (or **motor vehicle**) Fahrzeughalter; **K~ of the Great Seal** *Br* Großsiegelbewahrer (→*Lord Chancellor*); ~ **of the minutes** Protokollführer; ~ **of a prison** Gefängnisdirektor; **shop~** Ladeninhaber, Ladenbesitzer

Kennedy round Kennedy-Runde *(Zollsenkungsverhandlungen im Rahmen von →GATT)*

Kenya Kenia; **Republic of** ~ Republik Kenia
Kenyan Kenianer(in); kenianisch

kerb Straßenkante; **on the** ~ im Freiverkehr; ~ **dealing** *(Warenbörse)* inoffizieller Handel; ~ **market** *Br* Freiverkehrsmarkt; Nachbörse *(Handel in amtlich nicht notierten Werten)*; ~ **market price** *Br* Freiverkehrskurs; **~-stone broker** *Am* Freiverkehrsmakler *(kein Mitglied der Börse)*

key Schlüssel; Kennziffer; Haupt-; wichtig; ~ **ally** wichtiger Bündnispartner; ~ **currency** Leitwährung; ~ **date** Stichtag; ~ **feature** das Charakteristische; Hauptmerkmal; ~ **industry** Schlüsselindustrie; ~ **interest rates** Leitzinsen; ~ **issue** Kernproblem; ~ **job** *Am* Schlüsselarbeitsplatz *(der als Grundlage für Bewertung anderer Arbeiten dient, z.B. für Errechnung der Lohnsätze)*; ~ **man** Schlüsselkraft; Mann in e-r Schlüsselstellung; ~ **money** *Br* *(vom Mieter e-r Wohnung an Vermieter gezahlte)* Abstandssumme
key(-)note Grundgedanke (of a policy e-r Politik); ~ **address** (or **speech**) richtungsweisende (od. programmatische) Rede *(bes. bei Parteiversammlung)*
keynote *v* als Grundgedanke enthalten (od. verkünden)
key, ~number Kennziffer; ~ **of ratings** *Am* Schlüssel für die Bewertung von Unternehmen (od. Wertpapieren); ~ **official** Beamter in Schlüsselstellung; ~ **part** Schlüsselrolle; ~ **personnel** leitende Angestellte; ~ **position** (or **post**) Schlüsselstellung, Schlüsselposition; **~question** Schlüsselfrage; **~rate of interest** Leitzinssatz; **~role** Schlüsselrolle; ~ **to a cipher** Codeschlüssel; ~ **witness** Hauptzeuge; **to put under lock and** ~ hinter Schloß und Riegel setzen

keyed advertisement *Am* mit Kennziffer versehene (od. chiffrierte) Anzeige

Keys, House of ~ *Br* Parlament der Insel Man

Khadi Kadi *(Richter in islamischen Ländern)*; **~-justice** Kadijustiz

kickback (*freiwillige od. erzwungene*) Geldrückzahlung; Schmiergeld

kidnap attempt Entführungsversuch

kidnap *v (Kind od. Erwachsenen, bes. in erpresserischer Absicht)* entführen; Menschenraub begehen

kidnapper *(erpresserischer)* Entführer; Kindesentführer; Geiselnehmer; **to give in to the ~s' demands** den Forderungen der Entführer nachgeben; **to resist the ~s' demands** den Forderungen der Entführer nicht nachgeben

kidnapping *(erpresserische)* Entführung; Kindesentführung; Menschenraub; ~ **of hostages** Entführung von Geiseln; **attempted** ~ versuchte Entführung; **legal** ~ Entführung von Kindern aus gemischtnationalen Ehen

kill *v* töten; *parl (Gesetzesvorlage)* zu Fall bringen
killed in action *(im Kriege)* gefallen; **surviving dependants of a serviceman** ~ Kriegshinterbliebene
killing Tötung; hoher und ungewöhnlicher Spekulationsgewinn; **mercy** ~ Gnadentod, Euthanasie; **wilful** ~ vorsätzliche Tötung

kin 1. (Bluts-)Verwandtschaft; Verwandte(r), (die) Verwandten; Angehörige(r), (die) Angehörigen; Familie; **~sfolk** die Verwandten, Angehörigen; **~sman** der Verwandte; **~swoman** (die) Verwandte; **the next of** ~ der (die) nächste(n) Verwandte(n)
kin 2. (bluts-)verwandt; ~ **to** verwandt mit

kind Art, Gattung, Klasse, Sorte; **of average ~ and quality** von mittlerer Art und Güte
kind, in ~ in natura; **in cash or in** ~ in bar oder in Sachleistung(en); **allowance in** ~ Sachbezüge, Deputat; **equal in ~ and quality** von gleicher Art und Güte; **payment** (or **performance**) **in** ~ Naturalleistung, Sachleistung; **remuneration in** ~ Sachbezüge; **to make compensation in** ~ Schadensersatz in natura leisten
kind, of the same ~ gleichartig; von derselben Sorte; **of the same ~ and quality** von gleicher Beschaffenheit

kindred (Bluts-)Verwandtschaft; (Bluts-)Verwandte; *fig* verwandt, gleichartig; ~ **organizations** verwandte Organisationen

King König; **~'s Bench Division** →Queen's Bench Division (→*bench*); **~'s Counsel** (K. C.) →Queen's Counsel (→*counsel*); **~'s English** →Queen's English; **~'s evidence** →Queen's evidence (→ *evidence*); **~'s speech** →Queen's speech

kingdom Königreich; **United K~** Vereinigtes Königreich *(Großbritannien und Nordirland)*

kingship Königtum, Königswürde

kinship Verwandtschaft

kiosk Kiosk, Zeitungsstand; **telephone** ~ Telefonzelle

kirk *Scot* Kirche; **~-session** *Scot* Kirchengericht *(e-r Gemeinde)*

kite Gefälligkeitswechsel (accommodation bill); Kellerwechsel (fictitious bill); *Am* (noch) nicht gedeckter Scheck; gefälschter Scheck; ~ **flyer** Aussteller (od. Benutzer) nicht gedeckter Wechsel (od. Schecks); ~ **flying** →kiting; **to fly a** ~ e-en Gefälligkeitswechsel (od. Kellerwechsel) ausstellen (od. benutzen); Wechselreiterei betreiben

kite *v* sich durch wertlose Sicherheit *(z.B. Wechselreiterei)* Geld (od. Kredit) beschaffen; Wechselreiterei betreiben; **to** ~ **a cheque (check)** e-n (noch) nicht gedeckten Scheck ausstellen; e-n Scheckbetrag fälschen

kiting Ausstellung (od. Benutzung) e-s →kite; Wechselreiterei; Ausstellung e-s (noch) nicht gedeckten Schecks, Scheckreiterei; *Am* Scheckfälschung *(Einsetzung e-s höheren Betrages)*

kivi bond Neuseeland-Dollar Anleihe am Euromarkt

Knight Ritter; *Br* unterste Adelsstufe *(mit dem Titel „Sir" vor dem Vornamen) (nicht erbl. Titel des niederen Adels; cf. Baronet)*

knight derjenige, der e-e (Unternehmens-)-Übernahme beabsichtigt (→*white* ~)

knighthood, to confer a ~ *Br* die Ritterwürde verleihen *(Auszeichnung für öffentl. od. politische Verdienste)*

knock Schlag, Stoß; ~**-down price** Werbepreis; *(bei Auktionen)* Zuschlagpreis; ~**-for-**~ **agreement** *Br (Autovers.)* Abkommen *(zwischen Versicherungsgesellschaften)*, daß bei Unfällen jede Gesellschaft den Schaden an dem von ihr versicherten Wagen trägt *(unabhängig von der Schuldfrage)*

knock-out *Br sl.* fabrizierte Versteigerung *(auf Grund geheimer Verabredung e-s Händlerrings, den Ersteigerungspreis künstlich niedrigzuhalten und den Gewinn anschließend intern zu teilen)*; ~ **price** Schleuderpreis; **at a** ~ **price** spottbillig

knock *v* schlagen, stoßen, prallen (on, against gegen); **to** ~ **down** *(auf Auktionen)* zuschlagen, Zuschlag erteilen; *(Maschinen für Transport)* zerlegen; *(Preis)* stark drücken; *(Haus)* abbrechen

knock off *v colloq (vom Preis)* abziehen; **to** ~ **work** Arbeit einstellen

knock out *v Br (bei Auktionen)* unter sich verkaufen (→*knock-out)*

knocked down (K.D.) zerlegt

knocking advertising herabsetzende Werbung

knocking down Zuschlag *(auf Auktionen)*

knot Knoten (one →nautical mile per hour)

know, people in the ~ *colloq.* eingeweihte Kreise

know-how Know-how, Erfahrungswissen; **assignment of** ~ Know-how-Abtretung; **corporate** ~ *Am* Betriebs-Know-how; **industrial** ~ praktische Betriebserfahrung *(Produktionserfahrungen, Absatzerfahrungen etc)*; **manufacturing** ~ Spezialkenntnis(se) e-r Herstellungsmethode; **personal** ~ persönliches Know-how

know *v* wissen, kennen, erfahren; ~ **all men by these present** hiermit sei allen kundgetan; **to come to** ~ erfahren, in Erfahrung bringen; **to get to** ~ kennenlernen; **to** ~ **or to be chargeable with knowledge** kennen oder kennen müssen

known bekannt; **of** ~ **identity** von Person bekannt; **also** ~ **as ...** auch ... genannt; **be it** ~ **that** es sei kund und zu wissen, daß; **to be** ~ **to the police** der Polizei bekannt sein; **to come to be** ~ bekannt werden; **he knew or ought to have** ~ er wußte oder hätte wissen müssen; **to make** ~ *(etw.)* bekannt geben, zur Kenntnis bringen

knowingly wissentlich, bewußt; ~ **and wil(l)fully** wissentlich und absichtlich; **to make** ~ **false statements** wissentlich falsche Angaben machen

knowledge Kenntnis(se), Wissen; ~ **of business** Geschäftskenntnis(se); ~ **of line of business** Branchenkenntnis(se); ~ **of the facts** *(eigene)* Kenntnis der Tatsachen *(opp. information and belief)*; ~ **of the law** Rechtskenntnis(se); **actual** ~ tatsächliche (od. unmittelbare) Kenntnis; **business** ~ Geschäftskenntnis(se); **contrary to one's** ~ wider besseres Wissen; **from one's own** (or **from personal**) ~ aus eigener Kenntnis; aus eigenem Wissen; **general** ~ Allgemeinbildung; **lack of** ~ Unkenntnis; **specialized** (or **technical**) ~ Fachkenntnis(se); **to the best of one's** ~ **and belief** nach bestem Wissen und Gewissen; **to come to sb.'s** ~ jdm zur Kenntnis kommen; zu jds Kenntnis gelangen; **to get** ~ erfahren

Korea Korea; **Democratic People's Republic of** ~ Korea (Demokratische Volksrepublik) *(Nord-Korea)*; **of the Democratic People's Republic of** ~ Koreaner(in); koreanisch

Korea, Republic of ~ Korea (Republik) *(Süd-Korea)*; **of the Republic of** ~ Koreaner(in); koreanisch

Kremlin Kreml *(in Moskau)*

Kuwait Kuwait; **State of** ~ Staat Kuwait

Kuwaiti Kuwaiter(in); kuwaitisch

L

label (Waren-)Etikett, Aufschrift; (Anhänge- od. Aufklebe-)Zettel; Gepäckzettel; *(kurze)* Bezeichnung; Markierung; *(Zeitungen etc)* Impressum, Pflichteindruck; **address** ~ Adressenzettel; **baggage** ~ *Am* (**luggage** ~ *Br)* Gepäckanhänger; **gummed** ~ gummiertes Etikett, Aufklebezettel; **price** ~ Preiszettel; **stick-on-**~ Aufklebezettel; **tie-on** ~ Anhängezettel, Anhänger

label *v* etikettieren, mit Etikett (od. Aufschrift) versehen; beschriften, bezeichnen; markieren; *(mit Preis)* auszeichnen

label(l)ing Etikettierung; Bezeichnung; Markierung; (Preis-)Auszeichnung; ~ **machine** Etikettiermaschine; **grade** ~ Güteklassenbezeichnung; → **informative** ~

labo(u)r 1. Arbeit; ~ **arbitration** Schlichtung von Arbeitsstreitigkeiten; ~ **camp** (Zwangs-)Arbeitslager; Strafkolonie; ~ **conditions** Arbeitsbedingungen; ~ **contract** Tarifvertrag; ~ **cost** Arbeitskosten, Lohnkosten; ~ **court** *Am* Arbeitsgericht; ~ **dispute** arbeitsrechtliche Streitigkeit; ~ **exchange** *(früher:)* Arbeitsamt; Arbeitsnachweis; ~**-intensive** arbeitsintensiv; ~ **law** Arbeitsrecht; ~ **legislation** *Am* arbeitsrechtliche Gesetzgebung

labo(u)r market Arbeitsmarkt; **situation on the** ~ Arbeitsmarktlage

labo(u)r permit *Br (vom Ministry of Labour erteilte)* Arbeitsgenehmigung; **extension of** ~ Verlängerung der Arbeitsgenehmigung

labo(u)r, ~ **policy** Arbeitsmarktpolitik; ~ **saving** Arbeitsersparnis; arbeit(er)sparend; ~ **saving device** arbeitsparende Vorrichtung; ~ **statistics** Arbeitsstatistik

labo(u)r, allocation of ~ Zuteilung von Arbeit; **casual** ~ Gelegenheitsarbeit; **child** ~ Kinderarbeit; **convict** ~ Gefangenenarbeit; **Department of L**~ *Am* Arbeitsministerium; **direct** ~ Fertigungslöhne; **division of** ~ Arbeitsteilung; Spezialisierung der Arbeit; **farm** ~ Landarbeit; **forced** ~ Zwangsarbeit

labor, hard ~[1] *Am* Zwangsarbeit *(als Zusatzstrafe zum →penitentiary)*; **imprisonment at hard** ~ *Am* Zuchthausstrafe

labo(u)r, indirect ~ Fertigungsgemeinkostenlöhne; → **International L**~ **Organization; manual** ~ körperliche Arbeit; **to procure** ~ Arbeit verschaffen.

labo(u)r 2. Arbeitskräfte; Arbeitnehmer; Arbeiterschaft, Arbeiter; ~ **and capital** Arbeitnehmer und Arbeitgeber; ~ **bank** *Am* Gewerkschaftsbank; Arbeitnehmer und Arbeitgeber; ~ **copartnership** *Br* Gewinnbeteiligung der Arbeitnehmer; **L**~ **Day** *Am* Tag der Arbeit *(1. Montag im September)*; ~ **demand** Nachfrage nach Arbeitskräften; ~ **disturbances** Arbeiterunruhen; ~ **force** (Gesamtzahl der) Arbeitskräfte, Arbeitspotential *(entering the labour market; employed plus unemployed)*; ~ **leader** Gewerkschaftsführer; *Br* führender Mann in der →Labour Party

labo(u)r-management, ~ **committee** *bes. Am* gemischter Ausschuß der Arbeitgeber und Arbeitnehmer; ~ **relations** *bes. Am* Beziehungen zwischen Arbeitgebern und Arbeitnehmern; **L**~**-M**~ **Relations Act** (LMRA) *Am* →Taft-Hartley Act; **L**~**-M**~ **Services Administration** *Am* Behörde für Angelegenheiten des kollektiven Arbeitsrechts

labo(u)r, ~ **migration** Arbeitskräftewanderung; ~**mix** Verhältnis von Angestellten zu Arbeitern *(e-s Unternehmens)*; ~ **movement** Arbeiterbewegung; *Br* Entwicklung der Labour Party; ~ **negotiations** Verhandlungen zwischen den Tarifpartnern; ~ **organization** Arbeitnehmerorganisation; **L**~ **Party** *Br* Arbeiterpartei; ~ **piracy** (or **poaching**) Abwerbung von Arbeitskräften; **unfair** ~ **practices** unlautere Arbeitskampfmethoden; ~ **recruitment** Anwerbung von Arbeitskräften; ~ **relations** Beziehung zwischen den Sozialpartnern *(Betriebsführung und Arbeitnehmerorganisation, bes. Gewerkschaft)*; ~ **representation** Arbeitervertretung, Gewerkschaftsvertretung; ~ **requirement(s)** Bedarf an Arbeitskräften; ~ **reserve** Reserve an Arbeitskräften; ~ **scarcity** →~ shortage; ~ **shortage** Arbeitermangel, Mangel an Arbeitskräften; ~ **situation** *Am* Arbeitsmarktlage; ~ **stoppage** Arbeitseinstellung; ~ **supply** Angebot an Arbeitskräften; ~ **surplus** Überschuß an Arbeitskräften; ~ **troubles** Arbeiterunruhen; ~ **turnover** Arbeitskräftebewegung *(Personalveränderungen e-r Firma in Prozenten zur Durchschnittsbeschäftigung während e-r bestimmten Zeit)*; ~ **union** *Am* Gewerkschaft; ~ **union affiliation** *Am* Gewerkschaftszugehörigkeit; **L**~ **vote** *Br* Stimme (der Anhänger) der Labour Party

labo(u)r, allocation of ~ Zuteilung (od. Zuweisung) von Arbeitskräften; →**casual** ~; **conscription of** ~ Dienstverpflichtung; **Department of L**~ *Am* Arbeitsminsterium; **deployment of** ~ Einsatz der Arbeitskräfte; → **direction of** ~; **emergency** ~ Aushilfskraft; **employment of** ~ Beschäftigung von Arbeitskräften; **farm** ~ Landarbeiter; **female** ~ weibliche Arbeitskräfte; **foreign** ~ ausländische Arbeitskräfte, Fremdarbeiter; **free** ~ gewerkschaftlich nicht organisierte Arbeiterschaft; **hired** ~ Leiharbeitnehmer; **hire of** ~ Einstellung von Arbeitskräften; →**management and ~; mobility of ~** Freizügigkeit der Arbeitnehmer; **organized ~** gewerkschaftlich organisierte Arbeitnehmer; **protection of ~** Arbeiterschutz; **recruitment of ~** →~ recruitment; **scarcity** (or **shortage**) **of ~** Mangel an Arbeitskräften; **semi-skilled ~** angelernte Arbeiter; **skilled ~** gelernte Arbeiter, Facharbeiter; **unskilled ~** ungelernte Arbeiter; Hilfsarbeiter; **to direct ~** Arbeitskräfte lenken; **to import ~** ausländische Arbeitskräfte heranziehen; **the constituency has gone over to L~** *Br* der Wahlkreis ist zur Labour Party übergegangen

labo(u)rer *(bes. ungelernter)* Arbeiter; **agricultural ~** Landarbeiter; **casual ~** Gelegenheitsarbeiter; **day ~** Tagelöhner; **farm ~** Landarbeiter

Labourite *Br parl colloq.* Mitglied der Labour Party

laches *(schuldhafte)* Unterlassung; Versäumnis in der Geltendmachung e-s *(equitable)* Anspruchs; Verwirkung

lack Fehlen, Mangel (of an); **~ of agreement** Einigungsmangel; Dissens; **~ of business** Geschäftsstille; **~ of capital** Kapitalmangel; **~ of cash** Geldmangel; **~ of cause of action** fehlendes Rechtsschutzbedürfnis; **~ of compliance** (with the terms of a contract) Nichteinhaltung (der Vertragsbestimmungen)

lack of confidence Mangel an Vertrauen; **vote of ~** *parl* Mißtrauensvotum

lack, ~ of conformity (of the goods with the contract) Vertragswidrigkeit *(infolge von Sachmangel)*; **~ of consideration** Fehlen der Gegenleistung; **~ of education** Bildungsmangel; **for ~ of evidence** mangels Beweises; **~ of form** Formmangel, Formlosigkeit; **~ of funds** (or **means**) Mangel an Mitteln, Mittellosigkeit; **~ of jobs** Stellenmangel; **~ of jurisdiction** Mangel der Zuständigkeit; **~ of knowledge** Unkenntnis; **~ of money** Geldmangel, Geldknappheit; **~ of proof** →~ of evidence; **for ~ of** aus Mangel an

lack *v* ermangeln; fehlen an; nicht haben; **to ~ capital** nicht genug Kapital haben; **the court ~ed jurisdiction** das Gericht war nicht zuständig; **he ~ed the skills** ihm fehlten die Fähigkeit (und Kenntnisse)

lacuna Lücke *(z.B. im Gesetz)*

lade *v* →load *v*

lading Beladen *(e-s Schiffes)*; Verladen; Ladung, Fracht; **~ charges** Ladekosten, Ladegebühren; **~ port** Verladehafen, Versandhafen; **bill of ~** (B/L) →bill 1.

Ladyship, Your ~ *Br* Hohes Gericht *(Anrede hoher Richterinnen vor Gericht)*

laesae majestatis Majestätsbeleidigung

LAFTA →Latin-American Free Trade Association

lag Verzögerung, Zurückbleiben; Nachlaufen *(wirtschaftlicher etc Faktoren hinter anderen) (opp. lead)*; *sl. (alter)* Strafgefangener; **~ in investment** Stagnation der Investitionen; **cultural** (or **social**) **~** Zurückbleiben der kulturellen Entwicklung *(Diskrepanz zwischen Kultur und sozialer Struktur und der technisch-wirtschaftl. Entwicklung)*; **earnings ~** Verzögerung zwischen Entstehung und Ausbezahlung des Einkommens; **expenditure ~** Verzögerung zwischen Anfall und Verausgabung des Einkommens; **structual ~** struktureller Rückstand; **time ~** →time 1.

lag *v* verzögern; **to ~ (behind)** zurückbleiben (hinter); sich im Rückstand befinden; nachhinken

lagging, regions which are ~ behind in their development Gebiete, die e–n Entwicklungsrückstand aufweisen

lagan Lagan, *(mit Boje zur Wiederauffindung)* versenktes Schiffsgut *(cf. flotsam, jetsam)*

laid, the information must be ~ by or on behalf of the party aggrieved die Anzeige muß vom (od. im Namen des) Geschädigten erstattet werden

laid-off workers vorübergehend entlassene Arbeitskräfte *(z.B. wegen Auftragsmangels)* (→*lay off*)

laid up, to be ~ stilliegen *(Schiff)*

lairaging[02] Halten von Tieren in der Schlachtanlage

laissez-faire *Fr ("let [them] do [as they like]")* laissez-faire *(Schlagwort für wirtschaftl. Liberalismus; opp. state planning)*

laissez-passer *Fr ("let pass")* Passierschein; **delivery of ~** Ausgabe von (Grenz-)Passierscheinen

laicism Laizismus

laity Laienstand, Laien *(opp. clergy)*; Nichtfachleute, Laien

lake (Binnen-)See; **by ~** auf dem Binnenwege

lame duck *Br* sich in finanziellen Schwierigkeiten befindliches Unternehmen; *(Börse) sl.* ruinierter Spekulant, Zahlungsunfähiger; *Am parl* nicht wiedergewähltes Kongreßmitglied, dessen Amtszeit noch nicht abgelaufen ist; **~ argument** nicht überzeugendes Argument

lance, →**free ~**

land Land; (Grund und) Boden; Grundbesitz; Grundstück; Festland *(opp. sea)*; Land *(als politische Einheit, z.B. die USA im Ggs. zum Einzelstaat)*; **~s** Ländereien; Felder; **~ agent**

Grundstücksmakler; Gütermakler; *Br* Gutsverwalter, *Br (auch:)* Seehafenspediteur; ~ **and buildings** Grundstücke und Gebäude; ~ **and buildings, real estate** (*Bilanz*) unbebaute und bebaute Grundstücke (freehold); ~ **and chattels** Grundeigentum und bewegliche Sachen; ~**s and tenements** Grundbesitz (*Land und Gebäude*); ~**s, tenements and hereditaments** *Br* Grundstücke und Grundbesitz; ~ **bank** Bodenkreditanstalt, Hypothekenbank; *Am (staatl.)* Landwirtschaftsbank *(cf. Federal L~ Bank)*; ~ **bonds** *Am* landwirtschaftliche Pfandbriefe; ~**, buildings, plant and machinery** *Br (Bilanz)* Sachanlagen; ~ **carriage** Landtransport; Beförderung auf dem Landwege

land certificate *Br*[3] Eigentumsurkunde, Eigentumsbrief (title deed) *(über →registered land; enthält Grundbuchauszug)*; **depositing the** ~ (with the lender) *Br* formlose Bestellung e-r Hypothek

land charge[4] Belastung von Grundbesitz, Grundstücksbelastung; **L~ C~s Register** *Br* Register für Grundstücksbelastungen von nicht im Grundbuch (Land Register) registriertem Grundbesitz; →**local** ~

Br Die erste Hypothek wird nicht im Register eingetragen, vorausgesetzt, daß dem Darlehensgeber, wie üblich, die →title deeds übergeben sind. Die zweite und folgende Hypothek bedarf der Eintragung in dem Land Charges Register[5] oder, im Falle von registered land, im Land Register. Der Rang der Hypotheken (ohne title deeds) richtet sich nach dem Datum der Registrierung als land charges[5]

land, ~ **compensation** Entschädigung für enteigneten Grundbesitz; ~ **consolidation** Flurbereinigung; ~ **conveyance** →~ carriage; ~ **cost** Grundstückspreis; ~ **credit** Bodenkredit; ~ **credit company** Bodenkreditanstalt; ~ **development** Erschließung von Baugelände; ~ **suitable for development** *Br* Bauland; ~ **dispute** Grundstücksstreitigkeit; ~ **forces** *mil* Landstreitkräfte

land grant *Am (staatl.)* Landzuweisung; Übertragung bundeseigenen Grundvermögens; ~ **college** *Am* landwirtschaftliche Hochschule

land, ~**holder** Grundbesitzer, Grundeigentümer; Pächter; ~**holding** Grundbesitz, Landbesitz; Pacht; ~**-hungry** landhungrig, erpicht auf Landerwerb; ~ **improvement** Bodenverbesserung, Melioration; ~ **jobber** Grundstücksspekulant; Gütermakler; ~ **jobbing** Grundstücksspekulation; ~**lady** Hauswirtin; Vermieterin; Inhaberin *(e-s Fremdenheims etc)*; ~ **law** Grundstücksrecht; ~**-locked states** Binnenstaaten

landlord Hausbesitzer; Hauswirt; Vermieter; Verpächter, Pachtherr; Gastwirt; ~**'s right of distress** Vermieterpfandrecht; ~ **and tenant** Vermieter und Mieter; Verpächter und Pächter; **L~ and Tenant Act,** 1987 Mietgesetz; ~ **and tenant law** Mietrecht; Pachtrecht; ~ **and tenant relationship** Mietverhältnis, Pachtverhältnis; **agreement between** ~ **and tenant** Mietvertrag; Pachtvertrag; **ground** ~ *Br* Verpächter; Pachtherr

landmark Grenzstein, Grenzzeichen; *fig* Wendepunkt; Grundsatzentscheidung; *(SeeR)* Landmarke; **removal of a** ~ Grenzverrückung

land, ~ **on lease** Pachtland; ~**owner** Grundeigentümer, Grundbesitzer; Gutsbesitzer; ~ **patent** *Am* →patent 1.; ~ **planning** Raumordnung; ~ **price** Grundstückspreis, Bodenpreis; ~ →**reclamation**

land records *Am* Grundstücksregister *(öffentl. geführte, die Liegenschaften betreffende Übertragungs- und ähnliche Urkunden)*

Das amerikanische Liegenschaftsrecht kennt im allgemeinen keine Grundbücher im Sinne des deutschen Rechts. Die Eintragung (Registrierung) in den land records hat keine rechtsbegründende Wirkung. Von den in einer Anzahl von Einzelstaaten bestehenden Ausnahmen des Torrens-Systems abgesehen, ist sie nur für den Gutglaubenschutz erheblich *(cf. recording system)*. Die Handhabung der land records ist einzelstaatlich verschieden geregelt

land reform Bodenreform

Land Register *Br* Grundbuch; **office copy of the** ~ *Br* Grundbuchauszug *(im Ggs. zum land certificate kein title deed)*; **notice in the** ~ *Br* →notice 1.

Ein erheblicher Teil des Grundbesitzes in England und Wales ist im Land Register eingetragen *(cf. registered land)*. Die Eintragung hat rechtsbegründende Wirkung. Sie ist noch nicht überall zwingend vorgeschrieben, die Tendenz geht aber dahin, daß Registrierung überall obligatorisch wird. Nur in bestimmten Bezirken (compulsory registration areas) muß heute jede Eigentumsübertragung (change of ownership) registriert werden

Land Registrar, Chief ~ *Br* Leiter des Hauptgrundbuchamtes; **District** ~ →registrar

land registration Eintragung von Grundbesitz in das Grundbuch; **L~ R~ Act,** 1925 *Br* Gesetz, durch das die Eintragung von Eigentum an Grundbesitz im →Land Register eingeführt wurde

Land Registry *Br* Grundbuchamt

Es gibt das Land Registry in London[6] sowie mehrere District (Land) Registries

land, ~ **risk** *(VersR)* Landtransportrisiko; ~ **route** Landweg; ~**slide** *pol* Erdrutsch; ~**slide (victory)** überwältigender Wahlsieg; ~ **speculation** Grundstücksspekulation; ~ **speculator** Grundstücksspekulant; ~ **steward** *Br* Gutsverwalter; ~ **surveying** Landesvermessung; ~ **surveyor** Vermessungsbeamter

land, ~ **tax** *Am* Grundsteuer (*auf unerschlossene Grundstücke*); **L~s Tribunal** *Br* Grundstücks-Tribunal *(entscheidet über Entschädigung bei Enteignungen)*; ~ **value** Bodenwert, Grundstückswert; ~ **warfare** Landkrieg(sführung)

land, accretion of ~ →accretion; **adjacent** ~ Nachbargrundstück; **agricultural** ~ landwirtschaftlich genutztes Grundstück; **barren** ~ nicht anbaufähiges Land *(opp. arable ~)*; **building** ~ Bauland
land, by ~ auf dem Landwege; **by** ~ **and sea** zu Lande und zu Wasser; **carrier by** ~ Frachtführer; **conveyance** (or **carriage**) **of goods by** ~ Landtransport
land, charge on ~ →charge 2.; **derelict** ~ trokkengelegtes Land; **developed** ~ *Br* bebauter Grund und Boden; erschlossenes Baugelände; **development of** ~ Erschließung von Bauland; **flight from the** ~ Landflucht, **holdings of** ~ Landbesitz, Grundbesitz; **interest in** ~ Anteil (od. Recht) an Grundbesitz; **no-man's** ~ *pol* Niemandsland; **ownership of** ~ Grundeigentum, Grundbesitz; **parcel** (or **piece**) **of** ~ Grundstück, Parzelle; **speculation in** ~ Grundstücksspekulation; **speculator in** ~ Grundstücksspekulant; **title to** ~ Grundstückseigentum, Grundstücksrecht; **tract of** ~ Parzelle; **to charge one's** ~ s-n Grundbesitz belasten; **to hold** ~ Land besitzen; ~ **is dear** der Grund und Boden ist teuer

land *v* landen, an Land gehen; *(Ladung)* löschen, ausladen; *colloq.* erhalten; **to** ~ **a good job** e-e gute Stelle bekommen
landed, ~ **estate** →~ property; ~ **gentry** *Br* Landadel; ~ **interest(s)** Großgrundbesitz, Großgrundbesitzer *(als Interessengruppe)*; die Interessen des Großgrundbesitzes; ~ **nobility** *Br* Landadel; ~ **property** Grundbesitz, Grundeigentum, Landbesitz; Liegenschaften; ~ **proprietor** Grundeigentümer, Grundbesitzer; ~ **security** Sicherungsrechte an Grund und Boden; ~ **terms** franco Löschung
landing Landen, Landung *(opp. departure)*; Löschung *(e-r Ladung)*; ~ **and delivery** (ldg. & dely) Landung und Ablieferung; ~ **certificate** Löschbescheinigung, Löschschein; ~ **charges** Landungskosten; Löschungskosten; ~ **clearance** Landegenehmigung *(Flugzeug)*; ~ **order** (or **permit**) Löscherlaubnis; ~ **place** Landungsstelle; Landeplatz; ~ **prohibition** Landeverbot; **emergency** (or **forced**) ~ Notlandung *(e-s Flugzeugs)*; **to effect a** ~ landen

lane Fahrbahn *(e-r Autostraße)*; ~ **straddling** →straddling; **improper** ~ **usage** falsche Fahrbahnbenutzung; **three-**~ **traffic** dreispuriger Verkehr

language Sprache; Terminologie; ~ **block** Sprachbarriere; ~ **department** Sprachendienst; **business** (or **commercial**) ~ Geschäftssprache, Handelssprache; **command of a** ~ Beherrschung e-r Sprache; **crash** ~ **course** Intensivsprachkurs; **defamatory** ~ beleidigende Ausdrücke; **foreign** ~ Femdsprache; **legal** ~ Rechtssprache; Gerichtssprache; **official** ~ Amtssprache; **working** ~ Arbeitssprache; **to be proficient in** (or **to master**) **a** ~ e-e Sprache beherrschen

languishing trade stockender (od. darniederliegender) Handel

Lanham Act *Am*[7] Warenzeichengesetz *(von 1946)*
Bundesgesetzliche Regelung des amerikanischen Markenrechts *(cf. trade mark)*

Lao Laote, Laotin; laotisch
Lao People's Democratic Republic Laotische Demokratische Volksrepublik

lapidation Steinigung

lapse Erlöschen *(von Ansprüchen)*; Verfall, Heimfall *(e-s Rechts)*; Ablauf; *(kleiner)* Fehler (od. Irrtum); *(VersR)* Verfall der Versicherungspolice *(wegen Nichtzahlung der fälligen Prämie)*; ~ **notice** *(VersR)* *(schriftl.)* Benachrichtigung von der Beendigung des Versicherungsvertrages; ~ **of a contract** Ablauf e-s Vertrages; ~ **of a legacy** Wegfall (Hinfälligkeit) e-s Vermächtnisses *(wegen Vorversterbens des Bedachten)*; ~ **of a patent** Erlöschen e-s Patents; ~ **of a right** Erlöschen e-s Rechts; ~ **of time** Zeitablauf, Fristablauf; Verjährung; **to become barred by** ~ verjähren

lapse *v* erlöschen, verfallen, hinfällig werden; heimfallen; ablaufen, außer Kraft treten; *Br (Strafverfahren)* einstellen *(z.B. wegen Tod des Angeklagten)*
lapsed, ~→**devise;** ~ **legacy** *(durch den Tod des Bedachten)* hinfällig gewordenes Vermächtnis; ~ **patent** →patent 2.; ~ **policy** verfallene Versicherungspolice *(infolge Nichtzahlung der Prämie)*; ~ **policies book** *(VersR)* Versicherungsablaufregister; **the claim is** ~ der Anspruch ist erloschen
lapsing appropriation →appropriation 2.

larceny *bes. Am* Diebstahl *(cf. theft)*; ~ **and theft insurance** Diebstahlversicherung; ~ **by finder** *Am* Fundunterschlagung; **grand** ~ *Am* schwerer Diebstahl; **petty** ~ *Am* leichter Diebstahl *(bis zu bestimmter Wertgrenze)*; **to be indicted with** ~ wegen Diebstahls angeklagt sein

large groß; ~ **consumer** Großverbraucher; ~ **enterprise** (or **establishment**) Großunternehmen, Großbetrieb; ~ →**estate;** ~ **family** große (od. kinderreiche) Familie; ~ **income** hohes Einkommen; ~ **order** große Bestellung; ~ **profit** hoher Gewinn
large-scale in großem Ausmaß (od. Umfang); im großen; Groß-, Massen- *(opp. small-scale)*; ~ **enterprise** (or **establishment**) Großunternehmen, Großbetrieb; ~ **loan** Großkredit; ~ **manufacture** (or **production**) Massenfertigung, Massenproduktion; Serienfertigung, Serienherstellung; ~ **retail trade** Einzelhandel im großen

large, on a ~ scale in großem Umfang; **~ size** Großformat; **~ sum of money** große Geldsumme; **at ~** im allgemeinen; ausführlich; auf freiem Fuße; **the world at ~** die gesamte Welt

largely weitgehend

lash system Lash-System (→*lighter-aboard-ship*)

last, ~ bid letztes Gebot; **~ clear chance** *Am* →chance; **~ consumer** Letztverbraucher; **~-day business** *(Börse)* Ultimogeschäft *(am Monatsende abgeschlossenes Termingeschäft)*; **~-day money** Ultimogeld *(am Monatsende fälliges Leihgeld)*; **"~ hired, first fired"** *Am* zuletzt eingestellt, zuerst entlassen; **~-in-first-out** →lifo; **~-mentioned** letzterwähnt; **~ name** *Am* Familienname; **~ quotation** *(Börse)* Schlußnotierung; **as a ~ resort** als letzter Ausweg; **court of ~ resort** Gericht letzter Instanz; **~ speaker** Vorredner; **~ survivor annuity** →survivorship annuity; **~ will (and testament)** letztwillige Verfügung, Testament

lasting, ~ peace dauerhafter Frieden; **~ solution** Lösung von Dauer; **~ value** bleibender Wert

late spät, verspätet, nicht fristgemäß; kürzlich; *(kürzlich)* verstorben; ehemalig, früher; **the ~ 1970s** Ende der 70er Jahre; **~ fee** *Br (Post)* Spät(einlieferungs)gebühr; **the ~ minister** der frühere *(verstorbene od. zurückgetretene)* Minister; **~ of** ehemals wohnhaft in; **the ~ political troubles** die kürzlichen politischen Unruhen; **of ~** seit einiger Zeit; **to be ~ in paying** verspätet zahlen

later später; **at a ~ date** zu e-m späteren Zeitpunkt; **not ~ than** nicht später als (am)

latest spätest; neuest; zuletzt; **~ date** letzter Tag; äußerster Termin; **~ news** letzte (od. neueste) Nachrichten; **at the ~ on ...** spätestens am ..., bis ... spätestens

latent verborgen; **~ defect** (or **fault**) versteckter (od. verborgener) Mangel *(opp. patent defect)*; **~ reserves** →reserve 1.

Lateran Treaties Lateranverträge *(zwischen dem Heiligen Stuhl und Italien 1929 abgeschlossene Verträge)*

latifundia Latifundien

Latin America Latein-Amerika, Ibero-Amerika *(die [spanisch od. portugiesisch sprechenden] Länder Mittel- und Südamerikas)*

Latin-American Free Trade Association (LAFTA) Lateinamerikanische Freihandels-Assoziation

1980 durch die →Latin American Integration Association ersetzt

Latin American Integration Association (LAIA) (*spanisch* ALADI) Lateinamerikanische Integrationsassoziation (*Nachfolgeorganisation der →LAFTA*)

launch Gründung (*e-s Unternehmens*); Markteinführung (*e-s Produkts*); Stapellauf *(e-s Schiffes)*; **~ point** Abschußort *(e-r Rakete)*

launch *v* vom Stapel laufen; vom Stapel lassen; *(Rakete)* abschießen; in Tätigkeit setzen, starten; *(jdn)* lancieren; **to ~ an advertising campaign** e-n Werbefeldzug starten; **to ~ a drive** e-e Aktion starten; **to ~ an enterprise** ein Unternehmen anfangen; **to ~ a loan** e-e Anleihe auflegen; **to ~ (on the market)** auf den Markt bringen; **to ~ into politics** in die Politik einsteigen, Politiker werden

launcher Träger, Trägerrakete; (Raketen-) Abschußvorrichtung; **space vehicle ~** Raumfahrzeugträger; **European L~ Development Organization**[8] Europäische Organisation für die Entwicklung und den Bau von Raumfahrzeugträgern

launching Start; Stapellauf *(e-s Schiffes)*; Abschuß *(von Raketen)*; **~ base** Startbasis; **~ cost** Anlaufkosten; **~ facilities** Abschußanlagen *(für Raketen)*; **~ of a fund** Gründung e-s Fonds, Fondsgründung; **~ range for rockets** Raketenabschußplatz; **~ site** Abschußgelände

law Gesetz; Recht *(im objektiven Sinn; opp. right)*; das →Common Law *(opp. equity)*

law, to abide by a ~ ein Gesetz befolgen; **to abrogate a ~** ein Gesetz aufheben; **to apply a ~** ein Gesetz anwenden; **to be in the ~** Jurist sein; **to be good in ~** rechtlich begründet sein; **to be governed by a ~** unter ein Gesetz fallen; **to be subject to English ~** dem englischen Recht unterliegen; **to become ~** zum Gesetz werden; **to comply with a ~** ein Gesetz befolgen; **to contravene a ~** gegen ein Gesetz verstoßen; **to enact a ~** ein Gesetz erlassen; **to evade a ~** ein Gesetz umgehen; **to fall within the province of a ~** unter ein Gesetz fallen; **to go in for ~** *colloq.* Jura studieren; **to go to ~** vor Gericht gehen, den Rechtsweg beschreiten; prozessieren, klagen (against sb. gegen jdn); **to go to ~ with a p.** jdn verklagen, gegen jdn prozessieren; **to infringe a ~** ein Gesetz verletzen; **to observe a ~** ein Gesetz befolgen; **to practise ~** e-e Anwaltspraxis ausüben; **to read ~** *Br* Jura studieren; **to repeal a ~** ein Gesetz außer Kraft setzen; **to revise a ~** ein Gesetz abändern; **to study ~** Jura studieren; **to sue under a ~** aus e-m Gesetz klagen; **to violate a ~** ein Gesetz verletzen; **a ~ expires** ein Gesetz tritt außer Kraft

law, ~-agent *Scot* Rechtsanwalt (*solicitor*)

law and order öffentliche Ordnung; **maintenance of ~** Aufrechterhaltung der öffentlichen Sicherheit und Ordnung

law, ~s and regulations Gesetze und sonstige Rechtsvorschriften; **~ applicable** anwendbares Recht; **~ breaker** Gesetzesübertreter, Rechtsbrecher; **~ centre** *Br (gebührenfreie)*

Rechtsberatungsstelle; ~ **charges** *Am (Louisiana)* Gerichtskosten, Prozeßkosten

Law Commission *Br* Rechtskommission
Auf Grund des Law Commissions Act (1965) sind in England und Schottland aus 5 Mitgliedern bestehende ~s eingerichtet worden, die mit der systematischen Entwicklung und Reform des gesamten Rechts betraut sind

Law Commission, International ~ (ILC) Völkerrechtskommission *(der Vereinten Nationen) (cf. international)*

law, L~ Committee *Am* Rechtsbeirat der New Yorker Börse; ~ →**court**; **L~ Day** *Am* Rechtstag *(1. Mai mit öffentl. Veranstaltungen und Vorträgen in den Schulen)*; ~ **enforcement authorities** Vollstreckungsbehörden; **L~ Enforcement Assistance Administration** *Am (dem Justizministerium unterstelltes)* Bundesamt, das die örtlichen Polizeibehörden in ihrem Aufgabenbereich unterstützt; ~ **firm** (Rechts-)Anwaltssozietät; ~ **giver** *Am* Schöpfer des Rechts; ~ **in force** geltendes Recht

Law Institute, American ~ (ALI) private Organisation hervorragender amerikanischer Juristen *(Hauptzweck: Rechtsreform)*

law, ~ journal juristische Zeitschrift; **L~ List** *Br (jährl. amtl.)* Verzeichnis der Anwälte *(barristers, solicitors and other legal practitioners)*; **L~ Lords** *Br* Mitglieder des →House of Lords, die als Revisionsinstanz gewisse hohe Richterposten besetzen oder besetzt haben *(Lord Chancellor, Lords of Appeal in Ordinary, ex-Lord Chancellors etc)*

law-making Rechtsschöpfung; Rechtsetzung; ~ **power** Befugnis zur Gesetzgebung; ~ **treaty** *(VölkerR)* rechtsetzender Vertrag, normativer Vertrag *(opp. contractual treaty)*

law, ~ memorandum *Am (Zivilprozeß) (in Form e-s Gutachtens vorgebrachte)* schriftl. Stellungnahme zu den Rechtsgrundlagen des geltend gemachten Anspruchs; Rechtsausführungen *(e-r Prozeßpartei)*; ~ **merchant** Handelsrecht *(gerichtl. anerkanntes kaufmännisches Gewohnheitsrecht: commercial or mercantile law)*; ~ **of agency** Recht der Stellvertretung (und Auftragsrecht) (*cf. agency*); ~ **of conflict of ~s** *Am* internationales Privatrecht (IPR); ~ **of contract** Vertragsrecht, Recht der (Schuld-)Verträge; ~ **of decedents' estates** *Am* (*New York*) Erbrecht; ~ **of domestic relations** *Am* Familienrecht; ~ **of the domicile** (*IPR*) das am Wohnsitz e-r Person geltende Recht, Wohnsitzrecht (→*domicile*); ~ **of equity** Billigkeitsrecht (→*equity*); ~ **of evidence** Beweisrecht (→*evidence*); ~ **of the flag** (*VölkerR, IPR*) Flaggenrecht (*i. S. von Recht des Staates, dessen Flagge oder Hoheitszeichen ein Schiff oder Flugzeug führt*); ~ **of the forum** (*IPR*) →lex fori; ~ **of the land** Recht des Landes, Landesrecht; ~ **of libel** gesetzl. Bestimmungen über die Strafverfolgung von Ehrverletzungen; ~ **of master and servant** *Br* Arbeitsrecht; ~ **of nations Völkerrecht** (*jus gentium; s. international ~*); ~ **of peace** Recht des Friedens; Friedensvölkerrecht; ~ **of practice** (or **procedure**) Prozeßrecht; ~ **of prize** →prize 2.; ~ **of property** Sachenrecht (*einschließl. Liegenschaftsrecht*)

Law of Property Act, 1925 (L. P. A.) (as amended in 1926, 1929, 1964 and 1969) *Br* Gesetze über das Immobiliarrecht (mit abändernden Gesetzen)
Dieses Gesetz vereinfachte die Veräußerung von Grundbesitz. Nur 2 Formen von Eigentum an Land (→fee simple absolute in possession und →term 3. of years absolute) existieren als legal estates (→*estate*). Alle anderen Rechte an Grundbesitz gelten nur als →equitable interests. Erwerber eines legal estate (Käufer, Pächter, Mieter, gewisse Hypothekengläubiger) brauchen sich nicht mit den equitable interests zu befassen, soweit sie nicht Kenntnis oder zurechenbare Kenntnis davon haben (→*notice 2.*)

law, ~ of real property Liegenschaftsrecht; ~ **of the sea** Seerecht (→*sea*); ~ **of the staple** → ~ merchant; ~ **of succession** Erbrecht; ~ **of torts** Recht der unerlaubten Handlungen; **L~ of Treaties** →Vienna Convention on the **L~**; ~ **of war** Recht des Krieges, Kriegsvölkerrecht (*cf. Hague Convention, Geneva Convention*); ~ **office** *Am* Rechtsanwaltsbüro; **L~ Officer** (of the Crown) *Br* Rechtsberater der Krone (*Attorney-General and Solicitor-General; Scot Lord Advocate and Solicitor-General for Scotland*); ~ **reform** Rechtsreform

Law Reform (Contributory Negligence) Act *Br* s. contributory →negligence

Law Reform (Frustrated Contracts) Act *Br* →frustrated

Law Reform (Married Women and Tortfeasors) Act *Br (1935)*
Grundgesetz des englischen Ehegüterrechts[9] (mangels Vertrages gilt Gütertrennung kraft Gesetz). Das Gesetz bestimmt, daß verheiratete Frauen in gleicher Weise wie unverheiratete persönlich für ihre Verpflichtungen haften

law relating to employment Arbeitsrecht

law reports Urteilssammlung *(Sammlung von gerichtl. Entscheidungen mit Urteilsbegründung; Scot s. Session Cases)*
Br[10] Die Law Reports sind eine umfassende Urteilssammlung, die seit 1865 von dem Incorporated Council of Law Reporting for England and Wales herausgegeben wird. Jeder Band wird nach dem Veröffentlichungsjahr und dem Namen des entscheidenden Gerichts zitiert

law, ~ review (L. R.) juristische Zeitschrift; ~ **school** *Br* Rechtsakademie *(kein Teil der Universität); Am univ* juristische Fakultät

Law Society *Br* Berufsverband der →solicitors, *(etwa:)* Anwaltsverein *(cf. Bar Council)*; ~ **examination** Anwaltsprüfung *(der solicitors; cf. articled clerk)*; ~ **Gazette** Anwaltsblatt; ~ **of Scotland** schottischer Anwaltsverein

Aufgaben der Law Society: Ausbildung und Zulassung der solicitors, jährliche Genehmigung für Berufsausübung (durch Erteilung des →practising certificate); Interessenvertretung der solicitors; Auskunftserteilung über Standesfragen; Aufsichtsinstanz für Beschwerden gegen einen solicitor; konsultative Aufgaben bei Gesetzesreformen *(cf. Inns of Court and Bar Council).* Die Law Society ist zuständig für Erteilung des Armenrechts in Zivilsachen[11] *(cf. legal aid)*

law, ~ spiritual Kirchenrecht; **~ student** Student der Rechtswissenschaft, Jurastudent (stud. jur.); Rechtsgelehrter; **~ studies** Studium der Rechtswissenschaft; **~ term** Gerichts(sitzungs)periode *(außerhalb der Gerichtsferien; jetzt →sittings)*

law, according to ~ gesetzmäßig; von Rechts wegen; **act of ~** →act 2.; **by act of ~** kraft Gesetzes; **adjective ~** formelles Recht, Prozeßrecht *(opp. substantive ~);* **administrative ~** Verwaltungsrecht; **admiralty ~** Seerecht; **air ~** Luftrecht; **amendment to a ~** Gesetzesänderung; **at ~** nach →Common L~ *(opp. in equity);* **binding ~** bindendes (od. zwingendes) Recht; **binding in ~** rechtsverbindlich; **body of ~s** Gesetzessammlung; **branch of ~** Rechtsgebiet; **breach of the ~** Rechtsbruch, Gesetzesverletzung; **by ~** durch Gesetz; von Rechts wegen; **case ~** →case 1.; **circumvention of the ~** Umgehung des Gesetzes; **civil ~** Zivilrecht *(opp. criminal ~);* **Civil L~** römisches Recht; **codified ~** kodifiziertes Recht, gesetztes Recht; **→commercial ~; Common L~** →common 2.; **→company ~; comparative ~** Rechtsvergleichung; **compliance with a ~** Beachtung e-s Gesetzes: **conclusion of ~** Rechtsfolgerung; **conflict of ~s** Internationales Privatrecht (→*conflict*); **constitutional ~** Verfassungsrecht; **contrary to ~** rechtswidrig, gesetzeswidrig; **criminal ~** Strafrecht; Strafgesetz; **crown ~** *Br* Strafrecht; **customary ~** *(ungeschriebenes)* Gewohnheitsrecht; **denied on the ~** als rechtlich unbegründet abgewiesen; **domestic ~** innerstaatliches Recht; Heimatrecht *(opp. foreign ~);* **ecclesiastical ~** Kirchenrecht; **economic ~** Wirtschaftsgesetz; **enacted ~** Gesetzesrecht; **enforcement of a ~** Durchsetzung e-s Gesetzes; **equality before the ~** Gleichheit vor dem Gesetz; **established ~** bestehendes (od. geltendes) Recht; **evasion of a ~** Gesetzesumgehung; **exchange ~** Wechselrecht; Wechselordnung; **faculty of ~** juristische Fakultät; **family ~** Familienrecht; **federal ~** *Am* Bundesgesetz; Bundesrecht; **fiction of ~** gesetzliche Fiktion; **field of ~** Rechtsgebiet; **fiscal ~** Steuerrecht; **flexible ~** nachgiebiges Recht; **force of ~** Gesetzeskraft; **foreign ~** ausländisches Recht *(opp. domestic ~);* **game ~** Jagdrecht; Jagdgesetz; **history of ~** Rechtsgeschichte; **ignorance of the ~** Unkenntnis des Rechts (od. Gesetzes); **in ~ and in fact** rechtlich und tatsächlich; **industrial ~** *Br* Arbeitsrecht; **infringement of a ~** Verletzung e-s Gesetzes; **→international ~; interpretation of the ~** Gesetzesauslegung; **issue of ~** *(streitige)* Rechtsfrage; **judge-made ~** richterliches Recht *(opp. statute ~);* **knowledge of the ~** Rechtskenntnis(se); **maritime ~** Seerecht; **→martial ~; maxim of ~** Rechtsgrundsatz; **within the meaning of the ~** im Sinne des Gesetzes; **mercantile ~** Handelsrecht; **→military ~; mistake of ~** Rechtsirrtum; **→municipal ~; national ~** inländisches Recht, Landesrecht; **national ~s or regulations** innerstaatliche Gesetzgebung; **native ~** Eingeborenenrecht; **natural ~** Naturrecht; **by operation of ~** kraft Gesetzes; **→penal ~; permitted by ~** gesetzlich zulässig; **philosophy of ~** Rechtsphilosophie; **point of ~** Rechtsfrage, Rechtsargument; **→practice of ~; presumption of ~** Rechtsvermutung; **(established) principles of ~** (bestehende) Rechtsgrundsätze; **private ~** Privatrecht; **procedural ~** Verfahrensrecht; **promulgation of a ~** Verkündung e-s Gesetzes; **protected by ~** gesetzlich geschützt; **provision of a ~** Gesetzesbestimmung

law, public ~ öffentliches Recht *(Am Dachbegriff für Verfassungsrecht und administrative law; opp. private ~);* **public (international) ~** Völkerrecht; **public international ~ of the sea** Seevölkerrecht; **under public ~** öffentlich-rechtlich

law, question of ~ Rechtsfrage; **relevant in ~** rechtserheblich; **repeal of a ~** Aufhebung e-s Gesetzes; **required by ~** gesetzlich vorgeschrieben; **Roman L~** Römisches Recht; **rule of ~** →rule 2.; **source of ~** Rechtsquelle; **→statute ~; student of ~** →~ student; **substantive ~** materielles Recht *(opp. adjective ~);* **supremacy of ~** Vorherrschaft des Rechts *(cf. rule of ~);* **under the ~ of a country** nach dem Recht e-s Landes; **under the ~ in force** nach geltendem Recht; **unification of ~** Rechtsvereinheitlichung; **violation of a ~** Gesetzesverletzung; **written ~** geschriebenes (od. kodifiziertes) Recht

lawful gesetzlich, gesetzmäßig, rechtmäßig; rechtsgültig; **~ age** Volljährigkeit; **~ currency** gesetzliche Währung; im Lande gültige Münze; **~ goods** *Am* Waren, deren Ausfuhr gesetzlich nicht verboten ist; **~ holder** rechtmäßiger Besitzer (od. Inhaber); **~→representative**

lawfulness Gesetzmäßigkeit, Rechtmäßigkeit; Rechtsgültigkeit

lawless gesetzlos, ungesetzlich

lawsuit (Zivil-)Prozeß, Rechtsstreit; **costs of a ~** Prozeßkosten; **(unfavo[u]rable) issue of a ~** (ungünstiger) Ausgang e-s Prozesses; **party to a ~** Prozeßpartei; **→pending ~; to bring a ~ against a p.** gegen jdn e-n Prozeß anstrengen, jdn verklagen; **to conduct a ~ for a client** e-n

Prozeß für e-n Klienten führen; **to be involved in a** ~ in e-n Prozeß verwickelt sein; im Prozeß liegen; **to lose one's** ~ *bes. Am* s-n Prozeß verlieren, im Prozeß unterliegen; **to win one's** ~ *bes. Am* s-n Prozeß gewinnen

lawyer (Rechts-)Anwalt *(Br cf. barrister, counsel, solicitor; Am cf. attorney, counsel, counsellor);* Rechtsgelehrter; Jurist; **~'s opinion** *Am* Anwaltsgutachten; **international** ~ *(meist praktizierender)* Spezialist für internationales Recht; **to consult a** ~ e-n Anwalt befragen (od. zu Rate ziehen); **to engage (the services of) a** ~ e-n Anwalt nehmen; **to practice as a** ~ *(bes. EG und Ausland)* die Anwaltstätigkeit ausüben

lay 1. Laien-, weltlich *(opp. clerical);* nicht fachmännisch *(opp. professional);* ~ **judge** *Am* Laienrichter; **~man** Laie; Nichtfachmann; Nichtjurist; ~ **people** *Am* Laienrichter

lay 2., **~-by** Ausweichstelle *(für Fahrzeuge);* ~ **days** Liegetage; Löschzeit, Ladezeit *(e-s Schiffes im Hafen; cf. demurrage);* ~ **time** Liegezeit

lay *v* legen; vorbringen; **to** ~ **the blame on sb.** jdm die Schuld zuschieben; **to** ~ **claim** Anspruch erheben (to auf); *(etw.)* beanspruchen; **to** ~ **one's damages** *Am (im pleading)* seine Schadensersatzansprüche darlegen; **to** ~ **an indictment** *Am* e-e Anklage erheben; **to** ~ **an information against sb.** gegen jdn e-e Anzeige erstatten; jdn anzeigen (→*laid);* **to** ~ **sth. open** etw. aufdecken (od. offenlegen); **the Foreign Secretary will** ~ **papers (before the House)** *Br parl* der Außenminister wird das Unterhaus informieren; **to** ~ **great store on sth.** großen Wert legen auf etw.; **to** ~ **stress on** Nachdruck legen auf; betonen; **to** ~ **a tax on sth.** etw. mit e-r Steuer belegen, etw. besteuern; **to** ~ **the** →**venue**

lay *v*, **to** ~ **aside** *(Geld etc)* beiseite legen; **to** ~ **down** *(Amt, Posten, Waffen)* niederlegen; *(Regeln)* aufstellen; *(Schiff)* auf Stapel legen; **to** ~ **down a time-limit** e-e Frist setzen; **to** ~ **down one's tools** die Arbeit niederlegen, streiken; **to** ~ **in provisions** sich mit Vorräten eindecken; Vorräte anlegen; **to** ~ **an employee off work** das Arbeitsverhältnis mit e-m Arbeitnehmer aussetzen *(wegen mangelnder Beschäftigungsmöglichkeit unter Wegfall der Arbeitsvergütung);* **to** ~ **on** *(Gas, Wasser etc)* installieren; **to** ~ **on taxes** Steuern auferlegen; **to** ~ **on the table** *(Antrag etc)* auf unbestimmte Zeit zurückstellen; **to** ~ **out** auslegen, zur Schau stellen; *(Geld)* auslegen; *(Garten etc)* anlegen; **to** ~ **up a ship** ein Schiff außer Dienst stellen

lay(-)off (vorübergehende) Entlassung *(wegen mangelnder Beschäftigungsmöglichkeit unter Wegfall der Arbeitsvergütung);* ~ **rate** *Am* →separation rate

layout 1. Layout, Abriß *(für Werbedruck);* Anzeigenskizze, zeichnerische Unterlage; **~man** Layouter, Layout-Fachmann, Bildideengestalter *(für Werbedruck)*

layout 2. Anordnung *(von Einzelheiten);* Gestaltung *(innerhalb e-s Raumes od. Gebietes);* **departmental** ~ Anordnung der einzelnen Betriebsanlagen; **plant** ~ betriebliche Anlagenplanung; **workplace** ~ Arbeitsplatzgestaltung

l.c.l., ~ **freight** *Am* Stückgutfracht; ~ **rate** *Am* Stückguttarif; **to ship sth.** ~ *Am* etw. als Stückgut versenden (→*less than carload*)

lead 1. Führung, Leitung; Beispiel; Vorsprung (over vor); Vorauseilen von wirtschaftlichen (etc) Faktoren vor anderen *(opp. lag);* **~s** Richtlinien; **~s and lags in trade** *(unvorhergesehene)* Schwankungen im Handelsverkehr; ~ **time** Lieferzeit; **to be in the** ~ e-n Vorsprung haben (by von); **to have the** ~ die Führung haben; **to reduce the** ~ (of) aufholen; **to retain the** ~ die Führung (od. Vorrangstellung) (bei-) behalten; **to take the** ~ die Führung übernehmen

lead 2. Blei; Plombe; ~ (or **leaded**) **petrol** bleihaltiges Benzin; **~-free petrol** (*Am* **gas[oline]**) bleifreies Benzin; ~ **poisoning** Bleivergiftung; ~ **seal** Zollplombe, Zollsiegel; **to seal with** ~ plombieren, versiegeln

lead *v* führen, leiten; vorangehen; *Br* als erster Anwalt *(Queen's Counsel)* in e-m Prozeß auftreten *(cf. leading counsel);* **to** ~ **to** führen zu, zur Folge haben; entgegenführen; **to** ~ **a mutiny** e-e Meuterei anführen; **to** ~ **proof** *Scot* →proof 1.

leading, ~ **article** *com* Zugartikel; Leitartikel *(e-r Zeitung);* ~ **bank** führende Bank; Konsortialführerin

leading case wichtiger Präzedenzfall *(durch den ein Rechtsgrundsatz festgelegt wird);* **summary of ~s** Sammlung grundlegender Entscheidungen

leading, ~ **counsel** erster Anwalt *(Br opp. junior counsel);* ~ **currency** Leitwährung; ~ **decision** grundsätzliche *(gerichtl.)* Entscheidung *(über e-e Rechtsfrage);* ~ **employee** leitender Angestellter; ~ **price** Richtpreis; ~ **principle** oberster Grundsatz; ~ **question** Suggestivfrage; ~ **shares** *(Börse)* führende Werte, Spitzenwerte; ~ **underwriter** Erstversicherer

leader Führer, Leiter, Vorgesetzter; *Br* erster Anwalt *(Queen's Counsel);* Leitartikel *(e-r Zeitung);* **~s** *(Börse)* führende Werte, Spitzenwerte; ~ **of commerce and industry** Wirtschaftsführer; ~ **of the delegation** Delegationsführer; ~ **of a gang** Bandenführer, Rädelsführer; ~ **of industry** Wirtschaftsführer; **L~ of the Opposition** *Br parl* Oppositionsführer; ~ **of a parliamentary group** Fraktionsführer; ~ **writer** Leitartikler; **floor** ~ Fraktionsführer; **industrial** ~ *Am* Gewerkschaftsführer; →**loss ~;** **party** ~ Parteiführer; **ring** ~ Rädelsführer

leadership Führung, Führerschaft; führende Rolle; ~ **skill** Fähigkeit zur Führerschaft; **price** ~ →price 1.; **under the** ~ **of** unter der Führung von

leaflet *(kleiner)* Prospekt; Merkblatt; Flugblatt; (Werbe-)Broschüre; **instruction** ~**s** Anleitungen; **to distribute** ~**s** Flugblätter *(etc)* verteilen

league Bund, Bündnis; Liga; **world** ~ Weltbund, Weltliga; **in** ~ **with** verbündet mit; **to join a** ~ e-r Liga beitreten

League of Nations (L. N.) Völkerbund
1946 durch die Vereinten Nationen (United Nations) ersetzt

leak *(Presse)* undichte Stellen, durch die e-e Information nach außen dringt *(umfaßt echte und gezielte Indiskretion)*; →**radiation** ~

leak *v* nicht dicht sein; *(Informationen etc)* durchsickern lassen; **the information has** ~**ed out** die Information ist durchgesickert

leakage Leckage *(Ausfließen flüssiger Ladung)*; Auslaufen; *(Eisenbahn)* Rinnverlust; Durchsickern *(von Nachrichten)*; Versickern *(von Geldern)*; ~ **and breakage** Leckage und Bruch

lean *v* neigen, tendieren (to, towards zu), sympathisieren (to, towards mit)

leaning Neigung, Tendenz; **criminal** ~**s** kriminelle Neigungen

leap, ~**-frogging** Überspringen; ~**-frog appeal** Sprungrevision; ~ **year** Schaltjahr; **to rise by** ~**s and bounds** sprunghaft in die Höhe gehen *(Preise)*

leap *v*, **prices have** ~**t up** *colloq.* die Preise sind sprunghaft gestiegen

learn *v* lernen; erfahren; ersehen (from aus)

learned, my (very) ~ **friend** *Br* →friend; ~ **in the law** juristisch ausgebildet, rechtskundig; **the** ~→**professions;** ~**society** wissenschaftliche Gesellschaft; ~**societies and clubs** *Br* Idealvereine

learning, institution of ~ Lehranstalt

learner Anfänger, Anlernling; ~ **(driver)** Fahrschüler

lease[12] 1. Mietverhältnis; Mietvertrag, Pachtvertrag *(cf. lessee, lessor)*; Miete, Pacht; Vermietung, Verpachtung; Urkunde über den Miet- (od. Pacht)vertrag; ~ **agreement** Mietvertrag, Pachtvertrag; *(VölkerR)* Pachtabkommen; ~ **contract** →~agreement; ~ **for life** Pacht auf Lebenszeit; ~ **for a term of years** Pacht auf Zeit; ~ **form year to year** Pacht von Jahr zu Jahr; ~ **of livestock** Viehpacht; ~ **of reversion** Pachtvertrag (Mietvertrag), wonach der Pächter (Mieter) die Überlassung der Pacht- (Miet-)sache erst nach Ablauf e-s Pacht- (Miet-)verhältnisses mit dem Vorpächter (Vormieter) verlangen kann, aber sofort den Pachtzins (Mietzins) aus diesem vorhergehenden Pacht-(Miet-)vertrag erlangt; ~ **of a territory** *(VölkerR)* Verpachtung e-s Gebietes; ~**-purchase agreement** Mietkauf; ~ **with option to purchase** Mietkauf; **agreement for a** ~ Mietvorvertrag, Pachtvorvertrag; →**building** ~; **commercial** ~ Mietvertrag über gewerblich genutzte Räume; **contract for a** ~ Mietvorvertrag; Pachtvorvertrag; **currency of a** ~ Laufzeit e-s Miet- (od. Pacht)vertrages; **determination of a** ~ →determination 2.; **duration of (a)** ~ s. term of (a) →~; **on** (or **at**) **the expiration of the** ~ nach Ablauf des Miet- (od. Pacht)vertrages; **farming** ~ Pachtvertrag *(über landwirtschaftl. Grundstücke)*; **fixed-term** ~ *Br* zeitlich befristeter Mietvertrag; **ground** ~ →building ~; **life of a** ~ Laufzeit e-s Miet- (od. Pacht)vertrages; **long** ~ langfristiger Miet- (od. Pacht)vertrag; **object of** ~ Mietobjekt, Pachtobjekt

lease, on ~ zur Miete, mietweise; zur Pacht, pachtweise; **land (taken) on** ~ Pachtland

lease, period of (a) ~ s. term of (a) →~; **provisions of a** ~ s. terms of a →~; **renewal of** ~[13] Mietverlängerung; Pachtverlängerung; →**reversionary** ~; **signing of a** ~ Abschluß e-s Miet- (od. Pacht)vertrages; **sub-**~ Untermiete; Unterpacht; **tenure by** ~ Pachtbesitz; **term of (a)** ~ Mietzeit; Pachtzeit; Dauer e-s Miet- (od. Pacht)vertrages; →**termination of a** ~; **terms of a** ~ Bestimmungen e-s Miet- (od. Pacht-)vertrages; **under-**~ →sub~; **year of a** ~ Mietjahr; Pachtjahr

lease, to cancel a ~ →to terminate a ~; **to draw up a** ~ e-n Miet-(od. Pacht)vertrag aufsetzen; **to enter into a** ~ e-n Miet- (od. Pacht)vertrag abschließen; **the** ~ **expires** die Miete (od. Pacht) läuft ab; **to extend the** ~ →to renew the ~; **to grant sb. a** ~ an jdn *(auf bestimmte Zeit)* vermieten, verpachten; **to grant a** ~ **of business premises** Geschäftsräume vermieten; **to hold (land) under a** ~ in Pacht haben; **to renew the** ~ den Miet- (od. Pacht)vertrag erneuern (od. verlängern); **the** ~ **has run out** die Miete (od. Pacht) ist abgelaufen; **to sign a** ~ e-n Miet- (od. Pacht)vertrag abschließen; **the tenant takes a** ~ **of a shop** (or **store**) der Mieter mietet e-n Laden; **to take on a 99 year** ~ auf 99 Jahre pachten (od. mieten); **to terminate** (or **to give notice of termination of**) **a** ~ e-n Miet- (od. Pacht)vertrag kündigen; **a** ~ **which is not an overriding interest should be protected by an entry in the (land) register** *Br* e-e Miete, die *(wegen ihrer Dauer etc)* nicht als →overriding interest gilt, muß durch Eintragung im Grundbuch geschützt werden

lease 2. Leasing (→*leasing*); ~**back** →sale and lease back; ~ **broker** Leasing-Makler; **equipment** ~ →equipment leasing; **finance** ~ →leasing 2.; **gross** ~ der Vermieter (Leasing-

Geber) übernimmt die mit e-m Leasing-Geschäft verbundenen Nebenleistungen *(opp. net ~)*; **ground~** Grundstückspacht; **maintenance ~** s. maintenance →leasing; **net ~** der Mieter (Leasing-Nehmer) übernimmt die mit e-m Leasinggeschäft verbundenen Nebenleistungen *(Wartung, Reparaturen, Versicherung etc)*; **operating ~** s. operating →leasing; **plant ~** s. plant →leasing; **rent under a ~** Leasingzins; **(full) service ~** s. gross →~; **terms and conditions of ~** Leasing-Geschäftsbedingungen; **to offer ~s** Vermietungen anbieten

lease *v* mieten, vermieten; pachten, verpachten; leasen (→*leasing 2.*); **to ~ a farm** e-n Hof pachten (od. verpachten); **to ~ a shop** e-n Laden mieten (od. vermieten)

leased, ~ car *Am* Mietauto; **~ company** *Am* Pachtgesellschaft; **~ farm** gepachteter (od. verpachteter) Hof; **~ land** Pachtland; **~ property** Mietgegenstand; **~ territory** *(VölkerR)* Pachtgebiet

leasehold Pachtbesitz, Mietbesitz; Pacht-, Miet-; Pachtland, Mietgrundstück *(opp. freehold)*; **~ area** Pachtgebiet; **~ enfranchisement** *Br* Erwerb des Volleigentums an e-m Grundstück durch den Pächter od. Mieter (tenant) gegen Ablösung der Zinsverpflichtungen; **~ estate** pachtartiges (od. mietartiges) Besitzrecht *(term of years absolute)*; gepachteter Grundbesitz; Pachtgut; **~ improvements** Werterhöhung des gepachteten (od. gemieteten) Grundbesitzes *(durch Einbauten oder Ausbauten)*; **~ interest** aus der Landpacht fließendes Recht; Pachtrecht; Mietrecht; **~ land** gepachtetes Land, Pachtland; **~ land and buildings** *Br (Bilanz)* Pachtbesitz; **~ mortgage** Hypothek an gemietetem (od. gepachtetem) Grundbesitz; **~ property** Pachtland; gepachteter Grundbesitz; Mietgrundstück, gemieteter Grundbesitz *(opp. freehold property)*; **~ →reversion; ~ scheme perpetuity** räumlicher und zeitlicher Anteil an e-r (Ferien-)Wohnung; **~ tenure** Pachtbesitz; **~ territory** *(VölkerR)* Pachtgebiet

leaseholder Pächter; Mieter

leasing 1. Mieten; Pachten; Vermieten; Verpachten

leasing 2. Leasing *(Vermietung und Verpachtung von unbewegl. und bewegl. Gegenständen und industriellen Ausrüstungen, bes. durch ~ companies;)* **~ agreement** Leasing-Vertrag; **~ company** Leasing-Gesellschaft; **~ contract** Leasing-Vertrag; **~ of industrial equipment** s. equipment →~; **~ period** Dauer des Leasing; **~ rental** Leasingzins; **application for ~** Leasing-Antrag; **consumer goods ~** Konsumgütervermietung *(Vermietung von Kühlschränken, Waschmaschinen etc)*; **basic term ~** Leasing-Vertrag, der innerhalb e-r Grundmietezeit (basic term) nicht gekündigt werden kann; →**big ticket ~**; **cross-border ~** grenzüberschreitendes Leasing; Leasing-Vorgang, bei dem sich Leasing-Gesellschaften und Leasing-Nehmer in verschiedenen Staaten befinden; **direct ~** direktes Leasing *(zwischen Hersteller und Mieter ist keine Leasing-Gesellschaft eingeschaltet)*; **equipment ~** Ausrüstungsvermietung *(z. B. Büro-, Baumaschinen, Ladeneinrichtungen etc)*; **finance** (or **financial**) **~** Finanz-Leasing *(Vermietung von Investitionsanlagen mit unkündbarer Grundmietezeit; cf. basic term)*; **fleet ~** Vermietung ganzer Fahrzeug-Parks; *(mehr als 60 Kraftfahrzeuge)*; **gross ~** s. gross →lease *(lease 2.)*; **indirect ~** indirektes Leasing *(zwischen Hersteller und Mieter ist e-e Leasing-Gesellschaft eingeschaltet)*; **individual ~** Einzel-Leasing *(weniger als 10 Kraftfahrzeuge)*; **maintenance ~** Dienstleistungsleasing; Leasing, das auch Wartung einschließt; **net ~** s. net →lease *(lease 2.)*; **non-fleet ~** s. individual →~; **operating** (or **operational**) **~** *(meist kurzfristige)* Ausrüstungsvermietung *(Leasing-Vertrag kann unter Einhaltung e-r Frist jederzeit gekündigt werden)*; **plant ~** Vermietung (od. Verpachtung) ganzer Betriebsanlagen; Anlagenverpachtung; **real estate ~** Immobilien-Leasing; **revolving ~** der Leasingnehmer ist berechtigt, den Leasinggegenstand nach Ablauf e-r bestimmten Frist gegen e-n anderen Leasinggegenstand auszuwechseln; **second-hand ~** Leasing-Gegenstand ist ein gebrauchtes Wirtschaftsgut *(das bereits Gegenstand e-s Leasing-Vertrages mit e-m anderen Leasing-Nehmer war)*; **(full) service ~** s. gross →lease *(→lease 2.)*; **short ~** kurzfristiges Mietgeschäft; **truck** (or **vehicle**) **~** Fahrzeug-Leasing

least, ~ developed countries (LLDCs) am wenigsten entwickelte Länder; **~-favoured regions** am stärksten benachteiligte Gebiete

leather goods industry Lederwarenindustrie

leave 1. Erlaubnis, Genehmigung, Zustimmung, Zulassung *(für bestimmte Prozeßhandlungen)*; **~ to appeal** Zulassung der Berufungs- (od. Revisions)einlegung; **~ to speak** *parl* Worterteilung; **by ~ of the court** mit Genehmigung des Gerichts; **with the ~ and licence (~se) of the plaintiff** mit Erlaubnis des Klägers *(action of trespass)*; **to give** (or **grant**) **~** Erlaubnis erteilen; **to grant ~ for appeal** e-m Rechtsmittel (Berufung etc) stattgeben

leave 2. Urlaub; Abschied; **~ for education and training** Urlaub zu Bildungs- und Berufsbildungszwecken; **~ of absence** *mil* Urlaub; längerer Sonderurlaub *(meist ohne Gehalt)*; **~ schedule** *Am* Urlaubsplan; **~ with pay** bezahlter Urlaub; **~ without pay** unbezahlter Urlaub; →**absence without ~; additional ~**

Nachurlaub; **annual** ~ Jahresurlaub; **application for** ~ Urlaubsgesuch; **entitlement to (annual)** ~ Urlaubsanspruch; **extension** (or **prolongation**) **of** ~ Urlaubsverlängerung; **on** ~ beurlaubt; **paid** ~ bezahlter Urlaub; **sick** ~ Krankheitsurlaub; **special** ~ Sonderurlaub

leave, to ask for ~ um Urlaub bitten; **to be on** ~ auf Urlaub sein; **to exceed one's** ~ seinen Urlaub überschreiten; **to give** (or **grant**) **sb.** ~ **(of absence)** jdn beurlauben; **to go on** ~ auf Urlaub gehen; **to have a month's** ~ e-n Monat Urlaub haben; **to overstay one's** ~ seinen Urlaub überschreiten; **to take one's** ~ seinen Urlaub nehmen *(bes. von Beamten)*; sich verabschieden

leave *v* lassen; verlassen, abfahren, abreisen (for nach); auslaufen *(Schiff)*; abfahren *(Zug)*; hinterlassen, vermachen, vererben; (etw.) abgeben, aushändigen; **to** ~ **one's address** s-e Adresse hinterlassen; **to** ~ **blank** unausgefüllt lassen; **to** ~ **the cabinet** aus dem Kabinett ausscheiden; **to** ~ **the church** aus der Kirche austreten; **to** ~ **a country** auswandern; aus e-m Lande ausreisen *(opp. to enter)*; **to** ~ **a deposit** →deposit 1. und 2.; **to** ~ **to sb.'s →discretion; to** ~ **a large fortune** ein großes Vermögen hinterlassen; **to** ~ **off** aufhören; **to** ~ **off work** die Arbeit einstellen; **to** ~ **out of account** außer Betracht lassen; **to** ~ **a →port; to** ~ **a profit** e-n Gewinn abwerfen; **to** ~ **the service** aus dem Dienst ausscheiden

leaving, ~ **no heirs** (Sterben) ohne Erben; ~ **a port** Auslaufen aus e-m Hafen *(opp. entering a port)*; **entering and** ~ **the country** Ein- und Ausreise

Lebanese Libanes|e, ~in; libanesisch; ~ **Republic** Libanesische Republik

Lebanon Libanon

lecture Vortrag; Referat; *univ* Vorlesung (on über); ~ **with discussions** *univ* Seminar; ~ **list** *univ* Vorlesungsverzeichnis; ~ **room** *univ* Hörsaal; **attendance at a** ~ Besuch e-r Vorlesung (od. e-s Vortrages); **course of** ~**s** →course 2.; **inaugural** ~ *univ* Antrittsvorlesung; **open** ~ öffentliche Vorlesung; **series of** ~**s** Vortragsreihe; **to attend a** ~ e-e Vorlesung hören; e-n Vortrag besuchen; **to deliver** (or **give**) **a** ~ eine Vorlesung (od. e-n Vortrag) halten (on über); **to make** (or **take**) ~ **notes** Notizen bei e-r Vorlesung machen

lecture *v*, **to** ~ **on** e-n Vortrag halten über

lecturer Vortragender; *univ* Dozent; ~ **(without tenure)** *Am* Privatdozent

lectureship *univ* Lektorat; Dozentur; Lehrauftrag

ledger *com* Hauptbuch; ~ **abstract** Hauptbuchauszug; ~ **account** Hauptbuchkonto; ~**folio** Hauptbuchfolio; ~ **postings** Hauptbucheinträge *(cf. postings 2.)*; ~ **sheets** Kontoblätter; ~ **type journal** amerikanisches Journal *(in Tabellenform geführtes Hauptbuch)*; **clients'** ~ Mandantenbuch *(Br e-s solicitor)*; **creditors'** ~ Kreditorenbuch; **debtors'** ~ Debitorenbuch; **expenses** ~ Unkostenhauptbuch; **general** ~ Hauptbuch; **personal** ~ Privatkontenbuch; **plant** ~ Betriebs-Anlagenbuch; **property** ~ Sachanlagenbuch; **purchases** ~ Lieferantenbuch; **securities** ~ Effektenbuch; **shareholders'** (or **stockholders'**) ~ Aktienbuch; **subsidiary** ~ Nebenbuch, Hilfsbuch; **to balance the** ~ das Hauptbuch saldieren

leeway *fig* Rückstand; **financial** ~ finanzieller Spielraum; **to make up** ~ den Rückstand aufholen

left 1. links; ~ **bank** (of a river) linkes (Fluß-) Ufer; ~**-hand page** linke Seite *(e-s Buches)*; ~**-hand side** linke Seite *(e-s Kontos)*; **no** ~ **turn** Linksabbiegen verboten!; **improper** ~ **turn** *Am* falsches Einbiegen nach links; **to keep to the** ~ links fahren, die linke Straßenseite einhalten; **to overtake on the** ~ links überholen; **to turn** ~ links abbiegen

left 2. *pol* links *(opp. right)*; **the** ~ die Linke; ~ **wing** linker Flügel; linksstehend; ~**-wing coalition** Linkskoalition; ~**-wing opposition** Linksopposition; ~**-wing party** Linkspartei; ~**-wing press** Linkspresse; ~**-winger** jd, der dem linken Flügel e-r Partei angehört; **the extreme** (or **far**) **L**~ die äußerste Linke; **swing to the** ~ Umschwung nach links

left 3. ~ **till called for** postlagernd; ~ **at station till called for** bahnlagernd; ~ **luggage office** *Br* Gepäckaufbewahrung(sstelle); **he** ~ **me £ 500** er hinterließ mir £ 500

leftist *pol colloq.* Anhänger der Linken, Linkspolitiker, Linker; links orientiert; ~ **press** Linkspresse

legacy Legat, Vermächtnis (od. letztwillige Zuwendung) *(e-r bewegl. [im amerikanischen Recht mitunter auch unbewegl.] Sache od. e-r bestimmten Quote des Wertes des bewegl. Nachlasses)*; ~ **hunting** Erbschleicherei; **→abatement of a** ~; **→ademption of a** ~; **contingent** ~ bedingtes Vermächtnis; **cumulative** ~ zusätzliches Vermächtnis; **demonstrative** ~ beschränktes Gattungsvermächtnis *(das aus e-r bestimmten Vermögensmasse des Gesamtnachlasses zu entrichten ist)*; **general** ~ Gattungsvermächtnis *(das aus der gesamten Masse des Nachlaßvermögens zu entrichten ist)*; Geldsummenvermächtnis; Quotenvermächtnis; **particular** ~ s. specific →~; **pecuniary** ~ Geldvermächtnis, Vermächtnis in Geld; **→residuary** ~; **specific** ~ Vermächtnis *(e-r genau bezeichneten bewegl. Sache; entspricht etwa dem Vermächtnis des deutschen Rechts, § 1939 BGB)*; **to leave a** ~ **to a p.** jdm ein Vermächtnis aussetzen (od. e-e letztwillige Zuwendung machen); **to disclaim a ~** ein Vermächtnis (od. e-e letztwillige Zuwendung) ausschlagen

Dem anglo-amerikanischen Recht ist der Unterschied zwischen Erbeinsetzung und Vermächtnis unbekannt. Das liegt daran, daß der Nachlaß mit dem Tod des Erblassers nicht auf die Erben, sondern (*Am* meist) auf den →personal representative übergeht, und zwar mit gerichtlicher Ernennung rückwirkend auf den Erbfall. Alle durch letztwillige Verfügung Bedachten haben nur schuldrechtliche Ansprüche gegen den personal representative. Der Erblasser kann entweder nur eine bestimmte Sache vermachen (specific legacy), eine bestimmte Geldquote, Summe oder der Gattung nach bestimmte Sache des reinen Nachlasses (general legacy), oder den nach Tilgung aller Nachlaßverbindlichkeiten verbleibenden Überrest (residuary legacy)

legal gesetzmäßig, rechtmäßig, rechtsgültig *(opp. illegal);* juristisch, Rechts-, Gerichts-; gemäß dem →Common Law *(opp. equitable)*

legal action Prozeß; **to take ~ against a p.** gegen jdn gerichtlich vorgehen

legal advice *Br* unentgeltliche (oder kostenermäßigte) Beratungshilfe

legal, ~ adviser Rechtsberater, juristischer Berater; **~ agent** gesetzlicher Vertreter

legal aid *Br* Armenrecht (*jetzt:* Prozeßkostenhilfe); *Am* unentgeltliche Beratungshilfe *(cf. pauper); (PatR)* Verfahrenskostenhilfe; **~ certificate** *Br* Prozeßkostenhilfebescheinigung (*in Strafsachen*); **person in receipt of ~** *Br* Person, der das Armenrecht (Prozeßkostenhilfe) bewilligt ist; **to withdraw ~** *Am* jdm die Prozeßkostenhilfe (das Armenrecht) entziehen

Das Armenrecht ist in England und Wales durch die Legal Aid and Advice Acts von 1974 und 1979 geregelt, nach denen auch Ausländern Armenrecht gewährt werden kann. Über die Bewilligung des Armenrechts in Zivilsachen entscheiden nicht, wie im deutschen Recht, die Gerichte, sondern die →Law Society in London, die England und Wales in Legal Aid Areas aufgeteilt hat. Für Zivilsachen wird das Civil Aid certificate, für Strafsachen das Legal Aid certificate vom Gericht erteilt. Der Legal Aid Act 1982 bezieht sich nur auf Strafsachen.

Die Gegenseitigkeit bei der Bewilligung des Armenrechts ist im Verhältnis zu der Bundesrepublik durch Art. 14 des Deutsch-Britischen Abkommens über den Rechtsverkehr vom 20. 3. 1928[13a] verbürgt.

Im Verhältnis zwischen den Vereinigten Staaten und der Bundesrepublik ist das Armenrecht durch Art. VI Abs. 1 (in Verb. mit Nr. 7 des Protokolls) des Treaty of →Friendship, Commerce and Navigation[13b] geregelt

legal, ~ arguments Rechtsausführungen; **~→assignment, ~ assistance** Rechtshilfe; **~ authorities** Präzedenzentscheidungen; **~ (bank) reserves** →reserve 1.; **~ basis** Rechtsgrundlage; **~ branch** Rechtsabteilung; **~ capacity** Rechtsfähigkeit, Geschäftsfähigkeit (→*capacity); ~* **career** juristische Laufbahn; **~ cause** *Am (bei tort)* hinreichend enger Zusammenhang zwischen Verhalten des Beklagten und Schaden des Klägers; **~ certainty** Rechtssicherheit; **~ charge** →~mortgage; **~ charges** *Br* Anwaltsgebühren *(manchmal auch ungenau für ~ costs gebraucht); ~* **claim** Rechtsanspruch, gesetzlicher Anspruch; auf →Common Law beruhender Anspruch *(opp. equitable claim); ~* **clinic** *Am* Rechtsberatungsstelle; **~ commentary** juristischer Kommentar; **~ committee** Rechtsausschuß; **~ →competence; ~ conception** Rechtsauffassung, Rechtsbegriff; **~ consequence** Rechtsfolge;**~ costs** *Br* Rechtskosten *(court fees, solicitors' feewitnesses expenses); ~* **counsel** *Am* Rechtsberater; **~ currency** *Am* gesetzliches Zahlungsmittel; **~→custodian; ~ custom** *Am* Gewohnheitsrecht; **~ decision** Gerichtsentscheidung, richterliche Entscheidung; **~ defen|ce (~se)** Verteidigung vor Gericht; **~ department** (or **division**) Rechtsabteilung; **~ detriment** Rechtsnachteil; **~→disability**

legal, ~ dispute Rechtsfrage *(im Schiedsgerichtsverfahren); ~* **→domicile; ~ drafting** Entwurf von Rechtsdokumenten; **~ duty** gesetzliche Pflicht, Rechtspflicht; **~ education** juristische Ausbildung; **~ effect** Rechtswirksamkeit; **~ entity** juristische Person; **~ →estate; ~ ethics** Standespflichten des Juristen; **~ executive** *Br* Bürovorsteher e-s solicitor *(als eigener Berufsstand); ~* **expenses** Anwalts- und Gerichtskosten; **~ expenses insurance** Rechtsschutzversicherung; **~ expert** Jurist; **~ fees** Anwaltsgebühren; **~ fiction** Rechtsfiktion, gesetzliche Fiktion

legal force Rechtskraft, Rechtsgültigkeit; Gesetzeskraft; **without ~** (or **of no ~**) rechtsunwirksam; **to have ~** rechtskräftig sein, Rechtskraft haben; **to acquire ~** Rechtskraft erlangen, rechtskräftig werden

legal, ~ form Rechtsform; gesetzliche Form; **~ framework** Gesetzesrahmen; **~ government** rechtmäßige Regierung; **~ ground** Rechtsgrund; **~ heir** →heir at law; **~ history** Rechtsgeschichte; **~ holiday** *Am* gesetzlicher (od. öffentl.) Feiertag; **~ incapacity** Geschäftsunfähigkeit; **~ instrument** Rechtsdokument; **~ interest**[14] dingliches Recht an Immobilien; **~ interest rate** (or **~ rate of interest**) gesetzlicher Zinssatz; **~ investment** *Am* mündelsichere Kapitalanlage; **~ issue** Rechtsfrage; **~ knowledge** Rechtskenntnis(se); **~ liability** gesetzliche Haftpflicht; **~ list** *Am* Liste mündelsicherer Wertpapiere; **~ marriage** *Am* rechtsgültige Ehe; **~ matter** Rechtssache; **~ maxim** Rechtsgrundsatz; **~ →mortgage; ~opinion** →opinion 1. und 2.; **~ →owner; ~ →ownership; ~ person** juristische Person *(opp. natural person); ~* **personality** Rechtspersönlichkeit; **~ philosophy** Rechtsphilosophie; **~ position**

Rechtsstellung, Rechtslage; ~ →**possession;** ~ **practitioner** *Am* Rechtsanwalt; ~ **principle** Rechtsgrundsatz; ~ **procedure** gerichtliches Verfahren; ~ **proceedings** Gerichtsverfahren, Prozeß (→*proceedings*)

legal process Ladung *(vor das Gericht); (bes. hist.)* Prozeß; **by** ~ gerichtlich, auf dem Rechtswege; **immunity from** ~ Befreiung von der Gerichtsbarkeit; **to be immune from** ~ nicht der Gerichtsbarkeit unterworfen sein; **to proceed against a p. by** ~ gegen jdn gerichtlich vorgehen

legal, ~ **profession** juristischer Beruf; Anwaltsberuf, Anwaltschaft; ~ **protection** Rechtsschutz; ~ **provisions** gesetzliche Bestimmungen, Rechtsvorschriften; ~ **relationship** Rechtsverhältnis; ~ **remedy** →remedy 1.; ~ →**representative;** ~ **reserves** *(Bilanz)* gesetzliche Rücklagen; ~ **reserve ratio** →reserve 1.; ~ **rights** Rechte, die auf →Common Law beruhen *(opp. equitable rights)*

legal rule *Am* Rechtsnorm, Rechtssatz *(kasuistische Anweisung an den Richter, wie er im Einzelfall von e-r Rechtsnorm Gebrauch machen soll)*

legal, ~ **securities** *Am* mündelsichere Wertpapiere; ~ **sequence** Rechtsfolge; ~ **services** rechtliche Dienstleistungen; ~ →**status;** ~ **succession** Rechtsnachfolge; ~ **successor** Rechtsnachfolger; ~ **system** Rechtssystem; ~ **tender** gesetzliches Zahlungsmittel; ~ **term** juristischer (Fach-)Ausdruck; ~ **text** Gesetzestext; ~ **title** →title 2.; ~ **training** juristische Ausbildung; ~ **transaction** Rechtsgeschäft; ~ **uniformity** (or **unity**) Rechtseinheit; ~ **validity** Rechtsgültigkeit; ~ **view point** Rechtsstandpunkt

legally gesetzlich, rechtlich; auf dem Rechtswege; ~ **attested** amtlich beglaubigt; ~ **binding** rechtsverbindlich; ~ **effective** rechtswirksam; ~ **incapable** *Am* geschäftsunfähig; ~ **justifiable** rechtlich vertretbar; ~ **protected** gesetzlich geschützt; ~ **valid** rechtsgültig

legalese *Am sl.* Juristensprache *(meist im abfälligen Sinne)*

legalism strikte Einhaltung der Gesetze; Bürokratie, Amtsschimmel

legality Legalität, Gesetzmäßigkeit, Rechtmäßigkeit

legalization[15] Legalisierung, Beglaubigung *(e-r Unterschrift auf amtl. Urkunden, bes. zum Gebrauch im Ausland)*

legalize *v* legalisieren; *(Urkunde amtlich)* beglaubigen

legate *(VölkerR)* Legat *(e-m Botschafter gleichgestellter, aus besonderem Anlaß entsandter, nicht ständiger Vertreter des Vatikans; cf. nuncio, diplomatic agents)*

legatee Vermächtnisnehmer *(der aus e-m →legacy Begünstigte);* Testamentserbe *(von bewegl. Vermögen [cf. devisee], im amerikanischen Recht mitunter auch von unbewegl. Vermögen);* **particular** ~ s. specific →~

legatee, residuary ~ Vermächtnisnehmer (od. [Testaments-]Erbe) des Restnachlasses *(cf. residuary estate)*

Im anglo-amerikanischen Recht besteht rechtlich und praktisch kaum ein Unterschied zwischen (Testaments-)Erbe und Vermächtnisnehmer. Der residuary legatee ist als Empfänger des der Höhe nach meist unbestimmten Restnachlasses dem deutschen (Testaments-)Erben vergleichbar. Der Reinüberschuß der Erbschaft wird ihm aber im Ggs. zum deutschen Recht vom ~→executor ausbezahlt, er haftet also nicht für die Nachlaßschulden

legatee, sole ~ *Am (testamentarisch eingesetzter)* Universalerbe, Gesamterbe; **specific** ~ Vermächtnisnehmer e-r bestimmten bewegl. Sache

legation Gesandtschaft; Gesandtschaftsgebäude; **counsel(l)or (of** ~**)** Gesandtschaftsrat *(im deutschen dipl. Dienst als Titel abgeschafft)*

legator Vermächtnisgeber *(cf. legacy);* Testator; Erblasser

Legion, Foreign ~ Fremdenlegion

legislate *v* Gesetze geben (od. machen)

legislation Gesetzgebung; Gesetze; ~ **by reference** Gesetzgebung durch Verweisung *(auf bereits bestehende Gesetze);* ~ **(in force)** (geltende) Rechtsvorschriften; **channel of** ~ Gesetzgebungsweg; →**delegated** ~; **emergency** ~ Notgesetzgebung; →**municipal** ~; →**national** ~; **penal** ~ Strafgesetzgebung; **process of** ~ Gesetzgebungsverfahren; **promulgation of** ~ Gesetzesverkündung; **social** ~ Sozialgesetzgebung; **subordinate** ~ delegierte Gesetzgebung; Verordnung(en); **wartime** ~ Kriegsgesetzgebung; **to enact** ~ Gesetze erlassen; **to initiate** ~ Gesetze einbringen (od. vorschlagen)

legislative gesetzgebend; **by** ~ **act(ion)** auf dem Gesetzgebungswege; **L**~ **Assembly** gesetzgebende Versammlung; Parlament; ~ **authority** →~ power; ~ **body** gesetzgebende Körperschaft; ~ **budget** *Am* Haushaltsgesetz; ~ **control** Aufsicht der gesetzgebenden Gewalt; ~**department** *Am* Legislative *(cf. department);* **by** ~ **enactment** durch e-n Akt der Gesetzgebung; ~ **initiative** Gesetzgebungsinitiative; ~ **intent** Absicht des Gesetzgebers; ~ **investigation** *Am parl* Untersuchung durch e-n Ausschuß; ~ **jurisdiction** Gesetzgebungszuständigkeit; ~ **period** Legislaturperiode; ~ **power** gesetzgebende Gewalt; Legislative *(cf. executive, judicial power);* Gesetzgebungsbefugnis; ~ **provisions** Rechtsvorschriften; ~ **purpose**

Absicht des Gesetzgebers; ~ →**reciprocity;** ~ **recommendation** Empfehlung de lege ferenda; ~ **treaty** *(VölkerR)* normativer Vertrag

legislator Gesetzgeber

legislature Legislative *(opp. executive, judiciary),* gesetzgebende Körperschaft; **period of** ~ Legislaturperiode, Wahlperiode; **state** ~ *Am* Parlament e-s Einzelstaates

legitim *Scot* gesetzliches Pflichtteilsrecht der Kinder *(am bewegl. Teil des Nachlasses e-s Elternteils)*

legitimacy Ehelichkeit; Legitimität; Gesetzmäßigkeit *(opp. illegitimacy);* **L~ Acts** *Br*[16] Gesetze über die nichtehelichen Kinder; **declaration of** ~ *Br*[17] Erklärung der Ehelichkeit *(Erklärung, daß jemand das eheliche Kind s-r Eltern ist und [oder] daß die eigene Ehe oder die der Eltern od. Großeltern e-e rechtsgültige Ehe ist oder war);* **status of** ~ ehelicher Status; **to contest the** ~ die Ehelichkeit anfechten

legitimate *v* legitimieren; für rechtmäßig erklären; *(nichteheliches Kind)* für ehelich erklären; **to be(come) ~d by subsequent marriage** durch nachfolgende Eheschließung legitimiert werden

legitimate legitim, gesetzmäßig, rechtmäßig, berechtigt; ehelich; ~ **child** eheliches Kind; ~ **claim** berechtigter (od. rechtmäßiger) Anspruch; ~ **costs** rechtlich zulässige Kosten; ~ **descent** eheliche Abstammung; ~ **doubt** berechtigter Zweifel; ~ **interest** berechtigtes (od. legitimes) Interesse; **to declare a child (to be)** ~ ein Kind für ehelich erklären

legitimately, to be ~ interested ein berechtigtes Interesse haben

legitimation Legitimation; Legitimierung; ~ **of a child by subsequent marriage** Ehelichkeitserklärung e-s Kindes durch nachfolgende Heirat

legitimization →legitimation

legitimize *v* →legitimate *v*

leisure (time) Freizeit; ~ **activities** Freizeitgestaltung; ~ **pursuit** Freizeitbeschäftigung; **spending** (or **use**) **of** ~ Freizeitgestaltung

lend *v* (aus-, ver)leihen; Darlehen geben *(opp. to borrow);* **to** ~ **aid** Hilfe leisten; **to** ~ **on** (or **against**) **collateral (security)** lombardieren; **to** ~ **(out) money** Geld (ver)leihen; **to** ~ **money on goods** *(als Kreditgeber)* Waren beleihen (od. lombardieren); **to** ~ **money on an insurance policy** e-e Versicherungspolice beleihen; **to** ~ **money at** (or **on**) **interest (free of interest)** Geld auf Zinsen (zinsfrei) (aus)leihen; **to** ~ **money on mortgage** Geld unter hypothekarischer Sicherheit leihen, Hypothekendarlehen geben; **to** ~ **money on security** Geld gegen Sicherheit (aus-)leihen; **to** ~ **money on securities** *(als Kreditgeber)* Wertpapiere beleihen (od. lombardieren)

lender Ausleiher, Verleiher; Geldgeber, Darlehnsgeber, Kreditgeber *(opp. borrower);* ~ **on** →**bottomry;** ~ **of capital** Geldgeber, Kapitalgeber; ~ **of last resort** letzte Refinanzierungsinstanz *(Notenbank e-s Landes; Br Bank of England als Geldgeber an die discount houses);* ~ **of money** (or **money** ~) Geldverleiher

lending Ausleihen, Verleihen; Ausleihung; Darlehnsgewährung, Kreditgewährung *(opp. borrowing);* ~ **fee** Leihgebühr; ~ **library** Leihbücherei; **~on** (or **against**) **securities** Wertpapierbeleihung; Effektenlombardierung; ~ **on bills** Wechsellombard; ~ **on** (or **against**) **collateral** Gewährung e-s Lombardkredits *(gegen Effekten);* ~ **on goods** Warenbeleihung, Warenlombardgeschäft; ~ **operation** Darlehnsgeschäft; ~ **rate** Zinssatz für Ausleihungen; Lombardsatz; **ban on** ~ Kreditsperre; **direct** ~ **by credit institutions** Direktausleihungen der Kreditinstitute; **international** ~ internationaler Kreditverkehr

length Länge; ~ **of conversation** Gesprächsdauer; ~ **of a credit** Laufzeit e-s Kredits; ~ **of life** Lebensdauer; ~ **of service** Dienstzeit, Dienstalter; ~ **of term** (or **time**) (Zeit-)Dauer

lengthy langwierig; ~ **negotiations** langwierige Verhandlungen

lenienc|e, ~y Nachsicht, Milde; **to exercise** (or **show**) ~ Nachsicht walten lassen

lenient nachsichtig, milde; ~ **sentence** mildes Urteil

lese majesty Majestätsbeleidigung

lesion Schädigung

Lesotho Lesotho; **Kingdom of** ~ Königreich Lesotho

Lesotho, (of) ~ Lesother(in); lesothisch

less weniger, abzüglich; ~ **charges** abzüglich (od. nach Abzug) der Kosten (od. Spesen); ~ **developed countries** (LDC) Entwicklungsländer; ~ **discount** abzüglich Skonto; ~ **interest** abzüglich der Zinsen

less than carloads (l. c. l.) *Am* Stückgüter *(opp. bulk goods)*

less-than-carload, ~freight (l. c. l. freight) *Am* Stückgutfracht; ~ **lots** (l. c. l.) *Am* Stückgut; **shipment as** ~ **lot** *Am* Stückgutversand; ~ **rate** (l. c. l. rate) *Am* Stückgütertarif

less than fair value →LTFV

less than truckload (l. t. l.) *Am* Lkw-Stückgutladung

lessee Mieter, Pächter[12]; Leasingnehmer *(cf. leasing 2.)*

lessening of tension(s) *pol* Spannungsverminderung

lessor Vermieter, Verpächter[12]; Leasinggeber (→*leasing 2.*); **~'s lien** Pfandrecht des Vermieters

let *v* lassen, zulassen; überlassen; vermieten, verpachten; **to ~** *Br* zu vermieten; **to ~ a farm to a tenant** e-n Hof verpachten; **to ~ a flat** *Br* e-e Wohnung vermieten; **to ~ (out) on hire** *(bewegl. Sachen)* vermieten; **to ~ a prisoner escape** e-n Gefangenen entweichen lassen; **to ~ (furnished) rooms** (möblierte) Zimmer vermieten; **house (rooms) to ~** Haus (Zimmer) zu vermieten; **the house is easy to ~** das Haus läßt sich gut vermieten

letting Vermieten, Vermietung, Verpachten, Verpachtung; vermietete Wohnung, vermietetes Haus; **~ for hire** Vermietung *(bewegl. Sachen)*; **~ (out) of contracts** *Am* Auftragsvergabe; **non-commercial ~** nichtgewerbliche Vermietung; **rent from furnished or unfurnished ~** Miete aus möblierten oder unmöblierten Vermietungen

lethal weapon tödliche Waffe

letter 1. Buchstabe; **~ of the law** Buchstabe des Gesetzes; **in ~s** in Buchstaben, ausgeschrieben; **(in) block ~s** (in) Blockschrift

letter 2. Brief, Schreiben; **~ balance** *Br* Briefwaage; **~ book** Briefordner; **~ box** Briefkasten; **~ card** Briefkarte; **~ case** Brieftasche; **~ claiming responsibility for ...** Bekennerbrief *(z. B. bei Bombenanschlägen)*; **~ dated ... inst.** Brief (datiert) vom ... dt. Mts.; **~ file** Briefordner, Schnellhefter; **~gram** Brieftelegramm; **~head** (or **heading**) *(gedruckter)* Briefkopf; Briefbogen mit gedrucktem Kopf; **the ~ in hand** der vorliegende Brief; **~ of acceptance** *Br* →**~** of allotment; *Br (VersR)* Annahmeerklärung; **~ of acknowledgment** Bestätigungsschreiben; **~ of advice** *(schriftl.)* Anzeige, Benachrichtigung(sschreiben), Avis; **~ of allotment** *Br* Mitteilung über Zuteilung von Aktien *(opp. ~ of regret)*; **~ of application** Bewerbungsschreiben; *Br* Antrag auf Zuteilung von Wertpapieren; Zeichnungserklärung; **~ of appointment** Anstellungsschreiben *(des Arbeitgebers)*; **~ of attorney** *(schriftl.)* Vollmacht; **~ of authority** (L/A) *(Überseehandel)* Akkreditivermächtigung; **~ of complaint** Beschwerdebrief; **~ of condolence** Beileidsbrief, Kondolenzschreiben; **~ of congratulation** Glückwunschschreiben; **~ of consignment** Frachtbrief

letter of credit (L/C, l/c) Akkreditiv, Kreditbrief; **circular ~** Reisekreditbrief

letter of credit, commercial ~ (C. L. C., c. l. c.) *bes. Am (Exporthandel) (bes. Form des unwiderrufl., nicht bestätigten)* Akkreditiv(s); Handelsakkreditiv *(opp. standby ~)*

Beim commercial letter of credit kann der Exporteur (od. Begünstigte) eine beliebige Bank wählen, bei der er gegen Vorlage des ihm persönlich zugesandten Avisos zusammen mit den geforderten Dokumenten das Akkreditiv realisiert (od. die Negoziierung vornimmt)

letter of credit, confirmed (irrevocable) ~ bestätigtes (unwiderrufliches) Akkreditiv; **holder of a ~** Inhaber e-s Akkreditivs (od. Kreditbriefes); **issue of a ~** Eröffnung e-s Akkreditivs; Ausstellung e-s Kreditbriefes; **life of a ~** Laufzeit e-s Akkreditivs; **opening of a ~** Eröffnung e-s Akkreditivs; **revoking of a ~** Widerruf e-s Akkreditivs; **revolving ~** revolvierendes (sich erneuerndes) Akkreditiv; **→standby ~; travel(l)er's ~** Reisekreditbrief; **unconfirmed (revocable) ~** unbestätigtes (widerrufliches) Akkreditiv; **a ~ not yet utilized** ein noch nicht ausgenütztes Akkreditiv; **to cash a ~** e-n Kreditbrief einlösen; **to establish** (or **issue, open**) **a ~** ein Akkreditiv eröffnen; **the ~ expires** (or **becomes invalid**) das Akkreditiv wird ungültig

letter of hypothecation *Br* Verpfändungsbescheinigung; Pfandschein; Dokument, in welchem der Sicherungsgeber dem Sicherungsnehmer verspricht, nach Ankunft des Sicherungsgutes dieses für den Sicherungsnehmer aufzubewahren od. an ihn herauszugeben *(entspricht etwa dem amerikanischen trust receipt)*

letter, ~ of indemnity *(Außenhandel)* Indemnitätsbrief, Urkunde über e-e Entschädigungsgarantie *(wenn leichtverderbliche Ware ausgeliefert werden soll, aber die Papiere noch nicht vorliegen oder bei Beschädigung durch schlechte Verpakkung)*; **~ of →indication; ~ of inquiry** *(schriftl.)* Auskunftsersuchen; **~ of intent** Absichtserklärung; *Br (nicht bindende)* Bereitschaftserklärung e-r Partei, unter bestimmten Voraussetzungen e-n Vertrag schließen zu wollen; **~ of introduction** Einführungsschreiben, Empfehlungsschreiben; **~ of licence (~se)** Stundungsvereinbarung zwischen Gläubiger und Schuldner *(zur Vermeidung des Konkurses) (→deed of arrangement)*; **~ of lien** Pfandschein; Urkunde, in der der Importeur der Bank, die das Geschäft finanziert, bescheinigt, daß ihr die Ware als Pfand übertragen wurde; **~ of recommendation** Empfehlungsschreiben; **~ of regret** *Br* Mitteilung über Nichtzuteilung von Effekten *(opp. ~ of allotment)*; **~ of renunciation** *Br* Verzichtsschreiben betreffend die Ausübung von Bezugsrechten; **~ of resignation** *(schriftl.)* Rücktrittserklärung; **~ of rights** Bezugsrechtsangebot; **~ of safe conduct** Geleitbrief; **~ of sympathy** Beileidsschreiben; **~ of thanks** Dankschreiben

letter of trust *Br* Dokument, in welchem der Sicherungsgeber dem Sicherungsnehmer bestätigt, bestimmtes Sicherungsgut empfangen und für ihn innezuhaben und in welchem er verspricht, e-n Erlös für ihn entgegenzunehmen und alsbald an ihn abzuführen

letter, ~ rate Briefporto; **~ requesting** payment Mahnbrief; **~ stock** *Am* Aktien, die keine amtliche Zulassung für den Börsenhandel haben (*sie werden bei privaten Anlegern untergebracht, um die Kosten der Registrierungsgebühren bei der SEC zu sparen*); **~ telegram** Brieftelegramm; **~ to be called for** postlagernder Brief; **~ to the editor** Leserbrief; **~ to follow** Brief folgt

letter, business ~ Geschäftsbrief; **by ~** brieflich, schriftlich; **chain ~** Kettenbrief; **circular ~** Rundschreiben; **commercial ~** Geschäftsbrief; **covering ~** Begleitschreiben; →**dead ~; delivery of ~s** Briefzustellung; **draft ~** Briefentwurf; **exchange of ~s** Briefwechsel, Briefverkehr; **express ~** *Br* Eilbrief; **incoming ~** einlaufender Brief; **insured ~** *Br* Wertbrief; **mailing** *Am* (**posting** *Br*) **of a ~** Aufgabe e-s Briefes; **outgoing ~** auslaufender Brief; **prepaid ~** frankierter Brief

letter, private ~ privater Brief; **to disclose the contents of private ~s** das Briefgeheimnis verletzen

letter, registration of a ~ Aufgabe e-s Briefes als Einschreiben; **registered ~** Einschreibebrief; **secrecy of ~s** Briefgeheimnis; **sender of a ~** Absender e-s Briefes; **threatening ~** Drohbrief; **unclaimed ~** nicht abgeholter Brief; **unpaid ~** unfrankierter Brief; **to acknowledge receipt of a ~** den Empfang (od. Eingang) e-s Briefes bestätigen; **to confirm a ~** e-n Brief bestätigen; **to draft a ~** e-n Brief aufsetzen; **to file ~s** Briefe ablegen; **to mail** *Am* (**to post** *Br*) **a ~** e-n Brief zur Post aufgeben; **referring** (or **with reference**) **to your ~** unter Bezugnahme auf Ihren Brief; **replying to your ~** in Beantwortung Ihres Briefes; **to stamp a ~** e-n Brief frankieren

letters 3. (*amtl.*) Brief, Schreiben, Urkunde; **~ of administration** →administration 2.; **~ of business** *Br* Königl. Vollmacht an die →Convocation von York od. Canterbury (*in der diese ersucht wird, e-n bestimmten Gegenstand [special business] zu behandeln*); **~ of credence** (*VölkerR*) Beglaubigungsschreiben (*des Missionschefs*); **~ of guardianship** *Am* Urkunde über die Bestellung e-s →guardian; **~ patent** →patent 1. und 2.; **~ of recall** *dipl* Abberufungsschreiben

letters of request (to examine witness)[18] Rechtshilfeersuchen (*an ausländische Gerichte zur Zeugenvernehmung*); **execution of the ~** Erledigung des Rechtshilfeersuchens; **to transmit the ~** das Rechtshilfeersuchen übermitteln

Der Rechtshilfeverkehr in Zivilsachen (*cf. judicial assistance*) zwischen Großbritannien und Nordirland (einschließl. der Gebiete, deren internationale Beziehungen das Vereinigte Königreich wahrnimmt) und der Bundesrepublik ist durch Art. 8–12 des deutsch-britischen Abkommens über den Rechtsverkehr von 1928[18] geregelt. Das Abkommen ist nach 1945 mit beschränktem Anwendungsbereich wieder in Kraft gesetzt worden[19]

letters rogatory *Am* Rechtshilfeersuchen; **to draw up the ~** das Rechtshilfeersuchen abfassen; **to execute the ~** das Rechtshilfeersuchen erledigen

Der Rechtshilfeverkehr in Zivilsachen (*cf. judicial →assistance*) zwischen den Vereinigten Staaten und der Bundesrepublik wird auf vertragloser Grundlage gegenseitig geleistet. Soweit die deutschen Auslandsvertretungen in den Vereinigten Staaten Rechtshilfeersuchen nicht in eigener Zuständigkeit erledigen können, wird es in Form der →commission 2.[20] durchgeführt. Muß ein Rechtshilfeersuchen durch ein amerikanisches Gericht erledigt werden, wird es – unter Einschaltung der deutschen Auslandsvertretung – in Form der letters rogatory gestellt

letters testamentary *Am* →testamentary

letter *v* beschriften

lettering Beschriftung; Aufschrift; **~ of drawings** (*PatR*) Beschriftung der Zeichnungen

Levantine port Levante-Hafen (*Hafen der Levante-Länder des östl. Mittelmeeres*)

levée en masse *Fr* (*VölkerR*) Volksaufgebot (*bewaffnete Erhebung der Zivilbevölkerung gegen den eindringenden Feind*)

level Stand, Niveau, (*gleiche*) Höhe; **~ of armaments** Rüstungsstand; **~ of education** Bildungsniveau; **(high) ~ of employment** (hoher) Beschäftigungsstand; **~ of income** Einkommensniveau; **~ of invention** (*PatR*) Erfindungshöhe; **~ of living** *Am* Lebensstandard; **~ of output** Produktionsstand; **~ of performance** Leistungsstand; **~ of prices** (*allgemeines*) Preisniveau, Preisstand; Kursniveau, Kursstand; **low ~ of prices** niedriges Preisniveau; niedriger Stand der Preise (od. Kurse); **~ of production** Produktionsstand

level, A (= advanced) **~** *Br* Abschluß e-s Fachs der Oberstufe

Universitäten verlangen mehrere A-levels, d. h. den Oberstufenabschluß in mehreren Fächern (entspricht etwa dem deutschen Abitur) (→*General Certificate of Secondary Education*)

level, at the foreign ministers' ~ auf Außenministerebene; **at government ~** auf Regierungsebene; **at top ~** auf höchster Ebene; **high ~** hoher Stand; **authority at a higher ~** übergeordnete (od. vorgesetzte) Dienststelle; **highest ~** Höchststand (*Preise, Kurse etc*); **a conference on the highest ~** *pol* e-e Konferenz auf höchster Ebene; **authority at a lower ~** nachgeordnete Dienststelle; **lower ~ official** unterer Beamter; **lowest ~** Tiefstand (*Preise, Kurse*); **on a ~ with** in gleicher Höhe mit; auf gleicher Stufe; **on the ~** *colloq.* ehrlich; →**peak ~; pre-war ~** Vorkriegsstand;

price ~ →price 1. und 2.; **wage** ~ Lohnniveau, Lohnstand; **on the same** ~ auf gleicher Höhe (od. Stufe); **to maintain prices on the same** ~ Preise auf derselben Höhe halten; **to be placed on the** ~ **of** gleichgestellt werden mit; **to reach a** ~ e-n Stand erreichen

level gleich, gleichmäßig; ausgeglichen; ~ **crossing** *Br* schienengleicher Übergang; ~**headed** *(auch pol)* besonnen; ~ **premium** gleichbleibende (od. wiederkehrende) Prämie

levelheadedness, to show political ~ politische Besonnenheit zeigen

level *v* ausgleichen, gleichmachen, nivellieren; **to** ~ **down** nach unten ausgleichen; *(Löhne)* herabsetzen; **to** ~ **up** nach oben ausgleichen; *(Löhne)* erhöhen

levelling Ausgleichung, Gleichmachung, Nivellierung; ~ **down** Ausgleichung nach unten, Herabsetzung; ~ **of classes** Abschaffung der Klassenunterschiede; ~ **of premiums** *(VersR)* Bildung von Durchschnittsprämien; ~ **up** Ausgleichung nach oben, Erhöhung

leverage Hebelwirkung, Hebelkraft; Einfluß(nahme) (over auf); *Am* Verhältnis von Obligationen und Vorzugsaktien (bonds and preferred stock) zu Stammaktien (common stock) (wenn der Hauptteil des Gesellschaftskapitals sich aus bonds und preferred stock zusammensetzt, besteht ein high ~ factor); ~ **effect** Hebelwirkung; ~ **fund** Investmentfonds, der Kreditmittel zum Ankauf von Aktien verwendet; **bargaining** ~ Verhandlungsvorteil; **to have a high** ~ in hohem Maße fremdfinanziert sein

leveraged, ~ **buyout** (LBO) mit Hilfe von Krediten finanzierter Kauf e-s Unternehmens *(die Schulden werden mit Einnahmen aus dem erworbenen Unternehmen zurückgezahlt);* **highly** ~ vorwiegend mit Fremdkapital finanziert

leveraged firm verschuldete Firma *(die Fremdkapital aufgenommen hat)*

lev|y Erhebung *(von Steuern, Zöllen);* (Finanz-)Abgabe; Umlage; Pfändung *(auf Grund e-s Vollstreckungstitels); (EG)* Abschöpfung(sbetrag); *mil* Aushebung, Rekrutierung; ~ **of** →**attachment;** ~ **of execution** Betreibung der Zwangsvollstreckung; ~ **rate** Umlagesatz; **capital** ~ Kapitalabgabe; **export** ~**ies** *(EG)* Exportabgaben; **property** ~ Vermögensabgabe; **subsequent** ~ **of duties** Nacherhebung von Zöllen

levy *v (Steuern, Zölle)* erheben; **to** ~ **assessment** *Am* zur Zahlung *(auf das gezeichnete Grundkapital)* auffordern; **to** ~ **(a) distress upon a debtor's furniture** die Möbel des Schuldners im Wege der Selbsthilfe in Besitz nehmen *(vgl. § 561 BGB);* **to** ~ **(an) execution** die Zwangsvollstreckung durchführen; **to** ~ **execution against the debtor by seizure of his goods** Zwangsvollstreckung im Wege der Sachpfändung bei dem Schuldner durchführen; **to** ~ **execution against the debtor's goods** Zwangsvollstreckung in das bewegliche Vermögen des Schuldners durchführen; **to** ~ **a fi. fa.** e-n Pfändungsbefehl durchführen (→*fieri facias*); **to** ~ **a tax** e-e Steuer erheben; besteuern; **to** ~ **taxes by withholding** *Am* Steuern im Abzugsweg erheben; **to** ~ **war on a country** Krieg gegen ein Land führen

levied, charge ~ **(up)on** Umlage; **execution** ~ **(up)on the property of the judgment debtor** Zwangsvollstreckung in das Vermögen des Vollstreckungsschuldners; **execution** ~ **by seizure** Zwangsvollstreckung durch Pfändung und Wegnahme

levying, method of ~ **duties** Erhebungsverfahren für Zölle; ~ **of taxes** Erhebung von Steuern, Steuererhebung

lewd, to do a ~ **act** sich unzüchtig benehmen

lewdness, open ~ *Am*[21] öffentlich unzüchtiges Verhalten

lex *(IPR)* Gesetz; ~ **cartae sitae** *(IPR)* das am Lageort e-r Urkunde geltende Recht *(z.B. e-s Transportpapiers);* ~ **causae** *(IPR)* Wirkungsstatut *(das Recht, auf das die Kollisionsnormen verweisen);* ~ **domicilii** *(IPR)* Recht des Domizils *(cf. domicile);* ~ **fori** *(IPR)* Recht des Gerichtsortes, das am Gerichtsort geltende Recht

lex loci Ortsrecht; ~ **actus** *(IPR)* Recht des Handlungsortes *(z.B. des Abschlußortes bei Verträgen, des Errichtungsortes bei Testamenten);* ~ **contractus** *(IPR)* Recht des Vertragsortes (Abschlußortes od. Erfüllungsortes); ~ **delicti** *(IPR)* Recht des Ortes der unerlaubten Handlung; ~ **domicilii** Wohnsitzrecht *(das am Wohnsitz e-r Person geltende Recht);* ~ **laboris** *(IPR)* Recht des Arbeitsortes; ~ **monetae** *(IRP)* Recht der Währung (das die Währung e-r Schuld bestimmende Recht); ~**rei sitae** Recht der Belegenheit der Sache; ~ **solutionis** *(IPR)* Recht des Erfüllungsortes

lex, ~ **mercatoria** →law merchant; ~ **propria** →proper law; ~ **rei sitae** *(IPR)* →~ situs; ~ **scripta** *Am* Gesetzesrecht; ~ **non scripta** *Am* ungeschriebenes Recht; Richterrecht; ~ **situs** *(IPR)* Recht der belegenen Sache (od. des Lageortes)

LEXIS *(durch Telefonnetz zugängliche)* private Datenbank für sämtliche gerichtl. od. behördl. Entscheidungen, juristische Zeitschriften etc. *(weitgehend benützt)*

liabilities Verbindlichkeiten, Verpflichtungen; Schulden; Passiva *(opp. assets);* ~ **and shareholders' equity** *Am (Bilanz)* Verbindlichkeiten und Eigenkapital; ~ **incurred** eingegangene Verpflichtungen; ~ **in foreign currencies** Fremdwährungsverbindlichkeiten; ~ **of the estate** Nachlaßverbindlichkeiten; ~ **on bills of exchange** Wechselverpflichtungen, Wechselobligo; **assets and** ~ Aktiva und Passiva; **business** ~ Geschäftsschulden; **capital** ~ Kapitalverbindlichkeiten; **contingent** ~ Eventualverbindlichkeiten; *Br (Bilanz)* Rückstellungen für zweifelhafte Schulden; **current** ~ laufende Verpflichtungen; *(Bilanz)* kurzfristige Verbindlichkeiten; **discharge of** ~ Erfüllung von Verbindlichkeiten; **external** ~ Auslandsverbindlichkeiten; **internal** ~ Inlandsverbindlichkeiten; **foreign** ~ Auslandsverbindlichkeiten; **legal** ~ gesetzliche Verpflichtungen; **long term** ~ langfristige Verbindlichkeiten; **other** ~ *(Bilanz)* sonstige Verbindlichkeiten; **to contract** ~ Verbindlichkeiten eingehen; **to discharge** (or **meet**) **one's** ~ s-n Verpflichtungen nachkommen; **to incur** ~ Verpflichtungen eingehen; **to (fail to) meet one's** ~ s-n Verpflichtungen (nicht) nachkommen

liability Verbindlichkeit, Verpflichtung, Schuld; Verantwortlichkeit; Haftung, Haftpflicht; *(Bilanz)* Passivposten

liability, insurer's ~ **accrues** die Haftung des Versicherers tritt ein; **to assume** ~ die Haftung übernehmen; **to avail oneself of a clause excluding** ~ sich auf e-e Haftungsbeschränkungsklausel berufen; **to contract a** ~ e-e Verpflichtung eingehen; Haftung übernehmen; **to create** ~ die Haftung begründen; **to deny** ~ die Haftpflicht bestreiten; **to discharge a** ~ e-r Verpflichtung (od. Haftpflicht) nachkommen; **to be discharged from** ~ von der Haftung befreit sein; **to disclaim** ~ *(VersR)* die Haftung ablehnen; **to establish** ~ die Haftpflicht beweisen; **to exclude** ~ die Haftung ausschließen; **to exempt o. s. from** ~ s-e Haftung ausschließen; **to extend** ~ die Haftung erweitern; **to incur a** ~ e-e Verpflichtung übernehmen; e-e Verbindlichkeit eingehen; **to incur (legal)** ~ haftbar sein; **to join together in** ~ die Haftung gemeinsam übernehmen; **to limit** ~ die Haftung beschränken; **to release from** (or **relieve of**) **a** ~ von e-r Verpflichtung (od. Haftung) befreien; **to undertake a** ~ s. to contract a →~

liability, ~ **account** Passivkonto; ~ **based on fault** Verschuldenshaftung; ~ **certificate** *Am* Vollständigkeitserklärung (*hinsichtl. der dem Wirtschaftsprüfer eingereichten Unterlagen*); ~**created by statute** s. statutory →~; ~ **for animals** Tierhalterhaftung; ~ **for compensation** (Schadens-)Ersatzpflicht; ~ **for contributions** Beitragspflicht, Nachschußpflicht; ~ **for costs** Haftung für Prozeßkosten; ~ **for damage** Schadenshaftung; ~ **for damages** Schadenersatzpflicht; ~ **for debts** Schuldenhaftung; ~**for defects** Haftung für Mängel, Mängelhaftung; ~ **for loss** Haftung für Schaden (od. Verlust); ~ **for mortgage repayments** hypothekarische Haftung; ~ **for negligence** Haftung für Fahrlässigkeit; ~ **for support** *Am* Unterhaltspflicht

liability insurance Haftpflichtversicherung; →**employer's** ~; **personal** ~ Privathaftpflichtversicherung; →**professional** ~; →**public** ~

liability, ~ **in tort** Haftung aus unerlaubter Handlung, Deliktshaftung; ~ **of acceptor** (*WechselR*) Akzeptantenhaftung; ~ **of acceptor for hono(u)r** (*WechselR*) Haftung des Ehrenannehmers; ~ **of corporations** *Am*[22] Verantwortlichkeit von Körperschaften; ~ **of drawer** (*WechselR*) Ausstellerhaftung; ~ **of the estate** Nachlaßverbindlichkeit, Nachlaßschuld; ~ **of hotel-keepers**[23] Haftung der Gastwirte; ~ **of indorser** (*WechselR*) Indossantenhaftung; ~ **of an official** Amtshaftung; ~ **of →shipowners**; ~ **on a bill** Wechselverpflichtung; ~ **on a guarantee (guaranty)** Haftung aus e-r Garantie; ~ **over** *Am* Regreßpflicht; ~ **regardless of** (or **without**) **fault** Haftung unabhängig von Verschulden, Gefährdungshaftung; ~ **reserve** *Am* (*Bilanz*) Rückstellungen für Verbindlichkeiten; (*VersR*) Garantiereserven, Deckungsrücklagen; ~ **to (render) account** Rechenschaftspflicht, Rechnungslegungspflicht; ~ **to contribute** Beitragspflicht; Nachschußpflicht; ~ **to indemnify** Schadenersatzpflicht; ~ **to insure** Versicherungszwang; ~ **to make good a loss** Schadenersatzpflicht; ~ **to** (or **for**) **military service** Militärdienstpflicht, Wehrpflicht; ~ **to pay customs duties** Zollpflicht; ~ **to (pay) taxes** Steuerpflicht; ~ **to provide maintenance** Unterhaltspflicht; ~ **to put up additional cover** Nachschußpflicht; ~ **under a contract** Verpflichtungen aus e-m Vertrag; ~ **under mortgage** hypothekarische Haftung; ~ **waiver clause** Haftungsausschlußklausel

liability, absolute ~ unbeschränkte Haftung; Gefährdungshaftung; **acceptance** ~ *(WechselR)* Akzeptverpflichtung; **assumption of** ~ Schuldübernahme; **capacity to incur** ~ *(WechselR)* Verpflichtungsfähigkeit; →**carrier's** ~; **civil** ~ zivilrechtliche Haftung (od. Haftpflicht); **collective** ~ *(VölkerR)* Kollektivhaftung; **contingent** ~ Eventualhaftung, Eventualverbindlichkeit; **contractual** ~ vertragliche Verpflichtung (od. Haftung); →**criminal** ~; **discharge of a** ~ Erfüllung e-r Verbindlichkeit; →**employer's** ~ **(insurance); exclusion of** (or **exemption from**) ~ Haftungsausschluß; **extent of** ~ Umfang der Haftung; **fixed** ~ feste *(langfristige)* Verbindlichkeit; **floating** ~ laufende *(kurzfristige)* Verbindlichkeit; **free from** ~ ohne Obligo; unverbindlich; **government** ~ Staatshaftung; **indemnity against** ~ Haftungsausschluß; **individual** ~

persönliche Haftung; →**innkeeper's ~; joint ~** gemeinsame Verbindlichkeit, gemeinsame Haftung *(cf. joint debt);* →**joint and several ~; legal ~** gesetzliche Haftpflicht; **limitation of ~** →limitation 1; →**limited ~; noncontractual ~** außervertragliche Haftung; →**personal ~;** →**public ~; release from ~** Befreiung von der Haftung; **several ~** individuelle Haftung *(jeder einzelne haftet auf das Ganze);* **statutory ~** gesetzliche *(auf Parlamentsgesetz, nicht auf→Common Law beruhende)* Haftpflicht; **strict ~** Gefährdungshaftung, verschuldensunabhängige Haftung; **tax ~** Steuerpflicht; **third party ~ insurance** Haftpflichtversicherung; **unlimited ~** unbeschränkte Haftung; →**vicarious ~; without ~** s. free from →~

liable verantwortlich; haftbar, haftpflichtig (for für); verpflichtet; ausgesetzt, unterworfen (to a th. e-r Sache); **~ for compensation** (schadens)-ersatzpflichtig; **~ for** (or **in**) **damages** schadensersatzpflichtig; **~ for defects** für Mängel haftbar; **~ to contribution** beitragspflichtig; nachschußpflichtig; **~ to duty** zollpflichtig; abgabenpflichtig; **~ to execution** der Zwangsvollstreckung unterliegend; **~ to the extent of ...** haftbar bis ...; **~ to a fine** →fine; **~ to maintain** unterhaltspflichtig; **~ to make restitution** (rück)erstattungspflichtig, rückzahlungspflichtig; **~ to** (or **for**) →**military service; ~ to recourse** regreßpflichtig; **~ to stamp duty** stempelsteuerpflichtig; **~ to surcharge** *(Post)* zuschlagspflichtig; **~ to tax** steuerpflichtig; **~ under a contract** vertraglich verpflichtet; **~ up to his contribution** *(nur)* mit seiner Einlage haftbar *(cf. limited partner)*; **civilly ~** zivilrechtlich haftbar; **criminally ~** strafrechtlich haftbar; **individually ~** persönlich haftbar; **jointly and severally ~** gemeinsam *(als Gesamtschuldner)* haftbar; **party ~** →party 2.; **personally ~** persönlich haftbar; **severally ~** gesondert *(einzeln)* haftbar

liable, to be ~ (for) haften, haftbar sein (für); **to be ~ in one's individual capacity** (or **individually**) persönlich haften

liable, to be ~ (to) unterworfen sein, unterliegen; Gefahr laufen, riskieren; **to be ~ to a →fine; to be ~ to →imprisonment; to be ~ to a →penalty of £ 20; to be ~ to prosecution** sich der Bestrafung aussetzen, sich strafbar machen

liable, to be ~ with all one's assets (or **to the extent of one's property**) mit dem ganzen Vermögen haften; **to be ~ without limitation** unbeschränkt haften; **to be held ~** haftbar gemacht werden

liable, to become ~ on a bill wechselverpflichtet werden; **to hold a p. ~** jdn haftbar (od. verantwortlich) machen; **to make o.s. ~ to a penalty** (or **to render o.s. ~ to prosecution**) sich strafbar machen; **the rule is ~ to an exception** die Regel unterliegt e-r Ausnahme

liaison Verbindung; **~ committee** Verbindungsausschuß; **~ officer** Verbindungsmann; Verbindungsoffizier; **national ~ body**[24] staatliche Verbindungsstelle; **to establish ~ offices** Verbindungsstellen einrichten

libel 1. Beleidigung, Ehrverletzung, ehrenkränkende Behauptung, *(schriftl.)* Verleumdung, üble Nachrede

Libel ist Ehrverletzung in schriftlicher oder anderer dauerhafter Form, z. B. in Rundfunk[25] oder Film *(cf. slander)*.

Libel ist in gewissen Ausnahmefällen nicht nur als tort, sondern auch strafrechtlich verfolgbar (Geld- od. Gefängnisstrafe), im Ggs. zu slander

libel, ~ of goods *Am* →slander of goods; **~ of title** *Br* →slander of title; **~ suit** *bes. Am s.* action for →~; **action for ~** Beleidigungsklage; Verleumdungsklage; **to bring an action for ~ against a p.** jdn wegen Beleidigung (od. Verleumdung) verklagen; **trade ~** Anschwärzung; geschäftliche Verleumdung; **to publish a ~ against sb.** jdn durch schriftliche Mitteilung an e-n Dritten beleidigen (od. verleumden)

libel 2. *eccl (Am auch Schiffahrtsgericht)* Klage (-schrift); *Scot* Anklage; **to file a ~** e-e Klage einreichen

libel *v* beleidigen (od. verleumden) *(cf. libel 1.); eccl (Am auch Schiffahrtsgericht)* klagen (a p. gegen); *Scot* anklagen

libel(l)ant *eccl (Am auch Schiffahrtsgericht)* Kläger

libel(l)ee *eccl (Am auch Schiffahrtsgericht)* Beklagter

libel(l)er (or **libel[l]ist**) Verfasser e-r Schmähschrift, Verleumder

libel(l)ous beleidigend, ehrenrührig; verleumderisch, Schmäh-

liberal großzügig; *pol* liberal[26]; **L~** *Br pol* Liberaler, Mitglied der →Liberal Party

liberal arts *Am* Geisteswissenschaften; **Department of ~** *Am univ* philosophische Fakultät

liberal, ~ education Unterricht (od. Erziehung) zu umfassender Allgemeinbildung; **~ interpretation** weite (od. erweiternde) Auslegung *(opp. restrictive interpretation);* **L~ Party** *Br hist* Liberale Partei; **~ trade policies** liberale Handelspolitik; **to interpret ~ly** erweiternd auslegen

liberalization Liberalisierung (*Befreiung von Einschränkungen; durch →OEEC eingeführter Begriff für Befreiung der Einfuhr von mengenmäßigen Beschränkungen); ~* **of capital movements** Liberalisierung des Kapitalverkehrs; **~ of trade** Liberalisierung des Handels; **degree** (or **level**) **of ~** Liberalisierungsgrad; **progressive ~** schrittweise Liberalisierung

liberalize *v* liberalisieren *(von Einschränkungen frei machen)*; **~d capital account** liberalisiertes Kapitalkonto

liberalism Liberalismus

liberate *v* befreien; *(Gefangene)* freilassen

liberation Befreiung; Freilassung

Liberia Liberia; **Republic of ~** Republik Liberia
Liberian Liberianer, ~ in; liberianisch

liberticide Zerstörer (od. Zerstörung) der Freiheit

libert|y Freiheit; Sonderrecht, Vorrecht; **~ies clause** (termination contract of affreightment) *(Institute Cargo Clause)* Sonderrechtsklausel, Ende des Frachtvertrages; **~ of action** Handlungsfreiheit; **~ of conscience** Gewissensfreiheit; Glaubensfreiheit; **~ of contract** Vertragsfreiheit; **~ of movement** Freizügigkeit; **~ of the press** Pressefreiheit; **~ of speech** Redefreiheit; **~ of trade** Gewerbefreiheit; **civil ~ies** *Am (verfassungmäßig garantierte)* Bürgerrechte, Grundrechte; **deprivation of ~** Freiheitsberaubung; **individual** (or **personal**) **~** persönliche Freiheit; **religious ~** Religionsfreiheit; **to be at ~** frei sein; **to exercise a ~ (granted)** ein Recht ausüben; **to set a prisoner at ~** e-n Gefangenen freilassen; **I take the ~** ich erlaube mir

LIBID (London Interbank Bid Rate) Londoner Interbanken-Ankaufs(zins)satz *(für Eurodollar-Einlagen)*

LIBOR (London Interbank Offered Rate) Londoner Interbanken-Angebotssatz *(Basiszinssatz für Eurokredite)*

library Bibliothek, Bücherei; **circulating** (or **lending**) **~** Leihbücherei; **reference ~** Handbücherei; Nachschlagebücherei; Präsenzbibliothek

Libya Libyen
Libyan Libyer(in); libysch; **the ~ Arab Jamahiriya** Libysch-Arabische Dschamahirija

licen|ce (~se) 1. *(amtl.)* Erlaubnis (od. Genehmigung); Erlaubnisschein; *(amtl.)* Zulassung(sschein); Gewerbeberechtigung, Konzession *(zur Ausübung e-s Gewerbes, bes. zum Verkauf von Alkohol)*; Heiratserlaubnis; Führerschein; **~ application** Antrag auf Erteilung e-r Genehmigung; **~ fee** Konzessionsgebühr; *Br* Rundfunk- und Fernsehgebühr; *Am (einzelstaatl.)* Gebühr *(z. B. Zulassungsgebühr)* od. Steuer *(z. B. Gewerbesteuer, Kraftfahrzeugsteuer)*; **~ of marriage** →marriage ~; **~ plate number** *Am* Kraftfahrzeug-Zulassungsnummer; **~ tax** *Am* →~fee; **~ to carry fire arms** Waffenschein; **~ to practise medicine** ärztliche Approbation; **~ to operate** Zulassung zum Geschäftsbetrieb; Konzession

licen|ce (~se), applicant for a ~ Antragsteller *(auf Erteilung e-r amtl. Genehmigung)*; **building ~** Baugenehmigung; **common ~** *Br* allgemeine Erlaubnis (→*Kommentar zu marriage*); **dog ~** Erlaubnis zum Halten e-s Hundes; **driver's ~** *Am* Führerschein (→*driver*); **driving ~** *Br* Führerschein (→*driving*); **excise ~** *Br*[27] Lizenz zur Herstellung od. zum Verkauf gewisser Waren gegen Bezahlung e-r besonderen Steuer; Schankkonzession; **export ~** Ausfuhrgenehmigung; **game ~** *Br* Jagdschein; **general ~** allgemeine Genehmigung; **grant(ing) of a ~** Erteilung e-r Genehmigung (od. Konzession); **grantor of a ~** Verleiher e-r Genehmigung, Aussteller e-r Konzession; **gun ~** *Br* Waffenschein; **hack ~** *Am* Taxikonzession; **hawker's ~** Reisegewerbekarte; **holder of a ~** Inhaber e-r Konzession; **hunting ~** *Am* Jagdschein; **import ~** Einfuhrgenehmigung; **individual ~** Einzelgenehmigung; individuelle (Ein- bzw. Ausfuhr-)Bewilligung; **issuing of a ~** s. granting of a →~; **justices'** (or **magistrate**'s) **~** *Br* Konzession zum Verkauf von alkoholischen Getränken *(intoxicating liquors)*; **→liquor ~; →marriage ~; →motor vehicle ~; off-~** *Br* Schankkonzession über die Straße; **on-~** *Br* Schankkonzession im eigenen Betrieb; **revocation of a ~** s. withdrawal of a →~; **special ~** Sondergenehmigung; *Br* besondere Heiratserlaubnis (→*Kommentar zu marriage*); **subject to a ~** konzessionspflichtig; **→trading ~; withdrawal of a ~** Zurücknahme e-r Konzession; Entzug des Führerscheins

licence (~se), to cancel a ~ e-e Konzession entziehen; **to endorse a ~** e-e Strafe auf dem Führerschein vermerken; **a ~ is expired** e-e Konzession ist erloschen; **to file an application for a ~** um Erteilung e-r Konzession ersuchen; **to grant** (or **issue**) **a ~** e-e Genehmigung (od. Konzession) erteilen; **to hold a ~** e-e Konzession innehaben; die Zulassung haben; **to obtain a ~** e-e Konzession erhalten; **to revoke the ~** die *(amtl.)* Genehmigung (od. Konzession) zurücknehmen; den Führerschein entziehen; **to suspend the ~** *Am* die *(amtl.)* Genehmigung *(zeitweilig)* zurücknehmen; den Führerschein *(zeitweilig)* entziehen; **to take out a ~** sich e-e Konzession beschaffen; e-n Erlaubnisschein *(Jagdschein, Führerschein etc)* erwerben; **to withdraw the ~** s. to revoke the →~

licen|ce (~se) 2. *(das in der Regel jederzeit widerrufl.)* Recht, ein fremdes Grundstück zu benützen *(etwas zu tun, was sonst →trespass wäre)*

licen|ce (~se) 3. *(UrhR, PatR)* Lizenz *(Befugnis, das Recht e-s anderen zu benutzen)*; **~ agreement** Lizenzvertrag; **~ by estoppel** Lizenz kraft Verwirkung *(des Rechts des Patentinhabers, auf Unterlassung zu klagen)*; **~ fee** Lizenzgebühr; **~ holder** Lizenzinhaber; **~ of right** *Br*[28] *(unter bestimmten Voraussetzungen vom Patentgeber zu erteilende)* Zwangslizenz, Lizenzbereitschaft; ~

to manufacture Herstellungslizenz; ~ **to use** Benutzungslizenz; ~ **under a patent** Lizenz an e-m Patent; **bloc** ~ *(PatR)* En-bloc-Lizenz, Pauschal-Lizenz *(Vergebung aller Lizenzen in e-m geschlossenen Block)*

licen|ce (~se), compulsory ~ Zwangslizenz; **compulsory ~ for lack of exploitation** Zwangslizenz wegen Nichtausübung; **compulsory ~ for the public interest** Zwangslizenz aus Gründen des öffentlichen Interesses

licen|ce (~se), contractual ~ vertragliche Lizenz; →**cross ~; exclusive** ~ ausschließliche Lizenz, Alleinlizenz; **exploitation of a** ~ Lizenzverwertung, Lizenzauswertung; **express** ~ durch ausdrückliche Vereinbarung geschlossene Lizenz; **grantback** ~ Rücklizenz; **grantee of a** ~ Lizenznehmer; **granting of a** ~ Lizenzerteilung; **grantor of a** ~ Lizenzgeber; **holder of a** ~ Inhaber e-r Lizenz; **implied** ~ stillschweigend vereinbarte Lizenz *(die sich als Ergebnis der richterl. Auslegung od. Rechtsgestaltung ergibt)*; **issuance of a** ~ *Am* Erteilung e-r Lizenz; **manufacturing** ~ Herstellungslizenz; **non-exclusive** ~ nicht ausschließliche (od. einfache) Lizenz; **period of a** ~ Dauer e-r Lizenz, Lizenzdauer; **project** ~ Lizenz für ein bestimmtes Projekt; **renewal of a** ~ Erneuerung e-r Lizenz; **revocation of a** ~ Lizenzentzug; **royalty-free** ~ gebührenfreie Lizenz; **service supply** ~ erlaubte Nachlieferung von Ersatzteilen; **sub-**~ Unterlizenz; **subject to a** ~ lizenzpflichtig; **term of a** ~ s. period of a →~; **terms of a** ~ Lizenzbestimmungen; **trademark** ~ Warenzeichenlizenz; **withdrawal of a** ~ Lizenzentzug

licence (~se), to apply for a ~ e-e Lizenz beantragen; **to conclude the terms of a** ~ die Lizenzbestimmungen vereinbaren; **to exploit a** ~ e-e Lizenz verwerten; **to forfeit one's** ~ s-e Lizenz einbüßen; **to grant a** ~ e-e Lizenz erteilen; **to grant a ~ in respect of a copyright** e-e Lizenz zur Verwertung e-s urheberrechtlich geschützten Rechtsgutes einräumen; **to grant a ~ under a patent** e-e Patentlizenz erteilen; **to hold a** ~ e-e Lizenz innehaben; **to refuse a** ~ e-e Lizenz verweigern; **to revoke a** ~ e-e Lizenz entziehen (od. zurücknehmen); **to take out a** ~ sich e-e Lizenz beschaffen; **to withdraw a** ~ e-e Lizenz entziehen (od. zurücknehmen)

licen|se (~ce) *v (amtl.)* erlauben (od. genehmigen), *(behördl.)* Genehmigung erteilen; zulassen; Konzession (od. Lizenz) erteilen; konzessionieren; lizenzieren; **to ~ sb. to use a patent** jdm die Befugnis zur Benutzung e-s Patents erteilen

licensed amtlich zugelassen; konzessioniert; lizenziert; ~ **dealer** *Br* (*durch den Board of Trade*) zugelassener Wertpapierhändler; ~ **deposit-taking institution** *Br* Einlagen-Bank *(durch den Banking Act 1979 gegründetes zweitrangiges Bankgeschäft)*; ~ **house** (or **premises**) *Br* Lokal mit Schankkonzession; ~ **institution Br** Institut (*außer einer Bank*) mit Erlaubnis der →Bank of England für das Einlagengeschäft (*gemäß Banking Act 1979*); ~ **physician** *Am* approbierter Arzt; ~ **undertaking** konzessioniertes *(zum Geschäftsbetrieb zugelassenes)* Unternehmen; ~ **victualler** Gastwirt mit Schankkonzession; **to be** ~ zugelassen sein; Konzession (od. Lizenz) haben

licensing Zulassung; Konzessionserteilung *(bes. Erteilung von Schankkonzessionen)*; Lizenzerteilung; **L~ Act** *Br* Gaststättengesetz *(von 1953)*; ~ **agreement** Lizenzvereinbarung; ~ **authority** *Br* für die Erteilung von Schankkonzessionen zuständige Behörde; ~ **consultant** Lizenzberater; ~ **hours** *(gesetzl. begrenzte)* Ausschankzeiten *(für alkoholische Getränke)*; ~ **of motor vehicles**[29] Zulassung von Kraftfahrzeugen; ~ **period** Lizenzperiode; **cross-**~ *(PatR)* gegenseitige Lizenzerteilung, Austausch von Lizenzen; **cross-~ agreement** gegenseitiger Lizenzvertrag; **multiple** ~ *(PatR)* Erteilung von Parallellizenzen an mehrere Lizenznehmer; **package** ~ *(PatR)* Zusammenfassung von Lizenzen

licensee Inhaber e-r Genehmigung od. Konzession *(bes. e-r Schankkonzession)*; Lizenznehmer; *Am (auch:)* Inhaber e-s Führerscheins; Gast (od. Berechtigter), der nicht zu Zwecken der Förderung des Geschäftsbetriebes des Grundeigentümers das Land betritt *(cf. licen|ce [~se] 2.; opp. invitee)*; **sub-**~ Unterlizenznehmer

licenser *(Am* **licensor***)* Aussteller e-r Konzession; Lizenzgeber; **sub-**~ Unterlizenzgeber

lie Lüge; ~ **detector** Lügendetektor; **white** ~ Notlüge; **to tell ~s** lügen

lie *v* liegen; **to ~ →dormant; to ~ in grant** durch Urkunde übertragbar sein; **to ~ over** aufgeschoben werden; **an action ~s** e-e Klage ist zulässig (od. begründet); **an appeal ~s** (from a decision) e-e Berufung ist zulässig (gegen e-e Entscheidung); **the fault ~s with him** er trägt die Schuld

lying idle unergiebig, unrentabel

Liechtenstein Liechtenstein; **Principality of** ~ Fürstentum Liechtenstein; **(of)** ~ Liechtensteiner(in); liechtensteinisch

lien *(gesetzliches, gewohnheitsrechtl. entstandenes oder vertragl. vereinbartes, mit oder nicht mit Besitz verbundenes)* Zurückbehaltungsrecht *(mit Befriedigungsbefugnis)*; Pfandrecht *(an fremden Vermögensgegenständen zur Sicherung der Geldforderung des Gläubigers, die in Zusammenhang mit Handlungen entstanden ist, die sich auf die belasteten Vermögensgegenstände beziehen)*

lien, a ~ arises ein Pfandrecht (etc) entsteht; **to create a ~** ein Pfandrecht bestellen; **to enforce a ~** ein Pfandrecht verwerten (od. geltend machen); **a ~ is lost** ein Pfandrecht erlischt; **to waive a ~** auf ein Pfandrecht verzichten

lien, ~ by agreement Vertragspfandrecht; **~ by attachment** Pfändungspfandrecht *(aufgrund Arrestvollziehung)*; **~ by implication** (or **by operation of law**) gesetzliches Pfandrecht; **~ covenant** Zusicherung des Nichtbestehens e-r dinglichen Belastung *(bei Grundstücksübereignung)*; **~ created by statute** gesetzliches Pfandrecht; **~ creditor** *Am (beim →security interest)* Drittgläubiger mit Pfändungspfandrecht am Sicherungsgut; **~ on documents** Zurückbehaltungsrecht an Akten; **~ on a bill** Pfandrecht an e-m Wechsel; **~ on goods** (for freight) Pfandrecht an der Ladung; **~ on the instrument arising either from contract or by implication of law** *Am* vertragliches oder gesetzliches Pfandrecht am (Handels-)Papier; **~ on personal property** Fahrnispfandrecht; **~ on real estate** Grundpfandrecht; **~ on a ship** s. maritime →~; **~ perfected** Pfandrecht bei eingetretener Pfandreife; **~ theory** *Am* →mortgage *(Kommentar)*

lien, artisan's ~ *Am* Zurückbehaltungsrecht des Handwerkers an Mobilien; **attorney's →charging ~; attorney's →retaining ~; bailee's ~** Zurückbehaltungsrecht des berechtigten Fremdbesitzers an den ihm übergebenen Sachen *(zur Sicherung der Ansprüche gegen den Eigentümer aus dem Besitzmittlungsverhältnis)*; **carrier's ~** *(gesetzl.)* Pfandrecht des Frachtführers; **→charging ~; contractual** (or **conventional**) **~** Vertragspfandrecht; **enforcement of a ~** Verwertung (od. Geltendmachung) e-s Pfandrechts; **equitable ~** *(durch equity geschaffenes, besitzloses)* Pfandrecht *(z.B. des Käufers an der bewegl. oder unbewegl. Sache für die von ihm geleistete Anzahlung, oder wenn der Kaufvertrag rückgängig gemacht wurde. Es kann gutgläubigen Dritten gegenüber in der Regel nicht geltend gemacht werden)*; **factor's ~** Kommissionärspfandrecht *(→factor 2.)*; *(gesetzl.)* Sicherungsrecht des Factor am gesamten Lager in seinem jeweiligen Bestand *(→factor 3.)*; **floating ~** *Am* Sicherungsrecht an e-m Vermögensgegenstand mit wechselndem Bestand; **general ~** allgemeines Pfandrecht *(kann wegen aller dem Besitzer gegen den Eigentümer zustehenden Ansprüche geltend gemacht werden; opp. special ~)*; **→implied ~; innkeeper's ~** Pfandrecht des Gastwirts *(an den eingebrachten Sachen des Gastes)*; **judgment ~** *Am* durch Urteil begründetes Pfandrecht am pfändbaren Vermögen des Schuldners; Zwangshypothek; **junior ~** jüngeres *(im Rang nachstehendes)* Pfandrecht; **lessor's ~** Vermieterpfandrecht

lien, maritime ~ *(gesetzl.)* Schiffsgläubigerrecht; Schiffspfandrecht, seerechtliches Pfandrecht; **preferred maritime ~** *Am (gesetzl.)* Schiffsgläubigerrecht, das der vertraglichen Schiffshypothek gegenüber e-n Vorrang hat

lien, mechanic's ~ *Am (gesetzl.)* Pfandrecht des Bauhandwerkers od. Baustofflieferanten an e-m Bauwerk od. e-m Grundstück zur Sicherung von Ansprüchen auf Lohn und Forderungen aus Materiallieferungen; **particular ~** s. special →~; **possessory ~** Zurückbehaltungsrecht, das den Besitz der Sache voraussetzt *(opp. charging ~)*; **prior ~** *Am* älteres *(im Rang vorgehendes)* Pfandrecht; **purchaser's ~** Pfandrecht des Käufers *(an dem von ihm bezahlten od. angezahlten Kaufgegenstand)*; **→retaining ~; seller's ~** (for unpaid purchase money)[30] *(gesetzl.)* Zurückbehaltungsrecht des Warenverkäufers an der veräußerten Ware bis zur vollständigen Zahlung des Kaufpreises; **solicitor's →charging ~; solicitor's →retaining ~; special** (or **specific**) **~** Pfandrecht an e-r bestimmten Sache *(das nur die Forderung sichert, die mit der zurückbehaltenen Sache in rechtl. Zusammenhang steht; opp. general ~)*; **statutory ~** *(auf →statute law beruhendes)* gesetzliches Pfandrecht *(opp. Common Law ~)*; **vendor's ~** (for unpaid purchase money)[31] *(gesetzl.)* Sicherungsrecht des Verkäufers an dem veräußerten Grundstück *(das die Kaufpreisforderung sichert und wie ein Grundpfandrecht wirkt; auch gegenüber späteren entgeltlichen Grundstücksberechtigten wirksam, wenn im Grundbuch eingetragen)*

lienee Pfandschuldner, Verpfänder

lienholder →lienor

lienor Zurückbehaltungsberechtigter; Pfandgläubiger; *Am (beim →security interest)* Sicherungsnehmer

lieu, in ~ of an Stelle von, statt; **in ~ of an oath** an Eides Statt

lieutenant Stellvertreter; *mil* Leutnant; **~ colonel** Oberstleutnant; **~ general** Generalleutnant; **L~ Governor** *Am* Vizegouverneur *(e-s Einzelstaates)*; **Lord L~** *Br* →Lord

life Leben; Gültigkeitsdauer, Laufzeit *(e-r Versicherung, Anleihe etc)*; Lebensdauer *(s. useful →~)*; **~ and non-~ business** Lebens- und Sachversicherungsgeschäft; **~ annuitant** Leibrentenempfänger, Empfänger e-r Leibrente; **~ annuity** Leibrente, lebenslängliche Rente; **~ assurance** *Br* →~ insurance; **~ assured** *Br* Lebensversicherte(r); **~ births** Lebendgeburten; **~ boat** Rettungsboot; **~ contingency** *(VersR)* von der Lebensdauer abhängiges Risiko; **~ estate** Besitz auf Lebenszeit *(bes. von Immobilien) (entweder des tenant selbst od. e-s Dritten)*; Nießbrauch *(an unbewegl. Vermögen, auf [eigene od. fremde] Lebensdauer)*; **~ expectancy** Lebenserwartung; **~ guard** Leibwache; **~ history** Lebenslauf; ~ **imprisonment** lebenslängliche Freiheitsstrafe

life in being Lebenszeit, Dauer des Lebens e-r Person, die zur Zeit des Inkrafttretens e-s Testaments od. e-r Schenkungsurkunde lebt *(wichtig bei rule against perpetuities)*

life insurance Lebensversicherung; **L~I~Agency Management** (LIAMA) *Am* Dachorganisation von (über 500) Lebensversicherungsunternehmen *(mit Marktforschungs- und Ausbildungsaufgaben)*

life insurance company Lebensversicherungsgesellschaft; **joint stock** ~ Lebensversicherungs-AG; **mutual** ~ Lebensversicherungsgesellschaft auf Gegenseitigkeit

life insurance contract Lebensversicherungsvertrag

life insurance policy (L. I. P.) Lebensversicherungspolice; **to take out** (or **effect**) **a** ~ e-e Lebensversicherung abschließen

life insurance, ~ **premium** Lebensversicherungsprämie; ~ **with profits** *Br* Lebensversicherung mit Gewinnbeteiligung *(des Versicherungsnehmers);* ~ **without profits** *Br* Lebensversicherung ohne Gewinnbeteiligung *(des Versicherungsnehmers);* ~ **relief** *Br* →relief 3.; **industrial** ~ *Am* Kleinlebensversicherung; →**limited pay** ~; **non-**~ Nichtlebensversicherung; **ordinary** ~ *Am* Großlebensversicherung; Lebensversicherung auf den Todesfall; **whole** ~ s. ordinary →~; **to take out a** ~ e-e Lebensversicherung abschließen

life insured savings account *Am* (Kombination von) Lebensversicherung und Sparkonto

life interest auf *(eigene od. fremde)* Lebensdauer beschränktes Nutzungsrecht; lebenslänglicher Anspruch *(auf Früchte od. sonstige Rechte aus e-r beweglichen od. unbeweglichen Sache);* lebenslänglicher Nießbrauch *(bes. des überlebenden Ehegatten)*

Life interests werden oft unter Ehegatten begründet[32] und entstehen bei gesetzlicher Erbfolge. Sie haben eine dem deutschen Nießbrauch ähnliche Funktion

life, ~ **membership** lebenslängliche Mitgliedschaft; ~ **of an agreement** Laufzeit e-s Vertrages, Vertragsdauer; ~ **of a contract** →~ of an agreement; ~ **of a lease** Laufzeit e-s Miet- (od. Pacht-)vertrages; ~ **of a letter of credit** Laufzeit e-s Akkreditivs; ~ **of a loan** Laufzeit e-r Anleihe; ~ **of a patent** s. term of a →patent *(patent 2.)*; ~ **of a policy** Laufzeit e-r Police

life of a third party, contract on the ~ Vertrag über e-e Versicherung auf fremdes Leben, Lebensfremdversicherung; Drittlebensvertrag

Life Office *Br* Lebensversicherungsgesellschaft; **mutual and proprietary l~ o~s** Lebensversicherungsgesellschaften auf Aktien- und Gegenseitigkeitsbasis

life, ~ →**peer;** ~ →**peerage;** ~ **pension** →pension for ~; ~ **policy** →policy 2.; ~**-rent** *Scot* persönliche Dienstbarkeit; ~**-saving appliances** Rettungsmittel

life sentence (Verurteilung zu) lebenslängliche(r) Freiheitsstrafe; **to receive a** ~ zu lebenslänglicher Freiheitsstrafe verurteilt werden; **to serve a** ~ e-e lebenslängliche Freiheitsstrafe verbüßen

life, ~ **subscription** einmaliger Beitrag auf Lebenszeit; ~ **table** Sterblichkeitstabelle; ~ **tenancy** →tenancy for life; ~ **tenant** →tenant for life; ~ **tenure** lebenslängliche Anstellung

lifetime Lebenszeit; ~ **exemption** *Am* Freibetrag (des Schenkers) auf Lebenszeit; ~ **gift** Schenkung unter Lebenden (od. zu Lebzeiten); ~ **of a parliament** Legislaturperiode; ~ **of a patent** Laufzeit e-s Patents; ~ **transfer** (Vermögens-)Übertragung unter Lebenden; **during the** ~ **(of)** zu Lebzeiten (von)

life work Lebensarbeit, Lebenswerk

life, business ~ Geschäftsleben; **conditions of** ~ Lebensbedingungen, Lebensverhältnisse; **danger to** ~ Lebensgefahr; **duration of** ~ Lebensdauer; **economic** ~ Wirtschaftsleben; →**expectation of** ~

life, for ~ lebenslänglich, auf Lebenszeit; **appointment for** ~ Ernennung auf Lebenszeit; Lebensstellung; **income for** ~ lebenslängliches Einkommen, Einkommen auf Lebenszeit; →**pension for** ~; →**tenancy for** ~; →**tenant for** ~; **to hold office for** ~ auf Lebenszeit ein Amt innehaben

life, length of ~ Lebensdauer; **during his natural** ~ auf Lebenszeit; **presumption of** ~ Lebensvermutung; **professional** ~ Berufsleben; → **safety of** ~ **at sea; station in** ~ soziale Stellung; **(estimated) useful** ~ (geschätzte) Nutzungsdauer; **whole** ~ **annuity** lebenslängliche Rente; **to insure one's** ~ sein Leben versichern

lifeless lustlos, matt *(Börse)*

Liffe →London International Financial Futures Exchange

lifo ("last-in-first-out") „zuletzt eingekauft – zuerst verbraucht"

Methode der Bewertung des Vorrats

lift Lift, Aufzug; ~**-off** Abheben, Start *(e-r Rakete);* ~ **van** Möbeltransportbehälter *(für Überseeumzüge ohne Umladung)*

lift *v* aufheben; anheben; beseitigen; *sl.* stehlen; Plagiat begehen, plagiieren; **to** ~ **a ban** ein Verbot aufheben; **to** ~ **the blockade** die Blockade aufheben; **to** ~ **cattle** *Br* Vieh stehlen; **to** ~ **the censorship** die Zensur aufheben; **to** ~ **restrictions** Beschränkungen aufheben

lifting Aufhebung *(des Embargos, der Zensur etc);* Plagiat; *sl.* Stehlen; **cattle** ~ *Br* Viehdiebstahl; **shop** ~ Ladendiebstahl

lifter, cattle ~ *Br* Viehdieb; **shop** ~ Ladendieb

ligan →lagan

light Licht; ~ **dues** Leuchtturmgebühren, Leuchtfeuergebühren; ~**house** Leuchtturm; ~**ship** Feuerschiff, Leuchtschiff; **ancient** ~**s** *(durch mehr als 20jährige*[33] *Nutzung ersessenes)* Licht- und Fensterrecht; **(coast)** ~ Leuchtfeuer; **green** ~ freie Fahrt; offizielle Erlaubnis

light, in the ~ **of** angesichts (od. unter Berücksichtigung) von; **to consider in the** ~ **of . . .** unter dem Gesichtspunkt von . . . prüfen

light, →**neon** ~; →**red** ~; **traffic** ~**(s)** Verkehrslicht(er), Verkehrsampel

light leicht; unbeladen, leer *(Transport)*; ~ **cargo** Leichtgut; ~ **coin** *Am* Münze mit zu geringem Edelmetallgehalt *(opp. overweight coin)*; ~ **displacement** Leertonnage *(opp. load displacement)*; ~ **draught** Tiefgang des leeren Schiffes *(opp. load or laden draught)*; ~ **freight** (or **goods**) *(Schiffsfrachtverkehr)* Leichtgüter *(opp. heavy freight or goods)*; ~ **industries** Leichtindustrie *(opp heavy industries)*; ~ **punishment** (or **sentence**) leichte Strafe; ~ →**railway;** ~ **ship** →~ vessel; ~ **taxation** geringe Besteuerung; ~ **vessel** (Lt. V.) unbeladenes Schiff *(opp. laden vessel)*; ~ **work** leichte Arbeit

lighten *v* erleichtern; *(Schiff)* (ab)leichtern, teilweise entladen

lightening Erleichterung; (Ab-)Leichterung *(e-s Schiffes)*; ~ **of taxation** Steuererleichterung; **cost** (or **expenses**) **of** ~ **of a ship** Kosten der (Ab-)Leichterung

lighter Leichter; *(in Hamburg:)* Schute; ~**-aboard ship** Frachtschiff mit Leichtern an Bord

lighterage Leichterung; Leichterlohn; Transport durch Leichter

lighterhire Leichtermiete

lighterman Leichterschiffer

lighting Beleuchtung; ~ **equipment** Beleuchtungsanlage; ~ **expenses** Beleuchtungskosten; ~ **of vehicles**[34] Beleuchtung von Fahrzeugen; →**buoyage and** ~; **street** ~ Straßenbeleuchtung

lightning Blitzschlag; ~ **insurance** Versicherung gegen Blitzschlag; ~ **strike** Blitzstreik; ~ **war** Blitzkrieg

like gleich; ~ **grade and quality** gleiche Beschaffenheit und Güte *(von Waren)*; **of a** ~ **kind** von gleicher Art; ~**minded** gleichgesinnt; ~ **product** gleichartiges Erzeugnis

likelihood Wahrscheinlichkeit; ~ **of confusion** *(WarenzeichenR)* Verwechslungsgefahr

limb (Körper-)Glied; **damages allowed for the loss of a** ~ Schadensersatz für Verlust e-s (Körper-)Gliedes

LIMEAN (London Interbank Mean) Arithmetischer Mittelkurs aus →LIBOR und →LIBID

limelight, to be in the ~ im Mittelpunkt des Interesses stehen

limit Grenze; *com* Limit, Preisgrenze; *Am* Zinsobergrenze für Kredite von US-Banken gemäß →Regulation Q; *(VersR)* s. (office) →~; *(Börse)* Limit *(vom Auftraggeber angegebener Kurs)*; ~ **of credit** Kreditlimit; ~ **of indemnity** *(VersR)* Deckungsgrenze; Haftungsgrenze; ~ **order** *(Börse)* limitierter Auftrag *(cf. day order, market order)*; ~ **price** *(Kommissionsgeschäft)* Limitpreis; ~ **value** Grenzwert

limit, →**age** ~; **credit** ~ Kreditlimit; **debt** ~ Verschuldungsgrenze; **in** ~**s** *Am* Zutritt gestattet; **lower** ~ Mindestgrenze; untere Grenze; **off** ~**s** *Am* Zutritt verboten; **(office)** ~ *Br (vom Versicherer übernommener)* Höchstbetrag; Deckungsgrenze; **(price)** ~ →price 1. u. 2.; **speed** ~ Geschwindigkeitsgrenze; **time** ~ Frist (→*time 2.*); **up to the** ~ **of** bis zur Höhe von; **upper** ~ Höchstgrenze; obere Grenze; **within the** ~**s** innerhalb der Grenzen; im Rahmen von; **within the** ~**s of the court's jurisdiction** innerhalb der Zuständigkeit des Gerichts

limit, to be bound to a ~ an ein Limit gebunden sein; **to exceed the** ~ das Limit überschreiten; **to exceed the speed** ~ die *(zulässige)* Höchstgeschwindigkeit überschreiten; **to fix** (or **give**) **a** ~ ein Limit festsetzen; **to go beyond the** ~ das Limit überschreiten; **to keep within** (or **observe**) **the** ~ das Limit einhalten; **to raise the** ~ das Limit erhöhen; **to set a** ~ ein Limit festsetzen

limit *v* begrenzen; *com* limitieren, ein Limit vorschreiben; **to** ~ **an estate** ein zeitlich begrenztes Eigentumsrecht einräumen; **to** ~ **expenditure** Ausgaben beschränken; **to** ~ **a price** ein Preislimit setzen; **to** ~ **the time allotted to each speaker** die Redezeit begrenzen

limited begrenzt; beschränkt, limitiert; *(nach dem Namen e-r* ~ *liability company = Ltd)* mit beschränkter Haftung

Im englischen Recht[35] Zusatz bei Handelsfirmen, deren Teilhaber nur für die Bezahlung der von ihnen übernommenen shares haften (companies limited by shares; der deutschen AG od. GmbH entsprechend), oder auf Grund einer besonderen Garantie in Höhe eines bestimmten Betrages im Falle der Auflösung der Gesellschaft (companies limited by guarantee).

Am Während in einigen Einzelstaaten der Zusatz „Inc." *(cf. incorporated)* zum Namen einer AG zwingend ist, muß z. B. nach dem am 1. 9. 1963 in New York in Kraft getretenen Business Corporation Law der Name einer →corporation als Hinweis auf die Rechtsform die Bezeichnung Corporation (Corp.), Incorporated (Inc.) od. Limited (Ltd.) enthalten.

Die amerikanische Limited partnership, der das Wort „Limited" nachgestellt ist, darf nicht mit der britischen limited company verwechselt werden

limited, ~ administration *(sachl., zeitl. od. örtl.)* beschränkte *(vom Gericht bestimmte)* Erbschaftsverwaltung; **~ and reduced** *Br* →reduced, →reduction of capital; **~ (legal) competence** *Am* beschränkte Geschäftsfähigkeit; **~ condition (of a market)** Marktenge; **~ credit** Kredit in begrenzter Höhe; **~ dividend** limitierte Dividende; **contract of ~ duration** befristeter Vertrag; **~ executor** *(sachl., zeitl. od. örtl.)* beschränkter *(testamentarisch ernannter)* Erbschaftsverwalter; **~-function wholesaler** *Am* Großhändler, der nur einige Großhandelsfunktionen ausübt *(z.B. cash and carry wholesaler)*; **~ gold standard** Goldkernwährung; **~ guarantee** (or **guaranty**) befristete Garantie; **~ →jurisdiction**

limited legal capacity, person having ~ in der Geschäftsfähigkeit beschränkte Person

limited liability beschränkte Haftung (od. Haftpflicht); **~ company** *Br* Kapitalgesellschaft (→*company limited by shares*); Gesellschaft mit beschränkter Nachschußpflicht (→*company limited by guarantee*)

limited, ~ market enger (od. begrenzt aufnahmefähiger) Markt *(opp. free market)*; **~ means** begrenzte Mittel; **~ monarchy** konstitutionelle Monarchie; **~ order** *(Börse)* im Kurs limitierter Auftrag; **~ owner** Inhaber e-s dinglichen Rechts an Grundbesitz, das geringer ist als →fee simple *(z.B. tenant for life)*; **~ owner's charge** *Br*[36] Eigentümer-Grundschuld e-s life estate-Inhabers *(der Erbschaftssteuer für den Grundbesitz bezahlt hat)*; **~ →partner; ~ →partnership; ~ pay life insurance** *Am* Lebensversicherung mit abgekürzter Prämienzahlung *(der Versicherte bezahlt für e-e begrenzte Zahl von Jahren, ist aber für das ganze Leben versichert)*; **~ payment insurance →~** pay life insurance; **~ premium** *(VersR)* abgekürzte Prämienzahlung; **~ price** Limitpreis; Kurslimit; **~ price store** *Am* Kleinpreisgeschäft; **~ tax liability** beschränkte Steuerpflicht; **~ in time** befristet; **~ time offer** *Am* befristetes Angebot; **the time ~ in the contract** die vertraglich vorgesehene Frist; **the view is ~** *(Verkehr)* die Sicht ist behindert

limitedness of the market Marktenge

limiting value Grenzwert

limitation 1. Begrenzung, Beschränkung; Einschränkung; Kontingentierung; **~ of armament** Rüstungsbeschränkung; **~ of authority** Vollmachtsbeschränkung; **~ of damages** Begrenzung der Schadensersatzpflicht; **~ of dividends** Dividendenbegrenzung; **~ (of an estate or interest)** Befristung (zeitliche Beschränkung) bei der Zuwendung e-s Rechts oder e-r Befugnis *(z.B. wenn diese[s] mehreren Personen hintereinander nur auf Zeit zustehen soll)*; **~ of imports** Einfuhrbeschränkung; **~ of jurisdiction** Beschränkung der Zuständigkeit

limitation of liability Haftungsbeschränkung; **contractual ~** vertraglich vereinbarte Haftungsbeschränkung

limitation, ~ of membership Begrenzung der Mitgliederzahl; **~ of output** (or **production**) Produktionsbegrenzung, Produktionseinschränkung; **~ of the right of disposal** Verfügungsbeschränkung; **under a conditional ~** unter e-r einschränkenden Bedingung; **constitutional ~** verfassungsrechtliche Beschränkung; **imposition of ~s** Auferlegung von Beschränkungen; **→overall ~; words of ~** *Br*[37] *(bei Eigentumsübertragungen)* Worte, die das Eigentumsrecht *(des Käufers od. Erben)* bestimmen; **to impose ~s** Beschränkungen auferlegen

limitation 2. Verjährung; **L~ Act**[38] Verjährungsgesetz

limitation of actions 1. Verjährung *(die anders als im deutschen Recht als – prozeßrechtliche – Einrede angesehen wird und die Klag- und Aufrechenbarkeit des verjährten Rechts ausschließt). 2. Br*[39] Verjährung von Herausgabe- oder Zahlungsansprüchen in bezug auf Grundstücke *(führt zum Rechtsverlust; ähnelt also im deutschen Recht mehr der Ersitzung oder Versitzung als der Verjährung, die die Durchsetzbarkeit, nicht aber das Recht selbst beseitigt)*; **~ in respect of a claim** Anspruchsverjährung

limitation of criminal proceedings Strafverfolgungsverjährung

limitation, ~ of time *(StrafR)* Verjährung; **defen|ce (~se) of ~** Verjährungseinrede; **statute of ~s** Verjährungsgesetz; Verjährungsvorschriften *(→statute)*; **to be barred by ~** verjährt sein

limitation period Verjährungsfrist (→*period of limitation*); **extension of ~** (in case of disability) Hemmung der Verjährung

limping, ~ marriage hinkende Ehe *(deren Gültigkeit in mehreren Staaten unterschiedlich behandelt wird)*; **~ standard** hinkende Währung

Lincoln's Inn *Br* e-e der →Inns of Court

line 1. Verwandtschaftslinie; **~ of succession** Erblinie; **ascending ~** aufsteigende Linie; **collateral ~** Seitenlinie; **descending ~** absteigende Linie; **(relationship in the) direct ~** (Verwandtschaft in der) gerade(n) Linie; **to be next in ~ of succession** als nächster Verwandter nachfolgeberechtigt sein

line 2. Linie; **~ of demarcation** *(VölkerR)* Demarkationslinie; **~ of fire** Schußlinie; **~s of policy** →policy 1.; **above the ~ item** *Br* Posten des ordentlichen Haushalts; ordentlicher Etatposten; **assembly ~** Fließband; **below the ~ item** *Br* Posten des außerordentlichen Haushalts; **building ~** Fluchtlinie; **credit ~** Kreditlinie; **within the British ~s**[40] innerhalb der britischen Linien *(an den Einsatzorten britischer Streit-*

kräfte geschlossene Ehen); **to be in ~ with** entsprechen; **to draw the ~** die Grenze ziehen; **to draw hard and fast ~s** *fig* e-e scharfe Grenze ziehen; **to toe the ~** *colloq. (auch pol)* sich einfügen, sich unterwerfen; sich an die Parteilinie halten

line 3. Verkehrslinie; **~s of communication(s)** Nachrichtenweg; *mil* Nachschublinie; **~ navigation** Linienschiffahrt; →**air~; branch ~** Nebenlinie *(Bahn)*; **bus ~** Autobuslinie; **down ~** *Br* Strecke aus London heraus; **feeder** (or **local service**) **~** Zubringerlinie; **railway ~** Eisenbahnlinie; **shipping ~** Schiffahrtslinie; **steamship ~** Dampferlinie; **telegraph ~** Telegrafenverbindung; **telephone ~** Telefonverbindung; **tram(way) ~** Straßenbahnlinie; **trunk ~** Stammlinie *(verbindet die wichtigeren Verkehrszentren miteinander; cf. feeder ~); (Eisenbahn)* Hauptstrecke; *tel* Fernleitung; **up ~** *Br* Strecke nach London

line 4. Linie, Linienkräfte *(opp. staff)*; **~ and staff** *(verantwortliche)* Betriebsführung und *(nur)* beratende Mitarbeiter; **~ duties** Linienaufgaben; **~ management** Linienmanagement; **~ organization** Linienorganisation; **~ position** Linienstelle

line 5. *tel* Leitung; Anschluß; Verbindung; **exchange ~** Hauptanschluß; **extension ~** Nebenanschluß; **main ~** Hauptanschluß; **party ~** gemeinsamer Anschluß; **private ~** Privattelefon; **subscriber's ~** Teilnehmeranschluß; **the ~ is engaged** *Br* (**busy** *Am*) die Leitung ist besetzt; **to hold the ~** am Apparat bleiben

line 6. Zeile, Linie; **head~** Überschrift; Schlagzeile; **marriage ~s** *Br* Trauschein; **to drop a p. a ~** *colloq.* jdm e-e kurze Nachricht schreiben

line 7. Arbeitsgebiet, Tätigkeitsfeld; Fach, Gebiet; Branche; Produktionsprogramm; **to bring on ~** in Betrieb nehmen

line of business Geschäftszweig, Branche; **knowledge of the ~** Branchenkenntnis(se)

line, ~ of commerce *Am* Handelszweig, Wirtschaftszweig; **~ of industry** Industriezweig; **~ of insurance** Versicherungszweig; **~ of production** Produktionszweig; **in the food ~** in der Lebensmittelbranche; **full ~ forcing** *Am com* Zwang zur ganzen Auswahl *(verpflichtet den Zwischenhändler, alle Erzeugnisse s-s Lieferanten zu führen)*; **one ~ business** (or **shop**) Spezialgeschäft, Fachgeschäft; **that is not my ~** das schlägt nicht in mein Fach; **the insurance company writes property and casualty ~s** *Am* die Versicherungsgesellschaft betreibt Sach- und Schadensversicherungszweige

line 8. Artikel, Ware(nart), Posten; **~ of goods** Artikelserie; Warensortiment; **a cheap ~** e-e preiswerte Partie *(Waren)*; ein billiger Artikel; **a new ~** e-e neue Art von Ware; **side ~** Nebenartikel; **to drop a ~** e-e Warengattung fallenlassen; **to keep** (or **deal in**) **a ~** e-n Artikel führen

line 9. *(VersR) (vom Versicherer übernommener)* Höchstbetrag, Zeichnungsgrenze; **gross ~** Höchstgrenze der Annahme; **net ~** Höchstgrenze des Selbstbehalts

line(s) 10. Grundsatz; Richtlinie(n); Art und Weise; **~ of action** Handlungsweise, Vorgehen; **~ of argument** Argumentation, Beweisführung; **~ of conduct** Verhalten(sregel); Lebensführung; **the ~s of his policy** die Grundlinien s-r Politik, s-e politische Richtung; **along these ~s** nach diesen Richtlinien; **along commercial ~s** nach kommerziellen Gesichtspunkten; **guiding ~** Richtlinie; **to lay down ~s** Richtlinien geben; **to take the ~** die Ansicht (od. den Standpunkt) vertreten; **to take a strong ~** energisch vorgehen

line *v Am* grenzen (on an); **to ~ the streets** Spalier bilden; **to ~ up** sich arrangieren (with mit); *Am* anstehen, Schlange stehen, sich anstellen

lineage Abstammung; Vorfahren

lineal in gerader Linie (verwandt) *(opp. collateral)*; **~ consanguinity** Verwandtschaft in der geraden Linie; **~ descendant** Abkömmling in gerader Linie, direkter Abkömmling; **~→descent; to be ~ly descended from** in gerader Linie abstammen von

linear, ~ measure Längenmaß; **~ programming** lineare Programmierung, Linearplanung *(mathematische Methode zur Planung von Produktionsprozessen)*; **~ increase (reduction) of taxes** lineare Steuererhöhung (Steuersenkung)

liner Passagierdampfer, Linienschiff *(opp. tramp)*; **~ company** Linienreederei; **code of conduct for ~ conferences**[40a] Verhaltenskodex für Linienkonferenzen; **~ freighting** Stückgutbefrachtung; **~ rates** →rate 2.; **~ traffic** Linienschiffahrt; **~ train** →freight ~; **~ waybill** Seefrachtbrief; **air ~** Verkehrsflugzeug; **cargo ~** Linienfrachtschiff; →**freight ~; ocean ~** Überseedampfer

linguistic, ~ border Sprachgrenze; **~ problem** Sprachproblem; **~ work** *(UrhR)* Sprachwerk

link Verbindung(sstück); *fig* (Ketten-)Glied; Link *(Koppelung von Sonderziehungsrechten [SZR] mit der Gewährung von Entwicklungshilfe)*; **~ in a chain of evidence** Verbindungsstück in e-r Beweiskette; **~ road** Zubringer; **~-up** Zusammenschluß; Kontaktaufnahme; **capital ~** Kapitalverflechtung; →**genuine ~**

link *v* verbinden; **to ~ up** anschließen

linked, ~ sales system Kopplungskauf; **~ to gold** an das Gold gebunden; **equity-~** *(Lebensversicherung)* aktiengebunden; **index-~** indexgebunden; **unit-~** *Br (Lebensversicherung)* fondsgebunden

linkage Verflechtung; *pol* Gegenseitigkeit

linters Linters, *(kurze)* Baumwollfasern *(Rohstoff für künstl. Fasern, z. B. Zellulose)*

liquefied, ~ natural gas verflüssigtes Erdgas

liquid flüssig, liquid(e); ~ **assets** flüssige Mittel, flüssiges Vermögen; *(Bilanz)* Umlaufvermögen; ~ **debt** liquide (od. fällige) Forderung
liquid funds flüssige Mittel; Bargeld; **immobilization of** ~ Liquiditätsbindung
liquid, ~option note *Am* Null-Kupon Anleihe am US-Markt, die mit dem Recht auf Wandlung in Aktien ausgestattet ist; ~ **strength** kurzfristig liquidierbare Vermögenswerte

liquidate *v* liquidieren; *(aufgelöste Gesellschaft)* abwickeln *(üblicher:* to wind up*)*; in Liquidation gehen; *(Schuldbetrag od. Schadensersatz)* festsetzen; *(Schulden)* tilgen, begleichen, ablösen; *(Sachwerte)* flüssig machen; *(Börsentermingeschäfte)* abwickeln; glattstellen
liquidated, ~ assets veräußerte Vermögenswerte; ~ **claim** (or **demand**) Forderung auf e-e bestimmte (od. berechenbare) Summe; bezifferte Forderung; ~ **damages** bezifferter Schadensersatz; vereinbarte Vertragsstrafe (→*damages)*; ~ **demand** Forderung der Zahlung e-r bestimmten Geldsumme

liquidation Liquidation, Abwicklung; *Br* Konkurs (*e-r Kapitalgesellschaft*) (→*winding up*); Bezahlung, Tilgung *(e-r Schuld)*; Flüssigmachung *(von Sachwerten)*; *(Börse)* Glattstellung; ~ **of debts** Schuldentilgung; ~ **of a fund** Auflösung e-s Fonds; ~ **of reserves** Auflösung der Rücklagen; ~ **proceeds** Liquidationserlös; ~ **proceedings** *Am* Liquidationsverfahren *(die Aktiva des Schuldners werden verkauft und die Erlöse an die Gläubiger verteilt)*; ~ **sale** Liquidationsverkauf; ~ **subject to the supervision of the court** Liquidation unter Aufsicht des Gerichts; ~ **value** Liquidationswert; **compulsory** ~ zwangsweise Liquidation; **foreign ~s** Glattstellungen im Ausland *(z. B. bei Börsenverlusten)*; **inventory** ~ *Am* Lagerabbau; **voluntary** ~ Liquidation *(e-r Gesellschaft)* auf Grund Gesellschaftsbeschlusses; freiwillige Liquidation; ~ **is carried out** die Abwicklung wird durchgeführt; **to go into** ~ in die Liquidation gehen

liquidator Liquidator, Abwickler; *Br*[41] Konkursverwalter; **to appoint (remove) a** ~ e-n Liquidator bestellen (abberufen)

liquidity Liquidität, Flüssigkeit; ~ **afflux** Liquiditätszustrom; ~ **management** Liquiditätssteuerung; ~ **margin** Liquiditätsspielraum; ~ **position** Liquidität(slage); ~ **preference**[42] Liquiditätspräferenz; ~ **preference theory** *(von Keynes begründete)* Liquiditätspräferenztheorie; ~ **ratio** Liquiditätsgrad; ~ **reserves** Liquiditätsreserven *(der Banken)*; ~ **squeeze** Liquiditätsengpaß; **creation of** ~ Liquiditätsschaffung; **efflux of** ~ Liquiditätsabfluß; **excess** ~ Überliquidität; **influx of** ~ Liquiditätszufluß; **maintenance of** ~ Liquiditätserhaltung; **reduced** ~ Liquiditätseinengung; **strains on** ~ Liquiditätsanspannungen; **world** ~ internationale Liquidität

liquor Alkohol *(bes. Branntwein und Whisky)*; **~s** Spirituosen; ~ **excise** *Am* →~ tax; ~ **licen|ce (~se)** Schankkonzession *(für alkoholische Getränke)*; ~ **store** *Am* Geschäft mit alkoholischen Getränken; ~ **tax** *Am* Steuer auf alkoholische Getränke; ~ **traffic** Handel mit alkoholischen Getränken; →**intoxicating ~s**

lis pendens ("a pending suit") anhängiger Rechtsstreit
lis alibi pendens ("a suit pending elsewhere") (Einrede der) Rechtshängigkeit

list Liste; Verzeichnis, Aufstellung; *Br (Börse)* Kursblatt; *Am (Börse)* Liste der zum Börsenhandel zugelassenen Wertpapiere; *Br* Terminkalender (s. cause →~)
list, to add to a ~ in e-e Liste aufnehmen; **to be on the** ~ auf der Liste stehen; **to be on the short** ~ in die engere Wahl kommen; **to be at the head on the** ~ an der Spitze der Liste stehen; **to compile** (or **draw up**) **a** ~ e-e Liste aufstellen (od. anlegen); **to close a** ~ e-e Liste schließen; **to delete from the** ~ von der Liste löschen; **to enter in a** ~ in e-e Liste eintragen; **to head the** ~ als erster auf (od. an der Spitze) der Liste stehen; **to be included in a** ~ auf e-r Liste stehen; **to keep a** ~ e-e Liste führen; **to make out a** ~ ein Verzeichnis anfertigen; e-e Liste aufstellen; **to put on a** ~ auf e-e Liste setzen; **to strike off the** ~ von der Liste streichen; **to take a p.'s name off the** ~ jdn von der Liste streichen
list, ~ of applicants Bewerberliste; *Br* Zeichnungsliste; ~ **of articles** Warenliste; ~ **of assets** Vermögensverzeichnis; *(Konkursrecht)* Masseverzeichnis; Nachlaßverzeichnis; ~ **of bills for collection** Inkassowechselverzeichnis; ~ **of bills for discount** Diskontwechselverzeichnis; ~ **of classes of goods and services**[43] Klasseneinteilung von Waren und Dienstleistungen; ~ **of commodities** Warenliste, Warenverzeichnis; ~ **of contraband (articles)** Konterbandeliste; ~ **of correspondents** Korrespondentenverzeichnis; ~ **of creditors of a bankrupt** Konkurstabelle; ~ **of the crew** Musterrolle; ~ **of customers** Kundenliste; ~ **of →documents;** ~ **of drawings** Auslosungsliste; ~ **of electors** *Am* Wahlliste, Wählerliste; ~ **of fares** Eisenbahntarif; ~ **of foreign exchange** (Devisen-)Kurszettel; ~ **of names** Namensverzeichnis; ~ **(of names) of members** Mitgliederverzeichnis; ~ **of names of shareholders** (or **stockholders**) Liste der Aktionäre,

Gesellschafterverzeichnis; ~ **of orders** Bestelliste; ~ **of passengers** s. passenger→~; ~ **of those present** Anwesenheitsliste; ~ **price** Listenpreis, Katalogpreis; ~ **of prices** Preisliste; *Br* Kursblatt; ~ **of products** Warenliste, Warenverzeichnis; ~ **of quotations** *Br* Kursblatt; ~ **of sailings** Liste der Abgangsdaten; ~ **of salaries** Gehaltsliste; ~ **of authorized signatures** Unterschriftenverzeichnis; ~ **of speakers** Rednerliste; ~ **of stock exchange quotations** *Br* Kursblatt; ~ **of subscribers** Zeichnungsliste, Subskriptionsliste

list, active ~ *mil* Verzeichnis der Offiziere im aktiven Dienst; **officer on the active** ~ aktiver Offizier; **to be on the active** ~ im aktiven Dienst stehen

list, Air Force L~ *Br* Luftwaffenrangliste; **Army L**~ *Br* Heeresrangliste; **annual** ~ Jahresverzeichnis; **as per (enclosed)** ~ gemäß der (anliegenden) Liste; **attendance** ~ Anwesenheitsliste; **black** ~ schwarze Liste; **cargo** ~ Ladeverzeichnis; **cause** ~ *Br* Terminkalender; **check** ~ Kontrolliste; **Civil L**~ *Br parl* Zivilliste, Krondotation; **commercial** ~ Liste für *(gerichtl.)* Handelssachen; **deletion from the** ~ Löschung von der Liste; **duty** ~ Diensteinteilung; **electoral** ~ Wahlliste; **(foreign) exchange** ~ *(Börse)* (Devisen-)Kurszettel; **import** ~ Einfuhrliste; **Navy L**~ Marinerangliste; **official** ~ *Br*[44] *(Börse)* amtliches Kursblatt; *Am* Liste der börsenfähigen Aktien; **passenger** ~ Passagierliste; **price** ~ Preisliste; →**retired** ~; **salaries** ~ Gehaltsliste; **shopping** ~ Einkaufsliste; **stock exchange** ~ *Br* Kursblatt

list *v* auf die Liste setzen, in die Liste eintragen, listenmäßig erfassen (od. aufführen); katalogisieren, registrieren; *(Wertpapiere)* zum Börsenhandel zulassen, an der Börse notieren; *Am (das zu versteuernde Vermögen)* aufstellen; **to** ~ **a building** ein Gebäude unter Denkmalschutz stellen; **to** ~ **in a catalogue** in e-n Katalog aufnehmen; **to** ~ **property with a broker** *Am* e-n Makler beauftragen, Grundbesitz zu verkaufen (od. zu vermieten)

listed an der Börse eingeführt, notiert; ~ **building** unter Denkmalschutz stehendes Gebäude; ~ **market** *(Börse)* Markt mit notierten Papieren (*Br* →*Domestic Equity Market*); ~ **securities** *(zum Börsenhandel)* zugelassene Wertpapiere; börsennotierte Wertpapiere *(opp. unlisted securities)*; **securities not** ~ **on the stock exchange** Freiverkehrswerte

listing 1. Eintragung in e-e Liste; Aufnahme in ein Verzeichnis; Katalogisierung, Registrierung; ~ **fee** Aufnahmegebühr *(für Aufnahme in ein Verzeichnis)*

listing 2. *(Börse)* Zulassung *(von Wertpapieren)*; Börsennotierung; ~ **prospectus** *(Börse)* Einführungsprospekt; ~ **requirements** Börsenzulassungsvorschriften; **application for** ~ Antrag auf Börsenzulassung; **official** ~ **notice** Zulassungsbescheid *(für Wertpapiere zum Börsenhandel)*; **semi-official** ~ geregelter Freiverkehr

listing 3. ~ **property** (for taxation) *Am* Aufstellung des Vermögens *(für Steuererklärung)*

listing 4. *Am* Beauftragung e-s Maklers, Grundbesitz zu verkaufen (od. vermieten); →**general** ~

listen *v* hören, zuhören, anhören, **to** ~ **in** *(Telefongespräch)* heimlich mithören

listening, ~ **device** Abhörvorrichtung *(Telefon)*; ~ **public** *(Radio)* Hörerschaft

listenership *Am* Hörerschaft; ~ **research** *Am* Höreranalyse *(in der Funkwerbung)*

lite, pendente ~ während des Prozesses, solange der Prozeß schwebt

literal buchstäblich, wörtlich; ~ **meaning** wörtliche Bedeutung; ~ **proof** schriftlicher Beweis; ~ **translation** wörtliche Übersetzung

literary literarisch; ~ →**copyright;** ~ **piracy** literarischer Diebstahl, Plagiat; ~ →**property;** ~ **work** literarisches Werk; ~**, artistic and scientific works** *(UrhR)* Werke der Literatur, Kunst und Wissenschaft; **protection of** ~ **and artistic works**[45] Schutz von Werken der Literatur und der Kunst

literate *Br* Geistlicher der Church of England ohne Universitätsgrad

litigant Prozeßpartei, prozeßführende Partei; **successful** ~ obsiegende Partei

litigate *v* prozessieren; **to** ~ **a case** e-e Sache im Prozeßwege verfolgen, e-n Prozeß führen

litigation Prozeß, Rechtsstreit(igkeit); Prozeßführung; ~ **costs** Prozeßkosten *(einschließlich Anwaltsgebühren)*; ~ **department** *Am* Prozeßabteilung *(e-r Anwaltsfirma)*; **the claim which is the subject of the** ~ die eingeklagte Forderung; **conduct of** ~ Prozeßführung; **cost of** ~ →~ costs; **during** ~ s. pendente→lite; **in** ~ streitbefangen; **party to a** ~ Prozeßpartei; **to conduct** ~ **on behalf of a minor** e-n Prozeß für e-n Minderjährigen führen *(cf. guardian ad litem)*; **in England** ~ **is expensive** die Prozeßkosten sind in England hoch

litigator *Am* → litigant; auf Prozeßführung spezialisierter Anwalt *(e-r Anwaltsfirma)*

litigious streitig, strittig; prozeßfreudig; prozeßsüchtig; ~ **claim** strittige Forderung; ~ **person** Querulant

litispendence Rechtshängigkeit

little doing *colloq.* (or **little business**) wenig Geschäfte

littoral, ~ **sea** Küstenmeer; ~ **states of the Mediterranean** Anliegerstaaten des Mittelmeeres

live lebend(ig); ~ **animals** lebende Tiere; ~ **-births** Lebendgeburten *(opp. still-births)*; ~ **(broad-cast)** *(Radio)* Live-Sendung (→~ *transmission*); ~ **issue** aktuelle Frage
livestock[46] lebendes Inventar; Vieh(bestand); ~ **insurance** Viehversicherung; ~ **production** Tierzucht; **lease of** ~ Viehpacht
live, ~ **transmission** Livesendung; ~ **weight** Lebendgewicht *(opp. deadweight)*
lively discussion lebhafte Diskussion

live *v* leben, wohnen; **to ~ apart** getrennt leben *(Eheleute)*; **to ~ on one's capital** von s-m Kapital leben, sein Kapital verbrauchen; **to ~ beyond one's means** über s-e Verhältnisse leben

livelihood Lebensunterhalt, Existenz; **ability to earn one's** ~ Erwerbsfähigkeit; **major source of** ~ Hauptquelle des Lebensunterhalts; **to earn** (or **gain**) **one's** ~ s-n Lebensunterhalt verdienen

liveliness Belebtheit, Lebhaftigkeit *(des Marktes)*

livery Besitzübergabe, Besitzübertragung; **L ~ Companies** *Br* die (78) Gilden der City of London
liveryman *Br* Mitglied e-r Gilde der City of London

living Leben; Wohnen; Lebensunterhalt, Existenz; lebend; ~ **accommodation** Wohnung, Wohnraum; ~ **allowance** Unterhaltszuschuß
living conditions Lebensbedingungen; **constant improvement of** ~ ständige Besserung der Lebensbedingungen
living, ~ **expenses** Lebensunterhalt, Lebenshaltungskosten; ~ **habits** Lebensgewohnheiten; ~ **in** Wohnung beim Arbeitgeber; ~ **out** Wohnung außerhalb des Hauses des Arbeitgebers; ~ **resources** lebende Schätze *(z.B. des Meeres)*; ~ **space** Lebensraum; ~ **standard(s)** s. standard(s) of→~; ~ **trust** *Am* lebenslängliche Treuhandverwaltung; ~**wage** Mindestlohn, Existenzminimum *(für den Lebensunterhalt als angemessen angesehene Lohnhöhe)*; **cost of** ~ Lebenshaltungskosten (→*cost*)
living, standard(s) of ~ Lebensstandard, Lebenshaltung; **decline in (the) standard(s) of** ~ Sinken des Lebensstandards; **low standard(s) of** ~ niedriger Lebensstandard; **rise in (the) standard(s) of** ~ Steigen des Lebensstandards; **rising standard(s) of** ~ steigender Lebensstandard; **to raise the standard(s) of** ~ den Lebensstandard erhöhen
living, to earn (or **make**) **one's** ~ s-n Lebensunterhalt verdienen; **capable of earning one's** ~ erwerbsfähig; **unable to earn one's** ~ erwerbsunfähig

Lloyd's *Br* Lloyd's
Vereinigung von rund 6000 englischen, in etwa 300 syndicates zusammengeschlossenen Einzelversicherern (underwriting members), die verschiedene Zweige von Versicherungsgeschäften, bes. Seeversicherung, börsenmäßig betreiben
Lloyd's, ~ **agent** *Br* Havarie-Kommissar der Lloyd's Versicherer; ~ **brokers** *Br* Makler, denen die technische Durchführung des Lloyd's Versicherungsgeschäfts obliegt
Lloyd's List *Br* Lloyd's Liste, *(ein von Lloyd's herausgegebenes)* Schiffsnachrichtenblatt; ~ **Law Reports** Lloyd's List Urteilssammlung *(Veröffentlichung der seerechtlichen Rechtsprechung der obersten Gerichte)*
Lloyd's Register (of Shipping) (L.R.) *Br* Lloyd's Register
1. Selbständige Klassifikationsgesellschaft *(s. Society of →Lloyd's Register)*; 2. *(von der Society of Lloyd's Register herausgegebenes, jährl. veröffentlichtes) alphabetisches Verzeichnis aller Schiffe von mehr als 100 BRT*
Lloyd's Register, Society of ~ *Br* Lloyd's Registergesellschaft
Größte Organisation der Welt für Registrierung und Klassifikation von Seeschiffen des zivilen Sektors
Lloyd's unterwriter (or **underwriting member**) *Br* Einzelversicherer, der Mitglied von Lloyd's ist

load Last; Fracht, Ladung; Fuhre; Tragfähigkeit; Belastung; ~ **capacity** Ladefähigkeit, Tragfähigkeit; ~ **displacement** Ladetonnage *(opp. light displacement)*; ~ **draught** Tiefgang des beladenen Schiffes *(opp. light draught)*; ~ **funds** *Am* Investmentfonds, die e-e Gebühr berechnen
load line Ladelinie; Freibord; **International Convention of L~ L~s**[47] Internationales Freibordübereinkommen; **subdivision** ~ Schottenladelinie
load, ~ **of coal** Fuhre Kohle; ~ **of a ship** Schiffsladung; ~ **water line** Ladewasserlinie *(opp. light water line)*
load, additional ~ Beiladung; **cart** ~ Wagenladung; Fuhre; **financial** ~ finanzielle Belastung; **maximum** ~ Höchstbelastung; →**pay** ~; **peak** ~ Spitzenbelastung; **permissible** ~ Höchstbelastung; **sales** ~ *Am* Kosten bei Verkauf von Investmentfonds durch Vertriebsgesellschaften (→~*funds*); **(full) truck** ~ volle Waggonladung; **ship** ~ Schiffsladung; **useful** ~ Nutzlast

load *v* beladen; (auf-, ein-, ver-)laden; *Br (Börse) (Wertpapiere)* stark kaufen; **to ~ up** laden, Ladung einnehmen; **to ~ a cargo** e-e Ladung einnehmen; Fracht aufnehmen; **to ~ on a wag(g)on** auf e-n Waggon laden; e-n Waggon beladen
loaded beladen; ~ **to capacity** voll beladen; ~ **wine** gefälschter (od. verschnittener) Wein
loading Beladung, Verladung; (Auf-)Laden, Einladen, *(VersR)* (Prämien-)Aufschlag zu den Verwaltungskosten; *(bei Ratenzahlung)*

Aufschlag für Verwaltungskosten; ~ **and →unloading;** ~ **berth** Ladestelle, Ladeplatz; ~ **bridge** Verladebrücke; ~ **capacity** Ladekapazität; ~ **charge** *(VersR)* Zuschlaggebühr; ~ **charges** Ladegebühr; Verladungskosten; ~ **days** Ladetage; ~ **limit** Belastungsgrenze; ~ **of goods** Verladung der Ware; ~ **on the berth** Stückgutbefrachtung; ~ **port** Verladehafen, Versandhafen; ~ **risk** Verladerisiko; **maximum permissible** ~ höchst zulässige Beladung; **off** ~ *(bes. Südafrika)* Entladen; **place of** ~ Ladeplatz; **time for** ~ Ladezeit

loader Verlader, Auflader

loan 1. Darlehen (to an), Kredit; ~ **accommodation** Kreditgewährung; ~ **account** Darlehenskonto, Kreditkonto; ~ **against borrower's note** Schuldscheindarlehen; ~ **against security** Kredit gegen Sicherheit, gesichertes Darlehen; Lombardkredit; ~ **agreement** Darlehensvertrag, Kreditvertrag; Kreditvereinbarung; ~ **application** Kreditantrag; ~ **association** *Am* →building and ~ association; ~ **at call** kurzfristiges Darlehen; ~**s at concessionary rates** zinsgünstige Kredite; ~ **at interest** verzinsliches Darlehen; ~ **at notice** kündbares Darlehen; ~ **bank** *Br* Darlehenskasse, Kreditanstalt; ~ **broker** Finanzmakler; ~ **business** Lombardgeschäft; ~ **certificate** Darlehensschein; ~ **charges** Kreditgebühren; ~ **commitment** Darlehenszusage; ~ **cost** Kreditkosten; ~ **default** Kreditausfall; ~ **demand** Kreditnachfrage; ~ **diversification** Kreditstreuung; ~**s en bloc** Globaldarlehen; ~ **for consumption** Konsumentenkredit, Konsumkredit; ~**s for the purpose of investment** Investitionskredit; ~ **funds** Kreditmittel; ~ **given by a bank** Bankkredit; ~ **guarantee** Bürgschaft für ein Darlehen; ~ **holder** Obligationär; Hypothekengläubiger; ~ **insurance** Kreditversicherung; ~ **interest** Darlehenszinsen, Kreditzinsen; ~ **of general working capital** allgemeiner Betriebskredit; ~ **of money** (Geld-)Darlehen; ~**office** *Am* Darlehenskasse; ~ **on collateral** Lombarddarlehen

loan on goods (or **merchandise**) Warenlombard; **to take up a** ~ (*als Kreditnehmer*) Waren beleihen (od. lombardieren)

loan, ~ **on mortgage** durch Hypotheken gesichertes Darlehen; ~ **on overdraft** Kontokorrentkredit; ~ **on →pawn;** ~ **on a policy** Policedarlehen an Versicherte; ~ **on respondentia** Darlehen gegen Verpfändung der Schiffsfracht

loan on securities (or **stock**) Effektenlombard, Effektenkredit; **to take up a** ~ *(als Kreditnehmer)* Effekten lombardieren

loan, ~**s payable** Darlehensverbindlichkeiten; ~ **receipt** Darlehensquittung; ~**s receivable** Darlehensforderungen; ~ **repayable on demand** auf Anforderung rückzahlbares Darlehen; ~ **shark** wucherischer Geldverleiher, Kredithai; Zinswucherer; ~ **stock** festverzinsliche Wertpapiere; ~ **sub-participation** Unterbeteiligung an Darlehensforderungen; ~ **syndicate** Kreditkonsortium; ~ **value** Beleihungswert *(e-r Lebensversicherungspolice)*

loan, amount of the ~ Höhe des Darlehens; **application for a** ~ Kreditantrag; **as a** ~ als Darlehen, darlehensweise; **bank** ~**(s)** Bankdarlehen, Bankkredit; *(Bilanz)* Verbindlichkeiten gegenüber Banken; **bank rate for** ~**s** Lombardsatz; **bridging** ~ Überbrückungskredit; **broker's** ~ *Am* Maklerdarlehen; **call** ~ kurzfristiges Darlehen; **collateral** ~ Lombarddarlehen, Lombardkredit; **contract of** ~ Darlehensvertrag; **customer's** ~ Kundenkredit; **day-to-day** ~ *Br* Tagesgeld *(Leihgeld zwischen Banken für e-n Werktag);* **debtor of a** ~ Darlehensschuldner; **demand** ~ *Am* s. call →~; **duration of a** ~ Laufzeit e-s Darlehens; **farm** ~ *Am* →farm; **grant(ing) a** ~ Darlehensgewährung; **industrial** ~ Darlehen an die Industrie; **interest on** ~ Darlehenszinsen; **interim** ~ Zwischenkredit; **long-term** ~ langfristiges Darlehen; **marine** (or **maritime**) ~ Bodmereidarlehen, Bodmereigeld; **maturity of the** ~ Verfallzeit des Darlehens *(Zeitpunkt, zu dem es zurückgezahlt werden muß);* **mortgage** ~ Hypothekendarlehen; **personal** ~ Personalkredit; Kleinkredit *(e-r Bank);* **promise of a** ~ Darlehensversprechen; Kreditzusage; **→purchase money** ~; **redemption of a** ~ Tilgung e-s Darlehens; **repayment of a** ~ Rückzahlung e-s Darlehens; **short-term** ~ kurzfristiges Darlehen; **term** ~ befristetes Darlehen (→*term 2.);* **terms of a** ~ Darlehensbedingungen; **the terms of the** ~ **are 8 years with an interest rate of 9%** das Darlehen hat e-e Laufzeit von 8 Jahren und ist mit 9% zu verzinsen; **time** ~ Darlehen mit bestimmter Laufzeit, Zeitgeld *(opp. call ~)*

loan, to allow a ~ ein Darlehen bewilligen; Kredit gewähren; **to apply for a** ~ e-n Darlehensantrag stellen; **to contract a** ~ ein Darlehen aufnehmen; **the date on which a** ~ **falls due** der Fälligkeitstermin e-s Darlehens; **to grant a** ~ s. to allow a →~; **to pay off a** ~ s. to repay a →~; **to raise a** ~ ein Darlehen (od. Kredit) aufnehmen; **to recall a** ~ ein Darlehen kündigen; **to receive as a** ~ als Darlehen erhalten; **to redeem a** ~ ein Darlehen tilgen; **to repay a** ~ ein Darlehen zurückzahlen; **to take up a** ~ ein Darlehen (od. Kredit) aufnehmen

loan 2. Anleihe; ~ **(bearing interest) at 6%** sechsprozentige Anleihe; ~ **bearing interest at varied rates** Staffelanleihe; ~ **capital** *Br* Anleihekapital; ~**s in circulation** in Umlauf befindliche Anleihen; ~ **creditor** Anleihegläubiger; ~ **on debentures** Obligationsanleihe; ~ **debtor** Anleiheschuldner; ~**holder** (Anleihe-)-

Gläubiger; ~ **interest** Anleihezinsen; ~ **issue** Anleiheemission; ~**prospectus** Anleiheprospekt; ~ **redemption** Anleihetilgung; ~ **stock** *Br* Schuldverschreibungen; ~ **syndicate** Anleihekonsortium; ~ **yield** Anleiherendite

loan, corporation ~ *Br* Kommunalanleihe; **domestic** ~ Inlandsanleihe; **external** (or **foreign**) ~ Auslandsanleihe; **forced** ~ Zwangsanleihe; **government** ~ Staatsanleihe; **internal** ~ Inlandsanleihe; **issue of a** ~ Ausgabe (od. Begebung) e-r Anleihe; **local authority** ~ *Br* Kommunalanleihe; **municipal** ~ Kommunalanleihe; **national** ~ Staatsanleihe; **period of a** ~ Anleihelaufzeit; **perpetual (government)** ~ Rentenanleihe *(Staatsanleihe, bei der kein Tilgungszwang besteht);* **redemption** ~ Tilgungsanleihe; **redemption of a** ~ Tilgung e-r Anleihe; **subscriber to a** ~ Anleihezeichner

loan, subscription for (or **to**) **a** ~ Anleihezeichnung; **to invite subscription to a** ~ (or **to offer a** ~ **for subscription**) e-e Anleihe zur Zeichnung auflegen

loan, tied ~ zweckgebundene Anleihe; **war** ~ Kriegsanleihe

loan, ~ **to contract a** ~ e-e Anleihe aufnehmen; **to float** (or **issue**) **a** ~ e-e Anleihe ausgeben (od. begeben); **to place a** ~ e-e Anleihe unterbringen; **to redeem a** ~ e-e Anleihe tilgen; **to service a** ~ e-e Anleihe bedienen; **to subscribe to a** ~ e-e Anleihe zeichnen; **the** ~ **was fully subscribed** die Anleihe wurde voll gezeichnet; **the** ~ **was oversubscribed** die Anleihe wurde überzeichnet; **the** ~ **has been underwritten by a syndicate of banks** die Anleihe wurde von e-m Bankenkonsortium fest übernommen

loan 3. Leihe; Ausleihung; Leihgabe *(für Ausstellungen);* ~ **collection** Leihgabensammlung *(Kunstwerke)*

loan for use (Gebrauchs-)Leihe; **contract of** ~ Leihvertrag

loan hall (*Bibliothek*) Ausleihe

loan, as a ~ leihweise; als Leihgabe; **gratuitous** ~ →~ for use; **on** ~ leihweise; geliehen; **to have the** ~ **(of)** *(etw.)* borgen, ausleihen; *(etw.)* geliehen bekommen; **to put out on** ~ verleihen

loan *v bes. Am* (aus)leihen, entleihen; Darlehen (od. Kredit) geben

lobby Lobby; Gesamtheit der Lobbyisten *(cf. lobbyist); parl* Vorraum, Wandelhalle; **division** ~ *Br parl* Abstimmungsraum *(cf. division 2.)*

lobby *v (Abgeordnete)* zu beeinflussen versuchen *(um Gesetze durchzubringen);* politische Beeinflussung betreiben

lobbying Lobbyismus; (Versuch der) Beeinflussung von Abgeordneten durch Beauftragte von Interessengruppen *(cf. pressure groups)*

lobbyism *Am* Lobbyismus *(cf. lobbying)*

lobbyist Lobbyist; *(meist bezahlter)* Interessenvertreter, der im Vorraum (lobby) des Parlaments *(Am* Congress) versucht, die Abgeordneten zu beeinflussen

local örtlich, Orts-; Kommunal-; ortsansässig; ortsgebunden; *Am* örtliche (od. betriebliche) Abteilung e-r Gewerkschaft *(cf. union* ~, →*union 2.);* ~**s** Ortsansässige; ~ **action** *Am* Anspruch, der nur an Ort und Stelle eingeklagt werden kann *(z. B. action of trespass or replevin);* ~ **advertising** Anzeigenwerbung ortsansässiger Geschäfte; ~ **affairs** lokale Angelegenheiten, Kommunalangelegenheiten; ~ **agent** Bezirksvertreter; ~ **attorney** *Am* am Gerichtsort praktizierender Anwalt; ~ **authorities** Ortsbehörden, Kommunalbehörden; kommunale Gebietskörperschaften; ~ **authority** Kommunalbehörde *(Br*[48] *a county council, the Greater London Council, a district council, a London borough council, a parish council or [in Wales] a community council);* ~ **authority bonds** *Br* Kommunalobligationen; ~ **bill** (or **draft**) Platzwechsel *(opp. domestic bill);* ~ **bonus** Ortszulage; ~ **branch** Zweigstelle, Filiale; ~ **business** Platzgeschäft; ~ **by-laws** *Br* Ortsstatuten; ~ **call** *tel* Ortsgespräch; ~ **charge** *tel* Ortsgebühr; ~ **charges** Platzspesen; ~ **conditions** örtliche Verhältnisse (od. Gegebenheiten); Platzbedingungen; ~ **corporation** *Am* Gebietskörperschaft; ~ **council** Gemeinderat, Stadtrat; ~ **court** örtliches *(auf bestimmte Bezirke beschränktes)* Gericht *(county court, magistrates' court etc); Am (oft)* einzelstaatliches Gericht *(opp. U. S. court);* ~ **currency** Landeswährung, inländische Währung; ~ **custom** Orts(ge)brauch, Observanz (→*custom 1.);* ~ **dispute** *(VölkerR)* örtlicher Konflikt; ~ **elections** Kommunalwahlen

local government[49] Gemeindeverwaltung, Kommunalverwaltung; kommunale Selbstverwaltung *(Br parish [or in Wales, community], district and County Councils, the Greater London Council and the Common Council of the City of London); Am counties, cities, townships, villages and special areas [school districts]);* ~ **elections** Kommunalwahl, Gemeindewahl; ~ →**franchise;** ~ **law** Kommunalrecht; Gemeindeordnung; ~ **officer** Kommunalbeamter; ~ **stock** *Br* Kommunalobligationen; ~ **worker** *Br* kommunaler Angestellter

local, ~ **hotels** die Hotels am Ort; ~ **inhabitant** Ortsansässiger; ~ **inspection** Augenscheineinnahme, Ortsbesichtigung; ~ **land charge** *Br*[50] von e-r Behörde auferlegte Grundstücksbelastung *(die in dem local land charges register e-r Ortsbehörde eingetragen ist)*

local law örtliches Recht; *Am* Gemeindegesetz, Gemeindesatzung, Gemeindeverordnung; ~ **theory** *(IPR)* Theorie, die erklärt, daß die Anwendung fremden Rechts der inländischen Souveränität nicht widerspricht

local, ~ **manager** *Br* Bezirksdirektor; ~ **news**

Lokalnachrichten; ~ **option** →option 1.; ~ **paper** Lokalzeitung; ~ **patriotism** Lokalpatriotismus; ~ **rates** *Br* Ortsgesprächsgebühren; ~ **remedies rule** *(VölkerR)* →remedy 1.; **L~** →**Rent Officer;** ~ **resident(s)** Ortsbewohner; ~ **self-government** kommunale Selbstverwaltung; ~ **services** Kommunalleistungen; ~ **service line** Zubringerlinie; ~ **staff** ortsansässiges Personal; ~ **taxes** *Am* Kommunalsteuern; ~ **terms** Platzbedingungen; ~ **time** Ortszeit *(opp. standard time);* ~ **traffic** Ortsverkehr; Nahverkehr; innerstädtischer Verkehr; ~ **train** Lokalbahn, Nebenbahn; ~ **transaction** Platzgeschäft; ~ **union** *Am* →union 2.; ~ **usage** Ortsgebrauch, Platzusance

locally competent örtlich zuständig

localism örtliche (Sprach-)Eigentümlichkeit; Lokalpatriotismus

locality Lokalität, Örtlichkeit; Ort; Lage; ~ **classification** Ortsklasseneinstellung *(bei Tarifverträgen etc.)*

localization of a conflict *pol* Lokalisierung e-s Konfliktes

localize *v* lokalisieren, örtlich beschränken (od. begrenzen)

locate *v (Lage etc)* ausfindig machen, feststellen; *(Lage od. Platz)* bestimmen; *(an e-m bestimmten Ort)* errichten; ansiedeln; *(Grenzen)* abstecken; *Am (bewegliche Sachen)* vermieten; *Am colloq.* sich niederlassen; **to** ~ **errors** Fehler feststellen; **to** ~ **an industry** e-e Industrie ansiedeln; **to** ~ **the lines of property** *Am* die Grenzen e-s Grundstücks festlegen

located, to be ~ liegen, gelegen sein; belegen sein; Sitz haben; **assets** ~ **in a state** *(DBA)* in e-m Staat belegene Wirtschaftsgüter; **to be** ~ **in the area in which a law is valid** sich im Geltungsbereich e-s Gesetzes befinden

location Stelle, Platz, Lage *(bes. e-r Wohnung, Fabrik, e-s Geschäfts);* Ortsbestimmung, Lagebestimmung; Standort *(bes. e-r Industrie);* Ansiedlung; *bes. Am* Absteckung *(der Grenze); Am* abgestecktes (od. angewiesenes) Land; genaue Feststellung des Ortes *(z.B. e-s mining claim od. e-r Kernwaffen-Erschütterung* [cf. *detection*]*); Am* Vermietung *(von bewegl. Sachen);* ~ **factors** Standortfaktoren; ~ **notice** *(BergR)* Anschlag an der Fundstelle; **(industrial)** ~ **policy** Ansiedlungspolitik *(von Industrien);* Standortpolitik; **state of** ~ *(IPR)* Belegenheitsstaat

locator *Am* Vermieter *(von bewegl. Sachen)*

lock 1. Schloß; Verschluß; ~ **box-system** *Am* Postschließfächer bei US-Banken zum Clearing von Scheckzahlungen; **under** ~ **and key** hinter Schloß und Riegel, unter Verschluß

lock 2. Schleuse; ~ **dues** Schleusengeld; ~ **keeper** Schleusenwärter; **to pass a ship through a** ~ ein Schiff durchschleusen

lock *v* absperren, versperren; *(Schiff)* schleusen (through durch); **to** ~ **the baggage** das Gepäck abschließen; **to** ~ **out** *(Arbeiter)* aussperren; **to** ~ **up** *(etw.)* verschließen; *(Geld)* fest anlegen; festlegen; *(jdn)* einsperren

locked up, capital ~ **in land** in Grundbesitz fest angelegtes Geld

locking up of capital Festlegung von Kapital

lockage Schleusengeld

lockout Aussperrung *(der Arbeiter) (cf. strike);* **defensive** ~ (*against workers on strike*) Abwehraussperrung; **offensive** ~ (*against workers not on strike*) Angriffsaussperrung

lock(-)up Festlegung *(von Kapital); Am* Gefängnis *(für Untersuchungshaft);* ~ **shop** *Br* Laden, der nur Zugang von der Straße und keine Verbindung mit dem übrigen Gebäude hat

loco ... *com (mit Ortsbestimmung)* ab ... *(Käufer hat ab benanntem Ort Transportkosten zu zahlen)*

loco citato (loc.cit., l.c.) am angegebenen Ort *(e-s Buches)* (a. a. O.)

loco sigilli (L. S., l. s.) anstatt des Siegels

locum (tenens) Stellvertreter

locus in quo, view by the judge of the ~ Einnahme des Augenscheins; **to view** (or **inspect) the** ~ e-e Augenscheinseinnahme vornehmen

locus, ~ **regit actum** *(IPR)* das Ortsrecht (das Recht am Abschlußort) beherrscht das Rechtsgeschäft *(hinsichtlich des Inhalts und der Form; vgl. dazu Art. 11 EGBGB);* ~ **standi** *(bes. parl und PatR)* das Recht, gehört zu werden

lodemanage Lotsengeld

lodge (Freimaurer-)Loge

lodge *v* einreichen (with bei); hinterlegen, deponieren; *(in Untermiete, Hotel etc) (zeitweilig)* wohnen; *(als Mieter, Gast)* aufnehmen, unterbringen; **to** ~ **an appeal** ein Rechtsmittel *(Berufung etc)* einlegen; **to** ~ **a** →**caution; to** ~ **a claim** e-n Anspruch erheben; **to** ~ **a complaint** beanstanden, reklamieren; sich beschweren; **to** ~ **documents** Urkunden einreichen (with the appropriate official bei dem zuständigen Beamten); **to** ~ **at a hotel** in e-m Hotel wohnen; **to** ~ **one's proof** →proof 2.; to ~ **a protest** →protest 1.; **to** ~ **securities with a bank for safe custody** Wertpapiere bei e-r Bank hinterlegen

lodger (Zimmer-, Unter-)Mieter; zahlender Gast; **fellow** ~ Mitbewohner; **to live as a** ~ zur Miete wohnen; **to take in** ~**s** Untermieter nehmen

lodging Wohnung, Unterkunft; Unterbringung, Beherbergung *(cf. boarding);* Einlegung *(e-s Rechtsmittels, e-r Beschwerde etc);* ~**s** *Br* möblierte(s) Zimmer; ~ **allowance** Wohnungsgeldzuschuß; ~ **house** *(billige)* Pension; **common** ~ **house** *Br* Obdachlosenheim; **board and** ~ Unterkunft und Verpflegung; **to let** ~**s** *Br* Zimmer vermieten; **to live in** ~**s** *Br* möbliert wohnen

lodgment Hinterlegung *(von Dokumenten bei Gericht);* Anhäufung, Ansammlung

log →log-book

log *v (ins Logbuch)* eintragen

log(-)book Logbuch, Schiffstagebuch; *(Flugzeug)* Bordbuch; *(Auto)* Fahrtenbuch

logistical *mil* logistisch

logistics *mil* Unterbringungs- und Verpflegungswesen; Nachschubwesen

logroll *v Am (auch parl)* sich gegenseitig Hilfestellung leisten; *(Gesetz)* durch gegenseitige Hilfestellung durchbringen

logrolling *Am* gegenseitige Unterstützung; *parl colloq.* zeitweises Bündnis von Kongreßabgeordneten zur Durchsetzung von Gruppeninteressen

loiter[51] *v* bummeln, säumig sein *(bei der Arbeit);* sich herumtreiben, herumstehen, herumlungern

lombard, ~ **loan** Lombarddarlehen; Lombardkredit; ~ **rates** Lombardsätze

Lombard Street *Br (Straße in London, in der sich die großen Banken befinden)* Londoner Geldmarkt

Lomé Convention Abkommen von Lomé von 1986 (zwischen den Staaten der EG und den →ACP-Staaten)

London Agreement on German External Debts[52] Londoner Abkommen über deutsche Auslandsschulden (Londoner Schuldenabkommen) *(von 1953)*

London Boroughs die 32 Stadtteile von Greater London *(mit beschränkter Selbstverwaltung)*

London, ~ **Commodity Exchange** (LCE) Londoner Warenbörse; ~ **Gazette** *Br (zweimal wöchentl. erscheinendes)* Amtsblatt; ~ **interbank bid rate** →LIBID; ~ **interbank offered rate** →LIBOR; ~ **International Financial Futures Exchange** (Liffe) Londoner Internationale Finanzterminbörse; ~ **International Press Centre** Internationales Londoner Presseinstitut *(dem mehr als 2000 Verleger und Journalisten in rund 60 Ländern angehören);* ~ →**Metal Exchange;** ~ **Sessions** *Br* Sitzungen des Central Criminal →Court; ~ **Sittings** *Br* Sitzungen der Guildhall

London Stock Exchange s. London →International Stock Exchange

London, Greater ~ Groß-London

long 1. lang(dauernd); *com* langfristig, mit langer Laufzeit, auf lange Sicht; ~ **and short hauls** *Am* Güternah- und -fernverkehr

long-arm statute *(wörtl. etwa)* Gesetz mit langem Arm; ein über die Machtbefugnise e-s Staates hinausgreifendes Gesetz

Insbesondere in den USA verbreitete Gesetze, die (durch bes. geregelte Klageausstellung) die Zuständigkeit (→personal jurisdiction) für Kläger gegen nicht im Gerichtsstaat ansässige Beklagte (z. B. ausländische Unternehmen mit Geschäftstätigkeit im Gerichtsstaat) begründen; od. Gesetze des Gerichtsstaats (z. B. →antitrust laws), die sich auf ausländische Sachverhalte erstrecken. Gegen solche Gesetze wendet sich z. B. der britische Gesetzgeber mit dem →Protection of Trading Interests Act 1980

long, ~ **bill** Wechsel mit Laufzeit von mindestens 3 Monaten; ~ **credit** langfristiger Kredit

long-dated, ~ **bill** langfristiger Wechsel; ~ **investment** langfristige Kapitalanlage; ~ **securities** *(Börse)* Langläufer; *Br* langlaufende Staatspapiere *(ab 15 Jahren)*

long-distance, ~ **blockade** *(VölkerR)* Seesperre; ~ **call** *Am* Ferngespräch; ~ **flight** Langstreckenflug; ~ **goods traffic** *Br* Güterfernverkehr; ~ **hauling** *Am* Güterfernverkehr; ~ **lorry driver** *Br* Fernlastfahrer; ~ **road haulage** *Br* Güterfernverkehr; ~ **telephone charges** *Am* Fernsprechgebühren;~ **traffic** Fernverkehr; ~ **train** Fernzug

long, ~ **exchange** *Br* langfristiger Devisenwechsel; ~ **hand** Langschrift *(opp. shorthand);* ~ **haul** Langstrecken-; ~ **haul freight traffic** Güterfernverkehr; ~, **heavy or bulky articles** *(Bahntransport)* Sperrgut; ~ **lease** langfristige Miete (od. Pacht); ~**-lived assets** langlebige Wirtschaftsgüter; ~ **maturities** *(Börse)* Langläufer

long-range weitreichend; langfristig; weit vorausschauend; ~ **bomber** Langstreckenbomber; ~ **forecasts** weit vorausschauende Vorhersage; ~ **navigation** (Loran) Funkfernpeilung; ~ **planning** Planung auf lange Sicht; ~ **policy** Politik auf weite Sicht; ~ **transboundary air pollution** (LRTAP) weiträumige grenzüberschreitende Luftverschmutzung

long, ~ **rate** *(VersR)* Prämiensatz für e-e für länger als ein Jahr ausgestellte Versicherungspolice; ~ **shoreman** Schauermann, Hafenarbeiter; **of** ~ **standing** seit langer Zeit bestehend, alt; langandauernd

long-term langfristig; ~ **appointment** Einstellung für lange Zeit, Dauerstellung; ~ **benefit** *(VersR)* langfristige Leistung; ~ **borrowing** Aufnahme langfristiger Kredite; ~ **business** *Br* Personenversicherung(en) *(Großlebensversicherung, Kleinlebensversicherung und Sparversicherung; opp. general business);* ~ **(capital) gain**

(SteuerR) langfristiger Veräußerungsgewinn; ~ **contract** langfristiger Vertrag; ~ **credit** langfristiger Kredit; ~ **hedge** Termindekkungskauf; ~ **investment** langfristige Kapitalanlage; ~ **liabilities** langfristige Verbindlichkeiten *(opp. current liabilities);* ~ **loan** langfristiges Darlehen (*mehr als 5 Jahre*); ~ **planning** Planung auf lange Sicht; ~ **program(me)** langfristige Planung *(für Investitionen)*

long, ~ **ton** →ton 1; ~ **unemployed** Langzeitarbeitsloser; ~ **unemployment** Langzeitarbeitslosigkeit; ~ **vacation(s)** *Br* große Ferien *(Gerichts- od. Universitätsferien);* **to take the** ~ **view** →view 1.; **before** ~ bald, in absehbarer Zeit

long 2. Langläufer, langfristiges Wertpapier *(opp. medium, short);* eingedeckt *(mit Wertpapieren, die in Erwartung e-r Kurssteigerung gekauft sind); Am* Haussier *(opp. short);* ~**s** *Br* Staatspapiere mit Laufzeit ab 15 Jahren; ~ **account** (or **interest**) *Am* Hausseengagement; ~ **position** *Am* Hausseposition; ~ **side** *Am* Haussepartei; **buying** ~ *Am* Haussekauf; **to be** ~ **on the market** (or **to be on the** ~ **side of the market**) *Am* mit Wertpapieren eingedeckt sein *(für e-e Kurssteigerung);* **I am** ~ **100 U.S. Steel** *Am* ich habe e-n Bestand von 100 U. S. Stahlaktien

longer-range INF (LRINF) nukleare Mittelstreckensysteme größerer Reichweite

longevity Langlebigkeit, langes Leben; ~ **pay** *Am (jährl. od. periodische)* Lohn- od. Gehaltszulage *(auf Grund des Dienstalters);* Dienstalterzulage

look *v,* **to** ~ **after** sehen nach, sich kümmern um, betreuen; **to** ~ **after a p.'s interests** jds Interessen wahrnehmen; **to** ~ **for a place** (or **job**) Arbeit suchen; **to** ~ **forward** (to a th.) entgegensehen, sich *(auf etw.)* freuen; **to** ~ **into** untersuchen, prüfen; **to** ~ **through one's letters** s-e Briefe durchsehen; **to** ~ **up** nachschlagen

looking, to be ~ **for accommodation** *Br* auf Wohnungssuche sein *(möbl. Zimmer, Etage od. Haus);* **to be** ~ **for** *Am* **an apartment** (or *Br* **a flat**) auf Wohnungssuche sein *(Wohnung od. Etage in einem Haus)*

loophole *fig* Hintertür, Ausweg; ~ **in the legislation** Lücke in der Gesetzgebung; **tax** ~ *(meist unbeabsichtigte)* Lücke in der Steuergesetzgebung *(die es ermöglicht, Steuern zu vermeiden)*

loose lose; unverpackt; ~ **cash** Münzgeld, Kleingeld; ~ →**combinations; in** ~ **cover** broschiert; ~ **goods** unverpackte Waren; Schüttgut; ~**-leaf binders** Schnellhefter; ~**-leaf book** Loseblattbuch *(opp. bound book);* ~**-leaf ledger** Loseblatthauptbuch; ~ **or in packages** (or **packets**) lose oder verpackt; ~ **sheet** loses Blatt

loot (Kriegs-)Beute

loot *v* plündern; erbeuten

looted property Beutegut

looting Plünderung; ~ **of a corpse** Leichendiebstahl

Lord *Br* Lord *(Titel des hohen Adels, cf. Peer; Titel der anglikanischen Bischöfe und hohen Richter);* **the** ~**s** das Oberhaus *(opp. the Commons);* ~ **Advocate** *Scot* Kronanwalt *(entspricht dem →Attorney-General);* ~ **Chamberlain (of the Household)** Lord-Haushofmeister *(Beamter des Königl. Haushalts);* ~ **Great Chamberlain** Lord-Großkämmerer *(mit bestimmten offiziellen Aufgaben im Parlament, bei der Krönung etc)*

Lord (High) Chancellor *Br* Lordkanzler

Zu seinem Aufgabenkreis gehört die Ernennung der Richter und die Verwaltung der Gerichte (entspricht etwa den Aufgaben eines Justizministers). Kabinettsmitglied, Präsident des Oberhauses, Vorsitzender der →Chancery Division und des →Court of Appeal

Lord Chief Justice (of England) (L.C.J., C.J.) Lordoberrichter

Vorsitzender der Queen's →Bench Division, Richter des →Court of Appeal, stellvertr. Vorsitzender des High →Court

Lord, ~**'s Day Act** *Br*[53] Gesetz zur Einhaltung des Sonntags; ~ **High Commissioner** *Scot* Vertreter der Krone bei der General →Assembly der →Church of Scotland; ~**s High Commissioners of the Treasury** *Br* Finanzministerium *(the Prime Minister [who is also First Lord of the Treasury], the Chancellor of the Exchequer, and five Junior Lords);* ~**(s) Justice(s) of Appeal** Richter des →Court of Appeal; ~ **Justice-Clerk** *Scot* Vizepräsident des →Court of Justiciary; ~ **Justice General** *Scot* Präsident des High →Court of Justiciary; ~ **Lieutenant** *(auf Lebenszeit ernannter)* Vertreter der Krone in den Grafschaften; ~ **Mayor** *Br* →mayor; ~**s of the Admiralty** *Br* (leitende Beamte der) Admiralität; ~**s of Appeal in Ordinary**[54] *(auf Lebenszeit ernannte, besoldete)* richterliche Mitglieder des House of ~s; ~**of the manor** *Br hist* Gutsherr; ~ **of Session** *Scot* Richter des →Court of Session; ~**s of the Treasury** *Br* →~s (High) Commissioners of the Treasury; ~ **Ordinary** *Scot* e-r der fünf Richter des →Court of Session; ~ **President of the Court of Session** *Scot* Präsident des →Court of Session; ~ **President of the (Privy) Council** Lordpräsident des Geheimen Staatsrats; ~**Privy Seal** Lordsiegelbewahrer *(Kabinettsmitglied);* ~ **Provost** *Scot* Oberbürgermeister *(in großen Städten);* ~ **Rector** *Scot univ* (Ehren-)Rektor; ~**s Spiritual** geistliche Mitglieder des House of ~s *(Archbishops of Canterbury and York and 24 bishops);* ~ **Steward of the Queen's Household** Lord-Oberhofmeister *(überwacht das Personal);* ~**s Temporal** weltliche Mitglieder des House of ~s *(Dukes, Marquesses, Earls, Viscounts and Barons);* ~**s' veto** Veto(-recht) des Oberhauses; **First** ~ **of the Admiralty** *Br* Marineminister; **First L**~ **of the Treasury** →Treasury; →**Law** ~**s; My** ~ *Br* Anrede e-s Lord sowie der hohen Richter

Lordship, Your ~ *Br* Eure Lordschaft; Hohes Gericht *(Titel der Lords sowie Anrede der hohen Richter vor Gericht);* Eure Exellenz *(Bischof)*

loro account Lorokonto, Vestrokonto *(opp. nostro account)*

lorr|y *Br* Last(kraft)wagen, Lastauto (Lkw); ~ **driver** Lkw-Fahrer, **two ~loads of coal** zwei Lkw-Ladungen Kohle; ~ **pool** *Br* Fuhrpark; **ban on (driving) ~ies** Lkw-Verbot

lose *v* verlieren; *(Vermögen, Stellung etc)* einbüßen; Verlust erleiden; **to ~ an action** *Br* e-n Prozeß verlieren; **to ~ business** Kundschaft (od. Aufträge) verlieren; **to ~ ground** (an) Boden verlieren; (an) Einfluß verlieren (with bei); **to ~ one's job** (or **place**) s-e Stelle verlieren; **to ~ one's lawsuit** *bes. Am* →lawsuit; **to ~ a right** e-s Rechtes verlustig gehen; **to ~ in value** an Wert verlieren; **to ~ votes** Stimmen verlieren; **the investor lost heavily** der Anleger erlitt schwere Verluste

losing verlustbringend; unrentabel; ~ **bargain** (or **business**) Verlustgeschäft; ~ **party** die *(im Rechtsstreit)* unterliegende Partei *(opp. prevailing, successful, or winning party);* ~ **price** Verlustpreis

loss 1. Verlust; Einbuße, Ausfall; Schaden; Abgang, Schwund; **~es** *(Bilanz)* Abgänge; *mil* Verluste

loss, to apportion the ~ den Schaden aufteilen; **to assess the** ~ den Schaden abschätzen; **to avoid ~es** Verluste vermeiden; **to bear a** ~ e-n Schaden tragen; **to carry forward one's ~es** *Br (SteuerR)* die (Betriebs-)Verluste mit den Gewinnen späterer Jahre verrechnen; **to →cut one's ~es; the ~ falls upon X** den Schaden trägt X; **to have a share in the** ~ am Verlust teilnehmen; **to incur a** ~ e-n Schaden erleiden; **to incur heavy ~es** große Verluste erleiden; **~es have been incurred** Verluste sind entstanden; **to be liable for a** ~ für e-n Schaden haftbar sein; **to make good (or make up) for a** ~ e-n Verlust ausgleichen (od. decken); **to meet with a** ~ e-n Verlust (od. Schaden) erleiden; **a ~ occurred** ein Verlust ist eingetreten; **to recover one's ~es** sich schadlos halten; **to run one's business at a** ~ sein Geschäft so führen, daß Verluste entstehen, mit Verlust arbeiten; **to sell at a** ~ mit Verlust verkaufen; **to suffer** (or **sustain**) **a** ~ e-n Schaden (od. Verlust, Einbuße) erleiden; **substantiated** ~ nachgewiesener Schaden

loss, ~ **account** Verlustkonto; ~ **advice** Schadensanzeige; ~ **and gain account** *Am* →profit and loss account; ~ **assessment** Schadensfeststellung; Schadensabschätzung; ~ **by fire** Brandschaden; ~ **by leakage** (Gewichts-)Verlust durch Auslaufen; ~ **carried forward** Verlustvortrag; ~ **carryback** *Am* Verlustrücktrag *(steuerliche Verrechnung der [Betriebs-]Verluste mit Gewinnen aus früheren Jahren);* ~ **carry over** *Am* Verlustvortrag (→*carry over*); ~ **compensation** Verlustausgleich; ~ **in contribution** Beitragsausfall; **~es incurred in gambling** Spielverluste; ~ **in price** Preisverlust, Kursverlust; ~ **in transit** (Gewichts-)-Verlust auf dem Transport; ~ **in value** Wertverlust; ~ **in value due to age** Wertverlust durch Altern (*cf. deduction for depreciation*); ~ **in weight** Gewichtsverlust, Gewichtsschwund

loss leader Lockartikel; Lockvogel-Angebot *(Unterkostenangebot e-r Ware, das den Absatz anderer Waren günstig beeinflussen soll);* ~ **sales promotion** Lockvogelwerbung; ~ **selling** (Verlust-)Verkauf von Anreizwaren; **to use as a** ~ als Lockvogel verwenden

loss, ~ **of cash** Barverlust, Geldverlust; ~ **of clientele** Verlust der Kundschaft; ~ **of civil rights** Verlust der bürgerlichen Ehrenrechte; ~ **of consortium** Verlust (od. Beeinträchtigung) der Lebensgemeinschaft mit dem Ehegatten *(nur der Verlust der Arbeitskraft gibt Schadensersatzanspruch);* ~ **of customers** Kundenausfall, Kundenverlust, Kundenschwund

loss of earnings Verdienstausfall; **compensation for** ~ Entschädigung für Verdienstausfall; **to be entitled to appropriate compensation for** ~ Anspruch auf angemessene Entschädigung für Verdienstausfall haben; **to suffer** ~ Verdienstausfall haben

loss, ~ **of franchise** *Am* Verlust der Konzession; ~ **of the goods** Untergang der Ware; ~ **of income** Einkommensausfall, Einkommensverlust; Einnahmenausfall; ~ **of interest** Zinsverlust, Zinsausfall, Zinseinbuße; ~ **of a job** Arbeitsplatzverlust; ~ **of life** Verlust am Menschenleben; ~ **of a limb** Verlust e-s (Körper-)Gliedes; ~ **of markets** Verlust von Absatzgebieten; ~ **of money** Geldverlust; ~ **of nationality** Verlust der Staatsangehörigkeit (→ *nationality);* ~ **of orders** Verlust an Aufträgen; Auftragsausfall, Auftragsschwund; ~ **of pay** Lohnausfall; ~ **of production** Produktionsausfall; ~ **of profits** Gewinnverlust; Gewinnausfall; Ertragseinbuße; ~ **of (prospective) profits** entgangener Gewinn; ~ **of profit insurance** *Br (etwa)* Betriebsunterbrechungsversicherung *(z.B. bei Feuerschaden);* ~ **of property** Vermögensschaden, Vermögenseinbuße; Sachverlust; ~ **of rent** Mietverlust, Mietausfall; ~ **of rights** Rechtsverlust; Kursverlust; ~ **of services of the spouse** *Br* Verlust der Arbeitskraft des Ehegatten *(cf. ~ of consortium);* ~ **of a ship with all hands** Untergang e-s Schiffes mit der gesamten Besatzung; ~ **of sight** Verlust des Augenlichts; ~ **of time** Zeitverlust; ~ **of useful value** *Am (SteuerR)* unvorhergesehene Entwertung *(als Abschreibungsmöglichkeit; cf. obsolescence, wear and tear);* ~ **of work** *(caused by absenteeism or illness)* Arbeitsausfall; ~ **on the sale of shares** Verlust aus dem Verkauf von Aktien; ~**on securities** Kursverlust; ~ **set-off** Verlustausgleich

loss, advice of ~ Verlustanzeige; **amount of** ~ Schadenshöhe, Schadenssumme; **ascertainment of** ~ Feststellung des Schadens; **at a** ~ mit Verlust; **balance sheet showing a** ~ Verlustabschluß, Verlustbilanz; **book** ~ buchmäßiger Verlust; **business** ~ Geschäftsverlust; **calculation of** ~**es caused by operational deficiencies** Verlustquellenrechnung; **capital** ~ Kapitalverlust; **in case of** ~ im Verlustfalle; **cause of** ~ Schadensursache; **clear** ~ Nettoverlust, reiner Verlust; **corporate** ~**es** *Am* Verluste der Gesellschaft; Firmenverluste; **dead** ~ *sl.* Totalverlust; **gross** ~ Bruttoverlust, Rohverlust; **heavy** ~ schwerer Verlust; **interest** ~ Zinsverlust; **involving (a)** ~ verlustbringend; **irrecoverable** ~ unersetzlicher Verlust; **liability for** ~**es** Haftung für Schäden; **marine** ~ Verlust auf See; **natural** ~ natürlicher Schwund; **net** ~ Reinverlust, Nettoverlust; **normal** ~ s. natural → ~; **notice of** ~ Schadensanzeige, Verlustanzeige; **operating** ~ Betriebsverlust; **partial** ~ Teilverlust; **profit and** ~ Gewinn und Verlust *(→profit)*; **proof of** ~ Schadensnachweis; **risk of** ~ Gefahr des Verlustes (od. Untergangs); Gefahrtragung; **showing a** ~ e-n Verlust aufweisend; **total** ~ Totalverlust *(→loss 2.)*; **trading** ~ Betriebsverlust; **wage** ~ Lohnausfall

loss 2. *(VersR)* (Versicherungs-)Schaden; Schadensfall; ~ **adjustment** Schadenregulierung; Dispache; ~ **advice** Schadensanzeige; ~ **assessment** Schadensfeststellung *(der Höhe nach)*; Schadensabschätzung; ~ **assessor** *Br* Regulierungsbeamter; ~ **covered by insurance** durch Versicherung gedeckter Schaden; ~ **of specie** Denaturierung; ~ **ratio** Schadenquote *(Verhältnis zwischen Versicherungsleistung und den eingezahlten Prämien)*; ~ **recoverable under the policy** laut Versicherungspolice zu ersetzender Schaden; ~ **reserve** Schadenreserve; Rückstellung für laufende Risiken; ~ **settlement** Schadenregulierung; **all-**~ **insurance** *Am* Gesamtversicherung; **at the time of occurrence of the** ~ bei Eintritt des Versicherungsfalles; **first** ~ **insurance** Erstrisikoversicherung; **in case of** ~ bei Eintritt des Versicherungsfalles; **partial** ~ *(SeeversR)* Teilschaden, Teilverlust *(opp. total ~)*; **proof of** ~ Schadensnachweis; Nachweis des Eintritts des Versicherungsfalles

loss, total~ *(SeeversR)*[55] Totalschaden, Totalverlust; **actual total** ~ wirklicher Totalverlust; **constructive total** ~ konstruktiver (od. fingierter) Totalverlust, wirtschaftlicher Totalschaden *(als Totalschaden angenommener Teilschaden, wenn Wiederbeschaffung zu kostpielig sein würde)*

loss, to cover all ~**es** alle Schäden decken; **to make good any** ~ **covered by the insurance policy** jeden durch die Versicherungspolice gedeckten Schaden ersetzen; **a** ~ **occurs** ein Schaden tritt ein; **to pay full compensation for all** ~**es covered by the insurance** für alle durch die Versicherung gedeckten Schäden volle Entschädigung leisten; **to recover a** ~ e-n Schaden ersetzt bekommen

lost verloren, abhanden gekommen, in Verlust geraten; ~ **bill of exchange or cheque**[56] in Verlust geratener (od. verlorengegangener) Wechsel od. Scheck; ~ **cause** verlorene (od. aussichtslose) Sache; ~ **instrument** abhanden gekommene Urkunde; *Am*[57] verlorengegangenes (Handels-)Papier; ~ **opportunity** entgangene Gelegenheit; ~ **or not lost**[58] *(SeeversR)* Klausel für rückwirkenden Versicherungsschutz; ~ **profit(s)** entgangener Gewinn

lost property verlorene Sache; Fundsache(n); ~ **office** Fundbüro; **finder of** ~ Finder; **finding (of)** ~ Fund; **keeping (of)** ~ Fundunterschlagung; **piece of** ~ Fundsache

lost, days ~ **through strikes** durch Streiks verlorene Arbeitstage; **irretrievably** ~ **things** unwiederbringlich verlorene Sachen; **to be** ~ **at sea** auf See untergehen; **to get** ~ verlorengehen, abhanden kommen; **to give up for** ~ als verloren betrachten

lot 1. Los; ~ **number** Losnummer; **drawing (of)** ~**s** Losziehung; Auslosung; Verlosung; **by (drawing)** ~**s** durch Los; **to cast** ~**s** s. to draw →~s; **to be determined by** ~ durch das Los bestimmt werden; **to draw** ~**s** losen (for um); **to draw securities by** ~ Wertpapiere auslosen; **drawn by** ~ ausgelost

lot 2. *com* Partie, Posten *(Waren)*; *colloq.* Menge *(von Waren, Aktien etc)*; ~ **of goods** Warenposten; **a** ~ **of money** *colloq.* viel Geld; **auction** ~ Auktionsposten; **in** ~**s** partienweise, in Partien; **job** ~ Partieware(n); Ramschware(n); →**odd** ~; →**round** ~; **sale by** ~ Partieverkauf; **in small** ~**s** in kleinen Partien *(z. B. Wertpapiere)*; **to sell in** (or **by**) **small** ~**s** in kleinen Posten verkaufen

lot 3. *bes. Am* Stück Land, Parzelle; **building** ~ *bes. Am* Bauplatz, Baustelle; **parking** ~ *Am* Parkplatz; **pasture** ~ (Stück) Weideland; **to divide into** ~**s** *bes. Am (Land)* in Parzellen aufteilen, parzellieren

lot *v*, **to** ~ **(out)** verlosen, durch Los zuteilen; *(Land)* in Parzellen aufteilen; **to** ~ **out goods in parcels** →parcel 3.

lottery[59] Lotterie, Verlosung; ~ **bond** Losanleihe, Prämienanleihe; ~ **drawing** Losziehung, Verlosung; ~ **number** Losnummer; ~ **prize** Lotteriegewinn; ~ **sampling** *(Marktforschung)* Zufallsauswahl; ~ **ticket** Lotterielos; **charity** ~ Wohltätigkeitslotterie; **to take part in a** ~ in e-r Lotterie spielen

low niedrig; tief; billig; *(Börse)* Tief(stand); **L~ Church** *Br* puritanische und pietistische Richtung in der→Anglican Church; **~- class goods** Schundwaren; **~ cost** preiswert; **~-cost housing** billige Wohnungen, Sozialwohnungen; **the L~ Countries** die Niederlande; **~ demand** geringe Nachfrage; **~-duty goods** niedrig verzollte Waren; **~-emission car** abgasarmes Auto; **~ energy consumption** niedriger Energieverbrauch; **~ estimate** niedrige Schätzung; **~-grade** minderwertig, von minderer Qualität
low income niedriges Einkommen; **~ allowance** *Am (SteuerR)* Freibetrag für Steuerpflichtige von niedrigem Einkommen; **~ countries** einkommensschwache Länder
low interest niedrige Zinsen; **~ loan** Darlehen mit niedrigem Zinssatz; zinsgünstiges Darlehen; **~ rate countries** Niedrigzinsländer
low level Tiefpunkt, Tiefstand; **~ attack** Tieffliegerangriff; **~ flight** Tiefflug; **on a ~** auf niedriger Stufe
low price niedriger Preis; **~ countries** Billigpreisländer; **~ imports** Niedrigpreiseinfuhren
low, ~-priced niedrig im Preise; billig; **~-quality goods** Waren von minderer Qualität; **at a ~ rate of interest** zu niedrigen Zinsen; **~ speed** geringe Geschwindigkeit; **L~ Sunday** Weißer Sonntag *(erster Sonntag nach Ostern)*; **~-value assets** geringwertige Wirtschaftsgüter; **~ wages** niedriger Lohn; **~-water mark** Tiefwasserstandszeichen; *fig* Tiefstand; **~-yielding** ertragsschwach
low, prices are ~ die Preise sind niedrig; **the shares reached new ~s** die Kurse erreichten e-n neuen Tiefstand; **to buy ~ and sell high** billig einkaufen und teuer verkaufen; **to run ~** knapp werden; (nahezu) erschöpft sein *(Vorräte)*; **supplies** (or **stocks**) **are running ~** Vorräte werden knapp; **to sell sth. ~** etw. billig verkaufen

lower niedriger, tiefer; **~ bid** niedrigeres Gebot; Untergebot; **L~ Chamber** *parl*→L ~ House; **~ court** unteres Gericht, Vorinstanz
lower grade, ~ civil servant *Br* unterer Beamter; **the ~s of the Civil Service** *Br* der untere Beamtenstand *(im Dienste der Krone)*; **reduction to a ~** *Am mil* Rangverlust
lower, L~ House *parl* Unterhaus, Abgeordnetenhaus *(opp. Upper House)*; **~ income brackets** untere Einkommensstufen; **~ instance** niedrigere Instanz, Vorinstanz; **~-level official** unterer Beamter; **~ management** untere Führungskräfte, unteres Management; **~ middle class(es)** Kleinbürgertum; **~-priced** verbilligt; **L~ Saxony** *Ger* Niedersachsen

lower *v (Preise, Kosten etc)* herabsetzen, senken; fallen, sinken; *(Flagge)* niederholen; **to ~ the bank rate** den Diskontsatz senken; **to ~ the rate of interest** den Zinssatz herabsetzen (od. senken); **to ~ the rent** die Miete herabsetzen
lowering, ~ of prices Preissenkung; **~ of retirement age** Herabsetzung der Altersgrenze

lowest, ~ bid geringstes Gebot, Mindestgebot; **~ level** tiefster Stand; **~ price** niedrigster Preis (od. Kurs); **~ yield** Mindestertrag

loyalty Loyalität, Treue; Untertanentreue; **~ and good faith** Treu und Glauben; **~ arrangement**[60] Treueabmachung, Treuevertrag; **~ oath** (or **oath of ~**) *Am* Treueid *(bes. des Beamten)*; **~ rebate** Treuerabatt

LTFV (less than fair value), **~ sales** *Am* LTFV-Verkäufe *(von in die Vereinigten Staaten eingeführten Waren zu einem niedrigeren als dem angemessenen Wert, →anti-dumping duties)*

lucid interval lichter Augenblick

lucrative lukrativ, gewinnbringend, einträglich; **~ transaction** lukratives Geschäft

lucrum cessans *Am* entgangener Gewinn

luggage *bes. Br* (Reise-)Gepäck; **~ check** *Br* Gepäckschein; **~ insurance** *Br* (Reise-)Gepäckversicherung; **~ office** Gepäckaufgabe, Gepäckannahme, Gepäckaufbewahrung; **~ receipt** *Br* Gepäckschein; **~ registration office**→~ office; **~ van** *Br* Packwagen, Gepäckwagen; **excess ~** Übergepäck; **left-~ office** *Br* Gepäckaufbewahrung; **to send one's ~ in advance** sein Gepäck aufgeben

lull Geschäftsstille

lumber Bauholz, Nutzholz; **~ trade** Holzhandel

lump Masse, große Menge; Pauschal-; **in the ~** in Bausch und Bogen, im ganzen
lump sum einmalige Summe; Pauschalbetrag, Pauschale *(opp. instalment)*; Pauschal-; **~ charter** Pauschalcharter; **~ freight** Pauschalfracht; **~ guarantee** *(Zoll)* Pauschalbürgschaft; **~ order** *Br (Ehescheidung)* (Unterhalts-)Urteil auf Zahlung e-r Kapitalsumme; **~ payment** Pauschalzahlung, Zahlung e-r Pauschalsumme; Kapitalabfindung, Abfindungszahlung; **payment of a ~ in lieu of a pension** Kapitalabfindung anstelle von Rente; **to pay a ~** (durch Einmalzahlung) abfinden

lunacy[61] Geisteskrankheit

lunatic *Am* Geisteskranker *(Br→patient)*; geisteskrank

Lutheran World Federation (LWF) Lutherischer Weltbund (LWB)
Vereinigung fast aller lutherischer Kirchen der Welt. *Sitz:* Genf
Lutheran, National ~ Council *Am* Lutherischer Nationalrat
Umfaßt mit wenigen Ausnahmen die Lutheraner der Vereinigten Staaten

Luxemb(o)urg Luxemburg; **Grand Duchy of ~** Großherzogtum Luxemburg; **of ~** luxemburgisch

Luxemb(o)urger Luxemburger, ~in

LUXIBOR (Luxembourg Interbank Offered Rate) Zinssatz, zu dem international tätige Banken Geldmarktgeschäfte in Luxemburg abschließen

luxur|y Luxus; **~ies** Luxus; Luxuswaren; **~ and semi-~ goods** Güter des gehobenen Bedarfs; **~ articles** Luxusartikel; **~ flat** Luxuswohnung; **~ goods** Luxusgüter; **~ hotel** Luxushotel; **~ tax** Luxussteuer; **~ trade** Handel mit Luxusgütern

lying unwahr; **~ prospectus** Prospekt mit unwahren Angaben

lying idle unergiebig, unrentabel

lying in state *(öffentl.)* Aufbahrung

lynch-law Lynchjustiz

M

mace *bes. parl* Amtsstab, Zepter *(Hoheitszeichen beider Häuser des engl. Parlaments sowie des amerik. House of Representatives)*

machiavellism *pol* Machiavellismus

machination, to upset ~s Machenschaften vereiteln

machine Maschine; Apparat; *Am pol* nicht offizielle Organisation *(meist unter Leitung e-s boss)*, die Richtlinien e-r Partei, Nominierung der Wahlkandidaten etc kontrolliert und die Partei tatsächlich beherrscht *(aber mehr für private Zwecke, bes. Beschaffung von Posten)*; **~ accounting** (or **bookkeeping**) Maschinenbuchführung; **~ down time** *Am* Maschinenstillstandszeit; **~-made** maschinell hergestellt, Fabrik-, Maschinen- *(opp. handmade)*; **~ of government** Regierungsapparat; **~ operator** Bedienungsperson e-r Maschine; **~ production** maschinelle Herstellung; **~ tools industry** Werkzeugmaschinenindustrie; **~ works** Maschinenfabrik; **~-written** mit Schreibmaschine geschrieben *(opp. handwritten)*; **addressing ~** Adressiermaschine; **duplicating ~** Vervielfältigungsmaschine; **franking ~** Frankiermaschine; **invoicing ~** Fakturiermaschine; **to operate a ~** e-e Maschine bedienen

machinery Maschinerie; Maschinen; *fig* Apparat; **~ breakdown** Maschinenschaden; **~ fair** technische Messe; **~ of government** Regierungsapparat; **administrative ~** Verwaltungsapparat; **agricultural ~** landwirtschaftliche Maschinen; **manufacture of ~** Maschinenbau; **party ~** Parteiapparat

macroeconomics Makroökonomie *(opp. microeconomics)*

Madagascar Madagaskar; **Democratic Republic of ~** Demokratische Republik Madagaskar (→*Malagasy*)

made gemacht; hergestellt, angefertigt *(cf. make v)*; **~ in ...** hergestellt in ...; **~ to order** nach Angaben des Bestellers gefertigt; **~ up** fertiggestellt; Konfektions-, Fabrik-; **German-~ article** deutsches Fabrikat; →**home-~; to be ~ out in the name of the holder** auf den Inhaber lauten (od. ausgestellt sein)

Madrid CSCE follow-up conference Madrider KSZE-Folgetreffen

Madrid, the Arrangement of ~ for the Prevention of False Indications of Origin on Goods Madrider Abkommen über die Unterdrükkung falscher Herkunftsangaben auf Waren (Madrider Herkunftsabkommen) (MHA)

Die revidierte Fassung von Lissabon[1] des Madrider Herkunftsabkommens von 1891 ist von 18 Staaten unterzeichnet, darunter von der Bundesrepublik Deutschland und Großbritannien, nicht von den USA.

Das Abkommen wurde 1967 in Stockholm revidiert[2]. Jedes Erzeugnis, das eine falsche od. irreführende Herkunftsangabe trägt, wird, wenn in ihr einer der Vertragsstaaten als Ursprungsland angegeben ist, bei der Einfuhr in diesen Staat beschlagnahmt

Madrid, the Arrangement of ~ concerning the International Registration of Trade Marks Madrider Abkommen über die internationale Registrierung von Fabrik- und Handelsmarken (Madrider Markenabkommen) (MMA)

Die revidierte Fassung von Nizza[3] des Madrider Markenabkommens von 1891 ist von 17 Staaten unterzeichnet, darunter von der Bundesrepublik Deutschland, nicht von den USA. Das Abkommen wurde in Stockholm revidiert.[4]

Das MMA sichert den Angehörigen der Vertragsstaaten Schutz ihrer im Ursprungsland für Waren od. Dienstleistungen eingetragenen Marken in den übrigen Vertragsstaaten durch internationale Registrierung ihrer Marke[5]

magazine *mil* Magazin, Munitionsdepot; Zeitschrift; **M~ Advertising Bureau** *Am* Institut für Zeitungswerbung; **illustrated ~** illustrierte Zeitschrift, Illustrierte

Maghreb countries (Algeria, Libyan, Mauritania, Morocco and Tunisia) Maghreb-Länder (Algerien, Libyen, Mauretanien, Marokko und Tunesien)

magisterial obrigkeitlich; richterlich; Behörden-; maßgeblich *(Meinung);* ~ **law** *Br* das in den Magistrates' →Courts angewandte Recht

magistracy Obrigkeit, *(obrigkeitl.)* Amt; die Richter; Richterschaft; Amt e-s →magistrate

magistrate 1. Richter *(Br Berufs- und Laienrichter für Straf- und gewisse Zivilsachen niederer Ordnung und für Ermittlung von schweren Straftaten);* **M~s' Court** *Br* (**M~'s Court** *Am*) →court; **~'s licence** →licence 1.; **examining** (or **committing**) ~ Untersuchungsrichter; **investigating** ~ Untersuchungsrichter; **metropolitan (stipendiary)** ~ *Br* Berufsrichter *(in einigen größeren Städten);* **police** ~ *Am* Polizeirichter; **resident** ~ *(Nordirland)* Polizeirichter; **stipendiary** ~ *Br* s. metropolitan (stipendiary) →~
Am Richter mit Zuständigkeit für Strafsachen niederer Ordnung (police magistrate) oder für Straf- und Zivilsachen niederer Ordnung (magistrate)

magistrate 2. (Verwaltungs-)Beamter; *Scot* Bürgermeister (provost) od. Ratsherr (bailee); **chief** ~ oberster Verwaltungsbeamter (*Am* President, Governor, Mayor)

Magna Carta[6] wichtigstes altenglisches Grundgesetz von 1215 *(cf. constitution)*

magnate Magnat; **financial** ~ Finanzmagnat; **industrial** ~ Industriemagnat; Großindustrieller

maiden name Mädchenname, Geburtsname; **to resume one's** ~ s-n Mädchennamen wieder annehmen

maiden speech *Br parl* Jungfernrede, Antrittsrede; **he delivered his** ~ **in Parliament** er hielt s-e Jungfernrede im Parlament

maiden trip (or **voyage**) Jungfernfahrt *(e-s Schiffes)*

mail Postsendung(en); Postsache(n); **~bag** Postbeutel; ~ **ballot** Briefwahl; ~ **boat** Postschiff, Postdampfer; ~ **box** *Am* Briefkasten; ~ **collection** Postabholung; ~ **delivery** *bes. Am* Postzustellung

mail order Bestellung *(von Waren)* durch Postversand; ~ **article** Versandartikel; ~ **business** Versandhandel; ~ **department** Versandabteilung; ~ **firm** (or **house**) Versandhaus, Versandgeschäft; **~s for purchase and sale** *(Börse)* briefliche Kauf- und Verkaufsaufträge; ~ **insurance** Korrespondenzversicherung; ~ **selling** Versandverkauf

mail, passenger and parcel service Post-, Passagier- und Paketschiffahrt; ~ **plane** Postflugzeug; ~ **privilege** *Am* Portovergünstigung für bestimmte Klassen von Post; ~ **reply** briefliche Antwort; ~ **robbery** Postdiebstahl; ~ **service** Postdienst, Postverkehr; ~ **ship** Postschiff; ~ **stamp** Poststempel; ~ **steamer** Postdampfer; ~ **survey** schriftliche Befragung; ~ **theft** Postdiebstahl; ~ **train** Postzug; ~ **transfer** Postüberweisung, Geldüberweisung; ~ **transport (by air)** Postbeförderung (auf dem Luftweg); ~ **van** Postwagen; **by** ~ per Post; **(by) air** ~ (mit) Luftpost; **collection of** ~ Postabholung; **early** ~ Frühpost; **domestic** ~ inländische Post; **delivery** (or **distribution**) **of** ~ *Am* Postzustellung; **evening** ~ Abendpost; **first-class** ~ *Br* Inlandspost *(die schneller befördert wird, als second-class mail); Am* Briefpost *(letters, post[al] cards);* **foreign** ~ Auslandspost; **fourth-class** ~ *Am* Paketpost *(parcel post);* →**incoming** ~; **letter** ~ *Am* Briefpost; **morning** ~ Morgenpost; **by the next** ~ mit der nächsten Post; → **outgoing** ~; **by return** ~ postwendend; **second-class** ~ *Br* preisgünstige, aber langsamere Inlandspost; *Am* Zeitungspost *(newspapers, periodicals);* **third-class** ~ *Am* Drucksachen *(circulars, printed matter);* **by today's** ~ mit der heutigen Post; **to dispose of** (or **do**) **one's** ~ s-e Post erledigen; **to go through one's** ~ s-e Post durchsehen

mail *v* bei der Post aufgeben, zur Post geben; mit der Post (ver)senden

mailing Aufgabe bei der Post; Postversand; ~ **address** *Am* Postanschrift; ~ **certificate** *Am* (Post-)Einlieferungsschein; ~ **charges** (or **fees**) *Am* Postgebühren; ~ **deadline** *Am* letzter Termin für Postaufgabe; ~ **list** Adressenliste; Versandliste; **date of** ~ Tag der Aufgabe bei der Post

maim *v* verstümmeln; schwer am Körper verletzen; zum Krüppel machen; **~ing** Verstümmelung

main hauptsächlich, Haupt-; ~ **branch** Hauptfiliale, Hauptstelle; **~claim** *(PatR)* Hauptanspruch; ~ **concern** Hauptsorge, Hauptanliegen; ~ **contractor** Hauptlieferant; ~ **establishment** Hauptniederlassung; ~ **feature** Hauptmerkmal; ~ **land** Festland; ~ **line** *tel* Hauptanschluß; ~ **motion** *parl* Hauptantrag; ~ **office** *Am* Hauptbüro, Hauptgeschäftsstelle, Zentrale; ~ **point** Hauptsache; ~ **road** Haupt(verkehrs)straße; ~ **stream** Hauptendenz; Großteil der Anhänger; ~ **stream corporation fax** *Br* Körperschaftssteuer-Abschlußzahlung; ~ **street** *Am* Hauptstraße; **in the** ~ hauptsächlich, in der Hauptsache

maintain *v* (aufrecht)erhalten, beibehalten; *(Familie)* unterhalten; instand halten; *(Briefwechsel)* unterhalten, fortsetzen; *(Stellung)* halten, (weiterhin) behaupten; **to** ~ **an action** e-n Prozeß (durch)führen; **to** ~ **an attitude** e-e Haltung beibehalten; **to** ~ **one's candidature** *Br* s-e Kandidatur aufrechterhalten; **to** ~ **the contrary** das Gegenteil behaupten; **to** ~ **a correspondence** e-n Briefwechsel führen; **to** ~ **the deliveries** die Lieferungen aufrechterhalten; **to** ~ **diplomatic relations** diplomatische Beziehungen unterhalten; **to** ~ **one's ground** sich behaupten, standhalten; **to** ~ **an opinion**

bei e-r Meinung bleiben, e-e Meinung beibehalten (od. verteidigen); **to ~ order** die Ordnung aufrechterhalten; **to ~ peace** den Frieden (aufrecht)erhalten; **to ~ a point of view** →point 1.; **to ~ a policy** e-e Politik beibehalten, an e-r Politik festhalten; **to ~ one's position** sich in s-r Stellung behaupten; **he ~s his positions vis-à-vis increasing pressure from the Left** er behauptet seine Stellung gegenüber wachsendem Druck von der Linken; **to ~ possession** weiterhin im Besitz halten; **to ~ prices** Preise einhalten; **to ~ relations with** (Geschäfts-)Verbindungen unterhalten mit; **to ~ reserves** Reserven halten; **to ~ a suit** 1. *Am* e-n Prozeß (durch)führen; 2. →maintenance 4.

maintain *v*, **failure** (or **neglect**) **to ~ (a spouse or a child of the family)** Verletzung der Unterhaltspflicht (gegenüber e-m Ehegatten oder e-m Kind)

maintained, ~ prices gebundene Preise; **to be ~** unterhalten werden, Unterhalt beziehen; sich *(im Preise, Kurse)* halten; **the shares were well ~** die Aktien hielten sich gut; **the rise is ~** die Hausse hält an

maintainable haltbar, zu rechtfertigen, vertretbar

maintenance 1. (Lebens-)Unterhalt *(bes. für Kinder und getrennt lebende [Br auch geschiedene] Ehegatten); Br* Alimente; **~ agreement** Unterhaltsvereinbarung; **~ allowance** Unterhalt(szahlung); **~ arrears** Unterhaltsrückstände; **~ claim** s. claim for →~; **~ debtor** Unterhaltspflichtiger; **~ for children** *Br* Kindesunterhalt; **~ for spouse** *Br* Ehegattenunterhalt; **~ from the estate of a deceased spouse** *Br*[7] Unterhalt aus dem Nachlaß des verstorbenen Ehegatten

maintenance obligation, ~ in respect of adults Unterhaltspflicht gegenüber Erwachsenen; **~ in respect of children** Unterhaltspflicht gegenüber Kindern; **→Convention on the Law Applicable to M~ O~s; →Convention on the Recognition and Enforcement of Decisions Relating to M~ O~s**

maintenance of the crew Unterhalt (od. Verpflegung) der Mannschaft

maintenance order *Br* Unterhaltsurteil *(nach Ehescheidung:) (order for) →maintenance pending suit, secured →periodical payments order, →lump sum order and →property adjustment order)*; **failure to comply with a ~** Nichtbeachtung e-s Unterhaltsurteils; **to be liable to make payments under a ~** auf Grund e-s Unterhaltsurteils unterhaltspflichtig sein; **to fail to comply with a ~** ein Unterhaltsurteil nicht befolgen

maintenance pending suit *Br* Unterhalt während des (Scheidungs-)Prozesses

maintenance proceedings Unterhaltsprozeß, Verfahren auf Gewährung von Unterhalt; **institution of ~** Erhebung e-r Unterhaltsklage

maintenance, ~ suitable to a p.'s station in life standesgemäßer Unterhalt; **amount of ~** Unterhaltsbetrag; **arrears of ~** rückständige Unterhaltszahlungen; **award of ~** Zuerkennung (od. Gewährung) von Unterhalt

maintenance, claim for ~ Unterhaltsanspruch; **prosecution (enforcement) abroad of claims for ~** Verfolgung (Vollstreckung) von Unterhaltsansprüchen im Ausland

maintenance, duty of providing ~ Unterhaltspflicht; **entitled to ~** unterhaltsberechtigt; **(legal) liability to provide ~** (gesetzl.) Unterhaltspflicht

maintenance, obligation in respect of ~ Unterhaltspflicht; **to fail to meet one's obligation in respect of ~** s-e Unterhaltspflicht verletzen

maintenance, reasonable ~ angemessener Unterhalt; **wilful neglect to provide reasonable ~** *Br* vorsätzliche Verletzung der Unterhaltspflicht; **to fail to provide reasonable ~** s-r Unterhaltspflicht nicht nachkommen

maintenance, recovery of ~ Geltendmachung des Unterhaltsanspruchs; **Convention on the Recovery Abroad of M ~**[8] *(New Yorker)* Übereinkommen über die Geltendmachung von Unterhaltsansprüchen im Ausland *(von 1956)*

maintenance, right to ~ Unterhaltsanspruch; **secured ~** *Br* gesicherter Unterhalt *(Vermögen des Ehemannes wird sicherheitshalber nach dem Ermessen des Gerichts belastet)*; **separate ~ (payments)** *Am* Unterhalt(szahlungen) bei Getrenntleben der Ehegatten *(die Staaten, welche e-e →judicial separation nicht kennen, gewähren die Möglichkeit der Klage auf separate ~)*; **unsecured ~** *Br* ungesicherter Unterhalt *(entspricht weitgehend dem Unterhalt des deutschen Rechts)*

maintenance, to award (or **grant**) **~** Unterhalt zuerkennen; **the court awarded** (or **granted**) **the wife ~ at the rate of £ 5 a week** das Gericht billigte der Ehefrau Unterhalt in Höhe von £ 5 wöchentlich zu

maintenance, to be under an obligation to pay (or **responsible for**) **~** unterhaltspflichtig sein; **to claim ~** Unterhalt fordern (od. verlangen)

maintenance, to provide (~) (for a p) (jdm) Unterhalt gewähren, für jds Unterhalt sorgen *(cf. legal liability to provide ~, wilful neglect to provide reasonable ~, to fail to provide reasonable ~)*

maintenance 2. Wahrung, Erhaltung, Aufrechterhaltung; Behauptung, Verfechtung *(e-r Meinung)*; **~ of jobs** Erhaltung der Arbeitsplätze

maintenance of membership Aufrechterhaltung der Mitgliedschaft

Am In e-m Tarifvertrag zwischen Gewerkschaft und Arbeitgeber vereinbarte Klausel, wonach der Gewerkschaft bereits angehörende od. später beigetretene Arbeitnehmer Gewerkschaftsmitglieder bleiben müssen

maintenance, ~ of order Aufrechterhaltung der

Ordnung; ~ **of a patent** Aufrechterhaltung e-s Patents; ~ **of peace** →peace 1.; ~ **of one's rights** Wahrung s-r Rechte; **price** ~ (or **resale price** ~) Preisbindung der zweiten Hand

maintenance 3. Erhaltung; Instandhaltung; Wartung *(von Maschinen etc)*; ~ **of capital** Kapitalerhaltung; ~ **charges** (or **cost**) Instandhaltungskosten; Erhaltungsaufwand; ~ **leasing** →leasing 2.; ~ **personnel** Wartungspersonal; ~ **and repair** Unterhaltung und Instandsetzung; ~ **reserve** Rückstellung für Instandhaltungskosten; ~ **service** Wartung *(von Maschinen)*; ~ **work** Instandhaltungsarbeiten; → **cost of** ~; **current** ~ laufende Instandhaltung; **preventive** ~ vorbeugende Instandhaltung; **universal** ~ **standards** (UMS) universelle Instandhaltungsrichtwerte

maintenance 4. unzulässige Unterstützung e-r Prozeßpartei (od. beider) durch e-n Außenstehenden *(Am obs.)*

maintenor *Br* außenstehender Prozeßtreiber

maisonette *Br* kleine Wohnung *(abgeschlossener Teil e-s Hauses)*

Majesty Majestät, **by special appointment to Her** ~ *Br* Königl. Hoflieferant; **Her ~'s Commission** *Br* Königl. Offizierspatent; **during Her ~'s →pleasure; on Her ~'s Service** (O. H. M. S.) *Br* frei durch Ablösung *(portofreie Dienstsache)*

major Volljähriger, Mündiger; *mil* Major; *Am* Hauptfach; volljährig, mündig; größer *(opp. minor)*; ~ **damage** Großschaden; ~ **general** *mil* Generalmajor; ~ **objective** Hauptziel; ~ **part** größerer Teil; ~ **project** Großvorhaben; ~ **reason** Hauptgrund; ~ **repair** größere Reparatur; ~→**road**; ~ **shareholder** *(Am* **stockholder**) Hauptaktionär; Großaktionär; ~ **voice** gewichtige Stimme; ~ **war criminal** Hauptkriegsverbrecher

majority Volljährigkeit, Mündigkeit; Mehrheit, Majorität *(opp. minority)*; ~ **decision** Mehrheitsentscheidung; ~ **election** Mehrheitswahl; ~ **holding** (or **interest**) Mehrheitsbeteiligung; ~ **leader** *parl* Mehrheitsführer; ~ **of members** *(GesellschaftsR)* Mehrheit nach Köpfen *(opp. ~ of shares)*; ~ **of shares** Aktienmehrheit; (*GesellschaftsR*) Mehrheit nach Kapital (*opp. ~ of members*)

majority of votes Stimmenmehrheit, **a two-thirds** ~ e-e Zweidrittel-Stimmenmehrheit; **to receive the** ~ **cast** die Mehrheit der abgegebenen Stimmen erhalten; **the division resulted in a majority of 10 votes (cast)** →division 2.; **to win the election by a large** ~ **cast** die Wahl mit e-r großen Mehrheit der abgegebenen Stimmen gewinnen

majority, ~ **opinion** →opinion 1.; ~ **-owned subsidiary** Tochtergesellschaft, deren Aktienkapital zu mehr als 50% der Muttergesellschaft gehört; ~ **resolution** Mehrheitsbeschluß, mit Mehrheit gefaßter Beschluß; ~ **rights** Mehrheitsrechte *(der Aktionäre; opp. minority rights)*; ~ **rule** Herrschaft der Mehrheit

majority shareholding, Mehrheitsbeteiligung; **to acquire a** ~ die Aktienmehrheit erwerben

majority stockholders *Am* Besitzer der Aktienmehrheit

majority support, to (fail to) gain ~ die Unterstützung der Mehrheit (nicht) erringen

majority view Ansicht der Mehrheit

majority vote Mehrheitsbeschluß; Mehrheitswahl *(absolute Mehrheit)*; **to decide by a** ~ mit Stimmenmehrheit (od. durch Mehrheitsbeschluß) entscheiden

majority, absolute ~ absolute (Stimmen-) Mehrheit; **bare** ~ einfache (Stimmen-)Mehrheit; **by a** ~ **of** mit e-r Mehrheit von; **decision of the** ~ Mehrheitsbeschluß; **large** ~ große Mehrheit; **leader of the** ~ *parl* Mehrheitsführer; **narrow** ~ knappe Mehrheit; **overwhelming** ~ überwältigende Mehrheit; **parliamentary** ~ parlamentarische Mehrheit; **principle of** ~ Mehrheitsprinzip; **qualified** ~ qualifizierte Mehrheit; **upon reaching** ~ bei Erreichung der Volljährigkeit; **relative** ~ relative Mehrheit; **requisite** ~ erforderliche Mehrheit; **resolution of the** ~ Mehrheitsbeschluß

majority, simple ~ einfache (Stimmen-)Mehrheit; **simple distributed** ~ **vote** Abstimmung mit einfacher beiderseitiger Mehrheit; **to take a decision by a simple** ~ e-n Beschluß mit einfacher Mehrheit fassen *(Br cf. ordinary →resolution 2.)*

majority, three-fourths (or **three to one, three-quarters**) ~ Dreiviertelmehrheit *(Br cf. extraordinary or special →resolution 2.)*

majority, two-third ~ Zweidrittelmehrheit; **by a two-third** ~ mit Zweidrittelmehrheit; **the decision requires a two-third** ~ der Beschluß erfordert e-e Zweidrittelmehrheit

majority, vast ~ überwiegende Mehrheit; **to attain one's** ~ volljährig werden (at eighteen mit 18 Jahren); **on attaining one's** ~ bei Erreichung der Volljährigkeit; **to beat by a** ~ überstimmen; **to be elected by a** ~ **(of votes)** mit Stimmenmehrheit gewählt werden; **to command a** ~ **in the House of Commons** *Br* über e-e Mehrheit im Unterhaus verfügen; **to elect by an absolute (a simple)** ~ mit absoluter (einfacher) Mehrheit wählen; **to gain a** ~ e-e Mehrheit erringen; **to hold the** ~ die Mehrheit besitzen; **to join the** ~ sich der Mehrheit anschließen; **to obtain the necessary** ~ die erforderliche Mehrheit erzielen; **a** ~ **is obtained** *parl* es besteht Stimmenmehrheit; **to reach one's** ~ volljährig werden; **he is only a few votes short of a** ~ ihm fehlen nur wenige Stimmen an der Mehrheit

make (Fabrik-)Marke; Fabrikat, Erzeugnis; Bauart *(von Maschinen etc)*; ~ **of car** Automarke; **American** ~ amerikanisches Fabrikat; **foreign** ~ ausländisches Fabrikat; **own** ~ eigenes Fabrikat; **standard** ~ Normalausführung; **to be on the** ~ *sl.* auf Gewinn zielen; profitgierig sein; karrieresüchtig sein

makeshift Notbehelf; Not-, Behelfs-; behelfsmäßig

make-up Struktur, Zusammensetzung; Aufmachung, Ausstattung, Verpackung; *Br (Börse)* →making up; ~ **of the cabinet** *pol* Zusammensetzung des Kabinetts; ~ **of packets** Ausstattung (Verpackung) der Pakete; ~ **of the monthly reports** Ausstattung der Monatsberichte; ~ **pay** *Am (e-m Akkordarbeiter gezahlter)* Differenzbetrag zwischen garantiertem Mindestlohn und zu niedrigem Leistungslohn; **external** ~ Aufmachung (od. Ausstattung) von Waren; **(mental)** ~ Geisteshaltung, Einstellung

makeweight (Gewichts-)Zugabe; *fig* Ersatz, Notbehelf

make-work *Am* Gewerkschaftspraxis, die verhindern soll, daß sich durch technischen Fortschritt bedingte Arbeitszeitverkürzung negativ für den Arbeitnehmer auswirkt

make *v* machen; *(Vertrag)* (ab)schließen; herstellen, anfertigen; *(Urkunde)* aufsetzen; lassen, veranlassen, bewirken; ernennen zu; **to** ~ **an agreement** →agreement 1.; **to** ~ **an** → **allowance; to** ~ **an** →**assignment; to** ~ **a charge for sth.** für etw. e-e Gebühr erheben (od. berechnen); **to** ~ **charges against** Beschuldigungen erheben gegen; **to** ~ **one's choice** s-e Wahl treffen; **to** ~ **a claim on one's insurance** s-n Versicherungsanspruch geltend machen; **to** ~ **a decision** e-e Entscheidung treffen; e-n Entschluß fassen; **to** ~ **a declaration** e-e Erklärung abgeben; *Am* e-e (Zeugen-)Aussage machen; **to** ~ →**default in payment; to** ~ **good the damage**(or **loss**) den Schaden ersetzen; **to** ~ **headway** vorwärtskommen; **to** ~ **known** *(etw.)* bekanntgeben, zur Kenntnis bringen; **to** ~ **money** Geld verdienen; **to** ~ **(a)** →**payment; to** ~ **a point (of)** Wert darauf legen (zu); **to** ~ **a profit** e-n Gewinn erzielen; **to** ~**shift with (without) sth.** sich mit (ohne) etw. behelfen; **to** ~ **a speech** e-e Rede halten; **to** ~ **sure (of)** sich vergewissern; **to** ~ **war upon** Krieg führen gegen; **to** ~ **one's way** vorankommen; **to** ~ **a will** ein Testament machen

make away *v*, **to** ~ **with a document** *sl.* e-e Urkunde beiseite schaffen (od. verschwinden lassen); e-e Urkunde unterdrücken; **to** ~ **with a p.** *sl.* jdn beseitigen (od. töten)

make out *v* ausstellen; ausfindig machen; *(Handschrift etc)* entziffern; beweisen, nachweisen; **to** ~ **an account** e-e Rechnung ausstellen; **to** ~ **to bearer** auf den Inhaber ausstellen; **to** ~ **a bill** e-n Wechsel ausstellen; e-e Rechnung ausstellen; **to** ~ **in blank** in blanko ausstellen; **to** ~ **a case for (against)** argumentieren für (gegen); **to** ~ **a good case (for)** →case 1.; **to** ~ **a cheque (check) for £20** e-n Scheck auf £20 ausstellen; **to** ~ **a document** e-e Urkunde ausstellen; **to** ~ **an invoice** e-e Rechnung ausstellen (of über); **to** ~ **a** →**list;, to** ~ **to order** *(Wechsel, Scheck)* an Order ausstellen; **to** ~ **a statement of account** e-n Rechnungsauszug machen

make over *v* abtreten; übertragen (to sb. auf jdn); *(Vermögenswerte)* (ver)schenken; **to** ~ **a debt** e-e Forderung abtreten; **I made the house over to my daughter** ich schenkte das Haus meiner Tochter; **he made his business over to his son** (or **he made over his business to his son**) er übertrug sein Geschäft auf seinen Sohn

make up *v (Bilanz, Haushaltsplan, Liste, Tabelle etc)* aufstellen; *(Bericht, Warenproben etc)* zusammenstellen; *(Kommission etc)* zusammensetzen; **to** ~ **one's accounts** s-n (Jahres-) Abschluß machen; **to** ~ **the average** die Dispache aufmachen; **to** ~ **the deficit** den Fehlbetrag decken (od. ausgleichen)

make up, to ~ **for sth.** etw. ausgleichen, wiedergutmachen; etw. ersetzen, Ersatz leisten für etw.; etw. aufholen (od. einholen); **to** ~ **for a loss** e-n Verlust ausgleichen (od. decken); e-n Schaden ersetzen; **to** ~ **for lost time** die verlorene Zeit wieder einbringen

make up, to ~ **lost ground** *fig* verlorenen Boden wiedergewinnen; **to** ~ **one's mind** sich entschließen; **to** ~ **a quarrel** e-n Streit beilegen; **to** ~ **a shortage** e-n Fehlbetrag ausgleichen (od. decken, ergänzen); **to** ~ **statistics** e-e Statistik aufstellen

maker Hersteller, Fabrikant; Aussteller *(e-s Eigenwechsels)*; ~**'s number** Fabriknummer; **peace-**~ Friedensstifter

making Herstellung, Fertigung, Fabrikation; ~**s** Profit, Einnahmen, Verdienst; ~ **an entry** Eintragung, Buchung; ~ **a profit** Gewinnerzielung

making out Ausstellung *(e-s Schecks, e-r Rechnung etc)*; Aufstellung *(e-r Liste etc)*

making over Abtretung, Übertragung; ~ **a debt** Abtretung e-r (Geld-)Forderung

making up, ~ **the balance sheet** Bilanzaufstellung; ~ **the cash** Kassenabschluß; ~ **for losses** Verlustausgleich; ~ **(of) the monthly reports** Zusammenstellung (od. Abfassung) der Monatsberichte

making-up price *(Börse)* Abrechnungskurs *(von Effekten)*; Liquidationskurs *(im Termingeschäft)*

maladjusted child milieugestörtes Kind

maladjustment Mißverhältnis; schlechte (od. ungenügende) Anpassung; ~ **between supply and demand** Mißverhältnis zwischen Angebot und Nachfrage; ~ **of prices** *com* Preisschere

maladministration schlechte Verwaltung; unredliche Verwaltung

mala fide in bösem Glauben, bösgläubig *(opp. bona fide);* ~ **holder** bösgläubiger Inhaber; ~ **purchaser** bösgläubiger Käufer

mala fides böser Glauben *(opp. bona fides)*

Malagasy Madagasse, ~in; madagassisch (→*Madagascar)*

Malawi Malawi; **Republic of** ~ Republik Malawi
Malawian Malawier, ~in; malawisch

Malaysia Malaysia
Malaysian Malaysier, ~in; malaysisch

Maldives Malediven; **Republic of** ~ Republik Malediven
Maldivian Malediver, ~in; maledivisch

male männlich; ~ **child** Knabe; ~**s and females** männliche und weibliche Personen; ~ **issue** männliche Nachkommen; ~ **person** Person männlichen Geschlechts; **without** ~ **issue** ohne männliche Nachkommen; **in the** ~ **line** in der männlichen Linie

malefactor Täter, Verbrecher

malfeasance rechtswidriges Handeln, gesetzwidriges Verhalten *(z.B. trespass; cf. misfeasance, nonfeasance)*

Mali Mali, **Republic of** ~ Republik Mali
Malian Malier, ~in; malisch

malice Arglist, böse Absicht, (böser) Vorsatz; Böswilligkeit; ~ **aforethought** (or **prepense**) *(dolus praemeditatus) (StrafR)* vorbedachte böse Absicht *(besondere Vorsatzform bei Mord);* ~ **in fact** s. express →~; ~ **in law** s. implied →~; **actual** ~ s. express →~; **express** ~ ausdrücklich böse Absicht; **implied** ~ vermutete böse Absicht *(z.B. bei Tötungen, die unbeabsichtigt, aber mit dem Bewußtsein des tödlichen Ausgangs begangen sind)*
Bei Beleidigungen (defamation in Form von libel oder slander) schließt malice die Berufung auf gewisse Rechtfertigungsgründe (qualified privileges) aus

malicious in böser Absicht, böswillig *(vorsätzlich od. nicht absichtlich, aber im Bewußtsein der Möglichkeit des Erfolges herbeigeführt);* ~ **damage** böswillig zugefügter Schaden; ~ **falsehood** *Br*[9] böswillige Unwahrheit; Anschwärzung; ~ **injuries to property** böswillige Sachbeschädigung; ~ **injury to the person** böswillige Personenverletzung; ~ **mischief** *Am* und *Scot (böswillige)* Sachbeschädigung
malicious prosecution böswillige *(ohne Rechtsgrund vorgenommene)* Einleitung e-s Straf- od. Zivilverfahrens; böswillige Rechtsverfolgung; **action for** ~ zivile Schadensersatzklage gegen den böswilligen Kläger (od. Antragsteller, Anzeiger)
maliciously, ~ **inflicting grievous bodily harm** vorsätzliche schwere Körperverletzung; ~ **taking proceedings in bankruptcy** böswillige Einleitung e-s Konkursverfahrens

malinger *v (Krankheit)* simulieren *(bes. von Soldaten)*
malingering Simulation, Simulieren

malnutrition Unterernährung

malpractice Vernachlässigung der beruflichen Sorgfaltspflicht; ärztlicher Kunstfehler, *(fahrlässig)* falsche Behandlung; **liability for medical** ~ *Am* Arzthaftung
malpractice insurance Berufshaftpflichtversicherung; **legal** ~ Berufshaftpflichtversicherung der Rechtsanwälte; **medical** ~ Berufshaftpflichtversicherung der Ärzte; **professional** ~ Berufshaftpflichtversicherung

Malta Malta; **Republic of** ~ Republik Malta
Maltese Malteser, ~in; maltesisch

maltreatment of children Kindesmißhandlung

malversation korruptes Verhalten *(in e-r amtl. od. Vertrauensstellung; breach of trust, embezzlement, extortion, misappropriation etc)*

man Mensch; Mann; ~ **and wife** Mann und Frau; ~**-hour** Arbeits(kräfte)stunde; ~**-made fibres industry** Chemiefaserindustrie; ~ **in** *(Am auch* **on**) **the street** normal denkender Mensch, Durchschnittsbürger; ~ **of straw** Strohmann; ~**-of-war** Kriegsschiff; **business** ~ Geschäftsmann; **colo(u)red** ~ Farbiger; **key** ~ Mann in e-r Schlüsselstellung

man *v (Schiff)* bemannen; mit Personal besetzen; **to** ~ **(equip) and supply** *(Schiff)* ausrüsten
manned, M~ Orbiting Laboratory (MOL) *Am* bemanntes Laboratorium in Erdumlaufbahn; ~ **space flight** bemannter Raumflug
manning Bemannung *(e-s Schiffes);* Zusammensetzung des Fahrpersonals; Besetzung *(mit Arbeitskräften);* ~ **table** *Am* Stellenbesetzungsplan; Personalkartei

manage *v (Betrieb, Geschäfte)* führen, leiten; verwalten; *(Gut)* bewirtschaften; handhaben; behandeln; (es) einrichten, möglich machen; **to** ~ **a p.'s affairs** jds Angelegenheiten besorgen; **to** ~ **a business** e-n Betrieb führen; ein Geschäft betreiben; **to** ~ **an estate** ein Gut bewirtschaften; **to** ~ **a factory** e-e Fabrik führen; **to** ~ *Br* **property** (*Am* **real estate**) Grundbesitz verwalten; **to be authorized to** ~ **jointly** gemeinsam zur Geschäftsführung befugt sein
managed, ~ **currency** manipulierte (od. gesteu-

erte) Währung; ~ **economy** Planwirtschaft; ~ **fund** *Am* Investmentfonds, dessen Wertpapierbestand auswechselbar ist *(opp. fixed fund);* ~ **trust** *Am* Investmentgesellschaft mit wechselndem Effektenbestand; **ill** ~ schlecht geleitet; **well** ~ gut geleitet

managing leitend, geschäftsführend; führend; ~ **agent** Geschäftsführer; ~ **bank** konsortialführende Bank; ~ **board** Vorstand; ~ **body** geschäftsführendes Organ; ~ **chairman** geschäftsführender Vorsitzender; ~ **clerk** Disponent; Geschäftsführer; *Am* Bürovorsteher; ~ **committee** Vorstand; Verwaltungsausschuß; ~ **company** *Br* Gesellschaft, die als manager e-s →unit trust tätig ist; ~ **director** *Br* geschäftsführender Direktor; Generaldirektor; ~ **owner (of a ship)** Korrespondentreeder; ~ **partner** geschäftsführender Teilhaber (od. Gesellschafter); ~ **underwriter** Konsortialführer

management 1. Management; Unternehmensleitung, Unternehmensführung, Betriebsführung; Geschäftsleitung, Geschäftsführung; Direktion; leitende Angestellte; *(industrielle)* Führungskräfte; Arbeitgeber *(als Sammelbegriff)*

management, the ~ of the enterprise is located abroad die Geschäftsleitung des Unternehmens befindet sich im Ausland; **to resign from the** ~ von der Geschäftsführung zurücktreten; **to take over the** ~ die Geschäftsführung übernehmen

management, ~ **accounting** Rechnungswesen für besondere Bedürfnisse der Betriebsführung; ~ **and labo(u)r** Arbeitgeber *(Betriebsleitung)* und Arbeitnehmer; Sozialpartner; ~ **and union** Sozialpartner *(Vertreter der Arbeitgeber und Arbeitnehmer);* ~ **appraisal**→~audit; ~ **audit** Prüfung und Bewertung der Manager-Leistung; ~ **board** Geschäftsleitung *(e-s Unternehmens);* Vorstand; ~ **buyin** (MBI) *Am* Kauf e-s fremden Unternehmens durch ein Management; Übernahme durch Management-Experten außerhalb des Unternehmens; ~ **buyout** (MBO) Kauf (Übernahme) e-s Unternehmens durch dessen Management; Unternehmensverkauf an das eigene Management; ~ **by alternatives** Unternehmensführung mit Alternativlösungen; ~ **by delegation** Unternehmensführung durch Delegation von Kompetenzen an nachgeordnete Instanzen; ~ **by exception** Management nach Ausnahmeprinzipien *(das mittlere und untere ~ entscheidet selbständig, das top ~ nur in Ausnahmefällen);* ~ **by objectives** (MBO) Unternehmensführung mit Zielvorgabe; ~ **by results** ergebnisorientierte Methode der Unternehmensführung; ~ **cabinet** *Am* Management aus Führungsnachwuchskräften, denen die Aufgaben zur (Vor-)Behandlung zugewiesen werden *(cf. multiple ~);* ~ **committee** geschäftsführender Ausschuß; Direktorium; ~ **company** *Am*[10] Verwaltungsgesellschaft (Investmentgesellschaft); ~ **consultant** Betriebsberater, Unternehmensberater, Management-Berater; ~ **consultancy** (or **consulting**) Unternehmensberatung

management, ~ **decision** Entscheidung der Unternehmensleitung; ~ **development** Förderung der Führungskräfte e-s Unternehmens *(cf. on-the-job training, off-the-job training, →job training);* ~ **engineering** *Am* Betriebstechnik; ~ **expense(s)** Geschäftsführungskosten; ~ **game** *Am* Betriebs-(od. Unternehmens-)Planspiel; ~ **group** Konsortium

management of a corporation *Am (meist vom →board of directors ernanntes)* Management e-r AG, Verwaltungsspitze *(leitende Angestellte außerhalb od. innerhalb des board; executives od. officers, meistens bestehend aus president [cf. president 3.] [od. general manager], vice-president, secretary, treasurer)*

Dem management unterliegt praktisch die Führung des Unternehmens nach den policy determinations des board. Der board (directors) und das management (officers) sind oft identisch; board-Mitglieder sind oft managers

management, ~ **planning** Unternehmensplanung; ~ **ratio** *Am* Anzahl leitender Angestellter auf 1000 Beschäftigte; ~ **representatives** Vertreter der Unternehmensführung; ~ **reserve group** *Am* Führungsnachwuchsgruppe; ~ **science** Wissenschaft von der Betriebsführung; ~ **shares** Gründeraktien, Gründeranteile *(→share 2.);* ~ **stock** *Am* Mehrstimmrechtsaktien; ~ **team** Führungsgruppe; ~ **trainee course** Ausbildungskurs für Führungsnachwuchskräfte; **advanced** ~ **training program(-me)** Programm zur Ausbildung höherer Führungskräfte; ~ **trust** freier (od. flexibler) (Investment) Trust *(bes. Form des →investment trust; die Art der An- und Verkäufe der Effekten ist in das Ermessen der Geschäftsführer der Gesellschaft gelegt; opp. fixed trust)*

management, board of ~→board 1.; **business** ~ Geschäftsführung, Betriebsführung; **co-**~ Mitbestimmung; →**central** ~ **and control; industrial** ~ industrielle Führungskräfte; **junior** ~ s. lower →~; **levels of** ~ Stufen innerhalb e-s Management; **lower** ~ unteres Management, untere Führungskräfte; **middle** ~ mittlere Führungskräfte; **multiple** ~ mehrfache Führungskräfte *(Methode der Heranbildung des Nachwuchses von Führungskräften);* **under new** ~ unter neuer Geschäftsführung; **personnel** ~ Personalverwaltung; **place of** ~ *(Int. SteuerR)* Ort der Leitung; **plant** ~ Betriebsleitung, Betriebsführung; **scientific** ~ wissenschaftliche Betriebsführung; **top** ~ oberes Management, Unternehmensspitze; obere Führungskräfte; **workers' participation (in** ~**)** Mitbestimmung im Unternehmen

management 2. Verwaltung; Bewirtschaftung;

Handhabung; ~ **and control** *Am* Verwaltungsbefugnis am *(in manchen Staaten nur bewegl.)* →community property; ~ **committee** Verwaltungsausschuß; ~ **expenses** Verwaltungs(gemein)kosten; ~ **of currency** Währungsmanipulation; ~ **of the fair** Messeleitung; ~ **of fishing resources** Bewirtschaftung der Fischbestände; ~ **of land** Bodenbewirtschaftung; ~ **of securities** Verwaltung von Wertpapieren; ~ **of a ship** technische Bedienung e-s Schiffes; ~ **of waste** Abfallbewirtschaftung

management, Debt M~ *Am* Verwaltung der Bundesschuld *(durch das →Treasury)*; **general** ~ Geschäftsführung; **property** ~ Vermögensverwaltung; *Br* Grundstücksverwaltung, Hausverwaltung

manager Manager; leitender Angestellter *(e-s Unternehmens)*; Geschäftsführer; Konsortialführer; *Br parl* Mitglied e-s Ausschusses für Angelegenheiten, die beide Häuser betreffen; **~s** Direktion; **~'s authority** Geschäftsführungsbefugnis; **acting** ~ stellvertretender Leiter; geschäftsführender Leiter; **advertising** ~ Reklameleiter; Werbeleiter; **bank** ~ Bankdirektor; **branch** ~ Filialleiter; **(business)** ~ Geschäftsführer; **chief** ~ Hauptgeschäftsführer; **city** ~ *Am* Oberstadtdirektor; **departmental** ~ Abteilungsleiter; **deputy** ~ stellvertretender Geschäftsführer; **district** ~ Gebietsleiter; **estate** ~ Gutsverwalter; **factory** ~ Fabrikdirektor, Betriebsleiter; **farm** ~ (landwirtschaftl.) Verwalter, Gutsverwalter; **functional** ~ fachliche Führungskraft; **general** ~ leitender Angestellter; (Haupt-)Geschäftsführer *(der mit der Leitung des Unternehmens als Ganzem befaßt ist)*; *Am* Generaldirektor *(e-r AG)*; **hotel** ~ Hoteldirektor; **personal assistant (to the ~)** *(etwa)* Direktionsassistent; **personnel** ~ Personalchef; **promotion of prospective ~s** Förderung der Führungs-Nachwuchskräfte; Nachwuchsförderung für Betriebsführung; **property** ~ *Br* Grundstücksverwalter; Hausverwalter; **publicity** ~ Werbeleiter; **(receiver and)** ~ *Br* →receiver 2.; **sales** ~ Verkaufsleiter; → **special ~; staff** ~ Personalchef; **technical** ~ technischer Direktor; **works** ~ Betriebsleiter, Werksleiter; **to appoint a** ~ e-n Geschäftsführer bestellen; **to remove a** ~ die Bestellung e-s Geschäftsführers widerrufen

manageress Leiterin, Geschäftsführerin, Direktorin

managerial (geschäfts)leitend; Leitungs-, Führungs-, Direktions-; Manager-; ~ **accounting** →management accounting; **high** ~ **agent** *Am* Abteilungsleiter; ~ **authority** (Geschäfts-)Führungsbefugnis; ~ **body** →managing body; **in a** ~ **capacity** in leitender Stellung; ~ **economics** Betriebswirtschaftslehre, die sich mit Unternehmensführung befaßt; ~ **employee** leitender Angestellter; ~ **policy** Unternehmenspolitik; ~ **position** leitende Stellung *(in e-m Betrieb)*; ~ **problems** Probleme der Betriebsführung, Führungsprobleme; ~ **qualities** Führungsqualitäten; ~ **revolution** das Regime der Manager *(Verstärkung des Einflusses leitender Angestellter auf die Betriebsführung zuungunsten des Eigentümers)*; ~ **skills** Manager-Fähigkeiten; ~ **staff** leitendes Personal

managership Amt od. Stellung e-s →manager; Geschäftsführung, (Geschäfts-)Leitung; Direktion

managing →manage *v*

mandamus ("we command"), **order** (*Am* **writ**) **of** ~ *(an ein unteres Gericht, e-e Verwaltungsbehörde, e-e juristische Person des öffentlichen od. privaten Rechts gerichtete)* gerichtliche Verfügung zur Vornahme oder Unterlassung e-r Handlung; **interlocutory** ~ *Br*[11] einstweilige Verfügung

mandatary Mandatar; Beauftragter, Auftragnehmer, Bevollmächtigter *(opp. mandator)*

mandate Auftrag; *Am* gerichtl. Verfügung *(e-s oberen an ein unteres Gericht)*; Anweisung *(an e-e Bank, bes. bei Eröffnung e-s Kontos)*; (Bank-) Vollmacht *(zur Abhebung von Geld von jds Konto)*; *parl* Mandat *(des Abgeordneten)*; *(VölkerR)* Mandat(sgebiet) *(des Völkerbundes)*; **~s system** *(VölkerR)* Mandatssystem *(nach dem 2. Weltkrieg in das →trusteeship system umgewandelt)*; **allotment of ~s** *parl* Sitzverteilung; **dual** ~ *parl* Doppelmandat; **renewal of a** ~ *parl* Mandatsverlängerung; **territory under a** ~ *(VölkerR)* Mandatsgebiet; **third party** ~ Kontovollmacht; **→writ of ~; to contest a** ~ *parl* sich um ein Mandat bewerben

mandate *v (VölkerR) (Land)* unter ein Mandat stellen

mandated, ~ **area** Mandatsgebiet; ~ **territory** Mandatsgebiet *(des Völkerbundes; jetzt ersetzt durch →trusteeship der Vereinten Nationen)*; **ex-** ~ **territory** ehemaliges Mandatsgebiet

mandator Auftraggeber, Mandant; Vollmachtgeber *(opp. mandatary)*

mandatory 1. →mandatary

mandatory 2. obligatorisch, vorgeschrieben, zwingend, unabdingbar; ~ **conciliation** Zwangsschlichtung; ~ **injunction**[12] einstweilige Verfügung zur Vornahme einer Handlung; ~ **instructions** *Am* verbindliche Anweisungen; ~ **provision** zwingende Bestimmung; Mußvorschrift *(opp. directory provision)*; ~ **retirement** Zwangspensionierung; ~ **sign** *(Verkehr)* Gebotszeichen; **not** ~ abdingbar; **the written form is** ~ *Am* die Schriftform ist vorgeschrieben

maneuver *Am* →manoeuvre

manifest (Ladungs-)Manifest, Ladungsverzeichnis, (Schiffs-)Ladeliste *(für Zollzwecke); (Lufttransport)* Liste *(Passagiere, Bestimmungsort, Gepäckgewicht etc);* Kundgebung; Manifest *(→manifesto);* **inward** ~ Zolleinfuhrerklärung; **outward** ~ Zollausfuhrerklärung

manifest *v* darlegen, kundtun; *(im Ladungsmanifest)* aufführen

manifest offenbar, offensichtlich; augenscheinlich; ~ **injustice** offenkundige Ungerechtigkeit

manifestation Kundgebung, Offenbarung; Bekundung; *pol* öffentliche Kundgebung, Demonstration

manifesto Manifest, öffentliche Erklärung; *pol* Grundsatzerklärung, Programm *(e-r Partei);* **Communist M~** kommunistisches Manifest; **election** ~ Wahlprogramm

manifold *v* vervielfältigen; hektographieren

manifolder Hektograph

manipulate *v* handhaben; *(Preise, Wahlergebnisse)* manipulieren; *(unfair)* beeinflussen

manipulation Handhabung; Manipulation *(unfaire)* Beeinflussung; ~**s** unsaubere Praktiken, Machenschaften; ~ **of the currency** Währungsmanipulation; ~ **of elections** Wahlmanipulation; ~ **on the stock exchange** Börsenmanipulation, Börsenmanöver; **fraudulent** ~ betrügerisches Geschäftsgebaren

manner Art (und Weise); ~**s** Sitte(n); Manieren; ~ **of calculation** Berechnungsart; ~ **of conveyance** →mode of conveyance; ~ **of new manufacture** *(PatR)* Art neuer Herstellung, neuartige Herstellungsmethode; **business** ~**s** Geschäftsgebaren

manning →man *v*

manoeuv|re (-er) *mil* Manöver; *fig* Manöver, Kniff, Täuschungsversuch

manor *Br hist (großes)* Landgut, Rittergut; *Am* vom Staat verpachteter Großgrundbesitz; →**lord of the** ~

manpower Arbeitskräfte; ~ **cuts** Abbau von Arbeitskräften; ~ **establishment** Personalbestand; ~ **needs** Bedarf an Arbeitskräften; ~ **planning** Arbeitskräfteplanung *(Personalplanung e-s Unternehmens);* ~ **policy** Arbeitsmarktpolitik; ~ **requirement** Arbeitskräftebedarf; ~ **resources** Arbeitskräftepotential; ~ **shortage** Arbeitskräftemangel; ~ **situation** Lage am Arbeitsmarkt; ~ **surplus** Arbeitskräfteüberschuß; **allocation of** ~ Zuweisung von Arbeitskräften; **countries lacking** ~ Länder, die Mangel an Arbeitskräften haben

mansion *(herrschaftl.)* Wohnhaus; **the M~ House** *Br* Amtswohnung des Lord Mayor of London

manslaughter[13] *(StrafR)* Totschlag

Minderschwerer Fall der Tötung (without express or implied →malice); umfaßt vorsätzliche Tötung, die aber unüberlegt, z. B. auf Provokation hin, od. *Br*[14] mit verminderter Zurechnungsfähigkeit begangen ist, sowie Tötung aus Fahrlässigkeit *(criminal negligence)*

manslaughter, involuntary ~ fahrlässige Tötung *(dolus indirectus);* **misdemeanor** ~ *Am* Tötung anläßlich der Begehung e-s bloßen Vergehens *(die deshalb nicht als murder bestraft wird);* **voluntary** ~ vorsätzliche (aber unüberlegte) Tötung *(ohne →malice aforethought begangen; cf. murder)*

manu propria (m. p.) eigenhändig

manual Handbuch, Leitfaden; manuell, mit der Hand, Hand-; ~ **delivery** tatsächliche Übergabe; ~ **labo(u)r** (or **work**) körperliche Arbeit; ~ **worker** Arbeiter; →**army** ~; **Sign M~** →sign 1.

manufacture Fabrikation, *(fabrikmäßige)* Herstellung; Fabrikat, (Fabrik-, Industrie-)Erzeugnis; ~**s** (Fabrik-)Waren; Fertigwaren; ~ **to customer's specification** Einzelanfertigung; **article of** ~ Fabrikerzeugnis; **branch of** ~ Fabrikationszweig; **cost of** ~ Herstellungskosten; **course of** ~ Fabrikationsgang; **finished** ~ Fertigfabrikat(e), Fertigerzeugnis (-se); **foreign** ~ ausländisches Erzeugnis (od. Fabrikat); **home** (or **inland**) ~ einheimisches Erzeugnis, inländisches Fabrikat; **industrial** ~**s** gewerbliche Fertigwaren; **method of** ~ Herstellungsverfahren; **place of** ~ Herstellungsort, Fabrikationsstätte; **process of** ~ →process 2.; **semi-~(s)** Halbfabrikat(e), Halberzeugnis(se); **serial** ~ Serienherstellung; **supervision of** ~ Fertigungskontrolle; **wholesale** ~ Massenfabrikation, Massenherstellung; **year of** ~ Herstellungsjahr; **to discontinue the** ~ **of ...** die Herstellung von ... einstellen

manufacture *v* herstellen, produzieren; verarbeiten (into zu)

manufactured, ~ **articles** (or **goods**) Fabrikwaren, Industrieartikel; Fertigwaren, (Fertig-)Fabrikate; ~ **products** Industrieerzeugnisse; (Fertig-)Fabrikate; **semi-~ goods** Halbfabrikate, Halbfertigwaren; **product** ~ **in the United States** in den USA hergestelltes Erzeugnis

manufacturer Fabrikant; Hersteller; Industrieller; ~**'s agent** *Am* Industrievertreter, Generalvertreter; ~**'s brand** Fabrikmarke; ~**'s cost** Herstellungskosten; ~**'s excise** *Am* Herstellerumsatzsteuer *(Bundesumsatzsteuer auf der Her-*

stellerstufe; cf. retailer's excise); ~**'s export agent** *Am* Exportvermittler; ~**'s liability** Produzentenhaftung; ~**'s mark** Fabrikmarke; ~**'s price** Fabrikpreis; →**National Association of M~s**

manufacturing Fabrikation, *(fabrikmäßige)* Herstellung; verarbeitendes Gewerbe; Produktion; Fertigung; Fabrik-, Fabrikations-, Herstellungs-, Industrie-; ~ **agreement** Herstellungsvertrag; ~ **branch** Industriezweig; ~ **cent|re (-er)** Industriezentrum

manufacturing clause *Am (UrhR)* Klausel, die e-m amerikanischen Bürger od. in den Vereinigten Staaten wohnenden Ausländer den vollen Schutz des Urheberrechts nur dann gewährt, wenn s-e Bücher in Amerika gedruckt und gebunden worden sind

manufacturing, ~ **concern** Fabrikationsbetrieb; ~ **cost** Herstell(ungs)kosten; Fertigungskosten; ~ **country** Herstellungsland; Industrieland; ~ **defect** Fabrikationsfehler; ~ **district** Industriegebiet; ~ **efficiency** Produktionsleistung; ~ **enterprise** Herstellungsbetrieb; ~ **expense** Fertigungsgemeinkosten; ~ **industry** verarbeitende Industrie, Fertigungsindustrie; ~ **licen|ce (-se)** Herstellungslizenz; ~ **know-how** →know-how; ~ **planning** Fertigungsplanung; ~ **plant** Fabrikanlage, Fabrikationsbetrieb; ~ **price** Herstellungspreis

manufacturing process Herstellungsverfahren; Fertigungsverfahren; Fabrikationsprozeß; **inspection of the** ~ Fertigungsüberprüfung

manufacturing, for ~ **purposes** für Fabrikationszwecke; ~ **right** Herstellungsrecht, Fabrikationsrecht; ~ **secret** Fabrikationsgeheimnis; ~ **town** Fabrikstadt, Industriestadt

manuscript Manuskript; handschriftlich

map Karte; ~ **of the town** Stadtplan

maquis *Fr pol* Untergrundbewegung *(im 2. Weltkrieg);* Partisanen

mare clausum *(VölkerR)* geschlossenes Meer *(opp. open sea)*

marches Grenzen *(bes. zwischen England u. Wales und zwischen England u. Schottland)*

marchioness Marquise

Mareva injunction *Br* Arrestbeschluß, mit dem dem Schuldner die Wegschaffung von Werten aus dem Hoheitsbereich des Gerichts untersagt wird

margin 1. Rand, Abstand; ~ **stop** *(Schreibmaschine)* Randsteller; **in the** ~ am Rande; **noted in the** ~ am Rande vermerkt; **as per** ~ wie nebenstehend; **to write in the** ~ Randbemerkung machen

margin 2. Marge, Spanne, Spielraum, Verdienstspanne, Überschuß *(bei Kursen Unterschied zwischen An- und Verkaufspreisen, im Warenhandel zwischen Selbstkosten- und Verkaufspreisen); (Effektengeschäft)* Einschuß *(vom Auftraggeber für Wertpapierkauf auf Kreditbasis eingezahlter Betrag);* ~ **account** Einschußkonto *(des Effektenkäufers, der auf Kredit kauft);* ~ **buying** Margin-Kauf *(Effektenkauf unter Kreditierung e-s Teiles des Kaufbetrages);* ~ **call** Aufforderung zur Leistung e-r Nachschußzahlung *(zur Erhöhung der Mindestdeckung e-s Effektenkredites);* ~ **(of band) of the exchange rate** Bandbreite der Wechselkurse; ~ **of credit** Kreditspielraum; ~ **of** →**discretion;** ~ **of fluctuations** Schwankungsbreite *(e-s Wechselkurses)*

margin of preference Präferenzspanne; **maximum** ~ Präferenzhöchstspanne

margin, ~ **of profit** Gewinnspanne, Verdienstspanne; ~ **of safety** Sicherheitsmarge, Sicherheitsspanne; ~ **rate** *(Effektengeschäft)* Kreditgebühr; ~ **requirement** Einschußpflicht *(Mindesteinzahlungsbetrag, wenn Wertpapiere mit Makler- oder Bankdarlehen gekauft werden; "margin requirement of 70%" bedeutet, daß nur 30% des Kurswertes auf Kredit genommen werden können);* ~ **rules** *(Börse)* Kreditbeschränkungsregeln; ~ **trading** *Am* Wertpapierkäufe auf Kredit

margin, additional ~ weiterer Einschuß; **credit** ~ Kreditmarge, Kreditspielraum; **debt** ~ Verschuldungsspielraum; **fixed** ~**s (of the exchange rate)** feste Bandbreiten des Wechselkurses; **gross** ~ Bruttogewinn(spanne); Warenrohgewinn; **interest** ~ Zinsmarge, Zinsspanne; **liquidity** ~ Liquiditätsspielraum; **maximum** ~ Höchstspanne, Höchstspielraum; **minimum** ~ *(Effektengeschäft)* Mindesteinschuß; **narrow** ~ geringer Spielraum, geringe Spanne; **net** ~ (of an enterprise) Reingewinn(spanne); **trade** ~ Handelsspanne

margin, to buy on ~ *(Wertpapiere)* auf Einschuß kaufen; **to deposit a** ~ **in cash** e-n Bareinschuß leisten; **to leave a** ~ Spielraum gewähren; Gewinn abwerfen; **to sell on** ~ *(Wertpapiere)* auf Einschuß verkaufen

marginal Rand-, Marginal-; Grenz-; gerade noch rentabel; ~ **account** →margin account; ~ **analysis** Marginalanalyse; ~ **area** Randgebiet; ~ **case** Grenzfall; ~**constituency** *Br parl* Wahlbezirk mit knapper Stimmenmehrheit *(weniger als 3000 Stimmen)* für e-n von zwei führenden Kandidaten; ~ **cost** Grenzkosten; ~ **costing** Grenzkostenrechnung; ~ **earnings** Grenzertrag; ~ **efficiency of capital** Grenzleistungsfähigkeit des Kapitals; ~ **enterprise** Grenzbetrieb, unrentabler Betrieb; ~ **income** Deckungsbeitrag; ~ **labo(u)r** unrentable Arbeitskräfte; ~ **land** Grenzertragsboden *(Land, dessen Bestellung sich knapp lohnt);* ~ **mines** unrentable Zechen; ~ **note** Randbemerkung; ~ **product** Grenzprodukt; ~ **productivity**

Grenzproduktivität; ~ **profit** Grenzertrag, knapper Gewinn; ~ **rate of taxation** Grenzsteuersatz; ~ **rate of substitution** *Am* Grenzrate der Substitution *(Verhältnis der Austauschfähigkeit zweier Güter)*; ~ **relief** *Br (SteuerR)* Ermäßigung für e-n zu versteuernden Betrag, der knapp über der Steuergrenze liegt; ~ **revenue** Grenzeinnahmen *(Differenz zwischen Umsatz und variablen Kosten)*; ~ **sea** *(VölkerR)* Randmeer *(cf. territorial waters)*; ~ **seat** *Br parl* Sitz, der nur mit knappem Vorsprung gehalten wird; ~ **utility** Grenznutzen; ~ **value** Grenzwert; ~ **yield** Grenzertrag

marine See-, Schiffahrt-; Marine-; (Kriegs-, Handels-)Marine; *mil* Marineinfanterist *(Br Angehöriger der Royal M~s, Am Angehöriger des M~ Corps)*; ~ **adventure** Seeunternehmen; ~ **belt** *(VölkerR)* Randmeer *(→territorial waters)*; ~ **bill of lading** Seekonnossement; ~ **cable** Seekabel; **M~ Corps** *Am* Marine-Infanterie; ~ **engineering** Schiffsmaschinenbau; ~ **environment** Meeresumwelt; ~ **hull insurance** Seekaskoversicherung

marine insurance See(transport)versicherung *(Br cf. valued policy, open policy, voyage policy, time policy)*; **M~ I~ Act** (M. I. A.) *Br* Seeversicherungsgesetz *(1906)*; ~ **broker** Seeversicherungsmakler; ~ **policy** Seeversicherungspolice; **contract of** ~ Seeversicherungsvertrag; **inland** ~ *Am* Binnentransportversicherung *(Überlandtransport)*; *Br* Flußtransportversicherung; **ocean** ~ *Am* Seetransportversicherung

marine insurer, International Union of M~ I~s Internationale Seeversicherungs-Union

marine, ~ **interest** Bodmereizinsen; ~ **law** →maritime law; ~ **liability insurance** Seehaftpflichtversicherung; ~ **loan** Bodmerei(-darlehen); ~ **loss** Verlust auf See; ~ **navigation** Seeschiffahrt; ~ **peril(s)** See(transport)-gefahr; ~ **policy** Seeversicherungspolice

marine pollution Meeresverschmutzung; ~ **damage** Meeresverschmutzungsschaden; ~ **from land-based sources** Meeresverschmutzung vom Land aus; **prevention of ~ by dumping from ships and aircraft**[15] Verhütung der Meeresverschmutzung durch das Einbringen von Schiffen und Luftfahrzeugen; **prevention of ~ by dumping of wastes and other matters**[16] Verhütung der Meeresverschmutzung durch das Einbringen von Abfällen und anderen Stoffen

marine, ~ **rate** →rate 5.; ~ **registry** *Br* Eintragung ins Schiffsregister, ~ **registry office** *Br* Schiffsregisteramt

marine resources Meeresressourcen, Schätze des Meeres; **to exploit the** ~ die Meeresressourcen erschließen

marine, ~ **risk** See(transport)gefahr; ~ **science and technology** (MAST) Meereswissenschaften und -technologie (MAST); ~ **scientific research** wissenschaftliche Meeresforschung; ~ **station** Hafenbahnhof; ~ **store** Trödelladen *(für Schiffsgegenstände)*; ~ **stores** Vorräte an Schiffsbedarf; alte Schiffsgegenstände; ~ **transport** Seetransport, Beförderung auf dem Seewege; ~ **transport broker** Schiffsmakler; ~ **underwriter** Seeversicherer; ~ **warfare** Seekrieg(sführung); **mercantile** (or **commercial, merchant**) ~ Handelsmarine; **Royal M~s** *Br* Marine-Infanterie

mariner Seemann, Matrose; Seefahrer; **~s** Seeleute; **master** ~ Kapitän *(e-s Handelsschiffes)*

marital ehelich; ~ **→cohabitation;** ~ **deduction** (or **exemption**) *Am (für Erbschaft- und Schenkungsteuer)* Ehegattenabzug; Versorgungsfreibetrag (*des überlebenden Ehegatten*); ~ **deduction trust** *Am* Trust zur Verwaltung des erbschaftsteuerlichen Freibetrages des Ehegatten; ~ **infidelity** eheliche Untreue; ~ **intercourse** ehelicher Verkehr

marital property regime *Am* ehelicher Güterstand

marital relations eheliche Beziehungen; **extra-** ~ außereheliche Beziehungen

marital, ~ **rights and duties** eheliche Rechte und Pflichten; ~ **status** Familienstand

maritime See-, Schiffahrts-, Küsten-; **M~ Administration** *Am* Behörde für Schiffahrtsangelegenheiten; ~ **adventure** Seeunternehmen; ~ **affairs** Seewesen; Schiffahrtsangelegenheiten

maritime arbitration Seeschiedsgerichtsbarkeit; **Standing Committee on M~ A~**[16a] Ständiges Komitee für Seeschiedsgerichtsbarkeit

maritime, ~ **belt** → marine belt; ~ **blockade** (*VölkerR*) Seesperre

maritime cases, American M~ C~ *Am* Sammlung von seerechtl. Gerichtsentscheidungen

maritime casualty, state affected by the ~ durch den Seeunfall betroffener Staat

maritime claim (*VersR*) seerechtlicher Anspruch; **~s** Seeforderungen; **Convention on Limitation of Liability for M~ C~s**[16b] Übereinkommen über die Beschränkung der Haftung für Seeforderungen

maritime, ~ **commerce** Seehandel, Überseehandel; ~ **contract of affreightment** Seefrachtvertrag; ~ **custom** See(manns)brauch; ~ **disputes** seerechtliche Streitigkeiten; ~ **domain** See(hoheits)gebiet; ~ **fishing** Seefischerei; ~ **flag** Seeflagge; ~ **freight** Seefracht; ~ **hypothec(ation)** *Am* s. ~→ lien; ~ **insurance** →marine insurance; ~ **interest** →marine interest; ~ **law** Seerecht, Seeschiffahrtsrecht; ~ **international law** internationales Seerecht; ~ **→lien;** ~ **loan** Bodmerei(darlehen); ~ **matters** Seesachen, Schiffahrtsangelegenheiten; ~ **mortage** Schiffshypothek; ~ **peril(s)** See-

(transport)gefahr; ~ **policy** Seeversicherungspolice

maritime port Seehafen; **Convention and Statute on the International Regime of M~ P~s** Übereinkommen und Statut über die internationale Rechtsordnung der Seehäfen *(von 1923)*[17]

maritime, ~ **power** Seemacht; **M~ Provinces** Ostküste Kanadas; ~ **risk** See(transport)gefahr; ~ **safety** Sicherheit auf See

maritime search, International Convention on M~ S~ and Rescue[17a] Internationales Übereinkommen über den Such- und Rettungsdienst auf See

maritime, ~ **shipping** Seeschiffahrt; ~ **territory** *(VölkerR)* Staatsmeergebiet, Hoheitsgewässer (→*territorial waters*); ~ **town** Seestadt; ~ **trade** Seehandel, Überseehandel; ~ **transport (ation) of goods or passengers** Beförderung von Gütern oder Reisenden zur See; **means of ~ transport** Transportmittel des Seeverkehrs; ~ **warfare** Seekrieg(führung); **Federal M~ Commission** (FMC) *Am* Oberste Bundesbehörde für das Schiffahrtswesen; **international ~ arbitration** internationale Seeschiedsgerichtsbarkeit; →**International M~ Organization;** →**International M~ Satellite Organization**

mark 1. (Kenn-)Zeichen, Merkzeichen, Anzeichen (of für); Preiszettel, Auszeichnung *(an Waren);* Stempel; Kreuz *(als Unterschrift);* (Prüfungs-)Note; ~ **of origin** Herkunftszeichen, Ursprungszeichen; ~ **of quality** Gütezeichen; **boundary** ~ Grenzzeichen, Grenzmarke

mark, check ~ Kontrollzeichen; **to put check ~s** ankreuzen, anhaken

mark, distinctive ~ Unterscheidungsmerkmal, besonderes Kennzeichen; **identification** ~ Nämlichkeitszeichen; **price** ~ (ausgezeichneter) Preis; Preisbezeichnung; **reference** ~ Verweisungszeichen; **wide off the** ~ ganz unzutreffend; **to be up to the** ~ den Anforderungen entsprechen; **to put a ~ on** *(etw.)* mit e-m (Kenn-)Zeichen versehen

mark 2. Marke, Schutzmarke, Handelsmarke; Warenzeichen (→*trade* ~); **certification** ~ *Am*[18] Verbandszeichen, Güte- od. Verbandsmarke *(dient zur Garantie für Herkunft, Material, Herstellungsart etc von Waren);* **collective** ~ *Am* Verbandszeichen, Kollektivmarke *(Handels- od. Dienstleistungsmarke, die von den Mitgliedern e-s Verbandes benutzt wird);* **deceptive** ~ irreführendes (Waren-)Zeichen; **jointly owned ~s** Marken in gemeinschaftlichem Eigentum; **service** ~ *Am* →service 1.; **trade** ~ Warenzeichen (→*trade*)

mark 3. *Br (Börse)* Notierung; **to lodge objections to a** ~ gegen e-e Kursnotierung Einspruch erheben

mark *v* kennzeichnen, bezeichnen, beschriften; *(Waren)* mit Preis versehen, auszeichnen; *Br (Börse)* notieren; **to ~ down** *(Preis od. Kurs)* herabsetzen; niedriger notieren; mit e-m niedrigeren Preis versehen (od. auszeichnen); *(jdn. od. etw.)* vormerken, bestimmen; **he has been ~ed down for promotion** er ist für e-e Beförderung vorgemerkt; **to ~ out for** *(jdn)* bestimmen (od. ausersehen) für; **to ~ up** *(Preis od. Kurs)* heraufsetzen; höher notieren; mit e-m höheren Preis versehen (od. auszeichnen)

mark *v,* **to ~ one's ballot** seinen Stimmzettel ankreuzen; **to ~ boundaries** Grenzen bezeichnen (od. festsetzen); **to ~ a cheque** *Br* e-n Scheck bestätigen; **to ~ an examination paper** *(Schule, Universität, berufliche Prüfungen)* schriftliche Antworten auf Prüfungsfragen bewerten; **to ~ a price** *Br (Börse)* e-n Kurs notieren; **to ~ time** *fig* auf der Stelle treten; absichtlich nicht „vom Fleck" kommen

marked gekennzeichnet, bezeichnet; ausgezeichnet, mit Preisen versehen, markiert; ausdrücklich, merklich; ~ **check** *Am* →check 1.; ~ **cheque** *Br* bestätigter Scheck; ~ **goods** markierte Waren; ~ **improvement** merkliche Besserung; ~ **and numbered** mit Zeichen und Nummern versehen, gezeichnet und numeriert; ~ **price** ausgezeichneter Preis; **at ~-down price** zu ermäßigtem Preis; ~ **progress** merklicher Fortschritt; ~ **shares** *Br* abgestempelte Aktien; **to be** ~ *Br (Börse)* notiert werden; zur Notierung kommen; **to be ~ down** niedriger notiert werden; im Fallen sein; **to be ~ up** höher notiert werden; im Steigen sein

marking Kennzeichnung, Bezeichnung, Markierung; (Preis-)Auszeichnung; Bestätigung(svermerk) *(auf Scheck); Br (Börse)* Notierung, Kursfeststellung; ~ **and notification of patent rights** Patentberühmung; ~ **a cheque** *Br* Bestätigung e-s Schecks; ~ **clerk** *Br (Börse)* Kursmakler; ~ **out** Grenzziehung, Grenzabsteckung; Vermarkung; ~ **requirements** Vorschriften über die Kennzeichnung; **boundary** ~ Grenzbezeichnung; **false ~ of goods** falsche Bezeichnung von Waren; **national** ~ Hoheitsabzeichen *(e-s Flugzeugs);* →**road** ~

markdown Preisabschlag, Preisherabsetzung; niedrigere Auszeichnung *(e-r Ware);* Kursabschlag; *Am (Börse)* Disagio; ~ (on selling price) Handelsabschlag; *(bei Markenartikeln)* Handelsrabatt; ~ **on retail price** (or **retail** ~) Handelsabschlag

markup Preisaufschlag, Preiserhöhung; höhere Auszeichnung *(e-r Ware);* Gewinnaufschlag; Kursaufschlag; *Am (Börse)* Agio; ~ **(on purchase price)** Handelsaufschlag, Kalkulationsaufschlag; **import** ~ Aufschlag auf den Einfuhrpreis;**to charge a flat ~ on all items** bei allen Artikeln einheitlich denselben Preisaufschlag berechnen

market Markt; Marktplatz, Handelsplatz, Absatzgebiet, Absatzmarkt; Börse; Nachfrage (for nach); Geldmarkt; *colloq.* Marktpreis

market, to act on (or **to affect**) **the** ~ den Markt beeinflussen; **to apportion a** ~ e-n Markt aufteilen; **to be in the** ~ auf dem Markt sein, zum Verkauf angeboten werden; am Kauf interessiert sein, als Käufer auftreten (for für); **to bring on(to) the** ~ auf den Markt bringen; **to →bull the ~; to come into** (or **on**) **the** ~ auf den Markt (od. zum Verkauf) kommen; **to command the** ~ den Markt beherrschen; **to congest the** ~ den Markt überschwemmen; **to conquer the** ~ den Markt erobern; **to divide the** ~ den Markt aufteilen; **to dominate the** ~ den Markt beherrschen; **to find a** ~ Absatz finden; **to glut the** ~ den Markt überschwemmen; **to hold a** ~ e-n Markt abhalten; **to meet with a ready** ~ guten Absatz finden; **to open up new ~s** neue Märkte erschließen; **to play the** ~ *(Börse)* spekulieren; **to put on the** ~ auf den Markt bringen; **to regain a** ~ e-n Markt wiedergewinnen; **to sell at the** ~ *Am* zum Börsenkurs verkaufen; **to throw on the** ~ auf den Markt werfen; **the ~ is dead** der Markt ist sehr ruhig; **the ~ is lively** der Markt ist lebhaft

market, ~ **analysis** Marktanalyse, Marktuntersuchung; ~ **average** Durchschnittspreis am Markt; Durchschnittskurs; ~ **behavio(u)r** Marktverhalten; ~ **capitalization** Börsenwert; ~ **condition(s)** Marktlage, Marktverhältnisse; Konjunktur; ~ **conduct** Marktverhalten(sweise), Verhalten *(der Unternehmer)* auf e-m Markt; ~ **control** Marktbeherrschung; ~ **day** Markttag; Börsentag; ~ **dealer** Händler auf dem Markt; ~ **dealings** *Br* Börsenhandel; ~ **demands** Marktbedürfnisse; ~ **dominating enterprise** marktbeherrschendes Unternehmen; ~ **dues** Marktgebühren, Standgebühren

market economy Marktwirtschaft; **free (social)** ~ freie (soziale) Marktwirtschaft

market, ~ **floor** Börsensaal, ~ **fluctuations** Konjunkturschwankungen; ~ **forces** Marktkräfte; ~ **foreclosure** *Am*[18a] Marktzutrittsbeschränkung; ~ **gap** Marktlücke; ~ **garden** Handelsgärtnerei; ~ **investigation** Marktuntersuchung; ~ **leaders** führende Börsenwerte; ~ **letters** *Am (tägl.)* Marktberichte; ~ **loss** Kursverlust

market maker *Br* (*Börse*) Wertpapierhändler (*der durch Nennung von Ankaufs- und Verkaufskursen dem Markt die notwendige Liquidität bringt*); **gilt -edged** ~ (GEMM) Wertpapierhändler für Staatspapiere

market, M~News Börsenbericht (*als Überschrift in Zeitungen*); ~ **niche** Marktnische; ~ **of issue** Emissionsmarkt; ~ **order** unlimitierter Börsenauftrag, Bestensauftrag (*opp. limit order*); ~ **organization** (EG) Marktordnung, Marktorganisation (*→common organization of the market*); ~ **oriented** marktorientiert; ~ **outlet** Verkaufsstelle

market overt *bes. Br* offener Markt

Jeder Markt oder sonstiger Platz, dem durch besonderes Privileg oder Ortsgebrauch diese Sonderstellung eingeräumt ist (jedes Geschäft in der Londoner City gilt als ~ im Sinne von s. 22[1] des Sales of Goods Act, 1893). Beim gutgläubigen Kauf auf dem ~ ist Erwerb vom Nichteigentümer möglich (sofern es sich nicht um Crown property handelt oder um gestohlene Güter und der Bestohlene die Verurteilung des Diebes herbeigeführt hat)

market, ~ **penetration** Marktdurchdringung; ~ **performance** Marktleistung; ~ **place** Marktplatz; Handelsplatz; ~ **position** Marktlage, Marktposition; ~ **potential** Marktpotential, Absatzmöglichkeit

market power Marktmacht; Macht *(e-s Unternehmers)* auf dem Markt; **dominant** ~ marktbeherrschende Stellung

market price Marktpreis; Kurswert; **usual ~s** marktgängige Preise

market, ~ **profit** Kursgewinn; ~ **quotation** Kursnotierung; ~ **rally** Kurserholung; ~ **rate (of discount)** *Br* Diskontsatz der Geschäftsbanken; ~ **regulations** Marktordnung; ~ **report** Marktbericht; Börsenbericht, Kursbericht; ~ **research** Marktforschung; ~ **result** Marktergebnis; ~ **rigging** Kurstreiberei; ~ **saturation** Marktsättigung; ~ **segregation** Marktabriegelung; ~ **share** Marktanteil; ~ **share liability** (*Produkthaftpflicht*) Marktanteilshaftung; Haftung mehrerer (beklagter) Hersteller entsprechend ihrem Marktanteil; ~ **in ... shares** Markt für ... Aktien; ~ **sharing** Aufteilung des Marktes; ~ **sharing agreement** Marktaufteilungsabsprache; ~ **situation** Marktlage; ~ **splitting** Marktaufspaltung; ~ **stand** Marktstand; ~ **structure** Marktstruktur *(Anzahl und Größe der Unternehmen auf e-m Markt)*; ~ **support** Marktstützung; ~ **survey** Marktuntersuchung; ~**syndicate** Börsensyndikat; ~ **town** *bes. Br* Marktflecken; ~ **transactions** Börsengeschäfte, Börsentransaktionen

market value Marktwert; Kurswert; Verkehrswert; **fair** ~ (FMV) Marktwert, Tagespreis *(e-s Wirtschaftsgutes)*; **→foreign ~; present** ~ Zeitwert

market, absorptive capacity of the ~ Aufnahmefähigkeit des Marktes; **active** ~ lebhafter Markt; **agricultural** ~ Agrarmarkt; **assured** ~ sicherer Absatzmarkt; **at the** ~ *Am (Börse)* 1. zum Kurs; 2. *(bei Aufträgen)* bestens; **black** ~ schwarzer Markt *(→black)*; **bond** ~ Rentenmarkt; **brisk** ~ lebhafter Markt; **bull** ~ Haussemarkt; **buyers'** ~ Käufermarkt; **capital** ~ Kapitalmarkt *(opp. money ~)*; **cash** ~ *(Börse)* Kassamarkt; **commodity** ~ Warenmarkt, Rohstoffmarkt; **Common M~** →common 2.;

control of the ~ Marktbeherrschung; **covered** ~ Markthalle; **credit** ~ Kreditmarkt; **division of the** ~ Marktaufteilung; **domestic** ~ Binnenmarkt, Inlandsmarkt; **dull** ~ flaue (od. lustlose) Börse; **employment** ~ Arbeitsmarkt; **equity** ~ Aktienmarkt; **expansion of existing** ~**s** Ausdehnung bestehender Märkte; **export** ~ Exportmarkt; **fall in the** ~ Baisse; **flat** ~ s. dull → ~; **fluctuations of the** ~ Marktschwankungen, Konjunkturschwankungen; **(foreign) exchange** ~ Devisenmarkt; **forward** ~ *(Börse)* Terminmarkt *(opp. spot ~)*; **free** ~ *(Börse)* Freiverkehr *(→free)*; **futures** ~ *(Börse)* Terminmarkt; **grey** *Br (Am* **gray**) ~ grauer Markt; **heavy** ~ gedrückter Markt; **home** ~ s. domestic →~; **in the** ~ auf dem Markt (zum Verkauf) (s. *to be in the* →~); **inactive** ~ lustloser Markt; **inofficial** ~ *(Börse)* Freiverkehrsmarkt; **international** ~ Weltmarkt; **issue** ~ Emissionsmarkt; **labo(u)r** ~ Arbeitsmarkt; **lively** ~ lebhafter Markt; **money** ~ Geldmarkt *(→money)*; **off board** ~ *Am* Markt für nicht notierte Wertpapiere; **on the** ~ auf dem Markt (zum Verkauf)

market, open ~ 1. offener Markt *(Marktform, bei der jederzeit Mitbewerber auftreten können)*; *(Börse)* Freiverkehr(smarkt); **open** ~ **value** *Br (Erbschaftsteuer)* Marktwert, Wert auf e-m offenen Markt *(ein Vermögensgegenstand ist mit dem Wert anzusetzen, den er bei Verkauf zum Zeitpunkt des Todes auf e-m offenen Markt hat)*

market, open ~ 2. Offenmarkt-; **Open M~ Committee** *Am* Offenmarktausschuß *(vergleichbar dem Zentralbankrat der Deutschen Bundesbank; die Federal Reserve Banks dürfen nur mit Zustimmung des ~ Offenmarktgeschäfte durchführen)*; **open** ~ **considerations** s. open →~ policy; **open** ~ **operations** (or **transactions**) Offenmarktgeschäfte; **open** ~ **policy** Offenmarktpolitik *(Maßnahmen der Notenbank zur Regulierung des Geldmarktes durch An- und Verkauf von festverzinslichen Wertpapieren [meist Staatsanleihen])*

market, outside ~ *(Börse)*Freiverkehr *(→outside)*; **oversea** ~**s** Überseemärkte; **over-the-counter** ~ *Am* Markt für nicht notierte Wertpapiere, Freiverkehr(smarkt); **primary** ~ *Am* Vormarkt, Aufkaufmarkt *(dessen Hauptaufgabe es ist, Waren zu sammeln und weiterzugeben)*; **property** ~ *Br* Immobilienmarkt; **railway (railroad)** ~ *(Börse)* Markt für Eisenbahnwerte; **real estate** ~ Immobilienmarkt; **receptive** ~ aufnahmebereiter Markt; **rise in the** ~ Hausse; **in a rising** ~ bei anziehenden Kursen; **secondary** ~ (*Börse*) Umlaufmarkt; **sellers'** ~ Verkäufermarkt; **share** ~ Aktienmarkt; **share of the** ~ Marktanteil; **spot** ~ *(Börse)* Kassamarkt; **stagnant** ~ stagnierender Markt, Absatzstockung; **state of the** ~ Marktlage, Konjunktur; **steady** ~ fester Markt; **stock** ~ *Am* Aktienmarkt; Effektenbörse; →**street** ~; **at today's** ~ auf der heutigen Börse; **unofficial** ~ *Br* Freiverkehr(-smarkt); **weekly** ~ Wochenmarkt; **world** ~ Weltmarkt

market *v* auf den Markt bringen; in den Handel einführen

marketability Marktfähigkeit

marketable marktfähig, marktgängig; gangbar, absetzbar, *(gut)* verkäuflich; börsenfähig, börsengängig; ~ **equities** börsengängige Aktien

marketable securities börsenfähige Wertpapiere; Wertpapiere mit einem Börsenwert; **easily** ~ sofort realisierbare Wertpapiere

marketable title →title 2.; **M~ T~ Act** *Am* Gesetz zur Klärung der Rechtslage bei Grundeigentum *(cf. Recording Act)*

marketable value Marktwert, Verkaufswert

marketeer *Am* Verkäufer, Händler *(auf e-m Markt)*; →**black** ~

marketer *Am* Markthändler; Marktbesucher

marketing Marketing *(Gesamtheit der absatzfördernden Maßnahmen, umfaßt auch Marktforschung, Werbung etc)*;Vermarktung; Inverkehrbringen; Absatz(-); ~ **area** Absatzgebiet; ~ **association** Marketing-Verband, absatzwirtschaftlicher Verband; ~ **board** *Br (kartellartige)* Organisation zur Regelung des Absatzes bestimmter Agrarprodukte und zur Preiskontrolle; ~ **consultant** Berater für das Marketing; Absatzberater; ~ **cooperative** Absatzgenossenschaft; ~ **costs** Absatzkosten, Vertriebskosten; Vermarktungskosten; ~ **difficulties** Absatzschwierigkeiten; ~ **director** Marketing-Direktor, Leiter der Marketing-Abteilung; ~ **economy** Absatzwirtschaft; ~ **executive** leitender Angestellter für das Marketing; ~ **expert** →~ consultant; ~ **functions** absatzwirtschaftliche Funktionen; ~ **manager** Marketing-Direktor, Leiter der Abteilung Marketing *(in Großbetrieben)*; ~ **mix** gleichzeitige Einsetzung verschiedener Marketing-Instrumente *(Absatzförderung, Marktforschung, Preispolitik, Werbung etc)*; ~ **operations** absatzwirtschaftliche Maßnahmen; ~ **order** *Am* staatl. Absatzverordnung für Agrarprodukte; ~ **(policy)** Absatzpolitik, Vertriebspolitik; ~ **quotas** Absatzquoten; ~ **research** Marketingforschung

marketing, International M~ Federation (IMF) Internationale Absatzwirtschaftliche Vereinigung

marking →mark *v*

marksman *Am* Schreibunkundiger, der sein Kreuz *(als Unterschrift)* macht

marque, letters of ~ **and reprisal** *(älteres VölkerR)* Kaperbrief

marquis, -ess *Br* Marquis („Markgraf"), Marquise („Markgräfin") *(Adelsgrad zwischen duke und earl; Titel: most honourable)*

marriage Ehe; Eheschließung, Heirat; Hochzeit
Br Eine kirchl. Ehe (according to the rites of the Church of England) kann geschlossen werden: (a) nach erfolgtem Aufgebot (publication of banns of matrimony); (b) auf Grund einer vom Erzbischof von Canterbury erteilten besonderen Heiratserlaubnis *(special licence of marriage)*, die es Brautleuten ermöglicht, in jeder Kirche ohne Aufgebot zu heiraten; (c) auf Grund einer von einer zuständigen Kirchenbehörde erteilten allgemeinen Erlaubnis *(common licence)*; (d) auf Grund einer von einem →superintendent registrar ausgestellten Bescheinigung (certificate)[19] (auf Grund einer solchen Bescheinigung können nicht nur Church of England-Ehen, sondern auch standesamtliche Ehen [marriages in a registry] und Ehen der Katholiken, Juden, Quäker und →dissenters geschlossen werden)[20]

marriage, to annul a ~ e-e Ehe aufheben; **a** ~ **has broken down irretrievably**[23] e-e Ehe ist unheilbar zerrüttet; **to celebrate a** ~ e-e Ehe schließen, die Trauung vollziehen; **to contract** (or **enter into**) **a** ~ die Ehe eingehen (od. schließen); **to contract a new** ~ sich wiederverheiraten; **to give in** ~ *(jdn)* verheiraten (with mit); **to join in** ~ trauen; **to take a p. in** ~ jdn heiraten; **to solemnize a** ~ trauen, die Trauung vollziehen

Marriage Act *Br*[21] Ehegesetz
Zusammenfassung der gesetzlichen Vorschriften über Voraussetzung und Form der Eheschließung

marriage, ~ **articles** *(Hauptpunkte e-s)* Ehevertrag(es); ~ **broker** Ehemakler, Heiratsvermittler; ~ **brokerage** Heiratsvermittlung; Heiratsvermittlungsprovision; ~ **by proxy** Ferntrauung

marriage ceremony Trauung(sfeier); Eheschließung; **to perform the** ~ die Trauung vollziehen *(Standesbeamter od. Geistlicher)*; **to undergo a** ~ sich trauen lassen

marriage, ~ **certificate** Heiratsurkunde, Trauschein; ~ **contract** *Am* Ehevertrag; ~ **counselling** Eheberatung; ~ **failure** Scheitern der Ehe; ~ **guidance** Eheberatung; ~ **guidance counseller** *Br* Eheberater; ~ **in name only** Scheinehe; ~ **in a register office** (or **in the office of a superintendent registrar**) *Br* standesamtliche Trauung; ~ **licen|ce (-se)** *(Br kirchliche, Am amtliche)* Heiratserlaubnis *(auf Grund der Feststellung, daß kein Ehehindernis vorliegt; Br cf. common licence, special licence im Kommentar zu marriage)*; ~ **lines** *bes. Br* Trauschein; ~ **officer** *Br* Beamter, der im Ausland Ehen schließen kann *(z. B. ambassador, minister, consul etc)*; ~ **portion** Mitgift; ~ **rate** →rate 3.; **service** (kirchl.) Trauung, Traugottesdienst; ~ **settlement** Ehevertrag *(zwischen zukünftigen Ehegatten, in dem ein bestimmtes Vermögen für diese und deren zukünftige Familie festgelegt wird)*; ~ **within the prohibited degrees**[22] Ehe innerhalb der verbotenen Verwandtschaftsgrade

marriage, announcement of ~ Heiratsanzeige *(in e-r Zeitung)*; **annulment of** ~ Aufhebung der Ehe; **bar to** ~ Ehehindernis; **(irretrievable) breakdown of** ~ (unheilbare) Zerrüttung der Ehe; **by** ~ angeheiratet; **capacity to contract a** ~ Ehefähigkeit; **celebration of** ~ Eheschließung; kirchliche Trauung; →**ceremonial** ~; **church** ~ kirchliche Trauung

marriage, civil ~ standesamtliche Trauung; **to perform the civil** ~ standesamtlich trauen

marriage, →**common law** ~; **connected by** ~ s. related by →~; **connection by** ~ s. relation by →~; **consent to** ~ Heiratserlaubnis; Einwilligung zur Ehe; **covenant of** ~ Ehevertrag; **consummation of** ~ Vollziehung der Ehe; **dissolution of** ~ Auflösung der Ehe; **fictitious** ~ Scheinehe

marriage, Foreign M~ **Act** *Br* Gesetz über die Eheschließungen im Ausland
Der Foreign Marriage Act von 1892 regelt die Eheschließung im Ausland vor einem →marriage officer (einer der Brautleute muß die britische Staatsangehörigkeit besitzen).
Der Foreign Marriage Act von 1947 regelt die Eheschließung von im Auslandseinsatz befindlichen britischen Soldaten.
Der Marriage with Foreigners Act von 1906 regelt die Eheschließung eines englischen Staatsangehörigen mit einem Ausländer im Ausland od. in England

marriage, impediment to ~ Ehehindernis; **licen|ce (-se) of** ~ →~ licence; **mixed** ~ Mischehe; →**nullity of** ~; **party contracting a** ~ Eheschließender; **promise of** ~ Eheversprechen; **related by** ~ verschwägert; **relation by** ~ Schwägerschaft; **solemnization of a** ~ →solemnization; **valid** ~ rechtsgültige Ehe; **void** ~ Nichtehe *(bedarf keiner gerichtl. Auflösung)*; **voidable** ~ vernichtbare Ehe *(wegen fehlerhaften Zustandekommens; umfaßt die deutsche nichtige und aufhebbare Ehe)*; **witness to a** ~ Trauzeuge

marriageable heiratsfähig; ~ **age** heiratsfähiges Alter, Ehemündigkeit

married verheiratet (to mit); ehelich, Ehe-; ~ **allowance** *Br* persönlicher (Steuer-)Freibetrag *(für Eheleute)*; ~ **couple** Ehepaar; Eheleute; ~ **man** Ehemann; ~ **state** Ehestand; ~ **taxpayers filing separate returns** verheiratete Steuerpflichtige, die e-e getrennte Steuererklärung abgeben; ~ **woman** Ehefrau; ~ **woman in employment** berufstätige Ehefrau

Married Women's Acts *Am (einzelstaatl.)* Gesetze betr. das Vermögen von Ehefrauen
Diese Gesetze haben die nach Common Law bestehenden Beschränkungen der Vertragsfähigkeit der Ehefrau beseitigt und ihr die freie Verfügung über ihr Vermögen gegeben. Dies hat zur Gütertren-

nung in den Common Law-Staaten geführt, während in den 8 community property-Staaten der Güterstand weiterhin die allgemeine Gütergemeinschaft blieb *(cf. →community property)*

Married Women and Tortfeasors Act, 1935 *Br* →Law Reform (Married Women and Tortfeasors) Act

Married Women's Enabling Acts *Am* Gesetze, die der Ehefrau das Recht verleihen, Verträge zu schließen, über Eigentum zu verfügen etc

Married Women's Property Act, 1882 *Br* Gesetz betreffend das Vermögen von Ehefrauen
Br Das Gesetz führte die Gütertrennung ein. Es gilt heute noch, vor allem in der Bestimmung des s. 17[24], nach der ein Ehegatte in summary proceedings (d.h. schnell, unkompliziert) sein Eigentum von dem anderen Ehegatten herausverlangen kann, sowie in einigen Bestimmungen des →Law Reform (Married Women and Tortfeasors) Act
Am (einzelstaatl.) Gesetz, das der Ehefrau das Recht verlieh, in eigenem Namen Besitz zu erwerben und zu haben

Married Women (Restraint upon Anticipation) Act, 1949 *Br* Gesetz betreffend die Verfügungsbeschränkungen der Ehefrauen
Das Gesetz hat alle noch bestehenden Beschränkungen der testamentarischen und sonstigen rechtsgeschäftlichen Verfügungsmacht der verheirateten Frau abgeschafft

married, to get ~ sich verheiraten (to mit)

marry *v (jdn)* heiraten; (sich) verheiraten (to mit); trauen; **capacity to** ~ Ehefähigkeit; **engagement to** ~ Verlöbnis

marshal *mil* Marschall; *Br* Gerichtsbeamter, der den High Court-Richter auf der Rundreise begleitet; *Br* Vollstreckungsbeamter des High Court für Seerechtssachen; *Am* Dorfpolizist; Vollstreckungsbeamter *(der Bundesgerichte mit Funktionen e-s →sheriff)*; *Am (in einigen Städten)* Polizeidirektor; *Am (in einigen Städten)* Branddirektor *(der Feuerwehr)*; ~ **of the diplomatic corps** Zeremonienmeister; **Provost M~** *Am* Chef der Militärpolizei; **sky** ~ *Am* bewaffneter Flugbegleiter

marshal *v* ordnen; einordnen; aufstellen, zusammenstellen; *(feierl.)* (hinein)geleiten; **to** ~ **assets** e-n Verteilungsplan aufstellen zur Verteilung der Aktiven *(aus e-m Nachlaß od. e-r Konkursmasse)*; **to** ~ **facts** Tatsachen *(geordnet)* zusammentragen

marshalling gerichtl. Ordnung *(Regulierung der Haftung in Fällen, wo ein Schuldner mehrere Gläubiger hat, von denen der eine sich an mehrere Vermögensteile [funds], der andere nur an e-n Vermögensteil halten kann, zur möglichst gleichmäßigen Befriedigung der Gläubiger)*; ~ **yard** Verschiebebahnhof, Rangierbahnhof

Marshall Plan *Am* Marshall-Plan
Nach dem amerikanischen Außenminister Marshall benanntes Hilfsprogramm (European Recovery Program) für westeuropäische Staaten (von 1948)

martial court →court-martial

martial law Standrecht; Kriegsrecht; **according to** ~ standrechtlich; **lifting of** ~ Aufhebung des Kriegsrechts; **proclamation of** ~ Verhängung des Kriegsrechts; **to proclaim** ~ das Kriegsrecht verhängen; **to try by** ~ vor ein Kriegsgericht stellen

Mashreq countries *(Egypt, Jordan, Lebanon, and Syria)* Maschrik-Länder *(Ägypten, Jordanien, Libanon und Syrien)*

masonic lodge Freimaurerloge

mass Masse; ~ **arrests** Massenverhaftungen; ~ **circulation newspaper** Zeitung mit Massenauflage; **means of** ~ **communication** Massenkommunikationsmittel; ~ **demonstration** Massendemonstration; ~ **deportation** Massendeportation; **weapons of** ~ **destruction** Massenvernichtungswaffen; ~ **dismissals** Massenentlassungen; ~ **executions** Massenhinrichtungen; ~ **killings** Massenmord; ~ **media** Massenmedien *(Fernsehen, Radio, Presse etc.)*; ~ **meeting** Massenversammlung; ~ **merchandising** Warenhandel in großen Mengen; ~ **misery** Massenelend; ~ **observation** *Br (Meinungsforschung)* Massenbeobachtung, Beobachtung der gesamten Bevölkerung

mass-produce *v* in Massen (od. serienmäßig) herstellen; ~**d article** Massenartikel, Serienartikel

mass production Massenproduktion, Massenfertigung, Serienfertigung; ~ **goods** Massenartikel; ~ **industry** Massengüterindustrie

mass, ~ **survey** Reihenuntersuchung; ~ **unemployment** Massenarbeitslosigkeit

Massachusetts trust *Am (einzelstaatl. verschieden geregelter)* gesellschaftsähnlicher Zusammenschluß
Die Treugeber *(beneficiaries, die den Aktionären e-r AG entsprechen)* übertragen bestimmte Vermögenswerte auf ein Kollegium von Treuhändern *(trustees, die den directors of a corporation entsprechen)* gegen Entgegennahme von in der Regel übertragbaren Anteilscheinen *(shares trust certificates)*, mit denen die beneficiaries allein für die Schulden des Trust haften

master Meister, Handwerksmeister; Kapitän *(e-s Handelsschiffes)*; Dienstherr, Geschäftsherr *(opp. servant)*; *Br (aus der Reihe der barristers od. solicitors ernannter)* unterer Richter, Vorverfahrensrichter; *Am* Hilfsrichter *(im equity-Prozeß)*; *Am univ* Rektor *(e-s college)*; *Br* Lehrer; ~ **agreement** *Am* Mustertarifvertrag; *Br* Rahmenvertrag zwischen Händler und Finanzierungsinstitut bei Abzahlungskäufen *(cf. recourse agreement)*; ~ **and apprentice**

Meister und Auszubildender; ~ **and crew** (or **seamen**) Kapitän und Mannschaft

master and servant Geschäftsherr und Angestellter *(→employer and employee);* **law of** ~ *Br (individuelles)* Arbeitsrecht *(jetzt meistens employment law)*

master, ~ **budget** Gesamtetat; ~ **builder** Baumeister; ~**'s certificate** Kapitänspatent *(für Handelsschiff)*; ~ **contract** (*VersR*) Stammvertrag *(in der Gruppenlebensversicherung)*; ~ **craftsman** Handwerksmeister; ~ **file** Zentralkartei, Stammkartei; ~ **mariner** Kapitän *(e-s Handelsschiffes)*; **M~ of Laws** (LL.M.) höherer akademischer Grad der juristischen Fakultät; **M~ of the Rolls** (M.R.) *Br*[25] Richter des →Court of Appeal *(verantwortlich für die public records [Staatsarchive] und für Zulassung der solicitors)*

master, ~ **policy** Hauptpolice, Rahmenpolice *(bei Lebensversicherung für mehrere Leben); Br* Einheitspolice *(der solicitors für Schadenersatzansprüche wegen Fahrlässigkeit);* ~**'s protest** Seeprotest, Verklarung; ~ **schedule** Gesamtplan

master *v (Sprache etc)* beherrschen

mastery of the air Luftherrschaft

match monopoly Zündwarenmonopol

match *v* es aufnehmen mit; vergleichen (with mit); passen zu; passend zusammenstellen; **to** ~ **a th.** e-r Sache entsprechen (od. gleichkommen); **to** ~ **the sample** mit dem Muster übereinstimmen

matched, ~ **order** *Am (Börse)* Auftrag auf Kauf und Verkauf desselben Wertpapiers; ~ **samples** Vergleichsstichproben

matching Ausgleich (*z.B. Aktiva gegen Passiva*); gleich(kommend), entsprechend; ~ **principle** *Am (SteuerR)* Prinzip der Periodenzuordnung

mate (Arbeits-)Kamerad; (Handwerks-)Geselle; Schiffsoffizier *(unter dem captain); (Handelsmarine)* Steuermann; ~**'s certificate** (or **patent**) Steuermannspatent; ~**'s receipt** (M.R., m/r) *(internationales Seefrachtgeschäft) (der dem Versender ausgestellte provisorische)* Bordempfangsschein *(für die Übernahme von Ladungen);* **driver's** ~ Beifahrer

material 1. Stoff, Material; Baustoff; Unterlagen *(für Zeitungsartikel etc);* ~ **accounting** Materialabrechnung; ~ **assets** Sachwerte; ~ **consumption** Materialverbrauch

material costs Materialkosten; **direct** ~ direkte Materialkosten; **indirect** ~ Materialgemeinkosten

material, ~ **costing** Materialkostenermittlung; ~ **damage** Sachschaden; ~ **defect** Materialfehler *(→material 2);* ~ **handling** Materialtransport (*innerhalb e-s Betriebes*); ~ **issue** Materialausgabe; ~ **needs** (or **requirements**) Materialbedarf; ~**s requisition** Materialanforderung; ~ **testing** Materialprüfung; **basic** ~ Grundstoffe, Ausgangsstoffe; **building** ~ Baumaterial; **crude** ~ Rohmaterial; **defect in the** ~ Materialfehler; **direct** ~ Materialeinzelkosten; **faulty** ~ fehlerhaftes Material; **inferior** ~ schlechtes Material; schlechte Baustoffe; **investigating** ~ Ermittlungsmaterial; **issuance of** ~ *Am* Materialausgabe; **labo(u)r and** ~ Arbeitslohn und Material; **raw** ~ Rohstoff *(→raw);* **relevant** ~ Unterlagen; **sound** ~ gutes Material; **stock of** ~ Materialbestand; **writing** ~**s** Schreibmaterial

material 2. materiell; wesentlich; (rechts)erheblich; ~ **→alteration of an instrument;** ~ **benefit** materieller Vorteil; ~ **change of user** *Br* wesentliche Änderung im Gebrauch *(z.B. Umbau e-s Privathauses in ein Geschäftshaus);* ~ **circumstances** wesentliche Umstände; ~ **concealment** *(VersR)* Verschweigen e-s wesentlichen Umstandes; ~ **damage** wesentlicher Schaden; **non-**~ **damage** immaterieller Schaden; ~ **defect** wesentlicher Mangel *(→material 1.);* ~ **fact** wesentliche Tatsache; ~ **issue** wesentlicher Streitpunkt; ~ **→misrepresentation; in a** ~ **particular** in e-m wesentlichen Punkt; ~ **time** *(StrafR)* Tatzeit, entscheidungserheblicher Zeitpunkt

materially, ~ **altered** wesentlich geändert; ~ **injured** erheblich geschädigt

materiality Wesentlichkeit, Erheblichkeit

maternal relative Verwandte(r) mütterlicherseits

maternity Mutterschaft; ~ **allowance** *Br (wöchentliches)* Mutterschaftsgeld; ~ **benefits** *Br (Sozialvers.)* Mutterschaftsleistungen; ~ **leave** Mutterschaftsurlaub; **statutory** ~ **pay** *Br (vom Arbeitgeber zu zahlendes)* Mutterschaftsgeld

mathematical reserve *(VersR)* Deckungsrücklage, Prämienreserve

matricide Muttermord; Muttermörder *(cf. patricide)*

matriculate *v univ* (sich) immatrikulieren (lassen)

matriculation *univ* Immatrikulation

matrimonial ehelich; Ehe-; Heirats-; ~ **agency** Heiratsvermittlungsbüro; ~ **agent** Heiratsvermittler; ~ **causes** Ehesachen *(suits for divorce, nullity [of marriage], judicial separation und Br jactitation of marriage)*

Matrimonial Causes Act, 1973 (M.C.A.) *Br* zusammenfassendes Ehegesetz

Das Gesetz befaßt sich besonders mit Scheidung, gerichtl. Trennung und Nichtigerklärung der Ehe sowie mit →property (adjustment) orders, Unterhalt und Sorgerecht. Es gilt (abgesehen von einigen Vorschriften betr. →maintenance) nicht in Schottland und Nord-Irland

matrimonial, ~ **dispute** Ehestreitigkeit; ~ **home** eheliche Wohnung; ~ **home and contents** *Br* Familienheim und Mobiliar (Hausrat); ~ **jurisdiction** Zuständigkeit in Ehesachen; ~ **law** Eherecht; ~ **maintenance** *Br (von e-m Ehegatten an den anderen Ehegatten, aber auch an eheliche od. angenommene Kinder zu leistender)* ehelicher Unterhalt; ~ **matters** Ehesachen; ~ **obligations** eheliche Pflichten

matrimonial offen|ce (~se) Eheverfehlung, ehewidriges Verhalten; **to commit a** ~ e-e Ehewidrigkeit begehen

matrimonial, ~ **order** *Br (EheR)* gerichtl. Verfügung in e-r Ehesache *(betr. Unterhalt, Getrenntleben, Sorgerecht);* ~ **proceedings** Verfahren in Ehesachen

matrimonial property regime ehelicher Güterstand; **law applicable to the** ~ Güterrechtsstatut

matrimonial, ~ **suit** (Prozeß über) Ehesachen *(Br divorce, judicial separation, presumption of death and dissolution of marriage, and jactitation of marriage);* ~ **troubles** Eheschwierigkeiten

matrimony Ehe(stand); **contract of** ~ *Br* Ehevertrag; **to enter into** ~ in den Ehestand treten; **to join in** ~ trauen

matrix Matrize

matter Angelegenheit, Sache; **in the** ~ **of** (in re, Re) in Sachen; **in the** ~ **of the estate (of)** in der Nachlaßsache

matter, ~ **at hand** vorliegende Sache; ~ **at** (or **in**) **issue** Streitsache, Streitgegenstand; ~ **for discussion** Diskussionsgegenstand; ~ **in controversy** Streitgegenstand; ~ **in dispute** Streitgegenstand; ~ **of common concern** gemeinsame Belange; ~ **of consequence** wichtige Angelegenheit; Streitfall; ~ **of course** Selbstverständlichkeit; ~ **of discretion** Ermessensfrage; ~ **of fact** *bes. Am (strittige)* Tatfrage *(die von der →jury zu entscheiden ist; cf.* ~ *of law);* **as a** ~ **of fact** tatsächlich; ~ **of form** Formsache; ~ **of hono(u)r** Ehrensache; ~ **of law** Rechtsfrage *(die vom Gericht zu entscheiden ist; cf.* ~ *of fact);* ~ **of official concern** Dienstsache, amtliche Sache; ~ **of opinion** Ansichtssache; ~ **of prestige** Prestigefrage

matter of record aktenmäßig feststehende Tatsache; **to be a** ~ aktenmäßig feststehen

matter, ~**s of state** Staatsangelegenheiten; ~ **of substance** materiell-rechtliche Frage; **business** ~ geschäftliche Angelegenheit; **commercial** ~**s** Handelssachen; **to be a** ~ **for arrangement** besprochen (od. vereinbart) werden müssen; **to be a** ~ **of common knowledge** allgemein bekannt sein; **it is a** ~ **for concern** es ist beunruhigend; **to clear up a** ~ e-e Angelegenheit klären; **to handle a** ~ e-e Angelegenheit besorgen; **to settle a** ~ e-e Angelegenheit regeln; **as** ~**s stand** wie die Dinge liegen

matter *v* von Bedeutung sein, darauf ankommen, ausmachen

mature fällig *(bes. Wechsel);* reif; **after** ~ **deliberation** nach reiflicher Überlegung

matur|e *v* fällig werden; ablagern; **to** ~ **into a patent (grant)** zum Patent führen; **the policy** ~**s on** die Versicherungspolice wird am ... fällig

matured, ~ **bonds** *(zur Rückzahlung)* fällige Obligationen; ~ **claim** fällige Forderung; ~ **coupons** *Am (Bilanz)* noch nicht zur Zahlung eingereichte Kupons; **the obligation has** ~ die Verpflichtung ist fällig geworden

maturing on fällig (werdend) am

maturity Fälligkeit(stermin); Verfall(tag, -zeit) *(bes. e-s Wechsels od. e-r Obligation);* Laufzeit; Reife; ~ **age** *(VersR)* Endalter; ~ **date** s. date of→~; ~ **index** (or **tickler**) Verfallbuch; ~ **of the pledge** Pfandleihe; **at** ~ bei Verfall, bei Fälligkeit; **by** ~ *(VersR)* durch Ablauf *(opp. by death);* **date** (or **day**) **of** ~ Verfalltag, -datum; Fälligkeitstag, -termin; **date of** ~ **of a bill** Fälligkeitstag e-s Wechsels; **within the bill's** ~ innerhalb der Laufzeit des Wechsels; **on** ~ bei Fälligkeit, bei Verfall; **payment before** ~ **of the bill** Wechselzahlung vor Fälligkeit; **to pay a bill of exchange at** ~ (or **at its** ~ **date**) e-n Wechsel bei Fälligkeit zahlen

Mauritania Mauretanien; **Islamic Republic of** ~ Islamische Republik Mauretanien

Mauritanian Mauretanier, ~in; mauretanisch

Mauritius Mauritius

Mauritian Mauritier, ~in; mauritisch

maxim Maxime, (Rechts-)Grundsatz; ~ **of law** (or **legal**~) Rechtsgrundsatz, Rechtsmaxime

maximization of profits Gewinnmaximierung

maximize *v* maximieren

maximum Maximum; Maximal-, Höchst- *(opp. minimum);* ~ **amount** Höchstbetrag; ~ **benefit** (*VersR*) Höchstleistung; ~ **capacity** maximale Kapazität; ~ **carrying capacity** Höchsttragfähigkeit; ~ **discount** Höchstrabatt; ~ **duration of storage** Höchstlagerdauer; ~ **employment** Maximalbeschäftigung; Beschäftigungsoptimum; ~ **fee** Höchstgebühr; ~ **import duty** Höchstzoll bei der Einfuhr; ~ **liability** Höchsthaftung; ~ **limit** Höchstgrenze; ~ **load** Höchstbelastung; ~ **loan value** Beleihungsgrenze *(bei Wertpapieren);* ~ **number** Höchstzahl; ~ **output** (*Arbeit, Produktion*) Höchstleistung; ~ **penalty** (or **punishment**) Höchststrafe; ~ **permissible payload** höchstzulässige Nutzlast; ~ **price** Höchstpreis; *(Börse)* Höchstkurs; ~ **quota** Höchstkontingent;

~ **rate** Höchstsatz; *(Devisen)* Höchstkurs; ~ **rate of customs duties** Höchstzollsatz; ~ **salary** Höchstgehalt; ~ **sentence** Höchststrafe; ~ **speed** Höchstgeschwindigkeit; ~ **value** Höchstwert, obere Wertgrenze; ~ **wages** Höchstlohn, Spitzenlohn

mayhem *bes. Am* schwere Körperverletzung; Verstümmelung

mayor Bürgermeister; **Lord M~** *Br* Oberbürgermeister *(der City of London und einiger großer Städte)*; **L~ M~'s Show** *Br* Festzug des Oberbürgermeisters der City of London; ~ **and corporation** *Br* Bürgermeister und Rat (Stadtverwaltung)

mayor, to stand as a ~ sich als Kandidat für das Bürgermeisteramt aufstellen lassen

mayoralty Amt (od. Amtsperiode) e-s Bürgermeisters

McFadden Act *Am* Gesetz über das Verbot des Interstate-Banking zur Begrenzung der Geschäfte e-r Bank auf e-n Einzelstaat

McGuire Act *Am* (= Fair Trade Enabling Act) *(von 1925; cf. Miller-Tydings Act)*
Das Gesetz ermächtigte die Einzelstaaten, vertikale Preisbindungen auch für →nonsigners durch Gesetz verbindlich zu machen. Die meisten Einzelstaaten haben von dieser Ermächtigung durch Erlaß der →Fair Trade Acts Gebrauch gemacht

mean Mitte; Mittel-; Durchschnitt(swert); mittlere (-r, -s); durchschnittlich; gering, unbedeutend; ~ **due date** mittlerer Verfalltag; ~ **life** Durchschnittsleben; ~ **low water** (MLW) mittleres Niedrigwasser; ~ **number** Mittelwert; Durchschnittszahl; ~ **price** mittlerer Preis; Mittelkurs *(zwischen Kauf- und Verkaufskurs des Händlers)*; ~ **rate of exchange** Mittelkurs; ~ **spot rate** Kassa-Mittelkurs; ~ **time** mittlere (Sonnen-)Zeit; ~ **value** Durchschnittswert; Mittelwert; **arithmetical** ~ arithmetisches Mittel; Durchschnitt(swert)

meaning Sinn, Bedeutung; **prima facie** ~ *(MarkenR)* Unterscheidungskraft; **secondary** ~ *(WarenzeichenR)* Nebenbedeutung *(die aber zur Hauptbedeutung des Wortes im Verkehr wird; durch nachträgliche Verkehrsanerkennung erworbene Bedeutung)*; Verkehrsgeltung; **within the** ~ **of this law** im Sinne dieses Gesetzes

means (Geld-)Mittel, Vermögen; (Hilfs-)Mittel, Weg; ~ **of circulation** Umlaufmittel

means of communication Verkehrsmittel; Nachrichtenmittel; **rail, sea, air, telegraphic, radio and other** ~ Eisenbahn-, See-, Luft-, Draht-, Funk- und sonstige Verbindungen

means, ~ **of conveyance** Beförderungsmittel, Transportmittel; ~ **of evidence** Beweismittel; ~ **of payment** Zahlungsmittel; ~ **of production** Produktionsmittel; ~ **of subsistence** Existenzmittel; ~ **of transport(ation)** Transportmittel; Verkehrsmittel; Beförderungsmittel; ~ **test** Bedürftigkeitsprüfung; Feststellung der finanziellen Lage *(e-s Antragstellers)*; →**affidavit of** ~

means, ample ~ reichliche (od. genügende) Mittel; **to have ample** ~ **at one's disposal** über genügende Mittel verfügen

means, available ~ verfügbare Mittel; **limited** ~ begrenzte Mittel; **own** (or **private**) ~ Eigenmittel, Privatvermögen; **pecuniary** ~ Geldmittel; **of small** ~ minderbemittelt; **ways and** ~ →way 2.; **without** ~ unbemittelt, mittellos; **to be of independent** ~ finanziell unabhängig sein; **to find a** ~ e-n Weg finden; **to live beyond one's** ~ über s-e Verhältnisse leben; **to prove one's lack of** ~ s-e Bedürftigkeit nachweisen

measurable meßbar; *fig* absehbar; ~ **benefit to the enterprise** →benefit 1.

measure 1. Maßnahme, Maßregel; ~ **of assistance** Hilfsmaßnahme; ~ **of coercion** Zwangsmaßnahme; ~ **of control** Kontrollmaßnahme; ~ **of execution** Vollstreckungsmaßnahme; ~ **of precaution** Vorsichtsmaßregel; **coercive** (or **compulsory**) ~ Zwangsmaßnahme; **counter-**~ Gegenmaßnahme; **economizing** (or **economy**) ~ Sparmaßnahme; **emergency** ~**s** *pol* Notstandsmaßnahmen; **(as an) interim** ~ (als) Zwischenlösung; **precautionary** ~ Vorsichtsmaßregel; **as a precautionary** ~ vorsichtshalber; →**preliminary** ~**s**; **preventive** ~ vorbeugende Maßnahme; **security** ~ Sicherheitsmaßnahme; **to take (appropriate)** ~**s** (geeignete) Maßnahmen ergreifen (od. treffen), das Erforderliche veranlassen; **to take legal** ~**s** den Rechtsweg beschreiten

measure 2. Maß; Grad, Höhe; Ausmaß, Umfang; ~ **goods** →measurement goods; ~ **of damages** Bemessungsgrundlage für Schadensersatz, Höhe des Schadensersatzes; ~ **of value** Wertmesser; **cubic** ~ Hohlmaß; Raummaß; **in a great** ~ in hohem Maße; **linear** ~ Längenmaß; **made to** ~ nach Maß angefertigt; Maß-; **weights and** ~**s** Maße und Gewichte

measure 3. *Br* gesetzgeberische Maßnahme der →Church Assembly

measure *v* (ab-, aus-, ver)messen; **to** ~ **a ship** ein Schiff vermessen

measured, ~ **day rate** Tagesakkordsatz; **to be** ~ **by** berechnet werden nach; sich richten nach

measuring instruments Meßgeräte

measurement Messung, Vermessung; Maß; ~ **cargo** (or **goods**) sperrige Güter, Sperrgut *(opp. [dead] weight cargo)*; ~ **ton** Raumtonne; **certificate of** ~ (Schiffs-)Meßbrief; **(tonnage)** ~ **of a ship** Schiffsvermessung; **units of** ~ Einheiten im Meßwesen, Maßeinheiten

meat, ~ **inspection** Fleischbeschau; ~ **packing industry** Fleischkonservenindustrie

mechanic Handwerker; Mechaniker; Maschinenschlosser; ~**'s lien** →lien; **average** ~ **skilled in the art** *(PatR)* Durchschnittsfachmann; **motor** ~ Autoschlosser

mechanical mechanisch; maschinell; Maschinen-; ~ **bookkeeping** Durchschreibebuchführung; ~ **engineer** Maschinenbauingenieur; ~ **engineering (industry)** Maschinenbau(industrie); **mechanically propelled vehicle** Kraftfahrzeug

mechanization Mechanisierung, Technisierung; Umstellung auf Maschinenbetrieb

mechanize *v* mechanisieren, technisieren; auf Maschinenbetrieb umstellen

medal Medaille, Auszeichnung; Orden; **bar to a** ~ Ordensspange; **(Congressional) M~ of Honor** *Am* höchste Kriegsmedaille; **service** ~ Dienstauszeichnung; **to award a** ~ e-n Orden verleihen

meddle *v*, **to** ~ **in sb. else's business** (or **affairs**) sich in fremde Angelegenheiten mischen

media Werbeträger, Reklamemittel; (Nachrichten-)Medien *(Presse, Rundfunk, Fernsehen)*; ~ **advertising** Werbung durch Medien; ~ **analysis** Werbeträgeranalyse; ~ **landscape** Medienlandschaft; ~ **laws** Mediengesetze; ~ **research** Medienforschung, Werbeträgerforschung; **advertising** ~ Werbemittel, Werbeträger; **mass** ~ Massenmedien; **national** ~ *Am* Werbeträger, die über das ganze Land verbreitet sind; **(news)** ~ Nachrichtenmedien; **to run a** ~ **campaign** e-e Werbeaktion in den Massenmedien durchführen

mediate *v* vermitteln (between zwischen); **to** ~ **an armistice** e-n Waffenstillstand vermitteln (od. zustande bringen)

mediation Schlichtung, Vermittlung *(bes. in Arbeitsstreitigkeiten und internationalen Streitigkeiten; Am auch Ehestreitigkeiten)*; *(VölkerR) (spontane)* Vermittlung *(cf. conciliation)*; Güteverfahren, Schlichtungsverfahren *(opp. arbitration)*; ~ **agency** *Am* Schlichtungsstelle; ~ **committee** Vermittlungsausschuß, Schlichtungsausschuß; **Federal M ~ and Conciliation Service** (FMCS) *Am* Bundesschlichtungsamt für arbeitsrechtliche Streitigkeiten; **offer of** ~ Vermittlungsvorschlag

mediator Vermittler, Schlichter

Medicaid *Am* staatl. Gesundheitsdienst für Bedürftige *(cf. Medicare)*

medical ärztlich; ~ **advice** ärztlicher Rat; ~ **aircraft** *(VölkerR)* Sanitätsluftfahrzeug; ~ **attendance** ärztliche Betreuung; ~ **board** Gesundheitsamt; ~ **care** ärztliche Betreuung, Krankheitsfürsorge; ~ **certificate** (ärztl.) Attest; ~ **check-up** Gesundheitsüberprüfung; ~ **congress** Ärztekongreß; ~ **consultant** Facharzt

medical examination ärztliche Untersuchung; **compulsory** ~ Pflichtuntersuchung

medical, ~ **examiner** *Br* Amtsarzt, Vertrauensarzt; *Am* beamteter Arzt für die Leichenschau *(in Fällen gewaltsamen Todes oder Selbstmords; cf. coroner)*; ~ **(and surgical) expenses** Krankheitskosten; ~ **fee(s)** ärztliches Honorar; ~ **inspection** *Br* (amts)ärztliche Untersuchung; ~ **jurisprudence** Gerichtsmedizin; **M~ Officer of Health** (M.O.H.) *Br* Amtsarzt, Beamter des Gesundheitsdienstes *(der den lokalen Gesundheitsdienst unter sich hat)*; ~ **opinion** ärztl. Gutachten; ~ **payments coverage** *Am (VersR)* Deckung für Heilungskosten von Autoinsassen

medical practitioner praktischer Arzt; ~**'s liability** Arzthaftung

medical, ~ **referee** *Am* Amtsarzt, Vertrauensarzt; ~ **report** ärztlicher Bericht; ~ **service** Gesundheitsdienst; Sanitätswesen; ~ **specialist** Facharzt; ~ **superintendent (of a hospital)** Chefarzt; ~ **treatment** ärztliche Behandlung; **British M~ Association** (BMA) Britischer Ärzteverein; **General M~ Council** (GMC) *Br* Ärztekammer

Medicare *Am (auf Bundesgesetz beruhender)* Gesundheitsdienst (Krankheits- und Krankenhausversicherung) für Rentner *(cf. Medicaid)*

medicine Medizin; **M~s Act** *Br* Arzneimittelgesetz (*von 1968 und 1971*); **forensic** ~ Gerichtsmedizin; **licen|ce (~se) to practise** ~ ärztliche Approbation; **patent** ~ Markenmedizin; →**socialized** ~

Mediterranean, ~ **coastal states** Mittelmeeranrainerstaaten; ~ **countries** Mittelmeerländer; **protection of the** ~ **against pollution** Schutz des Mittelmeeres gegen Verschmutzung

medium 1. Mittel; Mittelsperson; Werbeträger, Reklamemittel *(cf. media)*; *med* Medium[26]; ~ **of exchange** Tauschmittel; ~ **of payment** Zahlungsmittel; **advertising** ~ Werbemittel, Reklamemittel; **through the** ~ **of** durch Vermittlung von

medium 2. mittlere(r, -s); Mittel-, Durchschnitts-; ~**s** mittelfristige Papiere *(opp. longs, shorts)*; ~ **and small(-scale) enterprises** Mittel- und Kleinbetriebe; ~**-dated** mittelfristig; ~ **income group** mittlere Einkommensgruppe; ~ **price** Mittelpreis, Durchschnittspreis; ~ **price range** mittlere Preislage; ~ **quality** mittlere Qualität; **good** ~ **quality** mittelfein *(Qualität)*; ~**-range nuclear missile** Mittelstreckenrakete; **car in the** ~ **range** Mittelklassewagen

medium-sized mittelgroß; ~ **concern** (or **establishment**) mittleres Unternehmen, Mittelbetrieb; ~ **town** mittlere Stadt
medium, ~-term mittelfristig; ~ **and long term debts** mittel- und langfristige Schulden; ~-**term loan** mittelfristiges Darlehen *(mit Laufzeit von 1–5 Jahren)*

meet *v* zusammentreffen, sich versammeln, zusammenkommen; treffen; sich treffen mit; tagen; *(Verpflichtung)* nachkommen; *(Wunsch)* erfüllen; entsprechen; **to ~ a bill** e-e Rechnung bezahlen; **to ~ a claim** e-n Anspruch erfüllen; **to ~ commitments** Verpflichtungen erfüllen (od. nachkommen); **to ~ competition** es mit der Konkurrenz zu tun haben; der Konkurrenz standhalten; **to ~ a condition** e-e Bedingung erfüllen; **to ~ the demand** die Nachfrage befriedigen; **to ~ one's engagements** →to ~ one's obligations; **to ~ sb.'s expenses** für jds Ausgaben aufkommen, jds Ausgaben decken; **to ~ one's liabilities** →to ~ one's obligations; **to ~ the needs** den Bedürfnissen (od. Erfordernissen) entsprechen; **to ~ an objection** e-m Einwand begegnen; **to ~ one's obligations** s-n Verpflichtungen nachkommen, s-e Verpflichtungen einhalten; **to ~ the payments** (Raten-) Zahlungen einhalten; **to ~ periodically** in regelmäßigen Abständen zusammenkommen; **to ~ a pledge** ein Versprechen einlösen; **to ~ sb.** jdn treffen; jdn kennenlernen; **to ~ sb. in a matter** jdm in e-r Angelegenheit entgegenkommen; **to ~ with an accident** e-n Unfall haben, verunglücken; **to ~ with approval** Billigung (od. Beifall) finden, gebilligt werden; **to ~ with a denial** bestritten werden; **to ~ with losses on the stock exchange** Verluste an der Börse erleiden; **to ~ with a refusal** e-e abschlägige Antwort erhalten, abschlägig beschieden werden; **to ~ the requirements** den Anforderungen entsprechen; die Voraussetzungen erfüllen; den Bedürfnissen entsprechen; **to ~ one's reward** s-e Belohnung erhalten; **the conference ~s in X** die Konferenz tritt in X zusammen; **the supply ~s the demand** →supply 2.

meeting (Zusammen-)Treffen, Zusammenkunft, Sitzung, Tagung; ~ **attendance fees** Sitzungsgelder; ~ **in camera** Sitzung unter Ausschluß der Öffentlichkeit; ~ **of creditors**[27] Gläubigerversammlung *(im Konkursverfahren)*; ~ **of members** Mitgliederversammlung; ~ **of minds** Willenseinigung; Übereinstimmung; ~ **of shareholders** Hauptversammlung *(e-r AG)*; Gesellschafterversammlung *(e-r GmbH)*; ~ **of stockholders** *Am* Hauptversammlung *(e-r AG)*; ~ **open to the public** öffentliche Sitzung; ~ **place** Tagungsort, Versammlungsort; Sammelplatz; Treffpunkt; ~ **room** Sitzungssaal
meeting, annual general ~ *Br* Jahreshauptversammlung, ordentliche Hauptversammlung *(e-r AG)*; **at a ~** auf e-er Sitzung; bei e-r Versammlung; **attendance at a ~** Teilnahme an e-r Sitzung; **calling** (or **convening, convoking**) **of a ~** Einberufung e-r Versammlung; **company ~** *Br* Gesellschafterversammlung; **corporate** (or **corporation**) ~ *Am* Gesellschafterversammlung; **extraordinary general ~** *Br* außerordentliche Hauptversammlung *(e-r AG)*; **first ~** *Br (KonkursR)* erste Gläubigerversammlung; **general ~** *Br* (ordentl.) Hauptversammlung *(e-r AG)*; **mass ~** Massenversammlung; **minutes of the ~** Sitzungsprotokoll; **notice of ~** Einberufung der Versammlung; **ordinary general ~** *Br* (ordentl.) Hauptversammlung *(e-r AG)*; **participation in a ~** Teilnahme an e-r Versammlung (od. Sitzung); **periodical ~s** regelmäßige Zusammenkünfte; →**place of ~; plenary ~** Plenarversammlung, Vollversammlung; **program(me) of ~** Sitzungsprogramm; **private ~** nicht öffentliche Sitzung; **regular ~** (of stockholders) *Am (ordentl.)* Hauptversammlung *(e-r AG)*; **special ~** Sondersitzung; **special ~** (of shareholders *Br*, stockholders *Am*) außerordentliche Hauptversammlung *(e-r AG)*; **statutory ~** *Br* konstituierende Hauptversammlung, Gründungsversammlung *(erste Hauptversammlung nach Gesellschaftsgründung)*
meeting, to address the ~ *(auf e-r Versammlung)* das Wort ergreifen; **to ask to address the ~** *(auf e-r Versammlung)* um das Wort bitten; **to withdraw the right to address the ~** *(jdm auf e-r Versammlung)* das Wort entziehen
meeting, to adjourn a ~ e-e Sitzung vertagen; **to appoint a day** (or **time**) **for a ~** e-e Sitzung anberaumen; **to arrange a ~** s. to fix a →~; **to attend a ~** e-e Versammlung (od. Sitzung) besuchen, an e-r Versammlung (od. Sitzung) teilnehmen; **to break up a ~** e-e Versammlung auflösen; e-e Sitzung aufheben; **to call** (or **convene, convoke**) **a ~** e-e Versammlung (od. Sitzung) einberufen (for 11 a.m. auf 11 Uhr); **to declare a ~ adjourned** e-e Sitzung vertagen; **to declare the ~ closed** die Sitzung schließen; **to discontinue a ~** e-e Sitzung abbrechen; **to fix a ~** e-e Sitzung anberaumen; **to hold a ~** e-e Versammlung (od. Sitzung) abhalten; **to open the ~** die Sitzung eröffnen; **to preside at a ~** in e-r Sitzung den Vorsitz führen; **to summon a ~** s. to call a →~; **a ~ was held** e-e Versammlung hat stattgefunden

meliorate *v* (sich) verbessern, *(Boden)* meliorieren

melioration Verbesserung; Melioration

melon *Am sl.* Riesengewinn; **to cut a ~** *Am* e-n Riesengewinn in Dividenden auszahlen

member Mitglied; ~ **as of right** Mitglied kraft

Rechts (od. kraft Amtes); ~ **bank** *Am* Bank, die Mitglied des →Federal Reserve System ist; ~ **country** Mitgliedstaat; ~ **country of the Convention** →Convention country; ~ **firm** *Am* broker-Firma, die Mitglied der Effektenbörse ist; ~ **government** Mitgliedsregierung; ~**s' meeting** Gesellschafterversammlung; ~ **nation** Mitgliedsstaat; ~ **of the board (of directors)** board-Mitglied; Mitglied des board of directors; ~ **of the cabinet** *pol* Kabinettsmitglied; ~ **of the committee** Ausschußmitglied; ~ **of a company** Gesellschafter; **M~ of Congress** *Am* Mitglied des Repräsentantenhauses; ~ **of the family** Familienangehöriger; ~ **of a firm** Teilhaber, Mitinhaber (e-r Firma); **M~ of Parliament** (M.P.) Parlamentsmitglied; *Br* Mitglied des Unterhauses; ~ **of the staff** Mitarbeiter; ~ **of a stock exchange** Börsenmitglied; ~**s present and voting** anwesende und abstimmende Mitglieder; ~**state** Mitgliedstaat

member, admission of ~s Aufnahme (od. Zulassung) von Mitgliedern; **affiliate** ~ angeschlossenes Mitglied; **alternate** ~ Ersatzmitglied; **associate** ~ assoziiertes Mitglied; **deputy** ~ stellvertretendes Mitglied; **expulsion of a** ~ Ausschluß e-s Mitglieds; →**founder ~; full** ~ Vollmitglied, ordentliches Mitglied; **honorary** ~ Ehrenmitglied; **life** ~ Mitglied auf Lebenszeit; **list of ~s** Mitgliederverzeichnis; **original** ~ Gründungsmitglied; **paying** ~ zahlendes (od. förderndes) Mitglied; →**private ~; withdrawal of ~s** Ausscheiden von Mitgliedern; **to accept** (or **admit**) **as a** ~ als Mitglied aufnehmen (od. zulassen); **to apply to become a** ~ Antrag auf Mitgliedschaft stellen; **to become a** ~ Mitglied werden; **to cease to be a** ~ (als Mitglied) ausscheiden (of aus); **to expel a** ~ ein Mitglied ausschließen; **to strike (a name) off the list of ~s** (jdn) als Mitglied ausschließen

membership Mitgliedschaft (in bei); Zugehörigkeit; Mitgliederzahl; ~ **association** *Am* nicht eingetragener Verein; ~ **card** Mitgliedskarte; ~ **corporation** *Am (nicht zu Erwerbszwecken gegründeter)* eingetragener Verein; ~ **dues** (or **fees**) Mitgliedsbeiträge; ~ **number** Mitgliedsnummer; ~ **register** Register der Mitglieder; **admission to** ~ Aufnahme (od. Zulassung) als Mitglied; **application for** ~ Beitrittsgesuch, -antrag; **cessation of** ~ Erlöschen der Mitgliedschaft; **compulsory** ~ Pflichtmitgliedschaft; **conditions of** ~ Aufnahmebedingungen; **declaration of** ~ Beitrittserklärung; **denial of** ~ Verweigerung der Aufnahme *(als Mitglied)*; **full** ~ volle Mitgliedschaft, Vollmitgliedschaft; **increase in** ~ Mitgliederzuwachs; **paid-up** ~ beitragsmäßiger Mitgliederstand, zahlende Mitglieder; **request for** ~ s. application for →~; **suspension of** ~ zeitweiliger Ausschluß aus der Mitgliedschaft; **withdrawal from** ~ Austritt *(als Mitglied)*

membership, to acquire ~ die Mitgliedschaft erwerben, Mitglied werden; **to admit to** ~ *(jdn)* als Mitglied aufnehmen; **to apply for** ~ Mitgliedschaft beantragen; **to cease** ~ als Mitglied austreten; **to commence** ~ als Mitglied eintreten; **to be ineligible for** ~ für die Mitgliedschaft nicht in Betracht kommen; **to lose** ~ die Mitgliedschaft verlieren; **to put a name down for** ~ Mitgliedschaft für jdn beantragen; **to withdraw from the** ~ **of** austreten aus; ~ **is open (to)** die Mitgliedschaft steht offen; ~ **is terminated** die Mitgliedschaft erlischt

memorandum (memo) *(kurze)* Aufzeichnung, Notiz, Vermerk *(über e-n Sachverhalt od. e-n Vertrag)*; Aktenvermerk; innerbetriebliche Mitteilung *(Anweisung der Abteilung e-er Behörde an e-e andere od. der Verwaltung e-r Gesellschaft an die verschiedenen Abteilungen)*; *(VölkerR)* Memorandum; *(SeeversR)* Haftungsbeschränkung *(hinsichtl. verderblicher Güter sowie kleinerer Schäden)*; ~ **book** Notizbuch, Vormerkbuch; ~ **check** *Am* vordatierter Scheck; ~ **clause** (*SeeversR*) Haftungsbeschränkungsklausel; ~ **decision** Entscheidung ohne Urteilsbegründung; ~ **endorsed on** Vermerk auf; ~ **for file** Aktenvermerk

memorandum in writing *(von den Parteien unterschriebener)* Vermerk über e-n Vertrag *(erforderlich zur Erzwingbarkeit bestimmter Verträge; Br*[28] *jetzt nur noch bei Grundstückskaufverträgen und Bürgschaftsverträgen)*

memorandum, ~ **of agreement** schriftlich abgefaßter Vertrag, Niederschrift e-s Vertrages; (*VölkerR*) Vereinbarung; ~ **of appearance** *Br* Anzeige des Beklagten, daß er sich vor Gericht verteidigen werde

memorandum of association *Br*[29] Satzung, Statut (*e-r Kapitalgesellschaft)*

Das memorandum regelt im wesentlichen das Außenverhältnis; es gibt insbesondere Namen und Zweck der Gesellschaft sowie Höhe und Stückelung des Nominal-Kapitals an (→*articles of association)*

memorandum, ~ **of deposit** *Br* Urkunde über die erfolgte Hinterlegung (*z. B. von Eigentumsurkunden; cf. deposit of title deeds*); ~ **of law** *Am* →law ~; ~ **of partnership** Gesellschaftsvertrag; ~ **of satisfaction** *Br (vom Registrar of Companies)* registrierte Erklärung, daß e-e Hypothek auf Grundbesitz der AG erloschen ist

memorandum of understanding (MOU) *(VölkerR)* Vereinbarung, Abmachung; *(EG)* Absichtserklärung; ~ **for cooperation in the field of liquid metal fast reactors**[30] Vereinbarung über Zusammenarbeit auf dem Gebiet der natriumgekühlten Brutreaktoren

memorandum, ~ **pad** Notizblock; **common** ~

Br Klausel der Lloyd's Policy, durch die für bestimmte Güterklassen der Bruchschaden von der Deckung ausgeschlossen wird

memorial Denkmal, Ehrenmal, Gedenkstätte; Gedächtnis-; Bittschrift, Eingabe, Petition; Klageschrift; *Br* Urkundenauszug *(für Registrierung der Urkunde);* **M~ Day** *Am* Volkstrauertag *(30. Mai);* ~ **park** *Am* Friedhof; ~ **plaque** Gedenktafel; ~ **publication** Gedächtnisschrift; ~ **service** Gedenkgottesdienst, Gedenkfeier; ~ **tablet** Gedenktafel; **to erect** (or **put up**) **a** ~ ein Denkmal (etc) errichten; **to submit a** ~ e-e Bittschrift überreichen; e-e Eingabe machen

memory Gedächtnis; Andenken; *(EDV)* Speicher; **in** ~ **of** zum Andenken an; **within living** ~ seit Menschengedenken

menace Drohung, Bedrohung

menial tasks untergeordnete Aufgaben

mens rea ("guilty mind") *(StrafR) (zur Strafbarkeit erforderliche)* Schuld *(cf. actus reus);* **requirement of** ~ Schulderfordernis

mental geistig, Geistes- *(opp. physical);* ~ **ability** geistige Fähigkeit; ~ **anguish** seelische Not; ~ **capacity** Zurechnungsfähigkeit; ~ **condition** Geisteszustand; ~ **cruelty** *Am* seelische Grausamkeit *(Eheverfehlung durch liebloses Verhalten);* ~ **defect**[31] Geistesstörung *(umfaßt krankhafte Störung der Geistestätigkeit und Geistesschwäche);* ~ **defectives** *Br* Geistesgestörte, Geistesschwache; ~ **deficiency** *Am*[31] →~ defect

mental disease Geisteskrankheit; ~ **or defect excluding responsibility** *Am*[32] die Verantwortung ausschließende Geisteskrankheit oder Geistesstörung; **hospital for ~s** *Am* psychiatrisches Krankenhaus

mental disorder[33] Geisteskrankheit; Geistesstörung; Geistesschwäche; **person suffering from (a)** ~ Geisteskranke(r); **suffering from (a)** ~ geisteskrank, geistesschwach; **to have sb. (medically) examined to ascertain whether he is suffering from (a)** ~ jdn auf s-n Geisteszustand untersuchen lassen

mental, ~ **disturbance** Geistesgestörtheit; ~ **element of an offen|ce (~se)** subjektiver Tatbestand e-r strafbaren Handlung

Mental Health, ~ **Act** *Br* Gesetz betr. Geisteskranke *(von 1983);* ~ **Review Tribunal** (MHRT) *Br* Anhörungsstelle (Beschwerdestelle) für alle Arten von zwangsweise eingewiesenen Geisteskranken; ~ **Review Tribunal Rules** *Br* Verfahrensgrundsätze des MHRT; **to apply to a** ~ **Review Tribunal (for discharge from detention)** *Br* sich an den MHRT wenden (zwecks Entlassung aus zwangsweiser Unterbringung in e-m psychiatrischen Krankenhaus)

mental, ~**home** →~ hospital; ~ **hospital** psychiatrisches Krankenhaus (*Br* →hospital); ~ **illness** Geisteskrankheit; **commitment to a** ~ **institution** *Am* zwangsweise Unterbringung in e-m psychiatrischen Krankenhaus; ~ **nursing** Krankenpflege der Geisteskranken; (~) **patient** *Br* Geisteskranke(r), Geistesschwache(r); ~ **reservation** →reservation 1.; ~ **strain** (or **stress**) geistige Belastung; ~ **work** geistige Arbeit

mentally, ~ **disordered** geisteskrank, geistesschwach; ~ **handicapped** geistig behindert; **physically and** ~ **handicapped** körperlich und geistig behindert

mention Erwähnung; Vermerk; ~ **of the inventor** *(PatR)* Erfindernennung; **hono(u)rable** ~ ehrenvolle Erwähnung; **to make** ~ **(of)** erwähnen

mention *v* erwähnen; **not to** ~ (ganz) abgesehen von; **to** ~ **sb. in one's will** jdn in seinem Testament bedenken

mentioned, ~ **above** s. above- →~; ~ **below** s. under- →~; **above-~** (a/m) oben erwähnt, obig; **hereinafter** ~ (or **under-~**) (u/m) unten erwähnt, nachstehend

mercantile kaufmännisch; Handels-; ~ **agency** (Handels-, Kredit-)Auskunftei; Handelsvertretung; Handlungsvollmacht; ~ **agent**[34] Handelsvertreter; *(auch)* Makler, Kommissionär; ~ **connection** Handelsbeziehung; ~ **custom** Handelsbrauch; ~ **establishment** Handelsniederlassung; Handelsfirma; ~ **law** Handelsrecht *(das gerichtl. anerkannte kaufmännische Gewohnheitsrecht; →law merchant);* ~ **marine** *Br* Handelsmarine; ~ **paper** *(börsengängiges od. marktfähiges)* Handelspapier; Warenwechsel; ~ **partnership** *Am* Handelsgesellschaft; ~ **practice** Handelsbrauch; ~ **system** Merkantilsystem; ~ **transaction** Handelsgeschäft

mercantilism Merkantilismus

mercenary, with ~ **intent** in gewinnsüchtiger Absicht

merchandise (mdse) Handelsware(n), Ware(n); Güter; Artikel; ~ **assortment** Warensortiment; ~ **in bond** Ware(n) unter Zollverschluß; ~ **broker** Warenmakler; ~ **exports** *Am* Warenexporte; ~ **for export** Exportware(n), Exportgüter; ~ **imports** *Am* Warenimporte; ~ **knowledge** Warenkunde; ~ **marking** Warenauszeichnung; ~ **trade balance** *Am* Handelsbilanz; ~ **traffic** Warenverkehr, Güterverkehr; ~ **turnover** Lagerumschlag; **article of** ~ Ware; Artikel; **stock of** ~ Warenlager

merchandise *v Am* Handel treiben; *(Ware)* kaufen und verkaufen

merchandising Merchandising; Warengestaltung und -darbietung *(im Rahmen der Vertriebs-*

taktik); Verkaufsförderung; ~ **(policy)** Verkaufspolitik, Absatzpolitik; **mass** ~ *Am* Warenhandel in großen Mengen

merchandiser *Am* beratender Verkäufer *(cf. merchandising)*

merchant (Groß-)Kaufmann, (Groß-)Händler; *Am* Einzelhändler, Ladeninhaber; ~**s** Kaufleute, Kaufmannschaft
merchant bank *Br* Merchant Bank
Die merchant banks widmen sich neben der Finanzierung des Groß- und Überseehandels auch dem Emissionsgeschäft; die bedeutendsten sind →accepting houses
merchant, ~**banking** *Am* Großkundengeschäft der Banken; ~ **flag** Handelsflagge; ~ **fleet** Handelsflotte; ~**man** Handelsschiff; ~ **marine** *Am*[35] Handelsmarine; ~ **navy** Handelsmarine; ~ **seaman** Matrose der Handelsmarine; ~ **seamen** Seeleute; ~ **service** Handelsschiffahrt; ~ **ship** (or **vessel**) Kauffahrteischiff; ~ **shipping** (M. S.) *Br*[36] Handelsschiffahrt
merchant, body of ~**s** Kaufmannschaft; **commission** ~ Kommissionär; **corporation of** ~**s** *Br* Handelsinnung; **coal** ~ Kohlenhändler; **export** ~ Exportkaufmann, Exporteur; **forwarding** ~ *Am* Spediteur; **import** ~ Importkaufmann, Importeur

merchantability marktgängige Qualität; Tauglichkeit *(für den Markt);* Marktgängigkeit; →**warranty of** ~

merchantable marktgängig, gangbar, gängig; ~ **quality** marktgängige (od. handelsübliche) Qualität *(Qualitätsbezeichnung für Ware mittlerer Güte)*

merchanting *Br* Handel, der darin besteht, daß Waren in einem Überseegebiet aufgekauft und in einem anderen verkauft werden; ~ **trade** Transithandel; ~ **transactions** Transithandelsgeschäfte

mercy Gnade; ~ **killing** Euthanasie, Tötung auf Verlangen; **appeal for** ~ s. petition for →~; **prerogative of** ~ *Br* →prerogative
mercy, petition for ~ Gnadengesuch; **to reject a** ~ ein Gnadengesuch ablehnen; **to submit a** ~ ein Gnadengesuch einreichen
mercy, petition for the exercise of Her Majesty's ~ *Br* Gnadengesuch

merge *v* aufgehen (lassen) (in in); (sich) verschmelzen (in, with mit); sich vereinigen; fusionieren; zusammenlegen
merged, ~ **companies** fusionierte Gesellschaften; **to be** ~ **into** aufgehen in

merger 1. Zusammenlegung; Aufgehen (in in); *(SchuldR)* Konfusion *(Vereinigung von Gläubiger und Schuldner in einer Person); (SachenR)* Konsolidation *(Aufgehen e-s geringeren Rechts an e-m Grundstück in ein weiteres); (StrafR) Am* Gesetzeskonkurrenz; ~ **of charges on property**[37] Vereinigung von Hypothekenschuld und -forderung in einer Hand; **M~ Treaty** *(EG)* Fusionsvertrag *(Vertrag zur Einsetzung e-s gemeinsamen Rates und einer gemeinsamen Kommission der Europäischen Gemeinschaften)*[38]
merger 2. Fusion, Verschmelzung, Unternehmenszusammenschluß *(durch Übernahme; cf. amalgamation, consolidation, take-over);* (Unternehmens-)Konzentration; ~ **authorization** Genehmigung von Unternehmenszusammenschlüssen; ~ **broker** Unternehmensmakler; ~ **clearance** *Am (AntitrustR)* Billigung der Konzentration; ~ **contract** Fusionsvertrag; ~ **control** Fusionskontrolle; Kontrolle von Zusammenschlüssen; **M~ Guidelines** *Am* Fusionsrichtlinien; ~ **negotiation** Verhandlung über Unternehmenszusammenschluß; ~ **of banks** Fusion von Banken; ~ **of enterprises** Unternehmenszusammenschluß; ~ **offer** Fusionsangebot; ~ **plan** Fusionsplan; ~**-type transaction** fusionsartiges Rechtsgeschäft
merger, bank ~ Bankenfusion; **business**[39] ~ Firmenzusammenschluß; Unternehmenszusammenschluß; **company** ~ Gesellschaftsfusion; **conglomerate** ~ konglomerater (Unternehmens-)Zusammenschluß (*Fusion [od. Zusammenschluß] von auf verschiedenen Märkten tätigen Firmen*); **corporate** ~ *Am* Fusion von Gesellschaften; **horizontal** ~ horizontaler (Unternehmens-)Zusammenschluß (*Zusammenschluß zweier konkurrierender Unternehmen*); **pre~ notification** *Am* Anzeige e-s geplanten Zusammenschlusses; **pre~ procedure** premerger-Verfahren *(wettbewerbsrechtl. Regelung über Unternehmenszusammenschlüsse);* **vertical** ~ vertikaler (Unternehmens-)Zusammenschluß (*die zur Erzeugung erforderlichen Zwischenprodukte sollen gemeinsam hergestellt werden*); **to advise a company on** ~**s** ein Unternehmen über Fusionen beraten

merit (das) Verdienst, (das) Berechtigte; *(günstige)* Tatsachen und Rechtspunkte; materielle Umstände *(die die Rechtsverteidigung e-r Person aussichtsreich erscheinen lassen; opp. procedural point);* ~ **bonus** *(einmalige)* Leistungszulage; ~ **goods** meritorische Güter; ~ **increase** Leistungszulage; ~**s of the case** das Wesen des Streitfalles *(im Ggs. zu den verfahrensrechtlichen Einzelheiten);* der entscheidungserhebliche Sachverhalt; ~**s of the defen**|**ce (~se)** wesentliche Punkte der Verteidigung; ~ **pricing system** *Am (Kraftfahrzeug-Vers.)* System, wonach die Haftpflichtversicherungsprämie bei unfallfreien Fahrern niedriger wird, von Fahrern mit Unfällen dagegen Aufzahlungen geleistet werden müssen; Bonus-Malus-System; ~ **rating** Leistungsbeurteilung *(von Beamten od. Angestellten); (etwa)* Personal- und Befähigungsnachweis; ~ **rating system** →~ pricing system; ~ **system** *Am* Verdienstsystem; Einstellung und Beförderung von Beamten nach Qualifikation *(opp. spoils system);* →**affidavit of ~s**

merit, (up)on the ~s in der Sache selbst; nach materiellem Recht; **on the ~s or in terms of amount** dem Grunde oder der Höhe nach; **decision on the ~s** Sachentscheidung; **dismissal on the ~s** Klageabweisung auf Grund e-r Sachentscheidung; **to admit the claim on the ~s** den Anspruch dem Grunde nach anerkennen; **to dismiss a complaint on the ~s** e-e Klage als unbegründet abweisen; **to deal with a case on its ~s** zur Hauptsache verhandeln; über den Grund des Anspruchs verhandeln; **to give a decision on the ~s of a case** e-e Sachentscheidung treffen; in der Hauptsache entscheiden

merit, the claim is devoid of ~ der Anspruch entbehrt jeder Grundlage; **the arguments were directed to the ~s or demerits of plaintiff's claim** die Vorbringen waren darauf gerichtet, ob der Anspruch des Klägers begründet sei oder nicht; **the petition has (no) ~** der Antrag ist (nicht) begründet; **the court regarded the appeal as being without ~s** das Gericht betrachtete den Einspruch (etc) als unbegründet; **to examine the ~s of a claim** e-n Anspruch auf s-e Berechtigung nachprüfen; **to have a defence (~se) upon the ~s** e-e Einwendung zur Hauptsache haben

merit *v* verdienen, wert sein; **to ~ special consideration** besondere Aufmerksamkeit verdienen; **an action is ~ed** e-e Klage ist geboten

meritocracy Leistungsgesellschaft

meritorious verdienstvoll; berechtigt, begründet

mesne dazwischenliegend, Zwischen-; in der Zwischenzeit erfolgt; ~ **process** *Am* Zwischenverfahren; ~ **profits** *Br* in der Zwischenzeit erlangter Gewinn *(Nutzungen, die ein unrechtmäßiger Inhaber von Grundbesitz bezog)*

mess, officers' ~ Offizierskasino

message Nachricht, Mitteilung; Botschaft; Botengang; *Am* amtliche Mitteilung *(des Präsidenten, der Gouverneure);* ~ **in code** (or **cipher**) verschlüsselte Nachricht; ~ **of good wishes** Glückwunsch(telegramm); **delivery of a ~** Übermittlung e-r Nachricht; **New Year's ~** *dipl* Neujahrsansprache; **radio ~** Radiomitteilung; **State of the Union M~** *Am* Bericht über die Lage der Nation *(dem Congress vom Präsidenten vorgelegter Rechenschaftsbericht);* **telephone ~** telefonische Mitteilung; **to address a ~ to** *dipl* e-e Botschaft richten an; **to carry a ~** e-e Botschaft überbringen; **to leave a ~** e-e Mitteilung hinterlassen; **to run ~s** Botengänge machen; **to take a ~** e-e Mitteilung entgegennehmen; e-e Mitteilung überbringen

messenger Bote; Kassenbote; Kurier; *Br* Gerichtsdiener *(beim Konkursgericht);* ~ **boy** Laufbursche, Botenjunge; **~'s fee** Botenlohn; ~ **service** Botendienst; **Foreign M~s' Service** *dipl* Kurierabteilung; **office ~** Bürobote; **Queen's M~** *Br* Königl. Kurier

Messrs. *(Abk. für Messieurs) Fr* Herren, Firma *(abgekürzt vor dem Namen e-r aus mehreren Personen bestehenden Firma)*

messuage Wohnhaus mit Hof und Grundbesitz; Anwesen

metage *(amtl.)* Messen (od. Wiegen) *(von Kohle, Getreide etc);* Meßgeld, Wiegegebühr

metal Metall; ~ **industry** Metallindustrie; ~ **manufacturing** (or **processing**) Metallverarbeitung; ~ **products** Metallwaren; **~-sheet** Blech; ~ **worker** Metallarbeiter; **European M~workers' Federation** (EMF) Europäischer Metallarbeiterverband (EMV)

metal, base ~ unedles Metall; **basic ~ industries** metallurgische Grundindustrien; **London M~ Exchange** (LME) Londoner Metallbörse *(für Kupfer, Zinn, Blei und Zink);* **nonferrous ~s** Nichteisenmetalle, NE-Metalle; **precious ~** Edelmetall

metallic Metall-; ~ **currency** Metallgeld, Hartgeld; Metallgeldumlauf; Metallwährung *(opp. paper currency);* ~ **money** Metallgeld, Hartgeld; ~ **standard** Metallwährung *(opp. paper standard);* **non-~ minerals industry** Industrie der Nichterz-Minerale

metallurgic Metall-, Hütten-; **~industry** Hüttenindustrie

mete *v*, **to ~ out punishment** Strafe zumessen

meteorological Wetter-; ~ **report** Wetterbericht; ~ **satellite** Wettersatellit; →**European Organization for the Exploitation of M~ Satellites;** ~ **service(s)** Wetterdienst

Meteorological, World M~ Organization (WMO) Weltorganisation für Meteorologie *(→world)*

meter Zähler; (Meß-)Uhr; *Am* Meter; **electricity ~** Stromzähler; **to read the gas ~** die Gasuhr ablesen

metes and bounds *Am* Grenzlinien *(e-s Grundstücks)*

method Methode; ~ **of calculation** Berechnungsart; ~ **of financing** Finanzierungsart; ~ **of manufacture** Herstellungsverfahren; ~ **of reference** Zitierweise; ~ **of voting** Abstimmungsart; ~ **of working** Arbeitsmethode; **~s study** Arbeitsmethoden-Untersuchung

Methodism *eccl* Methodismus

Methodist *eccl* Methodist; **M~ Ecumenical Conference** Methodistische Weltkonferenz

metric metrisch; ~**system** metrisches *(auf Meter und Kilogramm beruhendes)* Maß- und Gewichtssystem; ~ **ton** (M. T.) metrische Tonne *(1000 kg)*; ~ **units** metrische Einheiten; **to go** ~ *Br* sich auf das metrische System umstellen

metrication *Br* Umstellung auf das metrische System

metrology Meßwesen; →**International Organization of Legal** ~

metropolis Hauptstadt, Metropole; **commercial** ~ Handelsmetropole

metropolitan Großstadt-; hauptstädtisch, großstädtisch; Großstädter; *eccl* Metropolit; Erzbischof; erzbischöflich; ~ **and overseas territories** Heimat- und Überseegebiete; ~ **area** Großstadtgebiet, Gebiet großer Städte; ~ **country** Mutterland; ~ **districts** *Br* Stadtbezirke außerhalb Londons *(Unterabteilungen der →counties)*; **non-**~ **districts** *Br* weniger dicht besiedelte Bezirke; **M**~ **France** das französische Mutterland *(opp. dependencies overseas)*; **M**~ **Police districts** *Br* Polizeibezirke von Groß-London; ~ **(stipendiary) magistrate** *Br* →magistrate; ~ **territory** Mutterland; Heimatgebiet; **non-**~ **territories** außerhalb des Mutterlandes gelegene Gebiete; *(auch)* nichteuropäische Gebiete

Mexican Mexikaner, ~in; mexikanisch; **United** ~ **States** Vereinigte Mexikanische Staaten

Mexico Mexiko

MI 5, MI 6 *Br* Geheimdienst, Nachrichtendienst *(→Military Intelligence)*

Michaelmas *Br* Michaelistag *(29. September, Quartalstag)*

microchip cards *(EDV)* Karten mit Mikroschaltung

microeconomics Mikroökonomie *(opp. macroeconomics)*

mid mitten, in der Mitte befindlich; Mittel-; *(Bankwesen)* Medio *(der 15. e-s Monats)*; **the** ~ **1980s** Mitte der 80er Jahre; ~**-channel** *(VölkerR)* Talweg *(Mittellinie von Flüssen)*, **M**~ **Europe(an) Time** (M. E. T.) Mitteleuropäische Zeit (MEZ); ~**-June** Mitte Juni; **the M**~**lands** Mittelengland *(das Hauptindustriegebiet Englands)*, ~**-month** Medio-; ~**-month account** (or **settlement**) Medioabrechnung; ~**-term election** *Am* Zwischenwahl zum Kongreß *(während der Halbzeit der Amtsperiode)*; ~**-year dividend** Halbjahresdividende; ~**-year settlement** Halbjahresabrechnung

middle Mitte; mittlere (-r, -s); Mittel-; ~ **class (-es)** Mittelstand; Bürgertum; ~ **class car** Wagen der Mittelklasse; ~ **course** (in politics) mittlerer Kurs; **the** ~ **four** (or **4**) *Br (Produktenbörse)* die mittleren vier (warmen) Monate *(Mai, Juni, Juli, August)*; ~ **income group** mittlere Einkommensgruppe, Mittelstand

middleman *com* Zwischenhändler, Mittelsperson; Vermittler; ~**'s business** Zwischenhandel; ~**'s profit** Zwischengewinn

middle, ~ **management** mittlere Führungskräfte *(cf. top management)*; ~**-of the-road policy** Politik des Mittelweges; ~**-of the-roaders** Politiker, die auf dem gemäßigten Flügel ihrer Partei stehen; **in the** ~ **of his speech** mitten in s-r Rede; ~ **price** Mittelpreis; Mittelkurs; ~**-ranking states** Staaten mittlerer Größe; ~ **rate** Mittelkurs; ~**-sized** von mittlerer Größe; **M**~ **Temple** *Br* (Gebäude e-r) Barrister-Innung *(cf. Inns of Court)*

middling Mittelsorte, Ware(n) mittlerer Qualität

midnight deadline *Am*[40] Schlußtermin Mitternacht

Midsummer day *Br* Johannistag *(24. Juni, Quartalstag)*

midway *(VölkerR)* Talweg *(mittlere Fahrrinne)*

midwife[41] Hebamme

MIGA →Multilateral Investment Guarantee Agency

might Macht; **industrial** ~ industrielle Macht

migrant (Aus-, Ab-, Zu-)Wanderer; ab- und zuwandernd; ~ **for employment** →~ labo(u)r; ~ **labo(u)r** (or **worker**) Wanderarbeitnehmer; **organized transfer of** ~**s**[41a] organisierte Beförderung von Auswanderern

migration Wanderung; Abwanderung; Zuwanderung; ~ **of labo(u)r** Arbeitskräftewanderung; ~ **of money** Abwanderung des Kapitals; **Convention concerning M**~ **for Employment**[42] Übereinkommen über Wanderarbeiter; **International Organization for M**~[42a] Internationale Organisation für Wanderung; **right of free** ~ Freizügigkeit

mile Meile *(1,609 km)*; **nautical** ~ Seemeile *(1,852 km) (seit 1970 ersetzt durch:)* **international nautical** ~ Meile für See und Luftverkehr (1.50779 statute miles); **sea** ~ Seemeile; **statute** ~[43] (englische) Meile *(1,609 km)*; **three-**~ **limit** Dreimeilengrenze

mileage zurückgelegte Strecke *(in Meilen)*, Kilometerzahl; Meilengeld, Kilometergeld *(für Reisespesen)*; ~ **allowance** Meilengeld, Kilometergeld

militant militant, aktiv

militarism Militarismus

militarist Militarist

military Militär; militärisch; ~ **academy** Militärakademie; ~ **age** militärpflichtiges Alter; ~ **aid** →~ assistance; ~ **airfield** Militärflugplatz; ~ **alliance** Militärbündnis; ~ **area** Kriegsgebiet; *(SeekriegsR)* Seesperre; Sperrgebiet; **(furnishing of)** ~ **assistance** Militärhilfe, militärische Hilfeleistung; ~ **attaché** Militärattaché; ~ **authorities** Militärbehörden; ~ **balance** militärisches Gleichgewicht; ~ **base** Stützpunkt; ~ **budget** Militärhaushalt, Verteidigungshaushalt; ~ **cemetery** Soldatenfriedhof; ~ **code** Militärstrafgesetzbuch; ~ **commission** *Am* Militärgericht *(urteilt über Verstöße von Zivilpersonen nach →martial law)*; ~ **convention** *(älteres VölkerR)* Militärkonvention; ~ **coup (d'état)** Militärputsch; ~ **criminal law** Wehrstrafrecht; ~ **dictatorship** Militärdiktatur; ~ **court** Militärgericht, Kriegsgericht *(→court martial)*; ~ **establishment** stehendes Heer; ~ **execution** standrechtliche Erschießung; ~ **facilities** militärische Anlagen; ~ **federalism** *Am* verfassungsrechtlich festgelegtes Nebeneinanderbestehen der Bundesstreitmacht und einzelstaatl. Nationalgarde *(cf. National Guard)*; ~ **government** Militärregierung *(Militärverwaltung im besetzten Feindesland)*; ~ **hono(u)rs** militärische Ehrenbezeugungen; ~ **hospital** Lazarett; ~ **hospital ship** Lazarettschiff; ~ **identification card** *Am* Wehrpaß; ~ **installations** militärische Anlagen; ~ **integration** militärische Integration

Military Intelligence (M. I.) *Br* (Militärischer) Nachrichtendienst (MND); **MI 5** *Br* Amt für innere Sicherheit und Abwehr; **MI 6** *Br* Amt für Auslandsnachrichtendienst *(entspricht etwa dem BND)*

military, ~ **junta** Militärjunta; ~ **jurisdiction** Militärgerichtsbarkeit; ~ **law** Militärstrafrecht; Wehrstrafrecht; *(im weiteren Sinne:)* Militärrecht, Wehrrecht; ~ **leave** *Am* Urlaub; ~ **mission** Militärmission; ~ **objective** militärisches Ziel; ~ **offen|ces (~ses)** militärische strafbare Handlungen; ~ **pay** Wehrsold; ~ **pay book** Soldbuch; ~ **police** Militärpolizei; ~ **policy** Wehrpolitik; ~ **post** Feldpost; ~ **power** Militärmacht; Kriegsmacht

military service Militärdienst, Wehrdienst; **compulsory** ~ allgemeine Wehrpflicht (*Br* →National Service); **discharge from** ~ Entlassung aus dem Wehrdienst; **exempt from** ~ vom Wehrdienst befreit, unabkömmlich (uk); **fit for** ~ wehrdiensttauglich; **liability for** ~ Militärdienstpflicht, Wehrpflicht; **liable for** ~ militärdienstpflichtig, wehrpflichtig; **universal compulsory** ~ allgemeine Wehrpflicht; **to be called up for** ~ zum Militärdienst einberufen werden; **to be deferred** (or **postponed**) **from** ~ vom Militärdienst zurückgestellt werden; **to render** ~ Militärdienst leisten

military, ~ **sovereignty** Wehrhoheit; ~ **stores** (Vorräte an) Kriegsmaterial; ~ **target** militärisches Ziel; ~ **testament** formloses Testament e-r Militärperson *(im Krieg)*; ~ **training** militärische Ausbildung; ~ **tribunal** Militärgericht(shof); **para-**~ **organization** militärähnliche Organisation

military, to accede to a ~ **alliance** e-m Militärbündnis beitreten; **to grant sb.** ~ **hono(u)rs** jdm militärische Ehren erweisen; **to set up a** ~ **dictatorship** e-e Militärdiktatur errichten

militia[44] Miliz, Bürgerwehr *(opp. regular forces)*

mill Mühle; Spinnerei; Fabrik; ~**-owner** Mühlenbesitzer; Spinnereibesitzer; Fabrikbesitzer; **paper-**~ Papierfabrik; **rolling** ~ Walzwerk; **saw** ~ Sägewerk

millenium, the third ~ das 3. Jahrtausend

Miller-Tydings Act *Am* Gesetz zum Schutze vor Preisbindungen *(von 1937)*

Das Gesetz nahm gewisse Arten der vertikalen Preisbindung vom grundsätzlichen Verbot des →Sherman Act aus und ermächtigte die Einzelstaaten, die →Fair Trade Acts zu erlassen. Es ist durch den McGuire Act überholt, welcher die umstrittene Bindung von →nonsigners gestattete

milliard *Br* Milliarde *(Am billion)*

millinery Modewaren

milling industry, products of the ~ Müllereierzeugnisse

million Million

millionaire Millionär

mimeograph Vervielfältigungsapparat

mimeograph *v* vervielfältigen; ~**ing** Vervielfältigung; ~**ing department** Vervielfältigungsbüro

Mincing Lane Londoner Tee-, Kaffee-, Gummibörse

mind Verstand; Meinung, Ansicht; Gesinnung; Neigung, Absicht; **bearing in** ~ in dem Bewußtsein; **presence of** ~ Geistesgegenwart; **of sound** ~ →sound 2.; **state of** ~ Geisteszustand; **to my** ~ meiner Meinung nach; meines Erachtens; **of →unsound** ~; **to bear in** ~ Rechnung tragen, bedenken; **to bring** (or **call**) **to sb.'s** ~ jdn erinnern an; **to change one's** ~ s-e Ansicht ändern; **to make up one's** ~ sich entschließen

minded, feeble ~ geistesschwach; **like-**~ gleichgesinnt; **politically** ~ politisch gesinnt

mindful eingedenk, bewußt; **to be** ~ **(of)** sich bewußt sein, berücksichtigen

mine[45] 1. Bergwerk, Grube, Zeche; ~**s** Bergwerksaktien, Montanwerte; Kuxe; ~ **of information** *fig* Informationsquelle; Fundgrube an Informationen; ~ **owner** Bergwerkseigentümer; Zechenbesitzer; ~ **surveyor** Markscheider; ~ **worker** Bergarbeiter; **National Union of M~workers** (NUM) *Br* Bergarbeitergewerkschaft; **accident in a** ~ Grubenunglück; **coal** ~ Kohlenzeche; **gold** ~ Goldbergwerk; *fig* Goldgrube; **share in a** ~ Kux; **silver** ~ Silberbergwerk; **to apply for permission to work a** ~ Mutung einlegen, muten; **to be engaged in working ~s** Bergbau betreiben

mine 2. *mil* Mine; ~ **barrier** Minensperre; ~ **clearance** Minenräumung; ~ **field** Minenfeld; ~ **layer** Minenleger; ~ **sweeper** Minenräumboot; ~ **sweeping** Minenräumen; ~ **thrower** Minenwerfer; **contact** ~ Tretmine; **floating** ~ Treibmine; **risk of ~s** Minengefahr; **to lay ~s** Minen legen; **to strike a** ~ auf e-e Mine laufen; **to sweep ~s** Minen räumen

mine *v (Bodenschätze)* abbauen, gewinnen; mit Minen belegen, verminen

mined vermint; ~ **area** Minenfeld, Minensperrgebiet

miner Bergarbeiter, Grubenarbeiter, Kumpel; Minenleger; **~s' association** Knappschaft; **~s' benefit fund** Knappschaftskasse; **~s' insurance** Knappschaftsversicherung; **M~s' International Federation** (M. I. F.) Internationaler Bergarbeiterverband (*Sitz:* London)

mineral Mineral; Mineral-, mineralisch; ~ **coal** Steinkohle

mineral deposits Mineralvorkommen; **spot giving signs of** ~ Stelle mit Anzeichen für Mineralvorkommen *(→prospect)*

mineral, ~ **fuels** mineralische Brennstoffe; ~ **oil** Mineralöl, Erdöl; ~ **oil extraction** Erdölgewinnung; ~ **resources** mineralische Rohstoffe, Bodenschätze *(Erze, Kohle, Erdöl, etc);* ~ **right** Bergwerksrecht, Schürfrecht; ~ **rights duty** *Br* Bergwerkssteuer; **to work ~s** Mineralvorkommen gewinnen

minimal damage Bagatellschaden

mini-max floater →floater 2.

minimize *v* auf ein Mindestmaß verringern, möglichst niedrig halten

minimum Minimum; Mindestbetrag; Mindestmaß; Mindest-

minimum age Mindestalter; **Convention Concerning M~ A~ for Admission to Employment**[46] Übereinkommen *(der Intern. Arbeitsorganisation)* über das Mindestalter für die Zulassung zur Beschäftigung

minimum, ~ **amount** Mindestbetrag; ~ **capital** Mindestkapital; ~ **circulation** Mindestauflage; ~ **claim** Mindestforderung; ~ **commercial quantities** handelsübliche Mindestmengen; ~ **contribution** Mindestbeitrag; ~ **damage** geringfügiger Schaden, Bagatellschaden; ~ **demand** Mindestbedarf; ~ **(initial) deposit** Mindestanzahlung; ~ **income** Mindesteinkommen; ~ **inventory** Mindestbestand; ~ **lending rate** (MLR) *Br* „Mindestleihsatz", Diskontsatz (der Bank of England) *(ersetzte 1972 die bank rate, kam aber 1981 außer Gebrauch);* ~ **margin requirement** *Am* Mindesteinschußpflicht *(→margin 2.);* **~/maximum** mindestens/höchstens; ~ **number** Mindestzahl

minimum paid-in capital *Am* Mindestkapital

Zahlreiche Einzelstaaten fordern, daß ein bestimmter Mindestbetrag des Grundkapitals eingezahlt ist, bevor die corporation ihren Geschäftsbetrieb aufnimmt

minimum, ~ **participation** Mindestbeteiligung; ~ **pay** Mindestlohn; ~ **penalty** Mindeststrafe; ~ **period of coverage** Mindestversicherungszeit; ~ **premium** Mindestprämie; ~ **price** Mindestpreis; ~ **rate** Mindestsatz

minimum reserve Mindestreserve; ~ **ratio** Mindestreservesatz; **required** ~ Mindestreservensoll

minimum, ~ **sales** Mindestumsatz; ~ **sentence** Mindeststrafe; ~ **speed** Mindestgeschwindigkeit; ~ **stock(s)** Mindestvorräte; ~ **value** Mindestwert; ~ **wage** Mindestlohn; ~ **weight** Mindestgewicht; ~ **yield** Mindestrendite; **to stand at a** ~ *(Börse)* niedrig stehen

mining Bergbau; Montan-; ~ **academy** Bergakademie; ~ **claim** Mutung; ~ **company** Bergwerksgesellschaft; bergrechtliche Gewerkschaft; ~ **concession** Bergwerkskonzession; ~ **corporation** *Am* →~ **company;** ~ **disaster** Bergwerksunglück, Grubenunglück; ~ **engineer** Bergbauingenieur; ~ **industry** Montanindustrie, Bergbau; ~ **law** Bergrecht; ~ **lease** Bergwerkspacht; ~ **licence (~se)** Bergbaukonzession; ~ **market** Montanmarkt, Markt der Montanwerte; ~ **partnership** *Am* →partnership; ~ **right** Bergbaurecht; Abbaurecht; ~ **royalty** Förderabgabe; ~ **shares** (or **stocks**) Bergwerksaktien, Montanwerte; Kuxe; **coal** ~ Kohlenbergbau; **open cast** ~ Tagebau; **underground** ~ Untertagebau; **to apply for a** ~ **claim** (or **concession**) muten

minister 1. *bes. Br* Minister *(innerhalb und außerhalb des Kabinetts);* **M~ of the Crown** *Br*[47] Minister; ~ **without portfolio** Minister ohne Geschäftsbereich, Sonderminister; **Cabinet M~** *Br* Kabinettsminister; **at the foreign ~s' level** auf Außenministerebene; **junior** ~ **(Parliamentary Under-Secretary [of State])** →secretary 3.; **Prime M~** Premierminister *(→prime);* **the** ~ **has resigned** *Br* der Minister ist zurückgetreten

minister 2. *(VölkerR)* Gesandter *(im engeren Sinne);* **~-counsellor** Gesandter *(zugleich Vertreter des Botschafters);* ~ **plenipotentiary and envoy extraordinary**[48] außerordentlicher Gesandter und bevollmächtigter Minister *(förml.*

Bezeichnung für den Gesandten); ~ **resident**[49] Ministerresident; **public** ~ *Am* Angehöriger der oberen Rangklassen der diplomatischen Vertreter

minister 3. *eccl* Geistlicher, Pfarrer *(Br freikirchlicher Geistlicher, bes. der Presbyterian und Nonconformist Churches, cf. dissenters; Am protestantischer Geistlicher)*

ministerial 1. *bes. Br* ministeriell; Ministerial-, Minister-; *Br* Regierungs-; ~ **benches** *Br* Sitze der Regierungspartei, Regierungsbank *(im Unterhaus);* **in his** ~ **capacity** in s-r Eigenschaft als Minister; **M~ Committee** Ministerausschuß; **M~ Conference** Ministerkonferenz; **at** ~ **level** auf Ministerebene; ~ **meeting** Versammlung der Minister; Ministertreffen; ~ **office** *Br* Amt e-s Ministers; ~ **order** *Br* Verordnung; ~ **responsibility** *Br* Verantwortlichkeit der Minister *(gegenüber dem Parlament);* ~ **session** Tagung der Minister

ministerial 2. untergeordnet, (nur) mechanisch, Verwaltungs- *(opp. judicial or discretionary);* ~ **act** (or **duty**) an Weisungen gebundene Verwaltungstätigkeit; ~ **officer** Verwaltungsbeamter *(dessen Pflichten nur ministerial sind);* ~ **services** (nur) mechanische Verwaltungsdienste

ministerial 3. *eccl* geistlich, priesterlich *(cf. minister 3.);* ~ **duty** Seelsorge

ministry 1. *Br* (Gesamt-)Ministerium, Regierung *(weitergehend als cabinet, umfaßt das gesamte Ministerkollegium)*

ministry 2. *Br* (Ressort-)Ministerium; **M~ of Agriculture, Fisheries and Food** *Br* Landwirtschaftsministerium

ministry 3. geistliches Amt, Priesteramt, Geistlichkeit *(cf. minister 3.)*

minor 1. Minderjährige(r) *(Person unter 18 Jahren); Am* Nebenfach; **~s are subject to various disabilities** Minderjährige sind nicht voll geschäftsfähig; **~s lack testamentary capacity** (*Br*[50] unless they are members of the forces on active service or mariners at sea) Minderjährige sind testierunfähig; **to manage the affairs of a** ~ die Angelegenheiten e-s Minderjährigen besorgen

minor 2. minderjährig; unbedeutend, geringfügig, klein; geringer, kleiner *(opp. major);* ~ **amount** kleiner Betrag, Betrag geringer Höhe; ~ **clergy** niedere Geistlichkeit; ~ **damage** kleiner (od. geringer) Schaden; ~ **defects** kleinere Mängel; ~ **interests** *Br*[51] Rechte niederer Ordnung *(betr. Grundbesitz);* ~ **issue** Nebenfrage; ~ **loss** *(VersR)* Kleinschaden, Bagatellschaden; **of** ~ **interest** von untergeordnetem Interesse; ~ **→offen|ce (~se);** ~ **point** Nebensache; ~ **shareholder** Kleinaktionär

minority Minderjährigkeit, Unmündigkeit; Minorität, Minderheit *(opp. majority);* ~ **holding** Minderheitsbeteiligung; ~ **interests** Anteile in Fremdbesitz; ~ **of shareholders** (or **stockholders**) die Minorität der Aktionäre; ~ **opinion** Ansicht der Minderheit; ~ **partner** Minderheitsgesellschafter; ~ **report** Bericht der Minderheit; ~ **rights** Minoritätsrechte, Minderheitsrechte *(der Aktionäre);* ~ **share** Fremdanteil; ~ **shareholder (stockholder)** Minderheitsaktionär; konzernfremder Gesellschafter; ~ **shareholding** Minderheitsbeteiligung; ~ **vote** Stimmenminderheit *(weniger als die Hälfte der Stimmen)*

minorities *(VölkerR)* Minderheiten; ~ **problem** Minderheitenfrage; **exchange of** ~ Bevölkerungsaustausch; **protection of** ~ Minderheitenschutz

mint Münze; Münzanstalt; **~-mark** Münzzeichen; **~-master** Münzmeister; ~ **par (of exchange)** Münzparität; **Bureau of the M~** *Am* Münzamt

mintage Prägegebühr; geprägtes Geld

mint *v,* **to** ~ **coins** Münzen prägen (od. schlagen)

minting Ausmünzung, Münzprägung

minus, plus or ~ **→variation**

minute Minute; Entwurf; Vermerk, Notiz; Denkschrift; **~-book** Protokollbuch; **entry in the ~-book** Protokollaufnahme; **sworn ~-writer** beeidigter Protokollführer

Minuteman sehr aktiver Politiker

Minutemen *Am hist* rechtsradikale, antikommunistische, bewaffnete Organisation

minutes (Verhandlungs-)Protokoll, Niederschrift; ~ **of the meeting** Sitzungsprotokoll; ~ **(of an order or judgment)** *Br (von e-r Partei entworfener und von der anderen Partei genehmigter)* Entwurf e-r gerichtl. Verfügung od. e-s Urteils *(der Chancery-Division des High Court);* ~ **of the proceedings** Verhandlungsprotokoll; **agreed** ~ *(VölkerR)* vereinbarte Niederschrift; **board** ~ Protokoll über die →board-Sitzung; **drafting of the** ~ Abfassung des Protokolls; **entry in the** ~ Vermerk im Protokoll; **to adopt** (or **approve**) **the** ~ das Protokoll genehmigen, **to draw up the** ~ das Protokoll aufnehmen, protokollieren; **to enter in the** ~ im Protokoll vermerken; **to keep the** ~ Protokoll führen; **to record in the** ~ im Protokoll vermerken (od. aufnehmen); **to take the** ~ das Protokoll aufnehmen

minute *v,* **to have ~d** *(etw.)* zu Protokoll erklären

misadventure Unglücksfall, unglücklicher Zufall; **→homicide by** ~

misapplication falsche Anwendung; widerrechtliche Verwendung *(Veruntreuung von Geld)*; ~ **of deposit** Depotunterschlagung

misapply *v (etw.)* falsch anwenden; widerrechtlich verwenden; **to ~ funds** Gelder unterschlagen (od. veruntreuen)

misapprehension, under the ~ (that) in der irrigen Annahme (daß); **to be under a ~** sich im Irrtum befinden

misappropriate *v* widerrechtlich verwenden (od. sich aneignen); unterschlagen; veruntreuen

misappropriation widerrechtliche Verwendung (od. Aneignung); Unterschlagung; Veruntreuung; ~ **of clients' money** unrechtmäßige Verwendung von Mandantengeldern; ~ **of lost property** Fundunterschlagung; ~ **of public funds** Unterschlagung (od. Veruntreuung) von öffentlichen Geldern; ~ **of a trade mark** Markenverletzung

misbehave *v*, **to ~** sich schlecht benehmen

misbehavio(u)r schlechtes Benehmen; ungebührliches Verhalten; Amtspflichtverletzung

misbranded goods falsch bezeichnete Waren

miscalculate *v* falsch (be)rechnen, sich verrechnen; sich verkalkulieren

miscalculation falsche (Be-)Rechnung; Rechenfehler, Kalkulationsfehler; Fehlkalkulation

miscarriage Mißlingen, Scheitern; Fehlleitung (od. Irrlaufen) *(e-r Postsendung)*; Fehlgeburt; ~ **of justice** Fehlurteil; Justizirrtum; **to procure a ~** *(StrafR)* abtreiben

miscarr|y *v* mißlingen, scheitern; verlorengehen *(Briefe)*; **~ied** nicht angekommen

miscegenation Rassenmischung *(bes. von Weißen und Schwarzen)*

miscellaneous Verschiedenes; verschieden(artig); ~ **income** *(Bilanz)* sonstige Erträge; ~ **(shares)** *Br* sonstige Aktien

miscellany Sammelband, Sammlung *(z. B. von Staatsverträgen)*

mischief Unheil; Mißstand; Schaden; **criminal ~** *Am*[52] strafbare Sachbeschädigung; **malicious ~** *Am und Scot (böswillige)* Sachbeschädigung; **public ~** grober Unfug; **to remedy a ~** e-m Mißstand abhelfen, e-n Mißstand beseitigen

miscognisant nicht wissend, nicht vertraut (of mit)

misconceive *v* mißverstehen, falsch auffassen; **to ~ of** e-e falsche Vorstellung haben von

misconceived capital project Fehlinvestition

misconduct schlechtes (od. ordnungswidriges) Verhalten; ehewidriges Verhalten, *bes.* Ehebruch; Verletzung der Amtspflicht, schlechte Amtsführung *(z. B. des Konkursverwalters)*; ~ **in office by a public officer or employee** *Am*[53] *(StrafR)* Amtsdelikt; Pflichtverletzung e-s Beamten od. Angestellten; **professional ~** standeswidriges Verhalten; **to make an allegation of serious ~ against an official** e-m Beamten e-e schwere Pflichtverletzung zur Last legen

misconstruction falsche Auslegung

misconstrue *v* falsch auslegen

misdat|e *v* falsch datieren; **~ing** falsche Datumsangabe

misdeliver *v* falsch (od. irrtümlich) (an-, ab-)liefern

misdemeanant Täter; e-s Vergehens Schuldiger

misdemeanor *Am (StrafR)* Vergehen; **petty ~** *Am* leichtes Vergehen

Br hist leichteres →indictable offence. Der Unterschied zwischen misdemeanour und felony ist seit 1967[54] aufgehoben, der Begriff wird überhaupt nicht mehr gebraucht; die Bestimmungen für misdeameanours gelten für alle indictable offences[54].
Am strafbare Handlungen, die keine →felonies sind und die mit Gefängnis bis zu 1 Jahr (kein →penitentiary) oder mit Geldstrafe bis zu 500 Dollar geahndet werden. Nach dem neuen Model Penal Code wird misdemeanor auf Vergehen beschränkt. Er unterscheidet zwischen misdemeanor[55] (Vergehen; Gefängnis bis zu 1 Jahr) und petty misdemeanor[56] (leichtes Vergehen; Gefängnis bis 30 Tage)

misdescription falsche Beschreibung, falsche Angaben; **material** (or **substantial**) ~ *(in e-m Vertrag enthaltene)* grundlegende falsche Beschreibung *(macht in gewissen Fällen auf Wunsch der irregeführten Partei den Vertrag aufhebbar [voidable], auch wenn kein Betrug vorliegt)*

misdirect *v (Post)* an die falsche Adresse senden, *(Postsache)* falsch adressieren; fehlleiten; falsch unterrichten; *(Geschworene)* falsch belehren; **a judge sitting alone can ~ himself** ein Einzelrichter kann sich im Rechtsirrtum befinden

misdirection unrichtige Rechtsbelehrung *(der Geschworenen)*; falsche Adressierung; Fehlleitung; falsche Auskunft; Irreführung

misenter *v* falsch eintragen (od. buchen)

misfeasance *(schädigende)* Schlechtausführung e-r rechtlich an sich erlaubten Handlung *(cf. nonfeasance, malfeasance)*; ~ **proceedings** *Br*[57] summarisches gerichtliches Verfahren im Zuge e-r konkursmäßigen Liquidation (winding up) e-r Aktiengesellschaft (Handelsgesellschaft) gegen ein board-Mitglied, e-n Gründer, leitenden Angestellten oder Liquidator der Gesellschaft *(wegen Ersatzes veruntreuten* *oder verwirtschafteten Gesellschaftsvermögens an die Gesellschaft);* ~ **summons** *Br* Einleitung e-s →~ proceedings

misfeasor jd., der e-e →misfeasance begeht

misfile *v* falsch ablegen *(Akten, Schriftstücke usw.)*

misgovern *v* schlecht regieren (od. verwalten)

mishandling falsche Behandlung, falsche Handhabung

misinform *v* falsch unterrichten; falsche Auskunft geben; ~**ed** falsch informiert

misinformation falsche Information

misinterpret *v* falsch auslegen, mißdeuten

misinterpretation falsche Auslegung, Mißdeutung

misinvestment Fehlinvestition

misjoinder, ~ **of causes of action**[58] *(Zivilprozeß)* unzulässige Verbindung von mehreren Klagen; unzulässige objektive Klagehäufung; ~ **of inventor** *(PatR)* irrtümliche Angabe e-r Person als Miterfinder; ~ **of parties**[59] *(Zivilprozeß)* unzulässige Verbindung mehrerer Parteien *(als Kläger od. Beklagte),* unzulässige Streitgenossenschaft; unzulässige subjektive Klagehäufung

misjudgment Fehlurteil

mislabel *v* mit e-m falschen Etikett versehen; falsch bezeichnen

mislaid property verlegte (od. abhanden gekommene) Sache

mislead *v* irreführen, zu e-m Irrtum führen; **to** ~ **the buyer** den Käufer irreführen

misleading, ~ **advertising** irreführende (od. täuschende) Werbung; ~ **indications** irreführende Bezeichnungen; ~ **information** irreführende Auskunft; ~ **of the jury** falsche Belehrung der Geschworenen *(durch den Richter)*

mismanage *v* schlecht verwalten (od. führen); **to** ~ **one's business** seine geschäftlichen Angelegenheiten schlecht führen

mismanagement schlechte Verwaltung; ~ **(of a business)** schlechte Geschäftsführung; **the government's** ~ **of the economy** schlechte Wirtschaftsführung der Regierung

mismatch floater →floater 2.

misname *v* falsch benennen

misnomer falsche Benennung (od. Bezeichnung) *(e-r Person in e-r Urkunde etc);* unrichtige Namensangabe

mispleading grundlegend lücken- oder fehlerhafter Prozeßvortrag

misprision of felony (treason) *Am* Nichtanzeige (od. Unterlassung der Anzeige) e-r *(begangenen)* →felony (treason)

misquote *v* falsch anführen

misrepresent *v* falsch darstellen; unrichtig angeben

misrepresented by the press von der Presse falsch dargestellt

misrepresenting a fact Vorspiegelung e-r falschen Tatsache

misrepresentation falsche Darstellung *(von Tatsachen); (VertragsR)* den Tatsachen nicht entsprechende Angaben; Irreführung durch Vorspiegelung falscher Tatsachen *(durch e-n Vertragspartner bei der Vertragsanbahnung in e-r für den Vertragsschluß bestimmenden Weise) (sie berechtigt den Vertragsgegner grundsätzlich zur rückwirkenden Vertragsauflösung [→rescission] und weitgehend auch zum Schadensersatz, sei es neben, sei es an Stelle der Vertragsauflösung*[60]*); Am (WarenzeichenR)* Ausgeben e-r fremden Ware als eigene *(umgekehrtes →passing off); (VersR)* falsche Angaben *(bei der Erteilung der zur Beurteilung des Risikos durch den Versicherer erforderlichen Auskünfte);* Verletzung der vorvertraglichen Anzeigepflicht *(cf. concealment und nondisclosure)*

Misrepresentation Act 1967 *Br* Gesetz über die Rechtsfolgen von schuldloser Täuschung *(im Zusammenhang mit e-m Vertragsabschluß)*

misrepresentation, fraudulent ~ arglistig abgegebene unrichtige Tatsachendarstellung; wissentlich falsche Angaben *(in Betrugs- oder Täuschungsabsicht oder ohne Rücksicht auf ihren Wahrheitsgehalt);* (Irreführung durch Vorspiegelung falscher Tatsachen); **innocent** ~ schuldlos (in gutem Glauben) gemachte falsche Angaben, *(umfaßt als Oberbegriff sowohl)* schuldlose Falschdarstellung, *(als auch)* fahrlässige Falschdarstellung (→*negligent* ~) *(wird neuerdings aber auf schuldlose Falschdarstellung beschränkt);* **material** ~ *(VersR)*[61] unrichtige Angabe(n) über e-n *(für die Beurteilung des zu versichernden Risikos)* wesentlichen Punkt; **negligent** ~ fahrlässig gemachte falsche Angaben

misrule schlechte Regierung; Gesetzlosigkeit

miss *v* versäumen, verfehlen; **to** ~ **an opportunity** e-e Gelegenheit verpassen

missed profit(s) entgangener Gewinn

missing fehlend, abwesend; ~ **(in action)** *mil* vermißt; **search for** ~ **aircraft** Suche nach vermißtem Flugzeug; ~ **goods** fehlende Waren; ~ **items** fehlende (Post-)Sendungen; ~ **persons** vermißte Personen; **the dead, wounded and** ~ *mil* die Toten, Verwundeten und Vermißten; **to be** ~ abhandengekommen sein, fehlen; **to be reported** ~ *mil* als vermißt gemeldet werden

missing persons, Convention on the Declaration of Death of M~ P~[61a] Verschollenheitskonvention (Konvention der Vereinten Nationen über die Todeserklärung Verschollener)

missile Rakete(ngeschoß); ~ **deployment** Raketenstationierung; ~ **expert** (or ~**man**) Raketenfachmann; **anti-ballistic** ~ (ABM) *Am* Anti-Raketen-Rakete; **guided** ~ ferngesteuerte Rakete(nwaffe), Fernlenkwaffe; **intercontinental ballistic** ~ (I.B.M.) Interkontinentalrakete; **long-range** ~ Langstreckenrakete; **medium-range ballistic** ~ (M.R.B.M.) Mittelstreckenrakete; **short-range** ~ Kurzstreckenrakete; **surface-to-air** ~ (Sam) Boden-Luft-Rakete; **undersea long-range** ~ **system** (ULMS) Unterwasser-Langstreckenraketensystem; **to deploy** ~**s** Raketen stationieren (od. aufstellen)

mission 1. *(VölkerR)* Mission, ständige Vertretung im Ausland; **commercial** ~ Handelsmission; **diplomatic** ~ diplomatische Mission; **head of the** ~[62] Missionschef; **members of the staff of the** ~ Mitglieder des diplomatischen Personals; **military** ~ Militärmission; **premises of the** ~ Räumlichkeiten der Mission; **staff of the** ~ Personal der Mission; **trade** ~ Handelsmission

mission 2. Auftrag, Mission; **on a secret** ~ in geheimer Mission; **on a special** ~ in besonderer Mission; mit Sonderauftrag; **to perform** ~**s** Aufträge durchführen

mission 3. *eccl* Mission; Missionarstätigkeit; **foreign** ~ äußere Mission; **home** ~ innere Mission

missionary Missionar(in); Missions-; ~ **freedom** Missionsfreiheit; ~ **society** Missionsgesellschaft

misspell *v*, **to** ~ **a name** e-n Namen falsch schreiben

misstate *v* falsch angeben (od. darstellen)

misstatement falsche Angabe (od. Darstellung); **careless** ~ fahrlässig falsche Angabe; **deliberate** ~ **of fact** arglistige Täuschung

mistake Irrtum, Fehler; Versehen; ~ **as to the applicable law** *(IPR)* Irrtum über das anwendbare Recht *(z. B. jd errichtet ein Testament gemäß dem Recht des Staates A, obwohl nach dem maßgebenden IPR das Recht des Staates B anzuwenden ist);* ~ **as to expression** Irrtum in der Erklärung; ~ **as to the identity of the subject matter** Irrtum über die Identität des Vertragsgegenstandes; ~ **in calculation** Rechenfehler, Kalkulationsfehler; ~ **in the inducement** *Am* Irrtum im Motiv; ~ **of fact** Tatsachenirrtum; ~ **of fact (as to a** →**definitional element)** *(StrafR)* Tatbestandsirrtum; ~ **of intrinsic fact** wesentlicher Irrtum; ~ **of law** Rechtsirrtum; **by** ~ aus Versehen, versehentlich; **common** ~ allgemein verbreiteter Irrtum; gemeinsamer Irrtum *(beider Parteien);* **mutual** ~ gegenseitiger Irrtum *(beider Parteien);* **typographical** ~ Druckfehler; **unilateral** ~ einseitiger Irrtum; **to correct** (or **rectify**) **a** ~ e-n Irrtum richtigstellen (od. beheben)

mistake *v* sich irren; mißverstehen; verwechseln

mistaken irrtümlich, falsch; ~ **identity** Irrtum über die Person; Personenverwechslung; ~ **investments** Fehlinvestitionen; **to be** ~ sich irren, sich im Irrtum befinden

mistrial fehlerhaftes *(daher nicht zu e-r gültigen Entscheidung führendes)* Gerichtsverfahren *(in Zivil- od. Strafsachen)*

misuse Mißbrauch; mißbräuchliche Verwendung; falsche Benutzung; ~ **of authority** Mißbrauch der Amtsgewalt; Amtsmißbrauch; ~ **of discretionary power** Ermessensmißbrauch; ~ **of a flag** *(VölkerR)* Flaggenmißbrauch; ~ **of land** falsche Nutzung des Bodens; ~ **of product** Produktmißbrauch; ~ **of rights** Rechtsmißbrauch

misuse *v* mißbrauchen; falsch anwenden

misuser Mißbrauch e-s Rechts

mitigate *v (Strafe)* mildern; herabsetzen; **to** ~ **the damage** (or **loss**) den Schaden auf das Minimum beschränken *(Pflicht der durch Vertragsbruch geschädigten Partei)*

mitigating, to allow ~ **circumstances** *(StrafR)* mildernde Umstände zubilligen *(opp. aggravating circumstances);* **to plead** ~ **circumstances** mildernde Umstände geltend machen

mitigation Milderung; ~ **of damages** Herabsetzung des Schadensersatzes *(aus besonderen Gründen);* ~ **of a sentence** Herabsetzung e-r Strafe; Strafmilderung; **to consider in** ~ strafmildernd berücksichtigen; **to** →**plead in** ~; **to show facts in** ~ **of sentence** Tatsachen vorbringen zur Strafmilderung

mittimus ("we send") *(Br obs.)* gerichtliche Begleitverfügung zur Überweisung von (Gerichts-)Akten; *Am* Haftbefehl

mixed gemischt, vermischt; **of** ~ **blood** gemischter Abstammung; ~ **cargo** gemischte Ladung; Stückgutladung, Stückgüter; ~ **cargo rate** Stückgütertarif; ~ **carload** *Am* gemischte Ladung; Stückgutladung; ~ **carload rate** *Am* Stückgütertarif; ~ **commission** (or **committee**) gemischter Ausschuß; ~ **credit** Mischkredit *(e-e Mischung von Entwicklungshilfe und Handelsfinanzierung für Entwicklungsländer)*; ~ **duty** Mischzoll; ~ **economy** gemischte Wirtschaftsform *(an den maßgebl. Entscheidungen ist sowohl die Privatwirtschaft als auch der Staat durch die Unternehmen der öffentl. Hand be-*

teiligt; cf. private and public sector); ~ **enterprises** gemischtwirtschaftliche Unternehmen *(die private Wirtschaft und die öffentl. Hand sind nebeneinander beteiligt);* ~ **fund** ein aus den Einnahmen von real und personal property bestehender Fonds; ~ **(investment) fund** gemischter Fonds *(Aktien- und Rentenwerte);* ~ **policy** →policy 2.; ~ **property** aus personalty und realty bestehendes Vermögen, ~ **tariff** Mischzoll; ~ **tribunal** gemischter Gerichtshof

mob Pöbel, Mob; ~ **law** Lynchjustiz

mobile warfare Bewegungskrieg

mobility Beweglichkeit, Mobilität; ~ **allowance** *Br* Beihilfe für Personen, die außerstande sind zu gehen; ~ **of labo(u)r** (or **manpower**) Mobilität der Arbeitskräfte; **upward social** ~ sozialer Aufstieg

mobilization Mobilisierung; *mil* Mobilmachung; *com* Flüssigmachung

mobilize *v* mobilisieren; *mil* mobil machen; *(Geld)* flüssig machen

mock, ~ **auction**[63] Scheinauktion; ~ **purchase** Scheinkauf; ~ **trial** Scheinprozeß

modalities Abmachungen für Zahlungsart

mode Art (und Weise); ~ **of conveyance** (or **dispatch**) Beförderungsart, Versendungsart; ~ **of election** Wahlverfahren; ~ **of forwarding** → ~ of conveyance; ~ **of investment** Anlageart; ~ **of living** Lebensweise; ~ **of payment** Zahlungsweise; ~ **of transport** Beförderungsart

model Modell; Muster; Vorbild; vorbildlich; ~ **agreement** *Am* Muster-Tarifvertrag; ~ **farm** landwirtschaftlicher Musterbetrieb, Mustergut; ~ **convention** Musterabkommen; ~ **plant** Musterbetrieb

Model Act *Am* Gesetzesentwurf, Mustergesetz
Die 3 Institutionen, die eine große Anzahl von Mustergesetzen auf allen Gebieten geschaffen haben, die für die Gesetzgebung der Einzelstaaten als Vorbild dienen sollen, sind das American Law Institute, die American Bar Association sowie die National Conference of Commissioners on Uniform State Laws. Die beiden von den Einzelstaaten am häufigsten angenommenen Entwürfe sind der Model Business Corporation Act und der Model Penal Code

Model Business Corporation Act (Model Act) *Am* (Entwurf e-s) Muster-Aktiengesetz(es)
Dieser Model Act ist von der American Bar Association erarbeitet worden. Er ist eine wichtige Quelle für einzelstaatliche Gesetzgebung.
Die letzte komplette Fassung ist die von 1969, seitdem aber mehrfach ergänzt. 1983 ist eine neue Fassung entworfen worden

Model Penal Code (MPC) *Am* (Entwurf e-s) Muster-Strafgesetzbuch(es)
Vom American Law Institute als Modell eines Strafgesetzbuches aufgestellter Entwurf, der den Strafgesetzbüchern der 50 Einzelstaaten als Vorbild dient

moderate *pol* Gemäßigter *(opp. extremist); pol* gemäßigt; „Taube" *(opp. hawk);* mäßig, niedrig, mild *(Strafe);* ~ **income** mäßiges Einkommen; ~ **political views** gemäßigte politische Ansichten; ~ **prices** mäßige Preise

moderate *v* mäßigen, mildern; *(in e-r öffentl. Versammlung)* den Vorsitz führen

moderator *Am* Vorsitzender *(e-r öffentl. Versammlung); (unparteiischer)* Diskussionsleiter; *hist.* Schiedsrichter; *eccl (Presbyterianische Kirche)* Vorsitzender *(e-s Kirchengerichts); Br (Oxford, Cambridge)* Prüfungsvorsitzender

modernization plans Modernisierungspläne

modernize *v* modernisieren

modification (Ab-)Änderung, Abwandlung; Einschränkung; ~ **of the constitution** Verfassungsänderung; ~ **of the environment** Umweltveränderung (→*environmental* ~); ~ **of the terms of a contract** Änderung der Vertragsbedingungen; **proposed** ~ Änderungsvorschlag; **subject to ~s** Änderungen vorbehalten

modify *v (teilweise)* (ab)ändern; einschränken; **to ~ one's claims** s-e Forderungen abändern (od. einschränken)

moiet|y Hälfte; **in equal ~ies** je zur Hälfte

momentous steps wichtige Schritte, folgenschwere Maßnahmen

Monaco Monaco; **Principality of** ~ Fürstentum Monaco *(cf. Monegasque)*

monarchy Monarchie; **absolute** ~ absolute Monarchie; **constitutional** (or **limited**) ~ konstitutionelle Monarchie; **elective** ~ Wahlmonarchie; **hereditary** ~ Erbmonarchie

Monegasque Monegass|e, ~in; monegassisch

monetarism Monetarismus

monetary Geld-; Währungs-; Münz-; monetär, geldlich; ~ **agreement** Währungsabkommen *(cf. European M~ System);* ~ **area** Währungsgebiet; ~ **authorities** Währungsbehörden; ~ **base** Geldbasis; ~ **claim** Geldforderung; ~ **compensatory amount** (MCA) *(EG)* Währungsausgleichbetrag (WAB); ~ **contraction** Geldverknappung; ~ **convention** Münzkonvention; ~ **co-operation** monetäre Zusammenarbeit; ~ **crisis** Währungskrise; ~ **depreciation** Geldentwertung; ~ **difficulties** Währungsschwierigkeiten; ~ **disturbances** (or **disorder**) Währungsunruhen; ~ **fluctuations** Währungsschwankungen; ~ **gold** Münzgold; ~ **grant** (Geld-) Beihilfe; ~ **holdings** Geldbestand; ~ **law** Münzgesetz; ~ **management** Geldpolitik; ~ **matters** Geldangelegenheiten;

~ **measures** monetäre Maßnahmen, Währungsmaßnahmen; ~ **parity** Währungsparität

monetary policy Währungspolitik; Geld- und Kreditpolitik; **powers in the field of** ~ währungspolitische Befugnisse; **sound** ~ gesunde Währungspolitik; **in terms of** ~ währungspolitisch gesehen

monetary, ~ **power** *Am*[64] Währungskompetenz *(des Bundes);* ~ **proceeds of assets of the estate** *Am* Summenvermächtnis; ~ **reform** Währungsreform, Neuordnung des Geldwesens; ~ **rehabilitation** Währungssanierung

monetary reserves Währungsreserven *(der Zentralnotenbanken);* **decline in the** ~ Abnahme der Währungsreserven

monetary, ~ **reward** Belohnung in Geld; ~ **situation** Währungslage; ~ **sovereignty** Währungshoheit; Münzhoheit; ~ **stability** Währungsstabilität; ~ **standard** Währungsstandard, Währungseinheit *(cf. metallic standard, gold bullion standard, gold exchange standard, limping standard, paper standard);* Münzfuß; ~ **stock** *Am* gesamter Geldbestand *(e-s Landes);* ~ **transaction** Geldgeschäft; ~ **transactions** Zahlungsverkehr; ~ **turmoil** Währungsunruhen; ~ **union** Währungsunion; ~ **unit** Währungseinheit; Münzeinheit; **formation of** ~ **wealth** Geldvermögensbildung; ~ **problems have become less (more) acute** die Währungsschwierigkeiten haben nachgelassen (sich verschärft)

monetization Münzprägung; ~ **of the debt** *Am* Erhöhung des Zahlungsmittelumlaufs

monetize *v (Münzen)* prägen; zum gesetzlichen Zahlungsmittel machen

money Geld; Münze

money, to advance ~ Geld vorschießen (od. auslegen); **to advance** ~ **on securities** Wertpapiere beleihen (od. lombardieren); **to borrow** ~ Geld leihen (od. aufnehmen); **to call (in)** ~ Geld abrufen (od. kündigen); **to change** ~ Geld wechseln; **to create** ~ Geld schöpfen; **to deposit** ~ **at** (or **with**) **a bank** Geld bei e-r Bank einzahlen; **to draw** ~ **from an account** Geld von e-m Konto abheben; **to earn** ~ Geld verdienen; **to find the** ~ **for sb.** jdm das nötige Kapital verschaffen; **to furnish** ~ Geld beschaffen; **to get** ~ sich Geld beschaffen; **to grant** ~ Geld bewilligen; **to handle** ~ mit Geld umgehen; **to have** ~ **in** (or **with**) **a bank** Geld bei e-r Bank haben; **to invest one's** ~ **to good account** sein Geld gut anlegen; **to keep** ~ **with a bank** Geld bei e-r Bank haben; **to →lend** ~ **on goods (mortgage, security); to make** ~ Geld verdienen; **to put** ~ **in(to)** Geld stecken in, Geld anlegen; **to put up** ~ Geld aufbringen; **to raise** (or **take up**) ~ Geld aufnehmen; **to refund** ~ Geld zurückerstatten; **to remit** (or **transfer**) ~ Geld überweisen; **to withdraw** ~ Geld abheben; **the** ~ **comes in badly** das Geld geht schlecht ein; ~ **is lacking** das Geld fehlt; ~**is scarce** das Geld ist knapp

money, ~ **advance** Barvorschuß; ~ **at** (or **on**) **call** tägliches Geld; ~ **back** Geldrückgabe *(bei Nichtgefallen)*; ~ **bill** Finanzgesetz, Finanzvorlage; ~ **box** Sparbüchse; ~ **broker** Finanzmakler; Kreditvermittler; ~ **circulation** Geldumlauf; ~ **changer** (Geld-)Wechsler; ~ **claim** Geldforderung; ~ **collected by the post** Postnachnahme; ~ **compensation** Barabfindung, Geldentschädigung; ~ **consideration** Gegenleistung in Geld; ~ **damages** Schadensersatz in Geld; ~ **dealer** Devisenhändler; ~ **debt** Geldschuld; ~ **down** *sl.* bares Geld; ~ **due** ausstehendes Geld; ~ **flow** Geldstrom; ~ **grant** Geldbewilligung

money had and received, action for ~ Klage auf Herausgabe der ungerechtfertigten Bereicherung

money, ~ **held on** (or **in**) **trust** anvertrautes Geld; ~ **in account** *Br* Giralgeld, Buchgeld; ~ **interests** Finanzwelt; ~ **jobber** *Br* →~ changer; ~ **judgment** Urteil auf Zahlung e-r bestimmten Geldsumme; ~ **laundering** Geldwäsche; ~**lender** *(gewerbsmäßiger)* Geldverleiher, Geldgeber; ~ **letter** *Am* Wertbrief; ~ **loan** Bardarlehen, Kassendarlehen; ~ **lying idle** totes Kapital; ~**-making** Gelderwerb; gewinnbringend

money market Geldmarkt *(für kurzfristige Kredite; cf. capital market)*; ~ **certificates (of deposit)** *Am* Festgelder bei Depositenbanken *(deren Verzinsung sich an kurzfristigen →Treasury Bills orientiert)*; ~ **cumulative preferred stock** *Am* Vorzugsaktien mit Geldmarktcharakter *(bei denen alle 49 Tage die Dividende im Tenderverfahren neu festgelegt wird (s. adjustable rate →preferred stock)*; ~ **customs** Geldmarktusancen; ~ **(deposit) account** *Am* Geldmarkteinlagekonto amerikanischer Geschäftsbanken *(das nicht der Zinsobergrenze für Termingelder gemäß →Regulation Q unterliegt und über das begrenzt mit Scheck verfügt werden kann)*; ~ **fund** →~ mutual fund; ~ **indebtedness** Geldmarktverschuldung; ~ **(intelligence)** *Br (in Zeitung)* Börsennachrichten; ~ **loan** Geldmarktkredit; ~ **mutual fund** *Am* Investmentfonds, der ausschließlich in kurzfristigen Investmentpapieren investiert. (*Die Anteile an e-m solchen Fonds sind per Scheck übertragbar*); ~ **paper** Geldmarktpapier, Geldmarkttitel; ~ **rate** Geldmarktsatz; ~ **securities** Geldmarktpapiere; ~ **situation** Geldmarktlage

money, ~ **matters** Geldangelegenheiten; ~ **no object** Geld spielt keine Rolle; ~ **of exchange** Wechselgeld; ~ **of judgment** Urteilswährung; ~ **of payment** Zahlungswährung; ~ **office** Kasse(nbüro)

money order[65] (M.O.) *(vom Empfänger an e-m Postamt einzulösende)* Zahlungsanweisung, Postanweisung *(Br bes. für größere Beträge; cf. postal order)*; **M~ O~s and Postal Traveller's Cheques Agreement**[66] Postanweisungs- und Postreisescheckabkommen; ~ **telegram** telegrafische Geldüberweisung; **domestic** ~ *Am* Inlandspostanweisung; **foreign** (or **international**) ~ Auslandspostanweisung, Postanweisung auf das Ausland; **payee of a** ~ Zahlungsempfänger e-r Postanweisung; **telegraphic** ~ telegrafische Geldüberweisung; **trade charge** ~ Nachnahmepostanweisung

money, ~ **owed** Geldschuld; ~ **paid on account of costs** (Gerichts-)Kostenvorschüsse; ~ **procurement** Geldbeschaffung; ~ **put up** angelegtes Geld; ~ **rate** *(Börse)* Geldkurs *(Kurs, zu dem Nachfrage nach e-m Wertpapier besteht)*; **~s received** Geldeingänge; **~s received and expended** erhaltene und ausgegebene Gelder; vereinnahmtes und verausgabtes Geld; ~ **reserve** Geldreserve, Barreserve; ~ **stock** *Am* gesamter Geldbestand *(e-s Landes)*; Geldmenge; ~ **supply** Geldmenge, Geldvolumen; ~ **at long (medium, short) term** →term 2.; ~ **transactions** Geldgeschäfte; ~ **transfer** Geldüberweisung; ~ **transfers** Zahlungsverkehr; ~ **value** Geldwert; effektiver Wert *(bes. von Effekten; opp. nominal value)*; ~ **vault** *Am* Kassenschrank; ~ **volume** Geldvolumen; ~ **wages** Nominallohn *(opp. real wages)*; ~ **withdrawn from circulation** aus dem Verkehr gezogenes Geld; **~'s worth** Geld(es)wert

money, advance of ~ Vorschuß; **amount of** ~ Geldbetrag; **bank** ~ *Am* Giralgeld, Buchgeld; **bargain** ~ Draufgeld; **barren** ~ totes Kapital; **call** ~ →~ on call; **cheap** ~ billiges Geld; **claim for** ~ Geldforderung; **coined** ~ Hartgeld; **conduct** ~ Reisekosten *(z.B. für Zeugen)*; →**counterfeit** ~; **creation of** ~ Geldschöpfung; **current** ~ gängiges Geld, Kurantgeld; **day-to-day-**~ Tagesgeld; **dead** ~ totes Kapital; **demand for** ~ Geldnachfrage; **deposit** ~ *Br* Giralgeld, Buchgeld; **easy** ~ billiges Geld; leicht verdientes Geld; **excess** ~ Geldüberhang; **flow of** ~ Geldstrom

money, for ~ *(Börse)* netto Kasse; **dealing for** ~ Kassageschäft

mon|ey, glut of ~ Geldüberhang; **grant of** ~ Bewilligung von Geld; **hard** ~ Hartgeld, Metallgeld *(opp. paper ~)*; **hoarding of** ~ Geldhortung; **hot** ~ heißes Geld; **hush** ~ Schweigegeld; **immobilized** ~ festgelegtes Geld; **lack of** ~ Geldmangel; **long-term ~eys** langfristige Gelder; **loss of** ~ Geldverlust; **medium-term ~eys** mittelfristige Gelder; →**near** ~; →**overnight** ~; **paper** ~ Papiergeld; **pocket** ~ Taschengeld; **public** ~ öffentliche Gelder; **quasi-**~ *Am* →near ~

money, ready ~ bares Geld, Bargeld; **ready** ~ **only** nur gegen Barzahlung

mon|ey, regular ~ *Br* Tagesgeld, das jedoch nur selten zurückgerufen wird; **scarcity of** ~ Geldknappheit; **short of** ~ nicht bei Kasse, knapp an Geld; **short-term ~eys** kurzfristige Gelder; **shortage of** ~ Geldknappheit; **standard** ~ vollwichtige Münze; **sum of** ~ Geldsumme; **a sum certain in** ~ e-e bestimmte Geldsumme; →**supply of** ~; **tight** ~ knappes Geld; **time** ~ befristetes Darlehen, Festgeld; **want of** ~ Geldmangel

moneyed Geld-, Finanz-; vermögend; ~ **capital** Kapitalvermögen; flüssiges Anlagekapital; ~ **corporation** *Am* Gesellschaft, die bankmäßig Geschäfte betreibt (Bank, Versicherungsgesellschaft); **the** ~ **interest** die Finanzwelt; ~ **people** Geldleute, Kapitalisten

monger, fishm Fischhändler; **ironm** Eisenhändler; **war**~ Kriegshetzer

Mongolia Mongolei

Mongolian Mongole, ~in; mongolisch; ~ **People's Republic** Mongolische Volksrepublik

monition *(SeeR, Br obs.)* gerichtliche Ladung, Vorladung; *eccl* Mahnung; *eccl* Mahnschreiben

monitor *v*, **to** ~ **prices** Preise überwachen

monitoring Überwachung, Kontrolle; ~ **device** Mithöreinrichtung

monitory letter *Br eccl* Ermahnungsschreiben

monocracy Monokratie *(Regierung durch eine Person)*

monometallism Monometallismus *(auf ein Metall beschränkte Währung; opp. bimetallism)*

monopolism Monopolwirtschaft

monopolist Monopolist

monopolistic monopolistisch, marktbeherrschend; Monopol-; ~ **competition** monopolistische Konkurrenz; ~ **conditions** monopolistische (Wirtschafts-)Verhältnisse; ~ **position** Monopolstellung; ~ **use of patents** Monopolnutzung von Patenten; **improper use of** ~ **power** Monopolmißbrauch; **to discourage** ~ **business practices** monopolistische Geschäftspraktiken bekämpfen

monopolization Monopolisierung

monopolize *v* monopolisieren; allein beherrschen; für sich allein in Anspruch nehmen

monopoly Monopol; Monopolstellung; Ausschließlichkeitsrecht; Alleinverkaufsrecht; ~ **agreement** Monopolabsprache *(Preiskontrolle, Produktionskontrolle, Marktaufteilung)*

Die gesetzlichen Bestimmungen gegen Monopole

sind enthalten *Br* im →Restrictive Trade Practices Act 1976 und →Fair Trading Act 1973, *Am* im →Sherman Act (Sec. 2 des Sherman Act wendet sich gegen die Errichtung oder den Versuch der Errichtung eines Monopols. Nach dieser Bestimmung ist das Monopolisieren immer ein unreasonable restraint of trade)

Monopolies and Merger Commission (MsMC) *Br*[67] Monopol- und Fusionskommission; *(etwa)* Kartellbehörde

monopoly, ~ enterprise marktbeherrschendes Unternehmen; **~ on** (or **in**) **the market** →~ position; **~ position** Monopolstellung; **~ power** Monopolmacht; wirtschaftliche Machtstellung; **~ price** Monopolpreis; **~ profit** Monopolgewinn; **~ situation** Monopolsituation; **~ supplier** Angebotsmonopolist

monopoly, buyer's ~ Käufermonopol, Nachfragemonopol; **commercial ~** wirtschaftliches Monopol; **fiscal ~** Finanzmonopol *(z.B. Branntwein-, Zündwarenmonopol);* **foreign trade ~** Außenhandelsmonopol; **government ~** Staatsmonopol; **holder of a ~** Monopolinhaber; **legal ~** gesetzliches Monopol *(z.B. Monopol durch Patente);* **manufacturing ~** Alleinherstellrecht; **production ~** Fabrikationsmonopol; **promotive of ~** *Am* monopolfördernd; **public ~** *Am* Staatsmonopol *(z.B. postal services);* **(sales) ~** Alleinverkaufsrecht; **state ~** staatliches Monopol *(z.B. für Branntwein);* **state trading ~** staatliches Handelsmonopol; **improper use of ~ies** Monopolmißbrauch

monopoly, to assign a ~ ein Monopol übertragen; **to break a ~** ein Monopol brechen; **to establish a ~** ein Monopol errichten; **to grant a ~** ein Monopol verleihen (od. vergeben); **to have the ~ of** das Monopol haben für; **to hold a ~** ein Monopol haben

monopsony Nachfragemonopol

month (m., or mo., or mth) Monat; **~s after date** (m/d) Monate nach heute; **~s after sight** (m/s) Monate nach Sicht; **a ~'s credit** Kredit von e-m Monat, Einmonatskredit; **one ~'s notice** monatliche Kündigung; **subject to a ~'s notice** mit monatlicher Kündigung; **~ order** *Am* für einen Monat gültiger Börsenauftrag; **three ~s' paper** (or **bill at three ~s**) Wechsel mit e-r Laufzeit von drei Monaten, Dreimonatswechsel, **a ~'s pay** Monatsgehalt; **one ~'s rent** Monatsmiete; **a ~'s salary** Monatsgehalt; **~ under review** Berichtsmonat

month, by the ~ monatlich; **current ~** laufender Monat; **end of ~** Monatsende, Ultimo (→*end*); **of last ~** (ult.) vorigen Monats; **last day of the ~** ultimo; **mid-~** Medio (→*mid*); **money (lent) for one ~** Monatsgeld; **next ~** (prox.) nächsten Monats; **of the present** (or **this**) **~** (inst.) diesen Monats; **this day ~** heute vor e-m Monat; heute in e-m Monat; **within a ~** binnen Monatsfrist; **to pay by the ~** monatlich bezahlen

monthly monatlich; **~ account** Monatsrechnung; **~ →allowance; ~ average** Monatsdurchschnitt; **~ balance sheet** Monatsbilanz; **~ instalment** Monatsrate; **~ notice** monatliche Kündigung; **~ pay** monatlicher Lohn; Monatsgehalt; **~ report** Monatsbericht; **~ return** *(Bank)* Monatsausweis; **~season ticket** *(Bahn)* Monatskarte; **~ settlement** Monatsabschluß; **~ statement** monatliche Aufstellung; Monatsrechnung; *(Bank)* Monatsausweis; **semi-~** halbmonatlich

monument Denkmal; **protection of ancient ~s** Denkmalschutz; **to deface a ~** ein Denkmal beschädigen; **to raise** (or **set up**) **a ~** ein Denkmal errichten

mood at the stock exchange Stimmung an der Börse

Moody index *Am* Preisindexziffer für Stapelwaren des Welthandels

moonlight *v colloq.* nach Dienstschluß arbeiten; **~ing** *colloq.* Freizeitarbeit nach Dienstschluß

moor *v (Schiff)* festmachen, verankern; **to be ~ed** vor Anker liegen

moot *Br* Debattierübungen *(Diskussion angenommener Rechtsfälle der Studenten e-s →Inn of Court);* **~ case** (or **point**) strittiger Punkt

moot *v* zur Debatte stellen

moral moralisch, sittlich; **of good ~ character** charakterlich einwandfrei

moral hazard „moralische Gefährdung"; (*VersR*) subjektives Risiko, Risiko falscher Angaben des Versicherten; **~-phenomenon** (*VersR*) Phänomen, daß sich bei bestehender Versicherung die Schadenswahrscheinlichkeit erhöht, weil der Betroffene weniger achtsam ist

moral, ~ obligation moralische Verpflichtung; **~ pressure** moralischer Druck; **~ suasion** „gütliches Zureden", Einsatz der moralischen Autorität *(in der Bankensprache verwendeter Begriff, z.B. für Kontrolle der commercial banks durch die Bank of England im Interesse der Währungssicherung)*

moral turpitude, conduct involving ~ moralisch verwerfliches Verhalten

morale Moral; *bes. mil* (Kampf-)Moral *(Disziplin und zuverlässige Einstellung);* **decline of the ~ of the troops** Absinken der (Kampf-)Moral der Truppen; **the ~ is high** die Truppe od. Bevölkerung ist zuversichtlich eingestellt

morality Sittlichkeit, sittliches Verhalten; **busi-**

ness ~ Geschäftsmoral; **contrary to** ~ gegen die guten Sitten verstoßend; **international** ~ internationale Moral

moratorium Moratorium

morbid condition Krankheitszustand

mores, (transaction) contra bonos ~ gegen die guten Sitten (verstoßendes Rechtsgeschäft)

morning loan *Am* Darlehen für Börsenmakler zur Durchführung s-r Geschäfte während des Tages

Moroccan Marokkaner, ~ in; marokkanisch

Morocco Marokko; **Kingdom of** ~ Königreich Marokko

Morris plan bank *Am* Bank, die Lohnempfängern kleine Darlehen gibt

mortal remains sterbliche Überreste

mortality Sterblichkeit; Sterbewahrscheinlichkeit; ~ **rate** Sterblichkeitsziffer; ~ **risk** *(VersR)* Sterberisiko; ~ **table** *(Versicherung)* Sterblichkeitstafel; **excess** ~ *(VersR)* Übersterblichkeit; **infant** ~ Säuglingssterblichkeit; **light** ~ *(VersR)* Untersterblichkeit

mortgage Grundpfandrecht, Hypothek, Grundschuld; *(besitzloses)* Pfandrecht (→*chattel mortgage*); Verpfändung; **a** ~ **for ...** e-e Hypothek in Höhe von ...

In den USA begründet die mortgage in vielen Staaten nur eine Belastung *(lien theory)*, während in anderen der Hypothekengläubiger auflösend bedingtes Eigentum erhält *(title theory)*. Die Rechtsprechung kommt jedoch unter beiden Theorien vielfach zu den gleichen Ergebnissen.

In England gilt seit 1925 die lien theory auf Grund des Law of Property Act

mortgage, to borrow money on ~ Geld gegen hypothekarische Sicherheit aufnehmen; **to call in a** ~ e-e Hypothek kündigen *(Gläubiger)*; **to cancel (the registration of) a** ~ e-e Hypothek löschen; **the** ~ **term has come to an end** (or **expired**) die Laufzeit der Hypothek ist beendet; **to create a** ~ e-e Hypothek (od. ein Pfandrecht) bestellen; **to discharge a** ~ e-e Hypothek tilgen; **to encumber with** ~**s** mit Hypotheken belasten; **to** →**foreclose a** ~; **to give in** ~ *(bewegl. Sachen)* verpfänden; **to give notice of redemption of a** ~ e-e Hypothek kündigen *(Schuldner)*; **to grant a** ~ **on (one's) property as security for a loan** e-e Hypothek bestellen *(indem Schuldner Belastung s-s Grundbesitzes zuläßt)*; **to grant a loan secured by a** ~ e-e Hypothek geben; **to hold a** ~ Hypothekengläubiger sein; **to lend on** ~ Darlehen gegen Hypothek geben; **to pay** ~ **interest** Hypothekenzinsen zahlen; **to pay off a** ~ e-e Hypothek tilgen; **to register the** ~ **in the Land Register** *Br* die Hypothek in das Grundbuch eintragen; **to repay the** ~ die Hypothek zurückbezahlen; **the** ~ **is repayable by monthly instal(l)ments** die Hypothek ist in Monatsraten rückzahlbar; **to redeem the** ~ die Hypothek tilgen; **to secure a debt by** ~ e-e Forderung hypothekarisch sichern; **to take out a** ~ e-e Hypothek aufnehmen

mortgage, ~ **advance** Hypothekendarlehen; ~ **banking** Hypothekenbankgeschäft

mortgage bond hypothekarisch gesicherte Schuldverschreibung, Pfandbrief; **first** ~ durch erste Hypothek gesicherte Schuldverschreibung; **junior** ~ *Am* durch nachstellige Hypothek gesicherte Schuldverschreibung; **senior** ~ *Am* s. first →~

mortgage by deposit of title deeds *Br (formlose)* Hypothek durch Hinterlegung von Eigentumsurkunden *(cf. equitable mortgage)*

Diese Hypothek braucht nicht im →Land Register eingetragen zu werden

mortgage, ~ **certificate** Hypothekenbrief; Verpfändungsbescheinigung; ~ **charge** hypothekarische Belastung; ~ **claim** Hypothekenforderung; ~ **consolidation** Hypothekenzusammenlegung; ~ **creditor** Hypothekengläubiger; ~ **debenture** hypothekarisch gesicherte Schuldverschreibung; (Hypotheken-)Pfandbrief

mortgage debt Hypothekenschuld, Hypothekenforderung; **repayment of a** ~ Rückzahlung e-r Hypothek; **to pay off** (or **repay**) **the** ~ die Hypothek zurückzahlen (od. tilgen); **the mortgagor failed to pay off the** ~ **within the prescribed time** der Hypothekenschuldner zahlte die Schuld nicht innerhalb der vorgeschriebenen Zeit zurück *(cf. foreclosure)*

mortgage, ~ **deed** Hypothekenbrief, Verpfändungsurkunde; ~ **instrument** Verpfändungsurkunde; ~ **interest** Hypothekenzinsen; ~ **interest rate** Hypothekenzinssatz; ~ **loan** hypothekarisch gesichertes Darlehen, Hypothekarkredit; ~ **loan and investment company** *Am* Hypothekenbank

mortgage money Hypothekenbetrag; **to repay (the)** ~ die Hypothek zurückzahlen

mortgage, ~ **note** hypothekarisch gesicherte →promissory note; ~ **of the corporate property** Verpfändung von Vermögensstücken der Gesellschaft; ~ **of insurance** Hypothek, die sich auf die bei Verlust des Schiffes entstehende Versicherungsforderung erstreckt *(die ship mortgage erstreckt sich kraft Gesetzes nicht auf die Versicherungsforderung)*; ~ **on freehold and leasehold property** Hypothek auf →freehold und →leasehold Grundbesitz; ~ **on real estate** (or **real property**) (Grundstücks-)Hypothek; ~ **on ships** Schiffshypothek; ~**s payable** Hypothekenverbindlichkeiten; ~ **protection policy** Hypothekentilgungsversicherung; ~**s receivable** Hypothekenforderungen; ~ **recording office** *Am* Amt für die Eintragung von Hypotheken; ~ **redemption** Hypothekentilgung; ~ **redemption insurance** Rückzahlungslebensversicherung bei Grundstücksbelastung; *(etwa)* Bausparer-Lebensversicherung; ~ **register** *Am* Hypothekenregister; ~ **registry** *Am* Amt für die Eintragung von Hypotheken; ~ **term** Laufzeit e-r Hypothek

mortgage, aggregate ~ Gesamthypothek; **aircraft** ~ Pfandrecht an Luftfahrzeugen; **amortization** ~ Tilgungshypothek; **blanket** ~ Gesamthypothek; →**bulk** ~; **burdened with a** ~ hypothekarisch belastet; **by (way of a)** ~ hypothekarisch; durch Verpfändung; **cancellation of a** ~ *Am* Löschung e-r Hypothek; **certificate of** ~ *Br*[68] *(vom Registerbeamten ausgestelltes)* Zertifikat, in welchem e-e vom Schiffseigentümer benannte Person *(meist der Kapitän)* ermächtigt wird, während der Reise außerhalb des Heimathafens eine mortgage zu bestellen; **chattel** ~ Mobiliarhypothek, Pfandrecht *(an bewegl. Sachen; →chattel)*; **closed-end** ~ abgeschlossene Hypothek *(die bis zu ihrem Höchstbetrag in Anspruch genommen ist und keine weiteren Belastungen des gleichen Eigentums zuläßt; opp. open-end ~)*; **collateral** ~ **bonds** *Am* durch Hypothek gesicherte Schuldverschreibungen; **collective** ~ Gesamthypothek; →**consolidated** ~; →**consolidation of** ~**s**; **contributory** ~ für mehrere Gläubiger bestellte Hypothek; →**corporate** ~; **creation of a** ~ Bestellung e-r Hypothek; **debt secured by a** ~ hypothekarisch gesicherte Forderung; **defaulted** ~ in Verzug befindliche Hypothek; **discharge of a** ~ Tilgung e-r Hypothekenforderung; Löschung e-r Hypothek; →**endowment** ~

mortgage, equitable ~ Hypothek nach →equity-Recht *(opp. legal ~ or legal charge)*

Equitable mortgages entstehen in den Fällen, in denen die Errichtung einer legal mortgage nicht möglich oder unwirksam ist *(so bei nicht formgerechter oder noch nicht durchgeführter Bestellung, die aber nach equity- Recht besonders zwischen den Parteien als Belastung anerkannt ist, und bei formeller Übereignung e-s equitable estate*[69] *oder interest, etwa Verpfändung der Rechte des →beneficiary e-s trust, die nach equity-Recht nur ein Sicherungsrecht in der Form eines equitable interest verschafft)*, oder in Fällen, in denen die Parteien sich mit einem equitable right begnügen wollen.

Der gutgläubige Erwerber von nachstehenden Hypotheken (bona fide purchaser without notice) ist in beiden Fällen geschützt *(Br cf. notice 2)*.

Br Die Sicherungsgewährung einer equitable mortgage erfolgt durch Übergabe der Eigentumsurkunde (mortgage by deposit of title deeds) *(in den USA ungebräuchlich wegen eines anderen Übereignungssystems)*. *Br*[70] Im Schiffsrecht wird die equitable mortgage durch die unregistered mortgage vertreten

mortgage, first ~ erste Hypothek

Br Bei →unregistered land braucht die Hypothek nicht im →Land Charges Register eingetragen zu werden, vorausgesetzt, daß dem Darlehnsgeber die →title deeds übergeben werden. Außerdem wird über die Bestellung der nicht eingetragenen 1. Hypothek eine förmliche Urkunde (deed) ausgefertigt (sofern nicht nur eine →equitable mortgage gewollt ist)

mortgage, fleet ~ Hypothek an der gesamten Luftflotte e-s Luftverkehrsunternehmens; **general** ~ Gesamthypothek; Pfandrecht am gesamten Vermögen; **interest on** ~ Hypothekenzinsen; →**judicial** ~; **junior** ~ *Am* im Rang nachstehende Hypothek *(opp. senior ~)*

mortgage, legal ~ *Br*[71] *(gewöhnliche)* Hypothek *(des →Common Law; opp. equitable mortgage)*; **charge by way of legal** ~ *Br* Belastung mit einer Hypothek, Grundstücksbelastung

Eine (legal) mortgage (of land) wird entweder durch Einräumung eines Rechts auf Zeit (term of years) bestellt und findet durch Rückzahlung ihr Ende oder – gemäß gesetzlicher Vorschrift – durch Gewährung einer mittels gesiegelter Urkunde (deed) begründeten Grundstücksbelastung (charge by way of legal mortgage). Der mortgagee erhält nur ein lien, keinen legal litle.

Br[72] Im Schiffsrecht wird die legal mortgage durch die registered mortgage verkörpert.

Im Verhältnis zwischen der legal und der equitable mortgage ist die legal mortgage prima facie das stärkere Recht

mortgage, loan on ~ durch Hypothek gesichertes Darlehen; **maximum amount** ~ Höchstbetragshypothek; **on** ~ hypothekarisch; **open-end** ~ offene Hypothek *(ohne festen Schuldbetrag; opp. closed-end ~)*; **option** ~ Abzahlungshypothek (→*option*); **preferred** ~ *Am* s. preferred ship →~; **prior** ~ im Range vorgehende Hypothek; **priority** (or **ranking**) **of** ~**s** Rangordnung von Hypotheken; **real estate** ~ (Grundstücks-)Hypothek *(opp. chattel ~)*; **recording of a** ~ *Am* Eintragung e-r Hypothek; **redemption of a** ~ Tilgung (od. Ablösung) e-r Hypothek; **registered** ~ registrierte Hypothek; *Br*[72] ship ~ *(→mortgage)*; **registration of a** ~ *Br* Eintragung e-r Hypothek; **repayment** ~ Tilgungshypothek; **running account** ~ *Br* Höchstbetragshypothek

mortgage, second ~ zweite Hypothek *(cf. first ~)*

Br Die zweite (und folgende) mortgage (of land) bedarf zur Sicherung der Eintragung in einem Register (zweite Hypotheken von registered land werden im Land Register, zweite Hypotheken von unregistered land im Land Charges Register eingetragen)

mortgage, senior ~ *Am* im Rang vorgehende Hypothek *(opp. junior ~)*

mortgage, ship ~ Schiffshypothek

Im anglo-amerikanischen Recht findet die ship mortgage ihre Grundlage in dem allgemeinen mortgage-Recht.

Br Die legal mortgage wird durch die registered mortgage[72] an registrierten Schiffen, die equitable mortgage durch die unregistered mortgage[73] vertreten. Für die Bestellung der registered mortgage ist eine besondere Form und die Registrierung vorgeschrieben.

Am Die Schiffshypothek des Common Law wird nach einzelstaatlichem Sachenrecht beurteilt und steht den besonderen Schiffsgläubigerrechten (maritime liens) im Range stets nach.
Nur die preferred ship mortgage ist bundesrechtlich geregelt

mortgage, preferred ship ~ *Am (durch Bundesgesetz*[74] *geregelte, seerechtliche)* Schiffshypothek, die bei Einhaltung strenger Form und Publizitätsvorschriften dem Gläubiger den Vorrang vor nachfolgenden Schiffsgläubigerrechten (maritime liens) sichert

mortgage, subsequent ~ *(im Rang)* nachstehende Hypothek; **terms of the** ~ Bedingungen der Hypothek; Verpfändungsbedingungen

mortgage, unregistered ~ nicht registrierte Hypothek, *Br*[75] s. ship →~
Die Rechte aus unregistered ship mortgages gehen denjenigen aus registered ship mortgages und anderen Schiffsgläubigerrechten im Range nach

mortgage *v* mit e-r Hypothek (od. hypothekarisch) belasten; *(bewegl. Sachen)* verpfänden; **to** ~ **by deposit of title deeds** *Br* e-e Hypothek durch Hinterlegung e-r Eigentumsurkunde aufnehmen (→*mortgage by deposit of title deeds*); **to** ~ **a property** ein Grundstück (od. Haus) mit e-r Hypothek belasten

mortgaged, ~ **property** hypothekarisch belasteter Grundbesitz; verpfändetes Vermögen; **the property is** ~ **to the building society** *Br* das Haus ist zugunsten der Bausparkasse mit e-r Hypothek belastet

mortgaging property Belastung e-s Hauses mit e-r Hypothek; hypothekarische Belastung von Grundbesitz; Verpfändung von Vermögensgegenständen

mortgageable hypothekarisch belastbar; verpfändbar

mortgagee Hypothekengläubiger; Inhaber e-s Grundpfandrechts; Pfandgläubiger; ~ **clause** *(VersR)* Klausel zum Schutze des Hypothekengläubigers; ~ **in possession** *(das verpfändete Grundstück auf Grund des Grundpfandrechts)* besitzender Sicherungsgläubiger

mortgagor Hypothekenschuldner; Pfandgeber, Verpfänder; **the ~'s right to discharge the mortgage** (at any time on giving notice) Recht des Hypothekenschuldners, die Hypothek zu tilgen (zu jeder Zeit nach Kündigung); **the** ~ **has defaulted** der Hypothekenschuldner ist mit seinen Zahlungen in Verzug geraten; **the** ~ **failed to pay off the mortgage debt within the prescribed time** →mortgage debt

mortis causa von Todes wegen

mortmain[76] tote Hand; **alienation in** ~ *(verbotene)* Veräußerung an die tote Hand *(bes. von Land an e-e [wohltätige oder religiöse] corporation)*; ~ **statute** *Am* Gesetz, das die testamentarische Überlassung von Land an e-e corporation beschränkt oder den Betrag begrenzt, den ein Testator, der Frau und Kind hinterläßt, für wohltätige Einrichtungen hinterläßt

mortuary Leichenhalle; Toten-; ~ **dividend** *Am (VersR)* Todesfalldividende; ~ **table** *Am (VersR)* Sterblichkeitstabelle

mortuum vadium Hypothek

most favo(u)red nation meistbegünstigte Nation; ~ **clause** Meistbegünstigungsklausel; ~ **rate** Meistbegünstigungssatz; ~ **tariff** Meistbegünstigungstarif; ~ **treatment** Meistbegünstigung; **to be accorded** ~ **treatment** Meistbegünstigung genießen; **to grant each other** ~ **treatment** einander Meistbegünstigung einräumen

most seriously affected countries (MSAC) am schwersten betroffene Länder
Von den Vereinten Nationen vorgenommene Bezeichnung für Länder, die von einer Verschlechterung weltwirtschaftlicher Rahmenbedingungen am meisten betroffen sind

MOT[76a] **certificate** *Br (etwa)* TÜV-Bescheinigung

motel *Am* Motel *(Kraftfahrerhotel)*

mother, ~ **country** Mutterland *(opp. foreign possessions)*; **~'s pension** *Am* Rente für Mutter mit Kindern; ~ **tongue** Muttersprache; **working ~s** *(außerhalb des Hauses)* arbeitende Mütter, berufstätige Mütter

motion 1. Antrag *(in e-r Versammlung)*; ~ **for adjournment** (or **to adjourn**) (a meeting etc) Antrag auf Vertagung (e-r Sitzung etc); ~ **for closure** *parl* Antrag auf Debattenschluß

motion of censure (or **no-confidence**) *parl* Mißtrauensantrag; **to introduce** (or **present** or *Br* **table**) **a** ~ e-n Mißtrauensantrag einbringen; **to withdraw a** ~ e-n Mißtrauensantrag zurückziehen

motions on the agenda Anträge der Tagesordnung

motion, adoption of a ~ Annahme e-s Antrages; **mover of the** ~ Antragsteller; **order of precedence of ~s** *parl* Rangfolge der Anträge; **privileged** ~ *parl* Dringlichkeitsantrag; **procedural** ~ *parl* Antrag zur Geschäftsordnung; **rejection of a** ~ Ablehnung e-s Antrags; **substantive** ~ *parl* Antrag zur Sache

motion, to abandon a ~ e-n Antrag zurückziehen; **to adopt a** ~ e-n Antrag annehmen; **the** ~ **is adopted by 12 votes to 8** der Antrag ist mit 12 Stimmen gegen 8 angenommen; **the** ~ **was agreed upon** der Antrag wurde angenommen; **to bring forward a** ~ e-n Antrag stellen (od. einbringen); **to carry the** ~ den Antrag annehmen; **the** ~ **was carried** der Antrag ging durch (od. wurde angenommen); **to**

defeat a ~ e-n Antrag ablehnen; **to file a** ~ e-n *(schriftl.)* Antrag stellen; **to introduce a** ~ e-n Antrag stellen, beantragen; **to lay a** ~ **on the table** *parl* e-n Antrag auf unbestimmte Zeit zurückstellen; **to present** (or **propose**) **a** ~ e-n Antrag stellen, beantragen; **the** ~ **was put to the vote** der Antrag wurde zur Abstimmung vorgelegt; **to reject a** ~ e-n Antrag ablehnen; **to second a** ~ e-n Antrag unterstützen; **to withdraw a** ~ e-n Antrag zurückziehen

motion 2. Antrag *(an das Gericht durch e-e Partei od e-n Anwalt)*; ~ **denied on the law** *Am* als rechtlich unbegründet abgewiesener Antrag; ~ **for the admission of evidence** Beweisantrag; ~ **for dismissal** Antrag auf Klageabweisung; ~ **for injunction** Antrag auf Erlaß e-r einstweiligen Verfügung; ~ **for judgment** Antrag auf gerichtliche Entscheidung *(wenn keine Verhandlung stattgefunden hat, z.B. bei fehlender Klagebeantwortung)*; ~ **for reconsideration** Antrag auf erneute Überprüfung: ~ **for summary judgment** *Am* Antrag, ohne weitere Beweisaufnahme für den Kläger zu entscheiden; ~ **for a new trial** Antrag auf Wiederaufnahme des Verfahrens; ~ **of course** Antrag, auf den ohne mündliche Verhandlung entschieden werden kann; ~ **on notice** Antrag nach Benachrichtigung *(der betroffenen Partei; opp. ex parte ~)* ~ **to dismiss** Antrag (*des Beklagten*) auf Klageabweisung: ~ **to stay the action** Antrag auf Verfahrensaussetzung

motion, cross-~ Gegenantrag; **cross-~s** Antrag und Gegenantrag; **ex parte** ~ Antrag einer Partei *(ohne Anhörung der Gegenpartei; opp. ~ on notice)*; **originating** ~ *Br* Antrag, mit dem das Verfahren in der Chancery Division eingeleitet werden kann; **time for filing a** ~ Antragsfrist

motion, the ~ **must be argued** über den Antrag kann erst nach mündlicher Verhandlung entschieden werden; **to dismiss the** ~ den Antrag abweisen; **to file** (or **make**) **a** ~ e-n Antrag stellen; **to grant the** ~ dem Antrag stattgeben; **to vote for a** ~ für e-n Antrag stimmen

motion 3. Bewegung; Antrieb; ~ **picture industry** Filmindustrie; **in** ~ *(VerkehrsR)* in Fahrt befindlich; **at one's own** ~ aus eigenem Antrieb; **to set in** ~ in Gang setzen

motivate *v* motivieren, begründen; veranlassen

motivation Motivierung, Begründung; Antrieb; ~ **research** Motivforschung *(auf psychoanalytischen Methoden beruhender Zweig der Marktforschung)*

motive Beweggrund; **base ~s** niedrige Beweggründe; **improper** ~ unlauterer Beweggrund; sich als unbegründet erweisender Beweggrund; **interest ~s** eigennützige Beweggründe

motor Motor; Auto; **~s** *(Börse)* Kraftfahrzeugwerte; ~ **accident** Autounfall

motor-assisted bicycle, rider of a ~ Mofa-Fahrer

motorcade Autokolonne

motor-car *bes. Br* Auto, (Personen-)Kraftwagen (Pkw); **comprehensive** ~ **insurance** *Br* kombinierte Kfz-Versicherung; **output** (or **production**) **of ~s** *Br* Automobilproduktion; **to drive a** ~ ein Auto fahren

motor,~ **coach** Omnibus *(für Fernverkehr)*; (Reise-)Bus; ~ **court** *Am* Motel; **~cycle** Motorrad; ~ **hull insurance** *Br* Kraftfahrzeug-Kaskoversicherung; ~ **industry** *Br* Auto(mobil)industrie, Kraftfahrzeugindustrie

motor insurance *Br* Kraftfahrzeug-Versicherung, Kfz-Versicherung; ~ **policy** *Br* Kfz-Police; ~ **with no-claims bonus** (or **discount**) *Br* Kfz-Versicherung mit Schadenfreiheitsrabatt; **third party** ~ *Br* Kfz-Haftpflichtversicherung

motor, ~ **shares** (or **stocks**) Auto(mobil)aktien; ~ **show** *Br* Automobilausstellung; ~ **trade** *Br* Kraftfahrzeughandel; ~ **traffic** *Br* Kraftfahrzeug-Verkehr; ~ **traffic offence** Verstoß gegen die Vorschriften des Straßenverkehrs

motor vehicle Kraftfahrzeug (Kfz); ~ **equipment and parts**[77] Ausrüstungsgegenstände und Teile von Kraftfahrzeugen; ~ **(vehicle) insurance company** Kraftfahrzeug-Versicherungsgesellschaft; ~ **licence** *Br (schriftl. jährl.)* Erlaubnis, das Fahrzeug zu benutzen; ~ **licence duty** *Br* Kraftfahrzeugsteuer; ~ **licensing** Zulassung von Kraftfahrzeugen; ~ **passenger insurance** Insassenversicherung; ~ **registration number** Autokennzeichen; amtl. Kennzeichen für Kraftfahrzeuge; ~ **safety standards** *Am* Sicherheitsstandards für Kraftfahrzeuge *(Mindestanforderungen an die Sicherheit der Kfz)*; ~ **third party liability** Kraftfahrzeughaftpflicht; **driver of a** ~ Kraftfahrzeugführer; **driving or being in charge of a** ~ **when under the influence of drink** (or **drug**) *Br* **(operating a** ~ **[while] under the influence of liquor** *Am*) Führen e-s Kraftfahrzeuges unter Alkohol- *(Br* od. Rauschgift)einfluß; **operator of a** ~ *Am* Kraftfahrzeugführer; **owner of a** ~ Eigentümer e-s Kraftfahrzeugs; Kfz-Halter; **to operate a** ~ *Am* ein Kraftfahrzeug führen

motoring *bes. Br* Autofahren; **~cases** Verkehrsstrafsachen; ~ **offences** *Br* (Kraftfahrzeug-) Verkehrsdelikte

motorist Autofahrer, Kraftfahrer

motorway *Br* Autobahn

motu proprio („aus eigenem Antrieb") *eccl* Anfangsworte e-r päpstlichen Entscheidung

mourning Trauer; **court** ~ Hoftrauer; **national** ~ Staatstrauer

movable beweglich; *Scot* nicht vererblich; ~ **property** bewegliches Vermögen, Mobilien *(cf. movables);* Eigentum an beweglichen Sachen; *Scot* nicht vererbliches Vermögen *(opp. heritable property)*

movables bewegliches Vermögen, Mobilien; *Scot* alles Vermögen außer Erbschaft (heritage)
Movables[78] ist vor allem ein Begriff des Kollisionsrechts. Es entspricht in etwa personal property und chattels, umfaßt aber gewöhnlich nicht choses in action *(cf. immovables)*

move Schritt, Aktion, Maßnahme(n); *Am* Auszug *(aus e-m Haus)*

move *v (in Versammlungen und ProzeßR)* beantragen, Antrag stellen (od. einbringen); sich bewegen; ab- und zuwandern *(Arbeitskräfte);* **to ~ about freely** sich frei bewegen; **to ~ away** fortziehen; **to ~ down(wards)** fallen, sich abwärts bewegen *(Kurse, Preise);* **to ~ in(to)** einziehen; **to ~ out** ausziehen; **to ~ to** umziehen nach; **the shares ~d up** die Aktien stiegen (od. zogen an)

move *v*, **to ~ an affidavit** *Am* e-n Antrag auf Grund e-s anliegenden →affidavit stellen; **to ~ an amendment** e-n Abänderungsantrag einbringen; **to ~ the closure** *parl* Antrag auf Schluß der Debatte stellen; **to ~ the previous question** *parl* das Übergehen zur Tagesordnung beantragen *(→previous question);* **to ~ a resolution in a meeting** in e-r Versammlung e-e Entschließung einbringen

moving beweglich; in Bewegung (befindlich); Auszug *(aus e-m Haus);* Umzug; **~ allowance** *Am* Umzugskosten (Zuschuß); **~ company** *Am* Möbelspedition; **~ day** Umzugstag; **~ expenses** (or **expenses of ~**) Umzugskosten; **~ party** Antragsteller; **~ van** *Am* Möbelwagen; **~ violation** *Am* Verletzung e-r Verkehrsvorschrift *(→violation)*

movement Bewegung; *pol, eccl etc* Massenbewegung; *(Börse)* Kursbewegung; **~ certificate** *(EG)* Warenverkehrsbescheinigung; Präferenz-Ursprungsnachweis; **~ of capital** Kapitalbewegung; **~ of goods** Warenverkehr, Güterverkehr; **~ of prices** Preisbewegung; Kursbewegung; **downward ~** Fallen *(Kurse, Preise);* **freedom of ~** Freizügigkeit; **free ~ of labo(u)r** *(EG)* Freizügigkeit der Arbeitnehmer; **labo(u)r ~** Arbeiterbewegung; **resistance ~** Widerstandsbewegung; **underground ~** Untergrundbewegung; **upward ~** Aufwärtsbewegung, Steigen *(Kurse, Preise);* **youth ~** Jugendbewegung

mover *parl etc* Antragsteller; *Am* Möbeltransporteur; **chief** (or **prime**) **~** Hauptbetreiber

movie industry *Am* Filmindustrie

Mozambican Mosambikaner(in); mosambikanisch

Mozambique Mosambik; **People's Republic of ~** Volksrepublik Mosambik

mudslinging Verleumdung; Aufgabe von PR-Agenturen, den →raider bei den Aktionären unmöglich zu machen

mufti, in ~ *Br* in Zivil *(opp. in uniform)*

mugger Straßenräuber

mugging Raubüberfall *(auf offener Straße); sl.* Fotografieren für das Verbrecheralbum

mugshot *Am* Porträtfoto *(e-s Verbrechers)*, Polizeifoto

mulct Geldstrafe, Geldbuße

mulct *v* mit e-r Geldstrafe belegen

multiannual program(me) Mehrjahresprogramm

multicorporate enterprise *Am* Konzern

multicraft union *Am* Gewerkschaft, die mehrere handwerkliche Berufe umfaßt

multicurrency →pooling

multifariousness *(unzulässige)* Verbindung mehrerer Klagen in einer Klageschrift

Multifibre Arrangement (MFA) *(EG)* Multifaserabkommen; **to be covered by the ~** unter das Multifaserabkommen fallen

multigraph *Am* Vervielfältigungsapparat

multilateral multilateral, mehrseitig; **~ agreement** *(VölkerR)* multilaterales Abkommen *(opp. bilateral agreement)*

Multilateral Investment Guarantee Agency (MIGA), **Convention Establishing the ~**[78a] Übereinkommen zur Errichtung der Multilateralen Investitions-Garantie-Agentur; MIGA-Übereinkommen
Die MIGA hat die Aufgabe, durch Garantien gegen nichtkommerzielle Risiken *(z.B. Krieg)* Investitionen für produktive Zwecke, vor allem in den Entwicklungsländern, zu fördern

multilateral, ~ trade negotiations (MTN) multilaterale Handelsverhandlungen (MHV); **~ treaty** *(VölkerR)* multilateraler Vertrag

multiline telephone number *Am tel* Sammelnummer

multilingualism Mehrsprachigkeit

multinational, ~ company (or *Am* **corporation)** (MNC), multinationale Gesellschaft; **~ enterprise** (MNE) multinationales Unternehmen (MNU); internationaler (Groß-)Konzern; **~ state** *(VölkerR)* Nationalitätenstaat, Mehrvölkerstaat

multinationals multinationale Unternehmen, Multis

multi-option financing facility (MOFF) Rahmenkreditlinie für die Inanspruchnahme unterschiedlicher kurzfristiger Finanzierungsinstrumente am US- oder Euromarkt oder bei der Garantiebank

multipartite in mehrere Teile geteilt; *(VölkerR)* multilateral

multiple vielfach, mehrfach; **~s** *Br* Unternehmen mit Filialen; ~ **(address) telegram** (TM) Mehrfachtelegramm; ~ **applicants** *(PatR)* mehrere Anmelder; ~ **basing point system** *Am* kollektive Frachtsatzberechnung, Preisortsystem *(für Frachtberechnung werden mehrere Ausgangsorte festgesetzt; opp. single basing point system);* ~ **certificate** *Br* Zertifikat für mehr als eine Aktie; ~ **choice questions** Auswahlfragen; ~ **component facility** →multi-option financing facility; ~ **currency clause bond** Euroanleihe mit Währungsoption *(der Gläubiger kann zwischen zwei od. mehr Währungen für Zins- und Tilgungszahlungen wählen)*; ~ **entries** *Am* mehrmalige Einreisen; ~ **exchange rates** multiple Wechselkurse; ~ **family dwelling** Mehrfamilienhaus; ~ **firm** *Br* Kettengeschäft; ~ →**licensing;** **~-line (under)writer** *Am* Kompositversicherer, Mehrsparten-Versicherer; ~ **listing** →general listing; ~ **management** →management 1.; ~ **national** Mehrstaater

multiple nationality Mehrstaatigkeit; **Convention on Reduction of Cases of M~ N~ and Military Obligations in Cases of M~ N~**[78a] Übereinkommen über die Verringerung der Mehrstaatigkeit u. über die Wehrpflicht von Mehrstaatern; **holder of a** ~ Mehrstaater

multiple, ~ **office bank** Bank mit mehreren Filialen; ~ **party system** Mehrparteiensystem; ~ **poinding** *Scot* →interpleader; ~ **production** Serienherstellung; ~ **rate system** multiple Wechselkurse; ~ **risk insurance** kombinierte Versicherung; ~ **share certificate** Globalaktie; ~ **stages sales tax** *Am* Mehrphasen-Umsatzsteuer; ~ **store** Filialgeschäft *(Einzelladen e-s Filialnetzes; cf. chain store)*; ~ **store enterprise** Kettenunternehmen; ~ **taxation** mehrfache Besteuerung *(durch mehrere Staaten);* ~ **tenure** gemeinsamer Besitz *(Nutzung von Grundstükken durch mehrere Personen);* ~ **voting right** Mehrstimmrecht; ~ **voting shares** Mehrstimmrechtsaktien

multiplicity of actions[79] Einbringung mehrerer Klagen für den gleichen Anspruch

multipurpose Mehrzweck-; ~ **cooperative** Universalgenossenschaft

multi-role combat aircraft (MRCA) Mehrzweckkampfflugzeug

multis multinationale Unternehmen

multi-stage Mehrstufen-; ~ **group** mehrstufiger Konzern; ~ **rocket** Mehrstufenrakete; ~ **tax** Mehrphasensteuer; **tax calculated by a cumulative** ~ **system** Mehrphasensteuer[80]

multi-storey, ~ **block** Hochhaus; ~ **car park** Hochgarage, Parkhochhaus

multi-tier consolidation *Am* stufenweise Konsolidierung *(der Konzernunternehmen, wenn die Obergesellschaft unmittelbare und mittelbare Beteiligungen hält)*

municipal städtisch, kommunal, Gemeinde-; innerstaatlich, national; ~ **authorities** kommunale Behörden, Gemeindebehörden; ~ **bonds** *Am* Kommunalobligationen; ~ **border** Stadtgrenze; ~ **compensation** *Am* Abgabe an Gemeinde für Konzessionserteilung (franchise); ~ **corporation** kommunale Körperschaft; ~ →**court;** ~ **debts** Gemeindeschulden, Gemeindeverschuldung; ~ **election** *Am* Gemeindewahl, Kommunalwahl; ~ **employee** *Am* Kommunalangestellter; ~ **enterprise** Kommunalbetrieb; ~ **general obligation bond** *Am* allgemeine Kommunalobligation, die durch Steuereinnahmen bedient wird; ~ **government** Stadtverwaltung

municipal law *(VölkerR)* innerstaatliches Recht, Landesrecht *(opp. international law);* **approximation of the ~s** Angleichung der innerstaatlichen Rechtsvorschriften

municipal, ~ **legislation** innerstaatliche Gesetzgebung; ~ **loan** städtische Anleihe, Kommunalanleihe; ~ **officer** (or **official**) *Am* städtischer Beamter, Gemeindebeamter, Kommunalbeamter; Gemeindebediensteter; ~ →**ordinance;** ~ **property** städtisches Eigentum, Gemeindeeigentum; ~ **reception** Empfang durch die Stadtverwaltung; ~ **revenue bond** *Am* kommunale Ertrags-Obligation, die durch die Erträge konkreter Investitionen der Gemeinden bedient wird; ~ **securities** Wertpapiere der Gemeinden; ~ **services** städtische Einrichtungen; ~ **stock** →corporation stock; ~ **taxes** Kommunalsteuern

municipality Stadtgemeinde, Stadt mit Selbstverwaltung

municipalization Überführung in städtische Verwaltung

municipalise *v* in städtische Verwaltung überführen

muniment Urkunde *(die ein Recht od. e-e Forderung begründet);* **~s of title** Urkunden über das Eigentum an Grundbesitz

munition Kriegsmaterial, Munition; **~s industry** Rüstungsindustrie; ~ **works** Rüstungsbetrieb; **atomic demolition** ~ (ADM) Atomminen

murder[81] Mord *(Br rechtswidrige, mit →malice aforethought begangene Tötung e-s Menschen);* ~ **attempt**[82] Mordversuch; ~ **(attended) with robbery** Raubmord; ~ **in the first degree** *Am* schwerer (mit →malice aforethought begangener) Mord *(auf dem im allgemeinen die Todesstrafe [capital punishment] steht);* ~ **in the second degree** *Am* leichter Mord *(z.B. im Laufe e-s Streites);* Totschlag; ~ **trial** Mordprozeß; **attempted** ~[82] Mordversuch; **charged with** ~ angeklagt wegen Mordes; **on a charge of** ~ unter Mordanklage; **felony-**~ *Am* Verbrechen mit Todesfolge; **rape and** ~ Lustmord; **to commit a** ~ e-n Mord begehen; **a person not found guilty of** ~ **may be found guilty of manslaughter**[83] jd, der wegen Mordes nicht für schuldig befunden wurde, kann wegen Totschlags für schuldig befunden werden

Am Nach dem Model Penal Code (sec. 210.2) ist eine Straftat gegen das Leben Mord, wenn a) absichtlich od. wissentlich begangen, b) leichtfertig (recklessly) unter Umständen begangen, die ungewöhnliche Gleichgültigkeit gegenüber dem Wert menschlichen Lebens erkennen lassen

murder *v* (er)morden; **attempt to** ~[82] Mordversuch

murderer Mörder; **to hire a** ~ e-n Mörder dingen

mushroom enterprises Spekulationsbetriebe

mushroom *v* aus dem Boden schießen, schnell emporschießen

musical works *(UrhR)* Werke der Musik; **composer of** ~ Urheber von Werken der Tonkunst; **copyright in** ~[84] Urheberrecht an Werken der Tonkunst

must legislation *Am colloq.* unerläßlich notwendige Gesetze

muster *mil* Musterung, Appell; ~ **roll** Stammrolle; (Schiffs-)Musterrolle

mutatis mutandis ("the necessary changes being made") sinngemäß; **to apply** ~ entsprechend anwenden (od. gelten); entsprechende Anwendung finden

mutilated verstümmelt *(z.B. Telegramm);* beschädigt *(z.B. Wertpapier)*

mutilation *(auch UrhR)* Verstümmelung; Beschädigung; **self**~ (or **voluntary**) ~ *bes. mil* Selbstverstümmelung

mutineer Meuterer

mutiny *mil* Meuterei; **to institute a** ~ zu e-r Meuterei anstiften

mutiny *v* meutern

mutual 1. Versicherungsverein auf Gegenseitigkeit (VVaG); ~**s writing the windstorm and hail** *Am* VVaG, die Sturm- und Hagelschäden versichern; **farm** ~**s** *Am* landwirtschaftliche VVaG

mutual 2. gegenseitig, wechselseitig; auf Gegenseitigkeit; ~ **agreement** gegenseitiges Einvernehmen; gegenseitige Vereinbarung; ~ **agreement procedure** *(DBA)* Verständigungsverfahren; ~ **aid** →~ assistance; **M** ~ **and Balanced Reduction of Forces** (MBFR) *mil* gegenseitiger und ausgewogener Truppenabbau *(in Europa);* ~ **and proprietary life offices** *(Australien)* Lebensversicherungsgesellschaften auf Gegenseitigkeits- und Aktienbasis

mutual assistance gegenseitige Hilfe; ~ **between authorities** gegenseitige Amtshilfe; ~ **pact** *(VölkerR)* Beistandspakt; →**European Convention on M**~ **A**~ **in Criminal Matters**

mutual, ~ **association** Vereinigung auf Gegenseitigkeit; ~ **benefit society** Versicherungsverein auf Gegenseitigkeit; ~ **casualty insurance company** *Am* Versicherungsverein auf Gegenseitigkeit für Schadensversicherung

mutual company Versicherungsverein auf Gegenseitigkeit (VVaG); **incorporation of a** ~ Gründung e-r VVaG; **to incorporate a** ~ e-e VVaG gründen

mutual, by ~ **consent** in gegenseitigem Einvernehmen; ~ **credit** wechselseitig eingeräumter Kredit; ~ **dealings** wechselseitige Geschäfte; ~ **debts** wechselseitig bestehende Schulden; ~ **defen|ce (**~**se) agreement** *(VölkerR)* Abkommen über gegenseitige Verteidigungshilfe; ~ **fire insurance company** Feuerversicherungsgesellschaft auf Gegenseitigkeit

mutual fund *Am*[85] Investmentfonds *(mit unbeschränkter Emission von Anteilen; opp. closed-end fund);* **M**~ **F**~ **Directory** *Am* Nachschlagewerk für Investmentfonds; ~ **shares** *Am* Anteile e-r (→open-end) Investmentgesellschaft

mutual guarantee gegenseitiges Garantieversprechen; **treaty of** ~ *(VölkerR)* Garantievertrag

mutual insurance Versicherung auf Gegenseitigkeit *(zu deren Vermögen kein Aktienkapital gehört; opp. proprietary insurance);* ~ **company** Versicherungsverein auf Gegenseitigkeit (VVaG); **M**~ **I**~ **Companies' Association** *Br* Verband der Versicherungsvereine auf Gegenseitigkeit; ~ **society** *Br (und Australien)* Versicherungsverein auf Gegenseitigkeit; **American M**~ **I**~ **Alliance** (AMIA) Vereinigung amerikanischer Versicherungsvereine auf Gegenseitigkeit; **National Association of M**~ **I**~ **Companies** (NAMIC) *Am* Nationale Vereinigung von Versicherungsgesellschaften auf Gegenseitigkeit

mutual, ~ **investment trust** *Am* →~ fund; ~ **life assurance company** *Br* (~ **life assurance society** *[Australien]*) Lebensversicherungsgesellschaft auf Gegenseitigkeit; ~ **life insurance company** →~ life assurance company; ~ **life**

society *Am* Lebensversicherungsgesellschaft auf Gegenseitigkeit; ~ **loan association** *Am* →building and loan association; ~ **mistake** beiderseitiger Irrtum; ~ **office** *Br* Versicherungsverein auf Gegenseitigkeit *(opp. proprietary office)*; ~ **principle** Gegenseitigkeitsprinzip; ~ **property and casualty insurance company** *Am* VVaG für Sach- und Schadensversicherung; ~ **recognition of diplomas** gegenseitige Anerkennung der Diplome; ~ **savings bank** *Am* genossenschaftsähnliche Sparkasse; gemeinnützige Sparkasse; ~ **society** Versicherungsverein auf Gegenseitigkeit *(z. B. in Australien)*; **on** ~ **terms** auf Gegenseitigkeit; ~ **testament** gegenseitiges Testament; ~ **trust** *Am* Gemeinschaftsfonds, der auf den Grundsätzen des Investment Trust beruht und Sammelanlagen verwaltet; ~ **will** gegenseitiges Testament *(→will)*; **to be based on** ~ **trust** auf gegenseitigem Vertrauen beruhen

mutually, ~ **satisfactory arrangement** alle Teile befriedigende Abmachung; **to be** ~ **dependent** voneinander abhängig sein

mutuality of claims Gegenseitigkeit der Ansprüche *(als Voraussetzung der Aufrechnung [set-off])*

mutualization of a stock company *Am* Umwandlung e-r Aktiengesellschaft in e-n Versicherungsverein auf Gegenseitigkeit

mystic testament *Am (Lousiana)* geschlossenes (od. gesiegeltes) Testament, für das besondere Vorschriften gelten

N

nail, to pay on the ~ pünktlich bezahlen

naked (nked, nkd) lose *(von Öl) (opp. in barrels or in drums)*

naked, ~ **contract** *(wegen fehlender consideration)* unverbindlicher Vertrag (nudum pactum); ~ **debenture** *Br* ungesicherte Schuldverschreibung *(opp. mortgage debenture)*

name Name; ~, **address and →description;** ~ **and arms clause** *Br* Klausel in e-m Testament, in dem jdm Vermögen unter der Bedingung vermacht wird, daß er Namen und Wappen des Testators trägt, widrigenfalls das Vermögen auf den nächsten Erben (the next person in remainder) übergeht; ~ **brand** Markenartikel; ~**-day** *Br (Börse)* Skontrierungstag, Abrechnungstag; ~ **of a firm** →firm ~; ~ **of maker** Name des Ausstellers; ~ **plate** Türschild; Firmenschild; **assumed** ~ angenommener Name, Pseudonym, Deckname; **business** ~ Firmenname, Firma; **by** ~ mit Namen; **by the** ~ **of** unter dem Namen von, namens; **change of** ~ Namensänderung; **Christian** ~ Vorname; **collective** ~ Sammelname, Sammelbegriff; **confusion of** ~**s** Namensverwechslung; **corporate** ~ *Am* Firmenname *(e-r AG)*; **fictitious** ~ Deckname, Pseudonym; **first** ~ Vorname; **full** ~ Vor- und Zuname; **given** ~ Vorname; **index of** ~**s** Namensverzeichnis; **last** ~ *Am* Familienname; →**maiden** ~; **mistake in** ~ Namensirrtum; **sur**~ Familienname; →**trade** ~; **to ask for a p.'s** ~ nach jds Namen fragen; **to bear a** ~ e-n Namen führen; **to check off** ~**s on a list** Namen auf e-r Liste abhaken; **to enter one's** ~ sich eintragen (od. einschreiben); **to give one's** ~ s-n Namen nennen; **to keep one's** ~ **on the books** Mitglied *(e-s Vereins etc)* bleiben, s-e Mitgliedschaft beibehalten; **to be made out in the** ~ **of the holder** auf den Inhaber lauten; **to mention a p. by** ~ jdn namentlich erwähnen; **to put one's** ~ **to** s-n Namen setzen unter; **to put one's** ~ **down for** sich eintragen für; kandidieren für; **to refer to a p. by** ~ jdn mit Namen nennen (od. erwähnen); **to take one's** ~ **off the books** austreten *(aus e-m Verein etc)*, s-e Mitgliedschaft aufgeben

name *v* (be)nennen, bezeichnen, namhaft machen; *Am* ernennen; **to** ~ **the price** den Preis benennen (od. angeben)

named, ~ **policy** →policy 2.; **above-**~ (a/n) oben genannt

Namibia[1] Namibia; ~**n** Namibier, namibisch

naming Benennung, *(namentl.)* Bezeichnung, Namhaftmachung

narcotic Rauschgift, Suchtstoff; ~ **addict** Rauschgiftsüchtiger

narcotic drugs Rauschgifte, Suchtstoffe; **Commission on N~ D~** *(1946 vom Wirtschafts- und Sozialrat der Vereinten Nationen eingesetzte)* Rauschgiftkommission; **International Convention Relating to N~ D~**[1a] Internationales Opiumabkommen; **Single Convention on N~ D~**[2] Einheitsübereinkommen über Suchtstoffe

narcotics ring Bande von Rauschgifthändlern

narcotics, International N~ Control Board Internationales Suchtstoff-Kontrollamt (Suchtstoffamt); **smuggling of** ~ Rauschgiftschmuggel; **traffic in** ~ Rauschgifthandel; Handel mit Suchtstoffen; **habitual user of** ~**s** *Am* langjähriger Rauschgiftsüchtiger; **withdrawal of** ~ Entziehung (od. Entzug) von Suchtstoffen

narrate *v* berichten

narration of a journal entry Wortlaut e-r Buchung

narrow, by a ~ majority mit knapper Mehrheit

narrow *v* beschränken, einengen; **to ~ a claim** *(PatR)* e-n Anspruch einengen

narrowing, ~ amendment *(PatR)* einschränkende Änderung; **~ of claims** *(PatR)* Beschränkung der Ansprüche

nasciturus Nasziturus, Leibesfrucht

natality Geburtenziffer

nation Nation; Volk; **~-state** Nationalstaat; **~-wide** die ganze Nation (od. das ganze Land) umfassend; allgemein; *Am* bundesweit; **~-wide strike** *Am* Generalstreik; **community of ~s** Völkergemeinschaft; **industrial ~** Industriestaat; **law of ~s** Völkerrecht *(jus gentium)*; **member ~** Mitgliedsstaat; →**United N~s**

national 1. Staatsangehöriger, Inländer; **American ~ by birth** gebürtiger Amerikaner; **British ~ by virtue of citizenship**[3] britischer Staatsangehöriger auf Grund der Staatsangehörigkeit in den Mitgliedstaaten des Commonwealth; **dual ~** Doppelstaater, Inhaber von zwei Staatsangehörigkeiten; **foreign ~** ausländischer Staatsangehöriger, Angehöriger e-s fremden Staates; **French ~** französischer Staatsangehöriger; **local ~** einheimischer Staatsangehöriger *(e-r internationalen Organisation)*; **multiple ~** Mehrstaater, Inhaber mehrerer Staatsangehörigkeiten (→*multiple nationality*); **own ~** Angehöriger des eigenen Staates

national 2. national; staatlich; National-, Landes-, Staats-; *Am* gesamtamerikanisch, Bundes- *(opp. state)*; *(EG)* einzelstaatlich *(opp. Community)*; **N~ Academy of Sciences** (N. A. S.) *Am* Akademie der (Natur-)Wissenschaften *(in Washington)*; **~ accounting** volkswirtschaftliche Gesamtrechnung; **~ advertising** *Am* Werbung in den ganzen Vereinigten Staaten; **N~ Aeronautics and Space Administration** (NASA) *Am (zivile)* (Bundes-)Behörde für Luft- und Raumfahrt; **N~ Ambient Air Qualities Standards** *Am* Immissionsnormen; **~ anthem**[4] Nationalhymne; **~ application** *(europ. PatR)*[5] nationale Anmeldung; **~ assembly** Nationalversammlung; **N~ Assembly of the Church of England** (Church Assembly) *Br* Oberste Kirchenbehörde *(als gesetzgebende Versammlung, bestehend aus dem House of Bishops, dem House of Clergy und dem House of Laity)*

National Association, ~ for the Advancement of Colored People (NAACP) *Am* Nationale Vereinigung für die Förderung der farbigen Bevölkerung; **~ of Independent Insurers** (NAII) *Am* Nationale Vereinigung unabhängiger Versicherer; **~ of Insurance Commissioners** (NAIC) *Am* Nationale Vereinigung der Versicherungskommissare; **~ of Manufacturers** (N. A. M.) *Am* Nationaler Fabrikantenverband; **~ of Mutual Insurance Companies** (NAMIC) Nationale Vereinigung von Versicherungsvereinen auf Gegenseitigkeit; **~ of Securities Dealers** (NASD) *Am* Nationaler Verband der am außerbörslichen Handel (over-the-counter market) beteiligten Wertpapierhändler; **~ of Securities Dealers Automated Quotations** (NASDAQ) *Am* (elektronisches) System für Kursnotierung von Wertpapieren im →over-the-counter market; **~ of Security Dealers and Investment Managers** (NASDIM) *Br* Vereinigung der Wertpapierhändler und Investmentmanager und →self-regulatory organization der Londoner City für das Wertpapiergeschäft

national authority *(europ. PatR)*[6] nationales Amt *(die mit Erteilung von Patenten beauftragte Regierungsbehörde e-s Vertragsstaates)*

national banks *Am* Nationalbanken, Banken mit Bundeskonzession

Der Bundeskontrolle unterstehende private Depositenbanken; Mitglieder des →Federal Reserve System *(opp. state banks)*

national, ~ bankruptcy Staatsbankrott; **N~ Board for Prices and Incomes** *Br* staatl. Preis- und Einkommensüberwachungsstelle *(obs.)*; **~ boundary** *Am* Staatsgrenze; **~ brand** Schutzmarke *(e-s Artikels, der im ganzen Land verkauft wird)*; **N~ Broadcasting Corporation** (NBC) *Am* (größte private) Rundfunkgesellschaft; **~ call** *Br tel.* Ferngespräch; **~ centre (~er)** Landeszentrale

National Committee for the ICC Landesgruppe der Internationalen Handelskammer

national concern, matters of ~ nationale Belange

National Conference of Commissioners on Uniform State Laws *Am* Konferenz der Beauftragten für einheitliche Gesetze der Einzelstaaten

Die Konferenz erarbeitet einen Mustergesetzentwurf, der den Parlamenten der Einzelstaaten als eigenes Gesetz zur Annahme empfohlen wird. Zweck ist die Beseitigung von Unterschieden in den Rechten der Einzelstaaten *(cf. Uniform Acts)*

national consciousness Nationalbewußtsein

National Convention *Am* Nationalkonvent, Parteitag

Versammlung der Delegierten der einzelstaatl. Parteiorganisationen, um den Kandidaten für die Präsidenten- und Vizepräsidentenwahl zu nominieren und das Parteiprogramm festzulegen

National Council Nationalrat *(z.B. in Österreich, in der Schweiz)*; **~ of (the) Churches (of Christ)** *Am* Nationalrat der *(protestantischen, anglikanischen und orthodoxen)* Kirchen (Christi); **~ for Civil Liberties** (NCCL) brit. Bürgerschaftsvereinigung

national currency Landeswährung; **expressed in** ~ auf Landeswährung lautend

national custom Landesbrauch

national debt Staatsschuld *(Br funded od. unfunded; Am Schuld des Bundes);* **N~ D~ Commissioners** *Br* Staatsschuldenverwaltung

national defen|ce (~se) Landesverteidigung; **N~ D~ Contribution** *Br* Kriegsabgabe *(obs.);* ~ **expenses** Verteidigungsausgaben

national, ~ device Hoheitszeichen; ~ **economic accounting** volkswirtschaftliche Gesamtrechnung; **N~ Economic Development Council** (NEDC, „Neddy") *Br* Regierungsstelle zur Untersuchung der Wirtschaftsentwicklung auf dem öffentlichen und privaten Sektor; ~ **economy** Volkswirtschaft, Nationalökonomie; ~ **emblem** Hoheitszeichen; ~ **emergency** nationaler Notstand, Staatsnotstand; ~ **enterprise** Staatsbetrieb

National Enterprise Board (NEB) *Br* Behörde für staatliche Wirtschaftsförderung

Durch Industry Act 1980 mit National Research and Development Corporation fusioniert und als British Technology Group umbenannt, mit der Aufgabe neue Unternehmen zu fördern

National Environmental Policy Act (of 1969) (NEPA) *Am* Umweltschutzgesetz

national, N~ Executive (of the Labour Party) *Br* Parteivorstand; **N~ Executive Committee** (NEC) *Br* geschäftsführender Landesausschuß *(e-r Gewerkschaft);* **N~ Farmers' Union** (NFU) *Br* Wirtschaftsverband der Bauern; ~ **flag** Nationalflagge, Landesflagge *(opp. merchant flag);* **N~ Front** (NF) *Br* extrem rechte politische Partei *(deren Ziel es ist, die Zahl der in England ansässigen Farbigen zu verringern);* ~ **funeral** *Am* Staatsbegräbnis; **N~ Futures Association** (NFA) *Am* Aufsichtsorgan für den Terminhandel; ~ **gallery** Staatsgalerie

National Giro *Br* Postgirosystem; ~ **account** *Br* Postgirokonto; ~**bank** *Br* Postgiroamt; ~ **payment order** *Br* Zahlungsanweisung per Postgiro

national, ~ government *Am* Bundesregierung; **N~ Guard** *Am (den Gouverneuren der Einzelstaaten unterstehende)* Nationalgarde

National Health Service (NHS) *Br* Staatlicher Gesundheitsdienst

Der National Health Service sieht, von gewissen Ausnahmen abgesehen, freie (free of charge) Heilbehandlung (medical, dental, hospital or other services) für alle sich in Großbritannien aufhaltenden Personen vor

national, N~ Highway Traffic Safety Administration (NHTSA) *Am* Straßenverkehrsbehörde; ~ **holiday** nationaler Feiertag; **N~ Housing Act** *Am* Wohnungsbaugesetz; ~ **hymn** →~ anthem

national income Volkseinkommen; **average gross (net)** ~ durchschnittliches Brutto- (Netto-)Volkseinkommen; ~ **by distributive shares** *Am* Volkseinkommen nach Einkommensarten

national, ~ insignia Hoheitsabzeichen; ~ **insolvency** Staatsbankrott

national insurance (NI) *Br*[7] Sozialversicherung (→social security); ~ **contributions** Sozialversicherungsbeiträge

national, ~ interest Landesinteresse; ~ **issue** Inlandsemission; ~ **judge** *(VölkerR)* Richter, der die Staatsangehörigkeit e-r der Parteien besitzt; ~ **jurisdiction** inländische Gerichtsbarkeit; ~ **labo(u)r administration** *(EG)* einzelstaatliche Arbeitsverwaltung

National Labor Relations Act (NLRA) *Am*[8] Gesetz betr. die Arbeitsbeziehungen (Wagner Act) *(von 1935)*

National Labor Relations Board (NLRB) *Am* Bundesbehörde für Arbeitsbeziehungen

Durch den →NLRA geschaffene Verwaltungsbehörde mit quasi-richterlichen Funktionen und zwei Hauptaufgaben: Verfolgung unlauterer Arbeitspraktiken und Durchführung von Gewerkschaftswahlen *(für andere arbeitsrechtliche Probleme ist zuständig das Department of Labor)*

national, ~ language Landessprache; ~ **law** innerstaatliches Recht, inländisches Recht, Landesrecht; *(EG)* einzelstaatliches Recht *(opp. Community law);* ~ **laws and regulations** innerstaatliche Gesetzgebung

national legislation *(EG)* einzelstaatliche Rechtsvorschriften; **precedence of Community legislation over** ~ Vorrang der Gemeinschafts- gegenüber den einzelstaatlichen Rechtsvorschriften

national, ~ list Landesliste; ~ **marking** Hoheitsabzeichen *(e-s Flugzeugs);* ~ →**media;** ~ **mourning** Staatstrauer; **N~ Office** *Am (dem* →Commissioner of Internal Revenue unterstehende) Zentrale Steuerbehörde *(in Washington);* ~ **organization** *Am* Bundesorganisation; **N~ Over-the-Counter Index** US-Freiverkehrsindex (aus den Kursen der hundert größten im Freiverkehr gehandelten Unternehmen); ~ **park** Nationalpark, Naturschutzgebiet; ~ →**patent;** ~ **practices** innerstaatliche Gepflogenheiten; ~ **press** inländische Presse; **(gross, net)** ~ **product** (Brutto-, Netto-)Sozialprodukt; **N~ Radiation Protection Board** (NRPB) *Br* Behörde für Strahlenschutz; **N~ Railroad Passenger Corporation** *Am* (halbstaatl.) Bundesbahn; **N~ Reporter System** *Am* →reporter

national resident *Am* Einwohner, der die Staatsangehörigkeit des Wohnsitzlandes besitzt

national, ~ safety nationale (od. innere) Sicherheit; **N~ Safety Council** *Am* Gesellschaft *(wörtlich:* Rat) für Verkehrssicherheit

National Savings Bank (NSB) *Br* Postsparkasse; ~ **Investment Account** *Br* Sparkonto auf der Postsparkasse *(für Beträge ab £1);* ~ **Or-**

dinary Account *Br* Konto auf der Postsparkasse *(für Beträge ab 25p)*

national, N~ Savings Certificates *Br (vom Schatzamt ausgegebene, vom Postamt verkaufte)* staatliche Sparbriefe *(cf. index-linked ~);* **N~ Savings Stock Register** Verzeichnis der durch die →N~ Savings Bank verkauften Wertpapiere

National Science Foundation (N. S. F.) *Am*[9] (1950 gegründete) Bundesstiftung zur Förderung der Wissenschaften

national security nationale (od. innere) Sicherheit; Staatssicherheit; **N~ S~ Agency** (NSA) *Am (dem Pentagon unterstehender)* Nationaler Sicherheitsdienst *(Dachorganisation der Abwehreinheiten);* **N~ S~ Controls** *Am*[10] Kontrolle über Lieferungen von Waren und Technologie an dritte Staaten *(wenn dies die nationale Sicherheit der USA erfordert);* **N~ S~ Council** (NSC) *Am* Nationaler Sicherheitsrat *(in Washington);* **to be detrimental to** (or **to impair**) **the** ~ die nationale Sicherheit beeinträchtigen

national service *Br*[11] nationaler Wehrdienst (allgemeine Wehrpflicht) *(jetzt abgeschafft)*

National, ~ Socialism *Ger* Nationalsozialismus; ~ **Socialist** *Ger* Nationalsozialist (Nazi)

National Space Centre *Br* Nationales Raumfahrtzentrum

national state Nationalstaat; **multi-~** Nationalitätenstaat

national status Staatsangehörigkeit; **the jurisdiction of the court does not depend on the plaintiff's** ~ die Zuständigkeit des Gerichts hängt nicht von der Staatsangehörigkeit des Klägers ab

national, N~ Tax Association *Am* Steuerzahlervereinigung; ~ **team** Ländermannschaft; ~ **tendencies** nationale Strömungen; ~ **territory** Staatsgebiet

national treatment *(VölkerR)* Inländerbehandlung *(Gleichbehandlung e-s Ausländers mit den eigenen Staatsangehörigen);* **reciprocally accorded** ~ gegenseitig gewährte Inländerbehandlung

National Trust (for Places of Historic Interest or National Beauty) *Br*[12] *(gemeinnützige)* Nationale Institution für Naturschutzgebiete und Denkmalpflege

national, ~ union Zentralverband; *Am* Gewerkschaft mit Mitgliedern in allen Einzelstaaten; **N~ Union of Mineworkers** (NUM) *Br* Bergarbeitergewerkschaft; **N~ Union of Transport and General Workers** *Br* Transportarbeitergewerkschaft; ~ **waters** Eigengewässer, Binnengewässer

national wealth Volksvermögen; **elements of the** ~ Bestandteile des Volksvermögens

nationally televised *Am* im ganzen Land durch Fernsehen übertragen (worden)

nationality[13] Nationalität, Staatsangehörigkeit, Staatsbürgerschaft; Staatszugehörigkeit *(z. B. e-s Schiffes);* ~ **mark** Staatszugehörigkeitszeichen *(e-s Flugzeugs);* **acquisition of** ~ Erwerb der Staatsangehörigkeit; **certificate of** ~ *Am* Staatsangehörigkeitsausweis; **deprivation of** ~ Aberkennung der Staatsangehörigkeit; **→discrimination based on ~; double** ~ *Am* (**dual** ~*Br*) doppelte Staatsangehörigkeit

nationality, loss of ~ Verlust der Staatsangehörigkeit *(Br cf. deprivation or renunciation of →citizenship)*; **loss of ~ by native-born or naturalized citizens** *Am*[14] Verlust der Staatsangehörigkeit gebürtiger oder naturalisierter Amerikaner

nationality, original ~ ursprüngliche Staatsangehörigkeit; **person without a** ~ staatenlose Person; **proof of** ~ Nachweis der Staatsangehörigkeit; **release from** ~ Entlassung aus dem Staatsangehörigkeitsverhältnis; **(formal written) renunciation of** ~ *Am* (förmlicher) Verzicht auf die Staatsangehörigkeit; **retention of** ~ *Br* Beibehaltung der Staatsangehörigkeit

nationality, to acquire a ~ e-e Staatsangehörigkeit erwerben; **to adopt a** ~ e-e Staatsangehörigkeit annehmen; **to confer a ~ upon a p.** jdm e-e Staatsangehörigkeit verleihen; **to deprive a p. of his** ~ *bes. Am* jdm die Staatsangehörigkeit aberkennen; **to lose one's** ~ s-e Staatsangehörigkeit verlieren; **to reacquire one's** ~ s-e Staatsangehörigkeit wiedererlangen; **to renounce** ~ die Staatsangehörigkeit aufgeben

nationalization *bes. Br* Nationalisierung, Verstaatlichung; Vergesellschaftung; **intention of** ~ Verstaatlichungsabsicht; **to effect a ~ of an industry** e-e Industrie verstaatlichen

nationalize *v* nationalisieren, verstaatlichen; vergesellschaften

nationalized, ~ concern verstaatlichter Betrieb; volkseigener Betrieb *(Ausdruck der DDR,* →German Democratic Republic); ~ **industries** *Br* verstaatliche Industrien, Staatsindustrien

native Eingeborener; eingeboren; einheimisch, Landes-; gebürtig (of aus); **N~ American Rights Fund** (NARF) *Am* Organisation, die für die Rechte der Indianer eintritt; **~-born** eingeboren; gebürtig; **~-born American** gebürtiger Amerikaner; ~ **country** Heimatland, Vaterland, Geburtsland; ~ **labo(u)r** einheimische Arbeitskräfte; ~ **land** →~ country; ~ **language** Muttersprache; ~ **law** Eingeborenenrecht; **a ~ of France** ein gebürtiger Franzose; ~ **product** Landesprodukt; ~ **town** Heimatstadt, Vaterstadt; ~ **tribe** Eingeborenenstamm

NATO →North Atlantic Treaty Organization; ~ **armed forces** NATO-Streitkräfte

natural-born von Geburt; ~ **American citizen** amerikanischer Staatsangehöriger von Geburt, gebürtiger Amerikaner; ~ **British subject** britischer Staatsangehöriger von Geburt, geborener britischer Staatsbürger

natural, ~ **boundary** natürliche Grenze; ~ **calamity** Naturkatastrophe; ~ **child** nichteheliches Kind; ~ **death** natürlicher Tod; ~ **disaster** Naturkatastrophe; ~ **frontier** natürliche Grenze; ~ **gas** Erdgas (→*gas*); ~ **guardian** (Eltern als) Vormund; ~ **law** Naturrecht *(opp. man-made law)*; **during** (or **for**) **his** ~ **life** auf Lebenszeit; ~ **loss** natürlicher Schwund; ~ **person** natürliche Person *(opp. artificial or legal person)*; ~ **product** Rohprodukt; ~ →**resources;** ~ **right** 1. natürliches *(sich aus der Natur der Sache ergebendes)* Recht; 2. *Am* Grundrecht, *(durch die Verfassung gewährleistetes)* Freiheitsrecht; ~ **wastage of labo(u)r** natürlicher Abgang von Arbeitskräften *(retirement, death etc)*

naturalization Naturalisierung, Einbürgerung; ~ **of aliens**[15] Einbürgerung von Ausländern; ~ **of stateless persons**[16] Einbürgerung Staatenloser; ~ **proceedings** Einbürgerungsverfahren; **application for** ~ *Br* Einbürgerungsantrag; **certificate of** ~[17] Einbürgerungsurkunde (*Am* cf. first papers, second papers); **collective** ~ Kollektiveinbürgerung; **eligibility for** ~[18] Einbürgerungsfähigkeit

naturalization, petition for~ *Am*[19] Einbürgerungsantrag; **to file a petition for** ~ e-n Einbürgerungsantrag stellen

naturalization, qualifications for ~ *Br* Bedingungen für Einbürgerung; **revocation of** ~ Widerruf der Einbürgerung; **to be admitted to citizenship by** ~ *Am* eingebürgert werden

naturalize *v* naturalisieren, einbürgern

naturalized, ~ **American citizen** eingebürgerter Amerikaner; ~ **British subject** eingebürgerter britischer Staatsangehöriger; ~ **person** Eingebürgerter; **to become** ~ eingebürgert werden

nature Natur; Beschaffenheit, Art; **N**~ **Conservancy Council** (NCC) *Br* Naturschutzbehörde; ~ **conservation** (or **protection**) Naturschutz; ~ **of contents** Beschreibung des Inhalts *(e-s Pakets)*; ~ **reserve** Naturschutzgebiet; **crime against** ~ *(StrafR)* Sodomie

nautical nautisch, See-, Schiffs-; ~ **assessor** sachverständiger Beisitzer für Schiffahrtsfragen; ~→**mile;** ~ **will** Seetestament

naval Schiffs-, See-; Marine-; ~ **action** *mil* Seegefecht; ~ **affairs** Marineangelegenheiten, Marinewesen; ~ **agreement** Flottenabkommen; ~ **attaché** Marineattaché; ~ **base** *mil* Flottenstützpunkt; ~ **estimates** *parl* Marineetat; ~ **forces** Seestreitkräfte; ~ **officer** Marineoffizier; ~ **port** Kriegshafen; ~ **power** Seemacht; ~ **shipbuilding** Bau von Kriegsschiffen; ~ **station** Marinestation; ~ **stores** (Kriegs-)Schiffsvorräte; ~ **supremacy** Seeherrschaft; ~ **treaty** Flottenvertrag; ~ **vessel** Kriegsschiff; ~ **warfare** Seekrieg(führung)

navicert *(VölkerR)* Navicert, Geleitschein
Einem neutralen (Handels-)Schiff vom Kriegführenden ausgestellte Unbedenklichkeitsbescheinigung *(über das Nichtvorhandensein von Konterbandgütern zur Vermeidung der Durchsuchung des Schiffes)*

navigability Schiffbarkeit; ~ **licen|ce (~se) for inland waterway vessels** Schiffsattest für Binnenschiffe

navigable schiffbar; befahrbar; ~ **river** schiffbarer Fluß; ~ **waters** schiffbare Gewässer

navigation Schiffahrt, Seefahrt; Schiffsführung; ~ **agreement** Schiffahrtsabkommen; ~ **company** Schiffahrtsgesellschaft; ~ **dues** Schiffahrtsabgaben; ~ **law** Schiffahrtsrecht; ~ **mark** Seezeichen; ~ **route** Schiffahrtsstraße; **aerial** (or **air**) ~ Luftfahrt; **for the period of closed** ~ für die Zeit der Einstellung der Schiffahrt; **coasting** ~ Küstenschiffahrt; **commercial** ~ Handelsschiffahrt; **inland** ~ Binnenschiffahrt, Flußschiffahrt; **line** ~ Linienschiffahrt; **marine** ~ Seeschiffahrt; **treaty of** ~ Schiffahrtsvertrag; **Treaty of Friendship, Commerce and N**~ →friendship

navy (Kriegs-)Marine; (Kriegs-)Flotte; **N**~ **Bill** *parl* Flottenvorlage; **N**~ **Department** *Am* Marineministerium; **N**~ **Force** *Br* Marine; **N**~ **List** Marine-Rangliste *(Liste der Namen Br aller [Am der aktiven] Marineoffiziere)*; **N**~ **Register** *Am* Liste der Namen der Offiziere und Schiffe der US-Marine; ~ **regulations** *Am* Dienstvorschriften der Kriegsmarine; ~ **yard** Marinewerft; **Department of the N**~ *Am* →N~ Department; **merchant** ~ Handelsmarine

Nazi *Ger pol* Nazi (→National Socialist); ~ **victim** (or **victim of** ~ **persecution**) Opfer der Nazi-Verfolgung

near, ~ **banks** Quasibanken (*z. B. Versicherungen, Bausparkassen*); ~ **miss** Beinahezusammenstoß; ~ **money** Quasigeld; geldähnliche Forderungen, leicht liquidierbare Einlagen; ~ **relation** nahe(r) Verwandte(r)

nearest am nächsten gelegen; ~ **available market** nächst erreichbarer Markt; ~ **port** nächster Hafen; ~ **relative** nächste(r) Verwandte(r)

ne bis in idem ("not twice tried for the same offen|ce [~se]") Strafklageverbrauch (niemand kann zweimal wegen derselben Strafsache verurteilt werden) *(Grundgesetz Art. 103 [3]; Am cf. double jeopardy)*

necessaries Notwendigkeiten, lebensnotwendige Dinge, notwendiger Lebensbedarf; für den Lebensunterhalt notwendige Aufwendungen *(die abhängen von jds →station in life)*; **to pledge one's husband's credit for** ~ *Am* das Vermögen des Ehemannes durch Geschäfte zur Deckung des Lebensbedarfs der Familie verpflichten *(entspricht § 1357 BGB)*

necessary notwendig (to für); ~ **and proper** notwendig und geeignet; **if** ~ nötigenfalls; **to be** ~ erforderlich sein; **to consider** (or **deem**) ~ für notwendig erachten

necessitate *v* notwendig machen; erfordern

necessit|y Notwendigkeit; (dringendes) Bedürfnis; Not; Notstand; ~**ies** (of life) (zum Lebensunterhalt) notwendige Dinge, Lebensnotwendigkeiten; →**agency of** ~; →**agent of** ~; **articles of prime** ~ Artikel erstrangigen Bedarfs; **bare** ~ **of life** notwendiger Lebensbedarf; **excusing** ~ (*StrafR*) entschuldigender Notstand; **in case of** ~ erforderlichenfalls; **justifying** ~ (*StrafR*) rechtfertigender Notstand; **question of** ~ Bedürfnisfrage; **state of** ~ Notstand

necropsy Nekropsie, Leichenöffnung, Leichenschau

"Neddy" →National Economic Development Council

née *Fr (vor Mädchennamen der Ehefrau)* geborene

need dringende Notwendigkeit, Grund; Bedürfnis, Bedarf (for an); Mangel (for an); Not(lage), Armut; ~**s** Bedürfnisse; ~ **for capital** Bedarf an Kapital, Kapitalbedarf; ~ **of (foreign) exchange** Devisenbedarf; ~**s of the market** Marktbedarf; ~ **of** (or **for**) **money** Geldbedarf; ~**s test** →means test; **anticipated** ~ voraussichtlicher Bedarf; **basic** ~**s** Grundbedürfnisse; **borrowing** ~**s** Kreditbedarf; **capital** ~**s** Kapitalbedarf; **consumer** ~**s** Bedarf der Verbraucher; **a critical** ~ **has arisen** e-e dringende Notlage ist entstanden; **degree of** ~ Grad der Bedürftigkeit; **essential** ~**s** Lebensbedürfnisse; **for one's personal** ~**s** für den Eigenbedarf; **in** ~ **of assistance** hilfsbedürftig; **in** ~ **of repair** reparaturbedürftig

need, in case of ~ nötigenfalls, im Notfalle; **address** (or **referee**) **in case of** ~ Notadresse, Notanschrift; **in case of** ~ **apply to ...** nötigenfalls wenden Sie sich an ...

need, present ~ gegenwärtiger Bedarf; **proof of** ~ Bedürftigkeitsnachweis; **state of** ~ Notlage; **urgent** ~ dringender Bedarf; dringendes Bedürfnis; **if** ~ **arises** (or **if** ~ **be**) nötigenfalls, wenn nötig; **to be in** ~ (or **to have** ~) **(of)** Mangel haben (an), nötig haben, brauchen; **to fill** (or **meet**) **a** ~ e-m Bedürfnis entsprechen; den Bedarf decken; **to take account of the** ~**s** den Bedürfnissen Rechnung tragen

need *v* nötig haben, brauchen; **to** ~ **repairs** reparaturbedürftig sein; **when** ~**ed** im Bedarfsfalle, nötigenfalls

needy bedürftig; **the** ~ die Bedürftigen

ne exeat regno ("that he leave not the Kingdom") *Br* gerichtl. Verbot, das Vereinigte Königreich zu verlassen

negative negativ, verneinend *(opp. affirmative)*; ~ **answer** abschlägige Antwort *(opp. affirmative answer)*; ~ **clearance** *(EG und Am AntitrustR)* Negativattest; ~ **contract** Vertrag, der zu e-m Unterlassen verpflichtet; ~ **covenant** Unterlassungsversprechen; ~ →**easement;** ~ **injunction** gerichtliches Verbot; ~ **investment** *Am* →disinvestment; ~ **pregnant** *(Zivilprozeß)* formales Bestreiten, obwohl gleichzeitig e-e od. alle behaupteten Tatsachen darin zugestanden werden *(unzulässige Form des pleading)*; **(~)** →**prescription;** ~ →**reply;** ~ **taxes** negative Steuern (Transferzahlungen); ~ **vote** Nein-Stimme *(opp. affirmative vote)*; **to answer in the** ~ verneinend antworten, verneinen

negative *v* entgegenstehen; **to** ~ **a defen|ce** (~**se**) **under the statute of limitations** e-m Verjährungseinwand entgegenstehen; **to** ~ **the liability** die Haftpflicht ausschließen

neglect Vernachlässigung, Versäumnis; Unterlassung; ~ **of (official) duty** (Amts-)Pflichtverletzung; **benign** ~ *dipl* freundliche Vernachlässigung; **wilful** ~ **to maintain** vorsätzliche Verletzung der Unterhaltspflicht; ~ **to provide maintenance** Vernachlässigung der Unterhaltspflicht

neglect *v* vernachlässigen, versäumen; unterlassen; **to** ~ **children** Kinder vernachlässigen; **to** ~ **one's duty** s-e Pflicht verletzen; **to** ~ **a precaution** e-e Vorsichtsmaßregel außer acht lassen; **to** ~ **to pay one's debts** s-e Schulden nicht bezahlen

neglected child vernachlässigtes (od. verwahrlostes) Kind

neglectful nachlässig

negligence *(ZivilR)* Fahrlässigkeit; fahrlässig begangene unerlaubte Handlung; Verschulden; *(StrafR)*[20] *(unbewußte)* Fahrlässigkeit *(cf. recklessness)*; fahrlässiges (od. achtloses) Verhalten *(im Verkehr)*; ~ **clause** Freizeichnungsklausel *(Freizeichnung des Verfrachters von der Haftung für Fahrlässigkeit)*; ~ **without fault** *(objektive)* Fahrlässigkeit[21]; Fahrlässigkeit ohne subj. Schuldvorwurf[22]; ~ **per se** *Am* Haftung für Fahrlässigkeit, ohne daß subj. Vorwerfbarkeit (Verschulden) nachgeprüft wird; **action for** ~ Schadensersatzklage wegen fahrlässiger Schädigung; **active** ~ fahrlässiges Handeln; **comparative** ~ *Am (anspruchsvermindernde s) Mitverschulden (führt zu e-r Minderung des Schadensersatzanspruchs wie im deutschen Recht)*

negligence, contributory ~ Mitverschulden

Br (anspruchsvermindernde s) Mitverschulden (der Law Reform [Contributory Negligence] Act 1945 führte Schadenteilung nach dem Grad des Verschuldens ein)

Am (anspruchsvernichtendes) Mitverschulden (schließt e-n Schadensersatzanspruch des Geschädigten vollkommen aus; cf. comparative ~)

negligence, criminal ~ *(StrafR) (strafbare)* Fahrlässigkeit *(cf. manslaughter)*; **gross** ~ grobe Fahrlässigkeit; **hazardous** ~[23] Leichtfertigkeit; **→imputed** ~; **intentionally or through** ~ vorsätzlich oder fahrlässig; **law of** ~ Recht der (fahrlässigen) unerlaubten Handlung; **not due to** ~ unverschuldet; **ordinary** ~ *Am* (gewöhnliche) Fahrlässigkeit *(Außerachtlassung der im Verkehr erforderlichen Sorgfalt)*; **passive** ~ *Am* fahrlässiges Unterlassen; **slight** ~ *Am* leichte (od. geringe) Fahrlässigkeit *(Außerachtlassung des Maßes an Sorgfalt, das nur außergewöhnlich umsichtige od. vorsichtige Menschen anzuwenden pflegen)*; **statutory** ~ *Am* Verletzung gesetzlich vorgeschriebener besonderer Sorgfaltspflicht; **wanton** (or **wilful**) ~ *Am* bewußte (od. grobe) Fahrlässigkeit *(gewolltes Verhalten in dem Bewußtsein der Wahrscheinlichkeit e-s Schadenseintritts)*; **wilfully or by** ~ vorsätzlich oder fahrlässig; **the accident was due to the** ~ **of the defendant** der Unfall war auf Fahrlässigkeit des Beklagten zurückzuführen

negligent fahrlässig *(opp. intentional)*; nachlässig

negligent act, tort arising from a ~ fahrlässig begangene unerlaubte Handlung

negligent, ~ **escape** fahrlässiges Entweichenlassen *(e-s Gefangenen)*; ~ **handling of the matter by the solicitor** *Br* nachlässige Behandlung (od. Bearbeitung) der Angelegenheit durch den Anwalt; ~ **homicide** *Am*[24] fahrlässige Tötung; ~ **misrepresentation** fahrlässige Falschdarstellung; **grossly** ~ grob fahrlässig

negotiability Negoziabilität *(Eigenschaft als Order- oder Inhaberpapier)*; Begebbarkeit, Übertragbarkeit *(von Wertpapieren)*

negotiable negoziabel; *(durch Indossament od. Übergabe [delivery])* begebbar (od. übertragbar); aushandelbar; ~ **check** *Am* an Order od. auf den Inhaber lautender Scheck

negotiable instrument[25] *(durch Indossament od. Übergabe [delivery])* begebbares od. übertragbares Wertpapier

Umlauffähiges Papier des Geld- od. Kapitalmarktes, das ein Vermögensrecht verbrieft und mit oder ohne Indossament durch Übergabe des Papiers auf e-e andere Person übertragen und frei von Einwendungen aus dem Grundgeschäft oder Eigentumsmängeln gutgläubig erworben werden kann, entweder durch unveränderte Übergabe (Inhaberpapier) oder mittels Indossament (Orderpapier). Die wichtigsten negotiable instruments sind: bills of exchange, cheques (checks) und promissory notes

Negotiable Instruments, Uniform ~ **Law** (UNIL) *Am* Wertpapiergesetz *(Gesetz über Order- und Inhaberpapiere, das auch das Wechsel- und Scheckrecht umfaßt) (von 1896)*

Das Gesetz war in sämtlichen Einzelstaaten eingeführt worden. Die wertpapierrechtlichen Bestimmungen sind durch den von allen Einzelstaaten (außer Louisiana) angenommenen Uniform Commercial Code von 1959 (Art. 3: Commercial Paper) abgeändert worden

negotiable, ~ **notes** begebbare eigene Wechsel; ~ **on the stock exchange** börsenfähig; ~ **order of withdrawal** (NOW) *Am* übertragbare Zahlungsanweisung; Abhebungsauftrag *(s. NOW →account)*; ~ **papers** →~ instrument; ~ **quality** Eigenschaft der Begebbarkeit; ~ **securities** begebbare Wertpapiere; ~ **warehouse receipt** Orderlagerschein

negotiable, non(-) ~ *pol* nicht verhandelbar

negotiable, non-~ **bill** *Br*[26] unübertragbarer Wechsel, der die Übertragbarkeit durch den Vermerk "non-negotiable" oder ähnliche Worte verloren hat *(also nicht identisch mit dem deutschen Rektawechsel, der zwar nicht durch Indossament, aber immerhin durch Abtretung übertragen werden kann)*; *Am*[27] ein nicht durch Indossament, sondern lediglich durch Abtretung übertragbarer Wechsel *(er unterliegt – abgesehen von den Bestimmungen über das Indossament – dem Wechselrecht)*

negotiable, non-~ **cheque** *Br*[26] *(üblicher:* **cheque crossed not negotiable**) Scheck mit dem Vermerk "not negotiable"; durch ihn wird – anders als beim Wechsel *(s. non-→negotiable bill)* – die Übertragbarkeit des Schecks nicht eingeschränkt. Die Übertragung durch Indossament hat aber nur die Wirkung, daß auch der gutgläubige Erwerber nicht mehr Rechte erlangt als der Vormann. Also kein equity-Schutz. *(Der cheque crossed not negotiable entspricht also weder dem deutschen Order- noch dem deutschen Rektascheck vollkommen)*

negotiable, non~ **check** *Am*[28] ein nicht durch Indossament, sondern nur durch Abtretung übertragbarer Scheck *(er unterliegt – abgesehen von den Bestimmungen über das Indossament – dem Scheckrecht)*

negotiate *v* durch Verhandlung zustande bringen, aushandeln; verhandeln (über); negoziieren, begeben, übertragen; **to** ~ **an agreement** ein Abkommen (od. e-n Vertrag) aushandeln; **to** ~ **a bill (of exchange)**[29] e-n Wechsel begeben (od. weitergeben); **to** ~ **a contract** e-n

Vertrag aushandeln, über e-n Vertragsabschluß verhandeln; e-n Vertrag *(durch Verhandlung)* zustande bringen; **to ~ a draft** *(Außenhandel)* e-e Tratte ankaufen; **to ~ a loan** über die Aufnahme e-r Anleihe verhandeln; e-e Anleihe begeben *(im Wege der festen Übernahme durch e-e Bank);* **to ~ peace terms** Friedensbedingungen aushandeln; **to ~ a price** e-n Preis aushandeln, über e-n Preis verhandeln; **to ~ a settlement** →settlement 2.; **to ~ a transaction** ein Geschäft *(durch Verhandlung)* zustande bringen; **to ~ a treaty** *(VölkerR)* über den Abschluß e-s Vertrages verhandeln

negotiate *v*, **authority to** ~Verhandlungsvollmacht; Negoziierungskredit

negotiate *v*, **order to ~** (OtN) *(Außenhandelsfinanzierung)* Negoziierungsauftrag

Abart des Dokumentenakkreditivs. Bank des Importeurs beauftragt ihre Korrespondenzbank im Lande des Exporteurs, die auf erstere gezogene Tratte(n) des Exporteurs bei Vorlage geforderter Dokumente anzukaufen

negotiating, ~ bank *(beim letter of credit)* negoziierende Bank; Bank, die gemäß den Bedingungen des Akkreditivs zur Einlösung berechtigt ist; **~ brief** Verhandlungsmandat; **~ party** Verhandlungspartner; an der Verhandlung beteiligte Partei; **~ position** Verhandlungsposition; **~ power** Verhandlungsvollmacht; **~ table** Verhandlungstisch; **~ text** Verhandlungstext

negotiation Aushandlung; Verhandlung; Unterhandlung; *com* Begebung; Negoziation; **~ credit** Negoziierungskredit (*Wechselkredit zur Finanzierung von Außenhandelsgeschäften*); **~s for an armistice** Waffenstillstandsverhandlungen; **~s in progress** schwebende Verhandlungen; **~ of a bill (of exchange)**[29] Begebung (od. Übertragung) e-s Wechsels; **~ of a contract** Aushandlung e-s Vertrages; **~ of drafts** *(Außenhandel)* Ankauf (od. Diskontierung) von Tratten *(durch e-e Bank);* **~ of international agreements** Aushandlung internationaler Vereinbarungen; **~ of a loan** Verhandlung über die Aufnahme e-r Anleihe; Beschaffung e-s Darlehens; Begebung e-r Anleihe *(im Wege der festen Übernahme durch e-e Bank);* **~ of peace terms** Aushandlung von Friedensbedingungen; **~ package** Verhandlungspaket

negotiation, advice of ~ Negoziierungsanzeige; Begebungsaviso; **basis for ~s** Verhandlungsgrundlage; **breakdown of ~s** Scheitern der Verhandlungen; **breaking off of ~s** Abbruch der Verhandlungen; **by (way of) ~s** auf dem Verhandlungswege; **commercial ~s** Handelsbesprechungen; **conduct of ~s** Verhandlungsführung; **detailed ~s** Einzelbesprechungen; **forthcoming ~(s)** bevorstehende Verhandlung(en); **lengthy ~s** langwierige Verhandlungen; **matter of ~** Verhandlungssache; **open to ~** zu Verhandlungen bereit; **opening of ~s** Einleitung von Verhandlungen; **parties to the ~** Verhandlungspartner; **point for ~** Verhandlungspunkt; **preliminary ~s** Vorverhandlungen; **readiness to enter into ~s** Verhandlungsbereitschaft; **result of the ~s** Verhandlungsergebnis; **resumption of ~s** Wiederaufnahme der Verhandlungen; **round of ~s** Verhandlungsrunde; **stage of ~s** Stand der Verhandlungen; **tariff ~** Zollverhandlungen; **trade ~s** Wirtschaftsverhandlungen; **under ~** zur Verhandlung

negotiation, to be in ~ with sb. mit jdm in Verhandlung(en) stehen; **to break off ~s** Verhandlungen abbrechen; **to carry on** (or **conduct**) **~s** Verhandlungen führen; **to continue ~s** Verhandlungen fortsetzen; **to enter into ~s** in Verhandlungen (ein-)treten; Verhandlungen aufnehmen; **to initiate** (or **open**) **~s** Verhandlungen einleiten; **to re-open** (or **resume**) **~s** Verhandlungen wiederaufnehmen; erneut in Verhandlungen eintreten; **to settle by ~** durch Verhandlungen regeln (od. beilegen); **to take up ~s** Verhandlungen aufnehmen; **~s are in progress** Verhandlungen sind im Gange

negotiator Unterhändler; Vermittler; Verhandlungsführer

negotiorum gestio Geschäftsführung ohne Auftrag

negotiorum gestor Geschäftsführer ohne Auftrag

Nach englischem Recht wird dem Geschäftsführer ohne Auftrag kein Aufwendungsersatz zugebilligt, es sei denn, daß er eine gesetzl. Verpflichtung erfüllte

neighbo(u)r Nachbar; **~ state** Nachbarstaat; **good ~-policy** *(VölkerR)* Politik der guten Nachbarschaft; **good ~-relations** gutnachbarliche Beziehungen; **immediate ~** unmittelbarer Nachbar

neighbo(u)ring benachbart, angrenzend; **~ country** Nachbarland; **~ right** angrenzendes Recht; verwandtes Schutzrecht; **~ state** Nachbarstaat

neighbo(u)rly, good ~ relations gute Nachbarschaft; gutnachbarliche Beziehungen

nem. con. (nemine contradicente) ("no one saying otherwise") *Br (House of Commons)* einstimmig, mit großer Mehrheit

nem. dis. (nemine dissentiente) ("without anyone dissenting") *Br (House of Lords)* einstimmig

Neo, ~-Fascism Neo-Faschismus; **~-Nazism** Neonazismus

neon, ~ light Neonlicht *(Reklame);* **~ light advertising** Leuchtreklame

Nepal Nepal; **Kingdom of** ~ Königreich Nepal
Nepalese Nepales|e, ~in; nepalesisch

nepotism Vetternwirtschaft, Nepotismus

nervous shock Nervenschock *(Br bei torts Entschädigungsanspruch)*

net netto, rein; nach allen Abzügen *(opp. gross)*; ~ **amount** Nettobetrag, Reinbetrag; ~ **assets** Reinvermögen; ~ **asset value** Nettovermögenswert; Substanzwert *(e-s Unternehmens)*; ~ **avails** Reinertrag; *Am* Diskonterlös; ~ **balance** Nettosaldo, Reinüberschuß; ~ **borrowings** Nettokreditaufnahme; ~ **(prompt) cash** netto Kasse; (Zahlung) ohne Abzug; ~ **earnings** Nettoverdienst; Reingewinn; ~ **holdings** Nettobestände
net income Nettoeinkommen; Reinertrag; ~ **for the period** *Am* Jahresgewinn; ~ **per share** Reingewinn je Aktie; ~ **percentage of sales** Umsatzrendite
net, ~ **interest return** Nettoverzinsung; ~ **limit** (or **line**) *(VersR)* →line 9.; ~ **loss** Reinverlust; Nettoschaden; ~ **margin** Nettogewinnspanne; ~ **movement** *Am* Bilanz; ~ **national product** (NNP) Netto-Sozialprodukt (NSP); ~ **operating loss** Nettobetriebsverlust; ~ **premium** →premium 2.; ~ **present value method** Kapitalwertmethode (*Methode der Investitionsrechnung*); ~ **price** Nettopreis; ~ **proceeds (of sale)** Reinertrag, Reinerlös; ~ **profit(s)** Reingewinn, Nettogewinn; ~ **profits rule** *Am* Dividenden können nur aus dem →earned surplus gezahlt werden; ~ **U.K. rate** (of tax) *Br* →rate 2.; ~ **realizable value** *Br (Bilanz)* realisierbarer Verkaufserlös; ~ **receipts** Nettoeingänge, Nettoeinnahmen; ~ **register ton** (NRT) Nettoregistertonne (NRT); ~ **register (tonnage)** Nettotonnengehalt
net return Nettoertrag, Nettogewinn; Nettoverzinsung; **calculation of the** ~ Rentabilitätsrechnung
net, ~ **revenue** →~ income; ~ **sales** Nettoverkaufserlös, Nettoumsatz; *Am (Bilanz)* Umsatz; ~ **surplus** Reingewinn; ~ **value** Nettowert; ~ **wages** Nettolohn; ~ **(weight)** Nettogewicht; ~ **working capital** *Am (Bilanz)* Differenz zwischen Umlaufvermögen (current assets) und kurzfristigen Verbindlichkeiten (current liabilities); ~ **worth** Nettowert, Reinvermögen, reiner Wert *(e-s Geschäfts für den Inhaber: Vermögenswerte minus laufende Verbindlichkeiten)*; *Am (Bilanz)* Eigenkapital; ~ **worth of a group** Vermögenslage e-s Konzerns; ~ **yield** Nettoertrag, Reinertrag; **dividends** ~ *Br (Bilanz)* Dividende abzüglich Steuer

Netherlander Niederländer, ~in
Netherlands niederländisch; **the** ~ die Niederlande; **Kingdom of the** ~ Königreich der Niederlande

netting *Am* gegenseitige Verrechnung von Forderungen und Verbindlichkeiten

network Netz *(von Flüssen, Straßen etc.)*; *(Rundfunk)* Netz von *(miteinander verbundenen)* Radiostationen, Sendernetz; ~ **of branch offices** (or **branch**~) Filialnetz; ~ **of highways** (or **roads**) Straßennetz; ~ **of railways** Eisenbahnnetz; ~ **planning technique** Netzplantechnik; **intelligence** ~ Spionagenetz

neutral Neutraler, neutraler Staat; Angehörige(r) e-s neutralen Staates; neutral; ~ **asylum** →asylum 1.; ~ **ground** neutraler Boden; ~ **money** neutrales Geld; ~ **state** neutraler Staat; ~ **status** Neutralität; **to maintain a** ~ **attitude** (or **position**) e-e neutrale Haltung einnehmen; **they undertook to remain** ~ sie verpflichteten sich, neutral zu bleiben

neutrality Neutralität; ~ **agreement** Neutralitätsabkommen; **armed** ~ bewaffnete Neutralität; **benevolent** (or **friendly**) ~ wohlwollende Neutralität; **breach of** ~ Neutralitätsbruch *(von seiten e-s neutralen Staates)*; **declaration of** ~ Neutralitätserklärung; **permanent** ~ dauernde Neutralität; **policy of** ~ Neutralitätspolitik; **violation of** ~ Neutralitätsverletzung *(von seiten e-s anderen Staates)*; **to infract** (or **violate**) ~ die Neutralität verletzen; **to preserve** ~ die Neutralität bewahren

neutralization *(VölkerR)* Neutralisierung

neutralize *v (VölkerR)* neutralisieren; ~**d state** neutralisierter Staat *(z.B. Schweiz, Vatikan-Staat, Österreich)*; ~**d zone** neutralisierte Zone *(z.B. entmilitarisierte Zone)*

neutron bomb Neutronenbombe; **to defer production of the** ~ die Produktion der Neutronenbombe verschieben

never-never *sl.* Abstottern; Ratenkauf; **to buy sth. on the** ~ etw. auf Abzahlung kaufen

new neu; ~ **acquisition** Neuerwerbung, Neuanschaffung; ~ **borrowing** Neuverschuldung; ~ **building** Neubau
new business neue(s) Geschäft(e); *(VersR)* neuer Abschluß, neue Abschlüsse; ~ **commission** Abschlußprovision; ~ **department** Werbeabteilung; **to do** ~ Neuabschlüsse tätigen
New Community Instrument (NCI) *(EG)* Neues Gemeinschaftsinstrument *(neues Anleihe- und Darlehensinstrument der Gemeinschaft)*
new, ~ **construction** Neubau; ~ **deal** →deal; ~ **departure** *fig* neuer Weg, Neuorientierung; ~ **draft** neuer Entwurf; ~ **edition** Neuauflage; ~ **election** Neuwahl; ~ **establishment** Geschäftsneugründung; ~ **for old** neu für alt
new frontiers *fig* Neuland; **to open up** ~ neue Gebiete eröffnen
new, ~ **ground** *fig* Neuland; ~ **hirings** Neueinstellungen; ~ **issues** Neuemissionen; junge

Aktien (→*issue 3.*); ~ **order** Neuauftrag; ~ **publications** Neuerscheinungen; ~ **shares (stock)** junge Aktien; ~ **time dealing** *Br (Börse)* Wertpapiergeschäft; ~ **town** *Br*[30] Satellitenstadt; ~ **trial** *(Zivilprozeß)* Wiederaufnahmeverfahren; ~ **value part** *(VersR)* neuwertiger Teil *(opp. replaced part);* ~ **version of a law** Neufassung e-s Gesetzes

New Year's address (or **message**) *dipl* Neujahrsansprache, Neujahrsbotschaft

New York Futures Exchange (NYFE) *Am* Börse für Terminhandel, Terminbörse

New York Stock Exchange (N.Y.S.E.) *Am* New Yorker (Wertpapier-)Börse (Big Board)
Führende Wertpapierbörse der USA und größte der Welt. Sie stellt für Zulassung von Effekten strengere Anforderungen als die →American Stock Exchange und macht sie unabhängig von der Registrierung bei der →Securities and Exchange Commission

New Zealand Neuseeland; **of** ~ neuseeländisch

New Zealander Neuseeländer, ~in

newly industrialized countries (NICs) Schwellenländer *(die weder zu Entwicklungsländern noch zu Industrieländern gehören – z.B. Taiwan, Brasilien, Jugoslawien)*

news Nachrichten; Radio-, Fernsehnachrichten; ~ **advertisement** Zeitungsannonce; ~ **agency** Nachrichtenagentur; Zeitungsverkaufsstelle; ~ **agent** Nachrichtenagent; Zeitungshändler; ~ **ban** (or **blackout**) Nachrichtensperre; ~ **broadcast** Nachrichtensendung; ~ **bulletin** Nachrichtensendung; ~ **dealer** *Am* Zeitungs- (und Zeitschriften-)verkäufer; ~ **editor** Nachrichtenredakteur; ~ **item** Nachrichtenmeldung *(Radio od. Fernsehen)*

newspaper Zeitung *(cf. paper);* ~**s** Presse(wesen); ~ **advertising** Zeitungsreklame, Zeitungswerbung; ~**s and periodicals** Zeitungen und Zeitschriften; ~ **article** Zeitungsartikel; ~ **cutting** Zeitungsausschnitt; ~ **man** Journalist; Zeitungsmann; ~ **report** Zeitungsbericht; ~ **reporter** Berichterstatter; ~ **supplement** Zeitungsbeilage; ~**-wrapper** Kreuzband, Streifband

newspaper, American N~ Publishers Association (A.N.P.A.) Amerikanischer Zeitungsverlegerverband; **daily** ~ Tageszeitung; **financial** ~ Börsenblatt; **subscriber to a** ~ Zeitungsabonnent; **subscription to a** ~ Zeitungsabonnement; **Subscription to N~s and Periodicals Agreement** Postzeitungsabkommen; **to advertise in a** ~ in e-r Zeitung inserieren; **to discontinue a** ~ das Erscheinen e-r Zeitung einstellen; e-e Zeitung abbestellen; **to insert** (or **put**) **an advertisement in a** ~ in e-r Zeitung inserieren; **to publish a** ~ e-e Zeitung herausgeben; **to subscribe to** (or **to take**) **a** ~ e-e Zeitung abonnieren (od. halten, beziehen); **it was stated in the** ~ es stand in der Zeitung

news, ~ **photographer** Bildberichterstatter; ~ **reel** *(Film)* Wochenschau; ~ **release** Pressenotiz, Presseveröffentlichung; ~ **service** Nachrichtendienst; ~ **stand** Zeitungsstand, Zeitungskiosk; ~ **summary** kurze Zusammenfassung der (Radio-, Fernseh-)Nachrichten; ~ **vendor** Zeitungsverkäufer; **City N~** *Br* Börsennachrichten *(e-r Zeitung);* **collection of** ~ Einholung von Nachrichten; **commercial** ~ Handelsnachrichten, Börsennachrichten *(e-r Zeitung);* **domestic** ~ inländische Nachrichten; **foreign** ~ ausländische Nachrichten; **hot** ~ sensationelle Nachrichten; **illuminated** ~**band** Leuchtschrift; **latest** ~ letzte (od. neueste) Nachrichten; **local** ~ Lokalnachrichten; **to exercise censorship over** ~ Nachrichten zensieren

next friend[31] Prozeßpfleger *(prozessualer Vertreter des klagenden Minderjährigen od. beklagten nicht entmündigten Geisteskranken);* **a patient can only sue by his** ~ *Br* ein Geisteskranker kann nur durch seinen Prozeßpfleger klagen
Auf der Beklagtenseite heißt der Prozeßpfleger →guardian ad litem

next of kin nächste(r) Verwandte(r), nächste(r) Familienangehörige(r); **he is his father's** ~ er ist der nächste Verwandte seines Vaters; **his father's** ~ **are** ... die nächsten Verwandten seines Vaters sind ...

next, with the ~ **mail** mit der nächsten Post; ~ **month** nächsten Monats *(cf. proximo);* **end** ~ **(account)** *Br (Börse)* Ultimo nächsten Monats

NIBOR (New York Interbank Offered Rate) Referenzzinssatz für in New York international tätige Banken (→*FIBOR*, →*LIBOR*, →*LUXIBOR*)

Nicaragua Nicaragua; **Republic of** ~ Republik Nicaragua

Nicaraguan Nicaraguaner, ~in; nicaraguanisch

Nice, Arrangement of ~ **Concerning the International Classification of Goods and Services to which Trade Marks Apply**[32] Nizzaer Klassifikationsabkommen (NKA); Abkommen von Nizza über die internationale Klassifikation von Waren und Dienstleistungen für Fabrik- und Handelsmarken *(von 1957)*

nickel *Am* 5 cents

NIF →note issuance facility

Niger, Republic of the ~ Republik Niger; **(of the)** ~ Nigrer, ~in; nigrisch

Nigeria Nigeria; **Federal Republic of** ~ Bundesrepublik Nigeria

Nigerian Nigerianer, ~in; nigerianisch

night Nacht; ~ **charge** Nachttarif; ~ **duty**

Nachtdienst; ~ **flight** Nachtflug; ~ **letter (-gram)** *Am (verbilligtes)* Nachttelegramm *(opp. full rate telegram)*; ~ **safe** Nachttresor; ~ **school** Abendschule, Abendkursus; ~ **service** Nachtdienst; ~ **shift** Nachtschicht; ~ **watch** Nachtwache; ~ **watchman** Nachtwächter; ~ **work** Nachtarbeit; **first** (or **opening**) ~ Premiere

Nikkei Average Index der Tokio Börse

nil rate of duty *(Zoll)* Nullsatz; **tariff quota with a** ~ Zollkontingent zum Nullsatz

nil, ~ **return** Unpfändbarkeitsbescheinigung *(des Vollstreckungsbeamten; vermerkt auf der Rückseite des →writ of execution)*; ~ **tariff** Nulltarif

ninety, ~ **days loan(s)** Dreimonatsgeld; ~**-nine years' lease** Miete (od. Pacht) auf 99 Jahre

nisi, ~ **prius** *Am (untechnisch)* erste Instanz *(opp. appellate court)*; →**decree** ~

no, ~ **admittance** Eintritt verboten; ~ **agents** *Br (in Zeitungsinseraten unter "Houses for Sale")* keine Makler; ~ **business done** *(Börse)* ohne Umsatz; ~ **change given** Geld abgezählt bereithalten; ~ **claims bonus** *Br (Kraftfahrzeug-Haftpflichtvers.)* Prämiennachlaß für unfallfreies Fahren; Schadenfreiheitsrabatt; ~ **confidence vote** Mißtrauensvotum; ~ **fault liability** verschuldensunabhängige Haftung; ~ **funds** (N/F) *(ScheckR)* keine Deckung *(cf. refer to drawer)*; ~ **goods exchanged** Umtausch nicht gestattet; ~**-load funds** *Am* zuschlagfreier Investmentfonds; ~ **man's land** Niemandsland; ~ **names products** Gattungsprodukte *(z. B. Zucker, Mehl)*; ~ **par** ohne Nennwert, nennwertlos; ~ **par stock** *Am* nennwertlose Aktie(n), Quotenaktie(n); ~ **par value share** (or **stock**) →~ par stock; ~ **parking** Parken verboten; ~ **purpose loan** Kredit ohne nähere Zweckbindung; ~ **thoroughfare** Durchfahrt verboten; ~ **through road** Sackgasse

Nobel, ~ **Foundation** Nobelstiftung; **recipient of the** ~ **Prize** Empfänger des Nobelpreises; **to award the** ~ **Prize** den Nobelpreis verleihen

nobility *Br (hoher)* Adel *(dukes, marquesses, earls, viscounts, barons, and life peers who rank as barons)*; ~ **and gentry** hoher und niederer Adel; **landed** ~ Landadel; **patent of** ~ Adelsbrief; **title of** ~[33] Adelstitel

noble, the ~**s** *Br* der Adel; **of** ~ **birth** *Br* adlig

Noes *parl* Stimmen gegen; Neinstimmen *(opp. Ayes)*

noise Lärm; ~ **abatement**[34] Lärmbeschränkung; Lärmbekämpfung

noise emission, limitation of ~ **from subsonic aircraft** Begrenzung der Lärmemission von Unterschallflugzeugen

noise, ~ **level** Lärmpegel; ~**-maker** Ruhestörer; ~ **pollution** Lärmbelästigung; ~ **protection wall** Lärmschutzwand; **disturbing** ~ ruhestörender Lärm; **exposure to** ~ Lärmexposition

nolle prosequi ("to be unwilling to prosecute") (nol. pros.) *(Strafprozeß)* Einstellung des Verfahrens; *Am (auch Zivilprozeß)* Zurücknahme der Klage

nolo contendere ("I do not wish to contend") *Am (AntitrustR)* nicht bestreiten *(Beklagter erkennt das Urteil an, ohne Gesetzesübertretung zuzugeben)*

nol. pros. *v Am (colloq.)* das Verfahren einstellen

nomenclature Nomenklatur, Namensverzeichnis *(Verzeichnis der Wörter e-s bestimmten Sachgebietes)*; Benennungssystem, Bezeichnungsweise; Zolltarifschema; **N~ of Goods for the External Trade Statistics of the Community and Statistics of Trade between Member States** (NIMEXE) Warenverzeichnis für die Statistik des Außenhandels der Gemeinschaft und des Handels zwischen ihren Mitgliedstaaten (NIMEXE); **Convention on N~ for the Classification of Goods in Customs Tariffs**[35] Abkommen über das Zolltarifschema für die Einreihung der Waren in die Zolltarife; **(tariff)** ~ Zolltarifschema

nominal Nominal-, nominal; nominell, (nur) dem Namen nach; ~ **account** *Br* Sachkonto *(opp. personal account)*; ~ **amount** Nennbetrag, Nominalbetrag; ~ **assets** fiktive Aktiva; ~ **capital** →capital 1.; ~ **catch** (Fisch-)Fanggewicht; ~ **consideration** →consideration 1.; ~ **damage** *(lediglich)* nomineller Schaden *(ohne meßbaren Wert)*; ~ **damages** nomineller (nur symbolischer) Schadensersatz *(kann zuerkannt werden, wenn e-e Rechtsverletzung keinen substantiellen Schaden ausgelöst hat)*; ~ **fine** unbedeutende Geldstrafe; ~ **income** Nominaleinkommen *(opp. real income)*; ~ **interest (rate)** Nominalzins *(opp. real interest)*; ~ **list of shareholders** Liste der Aktionäre; Gesellschafterverzeichnis; ~ **owner** *(lediglich)* nomineller Inhaber *(z. B. trustee)*; ~ **partner** nicht aktiver Teilhaber; nomineller Gesellschafter *(→ostensible partner)*; ~ **party** nominelle (Prozeß-)Partei *(z. B. Prozeßvertreter für Minderjährigen, Geisteskranken etc.; Am opp. real →party in interest)*; ~ **party member** Mitläufer e-r Partei; ~ **price** nomineller Preis (od. Kurs) *(opp. market price)*; ~ **rank** Titularrang; ~ **rate** Nominalzinssatz; ~ **rent** *(nur der Form halber erhobene)* sehr geringe Miete (od. Pacht); ~ **roll** Namensverzeichnis; ~ **value** Nominalwert, Nennwert; ~ **wages** Nominallohn *(opp. real wages)*

nominate *v (jdn)* ernennen; *(jdn)* benennen, namhaft machen; bestellen; *(zur Wahl od. für* *ein Amt)* vorschlagen, nominieren; **to ~ an arbitrator** e-n Schiedsrichter ernennen; **to ~ a candidate** e-n Kandidaten *(zur Wahl)* aufstellen

nomination Ernennung; Benennung, Namhaftmachung; (Wahl-)Vorschlag, Nominierung; **~s committee** Ernennungsausschuß; Nominierungsausschuß; **~ of a candidate**[36] Aufstellung e-s Kandidaten; **~ papers** Bewerbungsantrag *(e-s Kandidaten für das Unterhaus)*; **entitled to make ~s** vorschlagsberechtigt; **to object to the ~** gegen die Nominierung *(e-s Kandidaten)* Einspruch erheben; **to submit ~s** Wahlvorschläge machen

nominative durch Ernennung eingesetzt *(opp. elective)*; **the ~ candidate** der benannte (od. vorgeschlagene) Kandidat

nominee *(für ein Amt od. e-e Wahl)* Vorgeschlagener, Benannter; vorgeschlagene Person; *(vorgeschlagener)* Kandidat; *com*[37] Strohmann, vorgeschobene Person, die regelmäßig nach den Weisungen e-s Hintermannes zu handeln hat *(ein Aktionär, der z.B. ausländischer Staatsangehöriger ist od. im Hintergrund bleiben will, bedient sich oft e-s ~ [shareholder] [Person od. Bank], der als Aktionär an s-r Stelle in den Aktienbüchern e-r Gesellschaft eingetragen ist)*; **~ shareholding** auf den Namen von Strohmännern eingetragener Aktienbesitz

nomocracy Nomokratie

non, ~(-)acceptance Nichtannahme; Annahmeverweigerung; **~-access**[38] Nichtbeiwohnung; **~active status** einstweiliger Ruhestand; **~age** *Am* Minderjährigkeit; Mangel des ehefähigen Alters; **~ aged** *Am* minderjährig

non, ~(-)agreement countries *(VölkerR)* Nichtabkommensländer; **~(-)aggression pact** *(VölkerR)* Nichtangriffspakt; **~(-)agricultural establishment** nichtlandwirtschaftlicher Betrieb; **~(-)aligned** politisch nicht gebunden; blockfrei; **~(-)aligned states** *pol* blockfreie Staaten; **~(-)alignment** Blockfreiheit; **~- allowable charges** *(SteuerR)* nicht absetzbare Ausgaben; **~(-)appealable** rechtskräftig; **~(-)appearance** Nichterscheinen (at a trial vor Gericht); **~(-)applicability** Nichtanwendbarkeit

non(-)assessable steuerfrei, abgabenfrei; **~ stock** *Am* nicht nachschußpflichtige Aktien

non, ~(-)assignability Nichtabtretbarkeit; **~-associated** *(EG)* nicht assoziiert; **~-attendance** Abwesenheit, Ausbleiben, Nichterscheinen; **~ bank-banks** *Am* Nichtbank-Banken *(Geldinstitute, die zur Umgehung von Bankaufsichtsnormen nur Teile e-s Bankservice anbieten)*; **~(-)belligerency** *(VölkerR)* Nichtkriegführung *(Bezeichnung für wohlwollende neutrale Haltung einiger Staaten während des 2. Weltkrieges)*; **~(-)belligerent** nicht am Krieg Teilnehmender *(Staat od. Person)*; nicht am Krieg teilnehmend; **~-binding offer** freibleibendes Angebot; **~-business days** arbeitsfreie Tage, Feiertage; **~(-) callable** unkündbar *(Effekten)*; **~(-)cash payment** bargeldlose Zahlung; **~-citizen** *Am* Nichtamerikaner

non(-)combattant Nichtkombattant, nicht an der Kampfhandlung Teilnehmender *(z.B. surgeon, chaplain, ambulance man)*; **~s** *(auch) (an Feindseligkeiten nicht beteiligte)* Zivilbevölkerung

non(-)commercial nicht gewerblich; **~ quantities** nicht zum Handel geeignete Mengen

non(-)commissioned nicht beauftragt; **~ officer** (N.C.O., non-com) Unteroffizier

non, ~(-)committal unverbindlich, sich nicht festlegend; ohne Bindung; **~-committed** *pol (noch)* ungebunden, blockfrei; **~-Community country** *(EG)* Drittland; **~(-)commutable investments** nicht ablösbare Kapitalanlagen; **~competition clause** Wettbewerbsklausel, Konkurrenzklausel; **~competitive bid** nicht wettbewerbsfähiges Angebot; **~completion** Nichtfertigstellung; **(in case of) ~compliance** (bei) Nichtbefolgung (od. Nichteinhaltung, Nichterfüllung); **~compliance with the time limit** Nichteinhaltung der Frist

non compos mentis ("not of sound mind") geisteskrank; unzurechnungsfähig; **person ~** Geisteskranker

non, ~ compulsory expenditure nichtobligatorische Ausgaben (NOA); **~conforming goods** nicht vertragsgemäße Waren; **~conformist** Nonkonformist; *Br* Dissenter *(bes. Protestant dissenter)*; **~-content** *Br (House of Lords)* Antragsgegner, mit „Nein" Stimmender; **~(-)contentious** →contentious; **~(-)contracting states** Nichtvertragsstaaten; **~(-)contractual liability** außervertragliche Haftung; **~contributory** nicht beitragspflichtig, beitragsfrei; **~contributory benefits** *Br (Sozialvers.)* nicht beitragsbezogene Leistungen; **~(-)cumulative** nichtkumulativ; **~(-)delivery** Nichtlieferung; Nichtübergabe; **~deterrables** *Am (StrafR)* diejenigen, auf die *(infolge ihres Geisteszustandes)* Strafandrohungen keine abschreckende Wirkung ausüben; **~-disclosure** Nichtoffenbarung, Unterlassen e-r Mitteilung (od. Anzeige), Verschweigen; **~(-) discretionary trust** *Br* Trust mit *(im trust deed)* festgelegten Anteilen; *Am* s. fixed →investment trust; **~(-)discrimination** Nichtdiskriminierung; Gleichbehandlung; **on ~(-)discriminatory terms** zu nicht diskriminierenden Bedingungen; **~(-)distinctive marks** →distinctive; **~(-)distributable property** *(KonkursR)* ausgesonderte Vermögensgegenstände; **~(-)durable goods** →durable; **~economic damage** immaterieller Schaden; **~(-) enforceability** Nichteinklagbarkeit; Rechtsschutzversagung; ~(-)**essential** nicht notwendig; ~(-)**essentials** nicht lebensnotwendige Güter

non est factum ("it is not his deed") Einrede des Beklagten gegenüber einer auf e-e Urkunde gestützten Klage, daß er durch seine Unterschrift nicht gebunden ist, weil er den Sinn der Urkunde nicht verstanden hatte

non, ~**-European** nichteuropäisch; ~**(-)execution** Nichtausführung; ~**-exclusive licen**ce **(~se)** einfache Lizenz; ~**-existent marriage** Nichtehe; ~**(-)extant** nicht vorliegend; ~ **facere** *(VölkerR)* Nichteingreifen; ~**-fatal injuries** nicht tödliche Verletzungen; ~**feasance** *(pflichtwidrige)* Unterlassung, Nichterfüllung *(e-r rechtl. Verpflichtung; cf. malfeasance, misfeasance);* ~ **(-)ferrous metals** Nichteisenmetalle (NE-Metalle); ~**forfeitability** Unverfallbarkeit (*e-r Lebensversicherungspolice*); ~**forfeitable** unverfallbar; ~**forfeiture** *(Lebensversicherung)* Unverfallbarkeit *(bei Nichtzahlung der Prämie verfällt die Versicherung erst dann, wenn die ausstehenden Prämien die technische Rücklage übersteigen);* ~**(-)fulfilment of a contract** Nichterfüllung e-s Vertrages; ~**(-)governmental organization** (NGO) Nicht-Regierungsorganisation (NRO); ~**immigrant** *Am*[39] Nichtimmigrant; ~**(-)independent** unselbständig; ~ **(-)indictable** →indictable; ~**(-) interest-bearing** zinslos, unverzinslich; ~**(-) interference** Nichteinmischung; ~**(-)intervention (policy)** Nichteinmischung(spolitik); ~**(-)joinder of party**[40] Nichtausdehnung e-r Klage auf notwendigen Streitgenossen; ~**(-) ledger assets** nicht buchungsfähige Wirtschaftsgüter *(z. B. künftige Forderungen)*

non(-)legal, in legal and ~ matters gerichtlich und außergerichtlich

non(-)liability Haftungsausschluß, Nichthaftung; ~ **clause** Freizeichnungsklausel

non-life, ~ **assurance** *Br* Nichtlebensversicherung; ~ **business** Sachversicherungsgeschäfte; ~ **companies** Versicherungsgesellschaften, die nicht die Lebensversicherung betreiben; ~ **mutuals** Versicherungen auf Gegenseitigkeit, die nicht die Lebensversicherung betreiben; ~ **policyholder** Versicherungsnehmer e-r Nicht-Lebensversicherung; **to do life and ~ business concurrently** gleichzeitig in der Lebens- und Sachversicherung tätig sein

non liquet (N.L.) ("it is not clear") *(VölkerR)* Unmöglichkeit der Entscheidung

non-material damage immaterieller Schaden

non(-)member Nichtmitglied; ~ **bank** *Am* dem →Federal Reserve System nicht angeschlossene Bank; ~ **countries** *(EG)* Drittländer; ~ **government** Nichtmitgliedsregierung; ~ **state** Nichtmitgliedstaat; **affiliates and ~s** Mitglieder und Nichtmitglieder

non, ~**(-)metallic minerals industry** Industrie der Nichterz-Minerale; ~**(-)metropolitan territories** →metropolitan; ~**-national labour** *(EG)* ausländische Arbeitskräfte; ~**-national resident** *Am* Einwohner, der nicht die Staatsangehörigkeit des Wohnsitzlandes besitzt; ~**(-)negotiable** →negotiable

non(-)nuclear, ~ **countries** Nichtatomländer; nicht atomare (od. nukleare) Länder; ~ **powers** Nichtnuklearmächte; ~ **weapon states** kernwaffenlose Staaten

non, ~**(-)observance** Nichtbefolgung, Nichtbeachtung; ~**-obviousness** *(PatR)* mangelnde Erfindungshöhe; ~**(-)occupational accident** Nichtberufsunfall, Nichtbetriebsunfall; ~**(-) official** nicht amtlich; inoffiziell

non(-)operating nicht in Betrieb befindlich; betriebsfremd; ~ **expense** betriebsfremder Aufwand; ~ **factory** stillgelegte Fabrik; ~ **revenue (or other income)** betriebsfremder Ertrag

non(-)participating *(VersR)* ohne Gewinnbeteiligung; nicht teilnehmend; ~ **government** Nichtteilnehmerregierung; ~ **policy** Versicherungspolice ohne Gewinnbeteiligung; ~ **state** Nichtteilnehmerstaat

non, ~**(-)participation in war** Nichtteilnahme am Krieg; ~**(-)partisan** zu keiner Partei Gehöriger; unparteiisch; ~**(-)party** parteilos, überparteilich; ~**(-)payment** Nichtzahlung; ~**(-)performance** Nichterfüllung, Nichtleistung; ~**performing loans** *Am* „notleidende" Kredite, für die Zins und/oder Tilgungszahlungen länger als 90 Tage nicht geleistet wurden; ~**(-)permanent member** nichtständiges Mitglied; ~**personal account** Sachkonto; ~**(-)prejudicial disclosure** *(PatR)* unschädliche Offenbarung; ~**(-)privileged** nicht bevorrechtigt; ~**(-)production bonus** von der Produktion unabhängige Sondervergütung

non(-)profit-making nicht auf Gewinn gerichtet, gemeinnützig; ~ **association** Idealverein; ~ **organization** nicht auf Gewinn(erzielung) gerichtete Organisation; gemeinnützige Organisation; ~ **policyholder** nicht gewinnberechtigter Versicherungsnehmer

non(-)proliferation (of nuclear weapons) Nichtweitergabe (von Atomwaffen); **N~ P~ Treaty** (NPT) Atomwaffen-Sperrvertrag *(s. Treaty on the N~ P~ of →Nuclear Weapons)*

non(-)quota nicht kontingentiert; im Kontingent nicht enthalten; ~ **immigrant** *Am* nicht unter die Kontingentierungsbestimmungen fallender Einwanderer; ~ **imports** nicht kontingentierte Einfuhrwaren

non(-)recognition *(VölkerR)* Nichtanerkennung

non-recourse financing Forfaitierung (→*forfaiting*)

nonrecurrent nicht wiederkehrend, einmalig; ~ **expenditure** einmalige Ausgabe; außerordentliche Aufwendungen; **income of ~ nature** *Br (Bilanz)* außergewöhnliche Erträge

nonrecurring →~recurrent; ~ **gains** Gewinne aus der einmaligen Veräußerung von Anlagevermögen

non, ~(-)residence Nichtansässigkeit; Abwesenheit *(von jds Wirkungskreis); (Devisen)* Ausländereigenschaft; *(Handelsgesellschaft)* Fehlen des (Haupt-)Geschäftssitzes in dem Staat, in dem die Gesellschaft inkorporiert ist

non(-)resident nicht *(dauernd)* ansässig; außerhalb (od. im Ausland) ansässig; auswärtig; gebietsfremd[41]; *(von jds Wirkungskreis)* abwesend; Nichtansässiger; jd, der nicht s-n (dauernden) Wohnsitz hat (of in); Gebietsfremder[41] *(früher: Devisenausländer);* Steuerausländer; *Br (bes. SteuerR)* nicht in Großbritannien ansässige natürliche Person; *Am* nicht in den USA ansässige Person; *Am* Person mit Wohnsitz außerhalb e-s Einzelstaates; ~ **alien** (NRA) im Ausland ansässiger Ausländer; *Am (DBA)* Ausländer ohne ständigen Wohnsitz in den USA *(der nur beschränkt steuerpflichtig ist);* ~ **citizen** *Am* Staatsbürger mit Wohnsitz im Ausland; ~ **company** *Br* Gesellschaft ohne (Haupt-)Geschäftssitz in England; ~ **corporation** *Am* Gesellschaft ohne (Haupt-)Geschäftssitz in den USA (od. e-m Einzelstaat); ~ **individual** nichtansässige ausländische natürliche Person; **a ~ partner in a partnership which does business in the U.S.** ein nichtansässiger Teilhaber e-r in den USA gewerblich tätigen Personengesellschaft; ~ **stockholder** *Am* auswärtiger Aktionär; **taxable as ~s engaged in trade or business in the United States** besteuerbar als in den USA gewerblich tätige nichtansässige Ausländer

non, ~(-)retroactivity Nichtrückwirkung; **~(-) self-executing treaty** *(VölkerR)* nicht unmittelbar anwendungsfähiger Vertrag; **~(-)self-governing territories** *(VölkerR)*[42] Gebiete ohne Selbstregierung *(cf. trusteeship system);* **~-signatory government** Nichtunterzeichnerregierung

nonsigner Nichtunterzeichner der Preisbindung der zweiten Hand *(cf. outsider);* **~s clause** Nichtunterzeichner-Klausel

Die nonsigners clause bindet unter bestimmten Voraussetzungen auch denjenigen an die vom Hersteller festgesetzten Wiederverkaufspreise, der bezüglich dieser Preise nicht in einem unmittelbaren Vertragsverhältnis mit dem Hersteller steht *(Br cf. Resale Prices Act 1976, s. 26; Am cf. McGuire Act in Verb. mit den Fair Trade Laws)*

nonstock-corporation *Am* rechtsfähige Gesellschaft auf persönlicher Basis, die keine aktienrechtlichen Anteile ausgibt *(z.B. rechtsfähiger Verein)*

non(-)stop durchgehend; *(Flug)* ohne Zwischenlandung; ~ **flight** Nonstopflug

non-substantive decision e-e nicht in der Sache selbst ergehende Entscheidung

nonsuit Klageabweisung *(öfter auf Antrag des Klägers, z.B. wenn er Klageantrag abändern will)*

nonsuit *v* die Klage abweisen; **the plaintiff was ~ed** die Klage wurde abgewiesen *(z.B. um Kläger zu ermöglichen, e-e neue, besser vorbereitete Klage einzureichen)*

nonsupport *Am* Verletzung der Unterhaltspflicht

non, ~-tariff barriers (NTB) nicht tarifäre Handelshemmnisse (NTH) *(z.B. Subventionen, Selbstbeschränkungsabkommen)*; **~(-)taxable** steuerfrei; **~(-)trader** Nichtkaufmann; **~-trading** nicht kaufmännisch tätig; nicht handeltreibend; **~-trading →corporation; ~-trading →partnership; ~-underwritten facility** Fazilität ohne Übernahmegarantie oder Deckungslinie e-r Bank

non(-)union nicht organisiert; keiner Gewerkschaft angehörig; **non-Union country** *Br* nicht dem Weltpostverein angehörendes Land; ~ **shop** gewerkschaftsfreier Betrieb; ~ **worker** Nichtgewerkschaftler

non(-)unionist e-r Gewerkschaft nicht Angehörender, Nichtmitglied von Gewerkschaften

non(-)user Nichtgebrauch; Nichtausübung *(e-s Rechtes [bes. e-s →easement] od. e-r Dienstpflicht);* ~ **of a patent** unterlassene Patentausübung

non, ~ vested pension right verfallbare Pensionsanwartschaft; **~-violence** Gewaltlosigkeit; **~-violent** gewaltlos; **~(-)voter** Nichtwähler

non(-)voting nichtstimmberechtigt; Stimmenthaltung; ~ **share** (or **stock**) stimmrechtslose Aktie

nonwaiver Nichtverzicht *(z.B. auf die Anwendung von Rechtsmitteln)*

non(-)warranty Haftungsausschluß; ~ **clause** Haftungsausschlußklausel, vertraglicher Ausschluß der Sachmängelhaftung

non(-)working of a patent Nichtausübung (od. Nichtverwertung) e-s Patents

no par stock →no

Nordic Council *(1953 von Dänemark, Norwegen und Schweden gegründeter)* Nordischer Rat *(zu dem seit 1955 auch Finnland gehört)*

norm Norm, Regel; Richtschnur

normal normal *(opp. exceptional);* **incidental to the ~ activity of a business** im Rahmen des üblichen Geschäftsverkehrs; ~ **loss** natürlicher Schwund; ~ **operator** *Am* Normalarbeiter, Durchschnittsarbeiter; ~ **output** Normalleistung; ~ **performance** Normalleistung; ~ **tax** *Am* Basissteuer der Einkommensteuer *(opp. surtax);* ~ **working hours** Normalarbeitszeit; **to reestablish ~ relations** normale Beziehungen wiederherstellen

normalization Normalisierung

North Atlantic Treaty Organization (NATO) Organisation des Nordatlantikpaktes[43]

Besteht seit 1949 und umfaßt 16 Mitglieder (einschließlich USA und Kanada)
Aufgabe: Verteidigung gegen einen bewaffneten Angriff auf einen od. mehrere Mitgliedstaaten[44]

North-East Atlantic Fisheries Commission (NEAFC) Kommission für die Fischerei im Nordostatlantik (NEAFC)

North Sea, ~ natural gas Erdgas der Nordsee; **~ oil** Nordseeöl; **~ pollution** Verschmutzung der Nordsee

North-South, ~ contrast Nord-Süd-Gegensatz; **~ Dialogue** Nord-Süd-Dialog *(zwischen den Industriestaaten und den Entwicklungsländern; →Conference on International Economic Cooperation)*; **~ divide** (or **differential**) Nord-Süd-Gefälle

North-West Atlantic Fisheries Organization (NAFO) Nordwestatlantische Fischereiorganisation

Norway Norwegen; **Kingdom of ~** Königreich Norwegen

Norwegian Norweger, ~in; norwegisch

Norwegian International Ship Register (NIS) Norwegisches Internationales Schiffsregister

nostro, ~ accounts Nostrokonten *(opp. loro accounts)*; **~ balances** Nostroguthaben *(e-r Bank)*; **~ liabilities** Nostroverpflichtungen *(e-r Bank)*; **~ securities** Nostroeffekten

not, ~ binding offer freibleibendes Angebot; **~ exceeding** nicht höher als; bis zu; **~ found** *Am* →found 2.; **~ guilty** unschuldig; **~ sufficient funds** (N. S., n. s. f.) keine Deckung *(Bankvermerk auf Schecks)*

notably insbesondere

notarial notariell, Notariats-; **~ act** Notariatsakt; **~ act of honour** *Br*[45] notarielle Ehrenhandlung; **~ charges not to be incurred** ohne Kosten *(Vermerk auf e-m Wechsel)*; **~ charges** (or **expenses**) →~ticket; **~ deed** notarielle Urkunde; **~ fees** Notariatsgebühren; **~ protest certificate** *Am* Protesturkunde; **~ seal** Dienstsiegel des Notars; **~ ticket** Notariatsgebühren *(auf nicht eingelösten Wechsel)*; **to obtain a ~ attestation to a document** e-e Urkunde vom Notar beglaubigen lassen (→*attestation*)

notarially, ~ certified notariell beglaubigt; **to get** (or **have**) **a document ~ attested** e-e Urkunde vom Notar beglaubigen lassen

notarize *v Am* notariell beglaubigen

notary (public) Notar
Br Gewöhnlich ein solicitor.[46] *Am* oft Nichtjurist, der sein Amt oft nur nebenberuflich ausübt. Die Haupttätigkeit des notary (public) besteht in der Beurkundung und Beglaubigung von Unterschriften (bes. für das Ausland), Ausfertigung beglaubigter Abschriften von Urkunden (bes. für das Ausland) sowie in der Aufnahme von Wechselprotesten

notary (public), ~'s clerk *Br* Büroangestellter e-s Notars; **~'s fees** Notariatsgebühren; **~'s office** Notariat; **~'s seal** Notariatssiegel; **attested** (or **certified**) **by a ~** notariell beglaubigt; **to strike a ~ off the roll** *Br* e-n Notar von der Liste streichen *(cf. →Court of Faculties)*

notation Vermerk; Aufzeichnung; **~ on a bill of exchange** (by a notary public) Protestvermerk auf e-m Wechsel

note 1. schriftl. Zahlungsversprechen, Schuldschein *(bes. IOU)*; eigener Wechsel, Solawechsel *(→promissory note)*; **~s** Schuldversprechen aller Art, bes. eigene Wechsel; *Am* mittelfristige *(3–15 Jahre)* ungesicherte Schuldverschreibungen; **~ and bonds** *Am* langfristige Obligationen; **~ broker** *Am* Wechselmakler; **~ brokerage** Wechselhandel; **~ issuance facility** (NIF) Fazilität zur revolvierenden Plazierung von Euronotes durch ein →tender panel (→*Euronote facility*); **~ maker** Aussteller e-s eigenen Wechsels; **~ of hand** Schuldschein; eigener Wechsel *(→promissory note)*; **~s payable** *Am (Bilanz)* Wechselschulden; Schuldwechsel; Wechselverbindlichkeiten; Schuldscheinverbindlichkeiten; ausgestellte Schuldversprechen; **~s receivable** *Am (Bilanz)* Wechselforderungen; Schuldscheinforderungen; **~ register** *Am* Wechselbuch; **~ tickler** *Am* Verfallbuch für Wechsel

note, bills and ~s Wechsel; **bill or ~** gezogener oder eigener Wechsel; **borrowers' ~s against ad rem security** dinglich gesicherte Schuldscheine; **cognovit ~** *Am* eigener Wechsel mit Unterwerfungsklausel; **collateral ~** *Am* durch Sicherheiten *(stocks, bonds, drafts etc)* gesicherter Schuldschein; **doubtful ~s and accounts** *Am (Bilanz)* dubiose Forderungen; **foreign ~** ausländischer eigener Wechsel; **inland ~** inländischer eigener Wechsel; **joint and several ~**[47] gesamtschuldnerisch verpflichtender eigener Wechsel; gesamtschuldnerisches Schuldversprechen; **→mortgage ~; →promissory ~**

note 2. Notiz, Vermerk; Anmerkung; **~s** *Am (in e-r juristischen Zeitschrift gebrachte)* Anmerkungen zu neuesten gerichtl. Entscheidungen; **~book** Notizbuch; Stenoblock; **~ for protest** *(WechselR)* Vormerkung zum Protest; **~ of blocking** Sperrvermerk; **~ of entry** Eintragungsvermerk *(in ein Register)*; **~ pad** Notizblock; **~ paper** Briefpapier; **~s to the financial statements** *Am* Anhang zum Jahresabschluß; **foot~** Fußnote; **head ~s** Leitsatz *(e-s Urteils)*; **marginal ~** Randbemerkung; **to keep a ~ of one's expenses** über s-e Ausgaben Buch führen; s-e Auslagen aufschreiben; **to make** (or **take**) **~s** sich Notizen machen (of über); notieren

note 3. kurzes Schreiben, schriftliche Mitteilung, Bescheid; **~ of issue** *Am (Zivilprozeß)*

Terminsnachricht; **advice** ~ Anzeige, Benachrichtung(sschreiben); **confirmation** ~ Bestätigungsschreiben; **cover** ~ *Br (VersR)* →cover; **delivery** ~ Lieferschein

note 4. Rechnung, Nota; ~ **of expenses** *Br* Auslagenrechnung, Spesenrechnung; **broker's** ~ Schlußschein; Schlußnote; **counsel's fee** ~ *Br* Gebührenrechnung des barrister; **credit** ~ Gutschriftanzeige; **debit** ~ Lastschriftanzeige, Belastungsaufgabe

note 5. Banknote; Geldschein; ~**s and small change** Banknoten und Kleingeld

notes and coins, circulation of ~ Bargeldumlauf; **foreign** ~ ausländische Banknoten und Münzen, Sorten

notes in circulation (Bank-)Notenumlauf; **cover of** ~ Notendeckung

note, ~ **issue** *Br* (Bank-)Notenausgabe; **counterfeit** ~ falscher Geldschein; **foreign exchange** ~**s** Banknoten in fremder Währung; **right of issuing** ~**s** Notenprivileg

note 6. *(VölkerR)* Note; ~ **in reply** Antwortnote; ~ **of protest** Protestnote; **circular** ~ Zirkularnote; **collective** ~ Kollektivnote; **exchange of diplomatic** ~**s** diplomatischer Notenwechsel; **verbal** ~ Verbalnote; **to deliver a** ~ e-e Note überreichen; **to reject a** ~ e-e Note zurückweisen

note *v* notieren, vermerken, aufschreiben; bemerken, zur Kenntnis nehmen; entnehmen; **to** ~ **(a protest of) a bill** auf e-m (ausländischen) Wechsel e-n notariellen Vermerk über die Nichtannahme od. Nichtzahlung des Wechsels *(zwecks späterer Protestaufnahme)* machen *(cf. noting);* **to** ~ **down** notieren; **to** ~ **a right on the record** ein Recht vormerken; **please** ~ **that** bitte nehmen Sie zur Kenntnis, daß; **to be pleased to** ~ mit Befriedigung zur Kenntnis nehmen

noted, ~ **for protest** *(WechselR)* zum Protest vorgemerkt *(cf. noting);* **be it** ~ **in passing** es sei nebenbei bemerkt

noting 1. in Anbetracht, angesichts; im Hinblick auf, in Kenntnis; ~ **the provisions of the treaty** im Hinblick auf die Bestimmung des Vertrags

noting 2. *Br*[48] Vermerk e-s Notars auf dem (ausländischen) Wechsel im Zeitpunkt der Annahme- od. Zahlungsverweigerung *(die förmliche Beurkundung der Annahme- od. Zahlungsverweigerung [→protest 2.] erfolgt auf Grund des noting);* ~ **and protest** Protestaufnahme; **delay in** ~ Verzug in der Vornahme des notariellen Vermerks; **expenses of** ~ Kosten des noting

nothing, ~ **in paragraph 1 shall be interpreted to mean that . . .** Absatz 1 ist nicht so auszulegen, als . . .; **for** ~ umsonst

notice 1. Kenntnis(nahme); Mitteilung, Bekanntmachung, Bekanntgabe; Anzeige, Benachrichtigung; (Zeitungs-)Anzeige; *(WechselR)* Notanzeige *(→~ of dishono[u]r);* ~ **in the Land Register** *Br* Vermerk im Grundbuch *(der verhindert, daß die Rangstelle bei späteren Belastungen an einen Gutgläubigen verloren geht);* ~ **in writing** schriftliche Mitteilung, schriftlicher Bescheid; ~ **of abandonment** *(SeeversR)* Abandonerklärung; ~ **of action** Klageandrohung *(Br nur erforderlich bei bestimmten Klagen gemäß local and personal Acts of Parliament);* ~ **of appeal** Rechtsmittelschrift; *(PatR)* Beschwerdeschrift *(→appeal 1.);* ~ **of appearance** Mitteilung der Einlassung an den Kläger *(→appearance 2.);* ~ **of appropriation** Mitteilung über Aussonderung einer für den Käufer bestimmten Ware *(→appropriation 1.);* ~ **of arrival** Eingangsbestätigung; ~ **of→assent;** ~ **of assessment** Steuerbescheid; *(Zoll)* Feststellungsbescheid; ~ **of assignment** Abtretungsanzeige; ~ **of bankruptcy** →bankruptcy ~; ~ **of birth** Geburtsanzeige; ~ **of blocking** Sperrvermerk; ~ **of claim** *(VersR)* Schadensanzeige; ~ **of consignment** Anzeige über die Absendung; ~ **of death** Todesanzeige; ~ **of defects** Mängelanzeige, Mängelrüge; ~ **of deficiency** *Am* Bescheid der Steuerbehörde, daß Überprüfung der Einkommensteuererklärung formale od. rechnerische Unrichtigkeiten ergab; ~ **of delivery** Erklärung der Lieferbereitschaft, Andienung; *Am* Empfangsbestätigung; ~ **of deposit** *Br* Vermerk über die Hinterlegung der Eigentumsurkunde *(s. deposit of title deeds, →deposit 1.)*

notice (of dishono[u]r)[49] Notanzeige *(Mitteilung von der Annahmeverweigerung od. Zahlungsverweigerung e-s Wechsels od. Schecks an den Aussteller und die Giranten);* **delay in giving** ~ Verzug bei Notanzeige; **to give** ~ Notanzeige erstatten; **to waive** ~ auf Notanzeige verzichten

notice of dishonor and protest *Am*[49a] Protestanzeige

notice, ~ **of dismissal** Entlassungsschreiben, Entlassungsbescheid; ~ **of engagement** Verlobungsanzeige

notice of intervention in opposition proceedings shall be filed in a written reasoned statement *(PatR)* der Beitritt zum Einspruchsverfahren ist schriftlich zu erklären und zu begründen

notice, ~ **of loss** Schadensanzeige, Verlustanzeige; ~ **of marriage** Heiratsanzeige; ~ **of meeting** *(AktienR)* Einberufung der Hauptversammlung; ~ **of motion**[50] Mitteilung an den Prozeßgegner, daß in e-m schwebenden Rechtsstreit ein bestimmter Antrag gestellt wird; ~ **of opposition** *(PatR)* schriftl. Einspruchseinlegung *(→opposition 2.);* ~ **of protest** *Am* Mitteilung *(des Notars)* über Wechselprotest; ~ **of→readiness;** ~ **of reference** Benachrichtigung über Verweisung *(e-s Rechts-*

streites, z.B. an e-n Schiedsrichter); Br[51] *(KartellR)* Benachrichtigung *(durch den registrar),* daß der Fall dem Gericht vorliegt *(entspricht in s-r Wirkung der Klageerhebung);* ~ **of rejection** Ablehnungsbescheid; ~ **of rescission** Anzeige des Rücktritts vom Vertrag; ~ **of suspension of payments** Anzeige der Zahlungseinstellung; ~ **of trial** *Am* schriftl. Benachrichtigung, daß in e-m schwebenden Verfahren zu e-r bestimmten Zeit Termin anberaumt wird; ~ **of withdrawal** Austrittserklärung; Rücktrittsanzeige *(cf. ~ 3.);* ~ **to admit documents** (or **facts**) *Br* schriftl. Aufforderung *(e-s solicitor an die Gegenpartei),* Beweismaterial oder Tatsachen vor der Verhandlung anzuerkennen; ~ **to pay** Zahlungsaufforderung; ~ **to proceed** Benachrichtigung des Gegners *(nachdem mindestens ein Jahr lang keine Schritte in e-m Prozeß unternommen wurden),* daß man gedenkt, den Prozeß fortzusetzen; ~ **to produce**[52] Aufforderung *(an die Gegenpartei),* Beweismittel zur Einsicht vorzulegen; ~ **to quit** Räumungsaufforderung; ~ **to third party** *Am* s. third party →~; ~ **to treat** *Br (im Enteignungsverfahren)* Benachrichtigung von der geplanten Enteignung an den Betroffenen und Bestätigung der Bereitschaft, über den Preis zu verhandeln; ~ **type statutes** *Am* →recording system

notice, advance ~ Voranzeige; vorherige Ankündigung; **consignment** ~ Versandanzeige; **D-N~s** (= defense notices) *Br* unverbindliche Richtlinien für die Nachrichtenmedien (*Presse, Rundfunk, Fernsehen*), in denen festgelegt wird, welche Vorgänge aus Gründen der nationalen Sicherheit zur Veröffentlichung nicht geeignet sind; **default** ~ *Br*[53] *(bei Abzahlungsgeschäften)* Mitteilung des Zahlungsverzuges *(hat der Käufer nach Ablauf e-r Frist von 7 Tagen seine Zahlungsverpflichtung [Ratenzahlung] nicht erfüllt, kann der Verkäufer vom Vertrag zurücktreten);* →**judicial** ~; **obituary** ~ Todesanzeige; **public** ~ öffentliche Bekanntmachung; **third party** ~ Streitverkündung *(→third party);* **till** (or **until**) **further** ~ bis auf weiteres; **without further** ~ ohne weitere Ankündigung; ohne weiteres

notice, without (previous or **prior)** ~ ohne vorherige Ankündigung (od. Benachrichtigung); **subject to change without** ~ freibleibend

notice, to be on ~ *Am* verständigt worden sein; davon unterrichtet sein; Kenntnis haben; **to bring to a p.'s** ~ zu jds Kenntnis bringen; jdm bekannt geben

notice, to give ~ **of** Kenntnis geben von, Mitteilung machen, bekanntgeben, benachrichtigen, anzeigen; *Am (vertragswidrige Beschaffenheit der Ware)* rügen; **obligation** (or **duty**) **to give** ~ **(of)** Mitteilungspflicht; Anzeigepflicht; **to give** ~ **of appeal** ein Rechtsmittel (Berufung etc) einlegen; **to give** ~ **of claim** (or **loss**) *(VersR)* Schaden anmelden; Schadensanzeige erstatten; **to give** ~ **of withdrawal** Austritt erklären; Rücktritt anzeigen; **to give due** ~ **(of)** formgerecht mitteilen; ordnungsgemäß anzeigen; **to give prompt** ~ umgehend benachrichtigen; **to give** ~ **to a third person** *Am* jdm den Streit verkünden; **to give** ~ **in writing within a reasonable time** e-e schriftliche Mitteilung in angemessener Frist machen; ~ **is hereby given** hierdurch wird bekanntgegeben; **to be given** ~ **(of)** Kenntnis erlangen (von); **to have been given inadequate** ~ **of** unzulängliche Kenntnis bekommen haben von

notice, to have ~ Kenntnis haben (of von); **to put up a** ~ e-e Bekanntmachung anschlagen; ein Schild aufstellen; **to receive** ~ Nachricht erhalten; Kenntnis erlangen; Beachtung finden; **to take** ~ zur Kenntnis nehmen, beachten; Kenntnis nehmen (of von); **to take no** ~ **(of)** nicht beachten

notice 2. Kenntnis (od. Kennenmüssen) *(der Rechte Dritter seitens e-s Erwerbers von bewegl. od. unbewegl. Vermögen od. Rechten);*[54] **actual** ~ tatsächliche Kenntnis *(der Rechte Dritter)* (Kennen); zurechenbare Kenntnis *(gewisser Rechte betr. Grundbesitz auf Grund von Registrierung);* **constructive** ~ zurechenbare Kenntnis *(der Rechte Dritter)* (Kennenmüssen) *(bes. auf Grund von Kenntnis seitens e-s Anwalts od. sonstigen Vertreters);* **imputed** ~ s. constructive →~

notice, without ~ gutgläubig; **purchaser without** ~ redlicher Erwerber; **to acquire for value without** ~ gutgläubig gegen Entgelt erwerben

notice, to be put on ~ auf Rechte Dritter aufmerksam gemacht werden

notice 3. Kündigung; ~ **deposits** *Am* Kündigungsgelder; ~ **in writing** schriftliche Kündigung; ~ **of cancellation** Kündigung, Rücktritt; ~ **of credit** Kreditkündigung

notice of denunciation of a convention (treaty) *(VölkerR)* Kündigung e-s Abkommens (Vertrages); **to give** ~ ein Abkommen (e-n Vertrag) kündigen

notice (of dismissal) Kündigung

notice of redemption of a mortgage Kündigung e-r Hypothek; **to give** ~ e-e Hypothek kündigen *(Schuldner)*

notice of repayment Kündigung *(durch die Bank)*

notice of termination of employment (or **service**)[54a] Kündigung des Arbeitsverhältnisses; **to give written** ~ das Arbeitsverhältnis schriftlich kündigen

notice of withdrawal Kündigung(sbenachrichtigung) *(cf. ~ 1.);* ~ **of credit** Kreditkündigung; ~ **of deposits** Kündigung von Einlagen

notice to quit Kündigung *(des Mieters, Pächters);* **to be under** ~ seine Kündigung erhalten; gekündigt sein; **to give a tenant** ~ e-m Mieter (od. Pächter) kündigen; **he was given** ~ ihm wurde gekündigt; **to receive 3 months'** ~ mit 3monatiger Frist gekündigt werden *(Mieter, Pächter)*

notice to terminate (agreement, employment, lease) Kündigung (e-s Vertrages, Arbeitsverhältnisses, Miet- od. Pachtvertrages)

notice to vacate Kündigung *(des Miet- od. Pachtverhältnisses durch den Vermieter, Verpächter)*

notice, at ~ kündbar; **at one month's** ~ mit e-r Kündigungsfrist von einem Monat; **at short** ~ kurzfristig kündbar *(→short 3.)*; **deposits at** ~ Einlagen mit Kündigungsfrist; Kündigungsgelder; **loan at** ~ kündbares Darlehen

notice, due ~ ordnungsgemäße (od. rechtzeitige) Kündigung; **expiration** (or **expiry**) **of** ~ Ablauf der Kündigungsfrist; **a fortnight's** ~ 14tägige Kündigung(sfrist); **incapable of being terminated by** ~ unkündbar

notice, monthly ~ monatliche Kündigung; **at** (or **subject to**) **a month's (3 months', 6 months')** ~ mit monatlicher (vierteljährlicher, halbjährlicher) Kündigung(sfrist); **upon six months'** ~ unter Einhaltung e-r Kündigungsfrist von sechs Monaten

notice, period of ~ Kündigungsfrist; **agreed period of** ~ vereinbarte Kündigungsfrist; **expiration of the period of** ~ Ablauf der Kündigungsfrist; **statutory (minimum) period of** ~[55] gesetzliche Kündigungsfrist; **the period of** ~ **expires** die Kündigungsfrist läuft ab

notice, reasonable~ angemessene Kündigung(sfrist); **receipt of** ~ Erhalt e-r Kündigung; **right to give** ~ Kündigungsrecht; **seven days'** ~ wöchentliche Kündigung(sfrist); **subject to** ~ kündbar; **subject to one year's** ~ mit einjähriger Kündigungsfrist; **term of** ~ Kündigungsfrist; **upon the** ~ unter Einhaltung e-r bestimmten Kündigungsfrist; **two weeks'** ~ vierzehntägige Kündigung(sfrist); **withdrawal of the** ~ Rücknahme der Kündigung

notice, without~ fristlos; **dismissal without** ~ fristlose Entlassung; **to terminate** *(employment etc)* **without any** ~ fristlos kündigen

notice, to give~ kündigen; **to give in one's** ~ s-e Kündigung einreichen; **to be given** ~ Kündigung erhalten; gekündigt werden; **ground for giving** ~ Kündigungsgrund; **right to give** ~ Kündigungsrecht; **without the right of giving** ~ unkündbar; **to give one month's** ~ **to one's employer** seinem Arbeitgeber mit monatlicher Kündigungsfrist kündigen; **to give one week's** ~ mit wöchentlicher Frist kündigen; **by giving three months'** ~ mit vierteljährlicher Kündigungsfrist; **to terminate a convention on giving six months'** ~ ein Abkommen mit sechsmonatlicher Frist kündigen

notice, the tenant received 3 months' ~ **to quit** dem Mieter (od. Pächter) wurde mit e-r Frist von 3 Monaten gekündigt; **to serve a** ~ **(up)on sb.** →serve *v* 4.

notice *v* zur Kenntnis nehmen, bemerken; erwähnen; **to** ~ **a p.'s services** jds Dienste *(in e-r Rede etc)* erwähnen

noticed facts *(vom Gericht ohne Beweis)* als offenkundig anerkannte Tatsache

notifiable disease meldepflichtige (od. anzeigepflichtige) Krankheit

notification *(förml.)* Mitteilung, Bekanntmachung, Anzeige; Zustellung; *(VölkerR)* Notifizierung, Notifikation; ~ **by delivery on the premises of the European Patent Office** Zustellung durch Übergabe im Europäischen Patentamt; ~ **by delivery by hand** Zustellung durch unmittelbare Übergabe; ~ **by post** Zustellung durch die Post; ~ **of an accident** Unfallanzeige; ~ **of birth** Bekanntgabe e-r Geburt *(beim Standesamt)*; ~ **of claim** (or **loss-**)*(VersR)* Schadensanzeige; ~ **of death** Bekanntgabe e-s Todesfalles *(beim Standesamt)*; ~ **of defects** *com* Mängelanzeige, Mängelrüge; ~ **of dividend** Dividendenankündigung; ~ **of the police** Benachrichtigung der Polizei; Erstattung e-r (Straf-)Anzeige; **official** ~ amtliche Bekanntgabe; **public** ~ öffentliche Bekanntmachung; öffentliche Zustellung

notify *v (förml.)* mitteilen, bekanntgeben, offiziell zur Kenntnis bringen, melden, anzeigen; zustellen; *(VölkerR)* notifizieren; **duty** (or **obligation**) **to** ~ **(sb. of sth.)** Anzeigepflicht; **to** ~ **a death** e-n Todesfall zur Kenntnis bringen (od. anmelden); **to** ~ **a defect** e-n Mangel anzeigen (ode. rügen); **to** ~ **the police** die Polizei benachrichtigen; **to** ~ **(sb.) of sth.** (jdn) von etw. benachrichtigen; **to** ~ **sb. promptly in writing** jdn unverzüglich schriftlich benachrichtigen

notified, the person ~ *Am* der Streitverkündete; **document to be** ~ *(PatR)* zuzustellendes Schriftstück; **to be** ~ Bescheid (od. Kenntnis) erhalten

notifying bank avisierende Bank

noting →note *v*

notion Auffassung, Begriff; ~**s** *bes. Am* Kurzwaren

notorious offenkundig; allgemein bekannt, gerichtsbekannt *(bes. im negativen Sinne)*, berüchtigt; ~ **prior use** *(PatR)* offenkundige Vorbenutzung

notour bankruptcy *Scot* offenkundig gewordener Bankrott

notwithstanding ungeachtet, unbeschadet, trotz; abweichend von; ~ **any provision to the contrary** unbeschadet irgendwelcher gegenteiliger Bestimmungen; ~ **the objections** ungeachtet der Einwände; ~ **the provisions of** in Abweichung von den Vorschriften des; ~ **this** in Abweichung hiervon

novation Novation, Schuldumschaffung *(bestehendes Schuldverhältnis wird durch ein anderes [neues Schuldverhältnis] ersetzt)*

novel *(PatR)* neu; ~ **feature** Neuheitsmerkmal; ~ **method** neuartiges Verfahren

novelties *com* Neuheiten

novelty *com* Neuheit; *(PatR)* Neuheit *(e-r Erfindung als Voraussetzung für Patentfähigkeit)*; ~ **search** *(PatR)* Neuheitsrecherche; **detrimental as to** ~ *(PatR)* neuheitsschädlich; **examination as to** ~ *(PatR)* Neuheitsprüfung, Prüfung der Neuheit; **objection for want of** ~ *(PatR)* Einspruch wegen mangelnder Neuheit; **technical** ~ technische Neuheit (od. Neuerung); **to constitute a bar as to** ~ (or **to be detrimental to** ~) *(PatR)* neuheitsschädlich sein; **the subject matter of the invention lacks** ~ *(PatR)* der Erfindung fehlt die Neuheit

no-victimization clause Maßregelungsklausel

NOW account →account 1.

noxious schädlich; ungesund (to für); giftig

nuclear Kern-, Atom-

nuclear accident nuklearer Unfall, Kernkraftunfall; **largest-scale** ~ größter anzunehmender Unfall (GAU)

nuclear, ~ **age** Atomzeitalter; ~ **armament(s)** (or **arming**) Atomrüstung

nuclear arms Atomwaffen; ~ **race** atomares Wettrüsten; **freezing of** ~ Einfrieren der A-Waffen

nuclear, ~ **attack** Angriff mit Atomwaffen; ~ **balance** atomares Gleichgewicht; ~ **blackmail** *pol* nukleare Erpressung *(gegenüber kernwaffenlosen Staaten)*; ~ **bomb** Atombombe; ~ **cargo ship** Reaktor-Frachtschiff

nuclear damage nuklearer Schaden; Atomschaden; **Vienna Convention on Civil Liability for N~ D~s**[56] Wiener Übereinkommen über die Haftung für nukleare Schäden *(21. 5. 1963)*

nuclear, ~ **deterrence** atomare (od. nukleare) Abschreckung; ~ **disarmament** atomare Abrüstung; Verzicht auf Atomwaffen; **~-driven** durch Kernenergie angetrieben

Nuclear Emergency Search Team (NEST) *Am* Spezialtruppe für gemeinsames Vorgehen im Falle e-s Unfalls mit US-Atomwaffen in der Bundesrepublik

nuclear energy Kernenergie; Atomenergie; ~ **plant** Atomkraftwerk

nuclear energy production, progressive reduction of ~ schrittweiser Abbau der Kernenergieerzeugung

nuclear energy, Convention on the Establishment of a Security Control in the Field of N~ E~[57] Übereinkommen zur Errichtung e-r Sicherheitskontrolle auf dem Gebiet der Kernenergie; →**European N~ E~ Agency; European N~ E~ Tribunal** (ENET)[58] Europäisches Kernenergie-Gericht; →**OECD's N~ E~ Agency** (NEA); **Paris Convention on Third Party Liability in the Field of N~ E~**[56] Pariser Übereinkommen über die Haftung gegenüber Dritten auf dem Gebiet der Kernenergie *(29. 7. 1960)* (mit Brüsseler Zusatzübereinkommen *[31. 1. 1963]*); **use of** ~ Kernenergienutzung; **to abandon** ~ den Ausstieg aus der Kernenergie vollziehen

nuclear, ~ **engineering** Kerntechnik; ~ **fission** Kernspaltung

nuclear force Atomstreitkraft; **tactical ~(s)** taktische Atomstreitkräfte

nuclear-free zone atomwaffenfreie Zone

nuclear freeze Einfrieren der nuklearen Aufrüstung

nuclear fuel Kernbrennstoff; ~ **storage** Lagerung von Kernbrennstoffen; ~ **supply** Versorgung mit Kernbrennstoffen; →**European Company for the Chemical Processing of Irradiated N~ F~s**

nuclear incident Atomunfall; **compensation for damage caused by a** ~ Entschädigung für durch e-n Atomunfall verursachten Schaden

nuclear industry Kern(energie)industrie, Atomindustrie

nuclear installations Nukleareinrichtungen, Kernkraftanlagen; **N~ I~ (Licensing and Insurance) Act** *Am* Gesetz über die Genehmigung und Versicherung von Kernenergieanlagen *(von 1959)*

nuclear, ~ **materials management** Bewirtschaftung von nuklearem Material (od. Kernmaterial od. von radioaktiven Abfallstoffen); ~ **missile** Atomrakete; **N~ Nonproliferation Act,** 1978 *Am* Gesetz über die Nichtverbreitung von Kernenergie *(das die Vorschriften für die amerikanischen Uranlieferungen nach Europa verschärft)*; ~ **passenger ship** Reaktor-Fahrgastschiff; ~ **physicist** Atomphysiker; ~ **physics** Atomphysik, Kernphysik; **N~ Planning Group** (NPG) *(NATO)* Nukleare Planungsgruppe

nuclear power Atomkraft; *pol* Kernwaffenmacht, Atommacht; **campaigner(s) against** (or **opponent[s] of**) ~ Atomkraftgegner; ~ **industry** Atomindustrie; ~ **plant** (or **station**) Atomkraftwerk; **non ~s** Nichtkernwaffenmächte

nuclear-powered atom(kraft)betrieben, kernkraftbetrieben; ~ **ship** Schiff mit Kernenergieantrieb

Nuclear Regulatory Commission (NRC) *Am* Behörde, die sich mit Planung und Bau neuer Kernkraftwerke sowie dem Schutz des nuklearen Materials vor dem Zugriff von Terroristen beschäftigt

nuclear research Kernforschung; →**European Organization for N~ R~**

nuclear, ~ safety nukleare Sicherheit; Sicherheit auf dem Gebiet der Kernenergie; **~ sharing** Kernwaffenmitbesitz

nuclear ship Atomschiff; Reaktorschiff; **Brussels N~ S~ Convention (Convention on the Liability of Operators of N~ S~s)**[59] Brüsseler Atomschiffskonvention (Übereinkommen über die Haftung der Inhaber von Atomschiffen *[von 1962]*)

nuclear, ~ site Kernenergieanlage; **~ stalemate** Atompatt; **~ states** atomare (od. nukleare) Staaten; **~ stockpile** Bestand an Atomwaffen; **~ submarine** Atom-U-Boot; **~ superiority** nukleare Überlegenheit

nuclear test Atom(waffen)versuch, Kernwaffenversuch *(→nuclear weapon test)*; **~ ban** Atom(waffen)versuchsverbot, Kernwaffentestverbot; **atmospheric ~s** Atomwaffenversuche in der Atmosphäre; **banning of ~ explosions** Verbot von nuklearen Versuchsexplosionen; **stopping (or suspension) of ~s** Einstellung der Atom(waffen)versuche; **to continue to hold ~s** Atom(waffen)versuche weiter durchführen

nuclear, ~ testing →~ test; **~ war** Atomkrieg; **~ warfare** nukleare Kriegführung; **~ warhead** Atomsprengkopf; **~ waste disposal** Beseitigung von Atommüll; Entsorgung; **~ waste dump** nukleares Endlager

nuclear weapon Atomwaffe, Kernwaffe; **non-~ states** kernwaffenlose Staaten

nuclear weapon test Atomwaffenversuch, Kernwaffenversuch; **~ explosion** Versuchsexplosion von Kernwaffen; **Treaty Banning N~ W~ T~s in the Atmosphere, Outer Space and Under Water**[60] (Moskauer) Vertrag über das Verbot von Kernwaffenversuchen in der Atmosphäre, im Weltraum und unter Wasser ([Atom-]Teststoppvertrag) *(von 1963)*; **to ban (suspend) ~s** Kernwaffenversuche verbieten (einstellen)

nuclear weapon, freezing of ~s Einfrieren der Kernwaffen; **renunciation of ~s** Verzicht auf Atomwaffen; **sharing of ~s** Kernwaffenmitbesitz; **Treaty on the Non-Proliferation of N~ W~s** (or **Non-Proliferation Treaty**) (NPT)[61] Vertrag über die Nichtverbreitung von Kernwaffen, Atomwaffensperrvertrag (ASV); **Treaty on the Prohibition of the Emplacement of N~ W~s and other Weapons of Mass Destruction on the Sea-Bed and the Ocean Floor and in the Subsoil thereof**[62] Vertrag über das Verbot der Anbringung von Kernwaffen und anderen Massenvernichtungswaffen auf dem Meeresboden und Meeresgrund; **use of tactical ~s** Einsatz von taktischen Atomwaffen

nuclear workers Arbeitnehmer in Kernkraftanlagen

nude contract →nudum pactum

nudum pactum mangels →consideration unverbindlicher Vertrag

nugatory unwirksam; wertlos

nuisance Belästigung, Beeinträchtigung, Störung *(z. B. vom Nachbargrundstück aus durch Rauch, Lärm etc)*; Lästigkeit; Umweltstörung; **~ abatement assessments** *Am* Sonderabgaben *(z. B. für Beseitigung von Schutt und Eis, Müllabfuhr etc)*; **abatement of ~** Beseitigung der Störung *(durch Selbsthilfe)*; →**attractive ~**; **common ~** s. public →~; **private ~** *(nachbarliche)* (Besitz-)Störung des einzelnen; verbotene Eigenmacht; **public ~** Störung der Allgemeinheit; öffentliches Ärgernis; öffentliche Gefahrenquelle; **to abate a ~** e-e Störung beseitigen (od. abstellen); **commit no ~** dieser Ort darf nicht verunreinigt werden; **to reduce ~s** Störungen (od. Umweltbelastungen) verringern

null nichtig, ungültig; **~ and void** (null und) nichtig; **the contract is ~ and void** der Vertrag ist nichtig

nulla bona ("no goods") Unpfändbarkeitsbescheinigung

nulla poena sine lege ("no punishment without a statute") *(StrafR)* keine Strafe ohne Gesetz *(cf. ex post facto law)*

nullification Ungültigmachung, Annullierung

nullify *v* ungültig machen, annullieren

nullity Nichtigkeit, Ungültigkeit; **~ action against a patent** *Am* Klage auf Nichtigkeit e-s Patents; **~ appeal** *(PatR)* Nichtigkeitsbeschwerde; **N~ Board** *(Europ. PatR)* Nichtigkeitssenat; **~ decree** s. decree of →~; **~ of marriage**[63] absolute Nichtigkeit (od. Vernichtbarkeit) der *(void or voidable)* Ehe; **~ suit** Nichtigkeitsverfahren; **decree of ~** (of marriage) Nichtigkeitsurteil *(wirkt grundsätzlich auf* den Zeitpunkt der Eheschließung zurück); **ground for ~** Nichtigkeitsgrund; **petition for ~**[64] (Ehe-)Nichtigkeitsklage; **to grant a decree of ~** e-e Ehe für nichtig erklären

number (No, no.) Nummer (Nr.), Zahl; Anzahl; **~ engaged** *Br tel* Nummer besetzt; **~ of employees** (or **personnel**) Personalstand; **~ plate** *Br (Auto)* Nummernschild; **back ~** alte Nummer *(e-r Zeitung)*; Ladenhüter; **check ~** Kontrollnummer; **consecutive ~** laufende Nummer; **even ~** gerade Zahl; **file ~** s. reference →~; **fractional ~** Bruchzahl; →**index ~**; **in large ~s** ingroßen Mengen; **invoice ~** Rechnungsnummer; **maximum ~** Höchstzahl; **minimum ~** Mindestzahl; **reference ~** Aktenzeichen, Geschäftszeichen *(→reference)*; **serial ~** Seriennummer, laufende Nummer; **specification of ~s** Nummernverzeichnis; **telephone ~** Telefonnummer; **to dial a ~** *tel* e-e Nummer wählen

number *v* numerieren; zählen; sich belaufen auf
numbered, ~ **account** Nummernkonto; **consecutively** ~ fortlaufend numeriert; **marked and** ~ mit Zeichen und Nummern versehen
numbering Numerierung

numeral Zahl, Ziffer, Nummer; ~ **mark** *Br (PatR)* Nummernzeichen

numerical, in ~ **orders** in zahlenmäßiger Reihenfolge, nach Nummern geordnet

nunciature *(VölkerR)* Nuntiatur; Amt(speriode) e-s Nuntius

nuncio *(VölkerR)* Nuntius *(e-m Botschafter gleichstehender ständiger Vertreter des Vatikans; cf. legate)*

nunc pro tunc ("now for then") rückwirkend

nuncupate *v* letztwillige Verfügung mündlich erklären

nuncupative will mündlich *(vor Zeugen)* erklärte letztwillige Verfügung

nuptial Ehe-; **ante-**~ **contract** Ehevertrag

nuptiality *(Statistik)* Heiratshäufigkeit

nurse (Kranken-)Schwester; **district** ~ Gemeindeschwester; **practical** ~ *Am (staatl. geprüfte, vorwiegend praktisch ausgebildete)* Krankenschwester; **registered** ~ *Am (staatl. geprüfte, theoretisch und praktisch ausgebildete)* Krankenschwester; **state-enrolled** ~ (S.E.N.) *Br* Hilfskrankenschwester; **state registered** ~ (S.R.N.) *Br* staatl. geprüfte Krankenschwester

nurse *v* pflegen; schonend umgehen mit; fördern *(z.B. persönliche Beziehungen)*
nursing Krankenpflege; ~ **allowance** Pflegegeld; ~ **home** Pflegeanstalt, Privatklinik; ~ **staff** Pflegepersonal

nutrition, ~ **level** Ernährungsstand; ~ **science** Ernährungswissenschaft

nutritional deficiency Unterernährung

O

oath[1] Eid *(umfaßt auch affirmation und Br*[2] *declaration)*
oath, ~ **for administrators** Eid des Erbschaftsverwalters (administrator) (*vor Erteilung der letters of* →*administration*); ~ **for executors** Eid des Erbschaftsverwalters (executor) (*vor Erteilung des* →*probate*); ~ **of allegiance** *(von gewissen hohen Beamten, Mitgliedern des Parlaments od. bei Einbürgerung zu leistender)* Treueid; *mil* Fahneneid; ~ **of disclosure** *Am* Offenbarungseid; ~ **of fidelity and secrecy** zu Treue und Verschwiegenheit verpflichtender Eid; ~ **of loyalty** *Am* →loyalty; ~ **of manifestation** *Am* Offenbarungseid; ~ **of office** *Br* Erbschaftsverwaltereid *(→~ for executors); Am* Amtseid; Diensteid; **administering** (or **administration of**) **an** ~ Abnahme e-s Eides, Vereidigung; **assertory** ~ *Am* Beteuerung unter Eid *(opp. promissory ~)*; **breaking of an** ~ Eidbruch; **coronation** ~ *Br (vom Erzbischof od. Bischof abgenommener)* Krönungseid; **false** ~ Meineid *(→false swearing)*; **form of** ~ Eidesformel; **judicial** ~ vom Richter abgenommener oder vor dem Richter geleisteter Eid; **loyalty** ~ *Am* Treueid *(bes. des Beamten)*; **official** ~ Amtseid, Diensteid
oath, on (or **upon**) ~ eidlich, unter Eid; **denial upon** ~ Abschwörung; →**discovery upon** ~; **evidence on** ~ eidliche (Zeugen-)Aussage; **statement on** ~ eidliche Erklärung; **testimony on** ~ s. evidence on →~; **to be on** ~ unter Eid aussagen; vereidigt sein; **he deposes upon his** ~ **and says** *Am* er erklärt unter Eid; **to give evidence on** ~ unter Eid aussagen; **to examine on** ~ *(Zeuge)* eidlich vernehmen; **to state** (or **make a statement**) **on** ~ unter Eid erklären, e-e Erklärung unter Eid abgeben
oath, parliamentary ~ *Br* von e-m Parlamentsmitglied geleisteter Eid; **promissory** ~ Gelöbnis unter Eid *(z.B. ~ of allegiance)*; **refusal to take an** ~ Verweigerung der Eidesleistung, Eidesverweigerung; **taking an** ~ Eidesleistung
oath, under ~ unter Eid, eidlich; **to affirm under** ~ eidlich versichern; **to make a false statement under** ~ e-e falsche Aussage unter Eid machen; **to testify under** ~ unter Eid aussagen
oath, violation of an ~ Eidesverletzung; **to administer an** ~ **to a p.** jdm e-n Eid abnehmen, jdn vereidigen; **to be bound by an** ~ eidlich gebunden sein; **to break one's** ~ eidbrüchig werden, s-n Eid brechen; **to confirm a statement by** ~ e-e Aussage eidlich erhärten; **to make** ~ schwören, e-n Eid leisten; **I, ..., make** ~ **and say as follows** ich, ..., erkläre unterEid; **to put sb. under** ~ jdn vereidigen; **to release a p. from his** ~ jdn von s-m Eid entbinden; **to take an** ~ e-n Eid ablegen (od. leisten), beeidigen

obedient, your ~ **servant** (or **yours** ~**ly**) Ihr sehr ergebener *(Briefschluß in amtl. Schreiben)*

obiit (ob.) *lat.* gestorben, verstorben

obiter →**dictum**

obituary (notice) Nachruf *(in Zeitungen);* Todesanzeige

object Gegenstand; Zweck, Ziel; **~s clause** *Br* Klausel der Gründungsurkunde (memorandum of association), in der der Gegenstand des Unternehmens anzugeben ist; **~ found** Fundsache; **~ of an action** Zweck des Verfahrens; **~ of art** Kunstgegenstand; **~s of a company** Gegenstand e-s Unternehmens; Ziele der Gesellschaft; Gesellschaftszweck; **with the ~ of gain** in gewinnsüchtiger Absicht; **~s of a power** *Br* die Personen, zu deren Gunsten e-e power of appointment *(→power 1.)* ausgeübt wird; **convincing ~** *(StrafR)* Beweisstück (corpus delicti); **expense is no ~** Kosten spielen keine Rolle; **immediate ~** Nahziel; **salary no ~** Gehalt Nebensache; **to achieve** (or **attain, gain**) **one's ~** sein Ziel erreichen

object *v* Einwendungen machen, einwenden, Einspruch (od. Widerspruch) erheben (to gegen); beanstanden; ablehnen; **to ~ to a juror (witness)** e-n Geschworenen (Zeugen) ablehnen; **to ~ to the members of a Board of Appeal if suspected of partiality** *(Europ. PatentR)* Mitglieder der Beschwerdekammer wegen Besorgnis der Befangenheit ablehnen

objected, the member ~ to das abgelehnte Mitglied; **a question to a witness is ~ to** gegen e-e Frage an e-n Zeugen wird Einspruch erhoben

objection Einwendung, Einwand, Einrede, Einspruch; Beanstandung; Bedenken (to gegen); Widerspruch; Ablehnung; **~ in (point of) law** Bestreiten der Schlüssigkeit der Klage; **~ to election** Wahleinspruch; **~ to an expert** Ablehnung e-s Sachverständigen; **~ to the jurisdiction** Einrede der Unzuständigkeit; **~ to a juror** Ablehnung e-s Geschworenen; **no ~** nichts einzuwenden; **preliminary ~**[3] prozeßhindernde Einrede; *(VölkerR)* Einrede in der Vorverhandlung; **reason for ~** Ablehnungsgrund; **right to ~** Einspruchsrecht; **to allow an ~** e-m Einspruch stattgeben; **to disallow an ~** e-n Einspruch verwerfen; **to grant an ~** e-m Einspruch stattgeben; **to make** (or **raise**) **an ~** e-n Einwand machen (od. erheben), e-e Einrede geltend machen; beanstanden; **to lodge an ~** Widerspruch erheben; **to offer ~** *dipl* Einspruch erheben; **to take ~s** s. to make →~s; **to withdraw an ~** e-n Einspruch zurücknehmen; **there are no ~s** es bestehen keine Bedenken, es ist nichts einzuwenden (to gegen)

objectionable zu beanstanden

objective Zweck; Ziel, Zielsetzung; objektiv, sachlich; **achievement** (or **attainment**) **of ~s** Erreichung von Zielen; **clear** (or **clearly defined**) **~** klar umrissenes Ziel; **company ~** Unternehmensziel; **major ~** Hauptziel; **military ~** militärisches Ziel; **primary ~** Hauptziel, oberstes Ziel; **to achieve** (or **attain**) **the ~** das Ziel erreichen

objector Gegner, Opponent; **conscientious ~** Wehrdienstverweigerer

oblations *Br* Zahlungen an die Kirche *(bei Hochzeiten, Beerdigungen etc)*

obligant *Scot* →obligee

obligate *v* verpflichten; zwingen; **to be ~d** *Am* verpflichtet sein

obligation Verpflichtung, Verbindlichkeit (to a p. jdm gegenüber); Schuldverhältnis; Schuldverschreibung; Auflage

obligation, to adhere to an ~ e-e Verpflichtung einhalten; **to assume an ~** e-e Verpflichtung übernehmen (od. eingehen); **to be under an ~** (to a p. jdm gegenüber) verpflichtet (od. gebunden) sein, die Verpflichtung haben; **to carry out one's ~s** s-e Verpflichtungen erfüllen; **to comply with ~s** Verpflichtungen nachkommen (od. einhalten); **to discharge one's ~s** s-e Verpflichtungen erfüllen; s-n Verpflichtungen nachkommen; **to enter into an ~** e-e Verpflichtung eingehen; **to fail in one's ~s** s-n Verpflichtungen nicht nachkommen; **to fulfil an ~** e-e Verpflichtung erfüllen; e-r Verpflichtung nachkommen; **to impose an ~ on a p.** jdm e-e Verpflichtung auferlegen; **to incur an ~** e-e Verpflichtung eingehen (od. übernehmen); **no ~s shall be incurred** keine Verpflichtungen sollen entstehen; **to meet** (or **perform**) **an ~** s. to fulfil an →~; **to put sb. under an ~** jdn verpflichten; jdm e-e Verpflichtung auferlegen; **to be released from one's ~s** von s-n Verpflichtungen befreit sein (od. entbunden werden); **to relieve of ~s** von Verpflichtungen entbinden

obligation, ~ arising from the contract die sich aus dem Vertrag ergebende Verpflichtung; **~ incumbent on a p.** jdm obliegende Verpflichtung; **~ in kind** Gattungsschuld

obligation of contracts, to impair the ~[4] in vertragliche Rechte eingreifen

obligation, ~ of secrecy Verpflichtung zur Geheimhaltung; **~ to accept (the goods)** Abnahmeverpflichtung; **~ to buy** Kaufverpflichtung, Kaufzwang; **~ to contract** Kontrahierungszwang; **~ to deliver** Lieferpflicht; **~ to disclose** (or **of disclosure**) Auskunftspflicht, Offenbarungspflicht; **~ to extradite** Auslieferungspflicht; **~ to give information** Auskunftspflicht; Anzeigepflicht; **~ to maintain a p.** (or **in respect of maintenance**) Unterhaltspflicht; **~ to notify** Anzeigepflicht; **~ to pay** Zahlungsverpflichtung; **~ to pay maintenance** Unterhaltspflicht; **~ to repay** Rückerstattungspflicht; **~ to support a p.** Unterhaltspflicht

obligation under a contract vertragliche Verpflichtung; **failure to perform an** ~ *(schuldhafte)* Nichterfüllung e-s Vertrags

obligation, assumption of an ~ Schuldübernahme; **business** ~ Geschäftsverbindlichkeit; **civic** ~**s** staatsbürgerliche Pflichten; →**contractual** ~; **creation of an** ~ Begründung e-s Schuldverhältnisses; **discharge of** ~**s** Erfüllung von Verpflichtungen; **equitable** ~ auf →equity-Recht beruhende Verpflichtung; **financial** ~ finanzielle Verpflichtung; **fulfilment of an** ~ Erfüllung e-r Verpflichtung; **imperfect** ~ nicht einklagbare Verpflichtung; **implied** ~ stillschweigend unterstellte Verpflichtung; **joint** ~ gemeinsame Verpflichtung; **joint and several** ~ gemeinsame (od. gesamtschuldnerische) Verpflichtung; **legal** ~ gesetzliche (od. rechtl.) Verpflichtung, Rechtspflicht; **long-term** ~ langfristige Verbindlichkeit; **moral** ~ moralische Verpflichtung; **performance of an** ~ Erfüllung e-r Verpflichtung; **short-term** ~ kurzfristige Verbindlichkeit; **specific** ~ Speziesschuld; **U.S. Government** ~**s** Schuldverschreibungen der Vereinigten Staaten; **without** ~ unverbindlich; freibleibend

obligator *Am* →obligor

obligatory obligatorisch, verpflichtend, verbindlich, zwingend vorgeschrieben *(opp. discretionary)*; ~ **disposition** Mußvorschrift *(opp. facultative disposition)*; ~ **insurance** Pflichtversicherung; ~ **law** zwingendes Recht; ~ **share** *Am* Pflichtteil

oblige *v* binden, verpflichten; gefällig sein; **you would greatly** ~ **us** Sie würden uns sehr zu Dank verpflichten; **an early reply would** ~ für baldige Antwort wäre ich dankbar

obliged, to be ~ **(to)** zu Dank verpflichtet sein; müssen

obliging verbindlich, entgegenkommend; kulant

obligingly entgegenkommenderweise

obligee (Obligations-)Gläubiger, (Forderungs-) Berechtigter

obligor (Obligations-)Schuldner, Verpflichteter

obliterate *v* (aus)löschen, ausradieren, (aus)streichen; *(Schrift)* unkenntlich machen; **to** ~ **a stamp** ein Postwertzeichen abstempeln (od. entwerten); **to** ~ **a trade-mark** ein Warenzeichen unkenntlich machen

obliteration Auslöschung, (Aus-)Streichung, Unkenntlichmachung; ~ **of a stamp** Abstempelung (od. Entwertung) e-s Postwertzeichens

obnoxious anstößig; belästigend

obrogation Novellierung e-s Gesetzes

obscene unzüchtig, obszön; ~ **literature** unzüchtige Literatur, Schmutzliteratur; ~ **publications**[5] pornographische Veröffentlichungen; **sending** ~ **articles through the post** *Br*[6] Versendung obszöner Artikel durch die Post

obscenity[7] Obszönität, Unanständigkeit

obsequies Trauerfeierlichkeiten

observance Be(ob)achtung, Befolgung, Einhaltung; *eccl* Observanz, Ordensregel; ~ **of the laws** Einhaltung der Gesetze; **non(-)** ~ **of the time limit** Nichteinhaltung der Frist; **Sunday O**~ **Acts** Gesetze über Einhaltung des Sonntags; **with due** ~ **of** unter gebührender Beachtung des (der)

observation Beobachtung; Bemerkung; ~ **period** Beobachtungszeitraum; ~ **satellite** Beobachtungssatellit; **behavio(u)r** ~ *(Marktforschung)* Verhaltensbeobachtung; **commitment for** ~ Überweisung *(in e-e Anstalt)* zur Beobachtung; **to be under** ~ beobachtet werden; **to keep sb. under** ~ jdn beobachten

observe *v* beobachten; befolgen, einhalten, erfüllen, nachkommen; bemerken; **to** ~ **a condition** e-e Bedingung einhalten (od. erfüllen); **to** ~ **a law** ein Gesetz befolgen; **to fail to** ~ **the time limit** die Frist nicht einhalten, die Frist versäumen

observer Beobachter; ~ **status** Beobachterstatus; **to admit** ~**s** Beobachter zulassen; **to send** ~**s** Beobachter entsenden; **to have the status of** ~**s** die Stellung von Beobachtern haben

obsolescence *(technische od. wirtschaftl.)* Überalterung; Veralterung; Wertminderung wegen Überalterung; *Br (SteuerR)* Abschreibungsursache wegen technologischer Veralterung; ~ **of seasonal goods** Überfälligkeit von Saisonware; **industry** ~ Industrieüberalterung; **method** ~ Überalterung des Produktionsverfahrens; **product** ~ Überalterung der Wirtschaftsgüter

obsolete (obs.) veraltet; außer Gebrauch; überholt; nicht mehr gültig; **to become** ~ veralten

obstacle Hindernis; **to be an** ~ **to** entgegenstehen; **to remove an** ~ ein Hindernis beseitigen

obstruct *v* hemmen, hindern; vereiteln; *(Verkehr)* versperren; *parl* Obstruktion leisten, verschleppen; **to** ~ **a constable in the execution of his duty** *Br*[8] **(to** ~ **an officer in the performance of his duty** *Am*) e-n (Polizei-)Beamten an der Ausübung s-r Pflichten *(bes. der Rechtsdurchsetzung)* hindern; **to** ~ **a highway** e-e Straße versperren; **to** ~ **traffic** den Verkehr behindern (od. blockieren); **to** ~ **sb.'s view** jdm die Aussicht versperren (od. verbauen); **attempt to** ~ **(the proceedings)** Verschleppungsversuch

obstructing, ~ governmental operations *Am*[9] Behinderung von Regierungsmaßnahmen; **~ highways**[10] Versperren von Landstraßen, Verkehrsbehinderung auf öffentl. Straßen; **~ a constable** *Br* (**an officer** *Am*) **in the execution (performance) of his duty** Widerstand gegen die Staatsgewalt

obstruction Behinderung; Versperrung; Hindernis (to für); *parl* Obstruktion *(Verschleppungstaktik zur Verhinderung e-r Abstimmung)*; **~ of an easement** Behinderung in der Ausübung e-r Grunddienstbarkeit; **~ of the highways** →obstructing highways; **~ of judicial proceedings** (rechtswidrige) Behinderung e-s Gerichtsverfahrens; **~ on the road** Hindernis auf der Straße; **~ of traffic** Behinderung des Verkehrs; **to practise ~** *parl* Obstruktion betreiben

obstructionism *parl* Obstruktionspolitik
obstructionist *parl* Obstruktionspolitiker

obtain *v* erhalten, erlangen, bekommen; (sich) beschaffen; erwirken; *(Preis)* erzielen; **to ~ acceptance** Akzept einholen; **to ~ an adjournment** e-n Aufschub erlangen; **to ~ advances of money** Vorschuß erhalten; **to ~ a commission** →commission 2.; **to ~ a p.'s consent** jds Zustimmung erhalten; **to ~ the contract** den *(ausgeschriebenen)* Auftrag erhalten; **to ~ credit by fraud** Kreditbetrug begehen; **to ~ employment** Arbeit erhalten; **to ~ by fraud** durch Betrug erlangen; betrügerisch erwerben; erschleichen; **to ~ goods** Waren beziehen; **to ~ information** Auskunft erhalten; **to ~ a judgment** ein Urteil erwirken (against gegen); **to ~ justice** Gerechtigkeit erfahren; **to ~ an order** e-n (Gerichts-)Beschluß erwirken; e-n Auftrag erhalten; **to ~ a price** e-n Preis erzielen

obtained, consent ~ by fraud durch Betrug erlangte Einwilligung; **details can be ~ from** Einzelheiten sind zu erfahren bei; **restitution of goods ~ by fraud** Zurückgabe von durch Betrug erworbenen Sachen

obtaining, ~ pecuniary advantage by deception[11] Erlangung e-s Vermögensvorteils durch Täuschung *(z. B. Kreditbetrug)*; **~ property by deception**[12] Erlangung von Vermögen durch Betrug; **the rules then ~** die damals geltenden Regeln

obtainable zu bekommen, erhältlich

obverse Vorderseite *(e-r Münze etc)*

obvious deutlich, offenkundig; naheliegend; **~ deficiencies** offensichtliche Mängel; **examination for ~ deficiencies** *(PatR)* Offensichtlichkeitsprüfung, Überprüfung auf offensichtliche Mängel; **non-~ defects** nicht offensichtliche Mängel

obviousness *(PatR)* Offenkundigkeit, Naheliegen *(e-r Erfindung)*; **non-~** Nichtoffensichtlichkeit; mangelnde Erfindungshöhe

occasion Gelegenheit; Fall, Vorfall; Anlaß (for zu); **on the ~ of** gelegentlich, anläßlich, bei; **on particular ~s** in besonderen Fällen, in Einzelfällen; **should ~ arise** gegebenenfalls; **as (the) ~ may require** nach Bedarf

occasion *v* verursachen, veranlassen; **expenditure ~ed to a p.** jdm entstandene Aufwendungen

occasional gelegentlich, Gelegenheits- *(opp. permanent)*; **~ labo(u)r** Gelegenheitsarbeiter; **~ purchase** Gelegenheitskauf

Occidental culture abendländische Kultur

occupancy Besitz, Innehabung; Besitzergreifung, Aneignung *(e-r herrenlosen Sache)*; **~ of a house** Bewohnen e-s Hauses; **ready for ~** schlüsselfertig

occupant Besitzer, Inhaber, Bewohner *(e-r Wohnung)*; *(VölkerR)* Okkupant; **~(s) of a house** Hausbewohner; **~ of an office** Inhaber e-s Amtes; **~ of a vehicle** Insasse e-s Fahrzeugs

occupation 1. Besitz, Innehabung, Bewohnen; Besitzergreifen; **~ of a house** Innehaben (od. Bewohnen) e-s Hauses; **ready for ~** bezugsfertig; **service ~** Besitz e-r Wohnung in Zusammenhang mit e-r Stellung; **to be in ~ of a house** ein Haus bewohnen

occupation 2. Beruf, *(derzeitige berufl.)* Beschäftigung (od. Tätigkeit); **~ group** Berufsgruppe; **by ~** von Beruf; **chief ~** Hauptberuf; Hauptbeschäftigung; **choice of ~** Berufswahl; **regular ~** Hauptberuf; **secondary ~** Nebenberuf; Nebenbeschäftigung; **to choose an ~** e-n Beruf wählen

occupation 3. *mil* Besetzung, Besatzung; **~ army** Besatzungsarmee; **~ authorities** Besatzungsbehörden; **~ costs** Besatzungskosten; **~ damage** Besatzungsschaden; **~ forces** Besatzungsstreitkräfte, Besatzungstruppen; **~ law** Besatzungsrecht; **~ power** Besatzungsmacht; **~ zone** Besatzungszone; **area of ~** Besatzungsgebiet; **costs of the ~** Besatzungskosten; **pre-~ law** Gesetz vor der Besetzung

occupation 4. *(VölkerR)* Okkupation; **belligerent ~** *(occupatio bellica)* kriegerische Besetzung *(fremden Staatsgebietes)*; **pacific ~** *(occupatio pacifica)* friedliche Besetzung *(staatenlosen Gebietes)*

occupational beruflich, Berufs-; Besatzungs-; **~ accident** Betriebsunfall; **~ adviser** *Am* Berufsberater; **~ category** Berufsgruppe; **~ choice** Berufswahl; **~ classification** Berufsaufgliederung; **~ disease** Berufskrankheit; **~ group** Berufsgruppe, Berufsverband; **~ guidance** Berufsberatung; **~ hazard** mit dem Beruf verbundene Gefahr, Berufsrisiko; **~ mobility** berufliche Mobilität; **~ pension** Betriebsrente; Pension, die von e-r Firma an frühere Arbeitnehmer gezahlt wird; ~ **pension scheme** betriebliche Altersversorgung; ~ **research** Berufsforschung; **O~ Safety and Health Act** (OSHA) *Am* Berufsschutz- und Gesundheitsgesetz; ~ **training** Berufsausbildung

occupationally, (person) ~ exposed (to radiation) beruflich strahlenexponiert(e Person)

occupier Bewohner; Wohnungsinhaber; Besetzer; **~'s liability**[13] Haftpflicht des Besitzers e-s Grundstücks gegenüber Personen, die das Grundstück betreten

occupy *v* in Besitz nehmen (od. halten); besitzen, innehaben, bewohnen; *(Wohnung)* beziehen; besetzen; *(jdn)* beschäftigen; *mil (Land)* besetzen; **to ~ the chair** den Vorsitz führen, vorsitzen; **to ~ an office** ein Amt bekleiden; **to ~ o. s.** sich beschäftigen (od. befassen) (with mit); **to ~ a post** (or **situation**) e-e Stellung (od. ein Amt) bekleiden; **to ~ rooms in a house** Räume in e-m Hause bewohnen

occupied, ~ building bewohntes Gebäude; besetztes Gebäude; ~ **territory** *mil* besetztes Gebiet

occupying authority (or **power**) Besatzungsmacht

occur *v* vorkommen, sich ereignen; **an accident ~red** ein Unfall ereignete sich (od. geschah); **a condition ~s** e-e Bedingung tritt ein; **difficulties are liable to ~** Schwierigkeiten können auftauchen; **an event ~s** ein Ereignis tritt ein; **a loss ~red** ein Schaden ist eingetreten (od. entstanden); **to pay any expenses that may ~** für etwaige Kosten aufkommen

occurrence Vorfall; Ereignis; Vorkommen; **~ of a condition** Eintritt e-r Bedingung; **~ of event insured against** (or **~ of the insurance contingency**) Eintritt des Versicherungsfalles; **to be of frequent ~** häufig vorkommen

ocean Ozean; See-; ~ **bill of lading** Überseekonnossement, Seefrachtbrief; **~-carrying trade** Hochseeschiffahrt; ~ **dumping** Versenkung von Industrieabfällen (etc) im Ozean; Verklappung; ~ **freight** Seefracht, Überseefracht; **O~ Freight Conference System** *Am* Seefrachtkonferenz-System *(cf. Shipping Act)*

ocean-going Hochsee-; ~ **steamer** Ozeandampfer; ~ **tug** Hochseeschlepper

ocean, ~ lane Schiffahrtsroute; ~ **liner** Überseepassagierschiff; ~ **marine insurance** *Am* (Über-)Seetransportversicherung; ~ **navigation** Seeschiffahrt; ~ **shipment** → ~ transport; ~ **trade** *Am* Überseehandel; ~ **transport** *Am* Überseetransport; **German O~** Nordsee

ochlocracy Ochlokratie, Herrschaft des Pöbels

ocular, ~ evidence Augenschein(seinnahme); ~ **witness** *Am* Augenzeuge

odd *(Zahl)* ungerade; einzeln; *(nach e-r Zahl)* etwas darüber; gelegentlich; ~ **day** Schalttag; ~ **jobs** gelegentliche *(kleine)* Arbeiten *(→job)*

odd lot ungerade Menge; Restpartie; Auktionsposten; weniger als 100 Aktien *(meist Aufträge über 1–99 shares; opp. round lot)*; ~ **broker** *(Börse)* Makler in kleinen Effektenabschnitten; ~ **business** Geschäfte in kleinen Effektenabschnitten; ~ **dealer** *Am (Börse)* Händler, der kleine Aufträge ausführt *(Auftrag für weniger als 100 Stück)*

odd, ~ money restliches Geld; ~ **month** Monat mit 31 Tagen; ~ **number** ungerade Zahl; vereinzelte Nummer; ~ **size** nicht gängige Größe; **10 pounds ~** etwas über 10 Pfund

odds (Gewinn-)Chancen; einzelne Stücke, Reste; **~ and ends** Reste, Abfälle; **the ~ are 2 to 1** die Chancen stehen 2 zu 1; **to be at ~ with sb.** sich streiten mit, uneinig sein mit

oddments Reste; übriggebliebene Waren, Einzelstücke, Restbestände, Ramschwaren

odious debts *(VölkerR)* anrüchige Schulden; Regimeschulden

OECD →Organization for Economic Cooperation and Development; ~ **Nuclear Energy Agency** (NEA)[13a] OECD-Kernenergie-Agentur

oecumenical ökumenisch; weltumfassend; **O~ Council** *eccl* Ökumenisches Konzil; **World O~ Conference** Weltkirchenkonferenz *(cf. World Council of Churches)*

of counsel *Am* Prozeßspezialist, verhandlungsführender Anwalt; Berater für e-e Anwaltsfirma

of course von Rechts wegen; **order ~** Verfügung auf Antrag (und Gefahr) e-r Partei, deren Ablehnung nicht im Ermessen des Gerichts steht
Br Ein Schritt in einem Verfahren wird als "of course" bezeichnet, wenn es nicht im Ermessen des Gerichts steht, ihn zu verweigern, vorausgesetzt, daß alle Formvorschriften befolgt wurden *(z.B. Erlaß e-s →writ of summons)*

off-balance transactions bilanzunwirksame Finanzierungsgeschäfte *(z.B. Fazilitäten, Optionen und Swaps)*

off, ~-board market *Am* Markt für nicht notierte Wertpapiere, Freiverkehr; **~-board securities** *Am* amtlich nicht notierte Werte, Freiverkehrswerte; ~ **the coast** vor der Küste; **for ~-consumption** (or **for consumption ~ the premises**) *Br*[14] zum Mitnehmen *(von alkoholischen Getränken)*; ~ **duty** dienstfrei; **~-floor trading** Freiverkehr; ~ **the →job training; ~-licence** *Br* →licence 1.; ~ **limits** *Am* Zutritt verboten; **~-loading** Entladung; ~ **peak hours** Stunden geringer Belastung *(Strom, Verkehr usw.)*; ~ **the record** →record 1.; ~ **season** außerhalb der Saison, Vorsaison, Nachsaison; tote Saison; ~ **season fares** (Luft-)Tarife außerhalb der Hochsaison; ~**-time** Freizeit; ~**-year elections** *Am* Zwischenwahlen

offen|ce (~se) strafbare Handlung, Straftat, Zuwiderhandlung; Gesetzesverletzung, Delikt *(kein technischer Begriff, umfaßt Br indictable offences und offences, die durch →summary proceedings ohne jury abgeurteilt werden können; Am felonies, misdemeanors und violations); mil* Angriff; **the ~ charged with** die zur Last gelegte Straftat; **~s against →property; ~ against public order** Ordnungswidrigkeit; **~s against public order and decency** *Am*[15] Straftaten gegen die öffentliche Ordnung und den Anstand; **administrative ~** Ordnungswidrigkeit; **coinage** (or **coining**) ~ Münzdelikt; **commission of an ~** Begehung e-r strafbaren Handlung; **criminal ~** strafbare Handlung; **currency ~** Devisenvergehen; **customs ~** Zollvergehen; **element of the ~** Tatbestandsmerkmal der Gesetzesverletzung; **federal ~** *Am* Straftat nach Bundesrecht; **first ~** strafbare Handlung e-r nicht vorbestraften Person; **fiscal ~** fiskalische strafbare Handlung; Zoll- und Steuervergehen; **in case of a fresh ~** im Wiederholungsfalle; **→ indictable ~; minor ~** (geringfügiges) Vergehen; Bagatelldelikt; **petty ~** *Am* Straftat mit geringer Strafandrohung; *(etwa)* Übertretung; **in the case of a second** (or **subsequent**) ~ bei Rückfall *(cf. previous conviction)*; **serious ~** Verbrechen (→*felony*); **weapons of ~** *mil* Angriffswaffen

offen|ce (~se), to commit an ~ e-e strafbare Handlung begehen; **an ~ is completed** e-e Straftat ist vollendet; **to constitute an ~** e-e strafbare Handlung darstellen; **all ~s are defined by statute** *Am*[16] alle Gesetzesverletzungen sind durch Gesetz begrifflich bestimmt; **to give ~** Anstoß erregen; beleidigen; **if the ~ is repeated** *(StrafR)* im Wiederholungsfalle; **to take ~** Anstoß nehmen (at an)

offend *v*, **to ~ (against)** verstoßen, zuwiderhandeln; **to ~ sb.** jdn beleidigen; bei jdm Anstoß erregen; **to ~ against the law** gegen das Gesetz verstoßen

offender Täter; Straftäter; Beleidiger; **first ~** (noch) nicht Vorbestrafter; Ersttäter; **habitual ~** Gewohnheitsverbrecher; **juvenile ~** jugendlicher Täter; **persistent ~** Gewohnheitsverbrecher; **petty ~** *Am* jd, der e-e Übertretung begeht; **political ~** politischer Verbrecher; **second ~** *Am* rückfälliger Täter; **third ~** *Am* zum zweitenmal rückfällig gewordener Täter; **to be a first ~** nicht vorbestraft sein, ein Ersttäter sein

offense *Am* →offence

offensive offensiv, Angriffs- *(opp. defensive)*; beleidigend; *mil* Offensive; **~ trade** *Br*[17] Anstoß erregendes *(genehmigungspflichtiges)* Gewerbe; **~ war** Angriffskrieg; **~ weapons** Offensivwaffen

offer Angebot *(opp. acceptance)*; Offerte; Anerbieten; *(Börse)* Brief, Angebot *(Preis, zu dem jd verkaufen will; opp. bid)*; **~ for sale by tender** *Br* Zeichnungsangebot durch Ausschreibung (→*tender 2)*; **~ of amends** *Br*[18] *(bei unbeabsichtigter Beleidigung)* Angebot der Genugtuung (od. Wiedergutmachung) *(in Form der Veröffentlichung e-r Entschuldigung und Richtigstellung)*; **~ of compromise** (or **compromise ~**) Vergleichsangebot; **~ of a contract** Vertragsangebot; **~ of employment** Stellenangebot; **~ of reward** Auslobung; **~ of shares**[19] Angebot von Aktien; **~ to buy** Kaufangebot; **~ to deliver** Lieferungsangebot; **~ without obligation** *Am* freibleibendes Angebot; **acceptance of an ~** Annahme e-s Angebots; **binding ~** festes Angebot; **non-binding ~** freibleibendes Angebot; **counter-~** Gegenangebot; **firm ~** festes Angebot *(opp. conditional ~)*; **general ~** öffentliches Angebot, Auslobung; **implied ~** stillschweigendes Angebot

offer, on ~ zu verkaufen, verkäuflich; im Angebot; **shares come on ~** Aktien werden angeboten

offer, person making an ~ Offerent; **rejection of an ~** Ablehnung e-s Angebots; **special ~** Sonderangebot; **verbal ~** mündliches Angebot; **to accept an ~** ein Angebot annehmen; **to decline** (or **refuse**) **an ~** ein Angebot ablehnen; **to entertain an ~** e-m Angebot nähertreten; **the ~ has expired** das Angebot ist erloschen; **to invite an ~** zur Abgabe e-s Angebots auffordern; **to make an ~ of a th. to a p.** jdm etw. anbieten; **to reject an ~** ein Angebot ablehnen; **to revoke** (or **withdraw**) **an ~** ein Angebot zurücknehmen (od. zurückziehen)

offer *v* anbieten, Angebot machen, offerieren; andienen; sich erbieten; **to ~ assistance** Hilfe anbieten; **to ~ o.s. as candidate** kandidieren; **to ~ a compromise** e-n Vergleichsvorschlag machen; **to ~ in evidence** als Beweis(stück) vorlegen; **to ~ an excuse** e-e Entschuldigung vorbringen; **to ~ a guarantee** Garantie bieten; **to ~ a price** ein Preisangebot machen; **to ~ resistance** Widerstand leisten; **to ~ for sale** zum Verkauf anbieten; **to ~ o.s. for a situation** sich für e-e Stelle anbieten

offered *(Börse)* Brief, Briefkurs; **~ price** Preisangebot; gebotener Preis; **~ rate** Verkaufs(zins)-satz *(→Libor)*; **~ subject to (prior) sale** Zwischenverkauf vorbehalten

offering Angebot(s-); Anerbieten; Kollekte *(während des Gottesdienstes)*; **~ of bribe** *(aktive)* Bestechung; **~ of investment (fund) certificates** Ausgabe von Investmentzertifikaten; **~ of a foreign issue** Auflegung e-r ausländischen Anleihe; **~ period** Zeichnungsfrist; **~ price** Angebotspreis, *(Börse)* Zeichnungskurs,

Emissionskurs; *(bei Investmentanteilen)* Ausgabepreis; **public** ~ öffentliches Zeichnungsangebot

offeree Empfänger e-s Angebots

offerer (or **offeror**) jd, der ein Angebot macht; Anbietender, Offerent; Auslobender

offhand aus dem Stegreif; kurz angebunden, unhöflich; **to speak** ~ aus dem Stegreif reden

office 1. *(bes. öffentl.)* Amt; Amtstätigkeit; amtliche Stellung; Dienst(leistung) *(→good ~s)*; (Gebäude und Personal e-r) Behörde; *bes. Br* Ministerium; **~-bearer** Amtsinhaber, Amtsträger

office copy amtlich erteilte Abschrift *(e-r Urkunde)*; Ausfertigung; ~ **of the →Land Register**; ~ **→probate**

office holder Amtsinhaber, Angehöriger des öffentlichen Dienstes; **federal** ~ *Am* Bundesbeamter; **local** ~ *Am* städtischer Beamter

Office, ~ **of Export Administration** (OEA) *Am* Amt, das über Exportgenehmigungsanträge entscheidet; ~ **of Fair Trading** *Br (auf Grund des →Fair Trading Act eingerichtetes)* Amt für Verbraucherschutz; ~ **of Trade and Investment Analysis** (OTIA) *Am* Amt zur Analyse von Außenhandel und Investitionen

office, abuse of ~[20] Amtsmißbrauch; **assumption of** ~ Amtsübernahme; **director's** ~ Direktorenposten; **discharge from** ~ Amtsenthebung; **eligibility for** ~ Qualifikation für ein Amt; **entry upon** ~ Amtsantritt; **upon entering into** ~ bei Dienstantritt; **Foreign O~** *Br* Auswärtiges Amt; **holder of an** ~ Inhaber e-s Amtes; **Home O~** *Br* Innenministerium; **loss of** ~ Amtsverlust; **period of** ~ s. term of →~; **predecessor in** ~ Amtsvorgänger; **President-in-~** amtierender Präsident; **public** ~ staatliches (od. öffentl.) Amt; **removal from** ~ Amtsentsetzung, Entfernung aus dem Amt; **successor in** ~ Amtsnachfolger; **taking** ~ Amtsantritt *(Am z. B. des Präsidenten)*; **tenure of** ~ s. term of →~

office, term of ~ Amtszeit, Dienstzeit, Amtsdauer; **renewal of term of** ~ Erneuerung der Amtsdauer; **his term of** ~ **has expired** s-e Amtszeit ist abgelaufen; **to extend the term of** ~ die Amtszeit verlängern

office, to appoint to an ~ *(jdn)* in ein Amt berufen; **to assume an** ~ ein Amt übernehmen; **to be in** ~ im Amt sein; *(polit. Partei)* an der Macht sein; **to be out of** ~ *(polit. Partei)* nicht an der Macht sein, in Opposition sein; **to come into O**~ *Br* ins Ministerium kommen, Minister werden; an die Regierung kommen (z. B. the Labour Party came into O~); **to continue in** ~ im Amt (ver)bleiben; **to dismiss** (or **discharge**) **from** ~ aus dem Dienst entlassen; **to enter upon (an)** ~ ein Amt (od. den Dienst) antreten; **to fill an** ~ s. to hold an →~; **to go out of** ~ aus dem Amt ausscheiden

office, to hold (an) ~ ein Amt innehaben (od. bekleiden); **disqualification to hold any** ~ Aberkennung der Fähigkeit, ein öffentliches Amt zu bekleiden; **to cease to hold** ~ aus dem Amt ausscheiden; **he shall hold** ~ **during a term of three years** s-e Amtszeit beträgt drei Jahre

office, to leave ~ aus dem Amt ausscheiden; **to put a p. in** ~ jdn in ein Amt einsetzen; **to remain in** ~ im Amte bleiben; **to resign one's** (or **retire from**) ~ sein Amt niederlegen, aus dem Dienst ausscheiden; vom Amt zurücktreten; **to run for an** ~ *Am* sich für ein Amt bewerben; **to succeed a p. in** ~ jds. Amt übernehmen; **to take an** ~ ein Amt übernehmen (od. antreten) *(z. B. Ministerposten)*; **the President takes** ~ *Am* der Präsident tritt sein Amt an; **to vacate one's** ~ aus dem Amt ausscheiden

office 2. Büro, Geschäftsstelle, Zweigstelle, Amtszimmer, Amtsraum, Dienstraum; *Br* Büro (od. Kanzlei) e-s solicitor; ~ **appliances** Bürobedarfsartikel; **pleasant** ~ **atmosphere** angenehmes Betriebsklima; ~ **automation** Automatisierung der Büroarbeit, Büroautomation; **~-boy** Bürohilfe, Laufbursche; ~ **circular** Dienstanweisung; ~ **equipment** Büroausstattung, Büroeinrichtung; ~ **expenses** Büro(un)kosten; ~ **fittings**→ ~ furniture; ~ **floater** *Am* Versicherung der Büroeinrichtung; ~ **furniture** Büroeinrichtung; Büromöbel; ~ **girl** Bürohilfe; ~ **hands** Büropersonal; ~ **hours** Bürostunden; Geschäftszeit, Geschäftsstunden; Dienstzeit; ~ **machine** Büromaschine; ~ **manager** Büroleiter (*Organisation, Kommunikation, Automatik*); ~ **of destination** *Br* Bestimmungspostamt; ~ **of issue** *Br (Post)* Ausgabestelle; ~ **of origin** *Br (Post)* Aufgabestelle, Abgangsstelle; ~ **of payment** *Br (Post)* Zahlstelle, Auszahlungsstelle *(money orders etc)*; ~ **of posting** *Br* Aufgabepostamt; ~ **of profit** *Br* staatl. bezahltes *Amt (bes. solches, das den Inhaber automatisch von der Mitgliedschaft des House of Commons ausschließt)*; ~ **personnel** Büropersonal; Büroangestellte; ~ **practise** *Am* Beratungspraxis *(e-s Anwalts)*; ~ **premises** Bürogebäude, Büroräume; ~ **rent** Büromiete; ~ **requisites** Büroartikel; ~ **salaries** Bürogehälter, Angestelltengehälter; ~ **staff** Büropersonal; ~ **supplies** Büromaterial, Bürobedarf; ~ **work** Büroarbeit

office, branch ~ Filiale, Nebenstelle, Zweigbüro; **central** ~ Zentrale; **→Central O~; court ~(s)** Geschäftsstelle(n) e-s Gerichts; **field** ~ Außenstelle, **→head ~; lawyer's** ~ *bes. Am* Anwaltsbüro; **main** ~ *Am* Hauptbüro, Hauptgeschäftsstelle, Zentrale; **principal** ~ Hauptsitz *(e-r Gesellschaft)*; **→registered ~; →statutory** ~

office 3. *Br* Versicherungsgesellschaft; **(~) limit** *(VersR)* →limit; ~ **premium** *(VersR)* Bruttoprämie; **fire** ~ Feuerversicherungsgesellschaft; **life** ~ Lebensversicherungsgesellschaft

officer[21] Beamter; Angestellter *(im öffentl.*

Dienst); leitender Angestellter *(e-s Unternehmens),* Direktor; ~ **in charge** vorübergehend verantwortlicher Leiter; **~s (of a company** *Br,* **corporation** *Am) leitende Angestellte (e-r AG),* Verwaltungsorgane; Vorstand (e-r AG) *(dem die laufende Geschäftsführung obliegt; Br directors, managers, secretaries; Am president, vice-president, treasurer, secretary);* **~s of the court** *Br* Justizbeamte, Richtergehilfen *(z.B. masters od. solicitors, die dem Gericht gegenüber bestimmte Pflichten haben)*

officer, ~ of a society Mitglied des Vorstandes e-s Vereins; **~s (of a society)** Vorstand

officer, administrative ~ *Br* Beamter *(höchste Stufe des Civil Service; cf. executive ~)*; **cabinet** ~ *Am* Minister; **clerical** ~ *Br* unterer Beamter; **customs** ~ Zollbeamter; **established** ~ planmäßiger Beamter; **executive** ~ →executive 2.; **fiscal** ~ Finanzbeamter; **insurance ~s** *Br* Beamte der Sozialversicherung mit (weitgehend) unabhängigen Entscheidungskompetenzen über Ansprüche der Sozialversicherten *(Beschwerden [appeals] gegen ihre Entscheidungen gehen an die →Social Security Appeal Tribunals);* **local government** ~ *Br* Kommunalbeamter; **police** ~ Polizist; **senior** ~ →senior 2.

officer 2. *mil* Offizier; **~s and men** Offiziere und Mannschaften; ~ **cadet** Offiziersanwärter; **~'s commission** Offizierspatent; ~ **commanding garrison** Standortältester; **~s' mess** Offizierskasino; ~ **on the active list** aktiver Offizier; ~ **replaced on the active list** re-aktivierter Offizier; **commanding** ~ Kommandeur; **half pay** ~ Offizier im Ruhestand (od. zur Disposition); **high ranking** ~ hoher Offizier; **junior** ~ Offizier mit jüngerem Patent; **non-commissioned** ~ Unteroffizier; **professional** *(Am* **regular***)* ~ Berufsoffizier; **reserve** ~ Reserveoffizier

official 1. Beamter; Funktionär; Angestellter *(im öffentl. Dienste) (cf. officer);* **customs** ~ Zollbeamter; **government** ~ Regierungsbeamter; Staatsbeamter; **senior** ~ hoher Beamter; **state** ~ *Am* Beamter e-s Einzelstaates

official 2. amtlich, dienstlich; offiziell; ~ **act** Amtshandlung; ~ **attire** Amtstracht; ~ **announcement** offizielle Verlautbarung; ~ **army communiqué** *mil* Heeresbericht; ~ **assistance** Amtshilfe; ~ **auhority** Amtsgewalt; ~ **authorization** amtliche Genehmigung; ~ **bodies** Regierungsstellen, Behörden; ~ **bond** →bond 3.; **O~ Bulletin** →O~ Gazette

official business Dienstsache, dienstliche Angelegenheit; Amtsgeschäfte; **O~ B~** *Am* Dienstpost *(Aufdruck auf Briefumschlag);* **on** ~ dienstlich

official, ~ call *tel* Dienstgespräch; **in one's ~ capacity** in amtlicher Eigenschaft, dienstlich; ~ **ceremony** feierlicher Staatsakt; **through ~ channels** auf dem Dienstwege; **matter of ~ concern** Dienstsache; **~copy** Ausfertigung; ~ **custodian for charities** *Br*[21a] Treuhänder für wohltätige Einrichtungen; ~ **denial** Dementi; ~ **description** Amtsbezeichnung; ~ **document** öffentliche Urkunde; ~ **dress** Amtstracht

official dut|y Amtspflicht, Dienstpflicht; **violation of ~ies** Amtspflichtsverletzung

official, ~ emoluments Dienstbezüge; ~ **exchange rate** amtlicher Wechselkurs; ~ **function** Amtshandlung, Amtsverrichtung; **O~ Gazette** *Am* Amtsblatt; Gesetzblatt

official hours Börsenzeit, Börsenstunden; **after** ~ nach Börsenschluß

official, ~ instructions Dienstvorschriften; **O~ Journal (of the European Communities)** Amtsblatt (der Europäischen Gemeinschaften); ~ **journey** Dienstreise; ~ **language** Amtssprache; ~ **language in court** Gerichtssprache; ~ **liability** Amtshaftung; **O~ →List;** ~ **listing** *Am* offizielle Zulassung zum Börsenhandel *(→listing 2.);* ~ **machinery** Behördenapparat; ~ **matter** dienstliche Angelegenheit, Dienstsache; ~ **paid** *Br* portofrei *(bei amtl. Schreiben)*

official position, loss of ~ Amtsverlust

official, ~ powers Amtsgewalt; ~ **principal** *Br (vom [Erz-]Bischof beauftragter)* Richter e-s geistlichen Gerichts; ~ **quotation** →quotation 3; ~ **rate of discount** Bankdiskont, Diskontsatz *(der Notenbanken; opp. private or market rate);* ~ **rate of exchange** amtlicher Wechselkurs; ~ **receiver** *Br*[22] *(bis zur Bestellung e-s →trustee in bankruptcy oder e-s →liquidator vom Department of Trade bestellter)* Konkursverwalter *(cf. receiving order);* ~ **records** amtliche Akten (od. Unterlagen); **O~ Register** *Am* →O~ Gazette; ~ **residence** Amtssitz; Dienstwohnung; ~ **robe** Amtsrobe

official secret[23] Dienstgeheimnis, Amtsgeheimnis; Staatsgeheimnis; **disclosure of ~s** Verrat von Dienstgeheimnissen

Official Solicitor (to the Supreme Court) *Br*[24] solicitor, der im Auftrag des Supreme Court in Verbindung mit bestimmten Personen *(z.B. persons under disability, persons committed for contempt)* tätig wird

official, from ~ sources aus amtlichen Quellen; ~ **statement** amtliche Verlautbarung; ~ **status** offizielle (od. amtliche) Stellung; ~ **strike** gewerkschaftlich organisierter Streik; ~ **travel** (or **trip**) Dienstreise; ~ **trip abroad** Auslandsdienstreise; ~ **use** Dienstgebrauch; **semi-~** halbamtlich, offiziös

officialdom Beamtenschaft; Beamtentum; Bürokratismus, Amtsschimmel

officialese Amtsjargon, Behördenjargon

officialism →officialdom

officiate *v* amtieren, ein Amt versehen; fungieren (as als); den Gottesdienst abhalten; **to ~ as chairman at a meeting** bei e-r Versammlung den Vorsitz führen

officiating president der amtierende Präsident

officio, ex ~ von Amts wegen, kraft Amtes

officious *dipl* offiziös, halbamtlich *(opp. official)*

offing, to be in the ~ nahe bevorstehen, sich anbahnen

offline (*EDV*) (not connected to a computer) rechnerunabhängig

offset Aufrechnung, Gegenrechnung, Verrechnung; Gegenposten; Ausgleich; Offsetdruck; **~ account** Verrechnungskonto; **~ agreement** Verrechnungsabkommen; Devisenabkommen; **~ countries** Offset-Länder *(die in e-m Zahlungsabkommen auf Verrechnungsgrundlage zusammengeschlossen sind)*; **~ dollar** Offset-Dollar, Verrechnungsdollar; **(foreign exchange) ~ payments** Devisenausgleich; **~ prohibition** Verrechnungsverbot

offset *v* aufrechnen, verrechnen (against mit), in Gegenrechnung bringen; ausgleichen, kompensieren; **to ~ against a claim** mit e-m Anspruch aufrechnen; **to ~ each other** sich gegeneinander aufheben; **the profits ~ the losses** die Gewinne gleichen die Verluste aus; **this decline has been fully ~** dieser Rückgang wurde völlig kompensiert

offsetting Aufrechnung, Verrechnung; **~ entry** Gegenbuchung; **foreign exchange ~** Devisenausgleich

offshore vor der Küste gelegen, küstennah; **~ fund** Off-Shore-Investmentfonds *(in e-r Steueroase ohne Investmentgesetzgebung beheimateter Fonds)*; **~ oil** Öl unter den Küstengewässern; **~ orders** *Am* Offshore-Aufträge *(für Lieferungen an andere Länder, die von den USA finanziert, aber außerhalb der USA erbracht wurden; cf. ~ purchases)*; **~ procurements**[25] *Am* Offshore-Beschaffungen; **~ purchases** *Am* Offshore-Käufe *(von den USA bezahlte Waffenlieferungen, die aber nicht die amerikanische Küste berühren)*

oil Öl; Erdöl, Mineralöl, Petroleum *(bes. in Österreich gebräuchlich)*; Olivenöl; **~s** →~ shares; **~ company** Erdölgesellschaft; **~ concession** Erdölkonzession; **~ deposit** Erdöllagerstätte; **~ exporting country** Erdölausfuhrland; **~ field** Erdölfeld; **~ futures market** Ölterminmarkt; **~ importing country** Erdöleinfuhrland; **~ industry** Erdölindustrie; **~ market** Mineralölmarkt; **~ occurrence** Erdölvorkommen; **~ pollution** Ölverschmutzung *(→pollution)*; **~ production** Erdölproduktion, Erdölgewinnung; **~ rig** Bohrinsel; **~ shares (stocks)** Wertpapiere der Erdölindustrie, Erdölaktien; **~ ship** (or **tanker**) (Öl-)Tanker; **~ supply** (Erd-)Ölversorgung

oil, crude ~ Rohöl; **dependence on ~ import(s)** Abhängigkeit von Erdöleinfuhren; **fuel ~** Heizöl; **heavy ~** Schweröl; **lubricating ~** Schmieröl; **waste ~** Altöl; **to discharge ~** (from a ship) Öl ablassen; **to prospect for ~** nach Öl bohren

oiler →oil ship

Oireachtas Parlament der Irischen Republik *(cf. Dail Eireann, Seanad Eireann)*

old age (hohes) Alter; **~ exemption** *Am (SteuerR)* Altersfreibetrag; **~ insurance benefit** *Am (Social Security)* Altersrente; **~ pension** *Am* Altersrente; **~ pensioner** Bezieher e-r Altersrente; Rentner; **~ provision** Altersvorsorge; **O~ A~, Survivors' and Disability Insurance** (OASDI) *Am* Alters-, Hinterbliebenen- und Invaliditätsversicherung

Old Bailey *Br* s. Central Criminal →Court

old established (or **of old standing**) althergebracht, seit langem bestehend; **~ firm** alteingesessene Firma

old people's home Altersheim

old stock Ladenhüter

older workers ältere Arbeitnehmer

oligarchy *pol* Oligarchie

oligopolist *com* Oligopolist *(Anbieter in e-r oligopolistischen Marktsituation)*

oligopolistic *com* oligopolistisch

oligopoly *com* Oligopol *(marktbeherrschende Stellung einiger weniger Unternehmen)*

oligopsony Oligopson, Nachfrageoligopol

olympic, O~ Games Olympische Spiele; →**International O~ Committee**

Oman, Sultanate of ~ Sultanat Oman

Omani Omaner, ~in; omanisch

Ombudsman *Br* Ombudsmann (*parlamentarischer Beauftragter, der die Beschwerden der Bürger entgegennimmt*)

omission Auslassung; *(bes. StrafR)* Unterlassung, Untätigbleiben; **acts** (or **commissions**) **and ~s** Handlungen und Unterlassungen; **errors and ~s excepted** (E. & O. E.) Irrtümer und Auslassungen vorbehalten

omit *v* unterlassen; auslassen, übergehen; **to ~ a dividend** e-e Dividende ausfallen lassen

omnibus Omnibus; Verschiedenes umfassend, Sammel-; **~ account** *Br* Sammelkonto *(verschiedener Inhaber od. Vermögensmassen)*; **~ claim** *Br* zusammenfassender Anspruch; **~ clause** Sammelklausel; *Am (Kraftfahrzeug-Haftpflichtversicherung)* Klausel, die den Versicherungsschutz auf jeden erstreckt, der rechtmäßig den Wagen mit Erlaubnis des Versicherten fährt; **~ deposit** Sammeldepot; **~ order** Sammelbestellung

Omnibus Trade and Competitiveness Act of 1988 *Am* Gesetz über Handel und Wettbewerbsfähigkeit
Neues amerikanisches Handelsgesetz, in welchem das gesamte Außenhandelsrecht reformiert und die Zielsetzung der amerikanischen Außenhandelspolitik formuliert ist

omnium *Br (Börse)* Gesamtwert der zur Sicherung e-s Darlehens herangezogenen Effekten od. Vermögenswerte

on account →account 1.; ~ **of** wegen

oncoming, ~ **generation** kommende Generation; ~ **pedestrian** entgegenkommender Fußgänger; ~ **traffic** Gegenverkehr

oncost *Br (Zuschlag zu den direkten Produktionskosten e-r Ware als Beitrag zu den)* Gemeinkosten

on licence *Br* →licence 1.

online *(EDV)* (connected to a computer) rechnerabhängig

on or after April 1 ab (od. mit Wirkung vom) 1. April

on or before April 1 bis zum (od. bis spätestens am) 1. April

on-stream, to go (or **be**) ~ *Am* Produktion beginnen, mit der Produktion begonnen haben *(chemische Industrie)*

on-the-job training Ausbildung am Arbeitsplatz

one-line business (or **shop**) Spezialgeschäft, Fachgeschäft

one-man, ~ **business** *Br* Einzelunternehmen, Einzelfirma; ~ **company** *(Am* **corporation***)* Einmanngesellschaft; ~ **or committee (management)** direktorial oder kollegial

one-off expenditure einmalige Ausgabe

one-party system Einparteiensystem

one-person household Einzelhaushalt

one-sided einseitig, parteiisch

one-way einseitig; *Am (Fahrkarte)* einfach, nur für die Hinfahrt; ~ **only** *Br* Einbahnstraße; ~ **street** Einbahnstraße; ~ **ticket** *Am* einfache Fahrkarte; einfacher Flugschein; ~ **traffic** Einbahnverkehr

onerous lästig, drückend *(hinsichtl. rechtl. Verpflichtungen);* ~ **clause** lästige Bedingung; ~ **devise** beschwertes Grundstücksvermächtnis *(→disclaimer);*~ →**gift;** ~ **property**[26] Vermögen mit Belastung(en) oder Auflage(n) *(die es lästig oder wertlos machen);* →**disclaimer of** ~ **property**

onus (of proof or **of proving** a fact or **probandi)** Beweislast *(cf. burden of →proof 1.);* **the** ~ **lies** (or **falls) on** (or **rests with) the defendant** die Beweislast trifft den Beklagten; **to discharge the** ~ den Beweis erbringen

onward, for ~ **transmission** zur Weiterleitung

op. cit. ("opere citato") im oben zitierten Werk, am angegebenen Ort (aaO)

open offen; öffentlich; zugänglich (to für); ~ **account** offenstehende Rechnung; Kontokorrentkonto; ~ **air assembly** Versammlung unter freiem Himmel; ~**-cast mining** Tagebau; ~ **cheque** *Br* Barscheck; ~ **city** *mil* offene Stadt; ~ **competition** freier Wettbewerb; ~ **contract** Kaufvertrag *(über Grundbesitz),* bei dem nur die Namen der Parteien, Kaufgegenstand und Kaufpreis festgelegt sind *(Br*[27] *bei e-m solchen Vertrag gelten bestimmte gesetzl. Bestimmungen betr. Nachweis des Eigentumsrechts [proof of title] und andere Verpflichtungen des Käufers und Verkäufers);* **in** ~ **court** in öffentlicher Verhandlung *(opp. in chambers);* ~ **cover** Deckung auf Grund e-r offenen Police; laufende Versicherung; ~ **credit** offener Kredit, Kontokorrentkredit; ~ **door policy** *(VölkerR)* Politik der offenen Tür

open-end investment company (or **trust**) *Am* Investmentgesellschaft, bei der die Zahl der für den Anlagefonds auszugebenden Aktien bzw. Anteile unbeschränkt ist, was heute die Regel ist *(opp. closed-end investment company [or trust])*

open-end fund *Am* Investmentfonds mit unbeschränkter Emissionshöhe *(opp. closed-end fund)*

open-end mortgage →mortgage

open, ~ **lecture** öffentl. Vorlesung; ~ **market** →market 1. und 2.; ~ **order** *Am (Börse)* bis auf Widerruf gültiger *(meist limitierter)* Auftrag; ~ **policy** (O.P.) →policy 2.; ~ **price association** *Am* Preismeldestelle

open price system (OPS) *Am* Preisinformationssystem, Preismeldesystem
Zur besseren Übersicht über die jeweilige Marktlage vereinbaren Unternehmen, sich laufend gegenseitig über eine Zentralstelle (Preismeldestelle) über ihre Preise oder Angebote zu unterrichten

open sea offenes Meer *(opp. closed sea);* **on the** ~ auf hoher See

open, ~ **season** Jagdzeit *(opp. closed season);* ~ **shop** Betrieb, der auch Nichtgewerkschaftsmitglieder beschäftigt *(opp. closed shop);* ~ **spaces** *Br* unbebautes Gelände; ~ **to the public** der Öffentlichkeit zugänglich; ~ **town** *(VölkerR)* offene Stadt; ~ **union** *Am* Gewerkschaft für Angehörige verschiedener Berufsgruppen; ~ **university** Fernuniversität; ~ **verdict** Feststellung e-r Straftat ohne Nennung des Täters; ~ **vote** offene Abstimmung; ~ **working** Tagebau

open, to be ~ **(to)** offen (od. zugänglich) sein (für); **to be** ~ **to inspection** zur Einsicht ausliegen

open, the present protocol shall be ~ **for accession by . . .** *(VölkerR)* dieses Protokoll liegt für

... zum Beitritt auf; **the present agreement shall be ~ for signature until ...** *(VölkerR)* dieses Abkommen liegt bis zum ... zur Unterzeichnung auf

open *v* öffnen, eröffnen; anfangen; **to ~ an account (at** or **with a bank)** ein Konto eröffnen (bei e-r Bank); **to ~ a branch** e-e Filiale eröffnen; **to ~ the budget** den Haushaltsplan vorlegen; **to ~ a business** ein Geschäft eröffnen; **to ~ the case** das Eröffnungsplädoyer in der Hauptverhandlung halten *(→opening the case)*; **to ~ the convention for signature** *(VölkerR)* das Abkommen zur Unterzeichnung auflegen; **to ~ up a country to trade** ein Land für den Handel erschließen; **to ~ a credit** e-n Kredit eröffnen; ein Akkreditiv erstellen; **to ~ the debate (discussion)** die Aussprache (Diskussion) eröffnen; **to ~ a default** *Am* Wiedereinsetzung nach Versäumnisurteil bewilligen; **to ~ a judgment** erneute Eröffnung der mündlichen Verhandlung in bereits entschiedener Sache zulassen; **to ~ a letter of credit** ein Akkreditiv eröffnen; **to ~ up new markets (abroad)** neue (ausländische) Märkte (od. Absatzgebiete) erschließen; **to ~ a meeting** e-e Sitzung eröffnen; **to ~ negotiations** Verhandlungen einleiten; **to ~ Parliament** *Br* das Parlament eröffnen; **to ~ (the) proceedings** das Verfahren eröffnen; **to ~ to the public** *Am (ein Patent)* zwangsweise der Öffentlichkeit zur Verfügung stellen; **to ~ a shop** e-n Laden eröffnen (od. aufmachen); **the shop ~s at 9 a.m.** der Laden macht um 9 Uhr morgens auf; **to ~ up** *(Märkte, Gelände)* erschließen

opening Eröffnung; einleitend; **~ of an account** Eröffnung e-s Kontos

opening address Eröffnungsansprache, Eröffnungsrede; **to deliver an ~** e-e Eröffnungsrede halten

opening, ~ balance Eröffnungsbilanz; **~ bank** Bank, die ein Akkreditiv eröffnet; **~ capital** Anfangskapital; Grundkapital; Stammkapital; **~ the case** Eröffnungsvortrag des Anwalts *(einleitende Übersicht des eigenen Standpunkts und der Beweismittel vor Aufruf der Zeugen)*; **~ ceremony** Eröffnungsfeier(lichkeit); Einweihungsfeier; **~ discussion** einleitende Besprechung; **(good) ~ for business** gute Geschäftsaussichten; **an ~ for trade** e-e günstige Gelegenheit für den Handel; **~ inventory** Eröffnungsinventur; **~ of a business** Geschäftseröffnung; **~ of a credit** Eröffnung e-s Kredits; Erstellung e-s Akkreditivs; **~ price** Eröffnungskurs, Anfangskurs; **~ quotation** erste Notierung *(Anfangskurs)*; **~ rate** Eröffnungskurs; **~ remarks** Einführungsworte; **(formal) ~ sitting** (feierliche) Eröffnungssitzung; **~ speech** Eröffnungsrede; Eröffnungsplädoyer *(des Anwalts des Klägers)*; **~ statement** einleitende Erklärung; **~ stock** Eröffnungsbestand; **~ talk(s)** einleitende Besprechung(en); **~ up** Erschließung *(neuer Märkte, von Gelände)*; **~ the vote** Eröffnung der Abstimmung

operate *v* (ein)wirken, sich auswirken; *(rechtl.)* Wirkung haben; bewirken, mit sich bringen; *(Maschine)* bedienen; handhaben, betreiben; funktionieren; arbeiten, tätig sein; *(Betrieb, Geschäft)* leiten, führen, betreiben; in Betrieb nehmen (od. setzen), in Gang bringen; *(Börse)* spekulieren; operieren; **to ~ an account** ein Konto unterhalten; **to ~ for one's personal account** für eigene Rechnung arbeiten; **to ~ an airline corporation** ein Luftverkehrsunternehmen betreiben; **to ~ another's automobile** *Am*[28] jds Auto benutzen; **to ~ a business** ein Geschäft betreiben; **to ~ at a deficit** (or **loss**) mit Verlust arbeiten; **the tax ~s to our disadvantage** die Steuer wirkt sich zu unserem Nachteil aus; **to ~ for a fall** *(Börse)* auf Baisse spekulieren, fixen; **to ~ against the public interest** sich gegen das öffentliche Interesse auswirken; den öffentlichen Interessen entgegenwirken; **to ~ a motor vehicle** *Am* ein Kraftfahrzeug führen; **to ~ at a profit** mit Gewinn arbeiten; **to ~ retroactively** rückwirkend in Kraft treten; **to ~ for a rise** *(Börse)* auf Hausse spekulieren; **to ~ an undertaking** ein Unternehmen betreiben; **a law ~s** ein Gesetz findet Anwendung; **licen|ce (~se) to ~** Zulassung zum Geschäftsbetrieb, Konzession

operated, privately ~ privat betrieben; **state ~** staatlich betrieben

operating Betriebs-; betrieblich; **→non-~**; **~ assets** Betriebsvermögen; **~ capital** Betriebskapital; **~ company** *Am* Gesellschaft, die tatsächlich Industrie- od. Handelsgeschäfte betreibt *(opp. holding company)*; *(auch)* Transportunternehmen; **~ concern** laufendes Unternehmen; **~ condition** betriebsfähiger Zustand, Betriebsfähigkeit; **~ conditions** Betriebsverhältnisse; **~ cost** Betriebskosten, Betriebsausgaben; **~ cycle** →cash flow cycle; **~ efficiency** betriebliche Leistungsfähigkeit; **~ equipment** Betriebseinrichtung; **~ expenses** Betriebsaufwendungen; **~ experience** Betriebserfahrung; **lease of ~ facilities** *Am* Betriebsüberlassungsvertrag; **~ funds** Betriebsmittel; Betriebskapital; **~ income** betriebliche Erträge; **~ instructions** Betriebsanleitung; Bedienungsvorschriften; **~ leasing** →leasing 2; **~ licen|ce (~se)** Betriebserlaubnis, Erlaubnis zum Geschäftsbetrieb; **~ loss** Betriebsverlust, Geschäftsverlust; **~ method** Arbeitsmethode; **~ of a motor vehicle** *Am* Führen e-s Kraftfahrzeuges; **~ permission** Betriebserlaubnis; **~ personnel** Bedienungspersonal; **~ principles** Geschäftsgrundsätze; **~ profit** Betriebsgewinn, Geschäftsgewinn; **~ revenue** betriebliche Erträge; **~ statement** *Am* Gewinn- und Verlustrechnung; Betriebsergebnisrechnung; ~ **subsidiary** *Am* tätige (arbeitende) Tochtergesellschaft; **insurance company ~ in ...** in ... tätige Versicherungsgesellschaft; **net ~ loss carryover** *Am*[29] Betriebsverlustvortrag; **to be ~** in Betrieb sein; arbeiten; **to be ~ at a loss** mit Verlust arbeiten

operation (Aus-)Wirkung; Arbeit; Arbeitsvorgang; Geschäft(svorgang); Transaktion; Betrieb, Gang; Bedienung *(e-r Maschine);* Funktionieren; *(auch mil)* Operation; **~s** Geschäfte, Transaktionen; Geschäftstätigkeit; ~ **authorization** Betriebsgenehmigung; ~ **in futures** *(Börse)* Termingeschäft; ~ **leader** Meinungsführer; **~s manager** *Am* Betriebsleiter; ~ **of air craft** Betrieb von Luftfahrzeugen; ~ **of a business** Betrieb e-s Geschäfts; ~ **of a convention** Wirksamsein (od. Geltung) e-s Abkommens; ~ **of a system** Funktionieren e-s Systems; **~s on the stock exchange** Börsengeschäfte; **~s research** (O.R.) *Am* Unternehmensforschung *(mathematische Methode zur Vorbereitung e-r optimalen Entscheidung bes. auf wirtschaftl. Gebiet);* **area of ~s** Tätigkeitsbereich, Arbeitsgebiet; **banking ~** *(das einzelne durchgeführte)* Bankgeschäft; **bear ~** Baissespekulation; **bull ~** Haussespekulation; **by ~ of** kraft, auf Grund von; **by ~ of law** kraft Gesetzes; **cash ~s** *(Börse)* Kassageschäfte; **check on the ~** *Am* Arbeitskontrolle; **coming into ~** Inkrafttreten *(e-s Gesetzes);* **credit ~s** Kreditgeschäfte; **field of ~s** s. area of →~s; **financial ~** Finanztransaktion, Finanzgeschäft; **in ~** in Betrieb; **marketing ~s** absatzwirtschaftliche Maßnahmen; **method of ~** Arbeitsmethode; **incidental to the normal ~ of a business** im Rahmen des üblichen Geschäftsverkehrs; **putting into ~** Inbetriebsetzung, Inbetriebnahme; **sphere of ~** Wirkungsbereich; **suspension of ~s** Einstellung der Geschäftstätigkeit; **to be in ~** in Kraft sein, gelten; in Betrieb (od. in Gang) sein; **to be out of ~** außer Betrieb sein; **to begin ~(s)** die Geschäftstätigkeit (od. den Betrieb) aufnehmen; **to cease ~(s)** die Geschäftstätigkeit (od. den Betrieb) einstellen; **to come into ~** in Kraft treten; **to commence ~s** in Betrieb nehmen; **to put in(to) ~** in Kraft setzen; in Betrieb (od. Gang) setzen; durchführen, verwirklichen; **to put out of ~** außer Betrieb setzen; **to suspend ~s** die Geschäftstätigkeit einstellen

operational Betriebs-; betrieblich; innerorganisatorisch; *mil* Operations-, Einsatz-; ~ **accounting** Betriebsabrechnung; ~ **audit** interne Revision; ~ **base** *mil* Aufmarschgebiet; **losses caused by ~ deficiencies** Verlustquellenrechnung; ~ **deficit** Betriebsdefizit; ~ **efficiency** Wirtschaftlichkeit *(e-s Betriebes);* ~ **experience** (or **know-how**) Betriebserfahrung; ~ **flight** *mil* Feindflug; ~ **hazards** Betriebsgefahren; ~ **gaming** *Br* Planspiele; ~ **leasing** →leasing 2.; ~ **loss** Betriebsverlust; ~ **procedure** Betriebsablauf; ~ **profit** Betriebsgewinn; ~ **research** *Br* →operations research; ~ **staff** *mil* Führungsstab; ~ **unit** Betriebsstätte; ~ **zone** *([See-]VölkerR)* Kriegsgebiet, Sperrgebiet; **to become ~** gebrauchsfähig (od. einsatzfähig) werden

operative wirksam, rechtswirksam; *bes. Am* (Fabrik-)Arbeiter; Handwerker; *Am* Detektiv; Betriebs-; ~ **effect** Wirksamkeit; ~ **expenses** *Am* betriebliche Aufwendungen; ~ **facts** *Am* Tatbestand(smerkmale); ~ **mistake** schwerwiegender Fehler *(der den Vertrag ungültig macht);* ~ **part of a deed** rechtsbegründender Teil e-r Urkunde *(im Anschluß an die →recitals);* ~ **provisions of a judgment** Urteilsformel, Urteilstenor; ~ **words** rechtsbegründende Worte *(in e-m deed);* **building ~** Bauarbeiter; **to be ~** Geltung haben, wirksam sein; **to become ~** in Kraft treten, wirksam werden; **to make ~** in Kraft treten lassen

operator Bedienungsperson *(e-r Maschine);* Betreiber e-r Kernkraftanlage; *Am* Unternehmer; *Am* Betriebsleiter; *(berufsmäßiger)* Börsenspekulant; *Am* Fahrer; ~ **for a fall** Baissespekulant; ~ **for a rise** Haussespekulant

operator's license *Am* Führerschein; Fahrerlaubnis; *Br*[30] Fahrerlaubnis für e-n Lkw-Fahrer; **to suspend the ~** den Führerschein (od. die Fahrerlaubnis) entziehen

operator, ~ of a motor vehicle *Am* Kraftfahrzeugführer; **machine ~** Bedienungsperson e-r Maschine; **(telephone) ~** Telefonist(in)

opinion 1. Meinung, Ansicht; Stellungnahme; *Am* Urteilsbegründung, Entscheidungsgründe e-s Urteils; **~s** *(technische Bezeichnung der)* Voten der Law Lords im House of Lords *(auch speeches genannt);* ~ **list** *Br* Auskunftbuch *(zur Eintragung von Auskünften über Kunden);* **(public) ~ poll** (or **research, survey**) Meinungsforschung, Meinungsbefragung, Erforschung der öffentlichen Meinung *(→poll 2.);* **O~ Research Centre** (ORC) *Br* Institut für Meinungsforschung

opinion, census of ~ Meinungsbefragung; **clash of ~s** Meinungsverschiedenheit; **concurring ~** zustimmendes Votum mit von der Mehrheit abweichender Begründung; **consensus of ~** übereinstimmende Meinung; **current ~** gegenwärtige (od. weit verbreitete) Meinung; **difference** (or **divergence, division**) **of ~** Meinungsverschiedenheit; **dissenting ~** *Am* Sondervotum mit abweichender Meinung zur Mehrheitsentscheidung *(vgl. im deutschen Recht § 30 Abs. 2 BVerfGG);* **endorsement of an ~** Zustimmung zu e-r Meinung; **expression of ~** Meinungsäußerung; **extreme ~s** *pol* radikale Ansichten; **favo(u)rable ~** gute Meinung; **free ~** freie Meinung; **free expression of ~**

Meinungsfreiheit; **in the** ~ **of** nach Ansicht von; **in my** ~ meiner Meinung nach; **legal** ~ *(allgemeine)* Rechtsauffassung; Rechtsmeinung; **majority** ~ Ansicht der Mehrheit; Mehrheitsvotum; **matter of** ~ Ansichtssache; **minority** ~ Ansicht der Minderheit; **political** ~ politische Ansicht; **prevailing** ~ herrschende Meinung *(→opinion 2.)*

opinion, public ~ öffentliche Meinung *(→public~)*; **reasoned** ~ mit Gründen versehene Stellungnahme; **separate** ~ eigene *(abweichende)* Meinung; **shift of** ~ Meinungswandel, Meinungsänderung; **statement of** ~ Meinungsäußerung; **suppression of** ~ Unterdrükkung der Meinungsäußerung; **widely held** ~ weit verbreitete Meinung

opinion, to advance an ~ e-e Meinung vorbringen; **to agree with** (or **assent to**) **an** ~ e-r Meinung beistimmen (od. zustimmen); **to ask (for) an** ~ e-e Stellungnahme einholen; **to ask for a p.'s** ~ jdn um s-e Meinung bitten; **to be of the** ~ der Meinung sein; **to change one's** ~ s-e Ansicht ändern; **to concur in an** ~ e-r Ansicht beitreten; **to deliver one's** ~ seine Stellungnahme abgeben, Stellung nehmen; seine Meinung äußern; **to be divided in** ~ geteilter Meinung sein (about über); **to differ in** ~ verschiedener Meinung sein; **~s differ** die Ansichten sind verschieden; **to express an** ~ e-e Meinung äußern; ein Urteil (od. e-e Stellungnahme) abgeben; **to form an** ~ sich e-e Meinung (od. ein Urteil) bilden; **to give an** ~ s. to express an →~; **to hold an** ~ e-e Meinung (od. Ansicht) vertreten; **to hold the** ~ **that** der Meinung sein, daß; **to maintain an** ~ bei e-r Ansicht bleiben; **to put forward an** ~ e-e Ansicht vorbringen

opinion 2. *(schriftl.)* Gutachten; Rechtsgutachten *(→counsel's ~)*; **→advisory ~; draft** ~ Entwurf e-s Gutachtens; **expert** ~ Gutachten des Sachverständigen *(→expert)*; **favo(u)rable** ~ günstiges (schriftl.) Gutachten; **lawyer's** ~ *Am* Anwaltsgutachten; **legal** ~ Rechtsgutachten *(e-s Anwalts, insbesondere über die Wirksamkeit e-s internationalen Vertrages nach e-m bestimmten Recht als Voraussetzung für Kreditvergabe)*; **medical** ~ ärztliches Gutachten; **technical** ~ *(PatR)* technisches Gutachten; **to deliver** (or **give, render**) **an** ~ ein Gutachten erstatten; begutachten; **to obtain** (or **seek, take**) **an** ~ ein Gutachten einholen

opium Opium; ~ **addict** Opiumsüchtige(r); ~ **stocks** Opiumbestände *(cf. dangerous →drugs)*

opponent Gegner, Gegenseite; *(Zivilprozeß)* Gegenpartei, Antragsgegner; gegnerisch; ~ **of the regime** *pol* Regimegegner

opportune günstig, opportun

opportunism Opportunismus

opportunist Opportunist

opportunity *(günstige)* Gelegenheit, Möglichkeit; Chance; ~ **for advancement** Aufstiegsmöglichkeit; ~ **of buying** Kaufgelegenheit; ~ **costs** Opportunitätskosten *(Kostenbegriff, der die Kosten negativ aus dem Nutzenentgang erklärt)*; **corporate** ~ *Am* Geschäftschance *(→corporate)*; **educational** ~ Bildungschance; Beschäftigungsmöglichkeit; **investment** ~ Investierungsmöglichkeit; **to afford** (or **give**) **a p. the** ~ jdm die Gelegenheit geben; **to avail o.s. of** (or **to seize, take**) **an** ~ e-e Gelegenheit ergreifen; **to miss an** ~ e-e Gelegenheit versäumen; **should the** ~ **arise** gegebenenfalls; **should an** ~ **offer** (or **present**) **itself** sobald sich e-e Gelegenheit bietet

oppose *v* sich widersetzen; widersprechen, Widerspruch (od. Einspruch) erheben; *(etw.)* bekämpfen; gegenüberstellen; **to** ~ **an application** *(PatR)* gegen e-e Anmeldung Einspruch erheben; **to** ~ **→execution; to** ~ **the grant of a patent** gegen e-e Patenterteilung Einspruch erheben; **to** ~ **a motion** e-m Antrag widersprechen; **to** ~ **the petition** *(KonkursR)* gegen den Antrag auf Konkurseröffnung Einspruch erheben *(→petition 2.)*

opposed entgegengesetzt; feindlich; **as** ~ **to** in Gegenüberstellung zu; im Gegensatz zu

opposing entgegengesetzt; gegnerisch; ~ **counsel** gegnerischer Anwalt, Gegenanwalt; ~ **expert opinion** Gegengutachten; ~ **party** *(Zivilprozeß)* Gegenpartei, Prozeßgegner; Antragsgegner; ~ **a patent** Einspruch gegen ein Patent

opposer Gegner, Opponent; *(PatR)* Einspruchsführer

opposite entgegengesetzt; gegenüberliegend, gegenüberstehend; Gegen-; Gegenteil; **the** ~ **benches** *parl* die Reihen der Opposition; ~ **opinion** entgegengesetzte Meinung; ~ **party** →opposing party; ~ **to** gegenüber

opposition 1. Widerstand (to gegen); Widerspruch (to zu); Gegensatz; ~ **procedure** Widerspruchsverfahren

opposition, in ~ **to** im Gegensatz zu; **to act in** ~ **to** zuwiderhandeln; **to be in** ~ **to** entgegenstehen, zuwiderlaufen

opposition, to encounter (or **meet with**) ~ auf Widerstand stoßen; **to offer** ~ Widerstand leisten (to gegen)

opposition 2. *(PatR)*[31] Einspruch *(gegen die Erteilung e-s Patents)*; *(WarenzeichenR)*[32] Widerspruch (to registration gegen die Eintragung); **O~ Division** *(Europ. PatR)* Einspruchsabteilung; ~ **fee** Einspruchsgebühr; ~ **period** Einspruchsfrist; Widerspruchsfrist

opposition proceedings *(PatR)* Einspruchsverfahren; *(WarenzeichenR)* Widerspruchsverfahren; **counterstatement in** ~ Einspruchserwiderung; **to intervene in the** ~ dem Einspruchsverfahren beitreten; **the patent has been revoked in** ~ das Patent ist im Einspruchsverfahren widerrufen worden

opposition, arguments in support of an ~ Einspruchsbegründung; **examination of** ~ Prüfung des Einspruchs; **grounds for** ~ Einspruchsgründe

opposition, notice of ~ *(PatR) (schriftl.)* Einspruchseinlegung; Einspruchsschrift; **rejection of the notice of** ~ **as inadmissible** Verwerfung des Einspruchs als unzulässig; **time for notice of** ~ Einspruchsfrist; **to act in common in filing notice of** ~ gemeinsam e-n Einspruch einreichen; **to file** (or **give**) **notice of** ~ *(gegen die Erteilung e-s Patents)* Einspruch einlegen (od. erheben); **to reject the notice of** ~ den Einspruch verwerfen

opposition, period for entering (or **filing**) **an** ~ *(PatR)* Einspruchsfrist

opposition *(PatR)*, **the** ~ **is admissible** der Einspruch ist zulässig; **to enter** (or **file**) **an** ~ **to an application** gegen e-e Anmeldung Einspruch einlegen (od. erheben); **to reject the** ~ den Einspruch zurückweisen (od. verwerfen); **to withdraw the** ~ den Einspruch zurücknehmen

opposition 3. *parl* Opposition; **O**~ **benches** *Br* Bänke der Opposition *(cf. front bench)*; ~ **from the left** (or **left-wing** ~) Linksopposition; ~ **party** Oppositionspartei; ~ **from the right** (or **right-wing** ~) Rechtsopposition; **leader of the O**~ Oppositionsführer; **Her Majesty's O**~ *Br* die Opposition; **to be in** ~ der Opposition angehören; **to go into** ~ in die Opposition gehen; **the Leader of the O**~ **was in possession of the House** *Br (House of Commons)* der Oppositionsführer hatte das Wort

oppression *(auch pol)* Unterdrückung; *Am* Mißbrauch der Stellung *(z. B. der Direktoren gegenüber den Aktionären)*; ~ **of minority shareholders** Unterdrückung der Minorität der Aktionäre; **official** ~ *Am*[33] *(StrafR)* Mißbrauch der Amtsgewalt

oppressive bedrückend; unzumutbar belastend; ~ **contract** Knebelungsvertrag; ~ **taxes** drükkende Steuern

oppressor and oppressed *pol* Unterdrücker und Unterdrückte

opt *v* optieren, sich entscheiden (for für); **to** ~ **out** herausgehen, aussteigen, den Rückzug wählen; **right to** ~ Optionsrecht; **to** ~ **for a nationality** für e-e Staatsangehörigkeit optieren

opting, ~ **out** Möglichkeit der Nichtteilnahme *(z. B. am Internationalen Währungsfonds)*; **person** ~ *(VölkerR)* Optant

optant *(VölkerR)* Optant

optimum Optimum; bestmöglich, optimal; ~ **size** optimale (Betriebs-)Größe; ~ **value** Optimalwert

option 1. Recht (od. Möglichkeit) zu wählen; Wahlrecht; Wahlmöglichkeit; *(freie)* Wahl; Option(srecht) *(das Recht, von e-m auf Grund e-s Vertrages bindenden Angebot – etwa zum Ankauf von Grundstücken od. Wertpapieren – Gebrauch zu machen)*; *(VölkerR)* Option *(Entscheidung für e-e bestimmte Staatsangehörigkeit)*; ~ **of exchange** Austauschrecht

option of a fine, imprisonment without the ~ Gefängnisstrafe ohne die Möglichkeit der Wahl e-r Geldstrafe

option, the court has the ~ **of imposing a fine** (or **may at its** ~ **impose a fine**) **or a term of imprisonment** das Gericht kann auf Geld- oder Gefängnisstrafe erkennen

option mortgage *Br* Optionshypothek *(weniger verbreitete komplizierte Hypothek neben →repayment mortgage und →endowment mortgage; ohne Gegenstück im deutschen Recht)*

option, ~ **of purchase** (in a lease) *Br* Recht des Mieters, die →reversion zu kaufen; ~ **on new stock** Bezugsrecht auf neue Aktien; ~ **right** Optionsrecht; ~ **to purchase land** *(vertragl.)* Optionsrecht auf Kauf e-s Grundstücks *(Br*[34] *begründet ein →equitable interest am Grundstück; nur bei Eintragung der Option im Grundbuch gegenüber späteren entgeltlichen Grundstücksberechtigten wirksam)*

option, at buyer's ~ nach Käufers Wahl; **first** ~ Vorhand *(beim Kauf)*; **local** ~ *Br* Ortsentscheid über Schankgerechtigkeit; **at seller's** ~ nach Verkäufers Wahl; **stock** ~ Bezugsrecht auf neue Aktien; Möglichkeit der Mitglieder der Verwaltung, während e-r bestimmten Zeit *(z. B. 5 Jahre)* Aktien zu e-m festen Preis zu erwerben; **to abandon one's** ~ s-e Option (od. sein Optionsrecht) aufgeben (od. verfallen lassen); **to exercise one's right of** ~ sein Optionsrecht ausüben; **to give** (or **grant**) **an** ~ e-e Option gewähren; *(jdm)* e-e Option einräumen; **to have an** ~ **on a piece of land** ein *(vertragl. eingeräumtes)* Optionsrecht auf Kauf e-s Grundstücks haben; **to stipulate an** ~ **right** ein Optionsrecht vereinbaren; **to take up an** ~ e-e Option (od. ein Optionsrecht) ausüben

option 2. *(Börse)* Option; ~ **bond** (or **issue**) Optionsanleihe *(die ein Bezugsrecht auf Aktien gewährt)*; ~ **bargain** Optionsgeschäft; Prämiengeschäft; ~ **contract** Optionsvertrag; ~ **(declaration) day** *Br* Prämienerklärungstag; ~ **dealer** *Br (Londoner Börse)* Prämienhändler; ~ **dealings** *Br* Prämiengeschäfte, Optionsgeschäfte; ~**s exchange** Optionsbörse; ~ **loan** Optionsanleihe

option money Prämie; **abandonment of the** ~ Aufgabe der Prämie

option, ~ **price** Optionspreis; Prämienkurs; **(~) rate** *Br* Prämiensatz, Prämienkurs; ~ **seller** Stillhalter; ~ **stock** Optionspapiere

option to buy Kaufoption; ~ **to double** Nochgeschäft *(Prämiengeschäft in Verbindung mit dem Kauf od. Verkauf fester Stücke);* ~ **to sell** Verkaufsoption; **buyer's** ~ Nochgeschäft in Käufers Wahl, Nochgeschäft auf Nehmen; **seller's** ~ Nochgeschäft in Verkäufers Wahl, Nochgeschäft auf Geben

option warrant Optionsschein *(der ein Bezugsrecht auf Aktien gewährt)*

option, buyer's ~ s. call →~; **call** ~ Kaufoption; Vorprämie(ngeschäft); **declaration of** ~ Optionserklärung; **dealings in** ~**s** Optionsgeschäfte, Prämiengeschäfte; Optionshandel; **double** ~ doppelte Option, Stellage (put and call option); **exercise of an** ~ Erklärung (od. Ausübung) e-r Option; **giver of an** ~ Prämienkäufer, Optionsgeber; **grantee of the** ~ Optionsberechtigter; **grantor of the** ~ Optionsverpflichteter, Optionsgeber; **put** ~ Verkaufsoption; Rückprämie(ngeschäft); **put and call** ~ Verkaufs- und Kaufoption; Vorprämie und Rückprämie; Stellage(geschäft); **seller's** ~ s. put →~; **taker of an** ~ Prämienverkäufer, Optionsnehmer; **to deal in** ~**s** Prämiengeschäfte machen; **to exercise the** ~ die Option ausüben (od. erklären); **to give an** ~ e-e Option einräumen

optional fakultativ, *(zur Wahl)* freigestellt, wahlfrei, nicht pflichtmäßig *(opp. obligatory);* ~ **bond** Optionsanleihe; ~ **clause** *(VölkerR)* Fakultativklausel; ~ →**conciliation;** ~ →**dividend;** ~ **equipment** (wahlweise) Extraausstattung *(gegen Aufpreis);* ~ **protocol** *(VölkerR)* Fakultativ-Protokoll; ~ **provisions** dispositive (od. durch Parteivereinbarung abänderbare) Vorschriften; Kannvorschriften; ~ **retirement** →retirement 1.; ~ **subject** Wahlfach; **to leave it** ~ **with a p.** es jdm freistellen; **a fine or jail sentence is** ~ **with the court** *Am* das Gericht kann auf Geld- od. Gefängnisstrafe erkennen

oral mündlich; ~ **agreement** mündliche Vereinbarung, mündlicher Vertrag; ~ **evidence** mündliche Zeugenaussage; ~ **examination** mündliche Prüfung; ~ **proceedings are held before the European Patent Office** e-e mündliche Verhandlung findet vor dem Europäischen Patentamt statt

oration, funeral ~ Grabrede

orator *Am* Kläger *(im equity-Prozeß)*

orbit *v (auf e-r Planetenbahn)* um die Erde kreisen; **O~ing Solar Observatory** (OSO) Sonnenobservatorium auf Erdumlaufbahn; **Manned O~ing Laboratory** (MOL) *Am* bemanntes Weltraumlaboratorium

orbital flight Erdumkreisung *(Umlaufbahn e-s Satelliten)*

orbital, Fractional O~ Bombing System (FOBS) partielles Kreisbahnraketensystem

ordain *v,* **to be ~ed priest** zum Priester geweiht werden

order 1. Anordnung, Reihenfolge; Ordnung, geordneter Zustand; Stand, Rang, Stellung; **~-book** *Br parl* Liste der *(dem House of Commons einzureichenden)* Anträge; **in** ~ **of age** nach dem Alter; ~ **of business** Tagesordnung

order of date, in ~ nach dem Datum, chronologisch

order of the day *parl* Tagesordnung; **to pass** (or **proceed) to the** ~ zur Tagesordnung übergehen

order of distribution Verteilungsordnung; **statutory** ~ gesetzliche Erbfolgeordnung

order, ~ **of merit** Rangordnung; ~ **of precedence** (or **rank**) Rangordnung, Rangfolge; ~ **of registration** Reihenfolge der Eintragung; ~ **of sequence** zeitliche Reihenfolge; ~ **of succession** Reihenfolge; *Am* Erbfolgeordnung; ~ **paper** *parl* schriftl. Tagesordnung; Sitzungsprogramm

order, in ~ in Ordnung; **in** ~ **of** in der Reihenfolge von; **in** ~ **of importance** nach Wichtigkeit; **in alphabetical** ~ in alphabetischer Reihenfolge; **in chronological** ~ chronologisch; **in good** ~ **(and condition)** in gutem Zustand; **in numerical** ~ in zahlenmäßiger Reihenfolge; nach Nummern geordnet

order, law and ~ Recht und Ordnung, öffentliche Sicherheit und Ordnung; **maintenance of law and** ~ Aufrechterhaltung der öffentlichen Sicherheit und Ordnung

order, out of ~ in Unordnung; defekt; nicht in der richtigen Reihenfolge, außer der Reihe; **to get out of** ~ in Unordnung geraten

order, point of ~ *parl* Antrag zur Geschäftsordnung; **to rise to a point of** ~ die Debatte mit der Anfrage unterbrechen, ob nicht e-e Verletzung der Geschäftsordnung vorliegt

order, public ~ öffentliche (Sicherheit und) Ordnung *(→public);* **rules of** ~ *parl* Geschäftsordnung; **social** ~ Gesellschaftsordnung; **standing** ~**(s)** *parl* Geschäftsordnung; **in working** ~ betriebsfähig

order, to be in ~ in Ordnung sein; **to call to** ~ *parl* zur Ordnung rufen; *Am (Versammlung)* eröffnen; **the meeting is called to** ~ ich eröffne hiermit die Sitzung; **to maintain** (or **preserve**) ~ die Ordnung aufrechterhalten; **to put in** ~ in Ordnung bringen, ordnen; **to put one's affairs in** ~ s-e Angelegenheiten in Ordnung bringen; sein Testament machen; **to restore** ~ die *(öffentl.)* Ordnung wiederherstellen

order 2. Befehl, Anordnung, (An-)Weisung; *(behördliche od. gerichtliche)* Verfügung;

Rechtsverordnung; *Br* Verfahrensregel *(das Verfahrensrecht des Supreme Court und der County Courts besteht aus orders, die in rules unterteilt sind);* ~ **for administration** →administration 2.; ~ **for confiscation** Einziehungsverfügung; Beschlagnahmeanordnung; ~ **for costs** (*gerichtl., von der Hauptentscheidung getrennte*) Kostenentscheidung; Kostenfestsetzungsbeschluß; ~ **for payment** gerichtl. Zahlungsbeschluß (*Br z.B. im Verfahren vor dem Magistrates' Court*); Mahnbescheid; ~ **for possession** *Br* (*gerichtl.*) Räumungsbefehl; ~ **for remittance** Überweisungsauftrag; ~**giving directions** *Br* Vorverhandlungsbeschluß (*zur Vorbereitung der Hauptverhandlung*); **O~ in Council** *Br* (Regierungs-)Verordnung (*seit 1948 als →statutory instruments veröffentlicht*); ~ **nisi** *Br (bes. hist.)* vorläufiger Gerichtsentscheid (*der nach e-r gewissen Zeit endgültig wird, wenn nichts dagegen unternommen wird*); ~ **of adjudication** Konkurseröffnungsbeschluß; ~**of →attachment;** ~ **of commitment** →commitment 1.; ~ **of the court** gerichtl. Verfügung (od. Anordnung); Gerichtsbeschluß (*jede gerichtl. Entscheidung, die nicht in der Form e-s judgment od. decree ergeht; umfaßt auch rules);* ~ **of the day** *mil* Tagesbefehl; ~ **of discharge** *Br (KonkursR)* Aufhebung des Konkursverfahrens; Entlastung des Gemeinschuldners; ~ **of execution** Anordnung der Zwangsvollstreckung; ~ **to dismiss the action** Klageabweisungsbeschluß; ~ **to →negotiate;** ~ **to pay costs** *(gerichtl.)* Kostenentscheidung *(→~ for costs);* ~ **to quit** *Br (gerichtl.)* Räumungsbefehl; ~ **to show cause** gerichtl. Verfügung, Einwendungen gegen e-e beabsichtigte Maßnahme des Gerichts vorzubringen

order, administrative ~ Verwaltungsverfügung; **by** ~ **of** auf Befehl (od. Anordnung) von; **contrary to** ~**s** befehlswidrig; **counter-**~ Gegenbefehl; **court** ~ →order of the court; **enforcement of an** ~ (by means of a writ of execution) Vollstreckung e-r gerichtl. Verfügung; **execution of an** ~ Ausführung e-r Anordnung; **executive** ~ *Am* →executive 1.; **failure to obey an** ~ Nichtbefolgung e-r Anordnung; **final** ~ Endverfügung; **until further** ~ bis auf weitere Anordnung; **interlocutory** ~ Zwischenverfügung *(des Gerichts vor dem Endurteil);* **maintenance** ~ *Br* Unterhaltsurteil *(→maintenance 1.);* **military** ~ militärischer Befehl; **money** ~ Zahlungsanweisung *(→money);* **on the** ~ **of** auf Anordnung (od. Befehl) von; **postal** ~ Postanweisung *(→postal);* **provisional** ~**s** *Br* vorläufige Verordnungen *(die der Genehmigung des Parlaments bedürfen);* **special** ~**s** *Br* Verordnungen mit Gesetzeskraft

order, to approve an ~ e-e Anordnung billigen; **to comply with an** ~ e-e Verfügung befolgen; **to discharge an** ~ e-e Verfügung aufheben; **to give an** ~ *mil* e-n Befehl erteilen; **to make an** ~ e-e Anordnung (od. Verfügung) erlassen; **to obtain an** ~ e-n (Gerichts-)Beschluß erwirken; **to revoke an** ~ e-e Anordnung widerrufen

order 3. *com* Bestellung, Auftrag; (*Börse*) Auftrag (of auf)

order, to attend to an ~ e-n Auftrag erledigen; **to be on** ~ bestellt sein; in Auftrag gegeben sein; **to book an** ~ e-n Auftrag annehmen; **to cancel an** ~ e-n Auftrag annullieren (od. stornieren); *(etw.)* abbestellen; **to canvass** ~**s** Aufträge hereinholen; **to collect** ~**s** Aufträge sammeln; **to confirm an** ~ e-n Auftrag bestätigen; **to countermand an** ~ s. to cancel an →~; **to execute** (or **fill**) **an** ~ (promptly) e-n Auftrag (schnell) ausführen; **to get** ~**s** Aufträge bekommen; **to give an** ~ (for goods) e-n Auftrag erteilen (od. vergeben); bestellen; **to give one's best attention to** ~**s** jds Aufträge bestens ausführen; **to obtain an** ~ e-n Auftrag erhalten; **to place an** ~ e-n Auftrag erteilen; e-e Bestellung aufgeben; **to place an** ~ **for an article with a firm** e-n Artikel bei e-r Firma in Auftrag geben (od. bestellen); **to receive an** ~ e-n Auftrag erhalten; e-e Bestellung entgegennehmen; **to renew** (or **repeat**) **the** ~ nachbestellen; **to solicit** ~**s** sich um Aufträge bemühen; **to take an** ~ e-e Bestellung (od. e-n Auftrag) annehmen (for auf)

order, ~ **(to buy or to sell) at best** (*Börse*) Auftrag bestens; ~ **backlog** Auftragsbestand, Auftragsüberhang; ~ **book** Bestellbuch, Auftragsbuch; ~ **for the account** *Br (Börse)* Terminauftrag; ~ **for collection** Inkassoauftrag; ~ **for collection of a debt on a bill of exchange by the post office** Postauftrag; ~ **for the settlement** *Br (Börse)* Terminauftrag

order form Bestellschein, Bestellzettel; **as specified on the attached** ~ wie auf beiliegendem Bestellschein angegeben

order, ~ **from abroad** Auslandsauftrag; ~ **from domestic customer(s)** (or **from within the country**) Inlandsauftrag; ~**s in** (or **on**) **hand** vorliegende Aufträge; Auftragsbestand; ~ **list** Bestelliste; ~ **number** Bestellnummer; ~ **pad** Bestellscheinblock; ~ **position** Auftragslage; ~ **processing** Auftragsbearbeitung; ~ **size** Bestellmenge; ~ **slip** Auftragszettel (des Börsenmaklers); ~ **to sell** Verkaufsauftrag

order, according to ~ laut Bestellung, auftragsgemäß; **acknowledgment of** ~ Auftragsbestätigung; **additional** ~ Nachbestellung; **as per** ~ laut Bestellung, auftragsgemäß; **awaiting your** ~**s** Ihren Aufträgen entgegensehend; **big** ~ großer Auftrag; **buying** ~ Kaufauftrag; **by** ~ **of** auf Bestellung von; **cancel(l)ation of an** ~ Annullierung (od. Stornierung) e-s Auftrags; Abbestellung; **carrying out of an** ~ Ausführung e-s Auftrags; **confirmation of**

(an) ~ Auftragsbestätigung; **dispatch** ~ Versandauftrag; **execution of an** ~ Ausführung e-s Auftrags; **falling off of** ~**s** Rückgang der Aufträge; **filled** ~ ausgeführter (od. erledigter) Auftrag; **firm** ~ fester Auftrag; feste Bestellung; **giving of** ~**s** Auftragsvergabe; **government** ~ Staatsauftrag; **heavy** ~**s** große Aufträge; **home-market** ~ Inlandsauftrag; **incoming** ~**s** eingehende Aufträge, Auftragseingang; **influx of** ~**s** Auftragszufluß

order, large ~ großer Auftrag; große Bestellung; **to give a large** ~ **for goods** e-e große Warenbestellung machen

order, list of ~**s** Bestelliste; **new** ~ Neuauftrag; **no** ~**s** (N/O) keine Aufträge; **on** ~ auf Bestellung; bestellt; **open** ~ *Am (Börse)* bis auf Widerruf gültiger Auftrag

order, placing of ~**s** Auftragsvergabe, Auftragserteilung; **on placing the** ~ bei der Bestellung

order, permanent ~ Dauerauftrag; **per** ~ laut Bestellung, auftragsgemäß; **public authorities'** ~**s** Aufträge der öffentlichen Hand; **purchase** ~ Kaufauftrag; **upon receipt of your** ~ nach Empfang Ihres Auftrags; nach Eingang Ihrer Bestellung; **repeat** ~ Nachbestellung; **second** ~ s. repeat →~; **standing** ~ Dauerauftrag; **stock exchange** ~ Börsenauftrag; **supplementary** ~ Nachbestellung; **trial** ~ Probebestellung; Probeauftrag

order, to ~ auftragsgemäß; auf Bestellung; nach Maß; **made to** ~ nach Bestellung angefertigt *(opp. ready-made)*; **to make to** ~ auf Bestellung anfertigen

order, unfilled ~**s** unerledigte Aufträge; Auftragsbestand; **backlog of unfilled** ~**s** Auftragsüberhang

order 4. Order *(wertpapiermäßige Zahlungsanweisung)*; ~ **bill (of exchange)** Orderwechsel; ~ **bill of lading** Orderkonnossement; ~ **bonds** Orderschuldverschreibungen; ~ **cheque (check)** Orderscheck *(opp. bearer cheque [check])*; ~ **clause** Orderklausel; ~ **instrument** Orderpapier; ~ **paper** *Am* Orderpapier; **bill of lading to** ~ Orderkonnossement; **cheque (check) to** ~ →~ cheque (check); **instrument to** ~ Orderpapier; **made out to** ~ an Order lautend; **payable to** ~ zahlbar an Order; **own** ~ eigene Order; **to be made out to** ~ an Order lauten; **to make a bill payable to** ~ e-n Wechsel an Order ausstellen; **to pay to a p.'s** ~ an jds Order zahlen

order 5. *eccl (geistl.)* Orden; **Holy** ~**s** geistlicher Stand *(→holy)*; **to take** ~**s** Geistlicher werden

order 6. Orden(szeichen); **O**~ **of the Garter** *Br* Hosenbandorden *(höchster engl. Orden)*; **O**~ **of the British Empire** Orden des Britischen Empire *(Verdienstorden)*; **to wear one's** ~**s** seine Orden tragen

order *v* befehlen, anordnen, anweisen; verfügen; ordnen, regeln; *(Waren etc)* bestellen, in Auftrag geben; **to** ~ **by telephone** telefonisch bestellen (od. ordern); **to** ~ **in advance** vorausbestellen; **to** ~ **one's affairs** s-e Angelegenheiten regeln (od. in Ordnung bringen); **to** ~ **to pay the costs** die Gerichtskosten auferlegen

ordered, as ~ laut Anordnung (od. Verfügung); laut Bestellung

ordering, ~ **costs** Bestellkosten; ~ **judgment** Leistungsurteil; ~ **quantity** Bestellmenge

orderly ordentlich; regelmäßig; *mil* Ordonnanz; ~ **behavio(u)r** ordnungsgemäßes Verhalten; ~ **(export) marketing** Wohlverhalten auf ausländischen Märkten *(auf denen Störung durch Exporte droht)*; Export-Selbstbeschränkung; **O**~ **Market Arrangement** (OMA) Selbstbeschränkungsabkommen *(für Export)*

ordinance Verordnung; Satzung *(von öffentl. rechtl. Körperschaften)*; **municipal** ~ *Am* städtische Verordnung; Gemeindeordnung, Gemeindesatzung; **to issue an** ~ e-e Verordnung erlassen

ordinaries *Br* Stammaktien *(→ordinary shares)*

ordinary 1. gebräuchlich, gewöhnlich, normal; Durchschnitts-; ~ **bill** Handelswechsel; ~ **budget** ordentlicher Haushalt; **O**~ **Business** (O. B.) Großlebensversicherungsgeschäft *(opp. Industrial Business)*; ~ **capital** Stammkapital; ~ **care** verkehrsübliche Sorgfalt *(→care)*; **in the** ~ **course of business** im Rahmen des üblichen Geschäftsverlaufs; ~ **court** ordentliches Gericht; ~ **creditor** gewöhnlicher *(nicht bevorrechtigter)* Konkursgläubiger *(opp. preferential creditor)*; ~ **→diligence; through** ~ **diplomatic channels** auf dem üblichen diplomatischen Weg; ~ **→director;** ~ **dividend** an den Inhaber von Stammaktien bezahlte Dividende; ~ **income** *Am (Körperschaftsteuer)* ordentliches Einkommen *(opp. capital gains)*; ~ **interest** gewöhnliche Zinsen *(auf der Basis von 360 Tagen berechnet; opp. exact interest)*; ~ **jurisdiction** ordentliche Gerichtsbarkeit; ~ **life assurance** *Br* (**insurance** *Am*) Großlebensversicherung; Lebensversicherung auf den Todesfall; ~ **meeting** *Br (ordentl.)* Hauptversammlung *(e-r AG)*; ~ **→negligence; man of** ~ **→prudence; of** ~ **quality** von durchschnittlicher Qualität; ~ **rate** *(Post)* gewöhnliche Gebühr; einfaches Porto; ~ **receipts** *Am* ordentliche (Staats-)Einnahmen; ~ **resolution** →resolution 2. und 3.; ~ **seaman** Leichtmatrose; ~ **session** ordentliche Sitzungsperiode; ~ **shares** (or *Am* **stock**) (ord., ordy) Stammaktien *(ohne Vorrechte)*; ~ **shareholder** Inhaber von Stammaktien, Stammaktionär; ~ **skill** gewöhnlich vorausgesetzter Grad von Geschicklichkeit; ~ **telegram** gewöhnliches Telegramm; ~ **term** *Am (StrafR)* →term 2.; ~ **treaty** *(VölkerR)* Vertrag

ordinarily, person ~ **skilled in the art** *(PatR)* Durchschnittsfachmann

ordinary 2. *Br* Richter *([Erz-]Bischof als Richter in kirchl. Sachen für e-e Provinz bzw. e-e Diözese); Am (in einigen Staaten)* Richter *(e-s Nachlaß- od. Vormundschaftsgerichts);* **~'s court** *Am (Georgia)* Nachlaßgericht

ordination Priesterweihe, Ordination

ordnance *mil* Ausrüstung, Waffen und Munition; **O~ Survey** *Br* amtliche Landesvermessung

ordre public *Fr* ordre public *(s. public →policy)*

ore-leave Schürfrecht

orientation Orientierung; Einweisung

organ Organ; **~ company** *Am* Organgesellschaft *(von e-m anderen Unternehmen abhängige Gesellschaft);* **~ of public opinion** Träger der öffentlichen Meinung; **~s of the United Nations** Organe der Vereinten Nationen *(cf. United Nations);* **administrative ~** Verwaltungsorgan; **donation of ~** Organspende; **party ~** Parteiorgan; **principal juridic ~** (of the United Nations) juristisches Hauptorgan (der Vereinten Nationen); **subsidiary ~** Hilfsorgan, Nebenorgan

organic verfassungsmäßig; **O~ Act** *Am* Grundgesetz für ein Territorium; **O~ Law** *Am* Staatsgrundgesetz

organization Organisation, Einrichtung; Gliederung; Gründung, Bildung; **~ certificate** *Am* Konzessionsurkunde, Gründungsurkunde *(für Kreditinstitute)*; **~ cost** (or **expenses**) *Am (Bilanz)* Organisationskosten; Gründungskosten *(e-s Unternehmens)*; **~ development** Organisationsentwicklung (OE)

Organization for Economic Cooperation and Development (OECD) Organisation für wirtschaftliche Zusammenarbeit und Entwicklung[35]

Mitglieder: 18 westeuropäische Staaten, dazu USA, Kanada, Japan, Finnland, Australien und Neuseeland.

Organe: Rat (Council), Exekutiv-Ausschuß (Executive Committee) und Generalsekretär (Secretary General).

Aufgaben: Koordinierung der Wirtschaftspolitik, besonders der Konjunktur- und Währungspolitik. Koordinierung der Wissenschaftspolitik. Finanzielle und technische Hilfe an die Entwicklungsländer. Koordinierung der Entwicklungshilfe in dem Ausschuß für Entwicklungshilfe (Development Assistance Committee), dem neben der EG-Kommission 14 OECD-Mitgliedstaaten angehören

organization meeting *Am* Gründungsversammlung

Organization of African Unity (OAU) Organisation für die Einheit Afrikas

Gegr. 1963.

Mitglieder: 50 afrikanische Staaten

Hauptorgan: Konferenz der Staats- und Regierungschefs (Conference of the Heads of State or Government) (muß jährlich einmal zusammentreten)

Organization of American States (OAS) Organisation der Amerikanischen Staaten[36]

Gegr. 1948. – *Mitglieder:* Alle nord-, mittel- und südamerikanischen Staaten mit Ausnahme von Kanada und Kuba.

Hauptorgan: (jedes Jahr tagende) Versammlung der Außenminister. Daneben bestehen ein Politischer Rat, ein Wirtschafts- und Sozialrat und ein Rat für Erziehung, Wissenschaft und Kultur.

Ziel: Friedliche Regelung interamerikanischer Streitigkeiten. Politische und wirtschaftliche Zusammenarbeit

Organization of Arab Petroleum Exporting Countries (OAPEC) Organisation der arabischen erdölexportierenden Staaten *(gegr. 1968; Sitz: Kuweit)*

Organization of Central American States (OCAS) Organisation der Zentralamerikanischen Staaten[37]

1951 gegründete Vereinigung der sechs zentralamerikanischen Staaten (Guatemala trat 1953 aus) mit dem Ziel einer engeren wirtschaftlichen und politischen Zusammenarbeit. *Sitz:* San Salvador

organization, ~ of the market *(EG)* Marktordnung; **O~ of Petroleum Exporting Countries** (OPEC) Organisation der erdölexportierenden Länder; **~ tax** *Am (New York)* Gründungssteuer *(e-r AG);* **affiliated ~** angeschlossene Organisation; **business ~** Unternehmensgliederung; **to join an ~** e-r Organisation beitreten; **to resign** (or **withdraw**) **from an ~** aus e-r Organisation austreten; **to set up an ~** e-e Organisation gründen (od. aufstellen)

organize *v* (sich) organisieren; gründen, einrichten, gestalten; veranstalten; **to ~ a corporation** *Am* e-e Aktiengesellschaft gründen; **to ~ a demonstration** e-e Demonstration veranstalten; **to ~ a fair** e-e Messe veranstalten

organized, ~ labo(u)r gewerkschaftlich organisierte Arbeitnehmer; **~ market** organisierter Markt *(in dem Geschäfte nach bestimmten Regeln abgewickelt werden)*

organizing committee Organisationsausschuß

organizer Organisator; Veranstalter; Gründer, gründendes Mitglied

origin Ursprung; Herkunft; *com* Provenienz; **~ brand** Herkunftsbezeichnung; **certificate of ~** Ursprungszeugnis, Herkunftsbescheinigung *(e-r Handelsware);* **country of ~** Herkunftsland, Ursprungsland; **designation** (or **indication**) **of ~** Herkunftsbezeichnung, Ursprungsbezeichnung *(e-r Handelsware);* **false indications of ~ on goods** falsche Herkunftsangaben auf Waren *(cf. Arrangement of →Madrid);* **goods of foreign ~** Waren ausländischer Herkunft; **mark of ~** Herkunftszeichen; **place of ~** Ursprungsort; **proof of ~** Herkunftsnachweis; **state of** ~ Heimatstaat, Ursprungsstaat

original 1. Urschrift; Original *(e-s Schriftstücks, e-s Kunstwerks etc);* ~ **agreement** Urschrift der Vereinbarung; ~**s and copies** Urschriften und Abschriften; ~ **invoice** Originalrechnung; ~ **of a document** Originalurkunde; ~ **of the document to be notified** *(europ. PatR)* Original des zuzustellenden Schriftstücks; ~ **supporting documents** Originalbelege, Originalunterlagen; ~ **(text)** Urschrift; Original(text); **in 3** ~ **texts** in 3 Urschriften; ~ **will** Originaltestament

original, in the ~ im Original, urschriftlich; **done at ... in 4** ~**s** *dipl* geschehen zu ... in 4 Urschriften; **in a single** ~ *dipl* in einer Urschrift

original, to compare the translation with the ~ die Übersetzung mit dem Original vergleichen; **to copy from the** ~ vom Original Abschrift nehmen

original 2. ursprünglich; originär; ~ **agreement** ursprüngliche Vereinbarung; ~ **application** *(PatR)* Erstanmeldung; ~ **assets** Anfangsvermögen; ~ **capital** *Am* Anfangskapital; Gründungskapital; Stammkapital

original, ~ **cost** Anschaffungskosten; Gestehungskosten; ~ **court**[38] *(IPR)* Gericht des Urteilsstaates; ~ **frustration** (or **impossibility**) anfängliche Unmöglichkeit *(der Leistung);* ~ **investment** erste Einlage *(e-s Gesellschafters);* ~ **invoice** Originalrechnung

original jurisdiction Zuständigkeit in erster Instanz *(opp. appellate jurisdiction);* **to have** ~ in erster Instanz zuständig sein

original, ~ **member** ursprüngliches Mitglied; Gründungsmitglied; ~ **nationality** ursprüngliche Staatsangehörigkeit; ~ **occupation** *(VölkerR)* originäre Okkupation; ~ **patent** Hauptpatent *(opp. supplemental patent);* ~ **price** Anschaffungspreis, Einkaufspreis; ~ **receipt** Originalquittung; ~ **share** (or **stock**) Stammaktie; ~ **value** Anschaffungswert, Neuwert; ~ **vote** Urabstimmung; ~ **works of** →**authorship**

originate *v* entstehen, seinen Ursprung haben, herstammen (in or from aus); entstehen; ins Leben rufen, hervorbringen; **to** ~ **from** (or **in**) **a country** aus e-m Lande stammen; **a circumstance which** ~**d after the conclusion of the contract** ein nach Vertragsschluß eingetretener Umstand

originating, ~ **motion** *Br* →motion 2.; ~ **summons** *Br*[39] Form der Klageerhebung in einem besonders beschleunigten Zivilverfahren; **products** ~ **in** (or **from**) Erzeugnisse mit Ursprung in

originator Urheber, Begründer

ornamental zur Verzierung dienend; Zier-; ~ **design** Geschmacksmuster; ~ **fixtures** bewegliche Sachen, die zum Zwecke der Verschönerung mit dem Hause verbunden sind *(cf. fixture)*

orphan Waise; ~**s' court** *Am (in einigen Staaten)* Nachlaßgericht; ~**'s pension** (or **benefit**) Waisenrente; **war** ~ Kriegswaise

orphanage Waisenhaus

ostensible anscheinend, angeblich; ~ **agency** (or **authority**) Anscheinsvollmacht; ~ **partner**[40] Scheingesellschafter, Gesellschafter nur nach außen hin *(ohne Eigeninteresse) (→partner)*

ostrich policy Vogel-Strauß-Politik

OTC market →over-the-counter market

other, ~ **assets** *(Bilanz)* sonstige Aktiva; **any** ~ **business** (AOB) *(Tagesordnung)* Verschiedenes; ~ **investments** *(Bilanz)* diverse Anlagewerte; ~ **payments** *(Bilanz)* sonstige Ausgaben; ~ **receipts** *(Bilanz)* sonstige Einnahmen; ~ **ranks** (O.R.) *Br* Unteroffiziere und Mannschaften; ~ **side** Gegenpartei; ~ **than** mit Ausnahme von

otherwise auf andere Weise, anderweitig, anderenfalls, sonst; **except as** ~ **provided** vorbehaltlich anderweitiger Regelung; **unless** ~ **agreed** mangels abweichender Vereinbarung; falls nichts anderes vereinbart ist; **unless** ~ **specified** sofern nichts anderes bestimmt ist

ounce (oz.) *Br* Unze *(28,35 g)*

oust *v (Mieter, leitenden Angestellten e-r Firma)* zwangsweise entfernen; den Immobiliarbesitz (freehold) entziehen; **to** ~ **the jurisdiction of a court** die Zuständigkeit e-s Gerichts *(vertraglich)* ausschließen, **to** ~ **from the market** vom Markt verdrängen; **to** ~ **sb. from office** jdn seines Amtes entheben

ouster zwangsweise Entfernung *(des Mieters od. e-s leitenden Angestellten);* Entziehung des Immobiliarbesitzes (freehold); Amtsenthebung

ousting of (the court's) jurisdiction Ausschluß der Zuständigkeit des Gerichts

out nicht mehr im Dienst (od. Amt); *parl* nicht am Ruder, in Streik; **the O**~**s** *Br* die Opposition(smitglieder) *(opp. the Ins);* ~**-clearing** *Br* das Herausnehmen von Wechseln und Schecks an ein clearing house zur Verrechnung; ~ **of bond** →bond 4.; ~ **of bounds** *Br (für bestimmte Personen, z.B. Militär, Schulen etc)* Zutritt verboten; ~ **of cash** nicht bei Kasse; ~ **of court** außergerichtlich; ~**-of-date** veraltet; *Br (auf Schecks)* Einlösungsfrist abgelaufen; ~ **of employment** arbeitslos; ~ **of fashion** aus der Mode, unmodern; ~ **of the jurisdiction** außerhalb der Gerichtshoheit *(im Ausland);* ~**-of-line** abweichend vom Üblichen; ~ **of money** nicht bei Kasse; ~**-of-pocket expenses** (Bar-)Auslagen, Spesen; ~ **of print** vergriffen; **to be** ~ **of the question** nicht in Frage kommen; ~ **of →repair**; ~ **of stock** nicht am Lager (od. vorrätig)

out of town verreist, abwesend; ~ **bill** *Br* Distanzwechsel; ~ **markets** *Am* Provinzbörsen *(außerhalb New Yorks)*

out of work arbeitslos; erwerbslos

outage Ausfall; **power** ~ Stromausfall

outbid *v* überbieten, höher bieten; **to ~ the prices** die Preise überbieten

outbidder *Am* Mehrbietender

outbound →outward bound *(opp. home bound)*

outbreak Ausbruch; ~ **of an epidemic (disease)** Ausbruch e-r Epidemie; ~ **of hostilities** Ausbruch der Feindseligkeit; ~ **of war** Kriegsausbruch

outbuilding Nebengebäude

outcome Ergebnis, Folge; ~ **of a conference** Ausgang e-r Konferenz; ~ **of a conversation** Ergebnis e-r Besprechung; ~ **of a division** Abstimmungsergebnis; ~ **of the election** Wahlergebnis

outdoor Außen-, im Freien; ~ **advertising** Außenwerbung; ~ **labo(u)r** Außenarbeit; ~ **patient** ambulant behandelter Patient; ~ **relief** *Br* Fürsorgeunterstützung für Arme *(außerhalb des Armenhauses)*; ~ **staff** im Außendienst tätiges Personal *(opp. indoor staff)*; ~ **work** Außenarbeit

outer, ~ **bar** *Br* →junior barrister *(who pleads outside the bar; opp. Queen's counsel)*; ~ **harbo(u)r** Außenhafen, Vorhafen; **O~ House** *Scot* →Court of Session als erstinstanzliches Gericht; ~ **office** Vorzimmer ~ **port** →~ harbo(u)r

outer space Weltraum; **Agreement on the Rescue of Astronauts, the Return of Astronauts and the Return of Objects Launched into O~ S~**[40a] Übereinkommen über die Rettung und Rückführung von Raumfahrern sowie die Rückgabe von den in den Weltraum gestarteten Gegenständen; **exploration and use of** ~ Erforschung und Nutzung des Weltraums; **Treaty on Principles Governing the Activities of States in the Exploration and Use of O~ S~, Including the Moon and Other Celestial Bodies**[40b] Vertrag über die Grundsätze zur Regelung der Tätigkeiten von Staaten bei der Erforschung und Nutzung des Weltraums einschließlich des Mondes und anderer Himmelskörper

outfit Ausrüstung, Ausstattung *(z. B. e-r Expedition, e-s Schiffes)*

outflow Abfluß *(opp. inflow)*; ~ **of gold** Goldabfluß, Abwanderung von Gold; **dollar** ~ Dollarabfluß; **foreign exchange** ~ Devisenabfluß *(ins Ausland)*

outgoings Ausgaben; (Kassen-)Ausgänge *(opp. receipts)*; ~ **on a property** wiederkehrende Auslagen für Grundbesitz *(bes. rates, mortgages, instalments)*

outgoing *(aus dem Amte etc)* ausscheidend; abtretend, weggehend *(opp. incoming)*; ~ **freight** Ausgangsfracht; ~ **goods** ausgehende Waren, Warenausgang; ~ **mail** ausgehende (od. abgehende) Post, Postausgang; ~ **member** ausscheidendes Mitglied; ~ **partner** ausscheidender Gesellschafter; ~ **tenant** ausziehender Pächter *(opp. incoming or ingoing tenant)*

outhouse Nebengebäude

outland bill *Br* im Außenhandel gebrauchter Wechsel

outlaw strike *Am* wilder Streik

outlaw *v* ächten; *Am* für unrechtmäßig erklären; *Am* für verjährt erklären; **to ~ war** den Krieg ächten

outlay (Geld-)Auslage(n), Ausgabe(n) (upon für); **cash** ~ Barauslagen, bare Auslagen; **professional** ~ *(SteuerR)* Werbungskosten; **reimbursement of** ~ Erstattung der Auslagen; **to make ~ of money** *Am* Geld auslegen; **to recover one's** ~ *Am* s-e Auslagen zurückerhalten

outlet Absatzgebiet; Verkaufs-Vertriebsstelle; ~ **for sales** Absatzgebiet, Absatzmarkt; Verkaufsstelle; ~ **store** Resteladen; ~ **to the sea** Zugang zum Meer; **to find an** ~ Absatz finden

outline Übersicht, Umriß; erste Entwurfsskizze; ~ **agreement** Rahmenabkommen; ~ **law** Rahmengesetz

outline *v* beschreiben, umreißen; darlegen; **to ~ a plan** e-n Plan skizzieren

outlook Aussicht, Ausblick; Anschauung(sweise); Standpunkt; ~ **for profits** Gewinnaussichten; **business** ~ Geschäftsaussichten, Konjunkturaussichten; **insularity (of)** ~ *Br* Engstirnigkeit; **political** ~ politische Aussichten

outlying, ~ **districts** entlegene Gebiete; ~ **possessions** *Am*[41] US-Samoa and Swains Island

outnumber *v* an Zahl übertreffen

outpatient ambulant behandelter Patient; **~s' department** (of a hospital) Poliklinik

outperform *v* übertreffen

outplacement *Am* Herausplazierung *(e-r Führungskraft)* und Finden e-r anderen Stellung *(faire Trennung und →replacement)*

outport Außenhafen *(der von den Linienreedereien nicht regelmäßig angelaufen wird)*

output (Gesamt-)Produktion, Produktionsmenge, *(mengenmäßiger)* Ertrag, Ausstoß; (Arbeits-,

Produktions-)Leistung; *(Bergbau)* Förderung, Fördermenge; *(EDV)* Ausgabe *(von Daten);* ~ **device** *(EDV)* Ausgabegerät; ~ **evaluation** Leistungsbewertung; ~ **figures** Produktionszahlen, Ausstoßzahlen; ~ **of coal** Kohleförderung; ~ **of labo(u)r** Arbeitsleistung; ~ **of the staff** Leistung des Personals; ~ **per hour** Stundenleistung *(e-s Arbeiters od. e-r Maschine);* ~ **rate** Ausstoßziffer; ~ **restriction** Produktionsbeschränkung; ~ **target** Produktionsziel, Produktionssoll; ~ **tax** *Br* (*von e-r steuerpflichtigen Person für gelieferte Waren od. sonstige Leistungen*) zu berechnende Umsatzsteuer (*opp. input tax*)

output, Produktionsmenge; **agricultural** ~ Gesamtproduktion der Landwirtschaft; **annual** ~ Jahresproduktion; **automobile** ~ Automobilproduktion; **the country's** ~ die volkswirtschaftliche Produktionsleistung; **daily** ~ Tagesproduktion; Tagesleistung; **decrease in** ~ Produktionsrückgang; Leistungsrückgang; **fall in** ~ Produktionsrückgang; **increase in** ~ Produktionsanstieg, Produktionssteigerung; Leistungssteigerung; **increased** ~ Mehrproduktion; **individual** ~ Einzelleistung; **industrial** ~ Industrieproduktion; **last year's** ~ vorjährige Produktion; **level of** ~ Produktionsstand; **limitation of** ~ Produktionsbegrenzung; **maximum** ~ Höchstproduktion, Produktionsoptimum; Höchstleistung; **minimum** ~ Mindestproduktion; Mindestleistung; **rise in** ~ s. increase in →~; **total** ~ Gesamtproduktion, Gesamtertrag; **world** ~ Weltproduktion

outputter *Am* Produzent, Erzeuger

outrage Gewalttätigkeit, Ausschreitung; gröbliche Verletzung; ~ **upon decency** *Am* Verletzung des Anstands; **anti-semitic ~s** antisemitische Ausschreitungen; **bomb** ~ Bombenanschlag; **terrorist** ~ Terroranschlag

outrageous unerhört, besonders ungehörig, empörend; ~ **conduct** unerhörtes *(grobes und rücksichtsloses)* Verhalten; ~ **price** übertrieben hoher Preis

outright völlig, gänzlich, total; geradewegs; ~ **denial** glatte Ablehnung; ~ **gift** bedingungslose Zuwendung *(Übertragung ins freie Eigentum);* ~ **refusal of payment** (or **to pay**) völlige Verweigerung der Zahlung

outrun *v* übersteigen; **to ~ one's credit** s-n Kredit überschreiten

outsell *v Am* mehr verkaufen als; e-n höheren Preis erzielen als

outside äußere(~r, ~s); Außen-; außenstehend; ~ **the United Kingdom** außerhalb des Vereinigten Königreichs

outside board (of directors) *Am* board, dessen Mitglieder sich aus den →outside directors zusammensetzen Führungsgremium, das etwa die Aufgaben des Aufsichtsrats der deutschen AG versieht. Die outside boards werden von Banken, Versicherungen und public utilities bevorzugt *(cf. inside board [of directors])*

outside, ~ **broker** nicht zur (offiziellen) Börse zugelassener Makler, Winkelmakler; ~ **broking** Betätigung als Winkelmakler

outside capital Fremdkapital; **financing with** ~ Fremdfinanzierung

outside, ~ **country** *(EG)* Drittland; ~ **director** außenstehendes *(unabhängiges, meist unternehmensfremdes)* Mitglied des →board of directors *(dem deutschen Aufsichtsrat ähnlich);* ~ **financing** Fremdfinanzierung *(e-s Unternehmens);* ~ **funds** fremde Mittel, Fremdkapital

outside market *(Börse)* Freiverkehr; ~ **securities** Freiverkehrswerte; ~ **transactions** (or **trading in the** ~) Geschäfte (od. Umsätze) im Freiverkehr; **rate in the** ~ Freiverkehrskurs

outside, ~ **one's official functions** außerdienstlich; ~ **person** *colloq.* Außenstehender; ~ **service** Außendienst; ~ **shareholder** konzernfremder Gesellschafter

outside sources, capital from ~ Fremdkapital

outsider Außenseiter; Unkundiger, Laie; Nichtmitglied; Nichtangehöriger e-s Kartells; Betrieb, der sich an marktregelnden Vereinbarungen, bes. Preisabsprachen, nicht beteiligt; vertraglich nicht gebundener Dritter, der den vorgeschriebenen Preis unterbietet *(cf. nonsigner); Am* →outside director; nicht gewerkschaftlich organisierter Arbeitnehmer; *(Seeschiffahrt)* ein außerhalb der Konferenz *(→conference 2.)* fahrender Reeder

outsize Übergröße; ~ **freight** übergroße Ladung

outskirts, ~ **of a town** (or **city** ~) Stadtrand(gebiete)

outstandings *Am* Außenstände

outstanding ausstehend, offenstehend, rückständig, unbezahlt, noch nicht bezahlt; hervorragend; ~ **account** offenstehende (od. unbezahlte) Rechnung; ~ **achievement** überragende Leistung; ~ **bonds** ausgegebene und in den Händen des Publikums befindliche Schuldverschreibungen; ~ **capital stock** *Am (AktienR)* nicht eingezahltes Grundkapital, ausstehende Einlagen; ~ **claim** *(VersR)* noch nicht abgewickelter Schaden, schwebender Schaden *(→claim 2.)*

outstanding debts ausstehende Forderungen, Außenstände; **collection of** ~ Einziehung von Außenständen; **to collect** ~ Außenstände einziehen

outstanding, ~ **experts** hervorragende Fachleute; ~ **interest** rückständige Zinsen; ~ **matter** unerledigte Sache; ~ **money** ausstehende Gelder; ~ **payment** ausstehende Zahlung; ~ **premium** Prämienaußenstände; ~ **shares** (or

stocks) in den Händen des Publikums befindliche Aktien; ~ **work** ausgezeichnete Arbeit; unerledigte Arbeit

outturn Ertrag

outvote *v (jdn)* überstimmen

outvoter *Br* nicht ortsansässiger (auswärtiger) Wähler

outward auswärts, nach außen; ~ **and homeward voyage** *Br* Hin- und Rückfahrt e-s Schiffes; ~ **appearance** äußere Aufmachung *(e-r Ware);* ~ **bill of lading** Exportkonnossement; ~**-bound vessel** (or ~ **bounder**) auf der Ausreise befindliches (od. auslaufendes) Schiff *(opp. homeward-bound vessel);* ~**-bound voyage** →~ voyage; ~ **cargo** →~ freight; ~ **freight** *Br* Hinfracht, abgehende Fracht *(opp. homeward or return freight);* ~ **half** (of a return ticket) *Br* Fahrkartenabschnitt für die Hinfahrt *(opp. return half);* ~ **and homeward voyage** *Br* Hin- und Rückfahrt *(e-s Schiffes);* ~ **journey** *Br* Hinreise *(opp. return journey);* ~ **mail department** Postversandabteilung, Expedition; ~ **manifest** Zollausfuhrerklärung *(opp. inward manifest);* ~ **passage** (or **voyage**) Ausreise, Hinreise *(opp. homeward or return passage or voyage);* ~ **processing** passiver Veredelungsverkehr

outworker Heimarbeiter

over Überschuß, Mehrbetrag; über, weiter; ~ **and above this** darüber hinaus; ~ **and short account** *Am* Kassendifferenzkonto; ~ **in (the) cash** *Am* Kassenüberschuß *(durch Irrtum);* ~ **or under** mehr oder weniger; ~ **spot** →spot 2.

over, cash shorts and ~**s** *Am* Kassenfehlbeträge und -überschüsse; **judgement** ~ *Am* Regreßurteil; **liability** ~ *Am* Regreßpflicht; **to recover** ~ *Am (bei e-m Dritten)* Regreß nehmen

overage (of cash) *Am* (Kassen-)Überschuß *(durch Irrtum)*

overall Gesamt-; einschließlich allem; insgesamt (gesehen); Global-; Pauschal-; ~ **agreement** Globalabkommen; ~ **balance of payments** Gesamtzahlungsbilanz; ~ **budget** Gesamtbudget; ~ **costs** Gesamtkosten; ~ **economy** Gesamtwirtschaft; ~ **economic development** (of a country) gesamtwirtschaftliche Entwicklung (e-s Landes); ~ **effect** Gesamtwirkung; ~ **limitation** *Am*[42] Anrechnung der in allen fremden Ländern bezahlten Steuerbeträge auf den Gesamtbetrag der auf ausländische Einkünfte entfallenden inländischen Steuerbeträge; ~ **plan** Gesamtplan; ~ **rate** Pauschalsatz; ~ **report** Gesamtbericht; ~ **risk** Gesamtrisiko; ~ **settlement** Gesamtregelung; ~ **situation** Gesamtlage; ~ **statement** *Am* Bilanz; ~ **survey** Gesamtübersicht; ~ **trade balance** Gesamthandelsbilanz

overassess *v (steuerl.)* zu hoch festsetzen (od. veranlagen)

overassessment zu hohe Festsetzung (od. [Steuer-]Veranlagung)

overbalance Übergewicht, Mehr (of an); ~ **of exports** Ausfuhrüberschuß

overbalance *v fig* überwiegen, übertreffen

overbid *v* überbieten, mehr bieten; **to** ~ **the prices offered** die angebotenen Preise überbieten

overbuilt zu dicht bebaut

overcapacity Überkapazität

overcapitalization Überkapitalisierung

overcapitalize *v* überkapitalisieren

overcarriage zu weit geführte Ladung; Mitnahme von Gütern über den Bestimmungshafen hinaus und spätere Ablieferung

overcertification *Am* Bestätigung e-s Schecks *(durch die Bank)*, der über e-n größeren Betrag lautet, als das Konto aufweist

overcharge (o/c.) Überforderung, zu hohe Berechnung; zu hoch berechneter Betrag, Überpreis; Überladung, zu hohe Belastung; ~ **of freight** zuviel berechnete Fracht

overcharge *v* zuviel fordern (od. berechnen); überladen, zu hoch belasten; **to** ~ **for one's goods** s-e Waren zu teuer verkaufen; für s-e Waren e-n zu hohen Preis fordern

overcharged, ~ **price** überhöhter Preis; **goods** ~ **in the invoice** zu hoch in Rechnung gestellte Waren

over(-)commitment Verpflichtung, die die (finanzielle) Leistungskraft des sich Verpflichtenden übersteigt; *Am pol* zu starke Belastung e-s Staates durch Verpflichtungen gegenüber anderen Staaten

overcrowd *v* überfüllen

overcrowded region Ballungsraum

overcrowding Überfüllung; Überbelegung *(e-r Wohnung)*[43]

overdependence übermäßige Abhängigkeit

overdraft (o/d.) Überziehung *(e-s Bankkontos od. Kredits);* Kontoüberziehung; überzogener Betrag; ~ **commission** (or **fee**) Überziehungsprovision; ~ **of credit** Kreditüberziehung; ~ **loan** Überziehungskredit, Dispositionskredit; ~ **(on current account)** Kontokorrentkredit; ~ **rate** Zinssatz für überzogene Konten; **to have an** ~ (with one's bank) sein Konto überzogen haben; **to make an** ~ *Am* ein Konto überziehen

overdraw *v (Konto, Kredit)* überziehen; **to** ~

one's account sein Konto überziehen; **~n account** überzogenes Konto; **to be ~n to the extent of...** bis zu e-r Höhe von ... überzogen sein; e-n Debetsaldo in Höhe von ... aufweisen
overdrawing, ~ (of an account) Überziehung e-s Kontos, Kontoüberziehung; **~ of a credit** Kreditüberziehung, Kreditüberschreitung

overdue überfällig *(Zahlung, Schiff)*; verfallen, abgelaufen *(z. B. Wechsel)*[44]; rückständig *(Zinsen, Dividende)*; **~ payment** rückständige Zahlung; **interest on ~ payments** Verzugszinsen; **~ premium** *(VersR)* rückständige Prämie; **when ~** *(WechselR)* nach Verfall; **to be ~** überfällig sein; Verspätung haben *(Zug)*

over(-)employment Überbeschäftigung

over(-)estimate Überbewertung; zu hohe Einschätzung

over(-)estimate *v (etw.)* überbewerten; *(etw.)* zu hoch einschätzen (od. veranschlagen)

overfish *v* zu stark ausfischen, überfischen
overfishing Überfischen, Überfischung

overflight Überflug

overflow Überschuß; Überfluß; **~ of population** Bevölkerungsüberschuß

overhanging branches Überhang

overhaul *v (Maschinen etc)* überholen, überprüfen und instand setzen; *(Schiff)* überholen; *(Schiff)* einholen

overhead, ~s (or **~ cost, expenses**) Gemeinkosten; laufende (od. allgemeine) (Geschäfts-)Kosten; **~ distribution** Gemeinkostenumlage; **~ rate** Gemeinkostensatz; **a firm's ~s consist of factory expense, administrative expense and selling expense** die Gemeinkosten e-s Unternehmens setzen sich zusammen aus Fertigungsgemeinkosten, Verwaltungsgemeinkosten und Vertriebsgemeinkosten

overheated economy überhitzte Konjunktur

overindebtedness Überschuldung

overinsurance Überversicherung

overinsure *v* überversichern

overinvest *v* zu hohe Investitionen vornehmen

overinvestment Überinvestition, zu hohe Investition

overissue Überemission, zu hohe Ausgabe *(von Wertpapieren, Banknoten)*

overissue *v (Banknoten, Wertpapiere)* zuviel ausgeben

overkill militärische Übervernichtung; Bestand an Atomwaffen, der über das zur Vernichtung des Gegners notwendige Potential hinausgeht

overkill *v Am sl.* über das Ziel hinausschießen; die Dinge zu weit treiben

overland über Land; auf dem Landwege; **~ journey** (or **travel**) Reise auf dem Landwege; **~ route** Landweg, Überlandweg

overlap *v fig* sich überdecken, überlappen, sich überschneiden; kumulieren
overlapping Überschneidung; Kumulierung; **~ provisions of a law** sich überschneidende Bestimmungen e-s Gesetzes; **to avoid ~** Überschneidung vermeiden

overleaf umseitig; wie auf der Rückseite angegeben

overlevered, the firm is ~ die Firma hat zuviel Fremdkapital aufgenommen

overload Über(be)lastung; zu hohes Gewicht

overload *v* über(be)lasten; überladen
overloading a ship Überladung e-s Schiffes

overmanned, to be ~ personell überbesetzt sein
overmanning Überbesetzung mit Arbeitskräften

overnight money *Br* kurzfristiges Darlehen von Banken an Wechselmakler; Tagesgeld

overpaid, return of an amount ~ Rückgabe e-s überzahlten (od. zuviel bezahlten) Betrages

overpay *v* zu hoch (od. zuviel) bezahlen, überzahlen; **to ~ a worker** e-n Arbeiter überzahlen

overpayment Überzahlung *(z. B. Steuern)*; zuviel gezahlter Betrag; **to claim ~ (of taxes)** geltend machen, zuviel Steuern gezahlt zu haben

overpeopled übervölkert

overpopulated übervölkert

overpopulation Übervölkerung

over(-)produce *v* überproduzieren; zuviel herstellen von

over(-)production Überproduktion

overrate *v* überschätzen; zu hoch einschätzen (od. veranlagen); *fig* überbewerten

overreach *v (jdn)* übervorteilen
overreaching conveyance *Br* lastenfreie Übertragung von Grundbesitz unter pfandmäßiger Belastung des Kaufpreises anstelle des Grundstücks

override *Am* Extrazahlung

override *v* außer Kraft setzen, sich hinwegsetzen über; **to ~ a veto** *parl* ein Veto überstimmen; **these conditions shall ~ any conditions referred to by the buyer** diese Bedingungen setzen die des Käufers außer Kraft
overriding vorrangig; überwiegend; **~ interests** ausschlaggebende Interessen; *Br*[45] nicht im →Land Register eintragungspflichtige Rechte

Dritter *(die aber den Käufer des Grundbesitzes binden; bezieht sich nur auf →registered land);* **a lease which is not an ~ interest should be protected by an entry in the Land Register** →lease 1.; ~ **trust** *Br* Trust, der e-m früher begründeten Trust vorangeht

overrule *v (Vorentscheidung)* außer Kraft setzen, aufheben, verwerfen; *(jdn)* überstimmen; **to ~ (the decision of) the lower court** die Entscheidung der unteren Instanz aufheben; **to ~ an objection** e-n Einspruch zurückweisen; **to ~ one's own holdings** (or **prior decisions**) *Am* von seiner eigenen Entscheidung abgehen; **to ~ a precedent** →precedent 1.; **a decision is ~d** ein Gericht *(höherer Instanz)* ist von e-r Entscheidung abgewichen

overruled *Am (AntitrustR) (der Einwand gegen das von der Gegenpartei vorgelegte Dokument wird vom Richter)* nicht anerkannt *(opp. sustained)*

overruling *Am* Abweichen von e-r Vorentscheidung; **prospective ~** *Am* zukünftig abweichende Rechtsprechung

overrun(s) *Am* Mehrkosten; Kostenüberschreitung

oversea(s) Übersee-; überseeisch; ausländisch; Auslands-; ~ **allowance** Auslandszulage; ~ **bank** Überseebank; ~ **branch** überseeische Filiale, Auslandsfiliale; **~s call** *tel* Auslandsgespräch; ~ **company** *Br*[46] ausländische Kapitalgesellschaft *(mit →place of business)* ~ **countries** Überseeländer, Ausland; **O~s Countries and Territories** (OCT) *(EG)* überseeische Länder und Gebiete (ÜLG); ~ **mail** Auslandspost *(Br bes. ausschließlich Europas);* ~ **market** überseeischer Markt, Überseemarkt; ~ **orders** Bestellungen aus Übersee; ~ **possessions** überseeische Besitzungen, Besitzungen in Übersee; ~ **postal rates** Auslandspostgebühren; Auslandsporto; **O~s Private Investment Corporation** (OPIC) *Am* staatliche Gesellschaft, die Auslandsinvestitionen gegen politische Risiken versichert; ~ **territories** überseeische Gebiete; ~ **trade** überseeischer Handel, Überseehandel; **~s trade corporation** (O.T.C.) *Br*[47] Übersee-Gesellschaft *(Gesellschaft mit Geschäftssitz in Großbritannien [U.K. resident company], die ihre gewerbliche Tätigkeit – entweder direkt oder durch e-e Tochtergesellschaft, ebenfalls mit Geschäftssitz in Großbritannien – im Ausland ausübt. Sie hat Steuervergünstigungen);* **buyer ~s** überseeischer (od. ausländischer) Käufer

overseer Aufseher, Vorarbeiter

oversell *v* über den Bestand verkaufen; mehr verkaufen, als man liefern kann

overshoot *v* hinausschießen über

overside über Schiffsseite, Überbord-; ~ **delivery clause** Überbord-Auslieferungs-Klausel *(Befrachter sichert sich das Recht, die Ladung zwecks Vermeidung der Kaikosten außenbords abnehmen zu dürfen);* **discharge ~** Ausladung über Schiffsseite

oversize Übergröße

oversman *Scot* Oberschiedsrichter, Obmann *(des Schiedsgerichts)*

overspend *v* zuviel ausgeben

overspending, budgetary ~ Haushaltsüberschreitung

overspill (of population) Bevölkerungsüberschuß

overstaffed mit zuviel Personal besetzt, personell überbesetzt

overstate *v* zu hoch angeben; übertreiben *(opp. to understate)*

overstay *v (Zeit, Urlaub)* überschreiten; **to ~ the market** *Am* den richtigen Zeitpunkt verpassen, am Markt zu kaufen od. zu verkaufen

overstep *v*, **to ~ the time-limit** die Frist überschreiten

overstock zu großer Vorrat, zu großes Lager

overstock *v* überfüllen, überbevorraten; **to ~ with goods** übermäßig mit Waren eindecken; **to ~ the market** den Markt überschwemmen

overstocked, to be ~ zu großes Lager führen; überbevorratet (od. zu hoch eingedeckt) sein; überfüllt sein *(Markt)*

overstocking Überbevorratung; Überfüllung

oversubscribe *v* überzeichnen; **the loan was heavily ~d** die Anleihe war hoch überzeichnet

oversubscription Überzeichnung *(e-r Anleihe) (cf. allotment letter, letter of regret)*

oversupply Überangebot, überreiche Zufuhr; ~ **of labo(u)r** Überangebot an Arbeitskräften

oversubsidized übermäßig subventioniert

overt offen; ~ **act** offenkundige Handlung; **letters ~** s. letters →patent; **→market ~**

overtake *v* überholen; einholen; (etw.) übertreffen; ~ **on the left** *Am* (**right** *Br*) links (rechts) überholen

overtaking, ~ prohibited (or **no ~**) Überholverbot

overtax *v* zu hoch besteuern, überbesteuern; *fig* zu sehr in Anspruch nehmen, überlasten

overtaxation Überbesteuerung

over the counter am Schalter, über den Ladentisch, gegen bar; *(Effektenhandel)* im freien Verkehr; außerhalb der Börse *(freihändiger Verkauf von Effekten);* **payable ~** am Schalter zahlbar; **to sell ~** *(Effekten)* im freien Verkehr verkaufen

over-the-counter (OTC), ~ **business** Schaltergeschäft, Tafelgeschäft; ~ **dealer** Freiverkehrshändler; ~ **market** Freiverkehr(smarkt) *(Handel in Wertpapieren, die nicht an e-r Börse zugelassen sind [→unlisted securities]);* Telefonverkehr *(zwischen den Banken); Am* Sammelbezeichnung für den Handel in Effekten außerhalb der Börsensäle; ~ **reports** *Am* Kursblatt der Freiverkehrswerte

overthrow Sturz *(e-r Regierung); pol* Umsturz

overthrow *v,* **to ~ a government** e-e Regierung stürzen

overtime (O.T.) Überstunden; ~ **allowance** (or **pay, payment**) Vergütung für Überstunden; ~ **parking** Überschreiten der Parkzeit; ~ **premium** Überstundenzuschlag; ~ **rate(s)** Überstundensatz; **to work** ~ Überstunden machen (od. leisten)

overtrade *v* über die eigenen Zahlungs- od. Verkaufsmöglichkeiten hinaus Handel treiben

overture Eröffnung *(von Verhandlungen);* (Verhandlungs-)Angebot; *pol* Annäherung (to an); ~ **of peace** Friedensangebot

overturn *v,* **to ~ a government** e-e Regierung stürzen

overvaluation Überschätzung, Überbewertung, zu hohe Bewertung

overvalue *v* überschätzen, überbewerten, zu hoch bewerten

overweigh *v* überwiegen, Übergewicht haben

overweight Übergewicht, zu hohes Gewicht; ~ **luggage** *Br* (**baggage** *Am*) Gepäck mit Übergewicht, Übergepäck

overwhelmed, ~ **with orders** mit Aufträgen überhäuft; ~ **with work** mit Arbeit überlastet
overwhelming majority überwältigende Mehrheit

overwork übermäßige Arbeit, Überbelastung

overwork *v* überanstrengen; **to ~ (o.s.)** sich überarbeiten; **to ~ one's employees** s-e Angestellten überlasten

owe *v* schulden, schuldig sein *(cf. IOU);* verdanken
owed, debt ~ by A to B Forderung des B an A
owing schuldig, geschuldet; **debts ~ and accruing** gegenwärtige und künftige Forderungen; **debts ~ to him** seine Forderungen; **rent** ~ geschuldete Miete, Mietrückstand; **to be ~ to sb.** jdm etw. schulden; **to have ~ to o.s.** ausstehen haben; **I have ~ to me £ 500** ich habe £ 500 ausstehen
owing to infolge von, wegen; ~ **circumstances** umständehalber; **to be** ~ herrühren von, zurückzuführen sein auf

owelty Gleichheit; **compensation given for** ~ Geldbetrag, der als Wertausgleich beim Tausch von nicht gleichwertigen Grundstükken gezahlt wird

own eigen; Eigen-; **on ~ account** auf eigene Rechnung
own, on one's ~ account für sich; **working on one's ~ account** für sich allein arbeiten *(opp. working in partnership)*
own, ~ **capital** Eigenkapital; ~ **consumption** Eigenverbrauch; ~ **costs** Selbstkosten; ~ **financing** Eigenfinanzierung; ~ **funds** Eigenmittel; **by one's ~ hand** eigenhändig; ~ **insurance** Selbstversicherung; ~ **insurer** Selbstversicherer; ~ **make** eigenes Fabrikat; ~ **resources** Eigenmittel
own, at one's ~ expense auf eigene Rechnung
own, in one's ~ right aus eigenem Recht; **to possess s.th. in one's ~ right** etw. als Eigentümer besitzen; **to have money in one's ~ right** eigenes Geld haben
own, of one's ~ eigen; **a house of one's** ~ ein eigenes Haus
own, on one's ~ *colloq.* allein, unabhängig; **to be** (or **work**) **on one's** ~ allein tätig sein *(opp. to work in partnership);* **on one's ~ account** für sich

own *v* Eigentum haben an, Eigentümer sein von; *(als Eigentümer)* besitzen; innehaben; zugeben, anerkennen; **to ~ a claim against sb.** *Am* e-n obligatorischen Anspruch gegen jdn haben; **to ~ a life estate** lebenslänglichen Nießbrauch haben; **to ~ a motor vehicle** ein Kraftfahrzeug halten
owned gehörend, gehörig, im Eigentum (by von); **family-~ enterprise** Familienunternehmen; **federally** ~ im Bundeseigentum (stehend); **foreign-~** in ausländischem Besitz (befindlich); **government** ~ s. state-→~; **jointly** ~ in gemeinsamem Eigentum (befindlich); **privately ~ enterprise** Privatbetrieb, privates Unternehmen; **publicly** ~ staatseigen; in öffentlichem Eigentum (befindlich); *(→publicly);* **state-~** staatseigen; in Staatseigentum (befindlich) *(→state 1.);* **to be ~ by** sich im Eigentum befinden von, gehören; **to be ~ by the state** im Staatseigentum stehen, Staatseigentum sein, dem Staate gehören

owner Eigentümer, Inhaber von Rechten; Unternehmer *(opp. worker);* ~**s** Reeder, Reederei; ~ **and charterer** Verfrachter und Befrachter; ~**'s equity** Eigenkapital *(e-s Unternehmens);* ~ **in fee simple** →~ of an estate in fee simple
owner-occupied, ~ **house** Eigenheim; vom Eigentümer bewohntes Haus; ~ **property** vom Eigentümer bewohnter Grundbesitz
ownerless herrenlos
owner, ~ **occupier** Eigenheimbesitzer *(Bewohner von eigenem Grundbesitz);* ~ **of an account**

Kontoinhaber; ~ **of a business** Geschäftsinhaber; ~ **of a car** Eigentümer e-s Kraftfahrzeuges; *(etwa)* Kfz-Halter; ~ **of a copyright** Inhaber e-s Urheberrechts

owner of an estate Inhaber e-s Rechts an Grundbesitz *(Eigentümer, Pächter oder Mieter)*; Gutsbesitzer; ~ **in fee simple (absolute)** Eigentümer e-s Grundstücks; *(genauer:)* Inhaber des höchstmöglichen Rechts an Grundbesitz *(cf. freehold)*

owner, ~ **of a factory** Fabrikbesitzer; ~ **of a firm** Firmeninhaber; ~ **of a house** Hauseigentümer, Hausbesitzer; ~ **of land** Eigentümer von Grundbesitz; (Groß-)Grundbesitzer; Gutsbesitzer; ~ **of large estates** Großgrundbesitzer; ~ **of a →motor vehicle**; ~ **of a patent** Patentinhaber; ~ **of real estate** (or **property**) Grundstückseigentümer; **~-operated farm** selbstbewirtschaftetes Gut

owner's risk (O.R.) Gefahrtragung des Eigentümers *(hinsichtl. e-r Ware während des Transports)*; ~ **of breakage** (o.r.b.) Bruchrisiko des Eigentümers; **at** ~ auf Gefahr des Eigentümers, auf eigene Gefahr

owner of a ship Reeder; **joint** ~ Mitreeder, Partenreeder

owner, ~ **pro tempore** (or **pro hac vice**) *(Seeschiffahrt)* Ausrüster *(e-s Schiffes)*; ~ **of a trademark** Inhaber e-s Warenzeichens

owner, adjacent (or **adjoining**) ~ Nachbareigentümer; Anlieger; **beneficial** ~ wahrer (od. wirtschaftlicher) Eigentümer *(opp. settlor, trustee, mortgagee, personal representative)*; **co-~** Miteigentümer *(jointly or in common, zur gesamten Hand od. nach Bruchteilen)*; Mitinhaber; (of a ship) Mitreeder, Partenreeder; **equitable** ~ Eigentümer (od. [Rechts-]Inhaber) nach equity-Recht *(dem das förml. Eigentum fehlt, z.B. wegen Fehler in der Übertragungsurkunde)*; wirtschaftlicher (od. wahrer) Eigentümer *(z.B. der beneficiary e-s trust; opp. legal ~)*; **estate** ~ →~ of an estate; **factory** ~ Fabrikbesitzer; **joint** ~ Miteigentümer, Mitinhaber *(der Begriff umfaßt alle Arten von Miteigentum, unabhängig von der Rechtsnatur, z.B. joint tenants und tenants in common)*; (of a ship) Mitreeder, Partenreeder; **land** ~ →~ of land; **lawful** ~ rechtmäßiger Eigentümer (od. Inhaber); **legal** ~ Eigentümer (od. Rechtsinhaber) kraft legal title *(→title 2.)*; formeller Eigentümer *(opp. equitable ~)*; **part** ~ Teileigentümer, Miteigentümer; (of a ship) Parteninhaber; **rightful** ~ s. lawful →~; **(ship)** ~ Reeder; **true** ~[48] wirklicher (od. rechtmäßiger) Eigentümer

ownership Eigentum(srecht); Inhaberschaft an Rechten; *(ungenau:)* Besitz

Während die h.M. im deutschen Recht ein Eigentumsrecht nur an Sachen, nicht aber auch an Rechten und Forderungen kennt, sondern hier von der Inhaberschaft desjenigen spricht, dem das Recht oder die Forderung gehört (zusteht), verwendet das anglo- amerikanische Recht überall den gleichen Begriff *(vgl. auch estate)*

ownership, ~ **combination** *Am* (Eigentums-) Zusammenschluß, Konzern; ~ **in common** →tenancy in common; ~ **in fee** *Am* unbeschränktes Eigentum; ~ **interest in a partnership** Anteil an e-r Personengesellschaft; Gesellschaftsanteil; ~ **of expiration** *Am (VersR)* freies Verfügungsrecht *(des Versicherungsvertreters)* über erneuerte Verträge; ~ **of land** Eigentum an Grundbesitz; ~ **of property** Eigentum an Grundbesitz (od. anderen Vermögenswerten); *(ungenau:)* Besitz an Grundvermögen

ownership of the state, to be transferred into the ~ in Staatseigentum überführt werden *(Br cf. nationalization)*

ownership reservation Eigentumsvorbehalt

ownership, absolute ~ unbeschränktes Eigentum *(z.B. im Falle e-s estate in fee simple; opp. restricted ~)*; **acquiring the** (or **acquisition of**) ~ Eigentumserwerb; **→beneficial ~; change in** ~ Eigentumswechsel; Besitzwechsel; **claim of** ~ Eigentumsanspruch; **→co-~**; **common** ~ Gemeineigentum; **creation of** ~ Eigentumsbildung *(in der Hand der Arbeitnehmer)*; **dispersal of** ~ Eigentumsstreuung; **divided** ~ geteiltes Eigentumsrecht *(beruht auf der Unterscheidung zwischen allgemeinem Recht [general title] und speziellem Eigentum [special property], z.B. des bailee, lienholder, mortgagee)*; **equitable** ~ Eigentumsrecht (od. Inhaberschaft an Rechten) nach equity-Recht; wirtschaftliches Eigentum *(z.B. des Empfängers der Einkünfte e-s trust)*; Nießbrauchrecht *(opp. legal ~)*; **evidence of** ~ Eigentumsnachweis; **government** ~ Staatseigentum *(als Recht)*; **joint** ~ gemeinsames Eigentum, Miteigentum, Mitinhaberschaft an Rechten *(cf. joint owner)*; (of a ship) Mitreederei, Partenreederei; **legal** ~ Eigentumsrecht (od. Inhaberschaft an Rechten) kraft e-s legal title *(→title 2.)*; formelles Eigentum *(opp. equitable~)*; **part** ~ →part 1.; **perfect** ~ *Am* unbeschränktes Eigentum; **proof of** ~ Eigentumsnachweis; **public** ~ *Br* Staatseigentum *(als Recht)*; **reservation of** ~ Eigentumsvorbehalt; **restricted** ~ beschränktes Eigentum *(z.B. e-s joint owner, lessee od. tenant for life)*; **right of** ~ Eigentumsrecht; **special** ~ beschränktes Eigentum *(z.B. e-s bailee, lienholder, mortgagee)*; **state** ~ *Am* Staatseigentum *(als Recht)*; **transfer of** ~ Eigentumsübergang, Eigentumsübertragung; **unlimited** ~ s. absolute →~; **to acquire (the)** ~ Eigentum erwerben (of an); **to pass into the** ~ **of** (als Eigentum) übergehen auf, in das Eigentum von ... übergehen; **to transfer** ~ Eigentum übertragen

oyer and terminer ("to hear and determine"); **court of** ~ *Am (altertüml. Name für)* Strafgericht erster Instanz

oyster, stealing ~s from ~ beds[49] Stehlen von Austern aus Austernbänken

ozone layer, Ozonschicht, Ozonschirm; **depletion of the ~ of the stratosphere** Verringerung der Ozonschicht der Stratosphäre; **gap in the** ~ Ozonloch; **Montreal Protocol on Substances that Deplete the O~ L~**[50] Montrealer Protokoll über Stoffe, die zu einem Abbau der Ozonschicht führen; **protection of the** ~ Schutz der Ozonschicht; **Vienna Convention for the Protection of the O~ L~**[51] Wiener Übereinkommen zum Schutz der Ozonschicht

P

pace Schritt, Tempo, Leistung; **to keep ~ with** *fig* Schritt halten mit

pacific friedlich, friedliebend; ~ **blockade** *(VölkerR)* →blockade

pacification Befriedung; Friedenstiftung

pacifism Pazifismus

pacifist Pazifist

pacify *v (Land)* befrieden; *(jdn)* beruhigen

pack Ballen, Bündel; Gesamtzahl der in e-r Saison hergestellten (Fisch-, Früchte- etc) Konserven; *Br* Gewicht für Mehl, Wolle od. Garne *(1 ~ Mehl = 280 pounds; 1 ~ Wolle = 240 pounds);* **a ~ of cigarettes** e-e Packung Zigaretten

pack *v* 1. (ver-, ein)packen; konservieren, eindosen

packed, ~ as usual in trade handelsüblich verpackt; **~ for exportation by sea** seemäßig verpackt; **~ for railway (railroad) transport** bahnmäßig verpackt; **to buy bulk or ~ goods** die Ware lose oder verpackt kaufen

packing (Ver-, Ein-)Packen; Verpackung; ~ **cardboard** Packkarton; ~ **charges** (or **cost**) Verpackungskosten; ~ **company** →~ house; ~ **credit** *bes. Br (im Dokumentenakkreditivverkehr)* Versandbereitstellungskredit *(Bankvorschuß an Exporteur auf Grund e-r besonderen Klausel für Verpackung und Versand);* ~ **extra** Verpackung wird extra berechnet; ~ **for shipment** →s. seaworthy →~; ~ **house** *Am* (Fleisch-)Konservenfabrik; ~ **included** einschließlich Verpackung, Verpackung frei; ~ **industry** *Am* Konservenindustrie; ~ **list** Versandliste; ~ **material** Verpackungsmaterial; ~ **paper** Packpapier; ~ **plant** *Am* →~ house; ~ **to be returned** Verpackung zurücksenden; ~ **slip** (or **ticket**) Packzettel; **no charge for** ~ Verpackung wird nicht berechnet; **cost of** ~ Verpackungskosten; **defective** (or **faulty**) ~ mangelhafte Verpackung; **seaworthy** ~ seetüchtige Verpackung; **to do one's ~** *colloq.* packen

pack *v* 2. *(e-e Geschworenenbank etc)* zur Sicherung e-r parteiischen Entscheidung zusammenstellen

package (pkg., pk.) Paket; Packung; Warenballen, Frachtstück, Kollo; *Am* (Post-)Paket; *bes. Am* in allen Einzelheiten ausgearbeitetes Programm; ~ **car** *Am* Waggon für Stückgutladung; ~ **deal** Gesamtvereinbarung, die mehrere (streitige) Verhandlungspunkte regelt *(z. B. Gesamtheit der durch →collective bargaining erreichten Vorteile);* Pauschalarrangement; ~ **freight** *Am* Stückgutfracht; ~ **insert** *Am* Packungsbeilage; ~ **licensing** *(PatR)* Zusammenfassung von Lizenzen; ~ **offer** *colloq.* Gesamtheit der zur Diskussion oder Annahme gestellten Vorschläge; ~ **policy** *(VersR)* Paketpolice; ~ **price** Pauschalpreis; ~ **store** *Am* Laden, in dem alkoholische Getränke nur in verschlossenen Behältern zum Verbrauch außerhalb des Landes verkauft werden; ~ **tour** *(durch Reisebüro veranstaltete)* Pauschalreise; **collect on delivery ~ (C.O.D. ~)** *Am* Nachnahmepaket; **express** ~ *Am* Eilpaket; **loose or in ~s** lose od. verpackt; **original** ~ Originalpackung; **to send the ~ collect** *Am* das Paket per Nachnahme senden; **to send a ~ by express** *Am* ein Eilpaket senden

package *v* einpacken, verpacken

packaging Verpackung; ~ **material** *Am* Verpakkungsmaterial; **cost of** ~ Verpackungskosten

packer Packer, Verpacker; Packmaschine; *Am* Konservenhersteller; **~'s wages** Packerlohn

packet Paket; *Br* Päckchen; ~ **(boat)** Paketboot, Postdampfer; ~ **line** Postschifflinie; **loose or in ~s** lose oder verpackt; →**postal** ~; **small** ~ Päckchen

packing →pack *v* 1.

pact Pakt; ~ **of non-aggression** Nichtangriffspakt; **mutual assistance** ~ Beistandspakt; **to make a** ~ e-n Pakt schließen

pacta sunt servanda ("contracts are to be kept") *(allgemeiner Rechtsgrundsatz)* Verträge müssen gehalten werden

pactum de contrahendo *(VölkerR)* Vertragsabschlußvereinbarung; Vorvertrag zu e-m völkerrechtlichen Vertrag

pad, (memorandum) ~ Notizblock; **stamp** ~ Stempelkissen; **(writing)** ~ Schreibblock, Briefblock

page Blatt, Seite; **foot of a** ~ Ende e-r Seite; **front** ~ Titelblatt, Vorderseite; **number of ~s** Seitenzahl

page *v* mit Seitenzahlen versehen, paginieren

paid bezahlt; ~ **cheque (check)** eingelöster Scheck; ~ **holidays** *Br* (**vacation** *Am*) bezahlter Urlaub

paid-in eingezahlt

paid-in surplus *Am (AktienR, Bilanz)* Reservekapital, das aus dem Verkauf von Aktien *(und nicht aus Gewinn)* stammt

1. Bei Nennwertaktien entsteht paid-in surplus durch Verkauf über pari.
2. Bei den in USA häufigen nennwertlosen Aktien entsteht paid-in surplus dadurch, daß nur ein Teil des Gegenwertes für die Aktien dem →stated capital (Grundkapital) zugeordnet wird.

Paid-in surplus ist die wichtigste Quelle des capital surplus (→*surplus* 2.)

paid-off creditor abgefundener Gläubiger

paid up bezahlt, *(voll)* eingezahlt; ~ **capital** *(von den Aktionären voll)* eingezahltes Kapital; ~ **insurance** voll eingezahlte *(daher in Zukunft prämienfreie)* Versicherung; ~ →**membership;** ~ **policy** beitragsfreie Police; ~ **shares in cooperative societies** Geschäftsguthaben bei Genossenschaften; ~ **stock** *Am* voll eingezahlte Aktien; ~ **value** *(VersR)* Umwandlungswert *(der Lebensversicherung, wenn Versicherungsnehmer Prämienzahlungen eingestellt hat)*

pain Schmerz(en); Strafe *(obs. außer in einigen Ausdrücken);* **~s of law** *Scot* Strafe

pain, mental ~ and suffering *Am* psychische Leiden; **compensation** *Am* **(damages** *Br*) **for ~ and suffering** Schmerzensgeld

pain, under ~ of death bei Todesstrafe; **under ~ of imprisonment** bei Gefängnisstrafe; **(up)on** (or **under**) ~ **of** bei (Vermeidung e-r) Strafe von

painting, works of ~ *(UrhR)* Werke der Malerei

pair, to work as an au ~ *Br* au pair *(als Haustochter)* arbeiten

pairing *parl* interfraktionelle Absprache, wonach bei erzwungener Abwesenheit von Abgeordneten bei Abstimmungen die gleiche Zahl Abgeordneter e-r anderen Partei auch nicht mit abstimmt

pais, →**estoppel in** ~; **trial in** (or **by**) ~ →trial by jury

Pakistan Pakistan; pakistanisch; **Islamic Republic of** ~ Islamische Republik Pakistan; **of** ~ pakistanisch

Pakistani Pakistaner, ~in

Palestine Liberation Organization (PLO) Palästinensische Befreiungs-Organisation

pallet[1] Palette *(Vorrichtung [device], auf deren Boden sich e-e gewisse Gütermenge zu e-r Verladeeinheit zusammenfassen läßt)*

palm-grease Schmiergeld(er)

palm off *v*, **to** ~ **on sb.** jdm etw. aufschwindeln (od. andrehen)

palmistry Wahrsagen aus der Hand

palpable error offensichtlicher Irrtum

pamphlet Broschüre; Flugblatt; Prospekt; ~ **copies** broschierte Ausgaben

Pan-Africanism Panafrikanismus
Pan-Americanism Panamerikanismus
Pan-Asianism Panasiatismus
Pan-Europeanism Paneuropäismus
Pan-Slavism Panslawismus

Panama Panama; **Republic of** ~ Republik Panama

Panama Canal, Treaty Concerning the Permanent Neutrality and Operation of the ~[1a] Vertrag über die dauernde Neutralität und den Betrieb des Panamakanals

Panamanian Panamaer, ~in; panamaisch

pandects Pandekten *(s. Corpus Juris Civilis)*

pander *(StrafR)* Kuppler

pander *v (StrafR)* Kuppelei betreiben; **~ing** Kuppelei

P & I Clubs (Protection and Indemnity Clubs) Gegenseitigkeitsversicherungsvereine der Reeder zur Deckung von Haftungs- und Kostenschäden

Entstanden in England zur Abdeckung sonst nicht versicherbarer Risiken. Jetzt auch in Norwegen und Schweden und ähnlich in Japan

panel Liste (od. Gruppe) von Personen *(die für bestimmte Aufgaben ausgewählt sind);* Sachverständigengruppe, Gremium; Ausschuß; Geschworenenliste; Geschworene, Schöffen; *(Meinungsforschung)* Befragtengruppe; Diskussionsgruppe; ~ **discussion** Forumsdiskussion; Podiumsdiskussion *(über ein bestimmtes Thema mit ausgewählten Rednern);* ~ **doctor** Kassenarzt; ~ **envelope** Fensterbriefumschlag; ~ **house** *Am* Bordell; ~ **(meeting)** *Am* Zusammenkunft ausgewählter Diskussionsredner; ~ **member** Diskussionsteilnehmer *(z. B. im Fernsehen);* **advisory** ~ beratender Ausschuß

Panhonlib(co) States Panhonlib(co)-Staaten, Billigflaggenländer

Die überseeischen Staaten Panama, Liberia, Honduras (und Costa Rica) verleihen ihre Flaggen (flags of convenience, cheap flags) gegen Zahlung e-r Registergebühr und e-r sehr niedrigen jährlichen Registersteuer ausländischen Schiffen. Zahlreiche Schiffe der Welthandelsflotte sind in diesen Staaten registriert, weil auf diese Weise bestimmte Sozialversicherungs- und Steuervorschriften umgangen werden können

panic, ~ **buying** Angstkauf, Angstkäufe; ~ **monger** Panikmacher; ~ **on the stock exchange** Börsenpanik; ~ **prices** Angstpreise; ~ **proof** krisenfest

pantomime, works of ~ *(UrhR)* pantomimische Werke

papal päpstlich; ~ →**brief**

paper 1. Papier; (Wert-)Papier; Wechsel; Schriftstück, Dokument; (Text e-s) Vortrag(s), Aufsatz, Abhandlung; ~**s** Papiere, Unterlagen, Urkunden, Akten; Examensfragen, Prüfungsarbeit; ~**s on appeal** *Am* Berufungsakten; ~**back** broschiertes Buch; Taschenbuch(ausgabe); ~→**blockade;** ~**-book** *Br* Zusammenstellung von Abschriften oder Auszügen der zwischen den Parteien ausgetauschten Schriftsätze; ~**-bound** broschiert; ~ **circulation** Papiergeldumlauf, Banknotenumlauf; ~ **clip** (or **fastener**) Büroklammer; ~ **company** Briefkastenfirma; Scheingesellschaft; ~ **credit** Kredit, der auf Grund e-r „papierenen" Sicherheit, d.h. ohne unmittelbare Bereitstellung von Vermögenswerten, gewährt wird *(z.B. Wechselkredit);* ~ **currency** Papiergeld; Papierwährung *(opp. metallic currency);* ~ **factory** (or **mill**) Papierfabrik; ~ **gold** Papiergold (→*special drawing rights*); ~ **holdings** Effektenbesitz; ~ **money** Papiergeld, Banknoten *(opp. coin);* ~ **profit** noch nicht realisierter Gewinn, rechnerischer Gewinn; ~ **rate** →rate 2.; ~ **securities** Papierwerte, Papiereffekten; ~ **standard** Papierwährung *(opp. metallic standard);* ~ **title** Schriftstück (od. Urkunde) über ein Recht *(z.B. Grundeigentum);* Wertpapier; **accommodation** ~ Gefälligkeitswechsel; **ballot** ~ Wahlzettel, Stimmzettel; **bank** ~ Bankwechsel *(opp. trade* ~*);* **bond** ~**s** Zollbegleitpapiere; **bundle of** ~**s** Aktenbündel; →**commercial** ~; →**financial** ~; **government** ~**s** Staatspapiere, Staatsanleihen; **official** ~**s** amtliche Schriftstücke; **ship's** ~**s** Schiffspapiere; **trade** ~ Handelswechsel, Warenwechsel *(opp. bank* ~*);* **three months'** ~ Dreimonatswechsel; **to produce** (or **present**) **one's** ~**s** s-e Papiere vorzeigen, sich ausweisen; **to read a** ~ e-n Vortrag halten (on über)

paper 2. Zeitung; ~**s and periodicals** Zeitungen und Zeitschriften; ~ **war(fare)** Zeitungskrieg, Pressekrieg; **daily** ~ Tageszeitung; **financial** ~ Handelsblatt, Börsenblatt; **local** ~ Lokalzeitung, Lokalblatt; **subscriber (subscription) to a** ~ Zeitungsabonnent (-abonnement); **trade** ~ Wirtschaftszeitung; Handelsblatt; **weekly** ~ Wochenzeitung, Wochenblatt; **to figure in the** ~**s** von der Presse erwähnt werden; **to take** (or **subscribe to**) **a** ~ e-e Zeitung halten, e-e Zeitung abonnieren

Papua New Guinea Papua-Neuguinea

Papua New Guinean Papua-Neuguineer(in); papua-neuguineisch

par Pari, Pariwert, Parikurs; ~ **collection** Inkasso zum Parikurs; ~ **issue** Pari-Emission; ~ **(of exchange)** Parikurs *(bei Währungen);*

par value Nennwert, Nominalwert; ~ **share** Aktie mit Nennwert; **no** ~ ohne Nennwert, nennwertlos; **no** ~ **share** *Am* nennwertlose Aktie, Quotenaktie

Im Ggs. zum deutschen Aktienrecht, das nur Anteile mit bestimmtem Nennwert zuläßt, kennt man in den USA und Kanada zwei Kategorien von shares: die par value shares, die e-n Nennwert haben, und die no-par (value) shares. Die nennwertlose Aktie ist nach englischem Recht unzulässig

par value of currencies Währungsparität

par value of shares, increase, decrease and change in the ~ Erhöhung, Verminderung und Änderung des Nennwertes der Aktien

par, above ~ über pari; über dem Nennwert; **above-**~ **price** (or **rate**) Überparikurs; **to be above** ~ über pari stehen

par, at ~ al pari, zum Nennwert; **exchange at** ~ Parikurs; **issue at** ~ Pari-Emission; **value at** ~ Wert al pari; **to be at** ~ al pari stehen; **to issue at** ~ zum Nennwert ausgeben

par, below ~ (or **at less than** ~) unter pari; unter dem Nennwert; **issue below** ~ Unterpariemission; **to be below** ~ unter pari stehen

par, no-~ **stock** *Am* nennwertlose Aktie, Quotenaktie

par, to be on a ~ gleich sein; auf gleichem Fuße stehen (with mit); **to put on a** ~ **with** gleichstellen mit

parade *mil* (Truppen-)Parade; Aufmarsch, Vorbeimarsch; **celebration** ~ Festaufmarsch; **fashion** ~ Modenschau; **identification** ~ *(StrafR)* Gegenüberstellung

paradigm (of an offence[~se]) (*StrafR*) Tatbestand; **prerequisite of the** ~ Tatbestandsmerkmal

paragraph (para) Absatz, Ziffer *(z.B. e-s affidavit);* **sub-**~ Unterabschnitt, Buchstabe; **the** ~ **reads** der Absatz lautet

Paraguay Paraguay; **Republic of** ~ Republik Paraguay

Paraguayan Paraguayaner, ~in; paraguayanisch

parajudicial außergerichtlich

paralegal (assistant) *Am* juristische Hilfskraft, Anwaltsassistent(in)

parallel standard Parallelwährung

parallel, consciously ~ business behavior *Am (AntitrustR)* bewußt gleichlautendes Geschäftsverhalten

parallelism, conscious ~ of action *Am (AntitrustR)* bewußte Parallelität des Handelns; bewußtes gleichgerichtetes Verhalten *(der Wettbewerber)*
Die von der Federal Trade Commission entwickelte "implied conspiracy doctrine" besagt, daß aus einer gewissen Parallelität des Handelns auf das Vorliegen einer →conspiracy geschlossen wird. Mit conscious parallelism of action versucht die F. T. C., das Verbot des § 1 Sherman Act auch auf solche Fälle auszudehnen, in denen mehrere Wettbewerber in Kenntnis des Verhaltens des anderen, wenn auch ohne Verständigung mit ihm, gleichartig handeln

para-military organization militärähnliche Organisation

paramount oberst, höchst, vorrangig; Haupt-; **~ consideration** oberster Gesichtspunkt; **of ~ importance** von höchster (od. überragender) Bedeutung; **it is of ~ importance** es kommt in erster Linie darauf an; **title ~** *(GrundstücksR)* stärkeres Recht

paraph Paraphe, Namenszug

paraphernal property (or **paraphernalia)** Vorbehaltsgut e-s Ehegatten

parcel 1. (Post-)Paket; *Am (auch)* Päckchen; **~ delivery** Paketzustellung; **~ issuing office** Paketausgabe(stelle); **~ mailing form** Paketkarte; **~(s) office** *Br* Paketannahme- und -ausgabestelle *(an e-m Bahnhof)*

parcel post Paketpost; **~ insurance** *Am* Paketversicherung; **~ office** *Am* Paketannahme- und -ausgabestelle; **~ window** *Am* Paketschalter; **by ~** als Postpaket; **by insured ~** *Br* als Wertpaket

parcel, ~ postage Paketporto; **~ receipt** Paketempfangsbescheinigung; **~(s) service** *Br* Paketzustelldienst; **air ~** Luftpostpaket; **C.O.D. ~** Nachnahmepaket; **express ~** Eilpaket; **insured ~** *Br* Wertpaket; **postal ~** Postpaket; **postage** (or **rate**) **for ~s** Paketgebühr; **small ~** Päckchen; **special handling ~** *Am* Schnellpaket

parcel 2. Stück Land, Parzelle, Grundstück; **~s** *Br (den →operative words folgender)* Teil e-r Urkunde *(bei Übertragungen Beschreibung des übertragenen Grundeigentums)*; **improved ~s** *Am* bebaute Grundstücke

parcel 3. Menge, Partie, Posten *(Ware)*; **~ goods** Stückgüter; **~ of goods** Partie Waren; **~ of shares** Aktienpaket; **bill of ~s** →bill 1.; **by** (or **in**) **~s** stückweise, in kleinen Posten; **to lot out goods in ~s** Waren in Einzelposten (od. Partien) aufteilen

parcel *v*, **to ~ (out)** parzellieren; *(Land)* in Parzellen aufteilen

parcelling (out) Parzellierung

parcenary →coparcenary

parcener →coparcener

pardon Begnadigung, Straferlaß *(im Einzelfalle; cf. amnesty)*; **Board of P~** *Am* Begnadigungsausschuß *(anstelle des Governor)*; **general ~** Amnestie; **grant of a ~** Begnadigung; **petition for a ~** Gnadengesuch; **power to grant a ~**[2] Begnadigungsrecht; **to deny a ~** ein Gnadengesuch ablehnen; **to grant a ~ to a p.** jdn begnadigen; **to petition for a ~** ein Gnadengesuch einreichen; um Begnadigung bitten; **to receive** (or **to be granted**) **a ~** begnadigt werden

pardon *v (jdn)* begnadigen; **~ed person** Begnadigter; **power of ~ing** Begnadigungsrecht *(Br cf. Royal prerogative of mercy)*

parens patriae action *Am (durch Hart-Scott-Rodino Antitrust Improvements Act 1976 geschaffene)* Klage der Regierungen der Einzelstaaten zugunsten der in ihrem Gebiet ansässigen Bürger auf dreifachen Schadensersatz bei Verletzungen des Antitrustrechts *(beschränkt auf Sherman Act)*

parent Elternteil; Stamm-; **~(s) and child cases** Kindschaftssachen; **~ application** *(PatR)* Hauptanmeldung; **~ body** Stammorgan; **~ company** (or **enterprise**) Muttergesellschaft, Obergesellschaft, Dachgesellschaft *(opp. subsidiary company)*; **~ house** Stammhaus *(opp. branch house)*; **~s' insurance benefits** *Am (Sozialvers.)* Hinterbliebenenrente für die Eltern e-s verstorbenen Erwerbstätigen; **~ organization** Dachorganisation; **~ store** Hauptgeschäft *(mit mehreren Filialen)*; **foster ~s** Pflegeeltern

parentage Abstammung; Herkunft

parental custody elterliche Sorge

parenticide Elternmord

pari delicto ("in equal guilt"), **to be in ~** *Am* mitschuldig sein *(Sonderform e-r Mitverantwortlichkeit, die Ersatzansprüche ausschließt)*

pari delicto, in ~ potior est conditio possidentis ("where both parties are equally at fault he who actually possesses any property in dispute is to be preferred") Rechtsgrundsatz, daß bei sittenwidrigem Geschäft über e-e Sache derjenige in der besseren Lage ist, der im Besitz der Sache ist *(vgl. im deutschen Recht z.B. § 817 BGB)*

pari passu ("on an equal footing") gleichrangig, gleichberechtigt; **~ mortgage** gleichrangige Hypothek; **ranking ~ with** gleichrangig mit

Paris Convention[2a] Pariser (Verbands-)Übereinkunft *(→convention 1.)*; **~ on Third Party Liability in the Field of →Nuclear Energy**

Paris Treaties Pariser Verträge
Das 1954 in Paris zwischen der Bundesrepublik einerseits und Frankreich, Großbritannien und den USA andererseits vereinbarte (1955 in Kraft getretene) Vertragswerk (Aufhebung des Besatzungsstatuts, Eingliederung der Bundesrepublik in die westliche Verteidigungsgemeinschaft [cf. NATO] etc)

Paris Union[2a] Pariser Verband *(der durch die →Paris Convention errichtete internationale Verband; cf. WIPO, Art. 2)*

Paris, Declaration of ~ Pariser Seerechtsdeklaration
1856 in Paris unterzeichnete Erklärung über Grundsätze des Seekriegsrechts (auf der 2. Haager Friedenskonferenz durch Zusatzabkommen ergänzt)

parish 1. *eccl* (Kirchen-)Gemeinde, Pfarrbezirk, Kirchspiel; ~ **clerk** *Br* Küster; ~ **office** *Br* Kirchenvorstand; ~**-pump politics** Kirchturmpolitik; ~ **register** Kirchenbuch *(christenings, marriages, burials)*

parish 2. *Br* Gemeinde(bezirk) *(die parishes sind die dritte Verwaltungsstufe innerhalb der counties);* ~ **council** *Br* Gemeinderat; ~ **councillor** Mitglied des Gemeinderats; ~ **meeting** *Br* Gemeindeversammlung

parish 3. *Am (Louisiana)* Kreis *(→county);* ~ **court** *Am (Louisiana)* Kreisgericht

parishioner Gemeindemitglied

parity 1. Parität, Gleichheit, Gleichwertigkeit; **on a** ~ **basis** paritätisch; ~ **of pay** (for men and women)[3] Lohngleichheit; ~ **of reasoning** Analogieschluß; ~ **of votes** Stimmengleichheit; **in the event of** ~ **of votes** bei Stimmengleichheit

parity 2. (Währungs-)Parität; Wechselkurs; ~ **change** Paritätsänderung; Wechselkursänderung; ~ **clause** Paritätsklausel; ~ **of a currency** Währungsparität; ~ **of exchange** (Wechsel-)Kursparität; ~ **point** Paritätspunkt; ~ **price** (or **rate**) Parikurs; ~ **table** Paritätstabelle; **at the** ~ **of** zur Parität von; **calculation of** ~ Paritätskalkulation; **exchange** ~ (Wechsel-)Kursparität; **gold** ~ Goldparität; **purchasing power** ~ Kaufkraftparität; **table of** ~**ies** Paritätstabelle; **to stand at** ~ al pari stehen

park 1. Park; **national** ~ Nationalpark, Naturschutzgebiet

park 2., **car** ~ *(größerer)* Parkplatz; **car** ~ **attendant** Parkwächter; **multi-storey car** ~ *Br* Park(hoch)haus

park *v* parken

parking Parken *(für Kraftwagen);* ~ **ban** Parkverbot; ~ **facilities** Parkmöglichkeiten; **special** ~ **facilities for the disabled** besondere Parkplätze für Behinderte; ~ **fee** Parkgebühr; ~ **fine** Geldbuße wegen falschen Parkens; ~ **garage** *Am* Park(hoch)haus; ~ **lot** *Am* Parkplatz; ~ **meter** Parkometer, Park(zeit)uhr; ~ **offences** *Br* das Parken betreffende Verstöße; ~ **place** Parkplatz; ~ **prohibited** Parken verboten; ~ **site** *Br* Parkplatz; ~ **ticket** Strafzettel für falsches Parken; ~ **violations** *Am* das Parken betreffende Verstöße; **no** ~ **(except for residents)** Parken verboten (außer für Bewohner der angrenzenden Straßen)

parlance Redeweise, Sprache; **commercial** ~ Geschäftssprache; **common** ~ Umgangssprache; **legal** ~ Rechtssprache, Gesetzessprache

parley *bes. mil* Verhandlung, Unterhandlung *(mit dem Feind)*

Parliament *Br* Parlament *(Am →Congress 1.);* ~ **Act** *Br* Parlamentsgesetz *(bes. von 1911 und 1949, die die Mitwirkung der Lords in der Gesetzgebung einschränken);* **Act of** ~ *Br* Gesetz; **dissolution of** ~ Parlamentsauflösung; **lifetime of a** ~ Legislaturperiode; **member of** ~ (M. P.) Parlamentsmitglied; *Br* Mitglied des Unterhauses; **opening of** ~ *(feierl.)* Parlamentseröffnung; **session of** ~ Tagung des Parlaments; ~ **adjourned** das Parlament vertagte sich; ~ **assembled** das Parlament trat zusammen; **to convoke** (or **summon**) ~ das Parlament einberufen; **to dissolve** ~ das Parlament auflösen; **to enter** (or **go**) **into** ~ ins Parlament gewählt werden; *Br* Mitglied des →House of Commons werden; **to prorogue** ~ das Parlament vertagen; **to stand for** ~ *Br* für das Unterhaus kandidieren; ~ **is in session** (or **sits**) das Parlament tagt

parliamentarian erfahrener Parlamentarier

parliamentarism Parlamentarismus

parliamentary Parlamentarier; parlamentarisch; ~ **agents** *Br* Personen *(meist solicitors),* denen die technische Durchführung der Verabschiedung von private bills *(→bill 3.)* obliegt; ~ **→borough; P**~ **Commissioner for Administration** *Br*[4] Beschwerdestelle *(für Beschwerden der Bürger in Verwaltungssachen);* ~ **committee** Parlamentsausschuß, parlamentarischer Ausschuß *(Br committees of the whole House, standing or sessional committees, select committees and joint committees);* ~ **constituency** Parlamentswahlkreis; **P**~ **Counsel** *Br* mit der Abfassung von Gesetzen beauftragte Regierungsstelle; ~ **debate(s)** *Br (gedruckte)* Parlamentsberichte *(cf. Hansard)*

parliamentary election *Br* Parlamentswahl; **to stand in the** ~ *Br* sich für das Parlament aufstellen lassen;

parliamentary, ~ **franchise** *Br*[5] Wahlrecht für Parlamentswahl; ~ **group** Fraktion *(→group 3.);* ~ **immunity** parlamentarische Immunität; **P**~ **Labour Party** *Br* Parlamentsfraktion der Labour Party; ~ **law** *Am* parlamentarische Geschäftsordnung; ~ **leader of a party** Fraktionsführer, Fraktionsvorsitzender; ~ **monarchy** parlamentarische Monarchie; ~ **→oath;** ~

party *Br* Parlamentsfraktion; ~ **practice** parlamentarischer Brauch; **P~ Private Secretary** (to the Secretary of State for Home Affairs) *Br (etwa)* Unterstaatssekretär (im Innenministerium); **breach of ~ privilege** Verletzung des Parlamentsfriedens; ~ **procedure** parlamentarisches Verfahren; ~ **publication** Parlamentsdrucksache; ~ **recess** Parlamentsferien; ~ **regime** →~system; ~ **report** Parlamentsbericht; ~ **seat** Abgeordnetensitz; ~ **sitting** Sitzung (od. Tagung) des Parlaments; ~ **statute** Parlamentsgesetz; ~ **system** parlamentarisches Regierungssystem; **P~ Under-Secretary (of State)** →secretary 3.; ~ **usage** →~ practice

parlor car *Am (Eisenbahn)* Salonwagen

parochial Pfarr-, Gemeinde-; eng, beschränkt; ~ **church council** *Br* Gemeindekirchenrat; ~ **elector** *Br*[6] Wähler von →parish councillors; ~ **politics** Kirchturmpolitik; **extra-~** außerhalb der Gemeinde

parochialism Lokalpatriotismus; Kirchturmpolitik

parochian *Br* →parishioner

parol(e) *(nur)* mündlich; schriftlich ohne Siegel; ~ **agreement** (or **contract**) formloser Vertrag *(mündlich od. schriftlich ohne Siegel)*

parol evidence mündlicher Beweis, Beweis schriftloser Verträge durch Zeugen- od. Parteiaussage *(Ggs. Urkundenbeweis e-s schriftl. geschlossenen Vertrages)*; ~ **rule** Regel, wonach bei Auslegung schriftlicher Erklärungen die außerhalb der Urkunde liegenden Umstände *(mündl. Nebenabreden etc)* nicht ermittelt und verwertet werden dürfen bei Vorliegen von schriftlichen Beweisstücken

parole 1. *Am*[6a] vorläufiger Aufenthalt; ~ **provision** gesetzliche Ermächtigung für die Gestaltung des vorläufigen Aufenthalts

parole 2. *mil*, ~ **(of hono[u]r)** Ehrenwort *(des Gefangenen)*; **to be on** ~ gegen Ehrenwort freigelassen sein; **to break one's** ~ sein Ehrenwort brechen

parole 3. *(StrafR)* bedingte Entlassung *(aus der Strafhaft vor Ablauf der Strafzeit bei gleichzeitiger Überwachung während e-r Bewährungszeit; cf. probation)*; ~ **administrator** *Am* Inspektor der bedingten Entlassung; **P~ Board** *Br*[7] Ausschuß für Gewährung der bedingten Entlassung; ~ **eligibility**[8] Infragekommen für bedingte Entlassung; ~ **hostel** *Am* Heim für bedingt Entlassene

parole supervision Aufsicht während der bedingten Entlassung; **person under** ~ jd, der als bedingt Entlassener unter Aufsicht steht

parole term Dauer der bedingten Entlassung; **balance of the** ~ Rest der bedingt erlassenen Freiheitsstrafe; **maximum** ~ Höchstdauer der bedingten Entlassung

parole, Board of P~[9] Ausschuß für Gewährung der bedingten Entlassung; **conditions of** ~ Bedingungen der bedingten Entlassung; **discharge from** ~ endgültige Entlassung; **field ~ officer**[10] Beamter des bedingten Entlassungsdienstes außerhalb der Anstalt; **field ~ service** bedingter Entlassungsdienst außerhalb der Anstalt; **length of** ~ Dauer der bedingten Entlassung

parole, release on ~[11] bedingte Entlassung *(aus der Strafhaft vor Ablauf der Strafzeit)*; **to be eligible for release on** ~ für bedingte Entlassung in Frage kommen

parole, re~ erneute bedingte Entlassung; **revocation of** ~[12] Widerruf der bedingten Entlassung; **to be released on** ~ bedingt entlassen werden; **to revoke the** ~ die bedingte Entlassung widerrufen

parole *v Am* vorläufigen Aufenthalt gestalten; *mil (Gefangenen)* gegen Ehrenwort entlassen; *(StrafR)* bedingt entlassen

parolee *Am mil* der gegen Ehrenwort freigelassene Gefangene; *(StrafR)* der bedingt Entlassene

parricide Mord (od. Mörder) des Vaters od. e-s nahen Verwandten

parson Pfarrer, Geistlicher

part 1. Teil; *(Buchhandel)* Lieferung, Nummer; (Schiffs-)Part; ~**(s)** Gegend, Bezirk; ~ **and parcel** wesentlicher Bestandteil; ~→**cargo;** ~ **damage** Teilschaden; ~ **delivery** Teillieferung

part exchange (Kauf unter) Inzahlungnahme; **to give in** ~ in Zahlung geben; **to take in** ~ in Zahlung nehmen

part load Teilladung; ~**s** Stückgüter; ~ **traffic** Stückgutverkehr

part of the contract Bestandteil des Vertrages

part owner Miteigentümer, Teileigentümer; ~ **(of a ship)** Parteninhaber, Partenreeder

part ownerhip Miteigentum, Teileigentum; ~ **(of a ship)** Parteninhaberschaft an e-m Schiff, Partenreederei

part-paid stock *Am* teileingezahlte Aktien

part payment Teilzahlung, Ratenzahlung, Abschlagzahlung; Anzahlung; ~ **terms** Teilzahlungsbedingungen; **in** ~ auf Abschlag; **to make a** ~ Teilzahlung (od. Anzahlung) leisten

part performance teilweise Erfüllung, Teilleistung; Anerkennungsleistung

Br Nach der equitable doctrine of part performance bewirkt eine Leistung, die im Vertrauen auf die Gültigkeit eines Vertrages erbracht worden ist (z. B. Reparatur des erworbenen Hauses), daß entgegen dem allgemeinen Grundsatz (Law of Property Act 1925, s. 40) aus dem betreffenden Vertrag auch dann geklagt werden kann, wenn kein schriftliches Beweismaterial vorliegt

part-time Teilzeit- *(halbtags, stundenweise etc; opp. full time)*; ~ **education** Teilzeitunterricht; ~

employee Teilzeitbeschäftigter; Teilzeitarbeitskraft; ~ **employment** (or **job**) Teilzeitbeschäftigung; Halbtagsbeschäftigung *(opp. full-time employment)*; ~ **unemployed** Teilzeitarbeitslose; ~ **work** Teilzeitarbeit; Halbtagsarbeit; ~ **worker** Teilzeitarbeitskraft; Teilzeitbeschäftigter; **to work** ~ (or **on a** ~ **basis**) halbtägig (od. halbtags, stundenweise etc) arbeiten

part, ~ **timer** →part-time worker; ~ **truck load** *Br (Eisenbahn)* Teilwaggonladung *(opp. [full] truck load)*; **component** ~ Bestandteil

part, in ~ teilweise, zum Teil; auf Abschlag; **in equal ~s** zu gleichen Teilen; **in foreign ~s** im Ausland; **payment in** ~ →~ payment; **wholly or in** ~ ganz oder teilweise

part, major ~ größerer Teil; **spare** ~ Ersatzteil

part, to form (a) ~ **of** e-n Teil bilden von; **to take** ~ **in** teilnehmen an

partly zum Teil, teilweise; **~-owned subsidiary** Tochtergesellschaft, die zu weniger als 100% im Besitz der Muttergesellschaft ist; ~ **paid (up)** (ptly pd) teilweise eingezahlt *(von Aktien, Neuemissionen)*; ~ **secured** teilweise gesichert *(opp. fully secured)*; **wholly or** ~ ganz oder teilweise

part 2. Partei, Seite; **on the** ~ **of** seitens, von seiten; **on your** ~ Ihrerseits; **to take sb.'s** ~ jds Partei ergreifen

part *v* teilen; sich trennen (with von); abgrenzen (with gegen); **to** ~ **with property** e-n Vermögensgegenstand (od. e-n Teil s-s Vermögens) aufgeben

partake *v*, **to** ~ **of the profits** am Gewinn teilnehmen

partial 1. teilweise, Teil-; ~ **acceptance** Teilakzept; teilweise (od. bedingte) Annahme; ~ **agreement** *(VölkerR)* Teilabkommen; ~ **amount** Teilbetrag; ~ **assignment** Teilabtretung; ~ **bond** *Br* Teilschuldschein; ~ **breach of contract** teilweiser Vertragsbruch; ~ **delivery** Teillieferung; ~ **→disability;** ~ **loss** (p.l.) *(SeeversR)* Teilschaden, Teilverlust *(opp. total loss)*; ~ **payment** →part payment; ~ **shipment** Teilverladung

partial 2. parteiisch, voreingenommen; befangen; ~ **award** parteiischer Schiedsspruch

partially →exempt

participant Teilnehmer, Teilhaber (in an); Konferenzteilnehmer, Teilnehmerland; ~ **in an offen|ce (-se)** *(StrafR)* Teilnehmer an e-r strafbaren Handlung

participate *v* teilnehmen, teilhaben, sich beteiligen (in an); beteiligt sein (in an); **to** ~ **in a business** sich an e-m Geschäft beteiligen; **to** ~ **in a loss** am Verlust beteiligt sein; **to** ~ **in committing an offen|ce (-se)** *(StrafR)* an e-r strafbaren Handlung teilnehmen; **to** ~ **in a plot** an e-r Verschwörung beteiligt sein; **to** ~ **equally in the profit** gleichen Anteil am Gewinn haben

participating beteiligt; gewinnbeteiligt, mit Beteiligung am Gewinn, gewinnberechtigt; **→non-~;** ~ **bond** Gewinnschuldverschreibung; ~ **capital stock** *Am* mit zusätzlicher Dividendenberechtigung ausgestattete Aktien; ~ **certificate** Genußschein; ~ **debenture** Gewinnschuldverschreibung; ~ **government** *(VölkerR)* Teilnehmerregierung; ~ **insurance** Versicherung mit Gewinnbeteiligung; ~ **mortgage** *Am* Hypothek, bei der bei Veräußerung des Grundbesitzes der Hypothekengläubiger Anspruch auf bestimmten Betrag aus Wertsteigerung hat; ~ **(life) policy** (Lebens-) Versicherungspolice mit Gewinnbeteiligung; ~ **preference shares** *Br* (~ **preferred stock** *Am*) Vorzugsaktien mit zusätzlicher Dividendenberechtigung; ~ **rights** Gewinnbeteiligungsrechte; Genußrechte; ~ **state** *(VölkerR)* Teilnehmerstaat

participation Beteiligung, Teilnahme, Teilhabe (in an); Mitwirkung; *(Bankwesen)* Konsortialbeteiligung; ~ **certificate** *Am* Anteilschein, Bescheinigung über den Anteil an e-m Wertpapier großer Stückelung; ~ **in an enterprise** Beteiligung an e-m Unternehmen; ~ **in a meeting** Teilnahme an e-r Versammlung (od. Sitzung); ~ **in an offen|ce (~se)** Teilnahme an e-r strafbaren Handlung; ~ **in profits** Gewinnbeteiligung; ~ **in a syndicate** Konsortialbeteiligung; ~ **loan** Konsortialkredit; Gemeinschaftsdarlehen; **electoral** ~ Wahlbeteiligung; **employee** ~ Mitbestimmung der Arbeitnehmer; **financial** ~ finanzielle Beteiligung; **general** ~ **clause** *(VölkerR)* Allbeteiligungsklausel; **workers'** ~ **in management** Mitbestimmung der Arbeitnehmer

participator Teilnehmer, Teilhaber; ~ **in an offen|ce (-se)** *(StrafR)* Teilnehmer an e-r strafbaren Handlung

particular besonders; einzeln; eingehend, ausführlich; ~ **average** →average 1.; ~ **case** besonderer Fall, Einzelfall; ~ **circumstances** besondere Umstände; ~ **estate** minderes Recht an Grundbesitz, an dem e-r dritten Person ein →remainder oder →reversion eingeräumt ist; ~ **fund** besonders bezeichneter Vermögensfonds; ~ **→legacy;** ~ **→lien;** ~ **→partnership;** ~ **place** bestimmter Ort; ~ **power** Spezialvollmacht *(opp. general power)*; ~ **tenant** tenant e-s ~ estate; **in general and in** ~ im allgemeinen und im besonderen; **in a material** ~ in e-m wesentlichen Punkt

particulars Einzelheiten, Näheres, nähere Angaben (of über); Schriftsatzergänzungen, Spezifizierungen *(der Klage od. Klageerwiderung im Schriftsatz)*; Personalien, Angaben zur Person *(z.B. in e-m Paß);* ~ **of an account** einzelne Posten e-r Abrechnung; ~ **of claim** *Br (County Court)* Klagebegründung *(im Schriftsatz);* ~ **of pleadings** *Br*[13] Einzelheiten im Schriftsatz; ~ **of the risk** *(VersR)* Gefahrenmerkmale; **bill of** ~ *Am* →bill 2.

particulars, full ~ genaue Einzelheiten, Näheres; **with full** ~ mit allen Einzelheiten

particulars, for further ~ **apply to** Näheres zu erfragen bei

particulars, application for further and better ~ *Br*[13] *(an die Gegenpartei gerichteter)* Antrag e-r Prozeßpartei auf Erteilung genauerer Angaben über den Inhalt des gegnerischen Schriftsatzes

particulars, personal ~ Personalbeschreibung; **written statement of** ~ schriftliche Bestätigung der Einzelheiten

particulars, to furnish ~ Einzelheiten angeben; Auskunft erteilen; **default in furnishing** ~ Nichtdarstellung von Einzelheiten *(im Tatsachenvortrag e-r Klage od. Klageerwiderung);* **failure to furnish** ~ Nichtmitteilung von näheren Einzelheiten

particulars, to give ~ spezifizieren; **as per** ~ **given below** wie unten im einzelnen ausgeführt; **to go into** ~ ins einzelne gehen, auf Einzelheiten eingehen

particularism Partikularismus

particularize *v* im einzelnen angeben, aufführen; spezifizieren

parties →party

partisan (Partei-)Anhänger; Partei-; *mil* Partisan; ~ **movement** Partisanenbewegung; **non-**~ zu keiner Partei Gehöriger

partisanship Parteinahme; Parteiwirtschaft; Parteianhängerschaft

partition Teilung, Aufteilung (among unter); Grundstücksteilung *(von Miteigentümern);* ~ **of a country** Teilung e-s Landes *(z.B. Teilung Deutschlands);* ~ **of a succession** Erbschaftsteilung; Erbauseinandersetzung; ~ **wall** Trennmauer, Brandmauer; **action for a** ~ Teilungsklage *(der Miteigentümer e-s Grundstücks);* **deed of** ~[14] schriftl. Teilungsvereinbarung; Teilungsurkunde *(der Miteigentümer e-s Grundstücks);* **distribution and** ~ *Am* Verteilung des bewegl. und unbewegl. Nachlasses; **scheme of** ~ Teilungsplan

partition *v (bes. Land)* teilen, aufteilen; **to** ~ **off** abteilen, abtrennen; abschotten; **to** ~ **an estate** ein Landgut (auf)teilen; **to** ~ **the market** den Markt aufteilen

partly →part 1.

partner Teilhaber, Gesellschafter *(bes. e-r offenen Handelsgesellschaft);* Associé, Sozius; Partner; *Am* Teilhaber e-r Anwaltsfirma, der *(im Ggs. zum associate)* Anteil am Gewinn erhält; ~ **by estoppel** Gesellschafter kraft Rechtsscheins; ~**'s capital** (or **contribution**) Einlagekapital; ~ **in joint account** Teilhaber auf gemeinsame Rechnung; ~**'s interest** Gesellschaftsanteil; **active** ~ aktiver *(sich offen an der Führung der Geschäfte beteiligender)* Gesellschafter *(opp. dormant, sleeping* or *silent* ~*);* **admission of a** ~ Aufnahme e-s Gesellschafters; **co-**~ Teilhaber, Mitgesellschafter

partner, dormant ~ stiller Gesellschafter; nicht an der Geschäftsführung beteiligter und nicht (allgemein) bekanntgemachter Gesellschafter

Der dormant partner ist zugleich →secret und →silent partner. Dormant und silent werden aber oft auch synonym gebraucht. Der dormant partner haftet (anders als der stille Gesellschafter des deutschen Rechts, dem er teilweise entspricht) grundsätzlich wie jeder andere Gesellschafter. Insbesondere für den ausgeschiedenen dormant partner gelten aber besondere Regeln

partner, expulsion of a ~ Ausschließung e-s Gesellschafters; **general** ~ unbeschränkt (persönlich) haftender Gesellschafter, Komplementär *(opp. limited* ~*);* **holding o.s. out as a** ~ *Br* →holding out; **inactive** ~ nicht tätiger Gesellschafter; **incoming** ~ (neu) eintretender Gesellschafter (od. Teilhaber); **individual** ~ einzelner Gesellschafter; **junior** ~ jüngerer Teilhaber; **limited** ~ beschränkt *(liable up to his contribution nur mit Einlage)* haftender Gesellschafter; Kommanditist *(→limited partnership);* **managing** ~ geschäftsführender Gesellschafter (od. Teilhaber); **nominal** ~ nicht aktiver Gesellschafter; **ordinary** ~ *Br* s. general →~; **ostensible** ~[15] Gesellschafter nach außen hin *(ohne Eigeninteresse);* vorgeschobener Gesellschafter; **outgoing** ~ ausscheidender Gesellschafter (od. Teilhaber); **quasi-**~ *Am* Scheingesellschafter; **retirement of a** ~ Ausscheiden e-s Gesellschafters (od. Teilhabers)

partner, secret ~ heimlicher (nicht bekanntgemachter) Gesellschafter *(der an der Geschäftsführung beteiligt sein kann und für die Gesellschaftsschulden haftet)*

partner, senior ~ Seniorpartner, Hauptteilhaber; **silent** ~ stiller Gesellschafter; an der Geschäftsführung nicht beteiligter *(nicht notwendig heimlicher, aber grundsätzlich voll haftender)* Gesellschafter *(opp. active partner);* **sleeping** ~ (meist synonym für) dormant →~, (vereinzelt auch für) secret →~; **special** ~ s. limited →~; **unlimited** ~ unbeschränkt haftender Gesellschafter; Komplementär; **withdrawing** ~ ausscheidender Gesellschafter; **working** ~ s. active →~; **to admit a p. as (a)** ~ **in a firm** jdn als Teilhaber in e-r Firma aufnehmen

partner, to be a ~ **in** Teilhaber sein an; **to cease to be a** ~ als Teilhaber ausscheiden

partner, to be personally liable as a ~ als Gesellschafter persönlich haften; **to buy out a** ~ e-n Teilhaber abfinden (od. auszahlen); **to enter (into)** (or **join**) **a firm as** ~ als Teilhaber in e-e Firma eintreten; **to hold o. s. out as a** ~ sich als Gesellschafter ausgeben (→*holding out*); **to take a p. into a firm as a** ~ s. to admit as (a) →~

partnership[16] Personengesellschaft; *(etwa:)* Offene Handelsgesellschaft (OHG); Gesellschaft des bürgerlichen Rechts; Teilhaberschaft, Sozietät *(Anwälte, Ärzte etc);* Partnerschaft

Gesellschaft (Sozietät), die jede – auf Gewinnerzielung gerichtete – gewerbliche und berufliche Tätigkeit zum Gegenstand haben kann. Sie ist hinsichtlich der Gründung, Rechtspersönlichkeit, Vertretung, Haftung etc im wesentlichen so ausgestattet wie die OHG, der sie weitgehend entspricht, wenn sie ein Handelsgeschäft betreibt.

Besonderheiten: *Br* Die Zahl der Gesellschafter ist auf 20, in Bankgeschäften auf 10 beschränkt. *Scot* Die partnership hat Rechtspersönlichkeit

partnership, to be in ~ with a p. mit jdm assoziiert sein; **to dissolve a** ~ e-e partnership auflösen; **to enter** (or **go**) **into** ~ **with** sich assoziieren (od. geschäftlich verbinden) mit; als Teilhaber eintreten bei; **to establish** (or **form**) **a** ~ e-e partnership gründen; **to join a** ~ als Gesellschafter (od. Teilhaber) eintreten; **to retire from a** ~ als Gesellschafter (od. Teilhaber) ausscheiden; **to take a p. into** ~ jdn als Gesellschafter (od. Teilhaber) aufnehmen; sich mit jdm assoziieren; **to withdraw from a** ~ s. to retire from a →~; **a** ~ **has expired** e-e Personengesellschaft (od. Sozietät) ist erloschen

partnership, ~ **agreement** (or **articles**) Gesellschaftsvertrag; Sozietätsvertrag; ~ **assets** Gesellschaftsvermögen; ~ **association** *Am* bes. Form der partnership *(Mitglieder sind nur beschränkt haftbar, können ihre Anteile frei übertragen);* ~ **assurance** *Br* Teilhaberversicherung; ~ **at will**[17] jederzeit kündbare partnership; ~ **by estoppel** Gesellschaft kraft Rechtsschein (*cf. holding out*)

partnership capital Gesellschaftskapital; **contribution to** ~ Einlage e-s Gesellschafters

partnership, ~ **debts** Gesellschaftsschulden, Firmenschulden; ~ **deed** Gesellschaftsvertrag; Sozietätsvertrag; ~ **firm** Firma e-r Personengesellschaft; Sozietät; ~ **funds** Gesellschaftskapital; ~ **income** Gesellschaftseinkommen; ~ **insurance** Teilhaberversicherung; ~ **interest** Beteiligung an e-r Personengesellschaft; Gesellschaftsanteil; ~ **loss(es)** Gesellschaftsverlust(e); ~ **property** Gesellschaftsvermögen; ~ **purpose(s)** Gesellschaftszweck(e); ~ **registration** Eintragung e-r Personengesellschaft; **articles of** ~ Gesellschaftsvertrag; Sozietätsvertrag; **certificate of** ~ *Am* Gründungsurkunde; **commercial** ~ Handel betreibende ~; Handelsgesellschaft; **deed of** ~ Gesellschaftsvertrag; Sozietätsvertrag; **dissolution of a** ~[18] Auflösung e-r Personengesellschaft; **dormant** ~ s. silent →~; **establishment of a** ~ Begründung e-s Gesellschaftsverhältnisses; **general** ~ (allgemeine) offene Handelsgesellschaft (OHG) *(zur Durchführung verschiedenartiger Geschäfte; opp. special* ~); →**industrial** ~

partnership, limited ~[19] Kommanditgesellschaft (KG)

Gesellschaft (Sozietät), die sich von der →partnership dadurch unterscheidet, daß einige Gesellschafter nur mit ihrer Einlage haften (limited [or special] partner; opp. general partner). Sofern die Gesellschaft ein Handelsgeschäft betreibt, entspricht sie weitgehend der deutschen KG

partnership, memorandum of ~ Gesellschaftsvertrag

partnership, mining ~ *Am (bes. Form e-r)* Bergwerksgesellschaft

Sie entsteht ohne ausdrückliche Vereinbarung dann, wenn Miteigentümer die Bodenschätze ihres Bergwerkseigentums gemeinsam ausbeuten und Gewinn und Verlust teilen. Ihre Anteile sind übertragbar. Besonderheiten bestehen hinsichtlich der Vertretungsbefugnis der einzelnen Miteigentümer

partnership, ordinary ~ *(gewöhnl.)* offene Handelsgesellschaft (OHG) *(opp. limited* ~*);* **particular** ~ s. special →~; **presumption of** ~ Vermutung, daß die Beteiligten ihr Kapital zur Gründung e-r ~ *(und nicht etwa als Darlehen)* hingegeben haben; **quasi-**~ Scheingesellschaft, Scheinsozietät *(jd wird hinsichtl. der Haftung so behandelt, als ob e-e* ~ *mit e-m anderen bestehe);* **share in a** ~ Anteil (od. Beteiligung) an e-r Personengesellschaft; **silent** ~ stille Gesellschaft; **special** ~ partnership zur Durchführung e-r bestimmten Transaktion (od. e-s einzelnen Geschäfts); Gelegenheitsgesellschaft *(opp. general* ~*);* →**sub**~

partnership, trading ~ Handelsgesellschaft; **nontrading** ~ nicht auf das Betreiben e-s Handelsgeschäfts ausgerichtete Gesellschaft (od. Sozietät); Gesellschaft des bürgerlichen Rechts

part|y 1. (Prozeß-)Partei *(in an action: plaintiff and defendant; in the case of a petition: petitioner and respondent);* ~ **and** ~ **costs** *Br* Prozeßkosten (→*costs*); ~ **appealing** →appellant; ~ **entitled to claim** Anspruchsberechtigter; ~ **in default** nicht erschienene (od. säumige) Partei; ~ **liable for costs** Kostenschuldner; ~ **to an action** Prozeßpartei; ~ **to a lawsuit** (or **litigation**) Prozeßpartei; ~ **to a suit** *bes. Am* Prozeßpartei; **act of** ~ Parteihandlung; Rechtsgeschäft; **adverse** ~ s. opposing →~; **contending** ~**ies** streitende Parteien; **defeated** (or **losing**) ~ unterliegende Partei; **moving** ~ Antragsteller; →**nominal** ~; **opposing** ~ Gegenpartei, Prozeßgegner; **real** ~ **in interest** *Am* wirkliche Prozeßpartei *(die als obsiegender Klä-*

ger unmittelbar durch das Urteil begünstigt wird; opp. nominal ~); **successful** ~ obsiegende Partei; **unsuccessful** ~ unterliegende Partei; **winning** ~ obsiegende Partei

part|y 2. (Vertrags-)Partei; Person, Beteiligter; *(mehreren Personen)* gemeinsam; **the ~ at fault in an accident** der Schuldige e-s Unfalls; ~ **concerned** Beteiligter (od. Betroffener), Interessent; ~ **contracting a marriage** Eheschließende(r); ~ **entitled** Berechtigte(r); ~ **in breach** (of contract) Partei, die den Vertrag verletzt hat; vertragsbrüchige Partei; ~ **in default** in Verzug befindliche Partei; zum Termin nicht erschienene Partei (→*default*); ~ **injured** s. injured →~

party liable Verpflichteter, Schuldner; ~ **on a bill** Wechselverpflichteter; ~ **under a contract** vertraglich verpflichtete Partei; ~ **to recourse** Regreßschuldner; ~ **to surrender** Herausgabeschuldner

part|y, ~ **line** *tel* gemeinsamer Anschluß, Gemeinschaftsanschluß; ~ **of the first (second) part** *Am (in Urkunden)* die zuerst (als zweite) erwähnte (Vertrags-)Partei; ~ **ticket** Sammelfahrschein *(zu ermäßigten Preisen);* ~ **to an agreement** Vertragspartei, Vertragspartner; (*KartellR*) an e-r Absprache Beteiligter; ~**ies to the present agreement** (*VölkerR*) Vertragsparteien dieses Abkommens; ~ **to a bill (of exchange)** Wechselbeteiligter (drawer, drawee, payee); ~ **to a contract** Vertragspartei, Kontrahent; ~ **to an instrument** *Am* Beteiligter e-s (Handels-)Papiers; ~**ies to the negotiation** Verhandlungspartner; ~ **to a sale** Partei e-s Kaufvertrages; ~ **to the trust** Trustbeteiligter; ~ **wall**[20] *(gemeinsame)* (Grenz-)Mauer, Brandmauer; **by agreement between the ~ies** durch Parteivereinbarung; **contracting** ~ vertragschließende Partei; Vertragspartei, Kontrahent; **immediate** ~ *(an e-m Wechsel)* unmittelbar Beteiligter *(opp. remote ~);* **injured** ~ der/die Verletzte, Geschädigte, Benachteiligte; **interested** ~ Interessent, Beteiligter; **third** ~ Dritter (→*third);* **to be a ~ to** beteiligt sein (od. teilnehmen) an; **unless the ~ies have otherwise agreed** mangels abweichender Vereinbarung der Parteien

party[21] 3. *(politische)* Partei; ~ **affiliation** Parteizugehörigkeit; ~ **badge** Parteiabzeichen; ~ **chief** *Am* Parteiführer; ~ **conference** (or **congress** *or Am* **convention**) Parteitag, Parteiversammlung; ~ **discipline** *bes. Br* Parteidisziplin, Fraktionsdisziplin; ~ **headquarters** Parteizentrale; ~ **leader** Parteiführer; ~ **leaders** (or **leadership**) Parteiführung

party line Parteilinie, Parteikurs; **across ~s** jenseits der Parteilinie; über Parteigrenzen hinweg; **deviation from the** ~ Abweichen von der Parteilinie; **fidelity to the** ~ Linientreue; **to follow the** ~ linientreu sein, Parteidisziplin halten

party, ~ **liner** Linientreuer *(bes. in Zusammenhang mit e-r Partei);* ~ **machinery** Parteiapparat; ~ **meeting** Parteiversammlung

party member Parteimitglied; **enrol(l)ed** ~ eingetragenes Parteimitglied

party, ~ **official** *Am* Mitglied des Parteivorstandes, Parteifunktionär; ~ **platform** Parteiprogramm; ~**-political** parteipolitisch; ~ **politician** Parteipolitiker; ~ **program(me)** Parteiprogramm; ~ **rally** Parteiversammlung; ~ **resolution** Fraktionsbeschluß; ~ **spirit** Parteigeist; ~ **split** Parteispaltung

party system Parteisystem; **multiple** ~ Mehrparteiensystem; **two** ~ Zweiparteiensystem

part|y, ~ **ticket** *Am* Parteiprogramm; ~ **truce** Burgfrieden der Parteien; ~ **whip** →whip; **above** ~ überparteilich; **chairman of the** ~ Parteivorsitzender; **coalition ~ies** Koalitionsparteien; **cohesion of a** ~ Zusammenhalt e-r Partei; **deputy** ~ **leader** *Br* stellvertretender Parteiführer; **exclusion from the** ~ Parteiausschluß; **executive committee of the** ~ Parteivorstand; **government** ~ *Br* Regierungspartei; **left-wing** ~ Linkspartei, Linke; **member of a** ~ →~ member; **moderate** ~ gemäßigte Partei; **non(-)**~ parteilos; überparteilich; **opposition** ~ Oppositionspartei; **right-wing** ~ Rechtspartei, Rechte; **statutes of the** ~ Parteistatuten, Parteisatzung; **subscription to a** ~ Parteibeitrag; **wing of the** ~ Parteiflügel

party, to ban a ~ e-e Partei verbieten; **to be affiliated to a** ~ e-r Partei angehören; **to be a member of a** ~ e-r Partei angehören; Parteimitglied sein; **to become a member of a** ~ Parteimitglied werden; **they constituted themselves a** ~ sie bildeten e-e Partei; **to desert a** ~ e-e Partei verlassen; **to form a** ~ e-e Partei gründen; **to give one's vote to a** ~ e-r Partei s-e Stimme geben; e-e Partei wählen; **to join a** ~ e-r Partei beitreten; in e-e Partei eintreten; **the** ~ **has split into factions** →faction; **to withdraw** (or **resign**) **from a** ~ aus e-r Partei austreten

pass Ausweis(karte); Passierschein; *mil* (Kurz-) Urlaubsschein; *Am* Dauerkarte, Jahresbillet; Freikarte

passbook Bankbuch; Sparkassenbuch; *Br* Zollscheinheft *(cf. Carnet de Passages en Douane);* Anschreibebuch *(des Kaufmanns)*

pass, ~ **degree** *univ* gewöhnlicher Grad ohne Auszeichnung; ~ **examination** *Br univ* Prüfung auf ein ~ degree; ~ **sheet** *Br* Grenzübertrittsschein für Kraftfahrzeuge *(cf. triptych); Br* Kontoauszug; ~**-through certificate** *Am* bundesstaatlich garantierter Finanzierungstitel der Hypothekenbanken

pass, annual ~ *Am* Jahreskarte *(z.B. für die Bahn);* **customs** ~ Zollpassierschein; **(free)** ~ Freikarte *(Theater, Bahn);* **frontier** ~ Grenzausweis; **(member's)** ~ Teilnehmerkarte,

Ausweiskarte; **visitor's** ~ Besuchererlaubnis *(Sprecherlaubnis für das Gefängnis)*; **to issue a** ~ e-n Ausweis ausstellen; e-n Passierschein ausgeben

pass *v* übergehen (to auf); übertragen, übergeben, weitergeben; eintragen, buchen; sich ereignen, eintreten; *(Prüfung)* bestehen; *(Gesetz)* annehmen (od. verabschieden); *fig* durchgehen, durchkommen; durchgehen, durchfahren; vorbeifahren an; *(Verkehr)* überholen; *fig* hinausgehen über, übertreffen; in Umlauf (od. Verkehr) bringen; **to** ~ **to a p.'s account** jdm in Rechnung stellen, jdn belasten; **to** ~ **an amendment** *parl* e-n Abänderungsantrag annehmen; **to** ~ **a Bill** *parl* ein Gesetz verabschieden *(opp. to defeat a Bill)*; **the Bill** ~**es through its various stages** der Gesetzesentwurf durchläuft die verschiedenen Stadien *(Lesungen etc)*; **the Bill was** ~**ed** →passed; **to** ~ **the border** (or **boundary**) über die Grenze gehen; die Grenze überschreiten; **to** ~ **the censor** durch die Zensur gehen; von der Zensur freigegeben werden; **to** ~ **a cheque through the clearing-house** *Br* e-n Scheck im Clearing verrechnen; **to** ~ **a forged cheque (check)** e-n gefälschten Scheck in den Verkehr bringen; **a contingency comes to** ~ e-e Bedingung tritt ein; **to** ~ **counterfeit money** gefälschtes Geld in den Verkehr bringen; **to** ~ **the customs** durch den Zoll gehen, den Zoll passieren; **to** ~ **a customs entry** e-e Zollerklärung abgeben, *(etw.)* zur Verzollung deklarieren; **to** ~ **a decision** e- e Entscheidung fällen (on über); **to** ~ **a dividend** e-e Dividende ausfallen lassen, keine Dividende zahlen; **to** ~ **an entry** e-e Eintragung machen, e-e Buchung vornehmen; **the estate** ~**es by (the) conveyance** das Eigentum an Grundbesitz geht durch die Übertragungsurkunde auf den neuen Eigentümer über; **to** ~ **an examination** e-e Prüfung bestehen; **to** ~ **an item to an account** *Br* e-n Posten auf e-m Konto (ver)buchen; **to** ~ **judgement** ein Urteil fällen, urteilen; **to** ~ **a resolution** beschließen, e-n Beschluß fassen; e-e Entschließung annehmen; **to** ~ **sentence** das Strafurteil fällen (od. verkünden); **to** ~ **sentence upon the accused** den Angeklagten verurteilen; **to** ~ **a statute** ein Gesetz verabschieden; **to** ~ **title** Eigentum übertragen (to auf); **to** ~ **a transfer** *Br (Buchführung)* e-n Übertrag machen; **to** ~ **goods in transit** →transit 1.

pass *v*, **to** ~ **for** (sb. or sth.) gelten als; **to** ~ **for military service** für diensttauglich erklären; **to** ~ **into the** →**ownership of; to** ~ **(o.s.) off as** (sich) ausgeben als (→*passing off*); **to** ~ **on** *Am (gerichtl.)* entscheiden (z. B. **the court** ~**ed on the issue of ...** das Gericht entschied über die Frage ...); **to** ~ **on (to sb.)** *(etw.)* weitergeben (od. weiterleiten) (an jdn); *(Steuern, Kosten)* (auf jdn) überwälzen; **to** ~ **over** *(etw.)* übertragen, weitergeben (to sb. jdm); *(jdn bei Beförderung etc)* übergehen; **to** ~ **over a country** ein Land überfliegen; **to** ~ **over sb.'s land** jds Grundstück betreten (od. befahren); **to** ~ **up** *Am sl.* ablehnen, zurückweisen; **property in the goods** ~**es to the buyer** das Eigentum an den Waren geht auf den Käufer über; **the risk** ~**es** die Gefahr geht über (to auf); **the title** ~**es** das Eigentum geht über

passed, ~ **by the censor** von der Zensur freigegeben; ~ **on tax** überwälzte Steuer; **the Bill was** ~ der Gesetzesentwurf wurde angenommen (od. ging durch); **the business** ~ **into other hands** das Geschäft ging in andere Hände über; **legislation** ~ **by Parliament** *Br* (**Congress** *Am*) die durch das Parlament *Br* (den Kongreß *Am*) verabschiedeten Gesetze; **the motion was** ~ der Antrag ging durch

passing, ~ **of a Bill** Verabschiedung e-s Gesetzes; ~ **of a dividend** Dividendenausfall; ~ **of entries** Vornahme von Eintragungen (od. Buchungen); ~ **of property** Eigentumsübergang; ~ **of (the) risk** Gefahrübergang; ~ **of title** Eigentumsübergang

passing off Ausgeben seiner eigenen Ware(n) als die e-s anderen; Unterschieben eigener Ware(n) als fremde *(zur Irreführung des Publikums)*; Kennzeichenmißbrauch

Wichtigste Form des unlauteren Wettbewerbs in Großbritannien und USA *(vgl. auch slander of title and slander of goods)*.

Die Voraussetzungen der Klage aus passing off sind in beiden Ländern die gleichen. Ein direktes Wettbewerbsverhältnis ist nicht erforderlich, es genügt die Möglichkeit einer Verwechslungsgefahr. Mit der Klage kann insbes. auch der Inhaber einer nicht eingetragenen Marke gegen die Verwendung eines verwechslungsfähigen Zeichens durch andere vorgehen

passing, ~ **on** Weiterleitung; Überwälzung (to auf); ~ **a resolution** Annahme e-r Entschließung; Beschlußfassung; **improper** ~ *Am (Verkehr)* falsches Überholen; **in** ~ nebenbei; **no** ~ *Am* Überholen verboten

passage Durchgang, Durchfahrt; Passage (Reise mit Schiff od. Flugzeug); (Über-)Fahrt, (See-)Reise; Fahrgeld *(für Schiff od. Flug)*; Recht der Benutzung e-s privaten Wasserweges *(als →easement)*; (Text-)Stelle; ~ **broker** *Br*[22] Auswanderungsagent; ~ **by air** Flug, Luftreise; ~ **contract** Passagevertrag, Überfahrtsvertrag; ~ **money** Passagegeld, Überfahrtsgeld; ~ **of a Bill** Verabschiedung (od. Annahme) e-s Gesetzes; Durchgang e-r Gesetzesvorlage; ~ **of the risk** Übergang der Gefahr; ~ **of title** Eigentumsübergang; ~ **ticket** Schiffskarte; **air** ~ Flug, Luftreise; →**innocent** ~**; (right of)** ~ Recht auf Benutzung e-s (privaten) Wasserweges; *(VölkerR)* Durchmarschrecht, Durchzugsrecht; **simple** ~ *(VölkerR)* bloße Durchfahrt; **to book one's** ~ s-e Schiffskarte (od.

Flugkarte) lösen (for nach); **to secure the ~ of a bill** ein Gesetz durchbringen

passenger Passagier, Reisender, Fahrgast, Fluggast; Insasse *(e-s Autos);* ~ **accident insurance** Insassen-Unfallversicherung; ~ **accommodation** Passagierräume; ~ **and goods traffic** Personen- und Güterverkehr; ~ **boat** →~ ship; ~ **car** *Am (Eisenbahn)* (Personen-)Wagen, Waggon; Personenkraftwagen (Pkw); ~**-cargo ship** Kombischiff; ~ **certificate** Zulassung für (Schiffs-)Personenbeförderung; ~ **coach** *(Eisenbahn)* (Personen-)Wagen; ~ **contract** Personenbeförderungsvertrag; ~ **fares** Personentarif; ~ **list** Passagierliste; ~**(s') luggage** (or **baggage**) Reisegepäck; Passagiergut; Fluggepäck; ~ **receipts** Einnahmen aus der Personenbeförderung; ~ **service** Personenverkehr; ~ **ship** Fahrgastschiff; ~ **space** Fahrgastraum; ~ **station** Bahnhof für den Personenverkehr; ~ **steamer** Fahrgastdampfer *(opp. cargo steamer);* ~ **ticket** Schiffskarte; Flugschein; ~ **traffic** (or **transport**) Personenverkehr

passenger, air (or **aircraft**) ~ Fluggast, Luftreisender; **carriage** (or **conveyance**) **of** ~**s** Personenbeförderung; **fellow** ~ Mitreisender; **to discharge** (or **put down**) ~**s** Fluggäste (od. Schiffsreisende) absetzen; **to take on** ~**s** Fluggäste (od. Schiffsreisende) aufnehmen

passing →pass *v*

passive passiv, untätig; nicht zinstragend, unverzinslich; ~ **bond** Obligation ohne Verzinsung; ~ **debt** nicht zinstragende Forderung *(opp. active debt);* ~ **negligence** *Am* fahrlässiges Unterlassen; ~ **resistance** *pol* passiver Widerstand; ~ **trade balance** passive Handelsbilanz; ~ →**trust**

pass-over, ~ **system** *Am (AntitrustR)* Art Finanzausgleich zwischen Händlern; **profit** ~ *Am (an den geschützten Händler gezahlter)* Teil des Verkaufsgewinns

passport (Reise-)Paß; ~ **control** Paßkontrolle; ~ **forgery** Paßfälschung; ~ **formalities** Paßformalitäten; ~ **holder** Paßinhaber; ~ **inspection** Paßkontrolle; ~ **office** Paßstelle; ~ **photo (-graph)** Paßbild; **bearer of a** ~ Inhaber e-s Passes; **collective** ~ Sammelpaß; **diplomatic** ~ Diplomatenpaß; **examination of** ~**s** Paßkontrolle; **extension of a** ~ Verlängerung e-s Passes; **forgery of** ~**s** Paßfälschung; **holder of a** ~ Paßinhaber; **inspection of** ~**s** Paßkontrolle; **issue of a** ~ Ausstellung e-s Passes; **renewal of a** ~ s. extension of a →~; **ship's** ~ Schiffspaß *(→sea letter);* **valid** ~ gültiger (Reise-)Paß; **to apply for a** ~ e-n Paß beantragen; **to check** (or **examine**) **a** ~ e-n Paß prüfen; **to extend a** ~ e-n Paß verlängern; **to forge or make false statements for procuring a** ~[23] e-n Paß fälschen oder falsche Angaben zur Erlangung e-s Passes machen; **to issue a** ~ e-n Paß ausstellen; **to have a** ~ **issued** sich e-n Paß ausstellen lassen; **to produce one's** ~ seinen Paß vorzeigen; **to take out a** ~ sich e-n Paß verschaffen; **the** ~ **has expired** der Paß ist abgelaufen

past consideration in der Vergangenheit liegende und daher für die Wirksamkeit des nunmehrigen Vertrags nicht ausreichende Gegenleistung

past, ~ **due** überfällig; ~ **jobs** bisherige Berufe; ~ **year** vergangenes Jahr

pastoral letter *eccl* Hirtenbrief

pasture Weiderecht; Weideland; ~ **lot** *(Stück)* Weideland; **common of** ~ Weiderecht *(gemeinsam mit dem Eigentümer des Weidelandes);* **right of** ~ Weiderecht; **several** ~ Weiderecht *(mit der Berechtigung, dem Eigentümer des Weidelandes das Weiden seines Viehs nicht zu gestatten)*

patent 1. Urkunde, durch die ein Recht od. Privileg verliehen wird *(s. letters →~ 1.);* ~ **of nobility** *Br* Adelsbrief; **(land)** ~ *Am* Urkunde, durch die der Staat e-r Einzelperson Bundesland überträgt; **letters** ~ *(Br vom Monarchen, Am von der Regierung ausgestellte)* Urkunde, durch die ein Recht, Privileg, Amt etc verliehen wird; Bestallungsurkunde, Ernennungsurkunde (→auch patent 2.); **(letters)** ~ **of** →**precedence**

patent 2. *(PatR)* Patent *(für e-e Erfindung);* patentiert; Patent-; Marken-

patent, to abandon a ~ ein Patent (ver)fallen lassen; **to apply for (the grant of) a** ~ ein Patent anmelden; *(etw.)* zum Patent anmelden; **to avoid a** ~ ein Patent *(als ungültig)* anfechten; **to cancel a** ~ (in the register) ein Patent löschen; **a** ~ **ceases to have effect** (or **a** ~ **expires**) ein Patent erlischt; **the** ~ **covers ...** das Patent betrifft ...; **the** ~ **is denied** das Patent wird versagt; **to exploit a** ~ ein Patent verwerten; **to extend a** ~ ein Patent verlängern; **to grant a** ~ ein Patent erteilen; *(etw.)* patentieren *(cf. novelty, utility);* **to infringe a** ~ ein Patent verletzen; **to invalidate a** ~ ein Patent für ungültig erklären; **to issue a** ~ ein Patent erteilen; **the** ~ **has lapsed** das Patent ist erloschen; **to obtain a** ~ ein Patent erlangen; **to reduce a** ~ **to practice** ein Patent praktisch verwertbar machen; **to refuse to grant a** ~ ein Patent versagen; **to revoke a** ~ ein Patent widerrufen (od. für nichtig erklären); **to surrender a** ~ auf ein Patent verzichten; **to take out a** ~ (for) sich patentieren lassen; **to utilize a** ~ ein Patent auswerten; **to withhold (the grant of) a** ~ ein Patent versagen

patent acquisition Patenterwerb

Patents Act (P. A.) *Br* Patentgesetz

Das Patentgesetz von 1977 hat das britische Patentrecht grundlegend geändert und internationale Übereinkünfte in Kraft treten lassen. Eine Reihe seiner Bestimmungen ist durch den neuen Copyright, Designs and Patents Act 1988 geändert worden

patent agent[24] Patentanwalt; **Chartered Institute of P~ A~s** *Br* Patentanwaltskammer

Patent and Trademark Office *Am* Bundespatentamt; Patent- und Warenzeichenamt

patent annuity Patenjahresgebühr

patent appeal, P~s A~ Tribunal *Br* Patentgericht; **Court of Customs and P~ A~s** *Am* →court

patent applicant Patentanmelder

patent application Patentanmeldung (→*application for [a] patent);* **common** ~ gemeinsame (Einreichung der) Patentanmeldung; **copending** ~ gleichzeitig anhängige Patentanmeldung; **date of filing of the** ~ Anmeldetag; **division of the** ~ Teilung der Patentanmeldung; **European** ~ Europäische Patentanmeldung *(→ European);* **Regulations for P~ A~s** Patentanmeldebestimmungen; **to process the** ~ die Patentanmeldung behandeln; **to refuse the** ~ die Patentanmeldung zurückweisen; **to withdraw the** ~ die Patentanmeldung zurücknehmen

patent, ~ **applied for** Patent angemeldet; ~ **attorney** *Am* Patentanwalt; **P~ Bar** *Am* Patentanwaltschaft; ~ **case** Patentstreitsache; ~ **category** Patentkategorie; ~ **charges** Patentkosten; ~ **claim** Patentanspruch

patent classification Patentklassifikation; **International P~ C~**[25] Internationale Patentklassifikation (→*European Convention on the International Classification of Patents for Invention;* → *Strasbourg Agreement Concerning the International P~ C~*)

Patent Cooperation Treaty (PCT)[26] Vertrag über die internationale Zusammenarbeit auf dem Gebiet des Patentwesens (Patentzusammenarbeitsvertrag)

35 Staaten, darunter die USA, die Sowjetunion, Japan und alle westeuropäischen Länder vereinbarten, das Anmeldeverfahren für Patente sowie die Vorarbeiten für die Erteilung zu straffen

patent, ~ **description** Patentbeschreibung; ~ **dispute** Patentstreitsache; ~ **division** Patentabteilung; ~ **document** Patenturkunde; ~ **drawing** Patentzeichnung; ~ **examiner** (Patent-)Prüfer; ~ **exchange agreement** Patentaustauschvertrag; ~ **exploitation** Patentverwertung; ~ **exploitation agreement** Patentverwertungsvertrag; ~ **fee** Patentgebühr; ~ **foods** Markennahrungsmittel; ~ **for designs** *Am* s. design →~; ~ **for an improvement** Verbesserungspatent

patent for invention Erfindungspatent; **Convention on the Unification of Certain Points of Substantive Law on Patents for Invention**[27] Übereinkommen zur Vereinheitlichung gewisser Begriffe des materiellen Rechts der Erfindungspatente (Straßburger Patentübereinkommen)

patent, ~ **grant** Patenterteilung; ~ **holder** Patentinhaber; ~ **in force** gültiges Patent; ~ **infringement proceedings** Patentverletzungsverfahren; ~ **interference proceedings** (*vom Patentamt eingeleitetes*) Verfahren zur Klärung von Prioritätsfragen

patent law Patentrecht; Patentgesetz; **substantive** ~ materielles Patentrecht

patent, ~ **legislation** Patentgesetzgebung; ~ **licen|ce (~se)** Patentlizenz; ~ **licensing agreement** Patentlizenzvereinbarung; ~ **litigation** Patentprozeß; ~ **marking** Patentberühmung; ~ **medicine** Markenarznei; ~ **monopoly** Patentmonopol; ~ **of addition** Zusatzpatent

Patent Office Patentamt; **European** ~ Europäisches Patentamt (→*European);* **to obtain a patent by making an application to the** ~ **accompanied by a specification** ein Patent erhalten durch Einreichung e-r von e-r Patentbeschreibung begleiteten Patentanmeldung

Das britische Patentamt[28] ist die für die Erteilung von Patenten sowie für die Eintragung von Mustern (designs) und Warenzeichen (trademarks) zuständige Behörde. Es steht unter der Leitung des Comptroller-General (of Patents, Designs and Trade Marks).

Das amerikanische Patentamt[29] ist eine Bundesbehörde in Washington, D.C. An seiner Spitze steht der Commissioner of Patents. Es ist zuständig für Aufgaben auf dem Gebiete des Patent- und Markenwesens, bei Erteilung der →design patents auch auf dem Gebiete des Musterwesens

patent, ~ **owner** Inhaber e-s Patents; ~ **pending** Patent angemeldet (*schwebende Patentanmeldung*); ~ **pool** Patentgemeinschaft *(Verbindung mehrerer Unternehmen zum Austausch von Patenten; cf. cross-licensing);* ~ **pooling agreement** Patentaustauschabkommen; ~ **reexamination** Patent-Überprüfung; ~ **register** *Am* Patentrolle; ~ **right** Patentrecht; ~ **rolls** *Br* Patentrolle; **P~ Rules** *Br* (**P~ Rules of Practice** *Am*) Ausführungsbestimmungen zum Patentgesetz

patent specification Patentbeschreibung; Patentschrift; **complete** ~ endgültige Patentbeschreibung; **printed** ~ Patentschrift; **provisional** ~ vorläufige Patentbeschreibung

patent, ~ **term** s. term of (a) →~; ~ **without examination** ungeprüftes Patent; ~ **year** Patentjahr

patent, additional ~ Zusatzpatent

patent, applicant for a ~ Patentanmelder; **joint applicants for a** ~ Mitanmelder e-s Patents

patent, application for (a) ~ Patentanmeldung, Anmeldung e-s Patents (→*application 2. und →patent application);* **filing of an application for (a)** ~ Einreichung e-r Patentanmeldung; **subject matter of an application for (a)** ~ Gegenstand der Patentanmeldung; **to file** (or **make**) **an application for (a)** ~ e-e Patentanmeldung einreichen; ein Patent anmelden

patent, arrangement ~ Anordnungspatent; **arrogation of** ~ Patentberühmung; →**classification of** ~**s**; →**Commissioner of P**~**s**; **Comptroller-General (of P**~**s, Designs and Trade Marks)** *Br* Präsident des Patentamtes; **defensive** ~ Sperrpatent; **design** ~ *Am* Geschmacksmuster-Patent *(eigenartige und ornamentale Muster e-s Fabrikationsgegenstandes)*; **device** ~ Vorrichtungspatent; **duration of a** ~ s. term of a →~; **European** ~ Europäisches Patent (→*European)*; **exclusive** ~ Ausschließlichkeitspatent; **expired** ~ erloschenes (od. abgelaufenes) Patent; **expiry of a** ~ Erlöschen e-s Patents; **exploitation of a** ~ Patentverwertung; **extension of (the term of) a** ~ Patentverlängerung; **foreign** ~ Auslandspatent; **forfeiture of a** ~ Verfall e-s Patents

patent, grant(ing) of a ~ Erteilung e-s Patents, Patenterteilung *(cf. novelty, utility)*; **opposition to the grant(ing) of a** ~ Einspruch gegen die Erteilung e-s Patents; **to file an application for the grant of a** ~[30] ein Patent anmelden; **to refuse the grant(ing) of a** ~ die Erteilung e-s Patents ablehnen

patent, grantee of a ~ Inhaber e-s Patents, Patentinhaber; **holder of a** ~ Patentinhaber; **improvement** ~ Verbesserungspatent; **independent** ~ selbständiges Patent, Hauptpatent; **infringement of a** ~ Patentverletzung *(→infringement)*; **interfering** ~ Kollisionspatent

patent, issue (or **issuing**) **of a** ~ Erteilung e-s Patents, Patenterteilung; **issue of a** ~ **without fees** gebührenfreie Erteilung e-s Patents; **fee for issue of a** ~ Patenterteilungsgebühr; **time of issue of a** ~ Zeitpunkt der Patenterteilung

patent, lapse of a ~ Erlöschen e-s Patents; **lapsed** ~ verfallenes Patent; **restoration of lapsed** ~**s** Wiederherstellung verfallener Patente

patent, letters ~ (for an invention) Patenturkunde, (Erfindungs-)Patent; **licen|ce (-se) under a** ~ Lizenz an e-m Patent; **life of a** ~ s. term of a →~; **main** (or **original**) ~ Hauptpatent *(opp. supplemental* ~*)*; **national** ~[30a] nationales Patent (granted by a →national authority)); **owner of a** ~ Inhaber e-s Patents, Patentinhaber; **plant** ~ *Am* Pflanzenpatent; **prior** ~ älteres Patent; **process** ~ Verfahrenspatent; **product** ~ Sachpatent; **proprietor of a** ~ Patentinhaber; **refusal of a** ~ Patentversagung; **regional** ~[30a] regionales Patent; **revocation of a** ~ Zurücknahme e-s Patents; **right derived from the** ~ Recht aus dem Patent; **right to the** ~ Recht auf das Patent; **scope of a** ~ (Schutz-)Umfang e-s Patents; **special pharmaceutical** ~ pharmazeutisches Patent; **subject of a** ~ Gegenstand e-s Patents; **subsequent** ~ jüngeres Patent; **supplemental** ~ Zusatzpatent *(opp. original* ~*)*; **surrender of a** ~ →surrender; **taker-out of a** ~ Patentinhaber

patent, term of (a) ~ (Schutz-)Dauer (od. Laufzeit) e-s Patents; Patentdauer; **expiration of term of (a)** ~ Ablauf der Schutzfrist e-s Patents; **extension of term of (a)** ~ Verlängerung der Patentdauer

Br[30b] Die Patentdauer beträgt 20 Jahre.

Am Die Patentdauer beträgt 17 Jahre mit Möglichkeiten der Verlängerung

patent, termination of the ~ Ende des Patents; **unexpired** ~ noch nicht abgelaufenes (od. erloschenes) Patent; **withdrawal of a** ~ Zurücknahme e-s Patents

patent offen, offenkundig *(opp. latent)*; ~ **ambiguity** offensichtliche *(aus dem Wortlaut der Urkunde sich ergebende)* Zweideutigkeit; ~ **defect** offener (od. erkennbarer) Mangel; ~ **dissent** offener Dissens

patent *v* patentieren; patentieren lassen

patented patentiert, durch Patent geschützt; Patent-; ~ **article** durch Patent geschützter Gegenstand; ~ **process** patentiertes Verfahren; **articles made by a** ~ **process** nach e-m patentierten Verfahren hergestellte Waren

patenting, double ~ Doppelpatentierung

patentability Patentfähigkeit, Patentierbarkeit; **bar to** ~ Patenthindernis; **lack of** ~ mangelnde Patentfähigkeit

patentable patentfähig, patentierbar; ~ **invention** patentfähige Erfindung; **an application contains a** ~ **subject matter** der Gegenstand e-r Anmeldung ist patentfähig

patentee Patentinhaber; **joint** ~**s** Mitinhaber e-s Patents

paternal väterlich; ~ **authority** (or **power**) *Am* väterliche (od. elterliche) Gewalt; **my** ~ **grandfather** mein Großvater väterlicherseits

paternalism Bevormundung nach Art der väterlichen Fürsorge; **industrial** ~ *Am* soziale Fürsorge des Unternehmers

paternity Vaterschaft; uneheliche Vaterschaft; ~ **case** (or **suit**) *Am* Vaterschaftsprozeß; ~ **test** *Am*[31] Blutgruppenuntersuchung *(zur Nachweisung der Vaterschaft)*; **acknowledgment of** ~ Vaterschaftsanerkenntnis; Anerkennung der nichtehelichen Vaterschaft; **establishment of** ~ Feststellung der Vaterschaft; **recognition of** ~ s. acknowledgement of →~; **to deny** ~ die *(außereheliche)* Vaterschaft bestreiten; **to determine** (or **establish**) **the** ~ **of an illegitimate child** die Vaterschaft e-s nichtehelichen Kindes feststellen (by means of a blood test durch Blutgruppenuntersuchung)

path Pfad, Weg; **cycle** ~ Radfahrweg

patient Patient; *Br*[32] Geisteskranke(r), Geistesschwache(r); **receiver for a** ~ →receiver 2.; **restricted** ~ *Br (in e-e psychiatrische Klinik eingewiesener)* Patient, der besonderen Beschränkungen unterliegt; Patient in e-r geschlossenen Abteilung; **to admit a ~ to a hospital** e-n Patienten in e-m Krankenhaus unterbringen; *Br (auch)* e-n Geisteskranken (od. Geistesschwachen) in e-r psychiatrischen Klinik unterbringen; **to appoint a guardian for a ~** *Br* e-n Geisteskranken entmündigen; **to be confined as a ~** *Br* in e-r psychiatrischen Klinik untergebracht sein; **to make a ~ subject to an order of the Court of Protection** *Br* e-n Geisteskranken entmündigen

patrial *Br*[33] jd, der das Recht des Wohnsitzes (right of abode) im Vereinigten Königreich hat und ohne Beschränkungen ein- und ausreisen kann

patricide Vatermord; Vatermörder *(cf. matricide)*

patrimonial ererbt, Erb-

patrimony väterliches Erbteil, Erbgut

patrol (Polizei- etc)Streife; Runde: *mil* Patrouille; ~ **duty** Streifendienst; ~ **man** *Br* Verkehrswacht *(der → Automobile Association); Am* Polizist im Streifendienst; ~ **vessel** Küstenwachboot; ~ **wagon** *Am* Gefangenentransportwagen *(der Polizei);* **frontier** ~ Grenzstreife, **ice ~ service** Eiswachdienst *(e-s Schiffes);* **(police) ~ car** Funkstreife(nwagen)

patrolling policeman Polizeistreife

patron Schirmherr; Gönner, Förderer; Mäzen; *colloq.* Kunde, Kundin; regelmäßiger Besucher *(z. B. e-s Theaters); Br eccl* Patron *(der das Vorschlagsrecht auf e-e Pfründe hat)*

patronage Schirmherrschaft, Schutz, Protektion; finanzielle Unterstützung; *colloq.* Kundschaft; Besucherkreis; *Br eccl* Patronatsrecht, Vorschlagsrecht für e-e Pfründe; *Am* Ämterpatronage, Vergebung von Ämtern an Anhänger der siegreichen politischen Partei *(cf. spoils system);* ~ **discount** Treuerabatt; ~ **dividends** Gewinnausschüttungen an Kunden *(bes. an Mitglieder von cooperative societies);* ~ **refund** *Am* Kundenrabatt; **under the ~ of** unter der Schirmherrschaft von

patronize *v* unterstützen; protegieren; *colloq. (Geschäft)* als Kunde besuchen, (Stamm-)Kunde sein bei; *(Theater)* regelmäßig besuchen; *(andere Völker)* gönnerhaft behandeln

pattern Muster *(auf Stoff, Tapete etc);* Modell, Probestück; Struktur; **articles** Massenwaren; ~ **bombing** Flächenbombardierung; ~ **book** Musterbuch; ~ **card** Musterkarte; ~ **designer** Modellzeichner; ~ **of forces** *fig* Kräftebild; ~**s of organization** Organisationsformen; ~ **parcel** Mustersendung; ~ **sample** Muster, Probestück; **according to ~** nach Muster (od. Probe); **assortment** (or **collection**) **of ~s** Musterkollektion; **behavio(u)r ~** Verhaltensmuster; **by ~** nach Muster (od. Probe); **change in the ~ of trade** Änderung in der Struktur des Handels *(in der regionalen Herkunft der Ware);* **(up) to ~** s. by →~; **to correspond to ~** dem Muster entsprechen; **to make to a ~** nach Muster herstellen

pattern *v*, **to ~ (up)on** ausrichten nach

pauper Armer; Bedürftiger; *Am* Unterstützungsempfänger; *Am* im Armenrecht[33a] (in forma pauperis) Klagender (od. Beklagter) *(cf. dispauper);* ~ **costs** *Am* Armenrechtskosten[33a]; ~ **petition** *Am* Armenrechtsantrag[33a]

pauperis, to sue (or **defend**) **(an action) in forma ~** *Am* im Armenrecht klagen (od. verklagt werden)

pauperism Pauperismus, Massenarmut

pave *v* pflastern; **to ~ the way** *fig* den Weg bahnen

pavement *Br* Bürgersteig; *Am* Fahrbahn; **wrong side of ~** *Am* falsche Straßenseite

paw, cat's ~ *(willenloses)* Werkzeug

pawn (Faust-)Pfand; Pfandsache
pawnbroker[34] Pfandleiher; ~**'s business** Pfandleihgeschäft, Pfandleihe; ~**'s shop** Pfandhaus, Leihhaus, Pfandleihanstalt
pawnbrokerage ~ → pawnbroking
pawnbroking Pfandleihe
pawn, ~-shop Leihhaus, Pfandleihanstalt; ~ **ticket** Pfandschein; **by ~** pfandweise; **debt on ~** durch Pfand gesicherte Schuld; **delivery of the ~** Übergabe der Pfandsache
pawn, in ~ verpfändet; **to hold in ~** *(etw.)* als Pfand halten; **to put in** (or **to**) **~** *(etw.)* als Pfand geben, verpfänden; **to take an article in ~** e-n Gegenstand als Pfand nehmen
pawn, loan on ~ Pfanddarlehen; durch Pfand gesichertes Darlehen; **to keep a ~** ein Pfand halten; **to lend on ~** gegen Pfandbestellung Darlehen geben; **to redeem a** (or **to take out of**) **~** ein Pfand auslösen

pawn *v* verpfänden, in Pfand geben; lombardieren; **to ~ securities** (or **stock**) Wertpapiere verpfänden (od. lombardieren)
pawned verpfändet; ~ **bill of exchange** verpfändeter Wechsel; ~ **object** Pfandgegenstand, Pfandsache
pawned property verpfändete Sachen (od. Vermögensgegenstände); **sale of ~** Pfandverkauf; **to redeem ~** verpfändete Gegenstände auslösen (od. einlösen)
pawned securities verpfändete (od. lombardierte) Wertpapiere
pawning Verpfändung, Pfandbestellung, Lombardierung

pawnable verpfändbar; lombardfähig

pawnee Pfandgläubiger, Pfandnehmer

pawner (or **pawnor**) Pfandgeber, Verpfänder

pay Bezahlung; Besoldung; (Arbeits-)Lohn, Gehalt; Wehrsold; ~ **account** Lohnkonto; ~ **agreement** Lohnabkommen; ~ **as-you-earn system** → pay 1. *(Imperativ)*; ~ **back period** *Am* →~ off period; ~ **bed** *Br* Privatbett *(in e-m Krankenhaus)*; ~ **bill** *Br* Zahlungsanweisung, Kassenanweisung; ~ **book** *mil* Soldbuch; Wehrpaß; ~ **by the hour** Stundenlohn; ~ **check** *Am* Gehaltsscheck, Lohnscheck; ~ **day** (Lohn-, Gehalts-)Zahltag; *Br (Terminbörse)* Abrechnungstag; ~ **envelope** Lohntüte; ~ **freeze** Lohnstop(p); ~ **grade** (or **group**) Besoldungsgruppe; ~ **increase** Gehaltserhöhung, Lohnerhöhung; ~ **level** *Am* Gehaltsstufe; ~**load** Nutzlast *(e-s Flugzeugs, Schiffs)*; *Am* finanzielle Belastung *(e-s Unternehmens)* durch Löhne und Gehälter

paymaster Zahlmeister; Schatzmeister; **P~ General** *Br* Beamter an der Spitze von Regierungsabteilungen *(bes. für Streitkräfte und Staatsdienst)*; *Am mil* Generalzahlmeister

pay-off *sl.* Abrechnung; Auszahlung; *Am* Bestechungsgeld; *Br colloq.* Anteil an durch Verbrechen erworbenem Gewinn

pay-off period *Am* Kapitalrückflußdauer; Zeitabschnitt, in dem sich e-e Investition bezahlt macht *(cf. cash flow, price-earnings ratio)*

pay office Zahlstelle; Lohnbüro

pay out Ausschüttung; Dividendenzahlung; ~ **ratio** ausgeschüttete Dividende in Prozenten des Bilanzgewinns

pay, ~ **packet** Lohntüte; ~ **phone** *Am* Münzfernsprecher; ~ **plan** *Am* Besoldungsordnung; ~ **rate** Stundenlohnsatz; Akkordlohnsatz; ~ **restraint** Zurückhaltung bei Lohnforderungen; ~ **rise** Lohnerhöhung, Gehaltserhöhung

pay(-)roll Lohnliste, Gehaltsliste; Löhne und Gehälter, Lohnsumme; ~ **account** *Am* Lohnkonto, Gehaltskonto; ~ **book** Lohnliste, Gehaltsliste; ~ **clerk** Lohnbuchhalter; ~ **deductions** *Am* Abzüge vom Lohn oder Gehalt *(gesetzliche Abzüge, z.B. Sozialversicherung; private Abzüge, z.B. Krankenversicherung)*; ~ **department** Lohnbüro; ~ **file** *Am* Lohndatei; ~ **period** *Am* Lohnzahlungszeitraum; ~ **records** *Am* Lohn- und Gehaltsunterlagen; ~ **robbery** *Am* Lohn- und Gehaltsunterlagen; ~ **robbery** Lohnkassenraub; ~ **sheet** Lohnliste, Gehaltsliste; ~ **tax** Sozialversicherungsbeitrag; **to be on the** ~ **of sb.** bei jdm angestellt sein; **to be off the** ~ arbeitslos (od. ohne Anstellung) sein; **to be taken off the** ~ entlassen werden

pay, ~ **scale** Lohntabelle; ~ **slip** *Br* Lohnzettel *(mit Lohnberechnung, Steuerabzügen etc.)*; **P~-TV** Abonnementfernsehen; ~ **voucher** Zahlungsanweisung, Kassenanweisung

pay, additional ~ Gehaltszulage, Zuschuß; **deduction from** ~ Lohnabzug; **dismissal** ~ *Am* Entlassungsabfindung; **equal** ~ **for equal work** gleicher Lohn für gleiche Arbeit; **extra** ~ Zulage *(zum Gehalt od. Lohn)*

pay, full ~ voller Lohn, volles Gehalt; **to restore to full** ~ *(Offizier)* reaktivieren; **to be retired on full** ~ mit vollem Gehalt pensioniert sein

pay, holiday(s) *Br* (**vacation** *Am*) **with (without)** ~ bezahlter (unbezahlter) Urlaub; **in the** ~ **of** beschäftigt bei; **military** ~ Wehrsold; **month's** ~ Monatsgehalt; **net** ~ Nettolohn, Nettogehalt; **weekly** ~ Wochenlohn; **without** ~ unbezahlt

pay *v* 1. *(Imperativ)* zahlen Sie; ~**-as-you-earn system** *(PAYE) Br* (~ **as you go system** *Am*) Quellenabzugsverfahren *(Arbeitgeber führt Steuer sofort bei Auszahlung des Gehalts od. Lohns ab)*; ~ **as-you-pollute principle** *(Umweltschutz)* Verursacherprinzip; ~ **cash** *Br (Ungültigmachung des crossing e-s Schecks)* gegen bar, in bar zahlbar; ~ **self** *(beim Scheck)* zahlen Sie an mich; ~ **selves** *(beim Scheck)* zahlen Sie an uns

pay *v* 2. (be)zahlen, begleichen; *(Gläubiger)* befriedigen; *(Wechsel)* einlösen; sich bezahlt machen (od. rentieren); **to** ~ **an account** e-e Rechnung bezahlen; **to** ~ **on account** *(etw.)* anzahlen; *Am* abbezahlen; **to** ~ **in advance** (or **in anticipation**) im voraus (be)zahlen, voraus(be)zahlen; **to** ~ **attention (to)** *(etw.)* beachten, aufpassen; **to** ~ **the balance** den Restbetrag bezahlen; **to** ~ **a p. through a bank** jdm Geld durch e-e Bank überweisen; **to** ~ **a bill** e-e Rechnung bezahlen; e-n Wechsel einlösen; **to** ~ **a bill for hono(u)r** e-n Wechsel ehrenhalber zahlen (od. einlösen); **to** ~ **by means of a bill** mit e-m Wechsel bezahlen; **to** ~ **by instal(l)ments** in Raten zahlen, Teilzahlung leisten; **to** ~ **by the month** monatlich bezahlen; **to** ~ **a call on sb.** jdm e-n Besuch machen; **to** ~ **a call on (partly paid) shares** (or **stock**) die geforderte Einlage (Teilzahlung) auf Aktien leisten; **to** ~ **(in) cash** bar (be)zahlen; **to** ~ **by cheque (check)** mit Scheck bezahlen; **to** ~ **one's compliments to sb.** jdm e-n Höflichkeitsbesuch machen; **to** ~ **one's contribution** s-n Beitrag leisten; **to** ~ **damages** Schadensersatz leisten; **to** ~ **one's debts** s-e Schulden bezahlen; **to** ~ **a deposit** anzahlen; Draufgeld bezahlen; **to** ~ **duty** (on) Zoll bezahlen (auf), verzollen; **to** ~ **the expense(s)** (of) die Kosten tragen (od. aufbringen) (für); aufkommen (für); **to** ~ **final homage** (or **one's final respects**) **to sb.** jdm die letzte Ehre erweisen; **to** ~ **promptly** umgehend zahlen; **to** ~ **sb. a visit** jdm e-n Besuch machen (od. abstatten); **to** ~ **one's way** ohne Verlust arbeiten; für s-n Unterhalt aufkommen (können); genug zum Lebensunterhalt verdienen

pay *v*, **to** ~ **back** zurückzahlen, zurückerstatten;

to ~ **down** anzahlen, Anzahlung leisten; **to ~ for** *(jdn od. etw.)* bezahlen; **to ~ (a bill of exchange) for hono(u)r** e-n Wechsel als Intervenient zahlen; zu Ehren (von) zahlen; **to ~ for oneself** für sich selbst zahlen (od. aufkommen); **to ~ in** einzahlen, *(auf Konto)* zahlen; *(Geld)* einschießen; **to ~ in full** ganz (od. voll) bezahlen; **to ~ in full or by instal(l)ments** im ganzen oder in Raten bezahlen; **to ~ into an account** auf ein Konto einzahlen; **to ~ into court** Geld bei Gericht hinterlegen; **to ~ off** *(vollständig)* abzahlen, tilgen; *Am (jdn)* auszahlen; *(Mannschaft)* abmustern; **to ~ off bonds** Obligationen einlösen; **to ~ off a creditor** e-n Gläubiger befriedigen; **to ~ off a debt** e-e Schuld abzahlen (od. tilgen); **to ~ off a dismissed employee** *Am* e-n entlassenen Angestellten auszahlen; **to ~ off a loan** ein Darlehen zurückzahlen; **to ~ off a mortgage** e-e Hypothek tilgen (od. ablösen); **to ~ on account** anzahlen; **to ~ out** aus(be)zahlen; *(Geld)* ausgeben; **to ~ up** voll bezahlen; **to ~ up shares (in full)** Aktien voll einzahlen; **to ~ well** sich gut rentieren (od. bezahlt machen); gut zahlen

pay *v*, **ability to ~** Zahlungsfähigkeit, Solvenz; **able to ~** zahlungsfähig; **failure to ~** Nichtzahlung; **failure to ~ on due date** (or **on time**) Zahlungsverzug; **committal to prison for failure to ~ a fine** Ersatzfreiheitsstrafe; **inability to ~** Zahlungsunfähigkeit; **notice to ~** Zahlungsaufforderung; **promise to ~** Zahlungsversprechen; **request to ~** Zahlungsaufforderung; **unable to ~** zahlungsunfähig; **it ~s (does not ~)** es rentiert sich (rentiert sich nicht)

paying zahlend; einträglich, rentabel; **~ agent** Zahlstelle *(e-r Bank)*; **~ bank** *(beim internationalen Zahlungsverkehr)* beauftragte Bank; **~ business** rentables (od. einträgliches) Geschäft; **~ cashier** auszahlender Schalterbeamter; **~ concern** gewinnbringendes (od. rentables) Unternehmen; **~ counter** (Auszahlungs-)Kasse; **~ guest** Pensionär

paying in Einzahlung; **~ book** *Br* Einzahlungsbuch; **~ slip** *Br* Einzahlungsbeleg

paying off Ab(be)zahlung, Tilgung; *Am* Auszahlung; **~ creditors** Befriedigung von Gläubigern; **~ a mortgage** Tilgung (od. Ablösung) e-r Hypothek

paying, ~ office *(money orders etc)* Zahlstelle *(opp. issuing office)*; **~ out** Auszahlung

paying, not ~ unrentabel

payable zahlbar, fällig; rentabel, lohnend; **~s** *Am (Bilanz)* Kreditoren, Verbindlichkeiten; **~ at (after) sight** (*Wechsel*) zahlbar bei (nach) Sicht; **~ in advance** im voraus zahlbar; vorauszahlbar; **~ in arrears** postnumerando zahlbar; **~ in cash** in bar zahlbar; **~ on delivery** zahlbar bei Lieferung; **~ on demand** (*Wechsel*) zahlbar bei Sicht; **~ on presentation** (*Wechsel*) zahlbar bei Vorlage; **~ to bearer** zahlbar an den Überbringer; **~ to order** zahlbar an Order; an Order lautend; **~ when due** (or **at maturity**) bei Fälligkeit zahlbar; **bills ~** →bill 4.; **mortgages ~** Hypothekenschulden; **notes ~** →note 1.; **the interest is ~ from** die Zinsen laufen vom

PAYE *Br* →pay-as-you-earn

payee Zahlungsempfänger; **~ of a bill (of exchange)** Wechselnehmer, Remittent; **~ of a cheque (check)** Zahlungsempfänger e-s Schecks; **~ of a money order** Empfänger e-r Zahlungsanweisung; →**fictitious ~**

payer Zahler; (Ein-, Aus-)Zahlender; **~ benefit** *Am (VersR)* Prämienbefreiung bei Tod od. Invalidität; **~ for hono(u)r** *(WechselR)* Ehrenzahler, Honorant; **prompt** (or **punctual**) **~** pünktlicher Zahler; **slow ~** säumiger Zahler; **tax~** Steuerzahler

payless vacation *Am* unbezahlter Urlaub

paymaster →pay

payment (payt, paymt, pt) (Be-)Zahlung; Zahlungsleistung; Begleichung *(von Schulden)*; Befriedigung *(von Gläubigern)*; Einzahlung, Auszahlung; Einlösung *(e-s Wechsels, Schecks)*; **~s** Zahlungsverkehr

payment, to anticipate a ~ im voraus (od. vor Fälligkeit) zahlen; **to be in arrears** (or **behind**) **with one's ~s** mit s-n Zahlungen im Verzuge sein; **to be punctual in one's ~s** s-e Zahlungen pünktlich erledigen; s-n Zahlungsverpflichtungen pünktlich nachkommen; **to cease ~s** Zahlungen einstellen *(Bank)*; **to claim** (or **demand**) **~** Zahlung verlangen, zur Zahlung auffordern; **to delay (in making) ~** mit der Zahlung im Verzug sein; **to effect (a) ~** s. to make a →~; **to enforce the ~ of debts** Schulden *(gerichtl.)* beitreiben; **to give in ~** in Zahlung geben; **to keep up one's ~s** s-e Zahlungsverpflichtungen einhalten

payment, to make (a) ~ Zahlung leisten, bezahlen; **to make a strong demand for ~** Zahlung nachdrücklich fordern; **to make a ~ a week in advance** e-e Woche im voraus zahlen; **failure to make a ~** Nichtzahlung; **~ is made in dollars** die Zahlung erfolgt in Dollar

payment, to meet the ~s die (Raten-)Zahlungen einhalten; **to postpone the ~** die Zahlung aufschieben; **to press for ~** Zahlung nachdrücklich fordern; **to receive ~s** Zahlungen entgegennehmen; **to refuse ~** Zahlung verweigern; **to request ~** Zahlung fordern; **to resume ~s** Zahlungen wieder aufnehmen; **to settle ~s in dollars** Zahlungen in Dollar durchführen; **to stop** (or **suspend**) **~s** Zahlungen einstellen; **to sue for ~** Zahlung einklagen, auf Zahlung klagen

payment, ~ against documents Bezahlung *(der*

Ware) gegen Aushändigung der Verschiffungsdokumente; ~**s agreement** Zahlungsabkommen; ~ **appropriation** (*EG*) Zahlungsermächtigung; ~**s arrangement** Zahlungsregelung; ~ **behavio(u)r** Zahlungsverhalten; ~ **bill** zur Zahlung vorgelegter Wechsel (*opp. acceptance bill*); ~ **bond** Zahlungsgarantie; ~ **by instal(l)ments** Ratenzahlung, Abschlagszahlung; ~ **by results** Leistungslohn (*z. B. piece rate system*); ~ **card** Zahlungskarte (*von Banken zum bargeldlosen Zahlungsverkehr, z. B. Eurocard*); ~ **countermanded** *(Scheckvermerk)* Zahlung gesperrt; ~ **date** Zahlungstermin; ~ **deadline** Zahlungsfrist; ~**s deficit** Defizit in der Zahlungsbilanz; ~**s due** fällige Zahlungen; ~ **for breakage** Refaktie; ~ **for hono(u)r**[35] Ehrenzahlung, Interventionszahlung (*für e-n notleidenden Wechsel*); ~ **(for hono[u]r) supra protest**[36] Ehrenzahlung nach Protest; ~ **guarantee (guaranty)** Zahlungsgarantie; ~ **in advance** Voraus(be)zahlung; ~ **in anticipation** Voraus(be)zahlung; ~ **in arrears** rückständige Zahlung; ~ **in cash** Bar(be)zahlung; ~ **in due course**[37] ordnungsmäßige Zahlung; ~ **in full** volle (Ein-)Zahlung; ~ **in kind** Naturalleistung, Sachleistung; ~ **in part** s. part →~; ~ **into a bank account** Einzahlung auf ein Bankkonto; ~ **into court** Hinterlegung (*e-s Geldbetrages*) bei dem (Prozeß-)Gericht; ~ **of (the) balance** Restzahlung; ~ **of a bill** Einlösung e-s Wechsels; ~ **of calls** *(AktienR)* Leistung der (*von der Gesellschaft*) geforderten Beträge auf gezeichnete Aktien; ~ **of dues** Beitragszahlung, Beitragsleistung; ~ **of duty** Verzollung; Versteuerung; ~ **of interest** Zinszahlung, Verzinsung; ~ **on account** Teilzahlung; Akontozahlung, Abschlagszahlung, Anzahlung; ~ **on account of costs** Kostenvorschuß (*auf Anwaltsgebühren*); ~ **on deferred terms** *Am* Ratenzahlung; ~ **on delivery** →cash on delivery; ~ **order** *(internationaler)* Zahlungsauftrag; ~ **receipt** Zahlungsquittung; ~ **received** Betrag erhalten; eingegangene Zahlung, Zahlungseingang; ~ **stop** Schecksperre; ~**s surplus** Zahlungsbilanzüberschuß; ~ **terms** Zahlungsbedingungen; ~**s to and from foreign countries** internationaler Zahlungsverkehr; ~ **transactions** Zahlungsverkehr; ~ **with order** →cash with order

payment, additional ~ zusätzliche Zahlung; Nach(be)zahlung; Nachschuß; **liability to make an additional** ~ Nachschußpflicht; **to call for an additional** ~ Nachschuß einfordern; **to make an additional** ~ nach(be)zahlen; nachschießen; Nach(be)zahlung (od. Nachschuß) leisten

payment, →advance ~; against ~ gegen Bezahlung, entgeltlich; **anticipated** ~ Vorauszahlung, Vorschuß; **application for** ~ Zahlungsaufforderung; **balance of** ~**s** Zahlungsbilanz (→*balance 2.)*; **cash** ~**(s)** Zahlung in bar, Barzahlung; **cessation of** ~ Zahlungseinstellung; **clean** ~ *(internationaler Zahlungsverkehr)* Bezahlung gegen offene Rechnung; **conditions of** ~ Zahlungsbedingungen, **confirmation of** ~ Zahlungsbestätigung; **countermand of** ~ Zahlungswiderruf; Schecksperre; **current** ~**s** laufende Zahlungen

payment, date of (or **for**) ~ Datum der Zahlung, Zahlungstermin; **to agree upon a date for (the)** ~ e-n Zeitpunkt für die Zahlung vereinbaren

payment, default in ~ Nichtzahlung, Zahlungsverzug; **deferred** ~ *Am* Ratenzahlung, Abzahlung; **deficit in** ~ Zahlungsausfall

payment, delay in ~ Zahlungsverzug; Zahlungsaufschub; **to grant a delay in** ~ Zahlungsaufschub gewähren, stunden; **to obtain a delay in** ~ Zahlungsaufschub (od. Stundung) erlangen; **there has been a delay in** ~ es wurde nicht pünktlich gezahlt

payment, demand for ~ Zahlungsaufforderung; Mahnung; **down** ~ Anzahlung (→*down); due* ~ ordnungsgemäße Bezahlung; **evading** ~ **of one's bill** Zechprellerei; **evidence of** ~ Zahlungsnachweis; **failing** ~ mangels Zahlung; **failure to make** ~ Nichtzahlung; **final** ~ Restzahlung, Abschlußzahlung; **form of** ~ Zahlungsweise; **in full and final** ~ als endgültige Abfindung; **the expenses incidental to the** ~ die Kosten der Zahlung; **incoming** ~ Zahlungseingang; **in lieu of a** ~ an Zahlungs Statt; **instead (by way) of** ~ an Zahlungs Statt; **instrument of** ~ Zahlungsmittel; **international** ~**s** internationaler Zahlungsverkehr; **late** ~ verspätete Zahlung; **lump sum** ~ Pauschalzahlung; **means of** ~ Zahlungsmittel; **method** (or **mode**) **of** ~ Zahlungsweise; **monthly** ~ monatliche Zahlung; **non(-)**~ Nichtzahlung; Nichteinlösung *(e-s Wechsels);* **on** ~ **of** gegen Bezahlung von; **order for** ~ (Aus-)Zahlungsanweisung; **part(ial)** ~ Teilzahlung, Ratenzahlung; **period allowed for** ~ Zahlungsziel; **periodical** ~**(s) (of maintenance)** regelmäßige (Unterhalts-)Zahlung(en); **place of** ~ Zahlungsort; **prompt** ~ schnelle Bezahlung; **receipt of a** ~ Eingang e-r Zahlung; **receipts and** ~**s** Einnahmen und Ausgaben *(e-r Bank);* **refusal of** ~ Zahlungsverweigerung; **regulation of** ~**s** Regelung des Zahlungsverkehrs; **request for** ~ Zahlungsaufforderung

payment, subsequent (or **supplementary**) ~ Nach(be)zahlung; Nachschuß; **to make a subsequent** (or **supplementary**) ~ nach(be)zahlen; nachschießen

payment, suspension of ~**s** Zahlungseinstellung; **term of** ~ Zahlungsfrist; →**terms of** ~

payment, time (fixed) for ~ Zahlungstermin, Zahlungsfrist; **to extend** (or **grant an extension of**) **the time for** ~ Zahlungsfrist gewähren, stunden

payment, upon ~ of gegen Zahlung von; **for want of ~** mangels Zahlung; **without ~** unentgeltlich, gratis; kostenlos

payola *bes. Am* (Bezahlung von) Bestechungsgeld *(für Werbung bes. im Radio od. Fernsehen)*

payor bank *Am*[38] zahlende Bank

payroll →pay

peace 1. *(VölkerR)* Frieden *(opp. war)*
peace approach, to make a tentative ~ Friedensfühler ausstrecken
peace, ~ conference Friedenskonferenz; **~ efforts** Friedensbemühungen; **~ establishment** (or **footing**) *mil* Friedensstärke
peace feelers, to put out ~ Friedensfühler ausstrecken
peaceful friedlich; **~ change** *(VölkerR)* friedliche Veränderung (od. Revision) *(Verfahren zur Änderung des status quo ohne Gewaltanwendung)*; **~ coexistence** *pol* friedliche Koexistenz; **~ penetration** *(VölkerR)* friedliche Durchdringung; **~ →pressure; ~ use of atomic energy** friedliche Nutzung der Kernenergie; **application of atomic energy to ~ pursuits** Anwendung der Atomenergie für friedliche Zwecke; **~ settlement of disputes** friedliche Beilegung von Streitigkeiten *(cf. European Convention for the P~ Settlement of Disputes)*

peace, ~ guarantee Friedensgarantie; **~ with hono(u)r** ehrenvoller Frieden; **~-keeping force** Friedensstreitmacht; **~-keeping operation** Friedensoperation; **~-loving** friedliebend; **~ movement** Friedensbewegung; **~ negotiations** Friedensverhandlungen; **~ offensive** Friedensoffensive; **~ offer** (or **overture**) Friedensangebot; **~ preliminaries** Friedensvorverhandlungen, Vorfrieden(svertrag); **~ research** Friedensforschung
peace, ~ settlement Friedensregelung, friedensvertragliche Regelung; **~ society** Friedensgesellschaft; **~ terms** Friedensbedingungen
peacetime Friedenszeit; in Friedenszeiten; **~ economy** Friedenswirtschaft; **~ needs** (or **requirements**) Friedensbedarf; **~ production** Friedensproduktion; **changing over** (or **conversion**) **of an industry from ~ production to production of war materials** Umstellung e-r Industrie von der Friedens- auf Kriegsproduktion; **in ~** im Frieden
peace treaty Friedensvertrag; **conclusion of a ~** Abschluß e-s Friedensvertrages; **to sign a ~** e-n Friedensvertrag unterzeichnen
peace, appeal for ~ Friedensappell; **at ~** im Frieden; **breach of the ~** (or **of a ~ treaty**) Friedensbruch; **conclusion of ~** Friedensschluß; **conditions of ~** Friedensbedingungen; **desire for ~** Friedenswunsch; Sehnsucht nach Frieden; **dictated ~** Diktatfrieden; **efforts to maintain ~** Friedensbemühungen; **enduring** (or **lasting**) **~** dauerhafter Frieden; **just ~** gerechter Frieden
peace, maintenance of (or **maintaining**) **~** Erhaltung (od. Wahrung) des Friedens; **to contribute to the maintenance of ~** zur Erhaltung des Friedens beitragen
peace, measures for maintaining ~ (Maßnahmen zur) Friedenssicherung
peace, mediation of ~ Friedensvermittlung; **negotiation of ~** Friedensverhandlung; **overture of ~** Friedensangebot; **preservation of ~** Erhaltung des Friedens; **prospects of ~** Friedensaussichten; **threat to (the) ~** Bedrohung des Friedens, Friedensbedrohung; **treaty of ~** → **~ treaty**; **violation of the ~** (or **of a ~ treaty**) Friedensbruch, Verletzung des Friedens; **will for ~** Friedenswille; **to be at ~ with a country** mit e-m Land im Frieden(szustand) leben; **to conclude ~** Frieden schließen; **to consolidate (the) ~** den Frieden festigen; **to endanger (the) ~** den Frieden gefährden; **to maintain ~** den Frieden erhalten; **to restore ~** den Frieden wiederherstellen; **to strengthen ~** den Frieden festigen
peace 2. *(innerstaatl.)* öffentliche Sicherheit und Ordnung; **~breaker** Störer der öffentl. Sicherheit und Ordnung; **~breaking** Störung der öffentl. Sicherheit und Ordnung; **~ officer** Beamter der öffentl. Sicherheit und Ordnung; Polizist *(Br constables, coroners, justices or sheriffs; Am constables, sheriffs, members of the police force)*; **breach of the ~** Störung der öffentl. Sicherheit und Ordnung *(cf. unlawful assemblies, riots, forcible entry and detainer)*; Bruch des Friedens[38a]; **Commission of the P~** *Br* der die →justices of the peace ernennende Ausschuß; **disturbance of** (or **disturbing the**) **~** Störung der öffentl. Sicherheit und Ordnung; **the Queen's ~** *Br* Landesfrieden; öffentl. Sicherheit und Ordnung; **to break the ~** (or **to commit a breach of the ~**) die öffentl. Sicherheit und Ordnung stören; **to keep the ~** die öffentl. Sicherheit und Ordnung wahren

peak höchster Stand, Höchststand; Konjunkturhoch(stand); Spitzen-; **~ demand** Spitzenbedarf; **~ hour(s) (of traffic)** Hauptverkehrsstunde(n)
peak level Höchststand *(Preise, Kurse)*; **to reach ~s** *(Börse)* Höchstkurse erzielen
peak, ~ load Spitzenbelastung; **~ output** Höchstproduktion; **~ performance** Spitzenleistung; **~ price** Höchstpreis; Höchstkurs; **~ sales** Spitzenverkaufszahlen; **~ season** Hauptsaison; Hochsaison; **~ traffic period** Verkehrsspitze; **~ wage** Spitzenlohn; **~ yield** Spitzenertrag; **to reach the ~** den Höchststand erreichen

peasantry Bauern(schaft), Landvolk

peculate *v (bes. öffentl. Gelder)* unterschlagen, veruntreuen

peculation Unterschlagung, Veruntreuung *(bes. öffentl. Gelder);* Amtsunterschlagung

peculiar 1. eigen(tümlich) (to für); besonder; ~ **characteristics** *Am (AntitrustR)* besondere Eigenschaften

peculiar 2. *Br* besondere Kirche (od. Kirchengemeinde), die nicht der Gerichtsbarkeit des zuständigen →ordinary untersteht *(z.B. Royal ~s = the sovereign's free chapel)*

peculiarity Besonderheit; **special ~ies** besondere Kennzeichen *(im Paß)*

pecuniary advantage Vermögensvorteil; **to gain a** ~ e-n Vermögensvorteil erlangen

pecuniary, ~ **aid** (or **assistance**) finanzielle Unterstützung; ~ **benefit** Vermögensvorteil; ~ **circumstances** Vermögensverhältnisse, Vermögenslage; ~ **claim** Geldforderung; vermögensrechtlicher Anspruch; ~ **compensation** Entschädigung in Geld; ~ **considerations** finanzielle Erwägungen; ~ **damage** Vermögensschaden, Vermögensnachteil; ~ **damages** Geldentschädigung; ~ **difficulties** Geldschwierigkeiten, finanzielle Schwierigkeiten; ~ **interest** finanzielles Interesse; finanzielle Beteiligung; ~ **legacy** Vermächtnis in Geld; ~ **loss** Vermögensschaden, finanzieller Verlust; ~ **obligations** finanzielle Verpflichtungen; ~ **prejudice** Vermögensnachteil; ~ **resources** Geldquellen, Geldmittel; **for (without)** ~ **reward** gegen (ohne) Entgelt

peddle *v* hausieren; Reisegewerbe betreiben

peddling Hausieren; Hausierhandel; Reisegewerbe

peddler →pedlar

peddlery *Am* →pedlary

pedestrian, ~ **crossing** Fußgängerübergang, Zebrastreifen; ~ **precinct** (or **zone**) Fußgängerzone

pedigree Stammbaum; Abstammung, Herkunft

pedlar Hausierer; Reisegewerbetreibender; **~'s certificate** *Br* (**~'s license** *Am*)Reisegewerbekarte

pedlary Hausieren; Hausierhandel; Reisegewerbe

peer *Br* Angehöriger des brit. Hochadels mit Anspruch auf Sitz im Oberhaus *(duke, marquis, earl, viscount, baron);* **life** ~ Peer auf Lebenszeit *(nicht erbl. Adelstitel);* **to create a p.** ~[39] jdn zum Peer ernennen

peerage *Br*[40] Gesamtheit der Peers; Peer-Würde; Adelsstand; Adelskalender; **life** ~[41] *(nicht erbl.)* Peerswürde auf Lebenszeit; **to raise to the** ~ in den (höheren) Adelsstand erheben

peeress *Br* Inhaberin der Peer-Würde; Ehefrau e-s →peer; **~-in-her-own-right** Peeress aus eigenem Recht *(wenn in Familien des Hochadels keine männl. Namensträger vorhanden sind, darf seit 1949 auch e-e Frau, der der Titel zusteht, den Oberhaussitz annehmen)*

peg *v (Markt, Kurse, Preise)* stützen (od. halten); ~ **ged price** gestützter (od. künstlich gehaltener) Preis (od. Kurs)

pejoration *Scot* Verschlechterung, Wertminderung *(opp. melioration)*

PEN (Club) (Poets, Essayists and Novelists) *(1921 gegr.)* Internationale Schriftstellervereinigung *(Sitz: London, Globe House)*

penal Straf-, strafrechtlich; strafbar *(weitergehend als criminal, bezieht sich nicht nur auf crimes);* ~ **act** strafbare Handlung; ~ **action** Klage auf Beitreibung e-r gesetzl. →penalty *(als Strafe, Ggs. Schadensersatzklage);* ~ **bond** Versprechen e-r Konventionalstrafe; ~ **clause** →penalty clause; ~ **code** Strafgesetzbuch (StGB) *(cf. Model P~ Code);* ~ **duty** Strafzoll; ~ **establishment** (or **institution**) Straf(vollzugs)anstalt, Gefängnis; ~ **interest** *Am* Verzugszinsen; ~ **jurisdiction** Strafgerichtsbarkeit; ~ **law** Strafrecht; Strafgesetz *(das e-e penalty verhängt);* ~ **legislation** Strafgesetzgebung; ~ **liability** *Am* strafrechtl. Verantwortlichkeit (od. Haftung); ~ **provision** (or **regulation**) Strafbestimmung; ~ **reform** Strafrechtsreform; ~ **servitude** *Br hist*[42] Zuchthaus(strafe); ~ **statute** Strafgesetz; ~ **suit** *Am* →~ action; ~ **sum** Vertragsstrafe, Konventionalstrafe; ~ **term** Strafzeit

penalization Bestrafung; strafrechtliche Verfolgung; Benachteiligung

penalize *v* mit Strafe belegen; bestrafen; schlechter stellen

penalt|y Strafe, *bes.* Geldstrafe; *Am (SteuerR)* Strafzuschlag; **~ies** Zwangsgeld *(z.B. Art. 172 EWG-Vertrag);* ~ **clause** Vertragsstrafeklausel; Strafklausel *(in e-m Vertrag);* Vereinbarung e-r Vertragsstrafe; ~ **duty** Strafzoll; ~ **envelope** *Am* Umschlag frei durch Ablösung, frankierter Dienstumschlag; ~ **for non-performance of a contract** Vertragsstrafe, Konventionalstrafe; ~ **rate** *Am* höherer Lohnsatz *(für Überstunden, Sonntagsarbeit od. gefährliche Arbeit);* Gefahrenzulage; ~ **tax** *Am*[43] Steuer mit Strafcharakter

penalty, abatement of ~ Strafermäßigung; **civil** ~ *Am* zivilrechtliche Strafe *(z.B. forfeiture, fine);* **contractual** ~ Vertragsstrafe, Konventionalstrafe; **customs** ~ Zollstrafe; **death** ~ Todesstrafe; **determination of the** ~ Strafzumessung; **extreme** ~ Todesstrafe; **fiscal** ~ Steuerstrafe; **when fixing the** ~ bei der Strafzumessung; **forbidden under** ~ **of a fine** bei Geldstrafe verboten; **forbidden under a** ~ **of**

£10 bei e-r Strafe von £10 verboten; **heavy** ~ schwere (od. hohe) Strafe; **imposition of a** ~ Verhängung e-r Strafe; **increase of** ~ Straferhöhung, Strafverschärfung; **increased** ~ verschärfte Strafe; **light** ~ leichte Strafe; **maximum** ~ Höchststrafe; **minimum** ~ Mindeststrafe; **on** ~ **of** bei (Androhung) e-r Strafe von; **on** ~ **of death** bei Todesstrafe; **pecuniary** ~ Geldstrafe; **recovery of a** ~ Beitreibung e-r Geldstrafe; **remission of a** ~ Straferlaß; **severe** ~ schwere Strafe; **under** ~ **of** s. on →~ of

penalty, to carry (or **entail**) **a** ~ e-e Bestrafung nach sich ziehen; **to fix a** ~ e-e Strafe festsetzen; das Strafmaß bestimmen; **to impose a** ~ **on a p.** jdn mit e-r Strafe belegen; e-e Strafe verhängen gegen jdn; **to incur a** ~ sich strafbar machen; e-e Strafe verwirken; **to inflict a** ~ e-e Strafe verhängen (on gegen); *(jdn)* bestrafen; **to be liable to a** ~ **of £20** mit e-r Geldstrafe von £20 zu bestrafen sein; **to make o.s. liable to a** ~ sich strafbar machen; **to remit a** ~ e-e Strafe erlassen; **to recover a** ~ e-e Geldstrafe beitreiben (od einziehen)

pendency Schweben, Schwebezeit; Anhängigsein *(e-s Prozesses)*; Rechtshängigkeit; ~ **of the application** *(PatR)* Anhängigkeit der Anmeldung

pendente lite so lange ein gerichtliches Verfahren anhängig ist

pending schwebend, noch nicht entschieden; *(bei Gericht)* anhängig; während, bis zu; ~ **action** anhängiger (od. schwebender) Rechtsstreit *(lis pendens)*; ~ **the action** während der Dauer des Prozesses; solange der Prozeß schwebt; ~ **application** *(PatR)* anhängige Anmeldung; ~ **at law** rechtshängig; ~ **bill** anhängige (od. schwebende) Gesetzesvorlage; ~ **in court** rechtshängig; ~ **debts** ungeregelte Schulden; ~ **delivery** bis zur Ablieferung; ~ **file** Akte für Unerledigtes; ~ **final decision** bis zur endgültigen Entscheidung; ~ **instructions** bis zum Eintreffen von Weisungen; bis auf weiteres; ~ **lawsuit** *(bes. Am)* schwebendes (od. anhängiges) Verfahren; ~ **litigation** anhängiger Prozess; ~ **loss** *(VersR)* noch nicht regulierter Schaden; ~ **(the) negotiations** während der Dauer der Verhandlungen; solange die Verhandlungen schweben; ~ **operations** schwebende Transaktionen; ~ **payment** bis zur Bezahlung; ~ **proceedings** schwebendes (od. anhängiges) Gerichtsverfahren; ~ **problems** (or **questions**) ungelöste Fragen; ~ **suit** →~ action; **cases** ~ schwebende Strafsachen; **to be** ~ anhängig sein, schweben

penetration *(StrafR)* Vereinigung der Geschlechtsteile *(Tatbestandsmerkmal von →rape)*

penitentiary *Am* Gefängnis

Am penitentiary wird in einigen Staaten statt prison gebraucht, in anderen für größere county jails. Es dient meist zur Vollstreckung von Strafen, denen die Verurteilung wegen e-r felony zugrunde liegt

penny (*pl.* pence) *Am* Eincentstück, *Br* **(new)** ~ (p) 1/100 e-s englischen Pfundes; ~ **bank** *Br* →savings bank; ~ **stock** *Am* Kleinaktien *(die zum Preise von weniger als 1 Dollar gehandelt werden)*

penological kriminalkundlich; Strafrechts-; ~ **research** Erforschung der Wirkung der Strafe

penology Pönologie, Lehre von den Strafen und ihrer Vollstreckung

pension Pension, Ruhegehalt, Ruhegeld; Rente; Altersversorgung; *Br* bestimmte bei der Universität Cambridge zu zahlende Gebühren; *Br* beratende Versammlung der Vorstandsmitglieder (benchers) der Gray's →Inn; ~**s** Versorgungsbezüge

pension benefit Pensionsleistung; **P~ B~ Guaranty Corporation** (PBGC) *Am* bundesstaatliche Gesellschaft zur Rückversicherung von betrieblichen Pensionsverpflichtungen; **right to future** ~**s** Pensionsanwartschaft, Versorgungsanwartschaft

pension, ~ **claim** Pensionsanspruch, Versorgungsanspruch; ~ **commitment** Pensionszusage; ~ **cost** (or **expense**) Aufwendungen für Altersversorgung; ~ **for life** Pension (od. Rente) auf Lebenszeit; ~ **for orphans** Waisenrente; ~ **fund** Pensionsfonds, Pensionskasse; ~ **increase** Pensionserhöhung; Rentenerhöhung; ~ **liabilities** *(Bilanz)* Pensionsverbindlichkeiten; ~ **(money)** Pension, Ruhegehalt; ~ **obligations** Verbindlichkeiten aus Altersruhegeld-Zusagen; ~ **payment** Pensionszahlung, Rentenzahlung; Versorgungsleistung; ~ **payments** Pensionsbezüge, Versorgungsbezüge; ~ **plan** *Am* Pensionsplan, Pensionsordnung; (betriebliche) Versorgungsordnung; ~ **pool** *Am* gemeinsame Pensionskasse mehrerer Arbeitgeber; ~ **recipient** Pensionsempfänger

pension reserve Pensionsrückstellung; **addition** (or **allocation**) **to the** ~ Zuführung zur Pensionsrückstellung; **creation** (or **formation**) **of a** ~ Bildung e-r Pensionsrückstellung; **release of the** ~ Auflösung der Pensionsrückstellung

pension right Pensionsanspruch, Versorgungsanspruch; **nonvested** ~ verfallbare Pensionsanwartschaft; **vested** ~ unverfallbare Pensionsanwartschaft

pension scheme Pensionsplan, Pensionskasse; **contributions under** ~**s** Beiträge zu Pensionskassen; **contributory** ~ Pensionsplan mit Beitragsleistung der Arbeitnehmer; **non(-)contributory** ~ Pensionsplan ohne Beitragsleistung der Arbeitnehmer; **terms of a** ~ Bedingungen e-r Pensionskasse; **to be a participant in the** ~ pensionsberechtigt sein

pension, claim to a ~ Pensionsanspruch, Versorgungsanspruch; Rentenanspruch; **contributory** ~ beitragspflichtige Pension; →**disability** ~; **eligible for** (or **entitled to**) **a** ~ pensionsberechtigt; **grant of a** ~ Bewilligung e-r Pension; **holder of a** ~ Pensionsempfänger, Pensionsberechtigter; **recipient of a** ~ Pensionsempfänger; Rentenempfänger; **retirement** ~ Pension, Ruhegehalt; *Br*[44] Altersrente; **compulsory retirement on a** ~ Zwangspensionierung; **right to a** ~ Pensionsanspruch, Versorgungsanspruch; **State Earnings-Related Pension Scheme** →state 1.; **survivors'** ~ Hinterbliebenenrente; **widow's** ~ Witwenpension, Witwenrente, Witwengeld

pension, to apply for a ~ e-e Pension (od. Rente) beantragen; **to calculate a** ~ e-e Pension (od. Rente) berechnen; **to draw a** ~ e-e Pension (od. Rente) beziehen; **to be entitled to a** ~ pensionsberechtigt (od. versorgungsberechtigt) sein; **to forfeit** (or **lose**) **one's right** (or **entitlement**) **to a** ~ einen Ruhegehaltsanspruch verlieren; **to go on a** ~ *colloq.* in den Ruhestand treten; **to receive a** ~ e-e Pension bekommen; **to retire on a** ~ sich pensionieren lassen, in den Ruhestand treten

pension (off) *v (jdn)* pensionieren, *(jdn)* in den Ruhestand versetzen; **~ing (off)** Pensionierung, Versetzung in den Ruhestand

pensionable pensionsfähig; pensionsberechtigt; ~ **age** Pensionsalter, pensionsfähiges (od. rentenfähiges) Alter; Rentenalter; ~ **post** (or **position**) pensionsberechtigte Stellung; **he retires after reaching** ~ **age** er tritt nach Erreichung der Altersgrenze in den Ruhestand

pensionary →pensioner

pensioner Pensionär; Pensions-, Ruhegehaltsempfänger; Versorgungsempfänger; Rentenempfänger, Rentner

Pentagon, the ~ *Am* das Verteidigungsministerium

pent-up, ~ **demand** Nachholbedarf; ~ **inflation** zurückgestaute (od. gesteuerte) Inflation

penuria testium *Scot* Fehlen von Zeugen

penury Mangel, Knappheit (of an); ungenügender Vorrat; Armut

people Volk; Menschen; Leute, man; Bevölkerung; **a ~'s Europe** (*EG*) Europa der Bürger; **colo(u)red** ~ Farbige; **moneyed** ~ Geldleute, Kapitalisten; **to go to the** ~ Neuwahlen abhalten

pep *v*, **to** ~ **up the economy** (or **economic activity**) *sl.* die Wirtschaft ankurbeln

peppercorn rent nominelle *(od. nur der Form halber gezahlte)* Miete (od. Pacht)

per, ~ **account rendered** laut ausgestellter Rechnung; ~ **annum** (p. a.) pro Jahr, jährlich; ~ (or **pur**) **autre vie** ("for the life of another") auf die Lebenszeit e-s Dritten; ~ **balance** per Saldo; ~ **capita** ("by heads") auf den Kopf *(der Bevölkerung);* pro Kopf; *(ErbR)* nach Köpfen *(opp. per stirpes)*

per cent (p. c.) Prozent, vom Hundert; prozentig; **4** ~ **per annum** 4 Prozent jährlich; **at what** **~?** zu wieviel Prozent?; **a loan at 4** ~ (or **a 4** ~ **loan**) e-e vierprozentige Anleihe; **below the 50** ~ **limitation** unter der 50-Prozent-Grenze; **to bear 10** ~ **interest** mit 10 Prozent verzinslich sein, 10 Prozent Zinsen tragen

percentage Prozentsatz; Prozent(e); Gewinnanteil *(z.B. Provision, Tantieme);* prozentualer Anteil

percentage basis, distribution on a ~ prozentuale Aufteilung

percentage, ~ **distribution** Tantiemeverteilung; ~ **figures** Prozentsätze; ~ **of distribution** Verteilungsschlüssel; ~ **of gold** Goldgehalt

percentage of profit(s) (prozentualer) Anteil am Gewinn, Tantieme; **to allow a** ~ e-e Tantieme geben

percentage, ~ **of recovery** *Am* Konkursquote; ~ **of voting** Wahlbeteiligung; ~ **quotation** Prozentkurs; ~ **share** prozentualer Anteil (of an); **calculation of** ~ Prozentrechnung; **contract** ~ vertraglicher Prozentsatz; **high** ~ hoher Prozentsatz; **to yield a** ~ Prozente abwerfen

percentaged (or **percental**) *Am* prozentual

per, ~ **contra entry** Gegenbuchung; ~ **curiam** (per cur.) ("by the court") durch das Gericht

perch Rute *(Längenmaß bes. für Land = 5½ yards od. 5,029 m)*

per diem ("by the day") pro Tag; ~ **allowance** *Am* Tagegeldvergütung, Reisespesenvergütung

peremptory peremptorisch; endgültig; unbedingt; zwingend *(opp. permissive);* ~ →**challenge;** ~ **plea** *Am* peremptorische (od. dauernde) Einrede *(opp. dilatory plea);* ~ **provision** zwingende Vorschrift, Mußvorschrift *(opp. optional provision);* ~ **term** *Am* Notfrist; ~ **writ** gerichtl. Verfügung *(Ladung zum persönlichen Erscheinen)*

per eundem ("by the same judge") durch denselben Richter

perfect vollkommen; vollendet; ~ **competition** vollkommener Wettbewerb, vollkommene Konkurrenz; ~ **trust** → executed trust

perfected security right *Am* registriertes Sicherungsrecht

perfection *Am*[44a] Wirksamwerden (od. Durchsetzbarkeit) e-s Sicherungsrechts gegenüber Dritten (→*attachment*)

perform *v* 1. *(Vertrag, Aufgabe, Versprechen etc)* erfüllen; leisten, verrichten

perform, to ~ a contract (wholly or in part) e-n Vertrag erfüllen (ganz od. teilweise); **failure to ~ a contract** Nichterfüllung e-s Vertrags

perform, to ~ one's duty s-e Pflicht erfüllen; **to ~ functions** Aufgaben wahrnehmen; **to ~ a marriage** e-e Eheschließung vornehmen; **to ~ one's obligations** s-n Verpflichtungen nachkommen; **to ~ a promise** ein Versprechen halten; **failure to ~** Leistungsunterlassung; **failure to ~ one's obligations** Nichterfüllung s-r Verpflichtungen; **incapable of being ~ed** nicht erfüllbar; **place where a contract is to be ~ed** Erfüllungsort; **promise to ~** Leistungsversprechen

perform *v* 2. aufführen, vortragen, darbieten

performing, ~ artist ausübender Künstler; **~ arts** darstellende Künste; **~ rights** Aufführungsrechte; **P~ Rights Society** (P.R.S.) *Br* Gesellschaft zum Schutze musikalischer Aufführungsrechte *(entspricht etwa der GEMA);* **P~ Rights Tribunal** *Br* Gericht zur Kontrolle der Ausübung der Rechte zur Lizenzierung öffentlicher Aufführungen

performance 1. Erfüllung; Leistung, Verrichtung; Durchführung, Ausführung; **~ appraisal** Leistungsbewertung; **~ bond** *(Exporthandel)* Urkunde über e-e Verpflichtung, die der Verkäufer bzw. s-e Bank zur Erfüllung e-s Kaufvertrages eingeht; Vertragserfüllungsgarantie; Leistungsversprechen; **~ efficiency** Leistungsgrad; **~ evaluation** Leistungsbewertung von Angestellten; **~ fund** Investmentfonds, der hohen Wertzuwachs des Vermögens anstrebt; **~ guarantee** *Br* Erfüllungsgarantie; **~ in kind** Naturalleistung, Sachleistung; **~ incentives** Leistungsanreize; **~ level** Leistungsgrad; **~ management** Einsatz aller Faktoren zur Optimierung der Leistung; **~ of a contract** Erfüllung e-s Vertrages, Vertragserfüllung; **~ of duties** Erfüllung von Pflichten

performance of functions Durchführung von Aufgaben; **continued ~** Fortführung von Aufgaben

performance, ~ of an obligation Erfüllung e-r Verpflichtung; **~ of a service** Erbringung e-r Dienstleistung; **~ rating** →merit rating

performance, collateral ~ Nebenleistung; **contemporaneous ~** Erfüllung Zug um Zug; **failure of ~** Nichterfüllung; **impediment to ~** Erfüllungshindernis; →**impossibility of ~**; **part ~** teilweise Erfüllung, Teilleistung *(→ part 1.);* **place of ~** Erfüllungsort, Leistungsort

performance, specific ~ (of a contract) vertragsgemäße Erfüllung, Leistung des vertraglich Geschuldeten; **action for specific ~** Klage auf Erfüllung des Vertrags; **to sue for specific ~** auf Erfüllung klagen

Das equity-Recht hat specific performance zugelassen, wenn der infolge Vertragsverletzung entstandene Schadensersatzanspruch den Gläubiger nicht in zumutbarer Weise befriedigt

performance, →substantial ~; → substituted ~; tender of ~ Anerbieten der Leistung; **time of ~** Leistungszeit

performance, to be liable for non(-)~ für Nichterfüllung haften; **to effect ~** Leistung bewirken (od. erbringen); leisten (to an); **to refuse ~** Leistung verweigern

performance 2. Aufführung, Vorstellung, Darbietung, **charity ~** Wohltätigkeitsvorstellung; **first ~** Uraufführung; Premiere; **public ~ of a work** öffentliche Aufführung e-s Werkes; **public stage ~** öffentliche Bühnen-Aufführung; **right of ~** Aufführungsrecht; **special ~** Sonderaufführung

performer[45] *(UrhR)* ausübender Künstler

peril Gefahr, Risiko; **~s insured against** versicherte Gefahren; **~s of the sea**[46] *(SeeversR)* Seerisiken, Gefahren der See *(zufällige Unfälle und Verluste durch die See: collision, foundering, shipwreck, stranding etc);* **~ of transportation** Transportgefahr; **~s of war** Kriegsgefahren, Kriegsrisiko; **at one's ~** auf eigene Gefahr; **excepted ~s** Freizeichnung für bestimmte Schadensursachen *(in Charterverträgen);* **excepted ~s clause** Freizeichnungsklausel; **extraneous ~s** *(VersR)* Sondergefahren; **fire ~** Brandgefahr; **imminent ~** drohende Gefahr; **in ~ of one's life** in Lebensgefahr; **marine** (or **maritime**) **~(s)** See(transport)gefahr

per, ~ incuriam ("through want of care") wegen mangelnder Sorgfalt *(des Gerichts);* **~ infortunium** ("by mischance") durch Mißgeschick

period Periode, Zeitabschnitt; Frist; Dauer; Laufzeit

period, to calculate a ~ e-e Frist berechnen; **to extend a ~** e-e Frist verlängern; **to fix** (or **lay down, set**) **a ~ (of time)** e-e Frist (fest)setzen; *(etw)* befristen; **the ~ commences to run** die Frist beginnt zu laufen; **the ~ has expired** die Frist ist abgelaufen; **a ~ runs** e-e Frist läuft; **the ~ shall run from** die Frist beginnt am; **the ~ shall start to run** die Frist beginnt zu laufen

period, ~ (allowed) for appeal Rechtsmittelfrist *(Berufungsfrist etc); (PatR)* Beschwerdefrist; **~ (allowed) for carriage** (or **conveyance**) Beförderungsfrist; **~ (allowed) for filing** *(PatR)* Anmeldefrist; **~ (allowed) for objection** Einspruchsfrist

period already served, to make allowance for the ~ *(StrafR)* die Untersuchungshaft anrechnen

period, ~ (set) for declaration Anmeldefrist; ~

for exchange Umtauschfrist; ~ **for initiating legal action** Klagefrist; ~ **for making a claim against one's insurance** Frist, innerhalb derer ein Versicherungsanspruch angemeldet werden muß; ~ **for presentation** Vorlegungsfrist; ~ **insured** Versicherungsdauer; ~ **of appointment** Amtsdauer; ~ **of assessment** Veranlagungszeitraum *(für Steuer)*; ~ **of availability** Gültigkeitsdauer *(z.B. e-s Fahrausweises)*; ~ **of computation** Berechnungszeitraum; ~ **of (possible) conception** Empfängniszeit; ~ **of copyright** Schutzfrist; ~ **of coverage** Versicherungszeit; ~ **of custody** →custody 3.; ~ **of delay in payment** Dauer des Zahlungsverzuges; ~ **for exchange** Umtauschfrist; ~ **of extension** Verlängerungszeitraum, Stundungsfrist

period of grace zusätzliche Frist, Nachfrist; ~ **for delivery** Nachfrist für die Lieferung; **expiry of the** ~ Ablauf der Nachfrist; **he is entitled to the** ~ ihm steht die Nachfrist zu; **to grant a** ~ e-e Nachfrist setzen

period, ~ **of guarantee** Garantiefrist; ~ **of insurance** Versicherungsdauer; ~ **of (a) lease** Mietzeit, Pachtzeit; Dauer e-s Miet- (od. Pacht)vertrages; ~ **of liability** Haftungsdauer; ~ **of a licen|ce (-se)** Dauer e-r Lizenz

period of limitation[47] Verjährungsfrist; **expiry of the** ~ Ablauf der Verjährungsfrist; **statutory** ~ gesetzliche Verjährungsfrist; **the** ~ **runs** (from) (or **the** ~ **begins** [or **commences**] **to run** [on]) die Verjährungsfrist beginnt (am); **the** ~ **does not run** die Verjährung ruht (ist gehemmt[48]); die Verjährungsfrist läuft noch nicht; **the claim is governed by the three-year** ~ der Anspruch fällt unter die dreijährige Verjährungsfrist; **to be subject to a** ~ **of 3 years** in 3 Jahren verjähren; **the** ~ **is subject to extension**[48] die Verjährung ist gehemmt

Während nach deutschem Recht die Verjährung eine Institution des materiellen Rechts ist, gehört sie nach anglo-amerikanischem Recht dem Prozeßrecht an.

Br Die wichtigsten Verjährungsfristen sind wie folgt: Alle Forderungen aus laufender Rechnung, Darlehen oder aus e-m formlosen Vertrag (simple →contract) sowie aus →tort verjähren in 6 Jahren seit Entstehung des Klaggrundes (Ansprüche wegen personal injuries verjähren im allgemeinen nach 3 Jahren). Für Forderungen aus gesiegelten Verträgen (contracts under seal) sowie Klagen auf Rückgabe eines Grundstücks ist eine 12jährige Verjährungsfrist vorgesehen. Urteilsschulden verjähren in 12 Jahren.

Am Jeder der 50 Einzelstaaten hat sein eigenes Verjährungsgesetz. Deliktsobligationen verjähren oft schon nach einem Jahr, vertragliche vielfach nach 2 od. 3 Jahren. Forderungen aus schriftlichen od. gesiegelten Verträgen wird gewöhnlich eine längere Verjährungsfrist (oft 20 Jahre) zugestanden

period, ~ **of a loan** Laufzeit e-r Anleihe; ~ **of one month** Monatsfrist; ~ **of notice** Kündigungsfrist (→*notice 3.*); ~ **of office** Amtsdauer, Amtszeit; ~ **of pendency** *(PatR)* Bearbeitungsdauer von Anmeldungen; ~ **of prescription** Ersitzungsfrist; Verjährungsfrist *(→prescription 2.)*; ~ **of probation** Bewährungsfrist; ~ **of service** Dienstzeit; ~ **of time** Zeitraum, Periode; Frist; ~ **of training** Ausbildungszeit; ~ **of transition** Übergangszeit; ~ **of validity** Gültigkeitsdauer, Laufzeit; ~ **of vocational adjustment** Einarbeitungszeit; ~ **of warranty** Gewährleistungsfrist; ~ **to run** Laufzeit; ~ **under review** Berichtszeitraum, Berichtsperiode; **accounting** ~ Abrechnungszeit

period, additional ~ Nachfrist; **to grant an additional** ~ **of reasonable length** e-e Nachfrist von angemessener Dauer setzen

period, assessment ~ Veranlagungszeitraum *(für Steuer)*; **comparable** ~ Vergleichszeitraum; **computation of** ~ Zeitberechnung, Fristberechnung; **contractual** ~ Vertragszeit; **copyright** ~ *(urheberrechtl.)* Schutzfrist; **credit** ~ Laufzeit e-s Kredits; **a 3 days'** ~ e-e Frist von 3 Tagen; **for a definite** ~ für e-e bestimmte Zeit

period, expiration (or **expiry**) **of (a)** ~ Zeitablauf; Fristablauf; **after the expiration of a reasonable** ~ nach Ablauf e-r angemessenen Frist

period, extension of a ~ Verlängerung e-r Frist, Fristverlängerung; **fixing of a** ~ Fristbestimmung; **fixed** ~ festgesetzte Zeit; **for a** ~ **of** auf die Dauer von; **guarantee** ~ Garantiefrist; Gewährleistungsfrist; **for an indefinite** ~ auf unbestimmte Zeit; **for a 3 months'** ~ auf die Dauer von 3 Monaten; **within a reasonable** ~ innerhalb e-r angemessenen Frist; **setting of a** ~ Fristsetzung, Befristung; **specified** ~ bestimmte Frist; **statutory** ~ **(of limitation)** gesetzliche (Verjährungs-)Frist; **subscription** ~ Zeichnungsfrist; **trial** ~ Probezeit; Versuchsstadium; **waiting** ~ Wartezeit; *(VersR)* Karenzzeit; **within a** ~ **of** innerhalb e-r Frist von; **within the set** ~ fristgemäß; **within the stipulated** ~ innerhalb der vereinbarten Zeit

periodical periodisch, regelmäßig wiederkehrend, in regelmäßigen Abständen; ~ **contribution** laufender Beitrag; ~ **meetings** regelmäßige Zusammenkünfte

periodical payments regelmäßig wiederkehrende Zahlungen; Geldrente; ~ **order** *Br (Ehescheidung)* Urteil auf Zahlung e-r Geldrente; **secured** ~ **order** *Br* Urteil auf Zahlung e-r Geldrente, gesichert durch Hinterlegung e-s Kapitalbetrages

periodical publications regelmäßig wiederkehrende Veröffentlichungen

periodically, to meet ~ in regelmäßigen Abständen zusammenkommen

peripheral, ~ **area** (or **region**) Randgebiet; ~ **state** Randstaat

perish *v* umkommen; *fig* untergehen; zugrunde gehen; verderben *(von Waren)*

perished, the goods have ~ die Ware ist verdorben (od. untergegangen); **hundreds of people** ~ **in the earthquake** Hunderte von Menschen kamen bei dem Erdbeben um

perishable leicht verderblich, nicht haltbar; ~ **goods** (or **merchandise**) leicht verderbliche Waren

perishables leicht verderbliche Waren

perjure *v*, **to** ~ **(oneself)** meineidig werden; e-n Meineid leisten; *(wissentl.)* falsch schwören

perjured meineidig; ~ **evidence** meineidige Zeugenaussage; **the witness** ~ **himself** der Zeuge leistete e-n Meineid

perjurer Meineidiger

perjury[49] Meineid; **subornation of** ~ Anstiftung zum Meineid; **to commit** ~ e-n Meineid leisten, Meineid begehen, meineidig werden
Die Strafbestimmungen von perjury beziehen sich auch auf affidavit, affirmation und *Br* declaration *(cf. false swearing)*

perks *sl.* →perquistes

permanency Dauerzustand

permanent (fort)dauernd, Dauer-; ständig, fest *(opp. temporary)*; ~ **abode** ständiger Aufenthalt(sort) (od. Wohnsitz); ~ **advisory board** (or **council**) ständiger Beirat; ~ **appointment** feste Anstellung, Dauerstellung; ~ **assets** feste Anlagen, Anlagevermögen *(opp. floating or circulating assets)*; ~ **body** ständiges Organ; ~ **committee** ständiger Ausschuß; **P**~ **Court of Arbitration** →arbitration; ~ **debt** fundierte (od. konsolidierte) Schuld; ~ **delegate** ständiger Delegierter; ~ **disability** (or **disablement**) dauernde Arbeitsunfähigkeit; Dauerschaden (lebenslänglicher Körperschaden)

permanent employee festangestellter Bediensteter *(opp. temporary employee)*; **to be a** ~ fest angestellt sein

permanent, ~ **employment** feste Anstellung; Dauerstellung; ~ **establishment** Betriebsstätte *(→establishment)*; ~ **funds** eiserner Bestand *(an Geld, Waren etc)*; ~ **home** *(DBA)* ständiger Wohnsitz; ~ **injunction** →perpetual injunction; ~ **investment** Daueranlage *(opp. temporary investment)*; ~ **labo(u)r** ständige Arbeitskräfte *(opp. seasonal labour)*; ~ **maintenance** *Br* ständiger Unterhalt *(opp. maintenance pending suit)*; ~ **member** ständiges Mitglied; ~ **neutrality** ständige (od. ewige) Neutralität; ~ **office** ständiges Büro; ~ **order** *Am* Dauerauftrag; ~ **position** (or **post**) Dauerstellung, Lebensstellung; feste Anstellung; ~ **representative** ständiger Vertreter; ~ **resident** *Am* Einwohner mit Daueraufenthaltsgenehmigung (*kein Staatsbürger*); ~ **situation** →~ position; ~ **staff** ständiges Personal *(opp. temporary staff)*; **P**~ **Under-Secretary (of State)** *Br* → secretary 3.

permissible zulässig, erlaubt; fakultativ; ~ **dose** *(AtomR)* zulässige Strahlendosis; ~ **expenses** *(von der Steuer)* abzugsfähige Unkosten; ~ **load** (zulässige) Höchstbelastung

permission Erlaubnis, Genehmigung; ~ **by the authorities** behördliche Genehmigung; ~ **to enter** Einreiseerlaubnis; ~ **to transact business** Geschäftserlaubnis; **government** ~ *Br* staatliche Erlaubnis; **grant of (a)** ~ Erlaubniserteilung; **by special** ~ mit besonderer Genehmigung; **to ask** (or **apply**) **for** ~ um Genehmigung bitten; **to get** ~ Erlaubnis erhalten; **to give** (or **grant**) ~ Erlaubnis erteilen, genehmigen; **to grant** ~ **to speak** *(jdm)* das Wort erteilen

permissive zulässig, erlaubt, statthaft, fakultativ *(opp. peremptory)*; ~ **provision** Kannvorschrift; **the** ~ **society** *Br* die (über)tolerante Gesellschaft *(sexual freedom, drug-taking etc)*; ~ **waste** →waste 3.

permit *(schriftl.)* Erlaubnis (od. Genehmigung), Erlaubnisschein; Zulassung; Zollabfertigungsschein; *bes. Br* Konzession *(→licence 1.)*; Passierschein; Ausweis(karte); ~ **card** *Am* Erlaubnisschein *(gewerkschaftl. Erlaubnis, als Nichtgewerkschafter [nonunion worker] vorübergehend in e-m gewerkschaftspflichtigen Betrieb [closed shop] zu arbeiten)*; ~ **holder** Inhaber e-r Erlaubnis, Erlaubnisscheininhaber (*Jagdschein, Führerschein etc.*); **(customs)** ~ Zollabfertigungsschein; **entry** ~ Einreiseerlaubnis; **exit** ~ Ausreiseerlaubnis; **export** ~ Ausfuhrerlaubnis; **fishing** ~ *Am* Fischereischein; **hunting** ~ *Am* Jagdschein; **import** ~ Einfuhrerlaubnis; **labo(u)r** ~ Arbeitserlaubnis; **withdrawal of a** ~ Zurückziehung (od. Widerruf) e-r Genehmigung; **to extend a** ~ e-e(n) Erlaubnis(-schein) verlängern; **to give** (or **grant**) **a** ~ e-e Genehmigung erteilen; **to issue a** ~ e-n Erlaubnisschein ausstellen; amtlich genehmigen

permit *v* erlauben, gestatten; **to** ~ **an appeal** e-e Berufung zulassen

permitted, ~ **by law** gesetzlich zulässig; ~ **use of a trade mark** zulässige Benutzung e-r Handelsmarke; **to be** ~ **to speak** das Wort erhalten

permittee jd, der e-e Erlaubnis erhalten hat; Berechtigter

per my et per tout ("by the half and by the whole") →joint tenancy

pernancy Annahme (od. Empfang) *(z.B. von tithe)*

perpetrate *v (strafbare Handlung)* begehen, verüben; **to ~ a fraud on the court** das Gericht irreführen

perpetration Begehung, Verübung *(e-r strafbaren Handlung)*; Täterschaft; **indirect ~** mittelbare Täterschaft

perpetrator *(StrafR)* Täter; **~ of an attempt on a p.'s life** Attentäter

perpetual (perp.) dauernd; fortwährend, ewig; unkündbar; **~ annuity** ewige (od. unkündbare) Rente; **~ bond** Annuitätenanleihe; **~ existence** uneingeschränkte Dauer; **~ injunction** endgültige gerichtliche Verfügung *(opp. interim, interlocutory, provisional, Am temporary injunction)*; **~ inventory** permanente Inventur, Buchinventur; **~ inventory card** laufende Bestandskarte; **~ lease** Miete (Pacht), die Mieter (Pächter) nach Ablauf verlängern kann; **~ loan** →loan 2.; **~ neutrality** ewige Neutralität

perpetual succession Fähigkeit e-r juristischen Person, unabhängig vom Wechsel der Mitglieder Träger von Rechten und Pflichten zu sein; **with ~** mit ständiger Rechtsnachfolge; von fortdauerndem Bestand; **to have ~** beständige Rechtsnachfolge haben; an keine Lebenszeit gebunden sein

perpetuate *v* verewigen; **to ~ testimony** Aussagen zur Beweissicherung aufnehmen; **action to ~ testimony** Beweissicherungsverfahren

perpetuation, proceedings for the ~ of testimony[50] Beweissicherungsverfahren *(bei Zeugenaussagen)*

perpetuity unbegrenzte Dauer, Dauerzustand; *(auch)* lebenslängliche Rente; **in ~** für unbegrenzte Zeit

perpetuities, rule against ~[51] Regel zur Verhütung zeitlich unbegrenzter Rechtszustände
(Sehr komplizierte) Regel, die verbietet, daß durch testamentarische od. rechtsgeschäftliche Anordnungen (bes. trust) die Verfügung über (Grund-)Eigentum über e-e bestimmte Zeit hinaus beschränkt wird *(21 Jahre nach dem eigenen Tod oder dem Tod anderer lebender Personen)*

per pro(curationem) ("as an agent") →procuration

perquisite(s) (*sl.* perks) Nebeneinkünfte, Nebenverdienst; Sondervergünstigung(en); *Am* Selbsterworbenes *(nicht Ererbtes)*

per se ("by itself") schlechthin, von selbst; automatisch; *Am (AntitrustR)* offenkundig (rechtswidrig); **negligence ~** *Am* Fahrlässigkeitshaftung unabhängig von Verschulden
Am (AntitrustR) Die per se rule ist eine von der amerikanischen Rechtsprechung entwickelte absolute Verbotsregel. Eine Verhaltensweise wird bereits ihrer wettbewerbsfeindlichen Natur wegen als rechtswidrig (gegen die Antitrustgesetze verstoßend) angesehen, ohne daß noch zu prüfen ist, ob sie reasonable ist *(cf. rule of reason)*. **Per se violations** sind bes. Preisvereinbarungen, Marktaufteilungen, Produktionsbeschränkungen, Gruppenboykott

persecute *v* verfolgen; **to be ~d** Verfolgungen ausgesetzt sein *(bes. aus religiösen od. rassischen Gründen)*

persecutee verfolgte Person, Verfolgte(r)

persecution Verfolgung; **~ of Jews** Judenverfolgung; **to be subject to ~** der Verfolgung ausgesetzt sein; **to suffer ~s** Verfolgungen erleiden (for wegen)

persecutor Verfolger

Persia Persien *(→Iran)*
Persian Perser, Perserin *(→Iranian)*

persist *v* beharren, bestehen (in auf); **to ~ in a demand** auf e-r Forderung bestehen

persistent beharrlich; anhaltend; **~ demand** anhaltende Nachfrage (for nach); **~ offender** Gewohnheitsverbrecher *(cf. extended term of imprisonment, →term 2.)*; **~ radiation** *(AtomR)* Dauerstrahlung

person Person; **~s and property** Personen und Sachen; **~ appearing** Erschienener; **~ carried over** *Br (Börse)* Reportgeber; **~ carrying over** *Br (Börse)* Reportnehmer; **~ charged with an offen|ce (-se)** Beschuldigter; **~ detained for hearing or trial** *Am*[52] Untersuchungsgefangener; **~ giving notice (to a third person)** *Am* Streitverkünder; **~ injured** Verletzter, Geschädigter, Beschädigter, Benachteiligter; **~ insured** Versicherter; **~ interested in the estate** *Br* Person mit Rechtsansprüchen gegen den Nachlaß; **~ international** Völkerrechtssubjekt; **~ liable for tax** Steuerpflichtiger; **~ non compos mentis** Unzurechnungsfähiger; Geisteskranker; **~ notified** *Am* Streitverkündeter; **~ of consequence** einflußreiche Person; **~ of full age (and capacity)** Volljähriger (und Geschäftsfähiger); **~ of independent means** finanziell Unabhängiger; **~ of →unsound mind; ~ sought** →wanted **~; ~ without a nationality** Staatenloser

person, artificial ~ juristische Person *(opp. natural ~)*; **→assisted ~; body of ~s** Personenmehrheit; **classes of ~s** Personengruppen; **damage to ~** Personenschaden *(opp. damage to property)*

person, offenses involving danger to the ~ *Am*[53] Straftaten gegen die Person

person, in ~ persönlich, in Person; nicht durch e-n Anwalt vertreten; **a party appears in ~ or by his counsel** e-e Partei erscheint persönlich oder wird durch ihren Anwalt vertreten

person, injury to ~ Personenschaden; **injury to ~ or property** Verletzung e-r Person od. e-s Vermögensguts; **insurance of** ~ Personenversicherung; **juridical** (or **juristic, legal**) ~ juristische Person; **movement of ~s** Personenverkehr; **natural** (or **physical**) ~ natürliche Person; **young** ~ Jugendlicher

persona grata *(VölkerR)* Persona grata *(als dipl. Vertreter erwünschte Person)*
persona non grata (or **ingrata**) *(VölkerR)* Persona ingrata *(als dipl. Vertreter unerwünschte Person)*

personage Persönlichkeit

personal persönlich; obligatorisch *(opp. real)*; Privat-; **~s** *Am (in Zeitungen)* Persönliches *(Nachrichten und Anzeigen)*; ~ **accident insurance** Unfallversicherung gegen Personenschäden; ~ **account** Personenkonto; Privatkonto, Kundenkonto; ~ **action** obligatorische Klage *(opp. real action)*; ~ **affair** →~ business; ~ **allowance** *Br (von Einkommensteuer abziehbarer)* persönlicher Freibetrag; ~ **announcement** *(in Zeitungen)* Familienanzeige
personal appearance, to make a ~ persönlich erscheinen *(Minister etc)*; **to put in a** ~ persönlich anwesend sein
personal assistant persönlicher Assistent; ~ **to the manager** *(etwa)* Direktionsassistent
personal, ~ **benefit** persönlicher Vorteil; ~ **business** persönliche Angelegenheit, Privatangelegenheit; ~ **call** *Br tel* Gespräch mit Voranmeldung; **in one's ~ capacity** persönlich, als Privatperson; ~ **characteristics** persönliche Eigenschaften; ~ **chattels**[54] persönliche Habe; *(zum persönlichen Gebrauch bestimmtes)* bewegliches Vermögen *(Hausrat, Juwelen, Kleidungsstücke, Auto etc)*; ~ **check** *Am* von e-r Privatperson ausgestellter Scheck, Privatscheck; ~ **computer** (PC) Personalcomputer; ~ **contribution to social insurance** *Am* Arbeitnehmeranteil zur Sozialversicherung (→*employee's contribution*); ~ **credit** Personalkredit
personal data Angaben zur Person, Personalien; *(EDV)* personenbezogene Daten *(→data 2.)* ~ **and testimonials** Bewerbungsunterlagen *(Angaben zur Person und Referenzen)*
personal, ~ **description** Personenbeschreibung; ~ **dossier** Personalakte; ~ **drawings** Privatentnahmen, Privatabhebungen; ~ **earnings** Einkünfte aus eigener Arbeit; ~ **effects** persönliche Gebrauchsgegenstände; ~ **estate** bewegliches Vermögen, Mobilien; beweglicher Nachlaß; ~ **exemption** *Am (Einkommensteuer)* persönlicher Freibetrag; ~ **files** Personalakten; ~ **finance company** *Am* Kundenkreditanstalt; ~ **holding company** *Am* personenbezogene Holding-Gesellschaft; ~ **identification number** (PIN) *(EDV)* Personenkennzahl (PK), Identifikationsnummer *(für Geldautomaten)*; ~ **income** persönliches Einkommen, Privateinkommen; ~ **income tax** *Am* Einkommensteuer; ~ **information** *(EDV)* personenbezogene Informationen (od. Daten)
personal injury Körperverletzung, Personenschaden; ~ **claim** Schadensersatzforderung wegen Körperverletzung; **to extend the time for bringing an action for** ~ die Frist für die Erhebung einer Klage wegen Personenschäden verlängern
personal, ~ **insurance** Personenversicherung; ~ **inviolability** *dipl* persönliche Unverletzbarkeit; ~ **→jurisdiction;** ~ **ledger** Privatkontenbuch
personal liability persönliche Haftung; ~ **insurance** Privathaftpflichtversicherung *(Versicherung für Privatpersonen gegen Schadensersatzforderungen)*; ~ **under a mortgage** persönliche Haftung für die Hypothekenforderung; **to exempt from** ~ persönliche Haftung ausschließen; **to incur** ~ sich persönlich haftbar machen; persönlich haftbar sein
personal, ~ **loan** Personalkredit; *Am* Kleinkredit *(e-r Bank)*; ~ **matter** Privatangelegenheit; ~ **particulars** Personalbeschreibung; ~ **→property;** ~ **record** berufliche Vergangenheit; Lebenslauf; ~ **relations** persönliche Beziehungen; ~ **relief** *Br* →~ allowance; ~ **representative**[55] Verwalter, Vertreter e-r Person; *bes.* Erbschaftsverwalter[56] (executor or administrator[57]); ~ **right** obligatorischer Anspruch; Persönlichkeitsrecht, Individualrecht; ~ **search** Leibesvisitation; ~ **security** persönliche Sicherheit *(ohne Hinterlegung von Werten)*; Bürgschaft; ~ **services** persönliche Dienstleistungen; ~ **service business** *Am* Dienstleistungsgewerbe *(ausschließlich der kaufmännischen Dienstleistungen)*; ~ **sovereignty** *(VölkerR)* Personalhoheit
personal status Personenstand, Familienstand; *(IPR)* Personalstatut *(Br und Am Domizilprinzip, deutsches Recht Staatsangehörigkeitsprinzip)*
personal, ~ **union** *(VölkerR)* Personalunion *(früher z. B. zwischen England und Hannover, Dänemark und Island)*; ~ **use** *(MietR)* Eigenbedarf; **articles for ~ use** Gegenstände des persönlichen Gebrauchs
personally persönlich; **to be ~ liable** persönlich (od. mit dem eigenen Vermögen) haften; **to deliver** ~ persönlich übergeben

personalit|y Persönlichkeit; ~ **cult** Personenkult, **to have international** ~ Völkerrechtspersönlichkeit haben; **the organization possesses juridical** ~ die Organisation besitzt Rechtspersönlichkeit; **company with legal** ~ rechtsfähige Gesellschaft; **a commercial company not possessing legal** ~ e-e Handelsgesellschaft ohne eigene Rechtspersönlichkeit; **right of** ~ Persönlichkeitsrecht; **well-known ~ies of stage and screen** bekannte Persönlichkeiten von Bühne und Film

personality of laws *(IPR)* Personalität der Gesetze (Beziehung der Gesetze auf eine Person)
Die Begriffe „Personalität" und „Realität" stammen aus der Zeit der Statutentheorie, die seit dem späten Mittelalter jahrhundertelang das Internationale Privatrecht (Kollisionsrecht) beherrscht hat. Personale Statuten waren solche Vorschriften, die sich auf die Person bezogen und z. B. die Geschäfts- oder Ehefähigkeit regelten. Sie hatten einen überörtlichen Anwendungsbereich, d. h. sie beherrschten die ihnen unterworfenen Personen auch in einem fremden Rechtsgebiet. Als reale Statuten galten die Bestimmungen, die sich auf Sachen bezogen. Sie waren nur auf die Sachen des Gebiets anwendbar, für das sie erlassen worden waren *(cf. reality of laws)*

personalty bewegliches Vermögen *(opp. realty)*

personam, action in ~ obligatorische Klage *(opp. action in rem)*; **right in ~** persönlicher (od. obligatorischer) Anspruch *(opp. right in rem)*

personate *v* sich (fälschlich) ausgeben für

personation[58], **(false) ~** Sichausgeben für e-n anderen *(→impersonate v)*

personnel Personal; Belegschaft; **~ accounting** Personalbuchhaltung; **~ administration** Personalverwaltung; **~ change** Personalveränderung; **~ consultant** Personalberater; **~ costs** Personalausgaben, Personalaufwand; **~ department** (or **division**) Personalabteilung, Personalbüro; **~ director** (or **manager**) Personalchef; **~ file** Personalakte; **~ management** Personalverwaltung; Personalführung; **in ~ matters** in Personalangelegenheiten, auf dem personellen Gebiet; **~ officer** Personalchef; **~ placement** Personaleinsatz; **~ policy** Personalpolitik; **~ records** Personalakten; **~ recruitment** Personalbeschaffung; Personaleinstellungen; **~ requirements** Personalbedarf; **change of ~** Personalwechsel, Personalveränderung; **engagement of ~** Einstellung von Personal; **executive ~** leitende Angestellte; **expenditure on ~** Personalausgaben; **number of ~** Personalbestand; **reduction of ~** Personaleinschränkung; **skilled** (or **trained**) **~** geschultes Personal, Fachpersonal

per stirpes ("by stocks") *(ErbR)* nach Stämmen *(opp. per capita)*

persuasion Überredung; Überzeugung, Glaube; **to be of Protestant ~** Protestant sein

persuasive authority Präzedenzfälle oder andere Rechtsquellen, die nicht bindend sind, aber dennoch vom Gericht in Betracht gezogen werden *(Br z.B. die Entscheidungen anderer Commonwealth-Gerichte, amerikanischer Gerichte, Gesetzeskommentare etc; Am Entscheidungen gleichgeordneter od. ausländischer Gerichte; cf. binding →precedents)*

pertain *v* gehören (to zu); betreffen, sich beziehen (to auf); dienen (to für)

pertinent zur Sache gehörig, zugehörig; sachdienlich; einschlägig; **~ data** entsprechende Unterlagen; **~ information** sachdienliche Angaben; **~ literature** einschlägige Literatur; **to be ~ to** Bezug haben auf, in Bezug stehen zu

per totam curiam ("by the whole court") als Plenarentscheidung des Gerichts

Peru Peru; **Republic of ~** Republik Peru
Peruvian Peruaner, Peruanerin; peruanisch

perusal *(sorgsames)* Durchlesen; *(genaue)* Durchsicht; **for ~** zur Einsichtnahme

perus|e *v (sorgsam)* durchlesen; **on ~ing** beim Durchlesen

perversion Entstellung, Verdrehung *(der Wahrheit)*; **~ of justice** Rechtsbeugung; **(sexual) ~** Perversität, Widernatürlichkeit

pervert (sexuell) perverser Mensch; jd., der widernatürliche Handlungen begeht (od. solche Neigungen hat)

pervert *v (Tatsachen)* entstellen, verdrehen; **to ~ the course of justice** den Lauf der Gerechtigkeit ablenken; das Recht beugen

petition 1. Eingabe, Gesuch, Bittschrift; Petition *(an staatl. Instanz: Staatsoberhaupt, Parlament, Behörden)*; *(förml.)* Antrag; Klage (-schrift) *(Am in gewissen →equity-Verfahren, Br in Scheidungs- und gewissen anderen Verfahren)*; **~ for clemency** Gnadengesuch; **~ for divorce** →divorce petition; **~ for the grant of a patent** Ersuchen auf Erteilung e-s Patents; **~ for nullity** Ehenichtigkeitsklage; **~ for a pardon** Gnadengesuch; **~ for review** Antrag auf Nachprüfung *(e-s Urteils)*; **~ for the winding up (of a company)** Antrag *(bei Gericht)* auf Liquidation e-r Gesellschaft; **~ in error** *Am* Antrag auf Wiederaufnahme des Verfahrens *(zur Nachprüfung von Rechtsfragen)*; **~ of appeal** *Br* Berufungsantrag, Berufungsschrift *(an →House of Lords od. →Privy Council)*; **~ of certiorari** Revisionsbegehren; **~ of course** *Br* Antrag bei der →Chancery Division zur Ergreifung e-r notwendigen Maßnahme; **→cross-~**; **election ~** *Br* Wahlprotest; **filing of the ~** Einreichung des (Ehescheidungs-)Antrags; **right of ~** Petitionsrecht; **to dismiss a ~** e-n Antrag ablehnen (od. abschlägig bescheiden); e-e Klage abweisen; **to draw up a ~** e-e Bittschrift aufsetzen; **to file a ~** e-n Antrag (od. ein Gesuch, e-e Klage) einreichen; **to file a (divorce) ~** e-e Scheidungsklage einreichen; **to grant a ~** e-m Antrag stattgeben, e-m Gesuch entsprechen; **to refuse a ~** ein Gesuch (od. e-e Bittschrift) abweisen; **the ~ has (no) merits** der Antrag ist (nicht) begründet

petition 2. ~ **(in bankruptcy)** (or **bankruptcy** ~) Antrag auf Konkurseröffnung, Konkurseröffnungsantrag; **involuntary** ~ *Am* Konkursanmeldung *(durch den Gläubiger)*; **voluntary** ~ *Am* Konkursanmeldung *(durch den Schuldner)*; **to dismiss the** ~ den Konkursantrag abweisen; **to file a** ~ Konkurseröffnung beantragen *(seitens des Gläubigers)*; **to file one's (own)** ~ (or *Am* **to file a** ~ **[in voluntary bankruptcy]**) den Konkurs anmelden *(seitens des Schuldners)*; **to present a** ~ **against sb.** gegen jdn die Konkurseröffnung beantragen *(seitens des Gläubigers)*

petition *v (schriftl.)* einkommen (to bei), Eingabe machen, ersuchen, beantragen, bitten; **to** ~ **for divorce** auf Scheidung klagen; den Scheidungsantrag einreichen; **to** ~ **for mercy** (or **a pardon**) ein Gnadengesuch einreichen

petitioning creditor[59] Gläubiger, der den Antrag auf Konkurseröffnung stellt

petitioner Antragsteller; Gesuchsteller, Bittsteller, Kläger *(bes. im Ehescheidungsprozeß; opp. respondent)*

petitory action *Scot* Klage auf Zahlung od. Erfüllung

petrodollar Petrodollar; **recycling of** ~**s** Rückfluß der Petrodollars *(in die Industrieländer)*

petrol *Br* Benzin; ~ **consumption** Benzinverbrauch; ~ **price** Benzinpreis; ~ **station** Tankstelle; **leaded** ~ verbleites (od. bleihaltiges) Benzin; **unleaded** ~ bleifreies (od. unverbleites) Benzin; **to fill up with** ~ tanken

petroleum Erdöl, Mineralöl, Petroleum; **P**~ **Cartel** Erdölkartell; ~ **prices** Erdölpreise; ~ **revenue tax** *Br* Steuern auf Einnahmen aus Erdölgewinnung *(z.B. aus der Nordsee)*; Erdölsteuer; **Organization of P**~ **Exporting Countries** (OPEC) Organisation der Erdöl-Exportländer; **manufacture of** ~ **products** Industrie der Mineralölerzeugnisse

pettifog *v* mit Schikanen arbeiten, Schliche anwenden; den Winkeladvokaten spielen

pettifogger Winkeladvokat

petties kleine Unkosten (od. Auslagen)

petty klein, geringfügig, unbedeutend; ~ **average** →average 1.; ~ **case** Bagatellsache

petty cash (P.C.) Kasse für kleine Auslagen; Portokasse; Handkasse; Bargeld; ~ **book** kleines Kassenbuch; Portobuch; ~ **receipt** Eingangsbeleg der Handkasse

petty, ~ **expenses** kleine Ausgaben (od. Spesen); ~ **jury** *Am* Urteilsjury (→*jury*); ~ **larceny** *Am* Bagatelldiebstahl; ~ **misdemeanor** *Am* leichtes Vergehen; ~ **→offen|ces (~ses);** ~ **→offender**

petty, ~ **officer** Maat *(entspricht dem N.C.O. = non-commissioned officer)*; ~ **sessions** summarisches Gericht von zwei od. mehreren Friedensrichtern *(Br*[60] *jetzt Magistrates' Courts genannt)*; ~ **theft** Bagatelldiebstahl; ~ **trader** kleiner Geschäftsmann

pharmaceutical, ~ **industry** Pharma-Industrie; ~**s** pharmazeutische Erzeugnisse, Arzneimittel

phase (Entwicklungs-)Phase, Stadium, Stufe; ~ **out** *(langsame)* (Produktions-, Arbeits- etc) Einstellung; *(stufenweiser)* Abbau, Auslaufen

phase *v* stufenweise durchführen; zeitlich staffeln; **to** ~ **out** *(Produktion etc) (langsam)* einstellen (od. auslaufen lassen); *(Zölle etc) (stufenweise)* abbauen, schrittweise aufheben

phasing out →phase-out; allmähliche Abschaffung; Auslaufen; ~ **of existing rights** Auslaufen bestehender Rechte

philanthropical activities Wohlfahrtstätigkeit; **to engage in** ~ sich auf dem Gebiete der Wohlfahrt betätigen

philanthropy, to practise ~ Wohlfahrtstätigkeit ausüben

Philippines Philippinen; **Republic of** ~ Republik der Philippinen

Philippine[61] philippinisch; (→*Filipino*)

philosophy, ~ **of law** (or **legal**~) Rechtsphilosophie

phon(e)y *colloq.* imitiert, (falsch) nachgemacht; ~ **papers** *sl.* gefälschte Papiere

phonogram Tonträger; **producer of** ~**s**[62] Hersteller von Tonträgern; **Convention for the Protection of Producers of P**~**s against Unauthorized Duplication of their P**~**s**[63] Übereinkommen zum Schutz der Hersteller von Tonträgern gegen unerlaubte Vervielfältigung ihrer Tonträger

phonograph record Schallplatte

phonorecord *Am (UrhR)* Tonträger; **coin operated** ~ **player** *Am (UrhR)* Münzautomat für Tonträger, Musikautomat

photocopier Fotokopiergerät

photocopy *v* fotokopieren

photocopy Fotokopie; **certified** ~ beglaubigte Fotokopie

photo(graph) Foto(grafie), Lichtbild; **full face** (or **front view**) ~ en-face-Aufnahme

photographic works Werke der Fotografie; Lichtbildwerke

Photostat (*Am auch* ~**ic copy**) Warenzeichen für ein Fotokopiergerät; *(ungenau auch:)* Fotokopie, Ablichtung

photostat *v* fotokopieren

phototelegram(me) Bildtelegramm

phraseology Ausdrucksweise, Wortlaut

physical physisch, körperlich *(opp. mental);* ~ **assets** Sachvermögen(swerte), Sachanlagen; ~ **condition** Gesundheitszustand; ~ **destruction of armaments** Verschrottung von Rüstungsgegenständen; ~ **education** Leibeserziehung; ~ **examination** körperliche Durchsuchung; ~ **fitness** körperliche Tauglichkeit; ~ →**inventory;** ~ **life** Lebensdauer, Nutzungsdauer; ~ **market** →spot market; ~ **person** natürliche Person; ~ **protection** Objektschutz
physically, ~ **disabled** Körperbehinderter; Versehrter; ~ **handicapped** körperbehindert

physician-patient privilege *Am* (die das Aussageverweigerungsrecht begründende) ärztliche Schweigepflicht

phytopathological control pflanzenrechtliche Kontrolle

phytosanitary certificate[64] Pflanzengesundheitszeugnis

pick *v (sorgfältig)* aussuchen; **to ~ a lock** ein Schloß mit dem Dietrich öffnen *(in der Absicht zu stehlen)*; **to ~ a p.'s pocket** bei jdm Taschendiebstahl begehen

pick-up *com sl.* Erholung; ~ **in orders** Auftragszunahme

pick up *v com* sich erholen; *(Fahrgäste)* aufnehmen (od. mitnehmen); **to ~ the goods** die Waren abholen; **to ~ a language** e-e Sprache durch Hören (ohne systematisches Studium) erlernen; **to ~ for a song** *sl.* billig erstehen

pickaback transport (*Am* **traffic**) Huckepackverkehr

picket Streikposten, Streikwache; ~ **line** Streikpostenkette; **to cross the ~ line** Streikposten nicht beachten

picket *v* Streikposten aufstellen vor; als Streikposten stehen
picketing[65] Aufstellung von Streikposten; Streikpostenstehen; **secondary ~** betriebsfremde Streikposten

pickpocket Taschendieb; **beware of ~s** Vorsicht, Taschendiebe!

pickpocketing Taschendiebstahl

pictorial advertising Bildwerbung

picture, a true and fair ~ ein den tatsächlichen Verhältnissen entsprechendes Bild

piece Stück; ~ **goods** (*Textil*) Meterware(n); ~ **meal price fixing** Preisfestsetzung von Fall zu Fall; ~ **number** Stückzahl; ~ **of evidence** Beweisstück, Beleg; ~ **of furniture** Möbelstück; ~ **of land** (or **ground**) Stück Land, Grundstück, Parzelle; ~ **of money** Geldstück; ~ **of news** Nachricht
piece rate Akkord(lohn)satz, Stück(lohn)satz *(opp. time rate)*; ~ **plan** Akkordsystem; **fixing of ~s** Festsetzung der Akkordsätze; **payment by ~s** Akkordlohn, Stücklohn; **work at ~s** nach Akkord bezahlte Arbeit
piece wages Akkordlohn, Stücklohn
piece(-)work Akkordarbeit; ~ **contract** Akkordvertrag; ~ **rate** Akkord(lohn)satz; **to do ~** im Akkord arbeiten
piece(-)worker Akkordarbeiter; **pieceworkers' guarantee clause** *Br* Verdienstsicherungsklausel für Akkordarbeiter *(→fall-back payment)*
piece, by the ~ stückweise, per Stück; **to pay by the ~** *(jdn)* im Akkord bezahlen; stückweise bezahlen; **to work by the ~** im Akkord arbeiten

pierage Hafengebühren; Kaigeld

piercing the corporate veil Durchgriffshaftung

pigeon(-)hole Ablegefach, Brieffach; Einordnung, Klassifizierung

pigeon(-)hole *v* in ein Fach legen, ablegen; beiseite legen; zurückstellen; klassifizieren; **to ~ a matter** die Erledigung e-r Sache verschleppen
pigeon(-)holed, the scheme was ~ der Plan war zurückgestellt

pig on pork *Br colloq.* auf eigene Niederlassung gezogene Wechsel

piggyback transport (or *Am* **traffic**) Huckepack- Verkehr

pile Haufen, Stoß; *(AtomR)* Reaktor; ~ **of money** große Menge Geld; ~**-up** Massenauffahrunfall *(z.B. auf der Autobahn)*

pilfer *v* stehlen, kleinen Diebstahl begehen, „mausen"; ~**ing** →pilferage

pilferage Stehlen, Diebstahl *(von geringerwertigen Sachen);* Notdiebstahl

pilferer Dieb *(der geringwertige Sachen gestohlen hat)*

pilgrim Pilger; ~ **traffic**[66] Reiseverkehr der Pilger

pillage Plünderung *(bes. im Krieg)*

pillag|e *v* plündern; ~**ing** Plünderung

pillory *v* dem Spott aussetzen

pilot 1. Lotse; Pilot; Flugzeugführer; ~ **boat** Lotsenboot; ~**-in-command** *Am* Flugzeugkommandant; ~**'s licen|ce (~se)** Lotsenpatent; Flugzeugführerschein; ~ **service** Lotsendienst; ~ **scheme** Pilotvorhaben; ~ **ship** (or **vessel**) Lotsenfahrzeug; ~ **trainee** Flugschüler; **commercial ~** Berufs-Flugzeugführer; **compulsory ~** Zwangslotse; **second ~** Kopilot

pilot 2. Versuchs-; ~ **lot** Versuchsserie; ~ **plant** Versuchsanlage; Versuchsbetrieb; ~ **project** (or **scheme**) Versuchsprojekt; ~ **study** (or **test, survey**) *(Marktforschung)* Probebefragung, Probeuntersuchung

pilot *v* lotsen; Flugzeug führen; *fig* führen, lenken; **to ~ in** einlotsen; **to ~ out** auslotsen; **to ~ a bill through Congress** *Am* ein Gesetz durchbringen

pilotage[67] Lotsen(dienst); *fig* Führung, Lenkung; ~ **(dues)** Lotsengeld, Lotsengebühren; ~ **inwards** (Lotsengeld für) Einlotsen; ~ **outwards** (Lotsengeld für) Auslotsen; ~ **waters** Lotsenstrecke, Lotsenrevier; **compulsory** ~ Lotsenzwang

pilotless aircraft unbemannte(s) Luftfahrzeug(e)

pimp *colloq.* Zuhälter, Kuppler

pin-money; Taschengeld; geringfügige Belohnung

pint Pinte *(⅛ Gallone; Br 0,568 l, Am 0,473 l)*

pioneer *mil* Pionier; *fig* Bahnbrecher; ~ **invention** *(PatR)* Pioniererfindung; ~ **work** Pionierarbeit

pioneer *v* den Weg bereiten (für); **~ing** Bahnbrechung

pipe Rohr, Leitung; Hohlmaß für Wein *(von unterschiedl. Größe, meist 105 gallons)*

pipeline[68] Rohrleitung; Pipeline; geheime Informationsquelle; *fig* üblicher Weg; **to be in the ~** auf dem Weg sein *(etw. herzustellen usw.)*

piracy *(VölkerR)* Piraterie, Seeräuberei; *(UrhR)* unzulässiger Nachdruck, Plagiat, Raubdruck *(cf. infringement of copyright)*; ~ **of a trademark** *(unzulässige)* Nachahmung e-s Musters; Markenpiraterie; **design** ~ sklavische Nachahmung; **labo(u)r** ~ Abwerbung von Arbeitskräften; **literary** ~ Plagiat

pirate *(VölkerR)* Seeräuber; *(UrhR)* Plagiator

pirate *v (UrhR)* unzulässig nachdrucken, ein Plagiat begehen; **to ~ employees** Arbeitskräfte abwerben; **to ~ a trademark** ein Warenzeichen nachahmen

pirated, ~ **edition** Raubdruck; ~ **goods** Piratenwaren, nachgeahmte Waren

pirating Plagiat; Raubdruck; Abwerbung von Arbeitskräften

piratical competition Ausnutzung der Arbeit und Gedanken des Konkurrenten

piscary, common of ~ Fischereiberechtigung *(→common 1.)*

pit 1. (Kohlen-)Grube, Bergwerk, Zeche; ~ **closure** Stillegung von Zechen; ~ **coal** Steinkohle; **~man** Bergmann

pithead Schachteingang; ~ **price** Preis ab Schacht; ~ **stocks** Kohlehalden; Haldenbestände

pit 2. *Am (Produktenbörse)* Maklerstand; ~ **trader** *Am (für eigene Rechnung spekulierender)* Produktenmakler; **wheat** ~ *Am* Weizenbörse

pitch Stand *(e-s Straßenhändlers); (Börse)* Maklerstand *(Br des jobber)*

placard Plakat, *(öffentl.)* Anschlag; **to post** (or **set up**) **a** ~ ein Plakat anschlagen

placard *v (öffentl.)* anschlagen; mit Plakat bekleben; durch Anschlag bekanntmachen

placarding Anschlag; Aushang

place 1. Platz, Ort; ~ **name** Ortsname; ~ **of abode** Aufenthaltsort, Wohnort; ~ **of accident** Unfallsort, Unfallstätte; ~ **of arrival** Ankunftsort; ~ **of birth** Geburtsort

place of business Geschäftssitz, geschäftliche (od. gewerbliche) Niederlassung; **fixed** ~ *(DBA)* feste Geschäftseinrichtung; **principal** ~ Hauptgeschäftsniederlassung; Sitz *(e-r Firma)*; **regular** ~ Betriebsstätte; **to establish a** ~ e-e geschäftliche Niederlassung begründen

place, ~ **of concealment** Versteck; ~ **of consignment** Versendungsort; ~ **of the crime** *(StrafR)* Ort des Verbrechens, Tatort; ~ **of custody** Verwahrungsort; ~ **of delivery** Liefer(ungs)ort; Erfüllungsort; ~ **of→departure;** ~ **of deposit** Hinterlegungsort; ~ **of destination** Bestimmungsort; ~ **of discharge** Ausladeort, Lösch(ungs)platz; ~ **of drawing** Ausstellungsort; ~ **of →employment;** ~ **of execution** Errichtungsort *(e-s Testaments)*; Ort der Ausfertigung *(e-r Urkunde)*; ~ **of fulfilment** Erfüllungsort; ~ **of hono(u)r** Ehrenplatz; ~ **of issue** Ausgabeort; Ausstellungsort; ~ **of loading** Ladeplatz; ~ **of manufacture** Herstellungsort; Fabrikationsstätte; ~ **of meeting** Tagungsort, Sitzungsort; ~ **of payment** Zahlungsort; ~ **of performance** Erfüllungsort; Leistungsort; ~ **of presentment** Vorlageort; ~ **of refuge** Zufluchtsort; ~ **of residence** Wohnort; Aufenthaltsort; ~ **of shipment** Verladeort; Versandort; ~ **of transshipment** Umladeplatz; Umschlageort; ~ **of unloading** Ausladeplatz

place of work Arbeitsplatz; **change of** ~ Arbeitsplatzwechsel

place view *(PatR)* Draufsicht

place, at this ~ am hiesigen Platz; **customary in a** ~ ortsüblich; **in** ~ **of** an Stelle von; **indication of** ~ Ortsangabe; **particular** ~ bestimmter Ort; **to take** ~ stattfinden

place 2. Stelle, Stellung; **permanent** ~ Dauerstellung; **to find a** ~ **for a p.** jdn unterbringen; **to lose one's** ~ s-e Stelle verlieren; **to take the** ~ **of sb.** jds Stelle einnehmen, an jds Stelle treten

place *v* setzen, stellen, legen; *(Geld)* anlegen;

(Wertpapiere) plazieren (od. unterbringen); *(jdn)* unterbringen; *(jdn)* anstellen; **to ~ to a p.'s account** jdm in Rechnung stellen; **to ~ on the agenda** auf die Tagesordnung setzen; **to ~ a ban** ein Verbot verhängen (on über); **to ~ bonds** Obligationen unterbringen (od. plazieren); **to ~ confidence** Vertrauen setzen (in auf); **to ~ a contract** *(bei Ausschreibungen)* e-n Auftrag vergeben (od. erteilen); **to ~ under sb.'s control** unter jds Aufsicht stellen; **to ~ to sb.'s credit (debit)** jdm gutschreiben (jdn belasten); **to ~ on deposit** deponieren, in Depot geben; **to ~ on the file** zu den Akten nehmen; **to be ~d in funds** *Br* Geld *(zur Deckung von Auslagen)* bekommen; **to ~ goods** Waren absetzen (od. verkaufen); **to ~ under guardianship** unter Vormundschaft stellen; **to ~ into the hands of a counsel** *(die Sache)* e-m Anwalt (*Br* e-m barrister) übergeben; **to ~ an issue** e-e Emission unterbringen; **to ~ a loan** (at 98%) e-e Anleihe (zum Kurse von 98%) unterbringen (od. plazieren); **to ~ money** (at interest) Geld (zinsbringend) anlegen; **to ~ an order** →order 3.; **to ~ on record** →record 1.; **to ~ to the reserve** dem Reservefonds zuführen; **to ~ shares with the public** Aktien beim Publikum unterbringen (od. plazieren); **to ~ workers** Arbeitnehmer vermitteln (od. unterbringen)

placing Arbeitsvermittlung; Plazierung (od. Unterbringung) *(von Wertpapieren)*; **~ of contracts** Auftragsvergebung *(→contract 2.)*; **~ of employees** Unterbringung von Arbeitnehmern; **~ of a loan** Unterbringung (od. Plazierung) e-r Anleihe; **~ of orders** →order 3.; **~ securities with the public** Unterbringung (od. Plazierung) von Wertpapieren bei dem Publikum; **private ~** *Br* private Effektenplazierung *(→private)*

placement *Am* Unterbringung *(von Arbeitskräften)*; *Am* Unterbringung (od. Plazierung) *(von Wertpapieren)*; **~ agency** *Am* Stellenvermittlung, Arbeitsvermittlung; **~ agent** *Am* Stellenvermittler; **~ of funds** Unterbringung von Geld; **~ service** *Am* Arbeitsvermittlung(sdienst); **~ test** *Am* Einstellungsprüfung; **private ~** *Am* private Effektenplazierung *(→private)*

plagiarism Plagiat, Diebstahl geistigen Eigentums; **to commit a ~** ein Plagiat begehen

plagiarist Plagiator

plagiarize *v (jds Werk)* plagiieren

plain clothes Zivil(anzug) *(opp. uniform)*; **~ man** Detektiv, Geheimpolizist

plain language, telegram in ~ nicht chiffriertes Telegramm

plain meaning rule Eindeutigkeitsregel *(eindeutiger Wortlaut schließt Auslegung aus)*

plain truth, to tell the ~ die reine Wahrheit sagen

plaintiff *(Zivilprozeß)* Kläger, Klägerin *(opp. defendant)*; **~'s claim** Klagebegehren; **~'s counsel** (or **counsel for the ~**) Anwalt (*Br* barrister) des Klägers; Prozeßbevollmächtigter; **~ in error** *Am* Kläger im Revisionsverfahren, Revisionskläger; **joint ~** Mitkläger; **to appear as ~** als Kläger auftreten; **to →find for the ~**

plan Plan, Entwurf, Vorhaben, Projekt; **~ of campaign** Feldzugsplan; **~ of distribution** Verteilungsplan; **~ (of reorganization)**[68a] Umorganisationsplan (Sanierungsplan, Vergleich); **~ of site** Lageplan; **according to ~** planmäßig; **financing ~** Finanz(ierungs)plan; **five-year ~** Fünfjahresplan; **formulation of a ~** Ausarbeitung e-s Plans; **general ~** Gesamtplan; **investment ~** Investierungsplan; **to abandon a ~** e-n Plan fallen lassen; **to alter one's ~s** s-e Pläne ändern; **to depart from one's ~** s-n Plan aufgeben; **to draw up a ~** e-n Plan aufstellen (od. entwerfen); **to interfere with a p.'s ~s** jds Pläne durchkreuzen; **to go ahead with one's ~s** s-e Pläne verwirklichen

plan *v* planen, entwerfen; *(Arbeit etc)* einteilen

planned, ~ economy Planwirtschaft *(opp. free market economy)*; **~ parenthood** Familienplanung *(Geburtenkontrolle)*

planning Planung; (Raum-)Planung; Einteilung *(der Arbeit)*; **~ agency** (or **board**) Planungsamt, Planungsstelle; **~ of industry** Industrieplanung; **~ legislation** *Br* Raumplanungsgesetzgebung; **~ permission** *Br*[69] *(behördliche)* Baugenehmigung; **~-programming-budgeting system** (PPBS) Programmbudget (*Hilfsmittel bei der Budgetaufstellung*); **~ restrictions** *Br* Baubeschränkungen; **city ~** *Am* Stadtplanung, städtebauliche Planung; **economic ~** Wirtschaftsplanung; **estate ~** Planung der Nachlaßabwicklung (*→estate*); **legal ~** *Am* juristische Tätigkeit, die Rechtsstreite verhindert; Kautelarjurisprudenz; **local ~ authority** *Br* örtliche Planungsbehörde; **long-range** (or **long-term**) **~** langfristige Planung, Planung auf lange Sicht; **manufacturing ~** Fertigungsplanung; **regional ~** Landesplanung; **short-range** (or **short-term**) **~** kurzfristige Planung, Planung auf kurze Sicht; **tax ~** Steuerplanung; **town** (or **urban**) **~** *Br* Stadtplanung; **town and country ~** Raumplanung; Raumordnung

plane 1. *colloq.* Flugzeug *(→aeroplane)*; **~ crash** Flugzeugabsturz; **mail ~** Postflugzeug; **special ~** Sonderflugzeug, Sondermaschine

plane 2. *fig.* Ebene; **on the international ~** auf internationaler Ebene

plank Einzelpunkt *(e-s politischen od. Parteiprogramms)*, Programmpunkt

plant 1. (Fabrik-, Betriebs-)Anlage; Betrieb; Fabrik; *(Bilanz)* Betriebseinrichtung, Maschinen; Betriebsgebäude; ~ **and equipment** *(Bilanz)* Betriebsgebäude und -einrichtungen; ~ **and machinery** (Betriebs-) Anlagen und Maschinen; ~ **capacity** Betriebskapazität, betriebliche Leistungsfähigkeit; ~ **closure** Betriebsschließung; ~ **extension** Betriebsvergrößerung; ~ **facilities** Betriebseinrichtungen; ~ **lease** (or **leasing**) Vermietung (od. Verpachtung) ganzer Betriebsanlagen; Anlagenverpachtung; ~ **ledger** (Betriebs-) Anlagenbuch; ~ **management** Betriebsführung, Betriebsleitung; ~ **manager** *Am* Betriebsleiter; ~ **regulations** Betriebsvorschriften; ~ **site** Fabrikgrundstück; ~ **size** Betriebsgröße; ~ **superintendent** *Am* Betriebsleiter; **expenditure for ~ assets** Investitionsaufwand; **factory ~** Fabrikanlage; **industrial ~** Industrieanlage, Fabrik; **manufacturing ~** Fabrikanlage, Fabrikationsbetrieb; **model ~** Musterbetrieb

plant 2. Pflanze; ~ **breeders' rights** Pflanzenzüchtungsrechte; ~ **breeding** Pflanzenzüchtung; ~ **patent** *Am* Pflanzenpatent

plant protection Pflanzenschutz; →**European P~ P~ Organization; International Convention for the Protection of New Varieties of Plants**[69a] Übereinkommen zum Schutz von Pflanzenzüchtungen; →**International P~ P~ Convention**

plant varieties (Pflanzen-)Sorten; **P~ V~ and Seeds Act** 1964 *Br* Gesetz über Pflanzen- und Samenarten; **animal breeds and ~** Tier- und Pflanzenzüchtungen; **protection of ~** Sortenschutz; **Register of P~ V~** Sortenkontrolle

plant 3. *Am (Presse)* „Pflanze" *(Information, die dem Reporter von interessierter Seite gegeben wird, damit er sie in s-r Zeitung „sprießen" läßt und sie e-e bestimmte Wirkung erzielt)*

plant *v* errichten, gründen; anbauen, (an-, be-)pflanzen; *sl. (jdm etw.)* unterschieben; jdn zu Unrecht belasten; **to ~ a bomb** e-e Bombe versteckt deponieren

planting, new ~ Neupflanzung

plastic, ~ arts Bildhauerkunst; **~s** (or **~ materials**) Kunststoff(e); **~s industry** Kunststoffindustrie; **~s processing industry** kunststoffverarbeitende Industrie

plat *Am* Parzellierungsplan, Bebauungsplan *(→platted land)*

plate (Metall-)Schild; ~ **glass insurance** (Spiegel- und Fenster-)Glasversicherung; **door ~** Namensschild, Türschild; **name ~** Türschild; Firmenschild; **license ~** *Am* Nummernschild *(e-s Autos)*; **(number) ~** Nummernschild *(e-s Autos)*

platform 1. Bahnsteig; ~ **car** *Am* offener Güterwagen; **goods ~** Güterladeplatz; **unloading ~** Güterabladeplatz

platform 2. Plattform; politische Basis, parteipolitischer Standpunkt; Wahlprogramm, Parteiprogramm; Rednertribüne, Podium; ~ **speaker** *Am* Redner; **common ~** *pol* gemeinsame Basis; **election ~** Wahlprogramm; **party ~** Parteiprogramm; **to erect a ~** e-e Tribüne errichten

platted land *Am* baureifes Land; Land, das in e-n Bebauungsplan aufgenommen worden ist

plea Einwand, Entschuldigung; dringende Bitte, Gesuch, Vorbringen; *(Zivilprozeß) Br hist*[70] Verteidigungsvorbringen *(des Beklagten)*, Klageerwiderung, Klagebeantwortung; Einrede; Einwendung; *(Strafprozeß)* Verteidigung, Einlassung *(des Angeklagten)*; ~ **bargaining** Verhandeln zwischen den Anklagevertretern *(Br prosecuting counsel, Am prosecuting attorney)* und dem Verteidiger *(defending counsel)*, daß der Angeklagte sich für schuldig bekennt und der Anklagevertreter e-e milde Strafe beantragt; ~ **for clemency** Gnadengesuch; ~ **in abatement** *Am* Antrag auf Prozeßabweisung (*ohne Entscheidung über den Sachantrag*); ~ **in bar** *Am* Antrag auf Sachabweisung; ~ **of confession and avoidance** *Am* Einrede *(ohne Leugnung des Klagevorbringens)*; ~ **of (not) →guilty;** ~ **of insanity** Einrede der Unzurechnungsfähigkeit; ~ **as to jurisdiction** Einrede der Unzuständigkeit *(des Gerichts)*; ~ **of justification** *(bei Beleidigungsklagen)* Geltendmachung, daß die behauptete Tatsache wahr ist; ~ **of prior publication** *(PatR)* Einrede der Vorveröffentlichung; ~ **of privilege** *Am* Geltendmachung des Zeugnisverweigerungsrechts; ~ **of res judicata** Einrede der Rechtskraft; ~ **of superior orders** *(VölkerR)* Einrede des höheren Befehls; **dilatory ~** *Am* dilatorische (od. aufschiebende) Einrede, Antrag auf Prozeßabweisung; **foreign ~** *Am* Einrede der Unzuständigkeit des Gerichts; **peremptory ~** *Am* peremptorische (od. rechtsvernichtende) Einrede, Antrag auf Sachabweisung; **the ~ is guilty** der Angeklagte erklärt sich für schuldig; **to put in a ~** e-e Einrede erheben (od. geltend machen); e-e Einwendung entgegensetzen; **to make a ~ in mitigation** *(das Gericht)* um milde(re) Beurteilung bitten; **to raise a ~** e-n Einwand erheben

plead *v (als Anwalt)* plädieren; *(als Partei od. Angeklagter vor Gericht)* vorbringen, geltend machen, einwenden; sich berufen auf; **to ~ for sb.** sich für jdn einsetzen; **to ~ for sth.** um etw. bitten; sich für etw. einsetzen (with sb. bei jdm); **to ~ at the bar** vor Gericht plädieren; **to ~ a case** (or **cause**) **before a** (or **in**) **court** e-e Sache vor Gericht vertreten; **to ~ as a** (or **in**) **defen|ce (~se)** als Einrede vorbringen, zur Verteidigung vorbringen; **to ~ one's good faith** sich auf s-n guten Glauben berufen; **to ~ (not) →guilty; to ~ one's ignorance** sich auf Unkenntnis berufen; **to ~ →justification; to ~ for mercy** um

Gnade bitten; **to ~ in mitigation** (or **to ~ mitigating circumstances**) *(StrafR)* mildernde Umstände geltend machen; **to ~ over** *(StrafR)* sich nicht für schuldig bekennen; **to ~ →prescription; to ~ →specifically; to ~ the statute of limitations** *(im Prozeß)* die Einrede der Verjährung erheben; sich auf Verjährung berufen

pleadable rechtlich zu verteidigen, vertretbar

pleader Verteidiger, Anwalt; Fürsprecher; *Br (common law-Prozeß)* jd, der Schriftsätze aufsetzt

pleading Schriftsatz; Parteivorbringen *(vor Gericht)*; Plädieren, Plädoyer *(des Anwalts)*; **~s** *(vorbereitende)* förmliche Schriftsätze *(die zwischen den Parteien gewechselt werden zur Festlegung aller strittigen Tat- und Rechtsfragen [i. e. until issue is joined]; die wichtigsten Schriftsatzformen sind Br statement of claim, defence, reply, petition and answer, Am complaint [or declaration], answer and reply)*; **~ to the charge** (or **indictment**) *(StrafR)* Einlassung auf die Anklage; **close of ~s** Schluß des Schriftsatzwechsels; **delivery of ~s** Einreichung von Schriftsätzen; Schriftsatzwechsel; **default of ~s** Schriftsatzversäumnis

pleading, special ~ 1. *Am* Eintreten für besondere Interessen; Förderung der Interessen e-r bestimmten Gruppe; **special ~ legislation** *Am* Gesetzgebung, die den Interessen e-r Gruppe (od. Einzelinteressen) dient

pleading, special ~ 2. s. to plead →specifically

pleading, to amend a ~ e-n Schriftsatz abändern; das Vorbringen ändern; **to answer one another's ~s** die Schriftsätze wechseln; **to draw** (or **settle**) **~s** Schriftsätze aufsetzen; **to deliver** (or **file**) **~s** Schriftsätze einreichen; **to strike out part of a ~** e-n Teil des Schriftsatzes *(auf Anordnung des Gerichts)* entfernen

please *v* gefallen, angenehm sein; **may it ~ Your Lordship** *Br (High Court etc)* (or **Your Hono[u]r**) *(Br County Court und Am)* Hohes Gericht *(Eröffnung des Vortrags des Anwalts)*; **Her Majesty has been graciously ~d** *Br* Ihre Majestät geruht

pleasure Vergnügen; **~ boat** Wasserfahrzeug zu Sport- und Vergnügungszwecken; **~ ground** *Br* Vergnügungspark; **~ navigation** Vergnügungsschiffahrt; **~ vessel** Vergnügungsschiff *(opp. trading vessel)*; **at one's ~** nach Belieben; **at the ~ of another** nach jds Belieben; widerruflich

pleasure, to be detained during Her Majesty's ~ *Br* →detain *v* 1.; **he holds office during Her Majesty's ~** *Br* s-e Amtszeit liegt im Ermessen Ihrer Majestät; er ist jederzeit kündbar; **to hold office at the ~ of the President** *Am* das Amt zur Verfügung des Präsidenten ausüben *(die Entlassung liegt im Ermessen des Präsidenten, z. B. bei höheren Verwaltungsbeamten der einzelnen Ressorts)*; **to serve at the ~ of the board** an die Weisungen des →board gebunden sein; **it gives me great ~ (to)** es ist mir e-e Freude (zu); **I have ~ in welcoming** ich habe das Vergnügen, zu begrüßen

plebiscite *(StaatsR)* Plebiszit, Volksabstimmung, Volksentscheid; *(VölkerR)* Volksabstimmung *(über Gebietszugehörigkeit)*; **~ zone** (or **territory subject to a ~**) Volksabstimmungsgebiet; **to conduct a ~** ein Plebiszit (od. e-e Volksabstimmung) durchführen; **a ~ is held** (or **taken**) ein Plebiszit wird vorgenommen; **to submit to a ~** e-r Volksabstimmung unterbreiten

pledge[71] (Faust-)Pfand; (Mobiliar-)Pfandrecht *(das durch Pfandvertrag und Übergabe der Pfandsache bestellt wird; es entsteht also nicht, wie lien, auch kraft Gesetzes)*; Verpfändung, Pfandsache, Pfandgegenstand; *(feierl.)* Versprechen, Zusage; **~ agreement**[72] Pfandvertrag; **~ given to the electorate** Wahlversprechen; **under ~ of secrecy** unter dem Siegel der Verschwiegenheit; **~ of securities** Verpfändung (od. Lombardierung) von Wertpapieren; **auction of the ~** Pfandversteigerung; **by way of a ~** pfandweise; **documentary ~** Dokumentenpfand *(der Schuldner übergibt dem Gläubiger an Stelle der Ware ein sie verkörperndes Wertpapier [z. B. Konnossement od. Lagerschein] als Sicherheit)*; **election ~** Wahlversprechen; **fit to serve as a ~** verpfändbar; **forfeited ~** verfallenes Pfand; **holder of a ~** Pfandgläubiger, Pfandnehmer, Pfandinhaber; **in ~ of** als Pfand für; **realization** (or **sale**) **of the ~** Pfandverwertung; Pfandverkauf; **redemption of a ~** Pfandeinlösung; **restitution of a ~** Pfandrückgabe; **unredeemed ~** nicht ausgelöstes Pfand; **to accept as** (or **in**) **~** als Pfand annehmen; **to be in ~** verpfändet sein; **to deposit a ~ with a p.** bei jdm ein Pfand hinterlegen; **to enforce the ~ by selling it** das Pfand durch Verkauf verwerten; **to fulfil ~s** *(feierl.)* Versprechen halten; **to give in ~** s. to put in →~; **to hold in ~** als Pfand haben (od. halten); **to meet a ~** ein Versprechen einlösen, zu e-m Versprechen stehen; **to put in ~** *(etw.)* verpfänden, als Pfand geben; **to redeem a ~** ein Pfand einlösen; **to take in ~** als Pfand nehmen; **to take out of ~** ein Pfand auslösen

pledge *v* verpfänden, in Pfand geben; *(feierl.)* versprechen, geloben, zusagen; **to ~ o.s.** sich verpflichten; **to ~ a chattel as security for a debt** e-e Sache als Sicherheit für e-e Schuld verpfänden; **to ~ the credit of sb.** jds Kreditwürdigkeit belasten (jdn mit seinen Schulden belasten); **to ~ one's hono(u)r** sich ehrenwörtlich verpflichten; **to ~ securities with a bank for payment of a loan** Effekten bei e-r Bank lombardieren lassen; **to ~ one's word** sein Ehrenwort geben

pledged, ~ **articles** (or **goods**) Pfandsachen, Pfandgut; ~ **securities** beliehene (od. lombardierte) Wertpapiere; **to be** ~ **to secrecy** zur Verschwiegenheit verpflichtet sein; **to redeem the** ~ **property** das Pfandgut einlösen

pledging Pfandbestellung, Verpfändung; ~ **of securities** Beleihung (od. Lombardierung) von Wertpapieren

pledgeable verpfändbar

pledgee Pfandgläubiger, Pfandnehmer, Pfandinhaber

pledger (or **pledgor**) Pfandschuldner, Pfandgeber, Verpfänder

plenary vollständig, Voll-, Plenar-; ~ **action** *Am* Klage im ordentlichen Verfahren; ~ **assembly** Plenarversammlung, Vollversammlung; ~ **debate** Plenardebatte; ~ **deliberation** Plenarberatung; ~ **decision** Plenarentscheidung; ~ **meeting** Plenartagung; ~ **power(s)** unbeschränkte Vollmacht; ~ **session** Plenarsitzung, Vollsitzung; **debate in** ~ **assembly** (or **session**) Plenarberatung

plene administravit ("he has fully administered") Einrede *(des executor od. administrator)* der Dürftigkeit des Nachlasses

plenipotentiar|y Bevollmächtigter; bevollmächtigt *(bes. in Verbindung mit diplomatischen Vertretern; cf. ambassador, minister)*; **to appoint as** ~ zum Bevollmächtigten ernennen; **the** ~**ies having exchanged their full powers found in good and due form, have agreed as follows** die Bevollmächtigten haben nach Austausch ihrer in guter und gehöriger Form befundenen Vollmachten folgendes vereinbart; **the** ~**ies have signed the present Treaty (and affixed thereto their seals)** die Bevollmächtigten haben diesen Vertrag unterschrieben (und mit ihren Siegeln versehen)

plentiful, money is ~ Geld ist reichlich vorhanden *(opp. scarce)*

plenum Plenum, Vollversammlung

plethora of money Überfluß an Geld, Geldfülle

plight schwierige Lage, Notlage; **affidavit of** ~ **and condition** eidliche Erklärung, daß ein Testament sich in demselben Zustand befindet wie beim Tode des Testators *(wenn dem äußeren Zustand nach Zweifel daran bestehen)*

plombé *Fr (amtl.)* plombiert

plot 1. Grundstück, Parzelle; ~ **of land** Stück Land; Grundstück, Parzelle; **building** ~ Baugrundstück

plot 2. *(geheimer)* Anschlag, Komplott, Verschwörung; **assassination** ~ Attentatsplan; **defeat of a** ~ Vereitelung e-s Anschlags; **exposure of a** ~ Aufdeckung e-r Verschwörung; **to defeat a** ~ e-n Anschlag vereiteln; **to devise a** ~ s. to lay a →~; **to discover a** ~ e-e Verschwörung aufdecken; **to lay a** ~ e-n Anschlag vorbereiten, e-e Verschwörung anzetteln

plot *v (im geheimen)* planen, e-n Anschlag machen, sich verschwören; e-n Plan anfertigen von; **to** ~ **(out)** *(Land)* in Parzellen aufteilen, parzellieren

plotting Verschwörung

plottage increment (or **value**) *Am* Mehrwert *(e-s Grundstücks)* durch Möglichkeit der Zusammenlegung mit angrenzenden Parzellen

plotter Verschwörer

plough *v*, **to** ~ **back earnings** (or **profits**) (Geschäfts-)Gewinne nicht entnehmen und wieder *(im Betrieb)* anlegen (od. reinvestieren)

plow back *v Am* →plough back *v*

plowing back of earnings *Am* Gewinnthesaurierung, Reinvestierung von Gewinnen

plug *v colloq. (im Fernsehen und Rundfunk)* Reklame machen für

plump for *v* wählen, sich entscheiden für

plunder Plünderung; (Kriegs-)Beute

plunge *v* stürzen *(z.B. Kurse, Preise)*; **to** ~ **a country into war** ein Land in den Krieg stürzen

plural mehrfach; ~ **marriage** Polygamie, Mehrehe *(Am früher bei den Mormonen üblich)*; ~ **tenure** gemeinsamer Besitz; ~ **vote** (or **voting**) (Wahl nach dem) Plural- (od. Mehrstimmen-) wahlrecht; Abgabe von mehr als e-r Stimme; Wahl in mehr als e-m Wahlbezirk; ~ **voter** Wähler mit Stimme in mehr als einem Wahlbezirk; ~ **voting share** Mehrstimmrechtsaktie

pluralist *eccl* jd, der mehr als eine Pfründe besitzt

plurality Mehrheit; *Am pol (bes. relative)* Stimmenmehrheit; *eccl* gleichzeitiger Besitz von mehreren Pfründen; ~ **of offices** Ämterhäufung; **to hold a** ~ **of offices** mehrere Ämter gleichzeitig haben, mehrere Ämter auf sich vereinigen

plus plus, zuzüglich; ~ **or minus** →**variation**

plutocracy Plutokratie, Geldherrschaft

pluvious policy Regenversicherungspolice

pneumatic, ~ **post** *Br* Rohrpost; ~ **tube items** Rohrpostsendungen

poach *v* Jagdwilderei (od. Fischwilderei) begehen, wildern; **to** ~ **labo(u)r** Arbeitskräfte abwerben

poaching[73] (Jagd-, Fisch-)Wilderei, Wildern; ~

of members *Br* Mitgliederabwerbung; **labo(u)r** ~ Abwerbung von Arbeitskräften

poacher Wilderer, Wilddieb

pocket Tasche; ~ **book** Taschenbuch; ~ **money** Taschengeld; ~ **supplement** (periodischer) Nachtrag *(der das Werk auf den neuesten Stand bringt)*; ~ **veto** *Am parl* Ausübung des Veto *(durch den Präsidenten od. den Gouverneur e-s Einzelstaates)* durch Nichtunterzeichnung e-r Gesetzesvorlage
pocket, out-of-~ expenses (Bar-)Auslagen für Unkosten; **with** ~ gegen Erstattung der Unkosten
pocket, to be in ~ *colloq.* Gewinn haben; **to be out of** ~ *colloq.* Verlust haben, verlieren (on an); **to pick sb.'s** ~ bei jdm Taschendiebstahl begehen

pocket *v* einstecken; *Am parl (Gesetzesvorlage)* nicht unterzeichnen (→*pocket veto*); **to** ~ **a profit** *sl.* e-n Gewinn einstecken (od. sich unrechtmäßig aneignen)

poinding *Scot* Zwangsvollstreckung in das bewegliche Vermögen *(des Schuldners)*

point 1. *(wesentl.)* Punkt; ~ **at issue** Streitpunkt, strittiger Punkt; entscheidende Frage; Beweispunkt; ~**s of claim** *Br (in Handelssachen)* (formlose) Klagebegründung *(anstelle des statement of claim)*; ~**s of defence** *Br (in Handelssachen)* (formlose) Klagebeantwortung *(anstelle von defence)*
point of departure Abfahrtsort; **agreed** ~ vereinbarter Absendungsort
point of entry Grenzübergangsstelle
point of fact Tatfrage; **in** ~ tatsächlich
point, ~ **of hono(u)r** Ehrensache; ~ **of intervention** Interventionspunkt
point of law Rechtsfrage; **appeal on a** ~ *(PatR)* Rechtsbeschwerde; **raising a** ~ Erhebung e-s Rechtseinwandes *(Br über den als →preliminary issue in e-r Vorverhandlung entschieden werden kann)*
point of order *parl* Antrag zur Geschäftsordnung (→*order 1.*)
point of purchase advertising Werbung am Verkaufspunkt
point of sale (POS) Ort des Verkaufs; ~ **banking** bargeldlose Zahlung an der Kasse e-s Einzelhandelsgeschäfts; ~ **system** bargeldloses Kassensystem (→POS); ~ **terminal** (*EDV*) Verkaufsstellenterminal (*elektronische Kassen für bargeldloses Einkaufen*)
point of view Gesichtspunkt, Standpunkt; **to maintain a** ~ auf e-m Standpunkt verharren, e-e Auffassung vertreten
point, ~**s rating** Punktbewertung; ~ **system** Punktsystem *(z. B. für Arbeitsbewertung)*
point, bullion ~ Goldpunkt; **case in** ~ vorliegender Fall; **chief** (or **main**) ~ Hauptpunkt, Hauptsache; →**crossing** ~; **discussion** ~ Verhandlungspunkt; **gold** (or **specie**) ~ Goldpunkt (→*gold*); **minor** ~ Nebensache; **off the** ~ nicht zur Sache gehörig; **on the same** ~ zu derselben Frage
point, to the ~ zur Sache gehörig, sachdienlich; **evidence (that is) not to the** ~ nicht sachdienlicher (od. unerheblicher) Beweis; **to speak to the** ~ zur Sache sprechen
point, to carry one's ~ mit s-r Ansicht durchdringen; **to come to the** ~ zur (Haupt-)Sache kommen; **to concede a** ~ in e-m Punkte nachgeben; **to drive home a** ~ mit Nachdruck darauf hinweisen; **that is not the** ~ darum handelt es sich nicht; **to make a** ~ **(of)** Wert darauf legen (zu)
point 2. *(Börse)* Punkt *(die e-r Kursnotierung zugrundeliegende Einheit)*; **to decline 3** ~**s** 3 Punkte nachgeben, um 3 Punkte fallen; **to gain 3** ~**s** 3 Punkte gewinnen; **to rise 2** ~**s** um 2 Punkte steigen

point out *v* hinweisen (to auf); bemerken

poison Gift; ~ **gas**[74] Giftgas; ~ **pills** Möglichkeiten, die Finanzierungspläne e-s →raiders durcheinanderzubringen *(z. B. Ausgabe neuer Aktien aus dem genehmigtem Kapital, Vorzugs- und Mehrstimmrechtsaktien)*; **to administer** ~ *(jdm)* Gift beibringen; *(jdn)* vergiften

poison *v* vergiften
poisoning Vergiftung; **murder by** ~ Giftmord

poisonous (or **toxic**) **waste** Giftmüll

Poland Polen (→*Polish People's Republic*)
Pole Pole, Polin

pole Rute (5,029 m)

polemics Polemik

police[75] Polizei; ~ **action** Polizeiaktion; ~ **area** Polizeirevier; ~ **cell** Haftzelle; ~ **constable** *Br (gewöhnlicher)* Polizist; ~ **cordon** Polizeikordon; ~ →**court**
police custody Polizeigewahrsam; **detention in** ~ Polizeihaft; **person detained in** ~ Person in polizeilichem Gewahrsam
police, ~ **detachment** Polizeiabteilung; Polizeiaufgebot; ~ **escort** Polizeieskorte, polizeiliche (Be-)Deckung; ~ **evidence as to character** polizeiliches Führungszeugnis; ~ **force** Polizei; ~ **headquarters** Polizeipräsidium; ~ **health precautions** gesundheitspolizeiliche Maßnahmen; ~ **informer** Polizeispitzel; ~ **inspector** *Br* Polizeikommissar; ~ **interrogation** polizeiliche Vernehmung; ~ **intervention** Einschreiten der Polizei; ~ **judge** *Am* Richter e-s ~ court; ~ **magistrate** *Am* Polizeirichter; ~**man** Polizist; ~**man on the beat** Polizei auf Streife; ~ **offense** *Am* Straftat mit geringer Strafandrohung; *(etwa)* Übertretung; ~ **officer** Polizeibeamter, Polizist; ~ **operation**

Polizeiaktion; ~ **patrol** Polizeistreife; ~ **photograph** *Br* Polizeifoto; ~ **power** *Am* Polizeigewalt *(Ordnungsgewalt der [Bundes- od. einzelstaatl.] Legislative)*; ~ **powers** Polizeibefugnisse; ~ **protection** Polizeischutz; ~ **raid** (Polizei-)Razzia

police record Strafregister; **abstract from the** ~ Strafregisterauszug; **to have a** ~ vorbestraft sein

police regulations polizeiliche Vorschriften; Polizeiverordnung; Polizeiverfügung; **contrary to** ~ polizeiwidrig

police, ~ **state** Polizeistaat; ~**-station** Polizeirevier, Polizeiwache

police supervision *Br*[76] Polizeiaufsicht; **to place** (or **put**) **sb. under** ~ jdn unter Polizeiaufsicht stellen; **to be subject to** ~ der Polizeiaufsicht unterstehen

police warning with on-the-spot fining (especially for minor traffic offences) *Am* gebührenpflichtige Verwarnung

police, border ~ Grenzpolizei; **chief of** ~ *Am* Polizeipräsident; **under control of the** ~ unter Polizeiaufsicht; →**detachment of** ~; **(strong) force of** ~ (starkes) Polizeiaufgebot; **frontier** ~ Grenzpolizei; **harbo(u)r** ~ Hafenpolizei; **local** ~ **authority** Ortspolizeibehörde; **military** ~ Militärpolizei; **political** ~ *Am* politische Polizei, Staatspolizei, Geheimpolizei; **railway** ~ *Br* Bahnpolizei; **secret** ~ *Br* Geheimpolizei, Staatspolizei; **traffic** ~ Verkehrspolizei

police, detained by the ~ von der Polizei festgenommen; **to be taken to the** ~ **station** zur Polizeiwache gebracht werden; **to give sb. into the custody of the** ~ (or **to give sb. over to the** ~) jdn der Polizei übergeben; **to give o.s. up to the** ~ sich *(freiwillig)* der Polizei stellen; **to hand** *(documents etc)* **over to the** ~ der Polizei übergeben; **to inform** (or **notify**) **the** ~ die Polizei verständigen (od. benachrichtigen); **to report to the** ~ sich bei der Polizei melden; **wanted by the** ~ von der Polizei gesucht, steckbrieflich verfolgt

police *v (Gebiet)* polizeilich überwachen; mit Polizei versehen

policy 1. *(praktisch befolgte)* Politik *(cf. politics)*; politischer Kurs, politische Richtung; Richtlinie, Grundsatz; Ziel(setzung), Programm; *Scot* Park e-s Landsitzes; ~ **decision** (rechts-) politische Entscheidung; ~ **determination** *Br (von der Regierung getroffene)* Entscheidungsfällung; ~ **discussion** Grundsatzbesprechung; **basic** ~ **issues** politische Grundsatzfragen

policy-making richtungweisend; ~ **official** *Am* Beamter in leitender Stellung; ~ **position** leitende Stellung

policy, ~ **of alliances** Bündnispolitik; ~ **of appeasement** Beschwichtigungspolitik; ~ **of attrition** Zermürbungspolitik; ~ **of containment** Eindämmungspolitik; ~ **of détente** Entspannungspolitik; ~ **of drift** Politik der Untätigkeit (des Sichtreibenlassens); ~ **of encirclement** Einkreisungspolitik; ~ **of a firm** Unternehmenspolitik; ~ **of the law** *Am* Zweck (od. Ziel) des Gesetzes; gesetzgeberische Absicht

policy, ~ **of the middle road** Politik der Mitte; ~ **of mutual understanding** Verständigungspolitik

policy of neutrality Neutralitätspolitik; **to practice a** ~ Neutralitätspolitik betreiben

policy, ~ **of non-intervention** Nichteinmischungspolitik; ~ **of rapprochement** (Wieder-)Annäherungspolitik; ~ **of the statute** →~ of the law; ~ **relating to economic trends** Konjunkturpolitik; ~ **statement** Grundsatzerklärung

policy, agricultural ~ Agrarpolitik; **new alignment of** ~ Neuorientierung der Politik; **ambiguous** ~ undurchsichtige Politik; **business** ~ Betriebspolitik, Geschäftstaktik; **business cycle** ~ Konjunkturpolitik; **change in** ~ Änderung der Politik; politischer Kurswechsel; **commercial** ~ Wirtschaftspolitik (→*commercial*); **currency** ~ Währungspolitik; **customs** ~ Zollpolitik; **deliberate** ~ gezielte Politik; **domestic** ~ Innenpolitik; **economic** ~ Wirtschaftspolitik; **exchange** ~ Devisenpolitik; **financial** (or **fiscal**) ~ Finanzpolitik; **foreign** (or **external**) ~ Außenpolitik

policy, general ~ allgemeine Richtlinie; **matters of general** ~ Angelegenheiten von grundlegender Bedeutung

policy, hands off ~ Nichteinmischungspolitik; **home** (or **internal**) ~ Innenpolitik; **(industrial) location** ~ Ansiedlungspolitik; **investment** ~ Investitionspolitik; **labo(u)r** ~ Arbeitsmarktpolitik; **legal** ~ Rechtspolitik; **lines of** ~ Grundlinien der Politik; **long-range** ~ Politik auf weite Sicht; **military** ~ Wehrpolitik; **monetary** ~ Währungspolitik (→*monetary*); **ostrich** ~ Vogel-Strauß-Politik; **population** ~ Bevölkerungspolitik; **price** (or **pricing**) ~ Preispolitik

policy, public ~[77] (= ordre public) die Grundsätze, durch die Vertrags- und Verfügungsfreiheit e-r Person zum besten der Allgemeinheit rechtlich eingeschränkt werden; Gemeinwohl; *(IPR)* ordre public als Inhalt e-r Vorbehaltsklausel[78], die bestimmt, daß das *(nach den inländischen Kollisionsnormen anwendbare)* ausländische Recht, das gegen den inländischen ordre public verstößt, nicht angewendet werden darf; **against** (or **contrary to**) **public** ~ gegen das Allgemeinwohl; gegen den ordre public; gegen die guten Sitten, sittenwidrig

policy, for reasons of ~ aus politischen Gründen; **retention of a** ~ Beibehaltung e-r Politik (od. e-s politischen Kurses); **social** ~ Sozialpolitik; **tariff** ~ Zollpolitik; **trade** ~ Handelspolitik; **wage** ~ (of the trade unions) Lohnpolitik (der Gewerkschaften)

polic|y, to adopt a ~ e-n Grundsatz anwenden; e-e Politik einschlagen; **to follow a** ~ s. to pursue a →~; **to formulate ~ies** Richtlinien aufstellen; **to maintain a** ~ an e-r Politik festhalten, e-e Politik beibehalten; **to pursue a (certain)** ~ e-e (bestimmte) Politik befolgen

policy 2. *(VersR)* Police, Versicherungsschein; ~ **applicant** Antragsteller; ~ **of assurance** *Br* Versicherungspolice; ~ **to bearer** Inhaberpolice

polic|y book Policenregister; **lapsed ~ies book** Versicherungsablaufregister

policy, ~ **conditions** Versicherungsbedingungen; ~ **date** Datum des Versicherungsbeginns; ~ **dividend** Gewinnanteil; ~ **drafting** Policenausfertigung; ~ **duty** Versicherungsgebühr, Versicherungssteuer; ~ **free of premium** prämienfreie Versicherung

policy holder Policeninhaber, Versicherungsnehmer; **~s' meeting** Mitgliederversammlung *(e-r →mutual insurance company)*; **non-profit** ~ nicht gewinnberechtigter Policeninhaber; **with-profit** ~ gewinnberechtigter Policeninhaber

policy, ~ **loan** Policendarlehen, Beleihung e-r (Lebens-)Versicherung; ~ **of insurance** s. insurance →~; ~ **of sea insurance** Seeversicherungspolice; ~ **number** Policennummer; ~ **owner** Versicherungsnehmer; ~ **proof of interest**[79] (P.P.I.) *(SeeversR)* Versicherungspolice ohne Nachweis e-s versicherbaren Interesses; ~ **provisions** Bestimmungen des Versicherungsvertrages; ~ **records** Versicherungsunterlagen; ~ **year** Jahr des Versicherungsbeginns

policy, additional ~ Nachtragspolice, Zusatzpolice; **all risks** ~ Universal(auto)versicherung; **assignment of a** ~ Abtretung e-r Versicherungspolice; **blank** ~ Policenformular; **blanket** ~ *Am* Pauschalpolice; **commencement of a** ~ Versicherungsbeginn; **compound** ~ *Am* Pauschalpolice; **declaration** ~ offene Police, Pauschalpolice; **expiration of a** ~ Ablauf e-r Versicherung(spolice); **expired** ~ abgelaufene Police; **→fleet** ~; **floating** ~ Abschreibepolice, offene Police, laufende Police; **free** ~ prämienfreie Police; **group** ~ Sammelpolice; **individual** ~ Einzelpolice; **insurance** ~ Versicherungspolice; **issuing of a** ~ Ausstellung e-r Police; **lapsed** ~ verfallene Police

policy, life ~ Lebensversicherungspolice; **whole life** ~ Lebensversicherung auf den Todesfall; **to take out a life** ~ sein Leben versichern lassen, e-e Lebensversicherung abschließen

policy, life of a ~ Laufzeit e-r Police; **loan on** ~ Policedarlehen; **loss recoverable under the** ~ laut Versicherungspolice zu ersetzender Schaden; **maritime** (or **marine**) ~ Seeversicherungspolice; **→master** ~; **mixed** ~[80] *(SeeversR)* Zeit- und Reisepolice; **named** ~ *(SeeversR)* Namenspolice *(opp. floating ~)*; **open** ~[81] (O.P.) offene Police, Police ohne Wertangabe *(opp. valued ~)*; **open** ~ **for a specific amount** Pauschalpolice; **paid-up** ~ prämienfreie Police; **participating** ~ Versicherung mit Gewinnbeteiligung; **standard** ~ Normalpolice, Einheitspolice *(mit gesetzl. festgelegtem Inhalt)*; **subsequent** (or **supplementary**) ~ Nachtragspolice; **surrender value of a** ~ Rückkaufswert e-r Police; **terms of the** ~ Versicherungsbedingungen; **time** ~ *(bes. SeeversR)*[80] Zeitpolice, zeitlich befristete Police; **unvalued** ~[81] offene Police, Police ohne Wertangabe; **valued** ~[81] taxierte Police, Police mit Wertangabe; **voyage** ~[81] Reiseversicherungspolice

policy, to borrow (or **lend money**) **on a** ~ e-e Police beleihen; **to issue** (or **make out**) **a** ~ e-e Police ausstellen; **to surrender a** ~ e-e (Lebensversicherungs-)Police zurückkaufen; **to take out a** ~ e-e Versicherung abschließen, sich versichern lassen; **to take out a** ~ **on one's life** e-e Lebensversicherung abschließen; **to underwrite a** ~ →underwrite *v* 2.

policy 3. *Am* Zahlenlotto; ~ **shop** Lotterieannahmestelle

Polish polnisch; ~ **People's Republic** Polnische Volksrepublik

politic, body ~ Staat(swesen)

political politisch; Staats-; **P~ Action Committee** (PAC) *Am (aus Extrabeiträgen finanziertes)* Sonderkomitee der Gewerkschaften zur Beteiligung an Wahlkämpfen

political activit|y politische Betätigung; **participation in illegal ~ies** Teilnahme an unerlaubter politischer Tätigkeit; **to be engaged in ~ies** sich politisch betätigen

political, ~ **agitator** politischer Agitator, (Volks-)Aufwiegler; ~ **ascendancy** politisches Übergewicht

political asylum politisches Asyl; **application for** ~ Antrag auf politisches Asyl; **to ask for** ~ um politisches Asyl bitten

political, ~ **attitude** politische Haltung; ~ **bargaining power** politische Verhandlungsstärke; ~ **circles** politische Kreise; ~ **climate** politisches Klima; ~ **colo(u)r** politische Einstellung (od. Tendenz) *(z.B. e-r Zeitung)*; ~ **consolidation** politische Konsolidierung; ~ **conviction** politische Überzeugung; ~ **cooperation** politische Zusammenarbeit; ~ **currents** politische Strömungen; ~ **dispute** politischer Streitfall; ~ **disturbances** politische Unruhen; ~ **economist** Volkswirt(schaftler); ~ **education** politische Bildung

political endorsement, selling ~ *Am*[82] politische Unterstützung gegen Vergütung

political, ~ **equality** politische Gleichberechtigung; ~ **events** politische Ereignisse; ~ **fund**[83] Sonderfonds e-r →trade union für politische Zwecke; ~ **gathering** politische Versammlung; ~ **goal** politisches Ziel; **on** ~ **grounds** aus politischen Gründen; ~ **group** (politische) Fraktion

political influence politischer Einfluß; **to deprive sb. of** ~ jdn politisch kaltstellen

political, ~ **meeting** politische Versammlung; ~ **offen|ce (~se)**[84] politisches Delikt, politische Straftat; ~ **offender** politischer Verbrecher; ~ **opinion** politische Meinung (od. Ansicht); ~ **opponent** politischer Gegner

political part|y politische Partei (→*party 3.*); **creation** (or **formation**) **of ~ies** Bildung politischer Parteien; **donation to ~ies** Parteienspende; **financing of ~ies** Parteienfinanzierung; **to vote for a** ~ e-e politische Partei wählen

political, ~ →**police;** ~ **prisoner** politischer Häftling; **for** ~ **reasons** aus politischen Gründen; ~ **refugee** politischer Flüchtling; Emigrant; ~ **rights** politische Rechte, staatsbürgerliche Rechte; ~ **risks** politische Risiken; ~ **science** politische Wissenschaften, Politologie; ~ **situation** politische Lage; ~ **society** Gesellschaft *(als polit.-soziol. Begriff)*; ~ **subdivision** Gebietskörperschaft; ~ **system** politisches System; ~ **tension** politische Spannung; ~ **thaw** politisches Tauwetter; **(moderate)** ~ **views** (gemäßigte) politische Ansichten

politically in politischer Hinsicht, vom politischen Standpunkt aus; ~ **clear** politisch unbelastet; ~ **not clear** politisch belastet; **~-minded** politisch gesinnt; ~ **reliable** politisch zuverlässig; ~ **unreliable** politisch unzuverlässig

politician (Berufs-)Politiker; Parteipolitiker; Geschäftemacher; **leading** ~ führender Politiker

politicize *v* politisieren; politisch informieren; sich als Politiker betätigen

politico, **~-economic** wirtschaftspolitisch; **~-geographical** geopolitisch; **~-social** sozialpolitisch

politics Politik, Staatskunst; politische Grundsätze (od. Ansichten); *Am* politische Taktik; **domestic** (or **internal**) ~ Innenpolitik; **in the field of** ~ auf politischem Gebiet; **foreign** ~ auswärtige Politik; **international** ~ Weltpolitik; **party** ~ Parteipolitik; **practical** ~ Realpolitik; **world** ~ Weltpolitik; **to deal in** ~ sich mit Politik beschäftigen; **to discuss** ~ s. to talk →~; **to be engaged in** ~ politisch tätig sein; **to enter** (or **go into**) ~ Politiker werden; **to launch into** ~ in die Politik einsteigen; Politiker werden; **to play** ~ taktieren; intrigieren; **to pursue** (or **steer**) **a middle course in** ~ e-n mittleren politischen Kurs einschlagen; **to talk** ~ über Politik sprechen, politisieren

polity Staatsform, Regierungsform; Staat

poll 1. *bes. pol* Wahl, Stimmenabgabe; Stimmenzählung; Liste der Wahlberechtigten, Wählerliste; Stimmenzahl; Wahllokal, Wahlort; Abstimmung; ~ **tax** *Br* Kommunalsteuer; **at the ~s** an der Wahlurne; →**challenge to the ~s;** →**deed ~; defeat at the ~s** Wahlniederlage; **heavy** ~ große Wahlbeteiligung; **light** ~ geringe Wahlbeteiligung; **result of the** ~ Wahlergebnis; **second** ~ zweite Abstimmung; **small** ~ s. light →~; **taking of (a)** ~ **(by secret ballot)**[85] *parl* Abstimmung (durch geheime Wahl); **to be at the bottom (head) of the** ~ die wenigsten (meisten) Stimmen erhalten (haben); **to declare the** ~ das Wahl- (od. Abstimmungs-)ergebnis bekanntgeben; **to defeat a p. at the ~s** über jdn e-n Wahlsieg erringen; **to be defeated at the ~s** e-e Wahlniederlage erleiden; **to go to the ~s** zur Wahl gehen, wählen; **to head the** ~ die meisten Stimmen erhalten (haben); **to take a** ~ abstimmen, wählen; **to top a** ~ die meisten Wählerstimmen bekommen

poll 2. *(Markt- und Meinungsforschung)* Umfrage, Befragung; **Gallup** ~ Gallup-Meinungsforschung (→*Gallup*); →**popularity ~; public opinion** ~ Meinungsbefragung; Umfrage zur Erforschung der öffentlichen Meinung; **to conduct a public opinion** ~ e-e öffentliche Meinungsumfrage durchführen

poll *v* wählen, s-e Stimme abgeben, abstimmen; *(Stimmen)* erhalten; *Am (einzeln)* befragen; **to** ~ **heavily** sehr viele Stimmen erhalten; **to** ~ **a jury** *Am* die Geschworenen hinsichtlich ihrer Entscheidung einzeln befragen; **to** ~ **a majority of votes cast** die Mehrheit der abgegebenen Stimmen erhalten

polling Wahl, Wählen, Stimmenabgabe, Abstimmung; Stimmenzählung; ~ **booth** Wahlzelle; ~ **clerk** Wahlbeisitzer; ~ **date** Wahltermin; ~ **day** Wahltag; ~ **district** Wahlbezirk; ~ **place** Wahllokal; Abstimmungsort; **~-station** Wahllokal; ~ **takes place** die Wahl findet statt

pollster *(Markt- und Meinungsforschung)* Fragesteller, Interviewer; **opinion** ~ Meinungsforscher

pollutant Schadstoff; Schmutzstoff; ~ **(product)** umweltbelastendes Erzeugnis; **emission of ~s** Schadstoffemission

pollute *v (Umwelt etc)* verschmutzen

polluter Umweltverschmutzer; ~ **pays principle** *(Umweltbelastung)* Verursacherprinzip; **civil liability of ~s** zivilrechtliche Haftung der Verursacher e-r Umweltverschmutzung

pollution Verschmutzung; Umweltverschmutzung

Pollution by Substances other than Oil, Pro-

tocol Relating to Intervention on the High Seas in Cases of ~ *(1973)*[86] Protokoll *(von 1973)* über Maßnahmen auf Hoher See bei Fällen von Verschmutzung durch andere Stoffe als Öl

pollution control Kontrolle der Verschmutzung der Umwelt, Umweltschutz *(z. B. Gewässerschutz)*; ~ **bonds** *Am* steuerfreie Kommunalanleihen zur Finanzierung behördlich vorgeschriebener Umweltschutzanlagen; ~ **standards** Umweltschutznormen

pollution, ~ of the air (or **air ~**)[87] Verunreinigung (od. Vergiftung) der Luft; Luftverschmutzung; ~ **of rivers** (or **streams**)[87a] Verschmutzung der Flüsse; ~ **of the (high) sea** Verschmutzung der See; ~ **of the sea from the land** Meeresverschmutzung vom Lande aus

pollution, ~ prevention Verhinderung der Verschmutzung; **anti~ investment** Umweltschutzinvestitionen; **anti-~ regulations** Umweltschutzvorschriften; **combatting ~** Kampf gegen die Verschmutzung; **environmental ~** Umweltverschmutzung, -belastung

Pollution, International Convention for the Prevention of P~ of the Sea from Ships[87b] Internationales Übereinkommen zur Verhütung der Meeresverschmutzung durch Schiffe

pollution, marine ~ Meeresverschmutzung *(→marine)*

pollution, oil ~ Ölverschmutzung (→*oil*); **International Convention on Civil Liability for Oil P~ Damage** (1984 Liability Convention)[88] Internationales Übereinkommen über die zivilrechtliche Haftung für Ölverschmutzungsschäden; (Haftungsübereinkommen von 1984); **International Convention for the Establishment of an International Fund for Compensation of Oil P~ Damage** (1984 Fund Convention)[89] Internationales Übereinkommen über die Errichtung e-s Internationalen Fonds zur Entschädigung für Ölverschmutzungsschäden; **International Convention Relating to Intervention on the High Seas in Cases of Oil P~ Casualties**[90] Internationales Übereinkommen über die Maßnahmen auf Hoher See bei Ölverschmutzungsunfällen; **International Convention for the Prevention of P~ of the Sea by Oil**[91] Internationales Übereinkommen zur Verhütung der Verschmutzung der See durch Öl; Ölverschmutzungsabkommen; **International Oil P~ Damage Compensation Fund**[89] Internationaler Fonds zur Entschädigung für Ölverschmutzungsschäden

pollution, →water ~

pollution, to stem ~ der Verschmutzung Einhalt gebieten

polyandry Polyandrie *(Ehe e-r Frau mit mehreren Männern zur gleichen Zeit)*

polygamy[92] Polygamie, Mehrehe

polygamous marriage polygamische Ehe, Mehrehe

polymetallic nodules of the deep sea bed (containing manganese, nickel, cobalt or copper)[93] polymetallische Knollen des Tiefseebodens (enthaltend Mangan, Nickel, Kobalt od. Kupfer); **Agreement Concerning Interim Arrangements Relating to ~** Übereinkommen über vorläufige Regelungen für polymetallische Knollen des Tiefseebodens

polypoly *com* Polypol *(diejenige Marktform, bei der viele Marktteilnehmer miteinander konkurrieren)*

pontage Brückengebühr *(zur Erhaltung der Brücke)*

pool Pool; *(lose od. vorübergehende)* Vereinigung von Unternehmen od. Personen zu e-m bestimmten Zweck *(zur Ausschaltung der gegenseitigen Konkurrenz; z. B. schlüsselmäßige Verteilung der Gewinne, Regelung der Produktionsmengen)*; Kartell, *(meist als)* Gewinnverteilungskartell; Zusammenfassung von Beteiligungen *(verschiedener Eigentümer an e-m Unternehmen zur Geltendmachung bestimmter Ansprüche, bes. des Stimmrechts)*; gemeinsamer Fonds des →International Monetary Fund *(→drawing rights)*; *(VersR)* Vereinigung mehrerer Versicherer zur Verteilung des Risikos; **~(s)** (Fußball)Toto; **~s** *(Seeschiffahrt)* Gewinnabrechnungsgemeinschaften; ~ **car service** *Am (Eisenbahn)* Zusammenfassung mehrerer kleinerer Sendungen in e-r Waggonladung zu verbilligter Frachtrate (→*carload rate*); ~ **selling** gemeinsamer Verkauf mehrerer Firmen; Verkauf im Rahmen e-s Kartells; ~ **support** *(Börse)* Stützungskäufe der Pool-Beteiligten; **bear (bull) ~** *(Börse)* Spekulantengruppe zur Herbeiführung e-r Baisse (Hausse); **patent ~** →patent 2.; **purchasing ~** Einkaufsgemeinschaft

pool *v* poolen; *(Unternehmen zur Verfolgung gemeinsamer Interessen [zu e-m Kartell])* zusammenlegen, kartellieren; *(Gewinne)* zusammenlegen und verteilen; *(Beteiligung am gleichen Unternehmen)* zusammenfassen *(cf. pool)*; *(Kräfte)* gemeinsam einsetzen; **to ~ funds** Gelder zusammenlegen; **to ~ orders** Aufträge zusammenfassen (od. kartellieren); **to ~ patents** Patente zusammenwerfen; **to ~ one's results** seine (Geschäfts-)Ergebnisse zusammenlegen

pooling 1. Poolung, Poolbildung *(cf. pool)*; Zusammenschluß, Kartellierung; Zusammenfassung *(bes. des Effektenbesitzes mehrerer Aktionäre)*; ~ **arrangement** Gewinnpoolungsvertrag; ~ **of efforts** gemeinsamer Einsatz von Kräften; ~ **of freight** *Am* Vereinbarung über gemeinsame Verfrachtung zum Zweck der gemeinsamen (billigeren) Frachtverrechnung; ~

of interests Interessenvereinigung, Interessengemeinschaft; ~ **of profits** Zusammenlegung und Verteilung der Gewinne, Gewinnpoolung; ~ **of risk** *(VersR)* Risikopoolung, Risikoverteilung; ~ **of votes** Stimmenvereinigung *(zwecks einheitlicher Geltendmachung von Aktionärsrechten)*; **patent ~ agreement** Patentaustauschabkommen

pooling 2. *Am* automatischer Übertrag mehrerer Kontensalden auf ein Zielkonto durch ein →cash management system; **multicurrency ~** Ausgleich von Kontensalden eines internationalen Konzerns in verschiedenen Währungen bei einer Bank

poor arm, dürftig; schlecht; unzulänglich; **the ~** die Armen; ~ **business** schlechtes Geschäft; ~ **debtor's oath** *Am* Offenbarungseid; ~ **investment** schlechte Kapitalanlage; ~ **litigant** *Am* im Armenrecht Klagender; ~ **quality** schlechte Qualität; **~s' roll** *Scot* Liste der Prozesse, in denen e-r Partei das Armenrecht bewilligt ist; ~ **work(manship)** schlechte Arbeit

POP-advertising →point of purchase advertising

popular volkstümlich, populär; Volks-; ~ **action** Popularklage; ~ **initiative** Volksbegehren; **~-priced** zu mäßigen (od. erschwinglichen) Preisen; ~ **votes** *Am* Stimmen der Wählerschaft, direkte Stimmen *(opp. electoral vote)*; ~ **will** Wille des Volkes; **to be very ~** *com* sehr gefragt sein

popularity poll *Am* Meinungsumfrage nach der Beliebtheit bestimmter Personen

populate *v* bevölkern

populated, densely ~ dicht bevölkert; **over-~** übervölkert; **sparsely (thickly) ~ areas** dünn (dicht) besiedelte Gebiete; **under-~** unterbevölkert

population Bevölkerung; ~ **census** Volkszählung; ~ **changes** *(VölkerR)* →~ transfers; ~ **decline** (or **decrease**) Bevölkerungsabnahme, -schrumpfung; ~ **density** Bevölkerungsdichte; ~ **explosion** Bevölkerungsexplosion; ~ **forecast** Bevölkerungsvorausschätzung, -prognose; ~ **growth** Anwachsen der Bevölkerung; Bevölkerungswachstum

population increase Bevölkerungszunahme; **annual rate of ~** jährlicher Bevölkerungszuwachs

population, ~ mobility (or **movement**) Bevölkerungsbewegung; ~ **policies** bevölkerungspolitische Maßnahmen; ~ **policy** Bevölkerungspolitik; ~ **projection** →~ forecast; ~ **pyramid** Bevölkerungspyramide; ~ **statistics**[94] Bevölkerungsstatistik; ~ **theory** Bevölkerungslehre, Bevölkerungskunde; ~ **transfers** *(VölkerR)* Bevölkerungsaustausch *(cf. minorities)*; ~ **trend** Bevölkerungsentwicklung; demographische Entwicklung; ~ **upsurge** Bevölkerungsaufschwung

population, actual (or **de facto**) ~ tatsächliche Bevölkerung; **census of ~** Volkszählung; **civilian ~** Zivilbevölkerung; **decline** (or **decrease) in ~** Bevölkerungsrückgang, Bevölkerungsabnahme; **density of ~** Bevölkerungsdichte; **dependent ~** die nicht erwerbstätige Bevölkerung; **employed ~** arbeitende Bevölkerung; **exchange of ~** →~ transfers; **frontier ~** Grenzbevölkerung; **increase in the ~** Bevölkerungszunahme; **movement of the ~ from country to city** (or **town**) Landflucht; **overspill of ~** Bevölkerungsüberschuß; **rural ~** Landbevölkerung

population, surplus of ~ Bevölkerungsüberschuß; **countries having surplus of ~** überbevölkerte Länder

population, total ~ Gesamtbevölkerung; Einwohnerzahl

population, urban ~ Stadtbevölkerung; **preponderance of urban ~** Überwiegen der Stadtbevölkerung

population, working ~ erwerbstätige Bevölkerung; **world ~** Weltbevölkerung

populous bevölkerungsstark, dicht bevölkert

pork *Am pol sl.* „fette Beute"; *(von der Regierung)* als political →patronage erlangte Sondervorteile; ~ **barrel** *Am sl.* aus politischen Gründen *(for local →patronage)* bewilligte Bundesgelder

pornography Pornographie, Schmutzliteratur

porrect *v (KirchenR)* zur Prüfung und Genehmigung vorlegen

port Hafen; ~ **administration** Hafenverwaltung; ~ **arrived from** letzter Verladehafen; ~ **authority** Hafenbehörde (→*P~ of London Authority*, →*P~ of New York Authority*); ~ **bill of lading** Hafenkonnossement; ~ **development** Hafenausbau; ~ **differential** *Am* Unterschied in den (Bahn-)Frachtgebühren für die gleiche Ladung zu verschiedenen Häfen; ~ **dues** Hafengebühren; ~ **equalization** *(Bahnverkehr)* Hafengleichstellung *(Schaffung von gleichen Frachtsätzen, unabhängig von der Entfernung, nach sämtlichen Häfen e-s Landes, zur Gleichstellung der Wettbewerbsverhältnisse der Häfen)*; ~ **equipment** (or **facilities, installations**) Hafenanlagen; ~ **of arrival** Ankunftshafen; Anlaufhafen; ~ **of call** Anlaufhafen; Orderhafen; ~ **of clearance** (Zoll-)Abfertigungshafen, Abgangshafen; ~ **of delivery** Löschhafen; ~ **of departure** Abgangshafen, Abfahrtshafen; ~ **of destination** Bestimmungshafen; ~ **of discharge** Löschungshafen, Entladehafen *(opp. ~ of loading)*; ~ **of disembarkation** Ausschiffungshafen; ~ **of distress** Nothafen; ~ **of entry** Zoll(abfertigungs)hafen; ~ **of loading,**

Verladehafen; **P~ of London Authority** (P.L.A.) Londoner Hafenbehörde; ~ **of necessity** (or **refuge**) Nothafen; **P~ of New York Authority** (PNYA) New Yorker Hafenbehörde; ~ **of registry** Heimathafen; ~ **of sailing** Abgangshafen; ~ **of shipment** Verschiffungshafen, Versandhafen; ~ **of survey** Hafen, in dem e-e Inspektion erfolgt; ~ **of trans(s)hipment** Umschlaghafen; ~ **of unloading** Entladehafen; ~ **regulations** Hafenordnung; ~ **risk** Hafenrisiko; ~ **sanitary authority** Hafengesundheitsbehörde

Port State Control, Memorandum of Understanding on ~[95] Vereinbarung über die Hafenstaatskontrolle

port, ~ toll *Am* Hafengebühr; ~ **warden** *Am* Hafenaufseher, Hafenmeister

port, air~ Flughafen; →**close ~; courtesy of the ~** *Am* Befreiung von der Zollrevision beim Gepäck; **customs of the** ~ Hafenusancen; **domestic** ~ Inlandshafen; **entry into a** ~ Einlaufen in e-n Hafen; **final** ~ letzter Bestimmungshafen, Endhafen; **free** ~ Freihafen; **home** ~ Heimathafen; **inland** ~ Binnenhafen; **intermediate** ~ Zwischenhafen; **lading** (or **loading**) ~ Verladehafen, Versandhafen; **maritime** ~ Seehafen; **naval** ~ Kriegshafen; **river** ~ Flußhafen; **sea** ~ Seehafen; **shipping** ~ Versandhafen

port, to call at a ~ e-n Hafen anlaufen, in e-n Hafen einlaufen; **to clear a** ~ aus e-m Hafen auslaufen; **to enter a** ~ in e-n Hafen einlaufen, e-n Hafen anlaufen; **to leave a** ~ aus e-m Hafen auslaufen; **to put into a** ~ s. to enter a →~; **to touch and stay at a** ~ e-n Hafen anlaufen und in e-m Hafen verweilen

portage Transport; Transportkosten

portal-to-portal-pay *Am* Lohn für die Zeit vom Betreten bis zum Verlassen des Betriebes

porter Pförtner, Portier; (Gepäck-)Träger; **~'s fee** *Am* Gepäckträgergebühr

portfolio 1. Portefeuille, (Minister-)Ressort, Geschäftsbereich *(e-s Ministers)*; **holder of a** ~ Ressortminister; **minister without** ~ Minister ohne Geschäftsbereich, Minister für Sonderaufgaben

portfolio 2. Aktenmappe, Aktentasche; (Effekten-)Portefeuille, Bestand *(an Wertpapieren)*; ~ **investment** Portefeuille-Investitionen, indirekte Investitionen; ~ **management** Effektenverwaltung, Vermögensverwaltung *(durch Banken, Kapitalsammelstellen etc)*; ~ **manager** Vermögensverwalter; ~ **of bills** (of exchange) Wechselbestand, Wechselportefeuille; ~ **of shares** (*Am* **stocks**) Portefeuille von Aktien; ~ **securities** Portefeuille-Effekten; Anlagepapiere; **insurance** ~ Versicherungsbestand; **investment** ~ Effektenportefeuille; **security** ~ Wertpapier-, Effektenportefeuille

portio legitima *Am* Pflichtteil

portion Teil, Anteil; *(durch letztwillige Verfügung od. aus e-m besonderen Anlaß [z.B. Eheschließung] gewährte)* besondere Zuwendung der Eltern an *(eigene od. angenommene)* Kinder; Mitgift, Aussteuer; Tranche *(Teilbetrag e-r Wertpapieremission)*; ~ **of the cost** Kostenanteil; ~ **of a loan** Teilbetrag e-r Anleihe; Tranche; ~ **of proceeds** Anteil am Ertrag; ~ **of profits** Gewinnanteil; **aggressive** ~ *Am* risikoreicher Teil der erworbenen Effekten *(e-s investment trust)*; **defensive** ~ *Am* risikoärmerer Teil der erworbenen Effekten *(e-s investment trust)*; **in equal ~s** zu gleichen Teilen; **legal** ~ *(ErbR)* gesetzlicher Erbteil; **marriage** ~ Mitgift, Aussteuer; **statutory** ~ **of the decedent's estate** gesetzlicher Erbteil

portion *v* einteilen; zuteilen, als Anteil zuweisen; **to ~ out** austeilen (to unter)

portrait[96] Porträt

Portugal Portugal

Portuguese Portugiese, Portugiesin; portugiesisch; **P~ Republic** Portugiesische Republik

POS-system (point of sale) automatisiertes Kassensystem *(elektronisches Bezahlen an der Ladenkasse)*

position 1. (Arbeits-)Stelle, Stellung, Position; ~ **bond** *Am* Kaution für Ausübung e-r bestimmten Tätigkeit *(unabhängig von der Person)*; ~ **classification plan** *Am* Stellenplan; ~ **for life** Lebensstellung; ~ **of authority** verantwortungsvolle Stelle; ~ **of influence** einflußreiche Stelle; ~ **of trust** Vertrauensstellung; ~ **offered** Stellenangebot

position, application for (appointment to) a ~ Bewerbung um e-e Stelle; **to invite applications for (appointment to) a** ~ e-e Stelle ausschreiben

position, change of ~ Stellenwechsel; **advertisement for a** ~ Stellengesuch *(in Zeitung)*; **fiduciary** ~ Vertrauensstellung; **holder of a** ~ Stelleninhaber; **honorary** ~ Ehrenamt; **in an inferior** ~ in untergeordneter Stellung; **leading** ~ leitende Stellung; **key** ~ Schlüsselstellung; **managerial** ~ *Am* leitende Stellung; **permanent** ~ Dauerstellung, feste Stellung; **unpaid** ~ Ehrenamt; **to apply for a** ~ sich um e-e Stelle bewerben; **to give up** (or **leave**) **one's** ~ s-e Stellung aufgeben; **to hold a** ~ e-e Stelle bekleiden; e-e Stellung innehaben; tätig sein (of als); **to lose one's** ~ s-e Stellung verlieren; **to maintain one's** ~ sich in s-r Stellung behaupten; **to occupy a** ~ s. to hold a →~; **to resign one's** ~ s-e Stellung aufgeben, von s-m Posten zurücktreten; **to take a** ~ e-e Stelle annehmen

position 2. Lage; Stand (as per vom); Standpunkt; Position; Tarifnummer; ~ **of an ac-**

count Kontostand; ~ **of constraint** Zwangslage; ~ **of the market** Marktlage; **bear** ~ *(Börse)* Baisseposition; **bull** ~ *(Börse)* Hausseposition; **cash** ~ Kassenstand; **competitive** ~ Wettbewerbslage, Konkurrenzfähigkeit; **creditor** ~ Gläubigerstellung; **debtor** ~ Schuldnerstellung; **exceptional** ~ Ausnahmestellung, Sonderstellung; **exchange** ~ Devisenlage; **factual** ~ Sachlage (*opp. legal* ~); **(sound) financial** ~ (gesunde) finanzielle Lage, Finanzlage; **food** ~ Ernährungslage; **legal** ~ Rechtslage; Rechtsstellung; **short** ~ s. bear →~; **to change one's** ~ s-e Lage verändern; s-e Lage verschlechtern *(im Vertrauen auf fremdes Verhalten; Voraussetzung für →estoppel)*; **to define one's** ~ s-n Standpunkt darlegen; Stellung nehmen (to zu); **to maintain one's** ~ s-n Standpunkt behaupten; **to take up a** ~ e-n Standpunkt vertreten

positive positiv; feststehend, bestimmt; *colloq.* sicher; ~ →**discrimination;** ~ →**easement;** ~ **evidence** eindeutiger Beweis; ~ **fact** feststehende Tatsache; ~ **law** positives Recht *(opp. natural law)*; **(~)** →**prescription**

posse Menge, Schar, Truppe; ~ **of police** *Am* Polizeiaufgebot

possess *v* besitzen, innehaben; **to** ~ **o.s. of a th.** etw. in Besitz nehmen

possessed, to be ~ **(of)** im Besitz sein (von), *(etw.)* in Besitz haben

possessing instruments of crime in Besitz von Werkzeugen, die zur Begehung von Verbrechen dienen

possession Besitz, Sachherrschaft, Innehabung; Besitzgegenstand; Besitzung; ~**s** Besitzungen; Besitz, Habe; ~ **action** s. action for →~; ~ **in fact** s. de facto →~; ~ **in law** s. legal →~; ~ **money** *Br* Gebühr für Verwahrung von Sachen, die durch Zwangsvollstreckung eingezogen wurden; ~ **order** *Br* s. order for →~; ~ **proceedings** *Br* Räumungsverfahren; ~ **with due title** s. legal →~; **action for** ~ *Br* Räumungsklage, Klage des Eigentümers auf Räumung; **actual** ~ s. de facto →~

possession, adverse ~ Ersitzung; **to acquire by adverse** ~ ersitzen

possession, concurrent ~ →joint ~; **constructive** ~ rechtlicher Besitz, fingierter Besitz, Besitz kraft gesetzlicher Vermutung *(z. B. des executor an den bewegl. Sachen des Verstorbenen beim Tode des Testators)*; **de facto** ~ tatsächlicher (od. unmittelbarer) Besitz; **delivery of** ~ Besitzübergabe; **disturbance of** (or **encroachment on**) ~ Besitzstörung; **quiet enjoyment of** ~ ungestörter Besitz; **faulty** ~ fehlerhafter Besitz; **foreign** ~**s** *Br (Einkommensteuer)* Vermögensgegenstände im Ausland; **in full** ~ **of his faculties** in vollem Besitz s-r geistigen Kräfte; **interference with a p.'s** ~ Besitzstörung; **joint** ~ Mitbesitz, gemeinsamer Besitz; **lawful** ~ rechtmäßiger Besitz; **legal** ~ rechtlicher Besitz, mittelbarer Besitz; **order for** ~ *Br (gerichtl.)* Räumungsbefehl; **oversea(s)** ~**s** Besitzungen in Übersee, überseeische Besitzungen; **right of** ~ Besitzrecht; **suit for** ~ s. action for →~; **taking** ~ **(of)** Besitzergreifung, Inbesitznahme; **transfer of** ~ Besitzübertragung; **unlawful** ~ **of firearms** unrechtmäßiger Waffenbesitz; **vacant** ~ sofort beziehbar; **writ of** ~ gerichtliche Besitzeinweisung *(in Grundbesitz)*; **to acquire** ~ Besitz erwerben; **to be in** ~ **of** besitzen, in Besitz sein von, innehaben; **to come into the** ~ **of a th.** in den Besitz e-r Sache gelangen; **to enter** (or **go**) **into** ~ in Besitz nehmen; **to have a th. in one's** ~ etw. in s-m Besitz haben; **to interfere with a p.'s** ~ jdn im Besitz stören; **to put in** ~ in Besitz setzen; **to recover** ~ **(of)** den Besitz (an) wiedererlangen; **to be restored to** ~ wieder in den Besitz eingesetzt werden; **to sue for** ~ *Br* auf Räumung klagen; **to take** ~ **(of)** *(etw.)* in Besitz nehmen; **to take** ~ **of an estate** e-e Erbschaft antreten

possessive right Besitzrecht

possessor Besitzer, Inhaber; ~ **of a driving-licence** *Br* Inhaber e-s Führerscheins; ~**'s agent** Besitzdiener; **adverse** ~ Ersitzer

possessory besitzend; besitzrechtlich, possessorisch; ~ **action** *Am* Besitz(schutz)klage; ~ **lien** →lien; ~ **title**[97] Besitztitel *(e-r Person, die 12 Jahre [Br in Ausnahmefällen, z. B. bei Krongütern, 30 Jahre] lang in Besitz von Land war, ohne Miete bezahlt od. auf andere Weise das Recht des wahren Eigentümers anerkannt zu haben)*

possibilit|y Möglichkeit; ~ **of confusion** Verwechslungsgefahr; **export** ~**ies** Exportmöglichkeiten; **reasonable** ~ begründete Möglichkeit

post 1. *bes. Br* Postsendung, Postsachen; Postamt; ~**-box** *Br* Briefkasten

postcard (p. c.) Postkarte; **picture** ~ Ansichtskarte; **reply-paid** ~ Postkarte mit Rückantwort

post, ~ **code** *Br* Postleitzahl; ~**-free** portofrei; frankiert; ~**man** *Br* Briefträger

postmark Poststempel; **date as** ~ Datum des Poststempels

postmark *v* abstempeln; ~**ed 3. 6. 19. .** Datum des Poststempels vom 3. 6. 19. .

postmaster Postamtsvorsteher

post office (P. O.) Postamt, Postanstalt; **P~ O~** *Br*[98] Behörde für Postwesen und National Girobank; ~ **address** *Am* Postanschrift; ~ **box** (P. O. B.) *Br* Postschließfach; ~ **clerk** Postbedienstete(r), Postangestellte(r); ~ **counter** Postschalter; **P~ O~ Department** (POD) *Am* Postministerium; **P~ O~ Guide** *Br* Postvorschriften; ~ **hours** Schalterstunden; ~ **receipt** Posteinlieferungsschein; Postquittung; ~ **regulation** *Br* Postordnung; **branch** ~ Zweigpostamt; **closing time of the** ~ Postschluß; **head** ~ Hauptpostamt; **sub-**~ *Br* Nebenpoststelle

post, by ~ *Br* per Post; **by to-day's** ~ mit der heutigen Post; **to send by** ~ mit der Post senden

post, letter ~ *Br* Briefpost; **military** ~ *Br* Feldpost; **morning** ~ *Br* Morgenpost; **parcel** ~ Paketsendung; *Br* Paketpost (→*parcel 1.*); **pneumatic** ~ *Br* Rohrpost; **by return of** ~ *Br* postwendend; **secrecy of the** ~ *Br* Postgeheimnis; Briefgeheimnis; **to deal with** (or **to go through**) **one's** ~ *Br* s-e Post erledigen

post 2. Stelle, Stellung; *(höherer)* Posten; Amt; ~ **of authority** einflußreiches Amt; **candidate for a** ~ Anwärter für e-e Stelle; **confidential** ~ Vertrauensstellung; **established** ~ Planstelle; **judicial** ~ Richteramt; **a good** ~ **in the public service** ~ e-e gute Stelle im Staatsdienst; **to advertise a** ~ e-e Stelle ausschreiben; **to fill a** ~ ein Amt innehaben (od. versehen); **to find a** ~ **for sb.** jdm e-e Stelle verschaffen; **to get** (or **be given, obtain**) **a** ~ e-e Stelle bekommen; **to resign** (or **retire from**) **a** ~ e-e Stelle aufgeben; **to take up a** ~ e-e Stelle antreten

post 3. Posten; Standplatz, Börsenstand; Buchungsposten; **P~ Exchange** (PX) *Am* Kaufhaus für Armeeangehörige, **first-aid** ~ Unfallstation

post 4. nach, später; ~**-acquisition** nach Beteiligungserwerb; nach der Übernahme; ~**-commitment hearing** *Am* (Straf-)Verfahren nach Einweisung *(in e-e psychiatrische Klinik)*; ~**(-)date**[99] *v (Scheck etc)* vordatieren; mit vorausliegendem Datum versehen *(opp. antedate)*; ~**-distribution trading** *Am* Sekundärhandel *(mit Effekten)*; ~**-doctoral fellow** (or **student**) *Am* jd, der nach Erlangung des Doktorgrades wissenschaftlich weiterarbeitet; ~**(-)entry** nachträgliche Zollerklärung; ~**-graduate** *Br* Doktorant

posthumous nachgeboren; ~ **child**[100] nach dem Tode des Vaters geborenes Kind; ~ **works**[101] nachgelassene Werke; nach dem Tode des Verfassers veröffentlichte Schriften

postliminium (or **postliminy**) *(VölkerR)* Postliminium; Wiederherstellung des früheren Rechtszustandes in e-m früher vom Feind besetzten Landesteil

post meridiem (p.m.) nachmittags

post(-)mortem nach dem Tode; ~ **(examination)** Leichenöffnung, Obduktion; **to hold a** ~ **(examination)** e-e Leichenschau vornehmen *(cf. coroner)*

post(-)natal nach der Geburt

post(-)nuptial nachehelich; ~ **settlement** nach Eheschließung getroffene Verfügung über Vermögen zugunsten der Ehepartner und/oder Nachkommen (→*settlement 3.*)

post-obit bond Schuldschein mit der Verpflichtung der Zahlung nach dem Tode e-r dritten Person

post(-)war Nachkriegs- *(opp. pre[-]war)*; ~ **demands** Nachkriegsbedürfnisse; ~ **period** Nachkriegszeit

post *v (e-n Brief)* in den Briefkasten tun; bei der Post aufgeben; *(öffentl.)* anschlagen, ankleben; eintragen, (ver)buchen; **to** ~ **bills** Zettel ankleben, Plakate anschlagen; **to** ~ **an entry** (or **item**) e-n Posten eintragen (od. verbuchen); **to** ~ **the journal into the ledger** (or **to** ~ **up the ledger from the journal**) Buchungen aus dem Journal in das Hauptbuch übertragen; **to** ~ **in a conspicuous place** an gut sichtbarer Stelle anschlagen; **to** ~ **(up)** durch Aushang bekanntmachen; *colloq. (jdn)* unterrichten (od. auf dem laufenden halten)

posted, well-~ *Am colloq.* gut unterrichtet; **the best-**~ **correspondent** *Am colloq.* der am besten informierte Korrespondent; **to be kept** ~ *colloq.* auf dem laufenden gehalten werden

posting 1. *Br* Aufgabe (od. Einlieferung) *(von Postsendungen)*; Anschlagen *(von Plakaten)*; ~ **of items** Einlieferung von Postsendungen; →**certificate of** ~; **latest time for** ~ Postaufgabeschluß

posting 2. Eintragung, (Ver-)Buchung; ~ **of items** Übertragung von Buchungen; ~**s from the journal to the ledger accounts** (or **ledger** ~**s**) Übertragung der Buchungen aus dem Journal in das Hauptbuch; ~ **medium** *Am* Buchungsunterlage; **double** ~ *Am* Doppelbuchung

postage Postgebühren; Porto(auslagen); ~ **book** Portobuch; ~**-due** Nachgebühr, Strafporto; ~ **envelope** *Am* Freiumschlag; ~ **expenses** Portoauslagen, Portospesen; ~**-free** (or **-paid**) freigemacht, frankiert; ~ **meter** *Am* Frankiermaschine; ~ **rates** *Br* Postgebühren, Posttarif; ~ **stamp** Briefmarke, Postwertzeichen; ~ **to be collected** unter Portonachnahme; ~ **underpaid** nicht genügend frankiert; ~ **unpaid** unfrankiert; **additional** ~ Nachgebühr, Strafporto; **exemption from** ~ Portofreiheit; **evasion of** ~ Portohinterziehung; **excess** ~ Nachgebühr, Strafporto; **free of** ~ *Am* portofrei; **inland** ~ **(rates)** *Br* Inlandporto; **liable to** ~ portopflichtig; **ordinary** ~ einfaches Porto; **overseas** ~ **(rates)** *Br* Überseeporto; **payment of** ~ Freimachung, Frankierung; **reduction of** ~ Portoermäßigung; **refunding of** ~ Portovergütung; **return** ~ Rückporto; **to pay the** ~ freimachen, frankieren

postal postalisch, Post-; ~ **address** Postanschrift; ~ **authorities** Postbehörde, Postverwaltung; ~ **car** *Am* Postwagen; ~ **charges** Postgebühren; ~ **clerk** Postbediensteter, Postangestellter; ~ **code** Postleitzahl; ~ **collection order** *Am* Postauftrag; ~ **communication** Postverbindung, Postverkehr; ~ **convention** Postabkommen; ~ **delivery** Postzustellung, Zustellung durch die Post; ~ **district** Post(zustell)-bezirk; ~ **fees** Postgebühren; **P~ Giro** *Br* →National Giro; ~ **item** Postsache; ~ **money order** *Am* Postanweisung; ~ **note** *(Kanada)* Postanweisung; ~ **order** (P.O.) *Br* Postanweisung *(für kleinere Beträge)*

postal packet *Br* Postpaket; Postsendung; **collection and delivery of ~s** Abholung und Zustellung von Postpaketen; **letters or other ~s** Briefe oder andere Postsendungen

Postal Parcels Agreement Postpaketabkommen

postal power *Am*[102] Posthoheit *(des Bundes)*

postal rates Posttarif, Postgebühren; **increase of ~** Erhöhung der Postgebühren; **overseas ~** Überseeporto

postal, ~ regulations postalische Bestimmungen, Postordnung; ~ **savings** Postsparguthaben; ~ **savings (depository) office** *Am* Postsparkasse; ~ **service** Postdienst; Postverkehr; ~ **system** Postwesen; ~ **traffic** Postverkehr; ~ **traveller's cheque** (*Am* ~ **travel[l]er's check**) Postreisescheck; **(Universal) P~ Union** (UPU) Weltpostverein (→*universal*); ~ **vote** Briefwahl; ~ **wrapper** Kreuzband, Streifband; ~ **zone number** *Am* Postleitzahl

poste restante postlagernd; *Br* Abteilung für postlagernde Sendungen

poster Plakat, Werbeplakat; Anschlag(zettel); Plakatankleber; ~ **advertising** Plakatwerbung; ~ **design** Plakatentwurf; ~ **panel** Anschlagtafel, Anschlagwand; ~ **pillar** Anschlagsäule, Litfaßsäule; **advertising ~** Reklameplakat; **(bill) ~** Plakatankleber, Zettelankleber; **election ~** Wahlplakat

posterity Nachkommenschaft; Nachwelt *(opp. ancestry)*

posthumous →post 4.

posting →post *v*

postliminium →post 4.

postpone *v* aufschieben, verschieben, verlegen; vertagen; *mil* zurückstellen; **to ~ the conference to next week** die Konferenz auf die nächste Woche vertagen; **to ~ payments for a year** die Zahlungen um ein Jahr hinausschieben; **to ~ trial** die Verhandlung vertagen

postponed, ~ creditor im Rang nachgehender Konkursgläubiger (→*priority of creditors*); ~ **debt** im Rang nachgehende Konkursforderung

postponement Aufschub, Verschiebung, Verlegung; Vertagung; ~ **of payments** Hinausschiebung der Zahlungen; ~ **of trial**[103] Vertagung der Verhandlung

pot *colloq.* Marihuana (soft drug)

potential Potential; (Aufstiegs-, Einfluß-, Leistungs-)Möglichkeit; **economic ~** Wirtschaftspotential; **war ~** Kriegspotential

potential potentiell, möglich; ~ **buyer** potentieller Käufer; ~ **competition** mögliche Konkurrenz; ~ **customer** möglicher Kunde; ~ **market** potentieller Markt, Absatzmöglichkeit(en)

Potsdam Agreement Potsdamer Abkommen
1945 zwischen USA, Großbritannien und der Sowjetunion abgeschlossenes Abkommen über Fragen einer gemeinsamen Nachkriegspolitik

pouch, diplomatic ~ Kuriergepäck

pound 1. Pfund *(Gewichtseinheit)* (lb) *(453,6 g); Br (Währungseinheit)* (£ vor e-r Zahl); ~ **sterling** (£stg) Pfund Sterling; **devaluation of the ~ (sterling)** Pfundabwertung; **fall of the ~** Pfundsturz; **forward ~** *(Börse)* Terminpfund
Seit 1971 besteht das Pfund nicht mehr aus 240 pence sondern aus 100 pence

pound 2. Pfandkammer; Pfandstall; **~(-)breach** (or **breach of ~**) *(StrafR)* Pfandbruch, Verstrickungsbruch *(hinsichtlich gepfändeten Viehs; cf. rescue of goods distrained)*; **to put distrained cattle in a ~** gepfändetes Vieh in e-n Viehstall tun

poundage *Br* Gebühr (od. Steuer) per Pfund Sterling; *Br* Pfändungsgebühr *(des sheriff)*; Bezahlung pro Pfund Gewicht

pourparler *Fr* Vorbesprechung

poverty Armut; ~ **affidavit** *Am* eidliche Erklärung, die notwendig ist, um im Armenrecht klagen zu können *(to sue in forma pauperis)*; ~ **line** (or *Am* **level**) Armutsgrenze *(Am Anspruchsvoraussetzung für Sozialleistungen)*; **below ~ level** unter dem Existenzminimum; **~-stricken** verarmt; **action to combat ~** Bekämpfung der Armut; **certificate of ~** *Am* Mittellosigkeitszeugnis

power 1. Befugnis; Vollmacht, Ermächtigung; Vermögen, Fähigkeit

power, to confer ~s on a p. jdm Befugnisse übertragen, jdm Vollmacht erteilen; **to exceed one's ~s** s-e Befugnisse überschreiten; **to exercise a ~** e-e Vollmacht ausüben; **to exercise ~s** Befugnisse ausüben; **to furnish** (or **invest**) **sb. with ~** jdn mit Vollmacht versehen, jdn bevollmächtigen; **to have ~** (to) ermächtigt sein; **to have sole ~** allein befugt sein

power, ~ of agency (or **of an agent**) Vertretungsbefugnis, Vertretungsmacht; ~ **to amend** (or **of amendment**) (Ab-) Änderungsbefugnis

power (of appointment) *(durch Rechtsgeschäft od. letztwillige Verfügung eingeräumte)* Befugnis, den Berechtigten oder Rechtsnachfolger e-s

Gegenstandes zu bestimmen; **donor of a** ~ Erteiler e-r ~; **general** ~ allgemeine Bestimmungsbefugnis; Recht zur Bestimmung eines oder mehrerer (beliebigen) Berechtigten oder Nacherben *(der donee ist in der Wahl der Zuwendungsempfänger frei);* **special** ~ Recht zur Bestimmung von Berechtigten oder Nacherben aus e-r beschränkten Gruppe von Personen

Diese sachenrechtliche Vollmacht muß von der gewöhnlichen Vollmacht des Stellvertretungsrechts unterschieden werden. Der Vollmachtgeber (sonst principal) heißt donor; der Bevollmächtigte (sonst attorney od. agent) heißt donee; die dritte Person, zu deren Gunsten die Vollmacht ausgeübt wird, heißt appointee (nicht grantee oder assignee).

Der donor (Erblasser od. Stifter e-s Treuhandverhältnisses) überträgt dem donee die Befugnis, über s-n Nachlaß od. das Treuhandgut (trust property) derart zu verfügen, daß der donee die Zuwendungsempfänger und ihre Anteile bestimmt (anders dagegen das deutsche Recht, § 2065 Abs. 2 BGB)

power (of attorney) *(P/A)*[104] *(schriftl.)* Vollmacht, Vollmachturkunde

Der Vollmachtgeber heißt principal od. constituent, der Bevollmächtigte agent od. attorney. Im schottischen Recht heißt die Vollmacht auch commission oder factory.

Der Bevollmächtigte setzt vor seine Unterschrift p.p.

power (of attorney), ~ **drawn up before a notary** *Br* notarielle Vollmacht; **as per** ~ laut Vollmacht; **collective** ~ Kollektivvollmacht; **expiration of a** ~ Erlöschen e-r Vollmacht; **extent of a** ~ Umfang e-r Vollmacht; **full** ~ s. general →~; **general** ~ Generalvollmacht *(opp. special ~);* **granting of a** ~ Erteilung e-r Vollmacht, Vollmachterteilung; **holder of a** ~ Vollmachtinhaber; **holding a** ~ bevollmächtigt; **irrevocable** ~ unwiderrufliche Vollmacht; **joint** ~ Gesamtvollmacht; **limited** ~ beschränkte Vollmacht; **permanent** ~ Dauervollmacht; **production of the** ~ Vorlegung der Vollmacht; **revocable** ~ widerrufliche Vollmacht; **revocation of** ~ Widerruf der Vollmacht; **scope of a** ~ Umfang e-r Vollmacht; **special** ~ Sondervollmacht, Einzelvollmacht *(für ein bestimmtes Rechtsgeschäft) (opp. general ~);* **substitute** ~ Untervollmacht; **unlimited** ~ Generalvollmacht; **withdrawal of** ~ Zurückziehung der Vollmacht; **to cancel a** ~ e-e Vollmacht entziehen (od. zurückziehen); **to execute a** ~ e-e Vollmacht ausstellen; **to give** (or **grant**) **sb.** ~ jdm Vollmacht erteilen; **to hold a** ~ e-e Vollmacht besitzen; Vollmacht haben; **to hold a** ~ **for sb.** von jdm bevollmächtigt sein; **to produce a** ~ e-e Vollmacht vorlegen; **to revoke a** ~ e-e Vollmacht widerrufen; **to withdraw a** ~ →to cancel a ~; **the** ~ **is extinct** die Vollmacht ist erloschen

power, ~ **of decision** Entscheidungsbefugnis, Entscheidungsgewalt; ~ **of discretion** Ermessensfreiheit; ~ **of disposal** Verfügungsgewalt, Verfügungsbefugnis; ~ **of distress** Recht *(des Vermieters von unbewegl. Sachen),* die vom Mieter eingebrachten Sachen zu beschlagnahmen

powers of entry Durchsuchungsrecht; Recht *(der öffentl. Gewalt),* in die räumliche Privatsphäre (Wohnung) einzudringen

power, (mortagee's) ~ **of sale**[105] Verkaufsberechtigung, *(gesetzl.)* Veräußerungsbefugnis *(bes. des Hypothekengläubigers [z.B. Bausparkasse, Bank] bei Nichtzahlung der fälligen Forderung ohne Mitwirkung des Gerichts oder des Hypothekenschuldners zum Zwecke der Befriedigung);* ~ **of substitution** Recht zur Unterbevollmächtigung, Untervollmacht; ~ **of termination** Befugnis, bei Eintritt e-r Bedingung ein Rechtsverhältnis zu beenden; ~ **to contract** Abschlußvollmacht; ~ **to negotiate** Verhandlungsbefugnis; ~ **to sign** Unterschriftsberechtigung, Zeichnungsvollmacht; ~ **to sue and to be sued** Prozeßfähigkeit (*e-r Handelsgesellschaft*) →**power,** →**borrowing** ~; **buying** ~ Kaufkraft; **collecting** ~ Inkassovollmacht; **competitive** ~ Konkurrenzfähigkeit; **corporate** ~**s** Handlungsfähigkeit e-r juristischen Person; →**discretionary** ~**s; economic** ~ Wirtschaftskraft; **in exercise of the** ~**s conferred** in Ausübung der übertragenen Befugnisse (od. Vollmacht); **excess of** ~**s** Überschreiten der Befugnisse; **express** ~ ausdrücklich erteilte Vollmacht

power, full ~**(s)** Vollmacht; **full** ~**s found in good and due form** *dipl* in guter und gehöriger Form befundene Vollmachten; **to invest a p. with full** ~**(s)** jdn mit Vollmacht versehen, jdn bevollmächtigen; **to have full** ~**(s)** Vollmachten haben, bevollmächtigt sein

power, general ~ Generalvollmacht *(cf. general →power [of appointment], general →power [of attorney]);* →**implied** ~**(s);** →**incidental** ~**s; within the limits of the** ~**s conferred** im Rahmen der Befugnisse; **plenary** ~**(s)** unbeschränkte Vollmacht; **productive** ~ Produktionskraft, Produktionsfähigkeit; **scope of** ~ Umfang der Vollmacht; **special** ~ Sondervollmacht *(cf. special →power [of appointment], special →power [of attorney]);* **substitute** ~**(s)** Untervollmacht; **unlimited** ~**(s)** Blankovollmacht

power 2. Macht, Gewalt, Herrschaft; Amtsgewalt; ~ **balance** *pol* Gleichgewicht der Kräfte; ~ **of the purse** *Br* Machtbefugnis der Exekutive gegenüber den Counties (*bei Gewährung von Staatszuschüssen*); *Am* Befugnis des Kongresses, darüber zu entscheiden, für welche Zwecke Bundesgelder verwandt werden dürfen; ~ **politics** Machtpolitik; **absolute** ~ unbeschränkte Macht; **abuse of** ~ Mißbrauch der Amtsgewalt; **advent to** ~ Zurmachtkommen; **assumption of** ~ Machtübernahme;

balance of ~ →~ balance; **coming into** ~ Machtübernahme; →**delegation of (legislative)** ~; **display of** ~ Machtentfaltung; **division of** ~**s** →division 1.; **economic** ~ Wirtschaftsmacht; **executive** ~ vollziehende Gewalt; Exekutive; **judicial** ~ richterliche (od. rechtsprechende) Gewalt
power, in ~ an der Macht, am Ruder; **party in** ~ Partei am Ruder
power, legislative ~ gesetzgebende Gewalt; Legislative; **official** ~**s** Amtsgewalt; **seizure** (or **seizing**) **of** ~ Machtergreifung, Machtübernahme; **sphere of** ~ Machtbereich
power, to assume ~ die Macht ergreifen (od. übernehmen); **to be in** ~ an der Macht (od. am Ruder) sein; **to come (in)to** ~ zur Macht kommen, an die Macht gelangen; **to continue in** ~ an der Macht bleiben; **to hold** ~ die Macht haben (od. besitzen), an der Macht sein; **all** ~ **emanates from** (or **originates in**) **the people** alle Gewalt geht vom Volke aus; **to remain in** ~ an der Macht bleiben; **to seize** ~ die Macht ergreifen
power 3. *pol* Macht *(Staat, Land)*; **air** ~ Luftmacht; **belligerent** ~ kriegführende Macht; **foreign** ~ ausländische Macht; **four-**~ **conference** Viermächtekonferenz; **the Great P**~**s** die Großmächte; **military** ~ Militärmacht, Kriegsmacht; **naval** (or **sea**) ~ Seemacht; **world** ~ Weltmacht
power 4. (Stark-)Strom; Energie; Leistung *(e-r Maschine)*; ~ **blackout** Stromausfall; ~ **consumption** Stromverbrauch; ~ **cut** Stromsperre; ~ **demand** →~ requirement; ~**-driven** motorgetrieben; ~ **economy** (or **industry**) Energiewirtschaft; ~ **plant** Elektrizitätswerk, Kraftwerk; ~ **requirement** Strombedarf; Energiebedarf; ~**-station** Elektrizitätswerk, Kraftwerk; ~ **supply (system)** Stromversorgung; **Federal P**~ **Commission** (FPC) *Am* Bundesbehörde für die Energiewirtschaft; **nuclear** ~ **plant** Atomkraftwerk

PR man →public relations man

practice Verfahren(sweise); Prozeßverfahren; Praxis *(bes. e-s Anwaltes, Arztes)*; Übung; Brauch, Praktik; Usance; Ausübung; ~**s** Praktiken, Gepflogenheiten; *(KartellR)* Geschäftspraktiken
Practice Act *Am* Prozeßordnung; **Civil** (or **General**) ~ *Am* Zivilprozeßordnung (ZPO)
practice, ~ **directions** *Br (von Richtern erlassene)* allgemeine Verfahrensanweisungen (od. -regeln); ~ **of law** Ausübung des Anwaltsberufes; ~ **of a profession** Ausübung e-s freien Berufes; **free** ~ **of religion** freie Religionsausübung; ~ **rules** *Am* Verfahrensvorschriften; (Zivil-)Prozeßordnung; ~ **to the contrary** entgegenstehender Brauch
practice, administrative ~**s** Verwaltungspraktiken; **Annual P**~ *Br (jährl. neu aufgelegte)* Sammlung von Prozeßvorschriften *(des Supreme Court)*; **banking** ~ Bankusance; **barrister's** ~ *Br* Anwaltspraxis
practice, business ~**s** *(KartellR)* Geschäftspraktiken; **deceptive business** ~**s** *Am (StrafR)* auf Täuschung angelegte geschäftliche Machenschaften; **to engage in a business** ~ *(KartellR)* e-e Geschäftspraktik anwenden
practice, commercial ~ auf Handelssachen spezialisierte Anwaltspraxis; **commercial** ~**s** Geschäftspraktiken
practice, common ~ allgemein übliches Verfahren; Verkehrssitte; **it is common** ~ es ist allgemein üblich; es ist handelsüblich
practice, unfair competitive ~**s** unlauterer Wettbewerb; **concerted** ~**s** *(KartellR)* (aufeinander) abgestimmte Verhaltensweisen (od. [Geschäfts-]Praktiken); →**corrupt** ~**s; electoral** ~**s** Wahlpraktiken
practice, established ~**(s)** bestehender Brauch; **it is established** ~ es ist üblich
practice, general ~ übliches Verfahren; allgemeine Praxis *(bes. des Arztes; opp. specialized* ~*)*; **General P**~ **Act** *Am* Zivilprozeßordnung; **illegal** ~**s** *Br* rechtswidrige (Wahl-) Praktiken; **in** ~ in der Praxis *(opp. in theory)*; in Übung *(opp. out of* ~*)*; **unfair labor** ~**s** *Am* unlautere Arbeitskampfmethoden; **large** ~ große Praxis; **lawyer's** ~ Anwaltspraxis; **law of** ~ *Am* Prozeßrecht; **medical** ~ Arztpraxis; **reduction to** ~ **of an invention** *(PatR)* praktische Verwertung e-r Erfindung; **solicitor's** ~ *Br* Anwaltspraxis; **specialized** ~ Praxis e-s Spezialisten *(bes. e-s Spezialarztes; opp. general* ~*)*; **trade** ~**s** Handelspraktiken (→*trade*)
practice, to be the normal (or **usual**) ~ üblich sein; **to buy a** ~ e-e Praxis kaufen; **to discontinue a** ~ e-e Praxis aufgeben; **to place** (or **put**) **into** ~ ausführen; **to reduce an invention to** ~ e-e Erfindung praktisch verwerten; **to retire from** ~ s-e Praxis aufgeben; **to take over a** ~ e-e Praxis übernehmen

practice *v Am* →practise *v*

practise *v (Beruf)* ausüben; praktizieren; *(Geschäft etc)* betreiben; in die Praxis umsetzen; **to** ~ **as an attorney** *Am* als Anwalt s-e Praxis ausüben (od. tätig sein); **to** ~ **at the bar** als Anwalt (*Br* als barrister) praktizieren; **to** ~ **bribery** bestechen; **to** ~ **in a court** *(regelmäßig) (als Anwalt)* vor e-m Gericht auftreten; **to** ~ **a fraud on the court** das Gericht täuschen; **to** ~ **before international authorities** vor internationalen Behörden *(als Anwalt)* auftreten; **to** ~ **an invention** e-e Erfindung praktisch durchführen; **to** ~ **law** e-e Anwaltspraxis ausüben, als Rechtsanwalt tätig sein
practise *v*, **to** ~ **medicine** als Arzt s-e Praxis ausüben (od. tätig sein); **licence (**~**se) to** ~ **medicine** ärztliche Approbation
practise *v*, **to** ~ **a profession** e-n Beruf ausüben;

to ~ as a solicitor *Br* als Anwalt s-e Praxis ausüben (od. tätig sein)

practising, ~ barrister *Br* praktizierender Anwalt; **~ certificate** *Br (dem solicitor von der →Law Society jährlich erteilte)* Erlaubnis zur Ausübung der Anwaltspraxis; **~ lawyer** praktizierender Anwalt; **~ solicitor** *Br* praktizierender Anwalt; **to prohibit from ~** (e-m Anwalt od. Arzt) die Berufsausübung untersagen

practitioner Praktiker; **general ~** (G.P.) praktischer Arzt; Allgemeinmediziner; **legal ~** *(praktizierender)* Rechtsanwalt

praecipe *(dem Gericht eingereichtes)* Stück Papier, das Einzelheiten e-s writ oder e-r Urkunde enthält, die das Gericht ausstellen soll

pratique Anlauf- bzw. Landeerlaubnis; **granting of free ~ to a ship or an aircraft**[106] Erteilung der Anlauferlaubnis an ein Schiff oder Landeerlaubnis an ein Luftfahrzeug

pray *v* bitten, ersuchen, beantragen

prayer 1. Klageantrag *(Br z.B. im Ehescheidungsverfahren); Am (AntitrustR)* Antrag des Justizministeriums; **~ for relief** Klagebegehren

prayer 2. Gebet; **P~ Book** (or **Book of Common P~**) *Br* Gebetbuch der Anglikanischen Kirche

preacher *Br* Prediger *(der →dissenters)*

preacquisition *(KonzernR)* vor Erwerb einer Beteiligung, vor Eingliederung, vor Übernahme; **~ losses** Verluste der Untergesellschaft, die sie vor dem Konzernzusammenschluß *(vor dem Zeitpunkt des Beteiligungserwerbs durch die Obergesellschaft)* erlitten hat; **~ profits** Gewinne, die von der Untergesellschaft vor ihrer Übernahme erzielt worden sind

preamble Präambel, Einleitung(ssätze), Eingangsformel

preaudience Recht, vor e-m anderen gehört zu werden und zu plädieren *(Br z.B. Queen's Counsel vor junior barrister)*

preaudit Vorprüfung

preauthorized credit *Am* Vereinbarung zwischen Gläubiger, Schuldner und Zahlstellen über regelmäßige Zahlungen (*dem deutschen Lastschriftverfahren vergleichbar*)

preauthorized debit *Am* Vereinbarung zwischen Bank und Kunde, daß die Bank regelmäßig Zahlungen zu Lasten des Kundenkontos ausführen soll (*dem deutschen Dauerauftrag vergleichbar*)

preauthorized electronic funds transfer *Am* elektronischer Zahlungsverkehr aufgrund vorheriger Vereinbarung zwischen Bank und Kunde (*vergleichbar mit dem deutschen Dauerauftrag und Lastschriftverfahren*)

prebend *eccl* Präbende, Pfründe

prebendary *eccl* Präbendar, Inhaber e-r Pfründe

precatory words e-e Bitte enthaltende Worte

precaution Vorsicht(smaßregel); Vorsorge für die Zukunft; **air raid ~s** Luftschutz; **to take ~s** Vorsichtsmaßnahmen ergreifen

precede *v (im Rang, in der Zeit, im Wert)* vor(an) gehen; den Vorrang haben (a p. vor jdm)

preceding vorhergehend *(opp. subsequent)*; **~ →endorser; the ~ paragraphs** die vorhergehenden Absätze; **~ speaker** Vorredner; **~ tax year** vorangegangenes Steuerjahr; **~ year** Vorjahr

precedence Vorrang, Vortritt (over vor); Rangordnung, Rangfolge; *Br* Vorfahrt (over vor); **~ of the members of the diplomatic staff** Rangordnung der Mitglieder des diplomatischen Personals; **ceremonial ~** protokollarische Rangordnung; **list of ~** Rangliste

precedence, order of ~ Rangordnung, Rangfolge; **order of ~ of motions** *parl* Rangfolge der Anträge

precedence, (letters) patent of ~ *Br (z.B. e-m barrister)* von der Krone erteilter höherer Rang; **table of ~** *Br* Rangordnung; **to give ~** (to vehicles coming from ...) *Br* Vorfahrt gewähren; **to take** (or **have**) **~ over** vor(an)gehen, den Vorrang (od. Vortritt) haben vor, rangieren vor; **to take ~ after** im Rang kommen (od. rangieren) nach

precedent 1. Präzedenzfall, Präjudiz *(als Quelle des geltenden Rechts für künftige Entscheidungen gleicher Art)*; **authoritative ~** bindender Präzedenzfall *(der vom Gericht befolgt werden muß; cf. stare decisis)*; **binding ~** s. authoritative →~; **binding force of a ~** bindende Kraft e-s Präzedenzfalles; **persuasive ~** Präzedenzfall, der nicht bindend ist, aber vom Gericht in Betracht gezogen wird *(cf. persuasive authority)*; **to become** (or **constitute**) **a ~** e-n Präzedenzfall bilden; **to cite a ~** e-n Präzedenzfall anführen; sich auf e-n Präzedenzfall berufen; **to create a ~** e-n Präzedenzfall schaffen (od. abgeben); **to disregard a ~** e-n Präzedenzfall nicht beachten; **to establish a ~** s. to create a →~; **to invoke a ~** s. to cite a →~; **to overrule a ~** sich über e-n Präzedenzfall hinwegsetzen; e-e Entscheidung als nicht mehr verbindlich betrachten *(die bisherige Rechtsprechung ausdrücklich aufgeben)*; **to quote a ~** s. to cite a →~; **to set a ~** e-n Präzedenzfall schaffen (od. abgeben)

precedent 2. Urkunde, die dem Anwalt als Muster beim Aufsetzen anderer Urkunden dient

precedent 3. vorher-, vorausgehend; **~ condition** Vorbedingung; aufschiebende Bedingung

precedented e-n Präzedenzfall habend

preceding →precede *v*

pre-censorship Vorzensur

precept gerichtl. Anordnung; *(schriftl.)* Anweisung an e-e Amtsperson zur Vornahme e-r Handlung *(Br z.B. des sheriff an den zuständigen Beamten, die Wahl e-s Member of Parliament durchzuführen)*

precinct *Am* Bezirk; Polizeibezirk; Wahlbezirk; ~ **caucus** *Am* Wählerversammlung des Wahlkreises; ~ **worker** *Am* Wahl(bezirks)helfer; **parliamentary ~s** *parl* Bannmeile; **shopping** ~ Geschäftsgebiet *(mit Kraftfahrverbot)*

precious metal futures *(Börse)* Edelmetall-Terminkontrakte

preclude *v* ausschließen (from von); **nothing in this agreement shall** ~ dieses Abkommen schließt nicht aus, daß; **a judgement ~s further argument** ein Urteil schließt weiteres Vorbringen aus

preclusion Ausschließung, Ausschluß (from von); ~ **clause** Ausschlußklausel; **term of** ~ Ausschlußfrist

preclusive ausschließend; ~ **period** Ausschlußfrist; **the time-limit is** ~ die Frist ist e-e Ausschlußfrist *(sie ist nicht verlängerungsfähig)*

precognition *Scot* Zeugenvernehmung vor der Verhandlung

precognose *v Scot* Zeugen vor der Verhandlung vernehmen

pre-collection letter *Am* letzte Mahnung

preconcerted vorher verabredet; abgekartet

precondition wesentl. Voraussetzung (of für); Vorbedingung

precontract Vorvertrag

predate *v* →antedate *v*

predatore raubgieriger Geschäftsmann

predatory räuberisch, raubgierig; ~ **actions** *Am* →~ practices; ~ **practices** *Am (AntitrustR)* Handelspraktiken, die darauf gerichtet sind, ein Konkurrenzunternehmen zugrunde zu richten; räuberische Methoden *(z.B. beim Boykott)*; ~ **price** Wucherpreis

predecease *v* früher sterben als; **~d** vorverstorben; **if the legatee ~s the testator, the legacy lapses** wenn der Vermächtnisnehmer vor dem Testator stirbt, wird das Vermächtnis hinfällig

predecessor Vorgänger *(opp. successor)*; ~ **company** Vorgesellschaft; ~ **in office** Amtsvorgänger; ~ **in title** Rechtsvorgänger, vorheriger Eigentümer *(von Grundbesitz)*

predetermined cost vorkalkulierte Kosten

predict *v* vorhersagen

predominance Vorherrschaft, Übergewicht

pre-election Vorwahl; ~ **promise** Wahlversprechen

pre-eminence, economic ~ wirtschaftliche Vorrangstellung

preempt *v* auf Grund e-s Vorkaufsrechts erwerben; *(auf Grund höherrangigen Rechts oder höherer Kompetenz)* ausschließen; *Am* das Vorkaufsrecht erwerben durch Siedlung auf staatl. Boden; *colloq. (Sitz, Parkplatz etc)* mit Beschlag belegen

preemption doctrine *Am* Vorrang des Bundesrechts vor dem Recht der Einzelstaaten

preemption, (right of) ~[107] Vorkaufsrecht *(Am bes. des Siedlers hinsichtl. des von ihm urbar gemachten staatl. Bodens)*; Bezugsrecht *(e-s Aktionärs auf neu ausgegebene Anteile)*; *Am* Recht des Bundes zur Gesetzgebung mit verdrängender Wirkung gegenüber gleichgerichteten einzelstaatlichen Gesetzen; *Am (Außenhandel)* das Recht e-r Regierung, Waren zu beschlagnahmen und sie zu dem von dem Importeur angegebenen Wert zu verkaufen, wenn Verdacht besteht, daß der Wert zu niedrig angegeben war; *(VölkerR)* Ankaufsrecht e-r Prise

preemptive, ~ **right** Vorkaufsrecht; Bezugsrecht *(e-s Aktionärs bei Ausgabe neuer Aktien)*; ~ **shares** *Am* Bezugsaktien; ~ **strike** *Am mil* Präemptivschlag *(opp. preventive strike)*

preemptor *Am* Erwerber *(von Grundbesitz)* auf Grund e-s Vorkaufsrechts; Vorkaufsberechtigter

pre-enactment explorer[108] (PEE) Pionierunternehmen

preestimate vorherige (Ein-)Schätzung; (Kosten-)Voranschlag

prefabricate *v (genormte)* Fertigteile *(für Häuser etc)* fabrikmäßig herstellen

prefabricated (prefab) in Fertigbauweise erstellt; vorgefertigt, Fertig-; ~ **house** Fertighaus

prefabrication *(serienmäßige)* Vorfertigung

prefer *v* vorziehen, bevorzugen; *(Forderung)* bevorzugt befriedigen; *(Klage etc)* einreichen, vorbringen; *(im Amt, Rang)* befördern; **to ~ an accusation against a p.** jdn anklagen; **to ~ a charge against a p.** e-e Anschuldigung gegen jdn erheben; jdn anklagen; **to ~ a claim** e-e Forderung geltend machen; Anspruch erheben (to auf), beanspruchen; **to ~ a complaint** e-e Beschwerde vorbringen; **to ~ one creditor over** (or **to**) **others** e-n Gläubiger bevorzugt befriedigen; **to ~ an officer to the rank of general** e-n Offizier zum General befördern

preferred bevorrechtigt, bevorzugt; ~ **bonds** →preference bonds; ~ **creditor** bevorrechtigter Konkursgläubiger; ~ **debt** →preferential debt; ~ **dividend** Vorzugsdividende; ~ **mortgage** *Am* s. ~ ship →mortgage; ~ **ordinary shares** *Br* bevorrechtigte Stammaktien; ~ **risk plan** *Am (KraftfahrzeugVers.)* Schadensfreiheitsrabatt; ~ **shareholder** *Am* Vorzugsaktionär

preferred stock (prefs.) *Am* Vorzugsaktien; **adjustable rate** ~ *Am* Vorzugsaktie, bei der die Dividende jeweils auf den gängigen Zinssatz für Geldmarktpapiere festgelegt wird *(durch Anlehnung an den Diskontsatz für→ Treasury bills, durch Tenderverfahren u. a.)*; **participating** ~ *Am* Vorzugsaktien mit zusätzlicher Dividendenberechtigung; **prior** ~ Sondervorzugsaktien (→*prior*)

preferred ship mortgage *Am s.* ship →mortgage

preferred, to be ~ **to** bevorzugt sein vor

preference Vorzug, Bevorzugung (to, over vor); Vorzugsstellung; *(KonkursR)* Gläubigerbegünstigung; **(avoidable)** ~ *Am (KonkursR)* Anfechtungstatbestand für bestimmte Konkurshandlungen, die vor Konkurseröffnung erfolgen; ~**s** Präferenzen; ~ **bonds** *Br* Prioritätsobligationen, Prioritäten *(mit Vorrang hinsichtl. Verzinsung und Rückzahlung ausgestattete Obligationen)*; ~ **dividend** Vorzugsdividende; ~ **freight** *Am* zu Vorzugsbedingungen beförderte Fracht *(verderblicher Waren)*; ~ **of creditors** *(KonkursR)* Gläubigerbegünstigung; ~ **offer** Vorzugsangebot, Sonderangebot; ~ **origin** *(Zoll)* Präferenzursprung

preference, ~ **shares** (prefs) *Br* Vorzugsaktien, Prioritätsaktien; ~ **share certificate** *Br* Vorzugsaktienzertifikat; **cumulative** ~ **shares** *Br* kumulative Vorzugsaktien (→*cumulative*); **participating** ~ **shares** *Br* Vorzugsaktien mit zusätzlicher Dividendenberechtigung; **redeemable** ~ **shares** *Br* tilgbare Vorzugsaktien (→*redeemable*)

preference shareholder *Br* Inhaber von Vorzugsaktien, Vorzugsaktionär

preference, elimination of ~**s** Beseitigung von Präferenzen; **fraudulent** ~ *(KonkursR)* Gläubigerbegünstigung; **in** ~ **to** unter Bevorzugung gegenüber; **margin of** ~ Präferenzspanne; **scheme of generalized** ~**s** (GSP) (EG) allgemeines Präferenzsystem; **undue** ~ unzulässige Bevorzugung; **voidable** ~ *Am (KonkursR)* Anfechtungstatbestand für bestimmte Rechtshandlungen, die vor Konkurseröffnung erfolgten; **to give** ~ (to one p. over another) (jdm) den Vorzug geben, (jdn) bevorzugen; **to be given** ~ bevorzugt sein

preferential bevorrechtigt, bevorzugt; Präferenz-, Vorzugs-; ~ **arrangements** Präferenzabmachungen, Präferenzregelungen; ~ **assignment** Vermögensübertragung zugunsten von Gläubigern *(durch den Konkursschuldner)*

preferential benefit *Am* Voraus; Vorwegentnahme; **by way of** ~ als Voraus

preferential claim bevorrechtigte Forderung

preferential consideration, to give a matter ~ etw. bevorzugt behandeln

preferential ~, ~ **countries** *(EG)* präferenzbegünstigte Länder; ~ **credit** Vorzugskredit

preferential creditor bevorrechtigter (Konkurs-) Gläubiger (→*priority of creditors*); →**pre-**~; ~**s rank before ordinary creditors** bevorrechtigte Gläubiger gehen gewöhnlichen Gläubigern im Rang vor

preferential debts[109] bevorrechtigte (Konkurs-) Forderungen

Während im allgemeinen die →secured creditors vor den →unsecured creditors befriedigt werden, ist durch Gesetz bestimmten Forderungen Vorrang eingeräumt (→*preferential payments, priority of creditors*)

preferential, ~ **dividend** Vorzugsdividende; ~ **duty** Präferenzzoll, Vorzugszoll; ~ **hiring** *Am* Bevorzugung von Gewerkschaftsmitgliedern bei der Einstellung; ~ **offer** Vorzugsangebot, Präferenzangebot

preferential payments bevorrechtigte (Aus-) Zahlungen *(Br z. B. aus der Konkursmasse, aus dem verschuldeten Nachlaß, bei der Liquidation e-r Gesellschaft oder von Sozialversicherungsbeträgen)*

preferential, ~ **price** Vorzugspreis; ~ **rate** (of customs duties) Vorzugs(zoll)tarif, Präferenzzollsatz; ~ **right** Vorzugsrecht; ~ **shop** *Am* Betrieb, der Gewerkschaftsmitglieder bei der Einstellung bevorzugt; ~ **tariff** (of customs duties) Präferenztarif, Vorzugszoll(tarif)

preferential treatment Vorzugsbehandlung, Bevorzugung *(opp. discrimination against)*; **to enjoy** ~ **in respect of tariffs** Zollpräferenzen genießen; **to give** ~ bevorzugt behandeln

preferential, to be ~ **(to)** vorzuziehen sein

preferentialism Präferenzsystem

preferred →prefer *v*

prefinance *v* vorfinanzieren

pregnancy Schwangerschaft; **assistance during** ~ **and confinement** Hilfe für werdende Mütter und Wöchnerinnen; **interruption of** ~ Schwangerschaftsunterbrechung; **prevention of** ~ Schwangerschaftsverhütung; **termination of** ~ *(bes. ärztliche)* Abtreibung

prejudge *v* im voraus (ver)urteilen; übereilt urteilen

prejudgment attachment *Am* Arrest zur Sicherung der Vollstreckung aus e-m künftigen Urteil

prejudication vorgefaßtes Urteil

prejudice Vorurteil, Voreingenommenheit, Befangenheit; Beeinträchtigung, Nachteil, Schaden; **to the** ~ **of sb.'s rights** zum Nachteil von jds Rechten; **class** ~ Standesvorurteil; **racial** ~ Rassenvorurteil; **no** ~ **to the plaintiff resulted** (or **the plaintiff has suffered no** ~) der Kläger hat (dadurch) keinen Nachteil erlitten; **to be of ~ to the interests** den Interessen abträglich sein; **to overcome a ~** ein Vorurteil überwinden

prejudice, with ~ *Am* Beschwer begründend *(von dem befaßten Gericht endgültig und zum Nachteil des Antragstellers entschieden)*

prejudice, without ~ freibleibend; ohne Schaden für die eigenen Rechte (od. Ansprüche); unbeschadet; ohne Verbindlichkeit, ohne Obligo; **without ~ negotiations** *(etwa)* Vergleichsverhandlungen; **to be without ~ (to)** unberührt lassen

Der Schutz vor Nachteilen aus without prejudice abgegebenen Erklärungen geht sehr weit. Haben die without prejudice geführten Verhandlungen nicht zu einer bindenden Abmachung geführt, so dürfen sie bei einer gerichtlichen Auseinandersetzung dem Gericht mit wenigen Ausnahmen nicht zur Kenntnis gebracht werden, damit das Gericht keinesfalls Folgerungen aus der Verhandlung zieht

prejudice *v* beeinträchtigen, benachteiligen, schädigen, abträglich sein; voreinnehmen; **to ~ a p.'s interests** jds Interessen beeinträchtigen (od. verletzen)

prejudiced voreingenommen, befangen; **~ opinion** vorgefaßte Meinung; **to be ~ (by)** benachteiligt werden; **to be ~ in favo(u)r of (against)** voreingenommen sein für (gegen); **to declare o.s. (to be) ~** sich für befangen erklären

prejudicial nachteilig, schädlich (to für); **to be ~** beeinträchtigen, sich nachteilig auswirken (to auf); **to be ~ to public order** die öffentliche Ordnung und Sicherheit gefährden

preliminaries Präliminarien; Vorverhandlungen; Vorbereitungen

preliminary Einleitung; vorläufig, einleitend, vorbereitend, Vor-; **~ act** *Br (von dem solicitor für jede Partei eingereichte)* gesiegelte Urkunde über Einzelheiten e-r Schiffskollision; **~ advice** Voranzeige; **~ agreement** *(VölkerR)* Vorvereinbarung; **~ and issue expenses** *Br (Bilanz)* Gründungs- und Unterparikosten; **~ answer** vorläufiger Bescheid; **~ audit** Vorprüfung *(e-s Rechnungsabschlusses)*; **~ calculation** Vorkalkulation, Voranschlag; **~ contract** Vorvertrag *(jd verpflichtet sich e-m anderen gegenüber, mit e-m Dritten e-n Vertrag zu schließen)*; **~ cost** *Am* Gründungs- und Organisationskosten; **~ decision** Vor(ab)entscheidung, vorläufige Entscheidung; **~ discussion** Vorbesprechung; **~ draft** Vorentwurf; **~ election** Vorwahl; **~ estimate** (Kosten-)Voranschlag

preliminary examination *(Strafprozeß)* gerichtliche Voruntersuchung *(vor e-m magistrate)*; *(Br jetzt meist committal proceedings genannt)*; Aufnahmeprüfung *(für bestimmte Berufsausbildungskurse)*; *Br (KonkursR)* vorläufige Vernehmung des Schuldners durch den →official receiver; *(PatR)* vorläufige Prüfung

preliminary, ~ expenses *Br*[110] Gründungs- und Organisationskosten *(e-r Handelsgesellschaft)*; **~ financing** Vorfinanzierung; **~ hearing** →~ examination; **~ injunction** *Am* einstweilige Verfügung; **~ inquiry** (or **enquiry**) *Br* gerichtliche Voruntersuchung (→~ *examination*); **~ issue** *Br*[111] schwierige Frage (bes. Rechtsfrage), mit der sich das Gericht in e-m Termin vor der Hauptverhandlung befaßt; **~ measures** vorläufige Maßnahmen; prozeßleitende Verfügungen *(des Internationalen Gerichtshofes)*; **~ negotiation** Vorverhandlung; **~ →objection; ~ proceedings** Vorverfahren

preliminary ruling *(EuGH)* Vorabentscheidung; **to refer a question to the European Court for a ~** e-e Rechtsfrage dem Europäischen Gerichtshof zur Vorabentscheidung vorlegen

preliminary, ~ talks Vorbesprechungen; **~ treaty** Vorvertrag

premarital intercourse vorehelicher Verkehr

premature verfrüht, vorzeitig; **~ birth** Frühgeburt; **~ death** vorzeitiger Tod; **~ election** vorgezogene Wahl; **~ retirement** vorzeitige Pensionierung

prematurely, to retire ~ vorzeitig ausscheiden; **to terminate ~** vorzeitig (be)enden

premeditated vorbedacht, vorsätzlich

premeditation Vorbedacht, Überlegung *(bes. Vorsatzform beim Mord)*

pre-merger notification (procedure) →merger 2.

premier *Br* Premierminister
premiership *Br* Amt des Premierministers

premise Prämisse, Vordersatz; Voraussetzung; **~s** das Obenerwähnte, das vorher Gesagte (od. Vereinbarte); Einleitung(ssätze) e-r Urkunde *(der Teil e-r Urkunde, der dem →habendum vorausgeht)*; Räumlichkeiten; Grundstück *(mit Nebengebäuden)*; Haus *(nebst Grund und Boden)*; Gebäude; Wohnung; Geschäft(sräume); Diensträume, Werkstatt; **~s of a conference** Räume e-r Konferenz; **~s of a mission** *dipl* Räumlichkeiten e-r Mission; **bank ~s** Bankgebäude; **exhibition ~s** Ausstellungsräume; **factory ~s** Fabrikgebäude; **licensed ~s** *Br* Lokal mit Schankkonzession; **official ~s** Diensträume; **on the ~s** auf dem Grundstück; im Gebäude; an Ort und Stelle; **shop ~s** Ladenräume; **to sell on the ~s** an Ort und Stelle verkaufen

premium (pm, prm) 1. Prämie, Preis, Auszeichnung, Belohnung; staatl. Zuschuß *(zur Förderung der Ausfuhr od. Einfuhr, z. B. Exportprämie)*; *Am* Zugabeartikel; Extrazahlung, Abstand(szahlung) *(des Mieters)*; *(bei Kursen)* Agio, Aufgeld; *(Börse) (Prämiengeschäft)* Prämie, Reugeld; ~ **bonds** *Br* →~ savings bonds; ~ **drawing** Prämienziehung; ~ **offer** *Am* Zugabeangebot; (Verkauf mit) Zugaben; ~ **on bonds** Anleiheagio; ~ **on exchange** Agio, Aufgeld; ~ **on gold** Goldagio; ~ **on a lease** Abstandszahlung; ~ **on shares** Agio der Aktien; ~ **pay** *Am* Zuschlag zum Lohn *(höherer Lohn für Überstunden, gefährl. Arbeit etc)*; ~ **reserve** Dekkungsrücklage; ~ **savings bonds** *Br* Sparprämienanleihen *(vom →Treasury durch die Post ausgegebene Staatsanleihen)*; ~ **wage system** Prämienlohnsystem

premium, at a ~ über pari; über dem Nennwert; mit e-m Aufgeld; **issue (of shares) at a** ~ Über-pari-Emission; **to be at a** ~ über pari stehen; sehr gesucht sein; **to sell at a** ~ mit Aufgeld verkaufen

premium, exchange ~ Agio, Aufgeld; **export** ~ Exportprämie; **gold** ~ Goldagio; **share** ~ Emissionsagio; **silver** ~ Silberagio; **to put a** ~ **on** e-e Prämie aussetzen für; **unlawful** ~**s may be recovered by action** *Br*[112] ungesetzliche Abstandszahlungen können durch Klage zurückgefordert werden

premium (pm, prm) 2. *(VersR)* (Versicherungs-)Prämie, Beitrag; ~ **amount** Höhe der Prämie; Prämienbetrag; ~ **bond** Prämienanleihe; ~ **due** ausstehende (od. fällige) Prämie, Sollprämie *(opp. ~ paid)*; ~ **for an additional insurance** Zusatzprämie; ~ **in arrears** rückständige Prämie; ~ **income** Prämieneinnahmen, Beitragseingang; ~ **instalment** Prämienrate; ~ **of insurance** s. insurance →~; ~ **paid** eingenommene Prämie, Istprämie; ~ **payment** Prämienzahlung; ~ **rate** Prämiensatz; ~ **rebate** Prämienrabatt, Beitragsermäßigung; ~ **receipt** Prämienquittung; ~ **receipts** Prämieneinnahmen; ~ **reminder** Mahnschreiben *(für Prämienzahlung)*; ~ **reserve** Prämienreserve; ~ **statement** Prämienabrechnung, Beitragsabrechnung

premium, additional ~ Prämienzuschlag; **amount of** ~ Höhe der Prämie; **annual** ~ Jahresprämie; **basic** ~ Grundprämie; **calculation** (or **computation**) **of** ~**s** Prämienberechnung, Beitragsberechnung; **charges additional to** ~ Nebenkosten zur Prämie; **collection of** ~**s** Prämieneinziehung, Beitragseinziehung; **extra** ~ erhöhte Prämie, Zusatzprämie *(für bes. Risiken)*; **earned** ~ verdiente (od. eingezahlte) Prämie; **first** ~ Erstprämie *(opp. renewal)*; **free of** ~ prämienfrei; **grading of** ~**s** Beitragsstaffelung; **gross** ~ Bruttoprämie; **increase of** (or **in the**) ~ Prämienerhöhung; **increasing** ~ steigende Prämie; **initial** ~ Anfangsprämie; **insurance** ~ Versicherungsprämie; **level** ~ gleichbleibende Prämie; **limited** ~ abgekürzte Prämienzahlung; **minimum** ~ Mindestprämie; **net** ~ Nettoprämie, Prämie frei von Unkosten; **office** ~ Bruttoprämie; **outstanding** ~ Prämienaußenstände; **overdue** ~ rückständige Prämie; **pure** ~ s. net →~

premium, payment of ~ Prämienzahlung, Beitragszahlung; **exemption from payment of** ~ Prämienbefreiung, Beitragsbefreiung

premium, rate of ~ Prämiensatz; **refund** (or **return**) **of** ~**(s)** Prämienrückzahlung; **renewal** ~ Folgeprämie *(opp. first ~)*; **respite of** ~ Prämienstundung; **semi-annual** ~ Halbjahresprämie; **single** ~ Einmalprämie *(opp. level ~)*; **tabular** ~ Tarifprämie

premium, unearned ~ (noch) nicht verdiente Prämie; **reserve for unearned** ~ *(Bilanz)* Prämienüberhang *(Rückstellung für am Bilanztag noch nicht verdiente Prämie)*

premium, waiver of ~**(s)** Prämienbefreiung

premium, to arrange a ~ e-e Prämie vereinbaren; ~**s are received by collectors** Prämien werden von Kassierern eingenommen (→*industrial assurance*); **to raise the** ~ die Prämie erhöhen

prepackaged (or **prepacked**) abgepackt; in Fertigpackungen

prepaid vorausbezahlt; ~ **expense** transitorische Aktiva; Rechnungsabgrenzungsposten; ~ **freight** vorausbezahlte Fracht; ~ **income** transitorische Passiva; ~ **letter** frankierter Brief; ~ **medicine** *Am* private Krankenversicherung; **postage** ~ frankiert, freigemacht

preparation Vorbereitung; Abfassung *(e-s Schriftstücks)*; Aufbereitung *(von Rohstoffen)*; *(StrafR)* Vorbereitungshandlung; ~**s for war** Kriegsvorbereitungen; ~ **of the budget** Aufstellung des Haushaltsplans; ~ **of a report** Abfassung (od. Ausarbeitung) e-s Berichts; **to make** ~**s** Vorbereitungen treffen

preparatory vorbereitend; ~ **acts** Vorbereitungshandlungen; ~ **committee** vorbereitender Ausschuß; ~ **work** Vor(bereitungs)arbeiten

prepare *v* vorbereiten; abfassen, ausarbeiten; aufbereiten; **to** ~ **the balance sheet** die Bilanz aufstellen; **to** ~ **a bill** e-e Rechnung ausstellen; **to** ~ **the budget** den Haushaltsplan aufstellen; **to** ~ **a case** e-e Rechtssache *(für die Verhandlung)* vorbereiten; **to** ~ **a contract** e-n Vertrag aufsetzen; **to** ~ **the estimates** *parl* den Etat aufstellen; **to** ~ **a paper** e-n Vertrag vorbereiten

prepared, ~ **in duplicate** in 2 Urkunden ausgefertigt, in 2facher Ausfertigung; ~ **foodstuff** Waren der Lebensmittelindustrie; Fertignahrung; **to be** ~ bereit sein

prepay *v* vorausbezahlen; vor Fälligkeit bezahlen; *(Brief etc)* frankieren (→*prepaid*); **to** ~ **the postage on a letter** e-n Brief frankieren; **to** ~ **a reply to a telegram** telegrafische Rückantwort bezahlen

prepayable, freight ~ Fracht vorauszahlbar

prepayment Voraus(be)zahlung; Frankierung; **~s** *Am (Bilanz)* Anzahlungen an Lieferanten; **~ clause** Klausel, daß Schuldner Darlehen vor Fälligkeit zurückzahlen darf; **~ of postage** Freimachung, Frankierung

prepense vorbedacht; vorsätzlich; **with→malice ~**

preponderance Übergewicht, Überwiegen; **upon the ~ of evidence** auf Grund des überzeugenden Beweises

prepossessor Vorbesitzer, früherer Besitzer

pre-preferential creditors *Br* sonderbevorrechtigte (Konkurs-)Gläubiger (*→priority of creditors*)

prerequisite Vorbedingung; Voraussetzung (of für); *(vorher)* erforderlich; **~ of the validity** Voraussetzung für die Gültigkeit; **to be ~** notwendig sein (to für); **to create the ~s** die Voraussetzungen schaffen

prerogative Vorrecht; Prärogative; **~ (of the Crown** or **Royal ~)** *Br* Königl. Hoheitsrecht *(unabhängig vom Parlament)*; **~ of mercy** *Br (vom Innenminister für die Krone ausgeübtes)* Begnadigungsrecht; **~ order** *Br*[113] (**~ writ** *Am*) Anweisung e-s höheren Gerichts an ein unteres Gericht, Tribunal oder e-e Verwaltungsstelle im Rahmen seiner Kontrollgerichtsbarkeit außerhalb des förmlichen Rechtsmittelzuges (supervisory jurisdiction) *(cf. Habeas Corpus, mandamus, prohibition und certiorari)*; **presidential ~s** *Am* Vorrechte (od. Befugnisse) des Präsidenten; **to exercise the Royal ~** *Br* das Königl. Begnadigungsrecht ausüben

presales service verkaufsfördernder Kundendienst *(z. B. persönlicher Verkauf)*

Presbyterian Church Presbyterianische Kirche *(reformiert-evangelische Kirche; bes. in USA und Schottland)*

Presbyterian (World) Alliance Reformierter Weltbund *(Zusammenfassung aller reformierten Kirchen)*

prescribe *v* vorschreiben; Rechte *(bes. an Grundbesitz)* auf Grund von Ersitzung beanspruchen (*→prescription 2.*); *med* verschreiben

prescribed, as ~ vorschriftsmäßig; **~ debt** verjährte Forderung (*→prescription 2.*); **~ dividend** verfallene (nicht rechtzeitig abgehobene) Dividende; **in the ~ form** in der vorgeschriebenen Form; **within the ~ period** (or **time**) fristgemäß, innerhalb der vorgesehenen Frist; **to become ~** *Am* verjähren

prescription 1. Vorschrift; *med* Rezept; **~ charges** Rezeptgebühren

prescription 2. Ersitzung *(Erwerb vornehmlich von Rechten und Berechtigungen an Grundstücken durch längere unwidersprochene Rechtsausübung kraft vermuteter Rechtseinräumung)* (sog. **positive ~** or **acquisitive ~**); Versitzung *(Rechtsverwirkung durch längere Nichtausübung)*; *(rechtsvernichtende materiellrechtliche)* Verjährung (sog. **negative ~** or **extinctive ~**); **~ of a claim** Verjährung e-s Anspruchs

Die Ersitzung (Versitzung) von Eigentum an Grundstücken unterliegt der →adverse possession und der →limitation

prescription, acquisitive →prescription 2.

prescription, by ~ durch Ersitzung (erworben); **corporation by ~** *Br* auf Gewohnheitsrecht beruhende Körperschaft *(z. B. City of London)*; **easement by ~** Grunddienstbarkeit kraft Ersitzung

prescription, extinctive ~ s. negative→~; **negative ~** Versitzung; *(anspruchsvernichtende)* Verjährung (*→prescription 2.*)

prescription, period of ~ Ersitzungsfrist *(bezieht sich nur auf →land)*; Verjährungsfrist; **expiration of the period of ~** Ablauf der Ersitzungs- (od. Verjährungs-)frist; **the period of ~ runs** (against a p.) die Ersitzungs- (od. Verjährungs-)frist läuft (zum Nachteil e-r Person)

prescription, positive ~ Ersitzung (*→prescription 2.*); **term of ~** s. period of→~; **to acquire by ~** ersitzen; **to become invalid** (or **void**) **by ~** durch Versitzung untergehen; verjähren (*→prescription 2.*); **to claim a right by ~** ein Recht *(bes. an Grundbesitz)* auf Grund von Ersitzung beanspruchen; **to plead ~** Ersitzung (od. Verjährung) geltend machen, sich auf Ersitzung (od. Verjährung) berufen

prescriptive Ersitzungs-; Verjährungs-; ersessen; durch Ersitzung (od. Verjährung) erworben; **~ debt** Verjährungsschuld; **~ right** durch Ersitzung (od. Verjährung) erworbenes Recht; ersessenes Recht; **to claim a ~ right** ein Recht auf Grund von Ersitzung beanspruchen

presence Anwesenheit, Gegenwart; Präsenz *(opp. absence)*; Vorhandensein; **~ chamber** (or **room**) *Am* Audienzzimmer; **in the ~ (of)** in Anwesenheit (von); **your ~ is requested** Sie werden gebeten zu erscheinen

present 1. Geschenk; **to make sb. a ~ (of a th.)** jdm ein Geschenk machen, jdm etw. schenken

present 2. anwesend, zugegen *(opp. absent)*; „hier" *(bei Namensaufruf)*; gegenwärtig, aktuell *(opp. future, past)*; vorliegend; laufend; **the ~ agreement** dieses Abkommen, dieser Vertrag; **~ and future property** gegenwärtiges und künftiges Vermögen; **the ~ article** dieser Artikel; **the ~ Cabinet** das gegenwärtige Kabinett; **in the ~ case** im vorliegenden Falle; **the ~ convention** dieses Abkommen; **~-day significance** gegenwärtige Bedeutung; **~ debt** bestehende Schuld; **of the ~ month** diesen Monats

present price Tagespreis; **at ~s** *(Börse)* bei dem gegenwärtigen Kursstand

present, at the ~ time gegenwärtig; **~ value** Gegenwartswert; Zeitwert; **~ year** laufendes Jahr

present, members ~ and voting anwesende und abstimmende Mitglieder

present, those (here) ~ die Anwesenden; **all those ~** alle Anwesenden; **among those ~** unter den Anwesenden; **list of those ~** Anwesenheitsliste

presents, these ~ vorliegendes Schriftstück, vorliegende Urkunde; **by these ~** hierdurch, durch diese Urkunde; **to all to whom these ~ shall come** an alle, denen diese Urkunde vorgelegt wird; **know all men by these ~** hiermit wird allen kundgetan (, daß)

present *v (Gesuch etc)* einreichen, überreichen; vorlegen; *(jdn)* vorstellen; *eccl (für e-e Pfründe)* vorschlagen; **to ~ sb. with** jdn *(in feierlicher Form)* beschenken mit; **to ~ accounts** Rechnungen vorlegen; **to ~ a bill** *parl* e-n Gesetzesentwurf einbringen; **to ~ a bill (of exchange) for acceptance (payment)** e-n Wechsel zur Annahme (Zahlung) vorlegen; **to ~ one's case** seinen Fall darstellen; **to ~ a certificate** e-e Bescheinigung vorlegen; **to ~ for collection** zum Inkasso vorzeigen; **to ~ a document** e-e Urkunde vorlegen (od. einreichen); **to ~ evidence** Beweismittel beibringen; **to ~ a gift** ein Geschenk überreichen; **to ~ a motion** e-n Antrag stellen (od. einbringen), beantragen; **to ~ a petition** ein Gesuch einreichen; **to ~ a report** e-n Bericht vorlegen; **to ~ a request** ein Gesuch stellen; **allow me to ~ Mr. X to you** darf ich Ihnen Herrn X vorstellen; **to ~ oneself for trial** *(StrafR)* zur Verhandlung erscheinen

presented, when ~ bei Vorlage; **to be ~ at Court** *Br* bei Hofe eingeführt werden

presenting, time for ~ bills *(WechselR)* Vorlegungsfrist

presentation Einreichung, Eingabe *(e-s Gesuches etc);* Vorlegung, Vorlage (od. Präsentation) *(z.B. e-s Wechsels, Schecks);* Darstellung; Beschenkung *(in feierlicher Form); (äußere)* Aufmachung *(der Ware); (Zoll)* Gestellung; Aufführung; *Br eccl* Vorschlag(srecht) *(für e-e Pfründe);* **~ at Court** *Br (förml.)* Vorstellung bei Hofe; **~ copy** Freiexemplar; **~ of the annual balance sheet** Vorlage des Jahresabschlusses; **~ of a bill (of exchange) for acceptance (payment)** Vorlegung (od. Präsentation) e-s Wechsels zur Annahme (Zahlung); **~ of a claim** Anspruchserhebung; Anmeldung e-r Forderung; **~ of credentials** Überreichung des Beglaubigungsschreibens (→*credentials 2.*); **~ of documents** Einreichung (od. Vorlegung) der Dokumente; **~ of foodstuffs** Aufmachung von Lebensmitteln; **~ paper** Festschrift; **~-to-customs charge** Gestellungsgebühren; **on ~** *(WechselR)* beim Vorlegen, bei Vorlage; **time (allowed) for ~** Vorlegungsfrist *(für Wechsel);* **upon ~** s. on →~

presentee jd, dem ein Wechsel vorgelegt wird; *Br (bei Hofe)* vorgestellte (od. eingeführte) Person; *eccl Br (für e-e Pfründe)* Vorgeschlagener; Schenkungsempfänger

pre-sentence investigation *Am*[114] der Straffestsetzung vorausgehende (gerichtl.) Nachforschung

presenter Vorleger, Präsentant *(e-s Wechsels etc);* jd, der etw. vorlegt; *Br eccl* jd, der e-n →presentee vorschlägt

presentment Vorlegung, Präsentation *(bes. e-s Wechsels, Schecks)*; Darstellung; *Am (von der →grand jury erhobene und dem öffentl. Ankläger übermittelte)* Anklage; Aufführung; **~ of a case** Darstellung e-s Falles; **~ for acceptance (for payment)** *(WechselR)* Vorlegung (od. Präsentation) zur Annahme (zur Zahlung); **delay in ~** Verzug bei Vorlage; **non-~** Nichtvorlegung, Nichtvorlage; **place of ~** Vorlegungsort; **time of ~** Vorlegungsfrist *(für Wechsel)*; **waiver of ~** Verzicht auf Vorlegung

preservation Erhaltung; Konservierung *(von Lebensmitteln)*; Beibehaltung; Aufbewahrung, Verwahrung; **~ of evidence** Beweissicherung; **~ of natural beauty** Naturschutz; **~ of peace** Erhaltung des Friedens; **~ of public order**[115] Aufrechterhaltung der öffentlichen Ruhe und Ordnung; **~ of testimony** Beweissicherung; **~ period** (for records etc) Aufbewahrungsfrist; **cost of ~** Erhaltungskosten; **forest ~** Erhaltung der Wälder, Waldschutz; **in a good state of ~** in gut erhaltenem Zustand, gut erhalten; **to be under a ~ order** *Br* unter Denkmalschutz stehen

preservatives (in foods) Konservierungsstoffe *(in Lebensmitteln)*

preserve (Jagd-, Fisch-)Gehege; *fig* Sondergebiet; **fishing ~** Fischgehege; **game ~** Jagdgehege, Wildpark

preserve *v* bewahren, schützen (from vor); *(in gutem Zustand)* erhalten; *(Lebensmittel)* konservieren; beibehalten; **to ~ employment** die Beschäftigungslage sichern; **to ~ the estate** den Nachlaß sichern; **to ~ game** Wild schützen und hegen; **to ~ jobs** Arbeitsplätze erhalten (od. sichern); **to ~ peace** den Frieden erhalten; **to ~ public order** die öffentliche Ruhe und Ordnung erhalten; **to ~ records** Akten erhalten (od. aufbewahren); **to ~ rights** Rechte wahren; **to ~ traces** Spuren sichern

preserved haltbar gemacht; **badly** (or **ill**) **~** schlecht erhalten; **well ~** gut erhalten

preside *v* vorsitzen, den Vorsitz führen (at, over a meeting in e-r Sitzung); Vorsitzender sein; **to ~ over** den Vorsitz führen bei

presiding, ~ arbitrator Obmann des Schiedsgerichts; **~ judge** den Vorsitz führender Richter, Vorsitzender; *(auch)* die Verhandlung führender Richter (Einzelrichter); **~ officer** Vorsitzender; den Vorsitz führendes Vorstandsmitglied *(e-s Vereins, e-r Handelsgesellschaft etc)*; *Br* Wahlvorsteher; **with Mr. X ~** unter dem Vorsitz von Herrn X

presidency Vorsitz, Präsidium; Amt (od. Amtsdauer) e-s Präsidenten, Präsidentschaft; **under the ~ of** unter dem Vorsitz von; **vice-~** stellvertretender Vorsitz; **to run** (or **stand**) **for the P~** *Am* sich als Präsidentschaftskandidat aufstellen lassen

president 1. Präsident, Vorsitzender; *Am univ* Rektor *(der nicht ausschließl. von den Fakultäten bestimmt wird und sein Amt dauernd innehat)* **~-in-office** amtierender Präsident; **honorary ~** ehrenamtlicher Präsident; **Lord P~ of the Council** *Br* Präsident des Geheimen Staatsrats; **vice-~** Vizepräsident; stellvertretender Vorsitzender; **to be elected ~** zum Präsidenten (od. Vorsitzenden) gewählt werden

President 2. *pol* Präsident *(als Staatsoberhaupt; Am*[116] *gleichzeitig Staatsoberhaupt und Regierungschef; cf. Chief →Executive)*; **the ~'s award** *Am* Friedensmedaille *(höchste zivile Auszeichnung)*; **~ elect** gewählter Präsident *(vor Amtsantritt)*; **~ of the Federal Republic (of Germany)** (deutscher) Bundespräsident; **Assistant to the ~** *Am* persönlicher Berater des Präsidenten *(ihm untersteht das →White House Office)*; **election of the ~**[117] Wahl des Präsidenten; **(Executive) Office of the ~** *Am* Präsidialkanzlei; **Vice-~** Vizepräsident

president 3. *Am* Unternehmensleiter, Generaldirektor *(e-r corporation)*; **executive vice-~** *Am* stellvertretender Generaldirektor

Der president ist in der Regel als oberster leitender Angestellter (chief executive officer) e-s →management Spitze der Verwaltung und vertritt die Gesellschaft nach außen *(entspricht etwa dem Vorsitzer des Vorstandes)*; er ist meist board-Mitglied. Zuweilen hat auch der Vorsitzende des board (chairman) die Funktion des president inne

presidential Präsidenten-, den Präsidenten (od. Vorsitzenden) betreffend, Präsidial-; **~ address** Ansprache des Präsidenten; **~ campaign** *Am* Wahlkampf vor der Präsidentenwahl; **~ candidate** Präsidentschaftskandidat; **~ election**[117] Präsidentenwahl; **~ electors** *Am* Wahlmänner *(cf. primary election)*; **~ message** *Am* Botschaft des Präsidenten an den Kongreß *(cf. State of the Union →Message)*; **~ primary** *Am (einzelstaatl.)* indirekte Wahl des Präsidenten *(cf. primary election)*; **~ privilege** Vorrecht des Präsidenten; **~ succession** *Am* Nachfolge in das Amt des Präsidenten; **~ system** *Am* Präsidialsystem *(nach welchem der für e-e bestimmte Zeit gewählte chief executive nicht dem Kongreß verantwortlich ist)*; **~ tenure** (or **term**)[118] Amtszeit des Präsidenten; **~ year** *Am colloq.* Jahr der Präsidentenwahl *(Jahr der Wahl der presidential electors durch das Volk)*

press Presse *(i. S. von)* Zeitungen, Zeitungswesen, Journalisten, Journalismus; (Buch-) Druck, Druckerei; Druck, Bedrängnis, Andrang, Gedränge; **~ advertisement** Anzeige in Zeitungen; **~ advertising** Anzeigenwerbung in der Presse; **~ agency** Presseagentur, Nachrichtenbüro; **~ agent** Presseagent; **~ announcement** Zeitungsanzeige; **~ attaché** Presseattaché; **~ campaign** Pressefeldzug; **~ censorship** Pressezensur; **~ clipping** *Am* →~ cutting; **~ commentary** Pressekommentar; **~ communications** Pressenachrichten

press conference Pressekonferenz; **to hold a ~** e-e Pressekonferenz abhalten

press, ~ controversy Pressepolemik; **~ coverage** Presseberichterstattung; **~ cutting** Zeitungsausschnitt; **~ department** Presseabteilung; **~ gallery** Pressetribüne *(Br im House of Commons)*; **~ guide** Zeitungskatalog; **~ hand-out** Pressemitteilung; **~ item** Zeitungsnotiz; **~ notice** Presseankündigung; Zeitungsnotiz; **~ office** Presseamt, Pressestelle; **~ officer** Pressereferent; **~ release** Pressemitteilung; **~ report** Zeitungsmeldung; **~ telegram** Pressetelegramm; **domestic ~** inländische Presse; **foreign ~** ausländische Presse; **freedom** (or **liberty**) **of the ~** Pressefreiheit; **gutter ~** Skandalpresse; **muzzling of the ~** Presseknebelung; **national ~** inländische Presse; **to go to ~** in Druck gehen; **to have a bad (good) ~** (un)günstig aufgenommen (od. beurteilt) werden

press *v (jdn)* (be)drängen, *(jdm energisch)* zusetzen; *(energisch)* betreiben *(an appeal, a campaign)*; geltend machen, verfolgen; **to ~ sth. on sb.** jdm etw. aufdrängen; **to ~ for sth.** auf etw. bestehen; auf etw. drängen; **to ~ a claim** auf e-r Forderung bestehen; **to ~ for payment** auf Zahlung drängen; Zahlung nachdrücklich fordern

pressed, to be (hard) ~ for sth. etw. (sehr) nötig brauchen; (sehr) knapp sein an etw.

pressing dringend; **the matter is ~** die Angelegenheit ist dringend (od. eilt)

pressure Zwang, Druck

pressure group *pol (organisierte)* Interessengruppe *(die e-n starken Druck ausüben kann)*

Vereinigungen und Verbände (Wirtschaftsverbände, Berufsverbände, Gewerkschaften etc), die zur Verfolgung ihrer Interessen auf die öffentl. Meinung, Parteien, Parlamentarier etc „Druck" (Einfluß) auszuüben versuchen *(cf. lobby)*

pressure, ~ **of business** Drang der Geschäfte; **under** ~ **of time** unter Zeitdruck; ~ **on prices** Preisdruck; **financial** ~ finanzieller Druck; **inflationary** ~ Inflationsdruck; **peaceful** ~ *(VölkerR)* Sanktionsmaßnahmen; **political** ~ politischer Druck; **to be under** ~ stark angespannt sein, unter Druck gesetzt werden; **to exert** (or **put**) ~ Druck ausüben (on auf); **to put a p. under** ~ jdn unter Druck setzen

prestige Prestige, Ansehen; **loss of** ~ Prestigeverlust; **matter of** ~ Prestigefrage

presume *v* vermuten, annehmen; unterstellen

presumption Vermutung, Annahme; Unterstellung; ~ **of advancement** *Br (ErbR)* Schenkungsvermutung

presumption of death Todesvermutung; **decree of** ~ **and dissolution of marriage** *Br (EheR)* gerichtliche Todeserklärung und Auflösung der Ehe

presumption, ~ **of fact** Tatsachenvermutung; ~ **of innocence**[118a] Unschuldsvermutung, Vermutung der Unschuld *(des Angeklagten, der bis zum Beweis der Schuld als unschuldig gilt)*; ~ **of law** Rechtsvermutung; ~ **of legitimacy** Vermutung der Ehelichkeit; ~ **of life** Lebensvermutung; ~ **of ownership** Eigentumsvermutung; ~ **of →partnership;** ~ **of paternity** Vaterschaftsvermutung; ~ **of survivorship**[119] Überlebensvermutung; **conclusive** ~ s. irrebuttable →~; **inconclusive** ~ s. rebuttable →~; **irrebuttable** (or **irrefutable**) ~ unwiderlegbare (Rechts-)Vermutung *(praesumptio juris et de jure)*; **rebuttable** (or **refutable**) ~ widerlegbare (Rechts-)Vermutung *(praesumptio juris; opp. irrebuttable or conclusive ~)*; **to raise a** ~ Anlaß zu e-r Vermutung geben, e-e Vermutung begründen

presumptive mutmaßlich; ~ **evidence** (or **proof**) Indizienbeweis; ~ **title** *(durch Besitz und Benutzung)* vermutetes Eigentum an Grundbesitz; →**heir** ~

presuppose *v* voraussetzen; zur Voraussetzung haben

presupposition Voraussetzung

pretax, ~ **income** Einkommen vor Abzug der Steuern; ~ **profit** Gewinn vor Abzug der Steuern, Vorsteuergewinn

preten|ce (~se) Vorspiegelung; Vorgeben, Vorwand; Anspruch(serhebung) (to auf); **under the** ~ **of** (or **that**) unter dem Vorwand von (od. daß); **under false** ~**s** unter Vorspiegelung falscher Tatsachen; **obtaining information under false** ~**s** *Am*[120] Erlangung von Informationen aufgrund Vorspiegelung falscher Tatsachen; **to make a** ~ **of s. th.** etw. vortäuschen

pretend *v* vorspiegeln, falsch behaupten; vortäuschen; **to** ~ **to be** sich (fälschlich) ausgeben als; **to** ~ **ignorance** Unkenntnis vortäuschen

pretender Heuchler, Täuscher; *bes. hist.* (Thron-)Bewerber, Prätendent

pretension Anspruch (to auf); (unberechtigte) Beanspruchung; **territorial** ~**s** territoriale Ansprüche

pretermission *Am*[121] Übergehung e-s Abkömmlings in gerader Linie (lineal heir) bei e-r letztwilligen Verfügung

pretermitted *Am (im Testament)* übergangen *(→pretermission)*

pretest *(bei Meinungsforschung etc)* Vortest; ~ **interview** Probeinterview

pretext Vorwand; **under** (or **on**) **the** ~ **of** (or **that**) unter dem Vorwand von (od. daß); **to make a** ~ **(of)** vorschützen, vorgeben

pretrial, ~ **detention** *Am* Untersuchungshaft; ~ **discovery** *Am (Zivilprozeß)* Verfahren zur Sachverhaltsermittlung vor der mündlichen Verhandlung *(den am Prozeß beteiligten Parteien soll vor der Hauptverhandlung Zugang zu allen Tatsachen und Beweismitteln verschafft werden; →discovery)*; ~ **examination** *Am* →examination 1.; ~ **order** (or **ruling**) im Vorverfahren erlassene Gerichtsverfügung, die die Regeln für die Hauptverhandlung trifft; ~ **procedure** *Am* Vorverfahren *(mündliche Vorbesprechung des Gerichts mit den Anwälten, die häufig zu e-m Vergleich führt)*; ~ **review** *Br* mündl. Vorbesprechung des Gerichts mit den (Anwälten der) Parteien zur Vorbereitung der mündlichen Verhandlung

pre- underwritten issue →issue 3.

prevail *v* herrschen, vorherrschen, überwiegen (in bei); ausschlaggebend (od. maßgebend) sein; obsiegen, den Sieg davontragen (over über); **to** ~ **against** sich durchsetzen gegen; **to** ~ **upon sb. to do sth.** jdn zu e-r Tat überreden; jdn bewegen, etw. zu tun; **conditions** ~ Zustände herrschen; **where there is a difference between the rules of common law and equity, the rules of equity** ~ wo ein Unterschied besteht zwischen common law und dem equity-Recht, ist das equity-Recht anzuwenden (od. maßgebend); **the plaintiff has** ~**ed** der Kläger hat obsiegt

prevailing herrschend; vorherrschend; allgemein geltend; üblich; ~ **case law** herrschende Rechtsprechung; **under the** ~ **circumstances** unter den gegebenen Verhältnissen; ~ **legal opinion** herrschende Meinung; *Am* Votum der Mehrheit; ~ **party** *(im Prozeß)* obsiegende Partei; ~ **price** gegenwärtiger (od. üblicher) Preis; ~ **rate** geltender Lohntarif; **the highest**

tax rate ~ from time to time der jeweils gültige höchste Steuersatz

prevalence Vorherrschen; Übergewicht; *(weite)* Verbreitung; ~ **of burglaries** Häufigkeit (od. Überhandnehmen) von Einbrüchen

prevaricate *v* die Wahrheit verdrehen, Ausflüchte machen; **a witness ~s** ein Zeuge macht Ausflüchte

prevarication Verdrehung der Wahrheit, Ausflucht; *fig* Ausweichen *(z. B. bei Zeugenaussage);* Prävarikation, Parteiverrat

prevent *v (etw.)* verhindern, verhüten; **to ~ sb. from doing sth.** jdn hindern, etwas zu tun

prevention Verhinderung; Verhütung, Vorbeugung; ~ **of accidents** Unfallverhütung; ~ **of crime** Verbrechensverhütung; ~ **of fiscal evasion** Verhinderung der Steuerverkürzung (*→fiscal evasion*)

Prevention of Fraud (Investments) Act *Br* Gesetz zur Verhütung von Kapitalanlagebetrug *(aufgehoben durch den →Financial Services Act)*

prevention, ~ **of hardship** Vermeidung von Härten; ~ **of loss** Schadensverhütung; ~ **of war** Verhütung des Krieges

preventive vorbeugend, verhütend; **to take ~ action** vorbeugende Maßnahmen treffen; ~ **detention** *Br hist*[122] Sicherungsverwahrung; ~ **effect** *(StrafR)* Präventivwirkung; ~ **→injunction;** ~ **maintenance** vorbeugende Instandhaltung; ~ **measures** vorbeugende Maßnahmen, Sicherungsmaßnahmen; ~ **strike** *mil* Präventivschlag *(opp. preemptive strike);* ~ **vaccination** Schutzimpfung; ~ **war** Präventivkrieg

previous vorhergehend, früher; ~ **application** *(PatR)* Voranmeldung, ältere Anmeldung; ~ **approval** vorherige Zustimmung; ~ **career** bisherige Tätigkeit *(im Lebenslauf etc)*; ~ **conviction** Vorstrafe (*→conviction 1.*); ~ **day** *(Börse)* vorhergehender (od. letzter) (Notierungs-)Tag; ~ **decision** frühere Entscheidung; ~ **endorser** Vorindossant *(e-s Wechsels)*; ~ **holder** Vorbesitzer, früherer Inhaber; ~ **illness** *(VersR)* frühere Krankheit, altes Leiden; ~ **indorser** →~ endorser; ~ **notice** Vorankündigung

previous question *parl* Vorfrage *(Frage, ob über die Hauptfrage sofort ohne weitere Debatte abgestimmt werden soll)*; **to move** (or **put**) **the ~** die Vorfrage stellen; das Übergehen zur Tagesordnung beantragen

previous, ~ **speaker** Vorredner; ~ **year** Vorjahr

previously vorher; ~ **convicted** vorbestraft

pre(-)war Vorkriegs-; ~ **level** Vorkriegsstand; ~ **prices** Vorkriegspreise

price 1. Preis; **at the ~ of** zum Preise von; ~ **action** Preismaßnahme; ~ **adjustment** Preisangleichung; ~ **administration** *Am (staatl.)* Preisüberwachung; ~ **advance** Preissteigerung; Preiserhöhung; ~ **agreed upon** vereinbarter Preis; ~ **agreement** (or **arrangement**) Preisvereinbarung, Preisabsprache; ~ **asked** geforderter Preis; ~ **basis** Preisbasis; ~ **boost** *(sprunghafte)* Preiserhöhung; ~ **calculation** Preiskalkulation, Preisberechnung; ~ **cartel** Preiskartell; ~ **catalogue** Preisliste, Preisverzeichnis; ~ **ceiling** *(amtl.)* festgesetzte (obere) Preisgrenze, Höchstpreis; ~ **change** Preisänderung; ~ **combination** *Am* Preiskartell; ~ **competition** Preiskonkurrenz; ~ **concession** Preiszugeständnis

price control *(staatl.)* Preiskontrolle, Preisüberwachung; ~ **authority** (or **board**) Preisüberwachungsstelle

price, ~**-controlled** preisgebunden; ~ **convention** Preisabkommen, Preisvereinbarung; ~ **cuts** Preissenkung; ~ **cutting** Preisschleuderei, Preisunterbietung; ~**-cutting** preissenkend; ~ **decline** Preisverfall; ~ **decontrol** Aufhebung der Preiskontrolle, Preisfreigabe; ~ **decrease** Preisherabsetzung, Preissenkung; Preisrückgang; ~ **determination** s. determination of→~s; ~ **development** Preisentwicklung; ~ **difference** Preisdifferenz, Preisunterschied; ~ **dumping** Preisdumping; ~ **discrimination**[123] Preisdiskriminierung; ~ **elasticity** Preiselastizität; ~**-enhancing** preistreibend; ~ **escalation clause** Preisgleitklausel; ~ **fixed by government (or trade organisations)** Richtpreis, Festpreis, gebundener Preis *(aufgrund einer Anordnung der Regierung oder der Verbände)*

price fixing Preisfestsetzung; Preisvereinbarung, Preisabsprache *(unter Wettbewerbern)*; Preisbindung; ~ **agreement** Vereinbarung zur Festlegung von Preisen; Preisabsprache; **resale** ~ *(Kanada)* Preisbindung der zweiten Hand

price fluctuations, to be subject to ~ Preisschwankungen unterliegen

price, ~ **floor laws** *Am* Gesetze, die Mindestpreise festsetzen; ~ **freeze** Preisstopp; ~ **gap** Preisgefälle

price increase Preiserhöhung, Preissteigerung; **general** ~ Teuerung

price index Preisindex; ~ **number** Preisindexziffer; **consumer** ~ Preisindex für die Lebenshaltung; **retail** ~ (RPI) →Index of Retail Prices; **wholesale** ~ Großhandelspreisindex, Index der Großhandelspreise

price indexation clause Preisindexklausel

price, ~ **indication** Preisangabe; ~ **influences** Preiseinflüsse; ~ **inquiry** Preisanfrage; ~ **label** Preiszettel; ~ **leader** Preisführer *(führendes Unternehmen e-s Industriezweiges, dessen Preispolitik von den anderen freiwillig befolgt wird; cf. ~ leadership)*

price leadership Preisführerschaft, Preisführung

(marktmäßig maßgebende Unternehmen bewirken durch ihre Preispolitik, daß ihre Wettbewerber ihren Preismaßnahmen folgen, ohne daß e-e Absprache vorliegt)

price level Preisniveau, Preisstand, Höhe der Preise; **to maintain prices on the same level** Preise auf demselben Stand halten

price limit Preisgrenze, Preislimit; **to observe a** ~ ein Preislimit einhalten

price line *Am* Einheitspreis

price list Preisliste, Preisverzeichnis; **prices shown in ~s** in Preislisten angegebene Preise; **to consult the** ~ in der Preisliste nachsehen; **to post up a** ~ e-e Preisliste aushängen

price, ~-maintained goods preisgebundene Waren; ~ **maintenance** Preisbindung der zweiten Hand; Einhaltung der Preise; ~ **maintenance agreement**[124] Preisbindungsvertrag, Vereinbarung der Preisbindung *(zwischen Hersteller und Einzelhändler, der den Wiederverkaufspreis festlegt)*; ~ **making** Preisfestsetzung, Preisbestimmung; ~ **margin** Preisspanne; ~ **mark** Preisauszeichnung; ausgezeichneter Preis; ~ **mechanism** Preismechanismus; ~ **movement** Preisbewegung; ~ **obtained** erzielter Preis; **~s of commodities** Warenpreise; ~ **of delivery** Lieferpreis, Bezugspreis; **~(s) offered** Preisangebot, gebotener Preis; ~ **per unit** Stückpreis; ~ **policy** Preispolitik; ~ **quoted in an offer** in e-m Angebot angegebener Preis, Angebotspreis; ~ **raising** Preiserhöhung; **~-raising** preiserhöhend, preissteigernd

price range Preislage, Preisspanne, Preisskala; **medium** ~ mittlere Preislage

price, ~ **rebate** Preisnachlaß; ~ **recession** Preisrückgang; **~s recommended** empfohlene Preise; ~ **recovery** s. recovery of →~; **~-reducing** preissenkend; ~ **reduction** Preissenkung, Preisherabsetzung *(beim Kauf)*; ~ **regulations** (or **rules**) Preisvorschriften; ~ **scissors** Preisschere; ~ **sensitive** preisempfindlich; ~ **slashing** Preisschleuderei; ~ **spread** Preisspanne; **~-stabilizing** preisstabilisierend; ~ **stability** Preisstabilität; ~ **stabilization** Preisstabilisierung; ~ **structure** Preisgefüge; ~ **subject to change without notice** Preis freibleibend; ~ **supplement** Preisaufschlag; ~ **support** Preisstützung *(durch den Staat)*; ~ **tag** (or **ticket**) Preisschild, Preiszettel; ~ **trend** Preisentwicklung; ~ **variance** Preisabweichung; ~ **variation clause** Preisgleitklausel; ~ **war** Preiskrieg; ~ **without engagement** Preis freibleibend

price, acceptable ~ annehmbarer Preis; **adequate** ~ angemessener Preis; **adjustable** ~ gestaffelter Preis; **advanced** ~ erhöhter Preis; **agreed** ~ vereinbarter Preis; **allround** ~ Gesamtpreis; **appreciation of** (or **in**) **~s** Steigen der Preise; **asking** ~ geforderter Preis; **at all ~s** in jeder Preislage; **average** ~ Durchschnittspreis; **base** (or **basic**) ~ Grundpreis; **booming ~s** schnell steigende Preise; **bottom** ~ niedrigster Preis; **break in ~s** Preissturz; **buying** ~ Kaufpreis; **calculation of ~s** Preisberechnung; **cash** ~ Barpreis, Preis bei Barzahlung; **ceiling** ~ *(amtl.)* Höchstpreis; **change in ~s** Preisänderung; **class of ~s** Preisklasse; **close** ~ scharf kalkulierter Preis; **collapse of ~s** Preissturz; **commodity ~s** Warenpreise; **competitive** ~ Konkurrenzpreis; **consolidation of ~s** Festigung der Preise; **at constant** ~ preisbereinigt; **consumer ~s** Verbraucherpreise; **current** ~ Tagespreis, gegenwärtiger Preis; **decline in ~s** Preisrückgang, Sinken der Preise; **decrease in** ~ Herabsetzung des Preises

price, delivered ~ Lieferpreis, Frankopreis; **delivered** ~ **system** *Am* Vereinheitlichung der Transportkosten der Produzenten *(cf. single basing point system, multiple basing point system, zone →pricing system, uniform delivered price)*; **uniform delivered** ~ *Am* Einheitspreis, der den Kunden ohne Rücksicht auf den Lieferort be- od. verrechnet wird

price, determination of ~s Preisbestimmung; Preisstellung; **difference in** ~ Preisunterschied, Preisdifferenz; Preisgefälle; **domestic** ~ Inlandspreis; **drop in ~s** Sinken der Preise, Preissturz; **dropping ~s** fallende Preise; **enhancement of ~s** Preissteigerung; **exceptional** ~ Sonderpreis; **excess(ive)** ~ Überpreis; **exorbitant** ~ Wucherpreis; **fair** ~ angemessener Preis; **fall in ~s** Preissturz, Sinken (od. Rückgang) der Preise; **falling** ~ sinkender Preis *(opp. rising ~)*; **fancy** ~ Liebhaberpreis; **final** ~ Endpreis; **firm** ~ fester Preis; **firmness of ~s** Stabilität der Preise; **first** ~ s. original →~

price, fixed ~ Festpreis, (staatl. od. privat) festgesetzter Preis; gebundener Preis; **officially fixed** ~ amtlich festgesetzter Preis

price, flat ~ Einheitspreis; **fluctuation of ~s** Preisschwankungen; **forcing up of ~s** Preistreiberei; **formation of ~s** Preisbildung; **graduated** ~ gestaffelter Preis; **gross** ~ Bruttopreis; **guiding** ~ Richtpreis

price, high ~ hoher Preis; **at a high** ~ zu hohem Preis, teuer; **to command a high** ~ hoch im Preise stehen

price, highest ~ Höchstpreis; **home (market)** ~ Inlandspreis; **identical ~s** gleiche Preise; **increase in ~s** Preissteigerung, Preiserhöhung; **indication of** ~ Preisangabe; **inquiry as to** ~ Preisanfrage; **invoice(d)** ~ Rechnungspreis; **leading** ~ Richtpreis; **losing** ~ Verlustpreis; **loss in** ~ Preisverlust

price, low ~ niedriger Preis; **at a low** ~ zu niedrigem Preise, billig; **lowest** ~ niedrigster Preis; **lump sum** ~ Pauschalpreis; **maintained ~s** gebundene Preise; **maladjustment of ~s** Preisschere; **manufacturer's** ~ Fabrikpreis,

Herstellerpreis; **marked** ~ ausgezeichneter Preis; **market** ~ Marktpreis; **matter of** ~ Preisfrage; **maximum** ~ Höchstpreis; **medium** (or **middle**) ~ Mittelpreis; **minimum** ~ Mindestpreis; **movement of** ~**s** Preisbewegung; **original** ~ Anschaffungspreis, Einkaufspreis; **peak** ~ Höchstpreis; **pegged** ~ s. supported →~; **prevailing** ~ s. ruling →~; **preferential** ~ Vorzugspreis; **quotation of** ~**s** Preisangabe; **raising of** ~**s** Preiserhöhung, Preissteigerung; **reasonable** ~ angemessener Preis; **receding** ~**s** fallende Preise; **recommended** ~ empfohlener Preis; **recovery of** ~**s** Erholen (od. Ansteigen, Anziehen) der Preise

price, reduced ~ ermäßigter Preis; **at reduced** ~**s** zu herabgesetzten Preisen

price, retail ~ Einzelhandelspreis (→*retail*); **rise in** ~**s** Ansteigen (od. Anziehen) der Preise, Preisanstieg, Preissteigerung; **rising** ~**s** steigende Preise *(opp. falling ~s)*; **ruinous** ~ Verlustpreis, Schleuderpreis; **ruling** ~ gegenwärtiger Preis; **selling** ~ Verkaufspreis; **special** ~ Sonderpreis, Ausnahmepreis; **stability of** ~**s** Preisstabilität; **stable** ~**s** stabile Preise; **statement of** ~**(s)** Preisangabe; Preisverzeichnis; **stationary** ~ stabiler Preis; **strengthening of** ~**s** Festigung der Preise; **suggested** ~ empfohlener Preis; **supported** ~ Stützungspreis; **top** ~ Höchstpreis; **uniform** ~**s** einheitliche Preise; **unreasonable** ~ unangemessener Preis; **wholesale** ~ Engrospreis, Großhandelspreis

price 2. *(Börse)* Kurs; ~ **advance** Kursanstieg; ~ **after hours** nachbörslicher Kurs; ~ **asked** Briefkurs *(Kurs, zu dem ein Angebot besteht)*; ~ **bid** *(buyers)* Geldkurs (G) *(Kurs, zu dem Nachfrage besteht; opp. ~[s] offered)*; ~ **change** Kursveränderung

price-earnings ratio (PER) Kurs-Gewinn- Verhältnis (KGV)

Bevorzugte Kennzahl zur Bewertung von Aktien, die aussagt, wie oft der Jahresgewinn *(der tatsächl. Unternehmensgewinn, der sich aus den Dividenden und den Zuweisungen zu offenen und stillen Rücklagen zusammensetzt)* je Aktie im Kurs dieser Aktie enthalten ist. Beispiel: Kurs je Aktie (450) dividiert durch Jahresgewinn je Aktie (30) = PER (15)

price, ~ **fall** Kursrückgang; ~ **for the account** *Br* Terminkurs *(opp. ~ for cash)*; ~ **for cash** Kassakurs, Kurs bei Barzahlung; ~ **for the settlement** *Br* Terminkurs *(opp. ~ for cash)*; ~ **fluctuations** Kursschwankungen; ~ **gain** Kursgewinn; ~ **improvement** Kursbesserung; ~ **level** Kursniveau, Kursstand; ~ **limit** Kursgrenze, Kurslimit; ~ **list** Kurszettel; ~ **loss** Kursverlust; ~ **movement** Kursbewegung; ~ **of call** Vorprämienkurs; ~ **of the day** Tageskurs; ~ **of option** Prämienkurs; ~ **of put** Rückprämienkurs; ~ **of shares** Aktienkurs, Börsenkurs; ~**(s) offered** *(sellers)* Briefkurs (B) *(Kurs, zu dem Angebot vorliegt; opp. ~ bid)*; ~ **pegging** Kursstützung; ~ **quotation** Kursnotierung; ~ **quoted** notierter Kurs, Kursnotierung; ~ **stabilization** Kursstabilisierung; ~ **support** Kursstützung; ~ **weakness** Kursabschwächung

price, advance in ~**s** →~ advance; **asked** ~ Briefkurs; **average** ~ Durchschnittskurs; **bid** ~ Geldkurs; **bottom** ~ niedrigster Kurs; **break in** ~**s** Kurssturz, Kurseinbruch; **buying** ~ Kaufkurs; **call** ~ Vorprämienkurs; **cash** ~ Kassakurs, Kurs bei Barzahlung; **closing** ~ Schlußkurs, letzter Kurs *(opp. opening ~)*; **crumbling of** ~**s** Abbröckeln der Kurse; **decline in** ~**s** Kursrückgang, Baisse; **depression of** ~**s** Kurseinbruch; **difference in** ~**s** Kursdifferenz; **drop** (or **fall**) **in** ~**s** Fallen der Kurse, Kursrückgang, Kurssturz; **firm** ~**s** feste Kurse; **fluctuation of** ~**(s)** Kursschwankungen; **forward** ~ *Br* (**future** ~ *Am*) Kurs für Termingeschäfte, Terminkurs *(opp. spot ~)*; **highest** ~ höchster Kurs; **increase in** ~ Kurssteigerung, Hausse; **issue** ~ Ausgabekurs, Emissionskurs; **jump in** ~**s** plötzlicher Kurssprung; **level of** ~**s** →~ level; **limited** ~ →~ limit; **list of** ~**s** *Br* Kursblatt; **loss in** ~ Kursverlust; **low** ~ niedriger Kurs; **lowest** ~ niedrigster Kurs; **making up** ~ *Br* Liquidationskurs; **market** ~ Börsenkurs; **maximum** ~ Höchstkurs; **medium** (or **middle**) ~ Mittelkurs; **minimum** ~ Mindestkurs; **movement of** ~**s** Kursbewegung; **offered** ~**(s)** →~(s) offered; **opening** ~ Eröffnungskurs, Anfangskurs, erster Kurs *(opp. closing ~)*; **peak** ~ Höchstkurs; **at present** ~**s** bei dem gegenwärtigen Kursstand

price, purchase ~**, difference between purchase and selling** ~ Kursspanne

price, put ~ Rückprämienkurs; **put and call** ~ Stellagekurs; **receding** ~**s** fallende Kurse; **recovery of** ~**s** Kurserholung; **rise in** ~**(s)** Kurssteigerung; **rising** ~**s** steigende Kurse; **selling** ~ Verkaufskurs; **share** ~**s** Aktienkurse, Börsenkurs; **slump (in** ~**s)** Kurssturz; **spot** ~ →spot 2.; **to-day's** ~ heutiger Kurs; **top** ~ Höchstkurs; **weakness in** ~ Kursabschwächung

price (1. und 2.), **to advance in** ~ im Preis (od. Kurs) steigen; **to advance the** ~ den Preis erhöhen; **to agree (up)on a** ~ e-n Preis vereinbaren; **to ascertain the** ~ den Preis festsetzen; **to ask the** ~ sich nach dem Preis erkundigen; **to beat down a** ~ e-n Preis herunterhandeln (od. drücken); **to bring down the** ~ s. to reduce the →~; **to calculate the** ~ den Preis berechnen; **to charge a p. a** ~ jdm e-n Preis berechnen, von jdm e-n Preis fordern; **to cut** ~**s** die Preise senken; **to demand a** ~ e-n Preis fordern; **to determine the** ~ den Preis bestimmen; **to establish a** ~ e-n Preis *(amtl.)* festsetzen; **to fall in** ~ im Preis (od. Kurs) fallen; **to fetch a (high)** ~ e-n (hohen) Preis erzielen; **to**

fix a ~ e-n Preis festsetzen; e-n Preis *(unter Wettbewerbern)* bestimmen (od. absprechen) *(für bestimmte Zeit unabänderlich machen); (Börse)* e-n Kurs feststellen; **to force down ~s** Preise (od. Kurse) drücken; **to force up ~s** Preise (od. Kurse) in die Höhe treiben; **to freeze ~s** Preisstopp durchführen; **to get a** ~ s. to realize a →~; **to go down in** ~ im Preise (od. Kurs) fallen; **to go up in** ~ im Preise (od. Kurs) steigen; **to increase in** ~ im Preise (od. Kurs) steigen, teurer werden; **to increase the** ~ den Preis erhöhen (od. heraufsetzen); **to inquire the** ~ nach dem Preis fragen, sich nach dem Preis erkundigen; **to keep down ~s** Preise niedrig halten; **to keep up ~s** Preise hoch halten; **to limit a** ~ ein Preislimit setzen; **to lower the** ~ s. to reduce the →~; **to maintain ~s** Preise (ein)halten; **to make a** ~ e-n Preis machen (od. bestimmen); **to name the** ~ den Preis nennen; **to negotiate a** ~ über e-n Preis verhandeln, e-n Preis aushandeln; **to obtain a** ~ s. to realize a →~; **to put a** ~ **on a p.'s head** s. to set a →~; **to quote a** ~ e-n Preis angeben; e-n Kurs notieren; **to raise ~s** Preise erhöhen; **to realize a** ~ e-n Preis erzielen; **to reduce the** ~ den Preis herabsetzen (od. senken); den Preis mindern; **to rise in** ~ im Preis (od. Kurs) steigen; **to set a** ~ **on a p.'s head** auf jds Kopf e-e hohe Belohnung aussetzen; **to suggest a** ~ e-n Preis empfehlen; **to undercut a p.'s** ~ jds Preis unterbieten; **the ~s are advancing** die Preise (od. Kurse) ziehen an (od. steigen); **the ~s have crumbled** s. the →~s have eased off; **~s are on the decline** die Kurse geben nach (od. gehen zurück); **~s depend on supply and demand** Preise richten sich nach Angebot und Nachfrage; **this** ~ **is liable to discount** von diesem Preise geht ein Rabatt ab; **~s have dropped** Preise (od. Kurse) sind gefallen; **the ~s have eased off** die Kurse haben nachgegeben (od. sind abgebröckelt); **the ~s are falling** (or **going down**) die Preise (od. Kurse) sinken (od. fallen); **~s are firm** die Kurse sind fest; **the ~s have gone up** (or **increased**) die Preise (od. Kurse) sind gestiegen; **the ~s are hardening** die Preise (od. Kurse) ziehen an; **the ~s jumped** die Preise gingen (sprunghaft) in die Höhe; ~ **is no object** der Preis spielt keine Rolle; **the ~s are rising** (or **on the rise**) die Preise (od. Kurse) steigen (od. gehen in die Höhe); **~s sag** →~s are on the decline

price *v* bewerten; den Preis festsetzen für; mit Preis(angabe) versehen; **to** ~ **goods** Waren mit Preis auszeichnen; **to** ~ **o.s. off the market** durch seine Preise wettbewerbsunfähig werden

priced, ~ **catalogue** Katalog mit Preisangaben; **low-**~ zu niedrigen Preisen, billig; **high-**~ zu hohen Preisen, teuer; **to be competitively** ~ im Preis konkurrenzfähig sein

pricing Preisfestsetzung, Preisbestimmung; Preiskalkulation; Preisauszeichnung; Feinabstimmung des endgültigen Emissionskurses e-r Anleihe während ihrer Zeichnungsfrist *(opp. bought deal);* ~ **policy** Preispolitik; ~ **system** Methode zur Preisberechnung; **dual** ~ Doppelpreissystem; **zone** ~ *Am* Preisbildung nach Zonen *(der Lieferpreis ist einheitlich für die Käufer innerhalb e-r Zone, wechselt aber von Zone zu Zone)*

pricking for sheriffs *Br* Ernennung der sheriffs

priest Priester, Geistlicher

prima facie ("at first sight") beim ersten Anschein

prima facie case prima-facie-Fall; glaubhaft gemachter Sachverhalt; **to establish** (or **make out**) **a** ~ *(vor Gericht)* glaubhaft machen

Fall, in dem auf Grund ihres prima facie bewiesenen Vorbringens zugunsten einer Partei zu entscheiden ist, wenn dieses nicht durch ein prima facie bewiesenes Vorbringen des Gegners erschüttert wird. Dann allgemeines Verfahren

prima facie evidence *(widerlegbarer)* Beweis des ersten Anscheins; Glaubhaftmachung; **to constitute** (or **establish**) **a** ~ glaubhaft machen; Beweis des ersten Anscheins darstellen

prima facie →meaning

primacy Primat, Vorrang; *eccl* Primat; **position of** ~ führende Stellung

primage Primage, *(kleiner prozentualer)* Frachtzuschlag *(des Reeders)*

primarily in erster Linie; in der Hauptsache; **person** ~ **liable** *(WechselR)* Erstverpflichteter; **to be liable** ~ **or secondarily** primär oder subsidiär haften

primary primär, hauptsächlich, Haupt-; Ur-; Anfangs-; *Am parl* Vorwahl (→~ *election*); ~ **assembly** →~ meeting; ~ →**boycott;** ~ **capital** *(Börse)* primäres Eigenkapital; ~ **commodities** Rohstoffe, Grundstoffe; ~ **concern** Hauptanliegen; ~ **contract** Hauptvertrag; ~ **dealers** *Am* Primärhändler *(Finanzinstitute, die bevollmächtigt sind, neue Staatspapiere direkt vom US Treasury zu kaufen);* ~ **demand** Hauptbedarf, vordringlicher Bedarf; ~ **deposits** effektive Einlagen *(durch Einzahlungen);* ~ →**documentary evidence;** ~ →**education**

primary (election) *Am* Vorwahl *(zur Wahl von Delegierten für den →National Convention);* **closed** ~ geschlossene Vorwahl *(Wähler nur einer politischen Partei können wählen);* **open** ~ offene Vorwahl *(Parteizugehörigkeit spielt keine Rolle)*

primary, ~ **evidence** Beweismittel erster Ordnung *(opp. secondary, hearsay ~);* ~ **examiner** *Am (PatentR, MarkenR)* Vorprüfer; **of** ~ **importance** von primärer (od. höchster) Wichtigkeit; ~ **industry** Grundstoffindustrie; ~ **in-**

surance amount *Am*[125] maßgeblicher Versicherungsbetrag; **~-line competition** *Am* Wettbewerb unter Verkäufern; ~ **line injury** *Am (WettbewerbsR)* Mitbewerber-bezogene Preisdiskriminierung *(opp. secondary line injury);* ~ **market** Primärmarkt; Markt für Neuemissionen; ~ **meeting** Vorwahl(versammlung) *(zur Nominierung von Kandidaten);* ~ **obligation** *Am (bei Bürgschaft)* Hauptverbindlichkeit; *(bei Wechseln etc)* primäre Verpflichtung; ~ **obligor** *Am (bei Bürgschaft)* Hauptschuldner; *(bei Wechseln etc)* in erster Linie (od. primär) Verpflichteter, Erstverpflichteter; ~ **point** *Am* Hauptumschlagplatz für landwirtschaftl. Erzeugnisse; Hauptgetreidemarkt; ~ **producing countries** Rohstoffländer; ~ **production** Urproduktion

primary products Grundstoffe, Rohstoffe; Hauptprodukte *(e-s Landes);* **prices of** ~ Rohstoffpreise

primary receipts *Am* tägl. Zufuhren an den Hauptgetreidemärkten *(→primary point)*

primary responsibility Hauptverantwortung; **area of** ~ *Am (AntitrustR)* Verkaufsgebiet mit primärer Verantwortlichkeit

primary, ~ **school** Grundschule (→*school*); ~ **shipment** *Am* tägl. Verschiffungen von den Hauptgetreidemärkten (→~ *point*); ~ **speech** *Am pol* Rede e-s Wahlkandidaten in der Vorwahl (→*primary election*) von Delegierten in den Partei-Konvent; ~ **strike** →strike

primate *eccl* Primas, Erzbischof; **P~ of all England** *Br* Erzbischof von Canterbury; **P~ of England** *Br* Erzbischof von York

prime Erst-, Haupt-; erstklassig; ~ **bank(er's) acceptances** Primadiskonten, Privatdiskonten; ~ **bill** erstklassiger Wechsel; ~ **contractor** Hauptlieferant; ~ **cost** (p.c.) Gestehungskosten *(e-s Unternehmers);* Herstellungskosten; *Am* Einzelkosten *(Kosten für Fertigungslohn und Material bei Herstellung e-s Artikels);* ~ **investment** erstklassige Kapitalanlage

Prime Minister Premierminister; Ministerpräsident *(e-s Landes)*

Br Offizieller Titel in Großbritannien. Der ~ hat das Amt des First Lord of the Treasury inne, ist Führer der Mehrheitspartei des Unterhauses und wird vom Souverän mit der Bildung der Regierung beauftragt

prime, ~ **paper** Primapapiere *(erstklassige Geldmarktpapiere);* ~ **quality** erstklassige Qualität; ~ **rate** *Am* Vorzugszins großer Geschäftsbanken für erstklassige Kreditnehmer; ~ **trade bill** *Br* erstklassiger Handelswechsel; ~ **underwriting facility** (PUF) Euronote-Fazilität, deren Preisbildung auf der Basis der US→~rate stattfindet

prime *v* in Gang bringen; *(jdn)* vorher informieren

primogeniture ("first-born") Primogenitur, Erstgeburt(srecht) *(opp. ultimogeniture)*

primo loco ("in the first place") an erster Stelle

prince Prinz; Fürst; **P~ Consort** Prinzgemahl; ~ **of the blood** *Br* Prinz von königlichem Blut; ~ **of the Church** Kirchenfürst; **P~ Regent** Prinzregent; **merchant** ~ Wirtschaftsführer

princedom Fürstenwürde; Fürstentum

princess Prinzessin; Fürstin; **P~ Royal** *Br* älteste Tochter e-s Souverän

principal Haupt-, hauptsächlich; Dienstherr; Geschäftsherr, Chef, Vorgesetzter; *(law of agency)* Auftraggeber; *(vom Handelsvertreter)* vertretener Unternehmer; *(bei Bürgschaft)* Hauptschuldner; Kapital *(opp. interest); (Börse)* Eigenhändler; *Br (etwa)* Ministerialdirigent; *(Außenhandelsfinanzierung)* auftraggebende Bank *(opp. agent);* Direktor, Rektor *(Br e-s college, Am e-r Schule);* ~ **administration** Haupterbschaftsverwaltung *(am Wohnsitz des Verstorbenen; opp. ancillary administration);* ~ **administrator** der im Domizilstaat ernannte Haupterbschaftsverwalter *(opp. ancillary administrator);* ~ **agreement** Hauptabkommen, Hauptvertrag; ~ **amount** Kapitalbetrag; ~ **and agent** Geschäftsherr und Vertreter; Vollmachtgeber und Bevollmächtigter; Unternehmer und Handelsvertreter; ~ **and interest** Kapital und Zinsen; ~ **argument** Hauptargument; ~ **cause** Hauptursache; ~ **creditor** Hauptgläubiger; ~ **contract** Hauptvertrag; ~ **(debtor)** *(bei Bürgschaft)* Hauptschuldner *(cf. surety);* ~ **defect** Hauptmangel; ~ **in the first degree** *(StrafR)*[126] Haupttäter; ~ **in the second degree** *(StrafR)*[126] Mittäter; ~ **of a firm** Firmeninhaber; Chef; ~ **offender** Haupttäter; ~ **office** Hauptsitz *(e-r Gesellschaft);* Hauptniederlassung, Hauptbüro, Zentrale; ~ **organs** (of UN) Hauptorgane (der Vereinten Nationen); ~ **place of business** Hauptbüro, geschäftliche Hauptniederlassung; Hauptgeschäftsstelle, Hauptsitz; **P~ →Register;** ~ **residence** Hauptwohnsitz; ~ **shareholder (stockholder)** Hauptaktionär, Großaktionär; ~ **value** *Br (SteuerR)* der *(der →estate duty zugrunde gelegte)* gemeine Wert; ~ **witness** Hauptzeuge; **→disclosed ~; undisclosed** ~ unbekannter Auftraggeber (→*undisclosed*); **to invade the** ~ *Am* das Kapital angreifen; **to be liable as a** ~ unmittelbar (od. selbstschuldnerisch) haften

principally hauptsächlich, grundsätzlich, im Prinzip

principality Fürstentum *(z. B. P~ of Liechtenstein, P~ of Monaco)*

principle Prinzip, Grundsatz; ~ **of efficiency** Leistungsprinzip; **~s of international law** völkerrechtliche Grundsätze; **(established) ~s of law** (bestehende) Rechtsgrundsätze; ~ **of legality** Legalitätsprinzip; ~ **of majority** Majoritätsprinzip; **declaration of ~s** Grundsatzerklärung; **in** ~ grundsätzlich; **legal** ~ Rechtsgrundsatz;

general(ly accepted) legal ~s allgemeine (allgemein anerkannte) Rechtsgrundsätze; **as a matter of ~** grundsätzlich; **statement of ~s** Grundsatzerklärung; **to adhere to a ~** e-n Grundsatz befolgen; **to lay down a ~** e-n Grundsatz aufstellen

print Druck; Ablichtung; *Am* gedruckte Veröffentlichung, bes. Zeitung; *Am* Auflage; **out of ~** vergriffen

print *v* drucken; **to ~ one's name** s-n Namen in Druckschrift schreiben

printed, ~ clause vorgedruckte Klausel *(opp. written clause)*; **~ description** *(PatR)* Patentschrift (→*description*); **~ form** (or **matter**) Vordruck, (vorgedrucktes) Formular; **~ form of receipt** Quittungsformular; **~ matter** *(Post)* Drucksache(n); *(PatR)* Druckschriften; **~ paper** *Br* Drucksache; **~ papers or samples of merchandise posted in bulk** Postwurfsendung; **~ paper rate** Tarif (od. Porto) für Drucksachen; **~ publication** *(PatR)* druckschriftliche Veröffentlichung

printing Druck; Drucken; Gedrucktes; **~ charges** (or **cost**) Druckkosten; **~ order** Druckauftrag; **~ works** Druckerei

printer Drucker; Druckereibesitzer; **~s** Druckerei; **~'s error** Druckfehler

prior vorhergehend, früher, vorrangig, bevorrechtigt; **~ to** vor; **~ applicant** *(PatR)* früherer Anmelder, Voranmelder; **~ application** *(PatR)* frühere Anmeldung; **~ approval** vorherige Genehmigung; **~ art** *(PatR)* Stand der Technik *(→art)*; **~ charge** *Br* vorrangige Hypothek; **~ charges** vorrangige Belastungen *(e-s Unternehmens hinsichtlich Kapitalrückzahlung od. Dividendenverteilung)*

prior claim früherer Anspruch; bevorrechtigte Forderung; **~ to satisfaction** Anspruch auf bevorrechtigte Befriedigung; **to have a ~** bevorrechtigt sein

prior, ~ conviction Vorstrafe (→*conviction*); **~ endorser** früherer Indossant, Vormann; **~ holder** Vorbesitzer, früherer Inhaber; **~ invention** frühere Erfindung; **~ lien** *Am* älteres *(im Rang vorgehendes)* Pfandrecht; **~ mortgage** im Range vorgehende Hypothek; **~ preferred stock** *Am* Sondervorzugsaktien *(die gegenüber anderen Vorzugsaktien der gleichen Gesellschaft bevorrechtigt sind)*; **~ printed publication** *(PatR)* *(neuheitsschädliche)* druckschriftliche Vorveröffentlichung; **~ public use** *(PatR)* offenkundige Vorbenutzung; **~ publication** *(PatR)* Vorveröffentlichung, frühere Veröffentlichung; **plea of ~ publication** Einrede der Vorveröffentlichung

prior right früheres (od. älteres) Recht, Vorzugsrecht; **holder of ~s** Inhaber von früheren Rechten; im Range vorgehender Gläubiger; **to have a ~** ein älteres Recht innehaben, bevorrechtigt sein

prior sale, subject to ~ Zwischenverkauf vorbehalten

prior to maturity vor Fälligkeit

prior use *(PatR)* Vorbenutzung; **prior public use** offenkundige Vorbenutzung; **acts of ~** Vorbenutzungshandlungen; **right to use based on ~** Vorbenutzungsrecht

priori, a ~ von vornherein

priorit|y 1. Priorität, *(zeitliches)* Vorhergehen, *(zeitlicher)* Vorrang (over, to vor) *(bes. e-r Hypothek od. e-s Pfandrechts vor e-r od. e-m anderen od. e-r Forderung im Konkurs)*; Dringlichkeit(sstufe); *Am* Vorfahrt; **~ies** *(KonkursR)* vorrangige Forderungen; **in ~ to** (mit Vorrang) vor

priority, to claim ~ Priorität (od. Vorrang) beanspruchen; **period for claiming ~** Prioritätserklärungsfrist

priority, to determine the ~ of an invention die Priorität e-r Erfindung bestimmen (→*interference proceedings*); **to give ~ (to)** den Vorrang geben (od. einräumen); *(GrundstücksR)* e-n Rang einräumen; vordringlich berücksichtigen; **to have ~ over** (im Rang) vorgehen; den Vorrang haben vor; **to have the benefit of a right to ~** das Prioritätsrecht genießen; **to promote with ~** bevorzugt befördern; **to rank in ~ to** (or **over**) den Vorrang haben vor; **to recognize a filing as giving right of ~** e-e Anmeldung als prioritätsbegründend anerkennen; **to take ~ over** den Vorrang haben vor; **to take advantage of the ~ of the previous application** *(PatR)* die Priorität e-r vorhergehenden Anmeldung in Anspruch nehmen

priority, ~ claim Prioritätsanspruch; *Am (KonkursR)* bevorrechtigte Forderung; **~ claimed** *(PatR)* beanspruchte Priorität; **~ creditor** *Am* bevorrechtigter (Konkurs-)Gläubiger *(opp. general creditor)*

priority date Prioritätsdatum; **claim of earlier ~** *(PatR)* prioritätsälterer Anspruch

priority, ~ documents Prioritätsbelege, -unterlagen; **~ list** Dringlichkeitsliste; **~ measures** vorrangige Maßnahmen; **~ notice** *Br*[127] Vormerkung

priority of creditors Rangordnung von (Konkurs-)Gläubigern

Das englische Konkursrecht kennt folgende Ranggruppen von Gläubigern im Konkurs des Gemeinschuldners:

1. Gläubiger von Konkurskostenforderungen einschließlich Auslagenersatz- und Vergütungsansprüchen (creditors entitled to bankruptcy costs and charges); sie entsprechen etwa den deutschen Massekosten-Gläubigern (§ 58 KO) und sind vorweg aus der Konkursmasse zu befriedigen; zur Rangordnung innerhalb dieser Ranggruppe s.R 117 der Bankruptcy Rules;

2. die mit einem Vorzugsvorrecht ausgestatteten Konkursgläubiger (pre-preferential creditors); dazu

gehören u. a.: im Nachlaßkonkurs der Testamentsvollstrecker oder Nachlaßverwalter (executor or administrator) wegen Begräbniskosten und notwendiger Auslagen (funeral and testamentary expenses); im Konkurs eines Beamten (officer) einer Friendly Society (Unterstützungskasse), der auf Grund seines Amtes Geld dieser Kasse verwahrt, die Unterstützungskasse wegen der ihr zustehenden Beträge (wenn sie sich nicht mehr abgesondert in der Masse befinden);
3. die einfachen bevorrechtigten Konkursgläubiger (preferential creditors); dazu gehören u. a.: Gläubiger von Gehalts- und Lohnansprüchen (salaries and wages), Sozialversicherungsbeiträgen (Social Security contributions), rückständigen Steuern (taxes) – jeweils unter zeitlicher Begrenzung des Anspruchs;
4. die gewöhnlichen Konkursgläubiger (ordinary creditors);
5. die nachgehenden Konkursgläubiger (postponed creditors); z. B. mit Anspruch aus einem dem Ehegatten für dessen Geschäft gegebenen Darlehen

priority, ~ of date zeitlicher Vorrang; **~ of debts** Rangordnung von (Konkurs-)Forderungen; **~ of filing date** Anmeldepriorität; **~ of invention** *(PatR)* Erfindungspriorität; **~ of liens** (on a property) Rangordnung von Pfandrechten *(an derselben Sache)*; **~ of mortgages** Rangordnung (Rangverhältnis) unter mehreren Hypotheken; **~ of rank** Vorrang

priority, ~ right Prioritätsrecht; **~ road ahead** *Am* Vorfahrt beachten; **~ treatment** Behandlung mit Vorrang; **to accord ~ treatment to a p.** jdn mit Vorrang behandeln

priority, according to ~ dem Range nach; nach der Rangfolge; **alteration** (or **change**) **of ~** *(GrundstücksR)* Rangänderung; **claim to ~** Beanspruchung der Priorität; **creditor by ~** *(KonkursR)* bevorrechtigter (od. im Rang vorgehender) Gläubiger; **date of ~** Prioritätstag; **declaration of ~** Prioritätserklärung; **degree of ~** Dringlichkeitsstufe; **of equal ~** gleichrangig; **persons of equal ~** gleichrangige Personen; **invention ~** Erfindungspriorität; **list of ~ies** Prioritätenliste; Dringlichkeitsliste; **loss of ~** Rangverlust; **motion having ~** vorrangig zu behandelnder Antrag; **multiple ~ies** mehrere Prioritäten; **order of ~ies of encumbrances** Rang(verhältnis) von Grundstücksbelastungen; **creditor next in order of ~** im Rang nächststehender Gläubiger; **right of ~** Prioritätsrecht; **sequence of ~** Rangfolge; **top ~** höchste Dringlichkeitsstufe; **with ~ over** mit Vorrang vor

priority 2. Unionsvorrang *(s. Paris or Union →Convention, the Arrangement of →Madrid)*; **~ period** Prioritätsfrist; **Convention ~** Verbandspriorität; **Union ~** Unionspriorität; **to claim ~** das Prioritätsrecht in Anspruch nehmen

prison Gefängnis, Strafvollzugsanstalt; **~ break** (or **breaking**) Ausbrechen aus dem Gefängnis; **~ breaker** Ausbrecher aus dem Gefängnis; **~ governor** *Br* Gefängnisdirektor; **~ guard** *Am* Gefängnisaufseher; **~ inmate** Gefängnisinsasse, Sträfling; **~ labo(u)r** Gefangenenarbeit; **~ officer** *Br* Strafvollzugsbeamter; Gefängnisaufseher; **~ riot** Gefangenenaufstand

prison sentence Gefängnisstrafe, Freiheitsstrafe; **to serve a ~** e-e Freiheitsstrafe absitzen (od. verbüßen)

prison, ~ term Strafzeit (→*term of imprisonment, term 2.*); **~ van** *Br* Gefangenen(transport)wagen; **~ warden** Gefängnisdirektor; **~ work** Gefangenenarbeit; **commitment to ~** Einlieferung in das Gefängnis; **discharge from ~** Entlassung aus dem Gefängnis; **escape from ~** Entweichen (od. Flucht) aus dem Gefängnis; **state ~** *Am* Staatsgefängnis *(Strafanstalt der Einzelstaaten für längere Freiheitsstrafen)*; **women's ~** Frauengefängnis; **to break out of ~** aus dem Gefängnis ausbrechen; **to commit to ~** in das Gefängnis einliefern; **to discharge from ~** aus dem Gefängnis entlassen; **to escape (from) ~** aus dem Gefängnis entkommen; **to get out of ~** aus dem Gefängnis kommen; **to put in** (or **send to**) **~** einsperren, ins Gefängnis setzen; **to release from ~** aus dem Gefängnis entlassen

prisoner Gefangener, Häftling, Sträfling; Angeklagter *(bei felony)*; **~ at the bar** Angeklagter *(der aus der Untersuchungshaft vorgeführt wird)*; **~ awaiting trial** Untersuchungsgefangener; **~ of state** politischer Gefangener

prisoner of war (POW) Kriegsgefangener; **treatment of ~s of war** Behandlung der Kriegsgefangenen (*cf. Geneva Convention[s] prisoner*

prisoner, ~ on remand Untersuchungsgefangener; **~ under sentence** (or **~ undergoing a sentence**) Strafgefangener; **custody of ~s** Bewachung von Gefangenen; **delivery of a ~** Einlieferung e-s Gefangenen; **Discharged P~s Aid Society** *Br* Gefangenenfürsorgeverein; **ex-~** ehemaliger Gefangener; **to hold a p. a ~** jdn gefangenenhalten; **to release a ~ on parole** e-n Gefangenen bedingt entlassen (→*parole 2.*); **to take a p. ~** jdn gefangennehmen

privacy (Recht auf) Privatleben (od. Intimsphäre); Privatsphäre; Geheimhaltung *(opp. publicity)*; **P~ Act** 1974 *Am* Datenschutzgesetz; **~ of an individual** (or **individual ~**) Persönlichkeitsrecht (rechtlich geschützte Individualsphäre) des Einzelnen; **infringement of** (or **intrusion upon**) **~** s. invasion of →~; **invasion of ~** Eingriff in die Intimsphäre; **invasion of personal ~** Verletzung des Persönlichkeitsrechts; **protection of data ~** Datenschutz; **right to ~** Recht (auf Achtung) der Privatsphäre (od. Intimsphäre) *(im englischen Recht noch nicht anerkannt)*; **violation of ~**[128] Verletzung der Privatsphäre (od. Intimsphäre); **to**

invade (or **intrude upon**) **sb.'s** ~ in jds Intimsphäre eindringen

private privat; nicht öffentlich; geheim; persönlich *(auch auf Briefen);* nicht amtlich
private, in ~ geheim; unter vier Augen; **a meeting held in** ~ e-e nicht öffentliche Sitzung; **trial in** ~ nicht öffentliche Verhandlung
private, to keep ~ geheim halten; **to mark a letter "~" (and confidential)** e-n Brief als „persönlich" (und vertraulich) bezeichnen; **the hearing shall be** ~ die Sitzung ist nicht öffentlich
private, ~ **account** (P/A.) Privatkonto; Geheimkonto; ~ **affairs** persönliche Angelegenheiten, Privatangelegenheiten; ~ **agreement** Privatabkommen; ~ **and confidential** vertraulich; ~ **arrangement** private Abmachung; gütliche Einigung; *(außergerichtlicher)* Vergleich; ~ **attorney** *Am* →attorney in fact; ~ **audience** Privataudienz; ~ **automatic branch exchange** (PABX) *(EDV)* Vermittlungsanlage, Nebenstellenanlage; ~ **bank** Privatbank(haus); ~ **bill** →bill 3.; ~ **box** *Br* Postschließfach; ~ **brand** Hausmarke, Eigenmarke
private business 1. →private affairs; 2. Privatwirtschaft; **he entered** ~ er ging in die Privatwirtschaft
private capacity, in one's ~ als Privatperson, privat, nicht amtlich
private, ~ **capital** Privatvermögen; ~ **car** Personenkraftwagen; ~ →**carrier;** ~ **chattels scheme** *Br*[129] Entschädigungsplan für Kriegsschäden an beweglichen Sachen; ~ **citizen** Privatperson; **in** ~ **clothes** in Zivil; ~ **company** *Br (etwa)* Gesellschaft mit beschränkter Haftung (GmbH) (→*company);* ~ **concern** Privatangelegenheit; ~ **consumption** Selbstverbrauch, Eigenverbrauch
private contract privater Vertrag; **by** ~ unter der Hand, freihändig
private, ~ **conversation** vertrauliche Unterredung (od. Besprechung); ~ **corporation** *Am* privatrechtliche Gesellschaft (→*corporation*); ~ **customer** Privatkunde; ~ **defen|ce (~se)** *(rechtmäßige, Haftung ausschließende)* Notwehr; ~ **documents** Privaturkunden; ~ **dwelling** Privatwohnung; ~ **enterprise (system)** Privatwirtschaft; freie Marktwirtschaft; ~ **estate** Siedlung mit Eigentumswohnungen
private hands, to pass into ~ in privaten Besitz (od. in Privathand) übergehen
private, ~ **house** Privathaus; Wohnhaus; ~ **income** Privateinkommen; ~ **individual** Privatperson; ~ **industry** Privatindustrie, Privatwirtschaft; ~ **information** vertrauliche Mitteilung; ~ **insurance** Privatversicherung; ~ **insurer** Privatversicherer; ~ **interests** Privatinteressen; ~ **international law** internationales Privatrecht (→*international law*); ~ **investments** private Kapitalanlagen (od. Investitionen); ~ **investor** privater Investor; ~ **law** Privatrecht, Zivilrecht *(opp. public law);* ~ **letter** →letter 2.; ~ **letter ruling** *Am (SteuerR)* Stellungnahme des →IRS zu e-m im Einzelfall unterbreiteten Sachverhalt *(Auskunft an den anfragenden Steuerpflichtigen)*
private life Privatleben; **intimate** ~ **of a person** Intimsphäre e-r Person
private, ~ **limited company** *Br* →~ company; ~ **line** Privattelefon; ~ **matters** Privatangelegenheiten; ~ **means** private Mittel, Privatvermögen; ~ **meeting** nicht öffentliche Sitzung
private member (of the House of Commons) *Br* Unterhausmitglied, das nicht der Regierung angehört; ~**'s bill** *Br* →bill 3.
private, ~ **negotiation** geheime Verhandlung; ~ →**nuisance;** ~ **office** Privatbüro
private ownership, to transfer (a nationalized industry) to ~ privatisieren
private, ~ **placing** *Br* (**placement** *Am*) private Effektenplacierung *(Direktverkauf von Emittenten z.B. an größere Versicherungsgesellschaften od. Pensionskassen; Am bedarf im Ggs. zur public issue keiner Genehmigung der SEC)*; ~ **property** Privateigentum, Privatbesitz; Privatvermögen; Privatgrundstück; ~ **rate** (or **discount**) *Br* Diskontsatz der Geschäftsbanken *(opp. official, or bank rate)*; ~ **sale** freihändiger Verkauf; ~ **school** Privatschule; ~ **secretary** Privatsekretär(in); ~ **sector (of economy)** privater Sektor (der Wirtschaft), Privatwirtschaft *(privately owned business enterprises; opp. public sector)*; ~ **(soldier)** einfacher Soldat *(ohne Dienstgrad),* Landser; ~ **sphere** Privatsphäre, Intimsphäre; ~ **talk** private Unterhaltung; Gespräch unter vier Augen
private treaty, sale by ~ freihändiger Verkauf *(opp. public sale);* **to sell by** ~ aus freier Hand (od. freihändig) verkaufen *(nicht durch Auktion)*
private, ~ **trust** →trust 1.; ~ **undertaking** Privatunternehmen, Privatbetrieb; **for** ~ **use** zum eigenen Gebrauch, zum Privatgebrauch; ~ **view** geschlossene *(nicht öffentl.)* Besichtigung *(e-r Ausstellung),* Besichtigung durch geladene Gäste
privately privat, als Privatperson; vertraulich; freihändig, unter der Hand; ~ **held corporation** *Am s.* close →corporation; ~ **operated** privat betrieben; ~ **owned** in Privatbesitz, in Privateigentum (befindlich); ~ **owned enterprise** (or **business,** or **concern** or **undertaking**) Privatbetrieb, privates Unternehmen; ~ **sold** privat verkauft; **publicly or** ~ **owned** in öffentlichem oder privatem Eigentum stehend; **to** →**sell** ~

privateer Kaperschiff

privatization Privatisierung

privatize *v* privatisieren

privation Not, Mangel (of an), Entzug

privies Personen, die zueinander in →privity stehen *(→privy)*

privilege Privileg, Sonderrecht, Vorrecht; Aussage- und Zeugnisverweigerungsrecht; Recht, im Prozeß die Offenlegung von Urkunden zu verweigern (→~ *from discovery*); Immunität *(Abgeordnete, Diplomaten etc)*; *(bei Beleidigungsklagen) (die Haftung des Beklagten ausschließender)* Rechtfertigungs- od. Entschuldigungsgrund; *Am (Börse)* Option(sgeschäft)

privilege, to accord (or **concede**) **a** ~ ein Vorrecht gewähren (od. einräumen); **to claim a** ~ ein Vorrecht beanspruchen; **to enjoy a** ~ ein Privileg (od. Vorrecht) genießen; bevorrechtigt sein; **to exercise a** ~ von e-m Privileg (od. Vorrecht) Gebrauch machen; **to hold special** **~s** im Besitz besonderer Vorrechte sein; besondere Vorrechte genießen; **to grant a** ~ →to accord a ~; **to waive a** ~ auf ein Vorrecht *(z.B. Zeugnisverweigerungsrecht)* verzichten

privilege against self-incrimination *Am* Zeugnisverweigerungsrecht *(bei Gefahr strafrechtlicher Verfolgung)*[130]

privileges and immunities (of citizens) *Am* Vorrechte und Befreiungen; ~ **clause** *Am*[130a] Bestimmung der Verfassung, wonach die Angehörigen der Einzelstaaten zu allen Freiheiten und Privilegien der übrigen Staaten berechtigt sind; ~ **of the United Nations**[130b] Vorrechte und Immunitäten der Vereinten Nationen

privilege ~ **broker** *Am* Prämienmakler; ~ **by reason of the occasion** *Br* →privileged occasions; ~ **from arrest** Immunität; ~ **from discovery** Recht der Verweigerung der Offenlegungspflicht; Befreiung von der Vorlagepflicht *(von Urkunden)*; ~ **from inspection** Recht der Verweigerung der Urkundenvorlage; ~ **of communications** (between a client and his lawyer) Aussageverweigerungsrecht *(s. legal professional →~)*; ~ **of (members of) Parliament** *Br* Immunität der Abgeordneten; ~ **of necessity** *(StrafR)* Notstand; ~ **of self-defen|ce(~se)** *(StrafR)* Notwehr; ~ **of a witness** (to decline to answer questions) Zeugnisverweigerungsrecht; *(bei bestimmten Fragen)* Auskunftsverweigerungsrecht; ~ **tax** *Am* Konzessionssteuer *(Steuer für konzessionspflichtige Betriebe)*

privilege, absolute ~ *(bei defamation)* absoluter Rechtfertigungsgrund *(absolut gerechtfertigt sind z.B. Erklärungen im Parlament od. in Gerichtsverhandlungen; Äußerungen zwischen Rechtsanwalt und Mandant; opp. qualified ~)*; **breach of** **~s** *Br* Verletzung der Parlamentsprivilegien; Privilegienbruch; Immunitätsverletzung; **commercial** ~ Konzession; **Committee for P~s** *Br parl* Ausschuß *(des House of Lords)* zur Regelung von Ansprüchen auf →peerages und Privilegien der →peers; **Committee of P~s** *Br parl* Ausschuß *(des House of Commons)* zur Untersuchung, ob ein Privilegienbruch vorliegt; **conditional** ~ s. qualified →~; **Crown** ~ *Br* Recht des Staates, Vorlage von Urkunden vor Gericht zu verweigern *(bei Gefährdung des öffentlichen Interesses)*; **diplomatic ~s and immunities** diplomatische Vorrechte und Immunitäten; **grounds of** ~ Gründe für die Gewährung von Vorrechten (od. Privilegien); **legal professional** ~ Aussageverweigerungsrecht des Anwalts *(Recht des Anwalts, als Zeuge die Aussage über ihm vom Mandanten anvertraute Dinge zu verweigern; Befreiung des Anwalts von der Pflicht der Vorlage von Urkunden)*; **personal** ~ persönliches Vorrecht *(des Botschafters, Abgeordneten, Anwalts etc)*; **plea of** ~ *Am* Geltendmachung des Zeugnisverweigerungsrechtes; **qualified** ~[131] *(bei defamation) (nur unter bestimmten Voraussetzungen durchgreifender)* Rechtfertigungsgrund *(der die Haftung dann ausschließt, wenn der Beklagte nicht in böswilliger Absicht [malice] gehandelt hat; hierunter fallen z.B. Äußerungen in Erfüllung e-r gesetzl., moralischen od. sozialen Pflicht, Äußerungen in Wahrnehmung berechtigter Interessen; opp. absolute ~)*; **special** ~ Sonderrecht; **tax** ~ Steuervergünstigung (→*tax*); **writ of** ~ *Br* gerichtl. Anordnung, e-e privilegierte Person aus der Haft zu entlassen

privilege *v* privilegieren; bevorrechten; Vorrecht (od. Sonderrecht) zugestehen; *(jdn)* befreien (from von)

privileged privilegiert; berechtigt, bevorrechtigt, sonderberechtigt; befreit (from von); unter das Berufsgeheimnis fallend; unter die Immunität fallend (→*privilege from arrest, diplomatic privileges*); unter das Zeugnisverweigerungsrecht fallend; *(bei defamation)* von der Haftung befreit; ~ **claim** *Am* bevorrechtigte Forderung

privileged communication *(zur Berufsverschwiegenheit verpflichtende, mündl.)* vertrauliche Mitteilung; Berufsgeheimnis *(hinsichtl. dessen ein Zeugnisverweigerungsrecht besteht, z.B. Mitteilungen zwischen Anwalt und Klienten, Ehegatten, Geistlichem und Beichtkind, Am [auch] Arzt und Patienten)*; *parl* Äußerung im Rahmen der Immunität; *(bei Beleidigungsklagen)* beleidigende Äußerung, die der Rechtsverfolgung entzogen ist; **written** ~ schriftl. vertrauliche Mitteilung *(deren Vorlegung nicht erzwungen werden kann)*

privileged, ~ **debt** bevorrechtigte Forderung; **legally** ~ **evidence** *Am*[132] *(StrafR)* Zeugnis, dessen Aussage verweigert werden darf; ~ **from disclosure** (or **discovery**) nicht offenlegungspflichtig; ~ **from distress** nicht pfändbar; ~ **motion** *parl* Dringlichkeitsantrag; ~ **occasions** *Br* privilegierte →defamatory statements, die im öffentlichen Interesse od. in

Verteidigung privater Rechte anderer gemacht werden; ~ **position** Vorzugsstellung; ~ **from production** nicht vorlegungspflichtig; ~ **statement** →~ communication; ~ **treatment** Vorzugsbehandlung; ~ **witness** Zeuge, der berechtigt ist, die Aussage zu verweigern; **to be** ~ **(from testifying)** das Zeugnisverweigerungsrecht haben

privity Mitwissen, Eingeweihtsein (to in); gemeinsame Interessenbeziehung; gemeinsame Rechtsbeziehung; ~ **in deed** vertragliche Rechtsbeziehung

privity of contract Rechtsbeziehung zwischen den unmittelbaren Vertragsparteien *(z.B. zwischen Mieter und Vermieter);* Vertragsbeziehung

Der Begriff besagt, daß grundsätzlich nur Vertragsparteien aus einem Vertrag berechtigt und verpflichtet werden können, nicht aber dritte Personen (Ausnahmen sind z.B. der trust od. die undisclosed agency)

privity of estate Rechtsbeziehung durch gemeinsame Rechte an Grundbesitz *(z.B. zwischen tenant for life und remainderman or reversioner)*

privy Mitinteressent; Beteiligter (to an); mitinteressiert, beteiligt (on an)

→privies sind z.B. Erblasser-Erbe, Verpächter-Pächter

Privy Council *Br* Geheimer Staatsrat, Kronrat

Hat nur noch Bedeutung als höchste Instanz für einige Commonwealth-Länder (→*Judicial Committee*) und Kirchengerichte

Privy Councillor (P.C.) *Br* Mitglied des Staatsrats

Privy Purse *Br* Königl. Privatschatulle *(der Teil der →Civil List, der für den persönlichen Gebrauch des Souveräns bestimmt ist)*

prize 1. Preis, Prämie; (Lotterie-)Gewinn; ~ **at an exhibition** Preis auf e-r Ausstellung

prize competition[133] Preisausschreiben; **to announce** (or **organize**) **a competition with prizes** ein Preisausschreiben veranstalten; **to take part in a** ~ an e-m Preisausschreiben teilnehmen

prize, ~ **fellow** *Br univ* Inhaber e-r Auszeichnung auf Grund s-s Examens; ~ **holder** Preisträger; ~ **list** Gewinnliste; ~**(-)man** Preisträger *(bes. e-s akademischen Grades);* ~ **medal** Preismedaille; ~ **money** Geldpreis; ~ **winner** Preisträger(in); ~**-winning** preisgekrönt; ~**-winning ticket** (in a lottery) Gewinnlos; **consolation** ~ Trostpreis; **distribution of** ~**s** Preisverteilung

prize, first ~ Hauptgewinn, großes Los; **to draw the first** ~ das große Los gewinnen

prize, lottery ~ Lotteriegewinn; **to award a** ~ e-n Preis verleihen (od. zuerkennen); prämieren; **to draw a** ~ **in a lottery** e-n Lotteriegewinn machen; mit e-m Lotteriegewinn herauskommen; **to receive a** ~ e-n Preis bekommen; **to win a** ~ e-n Preis gewinnen

prize 2. *(VölkerR)* Prise *(im Kriege aufgebrachtes Handelsschiff bzw. Frachtgut);* ~ **case** Prisensache; ~ **court**[134] Prisengericht, Prisenhof; ~ **crew** Prisenkommando; ~ **law** s. law of→~; ~ **money** (to captors) Prisengeld(er); ~ **salvage** Rettungsgeld des neuen Nehmers *(bei Zurückgewinnung e-s als Prise aufgebrachten Schiffes);* **bringing in of** ~ Einbringung e-r Prise; **condemnation as** ~ prisengerichtliche Einziehung; **law of** ~ Prisenrecht *(cf. capture, condemnation, continuous voyage);* **right of** ~ Recht auf das Machen von Prisen; **to condemn as** (or **declare a**) **lawful** ~ *(Schiff)* als gute Prise erklären; **to make (a)** ~ **(of)** Prise machen, als Prise aufbringen

pro ("for"; "for and on behalf of") *(auch vor Unterschriften)* für, an Stelle von; pro-; Ja-Stimme; ~**s and cons** (Gründe) für und wider

probability Wahrscheinlichkeit; ~ **calculus** *(Statistik)* Wahrscheinlichkeitsrechnung; ~ **check** Wahrscheinlichkeitsprüfung; ~ **of life** *(VersR)* Lebenserwartung; ~ **sampling** *(Meinungsforschung)* Wahrscheinlichkeitsauswahl; **in all** ~ aller Wahrscheinlichkeit nach

probable wahrscheinlich, mutmaßlich; glaubhaft; ~ **cause** vermutlicher Grund; hinreichender (Verdachts-)Grund; ~ **date of arrival** mutmaßlicher Ankunftstag; ~ **duration of life** *(VersR)* wahrscheinliche Lebenserwartung; ~ **error** (p.e.) wahrscheinlicher Fehler *(statistischer Mittelwerte)*

probate formelle Testamentsbestätigung und Bestellung des →executor durch das Gericht

Probate ist die dem Testamentsvollstrecker (executor proving the will) erteilte Bescheinigung über die Bestätigung des Testaments und des in ihm benannten Testamentsvollstreckers durch das Nachlaßgericht. Sie entspricht etwa der Eröffnungsverhandlung und der Erteilung des Erbscheins des deutschen Rechts

probate, ~ **action** Klage betr. Bestellung e-s →executor oder →administrator oder auf Feststellung der Gültigkeit e-s Testaments *(bei streitigen Nachlaßsachen);* ~ **advance** Bevorschussung e-s Nachlasses; ~ **bond** Kaution des Testamentsvollstreckers; **contentious** ~ **business** streitige Testamentssachen; ~ **in common form** *Br* gerichtl. Testamentsbestätigung in gewöhnlicher (od. einfacher) Form *(opp. ~ in solemn form);* ~ **copy** (of a will) *(vom Gericht erteilte)* Abschrift e-s Testaments; ~ **court** *Am (in einigen Staaten)* Nachlaßgericht; ~ **court judge** *Am (in einigen Staaten)* Nachlaßrichter; ~ **denied** Bestätigung des Testaments verweigert; ~ **estate** der Teil des Nachlasses, über den in der letztwilligen Verfügung verfügt wird; ~ **matters** Nachlaßsachen; Erbschaftsangelegenheiten; ~ **proceedings** Erbschaftsverfahren

Probate Registry *Br* Geschäftsstelle des Nachlaßgerichts; **District** ~ Nachlaßgericht außerhalb Londons *(für nicht streitige Nachlaßsachen)*; **Principal** ~ Nachlaßgericht in London *(für nicht streitige Nachlaßsachen)*

probate, ~ in solemn form *Br* gerichtl. Testamentsbestätigung in feierlicher Form *(wenn die Gültigkeit des Testaments bestritten und ein Gerichtsverfahren durchgeführt worden ist. Das Testament kann später nicht mehr angefochten werden; opp. ~ in common form)*; ~ **statute** *Am* Nachlaß- und Erbordnung; ~→**valuation; ancillary** ~ *Am* probate für Nachlaßwerte außerhalb des Staates des Wohnsitzes; **court of** ~ *Am (Connecticut)* Nachlaßgericht

probate, grant of ~ gerichtl. Testamentsbestätigung; Testamentsvollstreckerzeugnis *(Bestätigungsurkunde für den →executor)*; **application for a (grant of)** ~ Beantragung des →probate

probate, office copy ~ *Br* gerichtl. erteilte Abschrift des Testamentsvollstreckerzeugnisses; **to grant ~ of a will** (or **to make a grant of** ~) ein Testament *(und damit zugleich das Amt des Testamentsvollstreckers)* gerichtlich bestätigen; Testamentsvollstreckerzeugnis erteilen; **to take out ~ of a will** sich e-e gerichtl. Testamentsbestätigung erteilen lassen, sich ein Testament gerichtlich bestätigen lassen

probate *v bes. Am (ein Testament)* gerichtlich bestätigen

probation 1. Probezeit; ~ **year** Probejahr; **on** ~ auf Probe; **period of** ~ Probezeit; **to be on** ~ s-e Probezeit machen; **to be employed on** ~ auf Probe eingestellt sein

probation 2. *(StrafR)*[135] Bewährung; Strafaussetzung zur Bewährung *(unter Aufsicht e-s →~ officer)*

Die engl. und amerik. probation (Verbindung e-r bedingten Aussetzung der Bestrafung mit persönlicher Beaufsichtigung und Betreuung) ist das Vorbild der deutschen Bewährungshilfe

probation officer Bewährungshelfer; **to place a p. under the supervision of a** ~ jdn unter Aufsicht e-s Bewährungshelfers stellen

probation order gerichtl. Entscheidung, durch die auf Strafaussetzung zur Bewährung erkannt wird; **to make a** ~ auf Strafaussetzung zur Bewährung erkennen

probation, on ~ auf Bewährung; unter Zubilligung von Bewährungsfrist; **person on** ~ Person, deren Strafe zur Bewährung ausgesetzt ist; **suspension of sentence on** ~ *Am* Strafaussetzung unter Bewilligung e-r Bewährungsfrist; **to place a p. on** ~ die Strafe zur Bewährung aussetzen

probation, period (or **time**) **of** ~ Bewährungsfrist

probation, conditional discharge may be substituted for ~[136] bedingte Entlassung kann durch Strafaussetzung zur Bewährung ersetzt werden

probationary auf Probe eingestellt; Probe-; *(StrafR)* auf Bewährung; Bewährungs-; ~ **appointment** Einstellung auf Probe; ~ **driving licence** *Br* Führerschein auf Probe; ~ **employment** Probebeschäftigung, Probearbeitsverhältnis; ~ **period** Probezeit; *(StrafR)* Bewährungsfrist; ~ **rate** Lohnsatz während der Probezeit; ~ **time** →~ period; **the ~ period is dispensed** die Probezeit wird erlassen

probationer auf Probe Eingestellte(r); *(StrafR)* jd, dessen Strafe zur Bewährung ausgesetzt ist

probative als Beweis dienend; beweisrechtlich; ~ **force** Beweiskraft; ~ **value** Beweiswert

probatory *Am* als Beweis dienend; ~ **force** *Am* Beweiskraft; ~ **term** *Am* Termin zur Zeugenvernehmung

probe *Am* Untersuchung von Unregelmäßigkeiten *(bes. durch e-n besonderen Ausschuß)*

problem Problem; ~ **invention** *(PatR)* Aufgabenerfindung; **frontier** ~ Grenzproblem; **to handle a** ~ ein Problem behandeln; **to raise a** ~ ein Problem aufwerfen; **to solve pending ~s** schwebende Fragen lösen

procedural prozessual, verfahrensrechtlich; ~ **committee** Verfahrensausschuß; ~ **law** Verfahrensrecht, formelles Recht *(opp. substantial law)*; ~ **motion** *parl* Antrag zur Geschäftsordnung; ~ **principles** Prozeßmaximen; ~ **provision** Verfahrensbestimmung, Verfahrensvorschrift; ~ **question** Verfahrensfrage; ~ **rules** Verfahrensregeln; **substantial ~ violation** wesentlicher Verfahrensmangel; **to comply with ~ requirements** Verfahrensvorschriften erfüllen

procedure Verfahren; Vorgehen, Verhalten; ~ **on information** *Br* (erster Schritt im) Verfahren im Magistrates' Court nach Erhalt e-r Anzeige *(das Gericht hat zu entscheiden, ob die Straftat im →summary trial oder im →trial on indictment abzuurteilen ist)*; ~ **quo warranto** *Am* Entziehung der Rechtsfähigkeit *(von corporations)*; **Administrative P~ Act** (APA) *Am* Verwaltungsverfahrensgesetz *(von 1946)*; **appellate** ~ Rechtsmittelverfahren *(Berufungsverfahren etc)*

procedure, civil ~ Zivilprozeß; **code of civil** ~[137] Zivilprozeßordnung (ZPO); **Rules of Federal Civil P~** *Am* Bundes-Zivilprozeßordnung *(für District Courts und Courts of Appeals)*

procedure, course of ~ Verfahrensgang; **criminal** ~ Strafprozeß; **Code of Criminal P~** *Ger* Strafprozeßordnung (StPO); **election** (or **electoral**) ~ Wahlverfahren; **established uni-**

form ~ einheitlich festgelegtes Verfahren; **judicial or parajudicial** ~ gerichtliches oder gerichtsähnliches Verfahren; **law of** ~ Prozeßrecht; **legal** ~ Gerichtsverfahren *(Verfahrensweise)*; **legislative** ~ Gesetzgebungsverfahren; **parliamentary** ~ parlamentarisches Verfahren; **rules of** ~ Verfahrensregeln; Geschäftsordnung (→*rule 3.*)

proceed *v* vorgehen, verfahren, handeln; fortfahren (with mit, in); **to ~ against a p.** gegen jdn (gerichtl.) vorgehen (od. e-n Prozeß anstrengen); jdn verklagen; **to ~ by stages** schrittweise vorgehen; **to ~ from** herrühren von; hervorgehen aus; **to ~ on the voyage** die Fahrt fortsetzen *(Schiff)*

proceed *v*, **to ~ (to)** sich begeben (nach); *(zu etw.)* schreiten; **to ~ to a degree** *univ* e-n Grad erwerben; **to ~ to the election** zur Wahl schreiten; **to ~ to the next item on the agenda** zum nächsten Punkt der Tagesordnung übergehen; **to ~ to the order of the day** zur Tagesordnung übergehen; **to ~ to a vote** zur Abstimmung schreiten

proceed *v*, **to ~ with** fortfahren mit; *(etw.)* in Angriff nehmen, durchführen; **to ~ with an application** e-e Anmeldung bearbeiten; **to ~ with a case** e-e Sache verhandeln; **to ~ with one's speech** mit s-r Rede fortfahren; **to ~ with the trial** das Verfahren durchführen

proceeding Vorgehen, Verfahren; **~s** Prozeß, Gerichtsverfahren; Sitzungsberichte, Protokolle; **~s at trial** Hauptverhandlung; **~s in bankruptcy** Konkursverfahren (→*bankruptcy ~s*); **~s of a conference** (Bericht über den) Verlauf e-r Konferenz; **~s on appeal** Rechtsmittelverfahren (Berufungsverfahren etc.); **administrative ~s** Verwaltungsverfahren; **arbitration ~s** Schiedsgerichtsverfahren

proceedings, civil ~ Zivilprozeß, Verfahren in Zivilsachen; **to bring** (or **institute**) **civil** ~ ein Zivilverfahren anhängig machen, Klage erheben, im Klageweg vorgehen

proceedings, committal ~ *Br (StrafprozR)* Vorverfahren vor dem Magistrates' Court (→*preliminary examination*); **composition** ~ Vergleichsverfahren; **conduct of** ~ Verhandlungsführung; **costly** ~ kostspieliges Verfahren

proceedings, costs of (the) ~ Kosten des Verfahrens, Prozeßkosten; **to order to bear the costs of the** ~ die Prozeßkosten auferlegen

proceedings, criminal ~ Strafprozeß, Strafverfahren (→*criminal 1.*); **to render o.s. liable to criminal** ~ sich strafrechtlicher Verfolgung aussetzen; **to take criminal ~ against a p.** gegen jdn ein Strafverfahren einleiten

proceedings, (legal) defect in the ~ Verfahrensmangel; **delay of the** ~ Prozeßverschleppung; **disciplinary** ~ Disziplinarverfahren; **discontinuance of** ~ Einstellung des Verfahrens; **institution of** ~ Einleitung des Verfahrens; **judicial** ~ s. legal →~

proceedings, legal ~ Gerichtsverfahren; Prozeß; **to bring or defend legal** ~ e-e Klage einbringen oder den Klageanspruch bestreiten; **to carry on legal** ~ ein Gerichtsverfahren durchführen, prozessieren; **to institute legal** ~ gerichtlich vorgehen (od. klagen) (against gegen); ein gerichtliches Verfahren einleiten; e-n Prozeß anstrengen; **to take legal** ~ s. to institute legal →~; **to take legal ~ for the recovery of a debt** e-e Forderung einklagen; **to take or defend legal ~ on behalf of a p.** *(als Anwalt)* für Kläger oder Beklagten auftreten; **the organization may be a party to legal** ~ die Organisation ist parteifähig

proceedings, lengthy ~ langwieriges Verfahren; **minutes of the ~ (of a meeting)** Sitzungsprotokoll; **opening of the** ~ Eröffnung des Verfahrens; **party to the** ~ Prozeßpartei; **preliminary** ~ vorbereitendes Verfahren, Vorverfahren; **record of** ~ (gerichtl.) Verhandlungsprotokoll; **rules governing the** ~ Verfahrensbestimmungen; **stage of (the)** ~ Stand des Verfahrens; **stay of** ~ Einstellung des Verfahrens; **suspension of the** ~ Aussetzung des Verfahrens

proceedings, to adjourn the ~ die Verhandlung vertagen; **to bring ~ against sb.** jdn verklagen; gegen jdn gerichtlich vorgehen; **to close the** ~ das Verfahren einstellen; **to commence (the)** ~ das Verfahren einleiten; **to conduct the** ~ die Verhandlung führen; **to discontinue the** ~ s. to stay the →~; **to institute** ~ das Verfahren einleiten; **to institute ~ by way of appeal** ein Rechtsmittel einlegen; **to resume (the)** ~ das Verfahren wiederaufnehmen; **to stay** (or **stop**) **the** ~ das Verfahren einstellen; **to suspend the** ~ das Verfahren aussetzen; **to take** ~ s. legal →~

proceeds (Geld-)Ertrag, Erlös, Surrogat(e); **~ in cash** Barerlös; **~ from exports** Ausfuhrerlöse; **~ of an auction** Versteigerungserlös; **~ of collection** Inkassoerlös; **~ of a collection** Erlös e-r Sammlung; **~ of sale** Verkaufserlös; **~ of the winding up** Liquidationserlös; **annual** ~ Jahresertrag; **calculation of** ~ Ertragsberechnung; **cash** ~ Barerlös; **deficiency in the** ~ Mindererertrag; **gross** ~ Bruttoertrag; **net** ~ Nettoertrag, Reinertrag; **sale** ~ →~ of sale; **to remit the** ~ den Gegenwert anschaffen

procès-verbal *Fr* Protokoll; **to draw up a** ~ ein Protokoll erstellen (od. aufsetzen)

process 1. gerichtl. Verfügung *(z.B. Ladung)*[138]; Verfahren; **~ of legislation** Gesetzgebungsverfahren; **~ server** Zusteller *(e-r gerichtl. Verfügung)*; **abuse of** ~ *Br* Mißbrauch des Verfahrens, fehlendes Rechtsschutzbedürfnis *(das Gericht kann anordnen, daß ein [Teil e-s] Schrift-*

satz[es] entfernt wird, wenn mangelndes Rechtsschutzbedürfnis vorliegt oder das Verfahren skandalös, leichtsinnig oder Ärgernis erregend ist); →**due** ~ **of law**; →**legal** ~; **mesne** ~ *Am* Zwischenverfahren; **service of** ~ →service 3.; **summary** ~ summarisches Verfahren; **to serve a** ~ e-e gerichtl. Verfügung zustellen

process 2. (Arbeits-)Verfahren, Prozeß; Arbeitsgang; Arbeitsweise; Ablauf, Verlauf, Entwicklung, Fortgang, Fortschreiten; ~ **application** *(PatR)* Verfahrensanmeldung; ~ **chart** Arbeitsablaufdiagramm; ~ **control** Fertigungssteuerung; ~ **engineering** Verfahrenstechnik; ~ **of manufacture** Herstellungsverfahren, Fertigungsverfahren, Fabrikationsprozeß; ~ **patent** Verfahrenspatent; **finishing** ~ Veredelungsverfahren

process, in ~ im Gange; **in** ~ **of construction** im Bau (befindlich); **in** ~ **of development** in der Entwicklung begriffen; **in** ~ **of manufacture** in Herstellung; **in** ~ **of time** im Laufe der Zeit; **goods in** ~ *(Am [auch]* **work in**~) Halbfabrikate, Halberzeugnisse

process, industrial ~ industrielles Herstellungsverfahren; **manufacturing** ~ Herstellungsverfahren, Fertigungsverfahren; **operating** (or **working**) ~ Arbeitsverfahren; **production** ~ Produktionsprozeß, Produktionsverfahren; **secret** ~ Geheimverfahren; **special** ~ Spezialverfahren

process *v (jdn)* gerichtlich belangen; bearbeiten, (weiter)verarbeiten; veredeln; **to** ~ **data** *(Statistik)* Daten aufbereiten (od. auswerten); **to** ~ **a patent application** e-e Patentanmeldung behandeln (od. bearbeiten)

processed, ~ **foods** verarbeitete (od. veredelte) Nahrungsmittel; ~ **products** (weiter)verarbeitete Erzeugnisse; Verarbeitungserzeugnisse; Veredelungserzeugnisse

processing Bearbeitung, Verarbeitung *(von Waren)*; Veredelung; ~ **costs** Verarbeitungskosten; Fertigungskosten; ~ **country** Veredelungsland; ~ **enterprise** Verarbeitungsbetrieb; Veredelungsbetrieb; ~ **expenses** Verarbeitungskosten; Veredelungskosten; ~ **fee** Bearbeitungsgebühr; ~ **of data** (EDV) Verarbeitung der Daten; ~ **of goods** Veredelung von Waren; ~ **industry** verarbeitende Industrie, Verarbeitungsindustrie; Veredelungsindustrie; ~ **plant** Verarbeitungsanlage; ~ **stage** Verarbeitungsstufe; ~ **undertaking** →~ enterprise; **contract** ~ Lohnveredelung; **data** ~ *(EDV)* Datenverarbeitung; **degree of** ~ Verarbeitungsgrad; **further** ~ Weiterbehandlung; **products for further** ~ Vorerzeugnisse; **inward** ~ aktiver Veredelungsverkehr; **job** ~ Lohnveredelung; **outward** ~ passiver Veredelungsverkehr; **stage of** ~ Verarbeitungsstufe; **goods in the early stage of** ~ wenig veredelte Erzeugnisse; **textile** ~ Textilverarbeitung

processor Verarbeiter; **word** ~ Textverarbeiter

proclaim *v* proklamieren, öffentlich verkündigen (od. erklären); **to** ~ **a district** *Br* den Ausnahmezustand über ein Gebiet verhängen; **to** ~ →**martial law**; **to** ~ **a Republic** e-e Republik ausrufen; **to** ~ **war** den Krieg erklären

proclamation Proklamation, amtliche Verkündigung (od. Erklärung); Aufruf; ~ **of the Republic** Ausrufung der Republik; ~ **of a state of emergency** (or **siege**) Verhängung (od. Erklärung) des Ausnahmezustandes; **to issue** (or **make**) **a** ~ e-n Aufruf ergehen lassen

proctor *Br (Cambridge und Oxford)* Universitätsbeamter mit verschiedenen Pflichten, *(z.B.)* Universitätsrichter; Anwalt *(vor geistlichen und Seerechtsgerichten)*; **Queen's P**~ *Br* Beamter *(in der Family Division des High Court),* der bei Kollisionsgefahr in divorce und nullity cases eingreift oder als →amicus curiae das Gericht in schwierigen Fragen berät

procuration (proc.) 1. *(schriftl.)* Vollmacht *(bes. im WechselR)*; Vertretung; **by** ~ s. per →~

procuration, per ~ (or **per procurationem**) (p.p., per pro.) in Vollmacht, in Vertretung; **to sign a bill of exchange per** ~[139] e-n Wechsel per Vollmacht unterzeichnen

Procuration entspricht nicht der deutschen Prokura. Die in das Handelsregister einzutragende Handelsvollmacht des deutschen Prokuristen (Prokura) hat keine Parallele im anglo-amerikanischen Recht

procuration 2. Besorgung, Verschaffung; *(StrafR)*[140] Kuppelei; Zuhälterei; ~ **fee** (or **money**) Maklergebühr *(für Beschaffung e-s Darlehns)*; ~ **of a loan** Beschaffung e-s Darlehns; ~ **of a woman** *(StrafR)*[140] Kuppelei

procurator Bevollmächtigter; *Scot (selten)* Anwalt; ~**-fiscal** *Scot* Staatsanwalt *(im sheriff court)*; **P**~**-General** *Br* →Treasury Solicitor

Der procurator hat nicht die gleiche umfassende Vollmacht wie der Prokurist *(cf. procuration)*

procuratory *Am* und *Scot* Vollmacht

procure *v* (sich) beschaffen, verschaffen, beibringen, vermitteln; erwerben, erlangen; *(StrafR)* kuppeln, Kuppelei (be)treiben; **to** ~ **acceptance** Akzept einholen; **to** ~ **capital** Kapital beschaffen; **to** ~ **a p.'s consent** jds Zustimmung beibringen; **to** ~ **employment** Beschäftigung verschaffen; **to** ~ **employment for a p.** jdm Beschäftigung verschaffen; **to** ~ **evidence** Beweise beibringen; **to** ~ **funds** Kapital beschaffen; **to** ~ **goods** Waren beziehen; **to** ~ **a miscarriage** abtreiben; **to counsel and** ~ *(StrafR)* Beihilfe leisten

procuring Beschaffung, Vermittlung; *(StrafR)* Kuppelei; Zuhälterei; ~ **a breach of contract** Verleitung zum Vertragsbruch; ~ **goods** Beschaffung von Waren; Bezug von Waren; ~ **of a loan** Vermittlung e-s Darlehns

procurement Beschaffung, Beibringung, Vermittlung; ~ **agency** *Am* Beschaffungsstelle; ~ **of capital** Kapitalbeschaffung; ~ **of funds** Beschaffung von Mitteln, Kapitalbeschaffung; ~ **of a judgment** Erwirkung e-s Urteils; ~ **planning** Beschaffungsplanung; **contract for the ~ of services** Dienstverschaffungsvertrag; **government** ~ staatliches Beschaffungswesen (od. Auftragswesen)

procurer Beschaffer, Vermittler; *(StrafR)* Kuppler; Zuhälter

procuress *(StrafR)* Kupplerin

produce (Natur-)Erzeugnis(se), Produkt(e); Ertrag; ~ **broker** Warenmakler; ~ **business** Produktenhandel; ~ **dealer** Produktenhändler; ~ **exchange** Produktenbörse, Warenbörse; ~ **of the country** Landesprodukt(e); ~ **of Germany** deutsches Erzeugnis, deutsche Erzeugnisse; ~ **market** Produktenmarkt, Warenmarkt; ~ **trade** Produktenhandel; **agricultural** ~ landwirtschaftliche(s) Erzeugnis(se), Agrarprodukt(e); **dealer in** ~ Produktenhändler; **excess** ~ Überschußerzeugnis(se); **farm** ~ →agricultural ~; **foreign** ~ ausländische(s) Erzeugnis(se) *(opp. home ~)*; **gross** ~ Rohertrag; **home** (or **inland**) ~ inländisches Produkt, einheimische(s) Erzeugnis(se); **net** ~ Reinertrag

produce *v* erzeugen, produzieren, herstellen; vorlegen, beibringen, vorzeigen; *(Gewinn)* erzielen, einbringen; verursachen, bewirken, hervorbringen; **to ~ the accounts** die Rechnungen vorlegen; **to ~ an alibi** ein Alibi beibringen; **to ~ a certificate** e-e Bescheinigung vorlegen; **to ~ documents** Urkunden vorlegen (od. beibringen); **to ~ energy** Energie erzeugen; **to ~ evidence** Beweis antreten (od. erbringen); **to ~ an invention** *(PatR)* den Gegenstand der Erfindung herstellen; **to ~ a power of attorney** e-e Vollmacht vorlegen; **to ~ a prisoner** e-n Gefangenen *(zur Verhandlung)* vorführen; **to ~ reasons** Gründe anführen; **to ~ a witness** e-n Zeugen beibringen

producing Produzieren, Produktions-, Herstellungs-; ~ **area** Produktionsgebiet; ~ **cen|tre (~ter)** Produktionsstätte; ~ **cost** →production cost; ~ **country** Erzeugerland *(opp. consuming country)*; Förderland *(z. B. Erdöl)*; ~ **industries** erzeugende Industrie; produzierendes Gewerbe; **interest** ~ zinsbringend; **oil ~ country** Erdölförderland

producer Produzent, Hersteller, Fabrikant, Erzeuger *(opp. consumer)*; Filmproduzent; Regisseur; ~ **advertising** Herstellerwerbung; **~'s brand** Herstellermarke; **~s' cooperative (society)** Produktionsgenossenschaft; ~ **country** Erzeugerland; *(Öl)* Förderland; ~ **goods** Produktionsgüter *(opp. consumer goods)*; **~'s liability** Produzentenhaftung; ~ **price** Produzentenpreis, Herstellerpreis; **~s' surplus** Produzentenrente; **at the ~ stage** auf der Erzeugerstufe; **domestic** (or **home**) ~ inländischer Erzeuger

product Produkt, Erzeugnis; Fabrikat; Ware; ~ **analysis** Produktanalyse; ~ **claim** *(PatR)* Stoffanspruch; ~ **differentiation** Produktdifferenzierung; ~ **liability** Produkthaftung, Produzentenhaftung *(Haftung für fehlerhafte Produkte)*; ~ **liability insurance** Produkthaftpflichtversicherung; ~ **mix** gemischtes Sortimentsangebot; ~ **name** *Am (Warenzeichen)* Sachbezeichnung; ~ **of industry** Industrieprodukt; **~s of the soil** Bodenerzeugnisse, Bodenprodukte; **~s originating in** Erzeugnisse mit Ursprung in; ~ **patent** Sachpatent; ~ **placement** Markteinführung; Produkt-Plazierung *(Form der Werbung)*; **(chemical) ~ protection** *(PatR)* Stoffschutz; ~ **purchasing agency** Warenverkaufsagentur; ~ **quality specification** Qualitätsanforderungen für Produkte

product standards, defining of ~ Festlegung von Warennormen (od. Warentypen)

product test *(Marktforschung)* Produkttest

product, agricultural ~s s. farm →~s; **by-~** Nebenerzeugnis, Nebenprodukt; Abfallprodukt; **contractual** ~ Vertragserzeugnis; **farm ~s** landwirtschaftliche Erzeugnisse, Agrarerzeugnisse; **finished ~s** Fertigerzeugnisse, Fertigwaren; **foreign** ~ ausländisches Fabrikat (od. Erzeugnis) *(opp. home ~)*; **home** (or **inland**) ~ einheimisches Fabrikat, inländisches Erzeugnis; **industrial ~s** Industrieerzeugnisse; **joint ~s** Kuppelprodukte, Verbundprodukte; **manufactured ~s** Industrieerzeugnisse; **national** ~ Sozialprodukt *(cf. gross ~, net ~)*; **natural** ~ Rohprodukt; **primary ~s** Grundstoffe, Rohstoffe; **secondary** ~ Nebenprodukt; **semi-finished ~s** Halberzeugnisse, Halbfabrikate

production 1. Beibringung, Vorlegung, Vorlage; *Scot* Beweisstück; ~ **of a document** Vorlage e-r Urkunde; ~ **of evidence** Beweisantritt, Beibringung von Beweisen; ~ **of a prisoner** Vorführung e-s Gefangenen; ~ **of a witness** Beibringung e-s Zeugen

production 2. *(literarisches oder künstlerisches)* Werk; *(Film usw.)* Produktion

production 3. Produktion, Herstellung, Erzeugung, Fertigung; ~ **account** Produktionskonto; ~ **area** Produktionsgebiet; ~ **bonus** Produktionsprämie; Leistungsprämie; ~ **budget** Produktionsplan; ~ **capacity** Produktionskapazität; ~ **car** Serienwagen; ~ **cartel** Produktionskartell; ~ **cent|re (~er)** Produktionsstätte; ~ **control** Fertigungssteuerung; Produktionskontrolle; ~ **cooperative** Produktionsgenossenschaft

production cost Produktionskosten, Fertigungskosten; **indirect** ~ Fertigungsgemeinkosten

Production Credit Associations *Am* landwirtschaftliche Kreditgenossenschaften *(die kurz- oder mittelfristige Kredite gewähren)*

production, ~ **curve** Produktionskurve; ~ **cycle** Fertigungszeit; ~ **decrease** →decrease in ~; ~ **department** Fertigungsabteilung; ~ **engineer** Fertigungsingenieur; ~ **engineering** Produktionstechnik; ~ **equipment** Betriebseinrichtung, Fertigungseinrichtung; ~ **facilities** Produktionsanlagen; ~ **factors** Produktionsfaktoren; ~ **figures** Produktionszahlen; ~ **flow** Produktionsablauf; ~ **function** Produktionsfunktion; ~ **goal** Produktionsziel

production, ~ **grant** *Br (staatl.)* Beihilfe zur Förderung der Produktion; Produktionsprämie; ~ **in bulk** Massenproduktion, Massenherstellung; ~ **increase** s. increase in →~; ~ **index** Produktionsindex; ~ **level** Produktionsstand; ~ **loss** Produktionsausfall; ~ **machinery** Produktionsapparat; ~ **manager** Produktionsleiter; ~ **order** Fertigungsauftrag; ~ **plan** Produktionsplan, Fertigungsplan; ~ **planning** Fertigungsplanung; Produktionsplanung; ~ **plant** Produktionsanlage, Betriebsanlage; ~ **process** Fertigungsverfahren, Produktionsprozeß; ~ **program(me)** Fertigungsprogramm; ~ **program(me) planning** Fertigungsprogrammplanung; ~ **quota** Produktionsquote, -soll, -kontingent; ~ **schedule** →~ plan; ~ **surplus** Produktionsüberschuß; ~ **target** Produktionsziel; ~ **time** Herstellungsdauer

production, agricultural ~ landwirtschaftliche Erzeugung; **annual** ~ Jahresproduktion, Jahreserzeugung; **annual maximum** ~ jährliche Höchstproduktion; **area of** ~ *Am* Produktionsgebiet; **batch** ~ Serienproduktion, Serienfertigung; **branch of** ~ Produktionszweig; **commencement of** ~ Produktionsaufnahme; **cost of** ~ →~ cost; **daily** ~ Tagesproduktion; **curtailment of** ~ Produktionsdrosselung, Produktionsbeschränkung; **decline** (or **decrease**) **in** ~ Produktionsrückgang, Produktionsabnahme; **domestic** ~ Inlandsproduktion; **excess(ive)** ~ Überproduktion; Produktionsüberschuß; **extension of** ~ Produktionsausweitung; **increase in** ~ Produktionssteigerung, Produktionszunahme; **limitation of** ~ Produktionsbegrenzung; **line of** ~ Produktionszweig; **loss of** ~ Produktionsausfall; → **mass** ~; **means of** ~ Produktionsmittel; **method of** ~ Produktionsverfahren, Herstellungsverfahren; **over-**~ Überproduktion; **peace-time** ~ Friedensproduktion; **primary** ~ Urproduktion; **restriction of** ~ Produktionsbeschränkung; **serial** ~ Serienherstellung; **setback in** ~ Produktionsrückgang; **stoppage of** ~ *(vorübergehende)* Produktionseinstellung; **surplus** ~ Überproduktion; **termination of** ~ *(endgültige)* Produktionseinstellung; **total** ~ Gesamtproduktion; **war (-time)** ~ Kriegsproduktion; **world** ~ Weltproduktion

production, to be in good ~ genügend hergestellt werden; **to check** (or **put a check on**) ~ (or **to curb, curtail, cut down**) ~ die Produktion beschränken (od. drosseln); **to go into** ~ die Produktion aufnehmen; **to increase** ~ die Produktion steigern; **to reduce** ~ die Produktion einschränken (od. verringern); **to step up** ~ die Produktion steigern

productive produktiv, ertragreich, ertragsfähig, rentabel, ergiebig; ~ **assets** ertragbringende Anlagen; ~ **capacity** Produktionsfähigkeit, Produktionskapazität; Ertragsfähigkeit; ~ **capital** gewinnbringendes Kapital; ~ **efficiency** Leistungsfähigkeit, Produktivität; ~ **enterprise** ertragbringendes Unternehmen; **(capital)** ~ **of interest** zinsbringend(es Kapital); ~ **power** →~ capacity; ~ **soil** ertragreicher Boden

productiveness →productivity

productivity Produktivität, Ertragsfähigkeit, Rentabilität, Ergiebigkeit; ~ **agreement** (or **deal**) *Br* Produktivitätsvereinbarung *(Einigung über bessere Arbeitsbedingungen und höheren Lohn bei besseren Arbeitsleistungen)*; **increase in** (or **raising of**) ~ Produktivitätssteigerung; **increased** ~ erhöhte Produktivität; **to increase** (or **raise**) ~ die Produktivität steigern

profanation of a church Kirchenentweihung, Kirchenschändung

profess *v* gestehen, bekennen; *(freien od. akademischen)* Beruf ausüben

profession *(freier od. akademischer)* Beruf; freiberufliche Tätigkeit; *(gehobener)* Berufsstand; (Glaubens-)Bekenntnis; Versicherung, Beteuerung; ~ **of faith** Glaubensbekenntnis; ~ **or vocation** *Br (Einkommensteuer)* freie und sonstige selbständige Berufe; **by** ~ von Beruf, beruflich; **choice of** ~ Berufswahl; **crowded** ~ überfüllter Beruf; **exercise of a** ~ Ausübung e-s Berufes; **inability to practice one's** ~ Berufsunfähigkeit; **the (learned)** ~**s** die akademischen Berufe *(e.g. medicine, law, theology, teaching)*; **practice of a** ~ Ausübung e-s *(freien od. akademischen)* Berufes; **to carry on a** ~ e-n Beruf ausüben; **to enter (upon) a** ~ e-n Beruf ergreifen; **to enter the legal** ~ Jurist werden; **to practice a** ~ e-n Beruf ausüben; **to take up a** ~ s. to enter a →~; **this** ~ **has** (or **offers**) **good prospects** dieser Beruf ist aussichtsreich

professional beruflich, Berufs-; e-m *(freien od. akademischen)* Beruf angehörend; freiberuflich; berufsmäßig *(opp. amateur)*; fachlich, fachmännisch; Fach-; Fachmann; Börsenspekulant; Berufssportler; ~**s** *Br* sachverständige Berater, die für bestimmte Gebiete auf Dauer od. auf Zeit herangezogen werden; ~ **activity** *(freie)* Berufstätigkeit; ~ **association** Berufsverband, Berufsvereinigung; ~ **body** Berufsverband; ~ **career** Berufslaufbahn *(des Angehörigen e-s akademischen od. freien Berufes)*; **the** ~ **classes** die Angehörigen der freien (od. akademischen) Berufe *(als Gesellschaftsklasse)*; ~ **classification** Berufsgliederung; ~ **conduct** standesgemäßes Verhalten; ~ **confidentiality** Berufsgeheimnis; ~ **consul** Berufskonsul; ~ **corporation** *Am* Unternehmensform mit Rechtspersönlichkeit für freie Berufe *(die den frei praktizierenden Angehörigen höherer Dienstleistungsberufe [z.B. Ärzten, Anwälten] Steuervorteile von Angestellten verschafft)*; ~ **criminal** Berufsverbrecher; ~ **diplomat** Berufsdiplomat; ~ **earnings** Einkünfte aus freien (oder akademischen) Berufen; ~ **education** berufliche Ausbildung; ~ **employee**[141] beruflich besonders qualifizierter Arbeitnehmer *(leitender Angestellter, der nicht mit Routinearbeiten betraut ist)*; ~ **equipment** Berufsausrüstung

professional ethics Berufsethos; **canons of** ~ Standesregeln *(der Anwälte, Ärzte etc)*

professional etiquette Regeln des standesgemäßen Verhaltens *(bes. von Anwälten und Ärzten)*; **breach of** ~ standeswidriges Verhalten

professional, ~ **expenditure** →~ outlays; ~ **fees** Honorar; ~ **group** Berufsgruppe; ~ **hono(u)r** Standesehre; ~ **indemnity insurance** Berufshaftpflichtversicherung; ~ **journal** →~ magazine; ~ **liability** Haftung von Freiberuflern und fachkundigen Gewerbetreibenden; ~ **liabity insurance** Berufshaftpflichtversicherung; ~ **life** Berufsleben; ~ **magazine** Fachzeitschrift; ~ **man** Geistesarbeiter, Akademiker; freiberuflich Tätiger, Angehöriger e-s freien od. akademischen Berufes; **in a** ~ **manner** fachmännisch; ~ **misconduct** standeswidriges Verhalten; ~ **obligation** Standespflicht; ~ **officer** *Am* Berufsoffizier; ~ **organization** Berufsorganisation; ~ **outlays** *(SteuerR)* Werbungskosten; ~ **partnership** Sozietät; ~ **person** Angehöriger e-s freien Berufes; ~ **politician** Berufspolitiker; ~ **privilege** →privilege of communications; ~ **qualification** berufliche Qualifikation (od. Befähigung); ~ **risks indemnity insurance** *Br* Berufshaftpflichtversicherung; ~ **school** Fachschule*(→school 2.)*; ~ **secret** (or **secrecy**) Berufsgeheimnis

professional services freiberufliche Dienstleistungen; **income from** ~ Einkommen aus freiberuflicher Tätigkeit; **performance** (or **rendering**) **of** ~ Verrichtung (od. Ausführung) von freiberuflichen Tätigkeiten

professional, ~ **society** Berufsverband; ~ **soldier** Berufssoldat; ~ **speculator** *Am* berufsmäßiger Spekulant; ~ **standards** berufsethische Grundsätze; ~ **status** freiberuflicher Status (od. Rang); ~ **traders** *(Börse)* Berufshandel; ~ **training** Berufsausbildung; Fachausbildung; ~ **woman** freiberuflich tätige Frau; im freien od. akademischen Beruf stehende Frau; ~ **worker** Akademiker; Fachmann

professor *univ* Professor; **assistant** (or **associate** *Am*) ~ außerordentlicher Professor; **emeritus** ~ emeritierter Professor; **full** ~ ordentlicher Professor; Ordinarius; **guest** (or **visiting**) ~ Gastprofessor

professorial chair *univ* Lehrstuhl

professorship *univ* Professur; **establishment of** ~**s** Einrichtung von Lehrstühlen; **to be offered a** ~ **at a university** e-n Ruf an e-e Universität erhalten

proffer *v* anbieten; *com* andienen

proficiency Tüchtigkeit; Fertigkeiten; ~ **pay** Leistungszulage; **certificate of** ~ Befähigungsnachweis; **to pass an English** ~ **test** e-e Prüfung über genügende englische Sprachkenntnisse bestehen

profit Gewinn, Ertrag, Nutzen; ~**s** Erträge, Nutzungen, Früchte *(e-r Sache od. e-s Rechts)*

profit, ~**s accrue** die Gewinne fließen zu (od. fallen an); **to allocate the** ~ den Gewinn verteilen; **to appropriate a** ~ e-n Gewinn verwenden; **to ascertain the** ~ **(and loss)** den Gewinn (und Verlust) ermitteln; **to derive a** ~ Nutzen ziehen (from aus); **to distribute** ~**s** Gewinne verteilen (od. ausschütten); **to divide** ~**s** Gewinne (auf)teilen; **to draw** ~**s** Gewinne entnehmen; **to leave a** ~ e-n Gewinn abwerfen (od. bringen); **to make large** (or **big**) ~**s** große Gewinne erzielen; **to make a** ~ **on a transaction** an e-m Geschäft verdienen; **to operate at a** ~ mit Gewinn arbeiten; **to participate equally in the** ~**s** gleichen Anteil am Gewinn haben; **to realize a** ~ einen Gewinn erzielen; **to sell at a** ~ mit Gewinn verkaufen; **to share in the** ~**s** am Gewinn beteiligt sein; **to show a** ~ e-n Gewinn aufweisen, gewinnbringend sein; mit Gewinn abschließen; **to take** ~**s** *(Börse)* Gewinne mitnehmen; **to yield a** ~ e-n Gewinn abwerfen (od. ergeben)

profit and loss (P. & L.) Gewinn und Verlust; ~ **account** (P. & L. A/c.) *(jährliche)* Gewinn- und Verlustrechnung; Aufwands- und Ertragsrechnung; Gewinn- und Verlustkonto; ~ **pooling** (*Am* **sharing**) **agreement** Gewinngemeinschaftsvertrag, Gewinnpoolungsvertrag; ~ **statement** *Am* Gewinn- und Verlustrechnung; Ergebnisrechnung, Erfolgsrechnung; **to draw up** (or **prepare**) **a** ~ **account** Gewinn und Verlust berechnen

profit, ~ **account** Gewinnkonto; Gewinnrechnung; ~ **à prendre** Recht, die Nutzung aus e-m fremden Grundstück zu ziehen *(z.B. com-*

mom of fishery); ~ **balance** Gewinnsaldo; Gewinnüberschuß; ~ **carried forward** *(Bilanz)* Gewinnvortrag; ~ **contribution** Deckungsbeitrag; ~ **distribution** Gewinnverteilung, Gewinnausschüttung; ~**-earning** gewinnbringend, rentabel; ~ **forecast** Gewinnprognose; ~**s from business or profession** *(SteuerR)* Gewinne aus Geschäftsbetrieb od. freier Berufstätigkeit; ~ **from interest** Zinsgewinn; ~ **from operations** *Am* Betriebsgewinn; ~ **insurance** *Am* Betriebsunterbrechungsversicherung

profit-making, ~ **business** Erwerbsgeschäft; **the society operates on a non-~ basis** die Gesellschaft verfolgt keinen Erwerbszweck

profit, ~ **margin** Gewinnspanne, Gewinnmarge; ~ **maximization** Gewinnmaximierung; ~ **on exchange** Kursgewinn; ~ **on investments** Gewinn aus Kapitalanlagen; ~ **on realization** Veräußerungsgewinn; ~ **on a sale** Verkaufsgewinn; ~ **on sales** Umsatzrendite; ~ **participation** Gewinnbeteiligung; ~ **pass-over** *Am* →pass-over; ~ **planning** Gewinnplanung; ~ **pooling contract** (or **agreement**) Gewinngemeinschaftsvertrag

profit, ~ **realization** *(Börse)* Gewinnrealisation; Gewinnerzielung; ~ **realized** erzielter Gewinn; ~ **rise** Gewinnsteigerung; ~ **share** Gewinnanteil

profit-sharing Gewinnbeteiligung *(der Arbeitnehmer)*, Beteiligung am Betriebsergebnis, (materieller Teil der) Partnerschaft; am Gewinn beteiligt; ~ **agreement** Gewinnbeteiligungsvertrag; ~ **bond** Gewinnobligation, Gewinnschuldverschreibung; ~ **scheme** Gewinnbeteiligungsplan

profit, ~ **shrinkage** Gewinnschrumpfung; ~ **squeeze** Druck auf den Gewinn; Verminderung der Gewinnspanne; ~ **taking** *(Börse)* Gewinnmitnahme; ~ **transfer** Gewinnabführung; ~**-yielding** Gewinn abwerfend

profit, actual ~ tatsächlich erzielter Gewinn; **anticipated** ~ erwarteter Gewinn; **appropriation of the** ~ Verwendung des Gewinns; **assessment of** ~ Gewinnberechnung, Gewinnermittlung; **at a** ~ mit Gewinn; **balance of** ~ Restgewinn; **balance sheet showing a** ~ Gewinnabschluß; **big** ~ großer Gewinn; **book** ~ Buchgewinn; **business** ~ Geschäftsgewinn, Gewinn aus Gewerbebetrieb; Unternehmensgewinn; **calculation of** ~**s** Gewinnberechnung, Rentabilitätsberechnung; **casual** ~ gelegentlicher Gewinn; **chances of** ~ Gewinnchancen; **clear** ~**(s)** Reingewinn, Nettogewinn; **company** ~ Gesellschaftsgewinn; **commercial** ~ gewerblicher Gewinn; **contingent** ~ eventueller Gewinn; **disposition of** ~**s** Gewinnverwendung; **distributed** ~ ausgeschütteter Gewinn; **distribution of** ~**s** Gewinnverteilung, Gewinnausschüttung; **easy** ~ müheloser Gewinn; **excess** ~ Übergewinn, Wuchergewinn; **fair** ~ angemessener Gewinn; **gross** ~ Rohgewinn, Bruttogewinn; **illusory** ~ Scheingewinn; **incidental** ~ Nebengewinn; **industrial** ~ gewerblicher Gewinn; **interest** ~ Zinsgewinn

profit, interest in the ~**s** Gewinnbeteiligung; Interesse am Gewinn; **to have an interest in the** ~ am Gewinn beteiligt (od. interessiert) sein

profit, large ~ großer (od. hoher) Gewinn; **loss of** ~ Gewinnentgang, entgangener Gewinn, Gewinnausfall; **lost** ~ entgangener Gewinn; **with the intent of making a** ~ in gewinnsüchtiger Absicht; **margin of** ~ →~ margin; →**mesne** ~**s; net** ~ Reingewinn; **non-~ policy** nicht gewinnberechtigte Police; **operating** ~ Betriebsgewinn; **paper** ~ →paper 1.

profit, participation in ~**s** Gewinnbeteiligung; *(VersR)* Beteiligung am Überschuß; **to have a participation in** ~**s** gewinnbeteiligt sein

profit, →**percentage of** ~**s; ploughing** (*Am* plowing) **back of** ~**s** Gewinnthesaurierung (*e-s Unternehmens*); **realization of** ~**s** Gewinnerzielung; **reduction in** ~**s** Rückgang des Gewinns; **rentention of** ~**s** Thesaurierung; **rise in** ~**s** Gewinnanstieg; **share in (the)** ~**s** Gewinnanteil (→*share 1.*); **small** ~ kleiner (od. geringer) Gewinn; **source of** ~ Gewinnquelle; **surplus** ~**s** Gewinnüberschuß; **trading** ~ Geschäftsgewinn, Betriebsgewinn; **unappropriated** (or **undistributed**) ~ unverteilter Gewinn, nicht ausgeschütteter Gewinn; **with a view to** ~ in gewinnsüchtiger Absicht

profit *v* Nutzen (od. Vorteil) ziehen (by, from aus); sich etw. zunutze machen

profitability Ertragskraft, Rentabilität; Wirtschaftlichkeit; ~ **calculation** Rentabilitätsrechnung; **limit of** ~ Rentabilitätsgrenze; **overall** ~ Gesamtrentabilität *(e-s Unternehmens)*

profitable gewinnbringend, einträglich, rentabel; ~ **business** einträgliches (od. rentables) Geschäft; ~ **investment** gewinnbringende Anlage; **to be** ~ Gewinn (od. Vorteil) bringen; sich rentieren

profiteer Profitmacher, Preistreiber, Geschäftemacher; Schieber; **war** ~ Kriegsgewinnler

profiteering Profitmacherei; Schiebung, Schiebertum; Preistreiberei

pro forma ("as a matter of form") pro forma, nur der Form wegen, Schein-; ~ **invoice** Proformarechnung, fingierte Rechnung; ~ **transaction** Scheingeschäft

program(me) Programm; (Arbeits-)Plan; Sendefolge, Hörfolge; ~ **director** Sendeleiter; ~ **of meeting** Sitzungsprogramm; **according to** ~ programmgemäß; **change of** ~ Programmänderung; **electioneering** ~ Wahlprogramm;

exchange of ~s Programmaustausch; **financial ~** Finanz(ierungs)plan; **implementation of a ~** Durchführung e-s Programms; **party ~** Parteiprogramm; **political ~** politisches Programm; **relief ~** Hilfsprogramm; **working ~** Arbeitsplan; **to adhere strictly to a ~** sich streng an ein Programm halten; **to draw up** (or **formulate**) **a ~** ein Programm aufstellen; **to put a ~ on the air** *(im Fernsehen od. Rundfunk)* senden

program(me) *v* programmieren

program(m)ing Programmieren; Programmgestaltung

program(m)er *(EDV)* Programmierer

progress Fortschritt(e); (Fort-)Gang, Verlauf; **~ achieved** erzielte Fortschritte; **~ chaser** Terminjäger; **~ of events** Gang der Ereignisse; **~ of titles** *Scot* Reihe von Urkunden über Eigentum an Land; **~ of work** Fortschritt der Arbeit; **~ report** Tätigkeitsbericht; Bericht über den Stand der Angelegenheit(en); **economic ~** wirtschaftlicher Fortschritt (od. Aufschwung)

progress, in ~ im Gang; in Ausführung befindlich, in Arbeit; unfertig; **in full ~** in vollem Gang; **in ~ of time** im Laufe der Zeit; **negotiations in ~** schwebende Verhandlungen; **work in ~** Halberzeugnisse, Halbfabrikate; in Ausführung begriffene Arbeit; **to be in ~** im Gange sein *(Konferenz, Verhandlungen etc)*

progress, marked ~ merklicher Fortschritt; **promotion of ~** Förderung des Fortschritts; **to achieve (some) ~** Fortschritte erzielen; **he has made good ~** er machte gute Fortschritte; **to report ~** über den Stand der Angelegenheit(en) berichten

progression Progression, (fortschreitende) Steigerung; Stufenfolge; **saving clause as to ~ (to avoid double taxation)** *(DBA)* Progressionsvorbehalt; **tax ~** Steuerprogression

progressive progressiv, (stufenweise) fortschreitend *(opp. retrograde)*; schrittweise; fortschrittlich; **~ approximation** schrittweise Annäherung; **~ depreciation** progressive Abschreibung *(mit steigenden Jahresraten)*; **P~ Party** *Am* Progressisten *(1912 gegr. fortschrittlicher Flügel der Republikanischen Partei)*; **~ rate** progressiver Zinssatz; **~ removal of restrictions** schrittweiser Abbau von Beschränkungen; **by ~ stages** stufenweise; **~ tax** Progressivsteuer; **~ tendencies** fortschrittliche Tendenzen

pro hac vice ("for this occasion") (nur) für dieses eine Mal *(z. B. appointment)*

prohibit *v (behördl.)* verbieten, untersagen

prohibited, ~ aerial space *(VölkerR)* Luftsperrgebiet; **~ degree** (of relationship) *(für die Heirat)* verbotener Verwandtschaftsgrad; **~ goods** Schmuggelware, Konterbande; **~ transport** *(VölkerR)* Beförderungsverbot *(von kriegführenden Streitkräften auf neutralen Schiffen)*; **~zone** Sperrzone, Verbotszone

prohibition 1. Verbot, Untersagung; **~ of assembly** Versammlungsverbot; **~ of issue** Emissionssperre; **~ of trade** Handelsverbot, Handelssperre; **~ on exportation** Ausfuhrverbot; **~ on importation** Einfuhrverbot; **~ on trading** Gewerbeverbot; **~ procedure** Untersagungsverfahren; **export ~** Ausfuhrverbot; **import ~** Einfuhrverbot; **marriage ~** Eheverbot; **statutory ~** gesetzliches Verbot; **to impose a ~** ein Verbot verhängen (on über); **to remove a ~** ein Verbot aufheben; **to violate a ~** e-m Verbot zuwiderhandeln

prohibition 2., *Br*[142] **order of ~**, *Am* **writ of ~** bindende Anweisung e-r höheren Instanz *(Gericht od. Verwaltungsbehörde)* an e-e niedere Instanz *(Gericht od. Verwaltungsbehörde)*, ein anhängiges Verfahren wegen Unzuständigkeit einzustellen

prohibition 3. *Am*[143] Prohibition *(staatl. Verbot der Herstellung und des Verkaufs alkoholischer Getränke)*; **state ~ law** *Am* einzelstaatliches Prohibitionsgesetz

prohibitionist *bes. Am* Anhänger des gesetzl. Alkoholverbots; **~ country** Land mit Alkoholverbot; **~ measures** Maßnahmen zur Durchführung des Alkoholverbots

prohibitive verbietend, verhindernd, Sperr-; **~ duty** Prohibitivzoll, Sperrzoll; **~ price** unerschwinglicher Preis

prohibitory *bes. Br* verbietend; **~ duties** Schutzzölle; **~ →injunction**

project Vorhaben, Projekt, Plan; **~ finance** Projektfinanzierung; **~ manager** Projektmanager, Projektleiter; **~ management** Projektmanagement; **hush ~** Geheimprojekt; **industrial ~** Industrieprojekt; **investment ~** Investitionsvorhaben; **specific ~** bestimmtes Vorhaben; **to engage in a ~** ein Vorhaben in Angriff nehmen

project *v* planen, vorhaben; **~ing** Planung

prolicide Tötung der Leibesfrucht *(foeticide)*; Kindestötung *(infanticide)*

proliferate *v* stark an Zahl zunehmen, (sich) vermehren

proliferation Proliferation, starke Vermehrung (od. Ausbreitung); **Non-P~ Treaty** (or **Treaty on the Non-P~ of Nuclear Weapons**) (NPT)[143a] Vertrag über die Nichtverbreitung von Kernwaffen, Atomwaffensperrvertrag; **→Nuclear Non-P~ Act**

prolix weitschweifig

prolixity Weitschweifigkeit *(im pleading verboten)*

prolong *v* prolongieren; *(Frist)* verlängern; stunden; **to ~ (the time of) a bill** e-n Wechsel prolongieren; **to ~ the licen|ce (~se) until ...** die Konzession verlängern bis ...

prolongation Prolongation, (Frist-)Verlängerung; Stundung; **~ of a business** *(Börsentermingeschäft)* Prolongationsgeschäft; **~ of an agreement** Verlängerung e-s Vertrags; **~ of a bill** Prolongation e-s Wechsels; **~ of leave** Urlaubsverlängerung; **~ of payment** Zahlungsaufschub, Stundung

prominence Bedeutung, Wichtigkeit; **to achieve ~** Bedeutung erlangen; **he achieved ~ as a specialist in this field** er erlangte Bedeutung als Spezialist auf diesem Gebiete

promiscuity, (sexual) ~ häufiger Partnerwechsel

promise Versprechen, Zusage, Zusicherung *(meist in mündlicher Form; cf. covenant)*; **~ of finance** Finanzierungszusage; **~ of a loan** Darlehensversprechen; Kreditzusage; **~ of marriage** Eheversprechen; **~ of reward** Aussetzung e-r Belohnung; Auslobung; **~ to answer for the debt of another** Schuldübernahme; **~ to make a gift** Schenkungsversprechen; **~ to pay** Zahlungsversprechen, Zahlungszusage; **~ to perform** Leistungsversprechen; **breach of ~** Bruch des Versprechens; Wortbruch; **breach of ~ (to marry)** Verlöbnisbruch, Bruch des Eheversprechens; **collateral ~** kumulative (od. bestärkende) Schuldübernahme; Schuldbeitritt *(zu der Schuld e-s anderen; dieser bleibt primär leistungsverpflichtet)*; Interzession; **election ~** Wahlversprechen; **joint ~** Gesamthandverpflichtung; **joint and several ~** gesamtschuldnerische Verpflichtung; **to abide by a ~** ein Versprechen halten; **to break a ~** ein Versprechen brechen; **to keep** (or **fulfil, perform**) **a ~** ein Versprechen halten; **to make a ~** ein Versprechen geben; **to make good a ~** ein Versprechen halten (od. erfüllen)

promise *v* versprechen, zusagen, zusichern; **to ~ a reward** e-e Belohnung aussetzen; ausloben

promised, an expressly ~ quality e-e ausdrücklich zugesicherte Eigenschaft

promising vielversprechend, erfolgversprechend; **~ candidate** aussichtsreicher Kandidat

promisee Versprechensempfänger; jd, dem ein (Vertrags-)Angebot gemacht wird; **joint ~** →joint creditor

promiser →promisor

promisor Versprechensgeber, Versprechender; **joint ~** →joint creditor

promissory versprechend, ein Versprechen enthaltend; **~ →estoppel**

promissory note[144] (P/N, p.n.) Schuldanerkenntnis; Schuldschein; Eigenwechsel, Solawechsel; **~ made out to bearer** Inhaberwechsel; **maker of a ~** Aussteller e-s Eigenwechsels *(opp. payee)*; **to make a ~** e-n Eigenwechsel ausstellen

promissory, ~ →oath; ~ representation →representation 3.

promote *v* fördern, unterstützen, vorantreiben; gründen; *(jdn)* befördern; werben für, Reklame machen für, durch Reklame Verkauf *(e-s Artikels)* fördern; **to ~ a bill** *Br parl* die Verabschiedung e-s Gesetzes *(private bill; →bill 3.)* unterstützen; **to ~ a company** e-e (Handels-)Gesellschaft gründen; **to ~ sales** den Verkauf fördern

promoted, he was ~ to the rank of major er wurde zum Major befördert; **to be ~ with preference** (or **to be preferentially ~**) bevorzugt befördert werden

promoting, ~ syndicate *Br* Gründerkonsortium *(bes. Banken, die sich mit der Durchführung von Emissionsgeschäften zum Zwecke der erstmaligen Finanzierung e-s Unternehmens befassen)*; **cost of ~** Gründungskosten

promoter Förderer; Gründer *(e-s Unternehmens)*; Veranstalter; *Br parl* jd, der die Initiative für die Verabschiedung e-s Gesetzes *(private bill)* ergreift; **~s** *Br* Geschäftsleute, die Emissions- und Gründungsgeschäfte betreiben *(→promoting syndicate)*; **~s' shares** (or **stock**) Gründeraktien

promotion 1. Förderung, Unterstützung; Gründung, Errichtung *(e-r Handelsgesellschaft)*; Werbung, Reklame; **~ department** *Am* Werbeabteilung; **~ expense** Gründungskosten, Gründungsaufwand; **~ manager** *Am* Werbeleiter; **~ matter** *Am* Werbematerial; **~ money** *Br (dem promoter e-r Gesellschaft gezahlte)* Gründungskosten; **~ shares** Gründeraktien; **export ~** Ausfuhrförderung; **sales ~** Verkaufsförderung *(Verfahren zur Auftragserlangung)*

promotion 2. Beförderung; **~ according to** (or **by**) **ability** Beförderung nach Fähigkeiten; **~ according to** (or **by**) **seniority** Beförderung nach dem Dienstalter; **~ by selection** Beförderung außer der Reihe; **~ list** Beförderungsliste; **~ of prospective managers** (or **of managerial personnel**) Nachwuchsförderung für Betriebsführung; Förderung der Führungsnachwuchskräfte; **to get one's ~** befördert werden

promotional Beförderungs-; Werbe-, Reklame-; **~ classification change** *Am* Einstufung in e-e höhere Gehaltsstufe; **~ expenses** *Am* Werbungskosten; **~ prices** *Am* Werbepreise; **~ selling** Werbeverkauf

promotive of monopoly *Am* monopolfördernd

prompt (ppt) prompt, baldmöglichst, umgehend *(Handelsklausel, die besagt, daß die Leistung* *umgehend, d.h. binnen kürzester Frist, zu erfolgen hat);* ~**s** Br *(Warenbörse)* sofort lieferbare Ware(n); ~ **answer** →~ reply; ~ **attention to an order** sofortige Erledigung e-s Auftrags; ~ **cash** umgehende Zahlung *(innerhalb weniger Tage)*; ~ **delivery** sofortige Lieferung, Lieferung innerhalb kürzester Frist; ~ **forwarding** sofortiger Versand; ~ **note** *(dem Käufer vom Verkäufer übergebene)* Verkaufsnota mit Angabe der zu zahlenden Summe und der Zahlungsfrist; ~ **payer** pünktlicher Zahler; ~ **reply** umgehende Antwort; ~ **shipment** sofortiger Wechsel; **at a** ~ **of 3 months** gegen Dreimonatsziel: gegen e-e (Zahlungs-)Frist von 3 Monaten

promptly[145] prompt, innerhalb e-r kurzen Frist; **to attend to a matter** ~ e-e Sache umgehend erledigen

promulgate *v (öffentl.)* bekanntmachen; *(Gesetz)* verkünden, veröffentlichen; **to be** ~**d** verkündet werden, ergehen *(Gesetz)*

promulgation *(öffentl.)* Bekanntmachung; Verkündung, Veröffentlichung

prone geneigt (to zu); anfällig (to für); ~ **to crises** krisenanfällig

proneness to crises Krisenanfälligkeit

pronounce *v* aussprechen, verkünden, erklären; **to** ~ **an acquittal** e-n Freispruch verkünden, freisprechen; **to** ~ **a judgment** ein Urteil verkünden

pronouncement Verkündung, Erklärung; ~ **of judgment** Urteilsverkündung

proof 1. Beweis (of für); *(überzeugendes)* Beweismittel; ~ **of authenticity** Beweis der Echtheit

proof, ~ **of guilt** Schuldbeweis; ~ **of a witness** *Br (vom solicitor aufgenommene)* schriftl. Niederlegung der geplanten mündlichen Aussage e-s Zeugen vor Gericht

proof to the contrary Gegenbeweis; **to produce** ~ den Gegenbeweis führen

proof, as ~ **of** zum Beweis für; **burden of** ~ Beweislast; **reversal of the burden of** ~ Umkehr der Beweislast; **to place the burden of** ~ **on a p.** jdm die Beweislast auferlegen; **to shift the burden of** ~ die Beweislast umkehren; **the burden of** ~ **lies on** (or **rests with**) **plaintiff** der Kläger ist beweispflichtig (od. trägt die Beweislast)

proof, convincing ~ überzeugender Beweis; **documentary** ~ Urkundenbeweis, Beweis durch Urkunden; **failing** (or **for lack of**) ~ mangels Beweises; →**onus of** ~; **upon** ~ wenn bewiesen ist; **to adduce as** ~ als Beweis anführen; **to furnish** (or **give**) ~ Beweis liefern (od. erbringen), beweisen; **to lead** ~ *Scot* Beweis antreten (od. erbringen); **to produce** ~ Beweis liefern (od. erbringen); **to provide for** ~ s. to furnish →~; **he was put to strict** ~ er mußte ganz klar beweisen; **to supply** ~ Beweis liefern; **to take** ~**s** *Br* Zeugenaussagen *(vor der Verhandlung)* aufnehmen

proof 2. Nachweis, Beleg

proof (in bankruptcy) Nachweis (od. Anmeldung) e-r Konkursforderung; **admission (rejection) of** ~**s** Zulassung (Zurückweisung) von angemeldeten Konkursforderungen; **to lodge one's** ~ seine Konkursforderung anmelden

proof, ~ **of ability** Befähigungsnachweis; ~ **of authority** Nachweis der Vertretungsbefugnis

proof of (a) claim Forderungsnachweis; Nachweis e-r Forderung; *(VersR)* Anspruchsbegründung; **to file a** ~ e-e Konkursforderung anmelden

proof of (a) debt Nachweis e-r Forderung *(z.B. gegen e-n Konkursschuldner, e-e verstorbene Person, e-e partnership etc)*; Anmeldung e-r Konkursforderung; **to lodge** (or **make**) **a** ~ den Nachweis für e-e Forderung bringen; e-e Konkursforderung *(bei Gericht)* anmelden

proof of identity Nachweis der Identität; **submission of** ~ Vorlage des Personalausweises

proof, ~ **of loss** *(VersR)* Schadensnachweis; ~ **of nationality** Nachweis der Staatsangehörigkeit; ~ **of need** Nachweis der Bedürftigkeit; ~ **of origin** Herkunftsnachweis; ~ **of ownership** Eigentumsnachweis; ~ **of qualification** Befähigungsnachweis; ~ **of a right** Nachweis e-s Rechts; ~ **of service** Zustellungsnachweis; ~ **of title** Nachweis des Eigentumsrechts; ~ **of a will** →probate; **to furnish** (or **give**) ~ **(of)** Nachweis erbringen (od. führen) (für); **to require** ~ Nachweis(e) benötigen; **to show** ~ nachweisen

proof 3. Korrekturbogen; ~**-reading** Korrekturlesen; **revised** ~ Umbruch

proof 4. -sicher (against gegen); ~ **against corruption** unbestechlich; **burglar**~ diebessicher; **crisis-**~ krisenfest; **fire-**~ feuersicher; **judgment** ~ *Am* nicht eintreibbar

propaganda Propaganda; Reklame, Werbung; ~ **campaign** Reklamefeldzug; ~ **leaflet** Flugblatt; ~ **machinery** Propagandamaschine; ~ **for war** Kriegspropaganda; ~ **writings** Propagandaschriften, Reklameschriften; **atrocity** ~ Greuelpropaganda; **discontinuance of** ~ Einstellung der Propaganda; **election** ~ Wahlpropaganda; **to carry on** (or **make**) ~ Propaganda machen (od. treiben)

propagandist Propagandist

propensity Neigung, Hang (for zu); ~ **to consume** Konsumneigung, Konsumfreudigkeit; ~ **to import** Importneigung; ~ **to invest** Investitionsneigung, Anlagebereitschaft; ~ **to save** Sparneigung, Sparfreudigkeit

proper passend, geeignet, angemessen (to für);

ordnungsgemäß, sachgemäß, eigentlich; ~ **authority** zuständige Behörde; ~ **care** angemessene (od. nötige) Sorgfalt; ~ **custody** ordnungsgemäße Aufbewahrung; ~ **interpretation** richtige Auslegung; **the ~ law** (IPR) das angemessenerweise *(nach den objektiven Verknüpfungen des Falles)* anzuwendende Recht; ~ **law of contract** *(IPR)* das angemessenerweise auf e-n Vertrag anzuwendende Recht; ~ **meaning** eigentliche Bedeutung; ~ **measures** geeignete Maßnahmen; ~ **name** Eigenname; ~ **use** ordnungsgemäße Verwendung; **at the ~ time** zur gegebenen Zeit; zur rechten Zeit; **in the ~ form** formgerecht, in ordnungsmäßiger Form; **in the ~ sense** im eigentlichen Sinn; **through the ~ channels** auf dem Dienstwege

propert|y Eigentum; Eigentumsrecht; Vermögen, Vermögensgegenstand, Vermögenswert(e); *(bebautes oder unbebautes)* Grundstück; Grundbesitz, Grund und Boden, Landbesitz; (charakteristische) Eigenschaft; **~ies** *Br* Immobilien, Grundstücke, Liegenschaften; ~ **account** Anlagenkonto; Immobilienkonto

property, to acquire ~ Vermögen (od. Eigentum) erwerben; **to alienate ~** Vermögen veräußern; **to charge ~ as a security for a loan** *Br* Grundbesitz mit e-r Hypothek belasten; **to come into ~** Vermögen erben; **to convey (the title to) ~** Eigentum übertragen; **to enter the ~** das Grundstück betreten; **to hold ~** Eigentum haben; Vermögen besitzen; **to be liable to the extent of one's ~** mit s-m ganzen Vermögen haften; **to manage ~** *Br* Grundbesitz verwalten; **~ passes to** das Vermögen geht über auf; **to realize ~** Vermögen flüssig machen; **to remain the exclusive ~ of the vendor** ausschließliches Eigentum des Verkäufers bleiben; **to seize ~** Vermögen beschlagnahmen; **to transfer ~** Eigentum (od. Vermögen) übertragen; **the insurance company writes ~ and casualty lines** *Am* die Versicherungsgesellschaft betreibt Schadens- und Unfallversicherungszweige

property adjustment order *Br (EhescheidungsR)* Verfügung des Vermögensausgleichs

Übertragung von Vermögensgegenständen von einem Ehegatten auf den anderen oder auf die Kinder nach freiem Ermessen des Gerichts, das dabei die im Matrimonial Causes Act 1973, s. 25 aufgezählten Umstände in Betracht ziehen muß. Tatsächlich ist auf diese Weise mehr oder weniger – besonders bei länger bestehenden Ehen mit Kindern – der Güterausgleich bei der Ehescheidung eingeführt worden

property, ~ administration *Br* Häuserverwaltung; ~ **administrator** Hausverwalter; ~ **assets** Vermögenswerte; ~ **charges** *Am* Grundstückslasten; ~ **company** Immobiliengesellschaft; ~ **control** Vermögensaufsicht; ~ **crime** *Am* Eigentumsdelikt; ~ **damage** →damage to ~; ~ **damage (liability) insurance** Sachschaden- (Haftpflicht-) Versicherung; ~ **dealer** *Br* Grundstücksverkäufer; ~ **developer** *Br* Bauunternehmer, Grundstückserschließungs- und Verwaltungsgesellschaft; ~ **development** Grundstückserschließung; Entwicklung (Meliorisierung) e-s Bezirks durch die Errichtung von Läden, Schulen etc; ~ **dividend** Sachwertdividende *(statt Bardividende; z.B. Am Verteilung von Wertpapieren aus dem Bestand der Gesellschaft)*; ~ **divisible amongst creditors** *Br* Konkursmasse; ~ **fund** Immobilienfonds *(e-r Investmentgesellschaft)*; ~ **held on trust** Treuhandvermögen; ~ **holdings** Vermögenswerte; ~ **income** Einkommen aus Kapitalvermögen; ~ **insurance** Sachversicherung; ~ **interest** Vermögensinteressen; ~ **investment** Kapitalanlage in Grundbesitz; ~ **law** s. law of →~; ~ **ledger** Anlagenbuch; ~ **left** Nachlaß; ~ **levy** Vermögensabgabe; ~ **liability insurance** Sachhaftpflichtversicherung; ~ **loss** Vermögensverlust, Vermögensschaden; ~ **management** *Br* Vermögensverwaltung; Grundstücksverwaltung; Hausverwaltung; ~ **manager** *Br* Grundstücksverwalter; Hausverwalter; ~ **market** *Br* Grundstücksmarkt, Immobilienmarkt; ~ **of another** *Am (StrafR)* fremdes Eigentum; ~ **of state** *Am* Staatseigentum; ~ **owner** Grund(stücks)eigentümer, Hauseigentümer; (Haus- und) Grundbesitzer; ~ **passing on death** Vermögen, das beim Tode an die Erben übergeht; Erbschaft; ~ **plant and equipment** *Am (Bilanz)* Grundstücke und Gebäude, Maschinen und maschinelle Anlagen; ~ **prices** *Br* Grundstückspreise; ~ **register** *Br* Teil des Grundbuchblattes *(im →Land Register, neben proprietorship register, charges register)*; ~ **right** Eigentumsrecht, Vermögensrecht; **~, rights and interests** *(VölkerR)* Eigentum, Rechte und Interessen; ~ **settlement** Vermögensvertrag (→*settlement 3.*); ~ **speculation** Grundstücksspekulation; ~ **subject to a charge** (or **to charges**) belasteter Grundbesitz; ~ **tax** Grundsteuer; *Am* Vermögensteuer; ~ **tort** unerlaubte Handlung gegen das Eigentum od. Vermögen; Eigentums- od. Vermögensverletzung (durch unerlaubte Handlung); ~ **transactions** *Br* Grundstücksgeschäfte; **assessed ~ value** geschätzter Grundstückswert

property, accession of ~ Vermögenszuwachs; **accumulation of ~** Vermögensanhäufung; **acquisition of ~** Eigentumserwerb, Vermögenserwerb; **administration of ~** Vermögensverwaltung; **administrator of ~** Vermögensverwalter; **after-acquired ~** nach der Heirat erworbenes Vermögen; **alien ~** Ausländervermögen; **blocking of ~** Vermögenssperre; **built-on ~** bebautes Grundstück; **business** (or **commercial**) **~** Geschäftsgrundstück; **common ~** gemeinschaftliches Eigentum (od. Vermögen); Allgemeingut; **community ~** *Am (EheR)* Gütergemeinschaft; *(meist)* Errungenschaftsgemeinschaft (→*community 2.*); **company** ~ Gesellschaftsvermögen, Firmenvermögen; **conveyance of** ~ Übertragung von Vermögen; Eigentumsübertragung; **corporate** ~ *Am* Gesellschaftsvermögen; *Br* Gemeindevermögen; **cultural** ~ Kulturgüter; **division of** ~ Vermögensteilung; **enemy** ~ Feindvermögen; **exclusive** ~ ausschließliches Eigentum; **external** (or **foreign**) ~ ausländisches Vermögen, Auslandsvermögen; **freehold** ~ Grundeigentum, Grundbesitz (→*freehold*); **general** ~ unbeschränktes Eigentumsrecht *(which every absolute owner has; opp. special ~)*; **government** ~ Staatseigentum; **immovable** ~ *Am*[146] unbewegliches Vermögen, Immobilien; **industrial** ~ gewerbliches Eigentum (→*industrial*); **injury to** ~ Sachschaden; Sachbeschädigung; **intangible** ~ unkörperliche Vermögenswerte *(umfaßt nicht nur Bankguthaben od. Aktien sondern jede Art von Forderungen; opp. tangible ~)*; **intellectual** ~ *(UrhR)*[147] geistiges Eigentum; **inventory of** ~ Vermögensverzeichnis, Vermögensaufstellung; **items of** ~ Vermögensgegenstände; **joint** ~ Miteigentum *(zur gesamten Hand)*; gemeinsames Vermögen; **law of** ~ Sachenrecht *(einschließlich Liegenschaftsrecht; →law)*; **literary** ~ *(urheberrechtlich geschütztes)* geistiges Eigentum; **literary and artistic** ~ **rights** *(UrhR)* literarische und künstlerische Eigentumsrechte; **leasehold** ~ gemieteter (od. gepachteter) Grundbesitz; (→*leasehold*); **loss of** ~ Vermögensverlust, Vermögensschaden; **lost** ~ verlorene Sache, Fundsache(n) (→*lost*); **man of** ~ vermögender (od. wohlhabender) Mann; **mixed** ~ bewegliches und unbewegliches Vermögen; **movable** ~ bewegliches Vermögen (→*movable*); **offenses against** ~ *Am*[148] Straftaten gegen das Eigentum; **offence relating to entering and remaining on** ~ *Br* strafbare Handlung im Zusammenhang mit Betreten von und Verbleiben auf Grundbesitz; **partnership** ~ Gesellschaftsvermögen; **passing of** ~ Eigentumsübergang; Vermögensübergang

property, personal ~[149] bewegliches Vermögen, Mobiliarvermögen, Mobilien; beweglicher Nachlaß

Der Begriff personal property umfaßt die chattels personal (bewegl. Sachen) und die choses in action (heute alle Forderungsrechte, ferner Patent-, Warenzeichen-, Urheber- und Musterschutzrechte, Aktienrechte). Daneben gehören zu personal property die sog. →chattels real (z. B. Miet- und Pachtrechte)

property, possession of ~ Besitz von Vermögen; **present and future** ~ gegenwärtiges und künftiges Vermögen; →**private** ~; **qualified** ~ →special ~; **public** ~ Staatseigentum, Eigentum der öffentlichen Hand

property, real ~[149] Grundvermögen, Immobiliarvermögen, Immobilien, Grundstück(e), Liegenschaften; unbeweglicher Nachlaß; **real** ~ **holdings** Grundstücksbesitz; **real** ~ **interest** Anteil (od. Recht) an Grundbesitz; **real** ~ **law** Liegenschaftsrecht; **real** ~ **lien** *Am* Grundstücksbelastung; **real** ~ **tax** *Am* Grundsteuer *(Kommunalsteuer)*; **real** ~ **transfer tax** *Am* Grunderwerbssteuer; **credit on real** ~ Realkredit; Immobiliarkredit; **interest in real** ~ Anteil an Grundbesitz; **owner of real** ~ Grundstückseigentümer

Real property umfaßt alle Rechte an Grundstücken mit Ausnahme derjenigen, die als personal property gelten. Rechte an Grundstücken, die geringer als →freehold interests sind, gelten als →chattels real und gehören zu personal property

property, schedule of ~ Vermögensverzeichnis; →**separate** ~; **settlement of** ~ →settlement 3.; **special** ~ spezielles (od. beschränktes) Eigentum *(1. wenn e-e zweckgebundene Übergabe der Sache stattgefunden hat, z.B. erhält beim →bailment der →bailee special ~, während das general ~ beim bailor verbleibt; 2. wenn die Sache nicht im unbeschränkten Eigentum e-r Person stehen kann, z.B. bei wilden Tieren; opp. general ~)*

property, tangible ~ körperliche (od. greifbare) Vermögenswerte *(z.B. Maschinen, Warenvorräte)*; Sachvermögen; **taxation of** ~ Vermögensbesteuerung; **transfer of** ~ Eigentumsübertragung; Vermögensübertragung; **the whole of one's** ~ sein ganzes Vermögen

propone *v Scot* vorbringen *(z.B. e-e Einrede)*

proponent jd, der e-n Vorschlag macht; *Br* Antragsteller; *Am* jd, der dem Gericht ein Testament zur Bestätigung (probate) vorlegt

proportion Anteil, Teil; Verhältnis; ~ **of costs** Kostenanteil; ~ **of profit** Gewinnanteil; **in** ~ im Verhältnis (to zu), verhältnismäßig, anteilsmäßig; **out of** ~ unverhältnismäßig; **out of all** ~ in gar keinem Verhältnis stehend (to zu)

proportion *v* verhältnismäßig verteilen, umlegen; in das richtige Verhältnis bringen, anpassen; **to** ~ **one's expenditure to one's income** s-e Ausgaben dem Einkommen anpassen

proportional proportional, verhältnismäßig, anteilmäßig; ~**(ly) to** im Verhältnis zu; ~ **representation** (P.R.) Verhältniswahl(system); ~ **share** verhältnismäßiger Anteil, Quote; ~ **tax** Proportionalsteuer; ~ **vote** Verhältniswahl, Proportionalwahl

proportionality, principle of ~ Grundsatz der Verhältnismäßigkeit

proposal Vorschlag; Plan; (Versicherungs-)Antrag; Heiratsantrag; *Br*[150] *(dem master der Chancery Division eingereichter)* Antrag; ~ **for amendment** Änderungsvorschlag; ~**(s) for a composition** Vergleichsvorschlag, -angebot *(mit Gläubigern)*; ~ **for peace** Friedensangebot; **~(s) for a settlement** Vergleichsvorschlag, -angebot; ~ **form** *(VersR)* Antragsformular; Policenformular; ~ **of insurance** Antrag auf Abschluß e-r Versicherung; ~ **of marriage** Heiratsantrag; **~s received** eingegangene Anträge; **alternative** (or **counter-**) ~ Gegenvorschlag; **on the** ~ **of** auf Vorschlag von; **right of** ~ Vorschlagsrecht; **to adopt a** ~ e-n Vorschlag annehmen; **to approve** (or **agree to**) **a** ~ e-m Vorschlag zustimmen; **to decline a** ~ *(VersR)* e-n Antrag ablehnen; **to make a** ~ e-n Vorschlag machen; **to put forward appropriate ~s** geeignete Vorschläge unterbreiten; **to refuse** (or **reject**) **a** ~ e-n Vorschlag ablehnen; **to submit ~s** Vorschläge unterbreiten; **to submit a** ~ **for a policy** e-n Versicherungsantrag stellen

propose *v* vorschlagen; beantragen; *(Kandidaten)* aufstellen; **to** ~ **sb. for an office** jdn für ein Amt vorschlagen; jdn nominieren; **to** ~ **to a p.** jdm e-n Heiratsantrag machen; **to** ~ **an insurance** e-e Versicherung beantragen; **to** ~ **a motion** e-n Antrag stellen; **to** ~ **a resolution** e-e Entschließung einbringen; **to** ~ **terms of settlement** e-n Vergleichsvorschlag machen

proposed in Aussicht gestellt, geplant; ~ **amendment** Änderungsvorlage; ~ **modification** Änderungsvorschlag; ~ **budget** Haushaltsvorlage

proposer *(VersR)* Antragsteller

proposition Vorschlag; Antrag; *colloq.* Geschäft, Unternehmen; **to put forward a** ~ e-n Vorschlag einbringen

propound *v (Frage)* vorlegen, unterbreiten; **to** ~ **a will** *Br* auf Anerkennung e-s Testaments klagen (for obtaining probate in solemn form)

propria, in ~ **persona** ("in one's own person") *Am* in eigener Person *(nicht durch e-n Anwalt vertreten)*

proprietary Eigentums-; vermögensrechtlich; gesetzlich (od. patentrechtlich, urheberrechtlich) geschützt; ~ **account** Eigenkapitalkonto; ~ **article** Markenartikel; ~ **assurance** *Br* →~ insurance; ~ **capital** *Am* Eigenkapital *(e-s Unternehmens)*; ~ **classes** besitzende Klassen; ~ **company** *Am* Holdinggesellschaft, Dachgesellschaft; *(VersR)* Kapitalgesellschaft, Versicherungs-Aktiengesellschaft *(opp. mutual company)*; *(Australien und Südafrika: mit Zusatz Pty. Ltd. zu ihrem Namen)* GmbH (private limited company); ~ **goods** Markenwaren; ~ **insurance** *Br* Versicherung gegen Prämie *(opp. mutual insurance)*; ~ **insurance company** Versicherungsgesellschaft auf Aktienbasis *(opp. mutual insurance company)*; ~ **interest** Vermögensrecht; *(gewerbl.)* Eigentumsrecht; ~ **life office** *Br* Lebensversicherungsgesellschaft auf Aktienbasis; ~ **name** gesetzlich geschützter Name; **industrial property of a** ~ **nature** rechtlich geschütztes gewerbliches Eigentum; ~ **office** *Br* Versicherungsgesellschaft auf Aktienbasis

proprietary right Eigentumsrecht; **reservation of** ~ Eigentumsvorbehalt

proprietor Eigentümer, Besitzer; Inhaber; ~ **of a business** (or **firm**) Firmeninhaber, Geschäftsinhaber; **~'s capital** Eigenkapital; Kapital des Einzelunternehmers; ~ **of a design**[151] Inhaber e-s Musters; **~'s equity** *Am (Bilanz)* Eigenkapital; ~ **of a patent** Patentinhaber; ~ **of a trademark**[152] Inhaber e-s Warenzeichens; **joint ~s** Miteigentümer, Mitinhaber; *Br*[153] gemeinsame Markeninhaber; **landed** ~ Grundeigentümer, Grundbesitzer; →**registered** ~; **riparian** ~ Uferanlieger; →**sole** ~

proprietorship Eigentumsrecht, Eigentum; Inhaberschaft *(an Rechten)*; *Am (Bilanz)* Eigenkapital; ~ **register** *Br* Bezeichnung des Grundstückseigentümers im →Land Register; **corporate** ~ *Am* Gesellschaftskapital; **individual** (or **single**) ~ *Am* Einzelfirma, Einzelunternehmen; →**sole** ~

proprietress Eigentümerin, Inhaberin

propriet|y Angemessenheit; Anstand; **~ies** Anstandsformen; korrektes Verhalten

pro querente ("for the plaintiff") (pro quer.) für den Kläger

pro rata ("in proportion") verhältnismäßig, dem Anteil entsprechend, anteilig; ~ **apportionment** anteilmäßige Aufteilung (between zwischen); **on a** ~ **basis** anteilsmäßig; ~ **contribution** anteilmäßiger Beitrag, Anteil; ~ **freight** Distanzfracht; **freight paid** ~ anteilmäßige Fracht; ~ **share** verhältnismäßiger Anteil; ~ **temporis** (p.r.t.) entsprechend dem Zeitablauf, zeitanteilig

proratable *Am* anteilmäßig, verhältnismäßig; ~ **contribution** anteilmäßiger Beitrag

prorate *v Am* anteilmäßig (od. nach e-m bestimmten Schlüssel) aufteilen; umlegen; **to** ~ **profits** Gewinne anteilmäßig verteilen; **~d expense** Schlüsselgemeinkosten

proration *Am* anteilmäßige Aufteilung

prorogation *parl* Vertagung *(Br bis zur nächsten Sitzungsperiode, ohne das Parlament aufzulösen)*; *Scot* Unterwerfung unter ein nicht zuständiges Gericht

prorogue *v (Parlament)* (sich) vertagen

pros and cons Für und Wider

prosecute *v* 1. **to** ~ **sb. for sth.** jdn strafrechtlich verfolgen wegen, jdn anklagen wegen; **to** ~ **a company** gegen e-e Gesellschaft strafrechtlich vorgehen

prosecuted, bill-stickers will be ~ Zettelankleben ist bei Strafe verboten

prosecuting, ~ **attorney** *Am* (~ **counsel** *Br*) Anklagevertreter; ~ **authority** Strafverfolgungsbehörde; ~ **officer** *Am* Strafverfolgungsbeamter

prosecute *v* 2. betreiben, *(gerichtlich)* verfolgen; **to** ~ **an action** *(Zivilprozeß)* e-n Prozeß betreiben (od. führen); **to** ~ **a claim** e-e Forderung einklagen; e-n Anspruch *(gerichtl.)* verfolgen; **to** ~ **an inquiry** e-e Untersuchung durchführen; **to** ~ **a suit** *bes. Am (als Kläger)* e-n Prozeß führen

prosecuting, ~ **the law** Rechtsdurchsetzung; ~ **party** klagende Partei

prosecution 1. *(Strafprozeß)* Strafverfolgung; Anklage(erhebung); Anklagevertretung; **counsel for the** ~ Anklagevertreter

prosecution, criminal ~ strafrechtliche Verfolgung; **initiation of criminal** ~ Strafantrag; **to render o.s. liable to criminal** ~ sich strafrechtlicher Verfolgung aussetzen, sich strafbar machen

Prosecution, Crown ~ **Service** (CPS) *Br* Strafverfolgungsbehörde; Staatsanwaltschaft *(für England und Wales)*

Seit Oktober 1986 ist der CPS zuständig für die gerichtliche Verfolgung der meisten Straftaten; die Behörde beschäftigt fest angestellte Crown →Prosecutors

prosecution, Director of Public P~s (DPP) *Br* Leiter der Anklagebehörde *(cf. prosecutor)*

Dem Director of Public Prosecutions *(barrister od. solicitor mit wenigstens 10 Berufsjahren)* und seiner Behörde obliegt die Erhebung und juristische Vorbereitung der Anklage bei bes. wichtigen od. schwierigen Fällen. Für die Vertretung der Anklage vor dem Gericht engagiert diese Anklagebehörde aber von Fall zu Fall private Anwälte *(Anwälte können also sowohl als Verteidiger als auch als Ankläger auftreten)*. Seit Oktober 1986 leitet der DPP den Crown →*Prosecution Service*

prosecution, liable to ~ strafbar; →**malicious** ~; **statement of the** ~ Vortrag der Anklagebehörde, Anklagerede; **witness for the** ~ Belastungszeuge; **to discharge from** ~ *(den Angeklagten)* außer Verfolgung setzen; **to initiate a** ~ e-n Strafantrag stellen; **not to proceed with a** ~ die Strafverfolgung einstellen; **to render o.s. liable to** ~ sich strafbar machen

prosecution 2. Verfolgung, Fortsetzung, Durchführung *(e-s Plans od. Verfahrens)*; Betreiben *(e-r Tätigkeit)*; ~ **of an action** *(Zivilprozeß)* Rechtsverfolgung; Prozeßführung; ~ **of a claim** Verfolgung e-s Anspruchs; Einklagen e-r Forderung; ~ **of a right** Verfolgung e-s Rechts; Rechtsdurchsetzung; ~ **of the voyage** Fortsetzung der Fahrt *(e-s Schiffes)*; **want of** ~ mangelnde Prozeßverfolgung, Prozeßverschleppung

prosecutor Ankläger, Vertreter der Anklage, *(etwa)* Staatsanwalt *(Am cf. district attorney)*; **Crown** ~ *Br* Vertreter der Anklagebehörde; Staatsanwalt; **public** ~ öffentlicher Ankläger, Staatsanwalt

Im anglo-amerikanischen Recht ist wie im deutschen Recht die Strafverfolgung öffentlich. Ankläger ist immer der Staat (*Am* Bund od. Einzelstaat, je nachdem ob ein Bundesgesetz od. einzelstaatl. Gesetz verletzt wurde). Eine Strafsache wird deshalb bezeichnet *Br* R. (Regina or Rex) v. X; *Am* State (or People or US) v. X

prospect Aussicht; Schurf, Schürfstelle; voraussichtlicher Kunde, Reflektant, Interessent; ~**s for the future** (or **future** ~**s**) Zukunftsaussichten; ~**s of the market** Konjunkturaussichten; ~**s of success** Erfolgschancen; **cyclical** ~**s** Konjunkturaussichten; **crop** ~**s** Ernteaussichten; **spot giving** ~**s of mineral deposit** Stelle mit Anzeichen für Mineralvorkommen; **this profession has good** (or **favo[u]rable**) ~**s** (or **the** ~**s in this profession are good**) dieser Beruf ist aussichtsreich

prospect *v* schürfen (for nach); prospektieren; auf Mineralvorkommen prüfen; **to** ~ **for gold** nach Gold schürfen; **to** ~ **for oil** nach Öl bohren; **authority to** ~ Schürfgenehmigung; **freedom to** ~ Schürfgenehmigung

prospecting Prospektierung, Schürfen, Erkundung nutzbarer Bodenschätze; ~ **licen|ce(~se)** (or **permit**) Schürfgenehmigung

prospective in Aussicht stehend, voraussichtlich, zukünftig; (nur) in die Zukunft wirkend; ~ **buyer** (Kauf-)Interessent, Reflektant; ~ **customer** voraussichtlicher Kunde; ~ **damages** Ersatz für zukünftigen Schaden; ~ **legislation** zukünftige Gesetzgebung; ~ **managers** →promotion of ~ managers; ~ **overruling** *Am* zukünftig abweichende Rechtsprechung; ~ **subscriber** voraussichtlicher Zeichner

prospector Prospektor, Schürfer; großer Spekulant

prospectus Prospekt, Werbeschrift; (Emissions-) Prospekt[154] *(Offenlegung der Vermögensverhältnisse e-r Gesellschaft, verbunden mit Zeichnungseinladung vor Einführung von neuen Wertpapieren an der Börse)*; ~ **liability** Prospekthaftung; **to issue a** ~ **(of a company)** e-n Prospekt ausgeben (od. veröffentlichen)

prosper *v* blühen, florieren; gut gehen *(Geschäft)*

prosperity Prosperität, Wohlstand, *(wirtschaftliches)* Gedeihen; *(Konjunkturzyklus)* Aufschwung *(opp. depression)*; ~ **phase** Hochkonjunktur; **continuance of** ~ Anhalten der Konjunktur; **index of** ~ Wohlstandsindex; **national** ~ Wohlstand der Nation; **world** ~ Wohlstand in der Welt; **to adapt social security benefits to increasing** ~ die Sozialleistungen dem steigenden Wohlstand anpassen

prosperous blühend, erfolgreich; wohlhabend; ~ **years** Jahre des Wohlstandes, günstige Jahre

prostitute Prostituierte

prostitution[155] Prostitution, gewerbsmäßige Unzucht; **promoting** ~ Förderung der Prostitution

pro tanto ("for so much") insoweit, insofern

protect *v* 1. schützen, beschützen; protegieren; durch Schutzzölle schützen; **to** ~ **a bill** für e-n Wechsel einstehen *(dafür sorgen, daß er bei Fälligkeit bezahlt wird)*; **to** ~ **a p.'s interests** jds Interessen wahren (od. wahrnehmen)

protected, ~ **articles** durch Einfuhrzölle geschützte Waren; ~ **by law** gesetzlich geschützt; ~ **by (letters) patent** patentrechtlich geschützt; ~ **children** *Br*[156] versorgte Kinder, Kinder, für die e-e Adoption vorgesehen ist, sowie anderweitig untergebrachte Kinder, die keine Pflegekinder (→foster children) sind; ~ **person** Protegierter, Schützling; ~ **tenant** unter Kündigungsschutz stehender Mieter; ~ **works** *(UrhR)* geschützte Werke

protecting duty Schutzzoll

protect *v* 2. *(VölkerR)* schützen

protected, British ~ **person** britischer Schutzangehöriger *(Angehöriger der Protektorate, der geschützten Staaten, Mandats- und Treuhandsgebiete)*; **internationally** ~ **person** völkerrechtlich geschützte Person; ~ **state** *Br*[157] geschützter Staat *(unter brit. Schutzherrschaft stehender fremder Staat, dessen Außenpolitik vom Vereinigten Königreich geführt wird, der sich aber im übrigen selbst regiert)*

protecting, ~ **power** Schutzmacht; ~ **state** Schutzstaat

protection Schutz; Protektion, persönliche Förderung; Zollschutz, Schutzzoll(system) *(opp. free trade)*; Versicherungsschutz; ~ **against accidents** Unfallschutz; ~ **against dismissal**[158] Kündigungsschutz *(des Arbeitnehmers)*; ~ **against eviction** Kündigungsschutz *(des Mieters)*

protection and indemnity (P. & I.) *(VersR)* Reederhaftpflicht; **P~ and I~ Club** *Br* Reedervereinigung für die Versicherung von Risiken; ~ **risks** Reeder-Haftpflichtrisiken

protection, ~ **by (letters) patent** Patentschutz; ~ **during pregnancy and maternity** Mutterschutz; ~ **from execution** Vollstreckungsschutz; ~ **gang** Erpresserbande, die unter Androhung von Gewalt gegen Personen od. Vermögen Geld fordert *(cf.* ~ *money)*; ~ **money** *(als Schutz gegen Verfolgung)* von Privatpersonen an Verbrecher(organisation) gezahltes Geld, Schutzgeld; *Am (auch)* von Verbrechern an Polizei gezahltes Bestechungsgeld; ~ **of a bill** Einstehen für e-n Wechsel durch Einlösung (od. Bezahlung); ~ **of consumers** Verbraucherschutz; ~ **of creditors** *(KonkursR)* Gläubigerschutz; ~ **of the environment** Umweltschutz; ~ **of industrial property** gewerblicher Rechtsschutz; ~ **of interests** Wahrung der Interessen; ~ **of inventors** Erfinderschutz; ~ **of labo(u)r** Arbeitsschutz; ~ **of literary and artistic works** Schutz von Werken der Literatur und Kunst *(cf. Berne →Convention)*; ~ **of minorities** *(VölkerR)* Minderheitenschutz; ~ **of nationals abroad** Schutz der Staatsangehörigen im Ausland; ~ **of registered designs** *Br* (Gebrauchs-) Musterschutz (→*design 2.*); ~ **of third parties acting in good faith** Schutz gutgläubiger Dritter; ~ **of trade marks** Warenzeichenschutz

Protection of Trading Interests Act 1980 (PTIA) *Br* Gesetz zum Schutze der Handelsinteressen

Nach § 1 des Gesetzes kann der Handelsminister Unternehmen anweisen, bestimmte ausländische Anordnungen, die den internationalen Handel betreffen, nicht zu befolgen. Nach § 2 kann er die Weitergabe von Informationen an ausländische Stellen verbieten

protection, ~ **racket** Erpressung unter Androhung von Gewalt gegen Person od. Vermögen *(cf.* ~ *money)*; ~ **sought** *(PatR)* begehrter Schutz; **copyright** ~ Urheberrechtsschutz; **Court of P~** *Br* →court; **duration of** ~ Schutzdauer; **employment** ~[158] Arbeitnehmerschutz; **equal** ~ **of law**[159] Gleichheit vor dem Gesetz; **extent of the** ~ Schutzumfang; **functional** ~ *(VölkerR)* Schutz der internationalen Beziehungen; **interests warranting** ~ schutzwürdige Interessen (od. Belange); **legal** ~ Rechtsschutz; **means of** ~ Schutzvorrichtungen; **scope of** ~ Schutzbereich

protection, time (or **term**) **of** ~ *(UrhR, PatR)* Schutzdauer; **expiration of the time of** ~ Ablauf der Schutzfrist; **to compute the time of** ~ die Schutzdauer berechnen

protection, to afford ~ Schutz gewähren; **to buy** ~ sich Schutz kaufen (→~ *money*); **to enjoy** ~ Schutz genießen; **to give** ~ **to a bill** e-n Wechsel einlösen (od. bezahlen); **to place o.s. under the** ~ **of a p.** sich unter jds Schutz begeben

protectionism Protektionismus, Schutzzollsystem *(opp. free trade)*

protectionist Protektionist, Anhänger des Schutzzollsystems; protektionistisch; ~ **tendencies** protektionistische Tendenzen

protective schützend, Schutz-; ~ **aspect of duties** Schutzwirkung der Zölle; ~ **clause** Schutzklausel; ~ **custody** Schutzgewahrsam;

~ **device** Schutzvorrichtung; ~ **duty** Schutzzoll *(opp. revenue duty)*; ~ **labor legislation** *Am* Arbeiterschutzgesetzgebung; ~ **measures** Schutzmaßnahmen; ~ **order** Schutzanordnung; ~ **rights** Schutzrechte; ~ **system** Schutzzollsystem *(opp. free trade)*; ~ **tariff** Schutzzoll; ~ **trade measures** Handelsschutzmaßnahmen; ~ **trust** *Br*[160] Trust auf Lebenszeit (od. kürzere Zeit) des Begünstigten, der bei Eintritt e-s bestimmten Ereignisses *(z.B. Konkurs)* beendet wird; *Am* Bezeichnung für →spendthrift trust

protector Protektor; Schirmherr; Förderer, Gönner; *(VölkerR)* Schutzmacht, Protektor

protectorate Protektorat, Schutzherrschaft, Schutzgebiet; *Br*[157] Protektorat *(unter britischer Schutzherrschaft stehendes Staatsgebiet, dessen Außenpolitik vom Vereinigten Königreich wahrgenommen wird. Die Einwohner sind British →protected persons)*

pro tempore ("for the time being") (pro tem, p.t.) gegenwärtig, vorübergehend, für jetzt, stellvertretend

protest 1. Protest, Einspruch, Widerspruch, Verwahrung; Beteuerung, feierl. Erklärung; ~ **demonstration** Protestkundgebung; ~ **meeting** Protestversammlung; **captain's** ~ Verklarung, Seeprotest; **election** ~ Wahleinspruch; **note of** ~ *(VölkerR)* Protestnote; **payment under** ~ Bezahlung unter Vorbehalt; **ship's** ~ s. captain's →~; **to enter** (or **lodge, make**) **a** ~ Verwahrung einlegen, Protest erheben (with bei)

protest 2. *(WechselR)*[161] Protest *(notarielle Beurkundung der Annahme- od. Zahlungsverweigerung; cf. noting)*; ~ **certificate** Protesturkunde; ~ **charges** (or **expenses, fees**) Protestkosten; ~ **in due course** rechtzeitig erhobener Protest; ~ **in the case of a foreign bill**[162] Protest im Falle e-s ausländischen Wechsels *(nur in diesem Falle ist Protest zur Wahrung der Regreßansprüche erforderlich)*; ~ **for better security** *Br*[163] Protest mangels genügender Sicherheit *(z.B. beim Konkurs des →acceptor)* ~ **for non(-)acceptance** Protest mangels Annahme; ~ **for non(-)payment** Protest mangels Zahlung; ~ **waived** (in case of dishono[u]r) ohne Protest; ohne Kosten; **act of** ~ Protest(aufnahme); **cost of** ~ Protestkosten; **deed of** ~ Protesturkunde

protest, due ~ rechtzeitiger (od. rechtzeitig erhobener) Protest; **past due** ~ zu spät erhobener Protest

protest, expenses of ~ Protestkosten; **notice of** ~ *Am* Mitteilung *(des Notars)* über Wechselprotest; **noting and** ~ →noting 2.; **place of** ~ Ort des Protestes; →**supra** ~; **waiver of** ~ Verzicht auf Protest; **to draw up** (or **enter, make**) **a** ~ (of a bill of exchange) Protest aufnehmen (od. erheben)

protest 3. *Br parl (im Oberhaus von e-m Peer schriftl. vorgebrachter)* Minderheitsprotest *(gegen e-n Antrag)*

protest *v* 1. protestieren, Einspruch erheben, Verwahrung einlegen; widersprechen; beteuern, feierl. versichern; **to** ~ **against** beanstanden; **to** ~ **to a government** bei e-r Regierung Verwahrung einlegen (od. Einspruch erheben); **to** ~ **one's innocence** s-e Unschuld beteuern; **to** ~ **against a measure** gegen e-e Maßnahme protestieren; **to** ~ **a witness** *Am* gegen e-n Zeugen Einspruch erheben

protest *v* 2. *(WechselR)* Protest aufnehmen *(Notar)*; zu Protest gehen lassen *(Inhaber e-s Wechsels)*; **to** ~ **a bill (of exchange) for non-acceptance (non[-]payment)** e-n Wechsel mangels Annahme (Zahlung) zu Protest gehen lassen

protested, ~ **bill (of exchange)** protestierter Wechsel; **person** ~ **against** Protestat *(jd, gegen den protestiert wird)*; **to cause the bill to be** ~ (or **to have the bill** ~) den Wechsel zu Protest gehen lassen; Protest aufnehmen lassen; **to return the bill** ~ den Wechsel unter Protest zurückgehen lassen; **a bill is** ~ ein Wechsel ist zu Protest gebracht

protesting *(WechselR)* Protestaufnahme; **delay in** ~ Verzug bei Vornahme des Protestes; **expenses for** ~ Protestkosten; **person** ~ jd, der Protest erhebt; **time for** ~ Protestfrist

protestable protestfähig

Protestant Protestant; protestantisch; **P~ Episcopal Church** *Am* Anglikanische Kirche

Protestantism Protestantismus

protestation Beteuerung; Protest(erhebung), Einspruch(serhebung); ~ **of innocence** Beteuerung der Unschuld

protestator *Am* →protester

protester *Am* Protestierender; Beteuerer

prot(h)onotary *eccl* (Apostolischer) Protonotar; *Am* Justizbeamter

protocol Protokoll, Verhandlungsniederschrift; *(VölkerR)* Protokoll *(der Begriff umfaßt auch Gesamtheit der im diplomatischen Verkehr gebräuchlichen Formen)*; ~ **of amendment** Änderungsprotokoll; ~ **of extension** Verlängerungsprotokoll; ~ **of interpretation** Auslegungsprotokoll; ~ **of ratifications** Protokoll über den Austausch (od. die Hinterlegung) der Ratifizierungsurkunden; ~ **of rectification** Berichtigungsprotokoll; ~ **of signature** Unterzeichnungsprotokoll; **P~ on →Inspection; P~ Service** Protokoll(abteilung); **according to** ~ protokollgemäß; **additional** ~ Zusatzprotokoll; **Chief of P~** Chef des Protokolls; **final** ~ Schlußprotokoll; **secret** ~ Geheimprotokoll; **supplementary** ~ Zusatzprotokoll; **the present ~ shall be open for accession by ...** dieses Protokoll liegt für ... zum Beitritt auf; **to break the rules of** ~ gegen die Regeln des Protokolls verstoßen; **to draw up** (or **draft**) **a** ~ ein Protokoll aufnehmen (od. aufsetzen); protokollieren; **to record in a** ~ zu Protokoll nehmen, protokollieren

protocol *v* protokollieren, protokollarisch festhalten, Protokoll führen

protocolist *Am* Protokollführer

protonotary →prothonotary

prototype Vorbild; Muster, Modell; voll ausgearbeitet *(aber noch nicht in Serie gegangen)*

protract *v* verlängern, hinziehen, in die Länge ziehen; **to ~ a lawsuit** e-n Prozeß verschleppen

protracted, ~ debate langwierige Debatte; ~ **default** anhaltender (Zahlungs-)Verzug; ~ **loss** lang anhaltender Schaden

protraction Hinziehung, Hinausziehung, Verschleppung; ~ **of a lawsuit** Prozeßverschleppung

provable beweisbar, nachweisbar; ~ **debt** *(KonkursR)* anmeldbare Forderung

prove *v* beweisen, nachweisen, den Beweis erbringen; belegen; **to ~ (to be)** sich erweisen, sich herausstellen als; **to ~ one's alibi** sein Alibi nachweisen; **to ~ one's case** den Beweis erbringen; **to ~ one's claim** (or **a debt**) **in bankruptcy** seine Konkursforderung anmelden; **to ~ the contrary** das Gegenteil beweisen; den Gegenbeweis antreten; **to ~ (to be) correct** sich als richtig erweisen, zutreffen; **to ~ damage** Schaden nachweisen; **to ~ by means of documentary evidence** urkundlich belegen; **to ~ against the estate of a bankrupt** e-e Konkursforderung anmelden; **to ~ false** sich als falsch herausstellen; **to ~ one's identity** sich ausweisen (od. legitimieren); **to ~ to the satisfaction of the court** dem Gericht glaubhaft machen; **to ~ true** sich als wahr erweisen, sich als richtig herausstellen; **it is the executor's duty to ~ the will** es ist die Pflicht des Erbschaftsverwalters, das Testament anerkennen und bestätigen zu lassen; **proposals which ~ acceptable** Vorschläge, die sich als annehmbar erweisen

proved bewiesen; erwiesen; erprobt, bewährt; ~ **damages** nachgewiesener Schadensersatzanspruch; ~ **debt** nachgewiesene Forderung; ~ **will** als gültig bestätigtes Testament; **as** ~ erwiesenermaßen; **until the contrary be** ~ bis zum Beweis des Gegenteils

proven erwiesen; **not** ~ *Scot* Schuldbeweis nicht erbracht; **verdict of not** ~ *Scot* Freispruch mangels Beweisen

proving, ~ of a debt Forderungsanmeldung *(im Konkurs)*; **to be under the obligation of** ~ beweispflichtig sein

provenance (or **provenience**) Provenienz, Herkunft

provide *v* bestimmen, festsetzen; versorgen, versehen, (be)liefern; beschaffen; sorgen; Vorsorge treffen; bereitstellen; **to ~ against** Maßnahmen treffen gegen; *(etw.)* verhindern; **to ~ for** Maßnahmen treffen für; **to ~ for sb.** für jdn sorgen, jdn versorgen; **to ~ oneself with** sich versehen (od. eindecken) mit; **to ~ with acceptance** *(Wechsel)* mit Akzept versehen; **to ~ cover** Deckung anschaffen; **to ~ for an emergency** für e-n Notfall Vorsorge treffen; **to ~ (maintenance) for a p.** für jds Unterhalt sorgen; **to ~ the money to pay a bill (of exchange)** den Betrag für die Zahlung e-s Wechsels bereitstellen; **to ~ a person with money** jdm Geld besorgen, jdn mit Geld versehen; **to ~ for payment** für Zahlung sorgen; **to ~ security** Sicherheit leisten; Kaution stellen; **to ~ a time-limit** e-e Frist vorsehen; **to ~ in a will** in e-m Testament bestimmen; **the contract ~s** der Vertrag bestimmt (od. sieht vor); **failure to ~ for one's spouse and children** mangelnde Sorge für den Ehegatten und die Kinder

provided vorgesehen; versehen (with mit); vorausgesetzt, unter der Bedingung (that daß); sofern; ~ **for** versorgt; ~ **for in the contract** vertraglich (od. im Vertrag) vorgesehen; **not otherwise ~ for** (n.o.p.) nicht anderweitig vorgesehen; **except as otherwise ~ in section 5** soweit in § 5 nichts anderes bestimmt ist

provident vorsorglich, voraussehend; ~ **fund** Hilfskasse, Unterstützungskasse; ~ **reserve fund** außerordentliche Reserve; ~ **societies** *Br* →industrial and ~ societies

provider Lieferant, Lieferer; Ernährer *(der Familie)*

province Provinz *(bes. Übersetzung des kontinentalen Begriffes und der Einzelstaaten Kanadas)*; *fig* (Tätigkeits-)Gebiet, Aufgabenkreis, Fach(bereich), Geschäftsbereich, Ressort; *Br eccl* erzbischöflicher Gerichtsbezirk *(P~s of Canterbury and York)*; **it is not within my** ~ es gehört nicht zu meinem Aufgabenkreis; es schlägt nicht in mein Fach

provincial provinziell; Provinz-; Provinzbewohner; ~ **bank** Provinzbank; ~ **courts** *Br* geistliche Gerichte *(der Erzbischöfe von Canterbury und York)*; ~ **town** Provinzstadt

provision 1. *(in Gesetzen, Verträgen und Testamenten)* Bestimmung, Vorschrift; Klausel; ~**s of a contract** Vertragsbestimmungen *(→contract 1.)*; ~**s of an insurance policy** Versicherungsbestimmungen; ~**s of a lease** Bestimmungen e-s Miet- (od. Pacht)vertrages; ~ **of a statute** Gesetzesbestimmung; ~**s of a will** Bestimmungen e-s Testaments; ~ **relating to form** Formvorschrift; **according to the ~s of the statute** (or **Act**) nach den Bestimmungen des Gesetzes; **additional ~s** Zusatzbestimmungen; **breach of the ~s (of a law)** Verletzung der (gesetzlichen) Bestimmungen; **abolition of ~s** Aufhebung von Bestimmungen; **concluding ~** Schlußbestimmung; **final ~** Schlußbestimmung; **fiscal ~** steuerrechtliche Vorschrift; **legal ~** gesetzliche Bestimmung; **notwithstanding any ~ to the contrary** ungeachtet entgegengesetzter Bestimmungen; **penal ~** Strafbestimmung; **standard ~s** allgemeine Versicherungsbedingungen; **supplementary ~** Ergänzungsbestimmung; **transitional** (or **transitory**) ~ Übergangsbestimmung; **to apply a ~** e-e Bestimmung anwenden; **a ~ applies** e-e Bestimmung findet Anwendung; **to come** (or **fall**) **within the ~s of the Act** unter die Bestimmungen des Gesetzes fallen; **to conform with the ~s of the Act** in Übereinstimmung mit den Bestimmungen des Gesetzes handeln; **to contravene the ~s of the Act** den Vorschriften des Gesetzes zuwiderhandeln; **to infringe the ~s of the Act** die Bestimmungen des Gesetzes verletzen; **to observe ~s** Vorschriften beachten

provision 2. Vorkehrung, Vorsorge; Versorgung (of mit); Beschaffung, Bereitstellung; Zurverfügungstellung; ~**s** Lebensmittel, Vorrat, Proviant; ~ **dealer** →~merchant; ~ **for employment** Arbeitsbeschaffung; ~ **for the future** Vorsorge für die Zukunft; ~ **for old age** (or **retirement**) Altersversorgung; Altersvorsorge; ~ **industry** Nahrungsmittelindustrie; ~ **merchant** Lebensmittelhändler; ~ **of capital** Beschaffung (od. Bereitstellung) von Kapital; ~ **of electricity** Versorgung mit Elektrizität; ~ **of funds** Bereitstellung von Mitteln; ~ **of housing** Wohnungsbeschaffung; ~ **of services** Erbringen von Dienstleistungen; **adequate ~** genügende Vorsorge; **financial ~ for children of the family** *Br* Kindesunterhalt *(bei Scheidung etc)*; **financial ~ for spouse** *Br* Ehegattenunterhalt *(bei Scheidung etc)*; **to make ~ for** sorgen (od. Vorsorge, Vorkehrungen treffen) für; **to make ~ for cover** Deckung anschaffen

provision 3. *(Bilanz)* Rückstellung; ~**s** *(AktienR) (Bilanz)* Rückstellungen und Wertberichtigungen; ~ **for contingencies** Rückstellung für Eventualverbindlichkeiten; ~ **for depreciation** Rückstellung für Wertminderung; ~ **for doubtful debts** Wertberichtigung auf Forderungen; ~ **for outstanding losses** *(VersR)* Rückstellung für schwebende Schadensfälle; Schadensreserve; ~ **for renewals** *Br* Rückstellung für Ersatzbeschaffungen; ~ **for replacement of inventories** *Am* →replacement 1.; ~**s for superannuation** Pensionsrückstellungen; ~ **for taxation** Steuerrückstellung; ~ **for unearned premium** *(VersR)* Rückstellungen für *(am Bilanzstichtag)* noch nicht verdiente Prämien; **to make ~s** Rückstellungen bilden

provision *v*, **to ~ a ship** ein Schiff versorgen; ~**ing with raw materials** Versorgung mit Rohstoffen

provisional vorläufig, einstweilig, provisorisch; Interims-; ~ **account** vorläufiges Konto; ~→**administrator;** ~ **agenda** vorläufige Tagesordnung; ~ **agreement** →~ contract; ~ **application** *(PatR)* vorläufige Anmeldung; ~ **bond** Zwischenschein für e-e Obligation; ~ **committee** für vorübergehende Gelegenheit ernanntes Komitee; ad hoc-Ausschuß; ~ **contract** vorläufiger, noch nicht endgültig ausgearbeiteter und unterschriebener Vertrag; Vorvertrag; ~ **cover** *(VersR)* vorläufige Deckungszusage; ~ **driving licence** *Br* (~ **driver's license** *Am*) Führerschein auf Probe; ~ **government** vorläufige Regierung; Interimsregierung; ~ **injunction** einstweilige Verfügung; ~ **invoice** vorläufige Rechnung *(opp. final invoice)*; ~ **measure** vorläufige Maßnahme; ~ **orders** *Br*→order 2.; ~ **receipt** Interimsquittung; ~ **remedy** →remedy 1.; ~ **specification** *(PatR)* vorläufige Beschreibung *(opp. complete specification)*

provisionally, ~ **enforceable judgement** vorläufig vollstreckbares Urteil; ~ **invalid** schwebend unwirksam

proviso Klausel *(die e-e Bedingung od. einschränkende Bestimmung enthält, "provided that")*; ~ **clause** Vorbehaltsklausel; ~ **for cesser** Auflösungs- od. Rückerwerbsklausel *(bei Sicherungsrechten für den Fall der Befriedigung des Gläubigers)*; **with the ~ that** unter der Bedingung (od. mit der Einschränkung), daß; vorbehaltlich; **with the usual ~** unter dem üblichen Vorbehalt; **to make it a ~** zur Bedingung machen; sich vorbehalten

provocation Provokation, Herausforderung *(Br*[164] *[StrafR] ~ kann →murder auf →manslaughter reduzieren)*

provost *Br univ* Leiter e-s College *(in Oxford, Cambridge etc)*; *Am univ* hoher Verwaltungsbeamter; *Scot* Bürgermeister *(in großen Städten)*; **P~-Marshal** Chef der Militärpolizei; **Lord P~** *Scot* Oberbürgermeister

prowl car *Am* Streifenwagen der Polizei; Funkstreife

prowling[165] Umherstreifen, Umherlungern

proximate, ~ **cause** unmittelbare *(die Zurechnung e-s Schadens begründende)* Ursache *(opp. remote cause)*; ~ **in time** (Ursache, die dem Schaden) zeitlich am nächsten (steht)

proximity Nähe; nahe Lage (to an); ~ **of relationship** Nähe der Beziehungen der Parteien; Nähe der Verwandtschaft; ~ **of a town** Stadtnähe

proximo (prox.) ("of next month") nächsten Monats (n.M.) *(cf. ultimo, instant)*; **the 3rd** ~ der 3. nächsten Monats

prox|y[166] *(schriftl.)* Vollmacht *(für Stellvertretung, bes. zur Stimmausübung)*; *(vom Aktieninhaber erteilte)* Stimmrechtsvollmacht; Vollmachtsurkunde; (Stimmrechts-)Vertreter, Bevollmächtigter *(zur Stimmabgabe)*; Vertreter in der Stimmrechtsausübung; (Stimmrechts-)Vertretung *(auf Grund e-r Vollmacht)*; ~ **contest** (or **fight**) *Am* Stimmrechtskampf *(Kampf zwischen zwei Aktionärsgruppen innerhalb e-r Gesellschaft, wobei jede Seite versucht, durch Gewinnung möglichst vieler Vollmachten zur Vertretung von Aktien ihre eigene Stimmenzahl zu erhöhen)*; ~ **form** s. form of →~; ~ **giver** Vollmachtgeber; ~**holder** Stellvertreter (od. Bevollmächtigter) des Aktionärs; ~ **solicitation** (or **soliciting ~ies**) *Am (an die Aktionäre gerichtete)* Aufforderung zur Abgabe von Stimmrechtsvollmachten; ~ **solicitor** *Am* Bewerber um Stimmrechtsvollmacht; ~ **statement** Stimmrechtsvollmacht; ~ **vote** stellvertretend abgegebene Stimme; ~ **voting right** Vollmachtsstimmrecht

proxy, by ~ in Vertretung, in Vollmacht; **vote by** ~ in Vertretung abgegebene Stimme; **voting by** ~ Stimmrechtsausübung durch Stellvertreter; **to appear by** ~ s. to stand →~ for; **to be present at a meeting either personally or by** ~ e-r Versammlung persönlich oder durch Vertreter beiwohnen; **to vote by** ~ sich bei e-r Wahl vertreten lassen

proxy, form of ~ Vollmachtsformular, Formular für die Vollmachtserteilung; **general** ~ General(vertretungs)vollmacht *(zur Vertretung auf allen Gesellschaftsversammlungen)*; **irrevocable** ~ *Am* unwiderrufliche Vollmacht *(nur zulässig, wenn der Bevollmächtigte ein wirtschaftliches Interesse an den Aktien hat, aus denen er das Stimmrecht ausübt; cf. voting agreement, voting trust)*; **scope of** ~ Umfang der Vollmacht; **special** ~ besondere (Vertretungs-)Vollmacht *(zur Vertretung auf einer besonderen Gesellschaftsversammlung)*; **two-way** ~ Vollmacht mit zwei Entscheidungsmöglichkeiten *(to vote for or against the resolution)*; **to appoint** (or **authorize**) **a** ~ (to vote) e-n Bevollmächtigten ernennen, e-n Vertreter bestellen, sich vertreten lassen; **to appoint a p. as one's** ~ jdn zu s-m Vertreter bestellen, j-dn bevollmächtigen; **to send a** ~ e-n Vertreter entsenden, sich vertreten lassen; **to stand** ~ **for** als Vertreter fungieren für

prudence, man of ordinary ~ Mensch mit allgemeiner (od. normaler) Einsicht (od. Vorsicht); jd, der das übliche (od. normale) Maß von Sorgfalt aufwendet *(Maßstab für →negligence)*

prudent man vorsichtig (od. einsichtig) handelnder Mensch; **ordinary** ~ s. man of ordinary →prudence; ~ **rule** *Am* Standard für Anlagebeschränkungen zugunsten bestimmter, geschützter Vermögen *(analog etwa der mündelsicheren Anlage)*

pseudonym[167] Pseudonym, Deckname

psychiatric examination, remand for ~ Überweisung zur psychiatrischen Untersuchung

psychiatric hospital (or **institution**) *Am* psychiatrisches Krankenhaus; Nervenklinik

psychological warfare psychologische Kriegführung

psychology, industrial ~ Wirtschaftspsychologie

psychotherapist-patient privilege *Am* Aussageverweigerungsrecht bei Kommunikation zwischen Psychotherapeut und Patient

psychotropic substances[168] psychotrope (auf die Psyche einwirkende) Stoffe

public Öffentlichkeit, Publikum, Allgemeinheit; Staats-; **the general** ~ die breite Öffentlichkeit; **in** ~ öffentlich; **not open to the** ~ unter Ausschluß der Öffentlichkeit; **to appear in** ~ vor die Öffentlichkeit treten; **to make known to the** ~ öffentlich bekanntgeben; **to** →**open to the** ~

public öffentlich, allgemein *(opp. private)*; ~ **accounts** *Br* Konto für staatliche Gelder; **P~ Accounts Committee** (P.A.C.) *Br parl* Ausschuß für Prüfung der öffentlichen Ausgaben; ~ **accountant** *Am* Wirtschaftsprüfer *(cf. certified ~ accountant)*; ~ **acts** Gesetze allgemeinen Inhalts (→*act 1.*); ~ **address system** (P.A. system) öffentliche Lautsprecheranlage; ~ **administrator** *Am* öffentl. Erbschaftsverwalter; ~ **affairs** öffentliche Angelegenheiten, Staatsangelegenheiten; ~ **amenities** öffentliche Erholungsanlagen *(parks, swimming baths, childrens' playgrounds etc)*; ~ **and private bodies** öffentliche und private Stellen; ~ **appearance** Auftreten in der Öffentlichkeit; ~ **appointment** Staatsstellung; ~ **assistance** Sozialhilfe; ~ **assistance benefits** Leistungen der Sozialhilfe; ~ **attorney** *Am* →attorney at law; ~ **auction** öffentliche Versteigerung; Zwangsversteigerung; ~ **audience** öffentliche Audienz; ~ **authority** Staatsgewalt; ~ **authorities** Behörden, öffentliche Stellen; **for the** ~ **benefit** →benefit 1.; ~ **bill** →bill 3.; ~ **body** öffentlich-rechtliche Körperschaft; ~ **bonds** Staatsanleihen; ~ **building** öffentliches Gebäude; ~ **burdens** *Scot* auf Grundbesitz ruhende Abgaben *(Steuern etc)*; ~ **call** Kursfestsetzung durch Ausruf der Verkaufs- und Kaufangebote *(bes. im börsenmäßigen Warengeschäft)*; ~ **call box** *Br* öffentlicher (Münz-)Fernsprecher; ~ **charge** →charge 2.; ~ **communication** *(UrhR)* öffentliche Wiedergabe; ~ **company** *Br*→~ limited company; ~ **confidence** Vertrauen der Öffentlichkeit; ~ **contract** *(bei Ausschreibungen)* öffentlicher Auftrag *(→contract 2.)*

public convenience öffentliches Bedürfnis; öffentliche Bedürfnisanstalt; **certificate of ~ and necessity** *Am (Luft- und Omnibusverkehr)* Routenzertifikat *(für bestimmte Strecke)*

public, ~ →**corporation**; ~ **debt** *Am* öffentliche Schuld, Staatsschuld; ~ **defender** *Am* Offizialverteidiger; ~ **deposits** *Br* →deposit 3.; ~ **disturbances** Unruhen (→*disturbance*); ~ **document** öffentliche Urkunde; ~ →**domain**; ~ **employee** Arbeitnehmer des öffentlichen Dienstes; ~ **employment** Beschäftigung im öffentlichen Dienst; ~ **enemy** *Am* Nation (od. Angehöriger dieser Nation), mit dem ein Staat im Kriegszustand ist; Volksfeind; ~ **enterprise** staatliches Unternehmen, Staatsbetrieb; ~ **examination of the debtor** *Br* Vernehmung des Konkursschuldners in öffentlicher Sitzung; ~ **expenditure** Ausgaben der öffentlichen Hand, Staatsausgaben; ~ **expense** Staatskosten; (→*expense*); ~ **figure** Persönlichkeit des öffentlichen Lebens, allgemein bekannte Persönlichkeit; ~ →**finance**; ~ **funds** öffentliche Mittel (od. Gelder), *Br* fundierte Staatspapiere; ~ **gallery** *parl* Besuchertribüne; **P~ General Acts and Church Assembly Measures** *Br* amtliche Gesetzessammlung *(ab 1949)*

public health[169] öffentliches Gesundheitswesen; Volksgesundheit; ~ **service** *Am* Staatlicher Gesundheitsdienst

public, ~ **hearing** öffentliche Anhörung, öffentliche Verhandlung; ~ **holiday** gesetzlicher Feiertag; ~ **house** (pub) *Br* Gastwirtschaft, Gasthaus, Kneipe; ~ **indecency**[170] Erregung öffentlichen Ärgernisses; ~ **inquiry** *Br* amtliche Untersuchung; ~ **institution** öffentlich-rechtliche Anstalt, gemeinnütziges Unternehmen

public interest, to be in the ~ im öffentlichen Interesse liegen; **to be contrary to the** ~ dem öffentlichen Interesse zuwiderlaufen; gegen das öffentliche Interesse verstoßen; **the ~ is at stake** das öffentliche Interesse steht auf dem Spiel

public, ~ **international law** →international; ~ **issue** öffentliche Aufforderung zur Zeichnung von Effekten; ~ **investments** Investitionen der öffentlichen Hand; ~ **land** *Am* staatlicher Grundbesitz; ~ →**law;** ~ **liability** Haftung gegenüber der Öffentlichkeit; ~ **liability insurance** Betriebs-(od. Unternehmens-)haftpflichtversicherung *(deckt im Ggs. zur →employer's liability insurance Haftpflicht gegenüber betriebsfremden Personen)*; ~ **library** Volksbücherei; ~ **limited company** (plc) Aktiengesellschaft *(→company)*; ~ **loan** Anleihe der öffentlichen Hand, Staatsanleihe; ~ **meeting** öffentliche Versammlung; ~ **minister** *Am* →minister 2.; ~ **mischief** grober Unfug; ~ **money** öffentliche Gelder, Staatsgelder; ~ **notice** öffentliche Bekanntmachung; ~ **notice procedure** Aufgebotsverfahren; ~ **nuisance** Störung der Allgemeinheit; öffentliches Ärgernis; ~ **officer** Beamter; leitender Angestellter *(z. B. Direktor e-r AG)*; ~ **official** *Am* Beamter

public opinion[171] öffentliche Meinung; ~ **poll** (or **inquiry into** ~) Umfrage zur Erforschung der öffentlichen Meinung; Meinungsforschung *(cf. Gallup poll)*; ~ **research** Meinungsforschung; **American Association for P~ O~ Research** (A.A.P.O.R.) Amerikanischer Verband für Meinungsforschung; ~ **survey** Meinungsbefragung, -umfrage; **to conduct a ~ poll** die öffentliche Meinung erforschen, e-e Meinungsforschung durchführen

public order[172] öffentliche (Sicherheit und) Ordnung; **disturbance of** ~ Störung der öffentlichen Ordnung; **maintenance of** ~ Aufrechterhaltung der öffentlichen Ordnung; **offen|ce (~se) against** ~ Ordnungswidrigkeit; **offenses against ~ and decency** *Am*[173] Straftaten gegen die öffentliche Ordnung und den Anstand *(riot, disorderly conduct, etc)*

public, ~ **ownership** *Br* Eigentum der öffentlichen Hand, Staatseigentum *(cf. nationalization)*; ~ **part** der Öffentlichkeit zugänglicher Teil *(e-s Grundstücks)*; ~ **policy** →policy 1.; ~ **power district** *Am* Stromversorgungsbezirk; ~ **prior use** *(PatR)* offenkundige Vorbenutzung; ~ **procurement** öffentliches Auftragswesen; ~ **property** Staatseigentum, Eigentum der öffentlichen Hand; ~ →**prosecutor;** ~ **records** *Br (im →Record Office aufbewahrte)* öffentliche Akten

public relations (PR) Öffentlichkeitsarbeit, Kontaktpflege *(Bemühungen von Unternehmen, Einzelpersönlichkeiten od. Institutionen um Vertrauen in der Öffentlichkeit; moderne Form der Werbung)*; ~ **officer** (PRO) Berater für Public Relations; Public Relations-Fachmann

public, ~ →**revenue**; ~ **safety** öffentliche Sicherheit; ~ **sale** öffentliche Versteigerung, Auktion; ~ **school** →school 1.

public sector (of the economy) öffentlicher Sektor (der Wirtschaft) *(state-owned enterprises; opp. private sector)*

public sector borrowing requirement (PSBR) *Br* Kreditbedarf der öffentlichen Hand

Eine Möglichkeit für die Regierung, den PSBR zu decken, ist, Staatspapiere zu verkaufen

One of the ways the Government meets the PSBR is by selling Gilt-Edged Stocks

public, ~ **securities** Staatspapiere; ~ **servant** →servant 1.

public service 1. öffentlicher Dienst, Staatsdienst; Tätigkeit (od. Leistung) im öffentl. Interesse

public service 2. *Am* Bereitstellung von Versorgungsdiensten *(Gas, Elektrizität, Wasser, Transport etc)*; **P~ S~ Commission** (P.S.C.) *Am (einzelstaatl.)* Überwachungskommission für public utilities und transportation utilities; ~ **corporation** *Am* →~ utility

public, ~ **spending** Staatsausgaben, Ausgaben der öffentlichen Hand; ~ **supply contract** öffentlicher Lieferauftrag; ~ **taking of private property** Enteignung; ~ **(tele)phone** Fernsprechzelle, Münzfernsprecher

public transport öffentliches Verkehrswesen; **by** ~ mit öffentlichem Verkehrsmittel

public, ~ **trust** →charitable trust; **P~ Trustee** *Br* →trustee

public use Verwendung im öffentlichen Interesse *(als Rechtfertigung der Enteignung)*; ~ **proceedings** *Am (PatR) (etwa)* Einspruchsverfahren; **prior** ~ *(PatR)* offenkundige Vorbenutzung; **to expropriate property for** ~ *bes. Am* Privatbesitz zum Wohle der Allgemeinheit enteignen

public utilit|y, ~ies Versorgungsunternehmen, Versorgungsbetriebe, Unternehmen der öffentlichen Versorgung *(mit Elektrizität, Gas, Wasser, Verkehrsleistungen etc)*; *(Börse)* Aktien und Obligationen solcher Versorgungsbetriebe; Versorgungswerte; ~ **agency** *Am* Versorgungsbetrieb; ~ **bonds** Obligationen der Versorgungsbetriebe; **P~ U~ Commission** *Am* (PUC) *(einzelstaatl.)* Überwachungskommission für public utilities; ~ **company** (or **corporation**) Versorgungsunternehmen, Versorgungsbetrieb; ~ **district** (PUD) *Am* Versorgungsbezirk; **P~ U~ies Holding Company Act** (PUHCA) *Am* Bundesgesetz *(von 1935)*, das sich mit den Holding-Gesellschaften befaßt, die die Versorgung der Bevölkerung mit Elektrizität und Gas kontrollieren und sie der Kontrolle der Securities and Exchange Commission unterstellt; ~ **shares** (or **stocks**) Versorgungswerte; Werte von Versorgungsbetrieben; ~ **undertaking** Versorgungsunternehmen

public, ~ **warehouse** öffentl. Speicher; ~ **way** Landstraße; ~ **weal** allgemeines Wohl; ~ **works** öffentliche Bauarbeiten; **P~ Works Administration** (PWA) *Am* Behörde für öffentliche Arbeiten; **award of** ~ **works contracts** Vergabe öffentlicher Bauaufträge *(im Ausschreibungswege)*; **semi** ~ halböffentlich; **to become** ~ bekannt werden; **to go** ~ an die Börse gehen *(Aktien emittieren und anbieten)*; sich an der Börse einführen lassen; sich börsennotieren lassen; **to make** ~ öffentlich bekanntmachen; publizieren

publicly held corporation *Am* Kapitalgesellschaft mit breitgestreutem Aktienkapital

publicly owned staatseigen; in öffentlichem Eigentum (befindlich); ~ **enterprise** Staatsbetrieb; **to be** ~ im Staatseigentum (od. öffentlichen Eigentum) stehen

publicly, to appear ~ öffentlich erscheinen

publication Veröffentlichung, Bekanntmachung; Offenlegung; *(UrhR)* Veröffentlichung, Verbreitung[174], Erscheinen[174]; Publikation, veröffentlichtes Werk; *(PatR)* Druckschrift; *(BeleidigungsR)* Kundgebung *(der Mißachtung)*; Zurkenntnisbringung *(e-s defamatory statement an e-e vom Beleidigten verschiedene Person)*; *Am (ErbR)* mündliche Erklärung des Testators an Zeugen, daß die von ihnen unterschriebene Urkunde seinen letzten Willen darstelle; **~s made available to the public** *(PatR)* öffentliche Druckschriften; ~ **of the banns** (Erlaß des) (kirchl.) Aufgebot(s); ~ **of a book** Herausgabe (od. Erscheinen) e-s Buches; ~ **price** *(Buchhandel)* Ladenpreis; **annual** ~ Jahrgang; **in the course of** ~ im Erscheinen begriffen; **list of ~s** Verlagskatalog; Liste der Veröffentlichungen; **memorial** ~ Gedächtnisschrift; **monthly** ~ Monatsschrift; **new** ~ Neuerscheinung; **printed** ~ *(PatR)* druckschriftliche Veröffentlichung; **prior printed** ~ *(PatR) (neuheitsschädliche)* druckschriftliche Vorveröffentlichung; **to cease** ~ das Erscheinen *(e-r Zeitung)* einstellen

publicist Publizist; Völkerrechtler

publicity Publizität, (Bekanntwerden in der) Öffentlichkeit; Offenkundigkeit; Werbung, Reklame, Propaganda; ~ **agency** Werbeagentur, Reklamebüro; ~ **agent** Werbeagent; ~ **bureau** Werbebüro, Reklamebüro; ~ **campaign** Werbeaktion, Werbefeldzug; ~ **department** Werbeabteilung; Reklameabteilung; ~ **documents** Werbeschriften; ~ **drive** Werbefeldzug; ~ **expenses** Werbekosten; Reklamekosten; ~ **man** Werbeberater, Werbefachmann; ~ **manager** Werbeleiter; ~ **material** Werbematerial; ~ **office** Werbebüro; ~ **programme** Werbeprogramm; ~ **purposes** Werbezwecke; ~ **stunt** Werbegag; **broadcast** ~ Rundfunkwerbung; **export** ~ Exportwerbung

publicize *v (öffentl.)* bekanntgeben; publizieren; werben für; Reklame machen für; **to** ~ **a declaration** e-e Erklärung veröffentlichen

publish *v* veröffentlichen, (öffentlich) bekanntmachen; offenlegen; publizieren; *(UrhR)* veröffentlichen, herausgeben, erscheinen lassen; *(Buch)* verlegen; *(BeleidigungsR)* kundgeben (→*publication*); **to** ~ **the banns** (of marriage) das Aufgebot *(von der Kanzel)* verkünden; *(das Brautpaar)* aufbieten; **to** ~ **a (news)paper** e-e Zeitung herausgeben

published, ~ **by Beck** im Verlag Beck erschienen; ~ **price** Ladenpreis; ~ **works** erschienene Werke; **just** ~ soeben erschienen

publisher Verleger, Herausgeber; Verlagsbuchhändler; **contractual rights of a** ~ Verlagsrecht; **International P~s' Association** (IPA) Weltbund der Verleger

publishing Veröffentlichung, Herausgabe; Verlags-; ~ **agreement** Verlagsvertrag; ~ **business** Verlagsgeschäft; Verlagsbuchhandel; ~ **contract** →~ agreement; ~ **firm** (or **house**) Verlag(sbuchhandlung)

Im Gegensatz zum deutschen Recht fehlt im angloamerikanischen Recht eine gesetzliche Bestimmung für die Regelung des Verlagsverhältnisses; es gibt kein kodifiziertes Verlagsrecht

puff *(marktschreierische)* Anpreisung (od. Reklame)

puff *v (marktschreierisch)* anpreisen; *(bei Auktionen)* Scheingebot abgeben *(um den Preis höher zu treiben)*; **to** ~ **up prices** Preise hochtreiben

puffing *(marktschreierische)* Anpreisung; Abgabe von Scheingeboten; Preistreiberei; **harmless** ~ *Am* Übertreibung in der Werbung

puffer Marktschreier; Scheinbieter *(bei Auktionen)*; Preistreiber

puisne *(an Rang)* jünger; jünger(en Datums); nachstehend; Unter-; ~ **judge** *Am* rangniedriger Richter; beisitzender Richter; ~ **mortgage** *Br*[175] *(im Rang)* nachstehende Hypothek *(die nicht durch →deposit of title deeds geschützt ist)*

pull Zugkraft; Werbewirkung; *sl.* Protektion, Beziehungen; **inflation-induced** ~ **of imports** inflatorisch bedingter Einfuhrsog

pull *v* ziehen; **to** ~ **back** sich *(von e-m beabsichtigten Plan)* zurückziehen; **to** ~ **down** *(Gebäude)* abreißen; *(Preise, Kurse)* drücken; **to** ~ **off** Erfolg haben; **to** ~ **up** halten *(von e-m Wagen)*; **to** ~ **strings** *sl.* Beziehungen spielen lassen, Einfluß geltend machen *(um jdm od. sich selbst zu e-r Stelle zu verhelfen etc)*

pump priming *com* Ankurbelung *(charakterisiert durch die Forderung der Defizitfinanzierung in der Depression und des zyklischen Budgetausgleichs)*

punch Locher; ~ **card** Lochkarte; ~ **tape** Lochstreifen

punched, ~ **card** Lochkarte; ~ **card accounting department** Lochkartenabteilung; ~ **card method** Lochkartenverfahren; ~ **tape** Lochstreifen

punctual pünktlich; **to be** ~ **in paying** (or **to pay** ~**ly**) pünktlich zahlen; **to be** ~ **in one's payments** seine Zahlungen pünktlich erledigen

punish *v*[176] strafen, bestrafen (by mit); **to deserve to be** ~**ed** Strafe verdienen

punishable strafbar, straffällig; ~ **act** strafbare Handlung; ~ **by death** mit der Todesstrafe bedroht; ~ **offen|ce (~se)** strafbare Handlung; **an attempt is** ~ ein Versuch ist strafbar; **to be** ~ **by fine (imprisonment)** mit Geldstrafe (Gefängnis) zu bestrafen sein

punishment Strafe, Bestrafung; **arbitrary** ~ Strafe nach freiem Ermessen; **award of** ~ Strafzumessung; **capital** ~ Todesstrafe; →**corporal** ~; **exemplary** ~ als Abschreckung dienende Strafe; **immunity from** ~ Straflosigkeit; **inhuman or degrading treatment or** ~[176a] unmenschliche od. erniedrigende Behandlung od. Strafe; **lawful** ~ gesetzlich zulässige Strafe; **light** ~ leichte Strafe; **maximum** ~ Höchststrafe; **minimum** ~ Mindeststrafe; **mitigation of** ~ Strafminderung; **severe** ~ strenge Bestrafung; **to award a** ~ e-e Strafe zuerkennen; **to escape** ~ e-r Strafe entgehen; **to enable a p. to escape** (or **evade**) ~ jdn der Bestrafung entziehen; **to evade** ~ sich der Bestrafung entziehen; **to incur a** ~ sich strafbar machen, e-e Strafe verwirken; **to inflict a** ~ Strafe verhängen; *(jdn)* bestrafen; **to mitigate the** ~ die Strafe mildern

punitive (or **punitory**) strafend, Straf-; ~ **damages** Strafe einschließender Schadensersatz *(Am opp. compensatory →damages)*; ~ **expedition** (militärische) Strafexpedition; ~ **measures** Strafmaßnahmen; **to take** ~ **action against** Strafaktion unternehmen gegen

punter Börsenspekulant

pupil Schüler; Mündel; *Br* neu zugelassener barrister *(der mindestens für 1 Jahr bei e-m erfahrenen barrister [pupil master] arbeiten muß)*; *Scot* Kind bis 12 Jahre *(Mädchen)* od. 14 Jahre *(Junge)*

pupillage *Br* Lehrzeit *(bes. des neu zugelassenen barrister)*

puppet government Marionettenregierung, Schattenregierung

pur autre vie ("for another's life") auf Lebenszeit e-s Dritten; → **tenant** ~

purchase Kauf, Ankauf, Einkauf *(opp. sale)*; Anschaffung, Erwerb; gekaufte Sache; *(GrundstücksR)* (jede Art des) Erwerb(s) *(von real property außer durch Vererbung [descent])*

purchase, to acquire by ~ käuflich erwerben; **to conclude** (or **effect, make**) **a** ~ e-n Kauf machen (od. tätigen); **to withdraw from a** ~ von e-m Kauf zurücktreten, e-n Kauf rückgängig machen

purchase, ~**s account** Wareneinkaufskonto; ~ **agreement** Kaufvereinbarung; ~ **and sale** (An-, Ein-)Kauf und Verkauf; Erwerb und Veräußerung; ~**(s) books** (or ~**s day book**) →~journal; ~ **by description** Gattungskauf; ~ **contract** *(Börse)* Schlußnote; ~ **deed** Kaufvertrag; Kaufurkunde; ~ **for the account** *Br (Börse)* →~**for the settlement;** ~ **for cash** Kauf gegen bar, Barkauf; *(Börse)* Kassakauf; ~ **for future delivery** (Warenbörse) Terminkauf; ~ **for the settlement** *Br (Börse)* Terminkauf; ~ **for value without notice** gutgläubiger Erwerb gegen Entgelt; ~ **group** *Am (bei Wertpapieremissionen)* Konsortium; ~ **in auction** Ersteigerung; ~ **in bulk** Großeinkauf; ~ **invoice** Einkaufsrechnung, Eingangsrechnung; ~**(s) journal** Wareneingangsbuch; ~ **lease** *Am* Mietkauf; ~**(s) ledger** Kreditorenbuch; ~ **loan** *Am* →~ money loan

purchase money Kaufpreis, Kaufsumme; ~ **chattel mortgage** *Am* Sicherungseigentum des Verkäufers *(das der Käufer durch Rückübereignung bestellt)*; ~ **loan** Kaufpreisdarlehen; Warenbeschaffungskredit; ~ **mortgage** *Am* Restkaufgeldhypothek; ~ **security interest**[176b]; *Am* dingliches Recht am Kaufgegenstand zur Sicherung der Kaufpreisforderung; im Verhältnis zu Dritten ranggesichertes Sicherungsrecht

purchase, ~ **of assets** Kauf der Aktiva; ~ **of certain definite goods** Spezieskauf *(opp. quantity contract)*; ~ **of goods and services by customers** (**by government**) Güter- und Dienstleistungskäufe der privaten Haushalte (des Staates); ~ **of land** Grundstückserwerb; ~ **of securities** Ankauf von Wertpapieren; ~ **of services** →service 1.; ~ **of shares** Kauf von Aktien *(bei Firmenübernahme)*; ~ **of specified goods** (or **items**) Stückkauf, Spezieskauf; ~ **on account** Kauf auf Kredit; ~ **on approval** Kauf auf Probe; ~ **on commission** Kommissionseinkauf; ~ **on credit** Kreditkauf, Kauf auf Kredit; ~ **on inspection** Kauf auf Besicht; ~ **on margin** Wertpapierkauf gegen Kredit; ~ **on** (or **by sample**) Kauf nach Probe (od. Muster); ~ **on trial** Kauf auf Probe *(mit Rückgaberecht)*; ~ **order** Kaufauftrag, Bestellung(sschreiben)

purchase price Kaufpreis, Einkaufspreis, Ankaufspreis, Anschaffungspreis *(opp. selling price)*; **abatement of** (or **reduction in**) **the** ~ Herabsetzung des Kaufpreises, Minderung; **balance of** ~ Restkaufgeld; **claim for** ~ Kaufpreisforderung; **restitution of the** ~ Kaufpreiserstattung; **to abate** (or **reduce**) **the** ~ den Kaufpreis herabsetzen (od. mindern); **to allow a period of time to pay the** ~ e-e Frist für die Zahlung des Kaufpreises einräumen

purchase, ~ **quota** Einkaufskontingent; ~ **record** *Am* →~ journal, ~ **register** Kreditorenjournal, ~ **returns** Einkaufsretouren; ~**s returns book** (or **journal**) Rückwarenbuch, Retourenjournal

purchase, agreement of ~ **and sale** *Am* Kaufvertrag; **agreement of sale and** ~ **(of land)** *Br* (Grundstücks-)Kaufvertrag; **bona fide** ~ gutgläubiger Erwerb; **bulk** ~ Massenankauf; Mengeneinkauf; **by** ~ durch Kauf, käuflich; **cash** ~ Barkauf; *(Börse)* Kassakauf; **chance** ~ Gelegenheitskauf; **compulsory** ~ *Br* Enteignung *(von Grundbesitz gegen Entschädigung)*; **credit** ~ Kreditkauf *(opp. cash* ~*)*; **fictitious** ~ Scheinkauf; **firm** (or **fixed**) ~ fester Kauf; **forward** (*Am* **future**) ~ *(Börse)* Terminkauf; **a good** ~ ein guter Kauf; **governmental** ~ **of supplies** Beschaffungskäufe der Regierung; **hire-**~ *Br* Mietkauf, Teilzahlungskauf; **mock** ~ Scheinkauf; **occasional** ~ Gelegenheitskauf; **terms of** ~ Kaufbestimmungen, Kaufbedingungen; **wholesale** ~ Einkauf im großen, Engroskauf

purchase *v* kaufen, ankaufen, einkaufen; beziehen; käuflich erwerben; abnehmen; anschaffen, erstehen; *(GrundstücksR) (unter Lebenden)* erwerben *(opp. by descent)*; **authority to** ~ *(Exporthandel)* Ankaufsermächtigung (→*authority*); **to** ~ **at auction** ersteigern; **to** ~ **for cash** gegen Barzahlung kaufen; **to** ~ **compulsorily** *Br (Grundbesitz)* enteignen; **to** ~ **forward** (or **for future delivery**) *(Börse)* auf Termin kaufen; **to** ~ **on time** *Am* auf Abzahlung kaufen

purchaser Käufer, Ankäufer, Einkäufer; Erwerber; Abnehmer; *(GrundstücksR)*[177] Erwerber *(von real property auf jede Art außer by descent)*; ~**s' association** Einkaufsvereinigung; ~ **for value in good faith** gutgläubiger Erwerber, der gegen Entgelt erworben hat; ~ **for value without notice** gutgläubiger Erwerber gegen Entgelt *(cf. notice 2.)*; ~**'s** →**lien;** ~ **in bad faith** bösgläubiger Erwerber; ~ **in good faith** gutgläubiger Erwerber; **bona fide** (or **innocent**) ~ gutgläubiger Erwerber; **intending** (or **prospective**) ~ Käuferinteressent, Kaufinteressent, Reflektant; **to find a** ~ e-n Käufer finden

purchasing Kauf, Einkauf *(opp. selling)*; Anschaffung, Erwerb; (Waren-)Beschaffung

purchasing agent Einkaufsleiter *(Leiter e-r Einkaufsabteilung)*; Einkaufskommissionär; *(Außenhandel)* Einkaufsagent; **National Association of P**~ **A**~**s** *Am* Verband amerikanischer Einkäufer

purchasing, ~ **association** Einkaufsvereinigung; ~ **combine** Einkaufskartell, Einkaufsverband; ~ **cooperative** Einkaufsgenossenschaft; ~ **cost** Anschaffungskosten; ~ **country** Käuferland; ~ **department** Einkaufsabteilung; ~ **manager** Einkaufsleiter *(opp. sales manager)*; ~ **order** Kaufauftrag; ~ **pool** Einkaufsgemeinschaft

purchasing power (of money) Kaufkraft; ~ **parity** Kaufkraftparität; **decline in** (or **deterioration in** or **of**) **the** ~ **of money** Verschlechterung der Kaufkraft des Geldes; Geldentwertung; **to skim off surplus** ~ überschüssige Kaufkraft abschöpfen

purchasing, at the ~ **rate of exchange** zum Ankaufskurs; ~ **value** Anschaffungswert; **state** (or **government**) ~ Regierungskäufe

pure, ~ **competition** vollkommene Konkurrenz;

~ **economics** theoretische Volkswirtschaft; ~ **premium** *(VersR)* Nettoprämie *(opp. office premium, →office 3.)*

purge Reinigung; *pol* Säuberung(saktion)

purge *v* reinigen; *pol* säubern, beseitigen

purging *pol* Säuberung(saktion); ~ **contempt** Sühnen für ein →contempt of court *(durch Wiedergutmachung)*

purloin *v* stehlen

purport Inhalt, Sinn; erklärte Absicht

purport *v* besagen, zum Inhalt haben; bedeuten (wollen); vorgeben, behaupten; beabsichtigen; ~**ed** angeblich

purpose Absicht, Zweck, Ziel; ~ **saving** Zwecksparen; **achievement of** ~**s** Verwirklichung der Ziele; **for advertising** ~**s** zu Werbezwecken

purpose, general ~**s** Mehrzweck-; **to all** →**intents and** ~**s**; **on** ~ absichtlich, vorsätzlich; **to the** ~ zweckdienlich; **to achieve a** ~ e-n Zweck erreichen; **to answer the** ~ dem Zweck entsprechen, zweckentsprechend sein; **to be at cross** ~**s** *(unabsichtlich)* entgegenhandeln, sich mißverstehen

purse Geldbörse; *fig* Geld(summe), Fonds; ~-**snatching** *Am* Handtaschenraub; **common** (or **joint**) ~ gemeinsame Kasse; **power of the** ~ →power 2; →**Privy P**~; **public** ~ Staatskasse; **to hold the** ~ **strings** über die Geldmittel verfügen (od. Kontrolle ausüben)

purser Zahlmeister *(e-s Schiffes)*; **chief** ~ Oberzahlmeister

pursuance Fortführung, Verfolgung; **in** ~ **of** zufolge, gemäß; **in** ~ **of section 2** aufgrund von (od. gemäß) Abs. 2; **in** ~ **of the terms of a contract** gemäß den Bestimmungen e-s Vertrages

pursuant to zufolge, gemäß; im Sinne von; ~ **the statute** nach dem Gesetz

pursue *v (Verbrecher, Plan etc)* verfolgen; *(etw.)* betreiben; fortsetzen, fortfahren in; **to** ~ **one's business** s-n Geschäften nachgehen; **to** ~ **a claim** e-n Anspruch verfolgen; **to** ~ **a course** *fig* e-n Kurs (od. Weg) verfolgen (od. einschlagen); **to** ~ **a goal** ein Ziel verfolgen; **to** ~ **a policy** e-e Politik verfolgen; **to** ~ **one's studies** Studien betreiben; **to** ~ **a trade** ein Gewerbe betreiben

pursuing state das Recht der Nacheile ausübender Staat *(→hot pursuit)*

pursuer Verfolger; *Scot* Kläger; **to evade one's** ~**s** sich s-n Verfolgern entziehen

pursuit Verfolgung; Betreibung *(e-s Planes etc)*; Streben (of nach); ~**s** Geschäfte, Arbeiten, Studien; **right of (hot)** ~ *(VölkerR)* Recht auf Nacheile (*→hot*); **to take up the** ~ die Verfolgung aufnehmen

purvey *v (bes. Lebensmittel)* liefern; **to** ~ **for sb.** jdn beliefern

purveyance Lieferung *(bes. von Lebensmitteln)*

purveyor Lieferant *(bes. von Lebensmitteln)*; ~ **to the Royal Household** (or **to H.M. the Queen**) *Br* Hoflieferant

purview verfügender Teil e-s Gesetzes *(nach der preamble, er beginnt mit "be it enacted")*; Sinn e-s Gesetzes, gesetzgeberische Absicht; Geltungsbereich *(e-s Gesetzes)*; Wirkungskreis, Gebiet; **to come within the** ~ **of a statute** in den Geltungsbereich e-s Gesetzes fallen

push Stoß; *colloq.* Unternehmungsgeist, Schwung; ~ **boat** Schubschiff; ~-**button** automatisch; ~ **money** Verkäuferprämie für Ladenhüter; **to get the** ~ *sl.* entlassen werden, „rausfliegen"

push *v* stoßen; energisch betreiben; intensiv werben für, propagieren; **to** ~ **a claim** e-n Anspruch durchsetzen (wollen); **to** ~ **goods** Waren aufdrängen, Waren verkaufen wollen; **to** ~ **off** *(Waren billig)* abstoßen; *(Lager)* räumen; **to** ~ **through** *parl* durchbringen, durchpeitschen; **to** ~ **up money** Geld aufbringen; **to** ~ **up prices** Preise hochtreiben; **to be** ~**ed for money** in Geldverlegenheit sein

pusher Schubschiff; **drug** ~ *colloq.* Rauschgifthändler

put *(Börse) (Prämiengeschäft)* Rückprämie *(opp. call)*

put and call (p.a.c., Pac) Stellage, Stellgeschäft, Rück- und Vorprämie; ~ **option** Stellage; Stellagegeschäft; ~ **price** Stellkurs

put, ~ **of more** *Br* Rückprämie mit Nachliefern (Nochgeschäft); ~ **option** Verkaufsoption *(opp. call option)*; ~ **option business** (or **transaction**) Rückprämiengeschäft; ~ **price** Rückprämienkurs; **to give for the** ~ *Br* die Rückprämie verkaufen; **to take for the** ~ *Br* die Rückprämie kaufen

put *v* setzen, stellen, legen; *(Börse)* anbieten, liefern *(opp. to call)*; **to** ~ **it** es ausdrücken (od. formulieren); **to** ~ **an advertisement in a newspaper** e-e Anzeige in e-e Zeitung setzen; **to** ~ **the blame on sb.** jdm die Schuld zuschieben; **to** ~ **a clause in a contract** e-e Klausel in e-n Vertrag einfügen; **to** ~ **confidence in** Vertrauen setzen auf; **to** ~ **one's initials (to)** →initials 1.; **to** ~ **a name on a list** e-n Namen auf e-e Liste setzen; **to** ~ **pressure on sb.** auf jdn Druck ausüben; **to** ~ **the** →**question**; **to** ~ **a** →**resolution to a meeting**

put *v*, **to** ~ **back** *fig* verzögern; zurückkehren

(Schiff); (Geld) zurücklegen; **to ~ by** *(Geld)* beiseite legen

put (down) *v (Aufruhr etc)* niederschlagen, unterdrücken; *(Vorrat)* anlegen; aufschreiben, niederschreiben; **to ~ sb. down for** jdn vormerken für; **to ~ sth. down to sb.** jdm etw. zuschreiben; **to ~ down to a p.'s account** jdm in Rechnung stellen; **to ~ down to a customer's account** *Br* für e-n Kunden anschreiben; **to ~ (down) on the agenda** auf die Tagesordnung setzen; **to ~ one's name down on a list** sich in e-e Liste eintragen (lassen); **to ~ a name down for →membership**; **to ~ down passengers** Fahrgäste absetzen *(opp. to take on)*; **to ~ down a revolt** e-e Revolte niederschlagen; **to ~ down in writing** niederschreiben

put (forward) *v* vorbringen; *(Theorie etc)* aufstellen; **to ~ forward an argument** ein Argument vorbringen; **to ~ sb. forward as a candidate** jdn als Kandidaten in Vorschlag bringen; **to ~ forward a claim** e-n Anspruch geltend machen; **to ~ forward an opinion** e-e Ansicht vorbringen; **to ~ sb. forward for promotion** jdn für e-e Beförderung einreichen (od. vorschlagen); **to ~ forward reasons** Gründe vorbringen

put (in) *v (Antrag etc)* einreichen, vorlegen; einsetzen, einfügen; *(von Schiffen)* einlaufen; *(Hafen)* anlaufen; **to ~ in for sth.** *colloq. (förmlich)* bitten um etw.; etw. einreichen; **to ~ in a claim** Anspruch erheben (for auf); beanspruchen; **to ~ in a document** e-e Urkunde einreichen; **to ~ in for a job** sich um e-e Stelle bewerben; **to ~ in a plea of (not) guilty** sich für (nicht) schuldig bekennen; **to ~ in for a rise** *Br colloq.* um e-e Gehaltserhöhung bitten

put (into) *v* hinein-, einlegen; **to ~ money into a bank** Geld auf e-e Bank legen; **to ~ capital into a business** Kapital in ein Geschäft stekken; **to ~ into circulation** in Umlauf setzen; **to ~ into commission** *(Schiff)* in Dienst stellen; **to ~ into force** in Kraft setzen

put (off) *v* aufschieben, verschieben, vertagen; *(Schiff)* auslaufen, abfahren; **to ~ off one's creditors** s-e Gläubiger hinhalten; **to ~ off a matter for a month** e-e Sache um e-n Monat verschieben (od. vertagen)

put (on) *v (Kleidung)* anziehen; *(Summe)* aufschlagen (to the price auf den Preis); *(für etw. anderes)* einsetzen *(z. B. e-n Zug)*; **to ~ on file** zu den Akten nehmen; **to ~ on the market** auf den Markt bringen; **to ~ on oath** vereidigen; **to ~ on trial** vor Gericht bringen (od. stellen)

put (out) *v* hinauswerfen; *(Feuer)* löschen; auslaufen, in See stechen *(Schiff)*; **to ~ out of action** außer Betrieb setzen; **to ~ out money on a mortgage** Geld gegen e-e Hypothek ausleihen

put (over) *v (erfolgreich)* erklären, verständlich machen; **to ~ over a case** e-e Sache erklären *(um jdn davon zu überzeugen)*; **to ~ over a policy** für e-e Politik Verständnis gewinnen

put (to) *v*, **to ~ to sb.'s account** jdm etw. berechnen (od. in Rechnung stellen); **to ~ to (good) account** etw. verwerten; **to ~ sb. to great expense** jdm hohe Kosten verursachen; **to ~ to land** sich an Land begeben; **to ~ large sums to reserve** große Rücklagen machen; **to ~ to sale** zum Verkauf bringen (od. anbieten); **to ~ to sea** auslaufen, in See stechen; **to ~ to the vote** zur Abstimmung bringen (od. stellen)

put through *v* durchführen, zu Ende führen

put (up) *v* aufstellen, errichten *(z. B. Messestand)*; *(Plakat)* anschlagen; *colloq. (jdn)* aufnehmen, *(jdm)* Unterkunft geben; *(Preis etc)* erhöhen, heraufsetzen; **to ~ up a candidate for election** e-n Kandidaten zu Wahl aufstellen; **to ~ up funds** (or **money**) Geld aufbringen; **to ~ up the price** den Preis heraufsetzen; **to ~ up for sale** zum Verkauf anbieten; **the property was ~ up for auction** der Grundbesitz wurde versteigert

put upon *v* →to put on

putting, ~ in possession Einsetzung in den Besitz; **~ into force** Inkraftsetzung; **~ into operation** Inbetriebsetzung; Inbetriebnahme; **~ the question** *Br parl* Fragestellung *(Formulierung der Frage, über die zu entscheiden ist, durch den →speaker; hierdurch wird die Abstimmung eingeleitet)*; **~ up of funds** (or **money**) Kapitalaufbringung

putative mutmaßlich; **~ father**[178] mutmaßlicher Vater *(e-s nichtehelichen Kindes)*

pyramid scheme Plan, bei dem Gewinne aus einer Transaktion immer wieder zur Durchführung anderer Transaktionen verwandt werden

pyramid selling[179] Absatz durch Verkauf von – gestaffelten – Verkaufsrechten an e-m Produkt *(Erscheinungsform des Absatzes durch progressive Kundenwerbung)*; **~ system** Schneeballsystem

pyramiding *(Börse)* Anhäufung von Gewinnen durch Spekulationen *(z. B. durch mehrmaligen Kauf des gleichen Papiers bei e-r Hausse)*; Lohnsteigerung *(durch Zulagen etc)*

Q

Qatar Katar; **State of** ~ Staat Katar
Qatar, (of) ~ Katarer, ~in; katarisch

quadrennial vierjährig; vierjährlich

quadrilateral meeting Vierertreffen

quadrillion *Br* Quadrillion (10^{24}); *Am* Billiarde (10^{15})

quadripartite, Q~ Agreement *(von den vier Siegermächten ausgehandeltes)* Viermächteabkommen über Berlin (von 1971); ~ **conference** Viermächtekonferenz; ~ **meeting** Vierertreffen, Viermächtetreffen

quadruplicate vierfach(e Ausfertigung); **in** ~ vierfach

quadruplicate *v* vierfach ausfertigen

quaere ("inquire") man fragt sich, es ist die Frage (whether ob)

Quaker Quäker *(Br Mitglied der Society of Friends; Am Mitglied des American Friends Service Committee)*

qualification 1. Qualifikation, *(erforderl.)* Befähigung, Eignung, Tauglichkeit; Berechtigung; Vorbedingung, Voraussetzung (for für); *(IPR)* Qualifikation, Einordnung unter die Verweisungsbegriffe der Kollisionsnormen; ~ **for admission to a university** Voraussetzung für Zulassung zu e-r Universität; ~ **for citizenship** Voraussetzung für den Erwerb der Staatsangehörigkeit; ~ **for dividend** Dividendenberechtigung; ~ **for election** Wahlberechtigung; ~ **for an examination** *Am* (Erfüllung der Voraussetzungen für die) Zulassung zu e-r Prüfung; ~ **for naturalization** *Br* Voraussetzung für Einbürgerung; ~ **for pension** Pensionsberechtigung; ~ **for public office** Voraussetzung (od. Vorbedingung) für ein öffentliches Amt; ~ **of membership** Voraussetzung für den Erwerb der Mitgliedschaft; ~ **procedure** *Am* Zulassungsverfahren; ~ **shares** Qualifikationsaktien, Pflichtaktien *(Mindestzahl von Aktien, deren Übernahme Voraussetzung für Ernennung zum director e-r AG ist)*; ~ **test** Eignungsprüfung; Gütetest; **certificate of** ~ Befähigungszeugnis, Befähigungsnachweis; **occupational** (or **professional**) ~ berufliche Qualifikation; **proof of** ~ Befähigungsnachweis; **to hold the** ~ die (berufl.) Voraussetzung haben

qualification 2. Einschränkung; Vorbehalt; ~ **of an offer** Einschränkung e-s Angebots; **subject to** ~**s** Änderungen vorbehalten; **with the** ~ mit der Einschränkung; **without any** ~ ohne jede Einschränkung

qualified qualifiziert, befähigt, geeignet, tauglich; vorgebildet; berechtigt; eingeschränkt, bedingt; ~ **acceptance** *(WechselR)*[1] eingeschränktes Akzept *(opp. general acceptance)*; Annahme unter Vorbehalt; ~ **as to time** zeitlich beschränkt; ~ **(audit) certificate** eingeschränkter Bestätigungsvermerk *(des Wirtschaftsprüfers)* ~ **endorsement** *(WechselR)*[2] eingeschränktes Indossament, Indossament ohne Obligo; ~ **fee** von e-r Bedingung abhängiges Eigentumsrecht *(an Grundbesitz)*; ~ **for an appointment** für e-n Posten qualifiziert; ~ **indorsement** →~ endorsement; ~ **majority** qualifizierte Mehrheit; ~ **medical practitioner** approbierter praktischer Arzt; ~ →**privilege;** ~ **report** eingeschränkter Bericht *(des Wirtschaftsprüfers, z. B. durch die Erklärung, daß einige Posten unklar sind)*; **in a** ~ **sense** mit Einschränkungen; ~ **title** *Br*[3] Grundstücksrechtstitel, der gewissen (im →Land Register erwähnten) Beschränkungen unterliegt; ~ **to do business** *Am* Berechtigung zur Geschäftstätigkeit *(e-r corporation außerhalb des Gründungsstaates)*; ~ **voter** Wahlberechtigter, Abstimmungsberechtigter; **duly** (or **legally**) ~ **to practise medicine** *med* approbiert

qualify *v* qualifizieren, befähigen, berechtigen; die nötige Vorbedingung (od. Befähigung) besitzen, die nötigen Voraussetzungen erfüllen, in Frage kommen (for für); sich qualifizieren, sich als geeignet erweisen, s-e Befähigung (od. Eignung) nachweisen; *(e-e Erklärung)* einschränken; *(etw. durch Angabe der wesentl. Eigenschaften in e-e Klasse)* einordnen, kennzeichnen; *Scot* beweisen, nachweisen *(z. B. a title)*; **to** ~ **for citizenship** die nötigen Voraussetzungen für den Erwerb der Staatsangehörigkeit besitzen (od. nachweisen); **to** ~ **for an examination** die Voraussetzungen für die Zulassung zu e-r Prüfung erfüllen; **to** ~ **for an office** die nötigen Vorbedingungen für ein Amt besitzen (od. nachweisen); **to** ~ **as a physician** s-e Approbation als Arzt erhalten; **to** ~ **as a solicitor** *Br* als Rechtsanwalt zugelassen werden; **to** ~ **a statement** e-e Erklärung unter Einschränkungen abgeben; **to** ~ **the terms of a contract by a clause** die Bestimmungen e-s Vertrages durch e-e Klausel einschränken; **to** ~ **as a university lecturer** sich habilitieren

qualifying, ~ **certificate** Berechnungsnachweis; ~ **date** Stichtag; ~ **examination** Eignungsprüfung; ~ **participation** notwendige Mindestbeteiligung; ~ **period** *(VersR)* Wartezeit, Karenzfrist; ~ **shares** Pflichtaktien; **to complete the** ~ **period** die Wartezeit erfüllen

qualitative qualitativ; ~ **analysis** qualitative Untersuchung

quality Qualität, Eigenschaft, Beschaffenheit, Güte; ~ **as per sample** Qualität laut Muster; ~ **categories** Güteklassen; ~ **control** Qualitätskontrolle; Gütekontrolle;~ **goods** Qualitätswaren; ~ **grade** Qualitätsstufe; ~ **label** Gütezeichen; ~ **level** Qualitätsniveau; **improvement of the ~ of life** Verbesserung der Lebensqualität; ~ **mark** Gütezeichen; ~ **of the environment** Umweltqualität; ~ **of (an) estate** Umfang des Rechts an Grundbesitz *(ob zukünftiges oder gegenwärtiges, alleiniges oder gemeinschaftliches, volles oder partielles Eigentum [od. Besitz]);* ~ **or fitness** (on a sale of goods)[4] Qualität oder Tauglichkeit *(für den Zweck, für den die Ware bestimmt ist);* ~ **product** Qualitätserzeugnis; ~ **rating** Qualitätsbeurteilung; ~ **stabilization** *Am*[5] Qualitätsstabilisierung *(andere Bezeichnung für Preisbindung der zweiten Hand);* ~ **standards** Qualitätsnormen; ~ **test** Qualitätsprüfung, Güteprüfung

qualit|y, agreed ~ vereinbarte Qualität; **average** ~ Durchschnittsqualität; **of average kind and** ~ von mittlerer Art und Güte; **bottom** ~ schlechteste Qualität; **checking of** ~ Qualitätsprüfung; **choice** ~ erste Qualität; **complaint regarding the** ~ Qualitätsrüge; **defect as to** ~ Qualitätsmangel; Sachmangel; **fair average** ~ (f. a. q.) gute Durchschnittsqualität, gute Mittelqualität; **first (class)** ~ erste (od. prima) Qualität; **(of) high** ~ (von) gute(r) Qualität, hochwertig; **improvement of** ~ Qualitätsverbesserung; **(of) inferior** ~ (von) schlechte(r) Qualität, minderwertig; **managerial ~ies** Führungseigenschaften; **mark of** ~ Qualitätszeichen, Gütezeichen; **medium** ~ mittlere Qualität; **→merchantable ~; poor** ~ schlechte Qualität; **promised** ~ zugesicherte Eigenschaft; **required** ~ erforderliche Qualität; **second-class** ~ zweite Qualität; **(of) superior** ~ (von) beste(r) Qualität, hochwertig; **warranted** ~ s. promised →~; **warranty of** ~ Gewährleistung für Qualität (Sachmängelhaftung); **to check the** ~ die Qualität prüfen; **to guarantee ~ies** Eigenschaften zusichern

quango-quasi-autonomous non-governmental organization halbstaatliche Organisation *(z.B. ACAS)*

quantitative quantitativ, mengenmäßig; ~ **index** Mengenindex; **internal ~ regulations** inländische Mengenvorschriften; **to be subject to ~ restrictions** mengenmäßigen Beschränkungen (der Einfuhr od. Ausfuhr) unterliegen

quantit|ies, ~ y surveyor *Br* Baukostensachverständiger *(der bills of ~ aufstellt);* **bill of** ~ *Br* Aufstellung des benötigten Baumaterials, der Arbeitskräfte etc bei Errichtung e-s Gebäudes

quantity Quantität, Menge; ~ **bonus** *(ArbR)* Mengenprämie; ~ **buyer** Großabnehmer; ~ **buying** Mengenkauf; ~ **discount** (or **allowance**) Mengenrabatt; ~ **index** Mengenindex; ~ **of (an) estate** Dauer des Rechts an Grundbesitz *(in fee, for life, or for years);* ~ **of goods** Warenmenge; ~ **of production** Produktionsmenge; ~ **production** Massenherstellung; ~ **rebate** Mengenrabatt; ~ **sold** Absatzmenge; ~ **surveyor** →quantities; ~ **variance** Mengenabweichung

quantit|y, average ~ Durchschnittsmenge; **complaints regarding the** ~ Quantitätsrüge; **defect as to** ~ Quantitätsmangel; **difference in** ~ mengenmäßige Abweichung; **equal ~ies** gleiche Mengen; **excess** ~ zuviel gelieferte Menge; **in large ~ies** in großen Mengen; **maximum** ~ Höchstmenge; **minimum** ~ Mindestmenge; **non-commercial ~ies** nicht zum Handel geeignete Mengen; **to deviate from the ~ies** von den Mengen abweichen

quantum meruit ("as much as he has earned") angemessene Vergütung *(e-e der tatsächlichen Leistung entsprechende Vergütung)*

quantum of damages Betrag des Schadensersatzes; Entschädigungssumme

quarantinable, ~ diseases[6] quarantänepflichtige Krankheiten; ~ **immigrant** der Quarantänepflicht unterliegender Einwanderer

quarantine Quarantäne; *Am (Common Law)* Recht der Witwe, nach dem Tode ihres Mannes 40 Tage in s-m Haus zu leben; ~ **dues** Quarantänegelder; ~ **flag** Quarantäneflagge; ~ **harbo(u)r** Quarantänehafen; ~ **regulations** Quarantänebestimmungen; ~ **risk** Quarantänerisiko; **to be in** ~ in Quarantäne liegen; **to discharge from** ~ aus der Quarantäne entlassen; **to lift the** ~ die Quarantäne aufheben; **to put in** (or **under**) ~ unter Quarantäne stellen

quarantine *v* unter Quarantäne stellen

quare clausum fregit ("wherefore he broke the close") Hausfriedensbruch, Verletzung des Immobiliarbesitzrechts *(trespass to land)*

quarrel, to make up a ~ e-n Streit beilegen

quarry[7] Steinbruch; **~ing industry** Industrie der Steine und Erden

quart Quart(maß)

quarter 1. Viertel; Vierteljahr, Quartal; Viertelzentner (*Br* 28 lb. = 12,7 kg, *Am* 25 lb. = 11,34 kg); *Am* Vierteldollar, 25-cent(-Stück)

quarter day Quartalstag; *bes. Br* Mietzahltag
Br 25. 3. (Lady Day), 24. 6. (Midsummer Day), 29. 9. (Michaelmas), and 25. 12. (Christmas); *Scot* 2. 2. (Candlemas), 15. 5. (Whitsunday), 1. 8. (Lammas), 11. 11. (Martinmas), *Am (and Ger)* 1. 1., 1. 4., 1. 7., 1. 10.; **rent payable on ~s** *Br* an den Quartalstagen zahlbare Miete

quarter, ~**'s income** Vierteljahreseinkommen; ~**'s instal(l)ment** Vierteljahresrate; ~**s of coverage** *Am* Arbeitszeiten in buchmäßigen Vierteljahren *(zur Berechnung des Rentenanspruchs);* ~**'s payment** Quartalszahlung; ~**'s rent** Vierteljahresmiete; ~**'s salary** Vierteljahresgehalt; **to be paid by the** ~ vierteljährlich bezahlt werden

Quarter Sessions (Q. S.) Quartalgerichte
Br abgeschafft
Am (in einigen Einzelstaaten) vierteljährlich tagendes Gericht für leichtere Strafsachen

quarter stock Aktie mit e-m Nennwert von ‰ 25

quarter 2. Stadtviertel; **business** ~ Geschäftsviertel; **industrial** (or **manufacturing**) ~ Industrieviertel; **residential** ~ Wohnviertel, Wohnbezirk; **slum** ~**s** Elendsviertel

quarter 3. Stelle; *fig* Seite; **in diplomatic** ~**s** in diplomatischen Kreisen; **financial** ~**s** Finanzkreise; **from official** ~**s** von amtlicher Seite

quarter 4. ~**s** Quartier; Unterkunft; ~**master-general** (Q. M. G.) *mil* Generalquartiermeister; **to change one's** ~**s** umziehen

quarter 5. *bes. mil* Gnade; **no** ~ **was given** es wurde keine Gnade gezeigt

quarter *v mil* einquartieren; **to be** ~**ed** im Quartier liegen (at or in bei); ~**ing** Einquartierung; Unterkunft

quarterage Vierteljahreszahlung, Quartalszahlung; vierteljährliche (Miet-, Gehalts- etc) Zahlung; Quartalsbetrag

quarterly Vierteljahresschrift; vierteljährlich, quartalsweise; ~ **account** (or **bill**) Vierteljahresrechnung, Quartalsrechnung; ~ **disbursement** Quartalszahlung *(von Zinsen, Dividenden etc);* ~ **magazine** Vierteljahreszeitschrift; ~ **payment** vierteljährliche Zahlung, Quartalszahlung; ~ **period** Quartal; ~ **report** Vierteljahresbericht; ~ **salary** Vierteljahresgehalt; **to be paid** ~ vierteljährlich gezahlt werden

quash *v* aufheben, annullieren, für ungültig erklären; **to** ~ **a conviction** e-n Schuldspruch aufheben; **to** ~ **the indictment** die Anklage für nicht begründet erklären *(→indictment);* **to** ~ **the order of the inferior court** die Verfügung des unteren Gerichts aufheben; **to** ~ **the proceedings** das Verfahren niederschlagen; **to** ~ **a sentence** e-e Strafe aufheben

quasi Quasi-, Schein-; gewissermaßen; ~**- agreement** *Am*[8] *(AntitrustR)* Gruppendisziplin; aufeinander abgestimmtes Verhalten; ~**- contract** Quasivertrag, vertragsähnliches Schuldverhältnis *(Fälle ungerechtfertigter Bereicherung und Geschäftsführung ohne Auftrag);* ~**- contractual relationship** vertragsähnliches Rechtsverhältnis; ~**-corporation** *Am* Vereinigung, die wie e-e corporation behandelt wird, obgleich sie nicht "incorporated in proper form" ist *(z. B. labor unions);* ~**-crime** verbrechensähnliches Delikt *(das nicht mit Freiheits- od. Geldstrafe bestraft wird; z. B. Am gesetzwidrige Einwanderung, die mit →deportation geahndet wird);* ~ **in rem jurisdiction** *Am* fingierte in rem Zuständigkeit *(Zuständigkeit kraft fingierter Belegenheit e-s Rechts od. Rechtsverhältnisses; →jurisdiction quasi in rem);* ~**-judicial** gerichtsähnlich *(zwischen Justiz und Verwaltung stehend);* ~**-judicial agency** *Am* gerichtsähnliche Behörde *(z. B. Federal Trade Commission, die Rechtsschöpfung und Rechtsanwendung in gleicher Weise betreibt);* ~**-judicial functions** quasigerichtliche Tätigkeit *(bes. der Verwaltungsbehörden);* ~**-legislative international institutions** gesetzgebungsähnliche internationale Einrichtungen *(z. B. International Labour Organization);* ~ **money** →near money; ~ **municipal bonds** *Am* nicht vollwertige Kommunalanleihen; ~**-official** →semi-official; ~ **partner** *Am* Scheingesellschafter; ~ **partnership** →partnership; ~**-personalty** quasibewegliches Vermögen *(z. B. fixtures, chattels real, leases for years);* ~**-prosperity** Scheinkonjunktur; ~**-public corporation** *Am* Quasikörperschaft des öffentlichen Rechts *(privates Unternehmen, das e-e der Öffentlichkeit dienende Tätigkeit ausübt; z. B. Federal Reserve Banks und public utility companies);* ~**-realty** quasi-unbewegliches Vermögen *(bewegl. Vermögen, das wie unbewegl. Vermögen behandelt und als solches vererbt werden kann, z. B. heirlooms, title-deeds etc);* ~**-trustee** Quasitreuhänder *(jd, der sich als Treuhänder ausgibt und als solcher haftet);* **administrative** ~**-legislation** *Br* gesetzgebungsartige Verwaltungsanordnungen *(keine delegated legislation)*

quay Kai; Schiffs-Landeplatz; ~ **dues** Kaigebühren; ~ **receipt** Kaiempfangsschein; ~ **rent** Kailagergeld; **ex** ~ ab Kai; **to discharge at the** ~ am Kai löschen

quayage Kaigeld, Kaigebühr

Queen Königin; ~ **Anne's Bounty** *Br* Unterstützungsfonds für arme Geistliche; ~**'s Bench Division** (Q. B. D.) →bench 1.; ~ **Consort** Gemahlin e-s regierenden Königs; ~**'s Counsel (OC)** *Br* Anwalt der Krone (*→counsel 1.*); ~**dowager** Königinwitwe; ~**'s English** *Br* reines Englisch *(korrekte Anwendung der englischen Sprache);* ~**'s evidence** *Br* →evidence; ~ **regnant** regierende Königin; ~**'s proctor** *Br* →proctor; ~**'s speech** Thronrede

querulous person Querulant

query *v* in Frage stellen, bezweifeln, beanstanden

question Frage; *parl* Anfrage *(entspricht etwa der kleinen Anfrage);* **Q**~! Zur Sache! *(Zwischenruf*

im Parlament etc); ~ **at issue** Streitfrage; die zur Entscheidung stehende Frage; Kernfrage
question, ~ **in** (or **under**) **debate** zur Diskussion stehende Frage; ~ **in dispute** strittige Frage; ~ **of fact** Tatfrage; ~ **of confidence** *pol* Vertrauensfrage; ~ **of law** Rechtsfrage; ~ **of substance** Sachfrage; ~ **time** *parl* Fragestunde; **cross-**~ Kreuzfrage *(bei e-m Kreuzverhör);* **formulation of the** ~ Fragestellung; **in** ~ in Frage stehend, fraglich, vorliegend; **the person in** ~ der (die) Betreffende; **incidental** ~ Zwischenfrage; **leading** ~ Suggestivfrage; **legal** ~ Rechtsfrage
question, out of (the) ~ außer Frage; **to be out of the** ~ nicht in Frage kommen; **it is not out of the** ~ **that** es ist nicht ausgeschlossen, daß
question, to address a ~ *parl* Anfrage richten (to an); **to ask** ~**s** Fragen stellen; **to beg the** ~ der Frage (od. dem wahren Sachverhalt) ausweichen; **to broach a** ~ e-e Frage anschneiden; **to call for the** ~ *parl* um Abstimmung bitten; **to call in** ~ in Frage stellen, bezweifeln; **to come into** ~ in Frage (od. Betracht) kommen; **to depart from the** ~ vom Thema abweichen; **to put the** ~ (to the vote) *parl* Frage (zur Abstimmung) stellen, zur Abstimmung schreiten (→*putting the* ~); **to raise a** ~ e-e Frage aufwerfen; **the** ~ **arises** die Frage erhebt sich; **the** ~ **does not arise** die Frage ist belanglos (od. nicht zutreffend); **the** ~ **is** es handelt sich darum

question *v* befragen; verhören, vernehmen; in Zweifel ziehen
questioned, to be ~ **by the police** von der Polizei verhört werden
questioning Befragung; Verhör, Vernehmung; **upon** ~ **a p.** auf Befragen jds

questionary *Am* →questionnaire

questionnaire Fragebogen; ~ **surveys** *(MMF)* Umfragen an Hand von Fragebogen; **to complete** (or **fill in, prepare**) **a** ~ e-n Fragebogen ausfüllen; **to falsify** (or **forge**) **a** ~ e-n Fragebogen fälschen; **to submit a** ~ e-n Fragebogen einreichen

queu jumper *(Verkehr)* Kolonnenspringer

quick schnell; ~ **assets** flüssige Anlagen; *(Bilanz)* Umlaufvermögen; leicht realisierbare Aktivposten; ~ **returns** schneller Umsatz; **to make a** ~ **profit** in kurzer Zeit e-n Gewinn machen

quicky strike *Am* Blitzstreik, Kurzstreik

quid pro quo ("something for something") Gegenleistung

quiet ruhig; *com* lustlos, flau; ~ **enjoyment (of possession)** ungestörter Besitz

quiet *v*, **action to** ~ **title** *Am* Klage auf Feststellung der Eigentums- und Berechtigungsverhältnisse an Grundbesitz

quietus ("he has been relieved") Entlastung; Schulderlaß; **to give** ~ Entlastung erteilen

quinquennial fünfjährig, alle fünf Jahre

quintal Doppelzentner (100 kg)

quintuplicate fünffach

quisling Volksverräter, Kollaborateur *(Quisling war der Führer der norwegischen Nationalsozialisten)*

quit *v (Arbeitsplatz)* verlassen; aufgeben, verzichten auf; räumen, ausziehen *(Mieter);* **to** ~ **an employment** e-e Beschäftigung (od. Stelle) aufgeben; **to** ~ **office** ein Amt niederlegen; **to** ~ **the service** aus dem Dienst ausscheiden; **notice to** ~ Kündigung *(des Mieters od. Pächters;* →*notice 3.);* **order to** ~ *Br (gerichtl.)* Räumungsbefehl
quitting time *Am colloq.* Geschäftsschluß

quitclaim Verzicht(leistung); ~ **deed** *Am* Grundstücksübertragungsurkunde *(ohne Garantie für die Ordnungsmäßigkeit des übertragenden Rechtsanspruchs; Veräußerer überträgt nur die Rechte, die er selbst hat)*

quittance Entlastung, Quittung

quorum ("of whom") Quorum, beschlußfähige Anzahl, (Mindestzahl zur) Beschlußfähigkeit; *parl* Sitzungsfähigkeit; **absence** (or **lack**) **of** ~ Beschlußfähigkeit; **to ascertain that there is a** ~ (or **to establish that the** ~ **is present**) die Beschlußunfähigkeit feststellen; **to be without a** ~ beschlußunfähig sein; **to constitute** (or **form**) **a** ~ beschlußfähig sein; **to lack a** ~ beschlußunfähig sein; **there is a (no)** ~ die Versammlung ist (nicht) beschlußfähig; **a** ~ **is not present** es besteht keine Beschlußfähigkeit

quota Quote, prozentuale Beteiligung, (verhältnismäßiger) Anteil; Kontingent (on für); (Lieferungs-)Soll; ~ **agent** *com* Kontingentträger; ~ **agreement** (or **arrangement**) Quotenregelung; ~**-fixing cartel** Quotenkartell; ~ **goods** kontingentierte (od. bewirtschaftete) Waren; ~ **increase** Quotenerhöhung, Aufstockung der Quoten; ~ **litis** *Am* Erfolgshonorar *(e-s Anwalts) (cf. contingent fee);* ~ **of immigrants** *Am* Einwanderungsquote; ~ **of profit(s)** *(verhältnismäßiger)* Gewinnanteil; ~ **overrun** Quotenüberschreitung; ~ **provided for** vorgesehene Quote; ~ **restriction** Quotenkürzung, Kontingentierung; ~ **sample** (MMF) Quotenauswahl, Stichprobenanalyse; ~ **sampling** (MMF) Quotenauswahlverfahren *(festgelegt wird nur die Quote, d.h. die Anzahl der zu Befragenden, während die Auswahl dem Interviewer überlassen wird)*

quota share Kontingentanteil; *(VersR)* Quote *(bei Rückversicherung);* ~ **reinsurance** Quotenrückversicherung; ~ **reinsurance treaty** *(VersR)* Quotenrückversicherungsvertrag

quota system Quotensystem; Kontingentierungssystem *(z. B. für Einwanderer)*

quota, allocation of ~**s** Zuteilung von Quoten; **building** ~ Baukontingent; **buying** ~ Einkaufskontingent; **export** ~ Exportquote, Ausfuhrkontingent; **fixing of** ~**s** Festsetzung der Quoten, Kontingentierung; **foreign exchange** ~ Devisenkontingent; **global** ~ Globalkontingent; **goods** ~ Warenkontingent; **immigration** ~ Einwanderungsquote, Einwanderungskontingent; **import** ~ Importquote, Einfuhrkontingent; **increase of a** ~ Quotenerhöhung; Erhöhung e-s Kontingents; **maximum** ~ Höchstkontingent, Höchstquote; **marketing** ~ Absatzkontingent; **minimum** ~ Mindestkontingent, Mindestquote; **→non(-)** ~; **purchase** ~ Einkaufsquote, Einkaufskontingent; **reduction of a** ~ Quotenkürzung, Kürzung e-s Kontingents; **sales** ~ Verkaufsquote, Verkaufskontingent; Absatzkontingent; **subject to a** ~ kontingentiert; **tariff** ~ Zollkontingent; **yearly** ~ Jahreskontingent

quota, to allot ~**s** Quoten zuteilen; kontingentieren; **to dispose of a** ~ über ein Kontingent verfügen; **to exceed a** ~ e-e Quote überschreiten; **to exhaust a** ~ ein Kontingent erschöpfen; **to fix** (or **establish**) **a** ~ **(for)** *(etw.)* kontingentieren, ein Kontingent (od. e-e Quote) festsetzen (für); **to increase** (or **raise**) **the** ~ die Quote (od. das Kontingent) erhöhen; **to reduce the** ~ die Quote (od. das Kontingent) kürzen

quotable *(Börse)* notierbar; ~ **share** börsenfähige Aktie

quotation 1. Anführung, Zitierung; Zitat, zitierte Stelle; ~ **of one's authorities** Quellenangabe; ~ **of a case** Berufung auf e-e Entscheidung; **verbatim** ~ wörtliches Zitat

quotation 2. Preisangabe, Preisangebot, Kostenanschlag; **to ask sb. for a** ~ e-e Preisanfrage richten an jdn; von jdm ein Angebot mit Preis verlangen; **to submit a** ~ ein Preisangebot machen, e-n Kostenanschlag unterbreiten

quotation 3. *(Börse)* (Kurs-)Notierung; (Kurs-) Notiz; Kurs; ~ **for forward delivery** (or **for futures**) Terminnotierung; ~ **of the day** Tageskurs; ~ **of (foreign) exchange rates** Devisennotierung; ~ **of prices** Kursnotierung; ~ **on a foreign market** Auslandsnotierung; ~ **ticker** *Am* Börsenfernschreiber; **admission of shares** (or *Am* **stocks**) **to** ~ Zulassung von Aktien zur Börsennotierung; **application for** ~ **on the stock exchange** *Br* Antrag auf Zulassung zur Börsennotierung; **closing** ~ Schlußnotierung; Schlußkurs; **consecutive** ~ fortlaufende Notierung; **decline in** ~**s** Baisse; **difference in** ~**s** Kursunterschied, Kursdifferenz; **final** ~ Schlußkurs; **first** ~ Anfangskurs; **flat** ~ *Am* Kursnotierung ohne Zinsberücksichtigung; **foreign exchange** ~ Devisennotierung; **last** ~ Schlußnotierung; **the latest** ~**s** die letzten Kurse; **list of** ~**s** *Br* Kursblatt; **official** ~ amtliche Notierung; amtlicher Kurs; **official foreign exchange** ~ amtlicher Devisenkurs; **opening** ~ erste Notierung *(Anfangskurs);* **at the present** ~ zum gegenwärtigen Kurs, zum Tageskurs; **previous** ~ letzte Notierung *(vom Tage vorher);* **price** ~ Kursnotierung; **rise in** ~**s** Hausse; **share** ~ *Br* (**stock** ~ *Am*) Aktienkurs; Kursnotierung; **spot** ~ Kassakurs; **stock exchange** ~ Börsenkurs; **today's** ~ heutige Notierung; **unofficial** ~ Notierung im Freiverkehr; **to apply for official** ~ *Br (für ein Wertpapier)* Zulassung zur Börse beantragen; **to grant a** ~ zum Börsenhandel zulassen

quote *v* 1. anführen, zitieren; angeben; **to** ~ **as authority** als Quelle angeben; **to** ~ **a case** e-e Entscheidung *(als Präzedenzfall)* anführen; sich auf e-e Entscheidung berufen; **to** ~ **from a case** aus e-r Entscheidung *(wörtlich)* zitieren; **to** ~ **an instance** ein Beispiel anführen; **to** ~ **a precedent** e-n Präzedenzfall anführen; **to** ~ **a price** e-n Preis angeben; ein Preisangebot machen; **to** ~ **references** Referenzen angeben; **to** ~ **verbatim** wörtlich zitieren; **in your reply please** ~ in Ihrer Antwort bitte angeben

quoted, ~ **price** angegebener Preis, Preisangebot; **to be** ~ **in all communications** in allen Mitteilungen anzugeben

quote *v* 2. *(Börse)* notieren, Kurse (und Warenpreise börsenmäßig) feststellen und veröffentlichen; **to** ~ **a price** e-n Kurs notieren

quoted, ~ **company** börsennotierte Gesellschaft; ~ **investments** börsennotierte Anlagen; ~ **list** *Br* amtlicher Kurszettel *(opp. unquoted list);* ~ **price** *(Börse)* notierter Kurs; **officially** ~ **securities** zur amtlichen Notierung zugelassene Wertpapiere; ~ **shares** (börsen-)notierte Aktien; ~ **value** Kurswert; **to be** ~ **on the stock exchange** an der Börse notiert werden

quotient, election ~ Wahlquotient

quo warranto ("by what authority") *Am (einzelstaatl. verschieden geregeltes)* besonderes Verfahren, in dem die Rechtmäßigkeit der Ausübung des Privilegs e-r juristischen Person od. der Ausübung e-s öffentl. Amtes nachgeprüft wird

R

R&D →Research and Development

rabble-rouser *pol* (Volks-)Aufwiegler; Hetzagent; Agitator

race: 1. Rasse; ~ **discrimination** →racial discrimination; ~ **hatred** Rassenhaß; ~ **issue** Rassenproblem; ~ **relations**[1] Beziehungen zwischen den Rassen; ~ **riot** Rassenkrawall *(Am zwischen Weißen und Farbigen);* ~ **segregation** *Am* Rassentrennung, Rassenabsonderung *(in öffentl. Einrichtungen, Schulen etc)*; **without distinction of** ~ ohne Unterschied der Rasse; **human** ~ Menschengeschlecht

race 2. (Pferde, Boots- etc) Rennen; *fig* Wettlauf (for um); ~**course** Rennplatz, Rennbahn; ~ **between prices and wages** Lohn-Preis-Spirale; ~**s type statutes** *Am* →recording system; **armament** (or **arms**) ~ Wettrüsten; **to run a** ~ an e-m Rennen teilnehmen

race *v parl (Gesetze)* durchpeitschen

racial die Rasse betreffend, Rassen-; **removal of** ~ **barriers** Beseitigung von Rassenschranken; ~ **desegregation** Aufhebung der Rassentrennung; ~ **discrimination**[1] (or **discrimination on** ~ **grounds**) Rassendiskriminierung, unterschiedliche Behandlung von Rassen; ~ **equality** Rassengleichheit; ~ **intolerance** Unduldsamkeit in Rassenfragen; ~ **issue** Rassenfrage, Rassenproblem; ~ **minorities** Rassenminderheiten; ~ **persecution** Rassenverfolgung; ~ **policy** Rassenpolitik; ~ **prejudice** Rassenvorurteil; ~ **relations** →race relations; ~**segregation** →race segregation; ~ **supremacy** Rassenüberlegenheit; ~ **tension** Spannung in den Beziehungen zwischen den Rassen; ~ **unrest** Rassenunruhen; **multi-**~ aus vielen (verschiedenen) Rassen bestehend

racially homogeneous people rassisch einheitliches Volk

racialism *(übertriebenes)* Rassenbewußtsein

racialist Rassenfanatiker

racism →racialism

racist →racialist

rack jobber *Am* Regalgroßhändler, Großhändler, der Einzelhandelsgeschäfte mit kompletten Warengruppen *(außer Lebensmitteln)* beliefert *(und diese auf von ihm gemieteten Regalen zum Verkauf anbietet)*

rackrent *Br* 1. die volle auf dem Markt erzielbare Miete (od. Pacht); 2. Wuchermiete

racket auf Gewinn zielendes Unternehmen oder Tätigkeit, die sich unlauterer od. gesetzwidriger Mittel bedienen; unlautere Geschäftsmethode; Schiebung; **(blackmail)** ~ *Am* Erpressermethode *(nach der kein einmaliges Lösegeld sondern fortlaufende Gewinnbeteiligung verlangt wird)*

racketeer jd, der sich e-s →racket bedient, d. h. der an e-m unlauteren od. illegalen Geschäft od. Tätigkeit beteiligt ist; Schieber, Erpresser, Angehöriger e-r Gaunerbande, Gangster

racketeering *Am* organisierter Gelderwerb durch →rackets; gewerbsmäßige Anwendung von →rackets *(z. B. organisierte Erpressung von Geschäftsleuten);* **Anti-R**~ **Act** *Am* Bundesgesetz *(von 1940)* zur Bekämpfung gewerbsmäßiger Gangster, das Raub und Erpressung sowie gewalttätige Handlungen in Vorbereitung und Unterstützung von Raub und Erpressung *(im zwischenstaatl. Handel)* unter Strafe stellt

radar device Radaranlage

radiation *(AtomR)* radioaktive Strahlung; Strahlen-; ~ **barrier** Strahlungsabschirmung; ~ **detection instrument** (or ~ **detector**) Strahlennachweisgerät; Strahlendetektor; ~ **dose** Strahlendosis; ~ **exposure** Strahlenexponierung, Bestrahlung; ~ **hazard** Strahlengefahr, Strahlengefährdung; ~ **injury** Strahlenschädigung, Strahlenschaden; ~ **leak** undichte Stelle, an der radioaktive Strahlung austritt; ~ **lethality** Sterblichkeit infolge Bestrahlung; ~ **level** Strahlungshöhe; Strahlendosis

radiation protection Strahlenschutz; ~ **standards** Strahlenschutznormen

radiation, ~ **risks** Strahlenrisiken; ~ **sickness** Strahlenkrankheit, Strahlenerkrankung; ~ **survey meter** Strahlenüberwachungsgerät; **damage** (or **loss**) **caused by** ~ Strahlungsschaden; **occupational** ~berufsbedingte Bestrahlung; **(person) occupationally exposed to** ~ beruflich strahlenexponiert(e Person); **persistent** ~ Dauerstrahlung

radical *(auch pol)* Radikaler; radikal; ~ **measures** radikale (od. drastische) Maßnahmen; ~ **views** radikale Ansichten

radically tiefgreifend

radio Rundfunk, Radio; Funk; ~ **adaptation** Funkfassung, -bearbeitung; ~ **address** Rundfunkansprache; ~ **advertising** Rundfunkwerbung, Rundfunkreklame; ~ **and television program(me)s** Rundfunk und Fernsehprogramme; ~ **announcement** Radiodurchsage; Werbedurchsage im Rundfunk; ~ **broadcasting** (Rundfunk-)Sendung, (Rundfunk-)Übertragung; ~ **commentator** Rundfunkkommentator; ~**gram**→telegram; ~ **installation** Rundfunkanlage; ~ **licence dodger** *Br* Schwarzhörer; ~ **message** Funkspruch; ~ **pirate** Funkpirat; Schwarzsender; ~ **talk** Rundfunkansprache; ~ **telegram(me)** Funktelegramm; Funkspruch; ~ **telegraphy** Funktelegraphie; Telegraphiefunk; ~ **telephone** drahtlose Telefonie, Sprechfunk; **by** ~ drahtlos, durch Funk; über den Rundfunk; **coast-to-coast** ~ **speech** *Am* Radioansprache über alle Länder

radioactive radioaktiv; ~ **contamination** radioaktive Verseuchung; ~ **deposit** (or **fall-out**) radioaktiver Niederschlag; ~ **substance** radioaktiver Stoff

radioactive waste, disposal (or **final storage**) **of** ~ **in salt deposits**[1a] Endlagerung von radioaktiven Abfällen in Salzlagern; **management and storage of** ~ Behandlung und Lagerung radioaktiver Abfälle

radioactivity, maximum permitted ~ **level** erlaubte Höchstgrenze der Radioaktivität

radiological radiologisch; ~ **card** Strahlenpaß; ~ **protection** Strahlenschutz; ~ **warfare** radiologische Kriegsführung

radionuclides in drinking water and in air inhaled[1b] radioaktive Stoffe in Trinkwasser und Atemluft

rag, ~ **fair** Trödelmarkt; ~ **money** *Am* entwertetes Papiergeld

ragged bonds *Am* Obligationen mit abgetrennten, noch nicht fälligen Zinsscheinen

raid *(auch VölkerR) (feindl. od. räuberischer)* Überfall, Einfall; Razzia *(der Polizei)*; *(Börse)* Druck *(auf die Kurse)*; ~ **on a bank** s. bank →~; ~ **on the reserves** Angreifen der Reserven; **air** ~ Luftangriff; **bank** ~ Überfall auf e-e Bank, Bankraub; **bombing** ~ Bombenangriff; **police** ~ Polizeirazzia; **to make a** ~ überfallen, einfallen; e-e Razzia machen

raid *v* überfallen, einfallen in; e-n Überfall machen auf; e-e (Polizei-)Razzia machen auf; **to** ~ **a house** e-e (Polizei-)Razzia auf ein Haus machen; *(in räuberischer Absicht)* in ein Haus eindringen; **to** ~ **the market** *(Börse)* Kurse durch Verkäufe drücken; **to** ~ **the reserves** die Reserven angreifen; **to** ~ **the** →**sinking fund**

raider jd, der ein Zielunternehmen (→*target company*) mit der Absicht der Übernahme angreift; **corporate** ~ Gesellschaftsräuber *(als Übernahmeinteressent)*

raiding *Am* Mitgliederabwerbung *(z.B. bei Gewerkschaften)*; ~ **aircraft** Feindflugzeug; ~ **party** (Polizei-)Streife

rail Eisenbahn; Reling (→*ship's* ~); ~**s** Eisenbahnaktien; Eisenbahnobligationen; ~ **and water terminal** Umschlagplatz; ~**car** Triebwagen; ~ **carriage** Bahntransport; **combined** ~**/road carriage of goods** *Am* Huckepack-Verkehr; ~**/trailer shipment** *Am* Huckepack-Verkehr; ~ **transport** (Eisen-)Bahntransport; ~ **transportation insurance** *Am* Bahntransportversicherung; ~ **trip** *colloq.* Bahnfahrt

rail, British R~ Staatliche Britische Eisenbahn (-gesellschaft); **by** ~ mit der Eisenbahn, per Bahn; auf dem Schienenweg; **by an all-**~ **route** ausschließlich auf dem Schienenwege; **carriage** (or **conveyance**) **by** ~ Bahntransport; **dispatch by** ~ Bahnversand; **to go** (or **travel**) **by** ~ mit der (Eisen-)Bahn fahren (od. reisen)

rail *v (Güter)* mit der Bahn befördern; mit der Bahn fahren

railroad (Rr.)*Am* Eisenbahn; ~**s** *Am* Eisenbahnaktien; Eisenbahnwerte; ~ **accident** *Am* Eisenbahnunglück; ~ **bill of lading** *Am* (Bahn-) Frachtbrief; ~ **bonds** *Am* Eisenbahnobligationen; ~ **equipment** *Am* Eisenbahnzubehör

railroad freight *Am* (Eisen-)Bahnfracht; ~ **rates** *Am* Gütertarif; ~ **transportation** *Am* Eisenbahnfrachtverkehr

railroad, ~ **man** *Am* Eisenbahner; ~ **market** *(Börse)* Markt für Eisenbahnwerte; ~ **net** *Am* Eisenbahnnetz; ~ **passenger transportation** *Am* Eisenbahnpersonenverkehr; ~ **rates** *Am* Eisenbahntarif; ~ **station** *Am* Bahnhof; ~ **stocks** *Am* Eisenbahnaktien; **(**~**) ticket** *Am* (Bahn-)Fahrkarte; ~ **waybill** *Am* Frachtbrief

railroad *v Am (Güter)* mit der Bahn befördern; **to** ~ **a bill through Congress** *Am colloq.* e-n Gesetzesantrag im Kongreß durchpeitschen; **to** ~ **a country** *Am* in e-m Lande Eisenbahnen bauen

railway (Ry) *bs. Br (Am bes. in Zusammensetzungen)* Eisenbahn; ~**s** *Br* →~ shares; ~ **accident** Eisenbahnunglück; ~ **bonds** *Br* Eisenbahnobligationen; ~ **car** Eisenbahnwagen *(zur Personenbeförderung)*; Waggon; ~ **carriage** Eisenbahnwagen; ~ **connection** Bahnverbindung; ~ **employee** Bahnangestellter; ~ **engine** Lokomotive; ~ **equipment** Eisenbahnzubehör; ~ **freight rates** Gütertarif; ~ **goods traffic** *Br* Eisenbahngüterverkehr; ~ **guide** *Br* Kursbuch; ~ **journey** Reise per Bahn, Bahnfahrt; ~ **line** Eisenbahnlinie; ~**-man** Eisenbahner; ~ **market** *Br (Börse)* Markt für Eisenbahnwerte; ~ **passenger transportation** *Br* Eisenbahnpersonenverkehr; ~ **parcels service** *Br* Eisenbahnpaketdienst; ~ **police** *Br* Bahnpolizei; ~ **rates** *Br* Eisenbahntarif; ~ **service** Bahndienst; ~ **shares** (or **stock**) *Br* Eisenbahnaktien, Eisenbahnwerte; ~ **staff** Eisenbahnpersonal; ~ **station** *Br* Bahnhof; ~ **strike** *Br* Eisenbahnerstreik; ~ **system** *Br* Eisenbahnnetz

railway ticket *Br* (Bahn-)Fahrkarte; **production of the ~** Vorzeigen der Fahrkarte

railway traffic *Br* Eisenbahnverkehr; **~ regulations** Eisenbahnverkehrsordnung

railway transport *Br* (Eisen-)Bahntransport; **packed for ~** bahnmäßig verpackt

railway, ~ truck (or **wagon**) *Br* (Eisenbahn-) Waggon, offener Güterwagen; **~ workshop** Eisenbahnausbesserungswerk; **arterial ~** (Eisenbahn-)Hauptstrecke; **British R~s Board** Hauptverwaltung der britischen Eisenbahnen; **British R~s collecting vehicle** Zubringerfahrzeug der britischen Bahnen; **interurban ~** *Am* Stadtbahn; **light ~** *Br* Kleinbahn, Schmalspurbahn; **net of ~s** Eisenbahnnetz

rain insurance Regenversicherung

raise *Am* Gehaltserhöhung; Lohnerhöhung; **to get a ~** Gehalts-(od. Lohn-)erhöhung bekommen

raise *v* erheben; erhöhen, steigern; *(Geld)* aufbringen; *(Blockade etc)* aufheben; *(Volk)* aufwiegeln; *Am (Scheck etc)* durch Eintragung e-r höheren Summe fälschen; **to ~ an army** e-e Armee aufstellen; **to ~ the bank rate** den Diskontsatz erhöhen; **to ~ cattle** Vieh züchten; **to ~ a claim** e-n Anspruch erheben, e-e Forderung geltend machen; **to ~ a claim under a guarantee** e-e Garantie in Anspruch nehmen; **to ~ a collection** sammeln (→*collection 3.*); **to ~ a credit** e-n Kredit aufnehmen; e-n Kredit erhöhen; **to ~ the dividend** die Dividende erhöhen; **to ~ the embargo** das Embargo aufheben; **to ~ exports** die Ausfuhr steigern; **to ~ forces** Truppen aufstellen; **to ~ funds** Geldmittel aufnehmen (od. aufbringen); **to ~ the (rate of) interest** den Zinssatz erhöhen; **to ~ an issue** →issue 1.; **to ~ the limit** das Limit erhöhen; **to ~ a loan** ein Darlehen (od. e-e Anleihe) aufnehmen; **to ~ money** Geld aufnehmen (od. aufbringen); **to ~ a monument** ein Denkmal errichten; **to ~ a mortgage on leasehold property** e-e Hypothek auf gepachteten (od. gemieteten) Grundbesitz aufnehmen; **to ~ an objection** e-n Einwand erheben; e-e Einrede geltend machen; **to ~ a →presumption; to ~ the price** den Preis erhöhen (od. heraufsetzen); **to ~ a protest** Protest erheben (with bei); **to ~ the question** die Frage aufwerfen; **to ~ the rent** die Miete erhöhen; **to ~ sb.'s salary** jds Gehalt erhöhen; **to ~ a subject** e-e Sache zur Sprache bringen; **to ~ a tax** e-e Steuer erheben;

raised, ~ check *Am* durch Eintragung e-r höheren Summe gefälschter Scheck; **issues ~** aufgeworfene Fragen

raising, ~ an action *Scot* Klageerhebung; **~ of the bank rate** Diskonterhöhung; **~ of funds** (or **fund ~**) Aufnahme von Mitteln, Geldaufnahme; **~ of postal rates** Erhöhung der Postgebühren; **~ of the railway** *Br* (**railroad** *Am*) **rates** Erhöhung der Eisenbahntarife

rake off *sl.* Provision, Gewinnanteil *(an e-m unredlichen Geschäft)*

rally Zusammenkunft; *Am pol* Massenversammlung; *(Börse)* (Kurs-)Erholung, Auftrieb; **election ~** Wahlversammlung; **party ~** Parteiversammlung, Parteitag; **price ~** *(Börse)* Kurserholung

rally *v* sich (wieder) sammeln, sich scharen (round um); sich anschließen (to an); *com* sich erholen, anziehen *(Preise, Kurse)*

ram *v*, **to ~ a ship** ein Schiff rammen

ramification *fig* Verzweigung, Verästelung

ranch *Am* Farm; Viehwirtschaft

random Zufall; **~ sample** Zufallsstichprobe; **~ sampling** Zufallsstichprobenerhebung; **~ test** Stichprobe *(bes. in Zusammenhang mit breath tests on drivers suspected of being drunk)*; **to take ~ samples** Stichproben machen

random, at ~ zufällig, Zufalls-; **inspection at ~** (or **sample taken at ~**) Stichprobe; **to test at ~** Stichprobe machen

range Bereich, Umfang, Reichweite, Spielraum, Spanne, Aktionsradius; *mil* Schießplatz; (Waren-) Auswahl (of an); Sortiment, Kollektion; *(Außenhandel)* Reihe von Häfen, für die gleiche Frachtraten vereinbart sind *(sie werden nach dem geographisch ersten und letzten Hafen benannt, z.B. Antwerpen-Hamburg range)*; *(Börse)* Schwankung(sbreite) *(der Kurse)*; *(Statistik)* Spannweite; *(Raumfahrt)* Startzone, Startplatz, Startgelände; **~ of action** Tätigkeitsbereich; **~ of application** Anwendungsbereich

range, ~ of goods (or **articles in stock**) Sortiment; **to have a wide ~ of goods** e-e reiche Auswahl an Waren haben

range, ~ of patterns Musterauswahl, Musterkollektion; **~ of policies** Versicherungsarten; **~ of prices** Preisspanne *(innerhalb e-s Angebots)*; Kursspanne; **a good ~** e-e große Auswahl; **long-~** →long 1.; **price ~** Preisspanne; Kursspanne; **rate ~** Lohnspanne; **rocket ~** Raketen(versuchs)gelände; **salary ~** Gehaltsspanne; **short-~** →short 3.; **to move in a narrow ~** geringe (Preis-, Kurs-)Schwankungen aufweisen

range *v* (ein)ordnen, einreihen; sich erstrecken, reichen (from ... to von ... bis); *(im Preis etc)* sich bewegen, schwanken (from ... to von ... bis); **to ~ between** sich bewegen (od. liegen, schwanken) zwischen; **to ~ with** in gleichem Rang stehen mit

ranger *Am* Förster; *Br* Forstbeamter *(der Königl. Parks)*; *Am* Mondsonde

rank Reihe, Linie; Stand, Rang, Stellung; *mil* Dienstgrad; **the ~s** *mil* der Mannschaftsstand

rank and file gewöhnliche Mitglieder; Belegschaft; Masse der Anhänger e-r Partei; *parl* Masse der Hinterbänkler; *mil* (Unteroffiziere und) Mannschaften; ~ *(of workers etc)* Basis; ~ **union member** einfaches Gewerkschaftsmitglied; **remoteness from the** ~ Basisferne

rank, all ~s *mil* Offiziere, Unteroffiziere und Mannschaften; **badge of** ~ Rangabzeichen

rank, officials of comparable ~ in vergleichbarem Rang stehende Bedienstete

rank, of equal (or **equivalent**) ~ ranggleich, im Rang gleich(stehend); **equality of** ~ Ranggleichheit; **of high** ~ hohen Standes, hochgestellt; **insignia of** ~ *mil* Rangabzeichen; **lower in** ~ rangniedriger; →**other ~s; prior** ~ älterer (od. früherer) Rang; Priorität; **priority of** ~ Vorrang; →**seniority in** ~; **service** ~ Dienstgrad; **taxi** ~ *Br* Taxistand; **to reduce to the ~s** *(Offizier)* degradieren; **to take ~ with a p.** mit jdm in gleichem Rang stehen, mit jdm rangieren

rank *v* e-n Rang (od. e-e Stelle) einnehmen; *(im Rang)* gehören, rangieren (next to gleich hinter); einordnen, einreihen, Rangordnung bestimmen; **to ~ alike** gleichen Rang haben; **to ~ after** (or **below**) im Rang stehen nach, im Rang nachgehen (od. folgen); **to ~ before** im Range vorgehen, den Vorrang haben (od. rangieren) vor; **to ~ concurrently** →to ~ equally; **to ~ for dividend** dividendenberechtigt sein; **to ~ equally with** gleichen Rang haben wie, gleichstehen (od. gleichrangig sein) mit; **to ~ first** an erster Stelle stehen; **to ~ high** hoch stehen, e-e hohe Stellung einnehmen; **to ~ next to** im Range kommen nach; **to ~ pari passu** →to ~ equally; **to ~ prior to** den Vorrang haben vor; **to ~ with** den gleichen Rang haben wie, rangieren mit; **the debt ~s in priority (to)** die Forderung geht im Range vor

ranking Rang, Rangfolge, Rangordnung; *Am* führend; ~ **of claims** Rang (od. Rangordnung) der Forderungen; ~ **of creditors** Rangfolge der Gläubiger; ~ **for dividend** dividendenberechtigt; ~ **equally with** gleichrangig mit; ~ **first** an erster Stelle, erststellig; ~ **of mortgages** Rangordnung der Hypotheken, Hypothekenrang; ~ **pari passu with** gleichrangig mit; ~ **in priority to** mit Vorrang vor; ~ **system** *(Arbeitsbewertung)* Rangfolgeverfahren; **equally ~ creditors** gleichrangige Gläubiger; **high-~ officer** höherer Offizier

ransom Lösegeld; Freikauf *(e-s Gefangenen)*; ~ **demand** Lösegeldforderung; **to hold a p. to** ~ jdn bis zur Zahlung e-s Lösegeldes festhalten

ransom *v* freikaufen

rape[2] *(StrafR)* Notzucht, Vergewaltigung; **statutory** ~ *Am* Geschlechtsverkehr mit einem Mädchen, das noch nicht das einwilligungsfähige Alter hat

rapporteur *Fr parl* Berichterstatter

rapprochement *Fr* Wiederannäherung *(zweier Staaten)*

rasure ausradierte Stelle *(in e-r Urkunde etc)*

rat politischer Überläufer; Streikbrecher

rat *v colloq.* verraten

ratability →rateability

ratable →rateable

rate 1. (meist **~s)** *Br* Gemeindeabgabe(n), Gemeindesteuer(n), Kommunalsteuer(n), Steuer(n) für gewerblich genutzten Grundbesitz (→ *community charge*); **~-aided** *Br* mit Unterstützung aus Gemeindemitteln; **~s and taxes** *Br* Gemeinde- und Staatssteuern; ~ **capping**[3] staatliche Begrenzung der Gemeindesteuern; ~ **collection** s. collection of →~s; ~ **payer** *Br* (Gemeinde-)Steuerzahler; ~ **rebate** *Br* Herabsetzung der Gemeindesteuern für Personen mit geringem Einkommen; **~s receipt** *Br* Quittung e-r Behörde, daß Gemeindesteuern bezahlt sind; ~ **support grant** *Br*[4] staatliche Ausgleichszahlungen an finanzschwache Gemeinden; **bill for ~s** *Br* (Gemeinde-) Steueraufforderung; **church** ~ *Br* Kirchensteuer; **collection of ~s** *Br* Erhebung (od. Einziehung) von Gemeindeabgaben (od. -steuern); **general ~s** *Br* allgemeine Gemeindeabgaben (od. -steuern) *(für alle kommunalen Dienstleistungen außer Wasserversorgung, die den Bewohnern von →hereditaments gemäß dem →rateable value auferlegt werden)*; **local** (or **municipal**) **~s** *Br* →rate 1.; **water** ~ *Br* Wassergeld; **to levy a** ~ *Br* e-e Gemeindesteuer erheben

rate 2. *(fester)* Satz; Lohn(satz); Fracht(satz), Frachtrate; Zoll(satz); Zinssatz; *(VersR)* Beitragssatz, Prämiensatz (→*rate 5.*); Tarif; Gebühr; Anzeigenpreis; *Am (das von e-r →public utility erhobene)* Leistungsentgelt; Verhältnisziffer, Quote (→*rate 3.*); Devisenkurs (→*rate 4.*); ~ **card** Anzeigenpreisliste; **~change** Lohnänderung; ~ **cutting** *(Seeschiffahrt)* Frachtunterbietung; Tarifherabsetzung; Tarifunterbietung; *Am* Lohnkürzung, Kürzung bestehender Akkordsätze; ~ **for advances on securities** Lombardsatz; ~ **for day-to-day money** Tagesgeldsatz; ~ **for loans on collateral** Lombardsatz; ~ **increase** Anhebung der Tarife; ~ **s in force** geltende Tarife; **~-making** *Am* Tarifbestimmung; Gebührenfestsetzung; *(VersR)* Prämienfestsetzung; tarifbestimmend; ~ **of assessment** Veranlagungssatz, Steuersatz; *(bei Gemeindesteuer)* Hebesatz; ~ **of the benefit** Unterstützungssatz; Leistungshöhe; ~ **of charge** Gebührensatz; ~ **of commission** Provisionssatz; ~ **of contribution** Beitragssatz, Beitragshöhe; ~ **of depreciation** Abschreibungssatz; ~ **of dividend** Dividendensatz; ~ **of duties** Zollsatz; ~ **of erection** Montagesatz; ~ **of income tax** Steuersatz für Einkommensteuer (→*standard rate*); ~ **of insurance** →rate 5.

rate (of interest) Zinssatz, Zinsfuß; ~ **for advances on securities** Lombardsatz; **at a high (low)** ~ zu hohen (niedrigen) Zinsen; **cap** ~ Maximalzinssatz; **floor** ~ Mindestzinssatz; **lock** ~ Sperrzinssatz; **trigger** ~ Auslösezinssatz; **to lend money at the** ~ **of 5%** Geld zu 5% Zinsen (aus)leihen; **to increase** (or **raise**) **the** ~ den Zinssatz erhöhen; **to reduce the** ~ den Zinssatz senken

rate, ~ **(of option)** *Br (Börse)* Prämiensatz; ~ **of pay** Lohnsatz; ~ **of premium** *(VersR)* Prämiensatz (→*rate 5.*)

rate of return (on capital) (RoR) Rentabilität; Rendite; Zinssatz für Investitionen *(e-s Unternehmens)* (→*internal* ~); **estimate of** ~ Rentabilitätsrechnung

rate, ~ **of tax** Steuersatz; ~ **of wear and tear** Abnutzungssatz

rate, advertisement ~**s** Anzeigentarif; **average** ~ Durchschnittssatz; **basic** ~ Grundlohn; **bank** ~ Diskontsatz; **blanket** ~ Pauschalsatz; Pauschaltarif; **class** ~ Gruppen(fracht)tarif; **commodity** ~ *Am* Einzel(fracht)tarif; **at the contract** ~ zum Vertragspreis; **at the current** ~ zum geltenden Satz; **customs** ~ Zollsatz; **day** ~ Tagessatz; **deposit** ~ Zinssatz für Einlagen; **electric** ~ *Am* Strompreis, Stromtarif; **firm** ~ fester Satz; **at a fixed** ~ zu e-m bestimmten Satz; **at a favo(u)rable** ~ zinsgünstig; **flat** ~ Pauschalsatz; Grundgebühr (→*flat*); **foreign postage** ~**s** *Br (Post)* Auslandsporto; **freight** ~ Frachtrate; **full** ~**s** (of customs duties) allgemeiner Zolltarif *(opp. preferential* ~*s)*; **gas** ~ *Am* Gaspreis, Gastarif; **increase in** ~**s** Tariferhöhung; **interest** ~ Zinssatz (→*interest 4.*); **inland** ~ Binnentarif; **inland** ~ (of postage) Inlandporto; **letter** ~ Briefporto; **liner** ~**s** *(bei Charterverträgen)* Frachtraten nach den regulären Bedingungen des Linienverkehrs; **local** ~**s** *Am* Ortsgesprächgebühren; **long-distance calling** ~**s** *Am* Ferngesprächgebühren; **low-**~ **articles** Waren, die e-m geringen Zoll unterliegen; **maximum** ~ Höchstsatz; **minimum** ~ Mindestsatz; **mixed carload** ~ *Am* Stückgütertarif; **money market** ~**s** Geldzinssätze; **mortgage** ~ Hypothekenzinssatz; **net U. K.** ~ (of tax) *Br (für Zahlung der Steuer e-r Gesellschaft zugrundegelegter)* Steuersatz nach Abzug der Anrechnung für Doppelsteuer; **(option)** ~ *Br (Börse)* Prämiensatz; **ordinary** ~ *(Post)* gewöhnliche Gebühr; einfaches Porto; **paper** ~ nur auf dem Papier stehender Tarif; **parcel** ~ Paketgebühr; **postage** *Br* (or **postal**) ~**s** Postgebühren; **preferential** ~**s** (of customs duties) Vorzugs(zoll)tarif; **prevailing** ~ geltender Lohntarif; **private** ~ (of discount) *Br* Diskontsatz der Geschäftsbanken; **railway** (*Am* **railroad**) ~**s** Eisenbahntarif; **reduced** ~**(s)** ermäßigter Satz; ermäßigte Gebühr; ermäßigter Tarif; **regular** ~ Normalsatz; üblicher Lohnsatz; **released** ~ *Am* Tarif mit beschränkter Haftpflicht des Spediteurs; **scale of** ~**s** Tarif; **starting** ~ Anfangslohn; **(tax)** ~ Steuersatz (→*tax*); **telegram** ~ Wortgebühr; **telephone** ~**s** *Am* Telefongebühren; **time** ~**s** Zeitlöhne (→*time 1.*); **transit** ~ Frachttarif für Durchgangsgüter; **(wage)** ~ Lohnsatz; **to fix** ~**s** Sätze festsetzen; tarifieren

rate 3. (Verhältnis-)Ziffer, Rate, Quote, Anteil; Geschwindigkeit; ~ **of absenteeism** Abwesenheitsquote; ~ **of building** Bautempo; ~ **of consumption** Verbrauchsrate; ~ **of growth** Wachstumsrate; ~ **of increase** Zuwachsrate, Steigerungsrate; ~ **of inflation** Inflationsrate, Teuerungsrate; ~ **of investment** Investitionsrate; ~ **of mortality** Sterblichkeitsziffer; ~ **of production** Produktionsziffer; ~ **of turnover** Umsatzziffer; Umschlaggeschwindigkeit; **at the** ~ **of** mit der Geschwindigkeit von; **birth** ~ Geburtenziffer; **circulation** ~ Auflageziffer; **crime** ~ Kriminalitätsziffer; Verbrechensquote; **death** ~ Sterblichkeitsziffer; **divorce** ~ Scheidungsziffer; **marriage** ~ Heiratsziffer, Zahl der Eheschließungen

rate 4. (Wechsel-, Devisen-)Kurs; ~ **fixing** *Am* Kursfestsetzung; ~ **for cable transfers** Kurs für Kabelauszahlungen; ~ **gain** *Am* Kursgewinn; ~ **guarantee** Kurssicherung; ~**-hedged** kursgesichert; ~ **of conversion** *(Devisenmarkt)* Umrechnungskurs; ~ **of the day** Tageskurs; ~ **of exchange** Wechselkurs; Devisenkurs *(→ exchange rate)*; ~ **supporting** Kursstützung; **at the** ~ **of** zum Kurse von; **at the current** ~ zum Tageskurs; **at the present** ~ zum gegenwärtigen Kurs; **difference in** ~**s** Kursunterschied, Kursdifferenz; **exchange** ~ **mechanism** (ERM) Wechselkursmechanismus *(of the → European Monetary System)*; **fluctuations in the** ~ Kursschwankungen; **foreign exchange** ~ Devisenkurs; **forward** ~ Terminkurs; **forward exchange** ~ Devisenterminkurs; **with a high** ~ valutastark; **with a low** ~ valutaschwach; **mean** ~ Mittelkurs, Durchschnittskurs; **the** ~ **is falling** der Kurs fällt; **the** ~**s are going up** (or **are rising**) die Kurse steigen; **to hedge the** ~ den Kurs sichern

rate 5. (~ **of insurance**) Prämiensatz, Beitragssatz; ~**-making** Prämienfestsetzung; ~ **of premium** Prämiensatz; **annual** ~ Jahresprämie; **judgment** ~**s** *Am (Feuervers.)* nach eigenem Ermessen festgesetzte Prämien; **marine** ~ Prämiensatz der Seetransportversicherung; **short** ~ Prämie für e-n Zeitraum unter e-m Jahr

rate *v* (ein-, ab)schätzen, bewerten; bemessen; *(in e-e [Zoll-, Tarif-etc] Klasse)* einstufen; unter die →rate 1. fallen (od. eingestuft werden); *bes. Br* zur (Gemeinde-)Steuer heranziehen (od. veranlagen), besteuern; *Am (zu e-m bestimmten Tarif [rate])* transportieren; **to ~ a pension** e-e Pension festsetzen; **to ~ a ship** ein Schiff klassifizieren; **to ~ up** *(jdn)* höher versichern; in e-e höhere Prämiengruppe einstufen

rated, liability to be ~ *Br* (Gemeinde-)Steuerpflicht

rateability Abschätzbarkeit; *Br* (Gemeinde-) Steuerpflicht, Abgabepflicht (→*rate[s] 1.*)

rateable abschätzbar, zu bewerten; anteilmäßig; *Br* (gemeinde-)steuerpflichtig, -abgabepflichtig (→*rate[s] 1.*); **~ contribution** anteilmäßiger Beitrag; **~ freight** Distanzfracht; **~ property** *Br* steuerpflichtiger Grundbesitz (→*rate 1.*); **~ value** (R. V.) *Br (auf den tatsächlichen od. geschätzten Mieteinnahmen beruhender, für Zwecke der →rates 1. errechneter)* Steuerwert *(von Grundbesitz);* Einheitswert; **ascertainment of (the) ~ value of a hereditament** *Br*[5] Veranlagung zur Gemeindesteuer

rateably, to distribute ~ anteilsmäßig verteilen

ratification Genehmigung, Bestätigung; *(VölkerR)* Ratifikation, Ratifizierung; *Am* Heilung e-s unwirksamen Vertrages durch Genehmigung

ratification, instrument of ~ *(VölkerR)* Ratifikationsurkunde; **deposit (exchange) of the instrument of ~** Hinterlegung (Austausch) der Ratifikationsurkunde; **to deposit the instrument of ~** die Ratifikationsurkunde hinterlegen

ratification, the present treaty is subject to ~ *(VölkerR)* dieser Vertrag bedarf der Ratifikation; **~ is effected** die Ratifikation erfolgt

ratify *v* genehmigen, bestätigen; *(VölkerR)* ratifizieren

rating Einschätzung, Abschätzung, Bewertung *(Am auch von Effekten);* Bemessung, Einstufung; *Am* Leistungsbeurteilung; Einschätzung des Leistungsgrades; Tariffestsetzung, Tarifierung; *Br* Veranlagung zur (Gemeinde-)Steuer, Besteuerung; *Br* (Gemeinde-)Steuerbetrag; *Am* Krediteinschätzung, Bonitätsbewertung; **~ agency** *Am* Kreditauskunftei; **~ agreement** *(VersR)* Tarifvereinbarung; **~ area** *Br* (Gemeinde-) Steuerbezirk; **~ bureau** *Am* Kreditauskunftei; *Am (VersR)* Tarifierungsamt; Zweckverband von Versicherungsgesellschaften *(außer Lebensvers.)* zur Schaffung einheitlicher Versicherungsprämien sowie deren Durchsetzung bei der *(meist einzelstaatl.)* Aufsichtsbehörde; **~ compact** *Am (VersR)* Tarifkartell; **~ law** *Am (VersR)* Tarifierungsgesetz; **~ of unoccupied property** *Br* Veranlagung zur Gemeindesteuer (bes. Grundsteuer) von unbewohntem Grundbesitz; **~ system** Tarifsystem; *Am* Bewertungssystem *(für Effekten);* **~ table** Prämientabelle; **capital ~** *Am* →capital 1.; **classification ~** Tarifeinstufung; **credit ~** *Am* Einschätzung der Kreditfähigkeit; **efficiency ~** Leistungsbewertung; **employee ~** Beurteilung e-s Arbeitnehmers; **individual ~** *Br (VersR)* Anpassung der Prämie an das konkrete Risiko; **investment ~** *Am* Anlagebewertung; **job ~** Arbeitsbewertung

ratio Verhältnis(zahl), Quote; Meßzahl, Koeffizient; **~ between gold and silver** (Wert-)Verhältnis zwischen Gold und Silber; **~ of distribution** Verteilerschlüssel; **~ of sales to invested capital** Verhältnis von Umsatz zu Kapital; **~ of working expenses** Betriebskoeffizient; **cash position ~** Kassenstandskoeffizient; **cover ~** Deckungsverhältnis (→*cover*); **electoral ~** Wahlquotient; **equity ~** Verhältnis der Aktiva zum Eigenkapital (→*equity 2.*); **liquidity ~** Liquiditätskoeffizient; Liquiditätsgrad; **operating ~** Betriebskoeffizient; **price-earnings ~** (P/E R) Kurs-Gewinn-Verhältnis (→*price 2.);* **reserve ~** Liquiditätskoeffizient (*Am* →*Federal Reserve Banks)*

ratio decidendi ("the reason of a judicial decision") Entscheidungsgrund *(e-s Urteils) (das der Entscheidung zugrunde liegende Rechtsprinzip)*
Aus der richterlichen Entscheidung wird eine Rechtsregel hergeleitet, die ~, die im Ggs. zum obiter →dictum bindend ist (only the ~ operates as a precedent)

ration Ration, Zuteilung; **~ book** *Br (im 2. Weltkrieg)* Lebensmittelkarte; **~ card** Lebensmittelkarte; **~ coupon** Lebensmittelkartenabschnitt; **~ period** Zuteilungsperiode; **~ rate** (or **scale**) Rationshöhe; Zuteilungssatz; **extra ~** Sonderzuteilung; **food ~** Lebensmittelration; **putting on ~s** Rationierung

ration *v* rationieren, *(in Rationen)* zuteilen; bewirtschaften; mit Rationen versorgen

rationed, ~ goods bewirtschaftete (od. markenpflichtige) Waren; **de-~ goods** *(aus der Bewirtschaftung)* freigegebene Waren

rationing Rationierung, Zuteilung *(in Rationen);* Bewirtschaftung; **abolition of ~** Aufhebung der Rationierung (od. Bewirtschaftung)

rationale *Am* Beweggrund, Begründung, Grund, Grundsatzerklärung; Basis *(für e-e Entscheidung od. Handlung)*

rationalization Rationalisierung; **~ cartel** Rationalisierungskartell; **investments undertaken for ~ purposes** Rationalisierungsinvestitionen

ratione tenurae ("by reason or in respect of his tenure") auf Grund s-s Besitzes

ratten *v Br (Arbeiter)* an der Arbeit hindern (→*rattening)*

rattening *Br*[6] Hinderung e-s Arbeiters an der Arbeit *(durch Wegnahme od. Zerstörung des Arbeitsgeräts, um ihn zum Beitritt zu e-r Gewerkschaft od. zur Arbeitseinstellung zu zwingen)*

raw roh, unbearbeitet; ~ **or processed** unbearbeitet oder bearbeitet

raw material Rohmaterial, Rohstoff; ~ **agreement** Rohstoffabkommen; ~ **market** Rohstoffmarkt; ~**s and supplies** *Am (Bilanz)* Roh-, Hilfs- und Betriebsstoffe; **allocation of** ~**s** Zuteilung von Rohstoffen; **provisioning with** ~**s** Versorgung mit Rohstoffen; **requirements of** ~**s** Rohstoffbedarf; **scarcity of** ~**s** Rohstoffknappheit; **supply of** ~**s** Rohstoffversorgung

raw products (or **produce**) Rohstoffe

rayon Kunstseide

re ("in the matter of") in Sachen; ~ **X v. Y** in Sachen X ./. Y; *(in Geschäftsbriefen)* betrifft (betr.)

reach Reichweite; Bereich; **within** ~ erreichbar; ~**-me-down** *colloq.* Konfektions-(kleidung), (Kleidung) „von der Stange"

reach *v* erreichen; ankommen in; gelangen, zugehen; **to** ~ **(an) agreement** zu e-r Verständigung gelangen, e-e Einigung erzielen; **to** ~ **a** →**decision; to** ~ **one's goal** sein Ziel erreichen; **to** ~ **one's majority** mündig (od. volljährig) werden; **to** ~ **a high price** e-n hohen Preis erzielen

reached, the goods ~ **their destination** die Waren erreichten ihren Bestimmungsort; **your letter** ~ **me on** Ihr Brief erreichte mich am

reaching, on ~ **the age limit** bei Erreichung der Altersgrenze

reacquire *v* wiedererlangen, zurückerwerben; **to** ~ **one's nationality** s-e Staatsangehörigkeit wiedererlangen

reacquired stock *Am* →treasury stock

re-acquisition Wiedererlangung, Rückerwerb

reaction Reaktion; Rück-, Gegenwirkung; Rückschlag; *pol* Reaktion, reaktionäre Tendenz; ~ **time** Reaktionszeit; **forces of** ~ reaktionäre Kräfte

reactionary *pol* Reaktionär; reaktionär, rückschrittlich

reactor Reaktor; ~ **safety** Reaktorsicherheit; **nuclear** ~ **accident** Kernreaktorunglück; **operator of a nuclear** ~ Betreiber e-s Kernreaktors

read *v* lesen; lauten, heißen; *univ* studieren; **to** ~ **for the Bar** *Br* sich auf den Anwaltsberuf *(als barrister)* vorbereiten; **to** ~ **for an examination** sich auf e-e Prüfung vorbereiten; **to** ~ **law** *Br* Rechtswissenschaft (od. Jura) studieren; **to** ~ **a paper** e-n Vortrag (od. ein Referat) halten; e-e Zeitung lesen; **to** ~ **off** ablesen; **to** ~ **over** durchlesen; **to** ~ **over a copy with the original** e-e Abschrift mit dem Original vergleichen; **to** ~ **through** durchlesen; **the paragraph** ~**s** der Absatz lautet

read gelesen; ~ **and approved** vorgelesen und genehmigt; **the bill was** ~ **for the first time** der Gesetzesentwurf kam zur ersten Lesung

reading Lesen; Lesart, Auslegung; *parl* Lesung; ~ **as follows** mit folgendem Wortlaut; ~ **over** Durchlesen; **proof-**~ Korrekturlesen

readdress *v (Brief)* umadressieren, nachsenden

reader Leser; *univ* Dozent; Lektor *(e-s Verlags);* ~**s** Leserschaft; ~ **circle** Lesezirkel; ~ **in law** *Br (ordentl.)* Professor der Rechte; ~**s' interest research** Leserumfrage

readership Leserkreis; *univ* Dozentenstelle; ~ **survey** Leseranalyse

readiness Bereitschaft; ~ **to invest** Investitionsbereitschaft; **notice of** ~ Anzeige der Ladebereitschaft *(des Schiffes)*

readjourn *v* erneut vertagen

readjust *v* wieder in Ordnung bringen, neuordnen; *com* sanieren

readjustment Neuordnung, Neuregelung; *com* Sanierung

readmission Wiederzulassung (to zu), Wiederaufnahme (to in)

readmit *v* wiederzulassen, wiederaufnehmen

ready bereit; *com* verfügbar; prompt; ~ **assets** verfügbare Vermögenswerte; ~ **capital** umlaufendes Kapital; ~ **cash** bares Geld, Bargeld; **for** ~ **cash** gegen sofortige Barzahlung; ~ **for collection** abholbereit; ~ **for delivery** lieferbereit; auf Abruf; ~ **for dispatch** versandbereit; ~ **for occupation** bezugsfertig; ~ **for shipment** versandbereit; ~ **for use** gebrauchsfertig, betriebsfertig; ~**-for wear** *Am* →~-made

ready-made Fertig-, Konfektions- *(opp. made-to-order or custom-made);* ~ **clothes** Konfektion(skleidung)

ready market aufnahmefähiger Markt; **to find** (or **meet with**) **a** ~ schnellen Absatz finden

ready money Bargeld, bares Geld; ~ **business** Bargeschäft, Kassageschäft; **without** ~ bargeldlos

ready sale guter (od. schneller) Absatz (→*sale 1.)*

reaffirm *v* erneut bestätigen

reaffirmation *Am (KonkursR)* vertragliche Vereinbarung zwischen Gemeinschuldner und Gläubiger, wonach einzelne Forderungen, mit denen der Gläubiger im Konkurs ausgefallen ist, dem fortgesetzten Zugriff nach dem Konkurs ausgesetzt sein sollen

reafforest *Br v* wieder aufforsten

real wirklich, effektiv; echt; Sach-; dinglich *(bes. hinsichtlich freehold interests in land)*; ~ **account** Sachkonto; Bestandskonto; ~ **action** dingliche Klage *(s. action in →rem; opp. personal action)*; ~ **amount** Istbestand; ~ **assets** Immobiliarvermögen; ~ **burden** *Scot* Grundstücksbelastung; ~ **capital** Realkapital, Sachkapital; ~ **-chattels** →chattels ~; ~ **contract** *Am* Vertrag über Liegenschaften; ~ **covenant** ein sich auf Grundbesitz beziehendes →covenant; ~ **evidence** Augenschein

real estate *bes. Am* Grundeigentum, Grundbesitz, Grundstück(e), Immobilien; unbewegliches Vermögen; ~ **agency** *Am* Grundstücksvermittlung, Immobilienbüro; ~ **agent** (or **broker**) *Am* Grundstücksmakler; *Am* Immobilienmakler; ~ **company** *Am* Immobiliengesellschaft; ~ **development** Grundstückserschließung; ~ **fund** *Am* Immobilienfonds *(e-r Investmentgesellschaft)*; ~ **investment** *Am* Anlage in Grundbesitz; ~ **investment trust** (REIT) *Am* Immobilien-Investmentgesellschaft; ~ **lawyer** *Am* Anwalt, der sich vorwiegend mit Grundstückssachen befaßt; ~ **loan** *Am* Hypothekarkredit; ~ **management** Grundstücksverwaltung; ~ **market** Grundstücksmarkt, Immobilienmarkt; ~ **mortgage** *Am* Hypothek; ~ **price** *Am* Grundstückspreis; ~ **tax** *Am* Grundsteuer; ~ **value** *Am* Grundstückswert; ~ **venture** *Am* Grundstücksspekulation; **lien on** ~ *Am* Grundpfandrecht; **mortgage on** ~ *Am* Hypothek; **piece of** ~ *Am* Grundstück

real, ~ **income** Realeinkommen *(opp. nominal income)*; ~ **interest** Realzins *(opp. nominal interest)*; ~ **party in interest** *Am* →party 1.; ~ **property** Immobiliarvermögen, Grundbesitz *(→property)*; ~ **right** Recht an e-r Sache, dingliches Recht *(jus in re)*; ~ **security** dingliche Sicherheit, Realsicherheit; ~ **servitude** *Am* Grunddienstbarkeit; ~ **speculator** Immobilienspekulant; ~ **state of affairs** tatsächliche Sachlage; ~ **taxes** Realsteuern; **in** ~ **terms** effektiv; ~ **union** *(VölkerR)* Realunion; ~ **time** *(EDV)* Echtzeit-, Realzeit-; ~ **time processing** Echtzeit-Datenverarbeitung; ~ **value** effektiver Wert, Sachwert, Realwert *(opp. nominal value)*

reality of laws *(IPR)* Realität der Gesetze *(Beziehung der Gesetze auf Sachen; cf. personality of laws)*

realignment, ~ **of currency** Neufestsetzung der Wechselkurse zwischen 2 od. mehreren Staaten; ~ **of policy** Neuorientierung (od. Neuausrichtung) der Politik

realizable realisierbar; verwertbar; veräußerbar; flüssig zu machen(d); **securities** ~ **at short notice** kurzfristig realisierbare Wertpapiere; ~ **value** Veräußerungswert; Gegenwartswert

realization Realisierung; Verwertung; Veräußerung, Verkauf, Flüssigmachung; Verwirklichung; Liquidation; *(Börse)* Glattstellung; ~ **account** Liquidationskonto *(e-r Gesellschaft)*; ~ **of assets** Veräußerung von Vermögenswerten; ~ **of a plan** Verwirklichung e-s Plans; ~ **of a pledge** Pfandverwertung; Pfandverkauf; ~ **of profits** Gewinnerzielung; *(Börse)* Gewinnrealisierung; ~ **sale** Liquidationsverkauf; *(Börse)* Verkauf zwecks Glattstellung; ~ **value** Veräußerungswert, Realisationswert

realize *v* realisieren; verwerten; veräußern, verkaufen, flüssig machen, zu Gelde machen; verwirklichen; liquidieren; *(Börse)* glattstellen; sich *(über etw.)* im klaren sein, einsehen, verstehen; **to** ~ **one's assets** sein Vermögen flüssig machen (od. veräußern); **to** ~ **a price** e-n Preis erzielen; **to** ~ **a security** e-e Sicherheit verwerten, sich aus e-m Sicherungsgut befriedigen; ein Wertpapier verkaufen

realized, the land sold ~ **a fair price** das verkaufte Land brachte e-n angemessenen Preis; **the property was** ~ **to pay the capital transfer tax arising on the owner's death** *Br* der Grundbesitz wurde veräußert, um die beim Tode des Eigentümers angefallene Erbschaftsteuer zu bezahlen

realizing Veräußerung; im Hinblick darauf (that daß)

re(-)allocate *v* neu verteilen, neu zuteilen; *(Arbeiter)* umplazieren

re(-)allocation Neuverteilung, Neuzuteilung; Umplazierung *(von Arbeitern)*; ~ **of import quotas** Neuzuteilung von Einfuhrkontingenten; ~ **of land** Flurbereinigung

realm Reich, Königreich; Bereich, Gebiet; **custom of the** ~ *Br* Landesbrauch; **the Great Seal of the R**~ *Br* das große Reichssiegel; **estates of the** ~ *Br* die Reichsstände (*→estate*); **within the** ~ im Inland

realtor *Am* Grundstücksmakler, Immobilienmakler

realty Immobilien, Grundstück(e), Liegenschaften, Grundbesitz, Grundeigentümer *(opp. personalty)*; ~ **firm** *Am* Immobilienfirma; ~ **gains** *Am (SteuerR)* Gewinne aus der Veräußerung unbeweglichen Vermögens; ~ **transfer tax** *Am* Grunderwerbsteuer; **foreign** ~ *Am* ausländisches unbewegliches Vermögen; **to →convert** ~ **into personalty**

reanimate *v*, **to** ~ **trade** den Handel wieder in Gang bringen

reappointment, he shall (not) be eligible for ~ s-e Wiederernennung (od. Wiedereinstellung) ist (nicht) möglich

reappraisal Neueinschätzung, Neubewertung; Neubeurteilung *(der Lage)*

reappraise *v* neu abschätzen, neu bewerten

rear-end collision *(Auto)* Auffahrunfall

reargue *v Am (Zivilprozeß)* erneut verhandeln

reargument, motion for ~ *Am* Antrag auf neue Verhandlung *(in derselben Instanz)*

rearm *v* neu bewaffnen; (wieder-)aufrüsten

rearmament Neubewaffnung; (Wieder-)Aufrüstung

rearrange *v* neuordnen; erneut vereinbaren; umdisponieren

reason Grund; Vernunft; ~ **of arrest** Haftgrund; **for ~s of economy** aus Gründen der Sparsamkeit; **for ~s of health** aus gesundheitlichen Gründen; **by ~ of** wegen, auf Grund von; **compelling** (or **forcing**) **~s** zwingende (od. stichhaltige) Gründe; **decision supported by ~s** mit Gründen versehene Entscheidung; **main** (or **principal**) ~ Hauptgrund; **rule of** ~ →rule 2.; **sound** ~ stichhaltiger (od. triftiger) Grund; **statement of ~s** Darlegung (od. Angabe) der Gründe; **sufficient** ~ hinreichender Grund; **to advance ~s** Gründe vorbringen; **to give ~s for** begründen; **without giving ~s** ohne Angabe der Gründe; **to put forward ~s** s. to advance →~s; **to show** (or **state**) **~s** Gründe angeben

reasonable vernünftig; angemessen, zumutbar, gerechtfertigt *(im Verhältnis zwischen den Beteiligten angemessen und nicht das öffentliche Interesse verletzend; cf. rule of reason)*; ~ **belief** *(StrafR)*[7] vernünftiger *(durch die Umstände gerechtfertigter)* Glaube *(zu dem der Täter weder leichtfertig noch fahrlässig gelangte)*; ~ **care** angemessene (od. erforderliche) Sorgfalt; ~ **cause** triftiger Grund; hinreichender Anlaß; **without ~ cause** unbegründet; **with a ~ certainty** mit hinreichender Sicherheit; ~ **claim** begründeter Anspruch; ~ **deviation** gerechtfertigte Abweichung; ~ **diligence** angemessene (od. genügende) Sorgfalt; ~ **doubt** berechtigter Zweifel (→*doubt*); ~ **exchangeability** *Am (AntitrustR)* Austauschbarkeit *(von Waren)* nach vernünftigen Grundsätzen; ~ **expenses** angemessene Auslagen; ~ **grounds for believing** begründeter Anlaß zu der Vermutung; ~ **grounds for suspicion** hinreichende Verdachtsgründe; ~ **length of time** angemessener Zeitraum; ~ **maintenance** →maintenance 1.; ~ **man** *(Maßstab für →negligence)* vernünftiger (od. besonnener) Mensch *(jd, der das notwendige Maß an Sorgfalt aufwendet)*; ~ **(period of) notice** angemessene Kündigungsfrist; ~ **price** angemessener Preis; ~ **probability** hinreichende Wahrscheinlichkeit; ~ **relation doctrine** *(IPR) Am* Lehre, nach der e-e Rechtswahl nur anerkannt wird, wenn der Vertrag e-e sachliche (vernünftige) Beziehung zu dem gewählten Recht aufweist; ~ **relationship** vernünftige Beziehung; ~ **skill** angemessene Kenntnisse und Fähigkeiten

reasonable time, within a ~ innerhalb e-r angemessenen Frist; **to allow a ~** e-e angemessene Frist zubilligen

reasonably bei vernünftiger Betrachtungsweise, vernünftig(erweise); angemessen(erweise); ~ **prudent person** vernünftig handelnde Person

reasonableness Vernünftigkeit, Angemessenheit *(cf. rule of reason, →rule 2.)*

reasoned opinion mit Gründen versehene Stellungnahme

reasoning Argumentation; Schlußfolgerung

reassess *v* neu festsetzen; neu veranlagen

reassessment Neufestsetzung; Neuveranlagung

reassignment Rückübertragung; Rückabtretung

reassurance erneute Versicherung; Beruhigung; Rückversicherung

reassure *v* erneut versichern, beruhigen; rückversichern

reassured rückversichert; Rückversicherter

rebate Nachlaß, Preisnachlaß, Abzug, Rabatt (on auf); Bonifikation, Rückerstattung; ~ **of customs duty** Zollermäßigung; **dealers'** ~ Händlerrabatt; **freight** ~ Frachtrabatt, Frachtnachlaß; **quantity** ~ Mengenrabatt; **tax** ~ Steuernachlaß; **to allow** (or **grant**) **a** ~ e-n Rabatt gewähren

rebel *pol* Rebell, Aufrührer, Aufständiger

rebel *v pol* rebellieren, sich empören

rebellion *pol* Rebellion, Empörung, Aufruhr, Auflehnung, Aufstand

rebooking Umbuchung

reborrow *v* wieder borgen

rebuilding Wiederaufbau; Umbau *(e-s Hauses, Schiffes etc)*; ~ **of the economy** Wiederaufbau der Wirtschaft

rebuke *v* tadeln, zurechtweisen; **to be ~d** e-n Verweis bekommen

rebus sic stantibus ("under the circumstances"); ~ **clause** clausula rebus sic stantibus

rebut *v* widerlegen, entkräften

rebutting evidence Gegenbeweis *(zur Widerlegung der vom Gegner als Beweis angeführten Tatsachen)*; **to introduce** ~ den Gegenbeweis antreten

rebuttable widerlegbar; ~ →**presumption**

rebuttal Antritt (od. Führung) des Gegenbeweises; Gegenbeweis; **to offer evidence in** ~ (of an allegation) den Gegenbeweis antreten

rebuy *v* zurückkaufen

recall Zurückrufung; Rückruf *(z.B. von fehlerhaften Produkten)*; *(VölkerR)* Abberufung *(e-s diplomatischen Vertreters)*; *Am pol* vorzeitige Abberufung *(gewählter Repräsentanten durch qualifizierte Wahlmehrheit)*; Abberufung *(z.B. e-s Liquidators)*; (Auf-)Kündigung *(von Kapital, Kredit)*; ~ **test** *(Meinungsforschung)* Gedächtnistest; **letters of** ~ *(VölkerR)* Abberufungsschreiben

recall *v* zurückrufen, abberufen; *(Erklärung)* widerrufen, zurücknehmen; *(VölkerR) (e-n dipl. Vertreter)* abberufen; *(Kapital, Kredit)* kündigen; **to** ~ **goods** Waren rückrufen; **to** ~ **a loan** ein Darlehen kündigen

recalled, valid until ~ *(Börse)* bis auf Widerruf gültig

recant *v* förmlich widerrufen *(z.B. belastende Aussage)*; abschwören

recantation förmlicher Widerruf; Abschwören

recapitalization Neufinanzierung; Kapitalumschichtung; Sanierung

recapitalize *v* neu finanzieren; *(durch Veränderung der Kapitalverhältnisse e-r Gesellschaft)* sanieren

recapitulate *v (kurz)* zusammenfassen (od. wiederholen), rekapitulieren

recaption Wiederwegnahme; Wiederinbesitznahme *(e-s widerrechtl. vorenthaltenen Besitzes)*

recapture *Am* Rückgängigmachung von früheren Steuervorteilen *(z.B. Abschreibungen und Anrechnungen für Investitionen)*; *(VölkerR)* Wiederaufbringung *(e-s vom Feind aufgebrachten Handelsschiffes durch eigenes Kriegsschiff)*; Wiederergreifung *(e-s Gefangenen)*

recede *v* abstehen, Abstand nehmen (from von); (zu)rückübertragen; *com* zurückgehen, nachgeben *(Preise, Kurse)*; **to** ~ **from a demand** von e-r Forderung Abstand nehmen; **to** ~ **from a position** von e-r Stellung zurücktreten; **the shares** ~**d a point** die Aktien gingen um e-n Punkt zurück

receding prices fallende Preise; nachgebende (od. fallende) Kurse

receipt 1. Empfang, Erhalt, Eingang; Annahme, Entgegennahme *(der Ware durch den Käufer)*; ~**s** Eingänge, eingehende Gelder (od. Waren); Einnahme; ~**s and expenditure** Einnahmen und Ausgaben; ~**s book** Einnahmebuch; ~ **of goods** Warenannahme; ~ **of money** Eingang von Geld, Geldempfang; ~ **stamp** Eingangsstempel; ~ **voucher** Empfangsbescheinigung; **acknowledgment of** ~ Empfangsbestätigung; **actual** ~**s** Isteinnahmen; **additional** ~ Mehrerlös; **advice of** ~ Empfangsanzeige; **against** ~ gegen Empfangsbestätigung; **cash** ~ Kasseneingang; **certificate of** ~ Empfangsbescheinigung; **current** ~**s** *Am (Bilanz)* Umlaufvermögen; **daily** (or **day's**) ~**s** Tageseinnahmen; **date of** ~ Eingangsdatum; **deficiency in** ~**s** Mindereinnahmen; **excess of** ~**s over expenses** Einnahmeüberschuß; **falling off in the** ~**s** Rückgang der Einnahmen; **gross** ~**s** Bruttoeinnahmen; **increase of** ~**s** Mehreinnahmen; **net** ~**s** Nettoeinnahmen; **on** ~ s. upon →~; **other** ~**s** *(Bilanz)* sonstige Einnahmen; **revenue** ~**s** Steuereinnahmen; **sundry** ~**s** *(Bilanz)* verschiedene Einnahmen; **total** ~**s** Gesamteinnahmen; **upon** ~ nach Eingang, bei Empfang (od. Erhalt); **upon** ~ **of your order** nach Eingang Ihrer Bestellung, nach Empfang Ihres Auftrages; **yearly** ~**s** Jahreseinnahmen

receipt, we acknowledge ~ **of your letter** wir bestätigen den Empfang Ihres Schreibens; ~ **whereof is hereby acknowledged** worüber hierdurch quittiert wird; **we are in** ~ **of your letter of** wir erhielten Ihr Schreiben vom; **the expenses balance the** ~**s** die Ausgaben und Einnahmen decken sich; **the** ~**s do not cover the outlay** die Einnahmen decken die Ausgaben nicht; **the expenditure exceeds the** ~**s** die Ausgaben übersteigen die Einnahmen; **to take** ~ **(of)** in Empfang nehmen

receipt 2. Empfangsschein, Quittung; ~ **book** Quittungsbuch; ~ **for the balance** (or ~ **in full discharge**) Schlußquittung, endgültige Quittung; ~ **form** Quittungsformular; ~ **in duplicate** s. duplicate →~; ~ **in part** Teilquittung; ~ **of deposit** Depotschein; ~ **with consideration for payment stated** Quittung mit Angabe des Zahlungsgrundes; ~ **with consideration for payment not stated** Quittung ohne Angabe des Zahlungsgrundes; einfache Quittung.

receipt, accountable ~ Rechnungsbeleg, Buchungsbeleg; **acknowledgment of** ~ Empfangsbestätigung; **against (a)** ~ gegen Quittung; **application** ~ *Br (AktienR)* Zeichnungsbescheinigung; **as per** ~ laut Quittung; **blank** ~ Blankoquittung; **custom-house** ~ Zollquittung; **deposit** ~ Depotschein; **duplicate** ~ Duplikatquittung; Quittungsduplikat; **interim** ~ vorläufige Quittung; **luggage** ~ *Br* Gepäckschein; →**mate's** ~; **on** ~ bei Erhalt, beim Empfang; **warehouse** ~ Lagerschein; **to give a** ~ e-e Quittung geben (for über); quittieren; **to issue a** ~ e-e Quittung *(amtlich)* ausstellen; **to make** (or **write**) **out a** ~ e-e Quittung ausstellen, quittieren

receipt *v (Rechnung)* quittieren; Empfang bescheinigen (a th. e-r Sache); ~**ed bill** quittierte Rechnung

receivable ausstehen(d), noch zu fordern; zulässig; ~**s** Forderungen, Debitoren; **accounts** ~ Außenstände (→*accounts*); **bills** ~ einzulösende Wechsel, Besitzwechsel (Wechselforderungen) *(opp. bills payable)*; **notes** ~ s. bills →~; **current** ~**s** *Am (Bilanz)* Umlaufvermögen; **to be** ~ **in evidence** als Beweis(mittel) zugelassen werden

receive *v* erhalten, empfangen; in Empfang nehmen, entgegennehmen, annehmen; *(Geld)* einnehmen; (als gültig) anerkennen; **to** ~ **sb. into** jdn *(feierlich)* aufnehmen in; **to** ~ **approval** Genehmigung erhalten; **to** ~ **on credit** auf Kredit erhalten; **to** ~ **a distinction** e-e Auszeichnung erhalten; **to** ~ **dividends** Dividenden beziehen; **to** ~ **in evidence** als Beweis (-mittel) zulassen; **to** ~ **in exchange** eintauschen; **to** ~ **goods** Waren in Empfang nehmen; **to** ~ **information** Auskunft erhalten; **to** ~ **three month's notice** →notice 3.; **to** ~ **a proposal favo(u)rably** e-n Vorschlag günstig aufnehmen; **to** ~ **a refusal** e-e Ablehnung erfahren, abgelehnt werden; **to** ~ **a salary** ein Gehalt beziehen; **to** ~ **stolen goods** (or *Am* **property**) Hehlerei begehen, Diebesgut an sich bringen; **to** ~ **visitors** Besucher empfangen; **to** ~ **votes** Stimmen erhalten

received (rec'd, recd) *(Betrag)* erhalten; ~ **for shipment** übernommen zur Beförderung; ~ **for shipment B/L** Übernahmekonnossement; ~ **on account** als Akontozahlung erhalten; ~ **stamp** Eingangsstempel; ~ **with thanks** *(Betrag)* dankend erhalten *(als Quittungsvermerk)*; **money** ~ Geldeingang; **money** ~ **and expended** eingenommene und ausgegebene Gelder; **when** ~ nach Erhalt; bei Empfang; **to be** ~ **in audience** in Audienz empfangen werden

receiving Empfang; Annahme; ~ **agency**[8] Empfangsstelle; **authorized** ~ **agent** Empfangsbevollmächtigter; ~ **a bribe** passive Bestechung; ~ **cashier** Kassierer am Einzahlungsschalter; ~ **country** Aufnahmeland *(für Einwanderer)*; ~ **department** Warenannahme (-abteilung); **R**~ **Office** *(europ. PatR)* Anmeldeamt

receiving order (R.O.) *Br* Gerichtsbeschluß zur Einsetzung e-s Konkursverwalters (official receiver); **to have a** ~ **made against** *Br (etwa)* ein Konkursverfahren einleiten gegen

Verfügung des Gerichts auf den Konkursantrag hin (on presentation of the bankrupty petition), die zunächst bewirkt, daß der official receiver als interim receiver ernannt wird. In vielen Fällen kommt es danach zu einem Vergleichsverfahren (composition). Kommt kein Vergleich zustande, kann der Schuldner gerichtl. für zahlungsunfähig erklärt werden (the debtor may be adjudged bankrupt). Anmeldbar im Konkurs sind nur Forderungen, die vor dem Erlaß der ~ begründet worden sind.

Das amerikanische Recht kennt nicht wie das englische Recht das Vorverfahren zwischen receiving order und adjudication

Receiving Section, appeal from a decision of the ~ *(europ. PatR)* Beschwerde gegen die Entscheidung der Eingangsstelle

receiving, ~ **state** Empfangsstaat *(opp. sending state)*; ~ **stolen goods** (or *Am*[9] **property**) Hehlerei; ~ **teller** *Am* Kassierer *(am Einzahlungsschalter)*; **looking forward to** ~ **your reply** Ihrer Antwort entgegensehend

receiver 1. Empfänger *(opp. sender)*; *(Seefrachtgeschäft)* Ladungsempfänger; (Zoll-, *Am* Steuer-) Einnehmer; ~ **of stolen goods** (or *Am* **property)** *(StrafR)* Hehler; ~ **of wreck** Strandvogt *(für Strandungsfälle oder Schiffe in Seenot)*

receiver 2., *(gerichtlich, kraft Gesetzes*[10] *oder auf Grund e-r Vertragsurkunde [bes. Hypothekenurkunde] zugunsten bestimmter Gläubiger bestellter)* Zwangsverwalter *(der e-e Forderung einzieht oder Gesellschaften in Zahlungsschwierigkeiten oder Vermögen verwaltet, bis die Rechte der Interessenten geklärt sind)*; *Am* Konkursverwalter; Vermögensverwalter; Liquidator *(bei Auflösung e-r partnership)*; *Br* Vormund (→~ *for a patient)*; ~ **and manager** *Br (vom Gericht zugunsten von Gläubigern bestellter)* Vermögensverwalter mit Geschäftsführungsbefugnissen; ~**'s certificate** *Am (von e-m gerichtlich bestellten Verwalter ausgegebener)* Schuldschein; ~ **(for a patient)** *Br*[11] *(vom →Court of Protection bestellter und unter Aufsicht dieses Gerichts stehender)* Vormund über das Vermögen e-s Geisteskranken (od. Geistesschwachen); **interim** ~ *Br (vor Erlaß e-r →receiving order, sofern es zum Schutz des Vermögens des Konkursschuldners notwendig ist, ernannter)* zeitweiliger Konkursverwalter; **official** ~ *Br* (vorläufiger) Konkursverwalter (→*official)*

receiver 3. *(Radio, Fernsehen)* Empfänger, Empfangsgerät; *tel* Hörer

receivership Amt (od. Tätigkeit) e-s →receiver 2.; Zwangsverwaltung; Vermögensverwaltung *(z.B. auf Grund e-s Vergleichs zur Abwendung des Konkurses)*; Konkursverwaltung; *Br* Vormundschaft für das Vermögen e-s wegen Geisteskrankheit od. Geistesschwäche Entmündigten (→*receiver [for a patient]*); **under** ~ zwangsverwaltet; **to be put under** ~ unter Zwangsverwaltung gestellt werden

reception 1. Aufnahme; Annahme; Übernahme; ~ **area** (or **centre**) **for refugees** Auffanggebiet für Flüchtlinge; ~ **center** *Am (New York)* Gefängnis; ~ **of Roman Law** Rezeption des römischen Rechts; **to meet with a favo(u)rable** ~ e-e günstige Aufnahme finden

reception 2. *(offizieller)* Empfang; ~ **committee** Empfangskomitee; **civic** ~ *Br* Empfang durch die Stadtverwaltung; **farewell** ~ Abschiedsempfang; **state** ~ Staatsempfang; **to give** (or **hold**) **a** ~ e-n Empfang geben

receptive rezeptiv, aufnahmefähig; aufnahmebereit; ~ **market** aufnahmefähiger Markt

receptivity Rezeptivität; Aufnahmefähigkeit; Aufnahmebereitschaft *(z. B. des Marktes)*

recess (Gerichts-, Verhandlungs-, Sitzungs-) Pause; *(kurze)* Unterbrechung *(e-r Sitzung);* (Parlaments)Ferien; *Am* Gerichtsferien; ~ **appointment** *Am*[12] Befugnis des Präsidenten, frei gewordene Stellen zu besetzen, während der Senat nicht versammelt ist *(die so ernannten Personen müssen nach Ende der Senatsferien vom Senat im Amt bestätigt werden);* **Parliamentary** ~ *Br* Parlamentsferien; **to be in** ~ Sitzung unterbrechen; in Ferien sein

recession 1. *(VölkerR)* Rückabtretung, Rückgabe *(e-s abgetretenen Gebietes)*

recession 2. Rezession, *(leichter)* Konjunkturrückgang *(cf. depression);* **anti-~ policy** Politik der Konjunkturbelebung; **business** (or **trade**) ~ Geschäftsrückgang; *(kleiner)* Konjunkturrückgang; **period of** ~ Rezessionsphase

recessional *parl* Ferien-

recidivism Rückfall *(in ein Verbrechen)*

recidivist rückfälliger Täter *(cf. habitual offender)*

recipient Empfänger; **authorized** ~ Empfangsberechtigter; Zustellungsbevollmächtigter; ~ **country** Empfängerland *(Hilfe erhaltendes Land; opp. donor country);* ~ **of a dividend** Empfänger e-r Dividende; ~ **of a gift** Beschenkter; ~ **of a loan** Empfänger e-s Darlehns; ~ **of payment** Zahlungsempfänger; ~ **of a pension** Pensionsempfänger; Rentenempfänger

reciprocal gegenseitig, wechselseitig; ~ **agreement** Abkommen auf Gegenseitigkeit; ~ **contract** gegenseitiger Vertrag

reciprocal insurance Versicherung auf Gegenseitigkeit

Gegenseitige Gewährung von Versicherungsschutz durch eine Gruppe von Personen in der Weise, daß ein gemeinsamer Bevollmächtigter (attorney in fact) die Policen an und für die Mitglieder ausgibt. Die Mitglieder sind underwriters und insured zugleich

reciprocal protection of investments *(VölkerR)* gegenseitiger Schutz von Kapitalanlagen

reciprocal recognition and enforcement of foreign judgments gegenseitige Anerkennung und Vollstreckung ausländischer (Zivil-)Urteile *(→judgment)*

reciprocal rights, no ~ are found to exist die Gegenseitigkeit ist nicht verbürgt

reciprocal shareholding wechselseitige Beteiligung

reciprocal treatment, to grant ~ Gegenseitigkeit gewähren

reciprocal will *Am* gegenseitiges Testament

reciprocity *(auch VölkerR)* Gegenseitigkeit, Reziprozität; ~ **clause** Gegenseitigkeitsklausel; ~ **doctrine** *Am* Urteile ausländischer Gerichte werden in vielen Bundesstaaten nach dem Prinzip der Gegenseitigkeit anerkannt

reciprocity principle Reziprozitätsgrundsatz, Grundsatz der Gegenseitigkeit

Am Nach dem neuen US-Handelsgesetz (→ Omnibus Trade and Competitiveness Act) erhalten ausländische Unternehmen nur dann eine Zulassung in den USA, wenn US-Unternehmen die gleichen Rechte im jeweiligen Auslandsmarkt zugestanden werden

reciprocity, ~ **treaty** Gegenseitigkeitsvertrag; **in the absence of** ~ bei fehlender Gegenseitigkeit; **based upon** ~ auf Gegenseitigkeit beruhend; **legislative** ~ *(VölkerR)* Gegenseitigkeit der Gesetzgebung; **to guarantee** ~ Gegenseitigkeit verbürgen

recital 1. einleitende Erklärung (e-s Vertrags oder e-s Beschlusses), beginnt mit "whereas" und enthält die Geschäftsabsicht und die Tatsachen, auf denen die Geschäftsabsicht beruht

recital 2. Schilderung, Darstellung; Aufzählung; ~ **of details** Aufzählung von Einzelheiten; ~ **of facts** Darstellung des Sachverhalts

recital 3. Berufung (of auf); Zitat

recite *v* genau schildern, darstellen; zitieren; vortragen; **to** ~ **the facts** e-e Darstellung des Sachverhalts geben

recitation Vortrag; **right of** ~ Vortragsrecht

reckless rücksichtslos, leichtfertig; *(StrafR)* grob fahrlässig; ~ **driver** rücksichtsloser Fahrer; ~ **driving** rücksichtsloses Fahren; **he was booked by the police for** ~ **driving** er wurde von der Polizei wegen grob fahrlässigen Fahrens aufgeschrieben

recklessly endangering a p. *Am*[13] leichtfertige Gefährdung e-s anderen

recklessness Rücksichtslosigkeit, Leichtfertigkeit; *(StrafR)*[14] grobe Fahrlässigkeit

Recklessness ersetzt die deutsche bewußte Fahrlässigkeit, deckt dolus eventualis und jetzt auch unbewußte Fahrlässigkeit, wenn Täter sich des erhöhten Risikos bewußt war, bes. bei Verkehrsdelikten *(cf. negligence)*

reckon *v* rechnen; berechnen; errechnen; **to** ~ **up the cost** die Kosten (od. den Preis) ausrechnen; **to** ~ **with sth.** *fig* mit etw. rechnen

reclaim *v* zurückfordern; erneut fordern; *(Land)* urbar machen, *(Neuland)* gewinnen; *Scot* Berufung einlegen; **to** ~ **one's citizenship** s-e Staatsangehörigkeit wieder beantragen

reclamation Zurückforderung; *Am (KonkursR)* Aussonderungsanspruch; **land** ~ Urbarmachung von Land, Landgewinnung

reclassification Neueinstufung; Neuklassifizierung *(e-s Schiffes)*

reclassify *v* neu einstufen; *(Schiff)* neu klassifizieren

recognisance →recognizance
recognisee →recognizee
recognisor →recognizor

recognition Anerkennung; (Wieder-)Erkennen; *(VölkerR) (förml.)* Anerkennung *(cf. de facto ~, de jure ~); Am* Worterteilung *(im Parlament, bei offiziellen Gremien usw.)* ~ **of belligerency** *(VölkerR)* Anerkennung als kriegführende Partei; ~ **of foreign judgments** Anerkennung ausländischer Urteile; ~ **of paternity** Vaterschaftsanerkennung; ~ **of a state** Anerkennung e-s Staates; ~ **test** *(Meinungsforschung)* Wiedererkennungstest; **de-~** *(VölkerR)* Entziehung der Anerkennung; **de facto** ~ →de facto; **de jure** ~ →de jure; **in** ~ **of** als Anerkennung für; **mutual** ~ **of diplomas** →diploma; **non(-)~** Nichtanerkennung; **to refuse** ~ die Anerkennung verweigern (od. versagen)

recognizance Sicherheits-, Kautionsversprechen; *(gegenüber dem Gericht für sich oder einen anderen abzugebendes)* Versprechen, bei Zuwiderhandlung gegen gerichtliche Auflagen *(z.B. am Gerichtsort zu bleiben od. vor Gericht zu erscheinen)* e-n bestimmten Geldbetrag zu zahlen *(Am* in einzelnen Staaten wird ~ wie →bail bond gehandhabt); **conusee in a** ~ →recognizee; **conusor in a** ~ →recognizor; **to enter into a** ~ ein Sicherheitsversprechen abgeben

recognize *v* anerkennen *(cf. recognition);* erkennen (by an); (klar) erkennen; *Am* vor Gericht ein Schuldanerkenntnis abgeben *(→recognizance);* **to** ~ **a claim** e-n Anspruch anerkennen; **to** ~ **sb.** *Am* jdm das Wort erteilen

Recognized Investment Exchange (RIE) *Br* Anerkannte Investmentbörse *(klassifiziert durch den Financial Services Act)*
Der Betrieb des Handelsplatzes und die Aktivitäten der Investmentgesellschaften, die daran beteiligt sind, sind in die Verantwortung einer RIE gegeben

recognized, ~ **stock exchange** staatl. anerkannte Börse; **officially** ~ offiziell anerkannt; ~ **retail price** empfohlener Abgabepreis

recognizing in der Erkenntnis

recognizee derjenige, zu dessen Gunsten e-e →recognizance abgegeben worden ist

recognizor derjenige, der e-e →recognizance abgegeben hat

recommend *v* empfehlen, befürworten; **to** ~ **sb. as** jdn empfehlen als; **to** ~ **a price** e-n Preis empfehlen; **to** ~ **strongly** warm befürworten; **to** ~ **urgently** dringend empfehlen

recommended, ~ **practices** *(VölkerR)* Empfehlungen; ~ **price** empfohlener Preis, Richtpreis; ~ **retail price** empfohlener Abgabepreis

recommendable investment empfehlenswerte Kapitalanlage

recommendation Empfehlung, Befürwortung; **letter of** ~ Empfehlungsschreiben; **with a favo(u)rable** ~ befürwortend; **on** ~ **of** auf Empfehlung von; **to endorse a** ~ e-n Vorschlag befürworten; **to make a** ~ *(VölkerR)* e-e Empfehlung aussprechen (od. unterbreiten)

recommit *v (Gesetzesvorlage an e-n Ausschuß)* zurückverweisen; **to** ~ **oneself to a policy** sich erneut zu e-r Politik verpflichten; **to** ~ **to prison** wieder in das Gefängnis einliefern

recommitment *parl* Zurückverweisung *(e-r Gesetzesvorlage an e-n Ausschuß);* Wiedereinlieferung *(in das Gefängnis);* ~ **to a policy** erneute Verpflichtung zu e-r Politik

recommittal →recommitment

recompense *v* belohnen; entschädigen (for für); ersetzen; **to** ~ **a p. for a loss** jdn für e-n Verlust entschädigen

reconcile *v* versöhnen, aussöhnen; miteinander in Einklang bringen; **to** ~ **oneself to** sich aussöhnen (od. abfinden) mit

reconciled, to become ~ **to** sich abfinden mit

reconcilement →reconciliation 2.

reconciliation 1. Versöhnung, Aussöhnung; Wiederaussöhnung *(der Ehegatten; cf. condonation)*; **attempt at** ~ Sühneversuch *(Versuch der gütlichen Beilegung des Scheidungsverfahrens; vgl. § 614 ZPO)*; **to bring about** (or **effect**) **a** ~ e-e Versöhnung herbeiführen (od. zustandebringen)

reconciliation 2. Abstimmung *(von Konten)*; ~ **statement** Richtigbefundanzeige *(des Kunden)*

reconditioning Wiederinstandsetzung, Aufarbeitung; ~ **charges** Instandsetzungskosten

reconnaissance *mil* Aufklärung; ~ **aircraft** Aufklärungsflugzeug; ~ **patrol** Spähtrupp; ~ **satellite** Aufklärungssatellit

reconsider *v* nochmals erwägen, nachprüfen; erneut eingehen auf; *parl (früher beratenen Antrag)* nochmals beraten

reconsignment Umleitung, Weitersendung *(z.B. von Waren an neue Adresse)*

reconstruct *v* wiederaufbauen; umbauen; reorganisieren, sanieren

reconstruction Wiederaufbau; Umbau; Reorganisation (od. Sanierung) *(e-s Unternehmens);* ~ **loan** Wiederaufbaudarlehen; ~ **of a company** *Br*[15] Reorganisation (od. Sanierung) e-r Gesellschaft *(die freiwillig e-e Liquidation hat durchführen lassen);* ~ **programme** Sanierungsprogramm

reconversion Wiederumstellung *(z.B. e-s Fabrikbetriebes auf Friedensproduktion)*; Rückumwandlung (od. Rückumdeutung) *(e-r constructive →conversion, so daß das fiktiv umgewandelte Eigentum in s-r effektiven Gestalt erhalten bleibt; nach diesem equitable-Prinzip können Personen anstelle des ihnen vom Erblasser vermachten Erlöses aus Grundbesitz [proceeds of real estate devised upon trust] das Land selbst erhalten);* ~ **of unused foreign exchange** Rückwechselung nicht verbrauchter Devisen

reconveyance Rückübertragung *(des Grundbesitzes vom Hypothekengläubiger auf den Hypothekenschuldner)*

record 1. Aufzeichnung; *(schriftl.)* Bericht; Niederschrift; *(schriftl.)* Unterlage; Beleg; Verzeichnis; Akte(nstück); Protokoll *(des Parlaments od. der ordentlichen Gerichte)*; Gerichtsakte *(die bei e-m →court of ~ den protokollierten Gang des Verfahrens wiedergibt)*; *fig* Ruf, Leistungen in der Vergangenheit; Rekord, Höchstleistung (→*record* 3.); ~ **card** *Am* Karteikarte; ~ **copy** Aktenexemplar; ~ **date** *Am* Stichtag der Feststellung der Aktionäre *(für Dividendenzahlung etc)*; ~ **department** *(VersR)* Registratur; ~ **holder** *Am (im Aktienbuch der Gesellschaft)* eingetragener Aktionär; ~ **of attendance** Anwesenheitsliste; ~ **of interrogation** Vernehmungsprotokoll; ~ **of prior convictions** Aufstellung der Vorstrafen des Angeklagten *(zum Zwecke der Strafzumessung)*; ~ **sheet** Personalakte; ~ **of stockholders** *Am* Aktionärbuch; ~ **of the trial** Sitzungsprotokoll; **R~ Office** *Br* Staatsarchiv *(in London); Am* Grundbuchamt

record, bad ~ schlechte Vergangenheit; **he has a bad health** ~ er war oft krank

record, contract of ~ gerichtlich protokollierter Vertrag *(z.B. recognizance)*; **court of** ~ ordentliches Gericht (→*court)*; **criminal** ~ Vorstrafe(nverzeichnis) (→*criminal)*; **debt of** ~ gerichtlich festgestellte Forderung; **→estoppel by ~; for the** ~ *Am* für das Protokoll, zu Protokoll *(z.B. die Einwendung e-r Partei im Prozeß zu Protokoll geben, damit sie später im Rechtsmittelzug benutzt werden kann)*

record, good ~ gute Vergangenheit; **he has a good ~ of regular attendance** er ist (immer) regelmäßig zur Arbeit erschienen

record, of ~ eingetragen; **→matter of ~; owner of** ~ eingetragener Eigentümer; **stockholders of** ~ *Am* die im Aktienbuch *(am Stichtag)* eingetragenen Aktionäre

record, off the ~ *colloq.* inoffiziell; nicht für die Öffentlichkeit bestimmt; *(Presse)* nur der eigenen Unterrichtung dienend(e Information); **to speak off the** ~ nicht amtlich sprechen; **that is strictly off the** ~ das ist streng vertraulich zu behandeln

record, on ~ schriftlich niedergelegt; protokolliert; in (od. bei) den Akten; **on the** ~ nach Aktenlage; *(Presse)* offiziell verkündet(e Information); **to appear** (or **to be**) **on the** ~ in den Akten vermerkt sein; aktenmäßig feststehen; **to decide on the** ~ auf Grund der Akten (od. nach Aktenlage) entscheiden; **to enter on the** ~ in das Protokoll aufnehmen, im Protokoll vermerken; **to go on** ~ seine Stellungnahme zu Protokoll geben; *colloq.* bekannt sein als (od. für); **to place** (or **put**) **on** ~ zu Protokoll nehmen (od. geben); Protokoll aufnehmen; zu den Akten nehmen (od. geben); aufschreiben; *(etw.)* für die Zukunft festhalten; **to place it on** ~ (um) es aktenkundig (zu) machen, als Vermerk; **to take down on** ~ protokollieren

record, →personal ~; service ~ *mil* Wehrpaß; **trial** ~ Sitzungsprotokoll; **trial by** ~ *Am* Verfahren nach Aktenlage *(ohne Beweisaufnahme)*; **to draw up a** ~ ein Protokoll aufnehmen; **to keep a ~ of the proceedings** Protokoll in der Verhandlung führen

records 1. (Buchhaltungs-)Aufzeichnungen; Unterlagen; Belege; Verzeichnisse; Vorgänge; Protokolle; Akten; *Am* und *Scot* Register; ~ **of a bank** Bankunterlagen, Bankbelege; ~ **of a corporation** *Am* Gesellschaftsunterlagen *(Abschrift der charter, by-laws, minutes of meetings etc);* ~ **of the court** Gerichtskosten eines →court of record; **access to** ~ Zugang zu Akten; Akteneinsicht; **accounting** ~ Buchungsunterlagen; **books and** ~ Bücher und Geschäftspapiere; **case** ~ e-n Einzelfall betreffende (bes. behördliche) Akten *(z.B. beim Sozialamt);* **court** ~ Gerichtsakten; **deposit** ~ Depotunterlagen; **depository of** ~ Registratur, Archiv; **extract from** ~ Auszug aus den Akten; **inspection of the** ~ Akteneinsicht; **inventory** ~ (Buchhaltungs-)Aufzeichnungen über Vorräte; **judicial** ~ *Am* Prozeßakten; **land** ~ *Am* Grundstücksregister (→*land);* **personnel** ~ Personalakten; **private** ~ private Urkunden; **public** ~ öffentliche Urkunden; **Public R~ Office** *Br* Akten des Staatsarchivs *(Record Office);* **subsidiary** ~ Hilfsaufzeichnungen, Hilfsbücher; **transmission of** ~ Übersendung von Akten; **it appears by** (or **from**) **the** ~ es geht aus den Akten hervor; **to ask for** (or **to call in**) ~ Akten anfordern; **to consult** ~ Akten heranziehen (od. einsehen); **to enter the** ~ *Scot (bei Gericht)* registriert werden; **to inspect** ~ Akten einsehen; **to keep** ~ Akten (od. Vorgänge) führen; **to place a document with the** ~ e-e Urkunde zu den Akten legen (od. nehmen); **to request** ~ Akten anfordern

record(s) 2. *Am*[16] Daten; **access to** ~ Zugang zu Daten; **agency** ~ behördliche Daten; **archival** ~ Archivdaten; **disclosure of the** ~ Weitergabe der Daten; **statistical** ~ statistische Daten;

system of ~ Datenbank; **to have a copy made of the** ~ von den Daten e-e Abschrift machen lassen; **to maintain** ~ **on individuals** Daten über einzelne Personen speichern; **to review the** ~ in die Daten Einsicht nehmen

record 3. Rekord, Höchstleistung; ~**(-breaking)** Rekord-; ~ **attendance** Rekordbesuch, Rekordzahl von Besuchern; ~ **figure** Rekordzahl; **to beat** (or **break**) **a** ~ e-n Rekord schlagen (od. brechen); **to reach a** ~ **price** e-n Rekordpreis erzielen; **to hold the** ~ den Rekord halten

record 4. Schallplatte; Tonband; **right of communicating the work by means of sound or visual** ~ *(UrhR)* Recht der Wiedergabe durch Bild- oder Tonträger

record *v* aufzeichnen, *(schriftl. od. in den Akten)* festhalten (od. vermerken); *(in ein Register)* eintragen, registrieren; protokollieren, Protokoll führen, zu Protokoll nehmen; *(auf Schallplatten od. Tonband)* aufnehmen; **to** ~ **a deed** *Am* e-e (Grundstücks-)Übertragungsurkunde registrieren *(d.h. in ein öffentl. Register eintragen; →Recording Act)*; **to** ~ **in the minutes** im Protokoll vermerken (od. aufnehmen); **to** ~ **a mortgage** *Am* e-e Hypothek eintragen; **to** ~ **the proceedings of a court** bei e-r Gerichtsverhandlung Protokoll führen; **to** ~ **the requirements** den Bedarf schriftlich angeben; **to** ~ **on →tape; to** ~ **one's vote** wählen

recorded, ~ **delivery** *Br* Zustellung *(von Briefen od. Päckchen)* gegen Empfangsbestätigung; Einschreiben; **to have ...** ~ *(etw.)* zu Protokoll geben

recording Aufzeichnung; Eintragung; Registrierung; Protokollierung; *Am* Eintragung (od. Hinterlegung) e-r Grundstücksurkunde in den →land records *(cf.* ~ *system)*; amtl. Zählung; Tonaufnahme; **R~ Act** *Am (einzelstaatl.)* Gesetz, das e-e öffentl. Hinterlegung dinglicher Übertragungsurkunden *(deeds, mortgages, contracts or other written evidence of legal transactions)* vorschreibt; ~ **clerk** Protokollführer; ~ **fee** Registrierungsgebühr, Eintragungsgebühr; ~ **of a mortgage** *Am* Eintragung e-r Hypothek; ~ **office** *Am (etwa)* Grundbuchamt; ~ **officer** *Am* Beamter, in dessen Händen die Führung der →land records liegt;*(etwa)* Grundbuchbeamter

recording system *Am* Eintragungssystem *(cf. land records)*

Es gibt 3 Haupttypen des recording system:

1. races type statutes (nur in wenigen Staaten bestehende) Gesetze, die bestimmen, daß im Falle sich widersprechender Verfügungen derjenige das Recht erwirbt, der zuerst eingetragen wird. Der Zeitpunkt der Eintragung ist also maßgeblich. Der Erwerber eines Liegenschaftsrechts wird gegenüber zeitlich vorhergehenden Verfügungen, die das Grundstück betreffen, geschützt, wenn er „das Rennen zum recording office gewinnt";

2. notice type statutes (in etwa der Hälfte der Einzelstaaten geltende) Gesetze, die bestimmen, daß ein nicht eingetragenes dingl. Recht an einem Grundstück einem späteren entgeltlichen Erwerber nicht entgegengehalten werden kann, sofern dieser zur Zeit der Verfügung keine Kenntnis (notice) vom Bestehen dieses Rechtes hatte. Unkenntnis des späteren Erwerbers wird durch tatsächliche Kenntnis des Ersterwerbers oder durch Eintragung zerstört;

3. notice-race type statutes Gesetze, die bestimmen, daß der Erwerber eines Liegenschaftsrechts gegenüber zeitlich vorhergehenden Verfügungen, die das Grundstück betreffen, geschützt wird, wenn er „das Rennen zum recording office gewinnt" und keine tatsächliche oder durch Eintragung geschaffene Kenntnis von der vorhergehenden Verfügung hatte

recordable eintragungsfähig, registrierfähig; ~ **instrument** *Am* Urkunde, die in ein öffentl. Register aufgenommen werden kann

recordation *Am* Eintragung, Registrierung *(Übertragung des wesentl. [Vertrags-]Inhalts e-s eingereichten Schriftstücks in ein öffentl. Register)*; **office for** ~ **of personal status** (or **statistics**) (such as birth, death, marriage) *Am* Standesamt

recorder Protokollführer; Registerführer; Archivar; *Am* Standesbeamter; **R~** *Br*[17] nebenamtlicher Richter auf Zeit *(bes. im Crown Court; barristers und solicitors mit genügend Berufserfahrung können auf bestimmte Zeit als R~ ernannt werden)*; *Am* Strafrichter *(in einigen Städten)*; ~ **of deeds** *Am* →register of deeds; **R~ of London** *Br* beauftragter Richter (commissioner) des Central Criminal →Court

recording →record *v*

recount Nachzählung *(bes. von Wahlstimmen)*

recount *v* noch einmal zählen; nachzählen

recoup *v* (sich) entschädigen, schadlos halten; *Am* sich *(wegen Vertragsverletzung des Gegners)* schadlos halten; *(auch)* mindern *(→recoupment)*; **to** ~ **one's disbursements** s-e Auslagen wieder einbringen; **to** ~ **one's losses** (or **to** ~ **oneself for one's losses**) s-e Verluste wieder einbringen; sich für s-e Verluste schadlos halten

recoupment Entschädigung, Schadloshaltung; *Am* Schadloshaltung *(durch teilweises Zurückhalten oder Verweigern der Leistung aus e-m gegenseitigen Vertrag, weil der Gläubiger [Kläger] seine Vertragspflichten verletzt hat)*; *(auch)* Minderung

recourse Regreß, Rückgriff *(bes. im WechselR)*; Inanspruchnahme; Zuflucht (to zu); ~ **agreement** *Br* Rückgriffsvereinbarung (Garantieabrede zwischen Händler und Finanzierungsinstitut) *(in der sich der Händler verpflichtet, bei Ausfall des von ihm vermittelten Abzahlungskäu-*

fers die Ware vom Finanzierungsinstitut zurückzukaufen oder – häufiger – für den entstandenen Schaden aufzukommen gegen Abtretung der Rechte aus dem →hire-purchase agreement gegen den Käufer; häufig Bestandteil des →master agreement); ~ **claim** Regreßanspruch; ~**debtor** Rückgriffsschuldner; ~ **to the capital market** Beanspruchung des Kapitalmarktes; ~ **to the courts** Inanspruchnahme des Gerichts; ~ **to a credit** Inanspruchnahme e-s Kredits; ~ **to the endorser** *(WechselR)* Rückgriff auf den Indossanten; ~ **to a prior party** *(WechselR)* Sprungregreß; **claim of** ~ *(WechselR)* Regreßanspruch; **liable to** ~ regreßpflichtig; **liability to** ~ Regreßhaftung, Regreßpflicht; **person liable to** ~ Regreßpflichtiger, Regreßschuldner; **right of** ~ Rückgriffsrecht, Regreßanspruch; **without** ~ ohne Regreß, ohne Rückgriff; **to have** ~ Regreß nehmen (to, against gegen); sich halten (to an); **to have** ~ **to** in Anspruch nehmen; anrufen; **to have** ~ **to arbitration** das Schiedsgericht anrufen; **to have** ~ **to arbitration by the International Chamber of Commerce** das Schiedsverfahren der Internationalen Handelskammer in Anspruch nehmen *(s. ICC → Arbitration Clause);* **to have** ~ **to law** den Rechtsweg beschreiten

recover *v* 1. wiedererlangen, zurückerhalten; rückgewinnen; *(Geld)* eintreiben, beitreiben; *(Verlust od. Kosten)* wiedereinbringen; *(Schadensersatz)* erhalten; *(durch Urteil)* zugesprochen bekommen; *(KonkursR)* aussondern; **to** ~ **an amount** e-n Betrag einziehen; **to** ~ **average** Ersatz für Havarie erhalten; **to** ~ **costs** Prozeßkosten zugesprochen bekommen

recover *v*, **to** ~ **damages** Schadensersatz erhalten, entschädigt werden; **action to** ~ **damages** Schadensersatzklage

recover *v*, **to** ~ **a debt** e-e Forderung beitreiben (od. einziehen) *(→debt);* **to** ~ **one's disbursements** s-e Auslagen vergütet bekommen; **to** ~ **one's expenses** s-e Auslagen zurückerhalten; **to** ~ **any expenses properly incurred** Erstattung aller gerechtfertigten Auslagen erhalten; **to** ~ **fees** Gebühren beitreiben; **to** ~ **a fine** e-e Geldstrafe beitreiben; **to** ~ **as → input tax; to** ~ **interest (on)** Zinsen erhalten (auf); **to** ~ **judgment** ein Urteil erwirken; obsiegen

recover, to ~ **one's losses** s-e Verluste ersetzt bekommen; sich für s-e Verluste schadlos halten; **to** ~ **from A any loss (suffered by B)** von A Ersatz für den (durch B erlittenen) Schaden erhalten; **to** ~ **from the insurer the whole of the loss** vom Versicherer den ganzen Schaden ersetzt bekommen; **to** ~ **(from X) the amount of one's loss up to ...** (von X) Schadensersatz bis zu ... erhalten

recover *v*, **to** ~ **one's money** sein Geld zurückbekommen; **to** ~ **over** *Am (bei e-m Dritten)* Regreß nehmen; **to** ~ **a penalty** e-e Geldstrafe beitreiben (od. einziehen); **to** ~ **possession** den Besitz wiedererlangen; **to** ~ **in one's suit** s-n Prozeß gewinnen

recover *v* 2. sich erholen, ansteigen, anziehen *(Preise, Kurse);* ausgleichen; wieder erreichen

recovered, the prices ~ **their old level** die Preise (od. Kurse) erreichten ihren alten Stand wieder; **the stock-market** ~ die (Aktien-)Börse erholte sich; **the stock-market** ~ **its loss** die (Aktien-)Börse glich ihren Verlust wieder aus; **the shares** ~ **sharply** die Aktien zogen kräftig an

recoverable wiedererlangbar; zurückzugewinnen(d); einzutreiben; eintreibbar; aussonderungsfähig *(im Konkurs);* ~ **debt** beitreibbare Forderung; ~ **at law** (ein)klagbar; **amount** ~ **for non-delivery** Schadensersatz bei Nichtlieferung; **loss** ~ **under the policy** laut Versicherungspolice zu ersetzender Schaden; **rent** ~ **from the tenant** vom Mieter einziehbare Miete

recovery 1. Wiedererlangung; Rückgewinnung; Wiedereinräumung e-s früheren Rechts (od. Zurückgabe e-r Sache) durch Urteil; Einziehung, Eintreibung, Beitreibung; Ersatzleistung, Entschädigung; ~ **charges** Einziehungsspesen; ~ **deduction** *Am* Abschreibung; ~ **in prices** Preiserholung; ~ **of bad debts** Eingang von bereits als Verlust abgebuchten Forderungen; ~ **of damages** Erlangung (od. Erhalt) von Schadensersatz; ~ **of a debt** Eintreibung e-r Forderung; ~ **of land** *Am* Besitzentziehung; ~ **of maintenance** Geltendmachung des Unterhaltsanspruchs *(→maintenance);* ~ **of outstanding amounts** Eintreibung von Außenständen; ~ **of a penalty** Beitreibung e-r Geldstrafe; ~ **of property** Wiedererlangung des Eigentums; ~ **over** Regreß; ~ **property** *Am* nach dem →ACRS abgeschriebenes Anlagevermögen

recovery, action for the ~ **of land** *Br* Klage auf Herausgabe von Grundbesitz *(des Eigentümers gegen den nichtberechtigten Besitzer);* Räumungsklage; **action for the** ~ **of property** Herausgabeklage; **the amount of** ~ der beigetriebene Betrag; **enforced** ~ **procedure** *(europ. PatR)* Beitreibung *(von Gebühren);* **(final) judgment of** ~ *Am* (rechtskräftiges) obsiegendes Urteil

recovery, to sue (or **take legal proceedings**) **for the** ~ **of a debt** e-e Schuld einklagen

recovery 2. Aufschwung, Erholung *(im Konjunkturzyklus [business cycle] im Anschluß an e-e depression);* ~ **in business** Konjunkturbelebung, geschäftliche Wiederbelebung; ~ **of prices** *(langsames)* Anziehen der Preise; Kurserholung; ~ **of trade** Wiederbelebung des Handels; **economic** ~ Wirtschaftsbelebung; wirtschaftlicher (Wieder-)Aufstieg; wirtschaftliche Gesundung; **financial** ~ finanzieller (Wieder-)Aufstieg, Sanierung

recreation Erholung; **(organized)** ~ Freizeitgestaltung

recreational, ~ **facilities** Freizeiteinrichtungen; **for** ~ **purposes** für Erholungszwecke

recriminate *v* Gegenbeschuldigung vorbringen

recrimination Gegenbeschuldigung; *Am (EhescheidungsR)* Einrede des Beklagten, daß Kläger selbst e-s Scheidungsgrundes schuldig ist *(führt bei Beweis zur Klageabweisung)*

recrudescence Wiederaufleben *(z. B. der Arbeitslosigkeit)*

recruit *mil* Rekrut; Nachwuchs; **(new)** ~ neu eingestellte Arbeitskraft; ~**s to engineering** Ingenieurnachwuchs

recruit *v (Arbeitskräfte)* einstellen (od. anwerben, beschaffen)

recruitment, ~ **advertising** *Am* Stellenangebote *(in Zeitungen)*; ~ **of labo(u)r** Einstellung (od. Anwerbung) von Arbeitskräften; ~ **stop** Einstellungssperre

rectification Richtigstellung; Berichtigung, Verbesserung; *Br* Vertragsberichtigung *(Berichtigung rechtsgeschäftlicher Urkunden entsprechend dem wahren Willen der Parteien bei Vertragsabschluß [z. B. bei Vorliegen e-s Schreibfehlers]; Am cf. reformation)*; ~ **of boundaries** (or **frontiers**) Grenzberichtigung, Grenzbereinigung; ~ **of defects** Nachbesserung; ~ **of a document** Richtigstellung e-r Urkunde

rectify *v* berichtigen, verbessern, richtigstellen *(Br cf. rectification)*; e-n Mißstand beseitigen; **to** ~ **an entry** e-e Eintragung berichtigen; **to** ~ **an error** e-n Irrtum richtigstellen; **to** ~ **a grievance** e-r Beschwerde abhelfen

rectifying budget Nachtragshaushalt

rectitude, comparative ~ *Am (EhescheidungsR)* Abwägen der beiderseitigen Schuld

recurrent *(regelmäßig)* wiederkehrend; ~ **expenditure** fortlaufende Ausgaben; **non-**~ **expenditure** einmalige Ausgabe

recurring →recurrent; ~ **cost** *Am* laufende Geschäftskosten *(wages, raw material etc)*; **an often** ~ **error** ein oft wiederkehrender Fehler

recusatio testis *Am* Ablehnung e-s Zeugen

recycle *v* zurückfließen lassen, *(in den Kreislauf)* (zu)rückführen; *(Abfälle)* wiederverwerten (od. wiederverwenden); **to** ~ **surplus dollars** *(intern. Ölgeschäft)* Dollarüberschüsse wieder beim Kunden anlegen

recycling Rückgewinnung *(aus Abfallmaterial)*; Wiederverwertung; Wiederverwendung *(von Altmaterial)*; Rückfluß; ~ **of capital from the oil-producing countries** Rückschleusung des Kapitals der erdölerzeugenden Länder *(in die Industrieländer in Form von Beteiligungen)*; ~ **of petrodollars** Rückfluß der Petrodollar

red rot; ~ **book** *dipl* Rotbuch; ~ **carpet reception** „großer Bahnhof"; ~ **clause** *(im Dokumentenakkreditivverkehr)* rote Klausel *(in roter Schrift angegebene Zahlungsklausel, durch die e-e Überseebank ermächtigt wird, dem begünstigten Exporteur schon vor der Einreichung der Dokumente Vorschüsse zu gewähren)*; **R~ Crescent** Roter Halbmond *(z. B. in der Türkei; entspricht dem Roten Kreuz)*

Red Cross Rotes Kreuz; **donation to the** ~ Spende an das Rote Kreuz; **International Committee of the** ~ Internationales Komitee des Roten Kreuzes (IKRK); **League of** ~ **Societies** (LRCS) Liga der Rotkreuz-Gesellschaften *(bildet mit dem Internationalen Komitee des Roten Kreuzes und den nationalen Gesellschaften das Internationale Rote Kreuz)*; **the National** ~ **Societies** die nationalen Gesellschaften des Roten Kreuzes

red, ~ **ensign** *Br* rote Handelsflagge; ~**-handed** auf frischer Tat, in flagranti; **to be caught** ~**-handed** auf frischer Tat ertappt werden

red herring Ablenkungsmanöver; nicht zur Sache gehöriger Beitrag zu e-r Diskussion; ~ **(prospectus)** *Am (in roter Tinte gefertigte)* Vorankündigung des *(der S. E. C. einzureichenden)* Prospektes *(von e-r Wertpapieremission) (abgekürzte Fassung e-s →registration statement)*

red, ~ **interest** Sollzinsen; ~ **light** rotes Licht, Warnsignal; ~ **light district** Bordellviertel

redlining *Am (VersR, BankR)* Ausschluß bestimmter Personengruppen von Vertragsbeziehungen

Im VersR z. B. dadurch, daß Versicherer mit Hauseigentümern in von ihnen rot umrandeten Stadtbezirken wegen des schlechten Risikos keine Feuerversicherungen abschließen und dadurch Versicherung verhindern

red, ~ **tape** Bürokratismus, Amtsschimmel; ~ **tapist** Bürokrat; **to be in the** ~ in den roten Zahlen sein

reddendum Klausel in e-m Mietvertrag, die Höhe und Zahlungstermin der Miete näher bestimmt

redeem *v* zurückkaufen, zurückzahlen; einlösen, ablösen; amortisieren, tilgen; *(Pfand)* auslösen; **to** ~ **an annuity** e-e Rente ablösen; **to** ~ **banknotes** Banknoten einlösen; **to** ~ **a bond** (or **debenture**) e-e Schuldverschreibung zurückzahlen (od. tilgen); **to** ~ **a debt** e-e Schuld tilgen; **to** ~ **a loan** ein Darlehen (od. e-e Anleihe) tilgen; **to** ~ **a mortgage** e-e Hypothek tilgen; **to** ~ **a pledge** ein Pfand auslösen; **to** ~ **a promise** ein Versprechen erfüllen; **to** ~ **shares** *(eigene)* Aktien zurückkaufen (od. einziehen); Fondsanteile zurückkaufen (od. zurücknehmen)

redeemability Rückkaufbarkeit; Einlösbarkeit, Ablösbarkeit; Tilgbarkeit

redeemable (red.) rückkaufbar, rückzahlbar; einlösbar; ablösbar; amortisierbar, tilgbar *(opp. irredeemable)*; ~ **in advance** vorzeitig tilgbar; ~ **annuity** ablösbare Rente; ~ **bond** rückzahlbare (od. kündbare) Obligation; Tilgungsanleihe; ~ **in gold** in Gold rückzahlbar; ~ **preferred stock** *Am* (~ **preference shares** *Br*[18]) *(durch die Gesellschaft)* rückkaufbare (od. tilgbare) Vorzugsaktien

redelivery Rücklieferung; erneute Aushändigung

redemption Rückkauf, Rücknahme; Rückzahlung, Tilgung; Einlösung, Ablösung; Amortisierung; Auslösung *(e-s Pfandes)*; ~ **agreement** Tilgungsabkommen; ~ **date** Tilgungstermin; ~ **fund** Tilgungsfonds, Amortisationsfonds; ~ **in gold** Einlösung in Gold; ~ **loan** Tilgungsanleihe; ~ **moneys** Tilgungsbeträge; ~ **mortgage** Tilgungshypothek; ~ **of an annuity** Ablösung e-r Rente; ~ **of bonds** Tilgung von Schuldverschreibungen; ~ **of a debt** Tilgung e-r Schuld; ~ **of a loan** Tilgung e-s Darlehens; ~ **of a mortgage** Tilgung e-r Hypothek

redemption of a pledge, in default of ~ the pawnee has the power of sale bei nicht erfolgter Auslösung des Pfandes hat der Pfandinhaber das Recht des Verkaufs des Pfandes

redemption, ~ **of policy** Versicherungsrückkauf; ~ **of a promise** Einlösung e-s Versprechens; ~ **plan** Tilgungsplan; ~ **price** Rücknahmepreis *(bei Rückkauf von Anteilen)*; Rückzahlungskurs

redemption reserve Tilgungsrücklage; **capital ~ fund** *Br (Bilanz)* Kapitaltilgungsreservefonds

redemption, ~ **of shares** Rückkauf (od. Einziehung) von eigenen Aktien (od. Anteilen) *(durch die Gesellschaft)*; Rücknahme von (Investment-) Anteilen; ~ **of stocks** *Am* →~ of shares; ~ **suit** s. action for →~; ~ **table** Tilgungsplan; ~ **of units** *Br* Rücknahme von Fondsanteilen; ~ **value** Rückkaufswert; ~ **warrant** → warrant 3.

redemption, action for ~ Klage des Hypothekenschuldners auf Rückübertragung des Eigentums bei Bezahlung der Schuld; **equity of ~** Auslösungsrecht (→*equity 1.*); **statutory right of ~** *Am (einzelstaatl.)* gesetzliches Rückkaufsrecht *(der Schuldner, dessen Grundstück versteigert wurde, hat binnen e-r gewissen Frist, gewöhnl. ein Jahr, das Recht, sein Grundstück gegen Bezahlung des Versteigerungskaufpreises samt Zinsen und Kosten vom Erwerber des Grundstücks zurückzukaufen)*; **notice of ~ of a mortgage** Kündigung e-r Hypothek (→*notice 3.*); **subject to ~** tilgbar; **term of ~** Tilgungsfrist; **terms of ~** Rückzahlungsbedingungen; **to call up bonds for ~** Obligationen zur Tilgung aufrufen

redeploy *v (Arbeitskräfte, Truppen)* verlegen, umgruppieren; umstrukturieren

redeployment (Truppen-)Verschickung; ~ **of labo(u)r** Umgruppierung (od. Umsetzung) der Arbeitskräfte

redhibition *Am (Louisiana)* Rückgängigmachung e-s Kaufes; Wandlung *(wegen Gewährsmangel)*

redhibitory, ~ **action** *Am (Louisiana)* Wandlungsklage, Gewährleistungsklage; ~ **defect** *Am* Gewährsmangel

redirect *v* umleiten; *(Postsache)* umadressieren, nachsenden

redirection Umleitung; Umadressierung, Nachsendung; **application for ~** *(Post)* Nachsendeantrag

rediscount Rediskont; ~ **rate** *Am (Federal Reserve Banks)* Rediskontsatz

rediscount *v* rediskontieren

rediscounting Rediskontierung; ~ **of bills of exchange** Wechselrediskontierung; **to be eligible for ~** rediskontfähig sein

redispatch Weiterversendung

redispatch *v* weiterversenden

redistribute *v* neu verteilen, neu aufteilen, umverteilen

redistribution Neuverteilung, Neuaufteilung; Umverteilung; ~ **of electoral districts** Neueinteilung der Wahlbezirke; ~ **of wealth** Vermögensumverteilung; ~ **of work** Umverteilung der Arbeit

redistricting *Am* Neueinteilung der (Wahl-)Bezirke

redlining →red

redraft neuer Entwurf; Rückwechsel; ~ **charges** Rückwechselspesen

redraft *v* neu entwerfen, neu fassen

redraw *v* e-n Rückwechsel ziehen (on auf); **drawing and ~ing of bills** Wechselreiterei

redress Abhilfe, Behebung, Wiedergutmachung, Entschädigung; **legal ~** Rechtsschutz; **means of ~** Rechtsmittel; Hilfsmittel; **request for ~** *(VölkerR)* Aufforderung zur Abstellung der Rechtsverletzung *(Vorbedingung für Repressalien)*; **to give ~ (for a loss)** Schadensersatz leisten; **to have** (or **obtain**) ~ **(for one's losses)** Schadensersatz erhalten; **to seek ~ in court** das Gericht anrufen

redress *v* Abhilfe schaffen, abstellen, wiedergutmachen, entschädigen; **to ~ balance of trade**

eine Handelsbilanz ausgleichen; **to ~ a grievance** e-r Beschwerde (od. e-m Mißstand) abhelfen; **to ~ an injury** e-n Schaden wiedergutmachen, e-e Beschädigung beseitigen

reduce 1. *v* herabsetzen, ermäßigen, reduzieren, senken, vermindern, abbauen, verringern, (ver)kürzen; *Scot (gerichtl.)* für nichtig erklären; **to ~ the bank rate** den Diskontsatz senken; **to ~ the capital** *Br* (**capital stock** *Am*) *(AktienR)* das (Grund-)Kapital herabsetzen; **to ~ consumption** den Verbrauch einschränken; **to ~ the customs duties** die Zollsätze herabsetzen; **to ~ one's expenses** (or **expenditure**) s-e Ausgaben einschränken (od. vermindern); Einsparungen machen; **to ~ by half** um die Hälfte herabsetzen (od. kürzen); **to ~ imports** die Einfuhr beschränken; **to ~ the price** den Preis herabsetzen (od. mindern); **to ~ to the ranks** *mil (Offizier zum Soldaten)* degradieren; **to ~ (the) staff** Personal abbauen; **to ~ in value** entwerten; **to ~ wages** Löhne herabsetzen (od. kürzen)

reduced, ~ assessment niedrigere Bewertung; **~ costs** reduzierte (od. verminderte) Kosten; **~ liquidity** Liquiditätsbeengung; **at ~ fare** zu ermäßigtem Fahrpreis; **at ~ prices** zu ermäßigten (od. herabgesetzten) Preisen

reduced, ~ rate(s) ermäßigter Satz; ermäßigte Gebühr; ermäßigter Tarif; **~ rate ticket** *Br* verbilligte Fahrkarte

reduced, "and ~" *Br*[19] „und herabgesetzt", mit herabgesetztem (Grund-)Kapital *(Firmenzusatz bei e-r company limited by shares or guarantee; cf. reduction of capital)*

reduce *v* 2. zurückführen auf; anpassen an; umwandeln in; **the claim has been ~d to judgment** *Am* der Anspruch ist urteilsmäßig festgestellt; **to ~ to practice** *(etw.)* praktisch anwenden, in die Praxis umsetzen *(cf. invention)*; **to ~ to writing** *(etw.) schriftlich fixieren (od. niederlegen)*

reduction Herabsetzung, Ermäßigung, Reduzierung, Senkung, Verminderung, Abbau, Verringerung, Kürzung *(opp. increase)*; (Preis-) Nachlaß, Rabatt; Zurückführung (to auf); Umwandlung (to in); *Scot* Nichtigerklärung; **~ for children** Ermäßigung für Kinder; **~ in the bank rate** Diskontherabsetzung, Diskontsenkung; **~ in the damages** Herabsetzung des Schadensersatzes; **~ in the discount rate** Diskontherabsetzung, Diskontsenkung; **~ in duties** →**~** in the rate of duties; **~ in the number of employees** →**~** of staff; **~ in fares** Fahrpreisermäßigung; **~ in** (or **of**) **fees** Gebührenermäßigung; **~ in price** s. price →**~**; **~ in rank** *Br mil* Rangverlust, Degradierung; **~ in rates** Tarifsenkung; **~ in the (freight) rate** Frachtermäßigung, Frachtsenkung; **~ in the rate (of duties)** Senkung der Zollsätze, Zollsenkung; **~ in the rate (of interest)** Zinssenkung, Zinsnachlaß; **~ in** (or **of**) **salary** Gehaltskürzung; **~ in** (or **of**) **tariffs** Tarifsenkung; Abbau der Zölle; **~ in the trade deficit** Abbau des Handelsdefizits; **~ in value** Wertminderung; **~ in yield** Ertragsrückgang; **~ of capital** *Br*[19] Herabsetzung des Grundkapitals, Kapitalherabsetzung *(cf. "and reduced")*; **~ of capital stock** *Am* Herabsetzung des Grundkapitals; Kapitalherabsetzung; **~ of dividend** Dividendenkürzung; **~ of earning capacity** Erwerbsminderung; **~ of employment** Sinken der Beschäftigung; **~ of expenses** Kostenverringerung; **~ of rent** Miet- (od. Pacht-)herabsetzung; **~ of sentence** Herabsetzung e-r Strafe; Strafnachlaß; **~ of staff** Personalverringerung, Verringerung des Personalbestandes; **~ of stock** Lagerabbau; **~ of subsidies** Subventionsabbau; **~ of taxes** Steuersenkung; Steuerermäßigung; **~ of working hours** Arbeitszeitverkürzung; **~ to a lower grade** *Am mil* Rangverlust, Degradierung; **~ to practice of the invention** *(PatR)* Ausführung der Erfindung; **cost ~** Kostensenkung; **customs ~** Zollsenkung; **dividend ~** Dividendenkürzung; **freight ~** Frachtermäßigung, Frachtsenkung; **import ~** Einfuhrrückgang; **no ~s** feste Preise; **price ~** Preisnachlaß, Preisherabsetzung, Preissenkung; **staff ~** →**~** of staff; **with a ~ of 5%** mit 5% Rabatt; **to allow a ~** (vom Preis) ablassen; Rabatt geben; **to make a ~** e-e Ermäßigung eintreten lassen

redundancy Weitschweifigkeit *(z. B. im pleading)*; Überflüssigwerden *(von Arbeitskräften als Entlassungsgrund)*; *(betriebsbedingte)* Entlassung; **dismissal for** (or **by reason of**) **~** Entlassung wegen Arbeitsmangels; **R~ Fund** *Br* Entschädigungsfond für betriebsbedingte Entlassung oder Kurzarbeit; **~ insurance** *Br* Entschädigungsversicherung *(bei Entlassung wegen Arbeitsmangels)*; **~ notice** Mitteilung, daß Arbeitsplatz wegfällt; **~ payment** *Br*[20] Entlassungsabfindung *(Entschädigungszahlung an Arbeitnehmer, die wegen Arbeitsmangels nicht mehr gebraucht werden, z. B. bei Automatisierung des Betriebes)*; **~ rebate** *Br* Entschädigung aus dem R~ Fund für e-n Arbeitgeber, der **~** payment geleistet hat; **~ terms** Entlassungsbedingungen; **the workers feared further ~ies** die Arbeiter fürchteten weitere Entlassungen

redundant überflüssig; weitschweifend; **~ workers** freigewordene (od. entlassene) Arbeitskräfte; Arbeitnehmer, deren Arbeitsplatz wegfällt; **temporarily ~** vorübergehend *(von der Arbeit)* freigesetzt (→*lay-off*); **to make workers ~** Arbeiter entlassen *(wegen [geplanter] Betriebsstillegung oder Rationalisierung)*

reeducate *v* umerziehen; umschulen

reeducation Umerziehung; Umschulung

reelect *v* wiederwählen

reelection Wiederwahl; **... shall be eligible for ~** die Wiederwahl des ... ist zulässig; ... ist wiederwählbar

reeligibility Wiederwählbarkeit

reeligible wiederwählbar

reemploy *v* wiedereinstellen, wiederanstellen

reemployment Wiedereinstellung, Wiederanstellung; **order for ~** (of industrial tribunal) *Br* Anordnung der Wiedereinstellung e-s entlassenen Arbeitnehmers *(für die Zukunft zu angemessenen Arbeitsbedingungen)* (→*reinstatement order)*

reenact *v* wieder in Kraft setzen

reengage *v* wiedereinstellen

reengagement Wiedereinstellung

reenter *v* wieder betreten, wieder eintreten; neu eintragen; **to ~ upon** wieder Besitz nehmen von

reentry Wiederinbesitznahme *(bes. e-s Grundstücks durch den Vermieter od. Verpächter)*; Wiederbetreten; Wiedereintritt; Wiedereinreise; Neueintragung; **proviso for ~** Bedingung in e-m Miet- (od. Pacht-)vertrag, die dem Vermieter (od. Verpächter) bei Miet- (od. Pacht-) rückständen oder Verletzung anderer Vertragspflichten durch den Mieter (od. Pächter) die Wiederinbesitznahme des Grundbesitzes erlaubt

reestablish *v* wiederherstellen, wiederaufnehmen *(z.B. Handel)*; **to ~ diplomatic relations** diplomatische Beziehungen wiederherstellen; **to have one's right(s) ~ed** wieder in den vorigen Stand eingesetzt werden

reestablishment Wiederherstellung; Wiederansiedlung *(von Flüchtlingen)*; **~ of democracy** Wiederherstellung der Demokratie; **~ of full employment** Wiederherstellung der Vollbeschäftigung; **~ of rights** Wiedereinsetzung in den vorigen Stand

reeve *(Kanada)* Gemeindevorsteher

reexamination erneute Prüfung; *(Zivilprozeß)* erneute Zeugenvernehmung *(durch den Anwalt der Partei, die den Zeugen benannt hat, hinsichtl. neuer, erst im Kreuzverhör zutage getretener Tatsachen)*

reexamine *v* erneut überprüfen; *(Zeugen)* nochmals vernehmen (→*reexamination*)

reexchange[21] *(WechselR)* Rückrechnung *(Differenz des Wertes der Wechselsumme, verursacht durch die Zahlungsverweigerung im Ausland, wo er zahlbar war)*; **to recover the amount of the ~** den Betrag der Rückrechnung erhalten

reexport(ation) Reexport, Wiederausfuhr *(importierter Waren)*; **~ trade** Wiederausfuhrhandel

reexport *v* wiederausführen

ref.: Bezug (→*reference [number]*)

refer *v* verweisen (to an); (sich) beziehen, Bezug nehmen (to auf); hinweisen, verweisen (to auf); sich berufen (to auf); zurückbeziehen *(auf e-n früheren Zeitpunkt)*; **to ~ to sb. as** jdn bezeichnen als; **to ~ back** zurückverweisen (to an); **to ~ to an Act** sich auf ein Gesetz berufen; ein Gesetz zitieren; **to ~ to a dictionary** in e-m Wörterbuch nachschlagen; **to ~ to a document as proof** e-e Urkunde zum Beweis heranziehen; **~ to drawer** (R.D.) *(ScheckR)* an den Aussteller zurück *(wenn kein ausreichendes Guthaben vorhanden ist; cf. N/F)*; **to ~ a p. to a former employer** jdm s-n letzten Arbeitgeber als Referenz angeben; **to ~ to a p. by name** jdn mit Namen nennen (od. erwähnen)
referred to as bezeichnet als
referring, ~ a cause to a referee Verweisung e-r Sache an e-n →referee; **~ to your letter** Bezug nehmend auf Ihr Schreiben

referee Schiedsrichter; *(vom Gericht ernannter)* Sachverständiger; Sonderrichter *(Am pensionierter Richter od. Anwalt)*; Referenz(person); **~ (in bankruptcy)** *Am* Konkursrichter; **~ in case of need** *(WechselR)*[22] Notadressat

reference 1. Verweisung; *Br* Vorlage zur Entscheidung e-r Frage durch e-n →referee; **~ to arbitration** Verweisung an ein Schiedsgericht; **books of ~** benutzte Literatur; Quellen; **cross ~** Kreuzverweisung *(→cross)*
reference 2. Bezug(nahme), Hinweis, Berufung (to auf); Aktenzeichen; **~ to authorities** Quellenangabe; **~ book** Nachschlagewerk; **~ in case of need** *(WechselR)*[22] Notadresse; **~ files** Handakten; **~ library** Handbücherei
reference (number) (ref.) Aktenzeichen, Geschäftszeichen; **~ to be quoted in all communications** in jedem Schriftwechsel anzugebendes Aktenzeichen; **our ~** (Our Ref.:) unser Aktenzeichen; **your ~** (Your Ref.:) Ihr Aktenzeichen; **to put a ~ on a letter** e-n Brief mit e-m Aktenzeichen versehen; **to quote a ~** ein Aktenzeichen angeben
reference price *(EG)* Referenzpreis, Bezugspreis
reference, in (or **with**) **~ to** mit Bezug(nahme) auf; **→incorporation by ~**; **method of ~** Zitierweise; **notice of ~** *Br (KartellR)* Einleitung e-s formellen Verfahrens (→*notice 1.)*; **→ terms of ~; to have ~ to** sich beziehen auf
reference 3. Referenz, Empfehlung(sschreiben); Zeugnis *(für Angestellte)*; **bank(er's) ~** Bankauskunft, Bankreferenz; **first class ~s** erstklassige Referenzen; **indication of ~s** Angabe von Referenzen; **trade ~** Kreditauskunft; **to fur-**

nish ~s Referenzen beibringen; **to give** (or **quote**) **a p. as a** ~ jdn als Referenz angeben; **to state ~s** Referenzen angeben; **to take up sb.'s ~s** über jdn Referenzen einholen

referendum *pol* Referendum, Volksentscheid (on über); **petition for a** ~ Volksbegehren; **to hold a** ~ e-n Volksentscheid abhalten

referendum, ad ~ zur Berichterstattung

referral to a committee *parl* Überweisung an e-n Ausschuß

refinancing Refinanzierung; ~ **loan** Refinanzierungskredit

reflation Reflation

reflection, to grant period (or **time**) **for** ~ Bedenkzeit gewähren

refloating a ship Wiederflottmachung e-s Schiffes

reflux (Zu-)Rückfluß; ~ **of capital** Kapitalrückfluß

reforest *v Am* (wieder) aufforsten

reform Reform; Umgestaltung; ~ **of land tenure** Bodenreform; ~ **movement** Reformbewegung; ~ **school** *Am* Jugendgefängnis; **agrarian** ~ Bodenreform; **constitutional** ~ Verfassungsreform; **currency** ~ Währungsreform; **electoral** ~ Wahlreform; **fiscal** ~ Finanzreform; **land** ~ Bodenreform; **law** ~ Rechtsreform (→*law*); **monetary** ~ Währungsreform; **penal** ~ Strafrechtsreform; **proposal on** ~ Reformvorschlag; **sweeping** ~ durchgreifende Reform; **trenchant** ~ einschneidende Reform; **to carry out ~s** Reformen durchführen; **to initiate a** ~ e-e Reform einführen

reform *v* reformieren, neugestalten; **to** ~ **an instrument** *Am* e-e Urkunde *(dem Parteiwillen entsprechend)* berichtigen *(Br cf. to rectify)*

reformation Reformierung, Neugestaltung; *Am* Berichtigung *(e-r Urkunde, entsprechend dem wahren Willen der Parteien), (gerichtl.)* Vertragsänderung *(Br cf. rectification)*; ~ **of an offender** Besserung e-s Täters

reformatory Reform-; *Am* Jugendhaftanstalt *(Gefängnis für junge Rechtsbrecher bis zu 30 Jahren)*; ~ **efforts** Reformbestrebungen; **detention in a** ~ *Am* Unterbringung in e-r Jugendhaftanstalt

reforward *v* weiterbefördern

refrain *v* Abstand nehmen von; **to** ~ **from doing sth.** unterlassen, etwas zu tun; **to** ~ **from an action** sich e-r Tätigkeit enthalten; e-e Handlung unterlassen; **order to** ~ *Br (KartellR)* Unterlassungsanordnung

reformism Reformismus

refresher Sonderhonorar für den Anwalt (*Br* barrister) *(bei längerer Verhandlungsdauer)*; ~ **course** Wiederholungskurs; Fortbildungskurs

refreshing the memory *Br* Auffrischen des Gedächtnisses *(e-s Zeugen durch Verweisung auf e-e an sich als Beweis nicht zulässige von ihm erstellte Urkunde)*

refrigerated, ~ **traffic** Kühl(güter)transport; ~ **van** *Br* Kühlwagen; ~ **vessel** *Br* Kühlschiff

refrigeration, Agreement Concerning the International Institute of R~[23] Abkommen über das Internationale Kälteinstitut

refuge Zuflucht(sort, -stätte), Asyl; Verkehrsinsel; **house of** ~ Obdachlosenheim; **place of** ~ Zufluchtsort; **port of** ~ Nothafen; ~ **for battered women** Frauenhäuser; **to afford** (or **give**) ~ **to a p.** jdm Zuflucht gewähren; **to seek** (or **take**) ~ (in a country) (in e-m Lande) Zuflucht suchen

refugee *(polit.)* Flüchtling; Emigrant; Heimatvertriebener; ~ **camp** Flüchtlingslager; ~ **seaman**[24] Flüchtlingsseemann; ~ **status** Rechtsstellung als *(anerkannter)* Flüchtling; **admission of ~s** Aufnahme von Flüchtlingen; **assistance to ~s** Flüchtlingshilfe; **flood of ~s** Flüchtlingsstrom; **status of ~s**[25] Rechtsstellung der Flüchtlinge; **United Nations High Commissioner for R~s** (UNHCR) UNO-Hochkommissar für Flüchtlinge *(Sitz: Genf)*; **to be recognized as a** ~ als Flüchtling anerkannt werden

refund Rückerstattung, Rückvergütung, Rückzahlung

refund annuity Rentenversicherung(svertrag) mit Beitragsrückerstattung

Bei Tod des Versicherten erstattet Versicherer den Unterschiedsbetrag zwischen gezahlten Beiträgen (Prämien) und den bereits geleisteten Rentenbeträgen

refund, ~ **claim** (Rück-)Erstattungsanspruch; ~ **of travel expenses** Erstattung der Reisekosten; **application for** ~ Antrag auf Rückzahlung; **liable to** ~ (rück)erstattungspflichtig, rückzahlungspflichtig; **tax** ~ Steuerrückzahlung, Steuer(rück)vergütung; **to make a** ~ zurückzahlen

refund *v* zurückgeben, (zu)rückerstatten, (zu-)rückvergüten, (zu)rückzahlen; refinanzieren; umschulden; *(Anleihe)* neu fundieren; **to** ~ **the expenses** die Auslagen zurückerstatten

refunding Rückerstattung; Refinanzierung; Umschuldung; ~ **of debentures** Umwandlung von (kurzfristigen) Schuldverschreibungen *(z.B. durch Emission langfristiger Papiere)*; ~ **of expenses** Erstattung von Auslagen; ~ **of postage** Erstattung der Portokosten

refurbish *v* renovieren

refusal (Ver-)Weigerung, Ablehnung, Absage, Versagung; abschlägige Antwort, abschlägiger Bescheid (to auf); ~ **of an application** *(PatR)* Zurückweisung e-r Anmeldung; ~ **of an offer** Ablehnung e-s Angebots; ~ **of (grant of) a patent** Patentversagung; ~ **of a petition** Ablehnung e-s Gesuchs; ~ **of a proposal** Ablehnung e-s Vorschlags; ~ **to accept** Annahmeverweigerung; ~ **to buy** *(verbotene)* Bezugssperre

refusal to deal *Am (AntitrustR)* Liefersperre; Abschlußverweigerung; **collective** ~ Gruppenboykott; **concerted** ~ *Am* abgestimmte Lieferverweigerung *(Vereinbarung zwischen mehreren Unternehmen, mit e-m dritten Unternehmen keinen Handel zu treiben)*; **individual** ~ *Am* Abschlußverweigerung (od. Liefersperre) seitens e-s einzelnen *(stellt keinen Antitrust-Tatbestand dar)*

refusal, ~ **to give evidence** Aussageverweigerung, Zeugnisverweigerung; ~ **to pay** Zahlungsverweigerung; ~ **to sell** Liefersperre

refusal, first ~ **clause** *Am* Klausel, die ein Vorkaufsrecht einräumt; **right of first** ~ Vorkaufsrecht; **to give a p. the (right of) first** ~ jdm ein Vorkaufsrecht einräumen; jdm an Hand geben; **to meet with a** ~ e-e abschlägige Antwort erhalten, abschlägig beschieden werden

refuse Abfall, Abfälle, Müll; ~ **collection** (or **collection of** ~) Müllabfuhr; ~ **incinerating plant** Müllverbrennungsanlage; ~ **tip** *Br* Schuttabladeplatz

refuse *v* verweigern, (sich) weigern; ablehnen; absagen; versagen; **to** ~ **to accept (a bill)** Annahme (e-s Wechsels) verweigern; **to** ~ **an application** e-n Antrag ablehnen; *(PatR)* e-e Anmeldung zurückweisen; **to** ~ **a candidate** e-n Kandidaten ablehnen; **to** ~ **a claim** e-n Anspruch zurückweisen; **to** ~ **one's consent** s-e Zustimmung verweigern; **to** ~ **to take delivery** (of the goods) die Annahme verweigern; **to** ~ **to give evidence** die Aussage verweigern; **right to** ~ **to give evidence** Zeugnisverweigerungsrecht; **to** ~ **an invitation** e-e Einladung absagen; **to** ~ **liability** Haftpflicht ablehnen; **to** ~ **a licence (-se)** e-e Lizenz verweigern; **to** ~ **a patent** ein Patent versagen; **to** ~ **payment** Zahlung verweigern; **to** ~ **recognition** die Anerkennung versagen; **to** ~ **a request** ein Gesuch ablehnen

refutable widerlegbar

refutation Widerlegung

refute *v* widerlegen; **to** ~ **an assertion** e-e Behauptung widerlegen

regain *v*, **to** ~ **a market** einen Markt wiedergewinnen

regalia *Br* Vorrechte der Krone; Krönungsinsignien

regard Hinsicht, Bezug; Rücksicht; ~**s** Grüße, Empfehlungen; **with** ~ **to** hinsichtlich, in bezug auf; **with due** ~ **(to)** unter (gebührender) Berücksichtigung; **without** ~ **to cost** ohne Rücksicht auf die Kosten; **to give one's** ~**s to a p.** jdn grüßen; sich jdm empfehlen; **to have (particular)** ~ **(to)** (besonders) berücksichtigen; **to pay due** ~ **(to)** gebührend berücksichtigen, Rechnung tragen; **having** ~ **to** im Hinblick auf, mit Rücksicht auf; in Anbetracht daß; **having** ~ **to all the circumstances of the case** unter Würdigung aller Umstände des Falles

regard *v*, **as** ~**s** was anbetrifft

regarded, to be ~ **as** angesehen werden als, gehalten werden für

regarding hinsichtlich, bezüglich, betreffs

regardless of ohne Rücksicht auf, ohne Berücksichtigung; **liability** ~ **fault** Haftung unabhängig von Verschulden, Gefährdungshaftung

regency Regentschaft; **R**~ **Acts** *Br* Gesetze[26] betr. die Einsetzung e-s aus den nächsten Verwandten bestehenden Regentschaftsrates im Falle der Regierungsunfähigkeit des Monarchen *(Krankheit, längere Abwesenheit etc)*

regent Regent; *Am univ* Verwaltungsrat, Kurator; **Board of** ~**s** *Am univ* Kuratorium

regime 1. *pol* Regime, Regierung(sform); **imprisoned opponent of a** ~ inhaftierter Regimegegner; **loyal to the** ~ regimetreu; **supporter of a** ~ Anhänger e-s Regimes

regime 2. System von Regeln (Gesetzen, Verordnungen etc.); **community property** ~ *Am* Güterstand der Gütergemeinschaft (→*community 2.*); **matrimonial** (or **marital**) ~ *Am* ehelicher Güterstand; **statutory matrimonial property** ~ gesetzlicher Güterstand

regiment *v* in Gruppen einordnen; *(übermäßig)* organisieren; reglementieren *(bes. im kritischen Sinn)*

regimentation Zusammenschluß in Gruppen; *(übermäßige)* Organisation; Reglementierung

region Gebiet; *fig* Bereich; **border** ~ Grenzgebiet; **industrial** ~ Industriegebiet

regional regional, Regional-; örtlich, Orts-; ~ **agency** regionale Einrichtung; ~ **association** Regionalverband; ~ **development** regionale Entwicklung; ~ **office** regionale Geschäftsstelle; *(VersR)* Bezirksverwaltung; ~ **pact** *(VölkerR)* Regionalpakt; ~→ **patent;** ~ **planning** Raumplanung, Landesplanung; ~ **policy** Regionalpolitik; Raumordnung(spolitik); ~

representative Bezirksvertreter; ~ **research** Regionalforschung; Raumordnung; ~ **stock exchange** regionale Börse *(Am außerhalb New York City)*

regionalism Regionalismus

register Register; *(bes. amtlich geführtes)* Verzeichnis; *Am* Registerbeamter; Wählerliste, Wahlkartei

register, to enter in the ~ in das Register eintragen registrieren; **to keep a** ~ ein Register führen; **to record in the R** ~ **of European Patents** in das Europäische Patentregister eintragen; **to remove the trademark from the** ~ die Handelsmarke in der (Waren-)Zeichenrolle löschen; **to sign the** ~ *Br* e-e Eintragung im →register of births, deaths and marriages unterzeichnen; **to strike off the** ~ im Register löschen

register, ~ **book** *Br* Schiffshypothekenregister; ~ **of aircraft** Luftfahrzeugrolle; ~ **of births** Geburtenbuch; ~ **of births, deaths and marriages** *Br* Personenstandsbücher; ~ **of births, marriages and burials** *Am* Personenstandsbücher; ~ **relating to bonds** *Br* Register für Staatsanleihen (Government bonds); **R** ~ **of Business Names** *Br* Firmenregister

Register of Charges *Br*[27] Register der Belastungen *(e-r Gesellschaft)*

Der Ausdruck wird sowohl für das beim → Registrar of Companies als auch das von der Gesellschaft am → registered office zu führende Verzeichnis der Belastungen verwendet

register of companies *Br* Gesellschaftsregister; **to strike the company off the** ~ *Br* den Namen der Gesellschaft aus dem Register streichen

register of condolences, to sign the ~ sich in die Trauerliste eintragen

register, ~ **of (previous) convictions** *(etwa)* Strafregister; **R**~ **of Co-operative Societies** Genossenschaftsregister; **R**~ **of Copyrights** *Am* Urheberrechtsregister; **R**~ **of Corporations** *Am* Gesellschaftsregister; ~ **of deaths** Sterbebuch; **R**~ **of Deeds** *Am* Grundbuchamt; ~ **of (holders of) debentures** (or ~ **of debenture holders**) *Br* Liste der Schuldverschreibungsinhaber; **R**~ **of Designs** *Br* Musterregister; ~ **of directors' interests** *Br*[28] Register über die Interessen der Direktoren; ~ **of electors** Wählerliste

Register of European Patents Europäisches Patentregister; **extracts from the** ~ Auszüge aus dem Europäischen Patentregister; **to record in the** ~ in das Europäische Patentregister eintragen

register, R ~ **of Land Charges** *Br* s. Land Charges → R~; ~ **of marriages** Familienbuch; ~ **of members** *Br*[29] Aktienbuch, Verzeichnis der Aktionäre; Gesellschafterliste; **R**~ **of Membership Corporations** *Am* Vereinsregister

register, ~ **of patents** *Am* s. Patent →R~; **R**~ **of Plant Varieties** Sortenschutzrolle; **R**~ **of Sasines** *Scot* Grundbuch; ~ **of shareholders** Verzeichnis der Aktionäre; ~ **of ships** Schiffsregister; ~ **of stock and stockholders** *Br* Liste der Inhaber von →Government stock; **R**~ **of Trademarks** (Waren-) Zeichenrolle; **R**~ **of Vital Statistics** *Am* Personenstandsbücher; ~ **of voters** Wählerliste; ~ **of wills** *Am* Urkundsbeamter des Nachlaßgerichts

register office Registratur; Annahmestelle; *Br* Standesamt; **marriage at a** ~*Br* standesamtliche Trauung; **to get married at a** ~ *Br* sich standesamtlich trauen lassen

register, ~ **ton** →ton 2; ~ → **tonnage**

register, copy (of the) ~ Registerauszug; **deeds** ~ *Am* Sammlung von Abschriften oder Auszügen aus →deeds; **electoral** ~ Wählerliste; **entry in the** ~ Registereintragung; **extract from the** ~ Auszug aus dem Register; **Federal R**~ (Fed. Reg.) *Am*[30] Register, in dem die Rechtsverordnungen des Bundes chronologisch veröffentlicht werden; **General R**~ **Office** *Br* Hauptstandesamt; **inspection of the** ~ Einsicht in das Register; **Land R**~ *Br* Grundbuchamt (→*land*); **Land Charges R**~ *Br* Register für Grundstücksbelastungen (→*land*); **office copy (of the)** ~ amtlich erteilter Auszug aus dem Register *(bes. Land Register)*; **Official R**~ *Am* Amtsblatt; Gesetzblatt; **parish** ~ Kirchenbuch; **Patent R**~ *Am* Patentrolle; **Principal R**~ *Am (Warenzeichen)* Hauptregister *(steht nur solchen Marken offen, die über e-e ausreichende Unterscheidungskraft verfügen)*; **removal from the** ~ **of trademarks** Löschung in der (Waren-)Zeichenrolle; **share** ~ *Br* →~ of members; **ship's** ~ Schiffsregister; **stock** ~ *Am* Aktienbuch; *Br* Register für Local Authorities →stock; **Supplemental R**~ *Am (WarenzeichenR)* Nebenregister *(stellt an die Unterscheidungskraft der Marken nur geringe Anforderungen)*; **transfer** ~ *Br* Übertragungs- (od. Umschreibungs)register *(für Aktien)*

register *v* registrieren; *(in ein Register)* eintragen (lassen); sich eintragen, (sich) anmelden; sich *(amtl.)* eintragen lassen; *(Postsachen)* einschreiben (lassen); *(Aktien)* im Register umschreiben; ein Schiffszertifikat *(über Eigentum und Nationalität)* ausstellen *(cf. certificate of registry)*; *(Gepäck)* aufgeben; **to** ~ **births, marriages and deaths** Geburten, Eheschließungen und Sterbefälle eintragen (lassen) (od. anmelden); **to** ~ **bonds** Obligationen *(auf Namen)* eintragen; **to** ~ **a company (corporation)** e-e Handelsgesellschaft in das Gesellschaftsregister eintragen (lassen); **to** ~ **for a fair** sich zu e-r Messe anmelden; **to** ~ **a mortgage** *Br* e-e Hypothek *(in das Grundbuch)* eintragen (lassen); **to** ~ **a motor vehicle** ein Kraftfahrzeug registrieren (od. zulassen); **to** ~ **a treaty** *(VölkerR)* e-n Vertrag registrieren; **to ~ at a →university**

registered (reg.) *(in ein Register)* eingetragen; gesetzlich geschützt; *(in Verbindung mit Effekten)* auf den Namen lautend; *(auf Postsendungen)* „Einschreiben"; ~ **agent** *Am* Zustellungsbevollmächtigter, Vertreter *(für e-e corporation)*; ~ **agreement** *Br (KartellR)* registrierte Absprache; ~ **bond** auf den Namen lautende Schuldverschreibung, Namensschuldverschreibung; ~ **capital** Grundkapital *(e-r AG)*; Nominalkapital; ~ **certificate** auf den Namen lautendes Wertpapier *(opp. bearer certificate)*; ~ **charge** *Br* eingetragene Grundstücksbelastung *(cf. land charge)*; ~ **check** *Am* Bankscheck; ~ **company** eingetragene Gesellschaft (→*company*); ~ **coupon bond** *Am* Namensschuldverschreibung mit Zinsschein zahlbar an den Inhaber; ~ **debenture** →~ bond; ~ **design** *Br* eingetragenes (Gebrauchs-)Muster (→*design 2.*); ~ **design proceedings** *Br* Verfahren in Gebrauchsmustersachen; ~ **holder** *Br* eingetragener Inhaber *(von ~ securities)*; ~ **items** eingeschriebene (Post-)Sendungen; ~ **land** *Br (im →Land Register)* eingetragener Grundbesitz *(cf. land certificate)*; Am eingetragener Grundbesitz *(für den das →Torrens system gilt, im Ggs. zu dem traditionellen →recording system)*; ~ **letter** eingeschriebener Brief; **by ~ mail** als Einschreiben; ~ **mail receipt** Einlieferungsschein *(bei Einschreiben)*; ~ **member of a party** eingetragenes Parteimitglied; ~ **mortgage** *(in das Grundbuch)* eingetragene Hypothek; ~ **name** *Br* eingetragener Handelsname *(cf. business name)*; ~ →**nurse**; ~ **office** (eingetragener) (Haupt-)Sitz (e-r Gesellschaft, e-s Vereins); **by ~ post** *Br* als Einschreiben; ~ **proprietor** *Br* im Grundbuch (land register) eingetragener Eigentümer; ~ **representative** *Br (besonders qualifizierter)* Angestellter der → International Stock Exchange, der mit der Öffentlichkeit Kontakt hat; *Am (bei der → Securities and Exchange Commission registrierter, besonders qualifizierter)* Angestellter e-r broker-Firma, der Börsenaufträge entgegennimmt (→ *account executive*, → *customer's broker)*

registered securities Namenspapier; Namensaktien *(opp. bearer securities)*

Neben der Eintragung des Berechtigten im Register erfolgt die Ausgabe eines certificate auf den Namen des registered holder. Die Übertragung von Rechten aus ~ erfolgt durch Übertragungsurkunde (deed of transfer) und Umschreibung (registration) der Rechte auf den Namen des Erwerbers

registered, ~ share Namensaktie; *(Investmentanteil)* Namensanteil; ~ **share certificate** auf den eingetragenen Inhaber lautendes Zertifikat; ~ **shareholder** Inhaber von Namensaktien; ~ **societies** *Br (gemäß dem Industrial and Provident Societies Act)* registrierte Genossenschaften; ~ **stock(s)** *Am* Namensaktien; *Br* →inscribed stock; ~ **tonnage** s. register →tonnage; ~ **trader** *Am* →floor trader; ~ **trademark** eingetragenes *(gesetzlich geschütztes)* Warenzeichen; ~ **user** *Br*[31] *(in die Warenzeichenrolle)* eingetragener Lizenznehmer

registrable registrierfähig, *(auf den Namen)* eintragungsfähig

registrant Anmelder *(z.B. e-s Warenzeichens)*

registrar Registerbeamter, Registerführer; Registrator; *Br* richterlicher Hilfsbeamter *(e-s County Court)*; *Br* Gerichtsbeamter *(der Chancery Division)*; *Br* Standesbeamter; *Am* (*auch stock* ~) mit der Überwachung der Aktienausgabe beauftragte Stelle; **R~ General** (of Births, Deaths and Marriages) *Br* oberster Standesbeamter, Leiter des General →Register Office; **R~ of Companies** *Br*[32] Führer des Gesellschaftsregisters; **R~ of the Court of Justice** *(EG)* Kanzler des Gerichtshofs; ~ **of deeds** *Am* Führer der →land records; Grundbuchbeamter; ~ **of transfers** *Br* Umschreibungsbeamter *(für Aktien)*; ~**'s office** Registratur, Geschäftsstelle; *Br* Standesamt; **Chief Land R~** *Br* Leiter des Hauptgrundbuchamtes; **District Land R~** *Br* Leiter e-s Bezirksgrundbuchamtes; **superintendent ~** *Br* Hauptstandesbeamter (→*superintendent*)

registration Registrierung, (Register-)Eintragung, Einschreibung; Zulassung *(für Auto od. Br für bestimmte Berufe, z.B. Arzt)*; Anmeldung *(z.B. zu e-m Kongreß)*; Anmeldeverfahren; *Am univ* Immatrikulation; *Br (Post)* Einschreiben *(für Wertsendungen)*; (Gepäck-)Aufgabe; Umschreibung (→*registered securities*); ~ **certificate** Registrierungsbescheinigung *(s. certificate of →~)*; *(polizeil.)* Ausweis für Ausländer; *(etwa)* Aufenthaltsgenehmigung[33]; *Am (einzelstaatl.)* Registrierungsschein für Kraftfahrzeuge, *(etwa)* Kraftfahrzeugbrief; ~ **of aliens with the police** *Br* polizeiliche Anmeldung von Ausländern *(nur Ausländer brauchen sich polizeilich anzumelden und erhalten dann das →~ certificate)*; ~ **of births and deaths** Eintragung von Geburten und Todesfällen *(in das Register)*; ~ **of business names** *Br* Eintragung von Firmennamen; ~ **of charges in the Land Register** *Br* Eintragung von Belastungen in das Grundbuch; ~ **of a company** *Br* Eintragung e-r (Handels-)Gesellschaft in das Gesellschaftsregister

registration of a design Eintragung e-s Musters; **articles protected by the ~** Waren, die unter Musterschutz stehen

registration, ~ fee Eintragungsgebühr; Anmeldegebühr; Umschreibgebühr *(für Aktien)*; (Post-)Einschreibegebühr; *Am univ* Immatrikulationsgebühr; ~ **form** Meldeschein; ~ **label** (Klebe-)Zettel für Einschreibesendungen; ~ **number** Registrierungsnummer; *(Au-*

to) Zulassungsnummer; ~ **of land** Eintragung von Grundbesitz *(Br →Land Register, Am →Land Records)*; ~ **of luggage** *Br* Gepäckaufgabe; ~ **of marriage** Eintragung der Ehe *(in das Register)*; ~ **of a mortgage** Eintragung e-r Hypothek; ~ **of motor vehicles**[34] Registrierung (od. Zulassung) von Kraftfahrzeugen; ~ **of satisfaction** *Am* Eintragung der Löschung *(e-r Hypothek)*; ~ **of title (to land)** Eintragung der Eigentumsübertragung von Grundbesitz, Grundbucheintragung *(Am cf. Torrens system; opp. conveyancing by deed)*; ~ **of a trademark** Eintragung e-s Warenzeichens; ~ **of treaties** *(VölkerR)* Registrierung von Verträgen; ~ **office** Registeramt, Registerbehörde, Registratur; ~ **rules** Registrierungsvorschriften; ~ **statement** *Am* Registrierungsangaben *(der SEC bei Beantragung der Börsenzulassung einzureichende Unterlagen)*; ~ **with the police** Meldung bei der Polizei

registration, certificate of ~ Registrierungsbescheinigung; *(polizeil.)* Aufenthaltsgenehmigung (→~ *certificate)*; *Br* Bescheinigung über die Eintragung *(von Hypotheken und Belastungen e-r company)*; *Am (nach dem Torrens-System ausgestellte)* Beurkundung von Rechten an Grundbesitz; *Am (einzelstaatl.)* polizeil. Registrierschein *(für Kraftfahrzeuge)*; **compulsory** ~ Meldepflicht; **compulsory** ~ **areas** *Br* Gebiete, in denen Eigentumsübertragung an Grundbesitz registriert werden muß *(cf. Land Register)*; **concurrent** ~ *Am* gleiche Markeneintragung mehrerer Anmelder; →**deeds** ~; **defensive** ~ *Am (WarenzeichenR)* defensive Eintragung *(der im zwischenstaatl. Handel benutzten Marke)*; **office for** ~ **of personal status** *(such as birth, death, marriage)* Standesamt; **re-**~ Umregistrierung; Wiedereintragung; **state of** ~ Zulassungsstaat *(für Kraftfahrzeuge)*

registration, subject to ~ eintragungspflichtig; anmeldepflichtig; **agreement subject to** ~ *Br (KartellR)* der Meldepflicht unterliegende Absprache

registration, urgent ~ **by summary procedure** beschleunigte Eintragung *(e-s Warenzeichens)*

registration, to cancel (or **expunge**) **a** ~ e-e Eintragung löschen; **petition to cancel a** ~ Löschungsantrag; **to deny** ~ Antrag auf Eintragung zurückweisen; **to effect a** ~ e-e Eintragung vornehmen (od. machen); **to grant a p.** →**temporary** ~

registry Eintragung, Registrierung *(bes. e-s Schiffes)*; Registerbehörde; Registratur; *Br* Geschäftsstelle *(bestimmter Gerichte)*; ~ **books** Register; ~ **of deeds** *Am* Grundbuchamt; ~ **of a ship**[35] Registrierung e-s Schiffes, Eintragung e-s Schiffes in das Schiffsregister; **(ship's) certificate of** ~ →ship's registry certificate; **district** ~ *Br* Zweiggeschäftsstelle des High Court of Justice in den größeren Städten; **Land R**~ *Br* Grundbuchamt; **marine** ~ **office** *Br* Schiffsregisteramt; **port of** ~ Heimathafen

regnal year *Br* Jahr der Thronbesteigung *(wichtig für Datierung der Gesetze)*

regrading Neueinstufung

regrating An- und Verkauf von Waren auf demselben Markt; Aufkaufen von Lebensmitteln auf offenem Markt zum Zwecke des sofortigen Wiederverkaufs auf demselben Markt

regressive tax regressive Steuer

regret Bedauern; **letter of** ~ *Br* →letter 2.; **much to our** ~ zu unserem großen Bedauern; **to express one's** ~ sein Bedauern aussprechen

regret *v* bedauern; **we greatly** (or **much**) ~ wir bedauern sehr; **I** ~ **to inform you** es tut mir leid, Ihnen mitteilen zu müssen

regroup *v* umschichten; umgruppieren, neugruppieren; **to** ~ **investments** Anlagen umschichten

regular regulär, normal; regelmäßig, ständig; ordnungsgemäß, vorschriftsmäßig, satzungsgemäß; *(Zug)* fahrplanmäßig; Berufssoldat; ~ **agent** ständiger Vertreter; ~ **application** *(PatR)* ordnungsgemäße Anmeldung; ~ **army** Berufsheer; ~ **clergy** Ordensgeistlichkeit; ~ **course of business** normaler Geschäftsablauf; ~ **customer** Stammgast, Stammkunde; ~ **employee** festangestellter Bediensteter; ~ **employment** feste Anstellung *(opp. casual employment)*; ~ **hours** Normalarbeitsstunden; ~ **income** festes Einkommen

regular intervals, to meet at ~ in regelmäßigen Zeitabständen zusammenkommen

regular, ~ **meeting (of stockholders)** *Am (ordentliche)* Hauptversammlung; ~ **member** ordentliches Mitglied; ~ →**money;** ~ **officer** Berufsoffizier; ~ **payments** regelmäßige Zahlungen; Geldrente; ~ **place of business** Betriebsstätte; ~ **premium** *(VersR)* laufende Prämie; ~ **price** regulärer Preis; ~ **rate** üblicher Lohnsatz, Normalsatz; ~ **salary** festes Gehalt; ~ **service** fahrplanmäßiger Verkehr; Linienverkehr *(opp. shuttle service)*; ~ **services across the frontier** grenzüberschreitender Linienverkehr; ~ **session** ordentliche Sitzung; ~ **(soldier)** Berufssoldat; ~ **staff** ständiges Personal; ~ **time** normale Arbeitszeit; ~ **turn** geregelte Reihenfolge *(z. B. bei Beladung od. Löschung von Schiffen)*; ~ **way delivery** *Am (Börse)* normale und fristgerechte Lieferung *(von Wertpapieren)*; Lieferung am vierten Werktag *(bei Government bonds am folgenden Werktag)*; ~ **working time** Normalarbeitszeit

regularity Regelmäßigkeit; Ordnungsmäßigkeit; **for** ~**'s sake** der Ordnung halber

regularization Regelung; Regulierung; Bereinigung

regularize *v* regeln; regulieren; bereinigen

regulate *v* (sich) regulieren; regeln, lenken, ordnen; *(für etw.)* Regeln festsetzen, gesetzlich regeln; **power to** ~ *Am (dem Congress durch die Verfassung erteilte)* Ermächtigung, bestimmte Angelegenheiten *(z.B. interstate commerce)* gesetzlich zu regeln; **to** ~ **one's expenses according to one's income** s-e Ausgaben s-m Einkommen anpassen; **to** ~ **traffic** den Verkehr regeln

regulated, ~ **agreement** *Br*[36] Kreditvertrag; ~ **industries** *Am* geregelte Industriezweige; der besonderen Kontrolle der →Interstate Commerce Commission unterstellte Verkehrsunternehmen; ~ **investment company** *Am* gesetzlich geregelte (steuerbegünstigte) Investment-Gesellschaft

regulation 1. Regulierung, Regelung; (allgemeine) Vorschrift, Bestimmung; *(von den Verwaltungsbehörden auf Grund gesetzl. Ermächtigung erlassene Norm:)* (Rechts-)Verordnung; Ausführungsverordnung; Durchführungsverordnung; Verwaltungsvorschrift; *(EG)* Verordnung *(Beschluß des Ministerrats, der unverzüglich Gesetzeskraft in allen Mitgliedsländern erlangt)*; vorschriftsmäßig, richtig; ~**s** Satzung; ~ **of contractual relations** Anpassung von Verträgen (→ *Standing Committee for the R~ of Contractual Relations of the International Chamber of Commerce)*; ~ **of labo(u)r** Arbeitsregelung; ~ **of payments** Regelung des Zahlungsverkehrs; ~ **under Federal Law** *Am* bundesgesetzliche Regelung; **according to** ~**s** vorschriftsmäßig; satzungsgemäß; **air** ~**s** Luftverkehrsvorschriften; **building** ~**s** Bauvorschriften; **contrary to** ~**s** vorschriftswidrig; satzungswidrig; **customs** ~**s** Zollvorschriften; **domestic** ~**s** innerstaatliche Vorschriften; **foreign exchange** ~**s** Devisenbestimmungen; **export** ~**s** Ausfuhrbestimmungen; **factory** ~**s** Betriebsordnung; **harbo(u)r** ~**s** Hafenordnung; **import** ~**s** Einfuhrbestimmungen; **insurance** ~**s** Versicherungsbestimmungen; **issuance of** ~**s** Erlaß von Vorschriften; **internal** ~**s** Geschäftsordnung; **laws and** ~**s** Gesetze und sonstige (Rechts-)Vorschriften; →**police** ~**s; port** ~**s** Hafenordnung; **price** ~**s** Preisvorschriften; **staff** ~**s** Dienstordnung; **stock exchange** ~**s** Börsenordnung; **traffic** ~**s** (Straßen-)Verkehrsvorschriften; **working** ~**s** Betriebsvorschriften, Betriebsordnung; **to comply with** ~**s** Vorschriften befolgen (od. einhalten); **to evade** ~**s** Bestimmungen umgehen; **to lay down** ~**s** Vorschriften erlassen; **to observe a** ~ **strictly** sich streng an e-e Vorschrift halten

Regulation 2., ~s *Am* Finanzmarktregulierungen des →Federal Reserve Board; ~**Q** (Ceilings on Interest on Deposits) Zinshöchstgrenze

regulatory regelnd, regulativ; **R~ Agencies** (or **Commissions**) *(unabhängige, mit Befugnissen rechtsetzender, verwaltender od. richterl. Art ausgestattete)* Aufsichtsbehörden *(z.B. Interstate Commerce Commission)*; ~ **tax** Ausgleichssteuer *(z.B. hohe Steuer auf Öl, um den Verbrauch zu drosseln)*

rehabilitate *v* rehabilitieren; *(in e-n früheren Stand)* wiedereinsetzen; wiedereingliedern; resozialisieren; *(Firma)* sanieren; **to** ~ **prisoners**[37] Strafgefangene in die Gesellschaft wiedereingliedern

rehabilitation Rehabilitierung, Rehabilitation; Wiedereinsetzung *(in e-n früheren Stand)*; Wiedereingliederung; Resozialisierung; Sanierung; ~ **aid** Gefangenenfürsorge (Entlassenenfürsorge); **occupational** ~ **of the disabled** berufliche Wiedereingliederung der Behinderten; ~ **of prisoners** Wiedereingliederung von Strafgefangenen in die Gesellschaft; Resozialisierung von *(früheren)* Strafgefangenen; **programme for economic** ~ wirtschaftliches Sanierungsprogramm; **monetary** ~ Währungssanierung

rehear *v* noch einmal verhandeln; nochmals vernehmen

rehearing erneute Verhandlung; Berufung(sverfahren)

rehire *v* wieder einstellen

rehiring Wiedereinstellung

rehypothecate *v Am (Börse) (Effekten)* weiterverpfänden

reimbursable rückzahlbar; ~ **expenses** erstattungsfähige Auslagen

reimburse *v* zurückzahlen, (rück)erstatten; vergüten; *(mit Geld)* entschädigen; **to** ~ **oneself** sich schadlos halten (bei jdm); (rück)erstattet bekommen; **to** ~ **sb. his expenses** jdm die Kosten vergüten; jdm die Spesen erstatten; **liable to** ~ erstattungspflichtig; rückzahlungspflichtig

reimbursed, to be ~ **one's expenses** s-e Auslagen erstattet bekommen

reimbursing bank Remboursbank

reimbursement Zurückzahlung, (Rück-)Erstattung, Rückzahlung, (Rück-)Vergütung, (Geld-)Entschädigung; Rembours; ~ **claim** Remboursanspruch; ~ **credit** Rembourskredit

reimbursement of expenses (Rück-)-Erstattung der Auslagen (od. Spesen), Kosten(rück)erstattung; Spesenvergütung; **amount of** ~ **properly incurred** Höhe der Erstattung der gerechtfertigten Ausgaben; **to receive reimbursement of one's expenses** s-e Auslagen erstattet bekommen

reimbursement, ~ **of taxes** Rückzahlung von

Steuern; ~ **recourse** Remboursregreß; **bank entitled to claim** ~ remboursberechtigte Bank; **to provide** ~ Rembours leisten

reimport(ation) Reimport, Wiedereinfuhr *(ausgeführter Waren)*

reimport *v* wiedereinführen

reinforcement *mil* Verstärkung

reinstate *v (in ein Amt, in den vorigen Stand etc)* wiedereinsetzen; wiederherstellen; **to ~ an insurance** (or **a policy**) e-e Versicherung wieder in Kraft setzen; **to ~ workers** Arbeiter *(rückwirkend zu den früheren Arbeitsbedingungen)* wiedereinstellen

reinstatement Wiedereinsetzung *(in den vorigen Stand, in ein Amt etc)*; Wiederherstellung; Weiterbeschäftigung *(e-s entlassenen Arbeitnehmers zu den früheren Arbeitsbedingungen)*; *(VersR)* Wiederinkraftsetzung; Weiterversicherung; ~ **into the status quo ante** →restitutio in integrum; ~ **order** *Am* Verfügung, die e-n Arbeitgeber verpflichtet, e-n ungerechtfertigt entlassenen Arbeitnehmer *(rückwirkend zu den früheren Arbeitsbedingungen)* wiedereinzustellen *(s. order for →reemployment)*; ~ **value insurance** Neuwertversicherung

reinsurance Rückversicherung; ~ **commission** Rückversicherungsprovision; ~ **company** Rückversicherungsgesellschaft; ~ **contract** Rückversicherungsvertrag; **excess** ~ Exzedenten-Rückversicherung; **excess of loss** ~ Schadenexzedenten-Rückversicherung; **quota share** ~ Quotenrückversicherung; **surplus** ~ s. excess →~; **to take over in** ~ in Rückversicherung nehmen

reinsure (oneself) *v* (sich) rückversichern
reinsured rückversichert; Rückversicherter

reinsurer Rückversicherer

reintegration Reintegrierung; Wiedereingliederung; **social ~ of drug addicts** soziale Wiedereingliederung von Drogensüchtigen

reinvest *v* wiederanlegen, reinvestieren

reinvestment Wiederanlage *(von Kapital)*, Reinvestition; ~ **discount** Wiederanlagerabatt

reissue Wiederausgabe, Neuausgabe; Neuauflage; Neuemission; ~ **of a patent** erneute Erteilung e-s *(fehlerhaften)* Patents

reissue *v* wieder (od. erneut) ausgeben; neu ausstellen

reject(s) Ausschuß(waren)

reject *v* zurückweisen, ablehnen; nicht annehmen; verwerfen; **to ~ an appeal** ein Rechtsmittel *(Berufung etc)* zurückweisen; e-e Beschwerde verwerfen; **to ~ an application** e-n Antrag ablehnen; *(PatR)* e-e Anmeldung zurückweisen; **to ~ a bill** *parl* e-n Gesetzentwurf ablehnen; **to ~ a candidate** e-n Kandidaten nicht wählen; **to ~ a claim** e-n Anspruch zurückweisen (od. bestreiten) (as unfounded als unbegründet); e-e Reklamation zurückweisen; **to ~ a composition** e-n Vergleich ablehnen; **to ~ the goods which do not conform to the contract** die Abnahme vertragswidriger Ware(n) verweigern; **right to ~ the goods** Zurückweisungsrecht; **to ~ an offer** ein Angebot ablehnen; **to ~ a proposal** e-n Vorschlag ablehnen; **to ~ a request** ein Gesuch abschlägig bescheiden; **the Opposition Division ~s the notice of opposition** *(PatR)* die Einspruchsabteilung verwirft den Einspruch
rejected goods zurückgewiesene Waren

rejection Zurückweisung, Ablehnung; Nichtannahme, Annahmeverweigerung; Verwerfung; ~ **of the appeal as inadmissible** Verwerfung des Rechtsmittels als unzulässig; ~ **of the application** Ablehnung des Antrags; *(PatR)* Zurückweisung der Anmeldung; ~ **of a claim** Bestreiten e-s Anspruchs; Zurückweisung e-r Reklamation; ~ **of a motion** Ablehnung e-s Antrags; ~ **of the notice of opposition as inadmissible** *(PatR)* Verwerfung des Einspruchs als unzulässig; ~ **of proof (in bankruptcy)** Zurückweisung des Nachweises (od. der Anmeldung) e-r Konkursforderung (→*proof 2.*); **notice of** ~ Ablehnungsbescheid; **right of** ~ Zurückweisungsrecht; Abnahmeverweigerungsrecht *(des Käufers)*; **to move the ~ of a bill** die Ablehnung e-s Gesetzentwurfs beantragen

rejoinder Erwiderung; Duplik

relabel *v* neu etikettieren

relapse *(StrafR)* Rückfall; *(Börse)* Rückschlag

relapse *v* zurückfallen, wieder verfallen (into in); *(StrafR)* rückfällig werden; *(Börse)* wieder sinken (od. fallen); **the shares ~d a point** die Aktien fielen wieder um einen Punkt
relapsing *(StrafR)* rückfällig

relate *v* sich beziehen (to auf); berichten, erzählen; miteinander in Verbindung bringen; **to ~ back** zurückwirken
related verbunden (to mit); verwandt (to mit); ~ **by blood** blutsverwandt; ~ **company** angegliederte Gesellschaft, Beteiligungsgesellschaft; ~ **fields** verwandte Gebiete; ~ **in the collateral line** in der Seitenlinie verwandt; ~ **measures** flankierende Maßnahmen; ~ **patent** Bezugspatent; **closely** ~ nahe verwandt; **distantly** ~ entfernt verwandt
relating to in bezug auf, bezüglich

relation 1. Beziehung, Bezug; Verhältnis, Verbindung; ~ **back** Rückbeziehung, Rückwirkung *(e-s Rechts auf e-n früheren Zeitpunkt)*; ~ **between cause and effect** Kausalzusammenhang; **business** ~**s** Geschäftsverbindungen, Geschäftsbeziehungen; **commercial** ~**s** wirtschaftliche Beziehungen, Handelsbeziehungen; **deterioration of** ~**s** (with a country) Verschlechterung der Beziehungen (zu e-m Land); **diplomatic** ~**s** diplomatische Beziehungen (→*diplomatic*); **external** (or **foreign**) ~**s** auswärtige Beziehungen, Auslandsbeziehungen; **Foreign R~s Committee** *Am parl* Außenpolitischer Ausschuß *(des Senats)*; →**human** ~**s; improvement of** ~**s** Verbesserung der Beziehungen; **industrial** ~**s** →industrial 2.; **labo(u)r** ~**s** Beziehungen zwischen den Sozialpartnern (→*labour 2.*); →**public** ~**s; strained** ~**s** gespannte Beziehungen; **to break off** (or **discontinue**) ~**s** Beziehungen abbrechen; **to enter into** ~**s with** in Verbindung treten mit; **to establish** ~**s** Beziehungen herstellen; **to have business** ~**s with** in Geschäftsverbindung stehen mit; **to keep up** (or **maintain**) **friendly** ~**s with the Soviet Union** freundschaftliche Beziehungen zur Sowjetunion unterhalten; **to resume** ~**s** Beziehungen wiederaufnehmen

relation 2. Verwandte(r); ~**s by blood** Blutsverwandte *(cf. consanguinity)*; ~**s by marriage** Verschwägerte *(cf. affinity)*; ~**s in direct line** Verwandte in gerader Linie; ~**s in the second degree** Verwandte zweiten Grades; **close** (or **near**) ~ nahe(r) Verwandte(r)

relatione, ex ~ ("upon relation or information of") (ex rel.) 1. auf Anzeige *(e-r Person, die ein persönl. Interesse an der Angelegenheit hat [cf. relator], die die Grundlage e-r Klage od. Anklage [Br information] durch den Attorney-General bildet [Am eine solche Sache wird gewöhnl. bezeichnet: State ex rel. X v. Y])*; 2. auf Bericht *(über Gerichtsentscheidungen, die von e-m →reporter verfaßt wurden, der persönlich bei der Verhandlung nicht zugegen war und sein Material von e-m Anwalt bezog, der der Verhandlung beiwohnte)*

relationship 1. Beziehung, Verhältnis (to zu); **confidential** ~ Vertrauensverhältnis; **contractual** ~ Vertragsverhältnis; **external** ~ Außenverhältnis; →**fiduciary** ~; **internal** ~ Innenverhältnis; **legal** ~ Rechtsverhältnis

relationship 2. Verwandtschaft; **degree of** ~ Verwandtschaftsgrad; **to be within the prohibited degree of** ~ *(für die Heirat)* e-n verbotenen Verwandtschaftsgrad haben

relative 1. Verwandte(r), Angehörige(r); ~ **by blood** Blutsverwandte(r); ~ **by marriage** Verschwägerte(r); angeheiratete(r) Verwandte(r); **close** ~**s** nahe Verwandte; **collateral** ~ Verwandte(r) in der Seitenlinie; **distant** ~**s** entfernte Verwandte; **nearest** ~**s** nächste Verwandte; **to be a** ~ **on the father's (mother's) side** väterlicherseits (mütterlicherseits) verwandt sein

relative 2. relativ; bezüglich, sich beziehend (to auf); ~ **majority** relative Mehrheit; **supply is** ~ **to demand** das Angebot hängt von der Nachfrage ab

relatively verhältnismäßig

relator Person, auf deren Anzeige der Attorney-General Klage (od. Anklage) erheben läßt *(cf. ex →relatione)*

relax *v* lockern, mildern; sich erholen; entspannen; **to** ~ **a penalty** e-e Strafe mildern; **to** ~ **restrictions** Beschränkungen abbauen; **to** ~ **rules** Bestimmungen lockern; **to** ~ **tension** *pol* entspannen

relaxation Lockerung, Milderung; Erholung; Entspannung; ~ **of restrictive measures** Lokkerung einschränkender Maßnahmen; ~ **of tension** *pol* Entspannung

relay (Fernseh-, Radio-)Übertragung; Ablösung *(von Arbeitern)*; ~ **station** Relaisfunkstelle

release 1. Freilassung *(von Strafgefangenen, Kriegsgefangenen)*; Entlassung *(aus der Haft, Kriegsgefangenschaft etc.)*; ~ **date** Entlassungsdatum; ~ **from custody** Haftentlassung; ~ **from nationality** Entlassung aus dem Staatsangehörigkeitsverhältnis; ~ **from prison** Entlassung aus dem Gefängnis; ~ **on bail** Haftentlassung gegen Sicherheitsleistung; Freilassung gegen Kaution; ~ **on licence** *Br* bedingte Entlassung *(aus der Strafhaft vor Ablauf der Strafzeit)*; ~ **on parole** bedingte Entlassung *(→parole 3.)*; **conditional** ~ *Am*[38] bedingte Entlassung

release 2. Entbindung (from an obligation von e-r Verpflichtung); Erlaß (from a debt e-r Schuld); Entlastung *(bei Beendigung des Treuhandverhältnisses od. der Vormundschaft)*; Verzicht *(auf ein Recht od. e-n Anspruch)*; Verzichtsurkunde; Freigabe, Freigabeerklärung; *Am* (Freigabe zur) Veröffentlichung; Freistellung *(von der Arbeit)*; ~ **from bond** Zollfreigabe; ~ **from liability** Entbindung von der Haftung; ~ **of appropriations** Freigabe von Mitteln; ~ **of a blocked account** Freigabe e-s gesperrten Kontos; ~ **of an expectancy** *Am* Erbverzicht; ~ **of judgment** *Am* →satisfaction of judgment; ~ **of a mortgage** Tilgung e-r Hypothek; ~ **of the pension reserve** Auflösung der Pensionsrückstellung; ~ **of property** Freigabe des Vermögens; ~ **of a ship** Freigabe e-s Schiffes *(Aufhebung des Arrestes)*; ~ **of a tax** Erlaß e-r Steuer; **(temporary)** ~ **of workers** (zeitweilige) Freistellung von Arbeitern; ~ **under seal** förmlicher Erlaß; **first** ~ *(Film)* Uraufführung; **general** ~ Verzicht auf alle gegenwärtigen und künftigen Ansprüche; **press** ~ Pressemitteilung, freigegebene Mitteilung für die Presse; **to give** (or **grant**) ~ Entlastung erteilen

release 3. Übertragung des höheren Rechtes an Grundbesitz *(auch von remainder od. reversion)* an den Untereigentümer od. Nutznießer, der es in Besitz hat

release *v* 1. *(Gefangene)* freilassen, entlassen; *(von e-r Verpflichtung)* entbinden, entlasten; freistellen; *(jdn)* entlassen; *(etw.)* freigeben; der Öffentlichkeit zugänglich machen; *(auf Recht od. Anspruch)* verzichten, aufgeben; als Eigentum übertragen (→*release 3.*); **to ~ on bail** gegen Sicherheitsleistung (od. Kaution) aus der Haft entlassen; **to ~ from custody** aus der Haft entlassen; aus der treuhänderischen Verwahrung freigeben; **to ~ sb. from a debt** jdm e-e Schuld erlassen; **to ~ funds** *(gesperrte)* Gelder freigeben; **to ~ from a guarantee** aus e-r Garantieverpflichtung entlassen; **to ~ information to the press** e-e Nachricht an die Presse zur Veröffentlichung (frei)geben; **to ~ a mortgage** *Am* e-e Hypothek tilgen; **to ~ sb. from his oath** jdn von s-m Eid entbinden; **to ~ reserves** Rücklagen auflösen

released, to be ~ on parole *(StrafR)* bedingt entlassen werden; **to be ~ from prison** aus dem Gefängnis entlassen werden; **~ rate** *Am* Tarif mit beschränkter Haftpflicht des Spediteurs

release *v* 2. wieder vermieten (od. verpachten)

releasee jd, auf den Grundeigentum übertragen ist (→*release 3.*); jd, zu dessen Gunsten Verzicht geleistet ist

releasor jd, der Grundeigentum überträgt (→*release 3.*); jd, der Verzicht leistet

relegate *v* verbannen, relegieren; verweisen (to an)

relend *v* weiter verleihen

relevan|ce, ~cy Relevanz, Erheblichkeit, Wichtigkeit; **~ in law** Rechtserheblichkeit; **of legal ~** rechtserheblich; **plea to the ~** *Scot* →demurrer

relevant relevant, erheblich, wichtig (to für); ~→ **documents; ~ facts** rechtserhebliche Tatsachen; **~ information** wichtige Auskunft; **~ in law** rechtserheblich; **~ judicial decision** einschlägige Gerichtsentscheidung; **~ prior art** *(PatR)* einschlägiger Stand der Technik; **~ questions** sachdienliche Fragen; **~ statements made by the parties** rechtserhebliche Erklärungen der Parteien

reliability Zuverlässigkeit; Vertrauenswürdigkeit; Kreditwürdigkeit; **~ of the law** Rechtssicherheit; **~ of operation** Betriebssicherheit

reliable zuverlässig; vertrauenswürdig; kreditwürdig; **~ firm** reelle Firma; **from a ~ source** aus gut unterrichteter (od. zuverlässiger) Quelle; **~ witness** glaubwürdiger Zeuge

reliance Zutrauen, Vertrauen *(z. B. des Käufers)*; **detrimental ~** *Am* schadenbegründendes (vertrauendes) Verhalten *(e-r Vertragspartei)* (Vertrauensschaden); **to place ~ (up)on** Vertrauen setzen auf

reliction Anschwemmung *(Vergrößerung der Grundstücksfläche durch Zurückweichen e-s Gewässers od. durch Sinken des Wasserspiegels)*

relief 1. *(der durch die Klage verlangte)* Rechtsschutz; Rechtsbehelf; **~ against →forfeiture; ~ by way of interpleader** →interpleader ~; **~ sought** Klagebegehren; **equitable ~** Gewährung des Rechtsschutzes in equity (→*equitable*); **interlocutory ~** vorläufiger Rechtsschutz; **to grant the ~ sought in the petition** dem Klageantrag entsprechen

relief 2. Hilfe, Unterstützung; *Am* Sozialhilfe; Erleichterung, Abhilfe, Steuererleichterung; **~ agency** Hilfsorganisation, Hilfswerk; **~ committee** Hilfskomitee; **~ consignment** Hilfssendung; **~ for tax purposes** *(DBA)* Steuererleichterung; **~ from (customs) duty** *Br*[38a] Ermäßigung der Zollgebühren; Zollbefreiung; **~ fund** Unterstützungsfonds, Hilfsfonds *(z. B. für Opfer e-s Erdbebens)*; **~ measures** Hilfsmaßnahmen; **~ programme** Hilfsprogramm; **~ train** außerplanmäßiger Zug *(zur Entlastung des Verkehrs)*; **financial ~** *Br*[39] *(vom Gericht für Ehepartner od. Kinder festgesetzter)* Unterhalt, Vermögensübertragung od. Vermögensausgleich (→*property adjustment order) (bei Ehescheidung od. anderen Eheverfahren)*; **public ~** *Am* Sozialhilfe; **recipient of public ~** *Am* Empfänger von Sozialhilfe; **work ~** *Am* Beschaffung von Arbeitsplätzen *(zur Behebung der Arbeitslosigkeit)*; **to be on ~** *Am* Sozialhilfe beziehen; **to provide ~** *(DBA)* Steuererleichterung gewähren; **to provide ~ for refugees** für Unterstützung der Flüchtlinge sorgen

relief 3. *Br*[40] *(Einkommensteuer)* Steuerabzug, Freibetrag (→*allowance*); **double taxation** (or **tax**) **~** Anrechnung der ausländischen Steuern auf die britischen Steuern *(auf Grund von Doppelbesteuerungsabkommen)*; **life insurance ~** (Steuer-)Abzug für Lebensversicherungsbeiträge; **personal ~**→ personal allowance

relief 4. Ablösung *(auch mil)*; Aushilfe, Vertretung; **~ telephonist** Aushilfstelefonist

relieve *v* unterstützen, helfen; erleichtern, entlasten; *(jdn)* ablösen; **to ~ the common distress** die allgemeine Not lindern; **to ~ an emergency** e-e Notlage beheben; **to ~ hardship** Härten mildern; **to ~ of a liability** *(jdn)* von e-r Verpflichtung (od. Haftung) befreien; **to ~ a p. of a post** jdn s-s Amtes entheben; **to ~ the poor** die Armen unterstützen

religion Religion; **established ~** *Br* Staatsreligion; **freedom of** ~ Religionsfreiheit; **free exercise** (or **practice**) **of** ~[41] freie Religionsausübung; **minister of** ~ Geistlicher

religious religiös; ~ **belief** Glaube, Konfession; ~ **education** Religionsunterricht; ~ **freedom** (or **liberty**) Religionsfreiheit; ~ **privilege** *Am* Aussageverweigerungsrecht des Geistlichen; ~ **service** (or **worship**) Gottesdienst

relinquish *v* aufgeben; verzichten auf; **to** ~ **an action** e-e Klage zurücknehmen; **to** ~ **one's appointment** s-e Stelle aufgeben; **to** ~ **an inheritance** *Am* auf e-e Erbschaft verzichten; **to** ~ **a project** e-n Plan aufgeben; **to** ~ **a suit** e-e Klage zurücknehmen

relinquishment Aufgabe; Verzicht (of auf); *(VölkerR)* Rückgängigmachung *(e-r Annexion)*; ~ **of ownership** Eigentumsaufgabe; ~ **of a right** Aufgabe e-s Rechts, Verzicht auf ein Recht

reload *v* wieder verladen; umladen

reloading Wiederverladung, Wiederanbordbringen; Umladung

relocate *v* verlegen; verlagern; umsiedeln; *(e-n Angestellten)* versetzen; **to** ~ **a business** ein Geschäft verlegen

relocation Verlegung; Verlagern, Verlagerung; Umzug; (Zwangs-)Umsiedlung; *Scot* Wiedervermietung, Wiederverpachtung; Versetzung *(e-s Angestellten)*; ~ **assistance** Umzugsbeihilfe *(bei Versetzung)*; ~ **expenses** Umzugskosten; ~ **of industry** Verlagerung der Industrie; ~ **of a plant** Betriebsverlagerung

rely *v* sich verlassen, sich stützen, vertrauen (upon auf); sich berufen (on auf), geltend machen; **to** ~ **upon an award** e-n Schiedsspruch geltend machen; **to** ~ **upon a case** (or **decision**) (as →precedent) sich auf e-e frühere Entscheidung *(zur Geltendmachung e-s Rechtsstandpunktes)* berufen

relying upon im Vertrauen auf

rem, action in ~ dingliche Klage *(opp. action in personam)*; **right in** ~ dingliches Recht

remain *v* bleiben; übrig bleiben; **to** ~ **in effect** (or **force**) in Kraft bleiben, wirksam bleiben; **to** ~ **in existence** fortbestehen; **to** ~ **firm** fest bleiben, sich halten *(Preise, Kurse)*

remaining verbleibend; übriggeblieben, restlich; Rest-; ~ **amount** Restbetrag; ~ **assets** verbleibende Vermögenswerte; *(KonkursR)* Restmasse; ~ **useful life** Restnutzungsdauer; ~ **stock** Restbestand

remainder 1. Rest(betrag); Restbestand; ~ **of a debt** Restschuld; ~ **of stock** Restbestand

remainder[42] 2. *(SachenR)* Anwartschaft(srecht) *(auf Grundbesitz)*; **contingent** ~ bedingte(s) Anwartschaft(srecht) *(die Anwartschaft ist von e-m Ereignis abhängig, dessen Eintritt nicht bestimmt ist)*; Erbanwartschaft *(auf Grundbesitz)*; **vested** ~ unentziehbare(s) Anwartschaft(srecht) *(die Anwartschaft ist von e-m Ereignis abhängig, dessen Eintritt bestimmt ist)*

Ein remainder liegt vor, wenn durch Vertrag od. Testament die Anwartschaft auf das Recht an Grundbesitz für e-e Person nach dem Wegfall der zunächst berechtigten Person geschaffen wird. Im Gegensatz zur →reversion fällt der remainder nicht an den Veräußerer zurück, sondern geht an eine dritte Person.

Das komplizierte Institut des remainder ist im deutschen Recht zum größten Teil durch Eintragung ins Grundbuch (Vormerkung) ersetzt

remainderman die zum →remainder berechtigte Person; Anwartschaftsberechtigter; Nacherbe; *(beim trust)* „Schlußmann" *(an den das nach Trusterfüllung verbleibende Vermögen fällt)*

remand *(StrafR) Br* Überweisung (od. Zurücksendung) in die Untersuchungshaft oder Entlassung aus Untersuchungshaft gegen Kaution; *Am* Zurücksendung in die Haft; *Am* Zurückverweisung *(e-r Sache an die untere Instanz)*; ~ **centre** *Br* Jugendhaftanstalt *(für Jugendliche im Alter von 14 bis 21 Jahren)*; ~ **in(to) custody** Überweisung (od. Zurücksendung) in die Untersuchungshaft; ~ **home** *Br*[43] *(kommunale)* Jugendarrestanstalt; ~ **on bail** *Br* Freilassung gegen Kaution bis zur neuen Verhandlung *(nach Vertagung)*; **further** ~ **in custody** *Br* Haftfortdauer; **person held** (or **prisoner**) **on** ~ *Br* Untersuchungsgefangener; **period of** ~ (Zeit der) Untersuchungshaft; **review of a** ~ **in custody** *Br* Haftprüfung; **to appear on** ~ *Br* zur neuen Verhandlung *(nach Vertagung)* erscheinen; aus der Untersuchungshaft vorgeführt werden; **to be on** ~ *Br* in Untersuchungshaft sein

remand *v (StrafR)*, **to** ~ **a p.** *Br* →to ~ a p. on bail or to ~ a p. in custody; *Am* →to ~ a p. into custody; **to** ~ **a p. on bail** *Br* jdn gegen Kaution aus der Untersuchungshaft entlassen *(bis zum Termin der Hauptverhandlung)*; **to** ~ **a cause** *Am* e-e Sache zurückverweisen; **to** ~ **a p. in custody** *Br* jdn *(bei Vertagung e-r Verhandlung vor e-m magistrate od. justice of the peace bis zur neuen Verhandlung)* in die Untersuchungshaft (zurück)senden; **to** ~ **a p. into custody** *Am* jdn in die Haft zurücksenden *(bes. im habeas corpus-Verfahren)*; **the magistrate** ~**s the accused for a medical report** *Br* der Polizeirichter ordnet die ärztliche Untersuchung des Angeklagten an

remanded, person ~ **in custody** *Br* Untersuchungsgefangener; **to be** ~ **in custody** *Br* in die Untersuchungshaft zurückgesandt werden; in Haft bleiben; **to be** ~ **to a mental hospital** *Am* in e-e psychiatrische Klinik eingewiesen werden

remanet auf spätere Sitzung vertagter Prozeß; *Br* noch nicht erledigter Gesetzesentwurf

remanufacture Umarbeitung

remargin *v Am* nachschießen *(→margin 2.)*

remark Bemerkung; **opening ~s** Einführungsworte

remarriage Wiederverheiratung

remarry *v* (sich) wiederverheiraten, e-e neue Ehe eingehen

remeasure *v (Schiff)* wieder vermessen, neu vermessen

remedial Abhilfe gewährend, abhelfend; auf das Verfahren bezüglich, formell; ~ **measure** Abhilfemaßnahme; ~ **→statute**

remed|y 1. *(rechtliche od. prozessuale)* Abhilfe; Rechtsschutz; *(gerichtl. und außergerichtl.)* Rechtsbehelf; Rechtsmittel *(im weitesten Sinne)*; **civil ~ies** Rechtsmittel; ~ **of →defects; domestic ~ies** *(VölkerR)* innerstaatliche Rechtsbehelfe; **equitable ~ies** Mittel des Rechtsschutzes nach equity-Recht *(bes. specific performance of contracts, injunctions; opp. legal ~)*; **extrajudicial ~ies**[44] außergerichtliche Rechtsbehelfe; **judicial ~ies** gerichtliche Rechtsbehelfe *(action or suit)*; **legal ~** Rechtsschutz, Rechtsbehelf *(nach dem Common Law; opp. equitable ~)*

remed|y, local ~ *(VölkerR)* innerstaatliches Rechtsmittel; **local ~ies rule** Regel über die Notwendigkeit der Erschöpfung der innerstaatlichen Rechtsmittel; **exhaustion of local ~ies** Erschöpfung der innerstaatlichen Rechtsmittel

remedy, provisional ~ vorläufige Sicherungsentscheidung, einstweilige Verfügung *(die den Kläger davor bewahrt, daß die angestrebte endgültige Entscheidung infolge von unlauteren Machenschaften des Beklagten [z. B. Vermögensverfügungen] undurchsetzbar und damit wertlos wird; z. B. Ernennung e-s →receiver)*

remed|y, to find ~ies Abhilfe finden; **to resort to a ~** e-n Rechtsbehelf in Anspruch nehmen; **the ~ies have been exhausted** die Rechtsmittel sind erschöpft

remedy (of the mint) 2. Remedium, Toleranz *(gesetzl. zulässige Abweichung bei Ausprägung von Münzen)*; ~ **of** (or **for**) **fineness** zulässige Abweichung vom Feingehalt; ~ **of** (or **for**) **weight** zulässige Abweichung vom Gewicht

remedy *v* abhelfen, Abhilfe schaffen; abstellen, beheben, wiedergutmachen; **to ~ a complaint** e-r Beschwerde abhelfen; **to ~ a defect** e-n Mangel beheben (od. beseitigen); **to ~ the ineffectiveness** die Unwirksamkeit heilen; **to ~ a mischief** e-n Mißstand beseitigen; **to ~ an omission** etw. nachholen

remember *v* sich erinnern; **to ~ a p. in one's will** jdn in s-m Testament bedenken; ~ **me** (to) empfehlen Sie mich; **I wish to be ~ed** ich bitte um freundliche Empfehlungen

Remembrance Day *Br* Gedächtnistag *(für die Gefallenen der beiden Weltkriege; 11. November oder, wenn der Tag nicht auf e-n Sonntag fällt, der nächste Sonntag)*

Remembrancer, Queen's ~ *Br*[45] Master des Supreme Court mit verschiedenen Pflichten *(z. B. bestimmte, mit der Auswahl der sheriffs verbundene Funktionen, Vereidigung des Lord Mayor of London)*

remind *v* erinnern (of an), (an)mahnen; **to ~ a consignment** (or **shipment**) e-e Sendung anmahnen

reminder Mahnung, Anmahnung; Erinnerung(sschreiben); Mahnbrief; ~ **value** Erinnerungswert

remise *v (Recht, Anspruch etc)* aufgeben, überlassen

remission Zurückverweisung *(e-r Rechtssache von e-m höheren an ein unteres Gericht)*; Erlaß *(e-r Schuld, Strafe, Steuer etc)*; ~ **of arrears (of maintenance)** Erlaß der Unterhaltsrückstände; ~ **of charges** Gebührenerlaß; ~ **of customs duty** Erlaß der Zollgebühr; ~ **of a debt** Erlaß e-r Schuld, Schulderlaß; ~ **of a fee** Gebührenerlaß

remission of a sentence Erlaß e-r Strafe, Straferlaß; **automatic ~** *Br* automatischer Straferlaß

In England wird ein Verurteilter nach Verbüßung von zwei Drittel der Strafe aus dem Gefängnis entlassen, sofern er nicht durch schlechte Führung im Gefängnis die Verkürzung der Freiheitsstrafe verwirkt hat

remit *v* 1. *(Rechtssache an untere Instanz)* zurückverweisen; **to ~ a case for reconsideration** (or **for a full rehearing**) e-e Sache an den gleichen Richter zur erneuten Verhandlung und Entscheidung zurückverweisen

remitted case an das untere Gericht verwiesene Sache *(Br der High Court kann z. B. gewisse Sachen an den County Court verweisen)*

remit *v* 2. *(Schuld, Strafe etc)* erlassen; **to ~ arrears (of maintenance)** Rückstände (von Unterhaltszahlungen) erlassen; **to ~ fees** Gebühren erlassen; **to ~ a fine** e-e Geldstrafe erlassen; **to ~ a prison sentence for good conduct** e-e Freiheitsstrafe wegen guter Führung erlassen

remit *v* 3. überweisen, übersenden; Überweisung vornehmen; **to ~ a bill for collection** e-n Wechsel zum Inkasso übersenden; **to ~ by cheque (check)** durch (übersandten) Scheck bezahlen; **to instruct a bank to ~ money** e-e Bank anweisen, Geld zu überweisen

remitting bank überweisende Bank; Einreicherbank *(beim Inkasso)*

remittal *Am* Erlaß *(e-r Schuld, Strafe)*; Zurückverweisung *(e-r Rechtssache an die untere Instanz)*

remittance Überweisung; (Geld-)Sendung, überwiesene Summe, (übersandter) Wechsel, Scheck; Rimesse; ~ **advice** Überweisungsanzeige; ~ **basis** *Br (Einkommensteuer)* Besteuerung *(gewisser ausländischer Einkünfte)* nur der nach England überwiesenen Beträge; ~**s by foreign workers** Überweisungen der Gastarbeiter; ~ **to a bill (of exchange)** Wechselsendung; ~ **in cash** Barsendung; Baranschaffung; ~ **of funds** (or **money**) Geldsendung; **documentary** ~ dokumentäre Rimesse; **order for** ~ Überweisungsauftrag; **return** ~ Rücküberweisung; **to make a** ~ e-e Überweisung vornehmen

remittee Empfänger *(e-r Sendung von Geld, Wechseln, Schecks)*; Überweisungsempfänger

remitter Übersender *(e-r Überweisung)*, Geldsender

remittor *Am* →remitter

remnant Rest; Überrest; ~ **sale** Ausverkauf *(von Restbeständen)*

remodelling Umbau

remonetization Wiederinkurssetzung *(von Metallgeld; opp. demonetization)*

remonstrance Vorhaltung; Gegenvorstellung; Protest

remote entfernt; entlegen; ~ **cause** entfernte, für die Zurechnung des Schadens unbeachtliche Ursache *(cf. proximate cause)*; ~ **damage** entfernter *(daher nicht zurechenbarer)* Schaden; ~ **handling** Fernbedienung; ~ **parties** *(WechselR)*[46] mittelbare Beteiligte *(Wechselverpflichtete, die nicht in unmittelbaren Beziehungen zueinander stehen; opp. immediate parties)*

remoteness Entlegenheit, Ferne; ~ **of damage** Nichtzurechenbarkeit e-s Schadens

remoter issue entferntere Abkömmlinge *(grandchildren, great grandchildren etc)*

removable absetzbar; transportabel

removal 1. Fortschaffen, Beiseiteschaffen, Entfernen; Behebung, Beseitigung, Abstellung; *(VölkerR)* Herausnahme *(von Gebieten aus Vertragsbestimmungen)*; ~ **from the register** Löschung in der (Waren-)Zeichenrolle; ~ **from the stock exchange list** Absetzung *(e-s Wertpapiers)* von der amtlichen Notierung; ~ **jurisdiction** *Am* Zuständigkeit e-s Bundesgerichts kraft Verweisung *(in bestimmten Fällen der konkurrierenden Zuständigkeit kann Beklagter Verweisung e-r bei dem Gericht e-s Einzelstaates anhängigen Sache an den District Court beantragen)*; ~ **of causes**[47] Verweisung von Rechtssachen an ein anderes Gericht; *Am*[48] *bes.* Verweisung von Rechtssachen von e-m einzelstaatl. an ein Bundesgericht *(cf. diversity of citizenship)*; ~ **of difficulties** Behebung (od. Beseitigung) von Schwierigkeiten; **certificate of** ~ **of disabilities** →disability; ~ **of goods** Beiseiteschaffen von Waren *(z. B. vor Bezahlung des Zolls)*; ~ **of goods to prevent distress** Beiseiteschaffen von Sachen *(durch den Mieter)* zur Verhinderung der Beschlagnahme *(→distress 1.)* bei Mietrückständen; ~ **of refuse** *Am* Müllabfuhr; ~ **of restrictions** Aufhebung (od. Beseitigung) von Beschränkungen

removal 2. *Br* Umzug (from ... to von ... nach); *Br* Auszug (from a house aus e-m Haus); *(Wohnsitz etc)* Verlegung; ~ **contractor** *Br* Möbelspediteur; ~ **expenses** Umzugskosten; ~ **goods** *Br* Umzugsgut; ~ **of business** Geschäftsverlegung; ~ **of landmark** Grenzverrückung; **allowance for** ~ *Br* Umzugskostenbeihilfe; **notice of** ~ Umzugsanzeige

removal 3. Entlassung, Absetzung, Abberufung; (Straf-)Versetzung; ~ **from office** Entfernung aus dem Amt, Amtsenthebung, Dienstentlassung; ~ **of a director** Abberufung e-s Direktors; ~ **of a trustee** Abberufung e-s Treuhänders; ~ **without notice** fristlose Entlassung

remove Grad, Schritt, Stufe; Verwandtschaftsgrad *(bei cousins →removed)*

remove *v* 1. *(Vermögensgegenstände)* beiseiteschaffen, fortschaffen; entfernen, beseitigen; *(jdn)* beseitigen, töten; *(Rechtssache an ein anderes Gericht [Am bes. an ein Bundesgericht])* verweisen; *(Schwierigkeiten, Zweifel etc)* beheben; **to** ~ **from the agenda** von der Tagesordnung absetzen; **to** ~ **a blockade** e-e Blockade aufheben; **to** ~ **controls** Kontrollen aufheben; **to** ~ **goods** Sachen beiseiteschaffen *(z. B. um →distress bei Mietrückständen zu verhindern)*; **to** ~ **the seals** die Siegel (od. Plomben) entfernen; **to** ~ **the trade mark from the register** die Handelsmarke in der (Waren-)Zeichenrolle löschen; **to** ~ **traces** Spuren verwischen

removing, action for ~ *Scot* Klage auf zwangsweise Entfernung des Mieters/Pächters *(z. B. nach Ablauf der Miete/Pacht)*

remove *v* 2. umziehen (to nach), ausziehen; *(Wohnsitz etc)* verlegen; **to** ~ **a business** ein Geschäft verlegen; **to** ~ **furniture** *Br* Umzüge besorgen; **to** ~ **from a house** aus e-m Haus ausziehen

remove *v* 3. entlassen, absetzen, abberufen; (straf)versetzen; **to** ~ **a p. from office** jdn aus dem Dienst entlassen, jdn aus dem Amt entfernen, jdn s-s Amtes entheben; **to** ~ **a p.**

from his post jdn s-s Postens entheben; **to ~ a trustee** e-n Treuhänder abberufen

removed *(Verwandtschaftsgrad bei Vettern)* um eine, zwei etc Generationen auf- od. absteigend in der Verwandtschaft getrennt; **my first cousin once ~** das Kind meines Vetters od. der Vetter meiner Eltern *(e-s Elternteils)*; **my first cousin twice ~** der Enkel meines Vetters oder der Vetter meiner Großeltern *(e-s Großelternteils)*

remover Verweisung e-r Rechtssache an ein anderes Gericht (→*removal of causes*); *Br* Möbelspediteur

remunerate *v* vergüten, entlohnen, entgelten, bezahlen; **to ~ a p. for his services** jdn für s-e Dienste entlohnen; **ill ~d** schlecht bezahlt

remuneration Vergütung, Entlohnung, (Arbeits-)Entgelt; Bezahlung; Lohn, Gehalt, (Dienst-)Bezüge; Honorar; **~ for Members of Parliament** *parl* Diäten; **~ for salvage** Bergelohn; **~ for work** Arbeitsentgelt; **~ in cash and in kind** Geld- und Sachbezüge; **~ of staff** Besoldung des Personals; **fixed ~** Fixum; **for ~** gegen Entgelt; **non-cash ~** *Am* bargeldlose Gehaltszahlungen; **without ~** unentgeltlich; **to determine** (or **fix**) **the ~** die Vergütung festsetzen; **to receive an adequate ~ for one's work** e-e angemessene Vergütung für s-e Arbeit erhalten

remunerative ergiebig, einträglich, gewinnbringend; lohnend; **~ business** einträgliches Geschäft; **~ employment** Erwerbstätigkeit; **~ investment** gewinnbringende Kapitalanlage; **~ undertaking** rentables Unternehmen

rename *v* umbenennen; neu benennen

renationalization *Br* Wiederverstaatlichung

render *v* machen; zurückgeben; wiedergeben, *(in e-r fremden Sprache)* ausdrücken; **to ~ an account (of)** e-e Abrechnung vorlegen; Rechenschaft ablegen (über); **to ~ assistance** Hilfe (od. Beistand) leisten; **to ~ an award** e-n Schiedsspruch fällen; **to ~ a decision** e-e Entscheidung fällen; **to ~ information** Auskunft geben (od. erteilen); **to ~ judgment** *Am* ein Urteil fällen (od. verkünden); **to ~ a p. liable** jdn haftbar machen; **to ~ military service** Militärdienst leisten; **to ~ an opinion** e-e Meinung abgeben; ein Gutachten erstatten; **to ~ a profit** e-n Gewinn abwerfen; **to ~ a report** e-n Bericht erstatten; **to ~ services** Dienste leisten; **to ~ thanks** Dank sagen (od. abstatten); **to ~ void** nichtig machen

rendered, per account ~ laut *(früher ausgestellter)* Rechnung

rendering, ~ (of) accounts Rechnungslegung; **~ of services** (Erbringung von) Dienstleistungen; **~ of thanks** Danksagung

rendition *Br* Auslieferung *(e-r verdächtigen Person od. e-s Strafgefangenen zwischen Commonwealth-Staaten)*; **~ of judgment** *Am* Urteilsfällung, Urteilsverkündung; **~ of services** *Am* Dienstleistung

renegotiate *v* neu aushandeln, erneut verhandeln

renegotiation, ~ of an agreement Neuaushandlung e-s Abkommens; **~ of debt** Umschuldung

renew *v* erneuern; *(Vertrag)* verlängern; *(Wechsel)* prolongieren; **to ~ a contract implicitly** (or **tacitly**) e-n Vertrag stillschweigend verlängern; **to ~ a credit** e-n Kredit (od. ein Akkreditiv) verlängern; **to ~ a lease** e-n Miet- (od. Pacht)vertrag erneuern (od. verlängern); **to ~ an order** e-n Auftrag erneuern, nachbestellen; **to ~ a stock of goods** ein Warenlager wieder auffüllen

renewed erneuert, verlängert (to bis) *(z.B. Paß)*; **~ bill** →renewal bill

renewable erneuerbar, verlängerbar; prolongationsfähig; **~ term (life) insurance** Lebensversicherung mit steigender Prämie *(nach dem Lebensalter)*; **the agreement is ~** der Vertrag ist verlängerbar

renewal Erneuerung; (Vertrags-)Verlängerung; *(WechselR)* Prolongation; **~s** *Br (Bilanz)* Neuanschaffungen; **~ bill** Prolongationswechsel; **~ certificate** Erneuerungsschein, Talon; **~ clause** Verlängerungsklausel *(Vereinbarung, daß mangels Kündigung das Rechtsverhältnis auf unbestimmte Zeit forgesetzt wird)*; **~ date** *(VersR)* Erneuerungsdatum; **~ fee(s)** *(PatentR)* Jahresgebühr; **~ notice** *(VersR)* Aufforderung zur Prämienzahlung, Prämienrechnung; **~ of contract** Vertragserneuerung, Vertragsverlängerung; **~ of lease** Mietverlängerung, Pachtverlängerung; **~ of a passport** Verlängerung e-s Passes; **~ of a patent** Aufrechterhaltung e-s Patents; **~ of the term of office** Verlängerung der Amtsdauer; **~ premium** *(VersR)* Folgeprämie *(opp. first premium)*; **~ rate** Prolongationssatz

renounce *v* aufgeben, verzichten auf, ausschlagen *(bes. das Amt des Erbschaftsverwalters)*; **to ~ one's citizenship** *Br* (**nationality** *Am*) s-e Staatsangehörigkeit aufgeben; **to ~ a claim** auf e-n Anspruch verzichten, e-n Anspruch aufgeben; **to ~ one's interest in an estate** e-e Erbschaft ausschlagen; **the executor ~s probate** der Erbschaftsverwalter (→*executor*) lehnt das (executor-)Amt ab; **to ~ one's right** auf sein Recht verzichten *(bes. als Erbe od. Treuhänder)*; **to ~ one's right under a will** *Am* e-e testamentarische Verfügung ausschlagen

renovate *v* erneuern, renovieren

renowned angesehen, namhaft; renommiert; **world ~ firm** weltbekannte Firma

rent Miete, Mietzins; Pacht, Pachtzins; *Am (Bilanz)* Mieten und Pachten; **~s** Mieteinkünfte; Pachteinkünfte; **R~ Acts**[49] Mietgesetze; **~ in advance** Miet- (od. Pacht)vorauszahlung; **~ allowance** Mietzuschuß, Mietbeihilfe; **~ charge** *Am* Miete, Mietgebühr

rent-charge[50] *(reallastähnliche)* Belastung e-s Grundstücks mit wiederkehrenden Leistungen *(Gläubiger hat kein Rückfallsrecht [→reversion], aber bei Rückständen ein Recht zur Beschlagnahme [→distress]. Beispiel: Kauf auf Rentenbasis)*

rent, ~ collection Einziehung der Miete (od. Pacht); **~ control** Überwachung der Mietpreise; Mietüberwachung; **~-controlled flats** preisgebundene Wohnungen; **~ day** Mietzahlungstag *(cf. quarter day)*; **~ due** fällige Miete (od. Pacht); **~-free** mietfrei; pachtfrei; **~ increase** Mieterhöhung; Pachterhöhung; **~ insurance** Mietausfallversicherung; **R~ Officer** *Br* s. Local →R~ Officer; **~ paid in advance** (or **prepaid**) vorausbezahlte Miete (od. Pacht); **~s payable** Mietausgaben; **~ rebate** *Br* Mietermäßigung *(bei geringem Einkommen des Wohnungsmieters)*; **~ receipts** Mieteinnahmen; Pachteinnahmen; **~s receivable** Mieteinnahmen; **~ restriction** *Br* gesetzliche Überwachung der Mieten von Privatwohnungen; **~-roll** Register des vermieteten (od. verpachteten) Grundbesitzes und der Miet- (od. Pacht-) einnahmen; **~-service** wiederkehrende (Gegen-)Leistung aus e-m Grundstück *(des →tenant an den →landlord; dieser hat ein Rückfallrecht [→reversion] und bei Rückständen nach common law ein Recht auf Beschlagnahme [→distress])*; **~ subsidy** Mietzuschuß

rent, arrears of ~ Mietrückstände; Pachtrückstände; **back ~** rückständige Miete (od. Pacht); **claim for ~** Miet(zins)forderung; Pacht(zins-)forderung; **→dead ~; economic ~** *Br* wirtschaftliche Miete *(die z. B. die Ortsbehörde über die tatsächlichen Unkosten hinaus berechnet)*; **fair ~** angemessene Miete *(Br die von e-m Local →Rent Officer auf Antrag des Mieters od. Vermieters festgesetzt und registriert wird)*; **farm ~** Pacht(zins); **for ~** *Am (Haus, Zimmer)* zu vermieten; **ground ~** *Br* →ground 1.; **high ~** hohe Miete (od. Pacht); **imputed ~** Mietwert der vom Eigentümer genutzten Wohnung; **increase in ~** →~ increase; **Local R~ Officer** *Br* Beamter, der die s. fair →rent festsetzt *(gegen seine Entscheidung ist e-e Beschwerde beim Rent Assessment Committee möglich)*; **loss of ~** Mietausfall; Pachtausfall; **low ~** niedrige Miete (od. Pacht); **maximum ~ recoverable** erlangbare Höchstmiete *(Br under a regulated →tenancy)*; **a month's** (or **monthly**) **~** Monatsmiete; **office ~** Büromiete; **a quarter's ~** Vierteljahresmiete (*→quarter day*); **raising of ~** Miet- (od. Pacht-)erhöhung; **reduction of ~** Miet- (od. Pacht-)herabsetzung; **uncontrolled ~s** *Br* freie Mieten

rent, to be in arrears (or **behind[hand]**) **with one's ~** im Rückstand mit s-r Miete sein; mit der Mietzahlung im Verzug sein; **to collect a ~** e-e Miete einziehen; **to command a high ~** e-e hohe Miete erzielen; **to distress for ~** *(Sachen des Mieters)* wegen rückständiger Miete in Besitz nehmen; **he failed to pay the ~** (when it fell due) er geriet mit der Mietzahlung in Verzug; **certain ~s fall due on quarter days** *Br* bestimmte Mieten werden am Quartalstag fällig; **to fix a ~** e-e Miete (od. e-n Mietzins) festsetzen; **to increase the ~** s. to raise the →~; **to pay one's ~** s-e Miete bezahlen; **to raise the ~** die Miete erhöhen; **to recover a ~** e-e Miete erhalten (od. eintreiben); **to yield a ~** e-e Miete abwerfen; **~s have gone up** die Mieten sind gestiegen; **~s have leapt up** die Mieten sind sprunghaft gestiegen

rent *v* mieten, pachten *Am (auch)* vermieten, verpachten; **to ~ out** *Am* vermieten; **to ~ an apartment** *bes. Am* e-e Wohnung (ver)mieten; **to ~ a farm** e-n Hof pachten; **to ~ a flat** *Br* e-e Wohnung mieten; **to ~ a safe** ein Safe (od. Bankfach) mieten; **the apartment ~s for ‰ 500 a year** *Am* die Wohnung wird für 500 Dollar im Jahr vermietet; **rooms to ~** *Am* Zimmer zu vermieten; **he ~s his tenants low** *Br* er berechnet s-n Mietern (od. Pächtern) e-e niedrige Miete (od. Pacht)

rented gemietet, gepachtet; *Am (auch)* vermietet, verpachtet; **~ car** Leihwagen; **~ flat** *Br* Mietwohnung; **~ land** Pachtland

renting Mieten, Pachten; *Am (auch)* Vermieten, Verpachten

rentable zu mieten, zu pachten; *Am (auch)* vermietbar, verpachtbar

rental Betrag der *(gezahlten od. eingenommenen)* Miete (od. Pacht); Miete, Mietbetrag; Pacht, Pachtbetrag; *Am* Mietgegenstand *(z. B. Mietwohnung, Mietauto)*; **~ agreement** Mietvertrag *(für bewegl. Sachen, z. B. television sets od. beim → leasing)*; **~ assistance** Mietzuschuß; **~ charge** Mietgebühr *(für bewegl. Sachen)*; **~ contract** →~agreement; **~ income** Mieteinnahmen, Pachteinnahmen; **~ payments** Mietzahlungen; Leasingraten; **~ period** Mietzeit; **~ right** Recht zur Vermietung; **leasing ~** Leasingzins (*→leasing 2.*)

renter Mieter *(z. B. e-s Autos)*; Pächter, Filmleiher; **~ of a safe** Mieter e-s Safes

rentes *Fr* Rentenpapiere, Staatspapiere (French Government stocks)

rentier jd, der feste Einkünfte aus Kapitalvermögen (Grundbesitz oder Wertpapiere) hat (*→unearned income*)

renunciation Verzicht(leistung) (of auf); Verzichterklärung *(bes. Urkunde, durch die der Erbschaftsverwalter auf Erteilung der →probate od. der letters of administration [→administration 2.] verzichtet)*; ~ **of administration** Ablehnung des Amtes als Erbschaftsverwalter (→*administrator*); ~ **of agency** Widerruf des Vertretungs- od. Auftragsverhältnisses *(seitens des agent; cf. revocation)*; ~ **of citizenship** Verzichterklärung der Staatsangehörigkeit; ~ **of force** *pol* Gewaltverzicht; ~ **of guarantee** Garantieverzicht; ~ **of membership** Aufgabe der Mitgliedschaft; ~ **of nationality** *Am* Erklärung des Verzichts auf die Staatsangehörigkeit; ~ **of probate** Ablehnung des Amtes als Erbschaftsverwalter (→*executor*); ~ **of a right** Verzicht auf ein Recht; ~ **of a succession** *Am* Ausschlagung e-r Erbschaft; **letter of** ~ *Br* Verzichtleistungsschreiben *(bei Zuteilung neuer Aktien; cf. rights issue)*

renvoi *(IPR)* Rückverweisung *(durch die IPR-Normen des von den inländischen IPR-Normen bezeichneten Rechts)*; Weiterverweisung *(vgl. Art. 4 EGBGB)*

reopen *v* wiedereröffnen; wieder in Betrieb nehmen

reopening Wiedereröffnung; Wiederinbetriebnahme; ~ **(of) a case** Wiederaufnahme e-s Verfahrens; ~ **clause** *Am (in e-m Arbeitsvertrag)* Vertragsklausel, die Neuverhandlung e-s Vertragsteils vor Ablauf des Vertrages zuläßt

reorder Nachbestellung, Neubestellung

reorder *v* nachbestellen, neu bestellen

reorganization Umorganisation, Umstrukturierung, Betriebsumstellung; *Am* Umorganisation, Sanierung e-s Unternehmens *(mit od. ohne Mitwirkung des Gerichts); Am (etwa)* Vergleich *(e-s überschuldeten Unternehmens mit Gläubigern)*; *Am*[51] finanzielle Umorganisation e-s überschuldeten Unternehmens *(unter Aufsicht des Konkursgerichts)*; ~ **fund** Sanierungsfonds; ~ **measure** Sanierungsmaßnahmen; ~ **of working time** Neugestaltung der Arbeitszeit; ~ **proceedings** *Am* Umorganisationsverfahren; ~ **scheme** s. plan of →~; **plan of** ~ *Am*[51] Umorganisationsplan, Sanierungsplan; Vergleich; **private** ~ *Am* Umorganisation (od. Sanierung) *(ohne Mitwirkung des Gerichts)*

reorganize *v* umorganisieren, umstrukturieren; umordnen; sanieren

repackaging Umgestaltung von Anleihen am internationalen Kapitalmarkt durch Änderung der Laufzeit, des Zinssatzes, der Währung oder durch die Zerlegung in mehrere Tranchen

repair Reparatur, Instandsetzung, Ausbesserung; Nachbesserung; baulicher Zustand; ~**s** Reparaturen, Instandsetzungsarbeiten; ~**s to a building** Instandsetzung e-s Gebäudes; ~ **cost(s)** Reparaturkosten; ~ **order** Reparaturauftrag; **(quick)** ~ **service** (Schnell-)Reparaturdienst; ~ **shop** Reparaturwerkstatt; **beyond** ~ nicht mehr zu reparieren; **cost(s) of** ~ →~ cost(s); **emergency** ~ unbedingt notwendige Reparatur; **good** ~ gut ausgeführte Reparatur; **in good** ~ in gutem (baulichen) Zustand, gut erhalten; **maintenance and** ~ Unterhaltung und Instandsetzung; **major** ~**s** größere Reparaturen; **in need of** ~ reparaturbedürftig; **out of** ~ in schlechtem (baulichen) Zustand; reparaturbedürftig; **ordinary** ~**s** gewöhnliche *(regelmäßig notwendig werdende)* Reparaturen; **running** ~**s** laufende Reparaturen

repair, state of ~ baulicher Zustand; **the building is in a poor state of** ~ das Gebäude ist in e-m schlechten baulichen Zustand

repair, tenant's ~**s** dem Mieter (od. Pächter) obliegende Reparaturen; ~ **is required to be effected on site** die Reparatur hat am Aufstellungsort *(der Maschine etc)* zu erfolgen; **to carry out** ~**s (improperly)** Reparaturen (schlecht) ausführen; **to effect a** ~ s. to make a →~; **to keep in** ~ instandhalten; **to make** (or **perform**) **a** ~ e-e Reparatur vornehmen; **to need** ~**s** reparaturbedürftig sein; **to put in** ~ *(etw.)* reparieren (lassen), *(etw.)* instandsetzen (lassen)

repair *v* reparieren, instandsetzen; ausbessern

repairing, ~ **covenant** Klausel in e-m Miet- (od. Pacht)vertrag betr. Instandsetzung (od. Reparaturen); **the** ~ **obligations imposed on the tenant** die dem Mieter auferlegten Verpflichtungen zu Reparaturen

reparation Instandsetzung, Wiederherstellung; Wiedergutmachung *(durch Schadensersatz)*; Entschädigung; ~**s** *(VölkerR)* Reparationen, Kriegsentschädigung; ~ **demand** *(VölkerR)* Reparationsforderung; ~ **payments** *(VölkerR)* Reparationszahlungen; **to make** ~ **for** wiedergutmachen, Ersatz leisten

reparole *Am* erneute bedingte Entlassung *(cf. parole 2.)*

repatriate Repatriant, Heimkehrer; in die Heimat zurückgeführter (od. entlassener) Kriegs- od. Zivilgefangener

repatriate *v* repatriieren, in die Heimat zurückführen; wieder einbürgern *(opp. to expatriate)*; **to** ~ **gold** Gold in das Inland zurückführen

repatriated soldier Heimkehrer *(aus der Kriegsgefangenschaft)*

repatriation *(VölkerR)* Repatriierung; Rückführung in die Heimat *(von im Ausland Festgehaltenen)*; Wiedereinbürgerung *(opp. expatriation)*; ~ **of capital** Rückführung von Kapital in das Inland; ~ **of prisoners of war** Rückführung (od. Heimschaffung) von Kriegsgefangenen

repawn *v* wieder verpfänden

repay *v* zurückzahlen, zurückerstatten; nochmals bezahlen; tilgen; **to ~ o.s.** sich schadlos halten; **to ~ a credit** e-n Kredit zurückzahlen (od. tilgen); **to ~ a mortgage** e-e Hypothek zurückzahlen (od. tilgen); **liable to ~** rückerstattungspflichtig, rückzahlungspflichtig

repayable rückzahlbar; **debt ~ by annual instalments** in Jahresraten rückzahlbare Schuld; **loan ~ in 10 years** in 10 Jahren rückzahlbare Anleihe

repayment Rückzahlung, Rückerstattung, Rückvergütung; Tilgung; **~ commitments** Tilgungsverpflichtungen; **~ deferral** Tilgungsstreckung; **~ guarantee** Rückzahlungsgarantie (bezüglich der Rückzahlung geleisteter Zahlungen od. Anzahlungen) *(falls Garantieauftraggeber den Vertragsbedingungen nicht nachkommt;* **~ instal(l)ment** Rückzahlungsrate; **~ mortgage** Tilgungshypothek; **~ of a credit** Rückzahlung e-s Kredits; **~ of debts** Schuldenrückzahlung; **~ of a mortgage** Rückzahlung (od. Tilgung) e-r Hypothek; **~ of tax** Steuererstattung; **anticipated ~** vorzeitige Rückzahlung, Rückzahlung vor Fälligkeit; **conditions for ~** Rückzahlungsbedingungen; **full ~** Rückzahlung in voller Höhe; **obligation of ~** Rückzahlungsverpflichtung

repeal Aufhebung (od. Außerkraftsetzung) *(e-s Gesetzes) (revocation or abrogation)*; Widerruf

repeal *v (Gesetz)* aufheben (od. außerkraftsetzen); widerrufen

repealed, enactments ~ aufgehobene Rechtsvorschriften; **the Act is ~** das Gesetz tritt außer Kraft

repeat Wiederholung; **~ offender** Wiederholungstäter; **~ order** Nachbestellung; **to give** (or **place**) **a ~ order** e-e Nachbestellung machen, nachbestellen

repeat *v* wiederholen; noch einmal liefern; **to ~ an offer** ein Angebot wiederholen (od. erneuern); **to ~ an order for a th.** etw. nachbestellen; **in case of a ~ed offence(~se)** *(StrafR)* im Wiederholungsfalle

repeater *Am* Wähler, der (illegal) mehrere Stimmen abgibt *(cf. floater)*; *Am* rückfälliger Täter *(cf. recidivist)*

repel *v Scot (Einspruch etc)* zurückweisen

repercussion Rückwirkung (on auf); Auswirkung; **~s of war** Kriegsfolgen

repetition Wiederholung; *Scot* Rückerstattung irrtümlich gezahlten Geldes; **capable of ~** *(UrhR)* wiederholbar

repetitive work Routinearbeit

replace *v (etw.)* ersetzen (with or by durch), erneuern; *(jdn)* ersetzen (od. vertreten), an die Stelle treten von, *(j-s)* Stelle einnehmen; **to ~ the receiver** *tel* den Hörer wieder auflegen

replacement 1. Ersatz, Ersatzleistung, Ersatzlieferung, Ersatzbeschaffung, Wiederbeschaffung; Anlageerneuerung; **~ cost(s)** Wiederbeschaffungskosten; **~ demand** Ersatzbedarf; **~ in kind** Naturalersatz

replacement of inventories, provision for ~ *Am (Bilanz)* Rückstellung für die Auffüllung des Lagerbestandes

replacement, ~ (part) Ersatzteil; **~ price** Wiederbeschaffungspreis; **~ (purchase)** Ersatzbeschaffung; **~ reserve** *(Bilanz)* Erneuerungsrücklage, Rücklage für Ersatzbeschaffungen; **~ value** Ersatzwert; Wiederbeschaffungswert; **~ value insurance** Neuwertversicherung; **consignment of ~** Ersatzlieferung; **cost(s) of ~** →~ cost(s)

replacement, in ~ als Ersatz; **demand for other goods in ~** Verlangen nach Ersatzlieferung; **parts supplied in ~** (of defective parts) gelieferte Ersatzteile; **purchase of goods in ~** Deckungskauf; **to buy goods in ~** e-n Deckungskauf vornehmen; **to require goods in ~** Ersatzlieferung verlangen; **to resell goods in ~** e-n Deckungsverkauf vornehmen

replacement 2. Ersatz(person); Vertretung; Neubesetzung; **~ rate** Zu- und Abgangsrate; **cost of ~** Vertretungskosten; **holiday ~** *Br* (**vacation ~** *Am*) Urlaubsvertretung; **to get a ~** e-e Vertretung bekommen

repleader *Am* erneutes →pleading; Recht zu e-m erneuten →pleading

repledge *v* weiter verpfänden

replenish *v (Lager etc)* wieder auffüllen, *(Vorräte)* ergänzen; **to ~ one's reserves** s-e Reserven wieder auffüllen

replenishment Wiederauffüllung, Ergänzung; **~ of stocks** Lagerauffüllung; Wiederaufstokkung von Lagerbeständen; **~ of supplies** Ergänzung der Vorräte

repleviable wiedererlangbar *(durch →replevin)*

replevin[52] Herausgabeklage *(Klage auf Herausgabe von zu Unrecht gepfändeten Sachen gegen Sicherheitsleistung)*

replevin *v Am* →replevy *v*

replevisable →repleviable

replevisor Kläger in e-m replevin-Verfahren; jd, dem e-e bewegl. Sache *(Br widerrechtl.)* entzogen ist *(Br →distrainee)*; **the ~ can obtain a replevy of the goods unlawfully taken from him** der →replevisor kann die unrechtmäßig gepfändeten Sachen zurückbekommen

replevy →replevin

replevy *v (entzogene Sache im →replevin-Verfahren)* herausgeben (od. wiedererlangen)

repliant Kläger, der e-e Replik (reply) vorbringt

replica, to make a ~ of antiques Antiquitäten nachmachen

replicant *Am* Kläger, der e-e Replik (replication) vorbringt

replication *Am* Replik (des Klägers) *(formelle Bezeichnung für reply)*; **to deliver** (or **file**) **a ~** e-e Replik vorbringen

reply 1. Replik *(des Klägers auf Klagebeantwortung)*; **right of ~** *Br (Strafprozeß)* Recht des Anwalts auf das letzte Wort

reply 2. Antwort, Erwiderung; Antwortschreiben; **~ by return of post** *Br* (**by return mail** *Am*) postwendende Antwort; **~ (postal) card** *Am* Postkarte mit Rückantwort; **~ coupon** (Rück-)Antwortschein; **~ to a counterclaim** Entgegnung *(des Klägers)* auf e-e Widerklage

reply paid, ~ postcard *Br* Postkarte mit Rückantwort; **~ telegram** (RP.) Telegramm mit bezahlter Rückantwort

reply, ~ telegram Antworttelegramm; **affirmative ~** bejahende (od. zusagende) Antwort; **business ~ card** Werbeantwortkarte; **business ~ items** Geschäftsantwortsendungen; **early ~** baldige Antwort; **immediate ~** umgehende Antwort; **in ~ to your letter** in Beantwortung Ihres Schreibens; **in your ~ please quote** bei Beantwortung bitte *(Aktenzeichen)* angeben; **negative ~** abschlägige Antwort, abschlägiger Bescheid; **looking forward to receiving your ~** Ihrer Antwort entgegensehend; **right of ~** *Am (bei beleidigenden Äußerungen)* Anspruch auf Abdruck e-r Gegenerklärung; **without ~** unbeantwortet; **to expedite the ~** die Antwort beschleunigen; **to make a ~** antworten, erwidern; **we would be obliged by (your letting us have) an early ~** für baldige Antwort wären wir Ihnen dankbar; **all ~ies (will be) treated in confidence** die Antwort wird vertraulich behandelt

reply *v* antworten, erwidern; **~ing to your letter (inquiry)** in Beantwortung Ihres Briefes (Ihrer Anfrage)

repo →repurchase agreement

report Bericht (on über); Meldung; Rechenschaftsbericht; Geschäftsbericht (→*directors' ~*); Referat; *Br* (Zoll-)Deklaration; (Schul-)Zeugnis; Gerücht; **R~s** Sammlung gerichtlicher Entscheidungen; **~ of the auditor** Prüfungsvermerk des Wirtschaftsprüfers; **R~s of Cases before the Court of Justice** *(EG)* Sammlung der Rechtsprechung des Gerichtshofes; **~ period** Berichtszeitraum; **~ of proceedings** Verhandlungsbericht, Protokoll; **~ stage** *Br parl* Stadium der Beratung e-r Gesetzesvorlage *(in dem sie vom Ausschuß dem House of Commons vorgelegt wird [2. Lesung])*; **~ to the police** Anzeige bei der Polizei; **~ writing** Berichtsabfassung; **action ~** Tätigkeitsbericht; →**annual ~**; **auditor's ~** →~ of the auditor; **captain's ~** Seeprotest, Verklarung; **cash ~** Kassenbericht; **classified ~** *Am* Geheimbericht; **colo(u)red ~** gefärbter Bericht; **commercial ~** Handelsbericht; **comprehensive ~** umfassender Bericht; **confidential ~** vertraulicher Bericht; **consolidated ~** zusammengefaßter Bericht; **court expert's ~** Gutachten e-s vom Gericht ernannten Sachverständigen; **credit ~** Kreditauskunft; **current ~** laufender Bericht; **damage ~** *(VersR)* Schadensmeldung; Havariebericht; **date of ~** Berichtszeit(-punkt); **directors' ~** *(AktienR)* Geschäftsbericht des board of directors; **draft ~** Berichtsentwurf; **efficiency ~** Leistungsbericht; **factual ~** Tatsachenbericht; **final ~** Schlußbericht; **financial** (or **fiscal**) **~** Finanzbericht; **fortnightly ~** 14täglicher Bericht; **general ~** Gesamtbericht; **information ~** Informationsbericht; **interim ~** Zwischenbericht; → **law ~s**; **market ~** Marktbericht; Börsenbericht; **medical ~** ärztlicher Bericht; **by mere ~** vom bloßen Hörensagen; **meteorological ~** Wetterbericht; **month under ~** Berichtsmonat; **monthly ~** Monatsbericht; **sixmonthly ~** Halbjahresbericht

report, newspaper ~ Zeitungsbericht; **false newspaper ~** Zeitungsente

report, official ~ amtlicher Bericht; Protokoll; **overall ~** Gesamtbericht; **over the counter ~s** *Am* Kursblatt *(für die im geregelten Freiverkehr ermittelten Kurse)*; **period under ~** Berichtszeitraum; **press ~** Pressebericht; **progress ~** Bericht über den Stand e-r Angelegenheit; **quarterly ~** vierteljährlicher Bericht; **receiving ~** (Waren-)Eingangsmeldung; **stock market ~** *Am* Kursblatt *(für die →listed securities)*; **supplementary ~** Zusatzbericht, Ergänzungsbericht

report, to bring a ~ up to date e-n Bericht auf den neuesten Stand bringen; **to cook a ~** *sl.* e-n Bericht frisieren (od. fälschen); **to draw up a ~** e-n Bericht abfassen (od. erstellen); **to file a ~** e-n Bericht einreichen; **to frame a ~** e-n Bericht abfassen (od. formulieren); **to give a ~** e-n Bericht machen (od. erstatten), berichten (on über); **to include in a ~** in e-m Bericht aufnehmen; **to make a ~** s. to give a →~; *Am* e-e Anzeige erstatten; **to prepare a ~** e-n Bericht machen (od. abfassen)

report, to render a ~ e-n Bericht erstatten; **failure to render a ~** Nichterstattung e-s Berichtes

report, to request a ~ e-n Bericht anfordern; **to submit a ~** e-n Bericht einreichen; **from the ~**

it appears aus dem Bericht geht hervor; **there shall be included in the ~** der Bericht soll enthalten

report *v* berichten, Bericht erstatten (on über); *(für e-e Zeitung)* schreiben; melden, anzeigen (to bei); sich melden (to bei); ausweisen; **to ~ to** *(disziplinarisch)* unterstehen, unterstellt sein; **to ~ an accident** *(der Versicherung od. Polizei)* e-n Unfall (od. Schadensfall) melden; **to ~ for duty** sich zum Dienst melden; **to ~ (o.s.) to the police** (*Br [auch]* **to a police station**) sich bei der Polizei melden

report *v*, **to ~ an offen|ce(~se) to the police** die Polizei von e-r Straftat benachrichtigen; **to ~ a person to the police** jdn (bei der Polizei) anzeigen; **to ~ (sth.) to the police** e-e Anzeige erstatten *(Strafanzeige)*; **duty to ~ an offen|ce(~se) to the police** Anzeigepflicht

report *v*, **to ~ progress** über den Stand der Angelegenheit berichten; **to move to ~ progress** *Br parl* Schluß der Debatte beantragen *(oft um Obstruktion zu treiben)*

report *v*, **to ~ a trial** über e-n Prozeß berichten

reported earnings ausgewiesener Gewinn

reporting Berichterstattung; Meldung, Anzeige; **~ examiner** *(PatR)* Berichterstatter *(im Erteilungsverfahren)*; **~ pay** *Am* Anwesenheitslohn *(für Arbeiter, die sich zur regulären Arbeit gemeldet haben, aber keine Arbeit vorfinden)*; **~ sick** Krankmeldung; **~ to the police** Erstattung e-r Strafanzeige

reporter Berichterstatter; *Am* Protokollführer bei Gericht; Reporter, Zeitungsberichterstatter; *Am* Sammlung von Gerichtsentscheidungen; **Federal R~** (Fed.) *Am* Sammlung der Entscheidungen der Bundesberufungsgerichte; **National R~ System** *Am (in 7 regionale Bezirke*[53] *eingeteilte)* Sammlung der Entscheidungen der Gerichte der Einzelstaaten in fortlaufender Folge

repository Aufbewahrungsort; Ablage; (Waren-)Lager, Speicher

repossess *v* wieder in Besitz nehmen, zurücknehmen

repossession Wiederinbesitznahme; **judicial ~** Einweisung des Sicherungsnehmers in den Besitz des Sicherungsguts durch ein Gericht zur Durchführung der Verwertung *(opp. self-help repossession)*

represent *v* 1. vertreten; **to ~ a firm** e-e Firma vertreten; **to ~ the interests of a country** die Interessen e-s Landes vertreten; **authority to ~ (a person)** Vertretungsbefugnis; **to be instructed to ~ ...** mit der Vertretung von ... beauftragt sein

represented, ~ by counsel durch e-n Anwalt *(Br barrister mit solicitor; Am attorney)* vertreten; **to be (legally) ~** sich (durch e-n Anwalt) vertreten lassen

representing als Vertreter; **to withdraw from ~ the defendant** die Vertretung des Beklagten niederlegen

represent *v* 2. *(Tatsachen)* beschreiben, darstellen; hinstellen als; **to ~ o.s. as (an) expert** sich als Sachverständigen ausgeben; **to ~ falsely** den falschen Eindruck hervorrufen; **certificate ~ing shares** Zertifikat über Aktien

represent *v* 3. wiedervorlegen; **to ~ a bill for acceptance** e-n Wechsel erneut zum Akzept vorlegen

representation 1. Vertretung; Stellvertretung; **~ abroad** Auslandsvertretung; **~ before the Patent Office** Vertretung vor dem Patentamt; **~ by a lawyer** Vertretung durch e-n Anwalt; **~ cases** *Am* Streitfälle, bei denen es sich darum handelt, ob e-e Gewerkschaft zur Vertretung bestimmter Arbeitnehmer befugt ist; **~ order** *Br (KartellR)* Verfügung, wonach mehrere oder alle Beteiligten im Verfahren vertreten werden können; **~ of a state** (diplomatische) Vertretung e-s Staates; **diplomatic ~** diplomatische Vertretung; **employees' ~ in management** Mitbestimmung; **grant of ~** gerichtliche Erbschaftsverwaltungsbescheinigung *(umfaßt →probate und →letters of administration; cf. personal representative)*; **legal ~** Vertretung vor Gericht, Vertretung in e-m Prozeß; **legal and general ~** gerichtliche und außergerichtliche Vertretung; **parliamentary ~** parlamentarische Vertretung; **proportional ~** Verhältniswahl(system); **to maintain ~s** Vertretungen *(im Ausland)* unterhalten

representation 2. *(ErbR)*[54] Erbfolge nach Stämmen (od. Parentelen) *(Rechtsregel, nach der anstelle e-s fortgefallenen Erben dessen Abkömmlinge treten; entsprechend § 1924 BGB)*; **to take by ~** nach Stämmen *(per stirpes)* erben

representation 3. Darstellung, Schilderung; Aufführung, Vorführung, Vorstellung; *(VertragsR)* Erklärung, Angabe *(e-r Partei vor oder bei Vertragsabschluß; cf. misrepresentation)*; *Am (VersR)* Tatsachendarstellung bezüglich des zu übernehmenden Risikos; **~s and warranties** Zusicherungen und Gewährleistungen; **~ of a design** *(bildliche)* Darstellung e-s Musters; **estoppel by ~** Verwirkung durch Irreführung; **false ~s** falsche Angaben; Erregung e-r irreführenden Vorstellung; **fraudulent ~** Vorspiegelung falscher Tatsachen; **promissory ~** *(VersR)* sich auf die Zukunft beziehende Erklärung; **right of ~** *(UrhR)* Vorführungsrecht; **to make formal ~s** offiziell vorstellig werden (to bei); **to make written or oral ~s** schriftliche oder mündliche Erklärungen abgeben

representation 4. Vorhaltung, Vorstellung; **diplomatic ~** Demarche, (formeller) Protest; **upon the ~ of a claim** bei Geltendmachung e-s Anspruchs; **to make ~s** Vorhaltungen machen; Vorstellungen erheben; **to make dip-**

lomatic ~s to a state auf diplomatischem Wege bei e-m Staat vorstellig werden; Protest einlegen; **to make urgent ~s** *(jdm)* eindringliche Vorhaltungen machen

representative Vertreter; Stellvertreter; Repräsentant; Abgeordneter *(Am des Repräsentantenhauses)*; (stell)vertretend (of für); repräsentativ; bezeichnend, typisch (of für); **~ abroad** Auslandsvertreter; **~ action** Klage im Interesse e-r Gruppe von Beteiligten; Klage der einzelnen Gesellschafter (→*derivative action*); **~ by operation of law** gesetzlicher Vertreter; **in a ~ capacity** (or **character**) in vertretender Eigenschaft; **~ democracy** repräsentative Demokratie; **~ government** Repräsentativverfassung; **~ group member** *Br (Umsatzsteuer)* stellvertretendes Mitglied e-r Gruppe; **~ office** Repräsentanz; **~ period** *(GATT)* Grundsatz, daß das Einfuhrkontingent dem prozentualen Anteil der einzelnen Mitgliedstaaten an der Einfuhr der kontingentierten Ware in früheren Zeitabschnitten entspricht; **~ rates** *(EG)* repräsentative Kurse
Kurse für die Umrechnung der in der gemeinsamen Agrarpolitik verwendeten ECU in Landeswährung

representative, ~ sample repräsentative Stichprobe, Serienmuster; ~ →**sampling; authorized ~** bevollmächtigter Vertreter; **commercial ~** Handelsvertreter; **consular ~** konsularischer Vertreter; **diplomatic ~** diplomatischer Vertreter (to bei); **employers' ~** Arbeitgebervertreter; **foreign ~** Auslandsvertreter; **general ~** Generalvertreter; **House of R~s** *Am parl* Repräsentantenhaus (→*House 2.*); **lawful ~** rechtmäßiger *(ordnungsgemäß bevollmächtigter)* Vertreter; **legal ~** Vertreter in Rechtssachen *(bes. executor, administrator)*; Rechtsvertreter; *(auch)* ordnungsgemäß bevollmächtigter Vertreter; **personal ~** Erbschaftsverwalter *(executor or administrator; cf. personal)*; **professional ~** *(europ. PatR)* zugelassener Vertreter; **sales ~** (Handels-)Vertreter; **sole ~** Alleinvertreter; **special ~** *Am* Sonderbeauftragter; **to appoint a ~** e-n Vertreter bestellen; **to designate a ~** e-n Vertreter ernennen

repression *pol* Unterdrückung

repress *v*, **to ~ a revolt** e-e Revolte unterdrücken

repressed inflation zurückgestaute (od. gestoppte) Inflation *(s. suppressed* →inflation)

reprieve Strafvollstreckungsaufschub, bes. Aussetzung der Vollstreckung e-s Todesurteils; **to grant a ~** Vollstreckungsaufschub gewähren

reprieve *v* Strafvollstreckungsaufschub gewähren

reprimand Tadel, *(dienstl.)* Verweis; **severe ~** strenger Verweis; **to receive a ~** e-n Verweis erhalten

reprimand *v (dienstl.)* Verweis erteilen; *(jdn)* verwarnen

reprint Neudruck; *(unveränderte)* Neuauflage

reprisal Vergeltungsmaßnahme; *(VölkerR)* Repressalie *(z. B. embargo, retortion)*; Wiederwegnahme *(e-s aufgebrachten Schiffes; cf. recapture)*; **to make ~s** Repressalien ergreifen (on gegen)
(VölkerR) Vergeltung e-s Unrechts durch ein anderes, das aber wegen der vorangegangenen völkerrechtswidrigen Handlung des anderen Staates gerechtfertigt ist. Reprisal ist zuvor anzudrohen und muß verhältnismäßig sein; es gilt Verbot militärischer Gewalt (Art. 51 UN-Charta)

reprise, above all ~s *Br* nachdem alle *(jährl.)* Abgaben *(auf Grundbesitz)* gezahlt sind

reprivatization Reprivatisierung

reprivatize *v* reprivatisieren

reproach *v*, **to ~ sb. with** jdm Vorwürfe (od. Vorhaltungen) machen wegen

reprobate *v Scot* →approbate *v* and ~

reprocessing, ~ of nuclear materials Wiederaufbereitung von Kernmaterial; **~ plant** Wiederaufbereitungsanlage

reproduce *v* reproduzieren, nachdrucken, nachbilden, vervielfältigen; **to ~ a witness** e-n Zeugen wieder vorführen

reproduction Reproduktion, Nachdruck, Nachbildung, Wiedergabe *(durch Druck)*; Vervielfältigung; **right of ~** *(UrhR)* Vervielfältigungsrecht

reproductive debt *Br* durch Immobiliarvermögen (real assets) gedeckter Teil der Staatsschuld (national debt)

Republican Republikaner; *Am* Mitglied (od. Anhänger) der Republikanischen Partei; republikanisch; **~ form of government**[55] republikanische Regierungsform; **~ party** *Am* Republikanische Partei *(cf. Democratic party)*; **the House of Representative went ~** *Am* im Repräsentantenhaus gewannen die Republikaner die Mehrheit

republicanism republikanische Staatsform

republication 1., **~ of a will** erneute Testamentserrichtung *(nochmalige Abfassung e-s widerrufenen Testaments)*

republication 2. Neudruck, Neuauflage; Wiederveröffentlichung

repudiate *v* zurückweisen, nicht anerkennen; **to ~ a claim** e-n Anspruch zurückweisen; **to ~ a contract** den Vertrag nicht anerkennen; die Vertragserfüllung ablehnen; **to ~ a legacy** ein

Vermächtnis ausschlagen; **to ~ a public debt** e-e Staatsschuld nicht anerkennen, e-e Staatsschuld für nichtig erklären

repudiation Nichtanerkennung *(bes. e-r Staatsschuld)*; *Br eccl* Ausschlagung e-r Pfründe; **~ of a contract** Nichtanerkennung e-s Vertrages; Ablehnung der Vertragserfüllung, Erfüllungsverweigerung

repugnancy Unvereinbarkeit, Widerspruch

repugnant, to be ~ to im Widerspruch stehen zu

repurchase Rückkauf; Rücknahme *(von Investmentanteilen)*; **~ agreement** Rückkaufvereinbarung; (Wertpapier-) Pensionsgeschäft *(Verkauf e-s Postens zur sofortigen Auslieferung bei gleichzeitigem Wiederverkauf des gleichen Postens auf Termin)*; **~ price** Rückkaufpreis; Rücknahmepreis; Rücknahmekurs; **~ transactions** Pensionsgeschäfte; **right of ~** Rückkaufsrecht; **sale with option of ~** Verkauf mit Rückkaufsrecht

repurchase *v* zurückkaufen; **right to ~** Rückkaufsrecht

repurchaser Rückkäufer

reputation Ruf, (guter) Name; Leumund; Ansehen; **bad ~** schlechter Ruf; **business ~** geschäftliches Ansehen; **damage to ~** Schädigung (od. Beeinträchtigung) des Rufes; **defamation of a competitor's ~** Anschwärzung; **general ~** *(BeweisR)* allgemeine Ansicht; **injury to ~** s. damage to →~; **world-wide ~** Weltruf; **to damage** (or **injure**) **a p.'s ~** j-s Ruf schädigen; **to establish a ~ as a lawyer** sich e-n Ruf als Anwalt verschaffen

Br Der gute Ruf wird geschützt durch action for libel und action for slander

repute Ruf; Ansehen; **a doctor of ~** ein Arzt von Ruf (od. Ansehen); **to be held in bad** (or **ill**) **~** in schlechtem Ruf stehen, schlecht beleumdet sein; **to be held in good** (or **high**) **~** in gutem Ruf stehen, gut beleumdet sein; hoch angesehen sein

reputed angeblich, vermeintlich; bekannt, berühmt; **to be ~ to be** in dem Rufe stehen, zu sein; gelten für

reputed owner anscheinender Eigentümer (→*reputed ownership*)

reputed ownership anscheinendes Eigentum (Eigentumsvermutung)

Die "reputed ownership" Doktrin ist durch den Insolvency Act 1986 aufgehoben

request Bitte, Ersuchen (for um); Antrag, Gesuch, Verlangen; Aufforderung; Anforderung; **~ for admission** *Am (Zivilprozeß)* Aufforderung an die Gegenseite, bestimmte Behauptungen anzuerkennen; **~ for arbitration** Schiedsantrag, Schiedsklage (→*arbitration*); **~s book** Beschwerdebuch; **~ for documents** Anforderung von Unterlagen; **~ for examination** *(PatR)* Prüfungsantrag; **~ for (an extension of) time** Antrag auf Fristverlängerung; **~ for extradition** Auslieferungsersuchen; **~ for grant** *(PatR)* Erteilungsantrag; **~ for a holiday** *Br* Urlaubsgesuch; **~ for information** Bitte um Auskunft, Auskunftsersuchen; **~ note** Antrag auf Genehmigung zur Verlagerung zollpflichtiger Waren; **~ for an opinion** Einholung e-s Gutachtens; **~ for payment** Zahlungsaufforderung; Mahnung; **~ for quotation** Preisanfrage; **~ for →redress; ~ for respite** Stundungsgesuch; **~ stop** *Br* Bedarfshaltestelle; **at one's own request** auf eigenen Wunsch; **letters of ~** *Br* Rechtshilfeersuchen (→*letters 3.*); **party making the ~** antragstellende Partei; **person entitled to submit a ~** *(PatR)* Antragsberechtigter; **vacation ~** *Am* Urlaubsgesuch; **to comply with a ~** e-m Ersuchen stattgeben; e-r Bitte nachkommen; **to deal with a ~** e-n Antrag bearbeiten; **to deny a ~** s. to refuse a →~; **to draw up a ~** ein Gesuch abfassen; **to grant a ~** ein Gesuch bewilligen, e-m Ersuchen stattgeben; **to make a ~** e-n Antrag stellen; e-e Bitte (od. ein Gesuch) richten (to an); vorstellig werden (to bei); **to refuse** (or **reject**) **a ~** ein Gesuch ablehnen (od. abschlägig bescheiden); **to submit a ~** ein Gesuch (od. e-n Antrag) einreichen

request *v* bitten, ersuchen (for um); beantragen; verlangen, auffordern; anfordern; **to ~ an extension of time** um Fristverlängerung bitten; **to ~ information** um Auskunft bitten; **to ~ instructions** Anweisungen erbitten; **to ~ an opinion** ein Gutachten einholen; **to ~ payment** Zahlung verlangen; **to ~ permission** um Erlaubnis bitten

requested, the ~ authority die ersuchte Behörde; **as ~** wie erbeten (od. beantragt)

requesting, the ~ authority die ersuchende Behörde

require *v* fordern, verlangen; erfordern, notwendig machen; Bedarf haben an, brauchen; **to ~ a th. of a p.** von jdm etw. verlangen; **unless the context otherwise ~s** wenn sich aus dem Zusammenhang nichts anderes ergibt

required erforderlich; zu kaufen gesucht; **~ form** erforderliche Form; **~ (bank) reserves** *Am* → reserve 1.; **~ by law** gesetzlich vorgeschrieben; **the ~ money** das erforderliche Geld; **as (and when) ~** wie gewünscht, wunschgemäß; **if ~** wenn nötig, falls erforderlich; **a bond is ~** e-e Kaution muß gestellt werden

requirement Forderung, Verlangen; Anforderung; Erfordernis, Bedürfnis; Bedarf; Voraussetzung, Bedingung; erforderliche Eigenschaft; ~ **contract** *Am* Bedarfsdeckungsvertrag *(in dem sich der Käufer verpflichtet, s-n Bedarf an bestimmter Ware auf bestimmte Zeit bei dem Verkäufer zu decken)*; **~s for admission** Zulassungsbedingungen; **~s in goods** Warenbedarf; ~ **of form** Formerfordernis (→*form 1.*); **~s of raw materials** Rohstoffbedarf; **~s of traffic** Verkehrsbedürfnisse; **according to** ~ nach Bedarf; **anticipated** ~ voraussichtlicher Bedarf; **calculation of ~s** Bedarfsrechnung; **capital ~s** Kapitalbedarf; **current ~s** laufender Bedarf; **educational ~s** Bildungsvoraussetzungen; **export ~s** Exportbedarf; **financial** (or **financing**) **~s** Finanzbedarf; **formal** ~ Formerfordernis; **home ~s** Inlandsbedarf; **import ~s** Importbedarf; **labo(u)r ~s** Bedarf an Arbeitskräften; **legal ~s** gesetzliche Voraussetzungen; **own ~s** Eigenbedarf; **peacetime ~s** Friedensbedarf; **personal ~s** persönlicher Bedarf, Eigenbedarf; **total ~s** Gesamtbedarf; **yearly ~s** Jahresbedarf; **to comply with** (or **to fulfil[l]**) **the ~s** den Anforderungen entsprechen, die Voraussetzungen erfüllen; den Bedürfnissen entsprechen; **to meet the** ~ den Bedarf decken; **to satisfy the most urgent ~s** den dringendsten Bedarf decken

requisite Erfordernis; **~(s)** Bedarfsartikel; **office ~s** Büroartikel

requisite erforderlich, notwendig; ~ **capital** nötiges (od. erforderliches) Kapital; ~ **form** erforderliche Form; ~ **majority** erforderliche Mehrheit; **when** ~ erforderlichenfalls

requisition 1. *(förml.)* Ersuchen, *(förml.)* Aufforderung *(e-r Verpflichtung nachzukommen)*; Anforderung, Verlangen; *Scot (notarielle)* Zahlungsaufforderung; *Am* Auslieferungsersuchen, Auslieferungsantrag *(z.B. des Gouverneurs e-s Einzelstaates an den Gouverneur e-s anderen Einzelstaates)*; ~ **form** Bestellzettel; *Br* Auftragszettel *(für money order)*; ~ **number** Bestellnummer; **~s on title** *Br* Ersuchen um weitere Auskunft *(des Anwalts des Käufers od. Hypothekengläubigers von Grundbesitz an den Anwalt des Verkäufers od. Hypothekenschuldners nach Empfang des →abstract of title)*

requisition 2. *mil* Requirierung, Beschlagnahme, Erfassung (for von); **to make a ~ for** *(etw.)* beschlagnahmen

requisition *v* requirieren, beschlagnahmen

requisitioned property beschlagnahmte Vermögensgegenstände

requisitioning *mil*[56] Requisition, Requirierung, Beschlagnahme *(zugunsten der eigenen Armee)*; **de-~** Freigabe

requital, in ~ for als Belohnung (od. Entgelt) für

rerate *v* neu bewerten, neu einstufen

rerouting Umleitung; Umschreibung *(e-s Flugscheins)*; ~ **request** *Am (Post)* Nachsendeantrag

res Sache(n); ~ **furtivae** ("stolen goods") gestohlene Sachen; ~ **gestae** ("things done") Begleitumstände *(der entscheidungserheblichen Tatsachen eines Prozeßvortrags, auf die zum Beweise und zur Erläuterung dieser Tatsachen zurückgegriffen werden darf)*; ~ **in transitu** *(IPR)* Sachen auf der Reise *(die sich durch den Machtbereich mehrerer Rechtsordnungen bewegen, wobei die Frage entsteht, welches Recht sie beherrschen soll)*; ~ **ipsa loquitur** ("the thing speaks for itself") widerlegbare Vermutung, daß Beklagter fahrlässig handelte

res judicata *(zwischen den Parteien)* rechtskräftig entschiedene Sache; (materielle) Rechtskraft; ~ **effect** Rechtskraftwirkung; **plea of** ~ Einrede der Rechtskraft; **to become** ~ rechtskräftig werden

res, ~ **nova** ("a matter not yet decided") noch nicht entschiedene Sache; ~ **nullius** ("a thing which has no owner") herrenlose Sache

resal(e)able wiederverkäuflich

resale Wiederverkauf; Weiterverkauf, Weiterveräußerung; Verkauf aus zweiter Hand; Dekkungsverkauf; ~ **of goods** (by unpaid seller) Deckungsverkauf; ~ **price** Wiederverkaufspreis; Einzelhandelspreis; Ladenpreis

Resale Prices Act 1976 *Br*[57] Gesetz über Wiederverkaufspreise (Preisbindungsgesetz)

Das Gesetz gehört zusammen mit dem →Restrictive Trade Practices Act 1976, dem →Restrictive Practices Court Act 1976 und einigen Vorschriften des →Fair Trading Act 1973 zu der umfassenden neuen Gesetzgebung zum Wettbewerbsrecht

resale price fixing *(Kanada)* Preisbindung der zweiten Hand

(resale) price maintenance (RPM) Preisbindung der zweiten Hand, vertikale Preisbindung *(Festsetzung des minimalen Wiederverkaufspreises; Br cf. Resale Prices Act; Am durch die →Fair Trade Acts der Einzelstaaten gestattet)*

resale price, maintaining ~s Einhaltung von Wiederverkaufspreisen; **maintained minimum ~s** gebundene Mindestpreise; **to sell at a price below the** ~ unter dem Wiederverkaufspreis verkaufen

reschedule *v* (durch Umschuldung) ablösen, umschulden

rescheduled, countries with ~ debt(s) Umschuldungsländer

rescheduling Umschuldung; ~ **agreement** Umschuldungsvereinbarung

rescind *v* aufheben, für ungültig erklären, rückgängig machen, anfechten; **to ~ a contract** *(rückwirkend)* e-n Vertrag in beiderseitigem Einvernehmen auflösen; *(wegen wesentlicher*

Vertragsverletzung) durch einseitige Erklärung auflösen, vom Vertrag zurücktreten; wandeln; *(wegen Irrtums od. Irreführung [→misrepresentation],*[58] *Täuschung [→fraud, deceit])* durch einseitige Erklärung auflösen, den Vertrag anfechten *(to rescind setzt in der Regel voraus, daß Wiederherstellung des ursprünglichen Zustandes [→restitutio in integrum] noch möglich ist)*; **to ~ a guarantee** ein Garantieversprechen für ungültig erklären; **to ~ a judgment** ein Urteil aufheben; **to ~ a law** ein Gesetz außer Kraft setzen; **to ~ an order** e-e Anordnung aufheben; **to ~ a sale** e-n Kauf(vertrag) rückgängig machen, wandeln *(vgl. § 462 BGB)*

rescission Aufhebung, Ungültigkeitserklärung, Rückgängigmachung, Anfechtung; **~ for breach of warranty** *Am* Rückgängigmachung (od. Wandelung) wegen Gewährleistungsbruch; **~ for fraudulent misrepresentation** Auflösung (od. Beseitigung, Anfechtung) *(e-s Vertrages)* wegen arglistiger Täuschung *(→misrepresentation)*; **~ for innocent misrepresentation** *(rückwirkende)* Auflösung (od. Beseitigung, Anfechtung) *(e-s Vertrages)* wegen unbeabsichtigter Falschdarstellung; Irrtumsanfechtung *(→misrepresentation)*; Anfechtung wegen falscher Darstellung von Tatsachen; **~ of a contract** *(rückwirkende)* Auflösung (od. Beseitigung) e-s Vertrages in beiderseitigem Einvernehmen; *(wegen wesentlicher Vertragsverletzung)* Rücktritt vom Vertrag, Wandelung; *(wegen Irrtums od. Irreführung [→misrepresentation] und Täuschung [→fraud, deceit])* Anfechtung des Vertrages *(~ setzt in der Regel voraus, daß Wiederherstellung des ursprünglichen Zustandes [restitution in integrum] noch möglich ist)*; **~ of receiving order** *Br* Aufhebung der →receiving order; **~ of a sale** Rückgängigmachung e-s Kaufs (od. Kaufvertrages); Wandelung *(vgl. § 462 BGB)*; **~ proceedings** Anfechtungsverfahren; **action in ~** Anfechtungsklage, Aufhebungsklage; Klage auf Rückgängigmachung (od. Wandelung); **cause for ~** Anfechtungsgrund, Aufhebungsgrund, Rücktrittsgrund; **right of ~** Anfechtungsrecht, Aufhebungsrecht, Rücktrittsrecht; **to be subject to ~** der Anfechtung (od. Aufhebung, od. dem Rücktritt) unterliegen

rescissory action *Scot* Klage auf Nichtigerklärung e-s Vertrages, Aufhebungsklage, Anfechtungsklage

rescription *(Schweiz)* Reskription *(von der öffentlichen Hand ausgegeben)*, Schatzanweisung, Schatzwechsel

rescue Gefangenenbefreiung, *(gewaltsame)* Befreiung *(e-s Gefangenen)*; Rettung; Bergung; Rettungswesen, Rettungswerk; *com* Sanierung; **~ and return of astronauts**[59] Rettung und Rückkehr von Raumfahrern; **~ of goods seized in execution** Pfandbruch, Verstrikkungsbruch; **~ party** (or **team**) Rettungstrupp, Rettungsmannschaft; Bergungsmannschaft; **~ scheme** *com* Sanierungsprogramm; **~ work** Rettungsarbeiten

rescue *v (Gefangene) (gewaltsam)* befreien; retten; bergen; unter Pfandbruch an sich nehmen; *com* sanieren; **to ~ the market** den Markt stützen

research Forschung, Forschungsarbeit (on über); Nachforschung, Suche (for, after nach); *(MMF)* Erhebung, Umfrage; **R~ and Development** (R & D) Forschung und Entwicklung (F&E); **~ cent|re(~er)** Forschungszentrum, Forschungsstelle; **~ department** Forschungsabteilung; **~ funds** Forschungsmittel; **~ material** Forschungsmaterial; **joint ~ program(me)** gemeinsames Forschungsprogramm; **~ project** Forschungsvorhaben; **~ scholarship** Forschungsstipendium; **~ work** Forschungsarbeit; **~ worker** Forscher; **atomic ~** Atomforschung; **audience ~** *Br* Höreranalyse *(in der Funkwerbung)*; **business ~** Konjunkturforschung; **desk ~** Sekundärerhebung *(cf. field ~)*; **field ~** Felduntersuchung, Primärerhebung *(z.B. Marktforschung, Statistik)*; **International R~ Associates** (INRA) internationale Vereinigung von demoskopischen Instituten; **listenership ~** *Am* Hörerumfrage; **market ~** Marktforschung; **opinion ~** Meinungsforschung *(→public opinion ~)*; **readers interest ~** Leserumfrage; **space ~** Weltraumforschung; **to be engaged in** (or **to carry out**) **~** Forschungen betreiben, Forschungsarbeiten durchführen; **to make ~es** Nachforschungen anstellen

researcher Forscher; Ermittler

resell *v* wiederverkaufen, weiterverkaufen, weiterveräußern; **to ~ goods (in replacement)** e-n Deckungsverkauf vornehmen

resemblance, closest ~ größte Ähnlichkeit

reservation 1. Vorbehalt; Rechtsvorbehalt; Vorbehaltsklausel *(in e-m Vertrag)*; *Am* staatl. Grundbesitz, der bestimmten Zwecken vorbehalten ist *(Parks, Indian ~s etc)*
reservation of ownership Eigentumsvorbehalt; **sale with ~** Kauf unter Eigentumsvorbehalt
reservation, ~ of property →~ of title; **~ of a right** Rechtsvorbehalt; **~ of the right of disposal**[60] Vorbehalt der Veräußerungsbefugnis; **~ of right to rescind** (or **terminate**) Vorbehalt des Rücktritts vom Vertrag
reservation of title Eigentumsvorbehalt; **extended ~** verlängerter Eigentumsvorbehalt
Am Der Begriff „Eigentumsvorbehalt" fällt im Sinne des Article 3 des →Uniform Commercial Code unter den Oberbegriff →security interest
reservation, Indian ~ *Am* Reservat *(den Indianern zugewiesenes Wohngebiet)*; **mental ~** Men-

talreservation, geheimer Vorbehalt; **subject to certain** ~**s** mit gewissen Vorbehalten; **with** ~ unter Vorbehalt, vorbehaltlich; **without** ~ vorbehaltlos; ohne Bedenken; **to express** ~**s** Vorbehalte geltend machen; **to make a** ~ e-n Vorbehalt machen

reservation 2. *bes. Am* Reservierung, Vorbestellung; *(Schiff, Flugzeug)* Buchung; ~ **(of seats)** *(Eisenbahn etc)* Platzbestellung; ~ **fee** Gebühr für Platzbestellung; **room** ~ Zimmer(vor)bestellung; **to cancel a** ~ e-e Reservierung rückgängig machen; abbestellen

reserve 1. Reserve; Ersatz; *(VersR)* Prämienreserve; Zentralbankreserve; Währungsreserve; *(Bilanz)* Rücklage *(aus dem nicht ausgeschütteten Gewinn e-s Unternehmens oder der Einzahlung von Gesellschaftern stammende Reserven)*; *(Bilanz)* Rückstellung *(Passivposten für der Höhe oder dem Fälligkeitstermin nach unbestimmte Verbindlichkeiten)*; *Br* der Teil des Aktienkapitals, dessen Einzahlung nur bei Liquidation der Gesellschaft verlangt werden kann (→~ *liability*); ~ **assets** Reserveguthaben; Währungsreserven; ~ **assets ratio** *Br* Mindestreservesatz; ~ **balance** Mindesteinlagen der Banken bei e-r der 12 Federal R~ Banks; **R~ Bank** *Am* →Federal R~ Bank; ~ **capital** Reservekapital; ~-**carrying liabilities** *Am* mindestreservepflichtige Verbindlichkeiten; ~ **city** *Am* Stadt, in der sich e-e Federal R~ Bank befindet; ~ **currency** Reservewährung; ~ **for contingencies** Rückstellungen für Eventualverbindlichkeiten; ~ **for depletion** Rückstellung für Substanzverlust; ~ **for outstanding claims** *(VersR)* Rückstellung für schwebende Schadensfälle; ~ **for pension** Pensionsrückstellung; ~ **for sinking fund** Tilgungsrücklage; ~ **for taxation** Rückstellung für Steuern; ~ **for unearned premium** *(VersR)* Prämienüberhang *(Rückstellung für am Bilanztag noch nicht verdiente Prämie)*

reserve fund Reservefonds; Rücklage; **capital redemption** ~ *Br* Reservefonds zur Tilgung von Vorzugsaktien

reserve, ~ **liability** *Br*[61] Nachschußpflicht; ~ **maintained** Istreserve; ~ **part** Reserveteil, Ersatzteil; ~ **price** →reserve 2.; ~**s provided for by the articles of association** satzungsmäßige (od. statutarische) Rücklagen; ~ **ratio** Mindestreservesatz (s. legal →~ ratio); ~ **requirements** *Am* Mindestreserveanforderungen; ~ **stock** eiserner Bestand

reserve, building up of ~**s** Reservebildung; **capital** ~**s** Kapitalreserven; *(AktienR)* Rücklagen; **contingency** ~ Rückstellung für Eventualverbindlichkeiten; **creation of** ~**s** Reservenbildung; **depreciation** ~ Rückstellung für Wertminderung; **disclosed** ~**s** offene Rücklagen; **drawing on** ~**s** Rückgriff auf Reserven; **emergency** ~ Reserve für dringende Fälle; **excess (bank)** ~**s** *Am* Überschußreserven *(Einlagen der Mitgliedsbanken bei der Federal Reserve Bank über die Mindestreserven hinaus)*; **Federal R~ System (FRS)** *Am* Zentralbanksystem (→*federal*); **foreign exchange** ~ Devisenreserve; **free** ~**s** freie (od. freiwillige) Rücklagen; *Am* Guthaben der Mitgliedsbanken des FRS über die Mindestreserven hinaus; **general** ~**s** offene Rücklagen; **hidden** ~**s** stille Rücklagen; **latent** ~**s** stille Rücklagen; **legal** ~**s** gesetzliche Rücklagen; **legal (bank)** ~**s** gesetzliche Mindestreserven (s. *excess* →~*s*, s. *required* →~*s*); **legal** ~ **ratio** *Am (FRS)* gesetzlicher Mindestreservesatz; **loss** ~ *(VersR)* Schadensreserve; **pension** ~**s** Pensionsrückstellungen; **required (bank)** ~**s** *Am (von den Mitgliedsbanken des FRS)* geforderte Mindestreserven; **revenue** ~**s** *(für Dividendenzahlungen etc verfügbare)* freie Rücklagen; Gewinnrücklagen

reserves, secret ~ stille Rücklagen *(opp. visible* ~*)*; **creation of secret** ~[62] Schaffung stiller Rücklagen

reserve, statutory ~ statutarische (od. satzungsmäßige) Rücklage; **undisclosed** ~**s** stille Rücklagen; **unearned premium** ~ →premium 2.; **visible** ~**s** sichtbare (od. offene) Rücklagen; **voluntary** ~**s** freie Rücklagen

reserve, to accumulate ~**s** Reserven sammeln; **to allocate to the** ~**s** den Rücklagen zuführen; **to build up** (or **create**) ~**s** Reserven (od. Rücklagen) bilden; **to cancel** ~**s** *(IMF)* Reserven aus dem Verkehr ziehen *(IWF)*; **to draw on the** ~**s** die Reserven (od. Rücklagen) angreifen; **to maintain** ~**s** Reserven halten; **to transfer to the** ~ **fund** dem Reservefonds zuführen; **to put large sums to** ~ große Rücklagen machen

reserve 2. Vorbehalt; ~ **price** *(bes. bei Auktionen)* Vorbehaltspreis, Preislimit *(Mindestpreis, unter dem nicht verkauft werden kann)*; **under** ~ **(of)** vorbehaltlich; **under (the) usual** ~ unter dem üblichen Vorbehalt; **without** ~ ohne Vorbehalt; **to make a** ~ e-n Vorbehalt machen

reserve 3. *mil* Reserve *(opp. active)*; ~ **forces** *Br* Reservetruppen

reserve list, to be on the ~ der Reserve angehören

reserve, ~ **officer** Reserveoffizier; ~ **service** Reservedienst; **Army Emergeny R~** *Br* Heeresnotreserve; **Ready R~** *Am* Bereite Reserve

reserve, air force ~ Luftwaffenreserve; **army** ~ Heeresreserve; **Royal Naval** ~ *Br* Marinereserve

reserve *v* vorbehalten (to a p. jdm); sich vorbehalten (od. ausbedingen); reservieren; **to** ~ **one's decision** sich die Entscheidung vorbehalten; **to** ~ **judgment** die Urteilsverkündung aussetzen; **to** ~ **money for unforeseen contingencies** Geld für unvorhergesehene Ereignisse zurücklegen; **to** ~ **(a) part of the profit**

e-n Teil des Gewinnes zurücklegen; **to ~ a rent in a lease** sich in e-m Mietvertrag e-n bestimmten Mietzins ausbedingen; **to ~ (o.s.) the right** sich das Recht vorbehalten (to do or of doing); **to ~ a room** ein (Hotel-)Zimmer bestellen; **to ~ a seat** e-n Platz bestellen; **to ~ one's view** sich die Stellungnahme vorbehalten

reserved 1., **~ land** *Am* staatlicher Grundbesitz, der bestimmten Zwecken vorbehalten und unverkäuflich ist *(cf. reservation 1.)*; **~ list** *Br* Liste der Reserveoffiziere der Marine; **~ powers** *Am*[63] *(nicht in der Bundesverfassung erwähnte und daher)* den Einzelstaaten vorbehaltene Rechte *(z.B. police power)*; **~ seat** reservierter Platz; **~ seat ticket** (Bahn-)Platzkarte; **all rights ~** alle Rechte vorbehalten; Nachdruck verboten

reserved 2. *mil* unabkömmlich, u.k. (gestellt); **~ occupation** Unabkömmlichkeitsstellung (u.k.)

reserving, ~ the right vorbehaltlich des Rechts; **clause ~ errors** Irrtumsvorbehalt

resettle *v (jdn)* umsiedeln; *(Land)* wieder besiedeln

resettlement Umsiedlung; Neubesiedlung; Wiedereingliederung; **~ allowance** Umsiedlungsbeihilfe

resettlement fund[64] Wiedereingliederungsfonds *(des Europarates)*

Zweck des Fonds ist es, durch Darlehen oder Bürgschaften für Darlehen zur Lösung der sich aus Bevölkerungsüberschüssen für die europäischen Länder ergebenden Probleme beizutragen

resettlement, occupational ~ (Berufs-)Umschulung

resettler Umsiedler, Aussiedler

reship *v* wiederverladen; weiterversenden; als Rückfracht senden; *(von e-m Schiff auf ein anderes)* umladen

reshipment Wiederverladung, Weiterversendung; Umladung

reshuffle, Cabinet ~ *Br* Regierungsumbildung

reshuffle *v (Regierung)* umbilden; *(Unternehmen)* umgruppieren, umstrukturieren

reside *v (ständig)* wohnen, s-n Wohnsitz haben; ansässig sein, sich *(ständig)* aufhalten, Aufenthalt haben; *(Macht, Recht)* liegen (in bei); *(jdm)* zustehen

residing in Italy mit Wohnsitz in Italien

residence *(tatsächl.)* Wohnsitz, Wohnort *(cf. domicile)*; *(gewöhnl., nicht nur vorübergehender)* Aufenthalt(sort); Ansässigkeit; *Am* Steuer-Wohnsitz; *Br (herrschaftliches)* Wohnhaus; **~ allowance** *Am* Ortszuschlag, Wohngeld; **~ ban** Aufenthaltsverbot; **~ of a company (corporation)** (Verwaltungs-)Sitz e-r (Kapital-) Gesellschaft; **~ or principal place of business of the applicant** *(Europ. PatR)* Wohnsitz oder Geschäftssitz des Anmelders; **~ permit** Aufenthaltsgenehmigung *(für Ausländer)*; **~ requirement** *(DBA)* Wohnsitzvoraussetzung; **~ taxation** *(DBA)* Wohnsitzbesteuerung *(opp. source taxation)*; **change of ~** Wohnsitzverlegung; **family ~** Villa, Einfamilienhaus; **habitual ~** gewöhnlicher Aufenthaltsort; **→non(-)~**; **official ~** Amtssitz; Dienstwohnung; **ordinary ~** *Br* steuerlicher Wohnsitz; **permanent ~** *Am* unbegrenzte Aufenthaltsdauer

residence, place of ~ Wohnort, Aufenthaltsort; **second ~** Zweitwohnung; **state of ~** *(SteuerR)* Wohnsitzstaat

residence, to change one's ~ s-n Wohnsitz wechseln (od. verlegen); **to establish one's ~** s-n Wohnsitz begründen; **to take up one's ~** s-n Wohnsitz nehmen, sich niederlassen; **~ is required** es besteht Residenzpflicht (Pflicht, am Amtssitz zu wohnen)

residency Amtssitz, Residenz; *Am* Facharztausbildung

resident Person mit *(ständigem)* Wohnsitz (of in); ansässige Person; Ortsansässiger; Bewohner; Gebietsansässiger[65] *(früher: Deviseninländer)*; Steuerinländer; Insasse *(e-s Heims)*; *Am* Facharztvertreter *(Assistenzarzt, der in der Facharztausbildung steht)*; **R~** *Br* Resident, Regierungsvertreter; **→permanent ~**; **U.K. ~** in Großbritannien (und Nordirland) ansässige *(natürliche)* Person; **U.S. ~** in den USA (od. e-m Einzelstaat) ansässige *(natürliche)* Person

resident alien (im Inland) ansässiger Ausländer; *Am* Ausländer (Nichtamerikaner) mit ständigem Wohnsitz in den USA (der unbeschränkt steuerpflichtig ist); **non-~** im Ausland ansässiger Ausländer; *Am* nicht in den USA ansässiger Ausländer; Steuerausländer; **~ individuals** *Am* in den USA ansässige ausländische natürliche Personen

resident, ~ for tax purposes Steuerinländer; **R~-General** *Br* Generalresident; **~ of the Federal Republic** in der Bundesrepublik ansässige Person; **foreign ~** im Lande lebender Ausländer; **temporary ~** nur vorübergehend Ansässiger; **to be (a) ~ of a state** in e-m Staate ansässig sein; **to be bona fide ~ abroad** *Am* e-n echten Wohnsitz im Ausland haben

resident wohnhaft, (orts)ansässig; *Br (SteuerR)* in Großbritannien ansässig; **~ abroad** im Ausland wohnhaft; **U.K. ~ company** *Br* Gesellschaft mit (Geschäfts-)Sitz in Großbritannien (und Nordirland); **~ foreign corporation** *Am* ausländische Gesellschaft mit (Geschäfts-)Sitz in den Vereinigten Staaten; **~ magistrate** *(Nordirland)* Polizeirichter; **~ population**

Wohnbevölkerung *(opp. visitors, tourists etc.)*; ~ **taxpayer** inländischer (unbeschränkter) Steuerpflichtiger; Steuerinländer; →**non(-)** ~; **persons ordinarily** ~ **in ...** Personen mit gewöhnlichem Aufenthalt in ...; **to be (ordinarily)** ~ s-n Wohnsitz haben, ansässig sein; **to be** ~ **abroad** den Wohnsitz im Ausland haben; **to be** ~ **or established** s-n Wohn- od. Geschäftssitz haben

residential Wohn-; ~ **area** Wohngegend, Wohngebiet; ~ **construction** *Am* Wohnungsbau; ~ **customers** *Am* Haushaltungen *(Stromverbraucher)*; ~ **district** Wohngebiet, Wohnbezirk; ~ **estate** (or **property**) Wohngrundstück; Hausbesitz *(opp. commercial property)*; ~ **home for the elderly** Seniorenheim; ~ **qualification for voters** Wohnsitzerfordernis für Wähler; ~ **quarter** Wohnviertel, Wohnbezirk; **non-**~ **building** Nichtwohngebäude

residual Rest-; übrigbleibend; ~ **amount** Restbetrag; ~ **assets** Restvermögen(swert); Restmasse; ~ **claim** Restforderung; ~ **debt** Restschuld; ~ **estate** *Am* →residuary estate; ~ **powers** *Am* Gesetzgebungsbefugnisse der Einzelstaaten, die nicht dem Bund zugewiesen sind; ~ **product** Nebenprodukt; ~ **value** Rest(buch)wert

residuary restlich, übrig; ~ **beneficiary** (Testaments-)Erbe (od. Vermächtnisnehmer) des *(beweglichen und unbeweglichen)* Restnachlasses *(cf.* ~ *estate)*; ~ **bequest** letztwillige Zuwendung des beweglichen Restnachlasses; ~ **clause** Testamentsklausel, die über den Restnachlaß verfügt *(cf.* ~ *estate)*; ~ **devise** letztwillige Zuwendung des unbeweglichen Restnachlasses; ~ **devisee** (Testaments-)Erbe (od. Vermächtnisnehmer) des unbeweglichen Restnachlasses; ~ **estate**[66] Restnachlaß; der Teil des Nachlaßvermögens, der nach Bezahlung der Nachlaßschulden und Auszahlung aller besonderen Vermächtnisse übrigbleibt; *Br (auch)* der Teil des beweglichen Nachlasses, der in erster Linie für die Bezahlung der Schulden haftbar ist; ~ **gift** Vermächtnis des Vermögensrestes; (by will) Restvermächtnis; ~ **legacy** Restvermächtnis; letztwillige Zuwendung des beweglichen *(Am auch unbeweglichen)* Restnachlasses; ~ **legatee** (Testaments-) Erbe (od. Vermächtnisnehmer) des *(Br beweglichen)* Nachlasses (→*legatee*)

residue Rest, Reste, Restbetrag; restlicher Nachlaß *(das, was übrigbleibt von e-m testator's or intestate's estate nach Erfüllung aller Nachlaßverbindlichkeiten)*; ~**s** Rückstände

resign *v* verzichten auf; *(Amt, Forderung, Besitz etc)* aufgeben; *(Amt)* niederlegen; zurücktreten; ausscheiden; abdanken; **to** ~ **oneself to** sich abfinden mit; **to** ~ **an agency** e-e Vertretung niederlegen; **to** ~ **in a body** geschlossen zurücktreten; **to** ~ **from the Government** *Br* aus der Regierung ausscheiden; **to** ~ **a claim** auf e-e Forderung verzichten; **to** ~ **one's commission** *mil* s-n Abschied nehmen; **to** ~ **control of an estate** *Am* Nachlaßverwaltung abgeben; **to** ~ **membership** als Mitglied austreten (of aus); **to** ~ **(from office)** sein Amt niederlegen; aus dem Dienst ausscheiden; **to** ~ **one's position** s-e Stellung aufgeben, von s-m Posten zurücktreten; **the governor has** ~**ed** *Am* der Gouverneur ist zurückgetreten; **the minister has** ~**ed** *Br* der Minister ist zurückgetreten; **to** ~ **from the government** *Br* aus der Regierung ausscheiden

resignation Verzicht(leistung), Aufgabe, Amtsniederlegung; Rücktritt, Rücktrittsgesuch, Rücktrittserklärung; Ausscheiden *(aus dem Amt)*; *mil* Abdankung; Demission; ~ **of a benefice** *Br eccl* Aufgabe e-r Pfründe; ~ **of Cabinet** *Br* Rücktritt der Regierung; ~ **of one's rights** Verzicht auf s-e Rechte; **letter of** ~ Rücktrittsgesuch; *mil* Abschiedsgesuch; **to hand in** (or **tender**) **one's** ~ s-e Entlassung beantragen, sein Entlassungsgesuch einreichen; s-n Rücktritt anbieten (od. erklären); *mil* um s-n Abschied bitten

resignee jd, zu dessen Gunsten Verzicht geleistet wird

resigner Verzichtleistender

resins, artificial ~ (and plastic materials) Kunststoffe

resist *v* widerstehen, Widerstand leisten, sich widersetzen; **to** ~ **arrest** sich der Verhaftung widersetzen; **to** ~ **a claim** e-n Anspruch bestreiten; **to** ~ **a motion** e-n Antrag bekämpfen, Antragsgegner sein

resisting a constable *Br*[67] **(an officer** *Am***) in the execution of his duty** Widerstand gegen die Staatsgewalt

resistance Widerstand; Zurückhaltung *(beim Kauf)*; ~ **group** *pol* Widerstandsgruppe; ~ **movement** *pol* Widerstandsbewegung; ~ **to high prices** Käuferwiderstand; ~ **to wear and tear** Verschleißfestigkeit; **armed** ~ bewaffneter Widerstand; **attempt at** ~ Widerstandsversuch; **passive** ~ passiver Widerstand; **to meet with** ~ auf Widerstand stoßen; **to offer** ~ Widerstand leisten, sich widersetzen

resocialization Resozialisierung *(ehemaliger Strafgefangener)*

resocialize *v*, **to** ~ **prisoners** Gefangene resozialisieren (od. wiedereingliedern)

resolution 1. Beschluß, Entschließung; Resolution; ~ **of the majority** (or **majority** ~) Mehrheitsbeschluß; **adopting a** ~ Beschlußfassung; **competent to form a** ~ beschlußfähig; **draft** ~ Entschließungsentwurf; **passing a** ~ Annahme e-r Entschließung; Beschlußfassung

resolution 2. *(GesellschaftsR)* Beschluß(fassung); **corporate** ~ *Am* Beschluß der Hauptversammlung od. des →board of directors *(e-r AG);* **extraordinary** ~ *Br*[68] *(auf Hauptversammlung)* mit ¾ Mehrheit gefaßter Beschluß; **ordinary** ~ *Br*[68] *(auf Hauptversammlung)* mit einfacher Mehrheit gefaßter Beschluß; **special** ~ *Br*[68] *(auf Hauptversammlung)* Beschluß mit ¾ Mehrheit und besonderer Ankündigungsfrist *(21 Tage)*

resolution 3. *Br (KonkursR)* Beschluß der Gläubiger; **ordinary** ~ Beschluß der Mehrheit der *(persönlich od. durch Vertreter)* abstimmenden Gläubiger; **special** ~ Sonderbeschluß; Beschluß der Mehrheit der *(persönlich od. durch Vertreter)* abstimmenden Gläubiger, wenn deren Forderungen mindestens ¾ des Gesamtbetrages der in der Abstimmung vertretenen Forderungen erreichen

resolution 4. *parl* Resolution, Entschließung; **concurrent** (or **joint**) ~ *Am* gemeinsame Resolution *(des Senates und Repräsentantenhauses; joint ~ bedarf im Ggs. zu concurrent ~ zur Erlangung der Gesetzeskraft der Genehmigung des Präsidenten)*

resolution (1.-4.), **to adopt a** ~ e-n Beschluß fassen; e-e Entschließung annehmen; **to carry a** ~ e-n Beschluß *(in e-r Versammlung)* durchbringen; **to move a** ~ **at a meeting** e-e Resolution in e-r Versammlung einbringen (od. beantragen); **to pass a** ~ s. to adopt a →~; **to propose a** ~ e-e Entschließung einbringen; **to put a** ~ **to a meeting** e-e Entschließung zur Abstimmung bringen, über e-e Entschließung abstimmen lassen; **the** ~ **passed at the general meeting** der in der Hauptversammlung gefaßte Beschluß; **the** ~ **was passed unanimously** der Beschluß wurde einstimmig angenommen

resolutive (or **resolutory**) **condition** auflösende Bedingung

resolve *v* beschließen; sich entschließen; entscheiden; **to** ~ **a contract** e-n Vertrag *(ex nunc)* aufheben; **to** ~ **a matter** e-e Angelegenheit entscheiden; **the House** ~**s itself into a Committee** *Br parl* →Committee 2.; **the court** ~**d the issue against the defendant** *Am* das Gericht entschied gegen den Beklagten

resolved beschlossen; entschlossen, in dem Entschluß; ~ **that** *(auch parl)* es wurde beschlossen, daß

resort Zuflucht, Ausweg; *(allgemein)* besuchter Ort; Ferienort; ~ **to a court** Anrufung e-s Gerichts; ~ **to force** *(VölkerR)* Anwendung von Gewalt; ~ **to regional agencies** Inanspruchnahme regionaler Einrichtungen; **as a last** ~ als letzter Ausweg; **court of last** ~ Gericht letzter Instanz; **health** ~ Badeort, Kurort; **seaside** ~ Seebad; **to have** ~ **to** zurückgreifen auf

resort *v* regelmäßig aufsuchen (od. besuchen); **to** ~ **(to)** Zuflucht nehmen (zu), zurückgreifen (auf); **to** ~ **to arbitration** schiedsrichterliche Entscheidung in Anspruch nehmen; **to** ~ **to a court** ein Gericht anrufen, sich an ein Gericht wenden; **to** ~ **to force** Gewalt anwenden; **to** ~ **to a fund** auf e-n Fonds zurückgreifen; **to** ~ **to litigation** die Gerichte anrufen (od. in Anspruch nehmen)

resource Hilfsquelle; Zuflucht; ~**s** Ressourcen, *(wirtschaftl.)* Hilfsquellen, (Hilfs-)Mittel; (Geld-)Mittel; *(ungenutzte)* Naturschätze, Rohstoffquellen

Resource Conservation and Recovery Act of 1980 (RCRA) *Am (Umweltschutz)* Abfallbeseitigungsgesetz

Das Gesetz hat Lagerung und Transport von Abfällen nur auf dem Lande zum Gegenstand (→*Superfund*)

resources of the high seas, Convention on Fishing and Conservation of the Living R~ of the High Seas *(VölkerR) (auf der Internationalen Seerechtskonferenz in Genf abgeschlossene)* Konvention über Fischerei und Erhaltung von Naturschätzen in der hohen See *(Schonung der Fischbestände)*

resource, adequacy of ~**s** Zulänglichkeit von (Hilfs-, Geld-)Mitteln; **covering** ~**s** Dekkungsmittel; **creation of new** ~**s** Schaffung neuer Hilfsquellen; **credit** ~**s** Kreditquellen; **development of economic** ~**s** Erschließung der wirtschaftlichen Hilfsquellen; **financial** ~**s** finanzielle Mittel

resources, conservation of the fishing (or **fishery**) ~ Erhaltung der Fischbestände

resources, human ~ Arbeitskräftepotential; **liquid** ~ flüssige (Geld-)Mittel; **mineral** ~ mineralische Rohstoffe *(Erze, Kohle, Erdöl etc);* Bodenschätze; **national** ~ Reichtum (od. Schätze) des Landes *(Br e.g. North Sea oil; skilled labour)*

resources, natural ~ Naturschätze; **natural** ~ **royalties** Vergütungen für die Ausbeutung von Naturschätzen; **extraction of natural** ~ Ausbeutung von Bodenschätzen

resources, own ~ eigene Mittel, Eigenmittel; **out of one's own** ~ aus eigenen Mitteln

resources, real ~ *(Volkswirtschaft)* Güter- und Dienstleistungen; **utilization of the** ~ **of the oceans** Ausbeutung der Meeresschätze; **to open up new** ~ neue Hilfsquellen erschließen

respect Respekt, Achtung; Bezug, Hinsicht; **in all** ~**s** in jeder Hinsicht; **in this** ~ in dieser Hinsicht; **in** ~ **of** (or **with** ~ **to**) mit Bezug auf, bezüglich

respects Grüße, Empfehlungen; **to pay one's ~ to a p.** sich jdm empfehlen; **to pay one's final** (or **last**) **~ to a p.** jdm die letzte Ehre erweisen

respect *v* respektieren, achten; berücksichtigen; betreffen, sich beziehen auf; **to ~ a contract clause** e-e Vertragsklausel beachten

respected angesehen

respecting hinsichtlich, betreffend; **legislation ~ property** Gesetzgebung, die das Eigentum betrifft

respective bezüglich, betreffend; jeweilig; **~ly** beziehungsweise (bzw.)

respite Aufschub; Zahlungsaufschub, Stundung; **~ (of execution)** Aussetzung der Vollstreckung e-s (Todes-)Urteils; **to grant a ~** die Vollstreckung e-s (Todes-)Urteils aussetzen; **to grant a ~ (for payment) of a debt** die Zahlung von Schulden stunden

respite *v* Aufschub gewähren; Zahlungsfrist gewähren, stunden; Vollstreckung e-s Todesurteils aussetzen

respond *v* antworten; reagieren (to auf); *Am* haftbar sein, einstehen (to für); **to ~ in damages** *Am* schadensersatzpflichtig sein

respondeat superior ("let the superior be held responsible") Deliktshaftung des Arbeitgebers (master) für den Arbeitnehmer (servant), sowie des Auftraggebers (principal) für den Beauftragten (agent) für die in Ausführung der übertragenen Verrichtungen begangenen →torts *(→vicarious liability)*

respondent Beklagter *(in bestimmten Verfahren, bes. Ehescheidungssachen [opp. petitioner] od. Br in e-m Kartellverfahren; Am in equity- und admiralty-Verfahren);* Antragsgegner, Berufungsbeklagter; *(Meinungsforschung)* Befragter; Auskunftsperson; **co-~** mitbeklagter Ehebrecher

respondentia Bodmerei auf die Schiffsladung *(cf. bottomry);* →**loan on ~**

response Antwort; Reaktion (to auf); **flexible ~** *mil (dem jeweiligen Fall angepaßte und abgestufte)* elastische Abwehr, abgestufte Vergeltung

responsibility Verantwortung, Verantwortlichkeit; *(StrafR)*[69] Zurechnungsfähigkeit; Haftung, Haftbarkeit, Haftpflicht; **~ for an accident** Schuld an e-m Unfall; →**abdication of ~; criminal ~** strafrechtliche Verantwortlichkeit; Zurechnungsfähigkeit; **denial of ~** Ablehnung der Verantwortung

responsibility, diminished ~ *(StrafR)* verminderte Zurechnungsfähigkeit *(Br[70] führt zur Verurteilung wegen manslaughter anstelle von murder);* **person suffering from diminished ~** vermindert Zurechnungsfähiger

responsibility, discharge of one's ~ies Wahrnehmung von Aufgaben; **disclaimer of ~** s. denial of →~; **global ~ies** Verantwortlichkeit der Welt gegenüber; **limited ~ for torts** beschränkte Deliktfähigkeit; **on one's own ~** auf eigene Verantwortung; **to assume ~** die Verantwortung übernehmen (od. auf sich nehmen); **to bear ~** Verantwortung tragen; **to decline** (or **deny**) **all ~** jede Verantwortung ablehnen; **to discharge the directors from their ~ies** die Direktoren entlasten; **to disclaim ~** die Verantwortung ablehnen; **to incur ~** Verantwortung übernehmen; **to incur criminal ~** sich strafbar machen; **to involve ~** Verantwortung ablehnen; **to relieve a p. of his ~ies** jdn s-r Verantwortung entheben; **to take ~** s. to assume →~; **to withdraw from a ~** sich e-r Verantwortung entziehen; **the ~ lies** (or **rests**) **with** die Verantwortung liegt bei

responsible verantwortlich; haftbar, haftpflichtig; verantwortungsvoll; verantwortungsbewußt; **~ government** *Br* (Grundsatz der) Verantwortlichkeit der Regierung dem Parlament gegenüber; **~ partner** persönlich haftender Teilhaber; **~ position** verantwortungsvolle Stellung; Vertrauensposten; **to be ~ for** einzustehen haben für, zu verantworten haben; haften für; **to be ~ for an accident** an e-m Unfall Schuld haben; **to be ~ for maintenance** unterhaltspflichtig sein; **to hold ~** verantwortlich machen; **to make o.s. ~** die Verantwortung übernehmen, verantwortlich zeichnen (for für)

rest 1. Rest; Saldo; Rechnungsabschluß; Kontenabschluß; **~ capital** *Br* Reservefonds *(bes. der Bank von England);* **the date of the ~ of the current account** das Datum des Saldos des laufenden Kontos; **half yearly ~s** Halbjahresabschlüsse

rest 2. Ruhe; **~ home** Erholungsheim; **~ pause** Erholungspause

rest *v* ruhen; **to ~ (up)on** beruhen auf, sich stützen auf; **to ~ with sb.** bei jdm liegen, in jds Händen liegen; **to ~ (one's case)** *Am (ProzeßR)* erklären *(Erklärung e-r Partei),* daß die eigene Beweisführung abgeschlossen ist; **to let a matter ~** e-e Sache auf sich beruhen lassen

restate *v* neu darstellen, neu formulieren

restatement Neudarstellung, Neuformulierung

Restatement (of American Law) *(vom American Law Institute herausgegebene, nicht amtl.)* systematische Darstellung der Grundsätze des in den Einzelstaaten geltenden case law zur Förderung e-r Rechtsangleichung zwischen den Einzelstaaten

Jedes Sachgebiet[71] (z. B. Restatement of Torts, Restatement of Contracts) wurde getrennt von namhaften Sachverständigen bearbeitet und in Form einer Kodifikation mit Anmerkungen veröffentlicht. Manche Gebiete liegen bereits in zweiter Bearbeitung vor (z. B. Restatement 2nd of Agency)

restaurant Restaurant, Gaststätte, Lokal; ~ **car** Speisewagen; ~ **keeper** Gastwirt; **hotel and ~ business** Gaststättengewerbe; **to operate** *Am* (**to run** *Br*) **a** ~ ein Restaurant betreiben

restimulation of the economy Wiederankurbelung der Wirtschaft

restitutio in integrum ("restoration to the original position") Wiedereinsetzung in den vorigen Stand *(durch die e-n eingetretenen Rechtserfolg wieder aufhebende gerichtl. Verfügung);* Wiederherstellung des ursprünglichen Zustands

restitution Rückerstattung, Rückgabe, Herausgabe *(unrechtmäßig angeeigneten fremden Eigentums);* Wiederherstellung e-s früheren Rechtszustandes *(bes. nach Aufdeckung e-s Diebstahls, nach Anfechtung e-s auf e-m Willensmangel beruhenden Vertrages oder nach e-m erfolgreichen Berufungsurteil für den Unterlegenen der 1. Instanz; cf. rescission);* ~ **of a life insurance contract** Wiederherstellung e-r Lebensversicherung; ~ **of minors** *Scot* Wiedereinsetzung in Rechte, die durch während der Minderjährigkeit rechtsgültig ausgefertigte Urkunden verlorengingen; ~ **of possession** Wiedereinräumung des Besitzes; ~ **of property** Rückerstattung von *(unrechtmäßig angeeignetem)* Vermögen; ~ **order** *Br* gerichtl. Verfügung auf Herausgabe gestohlener Gegenstände an den Eigentümer; **writ of** ~ *(besondere)* gerichtl. Entscheidung, durch die zugunsten des obsiegenden Berufungsklägers der vor dem erstinstanzlichen Urteil bestehende Zustand wiederhergestellt wird; **liable to make** ~ rückerstattungspflichtig; **to be subject to** ~ der Rückerstattung unterliegen; **to make** ~ **(of)** wiederherstellen; rückerstatten; **to make** ~ **of the goods** die Ware zurückgeben

restock *v (Lager)* wieder auffüllen; den Vorrat ergänzen; wiederversorgen

restoration Rückgabe, Herausgabe, Rückerstattung; Wiederherstellung; Wiedereinsetzung (to in); Restaurierung; ~ **of a building** Wiederinstandsetzung (od. Restaurierung) e-s Gebäudes; ~ **of full employment** Wiederherstellung der Vollbeschäftigung; ~ **of lapsed patents** Wiederherstellung verfallener Patente; ~ **of order** Wiederherstellung der (öffentl.) Ordnung; ~ **of peace** Wiederherstellung des Friedens; Befriedung; ~ **of possession** Wiedereinräumung des Besitzes; ~ **to one's original position** Wiedereinsetzung in den vorigen Stand

restore *v* zurückgeben, rückerstatten; *(etw.)* wiederherstellen; *(jdn)* wiedereinsetzen (to in); *(Gebäude)* restaurieren, wiederinstandsetzen; **to** ~ **the equilibrium** das Gleichgewicht wiederherstellen; **to** ~ **to a level** wieder auf e-n Stand zurückbringen; **to** ~ **order** die (öffentl.) Ordnung wiederherstellen; **to** ~ **to full pay** *mil (Offizier)* reaktivieren; **to** ~ **a p. to his original position** jdn wieder in den vorigen Stand setzen; **to** ~ **peace** den Frieden wiederherstellen; **to** ~ **to possession** wieder in den Besitz setzen; **to** ~ **a text** e-n Text rekonstruieren

restow *v*, **to** ~ **the cargo** die Ladung neu verstauen

restrain *v* beschränken; hindern (from an); zurückhalten (from doing sth. etw. zu tun); **to** ~ **production** die Produktion drosseln; **to** ~ **trade** den Handel (od. Geschäftsverkehr) beschränken (→*restraint of trade*); **action to** ~ **interference** Klage auf Unterlassung der Störung; **injunction to** ~ **future infringement** *(PatR)* einstweilige Verfügung, weitere Patentverletzung zu unterlassen

restraining order *Am* richterl. Verbot; einstweilige Verfügung; *Br* Verfügung, durch die die Bank of England oder e-e Aktiengesellschaft an der Umschreibung von Aktien in ihren Büchern gehindert wird

restraining, agreements ~ **trade** Vereinbarungen, die den Wettbewerb beschränken

restraint Beschränkung, Einschränkung; Verhinderung; Zurückhaltung; **(voluntary)** ~ **agreement** Selbstbeschränkungsabkommen

restraint of competition Wettbewerbsbeschränkung; **agreement in** ~ wettbewerbsbeschränkende Vereinbarung *(s. horizontal, vertical →restraints)*

restraint of marriage, condition in ~ Bedingung *(in e-m Vertrag od. Testament),* durch die jds Eheschließung od. freie Gattenwahl ausgeschlossen werden soll

restraint(s) of princes (or rulers)[72] Verfügungen von hoher Hand

(Seevers. und Kriegsrisikopolice) Ausschluß der Haftung des Reeders für Verluste, die durch inländische od. ausländische Hoheitsakte (acts of government) entstanden sind

restraint of trade Wettbewerbsbeschränkung, wettbewerbsbeschränkendes Verhalten; **agreement in** ~ wettbewerbsbeschränkende Absprache; **combination in** ~ Zusammenschluß zur Beeinflussung des Handels; Kartell; **covenant in** ~ Konkurrenzklausel; **practices in** ~ →restrictive (trade) practices

Vertragliche Wettbewerbsbeschränkungen jeder Art sind grundsätzlich unzulässig.

Br Eine Wettbewerbsbeschränkung ist aber zulässig, wenn sie den vernünftigen Interessen der Parteien entspricht und der Gesamtheit nicht schadet. (Jede Art von restraint of trade wird daran gemessen, ob sie →reasonable ist; per se nichtige restraints, wie in den USA, gibt es nicht.) Für die Entscheidung ist ein besonderer Gerichtshof, der Restrictive Practices Court, zuständig.

Am Sec. 1 des Sherman Act erklärt als ungesetzlich

und strafbar „jede Vereinbarung, jeden Zusammenschluß in Form e-s Trusts od. in anderer Form, sowie jedes Zusammenwirken durch abgestimmtes Handeln *zur Beschränkung der wirtschaftlichen Betätigung* zwischen den Einzelstaaten oder mit anderen Ländern."[73] Nach der →Rule of Reason sind nur solche Maßnahmen als verbotene Beschränkung der Freiheit des Handels anzusehen, die den Wettbewerb in unvernünftiger Weise (unreasonably) beschränken. Im Ggs. zum englischen Recht kommt es nicht darauf an, ob ein Schaden für die Gesamtheit tatsächlich erwächst, sondern es genügt für die Ungültigkeitserklärung einer Vereinbarung in restraint of trade die Marktbeherrschungsabsicht

restraint on alienation Veräußerungsverbot

restraint, felonious ~ *Am*[74] *(StrafR)* bösartige Beschränkung der Handlungsfreiheit; **horizontal ~s** horizontale Wettbewerbsbeschränkungen *(Absprachen zwischen Beteiligten der gleichen Wirtschaftsstufe)*; **legal~(s)** Beschränkungen durch Gesetze; **vertical ~s** vertikale Wettbewerbsbeschränkungen *(Absprachen zwischen Beteiligten verschiedener Wirtschaftsstufen)*; **voluntary ~ agreement** Selbstbeschränkungsabkommen; **voluntary ~ of exports** Selbstbeschränkung bei Ausfuhren

restrict *v* beschränken, einschränken; *Am* Baubeschränkungen machen *(cf. zoning laws)*; **to ~ o.s.** sich beschränken (to auf); **to ~ one's expenses** s-e Ausgaben beschränken; **to ~ production** die Produktion drosseln

restricted beschränkt, eingeschränkt; nur für den Dienstgebrauch; ~ **application** begrenzte Anwendung; ~ **area** *mil* Sperrgebiet; *Am* Stadtteil mit Geschwindigkeitsbegrenzung

restricted data *Am* unter Geheimnisschutz stehende Angaben *(deren Preisgabe mit Strafe bedroht ist; z.B. Atominformationen)*; **to declassify** ~ *Am* Geheimmaterial freigeben

restricted, ~ district *Am* Stadtbezirk, in dem Baubeschränkungen bestehen *(cf. zoning laws)*; ~ **lands** *Am* Grundbesitz, dessen Verkauf Beschränkungen unterliegt *(z.B. zum Schutze der Indianer)*; ~ **(matter)** *Am* nur für den Dienstgebrauch; *mil* Verschlußsache; ~ **ownership** beschränktes Eigentum (→*ownership*)

restriction Beschränkung, Einschränkung; Restriktion; *Am* Baubeschränkung *(cf. zoning laws)*; *Br*[75] Vormerkung in das Land Register *(welche gewisse Eintragungen von Zustimmungserklärungen Dritter [z.B. trustees] abhängig macht oder die Auszahlung von Geldern an bestimmte Personen vorschreibt)*; *Am (AntitrustR)* Beschränkung *(in der Belieferung bestimmter Arten von Abnehmern;* s. *customer →~, territorial →~)*; einschränkende Bestimmungen *(bes. seitens der Regierung)*; ~ **of credit** s. credit →~; ~ **of production** Beschränkung der Produktion; ~ **on cultivation** Anbaubeschränkung; **~s on exportation** Ausfuhrbeschränkungen; **~s on importation** Einfuhrbeschränkungen; ~ **on trade** Handelsbeschränkung; **abolition of ~s** Aufhebung von Beschränkungen; **credit ~** Krediteinschränkung, Kreditrestriktion; **currency ~** Devisenbewirtschaftung; **customer ~** *Am (AntitrustR)* Kundenbeschränkung *(Verpflichtung des Alleinhändlers, bestimmte Kategorien von Abnehmern [Großabnehmer, öffentl. Hand etc] nicht od. nur mit Zustimmung s-s Lieferanten zu beliefern)*; **effect of ~s** Auswirkung von Beschränkungen; **government ~s** einschränkende Bestimmungen durch die Regierung; **quantitative ~s** mengenmäßige (Einfuhr-)Beschränkungen; **removal of ~s** Aufhebung von Beschränkungen; **territorial ~** *Am (AntitrustR)* Gebietsbeschränkung *(Verpflichtung des Alleinhändlers, außerhalb s-s Vertriebsgebietes ansässige Abnehmer nicht od. nur mit Zustimmung s-s Lieferanten zu beliefern)*; **to be subject to ~s** Beschränkungen unterliegen; **to impose ~s** (on) Beschränkungen auferlegen; **to institute ~s** Beschränkungen einführen; **to lift** (or **remove**) **~s** Beschränkungen aufheben (od. beseitigen)

restrictive restriktiv, beschränkend, einschränkend, einengend; ~ **agreement** *(KartellR)* beschränkende Absprache *(unter Unternehmern)*; ~ **business practices** restriktive Geschäftspraktiken *(→restricitve practices)*; ~ **condition** einschränkende Bedingung; ~**→covenant;** ~ **covenant insurance** Versicherung gegen Baubeschränkungen; ~ **credit policy** restriktive Kreditpolitik, Kreditdrosselungspolitik

restrictive endorsement einschränkendes Indossament; Rektaindossament

Br zur Wirkung s. Bill of Exchange Act 1882, s. 35 (1). *Am* Wirkung der Einschränkung, etwa "Pay A only", lange Zeit streitig. Klarstellung durch UCC, sec. 3–206 (1): Sie verhindert sowohl bei Wechseln als auch bei Schecks weder die Abtretung noch die Übertragung durch Indossament

restrictive, ~ injunction Verbotsverfügung; ~ **interpretation** restriktive (od. einschränkende) Auslegung *(opp. liberal interpretation)*

restrictive practices wettbewerbsbeschränkende Verhaltensweisen (od. Geschäftspraktiken), Wettbewerbsbeschränkungen; Kartelle; *Br* unwirtschaftliche Arbeitspraktiken, die wegen des Widerstandes der Beteiligten *(Gewerkschaften oder Betriebsführung)* schwer zu ändern sind *(z.B. unnötige Überstunden)*; ~ **agreement** Kartellvertrag; **ban on ~s** Kartellverbot

Restrictive Practices Court (R. P. C.) *Br* Gericht für Wettbewerbsbeschränkungen; Kartellgericht

Aus Berufs- und Laienrichtern zusammengesetztes Gericht, das wettbewerbeschränkende Absprachen, die gegen das öffentliche Interesse verstoßen, für nichtig erklären kann

Restrictive Practices Court Act 1976 Gesetz

über das Gericht für Wettbewerbsbeschränkungen (Kartellgericht) *(→Resale Prices Act 1976)*

restrictive trade practices wettbewerbsbeschränkende Geschäftspraktiken

Restrictive Trade Practices Act 1976 (R. T. P. A.) *Br*[76] Gesetz gegen Wettbewerbsbeschränkungen (Kartellgesetz) *(→Resale Prices Act 1976)*

restrictive trading agreement *Br* wettbewerbsbeschränkende Absprache

restrictively, to construe (or **interpret**) ~ einschränkend (od. eng) auslegen

restructure *v*, **to ~ a credit** e-n Kredit umschulden; **to ~ an enterprise** ein Unternehmen umstrukturieren (od. sanieren)

resubmission Wiedervorlage

resubmit *v* wieder vorlegen

result Ergebnis, Resultat; Folge, **~s** *(Bilanz)* Jahresergebnis; **~ crime** Erfolgsdelikt; **~ from ordinary activities** Ergebnis der gewöhnlichen Geschäftstätigkeit; **~ of evidence** Beweisergebnis; **~s of the group** Ertragslage des Konzerns; **~ of investigation** Untersuchungsergebnis; **~s of operations** Betriebsergebnis; **~s of the war** Kriegsfolgen; Auswirkungen des Krieges; **assessment of ~s** Ergebnisbeurteilung; **election ~** Wahlergebnis; **examination ~** Prüfungsergebnis; **final ~** Endergebnis; **total ~** Gesamtergebnis; **very close ~** sehr knappes Ergebnis; **a satisfactory ~ was achieved** ein zufriedenstellendes Ergebnis wurde erzielt; **to announce the election ~** das Wahlergebnis bekanntgeben; **to challenge an election ~** ein Wahlergebnis anfechten; **to show good ~s** gute Ergebnisse aufweisen

result *v* sich ergeben, hervorgehen (from aus), herrühren (from von); *(an den ursprüngl. Eigentümer)* zurückfallen *(cf. ~ing →trust)*; **to ~ in** zur Folge haben, hinauslaufen auf; **to ~ in a loss (profit)** e-n Verlust (Gewinn) ergeben, mit Verlust (Gewinn) abschließen

resulting, ~ powers *Am (StaatsR) (aus der Rechtsnatur abzuleitende, nicht auf einzelne Verfassungsbestimmungen gestützte)* resultierende Rechte; **~ →trust**

resume *v (Arbeit, Zahlungen etc)* wiederaufnehmen; *(Namen)* wiederannehmen *(cf. maiden name)*; *(Sitz)* wiedereinnehmen; resümieren, zusammenfassen; **to ~ one's duties** s-e Pflichten wiederaufnehmen; **to ~ diplomatic relations** diplomatische Beziehungen wiederaufnehmen; **to ~ negotiations** Verhandlungen wiederaufnehmen; **to ~ possession** (of) *(Grundbesitz)* wieder in Besitz nehmen *(Br bes. durch →letters patent übertragenes →crown land; der Eigentümer hat das Recht, die Erneuerung des Miet- [oder Pacht-] Vertrages abzulehnen, wenn er den Grundbesitz wieder in Besitz nimmt)*; **to ~ (the) proceedings** das Verfahren wiederaufnehmen

résumé *Fr* Resümee, Zusammenfassung

resummons erneute Ladung

resumption Wiederaufnahme; Wiederannahme; Wiederinbesitznahme; Zurücknahme *(e-r Bewilligung)*; **~ of business** Wiederaufnahme der Geschäftstätigkeit; **~ of dividends** Wiederaufnahme der Dividendenzahlungen; **~ of nationality** Wiederannahme der Staatsangehörigkeit; **~ of negotiations** Wiederaufnahme der Verhandlungen; **~ of payments** Wiederaufnahme der Zahlungen; **~ of possession** Wiederinbesitznahme *(von Grundbesitz; cf. to resume possession)*; **~ of a trial** Wiederaufnahme des Verfahrens; **~ of work** Wiederaufnahme der Arbeit

resurgence of nationalism Wiederaufleben des Nationalismus

resurrectionism Leichenraub

resurrectionist Leichenräuber

retail Einzelhandel *(opp. wholesale)*; **~ advertising** Einzelhandelswerbung, Ladenwerbung; **~ association →~ group**; **~ banking** *Am* Einzelkundengeschäft der Banken; **~ business** Einzelhandel(sgeschäft); **~ chain** *Am* Einzelhandelskette; **~ co-operative society** *Br* Konsumgenossenschaft; **~ credit** *Am* Kundenkredit; **~ (credit) card** *Am* Kundenkreditkarte; **~ dealer** Einzelhändler *(opp. wholesale dealer)*; **~ dealing** Einzelhandel; **~ discount** Einzelhändlerrabatt; **~ establishment** Einzelhandelsbetrieb; **~ firm** Einzelhandelsfirma; **~ group** *Am* Einzelhändlervereinigung

retail price Einzelhandelspreis; Ladenpreis; **~ index** Einzelhandelspreisindex; **R~ P~ Index** (RPI) *Br* Preisindex für die Lebenshaltung *(→Index of Retail Prices)*; **~ maintenance** Preisbindung der zweiten Hand

retail sales Einzelhandelsverkäufe; **~ tax** *Am (einzelstaatl., z.B. in New York)* Einzelhandelsumsatzsteuer

retail, ~ shop (or **store**) Einzelhandelsgeschäft; **~ trade** Einzelhandel; **~ trader** Einzelhändler *(opp. wholesale trader)*; **~ trading** Einzelhandel

retail, (*Br* **by**, *Am* **at**) ~ im kleinen, im Einzelhandel *(opp. [by or at] wholesale)*; **to buy (sell)** (*Br* **by** or *Am* **at**) ~ *(Waren)* in kleinen Mengen (od. im Einzelhandel) kaufen (verkaufen)

retail *v* im Einzelhandel verkaufen; im Einzelhandel verkauft werden; **the book ~s at** (or **for**) £2 das Buch kostet im Einzelhandel £2

retailer Einzelhändler *(opp. wholesaler)*; **~ cooperative** *Am* Einzelhändler-Einkaufsgenossenschaft; **~'s excise** *Am* (Bundes-)Einzelhandels-Umsatzsteuer *(cf. manufacturer's excise)*

retain *v* zurück(be)halten, einbehalten; beibehalten; sich vorbehalten; *(Plätze)* belegen; *com* thesaurieren; **to ~ an attorney** *Am* (**barrister** or **solicitor** *Br*) e-n Anwalt *(durch Zahlung e-s Vorschusses [retainer od. retaining fee])* verpflichten; e-n Anwalt nehmen; **to ~ books** Handelsbücher aufbewahren; **to ~ one's citizenship** *Am* (**nationality** *Br*) s-e Staatsangehörigkeit beibehalten; **to ~ files** *bes. Am* Akten aufbewahren; **to ~ one's position** s-e Stellung behalten; **to ~ possession** (of) in Besitz behalten; **to ~ a right** sich ein Recht vorbehalten

retained earnings (or **income**) *Am (Bilanz)* thesaurierter Gewinn; *(AktienR)* Gewinnrücklagen *(cf. earned surplus, →surplus 2.)*; **~ statement** *Am* Aufstellung des unverteilten Reingewinns; **legally ~** gesetzliche Rücklagen; **transfer to ~** *Am (AktienR)* Rücklagenzuweisung; **unrestricted ~** freie Rücklagen

retained, ~ premium *(Rückvers.)* Eigenbehaltsprämie: **~ profits** einbehaltene (nicht ausgeschüttete) Gewinne; Gewinnvortrag

retaining fee Anwaltsvorschuß

retaining lien Zurückbehaltungsrecht; **attorney's** *Am* (**solicitor's** *Br*) **~** Zurückbehaltungsrecht des Anwalts (*an Akten, Urkunden, Geld etc. bis zur Bezahlung seines Honorars*)

retainer 1. Verpflichtung e-s Anwalts *(durch Zahlung e-s Vorschusses)*; *(etwa)* Anwaltsbestellung (Vereinbarung zwischen Klienten und Anwalt [Br solicitor, Am attorney]); Mandat; *Br (auch)* Vereinbarung zwischen solicitor und counsel (barrister); Anwaltsvorschuß, vorläufiges Anwaltshonorar; **general ~** allgemeine Anwaltsbestellung *(für jeden möglichen Fall)*; Pauschalhonorar; **special ~** Anwaltsbestellung für e-n besonderen Zweck; Sonderhonorar

Br Solicitors übernehmen im allgemeinen ein Mandat ohne Prozeßvollmacht oder eine schriftliche Vereinbarung, bes. bei kleineren Sachen

retainer 2., **~ (of debts)**[77] Vorwegbefriedigungsrecht des Erbschaftsverwalters (personal representative)

Recht des executor od. administrator, sich aus dem in seinen Besitz gelangten Nachlaß wegen eigener ihm gegen den Erblasser zustehenden Forderungen zu befriedigen (aber erst nach Befriedigung einer bevorrechtigten Konkursforderung). *Br* Das Recht ist in Großbritannien beseitigt worden durch den Administration of Estates Act 1971, s. 10

retaliate *v (auch VölkerR)* Vergeltung üben, zu Vergeltungsmaßnahmen greifen

retaliation *(auch VölkerR)* Vergeltung, Vergeltungsmaßnahme; **in ~ for** als Vergeltung für; **to exercise (measures of) ~** Vergeltungsmaßnahmen ergreifen; **to suffer ~** Vergeltungsmaßnahmen hinnehmen

retaliatory, ~ duty Retorsionszoll, Kampfzoll; **~ forces** *mil* Schwerstreitkräfte *(mit hohem atomarem Wirkungsgrad)*; **~ measures** Vergeltungsmaßnahmen, Repressalien; **~ strike** *mil* Vergeltungsschlag; **~ tariff** Vergeltungszoll, Retorsionszoll; **to take ~ action** (or **to adopt ~ measures**) zu Vergeltungsmaßnahmen (od. Repressalien) greifen, Vergeltungsmaßnahmen ergreifen

retard *v* verzögern; **mentally ~ed child** geistig zurückgebliebenes Kind

retention Zurück(be)haltung, Einbehaltung; Beibehaltung; *(VersR)* Selbstbehalt, Eigenbehalt; *Scot* →lien; **~ in office** Belassung im Dienst; **~ manual** *Am* Handbuch über Aufbewahrungspflichten; **~ of an amount** Einbehaltung e-s Betrages; **~ of earnings** Gewinnthesaurierung *(e-s Unternehmens)*; Selbstfinanzierung; **~ of files** Aufbewahrung von Akten; **(declaration of) ~ of nationality** (Erklärung der) Beibehaltung der Staatsangehörigkeit; **~ of ownership** (or **title**) Eigentumsvorbehalt; **~ of wages** Einbehalten vom Lohn; **~ period** Aufbewahrungsfrist; **one copy for your ~** ein Exemplar zum dortigen Verbleib; **right of ~** Zurückbehaltungsrecht

retire *v* 1. zurücktreten; sich zurückziehen; ausscheiden; austreten; sich pensionieren lassen, in Pension gehen, in den Ruhestand treten; pensionieren, in den Ruhestand versetzen; *mil* verabschieden; **to ~ from an association** aus e-m Verband (od. Verein) austreten; **to ~ from business** sich vom Geschäft zurückziehen, aus dem Geschäft ausscheiden; sich zur Ruhe setzen; **to ~ from a firm** aus e-r Firma ausscheiden; **to ~ from office** →office 1.; **to ~ from a partnership** als Gesellschafter (od. Teilhaber) ausscheiden; **to ~ from service** aus dem Dienst ausscheiden; **to ~ from work** in den Ruhestand treten; **to ~ in rotation** turnusmäßig ausscheiden; **to ~ under the age limit** infolge der Erreichung der Altersgrenze in den Ruhestand treten; **to be due to ~** die Altersgrenze erreicht haben

retired zurückgetreten, ausgeschieden; pensioniert, im Ruhestand (i. R.); *bes. mil* außer Dienst (a. D.); **~ at one's own request** auf eigenen Wunsch pensioniert; **a ~ civil servant** ein pensionierter Beamter; **~ from public life** aus dem öffentlichen Leben zurückgezogen

retired list *mil* Verzeichnis der Offiziere außer Dienst; **to be on the ~** im Ruhestand (od. pensioniert, verabschiedet) sein; **to place** (or **put**) **on the ~** in den Ruhestand versetzen, pensionieren, verabschieden

retired, ~ partner ausgeschiedener Gesellschafter; **~ pay** Pension, Ruhegehalt

retiring, ~ **age** →retirement age; ~ **director** ausscheidender Direktor; ~ **partner** ausscheidender (od. austretender) Teilhaber

retire *v* 2. zurückziehen; einziehen, aus dem Verkehr ziehen; zurückzahlen; ausbuchen, *(buchmäßig)* aus dem Betrieb nehmen; **to** ~ **a bill** e-n Wechsel vor Fälligkeit einlösen; **to** ~ **bonds** Obligationen (tilgen und) aus dem Verkehr ziehen; **to** ~ **coins from circulation** Münzen aus dem Verkehr ziehen; **to** ~ **a loan** e-e Anleihe zurückzahlen

retirement 1. Rücktritt; Ausscheiden; Austritt; Pensionierung, (Versetzung in den) Ruhestand

retirement age Pensionsalter; **statutory** ~ gesetzliches Rentenalter; **to reach** ~ das Pensionsalter erreichen

retirement, ~ **annuity** *(VersR)* bei der Pensionierung ausgezahlte Altersrente; ~ **benefits** Pensionsbezüge; Altersruhegeld; ~ **fund** Pensionsfonds, Pensionskasse

retirement income Pensionseinkünfte, Ruhestandseinkünfte: ~ **credit** *Am*[78] *(SteuerR)* Freibetrag bei Pensionseinkünften

retirement, ~ **matters** Pensionsangelegenheiten; ~ **of an arbitrator** Ausscheiden e-s Schiedsrichters; ~ **of the jury** Zurückziehung der Geschworenen *(zur Beratung)*; ~ **of a partner** Ausscheiden e-s Teilhabers; ~ **on full (reduced) pension** Pensionierung mit vollem (herabgesetztem) Ruhegehalt; ~ **pay** Ruhegehalt

retirement pension Pension, Ruhegehalt; *Br (staatl.)* Altersrente (→*pension*); **non-contributory** ~ *Br*[79] beitragslose Altersrente (für bestimmte alte Leute)

retirement, ~ **plan** Pensionsplan; **compulsory** ~ **(on a pension)** Zwangspensionierung; **early** ~ vorzeitige Pensionierung; Vorruhestand; **optional** ~ freiwillige Pensionierung, Pensionierung auf eigenen Wunsch; **placing in** ~ Pensionierung, Versetzung in den Ruhestand; **voluntary** ~ freiwillige Pensionierung; **to go into** ~ in Pension gehen; **to live in** ~ im Ruhestand leben

retirement 2. Einziehung; Rückzahlung, Tilgung *(z. B. e-r Anleihe)*; ~**s** *(Bilanz) (buchmäßige)* Abgänge *(e-s Anlagegutes)*; ~ **of a bill** vorzeitige Einlösung e-s Wechsels; ~ **of bonds** Einlösung von Obligationen; ~ **of a loan** Rückzahlung e-r Anleihe

retool *v (Fabrik)* mit neuen Werkzeugen oder Maschinen versehen

retooling Neuausstattung *(mit Werkzeugen od. Maschinen)*

retort *(scharfe)* Erwiderung *(e-r Beleidigung)*

retort *v (Beleidigung)* erwidern; *(VölkerR)* Retorsion üben

retortion Erwiderung *(e-r Beleidigung)*; Vergeltung(smaßnahme); *(VölkerR)* Retorsion; *(IPR)* Anwendung von Vergeltungsrecht *(vgl. Art. 31 EGBGB a. F.)*

Vergeltung; Zwangsmittel, das als Antwort auf das Verhalten e-s anderen Staates e-n völkerrechtskonformen, aber unfreundlichen Akt darstellt (z. B. Einfuhrsperre, Abbruch diplomatischer Beziehungen)

retract *v* zurücknehmen, zurückziehen; widerrufen; **to** ~ **a confession** ein Geständnis widerrufen; **to** ~ **a promise** ein Versprechen zurücknehmen; **to** ~ **a testimony** e-e Zeugenaussage widerrufen

retraction Zurücknahme, Zurückziehung; Widerruf; *(probate practice)* Rücknahme der Verzichterklärung *(cf. renunciation)*; ~ **of a deposition** Widerruf e-r Zeugenaussage; ~ **statutes** *Am (einzelstaatl.)* Gesetze, die den Widerruf e-r beleidigenden Äußerung regeln

retrain *v* umschulen

retraining, (occupational) ~ **of handicapped persons** (Berufs-)Umschulung Körperbehinderter

retransfer Rückübertragung; Rücküberweisung *(von Geld)*

retransfer *v* rückübertragen, wieder abtreten; *(Geld)* rücküberweisen

retrench *v* einschränken; kürzen; Einsparungen vornehmen; **to** ~ **expenses** Ausgaben einschränken (od. herabsetzen), Einsparungen vornehmen; **to** ~ **a pension** e-e Pension kürzen

retrenchment (Ausgaben-)Einschränkung; Kürzung; Betriebsverkleinerung; ~ **in the budgetary expenditure** Einsparungen im Haushalt; ~ **of salary** Gehaltskürzung

retrial erneute Verhandlung; Wiederaufnahmeverfahren

retribution Vergeltung; Sühne *(als Strafzweck)*

retributive vergeltend, Vergeltungs-; ~ **damages** *Am* s. exemplary →damages

retrieval Wiedererlangung; Wiedergutmachung; ~ **of data** Abruf von Daten

retrieve *v* wiedererlangen; wiedergutmachen; **to** ~ **one's losses** s-e Verluste wieder einbringen; **to** ~ **one's reputation** s-n Ruf wiederherstellen

retroactive rückwirkend; **with** ~ **effect** mit rückwirkender Kraft, rückwirkend; **to have** ~ **effect** rückwirkende Kraft haben, rückwirken; ~ **law** (or **statute**) rückwirkendes Gesetz *(cf. ex post facto law)*

retroactively mit rückwirkender Kraft; **to tax** ~ rückwirkend besteuern

retroactivity Rückwirkung; rückwirkende Kraft

retrocede *v (Gebiet)* wieder abtreten, zurückübertragen; *(VersR)* retrozedieren, weiterrückversichern

retroceding insurer (or **company**) Retrozedent, Zweitrückversicherer

retrocession Wiederabtretung; *(VersR)* Retrozession *(Risikoübertragung des ersten auf den zweiten Rückversicherer)*; *Scot (selten)* →reconveyance; ~ **premium** Retrozessionsprämie

retrocessionary Retrozessionar

retrograde retrograd, rückläufig; rückschreitend *(opp. progressive)*; ~ **movement** rückläufige Bewegung *(z. B. der Kurse)*

retrogression Rückentwicklung, Rückfall

retrospective retrospektiv, rückwirkend; ~ **maintenance** Unterhalt für die Vergangenheit

retrospectivity Rückwirkung *(z. B. von Gesetzen)*

retry *v* erneut verhandeln; *(Verfahren)* wiederaufnehmen

return 1. *(offizieller)* Bericht; Bericht e-s Gerichtsbeamten *(z. B. e-s sheriff)* über Durchführung e-r gerichtlichen Verfügung *(unter Rückgabe der Unterlagen)*; *parl* Wahlbericht; *Br*[80] Bericht e-r Handelsgesellschaft *(an den →Registrar of Companies)*; Aufstellung, Übersicht; ~**s** statistische Angaben (od. Unterlagen); ~ **of expenses** Ausgabenaufstellung; **annual** ~ *Br*[80] Jahresbericht *(e-r Kapitalgesellschaft [ltd od. plc])*; **bank** ~ Bankausweis; **consolidated** ~ *Am*[81] Konzernbilanz; **election** ~**s** Wahlergebnisse; →**false** ~; **monthly** ~ *Br* Monatsausweis *(e-r Bank)*; **nil** ~ Fehlanzeige; **statutory** ~ gesetzlich vorgeschriebener Bericht; **traffic** ~**s** *(statistische)* Verkehrsziffern; **weekly** ~ Wochenausweis *(der Bank of England)*; **to file a** ~ **at the registry** bei der Registerbehörde e-n *(gesetzl. vorgeschriebenen)* Bericht einreichen

return 2. (Einkommen-)Steuererklärung; ~ **of (one's) income**[82] Einkommensteuererklärung; **delinquent** ~ *Am* rückständige Steuererklärung; **failure to file a** ~ Nichteinreichen der Steuererklärung; →**false** ~; **joint** ~ gemeinsame Steuererklärung *(von Ehegatten)*; **joint** ~ **privilege** Vergünstigung der gemeinsamen Steuererklärung; **separate** ~ getrennte Steuererklärung *(der Ehegatten)*; **tax** ~ Steuererklärung; **to file** (or **submit**) **a** ~ e-e Steuererklärung einreichen; **to fail to file the** ~ die Steuererklärung nicht einreichen; **to make one's tax** ~ seine Einkommensteuererklärung machen

return 3. Rückgabe; Rückerstattung, Rückvergütung; Gegenleistung; Rücklieferung, Rücksendung; Rück-; Gegen-; ~**s** Retouren, *(an den Verkäufer)* zurückgesandte Waren; *(Buchhandel)* Remittenden; *Br* Retouren, nicht eingelöste Wechsel od. Schecks; ~ **account** Rückrechnung; ~**s book** Retourenbuch, Buch für zurückgesandte Waren; ~ **card** *(an den →advertiser)* zurückgesandte Bestellkarte; ~ **cargo** Rückfracht, Rückladung; ~ **copies** *(Buchhandel)* Remittenden; ~ **freight** *Br* Rückfracht *(opp. outward freight)*; ~ **goods** →returned goods; ~**s inwards** *(von Kunden)* zurückgekommene Waren; ~ **load** Rückladung *(Ladung auf der Rückfahrt)*; ~ **of an amount overpaid** (or **of an excess amount**) Rückerstattung e-s zuviel gezahlten Betrages; ~ **of a charge** Gebührenrückerstattung; ~ **of contribution** Beitragsrückerstattung; ~ **of empties** Rücksendung von Leergut; ~ **of goods** Rücksendung der Waren; ~**s outwards** *(an Lieferanten)* zurückgesandte Waren; ~ **of premium(s)** *(VersR)* Prämienrückvergütung; ~ **of a visit** Gegenbesuch; ~ **premium** →returned premium; ~ **privilege** Rückgaberecht; ~ **receipt** *(Post)* Rückschein; ~ **remittance** Rücküberweisung; ~ **service** Gegendienst; **by** ~ **mail** *Am* postwendend; **by** ~ **(of post)** *Br* postwendend; **clause of** ~ *Scot* Klausel, durch die sich jd ausbedingt, daß das von ihm verliehene Recht unter gewissen Umständen an ihn zurückfällt; **demand for** ~ Rückforderung; **in** ~ **for** als Gegenleistung für; **purchase** ~**s** →~s outwards; **sales** ~**s** →~s inwards; **sale or** ~ →sale 1.

return 4. Rückfahrt; Rückkehr; Rück-; ~ **fare** Fahrgeld für Hin- und Rückfahrt; ~ **flight** Rückflug; ~ **freight** Rückfracht; ~ **half** (of a ticket) *Br* Fahrkartenabschnitt für die Rückfahrt *(opp. outward half)*; ~ **journey** Rückreise, Rückfahrt, Rückflug *(opp. outward journey)*; ~ **passage** Rückfahrt; ~ **ticket** *Br* Rückfahrkarte, Fahrkarte hin und zurück *(opp. single ticket)*; ~ **ticket fare** *Br* Fahrpreis für Hin- und Rückfahrt; ~ **trip** →~ journey; ~ **voyage** *(Seereise)* Rückreise, Rückfahrt *(opp. outward voyage)*; **immediately on my** ~ sofort nach meiner Rückkehr

return(s) 5. (Kapital-)Ertrag; Gewinn; Rendite; (Kapital-)Rentabilität; Verzinsung *(des eingesetzten Kapitals)*; ~ **on capital employed** →~ on investment; ~ **on equity** Rendite des Eigenkapitals; ~ **on investment** (R. o. I.) Ertrag aus Kapitalanlage (Investitionen), Kapitalrendite *(Kennziffer zur Analyse der Rentabilität e-s Unternehmens)*; ~ **on sales** Umsatzrendite; ~ **on securities** Wertpapierrendite; ~ **on shares** (*Am* **stock**) Aktienrendite; **gross** ~ Bruttoertrag; **interest** ~ Verzinsung; **normal** ~ landesübliche (Kapital-)Verzinsung; **rate of** ~**s** Zinssatz der Investitionen *(e-s Unternehmens)* (interner Ertragssatz); **rent** ~ Mietertrag; **sales** ~**s** Verkaufsergebnisse; **yielding a** ~ ertragsfähig, rentabel; **to get a good ~ on an investment** aus e-r Kapitalanlage e-e gute Rendite bekommen; **to bring** (or **yield**) **a ~** sich rentieren, e-n Gewinn bringen

return 6. *Br parl* Wahl *(e-s Kandidaten als M.P.; →return v 5.)*

return *v* 1. *(amtlich)* berichten; **to ~ a warrant** e-n Haftbefehl *(mit dem Bericht über die Durchführung)* vorlegen; **the sheriff ~s a writ of summons** der sheriff legt *(dem Richter)* die Ladung *(mit dem Bericht der Durchführung)* vor

return *v* 2. *(offiziell)* angeben, erklären; **liabilities ~ed at £ 3,000** mit £ 3000 angegebene Verbindlichkeiten; **he ~ed his income at £ 5,000** er gab sein Einkommen mit £ 5000 an; **the jury ~ed a verdict of guilty** die Geschworenen sprachen den Schuldspruch aus

return *v* 3. zurückgeben, zurücksenden; rückerstatten, rückvergüten, zurückzahlen; zurückkehren; **to ~ a bill unpaid** e-n Wechsel unbezahlt zurückgehen lassen; **to ~ a call** e-n Besuch erwidern; **to ~ the premium** *(VersR)* die Prämie zurückzahlen (od. rückvergüten); **if undelivered please ~ to** wenn nicht zustellbar, bitte zurücksenden an

returned, ~ bill Retourwechsel, Rückwechsel; **~ cheque (check)** Retourscheck, Rückscheck *(wegen fehlender Deckung)*; **~ empties** zurückgesandtes Leergut; **~ empty** leer zurück; **~ for want of acceptance** *(WechselR)* mangels Annahme zurück; **~ for want of funds** *(ScheckR)* mangels Deckung zurück; **~ goods** Retouren; *(Zoll)* Rückwaren; **R~ Letter Office** Büro für unzustellbare Briefe; **~ premium** *(VersR)* rückvergütete Prämie; **~ shipment rate** *Am* verbilligter Frachtsatz für Leergut; **to be ~ to sender** zurück(zusenden) an den Absender

return *v* 4. *(Gewinn)* einbringen; **the investments ~ed a good interest** die Kapitalanlagen brachten gute Zinsen ein

return *v* 5. *Br parl* wählen; **to ~ an M.P.** *Br* e-n Parlamentsabgeordneten wählen; **the constituency has ~ed a Conservative candidate** der Wahlkreis hat e-n konservativen Kandidaten ins Parlament gewählt

returning, ~ board *Am (einzelstaatl.)* Wahlausschuß; **~ officer** *Br* Wahlleiter *(sheriff od. mayor)*

returnable mit Bericht vorzulegen; zurückzugeben, rückgebbar; zurückzuzahlen, rückzahlbar; **the motion is ~ on ...** die Verhandlung über den Antrag findet statt am ...

reunification *(auch pol)* Wiedervereinigung; **~ of Germany** Wiedervereinigung Deutschlands; **family ~** *(VölkerR)* Familienzusammenführung

reunif|y *v* wiedervereinigen; **a ~ied Germany** ein wiedervereinigtes Deutschland

reunion →reunification

reunite *v* →reunify *v*

reusable wieder verwertbar, wieder verwendbar

reuse Wiederverwendung; **~ package** Mehrwegpackung

revalorization Revalorisierung, Aufwertung

revalorize *v* revalorisieren, aufwerten

revaluation Neubewertung, Neueinschätzung; Aufwertung *(e-r Währung; opp. devaluation)*; **~ of the pound (sterling)** Aufwertung des Pfundes; **~ of property** Neubewertung von Vermögen; **~ surplus** *Am* aus Höherbewertung von Anlagegütern entstandene Rücklagen; **~ (upward)** Aufwertung

revalue *v* aufwerten; neu bewerten, neu einschätzen; **to ~ (upward)** aufwerten

reveal *v* offenlegen

revenue (rev.) Einnahmen, Einkünfte, Ertrag, Erträge; Staatseinnahmen, Staatseinkünfte: *Am (Bilanz)* Umsatz; **~ account** Ertragskonto; **~ and expenditure** Staatseinnahmen und -ausgaben; **R~ (authorities)** *Br* Finanzbehörden; Fiskus; **~ bill** Steuervorlage; **~ bonds** *Am* kurzfristige Anleihen der öffentlichen Hand; **~ cases** Steuersachen; **~ cutter** Zollboot; **~ cutter service** *Am* Zolldienst; **~ duty** Finanzzoll *(opp. protective duty)*; **~-earning** gewinnbringend, einträglich; **~ expenditure** Kapitalaufwand zum Ersatz verbrauchter Werte *(opp. capital expenditure)*; **~ frauds** Steuer- od. Zollhinterziehung; **~ items** Einnahmeposten; **~ law** Steuerrecht; Steuergesetz; **~ offen|ce (~se)** Steuerdelikt; Zolldelikt; **~ office** Zollamt; **~ officer** Zollbeamter; **(inland** *Br***) ~ receipts** Steueraufkommen, Steuereinnahmen; **~ reserves** →reserve 1.; **R~ Ruling** (Rev. Rul.) *Am* verbindliche Auslegung e-s steuerrechtlichen Tatbestandes durch den →Internal Revenue Service; *(etwa)* Steuerrechtsbescheid; **R~ Service** *Am* →Internal R~ Service; **~ sharing** Beteiligung *(der Arbeitnehmer)* am Unternehmensgewinn; **~ stamp** Steuerstempel, Steuermarke, Banderole; **~ support grant** *Br*[83] staatliche Ausgleichszahlungen an finanzschwache Gemeinden; **~ tariff** Finanzzoll; **amount of ~** Betrag der Einnahmen; **customs ~** Zolleinnahmen; **defrauding the R~** *Br* Steuerhinterziehung; **government ~** *Br* s. public →~; **Inland R~** *Br* Finanzverwaltung (→Inland); **inland ~** *Br* Steuereinnahmen (→inland); **Internal R~ Service** (IRS) *Am* Bundessteuerbehörde; **internal ~** *Am* Staatseinkünfte (→*internal)*; **land ~** *Br* Einnahmen aus →crown lands; **local ~** Kommunaleinnahmen; **loss of ~** Einnahmeausfall; **→marginal ~**; **national ~** Volkseinkommen; **public ~** Staatseinkünfte; Einnahmen der öffentlichen Hand *(aus Steuern etc)*; Steuereinnahmen; **source of** ~ Einnahmequelle; **yearly** ~ Jahreseinnahmen; **to defraud the** ~ die Steuern hinterziehen

Reverend *Br eccl* Titel und Anrede e-s unteren Geistlichen; **Most** ~ Titel und Anrede e-s Erzbischofs; **Right** ~ Titel und Anrede e-s Bischofs; **Very** ~ Titel und Anrede e-s Dechanten

reversal Aufhebung *(des Urteils der Unterinstanz durch das Rechtsmittelgericht)*; Stornierung, Storno, Rückbuchung; Umkehr(ung); *fig* Umschwung, Kehrtwendung; ~ (of an entry or a posting) Stornierung, Stornobuchung; ~ **of opinion** Meinungsumschwung; ~ **of the burden of proof** Umkehr der Beweislast

reverse Rückseite *(e-r Münze etc)*; Rückschlag; entgegengesetzt, umgekehrt; ~ **charge call** *Am tel* R-Gespräch *(Empfänger zahlt die Gebühren)*; ~ **engineering** rückwärtige Konstruktion; Nachahmung e-s Produkts anhand des Originals und nicht anhand der Zeichnung; ~ **entry** →reversing entry; ~ **order** umgekehrte Reihenfolge; ~ **side** Rückseite *(z. B. e-r Münze)*; ~ **split** *Am* Zusammenlegung von Aktien *(Ausgabe e-r Aktie höheren Nennwerts anstelle mehrerer Aktien niedrigen Nennwerts; →stock split)*; ~ **takeover** *Br* Übernahme e-r public company (Aktiengesellschaft) durch e-e private company (GmbH); Übernahme e-r größeren durch e-e kleinere Gesellschaft; **on the** ~ umstehend; **to suffer a major** ~ e-n schweren Rückschlag erleiden

reverse *v (Urteil der unteren Instanz)* aufheben; *(Buchung)* stornieren, rückbuchen; umstoßen; umkehren; rückwärts fahren; **to** ~ **the charge** *tel* (Gespräch) durch das Amt als R-Gespräch anmelden lassen; **to** ~ **a decision** e-n Beschluß aufheben; **to** ~ **an entry** e-e Buchung stornieren; **to** ~ **the onus of proof** die Beweislast umkehren; **to** ~ **one's opinion** s-e Meinung völlig ändern; **to** ~ **a policy** e-e Politik revidieren

reversing entry Stornobuchung

reversible *(ProzeßR)* der Aufhebung unterliegend; umkehrbar

reversion Rückfallsrecht, Anwartschaft(srecht) *(auf Grundbesitz)*; Heimfall; **leasehold** ~ reversion des Vermieters (od. Verpächters) *(z. B. bei langfristigen Miet- od. Pachtverträgen)*

reversion ist das Recht des Grundeigentümers, der ein minderes Recht (particular estate) an seinem Grundbesitz eingeräumt hat (z. B. der Eigentümer eines estate in fee simple hat an seinem Grundbesitz einen lebenslängl. Nießbrauch [estate for life] eingeräumt), auf den Rückfall des particular estate nach Erlöschen des minderen Rechts

reversionary Anwartschafts-, Anwartschaft gebend; ~ **annuity** *(Lebensvers.)* Rente auf den Überlebensfall, Überlebensrente; ~ **bonus** *Br (VersR)* Summenzuwachs; ~ **claim** Heimfallsanspruch; ~ **dividend** *Am (VersR)* Summenzuwachs

reversionary heir Nacherbe; **estate of a** ~ Nacherbschaft; **right of a** ~ Nacherbenrecht

reversionary, ~ **interest** Rückfallanwartschaft; Anwartschaftsrecht *(reversion od. remainder; analog auch auf bewegl. Vermögen ausgedehnt)*; ~ **lease** *Br*[84] zukünftige Miete (od. Pacht), die nach Beendigung e-s vorhergehenden Miet- (od. Pacht-)Verhältnisses in Kraft tritt; ~ **succession** Nacherbfolge

reversioner jd, der e-e →reversion hat; *(im weiteren Sinne)* Anwärter auf ein future estate *(unbewegl. od. bewegl. Vermögen)*; Heimfallberechtigter

revert *v* zurückfallen (to an); anheimfallen, zurückkommen (to auf); **to** ~ **to a matter in due course** auf e-e Sache zu gegebener Zeit zurückkommen

reverted, property ~ Heimfallsgut

revesting Rückgabe von *(z. B. gestohlenem)* Vermögen an den ursprünglichen Eigentümer

review 1. Überprüfung, Nachprüfung, Revision, (nochmalige) Durchsicht; ~ **of a remand in custody** Haftprüfung; ~ **of taxation** *Br* nochmalige gerichtl. Überprüfung der Kostenrechnung des Anwalts; ~ **on appeal** *Am* und *Scot* Überprüfung e-s Urteils *(durch ein Rechtsmittelgericht)*; **board of** ~ Überprüfungsausschuß; Berufungsausschuß; **judicial** ~ *Am* Normenkontrolle *(Prüfung der Gesetze auf ihre Vereinbarkeit mit der Verfassung); (auch)* gerichtl. Überprüfung von Verwaltungsakten; Überprüfung der Entscheidung e-r Vorinstanz; **to be subject to** ~ der Nachprüfung unterliegen; **to come under** ~ überprüft werden; **to petition for** ~ Antrag auf Nachprüfung stellen

review 2. Bericht, Übersicht; ~ **of the market** (or **market** ~) Marktbericht; Börsenbericht; **month under** ~ Berichtsmonat; **period under** ~ Berichtszeitraum; **year under** ~ Berichtsjahr

review 3. Rezension, *(kritische)* Besprechung; Theaterkritik; Zeitschrift; ~ **copy** (of a book) Besprechungsexemplar; **book** ~ Buchbesprechung; **law** ~ juristische Zeitschrift

review 4. *mil* Truppenschau, Parade; **to hold a** ~ e-e Parade abhalten

review *v* überprüfen, nachprüfen, durchsehen, e-n Überblick geben über; rezensieren, besprechen; **to** ~ **a book** ein Buch besprechen; **to** ~ **taxation** *Br* die *(gerichtl. geprüfte)* Kostenrechnung des Anwalts nochmals gerichtl. überprüfen; **to** ~ **troops** e-e Parade abnehmen

reviewable nachprüfbar

revise *v* revidieren, durchsehen, nachprüfen; *(nach erfolgter Durchsicht od. Nachprüfung)* abändern (od. verbessern); *(Text)* überarbeiten; **to ~ boundaries** Grenzen revidieren; **to ~ a decision** e-e Entscheidung abändern; **to ~ a statute** ein Gesetz (überprüfen und) abändern

revised, ~ arrangement Neuregelung; **~ edition** neubearbeitete Auflage; **R~ Model Business Corporation Act** (RMBCA) *Am* Gesetzesmuster für Aktiengesetz *(Aktiengesellschaftsrecht)*; **~ proof** zweite Korrektur; **R~ Statutes** (Rev. Stat., Rev. St., R. S.) Sammlung neugefaßter Gesetze; **R~ →Uniform Reciprocal Enforcement of Support Act 1968** (URESA); **law as ~ on** Gesetz in der Fassung vom

revision Revision; *(nochmalige)* Durchsicht, Abänderung; Neuregelung

revision of a judgment[84a] Wiederaufnahmeverfahren; **application for ~**[84b] Antrag auf Wiederaufnahme des Verfahrens; **party claiming ~** die Wiederaufnahme beantragende Partei

revision, ~ of prices Abänderung der Preise; **~ of a treaty** *(VölkerR)* Revision e-s Vertrages; **frontier ~** Grenzberichtigung; **proceedings for ~** Wiederaufnahmeverfahren; **to undertake a ~** e-e Abänderung vornehmen

revisionism *pol* Revisionismus

revitalization of the capital market Wiederbelebung des Kapitalmarktes

revival Erneuerung, Wiederaufleben *(von Rechten)*; Wiederinkraftsetzung; *com* Wiederbelebung; Aufschwung, Erholung (→*recovery, upturn*); **~ in economic activity** Konjunkturbelebung; **~ of business** Geschäftsbelebung; Konjunkturaufschwung; **~ of a contract** Wiederauflebenlassen e-s Vertrages (od. Auftrages); **~ of a debt barred by limitation** Wiederaufleben e-r verjährten Forderung; **~ of a lapsed policy** Wiederinkraftsetzung e-r verfallenen Police; **~ of the market** Wiederbelebung (od. Erholung) des Marktes; **~ of sales** Absatzbelebung; **~ of trade** →**~** of business; **~ of a (revoked) will** Wiederinkraftsetzung e-s (widerrufenen) Testaments

revive *v* erneuern, wieder aufleben (lassen), wiederinkraftsetzen; sich beleben; sich erholen *(von Kursen)*; **to ~ an action** e-n Prozeß *(der z. B. wegen des Todes e-r Partei eingestellt war)* wiederaufnehmen; **to ~ an agreement** e-n Vertrag wiederaufleben lassen; **to ~ an industry** e-e Industrie beleben; **to ~ a will** ein *(widerrufenes)* Testament wieder aufleben lassen *(durch Neuerrichtung)*; **a statute-barred debt is ~d** (by acknowledgment or part payment) *Br* e-e verjährte Schuld lebt wieder auf

revocable widerruflich *(z. B. Vollmacht, Akkreditiv)*; zurücknehmbar; **~ →trust**

revocation Widerruf; Zurücknahme; Aufhebung, Entzug; *(PatR)* Nichtigerklärung; **~ action** *(PatR)* Nichtigkeitsklage; **~ division** *(PatR)* Nichtigkeitsabteilung; **~ in law** Widerruf kraft Gesetzes *(unabhängig vom Willen der Parteien)*; **~ of an Act** Aufhebung e-s Gesetzes; **~ of agency** Widerruf des Vertretungs- od. Auftragsverhältnisses *(seitens des principal; →renunciation)*; **~ of an authority** Widerruf e-r Vollmacht; **~ of a driving licence** *Br* (**driver's license** *Am*) Führerscheinentzug; **~ of (a) gift** Schenkungswiderruf; **~ of (a) grant of probate** (or **of letters of administration**)[85] Widerruf e-s Testamentsvollstreckerzeugnisses od. e-s Nachlaßverwalterzeugnisses; **~ of a letter of credit** Widerruf e-s Akkreditivs; **~ of a licen ce (~se)** Zurücknahme e-r Konzession; Lizenzentzug; **~ of an offer** Zurücknahme e-s (Vertrags-)Angebots; **~ of a patent** Zurücknahme e-s Patents; **~ of a power of attorney** Widerruf e-r Vollmacht; **~ of a probate** Widerruf e-s probate (of will); **~ of a will** Widerruf (od. Aufhebung) e-s Testaments; **constructive ~** →**~** in law; **judicial ~** Widerruf kraft gerichtl. Verfügung; **power of ~ and new appointment** *(urkundlich vorbehaltene)* Befugnis, e-e erfolgte Ernennung zu widerrufen und e-e neue vorzunehmen

revoke *v* widerrufen; zurücknehmen; aufheben; **to ~ an agency** ein Vertretungs- (od. Auftrags-)verhältnis widerrufen (→*revocation*); **to ~ an authority** e-e Vollmacht widerrufen; **to ~ one's consent** s-e Genehmigung zurückziehen; **to ~ a grant** e-e Schenkung widerrufen; **to ~ a law** ein Gesetz aufheben; **to ~ a letter of credit** ein Akkreditiv widerrufen; **to ~ a licen ce (~se)** →licence 1. und 3.; **to ~ an offer** ein Angebot zurücknehmen; **to ~ an order** e-n Auftrag (od. e-e Bestellung) zurücknehmen (od. annullieren); **to ~ a patent** ein Patent für nichtig erklären; **to ~ a power of attorney** e-e Vollmacht widerrufen; **to ~ a will**[86] ein Testament widerrufen

revolt Revolte, Aufruhr, Aufstand; **to crush a ~** e-e Revolte zerschlagen; **to keep** (or **put**) **down a ~** e-e Revolte unterdrücken; **to suppress a ~** e-e Revolte niederschlagen

revolt *v* revoltieren, sich empören (od. auflehnen) (against gegen)

revolution Revolution; **counter-~** Gegenrevolution; **→industrial ~**; **→managerial ~**; **world ~** Weltrevolution

revolutionary revolutionär, umstürzlerisch, umwälzend; Revolutionär

revolutionist Revolutionär

revolutionize *v* revolutionieren, umstürzen, umwälzen

revolve *v* sich drehen, umlaufen

revolving, ~ credit Revolvingkredit, d. h. sich bei Ablauf automatisch erneuernder Kredit; **~ Euronote issuance facility** (REIF) Variante der →note isuance facility; **~ fund** Umlauffonds, automatisch sich erneuernder Fonds *(dem Geld laufend entnommen und wieder zugeführt wird)*; **~ letter of credit** revolvierendes Akkreditiv, automatisch sich erneuerndes Akkreditiv; **~ -underwriting facility** (RUF) Fazilität zur revolvierenden Plazierung von Euronotes durch e-n →sole placing agent *(cf. note issuance facility [NIF])*

reward (Geld-)Belohnung; Vergütung; *fig* Lohn; **adequate** (or **due**) ~ angemessene Belohnung; **offer(ing)** (or **promise**) **of (a)** ~ Aussetzung e-r Belohnung; **person offering the** ~ Auslobender; **public offer of a** ~ Auslobung; **to advertise** (or **offer, promise**) **a** ~ e-e Belohnung aussetzen; **to offer a ~ publicly** ausloben

reward *v* belohnen; **the finder will be ~ed** der Finder wird e-e Belohnung erhalten

rewarehouse *v* wieder einlagern

rewarehousing Wiedereinlagerung

reweigh *v* nachwiegen

reweight nochmals ermitteltes Gewicht

rezoning Neueinteilung in Zonen

Rhine Rhein; **~ basin** Rheineinzugsgebiet; **~ boatman** Rheinschiffer; **~ Navigation Court** Rheinschiffahrtsgericht; **~ pollution** Rheinwasserverunreinigung

ribbon Band; Farbband *(e-r Schreibmaschine)*; **~ building** (or **development**) *Br* Serienbau, Stadtrandsiedlung *(längs der Landstraße)*

rich reich; **~ people** (or **the** ~) die Reichen; **~ soil** fruchtbarer Boden

Richard Roe fiktiver Name *(in Rechtsstreitigkeiten, wenn der richtige Name unbekannt ist)* (→John Doe)

riches, to amass ~ Reichtum (od. Reichtümer) ansammeln (anhäufen)

rid *v*, **to ~ one's property of debt** sein Vermögen entschulden; **to get ~ of** loswerden; **hard to get ~ of** schwer loszuwerden

ride Ritt; Fahrt; *Am* Mitfahrgelegenheit; **~ in a bus** (or **bus** ~) Omnibusfahrt; →**free** ~

ride *v* reiten; fahren; **to ~ a bicycle** radfahren; **to ~ in a bus** in e-m Bus fahren; **to ~ a motorcycle** Motorrad fahren

rider 1. Anhang *(zu e-r Urkunde)*; Nachtrag, Zusatz(klausel); Wechselallonge; *(VersR)* Policenanhang, Zusatz

rider 2. Reiter; (Rad- od. Motorrad-)Fahrer; **~ of a motor-assisted pedal cycle** Mofafahrer; **dispatch** ~ *mil* Meldefahrer; **free** ~ Spekulant

rig *v* betrügerisch handhaben; manipulieren; *(Schiff)* auftakeln; **to ~ an election** bei e-r Wahl Schiebungen machen; **to ~ the market** *(Börse)* e-e (künstl.) Kurssteigerung hervorrufen, die Kurse (künstl.) in die Höhe treiben

rigged, ~ bid Scheingebot; **participation in a ~ contest** *Am (StrafR)* Teilnahme an e-m Wettbewerb, dessen Ergebnis vorher verabredet war

rigging betrügerische Handhabung; **~ (the market)** Kurstreiberei; Kursmanipulation; **~ publicly exhibited contest** *Am (StrafR)* vorherige Verabredung des Ergebnisses e-s öffentlich veranstalteten Wettbewerbs

rigger Kurstreiber

right 1. Recht *(im subjektiven Sinne; cf. law)*; Anrecht, Berechtigung; (Rechts-)Anspruch; recht, richtig

right, to abandon a ~ ein Recht aufgeben; **to affect the ~s** die Rechte berühren; **to assert one's** ~ auf s-m Recht bestehen; sein Recht geltend machen; **to assign a** ~ ein Recht übertragen; **to →avail o.s. of a ~; to be** ~ recht haben; **to confer a** ~ ein Recht übertragen (on auf); **to constitute a** ~ ein Recht begründen; **to contest a p.'s** ~ jds Recht streitig machen; **to declare the** (preexisting) **~s** (of the litigants) durch Feststellungsurteil feststellen; **to deny a p. the** ~ jdm das Recht absprechen; **to disclaim a** ~ auf ein Recht verzichten; **to enforce a** ~ ein Recht durchsetzen (od. einklagen); **to exercise a** ~ ein Recht ausüben (od. geltend machen); **to forfeit a** ~ e-s Rechtes verlustig gehen, ein Recht verwirken; **to grant a** ~ ein Recht verleihen (od. einräumen); **to hold a** ~ ein Recht innehaben; **to infringe a** ~ ein Recht verletzen; **to lose a** ~ e-s Rechtes verlustig gehen; **to make a (binding) declaration of** ~[87] ein Feststellungsurteil erlassen; **to relinquish** (or **renounce**) **a** ~ auf ein Recht verzichten; **to reserve (to o.s.) the** ~ sich das Recht vorbehalten; **to stand on one's** ~ s. to assert one's →~; **to state the ~s** (of the litigants) s. to declare the →~s, **to sue in the ~ of the corporation** *Am* für die Aktiengesellschaft klagen; **to use a** ~ von e-m Recht Gebrauch machen; **to waive a** ~ auf ein Recht verzichten; **a ~ is extinct** ein Recht ist erloschen (od. untergegangen)

right, ~s and obligations Rechte und Pflichten; **R~ →Honourable; ~ in personam** obligatorisches Recht, schuldrechtlicher Anspruch; **~ in rem** dingliches Recht; **~ of action** Klagerecht, gerichtlich durchsetzbares Recht; *(auch* *identisch mit)* →chose in action; ~ **of assembly** Versammlungsrecht; ~ **of audience** Recht zum Auftreten in der mündlichen Verhandlung; Postulationsfähigkeit *(der Anwälte);* **by ~ of birth** kraft Geburt; ~ **of broadcasting** Senderecht; ~ **of common** gemeinschaftliches Nutzungsrecht (→*common 1.)*; ~ **of disposing** Verfügungsrecht; ~ **of election** Wahlrecht (→*election)*; ~ **of entry**[88] Recht der Inbesitznahme von Grundbesitz; ~ **of establishment** Niederlassungsrecht; ~ **of first refusal** Vorkaufsrecht; ~ **of →indemnity;** ~ **of notice** Kündigungsrecht; ~ **of preemption** Vorkaufsrecht; ~ **of recourse** Rückgriffsrecht, Regreßanspruch: ~ **of representation** Erbrecht nach Stämmen *(by stirpes; →representation 2.)*; ~ **of rescission** Anfechtungsrecht; ~ **of residence** Aufenthaltsrecht; ~ **of retention** Zurückbehaltungsrecht; ~ **of search** →search 1.; ~ **of separation** Aussonderungsrecht *(im Konkursverfahren)*; ~ **of →stoppage in transitu;** ~ **of →visit and search** →*visit 2.*; ~ **of way** Wegerecht (→*easement*); Vorfahrtsrecht; ~ **to benefit(s)** *(VersR)* Leistungsanspruch; ~ **to claim for damages** Schadenersatzanspruch; ~ **to drive** Fahrerlaubnis; ~ **to follow the asset** *Br* Folgerecht *(des beneficiary gegenüber Dritten; z.B. das Recht, Nachlaßgegenstände, über die der personal representative unzulässigerweise zugunsten e-s Dritten verfügt hat, von dem Erwerber herauszuverlangen)*[89]; ~ **to a hearing** Recht auf Anhörung, auf e-e mündliche Verhandlung; ~ **to vote** Stimmrecht, Wahlrecht; ~ **under a contract** Recht aus e-m Vertrag, vertragliches Recht

right, absolute ~ uneingeschränktes Recht *(opp. conditional ~);* **accrual of a** ~ Anfall (od. Entstehung) e-s Rechts; **acquired ~s and ~s in course of acquisition** erworbene Rechte und Anwartschaften; **all ~s reserved** alle Rechte vorbehalten *(cf. copyright)*

right, as of ~ von Rechts wegen; **member as of** ~ Mitglied kraft Rechts; **to meet as of** ~ automatisch zusammentreten

right, assertion of a ~ Geltendmachung e-s Rechts; **bearer of ~s and duties** Träger von Rechten und Pflichten; **Bill of R~s** →bill 3; **by** ~ von Rechts wegen; **by** ~ **of** kraft; auf Grund von; **civil ~s** (Staats-)Bürgerrechte; politische Rechte; **conditional** ~ bedingtes Recht *(opp. absolute ~)*; **contingent** ~ Anwartschaftsrecht; **contractual** ~ vertragliches Recht, obligatorisches Recht; **duly acquired ~s** wohlerworbene Rechte

right, enjoyment of a ~ Genuß (od. Ausübung) e-s Rechts; **equitable** ~ auf equity beruhendes Recht *(opp. legal ~)*; **exclusive** ~ ausschließliches Recht; Alleinberechtigung; **exercise of a** ~ Ausübung e-s Rechts; **existing** ~ gegenwärtiges Recht *(opp. future ~)*; **extent of a** ~ Umfang e-s Rechts; **extinguishment of a** ~ Erlöschen (od. Untergang) e-s Rechts; **forfeiture of a** ~ Rechtsverwirkung; Rechtsverlust; **fundamental ~s** Grundrechte; **future** ~ künftiges Recht *(opp. existing or present ~)*

right, in one's own ~ aus eigenem Recht; **peeress in her own** ~ *Br*[90] peeress durch Geburt od. Ernennung *(nicht durch Heirat)*; **she has a fortune in her own** ~ sie hat ein eigenes Vermögen

right, inchoate ~ noch in der Entstehung begriffenes Recht (→*inchoate*); **legal** ~ Recht, das auf Common Law beruht *(opp. equitable ~)*; **personal** ~ obligatorischer Anspruch; persönliches Recht, Individualrecht; **present** ~ gegenwärtiges Recht *(opp. future ~)*; **proprietary** ~ Eigentumsrecht; **real** ~ dingliches Recht *(opp. personal ~)*; **successor in** ~ Rechtsnachfolger; **vested** ~ wohlerworbenes Recht *(opp. inchoate ~)*

right 2. *(meist ~s) (AktienR) (den Aktionären gewährtes)* Bezugsrecht auf neue (junge) Aktien; ~ **(of application)** s. application →~s; ~ **dealings** Handel in Bezugsrechten; **~s issue** Bezugsrechtsemission *(von neuen Aktien)*; **~s market** Markt der Bezugsrechte; **~s offer** Bezugsrechtsangebot; **(application) ~s** *Br* Bezugsrecht; **cum ~s** mit Bezugsrecht; **ex ~s** ohne Bezugsrecht; **with ~s** mit Bezugsrecht; **to exercise a** ~ ein Bezugsrecht ausüben

right 3. a) rechts; ~ **bank** (of a river) rechtes (Fluß-)Ufer; **~-hand man** *fig* „rechte Hand"; **~-hand page** rechte Seite *(e-s Buches)*; **~-hand side** rechte Seite (e-s Kontos); **no ~ turn** Rechtsabbiegen verboten; **to keep to the** ~ rechts fahren, die rechte Straßenseite einhalten; **to overtake on the** ~ rechts überholen; **to turn** ~ rechts abbiegen

right 3. b) *pol* rechts; **the** ~ die Rechte; ~ **turn** Rechtswendung; ~ **wing** rechter Flügel; rechtsstehend; **~-wing coalition** Rechtskoalition; **~-wing opposition** Rechtsopposition; **~-wing party** Rechtspartei; **~-wing press** Rechtspresse; **extreme** ~ äußerste Rechte; **extreme ~ winger** Rechtsradikaler; **swing to the** ~ Umschwung nach rechts

rightful rechtmäßig; ~ **claim** berechtigter Anspruch; ~ **claimant** Anspruchsberechtigter; ~ **heir** rechtmäßiger Erbe; ~ **owner** rechtmäßiger Eigentümer

rightfulness Rechtmäßigkeit

rightist *pol colloq.* Anhänger der Rechten, Rechtsstehender; ~ **press** Rechtspresse

rightly mit Recht, richtig

rigid starr; ~ **trust** *Am* →fixed trust

rigidity Starrheit *(z.B. des Rechts)*

ring 1. Ring; (Unternehmer-)Ring; Bande; Börsenstand für Termingeschäfte; **the** ~ *Br* die Buchmacher; ~ **binder** Ringbuch; ~ **leader** Rädelsführer; Anführer e-r Bande; ~**-man** *Br* Buchmacher; ~ **of burglars** Einbrecherbande; ~ **trading** *Br* Auktionsverkäufe, bei denen die Händler e-n Ring um den Auktionator bilden; **narcotics** ~ Bande von Rauschgifthändlern; **price** ~ Preiskartell; **spy** ~ Spionagering, Spionageorganisation

ring 2. Telefonanruf; **to give a p. a** ~ jdn anrufen

ring *v*, **to** ~ **the changes on** die gleichen Tatsachen auf verschiedene Weise vorbringen; etw. in allen Tonarten versuchen; **to** ~ **(up) sb.** *tel* jdn anrufen

ringster *Am colloq. (meist verächtl.)* Mitglied e-r politischen Clique

riot *(StrafR)*[91] *(gesetzwidrige)* Zusammenrottung *(von wenigstens 3 Personen zur Störung der öffentl. Sicherheit und Ordnung)*; Aufruhr; Tumult, Krawall; ~**s** (innere) Unruhen, Ausschreitungen; **R**~ **Act** *Br* Gesetz *(von 1715)*, das riot unter Strafe stellt; **R**~ **(Damages) Act** *Br* Tumultschädengesetz *(von 1886)*; ~ **and civil commotions** (R. & C. C.) Aufruhr und bürgerliche Unruhen; ~**s, civil commotion and strike** (R. C. C. & S.) Aufruhr, Bürgerkrieg und Streik; ~ **squad** *Am* Überfallkommando; **damage by** ~ Tumultschaden; **prison** ~ Gefangenenaufstand, Gefangenenrevolte; **racial** ~ Rassenkrawall; **students'** ~**s** Studentenunruhen; **suppression of a** ~ Unterdrückung von Aufruhr; **serious** ~**s broke out** schwere Unruhen brachen aus; es kam zu schweren Ausschreitungen; **to put down a** ~ e-n Aufruhr unterdrücken

riot *v* sich zusammenrotten *(zur Störung der öffentl. Sicherheit und Ordnung)*; an e-m Aufruhr teilnehmen; randalieren

rioting, street ~ Straßenschlacht

rioter Aufrührer; Unruhestifter

riotous aufrührerisch; tumultuarisch; ~ **assembly** *Br (gesetzwidrige)* Zusammenrottung *(von wenigstens 12 Personen zur Störung der öffentl. Sicherheit und Ordnung)*

riparian Ufer-; Uferanwohner, Anlieger; ~ **owner** (or **proprietor**) Uferanlieger; ~ **right** Ufer(anlieger)recht; ~ **state** Uferstaat, Anliegerstaat

ripe for development entwicklungsreif, baureif

rip-off *colloq.* „Nepp"; Betrug; Diebstahl

ripped off, I got ~ ich wurde bestohlen

rise Steigen, Steigerung, Erhöhung, Anstieg; *(Börse)* Aufwärtsbewegung, Hausse; *Br colloq.* Gehaltserhöhung; Lohnerhöhung; Veranlassung; ~ **and fall of statesmen** Aufstieg und Sturz von Staatsmännern; ~ **in costs** Steigen der Kosten, Kostenanstieg; ~ **in exports** Exportsteigerung; ~ **in income** Einkommenssteigerung

rise in price(s) Preiserhöhung, Preisanstieg; Preisanhebung, Ansteigen der Preise; Kurssteigerung, Kursanstieg; **rise in the price of coal** Steigen der Kohlepreise; **to experience a** ~ e-e Preiserhöhung erfahren

rise, ~ **in salary** Gehaltserhöhung; ~ **in social position** sozialer Aufstieg; ~ **in (the) standard of living** Steigen des Lebensstandards; ~ **in wages** Steigen der Löhne, Lohnerhöhung; ~ **of 10 per cent** 10%ige Erhöhung; ~ **of postal rates** Erhöhung der Postgebühren; ~ **of railway** *Br* (**railroad** *Am*) **rates** Erhöhung der Eisenbahntarife; ~ **of shares** Steigen der Aktien *(opp. fall)*; ~ **to power** Machtübernahme; **dealing for a** ~ *(Börse)* Haussespekulation

rise, on the ~ im Steigen begriffen; **prices are on the** ~ die Preise (od. Kurse) steigen

rise, to ask for a ~ *Br colloq.* um Gehalts- (od. Lohn-)erhöhung bitten; **to be on the** ~ zunehmen, sich im Aufstieg befinden; im Preise (od. Kurs) steigen; **to buy for a** ~ *(Börse)* auf Hausse spekulieren; **to get a** ~ *Br colloq.* Gehalts- (od. Lohn-)erhöhung bekommen; **to give** ~ **to** Anlaß geben zu, veranlassen, verursachen

rise, to go for a ~ *(Börse)* auf Hausse spekulieren; **speculator who goes for a** ~ Haussespekulant

rise, to operate for a ~ *(Börse)* auf Hausse spekulieren; **to show a** ~ e-e Steigerung aufweisen; **to speculate for a** ~ auf Hausse spekulieren; **to undergo a** ~ e-e Steigerung erfahren; **the** ~ **is maintained** *(Börse)* die Hausse hält an; **substantial** ~**s were secured** *(Börse)* beträchtliche Kurssteigerungen wurden erzielt

rise *v* steigen, anziehen *(Preise, Kurse)*; aufstehen, sich erheben; *parl* die Sitzung beenden, sich vertagen; **to** ~ **against** sich erheben (od. rebellieren) gegen; **to** ~ **to the occasion** sich der Lage gewachsen zeigen; **to** ~ **to a point of order** →order 1.; **to** ~ **to power** an die Macht gelangen; **to** ~ **in price** im Preise (od. Kurs) steigen; **the market has** ~**n** die Kurse sind gestiegen; **the price rose to ...** der Preis (od. Kurs) stieg auf ...

rising 1. Steigen; Aufstehen; Aufstand; *parl* Vertagung; **vote by** ~ →vote 1.

rising 2. ansteigend; aufsteigend; *fig* aufstrebend; ~ **costs** steigende Kosten; ~ **generation** heranwachsende (od. kommende) Generation; ~ **lawyer** aufstrebender Anwalt

rising market, in a ~ bei anziehenden Kursen *(opp. on a falling market)*; **to be a** ~ im Preis (od. Kurs) steigen

rising, ~ **price** steigender (od. anziehender) Preis *(opp. falling price)*; ~ **prices** Teuerung;

R~ Sun *(Japan) (militärischer und ziviler)* Orden der aufgehenden Sonne; **to be** ~ im Preise (od. Kurs) steigen; **exports are** ~ die Ausfuhr steigt; **prices are** ~ die Preise (od. Kurse) steigen (od. ziehen an)

risk 1. Risiko, Wagnis, Gefahr; **~s** Risiken; ~ **assessment** Risikobeurteilung; **~- averse** *(finanziell)* risikoscheu; **~-bearer** Risikoträger; ~ **capital** Risikokapital; haftendes Kapital; ~ **excluded** ausgeschlossenes Risiko; ~ **inherent in an acquisition** mit e-m Kauf verbundenes Risiko; **~-money** Fehlgeld, Mankogeld *(des Kassierers)*; ~ **note** *Br (vertragl.)* Haftungsbeschränkung des Transportunternehmens; ~ **of carriage** Transportrisiko; ~ **of conveyance** Transportgefahr; ~ **of damage** Gefahr der Beschädigung; ~ **of escape** Fluchtgefahr; ~ **of fire** Brandgefahr; ~ **of loss** Gefahr des Verlustes (od. Untergangs); Gefahrtragung; ~ **of marketing** Absatzrisiko; ~ **premium** Risikoprämie; ~ **rating** Risikobewertung; ~ **spreading** Risikostreuung; ~ **taker** Risikoträger; **~-taking** Risikoübernahme; Gefahrtragung *(hinsichtl. des Untergangs von Sachen)*

risk, accident ~ Unfallrisiko; **for your account and** ~ auf Ihre Rechnung und Gefahr; **assumption of** ~ Risikoübernahme; Gefahrübernahme; **(voluntary) assumption of** ~ Handeln auf eigene Gefahr; **at the** ~ **of** auf Gefahr von; **at the** ~ **of one's life** unter Lebensgefahr; **at** ~ **rules** *Am*[92] Haftungsvorschriften *(zum Zweck der Begrenzung von Steuerabzügen)*; **attended with** ~ mit Gefahr verbunden; **bearer of** ~ Risikoträger; **business** ~ Geschäftsrisiko; **commercial** ~ wirtschaftliches Risiko; Unternehmerwagnis; **at consignor's** ~ auf Gefahr des Absenders; **contractor's** ~ Unternehmerrisiko; **cover on ~s** Deckung von Risiken; **credit** ~ Kreditrisiko; **customary ~s** handelsübliche Risiken; **decrease in** ~ Gefahrverminderung; **distribution of** ~ s. spreading of→~; **exchange (rate)** ~ Kursrisiko; **excluded** ~ ausgeschlossenes Risiko; **fire** ~ Brandgefahr; **loading** ~ Verladerisiko; **marine** (or **maritime**) ~ See(transport)gefahr; **at one's own** ~ auf eigene Gefahr; **passing of (the)** ~ Gefahrübergang; **pending ~s** laufende Risiken; **price** ~ Kursrisiko; **at receiver's** ~ auf Gefahr des Empfängers; **at sender's** ~ auf Gefahr des Absenders; **size of the** ~ Größe (od. Umfang) des Risikos; **spreading of** ~ Risikoverteilung, Risikostreuung; **transport** ~ Transportgefahr; **usual ~s** übliche Risiken; **war** ~ Kriegsrisiko

risk, to assume a ~ ein Risiko übernehmen; **to bear the** ~ die Gefahr tragen; **to incur a** ~ ein Risiko eingehen; sich e-r Gefahr aussetzen; **to run the** ~ Gefahr laufen, das Risiko eingehen; **to spread the** ~ das Risiko verteilen; **to take** (or **undertake**) **a** ~ ein Risiko übernehmen (od. eingehen); **the** ~ **is borne by ...** (or **lies with ...**) die Gefahr trägt ...; **the goods are at buyer's** ~ der Käufer trägt die Gefahr; **the** ~ **passes to the buyer** die Gefahr geht auf den Käufer über; **the time when the** ~ **passes (to the buyer)** der Zeitpunkt des Gefahrübergangs

risk 2. *(VersR)* Gefahr(enquelle); *(das vom Versicherer übernommene)* Risiko; versicherte Person; versicherter Gegenstand; ~ **aggravation** Risikoerhöhung; ~ **assessment** Risikobeurteilung; **~s book** Liste der übernommenen Risiken; ~ **covered** gedecktes Risiko, versicherte Gefahr; ~ **insured against** versicherte Gefahr; versichertes Risiko; ~ **markup** Risikoaufschlag; ~ **premium** Risikoprämie *(opp. gross or office premium)*; ~ **rating** Risikobewertung; **accumulation of** ~ Risikenhäufung; **against all ~s** (a.r.r.) gegen alle Gefahren; **aggravated** ~ erhöhtes Risiko; **all ~s policy** Universal(auto-)versicherung; **amount at** ~ Risikosumme (→*amount*); **amount of** ~ Größe des Risikos; **attachment of** ~ Beginn des Versicherungsrisikos; **category** (or **class**) **of ~s** Gefahrenklasse; **distribution of** ~ Risikoaufteilung; **exclusion of** ~ Risikoausschluß; **a good** ~ ein gutes Versicherungsobjekt; **particulars of the** ~ Gefahrenmerkmale; **preferred** ~ **plan** *Am* Schadensfreiheitsrabatt; **uninsured ~s** ungedeckte Risiken; **to cover a** ~ ein Risiko decken, sich gegen ein Risiko versichern; für ein Risiko die Versicherung übernehmen; **to share the** ~ das Risiko teilen (→*reinsurance*); **to underwrite marine ~s** e-e Seeversicherung unter Risikoverteilung übernehmen

risky speculation gewagte Spekulation

rival Rivale; Mitbewerber, Konkurrent; ~ **candidate** *parl* Gegenkandidat; ~ **firm** Konkurrenzfirma; ~ **trader** Konkurrent; ~ **union dispute** *Am* Streitigkeit zwischen zwei od. mehr Gewerkschaften über die Frage der Vertretung e-r bestimmten Gruppe von Arbeitnehmern bei Tarifverhandlungen; **business ~s** Konkurrenten

rivalry (between) Rivalität (zwischen); Konkurrenz, Wettbewerb

river Fluß; Strom; ~ **bank** Flußufer; ~ **bed** Flußbett; ~ **bill of lading** Ladeschein; ~ **craft** Flußfahrzeug; ~ **fishery** Flußfischerei, Binnenfischerei; **~side** Flußufer; **down the** ~ stromabwärts; **international** ~ internationaler Fluß; **navigable** ~ schiffbarer Fluß; **up the** ~ stromaufwärts

road (Land-, Fahr-)Straße; (Land-)Weg; **~(s)** Reede (→*roadstead*); ~ **accident** Verkehrsunfall, Autounfall; ~ **behavio(u)r** Verkehrsdisziplin; **~(-)block** Straßensperre; **~(-)book**

Straßenatlas; ~ **building** Straßenbau; ~ **carrying fast-moving traffic** *Br* Straße mit Schnellverkehr; ~ **charges** *Br* Erschließungsbeiträge *(für Straßenbau);* ~ **check** Straßenkontrolle, Verkehrsstreife; ~ **clear** *Am* freie Fahrt; ~ **closed** Straße gesperrt; ~ **construction** Straßenbau(arbeiten)

road haulage (of goods) *Br* Güterkraftverkehr; ~ **company** *Br* Güterkraftverkehrsunternehmen; ~ **operator** Kraftverkehrsunternehmer; **long distance** ~ *Br* Fernlastverkehr

road, ~ **hauler (haulier)** Güterkraftverkehrsunternehmer; ~ **hog** *Br. colloq.* rücksichtsloser (od. unbedachter) Fahrer, Verkehrsrowdy; ~ **house** Gasthaus *(an der Landstraße),* Kneipe; ~ **making** Straßenbau; Wegebau; ~ **map** Straßenkarte, Autokarte

road marking Straßenmarkierung; **European Agreement on R~ M~s**[93] Europäisches Übereinkommen über Straßenmarkierungen

road, ~ **narrows** Engpaß *(verengte Fahrbahn);* ~ **network** Straßennetz; ~ **passenger transport** Personenkraftverkehr; Beförderung von Personen im Straßenverkehr; ~ **passenger transport operator** Personenkraftverkehrsunternehmer; ~**, rail and inland waterway transport** Straßen-, Eisenbahn- u. Binnenschiffsverkehr; ~**/rail carriage of goods** Güterverkehr Schiene/Straße; ~ **repairs** Straßen(ausbesserungs-)arbeiten; ~ **safety** Verkehrssicherheit, Sicherheit im Straßenverkehr

road signs (Straßen-)Verkehrszeichen; **international** ~ internationale Verkehrszeichen; **prohibitive regulatory** (or **mandadatory**) ~ Vorschriftszeichen *(Verkehrszeichen)*

roadstead Reede *(bequemer Ankerplatz in Küstennähe)*; **ship lying in a** ~ Schiff, das auf Reede liegt

road toll Straßenbenutzungsgebühr

road traffic Straßenverkehr; **R~ T~ Act** (RTA) *Br* Straßenverkehrsgesetz *(Gesetz von 1972 und 1974)*; ~ **offence (~se)** Verkehrsdelikt; ~ **offender** Verkehrssünder

Road Traffic, Convention on ~[93a] Übereinkommen über den Straßenverkehr; →**European Agreement Supplementing the Convention on** ~

road ~ **transport** Straßenverkehr; ~ **under repair** Straße mit Baustellen; Straßenarbeiten; ~ **up** Straße *(wegen Baustelle)* gesperrt

road user Verkehrsteilnehmer; ~ **on foot** Fußgänger; ~ **on wheels** Kraftfahrer

roadway *Br* Fahrbahn

road works Straßenbauarbeiten

road, access ~ Zufahrtsstraße; **arterial** ~ Hauptverkehrsstraße; **by-**~ Nebenstraße; **by** ~ im Straßentransport, per Achse; **clear** ~ freie Straße; **cross~(s)** Straßenkreuzung; **in the** ~ auf der (Land-)Straße; **in the ~(s)** auf Reede (→*roadstead*); **main** ~ Hauptstraße; **maintenance of ~s** Straßenunterhaltung, Wegeunterhaltung; **major** ~ Fernverkehrsstraße; Vorfahrtstraße; **no through** ~ keine Durchfahrt

road, on the ~ unterwegs; **to be on the** ~ *(bes. geschäftl.)* unterwegs sein

road, private ~ nicht öffentliche Straße; Privatweg; **rules of the** ~ →rule 1.; **two-lane** ~ zweispurige Straße; **upkeep of ~s** s. maintenance of →~s; **use of a** ~ Benutzung e-r Straße; **the** ~ **is clear** die Straße ist frei; **to close a** ~ e-e Straße sperren; **to cross the** ~ die Straße überqueren

rob *v* (be)rauben; **to** ~ **sb. of sth.** jdm etw. rauben

robber Räuber

robbery[94] Raub, Raubüberfall; ~ **insurance** Beraubungsversicherung; **aggravated** ~ schwerer Raub; **armed** ~ bewaffneter Raubüberfall; **bank** ~ Bankraub, Banküberfall; **church** ~ Kirchendiebstahl; **highway** ~ Straßenraub; **mail** ~ Postdiebstahl; **to commit** ~ Raub begehen; **to take part in a gang** ~ sich an e-m Raubzug beteiligen

robe Robe, Amtstracht, Talar; **the (long)** ~ der Beruf der Juristen; **gentlemen of the** ~ Juristen (Anwälte od. Richter)

Robinson-Patman Act *Am* Antitrustgesetz *(von 1936),* welches Preis- und sonstige Diskriminierung zwischen gleichgestellten Abnehmern verbietet *(Erweiterung des Clayton Act, sec. 2.)*

rock-bottom price *colloq.* äußerst kalkulierter Preis; niedrigster Kurs

rocket Rakete; Raketen-; ~ **launching site** Raketen(abschuß)basis; ~ **range** Raketenversuchsgelände; **anti-aircraft** ~ Luftabwehrrakete; **intercontinental** ~ Interkontinentalrakete; **launching of ~s** Abschuß von Raketen; **multistage** ~ Mehrstufenrakete

rocketry Raketenwesen; Raketenwissenschaft

rogation, ~ **days** drei Tage vor Himmelfahrt (Ascension Day); ~ **week** die Woche, in der Himmelfahrt liegt

rogatory, letters ~ *bes. Am* Rechtshilfeersuchen (→*letters 3.*)

rogue Landstreicher; **~s' gallery** *Am* Verbrecheralbum

ROI →return on investment (→*return 5.*)

role, to play a ~ e-e Rolle spielen

roll Rolle; *(öffentl.)* Urkunde; Liste *(von Namen)*; (Gerichts-, Parlaments-)Protokoll; Anwaltsliste *(Br der zugelassenen solicitors)*; *Scot* Terminkalender; ~**-back** *Am colloq.* Preisherabsetzung *(durch Regierungsmaßnahme); (EG)* Abbau mengenmäßiger Beschränkungen

roll call Namensaufruf, Aufrufen der Namen; *mil* Anwesenheitsappell; ~ **vote** (or **vote by** ~) Abstimmung durch Namensaufruf, namentliche Abstimmung; **to take a** ~ **vote** namentlich abstimmen
roll ~ **of hono(u)r** Ehrentafel der Gefallenen
Roll of Solicitors, to be admitted to the ~ *Br* als Anwalt zugelassen werden
Rolls Series *Br* Sammlung britischer Urkunden und Quellen
roll, assessment ~ Steuerliste; **court** ~**s** Gerichtsakten; **death** ~ Verlustliste; **electoral** ~ Wahlliste, Wählerliste; →**Master of the R~s; muster** ~ *mil* Stammrolle; **nominal** ~ Namensverzeichnis, Namensliste; *mil* Stammrolle; **Parliament R~s** *Br* Parlamentsprotokolle *(bes. Gesetze)*; **Patent R~s** *Br* Patentrolle; **to be admitted to the** ~ als Anwalt (*Br* solicitor) zugelassen werden; **to call the** ~ die Namensliste verlesen, namentlich aufrufen; **to be struck off the** ~ von der Anwaltsliste *(Br als solicitor durch die Law Society)* gestrichen werden (→*disbar v*)

roll *v* rollen; **to** ~ **back** *Am colloq. (Preise durch Regierungsmaßnahmen)* senken; **to** ~ **forward** *(Steuer)* überwälzen
roll on/roll off (traffic) Ro-Ro-Verkehr *(im Ladehafen an Bord gestellt, im Bestimmungshafen von Bord gerollt)*
rolled, to be ~ **not tipped** nicht kanten, sondern rollen!
rolling, ~ **capital** Betriebskapital; ~ **mill** Walzwerk; ~ **rate note** zinsvariabler Schuldtitel, dessen Zins sich an den gleitenden Durchschnitten von drei aufeinanderfolgenden →LIMEAN-Sätzen orientiert; ~ **stock** *(Eisenbahn)* rollendes Material; Waggonbestand; **to be** ~ **in money** *sl.* im Geld schwimmen

rollover Darlehensverlängerung mit neu festgesetztem Zinssatz; *(auch)* Neufestsetzung des Zinssatzes selbst; ~ **credit** *(Eurokreditmarkt)* langfristiger Kredit zu kurzfristigen Zinssätzen *(die sich aus den Refinanzierungskosten der Bankdepositen ergeben)*

Romalpha clause[94a] Eigentumsvorbehaltsklausel *(des Lieferanten)*

Roman, ~ **Catholic** Katholik; ~ **Catholicism** Katholizismus; ~ **Law** römisches Recht; ~ **numerals** römische Ziffern

Romania Rumänien; **Socialist Republic of** ~ Sozialistische Republik Rumänien
Romanian Rumän|e, ~in; rumänisch

rood *(Flächenmaß)* ¼ e-s →acre

room Raum; Zimmer; ~**s to let** Zimmer zu vermieten; ~ **trader** *Am* →floor trader; **assembly** ~ Versammlungsraum; **auction** ~ Auktionslokal; **court** ~ Gerichtssaal; **furnished** ~ **(with attendance)** möbliertes Zimmer (mit Bedienung); **meeting** ~ Sitzungssaal; **show** ~ Ausstellungshalle; **vacant** ~ freies Zimmer; **to book** (or **reserve**) **a (hotel)** ~ ein (Hotel-)Zimmer bestellen; **to let (furnished)** ~**s** (möblierte) Zimmer vermieten; **to rent** (or *Br* **to take**) **a** ~ ein Zimmer mieten (with bei)

roomer *Am* Untermieter, Mieter e-s Zimmers

rooming house *Am* Pension, Logierhaus

Roosa-bonds *Am* Schuldverschreibungen des amerikanischen Schatzamtes

root of title älteste Urkunde, auf die Eigentumsrecht an Grundbesitz zurückgeführt wird *(Br wichtig für →unregistered land)*; **good** ~ Urkunde, aus der sich ein unangreifbares, fehlerfreies Eigentum am Grundstück ergibt

roster Dienstplan; (Anschriften-)Liste, Mitgliedsverzeichnis

rostrum Rednertribüne; **to come down from the** ~ die Rednertribüne verlassen; **to go up to the** ~ sich auf die Rednertribüne begeben; **to mount the** ~ die Rednertribüne besteigen

rota Turnus; Dienstplan

Rotarian Rotarier *(Mitglied e-s Rotary Club)*

rotating turnusmäßig wechselnd; ~ **shift** Wechselschicht

rotation turnusmäßiger Wechsel; Turnus; ~ **(in office)** turnusmäßiger Amtswechsel, Rotation; ~ **of crops** Fruchtwechsel; ~ **of ports** Reihenfolge, in der Häfen angelaufen werden; ~ **(period)** Turnus
rotation, by (or **in**) ~ turnusmäßig, im Turnus; **to retire by** (or **in**) ~ turnusmäßig ausscheiden
rotation, job ~ *Am (innerbetrieblicher)* Arbeitsplatzwechsel *(Methode des Austauschs von Abteilungsleitern untereinander; cf. multiple →management)*

rouble *Br* Rubel *(Währungseinheit der Sowjetunion)*

rough roh, grob; ungefähr; ~ **average** annähernder Durchschnitt; ~ **balance** Rohbilanz; ~ **calculation** Überschlag; Voranschlag; ~ **draft** erster Entwurf, Konzept; ~ **estimate of an expense** ungefährer Kostenvoranschlag; ~ **guess** ungefähre Schätzung

round Runde; Schuß, Ladung; ~ **of ammunition** Schuß Munition; ~ **of negotiations** Verhandlungsrunde; **to fire two** ~**s** zwei Schüsse abgeben; **to make the** ~ die Runde machen

round up of criminals Aushebung von Verbrechern; Razzia; **the police conducted a ~** die Polizei veranstaltete e-e Razzia

round *v*, **to ~ off** abrunden; **to ~ up** aufrunden; **to ~ up a gang of criminals** e-e Verbrecherbande ausheben

round rund; **in a ~about way** indirekt; **traffic at a ~about** *Br* Kreisverkehr; **in ~ figures** in runden Zahlen, rund; **~ lot** *(Börse)* 100 Stück e-r Aktie od. ein Vielfaches von 100 *(opp. odd lot)*; **in ~ numbers** s. in ~→ figures; **~ sum** runde Summe, glatter Betrag; **~ table conference** Konferenz am runden Tisch *(zwischen Gleichberechtigten)*; **~ trip** Rundreise; *Am* Hin- und Rückfahrt; **~ trip fare** *Am* Preis für Hin- und Rückfahrt; **~ trip ticket** *Am* Rückfahrkarte; **~ voyage** Schiffsrundreise; *Am* Hin- und Rückreise

roup *Scot* Auktion

roustabout *Am* Werftarbeiter, Arbeiter auf e-m Ölbohrturm

rout Zusammenrottung, Auflauf *(Delikt, das zwischen unlawful assembly und riot liegt)*

route Route, Weg, Strecke; Flugstrecke, Fluglinie; Schiffahrtsweg; **~ instructions** Leitvermerk; **~ of travel** Beförderungsweg *(Personenverkehr)*; **en ~** unterwegs; **forwarding ~** Beförderungsweg *(Güterverkehr)*; **to depart from the ~** von der *(vorgeschriebenen)* Route abweichen

route *v* die Route (od. die Reihenfolge der Arbeitsgänge) festlegen

routine Routine; gewohnheitsmäßiger Gang; üblich; **~ duties** laufende *(zum gewöhnl. Geschäftsbereich gehörende)* Pflichten; **~ expenditure** übliche Ausgaben; **~ matters** übliche Angelegenheiten; **~ work** Routinearbeit, alltägliche Arbeit; **as a matter of ~** routinemäßig; **office ~** üblicher Arbeitsgang *(im Büro)*; täglich anfallende Büroarbeit

Royal königlich; **~ Academician** *Br* Mitglied der ~ Academy; **~ Academy (of Arts)** *Br* Königl. Akademie der Künste; **~ Air Force** (R. A. F.) *Br* (Königl.) Luftwaffe; **~ Arms** *Br* Königl. Wappen; **~ Assent** *Br* Königl. Zustimmung *(die dem Gesetzesentwurf Gesetzeskraft verleiht)*; **~ Charter** *Br* Königliche Konzession *(→charter 1.)*; **~ Commission** *Br* Königliche Kommission *(von der Regierung ernannte Sachverständige ersten Ranges, die in grundlegenden Fragen sozialer, wirtschaftlicher und politischer Art richtungsweisende Berichte erstatten)*; **~ demesne** *Br* Krongüter, Staatsdomänen; **~ estate** *Br* Staatsdomäne; **~ fish** *Br* der Krone gehörende Fische *(in der Nähe der Küste gefangene Wale und Störe)*; **~ fishery** *Br* Fischereiregal der Krone an öffentlichen Gewässern; **Her ~ Highness** Ihre Königliche Hoheit; **~ Humane Society** *Br* (Königl.) Lebensrettungsgesellschaft; **~ Marines** *Br* (Königl.) Marine-Infanterie; **~ mines** *Br (der Krone gehörende)* Silber- od. Goldbergwerke; **~ Navy** (R. N.) *Br* (Königl.) Kriegsmarine; **~ personage** *Br* Mitglied der Königl. Familie; **~ prerogative** *Br* →prerogative

Royal Society (for the Advancement of Science) (R. S.) *Br* Königl. Akademie der (Natur-) Wissenschaften

Gegr. 1660. *Sitz:* London. Älteste naturwissenschaftliche Gesellschaft (umfaßt Naturwissenschaften, Mathematik und Medizin). Die Mitglieder der R. S. heißen Fellows (darunter ausländische Mitglieder)

Royal Society for the Prevention of Cruelty to Animals (R. S. P. C. A.) *Br* (Königl.) Tierschutzverein

Royal warrant *Br* Hoflieferantendiplom; **to hold a ~** das Diplom e-s Hoflieferanten besitzen

royalist Royalist, Anhänger des Königshauses

royalt|y Königtum; Königswürde; Mitglieder der königl. Familie *(meist* **~ies**); (vertragl. festgelegter) Ertragsanteil *(bes. an Autoren, Patentinhaber)*; (Autoren-)Tantieme, Honorar; *(PatentR)* Lizenzgebühren; *(BergR)* Förderabgaben, Bergwerksabgaben; **~ agreement** Lizenzvertrag; **on a ~ basis** gegen Zahlung e-r Lizenzgebühr; **~ cheque (check)** Rückscheck; **~-free licen|ce (~se)** gebührenfreie Lizenz; **~ies in respect of the operation of mines** *(DBA)* Vergütungen für die Ausbeutung von Bergwerken; **~ per unit** Stücklizenz; **~ rent** *Br* prozentuale Pacht im Verhältnis zum Ertrag e-s Bergwerks *(opp. dead rent)*; **copyright ~ies** Lizenzgebühren für Urheberrecht; **licen|ce (~se) subject to ~** gebührenpflichtige Lizenz; **percentage ~** Prozentlizenz; **recipient of the ~ies** Empfänger der Lizenzgebühren; **to derive ~ies** Lizenzgebühren beziehen; **to pay a ~** e-e Vergütung (Honorar etc) entrichten; **to tender ~ accounts** über die Lizenzgebühr(en) abrechnen

rubber (Natur-)Kautschuk, Gummi; Radiergummi; **~s →~** shares; **~ check** ungedeckter Scheck; **~ estate** (or **plantation**) Kautschukplantage; **~ shares (stock[s])** Gummiaktien, Gummiwerte; **~ stamp** Gummistempel; **Association of Natural R~ Producing Countries** (ANRPC) Vereinigung der Naturkautschuk-Erzeugerländer; →**International Natural R~ Agreement; natural ~**[94b] Naturkautschuk

rubble Trümmer(gestein), Schutt; **~ clearing** Schuttaufräumung

ruble →rouble

rubric Rubrik; Überschrift; **~ of a statute** Titel e-s Gesetzes; *Scot* Leitsatz *(e-r Entscheidung)*

RUF →revolving underwriting facility

ruin Ruine; Ruin, finanzieller Zusammenbruch; ~**s** Trümmer; **to bring to** ~ ruinieren, zugrunde richten

ruin *v* ruinieren, zugrunde richten

ruinous ruinös; baufällig; ~ **competition** ruinöser Wettbewerb; ~ **price** ruinöser Preis, Schleuderpreis; ~ **sale** Verkauf mit Verlust; **in a** ~ **state** baufällig

rule 1. Regel; Vorschrift; Richtlinie; Satzung; ~**s and regulations of a bank** allgemeine Geschäftsbedingungen e-r Bank; **R**~ **Committee** *Br* →rule 3.; **R**~**s Committee** *Am* Geschäftsordnungsausschuß *(des Repräsentantenhauses)*; ~**s of the air** Luftverkehrsregeln; ~**s of the club** Vereinssatzung; ~**s of conduct** Verhaltensmaßregeln; ~**s of the house** Hausordnung; ~**s of interpretation** Auslegungsregeln; ~**s of the road** *Am* Verkehrsregeln *(zu Wasser und zu Lande)*; **R**~**s of the Stock Exchange** Börsenordnung; ~ **of thumb** Faustregel, Erfahrungstatsache; **against the** ~**s** vorschriftswidrig; **as a** ~ in der Regel; **common** ~**s** Richtlinien; **exception to the** ~ Ausnahme von der Regel; **Fair Practices R**~**s** *Am (AntitrustR) (zwischen der Federal Trade Commission und den beteiligten Wirtschaftskreisen festgelegte)* Regeln zur Auslegung des zum Schutze des Wettbewerbs bestehenden Rechts; **formal** ~**s** Formvorschriften

rule, general ~ allgemeine Regel; Norm; **as a** ~ in der Regel

rule, guiding ~ Richtlinie; **standing** ~ feststehende Regel; **to be the** ~ vorgeschrieben sein; **to become the** ~ zur Regel werden; **to establish** ~**s** Vorschriften erlassen; Regeln aufstellen; **to lay down** ~**s** Regeln aufstellen; **to make it a** ~ es zur Regel machen; **the** ~ **is liable to exception** die Regel unterliegt e-r Ausnahme

rule 2. Rechtsregel, Rechtsgrundsatz; ~ **against accumulations** Regel, daß Einkünfte e-s trust nicht auf unbestimmte oder längere Zeit angesammelt werden können; ~ **against →competition;** ~ **against →perpetuities;** ~**s of evidence** Beweisregeln; ~**s of good husbandry** *Br*[95] Regeln der ordnungsgemäßen Bewirtschaftung; ~ **of law** Herrschaft des Rechts, Rechtsstaatlichkeit *(Vorherrschaft des Rechts über die Verwaltung)*; ~ **of precedent** Rechtsregel des bindenden Präzedenzfalles *(cf. stare decisis)*

rule of reason *Am (AntitrustR)* Vernunftsregel *(nach der ein Gesetz ausgelegt werden soll)*

Maßgeblicher Auslegungsgrundsatz für die Beurteilung der rechtlichen Zulässigkeit von Wettbewerbsklauseln und wettbewerbsbeschränkendem Verhalten. Nach der rule of reason sind (im Ggs. zur →per se-Regel) wettbewerbsbeschränkende Abreden zulässig, wenn sie vernünftig (reasonable) erscheinen und nicht gegen die public policy verstoßen. Eine Beschränkung des Wettbewerbs kann also nur dann als rechtswidrig (d. h. gegen die Antitrustgesetze verstoßend) angesehen werden, wenn sie unreasonable ist.

Die rule of reason, die dem Gericht weitgehendes Ermessen in der Beurteilung aller erheblichen wirtschaftlichen Umstände gibt, ist in der letzten Zeit von dem Obersten Gericht der Vereinigten Staaten mehr und mehr preisgegeben worden

rules on competition Wettbewerbsregeln

rule 3. *(meist* ~**s**) Verfahrensregel(n), Verfahrensvorschriften; (Zivil-)Prozeßordnung, Prozeßvorschrift(en); *Am (von den Verwaltungsbehörden auf Grund gesetzl. Ermächtigung erlassene Norm:)* Rechtsverordnung; Ausführungsverordnung; Verordnungsvorschrift

Br Das Verfahrensrecht ist nicht in einer einheitl. Verfahrensordnung kodifiziert, sondern vornehmlich in orders oder rules der einzelnen Gerichtshöfe niedergelegt

rule, R~ **Committee** *Br (aus Richtern und Anwälten bestehender)* Prozeßordnungsausschuß *(→Rules of the Supreme Court);* ~**-making** *Am* Erlaß von Verwaltungsvorschriften; **R**~**s of Conciliation and Arbitration** (of the International Chamber of Commerce)[96] Vergleichs- und Schiedsgerichtsordnung (der Intern. Handelskammer); ~**s of court** (or **court** ~**s**) gerichtl. Verfahrensvorschriften, Verfahrensregeln (→~*s of procedure*); Geschäftsordnung *(z. B. des Internationalen Gerichtshofs);* **ICC R**~**s of Optional →Conciliation;** ~**s of order** *parl* Geschäftsordnung, Verfahrensregeln *(Regeln über den ordnungsgemäßen Geschäftsverkehr in den Sitzungen)*; ~**s of practice** (or **practice** ~**s**) *Am* Verfahrensvorschriften, Verfahrensregeln; (Zivil-) Prozeßordnung

rules of procedure Verfahrensregeln; Verfahrensordnung, Prozeßordnung; Geschäftsordnung; **Federal Rules of Civil Procedure** *Am* Bundes-Zivilprozeßordnung; **Federal Rules of Criminal Procedure** *Am* Bundes-Strafprozeßordnung; **the organization shall adopt its own** ~ die Organisation erläßt ihre Verfahrensordnung selbst

Br Von Richtern und Anwälten (auf Grund der Bestimmungen des Judicature Act) geschaffenes Verfahrensrecht (das Verfahrensrecht des Supreme Court und der County Courts besteht aus orders, die in rules unterteilt sind)

rules of procedure, adoption of the ~ Annahme der Geschäftsordnung; **observance of the** ~ Einhaltung der Geschäftsordnung; **to adopt the** ~ die Geschäftsordnung annehmen (od. beschließen); **to adopt one's own** ~ sich s-e eigene Geschäftsordnung geben; s-e eigenen Verfahrensregeln beschließen; **to draw up the** ~ die Geschäftsordnung aufstellen; **to observe the** ~ die Geschäftsordnung einhalten

Rules of the Supreme Court (R. S. C.) *Br* Verfahrensregeln des Supreme →Court

Von dem Rule Committee aufgestellte, 1883 zusammengefaßte und 1965 geänderte Verfahrensvorschriften, die in dem „Annual Practice of the Supreme Court" zu finden sind

rule 4. **(~ of court)** gerichtl. Entscheidung *(in e-m Verfahren)*; ~ **absolute** *Br* endgültige Entscheidung; ~ **discharged** *Br* s. to discharge a →~; ~ **nisi** (or ~ **to show cause**) *Br* (vorläufige) Entscheidung, die endgültig wird, wenn es dem Beklagten nicht gelingt, triftige Gründe vorzubringen und die Aufhebung zu erwirken; **to discharge a** ~ *Br* die *(nachgesuchte)* Entscheidung verweigern, weil sie nicht hinreichend begründet ist, od. die Entscheidung aufheben, weil der Gegner e-n triftigen Gegengrund vorgebracht hat

rule 5. Herrschaft; **foreign** ~ Fremdherrschaft; **majority** ~ Herrschaft der Mehrheit; **mob** ~ Herrschaft des Pöbels

rule *v* regeln, anordnen, entscheiden, zu der Entscheidung kommen; (be)herrschen (over über); liniieren; **to** ~ **that** verfügen (od. e-n Gerichtsbeschluß erlassen), daß; **to** ~ **off an account** ein Konto abschließen; **to** ~ **sth. out** etw. ausschließen; **to** ~ **sb. out of order** *parl* jdm das Wort entziehen

ruling *(amtl. od. gerichtl.)* Entscheidung; Anordnung; Herrschaft; vorherrschend; geltend, bestehend; ~ **case** →leading case; **R~ Case Law** *Am* (Titel e-r) Sammlung von Entscheidungen; ~ **house** Herrscherhaus; ~ **price** gegenwärtiger Preis, Tagespreis, Marktpreis; **court** (or **judicial**) ~ gerichtl. Entscheidung; Gerichtsbeschluß; richterl. Verfügung; **price** ~ preisbestimmend; **to give** (or **make**) **a** ~ e-e Entscheidung fällen; e-n Bescheid erteilen

rummage Durchsuchen *(Br bes. e-s Schiffes durch Zollbeamte)*; Ramsch, Ausschuß; ~ **sale** *bes. Am* Ramschverkauf; Wohltätigkeitsbasar

rummaging of a ship *Br (zollamtl.)* Durchsuchung e-s Schiffes

rumo(u)r Gerücht (of über); **to disseminate** (or **spread**) **a** ~ ein Gerücht verbreiten; **the** ~ **is unfounded** (or **without foundation**) das Gerücht ist haltlos; **the** ~ **runs** es geht das Gerücht

rumrunner *Am* Alkoholschmuggler

rumrunning *Am* Alkoholschmuggel

run Lauf, Gang; Ansturm (on a bank auf e-e Bank); starke Nachfrage (on nach); Sorte, Klasse; zurückgelegte (Schiffs-)Strecke; Reihe, Folge, Dauer; **the** ~ **of events** der Gang der Ereignisse; ~ **of office** Amtsdauer; ~ **on shares** starke Nachfrage nach Aktien; **common** ~ durchschnittliche Art; **hit-and-~ driver** jd, der Fahrerflucht begangen hat; **in the long** ~ auf die Dauer, auf lange Sicht; **in the short** ~ auf kurze Sicht; **on the** ~ auf der Flucht; **trial** ~ Probefahrt; **to have the** ~ **of** freien Zutritt haben zu; etw. benutzen dürfen; **to have a long** ~ lange im Amt bleiben; **there was a great** ~ **on the article** der Artikel war stark gefragt

runabout ticket *Br (Eisenbahn)* Netzkarte

runaway durchgegangen, flüchtig; *com* schnellen Veränderungen unterworfen, schnell steigend; ~ **firms** *Am* Fluchtbetriebe *(die z.B. in Länder mit niedrigeren Arbeitslöhnen ausweichen)*; ~ **inflation** galoppierende Inflation; ~ **victory** Sieg mit großem Vorsprung, „Erdrutschsieg"

rundown Verringerung; Einschränkung; ~ **of staff** *Br* Personalabbau

runoff, ~ **election** Stichwahl; ~ **primary** *Am (in einigen Südstaaten)* endgültige Vorwahl

runup of prices in the stock market *Am* Steigen der Kurse am Aktienmarkt

run *v (Wechsel, Anleihe, Zinsen etc)* laufen; *(Geschäft, Maschinen)* laufen, in Betrieb sein; *(Ausgaben)* sich belaufen (to auf); *(Text, Brief)* lauten, den Wortlaut haben; *(Geld)* in Umlauf sein; *(öffentl. Verkehrsmittel)* verkehren; *(Verkehrsmittel etc)* betreiben; **to** ~ **against sb.** *(als Gegenkandidat)* gegen jdn auftreten; **to** ~ **aground** (or **ashore**) auflaufen, stranden; auflaufen lassen, auf Strand setzen; **to** ~ **the blockade** die Blockade brechen; **to** ~ **a business** ein Geschäft führen (od. leiten); **to** ~ **in connection with** *(Zug etc)* Anschluß haben an; **to** ~ **down sb.** jdn überfahren; *fig (jdn)* herabsetzen, in Verruf bringen; **to** ~ **down the goods of a competitor** die Ware des Konkurrenten anschwärzen; **to** ~ **down another ship** ein anderes Schiff *(nach Zusammenstoß)* in den Grund bohren; **to** ~ **errands** Botengänge machen; **to** ~ **a factory** e-e Fabrik leiten; **to** ~ **for** kandidieren für; **to** ~ **for a position** sich um e-n Posten bewerben; **to** ~ **for the Presidency** *Am* als Präsident kandidieren; **to** ~ **for the Senate** *Am* für den Senat kandidieren; **to** ~ **foul with a ship** mit e-m Schiff zusammenstoßen; **to** ~ **a hotel** ein Hotel führen; **to** ~ **into debt** sich in Schulden stürzen, in Schulden geraten; **to** ~ **into 10 editions** 10 Auflagen erleben; **to** ~ **into money** ins Geld gehen; e-e beträchtliche Summe betragen; **to** ~ **into thousands** in die Tausende gehen; **to** ~ **low** knapp werden, ausgehen; **to** ~ **messages** Botengänge machen; **to** ~ **out** ablaufen *(Pacht, Paß etc)*; zu Ende gehen, ausgehen *(Vorräte)*; **I have** ~ **out of this article** dieser Artikel ist mir ausgegangen; **the lease has** ~ **out** die Miete ist abgelaufen; **to** ~ **over** *(schnell)* durchlesen, überfliegen; noch einmal *(schnell)* durchgehen; *(jdn)* überfahren; **to** ~ **a risk** das Risiko eingehen; Gefahr laufen; **to** ~ **short** zu Ende gehen, knapp werden (of an); *(Waren)* nicht mehr vorrätig haben; **to ~ stock against one's client** Aktien seines Auftraggebers aufkaufen; **to ~ through** *(schnell)* durchlesen; **to ~ through a fortune** ein Vermögen durchbringen; **to ~ up** *(Preise, Kurse)* in die Höhe treiben; **to ~ up an account at** (or **with**) **a shop** (or **store**) e-e Rechnung in e-m Geschäft anwachsen lassen; auf Kredit kaufen; **to ~ up a flag** e-e Flagge hissen

run *v*, **the contract ~s for 5 years** der Vertrag läuft auf 5 Jahre; **the insurance ~s** die Versicherung läuft; **interest ~s from July 1** die Zinsen laufen ab 1. Juli; **period to ~** Laufzeit; **the period of limitation ~s from ...** die Verjährungsfrist läuft ab ...; **the period (of time) begins** (or **commences**) **to ~** die Frist beginnt zu laufen; **the period (of time) ~s** die Frist läuft; **the statutory period has ~ against the plaintiff** die Verjährungsfrist ist abgelaufen; **the train does not ~ on Sunday** der Zug verkehrt nicht am Sonntag

running 1. Laufen; Leitung; Führung; Laufzeit, Gültigkeitsdauer; Schmuggel

running down Zusammenstoß; Anschwärzung; **~ action** (or **case**) Schadensersatzklage wegen durch fahrlässiges Fahren oder Schiffskollision entstandenen Schadens; **~ clause** (R. D. C.) (Schiffs-)Kollisionsklausel *(regelt Deckung für Schäden bei Zusammenstoß von Schiffen)*

running, ~ into debt Verschuldung; **~ of an agreement** Funktionieren e-s Abkommens; **~ of the business** Geschäftsbetrieb; **~ of interest** Laufzeit der Zinsen; **~ of a period (of time)** Lauf e-r Frist; **~ of the statute of limitation** Lauf der Verjährungsfrist; **to be in the ~** Aussicht haben, in Betracht kommen *(für e-n Posten)*

running 2. (fort)laufend, ununterbrochen; in Betrieb, tätig; **~ account** laufendes Konto; Kontokorrentkonto; *Br* Anschreibkonto *(bei e-m Händler)*; **~ commentary** laufender Kommentar; Hörbericht; Rundfunkbericht; **~ costs** laufende Kosten; Betriebskosten; **~ days** laufende Kalendertage; **~ engagements** laufende Verpflichtungen; **~ expenses** laufende Ausgaben; **~ interest** Stückzinsen; **~ mate** Mitkandidat; Kandidat für das geringere von zwei politischen Ämtern; *Am* Vizepräsidentschaftskandidat; **~ number** laufende Nummer; **in ~ order** betriebsfertig; **~ yield** laufende Rendite; **~ with the land** e-m Grundstück anhaftend *(→covenant ~ with the land)*; **three days ~** drei Tage hintereinander; **a deed ~ to him** *Am* e-e Übertragungsurkunde zu seinen Gunsten; **during the ~ of the contract** während der Laufzeit des Vertrages

rupee (R.) Rupie *(Währungseinheit in Indien, Pakistan, Sri Lanka etc)*

rupture Bruch, Abbruch; **~ of an agreement** Vertragsbruch; **~ of diplomatic relations** Abbruch der diplomatischen Beziehungen

rural ländlich; landwirtschaftlich; Land- *(opp. urban)*; **~ cooperatives** *Am* landwirtschaftliche Genossenschaften; **~ exodus** Landflucht; **~ population** Landbevölkerung; **~ township** *Am* Landgemeinde; **~ workers** ländliche Arbeitskräfte

rush (Geschäfts-, Verkehrs-)Andrang; lebhafte Nachfrage (for nach); Ansturm (on auf); **~ hour(s)** Hauptverkehrszeit(en), Hauptgeschäftszeit(en); **~ of orders** hoher Auftragseingang; **~ order** Eilauftrag

rush *v*, **to ~ a bill through Parliament** *Br* ein Gesetz in Eile durchbringen; **to ~ up reinforcements** in aller Eile Verstärkungen heranbringen; **to ~ up prices** *Am* Kurse in die Höhe treiben

Rwanda Ruanda

Rwandese Ruander, -in; ruandisch

Rwandese Republic Republik Ruanda

S

sabbatical *Br (einjähriger)* bezahlter Bildungsurlaub

sabotage Sabotage; **~ activity** Sabotagetätigkeit; **act of ~** Sabotageakt; **counter-~** Sabotageabwehr; **economic ~** Wirtschaftssabotage; **to commit ~** Sabotage begehen

sabotage *v* Sabotage treiben, sabotieren

sack, to be given the ~ *sl.* entlassen werden

sack *v*, **to ~ a p.** *sl.* jdn entlassen

sacrifice Opfer; *com* Verlust; *(SeeversR)* Aufopferung; **cargo lost by ~** durch Aufopferung verlorengegangene Ladung; **general average ~s** Aufopferungen der großen Havarie, Havarie-Grosse-Opfer; **to sell at a ~** mit Verlust verkaufen

sacrificed goods *(SeeversR)* aufgeopferte Güter

sacrilege Kirchenraub, Kirchenschändung; **~ of** (or **on**) **a grave** Grabschändung

sacrosanct unverletzlich

sacrosanctity Unverletzlichkeit *(von Verträgen)*

safe 1. Safe, Schließfach, Tresorfach; **hire of a** ~ Safemiete; **hirer of a** ~ Mieter e-s Safe; **to force a** ~ ein Safe aufbrechen

safe 2. sicher; ~ **and sound** *colloq.* gesund und wohlbehalten; ~ **conduct** sicheres Geleit; Schutzbrief

safe custody (sichere) Verwahrung *(von Wertpapieren und Wertgegenständen)*; Depotverwahrung (→*custody 2.*); ~ **account** Depotkonto; ~ **agreement** Depotvertrag; ~ **fee** Depotgebühr

safe deposit Tresor, Stahlkammer; Aufbewahrung *(von Wertpapieren od. Wertsachen)* im Tresor; ~ **box** (Bank-)Schließfach, Safe; ~ **company** Gesellschaft zur Aufbewahrung von Wertgegenständen; ~ **vault** Stahlkammer

safeguard Schutz, Sicherung; **S**~ *Am mil* Abwehrraketenprojekt; ~**s** Schutzmaßnahmen; ~ **clause** Schutzklausel, Sicherungsklausel

safeguard *v* schützen, sichern; **to** ~ **interests** Interessen wahren (od. wahrnehmen)

safeguarding, ~ **national security** *Am* Schutz der nationalen Sicherheit; ~ **of the currency** Sicherung der Währung; ~ **of data** *(EDV)* Datenschutz; ~ **duty** *Br* Schutzzoll; ~ **of the peace** Sicherung des Friedens

safe investment sichere Kapitalanlage

safekeeping (sichere) Aufbewahrung (od. Verwahrung); ~ **of a will** (sichere) Verwahrung e-s Testaments; **fee for** ~ Aufbewahrungsgebühr

safety Sicherheit; ~ **appliances** *(gesetzl. vorgeschriebene)* Sicherheitsvorrichtungen; ~ **approval plate** Sicherheits-Zulassungsschild *(e-s Container)*; ~ **belt** *(Auto)* Sicherheitsgurt; ~ **bond** Kaution; Sicherheitsleistung; ~ **factor** Sicherheitsfaktor; ~ **margin** Sicherheitsspanne; ~ **measure** Sicherheitsmaßnahme; ~ **of life at sea**[1] Sicherheit des menschlichen Lebens auf See, Schiffssicherheit; ~ **regulations** Sicherheitsbestimmungen; ~ **standards** *(AtomR)* Sicherheitsnormen; **prejudicial to the** ~ **of the state** der Sicherheit des Staates abträglich; **road** ~ Sicherheit im Straßenverkehr

sag *v* sinken, nachgeben, abschwächen

sagging, ~ **market** abgeschwächter Markt *(mit nur geringem Kurs- od. Preisrückgang)*; ~ **of prices** Absinken der Kurse (od. Preise); ~ **prices** sinkende Kurse (od. Preise)

sail *v* abfahren *(Schiff)*; **expected to** ~ voraussichtliche Abfahrt

sailing Abfahrt, Auslaufen *(e-s Schiffes)*; ~ **date** Abfahrtsdatum; ~ **permit** Abfahrtserlaubnis, Abreiseerlaubnis; ~ **rules** Fahrtregeln *(e-s Schiffes)*; **arrival and** ~ Ankunft und Abfahrt; **list of** ~**s** Liste der Abgangsdaten; **time of** ~ Abfahrtszeit

salable verkäuflich; gangbar; absetzbar; ~ **value** Verkaufswert

salaried bezahlt, besoldet; Gehalt beziehend; ~ **employee** Gehaltsempfänger; *(höherer)* Angestellter; ~ **personnel** Gehaltsempfänger; ~ **worker** Gehaltsempfänger

salary Gehalt; Besoldung; ~ **account** Gehaltskonto; ~ **advance** Gehaltsvorschuß; ~ **and other emoluments** Gehalt und andere Bezüge; ~ **by arrangement** Gehalt nach Vereinbarung; ~ **assignment** Gehaltsabtretung; ~ **bracket** Gehaltsklasse; ~ **change** Gehaltsänderung; ~ **class** Gehaltsgruppe, Besoldungsgruppe; ~ **classification** Gehaltseinstufung; ~ **cut** Gehaltskürzung; ~ **demand** Gehaltsforderung; ~ **disparities** Gehaltsunterschiede; ~ **earner** Gehaltsempfänger, Gehaltsbezieher *(opp. wage earner)*; ~ **increase** Gehaltserhöhung, Gehaltsaufbesserung, Gehaltszulage; ~ **level** Gehaltsstufe; ~ **no object** Gehalt Nebensache; ~ **progression** Gehaltsentwicklung; **S**~ **Reduction Plan** *Am (privater und zusätzlicher)* Altersversorgungsplan *(Prämien werden vom Arbeitseinkommen einbehalten)*

salary required Gehaltsansprüche; **stating** ~ *(in Annoncen)* mit Angabe der Gehaltsansprüche

salar|y, ~ **rise** Gehaltserhöhung; ~ **scale** Besoldungsordnung; Lohn- od. Gehaltsordnung; ~ **slip** Lohn-, Gehaltszettel; Lohn-, Gehaltsabrechnung; **accrued** ~ Gehaltsrückstände; **addition to a p.'s** ~ Gehaltsaufbesserung, Gehaltszulage; **basic** ~ Grundgehalt; **commencing** ~ Anfangsgehalt; **cut in** ~ Gehaltskürzung; **deduction from** ~ Gehaltsabzug; **executive** ~**ies** *Am* Gehalt der leitenden Angestellten; **final** ~ Endgehalt; **fixed** ~ festes Gehalt; **increase in** ~ →~ increase; **initial** ~ Anfangsgehalt; **maximum** ~ Höchstgehalt; **M.P.s'** ~**ies** *Br* Diäten der Abgeordneten; **reduction in** (or **of**) ~ Gehaltskürzung; **regular** ~ festes Gehalt; **starting** ~ Anfangsgehalt; **rise in** ~ Gehaltserhöhung; **top level** ~ Spitzengehalt; **to anticipate one's** ~ Gehaltsvorschuß nehmen; **to ask for an advance on one's** ~ um Gehaltsvorschuß bitten; **to draw a** ~ ein Gehalt beziehen; **to fix the** ~ das Gehalt festsetzen; **to increase the** ~ das Gehalt erhöhen (od. aufbessern); **to receive a** ~ ein Gehalt beziehen; **to receive an advance on one's** ~ Gehaltsvorschuß bekommen

sale 1. Verkauf (und Übereignung) *(Vertrag zwischen seller/vendor und buyer/purchaser)*; Vertrieb, Absatz (→*sales*); Auktion (→*sale 3.*); Ausverkauf (→*sale 2.*); ~ **and lease back** Verkauf e-s Leasingobjektes an die Leasing-Gesellschaft und anschließende Rückvermietung an den Verkäufer (Leasingnehmer); ~ **by the bulk** Verkauf in Bausch und Bogen; ~ **by description** Verkauf nach Beschreibung; ~ **by lot** Partieverkauf; ~ **by private treaty** *Br* freihändiger Verkauf *(von Grundbesitz)*; ~ **by sample** Kauf nach Muster (od. Probe); ~ **by**

tender Verkauf durch Submission; ~ **contract** Kaufvertrag (→*contract of sale*); *Br (Börse)* Schlußschein; ~ **for the account** *(Börse)* Terminverkauf; ~ **for future delivery** *(Börse)* Terminverkauf; ~ **for prompt delivery** Verkauf zur sofortigen Lieferung; ~ **for quick delivery** Promptgeschäft; ~ **for the settlement** *(Börse)* Terminverkauf; ~ **invoice** Verkaufsrechnung

sale, ~ **of goods** Waren(ver)kauf, Warenabsatz; ~ **of specific goods** Spezieskauf; ~ **of unascertained goods** Gattungskauf

Sale of Goods Act 1979 (SGA) *Br*[2] Gesetz über den Warenkauf

Das Gesetz enthält eine Kodifikation des Rechts des Warenkaufs

sale of goods, formation of contracts for ~ Abschluß von Kaufverträgen über bewegliche Sachen

sale of goods, international ~ internationaler Warenkauf *(→United Nations Convention on Contracts for the International S ~ of G~)*

sale, ~ **of pledge** Pfandverkauf; ~ **of services** entgeltliche Leistung von Diensten; ~ **on approval** Kauf zur Ansicht; ~ **on commission** Verkauf auf Kommissionsbasis, Kommissionsverkauf; ~ **on credit** Verkauf auf Ziel; ~ **on trial** Kauf auf Probe

sale or return Verkauf mit Rückgaberecht (within a reasonable time); **on** ~ zur Ansicht

sale, ~ **with option of repurchase** Verkauf mit Rückkaufsrecht; ~ **terms** Verkaufsbedingungen; ~ **to arrive** (or ~ **subject to arrival)** Verkauf vorbehaltlich der Ankunft *(des Schiffes)*; ~ **value** Verkaufswert

sale, advertisement of a ~ Verkaufsanzeige; **after-**~ **service** Kundendienst; **agreement of purchase and** ~ *Am* Kaufvertrag; **agreement of** ~ **and purchase** *Br* (Grundstücks-)Kaufvorvertrag; **bill of** ~ Übereignungsurkunde *(insbesondere bei Sicherungsübereignung) (→bill 1.)*; **cash** ~ Bar(ver)kauf; *(Börse)* Kassageschäft; **casual** ~ Gelegenheits(ver)kauf; **commission on** ~ Verkaufsprovision; **→completion (of** ~**); conditions of** ~ Verkaufsbedingungen; **conditional** ~ Verkauf unter Eigentumsvorbehalt

sale, contract of ~[3] Kaufvertrag *(entweder sale = sofortige Eigentumsübertragung oder agreement to sell = zukünftige od. bedingte Eigentumsübertragung)*; **contract for the** ~ **of land** *Br* Grundstückskaufvertrag *(followed by conveyance or transfer)*

sale, credit ~ Kredit(ver)kauf, Abzahlungskauf, *(opp. cash ~)*; **duty-paid** ~ Verkauf nach erfolgter Verzollung; **exclusive (right of)** ~ Alleinverkaufsrecht

sale, for ~ zum Verkauf, zu verkaufen; **not for** ~ unverkäuflich; **offer for** ~ Verkaufsangebot; **to be for** ~ zum Verkauf stehen

sale, on ~ zum Verkauf, zu verkaufen; **to be on** ~ zu verkaufen (od. erhältlich) sein (at bei)

sale, party to a ~ Partei e-s Kaufvertrages; **period set for** ~ Verkaufstermin; **power of** ~ (over property without having the ownership of it) Verkaufsberechtigung (→*power 1.*); **proceeds of** ~ Verkaufserlös; **proforma** ~ Scheinverkauf; **public** ~ →sale 3; **purchase and** ~ **of a loan** Forderungskauf

sale, ready ~ schneller (od. leichter) Absatz; **of ready** ~ mit gutem Absatz, absatzfähig; **to have** (or **find, meet with**) **a ready** ~ guten (od. schnellen) Absatz haben (od. finden)

sale, rescission of a ~ Rückgängigmachung e-s Kaufs; Wandelung; **retail** ~ Verkauf im Einzelhandel, Kleinverkauf *(opp. wholesale ~)*; **short** ~ →short 2.; **slow** ~ langsamer Absatz; **spot** ~ Verkauf gegen sofortige Bezahlung; **subject to (prior)** ~ Zwischenverkauf vorbehalten; **terms of** ~ Verkaufsbedingungen; **wholesale** ~ Verkauf im großen, Großhandelsverkauf *(opp. retail ~)*

sale, to conclude (or **effect**) **a** ~ e-n Verkauf abschließen (od. tätigen); **to expose for** ~ zum Verkauf ausstellen; **to negotiate a** ~ e-n Verkauf aushandeln (od. zustande bringen); **to put up for** ~ zum Verkauf anbieten

sale 2. Ausverkauf; Schlußverkauf; **bargain** ~ Ausverkauf; **clearance** ~ (Räumungs-)Ausverkauf; **closing-down** ~ (Total-)Ausverkauf *(wegen Geschäftsaufgabe)*; **seasonal (clearance)** ~ Saisonschlußverkauf; **stock-taking** ~ Inventurausverkauf

sale 3. Versteigerung, Auktion; ~ **at** *Am* **(by** *Br***) auction** Versteigerung, Auktion; ~ **by order of the court** gerichtl. Versteigerung; ~ **catalogue** (or **catalogue of** ~) Auktionsliste; ~**s lot** Auktionspartie; ~ **ring** Käuferring; ~ **room** Auktionslokal, Auktionssaal; **execution** ~ *Am* Zwangsversteigerung; **forced** ~ Zwangsverkauf, Zwangsversteigerung; **judicial** ~ *Am und Scot* gerichtl. Versteigerung; Zwangsversteigerung; **public** ~ öffentl. Versteigerung, Auktion; **to put up for** ~ *Br* **by** *(Am* **at**) **auction** versteigern

sales Verkäufe; Umsatz; Absatz; Vertrieb; Warenverkauf; Ausverkauf; *(Börse)* Abschlüsse; ~ **account** Verkaufskonto; Warenausgangskonto; ~ **agent** (Handels-)Vertreter; Verkaufsagent; ~ **agreement** Kaufvertrag; ~ **analysis** Absatzanalyse; ~ **area** Verkaufsgebiet, Absatzgebiet; ~ **below cost** Verkäufe unter Selbstkosten; ~ **book** →~ day book; ~ **check** Kassenzettel; ~ **clerk** *Am* (Laden-)Verkäufer(in); ~ **commission** Verkaufsprovision; Abschlußprovision; ~ **contract** Kaufvertrag; ~ **day book** Warenausgangsbuch; Warenverkaufsbuch; ~ **department** Verkaufsabteilung; ~ **difficulties** Absatzschwierigkeiten; ~ **figures** Verkaufsziffern; Umsatzzahlen; ~ **finance company** *Am* Kundenkreditbank; Teilzahlungsinstitut; ~ **force** *Am* Verkaufspersonal; ~ **forecasting** Absatzprognose; Verkaufsvoraussage; ~ **guaran-**

tee Absatzgarantie; ~ **index** Umsatzindex; ~ **journal** →~ day book; ~**lady** →~woman; ~ **ledger** Debitorenbuch; ~ → **load;** ~**man** (Handels-)Vertreter, (Handlungs-)Reisender, Geschäftsreisender; Verkäufer; ~ **management** Verkaufsleitung; ~ **manager** Verkaufsleiter, Vertriebsleiter

salesmanship Verkaufsgewandtheit, –tüchtigkeit; **high pressure** ~ zielbewußte Verkaufsmethode

sales, ~ **monopoly** Vertriebsmonopol; ~ **office** Verkaufsbüro; ~ **order** *(Börse)* Verkaufsauftrag; ~ **planning** Verkaufsplanung; Umsatzplanung; ~ **promotion** Verkaufsförderung; ~ **publicity** Verkaufswerbung; ~ **quota** Verkaufskontingent, Absatzquote; ~ **reduction** Absatzrückgang; ~ **representative** (Handels-) Vertreter; (Handlungs-)Reisender; ~ **resistance** Zurückhaltung im Kauf; ~ **returns** Rücksendungen, Retouren; ~ **slip** *Br* Kassenzettel; ~ **staff** Verkaufspersonal; ~ **tax** *Am* Mehrwertsteuer; ~ **territory** Verkaufsgebiet, Absatzgebiet; ~ **volume** Absatz(menge); ~**woman** Verkäuferin

sales, all ~ **final** kein Umtausch; **annual** ~ Jahresumsatz; **cost of** ~ Absatzkosten, Vertriebskosten; **dullness in** ~ Absatzflaute; **gross** ~ Bruttoumsatz; →**net** ~; **rise in** ~ Umsatzsteigerung; Absatzerhöhung; ~ **declined heavily (slightly)** der Absatz ging stark (leicht) zurück; **to increase the** ~ den Umsatz steigern

saleable →salable

saloon Saal, Halle *(bes. e-s Hotels)*; *Am* Gastwirtschaft; Kneipe; ~ **car** *Br* Limousine; *(Eisenbahn)* Salonwagen; ~ **carriage** *Br* Salonwagen; **anti-**~ **league** *Am* Alkoholgegnerverband

SALT (Strategic Arms Limitation Talks) *(zwischen den USA und der Sowjetunion geführte)* Gespräche über Begrenzung der strategischen Waffen

salute Gruß; *mil* Salut; ~ **at sea** Gruß *(von Schiffen)* auf hoher See; **flag** ~ Flaggengruß; **a** ~ **of 10 guns was fired** ein Salut von 10 Schüssen wurde abgegeben; **to return a** ~ e-n Gruß erwidern

Salvador, El ~ El Salvador

Salvadorian Salvadorianer, ~in; salvadorianisch

salvage[4] Bergung, Rettung *(bes. aus Seenot, Feuer etc)*; Bergelohn; Bergungsgut; geborgenes Gut; Altmaterialverwertung; ~ **attempt** Bergungsversuch; ~ **bond** Kaution für (od. Versprechen der Zahlung von) Bergelohn; ~ **charges** (S. C.) Bergungskosten; ~ **company** Bergungsgesellschaft; ~ **loss** *(VersR)* Bergungsverlust *(Schaden nach Abzug des Verkaufserlöses der geretteten Sachen)*; ~ **(money)** Bergelohn; ~ **operations** Bergungsarbeiten; ~ **value** Schrottwert; Restwert, Veräußerungswert; **to assess the amount payable as** ~ die Höhe des Bergelohnes *(gerichtlich[5])* festsetzen

salvage *v (aus Seenot, Feuer etc)* retten; *(bes. Schiffe)* bergen; *(Altmaterial)* verwerten; **to** ~ **from the debris** aus den Trümmern bergen

salvaged property Bergungsgut

salve *v* →salvage *v*

salvor Berger, Retter

same case (S. C.) gleicher Fall *(bei aufeinanderfolgenden Hinweisen auf e-n und denselben Fall pflegt man diesen bei den Reports mit ~ zu bezeichnen)*

Samoa Samoa; **Independent State of Western** ~ Unabhängiger Staat Westsamoa

Samoan Samoaner, ~in; samoanisch

sample 1. Muster (Warenprobe); Probe; ~ **assortment** Musterkollektion; ~ **card** Musterkarte; ~ **collection** Musterkollektion; ~**, no commercial value** *Am (Post)* Muster ohne Wert; ~ **consignment** Ansichtssendung; ~ **(trade) fair** Mustermesse; ~ **of goods** Warenprobe; ~ **of handwriting** Schriftprobe; ~ **of the quality** Qualitätsprobe; ~ **packet** *(Post)* Mustersendung; Postwurfsendung; ~ **rate** *(Post)* Tarif für Mustersendungen; ~ **taking** Musterziehung; ~ **trunk** Musterkoffer; **according to** (or **as per**) ~ nach Probe (od. Muster); **commercial** ~ Warenmuster; **deviation from a** ~ Abweichung von e-m Muster; **to assort** ~**s** Muster zusammenstellen; **to be in accordance with** (or **up to**) ~ dem Muster entsprechen; **to draw** (or **take**) ~**s** Proben entnehmen; Muster ziehen; **to submit** ~**s** Muster vorlegen; **to supply** ~**s (of)** bemustern

sample 2. *(MMF, Statistik)* Stichprobe; (Objekt der) Auswahl; ~ **characteristics** Merkmale e-r Gruppe von Versuchspersonen; ~ **design** Auswahlplan, Stichprobenplan; ~ **make-up** Zusammenstellung e-r Gruppe von Versuchspersonen; ~ **of households** Haushaltsstichprobe; ~ **survey** Repräsentativerhebung; Stichprobenerhebung; ~ **taken at random** Stichprobe; **area** ~ Flächenstichprobe; **as a** ~ stichprobenweise; **proportionate** ~ ausgewogene Stichprobe; **random** ~ Zufallsstichprobe; **representative** ~ repräsentative Auswahl; repräsentative Stichprobe; **to take random** ~**s** Stichproben entnehmen (od. machen)

sample *v* Proben entnehmen, Muster ziehen; Proben geben, bemustern

sampled offer bemustertes Angebot

sampling Entnahme von Proben; Musterziehung; Bemusterung; *(MMF, Statistik)* Auswahl(verfahren); (Auswahl nach dem) Stichprobenverfahren; ~ **by taste** *Am* Gratisprobe; ~ **error** Auswahlfehler; Stichprobenfehler; ~

method (or **procedure**) Stichprobenverfahren; ~ **procedure** *(Statistik)* Auswahlverfahren; **area** ~ Flächenstichprobenverfahren; gebietsweises Auswahlverfahren; **quota** ~ Quotenauswahl (→*quota*); **random** ~ Entnahme von Stichproben; Zufallsauswahl; **representative** ~ Repräsentativerhebung; **stratified** ~ geschichtetes Stichprobenverfahren

sampler Musterzieher; Probennehmer; jd, der Stichproben macht

Samurai bond market Kaptialmarkt für von Nichtjapanern in Japan ausgegebene Yen-Anleihen

sanction *(offizielle)* Genehmigung, Billigung; *(VölkerR)* Sanktion *(als Unrechtsfolge bei Verstoß gegen e-e Völkerrechtsnorm)*; ~**s** Sanktionen, Zwangs-, Strafmaßnahmen (against gegen); **application of** ~ Anwendung von Strafmaßnahmen; **to give** ~ **(to)** *(etw.)* genehmigen (od. billigen); **to impose** ~**s** Sanktionen auferlegen

sanction *v (offiziell)* genehmigen, billigen; sanktionieren

sanctioned, the practice is ~ **by custom** die Handlungsweise ist kraft Gewohnheit sanktioniert

sanctity of treaties Heiligkeit der Verträge

sandwichman Sandwichmann, Träger von Werbeplakaten

sane geistig gesund

sanitary Gesundheits-, sanitär; ~ **arrangements** sanitäre Einrichtungen; ~ **control** Gesundheitskontrolle; ~ **facilities** sanitäre Anlagen; ~ **provisions** Gesundheitsvorschriften; **international** ~ **regulations** internationale Gesundheitsvorschriften (→*international)*

sanitation sanitäre Anlagen (od. Einrichtungen); **S~ Department** *Am* Müllabfuhr

San Marino, Republic of ~ Republik San Marino

San Marino, (of) ~ Sanmarine|se, ~sin; sanmarinesisch

sans recours *Fr* ("without recourse")[6] ohne Obligo

São Tomé and Príncipe, Democratic Republic of ~ Demokratische Republik São Tomé und Príncipe

sasine *Scot* Grundbesitz; **Register of S~s** *Scot* Grundbuch

satellite Satellit; Anhänger; Trabant; **S~ Business Systems** (SBS) firmeneigne satellitengestützte Datennetze; ~ **launching** Satellitenabschuß; ~ **state** Satellitenstaat; ~ **television** Satellitenfernsehen; ~ **town** *(am Rande e-r Großstadt gelegene)* Trabantenstadt, Satellitenstadt

satellite, communications ~[7] Fernmeldesatellit; Nachrichtensatellit; **communications** ~ **corporation** Satelliten-Fernmeldegesellschaft

satellite, International Telecommunication S~ Organization Internationale Fernmeldesatellitenorganisation *(→international)*; **meteorological** ~ Wettersatellit; **reconnaissance** ~ Aufklärungssatellit; **telecommunication** ~ Fernmeldesatellit

satiate *v*, **the market ist** ~**d** der Markt ist gesättigt

satisfaction Befriedigung; Zufriedenheit; Genugtuung; Tilgung, Bezahlung *(e-r Schuld)*; Erfüllung *(e-r Verpflichtung)*; ~ **of a claim** Befriedigung e-s Anspruchs; ~ **of judgment** Erfüllung e-s Urteils *(z.B. Zahlung auf Grund e-s Gerichtsurteils)*; ~ **of mortgage** *Am* Löschung e-r Hypothek; ~ **piece** Quittung über Erfüllung des Urteils *(Quittung, die die Befriedigung e-s Gläubigers bestätigt und die Befugnis zur Löschung seines Rechts enthält)*; **ademption of a legacy by** ~ Wegfall e-s Vermächtnisses durch entsprechende Zuwendung an den Begünstigten zu Lebzeiten des Testators; **certificate of** ~ Löschungsbestätigung; **entry of** ~ **of mortgage** *Am* (Eintragung der) Hypothekenlöschung; **job** ~ *Am* Arbeitsfreude; **memorandum of** ~ *Br*[8] Vermerk *(in dem vom → Registrar of Companies geführten →register of charges)* über die Löschung e-r die Gesellschaft betreffenden Belastung; **on proof of title to the purchaser's** ~ (or **to the** ~ **of the purchaser**) *(bei Grundstücksübertragungen)* bei e-m für den Käufer zufriedenstellenden Nachweis des Eigentumsrechts; **to enter a** ~ *Am* e-e Hypothek im Grundbuch löschen (lassen); **to establish** (or **show**) **to the** ~ **(of)** zufriedenstellenden Nachweis erbringen, glaubhaft machen; **to express one's** ~ sich zufrieden äußern; s-r Genugtuung Ausdruck geben

satisfactory zufriedenstellend; befriedigend; ~ **evidence** ausreichender Beweis; ~ **reply** befriedigende Antwort; **mutually** ~ **arrangement** alle Teile befriedigende Abmachung

satisf|y *v* befriedigen, zufriedenstellen; *(in befriedigender Weise)* überzeugen; *(Schuld)* tilgen, bezahlen; *(Verpflichtung)* erfüllen; **to** ~ **oneself** sich davon überzeugen (that daß); **to** ~ **sb.** jdn abfinden; **to** ~ **a claim** e-n Anspruch befriedigen, e-e Forderung erfüllen; **to** ~ **the court that** das Gericht davon überzeugen, daß; dem Gericht glaubhaft machen, daß; **to** ~ **one's creditors** s-e Gläubiger befriedigen; **to** ~ **the demand** die Nachfrage befriedigen; **to** ~ **a judgment** ein Urteil erfüllen; **to** ~ **the needs** den Bedarf befriedigen; **to be** ~**ied** zufrieden sein; zu der Überzeugung gelangen, überzeugt sein, sich überzeugt haben

saturation Sättigung; ~ **coefficient** Sättigungskoeffizient; ~ **point** Sättigungspunkt; **the market has reached ~ point** der Markt ist gesättigt

Saudi-Arabia, Kingdom of ~ Königreich Saudi-Arabien
Saudi-Arabian Saudiaraber, ~in; saudiarabisch

save *v* retten, bewahren (from von); *(Geld, Zeit etc)* sparen; sich vorbehalten; ~ **as you earn** (SAYE) *Br* (staatl.) Prämiensparsystem *(für kleine monatlich vom Lohn abgezogene Sparbeträge);* **to ~ sb. sth.** jdm etw. ersparen; **to ~ on sth.** an etw. sparen; **to ~ (up)** sparen; **to ~ expense** Kosten sparen; **to ~ one's face** sein Gesicht wahren; **to ~ labo(u)r** Arbeit sparen; **to ~ a p.'s life** jdm das Leben retten; **to ~ the statute of limitation** *Am* die Verjährung verhindern (od. ausschließen); **to ~ time** Zeit sparen(od. gewinnen); **to ~ o.s. the trouble** sich die Mühe sparen
saved, amount ~ gesparter (od. ersparter) Betrag

save außer, ausgenommen; ~ **for** abgesehen von; ~ **error and omission** (S. E. A. O.) Freizeichnungsklausel; ~ **as provided in paragraph 1** vorbehaltlich Art. 1; ~ **as provided otherwise** mangels gegenteiliger Vorschriften; ~ **as varied** (by) vorbehaltlich etwaiger Änderungen

saver Retter; Sparer; **life ~** Lebensretter

saving 1. Rettung; rettend; **life-~** lebensrettend
saving 2. (Rechts-)Vorbehalt; ~ **clause** Vorbehaltsklausel; Schutzklausel
saving 3. Sparen; Ersparnis; Einsparung (of an); sparsam, wirtschaftlich; sparend; **~s** Ersparnisse, ersparte Gelder; **~s account** Sparkonto; ~ **and loan association** *Am (genossenschaftl. organisierte)* Bausparkasse; ~ **of bail** Freiwerden der Sicherheitsleistung *(→bail)*
savings bank Sparkasse; ~ **book** Sparkassenbuch; ~ **deposits** Spareinlagen; ~ **depositor** Spareinleger; ~ **system** Sparkassenwesen
savings bank trust *Am* Sparkassentrust *(zugunsten e-s Dritten)*
Der savings bank trust entsteht durch die einseitige Willenserklärung des Kontoinhabers, er wolle sein Konto nunmehr als Treuhänder für den Begünstigten innehaben (Trustvermerk im Sparbuch: in trust for)
savings bank, →mutual ~; National S~ B~ (NSB) *Br* Postsparkasse; **Stock S~ B~** *Am* private Sparkasse *(die für Rechnung der Anteilseigner geführt wird)*; **Trustee S~ B~** *Br (über das ganze Land verbreitete)* große Sparkasse *(die 1986 eine public limited → company geworden ist); Am (von meist ehrenamtl. Treuhändern geleitete)* gemeinnützige Sparkasse
saving, ~s bonds *(staatl.)* Sparbriefe *(Am nicht übertragbare und nicht handelbare Sparanleihen des Bundes)*; **~s certificates** Sparbriefe; **~s deposits** Spareinlagen; ~ **of expense** Einsparung von Ausgaben, Kosteneinsparung; ~ **of labo(u)r** Arbeitsersparnis; Einsparung von Arbeitskräften; ~ **stamps** *(Br von der Post, e-r Trustee Savings Bank od. e-r National Savings Group, Am von e-r Savings Bank herausgegebene)* Sparmarken; **cost ~** Kosteneinsparung; **cost-~** kostensparend; **forced ~** Zwangssparen; **labo(u)r(-) ~** →labo(u)r 1.; **money-~** geldsparend; **→National S~s Certificates; premium ~ bonds** *Br* →premium 1.; **to draw on one's ~s** auf s-e Ersparnisse zurückgreifen; **to encourage ~s** das Sparen fördern; **to live on one's ~s** von s-n Ersparnissen leben

savo(u)r of *v* den allgemeinen Charakter haben von; *fig* Spuren zeigen von

sawmill Sägewerk

say *colloq.* sagen wir, nehmen wir an; ungefähr

scab *sl.* Streikbrecher

scale Skala; Tabelle; Tarif; Satz; Maßstab; Umfang; ~ **buying** *Am (spekulativer)* Aufkauf von Wertpapieren zu verschiedenen Kursen *(s. to buy on a →scale)*; ~ **charge →~** rate; ~ **graduation** Tarifstaffelung; ~ **of benefits** *(Sozialvers.)* Leistungstabelle; ~ **of charges** (or **fees**) Gebührentabelle, Gebührenordnung; **(official) ~ of fees** (amtl.) Gebührensätze; ~ **of pay** Lohntabelle; ~ **of premiums** *(VersR)* Prämienskala, Prämientarif; ~ **of prices** Preisskala; ~ **of rates** Tariftabelle; ~ **order** *Am* Auftrag an Makler, bestimmte Aktien zu verschiedenen Kurswerten zu kaufen od. zu verkaufen; ~ **rate** Gebühr nach Tarif; ~ **salaries** *Am* Tarifgehälter; ~ **selling** *(spekulativer)* Verkauf von Wertpapieren *(→to sell on a~); ~* **wage** *Am* Tariflohn
scale, →economies of ~
scale, on a ~ *(Börse)* zu verschiedenen Kurswerten; **to buy on a ~** s-e Käufe über e-e Baisseperiode verteilen; **to sell on a ~** s-e Verkäufe über e-e Hausseperiode verteilen
scale, on the agreed ~ tariflich; **on a large ~** in großem Umfang; **on a small ~** in kleinem Umfang; **pay ~** Lohntarif; **sliding ~** gleitende (Lohn-, Gebühren-, Preis-)Skala; **social ~** gesellschaftliche Rangordnung; **wage ~** Lohnskala; Lohnsätze; **to hold the ~s evenly** gerecht urteilen

scale *v (Löhne, Gehälter, Tarife etc)* staffeln; **to ~ down** verringern, herabsetzen, kürzen, reduzieren; *(Börse)* repartieren; **to ~ up** heraufsetzen, erhöhen, aufstocken
scaling down Kürzung, Reduzierung; *(Börse)* Repartierung
scaling up Erhöhung, Aufstockung

scalp *v (Börse)* mit kleinen Gewinnen spekulieren; *Am pol sl. (jdn)* kaltstellen

scalper *(Börse)* kleiner Spekulant

scan *v (EDV) (mit Licht)* abtasten; *(bes. schnell)* prüfen, untersuchen

scandal Skandal; öffentliches Ärgernis

scandalous, ~ **design** ärgerniserregende Darstellung *(im Warenzeichen)*; ~ **statement** *(in den pleadings)*[9] ärgerniserregende Erklärung

scanner Abtaster; Scanner *(mit e-m Laserstrahl arbeitendes Zusatzgerät an der Kasse. Mit Hilfe e-s Scanners können aus dem Strichcode [bar code] Artikelnummer und Preis gelesen werden; →European article number)*

scarce knapp *(opp. plentiful)*; ~ **articles** (or **goods**) Mangelwaren; **money is** ~ das Geld ist knapp

scarcity Knappheit, Verknappung, Mangel; ~ **of foreign exchange** Devisenmangel; ~ **of labo(u)r** Mangel an Arbeitskräften; ~ **of money** Geldknappheit; ~ **of raw materials** Rohstoffknappheit; ~ **value** Seltenheitswert

scare Panik; ~ **buying** Angstkäufe; ~ **on the stock exchange** Panik an der Börse

scene, ~ **of the accident** Unfallort; ~ **of the crime** Ort des Verbrechens, Tatort; ~ **of fire** Brandstelle; ~ **of operations** *mil* Operationsgebiet, Kriegsschauplatz

schedule Liste, Verzeichnis, Aufstellung, Tabelle; Anhang *(bes. zu e-m Gesetz od. e-r Urkunde);* Zeitplan, Terminplan, Arbeitsplan; Fahrplan; Kursbuch; *Br*[10] Einkommensteuergruppe *(für Berechnung der Einkommensteuer wird zwischen 6 Arten von Einkommen unterschieden [Schedule A–F])*; ~ **of the bank-rupt's creditors** Konkurstabelle; **S~s of Concessions** →concession; ~ **of costs** Kostentabelle; ~ **of documents** *Br* Liste der *(dem vendor's solicitor)* überreichten Urkunden mit Empfangsbestätigung *(bes. bei Grundstücksübertragungen) (→conveyancing)*; ~ **of investments** Verzeichnis der Anlagewerte; ~ **of property** Vermögensverzeichnis; ~ **of responsibilities** Geschäftsverteilungsplan; ~ **to a balance sheet** Anlage (od. Anhang) zu e-r Bilanz; **to a fixed** ~ nach e-m festen Zeitplan; **full** ~ vollbesetzter Zeitplan; **on** (or **up to**) ~ planmäßig; fahrplanmäßig, pünktlich; **vacation** ~ *Am* Urlaubsplan; **to compile** (or **make**) **a** ~ e-e Liste aufstellen; **to meet a** ~ *Am* e-n Terminplan einhalten

schedule *v (in e-m Plan [od. Fahrplan])* festlegen (od. vorsehen); *(in e-e Liste)* eintragen; *bes. Am* anberaumen (od. ansetzen) (for für); planen; *(als Anhang e-m Gesetz)* beifügen

scheduled festgelegt, vorgesehen; (ein)geplant, planmäßig; ~ **air service** planmäßiger Luftverkehr; Linienflugverkehr; ~ **depreciation** planmäßige Abschreibung; ~ **flight** Linienflug; ~ **price** Listenpreis; **as** ~ planmäßig; fahrplanmäßig; **the conference is** ~ **for** die Konferenz ist festgesetzt (oder anberaumt) für; **to be** ~ **to arrive** planmäßig ankommen (at um)

scheduling Planung; Terminplanung; **master** ~ Gesamtplanung

scheme Schema, Plan, Entwurf; Intrige; *Br (gerichtl.)* Vermögensverwaltungs- oder Vermögensverteilungsplan; *(gerichtl.)* Vergleichsplan (z. B. Verteilungsplan für e-n überschuldeten Nachlaß); ~ **of arrangement** *Br*[11] Vergleichsvorschlag *(→voluntary arrangement)*; ~ **of work** Arbeitsplan; **common plan and** ~ *Am* Komplott; **under a** ~ nach e-m Plan

scheme *v* planen, entwerfen; intrigieren

scholarship Gelehrsamkeit; Stipendium; ~ **to students studying abroad** Stipendium für Studierende im Ausland *(cf. European Agreement on Continued Payment of S~s to Students Studying Abroad)*; **close** ~ auf bestimmte Personen beschränktes Stipendium; **holder of a** ~ Inhaber e-s Stipendiums; **open** ~ nicht auf bestimmte Personen beschränktes Stipendium; **to award a** ~ ein Stipendium zuerkennen (od. verleihen); **to establish a** ~ ein Stipendium aussetzen

school 1. Schule; Lehrsystem, Richtung; *Am* College; Fakultät *(→school 2.)*

school age, (compulsory) ~ schulpflichtiges Alter; **of** ~ schulpflichtig

school, ~ **attendance** Schulbesuch; ~ **board** Schulaufsichtsbehörde; ~ **(crossing) patrol** Schülerlotse; ~ **enrol(l)ment** *Am* Schulanmeldung, Einschulung; ~ **fee(s)** Schulgeld; ~ **for the blind** Blindenschule; ~ **leaver** Schulabgänger; Absolvent e-r Schule; ~ **leaving certificate** Schulabgangszeugnis

school leaving examination, to take one's ~ *Br* sein Abschlußexamen (Abitur) machen

school, ~ **of industry** *Am (Nevada)* Jugendgefängnis; ~ **safety patrol** *Am* Verkehrssicherheitsdienst der Schüler, Schülerlotsendienst; ~ **training** Schulbildung; **at** ~ auf der Schule; **boarding** ~ *Br* Internat; **comprehensive** ~ *Br* Gesamtschule *(11–18 Jahre)*; **continuation** ~ Fortbildungsschule; **county** ~ *Br* staatl. Schule; **denominational** ~ Konfessionsschule; **grammar** ~ *Br (etwa)* Gymnasium; →**high** ~; →**industrial** ~; **night** ~ Abendschule; **nursery** ~ Kindergarten; **primary** ~ Grundschule *(Alter Br 5 bis 11 Jahre, Am 6–14 bzw. 12 Jahre)*; **private** ~ Privatschule; **public** ~ *Br* schulgeldpflichtige höhere Schule; *(zu e-m exklusiven Verband gehörende)* (Stiftungs-)Schule *(meist Internat)*; *Am und Scot* staatl. Schule (elementary or secondary ~); **secondary ~** Sekundarschule; Mittelschule; höhere Schule *(Br für Kinder über 11 Jahren; Am →high ~)*; **secondary ~ education** höhere Schulbildung; **selective ~** Ausleseoberschule, Gymnasium *(opp. comprehensive ~)*; **special ~ for educationally sub-normal children** Sonderschule; **state ~** *Br* staatliche Schule; **to attend ~** die Schule besuchen; **to enrol(l) in ~** *Am* einschulen; **to enter a child for a ~** *Br* ein Kind einschulen; **to go to ~** zur Schule gehen; **to leave ~** von der Schule abgehen

school 2. *univ* Fakultät; **S~ of Arts** Kunstakademie; **Law S~** juristische Fakultät; **Medical S~** medizinische Fakultät; **professional ~** Fachschule *(bes. für die Ausbildung der freien od. akademischen Berufe, z. B. law ~, medical ~)*

schooling Schulunterricht; Ausbildung; Schulung

science Wissenschaft, Naturwissenschaft; **~ of law** Rechtswissenschaft *(→jurisprudence)*; **big ~** Projektwissenschaft, *(die großes Kapital braucht)*; **political ~** Staatswissenschaft; Politologie; **social ~** Soziologie

scienter ("knowingly") wissentlich (begangene Handlung); *(im pleading)* Behauptung, daß etwas wissentlich getan ist; *(Tierhalterhaftung)* Haftung für gefährl. Tiere bei Kenntnis von deren Gefährlichkeit

scientific wissenschaftlich; **~ advance** wissenschaftl. Fortschritt; **S~ and Technical Research Committee** (Crest) Ausschuß für wissenschaftliche und technische Forschung (CREST); **~ discoveries**[12] wissenschaftl. Entdeckungen; **~ management** wissenschaftl. Betriebsführung; Betriebswissenschaft; **~ periodical** wissenschaftl. Zeitschrift; **~ research** wissenschaftl. Forschung

scientist Wissenschaftler; Naturwissenschaftler

scilicet (sc., scil.) ("that ist to say", "wit") nämlich; das heißt (d. h.)

scintilla of evidence kleinste Spur e-s Beweises

scire facias ("you may cause to know") *Br hist*[13] gerichtliche Anweisung, e-e öffentliche Urkunde anzuerkennen oder Gegengründe anzugeben

scofflaw *Am* Gesetzesübertreter

scoop *(Presse)* Erstmeldung; journalistischer Treffer

scope Bereich, Rahmen, Umfang; Anwendungsbereich, Geltungsbereich; Wirkungskreis, Aufgabenkreis; Gelegenheit; **~ of application** Anwendungsbereich; Geltungsbereich *(z. B. e-s Gesetzes)*; **~ of agent's authority** Umfang der Vertretungsbefugnis; **~ of business** Geschäftsrahmen *(Sortiment etc)*; **~ of a convention** Anwendungsgebiet (od. Geltungsbereich) e-s Abkommens; **~ of duties** Aufgabenkreis; **~ of the insurance** Versicherungsumfang; **~ of law** *(sachlicher)* Geltungsbereich e-s Gesetzes; Anwendungsgebiet e-s Gesetzes; **~ of liability** Haftungsumfang; **~ of power (of attorney)** Umfang der Vollmacht; Vollmachtsbereich; **~ of protection** Schutzumfang, Schutzbereich; **personal ~** persönlicher Geltungsbereich; **to act within the ~ of one's authority** im Rahmen s-r Vollmacht (od. Vertretungsmacht od. Amtsbefugnis) handeln; **to be beyond the ~ of sb.'s function** außerhalb jds Aufgabenkreis liegen; **to be local in ~** e-n örtlich begrenzten Wirkungskreis (od. Bereich) haben; **to come** (or **fall) within the ~ of a statute** unter ein Gesetz fallen

scorched earth policy *mil* Politik der verbrannten Erde

score *(erzielte)* Punktzahl; Rechnung, Zeche; 20 Stück; **to run up a ~** *Br colloq.* Schulden machen; anschreiben lassen

Scot Schotte, Schottin

scot free straffrei, ungestraft

Scotch schottisch *(→Scottish)*; **~man (~woman)** *(von Nichtschotten gebrauchte Bezeichnung für)* Schotte (Schottin) *(cf. Scotsman)*; **~marriage** *(nach schottischem Recht gültige)* formlose Eheschließung

Scotland Schottland; **~ Yard** *Br* (Zentrale der) Londoner Kriminalpolizei; **→Church of ~**

Scots schottisch

Scots law schottisches Recht

Schottland verfügt über ein eigenes Rechtssystem, das von dem Englands und Wales unabhängig ist. Es gibt bedeutende Unterschiede zwischen den beiden Systemen, z. B. im Grundstücksrecht, Vertragsrecht, Konkursrecht.

(EG) Das für Schottland anwendbare → national law ist das schottische und nicht das englische Recht

Scotsman (~ woman) *(von Schotten gebrauchte Bezeichnung für)* Schotte (Schottin)

Scottish schottisch

In Schottland wird "Scottish" oder seltener "Scots" bevorzugt und nicht das Wort "Scotch"

Scottish, ~ bank schottische Bank; **~ church** →Church of Scotland; **~ court** schottisches Gericht

Scottish, ~ legal system schottisches Rechtssystem; **~ Trades Union Congress** schottischer Gewerkschaftskongreß *(arbeitet eng mit dem englischen →TUC zusammen)*

scrap Schrott; Abfall; Ausschuß(ware); **~ metal** Altmetall, Schrott; **~ sales** Schrottverkäufe; Ausschußverkäufe; **~ value** Schrottwert, Abbruchwert

scrap *v* verschrotten, abwracken; *(alte Sachen)* ausrangieren

scratch *v*, **to ~ out** ausradieren; **to ~ the surface** (of a problem) (ein Problem) nur oberflächlich streifen

screen (Licht-, Wand-, Bild-)Schirm; **~ rights** Verfilmungsrechte; **~writer** Drehbuchautor, Scriptschreiber; **to bring to the ~** verfilmen

screen *v* abschirmen; *fig* schützen; *(jdn)* genau überprüfen *(bes. hinsichtlich politischer Vergangenheit od. zur Beurteilung der Qualifikation für e-e Anstellung)*; e-r Ausleseprüfung unterziehen; verfilmen

screening Abschirmung; Überprüfung; Aussonderung ungeeigneter Bewerber; **~ panel** *Am* Prüfungsausschuß; **~ process** (or **procedure**) Prüfungsverfahren; **~ test** Ausleseprüfung; **(health) ~** Vorsorgeuntersuchung

scrip Scrip; Zwischenschein *(bei Gründung e-r Aktiengesellschaft vor Ausstellung der Aktien oder für neu ausgegebene Obligationen)*; Bescheinigung über nicht gezahlte Zinsen von Schuldverschreibungen *(die den Zinsanspruch vorläufig aufheben)*; *Am* Berechtigungsschein auf Zuteilung von Staatsland; Papiergeld *(zum vorübergehenden Gebrauch)*; Besatzungsgeld; **~ certificate** vorläufiges Aktienzertifikat; **~ dividend** Dividende in Form von Zwischenscheinen; **~ issue** (Ausgabe von) Gratisaktien *(→bonus issue)*; **registered ~** auf den Namen lautender Interimsschein

script Handschrift *(opp. print)*; Erstausfertigung *(e-r Urkunde; cf. counterpart)*; *Br* Entwurf od. Abschrift bzw. Durchschlag e-s Testaments od. Kodizills *(die an die Stelle e-s zerstörten Testaments treten können)*; (Theater-)Manuskript; **(film) ~** Drehbuch; **~ writer** Drehbuchautor

scroll gedrucktes Zeichen an Stelle e-s Siegels; Liste, Rolle

scrutineer (Wahl-)Prüfer, Stimmenzähler

scrutinize *v* genau prüfen; *(Stimmen)* nachzählen

scrutiny genaue Prüfung; **~ (of votes)** Wahlprüfung

sculpture, works of ~ *(UrhR)* Werke der Bildhauerei

scuttle *v*, **to ~ a ship** ein Schiff anbohren *(um es zu versenken)*

SDI (Strategic Defence Initiative) Strategische Verteidigungsinitiative *(Raketenabwehrsystem im Weltall)*

SDR →special drawing right; **~ allocations** SDR-Zuteilungen

sea See, Meer; **~ accident** (or **accident at ~**) Seeunfall; **~ and land carriage** (or **transport**) See- und Landtransport; **~bed** Meeresgrund; **~bed mining** Tiefseebergbau; **~ board** Meeresküste

sea-borne auf dem Seeweg befördert; *(Schiff)* auf See befindlich; **~ goods** Seegüter; **~ trade** Überseehandel; **world ~ trade** Weltseehandel

seacoast Meeresküste; **states having no ~** Binnenstaaten

sea, ~ damage Seeschaden, Havarie; **~-damaged** (S./D.) seebeschädigt, havariert; **~drome** Fluginsel, *(schwimmender)* Flugstützpunkt; **~farer** Seemann; **~faring** seefahrend; Seefahrt; **~ forces** Seestreitkräfte; **~ frontier** Meeresgrenze *(opp. land frontier)*; **~ freight** Seefracht

sea-going seefahrend; (Hoch-)See-; **~ fleet** Hochseeflotte; **~ ship** (or **vessel**) Seeschiff; Ozeandampfer

sea, ~ insurance →marine insurance; **~-letter** *(VölkerR) (im Krieg mitzuführender)* Passierschein *(e-s neutralen Schiffes; →navicert)*; **~man** Seemann; Matrose; **~-mark** Seezeichen *(lighthouse, beacon etc)*

seamen Seeleute; **~'s employment agency** Heuerbüro; **~'s shore allowance** Landgangsgelder; **~'s wages** Seemannsheuer; **to engage ~** Seeleute anheuern (od. anmustern); **to discharge ~** Seeleute abmustern

sea, ~ mile Seemeile *(→nautical mile)*; **~ passage** →**~ voyage**; **~ peril** Seegefahr; **~ plane** Wasserflugzeug; **~port** Seehafen; **~ power** Seemacht, Seeherrschaft; **~-proof packing** seemäßige Verpackung, Überseeverpackung; **~ rescue service** Seenotdienst; **~'s resources** Meeresschätze; **~ risk** Seegefahr; **~ route** Seeweg, Seeschiffahrtsstraße; **~ shore** Seeküste; **~ trade** Seehandel, Überseehandel; **~ transport** Seetransport; Seeverkehr; **~ voyage** Seereise; **~ warfare** Seekrieg; **~ water** Seewasser *(opp. fresh water)*; **~ waybill** Seefrachtbrief

seaworthiness Seetüchtigkeit *(opp. unseaworthiness)*; **warranty of ~ of ship** *(VersR)* Zusicherung der Seetüchtigkeit des Schiffes

seaworthy seetüchtig; seemäßig

sea, access to the ~ *(freier)* Zugang zum Meer; **at ~** auf *(hoher)* See, auf dem Meer; zu See; **beyond the ~s** *Br* außerhalb Großbritanniens; *Am* außerhalb der USA; **countries beyond the ~s** überseeische Länder; **by ~** auf dem Seewege; **by land and sea** zu Lande und zu Wasser; **carriage by ~** Beförderung auf dem Seewege; Seetransport *(opp. carriage by land)*

sea, collision at ~ Zusammenstoß *(von Schiffen)* auf See; **Regulations for Preventing Collision at S~**[14] Seestraßenordnung (Regeln zur Verhütung von Zusammenstößen auf See)

sea, hazards of the ~ Seegefahr; **high ~(s)** offenes Meer, hohe See; **landlocked** (or **inland**) **~** Binnenmeer

sea, law of the ~ Seerecht; **Geneva Conferences on the Law of the S~** Genfer Seerechtskonferenzen; **public international law of the** ~ Seevölkerrecht, Meeresvölkerrecht; **UN Convention on the Law of the S~** (UNCLOS) Seerechtskonferenz der Vereinten Nationen *(von 1982)*

sea, →safety of life at ~; territorial ~ Küstenmeer; **to put to** ~ in See stechen, auslaufen *(Schiff)*

seal 1. Siegel; Siegelabdruck; Plombe *(→seal 2.)*; ~ **of a company** *Br*[15] Firmensiegel; ~ **of confession** Beichtgeheimnis; **common** ~ Firmensiegel; **contract under** ~ gesiegelter Vertrag (→contract 1.); **corporate** ~ *Am* Firmensiegel; *Br* Siegel e-r juristischen Person; **given under my hand and** ~ von mir eigenhändig unterschrieben und gesiegelt; **→Great S~; impressed** ~ Prägesiegel; **impression of a** ~ Siegelabdruck

seal, official ~ Amtssiegel, Dienstsiegel; **breaking official ~s** Siegelbruch

seal, under ~ gesiegelt, versiegelt; **under** ~ **of secrecy** unter dem Siegel der Verschwiegenheit; **to affix a** ~ (to) ein Siegel anbringen (od. beidrücken), (ver)siegeln; **to break a** ~ ein Siegel erbrechen; **to put a** ~ **on** versiegeln; **to remove** (or **take off**) **a** ~ ein Siegel abnehmen (od. entfernen)

seal 2. Plombe, Verschluß; **~s affixed** *(Zoll)* angelegte Verschlüsse; **customs** ~ Zollverschluß, Zollsiegel; **breaking of the (customs)** ~ Verschlußverletzung; **to affix a** ~ *(Zoll)* e-n Verschluß anlegen; **to break a** ~ e-n Verschluß (od. e-e Plombe) erbrechen; **to fix a** ~ **to** verplomben

seal 3. Robbe, Seehund; ~ **deaths** Robbensterben; **Convention for the Conservation of →Antarctic S~s**

seal *v* (ver)siegeln, mit e-m Siegel versehen; *(etw.)* besiegeln; verschließen, verplomben, plombieren; **to** ~ **off** abschotten; **to** ~ **officially** amtlich versiegeln; **to** ~ **up** versiegeln

sealed versiegelt, gesiegelt; verschlossen, plombiert; besiegelt *(z.B. ein Handel durch Handschlag)*; ~ **bid** *Am* →~ tender; ~ **by customs authorities** zollamtlich verschlossen; ~ **instrument** gesiegelte Urkunde; ~ **tender** Submissionsangebot in versiegeltem Umschlag; ~ **vehicle** plombiertes Fahrzeug

sealing Siegeln, Siegelung, Versiegelung; Verschluß, Plombierung; *Br (ZwangsvollstreckungsR)* (Erteilung e-r) Vollstreckungsklausel; **~-wax** Siegellack; **official** ~ *(Zoll)* amtlicher Verschluß

sealer (of weights and measures) *Am* Eichmeister

Seanad Eireann Oberhaus (oder Senat) des Parlaments der Irischen Republik *(cf. Oireachtas)*

SEAQ system *Br* (Stock Exchange Automated Quotations System) automatisches Kurs(informations)system

search 1. Suche (for nach); Durchsuchung; Haussuchung; Leibesvisitation; *(VölkerR)* Durchsuchung e-s Handelsschiffes durch ein Kriegsschiff in Kriegszeiten auf hoher See; Einsichtnahme in ein öffentl. Register; **~es**[16] Einsichtnahme e-s Käufers in öffentl. Register od. Anträge auf schriftl. Auskunft über den Stand von öffentl. Registern zur Feststellung, ob Lasten auf dem zu kaufenden Grundbesitz ruhen; ~ **and rescue service** Such- und Rettungsdienst; ~ **an seizure** Durchsuchung und Beschlagnahme; ~ **for accommodation** (or *Br* **flat**) Wohnungssuche; ~ **for a fugitive** Fahndung; ~ **for missing aircraft** →missing; ~ **of the luggage (baggage)** Durchsuchung des Gepäcks; ~ **of title** *Am* →title ~; **~-party** *Br* Suchtrupp, Rettungsmannschaft; ~ **warrant** *(gerichtl.)* Durchsuchungsbefehl; **body** (or **personal**) ~ Leibesvisitation; **official certificate of** ~ *Br* amtl. Bescheinigung über die Registerbelastung e-s Grundstücks; **house** ~ Haussuchung; **right of** ~ →visit and ~ *(→visit 2.)*; **title** ~ →title 2.; **to make a** ~ e-e Durchsuchung vornehmen (for nach); **to subject sb. to a personal** ~ jdn e-r Leibesvisitation unterziehen

search 2. *(PatR)* Recherche; ~ **as to a novelty** Neuheitsrecherche, Prüfung der Neuheit; **S~ Division** Recherchenabteilung *(des Europäischen Patentamtes)*; ~ **fee** Recherchengebühr; ~ **file** Prüfstoff; ~ **question** Recherchenanfrage

search, international ~ **report** *(europ. PatR)* internationaler Recherchenbericht; **the objective of the international** ~ **is to discover relevant prior art**[17] die internationale Recherche dient der Ermittlung des einschlägigen Standes der Technik

search, isolated ~ Einzelrecherche; **manual** ~ Handrecherche; **mechanized** ~ mechanische (od. Computer-)Recherche

search *v* suchen, forschen (for nach); *(Räume, Personen)* durchsuchen; prüfen (for auf); *(PatR)* recherchieren; **to** ~ **a house** ein Haus durchsuchen; e-e Haussuchung vornehmen; **to** ~ **the title** *Am* das Eigentum an Grundbesitz überprüfen *(→title 2.)*

searching, International S~ Authority[18] Internationale Recherchenbehörde; ~ **the register** Einsichtnahme in das Register *(→searches)*

searcher Untersucher, Prüfer; *(PatR)* Rechercheur; *Br* Zollbeamter, der auslaufende Schiffe nach unverzollten Waren durchsucht

season Saison; Jahreszeit

season ticket *(für Verkehrsmittel od. Veranstaltung)* Abonnementskarte, Zeitkarte, Dauerkarte *(für eine Saison)*; ~ **holder** Inhaber e-r Dauerkarte *(etc)*; **monthly** ~ Monatskarte; **to take out a** ~ e-e Dauerkarte nehmen

season, close ~ Schonzeit *(für Wild od. Fische; opp. open ~)*; **dead** ~ tote Saison; stille Jahreszeit; **end-of-~ sale** Saisonschlußverkauf; **at the height of the** ~ in der Hochsaison; **off** ~ außerhalb der Saison; Vorsaison; Nachsaison; **open** ~ Jagdzeit *(opp. close ~)*; **peak** ~ Hochsaison, Hauptsaison; **tourist** ~ Reisezeit; **the** ~ **is at its height** es ist Hochsaison

seasonal Saison-; saisonal, saisonbedingt, saisonüblich; ~ **allowance** Frühbezugsrabatt; ~ **article** Saisonartikel; ~ **business** Saisongeschäft; ~ **(clearance) sale** Saisonschlußverkauf; ~ **demand** saisonbedingte Nachfrage; ~ **employment** saisonale Beschäftigung; ~ **labo(u)rer** Saisonarbeiter; ~ **rates** Saisonsätze; ~ **sale** Saisonschlußverkauf; ~ **tariff** *Br* saisonbedingter *(im Winter höherer)* (Elektrizitäts-)Tarif; ~ **trade** Saisonhandel, Saisongeschäft; ~ **unemployment** saisonbedingte Arbeitslosigkeit; ~ **variations** Saisonschwankungen; ~ **worker** Saisonarbeiter(in); Saisonkraft; **subject to** ~ **influences** saisonabhängig

seasonally adjusted saisonbereinigt *(beim Index)*

seasoned securities gut eingeführte Wertpapiere

seat 1. Sitz; (Sitz-)Platz, Mitgliedschaft

seat belt Sicherheitsgurt; **compulsory wearing of** ~**s** Gurtanlegepflicht

seat, ~ **of a company** Sitz e-r Firma; ~ **of government** Regierungssitz; ~ **on a board** Sitz in e-m Verwaltungsrat *(→board 1.)*; ~ **on the stock exchange** Sitz (od. Mitgliedschaft) an der Börse; ~ **reservation** Platzbelegung; **country** ~ Landsitz; **to book** (or **reserve**) **a** ~ e-n Platz (voraus)bestellen, e-n Platz reservieren (lassen); **to have a** ~ **on a committee** e-m Ausschuß angehören

seat 2. **(parliamentary)** ~ Abgeordnetensitz, Mandat; ~ **allocation** (in the European Parliament) Sitzverteilung (im Europäischen Parlament); **to contest a** ~ kandidieren, als Kandidat auftreten; **to hold** (or **keep**) **one's** ~ *Br* ins Parlament wiedergewählt werden; **to lose one's** ~ **(on the Council)** *Br* (in den Gemeinderat od. Stadtrat) nicht wiedergewählt werden; **to obtain** ~**s** Sitze erhalten; **he lost his** ~ er wurde nicht wieder gewählt; **a** ~ **falls vacant** ein Sitz wird frei; **to resign** (or **vacate**) **one's** ~ sein Mandat niederlegen; **to win a** ~ *Br parl* als M. P. gewählt werden

seat *v* Sitzplätze haben für; fassen

seating, ~ **arrangement** Tischordnung; ~ **capacity** Anzahl der Sitzplätze *(in e-m Fahrzeug)*

secede *v* sich trennen, abfallen (from von)

secession Lossagung, Abfall (from von); *Am* Sezession *(Abfall der amerik. Südstaaten im Jahre 1861)*

secessionist Abtrünniger; Sezessionist

second *(im Duell)* Sekundant; ~**s** zweite Wahl, Waren zweiter Qualität

second *v* unterstützen; *bes. mil (jdn)* abordnen; **to** ~ **a motion** *parl* e-n Antrag unterstützen, e-m Antrag die *(erforderliche)* zweite Stimme geben

seconded official abgeordneter Beamter

second (2nd) zweite(r, -s); ~ **ballot** zweiter Wahlgang, Stichwahl *(→ballot)*; **S~ Chamber** *parl* zweite Kammer, Oberhaus

second-class zweitklassig, zweiten Ranges; ~ **mail** *Am* Zeitungspost; *Br* preisgünstigere, aber langsamere Inlandspost

second, ~ **cousin** Vetter zweiten Grades; ~ **creditor** nachrangiger Gläubiger; ~ **economy** Schattenwirtschaft

second(-)hand aus zweiter Hand; gebraucht, antiquarisch; ~ **bookshop** Antiquariat; ~ **car** *Br* Gebrauchtwagen; ~ **evidence** Beweis aus zweiter Hand; **to buy sth.** ~ etw. gebraucht (od. antiquarisch) kaufen; **to have** ~ **knowledge of sth.** etw. vom Hörensagen wissen

second, ~ **home** Zweitwohnung; ~ **issue** *(Wertpapieremission)* zweite Serie; ~ **lien** nachrangiges Pfandrecht; ~**-line shares** Nebenwerte; ~ **mortgage** zweite Hypothek *(→mortgage)*; ~ **of exchange** Sekundawechsel *(zweite Wechselausfertigung)*; ~ **→offender;** ~ **papers** *Am* die endgültige Einbürgerungsurkunde (certificate of naturalization) *(cf. first papers)*

second-rate von zweiter Qualität, zweitrangig; ~ **securities** zweitklassige Wertpapiere

second six months' interest Zinsen des zweiten halben Jahres

second strike capability *Am mil* Fähigkeit zum Gegenschlag

second-tier subsidiary Enkelgesellschaft

secondary sekundär, zweitrangig, untergeordnet *(opp. primary)*; ~ **boycott** mittelbare(r) Boykott(maßnahme) (gegen dritte Unternehmen); ~ **(capital) market** Sekundärmarkt *(bietet den Anlegern die Möglichkeit, mit ihren Wertpapieren zu handeln)*; ~ **cause** Nebenursache; ~ **credit** Gegenakkreditiv; ~ **(documentary) evidence** indirekter Urkundenbeweis *(→evidence)*; ~ **education** höheres Schulwesen; höhere Schulbildung; ~ **legislation** abgeleitetes Recht; ~ **liability** subsidiäre Haftung, Zweithaftung, Eventualhaftung; ~**-line competition** *Am* Wettbewerb unter Käufern *(opp. first-line competition)*; ~**-line injury** *Am (WettbewerbsR)* abnehmerbezogene Preisdiskriminierung *(opp. primary-line injury)*; ~ **liquidity** Sekundärliquidität

secondary, ~ **market** Sekundärmarkt, Umlaufmarkt *(opp. primary market)*; ~ **→meaning**

secondary mortgage market *Am* sekundärer Hypothekenmarkt

Markt, der aus der Weiterveräußerung von Hypotheken durch die ursprünglichen Hypothekare zwecks Kapitalbeschaffung an Investoren entsteht

secondary, ~ product Nebenprodukt; **~ residence** Zweitwohnsitz; ~ →**school; ~ strike** mittelbarer Streik

secondarily liable *(WechselR)* zweitverpflichtet, in zweiter Linie *(mit Regreßberechtigung)* haftpflichtig *(opp. primarily liable)*; **party ~** Zweitverpflichteter *(drawer or endorser)*

secondment, official on ~ →seconded official

secrecy Verschwiegenheit; Geheimhaltung; **~ of the ballot** Wahlgeheimnis; **~ of letters** Briefgeheimnis; **banker's duty of ~** Bankgeheimnis; **breach of official ~** (or **secret**) Bruch des Amtsgeheimnisses; **imposition of ~ of an invention** Geheimstellung e-r Erfindung; **official ~** Amtsverschwiegenheit; **duty** (or **obligation**) **to maintain** (or **preserve**) **~** Geheimhaltungspflicht; Verpflichtung zur Geheimhaltung; **placing under ~** Geheimstellung; **provisions for ensuring ~** Geheimhaltungsvorschriften; **removal of ~** Aufhebung der Geheimhaltung; **utmost ~** strengste Geheimhaltung; **to bind sb. to ~** jdn zur Verschwiegenheit verpflichten; **to impose ~ on an invention** e-e Erfindung unter Geheimschutz stellen; **to observe strict ~** strenge Verschwiegenheit wahren; **to be sworn to ~** zur (Amts-) Verschwiegenheit eidlich verpflichtet werden

secret Geheimnis; **~ of the confessional** Beichtgeheimnis; **business ~** Geschäftsgeheimnis; **manufacturing ~** Fabrikationsgeheimnis; **Official S~s Act** *Br* Gesetz über die Wahrung von Staatsgeheimnissen; **professional ~** Berufsgeheimnis; **top ~** strenges Geheimnis, „streng geheim"; **trade ~** Betriebsgeheimnis, Geschäftsgeheimnis; **to disclose a ~** ein Geheimnis preisgeben (od. verraten); **a solicitor is bound by law not to disclose his client's ~** *Br* ein Anwalt ist gesetzlich zur beruflichen Verschwiegenheit verpflichtet; **to keep** (or **safeguard**) **a ~** ein Geheimnis wahren

secret geheim; Geheim-; **~ agent** Geheimagent; Spion; **~ agreement** Geheimvertrag; **~ ballot** geheime Wahl; **~ deal** Geheimabkommen; **~ diplomacy** Geheimdiplomatie; **~ lien** heimliches Sicherungsrecht; **on a ~ mission** in geheimer Mission; ~→**partner**; **~ process** Geheimverfahren; **~ reserves** stille Rücklagen

Secret Service *Br* Geheimdienst *(MI 6; zuständig für Auslandsnachrichten,* →*Military Intelligence)*

secret societ|y Geheimbund; **offen|ce (~se) of membership of ~ies** Geheimbündelei

secret trust Trust, den ein Testator geschaffen hat, in dem er sich von dem Bedachten mündlich versprechen ließ, das Vermögen für bestimmte Personen oder bestimmte Zwecke zu verwalten

secret, to keep sth. ~ etw. geheimhalten

secretarial work Sekretariatsarbeit, Büroarbeit *(e-r Sekretärin)*

secretariat(e) Sekretariat; Geschäftsstelle; **S~ of the United Nations** Sekretariat der Vereinten Nationen *(oberste Verwaltungsbehörde unter dem Secretary-General)*

secretary 1. Sekretär, Sekretärin (to bei); **~'s office** Sekretariat, Geschäftsstelle; **assistant ~** *Br* zweite(r) Sekretär(in), Hilfssekretär(in); **private ~** Privatsekretär(in)

secretary 2. Schriftführer, Geschäftsführer *(e-r Gesellschaft, e-s Vereins etc)*; leitender Angestellter e-r AG; **~ and office** *Br* Sitz und Büro; **~-general** Generalsekretär; **company ~** leitender Angestellter e-r Kapitalgesellschaft; **executive ~** *Am* Geschäftsführer; Chefsekretär(in); **honorary ~** (hon. sec.) *Br* ehrenamtlicher Geschäftsführer

secretary 3. *Br* Minister *(Kurzform für S~ of State)*; *Am* (Bundes-)Minister; **S~ of Agriculture** *Am* Landwirtschaftsminister; **S~ of the Interior** *Am* Innenminister

Secretary of State *Am* (Bundes-)Außenminister; *(in Einzelstaaten)* Innenminister; *Br* Minister; **~ for Defence** *Br* Verteidigungsminister; **~ for Foreign and Commonwealth Affairs** *Br* Außenminister und Minister für Commonwealth-Angelegenheiten; **~ for Home Department** *Br* Innenminister; **~ for Scotland** *Br* Minister für Schottland; **~ for Trade and Industry** *Br* Wirtschaftsminister; **Parliamentary Secretary (of State)** *Br* s. Parliamentary Under-→Secretary (of State)

Secretary (of State), Parliamentary Under-~ *Br* parlamentarischer Staatssekretär, politischer Vertreter des Ministers im Parlament *(junior minister, Mitglied der Regierung)*; **Permanent Under-~** *Br* ständiger *(nichtpolitischer, fachlicher)* Staatssekretär

Secretary of Treasury *Am* Finanzminister

Secretary, Assistant ~ *Am* Ministerialdirektor; **Foreign ~** *Br* Außenminister; **Home ~** *Br* Innenminister; **Under-~** *Am* Staatssekretär

secretary 4. *(VölkerR)*, **First S~** Legationsrat 1. Klasse *(im Range e-s Regierungsdirektors)*; **Second S~** Legationsrat *(im Range e-s Oberregierungsrats)*; **Third S~** *Br* Legationssekretär *(im Range aber höher als der deutsche, weil bereits als planmäßiger Beamter lebenslänglich angestellt)*

secretaryship Amt e-s secretary

section Abschnitt; Paragraph *(e-s Gesetzes, e-r Urkunde; Gesetze sind in ~s[s] und sub-~s[ss] unterteilt)*; *Am* Landparzelle *(640 acres)*; Teil, Teilstück; Gruppe; *(Börse)* Effektengruppe; **~ 5 of the Act** § 5 des Gesetzes

sectional Teil-; Gruppen-; Lokal-; **~ furniture** Anbaumöbel; **~ interests** Lokalinteresse

sector Sektor, Bezirk; Bereich; ~ **boundary** Sektorengrenze; **economic** ~ Wirtschaftssektor; →**private ~ (of the economy);** →**public ~ (of the economy); public ~ borrowing** Kreditaufnahme der öffentlichen Hand

secular weltlich; hundertjährig; ~ **clergy** Weltgeistlicher *(opp. regular clergy)*; ~ **education** weltliche (schulische) Erziehung; ~ **or business day** Werk- od. Arbeitstag

secure sicher, gesichert; ~ **investment** sichere Kapitalanlage

secure *v* 1. sichern; *(jdn)* sicherstellen (by durch); *(jdm)* Sicherheit geben; **to ~ a debt by mortgage** e-e Forderung hypothekarisch sichern

secure *v* 2. sich *(etw.)* sichern; (sich) verschaffen, erhalten; **to ~ the agency of a company** sich die Vertretung e-r Gesellschaft sichern; **to ~ business** Geschäfte zustande bringen; **to ~ a contract** ein Geschäft zustande bringen; e-n Auftrag erhalten; **to ~ interests** Beteiligungen erwerben; **to ~ a majority of votes cast** die Mehrheit der abgegebenen Stimmen erhalten; **to ~ an order** e-n Auftrag erhalten; **to ~ possession** sich Besitz verschaffen; **to ~ profits** Gewinne erzielen

secured gesichert; sichergestellt; ~ **advance** Lombardkredit; ~ **bonds** *Am* gesicherte Obligationen *(cf. mortgage bonds, equipment trust bonds, collateral trust bonds; opp. debentures)*; ~ **credit** gesicherter Kredit *(opp. unsecured credit)*

secured creditor *(durch Hypotheken, Pfand etc)* gesicherter Gläubiger; *(KonkursR)* bevorrechtigter Konkursgläubiger *(der ein →mortgage, →charge oder →lien an einem dem Gemeinschuldner gehörenden Gegenstand hat) (opp. general creditor)*; **defrauding ~s** *Am (StrafR)* Täuschung von Gläubigern, für deren Forderungen Sicherheiten bestellt sind

secured, ~ loan gesichertes Darlehen; ~ **periodical payments order** *Br* →periodical payments

secured transactions *Am* Sicherungsgeschäfte *(sowohl bewegl. wie unbewegl. Vermögen betreffend)*

Durch Art. 9 des →UCC *(in allen Staaten außer Louisiana angenommen)* ist das Recht der Sicherungsgeschäfte an beweglichem Vermögen völlig neu gestaltet und tritt an die Stelle der bisher einzelstaatl. verschiedenen Regeln über Eigentumsvorbehalt, Mobiliarhypothek und andere Sicherungsrechte

securities[19] Effekten, Wertpapiere; Sicherheiten *(des Gläubigers)*; ~ **account** Wertpapierkonto; Depotkonto; **S~ Act** of 1933 (S. A.) *Am* Wertpapiergesetz *(reguliert die öffentliche Emission von Wertpapieren; cf. registration statement)*

Securities and Exchange Commission (SEC) *Am* (Bundes-)Börsenaufsichtsbehörde; **to be exempt from SEC-filing** *Am* keiner Genehmigung der SEC bedürfen

1934 geschaffene unabhängige, quasi-richterl. Bundesbehörde zum Zwecke der Überwachung des Effektenwesens. *Sitz:* Washington

Securities and Investments Board (SIB) *Br* Wertpapier- und Investitions(kontroll)behörde

Wer finanzielle Dienstleistungen erteilt, muß bei der SIB oder einer der von ihr anerkannten Organisation eingetragen sein *(→Self-Regulating Organization)*

Securities Association Ltd *Br* Überwachungsorganisation des Wertpapiermarktes

Sie ist eine →Self-Regulating Organization (SRO)

securities, ~ bearing interest verzinsliche Wertpapiere; ~ **business** Wertpapiergeschäft; ~ **dealer** *Am* Effektenhändler *(bes. am →over the counter market)*; ~ **department** Effektenabteilung; ~ **exchange** Wertpapierbörse; **S~ Exchange Act,** 1934 *Am*[20] Wertpapiergesetz *(regelt den Verkehr mit Wertpapieren)*

securities, ~ holder Inhaber von Wertpapieren; ~ **houses** *Am (Börse)* Händler am →over-the-counter market; **S~ Industries Association** *Am* Verband der Börsenmakler (brokers) und Emissionshäuser (investment banks); **S~ Investor Protection Corporation** (SIPC) *Am (nicht auf Gewinn gerichtete)* Gesellschaft zum Schutze von Anlegern, die bei e-m Zusammenbruch e-r Maklerfirma (brokerage house failure) Verluste erleiden; ~ **ledger** *Br* Effektenbuch; ~ **lodged as collateral** lombardierte Effekten; ~ **market** Effektenmarkt, Effektenbörse; ~ **portfolio** Wertpapierportefeuille, Wertpapierbestand; ~ **prices** Effektenkurse; ~ **quoted on the spot market** Kassawerte; ~ **regulatory body** *Br* Wertpapierbehörde; ~ **traded for future delivery** Terminpapiere; ~ **trading** Wertpapierhandel; ~ **transactions** Geschäfte mit Wertpapieren

securities, active ~ lebhaft gehandelte Effekten; **advances on ~** Effektenlombard; **bearer ~** Inhaberpapiere *(opp. registered ~)*; **collateral ~** beliehene (od. lombardierte) Wertpapiere; **custody of ~** Effektenverwahrung; **deposit of ~** Effektendepot; Hinterlegung von Effekten; **Federal S~ Acts** *Am* Bundeswertpapiergesetze *(→S~ Act, →S~ Exchange Act)*; **first-class ~** erstklassige Wertpapiere; **fixed interest-bearing ~** festverzinsliche Wertpapiere; **foreign ~** ausländische Wertpapiere, Auslandswerte; **gilt-edged ~** mündelsichere Wertpapiere; **Government ~** Staatspapiere, Staatsanleihen; *Am* Bundesanleihen; **investment ~** Anlagewerte *(opp. speculative ~)*; **investment in ~** Wertpapieranlage; **issue of ~** Ausgabe von Wertpapieren, Effektenemission; →**listed ~; loan on ~** →loan 1.; **management of ~** Verwaltung von Wertpapieren; **municipal ~** Kommunalanleihen; **public ~** Staatspapiere; **registered ~** Namenspapiere *(→registered)*; **return on ~** Wertpapierrendite; **schedule of ~** (listed with a bank) *Br* Depotauszug; **specula-**

tive ~ Spekulationspapiere *(opp. investment ~)*; **state** ~ *Am* Staatsanleihen *(der Einzelstaaten)*; **trader in** ~ Wertpapierhändler; **trading** (or **dealing**) **in** ~ Wertpapierhandel; **unlisted** ~ nicht notierte Wertpapiere *(→unlisted)*

securities, to advance money on ~ Wertpapiere beleihen (od. lombardieren); **to borrow on** ~ Effekten lombardieren lassen; **to deposit** (or **place**) ~ **in safe custody** *Br* (**to place** ~ **into a deposit** *Am*) Wertpapiere in ein Depot geben; **to place** ~ Wertpapiere placieren (od. unterbringen); **to pledge** ~ Wertpapiere beleihen (od. lombardieren) lassen; **to withdraw** ~ **from a deposit** Wertpapiere aus e-m Depot nehmen

securitization Verbriefung von Bankforderungen und Umwandlung in marktfähige Wertpapiere

Ersatz herkömmlicher Buchkredite und Bankeinlagen durch Emission von Wertpapieren. Beispiele für securitization sind →floating rate notes (FRNs), →certificates of deposit (CDs) oder auch verschiedene Arten von Euro-Fazilitäten wie →note issuance facilities (NIFs), →revolving underwriting facilities (RUFs) und andere

securitized assets verbriefte (und damit handelbare) Kreditforderungen

security 1. Sicherheit; Sicherheitsleistung; Sicherung *(gegen Rechtsbruch)*; Bürgschaft; Kaution; Garantie; Bürge, Pfand; Wertpapier; ~ **agreement** Sicherungsvereinbarung; Sicherheitsabrede; ~ **analysis** *Am* Anlageberatung; ~ **by mortgage** hypothekarische Sicherheit; ~ **deposit** Sicherheitsleistung *(des Pächters, durch die gewährleistet werden soll, daß er sich vertragstreu verhält)*; ~ **deposit account** Depotkonto; ~ **for costs**[21] Sicherheitsleistung für Prozeßkosten *(→costs)*; ~ **for a debt** Sicherheit für e-e Forderung; ~ **given by an employee** Kaution e-s Arbeitnehmers; ~ **holdings** Wertpapierbestand, Effektenbestand; ~ **identification number** Wertpapierkennummer; ~ **issue tax** *Am* Wertpapier-Emissionsteuer

security interest *Am* Sicherungsrecht an bewegl. od. unbewegl. Sachen, Forderungen und Rechten *(welches besitzlos oder an Besitz gebunden sein kann. Beispiele: Eigentumsvorbehalt, Hypothek, trust receipt, factor's lien)*; **filing of the** ~ Registrierung der Kreditsicherheit *(als Publizitätserfordernis der Wirksamkeit)*; **property subject to a** ~ *Am* Vermögensgegenstand, an dem ein Sicherungsrecht bestellt ist; **purchase money** ~ *Am* zur Sicherung e-s Kaufpreises bestelltes Sicherungsrecht

Im UCC, der heute in allen Staaten (außer Louisiana) gilt, ist security interest der Oberbegriff für die dort geregelten Sicherungsrechte. Er umfaßt also dort nicht die Sicherungsrechte an Immobilien

security, ~ **investment company** Wertpapier-Investment-Gesellschaft *(opp. property investment company)*; ~ **of employment** Sicherheit des Arbeitsplatzes *(hinsichtl. Entlassungen)*; ~ **of tenure** Mieterschutz; ~ **on property** *Am* s. real →~; ~ **prices** Effektenkurse; ~ **purchases** Effektenkäufe; ~ **sales** Effektenverkäufe; ~ **trading** Wertpapierhandel; ~ **transaction** *Am* Sicherungsgeschäft *(cf. secured transaction)*; ~ **transactions** Wertpapiergeschäfte; ~ **yield** Effektenrendite

security, able to give (or **furnish**) ~ kautionsfähig; **against** ~ gegen Sicherheitsleistung; **amount of** ~ Höhe der Sicherheitsleistung; Kautionshöhe; **ample** ~ genügende Sicherheit; →**collateral** ~; **heritable** ~ *Scot* Hypothek; **high-grade** ~ hochwertige Sicherheit; **joint** ~ →joint surety; **liable to give** ~ kautionspflichtig; **loan against** ~ →loan 1.; **on** ~ gegen Sicherheitsleistung; **personal** ~ persönliche Sicherheitsleistung *(→personal)*; **real** ~ dingliche Sicherheit; **rights in** ~ *Scot* Rechte *(die der Schuldner dem Gläubiger)* zu Sicherungszwecken *(einräumt)*; **sufficient** ~ ausreichende Sicherheit; **valid** ~ gültige Sicherheit

security, to furnish (or **give, provide**) ~ Sicherheit leisten; Kaution stellen; **to hold a** ~ ein Wertpapier besitzen; e-e Sicherheit (od. ein Sicherungsgut) haben; **to realize a** ~ e-e Sicherheit verwerten, sich aus e-m Sicherungsgut befriedigen; **to surrender the** ~ die Sicherheit aufgeben

security 2. *pol, mil* Sicherheit; Geheimhaltung; ~ **classification** Geheimhaltungseinstufung; ~ **clearance** *bes. mil* Berechtigung, geheime Dokumente und Nachrichten zu empfangen bzw. einzusehen

Security Council[22] (Welt-)Sicherheitsrat *(der Vereinten Nationen)*; **vote of the** ~ Abstimmungen im Sicherheitsrat; **to have recourse to the** ~ sich an den Sicherheitsrat wenden

security, ~ **grading** Geheimhaltungsgrad; ~ **measures** Sicherheitsmaßnahmen; ~ **pact** *(VölkerR)* Sicherheitspakt; ~ **precautions** Sicherheitsvorkehrungen; ~ **provisions** Geheimhaltungsvorschriften; ~ **rating** *Am* Geheimhaltungseinstufung; **for** ~ **reasons** aus Gründen der (öfftl.) Sicherheit; ~ **regulations** Verschlußsachenverordnung *(z.B. bei Euratom)*; Geheimschutzvorschriften; ~ **risk** jd, der wegen s-r politischen Ansichten für sein eigenes Land (als Spion) gefährlich ist; Sicherheitsrisiko; **S**~ **Service** *Br* Geheimdienst *(MI 5; zuständig für innere Sicherheit und Spionageabwehr; →Military Intelligence)*; **internal and external** ~ innere und äußere Sicherheit; **national** ~ nationale (od. innere) Sicherheit; Staatssicherheit; **to impair the** ~ die Sicherheit gefährden

secus ("otherwise") sonst anders

sedan *Am* Limousine

se defendendo, in ~ s. in →self-defen|ce (~se)

sedentary fishery sedentäre (od. stationäre) Fischerei, Grundfischerei *(sich ständig am Meeresgrund aufhaltender Fischarten)*

sedition umstürzlerisches (od. aufrührerisches) Verhalten; Aufwiegelung; (Rechts-)Staatsgefährdung; **incitement to ~** Anstiftung zum Aufruhr

seditious, ~ libel *Br* aufrührerische Schmähschrift; **~ meeting** zu aufrührerischen Zwekken einberufene Versammlung

seduction Verführung

see (erz)bischöflicher Stuhl; (Erz-)Bistum; **Holy S~** Heiliger Stuhl

see *v* sehen, ersehen (from aus); **to ~ a p. out** jdn hinausbegleiten; **to ~ to** sorgen für, achten auf; **to refuse to ~ a p.** jdn nicht vorlassen, jdn nicht empfangen

seen and approved gesehen und genehmigt

seek *v* suchen; erbitten, begehren *(cf. sought)*; **to ~ admission** um Zulassung nachsuchen; **to ~ a p.'s advice** jds Rat erbitten, sich beraten lassen; **to ~ legal advice** sich juristisch beraten lassen, e-n Anwalt befragen; **to ~ employment** e-e Stelle (od. Arbeit) suchen; **to ~ information** Auskünfte einholen; **to ~ work** →to ~ employment

segment Segment, Sparte

segregate *v* absondern, trennen; abschotten; isolieren

segregated *(bes. nach Rassen)* getrennt; **~ account** *Am* Sonderkonto *(zur Zahlung von Wechseln, Schecks etc)*; **~ school** *Am* Schule mit Rassentrennung *(opp. desegregated school)*

segregation Absonderung, Trennung; Isolierung; **(racial) ~** *bes. Am* Rassentrennung *(vor allem in öffentlichen Schulen, Verkehrsmitteln, Wohnbezirken)*; **de facto ~** *Am* Rassentrennung, die nicht durch den Staat *(sei es durch Gesetz od. Verwaltung)*, sondern durch die privaten Handlungen der Bürger begründet bzw. aufrechterhalten wird; **~ of prisoners** Absonderung von Gefangenen

segregationist Anhänger der Rassentrennung(spolitik)

seigniorage *Br* Münzerlöse

seisin →seizin

seizable der Beschlagnahme unterliegend; pfändbar; einziehbar

seize *v* in Besitz nehmen, ergreifen; *(bes. im Zusammenhang mit Gerichts- od. Verwaltungsverfahren)* beschlagnahmen, einziehen; pfänden; festnehmen; **to ~ on a case** aus e-m Fall Kapital schlagen; **to ~ (upon) a chance** (or **opportunity**) e-e Gelegenheit ergreifen; **to ~ contraband** Konterbande beschlagnahmen; **to ~ goods in execution under process of court** aufgrund gerichtlichen Vollstreckungsbefehls bewegliche Sachen in Besitz nehmen; **to ~ power** Macht ergreifen; **licence** (or **power**) **to ~** vertraglich eingeräumtes Recht, sich in den Besitz e-s Gegenstandes zu setzen und ihn zu verwerten *(begründet ein →equitable lien)*[23]

seized, to be ~ of im Besitz sein von; **the court ~ of the case** das angerufene Gericht; **release of property ~** Aufhebung e-r Beschlagnahme

seizin Besitz (an land by freehold), verbunden mit Eigentumsvermutung

seizure Inbesitznahme, Besitzergreifung; *(behördl.)* Beschlagnahme, Pfändung, Einziehung, Konfiszierung; dinglicher Arrest *(→anticipatory ~)*; Ergreifung, *(vorläufige)* Festnahme, Verhaftung; **unlawful ~ of an aircraft** widerrechtliche Inbesitznahme e-s Luftfahrzeuges; **Convention for the Suppression of Unlawful S~ of Aircraft**[24] Übereinkommen zur Bekämpfung der widerrechtlichen Inbesitznahme von Luftfahrzeugen; **~ in execution under process of court** Beschlagnahme *(von körperlichen Sachen)* aufgrund e-s gerichtlichen Vollstreckungsbefehles; **~ of crops** Pfändung der Früchte auf dem Halm; **~ of power** Machtübernahme, Machtergreifung; **~ of property** Vermögensbeschlagnahme, Vermögenseinziehung; **~ of a ship** (or **vessel**) *(VölkerR)* Beschlagnahme und Aufbringung e-s Schiffes *(in den Hafen e-s Kriegführenden als Prise)*; **~ on account of privacy** Aufbringung e-s Schiffes wegen Seeräuberei

seizure, actual ~ Beschlagnahme durch Wegnahme; **constructive ~** Beschlagnahme durch Verfügungsverbot; **execution levied by ~ (of debtor's goods)** Zwangsvollstreckung durch Pfändung und Wegnahme; **exempt(ed) from ~** s. protected from →~; **exemption from ~** Unpfändbarkeit; **protected from ~** von der Beschlagnahme (od. Pfändung) ausgenommen; **goods protected from ~ in execution** der Pfändung nicht unterworfene Gegenstände; **the state making the ~** *(bei Aufbringung e-s Schiffes)* der aufbringende Staat; **to be liable to ~** der Beschlagnahme unterliegen; **to effect a ~** e-e Beschlagnahme vornehmen, beschlagnahmen; **to effect ~ of a ship** ein Schiff beschlagnahmen (od. aufbringen); **to lift the ~** die Beschlagnahme aufheben

select *v* auswählen; **to ~ from** seine Auswahl treffen unter

selected investments ausgesuchte Anlageinvestitionen

select auserwählt; auserlesen; exklusiv; **~ audience** geladenes Publikum; **~ club** exklusiver Klub; **S~ Committee** *Br (House of Commons)* Sonderuntersuchungsausschuß

selection Auswahl, Auslese; ~ **interview** Vorstellungsgespräch; ~ **procedure** Auswahlverfahren; **assortment for** ~ Auswahlsendung; **promotion by** ~ Beförderung außer der Reihe; **to make a** ~ e-e Auswahl treffen

selective auswählend; ausgewählt; Auswahl-; gezielt; im einzelnen bestimmt; selektiv; ~ **distribution** (or **selling**) Vertrieb durch ausgewählte Händler; ~ **driver plan** *Am (VersR)* System, wonach unfallfreie Fahrer niedrigere Prämien zahlen; Schadensfreiheitsrabattsystem; ~ **placement** (of the handicapped in suitable employment) besondere Berufsunterbringung (der Behinderten); ~ **service** *Am* Wehrdienst *(des Einberufenen);* ~ **strike** Schwerpunktstreik

selectman *Am* Mitglied des Stadtrats

self, ~-appeal Werbewirkung *(e-r Ware)* für sich selbst; **~-appraisal** Selbstbeurteilung; **~-assessment** Selbstveranlagung *(des Steuerpflichtigen);* **~-contained flat** *Br* abgeschlossene Wohnung; **~-contracting** Selbstkontrahieren; **~-dealing** Selbstkontrahierung, Insichgeschäft

self-defen|ce (~se) Notwehr[25]; *(VölkerR)*[26] Selbstverteidigung; **individual and collective** ~ individuelle und kollektive Selbstverteidigung

self, ~ **determination** *(VölkerR)* Selbstbestimmung; **~-educated person** Autodidakt

self-employed selbständig (erwerbstätig); freiberuflich; ~ **(person)** Selbständiger; selbständig Tätiger (od. Erwerbstätiger)

self, ~-employment selbständige (Erwerbs-) Tätigkeit; **~-executing treaty** unmittelbar anwendbarer Vertrag, dessen Inhalt kein Ausführungsgesetz notwendig macht *(→executing);* **~-financing** Selbstfinanzierung, Eigenfinanzierung; **~-government** Selbstverwaltung

self-help Selbsthilfe; ~ **repossession** Inbesitznahme e-s Gegenstandes im Wege der Selbsthilfe
Durch den UCC zugelassen für den Sicherungsnehmer, der sich zur Vorbereitung der Verwertung in den Besitz des ihm verpfändeten Sicherungsguts setzen will *(Ggs. →judicial repossession)*

self-incrimination Selbstbezichtigung; **→privilege against** ~

self, ~ **insurance** Selbstversicherung, Eigenversicherung; **~-insurer** Selbstversicherer; **~-liquidating credit** *colloq.* sich selbst abdeckender Kredit; Warenkredit; **~-mutilation** Selbstverstümmelung; **~-preservation** Selbsterhaltung

self-protection, use of force in ~ *Am*[27] Gewaltanwendung im Falle von Notwehr

Self-Regulating Organization (SRO) *Br*[28] selbstregulierende Organisation *(die unterhalb des →SIB Investitionsgeschäfte autorisiert)*
Die SROs regeln und überwachen die Geschäfte von Anlageberatern und Effektenhändlern.
Die Vollmacht zur Führung e-r Investmentgesellschaft und die Überwachung der Geschäftsverhältnisse zwischen e-r solchen Gesellschaft und deren Klienten wird von e-r SRO übernommen *(cf. International Stock Exchange of the United Kingdom and the Republic of Ireland Ltd)*

self, ~ **restriction** Selbstbeschränkung; ~ **retention** *(VersR)* Selbstbehalt, Eigenbehalt

self-service Selbstbedienung; ~ **restaurant** Selbstbedienungs-, Automatenrestaurant; ~ **shop** (or **store**) Selbstbedienungsladen

self, ~-sufficiency Selbstversorgung, Autarkie; **~-sufficiency aid** (for refugee groups) Hilfe zur Selbsthilfe (an Flüchtlingsgruppen); **~-sufficient** (or **supporting**) nicht auf fremde Hilfe angewiesen, (finanziell) unabhängig; autark; **to be ~-supporting** sich selbst unterhalten (können)

sell *v* 1. verkaufen, veräußern (at a price zu e-m Preis); absetzen, vertreiben *(cf. sold)*; **to** ~ **for the account** *Br* →to ~ for the settlement; **to** ~ **to advantage** mit Gewinn verkaufen; **to** ~ **again** wiederverkaufen; **to** ~ **at** *Am* **(by** *Br***) auction** versteigern; **to** ~ **a bear** *(Börse)* auf Baisse spekulieren, fixen *(opp. to buy a bull)*; **to** ~ **for cash** gegen Barzahlung verkaufen; **to** ~ **on credit** auf Kredit verkaufen; **to** ~ **at a disadvantage** mit Verlust verkaufen; **to** ~ **forward** (or **for future delivery**) auf Termin verkaufen; **to** ~ **at a loss** mit Verlust verkaufen; **to** ~ **off** *(zu ermäßigten Preisen)* ausverkaufen; billig verkaufen; *(Börse)* glattstellen; **to** ~ **privately** (or **by private treaty**) unter der Hand (ohne Makler) verkaufen; **to** ~ **at a profit** mit Gewinn verkaufen; **to** ~ **at public sale** *Am* versteigern; **to** ~ **at a sacrifice** mit Verlust verkaufen; **to** ~ **by sample** nach Muster (od. Probe) verkaufen; *Br;* **to** ~ **on a scale** *(Börse)* seine Verkäufe über e-e Hausseperiode verteilen; **to** ~ **for the settlement** *Br (Börse)* auf Termin verkaufen; **to** ~ **short** *(Börse)* ohne Deckung verkaufen, fixen *(→short 2.)*; **to** ~ **up** die Waren e-s Schuldners verkaufen, um aus dem Erlös s-e Schulden zu bezahlen

sell *v*, **agreement to** ~[29] Kaufvertrag *(Verkäufer erklärt sich bereit, dem Käufer das Eigentum zu e-m späteren Zeitpunkt zu verschaffen)*

sell *v*, **right to** ~ Verkaufsrecht; **exclusive** (or **sole) right to** ~ Alleinvertriebsrecht

sell *v* 2. sich verkaufen lassen, Absatz finden; **to** ~ **badly** (or **hard**) sich schwer verkaufen lassen, **to** ~ **rapidly** reißend Absatz finden; **to** ~ **readily** (or **well**) sich gut verkaufen lassen, leicht verkäuflich sein; **to be hard to** ~ schwer verkäuflich sein

seller Verkäufer, Veräußerer *(opp. buyer, purchaser; für Grundbesitz ist vendor [opp. purchaser] üblicher)*; Lieferant; **~s** (S.) *Br (Kurszettel)* Verkäufer, Brief; **~s and buyers** *Br (Kurszettel)* Brief und Geld; **~'s lien (for unpaid purchase money)** →lien; **~s' market** Verkäufermarkt *(bei dem die Nachfrage größer ist als das Angebot; opp. buyers' market)*; ~ **of a call option** *Br (Börse)* Verkäufer e-r Vorprämie

seller's option *(Börse) (bei Termingeschäften)* Verkaufsoption, Rückprämie; ~ **to double** →option to double

sellers over *Br (Börse)* mehr Brief (Angebot) als Geld (Nachfrage) *(opp. buyers over)*

seller's rate *(Börse)* Briefkurs

seller, bear ~ Baissespekulant; **best**~ viel verlangtes Buch, Besteller; **intermediate** ~ Zwischenverkäufer; **short** ~ Baissier, Leerverkäufer, Fixer

selling Verkauf, Absatz; Vertrieb; ~**, administrative, and general expenses** *Am (Bilanz)* Verkaufs-, Verwaltungs- und allgemeine Kosten; ~ **agent** Verkaufskommissionär; Vertreter; ~ **and repurchase agreement** *Am* Pensionsgeschäft; ~ **below cost price** Verkauf unter Selbstkosten; ~ **commission** Verkaufsprovision; ~ **costs** Verkaufskosten; ~ **expense(s)** Verkaufsspesen; Vertriebs(gemein)kosten; ~ **group** →~ syndicate; ~ **hedge** Absicherung des Verkäufers; ~ **licence (~se)** Verkaufslizenz; ~ **off** (Saison-)Ausverkauf; ~ **off public assets** Privatisierung; ~ **office** Verkaufsbüro; ~ **order** Verkaufsauftrag, Verkaufsorder; ~ **out** zwangsweiser Verkauf von Effekten *(opp. buying in)*; ~ **point** Verkaufsargument; ~ **price** Verkaufspreis; Verkaufskurs; ~ **rate** *(Devisenmarkt)* Verkaufskurs, Briefkurs *(opp. buying rate)*; ~ **short** *(Börse)* Baissespekulation, Fixen; Leerverkäufe *(opp. buying long)*; ~ **syndicate** Plazierungskonsortium, Vertriebskonsortium; ~ **territory** Verkaufsgebiet; ~ **transactions** *(Börse)* Verkaufsabschlüsse; ~ **value** *(Börse)* Verkaufswert

semi, ~**-annual** halbjährlich; ~ **conductor** *(EDV)* Halbleiter; ~**-detached (house)** Hälfte e-s Doppelhauses, Doppelhaushälfte; ~**-durable goods** *Am* Konsumgüter mit e-r Lebensdauer von 6 Monaten bis 3 Jahren; ~→**flexible trust;** ~**-governmental** halbstaatlich; ~**-manufactures** (or ~**-manufactured goods**) Halbfabrikate, Halberzeugnisse; ~**-monthly** halbmonatlich; ~**-official** halbamtlich, offiziös; ~**-official trading** *(Börse)* geregelter Freiverkehr; ~**-public bodies** halbamtliche Stellen; ~**-skilled labo(u)r** angelernte Arbeitskräfte; ~**-trailer** Sattelanhänger

seminar Seminar; Kolloquium; **participant in a** ~ Seminarteilnehmer

semitic, anti-~ antisemitisch

semitism, anti-~ Antisemitismus

senate *pol* Senat *(erste Kammer des Parlaments in verschiedenen Staaten)*; *univ* Senat

Senate *Am*[30] Senat *(erste Kammer des Parlaments; cf. Congress)*; ~ **Foreign Relations Committee** Außenpolitischer Ausschuß des Senats; ~ **Judicial Committee** Rechtsausschuß des Senats; **State** ~ Senat e-s Einzelstaates

Die Mitglieder des Senats werden auf 6 Jahre von den wahlberechtigten Bürgern der Einzelstaaten gewählt. Jeder Staat wählt 2 Senatoren; alle zwei Jahre wird ⅓ des Senats neu gewählt.

Jedes Gesetz muß von beiden Kammern verabschiedet werden.

Auch die meisten Einzelstaaten besitzen einen Senat als Oberhaus ihrer Legislative

senator Senator; Senatsmitglied; **the** ~ **vacates his seat** der Senator tritt zurück

senatorial Senats-; ~ **courtesy** *Am* Übung der Senatoren, keiner Ernennung *(in e-m Einzelstaat)* zuzustimmen, die gegen den Willen des zuständigen Senators wäre; ~ **district** *Am* zur Wahl e-s Senators berechtigter Bezirk; ~ **duties** Pflichten e-s Senators; ~ **election** Wahl zum Senat; ~ **powers** Vollmachten des Senats; **the agreement is subject to a** ~ **ratification** das Abkommen muß vom Senat ratifiziert werden

send *v* senden, schicken; versenden, übersenden; **to** ~ **on approval** zur Ansicht senden; **to** ~ **cash** (or **collect**) **on delivery** (C. O. D.) gegen Nachnahme senden; **to** ~ **by mail** *Am* (**by post** *Br*) mit der Post schicken; **to** ~ **by rail** mit der Bahn versenden; **to** ~ **money** Geld überweisen; **to** ~ **a p. word** jdn benachrichtigen; jdm Bescheid sagen

send *v* **to** ~ **back** zurücksenden; **to** ~ **down** *Br univ* relegieren, von der Universität verweisen

send in *v* einreichen, einsenden; **to** ~ **accounts** Rechnungen einreichen; **to** ~ **one's card** (or **name**) sich (an)melden lassen; **to** ~ **one's resignation** s-n Rücktritt erklären; *mil* s-n Abschied einreichen

send on *v* weiterschicken; *(Brief)* nachsenden

send out *v* hinausschicken; veröffentlichen; **to** ~ **accounts** Rechnungen versenden (od. herausgehen lassen); **to** ~ **a prospectus** e-n Prospekt versenden (od. in Umlauf bringen)

sender Absender; Versender; Übersender; Einsender *(opp. receiver)*; Befrachter (→*shipper*); ~**'s certificate** *Am (Post)* Einlieferungsschein; ~ **of a money order** Einzahler e-r Zahlungsanweisung

sending Versendung, Versand, Übersendung; *dipl* Entsendung; ~ **of goods** Warenversand; ~ **state** Entsendestaat *(opp. receiving state)*; ~ **station** *(Eisenbahn)* Versandstation *(opp. receiving station)*

Senegal, Republic of ~ Republik Senegal

Senegalese Senegalelse, ~sin; senegalesisch

senior 1. Älterer; Dienstälterer, Dienstältester; Rangälterer, Rangältester; *Am* Student im letzten Studienjahr *(opp. freshman)*; *(nachgestellt nach e-m Namen)* der Ältere *(z. B. John Smith Sen.; opp. junior)*; **he is 5 years his ~** er ist 5 Jahre älter als er

senior 2. älter (to als); rangälter, rangältest; dienstälter; dienstältest *(opp. junior)*; **~ bond** erststellige Schuldverschreibung; **~ capital** *Br* Stammkapital *(e-s management trust)*; **~ civil servant** höherer (Staats-)Beamter; **~ clerk** Hauptbuchhalter; Bürovorsteher; **~ counsel** *Br* barrister, der ein Queen's →Counsel ist; **~ debt** vorrangige Verbindlichkeit; *(beim Unternehmenskauf)* vorrangig gesicherte (Bank-)Finanzierung; **~ executives** leitende Angestellte; höhere Führungskräfte; **~ lien** älteres (od. im Rang vorgehendes) Pfandrecht; **~ local government officer** *Br* höherer Kommunalbeamter; **~ member** amtsältestes Mitglied; **~ mortgage** *Am* im Rang vorgehende Hypothek *(opp. junior mortgage)*; **~ officer** höherer Beamter; *mil* höherer Offizier, Vorgesetzter; *Am* leitendes Firmenmitglied, leitender Angestellter; **~ official** höherer Beamter; **~ partner** Seniorpartner; Seniorchef; **~ personnel** (or **staff**) leitende Angestellte; **~ securities** Wertpapiere mit Vorrechten *(z. B. Vorzugsaktien)*

seniority höheres Alter; höheres Dienstalter; Rang(alter); Vorrang *(nach dem Alter od. Dienstgrad)*; Länge der Betriebszugehörigkeit; **~ allowance** *Am* Dienstalterszulage; **~ in rank** Dienst(vor-)rang; **~ list** *Am* Dienstrangliste; **~ pay** *Am* →~ allowance; **~ principle** Anciennitätsprinzip; **~ rule** *Am parl* Regel, daß den Vorsitz in e-m Ausschuß das dem Ausschuß am längsten angehörende Mitglied hat

seniority, according to (or **by**) **~** nach dem Dienstalter; **chairman by ~** Alterspräsident; **company ~** *Am* (Dauer der) Betriebszugehörigkeit; Dienstalter im Betrieb; **job ~** *Am* Dienstalter; **pay ~** *Am* Besoldungsdienstalter; **promotion by ~** Beförderung nach dem Dienstalter; **to rise (be promoted) by ~** nach dem Dienstalter aufrücken (befördert werden)

sensitive empfindlich; **~ area** gefährdetes (od. exponiertes) Gebiet; Sperrzone, Sicherheitsbereich; *fig* (besonders) empfindliches Gebiet; **~ information** geheim zu haltende Information; **~ to price changes** preisempfindlich

sentence Strafurteil; *(auferlegte)* Strafe *(im Sinne von Strafmaß)*; **~ involving imprisonment** Freiheitsstrafe; **~ of death** Todesurteil; **commencement of (the) ~** Strafantritt; **completion of ~** Beendigung der Strafverbüßung (od. Strafzeit); Strafende; **concurrent ~** *(durch Urteile angeordnete)* gleichzeitige Verbüßung zweier Freiheitsstrafen; **consecutive ~** *(durch Urteile angeordnete)* nacheinander erfolgende Verbüßung zweier Freiheitsstrafen; **custodial ~** Freiheitsstrafe; **excessive ~** übermäßig hohe Strafe; **execution of the ~** Vollstreckung des Strafurteils; **heavy ~** schwere Strafe; **imposition of a ~** Verhängung e-r Strafe; **inadequate ~** unzulängliche Strafe; **→indeterminate ~; jail ~** *Am* Gefängnisstrafe; **lenient ~** mildes Urteil; **→life ~**; **light ~** leichte Strafe; **maximum ~** Höchststrafe; **minimum ~** Mindeststrafe; **mitigation of ~** Strafmilderung; **prison ~** Freiheitsstrafe; **reasonable ~** angemessene Strafe; **remainder of a ~** Strafrest; **subsidiary ~** Nebenstrafe; **suspension of ~** Aussetzung der Vollstreckung e-s Urteils; **suspension of ~ (on probation)** Strafaussetzung (zur Bewährung) *(→probation 2.)*

sentence, to accept a ~ ein (Straf-)Urteil annehmen; **to appeal against a ~** gegen ein Urteil ein Rechtsmittel einlegen; **to award a ~** auf Strafe erkennen; **to carry out a ~** s. to execute a →~; **to complete one's ~** s-e Strafe verbüßen; **to determine the ~ (to be awarded)** die Strafe bestimmen; die Strafhöhe festsetzen; **to execute a ~** ein Urteil vollstrecken; **a ~ has expired** e-e Strafe ist verbüßt; **to impose ~** auf e-e Strafe erkennen; **to increase a ~** e-e Strafe erhöhen (od. verschärfen); **to pass ~** das Strafurteil fällen (od. verkünden); **to pass ~ on the accused** den Angeklagten verurteilen; **a ~ has been passed** ein Urteil ist ergangen; **to pronounce a ~** ein Urteil verkünden; **to reduce a ~** e-e Strafe herabsetzen; **to suspend a ~**[31] die Vollstreckung e-r Strafe aussetzen; **to uphold a ~** ein Urteil bestätigen

sentence *v (jdn)* verurteilen (to zu); die Strafe bestimmen (od. verhängen); **to ~ a p. to death** jdn zum Tode verurteilen; **to be ~d in one's absence** in Abwesenheit verurteilt werden; **to be ~d to one month (18 months) imprisonment** zu einem Monat (1½ Jahren) Gefängnis verurteilt werden

sentimental value Liebhaberwert; **~ damage** beeinträchtigtes Liebhaberinteresse; **articles of →intrinsic or ~**

separable (ab)trennbar

separate getrennt, gesondert; Sonder-; **~ account** Sonderkonto; **~ accounting** *(internationales SteuerR)* direkte Gewinnermittlungsmethode *(separate Betriebsstätten-Buchführung; opp. fractional apportionment)*; **~ action** selbständige Klage; **~ agreement** Sonderabkommen, Sondervertrag; **~ and common** (or **corporate**) **ownership** Privat- und Gesellschaftseigentum; **~ assessment of husband and wife** getrennte Veranlagung verheirateter Steuerpflichtiger; **~ book** Nebenbuch; **~ clause** *(VölkerR)* Separatartikel; **~ estate** Sondervermögen; Privatvermögen *(des Gesellschafters)* *(→estate)*; **~ jurisdiction** getrennte Gerichtsbarkeit *(→jurisdiction)*; **~ maintenance (pay-**

ments) *Am* →maintenance 1.; ~ **opinion** eigene (abweichende) Meinung; ~ **peace** Separatfriede, Sonderfriede; ~ **print** Sonderdruck; ~ **property** →~ estate; *Am (FamilienR)* Sondergut *(e-s Ehegatten; cf. community property, →community 2.)*; ~ **residence** Doppelwohnsitz; ~ **tax return** getrennte Steuererklärung; ~ **treaty** Separatvertrag; **under** ~ **cover** in besonderem Umschlag; mit gleicher Post; **to keep** ~ getrennt halten; **to live** ~ getrennt leben *(Eheleute)*

separate *v* (sich) trennen; aussondern; absondern; **to** ~ **from** (ab)trennen von; **to** ~ **from a church** aus e-r Kirche austreten

separation 1. Trennung; Abgang *(von Arbeitnehmern)*; Absonderung; ~ **allowance** Trennungsentschädigung; ~ **of Church and State** Trennung von Kirche und Staat; ~ **of powers** *(StaatsR)* Gewaltenteilung, Gewaltentrennung *(cf. executive, judicial, legislative power)*; ~ **of property** (Güterstand der) Gütertrennung; ~ **rate** *Am (monatl.)* Abgangsrate *(der Arbeitnehmer)*

separation 2. *(EheR)* Trennung, Getrenntleben; ~ **agreement** Vereinbarung des Getrenntlebens zwischen Ehegatten *(ohne Mitwirkung des Gerichts)*; **2 years** ~ **and consent** *Br* 2jährige Trennung und Einwilligung *(des/der Beklagten; cf. ground for divorce; →divorce)*; ~ **by consent** *Br* einverständliche Trennung *(von Ehegatten)*; ~ **deed** *Br* s. deed of→~; ~ **order** *Br*[32] *(von e-m Ehepartner auf Grund des Verhaltens des anderen Ehepartners erwirkte)* gerichtliche Anordnung *(des magistrates court)* des Getrenntlebens und Regelung der weiteren Rechtsbeziehungen zwischen den Ehegatten *(bes. Unterhalt und Sorgerecht)*; **decree of judicial** ~ *Br* gerichtliche Anordnung *(der Family Division des High Court)* des Getrenntlebens und Regelung der weiteren Rechtsbeziehungen zwischen den Ehegatten; **deed of** ~ *Br* schriftl. Vereinbarung des Getrenntlebens zwischen Ehegatten *(ohne Mitwirkung des Gerichts)*; **judicial** ~ gerichtliche Trennung e-r Ehe; gerichtliche Aufhebung der ehelichen Gemeinschaft (unter Aufrechterhaltung des Ehebandes); **voluntary** ~ *Am (durch ~ agreement erfolgte)* einverständliche Trennung

separatist Separatist; *eccl* Sektierer, Dissident

sequence Folge, Aufeinanderfolge; Reihenfolge; ~ **of priority** Rangfolge; **in** ~ aufeinanderfolgend; **order of** ~ zeitliche Reihenfolge

sequence *v (in e-r bestimmten Reihenfolge)* anordnen

sequentes, sequentia (seq. or seqq.) die folgenden (Seiten, Zeilen)

sequester *v* sequestieren; *(bis zur Befriedigung e-s Anspruchs)* zwangsverwalten; e-e →sequestration durchführen

sequestered estate Vermögen unter Zwangsverwaltung

sequestrate *v* →sequester *v*

sequestration Sequestration, Zwangsverwaltung *(bes. zur Erzwingung der Befolgung e-r gerichtl. Verfügung, z.B. e-r Unterhaltsverfügung)*; gerichtl. angeordnete Beschlagnahme von Vermögen des Schuldners; *Br eccl* Zwangsverwaltung der Einkünfte e-r Pfründe zur Befriedigung von Gläubigern od. bis zur Einführung des neuen Pfründeninhabers; *Scot* Verwertung der Konkursmasse unter Aufsicht des Gerichts; **execution by (writ of)** ~ Zwangsvollstreckung im Wege der Zwangsverwaltung; **to put under** ~ unter Zwangsverwaltung stellen

sequestration, writ of ~ *Br*[33] gerichtl. Anordnung an (meist 4) commissioners, jds Grundstück bis zur Befolgung e-r nichtbeachteten gerichtl. Verfügung zu betreten und Mieten, Nutzungen sowie Vermögensgegenstände in Zwangsverwaltung zu nehmen

sequestrator Sequester, Zwangsverwalter *(cf. sequestration)*

sergeant (Sergt) *mil* Unteroffizier *(non-commissioned officer above corporal)*; Polizeibeamter *(Br next in rank above constable)*; ~**-at-arms** →serjeant; **Common S~** →serjeant

serial Serien-, Reihen-; serienmäßig, in Lieferungen (erscheinend); ~ **bonds** in Serien unterteilte Obligationen, Serienanleihen; ~ **manufacture** (or **production**) Serienherstellung; ~ **number** Seriennummer, laufende Nummer; Fabrikationsnummer; ~ **publication** in Fortsetzungen erscheinende Veröffentlichung; ~ **work** Serienarbeit

seriatim der Reihe nach

series Serie, Reihe, Folge; ~ **of lectures** Vortragsreihe; ~ **of publications** Schriftenreihe; **in** ~ serienmäßig; **test** ~ Versuchsreihe

serious ernst; ~ **bodily injury** schwere Körperverletzung; ~ **concern** ernste Besorgnis; ~ →**offen|ce (-se)**

seriously disabled (person) Schwerbehinderter

seriousness of an offen|ce (-se) Schwere e-r Straftat

serjeant, ~-at-arms *Br* Beamter mit bestimmten zeremoniellen Pflichten *(z.B. Begleiter des Souveräns)*; parl Ordnungsbeamter; **Common S~** *Br* Gerichtsperson in der City of London *(fungiert als e-r der Richter [circuit judge] des Central Criminal Court)*

servant 1. Arbeitnehmer; Bediensteter *(e-r Be-*

hörde); Gehilfe; **master and ~** Dienstherr und Gehilfe *(im Sinne der deliktsrechtlichen Gehilfenhaftung)*

Nach dem anglo-amerikanischen Recht haftet der master Dritten gegenüber für Verschulden des servant, soweit dieser in seinem Interesse und nach seinen Weisungen tätig geworden ist

servant, ~ of a company Angestellter e-r Gesellschaft; **civil ~** Staatsbeamter *(→civil)*; **crown ~** *Br* Kronbeamter, Bediensteter der Krone; **public ~**[34] Staatsbeamter; Angestellter des öffentlichen Dienstes

servant 2. Hausangestellte(r); Diener; **~s** Dienstboten; **~ problem** Dienstbotenproblem; **domestic** (or **menial**) **~** Hausangestellte(r); Hausgehilfin; **man ~** Hausangestellter, (Haus-) Diener

serve *v* 1. dienen, Dienst leisten; im Dienst stehen, angestellt sein (with bei); *(Kunden etc)* bedienen; dienen, nützlich sein *(→serve 2.)*; *mil* dienen, Militärdienst (od. Wehrdienst) leisten; fungieren, amtieren (as als); *(Amt)* verwalten, innehaben; *(Ehrenamt, z. B. als Geschworener)* ausüben; versorgen (with mit) *(Wasser, Gas, Elektrizität etc)*; *Scot* (jdn gerichtl.) zum Erben erklären

serve *v*, **to ~ one's apprenticeship** (or **articles**) s-e Lehrzeit (od. Ausbildungszeit) durchmachen, absolvieren; in der Lehre sein; **he has ~d his apprenticeship** er hat ausgelernt

serve *v*, **to ~ in the armed forces** den Militärdienst (od. Wehrdienst) ableisten; **to ~ in the army** beim Heer Dienst tun; **to ~ with the colo(u)rs** den Militärdienst (od. Wehrdienst) ableisten; **to ~ on a committee** in e-m Ausschuß tätig sein; **to ~ a customer** e-n Kunden bedienen; **to ~ a customer with goods** Waren an e-n Kunden liefern; **to ~ as a juror** (or **on a jury**) (als) Geschworener (tätig) sein; **to ~ an office** ein Amt versehen; **to ~ in the police** bei der Polizei Dienst tun; **to ~ a term under articles** *Br* im Büro e-s solicitor s-e Lehrzeit durchmachen *(→articled clerk)*; **to ~ one's time in the army** →to ~ in the army

served, years ~ Dienstjahre

serve *v* 2. dienen; dienlich sein, nützen; **to ~ as collateral** (or **cover**) als Deckung *(e-s Kredits)* dienen; **to ~ one's end** den eigenen Zwecken dienen; **to ~ as guidance** als Richtlinie dienen; **to ~ as a pretext** als Vorwand dienen; **to ~ the purpose** den Zweck erfüllen; **to ~ various purposes** verschiedenen Zwecken dienen

serve *v* 3. *(Strafe)* verbüßen; **to ~ a (prison) sentence** (or **a term of imprisonment** or **a prison term**) e-e Freiheitsstrafe verbüßen; **to ~ time** *colloq.* s-e Freiheitsstrafe verbüßen (od. absitzen)

served, the sentence has been ~ die Strafe ist verbüßt

serving of a sentence Verbüßung e-r Freiheitsstrafe

serve *v* 4. zustellen; **to ~ on sb.** (or **to ~ sb. with**) jdm *(Ladung, Schriftstück etc)* zustellen; **to ~ the defendant** die Zustellung an den Beklagten vornehmen *(erfolgt meist durch die Gegenpartei od. durch den Anwalt, nicht durch das Gericht)*; **to ~ a notice on sb.** jdm e-e schriftliche Mitteilung *(Kündigung, Warnung etc)* zustellen; **to ~ a summons on sb.** (or **to ~ sb. with a summons**) jdm e-e Ladung zustellen

served, document to be ~ zuzustellendes Schriftstück; **person to be ~** Zustellungsempfänger

serving of a writ Zustellung e-r gerichtlichen Verfügung

server, process ~ Zustellungsbeamter

service 1. Dienst; Dienstleistung, Dienstverhältnis *(cf. master and servant)*; Bedienung, Service *(in e-m Hotel)*; Versorgung(sdienst) *(Gas, Elektrizität, Wasser etc)*; Militärdienst *(→service 2.)*; Zustellung *(→service 3.)*; Verkehrsdienst *(→service 4.)*; Gottesdienst *(→service 5.)*; (Gegen-)Leistung des →tenant *(→service 6.)*; **~s** Dienstleistungen; Verkehrsdienste *(→service 4.)*; **~ abroad** Auslandsdienst; **~ agency** Dienstleistungsagentur; **~ area** *(public utilities)* Versorgungsgebiet; *(Rundfunk)* Sendebereich; **~ charge** Vergütung für besondere Mühewaltung *(Bearbeitungsgebühr, Bedienungsgeld etc)*; *Am tel* Grundgebühr (einschließl. der Ortsgespräche); **~ charges** *Br* Dienstleistungskosten *(des Vermieters)*; **~ compartment** Dienstabteil

service contract Dienstvertrag; Wartungsvertrag; **to enter into a ~** e-n Dienstvertrag (od. Wartungsvertrag) abschließen

service, ~ flat *Br* Etagenwohnung mit Bedienung; **~ included** einschließlich Bedienung; **~ industry** Dienstleistungsgewerbe; **~ instructions** Betriebsvorschriften, Bedienungsanweisung; Dienstanweisung; **~ invention** Betriebserfindung, Diensterfindung; Arbeitnehmererfindung; **~ life** Nutzungsdauer; **~ management** (Dienst am) Kunden-Management; **~ mark** Marke zur Kennzeichnung von Dienstleistungen, Dienstleistungsmarke *(z. B. Am Greyhound für Omnibustransporte)*; **~ of an heir** *Scot* gerichtl. Anerkennung als Erbe; **~ organization** gemeinnützige Organisation *(z. B. Rotarier)*; **~ regulations** Dienstvorschriften; **~s rendered** geleistete Dienste, erbrachte Dienstleistungen; **~ sector** Dienstleistungssektor; tertiärer Sektor; **~ space** Wirtschaftsraum *(e-s Schiffes)*; **~ staff** *(dienstl.)* Hauspersonal *(z. B. e-r dipl. Mission)*; **~ station** Tankstelle; (Auto-)Reparaturwerkstätte; **~ till** Bankautomat; **~ (to customers)** Kundenbedienung; **~s transactions** Dienstleistungsverkehr; **~ undertaking** Dienstleistungsbetrieb

service, after-sales ~ Kundendienst; **car ~** Wagenpflege; **cartage ~** Rollfuhrdienst; **cessation of ~** Beendigung des Dienstverhältnisses; **Civil S~** öffentlicher Dienst, Staatsdienst *(→civil)*;

collection ~ Inkassodienst; **community** ~**s** Dienstleistungen für die Allgemeinheit; **contract for** ~**s** Dienstvertrag, Werkvertrag *(mit selbständigem Unternehmer oder freiem Mitarbeiter; opp. contract of ~, contract of employment)*; **contract of** ~ Arbeitsvertrag *(mit persönlich abhängigem Arbeitnehmer; opp. contract for ~)*; **diplomatic** ~ diplomatischer Dienst; **emergency** ~ Bereitschaftsdienst; **eminent** ~**s** hervorragende Dienste; **entering the** ~ Dienstantritt; **exchange of** ~**s** Dienstleistungsverkehr; **field** ~ Außendienst; **length of** ~ Dienstzeit, Dienstalter; **night** ~ Nachtdienst; **outdoor** (or **outside**) ~ Außendienst; **postal** ~ Postdienst; **press** ~ Pressedienst; **public** ~ →public service 1. und 2.; **purchase of** ~**s** entgeltliche Inanspruchnahme von Diensten; **return** ~ Gegendienst; **sale of** ~**s** entgeltliche Leistung von Diensten; **self-** ~ Selbstbedienung; **social** ~**s** soziale Dienstleistungen, soziale Einrichtungen; **years of** ~ Dienstjahre

service, to be in ~ *(als Hausangestellte)* beschäftigt sein; **to engage the** ~**s of a solicitor** *Br* (**an attorney** *Am*) e-n Anwalt nehmen; **to leave the** ~ aus dem Dienst ausscheiden; **to offer one's** ~**s** s-e Dienste anbieten; **to perform** (or **provide**) ~**s** Dienstleistungen erbringen; **to render a p. a** ~ jdm e-n Dienst erweisen; **to render** ~**s** Dienstleistungen erbringen; **to take into one's** ~ *(Hauspersonal)* einstellen

service 2. *mil* (Wehr-)Dienst *(cf. military ~)*; **the** ~**s** die Streitkräfte; das Militär *(Army, Navy, Airforce)*; ~ **in the field** Frontdienst; ~**man** Soldat, Angehöriger der Streitkräfte; ~ **medal** Dienstauszeichnung; ~ **order** Dienstbefehl; ~ **pay and allowances** Dienstbezüge; ~ **pension** Ruhegehalt für die Streitkräfte; ~ **rank** Dienstgrad; ~ **record** *Am* Wehrpaß; ~ **regulations** Dienstvorschriften; Dienstordnung; ~ **voter** *Br*[35] Wehrmachtsangehöriger, der sich bei e-r Wahl vertreten lassen kann; **on** →**active** ~; **armed** ~**s** (bewaffnete) Streitkräfte *(Army, Navy, Airforce)*; **branch of the** ~ Truppengattung; **field** ~ Frontdienst; **fit for** ~ diensttauglich; **in the** ~**s** beim Militär; **military** ~ Wehrdienst, Militärdienst *(→military)*; →**national** ~; **unfit for** ~ dienstuntauglich

service 3. Zustellung; ~ **by mail** *Am* (**post** *Br*)[36] Zustellung durch die Post; ~ **by publication** *Am* öffentliche Zustellung; ~ **(of the summons) by advertisement in the press** *Br*[37] Ladung durch öffentliche Zustellung in der Zeitung; ~ **of judicial and extrajudicial documents**[38] Zustellung gerichtlicher und außergerichtlicher Schriftstücke; ~ **of process** Zustellung der Ladung und der Klageschrift *(cf. personal ~ and substituted ~)*; ~ **out of the jurisdiction** Zustellung im Ausland; **acceptance of** ~ Annahme der Zustellung *(durch den Anwalt)*; **accepted** ~ *Br*[39] *(durch den solicitor des Beklagten)* angenommene (Ersatz-)Zustellung; **address for** ~[39] Zustellungsadresse; **endorsement of** ~ Vermerk über Zeit, Ort und Empfänger der Zustellung; **ordinary** ~ gewöhnliche (od. normale) Zustellung; **personal** ~ **of process** persönliche Zustellung zu eigenen Händen des Beklagten; **proof of** ~ Zustellungsnachweis; **substituted** ~[40] Ersatzzustellung; **within 2 weeks of** ~ binnen 2 Wochen nach Zustellung; **to accept** ~ die Zustellung annehmen *(durch den Anwalt)*; **to effect** ~ zustellen

service 4. Verkehrsdienst; (Linien-, Strecken-) Verkehr; **air** ~ Luftverkehr *(→air)*; **local** ~ lokale (Verkehrs-)Einrichtungen *(bus, train etc)*; **local** ~ **line** Zubringerlinie; **passenger** ~ Personenverkehr; **railway (railroad)** ~ Eisenbahnverkehr; **regular** ~ Linienverkehr; **shuttle** ~ Pendelverkehr

service 5. *eccl* Gottesdienst; **church** (or **divine**) ~ Gottesdienst; **funeral** ~ Trauergottesdienst; **marriage** ~ Traugottesdienst, Trauung; **memorial** ~ Gedenkgottesdienst; **to attend the** ~ den Gottesdienst besuchen; **to conduct** (or **take**) **the** ~ den Gottesdienst abhalten

service 6. (Gegen-)Leistung des →tenant an den →landlord wegen Grundstücksüberlassung

service *v*, **to** ~ **a loan** e-e Anleihe bedienen

serviceable, in (a) ~ **condition** in gebrauchsfähigem Zustand

servient *(mit e-r Grunddienstbarkeit)* belastet; ~ **tenement** dienendes (od. belastetes) Grundstück *(opp. dominant tenement)*

serving →serve *v* 3. und 4.

servitude *Am* und *Scot* (Grund-)Dienstbarkeit *(cf. easement)*; **international** ~**s**[41] Staatsdienstbarkeiten, völkerrechtl. Servituten; **personal** ~ persönliche Dienstbarkeit (*Scot* →life-rent); **praedial** ~ *Scot* (**real** ~ *Am*) Grunddienstbarkeit

session Sitzung *(e-s Gerichts, Parlament, e-r Kommission etc)*; Tagung; *parl* Sitzungsperiode; Börsentag, Börsenstunden; *Br* Studienjahr, akademisches Jahr *(1. 10.–30. 6.)*; *Am* Kurssemester *(z.B. summer ~)*; **S~ Cases** (S. C.) *Scot* Urteilssammlung *(Sammlung von gerichtl. Entscheidungen seit 1907)*; ~ **hall** Sitzungssaal; ~ **laws** *Am (chronologisch, nach Sitzungsperioden geordnete Sammlung der)* Gesetze e-r einzelstaatlichen Legislaturperiode *(opp. revised statutes)*; ~ **of a committee** Ausschußsitzung; ~ **of the Council** *(bes. EG)* Ratstagung; ~ **of a court** Gerichtssitzung; ~ **of legislature** *Am* Legislaturperiode; **closed** ~ nichtöffentliche Sitzung; **closing of a** ~ Schließung e-r Sitzung; →**Court of S**~; **full** ~ Plenarsitzung; **in the** ~ während der Sitzung; **joint** ~ *parl* gemeinsame Sitzung *(beider Häuser)*; **opening of the** ~

Eröffnung der Sitzung; **parliamentary** ~ *Br* Legislaturperiode; **plenary** ~ Plenarsitzung, Plenum; **regular** ~ ordentliche Sitzung *(opp. special ~)*; **secret** ~ Geheimsitzung; **special** ~ Sondersitzung; außerordentliche Sitzung *(→special)*; **to adjourn a** ~ e-e Sitzung vertagen; **to attend a** ~ an e-r Sitzung teilnehmen; **to be in** ~ tagen, e-e Sitzung abhalten; **to call** (or **convene, convoke**) **a** ~ e-e Sitzung einberufen; **to hold a** ~ e-e Sitzung (od. Tagung) abhalten; **to meet in ordinary** (or **regular**) ~ zu e-r ordentlichen Sitzung zusammentreten; **to meet in regular annual** ~ einmal im Jahr zu e-r ordentlichen Tagung zusammenkommen; **the committee is in** ~ die Kommission tagt; der Ausschuß hält e-e Sitzung ab; **the court is in** ~ das Gericht tagt; **the Senate is in** ~ *Am parl* der Senat hält e-e Sitzung ab (od. tagt); die Sitzungsperiode des Senats läuft

sessional Sitzungs-; ~ **expense allowance** *Parl* Diäten; **S~ Orders** *Br parl* nur für eine Sitzungsperiode geltende Geschäftsordnung *(opp. Standing Orders)*

set *(zusammengehörender)* Satz; Kollektion; Sortiment

set-aside Bereitstellung für künftigen Zweck; *(EG)* Stillegung von Ackerflächen

set, ~ of bills (of exchange)[42] Satz Wechsel *(verschiedene Ausfertigung des gleichen Wechsel)*; **bills (drawn) in a** ~[42] Wechsel in einem Satz *(in mehrfacher Ausfertigung)*; **to draw a bill in a** ~ **of three** e-n Wechsel in dreifacher Ausfertigung ausstellen

set, (full) ~ **of bills of lading** (vollständiger) Satz des Konnossements; ~ **of circumstances** Tatumstände, Tatbestand; ~ **of exchange** Satz Wechsel; ~ **of patterns** Musterkollektion; ~ **of printed forms** Formularsatz

set(-)back Zurückgang; Rückschlag; ~ **in production** Produktionsrückgang; **to have a** ~ e-n Rückschlag erleiden; **to have a** ~ **from ... to ...** zurückgehen von ... auf ...

set(-)off Aufrechnung im Prozeß[43] *(mit Gegenforderung gegen die Klagforderung)*; Verrechnung (against mit); Ausgleich (against für); **to plead a** ~ **by way of a defen|ce (~se)** die Aufrechnung e-s Anspruchs im Prozeß geltend machen

set(-)up Aufbau; Errichtung, Gründung; ~ **cost** Gründungskosten; Rüstkosten

set bestimmt, festgesetzt; feststehend, allgemein gebräuchlich; ~ **form of letter** Brief mit feststehendem Wortlaut (od. in feststehender Form); **at a** ~ **date** zu e-m bestimmten Termin; **within the** ~ **period** fristgemäß; ~ **speech** ausgearbeitete Rede

set *v* setzen, legen; bestimmen, festsetzen (at auf); **to** ~ **on fire** in Brand setzen; **to** ~ **one's hand** (to) *(Urkunde, Vertrag)* unterschreiben; **to** ~ **at liberty** →to ~ free; **to** ~ **a period (of time)** e-e Frist (fest)setzen; **to** ~ **a precedent** e-n Präzedenzfall schaffen (od. abgeben); **to** ~ **sail for** auslaufen nach; **to** ~ **one's signature to** s-e Unterschrift setzen unter; **to** ~ **a time limit to sth.** etw. befristen; Frist setzen für etw.

set aside (or **set apart**) *v* 1. beiseite legen; **to set goods aside** (or **apart**) Ware als für den Käufer bestimmt beiseitelegen (od. aussondern); **to** ~ **part of one's income** e-n Teil s-s Einkommens beiseite legen

set aside *v* 2. *(Entscheidung)* aufheben, außer Kraft setzen; **to** ~ **a composition** e-n Vergleich aufheben; **to** ~ **a judgment** ein Urteil aufheben *(durch das erlassende Gericht od. Rechtsmittelgericht)*; **to** ~ **a judgment in default**[44] ein Versäumnisurteil aufheben *(durch das erlassende Gericht unter Zulassung der Einlassung zur Hauptsache)*

set by *v* zurücklegen, auf die Seite legen, sparen

set down *v* niederschreiben; eintragen; **to** ~ **to a p.'s account** auf jds Rechnung setzen; **to set a case down for trial** e-e Sache in die Liste der anhängigen Verfahren eintragen; e-e Sache zur Hauptverhandlung ansetzen; e-n Termin anberaumen; **to** ~ **a meeting for ...** den Sitzungstermin anberaumen auf ...; **to** ~ **in writing** *(etw.)* schriftlich niederlegen

set forth *v* darlegen, erklären; vorbringen, anführen, zitieren; **to** ~ **grounds (for)** Gründe vorbringen (für); begründen; **to** ~ **a proposal** e-n Vorschlag vorbringen

set free *v*, **to set sb. free** jdn auf freien Fuß setzen, jdn freilassen; **to set capital free** (e. g. for investment) Kapital flüssig machen

set off *v* aufrechnen im Prozeß (mit Gegenforderung gegen die Klagforderung)[43]; verrechnen, aufrechnen (against mit); **to** ~ **gains against losses** Gewinne mit Verlusten aufrechnen

set out *v* darlegen, beschreiben; *(Ware)* auslegen, ausstellen

set up *v* *(Geschäft etc)* eröffnen, gründen; errichten; sich niederlassen; *(Meinung etc)* vorbringen; *(im pleading)* einwenden, geltend machen; **to set o.s. up** sich selbständig machen; **to set o.s. up as a lawyer** sich als Anwalt niederlassen; **to** ~ **a false alibi** ein unwahres Alibi vorbringen; **to** ~ **a breach of contract** sich auf Vertragsbruch berufen; **to** ~ **a business** ein Geschäft gründen; **to** ~ **a claim** e-e Forderung geltend machen; **to** ~ **a committee** e-n Ausschuß einsetzen; ein Komittee bilden; **to** ~ **a company** e-e Gesellschaft gründen (od. errichten); **to** ~ **a condition** e-e Bedingung stellen; **to** ~ **a defen|ce (~se)** e-e Einrede geltend machen; **to** ~ **a factory** e-e Fabrik gründen; **to** ~ **invalidity** Ungültigkeit geltend machen; **to** ~ **a monument** ein Denkmal errichten; **to** ~ **reserves** Rücklagen bilden; **to** ~ **the statute of limitations** Verjährung einwenden

setting aside, ~ an award Aufhebung e-s Schiedsspruches; **~ a gift** Schenkungsanfechtung; **~ judgment** Aufhebung e-s Urteils *(→to set aside)*; **~ (of) judgment in default**[44] Aufhebung e-s Versäumnisurteils
setting free of capital Flüssigmachung von Kapital
setting-up, ~ of a business Eröffnung (od. Gründung) e-s Geschäfts, Geschäftsgründung; **~ of a committee** Bildung (od. Einsetzung) e-s Ausschusses

settle *v* 1. regeln, ordnen, in Ordnung bringen; erledigen; bezahlen, begleichen; *(VersR)* regulieren; **to ~ an account** e-e Rechnung bezahlen; ein Konto abschließen; **to ~ accounts with sb.** *fig.* mit jdm abrechnen; **to ~ one's affairs** (before death) s-e Angelegenheiten ordnen; sein Testament machen; **to ~ the average** die Dispache aufmachen; **to ~ a balance** einen Saldo ausgleichen; **to ~ a bill** e-e Rechnung bezahlen (od. begleichen); **to ~ a claim** *(VersR)* e-n Schaden regulieren; **to ~ debts** Schulden bezahlen (od. begleichen); **to ~ a matter** e-e Angelegenheit regeln; **to ~ payments in dollars** Zahlungen in Dollar durchführen; **to ~ up** *colloq.* abrechnen (with mit)
settled fest, bestimmt; erledigt; bezahlt *(auf Rechnungen als Quittung)*; **~ account** beglichene (od. bezahlte) Rechnung; **~ by the contract** vertraglich geregelt; **~ income** festes Einkommen; **this issue is ~** diese Frage ist erledigt
settling Regelung, Erledigung; **~ agent** Schadenregulierer; **~ of an account**(or **bill**) Bezahlung e-r Rechnung; **way of ~ accounts** Zahlungsart
settle *v* 2. vereinbaren; sich einigen (for auf), sich vergleichen; *(Wortlaut e-r Urkunde)* festlegen; *(Streit)* beilegen, schlichten; *(meist außergerichtl.)* Vergleich schließen; **to ~ an affair amicably** e-e Sache gütlich beilegen; **to ~ an amount of compensation** e-e Abfindung vereinbaren; **to ~ by compromise** durch Vergleich erledigen; **to ~ a case** sich vergleichen; **to ~ the day** den Termin vereinbaren; **to ~ disputes by arbitration** Streitigkeiten auf schiedsrichterlichem Wege regeln; **to ~ the dispute out of court** den Streit außergerichtlich beilegen; **to ~ a document** den Wortlaut e-r Urkunde festlegen *(meist durch counsel)*; **to ~ an estate** *Am* e-n Nachlaß abwickeln; **to ~ an issue** →issue 1.; **to ~ an order** *Am* sich über den Wortlaut des Gerichtsbeschlusses einigen, den Wortlaut festlegen *(durch Anwälte nach Verkündigung der Entscheidung)*; **to ~ pleadings** Schriftsätze entwerfen; **to ~ the terms** die Bedingungen vereinbaren (od. festlegen)
settling, ~ (of) disputes out of court außergerichtliche Beilegung (od. Schlichtung) von Streitigkeiten; **~ pleadings** Entwurf von Schriftsätzen

settle *v* 3., **to ~ sth. (up)on sb.** jdm etw. aussetzen; **to ~ an annuity on a p.** jdm e-e Jahresrente aussetzen; **to ~ property** (upon a p.) über Vermögen zugunsten e-r Person *(od. mehrerer Personen)* verfügen, Vermögen mehreren nacheinander berechtigten Personen zuwenden *(oft durch Errichtung e-s Trustfonds mit Bestimmung des/der Begünstigten; cf. settlement 3.)*; **to ~ one's property on one's wife** e-n →trust über sein Vermögen zugunsten der Ehefrau begründen *(durch Schenkung unter Lebenden oder Testament)*
settled land *Br*[45] durch settlement (→*settlement 3.*) beschränkter Grundbesitz, der sich in der Hand e-s →tenant for life (od. →statutory owner) befindet
settling a sum Aussetzung e-r Summe
settle *v* 4. sich niederlassen; sich (od. jdn) ansiedeln; dauernden Wohnsitz nehmen; *(Land)* besiedeln; **to ~ down in a town** sich *(dauernd od. auf längere Zeit)* in e-r Stadt niederlassen; **to ~ refugees** Flüchtlinge ansiedeln
settled ansässig; besiedelt; **~ abode** fester Wohnsitz; **sparsely ~ area** dünn besiedeltes Gebiet

settlement 1. Regelung, Erledigung; Bezahlung, Begleichung; Ausgleich; Abfindung; *(VersR)* Regulierung; *(Börse)* Abrechnung, Liquidation *(→settlement 4.)*; **~s** Zahlungsausgleich *(→Bank for International S~s)*; **~ day** *(Terminbörse)* Börsenabrechnungstag; **~ of an account** Bezahlung e-r Rechnung; **~ of accounts** Abrechnung; **quarterly ~ of accounts** vierteljährliche Bezahlung von Rechnungen; **~ of a claim** *(VersR)* Regulierung e-s Schadens; **in ~ of all claims** zur Abfindung aller Ansprüche; **~ of a debt** Begleichung e-r Schuld; **~ of hardship cases** Härteregelung; **~ of transactions** Ausgleich des Zahlungsverkehrs *(→Bank for International S~s)*; **~ with withdrawing partner** Abfindung e-s ausscheidenden Teilhabers; **amicable ~** gütliche Regelung; **claim** (or **loss**) **~** *(VersR)* Schadensregulierung; **sum** (or **amount**) **paid in full ~ of all outstanding claims** pauschale Abfindung; **to accept a ~** sich abfinden lassen; **to make a ~ upon a p.** jdn abfinden; **to pay sb. a lump sum in ~ of his claim** jdn. abfinden
settlement 2. Vereinbarung; Beilegung, Schlichtung *(e-s Streites)*; *(meist außergerichtlicher)* Vergleich; vergleichsweise Erledigung; **~ by arbitration** →arbitration 1.; **~ of conflicts** (or **disputes**) Schlichtung (od. Beilegung) von Streitigkeiten; **~ negotiations** Einigungsverhandlungen; **~ of international disputes** friedliche Beilegung internationaler Streitigkeiten; **~ out of court** außergerichtlicher Vergleich; **~ procedure** Schlichtungsverfahren; **~ with one's creditors** Vergleich mit seinen Gläubigern; **compulsory ~** Zwangsvergleich; **proposal for a ~** Vergleichsvorschlag; **terms of ~** Vergleichsbedingungen; **to achieve** (or **effect**)

a ~ e-n Vergleich zustande bringen; **to negotiate a** ~ e-n Vergleich aushandeln, e-n Vergleich durch Verhandlungen zustande bringen; **to reach a** ~ e-e Einigung erzielen; zu e-m Vergleich kommen; **after protracted negotiations a** ~ **was reached by the parties** nach langen Verhandlungen einigten sich die Parteien (od. kam ein Vergleich zustande); **no** ~ **was reached** (or **resulted**) es kam kein Vergleich zustande

settlement (of property) 3. (urkundl.) Verfügung über *(bewegl. od. unbewegl.)* Vermögen *(die in Form e-s trust zugunsten einer od. mehrerer Personen vorgenommen wird; →settle v 3.)*; ~ **by will** testamentarische Verfügung, durch die Vermögen in e-m trust festgelegt wird; ~ **inter vivos** zu Lebzeiten des Errichters gegründeter Trust; **antenuptial** ~ vorehelicher güterrechtlicher Vertrag; vor Eheschließung abgeschlossener Ehevertrag; **deed of** ~ *bes. Am* Urkunde über die Übereignung von (Grund-) Vermögen *(oft bei feierl. Anlässen, z.B. der Heirat e-r Tochter, od. in Ausführung e-s Vermögensteilungsplanes)*; →**family** ~; →**marriage** ~; **post-nuptial** ~ nach Eheschließung abgeschlossener Ehevertrag; **strict** ~ Verfügung über Grundvermögen *(deren Zweck in der Festlegung der Erbfolge von Grundbesitz zugunsten der Familie des settlor liegt)*; **voluntary** ~ freiwillig, unentgeltlich *(ohne valuable consideration)* verfügtes settlement; **to make a** ~ **on a p.** jdm auf begrenzte Zeit oder bedingt Vermögen zuwenden

settlement 4. *(Börse)* Liquidation, Abrechnung *(Abwicklung der Termingeschäfte)*; ~ **account** Liquidationskonto; ~ **day** Abrechnungstag; ~ **price** Liquidationskurs; **dealing for future** ~ Terminkauf; **end month** ~ Ultimoliquidation, Ultimoabrechnung; **mid month** ~ Medioliquidation, Medioabrechnung; **special** ~ (S/S) Sonderliquidation *(für neu eingeführte Werte)*; **year-end** ~ Abrechnung per Jahresende

settlement 5. Siedlung; Ansiedlung; Besiedelung; ~ **area** *Am* Siedlungsgebiet; **Israel's** ~ **policy** israelische Siedlungspolitik

settler Siedler

settling →settle *v* 1., 2. und 3.

settlor Errichter e-s settlement *(→settlement 3.)*; Begründer e-s trust, Treugeber

sever *v* (ab)trennen; teilen; ausscheiden, sich trennen; **to** ~ **o.s. from the Church (to** ~ **connection with the Church)** aus der Kirche austreten; **to** ~ **a joint tenancy** Gesamthandseigentum in Bruchteilseigentum umwandeln; **to** ~ **relations** Beziehungen abbrechen

severable (ab)trennbar; teilbar

several einzeln, gesondert, getrennt *(opp. joint)*; ~ **creditor** Einzelgläubiger, einzelner von mehreren Mitgläubigern *(die nicht →joint creditors sind)*

several debt Einzelschuld, Einzelverpflichtung *(opp. joint debt)*

Gleiche (unabhängig voneinander bestehende) Verpflichtung mehrerer Personen, die einzeln belangt werden können. Der Gläubiger kann von jedem aber nur einen Teil der Schuld fordern (sind 3 Schuldner severally liable, braucht jeder nur ⅓ zu zahlen)

several debtor Einzelschuldner, einzelner Mitschuldner *(opp. joint debtor)*

Mehrere Personen verpflichten sich unabhängig voneinander zu derselben Leistung *(→several debt)*. Der Gläubiger kann einen einzelnen Schuldner aus der Haftung entlassen, ohne daß dadurch die anderen Mitschuldner befreit werden

several demand Einzelforderung

Ein Gläubiger hat gegen mehrere Schuldner selbständige Forderungen auf die gleiche Leistung

several, ~ **liability** Einzelhaftung; Individualhaftung *(jeder einzelne haftet auf das Ganze; opp. joint liability)*; ~ **promisee** einzelner Mitgläubiger *(jeder allein darf die Erfüllung verlangen)*; ~ **promisor** →~ debtor; ~ **tenancy** Einzelbesitz; →**joint and** ~

severally, ~ **liable** gesondert (od. einzeln) haftbar; →**jointly and** ~

severalty Bruchteilseigentum *(opp. joint ownership, ownership in common, and coparcenary)*; ~ **owner** Bruchteilseigentümer

severance Trennung (from von); Abtrennung; ~ **benefit** →~ pay; ~ **of diplomatic relations** Abbruch der diplomatischen Beziehungen; ~ **pay** Entlassungsabfindung *(e-s Arbeitnehmers)*; ~ **tax** *Am* Steuer auf die Konzession zur Gewinnung von Bodenschätzen

severe streng; hart; ~ **competition** scharfe Konkurrenz; ~ **illness** schwere Krankheit; ~ **punishment** schwere Bestrafung

sewage Abwässer; ~ **disposal** Abwässerbeseitigung; ~ **farm** Rieselfeld; ~ **plant** Kläranlage

sex discrimination unterschiedliche Behandlung nach dem Geschlecht; **S~ D~ Act** *Br*[46] Gleichberechtigungsgesetz

sexual, ~ **intercourse** Geschlechtsverkehr; ~ **offen|ces**[47] **(~ses)**[48] Sittlichkeitsdelikte, Straftaten gegen die Sittlichkeit

Seym, Sejm das polnische Parlament

Seychelles, Republic of ~ Republik Seschellen; **of** ~ seschellisch

Seychellois Sescheller(in)

shack, common of ~ *Br* Weiderecht der Eigentümer angrenzender Felder über die ganze Fläche nach der Ernte

shade *v* allmählich sinken *(von Preisen)*; **the**

shares ~d from ... to ... die Aktien sanken von ... auf ...

shading geringfügiger Kursrückgang

shadow, ~ cabinet *Br* Schattenkabinett; **~ director**[49] „Schattendirektor"; **~ economy** Schattenwirtschaft

shadow *v (jdn)* heimlich beobachten, beschatten

shady business dunkles (od. zweifelhaftes) Geschäft

shake out Personalabbau; Umstrukturierung; Gesundschrumpfung *(e-r Firma); (Börse)* Krise, in der die schwächeren Spekulanten aus dem Markt gedrängt werden

shake *v* **to ~ the confidence** das Vertrauen erschüttern; **the firm's credit was ~n** der Kredit der Firma war erschüttert

sham Schwindel, Trug, Täuschung; Schein-, fingiert; **~ bid** Scheingebot; **~ contract** Scheinvertrag, fingierter Vertrag; **~ dividend** Scheindividende; **~ pleading** mutwilliges, *(aus Verzögerungstaktik)* vorgebrachtes Parteivorbringen; **~ stock exchange transaction** Scheinverkauf an der Börse; **~ transaction** Scheingeschäft; **~ trial** Schauprozeß

SHAPE *(NATO)* (Supreme Headquarters of the Allied Powers Europe) Oberkommando der alliierten Streitkräfte in Europa

share 1. Teil, Anteil (in an); Beteiligung (in an); Quote; Kontingent; Schiffspart *(→~ in a ship)*; **~ and ~ alike** zu gleichen Teilen; **~cropper** *Am (bes. in den Südstaaten)* Pächter, der Pacht mit teilweiser Ablieferung der Ernte bezahlt; **~ in a business** Geschäftsanteil; **~ in the capital** Kapitalanteil; **~ in the estate** Erb(an)teil; Anteil an e-m Nachlaß; **~ in an inheritance** *Am* Erb(an)teil; **~ in the loss** Anteil am Verlust, Verlustanteil

share in (or **of**) **(the) profits** Gewinnanteil; Gewinnbeteiligung; **the ~ accrues to** der Gewinnanteil entfällt auf; **to be entitled to** (or **to have**) **a ~** am Gewinn beteiligt sein; **to give a p. a ~** jdn am Gewinn beteiligen; **to receive one's ~** s-n Gewinnanteil erhalten

share, ~ in a ship Schiffspart, Anteil e-s Mitreeders *(Br*[50] *jedes Schiff wird in 64 shares zerlegt)*; **~s trust certificates** *Am* →Massachusetts trust; **~-the-work plan** *Am* Plan, der anstelle von Entlassung Kurzarbeit aller Beteiligten vorsieht; **~ under an intestacy** gesetzlicher Erbteil

share, capital ~ Kapitalanteil; **in equal ~s** zu gleichen Teilen; **indefeasible ~** *Am (der Familie sichergestellter)* unangreifbarer Anteil am Nachlaß; **intestate ~** gesetzlicher Erbteil; **right to a ~** Anteilsrecht (in an); **statutory forced ~** *Am* bestimmte feste Quote am Nachlaß; Pflichtteil; **to be entitled to a ~ in an estate** zu e-m Anteil am Nachlaß berechtigt sein; **to fall to sb.'s ~** jdm zuteil werden; jdm als Anteil zufallen; **to go ~s with sb.** (in sth.) *(etw., z.B. Gewinn, Kosten)* mit jdm teilen; **to have a ~ in sth.** beteiligt sein (od. teilhaben) an etw.; **to have a half ~** zu 50% beteiligt sein; **to be held in undivided ~s** ungeteiltes gemeinsames Eigentum sein; **to take a ~ in the risk** sich am Risiko beteiligen

share 2. Aktie *(Anteilsrecht)*; Gesellschaftsanteil, Geschäftsanteil *(e-s Gesellschafters od. der Mitglieder e-r Genossenschaft)*; Investmentanteil

In Großbritannien ist das Aktienrecht in den →Companies Acts geregelt.

In den Vereinigten Staaten gibt es kein einheitliches Aktienrecht. Jeder der 50 Einzelstaaten hat sein eigenes Gesellschaftsrecht. Die Aktienemission unterliegt, soweit sie über die Grenzen eines Einzelstaates hinausgeht und eine gewisse Größenordnung überschreitet, der Kontrolle der →Securities and Exchange Commission des Bundes

shares, to allot ~ Aktien zuteilen; **to apply for ~** *Br* Aktien zeichnen; **to hold ~** (in a company) Aktien besitzen; Aktionär (e-r Gesellschaft) sein; **to issue ~** Aktien ausgeben; **to pay up ~** Aktien voll einzahlen; **to place ~ with the public** Aktien beim Publikum unterbringen (od. placieren); **to subscribe for ~** Aktien zeichnen; **the ~ advanced from ... to ...** die Aktien stiegen von ... auf ...; **the ~ are down** die Aktien stehen niedrig; **the ~ have fallen** (or **dropped**) die Aktien sind gefallen; **the ~ firmed up** die Aktien zogen an; **the ~ have gone up** (or **moved up**) die Aktien sind gestiegen (od. zogen an); **~ come on offer** Aktien werden angeboten; **the ~ recovered** die Aktien erholten sich; **the ~ are stationary** die Aktien sind fest geblieben

share, ~ acquisition *Am* →stock acquisition; **~s acquisition scheme** *Br* Plan, Arbeitnehmer durch die Ausgabe von Aktien am Gewinn zu beteiligen; **~ allotment** Aktienzuteilung; **~s and amounts owing from subsidiary companies** *Br (Bilanz)* Anteile und Geldbeträge, die von Tochtergesellschaften geschuldet werden; **~s applicant** Zeichner von Aktien; **~s applied for** gezeichnete Aktien; **~-based fund** Aktienfonds; **~ bonus** Aktienbonus *(opp. cash bonus)*; **~ capital** Aktienkapital, Grundkapital *(e-r AG)*; Betriebskapital *(e-r Genossenschaft)*; **~ certificate** *Br*[51] Aktienzertifikat, Aktien-Berechtigungsschein *(Urkunde darüber, daß der Inhaber des Scheins ein Anrecht auf die darin erwähnte Aktie hat; kein →negotiable instrument)*; Anteilschein; **~ circulation** Aktienumlauf; **~ deal** →~ acquisition; **~ denomination** Aktienstückelung; **~ dividend** (Dividende in Form von) Gratisaktien; **~ fund** Aktienfonds *(→fund 2.)*; **~s held in escrow** treuhänderisch verwaltete Aktien

shareholder Aktionär, Aktieninhaber; Anteilseigner; **~'s agreement** Vereinbarung zwischen Aktionären *(vertragliche Änderung der Aktionärsrechte)*; **~'s bill** *Am* Klage e-s Aktionärs anstelle der Gesellschaft; **~s' equity** *(Bilanz)* Eigenkapital; (Inbegriff der) Rechte des Aktionärs, die sich aus der Beteiligung an der Gesellschaft ergeben; **~s' meeting** Hauptversammlung e-r AG; Gesellschafterversammlung; **~'s right(s)** Bezugsrecht auf Aktien *(→rights 2.)*; **controlling ~** Mehrheitsaktionär; **ordinary ~** Inhaber von Stammaktien; Stammaktionär; **registered ~** Inhaber von Namensaktien; **to call the ~s together** (or **to convene the ~s**) die Aktionäre einberufen; **to call** (or **summon**) **~s to a general meeting** *Br* e-e Hauptversammlung einberufen

shareholding Aktienbesitz; Beteiligung; Anteilsbesitz; **acquisition of a ~** Beteiligungserwerb; **directors' ~** Aktienbesitz der Geschäftsleitung; **employee ~** Mitbeteiligung der Arbeitnehmer; **minority ~** Minderheitsbeteiligung; **to acquire a majority ~** e-e Aktienmehrheit erwerben

share, ~ in a mine Kux; **~ incentive scheme** Leistungsanreiz für leitende Angestellte durch die Möglichkeit des Aktienerwerbs; **~ index** Aktienindex; **~ (interest)** Geschäftsanteil; **~ issue** Aktienemission; **~ ledger** *Br* →**~** register; **~-list** *Br* (Aktien-)Kurszettel; **~ market** Aktienmarkt; **~s of beneficial interest** *Am* Treuhand-Anteilscheine *(cf. Massachusets trust)*; **~ of no par value** nennwertlose Aktie, Quotenaktie; **~s payable to bearer** Inhaberaktien; **~ premium**[52] Emissionsagio, Aktienagio

share prices Aktienkurse, Börsenkurse; **falling (rising) ~** fallende (steigende) Aktienkurse; **trend in ~** Aktienkursentwicklung; **~ went ahead** die Aktienkurse stiegen; **~ were maintained** (at yesterday's level) die Aktienkurse hielten sich

share, ~-pusher *Br*[53] *(gewerbmäßiger, von Haus zu Haus gehender)* Aktienaufdränger; **~ quotation** Kursnotierung; **~ rating** Bewertung e-r Aktie; **~ redemption** Aktieneinziehung; **~ register** Aktienregister, Aktienbuch; **~ speculation** Aktienspekulation; **~ split** Aktiensplit, Aktienaufteilung *(→splitting)*; **~ subscribed** gezeichnete Aktie; **~ transfer** Aktienübertragung; **~ warrant (to bearer)** *Br*[54] *(auf den Inhaber lautender)* Aktienschein *(der ein →negotiable instrument ist; cf. share certificate)*

share, allocation (or **allotment**) **of ~s** Zuteilung von Aktien; **applicant for ~s** *Br* Aktienzeichner; **application for (allotment of) ~s** Aktienzeichnung; **bank ~s** Bankaktien, Bankwerte; **block of ~s** Aktienpaket; **bonus ~** *Br* Gratisaktie; **cumulative preference ~s** *Br* kumulative Vorzugsaktien *(→cumulative)*; **deferred ~s** *bes. Br* Nachzugsaktien *(→deferred)*; Nachzugsanteile *(e-r Genossenschaft)*; **electricity ~s** Elektrowerte; **founders' ~s**[54] Gründeraktien *(→management ~s)*; **holder of ~s** Aktienbesitzer; **holding of ~s** Aktienbesitz; **inscribed ~s** *Br* Namensaktien; **interim ~s** Interimsscheine, Zwischenscheine; **issue of ~s** Aktienausgabe; **majority of ~s** Aktienmehrheit; **→management ~s**; **mining ~s** Bergwerksaktien, Montanwerte; **no par value ~s** nennwertlose Aktien, Quotenaktien; **non-voting ~s** stimmrechtslose Aktien; **oil ~s** Erdölaktien; **ordinary ~s** (ord.) Stammaktien *(opp. preference ~s)*; **parcel of ~s** Aktienpaket; **personal ~s** *Br* Namensaktien; **placing of ~s** Placierung (od. Unterbringung) von Aktien; **preference ~s** *Br* Vorzugsaktien, Prioritätsaktien *(Aktien mit besonderen Vorzugsrechten, z.B. im voraus e-e bestimmte Dividende zu beziehen)*; **redeemable preference ~s** *Br* rückkaufbare Vorzugsaktien

share, registered ~s Namensaktien

Anders als in Deutschland sind Aktien einer britischen company und einer amerikanischen corporation grundsätzlich keine Inhaberaktien, sondern Namensaktien

share, shipping ~s Schiffahrtswerte; **subscription to ~s** Aktienzeichnung; **transfer of ~s** Aktienübertragung; **transmission of ~s** *Br* Übergang der Inhaberschaft an Aktien kraft Gesetzes *(kraft Erbfolge, Konkurs)*; **unissued ~s** nicht ausgegebene Aktien; Vorratsaktien; **voting ~s** Aktien mit Stimmrecht

share *v (etw.)* teilen (among unter; with sb. mit jdm); aufteilen; **to ~ and ~ alike** gleich teilen; gleiche Teile bekommen; **to ~ in** sich beteiligen an; teilnehmen an; **to ~ (in) the costs** sich an den Kosten beteiligen; **to ~ in profits** am Gewinn beteiligt sein; **to ~ out** (ver-, auf-, aus)teilen; **to ~ out the costs** die Kosten verteilen (od. aufteilen) (among auf, between zwischen); **to ~ with** teilen mit, gemeinsam haben mit; **to ~ an office with sb.** ein Büro mit jdm teilen; **to ~ the risk** das Risiko teilen; **to ~ sb.'s view** jds Ansicht teilen; **to be entitled to ~ in the estate** zu e-m Anteil an der Erbschaft berechtigt sein

shared, ~ equity mortgage *Am* hypothekarisch gesichertes Darlehen unter Vereinbarung e-r Beteiligung des Gläubigers am Substanzwert des Grundstücks zwecks Verringerung des Zinssatzes; **~ responsibility** geteilte Verantwortung, Mitverschulden

sharing Teilung; Verteilung, Aufteilung; Beteiligung; **fair ~ of burdens** gerechte Verteilung der Lasten; **~ the market** Aufteilung des Marktes; **~ of nuclear weapons** Kernwaffenmitbesitz; **~ of profits** →profit **~**; **~ of the spoil** Teilung der Beute; **cost-~** Kostenbeteiligung; **gain-~** Gewinnbeteiligung *(der Arbeiter)*

shark Hai(fisch); *fig* Schwindler, Wucherer

shark repellents Maßnahmen zur Abwehr von Übernahmeangeboten

sharp, ~ **business** Schwindel, Gaunerei; ~ **practices** unsaubere (Geschäfts-)Praktiken; ~ **protest** scharfer Protest

shed Schuppen, (Lager-)Halle; **customs** ~ Zollschuppen; **freight** ~ *Am* Güterhalle

shed *v* abstoßen; **to** ~ **jobs** Mitarbeiter entlassen; ~**ding of labo(u)r** Abbau von Personal

sheet Blatt, Bogen; ~ **of drawings** *(PatR)* Zeichnungsblatt; ~ **of paper** Blatt Papier; **attendance** ~ Anwesenheitsliste; **balance** ~ Bilanz *(→balance 1.)*; **charge** ~ *Br* →charge 1.; **cost** ~ Kostenaufstellung; **coupon** ~ Couponbogen; **inventory** ~ Inventarverzeichnis; **loose** ~ loses Blatt; Flugblatt; **supplementary** ~ Extrabogen, Beiblatt

shelf Regal; (Wand-)Brett; ~ **life** Haltbarkeit; Aufbewahrungsdauer; ~ **registration** *Am* Vorausregistrierung von Anleihen bei der→Securities and Exchange Commission *(um diese periodisch, "off the shelf" zu verkaufen)*; **continental** ~ *(VölkerR)* Festlandsockel

shell Mantel *(e-r Kapitalgesellschaft)*; Firmenmantel; **formation of a** ~ **company** Mantelgründung; ~ **operation** Übernahme e-r Gesellschaft

shelter Schutz, Zuflucht; **air raid** ~ Luftschutzkeller; Bunker; **giving** ~ Unterschlupfgewährung; →**tax** ~

shelter *v*, **to** ~ **income** (from tax) das Einkommen *(rechtmäßig)* vor Steuerbelastung bewahren; *(rechtmäßige)* einkommensteuersparende Maßnahmen ergreifen

sheltered, ~ **accomodation** (for the elderly) Seniorenheim; ~ **employment** Arbeitsplätze für Behinderte mit besonderen Einrichtungen

shelve *v* auf ein Regal stellen; zu den Akten legen; ad acta legen; *fig* verschieben, zurückstellen; **to** ~ **a Bill** *Br* e-n Gesetzesentwurf *(auf unbestimmte Zeit)* zurückstellen

sheriff *Br (meist auf ein Jahr ernannter)* oberster Verwaltungsbeamter e-s county mit bestimmten Aufgaben *(bes. Leitung von Parlamentswahlen, Vollstreckung von Urteilen des High Court und der Strafgerichte)*; *Am* gewählter oberster Verwaltungsbeamter e-s county *(ihm untersteht die county-Polizei sowie die Vollstreckung strafrechtl. Urteile; des weiteren besorgt er die Zustellung von Ladungen, Urteilen, Beschlüssen etc.; Ladung der jury)*; *Scot* Richter; ~**-clerk** *Scot* Urkundsbeamter e-s sheriff court; ~ **court** *Scot (niederes)* Gericht *(mit Zuständigkeit in Zivil- und Strafsachen)*; ~**'s officer** Gerichtsvollzieher; **deputy** ~ *Am* Stellvertreter des örtlichen Polizeichefs; **goods taken in execution by a** ~ vom sheriff *(als Gerichtsvollzieher)* zur Vollstreckung beschlagnahmte Sachen

sheriffalty (or **sheriffdom**) Amt e-s sheriff

Sherman Act ("Act to Protect Trade and Commerce against Unlawful Restraints and Monopolies") *Am* grundlegendes Antitrustgesetz, Kartellgesetz *(von 1890)*

Das Gesetz enthält zwei Tatbestände eines wettbewerbswidrigen und ungesetzlichen Verhaltens. § 1[55] erfaßt nur Wettbewerbsbeschränkungen zwischen mehreren Unternehmen (Kartellverbot). § 2[56] betrifft auch das wettbewerbsbeschränkende Verhalten von Einzelunternehmen (Verbot des Monopolisierens). Der Sherman Act schuf u. a. die Möglichkeit, bei Gericht bestimmte Verfügungen gegen wettbewerbsbeschränkende Maßnahmen zu erwirken. Das Gesetz ist wesentlich geändert bzw. ergänzt durch Bestimmungen des Clayton Act, Robinson-Patman-Act, Miller-Tydings Act

shift 1. Veränderung, Wechsel, Verschiebung, Verlagerung; Umschichtung; *pol* Kursänderung; ~ **in supply** Angebotsverlagerung; ~ **of opinion** Meinungsumschwung

shift 2. Schicht *(Arbeitszeit od. Belegschaft)*; ~ **differential** (or **premium**) Schichtzulage *(für Arbeit außerhalb der normalen Arbeitszeit)*; **change of** ~ Schichtwechsel; **day** ~ Tag(es-)schicht; **extra** ~ Sonderschicht; **night** ~ Nachtschicht; **rotating** ~ Wechselschicht; **split** ~ nicht durchgehende (unterbrochene) Schicht; **to drop** ~**s** Feierschichten einlegen

shift 3. Ausweg, Notbehelf, Kniff, Trick; **to make** ~ sich behelfen

shift *v* (sich) verändern, wechseln, verschieben; **to** ~ **for o. s.** sich selbst helfen; **to** ~ **the burden of proof** die Beweislast umkehren; **to** ~ **investments** Anlagen umschichten; **to** ~ **the responsibility on a p.** jdm die Verantwortung zuschieben; **the cargo** ~**s** die Ladung verschiebt sich; **the prices have** ~**ed slightly** die Preise haben sich leicht geändert

shifting, ~ **the burden of proof** Umkehrung der Beweislast; ~ **of cargo** Verschiebung der Ladung; ~ **of risk** Risikoabwälzung; ~ **of taxation** (or **tax** ~) Steuerüberwälzung *(→tax)*

shilling Schilling

Br Seit 1971 aus dem Währungssystem verschwunden. Währungseinheit von Kenia, Uganda und Tansania

shingle *Am colloq.* Namensschild *(e-s Anwalts, Arztes)*; **to hang out one's** ~ e-e Praxis aufmachen

ship Schiff; ~**'s agent** Schiffsagent; ~**'s articles** Heuervertrag; ~ **broker** Schiffsmakler; ~**builder** Schiffsbauer, Werftunternehmer

shipbuilding[57] Schiffbau; ~ **industry** Schiffbau; ~ **yard** Schiffs(bau)werft

ship, ~ **canal** Schiffskanal; ~**'s certificate** →ship's registry certificate; ~ **chandler** Lieferant von Schiffsbedarf; Ausrüster; ~ **chandlery** Handlung für Schiffsbedarf; ~**'s clearance** →clearance 2.; ~ **collided with** angerammtes Schiff;

~'s **company** Schiffsbesatzung; ~'s **distress signal** Schiffsnotsignal; ~'s **equipment** Schiffsausrüstung; ~'s **fuel and stores** Brennmaterial und Vorräte des Schiffes; Schiffsbedarf; **(~'s) hold** Schiffsraum, Laderaum; **(~'s) hold required** Schiffsraumbedarf; ~'s **husband** Korrespondentreeder; ~ **in distress** Schiff in Seenot; ~'s **inventory** Schiffsinventar; ~**load** Schiffsladung; ~**master** Kapitän; ~ **mortgage** Schiffshypothek (→*mortgage)*

shipowner *(Seeschiffahrt)* Schiffseigentümer, Reeder; *(Binnenschiffahrt)* Schiffseigner; ~ **association** Reederverband; **liability of ~s**[58] Reederhaftung; ~'s **office** Reederei

ship, ~'s **papers** Schiffspapiere *(ship's registry certificate, bill of lading, bill of health, log book etc)*; ~'s **passport** →sea letter; ~'s **protest** Verklarung, Seeprotest

ship's rail Reling des Schiffes; **at** ~ längsseits des Schiffes

ship, ~'s **register** Schiffsregister; ~'s **registry certificate** *(Seeschiff)* Schiffszertifikat, Registerbrief; *(Binnenschiff)* Schiffsbrief; ~ **repair yard** Schiffsreparaturwerft; ~'s **stores** Schiffsvorräte, Vorräte an Bord; ~ **stores** Schiffsbedarfsmagazin; ~ **store dealer** Lieferant von Schiffsbedarf; ~'s **surgeon** Schiffsarzt; ~ **under average** havariertes Schiff

shipwreck Schiffbruch; **to suffer** ~ Schiffbruch erleiden

shipwrecked person Schiffbrüchiger

shipyard Werft

ship, all-freight ~ Mehrzweckfrachter, Kombischiff; **arrest of a** ~ Arrest(vollziehung) in ein Schiff; **on board (a)** ~ an Bord; auf dem Schiff; **cargo** ~ Frachtschiff; **convoy** ~ Begleitschiff; **entry and departure of a** ~ Ein- und Auslaufen e-s Schiffes; **equipment of a** ~ Schiffsausrüstung; **hospital** ~ Lazarettschiff; **loss of a** ~ **with all hands** Untergang des Schiffes mit der gesamten Besatzung; **management of a** ~ technische Bedienung e-s Schiffes; **merchant** ~ Handelsschiff, Kauffahrteischiff; **nuclear** ~ Atomschiff (→*nuclear)*; **passenger** ~ Fahrgastschiff; **share in a** ~ Schiffspart (→ *share 1.*); **space** ~ (Welt-) Raumschiff; **war**~ Kriegsschiff; **to board a** ~ an Bord e-s Schiffes gehen; *mil* ein Schiff entern; **to put a** ~ **in service** ein Schiff in Dienst stellen; **to unload a** ~ ein Schiff löschen; **a** ~ **is afloat** ein Schiff ist flott; **a** ~ **is ashore** ein Schiff ist gestrandet

ship *v (Waren)* verschiffen, versenden, befördern, verladen *(bes. Am auch zu Lande)*; *(Seeleute)* anheuern; sich anheuern lassen; *(Seefrachtgeschäft)* abladen; verfrachten; **to** ~ **in bulk** *(Waren)* lose (od. in loser Schüttung) verladen; **to** ~ **on deck** auf Deck verladen

shipped, ~ **bill (of lading)** Bordkonnossement; **goods** ~ (Fracht-)Sendung, Ladung

shipping Schiffahrt; Schiffe *(e-s Landes)*; Verschiffung, Versendung, Versand, Beförderung, Verladung *(bes. Am auch zu Lande)*; *(Seefrachtgeschäft)* Abladung; Verfrachtung; **S~ Act** 1916 *Am* Schiffahrtsgesetz *(regelt das Ocean Freight Conference System, →conference 2.)*[59]; ~ **advice** Versandanzeige; ~ **agency** Schiffsagentur; Speditionsfirma; ~ **agent** Schiffsagent; Seehafenspediteur; ~ **articles** Heuervertrag; ~ **bill** Verzeichnis verschiffter Waren; Zollfreischein; ~ **(business)** Schiffahrt; Seetransportgeschäft; ~ **charges** Verladekosten, Versandkosten; ~ **clerk** Expedient *(e-r Firma)*; ~ **commissioner** *Am* Beamter zur Überwachung der Dienstverhältnisse der Seeleute; Seemannsamt; ~ **company** Schiffahrtsgesellschaft; Reederei; **suitable ~ conditions** *Am* angemessene Transportbeschaffenheit; **S~ Conferences** Schiffahrtskonferenzen *(kartellartiger Zusammenschluß verschiedener Linienreedereien*[60]*)*; ~ **contract** *Am* Frachtvertrag; ~ **date** Versandtag; ~ **department** Versandabteilung; ~ **documents** Versanddokumente, Verladepapiere, Beförderungsdokumente; *(invoice, policy of insurance, bill of lading etc)*; ~ **exchange** Schiffahrtsbörse, Frachtbörse; ~ **expenses** Versandkosten, Transportkosten; ~ **firm** →~ house; ~ **house** Reederei; ~ **industry** Schiffahrt; ~ **instructions** Versandvorschriften; **S~Intelligence** →S~ News; ~ **line** Schiffahrtslinie; Linienreederei; ~**-master** *Br* Seemannsamtsleiter; **S~ News** Schiffahrtsberichte *(in Zeitungen)*; ~ **note** (S/N.) *(vom Ablader auszufüllender)* Schiffszettel; Verladeschein; ~ **notice** Versandanzeige; ~ **office** *Br* Speditionsbüro; Heuerbüro; ~ **order** Versandauftrag; ~ **papers** →~ documents; ~ **partnership** Partenreederei; ~ **port** Versandhafen; ~ **room** *Am* Versandraum, Verpackungsraum; ~ **shares** Schiffahrtswerte; ~ **space** Schiffsraum; ~ **terms** *Am* Versandbedingungen; ~ **trade** →~ business; ~ **traffic** Schiffsverkehr; ~ **weight** Verladegewicht, Versandgewicht

shipping, coastal ~ Küstenschiffahrt; **inland** ~ Binnenschiffahrt; →**International Chamber of S~;** →**International S~ Federation** Internationaler Reederverein; **maritime** ~ Seeschiffahrt; **merchant** ~ Handelsschiffahrt (→*merchant)*

shipment (shipt) 1. Verschiffung; Versendung, Versand, Verladung, Transport *(bes. Am auch zu Lande)*; *(Seefrachtgeschäft)* Abladung; Verfrachtung; ~ **as less (than) carload** *Am* Stückgutversand; ~ **made by post** Postversendung; ~ **on deck** Verladung auf Deck; **advice of** ~ Versandanzeige; **date of** ~ Verladedatum, Versandtermin; **evidence of** ~ Nachweis der (erfolgten) Verladung; **partial** ~ Teilverladung; **place of** ~ Verladeort; **port of** ~ Verladehafen, Versandhafen; **ready for** ~ versandbereit

shipment 2. Schiffsladung; Ladung; Frachtsendung; (Waren-)Sendung; ~ **against collection on delivery** (or **cash on delivery**) Nachnahmesendung; **collective** (or **consolidated**) ~ Sammelladung

shipper Befrachter; Ablader; Verlader; Spediteur

shipping →ship *v*

shoestring *colloq.* sehr kleines (ungenügendes) Kapital; ~ **company** *Am* finanzschwaches Unternehmen

shoo-in *Am* sicherer Kandidat, Spitzenkandidat

shoot Jagd(gebiet, -gruppe); **rent of a** ~ Jagdpacht; **to rent a** ~ e-e Jagd pachten

shoot *v* schießen; **to** ~ **dead** erschießen; **to** ~ **down an aircraft** ein Flugzeug abschießen; **to** ~ **up** *fig* emporschnellen

shooting Schießen, Schießerei; Jagd; ~ **incident** Schießerei; ~ **rights** Jagdrecht; ~ **season** Jagdzeit; ~ **war** heißer Krieg *(opp. cold war)*; **right of** ~ →~ rights

shop Laden, Geschäft; Werkstatt; Betrieb; ~ **agreement** Betriebsvereinbarung; ~ **assistant** *Br* Verkäufer(in), Ladenangestellte(r); ~**book** *Am* Geschäftsbuch, Journal; ~**book rule** *Am* Regel, nach der der Hinweis auf die eigenen Geschäftsbücher als Beweis zulässig ist; ~**(-) breaking** Ladeneinbruch; ~ **buying** *(Börse)* Berufskäufe; ~ **chairman** *Am* →~ steward; ~ **closing** Ladenschluß; ~ **committee** *Am* Betriebsausschuß; Betriebsrat; ~ **deputy** *Am* →~ steward; ~ **fittings** Ladeneinrichtung

shop floor Belegschaft; Betrieb; Arbeitsplatz *(in e-m Betrieb)*; Verkaufsfläche; **at the** ~ **level** arbeitsplatzbezogen, *pol* unter den Arbeitern in der Fabrik; **the men on the** ~ die Arbeiter *(opp. the management)*

shop, ~**keeper** Ladeninhaber, Ladenbesitzer; ~**keeping** Betreiben e-s Geschäfts; ~**lifter** Ladendieb; ~**lifting** Ladendiebstahl; ~ **premises** Ladenräume, Geschäftsräume; Werkstatt; ~ **price** Ladenpreis; ~ **rent** Ladenmiete; ~ **right** *Am* Arbeitgeberlizenz an der Erfindung des Arbeitnehmers; ~ **selling** *(Börse)* Berufsverkäufe; ~ **shares** Einführungsaktien; ~**-soiled** →~-worn; ~ **steward** gewerkschaftlicher Vertrauensmann (Personalvertreter); ~ **stewards committee** *Br (auch)* Betriebsrat; ~ **walker** Ladenaufsicht *(in e-m Warenhaus)*; ~ **window** Schaufenster; ~**-worn** *(von Ware)* angeschmutzt, angestaubt; **branch** ~ Zweiggeschäft; **closed** ~ gewerkschaftspflichtiger Betrieb (→*closed*); **contract** ~ Akkordbetrieb; **junk** ~ Ramschladen; → **open** ~**; repair** ~ Reparaturwerkstatt; **union** ~ *Am* gewerkschaftspflichtiger Betrieb (→ *union 2.)*; **to clear a** ~ ausverkaufen; **to close a** ~ ein Geschäft schließen; ein Geschäft verschließen; **to keep a** ~ ein Geschäft (einen Laden) haben; **to keep** ~ das Geschäft (den Laden) führen; **to lease a** ~ e-n Laden (ver)mieten; **to manage a** ~ s. to run a →~; **to patronize a** ~ in e-m Geschäft regelmäßig kaufen; **to rent a** ~ e-n Laden (ver)mieten; **to run a** ~ ein Geschäft führen; **to set up** ~ ein Geschäft eröffnen; **to talk** ~ fachsimpeln

shop *v* einkaufen, Einkäufe (od. Besorgungen) machen; **to** ~ **sb.** *colloq.* jdn bei der Polizei anzeigen

shopping Einkaufen; Einkäufe, Besorgungen; ~ **area** Einkaufsgegend; Geschäftsviertel; ~ **centre (center)** Geschäftszentrum; *Am* Ladenstadt *(am Rande e-r Großstadt zur Entlastung der city)*; ~ **district** →~ area; ~ **goods** *Am* Waren, die nicht zum dringlichen Bedarf gehören und erst nach Preisvergleich gekauft werden *(opp. convenience goods)*; ~ **list** Einkaufsliste; ~ **mall** Einkaufszentrum; ~ **street** Geschäftsstraße; →**forum** ~**;** →**treaty** ~

shore Küste *(am Meer)*; Ufer *(an Flüssen od. Seen)*; Strand; ~ **leave** Landurlaub; ~ **patrol** (S. P.) Küstenstreife *(Militärpolizei der Marine)*; **to go on** ~ landen *(von Personen)*

shore up *v fig* unterstützen, absichern

short 1. Fehlbetrag, Defizit; **cash** ~**s and overs** Kassenüberschüsse und -fehlbeträge

short 2. Kurzläufer, Papier mit kurzer Laufzeit *(opp. long, medium)*; *(Börse) Am* Baissier, Baissespekulant *(opp. long)*; ~**s** ohne Deckung verkaufte Wertpapiere od. Waren; Kurzläufer; ~ **account** Konto e-s Leerverkäufers; Baisseengagement; ~ **interest** (**or position**) Baisseengagement; ~**(sale)** Leerverkauf *(Verkauf von Wertpapieren, die der Verkäufer nicht besitzt, sondern später zu niedrigeren Kursen anschaffen will)*; ~ **seller** Baissier; Leerverkäufer, Fixer; ~ **selling** Fixen *(Abschluß e-s Leerverkaufs)*; ~ **side** Baissepartei; **to go** (or **sell**) ~ **securities** Wertpapiere ohne Deckung verkaufen, fixen

short 3. kurz; kurzfristig; knapp, unzureichend, fehlend

short of knapp an; zu wenig, fehlend; ~ **cash** (or **money**) nicht bei Kasse, knapp mit Geld; **to be** ~ **an article** e-n Artikel nicht vorrätig haben; **to be** ~ **shares** mit Aktien nicht genügend eingedeckt sein; gefixt haben

short, ~ **amount** Minderbetrag; ~ **bill** →~-dated bill; ~ **cause** im Schnellverfahren zu erledigende Rechtssache; ~ **covering** Deckungskauf; ~ **credit** kurzfristiger Kredit; ~ **crop** Ernte, die den Bedarf nicht deckt; ~ **delivery** unvollständige Lieferung

short-dated auf kurze Sicht *(opp. long-dated)*; ~ **bill** Wechsel auf kurze Sicht, kurzfristiger Wechsel; ~ **investment** kurzfristige Kapitalanlage

short distance, ~ goods traffic *Br* Güternahverkehr; ~ **hauling** *Am* Güternahverkehr
short entry *Br* vorläufige Gutschrift e-s noch nicht fälligen Wechsels durch die Bank; *(Zoll)* Unterdeklarierung
shortfall *bes. Am* Fehlbetrag, Defizit; Fehlmenge; Ausfall; Verknappung; ~ **in payments** Zahlungsausfall; ~ **in tax revenue** Steuerausfall
shorthand Kurzschrift; Stenografie; stenografisch *(opp. longhand)*; **official ~ note(s)** (or *Br* ~ **writer's notes**) stenografisch aufgenommenes Sitzungsprotokoll; **to take down in ~** Stenogramm aufnehmen; stenografieren
shorthanded, to be ~ Mangel an Arbeitskräften haben
short haul *Am* Güternahverkehr
short-haul aircraft Kurzstreckenflugzeug
short hours, working ~ *Am* Kurzarbeit
short lease Miet- od. Pachtvertrag bis zu 3 Jahren
short list *(engere)* Auswahlliste *(von Kandidaten)*; **to be put on the ~** in die engere Wahl kommen
short-list *v* in die engere Wahl ziehen; **to be ~ed** in die engere Wahl kommen
short-lived assets kurzlebige Wirtschaftsgüter
short notice kurze Ankündigung; **at ~** in kurzer Zeit; **deposits at ~** kurzfristige Einlagen
short order kurzfristiger Auftrag
short-range planning Planung auf kurze Sicht
short, ~ rate →rate 5.; **(in the) ~ run** auf kurze Sicht; **~-sighted policy** kurzsichtige Politik; **in ~ supply** → supply 1.; ~ **tap** *Br* laufend ausgegebene, kurzfristige Regierungsanleihe
short-term kurzfristig; ~ **benefit** *(VersR)* kurzfristige Leistung; ~ **(capital) gain** *(SteuerR)* kurzfristiger Veräußerungsgewinn; ~ **credit** kurzfristiger Kredit; ~ **gains** Vorteile in der nahen Zukunft; ~ **imprisonment** kurzfristige Freiheitsstrafe; ~ **investment** Geldanlage auf kurze Sicht; ~ **liabilities** kurzfristige Verbindlichkeiten; ~ **partnership** Gelegenheitsgesellschaft; ~ **prison sentence** kurzfristige Freiheitsstrafe
short time, ~ work Kurzarbeit; ~ **worker** Kurzarbeiter; ~ **working** Kurzarbeit; **to be on** (or **to work**) ~ kurzarbeiten
short, ~ title Kurztitel *(e-s Gesetzes)*; ~ **ton** → ton 1.; ~ **weight** Untergewicht, Fehlgewicht
short, to be ~ of Mangel haben an; **to come** (or **fall**) ~ **of** unzureichend sein; zurückbleiben hinter *(Erwartungen etc)*; **to cut ~** *(vorzeitig)* unterbrechen; **to run ~** zu Ende gehen, knapp werden (of an); *(Waren)* nicht mehr vorrätig haben

shortage Mangel, Knappheit (of an); Manko, Fehlbetrag; ~ **in the cash** Kassenfehlbetrag; ~ **of capital** Kapitalmangel; ~ **of foreign currency** Devisenknappheit; ~ **of goods** Warenknappheit; ~ **of money** Geldknappheit; ~ **of staff** Personalmangel; ~ **of transport** Fehlen von Transportmitteln; **food ~** Lebensmittelknappheit; **housing ~** Wohnungsmangel; **labo(u)r** (or **manpower**) ~ Mangel an Arbeitskräften, Arbeitskräftemangel; **to make up a ~** e-n Fehlbetrag ausgleichen (od. dekken); **to relieve a ~** e-n Mangel beheben

shorten *v* (ver-, ab)kürzen, verringern; kürzer werden; **to ~ a period of time** e-e Frist abkürzen
shortening of working hours Verkürzung der Arbeitszeit

shorter-range INF nukleare Mittelstreckensysteme kürzerer Reichweite

shortest, ~ route kürzester Weg; **in the ~ possible time** in kürzester Frist

shot, to be ~ erschossen werden

show Schau, Darbietung; (Waren-)Auslage; Ausstellung; Messe; *(Radio)* Programm; ~ **bill** Werbeplakat; ~ **business** Vergnügungsindustrie, Unterhaltungsindustrie; ~ **cause order** →order to show cause (→*order 2.*); ~ **of hands vote** *Am* (**vote by ~ of hands** *Br*) Abstimmung durch Handaufheben; **~room** Ausstellungsraum; ~ **trial** Schauprozeß; ~ **window** *Am* Schaufenster; **agricultural ~** Landwirtschaftsausstellung; **automobile** *Am* (**motor** *Br*) ~ Automobilausstellung; **on ~** zur Besichtigung; **to be on ~** *(in e-r Ausstellung)* zu besichtigen sein; ausgestellt sein

show *v* zeigen; aufweisen; *(Paß etc)* vorzeigen; dartun, beweisen, den Nachweis erbringen; vorführen; ausstellen; **to ~ a balance of** e-n Saldo von . . . aufweisen; **to ~ → cause; to ~ a deficit** ein Defizit aufweisen; **to ~ forth** darlegen; **to ~ one's hand** s-e Absichten verraten, s-e Karten aufdecken; **to ~ a loss (profit)** e-n Verlust (Gewinn) aufweisen; **to ~ proof** e-n Beweis liefern; **to ~ o. s. in public** sich in der Öffentlichkeit zeigen; **to ~ reasons** Gründe vorbringen (od. angeben); **it is incumbent on X to ~** dem X obliegt der Nachweis
shown, ~ below nachstehend aufgeführt; **as ~ by the books** buchmäßig

shrievalty Amt (od. Amtszeit) e-s →sheriff

shrink *v* (zusammen)schrumpfen, sich vermindern, abnehmen; *(Textilien)* einlaufen

shrinkage (Zusammen-)Schrumpfung, Schwund, Verminderung, Abnahme; Rückgang; *(Textilien)* Einlaufen; ~ **in value** Wertminderung; ~ **of exports** Exportschrumpfung; **profit ~** Gewinnschrumpfung

shunting 1. *(Börse)* Arbitrage *(zwischen zwei Parallelmärkten)*
shunting 2. Rangieren; ~ **yard** Rangierbahnhof, Verschiebebahnhof

shut-down *(vorübergehende od. dauernde)* Betriebseinstellung, Stillegung

shutdown *v (Fabrik)* stillegen; den Betrieb einstellen

shuttle, ~ service Pendelverkehr *(opp. regular)*; **space ~** Weltraumfähre

shyster *colloq.* zweifelhafter Anwalt *(der gegen das Berufsethos verstößt)*; Winkeladvokat

sick krank; **the ~** die Kranken
sick leave Krankheitsurlaub; **on ~** wegen Krankheit beurlaubt
sick list Krankenliste; **to be on the ~** krank geschrieben sein; **to put on the ~** krank schreiben
sick, ~ market *Am* flaue Börse; **~ pay** Krankengeld *(des Arbeitgebers an kranken Arbeitnehmer)*; **to report ~** *bes. mil* sich krank melden; **within 3 days of falling ~** innerhalb von 3 Tagen nach der Erkrankung

sickness Krankheit; **~ arising out of a p.'s employment** Berufskrankheit; **~ benefit**[61] Krankengeld; Leistungen bei Krankheit; **~ insurance** Krankenversicherung

side 1. Seite; **~ building** Nebengebäude; **~ issue** Nebenfrage, Frage von nebensächlicher Bedeutung
sideline Nebenbeschäftigung; Nebenartikel; *(Bahn)* Nebenlinie; **~ employment** Nebenbeschäftigung; **~ (leading to factory)** Nebenbahn
side, ~ note Randbemerkung; **~walk** *Am* Bürgersteig; **on the father's ~** väterlicherseits; **on the mother's ~** mütterlicherseits; **this ~ up** *(bei Verpackung)* oben! *(nicht stürzen!)*
side 2. Seite; Partei; **both ~s of industry** Sozialpartner; **to change ~s** auf die andere Seite übergehen; **to take a p.'s ~** (or **to take ~s with a p.**) jds Partei ergreifen, für jdn Partei ergreifen

side *v* Partei ergreifen (with für, against gegen)

siding Nebengleis; Anschlußgleis; Abstellgleis; **private ~** Privatanschlußgleis

siege Belagerung; →**proclamation of a state of ~**

Sierra Leone, Republic of ~ Republik Sierra Leone
Sierra Leonean Sierraleoner, ~in; sierraleonisch

sight 1. Anblick, Ansicht; Sicht; Sehvermögen; **~s** Sehenswürdigkeiten; **~seeing** Besichtigung von Sehenswürdigkeiten; **loss of ~** Verlust des Augenlichts; **to know sb. by ~** jdn vom Sehen kennen
sight 2. *com* Sicht, Vorzeigung, Vorlegung; **~ bill** Sichtwechsel; **~ deposits** Sichteinlagen, täglich fällige Gelder, Giroeinlagen; **~ draft** Sichttratte; **advice of international ~ drafts** Avisierung von internationalen Sichttratten; **~ payment** Sichtzahlung *(z.B. beim Akkreditiv)*; **~ rate** Sichtkurs, Kurs für Sichtpapiere; **bill of ~** vorläufige Zollangabe *(→bill 1.)*
sight, after ~ (a/s) nach Sicht; **30 days'** (or **days after**) **~** 30 Tage nach Sicht; **at ~** bei Sicht, bei Vorlegung; **bill (payable) at ~** Sichtwechsel; **due at ~** fällig bei Sicht

sight *v*, **to ~ a bill (of exchange**[62]**)** e-n Wechsel vorzeigen (od. vorlegen)

sign 1. Zeichen; Kennzeichen; Anzeichen (of für); (Aushänge-)Schild; **~board** Ladenschild; Firmenschild; **S~ Manual** Handzeichen *(Br bes. des Souveräns od. e-s hohen Beamten)*; **~-up** Beitritt; Unterstützung; **shop ~** Ladenschild
sign 2. (Verkehrs-)Zeichen; **~post** Wegweiser; **derestrictive ~** *Br* die Geschwindigkeitsbeschränkung aufhebendes Zeichen; **informative ~** Hinweiszeichen; **mandatory ~** Gebotszeichen; **prohibitive ~** Verbotszeichen; **stop ~** Haltesignal; **street ~** Straßenschild; **traffic ~** Verkehrszeichen; **warning ~** Warnzeichen; **to disobey a traffic ~** ein Verkehrszeichen nicht beachten

sign *v* unterzeichnen, unterschreiben, mit Unterschrift versehen; abzeichnen; **to ~ sth. away** etw. durch Unterschrift abtreten; **to ~ in full** mit dem vollen Namen unterschreiben; **to ~ off** *Am* kündigen; *(aus e-m Verband)* austreten; **to ~ on** (or **up**) *(jdn)* einstellen (od. anheuern); *(mit jdm)* e-n Arbeitsvertrag abschließen; sich einstellen (od. anheuern) lassen; sich *(vertraglich)* verpflichten; **to ~ on the crew of a ship** die Mannschaft e-s Schiffes anheuern
sign *v*, **to ~ the (ship's) articles** sich anheuern lassen; **to ~ an agreement** e-e Vereinbarung schließen; **to ~ a contract** e-n Vertrag unterschreiben; **to ~ for the firm** für die Firma zeichnen;**to ~ for the goods** den Empfang der Waren quittieren; **to ~ in one's own hand** eigenhändig unterschreiben; **to ~ a lease** e-n Miet- (od. Pacht)vertrag abschließen; **to ~ by a mark** (or **by making a cross**) durch ein Kreuz unterzeichnen; **to ~ in one's own name** mit eigenem Namen unterzeichnen; **to ~ the register** *Br* → register; **authority** (or **power**) **to ~** Zeichnungsberechtigung, Unterschriftsvollmacht; **authorized to ~** zeichnungsberechtigt, unterschriftsberechtigt; **person authorized to ~** Zeichnungsberechtigter
signed gezeichnet; **signed** (sgd.) **X** gezeichnet (gez.) X; **~ by the said X in the presence of** *(for documents under hand, i.e. not under seal)* unterschrieben von dem genannten X in Gegenwart von; **~, sealed and delivered by the said X in the presence of** *(for documents under seal)* unterschrieben, gesiegelt und ausgehän-

digt durch den genannten X in Gegenwart von

signing Unterzeichnung; ~ **authority** Unterschriftsberechtigung; Unterschriftsvollmacht; ~ **ceremony** Unterzeichnungsfeierlichkeit; ~ **of a contract** Unterzeichnung e-s Vertrags; ~ **on** Einstellung *(von Personal)*; ~ **power** Unterschriftsvollmacht

signal Signal, Zeichen; ~**s ahead** Verkehrsampel; **S~ Corps** *Am* **(Royal Corps of S~s** *Br*) *mil* Nachrichtentruppe; ~ **flasher** *Am* Warnblinkanlage; ~ **letters** Signalbuchstaben *(e-s Schiffes)*; ~ **of distress** Notsignal; **busy** ~ *Am* (or *Br* **engaged** ~) *tel* Besetzt-Zeichen; **cautionary** ~ Warnungssignal *(e-s Schiffes)*; **code of** ~**s** Flaggensignalsystem; **International Code of S~s** Internationales Signalbuch *(für den Nachrichtenverkehr auf See)*; **off-**~ Entwarnung; **on-**~ Warnsignal

signalment *Am* genaue (Personen-)Beschreibung zum Zweck der Identifizierung; Steckbrief; **descriptive** ~ Personenbeschreibung

signatory Unterzeichner; Signatar-; unterzeichnend; ~ **government** Unterzeichnerregierung; ~ **power** Unterzeichnungsvollmacht; ~ **state** Unterzeichnerstaat, Signatarstaat; ~ **to a contract** Unterzeichner e-s Vertrages; ~ **to a treaty** *(VölkerR)* Unterzeichner e-s Vertrages

signature Unterschrift, Unterzeichnung; Namenszug; ~ **book** (Bank-)Unterschriftenverzeichnis; ~ **by procuration** Unterschrift in Vollmacht; ~ **by authorized representative** Unterschrift durch bevollmächtigten Vertreter; ~ **card** Unterschriftenkarte; ~ **in blank** s. blank →~; ~ **missing** (sig.mis.) Unterschrift fehlt; ~ **on a bill** Wechselunterschrift; ~ **stamp** Unterschriftsstempel; ~ **verification** Unterschriftsprüfung; **attestation** (or **authentication**) **of** ~ Unterschriftsbeglaubigung; **blank** ~ Blankounterschrift; **certification of** ~ Unterschriftsbeglaubigung; **corporate** ~ *Am* Firmenzeichnung; **counter-**~ Gegenzeichnung; **facsimile** ~ Faksimileunterschrift; **forged** ~ gefälschte Unterschrift; **genuine** ~ echte Unterschrift; **genuineness of a** ~ Echtheit e-r Unterschrift; **joint** ~ gemeinschaftliche Unterschrift; Gesellschaftsunterschrift; Firmenzeichnung; **list of authorized** ~**s** Unterschriftenverzeichnis; **personal** ~ eigenhändige Unterschrift; **specimen** ~ Unterschriftsprobe; **unauthorized** ~ ohne Ermächtigung vorgenommene Unterschrift; Unterschrift ohne Vertretungsmacht; **verification of a** ~ (Nach-)Prüfung (od. Bestätigung) der Echtheit e-r Unterschrift; **to affix** (or **append**) **one's** ~ (to a document) (e-e Urkunde) mit seiner Unterschrift versehen; (e-e Urkunde) unterschreiben; **to attest** (or **authenticate**) **a** ~ e-e Unterschrift beglaubigen; **to bear the** ~ (of) die Unterschrift tragen, mit der Unterschrift versehen sein; **to certify a** ~ e-e Unterschrift beglaubigen; **to counterfeit a** ~ e-e Unterschrift fälschen; **to deny a** ~ e-e Unterschrift nicht anerkennen; **to forge a** ~ e-e Unterschrift fälschen; **to put** (or **set**) **one's** ~ (to) s-e Unterschrift setzen (unter), unterschreiben; **to put one's own** ~ (to) eigenhändig unterschreiben; **to verify a** ~ die Echtheit e-r Unterschrift (nach-)prüfen (od. bestätigen); **to →witness a** ~; **the above** ~ **is certified herewith** die Richtigkeit obiger Unterschrift wird hiermit beglaubigt; **the undersigned plenipotentiaries have affixed their** ~**s below the agreement** die unterzeichneten Bevollmächtigten haben ihre Unterschriften unter das Abkommen gesetzt

signer *Am* Unterzeichner; ~ **of a contract** Unterzeichner e-s Vertrages

signet Siegel; (Unterschriften-)Stempel; **writer to the** ~ *Scot* Rechtsanwalt (→*writer*)

significance (große) Bedeutung, Bedeutsamkeit; **act of legal** ~ Rechtsgeschäft

significant bezeichnend; bedeutsam; ~ **amount** erheblicher Betrag; beträchtliche Menge

signify *v* zum Ausdruck bringen, bekanntgeben; bedeuten

signing → sign *v*

silent still; ~ **march** *pol* Schweigemarsch; ~ **→partner**

silk Seide; *Br* Kurzbezeichnung für Queen's →Counsel; ~ **gown** *Br* Seidenrobe e-s Queen's → Counsel; ~ **mill** Seidenfabrik; **artificial** ~ Kunstseide; **to take** ~ *Br* Queen's Counsel werden

silver Silber; ~ **bullion** Barrensilber; ~ **certificate** *Am* Silberzertifikat *(Banknoten, die bis Juni 1968 in Barrensilber eingelöst werden konnten)*; ~ **coin** Silbermünze; ~ **coin and bullion** (Bank-)Silberbestand; ~ **currency** (or **money**) Silbergeld; ~ **point** Silberpunkt; ~ **standard** Silberwährung

similar ähnlich, gleichartig

similarity Ähnlichkeit, Gleichartigkeit (to mit); **substantial** ~ *(UrhR)* Ähnlichkeit (von 2 Werken) in wesentlichen Teilen; ~ **of trade marks** Übereinstimmung von Warenzeichen

simony[63] Simonie, Kauf oder Verkauf von geistlichen Ämtern

simple einfach; ~ **arbitrage** einfache (od. direkte) Devisenarbitrage *(bei Inanspruchnahme von nur 3 Börsen; opp. compound arbitrage)*; ~ **bond** hypothekarisch nicht gesicherte Obligation; ~ **bonus** *(VersR)* einfache Dividende

simple contract formloser *(mündl. od. schriftl.,*

aber nicht unter Siegel abgeschlossener) Vertrag *(opp. contract under seal)*; ~ **debts** aus e-m einfachen Vertrag herrührende Forderungen; gewöhnliche Forderungen *(mündl. od. schriftl. eingegangene Schulden, die keine →specialty debts sind; Br 6jährige Verjährungsfrist)*

simple, ~ **debenture** hypothekarisch nicht gesicherte Schuldverschreibung *(opp. mortgage debenture)*; ~ **interest** einfache Zinsen, Kapitalzinsen *(opp. compound interest)*; ~ **larceny** einfacher Diebstahl; ~ **majority** einfache (Stimmen-)Mehrheit (→ *majority*); ~ →**trust**

simplification Vereinfachung; Typenbeschränkung

simplify *v*, **to** ~ **the procedure** das Verfahren vereinfachen

simulate *v* simulieren, vorgeben

simulated, ~ **account** Proformarechnung; ~ **contract** Scheinvertrag

simulating objects of antiquity Nachmachen (od. Imitation) von Antiquitäten

simulation Simulation, Verstellung; Nachahmung

simultaneous gleichzeitig; ~ **death**[64] gleichzeitiger Tod *(Commorientenvermutung)*; ~ **interpretation** Simultandolmetschen; ~ **performance** Erfüllung Zug um Zug

sincere, yours ~**ly** *Br* (mit freundlichen Grüßen) Ihr; ~**ly (yours)** *Am (etwa)* Hochachtungsvoll *(häufig als Unterschrift unter Geschäftsbriefen)*

sinecure Sinekure, einträgliches Amt ohne Arbeit; Ehrenamt

sine die ("without day") ohne Anberaumung e-s neuen Termins; **to adjourn** ~ auf unbestimmte Zeit vertagen

sine prole (s. p.) ohne Nachkommenschaft

Singapore, Republic of ~ Republik Singapur

Singaporean Singapurer, ~in; singapurisch

single einzig; einzeln; einmalig; alleinstehend, ledig; **S**~ **Act** Einheitliche Europäische Akte; **S**~ **Administrative Document** (SAD) *(EG) (Zoll)* Einheitspapier (einheitl. EG-Warenbegleitpapier); ~ **allowance** *Br (SteuerR)* persönlicher Freibetrag; ~ **applicant** *(PatR)* Einzelanmelder; ~ **basing point system** *Am* System, nach dem die Frachtkosten für e-e Ware für jeden Käufer von e-m bestimmten Ort aus berechnet werden *(cf. multiple basing point system)*; ~ **cell** Einzelzelle; ~ **entry bookkeeping** einfache Buchführung *(opp. double entry bookkeeping)*; **S**~ **European Act** →~ Act; **S**~ **European Market** Europäischer Binnenmarkt; ~ **judge** Einzelrichter; ~**-line retail shop** (or **store**) Fachgeschäft, Spezialgeschäft; ~ **member private limited company** *(EG)* GmbH mit nur einem Gesellschafter; ~**-mindedly** zielstrebig; ~ **office bank** Bank mit nur einem Geschäftslokal; ~ **part** Einzelteil; ~ **part production** Einzelanfertigung; ~ **person** Unverheirate(r); Ledige(r); ~ **premium** *(VersR)* Einmalprämie *(opp. annual premium)*; ~ **proprietorship** *Am* Einzelfirma, Einzelunternehmen; ~ **residence** *Am* Einfamilienhaus; ~ **room** Einzelzimmer; ~ **state** lediger Stand; ~ **(ticket)** *Br* einfache Fahrkarte *(opp. return ticket)*; ~ **trader** *Br* Einzelkaufmann; ~ **woman** alleinstehende Frau; ledige (od. getrennt lebende) Frau

singular successor *Am und Scot* Einzelrechtsnachfolger, Singularsukzession

sink *v* sinken; sich senken *(Gebäude)*; versenken; tilgen, amortisieren; zurückgehen *(Preise)*; *(Preise)* herabsetzen; **to** ~ **a loan** e-e Anleihe tilgen; **to** ~ **money into a business** Geld in e-m Geschäft anlegen; **to** ~ **a ship** ein Schiff versenken

sinking Tilgung, Amortisation

sinking fund Tilgungsfonds, Amortisationsfonds; ~ **bonds** Obligationen mit Tilgungsplan; ~ **instal(l)ment** Tilgungsrate; ~ **loan** Darlehen (od. Anleihe) mit Tilgungsplan; ~ **reserve** Tilgungsrücklage; ~ **table** Tilgungsplan; **to raid the** ~ den Amortisationsfonds zu fremden Zwecken verwenden

Sir *Br* Titel des niederen englischen Adels *(Knight od. Baronet, immer mit Vornamen gebraucht)*; **Dear** ~ Sehr geehrter Herr *(in Briefen)*

sist *v Scot (Verfahren)* einstellen; *(Partei)* vorladen

sister, ~ **company** Schwestergesellschaft; ~**-in-law** Schwägerin; ~ **(ship)** Schwesterschiff; ~ **state** *Am* (anderer) Einzelstaat; **half-**~ Halbschwester

sit *v* sitzen; (Gerichts-)Sitzung halten; *parl* Sitzung abhalten; tagen; **to** ~ **on the bench** Richter sein; **to** ~ **in camera** unter Ausschluß der Öffentlichkeit verhandeln; **to** ~ **on a case** in e-r Sache verhandeln *(als Richter)*; **to** ~ **in chambers** → chambers 3.; **to** ~ **on a committee** Mitglied e-s Ausschusses sein, e-m Ausschuß angehören; **to** ~ **in conference** tagen; **to** ~ **in Congress** *Am* Kongreßmitglied sein; **to** ~ **for a constituency** e-n Wahlkreis *(im Parlament)* vertreten; **to** ~ **for an examination** →examination 4.; **to** ~ **on a jury** Geschworener sein; **the commission** ~**s** die Kommission tagt

sitdown strike Sitzstreik; Streik, in dem die Arbeiter sich weigern, den Arbeitsplatz zu verlassen

sit-in *colloq.* demonstratives Sich-auf-den-Boden-Setzen *(Am bes. Protestkundgebung im Kampf um Bürgerrechte [civil rights])*; studentische Protestdemonstration

sitting Sitzung; Tagung; ~ **member** *Br parl* Abgeordneter (M. P.), der vor Auflösung des Parlaments im Parlament seinen Sitz hatte; ~ **of a court** Gerichtssitzung, Gerichtstermin (→~s); ~ **tenant** (augenblicklicher) Mieter *(bes. in Zusammenhang mit Hausverkauf; →vacant possession)*; **at a** ~ in (od. bei) e-r Sitzung; **closing** ~ Schlußsitzung; **open** ~ öffentliche Sitzung; **to attend a** ~ e-r Sitzung beiwohnen; **to open a** ~ e-e Sitzung eröffnen; **the ~s are held in public** die Sitzungen werden öffentlich abgehalten

sittings *Br*[65] *(vier)* Sitzungen *(des Supreme Court)*; ~ **fee** Sitzungsgebühr

The *Hilary Sittings* (11. Januar bis Mittwoch vor Ostern); the *Easter Sittings* (Dienstag nach Ostern bis Freitag vor Pfingsten); *the Trinity Sittings* (Dienstag nach Pfingsten bis 31. Juli); *the Michaelmas Sittings* (beginnend an dem durch Order in Council festgesetzten Tag bis 21. Dezember)

site Lage *(e-s Grundstücks)*; Standort *(e-r Industrie)*; Baustelle, Baugrundstück; Ausstellungsgelände, Messegelände; ~ **development** Baulanderschließung; ~ **value** Wert des Baulandes *(ohne Berücksichtigung des darauf befindlichen Gebäudes)*; **(erection)** ~ Aufstellungsort *(z. B. e-r Maschine)*

site *v* an bestimmten Platz aufstellen, placieren

siting, ~ **policy of nuclear power stations** (or **policy on the** ~ **of nuclear power stations**) Standortpolitik für Kernkraftwerke; **industrial plant** ~ Ansiedlung von Industrieunternehmen

situ, in ~ an Ort und Stelle (→*situs*)

situated gelegen; in e-r Lage befindlich; **badly** ~ *(finanziell)* schlecht gestellt; in e-r schlechten Lage; *(örtl.)* schlecht gelegen; **well** ~ *(finanziell)* gut gestellt; in e-r guten Lage; *(örtl.)* gut gelegen; **for all others similarly** ~ für alle, die sich in der gleichen Lage befinden; **well** ~ **business** Geschäft in guter Lage

situation 1. *(örtliche)* Lage; (Sach-)Lage, Situation; ~ **on the labo(u)r market** Arbeitsmarktlage; **economic** ~ Wirtschaftslage; Konjunkturlage; **financial** ~ Finanzlage, finanzielle Lage; **labo(u)r** ~ Arbeitsmarktlage; **legal** ~ Rechtslage; **market** ~ Marktlage; **monetary** ~ Währungslage; **political** ~ politische Lage; **the** ~ **has aggravated** die Lage hat sich verschärft; **the** ~ **is deteriorating (improving)** die Lage verschlechtert (verbessert) sich

situation 2. Stellung *(untergeordneter Art)*; Stelle, Posten; ~ **for life** Lebensstellung; **~s vacant** Stellenangebote *(in Zeitungen)*; **~s wanted** Stellengesuche *(in Zeitungen)*; **applicant for a** ~ Bewerber um e-e Stelle; **permanent** ~ Dauerstellung; Lebensstellung; **to apply for a** ~ sich um e-e Stelle bewerben; **to find a** ~ **for a p.** jdm e-e Stelle verschaffen, jdn unterbringen; **to hold a** ~ e-e Stelle haben; **to look for a** ~ e-e Stelle suchen

situs Lageort, Belegenheit *(bes. von Grundbesitz; wird aber z. B. auch bei Forderungen verwendet, etwa bei der Beurteilung der Wirkungen e-r Enteignung durch e-n ausländischen Staat; im IPR ist ~ Anknüpfungspunkt vornehmlich für Immobilien)*; **law of the** ~ **of the land** *(IPR)* Recht des Ortes, wo das Grundstück belegen ist; **state of** ~ *(IPR)* Belegenheitsstaat; **to tax realty income at the state of** ~ *Am* Einkünfte aus unbeweglichem Vermögen im Staat der Belegenheit besteuern; **decisive is the** ~ **of the res** entscheidend ist, wo sich die Sache befindet

six sechs; **~monthly account** Halbjahresrechnung

size Größe; Format; Umfang; (Schuh-, Kleidungs-)Nummer, -größe; ~ **of the enterprise** Größe des Unternehmens, Unternehmensgröße; **commercial** ~ marktgängige Größe; **medium** ~ mittlere Größe; **odd** ~ nicht normierte Größe; nicht gangbare Größe; **pocket** ~ Taschenformat; **the smaller ~s** die kleineren Größen

skeleton Skelett; Rahmen; Gerüst; Umriß; Entwurf; ~ **agreement** Rahmenabkommen; ~ **bill** *(unausgefülltes)* Wechselformular; ~ **key** Nachschlüssel; Dietrich; ~ **law** Rahmengesetz; ~ **staff** auf e-e Mindestzahl reduziertes Personal; ~ **wage agreement** Manteltarifvertrag

sketch Entwurf, Skizze

skid mark Bremsspur

skill (Arbeits-)Geschicklichkeit; **~s** Fertigkeiten, Fähigkeiten und Kenntnisse; **occupational** (or **professional)** ~ berufliche Fähigkeit; **ordinary** ~ gewöhnlich vorausgesetzter Grad von Geschicklichkeit; **to acquire a** ~ e-e Fähigkeit erlangen

skilled geschickt; erfahren *(opp. unskilled)*; ~ **in the art** *(PatR)* →art 2.; **person ordinarily** ~ **in the art** *(PatR)* Durchschnittsfachmann; ~ **evidence** Sachverständigenbeweis; ~ **labo(u)r** gelernte Arbeiter (od. Arbeitskräfte), Facharbeiter *(opp. unskilled labo[u]r)*; **semi-~ labo(u)r** angelernte Arbeiter (od. Arbeitskräfte); ~ **personnel** Fachpersonal; ~ **witness** →expert witness; ~ **worker** Facharbeiter

skim *v* abschöpfen; flüchtig lesen, überfliegen; **to** ~ **off surplus purchasing power** überschüssige Kaufkraft abschöpfen

skimming off excess profit Gewinnabschöpfung

sky, ~ **advertising** Luftwerbung *(durch Himmelsschreiber)*; **~jacker** →hijacker; **~lab** experimentelle Erdaußenstation; Labor im Weltraum; ~ **marshal** *Am* „Himmelspolizist" *(zur Bewachung amerikanischer Verkehrsflugzeuge)*; ~**-rocketing** *colloq.* Emporschnellen *(von Preisen, Kursen)*; ~**-sign** Lichtreklame, hohes Reklameschild; ~**-writing** *(Reklame)* Himmelsschrift *(durch Flugzeuge)*

slack flau, geschäftslos; ~ **business** flaues (od. ruhiges) Geschäft; ~ **demand** schwache Nachfrage

slacken *v* nachlassen *(z.B. Nachfrage)*; abflauen; *(Börse)* nachgeben

slackening, ~ **of exports** Abflauen (od. Nachlassen) des Exports; ~ **tendency** Abschwächungstendenz

slackness Flaute

slander[66] (mündl.) Beleidigung *(Beleidigung durch ein gesprochenes Wort oder in einer anderen nicht dauerhaften Form)*; Verleumdung; üble Nachrede *(cf. libel)*

Slander ist ein Zivilunrecht (tort) und gibt im Gegensatz zu →libel nur Anspruch auf Schadensersatz bei Nachweis konkreten Schadens (special damage) *(mit Ausnahme der Fälle des slander per se, wo kein special damage nachgewiesen zu werden braucht)*

slander, ~ **of a competitor's title** Anschwärzung des Konkurrenten *(cf. injurious falsehood)*; ~ **of goods** *Br (böswillig [maliciously] geäußerte)* Herabsetzung der Ware des Konkurrenten; Anschwärzung durch Herabsetzung der Qualität fremder Waren; ~ **of title**[67] *(böswillig [maliciously] abgegebene)* falsche Behauptung zur Herabsetzung jds Rechtstitels an bewegl. od. unbewegl. Vermögen; ~ **per se**[68] zum Schadensersatz verpflichtende mündl. Beleidigung unabhängig davon, ob ein Schaden eingetreten ist; **to bring a** ~ **action against sb.** gegen jdn e-e Beleidigungsklage erheben; jdn wegen mündlicher Beleidigung verklagen

slander *v (mündlich od. in anderer nicht dauerhafter Form)* beleidigen, verleumden, in falschen Verdacht bringen

slanderous beleidigend, verleumderisch; ~ **per se** →slander per se

slashing criticism vernichtende Kritik

slate *Am* Kandidatenliste

slaughter Schlachten *(von Vieh)*; *(Börse)* Verkauf mit Verlust, Verschleuderung *(von Wertpapieren)*; ~ **house** Schlachthaus

slaughter *v (Vieh)* schlachten; *(Börse)* mit Verlust verkaufen, verschleudern

slave Sklave; ~ **dealer** Sklavenhändler; ~ **dealing** →~trade; ~ **trade** Sklavenhandel; **white** ~ **trade** (or **traffic**) Mädchenhandel; ~ **trader** Sklavenhändler; **to engage in the** ~ **trade** Sklavenhandel treiben

slavery, abolition of ~[69] Abschaffung der Sklaverei

slavish imitation *(UrhR)* sklavische Nachahmung (od. Wiedergabe)

sleeper Schlafwagen; **to book a** ~ *Br* e-n Schlafwagen bestellen

sleeping, ~ **car** Schlafwagen; ~→**partner**

slide *(Börse)* Absinken *(der Kurse)*

slide *v* gleiten, abgleiten *(Preise, Kurse)*

sliding, ~ **price clause** Gleitpreisklausel *(in Kaufverträgen)*; ~ **(wage) scale** gleitende (Lohn-)Skala *(cf. index of retail prices)*; ~ **scale tariff** Gleitzoll *(je nach den Einfuhrpreisen)*

slight geringfügig, unbedeutend, leicht; ~ **negligence** leichte Fahrlässigkeit (→*negligence*)

slip 1. Zettel; Beleg; *(z.B. an e-e Versicherungspolice angehefteter, e-e Klausel enthaltender)* Abschnitt; *(Bank)* Slip, Formularstreifen; (Druck-)Fahne; *Br*[70] *(VersR, insbesondere SeeversR und Lloyd's Vers.) (vom Versicherer unterzeichneter)* Vermerk über die beabsichtigte (See-)Versicherungspolice; ~ **book** *(Bank)* Belegbuch; ~ **law** *Am* Einzelveröffentlichung von Gesetzen nach ihrem Erlaß während e-s Jahres; ~ **road** Verbindungsfahrbahn; **betting** ~ Wettschein; **order** ~ Auftragszettel *(des Börsenmaklers)*; **paying-in** ~ *Br* (**deposit** ~ *Am*) Einzahlungsbeleg; **sales** ~ Kassenzettel

slip 2. Versehen; ~ **(of the pen)** Schreibfehler; ~ **rule** *Br*[71] Regel, nach der Schreibfehler in Urteilen etc durch das Gericht jederzeit auf Antrag berichtigt werden können

slip back *v*, **the shares** ~**ped back from ... to ...** die Aktien fielen von ... auf ...

slogan Slogan, (Werbe-)Schlagwort, Werbespruch

slot machine (Verkaufs-)Automat; **improper use** (or **misuse**) **of** ~ Automatenmißbrauch

slow langsam, säumig *(im Bezahlen)*; *com* flau

slowdown Verlangsamung, Nachlassen; Arbeitsverlangsamung; ~ **of** (or **in**) **demand** Nachlassen der Nachfrage; ~ **of economic activity** Rückgang der Konjunktur; ~ **(in production)** Produktionsverlangsamung; ~ **(strike)** *Am* Bummelstreik; **year of economic** ~ Flautejahr

slow, ~ **payer** säumiger Zahler; ~ **train** Personenzug; **go-**~ *Br* planmäßiges Langsamarbeiten; Bummelstreik; **to go** ~ in Bummelstreik treten

slow down *v* sich verlangsamen, nachlassen; langsamer fahren, Geschwindigkeit verringern; **to ~ investment** die Investitionsbremse ziehen

sluggish flau, stagnierend; ~ **demand** lustlose Nachfrage

sluggishness Stagnation, Flaute

sluicegate price *(EG)* Einschleusungspreis

slump *(plötzl.)* Kurs- od. Preissturz; *(plötzl. eintretende)* Baisse; *(starker)* Konjunkturrückgang, Rezession; Geschäftsflaute; ~ **in trade** Geschäftsrückgang; **~-proof** krisenfest

slump *v (plötzl.)* fallen; **the share ~ed ten points** die Aktie fiel um zehn Punkte

slums Slums, Elendsviertel; **~-clearance** Beseitigung von Elendsvierteln

slush money Bestechungsgeld, Schmiergeld

small, ~ advertisement Kleinanzeige; ~ **and medium-sized enterprises** (SMEs) Klein- und Mittelbetriebe (KMB)
small business[72] Klein- und Mittelbetriebe, gewerbl. Mittelstand *(opp. big business)*; **S~ B~ Administration** (SBA) *Am* Bundesbehörde zur Durchführung der Aufgaben der gewerbl. Mittelstandspolitik im Rahmen der S~ B~- Gesetzgebung; **S~ B~ Investment Companies** (SBIC) *Am*[73] Kapitalbeteiligungsgesellschaften für (entwicklungsfähige) Klein- und Mittelbetriebe
small change Kleingeld, Wechselgeld
small claim Bagatellsache; **S~ C~s Court** *Am (einzelstaatl.)* Gericht, dessen Zuständigkeit sich auf Geldansprüche aus Vertrag oder Delikt bis zu e-r bestimmten Grenze *(zwischen 200 und 1000 Dollar)* beschränkt; **~s procedure** *Br* vereinfachtes und beschleunigtes Prozeßverfahren *(betrifft Ansprüche mit Streitwerten von nicht über £500, die von e-m Schiedsrichter entschieden werden)*; **informal procedure for ~s** *Br* informelles Verfahren für Bagatellklagen
small, ~ coin Kleingeld; Scheidemünze; ~ **consignments** kleine Sendungen; Stückgut(sendungen); ~ **craft undertaking** kleiner Handwerksbetrieb; ~ **debts** geringfügige Schulden *(Schulden von geringer Höhe, für deren Beitreibung ein vereinfachtes Verfahren gilt)*
small, denominations (of banknotes) kleine Werte; ~ **deposits** kleine Einlagen; ~ **establishment** Kleinbetrieb; ~ **estate** kleiner Nachlaß; ~ **farmer** Kleinbauer; ~ **firms employment subsidies** (SFES) *Br* (staatl.) Beihilfe für Beschäftigung in Klein- und Mittelbetrieben; **~holder** *Br* Kleinbauer; **~holding** *Br*[74] Kleinlandbesitz *(Kleingrundbesitz zwischen 1 und 50 acres)*; ~ **loan** Kleinkredit; ~ **loan companies** *Am* Kleinkreditgesellschaften; **of ~ means** minderbemittelt; ~ **packet** Päckchen; ~ **profit** geringer Gewinn; **on a ~ scale** in kleinem Umfang; **medium and ~(-scale) enterprises** Mittel- und Kleinbetriebe; ~ **sum of money** kleiner Geldbetrag; ~ **trader** kleiner Geschäftsmann; kleiner Gewerbetreibender

smart money *Am* Zuschlag zum Schadensersatz *(der über den realen Schaden hinausgeht, Straffunktion hat und grobes Fehlverhalten voraussetzt)*

smash Zusammenbruch *(e-s Geschäfts)*, Bankrott; **~-and-grab-raid** Schaufenstereinbruch; **bank ~** Bankkrach

smooth functioning reibungsloses Funktionieren

smuggle *v* schmuggeln; **to ~ in** einschmuggeln
smuggled goods are liable to confiscation Schmuggelwaren unterliegen der Einziehung
smuggling[75] Schmuggel, Schleichhandel; ~ **of intoxicating liquor** Alkoholschmuggel; **currency ~** Devisenschmuggel; **drug ~** Rauschgiftschmuggel

smuggler Schmuggler, Schleichhändler; **band** (or **gang**) **of ~s** Schmugglerbande

snatching, handbag ~ Handtaschenraub

snowball *v* lawinenartig anwachsen

soar *v* emporschnellen, (an)steigen
soared, the expenditure has ~ die Ausgaben sind sprunghaft gestiegen
soaring inflation schnell steigende Inflation

social sozial; Sozial-; gesellschaftlich; Gesellschafts-; ~ **accounting** volkswirtschaftliche Gesamtrechnung; ~ **achievement** soziale Errungenschaft; ~ **activities** gesellschaftliche Veranstaltungen; ~ **adjustment** (of the convicted offender) Resozialisierung; ~ **benefits** soziale Erträge, sozialer Nutzen; ~ **capital** Sozialkapital, Sozialfonds; ~ **charges** soziale Abgaben; ~ **costs** soziale Kosten, volkswirtschaftliche Kosten *(die nicht direkt in die Kalkulation des Unternehmens eingehen, sondern von der Gesellschaft getragen werden; z.B. Kosten der Luft- und Wasserverschmutzung)*; ~ **decline** sozialer Abstieg; **S~ Democratic Party** (SDP) *Br* Sozialdemokratische Partei; ~ **disparities** soziale Unterschiede, **duties** gesellschaftliche Verpflichtungen; ~ **events** (gesellschaftl.) Veranstaltungen; ~ **evil** soziales Übel; ~ **expenditure** Sozialaufwendungen; **in the ~ field** auf sozialem Gebiet; ~ **gathering** gesellige Zusammenkunft; Empfang; ~ **goods** öffentliche Güter, Kollektivgüter; ~ **insurance** Sozialversicherung *(→Social Security Act)*; ~ **integration** soziale Eingliederung; ~ **intercourse** gesellschaftlicher

Verkehr; ~ **issue** Sozialfrage; ~ **legislation** Sozialgesetzgebung

social mobility, downward ~ *Am* sozialer Abstieg; **upward** ~ *Am* sozialer Aufstieg

social, ~ **obligations** gesellschaftliche Verpflichtungen; ~ **order** Sozialordnung, Gesellschaftsordnung; ~ **partners** Sozialpartner; ~ **policy** Sozialpolitik; Gesellschaftspolitik; ~ **position** gesellschaftliche Stellung; ~ **reform** Sozialreform; ~ **register** *Am* Nachschlagewerk der Angehörigen der obersten Gesellschaft; ~ **research** Sozialforschung; ~ **sciences** Sozialwissenschaften *(political economy, political science, sociology and history)*

social security soziale Sicherheit; Sozialversicherung; *Am* Rentenpflichtversicherung; **S~ S~ Act**[76, 77] Sozialversicherungsgesetz; **S~ S~ Administration** *Am* Sozialversicherungsbehörde *(Zentralbehörde der Social Security)*; **S~ S~ Appeal Tribunal** *Br* Ortstribunal (Ortsschlichtungsstelle) der Sozialversicherung; ~ **benefits** Sozialleistungen; Leistungen (od. Renten) aus Sozialversicherung *(contributory benefit, sickness benefit, Am z.B. old age insurance benefit, disability insurance benefit, survivors' benefit)*; Sozialhilfe (und andere Leistungen aus öffentlichen Mitteln) *(non-contributory benefits; Br z.B. supplementary benefits, family income supplement, child benefit)*; ~ **contributions** (or *Am* **taxes**) Sozialversicherungsbeiträge; soziale Abgaben; **contractual** ~ *Am* vertragliche soziale Sicherheit (→*employee-benefit plans*); **Agreement between the Federal Republic of Germany and the United States of America on S~ S~**[78] Abkommen zwischen der Bundesrepublik Deutschland und den Vereinigten Staaten über Soziale Sicherheit; **European Code of S~ S~**[79] Europäische Ordnung der Sozialen Sicherheit

social, ~ **services** Sozialleistungen und soziale Einrichtungen *(des Staates und der Ortsbehörden) (Br*[80] *z.B. für Körperbehinderte, alte Leute, Kinder und Familien mit besonderen Schwierigkeiten, "problem families")*; ~ **status** sozialer Status; gesellschaftliche Stellung; ~ **turmoil** (or **unrest**) soziale Unruhe(n); ~ **welfare benefits** *bes. Am* Sozialhilfe; ~ **(welfare) expenditure** *Am* Sozialausgaben; Sozialleistungen; ~ **welfare organization** *bes. Am* gemeinnützige Organisation

socialism Sozialismus; **construction of** ~ Aufbau des Sozialismus *(kommunistische Terminologie)*

socialist Sozialist; sozialistisch; ~ **achievement** sozialistische Errungenschaften *(kommunistische Terminologie)*; **S~ International** Sozialistische Internationale

socialite *colloq.* prominentes Mitglied der Gesellschaft; Angehöriger der High Society

socialization Sozialisierung, Vergesellschaftung

socialize *v* sozialisieren, vergesellschaften

socialized medicine *Am* staatl. Gesundheitsdienst

societ|y Gesellschaft, Verein, Vereinigung, Verband *(meist ohne eigene Rechtspersönlichkeit)*; Genossenschaft; Gesellschaft *(soziale Umwelt)*; **S~ for Worldwide Interbank Financial Telecommunication** (SWIFT) Gesellschaft *(mit Sitz in Brüssel)*, in der Banken zur Beschleunigung des internationalen Zahlungsverkehrs zusammenarbeiten; **banking ~ies** Genossenschaften, die Bankgeschäfte betreiben; **benefit** ~ Versicherungsverein auf Gegenseitigkeit; Unterstützungsverein; **building** ~ *Br* Bausparkasse

society, cooperative ~ *Br* Genossenschaft; Konsumverein; **Cooperative Wholesale S~** (CWS) *Br* Zentralgenossenschaft *(größtes genossenschaftl. Unternehmen der Welt, betätigt sich auf allen Wirtschaftsgebieten, einschließl. des Versicherungs- und Bankwesens)*; **member of a cooperative** ~ Genosse; Konsumvereinsmitglied

societ|y, fabric of ~ Gesellschaftsstruktur; → **friendly ~; incorporated** ~ eingetragener Verein; rechtsfähiger Verein; **industrial and provident ~ies** *Br* (Erwerbs- und Wirtschafts-) Genossenschaften (→*industrial*); → **Law S~; literary and scientific ~ies** *Br* literarische und wissenschaftliche Gesellschaften *(cf. learned ~, Royal S~)*; **loan** ~ *Br* Kreditgenossenschaft, Kreditverein; **officers of a** ~ Vorstand e-s Vereins; → **registered ~ies; to enter** (or **join**) **a** ~ in e-e Gesellschaft (etc) eintreten; e-r Gesellschaft (etc) beitreten; **to withdraw from a** ~ aus e-r Gesellschaft (etc) austreten

socio-economic sozialwirtschaftlich, sozioökonomisch

socio-economist Sozialwirtschaftler

sociological soziologisch

sociology Soziologie; **industrial** ~ Betriebssoziologie; **rural** ~ Agrarsoziologie

socio-political gesellschaftspolitisch

sodomy Sodomie; widernatürliche Unzucht

SOFFEX →Swiss Options and Financial Futures Exchange

soft currency weiche Währung; ~ **country** währungsschwaches Land, Weichwährungsland

soft, ~ **drink** alkoholfreies Getränk; ~ **loan** zins- und fristgünstiger Kredit *(bes. IMF)*

software Programmausrüstung *(e-r EDV-Anlage; opp. hardware)*; **S~ Tools** Computerprogramme, die die Erstellung von Software unterstützen

soil (Erd-)Boden; **improvement of the** ~ Melioration; **productive** ~ ertragreicher Boden; **products of the** ~ Bodenprodukte, -erzeugnisse; **to exhaust the** ~ *(landwirtschaftl.)* Raubbau treiben

sojourn *(vorübergehender)* Aufenthalt; **foreign** ~ Aufenthalt im Ausland

sojourner *Am* jd, der sich nur vorübergehend in den USA aufhält

Sola (Bill) *Br* Wechsel, von dem nur ein Exemplar im Umlauf ist

solatium Schmerzensgeld

sold verkauft; ~ **contract** *Br* →~ note; ~ **ledger** Verkaufsbuch, Verkaufsjournal; ~ **note** *Br (vom Makler dem Käufer übersandte)* Schlußnote, Schlußschein; ~ **out** ausverkauft, vergriffen, nicht mehr vorrätig; ~ **without resort to legal process** verkauft im Wege der Selbsthilfe *(bei Annahmeverzug des Käufers von verderbl. Waren)*

soldier Soldat; ~**'s pay** Wehrsold; **career** ~ *bes. Am* Berufssoldat; **fellow** ~ Kriegskamerad; **(private)** ~ einfacher Soldat *(ohne Dienstgrad)*

sole allein, einzig; ledig; ~ **agency** Alleinvertretung; ~ **agent** Alleinvertreter; ~ **and exclusive right** Ausschließlichkeitsrecht; ~ **arbitrator** Einzelschiedsrichter; ~ **bill** Solawechsel; ~ **buyer** alleiniger Abnehmer *(Vertragshändler, dem der Alleinvertrieb für ein bestimmtes Gebiet gewährt worden ist)*; ~ **heir** Alleinerbe; ~ **holder** Alleininhaber; ~ **inventor** Einzelerfinder *(opp. joint inventor)*; ~ **judge** Einzelrichter; ~ **legatee** *Am (testamentarisch eingesetzter)* Universalerbe; ~ **owner** alleiniger Eigentümer, Alleininhaber; ~ **placing agent** alleiniges Plazierungsinstitut *(Emissionsführer von Euronotefazilitäten, der allein die Bedingungen bestimmt, zu denen die →underwriters Papiere übernehmen müssen, die er nicht selbst plazieren konnte)*; ~ **proprietor** Alleininhaber; Einzelkaufmann; Einzelunternehmer; ~ **proprietorship** alleiniges Eigentumsrecht; *Am* Einzelfirma, Einzelunternehmen; ~ **representative** Alleinvertreter; ~ **right to sell** Alleinverkaufsrecht, Alleinvertriebsrecht; ~ **tenant** Alleinpächter; → **feme** ~; **to have** ~ **power** allein befugt sein

solemn feierlich, festlich; zeremoniell; ~ **ceremony** Festakt; **probate in** ~ **form** *Br* gerichtl. Testamentsbestätigung in feierlicher Form (→*probate*)

solemnization (~sation) of a marriage Trauung, Vollziehung der Eheschließung

solemnize (~se) *v* feierlich begehen; **to** ~ **a marriage** trauen, die Trauung vollziehen

solicit *v (dringend)* bitten, nachsuchen; sich um etw. bemühen (od. bewerben); *Am*[81] *(StrafR)* zu bestimmen versuchen; den Versuch der Anstiftung machen; *(von e-r Prostituierten)* ansprechen; **to** ~ **bids** *Am* s. to →~ tenders; **to** ~ **orders** sich um Aufträge bemühen; Aufträge hereinholen; **to** ~ **proxies** *Am* sich um Stimmrechtsvollmacht bewerben; **to** ~ **subscriptions** Abonnenten werben; **to** ~ **tenders** *(bei Ausschreibungen)* zur Abgabe von Angeboten auffordern, Angebote einholen; **to** ~ **votes** um Stimmen werben

solicitation Bitte(n), Anliegen, Ersuchen; *Am*[81] *(StrafR)* Versuch, zu einer Straftat zu bestimmen; versuchte Anstiftung; ~ **for bids** *Am (öffentl.)* Ausschreibung; ~ **of membership** Mitgliederwerbung; ~ **of (secret) agents** *pol* Agentenwerbung; **proxy** ~ *Am* Bewerbung um Stimmrechtsvollmacht

solicitor *Br*[82] Anwalt; *Am* (Abonnenten- etc) Werber; ~**'s bill** *Br* Gebühren- und Auslagenrechnung des Anwalts; ~**'s clerk** Kanzleikraft e-s solicitor; ~**'s costs** *Br* Anwaltskosten; **S~-General** *Br* zweiter Kronanwalt, Vertreter des Kronanwalts *(cf. Attorney-General)*; *Am* oberster Prozeßvertreter vor dem Supreme Court; ~**'s lien** (on his client's papers) *Br* Zurückbehaltungsrecht des solicitor *(an den Akten seines Mandanten bis zur Bezahlung des Honorars)*; ~ **of 4 years' standing** *Br* Anwalt mit vierjähriger Berufszeit; **S~ (of the Supreme Court)** *Br* (offizieller Titel des) Solicitor; ~**'s office** *Br* Anwaltsbüro; ~ **on the record** *Br* prozeßbevollmächtigter Anwalt; **adverse** ~ *Br* gegnerischer Anwalt; **City S~** *Am* städtischer rechtskundiger Beamter, Stadtsyndikus; → **Official S~**; **proxy** ~ *Am* Bewerber um Stimmrechtsvollmacht; → **Treasury S~**; **to be admitted as a** ~ *Br* als Anwalt zugelassen werden; **to place a matter into the hands of a** ~ *Br* die Sache e-m Anwalt (soliticor) übergeben; **to retain a** ~ *Br* e-n Anwalt *(durch Zahlung e-s Vorschusses)* nehmen

Der Anwaltstand ist in England in 2 Gruppen geteilt *(cf. barrister)*. Der Solicitor darf nicht vor den höchsten Gerichten plädieren. Wer einen Prozeß vor einem höheren Gericht auszutragen hat, muß sich einen Solicitor und einen Barrister nehmen. Der Klient kann sich nur durch Vermittlung des Solicitor an den Barrister wenden.

Die Hauptaufgaben des Solicitor sind: Rechtsberatung, Vorbereitung von Prozessen, Beurkundung von Rechtsgeschäften, Errichtung von Testamenten, Beglaubigung von Unterschriften und andere Aufgaben, die dem deutschen Notar zufallen.

Die Berufsorganisation der Solicitors ist die →Law Society

solid fest, haltbar, dauerhaft; ~ **argument** stichhaltiges Argument; ~ **vote** einstimmige Wahl; ~ **waste** feste Abfallstoffe

solidarity Solidarität; **declaration of** ~ Solidaritätserklärung; **to manifest one's ~** sich solidarisch erklären

solitary confinement Einzelhaft

solution of a problem Lösung e-s Problems

solvency (or **solvability**) Solvenz, Zahlungsfähigkeit; **~ ratio** Solvenzkennzahl *(für Kreditinstitute) (a bank's ability to cope with the risks it incurs);* **statutory declaration of ~** *Br*[82a] Solvenzerklärung

solvent solvent, zahlungsfähig *(opp. insolvent)*; **the estate is ~** der Nachlaß deckt alle Schulden

Somali Somalier, ~in; somalisch; **~ Democratic Republic** Demokratische Republik Somalia
Somalia Somalia

son Sohn; **~-in-law** Schwiegersohn

sophisticated hoch entwickelt; hoch differenziert; technisch ausgereift, hochtechnisiert

sophomore *Am* Student im zweiten Studienjahr; **~ year** zweites Studienjahr

sort Sorte, Art, Qualität; **medium ~** mittlere Qualität, Mittelsorte

sort *v* sortieren, ordnen; **to ~ letters** Briefe sortieren; **to ~ out** aussortieren

sought, ~ after gesucht, gefragt *(z.B. Effekten)*; **~ for** gesucht *(z.B. entwichener Gefangener)*; **person ~** Gesuchter

sound 1. Ton, Klang; Geräusch; **~ and television broadcasting** *Br* Rundfunk und Fernsehen; **~level** Lärmpegel; **~-record pirating** Raubkopien von Tonaufzeichnungen; **~ recorder** Tonwiedergabegerät; **~ recording** *(UrhR)* Tonaufnahme, Tonaufzeichnung
sound 2. gesund, unversehrt; fehlerfrei, unbeschädigt; vernünftig, stichhaltig; solide, sicher, kreditfähig; **~ argument** vernünftiges (od. stichhaltiges) Argument; **~ claim** begründeter Anspruch; **~ currency** gesunde Währung; **~ delivered** gesund ausgeliefert
sound, of ~ mind geistig gesund, zurechnungsfähig; **of ~ and disposing mind and memory** *Am* testierfähig; **being of ~ mind and memory** *Am* in vollem Besitz meiner geistigen Kräfte *(Eingangsformel e-s Testaments)*
sound, ~ reason stichhaltiger Grund; **~ value** *(VersR)* voller Wert, Verkehrswert *(opp. damaged value)*; *(Zoll)* Gesundwert; **safe and ~** wohlbehalten

sound *v* tönen; lauten; *fig* scheinen, den Eindruck machen (as if als wenn); (aus)loten, sondieren, erkunden; **the action ~s in contract (tort)** die Klage (od. der Anspruch) stützt sich auf Vertrag (Delikt); **the action ~s in damages** die Klage geht auf Schadensersatz

sounding rocket launching facilities Abschußanlagen für Höhenforschungsraketen

soundness Gesundheit, gesunder Geisteszustand; Fehlerfreiheit *(beim Kauf)*; **~ of mind** Zurechnungsfähigkeit; **financial ~** Bonität

source Quelle; *fig* Ursprung, Herkunft; **~ materials** *(AtomR)* Ausgangsstoffe; **~ of energy** Energiequelle; **~ of error(s)** Fehlerquelle; **~s of evidence** Beweismittel; **~ of funds** Mittelherkunft; **~ of income** Einkommensquelle; **~ of information** Informationsquelle; **~s of (the) law** Rechtsquellen; **~ of profit** Gewinnquelle; **~ of proof** Beweismittel; **~ of revenue** Einnahmequelle; **~ of supply** Bezugsquelle; Versorgungsquelle; **~ state** *(SteuerR)* Quellenstaat; **~ taxation** Quellenbesteuerung *(opp. residence taxation)*; **collection at ~** Steuererhebung an der Quelle (→*collection 1.)*; **country of ~** (of income) *(SteuerR)* Quellenstaat; **deduction of tax at ~** Steuerabzug an der Quelle (→*deduction 2.)*; **foreign ~ income** *Am* Einkommen aus ausländischen Quellen; **list of ~s used** Quellenverzeichnis; **from official ~s** aus amtlichen Quellen; **capital from outside ~s** Fremdkapital; **state of ~** *(SteuerR)* Quellenstaat; **tax (deducted) at ~** Quellensteuer; **US ~ income** *Am (SteuerR)* Einkommen, die aus amerikanischen Quellen stammen; **to collect taxes at ~** Steuern an der Quelle erheben; **to credit the tax of the ~ state against German tax** die Steuer des Quellenstaates auf die deutsche Steuer anrechnen; **to deduct taxes at ~** Steuern im Abzugswege erheben; **to indicate the ~** die Quelle angeben; **to learn from a reliable (well-informed) ~** aus zuverlässiger (gut unterrichteter) Quelle erfahren

South Africa Südafrika; **Republic of ~** Republik Südafrika[83]
South African Südafrikaner(in); südafrikanisch

South East Asia Treaty Organization Südostasienpakt (→*SEATO)*

South East Atlantic, Convention on the Conservation of the Living Resources of the ~[84] Übereinkommen zur Erhaltung der lebenden Schätze des Südostatlantiks

Southerner *Br* Südländer; *Am* Südstaatler

sovereign Souverän, Monarch(in); souverän *(Staat); Br* Goldmünze zu £1; souverän, unumschränkt; höchst; **~ emblem** Hoheitszeichen; **foreign ~→immunity; ~ power** Hoheitsgewalt; **~ right** Hoheitsrecht; **~ territory** Hoheitsgebiet

sovereignty Souveränität, Hoheitsgewalt;

Herrschaft; ~ **of the air** (or **over the air space**) Lufthoheit; ~ **of Parliament** *Br* Grundsatz des brit. Verfassungssystems, der besagt, daß das Parlament die oberste Rechtssetzungsgewalt hat; **financial** ~ Finanzhoheit; **judicial** ~ Gerichtshoheit; **military** ~ Wehrhoheit; **monetary** ~ Währungshoheit; Münzhoheit; **infringement of territorial** ~ Verletzung der Gebietshoheit

Soviet Sowjetbürger(in); sowjetisch; **~-American Arms Limitation Treaty** sowjetisch-amerikanischer Vertrag von 1977 über die Begrenzung der strategischen Waffen; ~ **Union** Sowjetunion; **(of the)** ~ Sowjetbürger (-in); sowjetisch; **the Supreme** ~ der Oberste Sowjet *(Volksvertretung)*; **Union of** ~ **Socialist Republics** (USSR) Union der Sozialistischen Sowjetrepubliken (UdSSR)

space 1. Platz, Raum; Zwischenraum; Zeitraum; Schiffsraum; ~ **occupied** (or **taken up**) besetzter (od. in Anspruch genommener) Raum; ~ **rate** Anzeigentarif; ~ **required** Platzbedarf; ~ **writer** nach der Zeilenzahl bezahlter Journalist; **advertising** ~ Raum für Anzeigen *(e-r Zeitung)*; Reklamefläche; **air** ~ Luftraum; **cargo** ~ Laderaum; **floor** ~ Hallenfläche, Ausstellungsfläche; **housing** ~ Wohnraum; **living** ~ Lebensraum; **open ~s** unbebautes Gelände; **for want of** ~ aus Platzmangel; **to book** ~ Schiffsraum bestellen; **to save** ~ Platz sparen

space 2. Weltraum; ~ **age** Raumfahrtzeitalter *(→European S~ Agency)*; ~ **arms** Weltraumwaffen; **~-based** im Weltraum stationiert; ~ **(communications) service** Weltraumfunkdienst; **~craft** (Welt-)Raumfahrzeug; ~ **flight** (Welt-)Raumflug; ~ **laboratory** (spacelab) Weltraumlabor; ~ **law** Weltraumrecht; **~man** Raumfahrer

space object Weltraumgegenstand; **Convention of International Liability for Damage Caused by S~ O~s**[85] Übereinkommen über die völkerrechtliche Haftung für Schäden durch Weltraumgegenstände

space, ~ **plane** Weltraumflugzeug; ~ **platform** →~ station; ~ **race** Wettlauf um die Erforschung des Weltraums

space research (Welt-)Raumforschung; **Committee for S~ R~** (COSPAR) *Am* Komitee für (Welt-)Raumforschung

space research, European S~ R~ Organization (ESRO)[86] Europäische Weltraumforschungs-Organisation

Sitz: Paris.

Organe: Rat (Council), Generaldirektor (Director-General), (Mitarbeiter-)Stab (staff)

Aufgabe: Durchführung eines Programms wissenschaftlicher Forschung und damit zusammenhängender technischer Tätigkeiten

space, ~ **satellite** (Raum-)Satellit; ~ **segment** Weltraumsegment *(→Intelsat)*; ~ **ship** (bemanntes) (Welt-)Raumschiff; ~ **shuttle** (Welt-) Raumfähre; Raumtransporter; ~ **station** (Welt-)Raumstation *(für Start und Landung von Raumschiffen)*; Weltraumfunkstelle; ~ **suit** Raumanzug

space technology, European S~ T~ Centre (ESTC) Europäisches Zentrum für Raumfahrt-Technologie

space, ~ **telemetering** Weltraumfernmessung; ~ **tracking** Weltraum-Bahnverfolgung; ~ **travel** (Welt-)Raumfahrt

Space Treaty Weltraumvertrag *(Vertrag zur Erforschung und friedlichen Nutzung des Weltraumes)*[87]

Etwa 60 Unterzeichnerstaaten (darunter die Bundesrepublik Deutschland).

Der Vertrag untersagt die Inanspruchnahme staatlicher Hoheitsrechte im Weltraum oder auf Himmelskörpern sowie das Verbringen von Waffen dorthin

space vehicle Raumfahrzeug; ~ **launcher** Raumfahrzeugträger; **European Organisation for the Development and Construction of S~ V~ Launchers**[88] Europäische Organisation für die Entwickung und den Bau von Raumfahrzeugträgern *(cf. European →Launcher Development Organisation; [ELDO])*

space weapons Weltraumwaffen

space, outer ~ Weltraum; **borderline between air space and outer** ~ Grenze zwischen Luftraum und Weltraum; **exploration and use of outer** ~ Erforschung und Nutzung des Weltraums; **law of outer** ~ Weltraumrecht; **return of objects launched into →outer** ~

space out *v*, **to** ~ **payments over 10 years** Zahlung auf über 10 Jahre verteilen

Spain Spanien

Spaniard Spanier, ~in

Spanish spanisch; **S~ State** Spanischer Staat

span Spanne; ~ **of control** Kontrollspanne *(Höchstzahl von Untergebenen, die geleitet werden können)*

spare übrig, Ersatz-, Reserve-; ~ **capacity** *Br* Reservekapazität; ~ **money** Notgroschen; ~ **part** Reserveteil, Ersatzteil

spare time Freizeit; ~ **activities** Freizeitgestaltung; ~ **job** Freizeitarbeit; Nebentätigkeit; ~ **occupation** Nebenbeschäftigung

spatial economy Raumwirtschaft

speak *v* sprechen, das Wort ergreifen; **to** ~ **extempore** improvisiert (od. aus dem Stegreif) sprechen; **to** ~ **in a p.'s favo(u)r** für j-n eintreten; **to** ~ **to the point** zur Sache sprechen; **to ask to** ~ sich zu Wort melden, um das Wort bitten; **I call upon Mr. X. to** *~Br* ich erteile Herrn X. das Wort; **to be permitted to** ~ das Wort erhalten

speaking, ~ **clock** *tel* Zeitansage; ~ **time** Redezeit; **generally** ~ allgemein genommen; **strictly** ~ genau genommen

speaker Sprecher, Redner, Wortführer; **S~** *parl* Vorsitzender, Präsident; **the last** (or **preceding** or **previous**) ~ der (Herr) Vorredner; **the list of ~s is exhausted** es liegt keine Wortmeldung mehr vor; **the S~ takes the chair** der Speaker eröffnet die Sitzung

Br Unter Speaker wird der vom Unterhaus gewählte Präsident des Unterhauses (House of Commons) verstanden, der offiziell Mr. Speaker heißt und im Ggs. zum Speaker of the House of Lords *(meist der Lord Chancellor)* parteipolitische Neutralität wahren muß. *Am*[89] Speaker ist der Präsident des Repräsentantenhauses, einzelstaatlich der Präsident einer oder beider Kammern des Parlaments

special besonders, Sonder-, Spezial-; speziell; ~ **account** Sonderkonto; ~ **acceptance** (of a bill of exchange) eingeschränktes Akzept *(zahlbar an e-m bestimmten Ort)*; **S~ Acts** (of Parliament) *Br* Sondergesetze *(local, personal or private acts)*; ~ **administration** *Br* →limited administration; ~ **agency** →agency 1. und 2.; ~→ **agent;** ~ **agreement** →agreement 1. und 3.; ~ **assessment** Sonderbesteuerung; Sonderumlage; *Am (vom Grundeigentum erhobene)* Sonderabgaben; ~ **assessment bond** *Am* Anleihe mit Deckung durch Einnahmen aus e-r besonderen Umlage; ~ **authorization** Sondergenehmigung; ~ **bargain** Sonderangebot; ~ **benefits** Sonderleistungen; ~ **bonus** Sonderzulage; *Br (VersR)* Sonderdividende; **S~ Branch** *Br* Staatssicherheitspolizei; ~ **buyer** *Br* Vertreter e-r Firma von Wechselmaklern (discount brokers), der Offenmarktgeschäfte in Treasury bills für die Bank of England durchführt; ~ **case**[90] besonderer Fall; Rechtssache, in der dem Gericht der Tatbestand zur Erlangung e-r gerichtl. Entscheidung in e-r Rechtsfrage vorgelegt wird; ~ **charges** *Am* außerordentliche Aufwendungen; Sondergebühren, Sonderkosten; ~ **checking account** *Am* gebührenpflichtiges Scheckkonto

Special Commissioners of Income Tax (S. C. I. T.) *Br* Sonderbeauftragte für Einkommensteuersachen

Beamte, die unabhängig über Beschwerden gegen Einkommensteuerveranlagung entscheiden. Gegen ihre Entscheidung kann zur lediglich rechtlichen Überprüfung (→*case stated*) der High Court angerufen werden

special, ~ **constable** Hilfspolizist; ~ **contingent account** Sonderkonto für Eventualfälle; ~ **crossing** *Br* →crossing 1.; ~ **damage**[91] konkreter Schaden *(der im Verfahren ausdrücklich vorgebracht und bewiesen werden muß; opp. general damage; cf. slander)*

special delivery *(Post)* Eilzustellung, Zustellung durch Eilboten; ~ **fee** *Am* Eilzustellgebühr; ~ **letter** *Am* Eilbrief; **by** ~ durch Eilboten

special, ~ **deposits** *Br (1960 eingeführte Form von)* Sondereinlagen *(die von den Londoner Clearing- und den schottischen Banken bei der Bank von England zu halten sind)*; *Am* zur sicheren Aufbewahrung bei e-r Bank hinterlegte Werte; ~ **discount** Sonderrabatt; ~ **dividend** *Am (VersR)* Sonderdividende

special drawing rights (SDR) Sonderziehungsrechte (SZR) *(Kunstwährung des Internationalen Währungsfonds, die sich aus e-m Korb von fünf wichtigen Weltwährungen zusammensetzt)*; **cumulative allocation of** ~[91a] kumulative Nettozuteilung von Sonderziehungsrechten; **to allocate** ~ Sonderziehungsrechte zuteilen; **to cancel** ~ Sonderziehungsrechte aus dem Verkehr ziehen (od. einziehen)

Die SDRs, die nach einem festen Schlüssel an die Mitgliedsländer des Internationalen Währungsfonds verteilt werden können, treten als Ergänzung bestehender Währungsreserven neben Gold und Dollar und dienen der Erhöhung der internationalen Liquidität

special, ~→**endorsement;** ~ **events** Veranstaltungen; ~ **examiner** jd. *(gewöhnl. ein Jurist)*, der im Auftrag des Gerichts in e-m besonderen Rechtsstreit Beweis erhebt; ~ **indorsement** → endorsement; ~ **fund** Sonderfonds; ~ **handling parcel** *Am* Schnellpaket; ~ **leave** Sonderurlaub; ~ **licence** *Br (vom Erzbischof von Canterbury erteilte)* Sondergenehmigung zur Eheschließung *(cf. Kommentar zu → marriage)*; ~ **lien** Pfandrecht an e-r bestimmten Sache (→*lien*); ~ **manager** *Br*[92] *(vom Gericht bestellter)* besonderer Verwalter; ~→ **meeting; on a** ~ **mission** in besonderer Mission; mit Sonderauftrag; ~ **orders** *Br* Verordnungen mit Gesetzeskraft; ~ **partner** beschränkt haftender Gesellschafter; ~→ **partnership;** ~ **pass** Sonderausweis; ~ **permit** Sondergenehmigung; ~ **personal representative** *Br*[93] Erbschaftsverwalter e-s →tenant for life hinsichtlich →settled land; ~ **pleading**[94] zusätzlicher Vortrag *(der sich nicht auf das Bestreiten des gegnerischen Vortrags beschränkt, sondern neue Gesichtspunkte einführt; cf. to plead →specifically)*; ~ **pleading legislation** *Am* Gesetzgebung, die den Interessen e-r Gruppe dient; ~ **power** (of appointment) Bestimmung von Berechtigten od. Nacherben aus e-r beschränkten Gruppe (→ *power 1.)*; ~ **power** (of attorney) Sondervollmacht (→*power 1.)*; ~ **privilege** Sonderrecht, Vorrecht; ~ **property** beschränktes Eigentum (→*property)*; ~→ **proxy;** ~ **quota** Sonderkontingent; ~ **representative** *Am* Sonderbeauftragter; ~ **resolution** →resolution 2. und 3.; ~ **risk policy** *(VersR)* kurzfristige Police für bestimmte Risiko; ~ **road** *Br*[95] Autobahn; ~ **rule** Sonderbestimmung; ~ **sale price** Ausverkaufspreis

special session außerordentliche Sitzung *(opp. regular session)*; ~**s** *Br* von zwei od. mehreren justices of the peace abgehaltenes Gericht zur Erledigung bestimmter Angelegenheiten *(z.B. Erteilung von Schankkonzession)*; **court of ~s** *Am (in einigen Einzelstaaten)* Gericht mit beschränkter Zuständigkeit in Strafsachen

special, ~ settlement *Br (Börse)* → settlement 4.; **~ situation fund** *Am* spekulativer (Investment-)Fonds *(mit hohem Verlustrisiko)*; **~ status** Sonderstellung; **~ supplement** Sonderbeilage; **~ trade** Spezialhandel; **~→trust**

specially, ~ crossed cheque *Br* →cheque; **~→ endorsed writ; generally and ~** im allgemeinen und besonderen; **to be endorsed ~** *(WechselR)* voll indossiert sein; **to plead ~** s. to plead →specifically

specialist Spezialist; Fachmann; *med* Facharzt; *Am (Börse)* Kursmakler *(Börsenmitglied der New Yorker Börse, der auf ein bestimmtes Wertpapier od. einzelne Effektenarten spezialisiert ist und – notfalls mit eigenen Mitteln – für geordnete Marktverhältnisse sorgen muß. Er ist als broker [d.h. auf Kommissionsbasis, meist für andere broker] und gleichzeitig als dealer tätig)*; **~ circles** (or **circle of ~s**) Fachkreise; **~ knowledge** Fachwissen; **to become a ~ in** sich spezialisieren auf; **to consult a ~** e-n Spezialisten zu Rate ziehen

specialit|y Besonderheit, Spezialität; Spezialgebiet; **~ies** *Br (Börse)* Spezialwerte; → **Federal ~ies**

specialization Spezialisierung

specialize *v* (sich) spezialisieren (in auf); einzeln aufführen

specialized spezialisiert; **~ agencies**[96] Sonderorganisationen *(der Vereinten Nationen)*; **~ education** Fachausbildung; **~ fair** Fachmesse; **~ knowledge** Fachkenntnisse; **~ practice** Praxis e-s Spezialisten; **~ worker** Facharbeiter

specialt|y 1. Besonderheit, Spezialität; Spezialartikel; Spezialfach, -gebiet; **~ies** *Am (Börse)* Spezialwerte; **~ gifts** Werbegeschenke; **~ goods** Spezialartikel; **~ store** *Am* Spezialgeschäft; Kaufhaus, Warenhaus; →**Federal ~ ies**

specialty 2., **~ (contract)** gesiegelter Vertrag *(der hinsichtl. consideration und Verjährung privilegiert ist; cf. contract under seal)*; **~ debt** Schuld aus gesiegeltem Vertrag od. kraft Gesetzes *(12jährige Verjährungsfrist)*

specie Metallgeld, Hartgeld, gemünztes Geld *(opp. paper money)*; **~ point** Goldpunkt; **gold ~** gemünztes Gold *(→gold)*; **in ~** in natura; in Hartgeld; **payment in ~** Zahlung in Metallgeld

species Art *(Tiere, Pflanzen etc)*; Gattung

specific bestimmt, konkret; spezifisch, kennzeichnend; **~ amount** bestimmter Betrag; **~ bequest** bestimmte letztwillige Zuwendung *(die sich von dem übrigen Nachlaß sondern läßt)*; **~ capital** zweckgebundenes Kapital; **~ cost** Einzelkosten, direkte Kosten; **~ denial** →denial 1.; **~ devise** letztwillige Verfügung über bestimmten Grundbesitz; **~ duty** spezifischer Zoll *(opp. ad valorem duty)*

specific goods[97] bestimmte (konkret ausgesuchte) Waren *(beim Spezieskauf; opp. unascertained goods)*; **purchase of ~** Spezieskauf

specific, ~→ legacy; ~→ legatee; ~ lien Pfandrecht an e-r bestimmten Sache (→*lien*); **~ obligation** Speziesschuld; **~ performance** Leistung des vertraglich Geschuldeten (→ *performance 1.*); **~ person** bestimmte Person; **~ restitution of property** Rückgabe e-s bestimmten Vermögensgegenstandes; **~ tariff** nach Menge, Stück od. Gewicht berechneter Zolltarif

specifically besonders; **to plead ~**[98] e-e bestimmte klagebegründende Tatsache oder *(seitens des Beklagten)* e-e Einrede od. Einwendung *(z.B. Verjährung, Verwirkung)* in e-m Schriftsatz angeben *(opp. general denial)*

specification Spezifizierung, genaue Angabe (od. Beschreibung); nähere Darlegung, (Einzel-)Aufstellung; Patentbeschreibung, Patentschrift (→*patent ~*); Ausfuhrerklärung; Spezifikation *(Herstellung e-r neuen bewegl. Sache durch Verarbeitung; Hersteller erwirbt das Eigentum, vgl. § 950 BGB)*; (Geld-)Sortenzettel; **~ cost** Standardkosten; **~ of disbursements** Auslagenaufstellung, Spesenaufstellung; **~ of the European patent** Europäische Patentschrift; **~ of numbers** Nummernverzeichnis; **abridg(e)ment of ~** *Br* Kurzfassung der Patentschrift; **(building) ~s** Baubeschreibung *(genaue technische Angaben des Architekten od. Bauingenieurs)*; **complete ~** *(PatR)* endgültige Beschreibung; **customs ~** Verzeichnis der zu verzollenden Waren; **(export) ~** *Br (Zoll)* Ausfuhrerklärung; **fee for the printing of a ~** *(PatR)* Druckkostengebühr für die Patentschrift; **job ~** Arbeitsbeschreibung; **manufacture to customer's ~** Einzelanfertigung; **provisional ~** *(PatR)* vorläufige Beschreibung; **to manufacture goods to ~** Waren nach Angabe anfertigen

specificity test *(IPR)* Untersuchung, ob Verjährungsregelung ausnahmsweise nicht der lex fori, sondern der das Recht beherrschenden Rechtsordnung zu entnehmen ist

specify *v* spezifizieren, näher angeben (od. bestimmen); einzeln aufführen (od. verzeichnen); **to ~ a period of time** e-e Frist bestimmen (od. setzen); **to ~ the place of payment** den Zahlungsort angeben

specified, ~ account spezifizierte Rechnung; **~ below** nachstehend aufgeführt; **~ date** bestimmter Zeitpunkt; **purchase of ~ goods** (or **items**) Spezieskauf, Stückkauf; **in ~ instal(l)ments** in festgesetzten Raten; **~ period** bestimmte (od. vereinbarte) Frist; **~ person** bestimmte Person; **for a ~ term** (or **time**) für e-e bestimmte Zeit; **unless otherwise ~** sofern nichts anderes bestimmt ist, mangels abweichender Vereinbarung

specimen Muster; Probe; Probestück; **~ contract** Mustervertrag; **~ copy** Probeexemplar; **~ page** Probeseite; **~ (of one's) signature** Unterschriftsprobe

speculate *v* spekulieren; **to ~ for differences** *Br* mit Kursunterschieden spekulieren; **to ~ for a fall** auf Baisse spekulieren; **to ~ for a rise** auf Hausse spekulieren; **to ~ in stocks and shares** in Wertpapieren spekulieren

speculating transactions Spekulationsgeschäfte

speculation Spekulation; **~ for a fall** Baissespekulation; **~ for a rise** Haussespekulation; **~ in futures** Terminspekulation; **~ in land** Grundstücksspekulation; **~ on the stock exchange** Börsenspekulation; **bear ~** Baissespekulation; **bull ~** Haussespekulation; **hazardous ~** gewagte Spekulation; **property** (or **land**) **~** Grundstücksspekulation; **wrong ~** Fehlspekulation; **to engage in (risky) ~s** sich auf (gewagte) Spekulationen einlassen

speculative spekulativ, Spekulations-; **~ buying** Spekulationskäufe, Meinungskäufe; **~ damages** →prospective damages; **~ dealer** Spekulant; **~ operations** Spekulationsgeschäfte; **~ profit** Spekulationsgewinn; **~ securities** (or **shares, stocks**) Spekulationspapiere *(opp. investment securities, shares or stocks)*; **~ selling** Spekulationsverkäufe, Meinungsverkäufe; **~ transactions** Spekulationsgeschäfte

speculator Spekulant; **~ for a fall** Baissespekulant; **~ for a rise** Haussespekulant; **~ in land** (or **land ~**) Grundstücksspekulant; **professional ~** berufsmäßiger Spekulant; **property ~ (or ~ in property)** Grundstücksspekulant

speech Rede, Ansprache; Sprache; **~es** *Br* Entscheidungsvoten der →Law Lords (→*opinion 1.)*; **~-day** *Br* (Jahres-)Schlußfeier *(an höheren Schulen)*; **~ from the throne** Thronrede; **closing ~** Schlußansprache; **counsel's ~** *Br* Anwaltsplädoyer; **election ~** Wahlrede; **extempore ~** Rede aus dem Stegreif; **farewell ~** Abschiedsrede; **freedom of ~** Redefreiheit; Recht der freien Meinungsäußerung; **inaugural ~** Antrittsrede; **liberty of ~** s. freedom of →~; **maiden ~** *parl* Jungfernrede; **in the middle of his ~** mitten in s-r Rede; **opening ~** Eröffnungsansprache; **to deliver** (or **make**) **a ~** e-e Rede (od. Ansprache) halten

speed Geschwindigkeit; **~ cop** *Am sl.* motorisierter Verkehrspolizist *(zur Überprüfung von Geschwindigkeitsüberschreitungen)*

speed limit Geschwindigkeitsbegrenzung; zulässige Höchstgeschwindigkeit; **~ zone** Zone mit *(polizeil.)* festgesetzter Höchstgeschwindigkeit; **to exceed the ~** die Geschwindigkeitsbegrenzung überschreiten

speed, ~ merchant *sl.* rücksichtsloser Fahrer; **~ restriction** Geschwindigkeitsbeschränkung; **~ trap** Autofalle; **~-up of production** Produktionssteigerung; **~ way** *Am* Schnellstraße; **low ~** geringe Geschwindigkeit; **maximum** (or **top**) **~** Höchstgeschwindigkeit; **to reduce (increase) ~** die Geschwindigkeit vermindern (erhöhen); **to resume ~** die Geschwindigkeit wieder aufnehmen

speed up *v* beschleunigen; **to ~ the proceedings** das Verfahren beschleunigen

speeding (violation) *Am* Überschreiten der zulässigen Geschwindigkeit; **ticket for ~** *Am* Strafzettel für Geschwindigkeitsüberschreitung

speedy reply schnelle Antwort

spell of unemployment Periode der Arbeitslosigkeit

spend *v (Geld)* ausgeben (on für); *(Zeit)* aufwenden, verschwenden; verbringen

spending (Geld-)Ausgabe; **~ behavio(u)r** Ausgabeverhalten; **~ capacity** Kaufkraft; **~ cuts** Ausgabenkürzung; **~ group** Käuferschicht; **~ money** Taschengeld; **~ policy** Ausgabepolitik *(der öffentl. Hand)*; **consumer ~** Verbraucherausgaben; →**deficit ~**; **government** (or **public**) **~** Staatsausgaben

spendthrift Verschwender; **~ trust** *Am* Trust, der dem Begünstigten (beneficiary) auf die Erträgnisse e-r Vermögensmasse beschränkt, die Vermögenssumme selbst gegen Gläubigerzugriffe sichert

sphere Sphäre, Bereich; (Wirkungs-)Kreis; **~ of activity** Wirkungskreis; Tätigkeitsbereich; **~ of business** Geschäftsbereich; **~ of duties** Aufgabenbereich; **~ of influence** *(VölkerR)* Einflußbereich, Einflußzone; **~ of interest** *(VölkerR)* Interessengebiet; **private ~** Privatsphäre, Intimsphäre

spin-off *Am* Übertragung des ausschlaggebenden Aktienkapitals an e-r Tochtergesellschaft durch die Muttergesellschaft an ihre Aktionäre *(cf. split-off)*; Ausgliederung und Verselbständigung e-s Unternehmensbereiches *(z. B. durch ein →management buyout)*; **~ product** Nebenprodukt, Abfallprodukt

spinning mill Spinnerei

spinster unverheiratete Frau; *Br (in Urkunden)* ledig *(von Frauen)*

spiral, inflationary ~ Inflationsschraube; **wage-price ~** Lohn-Preisspirale

spirit Geist; **within the ~ of the agreement** im Geiste des Abkommens

spirits[99] Spirituosen; ~ **monopoly** Branntweinmonopol; **licensing sale of** ~ Schankkonzession

spiritual geistig; geistlich *(opp. secular, lay)*; ~ **adviser** geistlicher Berater; Seelsorger; ~ **court** Kirchengericht; **the** ~ **heritage of Europe** das geistige Erbe Europas; ~ **sovereignty** Religionshoheit; **Lords S**~ →Lord

spiritualities of a bishop *Br* Einkünfte e-s Bischofs aus Pfründen *(opp. temporalities)*

spirituous liquors Spirituosen

spite fence *Am* Zaun, der errichtet ist, um den Nachbarn zu ärgern

splinter, ~ **group** Splittergruppe; ~ **party** Splitterpartei

split Spaltung, (Auf-)Teilung; Aktiensplit, Teilung e-s Investmentanteils (→*splitting*); *pol* abgespaltene Gruppe, Splittergruppe; *pol* geteilte Stimmabgabe; ~**-down** *Am* →reverse ~; ~**-off** *Am* Ausgabe von Aktien e-r *(neugegründeten)* Tochtergesellschaft an die Aktionäre der Muttergesellschaft im Austausch gegen Aktien der Muttergesellschaft; *(Art der)* Unternehmensentflechtung (*wie →spin-off, nur werden die Anteile der Tochter gegen Anteile der Mutter ausgetauscht*); ~ **order** *Am (Börse)* Kaufauftrag in mehreren Abschnitten zu verschiedenen Kursen; ~ **quotation** *Am* Notierung in Bruchteilen; ~ **re-export** *(Zoll)* Teilwiederausfuhr; ~ **shift** →shift 2.; ~ **tax rate** *Am* gespaltener Steuersatz; ~ **ticket** *Am* Wahlzettel e-s Wählers, der seine Stimme den Kandidaten verschiedener Parteien gibt; ~**-up** Teilung, Aufspaltung; *colloq.* Auseinandergehen, Auflösung *(z.B. e-r partnership)*; *Am* Austausch des gesamten Aktienkapitals der Aktionäre e-r Muttergesellschaft gegen Aktien e-r Tochtergesellschaft; *Am* Aktiensplit

split *v* spalten, (auf)teilen; zerlegen; sich spalten (od. teilen); **to** ~ **up** aufteilen; in kleinere Beträge zerlegen; sich spalten (od. teilen) (into in); **to** ~ **a cause of action**[100] e-n Klageanspruch auf mehrere Teilklagen verteilen; **to** ~ **the difference** sich auf halbem Wege treffen, sich den Differenzbetrag teilen; **to** ~ **the fee** das (Arzt-, Anwalts-) Honorar teilen; **to** ~ **the income** *Am (SteuerR)* das Einkommen *(von Eheleuten)* aufspalten (→*splitting*); **to** ~ **a party** e-e Partei spalten; **to** ~ **shares** (or *Am* **stocks**) Aktien splitten (od. teilen) (→*splitting*); **to** ~ **one's ticket** *Am* (or **vote**) s-e Stimme auf mehrere Kandidaten verteilen

splitting Spaltung, (Auf-)Teilung; bes. *Am* Splitting, Aktienaufteilung *(Aktien, deren Kurs sehr hoch gestiegen ist, werden in mehrere Aktien mit entsprechend kleinerem Nennwert aufgeteilt)*; Teilung e-s Investmentanteiles; *(EinkommensteuerR)* Splitting *(das Einkommen von Eheleuten wird zusammengerechnet, halbiert und jeder Ehepartner mit der Hälfte des errechneten Gesamtbetrages zur Steuer herangezogen)*; ~ **of a cause of action**[100] Einklagung e-s Teilanspruchs in der Absicht, den Restanspruch in e-m neuen Verfahren einzuklagen; ~ **of costs** (Auf-)Teilung der Kosten; ~ **up of a party** Spaltung e-r Partei; **fee** ~ Honorarteilung

spoils Beute; Diebesgut; ~**man** *Am* Postenjäger mit Hilfe der Partei; ~ **of war** Kriegsbeute; ~ **system** *Am* „Beutesystem", parteipolitische Ämterpatronage; *(entspricht etwa)* Parteibuchwirtschaft *(Besetzung der Beamtenstellen mit Mitgliedern der jeweils regierenden politischen Partei; cf. patronage; opp. merit system)*; **the thieves divided up the** ~ die Diebe teilten sich die Beute

spoil *v* verderben

spoilt (or **spoiled**), ~ **goods** verdorbene Waren; ~ **stamps** beschädigte Briefmarken (od. Stempel); ~ **voting paper** ungültige Stimme

spokesman Wortführer; *(offizieller)* Sprecher; ~ **for a group** Fraktionssprecher; **official** ~ *Am* Pressesprecher

spoliation Beraubung; Plünderung; Vernichtung (od. unbefugte Abänderung) e-r Urkunde durch e-n Dritten (→*alteration)*; *Br eccl* Wegnahme der Erträge e-r Pfründe auf Grund e-s angeblichen Rechts; *Br* Klage e-s Pfründeninhabers (incumbent) gegen den anderen

sponsion Verpflichtung, Bürgschaft; *(VölkerR)* von e-m nicht bevollmächtigten Vertreter *(z.B. General od. Admiral in Kriegszeiten)* übernommene Verpflichtung *(die ohne nachfolgende Ratifizierung durch den betr. Staat nichtig ist)*

sponsor Sponsor, Förderer, Schirmherr; Geldgeber; *Am* Bürge *(für Einwanderung)*; (Tauf-)Pate, Patin; Firma od. Privatperson, die für ein Radio- od. Fernsehprogramm e-e Summe bezahlt und dafür am Anfang od. Ende des Programms Werbung betreiben darf; *Am* Vertriebsgesellschaft für Investmentanteile; **fund** ~ Gründer e-s Investmentfonds; **to be** ~ (for) fördern, unterstützen; **to be** ~ **for a new employee** *Am* e-n neuen Angestellten einarbeiten; **to stand** ~ **to** Pate stehen bei

sponsor *v* fördern, unterstützen, befürworten; Garantie übernehmen für; Schirmherrschaft haben über; Rundfunk-, Fernsehprogramm finanzieren und dafür Werbung betreiben (→ *sponsor)*

sponsored gefördert (by durch, von); unter der Schirmherrschaft stehend; **government-**~ staatlich gefördert (od. unterstützt)

sponsoring Zurverfügungstellung von Geld und/oder Sachmitteln gegen e-e Gegenleistung, die den Marketing-Zielen e-r Unternehmung förderlich ist *(in Sport, Kultur od. im gesellschaftspolitischen Bereich)*

sponsorship Bürgschaft; Patenschaft; Förderung, Befürwortung; Schirmherrschaft

spontaneous spontan; freiwillig, aus eigenem Antrieb; ~ **combustion** Selbstentzündung *(als Gefahr für versicherte Gegenstände)*

sporting rights Jagdrecht

spot 1. Ort, Platz; *(Rundfunk, Fernsehen)* kurze Werbesendung; Werbedurchsage; ~ **announcement** *Am (Radio, Fernsehen)* Durchsage e-r (Geschäfts-)Reklame; ~ **check** Prüfung an Ort und Stelle; Stichprobe; **~-news reporter** *Am* Lokalberichterstatter; **on the** ~ an Ort und Stelle; zur Stelle

spot 2. *(Börse)* sofort lieferbar; sofort zahlbar *(bei Lieferung)*; Kassa- *(opp. forward)*; **~s** Lokowaren *(gegen sofortige Kasse gelieferte Waren)*; ~ **business** *(Effektenbörse)* Kassageschäft; *(Warenbörse)* Lokogeschäft; ~ **cash** sofortige Barzahlung; ~ **commodity** Lokoware

spot delivery sofortige Lieferung *(gegen Kasse)*; **to sell for** ~ loko verkaufen

spot exchange Bardevisen, Kassadevisen; ~ **transactions** (or **dealings**) Kassageschäfte in Devisen

spot goods Lokowaren (→*spots)*

spot market *(Effektenbörse)* Kassamarkt; *(Warenbörse)* Lokomarkt *(opp. forward or future market)*; ~ **rate of a currency** Kassakurs e-r Währung; **securities quoted on the** ~ Kassawerte

spot, ~ **price** *(Effektenbörse)* Kassakurs; *(Warenbörse)* Spotkurs, Lokopreis *(Preis bei sofortiger Lieferung; opp. forward or future price)*; ~ **purchase** Kassakauf; ~ **quotation** Kassanotierung; ~ **rate** *(Devisenmarkt)* Kassakurs; ~ **sale** Lokoverkauf, Verkauf am Kassamarkt *(opp. forward sale)*; ~ **trading** *Am* Verkäufe gegen sofortige Kasse und Lieferung *(opp. futures trading)*; ~ **transactions** Kassageschäfte; *(Warenbörse)* Lokogeschäfte, Spotgeschäfte *(gegen sofortige Kasse und Lieferung abgeschlossene Geschäfte; opp. forward or future transactions)*; **over** ~ *Br* Report *(Zuschlag zum Terminkurs)*; **under** ~ *Br* Deport *(Abschlag vom Terminkurs)*; **to buy** ~ *(Börse)* per Kasse kaufen; **to sell** ~ *(Börse)* per Kasse verkaufen

spousal support *Am (gerichtlich festgestellter)* Ehegattenunterhalt *(bei Getrenntleben od. nach der Scheidung)*

spouse Ehegatte, Ehegattin; **~'s exemption** *Am* (Steuer-)Freibetrag für den Ehegatten; ~ **support (payments)** *Am* Ehegattenunterhalt

spread 1. Verbreitung, Ausbreitung; Streuung; ~ **of epidemics** Verbreitung von Seuchen; ~ **of risk** Risikoverteilung

spread 2. ganzseitige Anzeige; **double** ~ doppelseitige Anzeige

spread 3. Marge, (Handels-, Kurs-, Zins-) Spanne; Preisdifferenz, Differenz zwischen zwei Preisen (od. Zahlen); Kursdifferenz *(z. B. zwischen →bid price und →asked price)*; Aufschlag auf den Kreditzinssatz; Konsortialprovision; **gross** ~ Bruttomarge

spread *v* verteilen; verbreiten; streuen; **to** ~ **an instal(l)ment over several months** e-e Ratenzahlung über mehrere Monate verteilen; **to** ~ **a risk** ein Risiko verteilen (od. streuen); **to** ~ **a rumour** ein Gerücht verbreiten

spring fair Frühjahrsmesse

spurious falsch; gefälscht, unecht

spurt (Kurs-)Sprung; plötzliches Steigen

spurt *v (Börse)* springen; plötzlich steigen

spy Spion; ~ **ring** Spionagering, Spionageorganisation; ~ **satellite** Überwachungssatellit; ~ **trial** Spionageprozeß; **master** ~ Chefspion; **police** ~ Polizeispitzel

spy *v* Spionage treiben; **to** ~ **out** ausspionieren; **to** ~ **(up)on a p.** jdm nachspüren, jdn bespitzeln

squad (Arbeits-)Trupp; *mil* Gruppe, Abteilung; ~ **car** *Br* Funkstreife(nwagen); **flying** ~ Überfallkommando *(der Polizei)*; **fraud** ~ *(Br)* Sondereinheit gegen Wirtschaftsverbrechen; **homicide** ~ Mordkommission; **police** ~ Polizeiabteilung; **traffic control ~s** *Am* Verkehrspolizei

squander *v*, **to** ~ **one's fortune** sein Vermögen verschleudern (od. verschwenden)

square Quadrat; ~ **foot** (ft^2) Quadratfuß (929,03 cm^2); ~ **inch** (in^2) Quadratzoll (6,4516 cm^2); ~ **mile** (mi^2) Quadratmeile (259 ha); ~ **yard** (yd^2) Quadratyard (0,83613 m^2)

square *v (Börse)* glattstellen; **to** ~ **accounts with sb.** *(auch fig)* mit jdm abrechnen; **to** ~ **sth. with** etw. in Übereinstimmung bringen mit

squat *v*[101] sich ohne Rechtstitel ansiedeln; unberechtigt ein Haus (od. e-e Wohnung, ein Stück Land) besetzen

squatting[101] Ansiedlung ohne Rechtstitel; rechtswidrige Besetzung von Grundbesitz *(um dort mietzins- und steuerfrei zu wohnen)*

squatter[101] Ansiedler ohne Rechtstitel; (illegaler) Hausbesetzer

squeeze Druck; (Geld-)Knappheit, Klemme; *(Warenterminmarkt)* Warenknappheit durch nicht abgedeckte Leerverkäufe; ~ **out** Verkauf von Aktiva der Gesellschaft an Mehrheitsaktionäre zu unangemessen niedrigeren Preisen; **bear** ~ *(Börse)* Zwang zu Deckungskäufen; **credit** ~ Kreditrestriktion (→*credit 1.*); **to have a close** (or **narrow**) ~ mit knapper Not davonkommen

squeeze *v*, **to** ~ **sb.** jdn unter Druck setzen; **to** ~ **the bears** zu Deckungskäufen zwingen; **to** ~ **money out of a p.** aus jdm Geld herauspressen

Sri Lanka, Republic of ~ Republik Sri Lanka; **(of)** ~ srilankisch

Sri Lankan Srilanker, ~in; srilankisch

stab *v (mit Dolch od. Messer)* (er)stechen, stoßen

Stabex *(EG)* →stabilization of export earnings

stability Stabilität; Beständigkeit; ~ **of exchange rates** Wechselkursstabilität; ~ **of the law** Rechtssicherheit; ~ **of prices** Preisstabilität, Festigkeit der Preise; Kursstabilität; ~ **of price levels** stabiles Preisniveau; ~ **of value** Wertbeständigkeit; ~ **ratio** *Am (Kapitalmarkt)* Index der Gewinn-(Dividenden-)Stabilität; **currency** (or **monetary**) ~ Währungsstabilität

stabilization Stabilisierung; ~ **fund** Währungsausgleichsfonds *(Br →Exchange Equalization Account)*; ~ **of (the) currency** Währungsstabilisierung; ~ **of export earnings** (Stabex) *(EG)* Stabilisierung der Ausfuhrerlöse (Stabex); ~ **of prices** Preisstabilisierung; Kursstabilisierung; →**quality** ~

stabilize *v* stabilisieren, festigen; **to** ~ **prices** Preise (od. Kurse) stabilisieren

stabilizer Stabilisator

stable fest, beständig, gleichbleibend; stabil; ~ **currency** stabile Währung; ~ **income** festes Einkommen; ~ **job** feste Stellung; **of** ~ **value** wertbeständig; **to keep** ~ stabil (od. unveränderlich) halten *(z.B. Löhne)*

stack Stapel, Haufen; *colloq.* große Menge; Bücherregal

stack *v (Container)* stapeln

staff 1. Mitarbeiter(stab); *(im Büro arbeitendes)* Personal, Angestellte; Belegschaft; Stab(skräfte) (→*staff 2.*); ~ **appraisal** Personalbeurteilung; ~ **bonus** Extrazahlung, Gratifikation; ~ **changes** Personalveränderungen; ~**-college** *mil* Kriegsakademie; ~ **costs** Personalaufwand; ~ **cuts** →~ reduction; ~ **manager** Personalchef; ~ **member** Mitglied des Personals *(z.B. e-r internationalen Organisation)*; ~ **movements** Einstellungen, Ernennungen und Kündigungen von Personal; ~ **of a diplomatic mission** Personal e-r diplomatischen Vertretung; ~ **officer** *mil* Stabsoffizier; ~ **planning** Stellenplan; ~ **provident fund** *Br* Angestelltenunterstützungskasse; ~ **reduction** Personalabbau, Verringerung des Personalbestandes; ~ **regulations** Dienstordnung; Personalstatut *(z.B. der UN)*; ~ **remuneration** (or **payment**) Besoldung des Personals; ~ **representative** Vertreter des Personals; *Am* Mitarbeiter, Vertreter *(e-r Behörde od. Firma)*; ~ **salaries** Gehälter des Personals; Angestelltengehälter; ~ **shares** *Br* an Angestellte und Arbeiter ausgegebene Aktien e-s Unternehmens; Belegschaftsaktien; ~ **shortage** Personalmangel; ~ **transfer** Versetzung von Personal; **addition to the** ~ Personalvermehrung; **administrative** ~ Verwaltungspersonal; **appointment and dismissal of** ~ Anstellung und Entlassung von Personal; **change in the** ~ Personalwechsel; **clerical** ~ Büropersonal; Schreibkräfte; **domestic** ~ (Haushalts-)Personal; **employment** (or **engaging**) **of** ~ Einstellung des Personals; Personaleinstellung; **field** ~ im Außendienst tätige Mitarbeiter; **local** ~ ortsansässiges Personal; **managerial** ~ Geschäftsleitung, Betriebsleitung; **member of the** ~ Mitarbeiter; **number of** ~ Personalbestand; **office** ~ Büropersonal; **outdoor** ~ im Außendienst tätiges Personal; **permanent** (or **regular**) ~ ständiges Personal, Stammpersonal *(opp. temporary* ~*)*; **service** ~ *(dienstl.)* Hauspersonal *(z.B. e-r diplomatischen Mission)*; **strength of the** ~ Personalbestand; **technical** ~ Fachpersonal; **temporary** ~ Aushilfspersonal; **to appoint** (or **employ, engage**) ~ Personal einstellen (od. anstellen); **to be on the** ~ **of** beschäftigt (od. Mitarbeiter) sein bei; zum Mitarbeiterstab (od. Personal) gehören; **to be short of** ~ an Personalmangel leiden; **to dismiss** ~ Personal entlassen; **to reduce (the)** ~ Personal abbauen, den Personalbestand verringern

staff 2. Stab, Stabskräfte *(e-s Unternehmens; opp. line,* →*line 4.)*; ~ **functions** mittelbare Aufgaben, Stabsaufgaben *(e-s Unternehmens, z.B. Personal-, Finanzwesen; opp. line duties)*; ~ **officer** leitender Angestellter e-s Unternehmens, der mit Stabsaufgaben betraut ist; ~ **organization** Stabsorganisation *(opp. line organization)*; ~ **position** Stabsstelle *(mit nur beratender Funktion, ohne Weisungsbefugnis)*

staff *v* mit Personal versehen (od. besetzen)

staffed, to be over~ (mit Personal) überbesetzt sein, zu viel Personal haben; **to be under**~ zu wenig Personal haben, Mangel an Personal haben; **to be well** ~ gut mit Personal versehen (od. besetzt) sein

staffing Versehung mit Personal; Personalplanung; ~**schedule** *Am* Stellen(besetzungs)plan

staffer Mitarbeiter

stag *Br (Börse)* Spekulant, der Aktien bei e-r Neuemission zum festen Preis zeichnet mit der Absicht, sie schnell mit Gewinn wieder zu verkaufen; Konzertzeichner

stag *v Br (bei Neuemissionen)* Aktien zum festen Preis zeichnen mit der Absicht, sie sehr schnell mit Gewinn wieder zu verkaufen

stagging *Br* Konzertzeichnung

stage 1. Stadium, Stufe, Entwicklungsstufe, Phase; Abschnitt; Tranche *(e-r Anleihe)*; Teilstrecke *(für Berechnung von Gebühren für öffentliche Verkehrsmittel)*; ~ **of appeal** Instanzenweg; ~ **of negotiations** Stadium der Verhandlungen; ~ **of proceedings** Stadium des Verfahrens; ~ **of processing** Verarbeitungsstufe; ~ **of rocket** Raketenstufe; **committee** ~→committee 2.; **fare** ~ Teilstrecke, Tarifgrenze; **in the initial** ~ im Anfangsstadium; **report** ~ *Br* Stadium der Beratung e-r Gesetzesvorlage (→*report*); **to proceed by** ~**s** schrittweise vorgehen

stage 2. Bühne, Theater; ~ **right** Aufführungsrecht

stagflation Stagflation *(Stagnation und Inflation)*

stagger *v* staffeln

Staggered Board *Am* Staffelung der Amtszeiten von Vorstand und Aufsichtsrat *(zur Abwehr von Übernahmen)*

stagnancy →stagnation

stagnant stagnierend, still, flau; ~ **market** stagnierender Markt, Absatzstockung

stagnate *v* stagnieren, stocken, darniederliegen

stagnation Stagnation, Stillstand, Stockung; ~ **of business** Geschäftslosigkeit, Geschäftsflaute

stake Wetteinsatz; Preis *(z.B. bei e-m Pferderennen)*; Einlage *(in e-e Gesellschaft)*; Beteiligung; Kapitaleinlage; **S~ (of Zion)** *Am* größere territoriale Einheit der Mormonenkirche

stakeholder Verwahrer e-s Wetteinsatzes; treuhänderischer Verwahrer *(für mehrere Personen)*; Herausgabeschuldner *(gegenüber mehreren sich streitenden Gläubigern)*; ~**'s interpleader** → interpleader; **the solicitor holds the deposit as** ~ *Br (bei Grundstücksverkäufen)* der Anwalt verwahrt die Anzahlung auf den Kaufpreis *(meist 10%, →deposit 2.)* treuhänderisch

stake, to be at ~ auf dem Spiele stehen; **to have a** ~ **in** beteiligt sein an; **in a limited company no member is liable beyond his** ~ in e-r limited company *(→company)* haftet kein Gesellschafter über seine Einlage (od. Beteiligung) hinaus

stake *v* (Geld) setzen (on auf); **to** ~ **out** *(Land)* abstecken

stale veraltet; nicht mehr frisch *(von Lebensmitteln)*; ~ **bill** verfallener Wechsel; ~ **cheque (check)** abgelaufener *(nicht rechtzeitig zur Zahlung vorgelegter)* Scheck *(der 6 Monate alt oder älter ist)*; ~ **demand** durch Zeitablauf *(unterlassene Geltendmachung)* verwirkter Anspruch; verjährter Anspruch; ~ **market** lustlose Börse; ~ **money order** verjährte Postanweisung

stalemate *(Schach)* Patt; *fig* ausweglose Situation; ~ **in progress** Stillstand im Fortschritt

stalemate *v*, **to be** ~**d** auf e-m toten Punkt angelangt sein

stalinisation, de-~ *pol* Entstalinisierung

Stalinism Stalinismus

stall Verkaufsstand; Marktstand; *Am* Parkplatz für einen Wagen; ~ **keeper** Standinhaber; **news**~ Zeitungsstand

stall off *v*, **to** ~ **one's creditors** seine Gläubiger hinhalten

stallage *Br* Recht, e-n Stand zu errichten; Standgeld; Marktgeld

stamp 1. Marke; Briefmarke, Postwertzeichen; ~ **affixing machine** Frankiermaschine; ~ **collection** Briefmarkensammlung; ~ **collector** Briefmarkensammler; ~ **dealer** Briefmarkenhändler; ~ **(dispensing) machine** Briefmarkenautomat; **adhesive** ~ aufklebbare (Brief-) Marke; **airmail** ~ Luftpostmarke; **commemorative** ~ Gedenkmarke; **impressed** ~ eingedruckte Marke; **insurance** ~ Versicherungsmarke; **issue of new** ~**s** Ausgabe neuer Briefmarken; **jubilee** ~ Jubiläumsmarke; **postage** ~ Postwertzeichen, Briefmarke; **savings** ~ Sparmarke (→*saving 3.*); **trading** ~ Rabattmarke; **unused** ~ nicht benutzte Freimarke; **to affix a** ~ **to** (or **to put a** ~ **on**) e-e Marke kleben auf

stamp 2. Stempel; ~ **pad** Stempelkissen; **coining** ~ Prägestempel; **date** ~ Tagesstempel, Eingangsstempel; Poststempel; **facsimile** ~ Faksimilestempel, Stempel mit Faksimileunterschrift; **firm** ~ Firmenstempel; **received** ~ Eingangsstempel; **rubber** ~ Gummistempel; **signature** ~ Unterschriftsstempel; Namensstempel

stamp 3. *(behördl.)* Stempel, Stempelmarke *(zur Erhebung von Steuern od. Gebühren)*; **S~ Act** *Br* Stempelsteuergesetz

stamp duty Stempelsteuer *(Steuermarke auf Urkunden etc)*

Br Die stamps werden meist eingeprägt (impressed). Die stamp duties sind entweder Feststempel (fixed in amount) oder Wertstempel (ad valorem)

stamp duty, ~ **on bills of exchange**[102] Wechsel(stempel)steuer; ~ **on conveyances and transfers** *Br* Stempelsteuer auf Übertragungsurkunden; ~ **on stock exchange transfers** *Br* Börsenumsatzsteuer; **exempt from** ~ stempel(steuer)frei; **liable** (or **subject**) **to** ~ stempel(steuer)pflichtig; **to be subject to** ~ e-r Stempelsteuer unterliegen

stamp, ~ **on a deed** s. deed →~; ~ **on securities** *Am* Effektenstempel(steuer); ~ **paper** Stempelpapier, Stempelbogen; ~ **tax** *Am* Stempelsteuer, Stempelgebühr; **adhesive** ~ aufklebbare Steuermarke; **deed** ~ Urkundensteuerstempel, Steuerstempel auf Urkunden; **impressed** ~ eingedruckter Stempel, Prägestempel; **inland** *Br* (**internal** *Am*) **revenue** ~ Steuermarke *(für Stempelsteuern)*; Banderole

stamp *v* (ab)stempeln; *(Post)* frankieren, freimachen; *(mit Prägeschrift)* einprägen

stamped, ~ **addressed envelope** (s. a. e.) Freiumschlag; ~ **paper** Stempelpapier, Stempelbogen; **insufficiently** ~ ungenügend frankiert; **to get a deed** ~ für e-e Urkunde die Stempelsteuer bezahlen

stamping Abstempelung; Frankierung

stand Stand(platz); (Verkaufs-)Stand; Stillstand; Stellungnahme, Ansicht, Meinung; *Am* Zeugenstand; ~ **in** (or **at**) **an exhibition** Stand in e-r Ausstellung; ~ **at a fair** Stand bei e-r Messe; **firm** ~ feste Stellungnahme (od. Meinung); **market** ~ Marktstand; **newspaper** ~ Zeitungskiosk; **on the** ~ *Am* bei der Zeugenvernehmung; **to make a** ~ für etw. einstehen; Widerstand leisten; **to put a p. on the** ~ *Am* jdn als Zeugen vernehmen; **to take the** ~ *Am* den Zeugenstand betreten; als Zeuge aussagen; **to take a** ~ (on) e-n Standpunkt vertreten; *fig* e-e Stellung einnehmen

stand *v* stehen; **to** ~ **adjourned** sich vertagen; **to** ~ **as it is** so (stehen)bleiben; **to** ~ **bail for a p.** für jdn Sicherheit leisten (od. Kaution stellen); **to** ~ **as a candidate** sich als (Wahl-)Kandidat aufstellen lassen, kandidieren; **to** ~ **convicted** überführt werden; **to** ~ **one's ground** sich behaupten; **to** ~ **guarantee for sb.** haften (od. einstehen, bürgen) für jdn; **he** ~**s first on the list** er steht als erster auf der Liste; **to** ~ **the loss** den Schaden tragen; **to** ~ **as a mayor** → mayor; **to** ~ **proxy for** → proxy; **to** ~ **on one's right** sich auf sein Recht berufen, auf s-m Recht bestehen; **to** ~ **surety** (or **security**) **for** Bürgschaft (od. Sicherheit) leisten für; **to** ~ **by the terms of a contract** sich an die Vertragsbedingungen halten; **to** ~ **trial** sich vor Gericht *(wegen e-r Straftat)* zu verantworten haben; **to adopt as it** ~**s** es unverändert annehmen; **the charge cannot** ~ die Anklage kann nicht aufrechterhalten werden; **the evidence will** ~ der Beweis wird anerkannt; **as matters** ~ wie die Dinge liegen

stand by *v*, **to** ~ **sb.** jdm beistehen; in Bereitschaft sein für jdn; *mil* bereitstehen, sich bereithalten; widerspruchslos zusehen

stand down *v (von e-m Kandidaten)* sich zurückziehen; den Zeugenstand verlassen

stand for *v* stehen für, bedeuten; eintreten für; *Br parl* als Kandidat auftreten für, kandidieren für; **to** ~ **a** →**constituency**

stand in *v* jdn *(in dessen Abwesenheit)* vertreten (od. ersetzen)

stand over *v* aufgeschoben (od. zurückgestellt) sein

stand up *v*, **to** ~ **for sb.** für jdn eintreten, für jdn Partei nehmen

standard 1. Norm, Regel, Richtlinie, Maßstab; Durchschnitt; Niveau; Leistungsniveau; (Mindest-)Anforderungen; Normal-, Einheits-, Durchschnitts-, Muster-, Standard-; Standard, Qualitätsmuster *(als Durchschnitt e-r bestimmten Qualität, z. B. im Baumwollhandel)*; Standard, Holzmaß *(für gesägte Ware)*; Standarte, Fahne; Währung (→*standard 3.)*; maßgeblich, führend; ~ **agreement** *Am* Mustertarifvertrag (→ *agreement 2.)*; **S~ and Poor's 500 Stocks Index** *Am* Aktienindex, der e-n Kursdurchschnitt von 500 Aktien darstellt; ~ **business conditions** allgemeine Geschäftsbedingungen; ~ **clause** standardisierte Formulierung; ~ **conditions** →condition 2.; ~ **contract terms** Standardvertragsbedingungen; ~ **cost** Standardkosten, Plankosten; ~ **deduction** *Am*[103] *(Einkommensteuer)* Pauschalabzug *(Pauschale für Sonderausgaben)*; ~ **deviation** *(Statistik)* Standardabweichung; ~ **earnings** *Br* Tarifverdienst; ~ **fire policy** Einheitsfeuerversicherungspolice

standard form Standardformular, Einheitsformular; ~ **contract** Einheitsvertrag; ~ **contract conditions** allgemeine Geschäftsbedingungen; **the policy is usually in a** ~ *(VersR)* die Police ist gewöhnlich einheitlich formuliert *(die Bedingungen können nicht – oder nur in beschränktem Umfange – abgeändert werden)*

standard, ~ **gauge** Normalspurweite; ~ **grade** Einheitssorte, Einheitsqualität; **S~ ICC Arbitration Clause** →arbitration 1.; ~**s in industry** Industrienormen; ~ **interest** üblicher Zinsfuß; **S~ International Trade Classification** (SITC) *(vom Wirtschafts- und Sozialrat der Vereinten Nationen ausgearbeitetes)* Internationales Warenverzeichnis für den Außenhandel; ~ **make** Normalausführung; ~ **measure** Normalmaß; Eichmaß; **general** ~ **of education** allgemeines Bildungsniveau; Allgemeinbildung; **highest** ~ **of efficiency** Höchstmaß an Leistung(sfähigkeit); **high** ~ **of ethics** hohes sittliches Niveau *(z. B. in der Werbung)*; ~ **of an examination** Anforderung bei e-r Prüfung; ~ **of invention** *(PatR)* Erfindungshöhe; ~**(s) of living** Lebensstandard (→*living*); ~**s of safety** Sicherheitsnormen; ~ **policy** Normalpolice, Einheitspolice; *Am (Feuerversicherung)* Einheitspolice *(meist mit gesetzl. festgelegtem Inhalt)*; ~ **practice** übliches Verfahren; ~ **provisions** allgemeine Versicherungsbedingungen

standard rate Einheitssatz, Normalsatz; *Br* Einheitssteuersatz *(Grundlage der Berechnung der Einkommensteuer. Er wird für jedes Steuerjahr durch das Finanzgesetz [Finance Act] neu festgesetzt)*; ~**s** *Br* Tariflohnsätze; ~**s of a benefit** Normalsätze für Renten, Krankengeld etc

standard, ~ **size** Normalgröße; ~ **stock(s)** *Am* Standardwerte, Spitzenwerte; ~ **terms of business** allgemeine Geschäftsbedingungen; ~ **time** Normalarbeitszeit, Standardzeit; ~ **trading conditions** *Br* Allgemeine Geschäftsbedingungen *(bes. der Spediteure)*; ~ **type contract** Einheitsvertrag; ~ **value** Normalwert, Einheitswert; ~ **wage** Tariflohn; ~ **weight** Normalgewicht, Eichgewicht; ~ **work** Standardwerk, maßgebliches Werk

standard, above ~ überdurchschnittlich; →**American National S~s Institute; below** ~ unter dem Durchschnitt; den Anforderungen nicht genügend; **British S~s Institution** (BSI) Britischer Normenverband *(e-e 1929 durch Royal Charter inkorporierte Vereinigung)*; **Bureau of S~s** *Am* Eichamt; **cotton** ~ Durchschnittsbaumwollqualität; **credit** ~**s** Kreditrichtlinien; **establishment** ~**s** anerkannte Normen; **by European** ~**s** nach europäischen Maßstäben; **general** ~**s** allgemeine Normen; **German Industrial S~** Deutsche Industrie-Norm (DIN); **health protection** ~**s** Normen für den Gesundheitsschutz; **international** ~**s** internationale Richtlinien; völkerrechtliche Verhaltensnormen; **National Bureau of S~s** (N.B.S.) *Am* Nationales Amt für Standardisierung *(staatl. oberste Eichbehörde und Normenausschuß)*; **product** ~**s** Warennormen; **professional** ~**s** berufsethische Grundsätze; **to be below** ~ den Anforderungen nicht entsprechen; dem Leistungsniveau nicht genügen; schlecht gearbeitet (od. hergestellt) sein (→ *poor workmanship)*; **to be up to** ~ den Anforderungen genügen; **to fix the** ~**s of weights and measures** Maße und Gewichte eichen; **to set** ~**s** Richtlinien aufstellen; Maßstäbe setzen; Normen festlegen

standard 2. Standard *(gesetzl. Feingehalt der Münzen)*; ~ **coin** Münze mit gesetzl. vorgeschriebenem Feingehalt; ~ **gold** Münzgold; ~ **mark** Feingehaltsstempel; ~ **money** vollwichtige Münze; ~ **of fineness** (gesetzl.) Feingehalt; ~ **silver** Münzsilber; ~ **weight (and fineness)** gesetzl. vorgeschriebenes Gewicht und Feingehalt *(von Münzen)*; ~ **weight coin** →~ coin

standard 3. Währung; ~ **money** Währungsgeld; **gold** ~ Goldwährung; **gold bullion** ~ Goldkernwährung; **gold exchange** ~ Golddevisenwährung; **gold specie** ~ Goldumlaufswährung; **metallic** ~ Metallwährung *(opp. paper ~)*; →**monetary** ~; **paper** ~ Papierwährung *(opp. metallic ~)*

standardization Standardisierung *(zur Schaffung e-r Norm)*; Vereinheitlichung, Normung; Typisierung; ~ **committee** Normenausschuß; ~ **of tariffs** Tarifvereinheitlichung; →**International S~ Organization** (ISO)

standardize *v* standardisieren, vereinheitlichen, normen, typisieren

standardized genormt; ~ **tenancy contract** Einheitsmietvertrag

standby Beistand; Bereitschaft; ~ **agreement of the underwriters** Garantie des Direktabsatzes von Wertpapieren durch Banken od. Makler *(die sich verpflichten, die nicht verkauften Wertpapiere e-r emittierenden Gesellschaft zu übernehmen)*; ~ **arrangement** Beistandsabkommen, Kreditvereinbarung zwischen IWF (International Monetary Fund) und Schuldnerland, die dieses verpflichtet, die in e-r Absichtserklärung (letter of intent) festgelegten Anpassungsmaßnahmen zur Verbesserung der Zahlungsbilanz einzuhalten; ~ **cost** Bereitschaftskosten; ~ **credit** Beistandskredit, Standby-Kredit *(an Mitgliedstaaten des Internationalen Währungsfonds zur Überbrückung von Zahlungsbilanzschwierigkeiten)*; ~ **letter of credit** *Am* Standby-Akkreditiv, Beistandsakkreditiv *(sehr häufig Garantieersatz; amerikanische Banken dürfen nur sehr beschränkt Garantie leisten)*; ~ **order** *mil* Bereitschaftsbefehl; ~ **ticket** *(verbilligter)* Flugschein ohne Platzreservierung für bestimmten Flug; ~ **time** Wartezeit; **to fly** ~ auf e-r Warteliste stehen *(um mit e-r Linienmaschine auf e-m freigebliebenen Platz zu fliegen)*

standing 1. Stellung, Ansehen; *(geschäftlicher etc)* Ruf; Kreditwürdigkeit; Dauer; ~ **to sue** *Am* Rechtsschutzinteresse, Klagebefugnis *(e-r Person, weil sie in ihren Rechten verletzt ist, bes. in verfassungsrechtlichen Streitigkeiten)*; **business** ~ Ansehen (od. Ruf) e-s Geschäfts; **credit** ~ Kreditstatus, Bonität; **financial** ~ Finanzlage, finanzielle Lage; **of high** ~ von hohem Ansehen; **of long** ~ seit langem bestehend; **a solicitor of 4 years'** ~ *Br* ein Solicitor mit 4jähriger Berufszeit; **to be of good** ~ angesehen sein; **to be of 10 years'**~ seit 10 Jahren bestehen; **the firm is of good** ~ die Firma hat e-n guten Ruf; **his** ~ **in the profession is not good** er ist in seinem Beruf nicht angesehen *(z.B. er ist kein angesehener Anwalt)*

standing 2. (be)ständig, dauernd, fest; stehend; *(Ernte)* auf dem Halm; ~ **army** stehendes Heer; ~**-by cases** *Am* Fälle widerspruchslosen Zusehens *(Unterlassen der Partei, wo sie vernünftigerweise hätte handeln sollen)*; ~ **charges** feste Unkosten; ~ **committee** ständiger Ausschuß; **S~ Committee for the Regulation of Contractual Relations** Ständiger Ausschuß für die Anpassung von Verträgen *(der Internationalen Handelskammer)*;~ **credit** laufender Kredit; ~ **crop** Ernte auf dem Halm; ~ **customer** fester Kunde, Stammkunde; ~ **data** *(EDV)* Stammdaten; ~ **order** Dauerauftrag; **S~ Orders** *parl* Geschäftsordnung *(Verfahrensregeln des Parlaments; Br opp. Sessional Orders)*; ~ **place** (or **room**) Stehplatz; ~ **rule** feststehende Regel; ~ **statement of fixed deductions** *Br (vom Arbeitgeber zu erstellende)* Aufstellung der festen (ständigen) Lohnabzüge

standpoint, to take a ~ e-n Standpunkt einnehmen

standstill Stillstand; ~ **agreement** Stillhalteabkommen; Moratorium; ~ **credit** Stillhaltekredit; **to be at a** ~ stocken; **the negotiations have come to a** ~ die Verhandlungen sind auf e-m toten Punkt angekommen (od. haben sich festgefahren)

stannary *Br* Zinngrube; Zinngrubengebiet

staple Haupthandelsartikel *(e-s Landes)*; Hauptgegenstand; Stapel-; (Baumwoll-, Woll- etc) Faser; **~s** Stapelwaren; ~ **commodities** Haupthandelsartikel *(e-s Landes)*; Stapelwaren; ~ **goods** Rohstoffe, Rohprodukte; ~ **industries** Hauptindustriezweige; ~ **places** Stapelplätze; ~ **products** →~ commodities

stapl|e *v (Papier etc)* (fest)klammern; *(mit Draht)* heften; **~ing machine** Heftmaschine

stapler (Baumwoll-)Sortierer; Heftmaschine

star, S~s and Stripes *Am* Sternenbanner *(Nationalflagge)*; **the S~-Spangled Banner** *Am* Sternenbanner *(Nationalhymne seit 1931)*

stare decisis ("to abide by former precedents") Grundsatz der bindenden Kraft der Präjudizien *(Gerichte sind durch Entscheidungen gewisser anderer Gerichte gebunden; cf. binding →precedent, overruling)*

START (Strategic Arms Reduction Talks) Gespräche über die Reduzierung strategischer Nuklearwaffen

start Start; günstige Ausgangsposition; **~-up** Existenzgründung; **~-up expenses** *Am* Gründungs- und Organisationskosten, Anlaufkosten; **~-up financing** Finanzierung der Gründung e-s Unternehmens; **to get a good ~ (on)** e-n Vorsprung bekommen (von)

start *v* anfangen (on mit); in Gang (od. Betrieb) setzen; abfahren, abgehen *(Zug)*; abfliegen *(Flugzeug)*, auslaufen *(Schiff)*; **to ~ the bidding** das erste Gebot machen (od. abgeben); **to ~ a business** ein Geschäft eröffnen; **to ~ a p. in business** jdm helfen, sich geschäftlich selbständig zu machen; jdn bei der Gründung e-s Geschäftes unterstützen; **to ~ a drive** e-e Aktion starten; **to ~ negotiations** Verhandlungen aufnehmen; **to ~ a rumour** ein Gerücht in Umlauf setzen; **to ~ on time** fahrplanmäßig abfahren

starting, ~ costs Anlaufkosten; ~ **credit** Anlaufkredit; ~ **date** Anfangsdatum; Einstellungsdatum; ~ **period** Anlaufzeit; ~ **point** Ausgangspunkt; ~ **price** Eröffnungspreis *(bei Auktionen)*; ~ **rate** Lohn bei der Einstellung; Anfangslohn; ~ **salary** Anfangsgehalt; ~ **station** Abgangsbahnhof; ~ **time** Anfangszeit *(opp. finishing time)*

starvation Verhungern; Hungertod; ~ **area** Hungergebiet

starve *v* Hunger leiden; verhungern (lassen)

state 1. Staat; *Am*[104] bes. Einzelstaat *(der USA)*, einzelstaatlich *(opp. federal)*; **the S~s** die (Vereinigten) Staaten (von Amerika); ~ **affairs** Staatsgeschäfte; ~ **aid** staatliche Unterstützung (od. Beihilfe); **~-aided** staatlich unterstützt; **S~ Annotations** *Am* Kommentare, aus denen hervorgeht, in welchem Umfange die Normen des → Restatement von den Einzelstaaten tatsächlich befolgt werden; ~ **attorney** *Am* Staatsanwalt e-s Einzelstaates; ~ **banks** *Am* →bank 1.; ~ **bonds** →bond 2.; ~ **boundary** Staatsgrenze; ~ **business** Staatsgeschäft; ~ **capital** *Am* Hauptstadt e-s Einzelstaates; ~ **capitalism** Staatskapitalismus; ~ **ceremony** feierlicher Staatsakt; ~ **chartered bank** *Am* einzelstaatlich zugelassene Bank; ~ **citizenship** *Am* Staatsangehörigkeit e-s Einzelstaates *(opp. federal citizenship)*; ~ **control** staatliche Kontrolle, Staatsaufsicht; **~-controlled** unter staatlicher Aufsicht; staatlich gelenkt; ~ **courts** *Am* →court 2.; **~craft** Staatskunst; ~ **criminal** *Am* politischer Verbrecher; jd, der e-s Verbrechens nach einzelstaatl. Recht überführt ist; **S~ Department** *Am* Außenministerium, Auswärtiges Amt; ~ **documents** amtliche Schriftstücke; **S~ Earnings-Related Pension Scheme** (SERPS) *Br* lohnbezogener Pensionsplan des Staates; ~ **enterprise** →~-owned enterprise; **S~'s → evidence; ~ expenditure** *Am* Ausgaben e-s Einzelstaates; ~ **funeral** *Br* Staatsbegräbnis; ~ **grant** staatlicher Zuschuß; **S~ house** *Am* Parlamentsgebäude *(e-s Einzelstaates)*; **S~ Immunity Act,** 1978 *Br* Gesetz über die Immunität der Staaten *(vor britischen Gerichten)*; ~ **indebtedness** Staatsverschuldung; **~→indemnity; ~ intervention** Eingreifen des Staates; ~ **lands** *Am* (bundes- od. einzel)staatlicher Grundbesitz *(der gemäß den general land laws von Privaten erworben werden kann)*; ~ **law** *Am* Recht der Einzelstaaten *(opp. federal law)*; ~ **legislature** *Am* Parlament e-s Einzelstaates

stateless staatenlos; ~ **person** Staatenloser; **expulsion of a ~ person**[105] Ausweisung e-s Staatenlosen; **naturalization of ~ persons**[106] Einbürgerung Staatenloser; **Convention Relating to the Status of S~ Persons**[107] Übereinkommen über die Rechtsstellung der Staatenlosen

statelessness Staatenlosigkeit; **Convention on the Reduction of S~**[108] Übereinkommen zur Verminderung der Staatenlosigkeit

state, ~ liability Staatshaftung; **~ line** *Am* Staatsgrenze *(zwischen zwei Einzelstaaten)*; **~ machinery** Staatsapparat; **~ member bank** *Am* Bank e-s Einzelstaates, die dem Federal Reserve System beigetreten ist; **~ monopoly** Staatsmonopol; **~ occasion** Staatsakt; **on ~ occasions** bei feierlichen öffentlichen Anlässen; **~ of residence** *(SteuerR)* Wohnsitzstaat; **~ of sites** *(IPR)* Belegenheitsstaat; **~ of source** *(SteuerR)* Quellenstaat; **~ of transit** Durchgangsstaat; **~ official** *Am* Staatsbeamter *(e-s Einzelstaates)*; **~-owned** staatseigen, in Staatseigentum (befindlich); **~-owned enterprise** Staatsunternehmen; staatliches Unternehmen; *(DDR-Terminologie)* volkseigener Betrieb (VEB) *(nach 1945 enteigneter und verstaatlichter Betrieb)*; **~-owned property** *(DDR-Terminologie)* Volkseigentum *(staatliches „sozialistisches" Eigentum; cf. ~-owned enterprise)*; **~ ownership** *Am* staatliches Eigentum, Staatseigentum *(als Recht)*; **~ papers** Staatsakten; **~ prison** *Am* einzelstaatliches Gefängnis; **~ property** *Am* Staatseigentum; **~ representative** *Am* Abgeordneter e-s Einzelstaates; **S~ rights** *Am* den Einzelstaaten vorbehaltene Rechte; **~ secret** Staatsgeheimnis; **~ securities** *Am* Wertpapiere der Einzelstaaten; **~ socialism** Staatssozialismus; **S~ Supreme Court** *Am* oberstes Gericht e-s Einzelstaates; **~ taxes** *Am* Steuern der Einzelstaaten; **~ trading countries** Staatshandelsländer; **~ trial** politischer Prozeß; **~ undertaking** staatliches Unternehmen; **~ welfare assistance** Sozialhilfe; **~'s witness** *Am* s. State's →evidence

state, act of ~ staatlicher Hoheitsakt; **Act of S~ doctrine** *(IPR)* Act of State-Lehre (→*act 2.*)

state, affairs of a ~ Staatsgeschäfte, öffentliche Angelegenheiten; **contracting ~** Vertragsstaat; **creditor ~** Gläubigerstaat; **federal ~** Bundesstaat; **foreign ~** ausländischer Staat; **Head of (the) S~** Staatsoberhaupt; **matters of ~** Staatsangelegenheiten; **member ~** Mitgliedstaat; **multi-nation ~** Nationalitätenstaat, Vielvölkerstaat; **receiving ~** Empfangsstaat; **Secretary of S~** → secretary 3.; **sending ~** Entsendestaat; **signatory ~** Signatarstaat

state 2. Zustand, Lage; Stand, (hoher) Rang; **~ly homes** *Br* Schlösser; **~ of an account** Kontostand; **~ of affairs** Stand der Dinge, Sachlage; *(ProzeßR)* Tatbestand, Sachverhalt; **~ of affairs of a company** Vermögens- und Finanzlage e-r Gesellschaft; **~ of (the) art** *(PatR)* →art 2.; **~ of business** Geschäftslage, Konjunktur; **~ of defence (~se)** Verteidigungszustand; **~ of emergency** *pol* Notstand; (staatlicher) Ausnahmezustand; **~ of health** Gesundheitszustand; **~ of the market** Marktlage; **~ of mind** Geisteszustand; **~ of need** Notlage; **~ of peace** Friedenszustand; **~ of→ repair**; **~ of the roads** Zustand der Straßen; **S~ of the Union Message** *Am* Ansprache zu Lage der Nation *(→message)*; **~ of war** Kriegszustand; **married ~** Ehestand; **mental ~** Geisteszustand

state *v* angeben, erklären, darlegen, feststellen; behaupten; berichten; aussagen; bestimmen, festsetzen; **to ~ the average** die Dispache aufmachen; **to ~ one's case** →case 1.; **to ~ a case for the determination of the High Court** *Br* → case 1.; **to ~ in detail** eingehend berichten; **to ~ expressly** ausdrücklich erklären; **to ~ facts** Tatsachen angeben (od. vorbringen); **to ~ one's grievance** Beschwerde führen; **to ~ the intention** die Absicht darlegen; **to ~ on oath** unter Eid erklären; **to ~ one's opinion** seine Meinung zum Ausdruck bringen; **to ~ full particulars** genaue Einzelheiten angeben; **to ~ a precise time** e-e genaue Zeit angeben

stated festgesetzt, festgelegt, bestimmt; **~ capital** *Am (in der Bilanz)* ausgewiesenes Grundkapital; **~ date** angegebenes Datum; **by ~ instal(l)ments** in festgesetzten Raten; **~ meeting** satzungsmäßige Sitzung *(des board of directors; opp. special meeting)*; **for a ~ term** für e-e ausdrücklich angegebene Zeit; **at the ~ time** zur festgesetzten Zeit; **as ~** wie angegeben; wie erwähnt; **it was ~ in the (news)paper** es stand in der Zeitung

stating the facts mit Angabe der Tatsachen

statement 1. Angabe, Erklärung, Darlegung; Verlautbarung; Ausführung *(e-s Redners)*, Referat; Feststellung; Aussage; **~ by prisoner** Gefangenenaussage; **~ by witness** Zeugenaussage; **~ in lieu of prospectus** *Br (erforderliche)* Aufstellung anstelle e-s Prospekts *(von der keinen Prospekt herausgebenden public company)* zur Zuteilung von Effekten; **~ (made) on oath** eidliche Erklärung

statement of affairs of a company *Br*[109] Vermögensaufstellung e-r →company im Abwicklungsverfahren *(→winding up)*

statement of (the) case Darlegung des Standpunktes; **written ~** Schriftsatz *(z. B. in e-m Schiedsverfahren)*; **to submit a ~** den Standpunkt darlegen

statement, ~ of claim *Br*[110] Klagebegründungsschrift (→*claim 1.*); **~ of contents** Inhaltsangabe

statement of defence *Br* Klagebeantwortung; **drawing up statements of claim and defence** *Br* Abfassung von Schriftsätzen zur Klagebegründung und Klagebeantwortung

statement, ~ of facts Sachverhalt; (Darstellung des) Tatbestand(es); **~ of opinion** Meinungsäußerung; **~ of particulars** nähere Angaben;

~ **of points** *Am* Feststellung der Streitpunkte *(durch die Parteien als Gegenstand der Verhandlung);* ~ **of principle** Grundsatzerklärung; ~**s of proof** *Br (Zivilprozeß)* Vorvernehmung von Zeugen durch den solicitor; ~ **of the prosecution** Vortrag der Anklagebehörde, Anklagerede; **S~s of Standard Accounting Practice** (SSAP) *Br (von den Berufsinstituten der Wirtschaftsprüfer erarbeitete)* Grundsätze der allgemeinen Rechnungslegung; **according to** (or **as per**) ~ laut Bericht; laut Angabe; **false** ~ unrichtige Angabe (od. Erklärung); Falschaussage; **sworn** ~ **in writing** schriftliche Erklärung unter Eid

statement, to bear out a ~ e-e Aussage bestätigen (od. bekräftigen); **to contradict a** ~ e-e Aussage für falsch erklären (od. widerrufen); **to make a** ~ e-e Erklärung abgeben; e-e Behauptung aufstellen; **to make a** ~ **(in court)** (vor Gericht) aussagen, e-e Aussage machen; **to make false** ~**s (in writing)** falsche (schriftl.) Angaben machen; **to make a** ~ **that one knows to be false or to make recklessly a** ~ **that is false** vorsätzlich oder fahrlässig falsche Angaben machen; **to retract a** ~ e-e Aussage widerrufen; **to take** ~**s** Aussagen abnehmen

statement 2. Bericht; Aufstellung; Liste, Verzeichnis; Übersicht; (Konto-)Auszug; Bankausweis; ~ **analysis** Bilanzanalyse

statement of account Rechnungsauszug; (Bank-)Kontoauszug; Rechnungsaufstellung, Abrechnung; **daily** ~ Tagesauszug; **to draw up** (or **make out**) **a** ~ e-n Rechnungsauszug machen

statement, ~ **of affairs** Finanzstatus; Übersicht (od. Bericht) über Vermögenslage *(e-r Person od. e-s Unternehmens)*; ~ **of affairs of the bankrupt** *Br*[111] Vermögenaufstellung des Konkursschuldners; Masseverzeichnis; ~ **of assets and liabilities** Aufstellung der Aktiven und Passiven; Bilanz; ~ **of average** Havarie, Dispache; ~ **of damage** Schadensaufstellung; ~ **of deposited securities** Depotauszug; ~ **of earned surplus** *Am* Teil der Gewinn- und Verlustrechnung, in dem die Veränderung des Gewinnvortrags dargestellt wird; ~ **of earnings** Gewinn- und Verlustrechnung; ~ **of expenses** Kostenaufstellung; ~ **of financial condition** Finanzstatus; ~ **of income** Ertragsrechnung; Teil der Gewinn- und Verlustrechnung, der zur Ermittlung des Periodengewinns dient; ~ **of income and surplus** *Am (AktienR)* jährl. Bericht nebst Bilanz und Gewinn- und Verlustrechnung; ~ **of operating results** *Am (Bilanz)* Ergebnisrechnung; ~ **of operations** *Am* Gewinn- und Verlustrechnung; Betriebsergebnisrechnung; ~ **of prices** Preisverzeichnis; ~ **of profit and loss** *Am* Gewinn- und Verlustrechnung *(enthält u. a. das →statement of income und das → statement of earned surplus)*; ~ **of retained earnings** *Am* →~ of earned surplus

statement, annual ~ Jahresabrechnung; **bank** ~ Kontoauszug e-r Bank; **cash** ~ Kassenabschluß; **corporate** ~ *Am* Bilanz *(e-r AG)*; **detailed** ~ detaillierte Aufstellung; **as per enclosed** ~ laut anliegendem Verzeichnis; **false** ~ falscher Bericht, falsche Behauptung; falsche Aufstellung

statement, financial ~ Finanzbericht; Rechnungsabschluß; **(annual) financial** ~ *Am* Jahresabschluß

statement, financing ~ *Am (beim → security interest) (e-e von den Parteien unterschriebene)* Finanzierungsanzeige *(Namen und Anschriften der Parteien und Angaben über die Art der sichernden Gegenstände)*

statement, interest ~ Zinsaufstellung; **monthly** ~ monatliche Aufstellung; monatliche Abrechnung; Monatsausweis *(e-r Bank)*; **weekly** ~ wöchentliche Aufstellung; wöchentliche Abrechnung; Wochenausweis *(e-r Notenbank)*; **to make a** ~ Bericht erstatten (on über)

statesman Staatsmann; Politiker; ~**like** staatsmännisch (klug); diplomatisch; ~**ship** Staatskunst, Politik

station 1. Stellung, Rang; ~ **in life** soziale (od. gesellschaftliche) Stellung; **maintenance suitable to a p.'s** ~ standesgemäßer Unterhalt

station 2. Bahnhof, Bahnstation; ~ **master** Bahnhofsvorsteher; ~ **of arrival** Ankunftsbahnhof; ~ **of departure** Abgangsbahnhof; ~ **of destination** Bestimmungsbahnhof; **central** (or **main**) ~ Hauptbahnhof; **forwarding** ~ Versandbahnhof; **goods-**~ *Br* Güterbahnhof; **railway-**~ *Br* (**railroad** ~ *Am*) Bahnhof; **terminal** ~ Endbahnhof, Sackbahnhof

station 3. Station, Posten, Stelle; Sender; *mil* Standort; *(Australien)* (Schafzucht-)Farm; ~ **hospital** *Am* Standortlazarett; ~ **house** *Am* s. police →~; **air** ~ Luftstützpunkt; **coastguard** ~ Küstenwachstation; **filling** ~ Tankstelle; **fire** ~ *Br* Feuerwache, Feuermeldestelle; **jamming** ~ Störsender; **naval** ~ Marinestation; **police** ~ Polizeiwache, Polizeirevier; **power** ~ Elektrizitätswerk, Kraftwerk; **radio** (or *Br* **wireless**) ~ Rundfunksender

station *v mil* stationieren

stationing *mil* Stationierung; **cost of** ~ **foreign troops** Stationierungskosten

stationary stillstehend; feststehend; stagnierend; gleichbleibend; stationär; ~ **population** stagnierende Bevölkerung; ~ **prices** gleichbleibende Preise; ~ **vehicle** stehendes Fahrzeug; **to be** ~ gleichbleiben, stagnieren

stationer Schreibwarenhändler; ~**'s (shop)** *bes. Br* Schreibwarengeschäft; **S~s' Company** *Br (Londoner)* Innung der Verleger, Buchhändler und Schreibwarenhändler; **S~s' Hall** *Br* Innungshaus der Verleger, Buchhändler und Schreibwarenhändler in London, wo ein Urheberrechtsregister (freiwillig) geführt wird

stationery Schreibwaren, Bürobedarf; ~ **clerk** Büromaterialverwalter; **(H. M.) S~ Office** (HMSO) *Br* staatliche Behörde für den Verkauf von Veröffentlichungen *(Gesetze, Verordnungen, →Hansard etc)* der Regierung, der Vereinten Nationen und anderer internationaler Organisationen sowie für den Verkauf von Schreibwaren

statistical statistisch; ~ **compilation** statistische Zusammenstellung; ~ **data** statistische Unterlagen; ~ **information** (or **material**) statistisches Material; statistische Unterlagen; ~ **reports** (or **returns**) statistische Berichte; Statistiken; ~ **statement** statistische Aufstellung; **Central S~ Office** *Br*[112] Zentrales Statistisches Amt; **International S~ Institute** (ISI) Internationales Statistisches Institut; **to make ~ inquiries** (or **to investigate ~ly**) statistische Erhebungen anstellen

statistician Statistiker

statistics[112] Statistik(en); ~ **of population** Bevölkerungsstatistik; **Central S~ Office** *Br* Statistisches Zentralamt; **criminal** ~ Kriminalstatistik; **demographic** (or **population**) ~ Bevölkerungsstatistik; **employment** ~ Statistik der Erwerbstätigkeit; **foreign trade** ~ Außenhandelsstatistik; **judicial** ~ Statistik im Rechtswesen; **official** ~ amtliche Statistik; **operational** (or **management**) ~ Betriebsstatistik; **sales** ~ Umsatzstatistik; **trade** ~ Handelsstatistik; **vital** ~ Personenstandstatistik; **to compile** ~ Statistiken (od. statistische Unterlagen) zusammenstellen (on über)

status Status; (soziale oder berufliche) Stellung; Rechtsstellung *(bes. bestimmter Personen, z. B. e-s Minderjährigen, e-r verheirateten Frau, e-s Geisteskranken, e-s Konkursschuldners)*; Finanzlage, Vermögenslage; geschäftl. Lage; ~ **inquiry** Bitte um Kreditauskunft; ~ **inquiry agency** Auskunftei; ~ **of aliens** Ausländereigenschaft; ~ **of diplomatic agents** besondere Stellung der Diplomaten; ~ **of legitimacy** ehelicher Status, Ehelichkeit; ~ **of refugees** Rechtsstellung der Flüchtlinge (→ *refugee)*; ~ **report** Kreditauskunft; ~ **symbol** Statussymbol; **civil** ~ Personenstand; →**equality of ~; →exterritorial ~; financial** ~ Finanzlage, Vermögenslage; Finanzstatus; **legal** ~ rechtliche Stellung, Rechtsposition; **marital** ~ Familienstand; **national** ~ Staatsangehörigkeit; → **personal ~; social** ~ sozialer Status; gesellschaftliche Stellung

status quo status quo, gegenwärtiger Zustand; **preservation of the** ~ Aufrechterhaltung des gegenwärtigen Zustandes; **to preserve the** ~ den gegenwärtigen Zustand aufrechterhalten

status quo ante status quo ante, vorheriger Zustand; **in statu quo ante bellum** in dem Zustand, in dem es sich vor dem Kriege befand

statutable →statutory

statute *(vom Parlament geschaffenes, kodifiziertes)* Gesetz *(opp. common law) (Am oft für →~ of limitations gebraucht)*; **~(s)** Statut(en), Satzung
Das statute law setzt weitgehend die Existenz des → Common Law voraus und ergänzt es oder ändert es ab. Soweit ein statute mit dem Common Law oder equity in Widerspruch steht, geht es diesen vor. Statutes sind in sections, diese in sub-sections unterteilt

Statues at Large (Stat.) *Am* amtliche Sammlung der Bundesgesetze; Bundesgesetzblatt

statute-barred verjährt; ~ **claim** verjährte Forderung; **to become** ~ verjähren; **personal injury claims are ~ after 3 years** Ansprüche wegen Körperverletzung verjähren nach 3 Jahren

statute, ~ **book** Gesetzbuch, Gesetzessammlung; ~ **law** Gesetzesrecht, kodifiziertes Recht *(vom Gesetzgeber geschaffenes Recht; opp Common Law)*; ~ **mile** Meile *(1,609 km)*; ~ **of descent** *Am* Gesetz bezügl. Intestaterbfolge in unbewegl. Vermögen *(jetzt in Vermögen jeder Art)*; ~ **of distribution** *Am* Gesetz bezügl. Intestaterbfolge in bewegl. Vermögen; **S~ of Frauds** →fraud

statute of limitation(s) Verjährungsgesetz, Verjährungsvorschrift(en); Verjährung(sfrist); **barred by the** ~ verjährt; **defence of** ~ Verjährungseinrede; **subject to the** ~ verjährbar; **suspension of the** ~ Hemmung der Verjährung; **waiver of the** ~ Verzicht auf Geltendmachung der *(bereits eingetretenen)* Verjährung *(z. B. durch Teilzahlung, wodurch die Verjährung unterbrochen wird)*; **to come** (or **fall**) **under the** ~ verjähren, der Verjährung unterliegen; **to plead the** ~ sich auf Verjährung berufen; die Einrede der Verjährung geltend machen; **to toll the** ~ *Am* die Verjährung hemmen; **the ~ starts to run again** *Am* die Verjährung beginnt wieder zu laufen; **the ~ is not a defense** *Am* die Klage ist nicht verjährt

statute, ~s of a political party Parteisatzung; **S~ of the Realm** *Br hist* Gesamtheit der Parlamentsgesetze; **~s of a university** Satzung e-r Universität; **S~ of Westminster** *Br* Westminster-Statut *(von 1931 zur Bestimmung der verfassungsrechtl. Stellung der Dominions)*; **~s personal** *(IPR)* Personalstatut; **~s real** *(IPR)* Realstatut; **the S~s Revised** *Br hist* amtliche Gesetzessammlung *(bis 1948)*; **according to the ~s** satzungsgemäß; **amending** ~ das statute law abändernde Gesetz *(cf. remedial →~)*; **Annual S~s** *Br* → annual; **circumvention of a** ~ Gesetzesumgehung; **collection of ~s** Gesetzessammlung; **consolidating** ~ Gesetz, das ein bisher verstreutes Gesetzesmaterial für ein bestimmtes Gebiet zusammenfaßt; **contrary to the** ~**s** satzungswidrig; **declaratory** ~ Ausführungsgesetz *(Gesetz, das den bisherigen Rechtszustand nicht ändern, sondern nur klarstellen will)*; **enabling** ~ Ermächtigungsgesetz *(Gesetz, das e-e bestehende Beschränkung beseitigt)*; **non-compliance with a** ~ Nichtbefolgung e-s Gesetzes; **penal** ~ Strafgesetz; **perpetual** ~ Gesetz, dessen Geltungsdauer nicht befristet ist *(opp. temporary* ~); **remedial** ~ das Common Law abändernde Gesetz *(cf. amending* →~*)*; **Revised S**~**s** Sammlung neugefaßter Gesetze; **university** ~**s** Universitätssatzung; **to come** (or **fall**) **under a** ~ unter ein Gesetz fallen; **to lay down the** ~**s** die Satzung niederlegen (od. festlegen)

statutory gesetzlich, Gesetz-; satzungsmäßig, statutenmäßig, statutarisch; ~ **agency** gesetzliche Vertretung; ~ **agent** gesetzlicher Vertreter; ~ **books** *Br* gesetzl. vorgeschriebene (Geschäfts-)Bücher *(z.B. register of members)*; ~ **claim** gesetzlicher *(auf e-m förmlichen Gesetz, nicht auf*→*Common Law beruhender)* Anspruch; ~ **company** *Br* ein durch besonderes Parlamentsgesetz gegründetes Versorgungsunternehmen (public utility company); ~ **damages** im Gesetz festgesetzter (od. vorgesehener) Schadensersatz

statutory declaration *Br* schriftliche eidesstattliche Versicherung (→*declaration 1.)*; **making a false** ~[113] Abgabe e-r falschen eidesstattlichen Erklärung

statutory, ~ **deductions** gesetzliche (Steuer-) Abzüge; ~ **dividend** satzungsmäßige Dividende; ~ **duty** gesetzliche Verpflichtung; **(~) factor's lien** (gesetzliches) Pfandrecht des Kommissionärs *(cf.* →*factor's lien)*; ~ **forced share** *Am* bestimmte feste Quote am Nachlaß; Pflichtteil; ~ **heir** *Am* gesetzlicher Erbe

statutory instruments *Br*[114] Verordnungen, Rechtsverordnungen; Ausführungsverordnungen

Section 1 des Statutory Instruments Act von 1946 bezeichnet als statutory instrument eine amtliche Anordnung, die nach parlamentarischer Ermächtigung als order, rule, regulation oder andere → subordinate legislation erlassen ist. Seit dem Statutory Instruments Act 1946 werden die statutory rules and orders statutory instruments genannt

statutory, ~ **interpretation** *Am* Auslegung von Gesetzen; ~ **law** →statute law; ~ → **liability;** ~ → **lien;** ~ **meeting** *Br (AktienR)* gesetzl. vorgeschriebene Gründungsversammlung; ~ **merger** *Am* Fusion; ~ **negligence** *Am* Verletzung der gesetzlich vorgeschriebenen besonderen Sorgfaltspflicht; ~ **obligation** gesetzliche Verpflichtung; ~ **office** *Am* Büro(adresse) *(e-r AG im Staate des Sitzes der corporation zur Erfüllung der gesetzl. Vorschrift, daß diese im Gründungsstaat anzugeben ist; Br* →*registered office)*; ~ **owner** *Br*[115] der trustee e-r Vermögensverfügung (→*settlement 3.)* od. e-e andere Person, die beim Fehlen e-s →tenant for life *(z.B. bei Minderjährigkeit)* die Rechte e-s tenant for life hat; ~ **period of limitation** gesetzliche Verjährungsfrist; ~ **(minimum) period of notice** *Br*[116] gesetzliche Kündigungsfrist; ~ **portion of the deceased's estate** *Am* gesetzlicher Erbteil; ~ **provisions** gesetzliche Vorschriften, Rechtsvorschriften; ~ **report** *Br (AktienR)* gesetzlich vorgeschriebener Gründungsbericht; ~ **right of succession** gesetzliches Erbrecht; ~ **tenant** *Br* unter Kündigungsschutz stehender Mieter (od. Pächter) *(umfaßt unter gewissen Umständen auch Angehörige des verstorbenen Mieters od. Pächters)*; ~ **trust** *Br* gesetzlich begründeter Trust (→ *trust 1.)*

stave off *v*, **to** ~ **bankruptcy** das Konkursverfahren abwenden

stay Aufenthalt; Aussetzung (od. Einstellung) *(e-s Verfahrens)*; ~ **abroad** Auslandsaufenthalt; ~ **in a port** Aufenthalt *(e-s Schiffes)* in e-m Hafen; ~ **of execution** *(einstweilige oder endgültige)* Einstellung der Zwangsvollstreckung; Gewährung von Vollstreckungsschutz *(durch gerichtliche Anordnung)*; ~ **of proceedings** Ruhen (od. Aussetzung, Einstellung) des Verfahrens *(durch Anordnung des Gerichts)*

stay *v* bleiben; sich (vorübergehend) aufhalten; *(Verfahren)* einstellen; *Am (e-r Partei)* die Vornahme e-r Prozeßhandlung verbieten; **to** ~ **execution** die Zwangsvollstreckung *(einstweilig oder endgültig)* einstellen; **to** ~ **proceedings** das Verfahren aussetzen (od. einstellen)

stead, to act in each other's ~ sich gegenseitig vertreten

steadiness Festigkeit, Stabilität *(der Kurse, Preise)*

steady *v* stabilisieren

steady (stdy) fest, beständig, stabil; ~ **demand** gleichbleibende Nachfrage; ~ **increase** ständige Zunahme; ~ **market** fester Markt; feste Börse; ~ **prices** feste (od. stabile) Preise; feste Kurse; **to remain** ~ sich halten, sich behaupten, fest bleiben *(Kurse, Preise)*

steal *v* stehlen, entwenden; **to** ~ **into** sich einschleichen in

stealing Stehlen; ~ **by finding** Fundunterschlagung; **cattle** ~ Viehdiebstahl; **child** ~ *(StrafR)* Kindesraub

steamer (str, sr, s.) Dampfer; **cargo** ~ Frachtschiff; **passenger** ~ Fahrgastschiff

steamship (s. s., S. S., s/s., ss.) Dampfer; ~ **line** Dampferlinie, Schiffahrtslinie

steel Stahl; **~s** *(Börse)* Stahlaktien, Montanaktien; **British S~ Corporation** (BSC) Dachgesellschaft der verstaatlichten britischen Stahlunternehmen; **~ group** *(Börse)* Stahlaktien, Montanaktien; **~ industry** (Eisen- und) Stahlindustrie; **~ mill** Stahl(walz)werk; **~ output** Stahlproduktion; **~-using industry** stahlverarbeitende Industrie; **~ vault** Stahlkammer; **~ works** Stahlwerk(e)

steerage Zwischendeck; **~ passenger** Zwischendeckpassagier, Passagier dritter Klasse

steering committee Lenkungsausschuß; **S~ C~ for Nuclear Energy**[116a] Direktionsausschuß für Kernenergie

stellionate *Scot (StrafR)* betrügerische Handlung

stem *v* hemmen, aufhalten, eindämmen

stencil Matrize

stencil *v* vervielfältigen

stenographer Stenograf(in)

stenographic(al) record stenografische Niederschrift

step 1. Schritt; Stufe; **~ by ~** schrittweise; stufenweise; **~-rate premium insurance** Lebensversicherung mit steigenden oder fallenden Prämien *(während der Laufzeit der Versicherung)*; **appropriate ~s** geeignete Maßnahmen (od. Schritte); **common ~s** gemeinsame Schritte; **introductory ~s** einleitende Schritte; **to take ~s** Maßnahmen ergreifen (against gegen)

step 2. Stief-; **~-child** Stiefkind; **~-daughter** Stieftochter; **~-father** Stiefvater; **~-mother** Stiefmutter; **~-parent** Stiefelternteil; **~-son** Stiefsohn

step-up Zunahme, Erhöhung; **~ in travel to Europe** Zunahme der Reisen nach Europa

step *v*, **to ~ up production** *colloq.* die Produktion erhöhen (od. steigern)

sterling *Br* Sterling; von richtigem Feingehalt; echt; **pound ~** (£ stg) Pfund Sterling; **~ balances** Sterlingguthaben; **~ certificate of deposit** *(seit 1968)* Sterling-Einlagenzertifikat; **~ invoice** in englischem Pfund zahlbare Rechnung; **~ silver** Sterlingsilber

stet ("let it stand") soll stehen bleiben

stevedore Stauer, Güterpacker; **~s** Schauerleute

steward (Haus- od. Grundstücks-)Verwalter; Haushalter, Küchenmeister *(e-s college, club etc)*; Steward *(e-s Schiffes, Flugzeugs)*; Festordner; **land ~** *Br* Gutsverwalter; → **Lord S~ of the Queen's Household; shop ~** Betriebsobmann; **union ~** *Am* s. shop →~

stewardess Stewardeß; Verwalterin

stewardship Verwalteramt; Stellung und Pflichten e-s →steward

stick-on label Aufklebezettel *(opp. tie-on label)*

stick-up *(bewaffneter)* Überfall

stick *v* befestigen; ankleben; anheften; **to ~ bills** Zettel ankleben; Plakate anschlagen; **to ~ down an envelope** e-n Briefumschlag zukleben; **to ~ to the text** sich genau an den Text halten; **to ~ up for a p.** *colloq.* für jdn Partei ergreifen; für jdn eintreten

sticker Aufklebezettel; *com* Ladenhüter, schwer verkäufliche Ware; **bill(-)~** Zettelankleber, Plakatankleber

stiffen *v* sich versteifen; *com* anziehen, fester werden *(Kurse, Preise)*; **~ing of the attitude** Versteifung der (politischen) Haltung

still Brennerei; **~(house)** Schnapsbrennerei

still, ~-birth Totgeburt *(opp. live birth)*; **~-born** totgeboren

stimulate *v* fördern, anregen; anreizen; beleben

stimulation of the economy Ankurbelung der Wirtschaft

stimulus Anreiz

stipend Besoldung, Gehalt *(bes. für →magistrates, Geistliche od. Lehrer)*

stipendiary bezahlt, besoldet; **~estates** *Am* als Belohnung für militärische und ähnliche Dienste gewährter Grundbesitz; **~→ magistrate**

stipulate *v* ausbedingen, *(vertragl.)* festsetzen, vereinbaren, abmachen; **to ~ for sth.** etw. ausbedingen, etw. zur Bedingung machen; **to ~ by contract** vertraglich festlegen (od. vereinbaren); **to ~ expressly** ausdrücklich vereinbaren; **to ~ a jurisdiction** e-n Gerichtsstand vereinbaren; **to ~ tacitly** stillschweigend vereinbaren; **to ~ (the) terms** Bedingungen festsetzen; **to ~ a time of** (or **for**) **delivery** e-e Lieferfrist festsetzen

stipulated, ~ by contract vertraglich vereinbart (od. festgelegt); **~ damages** *(für den Fall des Vertragsbruchs)* festgelegter Schadensersatz; Vertragsstrafe; **within the ~ period** innerhalb der vereinbarten Zeit; **within the period ~ by contract** innerhalb der vertraglich vereinbarten Frist; **~ premium** *(VersR)* Vertragsprämie; **~ quality** vereinbarte (od. ausbedungene) Qualität; **to deliver within the time ~** fristgerecht liefern; **the facts have been ~** *Am (Zivilprozeß)* ein bestimmter Sachverhalt wird durch Vereinbarung als unstreitig angesehen

stipulation Ausbedingung; *(vertragl.)* Festsetzung, Bestimmung; Vereinbarung, Abmachung; Parteiübereinkunft; Bedingung, Klausel; *Am* Vereinbarung unter den Prozeßanwälten *(cf. the facts have been →stipulated)*; ~ **as to time** Zeitbestimmung; ~ **in restraint of trade** Konkurrenzklausel; ~**s of a bill of lading** Bestimmungen e-s Konnossements; ~ **of a contract** Vertragsbestimmung; ~ **of the parties** Parteiabmachung; ~ **proceeding** *Am (AntitrustR)* Einigungsverfahren *(in dem sich die Parteien zur Aufgabe bestimmter Praktiken verpflichten)*; ~ **to the contrary** gegenteilige Bestimmung; **by** ~ einverständlich; **on the express** ~ mit der ausdrücklichen Bestimmung; **informal** ~ *Am (AntitrustR)* formlose Vereinbarung zwischen der → FTC und dem Betroffenen, daß e-e vorausgegangene Zuwiderhandlung nicht wiederholt werden darf *(noch formloseres Verfahren als → consent order)*; **supplementary ~s between the parties to the contract** ergänzende Vereinbarungen der Vertragsparteien

stipulator Vertragspartei, Kontrahent

stir *v*, **to ~ up** aufputschen, aufwiegeln (against gegen); **to ~ up disorder** (or **trouble)** *pol* Unruhe stiften

stirpes, succession per ~ Erbfolge nach Stämmen (od. Parentelen) *(opp. per capita)*

stitched broschiert

stock 1. *bes. Am* Aktie, Aktien *(e-r bestimmten Firma; cf. ~s)*; Wertpapier; Grundkapital *(e-r AG) (dessen Teilbeträge in die Bücher der betreffenden Gesellschaft auf den Namen des jeweiligen Eigentümers eingetragen werden)*; (Anteil am) Gesellschaftskapital; *Br* Anleiheschuld des Staates od. e-r Handelsgesellschaft *(Gesamtbetrag aller Anleihebeträge, die auf e-n bestimmten Betrag und auf den Namen lauten und im Schuldbuch des Staates od. e-r Gesellschaft eingetragen sind)*; ~**s** *bes. Am* Aktien *(verschiedener Gesellschaften)*; *Br*[117] Effekten, Wertpapiere, Schuldverschreibungen, Obligationen; *Br* Staatspapiere, Staatsanleihen *(Consols fallen unter ~s)*

Br die meisten Bestimmungen des Companies Act 1985[118] gelten sowohl für shares wie auch für stocks

stock, ~ account; *Br* Effektenkonto; ~ **acquisition** (or **deal)** *Am (bei Unternehmenskauf)* Kauf der Anteile der Zielgesellschaft *(opp. asset acquisition)*; ~**s and bonds** Effekten, Wertpapiere; ~ **arbitrage** *Br* Effektenarbitrage; ~ **assessment** *Am* →assessment

stockbroker Wertpapiermakler *(Am auf stocks und bonds spezialisiert)*

stockbroking Maklergeschäft, Effektengeschäft, Effektenhandel

stock certificate *Am (auf den Namen lautende)* Aktienurkunde *(über den gesamten Aktienbesitz e-s Gesellschafters)*; Globalaktie; *Br (auf den Namen lautende)* Bescheinigung über Besitz an Staatsanleihen (s. *government →~ stocks*)

Stock Clearing Corporation *Am* Tochtergesellschaft der New York Stock Exchange, die als Abrechnungsstelle fungiert

stock, ~ company (or **corporation)** *Am* Aktiengesellschaft; Kapitalgesellschaft; ~ **denomination** *Am* Aktienstückelung; ~ **department** *Br* Wertpapierabteilung *(e-r Bank)*; ~ **dividend** *Am* Dividende in Form von Gratisaktien

stock exchange Wertpapierbörse; ~ **account** Börsenbericht; **S~ E~ Automated Quotations System** →SEAQ system; ~ **broker** Börsenmakler; ~ **circles** Börsenkreise; ~ **commitment** Börsenengagement; **S~ E~ Council** *Br* Börsenaufsichtsbehörde; ~ **customer** Börsenbesucher; ~ **customs** Börsenusancen; ~ **dealings** Börsengeschäfte; ~ **holiday** *Br* Börsenfeiertag; ~ **hours** Börsenstunden; ~ **intelligence** *Br* Börsennachrichten; ~ **introduction** *Br* Einführung von Effekten an der (Londoner) Börse; ~ **list** *Br* Kurszettel, Kursblatt; ~ **loan** kurzfristiges Darlehen an Börsenmakler; ~ **money brokers** (SEMBs) Geldbroker für britische Staatspapiere; ~ **news** Börsennachrichten; **S~ E~ Official List** *Br* amtliches Kursblatt; ~ **operations** Börsengeschäfte; ~ **operator** Börsenspekulant; ~ **order** Börsenauftrag; ~ **parlance** Börsensprache; ~ **price** Börsenkurs

stock exchange quotation Börsenkurs; **list of ~s** *Br* Kurszettel, Kursblatt

stock exchange, ~ regulations Börsenordnung; ~ **seat** Börsensitz, Börsenmitgliedschaft; ~ **securities** Börsenwerte, an der Börse gehandelte Effekten; ~ **terminology** Börsensprache; ~ **tip** Börsentip; ~ **transactions** Börsengeschäfte, Börsenabschlüsse; **closing of the ~** Börsenschluß; **customs and usages of the ~** *Br* Börsenusancen; **listed on the ~** zum Börsenhandel zugelassen; börsengängig; **listing on the ~** Zulassung zum Börsenhandel; **member of the ~** Börsenmitglied; **provincial ~** *Br* Provinzbörse; **speculator on the ~** Börsenspekulant; **to be on the ~** Börsenmitglied sein; **to meet with losses on the ~** Verluste an der Börse erleiden

stockholder Aktieninhaber, Aktionär; Anteilseigner; *Br (auch)* Effekteninhaber, Besitzer von Wertpapieren; ~**'s derivative action** (or **suit)** *Am* Klage des Aktionärs an Stelle der Gesellschaft für sich und alle anderen Aktionäre *(Klage aus fremdem Recht)*; ~**'s equity** Eigenkapital; (Inbegriff der) Rechte des Aktionärs, die sich aus der Beteiligung an der Gesellschaft ergeben; Wert seiner Beteiligung am Reinvermögen der Gesellschaft; ~**s' ledger** *Am* Aktienbuch; ~**s' meeting** *Am* Hauptversammlung (→*meeting of ~s*); ~**s of record** *Am* die im Aktienbuch *(am Stichtag)* eingetragenen Aktionäre; ~**'s representative action** *Am* Klage des Aktionärs aus eigenem Recht für sich und alle Aktionäre *(z.B. wegen Vorenthaltung von*

Dividenden); ~'s **right** *Am* Bezugsrecht auf Aktien (→*right 2.)*; **common** ~ *Am* Stammaktionär; **preferred** ~ Vorzugsaktionär

stockholding *Am* Aktienbesitz; Aktienbeteiligung; **intercorporate** ~ *Am* Schachtelbeteiligung (→*intercorporate)*

stock, ~ **in treasury** eigene Aktien im Besitz der Gesellschaft; ~ **index futures** (SIF) *Am (Börse)* Terminkontrakte, die sich auf ein bestimmtes Aktienportefeuille beziehen; ~ **insurance companies** *Am* Versicherungsgesellschaften auf Aktien; ~ **issue** *Am* Aktienemission; ~ **jobber** *Br* Wertpapierhändler *(seit 1986 market maker genannt)*; ~→**jobbing**; ~ **ledger** *Am* Aktienbuch; ~ **list** *Am* (Aktien-)Kurszettel

stock market *Am* Aktienmarkt; Effektenbörse; ~ **boom** Aktienhausse; ~ **crash** Börsenkrach; ~ **crisis** Börsenkrise; ~ **prices** Börsenkurse; ~ **reports** *Am* Kursblatt *(der →listed securities)*; ~ **trader** *(Börse)* freier Wertpapierhändler; **official** ~ *(Börse)* Parkett

stock, ~ **note** *Am* durch Wertpapiere gesicherter Schuldschein; ~ **option** → option 1.; ~ **on option** *Br* Optionswerte; ~**owner** *Am* Aktienbesitzer; ~ **power** *Am* Vollmacht zum Verkauf von Aktien; ~ **price** *Am* Aktienkurs; ~ **purchase** *Am* Kauf von Aktien *(bei Firmenübernahme)*; ~**-purchase right** →option warrant; ~ **quotation** Aktiennotierung; ~ **receipt** *Am* vom Aktienverkäufer ausgestellte Quittung; ~ **redemption** *Am* Rückkauf der (eigenen) Aktien; ~ **register** *Am* Aktienbuch; *Br* Register für Kommunalpapiere; ~ **right** *Am* Bezugsrecht des Aktionärs zum Bezug junger Aktien; ~ **savings bank** *Am* → savings bank; ~ **scrip** *Am* Zwischenschein für den Bezug von Aktien; ~ **split** *Am* Aktiensplit, Aktienaufteilung (→*splitting*, →*split-up*, →*split-down)*; ~ **subscriber** *Am* Aktienzeichner; ~ **subscription** *Am* Zeichnung von Aktien; ~ **subscription right** Bezugsrecht des Aktionärs *(auf neu ausgegebene Aktien)*; ~ **takeover** *Am* Aktienübernahme; ~ **ticker** Börsentelegraf, Börsenfernschreiber; ~ **trading** *Am* Aktienhandel

stock transfer[119] Aktienübertragung; *Br*[120] Wertpapierübertragung; ~ **book** *Am* Buch für Aktienumschreibung(en); ~ **form** *Br* Formular zur Übertragung e-s Wertpapiers; ~ **tax** *Am* Börsenumsatzsteuer *(für Aktien)*

stock, ~ **valuation** *Am* Aktienbewertung; ~ **warrant** *Am* Aktienbezugsrechtsschein; *Br (auf den Inhaber lautendes)* Aktienzertifikat; ~ **watering** Kapitalverwässerung, Verwässerung des Aktienkapitals; ~ **yield** *Am* Aktienrendite

stock, assessable ~ *Am* nachschußpflichtige Aktien; **bank** ~ →bank 1.; **block of** ~**s** *Am* Aktienpaket; **bonus** ~ *Am* Gratisaktien (→ *bonus 1.)*; **capital** ~ *Am* Grundkapital *(e-r AG)* (→*capital 1.)*; **common** ~ *Am* (Summe der) Stammaktien *(ohne Vorrechte)*; **corporate** ~ *Am* Aktien; **corporate** ~**s** *Am* Kommunalobligationen (selten, z. B. der City of New York; sonst üblicher: municipal bonds); **corporation** ~**s** *Br* Schuldverschreibungen der städtischen Behörden, Kommunalobligationen; **curb** ~**s** *Am* Freiverkehrswerte; **dealer in** ~**s** *Am* Aktienhändler; **fall of** ~**(s)** *Am* Fallen der Aktien; **fancy** ~**s** *Am* unsichere Spekulationspapiere; **firm** ~ *Br* feste Werte *(opp. option ~)*; **foreign** ~**s** ausländische Aktien; ausländische Wertpapiere; **founders'** ~ *Am* Gründeraktien; **full-paid** ~ *Am* voll eingezahlte Aktien

stocks, government ~ *Br (festverzinsl.)* Staatspapiere, Staatsanleihen

Hierunter fallen z. B.: Consols, Annuities, Savings, Bonds, Treasury Stock, Guaranteed Stock, Funding Stock, Conversion Stock, Exchequer Stock. Die Papiere können durch das Post Office Savings Department gekauft oder verkauft werden

stock, guaranteed ~ *Am* Aktien mit Dividendengarantie; **income** ~ *Br* Wertpapiere mit hoher Rendite; **index of** ~**s** *Am* Aktienindex; **issued** ~ *Am* ausgegebene Aktien; **local authorities** ~**s** *Br* Kommunalpapiere; **mining** ~**(s)** Bergwerksaktien, Montanwerte; **motor** ~**(s)** Auto(mobil)aktien; **municipal** ~**s** *Br* s. corporation →~s; **new** ~**(s)** *Am* junge Aktien; **no par** ~ *Am* nennwertlose Aktien, Quotenaktien; **non-voting** ~ Aktien ohne Stimmrechte; **option** ~ *Br* Prämienwerte *(opp.* firm ~); **preferred** ~ Vorzugsaktien (→*preferred)*; **registered** ~**(s)** *Am* Namensaktien; *Br* Namenspapiere, auf den Namen lautende Aktien od. Obligationen; **return on** ~**s** Aktienrendite; **rise of** ~**(s)** *Am* Steigen der Aktien; **rubber** ~**(s)** Gummiaktien, Gummiwerte; **treasury** ~ *Am* eigene Aktien im Besitz der Gesellschaft (→*treasury)*; **voting** ~ Stimmrechtsaktien; **widely held** ~ *Am* Streubesitz; **to hold** ~**(s)** Aktien besitzen, Aktionär sein

stock 2. Vorrat, Bestand (of an); Warenbestand, Lagerbestand; (Waren-)Lager; ~**s** Vorräte, Bestände, Warenvorräte; ~ **account** Lagerkonto; Bestandskonto; ~ **accounting** (or **bookkeeping**) Lagerbuchhaltung, ~ **articles** stets vorrätige Artikel; ~ **book** Lagerbuch, Warenverzeichnis; Bestandsbuch; ~**building** Lagerauffüllung; Aufstockung der Bestände; ~ **clerk** Lagerverwalter; ~ **control** Lagerkontrolle, Bestandsüberwachung; ~**holder** Lagerhalter

stock in trade Waren und Vorräte *(Vorräte an Waren, Rohstoffen, Halb- od. Fertigfabrikaten)*; Warenbestände und Warenlager; Arbeitsmaterial

stock, ~**keeper** Lagerhalter; ~ **keeping** Lagerhaltung; ~ **list** Lagerliste, Bestandsliste; ~ **of bills of exchange** Wechselbestand; ~ **of goods** Warenlager; ~ **of money** *Am* gesamter Geldbestand *(e-s Landes)*; ~ **on commission** Kommissionslager; ~ **on hand** Lagerbestand; ~**-out costs** Fehlmengenkosten

stockpile *(übermäßig)* große Menge; Vorräte; Vorrat mit großen Reserven; Vorratslager *(von strategisch wichtigen Rohstoffen)*

stockpile *v (übermäßig)* große Vorräte anlegen; *(Rohstoffe)* horten

stockpiling Lagerbildung, Vorratsbildung *(Kauf und Lagerung)* von strategisch wichtigen Rohstoffen *(durch staatliche Stellen)*; Vorratswirtschaft; ~ **policy** Vorratspolitik *(Lagerhaltung von Reserven)*

stock, ~ **record** Lagerbuch; ~ **room** Lagerraum; ~ **sheet** Lagerliste, Bestandsliste

stocktaking Warenbestandsaufnahme, Inventur, Bevorratung; ~ **sale** Inventurausverkauf; **annual** ~ Jahresinventur

stock, ~ **turnover** Lagerumschlag; ~ **valuation** Bewertung des Lagerbestandes

stock, addition to ~**s** Erhöhung der Lagerbestände; **closing** ~ Schlußbestand *(opp. opening ~)*; **consignment** ~ Konsignationslager; **dead** ~ totes Inventar; unverkäufliche Waren; **exhaustion of** ~**s** Erschöpfung der Bestände; **foods** ~**s** Lebensmittelvorräte; **gold** ~ Goldbestand

stock, in ~ auf Lager; vorrätig; **goods in** ~ Warenbestand; Lagerbestand; **to be in** ~ vorrätig sein; **to lay** (or **take**) in ~ auf Lager nehmen, sich *(mit Waren)* eindecken

stock, low ~ geringer Vorrat; **old** ~ alte Warenbestände, Ladenhüter; **opening** ~ Anfangsbestand *(opp. closing ~)*; **out of** ~ nicht mehr vorrätig; ausverkauft; **reduction of** ~**s** Lagerabbau; **remainder of** ~ Restbestand; **replenishment of** ~**s** Lagerauffüllung; **reserve** ~ eiserner Bestand; **rolling** ~ Betriebsmittel; rollendes Material; **safety** ~ Sicherheitsbestand; **wag(g)on** ~ Wagenbestand; **world** ~ Weltvorrat

stock, to be out of ~ nicht mehr vorrätig sein; ausgegangen sein *(Ware)*; nicht mehr auf Lager sein; **to build up** ~**s** Lager auffüllen; Vorräte anlegen; **to clear the** ~ das Lager räumen; **to draw on a** ~ e-n Vorrat angreifen; **the** ~ **is exhausted** der Vorrat ist erschöpft; **to have in** ~ *(Ware)* führen; vorrätig (od. auf Lager) haben; **to have a** ~ **of** e-n Bestand (od. Vorrat) haben an; **to lay in a** ~ **of provisions** sich mit Lebensmitteln eindecken; **to take** ~ Bestand aufnehmen; Bestandsaufnahme machen (of von); Inventur machen; **to take** ~ **of the situation** die Lage überprüfen

stock 3. Vieh(bestand); ~ **breeder** Viehzüchter; ~ **breeding** Viehzucht; ~ **car** Viehwagen; ~ **farm** Zuchtfarm; ~ **farming** Viehzucht; ~ **market** Viehmarkt; ~ **raiser** *Am* Viehzüchter; ~ **raising** *Am* Viehzucht; ~**yard** Viehhof; **farm** ~ Viehbestand; **live** ~ lebendes Inventar; **to breed** (or *Am* **raise**) ~ Vieh züchten

stock *v (Ware)* auf Lager halten (od. nehmen); *(Ware)* führen, vorrätig haben; *(mit Waren)* versehen; **to** ~ **up on sth.** sich mit etw. eindecken

stocked auf Lager, vorrätig; ~ **goods** Warenbestände, Warenvorräte; **well** ~ gut versehen (with mit)

stockist Fachhändler mit größeren Auslieferungslagern

stolen goods (or **property**) Diebesgut; **innocent buying of** ~ gutgläubiger Erwerb gestohlenen Gutes; **handling** ~ *Br*[121] *(etwa)* Hehlerei

stone *Br* Gewichtseinheit *(= 14 pounds = 6,35 kg)*

stop Halt; Sperre, Sperrung; Einstellung; Haltestelle; ~**-go policy** Ankurbelung und Bremsen der Wirtschaftspolitik; ~ **list** schwarze Liste *(Br von Unternehmerverband über Händler, gegen die wegen Verstoßes gegen Preisabsprachen e-e Liefersperre verhängt worden ist)*[122]; ~**-loss order** Stop-Loss-Auftrag, limitierter kursgebundener Börsenauftrag *(Wertpapiere zu verkaufen oder zu kaufen, falls sie e-n bestimmten Kurs unterschreiten bzw. erreichen)*; ~**-loss reinsurance** Jahresüberschaden-Rückversicherung

stop order Stopp-Verfügung; 1. →stop loss order; 2. *Am* Verfügung *(der S. E. C. od. e-r einzelstaatl. Wertpapierstelle)* der Sperre e-r Effektenemission bis zur Vorlage e-s → registration statement; 3. *Br*[123] *(Chancery practice)* gerichtl. Verfügung, daß über bei Gericht hinterlegte Gelder od. Wertpapiere (funds in court) nicht ohne Kenntnis des Antragstellers durch Auszahlung od. auf andere Weise verfügt werden darf; 4. Anordnung der Schecksperre *(Anweisung des Kunden an e-e Bank, e-n von ihm unterzeichneten Scheck nicht zu honorieren)*; ~ **to buy** Kaufauftrag zur Sicherstellung e-s Kursgewinnes bei steigendem Kurs

stop, ~**over** *Am (Bahn)* Fahrtunterbrechung; *(Flugzeug)* Zwischenlandung; ~ **payment order** Anweisung *(an die Bank)* zur Zahlungssperre *(hinsichtl. e-s Schecks, Kontos etc)*; Schecksperre; ~ **press (news)** *Br (in e-r bes. Spalte gedruckte, nach Redaktionsschluß eingegangene)* letzte Nachrichten; ~ **price** Stoppreis; Stoppkurs, Kurslimit; ~ **sign** *(Verkehr)* Haltezeichen; **bus** ~ Omnibushaltestelle; **price** ~ Preisstopp; **wage** ~ Lohnstopp; **to put a** ~ (to) *(etw.)* zum Halten bringen; *(e-r Sache)* Einhalt gebieten; **to run without a** ~ durchgehend verkehren *(Zug)*

stop *v* anhalten, zum Stillstand bringen; beenden, aufhören; *(Zahlung, Verkehr etc)* einstellen; *(Scheck etc)* sperren; halten *(Zug)*; *(Maschine)* außer Betrieb setzen; **to** ~ **an account** *colloq.* ein Konto sperren; **to** ~ **bonds** Wertpapiere mit Sperre belegen; **to** ~ **business** den Betrieb einstellen; **to ~ over** Reise (od. Fahrt) unterbrechen; **to ~ payment(s)** Zahlung(en) einstellen; Auszahlung(en) sperren; **to ~ payment of a cheque** *(Am* **check)** e-n Scheck sperren lassen; **to ~ the period (of limitation) (from) running** die Verjährung hemmen; **to ~ the proceedings** das Verfahren einstellen; **to ~ selling** den Verkauf einstellen; **to ~ a p.'s wages** jds Lohn einbehalten; **to ~ working** die Arbeit niederlegen (od. einstellen); **failing to ~ after an accident** Fahrerflucht

stopped cheque (check) gesperrter Scheck

stopping, ~ distance Bremsweg *(e-s Autos)*; **~ place** *(Luftverkehr)* Zwischenlandestelle; **~ strip** Standstreifen

stoppage Anhalten; Stillstand; (Verkehrs- etc) Stockung; (Arbeits-, Betriebs-, Zahlungs-) Einstellung; Gehalts-, Lohneinbehaltung

stoppage in transitu, right of ~[124] Stoppungsrecht, Recht *(des unpaid seller of goods)* zum Anhalten unterwegs befindlicher Waren
Recht des Verkäufers, die auf dem Transport (in transitu) befindlichen verkauften Waren, sofern diese noch nicht in den Besitz des Käufers oder dessen Vertreters gelangt sind, vom Frachtführer zurückzuverlangen, wenn der Käufer zahlungsunfähig geworden ist (vgl. im deutschen Recht Art. 73 Abs. 2 und 3 EKG und § 44 KO sowie allgemein § 321 BGB)

stoppage, ~ of credit (or **lending)** Kreditsperre; **~ of payment(s)** Zahlungseinstellung; Auszahlungssperre; **~ of trade** Handelsembargo; **~ of traffic** Verkehrsstockung; **~ (on wages)** Einbehaltung von Löhnen

storable lagerfähig

storage Lagerung, Einlagerung *(bes. in e-m warehouse);* Lagerhaltung; Speicherung; Lagergeld, Lagergebühren; Lagerplatz; **~ agency bill** Vorratsstellenwechsel

storage charges (or **fees)** Lagergeld, Lagergebühren; **free of ~** lagergeldfrei

storage, ~ contract Lagervertrag; **~ facilities** Lagerungsmöglichkeiten; **~ of data** *(EDV)* Datenspeicherung; **~ place** Lagerplatz; **~ room** Lagerraum, Speicher *(für Waren)*

storage, cold ~ Lagerung im Kühlraum; **cold ~ vessel** Gefrierschiff; **files in ~** *Am* abgelegte Aktien; **final ~ of radioactive waste** Endlagerung von radioaktiven Abfällen; **public ~** *(EG)* öffentliche Lagerhaltung; **to keep in cold ~** im Kühlhaus lagern

store 1. Vorrat, Bestand (of an); Lager; *Br* Lagerhaus, Speicher; **~s** Vorräte; Bestände; Lagerbestände; Vorratslager; *(bes.* Schiffs-)Ausrüstung(sgegenstände); Warenhausaktien; **~ account** Lagerkonto; **~ accounting** (or **bookkeeping)** Lagerbuchführung; **~ book** Lagerbuch, Bestandsbuch; **~(-)house** Lagerhaus; Speicher; **~keeper** Lagerhalter, Lagerverwalter; **~man** *Am* →~keeper; **~ of arms** Waffenlager; **~ room** Vorratsraum

store, bill of ~s →bill 1.; **bonded ~** *Br* → bonded warehouse; **ex ~** ab Lager; **in ~** vorrätig, auf Lager; **marine ~s** Vorräte an Schiffsbedarf; alte Schiffsgegenstände; **military ~s** Vorräte an Kriegsmaterial; **naval ~s** (Kriegs-)Schiffsvorräte; **ship's ~s** Vorräte an Bord; Schiffsproviant; **ship ~s** Schiffsbedarfsmagazin; **to lay** (or **take) in a ~** e-n Vorrat anlegen (of von); **to put in ~** einlagern; **to take out of ~** auslagern

store 2. *bes. Am* Laden, Geschäft; **~(s)** *Br* s. department →~; **~ card** *Am* Reklamekärtchen *(zur Beschreibung der Ware)*; **~keeper** *Am* Ladeninhaber, Geschäftsinhaber; **~ rental** *Am* Ladenmiete; **~s shares** *Br* Warenhausaktien; **~ sign** *Am* →~ card; **~ window** *Am* Schaufenster; **branch ~** *Am* Zweiggeschäft; **chain ~** Filialgeschäft (→*chain)*; **department ~** Warenhaus, Kaufhaus; **specialty ~** *Am* Spezialgeschäft

store 3., **to set great (little) ~ by sth.** großen (geringen) Wert legen auf etw.

store *v* lagern, einlagern; auf Lager nehmen, aufbewahren; mit Vorräten versorgen; speichern; **to ~ a ship** ein Schiff verproviantieren; **to ~ sth. (up)** etw. einlagern (od. speichern)

stored, ~ data *(EDV)* gespeicherte Daten; **~ files** *Am* abgelegte Akten

storing (Ein-)Lagerung; Lagerhaltung; Aufbewahrung *(von Vorräten)*; Speicherung; Verproviantierung; **~ business** Lagergeschäft; **~ charges** (or **cost for ~)** Lagerkosten

Stort(h)ing Storting *(norwegisches Parlament)*

stow *v (Güter, Ladung)* stauen; **to ~ sth. (away)** etw. verstauen; **~ing** Stauen *(sachgemäßes Stapeln der Ladung)*

stowage Stauen, Stauung; Verstauung; Laderaum; Stauerlohn; **~ plan** Stauplan

stowaway blinder Passagier

stower Stauer *(jd., der Schiffe be- und entladet)*

straddle *(Effektenbörse)* Stellage(geschäft)

straddling, lane ~ Inanspruchnahme zweier Fahrbahnen; *(ordnungswidriger)* Fahrbahnwechsel

straight gerade; unmittelbar, direkt; ehrlich, reell; in Ordnung, ordentlich; *Am pol* linientreu *(z. B. a ~ Republican)*; **~ bankruptcy** *Am* Konkurs *(opp. reorganization)*; **~ bill of lading** auf den Namen ausgestelltes *(nicht übertragbares)* Konnossement; **~ bonds** festverzinsliche Anleihen *(opp. convertible bonds); ~* **credit** *Am* Dokumenten-Akkreditiv, das nur bei bestimmten Banken benutzbar ist *(opp. commercial*

letter of credit); ~**forward procedure** unkompliziertes Verfahren; ~ **life insurance** Todesfallversicherung; ~**-line (method of) depreciation** *(Einkommensteuer)* gleichbleibende (od. lineare) Abschreibung(smethode) *(cf. sum-of-the-years-digitdepreciation)*; ~**-line rate** linearer Abschreibungssatz; ~ **mortgage** *Am* gewöhnliche Darlehenshypothek *(ohne Tilgungsraten auf das Kapital; dieses wird am Ende der Laufzeit insgesamt fällig)*
straight ticket *Am* Stimmzettel e-s Wählers, der s-e Stimme den Kandidaten einer Partei gibt *(opp. split ticket)*; **to vote the** ~ *Am* die Kandidaten nur einer Partei wählen; bei der Abstimmung der Parteilinie folgen
straight time *Am* normale Arbeitszeit *(opp. piecework, overtime)*

strain Spannung, Anspannung, Beanspruchung; ~ **on credit** Kreditanspannung, Kreditbeanspruchung; ~ **on liquidity** Liquiditätsanspruch; **financial** ~ finanzielle Beanspruchung; **internal** ~**s** innerpolitische Spannungen; **political** ~**s** politische Spannungen; **social** ~**s** soziale Spannungen

strain *v* (an)spannen; **to** ~ **a point** zu weit gehen; **to** ~ **one's powers** s-e Befugnisse überschreiten; **to** ~ **relations** Beziehungen e-r Belastung aussetzen
strained, ~ **interpretation of a statute** überdehnte Auslegung e-s Gesetzes; ~ **relations** gespannte Beziehungen

strait 1., ~**s** Meerenge, Straße; **the S**~**s of Dover** die Straße von Dover
strait 2.; ~**s** schwierige Lage, Not; ~ **jacket** Zwangsjacke; **to be in financial** ~**s** in finanziellen Schwierigkeiten (od. in Geldnot) sein

strand *v auch fig* stranden (lassen)
stranded goods (or **property**) Strandgut
stranding (of a ship) Strandung

stranger Fremder; Neuling; Unbeteiligter; Dritter *(weder Partei noch →privy)*; **to spy** (or **see**) ~**s** *Br* die Räumung der Galerie des House of Commons beantragen

Strasbourg Agreement Concerning the International Patent Classification[124a] Straßburger Abkommen über die internationale Patent-Klassifikation

strata of the population Bevölkerungskreise, Bevölkerungsschichten *(→stratum)*

strategic, S~ **Air Command** (SAC) strategisches Luftwaffenkommando *(der NATO)*; **S**~ **Arms Limitation Talks** →SALT; **S**~ **Arms Reduction Talks** →START; ~ **balance** strategisches Gleichgewicht; **S**~ **Defense Initiative** →SDI; ~ **goods** kriegswichtige Güter; ~ **plan** Planspiel; ~ **planning** strategische Planung

strategy Strategie, Kriegskunst; →**forward** ~

stratification, social ~ soziale Schichtung

stratified sample geschichtete Stichprobe

stratum (Bevölkerungs-)Schicht; *(Statistik)* Erhebungsschicht; ~ **of buyers** Käuferschicht

straw, ~ **bail** *Am* wertlose (od. ungenügende) Kaution; ~ **bid** *Am colloq.* Scheingebot; ~ **bond** *colloq.* wertloser Verpflichtungsschein; ~ **man** (or **man of** ~) Strohmann, vorgeschobene Person; ~ **vote** *Am* Probeabstimmung

stray entlaufenes (od. verirrtes) (Haus-)Tier; verirrt; vereinzelt; ~ **customer** vereinzelter Kunde; **waifs and** ~**s** verwahrloste Kinder; **to impound** ~ **cattle** entwichene (od. verirrte) Tiere einsperren

stream, ~ **of refugees** Flüchtlingsstrom; ~ **of traffic** Verkehrsstrom; **in-**~ **investments** Investitionen in branchenverwandten Unternehmen; **off-**~ **investments** Investitionen in branchenfremden Unternehmen; **to bring on** ~ in Betrieb nehmen; **to come on** ~ in Betrieb gehen

streamline *v fig* modernisieren; rationalisieren; vereinfachen
streamlined procedure vereinfachtes Verfahren
streamlining Rationalisierung; ~ **the customs formalities** Vereinfachung der Zollformalitäten

street Straße; →**Wall S**~; ~ **accident** *Am* Verkehrsunfall; Autounfall; ~ **brawl** Straßenauflauf; ~ **broker** *Am* freier Makler; ~ **car** Straßenbahn(wagen); ~ **cleaning** Straßenreinigung; ~ **certificate** *Am* Aktienzertifikat mit e-m Blankoindossament des Inhabers *(das e-e formlose Übertragung ermöglicht)*; ~ **collection** Straßensammlung; ~ **lighting** Straßenbeleuchtung; ~ **loan** *Am* kurzfristiges Darlehen an Börsenmakler; ~ **market** Freiverkehr(smarkt); *Br* Nachbörse; ~ **number** Hausnummer; ~ **price** Freiverkehrskurs; *Br* Kurs an der Nachbörse; ~ **railway** *Am* Straßenbahnlinie; ~ **sale** Verkauf auf der Straße; ~ **trader** Straßenhändler; ~ **trading** Straßenhandel; ~ **vending** →~sale; ~**walking** Prostitution
street, in the ~ *Br (Börse) (Geschäft)* nach Börsenschluß (od. nachbörslich) erledigt; **man in** *(Am auch* **on***)* **the** ~ Durchschnittsbürger; **price in the** ~ Freiverkehrskurs
street, one-way ~ Einbahnstraße; **side** ~ Seitenstraße; **the** ~ **is closed** (or **barred**) die Straße ist gesperrt

strength Kraft, Stärke; Festigkeit; *bes. mil* (Personal-, Truppen-)Stärke, Bestand; ~ **of an argument** überzeugende Kraft e-s Arguments; ~ **of the establishment** *Br* Personalbestand *(im Civil Service)*; ~ **of the forces** Truppenstärke;

actual (or **effective**) ~ *mil* Iststärke, Istbestand; **competitive** ~ Wettbewerbsfähigkeit; **economic** ~ Wirtschaftskraft; **on the** ~ *Br mil* in der Stammrolle; **on the** ~ **of** auf Grund von, im Vertrauen auf; **staff** ~ Personalbestand; **prices show greater** ~ die Kurse haben sich gefestigt

strengthen *v* verstärken; festigen; stark (od. stärker) werden; *(Börse)* sich festigen; **to** ~ **the friendly relations** die freundschaftlichen Beziehungen enger gestalten

strengthening Verstärkung; *(auch Börse)* Festigung; ~ **of peace** Festigung des Friedens; ~ **of a regime** *pol* Festigung e-s Regimes

stress *fig* Gewicht, Nachdruck; Stress, Beanspruchung, Überlastung; ~ **of competition** Wettbewerbsdruck; **capacity for** ~ Belastbarkeit *(e-s Menschen)*; **times of political** ~ politische Krisenzeiten; **to lay** ~ **on** Nachdruck legen auf, betonen

stretch (Aus-)Dehnung; (Über-)Spannen; *fig* Überschreiten *(der Befugnisse, Macht etc)*; Strecke; Zeitspanne; *colloq.* Strafzeit; **~-out** *Am* vermehrte Arbeit ohne entsprechende Bezahlung; **at a** ~ ununterbrochen, ohne Unterbrechung; **to be near to full** ~ fast an der Belastungsgrenze stehen; **to do a** ~ *Br sl. (Häftling)* „sitzen"

stretch *v* (sich) (aus)dehnen; (über)spannen; *fig* überschreiten; sich erstrecken; **to** ~ **a point** etwas zu weit gehen; **to** ~ **a rule** e-e Vorschrift zu weit auslegen

strict streng, genau; ~ **censorship** strenge Zensur; **in** ~ **confidence** streng vertraulich; ~ **construction** enge Auslegung *(opp. liberal →construction)*; ~ **liability (in tort)** strenge (verschuldensunabhängige) Haftung; Gefährdungshaftung; ~ **liability for misrepresentation** verschuldensunabhängige Haftung für falsche Angaben; ~ **observance** genaue Befolgung; ~ **settlement** →settlement 3.

strictly, ~ **confidential** streng vertraulich; ~ **construed** eng ausgelegt; ~ **net** (Bezahlung) rein netto; ~ **speaking** genau genommen; **to adhere** ~ **to the terms of a contract** sich genau an die Vertragsbestimmungen halten

stride, to make great ~**s** *fig* große Fortschritte machen

strife, the country's economy was disrupted by industrial ~ die Wirtschaft des Landes wurde durch Unfrieden in der Industrie erschüttert

strike[125] Streik, Ausstand *(opp. lock- out)*; Stoß, Schlag; ~ **ballot** Urabstimmung; ~ **benefits** *(von der Gewerkschaft gezahlte)* Streikgelder; ~ **(benefit) fund** Streikfonds; **~bound** bestreikt, vom Streik betroffen; **~(-)breaker** Streikbrecher; ~ **committee** Streikausschuß; ~ **forces** *mil (NATO)* Eingriff- und Unterstützungsstreitkräfte; ~ **fund** Streikfonds, Streikkasse; **~-hit** bestreikt; ~ **leader** Streikführer; ~ **leadership** Streikleitung; ~ **money** →~ benefits; ~ **pay** Streikgelder; **~, riots and civil commotions** (S. R. C. C.) Streik, Aufruhr und innere Unruhen; ~ **vote** Abstimmung über e-n Streik; Urabstimmung; ~ **warning** Streikandrohung; ~ **without (giving) notice** Streik ohne Ankündigung

strike, ban on ~ Streikverbot; **danger of a** ~ Streikgefahr; **general** ~ Generalstreik; **illegal** ~ illegaler Streik, wilder Streik; **national** (or **nation-wide**) ~ landesweiter Streik; →**official** ~; **on** ~ streikend, ausständig; **primary** ~ unmittelbarer Streik *(zur Durchsetzung von Forderungen in dem Betrieb der streikenden Arbeitnehmer)*; **prohibition of** ~**s** Streikverbot; **protest** ~ Proteststreik; **quicky** ~ *Am* s. wildcat →~; **secondary** ~ mittelbarer Streik *(gegen e-n Unternehmer, der mit bestreiktem Betrieb in Geschäftsverbindung steht, z. B. dessen Materialien verwendet)*; **sit down** (or **sitin**) ~ Sitzstreik; **sympathy** ~ Sympathiestreik; **threat of a** ~ Streikdrohung; **token** ~ Warnstreik; →**unofficial** ~; **warning** ~ Warnstreik; **wave of** ~**s** Streikwelle; **wildcat** ~ wilder *(gewerkschaftl. nicht genehmigter)* Streik; **to be on** ~ streiken, ausständig sein; **to break a** ~ e-n Streik brechen; streikbrüchig werden; **to call a** ~ e-n Streik ausrufen; zu e-m Streik aufrufen; **to call off a** ~ e-n Streik abrufen; **to call out on** ~ zum Streik aufrufen; **to come out** (or **go**) **on** ~ in Streik treten, streiken; **a** ~ **has broken out** ein Streik ist ausgebrochen; **the** ~ **has been settled** der Streik ist beigelegt

strike *v* 1. streiken; **order to** ~ Streikbefehl; **right to** ~ Streikrecht

strike *v* 2. stoßen, schlagen, treffen; **to** ~ **an average** den Durchschnitt nehmen *(→average 2.)*; **to** ~ **a balance** die Bilanz ziehen; den Saldo ziehen, saldieren; *fig* e-n Ausgleich finden; *(Sachen)* gegeneinander abwägen; **to** ~ **a bargain** e-n Handel (od. ein Geschäft) abschließen; handelseinig werden; **to** ~ **coins** Münzen prägen (od. schlagen); **to** ~ **one's flag** seine Flagge streichen (od. niederholen); **to** ~ **a jury** *Am* →striking a jury; **to** ~ **oil** auf Erdöl stoßen

strike off *v*, **to** ~ **an item off the list** e-n Posten von der Liste streichen; **to** ~ **the register** im Register löschen; **to** ~ **the roll** *Br* →striking off the roll; **to** ~ **3%** 3% abziehen, e-n Abzug von 3% machen

strike out *v* ausstreichen, durchstreichen; **to** ~ **the action** die Klage aus dem Prozeßregister streichen; **to** ~ **a pleading** →striking out of pleadings; ~ **words not applicable** Nichtzutreffendes bitte streichen

striking, ~ **a balance** Bilanzziehung, Saldierung;

~ **a jury** *Am* Bildung e-r Geschworenenbank aus 12 Geschworenen *(nach Streichung [abwechselnd durch die Parteien] der übrigen auf der Liste stehenden Geschworenen)*; ~ **off a case** (*or* **cause**) *Am* Streichung e-s Prozesses im Prozeßregister; Abweisung e-s Prozesses *(ohne Sachentscheidung) (z. B. wegen Unzuständigkeit des Gerichts)*; ~ **off the roll** *Br* Streichung *(e-s solicitor)* von der Anwaltsliste *(cf. disbarring)*; ~ **out an action** *Br* Streichung e-r Klage im Prozeßregister; Abweisung des Prozesses *(ohne Sachentscheidung) (z. B. wegen Unzuständigkeit des Gerichts, wegen Verfahrensmißbrauchs oder Prozeßverschleppung)*; ~ **out of pleadings** (or **part thereof**) *Br*[126] Streichung e-r Klagebegründung oder -beantwortung (ganz oder zum Teil) als unzulässig *(es wird so entschieden, als wenn das Gestrichene überhaupt nicht geschrieben worden wäre)*; ~ **out proceedings** *Br* →~ out an action; ~ **power** *mil* Schlagkraft

striker Streikender, Ausständiger

stringency Strenge, Schärfe; zwingende Kraft *(z. B. e-s Arguments)*; (Geld- *etc*) Knappheit; ~ **on the money market** Verknappung am Geldmarkt; **credit** ~ Kreditknappheit; **(foreign) exchange** ~ Devisenknappheit

stringent *(von Regeln, Vereinbarungen)* streng; *(von Argumenten)* überzeugend, zwingend; *(Geldmarkt)* knapp, angespannt; ~ **form** strenge Form

strings, (with) no ~ **attached** (or **without** ~) ohne (zusätzliche einschränkende) Bedingungen

stripped bonds Anleihen, bei denen die Zinsscheine von der Schuldurkunde getrennt werden

stripping, →**asset** ~

stroke of the pen Federstrich

strong stark, kräftig *(opp. weak)*; triftig *(Grund)*; überzeugend, zwingend *(Argument)*; dringend *(Verdacht)*; fest *(Börse, Kurse)*; ~**-arm clause** *Am*[126a] Recht des Konkursverwalters, im Konkurs des Schuldners bestimmte nicht abgeschlossene Rechtsübertragungen des Schuldners für unwirksam zu erklären; ~ **box** Tresorfach; Safe; Stahlkassette; ~ **currency** starke Währung; ~ **currency country** Starkwährungsland; ~**hold** *fig* Bollwerk, Hochburg *(z. B. ~hold of Protestantism)*; ~ **market** feste Börse; ~ **measures** drastische Maßnahmen; ~**-room** (Bank-)Tresor, Stahlkammer

struck, ~ **factory** *Am* bestreikte Fabrik; ~ **jury** *Am* e-e aus 12 Geschworenen bestehende, in e-m bes. Verfahren gebildete Geschworenenbank *(cf. striking a jury)*

struck out, order that an action be ~ *Br* →striking out an action; **order that pleadings (or part thereof) be** ~ *Br* →striking out of pleadings

structural strukturell, Struktur-; Bau-, baulich

structural adjustment strukturelle Anpassung; ~ **facility** (SAF) Strukturanpassungsfazilität (SAF) *(des IWF/IMF)*
Im Jahre 1980 eingeführter längerfristiger Kredit der Weltbank. Voraussetzung ist ein Anpassungsprogramm

structural adjustment facility, enhanced ~ (ESAF) erweiterte Strukturanpassungsfazilität *(→enhanced)*

structural alterations (to a building) Umbau; **to carry out** ~ umbauen

structural, ~ **change** Änderung der Struktur, strukturelle Veränderung; Strukturwandel

structural crisis, to suffer from a ~ unter e-r Strukturkrise leiden

structural, ~ **defect** Baufehler; Konstruktionsfehler; ~ **disparities** strukturelle Unterschiede; ~ **engineering** Bautechnik; ~ **fund** *(EG)* Strukturfonds; ~ **improvement** Strukturverbesserung; ~ **shift** Strukturanpassungsdruck; ~ **unemployment** strukturelle Arbeitslosigkeit

structurally backward strukturell rückständig

structure Struktur, Gefüge; Aufbau; Bau; *(großes)* Gebäude; ~ **of a house** Bauart e-s Hauses; ~ **of an organization** Aufbau e-r Organisation; ~ **of society** Gesellschaftsstruktur; **agricultural** ~ Agrarstruktur; **economic** ~ Wirtschaftsstruktur; **market** ~ Marktstruktur *(→market)*; **population** ~ Bevölkerungsaufbau; **price** ~ Preisgefüge

struggle Kampf; ~ **for power** Machtkampf; **class** ~ Klassenkampf; **domestic** ~**s** innenpolitische Kämpfe; **to conduct a** ~ e-n Kampf austragen

stub Kontrollabschnitt; Coupon

student Student(in); Schüler(in); Kursteilnehmer; Gelehrter; ~ **employee**[127] Gastarbeitnehmer; ~ **exchange** Studentenaustausch; ~**s' hostel** Studentenheim; ~ **of law** s. law-→~; ~ **unrest** Studentenunruhen; **elementary** ~ *Am* Grundschüler; **exchange** ~ Austauschstudent; **fellow** ~ Kommilitone; **law** ~ Student der Rechte, Jurastudent; **to be a** ~ **(of)** studieren

stud|y Studium; Studie; wissenschaftliche Arbeit; Untersuchung; ~ **committee** Studienkommission; ~ **group** Studiengruppe; Arbeitsgemeinschaft; **comparative** ~ Vergleichsuntersuchung; **to pursue one's** ~**ies** Studien betreiben

study *v* studieren; **to** ~ **for the bar** (or **to** ~ **law**) Jura (od. Rechtswissenschaften) studieren

stuff gown *Br* Wolltalar *(des junior counsel; →counsel 2.)*; der junior counsel *(cf. silk gown)*

stuffer *Am* Reklamebeilage

stumer *Br sl.* gefälschter (od. ungedeckter) Scheck; gefälschte Münze (od. Banknote)

stump *Am* öffentl. (bes. politische) Rede, Wahlrede; ~ **orator** Wahlredner; ~ **speech** *Am* Wahlrede, parteipolitische Rede; **on the** ~ *Am pol* auf Wahlreise; **to go on the** ~ *Am* öffentliche (bes. politische) Reden halten

stump *v Am colloq.* Wahlreden halten; **to** ~ **the country** *Am* als Wahlredner umherfahren; im ganzen Lande Wahlreden halten

stumper *Am colloq.* Wahlredner

stunt *colloq.* (Reklame-)Trick

style 1. Stil, Ausdrucksweise; (Bau-, Kunst-) Stil; Mode; **business** (or **commercial**) ~ Geschäftsstil; **concise** ~ knapper Stil; **the latest** ~ die neueste Mode; **to be in** ~ in Mode sein

style 2. Bezeichnung, Name; Titel, Anrede; ~ **(of a firm)** *Br* Firmenbezeichnung; Firmenname; ~ **of address** Anrede; **under the** ~ **of** unter dem Namen; unter der Firma

style *v* benennen, anreden; entwerfen, gestalten

styling industrielle Formgebung *(cf. industrial design)*

suability *bes. Am* (Ver-)Klagbarkeit, Einklagbarkeit

suable *bes. Am* auf dem Klageweg verfolgbar, einklagbar; **to be** ~ verklagt werden können

suasion, moral ~ gütliches Zureden *(→moral)*

sub Unter-, Teil-, Hilfs-; *Br colloq.* Vorschuß; (Mitglieds-)Beitrag; ~**(-)agency** Untervertretung; Unterbevollmächtigung; Unteragentur; *Am* Nebenstelle; ~**(-)agent** Untervertreter; Unterbevolmächtigter; Subagent; ~**branch** Zweigstelle; Fachgruppe; ~**-classification** Untergliederung; ~ **colore juris** s. under →colo(u)r of law; ~**(-)committee** Unterausschuß; ~**contract** Untervertrag; Vertrag mit e-m Zulieferer

subcontract *v* e-n Untervertrag (od. Zuliefervertrag) abschließen; *(beim Werkvertrag)* die Arbeit (od. den Auftrag) weitervergeben

subcontracted, in building contracts part of the work is ~ in Bauverträgen wird ein Teil der Arbeit weitervergeben *(cf. vicarious performance)*

subcontracting Abschluß e-s Untervertrages (od. Zuliefervertrages); Vergabe von Unteraufträgen; Zulieferung; *(beim Werkvertrag)* Weitervergabe von Arbeit; ~ **agreement** Zuliefervertrag

subcontractor Unterauftragnehmer, Subunternehmer; Unterlieferant, Zulieferer

subdelegation Subdelegation, Weiterdelegierung *(cf. delegated legislation)*

subdivide *v* unterteilen, noch einmal teilen; *(in kleinere Teile)* aufteilen; *(Grundstücke in Parzellen)* aufteilen, parzellieren

subdivision Unterabteilung, Untergruppe; *Am* Aufteilung *(in Parzellen)*; **political** ~ Gebietskörperschaft

sub, ~**duct** *v Br (probate proceedings) (ein caveat)* zurückziehen; ~**editor** zweiter Schriftleiter; Hilfsredakteur; ~**-group** Teilkonzern; ~**group accounts** Teilkonzernabschluß; ~**heading** Untertitel; *(Zoll)* Tarifstelle; ~**(-)hire** *v (bewegl. Sachen)* untervermieten; ~**-item** Unterposition, Nummer; ~**jacent state** *(WeltraumR)* Bodenstaat

subject 1. Gegenstand; Sachgebiet; ~**(s)** *Scot* Vermögen, *bes.* Grundbesitz *(heritable property)*; ~ **catalogue** Sachkatalog; ~ **index** Sachverzeichnis, Sachregister

subject matter Gegenstand; ~ **insured** versicherter Gegenstand; ~ **jurisdiction** *Am* sachliche Zuständigkeit; ~ **of the action** Gegenstand der Klage; Streitgegenstand; ~ **of the application** *(PatR)* Anmeldungsgegenstand; ~ **of the contract** Gegenstand des Vertrages, Vertragsgegenstand; ~ **of the insurance** Gegenstand (Schutzobjekt) der Versicherung; ~ **of the invention** Gegenstand der Erfindung

subject, ~ **of conversation** Gesprächsthema; ~ **of discussion** Diskussionsgegenstand; Verhandlungsthema; **to change the** ~ das Thema wechseln; **to deviate from the** ~ vom eigentlichen Thema abkommen; **to file under** ~**s** nach Sachgebieten einordnen

subject 2. Untertan, Staatsbürger; **British** ~ britischer Staatsbürger *(→British)*; **foreign** ~ Ausländer

subject 3. Person; ~ **of international law** Völkerrechtssubjekt; ~ **of rights and duties** Träger von Rechten und Pflichten; **to be a** ~ **of law** Rechtspersönlichkeit haben

subject *v*, **to** ~ **to** unterwerfen, aussetzen; **the contract is** ~ **to German law** der Vertrag unterliegt dem deutschen Recht

subject to ausgesetzt, unterworfen; abhängig von, vorbehaltlich; ~ **alteration(s)** Änderungen vorbehalten; ~ **amendments** vorbehaltlich etwaiger Abänderungen; ~ **appeal** der Berufung (etc) unterliegend; ~ **approval** genehmigungspflichtig; ~ **Art. 50** vorbehaltlich des Art. 50; ~ **availability of funds** unter dem Vorbehalt, daß Mittel vorhanden sind; ~ **call** *(Einlagen)* täglich kündbar; ~ **censorship** zensurpflichtig; ~ **change** Änderungen vorbehalten; ~ **change without notice** freibleibend; ~ **(a) commission** provisionspflichtig; ~ **compulsory insurance** versicherungspflichtig; ~

the conditions vorbehaltlich der Bedingungen; ~ **contract** vorbehaltlich e-s Vertragsabschlusses; ~ **control** kontrollpflichtig; ~ **correction** Irrtum vorbehalten, ohne Gewähr; ~ **denunciation** *(VölkerR)* kündbar; ~ **distress** pfändbar; ~ **duty** zollpflichtig; ~ **execution** der Zwangsvollstreckung unterliegend; ~ **explicit provisions to the contrary** soweit nicht ausdrücklich etwas anderes bestimmt ist; ~ **a fee** gebührenpflichtig; ~ **fluctuations** Schwankungen unterworfen; ~ **licen|ce (~se)** lizenzpflichtig; genehmigungspflichtig; ~ **modification(s)** Änderungen vorbehalten; **property ~ a mortgage** mit e-r Hypothek belasteter Grundbesitz; ~ **notice** kündbar; ~ **prior sale** Zwischenverkauf vorbehalten; ~ **redemption** tilgbar; kündbar; ~ **reservation** unter Vorbehalt; ~ **taxation** steuerpflichtig, der Steuer unterliegend; ~ **the terms of the contract** vorbehaltlich der Bestimmungen des Vertrags; ~ **this** unter diesem Vorbehalt; **to be ~** unterworfen sein, unterliegen; abhängen von; **to be ~ an Act** unter ein Gesetz fallen; **to be ~ an appeal** e-m Rechtsmittel *(Berufung etc)* unterliegen; **to be ~ the jurisdiction** der Gerichtsbarkeit unterstehen; **he is ~ the provisions of the Act** auf ihn finden die Bestimmungen des Geseztes Anwendung; **to be ~ ratification** der Ratifikation bedürfen

subjection Unterwerfung; Unterworfensein; Abhängigkeit (of von)

subjoin *v* (noch) beifügen

sub judice ("in course of trial") (noch) anhängig, (noch) nicht entschieden

sublease Untermiete; Unterpacht; Untervermietung; Unterverpachtung; **to enter into a ~** →sublet *v*

sublease *v* untervermieten; unterverpachten
subleasing Untervermietung; Unterverpachtung

subledger s. subsidiary →~ ledger

sublessee Untermieter; Unterpächter

sublessor Untervermieter, Unterverpächter

sublet *v* untervermieten; unterverpachten, in Unterpacht geben; Teil e-s Auftrags weitervergeben
subletting Untervermietung; Unterverpachtung

sublicen|ce (~se) Unterlizenz

sublicence *v* Unterlizenzen vergeben

sublicensee Unterlizenznehmer

sublicens|er (~or) Unterlizenzgeber

submanager stellvertretender Direktor

submarine U(ntersee)boot; unterseeisch; ~ **base** U-Boot-Stützpunkt; **~-launched ballistic missiles** (SLBM) Langstreckenraketen mit Reichweiten über 4000 km, die von atomar angetriebenen U-Booten gestartet werden; ~ **warfare** U-Bootkrieg; **nuclear(-powered)~** Atom-U-Boot; **anti-~ system** U-Boot-Abwehrsystem

submarket *Am* Teilmarkt

subminimum unter dem Minimum; ~ **rate** untertariflicher Lohn

submission 1. Unterwerfung (to unter); ~ **(to arbitration)** *(schriftl.)* Schieds(gerichts)vereinbarung; ~ **to an award** Unterwerfung unter e-n Schiedsspruch; ~ **bond** Kaution für die Einhaltung e-r Schiedsvereinbarung

submission 2. Einreichung, Vorlegung, Vorlage; Vorbringen, *(zur Entscheidung durch das Gericht vorgebrachte)* Behauptung *(e-r Partei)*; ~ **of evidence** Vorlage von Beweisen; ~ **of a party** Vorbringen e-r Partei; ~ **of a passport for inspection** Vorlegung e-s Passes zur Kontrolle; ~ **of proof** Beweisantritt, Vorlage von Beweismitteln; ~ **of a proof** *Br* Anmeldung e-r Konkursforderung; ~ **of samples** Vorlegung von Mustern; ~ **of tenders** Einreichung von Angeboten *(bei Ausschreibung)*

submit *v* einreichen, vorlegen; anheimstellen, zu bedenken geben; sich unterwerfen, sich fügen; darlegen, vortragen; **to ~ oneself (to)** sich unterwerfen, sich fügen (in); **to ~ to adjudication** sich e-m *(internationalen)* Rechtsspruch unterwerfen; **to ~ an application** ein Gesuch (od. e-n Antrag) einreichen; **to ~ to arbitration** sich dem schiedsrichterlichen Verfahren unterwerfen; **to ~ a case to the court** dem Gericht e-n Fall *(zur Entscheidung)* vortragen; **to ~ a claim** e-n Anspruch vorbringen (od. einreichen); **to ~ for decision** zur Entscheidung vorlegen; **to ~ to a decision** sich mit e-r Entscheidung abfinden; **to ~ evidence** Beweise vorbringen; **to ~ goods to a careful** (or **detailed**) **examination** Waren e-r genauen Untersuchung unterwerfen; **to ~ information** Auskunft geben; **to ~ to the jurisdiction of a foreign court** die Zuständigkeit e-s ausländischen Gerichts anerkennen; **to ~ proposals** Vorschläge unterbreiten; **to ~ to a sentence** sich mit e-m (Straf-)Urteil abfinden; **to ~ for signature** zur Unterschrift vorlegen; **to ~ a statement of one's affairs** *Br (KonkursR)* e-e Vermögensaufstellung vorlegen; **to ~ vouchers** Belege einreichen

sub modo ("under condition or restriction") unter der Bedingung; mit der Einschränkung

sub nom. ("sub nomine") unter dem Namen

subnormality[128] Subnormalität

sub-office Nebenstelle, Zweigstelle *(e-r Bank)*; Geschäftsstelle

subordinate Untergebener *(opp. superior)*; untergeordnet (to a p. jdm); nachgeordnet; ~ **attachment** Anschlußpfändung; ~ **bodies** nachgeordnete Stellen; ~ **legislation** delegierte Gesetzgebung; Verordnung(en); ~ **official** unterer Beamter; ~ **post** (or **situation**) untergeordnete Stellung; ~ **question** untergeordnete (od. nebensächliche) Frage; **to be ~ to sb.** jdm unterstehen (od. unterstellt sein)

subordinate *v* zurückstellen (to hinter); unterordnen; **to ~ one's own claim to that of another creditor** den Nachrang e-r Forderung hinter der e-s anderen Gläubigers erklären

subordinated, ~ creditor im Range nachstehender Gläubiger; ~ **debt** nachrangige Schuld; ~ **liabilities** *Am* nachrangige Verbindlichkeiten *(z. B. im Konkurs)*; **this claim is ~ to that of the Inland Revenue for arrears of income tax** *Br* der Anspruch des Finanzamts auf Einkommensteuer-Rückstände geht diesem Anspruch vor

subordination Unterordnung; Zurückstellung; Rangrücktritt; Rangnachfolge; ~ **agreement** Rangrücktrittsvereinbarung

suborn *v (jdn zu e-m Verbrechen, bs. zum Meineid)* anstiften; **to ~ witnesses** Zeugen bestechen, bes. Zeugen zum Meineid anstiften

subornation of perjury[129] Anstiftung zum Meineid

subparagraph Unterabschnitt, Buchstabe; Absatz

subparticipation Unterbeteiligung

subpartner *Br* persönlich nicht haftender Gesellschafter

subpartnership Unterbeteiligung an e-r → partnership *(ohne Gesellschafter [od. Sozius] zu sein, also etwa auf Grund e-r Vereinbarung mit e-m Gesellschafter, wonach subpartner an dem auf diesen Gesellschafter entfallenden Gewinn beteiligt ist)*

subpoena[130] Zeugenvorladung vor Gericht *(unter Strafandrohung)*; ~ **ad testificandum**[131] Zeugenladung *(unter Strafandrohung)*; ~ **duces tecum**[131] mit Strafandrohung versehene Anweisung an e-n Zeugen, bestimmte Urkunden *(Briefe, Geschäftsbücher etc)* vorzulegen; **to issue a ~ requiring the attendance of witnesses** e-e Ladung *(unter Strafandrohung)* für das Erscheinen von Zeugen erlassen

subpoena *v (jdn unter Strafandrohung für den Fall des Ausbleibens)* (vor)laden; **to ~ bank records** Vorlage von Bankauszügen *(durch ein writ of subpoena)* unter Strafandrohung verlangen; **to ~ a witness** e-n Zeugen *(unter Strafandrohung)* laden

subpurchaser Käufer aus zweiter Hand, mittelbarer Käufer; Endabnehmer

subreption Erschleichung *(durch falsche Darstellung od. Verschweigung von Tatsachen)*

subrogate *v* an die Stelle setzen, *(in jds Rechte)* einsetzen *(cf. subrogation)*

subrogated, to be ~ an die Stelle treten (to von); **the insurer is ~ to the rights of the insured on paying his claim** der Versicherer, der die Versicherungssumme gezahlt hat, wird in die Rechte des Versicherten eingesetzt *(er erwirbt also die Schadensersatzforderung gegen den Schädiger)*

subrogation Subrogation, Rechtseintritt; Eintritt (od. Einsetzung) e-r anderen Person an die Stelle des ursprünglichen Gläubigers in die Forderung und ihre Sicherungsrechte *(entweder kraft Rechts [by operation of law]:)* Legalzession, gesetzlicher Forderungsübergang; *(oder kraft Vereinbarung [by contract]:)* Abtretung aufgrund rechtlicher Verpflichtung; **letter of ~** Abtretungserklärung

subscribe *v* 1. unterschreiben, unterzeichnen *(am Ende e-r Urkunde)*; **to ~ one's name to a document** e-e Urkunde unterzeichnen

subscribing witness Unterschriftszeuge *(z. B. bei Errichtung e-s Testaments)*

subscribe *v* 2. *(gemeinsam mit anderen e-n Geldbetrag)* zeichnen (od. spenden) *(z. B. für karitativen Zweck)*; Mitgliedsbeitrag *(für Klub etc)* zahlen; *(Buch)* subskribieren; **to ~ to** *(e-r Sache)* beistimmen; **to ~ to** *(Am* **for) a newspaper** e-e Zeitung abonnieren; **to ~ to a (***Br* **private) health insurance (scheme)** e-r Krankenkasse angehören

subscribed, the sum needed was over-~ die benötigte Summe war überzeichnet

subscribing member förderndes Mitglied

subscribe *v* 3. *(Aktien, Anleihen etc)* zeichnen; **to ~ in excess** (or **to over~**) überzeichnen; **to ~ for shares** Aktien zeichnen; **right to ~ for new shares** Bezugsrecht auf junge Aktien

subscribed, ~ capital *Am (von den Gründern [incorporators] od. dem Publikum [investing public])* gezeichnetes Kapital; **amount ~** (to a loan issue) Zeichnungsbetrag; **the issue was fully ~** die Anleihe war überzeichnet; **the loan was ~ several times over** die Anleihe war mehrfach überzeichnet

subscribe *v* 4. *(VersR)*, **to ~ a policy** e-e Versicherung übernehmen; **~d risk** übernommene Gefahr

subscriber 1. Unterzeichner (to a document e-r Urkunde); *(Buchhandel)* Subskribent; ~ **to the memorandum of association** *Br* Unterzeichner der Gründungsurkunde *(e-r Aktiengesellschaft)*; Gründungsgesellschafter

subscriber 2., **~'s line** *tel* Teilnehmeranschluß; **~'s number** *tel* Teilnehmernummer, Fernsprechnummer; ~ **(to charity)** Spender; ~ **to** (*Am* **for**) **a newspaper** Abonnent auf e-e Zeitung, Bezieher e-r Zeitung; ~ **to a telephone line** Fernsprechteilnehmer; ~ **to** *(Am* **for) a periodical** Zeitschriftenabonnement; **list of ~s** Abonnentenliste

subscriber 3. Zeichner *(von Wertpapieren)*; ~ **to a loan** Anleihezeichner; ~ **for shares** Aktienzeichner; **list of ~s** Zeichnungsliste

subscription 1. Unterzeichnung, Unterschrift (to a document unter e-e Urkunde); *(Buchhandel)* Subskription

subscription 2. Zeichnung *(e-r Geldsumme)*; gezeichnete Summe, Zeichnungsbetrag; Mitgliedsbeitrag; ~ **in kind** Sacheinlage; ~ **list** Zeichnungsliste; ~ **to a charity** (or **charitable** ~) Spende für e-e wohltätige Einrichtung; Zusage, an e-m Wohltätigkeitswerk teilzunehmen; ~ **to a party** Parteibeitrag; **amount of the** ~ Höhe des Beitrags; **annual** ~ Jahresbeitrag; **cash** ~ Bareinlage *(bei Firmengründung)*; **club** ~ Klubbeitrag; **life** ~ einmaliger Beitrag auf Lebenszeit; **monthly** ~ Monatsbeitrag; **yearly** ~ Jahresbeitrag; **to pay one's** ~ s-n Beitrag entrichten; **to raise the** ~ den Beitrag erhöhen

subscription 3. Abonnement; ~ **agent** *Am* Abonnentenwerber; ~ **card** Abonnementskarte, Dauerkarte; ~ **fee** Abonnentenpreis; ~ **to** *(Am* **for**) **a (news)paper** (or **periodical**) Abonnement auf e-e Zeitung (od. Zeitschrift); ~ **price** Abonnementspreis; Bezugspreis; ~ **rental** *Br tel* Grundgebühr; ~ **ticket** Abonnementskarte; **annual** ~ Jahresabonnement; **by** ~ im Abonnement; **discontinuance of** ~ Abbestellung e-r Zeitung (od. e-s Abonnements); **quarterly** ~ Vierteljahresabonnement; **rate of** ~ Abonnementspreis; **to cancel** (or **discontinue**) **one's** ~ sein Abonnement aufgeben, seine Zeitung abbestellen; **to renew a** ~ ein Abonnement erneuern; **to solicit (newspaper) ~s** Abonnenten werben; **to take out a** ~ **to** *(Am* **for**) **a (news-)paper** e-e Zeitung abonnieren (od. bestellen); **the** ~ **expires on** das Abonnement läuft ab am

subscription 4. Subskription, Zeichnung *(bei der Emission von Aktien od. Obligationen)*; ~ **agent** Annahmestelle für Zeichnung *(von Aktien etc)*; ~ **agreement** *(Eurokapitalmarkt)* Subskriptionsvereinbarung (od. Zeichnungsvertrag) *(bei e-r Euroanleihe zwischen emissionsführender Bank und Schuldner)*; ~ **blank** *Am* → ~ form; ~ **form** Zeichnungsformular; ~ **ledger** *Am* Aktienzeichnungsbuch; ~ **list** Zeichnungsliste; ~ **offer** Zeichnungsangebot; ~ **period** Zeichnungsfrist; ~ **price** Ausgabekurs; ~ **receipt** Zeichnungsbescheinigung; ~ **right** *(AktienR)* Bezugsrecht; ~ **to a loan** Anleihezeichnung; ~ **to** *(Br a.* **for**) **shares** (or **stock**) Aktienzeichnung; ~ **warrant** Bezugsberechtigungsschein (→ ~ *right*); **amount of the** ~ Zeichnungsbetrag; **closing of the** ~ Zeichnungsschluß; **day of** ~ Zeichnungstag; **initial** ~ Erstzeichnung; **offer for** ~ Zeichnungsangebot; **(securities) offered for** ~ zur Zeichnung aufgelegt(e Wertpapiere); **over-**~ Überzeichnung; **terms of** ~ Zeichnungsbedingungen, Bezugsbedingungen; **to invite** ~ **for shares** Aktien zur Zeichnung auflegen; **to offer a loan for** ~ e-e Anleihe zur Zeichnung auflegen; **to be offered for** ~ zur Zeichnung aufliegen

subsection Absatz

subsequent (nach)folgend (to auf); später (to als); nachträglich, Nach-; anschließend (to an); ~ **action** weiteres Vorgehen; ~ **additions** *(Bilanz)* Zugänge; ~ **applicant** *(PatR)* späterer Anmelder; ~ **condition** auflösende Bedingung; ~ **delivery** Nachlieferung; ~ **entry** Nachtragsbuchung; ~ **event** *Am* Ereignis nach dem Bilanzstichtag; ~ **holder** nachfolgender (od. späterer) Inhaber; ~ **indorser** nachfolgender Indossant, Nachmann; ~ **insurance** Nachversicherung; ~ **levy of duties** Nacherhebung von Zöllen; ~ **mortgage** *(im Rang)* nachfolgende Hypothek; ~ **patent** jüngeres Patent; ~ **payment** Nach(be)zahlung; Nachschuß; ~ **performance** Nachleistung; ~ **policy** Nachtragspolice; ~ **premium** (VersR) Folgeprämie; **to deliver ~ly** nachliefern

subsidiar|y 1. Tochtergesellschaft; Filiale; ~ **(company)**[132] Tochtergesellschaft; abhängige Gesellschaft, beherrschte Gesellschaft; **foreign** ~ Tochtergesellschaft im Ausland; **income from ~ies** Erträge aus Beteiligungen an Tochtergesellschaften; **fully-owned** ~ Tochtergesellschaft, die zu 100% im Besitz der Muttergesellschaft ist; **sub-**~ Enkelgesellschaft

subsidiary 2. Hilfs-, Neben-; subsidiär; untergeordnet; ~ **account** Hilfskonto; ~ **agreement** Nebenabrede; ~ **body** Nebenorgan; nachgeordnetes Organ; ~ **committee** Nebenausschuß, nachgeordneter Ausschuß; ~ **earnings** Nebenverdienst; ~ **employment** Nebenbeschäftigung; ~ **law** *(IPR)* subsidiär geltendes Recht; ~ **organs** nachgeordnete Organe; ~ **sentence** Nebenstrafe

subsidization Subventionierung

subsidize *v* subventionieren; durch *(zweckgebundene)* öffentliche Mittel unterstützen; bezuschussen; **to ~ a steamship line** e-e Schifffahrtslinie subventionieren

subsidized, ~ **export** subventionierter Export; ~ **housing** Sozialwohnungen; ~ **loan** zinsverbilligtes Darlehen *(z. B. der EIB)*; ~ **price** subventionierter Preis

subsidizing of exports Exportsubventionierung

subsid|y Subvention, *(staatl.)* Beihilfe, *(öffentl. zweckgebundener)* Zuschuß *(z. B. an Industriezweige, an in der Landwirtschaft tätige Perso-*

nen[133] *oder an örtl. Behörden für Wohnungsbeschaffung*[134]); **~system** *(EG)* Beihilfesystem; **export ~ies** Exportbeihilfen, Exportsubventionen; **industrial ~ies** Industriesubventionen; **price ~** Subvention von Preisen; **rent ~** Mietbeihilfe, Mietzuschuß; **to grant ~ies** Subventionen gewähren

subsist *v* bestehen, weiterbestehen; sich ernäheren, leben (on von); *(jdn)* unterhalten; **the custom still ~s** es besteht noch der Brauch

subsisting, ~ bill noch gültiger Wechsel; **to be ~** von Bestand sein

subsistence (Lebens-)Unterhalt, Auskommen; Existenz; Versorgung; **~ allowance** Unterhaltszuschuß; **~ expenses** Aufenthaltskosten; **allowance for ~ expenses** Tagegelder; **~ level** Existenzminimum; **~ of troops** Truppenversorgung; **means of ~** Unterhaltsmittel; Erwerbsquelle; **reasonable ~** angemessener Unterhalt

subsoil of the ocean Meeresuntergrund

subsonic aircraft Unterschallflugzeug(e)

substance Substanz; Wesen, Kern e-r Sache; *(PatR)* Stoff; Geld, Vermögen; **~ or composition** *(PatR)* Stoffe oder Stoffgemische; **fissionable ~** spaltbarer Stoff; **loss of ~** Substanzverlust; **matter of ~** materielle (materiellrechtliche) Frage; **persons of ~** bemittelte Personen

substandard unterdurchschnittlich, unter der Norm; *Am*[135] unter der gesetzl. festgelegten Mindestqualität *(und nicht als solche bezeichnet)*; **~ goods** Ausschußware, Partiewaren; **~ risk** (VersR) erschwertes Risiko

substantial wesentlich; wirklich; erheblich, nennenswert; vermögend; **in ~ agreement** im wesentlichen übereinstimmend; **~ damage** erheblicher Schaden; **~ damages** Schadensersatz für tatsächlich eingetretenen Schaden *(opp. nominal damages)*; **~ evidence** hinreichender Beweis; **~ harm** beträchtlicher Schaden; **~ interest** wesentliches Interesse; **~ part** wesentlicher Teil; **~ performance** im wesentlichen erbrachte Leistung *(vgl. § 320 Abs. 2 BGB); (Werkvertrag)* die im wesentlichen dem Vertrag entsprechende Vollendung des Werkes; **~ risk** erhebliche Gefahr; **~ value** erheblicher Wert

substantially im wesentlichen; **to be ~ interested** ein wesentliches Interesse haben

substantiate *v* substantiieren, dartun, nachweisen, begründen; **to ~ a claim** e-n Anspruch (näher) begründen

substantiated damage (or **loss**) nachgewiesener Schaden

substantiation Substantiierung; (nähere) Begründung; Nachweis

substantive wesentlich; selbständig; **~ law** materielles Recht *(opp. adjective law or procedural law)*; **~ motion** *parl* Antrag zur Sache; **~ patent law** materielles Patentrecht; **non-~ decision** nicht in der Sache selbst ergehende Entscheidung

substitute Stellvertreter, Vertreter *(bes. in jds Abwesenheit)*; Ersatz(-); Ersatzmann, Substitut, Surrogat, Ersatzstoff, Ersatzmittel; **~ delivery** Ersatzlieferung

substitute goods Substitutionsgüter; **to require delivery of ~** Ersatzlieferung verlangen

substitute, ~ power of attorney Untervollmacht; **~ to a legatee** Ersatzvermächtnisnehmer; **to act as ~ for sb.** jdn vertreten; **to provide a ~** sich vertreten lassen, Ersatz stellen

substitute *v (jdn, etw.)* an die Stelle setzen (for von); *(jdn, etw.)* ersetzen (for durch); **to ~ for sb.** jdn vertreten, als jds Stellvertreter handeln; **to ~ B for A** A durch B ersetzen; **to ~ an heir** *Am* e-n Ersatzerben bestellen

substituted, ~ contract neuer Vertrag; Novationsvertrag; **~ debtor** neuer Schuldner, Übernehmer e-r Schuld *(bei Schuldübernahme)*; **~ executor** Ersatz-Testamentsvollstrecker; **~ expenses** *(SeeversR)* stellvertretende Kosten *(bei der Havariegrosse)*; **~ heir** *Am* Ersatzerbe; **~ legatee** Ersatzvermächtnisnehmer; **~ performance** Leistung an Erfüllungsstatt; Ersatzleistung; **~ service** Ersatzzustellung

substitution Substitution, Substituierung; Ersatz; Ersetzung (for durch); Einsetzung (for für); Stellvertretung, Vertretung; **~ of a child** Kindesunterschiebung; **~ of an heir** *Am* Einsetzung e-s Ersatzerben; **~ of a legatee** Einsetzung e-s Ersatzvermächtnisnehmers; **in ~ for** als Ersatz für; an Stelle von; **power of ~** Recht zur Unterbevollmächtigung

substitutional (or **substitutionary**) stellvertretend; Ersatz-; **~ gift** Ersatzvermächtnis

substratum Grundlage, Basis

sub-subsidiary Enkelgesellschaft

subtenancy Untermiete; Unterpacht

subtenant Untermieter; Unterpächter

subtitle Untertitel

subtotal Teilsumme, Zwischensumme

subunderwriter Unterversicherer

suburban, ~ housing estate Stadtrandsiedlung; **~ line** Vorortbahn; Vorortstrecke; **~ traffic** Vorortverkehr

subvention Subvention, Beihilfe, staatl. Zuschuß (→*subsidy*)

subversion Umsturz, gewaltsame Beseitigung

(der Regierung, Verfassung etc); Unterwanderung

subversive (or **subversionary**) subversiv, umstürzlerisch; ~ **activities** subversive (od. staatsgefährdende) Tätigkeiten; ~ **forces** umstürzlerische Kräfte (→*fifth column*)

subvert *v* umstürzen, untergraben

subway Unterführung, Tunnel für Fußgänger; *Am* Untergrundbahn, U-Bahn

succeed *v* 1., **to ~ a p.** jdm folgen, auf jdn folgen; jds (Rechts-)Nachfolger sein; **to ~ a p. in office** jdm im Amt folgen; jds Amt antreten (od. übernehmen); **a Democrat ~s a Republican as President** *Am* ein Demokrat folgt e-m Republikaner als Präsident; **to ~ in**→ succeed *v* 2.; **to ~ to a deceased's** *Br* (**decedent's** *Am*) **estate** jdn beerben; **to ~ to the estate of a deceased** *Br* (**decedent** *Am*) **(person) on intestacy or under a will** als gesetzlicher Erbe oder Testamentserbe erben; auf Grund gesetzlicher Erbfolge oder letztwilliger Verfügung erben; **to ~ to land under a will** Grundbesitz auf Grund letztwilliger Verfügung erben; **to ~ to (a p.'s) property** Vermögen erben; jdn beerben; **to ~ to real property**.Grundbesitz erben; **to ~ to a p.'s rights** in jds Rechte eintreten; **to ~ a p. to the throne** jdm auf den Thron folgen; **to ~ to the title** den Titel erben; **right to ~ (to a decedent's estate)** *Am* Erbrecht, Erbberechtigung; **the illegitimate child has a right to ~ on the intestacy of either parent** *Br*[136] das nichteheliche Kind hat ein gesetzliches Erbrecht gegenüber beiden Elternteilen

succeeding, the next ~ day der nächstfolgende Tag

succeed *v* 2., **to ~ in** Erfolg haben, erfolgreich sein mit (od. bei); **to ~ in one's claim** mit s-r Forderung durchdringen, mit e-r Klage Erfolg haben; **he ~ed in his plans** er war mit seinen Plänen erfolgreich

success Erfolg; ~ **factors** Erfolgsfaktoren; ~ **in business** Geschäftserfolg; **chances of ~** Erfolgsaussichten; **to meet with ~** erfolgreich sein; Erfolg erzielen

successful erfolgreich; ~ **party** (or **litigant**) *(Zivilprozeß)* obsiegende Partei *(opp. losing party)*

succession 1. (Aufeinander-) Folge, Reihe, Reihenfolge, ~ **of crops** Fruchtwechsel; **in ~** nacheinander, hintereinander

succession 2. Nachfolge; Amtsnachfolge; Rechtsnachfolge; Erbfolge; ~ **ab intestato** *Am* gesetzliche Erbfolge; ~ **by inheritance** *Am* Erbfolge; ~ **duty** *Am* Erbschaftsteuer; ~ **in title** Rechtsnachfolge; ~ **of states** Staatennachfolge, Staatensukzession; ~ **on intestacy** gesetzliche Erbfolge; ~ **per stirpes** (or **by stocks**) Erbfolge nach Stämmen; ~ **tax** *Am* Erbschaftsteuer; ~ **to an estate** Erbanfall; ~ **to an office** Amtsnachfolge, Nachfolge im Amt; ~ **(to the throne)** Thronnachfolge

succession, by way of ~ im Wege der Erbfolge; **in ~ to** als Nachfolger von; **intestate ~** Intestaterbfolge, gesetzliche Erbfolge (→*intestate*); **law of ~** Erbrecht (→*intestate~*, →*testamentary ~*); **legal ~** Rechtsnachfolge; **line of ~** Erblinie; **to be next in line of ~** als nächster Verwandter nachfolgeberechtigt sein *(Br to the Crown or title of peerage)*; **order of ~** Erbfolgeordnung; **order of ~ (to the throne)** Thronfolgeordnung; **partial ~** *(VölkerR)* Teilrechtsnachfolge *(opp. universal ~)*; →**perpetual ~**; **right of ~** Erbfolgerecht; **singular ~** *Am und Scot* Einzelrechtsnachfolge; **testamentary ~** testamentarische Erbfolge; →**universal ~**; **vacant ~** herrenloser Nachlaß; **to renounce** (or **disclaim**) **the statutory right of ~** auf das gesetzliche Erbrecht verzichten

successive(ly) aufeinanderfolgend, nach und nach, nacheinander *(opp. concurrent[ly])*

successor Nachfolger *(opp. predecessor)*; Amtsnachfolger; Rechtsnachfolger; ~ **in** (or **to an**) **office** Amtsnachfolger; ~ **in title** Rechtsnachfolger; ~ **to the throne** Thronfolger; **intestate ~** gesetzlicher Erbe; **legal ~** Rechtsnachfolger; **singular ~** *Am und Scot* Einzelrechtsnachfolger; **universal ~** *Am und Scot* Gesamtrechtsnachfolger; **to appoint a p. one's ~** jdn zu s-m Nachfolger ernennen; **to designate a ~** e-n Nachfolger bestimmen

Sudan Sudan; **Republic of the ~** Republik Sudan

Sudanese Sudanese, ~sin; sudanesisch

sue *v (Zivilprozeß)* klagen, prozessieren; ~ **and labour clause** (S/L.C.) *Br*[137] *(SeeversR)* Klausel betr. Schadensabwendung und Schadensminderung; **to ~ for** klagen auf, *(etw.)* einklagen; bitten um; **to ~ a p.** gegen jdn klagen; jdn verklagen; gegen jdn gerichtl. vorgehen; **to ~ for an armistice** um Waffenstillstand bitten; **to ~ for damages** auf Schadensersatz klagen; **to ~ for a debt** e-e Forderung einklagen; **to ~ for a divorce** auf Scheidung klagen; **to ~ for infringement of copyright** wegen Verletzung des Urheberrechts klagen; **to ~ for performance** auf Erfüllung klagen; **to ~ for rescission** (of a contract) auf Aufhebung (e-s Vertrags) klagen; **to ~ in forma pauperis** *Am* im Armenrecht klagen; **to ~ on a bill (of exchange)** Zahlung e-s Wechsels einklagen, e-e Wechselforderung einklagen; **to ~ on a contract** aus e-m Vertrag klagen; **to ~ out** *(auf dem Rechtsweg)* erwirken (writ, pardon, etc)

sued, amount ~ for eingeklagter Betrag

suing, ~ and labouring clause →sue and labour clause; **a p. ~ or defending** (or **a p. ~ or being sued**) Kläger oder Beklagter

suffer *v* leiden, erleiden; dulden, zulassen; **to ~ a decline** *(Börse)* e-n Rückgang erfahren; **to ~ a defeat** e-e Niederlage erleiden (→*defeat*); **to ~ a loss** e-n Verlust (od. Schaden) erleiden; **to ~ a loss in exchange** e-e Kurseinbuße erleiden; **trade is ~ing from the war** der Handel leidet unter dem Krieg

sufferance *(stillschweigende)* Duldung; **bill of** ~→ bill 1.; **estate** (or **tenancy**) **at** ~ geduldeter Besitz *(von Immobilien nach Ablauf des ursprünglich bestandenen Rechts zum Besitz)*; **tenant at** ~ geduldeter Mieter (od. Pächter)

sufficiency genügende Menge (of an); Suffizienz; Hinlänglichkeit; *mil* genügende Anzahl *(von Vergeltungswaffen)*; hinreichende Schlagkraft

sufficient genügend, hinreichend; ~ **cause** triftiger Grund; ~ **evidence** hinreichende(r) Beweis(e); ~ **funds** ausreichendes Guthaben *(beim Scheck)*; genügende Deckung; **the pleading is** ~ das Parteivorbringen ist schlüssig

suffragan *(Anglikanische Kirche)* Weihbischof

suffrage *pol* (aktives) Wahlrecht; Zustimmung; **universal** ~ allgemeines Wahlrecht; **election by direct universal** ~ Direktwahl *(des Europäischen Parlaments)*; **women's** ~ Frauenwahlrecht

sugar Zucker; ~ **exchange** Zuckerbörse; ~**-refinery** Zuckerraffinerie; ~ **works** Zuckerfabrik; **countries importing** ~ Zuckerimportländer

sugar, International S~ Agreement Internationales Zuckerübereinkommen; **International S~ Council** (ISC) Internationaler Zuckerrat *(vgl. Internationales Zuckerabkommen von 1953, Kap. XIII)*[138]

suggest *v* anregen, vorschlagen, nahelegen, empfehlen; **~ed (retail) price** empfohlener Preis, Richtpreis

suggestion Anregung, Vorschlag; Empfehlung; ~ **box** *Am* Kasten für (anonyme) Verbesserungsvorschläge; ~ **scheme** *Am* Vorschlagswesen für betriebliche Verbesserungen; ~ **selling** *Am* Suggestivverkauf *(Kundenbeeinflussung)*

suicidal selbstmörderisch; Selbstmord

suicide[139] Selbstmord; Selbstmörder; **attempted** ~ Selbstmordversuch; **causing or aiding** ~ *Am*[140] Verursachen e-s Selbstmords oder Beihilfe zum Selbstmord; **to commit** ~ Selbstmord begehen

sui generis ("of its own kind") eigener Art; **a case** ~ ein besonderer Fall

sui juris ("of his own right") geschäftsfähig *(jd. der mündig geworden ist und nicht unter Vormundschaft steht)*

suit (Zivil-)Prozeß, Rechtsstreit, Klage *(Br*[141] *bes. im equity- od Ehescheidungsprozeß)*; Gesuch, Antrag, Eingabe; ~ **at law** *Am* (Zivil-) Prozeß; ~ **for a debt** *Am* Einklagung e-r Schuld; ~ **in equity** Klage im equity-Recht *(betr. Rechtsgebiete, in denen das →equity-Recht vorherrschend ist, z.B. Trusts, Nachlaßsachen)*; ~ **on a bill** (of exchange) *Am* Wechselklage; **civil** ~ *bes. Am* Zivilprozeß; **criminal** ~ *Am (selten)* Strafprozeß; **divorce** ~ Ehescheidungsprozeß; **interest** ~ *Br* →interest 1.; **party to a** ~ *bes. Am* Prozeßpartei; **to bring a** ~ **against a p.** gegen jdn klagen (od. gerichtl. vorgehen); mit jdm prozessieren; **to carry on a** ~ *bes. Am* e-n Prozeß führen; **to commence a** ~ *bes. Am* klagen, e-e Klage erheben; **to defend a** ~ sich gegen e-e Klage verteidigen; den Klaganspruch bestreiten; **to enter a** ~ *bes. Am* e-r Prozeßpartei *(zum Zwecke ihrer Unterstützung)* beitreten; **to file** (or **institute**) **a** ~ *Am* Klage einreichen, gerichtlich vorgehen; **a bond given as security of costs is put in** ~ *Br* ein als Sicherheitsleistung gegebener Verpflichtungsschein wird verwertet

suit *v*, **to be ~ed to** (or **for**) geeignet sein (od. sich eignen) für

suitability Eignung

suitable geeignet, angemessen, passend; **maintenance** ~ **to a p.'s station in life** standesgemäßer Lebensunterhalt; **to be** ~ **for** sich eignen für

suite *dipl* Gefolge; **official** ~ offizielles Gefolge; **private** ~ privates Gefolge, privates Dienstpersonal

suitor Prozeßpartei, Prozeßführender, Kläger

sum Summe, (Geld-)Betrag; ~ **assured** → ~ insured; **a** ~ **certain (of money)** e-e bestimmte Geldsumme; ~ **deposited** (or ~ **on deposit**) hinterlegter Betrag; ~ **due** geschuldete Summe; fälliger Betrag; **the** ~ **due to me** der mir geschuldete Betrag; ~ **exceeding** Betrag über, Betrag von mehr als; ~ **in dispute** Streitwert; ~ **in words** Betrag in Worten; ~ **insured** Versicherungsbetrag, Versicherungssumme; ~ **of less than** Betrag unter; ~ **of money** Geldsumme, Geldbetrag; **~-of-the-years-digit (method of) depreciation** *(Einkommensteuer)* digitale Abschreibung(smethode); Abschreibung nach der Jahressumme, *(cf. straight-line (method of) depreciation)*; ~ **paid in** Einlage; ~ **total** Gesamtsumme, Gesamtbetrag

sum, agreed ~ vereinbarter Betrag; **big** ~ hohe Summe; **definite** ~ bestimmte Summe; **equivalent** ~ Gegenwert; **even** ~ runde Summe; **fixed** ~ bestimmte Summe, Fixum; **flat** ~ Pauschalbetrag; **given** ~ bestimmte Summe; **gross** ~ Gesamtsumme; → **lump** ~; **round** ~ auf- (od. ab-)gerundeter Betrag, runde Summe

sum up *v (Ergebnis)* zusammenfassen; addieren,

zusammenzählen; Schlußplädoyer halten; **to ~ evidence** das Ergebnis der Beweisaufnahme zusammenfassen

summing up Zusammenfassung; Schlußplädoyer; Rechtsbelehrung *(des Richters an die Geschworenen, enthaltend e-e Zusammenfassung der erhobenen Beweise, deren Würdigung ausschließl. den Geschworenen überlassen wird, und e-e Belehrung über die maßgeblichen rechtl. Fragen)*

summarize *v (kurz)* zusammenfassen, zusammenfassende Darstellung geben

summarized balance sheet Bilanzauszug

summarizing it can be stated zusammenfassend ist festzuhalten

summary 1. Auszug, *(kurze)* Übersicht; Zusammenfassung, zusammenfassende Darstellung; **~ of contents** Inhaltsangabe; **~ of evidence** *(Zivilprozeß)* Ergebnis der Beweisaufnahme; *(Strafprozeß)* Ergebnis der Ermittlungen; **~ of the facts** kurze Darstellung des Sachverhalts; **to give** (or **make**) **a ~ of** e-n Überblick (od. e-e Übersicht) geben über

summary 2. summarisch, kurz zusammengefaßt; abgekürzt, Schnell-; **~ account** zusammenfassender Bericht; Abschlußrechnung; **~ administration** Verwaltung von Bagatellnachlässen; **~ conviction** Verurteilung im summarischen Verfahren (→ *conviction 1.*); **~ court (martial)** *Am* einfaches Kriegsgericht *(mit beschränkter Strafbefugnis und keiner Zuständigkeit für Offiziere)*; **~ dismissal** fristlose Entlassung; **~ judgment** *(Br*[142] *High Court)* Urteil im summarischen (od. beschleunigten) Verfahren *(das auf dem affidavit des Klägers basiert; cf. ~ procedure)*

summary jurisdiction summarische Gerichtsbarkeit *(in Straf- und Zivilsachen)*; Befugnis e-s (Straf-)Gerichts, Personen durch →conviction zu bestrafen; **court of ~** →court

summary offen|ce (~se) summarisch verfolgbare (leichtere) Straftat, die ohne Mitwirkung von Geschworenen *(Br von e-m Magistrates' Court)* abgeurteilt wird *(cf. non-indictable offen|ce [~se])*

summary process summarisches Verfahren, Schnellverfahren

summary proceedings (or **procedure**) summarisches Verfahren, Schnellverfahren *(in dem nach Lage der Akten ohne Durchführung e-r förml. Beweisaufnahme entschieden wird [cf. ~ judgment]; Am z.B. Verfahren, den Mieter zur Räumung zu zwingen [bes. bei Mietzinsrückstand])*; **~ for debt** Mahnverfahren

summary, ~ schedule kurze Aufstellung; **~ statement of the position** zusammenfassende Darstellung der Lage; **~ trial** summarisches (od. beschleunigtes) Strafverfahren

summarily, to dismiss an employee ~ e-n Angestellten fristlos entlassen; **person ~ →detained; ~ sentenced** summarisch (od. im Schnellverfahren) abgeurteilt

summation *Am* Schlußplädoyer *(des Anwalts)*

summer, ~ holidays *Br* Sommerferien, große Ferien; **~ school** Ferienkurs *(in den Sommerferien)*; **to introduce ~ time** die Sommerzeit(regelung) einführen

summing up →sum up *v*

summit, ~ agreement *pol* Gipfelabkommen; **~ conference** Gipfelkonferenz; **~ meeting** Gipfeltreffen

summon *v (bes. Beklagten od. Zeugen) (vor Gericht)* laden, vorladen; *(behördlich)* auffordern; *(Parlament, Akionäre, Tagung etc)* einberufen; **to ~ a meeting** e-e Sitzung (od. Versammlung) einberufen (od. anberaumen); **to ~ a witness** (or **to ~ sb. to appear as a witness**) e-n Zeugen laden

summoned, to be ~ to appear before a court (or **in court**) vor Gericht geladen werden; **duly ~** ordnungsgemäß geladen

summoning Ladung; Vorladung *(vor Gericht)*; *(behördl.)* Aufforderung; Einberufung *(z.B. zu e-r Versammlung)*; **~ of witnesses** Ladung von Zeugen

summons 1. *(schriftl.)* Ladung, Vorladung *(vor Gericht)*; Zeugenladung; Aufforderung; Einberufung *(Br des Parlaments)*; **~ and complaint** Ladung und Klageschrift; **~ to pay** Mahnung; **default ~** *(ungefähr)* Mahnbescheid; Ladung zum Mahnverfahren *(wenn der Geladene nicht erscheint, wird ein →default judgment erlassen)*; **failure to comply with a ~** Nichterscheinen, Ausbleiben *(vor Gericht)*; **→judgment ~; →originating ~; request for ~** Ladungsgesuch; **service of a ~** Zustellung e-r Vorladung; **writ of ~** Klageschrift mit Prozeßladung (→*writ*); **to answer** (or **comply with**) **a ~** e-r Ladung Folge leisten; **to issue a ~** (vor-) laden; e-e Ladung ergehen lassen; **to serve a ~ (up)on a p.** (or **to serve a p. with a ~**) jdm e-e Ladung zustellen; **to take out a ~ against a p.** jdn (vor)laden lassen

summons 2. *Br (High Court)* Antrag an e-n Richter od. master in chambers in e-m schwebenden Verfahren; **~ for directions** *Br* Antrag auf prozeßleitende Verfügung (→ *directions)*
Der Antrag wird vom Kläger nach Abschluß des förmlichen Schriftsatzwechsels an den Richter des Vorverfahrens gestellt

sumptuary laws *Br hist.* Gesetze gegen übertriebenen Luxus

sumptuous living aufwendige Lebenshaltung

sunday, ~ edition Sonntagsausgabe; **S~ Observance Act** Gesetz zur Einhaltung der Sonntagsruhe

sundries Verschiedenes, Diverses; verschiedene

Artikel; ~ **account** Konto „Verschiedenes"; ~ **journal** Journal „Verschiedenes"; **invoice of** ~ Rechnung über verschiedene Waren

sundry verschieden, divers; ~ **creditors** diverse Kreditoren; ~ **debtors** diverse Debitoren; verschiedene Forderungen; ~ **expenses** Ausgaben für Verschiedenes; ~ **receipts** verschiedene Einnahmen

superannuate *v (wegen Erreichung der Altersgrenze)* in den Ruhestand versetzen, pensionieren; in den Ruhestand treten, in Pension gehen; ~**d** pensioniert; veraltet

superannuation Pension, Ruhegehalt *(bes. für Beamte)*; Pensionierung, Versetzung in den Ruhestand; Überalterung; **S~ Acts** *Br* Gesetze über die Altersversorgung von Beamten; ~ **contribution** Pensionsbeitrag; Beitrag zur Altersversicherung *(zum →~ fund)*; ~ **fund** Pensionsfonds *(aus dem [Betriebs-, Zusatz-] Pensionen gezahlt werden)*; ~ **payment** Abzug vom Gehalt für beitragspflichtige Pension; ~ **provisions** *(Bilanz)* Pensionsrückstellungen; ~ **scheme** Pensionsplan *(für Beamte)*; **entitled to** ~ pensionsberechtigt

supercargo Superkargo, Kargador *(bevollmächtigter Begleiter der Ladung auf See)*

superdividend Superdividende, Zusatzdividende

superfine extrafein

Superfund Amendments and Reauthorization Act of 1986 *Am* Umweltschutzgesetz
Dieses Gesetz erweitert CERCLA (Comprehensive Environmental Response, Compensation and Liability Act of 1980). CERCLA begründete den Superfund und wird nach dem in ihm geregelten System der Mittelbeschaffung colloq. *Superfund Act* genannt. Im Gegensatz zum Abfallbeseitigungsgesetz (→RCRA) regelt der Superfund auch die Abfälle der Luft und des Wassers

superhighway *Am* Autobahn

superimpose *v* hinzufügen (on zu); ~**d clauses** zusätzliche Klauseln

superintend *v* die Oberaufsicht führen, beaufsichtigen, überwachen

superintendence Oberaufsicht; Betriebsleitung

superintendent die Aufsicht führende Person; Aufsichtsbeamter; Leiter, Direktor; Betriebsleiter; *Br* Polizeidirektor; *Am* Gefängnisdirektor; ~ **of agents** *(VersR)* Bezirksdirektor

superintendent registrar *Br* Hauptstandesbeamter *(der die Aufsicht über die registrars of births, deaths and marriages in dem ihm unterstehenden registration district ausübt)*; ~**'s licence** *Br* von e-m Hauptstandesbeamten ausgestellte Bescheinigung (→ *marriage, Ziffer [d])*; **marriage in the office of a** ~ *Br*[143] standesamtliche Trauung; **office of a** ~ *Br* Standesamt; **to get married before a** ~ *Br* sich standesamtlich trauen lassen

superior 1. (Dienst-)Vorgesetzter; **immediate** ~ unmittelbarer Vorgesetzter; **his** ~ **in rank** sein Dienstvorgesetzer

superior 2. höher(er, -e, -es); höher(stehend); vorgesetzt, rangälter; *com* höherwertig, besser (to als) *(opp. inferior)*; ~ **(to)** überlegen; ~ **authority** vorgesetzte Behörde; **S~ Court** → court; ~ **forces** *mil* überlegene Streitkräfte, Übermacht; ~ **mortgage** im Range vorgehende Hypothek; ~ **officer** höherer (od. dienstvorgesetzter) Offizier (od. Beamter); Vorgesetzter; ~ **order** *mil* höherer Befehl *(als Rechtfertigung für Kriegsverbrechen)*; ~ **right** vorrangiges Recht; ~ **title** (to an estate) besserer Rechtsanspruch

superiority Überlegenheit; **air** ~ Luftüberlegenheit; **economic** ~ wirtschaftliche Überlegenheit

supermarket Supermarkt; großes (Lebensmittel-) Geschäft mit Selbstbedienung

super NOW-account *Am* →account 1.

supernumerary überzählig; außerplanmäßig; Hilfsangestellte(r); außerplanmäßiger Beamter (od. Offizier); ~ **clerk** *Am* Volontär

superpower Supermacht

supersede *v (jdn od. etw.)* ersetzen; an die Stelle setzen von; an die Stelle treten von; aufheben; **the Governor** ~**d Judge A with Judge B** *Am* der Gouverneur ersetzte den Richter A durch den Richter B

supersedeas ("that you may disregard") gerichtl. Verfügung (writ) zur Einstellung e-s Verfahrens

supersonic Überschall-; ~ **aircraft** Überschallflugzeug(e)

supertare Supertara, Übertara *(zusätzl. Taravergütung)*

supertax →surtax

supervening impossibility of performance nachträgliche Unmöglichkeit der Leistung *(→frustration)*

supervise *v* beaufsichtigen, überwachen, die Aufsicht haben (od. führen) über

supervising, ~ **authority** Aufsichtsbehörde; ~ **duty** Aufsichtspflicht

supervision Beaufsichtigung, Überwachung; (Ober-)Aufsicht, Kontrolle (of über); Dienstaufsicht; ~ **of the frontier** Grenzüberwachung; ~ **of manufacture** Fertigungskontrolle; ~ **order** *Br*[144] gerichtliche Verfügung der Aufsicht *(z.B. über jugendliche Täter durch e-n*

Bewährungshelfer) (s. *police* →~); **duty of** ~ Aufsichtspflicht; **government** ~ Staatsaufsicht; **police** ~ *Br* Polizeiaufsicht (→ *police*); **power of** ~ Aufsichtsbefugnis; **to be subject to the** ~ **(of)** der Aufsicht unterstehen; **to have the** ~ **(of)** beaufsichtigen

supervisor Aufsichtsperson, Aufseher; mit e-r Überwachungstätigkeit betraute Person: Vorgesetzter; *Am* leitender Angestellter *(steht in etwa dem Personalchef e-s deutschen Unternehmens gleich)*; ~ **of elections** *Am* Wahlprüfer *(der die Registrierung der Wähler überwacht)*; **Board of S~s** *Am* oberstes Selbstverwaltungsorgan e-s Kreises

supervisory Aufsichts-, Überwachungs-; aufsichtführend; ~ **authority** Aufsichtsbehörde; ~ **body** Aufsichtsorgan, Überwachungsstelle; ~ **committee** Überwachungsausschuß; ~ **duty** Aufsichtspflicht; ~ **employee** →supervisor; ~ **jurisdiction** Kontrollgerichtsbarkeit *(der höheren Gerichte über untere Gerichte, Tribunale [und auch Verwaltungsstellen] außerhalb des förmlichen Rechtsmittelzuges, vornehmlich gerichtet auf Einhaltung von Zuständigkeit und Verfahrensgrundsätzen im Wege des Erlasses e-s →prerogative order [or writ], writ of →habeas corpus, →mandamus, →prohibition 2. od. → certiorari)*; ~ **staff** Aufsichtspersonal

supplant *v* ersetzen (by durch); jds Stelle einnehmen

supplement Ergänzung, Nachtrag; Anhang; Ergänzungsband; Beiheft; Zuschlag, Aufschlag; (Zeitungs-)Beilage; **~s to an agreement** Ergänzungen (od. Nebenabreden) zu e-m Vertrag; **commercial** ~ Handelsbeilage; **earnings-related** ~ *Br (Sozialvers.)* lohnbezogener Zuschlag; **Exchequer S~s** *Br* Staatszuschüsse; **Federal S~** *Am* inoffizielle Sammlung von Entscheidungen der → District Courts; **income** ~ *Am* staatlicher Zuschuß zum Einkommen *(als anti-poverty-Maßnahme)*; **literary** ~ Literaturbeilage; **women's** ~ Frauenbeilage

supplement *v* ergänzen; e-n Nachtrag liefern; **to** ~ **a law** ein Gesetz ergänzen; **~ing** in Ergänzung zu

supplemental →supplementary; ~ **annuity** Zusatzrente; ~ **deed**[145] Nachtragsurkunde; ~ **patent** Zusatzpatent; ~ **pleading** *Am* ergänzender Schriftsatz *(Klageänderung, Klageerweiterung etc)*; **S~ Register** *Am* →register; **S~ Security Income** (SSI) *Am* zusätzliche Einkommenssicherung *(besonders Bedürftiger)*; **S~ Unemployment Benefits** (SUB) *Am (zur öffentl. Arbeitslosenversicherung aus e-m betrieblichen Sonderfonds gezahltes)* zusätzliches Arbeitslosengeld

supplementary ergänzend, Ergänzungs-; Nachtrags-, nachträglich, Zusatz-; ~ **agreement** → agreement 1. und 3.; ~ **allowance** Zusatzrente; ~ **appropriation** *Am parl* Nachtragsbewilligung; ~ **banking functions** irreguläre Bankgeschäfte; ~ **benefits** Sozialhilfe *(jetzt: →income support)*; ~ **bonus** *Br (VersR)* Zusatzdividende; ~ **budget** Nachtragshaushalt(splan); ~ **charge** (Zug-)Zuschlag; ~ **claim** Nachforderung; ~ **convention** Zusatzabkommen; ~ **entry** Nachtragsbuchung; ~ **estimates** *Br parl* Nachtragsetat; ~ **files** Beiakten; ~ **financing** Nachfinanzierung; ~ **insurance** Zusatzversicherung; ~ **list** *Br* Beilage zum amtl. Kursblatt; ~ **load** Beiladung; ~ **order** Nachbestellung; ~ **payment** Nachzahlung, Nachschuß; ~ **policy** *(VersR)* Nachtragspolice

supplementary proceedings (or **procedure**) *Am* Offenbarungsverfahren *(zur Ermittlung des Vermögens des Urteilsschuldners, wenn Pfändung nicht zur Befriedigung des Gläubigers geführt hat)*; **examination of the judgment debtor in** ~ Offenbarungseid

supplementary, ~ **protocol** Zusatzprotokoll; ~ **provisions** ergänzende Bestimmungen; ~ **report** Zusatzbericht, Ergänzungsbericht; ~ **sheet** Beiblatt, Extrabogen; ~ **sickness insurance** Krankenzusatzversicherung; ~ **sum** Zuschlag; ~ **unemployment benefits** (SUB) *Am* zusätzliches Arbeitslosengeld; ~ **volume** Ergänzungsband; ~ **vote** *parl* Nachbewilligung; **to be** ~ **(to)** ergänzen

suppliant Bittsteller

supplier Lieferant; Lieferer; Anbieter; Zulieferant; ~ **debts** Lieferantenschulden; **(long-term)** ~**'s declaration** *Br (Zoll)* (Langzeit-) Lieferantenerklärung; **~s' ledger** Lieferantenbuch; ~ **of goods** Warenlieferant; ~ **of services** derjenige, der Dienste leistet; Erbringer von Dienstleistungen; **credit granted by** ~ Lieferantenkredit

supplies Lieferungen; Zulieferungen; Vorräte, (Lager-)Bestände; *bes. mil* Nachschub; *parl* bewilligte (Haushalts-)Gelder; **base of** ~ *mil* Nachschubbasis; **office** ~ Büromaterial; **operating** ~ Betriebsstoffe; **replenishment of** ~ Ergänzung der Vorräte; **war** ~ Kriegslieferungen; **withholding** ~ **of goods** (from a dealer) Lieferverweigerung; **to depend on foreign** ~ von ausländischen Lieferungen abhängig sein; **the** ~ **failed** die Vorräte gingen aus; **to lay in** ~ **for the winter** Vorräte für den Winter anlegen; **to obtain one's** ~ **from X** sich von X beliefern lassen; **to vote** ~ *parl* (Haushalts-)Gelder bewilligen; **to withhold** ~ **of goods from a dealer** die Belieferung e-s Händlers mit Waren verweigern

supply 1. Versorgung (of mit); Belieferung; Lieferung (to an); Beschaffung; Zufuhr; Vorrat (of an); (Lager-)Bestand; *mil* Nachschub; Ersatzmann (→*supply 3.*); **S~ Agency** *(Euratom)* Versorgungsagentur; ~ **area** Versorgungsgebiet; ~ **bottleneck** Lieferengpaß; Versorgungsengpaß; ~ **conditions** Lieferungsbedingungen; Versorgungsbedingungen

supply contract Liefervertrag; *(bei Ausschreibungen)* Lieferauftrag; **public ~s** öffentliche Lieferaufträge; **to award a ~** e-n Lieferauftrag vergeben

supply, ~ contractor Heereslieferant; **S~ days** → supply 4; ~ **difficulties** Lieferschwierigkeiten; Versorgungsschwierigkeiten; ~ **industry** Zulieferindustrie; ~ **lines** *mil* Nachschubverbindungen; ~ **of goods** Warenlieferung; **S~ of Goods and Services Act 1982** *Br* Gesetz für Warenkauf-, Warenlieferungs- und Dienstleistungsverträge *(wichtige Ergänzung zum →Unfair Contract Terms Act)*; ~ **of money** Geldversorgung *(e-s Landes)*; ~ **of raw materials** Rohstoffversorgung

supply of services Erbringung von Dienstleistungen; **free ~** freier Dienstleistungsverkehr

supply requirements Versorgungsbedarf

supply, claim for ~ *Am* Unterhaltsanspruch; **Committee of S ~** →supply 4.; **credit ~** Kreditbeschaffung; **difficulties of ~** →~ difficulties; **electricity ~ industry** Elektrizitätswirtschaft; **energy ~** Energieversorgung; **essential ~** lebenswichtiger Bedarf; **food ~** Nahrungsmittelversorgung; Nahrungsmittelzufuhr; **fuel ~** Kraftstoffvorrat; **gas ~ industry** Gaswirtschaft, **market ~** Marktbelieferung; **money ~** Geldvorrat; **month's ~** Monatsbedarf; **object of ~** Liefergegenstand; **power ~** Energieversorgung; Versorgung mit Strom; **in short ~** knapp, beschränkt lieferbar; **source of ~** Lieferquelle, Versorgungsquelle; **water ~** Wasserversorgung; **to cut off (the) ~** die Zufuhr abschneiden; **to lay** (or **take**) **in a ~** e-n Vorrat anlegen (of an)

supply 2. Angebot; ~ **and demand** Angebot und Nachfrage; ~ **curve** Angebotskurve; ~ **of labo(u)r** Angebot an Arbeitskräften; ~ **of money** Geldangebot *(am Geldmarkt)*; **capital ~** Kapitalangebot; **excess(ive) ~** Überangebot; **floating ~** laufendes Angebot; **labo(u)r ~** →~ of labo(u)r; **short ~** Unterangebot; **the demand exceeds the ~** die Nachfrage übersteigt das Angebot; **the ~ meets the demand** das Angebot entspricht der Nachfrage

supply 3. Ersatzmann, *(vorübergehender)* Vertreter *(bes. für e-n Lehrer od. Geistlichen)*; ~ **teacher** Aushilfslehrer(in); **to hold a post on ~** e-e Stelle vorübergehend innehaben

supply 4. *Br parl* bewilligter Etat; **S~ Days** *Br* Sitzungstage des →Committee of S~; **Committee of S~** *Br* Haushaltsausschuß

supply *v* liefern, beschaffen; *(jdn)* beliefern, versorgen; *(Nachfrage etc)* befriedigen; ergänzen; ausgleichen, ersetzen; *(Amt)* vorübergehend versehen; **to ~ the deficiency** den Fehlbetrag ausgleichen; **to ~ a document** e-e Urkunde beschaffen; **to ~ evidence** Beweismaterial beibringen; **to ~ a family** e-e Familie versorgen; **to ~ information** Auskunft geben; **to ~ an interpreter** e-n Dolmetscher stellen; **to ~ the market** den Markt beliefern; **to ~ an omission** e-e Auslassung ergänzen; nachtragen, was übersehen wurde; **to ~ a p.'s place** jdn vertreten; **to ~ a ship** ein Schiff mit Lebensmitteln versorgen (→*to man and ~*)

supplying Lieferung, Versorgung, Belieferung

support 1. Unterstützung, Beistand, Hilfe; Bestätigung; **deserving ~** unterstützungswürdig, förderungswürdig; **in ~** *mil* in Reserve; **in ~ of** als Beleg für; als Bestätigung für; **affidavit in ~ of an application** *Br* schriftl. eidliche Aussage zur Unterstützung e-s *(gerichtl.)* Antrags; **documents in ~ of** Belegstücke für; **majority ~** Unterstützung der Mehrheit; **to give ~ to sb.** jdn unterstützen; **to obtain ~ in the election** bei der Wahl Unterstützung erhalten; **to receive financial ~** finanziell unterstützt werden

support 2. (Lebens-)Unterhalt; *Am* Alimente; ~ **agreement** *Am* Unterhaltsvereinbarung; ~ **at the subsistence level** *Am* notdürftiger Unterhalt; ~ **award** *Am* Unterhaltsurteil; ~ **claim** *Am* Unterhaltsanspruch; ~ **of an illegitimate child** *Am* Unterhalt e-s nicht ehelichen Kindes; ~ **of a spouse during separation** *Am* Unterhalt e-s Ehegatten bei Getrenntleben

support payment *Am* Unterhaltsbetrag; **regular ~s** *Am* Unterhaltsrente; **to calculate the ~s** *Am* den Unterhalt berechnen

support proceedings *Am* Verfahren auf Gewährung von Unterhalt; Unterhaltsprozeß

support, action for ~ *Am* Unterhaltsklage; **affidavit of ~** *Am* Bürgschaftserklärung (→*affidavit*); **duty to furnish ~** *Am* Unterhaltspflicht; **liability for ~** *Am* Unterhaltspflicht; **means of ~** Existenzmittel; **in need of ~** unterhaltsbedürftig; **obligation to pay ~** *Am* Unterhaltspflicht; **order awarding ~** *Am* Unterhaltsurteil; **permanent ~** *Am* laufender Unterhalt; **reasonable (amount of) ~** *Am* angemessener Unterhalt; **Uniform Civil Liability for S~ Act** *Am* Einheitl. Gesetz über die Unterhaltspflicht; **Uniform Reciprocal Enforcement of S~ Act** *Am (in fast allen Einzelstaaten angenommenes)* Einheitliches Gesetz über die gegenseitige Vollstreckung von Unterhaltsansprüchen; **to award ~** *Am* Unterhalt zuerkennen; **to provide ~** Unterhalt gewähren

support 3. *techn* Abstützung, Absteifung; **right of ~** Recht auf Abstützung des eigenen Grund und Bodens *(die Erdarbeiten des Nachbarn dürfen ihn nicht zum Einsturz bringen; vgl. § 909 BGB)*

support 4. *com* Stützung; *(Börse)* Stützungsaktion; ~ **buying** Stützungskäufe *(Käufe zur*

Stützung von Wertpapierkursen); ~ **price** Stützungspreis *(Am bes. für landwirtschaftl. Erzeugnisse)*; Interventionskurs; ~ **purchases** →~ buying; **banking** ~ Stützungsaktion (od. Intervention) der Banken; **price** ~ Preisstützung *(durch den Staat)*

support *v* 1. unterstützen; *(jdm)* helfen, beistehen; bestätigen, rechtfertigen; unterhalten, ernähren; **to** ~ **oneself** seinen Unterhalt selbst verdienen; **to** ~ **sb.** für jdn eintreten; **to** ~ **sth.** sich für etw. einsetzen; **to** ~ **a candidate** e-n Kandidaten unterstützen; **to** ~ **a cause** für e-e Sache eintreten; e-e Sache finanziell unterstützen; **to** ~ **a charity** e-e karitative Organisation *(durch Geld)* unterstützen; **to** ~ **a deduction** e-e Schlußfolgerung rechtfertigen; **to** ~ **by documents** mit Urkunden belegen, urkundlich belegen; **to** ~ **a family** e-e Familie ernähren (od. unterhalten); **to** ~ **a political party** e-e politische Partei unterstützen; **liable to** ~ *Am* unterhaltspflichtig

supported, to be ~ *Am* Unterhalt beziehen; **entitled to be** ~ unterhaltsberechtigt

supporting, ~ **authorities** Belegstellen, ~ **documents** (or **material**) Belege, Unterlagen; **to be incapable of** ~ **oneself** außerstande sein, sich selbst zu unterhalten

support *v* 2. *com (Preise)* stützen; *(Kurse)* durch Käufe stützen

supported, ~ **price** Stützungspreis; gestützter Preis; Stützkurs; **mines were** ~ die Montanwerte wurden durch Käufe gestützt

supporting purchase *(Börse)* Stützungskauf

supporter Anhänger *(e-r Bewegung, Partei etc)*; Sympathisant, Fan; Verfechter *(e-r Meinung etc)*; ~ **of a family** Ernährer e-r Familie; ~ **of a regime** Anhänger e-s Regimes

suppose *v* voraussetzen, annehmen, vermuten

supposed angeblich, vermutet; ~ **deceased** *Am* Verschollener; **let it be** ~ **that** nehmen wir den Fall an, daß

supposing angenommen

supposition Voraussetzung; Annahme, Vermutung; **(up)on the** ~ **that** unter der Voraussetzung (od. in der Annahme), daß

suppress *v* unterdrücken; verheimlichen; abschaffen; **to** ~ **a document** e-e Urkunde unterdrücken; **to** ~ **evidence** Beweismaterial unterdrücken; Beweis(e) unterschlagen; **to** ~ **a fact** e-e Tatsache verschweigen; **to** ~ **a revolt** e-e Revolte niederschlagen; **to** ~ **the truth** die Wahrheit vertuschen; **to** ~ **a will** ein Testament verheimlichen

suppression Unterdrückung; Verheimlichung; Abschaffung; ~ **of crime** Verbrechensbekämpfung; ~ **of documents** Urkundenunterdrückung; ~ **of evidence** Unterdrückung von Beweismaterial; Beweisunterschlagung; ~ **of a find** Fundunterschlagung; ~ **of information** Verheimlichung von Informationen; ~ **of opinion** Unterdrückung der Meinungsäußerung

suppressio veri ("suppression of the truth") Verschweigung der Wahrheit

supranational supranational, übernational; ~ **organization**[146] supranationale Organisation *(die – im Ggs. zu den internationalen Organisationen – mit unmittelbarer Entscheidungsbefugnis gegenüber ihren Mitgliedstaaten ausgestattet ist)*

supra protest (S. P.) *(WechselR)* nach Protest; **acceptance (for hono[u]r)** ~[147] Ehrenannahme nach Protest; →**payment (for hono[u]r)** ~

supremacy höchste Gewalt; Oberhoheit; Vorherrschaft, Vorrang; ~ **clause** *Am*[148] Vorrangklausel *(nach der ein Bundesgesetz dem Gesetz e-s Einzelstaates vorgeht)*; ~ **of law** Vorrang des Rechts; Vorherrschaft des Rechts *(cf. rule of law)*; **air** ~ *mil* Luftherrschaft; **naval** ~ *mil* Seeherrschaft

supreme höchst, oberst; **S~ Allied Commander Atlantic** (SACLANT) Oberster Alliierter Befehlshaber-Atlantik *(cf. NATO)*; **S~ Allied Commander Europe** (SACEUR) Oberster Alliierter Befehlshaber-Europa *(cf. NATO)*; ~ **authority** Regierungsgewalt; ~ **command** Oberkommando; ~ **commander** oberster Befehlshaber

Supreme Court →court

Supreme Court (of the United States) →court

Supreme Court of Judicature →court

supreme, S~ Headquarters of the Allied Powers in Europe →SHAPE; **S~ Soviet** *parl* Oberster Sowjet

surcharge Aufschlag, Zuschlag(sgebühr); (See-) Frachtzuschlag *(für Mehrkosten und Schiffsabgaben)*; Nachgebühr, Strafporto; *(Kraftfahrzeugvers.)* Malus; Überladung; Überbelastung; Belastung mit e-m bestimmten Betrag, der zu ersetzen ist *(z. B. bei Nachweis von unvollständiger od. fehlerhafter Rechnungslegung oder Br unrechtmäßiger Ausgabe öffentl. Gelder)*; **items liable to** ~ *Br* nachgebührpflichtige Sendungen

surcharge *v* aufschlagen; zusätzl. od. zuviel belasten (od. fordern); mit Zuschlag *(Nachporto, Steuerstrafe etc)* belegen; *(Postwertzeichen)* überdrucken; *(equity) (Rechnungsleger)* mit bestimmtem Betrag belasten *(bei unvollständiger od. fehlerhafter Rechnungslegung)*; **to** ~ **and falsify** *(vor Gericht)* den Nachweis bringen, daß ein Kasseneingang nicht gebucht od. ein Rechnungsposten falsch eingesetzt ist und den Rechnungsleger dafür persönl. haftbar machen

surcharged letter Brief mit Nachgebühr

sure, to make ~ **(of)** sich vergewissern

suret|y Garant *(für e-e fremde Schuld)*; Bürge; Schuldmitübernehmer; Pfandbesteller *(für e-e fremde Schuld)*; Interzedent *(jeder, der in irgendeiner Form zur Sicherung e-r fremden Schuld e-e Verpflichtung übernommen hat, sofern dieses Verhältnis der beiden Verpflichteten dem Gläubiger bekannt ist)*; *(untechnisch:)* Sicherheit, Sicherheitsleistung, Garantie, Bürgschaft, Kaution; ~ **bond** Bürgschaftsurkunde; schriftliche Garantieerklärung *(für e-n anderen)*, schriftliche Kautionserklärung (→*bond 3.*); ~ **company** *Am* Garantieversicherungsgesellschaft; Kautionsversicherungsgesellschaft; ~ **for (payment of) a bill** Wechselbürge; Wechselbürgschaft; ~ **for a** ~ Rückbürgschaft; ~ **insurance** Kautionsversicherung; ~**ies of the peace and good behaviour** *Br* Bürgen für Bewährungsfrist (→*bound over*); **co-**~ Mitbürge; **compensated** ~ bezahlter Bürge; **counter-**~ Rückbürge; Rückbürgschaft; **defen|ces (~ses) pleaded by the** ~ Einreden des Bürgen; **discharge of a** ~ Entlastung e-s Bürgen; **to apply to one's** ~ s-n Bürgen in Anspruch nehmen; **to be** (or **become**) ~ **for** Bürgschaft leisten für, bürgen für; **to find a** ~ sich e-n Bürgen (od. Sicherheit) verschaffen; **to offer** ~ e-n Bürgen stellen; **to stand** ~ **for** s. to be →~ for

suretyship Bürgschaft; Garantie *(für fremde Schuld)*; Schuldbeitritt; Pfandbestellung *(für fremde Schuld)*; Interzession; ~ **insurance** *Am* Personengarantieversicherung; Vertrauensschadenversicherung; **contract** (or **deed) of** ~ Bürgschaftsvertrag; Garantievertrag
Die Bürgschaft muß nach dem Statute of → Frauds schriftl. eingegangen werden

surf risk Brandungsrisiko

surface Oberfläche; ~ **craft** Überwasserfahrzeuge; ~ **mail** *Br* gewöhnliche Post *(opp. air mail)*; ~ **marking** Fahrbahnmarkierung; ~-**to-air missile** (SAM) vom Boden ferngelenktes Flakgeschoß; Flugkörper zur Bekämpfung von Flugzielen vom Boden od. Schiff aus; ~ **water** Oberflächenwasser *(opp. subsurface or ground water)*; ~ **working** Tagebau; **on the** ~ über Tage, im Tagebau; *fig* oberflächlich betrachtet

surgery (*bes.* Arzt-)Sprechstunde

surgical chirurgisch; ~ **(fees) insurance** *Am* Operationskostenversicherung

Surinam Surinam; **Republic of** ~ Republik Surinam

Surinamese Surinamer, ~ in; surinamisch

surname Familienname, Nachname

surplice fees *Br eccl* übliche Zahlungen an Geistliche bei Trauungen, Taufen und Begräbnissen

surplus 1. Überschuß, Mehrbetrag; Gewinn; Rest(betrag); überschüssig; ~ **account** Gewinnkonto; ~ **area** Überschußgebiet; ~ **assets** *Br* Liquidationswert e-r Gesellschaft; ~ **brought forward** *Am* Gewinnvortrag; ~ **commodities** Überschußerzeugnisse; ~ **copies** überschüssige Durchschläge (od. Exemplare); ~ **country** Überschußland; ~ **dividend** *Am* Superdividende, außerordentliche Dividende; ~ **in the balance of payments** Aktivsaldo der Zahlungsbilanz; Zahlungsbilanzüberschuß; ~ **in the cash** Kassenüberschuß *(opp. shortage)*; ~ **in taxes** Steuermehreinnahmen *(opp. deficit in taxes)*; ~ **of assets over liabilities** Überschuß der Aktiven über die Passiven; Bilanzüberschuß *(opp. deficiency)*; ~ **of births over deaths** Geburtenüberschuß; ~ **of imports** Importüberschuß; ~ **population** Bevölkerungsüberschuß; ~ **profit** Mehrgewinn; ~ **receipts** Mehreinnahmen; ~ **reinsurance** Exzedenten-Rückversicherung; ~ **revenue** Einnahmeüberschuß, Mehreinkommen; ~ **statement** *Am* Aufstellung über den Gewinn; ~ **value** Mehrwert; ~ **weight** Übergewicht; **export** ~ Ausfuhrüberschuß; **labo(u)r** ~ Überschuß an Arbeitskräften; **producers'** ~ Herstellergewinn; **production** ~ Produktionsüberschuß; **to eliminate** ~**es** Überschüsse abbauen

surplus 2. *Am (AktienR)* Reingewinn und Rücklagen aller Art; ~ **reserves** Sonderrücklagen; ~ **treaty reinsurance** Exzedentenrückversicherung; **appropriated** ~ den Rücklagen zugewiesener Gewinn; **capital** ~ Rücklagen, die nicht aus Jahresüberschüssen stammen; **donated** ~ Rücklagen aus unentgeltlichen Zuwendungen von Aktionären oder anderen; **earned** ~ thesaurierter Gewinn; Gewinnrücklagen; *(entspricht etwa den)* freie(n) Rücklagen *(des deutschen AktienR)*; →**paid-in** ~; **reduction** ~ *Am* aus Kapitalherabsetzungen entstandene Rücklagen; →**revaluation** ~; → **unappropriated** ~

surplusage Überschuß; *(im pleading)*[149] überflüssiges Vorbringen (→*striking out of pleadings*)

surprise attack *mil* Überraschungsangriff

surrebut *v Am* der Quadruplik des Beklagten antworten

surrebutter *Am* Quintuplik, Antwort des Klägers auf e-e Quadruplik

surrejoin *v Am* der Duplik des Beklagten antworten *(cf. rejoinder)*

surrejoinder *Am* Triplik, Antwort des Klägers auf die Duplik

surrender 1. Aufgabe, Verzicht, Rückgabe; Übergabe, Herausgabe; Aushändigung; Aufgabe e-s Besitzrechts *(estate for life or for years)* an jdn, der ein →reversion od. →remainder daran hat *(so daß das geringere estate in ein größeres übergeht [merges])*; *(VölkerR)* Übergabe *(e-r auszuliefernden Person)*; Auslieferung; *mil* Kapitulation (→ *surrender 3.*); ~ **of a criminal** Übergabe e-s Häftlings *(zur Aburteilung in e-m anderen Gerichtsbezirk)*; ~ **of lease**[150] Verzicht auf ein Miet- (od. Pacht-)recht *(vor Ablauf des Miet- od. Pachtvertrages)*; Räumung; ~ **of a patent** Verzicht auf ein Patent; Zurückgabe e-s Patents *(durch den Nichtberechtigten)*; ~ **of a preference** *Am*[151] *(KonkursR)* Verzicht auf e-e Vorzugsstellung *(um andere Forderungen anmelden zu können)*; ~ **of rights** Aufgabe von Rechten, Verzicht auf Rechte; ~ **of a security** Aufgabe e-s Sicherungsrechtes (od. e-r Sicherheit); ~ **of shares** *Br* Rückgabe von Aktien an die Gesellschaft; **compulsory** ~ *Scot* Enteignung; **person liable to** ~ Herausgabeschuldner

surrender 2. *(VersR)* Rückkauf *(Aufgabe e-r Versicherung gegen Rückzahlung e-s Teiles der eingezahlten Prämiensumme)*; ~ **charge** Gebühr bei Aufgabe e-r Versicherung; ~ **value** Rückkaufswert *(e-r Versicherungspolice)*; **including ~s of bonus** Rückkäufe, einschließl. der darauf entfallenen Gewinnanteile

surrender 3. *mil* Übergabe, Kapitulation; ~ **terms** (or **terms of** ~) Übergabebedingungen, Kapitulationsbedingungen; **unconditional** ~ bedingungslose Kapitulation

surrender *v* aufgeben, verzichten, zurückgeben; übergeben, herausgeben; sich stellen; *(VölkerR) (e-n auszuliefernden Täter)* übergeben; ausliefern; *mil* kapitulieren; **to** ~ **one's bail** sich dem Gericht wieder stellen *(nachdem man gegen Sicherheitsleistung aus der Haft entlassen war)*; **to** ~ **an estate** ein Besitzrecht aufgeben *(so daß der → reversioner od. →remainder den Besitz erhält)*; **to** ~ **a lease** auf ein Miet- (od. Pacht-)recht verzichten, räumen (→*surrender 1.)*; **to** ~ **a patent** auf ein Patent verzichten; **to** ~ **to the police** sich der Polizei stellen; **to** ~ **a policy** e-e Versicherungspolice zurückkaufen (→*surrender 2.)*; **to** ~ **a right** auf ein Recht verzichten; **to** ~ **a security** ein Sicherungsrecht (od. e-e Sicherheit) aufgeben; **to** ~ **unconditionally** *mil* bedingungslos kapitulieren

surrenderee derjenige, an den herausgegeben wird; Übernehmer

surrenderor derjenige, der herausgibt

surreptitious unter der Hand, erschlichen, heimlich; unecht, gefälscht; ~ **edition** unerlaubter Nachdruck; **to obtain ~ly** erschleichen

surrogacy Leihmutterschaft

surrogate Surrogat, Ersatz; *Br* Vertreter *(bes. e-s Bischofs)*; *Am* Nachlaßrichter; *Scot* Ersatz; ~ **baby** Baby von e-r Leihmutter; **S~'s Court** *Am* Gericht für Nachlaß- (und oft Pflege-)sachen; ~ **mother** Leihmutter, Mietmutter

surrounding, ~s Umgebung, ~ **circumstances** Begleitumstände

surtax Zusatzsteuer *(zur Einkommensteuer)*; ~ **exemption** *Am* Zusatzsteuerfreibetrag

Br Die surtax wurde durch den Finance Act 1971 abgeschafft und durch eine gestaffelte Einkommensteuer für alle Einkommensstufen ersetzt.

Am Zusätzlich zur Einkommensteuer (normal tax) erhobene Ergänzungssteuer mit Steuerprogression

surtax *v Am* mit e-r Zusatzsteuer belegen

surveillance Überwachung, Beaufsichtigung, Aufsicht, Kontrolle; ~ **action** Lauschoperation; ~ **of imports** Einfuhrüberwachung; ~ **satellite** Überwachungssatellit; **under police** ~ unter Polizeiaufsicht; **space** ~ Weltraumüberwachung

survey 1. *(allgemeiner)* Überblick, Übersicht; Besichtigung, Prüfung, Begutachtung *(z.B. des Zustandes e-s Hauses od. von Waren)*; (Sachverständigen-)Gutachten *(bes. das das Resultat e-r Besichtigung od. Vermessung enthält)*, Expertise; Vermessung *(e-s Grundstücks)*; ~ **certificate** Besichtigungsschein; ~ **fee** Honorar für Gutachten; Besichtigungsgebühr *(z.B. für ein Schiff)*; ~ **of land** Landvermessung; ~ **report** Sachverständigengutachten; Besichtigungsbericht; *(Schiff)* Havariezertifikat; **damage** ~ Havarieuntersuchung, -besichtigung; **Ordnance S~** (OS) *Br* amtliche Landvermessung; **political** ~ Übersicht über die politische Lage; **special** ~ *Br (alle 4 Jahre erforderliche)* Begutachtung der Beschaffenheit e-s Schiffes

survey 2. *(MMF)* Meinungsumfrage, Befragung, Erhebung; ~ **data** Umfrageergebnisse; **consumer** ~ Verbraucherumfrage; **dealer** ~ Händlerbefragung; **factual** ~ Untersuchung von Tatsachen; Marktforschung an Ort und Stelle (→*field research)*; **habit** ~ Untersuchung von Verbrauchergewohnheiten; **mail** ~ Befragung auf dem Postweg; **market** ~ Marktuntersuchung; **opinion** ~ Meinungsumfrage; **to conduct a** ~ e-e Erhebung durchführen

survey *v* überblicken, übersehen; besichtigen; *(Zustand, z.B. e-s Hauses oder von Waren, zur Feststellung von Mängeln)* prüfen, begutachten; *(Land)* vermessen; **to the situation** die Lage überblicken

surveyed, to have a house ~ ein Haus begutachten lassen

surveying Vermessung(swesen); Begutachtung; ~ **a new building** Bauabnahme; **land** ~ Landvermessung

surveyor Landvermesser, Geodät; Sachverständiger, Gutachter *(bes. für Beschaffenheit e-s Hauses oder Schiffes oder von Waren)*; Schadensbesichtiger; Havariekommissar; Aufsichtsbeamter, Inspektor; ~ **of customs** *(aufsichtsführender)* Zollbeamter; ~ **of the port** *Am (aufsichtsführender)* Zollbeamter; ~ **of weights and measures** *Br* Eichmeister; ~**'s office** Hochbauamt; **land** ~ Vermessungsbeamter; **quantity** ~ →quantities

survival Überleben; ~ **of action** Weiterbestehen des Klaganspruchs; **chance of** ~ Überlebenschance; **on** ~ *(VersR)* im Erlebensfalle

survive *v* überleben, fortdauern

surviving überlebend, hinterblieben; ~ **corporation** *Am (bei Zusammenschluß von zwei Kapitalgesellschaften)* übernehmende Gesellschaft

surviving dependants Hinterbliebene; Überlebende; ~ **allowance** *Am* Hinterbliebenenbezüge; ~ **of a serviceman killed in action** Kriegshinterbliebene

surviving spouse überlebender Ehegatte

survivor der/die Überlebende; der/die Hinterbliebene; ~**s' benefit** *Am (Social Security)* Hinterbliebenenrente; ~**s' insurance** *Am* Hinterbliebenenversicherung; ~**s' pensions** Hinterbliebenenbezüge; **Old Age, S~s' and Disability Insurance** (OASDI) *Am* Alters-, Hinterbliebenen- und Invalidenversicherung; **on the death of one of two → joint tenants the whole property vests in the** ~ beim Tode eines der beiden Miteigentümer geht das Eigentum auf den Überlebenden über

survivorship Überleben; Recht des Überlebenden, den Anteil e-s od. mehrerer Verstorbener e-r →joint tenancy für sich zu beanspruchen; Anwachsungsrecht (jus accrescendi); ~ **annuity** Überlebensrente, Rente auf den Überlebensfall *(für e-n →beneficiary nach dem Tode des → annuitant)*; **non-~ between partners** Nichtanwachsung des Anteils zwischen Gesellschaftern *(vgl. Kommentar zu →joint tenancy)*; **presumption of** ~ Überlebensvermutung; **right of** ~ Anwachsungsrecht

susceptible fähig (of zu); ~ **of proof** beweisbar; **to be** ~ **of** zulassen

sushi bond Dollarbond japanischer Emittenten

suspect verdächtige Person; Tatverdächtiger; ansteckungsverdächtige Person[152]; verdächtig (of a th. e-r Sache); **political** ~**s are kept under surveillance** politisch verdächtige Personen werden überwacht

suspect *v* verdächtigen, in Verdacht haben (of wegen)

suspected, ~ **bill (of health)** Gesundheitspaß mit dem Vermerk „ansteckungsverdächtig"; ~ **of an escape attempt** fluchtverdächtig; ~ **ship** seuchenverdächtiges Schiff; **to be** ~ **of having committed an offen|ce (~ se)** tatverdächtig sein

suspend *v (vorübergehend)* einstellen, aussetzen; *(einstweilig)* aufheben (od. außer Kraft setzen); *(jdn)* suspendieren; *(jdn zeitweilig)* ausschließen; **to** ~ **execution** die Zwangsvollstreckung *(einstweilig)* einstellen; **to** ~ **the license** *Am* die *(amtl.)* Genehmigung *(zeitweilig)* zurücknehmen; den Führerschein *(zeitweilig)* entziehen; **to** ~ **nuclear weapon tests** Kernwaffenversuche einstellen; **to** ~ **an order** e-n Befehl aufheben; **to** ~ **payment of one's debts** Zahlung einstellen *(Konkursgrund)*; **to** ~ **performance** die Erfüllung *(e-s Vertrages etc)* aussetzen; **to** ~ **proceedings** das Verfahren aussetzen; **to** ~ **a sentence** die Vollstreckung e-r Strafe aussetzen; **to** ~ **sb. (from office)** jdn *(einstweilig)* des Amtes entheben, jdn suspendieren; **to** ~ **the traffic** den Verkehr unterbrechen; **to** ~ **work** die Arbeit einstellen

suspended (prison) sentence zur Bewährung ausgesetzte Freiheitsstrafe; **to give a p. a six-month** ~ jdn zu 6 Monaten mit Bewährung verurteilen

suspended, to be ~ ruhen *(Rechte, Pflichten)*; **to be** ~ **(from office)** *(vorläufig)* des Dienstes enthoben sein, suspendiert sein; **the benefits have been** ~ *(VersR)* die Leistungen ruhen; **the statute of limitation is** ~ die Verjährung ist gehemmt

suspense Ungewißheit; Schwebe; ~ **account** transitorisches Konto, Interimskonto; ~ **entry** vorläufige Buchung; Zwischeneintragung; ~ **items** vorläufige Posten, Übergangsposten; **to be (keep) in** ~ in der Schwebe (od. im Ungewissen) sein (lassen); **the matter is in** ~ die Angelegenheit ist in der Schwebe

suspension Einstellung, Aussetzung; *(einstweilige)* Aufhebung (od. Außerkraftsetzung); *(vorläufige)* Ausschließung; Suspension, *(vorläufige)* Amtsenthebung; ~ **agreement** *Am* Einstellungsübereinkommen mit ausländischen Regierungen betr. Beendigung von Subventions- od. Antidumping-Verfahren; ~ **(from office)** Suspension, *(einstweilige)* Dienstenthebung; ~ **of arms** Waffenruhe *(für vereinbarte Zeit od. vereinbarten Ort)*; ~ **of customs duties** Zollaussetzung; ~ **of diplomatic relations** Einstellung der diplomatischen Beziehungen; ~ **of a driver's license** *Am (zeitweilige)* Entziehung des Führerscheins; ~ **of earnings** (or **salary**) *Am (zeitweilige)* Aussetzung der Lohn- oder Gehaltszahlung *(z. B. als Disziplinarmaßnahme)*; ~ **of execution** Aussetzung der Zwangsvollstreckung; ~ **of gold standard** Aufhebung des Goldstandards; ~ **of hostilities** Einstellung der Feindseligkeiten; ~ **of the insurance** Ruhen der Versicherung; ~ **of members** *(vorübergehender)* Mitgliederausschluß; ~ **of military operations** Einstellung der Kampfhandlungen; ~ **of nuclear tests** Einstellung der Atom(waffen)versuche; ~ **of**

payment(s) Zahlungseinstellung; ~ **of privileges** Aufhebung von Vorrechten; ~ **of proceedings** Aussetzung des Verfahrens; ~ **of sentence** Aussetzung der Strafvollstreckung; ~ **of sentence (on probation)** Strafaussetzung (zur Bewährung) (→*probation 2.*); ~ **of a statute** *(vorläufige)* Außerkraftsetzung e-s Gesetzes; ~ **of the statute of limitations** Hemmung der Verjährung; ~ **of work** Aussetzung der Arbeit; ~ **without salary** vorläufige Dienstenthebung mit Einbehaltung der Dienstbezüge

suspensive aufschiebend; ~ **condition** *Am* und *Scot* Suspensivbedingung, aufschiebende Bedingung; ~ **effect** Suspensiveffekt, aufschiebende Wirkung

suspensory, ~ **condition**→suspensive condition; ~ **veto** *Am* die Gesetzeswerdung aufschiebendes Veto

suspicion Verdacht (of a p. gegen jdn); **reasonable (grounds for)** ~ hinreichender Verdacht; **unfounded** ~ grundloser Verdacht; **upon strong** ~ wegen dringenden Verdachts; ~ **is (up)on him** es besteht Verdacht gegen ihn; **to be under** ~ im Verdacht stehen; **to cast** (or **draw**) ~ **on** Verdacht lenken auf; **to entertain** (or **have**) **a** ~ Verdacht hegen; **to be held on** ~ **of theft** (or *Am* **larceny**) (at a police station) wegen Diebstahlsverdacht festgenommen sein

suspicious verdächtig; ~ **fact** Verdachtsmoment

sustain *v* 1. *(als richtig)* bestätigen, als rechtsgültig anerkennen; *(etw.)* rechtfertigen, erhärten; *(e-m Antrag, Einwand, Klagebegehren etc)* stattgeben; *(Anspruch etc)* aufrechterhalten; *(jdn od. jds Anspruch)* unterstützen; ~**ed** *Am (vom Richter)* anerkannt *(opp. overruled)*; **the court** ~**ed the motion (objection)** das Gericht gab dem Antrag (der Einwendung) statt; **the evidence** ~**ed his allegation** der Beweis rechtfertigte s-e Behauptung

sustain *v* 2. *Am* unterhalten, für den Unterhalt sorgen; **to** ~ **a family** e-e Familie unterhalten

sustain *v* 3. *(etw.)* (aufrecht)erhalten, fortsetzen; **to** ~ **a conversation** e-e Unterhaltung fortführen; ~**ed interest** anhaltendes Interesse; ~ **ed growth** dauerhaftes Wachstum

sustain *v* 4. ertragen, ausstehen; **to** ~ **the burden of proof** den e-m obliegenden Beweis erbringen; **to** ~ **comparison** e-m Vergleich standhalten; **whatever costs and expenses he may have reasonably** ~**ed** die ihm vernünftigerweise entstandenen Kosten und Auslagen

sustain *v* 5. erleiden; **to** ~ **damage** Schaden erleiden; **to** ~ **a defeat** e-e Niederlage erleiden; **to** ~ **an industrial injury** e-n Arbeitsunfall erleiden; **to** ~ **injuries** Verletzungen davontragen; **to** ~ **a loss** e-n Verlust erleiden

sustaining program *Am (Radio)* Programm *(ohne Reklameeinschaltung)*

sustenance (Lebens-)Unterhalt; Versorgung; Nährwert

sustentation fund Untersützungsfonds *(bes. für bedürftige Geistliche)*

suzerain *(VölkerR)* Suzerän, (souveräner) Oberstaat

suzerainty *(VölkerR)* Suzeränität, Schutzhoheit *(e-s Oberstaates)*; **state under** ~ Vasallenstaat

swap Tausch; *(Devisenhandel)* Swap, Swapgeschäft *(zur Kurssicherung); colloq.* Tausch(handel)

Das Swapgeschäft ist eine Devisentransaktion unter Banken, wobei der Verkäufer der Devisen diese per Kasse abgibt und sie gleichzeitig auf Termin wieder zurückkauft oder umgekehrt. Dadurch wird der Rücktausch in die eigene Währung ohne Kursrisiko möglich

swap, ~ **agreement** Swapabkommen; ~ **dealer** Swap-Händler (→*International S~ Dealers Association*); ~ **offer** Umtauschangebot; ~ **rate** Swapsatz *(Unterschied zwischen Devisenterminkurs und Devisenkassakurs)*; ~ **transaction** Swapgeschäft; **to engage in** ~ **transactions** Swaptransaktionen *(Kurssicherungsgeschäfte)* vornehmen

swap, asset-equity ~ Schuldenswap

Beitrag zur marktgerechten Lösung des internationalen Schuldenproblems. Mit seiner Hilfe können Auslandsschulden in Direktinvestitionen umgewandelt werden

swap, currency ~ Währungsswap

Devisenswapgeschäft z. B. zwischen zwei Unternehmen oder zwei Zentralbanken. Tausch und Verbindlichkeiten in unterschiedlicher Währung einschließlich der anfallenden Zinsen

swap, cross-currency interest rate ~ Tausch fester Zinszahlungen in einer Währung gegen feste Zinszahlungen in anderer Währung *(Kombination von currency swap und interest rate swap)*

swap, debt ~ Schuldenswap *(cf. loan →~)*

swap, debt-equity ~ Umwandlung von Forderungs- in Beteiligungskapital

swap, financial ~ Finanzswap

Austausch von Zahlungsströmen zwischen zwei oder mehr Vertragsparteien für eine bestimmte Zeit. Sie dienen im wesentlichen dazu, das Währungs- und/oder Zinsrisiko offener Positionen zu schließen, Finanzierungskosten zu senken bzw. die Erträge aus Anlagen zu verbessern (interest rate →~, currency →~, cross-currency interest rate →~)

swap, interest rate ~ Zinsswap

Tausch unterschiedlicher Zinsarten in einer Währung *(z. B. feste gegen variable Zinsen)*

swap, loan ~ Forderungstausch *(zwischen Banken zum Management ihrer Kreditportefeuilles)*

swap *v* tauschen; *(Devisenhandel)* ‚swappen' *(per Kasse verkaufen und auf Termin wieder zurück-*

kaufen oder umgekehrt); Swapgeschäft(e) durchführen

swapping Swapgeschäft; **house** ~ Haus- od. Wohnungstausch

SWAPO (South West African People's Organization) Organisation des Südwestafrikanischen Volkes *(von Namibia)*

Swaption Option aus Ausübung e-s Swap; **extendable** ~ Option auf Verlängerung e-s Swapkontrakts

Swaziland, Kingdom of ~ Königreich Swasiland

Swazi Swasi; swasiländisch

swear *v* schwören; *(jdn)* vereidigen; *(jdn od. etw.)* beeid(ig)en (→*sworn*); fluchen; **to** ~ **at sb.** jdn beschimpfen; **to** ~ **falsely** falsch schwören *(→false swearing)*; **to** ~ **sb. in** jdn vereidigen (od. beeid[ig]en); **to** ~ **in an official** e-n Beamten vereidigen; e-m Beamten den Dienstеid abnehmen; **to** ~ **in a witness** e-n Zeugen beeidigen; **to** ~ **out a warrant of arrest** e-n Haftbefehl durch beschworene Strafanzeige erwirken; **to** ~ **to sth.** etw. beschwören (od. beeid[ig]en); ~ **an affidavit** e-e schriftliche eidliche Versicherung abgeben; **to** ~ **an oath** e-n Eid leisten; (etw.) beeid(ig)en; **to** ~ **the peace** *Br* schwören, daß einem Körperverletzung droht (against von); **to** ~ **a p. to secrecy** jdn eidlich zur Verschwiegenheit verpflichten; **to** ~ **to the truth of a statement** die Wahrheit e-r Aussage beschwören; **I solemnly** ~ **to tell the truth, the whole truth and nothing but the truth** ich schwöre feierlich, die reine Wahrheit zu sagen, nichts zu verschweigen und nichts hinzuzufügen

swearing Schwören; Eidesleistung; Fluchen; ~ **in** Vereidigung, Beeidigung; ~ **in of witnesses** Zeugenbeeidigung; **false** ~ Falschbeschwören (→ *false*)

sweat damage Schiffsdunstschaden, Kondenswasserschaden *(durch Bildung von „Schiffs-" oder „Ladungsschweiß")*; **liable for** ~ haftbar für Schiffsdunstschaden

sweat-shop Ausbeutungsbetrieb, Betrieb(sraum) mit schlechten Arbeitsbedingungen (→ *sweating system)*

sweat *v* für Hungerlohn arbeiten; *(Arbeiter)* ausbeuten, für Hungerlohn arbeiten lassen

sweated, ~ **labo(u)r** ausgebeutete *(schlechtbezahlte etc)* Arbeiter; ~ **money** Hungerlohn

sweating system Ausbeutungssystem *(bes. durch Zwischenunternehmer oder Zwischenmeister [vgl. § 2 HeimarbG] vermittelte Beschäftigung von ungelernten Arbeitern od. Heimarbeitern gegen geringen Stücklohn)*

Swede Schwede, Schwedin

Sweden Schweden; **Kingdom of** ~ Königreich Schweden

Swedish schwedisch

sweep account *Am* →account 1.

sweeping reform weitreichende Reform

SWIFT ~ Society for Worldwide Interbank Financial Telecommunication

Swiftair *Br* Schnellsendungen durch Luftpost

swindle Schwindel, Betrug; **insurance** ~ Versicherungsbetrug

swindle *v* beschwindeln, betrügen

swindler Schwindler, Betrüger, Hochstapler

swing 1. Schwung; *fig* Umschwung; *Am sl.* Konjunkturperiode; *Am* Wahlreise durch die verschiedenen Wahlkreise; ~**back** *Am pol* Umschwung; ~ **shift** *Am* (8-Stunden-)Schicht *(ab 16 Uhr)*; ~ **to the left** *pol* Umschwung nach links

swing 2. Swing, Kreditmarge *(wechselseitig eingeräumte Kreditlinie im internationalen Zahlungsverkehr)*; gegenseitig eingeräumter, zinsloser Überziehungskredit im innerdeutschen Handel; ~ **credit** *(zinsloser)* Überziehungskredit; ~ **line** *Am* kurzfristiger Überziehungskredit

swing *v Am* erfolgreich durchführen

Swiss Schweizer, ~in; schweizerisch; ~ **Confederation** Schweizerische Eidgenossenschaft (→ *Switzerland*); ~ **Options and Financial Futures Exchange** (Soffex) Schweizer Börse für Optionen und Finanzterminkontrakte (Schweizer Terminbörse)

switch 1. *(Außenhandel)* Switchgeschäft

Warengeschäft, das aus devisenwirtschaftl. Gründen nicht unmittelbar mit dem Empfangsland getätigt, sondern über ein drittes Land geleitet wird. (Beim Importswitch werden die Waren in einem anderen als dem Herstellerland gekauft, beim Exportswitch gehen die Ausfuhrgüter in ein anderes als das endgültige Käuferland)

switch 2. *(Effektenhandel)* Switch *(Verkauf e-s Wertpapieres, dessen Anlage nicht günstig erscheint, und Anlage des Erlöses in e-m anderen Wertpapier)*; ~ **funds** Anlagemittel

switch-board Schalttafel; Telefonzentrale, Vermittlung

switch *v* (um)schalten; umlenken, umleiten; *(Eisenbahn)* rangieren; *(Außenhandel)* ein Switchgeschäft machen, switchen (→ *switch 1.*); **to** ~ **(over) to** hinüberwechseln zu; **to** ~ **over production** die Produktion umstellen (to auf); **to** ~ **cargo** Güter umleiten

switching *(Investmentgeschäft)* Überwechseln von einem Fonds zum anderen; ~ **of securities** Umschichtung (od. Austausch) von Wertpapieren *(gegen Wertpapiere anderer Unternehmen zum Zwecke der Werterhaltung e-s Portefeuille)*; **tax** ~ Portefeuilleumschichtung aus steuerlichen Gründen

Switzerland Schweiz (→*Swiss*)

sworn vereidigt, beeidigt; beschworen; ~ **before me** vor mir beschworen; ~ **certificate** *Am* Urkunde in „beschworener" Form *(für die Gründung e-r limited partnership erforderlich)*; ~ **evidence** eidliche Zeugenaussage; ~ **expert** beeidigter Sachverständiger; ~ **statement** eidliche Erklärung; ~ **witness** beeidigter Zeuge; **being duly** ~ nach ordnungsgemäßer Vereidigung; **to be** ~ **in** vereidigt werden; **he was** ~ **in as a member** er wurde als Mitglied vereidigt; **to be** ~ **to secrecy** zur (Amts-)Verschwiegenheit eidlich verpflichtet werden

syllabus Lehrplan; Zusammenfassung, Inhaltsangabe; *Am* kurze Darstellung der entschiedenen od. erörterten Rechtsfragen in e-r (später) veröffentlichten Entscheidung (reported case)

symbol Symbol, Kennzeichen; Signatur *(bei Büchern)*; **official** ~ **of a state** staatliches Hoheitszeichen

sympathetic, ~ **strike** Sympathiestreik; **to accord** (or **give**) ~ **consideration (to)** *(etw.)* wohlwollend in Betracht ziehen (od. prüfen)

sympathetically, to examine ~ wohlwollend prüfen

sympathizer Anhänger (with a policy e-r Politik); Sympathisant; Mitläufer *(e-r Partei, ohne Mitglied zu sein)*

sympathy Sympathie; Mitgefühl; Beileid; ~ **strike** Sympathiestreik; **letter of** ~ Beileidsschreiben; **to express** (or **offer**) **one's** ~ **to a p.** jdm sein Beileid aussprechen, jdm kondolieren

symposium Symposium; Sammlung von Beiträgen über ein Thema von verschiedenen Verfassern; Kolloquium, Diskussionsveranstaltung

symptom Symptom; ~**s of (an) inflation** Anzeichen für e-e Inflation

synallagmatic contract synallagmatischer (od. gegenseitiger) Vertrag

synchronize *v (zeitlich)* übereinstimmen

synchronization *(zeitliche)* Übereinstimmung

syndic Syndikus, Rechtsberater

syndicalism Syndikalismus *(sozialrevolutionäre Arbeiterbewegung, deren Ziel die Übernahme der Produktionsmittel durch die gewerkschaftl. Verbände ist)*; **criminal** ~ *Am* →criminal

syndicate[153] Interessengemeinschaft, Konsortium *(vorübergehender Zusammenschluß mehrerer Banken od. anderer Unternehmen zur Durchführung e-s gemeinsamen Geschäftes, z.B. zur Ausgabe e-r neuen Anleihe)*; Konsortial-; *Br* Zusammenschluß mehrerer →underwriters von →Lloyd's *(zwecks Risikenausgleich)*; Nachrichtenagentur *(die Artikel etc zur gleichzeitigen Veröffentlichung in verschiedenen Zeitungen verkauft)*; *Am* geschäftlich getarnte Verbrecherorganisation; ~ **account** Konsortialkonto; ~ **agreement** Konsortialvertrag; ~ **of American banks** amerikanisches Bankenkonsortium; ~ **banking** *Am* Bank-Konsortialgeschäft; ~ **credit** (or **loan**) Konsortialkredit; ~ **manager** führende Bank e-s Konsortiums; ~ **member** Konsortialmitglied, Konsorte; ~ **participation** Konsortialbeteiligung; ~ **transactions** Konsortialgeschäfte; **banking** ~ Bankenkonsortium; **financial** ~ Finanzkonsortium; **issue** ~ Emissionskonsortium; **market** ~ Börsenkonsortium; **member banks of a** ~ Konsortialbanken; **original** ~ *Am* Übernahmekonsortium; **participant in a** ~→~ member; **participation in a** ~ Konsortialbeteiligung; **promoting** ~ Gründerkonsortium (→ *promoting*); **underwriting** ~ →underwriting 1.; **to form a** ~ ein Konsortium bilden

syndicate *v* ein Konsortium bilden; sich zu e-r Interessengemeinschaft zusammenschließen; *(Artikel)* an verschiedene Zeitungen gleichzeitig verkaufen

syndicated, ~ **article** in mehreren Zeitungen gleichzeitig erscheinender Artikel; ~ **bid** *Br* Abgabe von Angeboten der Diskontbanken bei der wöchentlichen Ausschreibung von Schatzwechseln *(→weekly tender)*; ~ **Eurocurrency credit** unverbriefter Eurokonsortialkredit; ~ **loan** Konsortialkredit

synthetic fibres Chemiefasern

synetics *Am* Methode für schöpferisches Gruppen-Denken *(e-s Teams)*
Bes. von großen Firmen benutztes System, die Lösung bestimmter Probleme einer Gruppe meist aus verschiedenen Berufen stammender Persönlichkeiten zu übertragen, die innerhalb einer Firma od. freiberuflich arbeitet und sich für ihre Tätigkeit u. a. der Erkenntnisse der Denk-, Persönlichkeits- und Sozialpsychologie bedient

synod *eccl* Synode, Kirchenversammlung *(Br cf. Convocation)*

synopsis Synopsis; *(kurze)* Zusammenfassung, vergleichende Übersicht

synoptic report zusammenfassender Bericht

synthetic synthetisch; ~**s** Kunststoff(e)

Syria Syrien

Syrian Syrer, ~in; syrisch; ~ **Arab Republic** Arabische Republik Syrien

system System; Anordnung; ~ **of government** Regierungssystem; ~ **of roads** Straßennetz; **accounting** ~ Buchungssystem; Buchführungssystem; **cash** ~ Barzahlungssystem;

clearing ~ Verrechnungssystem; **credit** ~ Kreditwesen; **currency** ~ Währungssystem; **economic** ~ Wirtschaftssystem; **electoral** ~ Wahlsystem; **fiscal** ~ Steuersystem; Finanzsystem; **government** ~ Regierungssystem; **legal**~ Rechtssystem; Rechtsordnung; **railway (railroad)** ~ Eisenbahnnetz; **to follow a** ~ ein System befolgen

systematize *v* systematisieren, in ein System bringen, planmäßig ordnen

T

tab Schildchen, (Kartei-)Reiter; *colloq.* Rechnung; Kontrolle; **to keep ~s on sb.** jdn überwachen

table Tisch; Tabelle, Verzeichnis, Liste; **T~ A** *Br*[1] Muster der Satzung (articles of association) e-r AG; ~ **of authorities consulted** Verzeichnis der benutzten Quellen; ~ **of contents** Inhaltsverzeichnis; ~ **of charges** Gebührentabelle; ~ **of events** Festprogramm; ~ **of par values** Paritätentabelle; **conversion** ~ Umrechnungstabelle; **interest** ~ Zinstabelle; **mortality** ~ *(VersR)* Sterbetafel; **redemption** ~ Tilgungsplan; **to compile ~s** Tabellen aufstellen; **to lay on the** ~ *parl (Antrag etc)* auf unbestimmte Zeit zurückstellen

table *v* auf den Tisch legen; tabellarisch eintragen; **to ~ a Bill** *Br* e-n Gesetzesentwurf einbringen; *Am* e-n Gesetzesentwurf auf unbestimmte Zeit vertagen; **to ~ a question** *Br parl* e-e Anfrage *(schriftl.)* einbringen

tabled, ~ **amendment** *Br parl* beantragte Änderung *(e-s Gesetzesentwurfs)*; Änderungsantrag; **amendments ~ by the group** *Br* von der Fraktion vorgelegte Änderungsanträge

tabular tabellarisch, Tabellen-; ~ **bookkeeping** amerikanische Buchführung; **in ~ form** tabellarisch, in Tabellenform; ~ **premium** Tarifprämie; ~ **statement** Aufstellung in Tabellenform, tabellarische Aufstellung

tabulate *v* in Tabellen bringen (od. aufstellen); tabellieren

tabulation Aufstellung in Tabellenform; tabellarische Anordnung; Tabellierung

tacit stillschweigend; ~ **agreement** stillschweigende Vereinbarung *(opp. express agreement)*; ~ **approval** stillschweigende Genehmigung; ~ **mortgage** *Am* Hypothek kraft Gesetzes; Zwangshypothek; ~ **renewal of a contract** stillschweigende Verlängerung e-s Vertrages; **to agree ~ly** stillschweigend zustimmen

tack *v* anheften, anfügen; anrechnen; zusammenheften, zusammenfügen, aneinanderreihen, verbinden, vereinigen; **to ~ mortgages, possessions** *(etc)* →tacking

tacking Anheftung, Anfügung; Anrechnung; Zusammenheftung, Zusammenfügung, Aneinanderreihung, Verbindung, Vereinigung; ~ **of mortgages**[2] Vereinigung e-r nachrangigen *(meist dritten)* mit e-r vorrangigen *(meist ersten)* Hypothek unter rangmäßiger Zurückdrängung von Zwischenrechten *(meist zweite Hypothek)*; ~ **of possessions** *(in the law of prescription) Am* Anrechnung von Besitzzeiten von Vorbesitzern auf die Besitzzeit des gegenwärtigen Besitzers *(um die zum Rechtserwerb erforderliche Ersitzungszeit zu erreichen)*; ~ **of provisions to money bill** *Br (rechtsmißbräuchliche)* Einfügung von Bestimmungen in den →money bill *(die mit diesem nichts zu tun haben, um sie im House of Lords durchzubringen, das money bills nicht abändern darf)*; ~ **of (successive) disabilities** *(in the law of limitation to actions) Am* Zusammenrechnung verschiedener *(in der Person der Partei und ihrer Rechtsvorgänger begründeter)* Hemmungszeiten der Verjährung *(um die Klageverjährung auszuschließen)*

tactical atomic (or **nuclear**) **weapons** taktische Atomwaffen

Taft-Hartley Act 1947 *Am*

Amerikanisches Arbeitsgrundgesetz *(offizieller Titel:* Labor Management Relations Act), das die Beziehungen zwischen den Sozialpartnern regelt und verschiedene Gewerkschaftspraktiken für ungesetzlich erklärt. Das Gesetz sieht u.a. eine →cooling-off period vor jeder Streikaktion vor sowie das Recht des Präsidenten, e-n Streik für 80 Tage auszusetzen, wenn er die nationale Sicherheit und die wirtschaftl. Stabilität der USA gefährden könnte

tag Anhänger, Anhängezettel, Etikett; ~ **label** Anhängezettel *(opp. gummed label)*; **identification ~** *mil* Erkennungsmarke; **price** ~ Preiszettel, Preisschild

tag *v* mit e-m Anhängezettel versehen; *(Ware)* auszeichnen

tail erbrechtliche Beschränkung von Eigentum *(Beschränkung in der Erbfolge)*; **~(-) back** Verkehrsstau; ~ **female** Beschränkung auf weibliche Nachkommen; ~ **male** Beschränkung auf männliche Nachkommen; **estate in (fee)** ~ erbrechtlich gebundenes Grundeigentum *(Br existiert seit dem Law of Property Act 1925 nur noch als →equitable interest; →estate)*; **issue in** ~ *(GrundstücksR)* Nachkommen(schaft) als Erben von erbrechtlich gebundenem Grundbesitz (→*issue 2.*); **tenant in** ~ (Grundstücks-)Eigentümer, dessen Rechte durch Nacherbenbestimmungen beschränkt sind

tailgate, don't ~ *Am (Verkehr)* Abstand halten

taint, hereditary ~ erbliche Belastung

take (Geld-)Einnahme; Menge *(Fischfang etc)*; ~ **(-)away meals** Mahlzeiten zum Mitnehmen; ~**-home pay** Nettolohn; ~**-off** Start; Abflug

takeover Übernahme; Geschäfts-, Firmenübernahme; Übernahme e-r AG durch Erwerb ihrer Aktien; ~ **agreement** Übernahmevertrag

takeover bid (TOB)[3] Übernahmeangebot

Die übernehmende Gesellschaft macht den Aktionären der einzugliedernden Gesellschaft das Angebot, ihre Aktien zu erwerben, entweder im Wege des Kaufes gegen Barzahlung oder im Wege des Tausches gegen Aktien der übernehmenden Gesellschaft. Als Ergebnis wird die übernehmende Gesellschaft die Muttergesellschaft der einzugliedernden Gesellschaft. Normalerweise bleiben die beiden Gesellschaften als Rechtspersönlichkeiten bestehen und sind dann verbundene Gesellschaften. In Großbritannien zieht man den take-over der Verschmelzung (amalgamation) vor

takeover, T~ Code *Br* Regeln für die Übernahme von Unternehmen; ~ **negotiations** Übernahmeverhandlungen; ~ **of a firm** Übernahme e-r Firma; **T~ Panel** *Br* Kontrollorgan für Übernahmen und Fusionen *(Abkürzung für: City of London's Panel on Takeovers and Mergers)*; ~ **price** Übernahmepreis; ~ **target** Übernahmeziel; ~ **terms** Übernahmebedingungen; **friendly** ~ freundliche (od. einvernehmliche) Übernahme *(Übernahme mit Billigung der Zielgesellschaft)*; **hostile** ~ feindselige, nicht einvernehmliche Übernahme *(gegen den Willen der Zielgesellschaft durchgeführte Übernahme)*

take *v* nehmen, entgegennehmen, abnehmen, annehmen, wegnehmen, mitnehmen; **to ~ account of sth.** etw. berücksichtigen; **to ~ action** etw. veranlassen; Schritte unternehmen; **to ~ advantage of the opportunity** (to) die Gelegenheit benutzen, (um); **to ~ advantage of sb.** jdn ausnützen, jdn übervorteilen; **to ~ an affidavit** e-e (schriftl.) eidliche Erklärung entgegennehmen; **to ~ a chance** wagen, riskieren; **to ~ charge of**→charge 3.; **to ~ sb. in charge** jdn festnehmen

take *v*, **to ~ delivery of the goods** die Ware(n) abnehmen; **failure to ~ delivery** Nichtabnahme *(der Lieferung)*

take *v*, **to ~ sb. at a disadvantage** jdn in ungünstiger Situation treffen; **to ~ evidence** → evidence; **to ~ the floor** *parl* das Wort ergreifen; **to ~ sth. for granted** etw. als Tatsache hinnehmen; etw. als selbstverständlich ansehen; **to ~ information** Auskunft (od. Informationen) einholen; **to ~ an interest in an enterprise** sich für ein Unternehmen interessieren; sich an e-m Unternehmen *(finanziell)* beteiligen; **to ~ an inventory** ein Inventar (od. Bestandsverzeichnis) aufstellen; inventarisieren; **to ~ issue with sb. (on sth.)** sich mit jdm in e-e Auseinandersetzung (über e-n Punkt) einlassen; **to ~ legal advice** sich juristisch beraten lassen; **to ~ measures** Maßnahmen ergreifen; **to ~ a p.'s name and address** jds Namen und Anschrift notieren; **to ~ notes** sich Notizen machen (of über); notieren; **to ~ notice** beachten; Kenntnis nehmen (of von); **to ~ an order** e-e Bestellung (od. e-n Auftrag) annehmen; **to ~ a paper** e-e Zeitung halten; **to ~ part** sich beteiligen (in an); **to ~ place** stattfinden; **to ~ the place of sb.** jdn ersetzen; **to ~ a poll** abstimmen, e-e Abstimmung vornehmen; **to ~ possession of sth.** etw. in Besitz nehmen; **to ~ possession of the completed work** *(beim Werkvertrag)* das Werk abnehmen; **to ~ power** die Macht ergreifen; **to ~ (legal) proceedings** e-n Prozeß anstrengen; gerichtlich vorgehen (against gegen); **to ~ a record of a speech** e-e Rede mitschreiben; **to ~ the risk** das Risiko auf sich nehmen, riskieren; **to ~ steps** Schritte unternehmen; **to ~ sb.'s testimony** jdn als Zeugen vernehmen; **to ~ time** Zeit benötigen (od. brauchen); dauern; **to ~ title** *Am* Eigentum erwerben; **to ~ a vote** abstimmen (lassen) (on über); **to ~ under a will** auf Grund e-s Testaments erben

take *v*, **to ~ away** wegnehmen, mitnehmen; **to ~ back** *(Waren, Versprechen etc)* zurücknehmen; **to ~ down** aufschreiben, niederschreiben, notieren; herunternehmen (from von); **to ~ down a speech in shorthand** e-e Rede stenografisch aufnehmen; **to ~ for** *(jdn) (irrtümlich)* halten für; **to ~ in** *(Gäste etc)* aufnehmen; *(Arbeit für zu Hause)* übernehmen *(washing, typewriting etc)*; einschließen, einbegreifen; *(Waren)* hereinnehmen; *(Ladung)* einnehmen; *(Geld)* einnehmen; *colloq.* anführen (→*to be taken in*); *Br (Börse) (Termingeschäft)* in Report nehmen; hereinnehmen; **to ~ into consideration** in Betracht ziehen; **to ~ a p. into → partnership**

take *v*, **to ~ off** wegnehmen; *(Skonto, Rabatt)* abziehen; abfliegen, starten; **to ~ a p.'s name off the list** jdn von der Liste streichen; **to ~ off the price** vom Preise nachlassen; **to ~ off the seals** die Siegel abnehmen, entsiegeln; **to ~ off a train** e-n Zug aus dem Verkehr ziehen

take *v*, **to ~ on** *(Arbeit, Verantwortung)* übernehmen; *(Arbeiter)* einstellen; *(als Mitglied)* aufnehmen; **to ~ on charter** chartern, *(Schiff od. Flugzeug)* mieten; **to ~ on credit** auf Kredit kaufen, anschreiben lassen; **to ~ on hire** mieten; **to ~ on a job** e-e Arbeit übernehmen; **to ~ (a house) on lease** (ein Haus) mieten

take *v*, **to ~ out** *v* herausnehmen; *(Patent, Vorladung)* erwirken; *(Versicherung)* abschließen; **to**

~ **out a certificate** sich e-e Bescheinigung ausstellen lassen; **to ~ out citizenship papers** *Am* die Einbürgerung erwirken; **to ~ out a licen|ce (~se)** →licen|ce (~se) 1. und 3.; **to ~ out a life insurance** sein Leben versichern lassen; e-e Lebensversicherung abschließen; **to ~ out a mortgage** e-e Hypothek aufnehmen; **to ~ out a passport** sich e-n Paß beschaffen; **to ~ out a patent** (for) sich patentieren lassen; **to ~ out a policy** e-e Versicherung abschließen; sich versichern lassen; **to ~ out probate of a will** → probate; **to ~ out a summons against sb.** jdn (vor)laden lassen

take *v*, **to ~ over** *(Aufgabe, Amt, Ware etc)* übernehmen; **to ~ over a business** (or **a firm**) ein Geschäft (od. e-e Firma) übernehmen; **to ~ over the management** die Leitung übernehmen (of von)

take *v*, **to ~ up** übernehmen; aufnehmen; *(Posten)* antreten; *(Laufbahn)* einschlagen; *(Passagiere)* mitnehmen; **to ~ up an agency** e-e Vertretung übernehmen; **to ~ up a bill** e-n Wechsel einlösen; e-n Wechsel akzeptieren; **to ~ up the documents** die Dokumente übernehmen (od. in Empfang nehmen); **to ~ up employment** Beschäftigung aufnehmen; **to ~ up a loan** ein Darlehen (od. Kredit) aufnehmen; **to ~ up money** Geld aufnehmen; **to ~ up an option** ein Optionsrecht ausüben; **to ~ up a profession** e-n Beruf ergreifen; **to ~ up shares** Aktien beziehen, Aktien zeichnen

taken genommen; besetzt; ~ **as a whole** im ganzen betrachtet; **not to be ~ away** nicht mitnehmen *(z.B. Bücher in Bibliothek)*; **to be ~ in** getäuscht (od. hereingefallen) sein; **he was ~ off to prison** er wurde ins Gefängnis abgeführt

taken over, company ~ übernommene Gesellschaft

taker 1. Abnehmer, Käufer; *Am* Erbe *(auf Grund letztwilliger Verfügung)*, Vermächtnisnehmer; ~ **of a bill** Wechselnehmer; **~-out of a patent** Patentinhaber

taker 2. *Br (Börse)* Hereinnehmer *(opp. giver; cf. to take in)*; ~ **for a call** Verkäufer e-r Vorprämie; ~ **for a call of more** Verkäufer e-s Rechts zur Nachforderung; ~ **for a put** Käufer e-r Rückprämie; ~ **of an option** *Br* Optionsnehmer, Prämiennehmer; **the market is all ~s** es herrscht Baissestimmung am Markt

taking Wegnahme; Nehmen; **~s** Einnahmen; **to check the day's ~s** die Tageseinnahmen nachprüfen

taking, ~ delivery of the goods Abnahme der Ware(n); ~ **effect** Inkrafttreten; ~ **evidence** Beweisaufnahme, Beweiserhebung; ~ **an inventory** Inventur, Bestandsaufnahme; ~ **an oath** Eidesleistung; ~ **possession** Besitzergreifung, Besitznahme; ~ **samples** Musterziehung; ~ **testimony** Zeugenvernehmung; **profit ~** *(Börse)* Gewinnrealisierung; **unlawful ~** unrechtmäßiges Wegnehmen

taking, ~ off the seals Siegelabnahme, Entsiegelung; ~ **out an insurance contract** Abschluß e-s Versicherungsvertrages; ~ **out a patent** Erlangung e-s Patents; ~ **out of pawn** Pfandeinlösung

taking over Abnahme, Übernahme; ~ **a business** Übernahme e-s Geschäfts, Geschäftsübernahme; ~ **price** Übernahmekurs; **company ~** übernehmende Gesellschaft; **delayed ~** Abnahmeverzug *(beim Werkvertrag)*

taking up, ~ of capital Kapitalaufnahme; ~ **a loan** Darlehnsaufnahme; ~ **an office** Dienstantritt; ~ **of stock** Abnahme der Aktien; **(up)on ~ one's post** bei Dienstantritt

tale quale (t/q., T. Q.) →tel quel

tales Ersatzmänner e-r jury; Ersatzgeschworene

talesman Ersatzgeschworener

Talisman *Br (Börse) (1979 eingeführtes)* computergesteuertes Abrechnungssystem, das Büros auf der ganzen Welt unterhält *(Clearinghaus für Wertpapiere)*

talk Gespräch; Unterredung, Besprechung; *(zwangloser)* Vortrag (on über); **~s about ~s** *Am pol* (Sondierungs-)Gespräche, in welchem Rahmen und mit welchem Ziel Verhandlungen möglich sind; **confidential ~** vertrauliche Unterredung; **informal ~** zwangloses Gespräch; **preliminary ~s** Vorbesprechungen; **to give a ~** e-n Vortrag halten; **to hold ~s with** Besprechungen abhalten mit; **to resume political ~s** politische Gespräche wiederaufnehmen

talk *v* reden (of or about über); sich besprechen; **to ~ business (politics)** über Geschäfte (Politik) sprechen; **to ~ a matter over** (or **to ~ over a matter**) *colloq.* e-e Sache besprechen; **to ~ out** *parl* durch lange Debatten Abstimmung verhindern; **to ~ shop** *colloq.* fachsimpeln

tally Gegenrechnung; (Konto-)Gegenbuch *(e-s Kunden)*; Gegenstück; Abhaken, Kontrolle (→ *tallying*); Etikett, Kennzeichen *(z.B. auf Kisten)*; **~clerk** Kontrolleur; *(Seefrachtgeschäft)* Ladungskontrolleur; *Am* Stimmenzähler *(bei Wahlen)*; **~man** Tallyman; Kontrolleur, Nachprüfer der Stückzahlen *(beim Be- und Entladen von Schiffen)*; ~ **sheet** Kontrolliste; ~ **trade** *Br* Teilzahlungsgeschäft

tally *v* kontrollieren, nachzählen; abhaken; *(Waren)* auszeichnen, etikettieren; übereinstimmen (with mit)

tallying Abhaken *(der Zahl der Stücke)*; Tallieren *(Kontrolltätigkeit beim Be- und Entladen der Schiffe)*

talon *Br* Talon, Erneuerungsschein *(zum Bezug e-s neuen Couponbogens)*

tamper *v,* **to ~ with sth.** *(in betrügerischer Absicht)* Veränderungen vornehmen an etw.; etw. fälschen; **to ~ with sb.** jdn bestechen; **to ~ with a document** e-e Urkunde fälschen
tampering, ~ with mail unbefugtes Handhaben der Post; **~ with records**[4] Vornahme von Fälschungen an Eintragungen; **~ with witnesses**[5] (Versuch der) Zeugenbeeinflussung

tandem measure Junktim

tangible greifbar, körperlich; **~s** →~assets *(opp. intangibles)*; **~ assets** materielle Vermögenswerte (od. Wirtschaftsgüter) *(e-s Unternehmens)*; Sachvermögen; **~ fixed assets** Sachanlagevermögen; **~ property** →~ assets; **~ result** greifbares Ergebnis

tank Tank; *mil* Panzer; **~ battle** Panzerschlacht; **~ car** *(Eisenbahn)* Tankwagen, Kesselwagen; **~ ship** (or **vessel**) Tankschiff, Tanker; **~ shipping** Tankschiffahrt; **~ steamer** Tankdampfer

tanker Tanker, Tankschiff; Tankflugzeug; **~ fleet** Tankerflotte; **~ owner** Tankreeder

tantamount gleichbedeutend (to mit)

Tanzania Tansania; **United Republic of ~** Vereinigte Republik Tansania
Tanzanian Tansanier, ~in; tansanisch

tap 1. (Wasser-, Faß-, Gas-)Hahn
tap 2. *Br* jederzeit verfügbares Wertpapier *(bezieht sich nur auf Schatzwechsel und auf staatl. Schuldverschreibungen, nicht auf Aktien)*; **short ~** *Br* kurzfristige Regierungsanleihe; **~ bills** *Br* →~ **Treasury bills; ~ bonds** *Am* in unbegrenzter Höhe und auf unbestimmte Zeit ausgegebene Staatspapiere; **~ issue** *Br* vom →Treasury laufend *(unter Ausschaltung der Börse)* an Regierungsstellen und andere Käufer ausgegebene Wechsel und Wertpapiere; **~ stock** *Br* laufend ausgegebene staatl. Schuldverschreibungen; **~ Treasury bills** *Br* laufend ausgegebene Schatzwechsel

tap *v (auch fig)* anzapfen; erschließen; **to ~ a line** (or **wire**) ein Telefongespräch abhören; **to ~ new resources of energy** neue Energiequellen erschließen; **to ~ a telegraph wire** ein Telegramm abfangen
tapping, telephone ~ Abhören von Telefongesprächen; →**wire ~**

tape (Stoff-, Metall-)Band; Tape, Papierstreifen *(zum Aufschreiben der empfangenen Morsezeichen)*; *(Börse)* Papierstreifen *(auf dem laufend die Kurse verzeichnet werden)*; Tonband; **~ abbreviations** Börsenabkürzungen *(für den Börsenfernschreiber)*; **~ price** durch den Börsenfernschreiber (od. telegrafisch) mitgeteilter Kurs; **~ quotation** *(Börse)* Tape-Notierung; **~ recorder** Tonbandgerät; **~ recording** (Ton-) Bandaufnahme; **blank ~** Leerband; **(recording) ~** Tonband; **red ~** Bürokratismus; Amtsschimmel; **to record on ~** auf Tonband aufnehmen; ein Tonband besprechen

tape *v* auf Band sprechen; auf Tonband aufnehmen

taper off *v* auslaufen, zu Ende gehen

tardy *bes. Am* säumig; verspätet *(opp. prompt)*; **~ payer** säumiger Zahler

tare Tara (T, Ta) *(Gewicht der Verpackung)*; Taravergütung; **~ assumed by the customs** Zolltara; **~ weight** Taragewicht; **actual** (or **real**) **~** wirkliche Tara, Nettotara; **customary ~** Usotara; **customs ~** Zolltara; **super ~** zusätzliche Taravergütung; **to make allowance for ~** Tara vergüten; **to state the ~** tarieren

tare *v* tarieren, die Tara (od. das Verpackungsgewicht) bestimmen; die Tara vergüten

target Ziel; (Produktions-)Ziel, Soll; Zielgesellschaft *(→takeover)*; Adressat *(e-r Zustellung)*; **~ account** → *account 1.*; **~ area** *mil* luftgefährdetes Gebiet; **bombing of ~ areas** Flächenbombardierung; **~ company** Zielgesellschaft, Gesellschaft, die zum Ziel e-s Übernahmeangebots wird; **~ model** Entscheidungsmodell; **~ price** angestrebter Preis; Richtpreis; **sales ~** Verkaufsziel; **to achieve the ~** das Soll erfüllen

tariff 1. Zolltarif; Zoll, Zoll-; **T~ Act** *Am* Zollgesetz; **~ adjustment** Zoll(tarif)anpassung; **~ agreement** Zollabkommen; Zollvereinbarung; **~ barriers** Zollschranken; **~ classification** Tarifeinstufung, Tarifierung
tariff concessions Zugeständnisse auf dem Gebiete des Zollwesens; **schedules of ~** Zollzugeständnislisten; **to be accorded ~** Zollzugeständnisse erhalten
tariff, ~ cut(ting) Zollsenkung; **~ differential** Zollunterschied, Unterschied in den Zollsätzen; **~ discrimination** benachteiligende Zollbehandlung; **~ headings** Tarifstellen; **~ increase** Zollerhöhung; **~ item** Tarifposition; **~ law** Zollgesetz; **~ legislation** Zollgesetzgebung; **~ maker** *Am* Zollgesetzgeber; Zoll festsetzende Stelle; **~ making** *Am* Zollfestsetzung; **~ negotiations** Zoll(tarif)verhandlungen; **~ nomenclature** Zolltarifschema; **~ policy** Zollpolitik; **~ preferences** Zollpräferenzen; **~-protected** durch Zölle geschützt; **~ protection** Schutz durch Zölle; **~ quota** Zollkontingent
tariff rate Zollsatz; **lowering** (or **reduction**) **of ~s** Senkung der Zollsätze; **raising** (or **increase**) **of ~s** Erhöhung der Zollsätze
tariff, ~ reduction Zollherabsetzung, Zollsenkung; **~-regulating** zollregelnd; **~ regulations** Zollbestimmungen; **~-ridden** mit hohen Zöllen belastet; **T~ Schedules of the**

United States (TSUS) Zolltabellen der Vereinigten Staaten *(der Zoll wird nach den US-Zolltabellen festgesetzt; cf. →Harmonized Commodity Description and Coding System)*; ~ **treatment (applicable to goods)** zolltarifliche Behandlung (von Waren); ~ **union** Zollverband, Zollunion; ~ **wall** Zollschranke

tariff, according to (or **as per**) laut Zolltarif, tarifmäßig; **ad valorem** ~ Wertzoll *(opp. specific ~)*; **agricultural** ~ Agrarzoll; **compensating** ~ Ausgleichszoll; **compound** ~ gemischter (od. kombinierter) Zolltarif *(entweder →ad valorem duty plus →specific duty od. einer von beiden, und zwar der höhere)*; **countervailing** ~ Ausgleichszoll; **customs** ~ Zolltarif; **differential** ~ *(Zoll)* Differentialtarif, Staffeltarif; **export** ~ Ausfuhrzoll(tarif); **flexible** ~ *(im Ermessen der Zollbeamten liegender)* flexibler (od. der Situation angepaßter) Zolltarif *(z.B. bei e-m in Aussicht stehenden →dumping)*; **import** ~ Einfuhrzoll(tarif)

tariff, the Community's integrated ~ (Taric) *(EG)* der integrierte Tarif der Europäischen Gemeinschaften (Taric)

Grundlage für alle Einfuhrmaßnahmen der Gemeinschaft

tariff, internal ~ Binnenzoll(tarif); **mixed** ~ s. compound →~; **multiple** ~ Mehrfachzoll; **preferential** ~ Vorzugszoll(tarif); **protective** ~ Schutzzoll; **retaliatory** ~ Vergeltungszoll; **revenue** ~ Finanzzoll *(opp. protective ~)*; **sliding-scale** ~ Gleitzoll; **specific** ~ nach Menge, Stück od. Gewicht berechneter Zolltarif; **to decrease** (or **lower**) **the** ~**s** die Zölle senken; **to increase** (or **raise**) **the** ~**s** die Zölle erhöhen

tariff 2. Tarif; Liste von Preisen od. Gebühren; Preisliste *(Br bes. e-s Hotels)*; Versicherungstarif; ~ **agreement** Tarifabsprache; ~ **business** *Br* Versicherungsgeschäfte, die unter die Abmachungen der →tariff companies fallen; ~ **companies** (or **offices**) *Br* Versicherungsgesellschaften, die zu e-m Kartell gehören, das die Versicherungsbedingungen und Prämien für die Mitgliedsgesellschaften festlegt; ~**-free** zollfrei; ~ **in force** gültiger Tarif; ~ **making** *Am* Tariffestsetzung; ~ **of fares** Fahrpreistarif; ~ **raising** Tariferhöhung; ~ **rate** Tarifsatz, ~ **reduction** Tarifermäßigung, Tarifsenkung; ~ **ring** Versicherungskartell; ~ **war** Tarifkrieg

tariff, electricity ~ Stromtarif *(Br. cf. time-of-day-~)*; **gas** ~ Gastarif; **graduated** ~ Staffeltarif; **hotel** ~ *Br* Zimmerpreise in e-m Hotel; **increase in** ~ Tariferhöhung; **insurance** ~ Versicherungstarif, Prämientarif; **local** ~ Binnentarif; **passenger** ~ Personentarif; **railway** ~ Eisenbahntarif; **raising of the** ~ Tariferhöhung; **reduction of the** ~ Tarifsenkung, Herabsetzung des Tarifs; **to fix the** ~ den Tarif festsetzen, tarifieren

tariffication Tariffestsetzung, Tarifierung

task Aufgabe; *(bes.* schwere) Arbeit; ~ **force** Arbeitsgruppe, Gruppe von Personen mit verschiedenem Fachwissen zur Lösung e-s Problems; *mil* Sonder-Kampfgruppe; ~ **wage(s)** →piece wage(s); ~ **work** →piecework; **assignment of** ~**s** Zuweisung von Arbeiten; **to assign a** ~ **to a p.** (or **to assign a p. to a** ~) jdm e-e Aufgabe zuweisen; jdn für e-e Aufgabe einsetzen

TASS amtliche sowjetische Nachrichtenagentur

tax Steuer; *(öffentl.)* Abgabe

tax, to abate a ~ e-e Steuer herabsetzen (od. ermäßigen); **to abolish a** ~ e-e Steuer aufheben; **to appeal a** ~ **assessment** gegen e-n Steuerbescheid Einspruch erheben; **to be in arrears with the payment of (one's)** ~**es** mit der Zahlung von Steuern im Rückstand sein; **to collect** ~**es** Steuern erheben (od. einziehen); **to compute the amount of a** ~ die Steuerhöhe berechnen; **to cut** ~**es** Steuern senken; **to deduct** ~**es at source** Steuern im Abzugswege erheben; **to evade** ~**es** Steuern hinterziehen; **to file a** ~ **declaration** s. to make a →~ return; **to impose a** ~ **on sth.** etw. mit e-r Steuer belegen; etw. besteuern; **to increase a** ~ e-e Steuer erhöhen; ~**es have increased** die Steuern sind höher geworden; **to levy a** ~ **on sth.** e-e Steuer erheben auf etw.; etw. besteuern; **to levy** ~**es by withholding** *Am* Steuern im Abzugsweg erheben; **to lower a** ~ s. to reduce a →~; **to make a** ~ **return** e-e Steuererklärung abgeben (od. einreichen); **to raise a** ~ e-e Steuer erheben; **to recover a** ~ e-e Steuer eintreiben; **foreign** ~**es are not recoverable by action** ausländische Steuern sind nicht einklagbar; **to reduce a** ~ e-e Steuer herabsetzen (od. senken); **to shift a** ~ e-e Steuer überwälzen (→ *tax shifting*); **to be subject to a** ~ e-r Steuer unterliegen, steuerpflichtig sein *(z.B. Einkommen)*; **to withhold a** ~ *Am* e-e Steuer *(vom Lohn etc)* einbehalten

tax, ~ **abatement** Steuernachlaß, Steuersenkung, Herabsetzung der Steuer; ~ **accounting** Steuerbuchhaltung; ~ **accruals** Steuerrückstellungen; ~ **advantage** Steuervorteil; ~ **adviser** Steuerberater

tax allocation, ~ **among consolidated companies** *Am* Verteilung des Steueraufwands auf die Konzerngesellschaften; **interperiod** ~ *Am* Zuordnung des Steueraufwands zur Steuerschuld verschiedener Perioden

tax, ~ **allowance** *Br* (Steuer-)Freibetrag; ~ **anticipation certificate** (or **warrant**) *Am* Steuergutschein[6]; ~ **appeal** Steuereinspruch; ~ **arrears** Steuerrückstände; ~ **assessment** Steuerveranlagung; ~ **assessment notice** *Am* Steuerbescheid; ~ **assessor** *Am* Steuerveranlagungsbeamter; Behörde, die die (jährl.) Grundsteuer festsetzt; ~ **at source** Quellensteuer; ~ **attor-**

ney *Am* Anwalt für Steuersachen; ~ **audit** *Am* Steuerprüfung; ~ **auditor** *Am* Steuerprüfer; ~ **authorities** Steuerbehörden; ~ **avoidance** *(erlaubte)* Steuerausweichung, *(legale)* Steuerumgehung *(cf. ~ evasion)*; ~ **avoider** Steuerausweicher *(jd, der versucht, unter Ausnutzung aller legalen Mittel so wenig Steuern wie möglich zu bezahlen)*; ~ **balance sheet** *Am* Steuerbilanz; ~ **base** Steuerbemessungsgrundlage; ~ **benefits** Steuervergünstigungen, steuerliche Vergünstigungen; ~ **bill** *Br sl.* Steuerbescheid, Steuerschuld; *parl* Steuervorlage; ~ **bond** *Am* →~ anticipation certificate; ~ **book** *Am* →~ roll; ~**- bought** *Am* aus Steuergründen erworben; ~ **bracket** Steuerklasse, Steuerstufe; ~ **break** *Am* Steuervorteil; Steuervergünstigung; ~ **burden** Steuerlast, Steuerbelastung; ~ **certificate** *Am* Bescheinigung über den Kauf von Land in e-m →~sale; ~ **claim** Steuerforderung; ~ **collected at source** Quellensteuer; ~ **collection** Steuereinziehung; Steuerbeitreibung; ~ **collector** *Br* Beamter des Finanzamtes; ~ **computation** Selbstveranlagung des Steuerpflichtigen; ~ **concession** Steuervergünstigung; ~ **consultant** Steuerberater

tax convention Steuerabkommen; **United States - German T~ C~** Deutsch-Amerikanisches Doppelbesteuerungsabkommen

Tax Court (T. C.) *Am* Steuergericht; *Am* offizielle Sammlung der Entscheidungen des Bundessteuergerichts; ~ **(of the U. S.)** *Am* Bundessteuergericht *(Berufungsinstanz für fast alle bundessteuerl. Entscheidungen des Bureau of Internal Revenue)*

tax credit[7] Steuergutschrift; *(von der Steuerschuld abgezogene)* Steueranrechnung; ~ **system** *(DBA)* Steueranrechnungsmethode *(→credit 3.)*; **direct** ~ direkte Steueranrechnung; **foreign** ~ Anrechnung von im Ausland gezahlten Steuern; **indirect** ~ indirekte Steueranrechnung; **investment** ~ Anrechnung von Investitionskosten; **matching** ~ *(DBA)* Anrechnung fiktiver ausländischer Steuern

tax, ~ **cut** Steuersenkung, Steuerermäßigung; ~**-cutting** steuermindernd; ~ **declaration** Steuererklärung; ~ **deductability** Abzugsfähigkeit von Steuern; ~ **deducted** *Br (vom Lohn, von Dividenden etc)* einbehaltene Steuern; ~ **deducted at source** Steuerabzug an der Quelle, Quellensteuerabzug; ~ **deduction** Steuerabzug *(durch Einbehaltung der Steuer an der Einkunftsquelle)*; ~ **deed** *Am* Übertragungsurkunde an den Erwerber (od. Ersteigerer) von Grundbesitz bei e-m →tax sale; ~ **deferment** *Br* (~ **deferral** *Am*) Steuerstundung; ~ **deficit** Steuerfehlbetrag; ~ **delinquency** *Am* Steuersäumnis, verspätete Zahlung der Steuer; ~ **disadvantage** Steuernachteil, steuerlicher Nachteil; ~ **discrimination** Steuerdiskriminierung; ~ **dodging** *colloq.* Steuerausweichung, Steuerumgehung; ~ **domicile** steuerlicher Wohnsitz; ~**es due** fällige Steuern; Steuerschuld; ~**es eligible for credit** *(DBA)* anrechenbare ausländische Steuern; ~ **equalization account** *Br* Steuerausgleichskonto; ~ **equity** Steuergerechtigkeit; **T~ Equity and Fiscal Responsibility Act** 1982 (TEFRA) *Am* Gesetz über Steuerausgleich und fiskalische Verantwortung *(Einkommensteueränderungsgesetz mit Mehrbelastung für Private und Unternehmer)*; ~ **evader** Steuerhinterzieher; ~ **evasion** *(unerlaubte)* Steuerhinterziehung *(z. B. Steuerverkürzung, Steuerflucht)*

tax-exempt *bes. Am* steuerfrei; ~ **amount** Steuerfreibetrag; ~ **bonds** *Am* steuerfreie Wertpapiere *(von der Bundeseinkommensteuer freie Staats- od. Kommunalanleihen)*; ~ **income** steuerfreies Einkommen

tax, ~ **exemption** Steuerbefreiung, Steuerfreiheit; *Am* Freibetrag; ~ **expenditure** Steueraufwendungen; ~**-filing date** Termin für Abgabe der Steuererklärung; ~ **form** Steuererklärungsformular; ~ **fraud** Steuerhinterziehung

tax-free steuerfrei; ~ **allowance** *Br* (Steuer-)Freibetrag; ~ **income** steuerfreies Einkommen

tax, ~ **guidelines** Steuerrichtlinien; ~ **harmonization** *(EG)* Steuerharmonisierung; ~ **haven** Steueroase *(z. B. Monaco, Liechtenstein)*; ~ **incidence** Steuerinzidenz, Steuerwirkung, Steuereffekt; ~ **inspector** →inspector of taxes; ~ **instalment** (*Am* **installment**) Steuerrate; ~**-laden** *Am* mit Steuern überladen; ~ **law** Steuergesetz; ~ **lawyer** *Am* Anwalt für Steuersachen; ~ **levy** Steuererhebung; ~ **liability** Steuerpflicht, Steuerschuld, ~ **lien** *Am* Steuerpfandrecht *(Pfandrecht zugunsten des Bundes od. e-s Einzelstaates zur Sicherung e-r Steuerforderung)*; ~ **load** Steuerlast; ~ **loss** Steuerausfall; ~ **loss company** *(vergleichbar mit)* Abschreibungsgesellschaft; ~ **management** Steuermanagement; ~ **option corporation** *Am* Kapitalgesellschaft, die unter bestimmten Voraussetzungen steuerlich als Personengesellschaft behandelt wird; ~ **package** Steuerpaket; ~**-paid** versteuert

taxpayer Steuerzahler; Steuerpflichtiger, Steuersubjekt; ~ **in arrears** rückständiger Steuerpflichtiger; **foreign** ~ Steuerausländer

tax, ~ **payment date** Steuer(zahlungs)termin; ~ **penalty** Steuersäumniszuschlag; ~ **planning** Steuerplanung *(unter legaler Umgehung belastender Bestimmungen)*; ~ **practitioner** *Br* Steuerberater

tax privilege Steuervergünstigung; Steuerbegünstigung; **with** ~**s** (or **tax privileged**) steuerbegünstigt; **to enjoy** ~**s** Steuervergünstigungen genießen

tax, ~ **progression** Steuerprogression; ~ **purchaser** *Am* Erwerber (meist Ersteigerer) bei zum Zwecke der Bezahlung von Steuern vorgenommenem →~ sale

tax rate Steuersatz; **reduced** ~ ermäßigter Steuersatz; **cut** (or **reduction**) **in** ~**s** Senkung der Steuersätze, Steuersenkung

tax, ~ **rebate** Steuernachlaß; ~ **receipts** Steuereinnahmen; ~ **receiver** *Am* Steuereinnehmer; ~ **reduction** Steuerermäßigung, Steuersenkung; ~ **reform** Steuerreform

Tax Reform Act of 1986 *Am* Steuerreformgesetz
Abbau einer Vielzahl von Steuervergünstigungen und Herabsetzung der Spitzensteuersätze bei der Einkommensteuer und Körperschaftsteuer

tax, ~ **refund** Steuerrückerstattung; ~ **regulations** steuerliche Vorschriften, Steuervorschriften

tax relief Steuerbefreiung, Steuervergünstigung; **entitled to** ~ steuerbegünstigt

tax reserve Steuerrückstellung; ~ **certificates** *Br* nicht übertragbare Wertpapiere für angelegte Steuerrücklagen

tax, ~ **return** (Einkommen-)Steuererklärung (→ *return 2.)*; ~ **revenue** Steueraufkommen, Steuereinnahmen; ~**-ridden** *Am* mit Steuern überladen; ~ **roll** Steuerliste; ~ **sale** *Am* Zwangsverkauf od. Zwangsversteigerung von Grundbesitz zur Eintreibung der Steuerschuld; ~ **saving** Steuerersparnis; ~ **scale** Steuertarif; ~ **shelter** Steuerersparnis; steuersparende Maßnahme od. Unternehmung *(z.B. Abschreibungsgesellschaft)*; ~ **shifting** Steuerüberwälzung (shifting forward Steuervorwälzung; shifting backward Steuerrückwälzung); ~ **source** Steuerquelle; ~ **sovereignty** Steuerhoheit; ~ **stamp** Steuermarke, Banderole; ~ →**switching;** ~ **table** Steuertabelle; ~ **title** *Am* Rechtstitel des →~ purchaser; ~ **voucher** Steuerbeleg; ~ **withheld** *Am (vom Lohn)* einbehaltene Steuer; ~ **withheld on dividends** *Am* im Abzugswege erhobene Steuern auf Dividenden; ~ **withholding at the source** *Am* Steuerabzug an der Quelle; ~ **year** Steuerjahr *(Br 6. April–5. April)*; ~ **yield** Steueraufkommen; Steuerertrag

tax, accrued ~**es** *(Bilanz)* Steuerschulden; **accumulated earnings** ~ *Am*[8] (Sonder-)Steuer *(für corporations)* auf angesammeltem *(nicht ausgeschüttetem)* Gewinn; **additional** ~ Steuerzuschlag; **advance payment of** ~**es** Steuervorauszahlung; **after** ~**es** nach Abzug von Steuern; **amount of** ~ Steuerbetrag; **arrears of** ~ Steuerrückstände; **assessable to** ~ steuerpflichtig; **assessment of** ~**es** Steuerveranlagung; **automobile** ~ *Am* Kraftfahrzeugsteuer; →**avoidance of** ~**es; capital** ~ Vermögensteuer; **capital gains** ~ (CGT) Steuer auf Veräußerungsgewinne; **capital transfer** ~ (CTT) *Br* Vermögensübertragungssteuer *(1986 abgeschafft und durch Inheritance Tax ersetzt)*; **collection of** ~**es** Einziehung (od. Beitreibung) von Steuern; **collector of** ~**es** Steuereinnehmer; **corporation** ~[9] (C. T.) Körperschaftsteuer; **deduction of** ~ **at source** → deduction 2.; **deferred** ~**es** latente Steuern; **delinquent** ~ *Am* rückständige Steuer; **direct** ~**es** direkte Steuern *(opp. indirect taxes)*; **estate** ~ *Am*[10] Nachlaßsteuer, Erbschaftsteuer; **estimated** ~ *(auf Grund der → declaration of income)* geschätzte (Einkommen-)Steuerschuld des laufenden Jahres; **evasion of** ~**es** →~ evasion

tax, excise ~ 1. Verbrauchssteuer; 2. *Am* Sonderumsatzsteuer des Bundes für bestimmte Güter *(z.B. Automobile, Fernseh-, Film- und Fotoapparate, Juwelen, Pelze)*
Die excise tax (2.) wird auf der Einzelhandelsstufe (retailer's excise) wie auf der Herstellerstufe (manufacturer's excise) erhoben

tax, exempt from ~**es** *Am* steuerfrei; **federal** ~**es** *Am* Bundessteuer; **federal** ~ **legislation** *Am*[11] Bundessteuer-Gesetzgebung; →**foreign** ~; **franchise** ~ *Am* Konzessionsteuer (→*franchise*); **free of** ~ (F. O. T.) (or **from** ~**es**) steuerfrei; **general property** ~ *Am* Vermögensteuer (→*general*); **gift** ~ *Am* Schenkungsteuer; **graduated** ~ gestaffelte Steuer; **imposition of** ~**es** Besteuerung

tax, income ~[12] Einkommensteuer (→*income*); **individual income** ~ *Am* Einkommensteuer e-r natürlichen Person

tax, increase in the ~**es** Steuererhöhung; **indirect** ~**es** indirekte Steuern; **inheritance** ~ *Am (einzelstaatl.)* Erbschaftsteuer; **input** ~ *Br (Mehrwertsteuer)* Vorsteuer; **interest equalization** ~ *Am* Zinsausgleichsteuer (→*interest 4.)*; **levy(ing) of** ~**es** Steuererhebung, Besteuerung; **liable to a** ~ steuerpflichtig; **local** ~**es** Kommunalsteuern; **municipal** ~**es** *Am* Kommunalsteuern; **National T~ Association** *Am* Vereinigung der Steuerzahler; **normal** ~ *Am* normale Bundes-Einkommensteuer *(opp. surtax)*; →**payroll** ~; **petroleum revenue** ~ *Br*[13] Steuer auf Einnahmen aus Gewinnung von Erdöl *(z.B. in der Nordsee)*; **property** ~ *Br* Grundsteuer; *Am* Vermögenssteuer; **provision for** ~**es** Rückstellung für Steuern; **rate of** ~**es** Steuersatz *(cf. rate of income tax,* →*rate 2.)*; **rates and** ~**es** *Br* Kommunal- und Staatssteuern; **real estate** ~ *Am* Grundsteuer; **receiver of** ~**es** *Am* Steuereinnehmer; **reduction of** ~**es** →~ reduction; **refund** (or **reimbursement**) **of** ~**es** Steuererstattung; **regressive** ~ regressive Steuer; **remission of** ~**es** Steuererlaß; **sales** ~ Umsatzsteuer; **social security** ~**es** *Am* Sozialversicherungsbeiträge; **state** ~ *Am* einzelstaatliche Steuer *(opp. federal* ~*)*; **stock transfer** ~ *Am* Börsenumsatzsteuer *(für Aktien)*; **turnover** ~ *Am* Umsatzsteuer; **use** ~ *Am* Verbrauchsteuer *(auf die Artikel, auf denen keine sales tax liegt)*; **value added** ~ (VAT) Mehrwertsteuer; **wealth** ~ Vermögensteuer; **withheld** ~**es** einbehaltene Steuern; → **withholding** ~

tax *v* 1. *(jdn od. etw.)* besteuern; *(jdm)* e-e Steuer auferlegen; *Am colloq.* als Preis fordern; **to** ~

heavily hoch besteuern; **to ~ income** Einkommen besteuern; Einkommensteuer erheben; **right to ~** Besteuerungsrecht

taxed, object ~ Steuerobjekt, Steuergegenstand

taxing Besteuerung; **~ authority** Steuerbehörde; **~ competence** *(DBA)* Steuerkompetenz; **~ district** *Am* Steuerbezirk; **~ power** *Am*[14] Steuerhoheit *(des Bundes)*; **~ state** besteuernder Staat

tax *v* 2., **to ~ the costs** die Kosten festsetzen; *Br* die Gebührenrechnung des solicitor (bill of costs) überprüfen und anerkennen od. abändern *(cf. taxation of costs)*; die *(von der unterliegenden Partei zu erstattenden)* Prozeßkosten festsetzen

taxing, ~ masters *Br* Gerichtsbeamte des → Supreme Court, die persönlich unabhängig das →T~ Office leiten und als →~ officers die →taxation of costs durchführen; **T ~ Office** *Br* Abteilung des Central Office des Supreme Court, in der die Kostenfestsetzungsverfahren des →High Court (mit Ausnahmen) und des → Court of Appeal durchgeführt werden; **~ officer** Kostenfestsetzungsbeamter

taxable besteuerbar, steuerpflichtig; Steuer-; **~ capacity** Steuerkraft; **~ capacity principle** *(SteuerR)* Leistungsfähigkeitsprinzip; **~ costs** *Am* vom Prozeßgegner zu erstattende Kosten; **~ estate** *Am* zu versteuernder Nachlaß; **~ event** Steuertatbestand; **~ income** steuerpflichtiges Einkommen; **~ object** Steuergegenstand, Steuerobjekt; **~ pay** steuerpflichtiger Lohn; **~ period** Steuerperiode, Veranlagungszeitraum; **~ profit** zu versteuernder Gewinn; **~ value** Steuerwert; **~ year** *Am* Steuerjahr, Veranlagungsjahr

taxation 1. Besteuerung; Steuern; **~ at source** *(DBA)* Quellenbesteuerung; **~ equalization reserve** *Br (Bilanz)* Steuerausgleichsrücklage; **~ of income** Besteuerung des Einkommens; **~ of profits** Besteuerung des Gewinns; **~ of property** Vermögensbesteuerung; Substanzbesteuerung; **burden of ~** Steuerlast; **cut in ~** Senkung der Steuern

taxation, double ~ Doppelbesteuerung; **Double T~ Convention** Abkommen zur Vermeidung der Doppelbesteuerung (→*double*); **double ~ relief** Befreiung von der Doppelbesteuerung (→*relief 3.*)

taxation, exempt from ~ steuerfrei; **future ~** *Br (Bilanz)* Steuerrückstellung; **high ~** hohe Besteuerung; **increase in ~** Steuererhöhung; **law of ~** Steuerrecht; **liable to ~** steuerpflichtig; **light ~** geringe Besteuerung; **multiple ~** mehrfache Besteuerung *(durch mehrere Staaten)*; **provision for ~** Rückstellung für Steuern; **rate of ~** Steuersatz; **resistance to ~** Steuerwiderstand; **shifting of ~** → tax shifting; →**unitary ~**; **to be liable to ~** der Steuer unterliegen; **to reduce the (level of) ~** die Steuern senken

taxation 2., **~ of costs** Kostenfestsetzung; *Br* Prüfung (und eventuell Herabsetzung) der Gebührenrechnung (bill of costs) des solicitor *(im High Court durch →taxing masters, in den County Courts durch →registrars)*; gerichtl. Festsetzung der *(von der unterliegenden der obsiegenden Partei zu zahlenden)* Prozeßkosten; **to review ~** *Br* die Gebührenrechnung des solicitor nochmals gerichtlich überprüfen

taxi rank *Br* (or **stand**) Taxistand

taxing → tax *v* 1. und 2.

teach-in Podiumsdiskussion; öffentliches Gespräch; *(politisch orientierte)* studentische Protestversammlung

teaching Unterricht; Lehre, Doktrin; **~ aids** Lehrmaterial; **~ appointment** *univ* Berufung auf e-n Lehrstuhl; *(Schule)* Stelle e-s Lehrers; **~ method** Lehrmethode; **~ staff** Lehrkörper

team Mannschaft; Arbeitsgruppe, (Personen-) Gruppe *(für bestimmte Arbeit)*; **~ spirit** Gemeinschaftsgeist; **~work** Gruppenarbeit, Zusammenarbeit e-r Gruppe; **management ~** Führungsgruppe; **national ~** *(Sport)* Nationalmannschaft

team up *v*, **to ~ with** *colloq.* zusammenarbeiten mit

teamster *Am* Transportarbeiter; Lkw-Fahrer

tear gas Tränengas; **~ bomb** Tränengasbombe

tear, ~-off calendar Abreißkalender; **~-open wrapper** Aufreißpackung; **~ sheet** *Am (dem Annoncierenden zugesandte)* Belegseite

tear *v* zerreißen; **to ~ down** *(Haus, Plakat etc)* abreißen; **to ~ a cheque (check) out of the book** e-n Scheck aus dem Heft abtrennen; **to ~ up** *(Brief etc)* zerreißen

teaser *Am sl.* Neugierde erregendes Werbemittel

teasing campaign *Am sl.* Werbung, die durch Anwendung von Tricks Neugierde erregt

technical technisch, fachlich, Fach-; *Am (Börse)* durch Manipulationen beeinflußt, manipuliert; **~ adviser** technischer Berater, Fachberater; **~ aid** technische (Entwicklungs-)Hilfe

Technical and Miscellaneous Revenue Act of 1988 (TAMRA) Korrekturgesetz zum Steuerreformgesetz 1986

Die kürzlich in Kraft getretene Nachlaßsteuergesetzgebung kann sowohl für Deutsche, die Vermögen in den USA haben oder dort wohnen, als auch für in Deutschland lebende amerikanische Staatsangehörige zu einer beträchtlichen Erhöhung der Steuerbelastung des Nachlasses führen

technical, T~ Assistance Board (TAB) Amt für Technische Hilfe *(der Vereinten Nationen)*; **~ bodies** Fachgremien; **~ committee** Fachausschuß; ~ **consultant** technischer Berater; ~ **data** technische Unterlagen

technical expertise technisches Gutachten; **ICC International Centre for T~ E~** ICC Internationale Zentralstelle für technische Gutachten;[15] **ICC Rules for T~ E~** ICC Verfahren zur Einholung technischer Gutachten

technical, ~ **high school** *Am (etwa)* Gewerbeschule; ~ **improvement** technische Verbesserung; ~ **knowledge** Fachkenntnis(-se); ~ **manager** technischer Direktor; ~ **question** technische Frage; verfahrensrechtliche Frage; ~ **prerequisites** technische Voraussetzungen; ~ **progress** technischer Fortschritt; ~ **staff** Fachpersonal; ~ **term** Fachausdruck; ~ **training** Fachausbildung

technically advanced hochtechnisiert

technocracy Technokratie *(Herrschaft der Technik)*

technocrat Technokrat

technocratic technokratisch

technological technologisch; ~ **advance** technologischer Fortschritt; ~ **cooperation** technologische Zusammenarbeit; ~ **forecasting** (T/F) *Am* technologische Vorausschau; ~ **gap** technologische Lücke; ~ **unemployment** technologische *(durch Änderung der Produktionsmethoden bedingte)* Arbeitslosigkeit

technologically advanced country technologisch fortgeschrittenes Land

technology Technologie; **high** ~ (high tech) Hoch- od. Spitzentechnik (od. -technologie); **the most advanced** ~ der neueste Stand der Technik; **transfer of** ~ Technologietransfer

Telecom, →**British** ~

telecommunication Telekommunikation, Nachrichtenübermittlung; ~**s** Fernmeldewesen; Fernmeldeverkehr; **global** ~ **network** Welt-Fernmeldenetz; ~ **satellite** Fernmeldesatellit; ~ **service** Fernmeldedienst; →**European T~s Satellite Organization** (EUTELSAT); **International T~ Convention** Internationaler Fernmeldevertrag; **International T~ Satellite Organization** Internationale Fernmeldesatellitenorganisation (→ *Intelsat*); **International T~ Union** (ITU) Internationaler Fernmeldeverein (→ *international)*

telecopier Telekopierer

telecopy *v* fernkopieren

telecopying Fernkopieren

telefax *(EDV)* Telefax *(Kopie, die über das Telefonnetz kommt)*

telegram Telegramm; ~ **address** Telegrammanschrift, Drahtanschrift; ~ **addressed poste restante** postlagerndes Telegramm; ~ **by telephone** telefonisch zugestelltes Telegramm; ~**s counter** *Br* Telegrammschalter; ~ **delivered by mail** *Br* Brieftelegramm; ~ **form** Telegrammformular; ~ **in cipher** (or **code**) Telegramm in Geheimschrift; Chiffretelegramm; ~ **in plain language** nicht chiffriertes Telegramm; ~ **of condolence** Beileidstelegramm; ~ **of congratulation** Glückwunschtelegramm;~ **rate** Telegrammgebühr, Wortgebühr; ~ **to be redirected** nachzusendendes Telegramm; ~ **to follow addressee** nachzusendendes Telegramm; ~ **with notice of delivery** (by telegraph) Telegramm mit Empfangsbenachrichtigung; telegrafische Empfangsanzeige; ~ **with repetition** Telegramm mit Wiederholung

telegram, by ~ telegrafisch; **charge for** ~ Telegrammgebühr; **cipher** ~ → ~ in cipher; **code** ~ → ~ in code; **exchange of** ~**s** Telegrammwechsel; **greetings** ~ Glückwunschtelegramm; Schmuckblattelegramm; **letter** ~ Brieftelegramm; **money order** ~ telegrafische Geldüberweisung; **multiple (address)** ~ (TM) Mehrfachtelegramm; **mutilated** ~ verstümmeltes Telegramm; **prepaid** (or **reply paid**) ~ Telegramm mit bezahlter Rückantwort; **reply by** ~ telegrafische Antwort; **service** ~ Diensttelegramm; **urgent** ~ dringendes Telegramm; **to deliver a** ~ ein Telegramm zustellen; **to hand in** (or *Am* **file**) **a** ~ ein Telegramm aufgeben; **to inquire by** ~ telegrafisch anfragen; **to send a** ~ telegrafieren, ein Telegramm schicken

telegraph Telegraf; ~ **boy** (or **messenger**) Telegrammbote; ~ **office** Telegrafenamt, Telegrafenstelle; **by** ~ telegrafisch

telegraph *v* telegrafieren

telegraphese *colloq.* Telegrammstil

telegraphic telegrafisch; ~ **address** (T. A.) Telegrammanschrift, Drahtanschrift; ~ **answer** Drahtantwort; ~ **code** Telegramm-Code; Telegrafenschlüssel; ~ **message** telegrafische Mitteilung; ~ **money order** telegrafische Geldüberweisung; ~ **remittance** telegrafische Überweisung; ~ **reply** Drahtantwort; ~ **transfer** (T. T.) telegrafische Auszahlung *(telegrafische Banküberweisung von Geld ins Ausland)*

telemessage *Br (durch Telefon od. Telex)* aufgegebenes Telegramm

telephone Telefon, Fernsprecher; ~ **answering machine** Fernsprechaufnahmegerät; ~ **answering service** Fernsprechauftragsdienst; ~ **bill** Telefonrechnung; ~ **bill-paying** *Am* telefonischer Zahlungsauftrag; ~ **booth** (or **box**) Telefonzelle, Fernsprechzelle; **(~)call** Telefongespräch (→*call 5.*); ~ **charges** Fernsprechgebühren; ~ **communication** telefonische

Mitteilung; ~ **connection** Telefonverbindung; Fernsprechanschluß; **our ~ conversation of this day** unser heutiges Telefongespräch; ~ **directory** Fernsprechbuch; ~ **exchange** Fernsprechzentrale; Vermittlung; ~ **extension** Nebenanschluß; ~ **facilities** Fernsprechanlage; ~ **message** telefonische Benachrichtigung; ~ **network** Fernsprechnetz; ~ **number** Telefonnummer, Rufnummer; ~ **rates** *Am* Fernsprechgebühren; ~ **redemption privilege** *Am* Liquidation von Anteilen an →money market funds durch telefonische Anweisung; ~ **subscriber** Fernsprechteilnehmer; ~ **tapping equipment** (Telefon-) Abhöranlage; ~ **trade** *(Börse)* Telefonhandel; **automatic** ~ Selbstanschluß(fernsprecher)

telephone, by ~ telefonisch, fernmündlich; **inquiry by** ~ telefonische Anfrage; **to inquire by** ~ telefonisch anfragen

telephone, installation of a ~ Einrichtung e-r Telefonanlage; **to be on the** ~ Fernsprechanschluß haben; am Apparat sein; **to be wanted on the** ~ telefonisch verlangt werden; **to intercept** ~ **calls** (or **to tap the** ~ **wire**) Telefongespräche abhören

telephone *v* telefonieren, anrufen

telephony Fernsprechwesen

teleprint *v Br* fernschreiben; mit Fernschreiben durchgeben an

teleprinter *Br* Fernschreiber *(Gerät)*; ~ **line** Fernschreibleitung; ~ **network** Fernschreibnetz; ~ **user** Fernschreibteilnehmer

teletype *Am* Fernschreiber *(Gerät)*; **international** ~ **code** internationaler Fernschreibcode; ~ **message** Fernschreiben; ~ **operator** Fernschreiber *(Person)*

teletyper *Am* Fernschreiber *(Gerät)*; ~ **line** Fernschreibleitung

teletypist *Am* Fernschreiber *(Person)*

televise *v* im Fernsehen senden; *(durch Fernsehen)* übertragen

televised speech Fernsehansprache

televising Fernsehübertragung

television[16] (T. V.) Fernsehen; ~ **adaptation** Fernsehbearbeitung; ~ **address** Fernsehansprache; ~ **advertising** Fernsehwerbung, Werbefernsehen; ~ **broadcast**[17] Fernsehsendung; ~ **by satellite** Satellitenfernsehen; ~ **charges** Fernsehgebühren; ~ **commercial** Fernsehwerbesendung; ~ **coverage** Fernsehberichterstattung; ~ **licence fee** *Br* Fernsehgebühr; ~ **network** Fernsehnetz; ~ **news (broadcast)** Nachrichten im Fernsehen; ~ **programme** Fernsehprogramm, Fernsehsendung; ~ **rental** *Br* Miete für Fernsehgeräte; ~ **right** Fernsehsenderecht; ~ **set** Fernsehapparat; **coin** ~ Münzfernsehen; **colo(u)r** ~ Farbfernsehen; **commercial** ~ Werbefernsehen (→*commercial*); **Education T**~ (ETV) *Am* Bildungsfernsehen; **to speak on** ~ im Fernsehen sprechen

telex[18] Telex, Fernschreiben; Fernschreiber *(Gerät)*; ~ **bill** Fernschreibrechnung; ~ **call charge** Fernschreibgebühr; ~ **charges** Fernschreibgebühren; ~ **connection** Fernschreibverbindung; ~ **directory** Verzeichnis der Fernschreibteilnehmer; ~ **exchange** Telex-Zentrale; ~ **line** Fernschreibleitung; ~ **(line) rental** Fernschreibgrundgebühr; ~ **machine** Fernschreibgerät; ~ **message** Fernschreiben; ~ **number** Fernschreibnummer; ~ **operator** Fernschreiber *(Person)*; ~ **subscriber** Fernschreibteilnehmer; ~ **traffic** Fernschreibverkehr; **by** ~ durch Fernschreiben, fernschriftlich

telex *v*, **to** ~ **sth.** etw. fernschriftlich mitteilen

tell *v* zählen; erzählen, sagen; **to** ~ **a lie** lügen; **to** ~ **the truth** die Wahrheit sagen; **to** ~ **the votes** *parl* die Stimmen zählen

teller (Bank-)Kassierer; Kassenbeamter; *parl* Stimmenzähler *(Br bei e-r →division 2.)*; **automatic** ~ *Am* Geldautomat

tel quel (t/q., T. Q.) „so beschaffen wie beschaffen"; ~ **clause** Telquel-Klausel

Handelsklausel (bes. im Überseeverkehr), durch deren Vereinbarung der Verkäufer die Haftung für Verlust und Beschädigung der Waren auf dem Transport ausschließt

tel quel rate *Br* Telquel-Kurs *(Devisenkurs, in den Zinsen und Spesen bereits eingerechnet sind)*

Templar *Br* Anwalt (barrister) od. Student der Rechte mit Büro (chambers) oder Wohnung im →Temple, London

Temple *Br* (Residenz von zwei der vier) Rechtsinnungen (→*Inns of Court)* in London, und zwar →Middle ~ und →Inner ~

temporal zeitlich, weltlich *(opp. spiritual)*; ~**s** → temporalties; **Lords T**~ →Lord

temporalities *eccl* Temporalien; Kirchenvermögen und Kircheneinkünfte; ~ **of a bishop** *Br* mit e-m Bischofsamt verbundener weltlicher od. zeitlicher Besitz *(opp. spiritualities)*

temporary zeitweilig, vorläufig, vorübergehend; provisorisch; Aushilfs-; ~ **admission** *(Zoll)* vorübergehende (zollfreie) Einfuhr *(von Gütern, die später wieder ausgeführt werden sollen)*; *(→Customs Convention on the A.T.A. Carnet for the ~ admission of goods)*; ~ **allowance** vorübergehende geldliche Zuwendung; ~ **annuity** Zeitrente; ~ **appointment in the Civil Service** *Br* vorübergehende Stelle im Civil Service; ~ **bond** vorläufige Obligation;

~ **credit** Zwischenkredit; ~ **disability** zeitweilige Erwerbsunfähigkeit *(opp. permanent disability)*; ~ **driver's license** *Am* Führerschein auf Probe

temporary employment vorübergehende Beschäftigung, Zeitarbeit *(opp. permanent employment)*; ~ **agency** *(bei Arbeitnehmerüberlassung)* Verleihfirma, Leiharbeitunternehmen; ~ **business** gewerbsmäßige Arbeitnehmerüberlassung

temporary, ~ **importation papers** Zollpapiere für die vorübergehende Einfuhr; ~ **injunction** *Am* einstweilige Verfügung; ~ **insurance** zeitlich begrenzte Versicherung; ~ **investment** kurzfristige Kapitalanlage; *(Bilanz)* Wertpapiere des Umlaufvermögens; ~ **provision** Übergangsbestimmung; ~ **receipt** Zwischenquittung

temporary registration, to grant a p. a ~ *Br* jdm e-e vorläufige Zulassungsgenehmigung als Arzt erteilen

temporary, ~ **repairs** provisorische Reparaturen; ~ **restraining order** (T.R.O.) *Am* befristete einstweilige Verfügung *(für die Zeit bis zur mündl. Verhandlung)*; ~ **staff** Aushilfspersonal; Angestellte auf Zeit *(opp. permanent staff)*; ~ **use** vorübergehender Gebrauch; ~ **work** Gelegenheitsarbeit; Zeitarbeit, Leiharbeit

temporary worker Gelegenheitsarbeiter; Leiharbeiter, Zeitarbeitnehmer; **to hire out** ~**s** Leiharbeitnehmer verleihen

tenancy Besitz, Eigentum; Grundeigentum *(im Sinne von freehold tenancy)*; Mietbesitz, Pachtbesitz[19] *(an Immobilien)*; Mietverhältnis, Pachtverhältnis; Mietdauer, Pachtdauer; *Br* Besitz *(an bewegl. Vermögen auf Grund e-s → settlement 3.)*; ~ **agreement** (or **contract**) Mietvertrag, Pachtvertrag; ~ **at sufferance** geduldeter Besitz *(→sufferance)*; ~ **at will** nach Belieben *(des landlord od. des tenant)* jederzeit kündbares Miet- (od. Pacht)verhältnis

tenancy for life *Br*[20] *(durch ein → settlement 3. geschaffenes)* zeitlich auf die Dauer e-s Lebens beschränktes Eigentumsrecht *(bes. an Grundbesitz)*; lebenslängl. Miet- od. Pachtverhältnis

tenancy, ~ **for years** Miet- (od. Pacht)verhältnis, das nach Ablauf e-r bestimmten Zeit endet; ~ **from month to month** monatl. laufendes Miet- (od. Pacht-)verhältnis; ~ **from year to year** von Jahr zu Jahr laufendes Miet- (od. Pacht-)verhältnis *(das zum Ablauf e-s Miet- oder Pachtjahres gekündigt werden kann; meist mehrmonatl. Kündigungsfrist)*; ~ **in common** Miteigentum *(an Grundbesitz)* nach Bruchteilen, Bruchteilsgemeinschaft *(→common 2., in →common; opp. joint tenancy)*; ~ **year** Mietjahr; Pachtjahr

tenancy, agricultural ~ Pacht e-s landwirtschaftlichen Grundstücks; landwirtschaftliches Pachtverhältnis; **assured** ~ *(nach dem Housing Act 1988)* preisüberwachter Mietbesitz; **expiration of** ~ Ablauf des Miet- (od. Pacht-)verhältnisses; **extension of** ~ Mietverlängerung, Pachtverlängerung; **farm** ~ Pacht e-s Hofes; landwirtschaftliches Pachtverhältnis; **joint** ~ Miteigentum zur gesamten Hand *(→joint)*; **life** ~ →~for life

tenancy, regulated ~ preisüberwachter Mietbesitz an Wohnungen, deren →rateable value unter bestimmten Grenzen liegt, und der vor dem Housing Act 1988 begründet ist

tenancy, periodic ~ fortlaufendes *(sich jeweils um e-n bestimmten Zeitraum verlängerndes)* Mietverhältnis *(z.B. weekly →~)*; **sub-**~ Untermiete, Unterpacht; **a** ~ **terminable by half a year's notice** Miete (od. Pacht) mit halbjähriger Kündigung; **on the termination of the** ~ bei Beendigung der Miete (od. Pacht); **weekly** ~ wochenweise festgesetztes Mietverhältnis; **to extend a** ~ e-e Miete (od. Pacht) verlängern; **the** ~ **has run out** die Miete (od. Pacht) ist abgelaufen

tenant Mieter, Pächter[19] *(opp. landlord)*; Inhaber, Besitzer *(auch von bewegl. Vermögen, z.B. e-r Rente)*; Grundeigentümer *(→~ in fee simple, ~ in →tail)*; ~ **at sufferance** geduldeter Mieter (od. Pächter) *(→tenancy at sufferance)*; ~ **at will** jederzeit kündbarer Pächter (od. Mieter); Pächter (od. Mieter), der jederzeit kündigen kann; ~**'s default** Verzug des Mieters; ~ **farmer** (Guts-)Pächter

tenant for life[21] Besitzer *(bes. von Immobilien)* auf eigene Lebenszeit (od. Lebenszeit e-s Dritten); Nutznießer auf Lebenszeit; ~ **of a trust fund** lebenslänglicher Nutznießer e-s Stiftungsvermögens

tenant, ~ **for years** Pächter (od. Mieter) auf Zeit *(lessee)*; ~ **from year to year** →tenancy from year to year; ~ **in common** Miteigentümer *(an Grundbesitz) (Bruchteilseigentum; opp. joint ~)*; ~ **in fee simple** Grundeigentümer *(freeholder)*; ~ **in (fee) tail** →tail; ~ **pour autre vie** (Grund-)Besitzer auf Lebenszeit e-s Dritten; ~**'s repairs** vom Mieter (od. Pächter) zu tragende Reparaturen; ~**-right** *Br*[22] Verlängerungs- oder Erstattungsansprüche des Landpächters nach Ablauf der Pachtzeit *(z.B. Anspruch auf Erstattung der Kosten für verwendete, über die Pachtzeit hinaus wirkende Düngemittel)*; ~**'s (third party) risk** Mieterhaftung

tenant, agricultural ~ (landwirtschaftl.) Pächter; **cash** ~ *Am* Pächter, der Pacht in bar entrichtet; **cash-share** ~ *Am* Pächter, der Pacht in bar od. Ernteerzeugnissen entrichtet *(cf. share ~)*; **farm** ~ →agricultural ~; **game** ~ Jagdpächter; **incoming** ~ neuer Mieter (od. Pächter); **joint** ~ *(gesamthänderisch gebundener)* Miteigentümer; Mitmieter; Mitpächter; **land let to a** ~ Pachtland; →**landlord and** ~; **life** ~→

~ for life; **outgoing** ~ ausziehender Mieter (od. Pächter); **share** ~ *Am* Pächter, der Pacht in Ernteerzeugnissen (in shares of produce) entrichtet; →**statutory** ~; **sub**~ Untermieter, Unterpächter; **to let to a** ~ vermieten, verpachten; **to let a farm to a** ~ e-n Hof verpachten

tenant *v* in Miete (od. Pacht) haben; Mieter (od. Pächter) sein von

tenanted, a house ~ **by 4 families** ein von 4 Familien bewohntes Haus

tenantable mietbar, pachtbar; ~ **repair** bewohnbarer baulicher Zustand

tend *v* Tendenz (od. Neigung) zeigen, tendieren, neigen (to zu); abzielen, gerichtet sein (to auf)

tendenc|y Tendenz, Neigung; jeweilige Entwicklungsrichtung; ~**ies of the market** Börsentendenz; ~ **towards higher prices** *(Börse)* Hausseneigung; **bearish** (or **downward**) ~ fallende Tendenz; Baissetendenz; **bullish** (or **upward**) ~ steigende Tendenz; Haussetendenz; **stronger** ~ **in prices** Befestigung der Kurse; **weaker** ~ **in prices** Abschwächung der Kurse

tendentious report tendenziöser (od. gefärbter) Bericht

tender 1. Angebot, Anerbieten *(von Zahlung od. Leistung zur Begleichung e-r Schuld od. Erfüllung e-r Verpflichtung)*; Zahlungsangebot; Leistungsangebot; Lieferungsangebot; Andienung; die angebotene Geldsumme; Kostenanschlag; *Scot* Zahlungsangebot *(durch den Beklagten nicht vor, sondern während des Prozesses)*; ~ **of amends**[23] Angebot e-r Entschädigung *(für ein e-m zur Last gelegtes Unrecht)*; ~ **of documents** Vorlage von Dokumenten; ~ **of issue** *Br* →joinder of issue; ~ **of rent due** Anerbieten der Zahlung der fälligen Miete; ~ **of resignation** Rücktrittsgesuch; ~ **of services** Anerbieten von Diensten; ~ **solicitation** Übernahmeangebot; **legal** ~ gesetzl. Zahlungsmittel *(das zur Bezahlung e-r Schuld nicht zurückgewiesen werden kann)*; **perfect** ~ **rule** *Am*[23a] Verkäufer muß Ware in vertragsgemäßem Zustand anbieten; **plea of** ~[24] Einwand des Beklagten, daß er zur Zahlung bereit war und die geforderte Summe jetzt bei Gericht hinterlegt; **to make** (or **submit**) **a** ~ ein Angebot abgeben; **to make a** ~ **(of)** *(als Zahlung od. Leistung)* anbieten

tender 2. Zeichnungsangebot; ~ **bills** *Br* Schatzwechsel, die wöchentlich im →~system dem Meistbietenden zugeteilt werden; ~ **for public loans** Zeichnungsangebot auf öffentl. Anleihen

tender offer, *Am (AktienR)* Übernahmeangebot; Angebot an die Aktionäre, ihre Aktien zwecks Übernahme der Gesellschaft zu veräußern (→*takeover bid*); **cash** ~ Angebot an die Aktionäre, Aktien gegen bar zu verkaufen; **hostile** ~ gegen das Management durchgesetztes Übernahmeangebot

tender panel Bietungskonsortium; ~ **procedure** Tenderverfahren *(Verfahren zur Überbringung e-r Wertpapieremission im Rahmen e-r Auktion)*

tender, ~ **rate** Emissionssatz *(im Tenderverfahren)*; ~ **system** *Br (Emissionsmethode)* Tenderverfahren; Zeichnungsangebot mit unbestimmtem Kurs *(die Effekten werden dem Meistbietenden zugeteilt)*; **weekly** ~ *Br (Geldmarkt)* wöchentliche Auktion von Schatzwechseln *(im Tenderverfahren)*; **to invite** ~**s for** zur Abgabe von Zeichnungsangeboten auffordern

tender 3. *(bei Ausschreibungen)* Angebot *(für Leistungen od. Lieferungen)*; Anbieten; ~ **agreement** Bietungsabsprache; Submissionsvertrag; ~ **documents** Ausschreibungsunterlagen; ~ **guarantee** Bietungsgarantie; ~ **procedure** Ausschreibungsverfahren; **acceptance of** ~ Zuschlag *(Erteilung e-s Auftrags)*; **allocation to the lowest** ~ Vergebung an das niedrigste Angebot; **by** ~ durch Ausschreibung im Submissionswege; **call for** ~**s** *Am* Ausschreibung; **party inviting a** ~ ausschreibende Partei; **sealed bid** ~ *Br* Submissionsangebot in versiegeltem Umschlag; **terms of the** ~Ausschreibungsbedingungen; **to accept the** ~ den Zuschlag erteilen; **to invite** ~**s** ausschreiben, die Ausschreibung vornehmen; ~**s are invited for ..** Angebote sind einzureichen bis zum ..; **to make** (or **send in**) **a** ~ ein Angebot abgeben; sich um e-n *(ausgeschriebenen)* Auftrag bewerben; **to put out to** ~ ausschreiben; **to solicit** ~**s** Angebote einholen

tender *v* anbieten, ein Angebot machen; einreichen, beantragen; *(Zahlung, Leistung zur Begleichung e-r Schuld od. Erfüllung e-r Verpflichtung)* anbieten; andienen; **to** ~ **for** *(bei Ausschreibungen)* sich bewerben um; ein Angebot abgeben; **to** ~ **for a contract** *Br* sich um e-n *(ausgeschriebenen)* Auftrag bewerben; **to** ~ **for a supply of goods** *(bei Ausschreibungen)* sich um e-n Liefervertrag bewerben; **to** ~ **for a public loan** ein Zeichnungsangebot auf e-e öffentl. Anleihe abgeben; **to invite the public to** ~ **for a loan** die Öffentlichkeit durch Abgabe von Zeichnungsangeboten zu e-r Anleihe auffordern

tender *v*, **to** ~ **a bid** *Am (bei Ausschreibungen)* ein Angebot abgeben; **to** ~ **delivery** Lieferung anbieten; **to** ~ **documents** Urkunden vorlegen; **to** ~ **evidence** Beweis antreten (od. vorbringen); **to** ~ **goods** Waren zum Verkauf anbieten; **to** ~ **an issue** in e-m pleading die Behauptung(en) der Gegenpartei bestreiten *(ohne Vorbringung neuer Tatsachen)* und die Entscheidung dem Gericht überlassen; **to** ~ **an oath to a p.** jdm e-n Eid zuschieben; **to** ~ **a plea** e-e

Einrede (etc) vorbringen; **to ~ (a) proof** Beweis erbringen; **to ~ the amount of rent** die Bezahlung der Miete anbieten; **to ~ one's resignation** s-n Rücktritt anbieten; s-e Entlassung einreichen; **to ~ one's services** s-e Dienste anbieten; **to ~ one's thanks** s-n Dank aussprechen

tenderee *(bei Ausschreibungen)* Auftrag vergebende Stelle, Ausschreibender, Auftraggeber *(dem ein Angebot gemacht wird)*

tenderer *(bei Ausschreibungen)* Submittent *(der sich um e-n Auftrag bewirbt)*; Bieter; **the ~ is bound to keep open his tender during a period** der Submittent ist während e-r Frist an sein Angebot gebunden

tendering Angebotsabgabe; **~ procedure** Ausschreibungsverfahren

tenement Wohnhaus; Grundbesitz; *Br* Wohnung in e-m Mietshaus; **~(house)** Mietskaserne; **dominant ~** *(bei Grunddienstbarkeit)* herrschendes Grundstück; **lands and ~s** Grundbesitz *(Land und Gebäude)*; **servient ~** *(bei Grunddienstbarkeit)* dienendes (od. belastetes) Grundstück

tenet Grundsatz; Lehre, Doktrin

tenor *(wesentl.)* Inhalt; Wortlaut; Sinn, Bedeutung; genaue Abschrift; Laufzeit; **~ of a bill**[25] Laufzeit e-s Wechsels; **~ of a deed** *(im Rechtsgebrauch:)* genauer Wortlaut e-r Urkunde; *(im allgemeinen Sprachgebrauch:) (wesentl.)* Inhalt (od. Sinn) e-r Urkunde; **executor according to the ~** Testamentsvollstrecker nach dem wahren Sinn des Testaments; **proving the ~** *Scot* Beweis des Inhalts e-r verlorengegangenen Urkunde

tense situation *pol* gespannte Lage

tension, easing (or **relaxation**) **of ~** *pol* Entspannung; **international ~s** internationale Spannungen; **to decrease ~s** Spannungen verringern; **to ease ~** *pol* entspannen

tentative versuchsweise, Probe-; **~ agreement** Probevereinbarung; **~ draft** Probeentwurf; **~ tax** *Am* vorläufige Steuer (Nachlaßsteuer); **to make a ~ offer** probeweise ein Angebot machen

tenure *(allgemein:)* Besitz, Innehabung *(von Grundbesitz, e-s Amtes)*; *(technisch:)*[26] Recht zum Besitz *(die Gesamtheit der Rechte, die jd an e-m Grundstück haben kann)*; **~ of a chair** Innehaben e-s Lehrstuhls; **~ under a lease** Pachtbesitz

tenure for life, appointment as civil servant with ~ *Am* Ernennung zum Beamten auf Lebenszeit; **to be appointed a civil servant with ~** *Am* zum Beamten auf Lebenszeit ernannt werden

tenure of office Dienstzeit, Amtsdauer; **to have a ~ of 5 years** für die Dauer von 5 Jahren (für ein Amt) gewählt werden

tenure, freehold ~ Eigenbesitz *(von Grundstükken)*; **leasehold ~** Pachtbesitz; **permanent ~** *Am* feste Anstellung; **security of ~** Mieterschutz; Pachtschutz; **statutory ~** *Am* gesetzliche Dienstzeit

term 1. Wort(laut), Ausdruck; (Fach-)Begriff, Terminus; **~ of art** Fachausdruck; **by the ~ of the contract** nach dem Wortlaut des Vertrages; **the ~ employee** der Arbeitnehmerbegriff; **business ~** kaufmännischer Ausdruck; **commercial ~** Handelsausdruck; **descriptive ~** *Am (WarenzeichenR)* beschreibende Angabe *(die e-e Eigenschaft der Ware nennt)*; **exact ~s** genauer Wortlaut; **in ~s of** →terms; **legal ~** juristischer Ausdruck; **technical ~** Fachausdruck

term 2. Bedingung (→*terms*); Frist; Dauer, Laufzeit; Zeitabschnitt, Zeitraum; *Br* Zahltag; *Am* Sitzungsperiode *(e-s Gerichts)*; Amtsperiode; **~ assurance** *Br* → **~** insurance; **~ bill** *Br* Wechsel mit bestimmter Frist; **~ bonds** Obligationen e-r Emission mit einheitlichem Fälligkeitsdatum *(opp. serial bonds)*; **~ contract** Zeitvertrag; **~ days** Fälligkeitstage, Zahltage *(z.B. für Miete, Zinsen)*; **~ debt** später fällig werdende Forderung; **~ deposits** *Br* Termineinlagen; **~ fee** *Br (vom solicitor von s-m Klienten zu fordernde)* Prozeßgebühr *(für Sitzung im Supreme Court)*; **~ insurance** Risikolebensversicherung (abgekürzte Todesfallversicherung); **~ loan** mittelfristiger Kredit; Darlehen füe e-e bestimmte Zeit *(meist für 1 bis 10 Jahre, das gewöhnlich in Raten rückzahlbar ist;* **~ of a bill** Laufzeit e-s Wechsels; **~ of a contract** Vertragsbedingung; Laufzeit e-s Vertrages; **~ of copyright** *(UrhR)* Schutzfrist; **~ of court** *Am* Sitzungsperiode e-s Gerichts *(die Zeit, während der das Gericht e-e session halten kann)*

term of delivery Lieferfrist; **to adhere to** (or **keep**) **the ~** die Lieferfrist einhalten; **to exceed the ~** die Lieferfrist überschreiten

term of a guarantee Dauer e-r Garantie, Garantiefrist

term (of imprisonment) Gefängnisstrafe, Strafzeit (→*imprisonment)*; **concurrent and consecutive ~s** *Am*[26a] gleichzeitige und aufeinanderfolgende Vollstreckung von Freiheitsstrafen; **extended ~**[27] verlängerte Strafzeit; Sicherungsverwahrung; **maximum ~** Höchststrafe; **minimum ~** Mindeststrafe; **ordinary ~** *Am*[28] in der Regel anzuwendende Freiheitsstrafe *(gewöhnlicher Strafrahmen)*; **special ~** *Am*[29] Sonderstrafmaß; **to impose a sentence of imprisonment for an extended ~** auf e-e verlängerte Freiheitsstrafe erkennen

term, ~ of a lease Bedingung (od. Dauer) e-s Miet- (od. Pacht-)Vertrages; Mietzeit, Pachtzeit; ~ **of a licen|ce (~se)** Lizenzdauer; ~ **of life** Lebensdauer, Lebenszeit; ~ **of limitation** Verjährungsfrist; ~ **of a loan** Laufzeit e-s Kredits; ~ **of notice** Kündigungsfrist; ~ **of office** Amtszeit, Amtsdauer; Mandat; ~ **of (a) patent** Schutzfrist e-s Patents (→*patent 2.*); ~ **of payment** Zahlungsfrist; ~ **of validity** Gültigkeitsdauer

term, beginning (or **commencement**) **of the** ~ Fristbeginn; **expiration** (or **expiry**) **of the** ~ **(fixed)** Fristablauf; **on expiration of the** ~ nach Ablauf der Frist; **expired** ~ abgelaufene Frist; **fixed** ~ bestimmte Dauer *(z.B. e-s Vertrages)*; fester Termin; →**inominate** ~; **legal** ~**s** *Scot* →~ days; **length of** ~ Zeitdauer; **long-**~ langfristig (→*long 1.*); **medium** ~ mittelfristig *(→medium 2.)*; **moneys at long** ~ langfristige Gelder; **moneys at medium** ~ mittelfristige Gelder

term, prison ~ Strafzeit (→~ *of imprisonment*); **to serve a prison** ~ e-e Freiheitsstrafe verbüßen

term, running of a ~ Lauf e-r Frist; **short-**~ kurzfristig (→*short 3.*); **monies at short** ~ kurzfristige Gelder

term, to adhere (or **comply with**) **a** ~ e-e (Zahlungs-)Frist wahren (od. einhalten); **to adhere to** (or **keep**) **the** ~ **of delivery** die Lieferfrist einhalten; **to extend a** ~ e-e (Zahlungs-)Frist verlängern; **to keep a** ~ e-e (Zahlungs-)Frist einhalten; **to set a** ~ e-e (Zahlungs-)Frist (fest-)setzen; e-e Grenze setzen (to für); **the** ~ **expires** die (Zahlungs-)Frist läuft ab

term 3., ~ **(of years)** zeitlich begrenztes miet- od. pachtartiges Grundstücksrecht; ~ **of years absolute** pachtartiges Besitzrecht für e-e bestimmte Zeit *(cf. legal → estate)*

term 4. *(Universität od. Schule)* Semester, Trimester; ~ **papers** *Am univ* Seminaraufgaben; schriftl. Arbeit für e-e Vorlesung od. ein Seminar; **end of (the)** ~ Semesterschluß; **in** ~ **(-time)** (or **during** ~) im Semester; **to enter one's name for the** ~ sich immatrikulieren lassen; **to keep one's** ~**s** Pflichtvorlesungen belegen

terms Bedingungen, Bestimmungen; Klauseln; *(gefordertes)* Honorar; Termine (→ *term 2.*); Begriffe (→ *term 1.*)

terms, to accept ~ Bedingungen annehmen; **to adhere to the** ~ die Bedingungen einhalten; **to agree (up)on the** ~ sich über die Bedingungen einigen; **to bring a p. to** ~ jdn zur Annahme der Bedingungen zwingen (od. veranlassen); **to come to** ~ sich einigen; zu e-m Vergleich kommen, sich vergleichen; **to come within the** ~ **of a contract** unter die Bestimmungen e-s Vertrages fallen; **to comply with the** ~ die Bedingungen erfüllen; **to embody** ~ **in an agreement** Bestimmungen in e-m Vertrag aufnehmen; **to fix the** ~ die Bedingungen festsetzen

terms, ~ **inclusive** alles inbegriffen; ~ **of admission** Zulassungsbedingungen; ~ **of an agreement** Vertragsbedingungen, Vertragsbestimmungen; *(KartellR)* Bestimmungen e-r Absprache; ~ **of amortization** Tilgungsbedingungen; ~ **(and conditions) of business** Geschäftsbedingungen; ~ **of composition** Vergleichsbedingungen; ~ **of a contract** →contract 1.; ~ **(and conditions) of a guarantee** Gewährleistungs-bedingungen; Garantiebedingungen; ~ **(and conditions) of employment** Arbeitsbedingungen; Anstellungsbedingungen; ~ **(and conditions) of a loan** →~ of a loan; ~ **of financing** Finanzierungsbedingungen; ~ **of interest** Zinsbedingungen; ~ **of a lease** Bedingungen (od. Bestimmungen) e-s Miet- (od. Pacht-)vertrages (→*lease 1.*); Leasingbedingungen, Leasingbestimmungen (→*lease 2.*); ~ **of a licen|ce (~se)** Lizenzbestimmungen; ~ **of a loan** Darlehensbedingungen; Anleihebedingungen

terms of payment (ToP) *(Außenhandel)* Zahlungstermine, zeitliche Zahlungsgewohnheiten; *(privatwirtschaftlich)* Zahlungsbedingungen, Zahlungsmodalitäten *(e.g. cash on delivery, prompt cash, Br hire-purchase terms, credit terms)*; ~ **customary to international trade** im internationalen Handel übliche Zahlungsziele; **establishment of the** ~ Festsetzung der Zahlungsbedingungen

terms of peace, to negotiate ~ Friedensbedingungen aushandeln

terms of reference Gegenstände e-r Untersuchung; *(e-r od. mehreren Personen)* zur Entscheidung od. zum Bericht übertragene Punkte; Aufgabenbereich; **arbitrator's** ~[29a] Aufgaben des Schiedsrichters *(die er in e-m Schriftstück vor Beginn des Schiedsverfahrens festlegt)*; **to define the** ~ den Gegenstand e-r Untersuchung (od. die Aufgaben) bestimmen

terms, ~ **of a sale** Verkaufsbedingungen; ~ **of settlement** Vergleichsbedingungen *(→ settlement 2.)*; ~ **of subscription** Zeichnungsbedingungen (→*subscription 4.)*

terms of trade (ToT) *(Außenhandel)* Austauschverhältnis, Austauschrelationen *(in e-r Währungseinheit ausgedrücktes Preisverhältnis zwischen Exporten und Importen e-s Landes)*

terms strictly cash nur gegen Barzahlung

terms, on accommodating (or **advantageous**) ~ zu günstigen Bedingungen; **amendment of** ~ Änderung der Bedingungen; → **cash** ~; **compliance with the** ~ Einhaltung der Bedingungen; **contract** ~ Vertragsbedingungen, Vertragsbestimmungen; **credit** ~ Kreditbedingungen; **easy** ~ **(of payment)** günstige Zahlungsbedingungen; Zahlungserleichterungen *(z.B. Ratenzahlungen)*; **on equal** ~**s** unter den gleichen Bedingungen; **exact** ~ genaue Bedingungen; **fair** ~ angemessene Bedingungen; → **gross** ~; **implied** ~ stillschweigend mit eingeschlossene (Vertrags-)Bedingungen (→ *implied)*

terms, in ~ of im Sinne von, inbegriffen; in bezug auf, hinsichtlich; gemessen an; was ... anbetrifft; **in ~ of defen|ce (~se)** was die Verteidigung anbetrifft; **in ~ of dollars** in Dollar ausgedrückt (od. umgerechnet)

terms, International Commercial T~ →Incoterms; **local ~** Platzbedingungen; **on mutual ~** auf Gegenseitigkeit; **peace ~** Friedensbedingungen; **in real ~** effektiv; **special ~** Sonderbedingungen; **in set ~** festgelegt; **strained ~** gespannte Beziehungen; **Trade T~** handelsübliche Vertragsformeln (→ *trade*); **on usual ~** zu den üblichen Bedingungen

terminable zeitlich begrenzt; kündbar; **~ annuity** *Br* befristete (od. befristbare) Rente; Zeitrente; **~ contract** kündbarer Vertrag; **a tenancy ~ by half a year's notice** → tenancy; **not ~** unkündbar

terminal 1. End-, Abschluß-; Grenz-; Semester; Umschlagstelle; Endstation; *Br (Produktenbörse)* Termin- *(opp. spot)*; **~ charges** (Fracht-) Zustellgebühren; **~ illness** Krankheit mit tödlichem Ausgang; **~ job** *Am (höchste erreichbare)* Endstellung *(ohne Beförderungsmöglichkeit)*; **~ market** *Br (Produktenbörse)* Terminmarkt; Warenterminbörse; **~ payment** *Am* Zahlung der letzten Rate *(in e-m Abzahlungsvertrag)*; **~port** Endhafen; **~ price** *Br (Produktenbörse)* Preis für künftige Lieferung; **~ station** Endbahnhof, Sackbahnhof; **~ utility** Grenznutzen; **~ wage** *Am* Entlassungsabfindung; **air ~** *(Flughafen)* Abfertigungsgebäude; **rail and water ~** Umschlagplatz

terminal 2. *(EDV)* Terminal *(Gerät zur Eingabe von Daten und/oder Ausgabe von Ergebnissen)*; **point-of-sale ~** Verkaufsstellenterminal

terminate *v* beenden, beendigen; abschließen; kündigen; ablaufen, enden; erlöschen: **to ~ an agreement without prior notice** e-n Vertrag fristlos kündigen; **to ~ one's contract of employment** seinem Arbeitgeber kündigen; **to ~ a p.'s employment** jdm kündigen; **to ~ a lease** e-n Miet- (od. Pacht-)vertrag kündigen; **to ~ the proceedings** das Verfahren einstellen; **to ~ without notice** fristlos kündigen; **notice to ~ (agreement, employment, lease)** →notice 3.

terminated, the agreement is ~ das Abkommen läuft ab; **the obligations have ~** die Verbindlichkeiten sind erloschen

termination Beendigung; Ende, Ablauf; Erlöschen; Kündigung; **~ of an agreement** Beendigung (od. Kündigung) e-s Vertrags; Auflösung e-s Kartells; Aufhebung e-r Absprache; **~ of sb.'s appointment** jds. Abberufung; **~ of →bankruptcy proceedings; ~ of a contract of employment** Beendigung (od. Kündigung) e-s Arbeitsvertrages; **~ of employment by notice** Beendigung des Arbeitsverhältnisses durch Kündigung; **~ of membership** Erlöschen der Mitgliedschaft; **~ of a partnership** Beendigung (od. Auflösung) e-r Personengesellschaft; **~ of pregnancy** Abtreibung; **~ of a right** Erlöschen e-s Rechts; **~ of a treaty** *(VölkerR)* Außerkrafttreten (od. Außerkraftsetzen) e-s Vertrages; **~ payment** Abfindung *(bei Kündigung von Arbeitnehmern)*; **~ without notice** fristlose Kündigung; **power of ~** Befugnis, bei Eintritt e-r Bedingung ein Rechtsverhältnis zu beenden; **subject to ~** kündbar; **to bring to a ~** (or **to put [a] ~ to**) *(etw.)* beendigen (od. zum Abschluß bringen)

terminology Terminologie, Fachsprache; **legal ~** Rechtssprache

terminus Ende; *bes. Br* Endstation; **~ a quo** ("starting point") Ausgangspunkt *(e-s Arguments)*; **~ ad quem** ("finishing point") Endpunkt

termor Besitzer (od. Nutznießer) von Grundbesitz auf Zeit (for a term of years or for life)

terra nullius *(VölkerR)* staatenloses Gebiet, Niemandsland

terraced houses *Br* Reihenhäuser

territorial Territorial-; Hoheits-; Gebiets-; *Am* ein Territorium betreffend; *Br* Landwehrmann *(Mitglied der T~ Army)*; **~ air space** Lufthoheitsgebiet; **~ application** räumlicher Geltungsbereich; **~ area** Hoheitsgebiet; **T~ Army** *Br*[30] Landwehr; **~ authorities** Gebietskörperschaften; **~ changes** Gebietsveränderungen; **~ claim** territorialer Anspruch, Gebietsanspruch; **~ courts** *Am* in den Territorien *(→territory)* errichtete Gerichte; **~ gains** territoriale Gewinne; **~ invasion** Eindringen in das Hoheitsgebiet; **~ jurisdiction** Territorialhoheit, Gebietshoheit; örtliche Zuständigkeit *(z. B. e-s Konsuls)*; **~ law** →municipal law; **~ protection** Gebietsschutz; **~ restraints** *Am* Gebietsbeschränkungen (→*vertical restraint guidelines*); **~→restriction; ~ sea** Küstenmeer; **~ sovereignty** Gebietshoheit; **~ unit** Gebietseinheit; **~ waters** Hoheitsgewässer, Territorialgewässer; Eigengewässer; **to violate ~ waters** in Küstengewässer eindringen

territoriality Territorialität, Zugehörigkeit zu e-m Staatsgebiet

territor|y Gebiet; Staatsgebiet, Hoheitsgebiet; *com* Gebiet e-s Vertreters (commercial travel[l]er); **T~** *Am*[31] Territorium *(Gebiet unter Souveränität der Vereinigten Staaten, das noch nicht zum Einzelstaat [State] erhoben wurde; z. B. Alaska bis 1958, Hawaii bis 1959. In Kanada und Australien gibt es ähnliche Teilgebiete, die noch* *nicht "Province" oder "State" sind)*; ~ **allocation** Marktaufteilung; **acquisition of** ~ *(VölkerR)* Gebietserwerb; **allocation of ~ies or customers** Aufteilung von Märkten oder Kunden; **cession of a** ~ *(VölkerR)* Abtretung e-s Gebietes; **customs** ~ Zollgebiet; **exchange of ~ies** Gebietsaustausch; **in German** ~ auf deutschem (Staats-)Gebiet; **loss of** ~ *(VölkerR)* Gebietsverlust; **maritime** ~ maritimes Hoheitsgebiet, Hoheitsgewässer; → **metropolitan ~; national** ~ Staatsgebiet; **non-self-governing ~ies** →governing; **trusteeship ~ies** Treuhandgebiete (→*trusteeship*); **to enter (leave) the** ~ das Hoheitsgebiet betreten (verlassen)

terror Terror, Schreckensherrschaft; **to suppress** ~ Terror unterdrücken

terrorism Terrorismus; **acts of** ~ Terrorakte, Terroranschläge; **combatting** (or **fight against**) ~ Bekämpfung des Terrorismus; →**European Convention on the Suppression of T~; to curb** ~ den Terrorismus eindämmen

terrorist Terrorist; terroristisch; ~ **act** Terrorakt; ~ **attack** Terroristenangriff (od. -anschlag); ~ **attempt at blackmail** terroristischer Erpressungsversuch; ~ **bombing** terroristische Bombenanschläge; ~ **hide-out** Terroristenversteck; ~ **murder** von Terroristen verübter Mord

terroristic terroristisch; ~ **threats** *Am*[32] *(StrafR)* terroristische Drohungen

tertiary sector tertiärer Sektor, Dienstleistungssektor *(bes. Handelsbetriebe, Bank- und Versicherungsbetriebe)*

test Probe, Prüfung, Versuch, Untersuchung; Test; ~ **action** →~case; ~ **audit** stichprobenweise Prüfung; ~ **ballot** Probeabstimmung; **T~ Ban Treaty** Teststopp-Vertrag *(s. Treaty Banning →Nuclear Weapon T~s)*; ~ **case** Musterklage, Musterprozeß, Leitverfahren *(dessen Ausgang auch für andere, zunächst ausgesetzte, gleichartige Prozesse bestimmend sein soll)*; Präzedenzfall; ~ **drive** *(Auto)* Probefahrt; ~ **flight** *(Flugzeug)* Probeflug; ~ **on site** (Abnahme-) Prüfung am Aufstellungsort *(z. B. e-r Maschine)*; ~ **purchase** Testkauf, Kauf zu Untersuchungszwecken; ~ **series** Versuchsserie; ~ **site** Versuchsgelände; ~ **stage** Versuchsstadium; ~**-tube baby** Retortenbaby; ~ **weighing** *(Zoll)* Nachwiegen, Gewichtskontrolle; **acceptance** ~ Abnahmeprüfung; **blood** ~ Blutprobe, Blutgruppenuntersuchung *(zum Nachweis der Vaterschaft; cf. paternity)*; **capacity** ~ Eignungsprüfung; **check** ~ Gegenprobe; **driving** ~ *Br* Fahrprüfung *(zur Erlangung e-r →driving licence)*; **goods** ~ Warentest; **grading** ~ Test zur Einstufung; **means** ~ Bedürftigkeitsprüfung; **nuclear weapon** ~ Atomwaffenversuch (→*nuclear*); **same-statute** (or **specificity**) ~ *(IPR)* →specificity; **to put sth. to the** ~ etw. prüfen (od. e-m Test unterwerfen); **to take a** ~ sich e-r Prüfung (od. e-m Test) unterziehen

test *v* untersuchen, prüfen; testen, e-m Test unterwerfen; **to** ~ **a coin for weight** e-e Münze auf das vorschriftsmäßige Gewicht prüfen

test-market *v* versuchsweise auf den Markt bringen

tested getestet, erprobt; **to have sth.** ~ etw. testen lassen

testing Untersuchung, Prüfung; Test; Erprobung; ~ **of goods** Warentest; **material** ~ Materialprüfung; **quality** ~ Qualitätsprüfung

testacy Zustand e-s →testate; (Rechtszustand bei Sterben unter) Hinterlassung e-s gültigen Testaments *(opp. intestacy)*

testament Testament, letztwillige Verfügung *(testament ist meist in der Verbindung last will and ~ gebraucht)*; ~**-dative** *Scot* Bestätigung als → executor-dative; ~**-testamentar** *Scot* Bestätigung als →executor-nominate; **inofficious** ~ *Am* pflichtwidriges Testament *(→inofficious)*; **last will and** ~ Testament, letztwillige Verfügung; **military** ~ →military; **mutual** ~ gegenseitiges Testament

testamentary testamentarisch, letztwillig; Testier-; ~ **burden** testamentarische Auflage

testamentary capacity Testierfähigkeit, Fähigkeit zur Errichtung e-s Testaments; **to have** ~ testierfähig sein; **minors lack** ~ Minderjährige sind nicht testierfähig

testamentary, ~ **causes** die Gültigkeit od. Errichtung e-s Testaments betreffenden Rechtssachen; ~ **clause** Testamentsbestimmung

testamentary disposition letztwillige Verfügung; Verfügung von Todes wegen; **Convention on the Conflict of Laws Relating to the Form of T~ D~s**[33] Übereinkommen über das auf die Form letztwilliger Verfügungen anzuwendende Recht; **to make a** ~ letztwillig verfügen

testamentary, ~ **expenses** Kosten der Erbschaftsverwaltung durch den → executor; ~ **gift** Vermächtnis; ~ **guardian**[34] durch Testament eingesetzter Vormund; ~ →**guardianship;** ~ **heir** *Am* testamentarischer Erbe *(cf. personal representative)*, ~ **provision** letztwillige Verfügung; ~ **succession** testamentarische Erbfolge; ~ **trust** →trust 1.; ~ **trustee** durch Testament eingesetzter Treuhänder

testamentary, letters ~ *Am* Testamentsvollstreckerzeugnis *(gerichtl. Bestellung als → executor)*; **to grant letters** ~ ein Testamentsvollstreckerzeugnis erteilen

testate Erblasser, der ein gültiges Testament

hinterlassen hat; ein gültiges Testament hinterlassend *(opp. intestate)*; **by ~ or intestate succession** durch testamentarische oder gesetzliche Erbfolge; **to die ~** unter Hinterlassung e-s gültigen Testaments sterben

testator Testator; Erblasser, der ein Testament hinterlassen hat; **competent as ~** testierfähig; **~'s intention** Absicht des Testators

testatrix Erblasserin, die ein Testament hinterlassen hat

testatum Ende der Einleitung e-r förmlichen Vertragsurkunde *(cf. now this deed → witnesseth)*

teste ("witness") letzter Satz e-s →writ *(beginnend mit "witness")*, aus dem Datum und Ort der Ausstellung hervorgeht

tester Prüfer; Prüfgerät

testify *v (unter Eid od. unter förml. Versicherung an Eides Statt [under oath or on affirmation])* als Zeuge aussagen, bezeugen; **to ~ against a p.** gegen jdn aussagen; Zeuge sein gegen jdn; **to ~ in** (or **before a**) **court** vor Gericht aussagen; **to ~ in a p.'s favo(u)r** zugunsten jds aussagen; **to ~ on behalf of a p.** für jdn aussagen; **to ~ on** (or **under**) **oath** e-e eidliche Zeugenaussage machen; **to ~ to sth.** etw. bezeugen; **refusal to ~** Aussageverweigerung; **to refuse to ~** die (Zeugen-)Aussage verweigern

testifying, privileged from ~ das Zeugnisverweigerungsrecht haben

testimonial Zeugnis *(bes. über Dienstleistungen, gutes Verhalten etc)*; Empfehlungsschreiben; Ehrengabe

testimonium clause Beglaubigungsvermerk am Ende e-r Urkunde (od. e-s Testamentes) *(z.B. "In witness whereof, we have hereunto set our hands and seals this ... day of ...")*

testimon|y Zeugenaussage *(vor Gericht)* (unter Eid od. an Eides Statt under oath or on affirmation); **conflicting** (or **divergent**) **~ies** voneinander abweichende (od. sich widersprechende) Zeugenaussagen; **expert ~** Sachverständigengutachten; **preservation of ~** Beweissicherung; **proceedings for the perpetuation of ~** Beweissicherungsverfahren; **recording of ~** Beweisaufnahme; **right to withhold ~** Zeugnisverweigerungsrecht

testimony, to bear ~ bezeugen, Zeugnis ablegen (to für); **to give ~ as a witness** als Zeuge aussagen; **to perpetuate ~** Aussagen zur Beweissicherung vornehmen; **to take sb.'s ~** jdn als Zeugen vernehmen; **a ~ is taken** e-e Zeugenvernehmung findet statt; **to withdraw ~** e-e Zeugenaussage widerrufen

text Text, Wortlaut; **~book** Hand- od. Lehrbuch, Fall- od. Entscheidungssammlung *(für ein bestimmtes Rechtsgebiet)*; **~ of the contract** Vertragstext; **~ of the law** Gesetzestext; **~ of an oath** Eidesformel; **~ of a patent application** Wortlaut e-r Patentanmeldung; **~ processing** *(EDV)* Textverarbeitung; **authentic ~** maßgebender Text; **coded ~** verschlüsselter Text; **draft ~** Textentwurf; **official ~** amtlicher Wortlaut; **original ~** Originaltext; **the English ~ will prevail** der englische Text ist maßgeblich

textile, ~s Textilien, Textilwaren; **~ finishing** Textilveredelung; **~ goods fair** Textilmesse; **~ industry** Textilindustrie; **~ shares** Textilwerte

Thai Thailänder, ~in; thailändisch

Thailand Thailand; **Kingdom of ~** Königreich Thailand

thanking you in advance Ihnen im voraus dankend

thanks, letter of ~ Dankschreiben; **rendering of ~** Danksagung; **returned with ~** mit Dank zurück; **I would like to take this opportunity to express my ~ to you** (for ...) darf ich Ihnen meinen besten Dank aussprechen

Thanksgiving Day *Am* Erntedanktag *(gesetzl. Feiertag am 4. Donnerstag im November)*

theatre *(Am* **theater**), **~ of operations** *mil* Operationsgebiet; **~ of war** Kriegsschauplatz

theft[35] Diebstahl *(Am umfaßt in manchen Einzelstaaten auch Veruntreuung und Betrug)*; **~ by breaking and entering** Einbruchsdiebstahl; **~ by climbing into premises** Einsteigediebstahl; **~ by finding** Fundunterschlagung; **~ in a hotel** Hoteldiebstahl; **~ insurance** Diebstahl-Versicherung; **~, pilferage and non-delivery** (T. P. N. D.) Diebstahl und Nichtablieferung; **aggravated ~** schwerer Diebstahl; **insurance against burglary and ~** Einbruchs- und Diebstahlversicherung; **car ~** Autodiebstahl; **mail ~** Postdiebstahl; **to charge sb. with ~** jdn des Diebstahls beschuldigen; **to commit a ~** Diebstahl begehen

then damals; damalig; künftig

therapeutic abortion Schwangerschaftsabbruch aus medizinischer Indikation

thereafter danach

there and back *Br* hin und zurück

thereinafter nachstehend

thereinbefore vorstehend

thermal power station Wärmekraftwerk

thermonuclear bomb Wasserstoffbombe

theory Theorie; **in ~** in der Theorie *(opp. in practice)*; **to advocate a ~** e-e Theorie verfechten; **to put forward a ~** e-e Theorie aufstellen

thesis These, Dissertation

thief Dieb; ~**-proof** diebessicher

thin market *(Börse)* flauer Markt

thing Sache; ~ **in action** →chose in action; ~**s personal** bewegl. Sachen; ~**s in possession** Sachen; ~**s real** unbewegl. Sachen, Grundstücke

third 1. (der/die/das) Dritte; Drittel (→*third 2.)*; ~**-class** drittklassig; ~**-class mail** *Am* Drucksachen (→*mail*); ~ **degree** *Am* intensives polizeil. Verhör, um e-n Häftling zum Geständnis zu bringen; **T~ Market** *Br (Börse)* Dritter Markt *(begrenzter Markt, der im Januar 1987 eingeführt wurde, um jungen, noch im Wachstum begriffenen britischen Unternehmen zu helfen, auf einfache und kosteneffektive Weise Kapital zu beschaffen; →Domestic Equity Market)*; ~ **market** *Am* außerbörslicher Handel in börsennotierten Aktien (→*OTC market*); ~ **of exchange** Tertiawechsel; ~ **offender** *Am* zum zweitenmal rückfällig gewordener Täter

third party a) *(allgemein)* Dritter; ~ **accident insurance** *Br* Unfall-Fremdversicherung; ~ **acting in good faith** gutgläubiger Dritter; ~ **beneficiary** Begünstigter aus e-m Vertrage zugunsten Dritter; Drittbegünstigter; ~ **beneficiary contract** (or **contract for the benefit of a** ~) Vertrag zugunsten Dritter; ~ **funds** Fremdgelder; ~ **indemnity insurance** Haftpflichtversicherung; ~ **insurance** Fremdversicherung; Haftpflichtversicherung; ~ **liability insurance**[36] Haftpflichtversicherung; ~ **mandate** Kontovollmacht; ~ **rights** Rechte Dritter

Third Parties (Rights against Insurers) Act 1930 *Br* Gesetz mit dem Zweck, im Falle des Konkurses e-s Haftpflichtversicherten den Geschädigten zu schützen und ihm die Rechte gegen die Versicherung zu übertragen

third party risk *Br* Drittschadenhaftpflichtrisiko; ~ **policy** *Br*[37] Kraftfahrzeughaftpflichtversicherungspolice; **to insure against** ~ **only** (not to take out a comprehensive [motor] policy or insurance) nur e-e Kraftfahrzeug-Haftpflichtversicherung abschließen (sich nicht gegen alle Gefahren versichern)

third party, contract on the life of a ~ Vertrag über e-e Versicherung auf fremdes Leben; Drittlebensversicherungsvertrag; Lebensfremdversicherungsvertrag

third party b) Dritter *(der sich an e-m anhängigen Prozeß beteiligt)*; ~ **answer** *Am* Streitverkündungsbeantwortung des →third party defendant; ~ **claim** Streitverkündung; ~ **complaint** *Am* Streitverkündungsschrift des *(ursprünglich)* Beklagten (nunmehr third party plaintiff) gegen e-n Dritten (third party defendant) auf Einbeziehung in den Rechtsstreit als *(weitere)* Partei; ~ **defendant** Streitverkündeter, Nebenintervenient, Streitverkündungsempfänger

third party notice[38] Streitverkündung; ~ **procedure** *(etwa)* Streitverkündungsverfahren; **person served with a** ~ *Br* Streitverkündungsempfänger, Streitverkündeter; **person serving a** ~ *Br* Streitverkündender; **to issue a** ~ den Streit verkünden; **to serve a** ~ **on sb.** *Br* jdm den Streit verkünden

third party petition *Am* →third party complaint

third, ~ **person** →third party a); **T~ World** Dritte Welt *(Entwicklungsländer)*

third 2. Drittel; **two-~s majority** Zweidrittelmehrheit; **by two-~s of the votes cast** mit zwei Drittel der abgegebenen Stimmen

this day six (or three) months *Br parl* nicht in dieser Sitzung *(e-e Möglichkeit der Ablehnung e-s Gesetzesentwurfs)*

thorough eingehend, gründlich; durch und durch; **to receive a** ~ **training** e-e gründliche Ausbildung erhalten

thoroughfare Durchgang, Durchfahrt; (Haupt-) Verkehrsstraße; **no** ~ Durchfahrt verboten

those present die Anwesenden

threat Drohung (of mit); Bedrohung; ~**s action** *Br*[39] Klage desjenigen, der von e-m anderen grundlos wegen Patentverletzung bedroht wurde; ~ **of (legal) proceedings** Klagedrohung; ~ **of war** Kriegsdrohung; Kriegsgefahr; ~ **to peace** Bedrohung des Friedens; ~**s with intent to extort money or other things** *(StrafR)* erpresserisches Unternehmen *(schließt den Versuch des § 253 StGB ein)*; **hidden** ~ versteckte Drohung; **to carry out a** ~ e-e Drohung ausführen; **to constitute a** ~ **to the security of the state** e-e Gefahr für die Sicherheit des Staates darstellen

threaten *v* drohen; bedrohen; androhen; **to** ~ **peace** den Frieden gefährden; **to** ~ **a p. with legal proceedings** jdm ein Gerichtsverfahren androhen

threatened, he was ~ **with punishment** ihm wurde Strafe angedroht

threatening letter[40] Drohbrief

three, ~**-cornered arrangement** Dreiecksvereinbarung; ~**-D-policy** *Am* Vertrauensschaden-Versicherung (gegen dishonesty [Unehrlichkeit], disappearance [Verschwinden], destruction [Zerstörung]); ~**-mile limit** Dreimeilengrenze *(→ territorial waters)*; ~ **-mile zone** *(VölkerR)* Dreimeilenzone; ~ **months' bill** Dreimonatswechsel; ~ **per cents** *Br* dreiprozentige Papiere; ~ **to one majority** (or ~ **fourths majority,** ~ **quarter majority)** Dreiviertelmehrheit

threshold *auch fig.* Schwelle; Schwellen-; Anfang, Beginn; ~ **countries** Schwellenländer; ~ **payment** indexgebundene Lohnerhöhung; ~ **worker** *Am* berufsunerfahrener Arbeiter

thrift Sparsamkeit, Wirtschaftlichkeit; **~s** →~institutions; ~ **account** *Am* Sparkonto; ~ **deposits** *Am* Spareinlagen; ~ **institutions** *Am* Bausparkassen; Sparkassen *(für Einzelhandelsgeschäfte)*; **to promote** ~ das Sparen fördern

thriving blühend, florierend; **business is** ~ die Geschäfte gehen gut

throne Thron; **abdication of the** ~ Abdankung; **accession to the** ~ Thronbesteigung; **disclaimer of the** ~ Thronverzicht; **heir to the** ~ Thronerbe; **speech from the** ~ Thronrede; **succession to the** ~ Thronfolge; **successor to the** ~ Thronfolger; **to abdicate the** ~ abdanken; **to ascend (to) the** ~ den Thron besteigen; **to come to the** ~ auf den Thron kommen; **to succeed a p. to the** ~ jdm auf den Thron folgen

throttle *v* erdrosseln; **to** ~ **freedom in a country** Freiheit in e-m Lande unterdrücken

through durch; *Am* bis einschließlich (from Thursday ~ Tuesday); *(Verkehrsverbindung)* durchgehend; ~ **bill of lading (~ B/L)** Durchkonnossement; ~ **bookings** Pauschalreisen; ~ **car** (or *Br* **carriage, coach**) Kurswagen; ~ **rate** Durchgangstarif; ~ **registration of luggage** *Br* Gepäckaufgabe zur durchgehenden Beförderung; ~ **traffic** durchgehender Verkehr; ~ **train** durchgehender Zug; **~way** *Am* Autobahn

throw *v* (ab-, auf-, zu-)werfen; **to** ~ **goods on the market** Waren auf den Markt werfen; **to** ~ **an obligation on a p.** jdm e-e Verpflichtung auferlegen; **to** ~ **on a tenant the obligation to keep the building in good repair** dem Mieter die Pflicht auferlegen, das Gebäude in gutem Zustand zu halten; **to** ~ **out a bill** *parl* e-n Gesetzesentwurf ablehnen; **to** ~ **over board** über Bord werfen; **to** ~ **up a post** e-n Posten aufgeben

thrown, to be ~ **back upon** *fig* zurückgeworfen sein auf; **to be** ~ **out of work** arbeitslos werden

throwaway *colloq.* Handzettel; ~ **society** Wegwerfgesellschaft

throwback rule *Am*[41] Rückbezugsregel

thru *Am* →through

tick Häkchen *(Vermerkzeichen)*; *colloq.* Kredit, Pump; **to mark (off) with a** ~ abhaken; **to put a** ~ **against an item** e-n Posten abhaken

tick *v Am colloq.* auf Kredit kaufen; **to** ~ **(off)** *(Wort)* anstreichen; *(Posten, Namen etc)* abhaken; abzeichnen

ticker Börsentelegraf, Börsenfernschreiber *(mit Kursen und Umsatzangaben)*; ~ **service** *Am* Tickerdienst *(in dem für jede Aktie e-e Abkürzung, Ticker-Symbol, verwendet wird)*

ticket 1. Fahrkarte, Fahrausweis; Billet; Flugschein; Buskarte; Schiffskarte; Eintrittskarte; Konzert-, Theater-, Kinokarte; (Lotterie-) Los; (Preis-)Zettel, Etikett; *Br (Börse) (dem Verkäufer vom Makler ausgehändigter)* Vermerk über Wertpapiergeschäfte *(für die Abrechnung)*; *Am (als Stimmzettel benutzte)* Liste der Wahlkandidaten; Wahlliste; Strafzettel *(→ticket 2.)*; *Br mil* Entlassungsschein; ~ **agent** *Am* Fahrkartenverkäufer; Vorverkaufsstelle *(für Theaterkarten)*; ~ **at reduced rate** verbilligte Fahrkarte *(opp. ~ at full rate)*; ~ **collector** Fahrkartenkontrolleur; **~-day** *Br (Börse)* Tag vor dem Abrechnungstag (account or settlement day), an dem die tickets eingereicht werden; ~ **inspection** Fahrkartenkontrolle; ~ **number** Losnummer; ~ **(of admission)** Eintrittskarte

ticket of leave *Br* Bescheinigung über bedingte Entlassung *(aus der Strafhaft vor Ablauf der Strafzeit; entspricht etwa dem →parole)*; ~ **man** *Br* der bedingt Entlassene

ticket, ~ **office** Fahrkartenschalter; (Theater-, Kino-)Kasse; ~ **sale** Karten(vor)verkauf; ~ **window** *Am* Fahrkartenschalter

ticket, admission ~ Eintrittskarte; **advance** ~ **sale** Kartenvorverkauf; **banker's** ~ *(beim Wechselregreß)* Rückrechnung; **cloakroom** ~ *Br* Gepäck(aufbewahrungs)schein; Garderobenmarke; **collective** ~ Sammelfahrschein; **commutation** ~ *Am* Abonnementsfahrkarte, Zeitkarte; **complimentary** ~ Freikarte, Ehrenkarte; **delivery** ~ Lieferschein; **free (admission)** ~ Freikarte; **job** ~ Arbeitslaufzettel; **lottery** ~ Lotterielos; **luggage** ~ Gepäckschein; **mixed** ~ *Am* Kompromißwahlliste; **monthly season** ~ monatliche Abonnementskarte; **one-way** ~ *Am* einfache Fahrkarte; **party** ~ Sammelfahrschein; *Am pol* Liste der Parteikandidaten für e-e Wahl; **pawn** ~ Pfandschein; **railroad** *Am* (**railway** *Br*) ~ (Bahn-) Fahrkarte; **rail season** ~ Bahnabonnementskarte; **reduced-rate** ~ *Br* →~ at reduced rate; **reserved seat** ~ Platzkarte; **return** ~ Rückfahrkarte; **round trip** ~ *Am* Rückfahrkarte; **season** ~ Abonnementskarte, Dauerkarte; **single** ~ einfache Fahrkarte; **to vote the** → **straight** ~

ticket 2. *(bei leichteren Verkehrsdelikten)* Strafzettel; *(etwa)* gebührenpflichtige Verwarnung; Strafmandat; **parking** ~ Strafzettel für ordnungswidriges Parken; **speeding** ~ Strafzettel für Überschreiten der Geschwindigkeit; **to get a** ~ e-n Strafzettel *(von der Verkehrspolizei überreicht od. an den Wagen geheftet)* bekommen

ticket *v* etikettieren, mit Etikett versehen; *(Ware)* auszeichnen

tickler *Am colloq.* Terminkalender; ~ **file** *Am* Fälligkeitsverzeichnis; **note** ~ *Am* Verfallbuch für Wechsel

tidal harbo(u)r Tidehafen *(unter Einwirkung von Ebbe und Flut stehender Hafen)*

tide Ebbe und Flut; *fig* Strömung, Tendenz; ~ **of events** Zeitströmung; ~**sman** *Am* →~ waiter; ~ **waiter** *Am* Zollbeamter, der den einlaufenden Schiffen entgegenfährt und an Bord bleibt, bis die Ladung gelöscht ist; **turn of the** ~ *fig* Umschwung *(z.B. der öffentlichen Meinung)*

tide-over credit Überbrückungskredit

tie Band; Bindung, Verpflichtung; *parl* Stimmengleichheit; *Br* Verpflichtung e-s →tied house, s-e Waren von e-r bestimmten Firma zu beziehen, (Allein-)Bezugsverpflichtung; ~**-break** *Am* Stichwahl; ~ **division** unentschiedene Abstimmung *(mit je gleich vielen Stimmen)*; **in the event of a** ~ bei Stimmengleichheit

tie-in Verbindung; zwei miteinander verbundene Werbungen *(z.B. e-s Einzelhändlers und e-s Fabrikanten)*; ~ **agreement** Kopplungsvertrag; ~ **clause** *Am* Kopplungsklausel (→*tying clause*); ~ **sale** *Am* Kopplungsverkauf; ~ **transaction** Kopplungsgeschäft

tie-on label Anhängezettel, Anhänger *(opp. gummed →label)*

tie-up Vereinigung, Verbindung; (Unternehmens-)Zusammenschluß; Junktim; *Am* Stokkung, Stillstand; *Am* Verkehrseinstellung; Betriebseinstellung *(z.B. durch Streik)*

tie *v* binden, befestigen (to an); verpflichten; **to** ~ **down** einschränken, beschränken (to auf); **to** ~ **in** passen zu, entsprechen; **to** ~ **up** *(Paket)* verschnüren; *(Kapital)* blockieren, festlegen; **to** ~ **up a factory** *Am* e-e Fabrik stillegen; **to** ~ **up one's money in land** sein Geld in Grundbesitz festlegen; **to** ~ **up property** Vermögen (od. Grundbesitz) e-r Verfügungsbeschränkung unterwerfen; **to** ~ **up with** sich verbinden (od. zusammenschließen) mit

tied, ~ **cottage** mietrechtlich gebundene Werkswohnung *(die nur der Arbeitnehmer vom Arbeitgeber mieten kann)*; ~ **grant** (zweck)gebundener Zuschuß; ~ **house** *Br* von e-r Brauerei kontrollierte Gaststätte *(opp. free house)*; ~ **loan** (zweck)gebundener Kredit; ~ **sale** *Am* Kopplungsverkauf; ~ **share** vinkulierte Aktie; ~ **to the index** indexgebunden, an den Index gebunden; **the will** ~ **up the estate** das Testament legte den Nachlaß fest *(unterwarf ihn bestimmten Beschränkungen)*

tier subsidiary *Am* Enkelgesellschaft

tight eng; knapp, angespannt; **money is** ~ Geld ist knapp *(schwer zu bekommen)*; ~ **money market** angespannter Geldmarkt *(opp. easy money market)*

tighten *v* enger machen (od. gestalten); **to** ~ **(up) the blockade** die Blockade verschärfen; **to** ~ **(up) the censorship** die Zensur verschärfen; **to** ~ **conditions** Bedingungen verschärfen; ~**ing of the money market** Versteifung des Geldmarktes

tightness Verknappung, Knappheit; ~ **of money** Geldknappheit

TIGR →treasury investment growth receipt

till Ladenkasse; ~ **money** Geld in der Ladenkasse; Kassenbestand; Bargeld e-r Bank für den täglichen Geldbedarf; *Am (von der zuständigen Reservebank für erforderlich gehaltener)* Mindestsatz an liquiden Reserven in bar; ~**-tapping** Diebstahl aus der Ladenkasse; **shop** ~ Ladenkasse

till bis zu; ~ **further advice** (or **notice**) bis auf weiteres

till *v*, **to** ~ **the soil** den Boden bestellen

timber Bauholz, Nutzholz *(Br im engeren Sinne: schlagfähige Eiche, Esche und Ulme)*; Baumbestand, Wald; ~ **(land)** *Am* Wald *(der Nutzholz liefert)*; ~ **merchant** Holzhändler; ~ **trade** Holzhandel

time 1. Zeit; Zeitpunkt; Zeitdauer; Termin; Frist *(→time 2.)*; *(Fernsehen, Radio)* Sendezeit

time, to do ~ s-e Zeit *(im Gefängnis)* „absitzen"; **to fix a** ~ e-n Termin ansetzen; **to pay on** ~ pünktlich bezahlen; **to purchase on** ~ *Am* auf Abzahlung kaufen; **to save** ~ Zeit sparen; **to serve one's** ~ *mil* s-e Zeit abdienen; s-e Lehrzeit durchmachen; **to specify a** ~ e-n Zeitpunkt festsetzen; **to take** ~ Zeit benötigen (od. brauchen)

time, ~ **allowance** *(EDV)* Zeitvorgabe; ~ **and materials contract** Werklieferungsvertrag; ~ **and motion studies** Zeit- und Bewegungsstudien *(Arbeitsablauf)*; ~ **bargain** *(Börse)* Termingeschäft; ~ **barred** verjährt

time basis, erection (etc) **on a** ~ Montage nach Zeitberechnung

time, ~ **bill** Wechsel mit Laufzeit; Nachsichtwechsel; ~ **bomb** Zeitbombe; ~ **book** Arbeits(stunden)buch; ~ **card** *(Arbeitszeit)* Kontrollkarte; ~ **charter** Zeitcharter, Zeitfrachtvertrag *(opp. trip →charter)*; ~ **clock** Stechuhr; ~**s covered** Verhältnis Gewinn/Dividende; ~ **deposit rate** Termingeldsatz; ~ **deposits** Termineinlagen, befristete Einlagen *(Festgelder und Spareinlagen mit e-r Kündigungsfrist von mindestens 30 Tagen)*; ~ **draft** →~ bill; ~ **expired** *Br mil* ausgedient *(von Soldaten und Unteroffizieren)*; ~ **fixed for payment** Zahlungstermin; ~ **for consideration** Bedenkzeit; ~ **for loading** Ladezeit; ~ **immemorial** *Br* unvordenkliche Zeiten; ~ **insurance** Versicherung auf Zeit; ~**keeper** (Arbeits-)Zeitkontrolleur; ~**keeping** (Arbeits-)Zeitkontrolle; ~ **lag** Verzögerung *(zwischen dem Eintreten e-s Ereignisses und den sich daraus ergebenden Folgen)*; ~ **limit**

Zeitbeschränkung (→time 2.); ~ **limitation** *Am*[42] *(StrafR)* Verjährung; ~ **loan** Darlehen mit bestimmter Laufzeit *(opp. demand loan; →loan 2.)*; ~ **management** Zeitplanung; ~ **money** befristetes Darlehen; ~ **note** →~ bill; ~ **of arrival** Ankunftszeit; ~ **of conclusion of the contract** Zeitpunkt des Vertragsabschlusses; ~**-of-day-tariff** *Br* Stromtarif mit hoher Tages- und niedriger Nachtgebühr; ~ **of delivery** Lieferzeit; Zeit der Zustellung; ~ **of departure** Abfahrtzeit; Abflugzeit; ~ **of flight** Flugzeit; ~ **of maturity** Verfallzeit; ~ **of payment** Zahlungstermin; ~ **of protection** →protection; ~ **of validity** Gültigkeitsdauer; ~ **of waiting** Wartezeit; ~ **off** Freizeit

time payment *Am* Ratenzahlung; **to buy on a ~ plan** *Am* auf Abzahlung kaufen

time, ~ **policy** → policy 2.; ~ **premium** Zeitprämie; ~ **purchase** Terminkauf; ~ **rates** Zeitlöhne *(Arbeiter erhält e-e bestimmte Summe pro Stunde; opp. piece rates)*; ~**-saving** zeitsparend; ~**(-)server** Opportunist; ~**(-)serving politician** opportunistischer Politiker

time-sharing (T. S.) *(EDV)* „Zeitteilung" *(Verfahren, bei dem die Zeit, in der ein Großcomputer für die Datenverabeitung zur Verfügung steht, auf mehrere „Teilnehmer" aufgeteilt wird); (auch)* Immobilienkauf auf Zeit; Plan, nach dem das Eigentum an e-r Ferienwohnung nach Zeit geteilt wird; ~ **charge** Gebühr für in Anspruch genommenen Zeitanteil

time, ~ **sheet** →~ card; ~ **stamp** Zeitstempel; ~**table** Zeitplan, Stundenplan; Kursbuch; Fahrplan, Flugplan; ~ **ticket** *Am* →~ card; ~ **wage(s)** Zeitlohn; ~ **work** Zeitarbeit; nach der Zeit bezahlte Arbeit *(opp. piece work)*; ~ **worked** die geleisteten Arbeitsstunden

time, appointed~ Termin; at any ~ zu jeder (beliebigen) Zeit; **at the appropriate** ~ zur gegebenen Zeit; **at a definite** ~ zu e-r bestimmten Zeit; **at the fixed** ~ zur festgesetzter Zeit; **at the present** ~ gegenwärtig: **at the proper** ~ zur gegebenen (od. rechten) Zeit; **at the** ~ **provided for by the contract** zum vertraglich vereinbarten Zeitpunkt; **by passage of** ~ durch Zeitablauf; **calculation of** ~ Zeitberechnung; → **closing** ~; **computation of** ~ Zeitberechnung; **dead** (or **delay**) ~ *(betriebl. bedingte)* Verlustzeit; **for the** ~ **being** zur Zeit (z. Zt.); gegenwärtig; **for some** ~ seit einiger Zeit; für einige Zeit; →**full-**~; →**half-**~; **in** ~ rechtzeitig; **in due** ~ rechtzeitig; termingemäß; **lack of** ~ Zeitmangel; **lapse of** ~ Zeitablauf; **length of** ~ Zeitdauer; **limitation of** ~ *Am (StrafR)* →~ limitation; **local** ~ Ortszeit; **mean** ~ mittlere Sonnenzeit; **off-**~ Freizeit; **on** ~ pünktlich; termingemäß; *Am* auf Abzahlung; → **part-**~; **saving of** ~ Zeitgewinn; **shipping** ~ Versandtermin; →**short-** ~; **spare** ~ Freizeit *(→ spare)*; **speaking** ~ Redezeit; **standard**~ Normalzeit; **up to the present** ~ bis heute; **within a given** ~ innerhalb e-r bestimmten Zeit; **within the shortest possible** ~ in kürzester Zeit

time 2. Frist; **to abridge the** ~ die Frist verkürzen; **to allow** ~ e-e Frist bewilligen; **to enlarge** (or **extend**) **the** ~ die Frist verlängern; **to exceed the** ~ **allowed** die Frist überschreiten; **to extend the** ~ **for bringing an action (for personal injuries)** die Frist für die Erhebung e-r Klage (wegen Personenschäden) verlängern; **to fix** (or **set**) **a** ~ e-e Frist festsetzen; **to stipulate a** ~ **for delivery** e-e Lieferfrist festsetzen; ~ **begins** (or **starts**) **to run** die Frist beginnt; ~ **begins to run** (against) die Verjährung beginnt; **the** ~ **for institution of proceedings begins to run** die Klagefrist beginnt zu laufen; ~ **is (of) the essence of the contract** die Einhaltung der Frist ist wesentliche Vertragsbedingung

time, ~ **allowed** (for) gewährte (od. vorgesehene) Frist; ~ **for acceptance** *(WechselR)* Annahmefrist; ~ **for appeal** → appeal 1.; ~ **for application** Anmeldefrist, Antragsfrist; ~ **for delivery** Lieferfrist *(→delivery)*; ~ **for entering an appearance** Einlassungsfrist; ~ **for filing (a pleading)** Frist zur Einreichung (e-s Schriftsatzes); ~ **for payment** Zahlungsfrist

time for service of defence (~se) Klagebeantwortungsfrist; **extension of** ~ Verlängerung der Klagebeantwortungsfrist

time limit Frist; ~ **for claims** Rügefrist; ~ **of an award** Frist, innerhalb welcher ein Schiedsspruch ergehen muß; **the** ~ **of June 30** die Frist bis zum 30. Juni; **adherence to** (or **compliance with**) **a** ~ Einhaltung e-r Frist; **after the expiry** (or **expiration**) **of the** ~ nach Fristablauf; **failure to meet a** ~ Fristüberschreitung; **observance of a** ~ Einhaltung e-r Frist; **within the** ~ fristgemäß; **within a specified** ~ innerhalb e-r bestimmten Frist; **to adhere to** (or **comply with**) **a** ~ e-e Frist einhalten; **to enlarge** (or **extend**) **a** ~ e-e Frist verlängern; **to fix** (or **lay down**) **a** ~ e-e Frist festsetzen (od. bestimmen); **to observe a** ~ e-e Frist einhalten (od. wahren); **to fail to observe the** ~ die Frist versäumen; **to provide for a** ~ e-e Frist vorsehen; **to set a** ~ e-e Frist setzen; *(etw.)* befristen; **within the** ~ **stipulated in the contract** innerhalb der vertraglich vorgesehenen Frist

time, ~ **limited (for)** →~ allowed; **the** ~ **limited in the contract** die vertraglich vorgesehene Frist

time stipulated, to deliver within the ~ fristgemäß liefern

time, computation of ~ Fristberechnung; **expiration** (or **expiry**) **of** ~ Fristablauf; **extension of** ~ Fristverlängerung; **limited in** ~ befristet; **on** ~ fristgemäß; **out of** ~ nicht fristgerecht; verspätet; → **period of** ~; **reasonable** ~ angemessene Frist; **within the ~ allowed by law** innerhalb der gesetzlichen Frist; **within a fixed** (or **given**) ~ innerhalb e-r bestimmten Frist, fristgemäß

time *v* den (richtigen) Zeitpunkt wählen; feststellen, wie lange man braucht (od. wie lange etw. dauert); zeitlich aufeinander abstimmen; **to ~ investments** den geeigneten Zeitpunkt für Anlagen suchen

timed zeitlich festgelegt auf; **well-~** mit gut gewähltem Zeitpunkt

timing Bestimmung (od. Finden) des richtigen Zeitpunktes *(z. B. beim Kauf oder Verkauf von Aktien);* Terminplanung; **bad ~** Wählen e-s schlechten Zeitpunkts

timely rechtzeitig, im rechten Augenblick

tin Zinn; Konservendose; **~s** →~ shares; **~lined case** mit Blech ausgelegte Kiste; **~ shares** Zinnaktien; **Sixth International T~ Agreement**[42a] 6. Internationales Zinnübereinkommen

tinned food *Br* Lebensmittelkonserven; Dosennahrung

tip Trinkgeld; Tip, Wink, vertrauliche Information; **(refuse) ~** *Br* Müllabladeplatz; **stock exchange ~** Börsentip

tip-off Warnung, Hinweis; **to give the police a ~** der Polizei e-n Hinweis geben

tippee Empfänger vertraulicher, unter Geheimnisbruch gegebener Informationen

tipstaff Justizwachtmeister *(Br des Supreme Court, der jdn, der sich des →contempt of court schuldig gemacht hat, festnimmt)*

TIR (*Fr* Transport International Routier = international road transport); **~ Convention**[43] TIR-Übereinkommen; **Customs Convention on the International Transport of Goods under Cover of ~ Carnets** Zollübereinkommen über den internationalen Warentransport mit Carnet TIR

tithe *Br eccl* der Zehnte *(Abgabe der Bewohner e-s → parish an die Kirche)*

title 1. Titel, Überschrift; Amtstitel; Adelstitel; **~ catalogue** Titelkatalog; **~ of an Act** Name e-s Gesetzes *(cf. short ~)*; Name e-s Kapitels in e-m Gesetz; **~ of an action** (or **cause**) einleitende Angaben des Gerichts und der Parteien in e-r Klageschrift; Rubrum; **~ of the invention** *(die e-r Patentbeschreibung vorangesetzte)* kurze Bezeichnung der Erfindung; **~ of nobility** Adelstitel (→*nobility*); **~ page** Titelblatt; **official ~** Amtsbezeichnung; **short ~** Kurztitel *(e-s Gesetzes);* **sub-~** Untertitel; **to assume a ~** e-n Titel *(unberechtigt)* annehmen; **to bear a ~** e-e Überschrift tragen; **to hold a ~** e-n Titel führen

title 2. Eigentum(srecht) *(im Sinne von ownership*[44]); Eigentum an Grundstück(en) *(colloq.* an Grundbesitz); Rechtsanspruch auf Grundstück(e) (Grundbesitz); Rechtstitel; urkundlicher Nachweis e-s dingl. Rechts *(bes. an Grundbesitz);* **~ by descent** *Am* Rechtstitel auf Grund von gesetzl. Erbfolge; **~ certificate** (or **deed**) Eigentumsurkunde *(Urkunde, die den Nachweis des Rechtstitels an Grundbesitz enthält; Br cf. deposit of ~deeds)*

title insurance Versicherung der Eigentumsrechte; *Am* Versicherung des Käufers gegen Rechtsmängel bei Immobiliarerwerb; **~ companies** *Am* Versicherungsgesellschaften, die gegen Prämienzahlung für die Rechtsbeständigkeit des erworbenen Grundeigentums und von Hypothekenforderungen haften

title registration *Am* Grundbucheintragung (→ *Torrens system)*; **~ office** *Am* Grundbuchamt
Im Gegensatz zur herkömmlichen →deeds registration haben einige amerikanische Staaten das Grundbuchsystem eingeführt

title, ~ retention Eigentumsvorbehalt *(→retention of title);* **~ search** *Am* (Grundstücks-) Rechtstitelüberprüfung *(Feststellung des Eigentums an e-m Grundstück durch Prüfung der Kette der Übereignungsurkunden)*; **~ standards** *Am* Richtlinien zur Vereinheitlichung der (Grundstücks-)Titelprüfungspraktiken

title theory *Am (in mehreren Einzelstaaten geltende)* Theorie, wonach der Hypothekengläubiger anstelle e-r bloßen Belastung (lien) das *(allerdings bedingte)* Eigentum (title) an dem als Sicherheit dienenden Grundstück erhält *(cf. Kommentar zu mortgage)*

title, ~ to a benefit Anspruch auf e-e (Versicherungs-)Leistung; **~ to goods** Eigentum an Waren; **~ to land** Eigentum an Grundbesitz; Rechtsanspruch auf Grundbesitz

title, → absolute ~; bad ~ mangelhafter Rechtstitel; **certificate of ~** *Br*[45] Zertifikat *(z. B. share certificate, stock certificate, debenture certificate); Am* Eigentumsurkunde; Eigentümerzeugnis *(z. B. an Kraftfahrzeugen); (etwa)* Kraftfahrzeugbrief; Doppel des Grundbuchblattes; **clear ~** s. good →~; **colo(u)r of ~** Anschein e-s Rechts (→*colo(u)r)*; **covenants for ~** *(Br*[46] *stillschweigend eingeschlossene)* Zusicherungen der Rechtsmängelfreiheit bei Grundstücksübertragungen; **defect in ~** Rechtsmangel (→*defect*); **defective ~** fehlerhafter Rechtstitel; mit Mängeln behaftetes Recht; **devolution of ~** Eigentumsübergang, Rechtsübergang; **→document of ~; equitable ~** Eigentumsrecht nach equity-Recht *(cf. equitable →ownership; opp. legal ~)*; **evidence of ~** Beweisurkunde über Eigentumsrechte *(im Grundstücksrecht)*

title, good ~ hinreichender Rechtstitel; unbestreitbares Eigentum; **to have a good ~** hinreichend berechtigt sein *(das Grundstück ohne Rechtsmängel zu verkaufen)*

title, imperfect ~ fehlerhafter Eigentumstitel; **insurance of ~** *Am* →~ insurance; **investiga-**

tion of ~ Prüfung der Eigentums- und Belastungsverhältnisse von Grundbesitz *(beim Grundstückskauf)*; **legal** ~ formelles Eigentumsrecht *(opp. equitable ~)*; **marketable** ~ *(vom Verkäufer von Grundbesitz nachgewiesenes)* hinreichendes Eigentumsrecht *(das auf genügende urkundliche Grundlage gestützt ist; Br*[47] *Verkäufer muß e-e Kette von Rechtstiteln nachweisen, die wenigstens 15 Jahre zurückgeht; Am cf. Marketable T~ Acts)*; **passage** (or **passing**) **of** ~ Eigentumsübergang; **plaintiff's** ~ Klagerecht des Klägers; →**possessory** ~; **predecessor in** ~ Rechtsvorgänger; **proof of** ~ Nachweis des Eigentumsrechts *(an Grundbesitz)*; → **qualified** ~; **registered** ~ *Br* im →Land Register eingetragenes Eigentum an Grundbesitz; **registration of** ~ **to land** *Br* Grundbucheintragung; **reservation of** ~ Eigentumsvorbehalt; →**root of** ~; **successor in** ~ Rechtsnachfolger; **transfer of** ~ Eigentumsübertragung; **warranty of** ~ Gewährleistung wegen Rechtsmängeln; **to acquire** ~ Eigentum erwerben; **to search the** ~ *Am* das öffentliche Register zur Feststellung des Eigentums an Grundbesitz und der auf dem Eigentum ruhenden Lasten einsehen; **to take** ~ *Am* Eigentum erwerben; **the** ~ **passes to** das Eigentum geht über auf

tobacco duty (or **tax**) Tabaksteuer; ~ **products duty** Tabakwarensteuer

today's rate (of exchange) Tageskurs

toe *v*, **to** ~ **the line** →line 2.

toft verfallenes, verlassenes Anwesen

Togo Togo
Togolese Togoer, ~in; togoisch; ~ **Republic** Republik Togo

token Zeichen; Symbol; Gutschein; Bon; Schein-; ~ **coin** Scheidemünze; (Metall-) Wertmarke; ~ **imports** symbolische Einfuhr; ~ **money** Notgeld; Scheidemünze *(opp. standard money)*; ~ **payment** symbolische Zahlung, Handgeld *(zum Zeichen der Anerkennung e-r Schuld)*; ~ **strike** Warnstreik; ~ **vote** *parl* Bewilligung e-r Summe, die überschritten werden kann

Tokyo round Tokiorunde *(1976–79) (die siebente Runde der →Gatt Gespräche, die den Zweck hatte, Zölle und Handelshemmnisse herabzusetzen)*

tolerance Toleranz; zulässige Abweichung; ~ **of the mint** Münztoleranz, Remedium

toll (Benutzungs-)Gebühr, Wegegeld, Brückengeld, Straßenbenutzungsgebühr, Maut; *(Markt)* Standgeld; *Am* Gebühr für Ferngespräch; *fig* Tribut; ~**(-)bar** Schranke, Schlagbaum; ~ **call** *Am* Ferngespräch; ~**gate** Schlagbaum; ~ **of the roads** (Ziffer der) Verkehrsunfälle; ~ **road** *Am* gebührenpflichtige (od. mautpflichtige) Autobahn; Mautstraße; **death** ~ Zahl der Todesopfer; **port** ~ *Am* Hafengebühr

toll *v*, **to** ~ **the statute of limitations** *Am* die Verjährung hemmen

tollage Bezahlung (od. Erhebung) e-r Gebühr *(→ toll)*

tombstone Anzeige in der Finanzpresse, mit der Schuldner sowie Einzelheiten e-r Emission oder e-s Konsortialkredits bekannt gegeben werden, einschließlich der Mitglieder des Konsortiums *(die aber kein konkretes Verkaufs- od. Plazierungsangebot darstellt)*

ton 1. Tonne *(Gewichtseinheit)*; ~ **mile** (T. M.) *(Eisenbahn)* Tonnenmeile *(Transport einer → ton Güter auf e-e Entfernung von einer → mile; entsprechend dem Tonnenkilometer)*; **long** ~ *bes. Br* Tonne *(2240 pounds od. 1016 kg)*; **metric** ~ metrische Tonne *(2204,6 pounds od. 1000 kg)*; **short** ~ *bes. Am* Tonne *(2000 pounds od. 907,2 kg)*

ton 2. Tonne *(Raummaß)*; ~**s deadweight** (tdw) Tragfähigkeit; **measurement** ~ Raumtonne, Frachttonne

ton, register ~ Registertonne; **gross register** ~ (g. r. t.) Bruttoregistertonne (BRT); **net register** ~ (n. r. t.) Nettoregistertonne (NRT)

tone *(Börse)* Stimmung, Haltung; **prevailing** ~ vorherrschende Stimmung, Grundhaltung

tonnage Tonnage, Raumgehalt *(e-s Schiffes)*; Schiffsraum; *(in tons berechnete)* Tragfähigkeit; Gesamtschiffsraum *(der Handelsflotte e-s Landes)*; Ladungsgewicht *(in Tonnen)*; ~ **certificate**[48] Schiffsmeßbrief; ~ **(duty)** Tonnengebühr, Tonnengeld; ~ **length** Vermessungslänge; ~ **mark** Vermessungsmarke; ~ **measurement (of ships)**[49] Vermessung von Schiffen, Schiffsvermessung; ~ **rate** *Am* Lohnsatz pro Tonne *(im Bergbau)*; **deadweight** ~ Tragfähigkeit, Ladefähigkeit; **displacement** ~ Wasserverdrängung in Tonnen *(bei Kriegsschiffen)*; **gross** ~ Bruttotonnengehalt, Bruttoraumgehalt; **net** ~ s. register →~; **parcels** ~ *Br* Paketfahrttonnage; **register** ~ (Netto-)Registertonnage, Nettotonnengehalt *(gross ~ abzüglich des durch Maschinen, Mannschaftsräume etc besetzten Platzes)*

tontine Tontine; *(seit dem 17. Jahrhundert bekannte)* lotterieähnliche Rentenversicherung auf den Erlebensfall

tool Werkzeug, Gerät; *fig* Werkzeug; **to lay down** ~**s** die Arbeit niederlegen; streiken

top 1. Gipfel; Spitzen-; ~ **copy** Original; **in 2** ~ **copies** in 2 Urschriften; ~ **executive** *Am* Leiter e-s Unternehmens; ~ **gains** *(Börse)* Spitzengewinne; ~ **grade civil servant** *Br* höherer Beamter

top-heavy *(Wertpapiere)* überbewertet; *(Unternehmen)* in der Spitze überorganisiert; ~ **market** Markt, auf dem die Aktienpreise im Verhältnis zu ihrem wahren Wert zu hoch sind und fallen müssen

top, ~-level conference Konferenz auf höchster Ebene; **~-level executive** oberste Führungskraft; ~ → **management;** ~ **manager** *Am* oberster Betriebsleiter; ~ **price** Höchstpreis, Höchstkurs

top priority höchste Priorität; Vorrang vor allem anderen; ~ **aim** an erster Stelle stehendes Ziel

top, ~ **salary** Spitzengehalt; ~ **secret** streng geheim

top 2. oben *(Aufschrift auf Kisten etc; opp. bottom)*; ~ **left-hand corner** links oben; **~side up** oben

top *v*, **to** ~ **a list** an der Spitze e-r Liste stehen

topic Thema; Diskussionsgegenstand

topical aktuell

torchlight procession Fackelzug

Torremolinos Convention for the Safety of Fishing Vessels[49a] Internationales Übereinkommen von Torremolinos über die Sicherheit von Fischereifahrzeugen

Torrens system *(GrundstücksR)* Registrierungssystem *(ähnlich dem deutschen Grundbuchsystem)*

Br Das von dem Australier Sir Robert Torrens 1858 eingeführte und in Australien, Kanada und einigen US-Staaten geltende Registrierungssystem ist die Grundlage der gemäß der Land Transfer Acts in England eingeführten Eintragung *(cf. Land Register)*. *Am* Das Torrens-System ist in mehreren Einzelstaaten als wahlweise benutzbares System zugelassen *(cf. land records)*.

Der grundlegende Unterschied zum herkömmlichen → recording-system liegt darin, daß nicht nur das Beweismaterial bezügl. des Eigentums protokolliert wird, sondern daß das Eigentum selbst Gegenstand des Registers ist. Dem Erwerber von Grundstücksrechten werden durch die Ausgabe e-s certificate of → registration seine Rechte von Amts wegen beurkundet

tort unerlaubte Handlung, zivilrechtl. Delikt *(rechtswidrige Handlung, die schadensersatzpflichtig macht [cf. Kommentar zu law of→torts])*

tort, to commit a ~ e-e unerlaubte Handlung begehen; **an action lies in** ~ e-e Klage ist aus unerlaubter Handlung begründet; **to obtain damages in** ~ Schadensersatz wegen unerlaubter Handlung erlangen; **to sue in** ~ aus unerlaubter Handlung klagen

tort, ~ **arising out of contract** unerlaubte Handlung aus e-m Vertragsverhältnis *(z. B. haftet der Arzt für Fahrlässigkeit bei der Behandlung e-s Patienten)*; ~ **cause of action** *Am* Anspruch aus unerlaubter Handlung

tort claim *Am* Anspruch aus unerlaubter Handlung; **Federal T~ C~s Act** *Am* Bundesschadensersatzgesetz *(von 1946; unterwirft die Bundesverwaltung der Schadensersatzpflicht für fahrlässige Handlungen ihrer Organe)*

tortfeasor (deliktischer) Täter, Begeher e-r unerlaubten Handlung; Schadensersatzpflichtiger; *(AtomR)* jd, der für Atomschäden haftet; **joint ~s** Mittäter; mehrere am Delikt Beteiligte

tort, ~ **liability** Deliktshaftung; ~ **of negligence** fahrlässige Rechtsverletzung

tort, action in ~ Klage aus unerlaubter Handlung; **business ~s** unerlaubte Handlungen im Geschäftsverkehr; **cause of action in** ~ (or **claim in** ~) Anspruch aus unerlaubter Handlung; **damages in** ~ Schadensersatz wegen unerlaubter Handlung; **intentional** ~ vorsätzlich begangene unerlaubte Handlung; **joint** ~ gemeinsam begangene unerlaubte Handlung

tort, law of ~s Recht der unerlaubten Handlungen, Deliktsrecht

Das anglo-amerikanische law of torts kennt keinen allgemeinen Begriff der unerlaubten Handlung *(vgl. § 823 BGB)*. Es gibt kein allgemeines law of tort, nur ein law of torts. Voraussetzung für ein tort ist ein Eingriff in ein geschütztes Rechtsgut. Die wichtigsten torts sind: negligence, fraud, libel, slander, false imprisonment, malicious prosecutions, nuisance, assault and battery, deceit, conversion, interference with contractual relations

tort, liability in ~ Haftung aus unerlaubter Handlung; Deliktshaftung; **maritime** ~ *Am* unerlaubte Handlung, die auf schiffbaren Gewässern begangen ist; **personal** ~ Verletzung persönlicher Rechtsgüter *(opp. property ~)*

tort, property ~ Vermögensverletzung, unerlaubte Handlung gegen Eigentum od. Vermögen *(opp. personal ~)*

Torts to personal property umfassen z. B. infringement of a patent, trade mark, copyright; torts to real property umfassen z. B. ouster, trespass, nuisance, waste

tortious, ~ **act** unerlaubte Handlung; ~ **liability** Haftung aus unerlaubter Handlung, deliktische Haftung *(opp. contractual liability)*

torture Folterung; ~ **methods** Foltermethoden

Tory *Br* Konservativer; ~ **member** konservativer Abgeordneter; **the constituency has gone** ~ *colloq.* der Wahlbezirk hat jetzt e-n konservativen Abgeordneten

Tories *Br*[50] *parl (heute noch gebrauchte Bezeichnung für die)* Anhänger der konservativen Partei

toryism *Br* Torytum, Konservatismus

tot *v*, **to** ~ **(up)** addieren, zusammenzählen

total Gesamtsumme, Gesamtbetrag; Gesamt-; gesamt; ~ **allowable catches** (TACs) zulässige Gesamtfangmenge *(von Fischen)*; ~ **amount** Gesamtbetrag, Gesamtsumme; ~ **assets** Gesamtvermögen, Gesamtwert der Aktiva; ~ **casualties** *mil* Gesamtverluste; ~ **claim** Gesamtforderung; ~ **damage** Gesamtschaden; ~ **debt** gesamte Schuldsumme; ~ **dependency** *Am (Workmen's Compensation Acts)* völlige Abhängigkeit *(des Familienangehörigen von dem Verdienst des Arbeiters)*; ~ **disability** (or **disablement**) vollständige Arbeitsunfähigkeit, Vollinvalidität; ~ **expenditure** Gesamtausgaben; ~ **income** Gesamteinkommen; ~ **loss** (T. L., t. l.) Gesamtverlust, Totalverlust *(opp. partial loss, →loss 2.)*; ~ **loss only** (T. L. O.) nur bei Totalverlust; ~ **output** Gesamtleistung; ~ **population** Gesamtbevölkerung; ~ **receipts** Gesamteinnahmen; ~ **requirements** Gesamtbedarf; ~ **sales** (or **turnover**) Gesamtumsatz; ~ **votes cast** Gesamtstimmenzahl; ~ **war** totaler Krieg; ~ **yield** Gesamtertrag; Gesamtrendite

total *v* im ganzen betragen; sich belaufen (to auf); **to ~ one's car** *Am colloq.* Totalschaden haben

totalitarian state totaler Staat, totalitärer Staat

totalitarianism Totalitarismus *(Tendenz zum totalen Staat)*

totalizator Totalisator *(beim Renn- oder Turniersport)*

toties quoties ("as often as occasion arises") so oft sich die Gelegenheit bietet

touch Verbindung, Kontakt; *(Börse) Br* der beste Geldkurs und Briefkurs *(für bestimmte Wertpapiere)*; **to get into ~ with a p.** mit jdm in Verbindung treten (od. sich ins Benehmen setzen); **to keep in ~ with a p.** mit jdm in Verbindung bleiben; **to lose ~ with a p.** mit jdm die Verbindung verlieren

touch *v (Thema etc)* berühren; in Kontakt kommen; **to ~ bottom** den niedrigsten (Kurs-) Stand erreichen; **to ~ the capital** das Kapital angreifen; **to ~ at a port** e-n Hafen anlaufen

tour (Rund-)Reise; Rundgang (of durch); ~ **of Germany** Reise durch Deutschland; ~ **operator** Reiseveranstalter; **business ~** Geschäftsreise; **circular ~** *Br* Rundreise; **conducted** (or **guided, organized**) ~ Gesellschaftsreise; **official ~** Dienst(rund)reise; **package ~** Pauschalreise

touring Tourismus, Touristik; Fremdenverkehr

tourism Reiseverkehr; Fremdenverkehr(swesen); Tourismus, Touristik; ~ **advertising** Fremdenverkehrswerbung; ~ **exchange** Tourismusbörse; **World T~ Organization** (W. T. O.)[51] Weltorganisation für Tourismus

tourist (Vergnügungs-)Reisender; ~ **advertising** Fremdenverkehrswerbung; ~ **agency** (or *Am* **bureau**) Reisebüro; Verkehrsbüro; ~ **authority** Fremdenverkehrsamt; ~ **class** Touristenklasse; **(~) guide** Fremdenführer; ~ **industry** Fremdenverkehrsgewerbe; ~ **office** *Br* Reisebüro; ~ **publicity documents and material** Werbeschriften und Werbematerial für den Fremdenverkehr; ~ **spending** Ausgaben im Reiseverkehr; ~ **trade** (or **traffic**) Fremdenverkehr; **International T~ Association** (I. T. A.) Internationale Touristenvereinigung

tout Kundensucher, Kundenwerber

tout *v (Kunden od. Stimmen)* werben; **~ing for customers** Kundenwerbung

tow Schleppen; **~-away zone** Parkverbot(szone) *(Gebiet, in dem widerrechtlich parkende Kraftfahrzeuge von der Polizei abgeschleppt werden)*; ~ **truck** *Am* Abschleppfahrzeug

tow *v* schleppen; *(Auto)* abschleppen; *(Schiff)* bugsieren

towing (Ab-)Schleppen, Schleppschiffahrt

towage Schleppen, Bugsieren; Schlepplohn, Bugsierlohn

tower (Wohn-, Büro-)Hochhaus; ~ **block** *Br* Hochhaus

to wit ("that is to say") nämlich

town Stadt *(Br große und kleine Stadt; Am Gemeinde unter dem Rang e-r Stadt)*; ~ **and country planning** *Br*[52] Raumplanung, Raumordnung; ~ **and →gown;** ~ **bill** *Br* Platzwechsel; ~ **clerk** *Br* städtischer Verwaltungsbeamter; *Am* Gemeindeverwaltungsbeamter; ~ **council** *Br* Stadtrat; *Am* Gemeinderat; ~ **councillor** *Br* Stadtratsmitglied, Ratsherr; Gemeinderatsmitglied; ~ **hall** *Br* Rathaus; ~ **management** *Am* Gemeindeverwaltung; ~ **meeting** *Am* Gemeindeversammlung; ~ **planning** Stadtplanung, städtebauliche Planung; ~ **property** *Br* städtischer Grundbesitz; **(~) → twinning; company ~** *Am* Firmensiedlung *(von e-r privaten [Aktien-]Gesellschaft gegründete Stadt für die Belegschaft ihres Werkes)*; **incorporated ~** *Am* zur Stadt erhobene Gemeinde *(town mit den Rechten e-r city)*; **manufacturing ~** Industriestadt; **medium-sized ~** mittlere Stadt; **→satellite ~**

township *Br* kleine Stadt; *Am* (Stadt-)Gemeinde *(unter dem Rang e-r city)*; Kommunalbezirk *(als Unterteilung e-s county)*; **rural ~** *Am* Landgemeinde

toxic giftig; Gift-; **T~ Substances Control Act** *(von 1976)* (TSCA) *Am* Gesetz betr. die Überwachung toxischer chemischer Stoffe *(vergleichbar dem deutschen Gesetz zum Schutz von gefährlichen Stoffen; Chemikaliengesetz)*

toxic waste Giftmüll; **export of ~** Giftmüllexport

toxic weapons toxische Waffen; **Convention on the Prohibition of the Development, Production and Stockpiling of Bacteriological and T~ W~ and on their Destruction**[53] Übereinkommen über das Verbot der Entwicklung, Herstellung und Lagerung bakteriologischer (biologischer) und toxischer Waffen sowie über die Vernichtung solcher Waffen

trace Spur, Fährte; **~s of poison** geringe Mengen von Gift; **preserving ~s** Spurensicherung; **to leave ~s** Spuren hinterlassen; **to preserve ~s** Spuren sichern; **to remove ~s** Spuren verwischen

trace *v* nachspüren, ausfindig machen; **to ~ (back)** zurückverfolgen auf; **right to ~** Verfolgungsrecht *(bei unberechtigten Vermögensverschiebungen; →tracing)*

tracing Suchen, Nachforschung; *Br* Verfolgungsrecht (right to follow assets) des Begünstigten (beneficiary) gegenüber Treuhänder *(z.B. bei Treubruch, Konkurs od. Tod des trustee)* und Dritten

track Spur, Fährte; (Eisenbahn-)Gleis; **to be on the ~ of sb.** jdm auf der Spur sein

track down *v* aufspüren, ausfindig machen

tract Broschüre, Abhandlung; Strecke, Gebiet; **~ (of land)** Grundstücksparzelle

trade Handel; Handelsverkehr, Wirtschaftsverkehr; Branche; Gewerbe, gewerbl. Tätigkeit; Handwerk; (handwerklicher od. kaufmännischer) Beruf *(opp. profession)*

trade, to be in the ~ *(in e-r bestimmten Branche)* als Kaufmann tätig sein; ein Geschäft haben; **to carry on a ~** ein (Handels-)Gewerbe betreiben (od. ausüben); **to differ from ~ to ~** je nach Branche verschieden sein; **to follow** (or **pursue**) **a ~** ein Gewerbe (od. Handwerk) betreiben; **to restrain ~** →restrain *v*; **to sell to the ~** an Wiederverkäufer verkaufen; **~ is bad** (or **dull**) die Geschäfte gehen schlecht; **~ is brisk** die Geschäfte gehen gut

trade, the ~ *Br. colloq.* der Handel in Spirituosen; **~ acceptance** Handelsakzept *(Akzept, dem ein Warengeschäft zugrunde liegt);* Warenwechsel; **~ accounts payable** *(Bilanz)* Verbindlichkeiten aus Warenlieferungen und Dienstleistungen; **~ accounts receivable** *(Bilanz)* Forderungen aus Warenlieferungen und Dienstleistungen; **~ adjustment assistance** *Am* strukturelle Anpassungshilfen *(für Wirtschaftsteilnehmer, die infolge von angestiegenen Importen Schaden erlitten haben);* **~ agreement** Handelsabkommen; *Am* Tarifvertrag (→*collective agreement)*

Trade Agreements Act of 1979 *Am* Gesetz über (internationale) Handelsvereinbarungen

Heute gültiges Recht auf dem Gebiet des intern. Warenhandels. Umfangreiche Änderungen amerikanischer Rechtsvorschriften, insbes. auf dem Gebiet des Zollwesens, des Antidumpingrechts und des Rechts der Ausgleichszölle

trade, ~ allowance Handelsrabatt; **~ and business expenses** *Am*[54] Betriebsausgaben und Werbungskosten; **~ and commerce** Handel und Gewerbe; **T~ and Development Board** Handels- und Entwicklungsrat (Welthandelsrat) *(ständiges Organ von* →UNCTAD); **~ association**[55] Unternehmerverband, Wirtschaftsverband, Fachverband *(der Wirtschaft);* **~ balance** *(Außenhandel)* Handelsbilanz *(→ balance of trade)*

trade barriers, removal of ~ Beseitigung der Handelshemmnisse

trade, T~ Bill *Am* Gesetzesvorlage für ein Handelsabkommen; **~ bill** Warenwechsel, Handelswechsel *(opp. finance bill)*; **~ channels** Handelswege; Absatzwege

trade charge *Br* Nachnahmebetrag; **~ letter** *Br* Nachnahmebrief; **~ money order** *Br* Nachnahmepostanweisung

trade conference, United Nations T~ C~ → United Nations Conference on Trade and Development

trade, ~ connections Handelsbeziehungen; **~ credit** Warenkredit; **~ creditor** Lieferantenkreditgeber; **~ creditors** Verbindlichkeiten aus Warenlieferungen und Leistungen; **~ currents** Handelsströme; **~ customs** →custom 1.; **~ cycle** *Br* Konjunkturzyklus; **~ debtors** Forderungen aus Warenlieferungen und Leistungen; **~ deficit** Außenhandelsdefizit; **~ delegation** Handelsdelegation

trade description[56] Handelsbeschreibung, Warenbeschreibung *(Angaben hinsichtlich Zahl, Menge, Gewicht, Herstellungsort von Waren etc)*

Br Der Trade Descriptions Act 1968 hat zum Verbraucherschutz beigetragen durch die Möglichkeit der Strafverfolgung im Falle irreführender Beschreibung von Waren und Dienstleistungen. Die Regelung ist jetzt im →Consumer Protection Act enthalten

trade, ~ directory Branchenadreßbuch; **~ discount** Rabatt für Wiederverkäufer; **~ disparagement** Verleumdung im geschäftlichen Verkehr

trade dispute[57] Arbeitsstreitigkeit *(zwischen Arbeitgebern und Arbeitnehmern oder zwischen Arbeitnehmern untereinander)*; **settlement of international ~s** Beilegung internationaler Handelsstreitigkeiten

trade, ~ effluent Abwässer aus Gewerbebetrieben; **~ fair** (Handels-)Messe; Fachmesse; **~ figures** Außenhandelszahlen; **~ fixtures** Betriebsausstattung *(→ fixture)*; **~ flows** Handelsströme; **~ gap** Handelslücke, Handelsbilanzdefizit *(Differenz zwischen Importen und Exporten e-s Landes)*

trade-in in Zahlung gegebene (gebrauchte) Ware

(z.B. Gebrauchtwagen); ~**value** Eintauschwert, Verrechnungswert *(e-r in Zahlung gegebenen Sache)*; **to make an allowance for a ~** e-e gebrauchte Sache in Zahlung nehmen

trade, ~ investment *Br (Bilanz)* Vermögensanlagen im Interesse des Geschäftsbetriebs; Beteiligungen; ~ **journal** Handelsblatt; ~ **libel** *Am* Verleumdung im Geschäftsverkehr; Anschwärzung *(cf. injurious →falsehood)*; ~ **losses** *(SeeversR)* gewöhnlicher Gewichtsabgang und Schwund unterwegs; ~ **margin** Handelsspanne

trademark[58] Warenzeichen; Handelsmarke, Fabrikmarke

Br Das Warenzeichenrecht ist in dem Trade Marks Act 1938 geregelt. Die Eintragung e-s Warenzeichens erfolgt bei dem Comptroller-General of Patents, Designs and Trade Marks *(cf. Patent Office)*. Der Trade Marks Act 1938 unterscheidet eine Eintragung in Part A und Part B. Letztere Eintragung stellt geringere Anforderungen an die für jedes Zeichen notwendige Unterscheidungskraft. Der nicht eingetragene Warenzeicheninhaber ist geschützt durch die Klage aus → passing off.

Am Warenzeichen werden nur durch Benutzung (adoption and use) eines Zeichens beim Verkauf von Waren erworben. Ein solches Zeichen kann in ein Bundesregister od. in die Register der Einzelstaaten eingetragen werden. Die bundesgesetzliche Regelung des Markenrechts befindet sich im Lanham Act von 1946, der ein Hauptregister (Principal Register) und ein Ergänzungsregister (Supplemental Register) einführte. Die Eintragung erfolgt beim Patentamt *(cf. Patent Office)*. Durch diese Eintragung (Trade Mark registered US Patent Office) ist die Marke in der Regel in allen Einzelstaaten geschützt; die einzelstaatl. Registrierung bewirkt nur Schutz in dem betreffenden Einzelstaat

trademark, ~ application Warenzeichenanmeldung; ~ **article** durch Warenzeichen geschützter Artikel; Markenartikel; ~ **examiner** Warenzeichenprüfer; ~ **infringement** Warenzeichenverletzung; ~ **licen|ce (~se)** Warenzeichenlizenz; ~ **litigation** Warenzeichenstreitsachen; ~ **opposition** Warenzeichenwiderspruch (→*opposition 2.*); ~ **owner** Markeninhaber; ~ **piracy** Markenpiraterie; ~ **pirate** Markenpirat; ~ **protection** Warenzeichenschutz; ~**register** Zeichenrolle

Trademark Registration Treaty (TRT)[58a] Vertrag über die internationale Registrierung von Marken von 14 Unterzeichnerstaaten *(z.B. USA, Großbritannien, BRD und Sowjetunion)*

trademark, action for infringement of a registered ~ Warenzeichenverletzungsklage; **alteration of a ~** Warenzeichenabänderung; **arbitrary ~** willkürlich gewähltes Zeichen *(das keinerlei Sinn zum Ausdruck bringt)*; **association of ~s** Verbindung von Warenzeichen; **associated ~s** *Br*[59] verbundene Warenzeichen *(gleiche od. verwechslungsfähige Marken desselben Zeicheninhabers werden gemeinsam in das Register eingetragen)*; **cancellation of a ~** Löschung e-s Warenzeichens; **certification ~s**[60] Güte- od. Verbandsmarken; Gütezeichen; **collective ~** Verbandszeichen; **common law ~s** *Am* nicht eingetragene Warenzeichen; **deceptive ~** irreführendes Warenzeichen; **defensive ~** *Br* Defensivmarke; **distinctive ~** unterscheidungskräftiges Warenzeichen; **lapse of a ~** Erlöschen e-s Warenzeichens; **non-distinctive ~** Warenzeichen ohne Unterscheidungskraft; **owner** (or **proprietor**) **of a ~** Inhaber e-s Warenzeichens; Zeicheninhaber; **Register of T~s** *Br* (Waren-)Zeichenrolle; **registered ~** eingetragenes (gesetzl. geschütztes) Warenzeichen; **registration of ~s**[61] Eintragung von Warenzeichen; **similarity between two ~s** Übereinstimmung zwischen zwei Warenzeichen; **unregistered ~** nicht eingetragenes Warenzeichen

trademark, to assign a ~ ein Warenzeichen übertragen; **to expunge the registration of a ~** die Eintragung e-s Warenzeichens löschen; **to infringe a ~** ein Warenzeichen verletzen; **to label with a ~** (or **to put a ~ on**) mit e-m Warenzeichen versehen; **to register a ~** ein Warenzeichen eintragen (lassen); **to use a ~** ein Warenzeichen benutzen

trademark *v Am* mit e-m Warenzeichen versehen; ein Warenzeichen eintragen; ~**ed goods** *Am* Markenartikel, Markenwaren

trade, ~ mart Großhandelszentrum; ~ **measures** handelspolitische Maßnahmen; ~ **mission** Handelsmission; ~ **name** Firmenname, Firma *(des Einzelkaufmanns)*; Handelsname, handelsübliche Bezeichnung; ~ **negotiations** Handelsverhandlungen; ~**-off** (gegenseitige) Abstimmung; Maßnahme zur Abstimmung (od. Koordinierung) *(z.B. zwischen Inflation und Arbeitslosigkeit)*

trade, ~ or business *Am* Geschäftstätigkeit; ~ **or business income** *Am (SteuerR)* Einkünfte aus gewerblicher Tätigkeit

trade, ~ organization Berufsorganisation; ~ **paper** Warenwechsel; Handelsfachzeitschrift; ~ **payables** →~ creditors; **T~ Pledge** *(von den Regierungen der OECD-Staaten 1974 unterzeichnetes)* handelspolitisches Stillhalteabkommen; ~ **policy** Handelspolitik

trade practice, ~s Handelspraktiken, Handelsgewohnheiten; **T~ P~ Conferences** *Am (AntitrustR)* Konferenzen unter Leitung der → F.T.C., auf denen die ~ rules ausgearbeitet werden; **T~ P~ (Conference) Rules** *Am (von der →F.T.C. und einzelnen Unternehmergruppen festgelegte)* Wettbewerbsregeln *(durch die unlautere Wettbewerbsmethoden für ungesetzl. erklärt werden können)*; → **unfair ~s**

trade, ~ price Preis für Wiederverkäufer, Großhandelspreis; ~ **promotion** Absatzförderung; ~ **protection society** *Br* Kreditschutzverein; ~ **receivables** →~ debtors

trade reference Kreditauskunft; Handelsreferenz; **to ask someone for a ~** jdn um Benennung e-r Handelsreferenz bitten

trade, ~ register Handelsregister; **~ regulation rules** Wettbewerbsregeln; **~ relations** Handelsbeziehungen; →**US T~ Representative;** **~ returns** Handelsstatistiken; **~ school** Handelsschule; Berufsfachschule

trade secret Betriebsgeheimnis, Geschäftsgeheimnis; **disclosure of ~s** Verrat von Geschäftsgeheimnissen; Geheimnisverrat; **preservation of ~s** Wahrung von Betriebsgeheimnissen; **to disclose** (or **divulge**) **~s** Betriebsgeheimnisse verraten; **to exploit (preserve) ~s** Betriebsgeheimnisse verwerten (wahren)

trade, ~ settlement Handelsniederlassung *(im Ausland)*; **~ stamps** *Am* →trading stamps; **~ statistics** Handelsstatistiken; **~ supervision** Gewerbeaufsicht; **~ talks** Handelsgespräche; **~ terms** Handelsklauseln

Trade Terms *(von der Internationalen Handelskammer 1923 und zuletzt 1953 veröffentlichte)* handelsübliche Vertragsformeln *(anders → terms of trade)*

Synoptische Gegenüberstellung von Lieferklauseln wie fob, cif etc und deren unterschiedliche Auslegung in 18 verschiedenen Ländern *(cf. Incoterms)*

trade union[62] Gewerkschaft *(es gibt zwei Hauptarten von Gewerkschaften: craft unions und industrial unions; → union 2.)*; **~ affiliation** Gewerkschaftszugehörigkeit; **T~ U~ Congress** (TUC) *Br* Gewerkschaftskongreß *(Dachverband der britischen Gewerkschaften)*; **~ delegate** Gewerkschaftsvertreter; **~ dues** Gewerkschaftsbeiträge; **~ leader** Gewerkschaftsführer; **~ member** Gewerkschaftsmitglied; **~ movement** Gewerkschaftsbewegung; **(full time) ~ official** (hauptamtl.) Gewerkschaftsfunktionär; → **International Confederation of Free T~ U~s;** → **World Federation of T~ U~s** (WFTU) *(unter kommunistischem Einfluß stehender)* Weltgewerkschaftsbund (WGB)

trade unionism Gewerkschaftswesen; **international ~** internationales Gewerkschaftswesen (→*International Confederation of Free Trade Unions, World Federation of →Trade Unions)*

trade, ~ unionist Gewerkschafter; **~ usage** Handelsbrauch, Usance; **~ value** Handelswert, Verkehrswert; **~ volume** Handelsvolumen; **~ war** Handelskrieg

trade, balance of ~ Handelsbilanz (→*balance 2.)*; **active** (or **favo[u]rable**) **balance of ~** aktive Handelsbilanz; **passive** (or **unfavo[u]rable**) **balance of ~** passive Handelsbilanz

trade, balanced ~ ausgewogener Handelsverkehr; **branch of ~** Wirtschaftszweig; **carrying ~** Spedition *(bes. von e-m Land in ein anderes)*; **commodity ~** Rohstoffhandel; **custom of (the) ~** Handelsbrauch, Usance (→*custom 1.)*; →**Department of T~ and Industry; domestic ~** inländischer Handel, Binnenhandel; **European Free T~ Association** →EFTA; **expansion of ~** Ausweitung des Handels; **export ~** Ausfuhrhandel; **external ~** Außenhandel; **fair ~** *Am* Preisbindung zweiter Hand (→*fair*); **foreign ~** Außenhandel (→*foreign*); **home ~** s. domestic →~; **import ~** Einfuhrhandel; **inland ~** Binnenhandel; inländischer Handel; **intermediate ~** Zwischenhandel; **internal ~** Binnenhandel; **international ~** Welthandel; **itinerant ~** Wandergewerbe; **maritime ~** Seehandel, Überseehandel; **ocean ~** *Am* Überseehandel; **restraint of ~** Wettbewerbsbeschränkung (→*restraint*); **retail ~** Einzelhandel; Kleinhandel; **telephone ~** *(Börse)* Telefonhandel; → **terms of ~**; **usual in ~** handelsüblich, geschäftsüblich; **well up in the ~** branchenkundig; **wholesale ~** Großhandel

trade *v* Handel treiben, handeln (in a th. mit etw.); **the firm ~s with China** die Firma treibt Handel mit China; die Firma steht in Geschäftsverbindung mit China; **to ~ down** *Am* mit billigeren Artikeln zur Erhöhung des Umsatzes handeln; **to ~ in** in Zahlung geben; **to ~ in futures** Termingeschäfte betreiben; **to ~ off the floor** außerbörslich handeln; **to ~ over the counter** im Freiverkehr handeln; **to ~ up** mit Waren höherer Preislage und Qualität zur Umsatzsteigerung handeln

traded, T~ Options Market *Br (Börse)* Markt für Optionsgeschäfte *(Geschäfte mit gehandelten Optionen)*; **the shares are ~ on the stock exchange** die Aktien werden an der Börse gehandelt

trader Händler; Geschäftsmann; Gewerbetreibender; Handelsschiff; *Am (Börse)* Wertpapierhändler; **~s** Kaufleute; **floor ~** *Am* Börsenmitglied, das für eigene Rechnung spekuliert; **professional ~s** *(Börse)* Berufshandel; **retail ~** Einzelhändler; **street ~** Straßenhändler; **wholesale ~** Großhändler

tradesman (Einzel-)Händler; Geschäftsmann; Ladeninhaber (od. dessen Angestellter); Handwerker

tradesmen Geschäftsleute; Gewerbetreibende; **~'s entrance** Eingang für Lieferanten

trading Handel; Handeln; Börsenhandel; Geschäfts-, Betriebs-; **~ account** Verkaufskonto *(Geschäftskonto, das nur den Bruttogewinn aus dem Handel anzeigt, ohne Berücksichtigung der Gemeinkosten)*; **~ agreement** *(KartellR)* Absprache; **~ area** Absatzgebiet, Verkaufsgebiet; **~ bank** *(Australien)* s. commercial →bank; **~ capital** Betriebskapital, Betriebsmittel; **~ certificate** *Br (vom →Registrar of Companies erteilte)* Handelserlaubnis *(ohne die e-e Kapitalgesellschaft ihre Geschäftstätigkeit nicht aufnehmen kann)*; **~ concern** Handelsunternehmen; **~ conditions** Geschäftsbedingungen; **~ →cor-**

poration; ~ **day** Börsentag; ~ **down** Handeln mit billigeren Artikeln zur Erhöhung des Umsatzes; ~ **enterprise** Handelsunternehmen; Gewerbebetrieb; ~ **estate** *Br* Industriesiedlung; Industriepark; ~ **floor** Börsensaal; ~ **in calls** *Br (Börse)* Vorprämienhandel; Abschlüsse in Kaufoptionen; ~ **in futures** *(Börse)* Termingeschäft; ~ **in puts** *Br (Börse)* Rückprämienhandel; Abschlüsse in Verkaufsoptionen; ~ **licen|ce (~se)** Handelserlaubnis; Gewerbekonzession; ~ **loss** Betriebsverlust; ~ **market** stagnierende Börse, in der die Beteiligten meist Berufshändler sind; ~ **of securities** Handel mit Wertpapieren; ~ **on the equity** Fremdfinanzierung; ~ **on margin** *Am* →margin buying; ~ **partner** Handelspartner; ~ →**partnership;** ~ **post** *Am* Börsenstand, Maklerstand; ~ **profit** Betriebsgewinn, Geschäftsgewinn

trading rate Wechselkurs für Transaktionen der Leistungsbilanz; **non-~** Wechselkurs für Transaktionen der Kapitalbilanz

trading, ~ **results** Betriebsergebnisse; ~ **stamps** Rabattmarken *(gegen Ware einlösbare Gutscheine)*; ~ **standards department** *Br* Kommunalbehörde, die die Einhaltung der Handelsregeln überwacht; ~ **up** Handeln mit Waren höherer Preislage und Qualität zur Erhöhung der Gewinnspanne; ~ **vessel** Handelsschiff, Kauffahrteischiff *(opp. pleasure vessel)*; ~ **year** Geschäftsjahr

trading, →**fair** ~; →**fraudulent** ~**; illicit** ~ unerlaubter Handel, Schwarzhandel *(z.B. mit Suchtstoffen);* →**wrongful** ~

traduce *v* verleumden

traffic 1. (Straßen-, Eisenbahn-, Schiffs-, Güter-, Personen-)Verkehr; Verkehrswesen

traffic, to block the ~ den Verkehr behindern; **to direct** (or **regulate**) **the** ~ den Verkehr regeln; **to divert (the)** ~ den Verkehr umleiten; **to obstruct the** ~ den Verkehr behindern

traffic, ~ **accident** Verkehrsunfall; ~ **beacon** Verkehrssignal *(für Fußgänger);* ~ **block** →~ congestion

traffic cases, increase in ~ Zunahme der Verkehrs(straf)sachen

traffic, ~ **census** Verkehrszählung; ~ **circle** *Am* Kreisverkehr; **T~ Code** *Am* → Uniform T~ Code; ~ **congestion** Verkehrsstau, Verkehrsstockung; ~ **direction** Verkehrslenkung; ~ **diversion** *Br* Umleitung des Verkehrs; ~ **engineer** *Am* Verkehrsingenieur; ~ **flow** Verkehrsstrom; ~ **hold up** Verkehrsstockung; ~ **in transit** Transitverkehr; ~ **island** Verkehrsinsel; ~ **jam** →~ congestion; ~ **junction** Verkehrsknotenpunkt

traffic light(s) Verkehrsampel; **linked** (*Am* **synchronized**) ~ grüne Welle *(bei Verkehrsampeln)*

traffic, ~ **of the port** die ein- und ausgehenden Schiffe; ~ **offence (-se)** Verkehrsdelikt, Ordnungswidrigkeit im Verkehr; ~ **offender** Verkehrssünder; ~ **pacer** grüne Welle *(bei Verkehrsampeln);* ~ **peak** Verkehrsspitze

traffic policy, problems of ~ verkehrspolitische Fragen

traffic, ~ **planning** Verkehrsplanung; ~ **regulation** Verkehrsregelung; ~ **regulations** Verkehrsregeln, (Straßen-)Verkehrsvorschriften; ~ **requirements** Verkehrsbedürfnisse; ~ **returns** Verkehrsziffern; ~ **sign** Verkehrszeichen; ~ **statistics** Verkehrsstatistik; ~ **stream** Verkehrsstrom; ~ **turning the corner** Einbiegeverkehr; ~ **violation** *Am* Verletzung der Verkehrsvorschriften; ~ **warden** *Br* Politesse; Hilfspolizist *(zur Überwachung des Parkwesens)*

traffic, air (or **aerial)** ~ Luftverkehr; **border** ~ Grenzverkehr; **city** ~ großstädtischer Verkehr; Verkehr in der Innenstadt; **density of** ~ Verkehrsdichte; **dislocation of** ~ Verkehrsdurcheinander; **endangering of** ~ Verkehrsgefährdung; **flow of** ~ Verkehrsstrom; **freight** ~ *Am* Güterverkehr; **frontier** ~ Grenzverkehr; **goods** ~ *Br* Güterverkehr; **heavy** ~ starker Verkehr; **highway** ~ Straßenverkehr *(über Land)*; **increase in** ~ Verkehrszunahme; **inland** ~ Binnenverkehr, Inlandsverkehr; **local** ~ Nahverkehr; Ortsverkehr; innerstädtischer Verkehr; **long-distance** ~ Fernverkehr; **maritime** ~ Seeverkehr; **motor** ~ Autoverkehr; **obstruction of** ~ Behinderung des Verkehrs; **oncoming** ~ Gegenverkehr; **one-way** ~ Einbahnverkehr; **passenger** ~ Personenverkehr; **postal** ~ Postverkehr; **railway** ~ *Br* (**railroad** ~ *Am*) (Eisen-)Bahnverkehr; **road** ~ Straßenverkehr (→*road*); **short-distance** ~ Nahverkehr; **through** (or **transit**) ~ Durchgangsverkehr; **tourist** ~ Fremdenverkehr; **volume of** ~ Verkehrsaufkommen

traffic 2. Handel, Handelsverkehr; illegaler Handel; ~ **in arms** Waffenhandel, Waffenschmuggel; ~ **in votes** Stimmenkauf; **commercial** ~ Handelsverkehr; **drug** ~ Rauschgifthandel; Handel mit Suchtstoffen; **illegal** ~ Schleichhandel, Schmuggel; Schwarzhandel; **liquor** ~ Handel mit alkoholischen Getränken; **white slave** ~ Mädchenhandel

traffic *v*, **to** ~ **in drugs** mit Rauschgift handeln

trafficker Schwarzmarkthändler; Schmuggler; **drug** ~ *(illegaler)* Rauschgifthändler, Dealer

trailer Anhänger *(zu e-m Kfz.; opp. tractor)*; Wohnwagen; **~-on-flat-car transport** (TOFC) *Am* Huckepackverkehr

train (Eisenbahn-)Zug; ~ **accident** Eisenbahnunglück; ~ **collision** Eisenbahnzusammenstoß; ~ **connection** Zugverbindung; ~ **ferry** Eisenbahnfähre, Trajekt; ~ **schedule** Fahrplan; **commuter** ~ Vorortzug; **direct** ~

durchgehender Zug; **express** ~ D-Zug; **fast** ~ Schnellzug, D-Zug; **freight** ~ *Am* Güterzug; **goods** ~ *Br* Güterzug; **hospital** ~ Lazarettzug; **passenger** ~ Personenzug; **through** ~ durchgehender Zug, D-Zug; **to change ~s** umsteigen; **to go by** ~ mit dem Zug fahren; **to lay on a special** ~ e-n Sonderzug einsetzen

trainee in der Ausbildung stehende Person; Auszubildende(r); Anlernling; Praktikant; Nachwuchskraft; **industrial** ~ (or *Am* **on the job** ~) Firmenpraktikant; **management** ~ Führungsnachwuchskraft

training Ausbildung; Schulung; Anlernen; ~ **cent|re (~er)** Ausbildungsstätte; ~ **course** (Schulungs-)Kursus, Lehrgang; ~ **facilities** Ausbildungsmöglichkeiten; ~ **farm** landwirtschaftl. Lehrbetrieb; ~ **grant** Ausbildungsbeihilfe; ~ **leave** Bildungsurlaub; ~ **off the job** Ausbildung außerhalb des Arbeitsplatzes; ~ **on the job** Ausbildung am Arbeitsplatz; ~ **program(me)** Ausbildungsprogramm *(cf. advanced →management ~ program)*; ~ **school** *Am (in einigen Staaten)* Jugendstrafanstalt; ~ **subsidy** Ausbildungsbeihilfe; ~ **within industry** (TWI) *Am* Form der Ausbildung betrieblicher Führungskräfte; **commercial** ~ Ausbildung als Kaufmann; kaufmännische Ausbildung; **continuation** (or **further**) ~ Weiterbildung; Berufsfortbildung; **period of** ~ Ausbildungszeit; **professional** ~ s. vocational →~; **re**~ Umschulung; **recurrent** ~ ständige Weiterbildung; **technical** ~ Fachausbildung; **vocational** ~ Berufsausbildung; **to complete a** ~ e-e Ausbildung beenden; **to receive (a)** ~ e-e Ausbildung bekommen

tram(car) *Br* Straßenbahn

tramp Trampschiff *(Frachtdampfer ohne feste Route; opp. liner)*; ~ **corporation** *Am* Briefkastengesellschaft; ~ **navigation** (or **shipping**) Trampschiffahrt; ~ **steamer** Trampschiff

tramping Trampschiffahrt, Charterschiffahrt

tranche Tranche; **splitting of a loan into ~s** Aufteilung e-r Anleihe in Tranchen

transact *v* durchführen, zustandebringen, abschließen; **to ~ a bargain** e-n Handel abschließen; **to ~ business** Geschäfte tätigen (od. machen); **to ~ business for one's own or for another's account** für eigene oder für fremde Rechnung Geschäfte machen; **to ~ a deal** e-e Abmachung zustande bringen; **to ~ insurance business** das Versicherungsgeschäft betreiben; **to ~ negotiations** Verhandlungen führen

transacted, to put down on the agenda the business to be ~ die zu erledigenden Geschäfte auf die Tagesordnung setzen

transaction Durchführung, (Geschäfts-)Abschluß; Geschäft; Geschäftsvorgang, Geschäftsvorfall; Transaktion; **~s** Geschäfte; Umsätze; *(Börse)* Abschlüsse; Sitzungsprotokoll *(bes. e-r wissenschaftlichen Gesellschaft)*; ~ **at an undervalue** *Br*[63] *(die Gläubiger benachteiligendes)* Geschäft unter Wert *(z.B. vor Konkurs e-r natürlichen Person od. Liquidation e-r company)*; **~s between related taxpayers** *Am*[64] Umsätze (od. Transaktionen) zwischen verbundenen Steuerpflichtigen; **~s for one's own account** Eigengeschäfte; ~ **for cash** Kassageschäft; ~ **for future delivery** *(Produktenbörse)* Termingeschäft; ~ **for the settlement** *Br (Bröse)* Termingeschäft; ~ **in foreign exchange** Devisengeschäft; **the bank's ~s in securities** Wertpapiergeschäfte des Kreditinstituts; ~ **on credit** Kreditgeschäft; **~s on the stock exchange** Börsengeschäfte; **~s tax** *Am* Umsatzsteuer; **banking** ~ Bankgeschäft; **bear** ~ Baissespekulation; **bull** ~ Haussespekulation; **business** ~ Geschäft(svorfall) (→*business*); **capital** ~ Kapitaltransaktion; **capital ~s** Kapitalverkehr; →**cash ~(s)**; **financial** ~ Finanztransaktion; **(foreign) exchange ~s** Devisengeschäfte; **forward** ~ *(Produktenbörse)* Termingeschäft; **legal** ~ Rechtsgeschäft, Rechtsvorgang, rechtlich erhebliches Geschehen *(durch das Rechtsbeziehungen begründet werden)*; **market** ~ s. stock exchange →~; **money** (or **monetary**) **~s** Geldgeschäfte; **stock exchange** ~ Börsengeschäft; **to enter into a** ~ ein Geschäft vornehmen (od. abschließen); **~s in ... were few** *(Börse)* es wurden in ... wenig Abschlüsse getätigt; **the ~ took place in England** das Geschäft ist in England vorgenommen worden

transborder data flow (TDF) grenzüberschreitender Datenfluß (od. Datenverkehr [GDV])

transboundary grenzüberschreitend; ~ **air pollution** grenzüberschreitende Luftverunreinigung; ~ **water pollution** grenzüberschreitende Gewässerverunreinigung

transcribe *v* abschreiben; **to ~ a program(me)** ein Rundfunkprogramm auf Schallplatten übertragen *(für Sendezwecke)*; **to ~ shorthand notes** ein Stenogramm *(in Langschrift)* übertragen

transcript Abschrift; Kopie *(z.B. e-s Wechsels)*; *(e-r Partei erteilte)* Ausfertigung e-s Gerichtsprotokolls; Tonaufnahme *(auf Schallplatten für Sendezwecke)*; ~ **of evidence** Beweisaufnahmeprotokoll; ~ **of record** *Am* Bescheinigung über Eintragung e-s Urteils *(cf. entry of →judgment)*; *Am* Ausfertigung e-s Gerichtsprotokolls *(einschließlich der Schriftsätze der Parteien, des Urteils etc, zur Vorlage bei Einlegung e-s Rechtsmittels)*

transcription Abschrift, Kopie; *(Radio)* Tonband- od. Schallplattenaufnahme *(für Sendezwecke)*

transfer 1. *(rechtsgeschäftl.)* Übertragung (von Rechten und Vermögensgegenständen) *(z.B. auf Grund e-s Kaufs od. e-r Schenkung)*; Grundstücksübertragungsurkunde (→~ *deed*, →~ *of land)*; Rechtsübergang (to auf); *(gesetzl.)* Übergang von Rechten und Vermögensgegenständen *(z.B. im Konkurs des Inhabers od. bei Erbfolge)*; ~ **by operation of law** gesetzlicher Übergang; ~ **by way of gift** Schenkung; ~ **by way of security** Sicherungsübereignung; ~ **(deed)** Grundstücksübertragungsurkunde *(Br hinsichtlich →registered land) (s. auch transfer 4.)*; ~ **in bulk** *Am* Geschäftsübertragung *(→bulk transfer)*; ~ **of business** Übertragung e-s Geschäfts; Geschäftsübergang; ~ **of claim** Forderungsübertragung; ~ **of a debt** Abtretung e-r Forderung; ~ **of expectancy** Übertragung e-r Erbanwartschaft; ~ **(of land)** Grundstücksübertragung(surkunde) *(Br*[65] *Urkunde, in der Vollzug des Kaufvertrages niedergelegt wird und zwar hinsichtlich →registered land; cf. conveyance)*; ~ **of ownership** Eigentumsübertragung; ~ **of real estate** *Am* Grundstücksübertragung(surkunde); ~ **of rights** Übertragung von Rechten; ~ **of technology** Technologietransfer; ~ **of title** Eigentumsübertragung; ~ **of title to property** Übertragung von Eigentum an Grundbesitz; ~ **taxes** *Am* Vermögensübertragungssteuern *(z.B. Erbschaft-, Schenkungsteuern)*; ~ **to the pension reserve** Zuführung zur Pensionsrückstellung; ~ **to the reserve** Zuführung zur Rücklage

transfer, absolute ~ uneingeschränkte Übertragung; **conditional** ~ an Bedingungen geknüpfte Übertragung; **fraudulent** ~**s** *Am*[65a] (anfechtbare) Vermögensübertragung vor Konkurseröffnung mit dem Vorsatz, Gläubiger zu hintergehen; **instrument of** ~ Übertragungsurkunde, **involuntary** ~ gesetzlicher Übergang

transfer 2. (Geld-)Überweisung; ~ **account** Girokonto; ~ **in(to) an account** Überweisung auf ein Konto; ~ **income** Transfereinkommen *(Einkommen der Empfänger staatlicher Unterstützungen)*; ~ **payments** Transferzahlungen *(Unterstützungszahlungen staatl. Stellen, z.B. Bezüge aus Br Income Support, Am Social Security, Arbeitslosenunterstützung, Studienbeihilfen)*; *(Zahlungsbilanz)* unentgeltliche Leistungen; ~ **payments account** Übertragungsbilanz; **bank** ~ Banküberweisung, Giroüberweisung; **cable** ~ (C.T.) telegrafische Überweisung; **money** ~ Geldüberweisung; **telegraphic** ~ (T.T.) telegrafische Überweisung; **to make a** ~ überweisen; **to make a** ~ **to the credit of a p.'s account** Geld auf jds Konto überweisen; **to pay by** ~ durch Überweisung (bargeldlos) zahlen

transfer 3. *(internationaler Zahlungsverkehr)* Transfer *(Zahlung von e-m Währungsgebiet in ein anderes)*; ~ **agreement** Transferabkommen; ~ **licen|ce (~se)** Transferbewilligung; ~ **of capital** Transfer(ierung) von Kapital; Kapitaltransfer; **(foreign) currency** ~ Devisentransfer; **prohibition of** ~ Transferverbot; **restrictions on** ~ Transferbeschränkungen

transfer 4. Verlegung; Verlagerung; Versetzung; ~ **allowance** *Am* Umzugskostenbeihilfe; ~ **for disciplinary reasons** Strafversetzung; ~ **of actions** (or **causes**)[66] Verweisung von Klagen *(an ein anderes Gericht od. e-e andere Abteilung)*; ~ **of business** Geschäftsverlegung; ~ **of domicil(e)** *(etwa)* Wohnsitzverlegung; ~ **of prisoners** Verlegung von Gefangenen; ~ **of profits** Gewinnverlagerung; ~ **of the seat of the company** Verlegung des Sitzes der Gesellschaft; ~ **ticket** Umsteigekarte; Anschlußfahrkarte; ~ **to another flag** Wechsel des Flaggenstaates (od. der Staatsangehörigkeit von Schiffen)

transfer, forcible ~ *(VölkerR)* Vertreibung; **(staff)** ~**s** Versetzungen; **to get a** ~ versetzt werden, sich versetzen lassen

transfer 5. (tfr) Übertragung (od. Umschreibung) *(von Aktien)*; *Br* Übertragungsurkunde (→~ *deed)*; ~ **agent** *Am* Transferagent *(Stelle, oft Bank od. Trust Company, die die Umschreibung der Namensaktien, bei Aktienübertragungen oft auch die Auszahlungen von Dividenden an die Aktionäre, vornimmt)*; ~ **book** (Aktien-)Umschreibungsbuch; ~ **(deed)** Übertragungsurkunde *(Br → registered securities)*; ~ **duty** *Br* Börsenumsatzsteuer; ~ **fee** Gebühr für Übertragung von Aktien; ~ **form** *Br* Formular zur Übertragung e-s Wertpapiers; Umschreibungsformular; ~ **in blank** s. blank →transfer; ~ **journal** *Am* Buch für Aktienumschreibungen; ~ **of debentures** *Br*[67] Übertragung von Obligationen; ~ **of (registered) shares** *Br*[68] Aktienübertragung, Aktienumschreibung; ~ **receipt** *Br* Quittung über erfolgte Übertragung (od. Umschreibung) von Aktien; ~ **register** *Br* Übertragungs- (od. Umschreibungs)register *(für Aktien)*

transfer, blank ~ *Br* in blanko ausgestellte Aktien-Übertragungsurkunde; Aktien-Blankoindossament *(auf getrennter Urkunde)*

Wird mit der Aktie vornehmlich zu Sicherungszwecken übergeben. Der Erwerber hat es in der Hand, nach Vervollständigung des Blanketts seine Eintragung in die Bücher der Gesellschaft und dadurch die Vollrechtsübertragung auf ihn herbeizuführen

transfer, instrument of ~ *Br* Übertragungsurkunde; **registrar of** ~**s** *Br* Umschreibungsbeamter *(für Aktien)*; **registration of** ~**s** *Br* Umschreibungen im Aktienbuch; **share** ~ *Br* →~ of shares; **stock** ~ Aktienübertragung; *Br* Wertpapierübertragung (→*stock 1.)*; **to effect a** ~ e-e Übertragung (od. Umschreibung) *(von Aktien)* vornehmen

transfer 6. *(Buchführung)* (tfr) Übertrag; Umbuchung; ~ **of an amount from one account to another** Umbuchung; ~ **of balance** Saldoübertrag; ~ **of an entry** Umbuchung; **to pass a** ~ e-n Übertrag machen

transfer *v (Recht, Vermögen)* übertragen; abtreten, zedieren; transferieren *(Zahlungen an das Ausland leisten); (Geld)* überweisen; *(Wertpapiere)* übertragen, umschreiben; verlegen (from ... to von ... nach); verlagern; *(jdn)* versetzen; *(Buchführung)* übertragen, vortragen; umbuchen; *(Eisenbahn)* umsteigen; **to ~ a case** e-e Rechtssache *(an ein anderes Gericht)* verweisen; **to ~ for disciplinary reasons** *(jdn)* strafversetzen; **to ~ foreign currency** Devisen transferieren; **to ~ an instrument for value** ein (Handels-)Papier entgeltlich übertragen; **to ~ money to an account** Geld auf ein Konto überweisen; **to ~ money by cable** Geld telegrafisch überweisen; **to ~ property** Eigentum (od. Vermögen) übertragen; **to ~ to the reserves** den Rücklagen zuführen; **to ~ shares** Aktien umschreiben; **to ~ title** das Eigentum übertragen

transferability Übertragbarkeit; ~ **by succession** (or **inheritance**) Vererblichkeit; ~ **of a debt** Abtretbarkeit e-r Forderung; ~ **of possession by succession** Vererblichkeit des Besitzes; ~ **of a share** Umschreibbarkeit e-r Aktie

transferable übertragbar (to auf); abtretbar, transferierbar; transferabel; umschreibbar *(von Aktien)*; ~ **loan certificates** (TLC) *(Finanzinstrument zur Forderungsübertragung)* übertragbarer Darlehensschein; ~ **loan facility** übertragbare Kreditfazilität

transferee (Übertragungs-)Empfänger; Zessionar; Erwerber *(durch Übertragung)*; Übernehmer, Transfer-Begünstigter; ~ **company** übernehmende Gesellschaft; ~ **of a bill (of exchange)** Übernehmer e-s Wechsels; ~ **of a share** Erwerber (od. Käufer) e-r Aktie

transference Übertragung; Umschreibung; Versetzung

transferor Übertragender; Veräußerer; Zedent; ~ **company** übertragende Gesellschaft; ~ **of shares** Veräußerer (od. Verkäufer) von Aktien (od. Anteilen)

transform *v* umformen, umwandeln; umgestalten

transformation Umformung; Umwandlung; *(UrhR)* Umgestaltung; ~ **of a corporation into a partnership** *Am* Umwandlung e-r Kapital- in e-e Personengesellschaft

transfrontier grenzüberschreitend; ~ **shipment of hazardous waste** grenzüberschreitende Verbringung gefährlicher Abfälle

transgress *v (Gesetz)* übertreten, verletzen

transgression Übertretung, Verletzung *(e-s Gesetzes)*

tranship *v (Güter)* umladen; umschiffen, umschlagen, umstauen

transhipment Umladung; Umschiffung *(von e-m Schiff auf ein anderes)*; ~ **bill of lading** Umladekonnossement; ~ **charges** Umladegebühren; Umschlaggebühren; **port of** ~ Umschlaghafen

transient vorübergehend; ~ **(visitor)** *Am* Durchreisender

transire *Br*[69] (Zoll-)Begleitschein, Passierschein *(ohne den das Schiff nicht abfahren darf)*

transit 1. Transit *(Durchgang von Personen od. Waren durch das Gebiet e-s Staates)*; Durchfuhr(-); Durchgang(s-); Durchflug; ~ **agent** Transitspediteur; Zwischenspediteur; ~ **bond** *Br* Transitschein; ~ **cargo** Transitladung; ~ **charges** Durchfuhrabgaben, Transitgebühren; ~ **country** Durchfuhrland; ~ **dispatch** Transitversand; ~ **duties** Transitzölle; Durchfuhrabgaben; ~ **entry** *(Zoll)* Durchfuhrerklärung; ~ **flight** →flight 2.; ~ **freight** Durchfuhrfracht; ~ **goods** Transitgüter, Transitwaren; ~ **number** *Am* Bankleitzahl *(auf Schecks)*

transit of goods Durchfuhr von Waren, Warentransit; →**Customs Convention on the International T~ of G~**

transit, ~ **permit** Durchfuhrbewilligung; ~ **rate** Frachttarif für Durchgangsgüter; Transittarif; ~ **store** Transitlager, ~ **trade** Transithandel; ~ **traffic** Transitverkehr; ~ **visa** Transitvisum; Durchreisevisum

transit, goods in ~ Transitwaren; **right of** ~ Recht der Durchfuhr von Waren; **right of air** ~ Durchflugrecht; **to pass in** ~ transitieren; durchgehen, durchlaufen; **to pass goods in** ~ Waren durch ein Land führen

transit 2. Transport *(bes. der Ware vom Verkäufer zum Käufer)*; ~ **bill** Transportrechnung; ~ **by rail** Bahntransport; ~ **documents** *(EG)* Versandpapiere

transit, in course of ~ unterwegs; **ordinary course of** ~ gewöhnliche Route; **damage in** ~ Beschädigung auf dem Transport; Transportschaden; **damaged in** ~ unterwegs beschädigt; **during** (or **in**) ~ auf dem Transport; unterwegs; **(goods in)** ~ **insurance** Gütertransportversicherung; **loss in** ~ Transportschaden; (Gewichts-)Verlust auf dem Transport; **sea** ~ Seetransport, Überseetransport; **to insure goods in** ~ Waren auf dem Transport versichern

transit 3., ~ **in rem judicatam** ("it passes into [or becomes] a res judicata") es erwächst in Rechtskraft *(wodurch e-e zweite Klage zur Durchsetzung des gleichen Anspruchs verhindert wird)*

transition Übergang; ~ **period** Übergangszeit; **state of** ~ Übergangsstadium

transitional, ~ **benefit** *Am* Übergangsrente; ~ **period** Übergangszeit; ~ **provision** Übergangsbestimmung

transitory vorübergehend, transitorisch; ~ **action** *Am* Klage, die keinen ausschließlichen Gerichtsstand hat *(z.B. Schadensersatzklage; opp. local action)*; ~ **items** transitorische Posten *(der Rechnungsabgrenzung)*; ~ **period** Übergangszeit; ~ **provision** Übergangsbestimmung

transitu, in ~ unterwegs; → **stoppage in** ~

translate *v* übersetzen (from ...into von ... in); *(Währungen)* umrechnen; *eccl (Bischof)* versetzen; **to** ~ **a currency** e-e Währung umrechnen; **to** ~ **a telegram** ein Telegramm dechiffrieren

translation Übersetzung; Umrechnung *(ausländischer Währungen)*; *eccl* Versetzung e-s Bischofs; ~ **agency** (or **bureau**) Übersetzungsbüro; ~ **charge** Übersetzungsgebühr; **close** ~ wortgetreue Übersetzung; **inaccuracy of a** ~ Ungenauigkeit e-r Übersetzung; **literal** ~ wörtliche Übersetzung; **the** ~ **corresponds to the original text** die Übersetzung stimmt mit dem Urtext überein

translator Übersetzer; **free-lance** ~ freiberuflicher Übersetzer; **full-time** ~ hauptberuflicher Übersetzer; **sworn** ~ *Ger* vereidigter Übersetzer
In England und den USA gibt es keine allgemein vereidigten Übersetzer. Die Richtigkeit e-r Übersetzung in e-m Gerichtsverfahren muß von dem Übersetzer durch ein affidavit bestätigt werden

transmission Übertragung *(kraft Gesetzes)*; Übergang; Übersendung, Übermittlung; Versand; Durchleitung; *(IPR)* Weiterverweisung; (Rundfunk-, Fernseh-)Sendung; *(EDV)* Datenübertragung, Datenübermittlung; ~ **by operation of law** Übergang kraft Gesetzes *(z.B. durch Erbfolge, Konkurs)*; ~ **of goods** Warenversand; ~ **of shares** *Br* Übergang von Aktien (od. Anteilen) *(infolge von Erbschaft [an den personal representative] oder von Konkurs)*; ~ **on death** Übergang von Todes wegen

transmission, broadcast (or **radio**) ~ Rundfunkübertragung; **for onward** ~ zur Weiterleitung (to an); **secondary** ~ *Am* Kabelfernsehen

transmit *v* übertragen, überlassen; übersenden, übermitteln; versenden; *(Rundfunk)* senden; (Fernseh-)Sendungen durchführen; **to** ~ **by operation of law** übertragen kraft Gesetzes; **to** ~ **instructions** Weisungen erteilen; **to** ~ **onward** weiterleiten (to an); **to** ~ **an order** e-n Auftrag übermitteln

transmitting, ~ **agency**[70] Übermittlungsstelle; ~ **station** Sendestelle, Sender *(opp. receiving station)*

transmittal Übersendung; Übertragung; ~ **of the international application** *(Europ. PatR)* Weiterleitung der internationalen Anmeldung

transnational, ~ **corporation** (TNC) *Am* multinationale Gesellschaft; internationaler (Groß-) Konzern; ~ **enterprise** (TNE) *Am* transnationales (od. multinationales) Unternehmen

transplant Transplantation; das transplantierte Organ

transplant *v (Menschen)* verpflanzen, umsiedeln (to nach); *(Gewebe, Organ)* transplantieren

transplantation Transplantation, Organverpflanzung

transport Transport, Beförderung; Transportwesen; Transportmittel; Verkehr, Verkehrswesen; Verkehrsmittel; Verkehrsbetrieb; **T~ Act** *Br*[71] Verkehrsgesetz; ~ **agency** Speditionsfirma; ~ **agent** Spediteur; **T~ and General Workers' Union** (TGWU) *Br* Transportarbeitergewerkschaft; ~ **authorities** *Am* Verkehrsbehörden; ~ **by air** s. air →~; ~ **by land** Beförderung auf dem Landwege; ~ **by rail** s. rail →~; ~ **by road** Straßengüterverkehr, Güterverkehr mit Lkw; ~ **charges** Transportkosten, Beförderungskosten; ~ **company** *Br* Speditionsgesellschaft; ~ **contract** Beförderungsvertrag; ~ **costs** →~ charges

transport document, ~**-s** Transportdokumente *(Linienschiffahrt)*; **clean** ~ reines Transportdokument *(ohne Klauseln od. Vermerk)*

transport; ~ **facilities** Verkehrseinrichtungen; Transportmöglichkeiten; ~ **industry** Transportgewerbe; ~ **infrastructure** Verkehrsinfrastruktur; ~ **insurance** Transportversicherung; ~ **insurance on valuables** Valorenversicherung; ~ **of goods** Warentransport, Warenbeförderung; ~ **of goods by road** Güterverkehr; ~ **on inland waterways** Transport im Binnenschiffahrtsverkehr; ~ **planning** Verkehrsplanung; ~ **policy** Verkehrspolitik; ~ **risk** Transportgefahr, Transportrisiko; ~ **services** Verkehrsdienstleistungen; ~ **trade** Transportgewerbe; ~ **worker** Transportarbeiter

transport, air ~ Luftverkehr; Beförderung auf dem Luftwege; **air** ~ **agreement** Abkommen über den Luftverkehr; **commercial scheduled air** ~ planmäßiger gewerblicher Luftverkehr

transport, city ~ städtische Verkehrsbetriebe; **collective** ~ Sammeltransport; **conditions of** ~ Beförderungsbedingungen; **goods** ~ Gütertransport; **inland** ~ Binnentransport; Binnenverkehr; **inland water** ~ (IWT) *Am* (Beförderung im) Binnenschiffahrtsverkehr; **interstate** ~ *Am* zwischenstaatlicher (Güter-)Verkehr; **London Regional T~** Behörde für das Verkehrswesen (public transport) in London und

Umgebung; **mail** ~ Postbeförderung; **marine** (or **maritime**) ~ Seetransport; Beförderung auf dem Seewege; **means of** ~ Transportmittel, Beförderungsmittel; Verkehrsmittel; **method** (or **mode**) **of** ~ Beförderungsart, Verkehrsart; **motor truck** ~ *Am* Güterverkehr mit Lkw; **passenger** ~ Personenverkehr

transport, by public ~ mit öffentliche|m(-n) Verkehrsmittel(n); **public** ~ **system** öffentliches Verkehrswesen

transport, rail (or **railway**) ~ *Br* (Eisen-)Bahntransport; (Eisenbahn-)Güterverkehr; **rail(way) passenger** ~ *Br* Eisenbahnpersonenverkehr; **road** ~ *Br* Güterkraftverkehr; Straßen(güter)verkehr; **sea** ~ Seetransport; Beförderung auf dem Seewege; **Secretary of State for T~** *Br* Verkehrsminister; ~ **shall be effected at buyer's risk** der Transport geschieht auf Gefahr des Käufers

transport *v* transportieren, befördern; versenden; **to** ~ **goods by rail** Waren per Bahn versenden

transportable transportierbar; versandfähig

transportation Transport, Beförderung; Versendung; *Am* Transportwesen; *Am* Verkehrswesen; *Am* Verkehrsmittel; ~ **advertising** *Am* Verkehrs(mittel)werbung; ~ **agency** *Am* Speditionsfirma; ~ **conditions** *Am* Beförderungsbedingungen; ~ **costs** Transportkosten, Beförderungskosten; ~ **equipment** *Am* Transporteinrichtungen; ~ **rate** Transporttarif; **highway** ~ *Am* Güterverkehr mit Lastwagen; **interference with** ~ Transportgefährdung; **means of** ~ Transportmittel, Beförderungsmittel; Verkehrsmittel; **public** ~ *Am* öffentliches Verkehrsmittel; **railroad freight** ~ *Am* (Eisen-)Bahnfrachtverkehr; **railroad passenger** ~ *Am* (Eisen-)Bahnpersonenverkehr

transship →tranship

transshipment →transhipment

trap *auch fig* Falle; ~ **orders** Bestellungen durch e-n → agent provocateur, um e-n beweisbaren Verletzungsfall herbeizuführen; **police** ~ Autofalle

trap *v* Falle(n) stellen

trash wertlose Waren; Ausschuß(waren); *Am* Abfall, Müll; ~ **incinerating plant** *Am* Müllverbrennungsanlage

travel Reisen; Reise-; ~**s** (Auslands-)Reisen; **international** ~ grenzüberschreitender Reiseverkehr; ~ **abroad** Reisen ins Ausland; ~ **advance** *Am* Reisekostenvorschuß; ~ **agency** Reiseagentur; ~ **agent(s)** Reisebüro; ~ **document** Reisedokument, Reisepapier

travel expenses Reisekosten; Reisespesen; ~ **statement** Reisespesenabrechnung; **refund of** ~ Erstattung der Reisekosten; **to be reimbursed for** ~ die Reisekosten ersetzt bekommen

travel, ~ **guide** Reiseführer; ~ **insurance** Reiseversicherung; ~ **on official business** Reisen in dienstlicher Angelegenheit

travel *v* reisen; fahren; **to** ~ **on business** geschäftlich reisen

travelling (*Am* **traveling**) Reisen; ~ **agent** Vertreter; Handelsvertreter (selbständiger Gewerbetreibender); Handlungsreisender; ~ **allowance** Reisekostenpauschale; ~ **buying agent** *Am* für Importeure in fremden Märkten reisender Einkäufer; ~ **exhibition** Wanderausstellung

travel(l)ing expenses Reisekosten, Reisespesen; **advance for** ~ *Br* Reisekostenvorschuß; **compensation for** (or **reimbursement of**) ~ Reisekostenerstattung; Vergütung der Reisespesen; **to reimburse** ~ Reisekosten erstatten

travel(l)ing salesman (Handels-)Vertreter; Handlungsreisender

traveller (*Am* **traveler**) Reisender; ~**'s accident insurance** Reiseunfallversicherung; ~**'s cheque (check)** Reisescheck; ~**'s letter of credit** Reisekreditbrief; ~ **on commission** Provisionsreisender; **commercial** ~ Vertreter; Handlungsreisender; → **fellow** ~

traverse *(im pleading)* Leugnen, Bestreiten *(des klägerischen Vorbringens; →denial)*; ~ **jury** *Am* s. petty →jury

traverse *v (im pleading)* leugnen, *(Tatsache)* bestreiten (*→deny v*)

trawling, to be engaged in ~ Schleppnetzfischerei betreiben

treachery Verrat *(Br mit der Absicht, dem Feind zu helfen)*

treason[72] Landesverrat; Hochverrat *(Br Verletzung der Untertanentreue [breach of allegiance]; bes. gegen den Souverän gerichtete strafbare Handlung)*; ~ **felony** *Br*[73] gewisse leichtere Fälle von treason; ~ **trial** Landesverratsprozeß; Hochverratsprozeß; **high** ~ →treason; **misprision of** ~ Nichtanzeige (od. Unterlassung der Anzeige) e-s *(geplanten od. begangenen)* Hochverrats (od. Landesverrats); **to commit** ~ Landesverrat (od. Hochverrat) begehen

treasonable verräterisch; Landesverrats-; Hochverrats-

treasure Schatz; ~ **trove** Schatzfund *(betreffend Gold- od. Silberstücke in Münzen, Platten od. Barren; Br gehört der Krone; Am ist dem Fund gleichgestellt)*; **art** ~**s** Kunstschätze; **national** ~**s of artistic value** nationales Kulturgut von künstlerischem Wert

treasure up *v* (an)sammeln, horten

treasurer Schatzmeister; Kassenführer, Kassenwart *(e-s Vereins, Klubs etc)*; *Br* (Stadt-)Kämmerer; ~ **(of a corporation)** *Am* Leiter der Finanzabteilung *(e-r AG; vergleichbar mit dem deutschen kaufmännischen Vorstandsmitglied)*; **T~ of the Household** *Br* Finanzbeamter des Königl. Haushalts *(im Range nach dem Lord Steward)*; **T~ of the United States** *Am* Beamter des Finanzministeriums, der u.a. für die Verwaltung öffentl. Gelder verantwortlich zeichnet

Treasurership *Am* Gesamtheit der finanzwirtschaftlichen Aufgaben

treasury Schatzamt, Finanzministerium *(Br →Lord High Commissioners of the T~; Am →T~ Department)*; Staatskasse; Fiskus; ~ **authorities** Finanzbehörden; **T~ Bench** *Br parl* Regierungsbank

Treasury bills *(auf Diskontbasis angebotene)* (kurzfristige) Schatzwechsel *(Br die jeden Freitag im Submissionswege zugeteilt werden [s. market →~] und e-e Laufzeit normalerweise bis zu 3 Monaten haben; Am mit e-r Laufzeit von üblicherweise 3–6 Monaten)*; **market** ~ *Br* Schatzwechsel, deren Ausgabe wöchentlich auf abgegebene Angebote (tenders) erfolgt; **tap** ~ *Br* laufend ausgegebene Schatzwechsel *(→tap issue)*

Treasury Board *Br* cf. Lord High Commissioners of the →Treasury

Treasury, ~ **bonds** (Treas. Bds.) *Br* →~stock; *Am (langfristige verzinsl.)* Staatsschuldverschreibungen *(mit e-r Laufzeit von mehr als 5 Jahren)*; *Am (von der Gesellschaft zurückerworbene)* eigene Schuldverschreibungen; ~ **bond futures** auf →T~ bonds basierende Zinstermingeschäfte

Treasury certificate *Am (kurzfristiger, auf Couponbasis angebotener)* Schatzwechsel (Schatzanweisung) *(mit e-r Laufzeit bis zu 12 Monaten)*

Treasury consent *Br* Sondergenehmigung der Steuerverwaltung

Treasury Department *Am* (Bundes-)Finanzministerium; **Secretary of the** ~ *Am* (Bundes-)Finanzminister

treasury, T~ Directive *Br* Anweisung des Treasury an die Banken hinsichtl. des Umfanges der Bankdarlehen (bank advances); **T~ Exchange Stabilization Fund** *Am* Währungsausgleichsfonds; **T~ investment growth receipt** (TIGR) *Am (von e-m brokerage house verkauftes)* Recht auf ein US →Treasury bond *(→zerobonds)*; **T~ loan** *Br* Schatzanleihe; **T~ notes** *Br* →currency notes; *Am (mittelfristige)* Schatzwechsel (Schatzanweisungen) *(mit e-r Laufzeit von 1–5 Jahren)*; **T~ Regulations** (Treas. Reg.) *Am* Steuerrichtlinien; **T~ Secretary** *Am* Finanzminister; ~ **shares** eigene Aktien; **T~ Solicitor** *Br* Rechtsberater des Treasury und einiger anderer Ministerien *(meist ein barrister)*; ~ **stock** *Am (von der Aktiengesellschaft durch Kauf, Geschenk etc zurückerworbene)* eigene Aktien; *Br* gesamte Schatzanweisungsemission; **T~ warrant** *Br* Schatzanweisung; *Am* Zahlungsanweisung des Finanzministeriums (in ordinary bank check form)

Treasury, Department of the ~ →~ Department

Treasury, First Lord of the ~ *Br (nomineller)* Leiter des Treasury *(der Premierminister; Finanzminister ist der Chancellor of the Exchequer)*

Treasury, → **Lord High Commissioners of the** ~

treat *v* behandeln; handeln (of von); verhandeln (with mit); **to** ~ **to sth.** mit etw. bewirten; etw. zugute kommen lassen; **to** ~ **with sb.** mit jdm verhandeln; **invitation to** ~ *Br* Aufforderung zur Abgabe e-s Angebots; **notice to** ~ *Br* →notice 1.

treating *Br*[74] Bewirtung *(vor, während od. nach e-r Wahl; cf. corrupt practices)*

treatise Abhandlung; Lehrbuch; Monographie

treatment Behandlung; ~ **of aliens** (or **foreigners**) Ausländerbehandlung; **customs** ~ zollrechtliche Behandlung; **discriminative** ~ unterschiedliche Behandlung; **medical** ~ ärztliche Behandlung; **most-favo(u)red nation** ~ Meistbegünstigung; **national** ~ Inländerbehandlung *(→ national)*; **preferential** ~ Vorzugsbehandlung *(→ preferential)*

treaty[75] 1. *(VölkerR)* (Staats-)Vertrag; ~ **collection** Vertragssammlung; ~ **duties** Vertragszölle; ~ **duty** Vertragspflicht; ~ **investor** *Am*[75a] Kapitalanleger aus e-m Land, mit dem ein Staatsvertrag abgeschlossen wurde; **~-making power**[76] Berechtigung zum Abschluß von Staatsverträgen; **T~ of Accession** *(EG)* Beitrittsvertrag; ~ **of arbitration and conciliation** Schieds- und Schlichtungsvertrag; ~ **of commerce** Handelsvertrag; **T~ of Friendship, Commerce and Navigation** (FCN Treaty) *Am* Freundschafts-, Handels- und Schiffahrtsvertrag *(→ friendship)*; ~ **of guarantee** Garantievertrag; ~ **of limits** Grenzvertrag; **Treaties of Rome** Römische Verträge *(zur Gründung der ECC/EWG und EAEC/Euratom)*; ~ **powers** Vertragsmächte

treaty shopping Versuche von Steuerpflichtigen, Vorteile aus Doppelbesteuerungsabkommen *(→double taxation)* zu erlangen, die ihnen nicht zustehen; Steuergestaltungsmöglichkeiten

In der Literatur ist umstritten, ob treaty shopping als →tax avoidance oder →tax evasion einzustufen ist

treaty, ~ trade *Am*[76a] Geschäftsmann aus e-m Land, mit dem ein Staatsvertrag abgeschlossen wurde

treaty, bound by ~ vertraglich gebunden; **by virtue of a ~** kraft e-s Vertrages; **collective ~** Kollektivvertrag; **commercial ~** Handelsvertrag; **conclusion of a ~** Abschluß e-s Vertrages; **contractual ~** *(VölkerR)* rechtsgeschäftlicher Vertrag *(opp. law-making ~)*; **contrary to ~** vertragswidrig; **draft (of a) ~** Vertragsentwurf; **law(-)making ~** *(VölkerR)* rechtsetzender Vertrag, normativer Vertrag; **non-law(-)making** (or **ordinary**) **~** rechtsgeschäftlicher Vertrag; **Non-Proliferation T~** (NPT) Atomsperrvertrag; **peace ~** Friedensvertrag; **preliminary ~** Vorvertrag; **→self-executing ~**; **signatory to a ~** Unterzeichner e-s Vertrags; **Space T~** Weltraumvertrag; **state party to the ~** Vertragsstaat; **Test-Ban T~** Teststoppvertrag; **violation of a ~** Vertragsverletzung, Vertragsbruch; **to conclude a ~** e-n (Staats-)Vertrag abschließen; **to denounce a ~** e-n Vertrag kündigen (with 3 months' notice mit 3monatiger Frist); **to enter into a ~** e-n (Staats-)Vertrag abschließen; **to join a ~** e-m Vertrag beitreten; **to make a ~** e-n Vertrag abschließen; **to negotiate a ~** e-n Vertrag aushandeln; den Abschluß e-s Vertrages *(durch Verhandlung)* zustandebringen; **to sign a ~** e-n Vertrag unterzeichnen; **the ~ is terminated** der Vertrag ist abgelaufen

treaty 2. *(PrivatR)* Vorverhandlung *(über einen Vertrag od. ein sonstiges Rechtsgeschäft)*; Ausarbeitung des abzuschließenden Rechtsgeschäfts; *(auch)* Vertrag; Verhandlung, Abmachung *(zwischen Personen)*; **~ reinsurance** obligatorische Rückversicherung; **sale by private ~** *Br* freigestalteter Verkauf von Grundbesitz; **to be in ~ with sb.** mit jdm in Verhandlung stehen (for wegen); **to sell a house by private ~** *Br* ein Haus freihändig verkaufen

treble *v* (sich) verdreifachen

treble dreifach; **~ damages** *Am (über den tatsächl. Schaden hinausgehender)* Schadensersatz in dreifacher Höhe *(z.B. bei Verletzung der Antitrustgesetze; cf. Clayton Act, sec. 4)*

trend Trend; Richtung, Tendenz; **~ in** (or **of**) **prices** Preistendenz; Kurstendenz; **~ of business** Geschäftsgang; Konjunkturentwicklung; **~ reversal** Tendenzwende; **cyclical** (or **economic**) **~** Konjunkturentwicklung; **upward ~** steigende Tendenz; **the steady ~ was maintained on the share (stock) market** auf dem Aktienmarkt blieb die stabile Tendenz erhalten

trespass Besitzstörung; (bes.) unbefugtes Betreten *(e-s fremden Grundstücks)*; Hausfriedensbruch; Verletzung des Eigentums (od. der Rechte) *(e-r Person)*; **~ on the case** *Am (der action for ~ nachgebildete)* allgemeine Schadensersatzklage wegen rechtswidrig od. fahrlässig begangener Handlungen, durch die dem Kläger Schaden entstanden ist; **~ to chattels** →~ to goods; **~ to goods** Besitzstörung von Sachen *(e.g. damaging or destroying goods)*; **~ to land** unbefugtes Betreten fremden Grundbesitzes; Störung des Besitzes an Liegenschaften; **~ to the person** Verletzung (der Rechte) e-r Person *(assault, battery, false imprisonment)*; **action for ~**[77] Schadensersatzklage wegen Besitzstörung (od. Personen- od. Eigentumsverletzung); **criminal ~** *Am*[78] strafbares Eindringen; **to commit a ~** →trespass *v*

trespass *v* ("to pass beyond") Besitz stören; in jds Rechte (od. Eigentum) eingreifen; **to ~ on a p.'s land** (or **property**) jds Grundbesitz unbefugt betreten; **to ~ on a p.'s time** jds Zeit ungebührlich in Anspruch nehmen

trespasser Besitzstörer; Rechtsverletzer; jd, der unbefugt ein Grundstück betritt; **defiant ~** *Am (StrafR)*[78] mutwilliger Rechtsbrecher; **~s will be prosecuted** Betreten bei Strafe verboten

trespassing, No T~! Betreten verboten!

triable verhandelbar; *(StrafR)* verfolgbar; **crimes (not) ~ on indictment** →crime; **a ~ issue** e-e Tatfrage, über die durch →trial entschieden werden muß

trial 1. (Gerichts-)Verhandlung; (Gerichts-)Verfahren; Hauptverhandlung

trial, to appoint (or **assign**) **a day for ~** e-n Termin (für die Verhandlung) anberaumen; **to be on ~** vor Gericht stehen; unter Anklage stehen; **to bring sb. to ~** jdn vor Gericht bringen; **to commit for ~** →commit *v*; **to dispose of a case without ~** ein Verfahren ohne mündliche Verhandlung erledigen *(cf. settlement 2., compromise, Br default procedure, summary judgment, Am striking off a case, Br striking out an action)*; **to fix a day for ~** s. to appoint a day for →~; **to go on ~** vor Gericht kommen; **to proceed with the ~** die Verhandlung fortsetzen; **to put sb. on ~** s. to bring sb. to →~; **to stand ~** sich vor Gericht zu verantworten haben; unter Anklage stehen

trial, ~ at bar Verhandlung vor dem Gericht in vollständiger Besetzung; **~ brief** *Am* Verhandlungsschriftsatz *(des Anwalts)*; **~ by the country** *Am* Verhandlung mit Geschworenen (Schöffen) *(→jury)*; **~ by court-martial** Verhandlung vor e-m Kriegsgericht; **~ by jury** Schwurgerichtsverfahren; Verhandlung vor e-m Gericht mit Geschworenen (Schöffen); ~ **centres** *Br* Außenstellen des High Court; ~ **court** Prozeßgericht 1. Instanz; *(opp. appellate court)*; *Am (einzelstaatl.)* erstinstanzliches Gericht mit allgemeiner Zuständigkeit; ~ **date** Verhandlungstermin *(in Strafsachen)*; ~ →**docket;** ~ **in the absence of the defendant** Versäumnisverfahren *(bei Säumnis des Beklagten);* ~ **in camera** nicht öffentliche Verhandlung *(opp. ~ in open court);* ~ **judge** Richter der ersten Instanz; Hauptverhandlungsrichter; Tatrichter; ~ **jury** Geschworene (Schöffen) in e-m Prozeß; Urteilsjury *(→jury)*; ~ **lawyer** *Am* Prozeßanwalt *(der sich auf streitige Verfahren, bes. jury trials, spezialisiert hat);* ~ **list** *Am* Terminkalender *(des Gerichts)*; ~ **of an action** Verhandlung e-r Zivilsache; ~ **of a case** →~ of an action; ~ **of issue of facts** *(gesonderte)* Verhandlung über Tatfragen; Beweisaufnahme; ~ **on indictment** Hauptverhandlung mit →jury *(wegen e-s →indictable offence);* ~ **record** Beweisaufnahmeprotokoll

trial, adjournment of ~ Vertagung der Verhandlung; **civil** ~ Zivilverfahren; **committal for** ~ **(of)** Anklageerhebung (gegen); **criminal** ~ Strafverfahren; **date of** ~ Verhandlungstermin; **department** ~ *Am* Disziplinarverfahren gegen e-n Beamten; **mock** ~ Scheinprozeß

trial, new ~ *(Zivilprozeß)* Wiederaufnahmeverfahren; **application** (to the court of appeal) **for a new** ~ Antrag auf Wiederaufnahme des Verfahrens

trial, notice of ~ *Am* →notice 1.; **person detained for** ~ *Am* (or **prisoner awaiting** ~) Untersuchungsgefangener; →**pre-**~ **discovery; setting down for** ~ *Br* Terminanberaumung; **show** ~ Schauprozeß; **state** ~ politischer Prozeß; **summary** ~ Hauptverhandlung ohne →jury; **without** ~ s. to dispose of a case without →~

trial 2. Versuch, Probe; ~ **balance** (T. B.) Probebilanz; ~ **balance book** Zwischenbilanzbuch; ~ **buying** Testkauf; ~ **engagement** Anstellung auf Probe; ~ **flight** Probeflug; **T~ of the Pyx** *Br (jährliche)* Prüfung neu geprägter Münzen *(durch die jury of Goldsmiths' Company)*; ~ **offer** Werbeangebot; ~ **order** Probebestellung; ~ **period** Probezeit; ~ **rate** Werbepreis; ~ **trip** Probefahrt *(bes. e-s Schiffes)*; **by way of** ~ s. on →~

trial, on ~ auf (od. zur) Probe, **employment on** ~ Anstellung auf Probe; **goods sent on** ~ Probesendung; **a month on** ~ e-e Probezeit von einem Monat; **purchase on** ~ Kauf auf Probe

triangular, ~ **talk** *pol* Dreierbesprechung; ~ **trade** *com* Dreiecksverkehr *(zwischen drei Ländern)*; ~ **transaction** Dreiecksgeschäft

tribal law Stammesrecht

tribunal Gerichts(hof); Sondergericht; *Br* Tribunal *(das auf bestimmten Sachgebieten gerichtl. od. quasigerichtl. Funktionen ausübt)*; **Administrative T~** Verwaltungsgericht *(der Vereinten Nationen)*; **arbitration** ~ Schiedsgericht; **Copyright Royalty T~** *Am* Schiedsstelle für Urheberrechtsvergütungen; **Council on T~s** *Br*[79] Rat für Tribunale; →**Employment Appeal T~;** →**Industrial T~; Lands T~** *Br* Grundstücks-Tribunal *(entscheidet u.a. über die Entschädigungssumme bei Zwangsenteignung [compulsory purchase])*; **Pension Appeal T~** *Br* Pensions-Tribunal *(zuständig für von den Behörden abgewiesene Versorgungsansprüche)*; **Transport T~** *Br* Transport-Tribunal *(zuständig für Einsprüche gegen e-e Erhöhung der Tarife der Eisenbahn)*; **may it please the T~** „Hoher Gerichtshof"; **the Supreme Court is the highest** ~ **of the United States** der Supreme Court ist das oberste Gericht der Vereinigten Staaten; **to constitute** (or **establish**) **a** ~ ein Tribunal (od. ein Gericht) errichten

tribute *fig* Hochachtung, Anerkennung; **to pay** ~ **to sb.** Anerkennung (für jds Verdienste) aussprechen; jdm Anerkennung (für Verdienste) aussprechen; **the House paid** ~ **to X who died on ...** das Parlament gedachte ehrend des am ... verstorbenen X

trick Trick, Kunstgriff; **confidence** ~ Schwindeltrick

tried →try *v*

triennial dreijährlich; Dreijahres-

triers (or **triors**) *Br* vom Gericht zur Prüfung der Ablehnung von Geschworenen bestellte Personen

trigger action, a lower (upper) ~ **price**[79a] ein unterer (oberer) Auslösepreis

trigger rate (of interest) Auslösezinssatz

trillion *Br* Trillion, *Am* Billion

trim *v (Ladung im Schiffsraum)* trimmen; *auch fig* beschneiden, kürzen; *pol (zwischen den Parteien)* lavieren; **to** ~ **the budget funds** die Haushaltsmittel kürzen

Trinidad and Tobago, Republic of ~ Republik Trinidad und Tobago

Trinity House, Corporation of ~ *Br* Behörde zuständig für Navigationshilfe an den englischen Küsten *(Leuchttürme, Lotsen, Bojen etc)*

trip Fahrt, Reise; ~ **there and back** *Br* Hin- und Rückreise; **air** ~ Flug; **business** ~ Geschäftsreise; **pleasure** ~ Vergnügungsreise; **rail** (or **train**) ~ *Am colloq.* Bahnfahrt; **round** ~ Rundreise; *Am* Hin- und Rückfahrt

tripartite dreifach (ausgefertigt); *(VölkerR)* zwischen drei Mächten abgeschlossen; dreiseitig; ~ **agreement** Dreimächteabkommen, Dreierabkommen; ~ **indenture** Vertragsurkunde in dreifacher Ausfertigung; ~ **treaty** Dreimächtevertrag

triple dreifach; ~ **damages** dreifacher Schadensersatz

triplicate dreifach; in dreifacher Ausfertigung; dritte Ausfertigung; **bill of lading in** ~ Frachtbrief in drei Ausfertigungen; **drawn up in** ~ dreifach ausgefertigt

triptych[80] Triptyk, Zollpassierschein *(für zollfreien Grenzübertritt von Kraft- und Wasserfahrzeugen; cf. carnet de passage)*

trivial loss geringfügiger Schaden, Bagatellschaden

troop Truppe(n); ~**ship** *mil* Truppentransportschiff; ~ **strength** Truppenstärke; **dispatch of** ~**s** Entsendung von Truppen; **withdrawal of** ~**s** Truppenabzug

troop *v*, **to** ~ **the colour** *Br* die Fahnenparade abnehmen; ~**ing the colours** *Br* Fahnenparade *(am offiziellen Geburtstag der Königin)*

tropical countries, fit for service in ~ tropentauglich

tropical timber Tropenhölzer; →**International T~ T~ Organization** (ITO)

trouble Sorge, Ärger, Schwierigkeiten; *pol* Unruhe; ~**-maker** Unruhestifter; ~**-shooter** Schlichter *(bei Streitigkeiten; z.B. in der Industrie);* Krisenmanager; ~**spot** Krisenherd; **domestic** ~**s** häuslicher Unfrieden; **labo(u)r** ~**s** Arbeiterunruhen

trough Tief *(am Aktienmarkt)*

trover rechtswidrige Aneignung fremder beweglicher Sachen; **action of** ~ *ursprüngl. Klage auf Herausgabe des Wertes e-r rechtswidrig angeeigneten Sache; heute gleichbedeutend mit action of conversion* (→*conversion 2.*)

troy weight Troygewicht *(für feinere Wägungen, z.B. Gold, Silber, Juwelen und Chemikalien; 1 lb. = 12 oz. = 372,25 g)*

truce *(zeitweiliger)* Waffenstillstand; Waffenruhe; **expiration** (or **expiry**) **of** ~ Ablauf (od. Ende) des Waffenstillstandes; **flag of** ~ Parlamentärsfahne; **party** ~ →party 3.; **to make** ~ **with** Waffenstillstand schließen mit

truck 1. Tausch(handel); *Am* Produkte e-r Handelsgärtnerei; **T~ Acts** *Br*[81] Gesetze zur Abschaffung des →~ system; ~ **farming** Gemüseanbau für den Markt; ~ **gardener** *Am* Handelsgärtner, Gemüsegärtner; ~ **system** *hist* Trucksystem; System, nach dem Lohnzahlungen nicht in barem Geld erfolgten, sondern als Naturallohn *(in Waren des eigenen Unternehmens)*

truck 2. Lastkraftwagen (Lkw); *Br (offener)* Güterwagen, Waggon *(opp. van)*; ~ **driver** Lkw-Fahrer

truck load Lkw-Ladung; *Br* Waggonladung; **full** ~ ganze Waggonladung *(opp. part ~)*

truck, ~ **pool** Fuhrpark; ~ **requirement** *Br* Bedarf an Waggonraum; ~ **shop** *Am* Tankstelle *(mit Restauration)* für Lkw-Fahrer; ~ **trailer** Lkw-Anhänger; ~ **wholesaler** *Am* Großhändler, der kein Lager hat, sondern seine *(meist verderblichen)* Waren direkt an die Einzelhändler ausliefert; **free on** ~ (F. O. T., f. o. t.) frei Lkw; *Br* frei Waggon; **long distance** ~ *Am* Fernlaster; **motor** ~ *Am* Lastkraftwagen (Lkw); **motor** ~ **transport** *Am* Beförderung (od. Güterverkehr) mit Lastkraftwagen; **to ship by** ~ *Am* im Lkw befördern

truck *v* tauschen, Tauschhandel treiben; Lohn in Waren (od. Naturalien) zahlen (→*truck 1.*); mit Lastkraftwagen befördern; *Br* in Güterwagen befördern (od. verladen); *Am* Lkw-Fahrer sein

trucking *Am* Güterkraftverkehr; Straßengüterverkehr; ~ **company** (or **firm**) *Am* Güterkraftverkehrsunternehmen

truckage Tausch(handel); Beförderung durch Lkw; Beförderungskosten

true wahr, wahrheitsgetreu; ~ **and fair view** → view 1.; ~ **bill** →bill 2.

true copy gleichlautende *(mit dem Original übereinstimmende)* Abschrift; **I certify that this is a** ~ die Richtigkeit dieser Abschrift wird bescheinigt

true, ~ **heir** rechtmäßiger Erbe; ~ **lease** *Am* steuerbegünstigtes Leasing *(der Leasinggeber ist Eigentümer);* ~→**owner;** ~ **report** wahrheitsgetreuer Bericht; ~ **weight** genaues Gewicht; **to prove (to be)** ~ sich als wahr erweisen

truly, *Br* **yours (very)** ~ (*Am* **very** ~ **yours**) *(formeller Briefschluß)* hochachtungsvoll; Ihr sehr ergebener

truncheon (Polizei-)Gummiknüppel, Schlagstock

trunk Hauptlinie *(e-r Eisenbahn, e-s Kanals etc)*; ~**-line** *(Eisenbahn)* Hauptstrecke; *tel* Fernleitung; ~**-road** Fernverkehrsstraße *(die große Städte verbindet)*; ~**-traffic** Fernverkehr

trust 1. Treuhandverhältnis; ~**(s)** Treuhandvermögen (→*settlor,* →*trustee,* →*beneficiary*)

Ein trust ist eine auf →equity beruhende Rechtsbeziehung zwischen dem Treuhänder (trustee) und dem Begünstigten (beneficiary; früher cestui que trust) (auf beiden Seiten kann e-e Mehrheit von Personen auftreten), durch die das von dem Besteller des trust (settlor od. *Am* trustor) auf den Treuhänder zugunsten des Begünstigten übertragene Vermögen von diesem verwaltet wird. Während der Begünstigte der equitable →owner des Treuhandgutes ist, wird der Treuhänder der legal →owner. Der settlor und der

trustee können identisch sein (wenn sich der settlor im trust agreement selbst zum trustee ernennt). Ein trust wird entweder durch Rechtsgeschäft begründet oder entsteht kraft Gesetzes *(cf. implied trust)*.
Der trust ist eines der bedeutendsten Rechtsinstitute des englischen und amerikanischen Rechts, das in fast jedem Rechtsgebiet vorkommt. So wird es z. B. im Vormundschaftsrecht verwandt (der guardian ist trustee für den ward); der Erbschaftsverwalter (personal representative) ist rechtlich ein trustee; der Konkursverwalter (trustee in bankruptcy) hat die Konkursmasse zugunsten der Gläubiger in Eigentum; das Vermögen von Vereinen ohne Rechtspersönlichkeit, bes. der unzähligen Klubs, Kirchen und Gewerkschaften wird üblicherweise von trustees verwaltet. Gegenstand des trust kann grundsätzlich jedes Vermögensrecht sein (Grundstück, Aktien, Hypothek, Bankkonto, Patent, Urheberrecht etc). Der trust ist die häufigste Form der Vermögensbindung über den Tod hinaus. Durch die Errichtung eines trust sind die Interessen des Begünstigten in mehrfacher Beziehung gewahrt. Er kann z. B. das →tracing gegenüber dem trustee od. Dritten geltend machen. Der Treuhänder haftet persönlich wegen Treubruchs (breach of trust)

trust, to constitute (or **create, declare, establish**) **a** ~ ein Treuhandverhältnis begründen; e-n Trust errichten; **he created ~s by will in favo(u)r of his children** er hinterließ Vermögen an Treuhänder zur Verwaltung für seine Kinder *(übliche Form e-s Vermächtnisses an minderjährige Nachkommen)*; **~s can be created by will or by deed** ein Treuhandverhältnis kann durch Testament oder Schenkungsurkunde begründet werden; **to hold in** ~ als Treuhänder (od. treuhänderisch) verwalten; **to resign from the** ~ als Treuhänder zurücktreten; **to transfer property into** ~ Vermögensgegenstände auf den Trust übertragen

trust agreement 1. Treuhandvertrag; 2. *Am*[82] Vertrag, der ein besitzloses Sicherungsrecht an Fahrnis (security interest) schafft

trust assets Treuhandvermögen

trust certificate *Am* 1. →equipment ~; 2. shares ~ (→*share 1.*)

trust company *Br* Investmentgesellschaft; *Am* Treuhandgesellschaft, Treuhandbank *(die Vermögen ihrer Auftraggeber verwaltet)*

trust corporation *Br*[83] öffentliche Treuhandstelle

Trust corporation ist der Public →Trustee od. e-e juristische Person (corporation), die entweder für einen besonderen Fall als Treuhänder gerichtlich ernannt ist od. die kraft Gesetzes[84] berechtigt ist, als custodian trustee tätig zu werden (z. B. e-e Gesellschaft nach dem Companies Act, 1948). Nach dem Law of Property (Amendment) Act, 1926, s. 3, schließt der Begriff "trust corporation" ein: den Treasury Solicitor, den Official Solicitor, Konkursverwalter (trustees in bankruptcy) und bestimmte juristische Personen, die gemeinnützige, kirchliche od. öffentl. trusts verwalten

trust, ~ **deed** (Urkunde über) Errichtung e-s Treuhandverhältnisses; Vertrag zur Trusterrichtung; (Urkunde über) Übereignung von Vermögen an e-n Treuhänder zur Sicherung (e-r Vielzahl) von Gläubigern *(z. B. aus Schuldverschreibungen)*; ~ **deed mortgage** *Am* →deed of trust; ~ **department** *Am* Treuhandabteilung *(e-r Bank)*; ~ **estate** →~ property

trust for sale *Br*[85] unmittelbar bindender Trust zum Verkauf *(bes. von Grundbesitz; meist nicht auf alsbaldigen Verkauf ausgerichtet)*

Ein trust for sale entsteht in gewissen Fällen kraft Gesetzes, z. B. Law of Property Act 1925, s. 36 (1) betr. gemeinsamen Grundbesitz, Administration of Estates Act 1925, s. 33 (1) betr. gesetzliche Erbfolge

trust fund(s) Treuhandfonds; treuhänderisch verwaltetes Vermögen *(Geld, Wertpapiere od. Mündelgelder)*; **personal** ~ *Am* bankverwaltetes Privatvermögen

trust in favo(u)r of a charity Schenkung (od. Vermächtnis) zu treuen Händen für wohltätige Zwecke; *(etwa)* wohltätige Stiftung

trust income Einkommen aus Treuhandvermögen; **owner of the** ~ Bezieher des Treuhandeinkommens

trust, ~ **indenture** Treuhandvertrag; *Am*[86] Vertrag zwischen e-r Aktiengesellschaft, die Obligationen ausgegeben hat, und e-r Bank, die als Treuhänder für die Obligationsbesitzer fungiert; Trusturkunde, Treuhandurkunde; ~ **instrument** *Br*[87] Urkunde, durch die *(mit dem →vesting deed)* ein trust über →settled land begründet wird; ~ **inter vivos** *Am* s. inter vivos →~; ~ **investment** *Am* mündelsichere Kapitalanlage; ~ **letter** *Br* →letter of ~ (→*letter 2.*); ~ **money** treuhänderisch verwaltetes Geld; ~ **money (for ward)** Mündelgeld; ~ **officer** *Am* Mitglied (od. Angestellter) der Treuhandabteilung e-r Bank; ~ **property** Treuhandvermögen, Trustvermögen; fiduziarisches Eigentum; ~ **purpose** Trustzweck

trust receipt *Am* Treuhandquittung

Besitzloses Sicherungsrecht an bewegl. Sachen (od. Fahrnis) *(neben Mobiliarhypothek, Eigentumsvorbehalt und factor's lien)*. Beim trust-receipt-Geschäft für den Warenkauf stellt der Käufer als Sicherungsgeber dem Sicherungsnehmer, der die Kaufpreisforderung finanziert, ein trust receipt aus, welches ein Sicherungsrecht an den gelieferten Waren bzw. den Traditionspapieren zugunsten des Sicherungsnehmers begründet. Die trust receipt-Sicherung hat sich im amerikanischen Importhandel entwickelt und zwar als Sicherungsmittel bei der Drittfinanzierung des Kaufpreises, wurde dann aber auch in erheblichem Umfange im Binnenhandel, insbes. im Kraftfahrzeug-Großhandel benutzt.
Eine einheitliche Regelung der trust receipt-Finanzierung fand sich zuerst im Uniform Trust Receipts Act (U. T. R. A.) von 1933. Dieser ist überholt durch Art. 9 des →UCC, welcher alle besitzlosen Sicherungsrechte an bewegl. Sachen mit dem Sammelnamen "security interest" bezeichnet und das trust receipt durch das "trust agreement" ersetzt

trust, ~ stock *Am colloq.* mündelsichere Wertpapiere; **~ territory** *Am (VölkerR)* Treuhandgebiet *(cf. trusteeship system)*; **~ transaction** Treuhandgeschäft

trust, bare ~ s. simple →~; →**Brain T~; breach of** ~ Verletzung der Pflichten als Treuhänder; **business** ~ *Am* →Massachusetts ~; **charitable** ~ gemeinnütziger Trust *(zur Förderung gemeinnütziger [od. wohltätiger] Zwecke errichteter Trust; entspricht der wohltätigen Stiftung des deutschen Rechts)*; →**collateral ~ bonds (certificates); community** ~ *Am* →community 1.

trust, constructive ~ fingierter Trust *(auf Grund e-r construction of equity; opp. express ~)*

Der constructive trust wird entgegen dem Parteiwillen vom Richter dann auferlegt, wenn das Eigentumsrecht (title) zugunsten einer Person besteht, der es nach Billigkeit (equity) nicht zustehen dürfte. Eine solche Person wird kraft Fiktion wie ein trustee behandelt. Auf diese Weise können z. B. die Folgen der ungerechtfertigten Bereicherung aus fiduziarischen Rechtsverhältnissen od. aus betrügerischem Verhalten e-r Vertrauensperson verhindert werden. – Constructive trust im weiteren Sinne wird auch anstelle von implied trust gebraucht. Anwendungsbereich des ~ im amerikanischen Recht weiter als im englischen Recht

trust, contingent ~ bedingtes Treuhandverhältnis; **court** ~ *Am* Treuhandgut, das auf Grund e-r gerichtl. Entscheidung von e-r Treuhandgesellschaft verwaltet wird; **declaration of** ~ Trust-Errichtung durch Erklärung *(wodurch sich ein Vermögensinhaber selbst zum trustee seines Vermögens erklärt)*; **deed of** ~→deed; **directory** ~ Treuhandverwaltung nach Anweisung *(ohne eigenes Ermessen)*

trust, discretionary ~ ins Ermessen des trustee gestellter Trust

Trust, bei dem dem trustee auferlegt wird, das Treuhandvermögen (bes. das Einkommen) nach freiem Ermessen unter eine festgelegte Gruppe (z. B. Kinder od. Nachkommen des settlor) zu verteilen. Discretionary trusts sind beliebt wegen der Möglichkeit der Erlangung von Steuervorteilen

trust, →**equipment** ~; **executed** ~ genau festgelegtes Treuhandverhältnis; ausgeführtes Treuhandverhältnis; **execution of a** ~ Erfüllung des Zweckes e-s trust (und damit Auflösung); **executory** ~ später noch festzulegendes Treuhandverhältnis; **express** ~ ausdrücklich *(durch Vertrag, letztwillige Verfügung etc, also rechtsgeschäftl.)* geschaffenes Treuhandverhältnis *(opp. ~ arising by operation of law, e.g. implied ~)*; **family** ~ Familienstiftung;→**fixed** ~; →**flexible** ~; **grantor of a** ~ *Am* Stifter (od. Besteller) e-s Treuhandverhältnisses; **imperfect** ~ s. executory →~

trust, implied ~ (als beabsichtigt) vermutetes Treuhandverhältnis; *(constructive trust oder resulting trust; opp. express ~)*

Der implied trust, ein kraft Gesetzes fingierter Trust, ist ein sich (stillschweigend) aus den Handlungen einer Partei od. aus dem Charakter einer Urkunde ergebender trust

trust, in ~ in treuhänderischer Verwaltung; **in ~ for** zu treuen Händen für, als Treuhänder für *(vgl. z.B. Kommentar zu →savings bank trust)*; **property held in** ~ Vermögen in treuhänderischer Verwaltung; **I hold this property in ~ for my nephew** ich verwalte dieses Vermögen als Treuhänder für meinen Neffen

trust, industrial ~ *Am* Finanzierungsgesellschaft für Industriebedarf; **inter vivos** (or **living**) ~ Trust zu Lebzeiten des Verfügenden (settlor) *(opp. testamentary ~)*

trust, investment ~ Investmentfonds, Kapitalanlagegesellschaft *(→investment)*; **investment ~ manager** Fondsverwalter

Nach englischem und amerikanischen Recht wird das Investmentgeschäft in Trustform durchgeführt *(cf. fixed trust, management trust, unit trust)*. Der Investmenttrust ist eine Vereinbarung zwischen einer kleinen Personenzahl (trustees) und einer verhältnismäßig großen und fluktuierenden Zahl von Personen (gewöhnlich subscribers genannt oder certificate holders etc)

trust, irrevocable ~ unwiderruflicher Trust *(der vom settlor nicht mehr abgeändert werden kann)*; **land** ~ *Am* Grundbesitz-Trust; **letter of** ~ *Br* →letter 2.; →**Massachusetts** ~; →**National T~; overriding** ~ Trust, der e-m früher begründeten Trust vorgeht; **passive** ~ Trust, in dem der trustee keine aktiven Pflichten zu erfüllen hat; **perfect** ~ s. executed →~; **presumptive** ~ s. implied →~

trust, private (express) ~ *(durch Parteiakt ausdrückl. geschaffener)* privater Trust *(bei dem die Begünstigten individuell bezeichnet sind; opp. public ~)*; Familienstiftung

Der private trust schließt jede fiduziarische Tätigkeit ein, wie die e-s administrator, executor, guardian, committee, assignee etc

trust, property held in (or **on**) ~ Treuhandgut; →**protective** ~

trust, public (express) ~ öffentlicher Trust *(im Interesse der Allgemeinheit; opp. private ~)*

Der public trust, z. B. der charitable trust, ist meist steuerrechtlich begünstigt

trust, resulting ~ *(kraft Gesetzes)* an den ursprünglichen Eigentümer zurückfallender Trust

Ein →implied trust, bei dem das →beneficial interest an dem Vermögen an die Person, die es an den trustee übertrug oder die Mittel dazu verschaffte, oder an ihre Vertreter, zurückfällt (results); z. B. wenn ein ausdrücklicher Trust aus irgendwelchen Gründen nicht wirksam entstehen konnte (wenn z. B. der Begünstigte zur Zeit des Inkrafttretens der Trusturkunde nicht mehr am Leben war)

trust, revocable ~ widerrufbarer Trust *(der vom settlor abgeändert werden kann; ähnelt dem deutschen Treuhandverhältnis)*; → **savings bank** ~; **secret** ~ geheimer Trust *(→secret)*; **shares ~ certificates** *Am* übertragbare Anteilscheine e-s

→Massachusetts trust; **simple** ~ *Am* einfacher Trust *(der dem Begünstigten keine Verwaltungspflichten auferlegt und dessen gesamtes Einkommen laufend an den Begünstigten ausgeschüttet werden muß)*; **special** ~ Trust, der dem Begünstigten bestimmte Pflichten auferlegt; **spendthrift** ~ *Am* Verschwendertrust (→*spendthrift)*

trust, statutory ~ *Br* gesetzlich begründeter Trust

Hierunter fallen bes. 1. der → trust for sale; 2. der trust zugunsten des Erben bei gesetzl. Erbfolge[88]. Er bewirkt u. a., daß minderjährige Erben ihren Anteil erst nach Vollendung des 18. Lebensjahres oder nach Eheschließung erhalten

trust, subject matter of the ~ Treuhandvermögen, Treugut; **terms of the** ~ Bedingungen des Treuhandverhältnisses; **testamentary** ~ *Am* Trust durch Verfügung von Todes wegen *(der erst mit dem Tode des settlor wirksam wird; opp. inter vivos ~)*; **upon** ~ **(to)** (or **upon the following** ~**s**) *(in e-m Testament)* um wie folgt darüber zu verfügen *(cf. I give all my property to my →trustee upon the following ~s)*; **voluntary** ~ *Am* rechtsgeschäftlich errichteter Trust *(opp. implied or constructive ~)*; →**voting** ~

trust 2. *com* Trust; ~ **busting** *Am* Zerschlagung e-s trust *(nach den antitrust laws)*

Sonderform des Konzerns, bei der e-e Verwaltungsgesellschaft (Holdinggesellschaft) die Aktien der zusammengefaßten Unternehmen im Austausch gegen ihre eigenen Anteile erwirbt.

Im Sprachgebrauch wird jedoch vielfach jeder mächtige Konzern od. auch eine aus der Fusion aus mehreren Gesellschaften hervorgegangene Einzelunternehmung als trust bezeichnet.

In den Vereinigten Staaten wurde durch die Antitrustgesetzgebung (→*antitrust law)*, bes. den →Sherman Act, versucht, die Trustbildung zu hindern

trust 3. Vertrauen (in auf); Zutrauen (in zu); ~ **card** *Br* Kreditkarte; → **breach of** ~

trust, in ~ zu treuen Händen; **money in** ~ anvertrautes Geld

trust, on ~ ohne Nachprüfung (od. Beweis); *com* auf Kredit; **to buy goods on** ~ Waren auf Kredit kaufen; **to take a statement on** ~ e-r Behauptung ohne Beweis glauben

trust, position of ~ Vertrauensstellung; verantwortungsvolle Stellung; **to place** (or **put**) ~ **in** Vertrauen setzen auf

trust *v* vertrauen (sb. jdm); vertrauen (od. sich verlassen) (in or to auf); **to** ~ **sb. with money** jdm Geld anvertrauen

trustee[89] Treuhänder; Fiduziar; Vermögens-Verwalter, Beauftragter, Betrauter *(der im Vertrauensverhältnis [in a fiduciary relation] zu jdm steht, z.B. attorney, bailee etc)*; *Am (beim trust receipt)* Sicherungsnehmer *(opp. entruster)*

Trustee im engeren Sinne ist eine natürl. od. juristische Person, die in eigenem Namen für den (od. die) Begünstigten Vermögen treuhänderisch verwaltet (holds in trust), an dem ihm der legal title, dem beneficiary der equitable title zusteht *(cf. trust 1.)*

trustee in bankruptcy Konkursverwalter *(Br*[90] *auf der ersten Gläubigerversammlung statt des →official receiver ernannter außeramtl. Konkursverwalter); Am (vom Konkursgericht bestellter)* Treuhänder in e-m Reorganisationsverfahren

Der Konkursverwalter ist Treuhänder und hat die Konkursmasse als Treuhandgut zugunsten der Gläubiger in Eigentum

trustee, ~**'s certificate** *Br* Verwahrungsschein, Hinterlegungsschein; ~ **de son tort** jd, der sich unrechtmäßig in die Abwicklung e-s Nachlasses einmischt *(und sich dadurch gegenüber dem rechtmäßigen executor od. administrator und Erben und Gläubiger des Erblassers haftbar macht; → executor de son tort)*; ~ **of an estate** Nachlaßverwalter; ~**'s indemnity** Recht des Treuhänders auf Entschädigungsbetrag für Aufwendungen aus dem Treuhandvermögen; ~ **investment** *Br*[91] mündelsichere Kapitalanlage; ~ **process** *Am (in einigen Staaten)* (Forderungs-)Pfändungsbeschluß; Zahlungsverbot an den Drittschuldner; **T**~ →**Savings Bank;** ~ **security** (or **stock**) mündelsicheres Wertpapier; **appointment of a** ~ Einsetzung (od. Ernennung) e-s Treuhänders; **board of** ~**s** Treuhänderausschuß; Kuratorium; **co-**~ Mittreuhänder; **custodian** ~ Treuhänder, dessen Aufgabe nur in der Verwahrung des Treuhandvermögens besteht *(cf. managing ~)*; **discharge of a** ~ Entlastung e-s Treuhänders; **judicial** ~[92] gerichtlicher Treuhänder, amtlicher Treuhänder; **managing** ~ Treuhänder, dessen Aufgabe nur in der Verwaltung des Treuhandvermögens besteht *(das vom custodian ~ verwahrt wird)*; **private** ~ durch Privatperson ernannter Treuhänder; **Public T**~ *Br*[93] staatl. Treuhandstelle, öffentl. Treuhänder *(Staatsbeamter, der auftritt, wo ein anderer Treuhänder fehlt, und der gegen geringes Entgelt meist kleinere Vermögen verwaltet)*; **resignation of a** ~ *(freiwilliger)* Rücktritt e-s Treuhänders; **testamentary** ~ *Am* durch Testament eingesetzter Treuhänder; **under** ~ treuhänderisch verwaltet

trustee, to act as ~ als Treuhänder tätig sein; **to appoint a** ~ e-n Treuhänder ernennen; **I give all my property to my** ~ **upon the following trusts** ich gebe mein ganzes Vermögen meinem Treuhänder, der darüber wie folgt verfügen soll; **to remove a** ~ e-n Treuhänder entlassen (od. abberufen)

trusteeship Amt e-s →trustee; Treuhandverwaltung; Kuratorium; Treuhand-; *(VölkerR)* Treuhandverwaltung *(durch die Vereinten Nationen)*; ~ **agreement** *(VölkerR)*[94] Treuhandabkommen; **T**~ **Council**[95] Treuhandrat *(cf. United Nations)*; ~ **system**[96] *(VölkerR)* Treuhandsystem; ~ **territories** *(VölkerR)* Treuhandgebiete *(ehemalige Mandate des Völkerbundes, die in das Treuhandsystem der Vereinten Nationen überführt sind)*; **territories administered under the ~ system** Gebiete, die treuhänderisch verwaltet werden

truster *Scot* jd, der Vermögensgegenstände auf den Trust überträgt

trustor *Am* Begründer e-s trust, Treugeber (→*settlor*)

trustworthiness Vertrauenswürdigkeit; Glaubwürdigkeit

trustworthy vertrauenswürdig; glaubwürdig

truth Wahrheit; **~ in advertising** Wahrheit in der Werbung
truth in lending *Am* Wahrheit bei Kreditgeschäften *(durch ordnungsmäßige Angaben [Zinshöhe etc.] des Kreditgebers)*; **T~-in-Lending Act** *Am (bundesrechtl.)* Gesetz zum Schutz von Kreditnehmern (einschließlich Abzahlungsgeschäften)
truth of a statement Richtigkeit e-r Aussage; **to swear or affirm the ~** die Wahrheit (od. Richtigkeit) e-r Aussage beschwören od. bekräftigen; **to prove the ~ of one's statement** den Wahrheitsbeweis erbringen *(z.B. in Beleidigungsklagen)*
truth, contrary to the ~ wahrheitswidrig; **defense of ~** *Am* →defense 1.; **the plain ~** die reine Wahrheit; **to admonish to tell the ~** zur Wahrheit ermahnen; **to ascertain the ~** die Wahrheit ermitteln; **to suppress the ~** die Wahrheit verheimlichen; **I swear before Almighty God that the evidence I shall give shall be the ~, the whole ~ and nothing but the ~** *Br (Voreid) (etwa)* ich schwöre bei Gott dem Allmächtigen, daß ich die reine Wahrheit sagen und nichts verschweigen werde

tr|y *v* versuchen; erproben; *(gerichtl.)* untersuchen, verhandeln, verhören; **to ~ a case** über e-e Zivil- od. Strafsache gerichtl. verhandeln; **to re~** erneut verhandeln; **he was tried for murder** er wurde wegen Mordes vor Gericht gestellt

tub *Br* Tub, Faß *(Gewichtsmaß für Butter: 38,102 kg; für Tee: 27,216 kg)*

tube *Br* Untergrundbahn

tug (-boat) Schlepper, Schleppdampfer

tuition fee Studiengebühr; **~ waiver** Studiengebührenerlaß

tumble *v (von Preisen, Kursen)* fallen, stürzen (to auf)

tumble-down baufällig

Tunisia Tunesien; **Republic of ~** Tunesische Republik

Tunisian Tunesier, ~in; tunesisch

turbary, (common of) ~ Recht, Torf abzustechen; Torfgerechtigkeit

Turk Türke, Türkin
Turkey Türkei; **Republic of ~** Republik Türkei
Turkish türkisch

turmoil Tumult, Aufruhr; **political ~** politische Unruhen

turn 1. Wendung, Wende; Veränderung, Umschwung; Reihenfolge, Turnus; (Arbeits-) Schicht; Provision e-s Wertpapierhändlers; Handelsgewinn; *Am (auch)* Umsatz; **~ for the better** Wendung zum Besseren; **~ for the worse** Wendung zum Schlechteren; **~ in the market** Umschwung am Markt; **~ of the year** Jahreswende; Jahreswechsel; **bank's ~** Gewinn e-r Bank durch die Zinsspanne; **by ~s** nacheinander, abwechselnd; **for a ~** kurzfristig angelegt *(Effekten)*; als kurzfristige Effektenanlage *(in Erwartung e-s baldigen Kursgewinns)*; **in ~** der Reihe nach; **jobber's ~** *Br* Kursgewinn des Effektenhändlers; **out of ~** außer der Reihe; **to take ~s** (at sth.) sich miteinander abwechseln (bei); **to take one's ~** an die Reihe kommen
turn 2. Richtungsänderung; (Straßen- etc) Biegung; **~ left signal** Linksabbiegerzeichen; **~off** (Straßen-)Abzweigung; **no left (right) ~** Links-(Rechts-)abbiegen verboten!

turnabout Kehrtwendung; *pol* (völliger) Kurswechsel

turnaround Tendenzumschwung, Wende

turncoat Abtrünniger, Überläufer *(jd, der s-e Partei od. s-e Grundsätze aufgibt)*

turning →turn *v*

turnkey schlüsselfertig; **~ contract** Bauvertrag, der die schlüsselfertige Übergabe des Gebäudes vorsieht; **~ project** schlüsselfertiges Projekt

turn(-)out Ausstattung; (Gesamt-)Produktion, Ertrag; Leerung, Räumung; Teilnahme, Besucherzahl; **~ (at the election)** Wahlbeteiligung; **there was a good ~ for his speech** sein Vortrag war gut besucht

turnover (Geschäfts-)Umsatz; (Lager-)Umschlag; **~ figures** Umsatzzahlen; **~ commission** Umsatzprovision; **~ of capital** Umschlag des Kapitals; **~ order** *Am*[97] *(KonkursR)* Anordnung e-s amerikanischen Konkursgerichts, das in den USA belegene Vermögen des Gemeinschuldners an den ausländischen Konkursverwalter zur Verteilung im Auslandsverfahren abzuführen; **~ rate** Umschlaggeschwindigkeit; Umsatzhäufigkeit; **~ in stock** Lagerumschlag; **~ tax** *Am* Umsatzsteuer; **ac-**

tive ~ reger Umsatz; **annual** ~ Jahresumsatz; **average** ~ durchschnittlicher Umsatz; **capital** ~ Kapitalumschlag; **goods** ~ Güterumschlag; **finished goods** ~ Umschlaggeschwindigkeit des Warenbestandes; **gross** ~ Bruttoumsatz; **inventory** ~ Lagerumschlag; **labo(u)r** ~→labo(u)r 2.; **large** ~ großer Umsatz; **merchandise** ~ Warenumsatz; **minimum** ~ Mindestumsatz; **rate of** →~ rate; **raw material** ~ Umschlaggeschwindigkeit des Rohstoffbestandes; **stock** ~ Lagerumschlag; **to do a large** ~ e-n großen Umsatz erzielen; **there was a small** ~ es wurde wenig umgesetzt

turnpike *Am* gebührenpflichtige Autobahn; Schranke, an der die Gebühr erhoben wird

turn *v* drehen, wenden; verändern; Richtung nehmen; **to ~ sth. to account** etw. verwerten; sich etw. zunutze machen; **to ~ left (right)** links (rechts) abbiegen; **to ~ a partnership into a company** *Br* e-e Personengesellschaft in e-e Kapitalgesellschaft umwandeln; **to ~ to profit** →to ~ to account; **to ~ the tables** die Lage zum Gegenteil verändern

turn *v*, **to ~ a p. back at the border** jdn an der Grenze zurückweisen (od. zur Rückkehr veranlassen); **to ~ down a proposal** e-n Vorschlag zurückweisen; **to ~ sb. in** (to the police) *colloq.* jdn der Polizei übergeben; **to ~ into money** zu Gelde machen; **to ~ off** *(Verkehr)* abbiegen; *(Gas, Licht, Radio etc)* abstellen; **to ~ on sth.** abhängen von etw.; **to ~ sth. on** *(Gas, Licht, Radio etc)* anstellen; **to ~ out** *(Waren)* herstellen, produzieren; ausräumen, leeren; *(jdn)* hinauswerfen; **to ~ out (to be)** sich erweisen (als); sich herausstellen (als); **to ~ out well** e-n guten Ausgang nehmen; **to ~ over** *(Waren)* umsetzen; **to ~ over per annum** e-n Jahresumsatz haben (von)

turning, ~ to account (or **profit**) Verwertung; ~ **point** Wendepunkt; **second ~ to the left** zweite Abbiegung links

turpitude, conduct involving moral ~ moralisch verwerfliches Verhalten

tutelage Vormundschaft; Pflegschaft (→ *guardianship*); **to place** (or **put**) **a p. under** ~ jdn unter Vormundschaft stellen; jdn entmündigen

tutor Privatlehrer, Hauslehrer; *Scot* Vormund *(e-s Minderjährigen)*; *Br univ* Studienleiter; *Am univ* Assistent, Lektor; **~-dative** *Scot* durch Gericht ernannter Vormund; **~-nominate** *Scot* von den Eltern ernannter Vormund

tutor *v* Privatunterricht geben

TV-advertising Fernsehwerbung (→*television)*

twice, the magazine appears ~ a month (or ~ **monthly**) die Zeitschrift erscheint zweimal monatlich

twin, ~ ship Schwesternschiff; ~ **towns** Partnerstädte

twinning, (town-)~ Gründung von Partnerschaften zwischen Städten

twist *v (Sinn)* verdrehen, entstellen; **to ~ the law** das Recht verdrehen; **to ~ the truth** die Wahrheit entstellen; **~ing** *Am* Überreden e-s Versicherungsnehmers, e-e Versicherung fallen zu lassen und dafür e-e andere abzuschließen

two, ~ career family Familie, in der beide Partner berufstätig sind; **~-dollar broker** *Am* Börsenmakler, der Geschäfte für e-n anderen Makler vornimmt; **~-job man** *Am* Doppelverdiener; **~-party system** Zweiparteiensystem; ~ **sides of industry** Sozialpartner; **~-thirds majority** Zweidrittelmehrheit; **~-tier gold price** gespaltener (od. zweigeteilter) Goldpreis; **~-tier offer** *(bei Fusion) Am* zweigeteiltes Übernahmeangebot e-s Unternehmers, der e-n günstigen Kurspreis für e-e Mehrheitsbeteiligung, aber nur e-n geringeren Preis für den Rest bezahlt

tycoon *colloq.* mächtiger Industrieller, Großindustrieller; Wirtschaftskapitän

tying, ~ agreement →~ contract; ~ **arrangement** Kopplungsvereinbarung; ~ **clause** *Am (AntitrustR)* Kopplungsklausel (fällt unter die →*per se violations)*; ~ **contract** *Am*[98] *(AntitrustR)* Kopplungsvertrag *(der den Abnehmer e-r Ware verpflichtet, auch Waren anderer Art vom Lieferer der Hauptwaren zu beziehen)*; ~ **product** *Am* Kopplungsprodukt, die Kopplung ermöglichendes Erzeugnis; ~ **sale** *Am* Kopplungsverkauf; ~ **up of capital** Festlegung von Kapital

type Art, Typ; Muster; Type, (gedruckter) Buchstabe

type-approval Typengenehmigung, Bauartgenehmigung; ~ **of motor vehicles** *(EG)* Betriebserlaubnis für Kraftfahrzeuge

type, ~ faces[99] typographische Schriftzeichen; ~ **of construction** Bauart; ~ **of enterprise** Unternehmensform; ~ **of risk** *(VersR)* Risikoart; **~script** Schriftstück in Maschinenschrift; **to determine the** ~ typisieren, typen

type *v* mit der Maschine schreiben, *com* typisieren, typen

typed letter maschinengeschriebener Brief

typing Maschineschreiben; *com* Typung, Typisierung; ~ **error** Tippfehler; ~ **pool** Schreibsaal

typewrite *v* auf der Maschine schreiben; tippen

typewriting Maschineschreiben, Tippen

typewritten mit der Maschine geschrieben

typewriter Schreibmaschine; **portable** ~ Reiseschreibmaschine

typical typisch, charakteristisch (of für)

typify *v com* typisieren

typist Maschinenschreiber(in); Schreibkraft; **shorthand** ~ Stenotypistin

typographer (Schrift-)Setzer

typographical mistake (or **error**) typographischer Fehler

tythe *Br* →tithe

U

uberrima fides ("utmost good faith") Höchstmaß an Treu und Glauben; Gebot gesteigerter Ehrlichkeit, Offenheit und Offenbarung

uberrimae fidei, contract ~ vom Gebot gegenseitiger, uneingeschränkter Ehrlichkeit, Offenheit und Offenbarung beherrschter Vertrag

Verstoß führt zur Vernichtung des Vertrages. Beispiel: Lebensversicherungsvertrag mit seinen weitreichenden (vor)vertraglichen Aufklärungspflichten des Versicherungsnehmers

Uganda Uganda; **Republic of** ~ Republik Uganda

Ugandan Ugander, ~in; ugandisch

Ukrainian Ukrainer, ~in; ukrainisch; ~ **Soviet Socialist Republic (Ukrainian SSR)** Ukrainische Sozialistische Sowjetrepublik

ullage Flüssigkeitsverlust *(im Faß etc)*

Ulster Unionist Party Unionistische (protestantische) Partei *(tritt für die bestehende Union von Nordirland mit Großbritannien ein)*

ultimate (aller)letzt; endlich, schließlich; Grund-; ~ **beneficiary** Letztbegünstigter; **the** ~ **cause** die eigentliche Ursache; ~ **consumer** Endverbraucher; **the** ~ **facts** *(Zivilprozeß)* die rechtserheblichen bestrittenen Tatsachen *(von deren Beweis der Ausgang des Rechtsstreites entscheidend abhängt)*; ~ **parent company** *Am* Konzernspitze; ~ **waste disposal** Endlagerung *(von radioaktiven Abfällen)*

ultimately schließlich, letzten Endes, im Grunde

ultimatum Ultimatum; **in the form of an** ~ ultimativ; **to issue an** ~ ein Ultimatum stellen

ultimo (ult.) vorigen Monats (v. Mts.) *(cf. proximo, instant)*; **your letter of the 26th ult.** Ihr Schreiben vom 26. v. Mts.

ultimogeniture Erbfolge an den jüngsten Sohn *(opp. primogeniture)*

ultra hazardous activity außergewöhnlich gefährliche Tätigkeit *(Sprengung etc)*

ultra vires ("beyond the powers") über die Befugnisse hinausgehend *(opp. intra vires)*; ~ **action** Überschreitung der Befugnisse; ~ **doctrine** Ultravires-Lehre; **to act** ~ die Befugnisse (od. Grenzen nach der ~ doctrine) überschreiten

Unter der ultra-vires-doctrine wird die Lehre verstanden, nach der die rechtsgeschäftl. Bewegungsfreiheit von Gesellschaften durch den satzungsmäßig festgesetzten Geschäftszweck begrenzt wird. Die wichtigsten Folgen für die Überschreitung dieser Grenzen: Nichtigkeit bzw. Anfechtbarkeit des Rechtsgeschäfts, Möglichkeit der Löschung der Gesellschaft durch den Staat, volle Haftung der Mitglieder der Verwaltung gegenüber der Gesellschaft. Diese Wirkung wird in der Praxis vielfach durch eine sehr weitgehende Fassung des Geschäftszweckes verhindert. In den USA ist außerdem durch Rechtsprechung und Gesetz[1] weitgehend durchgesetzt worden, daß ultra-vires-Geschäfte im Außenverhältnis nicht nichtig sind.

Das Gesetz über die Angleichung des englischen Rechts an das EG-Recht[2] hat die ultra-vires-Lehre für Großbritannien zwar nicht aufgehoben, jedoch erheblich eingeschränkt: Die Gesellschaft kann gegenüber einem gutgläubigen Geschäftspartner die Ultra-vires-Nichtigkeit eines von ihrem Vorstand (directors) gebilligten Geschäfts nicht geltend machen

umbrella *fig* (bes. politischer) Schutz; Deckung; **under the** ~ **of the UN** unter dem Schutz der Vereinten Nationen; ~ **advertising** Verbundwerbung *(branchengleicher Unternehmen)*; ~ **liability insurance** Haftpflichtausfallversicherung *(Haftpflichtversicherung zur Abdeckung von Risiken, die durch bereits vorhandene reguläre Haftpflichtversicherungen nicht gedeckt sind)*; ~ **organization** Dachorganisation

umpire Schiedsrichter; *bes.* Oberschiedsrichter, Obmann *(der beigezogen wird, wenn zwei Schiedsrichter sich nicht einigen können)*[3]; **to appoint an** ~ e-n Schiedsrichter bestellen

umpirage Ausübung des Amtes des (Ober-)Schiedsrichters; Entscheidung durch Schiedsspruch

UN →United Nations

una voce ("with one voice") einstimmig

unable, ~ **to pay** zahlungsunfähig; ~ **to plead** verhandlungsunfähig; ~ **to work** arbeitsunfähig

unaccounted for, to be ~ ungeklärt geblieben sein

unaddressed ohne Adresse; ~ **mailing** Postwurfsendung

unadjusted *(VersR)* unerledigt, schwebend

unadulterated unverfälscht, rein

unadvanced member *Br* Bausparer, dessen Zuteilungsdarlehen noch nicht ausgezahlt ist *(opp. advanced member)*

unaffected unberührt, unbeeinflußt (by von); **the rights of third parties remain** ~ die Rechte Dritter bleiben unberührt

unaffiliated company nicht angegliederte Gesellschaft

unalienable →inalienable

unaltered, the price remains ~ der Preis bleibt unverändert

unanimity Einstimmigkeit; **with** ~ einstimmig

unanimous einstimmig; ~ **vote** einstimmig gefaßter Beschluß; **in the absence of** (or **failing**) **a** ~ **decision** (or **vote**) falls keine Einstimmigkeit erzielt wird; **to give a** ~ **decision** einstimmig entscheiden

unanimously, ~ **reelected** einstimmig wiedergewählt; **the resolution was adopted** (or **carried, passed**) ~ der Beschluß wurde einstimmig gefaßt; die Entschließung wurde einstimmig angenommen

unanswerable unwiderleglich; **his case is** ~ seine Argumente sind unwiderlegbar

unanswered, to leave ~ unbeantwortet lassen

unappealable nicht rechtsmittelfähig, keine Rechtsmittel zulassend; ~ **judgment** rechtskräftiges Urteil

unappropriated, ~ **(retained) earnings** (or **income**) *Am* →~ (earned) surplus; ~ **funds** *(öffentl. Haushalt)* (noch) nicht verwendete Mittel; ~ **profit** unverteilter Reingewinn; Bilanzgewinn; ~ **(earned) surplus** *Am (AktienR)* nicht ausgeschütteter Gewinn; freie Rücklagen

unascertained goods Gattungssachen *(opp. specified goods)*; **purchase of** ~ Gattungskauf; **the contract relates to the sale of** ~ der Kaufvertrag betrifft Gattungssachen

unassignable nicht übertragbar

unassisted person (or **party**) *Br (Zivilprozeß)* Person (od. Partei), der das Armenrecht nicht bewilligt ist *(opp. assisted person)*

unattached nicht zugehörig; unabhängig, parteilos; nicht beschlagnahmt (od. gepfändet)

unauthorized nicht ermächtigt; unbefugt; ~ **agency** Vertretung ohne Vertretungsmacht; ~ **agent** Vertreter ohne Vertretungsmacht; ~ **broadcasting of radio or television signals** widerrechtl. Ausstrahlen von Rundfunk- und Fernsehsendungen, "Funkpiraterie"; ~ **clerk** *Br* Angestellter e-s Börsenmaklers, der keine Abschlüsse tätigen darf; ~ **insurer** *Am* nicht (zum Geschäftsbetrieb) zugelassenes Versicherungsunternehmen; ~ **reprint** unberechtigter Nachdruck; ~ **signature** ohne Ermächtigung vorgenommene Unterschrift; Unterschrift ohne Vertretungsmacht; ~ **strike** wilder Streik; ~ **use** unbefugte Benutzung

unavailability (or **unavailableness**) Nichtverfügbarkeit

unavailable nicht verfügbar

unavoidable unvermeidbar; ~ **accident** unvermeidbarer Unfall; ~ **costs** feste Kosten, Fixkosten

unaware, to be ~ in Unkenntnis sein (of über)

unbalanced unausgeglichen; ~ **budget** unausgeglichener Haushalt

unbankable paper nicht bankfähiger (od. diskontierbarer) Wechsel

unbecoming unziemlich; ungebührlich; ~ **conduct** ungebührliches Verhalten

unbiased unparteiisch; unvoreingenommen

unblock *v (gesperrtes Konto)* freigeben (od. entsperren); ~**ing** Freigabe, Entsperrung *(des gesperrten Kontos)*

unborn child Kind im Mutterleib

unbound ungebunden, broschiert

unbribable unbestechlich

unbroken, ~ **line of authorities** ständige Rechtsprechung; ~ **seal** unverletztes Siegel

uncallable loan unkündbares Darlehen

uncalled capital *(von der Gesellschaft)* noch nicht aufgerufenes (od. eingefordertes) Kapital

uncertain unbestimmt; unklar, unsicher

uncertainty Unbestimmtheit; Unklarheit, Mangel an Genauigkeit *(z. B. in der Formulierung e-s Testaments)*; Unsicherheit, Ungewißheit; nicht versicherbares Risiko; **legal** ~ Rechtsunsicherheit; **void for** ~ wegen Unklarheit *(bes. unklarer Formulierung)* nichtig

unchanged, the prices remain ~ die Preise bleiben unverändert

unchecked baggage nicht aufgegebenes Gepäck

UNCITRAL →United Nations Commission on International Trade Law; ~ **Arbitration Rules** UNCITRAL-Schieds(gerichts)ordnung; ~ **Conciliation Rules** UNCITRAL-Schlichtungsordnung

unclaimed nicht beansprucht; nicht abgeholt, nicht abgenommen; ~ **dividend** nicht abgehobene Dividende; ~ **letter** nicht abgeholter (od. unzustellbarer) Brief; ~ **lost property** Fundsache(n); ~ **wreck** herrenloses Wrack

unclean hands „unreine Hände"; Einwand *(des →equity-Rechts),* der Kläger handele selbst unlauter (od. unredlich, rechtswidrig) und verdiene deshalb keinen gerichtlichen Rechtsschutz *(cf. with →clean hands)*

uncleared goods zollamtlich noch nicht abgefertigte Waren

uncollected goods[4] nicht abgeholte Waren

uncollectible nicht beitreibbar, nicht einziehbar; ~ **accounts** (or **receivables**) uneinbringliche Forderungen

uncommitted nicht gebunden, ungebunden; *pol* blockfrei; ~ **funds** frei verfügbare *(nicht zweckgebundene)* Mittel

unconcerned uninteressiert (with an); unbeteiligt (in an)

unconditional bedingungslos; ~ **→acceptance;** ~ **discharge** *Br (StrafR)* bedingungslose Entlassung *(→discharge 2.)*; ~ **offer** vorbehaltloses Angebot; ~ **surrender** *mil* bedingungslose Kapitulation

unconfirmed letter of credit unbestätigtes Akkreditiv

unconfutable unwiderlegbar

unconscionability Sittenwidrigkeit; *(etwa)* Verstoß gegen Treu und Glauben; Unzumutbarkeit

unconscionable *(objektiv)* sittenwidrig, unzumutbar; gegen Treu und Glauben verstoßend; ~ **bargain** →catching bargain; ~ **clause** unzumutbare Klausel; *(wegen ihres sittenwidrigen oder unzumutbaren Inhalts) (gerichtlich)* nicht durchsetzbare (Vertrags-)Klausel; ~ **contract** sittenwidriger Vertrag; *(gerichtlich)* nicht durchsetzbarer Vertrag (*→~ clause*)

unconstitutional verfassungswidrig

unconstitutionality Verfassungswidrigkeit; **complaint or** ~ Verfassungsbeschwerde

uncontestable unbestreitbar; unangreifbar

uncontested unbestritten; unangefochten; ~ **election** Wahl ohne Gegenkandidaten

uncontrolled unbeaufsichtigt; ~ **economy** freie Wirtschaft; ~ **rents** freie Mieten

unconvicted prisoner *Br* Untersuchungsgefangener

uncover *v*, **to ~ a plot** e-e Verschwörung aufdecken

uncovered ungedeckt; ~ **advance** nicht gedeckter Kredit; ~ **bear** *(Börse)* Blankoverkäufer; ~ **cheque (check)** Scheck ohne Deckung; ~ **circulation** *(z.B. durch Gold)* ungedeckter Notenumlauf; ~ **risk** *(durch Versicherung)* nicht gedecktes Risiko

uncrossed cheque *Br* nicht gekreuzter Scheck, Barscheck

UNCTAD →United Nations Conference on Trade and Development; ~ **Trade and Development Board** Handels- und Entwicklungsrat der UNCTAD, Welthandelsrat

uncustomed goods zollfreie Waren; unverzollte Waren

undated nicht datiert, ohne Datum; ~ **loan** unbefristetes Darlehen; ~ **stocks** *Br* ewige Rente *(z.B. consols)*

undeclared cargo *(Zoll)* nicht deklarierte Ladung

undefended *(im Prozeß)* nicht verteidigt, nicht durch e-n Verteidiger vertreten; ~ **town** *(VölkerR)* offene Stadt

undeliverable *(Post)* unzustellbar

undelivered *(Post)* nicht zugestellt; ~ **goods** noch nicht gelieferte Waren

undenominational school konfessionslose Schule

under, ~ **an Act** gemäß e-m Gesetz, auf Grund e-s Gesetzes; ~ **age** minderjährig; ~ **bond** unter Zollverschluß; ~ **construction** im Bau (befindlich); ~ **sb.'s name** unter jds Namen; ~ **repair** in Reparatur; ~ **the rule** (UR) *Am (Börse)* („auf Grund der Börsenordnung") zwangsweiser Kauf od. Verkauf durch e-n Beamten der Börse *(zur Durchführung der Transaktion e-s insolventen →trader)*; **contract** ~ **seal** gesiegelter Vertrag *(→contract)*

underassessment zu niedrige Veranlagung

underbid *v (bei e-r Versteigerung)* unterbieten

underbill *v Am (Waren)* zu niedrig in Rechnung stellen

undercharge zu geringe Berechnung (od. Belastung); zu niedrig berechneter Betrag *(opp. overcharge)*

undercharge *v* zu wenig berechnen (od. in Rechnung stellen); zu gering belasten

undercover geheim; ~ **agent** Geheimagent *(der zur Aufklärung von Verbrechen in e-e kriminelle Organisation eindringt)*; Polizeispitzel; verdeckt arbeitender Polizeibeamter; Detektiv; ~ **payments** Bestechungsgelder

undercut *v* unterbieten

underdog Benachteiligter, Unterprivilegierter

underemployed unterbeschäftigt

underemployment Unterbeschäftigung, nicht volle Beschäftigung

underestimate Unterschätzung, Unterbewertung

underestimate *v* zu niedrig einschätzen (od. veranschlagen), unterbewerten

undergo *v* durchmachen, erfahren, sich unterziehen; **to ~ a change** e-e Änderung erfahren; **to ~ an examination** vernommen (od. verhört) werden; **to ~ a prison sentence** e-e Gefängnisstrafe verbüßen; **to ~ repairs** in Reparatur sein; **to ~ a trial** vor Gericht gestellt werden

undergraduate *Br* Student vor Erwerb des ersten akademischen Grades; *Am* Student während der ersten 4 Jahre s-s Studiums am College

underground *(auch pol)* Untergrund; *(Bergwerk)* unter Tage; *Br* Untergrundbahn, U-Bahn; **~ car park** *Br* Tiefgarage; **~ economy** Schattenwirtschaft, Untergrundwirtschaft; **~ engineering** Tiefbau(wesen); **~ mining** Untertagebau; **~ parking lot** *Am* Tiefgarage; **~ (railway)** *Br* U-Bahn; **~ testing** unterirdische (Kernwaffen-)Versuche; **~ train** *Br (einzelne[r])* U-Bahn (-zug); **~ worker** Untertagearbeiter; *pol* jd, der im Untergrund arbeitet; **~ working** Untertagebau; **to go ~** *pol* in den Untergrund gehen; **to go by ~** *Br* mit der U-Bahn fahren

underinsurance Unterversicherung

underinsure *v* unterversichern; **to be ~d** unterversichert sein

underlease *v* →sublease *v*

underlessee →sublessee

underlessor →sublessor

underlet *v* →sublet *v*

underline *v* unterstreichen

underlying zugrundeliegend; **~ bonds** *Am (bei Ausgabe von mehreren Obligationen hinsichtl. Verzinsung und Sicherheit)* bevorrechtigte Obligationen; **~ company** *Am colloq.* Tochtergesellschaft, die nur wegen nicht übertragbarer Rechte od. Konzessionen (franchises) fortbesteht; **~ contract** als Grundlage dienender Vertrag; **~ lien** *Am* vorrangiges Pfandrecht; **~ mortgage** *Am* dem Range nach bevorrechtigte Hypothek; **~ policy** *Am* →master policy

undermanned (personell) unterbesetzt *(Fabrik etc)*; ungenügend bemannt *(Schiff)*

undermentioned (u/m) unten erwähnt, nachstehend

undermine *v fig* untergraben, zersetzen; **to ~ the morals** *mil* die Moral zersetzen

underpay *v* schlecht (od. ungenügend) bezahlen; **postage underpaid** nicht genügend frankiert

underpayment Unterbezahlung, nicht genügende Bezahlung; zu wenig entrichteter Betrag

underpopulated unterbevölkert

underprice unter dem allgemeinen Preisniveau liegender Preis; Schleuderpreis

underprice *v*, **to ~ a competitor** *Am* e-n Konkurrenten unterbieten

underpricing Unterbietung

underprivileged (sozial od. wirtschaftlich) benachteiligt, schlecht(er) gestellt; **the ~ classes** die (sozial od. wirtschaftlich) Schlecht(er)gestellten

underrate *v* unterbewerten; untertarifieren; *fig* unterschätzen

undersea Unterwasser-; **~ long-range missile system** (ULMS) Unterwasser-Langstreckenraketensystem; **~ missile fleet** Unterwasserraketen-Flotte

Undersecretary of State Staatssekretär; **Deputy ~** *Am* Unterstaatssekretär; **Parliamentary ~** *Br* Parlamentarischer Staatssekretär; **Permanent ~** *Br* →secretary 3.

undersell *v (etw.)* unter (dem) Wert verkaufen; billiger verkaufen *(als ein anderer)*; verschleudern; *(jdn)* unterbieten

underselling price Schleuderpreis

under-sheriff Vertreter e-s →sheriff

undersign *v* unterschreiben, unterzeichnen; **the ~ed** der (die) Unterzeichnete(n)

understaffed (personell) unterbesetzt *(→staff v; opp. overstaffed)*

understand *v* verstehen; erfahren, hören; als sicher annehmen, voraussetzen *(cf. understood)*

understanding Verstehen, Verständnis (of für); Verständigung, Einvernehmen; *(VertragsR)* Vereinbarung, Abmachung; *(VölkerR)* Vereinbarung, Absprache; **hono(u)rable ~s** formlose Absprachen über Wettbewerbsbeschränkungen; **international ~** internationale Verständigung; **on the ~ that** mit der Maßgabe (od. unter der Voraussetzung), daß; **policy of mutual ~** Verständigungspolitik; **to come to** (or **reach**) **an ~** e-e Verständigung erzielen, zu e-r Verständigung gelangen

understate *v* zu niedrig angeben, unterbewerten *(opp. to overstate)*

understatement Unterbewertung; ungenügende Angabe; Untertreibung

understock *v* e-e zu kleine Menge auf Lager nehmen *(opp. overstock v)*
understocked, to be ~ with zu wenig Vorrat haben an

understocking Unterbevorratung

understood verstanden; übereingekommen, vereinbart; **at the ~ price** zu dem vereinbarten Preis; **it is ~** man kann (als sicher) annehmen; es wird davon ausgegangen, daß; **it is further expressly ~** es wird weiter ausdrücklich vereinbart (that daß)

undersubscribed issue nicht in voller Höhe gezeichnete Emission

undertake *v (etw.)* übernehmen, auf sich nehmen; sich verpflichten, versprechen, garantieren; *(etw.)* unternehmen; **to ~ a business** die Besorgung e-s Geschäftes übernehmen; **to ~ the collection of a bill** das Inkasso e-s Wechsels übernehmen (od. besorgen); **to ~ a liability** e-e Verpflichtung eingehen; Haftung übernehmen; **to ~ obligations** Verpflichtungen eingehen (od. übernehmen); **to ~ a risk** ein Risiko übernehmen (od. eingehen)

undertaker Beerdigungsinstitut; **statutory ~s** *Br (gesetzlich autorisierte)* Unternehmer öffentlicher Betriebe

undertaking 1. Versprechen, bes. ein im Laufe des Prozesses von e-r Partei od. ihrem Anwalt gegebenes Versprechen *(durch das vom Gericht od. der Gegenpartei Konzessionen erwirkt werden)*; Verpflichtung(serklärung), *(verbindliche)* Zusage, Zusicherung; **~ to appear in an action** *Br* Versprechen *(des solicitor für s-n Klienten)*, sich auf die Klage einzulassen (to enter an appearance); **~ to pay** Zahlungsversprechen, Zahlungszusage; **~ as to quality** Zusicherung e-r Eigenschaft *(Sachmängelhaftung)*; **contractual ~** vertragliches Versprechen; **formal ~** förmliche Verpflichtung; **on the ~** auf die Zusicherung (od. das bindende Versprechen) hin; **voluntary ~** freiwillige Verpflichtung; **to enter into an ~** e-e Verpflichtung eingehen; **to give an ~** sich verpflichten, e-e Verpflichtung übernehmen
undertaking 2. Unternehmen; Unternehmung; Betrieb; **~s for collective investment in transferable securities** (Ucits) *(EG)* Organismen für Anlagen in Wertpapieren; **agricultural ~** landwirtschaftlicher Betrieb; **commercial ~** (Handels)Unternehmen; Handelsbetrieb; **industrial ~** Industrieunternehmen; **joint ~** gemeinsames Unternehmen, Gemeinschaftsunternehmen *(→joint)*; **private ~** Privatunternehmen; **to operate an ~** ein Unternehmen betreiben

under(-)tenancy →subtenancy

under(-)tenant →subtenant

undervaluation zu niedrige Schätzung, Unterbewertung

undervalue, →transaction at an ~

undervalue *v* zu niedrig schätzen, unterbewerten

underweight Untergewicht

underworld Unterwelt

underwrite *v* 1. *(bestimmte Teile e-r Effektenemission)* garantieren *(durch Verpflichtung zur Übernahme des nicht unterzubringenden Teiles e-r Emission; cf. underwriter 1.)*; *(Effektenemission)* fest übernehmen; **to ~ an issue** die Unterbringung e-r Emission garantieren
underwriting 1. Garantie (od. Übernahme) e-r Effektenemission; **~ agreement** Übernahmevertrag, Konsortialvertrag *(betr. Übernahme und Plazierung von Wertpapieren durch ein Emissionskonsortium)*; **~ bank** Konsortialbank; **~ business** Effektenemissionsgeschäft; Konsortialgeschäft; **~ commission** Provision für Übernahme der Effektenemission; **~ commitment** Konsortialverpflichtung; **~ contract** →**~** agreement; **division** Emissionsabteilung; **~ group** Übernahmekonsortium; **~ guarantee** Garantie der Unterbringung e-r Emission; **~ houses** *Am* Emissionshäuser *(übernehmen die gesamte Abwicklung des Emissionsgeschäftes)*; **~ risk** Übernahmerisiko; **~ share** Konsortialquote; **~ syndicate** Emissionskonsortium; **firm ~** feste Übernahme e-r Effektenemission
underwritten *(Effektenemission)* fest übernommen; **the loan was ~ by a consortium of banks** die Anleihe wurde von e-m Bankenkonsortium fest übernommen

underwrite *v* 2. versichern; *(bes. SeeversR) (gemeinsam mit anderen Versicherern)* e-e Versicherung übernehmen *(→underwriter 2.)*; **to ~ marine risks** e-e Seeversicherung unter Risikobeteiligung übernehmen; **to ~ a policy** e-e Police *(als Versicherer)* unterzeichnen; e-e Versicherung übernehmen
underwriting 2. (bes. See-)Versicherung(sgeschäft); Abschluß *(des Versicherungsvertrages)*; **cash flow-~** Versicherungs- und Prämienkalkulation unter strikter Berücksichtigung der Zinserträge; **~ agent** *Br* Abschlußagent, Versicherer *(Bevollmächtigter, der für mehrere Lloyd's-Mitglieder das Versicherungsgeschäft ausübt)*; **~ business** (See-)Versicherungsgeschäft; **~ contract** Versicherungsvertrag; **~ group** Versicherungskonsortium; **~ limit** Zeichnungsgrenze; **~ member** *Br* Einzelversicherer *(von →Lloyd's)*; **non-~ member** *Br* inaktives Mitglied *(von →Lloyd's)*; **~ office** *Br* Versicherungsgesellschaft; **~ of a policy** Übernah-

me e-r Versicherung *(cf. underwrite 2.)*; ~ **profit or loss** Gewinn od. Verlust des Geschäftsjahres *(e-r Versicherung)*; ~ **reserve** Schadenreserven, Schadenrückstellung; ~ **a risk** Übernahme e-s Versicherungsrisikos *(gemeinsam mit anderen underwriters)*

underwriter 1. *(Effektenhandel)* Garant (od. Übernehmer) e-r Effektenemission *(Einzelperson, Bank od. Konsortium, die sich gegen e-e Provision verpflichten, den nicht unterzubringenden Teil e-r Effektenemission zu übernehmen)*; Konsortialmitglied; Emissionsbank, Emissionsfirma; ~**s** Emissionshäuser; **national** ~**s** *Am* Emissionsfirmen, deren Geschäftsbereich sich über die ganzen Staaten erstreckt

underwriter 2. Versicherer; *(bes. [See-]Versicherer, der meist gemeinsam mit anderen – zur Teilung des Risikos – e-e Versicherung übernimmt)*; Einzelversicherer *(Br cf. Lloyd's)*; **U~s' Laboratories** (UL) *Am* private Vereinigung, die etwa dem TÜV entspricht; **cargo** ~ Frachtenversicherer; **fire** ~ Feuerversicherer; **leading** ~ Erstversicherer; **life** ~ *Am colloq.* Lebensversicherungsagent; →**Lloyd's** ~; **marine** ~ Seeversicherer

underwriting →underwrite *v* 1. und 2.

undesirable alien, to deport an ~ e-n unerwünschten (od. lästigen) Ausländer abschieben

undeveloped nicht entwickelt *(opp. developed)*; ~ **land** *Br* nicht erschlossenes (Bau-)Gelände; ~ **parcel of land** *Am* nicht bebautes Grundstück

undischarged nicht bezahlt; unerledigt; nicht entladen *(Schiff)*; ~ **bankrupt**[5] (noch) nicht entlasteter Gemeinschuldner; ~ **debt** nicht bezahlte (od. beglichene) Schuld

undisclosed geheimgehalten, nicht bekanntgegeben; ~ **agency** verdeckte (od. mittelbare) Stellvertretung; ~ **agent** mittelbarer Stellvertreter; ~ **buyer** ungenannter Käufer; ~ **channelling of profits** *(SteuerR)* verdeckte Entziehung von Gewinnen; ~ **reserves** stille Rücklagen

undisclosed principal verdeckt vertretener Unternehmer (→*disclosed principal*)
Der ~ wird aus einem Vertrag berechtigt und verpflichtet, auch wenn die Vertreterstellung seines Vertreters nicht erkennbar war, sofern der (Handels-) Vertreter nur innerhalb seiner Vertretungsmacht gehandelt hat

undiscountable bill nicht diskontierbarer Wechsel

undisposed application *(PatR)* schwebende Anmeldung

undistorted competition unverfälschter Wettbewerb

undistributed profit unverteilter (nicht ausgeschütteter) Gewinn

undivided right Anteilsrecht an e-m Vermögensgegenstand, der mehreren Teilhabern in ungeteilter Gemeinschaft zusteht

undivided share (in land) ungeteiltes gemeinsames Eigentum an e-r Liegenschaft *(jointly or in common)*
Betrifft sowohl Gesamthands- als auch (ideelle) Bruchteilsberechtigung. *Br*[6] ~ kann seit 1925 nur noch als →settled land *(settle v 3.)* od. durch einen →trust for sale begründet werden

undivided shares, community by ~ Gemeinschaft nach Bruchteilen

undo *v*, **to** ~ **a bargain** ein Geschäft rückgängig machen

undrawn profit nicht entnommener Gewinn

undue ungehörig, ungebührlich; nicht geschuldet; ~ **debt** zu hohe Forderung; ~ **delay** ungehörige Verzögerung; ~ **hardship** unbillige Härte; ~ **influence** ungebührliche Beeinflussung *(z.B. bei Errichtung e-s Testaments od. bei Wahlen*[7]*)*; ~ **preference** *Br (KonkursR)* Gläubigerbegünstigung; **without** ~ **delay** unverzüglich; **to take** ~ **advantage (of)** ausnützen

unearned nicht *(durch Arbeit)* verdient; ~ **income** Einkommen aus Vermögen, Besitzeinkommen *(opp. earned income)*; *Br (steuerlich höher bewertetes)* Kapitaleinkommen; ~ **increment** Wertzuwachs von Grundbesitz *(unabhängig von den Aufwendungen des Eigentümers, z.B. durch Wertsteigerung des Bodens)*; ~ **premium** *(VersR)* (noch) nicht verdiente Prämie *(→premium 2.)*

uneconomic(al) unwirtschaftlich, unrentabel

unemployability supplement *Br*[8] Zuschlag zu den Leistungen der Arbeitslosenversicherung *(bei lebenslänglicher Arbeitsunfähigkeit)*

unemployable Arbeitsunfähige(r); arbeitsunfähig

unemployed arbeitslos, erwerbslos; **the** ~ die Arbeitslosen; ~ **capital** ungenütztes (od. totes) Kapital; ~ **person** Arbeitsloser; ~ **or underemployed** arbeitslos oder unterbeschäftigt

unemployment Arbeitslosigkeit, Erwerbslosigkeit; ~ **among young people** Jugendarbeitslosigkeit

unemployment benefit *Br*[9] (**compensation** *Am*) Arbeitslosengeld; **recipient of** ~ Empfänger von Arbeitslosengeld; **to draw** ~ Arbeitslosengeld beziehen

unemployment figures Arbeitslosenzahlen

unemployment insurance[10] Arbeitslosenversicherung; **Federal** ~ **taxes** *Am* Beiträge für die Bundesarbeitslosenversicherung

unemployment, U~ Payroll Tax *Am* Arbeitslosenversicherungsbeitrag; ~ **rate** Arbeitslosenquote; ~ **trap** Lücke zwischen den Sozialleistungen, die ein Arbeitsloser erhält, und seinem Lohn

unemployment, concealed ~ versteckte Arbeitslosigkeit; **cyclical** ~ konjunkturelle Arbeitslosigkeit; **decrease** (or **decline**) **in** ~ Rückgang der Arbeitslosigkeit; **disguised** ~ versteckte Arbeitslosigkeit; **frictional** ~ friktionelle (od. temporäre) Arbeitslosigkeit; **increase in** ~ Anstieg der Arbeitslosigkeit; **prolonged** ~ s. sustained →~; **seasonal** ~ saisonbedingte Arbeitslosigkeit; **structural** ~ strukturelle Arbeitslosigkeit; **sustained** ~ anhaltende Arbeitslosigkeit; **to combat** ~ die Arbeitslosigkeit bekämpfen; ~ **declines** die Arbeitslosigkeit nimmt ab; **to eliminate** ~ die Arbeitslosigkeit beseitigen; **threatened with** ~ von Arbeitslosigkeit bedroht

unencumbered unbelastet, hypothekenfrei; ~ **property** nicht belasteter Grundbesitz

unenforceability Nichteinklagbarkeit, Unmöglichkeit der Geltendmachung; Prozeßhindernis

unenforceable nicht erzwingbar; nicht (ein-) klagbar

unentered *(Zoll)* nicht deklariert

unequal ungleich; ~ **terms** unterschiedliche Bedingungen; ~ **treaties** *(VölkerR)*[11] ungleiche Verträge; **to be** ~ **to a th.** e-r Sache nicht gewachsen sein

UNESCO →United Nations Educational, Scientific and Cultural Organisation

unestablished civil servant (or **local government officer**) *Br* außerplanmäßiger Beamter

unethical unmoralisch; standeswidrig

uneven distribution ungleichmäßige Verteilung

unexpected profit unerwarteter Gewinn

unexpended appropriations nicht verbrauchte Haushaltsmittel

unexpired (noch) nicht abgelaufen; ~ **bill** noch nicht fälliger Wechsel; ~ **patent** →patent 2.

unexploited invention *(PatR)* nicht verwertete Erfindung

unfair unbillig, unredlich; mißbräuchlich; ~ **business practices** unlautere Geschäftsmethoden; ~ **competition** unlauterer Wettbewerb *(→competition)*

Unfair Contract Terms Act, 1977 *Br* Gesetz gegen die Verwendung unlauterer Vertragsbedingungen

Das Gesetz hat grundlegende Änderungen hinsichtlich des Vertragsrechts und der Haftung für Fahrlässigkeit (liability in tort for negligence) herbeigeführt. Insbesondere hat es die Freizeichnungsklausel (→exemption clause) eingeschränkt sowie den Umfang des Haftungsausschlusses (exclusion of liability).

Nach Struktur und Inhalt ist das Gesetz dem deutschen AGBG vergleichbar, aber komplizierter und eher strenger

unfair dismissal[12] unfaire Entlassung; ~ **compensation** *Br* Entschädigung bei ungerechtfertigter Entlassung

unfair labor practices *Am* unfaire Praktiken im Arbeitsleben *(entweder durch den Arbeitgeber [→National Labor Relations Act] oder durch die Gewerkschaften [→Taft Hartley Act])*; **to engage in** ~ unbillige (od. unlautere) Arbeitspraktiken begehen

unfair, ~ **list** *Am* schwarze Liste *(Gewerkschaftsliste von als unfair bezeichneten Arbeitgebern)*; ~ **methods of competition** unlautere Wettbewerbsmethoden; ~ **terms** mißbräuchliche Klauseln; ~ **trade practices** *Am* unlautere Handelspraktiken *(cf. →Price Floor Laws, →Fair Trade Acts, →Unfair Trade Practices Acts)*; **U~ Trade Practices Acts** *Am (einzelstaatl.)* Gesetze gegen den unlauteren Wettbewerb

unfavo(u)rable ungünstig; ~ **exchange rate** ungünstiger (Wechsel-, Devisen-)Kurs; ~ **trade balance** passive Handelsbilanz; **to form an** ~ **opinion (of)** e-n ungünstigen Eindruck gewinnen (von); **to have an** ~ **effect (on)** sich ungünstig auswirken (auf)

unfilled, ~ **orders** unerledigte Bestellungen (od. Aufträge); ~ **vacancies** offene Stellen

unfinished business *parl* Unerledigtes

unfit untauglich, ungeeignet; ~ **for human consumption**[13] für die menschliche Ernährung ungeeignet; ~ **for service** dienstunfähig; ~ **for work** arbeitsunfähig; ~ **to plead** *(Strafprozeß)* verhandlungsunfähig

unfitness for work Arbeitsunfähigkeit

unforeseen circumstances excluded (u.c.e.) ausgenommen nicht vorhergesehene Umstände

unforgeable document fälschungssicherer Ausweis

unfounded, ~ **complaint** unbegründete Beschwerde; ~ **suspicion** unbegründeter Verdacht

unfriendly, ~ **act** *(VölkerR)* unfreundlicher Akt; ~→**takeover**

unfreeze *v (Preis-, Lohnstopp etc)* aufheben *(opp. freeze v)*; **to** ~ **funds** Guthaben freigeben

unfunded unfundiert; ~ **debt** *Br* unfundierte (od. schwebende) *(kurzfristige öffentl.)* Schuld *(opp. funded debt)*

unfurnished, the house is let ~ das Haus wird unmöbliert vermietet

ungeared fund *Br* Versicherungsfonds ohne Fremdmittel

unicameral legislation aus einer Kammer bestehendes Parlament *(Am z.B. in Nebraska)*

unidentifiable nicht identifizierbar

unidentified, ~ **flying object** (UFO) unbekanntes Flug-Objekt (UFO); ~ **goods** gattungsmäßig bezeichnete Ware

unification Vereinheitlichung; (Ver-)Einigung; Unifizierung, Konsolidierung; ~ **of law** Vereinheitlichung des Rechts; **International Institute for the U~ of Private Law** Internationales Institut für die Vereinheitlichung des Privatrechts; ~ **of different loans** Unifizierung (od. Zusammenziehung) mehrerer Staatsanleihen in e-e einheitliche

unified →unify *v*

uniform 1. einheitlich, gleichmäßig; Einheits-

Uniform Acts *Am (von der →National Conference of Commissioners on Uniform State Laws ausgearbeitete und den einzelstaatl. Gesetzgebern zur Einführung empfohlene)* Modellkodifikationen *(cf. Model Act)*

Die wichtigsten, von vielen Einzelstaaten – zum Teil mit Abänderungen – angenommenen Gesetze sind: →Uniform Commercial Code (UCC); →Uniform Partnership Act (UPA); Uniform Reciprocal Enforcement of→Support Act (URESA)

uniform application of the law einheitliche Rechtsanwendung

Uniform Commercial Code (UCC) *Am* Einheitliches Handelsgesetz *(cf. Uniform Acts)*

Unter Mitwirkung vieler Sachverständiger verfaßt und vom American Law Institute und der National Conference of Commissioners on Uniform State Laws herausgegeben. Der UCC ist von allen Einzelstaaten (außer Louisiana) angenommen, z.T. mit Änderungen durch die einzelstaatlichen Gesetzgeber.

Art. 1 – General Provisions (Allgemeiner Teil)
Art. 2 – Sales (Warenkauf)
Art. 3 – Commercial Paper (Wertpapierrecht)
Art. 4 – Bank Deposits and Collections (Bankeinlagen und Bankinkasso)
Art. 5 – Letters of Credit (Akkreditiv)
Art. 6 – Bulk Transfers (Geschäftsübertragungen)
Art. 7 – Warehouse Receipts, Bills of Lading and other Documents of Title (Lagerschein, Ladeschein und andere Traditionspapiere)
Art. 8 – Investment Securities (Anlagepapiere) (Schuldverschreibungen, Aktien etc)
Art. 9 – Secured Transactions; Sales of Accounts, Contract Rights and Chattel Paper (Mobiliarsicherungsrecht)
Art. 10 – Aufhebung der durch den UCC überholten Uniform Laws auf dem Gebiete des Handelsrechts; nämlich
Uniform Negotiable Instruments Acts (UNIL)
Uniform Warehouse Receipts Act (UWRA)
Uniform Sales Act (USA)
Uniform Bills of Lading Act (UBLA)
Uniform Stock Transfer Act (USTA)
Uniform Conditional Sales Act (UCSA)
Uniform Trust Receipts Act (UTRA)

Uniform Customs and Practice for →Documentary Credits

uniform delivered price *Am* einheitlicher Lieferpreis *(Einheitspreis, der den Kunden ohne Rücksicht auf den Lieferort berechnet wird)*

Uniform Enforcement of Foreign Judgments Act *Am* Einheitliches Gesetz zur Vollstreckung einzelstaatlicher Urteile *(s. foreign →judgments)*

Uniform Foreign Money-Judgments Recognition Act *Am* Einheitliches Gesetz über die Anerkennung ausländischer Geldurteile *(s. foreign →judgments)*

Dieses Gesetz läßt den Gegenseitigkeitsgrundsatz fallen

uniform law einheitliches Gesetz *(Am cf. Uniform Acts)*; **U~ L~s Annotated** (U.L.A.) *Am* Sammlung der Uniform Laws mit Anmerkungen sowie Entscheidungsverzeichnis

Uniform Law on the Formation of Contracts for the International Sale of Goods *Br* Einheitliches Gesetz über den Abschluß von internationalen Kaufverträgen über bewegliche Sachen

Uniform Laws on International Sales Act 1967 *Br* Gesetz über die Einheitlichen Gesetze für den internationalen Warenkauf

Das Gesetz setzt die beiden Haager Übereinkommen über den internationalen Kauf beweglicher Sachen *(→Hague Convention Relating to a Uniform Law of the International Sale of Goods und →Hague Convention Relating to a Uniform Law on the Formation of Contracts for the International Sale of Goods)* in innerstaatliches Recht um. Es enthält als Anlagen zwei Einheitsgesetze, nämlich das →Uniform Law on the International Sale of Goods und das →Uniform Law on the Formation of Contracts for the International Sale of Goods, die 1972 in Kraft getreten sind.

Die entsprechenden deutschen Einheitsgesetze von 1973 *(BGBl I S. 856 und 868)* sind 1974 in Kraft getreten

Uniform Law on the International Sale of Goods *Br* Einheitliches Gesetz über den internationalen Kauf beweglicher Sachen

Uniform, ~ **Limited Partnership Act** (ULPA) *Am* Einheitliches Gesetz über die Kommanditgesellschaft; ~ **Partnership Act** (UPA) *Am* Einheitliches Gesetz über Personengesellschaften mit unbeschränkter Haftung (etwa OHG); **u~ price** Einheitspreis; ~ **Probate Code** *Am* Gesetzesmuster für Gesetze über Nachlaßverwaltung; ~ **Product Liability Act** (UPLA) Einheitliches Gesetz für Produzentenhaftung; **u~ quotation** Einheitskurs; **u~ rate** Einheitssatz; Einheitskurs

Uniform, Revised ~ Reciprocal Enforcement of Support Act of 1968 (URESA) *Am* Gesetzesmuster für Gesetze über die Anerkennung ausländischer Unterhaltsurteile
Danach werden ausländische Unterhaltsurteile anerkannt, sofern im Verhältnis zu dem ausländischen Staat die Gegenseitigkeit festgestellt ist
Uniform Rules, (ICC) ~ for →Collections; (ICC) ~ for →Contract Guarantees
Uniform, ~ Securities Act *Am (einzelstaatl.)* Einheitliches Wertpapiergesetz; **u~ tariff** Einheitstarif
Uniform Traffic Code *Am* Einheitliches Verkehrsgesetz
Modellverordnung eines Einzelstaates zur Annahme seitens der Gemeinden, Kreise etc.

uniform 2. Uniform; **in ~** in Uniform *(opp. in plain clothes; Br. auch in mufti)*

uniformity Einheitlichkeit; Gleichmäßigkeit; **~ in taxation** gleichmäßige Besteuerung
uniformity, Acts of U~ *Br* Gesetze zur einheitlichen Regelung des Gottesdienstes *(bes. das Gesetz von 1662)*

unify *v* vereinigen, vereinheitlichen; unifizieren, zu e-r Einheit zusammenschließen, konsolidieren
unified, ~ bond konsolidierte Anleihe; **~ credit** *Am*[14] pauschale Steuergutschrift; **~ debt** konsolidierte Schuld

unilateral einseitig; nur auf e-r Seite; **~ contract** einseitig verpflichtender Vertrag; **~ parking** auf eine Straßenseite beschränktes Parken

unimpeded access *(VölkerR)* ungehinderter Zugang

unimproved, ~ goods unveredelte Waren; **~ land** (or **real estate**) *Am* nicht bebautes (od. erschlossenes) (Bau-)Gelände

unincorporated *Am* nicht eingemeindet; außerhalb der Gemeindegrenzen *(Gebiet, Ortschaft)*
unincorporated association nicht rechtsfähige Vereinigung; nicht eingetragener Verein
Körperschaftlich organisierte Gesellschaft, die nicht in das Handelsregister eingetragen ist und keine eigene Rechtspersönlichkeit hat. *Br* In der Wirtschaft sind vor allem die Gewerkschaften und die Unternehmerverbände als ~ organisiert
unincorporated, ~ bank *Am* Privatbank; **~ enterprise** Unternehmen ohne eigene Rechtspersönlichkeit *(Personengesellschaften und Einzelkaufleute)*

uninsurable risk nicht versicherungsfähiges Risiko

uninsured nicht versichert; **~ employment** versicherungsfreie Beschäftigung; **~ motorist protection insurance** Kfz-Versicherung gegen Schäden durch nicht versicherte Fahrer; **~ parcel** nicht versichertes Paket; **~ risk** ungedecktes Risiko

union 1. Vereinigung, Zusammenschluß; Staatenverbindung; die USA; Union, Verband *(cf. Berne →Convention, Paris →Convention)*; *Br eccl* Verbindung von zwei od. mehreren Pfründen (benefices); **U~ Convention** Pariser (Verbands-)Übereinkunft, Unionsvertrag *(→convention 1.)*; **U~ country** Land im Weltpostverein *(Universal Postal Union)*; Verbandsland *(cf. country of the U~)*; **U~ Jack** Nationalflagge von Großbritannien; **U~ of International Fairs** Internationaler Messeverband[15]; **U~ of Soviet Socialist Republics** (USSR) Union der Sozialistischen Sowjet-Republiken *(→Soviet Union)*; **U~ priority** →priority 2.; **country of the U~** Verbandsland *(cf. Berne →Convention, Paris →Convention)*; **country outside the U~** verbandsfremdes Land; **customs ~** Zollunion; **international ~** internationaler Verband; **monetary ~** Währungsunion; **Office of the International U~ for the Protection of Literary and Artistic Works**[16] Büro des Internationalen Verbandes zum Schutze von Werken der Literatur und Kunst *(cf. Berne →Convention)*; **Universal Postal U~** (U. P. U.) Weltpostverein (→Universal)
union 2. Gewerkschaft *(→trade union)*; **~ agreement** *Am* Tarifvertrag; **~ card** *Br* Mitgliedsausweis e-r Gewerkschaft; **~ certification** *Am (vom National Labor Relations Board od. e-r ähnl. Behörde ausgestellte)* Bescheinigung, daß e-e Gewerkschaft die gesetzl. Voraussetzungen als Arbeitnehmervertretung erfüllt hat
union contract *Am* Tarifvertrag; **~ negotiations** *Am* Tarifverhandlungen; **~ termination** *Am* Tarifkündigung
union dues Gewerkschaftsbeiträge; **deduction of ~ from wages** *Br* Erhebung der Gewerkschaftsbeiträge durch Lohnabzug
union, ~ jurisdiction *Am* Zuständigkeit der Gewerkschaft; **~ label** *Am* Gewerkschaftsetikett *(an Waren)*; **~ labo(u)r** gewerkschaftlich organisierte Arbeitskräfte; **(trade) ~ leader** Gewerkschaftsführer; **~-management cooperation** Zusammenarbeit zwischen Gewerkschaften und Unternehmer; **~ member** Gewerkschaftsmitglied; **compulsory ~ membership** Gewerkschaftsmitgliedschaft als Voraussetzung der Einstellung *(bei →closed shop oder →union shop; →open shop)*; **~ official** Gewerkschaftsfunktionär; **~ rate** Tariflohn, Tarifsatz; **~ relations** Beziehungen e-s Unternehmens zur Gewerkschaft; **(trade) ~ representative** Gewerkschaftsvertreter; **~ security clauses** *Am (im Tarifvertrag aufgenommene)* Schutzklauseln für die gewerkschaftliche Vertretung im Betrieb; **~ shop** gewerk-

schaftspflichtiger Betrieb *(Unternehmen, das auch nichtorganisierte Arbeitskräfte einstellt, die aber nach e-r bestimmten Zeit Gewerkschaftsmitglieder werden müssen)*; **U~ of Shop, Distributive, and Allied Workers** (USDAW) *Br* Gewerkschaft der im Laden, Handel und verwandten Gebieten Tätigen; ~ **steward** *Am* Betriebsobmann; ~ **subscription** Gewerkschaftsbeitrag; ~ **wage rate** Tariflohn

union, anti-~ gewerkschaftsfeindlich; **branch** ~ *Am* s. local →~; **closed** ~ Gewerkschaft mit Mitgliederbeschränkung; **company** ~ *Am* Betriebsgewerkschaft; **craft** ~ Fachgewerkschaft; berufsgebundene Gewerkschaft; **denominational** ~ konfessionelle Gewerkschaft; **horizontal** ~ s. craft →~; **independent** ~ unabhängige *(keinem Gewerkschaftsverband [Am nicht der AFL/CIO] zugehörige)* Gewerkschaft; **industrial** ~ Industriegewerkschaft; **international** ~ *Am* Gewerkschaft mit Mitgliedern in anderen Ländern *(bes. in Kanada)*; **labor** ~ *Am* Gewerkschaft; **local** ~ *Am* örtliche Abteilung e-r Gewerkschaft, Ortsverband; **national** ~ *Am* zentrale Gewerkschaft *(mit Mitgliedern in allen Einzelstaaten)*; →**non-~; non-~ worker** Nichtgewerkschafter, nicht gewerkschaftlich organisierter Arbeiter; **trade** ~ Gewerkschaft *(→trade)*; **vertical** ~ s. industrial →~; **to join a** ~ e-r Gewerkschaft beitreten

unionism Unionismus; *Br* Gegnerschaft gegen die →Home Rule; Gewerkschaftswesen, Gewerkschaftspolitik

unionist Gewerkschafter; Gewerkschaftsmitglied; *Br* Gegner der →Home Rule; →Ulster U~ **Party**

unioni|ze *v (Arbeitnehmer)* gewerkschaftl. organisieren, der Zugehörigkeit zu e-r bestimmten Gewerkschaft unterwerfen; **~d workforce** gewerkschaftlich organisierte Arbeitskräfte

unique copy Unikat

unissued, ~ capital *Br* (**capital stock** *Am*) genehmigtes, noch nicht ausgegebenes Grundkapital; ~ **shares** (or **stock**) zur Ausgabe genehmigte, aber noch nicht emittierte Aktien

unit 1. Einheit; Stück; Betrieb; Einzelteil; Anbauteil *(Möbel)*; *mil* Truppenverband; ~ **amount** Betrag pro Einheit; ~ **bank** *Am* filiallose Bank, Bank ohne Zweigstellen; ~ **banking states** *Am* (Einzel-)Staaten, in denen Gründung von Bankfilialen *(→branch banking)* verboten ist; ~ **cost** Kosten pro Einheit; Stückkosten; ~ **of account** (u. a.) Rechnungseinheit (R.E.); ~ **of charge** Gebühreneinheit; ~ **of currency** Währungseinheit; ~ **of measurement** Maßeinheit; ~ **price** Preis pro Einheit; Stückpreis; ~ **quotation** *(Börse)* Stücknotiz; **monetary** ~ Währungseinheit

unit 2. *Br* Fondsanteil, Anteil an e-m →~ trust; ~ **certificate** *Br* Anteilsschein: ~ **holder** *Br* Anteilseigner; **~-linked (life) assurance** *Br* fondsgebundene Lebensversicherung; **bonus** ~ Gratisanteil

unit trust *Br*[17] Investmentfonds; ~ **price** Kurs e-s Fondsanteils

Bei dem unit trust, der seit den 50er Jahren in Großbritannien für den kleinen Anleger an Bedeutung gewonnen hat, kauft die Trustleitung (management company) aus eigenen Mitteln Effekten, die sie bei einem Treuhänder (trustee, meist Bank oder Versicherungsgesellschaft) deponiert und von denen sie dann Anteilsscheine (units) an die Anteilseigner (unit holders) ausgibt. Der unit trust, in etwa vergleichbar dem amerikanischen →mutual fund, ist nicht zu verwechseln mit einem investment trust. Die Anteilseigner sind unit holders, nicht shareholders. Die management company und der trustee unterliegen den Bestimmungen eines Treuhandvertrages (trust deed).

Beim **flexible unit trust** können im Ggs. zum **fixed unit trust** die Wertpapiere des Fonds jederzeit ausgetauscht werden

Unitarian *eccl* Unitarier *(Protestant, der die Trinitätslehre ablehnt)*; unitarisch; *pol* Anhänger des Unitarismus

unitarianism *eccl* die Glaubensbewegung der Unitarier; *pol* Unitarismus *(Bestreben nach Stärkung der Rechte des Gesamtstaates [Bundesstaats od. Staatenbundes] gegenüber den Einzelstaaten [Ländern]; opp. federalism)*

unitary patents *(Europ. PatR)* einheitliche Patente

unitary taxation (UT) *Am* Einheitlichkeit der Besteuerung

Danach stellt der selbst erwirtschaftete Gewinn für die Besteuerung einer Tochtergesellschaft nur einen Beitrag zum Gesamtgewinn des Unternehmensverbundes dar.

Die Unitary Taxation Method (UTM) sieht für die Besteuerung des Gewinns eines Unternehmens in einem Staat die Berücksichtigung sämtlicher weltweiter Gewinne des Unternehmens vor

united vereint; vereinigt

United Arab Emirates Vereinigte Arabische Emirate

Abu Dhabi, Ajman, Dubai, Fujairah, Ras al Khaimah, Sharjah, Umm al Qaiwain.

Abu Dhabi, Adschman, Dubai, Fudschaira, Ras al Chaima, Schardscha, Umm al Kaiwain

united front Einheitsfront

United Kingdom (UK) Vereinigtes Königreich; ~ **of Great Britain and Northern Ireland** Vereinigtes Königreich Großbritannien und Nordirland; ~ **national** britischer Staatsangehöriger; **person resident in the** ~ Person mit Wohnsitz in dem Vereinigten Königreich

United Nations (UN) Vereinte Nationen; ~ **Organization** (UNO) Organisation der Vereinten Nationen (UNO); **Charter of the** ~[18] Satzung der Vereinten Nationen; **specialized agencies of the** ~ Sonderorganisationen der Vereinten Nationen *(→specialized agencies)*
Staatenvereinigung, die 1945 an die Stelle des Völkerbundes trat. *Sitz* (headquarters): New York. Mehr als 150 Mitglieder.
Hauptorgane (principal organs):
1. Generalversammlung (Vollversammlung) (General Assembly) als oberstes Organ, bestehend aus Vertretern aller Mitglieder, die jeder 1 Stimme haben
2. (Welt-)Sicherheitsrat (Security Council)
3. Wirtschafts- und Sozialrat (Economic and Social Council (ECOSOC), der durch Ausschüsse mit bestimmten Aufgabenbereichen arbeitet (8 Fachkommissionen [z. B. Transport- und Nachrichtenwesen, Statistik, Menschenrechte, Rauschgifte] und 4 Regionalkommissionen) *(cf. ECA, ECAFE, ECE, ECLA)*
4. Treuhandrat (Trusteeship Council), dem die Aufsicht über die Treuhandgebiete (→trusteeship territories) zusteht
5. Internationaler Gerichtshof (→International Court of Justice)
6. Generalsekretariat unter Leitung e-s Generalsekretärs (Secretary General)

(Haupt-)Aufgaben: Sicherung des Weltfriedens. Förderung der internationalen Zusammenarbeit auf wirtschaftl., sozialem, kulturellem und humanitärem Gebiet

United Nations Administrative Tribunal (UNAT)[19] Verwaltungsgericht der Vereinten Nationen

United Nations Center on Transnational Corporations (UNCTC) Zentrum der Vereinten Nationen für transnationale Unternehmen

United Nations Children's Fund[20] (UNICEF) Weltkinderhilfswerk der Vereinten Nationen
Gegr. 1946 zur Unterstützung hilfsbedürftiger Kinder in den von Krieg heimgesuchten Ländern Europas und Asiens. Seit 1950 liegt der Schwerpunkt der Arbeit in den Entwicklungsländern (Verteilung von Medikamenten und Nahrungsmitteln, Bekämpfung von Kinderkrankheiten, Schutzimpfungen, Mütterberatungen etc)

United Nations Commission on International Trade Law (→UNCITRAL) Kommission der Vereinten Nationen für internationales Handelsrecht
Die Aufgabe der UNCITRAL besteht darin, die fortschreitende Harmonisierung und Vereinheitlichung des Rechts des internationalen Handels zu fördern

United Nations Conference on the Law of the Sea (UNCLOS) Seerechtskonferenz der Vereinten Nationen, UN-Seerechtskonferenz

United Nations Conference on Trade and Development (UNCTAD) Welthandels- und Entwicklungskonferenz der Vereinten Nationen, Welthandelskonferenz
Gegr. 1964 als ständiges Organ der Generalversammlung der Vereinten Nationen. 168 Mitgliedstaaten, zu denen auch die Staatshandelsländer gehören. Die Unctad kann nur „Empfehlungen" aussprechen.
Ständiges Organ: Handels- und Entwicklungsrat (Welthandelsrat) (Trade and Development Board). Der Rat hat 4 Ausschüsse: Grundstoffe (Committee on Commodities), Fertigwaren (Committee on Manufactures), Schiffahrt (Committee on Shipping), Handelsfragen und Finanzen (Committee on Invisibles and Financing Related to Trade).
Ziele: Förderung des internationalen Handels, besonders im Hinblick auf eine Beschleunigung der wirtschaftl. Entwicklung der Entwicklungsländer; Ausarbeitung von Grundsätzen und Richtlinien für internationalen Handel und wirtschaftl. Entwicklung; Harmonisierung unterschiedlicher Handels- und Entwicklungsstrategien der Industrie- und Entwicklungsländer; Schaffung einer neuen Weltwirtschaftsordnung

United Nations Convention on Contracts for the International Sale of Goods[21] Übereinkommen der Vereinten Nationen über den internationalen Warenkauf (VN-Kaufrechtsübereinkommen [VNKÜ])
Das Übereinkommen wurde 1980 von ca. 60 Staaten beschlossen, von 20 Staaten gezeichnet und bislang von 11 Staaten ratifiziert. Es ist am 1. 11. 1988 in Kraft getreten.
Das Übereinkommen stellt eine grundlegende Revision des Haager Kaufrechtsübereinkommens dar *(→Hague Sales Convention, →Hague Formation Convention),* an dessen Stelle es treten soll

United Nations Convention on the Law of the Sea Seerechtsübereinkommen der Vereinten Nationen *(von 1982)*

United Nations Development Programme (UNDP) Entwicklungsprogramm der Vereinten Nationen, UN-Entwicklungsprogramm *(mit dem Ziel, den Lebensstandard und das Wirtschaftswachstum vor allem in den ärmsten Ländern der Welt zu fördern)*

United Nations Educational, Scientific and Cultural Organization (UNESCO)[22] Organisation der Vereinten Nationen für Erziehung, Wissenschaft und Kultur, UN-Erziehungs-, Wissenschafts- und Kulturorganisation
Gegr. 1945 (in Kraft getreten 1946).
Organe: Generalkonferenz (General Conference) als oberstes Organ; Exekutivrat (Executive Board), der für die Durchführung des Arbeitsprogramms verantwortlich ist; Sekretariat (Secretariat) unter Leitung e-s Generaldirektors. Länderkommissionen (National Commissions) in allen Mitgliedstaaten.
Aufgabe: Internationale Zusammenarbeit auf geistig-moralischer Basis. Verbesserung des Erziehungswesens in den Mitgliedstaaten, Abbau des Analphabetentums; Förderung der Wissenschaft, bes. der Naturwissenschaft, Unterstützung wissenschaftl. Forschungsinstitute; Unterstützung der internationalen kulturellen Beziehungen

United Nations Emergency Forces (UNEF) Einsatzstreitkräfte der Vereinten Nationen

United Nations Environment Programme (UNEP) Umweltprogramm der Vereinten Nationen, UN-Umweltprogramm

United Nations Fund for Population Activities (UNFPA) UN-Fonds für bevölkerungspolitische Aktivitäten

United Nations General Assembly Vollversammlung der Vereinten Nationen *(→assembly)*

United Nations High Commissioner for Refugees (UNHCR) Hochkommissar der Vereinten Nationen für Flüchtlinge

United Nations Industrial Development Organization (UNIDO) Organisation für industrielle Entwicklung der Vereinten Nationen
Sitz: Wien.
Oberstes Organ: Rat für industrielle Entwicklung (Council for Industrial Development).
(Haupt-)Aufgabe: Beratung der Entwicklungsländer in allen Industrialisierungsfragen durch ca. 400 UNIDO-Experten; Vermittlungsagent für die Finanzierung der Industrialisierungsprojekte

United Nations Organization (UNO) Organisation der Vereinten Nationen (UNO)

United Nations Refugee Fund (UNREF) Flüchtlingshilfsfond der Vereinten Nationen

United Nations Relief and Works Agency for Palestine Refugees (UNRWA) Hilfswerk der Vereinten Nationen für die Palästinaflüchtlinge

United Press International (UPI) Nachrichtenbüro *(in New York)*
Vereinigung von United Press Association (UP) und International News Service (INS) *(1958)*

United States (U. S.) Vereinigte Staaten; ~ **of America** (USA) Vereinigte Staaten von Amerika (USA); ~ **citizen** amerikanischer Staatsangehöriger; ~ **citizenship** amerikanische Staatsangehörigkeit

United States Code (U. S. C.) *Am* offizielle Sammlung von Bundesgesetzen *(entspricht dem deutschen Bundesgesetzblatt Teil III)*
15 U. S. C. § 14 bedeutet z. B. United States Code, Bd. 15, § 14

United States Code Annotated (U. S. C. A.) *Am* mit Anmerkungen versehener U. S. C. *(enthält vor allem Hinweise auf Entscheidungen, in denen das Gesetz ausgelegt wird)*

United States, ~ Commissioners *Am (vom Federal District Court ernannte)* untere Gerichtsbeamte; **(~) District →Court; ~ national** Staatsangehöriger der Vereinigten Staaten; ~ **Pharmacopoeia** (USP) amerikanisches Pharmakopöe *(amtl. Zusammenstellung von Arzneimitteln und Chemikalien mit Zusammensetzungen, Reinheits- und Gütevorschriften; entsprechend dem Deutschen Arzneibuch [D. A. B.])*

United States Real Property Holding Company *Am* Kapitalgesellschaft, deren Vermögen zu mehr als 50% aus amerikanischen Immobilien besteht

United States Real Property Interest *Am* Immobilienrecht *(i. S. des Internal Revenue Code)* (schließt auch bewegliches Vermögen ein, welches im Zusammenhang mit dem Grundstück gebraucht wird)
Beide Begriffe wurden im →Foreign Investment in Real Property Tax Act of 1980 geschaffen zum Zweck der Besteuerung von Gewinnen aus Grundstücksverkäufen durch Ausländer

United States (Supreme Court) Reports (U. S.) *Am* amtliche Sammlung der Entscheidungen des Supreme Court *(→court)*; **Lawyers' Edition of ~** (L. Ed.) *(privat herausgegebene)* Sammlung der Entscheidungen des Supreme Court

unity Einheit; Einigkeit (among unter); Einheitlichkeit *(bes. zur Betonung des Gesamthandcharakters e-r →joint tenancy)*; ~ **of action** Aktionseinheit; ~ **of Europe** Einheit Europas; ~ **of interest** Gleichheit der Beteiligung *(mehrerer joint tenants)*; ~ **of invention** Einheitlichkeit der Erfindung; ~ **of possession** 1. einheitlicher Besitz *(mehrerer joint tenants)*; 2. zweifaches Rechtsverhältnis e-r Person an e-r Sache, bei dem das geringere Recht in dem höheren Recht aufgeht *(z. B. derjenige, zu dessen Gunsten e-e Grunddienstbarkeit bestellt ist, pachtet das herrschende Grundstück)*; ~ **of title** einheitlich begründeter Rechtsanspruch *(mehrerer joint tenants)*; **economic ~** Wirtschaftseinheit

universal universal, universell, allgemein; Gesamt-, weltumfassend; ~ **agent** Generalbevollmächtigter; ~ **bank** Universalbank; *Br* Allzweck-Bank, die Emissions- sowie Depositengeschäfte anbietet; ~ **beneficiary** *Br* Alleinerbe

Universal Copyright Convention[23] Welturheberrechtsabkommen (WUA)
Das Welturheberrechtsabkommen (WUA), das im Jahre 1952 in Genf mit dem Ziele abgeschlossen wurde, auch im Verhältnis zu Staaten, die nicht der Berner Union angehören, insbes. den USA, den Urheberrechtsschutz durch ein multilaterales Abkommen sicherzustellen, dient, wie es in Art. I heißt, dem Schutze der „Werke der Literatur, der Wissenschaft und der Kunst" (literary, scientific and artistic works). Im Ggs. zur Berner Übereinkunft begründet das WUA nur völkerrechtl. Verpflichtungen; man spricht hier nicht von Verbandsländern (Union Countries), sondern von Vertragsstaaten (Contracting States).
Die Bundesrepublik ist dem WUA beigetreten[24].
Durch den →Berne Implementation Act of 1988 sind die USA der Revidierten Berner Übereinkunft *(Revised Berne →Convention)* beigetreten

universal, U~ Declaration of Human Rights Allgemeine Erklärung der Menschenrechte (UNO-Menschenrechtsdeklaration) *(s. Kom-*

mentar zu →human rights); ~ **maintenance standards** →maintenance 3. ~ **military training** (U. M. T.) *Am*[25] allgemeine Wehrpflicht

Universal, ~ **Postal Convention**[26] Weltpostvertrag; ~ **Postal Union** (U. P. U.)[27] Weltpostverein *Am;* ~ **Postal Union Congress** Weltpostkongreß *(gesetzgebendes Organ des Weltpostvereins, der alle Mitgliedstaaten umfaßt und in der Regel alle 5 Jahre zusammentritt)*

universal, ~ **product code** (UPC) *Am* Artikelnumerierung; ~ **standards** Qualitätsbezeichnung für Baumwolle; ~ **succession** *Am und Scot* Gesamt(rechts)nachfolge, Universalsukzession; ~ **suffrage** allgemeines Wahlrecht

universe *Am* Grundgesamtheit

university Universität, Hochschule; ~ **circles** Universitätskreise; ~ **degree** akademischer Grad; ~ **education** Hochschul(aus)bildung, akademische Bildung; ~ **extension courses** Universitätskurse für breite Volksschichten; Volkshochschulkurse; ~ **fees** Studiengebühren

university lecturer (Hochschul-)Dozent; **to qualify as a** ~ sich habilitieren

university, ~ **statutes** Universitätssatzung; ~ **teacher** Hochschuldozent; **admission to a** ~ Zulassung zu e-r Universität; **at the** ~ auf der Universität *(Studenten)*; an der Universität *(Lehrkörper)*; in der Universität *(im Gebäude)*; →**International Association of U~ Professors and Lecturers; open** ~ Fernuniversität; **to be admitted to a** ~ *Br* (to **enroll** [or **register**] **at a** ~ *Am*) sich immatrikulieren lassen; **to enter** (or **go up to** *Br*) **a** ~ an e-e Universität gehen

unjust ungerecht, unbillig; ~ **enrichment** *Am und Scot* ungerechtfertigte Bereicherung; **to benefit ~ly** sich ungerechtfertigt bereichern

unjustifiable nicht zu rechtfertigen

unjustified ungerechtfertigt

unknown unbekannt; ~ **risk** unbekanntes (nicht bestimmtes) Risiko

unlade *v* →unload *v*

unlawful ungesetzlich, rechtswidrig, widerrechtlich, unrechtmäßig; ~ **assembly** unzulässige Zusammenrottung, Auflauf; ~ **detention** ungesetzliche Haft

unlawfulness Rechtswidrigkeit

unleaded petrol (*Am* gas(oline) bleifreies Benzin

unless wenn nicht; vorausgesetzt, daß nicht; ~ **countermanded** mangels gegenteiliger Nachricht; Abbestellung vorbehalten; ~ **otherwise agreed** (or **provided**) mangels abweichender Vereinbarung; vorbehaltlich anderer Vereinbarung; ~ **otherwise specified in ...** sofern in ... nichts anderes bestimmt ist; ~ **and until** solange nicht

unlevered firm schuldenfreie Firma *(die ausschließlich mit Eigenkapital finanziert ist)*

unlicensed unkonzessioniert; ~ **insurer** *Am* →unauthorized insurer

unlimited unbeschränkt; unbegrenzt; ~ **claim** ziffernmäßig nicht begrenzte Forderung; ~ →**company;** ~ **credit** unbeschränkter Kredit; ~ **liability** unbeschränkte Haftung; ~ **order** unlimitierter (Börsen-)Auftrag; ~→**partner; for an** ~ **period** auf unbegrenzte Zeit; unbefristet; ~ **policy** Generalpolice

unliquidated damages *(der Höhe nach)* (noch) unbestimmter Schadensersatz *(opp. liquidated damages)*

Schätzungsbedürftiger Schadensersatz, der nicht ziffernmäßig festgesetzt werden kann, sondern unter Berücksichtigung der Umstände des Schadensfalls von den Parteien, oder falls sie sich nicht einigen können, vom Gericht nach Schätzung festgesetzt werden muß (vgl. hierzu § 287 ZPO)

unliquidated demand *(der Höhe nach)* unbestimmte Forderung

unlisted securities *(an der Börse)* nicht notierte Wertpapiere *(die im privaten Maklergeschäft [Am over the counter] gehandelt werden)*; Freiverkehrswerte *(opp. listed securities)*; ~ **market** (USM) Markt für nicht notierte Wertpapiere; *(geregelter)* Freiverkehr *(Br →Domestic Equity Market)*

unload *v* ent-, ab-, ausladen; *(Ladung)* löschen; *sl. (Wertpapiere)* auf den Markt werfen, abstoßen; **to** ~ **a ship** ein Schiff löschen

unloading, ~ **berth** Ausladeplatz, Löschplatz; ~ **charges** Ausladekosten, Abladekosten; Kosten für Löschung; ~ **risk** *(VersR)* Löschrisiko; **costs of** ~ →~ charges; **days for** ~ Ausladezeit; Entladezeit, Löschzeit; **loading and** ~ Laden und Entladen; *(Schiff)* Laden und Löschen

unmarketable securities nicht börsengängige Wertpapiere

unmatured claim noch nicht fälliger Anspruch

unmerchantable *(für den Gebrauch od. Verkauf)* nicht geeignet; unverkäuflich *(opp. merchantable)*

unmortgaged nicht verpfändet; nicht hypothekarisch belastet

unnamed donor ungenannter Spender

unnatural offen|ce (~se)[28] widernatürliche Unzucht

unneutral service *(VölkerR)* neutralitätswidrige Dienste *(e-s Schiffes)*

unobvious *(PatR)* unvorhersehbar

unoccupied unbewohnt, leerstehend; unbeschäftigt; ~ **property** unbewohnter Grundbesitz

unofficial nicht amtlich, inoffiziell; ~ **broker** *Br* Freiverkehrsmakler; **in an ~ capacity** inoffiziell, nicht amtlich; ~ **market** *Br (ungeregelter)* Freiverkehr; Telefonverkehr; ~ **quotation** Notierung im *(ungeregelten)* Freiverkehr; ~ **strike** *Br* gewerkschaftlich nicht genehmigter Streik

unopposed unwidersprochen; ohne Gegenkandidaten; ~ **candidate** alleiniger Kandidat

unorganized labo(u)r gewerkschaftlich nicht organisierte Arbeitnehmer

unpaid unbezahlt; rückständig; ehrenamtlich; unfrankiert *(Brief)*; ~ **bill** unbezahlte Rechnung; ~ **bill (of exchange)** nicht eingelöster Wechsel; ~ **capital** *(AktienR)* noch nicht eingezahltes Kapital *(cf. paid-up capital)*; ~ **cheque (check)** nicht eingelöster Scheck; ~ **dividend** noch nicht ausgezahlte (od. rückständige) Dividende

unpaid seller, ~'s lien s. seller's →lien (for unpaid purchase money); **remedies of the ~ against the buyer** Rechtsbehelfe gegen den Käufer bei *(ungerechtfertigter)* Zahlungsverweigerung; **rights of the ~ against the goods** Rechte *(des Verkäufers)* auf die Kaufsache bei Nichtzahlung des Kaufpreises

unpaid, to leave a bill ~ e-e Rechnung unbezahlt lassen; e-n Wechsel nicht einlösen; **to return a bill ~** e-e Rechnung (od. e-n Wechsel) unbezahlt zurückgehen lassen

unpatented nicht patentiert

unplatted land *Am* unerschlossenes Land

unpolled electors Nichtwähler

unprecedented ohne Präzedenzfall; beispiellos

unprejudiced unvoreingenommen, vorurteilsfrei; unparteiisch

unproductive, ~ capital totes Kapital; ~ **wage** unproduktiver Lohn

unprofessional conduct standeswidriges Verhalten

unprofitable unrentabel; ~ **investment** Fehlinvestition

unprovided for unversorgt; **the widow was left ~** die Witwe blieb unversorgt zurück

unpublished works nicht veröffentlichte Werke

unpunished unbestraft; **to go ~** straflos ausgehen

unqualified nicht qualifiziert, ungeeignet; uneingeschränkt, unbedingt; ~ **acceptance** *(WechselR)* unbeschränktes Akzept; bedingungslose Annahme

unquoted nicht angeführt (od. zitiert); nicht börsennotiert; ~ **company** Gesellschaft, deren Aktien noch nicht börsennotiert sind; ~ **list** *Br* Freiverkehrsnotierung *(opp. quoted list)*; ~ **shares** nicht notierte Aktien

unrealized profits nicht realisierte Gewinne

unreasonable unvernünftig, unangemessen; *Br (in Zusammenhang mit contracts in restraint of trade), Am (AntitrustR)* den Wettbewerb in unvernünftiger Weise beschränkend *(und deshalb nicht unter die →rule of reason fallend)*; ~ **conduct** *Br (EhescheidungsR)* unzumutbares Benehmen des/der Beklagten *(cf. ground for →divorce)*; ~ **expense** unverhältnismäßige Kosten; ~ **length of time** unangemessene Zeitdauer; ~ **price** unangemessener Preis; **on ~ terms** unter unangemessenen Bedingungen

unrebuttable unwiderlegbar

unreceipted bill nicht quittierte Rechnung

unreceptive attitude wenig entgegenkommende Haltung

unrecognizable, to render ~ unkenntlich machen

unrecognized state *(VölkerR)* nicht anerkannter Staat

unrecorded mortgage *Am* nicht eingetragene Hypothek

unrecoverable debt nicht beitreibbare Forderung

unredeemable bonds untilgbare Obligationen

unredeemed nicht eingelöst *(Versprechen)*; nicht ausgelöst *(Pfand)*; nicht getilgt *(Schuld)*

unregistered nicht registriert, nicht eingetragen; *(Post)* nicht eingeschrieben; ~ **companies** *Br*[29] nicht eingetragene Gesellschaften; ~ **land** *Br* nicht im →Land Register eingetragener Grundbesitz *(cf. first →mortgage)*; ~ **letter** einfacher *(nicht eingeschriebener)* Brief; ~ **→mortgage; ~ society** nicht eingetragener Verein

unremovable unabsetzbar *(z. B. Richter)*

unrest, focus of ~ Unruheherd; **political ~** politische Unruhen; **social ~** soziale Unruhen; **student ~** Studentenunruhen

unrestricted unbeschränkt; *(Straße)* ohne Geschwindigkeitsbegrenzung

unrevoked nicht widerrufen

unroadworthiness Unbefahrbarkeit *(der Straße für Fahrzeuge)*

unrouted telegram Telegramm ohne Leitvermerk

unsalaried unbesoldet, unbezahlt; ehrenamtlich; ~ **clerk** Volontär

unsal(e)able unverkäuflich; ~ **article** Ladenhüter

unsatisfactory unbefriedigend

unsatisfied unbezahlt, unbeglichen *(Schuld)*; nicht befriedigt *(Gläubiger)*; ~ **execution** erfolglose Zwangsvollstreckung

unseal *v* entsiegeln, das Siegel entfernen
unsealed unversiegelt; ohne Siegel
unsealing Siegelabnahme, Entsiegelung

unseaworthiness Seeuntüchtigkeit

unseaworthy ship[30] seeuntüchtiges Schiff

unscheduled depreciation außerplanmäßige Abschreibung

unsecured ungesichert, nicht sichergestellt; ohne Deckung; ~ **credit** ohne Sicherheit gegebener Kredit (z. B. Personalkredit); ~ **creditor** nicht gesicherter (od. sichergestellter) Gläubiger; *(KonkursR)* nicht bevorrechtigter Gläubiger; ~ **loan** ungesichertes Darlehen; Anleihe ohne Deckung; ~ **maintenance** *Br* →maintenance 1.; ~ **overdraft** ungesicherter Kontokorrentkredit

unseizable unpfändbar

unserviceable unbrauchbar *(von Sachen)*

unsettled unerledigt; nicht bezahlt; unbesiedelt *(Land)*; wechselnd; schwankend *(z. B. politisches Klima)*; ~ **account** offenstehende Rechnung; ~ **application** *(PatR)* unerledigte Anmeldung; ~ **claims** *(VersR)* unerledigte Schadensfälle *(→claim 2.)*

unship *v (Ladung)* löschen, ausladen; *(Passagiere)* ausschiffen

unshipment Löschung, Ausladung

unsigned nicht unterzeichnet, ohne Unterschrift

unsized nicht *(nach Größen)* sortiert

unskilled, ~ **labo(u)r** ungelernte Arbeiter (od. Arbeitskräfte), Hilfsarbeiter *(opp. skilled labo[u]r)*; ~ **worker** ungelernter Arbeiter, Hilfsarbeiter

unsocial hours *Br* unsoziale Stunden *(z. B. Nachtschicht von Busfahrern, Polizei etc)*

unsold unverkauft; **subject to being** ~ Zwischenverkauf vorbehalten

unsolicited unaufgefordert; unerbeten; ~ **call** unaufgeforderter Anruf (od. Besuch); ~ **goods**[31] unaufgefordert zugesandte (od. unbestellte) Waren

unsound ungesund; ~ **financial condition** ungesunde Finanzlage; **the building is** ~ das Gebäude ist in schlechtem Zustand

unsound, of ~ **mind** geisteskrank, geistesgestört, geistesschwach *(der Begriff umfaßt insanity, idiocy and imbecility)*; **person of** ~ **mind** Geisteskranker, Geistesgestörter, Geistesschwacher *(umfaßt insane person, idiot and imbecile; Br im amtl. Sprachgebrauch jetzt: person suffering from mental disorder)*; **in a state of** ~ **mind** in e-m Zustand krankhafter Störung der Geistestätigkeit; **to declare sb. of** ~ **mind** *Am* jdn wegen Geisteskrankheit entmündigen

unsoundness of mind Geisteskrankheit, Geistesgestörtheit, Geistesschwäche

unspecified nicht näher spezifiziert, nicht einzeln angegeben

unstable →unsteady

unstamped ungestempelt; unfrankiert *(Brief)*

unsteadiness Unbeständigkeit *(Markt, Preise, Kurse)*

unsteady unbeständig; schwankend *(Kurse)*

unsubscribed stock nicht gezeichnete Aktie(n)

unsuccessful ohne Erfolg, erfolglos; ~ **execution** erfolglose Zwangsvollstreckung; ~ **party** unterliegende (Prozeß-)Partei; **to be** ~ *(Prozeß)* verlieren

unsufficiency *(Zivilprozeß)* Mangel an Schlüssigkeit

unsufficient, the evidence is ~ das Beweismaterial ist unzulänglich, reicht nicht aus

unsuitable ungeeignet

unsworn, ~ **testimony** nicht beeidigte Zeugenaussage; **to leave a witness** ~ e-n Zeugen unbeeidigt lassen

untapped applicant nicht berücksichtigter Bewerber

untaxed unbesteuert, steuerfrei

untenable, ~ **argument** unhaltbares Argument; ~ **condition** untragbarer Zustand; ~ **view** nicht vertretbare Ansicht

untenanted unbewohnt; unvermietet; unverpachtet

unthrifty verschwenderisch

untied loan (or **credit**) *(Entwicklungshilfe)* ungebundener Kredit

until bis; ~ **February 1** bis zum 1. Februar; ~ **cancel(l)ed** bis auf Widerruf; ~ **the contrary is proved** bis zum Beweis des Gegenteils; ~ **countermanded** (or **recalled**) bis auf Widerruf; ~ **further advice** (or **notice**) bis auf weiteres

untimely unzeitig, ungelegen; vor der Zeit, verfrüht

untransferable nicht übertragbar

untrue, ~ **statement** unwahre (od. falsche) Aussage; **to prove to be** ~ sich als unwahr erweisen

untrustworthy unzuverlässig; nicht vertrauenswürdig

unused unbenutzt; ungebraucht; nicht gewöhnt (to an); ~ **credit** nicht in Anspruch genommener Kredit; ~ **ticket** nicht benutzte Fahrkarte

unvalued nicht abgeschätzt; nicht taxiert; ~ **policy** →policy 2.; ~ **stock** *Am* nennwertlose Aktie *(→no par stock)*

unveil *v*, **to ~ a monument** ein Denkmal enthüllen

unveiling ceremony Einweihungsfeier *(für ein Denkmal)*

unvouched funds *Am* Gelder, die ohne Belege verausgabt werden dürfen; Reptilienfonds

unwarranted unverbürgt, ohne Gewähr, unberechtigt

unwilling to pay zahlungsunwillig

unworkable nicht durchführbar *(Plan)*; nicht zu bearbeiten *(Material)*; nicht abbaufähig

unworthy of credit unglaubwürdig, kreditunwürdig, nicht kreditwürdig

unwritten law ungeschriebenes Recht *(Gewohnheitsrecht und case law)*

up *(auch fig)* oben; hoch *(im Kurse)*; ~ **against** (Schwierigkeiten etc) gegenüberstehend; ~**s and downs** Schwankungen *(z.B. der Aktienkurse)*

up before, to be ~ the court vor Gericht verhört (od. verhandelt) werden

up for bereit zu; **to be ~ discussion** zur Diskussion stehen; **to be ~ election** auf der Wahlliste stehen; **to be ~ exceeding the speed limit** wegen Überschreitung der Geschwindigkeitsbegrenzung vor Gericht stehen; **my insurance is ~ renewal** *colloq.* meine Versicherungspolice muß verlängert werden

up in, to be ~ bewandert sein in

up till bis

up to bis zu; bis zum Betrage von; ~ **London** (bis) nach London; ~ **now** bisher, bis jetzt; ~ **(-)date** →up-to-date; ~ **this day** bis zum heutigen Tage; ~ **standard** vollwertig; **to be ~** *(e-r Sache)* gleichkommen, gewachsen sein

up with, to keep ~ Schritt halten (mit)

up, to go ~ steigen, in die Höhe gehen (mit) *(Preise, Kurse)*; **prices are ~** die Preise sind hoch (od. gestiegen); **prices are still going ~** die Preise steigen noch

update, financial ~ letzter Stand der Kursnotierungen

update *v* auf den neuesten Stand bringen; aktualisieren, modernisieren; fortschreiben

updating Aktualisierung

upgrade *v* höher einstufen; *(im Beruf)* befördern *(opp. downgrade v)*

upgrading höhere Einstufung; Höhergruppierung; Beförderung *(opp. downgrading)*

upheaval Umwälzung, Umschwung, Umsturz; **social ~s** soziale Umwälzungen

uphold *v* aufrechterhalten, bestätigen; stützen; **to ~ a cause** e-e Sache vertreten; **to ~ a conviction** e-n Schuldspruch bestätigen; **to ~ a →judgment; to ~ an objection** e-m Einspruch stattgeben; **to ~ a right** ein Recht geltend machen; **to ~ a sentence** ein Strafurteil bestätigen

upkeep Instandhaltung(skosten); Unterhalt(skosten); ~ **of a historic building** Erhaltung(skosten) e-s historischen Gebäudes; ~ **of roads** Instandhaltung(skosten) von Straßen

upper ober, höher, Ober-; **the ~ classes** die Oberschicht; ~ **intervention point** *(Devisenhandel)* oberer Interventionspunkt *(→floating 1.)*; ~ **limit** Obergrenze, Höchstgrenze; **the ~ ten (thousand)** die oberen Zehntausend

Upper Volta Obervolta; **Republic of the ~** Republik Obervolta; **(of the) ~** Obervoltaer, ~in; obervoltaisch

uprate *v* höher ansetzen

upright 1. aufgerichtet, senkrecht; ~ **size** Hochformat; **keep ~** nicht stürzen *(z.B. auf Kisten)*

upright 2. aufrichtig, ehrlich

uprising Erhebung, Aufstand, Revolte

uproar Tumult

upset price *(bei Auktionen)* Mindestpreis *(unter dem kein Angebot angenommen werden darf)*

upset *v* umstoßen; *(Plan)* vereiteln

upstream subsidies *Am* Beihilfen an Zulieferunternehmen der ausländischen Hersteller, die ihre Waren in die Vereinigten Staaten ausführen

upsurge *fig* steiler Aufstieg (od. Anstieg); Aufwallung

upswing *fig* Anstieg; Aufschwung, Aufwärtstrend *(opp. downswing)*; ~ **in prices** Preisanstieg; Kursaufschwung; **(cyclical) ~** Konjunkturaufschwung; **economic ~** Wirtschaftsaufschwung

up to date →date

uptrend Aufwärtsbewegung, -trend *(opp. downtrend)*; ~ **of prices** Aufwärtsbewegung der Preise; Preisauftrieb

upturn Aufschwung, Besserung *(opp. downturn)*; ~ **in demand** Nachfragebelebung; ~ **in prices** (or **quotation**) Kursaufschwung;

economic ~ Wirtschaftsaufschwung, wirtschaftlicher Aufschwung; Konjunkturbelebung

upvaluation Aufwertung *(e-r Währung);* höhere Bewertung

upvalue *v* aufwerten

upward nach oben, aufwärts *(opp. downward);* ~ **movement** Aufwärtsbewegung; ~ **social mobility** sozialer Aufstieg

upward tendency (or **trend**) steigende Tendenz; Hausse; ~ **of prices** Preisauftrieb; Kursauftrieb; ~ **of wages** Lohnauftrieb

uranium Uran; ~ **exploration** (or **extraction**) Urangewinnung; ~ **(re)sources** Uranvorkommen; **enriched** ~ angereichertes Uran

urban städtisch; Stadt- *(opp. rural);* ~ **area** Stadtgebiet; ~ **cent|re (~er)** Stadtzentrum; ~ **development** städtebauliche Entwicklung; ~ **district** Stadtbezirk; ~ **guerilla** Stadtguerilla; ~ **population** Stadtbevölkerung; ~ **renewal** Städtesanierung; ~ **servitude** *Scot* mit e-m Haus verbundene Grunddienstbarkeit *(z.B. auf Licht und Luft);* ~ **sprawl** Zersiedlung

urbanization Urbanisierung, Verstädterung

urbanize *v* urbanisieren, verstädtern; **highly ~d region** Ballungsgebiet

urge *v* dringend ersuchen (od. nahelegen); *(auf etw.)* drängen; geltend machen; **to ~ sb. to do sth.** jdm dringend nahelegen, etw. zu tun

urgency Dringlichkeit; ~ **measure** Dringlichkeitsmaßnahme; ~ **motion** *parl* Dringlichkeitsantrag; **in case of** ~ im Dringlichkeitsfalle; **degree of** ~ Dringlichkeitsstufe; **to propose an ~ motion** e-n Dringlichkeitsantrag stellen

urgent dringend, dringlich, eilig; *(auf Briefen)* „eilt"; ~ **items** dringende (Post-)Sendungen; ~ **need** dringender Bedarf; ~ **order** Eilauftrag; ~ **telegram** dringendes Telegramm; **very** ~ eilt sehr; **to give ~ attention** (or **consideration**) (to) *(etw.)* vordringlich behandeln; **to make ~ representations** *(jdm)* eindringliche Vorhaltungen machen

urgently, to request ~ dringend bitten

Uruguay Uruguay; **Eastern Republic of** ~ Republik Östlich des Uruguay

Uruguayan Uruguayer, ~in; uruguayisch

US →United States; ~ **Trade Representative** (USTR) *(durch US-Omnibus Trade and Competitiveness Act eingeführter)* amerikanischer Handelsbeauftragter

usable brauchbar, verwendbar

usage Brauch, Gebräuche; Handelsbrauch, Usance; Verkehrssitte; Börsenbrauch; Sprachgebrauch; Benutzung; ~ **of the port** Hafenusance; ~ **of trade** Handelsbrauch, Usance; **according to** ~ dem (Handels-)Brauch entsprechend; usancenmäßig

usage, commercial ~ Handelsbrauch; Usance; **in accordance with commercial** ~ handelsüblich; usancenmäßig

usage, international ~ internationaler Brauch; **local** ~ örtlicher Brauch, Ortsgebrauch; Platzusance

usance *(übliche)* Wechselfrist; **bill at** ~ Usowechsel

use 1. Gebrauch, Benutzung, Anwendung, Verwendung; Ausübung *(e-s Rechts);* Verbrauch; ~ **and occupancy insurance** *Am* Betriebsunterbrechungsversicherung *(wegen Zerstörung des Gebäudes durch Feuer, Tornado etc);* ~ **and occupation** →use 2.; ~ **classes**[32] Art der Bodennutzung *(z.B. residential [Wohnungen], shopping [Läden], green belt [Grüngürtel]);* ~ **of force** Anwendung von Gewalt; ~ **of a fund** Inanspruchnahme e-s Fonds; ~ **of funds** Mittelverwendung; ~ **of immovable property** *(DBA)* Nutzung unbeweglichen Vermögens; ~ **of the invention** Benutzung der Erfindung; ~ **of proceeds** Erlösverwendung; ~ **of resources** Mittelverwendung; ~ **of a right** Ausübung e-s Rechts; ~ **of a road** Benutzung e-r Straße; ~ **of a sum of money** Verwendung e-r Geldsumme; ~ →**tax;** ~ **value** Gebrauchswert

use, compensation for ~ Nutzungsentschädigung; **concurrent** ~ *(WarenzeichenR)* konkurrierender Gebrauch; **continuation of** (or **continued**) ~ *(PatR)* Weiterbenutzung; **for daily** ~ zum täglichen Gebrauch; **exclusive** ~ ausschließliche Benutzung; **fair** ~ *(UrheberR)* freie Benutzung *(e-s urheberrechtlich geschützten Werkes);* **for home** ~ zum Verbrauch im Inland; **for one's own** ~ für eigene Verwendung; zum eigenen Gebrauch; **joint** ~ Mitbenutzung, gemeinsame Benutzung; **official** ~ Dienstgebrauch

use, personal ~ *(MietR)* Eigenbedarf; **for personal** ~ zum persönlichen Gebrauch

use, prior ~ *(PatR)* Vorbenutzung; *(WarenzeichenR)* vorherige Benutzung *(im amerikanischen Recht ist nicht die Marke als solche, sondern deren erste Verwendung im Handelsverkehr geschützt);* **prior public** ~ *(PatR)* offenkundige Vorbenutzung; **acts of prior** ~ *(PatR)* Vorbenutzungshandlungen; **notorious prior** ~ *(PatR)* offenkundige Vorbenutzung

use, public ~ Verwendung im öffentlichen Interesse *(als Rechtfertigung der Enteignung; →public);* **for public** ~ für die Öffentlichkeit, für alle; **re-~** Wiederverwendung; **unauthorized** ~ unbefugte Benutzung

use, to be of no ~ keinen Zweck haben; **to convert to one's own** ~ *(etw.)* unrechtmäßig für sich verwenden; **to make** ~ (of) *(etw.)* gebrauchen (od. benutzen); *(von etw.)* Gebrauch machen; **to make good** ~ **of one's money** sein Geld gut verwenden; **to make** ~ **of a right** ein Recht ausüben, von e-m Recht Gebrauch machen; **to make improper** ~ (of) *(etw.)* mißbrauchen; **to take for one's own** ~ für sich verwenden

use 2. *(bis an die Grenzen des Eigentums erweitertes)* Nutzungsrecht

Der use, Vorgänger des späteren trust, bestand im Mittelalter in dem equitable right des cestui que use auf weitgehende Nutzung des Grundbesitzes, während das Eigentum (legal right) auf einen Strohmann, den feoff to uses, übertragen wurde, der im Ggs. zum späteren trustee keine Pflichten zu erfüllen hatte.

Das Statute of Uses (1535) schaffte diese mißbräuchliche Spaltung weitgehend ab, indem es den formalen Rechtstitel dem Nutzungsberechtigten zuwies. Von dem Statute of Uses waren u. a. nicht berührt die sog. "active uses", für die die Bezeichnung "trust" aufkam.

Das Statute of Uses wurde in England durch den Law of Property Act 1925, sec. 207 and Sched. VII, aufgehoben. Es hat in Amerika Gesetzgebung und Rechtsprechung u. a. entscheidend beeinflußt hinsichtlich der passive trusts, die mit Ausnahme der kraft Gesetzes entstandenen trusts (constructive and resulting trusts) weitgehend als ungültig behandelt werden

use and occupation Gebrauch und Innehabung *(e-s Grundstücks)* aufgrund e-s ausdrücklich od. stillschweigend abgeschlossenen Vertrages, der keine Abmachung über die Vergütung enthält; **action for** ~ Klage *(des Grundstückseigentümers)* auf Herausgabe der durch ~ aus dem Grundstück gezogenen Nutzungen

use *v* gebrauchen, benutzen, anwenden, verwenden; **to** ~ **(up)** verbrauchen; **to** ~ **a credit** e-n Kredit in Anspruch nehmen; **to** ~ **a dictionary** ein Wörterbuch benutzen; **to** ~ **one's own discretion** nach eigenem Ermessen handeln; **to** ~ **force** Gewalt anwenden; **to** ~ **one's influence** s-n Einfluß geltend machen; **to** ~ **an invention** e-e Erfindung nutzen; **to** ~ **an opportunity** e-e Gelegenheit benutzen; **to** ~ **the railway (railroad)** die (Eisen-)Bahn benutzen; **to** ~ **a sum of money** e-n Geldbetrag verwenden; **bona fide intention to** ~ *(WarenzeichenR)* ernsthafte Benutzungsabsicht; **right to** ~ Benutzungsrecht

used gebraucht; ~ **car** Gebrauchtwagen; **to get** ~ **to** sich gewöhnen an

useful nützlich; brauchbar; Nutz(ungs)-; ~ **capacity** Nutzlast; ~ **life** Lebensdauer *(von Sachen)*; Nutzungsdauer; ~ **load** Nutzlast; **loss of** ~ **value** *Am (SteuerR)* unvorhergesehene Entwertung (→*loss 1.)*

usefulness Nützlichkeit; Brauchbarkeit; **period of** ~ Nutzungsdauer

useless nutzlos; unbrauchbar; sinnlos

user Benutzer; Gebraucher, Verbraucher; Drogenverbraucher; Benutzung (od. Gebrauch) von Grundbesitz *(für e-n bestimmten Zweck)*; Ausübung *(e-s Rechts)*; ~ **costs** Nutzungskosten; **business** ~ gewerbliche Benutzung *(von Grundbesitz)*; **concurrent** ~**s** *(WarenzeichenR)* konkurrierende (od. nebeneinander bestehende) Benutzer; **end** ~ Endverbraucher; **joint** ~ Mitbenutzer; **non-**~ Nichtgebrauch; Nichtausübung *(e-s Rechts)* (→*non)*; **previous** (or **prior**) ~ Vorbenutzer; **registered** ~ *Br*[33] *(in die Warenzeichenrolle)* eingetragener Lizenznehmer; **road** ~ Benutzer e-r Straße; Verkehrsteilnehmer

usher Gerichtsdiener; Saaldiener; Platzanweiser; **(court)** ~ *Br (etwa)* Justizwachtmeister

USSR UdSSR (→*Union of Soviet Socialist Republics)*

usual üblich, gewöhnlich; ~ **conditions** (u. c.) übliche Bedingungen; **under (the)** ~ **reserve** (u. u. r.) unter dem üblichem Vorbehalt; ~ **in trade** handelsüblich, geschäftsüblich; branchenüblich

usufruct Nutzungsrecht; Nießbrauch; ~ **of immovable property** *(DBA)* Nutzungsrecht an unbeweglichem Vermögen; **to create** (or **grant**) **a** ~ e-n Nießbrauch bestellen

usufructuary den Nießbrauch betreffend; Nießbraucher; Nutznießer; ~ **right** Nutzungsrecht, Nießbrauch(srecht)

usurer Wucherer

usurious wucherisch; Wucher-; ~ **interest** Wucherzinsen; ~ **money lending** Wucher

usurp *v* usurpieren; *(widerrechtl.)* an sich reißen *(Recht, Macht, Thron etc)*; sich *(widerrechtl.)* anmaßen

usurpation widerrechtliche Aneignung (od. Besitzergreifung); Usurpation

usurper Usurpator

usury Wucher; Wucherzinsen; ~ **law** *Am* Wuchergesetz; **to practise** ~ Wucher treiben

utilities *Am* (Strom-, Gas-, Wasser-)Versorgungsunternehmen; *(Börse)* Versorgungswerte, Tarifwerte; →**public** ~

utility Nutzen, Nützlichkeit, Brauchbarkeit; (Eignung zur) gewerbliche(n) Anwendbarkeit *(im PatentR sind utility und novelty Voraussetzung für Erteilung e-s Patents)*; öffentlicher Versorgungsbetrieb *(Strom, Gas, Wasser etc)* (→*public* ~); ~ **certificate** Gebrauchsmusterzertifikat; ~ **company** Versorgungsunternehmen, Unternehmen der Versorgungsindustrie; ~ **goods** Gebrauchsgüter; ~ **invention** gewerblich verwertbare Erfindung

utility model Gebrauchsmuster; ~ **disputes** Gebrauchsmusterstreitsachen; ~ **infringement** Gebrauchsmusterverletzung; ~ **register** Gebrauchsmusterrolle
utility, ~-operated stores *Am* betriebseigene Läden der Versorgungsunternehmen; ~ **patent** gewerblich verwertbares Patent; ~ **rates** Abgaben und Gebühren an die (städtischen) Versorgungsbetriebe; **(public)** ~ (Unternehmen der) öffentliche(n) Versorgung *(mit Elektrizität, Gas, Wasser, Verkehrsleistungen)*; ~ **value** Nutzwert

utilization Nutzbarmachung; Ausnutzung, Auslastung; Nutzung, Verwertung; ~ **of appropriations** Inanspruchnahme (od. Verwendung) der Haushaltsmittel; ~ **of resources** Ausnutzung der Hilfsquellen; ~ **of scrap** Abfallverwertung; ~ **rate** (or **ratio**) (Kapazitäts-)Ausnutzungsgrad

utilize *v* nutzbar machen; (aus)nutzen, verwerten; verwenden; **to ~ a credit** e-n Kredit in Anspruch nehmen; **a letter of credit not ~d** ein noch nicht ausgenutztes Akkreditiv; **to ~ a patent** ein Patent auswerten

utmost äußerst; **matter of (the) ~ concern** (or **importance**) Sache von äußerster Wichtigkeit; ~ **secrecy** strengste Geheimhaltung

utopian utopisch, wirklichkeitsfremd

utter barrister *Br* →junior barrister *(opp. Queen's Counsel)*

utter *v* äußern, aussprechen; *(StrafR) (gefälschte Urkunde od. Falschgeld)* in Umlauf setzen; **to ~ calumnies** verleumden
uttering false coin Inverkehrbringen (od. Weitergabe) von Falschgeld; Münzbetrug

utterer of counterfeit coin Verausgaber von Falschmünzen

U-turn *(auch pol)* (völlige) Kehrtwendung; **to make a ~** e-e Kehrtwendung machen

V

vacancies Stellenangebote, freie Stellen *(e-s Betriebes)*; freie Räume; **three ~ies in this appartment house** *Am* drei leerstehende Wohnungen in diesem Mietshaus
vacancy 1. freie (od. offene, unbesetzte) Stelle; Vakanz; frei werdender (od. gewordener) Sitz; **to advertise a ~** e-e freie Stelle ausschreiben; **to fill a ~** e-e (freie) Stelle neu besetzen; e-n Sitz neu besetzen; **a ~ arises** (or **occurs**) e-e Vakanz tritt ein; e-e Stelle wird frei; ein Sitz wird frei; **to fill a ~ in Congress** *Am* im Kongreß e-n Sitz neu besetzen
vacancy 2. Leerstehen *(e-r Wohnung)*; Unbewohntsein *(e-s Hauses)*; Zimmer frei *(Hotel)*; ~ **clause** *Am (bes. VersicherungsR)* Bestimmung in e-m Vertrag, die Leerstehen e-r Wohnung während e-r bestimmten Zeit erlaubt; **no ~ies in this hotel** in diesem Hotel sind keine Zimmer frei

vacant 1. frei, unbesetzt; vakant; ~ **succession** herrenlose Erbschaft; **situations ~** Stellenangebote, offene Stellen *(in Zeitungen)*; **to apply for a ~ post** sich um e-e freie Stelle bewerben; **a position becomes ~** e-e Stelle wird frei; **a seat falls ~** *parl* ein Sitz wird frei
vacant 2. unbewohnt, leerstehend; ~ **lot** *Am* unbebautes Grundstück; ~ **possession** verlassener Grundbesitz; ~ **room** Leerzimmer; **to give ~ possession on completion** bei Abschluß des Kaufvertrags das Haus (od. die Wohnung) sofort beziehbar übergeben

vacate *v* 1. *(Wohnung etc)* räumen; ausziehen; *(Stellung)* aufgeben; **to ~ an office** ein Amt niederlegen (od. aufgeben); aus dem Amt ausscheiden; **to ~ one's residence** s-n Wohnsitz aufgeben; **to ~ one's seat** *parl* sein Mandat niederlegen; **notice to ~** Kündigung *(→notice 3.)*
vacate *v* 2. aufheben, annullieren, für ungültig erklären; **to ~ a judgment** *Am* ein Urteil aufheben

vacation 1. *Br* Gerichtsferien; *Br* Universitätsferien; *Am* Schulferien; *Am* (Erholungs-)Urlaub, Ferien; ~ **allowance** *Am* Urlaubsgeld; ~ **business** *Br* Feriensachen *(des Gerichts)*; ~ **court** *Br* Ferienkammer; ~ **judge** *Br* Richter während der Gerichtsferien; ~ **of the court** *Br* Gerichtsferien; ~ **replacement** *Am* Urlaubsvertretung; ~ **request** *Am* Urlaubsgesuch; ~ **schedule** *Am* Urlaubsplan; ~ **sittings** *Br* Sitzungen von 2 Richtern des High Court (vacation judges) während der Gerichtsferien; ~ **with pay** *Am* bezahlter Urlaub; ~ **without pay** *Am* unbezahlter Urlaub; **to be on ~** *Am* auf Urlaub sein; **to take a ~** *Am* Urlaub nehmen, Ferien machen
vacation 2. Niederlegung *(e-s Amtes)*; Räumung *(e-s Hauses)*

vaccinate *v* impfen (against gegen)

vaccination Impfung; ~ **certificate** Impfschein, Impfbescheinigung; **compulsory ~** Impfzwang; **international certificate of ~ or re~ against smallpox**[1] internationale Bescheinigung über Impfung oder Wiederimpfung gegen Pocken; **preventive ~** Schutzimpfung

vagabond (or **vagrant**)[2] Landstreicher, Gammler

vagrancy Landstreicherei; Gammlerei

valid gültig, rechtsgültig; triftig, stichhaltig; richtig, berechtigt; ~ **argument** stichhaltiges Argument; ~ **claim** berechtigter Anspruch; ~ **contract** (or **deed**) rechtsgültiger Vertrag; ~ **marriage** (rechts)gültige Ehe; ~ **objection** berechtigter Einspruch; ~ **passport** gültiger Paß; ~ **reason** triftiger Grund; ~ **until recalled** *(Börse)* bis auf Widerruf gültig; ~ **up to and including** gültig bis einschließlich; ~ **will** gültiges Testament; **to become** ~ rechtswirksam werden

validate *v* gültig machen; für (rechts)gültig erklären; bestätigen; bereinigen

validation Gültigkeitserklärung; Bestätigung; ~ **certificate** Gültigkeitsbescheinigung

validity Gültigkeit, Rechtsgültigkeit; Richtigkeit, Berechtigung; Gültigkeitsdauer; ~ **of an argument** Stichhaltigkeit e-s Arguments; ~ **of a contract** (or **deed**) Rechtsgültigkeit e-s Vertrages; ~ **of an election** Gültigkeit e-r Wahl; **expiration of (the period of)** ~ Ablauf der Gültigkeitsdauer; **extension of (the period of)** ~ Verlängerung der Gültigkeitsdauer; **of general** ~ allgemeingültig; **legal** ~ Rechtsgültigkeit; **run of** ~ Gültigkeitsdauer; **period** (or **time**) **of** ~ Gültigkeitsdauer; **to contest** (or **dispute**) **the** ~ die Gültigkeit bestreiten (od. anfechten); **to extend the (duration of)** ~ die Gültigkeitsdauer verlängern

valorem, ad ~ **duty** Wertzoll; vom Wert abhängende Stempelsteuer (stamp duty); **ad** ~ **rates** Wertfracht *(Fracht nach Prozentsätzen des Warenwertes)*; **ad** ~ **tax** *Am* Vermögenssteuer

valorization Valorisation *(staatl. Maßnahmen zur Stabilisierung der Marktpreise, z.B. planvolle Vernichtung nicht absetzbarer Rohstoffe od. landwirtschaftl. Erzeugnisse mit dem Ziel, den Preis des verbleibenden Restes zu erhöhen)*

valorize *v* valorisieren *(Preise durch staatl. Maßnahmen zugunsten der Produzenten beeinflussen; cf. valorization)*

valuable wertvoll, kostbar; abschätzbar; ~ **articles** Wertsachen; ~ **assets** Wertgegenstände, Valoren; ~ **consideration** entgeltliche (geldwerte) Gegenleistung; **for** ~ **consideration** (without notice) gegen Entgelt, entgeltlich (ohne Kenntnis der Unzulässigkeit)

valuables Wertsachen, Valoren; ~**insurance** Valorenversicherung

valuation Bewertung, Wertbestimmung; geschätzter Wert, Taxwert; *(Bilanz)* Wertansatz; *Br* Festsetzung des Steuerwertes von Grundbesitz *(→rateable value)*; *Am* Bestimmung des Gegenwartswerts e-r Lebensversicherungspolice; ~ **allowance** Wertberichtigung; ~ **at cost** Bewertung zu den Anschaffungskosten; ~ **basis** Bewertungsgrundlage; ~ **charge** Wertzuschlag *(für erhöhte Haftung bei Luftfracht)*; ~ **for customs purposes** Zollwertermittlung; ~ **for rating** *Br* Abschätzung des Grundbesitzes zur Berechnung der Kommunalsteuer; ~ **list** *Br*[3] *(von Beamten des Inland Revenue in e-m Kommunalsteuerbezirk angelegtes)* Verzeichnis der Grundstücksverhältnisse; *(etwa)* Kataster *(zur Bestimmung des →rateable value)*; ~ **of an enterprise** Unternehmensbewertung; ~ **of fixed assets** Bewertung des Anlagevermögens; ~ **of property** Abschätzung (od. Bewertung) von Grundbesitz; *Br* Festsetzung des →rateable value von Grundbesitz; ~ **reserve** Rückstellung für Wertberichtigungen; ~ **roll** *Scot (etwa)* Kataster *(für Steuerzwecke)*; **basis of** ~ Bewertungsgrundlage; **inventory** ~ Bestandsbewertung; **objection to** ~ Einspruch gegen die Wertbestimmung; *Br* Einspruch gegen die Festsetzung des →rateable value; **probate** ~ *Br* Wertbestimmung des Nachlasses *(zur Festsetzung der →inheritance tax)*; **to undertake the** ~ **of property** Grundbesitz bewerten *(Br auch zur Festsetzung des →rateable value)*

valuator Taxator, Taxierer, Schätzer

value 1. Wert; *bes. Br* Valuta (*Geld in ausländischer Währung*)

value, to assess the ~ den Wert festsetzen; **to attach** ~ **to sth.** e-r Sache Wert (od. Bedeutung) beimessen; **to compute the** ~ den Wert berechnen; **to declare the** ~ den Wert angeben; **to decline** (or **fall**) **in** ~ im Werte sinken, Wertminderung erfahren; **to increase in** ~ s. to rise in **→~; to lose in** ~ an Wert verlieren; **to reduce in** ~ entwerten; **to rise in** ~ im Wert steigen; **to set (great)** ~ **on** (großen) Wert legen auf

value-added Wertschöpfung; ~ **tax** Mehrwertsteuer *(→VAT)*

value, ~ **adjustments** *(Bilanz)* Wertberichtigungen; ~ **analysis** Wertanalyse (*Methode zur Ergebnisverbesserung in allen Bereichen e-r Unternehmung*); ~ **as a going concern** Unternehmenswert; ~ **assessed** geschätzter Wert; ~ **compensated** (*Devisenhandel*) Valuta kompensiert

value date *bes. Br* Tag der Wertstellung (*auf dem Bankkonto*); Valutierungstag (*an dem e-e Gut- od. Lastschrift für den Kunden erfolgt*); Abrechnungstag (*im Devisenhandel*); **to state the** ~ valutieren

value, ~**engineering** Wertanalyse auf Untersuchungsobjekte im Entstehungsstadium; ~ **for collection** Inkassowert; ~ **given clause** Valutaklausel; ~ **in exchange** Tauschwert; ~ **involved in litigation** Streitwert; ~ **1. June** Valuta 1. Juni; ~ **of money** Wert (od. Kaufkraft) des Geldes

value, above the ~ über dem Wert; **acquisition** ~

Anschaffungswert; **actual** ~ tatsächlicher Wert, Effektivwert *(opp. nominal ~)*; **agreed** ~ vereinbarter Wert; **aggregate** ~ Gesamtwert; **amateur** ~ Liebhaberwert; →**annual** ~ **appraised** ~ Schätzwert, Taxwert; **appreciation in** ~ Wertsteigerung, Werterhöhung; **arbitrary** ~ willkürlich angenommener Wert; **ascertainment of** ~ Wertermittlung; **below** ~ unter dem Wert; →**book** ~; **calculation of** ~ Wertberechnung; **cash** ~ Barwert; **certificate of** ~ Bescheinigung des Wertes *(Br bes. in der Übertragungsurkunde [conveyance, transfer] bei Veräußerung von Grundbesitz. Zweck: Vermeidung oder Niedrighaltung der →stamp duty)*; **declared** ~ angegebener Wert; *(Zoll)* angemeldeter Wert; **declaration of** ~ Wertangabe; **decline** (or **decrease**) **in** ~ Werteinbuße, Wertminderung; **depreciation in** (or **diminuation of**) ~ Wertminderung; Entwertung; **determination of** ~ Wertfeststellung; Wertfestsetzung; **enhancement in** ~ Wertsteigerung, Werterhöhung; **estimated** ~ s. appraised →~; **exchange** ~ (Ein-)Tauschwert; **face** ~ Nennwert, Nominalwert; **fair** ~ angemessener Wert; **good** ~ **(for money)** preiswert; **increase in** ~ Wertsteigerung; **increment in** ~ Wertzuwachs; **insurable** ~ versicherbarer Wert; **insured** ~ Versicherungswert; **letting** ~ Mietwert; Pachtwert; **loan** ~ Beleihungswert; **loss in** ~ Wertverlust; Entwertung; **market** ~ Marktwert; Verkehrswert; **new** (or **original**) ~ Neuwert, Anschaffungswert; **nominal** ~ nomineller Wert; Nominalwert *(→nominal)*; **object of** ~ Wertgegenstand; **of good** ~ preiswert; **of small** ~ geringwertig; **of stable** ~ wertbeständig; **purchasing** ~ Anschaffungswert; **real** ~ effektiver Wert, Sachwert; **reduction in** ~ Wertminderung; Entwertung; **replacement** ~ Wiederbeschaffungswert; **scarcity** ~ Seltenheitswert; **scrap** ~ Schrottwert; **sentimental** ~ Liebhaberwert; →**sound** ~; **surrender** ~ Rückkaufswert *(e-r Lebensversicherung)*; **to the** ~ **of** bis zu, im Werte von; **total** ~ Gesamtwert; **trade** ~ Handelswert, Verkehrswert; **use** ~ Gebrauchswert

value, loss of useful ~ *Br (SteuerR)* unvorhergesehene Entwertung *(als Abschreibungsmöglichkeit; cf. obsolescence, wear and tear)*

value 2. Gegenleistung *(→valuable consideration)*; **for** ~ gegen Entgelt, entgeltlich; **holder for** ~ entgeltlicher Inhaber; Inhaber, der ein Wertpapier (od. e-n Wechsel) entgeltlich erworben hat; **purchaser for** ~ **without notice** gutgläubiger Erwerber gegen Entgelt; **bona fide purchaser for** ~ gutgläubiger Erwerber gegen Entgelt; **to acquire for** ~ **without notice** gutgläubig gegen Entgelt erwerben; **to take an instrument for** ~ *Am* ein Papier entgeltlich erwerben

value *v (Wert)* (ab)schätzen; bewerten, taxieren (at auf); valutieren; **to** ~ **sb.'s advice** jds Rat schätzen; **to** ~ **land** (or **property**) den Grundstückswert abschätzen

valued, ~ **customer** geschätzter Kunde; ~ **policy** Police mit Wertangabe, taxierte Police *(opp. open policy)*

valuing Schätzung; Bewertung, Taxierung

valueless wertlos; **to render** ~ wertlos machen, entwerten

valuer Taxator, Taxierer, Schätzer; ~**'s office** Katasteramt

valuta Valuta

van *bes. Br* Lieferwagen; *Br (geschlossener)* Güterwagen; Lastkraftwagen; **furniture** ~ *bes. Br* Möbelwagen; →**lift** ~; **luggage** ~ *Br* Packwagen; **moving** ~ *Am* (**removal** ~ *Br*) Möbelwagen

vandalism Rowdytum; böswillige Sachbeschädigung; Vandalismus

vandalize *v* böswillig zerstören

variability Veränderlichkeit *(Kurse, Preise etc)*

variable veränderlich, schwankend *(opp. fixed)*; ~ **annuity** Rente mit veränderlichen Auszahlungsbeträgen *(Kombination von Lebensversicherung und Investmentanlage)*; ~ **costs** variable Kosten; ~ **(exchange) rate** variabler Kurs; ~ **(interest) rate** variabler Zins; ~ **life insurance** *Am* fondsgebundene Lebensversicherung; ~ **or fixed payments** (*DBA*) veränderliche od. feste Vergütungen; ~ **premium** veränderliche Prämie; ~ **price** variabler Kurs; ~**-price market** variabler Markt; ~ **rate mortgage** *Am* hypothekarisch gesichertes Darlehen mit variablem Zinssatz; ~**-yield interest-bearing securities** Wertpapiere mit schwankendem Ertrag, variable Werte

variance Abweichung, Veränderung; Widerspruch; Uneinigkeit, Streit; *(im pleading)* widersprüchlicher Vortrag *(Widerspruch zwischen Klagebehauptung und dem Ergebnis der Auswertung der Beweismittel, die zur Unterstützung der Klagebehauptung vorgetragen wurden)*; ~ **between reports** Widerspruch zwischen Berichten; ~ **in values** Wertabweichung; **cost** ~ Kostenabweichung; **price** ~ Preisabweichung; **quantity** ~ Mengenabweichung; →**zoning** ~; **at** ~ **with** in Abweichung von; im Widerspruch zu

variation Veränderung; Abweichung; Schwankung; *(Statistik)* Streuung; ~ **in prices** Preisschwankung; ~**s in public opinion** Wandel in der öffentlichen Meinung; **allowed** ~ zulässige Abweichung; Toleranz; **plus or minus** ~ Abweichung nach oben *(z. B. Preiserhöhung)* oder unten *(z. B. Preisminderung)*

variet|y Mannigfaltigkeit, Vielfalt; *(breites)* Sortiment; Auswahl; Art, Sorte; Varieté; ~ **reduction** Sortimentsbeschränkung; **list of ~ies** Sortenkatalog

vary *v* abändern; abweichen (from von); sich (ver)ändern; variieren, verschieden sein; **the prices ~ widely** die Preise sind sehr unterschiedlich; **to ~ the terms of a contract** die Vertragsbestimmungen abändern

vast majority überwiegende Mehrheit

VAT (value-added tax) Mehrwertsteuer; ~ **accounting period** Voranmeldezeitraum *(für Mehrwertsteuer)*; ~ **base** Mehrwertsteuerbemessungsgrundlage; ~ **Directive** Mehrwertsteuerrichtlinie; ~ **increase** Mehrwertsteuererhöhung; ~ **rate** Mehrwertsteuersatz; ~ **refund** Mehrwertsteuerrückerstattung; ~ **revenues** Mehrwertsteuereinnahme; ~ **zero-rating** Mehrwertsteuersatz Null

VAT, collection of ~ Mehrwertsteuererhebung; **exempted from** ~ von der Mehrwertsteuer befreit; **exemption from** ~ Mehrwertsteuerbefreiung; **flat-rate** ~ Mehrwertsteuerpauschale; **rise in** ~ →~increase; **subject to** ~ mehrwertsteuerpflichtig

Vatikan Vatikan; ~ **City** Vatikanstadt; ~ **City State** Staat Vatikanstadt

vault Tresor, Stahlkammer *(e-r Bank)*; Gruft; ~ **cash** Bargeld e-r Bank für den täglichen Bedarf; **bank** ~ Banktresor; **family** ~ Familiengruft; **safe deposit** ~ *Am* Stahlkammer

vegetable, ~ **products** Waren pflanzlichen Ursprungs; **processed fruit and** ~**s** Verarbeitungserzeugnisse aus Obst und Gemüse

vehicle Fahrzeug; (Hilfs-)Mittel; ~ **and traffic laws** *Am* Verkehrsvorschriften; ~ **licence duty** *Br* Kraftfahrzeugsteuer; ~ **pool** Fuhrpark; ~ **registration** Kraftfahrzeugzulassung; ~ **registration document** *Br* Kraftfahrzeugbrief; ~ **test** Fahrzeugüberwachung; **commercial** ~ Nutzfahrzeug; **motor** ~ Kraftfahrzeug *(→motor)*; **passing and overtaking** ~**s** vorbeifahrende und überholende Fahrzeuge; **public** ~ öffentliches Verkehrsmittel

vehicular, ~ **hazard warning** Warnblinkanlage; ~ **traffic** Fahrzeugverkehr

veil, under the ~ **of** *fig* unter dem Deckmantel von; **to pierce the corporate** ~ den Deckmantel (od. Schleier) der Rechtspersönlichkeit e-r Gesellschaft durchstoßen (od. lüften) *(zum Zwecke der persönlichen Haftung des Gesellschafters)*; Durchgriffshaftung annehmen

veiled balance sheet verschleierte Bilanz

velocity of circulation of money Umlaufgeschwindigkeit des Geldes

venal käuflich, bestechlich

vend *v* verkaufen
vending machine (Verkaufs-)Automat

vendee *Am* Käufer(in), Erwerber(in) *(bes. von Grundbesitz)*

vendible verkäuflich

vendor Verkäufer(in) *(bes. im Liegenschaftskauf)*; ~ **company** einbringende Gesellschaft; ~**'s lien** *Am* Sicherungsrecht des Verkäufers an der veräußerten Sache; ~**'s mortgage** *Br* Restkaufgeldhypothek; ~**s' shares** eingebrachte Aktien; Gründeraktien

vendue *Am* Auktion

veneral disease Geschlechtskrankheit

Venezuela, Republic of ~ Republik Venezuela
Venezuelan Venezolaner, ~in; venezolanisch

venire ("to come") *Am* Geschworenenvorladung; die zur Auswahl für die →jury vorgeladenen Bürger
venireman *Am (auf der Liste stehender)* zum Geschworenendienst vorgeladener Bürger

venture Wagnis, Risiko; risikoreiches Unternehmen; ~ **capital** Risikokapital; Wagniskapital; ~ **financing** Wagnisfinanzierung; **business** ~ geschäftliches Vorhaben; **high-risk** ~ mit hohem Risiko verbundenes Unternehmen; →**joint** ~; **real estate** ~ *Am* Grundstücksspekulation; **to join a** ~ e-m Unternehmen (od. Vorhaben) beitreten; **to start a new** ~ ein Unternehmen gründen

venue *(örtliche)* Zuständigkeit *(e-s Gerichts)*; Gerichtsstand; Treffpunkt, Zusammenkunftsort; **to change the** ~ die Rechtssache an das Gericht e-s anderen Bezirks abtreten; **to lay the** ~ den Ort für die Durchführung des Verfahrens bestimmen; die Klage einbringen (in); **to dismiss the complaint for improper** ~ die Klage wegen örtlicher Unzuständigkeit abweisen; **to fix the** ~ bestimmen, vor welchem zuständigen Gericht die Verhandlung stattfinden soll

verbal mündlich *(opp. written)*; wörtlich, wortgetreu; ~ **agreement** mündliche Vereinbarung (od. Absprache); ~ **note** *(VölkerR)* Verbalnote; ~ **offer** mündliches Angebot

verbatim wörtlich, Wort für Wort; ~ **quotation** wörtliches Zitat; ~ **record of the proceedings** wortgetreues Protokoll (od. Wortlautprotokoll) des Verfahrens; **to quote** ~ wörtlich zitieren

verbose weitschweifig

verdict Wahrspruch *(der Geschworenen in e-r Tatfrage im Straf- od. Zivilprozeß)*; Jury-Urteil; *(allgemeines)* Urteil, Meinung, Ansicht; ~ **for the defendant (plaintiff)** *(Zivilprozeß)* Verneinung (Bejahung) des Klageanspruchs; ~ **of guilty** *(Strafprozeß)* Schuldspruch; ~ **of not guilty** Erkennen auf „nicht schuldig" *(durch die Schöffen)*[4]; ~ **of the jury** Urteilsspruch der Geschworenen; **general** ~ *(Zivilprozeß)* Entscheidung für den Kläger od. den Beklagten; *(Strafprozeß)* Schuldspruch od. Freispruch; **special** ~ Feststellung des Tatbestandes *(die rechtliche Entscheidung wird dem Gericht überlassen)*; **to give** (or **return**) **a** ~ e-n Spruch fällen; **the jury returned** (or **brought in, delivered, gave**) **a** ~ **of guilty/not guilty** die Geschworenen (Schöffen[4]) erkannten auf schuldig/ nicht schuldig

verifiable verifizierbar, nachprüfbar

verification Verifizierung; Bestätigung *(der Richtigkeit od. Wahrheit)*; Überprüfung, Nachprüfung; *Am* eidliche Beteuerung am Ende e-s Schriftsatzes, daß die darin enthaltenen Vorbringen wahr sind; ~ **of the cash** Kassenrevision; ~ **of a flag** *(VölkerR)* Prüfung e-r Flagge, Flaggenprüfung; ~ **of a →signature;** ~ **statement** *(Bank)* Saldenbestätigung; **after** ~ nach Richtigbefund; **delivery** ~ Wareneingangsbescheinigung

verify *v* verifizieren; *(Richtigkeit etc)* bestätigen, nachprüfen; *Am* eidlich bestätigen; **to** ~ **an account** e-e Rechnung nachprüfen; die Richtigkeit e-s Kontensaldos bestätigen; **to** ~ **the cash** die Kasse prüfen (od. revidieren); **to** ~ **an oath** eidlich bestätigen; **to** ~ **a signature** die Echtheit e-r Unterschrift nachprüfen (od. bestätigen); **to** ~ **a statement** die Richtigkeit e-r Aussage bestätigen; e-e Aussage als wahr nachweisen

verified by affidavit durch eidliche Erklärung bestätigt (od. bekräftigt)

verifying, a translator's affidavit ~ **the translation** das die Richtigkeit der Übersetzung bestätigende Affidavit e-s Übersetzers

Veritas, (Bureau ~**)** Schiffsklassifizierungsgesellschaft

versatility Vielseitigkeit; Anpassungsfähigkeit

versed erfahren, bewandert; **to be** ~ **in business** geschäftserfahren sein, ein versierter Geschäftsmann sein

version Version, Fassung, Darstellung; Übersetzung; **amended** (or **revised**) ~ **of a law** Neufassung e-s Gesetzes

versus (v.) gegen; **re X v. Y** in Sachen X./.Y

vertical vertikal *(opp. horizontal)*; ~ **combination** vertikaler Zusammenschluß, Vertikalkonzern; ~ **integration** vertikale Integration *(Zusammenschluß mehrerer Unternehmer verschiedener Produktionsstufen)*; ~ **→merger;** ~ **price-fixing** vertikale Preisvereinbarung, Preisbindung der zweiten Hand *(Vereinbarung zwischen Produzenten und Großhändler oder Großhändler und Einzelhändler)*; ~ **restraint guidelines** vertragliche Wettbewerbsbeschränkungen in der Vertikalebene *(bes. Gebiets- und Kundenbeschränkungen)*; ~ **→restraints;** ~ **trust** Vertikaltrust; ~ **union** Industriegewerkschaft *(Mitglieder nur einer Industrie)*, vertikale Gewerkschaft

vessel Schiff; Fahrzeug; ~ **of inland navigation** Binnenschiff; **cargo** ~ Frachtschiff; **coasting** ~ Küstenschiff; **cold storage** ~ Kühlschiff, Schiff mit Gefrieranlage; **entry and departure of a** ~ Ein- und Auslaufen e-s Schiffes; **escort** ~ Geleitschiff; **factory** ~ Fischverarbeitungsschiff; **fishing** ~ Fischereifahrzeug; **idle** ~ stilliegendes Schiff; **laden** (or **loaden**) ~ beladenes Schiff; **light** ~ unbeladenes Schiff; **merchant** ~ Handelsschiff, Kauffahrteischiff; **passenger** ~ Passagierschiff; **pilot** ~ Lotsenfahrzeug; **sailing** ~ Segelfahrzeug; **sea-going** ~ (Hoch-)Seeschiff; **trading** ~ Handelsschiff; **war** ~ Kriegsschiff

vest *v (Recht)* verleihen, übertragen (in sb. auf jdn); zufallen, übertragen werden, übergehen (auf); *(Vollmacht)* erteilen, *(mit Vollmacht)* ausstatten; **to** ~ **sb. with authority** jdm Vollmacht erteilen; jdn ermächtigen; **as soon as a p. is adjudicated bankrupt, his property** ~**s in the trustee in bankruptcy** bei Konkurseröffnung geht das Vermögen des Gemeinschuldners auf den Konkursverwalter über

vested verliehen, bekleidet; festbegründet; eingesetzt; ~ **interest** sicher begründetes Anrecht *(opp. expectancy)*

vested, ~ **in interest** bekleidet mit e-m gegenwärtigen (bestehenden) Recht auf zukünftigen Besitz *(e-s Grundstückes)*; ~ **in possession** bekleidet mit e-m Recht auf unmittelbaren Besitz *(e-s Grundstücks)*

Beispiel: Wenn ein Grundstück zunächst an A und nach dessen Tode bedingungslos an B fällt, dann ist das Recht des A vested in possession und das des B vested in interest

vested, ~ **pension right** unverfallbare Pensionsanwartschaft; ~ **remainder** unentziehbare(s) Anwartschaft(srecht) *(→remainder 2.)*

vested right feststehendes *(d.h. nicht von e-r Bedingung abhängiges)* Recht; wohlerworbenes (unverfallbares) Recht; ~ **theory** *(IPR)* Lehre von der Anerkennung der in e-m anderen Staat begründeten, also wohlerworbenen Rechte

vested with powers mit Vollmacht versehen

vested, body (or **person**) ~ **with authority** mit Vollmacht versehene (od. ermächtigte) Körperschaft (od. Person); **to be ~ in a p.** in jds Händen liegen; **the court is ~ with discretion** das Gericht hat nach freiem Ermessen zu entscheiden; **the executive power shall be ~ in the President** *Am*[5] die vollziehende Gewalt liegt beim Präsidenten

vesting Verleihung, Übertragung; Übernahme, Anfall; Unverfallbarkeit *(z.B. e-s Pensionsanspruchs)*; **~ assent** *Br*[6] Urkunde, durch die ein Erbschaftsverwalter (personal representative) nach dem Tode e-s →tenant for life oder →statutory owner →settled land auf den neuen Berechtigten überträgt; **~ deed** *Br*[6] Urkunde, durch die →settled land auf e-n →tenant for life od. →statutory owner übertragen wird *(cf. trust instrument)*; **~ instrument** *Br*[6] Übertragungsurkunde *(vesting deed, vesting assent od. vesting order)*; **~ of powers** Übertragung von Vollmachten; **~ order** *Br*[7] gerichtl. Verfügung, die das Eigentum an Grundbesitz e-r bestimmten Person *(z.B. e-m trustee)* überträgt ohne Aushändigung e-s deed; *Am* Beschlagnahmeverfügung des →Custodian of Enemy Property

vestibule training *Am* Ausbildung in eigener Lehrwerkstatt *(e-s Industriebetriebes)*

vet *v Br fig (genau)* (über)prüfen; **~ting of an application** Prüfung e-s Antrags

veteran *bes. Am* ehemaliger Kriegsteilnehmer, ehemaliger Angehöriger der Streitkräfte; **V~s' Administration** *Am (etwa)* Versorgungsverwaltung *(für den Personenkreis ehemaliger Kriegsteilnehmer)*; **~s' benefits** *Am (umfangreiches Programm verschiedenartiger)* Leistungen an ehemalige Kriegsteilnehmer; **V~s' Day** *Am* Tag der ehemaligen Kriegsteilnehmer *(gesetzl. Feiertag am 4. Montag im Oktober)*

veterinary tierärztlich; Veterinär-; **~ legislation** Veterinärgesetzgebung; **~ research** Veterinärforschung; **~ surgeon** (vet) Tierarzt

veto Veto, Einspruch(srecht); **~ message** *Am* Vetobotschaft *(Begründung des Veto durch the →Executive; cf. ~ power)*; **~ power** *Am*[8] Einspruchsrecht *(des Präsidenten od. e-s Gouverneurs gegen e-n Gesetzgebungsbeschluß der Legislative)*; →**pocket ~; right of ~** Vetorecht; **to exercise one's right of ~** sein Vetorecht ausüben (against gegen); **to override a ~** sich über ein Veto hinwegsetzen; **the President's ~ may be overridden** (by a two-thirds majority of the two Houses of Congress) *Am* das Veto des Präsidenten kann außer Kraft gesetzt werden; **to put a ~** Einspruch erheben, ein Veto einlegen (on gegen)

veto *v* Veto einlegen gegen; Einspruch erheben gegen; verbieten

vetoed, the police ~ the demonstration die Polizei verbot die Demonstration; **the President ~ the bill** *Am* der Präsident legte ein Veto gegen den Gesetzesantrag ein

vetoer *Am* Vetoeinlegender

vexatious action[9] (or *Am* **suit**) schikanöse (od. mutwillige) Klage *(cf. abuse of process)*

viability Lebensfähigkeit; Durchführbarkeit *(e-s Planes etc) (vom wirtschaftlichen Standpunkt aus gesehen)*; **financial ~** *Am* Rentabilität

viable lebensfähig; **economically ~ farming** wirtschaftlich existenzfähige Landwirtschaft; **a country is ~ if it is able to pay its way unaided** ein Land ist „lebensfähig", wenn es in der Lage ist, ohne fremde Hilfe auszukommen

vicar Pfarrer; *Br* Gemeindepfarrer *(der anglikanischen Kirche)*

vicarious stellvertretend; **~ agent** Verrichtungsgehilfe, Erfüllungsgehilfe; **~ liability** Haftung für ein Verhalten Dritter *(z.B. des Geschäftsherrn für das Verhalten seiner Gehilfen) (→respondeat superior) (ähnlich § 831 BGB)*; **~ performance** stellvertretende Ausführung *(z.B. weitervergebene Arbeit bei e-m Bauvertrag)*

vicariously, a principal may be ~ liable for the tort committed by his agent ein Geschäftsherr kann für die unerlaubte Handlung seines Vertreters (Gehilfen) haftbar sein

vice 1. Vize-, stellvertretend; **~-chairman** stellvertretender Vorsitzender; Vizepräsident; **V~-Chamberlain** *Br* Vertreter des Lord Chamberlain; **~-chancellor** Vizekanzler; *Br univ (geschäftsführender)* Rektor; **~-consul** Vizekonsul; **~-president** Vizepräsident; stellvertretender Vorsitzender; *Am (bei großen Gesellschaften [corporations] dem Präsidenten nachgeordneter)* Direktor; **V~-President of the United States** *Am*[10] Vizepräsident der Vereinigten Staaten; **~roy** Vizekönig; **executive ~-president** *Am* stellvertretender Generaldirektor *(e-r corporation)*

vice 2. Laster; Fehler *(e-r Ware etc)*; **~ squad** *Am* Sittenpolizei; **inherent ~** innerer Verderb

vice versa ("by the other way round") umgekehrt

vicinity Nachbarschaft; Nähe

vicious korrupt, lasterhaft; **~ circle** Circulus vitiosus; Teufelskreis

victim Opfer; **~ of a disaster** Opfer e-r Katastrophe; **war ~** Kriegsopfer

victimization unfaire, schikanöse Maßregelung, Schikanierung; →**no-~ clause; prohibition of ~** Maßregelungsverbot

victimize *v (jdn)* schikanieren; *(jdn)* unfair maßregeln

victorious powers Siegermächte

victory Sieg (over über) *(opp. defeat);* ~ **at the elections** (or **polls**) Wahlsieg; **electoral** ~ Wahlsieg; **to gain a** ~ e-n Sieg erringen

victuals *bes. Br* Lebensmittel, Eßwaren; Vorräte

victualler Lebensmittellieferant; **licensed** ~ *Br* Gastwirt mit Schankkonzession

victualling bill *Br* Zollschein für Schiffsproviant

videlicet (viz.) nämlich

video Video; *Am* Fernsehen; Fernseh-; ~**s** Videofilme; ~ **cassette** Videokassette; ~ **film** Videofilm; ~ **piracy** Videopiraterie; ~ **recorder** Videorecorder *(Speichergerät zum Wiedergeben von Fernsehsendungen und Videofilmen);* ~ **screen** *(EDV)* Bildschirm; ~ **tape recording** Videoaufzeichnung; ~ **telephone** Bildfernsprecher; ~ **text** *(EDV)* Bildschirmtext (Btx)

vidimus ("we have seen") Einsichtnahme *(z.B. in Geschäftsbücher);* Auszug *(e-r Urkunde);* beglaubigte Abschrift

vie, pour autre ~ für Lebenszeit e-s Dritten

Vienna Convention on Civil Liability for →Nuclear Damages
Vienna Convention on Consular Relations[11] (VCCR) Wiener Übereinkommen (od. Konvention) über konsularische Beziehungen (VCCR)
Vienna Convention on Diplomatic Relations[11a] Wiener Übereinkommen (od. Konvention) über diplomatische Beziehungen
Vienna Convention on the Law of Treaties[11b] Wiener Übereinkommen (od. Konvention) über das Recht der Verträge (oder Wiener Vertragskonvention)

Viet Nam (Vietnam) Vietnam; **Socialist Republic of** ~ Sozialistische Republik Vietnam
Vietnamese Vietnames|e, ~in; vietnamesisch

view 1. Sicht; (Recht auf) Aussicht; Besichtigung; *(ProzeßR)* Besichtigung, Augenschein(seinnahme) *(durch das Gericht);* Bild; **aerial** ~ Luftbild
view, the ~ **is limited** (or **restricted**) die Sicht ist behindert; **to take the long** ~ auf lange Sicht planen
view, a true and fair ~ *Br*[11c] ein wahres und angemessens Bild
Die Bilanz muß ein wahres und angemessenes Bild der Vermögens- und Finanzlage (state of affairs) der company am Bilanztag und die Gewinn- und Verlustrechnung ein wahres und angemessenes Bild der Ertragslage der company während des Geschäftsjahres vermitteln
view, to give a true and fair ~ **of the company's position** e-n getreuen Einblick in die Lage der Gesellschaft geben
view 2. Ansicht, Meinung (of über); **exchange of** ~**s** Meinungsaustausch; **extreme** ~**s** *pol* radikale Ansichten; **legal** ~ **point** Rechtsstandpunkt; **majority** ~ Ansicht der Mehrheit; **point of** ~ →point 1.; **political** ~**s** politische Ansichten; →**private** ~; **to agree with a p.'s** ~**(s)** jds Ansicht beipflichten; **to exchange** ~**s** Meinungen austauschen; **to express one's** ~**(s)** s-e Ansicht äußern; **to hold the** ~ die Ansicht vertreten; auf dem Standpunkt stehen; **to share a p.'s** ~**s** jds Meinung teilen; **to state one's** ~**(s)** s-e Ansicht äußern; Stellung nehmen (on zu); **to take the** ~ s. to hold the →~; **to take a different** ~ anderer Meinung sein
view 3. Absicht, Zweck; Motiv; **the dominant** ~ das vorwiegende (od. leitende) Motiv; **with a** ~ **to** in der Absicht (doing zu tun); **with a** ~ **to profit** in Gewinnabsicht; **to have in** ~ beabsichtigen

view *v* besichtigen, prüfen, in Augenschein nehmen; betrachten, beurteilen; fernsehen; **to** ~ **the scene of the crime** den Tatort besichtigen; **the proposal is** ~**ed favo(u)rably** der Vorschlag ist günstig aufgenommen
viewing figures *(Fernsehen)* Einschaltquote

viewer Fernsehzuschauer; *Am* vom Gericht zur Inspektion und Begutachtung *(z.B. bei Trassenführung von Straßen)* beauftragte Person

vigilance Wachsamkeit *(opp. laches);* ~ **committee** Bürgerwehr-Ausschuß *(zur eigenmächtigen Gefahrenabwehr durch Selbsthilfe an Stelle von fehlender oder versagender staatlicher Polizeigewalt)*

vigilantes Mitglieder e-r Art Bürgerwehr

vilify *v* herabsetzen, schmähen; *(durch Worte)* beleidigen

village Dorf, Ortschaft; *Am* ländliche Gemeinde; ~ **council** *Am* Gemeinderat

vindicate *v* rechtfertigen, schützen, verteidigen; beanspruchen, behaupten; **to** ~ **a claim** e-n Anspruch geltend machen

vindication Rechtfertigung, Verteidigung; Beanspruchung, Behauptung; ~ **of one's rights** Geltendmachung seiner Rechte

vindictive damages s. exemplary →damages

viniculture Weinbau

vintner Weinhändler

violate *v* verletzen; übertreten; **to** ~ **a frontier** e-e Grenze verletzen; **to** ~ **a law** ein Gesetz übertreten, gegen ein Gesetz verstoßen; **to** ~ **an oath** e-n Eid brechen; **to** ~ **sb.'s privacy** jds Intimsphäre verletzen; **to** ~ **a treaty** e-n Vertrag verletzen

violation Verletzung; Verstoß (of gegen); Übertretung[12]; ~ **of the border** Grenzverletzung; ~ **of a contract** Vertragsverletzung; ~ **of the**

covenants Verletzung der Vereinbarungen; ~ **of human rights** Menschenrechtsverletzung; ~ **of a law** Gesetzesverletzung; ~ **of international law** Völkerrechtsverletzung; ~ **of neutrality** Neutralitätsverletzung; ~ **of an oath** Eidbruch; ~ **of the peace** Friedensbruch, Verletzung des Friedens; ~ **of the privacy of a p.'s house** Hausfriedensbruch; ~ **of professional secrecy** Verletzung des Berufsgeheimnisses; ~ **of sb.'s rights** Verletzung jds Rechte; ~ **of section 10** Verstoß gegen § 10; ~ **of a treaty** *(VölkerR)* Vertragsverletzung, Vertragsbruch; ~ **of trust** Vertrauensbruch; ~ **per se** *Am* →per se ~; **frontier** ~ Grenzverletzung; **moving** ~ *Am* Verletzung e-r Verkehrsvorschrift *(hinsichtl. des sich bewegenden Verkehrs; opp. parking ~)*; **traffic** ~ *Am* Verkehrsverletzung; **to be in** ~ **of a provision** e-e Bestimmung verletzen; **to commit a** ~ *Am* e-e Übertretung begehen

violator Verletzer; Übertreter

violence Gewalt, Gewaltsamkeit *(einschließlich intimidation und assault)*; Gewalttätigkeit (towards gegen); **domestic** ~[13] Gewalttätigkeit innerhalb der Familie (od. Haushaltsgemeinschaft); **non-**~ Gewaltlosigkeit; **renunciation of** ~ Gewaltverzicht; **victims of acts of** ~ Opfer von Gewalttätigkeiten; **to use** ~ Gewalt anwenden

violent, ~ **attack** gewaltsamer Angriff; ~ **crime** Gewaltverbrechen; ~ **presumption** starke (od. erdrückende) Vermutung *(e-s Umstandes) (höchste Stufe der Wahrscheinlichkeit)*; **to die a** ~ **death** e-s gewaltsamen Todes sterben

virement Virement; Befugnis der Übertragung e-s Etatpostens (item) auf e-n anderen Titel od. ein anderes Haushaltsjahr

vires, intra ~ innerhalb der Handlungsmacht; **ultra** ~ über die Befugnisse hinausgehend *(→ultra)*

virtual wirklich, tatsächlich, im Grunde (genommen); **he is the** ~ **manager of the firm** er ist der eigentliche Leiter der Firma

virtually tatsächlich, so gut wie; ~ **the whole of August** praktisch den ganzen August (hindurch)

virtue, by (or **in**) ~ **of** kraft, auf Grund von; **in** ~ **of my authority** auf Grund meiner Ermächtigung; **in** ~ **of an office** kraft e-s Amtes

vis major ("greater force") höhere Gewalt *(→Act of God)*

visa (or *Am* **vise**) Visum, Sichtvermerk; **entry** ~ Einreisevisum; **issue of** ~**s** Erteilung von Visa; **transit** ~ Durchreisevisum; **visitor's** ~ *Am* Visum für vorübergehenden Aufenthalt; **to abolish** ~**s** den Visumzwang aufheben; **to mark a passport with a** ~ (or **to put a** ~ **on a passport**) e-n Paß mit dem Visum versehen; ~**s are compulsory** es besteht Visumzwang

visa *v (Paß)* mit e-m Visum versehen

vis-à-vis third parties Dritten gegenüber

viscount *Br* Vicomte *(zwischen Graf [earl] und Baron [baron] stehender Adelstitel)*

visibility Sichtweite; *(Verkehr)* Sichtverhältnisse; **poor** ~ schlechte Sichtverhältnisse

visible sichtbar; ~**s** →~ items *(opp. invisibles)*; ~ **exports** sichtbare Ausfuhren, Warenausfuhren; ~ **imports** sichtbare Einfuhren, Wareneinfuhren; ~ **items** *(Zahlungsbilanz)* sichtbare Posten; ~ **reserves** sichtbare (od. offene) Reserven *(opp. secret reserves)*; ~ **trade** sichtbarer (Außen-)Handel *(mit Gütern im Ggs. zu Dienstleistungen)*; Warenhandel

visit 1. Besuch; ~ **of condolence** Beileidsbesuch; **congratulatory** ~ Gratulationsbesuch; **farewell** (or **leave-taking**, or **parting**) ~ Abschiedsbesuch; **first** ~ Antrittsbesuch; **to pay a** ~ **to a p.** jdm e-n Besuch machen; **to pay an official** ~ **to sb.** jdm e-n offiziellen Besuch abstatten; **to return a** ~ e-n Besuch erwidern

visit 2. *(behördlicher)* Besuch *(zum Zwecke der Besichtigung oder Durchsuchung)*; ~ **and search** *(VölkerR)* Durchsuchung *(e-s Handelsschiffes; s. right of →~ and search)*; **domiciliary** ~ Haussuchung; **right of** ~ *(VölkerR)* Recht der Flaggenkontrolle *(Feststellung der rechtmäßigen Führung e-r nationalen Flagge durch Prüfung der Schiffspapiere)*; **right of** ~ **and search** *(VölkerR)* Durchsuchungsrecht *(Recht e-s Kriegsschiffes, ein neutrales Handelsschiff in Kriegszeiten auf hoher See bes. auf Konterbande zu durchsuchen)*

visit *v* besuchen; besichtigen; durchsuchen; **to** ~ **and search** *(VölkerR) (ein Handelsschiff)* durchsuchen *(→visit 2.)*; **permission to** ~ **a prisoner** Erlaubnis, e-n Gefangenen zu besuchen

visiting, ~ **card** Visitenkarte; ~ **forces** besuchende *(ausländische)* Streitkräfte; ~ **hours** Besuchszeit (at a hospital in e-m Krankenhaus); ~ **professor** Gastprofessor; ~ **teacher** Gastlehrkraft

visitation Visitation; Besuch; *eccl* (periodischer) Besuchsdienst, Prüfungsbesuch *(z.B. des Bischofs in e-r Diözese)*; *Br* Inspektion *(e-r gemeinnützigen Organisation [eleemosynary corporation])*; **right of** ~ **and search** *(VölkerR)* s. right of →visit and search

visitatorial power Aufsichtsrecht, Inspektionsrecht

visitor 1. *(allgemein)* Besucher; (Kur-)Gast; ~ **of the Stock Exchange** Börsenbesucher; ~**'s**

→**pass;** ~**'s permit** schriftl. Besuchserlaubnis; **distinguished** ~**s** *Br parl* Vorzugsgäste; **influx of** ~**s** Besucherstrom; **to receive** ~**s** Besucher empfangen

visitor 2. Visitator; Inspekteur; Beamter, dem e-e Prüfung (od. Aufsicht) obliegt (*z.B. Br*[14] *für Geisteskranke:* **Lord Chancellor's** ~); *Br* Inspekteur für alle gemeinnützigen (eleemosynary), viele kirchliche und andere Organisationen *(z.B. colleges); Br* Gefängnis-Visitator *(zur Kontrolle der Gefängnisverwaltung und Unterbreitung von Anträgen der Häftlinge an das Innenministerium)*

visitorial →visitatorial

visual, ~ **display unit** (VDU) Bildschirmgerät; ~ **flight rules** (VFR) Sichtflugregeln *(opp. Instrument Flight Rules [IFR])*

visualization bildliche Darstellung

visualizer Visualizer, Ideengestalter *(für Werbung)*

vital lebenswichtig; unbedingt erforderlich (to für); vital; ~ **interests** lebenswichtige Interessen; **cent|re (**~**er) of** ~ **interests** *(DBA)* Mittelpunkt der Lebensinteressen

vital statistics Personenstandsstatistik; *Am* Standesamtswesen; **V**~ **S**~ **Office** *Am* Standesamt; **Bureau of V**~ **S**~ *Am* Standesamt; **documents of** ~ standesamtliche Urkunden; **Register of V**~ **S**~ Personenstandsbücher; **Registrar of V**~ **S**~ *Am* Standesbeamter

vitiate *v* ungültig machen; für ungültig erklären; **this admission** ~**s the claim** dieses Zugeständnis entkräftigt den Anspruch; **fraud** ~**s a contract** Betrug macht e-n Vertrag ungültig

viticultural land register Weinbaukataster

viva voce mündlich; ~ **examination** mündliche Prüfung

vivary Tiergehege; Fischteich; *(auch)* Vivarium, Aquarium

vivisection Vivisektion

vivos, inter ~ unter Lebenden; **gift** (or **disposition**) **inter** ~ Schenkung (od. Verfügung) zu Lebzeiten *(d.h. nicht durch Testament)*

vocation Beruf; Berufung; Neigung; **profession or** ~ *Br (SteuerR)* freie und sonstige selbständige Berufe; **to practise a** ~ e-n Beruf ausüben; **to pursue one's** ~ s-m Beruf nachgehen

vocational beruflich; Berufs-; ~ **adjustment** Einarbeitung; **period of** ~ **adjustment** Einarbeitungszeit; ~ **adviser** Berufsberater; ~ **aptitude** berufliche Eignung; ~ **association** Berufsverband, Fachverband; ~ **choice** Berufswahl; ~ **counsel(l)ing** Berufsberatung; ~ **counselor** *Am* Berufsberater; ~ **education** berufliche Bildung; Berufsausbildung; ~ **guidance** Berufsberatung; ~ **institution** *Am* Jugendstrafanstalt *(z.B. in New York, Tennessee);* ~ **rehabilitation** berufliche Wiedereingliederung *(z.B. von Körperbehinderten);* ~ **retraining** berufliche Umschulung; ~ **school** *Am* Jugendstrafanstalt *(z.B. in Michigan, Montana)*

vocational training Berufsausbildung, berufliche Ausbildung; ~ **centre** *Br* Berufsschule; ~ **institute** *Am* Jugendgefängnis; ~ **policy** Berufsbildungspolitik; **advanced** ~ berufliche Fortbildung; **to undergo a** ~ sich e-r Berufsausbildung unterziehen

voice Stimme; ~**-printing** elektronische Sprachbildaufzeichnung *(zur Identifizierung von Personen, z.B. im Zusammenhang mit Entführungen)*

void nichtig; ungültig; ~ **ab initio** von Anfang an nichtig; ~ **contract** nichtiger Vertrag; ~ **marriage** Nichtehe *(→marriage);* ~ **voting paper** ungültiger Stimmzettel; **null and** ~ null und nichtig; **a contract may be** ~ **on the face of it** ein Vertrag kann auf Grund des Wortlautes nichtig sein; **to declare sth.** ~ etw. für nichtig erklären

void *v* ungültig machen; *(einseitig)* aufheben, auflösen; *(im weiteren Sinne)* anfechten

voidability Vernichtbarkeit, *(einseitige)* Aufhebbarkeit, Auflösbarkeit; Anfechtbarkeit; ~ **due to error** Anfechtbarkeit wegen Irrtums

voidable vernichtbar, *(einseitig)* annullierbar, aufhebbar, anfechtbar; ~→**contract;** ~→**marriage**

voidance *eccl* Unbesetztsein e-r Pfründe

voidness Nichtigkeit; ~ **of marriage** Nichtigkeit der Ehe

voir(e) dire ("to speak the truth") Vorvernehmung unter Eid e-s Geschworenen oder Zeugen zur Feststellung seiner Eignung *(dient z.B. dem Ausschluß von Geisteskranken)*

volenti non fit injuria ("that to which a man consents cannot be considered an injury") niemand kann e-e Klage wegen e-r unerlaubten Handlung (tort) erheben, der er ausdrücklich oder stillschweigend zugestimmt hatte; niemand kann ein Recht einklagen, auf das er freiwillig verzichtet hatte

volte-face völlige Abkehr *(von e-r Meinung, e-r Politik etc)*

volume Band, Buch; Volumen; *(großer)* Umfang; ~ **discount** Mengenrabatt; ~ **of aid** Umfang der Hilfe; ~ **of building** Bauvolumen; ~ **of business** Umfang der Geschäfte, Geschäftsumfang; ~ **of production** Produktionsvolumen; ~ **of trade** Handelsvolumen; ~

of traffic Verkehrsaufkommen; ~ **of work (arising)** Arbeitsanfall; **export** ~ Exportvolumen

voluntar|y freiwillig; unentgeltlich (without valuable consideration); ~ **acceptance of risk** Handeln auf eigene Gefahr; ~ **allowance** *Br* →~ payments; ~ **arrangement** *Br*[14a] *(gerichtlich überwachter)* freiwilliger Vergleich *(zur Abwendung des Konkurses)*; ~ **association** *Am com* Zusammenschluß für bestimmten Zweck *(ohne eigene Rechtspersönlichkeit)*; ~ **bankruptcy** Konkurs (-eröffnung) auf Antrag des Gemeinschuldners; ~ **chain** freiwillige Ladenkette *(Zusammenschluß von Einzelhändlern unter der Führung e-s Großhändlers)*; ~ **confession** freiwilliges Geständnis; ~ **contribution** freiwilliger Beitrag, Spende; ~ **contributor** *(Sozialvers.)* freiwillig Versicherter; ~ **conveyance**[15] unentgeltliche (Eigentums-)Übertragung; Schenkung; ~ **cooperatives** freiwillige Einkaufsgenossenschaften *(z. B. Spar)*; ~ **export restraint** (VER) *(nur von dem Exportland überwachte)* Selbstbeschränkungsvereinbarung *(→orderly marketing arrangement)*; ~ **group** Einkaufsvereinigung; ~ **homes** *Br*[16] *(ganz od. teilweise)* durch Spenden unterhaltene Jugendheime; ~ **hospital** durch Spenden unterhaltenes Krankenhaus; ~ **ignorance** *Am* schuldhaftes Nichtwissen; ~→**insolvency;** ~ **insurance** freiwillige Versicherung; ~ **jurisdiction** freiwillige Gerichtsbarkeit; ~ **liquidation** freiwillige Liquidation *(e-r Gesellschaft; s. ~→winding up)*; ~ →**manslaughter;** ~ **organization** Wohltätigkeitsorganisation; ~ **patient** *Br* sich freiwillig wegen Geisteskrankheit behandeln lassender Patient; ~ **payments** *Br* freiwillige Geldzahlung des Ehemannes an die von ihm getrennt lebende Ehefrau; ~ **petition** (in bankruptcy) *Am* →petition 2.; ~ **restraint agreement** *Am* Selbstbeschränkungsabkommen *(das den Export von bestimmten Waren aus einzelnen Exportstaaten in die USA auf bestimmte Prozentsätze des US-Verbrauchs beschränkt)*; ~ **school** *Br*[17] von e-r örtl. Behörde unterhaltene (Konfessions-)Schule; ~ **separation** *Am* →separation 2.

Voluntary Service Overseas (VSO) Entwicklungshilfe; **VSO worker** Entwicklungshelfer

voluntary, ~ **settlement** freiwilliger außergerichtlicher Vergleich; *(auch)* →settlement 3.; ~ **staff** unbezahlte (od. ehrenamtliche) Mitarbeiter; ~ **trust** *Am* rechtsgeschäftl. errichteter Trust *(opp. implied or constructive trust)*; ~ **undertaking** *Br*[18] Verpflichtung zur freiwilligen Aufgabe des beanstandeten Verhaltens e-s Monopols; ~ **waste** →waste 3.; ~ →**winding up**

volunteer freiwilliger, unbesoldeter Mitarbeiter; ohne od. nur gegen e-e kleine Vergütung Tätiger; unentgeltlicher Besorger fremder Geschäfte; Geschäftsführer ohne Auftrag; *Br* Entwicklungshelfer; *mil* Freiwilliger *(opp. conscript)*; unentgeltlicher (Eigentums-)Erwerber (od. Rechtsnachfolger) *(auf Grund e-s Testaments od. Br e-s →settlement; opp. one who gives valuable consideration)*; **overseas** ~ Entwicklungshelfer

volunteer *v* sich freiwillig melden (for zu); *(Dienste)* freiwillig übernehmen (od. anbieten); *(Information)* unaufgefordert geben

vostro account Vostrokonto *(opp. nostro account)*

vote 1. (Wahl-)Stimme; Abstimmung, Stimm(en)abgabe; Stimmrecht, Wahlrecht; Votum; **5 ~s against** 5 Gegenstimmen; **the motion was carried by** (or **with**) **a large majority, with 3 ~s against and 5 abstentions** der Antrag wurde mit großer Mehrheit angenommen, mit 3 Gegenstimmen und 5 Enthaltungen

vote, to cancel a ~ e-e Abstimmung für ungültig erklären; **to cast one's** ~s-e Stimme abgeben; wählen; **to declare a** ~ **invalid** e-e Abstimmung für ungültig erklären; **to defeat by** ~ überstimmen; **to give a** ~ **(for, against)** stimmen (für, gegen); **to give one's** ~ **to** (or **for**) **a candidate** e-m Kandidaten s-e Stimme geben; **to have a** ~ Stimmrecht haben, stimmberechtigt sein; **to lose a** ~ e-e Abstimmung verlieren; **to participate in a** ~ an e-r Abstimmung teilnehmen; **to poll** (or **receive**) **5** ~**s** 5 Stimmen erhalten; **to proceed to a** ~ zur Abstimmung schreiten; **to protest against a** ~ e-r Abstimmung widersprechen; **to put (a question) to the** ~ (e-e Frage) zur Abstimmung bringen; **the motion was put to the** ~ der Antrag wurde zur Abstimmung vorgelegt (od. gestellt); **to split one's** ~ panaschieren; **to take a** ~ e-e Abstimmung durchführen; abstimmen (lassen) (on über); **to withhold one's** ~ sich der Stimmabgabe enthalten; **a** ~ **is taken** es wird abgestimmt

vote, ~ **by acclamation** Abstimmung durch Zuruf; ~ **by correspondence** schriftl. Stimmenabgabe; ~ **by division** Abstimmung durch Hammelsprung *(→division 2.)*; ~ **by open ballot** offene Abstimmung; ~ **by proxy** in Vertretung abgegebene Stimme; ~ **by rising** Abstimmung durch Sicherheben von den Sitzen; ~ **by rising or remaining seated** Abstimmung durch Aufstehen oder Sitzenbleiben; ~ **by secret ballot** geheime Abstimmung; ~ **by show of hands** Abstimmung durch Handaufheben

votes cast abgegebene Stimmen; **majority of** ~ Mehrheit der abgegebenen Stimmen; **number of** ~ Stimmenzahl; **total number of** ~ Gesamtstimmenzahl; **to receive** (or **poll**) **a majority of the** ~ die Mehrheit der abgegebenen Stimmen erhalten

vote, ~ catching Stimmenfang; **~ of censure** *parl* Mißbilligungsvotum *(→censure)*; **~ of confidence** *parl* Vertrauensvotum *(→confidence)*; **~ of no confidence** *parl* Mißtrauensvotum *(→confidence)*; **~ of thanks** Dankesworte *(nach e-m Vortrag)*; **~s polled** abgegebene Stimmen; **affirmative ~** Ja-Stimme *(opp. negative ~)*; **buying of ~s** Stimmenkauf

vote, by ~ durch Abstimmung; **by 7 ~s to 5** mit 7 gegen 5 Stimmen; **agreed to** or **adopted (rejected) by 7 ~s to 5** mit 7 gegen 5 Stimmen angenommen (abgelehnt)

vote, casting ~ ausschlaggebende Stimme; **casting of ~s** Stimmabgabe; **close ~** knappes Abstimmungsergebnis; **counting of ~s** Stimmenzählung; **decisive ~** s. casting →~; **electoral ~s** *Am* Stimmen der Wahlmänner *(opp. popular ~s)*

vote, equality of ~s Stimmengleichheit; **in the event of equality of ~s** bei Stimmengleichheit

vote, final ~ Schlußabstimmung; **floating ~** Stimmen der Parteilosen; **free ~** *parl* Abstimmung ohne Fraktionszwang; **gain** (or **increase**) **in ~s** Stimmengewinn; **invalid ~** ungültige Stimme; **Labour ~** *Br* Stimmen der Labour Party; **loss of ~s** Stimmenverlust, Stimmeneinbuße; **majority of ~s** Stimmenmehrheit *(→majority)*; **minority of ~s** Stimmenminderheit; **negative ~** Nein-Stimme *(opp. affirmative ~)*; **(requisite) number of ~s** (erforderliche) Stimmenzahl; **original ~** Urabstimmung; **→plural ~; popular ~s** *Am* Stimmen der Wählerschaft, direkte Stimmen *(opp. electoral ~s)*; **postal ~** Briefwahl; **proportional ~** Verhältniswahl; **result of the ~** Abstimmungsergebnis

vote, rising ~ *Am* →~ by rising; **show of hands ~** *Am* →~ by show of hands; **taking a ~** Abstimmung; Stimmenabgabe; Wahl; **total ~s** Gesamtstimmenzahl; **written ~** schriftl. Abstimmung

vote 2. *parl* Bewilligung, bewilligter Betrag; **~ on account** *Br parl* vorläufige Abschlagsbewilligung *(bis zur endgültigen Annahme des Budget)*; **supplementary ~** *parl* Nachbewilligung

vote *v* abstimmen (on über); wählen; beschließen; *(Geld)* bewilligen; **to ~ against** stimmen gegen; votieren gegen; **to ~ by acclamation** durch Zuruf abstimmen; **to ~ by ballot** in geheimer Wahl (od. durch Stimmzettel) abstimmen; **to ~ by proxy** sich bei der Abstimmung vertreten lassen; **to ~ down** überstimmen, *(Antrag etc)* (durch Abstimmung) ablehnen; **to ~ for sb.** jdn wählen, für jdn stimmen; s-e Stimme für jdn abgeben; **to ~ for sth.** für etw. stimmen; für etw. votieren; **to ~ in** durch Abstimmung wählen; **to ~ on a resolution** über e-e Entschließung abstimmen; **to ~ sb. out of office** jdn abwählen

vote *v*, **to ~ the adjournment of a meeting** die Vertagung e-r Versammlung beschließen; **to ~ the appropriation** *Am parl* Mittel bewilligen; **to ~ on a bill** über e-e Gesetzesvorlage abstimmen; **to ~ the budget** *parl* den Haushaltsplan verabschieden; **to ~ funds** Gelder *(durch Abstimmung)* bewilligen; **to ~ Republican** *Am* für die Republikaner stimmen; **to ~ a resolution** e-n Beschluß *(durch Abstimmung)* fassen; **to ~ supplies** *parl* Gelder bewilligen; **entitled to ~** stimmberechtigt; wahlberechtigt; **legal incapacity to ~** gesetzl. Unfähigkeit zu wählen *(Fehlen des aktiven Wahlrechts)*; **qualified to ~** wahlberechtigt

vote *v*, **right to ~** Stimmrecht; Wahlrecht; **exercise of the right to ~** Ausübung des Stimmrechts; **in England women were given the (right to) ~ in 1918** in England erhielten die Frauen das Stimmrecht im Jahre 1918

voter Stimmberechtigter, Wahlberechtigter; Abstimmender, Wähler; **absent ~** Briefwähler; jd, der durch e-n Stellvertreter (proxy) wählt *(z. B. Blinder)*; **floating ~** nicht parteigebundener Wähler; Wechselwähler; **register of ~s** Wählerliste; **service ~** *Br mil* →service 2.

voting Stimmen; Abstimmung, Wahl; Stimm(en)abgabe; Wahl-, Stimm-; **~ age** Wahlalter; **~ agreement** *Am (AktienR)* Stimmrechtsbindungsvertrag *(im Ggs. zum →trust agreement verbleibt dem Aktionär das Stimmrecht, er ist nur durch die Bestimmung des ~ agreement gebunden)*; **~ booth** Wahlzelle; **~ box** Wahlurne; **~ by →acclamation; ~ by (secret) ballot** geheime Wahl; **~ by correspondence** schriftl. Stimmabgabe; **~ by mail** Briefwahl; **~ by proxy** Stimmrechtsausübung durch (bevollmächtigten) Vertreter; **~ by show of hands** Wahl durch Handaufheben; **~ capital** stimmberechtigtes Kapital; **~ member** stimmberechtigtes Mitglied

voting paper Stimmzettel; **~ left blank** nicht ausgefüllter Stimmzettel; **to deposit a ~ in the ballot-box** e-n Stimmzettel in die Wahlurne werfen

voting power Stimmrecht; **shares without ~** stimmrechtslose Aktien

voting, ~ procedure Abstimmungsverfahren; **~ proxy** Stimmrechtsvollmacht; **~ public** Wählerschaft

voting right Stimmrecht; Wahlrecht; **to exercise the ~** das Stimmrecht ausüben

voting, ~ rules Abstimmungsvorschriften; **~ shares** (or *Am* **stock**) Stimmrechtsaktien; stimmberechtigte Aktien (od. Anteile); **common ~ shares** stimmberechtigte Stammaktien; **~ slip** →~paper

voting strength Wahlstärke; **the ~ of . . . is about . . . . . .** hat etwa . . . Stimmberechtigte

voting system Abstimmungsmodus

voting trust *(AktienR)* auf das Stimmrecht *(von Aktionären)* beschränkter Trust
Einige od. alle Aktionäre einer od. mehrerer Gesell-

schaften übertragen ihre Aktien auf einen od. mehrere voting trustees (natürl. od. juristische Personen) für einen begrenzten Zeitraum und erhalten dafür →voting trust certificates, die im Verkehr wie Aktien behandelt werden. Den Aktionären verbleibt das Recht auf Dividende, Anteil am Liquidationserlös etc., während die trustees als legal owners der Aktien aus eigenem Recht heraus stimmberechtigt sind. *Zweck:* Stimmrechtsballung, um die Aktionärsrechte geschlossen zur Geltung zu bringen. Die voting trusts sind, wie das gesamte Gesellschaftsrecht, durch einzelstaatl. Gesetze geregelt

voting trust agreement *Am* Vertrag *(zwischen Aktionären und voting trustees),* durch den ein →voting trust begründet wird; Stimmbindungsvertrag

voting trust certificate *bes. Am (von e-m →voting trustee ausgegebenes)* Stimmbindungs-Treuhandzertifikat *(das die Ansprüche des Aktionärs gegen den Treuhänder verbrieft, wobei das Stimmrecht ausdrücklich ausgenommen wird; cf. voting trust)*; ~ **holder** Inhaber e-s ~; *(durch das voting trust agreement)* gebundener Aktionär

voting trustee *bes. Am* Treuhänder (legal owner) der ihm übertragenen Aktien *(der das Stimmrecht nach Maßgabe des →voting trust agreement ausübt)*

voting, absentee ~ Briefwahl; **abstention (from ~)** Stimmenthaltung; →**cumulative ~; direct** ~ direkte Wahl; **method of** ~ Abstimmungsart, Abstimmungsverfahren; **non-~ member** nicht stimmberechtigtes Mitglied; **open** ~ offene Wahl *(opp. secret ~)*; **percentage of** ~ Wahlbeteiligung; →**plural ~; right of** ~ s. right to →vote; **secret** ~ geheime Abstimmung (od. Wahl); **to abstain from** ~ sich der Stimme enthalten

voteless shares stimmrechtslose Aktien

vouch *v*, **to ~ for** einstehen für, sich verbürgen für; **to ~ to warranty** (or **guaranty**) *Am* den Veräußerer *(e-s Grundstücks)* aufgrund seiner Gewährleistung auffordern, das dem Erwerber bestrittene Eigentum zu verteidigen

vouching in *Am* Nachricht des Beklagten an den Dritten von der Anhängigkeit des Verfahrens; Streitverkündung

voucher Beleg, Zahlungsbeleg; Quittung; *(schriftl.)* Unterlage; Schein, Bescheinigung; Gutschein; ~ **attached** (V/A) Beleg anliegend; ~ **copy** Belegexemplar, Belegnummer *(e-r Zeitung)*; ~ **for payment** Zahlungsbeleg; ~ **for receipt** Quittungsbeleg, Quittung; ~ **in support of an account** Beleg für e-e Rechnung (od Abrechnung); ~ **register** Belegverzeichnis; **audited** ~ geprüfter Beleg; **baggage** ~ Gepäckschein; **cash** ~ Kassenbeleg; **check** ~ *Am* Belegabschnitt an e-m Scheck; **credit** ~ Gutschein; Gutschrift(zettel); **expense** ~ Ausgabenbeleg; **gift** ~ Geschenkgutschein; **luggage** ~ Gepäckschein; **luncheon** ~ *Br* Gutschein für Mittagessen; **tax** ~ Steuerbeleg; **to support by** ~ *(Auslagen etc)* belegen

voyage *(lange)* Seereise, Flug(reise); ~ **charter** Reisecharter (→*charter 2.*); ~ **freight** Frachtkosten für die ganze Reise; ~ **insurance** *(Seevers.)* Reiseversicherung *(für Ladung und Schiff für e-e besondere Fahrt)*; ~ **out** Hinreise; ~ **out and home** *Br* Hin- und Rückfahrt; ~ **policy** Reiseversicherungspolice (→*~insurance)*; ~ **premium** Reiseversicherungsprämie; **foreign** ~ Auslandsreise, Überseereise; **homeward** ~ Rückfahrt *(e-s Schiffes)*; **outward and homeward** ~ Hin- und Rückfahrt *(e-s Schiffes)*; **on a** ~ auf Reisen; **prolongation of the** ~ Verlängerung der Reise; **prosecution of the** ~ Fortsetzung der Reise; **return** ~ *Br* Rückreise, Rückfahrt

W

wage (Arbeits-)Lohn; Heuer

wage, to adjust ~s Löhne anpassen (od. angleichen); **to attach ~s** Löhne pfänden; **~s may be attached by order of court to satisfy maintenance orders or judgment debts** *Br*[1] Löhne können durch gerichtliche Verfügung für Unterhaltszahlungen und urteilsmäßig festgestellte Schulden gepfändet werden; **to curb ~s** Löhne drosseln; **to cut ~s** Löhne kürzen; **to deduct from the ~s** vom Lohn abziehen; **to freeze ~s** Lohnstop(p) durchführen; **to increase ~s** die Löhne erhöhen; **to reduce ~s** die Löhne herabsetzen (od. kürzen); **to retain ~s** Löhne einbehalten

wage, W~s Act 1986 *Br* Lohngesetz; ~ **accounting** Lohnbuchhaltung; ~ **adjustment** Lohnangleichung; ~ **advance** (Lohn-)Vorschuß; **~(s) agreement** Lohnvereinbarung; Tarifvertrag; **~s and salaries** Löhne und Gehälter; ~ **arbitration** Schlichtung von Lohnstreitigkeiten; ~ **bargaining** *(tarifliche)* Lohnverhandlung(en); ~ **based on the output** Leistungslohn; ~ **check** *Am* Lohnscheck; ~ **ceiling** *(gesetzl. zugelassener)* Höchstlohn; ~ **claims** Lohnansprüche, Lohnforderungen; **W~s Council** *Br*[2] Lohnausschuß *(zur Festsetzung von Mindestlöhnen)*; ~ **demand** Lohnforderung; ~ **determination** Lohnfestsetzung; ~ **differentials** Lohnunterschiede (→*differential)*; ~ **dispute** Lohnstreitigkeit; ~ **drift** *Br* Lohndrift *(Unterschied zwischen Tariflohn und dem gezahlten Lohn)*; ~ **earner** Lohnempfänger, Arbeiter *(opp. salary earner)*; ~**-earning employment** nicht selbständige Beschäftigung; ~ **fixing** Lohnfestsetzung, Lohnbestimmung; ~ **freeze** Lohnstop(p); ~ **fund** Lohnfonds; ~ **incentive** Lohnanreiz *(→incentive)*; ~ **increase** (or **increment**) Lohnerhöhung; ~ **indexation** Lohnindexbindung; ~**s in kind** Naturallohn; ~ **intensive** lohnintensiv; ~ **labor** *Am* Lohnempfänger; ~ **leadership** Lohnführerschaft *(tarifpolitische Führerstellung)*; ~ **level** Lohnniveau; Lohnhöhe; ~ **on piece-work basis** Stücklohn; ~ **packet** Lohntüte

wage payment Lohnzahlung; **advance** ~ Lohnvorauszahlung; **continued** ~ Lohnfortzahlung *(bei Krankheit)*

wage, ~ **policy** Lohnpolitik; *(→wage restraint)*; ~**-price spiral** Lohn-Preis-Spirale; ~**-push inflation** Lohndruckinflation

wage rate Lohnsatz; Tarifsatz; ~ **autonomy** Tarifautonomie; **hourly** ~(or ~ **per hour**) Stundenlohnsatz; **standard** ~ Tarifsatz; **weekly** ~ Wochenlohnsatz

wage, ~ **regulation** Lohnregelung; ~**-related pension** dynamische Rente; ~ **restraint** (Politik der) Niederhaltung von Löhnen *(zur Bekämpfung der Inflation)*; *(freiwillige od. auferlegte)* Zurückhaltung bei Lohnforderungen; ~ **rise** Lohnerhöhung; ~ **rounds** Lohnrunden; Zyklus von Lohnforderungen und Regelungen in e-r Volkswirtschaft; ~**scale** Lohnskala; Lohntarif; ~ **schedule** Lohntabelle; ~**s sheet** Lohnliste; ~ **slave** jd, der für e-n Hungerlohn arbeitet; ~ **slip** Lohn(abrechnungs)zettel; ~ **stop** Lohnstop(p); Begrenzung von Sozialhilfeleistungen durch das allgemeine Lohnniveau; ~**structure** Lohngefüge; ~**worker** *Am* Lohnempfänger

wage, actual ~ Reallohn; **adjustment of** ~**s** Anpassung der Löhne; **advance** ~ **payment** Lohnvorauszahlung; **agreed** ~**(s)** Tariflohn; **assignment of** ~**s**[3] Vorausabtretung des Lohns *(oft in Zusammenhang mit Abzahlungsgeschäften)*; **basic** ~ Grundlohn; **contractual** ~**(s)** vertragsmäßiger Lohn, Tariflohn; **daily** (or **a day's**) ~ Tageslohn; **garnishment of** ~**s** *Am* Lohnpfändung; **guaranteed minimum** ~ garantierter Mindestlohn; **hourly** ~**(s)** Stundenlohn; **increase in** ~**s** Anstieg der Löhne; Lohnerhöhung; **industrial** ~**s** Industriearbeiterlöhne; **job** ~**(s)** Akkordlohn, Stücklohn; **living** ~ *(für das Existenzminimum)* ausreichender Lohn; **local** ~**(s)** ortsüblicher Lohn; **loss of** ~**s** Lohnausfall; **monthly** ~**(s)** Monatslohn; **peak** ~ Spitzenlohn; **piece(-)work** ~**(s)** Stücklohn, Akkordlohn; **real** ~**(s)** Reallohn; **reduction of** ~**s** Lohnherabsetzung; **rise in** ~**s** Lohnerhöhung, Steigen der Löhne; **seamen's** ~**s** Seemannsheuer; **standard** ~**s** Tariflohn; **time** ~**(s)** Zeitlohn; **weekly** ~ Wochenlohn

wage *v*, **to** ~ **war against a country** Krieg gegen ein Land führen; **to** ~ **war on want** Krieg gegen die Not (od. Armut) führen

wager Wette; Wetteinsatz; ~ **policy** →wagering policy; **to lay** (or **make**) **a** ~ e-e Wette eingehen, wetten

wager *v (als Einsatz)* setzen (on auf); **to** ~ **a p. £5** mit jdm um £5 wetten

wagering, ~ **contract** Spielvertrag (Spielwette, Rennwette); Wettvertrag; ~ **debts** Spielschulden; ~ **policy**[4] *(verbotene)* Wettversicherung *(Versicherungspolice, bei der der Versicherte an dem Versicherungsgegenstand kein Interesse hat)*

Wagner Act *Am* Gesetz über die Regelung der Arbeitsbeziehungen *(von 1935) (→National Labor Relations Act)*

wag(g)on *(Am* **wagon**) Wagen; *Br* Güterwagen, Waggon; ~ **→jobber;** ~ **load** Wagenladung; *Br* Waggonladung

wag(g)onage Transport mit Wagen; Transportkosten

waif herrenloses Gut; *(untechnisch:)* Obdachloser; verwahrlostes Kind; *Scot* Landstreicher; ~**s** vom Dieb auf der Flucht *(aus Furcht vor Entdeckung)* weggeworfene gestohlene Güter; ~**s and strays** verwahrloste Kinder

wait-and-see-policy Politik des Abwartens; abwartende Haltung

waiter Kellner; *Br* Börsendiener

waiting, ~ **period** Wartezeit; *(VersR)* Karenzzeit; ~ **room** Wartezimmer; *(Bahnhof)* Wartesaal; **no** ~ Halteverbot; **to keep a p.** ~ jdn warten lassen; **to put sb. on the** ~ **list** jdn auf die Warteliste setzen

waive *v* aufgeben, verzichten auf; erlassen; **to** ~ **a claim** auf e-n Anspruch verzichten; **to** ~ **customs duties** Zollabgaben erlassen; **to** ~ **a defence (~se)** auf die Geltendmachung e-r Einwendung (etc) verzichten; **to** ~ **fees** Gebühren erlassen; **to** ~ **notice** auf Ankündigung (od. vorherige Mitteilung) verzichten; **to** ~ **a privilege** auf ein Vorrecht *(z. B. Zeugnisverweigerungsrecht)* verzichten; **to** ~ **one's rights under a contract** auf seine vertraglichen Rechte verzichten; **to** ~ **a tort** e-n deliktsrechtlichen Anspruch aufgeben *(→waiver of tort)*

waiving Verzicht auf

waiver Aufgabe *(e-s Rechts)*; Verzicht, Verzichtleistung, Verzichterklärung; Befreiung *(von der Einhaltung bestimmter Verpflichtungen)*; Erlaß, Erlassen; ~ **clause** Verzichtklausel; ~ **of a fee** Gebührenerlaß; ~ **of interest** Zinsverzicht; ~ **of premium** *(VersR)* Beitragsbefreiung; ~ **of privilege** Verzicht auf ein Vorrecht *(bes. Zeugnisverweigerungsrecht und Recht auf Offenle-*

gung prozeßwichtiger Urkunden); ~ **of protest** Verzicht auf Protest *(→protest 2.)*; ~ **of a right** Verzicht auf ein Recht; ~ **of the statute of limitations** Verzicht auf Geltendmachung der *(bereits eingetretenen)* Verjährung *(→statute of limitations)*; ~ **of title** Rechtsverzicht; ~ **of tort** Aufgabe e-s deliktsrechtlichen Anspruchs *(indem man das schädliche Verhalten nachträglich billigt und dadurch günstigere quasivertragliche Ansprüche eröffnet)*

Vergleichbares Vorgehen ermöglichen im deutschen Recht § 687 Abs. 2 und § 816 BGB

walk Route, Runde *(e-s Postbeamten etc)*; **~s** *Br* Inkassi auf nicht dem Clearing angeschlossene Banken *(z.B. Overseas and Foreign Banks)*; **~(s) clerk** *Br* Bankbote, Inkassobote *(e-r Bank, der mit dem Inkasso von ~s beauftragt ist)*; ~ **of life** soziale Stellung (od. Schicht); Beruf; **from all ~s of life** aus allen Berufskreisen od. Schichten; **~-out** *colloq.* Arbeitsniederlegung, Streik *(opp. lockout)*; Verlassen des Sitzungssaales *(als Zeichen des Protests)*

walk out *v* die Arbeit niederlegen, streiken; *(als Zeichen des Protests)* den Sitzungssaal verlassen

wall Mauer; **Berlin W~** *pol* Berliner Mauer *(am 9. 11. 1989 geöffnet)*; **→Chinese W~; customs ~s** Zollschranken

Wall Street *Am* Straße in New York, in der das Finanzviertel liegt; *fig* amerik. Geld- und Kapitalmarkt; *fig* amerik. Hochfinanz

wallet Brieftasche

want Mangel (of an); Bedarf, Bedürfnis (of an); ~ **ad** *colloq.* Kleinanzeige, Suchanzeige *(im Inseratenteil)*; **(for)** ~ **of advice** mangels Bericht; ~ **of capital** Kapitalmangel; ~ **of care** (or **diligence**) mangelnde Sorgfalt; ~ **of confidence** Mangel an Vertrauen; **for** ~ **of consideration** mangels Gegenleistung; **for** ~ **of evidence** mangels Beweises; **for** ~ **of funds** wegen fehlender Mittel; **returned for** ~ **of funds** *(ScheckR)* mangels Deckung zurück; ~ **of jurisdiction** fehlende Zuständigkeit; ~ **of novelty** *(PatR)* mangelnde Neuheit; **dismissal of an action for** ~ **of prosecution** Abweisung der Klage wegen Prozeßverschleppung; **in** ~ **of repair** reparaturbedürftig; **to be in** ~ **of a th.** etw. benötigen (od. brauchen); Bedarf haben an etw.; **to meet a** ~ e-m Bedürfnis abhelfen, ein Bedürfnis befriedigen; **to plead** ~ **of jurisdiction** die fehlende Zuständigkeit geltend machen

want *v* fehlen; brauchen, benötigen; verlangen

wanted verlangt; gesucht; ~ **advertisement** Suchanzeige; ~ **immediately** für sofort gesucht; ~ **person** *(von der Polizei)* Gesuchte(r) *(der/die auf der Fahndungsliste steht)*; ~ **by the police** von der Polizei gesucht; steckbrieflich verfolgt; **situations** ~ Stellengesuche *(in Zeitungen)*

wanting fehlend, nicht vorhanden; ohne, in Ermangelung von; **to be** ~ fehlen, nicht haben (in sth. etw.)

wantage *Am* Fehlbetrag; Defizit

wanton rücksichtslos, böswillig; ~ **insult** mutwillige Beleidigung; ~ **negligence** *Am* bewußte (od. grobe) Fahrlässigkeit *(s. ~→negligence)*

war Krieg *(opp. peace)*

war, when the ~ **broke out** bei Kriegsausbruch; ~ **has broken out** der Krieg ist ausgebrochen; **to be engaged in a** ~ in e-n Krieg verwickelt sein; **to declare** ~ den Krieg erklären (on a country e-m Land); **to drift into** ~ dem Krieg zutreiben; **to enter (the)** ~ (against) in den Krieg eintreten (gegen); **to levy** (or **make, wage**) ~ **on a country** Krieg gegen ein Land führen; **to make** (or **wage**) ~ Krieg führen (on, against gegen)

war, ~ **of aggression** Angriffskrieg; ~ **atrocities** Kriegsgreuel; ~ **of attrition** Zermürbungskrieg; ~ **bonds** Kriegsanleihen; ~ **casualties** Kriegsverluste; ~ **charities** *Br*[5] wohltätige Einrichtungen *(Fonds, Vereine etc)* zur Linderung der Not der vom Krieg Betroffenen; ~ **chemicals** chemische Kampfstoffe; ~ **correspondent** Kriegsberichterstatter; ~ **crime** Kriegsverbrechen

war criminal *(VölkerR)* Kriegsverbrecher; **major** ~ Hauptkriegsverbrecher; **trial of ~s** Kriegsverbrecherprozeß

war damage[6] **(sustained)** (erlittener) Kriegsschaden; **reparation** (or **compensation**) **for** ~ Kriegsentschädigung; Reparationen; **to assess ~s** Kriegsschäden feststellen

war, ~ **dead** Kriegstote; ~ **debts** Kriegsschulden; ~ **decoration** Kriegsauszeichnung; ~ **disabled** Kriegsbeschädigter; kriegsbeschädigt; ~ **disablement** Kriegsbeschädigung; ~ **economy** Kriegswirtschaft; ~ **effort** Kriegsanstrengung; ~ **establishment** (or **footing**) Kriegsstärke; ~ **expenses** Kriegskosten; ~ **factory** Rüstungsfabrik

warfare Krieg(führung); **aerial** ~ Luftkrieg; **chemical** ~ Kriegführung mit Chemikalien; **economic** ~ Wirtschaftskrieg; **germ** ~ Kriegführung mit Bakterien; **maritime** ~ Seekrieg; **nuclear** ~ Atomkrieg

war graves Kriegsgräber; **W~G~ Commission** Kriegsgräberfürsorge, Kriegsgräberkommission

war, ~ **guilt (clause)** *(VölkerR)* Kriegsschuld (-klausel); **~head** Sprengkopf; ~ **industry** Kriegsindustrie; ~ **injury** Kriegsverletzung; **~like operations** kriegsähnliche Handlungen; ~ **loan** *Br* Kriegsanleihe; ~ **losses** Kriegsverluste; ~ **material** Kriegsmaterial; ~ **me-**

morial Kriegerdenkmal; ~**monger** Kriegstreiber, Kriegshetzer; ~**mongering** Kriegshetze; ~ **order** Rüstungsauftrag; ~ **orphan** Kriegswaise; ~ **pension** Kriegsopferrente; ~ **plant** Rüstungsbetrieb; ~ **preparations** Kriegsvorbereitungen; ~ **profiteer** Kriegsgewinnler; ~ **profits** Kriegsgewinn; ~ **reserve** *(VersR)* Kriegsreserve, Kriegsrücklage

war risk Kriegsrisiko; ~ **clause** Kriegsklausel; ~ **insurance**[7] Kriegsrisikoversicherung

war strength Kriegsstärke

wartime, ~ **economy** Kriegswirtschaft; ~ **legislation** Kriegsgesetzgebung; ~ **measures** Kriegsmaßnahmen; ~ **needs** Kriegsbedarf; ~ **production** Kriegsproduktion; ~ **propaganda** Kriegspropaganda; ~ **wedding** Kriegstrauung

war, ~ **victim** Kriegsopfer; ~**-weariness** Kriegsmüdigkeit; ~**-weary** kriegsmüde; ~ **widow** Kriegerwitwe; ~**-worn countries** kriegszerstörte Länder; ~ **zone** *(VölkerR)* Kriegsgebiet, Sperrgebiet *(bes. auf hoher See)*; **act of** ~ Kriegshandlung; **aerial** (or **air**) ~ Luftkrieg; **articles of** ~ *Am* Militärstrafgesetze

war, at ~ im Krieg(szustand) (with mit); **country at** ~ kriegführender Staat; **to be at** ~ **with** Krieg führen gegen

war, breaking out of ~ Kriegsausbruch; **burdens of** ~ Kriegslasten; **in case of** ~ im Kriegsfalle; **civil** ~ Bürgerkrieg; **cold** ~ kalter Krieg; **conduct of a** ~ Kriegsführung; **consequences of** ~ Kriegsfolgen; **customs of** ~ Kriegsbräuche; **danger of** ~ Kriegsgefahr; **declaration of** ~ Kriegserklärung; **defensive** ~ Verteidigungskrieg; **due to the** ~ kriegsbedingt; **effect of** ~ Kriegsfolge, Kriegsauswirkung *(z. B. auf e-n Vertrag)*; **entering** (or **entry into**) **the** ~ Kriegseintritt; **hono(u)rs of** ~ Kriegsauszeichnungen; **lightning** ~ Blitzkrieg; **maritime** (or **naval**) ~ Seekrieg; **outbreak of** ~ Kriegsausbruch; **outlawing of** ~ Kriegsächtung; **post(-) war** Nachkriegs- (→*post 4.)*; **prevention of** ~ Verhütung des Krieges; **preventive** ~ Präventivkrieg; **prisoner of** ~ Kriegsgefangener *(→prisoner)*; **as a result of the** ~ kriegsbedingt; **state of** ~ Kriegszustand; **theat re (~er) of** ~ Kriegsschauplatz

ward 1. Mündel *(Minderjähriger, der unter Vormundschaft steht; cf. guardian)*; ~ **of court**[8] jd. *(Minderjähriger, Am auch Geisteskranker etc)*, der unter gerichtlicher Vormundschaft steht; ~**'s money** (or **patrimony**) Mündelgeld

ward[9] 2. Stadtbezirk *(für Verwaltungszwecke) (Br z. B. die City of London ist in ~s eingeteilt)*; *Br* Wahlbezirk *(für Kommunalwahlen)*

ward 3. Abteilung *(e-s Krankenhauses, Gefängnisses etc)*; Station *(e-s Krankenhauses)*

ward off *v*, **to** ~ **a danger** e-e Gefahr abwenden

warden Vorsteher, Leiter; *Br* Rektor e-s College; *Am* Aufsichtsbeamter; **(air raid)** ~ Luftschutzwart; →**church** ~; **fire** ~ *Am* Feuerwache; **game** ~ Jagdaufseher; **port** ~ *Am* Hafenaufseher; **prison** ~ *Am* Gefängnisdirektor; →**traffic** ~

wardship Vormundschaft; Amt e-s →guardian

warehouse 1. Lagerhaus, (Lager-)Speicher; (Waren-)Lager; Zollgutlager (→*warehouse 2.)*; ~ **account** Lagerkonto; ~ **book** Lagerbuch; Bestandsbuch; ~ **certificate** *Am* →~ receipt; ~ **charges** Lagergeld, Lagergebühren; ~ **goods** Lagergut, Waren auf Lager; ~ **keeper** →~man; ~**man** Lagerhalter; Lagerverwalter; ~ **receipt** (W/R)[10] *(vom Lagerhalter ausgestellter)* Lagerempfangsschein, Lagerschein; ~ **rent** Lagermiete; ~**-to-**~ **clause** *(Institute Cargo Clause)* von-Haus-zu-Haus-Klausel; ~**-to-**~ **insurance** Versicherung von Haus zu Haus; ~ **warrant** (W/W) →~receipt; **to deposit** (or **store**) **in a** ~ in e-m Lagerhaus einlagern

warehouse[11] 2., **(bonded)** ~ Zollgutlager, Zollniederlage *(wo zollbare Waren bis zur Wiederausfuhr od. bis zum Übergang in den freien Inlandsverkehr [for home consumption] unverzollt gelagert werden)*; **free** ~ Freilager; **storing in a** ~ (Ein-)Lagerung unter Zollverschluß

warehouse *v* einlagern; auf Lager geben (od. nehmen); unter Zollverschluß geben (od. [ein-]lagern)

warehousing (Ein-)Lagerung; Lagerhaltung; Lagergeschäft; Verschleierung der Aktienkäufe durch Strohmänner und andere *(Zweck: überraschender Übernahmeangriff gegen ein Unternehmen)*; ~ **(in bond)** (Ein-)Lagerung unter Zollverschluß; ~ **charges** Gebühren der Einlagerung unter Zollverschluß; ~ **entry** (Zoll-)Deklaration zur Einlagerung unter Zollverschluß; ~ **system** Zollverschluß(system) *(vorübergehende unverzollte Lagerung von Waren; →warehouse 2.)*; **field** ~ *Am* (Ein-)Lagerung sicherungsübereigneter Waren

warn *v (jdn)* warnen (against vor); *(jdn)* verwarnen; *Scot* kündigen; **to** ~ **against** abmahnen von; **to** ~ **(of)** hinweisen (auf)

warning Warnung; Verwarnung; *Scot* Kündigung; ~ **shot** Warnschuß; ~ **sign** *(Verkehr)* Warnzeichen; ~ **triangle** Warndreieck; **air raid** ~ Fliegeralarm; **to give a** ~ **to sb.** jdn verwarnen

warrant 1. *(e-r Gerichtsperson, z. B. sheriff, bailiff etc, erteilter)* schriftl. Befehl; Haftbefehl; Durchsuchungsbefehl; Beschlagnahmeverfügung; Anordnung der zwangsweisen Vorführung vor Gericht *(e-s Zeugen od. Angeklagten)*; ~ **of arrest** *(während e-r Verhandlung erlassener)* Haftbefehl *(→arrest)*; Beschlagnahmeverfügung *(für ein Schiff)*; ~ **of commitment** *Am* Einlieferungsbefehl; ~ **of distress** gerichtliche

Ermächtigung zur Beschlagnahme; *(ungenau)* Pfändungsbeschluß; ~ **of execution** *Br* Vollstreckungsbefehl e-s County →Court an den sheriff *(entspricht dem writ of→fieri facias des High →Court)*; ~ **under his hand and seal** *Br* von ihm unterzeichneter und gesiegelter Gerichtsbefehl *(Haftbefehl, Durchsuchungsbefehl etc)*; **bench** ~ richterlicher Haftbefehl *(→bench 1.)*; →**death** ~; →**justice's** ~; **search** ~ gerichtl. Anordnung der Durchsuchung, Durchsuchungsbefehl; **to issue a** ~ e-n Haftbefehl erlassen; **to serve a** ~ **on a p.** (or **to serve a p. with a** ~) jdm e-n Gerichtsbefehl zustellen; **to take out a** ~ **against a p.** gegen jdn e-n Haftbefehl erwirken; **a p. is wanted on a** ~ jd wird steckbrieflich gesucht

warrant 2. Ermächtigung; besondere Prozeßvollmacht; ~ **of attorney** besondere schriftliche Prozeßvollmacht für e-n Anwalt *(durch die er bevollmächtigt wird, für den Aussteller vor Gericht den Anspruch e-s in dem ~ genannten Gläubigers ohne Verteidigung anzuerkennen. Zweck: Sicherung des Gläubigers)*; **royal** ~ *Br* Hoflieferantendiplom

warrant, this shall be sufficient ~ **for doing** diese Urkunde ermächtigt zur Vornahme dieser Handlung

warrant 3. Bescheinigung, Berechtigungsschein; Optionsschein, Bezugsrechtsschein; ~ **exercise price** Kurs, zu dem der Inhaber e-s Optionsscheins Aktien erwerben kann; ~ **issue** Emission von Optionsscheinen; Optionsanleihe

warrant, bearer ~ Inhaberoptionsschein; **bond** ~ Anleiheoptionsschein; Optionsschein für Anleihen desselben Emittenten; **dividend** ~ Dividenden-Zahlungsanweisung; **dock** ~ *Br* Docklagerschein; **harmless** ~ Optionsschein, bei dem die Ausübung des Rechts an die vorzeitige Kündigung der Originalanleihe *(→host bond)* durch den Emittenten geknüpft ist; **interest** ~ Zinsberechtigungsschein; **naked** ~ Optionsschein ohne Optionsanleihe; **redemption** ~ Tilgungs-Optionsschein, der gegen e-n fixen Preis an den Emittenten zurückgegeben werden kann; **share** ~ →share 2.; **stock** ~ →stock 1.; **stock purchase** ~ Optionsschein; **subscription** ~ →subscription 4.; **with** ~**s** (ww) inklusiv Bezugsrechte; **without** ~**s** (w) ausschließlich (od. ohne) Bezugsrechte

warrant 4. *Br com* Lagerschein *(bes. Orderlagerschein)*; *Br (neben dem Lagerschein ausgestellter)* Lagerpfandschein *(zur Verpfändung der eingelagerten Güter)*; **advance on** ~ Lagerscheinvorschüsse; **bearer of the** ~ Inhaber des Lagerscheins; **goods covered by** ~ durch Lagerschein gesicherte Güter; **to secure by** ~ durch Lagerschein sichern

warrant 5. *mil* Bestallungsurkunde; ~ **officer** *Br* höchster Rang des non-commissioned officer; *Am* Dienstgrad in der Marine entsprechend dem Unteroffizier im Heer

warrant *v* zusichern, garantieren, gewährleisten, einstehen für; ermächtigen; rechtfertigen; **to** ~ **impliedly** stillschweigend zusichern; **to represent and** ~ ausdrücklich erklären, zusichern

warranted gerechtfertigt; zugesichert; ~ **free of** garantiert frei von; ~ **free from adulteration** *(bei Nahrungsmitteln)* Reinheit garantiert; ~ **pure** *com* garantiert rein; ~ **quality** zugesicherte Eigenschaft

warrantable title Rechtstitel, für den e-e Garantie abgegeben werden kann *(Am cf. warranty deed)*

warrantee Zusicherungs- (od. Gewährleistungs-, Garantie-)empfänger, Garantienehmer

warrantor Zusicherungsgeber, Gewährleistender, Garantiegeber

warranty *(im Liegenschafts- und Warenkaufrecht)* vertragl. Zusicherung, Zusicherungsabrede, Garantie für Sach- od. Rechtsmängel; *Br* unwesentliche Vertragsbestimmung *(Nebenpflicht; zu unterscheiden von→condition 1.; cf. breach of ~)*; Gewährleistung; *(VersR) (vom Versicherungsnehmer abgegebene)* Zusicherung der Richtigkeit seiner Angaben, Garantie für den Eintritt oder Nichteintritt bestimmter *(risikoerheblicher)* Tatsachen *(cf. breach of ~ 2.)*

warranty, to break a ~ e-e Zusicherung (od. Gewährleistung) nicht einhalten; **to give** (or **make**) **a** ~ e-e Gewährleistung übernehmen

warranty, ~ **claim** Gewährleistungsanspruch; ~ **clause** Garantieklausel, Gewährleistungsklausel; ~ **deed** *Am* Grundstücksübertragungsurkunde *(mit bestimmten Zusicherungen)*; ~ **for hidden defects** Garantie (od. Gewährleistung) wegen verborgener Sachmängel; ~ **liability** Garantiehaftung

warranty of authority Garantie für die eigene Verfügungs- od. Vertretungsmacht; **liability for breach of** ~ (Garantie-)Haftung für das Handeln ohne Vertretungsmacht; Haftung des vollmachtlosen Vertreters (falsus procurator)

warranty, ~ **of fitness for a particular purpose** *Am*[12] Gewährleistung der Eignung für e-n bestimmten Zweck *(sie wird vom Gesetz auferlegt, falls der Verkäufer den bestimmten Zweck kannte und der Käufer sich auf die fachmännische Wahl der Ware seitens des Verkäufers verließ)*; ~ **of goods** *Am* →~ of quality; ~ **of merchantability** *Am*[13] Gewährleistung, daß die Waren von durchschnittlicher Qualität und für den normalen Gebrauch geeignet sind; ~ **of quality** Gewährleistung, daß Waren e-e bestimmte Qualität haben (Sachmängelhaftung); ~ **of quiet enjoyment** Zusicherung des ungestörten Besitzes; ~ **of title** Gewährleistung wegen Rechtsmängel (Rechtsmängelhaftung)

warranty, breach of ~ 1. *(im Liegenschafts- und Warenkaufrecht)* Gewährleistungsbruch, Verletzung e-r vertragl. Zusicherung (od. Zusicherungsabrede) *(vgl. § 463 BGB)*

Br[14] Der Käufer hat lediglich Anspruch auf Schadensersatz, kann also die Ware nicht zurückweisen und den Vertrag nicht als fehlgeschlagen behandeln (he cannot reject the goods and treat the contract as repudiated). Anders, wenn die Zusicherung nicht als warranty sondern als →condition zu qualifizieren ist. Die Qualifikation ist Auslegungssache.
Am[15] Der Käufer kann Schadensersatz verlangen oder vom Vertrag zurücktreten

warranty, breach of ~ 2. *(im Versicherungsrecht)* Zusicherungsverletzung, Garantieverletzung *(der Obliegenheitsverletzung des deutschen Rechts vergleichbar)*
Br (VersR) Im Gegensatz zum allgemeinen Vertragsrecht *(cf. breach of warranty 1.)* ist hier breach of warranty gleichbedeutend mit breach of condition. Ob warranty = condition oder eine andere →stipulation vorliegt, deren Verletzung nur zum Schadensersatz berechtigt, ist Auslegungssache

warranty, express ~ ausdrückliche Zusicherung; vertragliche Gewährleistung *(Am*[16] *entsteht durch ausdrückliche Zusicherung, durch Beschreibung der Ware od. durch Kauf nach Muster) (opp. implied ~)*

warranty, implied ~[17] konkludente Zusicherung; stillschweigende Zusage der Freiheit von Mängeln *(Br cf. implied →condition)*; gesetzliche Gewährleistung *(Am nach dem in allen Einzelstaaten angenommenen UCC fallen hierunter ~ of merchantability und ~ of fitness for a particular purpose) (opp. express ~)*; *(VersR)* stillschweigende (od. kraft Gesetzes), als Versicherungsbedingungen geltende Zusicherung (od. Garantie) *(des Versicherungsnehmers)*

warranty, non-~ Haftungsausschluß

warren Wildgehege; *hist* Jagd-, Hegerecht

warring countries kriegführende Länder

Warsaw Convention for the Unification of Certain Rules Relating to International Carriage by Air Warschauer Abkommen zur Vereinheitlichung von Regeln über die Beförderung im internationalen Luftverkehr *(von 1929)*
Das Warschauer Abkommen, ergänzt durch das Haager Protokoll von 1955[18] und das Zusatzabkommen von Guadalajara (Mexiko) von 1961[19], regelt u. a. die Haftung des Luftfrachtführers bei der internationalen Personen-, Reisegepäck- und Güterbeförderung

Warsaw-Oxford Rules for C.I.F. Contracts Warschau Oxford Regeln für CIF-Geschäfte *(von 1932) (abgeänderte CIF-Regeln)*

Warsaw Pact Warschauer Pakt *(genaue Bezeichnung:* Treaty of Friendship, Cooperation and Mutual Assistance Pakt über Freundschaft, Zusammenarbeit und gegenseitigen Beistand)
Gegr. 1955. *Mitgliedstaaten*[20]: Sowjetunion, Bulgarien, Deutsche Demokratische Republik, Polen, Rumänien, Tschechoslowakei und Ungarn.
Zweck: Gemeinsame Verteidigung im Falle eines bewaffneten Angriffs auf einen Partnerstaat

wash sale *Am (Börse)* Scheinkauf und -verkauf *(von Wertpapieren zur Beeinflussung des Marktes od. zur Steuerumgehung)*

wash *v*, ~ **and wear** pflegeleicht; **to be ~ed ashore** (or **on shore**) ans Land getrieben (od. geschwemmt) werden; **to be ~ed overboard** über Bord gespült werden

washing *Am* Börsenscheingeschäft; ~ **overboard** Überbordspülen

Washington Convention on International Trade in Endangered Species of Wild Flora and Fauna Threatened with Extinction (of 1973) Übereinkommen über den internationalen Handel mit gefährdeten Arten freilebender Tiere und wildwachsender Pflanzen (Washingtoner Übereinkommen)

wastage Schwund; Vergeudung, Verschwendung; Verschleiß; ~ **of energy** Energieverschwendung; **natural ~ of labo(u)r** natürlicher Abgang von Arbeitskräften

waste 1. Verschwendung; übermäßiger Verbrauch; ~ **of money** Geldverschwendung; ~ **of paper** Papierverschwendung; ~ **of time** Zeitverschwendung; ~ **society** Wegwerfgesellschaft

waste 2. Abfall, Abfälle, Abfallstoffe, Schwund, Verlust; öde, verlassen; unbrauchbar; Alt-, Abfall-; ~ **avoidance** Abfallvermeidung; ~ **disposal** Abfallbeseitigung; Entsorgung; ~ **incineration plant** Müllverbrennungsanlage; ~ **land** unbebautes (od. nicht anbaufähiges) Land; Ödland, Brachland *(opp. arable land)*; *(durch Krieg etc)* verwüstetes Land; ~ **management** Abfallwirtschaft; ~ **material** Abfallstoffe; ~ **oil** Altöl; ~ **paper** Papierabfälle; ~ **treatment** Abfallbehandlung; ~ **waters** Abwässer; **hazardous** ~ gefährliche Abfälle; **natural** ~ natürlicher Schwund; **nuclear** ~ Atommüll; **recycling of** ~ Rückführung von Abfallstoffen; **solid** ~ feste Abfallstoffe; **urban** ~ städtische Abfälle; **to dispose of radioactive** ~ radioaktive Abfallstoffe beseitigen; **to lay** ~ zerstören, verwüsten; **to lie** ~ brachliegen

waste 3. Wertminderung *(von Grundbesitz)*; →**impeachment of ~**; **permissive** ~ Wertminderung durch Unterlassen *(z.B. Vernachlässigung notwendiger Reparaturen)*; **voluntary** ~ absichtlich herbeigeführte Wertminderung *(z.B. Abreißen e-s Hauses)*

waste *v (Grundbesitz)* vernachlässigen, in Verfall geraten lassen *(→waste 3.)*; *(Geld, Zeit)* verschwenden; vergeuden

wasting assets kurzlebige (verbrauchbare) Vermögenswerte *(aus der Landpacht fließende Rechte, Ölvorkommen, Holz, Patente etc)*

wasteful, ~ **economy** Abfallwirtschaft; ~ **exploitation** Raubbau

waste land →waste 2.

watch and ward Wachpflicht *(von Polizisten)* bei Tag und bei Nacht

watching, to hold a ~ brief for a p. *Br* jds Interesse *(bei Gericht)* als Beobachter vertreten

water Wasser; **~s** Gewässer; **~ bailiff** *Br*[21] Fischereiaufseher; **~borne** auf dem Wasserwege befördert; **~ carriage** Wassertransport; **~ charges** *Am* Wassergeld; **~ contamination** Verschmutzung der Gewässer; **~course** Wasserlauf; *(künstl.)* Kanal; **~ craft** Wasserfahrzeug(e); **~ damage** Wasserschaden; **~ divide** *(VölkerR)* Wasserscheide; **~fowl habitat** cf. Convention on →Wetlands; **~ front** am Wasser gelegener Landstreifen; **~ line** Wasserlinie, Ladelinie *(e-s Schiffes)*; **~ management** Wasserwirtschaft; **~mark** Wasserzeichen *(z.B. e-r Banknote)*; **~ pollution** Wasserverunreinigung; Verschmutzung der Gewässer; **~ rate** Wassergeld; **~ right** Wassernutzungsrecht; Wasserentnahmerecht; Wassergerechtsame; **~ route** →~way; **~shed** →~ divide; **~ supply** Wasserversorgung

waterway[22] Wasserweg; Schiffahrtsweg *(Fluß und Kanal)*; →**inland ~**

waterworks Wasserwerke *(e-r Stadt)*

water, boundary ~s Grenzgewässer; **by ~** zu Wasser, auf dem Wasserwege; **carriage by ~** Beförderung zu Wasser (od. auf dem Schiffswege); **coastal ~s** Küstengewässer; **domestic ~s** Binnengewässer; **fresh ~** Frischwasser *(opp. sea ~)*; **ground ~** Grundwasser; **high ~** Hochwasser, Flut, Tide; **high ~- mark** Hochwasserstandszeichen, *fig.* Hochstand

water, inland ~s Binnengewässer, Eigengewässer; **inland ~(s) navigation** Binnenschiffahrt; →**inland ~(s) transport**

water, low ~ Niedrigwasser, Ebbe; **low-~mark** Niedrigwasserstandszeichen, *fig* Tiefstand; **national ~s** s. inland →~s; **sea ~** Seewasser *(opp. fresh ~)*; **sub-surface ~** Grundwasser; **supply of ~** Wasserversorgung; **surface ~** Oberflächenwasser; **territorial ~s** Hoheitsgewässer

water *v fig* verwässern

watered, ~ shares *(durch Ausgabe neuer Aktien)* verwässerte *(nur teilgedeckte)* Aktien; **~ stock** *Am (AktienR)* verwässertes Grundkapital *(verursacht durch Unter-Pariemission)*

watering of stock *Am (AktienR)* Kapitalverwässerung

wave, ~ of strikes Streikwelle; **buying ~** Ansturm der Käufer

waver *v*, **to ~ in one's resolution** in s-m Entschluß schwanken

way 1. Weg; Wegerecht *(s. right of →~)*; **~s and means** →way 2.

waybill (W. B.) Passagierliste; Frachtbrief, Warenbegleitschein; **air ~** Luftfrachtbrief; **duplicate ~** Frachtbriefduplikat; **sea ~** Seefrachtbrief

way, ~(-)going crop abgehende Ernte *(Ernte, die erst nach Ende der Pachtzeit reif wird) (→away- going crop)*; **~ in** *Br* Eingang *(für Reisende)*; **~(-) leave** Wegerecht, Durchgangsrecht *(für Zechenbesitzer etc)*; **~ of necessity** Notweg; gesetzl. begründetes Wegerecht *(vgl. § 917 BGB)*; **~(-)out** *Br* Ausgang *(für Reisende)*; *fig* Ausweg; **~ station** Zwischenstation; **~ward child** *Am* moralisch gefährdetes Kind; **by the nearest ~** auf dem nächsten Wege; **give ~** *Br (Verkehrszeichen)* Vorfahrt beachten

way, right of ~ Wegerecht *(als Dienstbarkeit)*; Vorfahrt(srecht); **to have the right of ~** Vorfahrt haben; *(Fußgänger)* Vorrang haben

way, to give ~ den Vorrang lassen; nachgeben; **to give ~ to sb.'s demands** jds Forderungen nachgeben; **to make one's ~** vorankommen; **to pay one's ~** →pay *v*

way 2. Weg; Art und Weise

ways and means Mittel und Wege *(bes. für Geldbeschaffung)*; **~ advances** *Br* von der Bank von England dem Staat (Schatzamt) gewährte kurzfristige Kredite; **Committee** *Br* **of** *(Am* **on) W~ and M~** →Committee 2.

way, by ~ of auf dem Wege über, durch; als; **by ~ of excuse** als Entschuldigung; **by ~ of gift** schenkungsweise; **by ~ of negotiation** auf dem Verhandlungswege

weak schwach; flau; **~ currency** schwache Währung; **~-currency countries** währungsschwache Länder; **~ market** *(Börse)* schwacher (od. lustloser) Markt; **financially ~** kapitalschwach

weaken *v (Börse)* abschwächen, schwächer werden; **the shares ~ed from ... to ...** die Aktien fielen von ... auf ... zurück

weakness of the market schwache Marktlage

weal, for the public (or **general**) **~** für das Gemeinwohl, für das Wohl der Allgemeinheit

wealreaf Leichenfledderei, Totenberaubung *(im Grab)*

wealth Reichtum; Vermögen; **~ creation** Vermögensbildung; **~ of a nation** (or **national ~**) Volksvermögen; **~ tax** Vermögenssteuer; **to amass great ~** große Reichtümer ansammeln

wealthy reich, vermögend, wohlhabend

weapon Waffe; **~s of defen|ce (~se) and offen|ce (~se)** Angriffs- und Verteidigungswaffen; **~ of mass destruction** Massenvernichtungswaffen; **atomic ~s** Atomwaffen; **carrying (of) ~s** Tragen von Waffen; **conventional ~** konventionelle Waffe; **Convention on the Prohibition of the Development,**

Production and Stockpiling of Bacteriological (Biological) and Toxic W~s and on their Destruction[22a] Übereinkommen über das Verbot der Entwicklung, Herstellung und Lagerung bakteriologischer (biologischer) Waffen und von Toxinwaffen sowie über die Vernichtung solcher Waffen; **deadly** ~[23] tödliche Waffe; **tactical nuclear ~s** taktische Kernwaffen

wear and tear Abnutzung *(durch Gebrauch)*; *(natürlicher)* Verschleiß; **depreciation for** ~ *Br (SteuerR)* Absetzung für Abnutzung (AfA)

wearing apparel *(nicht der Pfändung unterworfene)* Kleidungsstücke; **necessary ~ and bedding** *(KonkursR)* notwendige Kleidungsstükke und Betten

weary of office amtsmüde

weather, ~ forecast Wettervorhersage; ~ **insurance** Reisewetterversicherung; ~ **permitting** (w. p.) bei günstigem Wetter; ~ **working day(s)** (W. W. D.) nach Wetterlage mögliche(r) Arbeitstag(e)

weather *v*, **to ~ a difficult period** e-e schwierige Zeit überstehen

Webb Pomerene, ~ Act *Am* Webb Pomerene-Gesetz *(amtl. Bezeichnung*: Export Trade Act) *(von 1918)*; ~ **association** *Am* gesetzl. erlaubtes Exportkartell
Das Gesetz befreite die Exportkartelle von dem allgemeinen Kartellverbot der Antitrustgesetze, sofern sie den Wettbewerb auf dem Inlandsmarkt nicht beeinflussen

wedding Hochzeit(sfeier); ~ **announcement** (or **card**) Heiratsanzeige; ~ **day** Hochzeitstag; ~ **presents** Hochzeitsgeschenke

wedlock Ehe(stand); **out of** ~ nicht ehelich; **child born out of** ~ nichteheliches Kind; **to be born in lawful** ~ ehelich geboren sein

week Woche; ~ **order** *Am* für e-e Woche gültiger Börsenauftrag; ~ **under review** Berichtswoche; **two ~s' notice** 14tägige Kündigung(sfrist)

weekly wöchentlich; Wochenzeitschrift; ~ **benefit** Wochengeld *(für Zeit der Arbeitslosigkeit)*, ~ **loans** (or **fixtures**) *(Börse)* Geld auf eine Woche, wöchentliche Darlehen; ~ **(paper)** wöchentliche Zeitung; ~ **return** Wochenausweis *(der Bank of England)*; ~ **season ticket** Wochenkarte; ~ →**tenancy**

weekly tender *Br (Geldmarkt)* wöchentliche Auktion
Die britischen Schatzwechsel werden im Tender- oder Auktionsverfahren emittiert

weigh *v* wiegen, Gewicht feststellen (od. haben); abwägen; **to ~ (up)** abwägen, gut überlegen; **to ~ evidence** den Beweis würdigen

weighing Wiegen; Abwägen, Erwägen; **check** ~ Nachwiegen

weigher Wiegender; Waagemeister; **check** ~ Gewichtskontrolleur

weight 1. Gewicht; ~ **allowed free** Freigewicht
weights and measures[24] Maße und Gewichte; **inspector of** ~ *Br* Eichmeister; **Office of W~ and M~** *Br* Eichamt
weight, ~ goods (or **cargo**) Schwergut *(opp. measurement goods or cargo)*; ~ **limit** Gewichtsgrenze, Höchstgewicht; ~ **note** Wiegeschein; ~ **of fine gold** Feingoldgehalt; ~ **slip** Wiegezettel; ~ **stamp** Wiegestempel; ~ **when empty** Leergewicht
weight, by ~ nach Gewicht; **certificate of** ~ Gewichtsbescheinigung; **commercial** ~ Handelsgewicht; **dead** ~ Eigengewicht; **declaration of** ~ Gewichtsangabe; **deficiency in** ~ Fehlgewicht, Gewichtsmanko; **deficient in** ~ untergewichtig, zu leicht; **excess ~ charges** *(Flugzeug)* Gebühren für Übergewicht; **gross** ~ Bruttogewicht; **indication of** ~ Gewichtsangabe; **loss in** (or **reduction of**) ~ Gewichtsverlust; **net** ~ Nettogewicht; **remedy of** ~ zulässige Abweichung vom Gewicht (→*remedy 2.*); →**short** ~; **shortage in** ~ s. deficiency in →~; **surplus** ~ Mehrgewicht; Übergewicht; **to adjust a** ~ ein Gewicht eichen; **to be deficient in** ~ kein volles Gewicht haben; **to exceed the** ~ das Gewicht überschreiten
weight 2. Gewicht; Bedeutung, Wichtigkeit; **the ~ of authority** *(etwa)* die herrschende Meinung; ~ **of evidence** Gewicht des Beweismaterials; **man of** ~ maßgebliche Persönlichkeit; **to carry** ~ Einfluß haben; von Bedeutung sein; **to give due ~ to a th.** etw. gebührend würdigen

weight *v* belasten, beschweren; bewerten; *(Statistik)* gewichten
weighted average gewogener Durchschnitt(swert)
weighting *(Statistik)* Gewichtung; ~ **allowance** *Br* Ortszuschlag

weir Damm, Wehr, Stauwehr

welcome Empfang, Begrüßung; ~ **address** Begrüßungsansprache; **to extend a ~ to a p.** jdn willkommen heißen, jdn begrüßen

welcome *v*, **to ~ a p.** jdn begrüßen; **he ~d those present** er hieß die Anwesenden willkommen

welfare Wohlergehen; Wohlfahrt, Fürsorge(tätigkeit); Sozialhilfe; ~ **activity** Fürsorgetätigkeit, Sozialarbeit; ~ **agency** *Am* Sozialbehörde; ~ **benefits** Fürsorgeleistungen, Sozialleistungen; ~ **economics** Wohlfahrtsökonomik, Wohlfahrtstheorie; ~ **expenditure** *Am* Sozialausgaben; ~ **facilities** Sozialeinrichtungen; ~ **fund** Wohlfahrtsfonds; ~ **institution** Wohlfahrtseinrichtung; soziales Hilfswerk; ~ **officer** Sozialarbeiter(in); ~ **recipient** *Am* Bezieher von Sozialleistungen; Sozialhilfeempfänger; ~ **roll** Liste der Sozialhilfeempfänger; ~ **services** Wohlfahrtseinrichtungen; Sozialleistungen; ~ **state** Wohlfahrtsstaat; ~ **visitor** Hausfürsorgerin

welfare work Wohlfahrtspflege; Sozialarbeit; **associations of private** ~ Verbände der freien Wohlfahrtspflege; **industrial** ~ betriebliche Sozialarbeit; **to do** ~ Wohlfahrtstätigkeit ausüben

welfare worker Sozialarbeiter(in)

welfare, infant ~ Säuglingsfürsorge; **maternity and child** ~ Fürsorge für Mutter und Kind; **occupational** ~ betriebliche Sozialleistungen; **public** ~ Wohlergehen der Allgemeinheit; *bes. Am* Sozialhilfe; **public** ~ **offenses** *Am* um des Wohlergehens der Allgemeinheit willen verbotene Handlungen oder Unterlassungen; **to be on** ~ *Am* Sozialhilfe beziehen

well-being Wohlergehen; **economic** ~ Wohlstand

well, ~-connected mit guten Beziehungen; **~-established** etabliert; **~-founded complaint** begründete Beschwerde (od. Reklamation); **~-founded suspicion** begründeter Verdacht; **from a ~-informed source** aus gut unterrichteter Quelle; **~-off** wohlhabend, in guten Verhältnissen (lebend); **~-priced** preisgünstig; **~-situated business** Geschäft in guter Lage; **~-to-do** *Br* wohlhabend; ~ **up in the trade** branchenkundig

Welsh walisisch; **W~ Office** *Br* Regierungsbehörde für walisische Angelegenheiten

welsh mortgage Hypothek, kraft derer dem Gläubiger das Pfandgrundstück übertragen wird und ihm die Nutzungen ohne Anrechnung auf s-e Forderung gebühren, bis der Schuldner das Pfandgrundstück durch Tilgung der Forderung zurückerwirbt, was er jederzeit kann *(Br selten; Am obs.)*

welsher (or **welcher**) betrügerischer Buchmacher

West Africans (or **West African shares**) *Br* westafrikanische Werte

Western European Union[25] (WEU) Westeuropäische Union

Mitglieder: Die Bundesrepublik Deutschland, Großbritannien, Frankreich, Italien und die Benelux-Staaten. Kollektiver Beistandspakt im Rahmen der →NATO. Zuständig für Fragen der westeuropäischen Sicherheit. *Sitz:* London

westernize *v* verwestlichen

WESTLAW *Am (durch Telefonnetz zugängliche)* Datenbank für juristische Daten *(gerichtl. und behördl. Entscheidungen, Aufsätze)*

Westminster Sitz des englischen Parlaments; →**Statute of** ~

wet naß; *Am colloq.* nicht unter Alkoholverbot stehend *(opp. dry; cf. prohibition 3.)*; ~ **dock** Schwimmdock *(opp. dry dock)*; ~ **goods** flüssige Waren *(opp. dry goods)*

wetting by sea-water Naßwerden (od. Durchnässung) durch Seewasser

wetland Feuchtgebiet; **Convention on W~s of International Importance, Especially as Waterfowl Habitat**[26] Übereinkommen über Feuchtgebiete, insbesondere als Lebensraum für Wasser- und Wattvögel von internationaler Bedeutung

whack *v* aufteilen, parzellieren, auseinandersetzen

whale-fishing Walfang

whaler Walfänger; **~y** *Am* Walfang; Walfangindustrie

whaling Walfang; ~ **industry**[27] Walfangindustrie; **International Convention for the Regulation of W~**[27a] Internationales Übereinkommen zur Regelung des Walfangs; **International W~ Commission** Internationale Walfangkommission

wharf Kai; Lade- und Löschplatz *(von Schiffen)*; Pier; ~ **dues** Kaigeld, Kaigebühr(en); Lade- und Löschgebühren; **approved ~ves** *Br*[28] *(von den Commissioners of Customs and Excise)* als geeignet genehmigte Plätze zum Beladen und Löschen zollpflichtiger Waren

wharf *v (Schiff)* an e-m Kai anlegen; *(Ladung)* löschen

wharfage →wharf dues

wharfinger[29] Kaibesitzer, Kaimeister *(owner or lessee of a wharf)*; **~'s certificate** (or **receipt**) Kaiquittung *(Bescheinigung des ~ über Empfang der Ware)*; ~ **warrant** *Br* Kailagerschein

wheat Weizen; ~ **flour** Weizenmehl; ~ **shipments** Weizenverschiffungen, Weizenlieferungen; **W~ Trade Convention**[30] Weizenhandels-Übereinkommen

wheat, bulk ~ loser Weizen; **quantities of** ~ Weizenmengen; **sample** ~ Musterweizen; **seed** ~ Weizensaatgut; **supply of** ~ Versorgung mit Weizen; **trade in** ~ Weizenhandel

wheelage Wegegeld, Rollgeld

wheeler, ~-dealer *colloq.* Intrigant; **W~ Lea Act** *Am* Zusatz zum →Federal Trade Commission Act von 1938 *(umfaßt bes. den Kampf gegen fal-*

sche od. irreführende Werbung hinsichtlich Lebensmittel, Arzneimittel und Kosmetika)

when due bei Fälligkeit, bei Verfall

when issued (w.i.) bei Erscheinen *(der Wertpapiere)*

whereabouts *(derzeitiger)* Aufenthalt(sort)

whereas in Anbetracht *(der Tatsache)*, daß; angesichts; da nun; ~ **clause** einleitender Teil e-r Urkunde *(mit Wiedergabe der zugrundeliegenden Tatsachen)*

wherefore weshalb

whip *bes. Br parl* Einpeitscher *(hält die Parteidisziplin bzw. den Fraktionszwang bei Abstimmungen aufrecht)*; Fraktionsrundschreiben, Fraktionszwang; **chief** ~ Fraktionsführer; **one line** ~ Aufforderung, zur Abstimmung zu erscheinen; **two line** ~ dringende Aufforderung, zur Abstimmung zu erscheinen; **three line** ~ absoluter Abstimmungszwang *(3mal unterstrichene Aufforderung zur Anwesenheit)*; **the ~s are off** der Fraktionszwang ist aufgehoben; **to be under the party** ~ unter Fraktionszwang stehen

whip *v* peitschen; *(mit Gewalt)* treiben, nötigen; **to ~ in** *Br (Parteimitglieder zur Abstimmung)* zusammentrommeln

whipped vote Stimmabgabe unter Fraktionszwang

whipping Peitschen; Prügelstrafe

whispering propaganda Flüsterpropaganda

Whit Sunday Pfingstsonntag

White Book *Br* Weißbuch
Es umfaßt alle Prozeßmaximen und Richtlinien für die Rechtspflege beim Supreme →Court of England and Wales

white-collar *colloq.* Kopf-, Geistes-; Büro-; ~ **crime** Wirtschaftsverbrechen; ~ **job** Beschäftigung als Büroangestellter, Bürotätigkeit, Schreibtischarbeit; ~ **offenses** *Am* Wirtschaftsstraftaten; ~ **union** Angestelltengewerkschaft; ~ **worker** (Büro-)Angestellte(r)

white, W~Ensign *Br* Flagge der Kriegsmarine; ~ **flag** *mil* weiße Fahne, Parlamentärsflagge

Whitehall (Straße in London mit dem) Regierungsviertel; britische Regierung

White House, the ~ *Am* das Weiße Haus *(Regierungssitz des Präsidenten)*; ~ **Office** persönlicher Mitarbeiterstab des Präsidenten

white, ~ **knight** („edler Ritter") Investor, der Aktionären ein Übernahmeangebot mit Zustimmung der Zielgesellschaft unterbreitet, nachdem dem Unternehmen ein unerwünschtes Übernahmeangebot (hostile →takeover) angedroht worden war; **W~ Paper** *pol bes. Br* Weißbuch *(Informationsbericht über Regierungspolitik für Parlament und Öffentlichkeit)*; **W~ Russian** Weißrusse *(→Byelorussian)*; ~ **slavery** →~ slave trade; ~ **slave trade** (or **traffic**) Mädchenhandel; ~ **trash** *Am colloq.* arme weiße Bevölkerung *(bes. im Süden der USA)*

Whitley Council *Br* aus Arbeitgebern und -nehmern bestimmter Industrien zusammengesetzter Ausschuß zur Regelung bestimmter Fragen; Schlichtungsausschuß

whiz(z) kid Senkrechtstarter, hochbegabte junge Person

whole ganz; **of the** ~ →**blood;** ~ **coverage** vollständige Deckung; ~ **life insurance** Lebensversicherung auf den Todesfall, Todesfallversicherung; **the ~ or (a) part** das ganze od. ein Teil; **the ~ of one's property** sein ganzes Vermögen; **on the** ~ im ganzen gesehen, im großen und ganzen

wholesale Großhandel; Großhandels-, Engros-; in Massen; im großen *(opp. retail)*; ~ **banking** Bankgeschäfte mit großen Unternehmen; Großkundengeschäfte e-r Bank; ~ **business** Großhandelsgeschäft, Großhandel; Großkundengeschäft; ~ **commerce** →~ trade; ~ **dealer** Großhändler, Grossist; **(by way of)** ~ **dealing** (im) Großhandel; ~ **discount** Großhandelsrabatt; ~ **distributor** Großhandelsverteilerstelle; ~ **enterprise** (or **establishment**) Großhandelsunternehmen; ~ **firm** (or **house**) Großhandelsfirma, Großhandlung

wholesale grocer Lebensmittelgroßhändler; **U.S. W~G~s' Association** Verband der amerikanischen Lebensmittelgroßhändler

wholesale, ~ **insurance** Gruppenversicherung; ~ **investor** Großanleger; ~ **merchant** →~ dealer; ~ **price** Großhandelspreis; ~ **price index** Index der Großhandelspreise; ~ **purchase** Einkauf im großen; Engroseinkauf; ~ **sale** Verkauf im großen, Engrosverkauf; **(cooperative)** ~ **society** *Br* Großeinkaufsgenossenschaft; ~ **store** *Am* Großhandelsgeschäft

wholesale trade Großhandel (in mit); **to do** ~ Großhandel treiben

wholesale, ~ **trader** →~ dealer; **by** ~ en gros; in großen Mengen; **by ~ or by retail** im Groß- od. Einzelhandel; **to deal** ~ Großhandel treiben

wholesaler Großhändler, Grossist *(opp. retailer)*

wholetime employment ganztätige Beschäftigung

wholly ganz, gänzlich, vollständig; ~ **or in part** (or **partly**) ganz oder teilweise; **~-owned subsidiary** 100%ige Tochtergesellschaft; **to agree with sb.** ~ mit jdm völlig übereinstimmen

whore Prostituierte, Hure, Dirne; ~ **master** Zuhälter

wide, ~ **choice** große Auswahl; ~ **circulation** große Auflage; ~ **experience** große Erfahrung; ~ **prices** *(Börse)* Kurse mit großer Spanne zwischen Geld- und Briefkurs; ~**-ranging** (or **reaching**) weitreichend; ~**spread** weitverbreitet; **country**~ (or **nation**~) über das ganze Land verbreitet; **world-**~ weltweit

widely weit (auseinander); in hohem Maße, sehr; ~ **held opinion** weit verbreitete Meinung; ~ **spread shareholdings** Aktienstreubesitz; **to differ** ~ sehr unterschiedlich sein; **to differ** ~ **in opinion** sehr verschiedener Meinung sein

widow Witwe; ~**'s annuity** Witwenrente; ~ **and orphan stock** *Am* Wertpapiere mit hoher Sicherheit; mündelsichere Wertpapiere

widow's benefits Sozialversicherungsleistungen an Witwe

Br[31] In der Sozialversicherung (social security) gibt es 3 Arten von widow's benefits: →widow's payment, →widowed mother's allowance, →widow's pension. Ab April 1979 sind widow's benefits abhängig von dem Verdienst des verstorbenen Ehemannes (earnings-related)

widow, ~**'s payment** *Br (zeitweilige)* Witwenbeihilfe; ~**'s pension** *Br (ständige)* Witwenrente; ~**'s terce** *Scot* →terce

widowed verwitwet; ~ **mother's allowance** *Br* Beihilfe für verwitwete Mutter

widower Witwer; ~**'s (insurance) benefit** *Am (Sozialversicherung)* Hinterbliebenenrente für Witwer *(der verstorbenen Erwerbstätigen)*

widowhood Witwenschaft, Witwenstand

wife Ehefrau; ~**'s insurance benefit** *Am (Sozialversicherung)* Zusatzrente für Ehefrau des Hauptbezugsberechtigten; **husband and** ~ Eheleute, Ehegatten; **husband's responsibility for** ~**'s expenditure** Haftung des Ehemannes für die Verpflichtungen der Ehefrau

wildcat unreell, unseriös; Schwindel-; *(bei Erdölbohrungen)* unsicher, riskant; ~ **company** *Am* Schwindelfirma; ~ **securities** hochspekulative und zumeist wertlose Effekten; ~ **strike** wilder Streik

wilderness, to be sent (off) into the ~ *fig* in die Wüste geschickt werden

wild fauna freilebende Tiere; **Convention on the International Trade in Endangered Species of W**~ **F**~ **and Flora**[32] Übereinkommen über den internationalen Handel mit gefährdeten Arten freilebender Tiere und Pflanzen (Washingtoner Artenschutzübereinkommen)

wildlife, ~ **sanctuary** Schutzgebiet für freilebende Tiere; → **World W**~ **Fund**

wilful absichtlich, vorsätzlich *(→intentional)*; ~ **deceit** arglistige Täuschung; ~ **negligence** bewußte Fahrlässigkeit *(→negligence)*

wilfully or by negligence vorsätzlich oder fahrlässig

will 1. Wille; ~**-call purchase** *Am* Kauf, bei dem e-e Anzahlung gemacht und die Ware zurückgelegt wird; ~ **for peace** Friedenswille; ~ **of the parties** Parteiwille; **of one's free** ~ aus freiem Willen, freiwillig

will, at ~ nach Belieben; auf Widerruf; jederzeit und grundlos (*Kündigung*); **estate at** ~ →tenancy at will; **freedom of the** ~ Willensfreiheit; **partnership at** ~ [33] jederzeit kündbare Personengesellschaft; →**tenancy at** ~; →**tenant at** ~

will 2. Testament, letztwillige Verfügung *(cf. testator)*; **W**~**s Act** (WA) *Br*[34] Testamentsgesetz

Ein Testament ist nur gültig, wenn der Testator volljährig (of legal age) sowie zurechnungsfähig (of sound mind) war und es in Gegenwart von Zeugen errichtet wurde.[35] *Am* Diese Voraussetzungen sowie auch die Zahl der gesetzl. erforderlichen Zeugen sind einzelstaatl. verschieden geregelt

will, to administer a ~ ein Testament zur Ausführung bringen; **to benefit by** (or **under**) **a** ~ in e-m Testament bedacht werden; **to carry out the provisions of a will** die Testamentsbestimmungen ausführen; **to contest** (or **dispute**) **a** ~ ein Testament anfechten; **to dispose by** ~ *(über etw.)* letztwillig verfügen; *(etw.)* vermachen; **to draft** (or **draw up**) **a** ~ ein Testament aufsetzen; **to execute a** ~ ein Testament *(rechtsgültig)* ausfertigen (*→execute v*); **to forge a** ~ ein Testament fälschen; **to include a p. in a** ~ jdn im Testament bedenken; **to invalidate a** ~ ein Testament ungültig machen; **to leave by** ~ testamentarisch vermachen; **to make one's** ~ sein Testament machen; **to mention a p. in one's** ~ jdn in s-m Testament bedenken; **to probate a** ~ ein Testament gerichtlich bestätigen; **to prove a** ~ ein Testament gerichtlich anerkennen und bestätigen lassen *(Aufgabe des →executor)*; **to provide in a** ~ in e-m Testament bestimmen; **to read a** ~ ein Testament eröffnen; **to register a** ~ *Am* ein notarielles Testament errichten; **to remember a p. in one's** ~ jdn in s-m Testament bedenken; **to revoke a** ~ ein Testament widerrufen; **to take by** (or **under**) **a** ~ auf Grund e-s Testaments erben; **to witness a** ~ die Errichtung e-s Testamentes bezeugen

will, able to make a ~ s. capable of making a →~; **agreement to make a** ~ s. contract to make a →~; **ambulatory** ~ *(bis zum Tode des Erblassers)* jederzeit widerrufliches Testament; **assets under a** ~ Nachlaß; **attested** ~ von Zeugen unterschriebenes Testament; **by** ~ testamentarisch, durch letztwillige Verfügung; **beneficiary under a** ~ Testamentserbe; Vermächtnisnehmer *(nach engl. und amerik. Recht ist nicht der Erbe als solcher, sondern der →executor für die Abwicklung des Nachlasses verantwortlich)*; **capacity to make a** ~ Testierfähigkeit; **capable of making a** ~ testierfähig; **clause of a** ~ Testamentsbestimmung; **contesting (of) a** ~ Testamentsanfechtung; **contract to make a** ~ erbrechtlicher Verpflichtungsvertrag *(hat nach Billigkeitsrecht etwa die Funktionen, die im deutschen Recht dem im anglo-amerik. Recht unbekannten Erbvertrag zukommen)*; **duly authenticated copy of a** ~ ordnungsgemäß beglaubigte Abschrift e-s Testaments; **properly executed** ~ ordnungsgemäß errichtetes Testament; **execution of a** ~ *(rechtsgültige)* Ausfertigung e-s Testaments (s. *to execute a* →~); **place of execution of a** ~ Ort der Errichtung e-s Testamentes; **holographic** ~ eigenhändig geschriebenes *(ohne Zeugen unterschriebenes)* Testament; **incapable of making a** ~ nicht testierfähig; **informal** ~ formloses Testament; **interpretation of a** ~ Auslegung e-s Testaments; **joint** ~ gemeinschaftliches Testament *(Testament mehrerer in e-r Urkunde, wobei jeder s-e Verfügungen bis zu s-m Tode widerrufen kann) (vgl. dazu auch § 2265ff. BGB)*; **joint and mutual** ~ gemeinschaftliches und gegenseitiges (od. wechselbezügliches) Testament *(Testament mehrerer in einer Urkunde, wobei jeder Testierender den anderen bedenkt, sei es in korrespektiver, sei es in reziproker Weise) (vgl. etwa §§ 2269, 2270 BGB)*; **last** ~ **and testament** *(formeller Ausdruck für)* Testament, letztwillige Verfügung; **mutual** ~ *(nicht gemeinschaftliches)* gegenseitiges *(und zwar korrespektives od. reziprokes)* Testament; **nuncupative** ~[36] mündlich *(vor Zeugen)* erklärte letztwillige Verfügung; **probate of a** ~ Testamentsbestätigung *(→probate)*; **proved** ~ als gültig bestätigtes Testament; **provisions of a** ~ Bestimmungen e-s Testaments; **reciprocal** ~ *Am* gegenseitiges Testament; **→register of ~s; revocation of a** ~ Widerruf (od. Aufhebung) e-s Testaments; **terms of a** ~ Testamentsbestimmungen; **at the time of making the** ~ zur Zeit der Testamentserrichtung

will *v* wollen; durch Testament bestimmen (od. vermachen)

willful *Am* →wilful

win *v* gewinnen, (ob)siegen; *(BergR)* gewinnen, abbauen; **to** ~ **one's case** (or **lawsuit**) s-n Prozeß gewinnen; obsiegen; **to** ~ **a competition** ein Preisausschreiben gewinnen; **to** ~ **a mineral** ein Mineral abbauen; **to** ~ **ore or coal by mining** Erz od. Kohle durch Abbau gewinnen; **to** ~ **a seat** *parl* e-n (Abgeordneten-)Sitz erringen; **to** ~ **a p. over** jdn gewinnen für; jdn für sich gewinnen

winning, ~ **ore** Erzgewinn, Erzabbau; ~ **party** obsiegende (Prozeß-)Partei; ~ **ticket** Lotteriegewinn(los)

windfall Fallobst, Windwurf; *fig* Glücksfall; ~ **profit** Zufallsgewinn; unerwarteter Gewinn; ~ **receipts** *(SteuerR)* Zufallseinnahmen *(Schenkungen, Vermächtnisse etc)*

wind up *v* abschließen; Schluß machen; *(Unternehmen)* liquidieren, *(Rechtsverhältnisse e-r aufgelösten Gesellschaft)* abwickeln; **to** ~ **one's affairs** seine Geschäfte *(endgültig)* abwickeln; **to** ~ **a company** *Br*[37] (**corporation** *Am*) die Liquidation e-r (Handels-)Gesellschaft durchführen *(cf. winding up)*; **to** ~ **an estate** *bes. Br* e-n Nachlaß abwickeln; **petition to** ~ Liquidationsantrag

winding up Liquidation, Abwicklung *(der Rechtsverhältnisse e-r aufgelösten Gesellschaft)*; Liquidation, Abwicklung; *Br* Konkurs *(e-r Kapitalgesellschaft)*; ~ **costs** Liquidationskosten; ~ **by the court** *Br*[38] zwangsweise Liquidation durch das Gericht; *(etwa)* Gesellschaftskonkurs

winding up of a company *Br*[39] Abwicklung e-r Gesellschaft

Im englischen Recht heißt nur die Liquidation e-r company (→ltd, →plc) winding up. Es gibt die freiwillige Abwicklung *(s. voluntary →winding up)* und die Abwicklung durch das Gericht *(→winding up by the court)*. Der Konkurs von natürlichen Personen und Personengesellschaften heißt bankruptcy

winding up of a fund Auflösung e-s Fonds

winding up order (of the court) Gerichtsbeschluß auf Eröffnung des Liquidationsverfahrens; **to make the** ~ den Liquidationsbeschluß ergehen lassen

winding up, ~ **petition** Liquidationsantrag, Antrag auf Eröffnung des Liquidationsverfahrens; ~ **proceedings** Liquidationsverfahren; ~ **proceeds** Liquidationserlös; ~ **resolution** Liquidationsbeschluß *(der Gesellschafter)*; ~ **sale** Ausverkauf wegen Geschäftsaufgabe; Totalausverkauf; **application for** ~ Liquidationsantrag; **compulsory** ~ →~ by the court

winding up, voluntary ~ *Br*[40] freiwillige Abwicklung

Bei der freiwilligen Abwicklung wird unterschieden zwischen creditors' voluntary →winding up und members' voluntary →winding up.

Die freiwillige Abwicklung erfolgt bei Ablauf der im Gesellschaftsvertrag festgelegten Zeit für das Bestehen der Gesellschaft oder bei Beschluß der Gesellschafter (z. B. wegen Überschuldung)

winding up, creditors' voluntary ~ *Br*[41] freiwillige Abwicklung zugunsten der Gläubiger

winding up, members' voluntary ~ *Br*[41a] freiwillige Abwicklung durch die Gesellschafter

Bei einer freiwilligen Abwicklung durch die Gesellschafter müssen die Direktoren eine Erklärung abgeben, daß die Gesellschaft innerhalb von max. 12 Monaten ab Beginn der Abwicklung ihre Schulden einschließlich Zinsen vollständig bezahlen kann *(cf. stat-*

utory declaration of→*solvency).* Wenn diese Erklärung nicht abgegeben wird bzw. wenn der von den Gesellschaftern bestellte Liquidator der Auffassung ist, daß die Gesellschaft die Zahlungen nicht gemäß der Solvenzerklärung einhalten kann, so heißt die Abwicklung creditors' voluntary →winding up

windmill Windmühle; *com sl.* Reitwechsel; Kellerwechsel *(cf. kite)*

window, ~ advertising Schaufensterreklame; **~ card** Schaufensterplakat; **~ clerk** *Am (Post)* Schalterbeamter; **~ display** Schaufensterauslage; **~ dressing** Schaufensterdekoration; **~ dressing (of the balance-sheet)** *(gesetzl. erlaubtes)* Frisieren der Bilanz; Bilanzfrisur; **~ envelope** Fenster(brief)umschlag

windstorm insurance Sturmschädenversicherung

wine, ~ growing Weinbau; **adulteration of ~** Weinfälschung; **importation of ~** Einfuhr von Wein; **trade in ~**(or **~trade**) Weinhandel

wing *pol* Flügel *(e-r Partei)*; **left ~**→left 2.; **right ~**→right 3b.

winner obsiegende Partei

winning →win *v*

wipe off *v*, **to ~ a debt** e-e Schuld abtragen (od. tilgen); **to ~ a debit balance** ein Debetsaldo ausgleichen

wire Draht; *colloq.* Telegramm; **~ answer** Drahtantwort; telegrafische Antwort; **~ collect** *Am* Telegramm mit bezahlter Rückantwort; **~puller** *bes. pol (unsichtbarer)* Drahtzieher; **~pulling** *bes. pol* Drahtziehen, Machenschaften; **~ tap** *v* abhören, mithören *(durch Anzapfen e-r Telefonleitung)*; **~ tapper** Abhörer; **~ tapping** Abhören von Telefongesprächen; **~ tapping scandal** Abhörskandal; **~ transfer** *Am* telegrafische Geldüberweisung; **by ~** telegrafisch; **hot ~** *pol* heißer Draht; **reply by ~** →~ answer; **to countermand by ~** abtelegrafieren; **to hand in a ~** ein Telegramm aufgeben; **to send a ~** telegrafieren, drahten; **to telephone a ~** ein Telegramm telefonisch durchsagen

wire *v colloq.* drahten, telegrafieren; **to ~ back** zurücktelegrafieren; **~ fate** geben Sie telegrafische Nachricht über das Schicksal e-s Wechsels (od. Schecks)

wireless drahtlos, Funk-; *Br* →radio

wiretap *v* abhören

wish, message of good ~es Glückwunschtelegramm; **to express the ~** den Wunsch äußern

wit, to ~ das heißt (d. h.); nämlich

witam Freispruch aufgrund gelungenen Zeugen(gegen)beweises

with costs *Br (in e-m Urteil)* mit Kosten *(die obsiegende Partei ist berechtigt, von der Gegenpartei die taxed costs ersetzt zu erhalten,* →*tax v 2.)*

with rights mit Bezugsrecht *(*→*right 2.)*

withdraw *v* 1. zurückziehen, zurücknehmen; abberufen; entziehen, widerrufen; *(Geld)* abheben, entnehmen; **to ~ an action** e-e Klage zurücknehmen (od. zurückziehen); **to ~ an appeal** ein Rechtsmittel zurücknehmen; **to ~ an application** →application 1. und 2.; **to ~ one's candidature** s-e Kandidatur zurückziehen; **to ~ from a case** sein Mandat niederlegen *(als Anwalt)*; **to ~ the charge** die Anklage zurücknehmen *(das Strafverfahren einstellen)*; **to ~ coins from circulation** Münzen aus dem Verkehr ziehen; Münzen außer Umlauf setzen (od. einziehen); **to ~ one's confidence from a p.** jdm sein Vertrauen entziehen; **to ~ a credit** e-n Kredit zurückziehen (od. kündigen); **to ~ immunity from sb.** jds Immunität aufheben; **to ~ a juror** e-n Geschworenen abberufen *(*→*withdrawal of juror)*; **to ~ a licen|ce (~se)** e-e *(amtl.)* Genehmigung (od. Konzession) zurücknehmen; e-e Lizenz entziehen; **to ~ a measure** e-e Maßnahme rückgängig machen; **to ~ money from an account** Geld von e-m Konto abheben; **to ~ money from a business** Geld aus e-m Geschäft herausziehen; **to ~ the patent application** die Patentanmeldung zurücknehmen; **to ~ a power of attorney** e-e Vollmacht widerrufen; **to ~ one's promise** sein Versprechen zurücknehmen; **to ~ restrictions** Beschränkungen aufheben; **to ~ securities from a deposit** Effekten aus e-m Depot nehmen; **to ~ a sum of money** e-n Geldbetrag abheben; **to ~ a statement** e-e Aussage zurücknehmen (od. widerrufen); **to ~ troops** Truppen zurücknehmen; Truppen abziehen

withdraw *v* 2. sich zurückziehen; zurücktreten (from von); ausscheiden; austreten (from aus); *mil* sich absetzen; **to ~ from an agreement** von e-m Vertrag zurücktreten; *(VölkerR)* ein Abkommen (od. Übereinkommen) kündigen; **to ~ from an association** aus e-m Verband austreten; **to ~ from business** sich vom Geschäftsleben zurückziehen; **to ~ from a contract** von e-m Vertrag zurücktreten; **to ~ from membership of** *(als Mitglied)* austreten aus; **to ~ from a partnership** als Gesellschafter (od. Teilhaber) ausscheiden; **to ~ from a party** aus e-r Partei austreten; **to ~ from a purchase** von e-m Kauf zurücktreten; e-n Kauf rückgängig machen; **to ~ from respresenting** die Vertretung des Beklagten niederlegen

withdrawal 1. Zurückziehung, Rücknahme(erklärung); Abberufung; Widerruf; Bankabhebung, (Geld-)Abhebung, Entnahme; **~s** Abhebungen, (Privat-)Entnahmen; **~ form** Abhebungsformular; ~ **from an agreement** →withdrawal 2.; ~ **from a case** Mandatsniederlegung *(e-s Anwalts)*; ~ **from a contract** →withdrawal 2.; ~ **notice** s. notice of→withdrawal 1. und 2.; ~ **of the authorization to operate** Konzessionsentzug; Entzug der Bewilligung zum Geschäftsbetrieb; ~ **of banknotes** Einziehung von Banknoten; ~ **of a bill (of exchange)** Zurücknahme e-s Wechsels; ~ **of capital** Kapitalentnahme; ~ **of credit** Zurückziehung des Kredits, Kreditkündigung; ~ **of deposits** Abhebung von (Spar-)Einlagen; ~ **of funds** Mittelabzug; ~ **of a p.'s immunity** Aufhebung jds Immunität; ~ **of (a) juror** Abberufung e-s Geschworenen *(Methode zur Beendigung e-s trial; im Zivilprozeß gleichbedeutend mit discontinuance)*; ~ **of a licen|ce (~se)** Zurücknahme e-r *(amtl.)* Genehmigung (od. Konzession); Lizenzentzug; ~ **of members** →withdrawal 2.; ~ **of money from an account** Geldabhebung von e-m Konto; ~ **of motion** Zurücknahme des Antrags; ~ **of narcotics** Entzug von Suchtstoffen; ~ **of the notice** Rücknahme der Kündigung; ~ **of an order** Zurückziehung e-s Auftrags; Rückgängigmachung e-r Bestellung, Abbestellung; ~ **of a permit** Zurückziehung (od. Widerruf) e-r Genehmigung; ~ **of power of attorney** Zurückziehung (od. Widerruf) der Vollmacht; ~ **of a request** Zurückziehung (od. Zurücknahme) e-r Bitte; ~ **of troops** Zurücknahme von Truppen *(hinter e-e bestimmte Linie)*; Abzug von Truppen *(aus e-m Land)*; ~ **warrant** *(Sparkasse)* Auszahlungsermächtigung; **day-to-day ~s** tägliche Abhebungen

withdrawal, notice of ~ Kündigung(sbenachrichtigung) *(cf. withdrawal 2.)*; **notice of ~ of bonds** Kündigung von Obligationen; **to give notice of ~ of bonds** die Rückzahlung von Obligationen ankündigen

withdrawal 2. Zurückziehen, Rücktritt; Ausscheiden; Austritt (from aus) *(→withdraw v 2.)*; ~ **from an agreement** Rücktritt von e-m Vertrag; *(VölkerR)* Kündigung e-s Abkommens (od. Übereinkommens); ~ **from a contract** Rücktritt von e-m Vertrag; ~ **from membership** Austritt als Mitglied; ~ **of members** Ausscheiden von Mitgliedern; **notice of** ~ Austrittserklärung; Rücktrittsanzeige; **voluntary** ~ freiwilliger Rücktritt; **to declare one's** ~ s-n Rücktritt erklären

withheld, tax ~ on dividends im Abzugswege erhobene Steuer auf Dividenden; **taxes ~ are considered as paid for and by the taxpayer** *Am*[42] einbehaltene Steuern gelten als für und vom Steuerpflichtigen bezahlt

withhold *v* zurückhalten, einbehalten; verhindern, versagen; **to ~ sth. from sb.** jdm etw. vorenthalten; **to ~ an amount from sb.'s pay** e-n Betrag von jds Lohn einbehalten; **to ~ one's assent** s-e Zustimmung versagen; **to ~ (the grant of) a patent** ein Patent versagen; **to ~ supplies of goods from a dealer** die Belieferung e-s Händlers mit Waren verweigern; **to ~ a tax** *Am* e-e Steuer einbehalten; **to ~ the truth** die Wahrheit verschweigen; **to ~ one's vote** sich der Stimmabgabe enthalten; **to add and to ~ nothing** nichts hinzufügen und nichts verschweigen; **anyone who makes payments of salaries, wages, compensations, remunerations or emoluments from U.S. sources to a non-resident alien, foreign partnership or foreign corporation must ~ tax at the rate of 30 per cent of the gross amount paid** *Am*[43] jeder, der aus amerikanischen Quellen an e-n in den USA nicht ansässigen Ausländer, e-e ausländische Personengesellschaft oder Körperschaft Gehälter, Löhne oder sonstige Vergütungen zahlt, hat davon e-n Steuerabzug von 30% des Bruttobetrages einzubehalten *(→withholding)*

withholding Zurückbehaltung, Einbehaltung *(Am bes. vom Einkommen für Steuern)*; Versagen; Vorenthaltung; ~ **exemption** *Am* Freistellung von der Abzugssteuer; Lohnsteuerfreibetrag; ~ **of a patent** Versagung e-s Patents; ~ **of tax** *Am* Steuereinbehaltung; ~ **of wages** Einbehaltung von Löhnen

withholding requirement *Am* Erfordernis des Steuerabzugs; **to be exempt from the ~** *Am* von der Abzugssteuer ausgenommen sein

withholding, ~ rules *Am* Abzugssteuervorschriften; ~ **statement** *Am* Bescheinigung über einbehaltene Lohnsteuer; ~ **supplies of goods** (from a dealer) Lieferverweigerung; ~ **system** *Am* System der Quellenbesteuerung

withholding tax *Am* Abzugssteuer, Quellensteuer; ~ **at source** Steuerabzug an der Quelle; ~ **on dividends** *Am* Abzugssteuer (od. Quellensteuer) auf Dividenden *(z.B. Kapitalertragssteuer)*; **~es on salaries and wages** Abzugssteuer (Steuerabzug) bei Gehältern und Löhnen *(entspricht der deutschen Lohnsteuer)*; ~ **table** *Am (etwa)* Lohnsteuertabelle; **to subject dividends to a ~** Dividenden e-r Quellensteuer unterwerfen

withholding, to impose (or **levy**) **taxes by (way of) ~** *Am* Steuern im Abzugswege erheben

within binnen, innerhalb; ~ **the meaning of the Act** im Sinne des Gesetzes; ~ **three days** binnen drei Tagen; ~ **a reasonable time** innerhalb e-r angemessenen Frist; ~ **a short time** binnen kurzem; **to live ~ one's income** in den Grenzen seines Einkommens leben

without ohne; ~ **(other) advice** *(auf Wechsel)* ohne Bericht *(opp. as per advice)*; ~ **debt** schuldenfrei; ~ **delay** unverzüglich; ~ **engagement** ohne Verpflichtung, freibleibend; ~ **extra charge** ohne Preisaufschlag; ~ **notice** ohne vorherige Benachrichtigung; fristlos; gutgläubig *(→notice 2.)*; ~ →**prejudice;** ~ **recourse** *(WechselR)* ohne Regreß(möglichkeit), ohne Gewähr *(ein mit dem Zusatz ~ recourse versehenes Indossament besagt, daß der Indossant nicht haftet)*; ~ **reserve** ohne Vorbehalt *(e-s Mindestpreises bei Auktionen) (der Verkäufer, der e-e Sache im Wege der Auktion veräußert hat, hat keinen Mindestpreis festgesetzt)*; ~ **sufficient cause** ohne ausreichenden Grund, unbegründet; **to dispose of a case** ~ **trial** →trial 1.

withstand *v* widerstehen; aushalten; **not ~ing the provisions of section 2** unbeschadet der Bestimmungen des Absatz 2

witness 1. *(in e-m Gerichts- od. anderem Verfahren)* Zeuge *(der [in der Regel] unter Eid mündlich aussagt: who gives testimony under oath)*[44]

witness, to adduce ~es Zeugen beibringen; **to appear as** ~ als Zeuge erscheinen; **to call a** ~ e-n Zeugen laden; e-n Zeugen aufrufen; **to call a p. as a** ~ jdn als Zeugen benennen; **to compel the attendance of a** ~ das Erscheinen e-s Zeugen erzwingen *(cf. subpoena)*; **to confront ~es** Zeugen gegenüberstellen; **to examine a** ~ e-n Zeugen *(eidlich)* vernehmen; **the ~es are not examined by the Court but by the parties** die Zeugen werden nicht vom Gericht, sondern von den Parteien vernommen; **to hear a** ~ e-n Zeugen vernehmen; **to object to a** ~ e-n Zeugen ablehnen; **to produce a** ~ e-n Zeugen stellen (od. beibringen); e-n Zeugen vorführen; **to summon a** ~ e-n Zeugen *(gerichtl.)* vorladen; **to swear in a** ~ e-n Zeugen vereidigen; **to take statements from ~es** Zeugenaussagen aufnehmen; **the** ~ **described the incidence** (or **occurrence, event**) der Zeuge schilderte den Vorfall; **the ~es differ** die Zeugen machen verschiedene Aussagen; die Zeugenaussagen widersprechen sich

witness, ~ **against a p.** Belastungszeuge; ~ **box** Zeugenbank; ~ **expenses** (or **fees**) Zeugengebühren; ~ **for the Crown** *Br* s. Crown →~; ~ **for the defence (~se)** Zeuge der Verteidigung, Entlastungszeuge; *(Zivilprozeß)* vom Beklagten benannter Zeuge; *(Strafprozeß)* vom Angeklagten benannter Zeuge; ~ **for the prosecution** Zeuge der Anklage, Belastungszeuge; Kronzeuge; ~ **stand** *Am* Zeugenstand; ~ **summons** *Br* Zeugenladung; ~ **to a marriage** →witness 2.; ~ **to a will** →witness 2.

witness, adverse ~ Zeuge der Gegenseite; feindlicher Zeuge; **appearance of ~es** Erscheinen von Zeugen *(ein Zeuge kann freiwillig erscheinen od. wird unter Strafandrohung geladen; cf. subpoena)*; **attendance of ~es** Erscheinen von Zeugen; Zeugenanwesenheit; **bribing of ~es** Zeugenbestechung; **coercion of ~es** Zeugennötigung; **commission to examine ~es** *Am* Rechtshilfeersuchen zur Vernehmung von Zeugen; **competence of a** ~ Fähigkeit, Zeuge zu sein; **competent** ~ *(rechtl.)* zulässiger Zeuge; **contumacious** ~ *(trotz Ladung)* nicht erschienener Zeuge; **corruption of ~es** Zeugenbestechung; **credible** ~ glaubwürdiger Zeuge; **crown** ~ *Br* Kronzeuge *(der gegen Zusicherung der Straffreiheit gegen seine Mitschuldigen aussagt; cf. to turn Queen's evidence, →evidence)*; **evidence by ~es** Zeugenbeweis; **examination of a** ~Zeugenvernehmung; **expert** ~ sachverständiger Zeuge *(→expert)*; **eye(-)** ~ Augenzeuge; **friendly** ~ eigener Zeuge; **hearing of a** ~ Zeugenvernehmung; **hostile** ~[45] *(eigener)* Zeuge, der sich *(unerwartet)* als feindlich erweist; **interested** ~ parteiischer Zeuge; **non-compellable** ~ zur Verweigerung der Aussage berechtigter Zeuge; **principal** ~ Hauptzeuge; **privilege of a** ~ **to decline to answer questions** Zeugnisverweigerungsrecht; **privileged** ~ Zeuge, der berechtigt ist, die Aussage zu verweigern; **production of a** ~ Beibringung e-s Zeugen; Vorführung e-s Zeugen; **proof of a** ~ *Br* →proof 1.; **prosecution** ~ →~ for the prosecution; **skilled** ~ sachverständiger Zeuge; **statement (made) by (a)** ~ Zeugenaussage; **swearing of a** ~ Zeugenvereidigung; **unsworn** ~ nicht beeidigter Zeuge

witness 2. Zeuge *(der Errichtung e-r Urkunde)*; ~ **to a marriage** Trauzeuge; ~ **to (a) will** Testamentszeuge *(der das Testament mit s-m Namen unterschreibt; cf. will)*; **attesting** (or **subscribing**) ~ Zeuge bei Errichtung e-r Urkunde *(der die Urkunde mit s-m Namen unterschreibt)*

witness 3. Zeugnis; **false** ~ falsches Zeugnis; **in** ~ **whereof I have hereunto set my hand** zum Zeugnis dessen habe ich diese Urkunde eigenhändig unterschrieben; **to bear** ~ **to** (or **of**) *(etw.)* bezeugen

witness *v* Zeuge sein von; *(Errichtung e-r Urkunde)* als Zeuge unterschreiben *(→witness 2.)*; **to** ~ **to sth.** *(vor Gericht)* als Zeuge aussagen über etw.; etw. bezeugen; **to** ~ **an accident** Zeuge e-s Unfalles sein; **to** ~ **a signature** durch Unterzeichnung der Urkunde bestätigen, daß man Zeuge der Unterzeichnung der Urkunde war; e-e Unterschrift bestätigen; **(now this deed) ~eth** nun bezeugt dieser Vertrag *(Einführungsformel in dem →operative part of a deed)*

wittingly or through negligence vorsätzlich oder fahrlässig

witword Herausgabeanspruch aufgrund eidlicher Bekräftigung

woman, ~ **engaged in business** Geschäftsfrau; ~ **executive** weibliche Führungskraft; Unternehmensleiterin; **career** ~ berufstätige Frau; **professional** ~ berufstätige Frau, im freien (od. akademischen) Beruf stehende Frau; **single** ~ alleinstehende Frau; ledige (od. getrennt lebende) Frau

women, W~'s Lib(eration) movement Freiheits-, Emanzipationsbewegung der Frauen *(seit dem 2. Weltkrieg)*; **~'s refuge** Frauenhaus; **~'s suffrage** Frauenwahlrecht; **~'s supplement** Frauenbeilage

wood Wald; Holz; ~ **coal** Braunkohle; ~ **industry** Holzindustrie; **~land** Waldgebiet, Forsten; **~lands managed on a commercial basis** *Br (SteuerR)* gewerblich genutzter Forstbesitz; ~ **manufacture** (or **processing** or **working**) Holzverarbeitung; **fuel** ~ Brennholz

woolsack *Br* Wollsack *(Sitzkissen des Lordkanzlers in s-r Eigenschaft als Speaker des →House of Lords)*; **to reach the** ~ Lordkanzler werden; **the Lord Chancellor takes his seat on the** ~ der Lordkanzler eröffnet die Oberhaussitzung

word Wort; **~s** *(im Beleidigungsprozeß)* Äußerung; ~ **of art** Fachausdruck; ~ **of hono(u)r** Ehrenwort; **~s of limitation** →limitation 1.; **~s of welcome** Begrüßungsworte; ~ **processing** *(EDV)* Textverarbeitung; ~ **processor** *(EDV)* Textverarbeiter

word, action for ~s *Am* Beleidigungsklage *(action of slander)*; **concluding** ~ Schlußwort; **identification ~s** *tel* Buchstabierwörter; **key** ~ Stichwort; **in other ~s** mit anderen Worten; **sum in ~s** Betrag in Worten

word *v (etw.)* in Worte fassen, formulieren; abfassen; **a speech ~ed as follows** e-e Rede folgenden Wortlauts

wording Wortlaut, Formulierung; ~ **of the bill** Wechseltext, Wortlaut des Wechsels; **according to the** ~ **of the contract** nach dem Wortlaut des Vertrages; ~ **of the law** Gesetzestext; ~ **of the oath** Eidesformel

work 1. *(körperl. od. geistige)* Arbeit

work, to be in arrears (or **behind**) **with one's** ~ mit s-r Arbeit im Rückstand sein; **to cease** ~ Arbeit einstellen (od. niederlegen); **to contract for** ~ Arbeit *(im Werkvertrag)* übernehmen (od. vergeben); **to do** ~ Arbeit leisten; **to find** ~ **for sb.** jdm Arbeit vermitteln; **to get to** ~ den Arbeitsplatz erreichen; **to look for** ~ Arbeit suchen; **to perform** ~ Arbeit verrichten; **to resume** ~ Arbeit wieder aufnehmen; **to start** (or **take up**) ~ Arbeit aufnehmen

work, ~ **according to the book** *Am* →~ to rule; **~aholic** Arbeitsbesessener; arbeitsbesessen

work by contract, to give out ~ Arbeit ausschreiben, Arbeitsauftrag *(im Submissionswege)* vergeben *(→contract 2.)*

work, ~ **creation** Arbeitsbeschaffung; ~ **ethic** Arbeitsmoral; ~ **farm** *Am (Strafvollzug)* landwirtschaftliche Arbeitsstätte; **~force** Belegschaft; Personalbestand *(e-s Unternehmens)*; ~ **in hand** Auftragsbestand; laufende Arbeiten; ~ **in process** (WIP) in Gang befindliche Arbeit; unfertige Erzeugnisse; ~ **in process inventory** *Am* Bestand an unfertigen Erzeugnissen; ~ **in progress** →~ in process; ~ **load** Arbeitspensum, Arbeitslast; **~man** Arbeiter

workmanship (Art der) Arbeitsausführung; Arbeit; **defect in** ~ Bearbeitungsmangel, Arbeitsfehler; **poor** ~ schlechte Arbeit

workmen's compensation *Am* Unfallentschädigung *(für Betriebsunfälle und Berufskrankheiten; accidents or injuries arising out of employment and occupational diseases)*; **W~ C~ Act** (WCA) *Am* Gesetz betr. Unfallversicherung der Arbeiter; Betriebsunfallgesetz; ~ **insurance** *Am* Unfallversicherung der Arbeiter, Betriebsunfallversicherung

work, ~ **on contract** vertraglich übernommene (od. vergebene) Arbeit; **~people** Arbeiter, Arbeitnehmerschaft; **~place** Arbeitsplatz, Arbeitsstätte *(Laden, Fabrik etc)*; ~ **at piece rates** nach Akkord bezahlte Arbeit; ~ **at time rates** nach Zeit bezahlte Arbeit; **~-sharing** Arbeitsumverteilung; (bessere) Aufteilung der *(vorhandenen)* Arbeit *(um Entlassungen zu vermeiden)*; **~shop** Werkstatt, Werkstätte; Arbeitstagung; Kurs; Seminar; ~ **study** Arbeitsstudie (REFA); ~ **to rule** *Br* Dienst nach Vorschrift; Bummelstreik

work, at ~ bei der Arbeit; **accident at** ~ Betriebsunfall; **to be at** ~ **on** beschäftigt sein mit; arbeiten an

work, brain ~ geistige Arbeit; **casual** ~ Gelegenheitsarbeit; **cessation of** ~ Niederlegung (od. Einstellung) der Arbeit; **clerical** ~ *(untergeordnete)* Büroarbeit; **contract** ~ *(im Werkvertrag)* übergebene (od. übernommene) Arbeit; **contract for** ~ **and labo(u)r** Werkvertrag; **contract for** ~ **and materials** Werklieferungsvertrag; **desk** ~ Büroarbeit; **domestic** ~ Haus(halts)arbeit; **fit for** ~ arbeitsfähig; **flow of** ~ Arbeits(ab)lauf; **home** ~ Heimarbeit; **illicit** ~ Schwarzarbeit; **job-~** s. piece—→~; **office** ~ Büroarbeit; **out of** ~ arbeitslos; **part-time** ~ Teilzeitarbeit; **piece-~** Akkordarbeit, Arbeit im Stücklohn; **remuneration for** ~ Arbeitsentgelt; **resumption of** ~ Wiederaufnahme der Arbeit; **scheme of** ~ Arbeitsplan; **short-time** ~ Kurzarbeit; **skilled** ~ Facharbeit; **suspension of** ~ Arbeitseinstellung; **temporary** ~ Zeitarbeit, Leiharbeit; Gelegenheitsarbeit; **time** ~ nach der Zeit bezahlte Arbeit *(opp. piece-~)*; Zeitarbeit, Leiharbeit; **unfit for** ~ arbeitsunfähig; **volume of** ~ Arbeitsanfall; **vacation** ~ Ferienarbeit

work 2. *(UrhR)* Werk; ~ **for hire** *Am* Arbeitnehmerwerk, Auftragswerk; ~ **made on commission** *Am* Auftragswerk; **~s of applied art** Werke der angewandten Kunst; **~s of art** Kunstgegenstände; **~s of drawing** Werke der zeichnenden Kunst; ~ **of reference** Nachschlagewerk; **artistic ~s** Werke der bildenden Kunst; **collected ~s** gesammelte Werke; **collective** (or **contributed**) ~ Sammelwerk *(z.B. Zeitschrift, Anthologie, Enzyklopädie)*;

copies of the ~ Werkstücke; **derivative** ~ Bearbeitung; **literary** ~ literarisches Werk; **musical** ~ Werk der Tonkunst; **published** ~ erschienenes Werk; **scientific** ~ wissenschaftliches Werk

works 1. *(oft im Singular)* Fabrik(anlage), Werk, Betrieb; ~ **agreement** Betriebsvereinbarung; ~ **committee** →~council; ~ **council** Betriebsrat *(nicht gesetzlich institutionalisierte Funktionen des deutschen Betriebsrats werden weitgehend von den →shop stewards wahrgenommen)*; ~ **invention** Betriebserfindung; ~ **manager** Betriebsleiter, Werksdirektor; ~ **representative** Betriebsobmann; **ex** ~ ab Werk *(cf. Incoterms 1980)*; **iron** ~ Eisenhütte, Eisenwerk; **the owner of a glass** ~ der Eigentümer e-r Glashütte

works 2. Anlagen, Bauten; bauliche Arbeiten; ~ **of construction** Bauarbeiten; ~ **of demolition** Abbrucharbeiten; **capital** ~ Großbauten, öffentl. Bauten; **clerk of the** ~ Bauaufseher; **public** ~ öffentliche Bauarbeiten; **public** ~ **contracts** öffentliche Bauaufträge *(bei Ausschreibungen)*

work *v* arbeiten; *(von e-r Maschine, Methode etc)* funktionieren; bewirken, wirksam sein, sich auswirken; bearbeiten; *(Land)* bebauen; fördern, gewinnen; *(Aufgabe)* erledigen; **to** ~ **by the job** (or **piece**) im Akkord arbeiten; **to** ~ **a change** e-e Veränderung bewirken (od. hervorrufen); **to** ~ **a district** e-n Bezirk geschäftlich bearbeiten (od. bereisen); **to** ~ **a farm** e-n Hof bewirtschaften; **to** ~ **a mine** e-e Grube abbauen; Bergbau betreiben; **to** ~ **minerals** Mineralien abbauen; **to** ~ **overtime** Überstunden machen; **to** ~ **a patent** ein Patent verwerten; **to** ~ **to rule** *Br* nach Vorschrift arbeiten, in Bummelstreik gehen; **to** ~ **short hours** Kurzarbeit leisten

work *v*, **to** ~ **at** arbeiten an; **to** ~ **in(to)** einarbeiten; **to** ~ **off a debt** e-e Schuld abarbeiten; **to** ~ **out the interest** die Zinsen berechnen; **to** ~ **out a plan** e-n Plan ausarbeiten; **to** ~ **up** *colloq.* aufarbeiten; **to** ~ **up a business** ein Geschäft auf e-n besseren Stand bringen

worked, time (or **hours**) ~ geleistete Arbeitsstunden; **capable of being** ~ *(Bergwerk)* abbaufähig

working Arbeiten; arbeitend; Arbeit(s-); Betriebs-; Funktionieren; funktionierend; (Aus-) Wirkung; Bearbeitung, Verarbeitung; Ausbeutung, Abbau; Grube(nanlage); ~ **of an agreement** Funktionieren e-r Vereinbarung; ~ **arrangement** sich bewährende Abmachung; ~ **by the book** (or **by the rule**) *Am* Arbeit nach Vorschrift; Bummelstreik; ~ **capacity** Arbeitskraft, Arbeitsfähigkeit; ~ **capital** Betriebskapital, Nettoumlaufvermögen *(Differenz zwischen Umlaufvermögen und kurzfristigen Verbindlichkeiten)*; ~ **card** *Am* Mitgliedsausweis e-r Gewerkschaft; ~ **classes** Arbeiterklasse; ~ **climate** Betriebsklima; ~ **community** Arbeitsgemeinschaft; ~ **conditions** Arbeitsbedingungen; ~ **day** Arbeitstag; ~ **expenses** Betriebskosten; ~ **funds** Betriebsmittel; ~ **group** Arbeitsgruppe, Arbeitskreis

working hours Arbeitsstunden, Arbeitszeit; **collectively agreed** ~ tarifliche Arbeitszeit; **flexible** ~ gleitende Arbeitszeit *(→flex[i]time)*; **reduction in** (or **shortening of**) ~ Verkürzung der Arbeitszeit

working, ~ **language** *(offizielle)* Arbeitssprache *(z.B. bei der EG)*; ~ **life** Berufsleben; Nutzungsdauer *(e-r Maschine)*; ~ **majority** arbeitsfähige (od. ausreichende) Mehrheit; ~ **men's club** *Br*[46] Arbeiterverein *(für Geselligkeiten, gegenseitige Hilfe etc)*; ~ **(of) a patent** Verwertung e-s Patents

working order, to be in ~ in betriebsfähigem Zustand sein; (gut) funktionieren

working, ~ **papers** Arbeitspapiere; ~ **partner** aktiver Gesellschafter; ~ **party** Arbeitsgruppe; ~ **population** erwerbstätige Bevölkerung, Erwerbsbevölkerung; ~ **practise** Arbeitsweise, Arbeitsmethode; *(Bergwerk)* Abbauverfahren; ~ **program** *(EDV)* Arbeitsprogramm; ~ **regulations** Betriebsvorschriften; Betriebsordnung; ~ **short hours** *Am* Kurzarbeit; ~ **time** →~ hours; ~ **to rule** *Br* Bummelstreik; ~ **wife** erwerbstätige Ehefrau; **to be engaged in** ~ **mines** Bergbau betreiben

workable praktisch durchführbar; brauchbar; *(Bergbau)* abbaubar; ~ **competition** *Am* funktionsfähiger Wettbewerb; wirksame Konkurrenz

worker Arbeiter(in); Arbeitnehmer(in); **W~s' Compensation Laws** *Am (einzelstaatl.)* Gesetze für Entschädigung bei Arbeitsunfall und Arbeitsunfähigkeit; **~s' dwellings** Arbeiterwohnungen; **W~s' Education Association** (WEA) *Br (etwa)* Volkshochschule; **W~s' Educational Trade Union Committee** (WETUC) *Br* Gewerkschaftsausschuß für Arbeiterbildung; **~s' housing estate** Arbeitersiedlung; **~s' participation** Arbeitnehmermitbestimmung; **~s' participation in the management of the enterprise** Arbeitnehmerbeteiligung an der Unternehmensführung; Mitbestimmung der Arbeitnehmer im Unternehmen; **~s' quarters** Arbeitersiedlung; **~s' representative(s)** Arbeitnehmervertreter; **agricultural** ~ Landarbeiter; **auxiliary** ~ Hilfsarbeiter; **blue-collar** ~ *Am* Arbeiter; **building** ~ Bauarbeiter; **casual** ~ Gelegenheitsarbeiter; **domestic** ~ inländischer Arbeiter; **factory** ~ Fabrikarbeiter(in); **fellow** ~ Arbeitskamerad(in); **foreign** ~ ausländischer Arbeitnehmer; Fremdarbeiter; Gastarbeiter; **frontier** ~ Grenzarbeitnehmer; **guest** ~ Gastarbeiter(in); **heavy** ~ Schwerarbeiter; **home** ~ Heimarbeiter(in); **industrial** ~ Industriearbeiter; **job** ~ Akkordarbeiter; **piece** ~ Akkordarbeiter; **salaried** ~ Angestellte(r); **seasonal** ~ Saisonarbeiter; **skilled** ~ gelernter Arbeiter, Facharbeiter; **unskilled** ~ ungelernter Arbeiter, Hilfsarbeiter; →**white-collar** ~

working →work *v*

workman →work 1.

world Welt; ~ **agreement** Weltabkommen; ~ **alliance** Weltbund; **W~ Association for Public Opinion Research** (WAPOR) Internationaler Verband für Meinungsforschung; **W~ Bank** Weltbank (→International Bank for Reconstruction and Development); **W~ Confederation of Labour** (WCL) Weltverband der Arbeitnehmer (WVA); **W~ Council of Churches** (WCC) Weltkirchenrat (Ökumenischer Rat der Kirchen) *(dem die meisten christlichen Kirchen, nicht aber die röm.-kath. Kirche angehören) (Sitz: Genf)*; ~ **consumption** Weltverbrauch; ~ **demand** Weltbedarf; Weltnachfrage; ~ **depression** weltweiter Konjunkturtiefstand; ~ **domination** Weltherrschaft; ~ **economic crisis** Weltwirtschaftskrise; ~ **economic condition** Weltwirtschaftslage; ~ **(-wide) economy** Weltwirtschaft; ~ **fair** Weltausstellung

World Federation for the Protection of Animals (WFPA) Welttierschutzbund

World Federation of Scientific Workers (WFSW) Weltbund der Wissenschaftler

World Federation of Trade Unions (WFTU) *(kommunistischer)* Weltgewerkschaftsbund (WGB) *(cf. International Confederation of Free Trade Unions) (Sitz:* Prag*)*

World Food, ~ Council Welternährungsrat *(→Food Aid Convention)*; ~ **Program(me)** (WFP) Welternährungsprogramm (WEP) *(Sonderaktion der FAO der Vereinten Nationen)*

World Health Organization (WHO) Weltgesundheitsorganisation[47]

Sonderorganisation der Vereinten Nationen. Gegr. 1948. *Sitz:* Genf.

Ziel: Bester erreichbarer Gesundheitszustand aller Völker (highest possible levels of health); Seuchenbekämpfung, vorbeugender Gesundheitsschutz.

Organe: Gesundheitsversammlung ([World] Health Assembly); Sekretariat (Secretariat with the Director-General)

World Intellectual Property Organization (WIPO) Weltorganisation für Geistiges Eigentum; **Convention Establishing the** ~[48] Übereinkommen zur Errichtung der Weltorganisation für geistiges Eigentum.

Gegr. 1967. *Sitz:* Genf.

Zweck: a) Weltweite Förderung des Schutzes des geistigen Eigentums durch Zusammenarbeit der Staaten, gegebenenfalls im Zusammenwirken mit einer anderen internationalen Organisation;

b) Gewährleistung der verwaltungsmäßigen Arbeit zwischen den Verbänden (Unions).

Organe: Generalversammlung (General Assembly) (bestehend aus den Vertragsstaaten des Übereinkommens, die Mitglied mindestens eines Verbandes sind); Konferenz (Conference) (bestehend aus den Vertragsstaaten des Übereinkommens); Koordinierungsausschuß (Coordination Committee); Internationales Büro (International Bureau with the Director-General)

world, W~ Jewish Congress (WJC) Jüdischer Weltkongreß *(Sitz:* New York); ~ **language** Weltsprache; **the** ~ **at large** die gesamte Welt; **W~ League** Weltbund; ~ **market requirements** Bedürfnisse des Weltmarktes; **W~ Medical Association** (WMA) Weltärztebund *(Sitz:* New York)

World Meteorological Congress[49] Meteorologischer Weltkongreß

World Meteorological Organization[50] (W. M. O.) Weltorganisation für Meteorologie

Sonderorganisation der Vereinten Nationen. *Sitz:* Genf.

Aufgabe: Internationale Zusammenarbeit auf dem Gebiet der Wetterforschung

world, ~ **opinion** Weltmeinung; ~ **output** Weltproduktion; ~ **politics** Weltpolitik; ~ **power** Weltmacht; ~**-renowned firm** weltbekannte Firma; **on a** ~ **scale** weltweit; ~ **seaborne trade** Weltseehandel; ~ **trade** Welthandel; **W~ Tourism Organization** (WTO)[51] Weltorganisation für Tourismus; **W~ Veterinary Association** (WVA) Welttierärztegesellschaft; **W~ War** Weltkrieg; ~**-wide** weltweit, weltumfassend; ~**-wide reputation** Weltruf; **W~ Wildlife Fund** (WWF) Weltverband zum Schutz wildlebender Tiere

world, banking ~Bankwelt, Bankleute; **business** (or **commercial**) ~ Geschäftswelt; **financial** ~ Finanzwelt; **throughout the** ~ weltweit

worn verbraucht, abgenutzt; ~ **coin** abgegriffene Münze

worse, business is getting ~ die Geschäftslage verschlechtert sich

worsen *v* (sich) verschlechtern; ~**ing of political relations** Verschlechterung der politischen Beziehungen

worship, religious (or **public**) ~ Gottesdienst; **Your W~** *Br (etwa)* Hochwürden *(Anrede e-s magistrate)*

worth wert; Wert; ~ **mentioning** erwähnenswert; ~ **the money** preiswert; →**net** ~; **to be** ~ wert sein; kosten; *colloq.* Einkommen haben von

worthy, ~ **of credit** kreditwürdig; glaubwürdig *(Zeuge)*; **air**~ lufttüchtig; **sea**~ seetüchtig

wound up, the company is being ~ die Gesellschaft befindet sich in Liquidation *(→winding up)*

wounded, ~ (person) Verwundeter; Verletzter; **collection** (or **removal**), **exchange, transportation of the ~** Bergung, Austausch, Abtransport der Verwundeten

wrap *v,* **to ~ (up)** einwickeln, einpacken; **to ~ up a deal** *colloq.* ein Geschäft abschließen

wrapping Verpackung; **~ material** Verpackungsmaterial; **~ paper** Packpapier

wrapper Packer; *(Buch)*Schutzumschlag; Streifband; Kreuzband; **to post in ~s** unter Streifband senden

wreck Schiffbruch; Zerstörung, Ruin; (Schiffs-, Flugzeug-, Auto-)Wrack; Wrackteil, Schiffstrümmer; Strandgut *(Br*[52] *umfaßt jetsam, flotsam, lagan und derelict)*; **W~ Commissioners** *Br*[53] Personen, die Schiffsunfälle untersuchen; **~-master** Strandvogt; **cutting away ~** Kappen von Wrackteilen; **receiver of ~** *Br* Strandvogt *(→receiver 1.)*; **to suffer ~** Schiffbruch erleiden

wreck *v* zerstören; abreißen, abbrechen; abwracken; *fig* zugrunde richten; *(Zug)* entgleisen lassen; *Am* mit verschrotteten Fahrzeugen handeln; **to ~ sb.'s plans** jds Pläne zum Scheitern bringen

wrecked zerstört, vernichtet; gescheitert; gestrandet; schiffbrüchig; **~ cargo** (or **freight**) durch Schiffbruch verlorengegangene (od. beschädigte) Fracht; Wrackgut; **~ ship** schiffbrüchiges Schiff *(umfaßt auch gesunkenes Schiff)*; **to be ~** Schiffbruch erleiden; scheitern; **the train was ~** der Zug wurde zum Entgleisen gebracht

wrecking, ~ firm *Am* Abbruchunternehmen; **~ of a train** Verursachung der Entgleisung e-s Zuges (Eisenbahnattentat)

wreckage Wrackteil(e); Wrackgut, Strandgut; Trümmer *(z. B. e-s abgerissenen Hauses)*

wrecker Bergungsdampfer; *Am* (Haus-)Abbruchsunternehmer; *Am* Abschleppwagen *(für beschädigte Kraftfahrzeuge)*

writ[54] *(mit dem Siegel e-s Gerichts, Br oder der Krone, versehene, an e-e Gerichtsperson [z. B. sheriff, marshal] od. Br e-e Privatperson gerichtete, ein Tun od. Unterlassen vorschreibende)* gerichtl. Anweisung, gerichtl. Befehl, gerichtl. Verfügung; *Br* Prozeßladung mit Klageschrift *(→~ of summons)*; Vollstreckungsbefehl *(→~ of execution)*; *Scot* Schriftstück, Urkunde *(deed, bond, contract etc)*; *Br parl* Wahlausschreibung; **~ne exeat regno** *Br* gerichtliche Anordnung, die dem Beklagten *(zur Sicherung e-s Prozesses)* das Verlassen Englands verbietet *(bei Klagen in →equity)*; **~ of assistance** *Am* Räumungsbefehl; *(an den sheriff gerichtete)* gerichtl. Verfügung, Zwangsräumung zu betreiben und den Kläger in den Grundbesitz einzuweisen; **~ of attachment** *(Strafprozeß)* Haftbefehl *(bes. wegen contempt of court)*; *(Zivilprozeß)* Arrestbefehl; Pfändungs-, Beschlagnahmebeschluß; **~ of capias** *Am (Zivilprozeß)* Haftbefehl gegen den Beklagten zur Durchsetzung e-r gerichtl. Ladung, Verfügung od. e-s Urteils *(nur in bestimmten Fällen anwendbar)*

writ of certiorari *Am*[55] Verfügung, mit der die Revision zugelassen wird *(bezieht sich vorwiegend auf den US Supreme Court)*; **petition for a ~** *Am* Antrag auf Zulassung der Revision *(meist in Bezug auf den US Supreme Court)*

writ, ~ of debt *Am* Zahlungsbefehl; gerichtl. Anweisung zur Zahlung e-s nach Behauptung des Gläubigers geschuldeten, bestimmten oder berechenbaren Geldbetrages; **~ of delivery** *Br* richterlicher Vollstreckungsbefehl *(auf Herausgabe e-r Sache)*; **~ of ejectment** *Am* richterl. Anweisung zur Durchführung e-r Räumung od. Entsetzung e-s nicht berechtigten Besitzers von Liegenschaften; **~ of error coram nobis** (or **vobis**) *Am* richterl. Anweisung zur Übersendung der Prozeßakten zur Überprüfung von Tatsachenfragen

writ of execution Vollstreckungsanweisung; *(an den sheriff vom Urteilsgläubiger gesandte)* richterl. Anweisung zur Vollstreckung e-s Urteils *(z. B. writ of fieri facias, writ of possession)*

writ, ~ of →fieri facias; ~ of →Habeas Corpus; ~ of →mandamus; ~ of mandate *Am* Anweisung e-s höheren an ein ihm untergeordnetes Gericht *(z. B. das Verfahren auszusetzen, ein Rechtsmittel zu gewähren)*; **~ of possession** gerichtl. Besitzeinweisung *(in Grundbesitz) (Vollstreckungsmittel bei Besitz- und Räumungsklagen)*; **~ of →privilege**; **~ of prohibition** *Am* →prohibition 2.; **~ of →restitution; ~ of review** *Am* richterl. Anweisung an e-e untere Instanz (auch Verwaltungsinstanz), die Entscheidung zur Überprüfung vorzulegen; **~ of →sequestration**

writ of summons[56] *(die den Prozeß einleitende)* Prozeßladung mit Klageschrift *(Beklagter wird aufgefordert, innerhalb der vorgeschriebenen Frist sich auf die Klage einzulassen, anderenfalls er mit e-m Versäumnisurteil zu rechnen hat)*

Br Ein writ of summons ergeht in allgemeiner Form oder specially →endorsed. Die Klagebegründung (statement of claim) kann entweder auf dem writ vermerkt oder gleichzeitig (oder innerhalb von 14 Tagen nach erfolgter Einlassung) zugestellt werden.
Am Einzelstaatlich verschieden geregelt

writ, ~ of →supersedeas; concurrent ~ weitere Ausfertigung e-s writ (of summons); **peremptory ~** *(besonders geartete, selten gebrauchte)* gerichtl. Verfügung (die in Ladung zum persönlichen Erscheinen besteht); **→prerogative ~; service of the ~** Zustellung des writ; **to serve a ~ (up)on a p.** jdm e-n writ *(Ladung etc)* zustellen; **to take out a ~ against a p.** jds Ladung erwirken; **a ~ issues** e-e richterl. Anweisung ergeht

write-down (Teil-)Abschreibung
write-off (vollständige) Abschreibung; Forderungsabschreibung; Abbuchung; als wertlos abzuschreibende Sache
write-up (Presse-)Bericht; schriftl. Anpreisung; Höherbewertung; Zuschreibung

write *v* schreiben; *(als Versicherer)* Versicherungsvertrag abschließen; **to ~ a cheque (check)** e-n Scheck ausstellen; **to ~ one's will** sein Testament aufsetzen
write *v*, **to ~ back an item** e-n Eintrag rückbuchen (od. stornieren); **to ~ back reserves** Rücklagen auflösen; **to ~ down** *(etw.)* niederschreiben (od. notieren); *com (nach und nach)* abschreiben; **to ~ in for sth.** *colloq.* etw. schriftl. bestellen, etw. kommen lassen; **to ~ off** *com (vollständig)* abschreiben; **to ~ off a bad debt** e-e zweifelhafte Schuld abbuchen; **to ~ (out)** *(Wechsel, Scheck etc)* ausschreiben; **to ~ up** *(etw.)* auf den neuesten Stand bringen; höher bewerten, zuschreiben; *(Ereignis)* genau beschreiben; *(schriftl.)* lobend erwähnen

writer Schreiber; Schriftsteller; *Br (Börse)* Verkäufer e-r Option; Versicherer; **~ (to the signet)** *Scot* Anwalt; **~s' union** Schriftstellerverband

writing Schreiben; schriftliche Abfassung; Schriftwerk; (Hand-)Schrift; Schriftform; Schriftstellern, Schriftstellerei; **~s** literarisches Werk; **~ company** *Am* Versicherungsgesellschaft; **~ down** (or **off**) Abschreibung; **~ limit** *(Rückvers.)* Zeichnungsgrenze; **~ pad** Schreibunterlage; Schreibblock; **~ paper** Schreibpapier; **illegible ~** unleserliche Schrift; **legal ~** juristischer Aufsatz
writing, in ~ schriftlich; **agreement in ~** schriftl. Vereinbarung; schriftl. Vertrag; **to confirm in ~** schriftlich bestätigen; **to inquire in ~** schriftl. anfragen; **to put sth. (down) in ~** etw. niederschreiben; etw. schriftlich aufsetzen; **~ is essential to the validity of certain contracts** Schriftform ist Wirksamkeitsvoraussetzung bestimmter Verträge

written geschrieben, schriftlich; **~ agreement** schriftliche Vereinbarung, schriftlicher Vertrag; **~ censure** schriftl. Verweis *(als Disziplinarmaßnahme)*; **~ communication** schriftl. Benachrichtigung; **~ confirmation** schriftl. Bestätigung *(opp. verbal confirmation)*; **~ evidence** Urkundenbeweis *(opp. oral evidence)*; **~ examination** schriftl. Examen; **~ law** geschriebenes (od. kodifiziertes) Recht; **~ notice** schriftl. Mitteilung (od. Kündigung); **~ statement** schriftl. Erklärung

wrong Unrecht; **~doer** Übeltäter, Missetäter; **private ~** zivilrechtl. Delikt; rechtswidrige Handlung gegen Einzelperson(en) *(breach of contract, tort etc)*; **public ~** strafbare Handlung gegen die Allgemeinheit *(crimes and other offences [-ses])*

wrong *v (jdn)* ungerecht behandeln; *(jdm)* Unrecht (od. Schaden) tun; **consumers who have been ~ed** geschädigte Verbraucher

wrong unrichtig, falsch; **~ address** falsche Anschrift; **~ conclusion** (or **inference**) Fehlschluß; **~ decision** Fehlentscheidung; **~ flag** falsche Flagge; **~ number** *tel* falsche Nummer; falsch verbunden; **~-way driver** Geisterfahrer
wrongly falsch, zu Unrecht; **~ accused** zu Unrecht angeklagt; **~ issued patent** zu Unrecht erteiltes Patent

wrongful unrechtmäßig, rechtswidrig; **~ death statutes** *Am* →death; **~ dismissal** ungerechtfertigte Entlassung; **~ trading** *Br*[57] Betreiben unrechtmäßiger Geschäfte *(vor Liquidation e-r company)*

X

xenodochy Gastfreundschaft; Aufnahme von Fremden
xenophobia Fremdenfeindlichkeit, Ausländerfeindlichkeit

xenophobic fremdenfeindlich, ausländerfeindlich

Xerox (copy) *Br* Xerokopie *(Fotokopie durch xerografische Geräte von Rank-Xerox Plc und Xerox Corporation)*

X-rating Einstufung als Film mit Jugendverbot

X-ray Röntgen-

Y

Yalta Conference Konferenz von Jalta (Krim-Konferenz) *(1945)*
Besprechung in Jalta zwischen Roosevelt (USA), Churchill (Großbritannien) und Stalin (UdSSR) über die gemeinsame Nachkriegspolitik

Yankee bonds *Am* Anleihen ausländischer Emittenten *(am US Kapitalmarkt)*

Yankee certificates of deposit *Am (von amerikanischen Zweigniederlassungen ausländischer Banken ausgestellte)* übertragbare Zertifikate (Quittungen) über Depositen

yard 1. (yd.)[1] Yard, Elle *(3 feet or 36 inches = 91,44 cm)*

yard 2. Hof; Werkplatz; Lagerplatz; **navy** ~ Marinewerft; **prison** ~ Gefängnishof; **railway** ~ Rangierbahnhof; **ship** ~ Schiffswerft

yard 3. *Br,* **the Y**~→Scotland Yard

yardage (Bezahlung für) (Werk-, Lager-) Platznutzung

year Jahr; **the ~s ahead** die kommenden Jahre; ~ **of assessment** *Br* Veranlagungsjahr, Steuerjahr *(cf. fiscal →~)*; **~book** Jahrbuch; **Y~ Books** (Y. B.) *Br* Jahrbücher *(amtl. Sammlung von Gerichtsentscheidungen aus den Jahren 1290 bis 1535)*; **~-end** Jahresende; **~-end closing** *Am* Jahresabschluß; **~-end dividend** *Am* am Ende des Geschäftsjahres zusätzlich zur regulären Dividende gezahlte Sonderdividende; **a ~'s guarantee** ein Jahr Garantie; **3 ~s hence** (heute) in 3 Jahren; ~ **of manufacture** Herstellungsjahr; Baujahr *(e-s Autos)*; **~s of office** Dienstjahre; ~ **under review** Berichtsjahr; **~s served** (or **~s of service**) Dienstjahre; **~'s support** *Am* Jahresunterhaltsanspruch *(der Ehefrau und der minderjährigen Kinder im 1. Jahr nach dem Tode des Erblassers)*; **~- to-~ growth ratio** jährliche Zuwachsrate; **all the ~ (round)** ganzjährig, das ganze Jahr über; **company's ~** *Br* Geschäftsjahr *(1. 1. bis 31. 12.)*; **financial** ~ *Br* Haushaltsjahr, Rechnungsjahr *(der öffentl. Haushalte) (1. 4. bis 31. 3.)*; **fiscal** ~ *Br*[2] Steuerjahr *(6. 4. bis 5. 4.)*; *Am* Haushaltsjahr, Rechnungsjahr *(der öffentl. Haushalte) (nicht unbedingt gleichlaufend mit dem Kalenderjahr; das US-Bundesrechnungsjahr läuft vom 1. Juli bis 30. Juni)*; **leap** ~ Schaltjahr; →**mid ~; present** ~ laufendes Jahr; **preceding** (or **previous**) ~ Vorjahr; **(open) throughout the** ~ ganzjährig (geöffnet)

yearly jährlich; ~ **accounts** Jahresabschluß; ~ **income** Jahreseinkommen; ~ **output** Jahresertrag; Jahresleistung; ~ **receipts** Jahreseinnahmen; ~ **requirements** Jahresbedarf; ~ **revenue** Jahreseinnahmen; ~ **subscription** Jahresbeitrag; ~ **tenancy** →tenancy from year to year; **half-~** halbjährlich; Halbjahres- *(→half)*

yellow, ~-dog *Am* gewerkschaftsfeindlich; **~-dog contract** *Am*[3] Anstellungsvertrag, in dem Arbeitnehmer sich verpflichten, keiner Gewerkschaft beizutreten oder e-e bereits bestehende Mitgliedschaft aufzugeben; ~ **flag** *(VölkerR)* Quarantäneflagge; ~ **jack** →~ flag; ~ **lines** *Br* gelbe Linien *(zur Kennzeichnung der Parkbeschränkung)*; **Y~ Pages** Fernsprech-Branchenbuch; ~ **press** *Am* Sensationspresse; Hetzpresse

Yemen Jemen; ~ **Arab Republic** Jemen, Jemenitische Arabische Republik

Yemenite Jemenit(in)

Yemeni jemenitisch

Yemen, People's Democratic Republic of ~ Demokratische Volksrepublik Jemen; **Democratic** ~ Demokratischer Jemen

Yemen, (of) Democratic ~ Jemenit(in); jemenitisch

yen Yen *(japanische Währungseinheit)*

yeoman *(Lehensrecht)* freier Bauer *(mit kleinem Grundbesitz) (→freeholder)*

yield Ertrag; Ausbeute; Ernte; Rendite; effektive Verzinsung; ~ **curve** Zinsertragskurve *(Spanne zwischen kurz- und langfristigen Zinssätzen)*; ~ **forecasting** Ertragsvorausberechnung; ~ **gap** Renditenlücke *(Unterschied zwischen dem Ertrag der Stammaktien und staatlichen Wertpapieren)*; ~ **of taxes** s. tax →~; ~ **on capital** (or **on invested funds**) Kapitalertrag; ~ **on shares** Aktienrendite; ~ **oriented** ertragsorientiert; ~ **table** →bond table *(→bond 2.)*; ~ **tax** *Am* Kapitalertragssteuer; **crop** ~ Ernteertrag; **fixed** ~ **investment** Anlage mit festem Ertrag; **high-~ share** Aktie mit hoher Rendite; **net** ~ Nettoertrag, Reinertrag; **peak** ~ Ertragsspitze; **reduction in** ~ Ertragsrückgang; **stock** ~ *Am* Aktienrendite; **tax** ~ Steueraufkommen; **total** ~ Gesamtrendite; **variable** ~ **investment** Anlage mit schwankendem Ertrag; **to obtain ~s** Rendite erzielen; **to produce a** ~ e-n Ertrag abwerfen

yield *v (Gewinn)* (ein)bringen, abwerfen; (Ernte- etc) Ertrag geben; gewähren, zugestehen; die Vorfahrt lassen; *Am (jdm)* das Wort überlassen; **to ~ to sb.** jdm nachgeben; **to ~ to sth.** sich in etw. fügen; **to ~ 4%** sich mit 4% verzinsen; e-e Rendite von 4% ergeben; **to ~ to conditions** auf Bedingungen eingehen; **to ~ high interest** hochverzinslich sein; *(Aktien)* hohe Rendite bringen; **to ~ interest** Zinsen bringen; sich verzinsen; **to ~ a return** e-n Ertrag abwerfen; etw. einbringen; sich rentieren; **to ~ a small return** wenig einbringen; **to ~ up possession** Besitz *(an Grundbesitz)* aufgeben; **~ (right of way)** *Am* Vorfahrt beachten!

yielding, ~ and paying Einleitungsklausel in Miet- od. Pachtverträgen mit Vorbehalt des zu zahlenden Miet- od. Pachtzinses; **~ a dividend of** mit e-r Dividende von; **~ high interest** hochverzinslich; **~ no interest** unverzinslich; **~ of a right** Aufgabe e-s Rechts; **profit ~** ertragreich

York-Antwerp rules (Y. A. R) *(SeeversR)* York-Antwerpener Regeln
Auf den Konferenzen der Internationalen Law Association in York (1864) und Antwerpen (1877) ausgearbeitete, später mehrfach revidierte[4] private, aber international anerkannte Regeln über die wichtigsten Fragen der Großen Haverie.
Sie gelten nur, wenn sie im Seefrachtvertrag vereinbart sind

young bond Euroanleihe mit Wertsicherungsklausel *(Sicherung des Anlegers gegen Kursverluste bei sinkenden Devisenkursen durch Bindung der Anleihewährung an e-e Bezugswährung)*

Young Christian Workers (YCW) Christliche Arbeiterjugend

Young Men's Christian Association (YMCA) Christlicher Verein Junger Männer (CVJM); **World Alliance of ~s** (WYMCA) Weltbund der YMCA (*Sitz:* Genf)

young people seeking employment Arbeit suchende Jugendliche

young person Jugendlicher *(Br[5] zwischen 14 und 17 Jahren)*

Young Plan Young-Plan *(zur Regelung der deutschen Reparationsverpflichtungen nach dem Ersten Weltkrieg)*

Young Women's Christian Association (YWCA) Christlicher Verband Junger Frauen; **World Alliance of ~s** (WYWCA) Weltbund der YWCA (*Sitz:* Genf)

youth Jugend; Jugendliche(r)

youth custody *Br[6]*, **(sentence of) ~** Jugendstrafe *(für Täter zwischen 15 und 21 Jahren)*; **Y~ C~ Centre** *Br* Jugendstrafanstalt

youth, ~ detention Jugendarrest; **~ exchange** Jugendaustausch; **~ hostel** Jugendherberge; **International Y~ Hostel Federation** (IYHF) Internationaler Jugendherbergsverband (*Sitz:* Kopenhagen); **~ meeting** Jugendtreffen; **~ movement** Jugendbewegung; **~ officer** Jugendpfleger; **~ services** Jugendarbeit; **Y ~ Training Scheme** (YTS) *Br* Projekt *(der Regierung)* zur Ausbildung von Jugendlichen; **~ unemployment** Jugendarbeitslosigkeit; **~ welfare** Jugendfürsorge; **~ welfare department** Jugendamt; **~ work** Jugendarbeit

youthful offender jugendlicher Täter

Yugoslav Jugoslaw|e, ~in; jugoslawisch

Yugoslavia Jugoslawien; **Socialist Federal Republic of ~** Sozialistische Föderative Republik Jugoslawien

yuppie (young urban professional) junger leistungsbewußter Aufsteiger

Z

Zaire Zaire; **Republic of ~** Republik Zaire

Zairian Zairer, ~in; zairisch

Zambia Sambia; **Republic of ~**[1] Republik Sambia

Zambian Sambier, ~in; sambisch

zebra crossing *(Verkehr)* Zebrastreifen

zero, ~ base budgeting (ZBB) *Am* Budgetierung auf Nullbasis *(alle Ausgaben müssen jährlich gerechtfertigt werden, bevor sie in den Haushaltsplan aufgenommen werden)*

zero bonds (or **~ coupon bonds**) Null-Coupon-Anleihen *(Zins und Zinseszins werden erst am Ende der Laufzeit gezahlt)*
Zerobonds auf dem US-Markt können je nach Depotbank Tiernamen tragen *(z. B. →CATs, →TIGR)*

zero, ~ growth Nullwachstum; **~ option** *pol* Nullösung; **~ rate** Nullsatz

zero-rated *Br[2]* *(UmsatzsteuerR)* mit dem Nullsatz besteuert; von der Mehrwertsteuer befreit
Im britischen Umsatzsteuerrecht wird eine Leistung als "zero-rated" bezeichnet, wenn sie zwar steuerpflichtig ist, aber mit 0% besteuert wird. Der Unterschied zu den →"exempt supplies" liegt darin, daß der mit dem Nullsatz besteuerte Leistungen erbringende Unternehmer zum Vorsteuerabzug (→deduction of input tax) berechtigt ist. *(Entspricht in etwa „Steuerbefreiung mit Vorsteuerabzugsberechtigung" – §§ 4 i. V. m. 15 Abs. 3 UStG)*

zero rating *Br* Nulltarifierung; **(VAT) ~** Mehrwertsteuersatz Null; Mehrwertsteuerbefreiung; Besteuerung zum Nullsatz

zero, →double ~ option

Zimbabwe Simbabwe; **Republic of ~** Republik Simbabwe

Zimbabwean Simbabwer, ~in; simbabwisch

zip, ~ area *Am* Postleitzone; **~ code** *Am* Postleitzahl

zloty Zloty *(polnische Münze)*

zonal Zonen-; **~ border** (or **boundary**) (with check point) *pol* Zonengrenze (mit Übergangsstelle)

zone 1. Zone; Landstrich; *fig* Bereich, Gebiet; *Am* (Gebühren-)Zone *(für Eisenbahn, Post etc)*; ~ **of influence** *pol* Einflußzone, Einflußbereich; ~ **of occupation** (or **occupation** ~) Besatzungszone; ~ **pricing** *Am* Preisbildung nach Zonen; ~ **rate** *Am (public utilities)* Zonentarif; **operational** ~ *(VölkerR)* Kriegsgebiet, Sperrgebiet; **postal** ~ Post(zustell)bezirk; **prohibited** ~ Sperrgebiet

zone 2. *Am (durch Verordnung auf bestimmte Bauvorhaben beschränktes)* Stadtgebiet (od. Kreisgebiet); ~ **change** *Am* Änderung e-s Gebietes von e-r Zone in e-e andere; **business** ~ Geschäftsbezirk; **residential** ~ Wohnbezirk; **unrestricted** ~ Gebiet mit den geringsten Baubeschränkungen *(bes. Fabrikgegend)*

zone *v* in Zonen einteilen; *Am (Bauplanung)* in Bezirke mit verschiedenen Verwendungszwecken einteilen *(→zone 2.)*

zoning Einteilung in Zonen; Flächenaufteilung *(bei Städteplanung)*; territoriale Marktaufteilung; ~ **administrator** *Am* Beamter, der mit der Durchführung der ~ ordinance(s) beauftragt ist; **(Planning and) Z~ Commission** *Am* Bürgerausschuß, der alle wesentlichen Planungs- und "zoning"-Entscheidungen trifft; ~ **laws** (or **ordinances**) *Am* Bauordnungen *(die bestimmte Beschränkungen auferlegen; cf. zone 2.)*; ~ **plan** *Am* Bebauungsplan; ~ **restrictions** Bebauungsbeschränkungen; ~ **variance** *Am (auf Antrag behördlich genehmigte)* Ausnahme von örtlichen Bebauungsvorschriften

Footnotes – Fußnoten

Zu A

[1] *Am* Lanham Act, Section 45
[2] *Br* obs.
[3] MPC s. 230. 3(2)
[4] MPC s. 230. 3(1)
[5] *Br* Land Registration Act 1925, s. 5
[6] *Br* Sixth Schedule, Law of Property Act 1925, s. 206 (2)
[7] *Br* Art. 28 BEA; *Am* UCC s. 3–415
[8] Parteien vereinbaren, daß Gläubiger anstelle der geschuldeten Leistung eine andere annimmt (accord), die erfüllt werden muß (satisfaction)
[9] UCC s. 9–102 (1) (b)
[10] *Br* zur Tätigkeit der accountants gehört auch die des Steuerberaters (keine gesonderte Berufsorganisation in England)
[11] Mitglied der Association of Certified Accountants
[12] Mitglied des Institute of Chartered Accountants
[13] Mitglied des American Institute of Certified Public Accountants (New York) (AICPA)
[14] *Am* IRC s. 446
[15] *Am* IRC ss. 531–537
[16] Beschluß des Rates der Europäischen Gemeinschaften vom 1. 1. 1973 zur Anpassung der Dokumente betreffend den Beitritt neuer Mitgliedstaaten (Amtsblatt der Europäischen Gemeinschaften Nr. L 2 vom 1. 1. 1973, S. 1)
[17] *Am* IRC s. 62
[18] Bankruptcy Code Chapter 13
[19] cf. Chapters XII, XIII of the Charter of the United Nations
[20] besondere wirtschaftsregelnde (Bundes-) Behörde, oft mit Funktionen zwischen Verwaltung und Gericht; sie ist dann independent, d. h. nur dem Parlament verantwortlich (→Independent Regulatory Agency)
[21] das Gesetz enthält einheitliche Vorschriften über den Erlaß von Rechtsverordnungen
[21a] Insolvency Act 1986, s. 29
[22] innerhalb der Queen's Bench Division
[23] *Br* Mental Health Act 1959, s. 25
[24] *Br* Children Act 1975, Adoption Act I 1976, Adoption (Scotland) Act 1978; *Am* Uniform Adoption Act 1953 (ist nur von einigen Einzelstaaten angenommen)
[25] Inland Revenue stamp auf bestimmten Urkunden gemäß dem Wert des Rechtsgeschäfts (amount depending on value of transaction evidenced by document)
[26] *Br* Limitation Act 1939, ss. 10, 16
[27] bes. im Zivilprozeß. Entsprechende Begriffe im Strafprozeß: →information und → deposition
[28] Offenbarungseid in der BRD abgeschafft und ersetzt durch eidesstattliche Versicherung
[29] lockerer als subsidiary
[30] *Br* the Oaths Act 1888 and the Oaths Act 1961 lassen eine affirmation anstelle des Eides zu
[31] American Federation of Labor and Congress of Industrial Organizations
[32] BGBl 1981 II S. 254
[32a] BGBl 1973 II S. 1794
[33] der Family Law Reform Act 1969 setzte die Volljährigkeit von 21 auf 18 Jahre herab (für England und Wales, nicht für Schottland oder Nordirland)
[34] vgl. Art. 4 des Wiener Übereinkommens über diplomatische Beziehungen – BGBl 1964 II S. 957
[35] Convention for the Suppression of Unlawful Seizure of Aircraft Übereinkommen zur Bekämpfung der widerrechtlichen Inbesitznahme von Luftfahrzeugen – BGBl 1972 II S. 1506
[36] BGBl 1982 II S. 374; 1988 S. 422
[37] Multilateral Agreement on Commercial Rights of Non-Scheduled Air Services in Europe Mehrseitiges Abkommen über gewerbliche Rechte im nichtplanmäßigen Luftverkehr in Europa – BGBl 1959 II S. 822
[38] Multilateral Agreement relating to Certificates of Airworthiness for Imported Aircraft Mehrseitiges Übereinkommen über Lufttüchtigkeitszeugnisse eingeführter Luftfahrzeuge – BGBl 1962 II S. 24
[39] *Br* British Nationality Act 1948, s. 32; *Am* Immigration and Nationality Act 1952, s. 101 (3)
[40] Aliens' Employment Act 1955
[41] *Br* Bills of Exchange Act, s. 64
[42] *Br* Companies Act 1985, ss. 425–427
[43] Internal Revenue Code s. 179
[44] *Br* durch den Rights of Light Act von 1959 auf 27 Jahre erweitert
[45] Companies Act 1985, ss. 363–365 und Schedule 15
[46] BGBl 1978 II S. 1518
[47] BGBl 1982 II S. 421
[48] BGBl 1987 II S. 92
[49] MPC s. 224.2
[50] *Am* IRC s. 1491 ff
[51] neuer Begriff des Berufsbildungsgesetzes
[52] *Am* Uniform Sales Act, s. 19, Rule 4

[53] Administration of Estates Act 1925, s. 41
[54] BGBl 1961 II S. 122; 1962 II S. 102
[55] Art. 1 Abs. 2 (a) – BGBl 1964 II S. 426; 1965 II S. 271
[56] International Chamber of Commerce
[57] vgl. Vergleichs- und Schiedsgerichtsordnung der Intern. Handelskammer (Rules of Conciliation and Arbitration)
[58] Internationale Handelskammer
[59] →European Convention on International Commercial Arbitration
[60] BGBl 1987 II S. 624
[61] geschützt durch Art. 4 der Pariser Fassung der Berner Übereinkunft (Berne →Convention)
[62] BGBl 1957 II S. 782
[63] nach Art. III Abs. 2 des Deutsch-Amerikanischen Doppelbesteuerungsabkommens (United States-German Tax Convention) dürfen der einzelnen Betriebsstätte steuerrechtlich nur die Gewinne zugerechnet werden, welche die Betriebsstätte als selbständiges Unternehmen erzielt hätte (dealing at arm's length with the enterprise of which it is a permanent establishment)
[64] International Convention relating to the arrest of seagoing vessels Internationales Übereinkommen zur Vereinheitlichung von Regeln über den Arrest in Seeschiffe – BGBl 1984 II S. 209
[65] *Am* MPC s. 220.1
[66] üblicher: objet d'art
[67] *Br* Companies Act 1985, ss. 7–9
[68] BGBl 1966 II S. 617, 1968 II S. 906
[69] *Br* nach dem Theft Act ist asportation als Vorbedingung für larceny ersetzt durch appropriation
[70] MPC s. 211.1
[71] MPC s. 211.1 (2)
[72] MPC s. 213.4
[73] Administration of Estates Act s. 36 (4)
[74] Judicature Act 1925, ss. 33 (3), 98
[75] Rechtshilfe in Strafsachen im Verhältnis zwischen Großbritannien und der Bundesrepublik – BGBl 1961 II S. 573. Rechtshilfe in Strafsachen (sowie Erteilung von Auskünften aus dem Strafregister) im Verhältnis zwischen den Vereinigten Staaten und der Bundesrepublik – BGBl 1961 II S. 472
[76] vgl. EWG-Vertrag Art. 131
[77] in älteren Urkunden vorkommendes Wort für das gebräuchlichere ,,conveyance" bzw. ,,to convey"
[78] diese Gesetze entsprechen etwa dem deutschen Versicherungsaufsichtsgesetz
[79] BGBl 1958 II S. 4
[80] Übereinkommen zwischen den Parteien des Nordatlantikvertrages über die Zusammenarbeit auf dem Gebiete der Atominformationen – BGBl 1971 II S. 545
[81] Attachment of Earnings Act 1971
[82] unter dem Comptroller and Auditor-General
[83] the amount of capital stated in *Br* the Memorandum of Association of a company (*Am* the charter of a corporation)
[84] entspricht dem deutschen ADAC
[85] der bekannteste Kursdurchschnitt ist der Dow-Jones Average

Zu B

[1] *Br* Bail Act 1976
[2] a magistrate in a Scottish →burgh
[3] RGBl 1930 II S. 289; BGBl 1953 II S. 117; 1956 II S. 331, 746
[4] eine Kombination des commercial banking and investment banking ist den amerik. Banken nicht erlaubt
[5] kodifiziert in Title 11 of the United States Code
[6] besteht seit 1922
[7] früher ,,cestui que trust"
[8] Friendly Societies Act 1896, s. 8 (3)
[9] Convention Concerning Protection Against Hazards of Poisoning Arising from Benzene – BGBl 1973 II S. 958
[10] World Intellectual Property Organization, Art. 2 VI – BGBl 1970 II S. 295
[11] *Am* MPC s. 230.1
[12] cf. International Convention for the Unification of Certain Rules of Law Relating to Bills of Lading
[13] Abkommen zur Vereinheitlichung des Wechselrechts (RGBl 1933 II S. 377, 974; BGBl 1960 II S. 2315): 1. Abkommen über das Einheitliche Wechselgesetz (Convention Providing a Uniform Law for Bills of Exchange and Promissory Notes) (RGBl 1933 II S. 378; BGBl 1953 II S. 116, 148, 592); 2. Abkommen über Bestimmungen auf dem Gebiete des internationalen Wechselprivatrechts (Convention for the Settlement of Certain Conflicts of Laws in Connection with Bills of Exchange and Promissory Notes) (RGBl 1933 II S. 444; BGBl 1953 II S. 116, 148, 592); 3. Abkommen über das Verhältnis der Stempelgesetze zum Wechselrecht (Convention on the Stamp Laws in Connection with Bills of Exchange and Promissory Notes) (RGBl 1933 II S. 468; 1936 II S. 322; 1938 II S. 856; 1939 II S. 752; BGBl 1953 II S. 148)
von den 3 Abkommen der Genfer Wechselrechtskonferenz hat Großbritannien nur das Stempelabkommen unterzeichnet
[14] der Bills of Exchange Act 1882, durch die Amending Acts of 1906, 1907 und 1932 sowie

den Cheques Act 1957 teilweise abgeändert od. ergänzt, gilt im ganzen Vereinigten Königreich (England, Irland und Schottland)
[15] Vereinbarung zwischen USA und BRD – BGBl 1976 II S. 1733
[16] BGBl 1988 II S. 469
[17] Criminal Justice Act 1948, s. 48 (1) (c), Criminal Justice Act 1961, s. 1
[18] Institute Cargo Clause
[19] Art. 39 der UN Charta
[20] Br action for breach of promise abolished by Law Reform (Miscellaneous Provisions) Act 1970
[21] einziger Scheidungsgrund nach dem Matrimonial Causes Act 1973, s. 1
[22] *Am* cf. MPC s. 240.1
[23] British Nationality Act 1949, s. 3
[24] Mental Health Act 1959, ss. 97, 98
[25] BGBl 1952 II S. 1
[25a] BGBl 1983 II S. 77
[26] die buffer stocks dienen dazu, Fluktuationen des Angebots und damit der Preise durch Aufkauf des Überangebots bzw. Verkauf bei Übernachfrage auszugleichen
[26a] International Monetary Fund
[27] Law of Property Act 1925, s. 99 (3) (ii); Settled Land Act 1925, ss. 44, 46
[28] Building Societies Act 1986
[29] UCC s. 6–102
[30] z. B. Bureau of Internal Revenue (Teil des Treasury Department)
[31] *Br* neugefaßt durch Theft Act 1968, s. 9. Danach umfaßt burglary auch das frühere Delikt des housebreaking und beschränkt sich nicht mehr auf den nächtlichen Einbruch
[32] *Am* 8 gallons = 33,35 l
[33] vgl. Vergleichs- und Schiedsordnung der Internationalen Handelskammer
[34] Consumer Credit Act 1974

Zu C

[1] Lanham Act, s. 14
[2] *Br* vor dem Administration of Estates Act 1925
[3] IRC s. 263
[3a] *Am* § 1201 IRC
[4] IRC s. 1203
[5] IRC s. 1202
[6] Seit dem Finance Act 1986 ersetzt durch inheritance tax
[7] Children and Young Persons Act 1969, ss. 1, 20
[8] Children Act 1959, s. 59.
[9] Road Traffic Act 1972, s. 3
[10] BGBl 1989 II S. 299
[11] BGBl 1964 II S. 109
[12] BGBl 1956 II S. 1988, 2006
[13] BGBl 1965 II S. 917
[14] Convention on the Contract for the International Carriage of Goods by Road (CMR) Übereinkommen über den Beförderungsvertrag im internationalen Straßengüterverkehr (CMR) – BGBl 1961 II S. 1120; 1980 S. 733
[15] IRC s. 904 (f) (4)
[16] Communidad Centro-Americana
[17] UCC s. 3–104
[18] *Br* nach Registrierung der Gründungsurkunde (memorandum of association) und *(eventuell)* der Satzung (articles of association) und Bezahlung der Gebühren erteilt der Registrar das certificate of incorporation; Companies Act 1985, s. 13
[19] Companies Act 1985, s. 186
[20] Employment Protection Act, 1975, S. 7 (1)
[21] UNIL s. 187; UCC s. 3–411
[22] Administration of Justice (Miscellaneous Provisions) Act, 1938, s. 7. Courts Act, 1971, s. 10 (5); Sched. 8, para 40.
[23] heute ersetzt durch beneficiary
[24] Law of Property Act 1925, s. 85 (1)
[25] Wiener Übereinkommen über diplomatische Beziehungen, Art. 14c – BGBl 1964 II S. 968
[26] *Am* IRC s. 170, s. 873 (b) (2), s. 882 (e) (1)
[27] BGBl 1973 II S. 430, 505; 1974 S. 769; 1980 II S. 1252; 1985 II S. 306
[28] UCC §§ 9–104
[29] neuer Begriff nach dem Financial Services Bill
[30] Cif wird häufig in Lieferverträgen mit Partnern in Übersee bei Benutzung des Seeweges vereinbart
[31] *Br* es gibt 6 circuits: Midland and Oxford Circuit, North Eastern Circuit, Northern Circuit, South Eastern Circuit, Wales and Chester Circuit, Western Circuit (die meisten befassen sich nur mit Strafsachen, einige auch mit Zivilsachen)
[32] Courts Act 1971, s. 16
[33] British Nationality Act 1982, ss. 30,31
[34] British Nationality Act 1948, s. 19
[35] Federal Trade Commission Act. s. 20
[36] Bureaux Internationaux Réunis pour la Protection de la Propriété Industrielle Littéraire et Artistique, Genf, 32 Chemin des Colombettes
[37] sie wird unter bestimmten Umständen steuerlich benachteiligt
[38] *Am* durch den Taft-Hartley Act für ungesetzlich erklärt
[38a] BGBl 1988 II S. 303 ff.
[39] *Am* MPC s. 212.5

[40] *Br* Coinage Acts of 1891, 1920 and 1946
[41] *Am* UCC ss. 9–105 (1) (c)
[41a] BGBl 1986 II S. 374
[41b] Publikation Nr. 322 der Internationalen Handelskammer (englisch und deutsch)
[42] BGBl 1965 II S. 742; 1976 II S. 1018; 1983 II S. 303; 1989 II S. 542
[43] Commerce ist weitergehend als trade; der Begriff umfaßt auch kaufmännische Dienstleistungen (Lagerung, Transport, Bank- und Versicherungsgeschäfte)
[44] der 98 lokale Handelskammern und eine größere Anzahl von solchen angehören, die im Exportgeschäft tätig sind
[44a] Handelsvertretung, Leitfaden für den Abschluß von Verträgen. Publikation Nr. 410 der Internationalen Handelskammer (englisch und deutsch)
[45] *Am* Uniform Commercial Code, Art. 3
[46] vgl. Broschüre 192 der Internationalen Handelskammer (→ICC): "Uniform rules for the collection of commercial paper" („Einheitliche Richtlinien für das Inkasso von Handelspapieren"). Im Sinne dieser Richtlinien gelten als Handelspapiere: Wechsel (bills of exchange), Solawechsel (promissory notes), Schecks (cheques), dokumentäre Rimessen (documentary remittances), Quittungen (receipts) und alle anderen Abschnitte, die für ein Inkasso in Frage kommen (and any other documents likely to provide instruments for collections)
[47] BGBl 1955 II S. 634; 1956 II S. 29; 1957 II S. 1688
[48] Administration of Justice Act 1970
[49] Nach Schedule 4 des Administration of Justice Act gehören hierzu "Income Tax, National Insurance contributions, National Health Service contributions, Redundancy Fund contributions"
[49a] BGBl 1985 II S. 718
[50] British Nationality Act 1982, s. 37; Immigration Act 1971, Part I
[50a] Community charge ab 1. 4. 1990 Steuer für Wohngrundstücke
[51] Arizona, Idaho, Kalifornien, Louisiana, Nevada, Neumexiko, Texas und Washington
[52] Europäische Gemeinschaften
[53] Europäische Wirtschaftsgemeinschaft
[54] Companies Act 1985, s. 1
[55] Companies Act 1985, s. 704
[56] Companies Act 1985, ss. 1, 3; ss. 117, 118
[57] Employment Protection Act 1975, s. 73
[58] MPC s. 242.5
[59] Acquisition of Land (Authorization Procedure) Act, 1946
[60] § 25 GWB; vgl. auch Art. 85 EWG-Vertrag
[61] Anhang III der ICC Vergleichsordnung S. 36 – Publikation Nr. 447 der Internationalen Handelskammer (englisch und deutsch)
[62] ICC Vergleichsordnung S. 8ff. – Publikation Nr. 447 der Internationalen Handelskammer (englisch und deutsch)
[62a] BGBl 1983 II S. 99
[63] ICC Vergleichsordnung S. 5 und 8ff. – Publikation Nr. 447 der Internationalen Handelskammer (englisch und deutsch)
[64] Consumer Credit Act 1974, s. 189
[65] *Br* Condonation als Einwand gegen die Ehescheidungsklage (as bar to divorce) wurde durch den Divorce Law Reform Act, 1969, abgeschafft
[66] „Bei amerikanischen Investmentfonds ist zwischen ‚Regulated Investment Companies' im Sinne der §§ 851ff IRC und nicht als solche qualifizierten investment companies zu unterscheiden. Während die erstere nach US-Steuerrecht im wesentlichen als transparent behandelt wird mit der Folge, daß der Fonds selbst nicht steuerpflichtig ist und die vom Fonds bezogenen Dividenden und capital gains dem Anteilhaber mit allen steuerlichen Konsequenzen eines unmittelbaren Bezugs zugerechnet werden, stellen die Ausschüttungen der letzteren nach amerikanischer Auffassung Dividenden dar, die der Fonds als solcher verteilt; sie sind daher nicht transparent." Debatin-Walter „Handbuch zum Deutsch-Amerikanischen Doppelbesteuerungsabkommen" B VI Ziffer 94 und 99.
[67] die Confederation of British Industry (CBI) ist der wichtigste britische Unternehmerverband. Er übernahm die Aufgaben der früheren „British Employers Confederation", „Federation of British Industries" sowie „National Association of British Manufacturers"
[68] *Am* Lanham Act, s. 23
[69] Lanham Act, s. 32
[70] Art. I s. 8 of the Constitution of the United States
[71] IRC s. 1501ff
[72] IRC ss. 1501–1505
[73] nach dem Sherman Act, section 1 ist verboten der Zusammenschluß von zwei od. mehr Personen, um durch abgestimmtes Verhalten (concerted action) e-e illegale Handlung oder e-e legale Handlung mit verbotenen Mitteln zu tun. Die Bestimmung richtet sich vor allem gegen „Kartelle".
[74] Konsularvertrag zwischen der Bundesrepublik Deutschland und dem Vereinigten Königreich von Großbritannien und Nordirland – BGBl 1957 II S. 285
[75] Wiener Übereinkommen über konsularische Beziehungen – BGBl 1969 II S. 1585
[76] *Br* im allgemeinen auf folgende 2 Fälle beschränkt: a) im Nachlaßgericht (Erteilung von →probate in common form und →letters of administration); b) in der → Chancery Division (Auslegung von Rechtsfragen oder Unklarheiten in Urkunden sowie Anweisungen an → trustees)
[77] Bundesverfassung Art. I s. 10
[78] *Br* Sale of Goods Act, 1979

[78a] Publikation Nr. 325 der Internationalen Handelskammer (englisch und deutsch)
[79] UCC ss. 9–106
[79a] BGBl 1985 II S. 590
[80] BGBl 1973 II S. 1071
[80a] BGBl 1965 II S. 1213
[80b] BGBl 1970 II S. 293, 391
[81] BGBl 1985 II S. 666
[82] Convention relative aux transports internationaux ferroviaires
[82a] BGBl 1987 II S. 252
[82b] BGBl 1967 II S. 1233
[82c] BGBl 1985 II S. 539
[82d] BGBl 1977 II S. 215
[82e] BGBl 1967 II S. 2435; 1971 II S. 1377; 1986 II S. 1142
[82f] BGBl 1986 II S. 840
[82g] BGBl 1986 II S. 837
[82h] BGBl 1982 II S. 374; 1986 II S. 1397; 1988 II S. 422
[82i] BGBl 1986 II S. 826; 1986 I S. 1156
[83] IRC s. 1231
[84] das Genossenschaftsrecht ist in den Industrial and Provident Societies Acts, 1893 to 1961 enthalten
[85] z. B. in Art. 8 des Übereinkommens zur Errichtung der Weltorganisation für geistiges Eigentum – BGBl 1970 II S. 309
[86] BGBl 1973 II S. 1069, 1111
[87] IRC § 7701 (a) (3)
[88] nach dem MPC s. 401. 1 (1) fallen unter correctional institution z. B. Gefängnisse (prisons), Jugendgefängnisse (reformatories), ,,Herbergen" für bedingt Entlassene und für diejenigen, deren Strafe zur Bewährung ausgesetzt ist (parole and probation hostels)
[89] RGBl 1928 II S. 624; BGBl. 1953 II S. 116
[90] BGBl 1956 II S. 488
[91] BGBl 1956 II S. 502
[92] RGBl 1933 II S. 913; BGBl 1961 II S. 566
[93] Local Government Act 1972
[94] 28 U. S. A. § 171
[95] 28 U. S. C. A. § 211
[96] durch den Court Act 1971 sind die Courts of Quarter Sessions und die Courts of Assize abgeschafft. An ihrer Stelle ist der →Crown Court getreten
[97] der Crown Court trat 1971 an die Stelle der Courts of Assize und der quarter sessions (als Teil des Supreme Court)
[98] 28 U. S. C. A. § 251
[99] 28 U. S. C. A. § 1251
[100] 18 U. S. C. A. § 3231
[101] 28 U. S. C. A. § 1332
[102] 28 U. S. C. A § 1331
[103] 28 U. S. C. A. § 1333
[104] 28 U. S. C. A. § 1334
[105] 28 U. S. C. A. § 1338
[106] 28 U. S. C. A. § 1346 (b)
[107] 28 U. S. C. A. § 1351
[108] BGBl 1952 II S. 691, 695; 1963 II S. 351
[109] Article III Section 2 of the Constitution
[110] 28 U. S. C. A. § 1251 ff.
[111] Judicature Act 1925, s. 1
[112] Courts Act, 1971, s. 1 (1)
[113] Consumer Credit Act 1974, s. 189
[114] *Am* IRC ss. 901–906
[115] Model Penal Code s. 1.04 (1)
[116] BGBl 1967 II S. 1235
[117] BGBl 1970 II S. 461
[118] Admission Temporaire – Temporary Admission
[119] BGBl 1965 II S. 949
[120] Echantillons Commerciaux – Commercial Samples
[121] BGBl 1965 II S. 918
[122] BGBl 1967 II S. 745
[123] BGBl 1979 II S. 445
[124] BGBl 1961 II S. 922
[124a] BGBl 1971 II S. 1102
[125] BGBl 1960 II S. 1515
[126] BGBl 1965 II S. 1097
[126a] BGBl 1969 II S. 1076
[127] BGBl 1969 II S. 1914
[128] BGBl 1959 II S. 1501
[129] BGBl 1960 II S. 1511

Zu D

[1] BGBl 1985 II S. 900
[1a] Criminal Damage Act 1971
[1b] BGBl 1985 II S. 539f.
[2] Fair Deal 1. Grundsatz einer liberalen Wirtschaftspolitik, nach der jeder Nation ein gerechter Anteil an den Rohstoff- und Energiequellen der Welt zusteht *(Fortentwicklung des →New Deal)*; 2. *Am* das 1949 von Präsident Truman verkündete Wirtschafts- und Sozialprogramm
[3] New Deal *Am* ursprünglich Roosevelts neue Wirtschaftspolitik (von 1933 zur Bekämpfung der Weltwirtschaftskrise). Die New Deal- Gesetzgebung (→NIRA) wurde durch den Supreme Court außer Kraft gesetzt
[4] *Br* Abschaffung der Todesstrafe für Mord cf. Murder (Abolition of Death Penalty) Act 1965; *Am* 1972 vom Obersten Gerichtshof als verfassungswidrig erklärt
[5] nach Verurteilung wegen e-r →felony
[6] BGBl 1955 II S. 706; 1958 II S. 166
[7] BGBl 1953 II S. 333, 473
[8] Stichtag für die Umstellung der Währung war der 15. 2. 1971. Seit dieser Zeit besteht das Pfund Sterling aus 100 (statt 240) pence und der shilling ist abgeschafft

[9] die D. o. I. ist nach s. 334 (f) of INA nur noch freiwillig abzugeben. Einige Einzelstaaten machen die Ausübung gewisser Berufe von dem Besitz der →first papers abhängig

[10] Statutory Declaration Act 1835; s. 5 of the Perjury Act 1911

[11] IRC s. 167

[12] Matrimonial Causes Act 1973, s. 1 (5)

[13] *Br* abgeschafft durch Matrimonial Proceedings and Property Act 1970

[14] im Gegensatz zur herkömmlichen deeds registration haben einige amerikanische Staaten das Grundbuchsystem eingeführt. Die deeds registration hat lediglich Sicherungsfunktion, indem sie den Vorrang der registrierten Verfügung vor späteren Verfügungen begründet

[14a] BGBl 1988 II s. 805

[15] *Br* Defamation Act 1952

[16] *Br* Defamation Act, s. 4

[17] Mental Health Act 1959, s. 127

[18] 1939–1964. An ihre Stelle traten die →National Development Bonds

[19] der Empfänger des Briefes muß ebenfalls eine Empfangsbescheinigung unterzeichnen. Im Falle des Verlustes wird im Ggs. zum registered letter von der Post keine Entschädigung (compensation) gezahlt

[20] Housing Act 1957, ss. 4, 21

[21] nicht gleichbedeutend mit den Aufgaben des deutschen Innenministeriums

[22] National Insurance (Industrial Injuries) Act 1946 to 1957.

[23] Law of Property Act 1925, ss. 2 (3) and 13.

[24] *Br* Law of Property Act 1925, s. 49 (2).

[25] Mindestreserven, die von den Londoner Clearing- und den schottischen Banken bei der Bank von England zu halten sind

[26] *Br* British Nationality Act 1948, s. 19

[27] *Br* Supply of Goods (Implied Terms) Act 1973, s. 2; Sale of Goods Act 1979, s. 13.

[28] es können für den Schutz der industriellen Formgebung einerseits die Regeln über das Musterrecht, andererseits die über das Urheberrecht in Betracht kommen

[29] Registered Designs Act 1949 und Copyright, Designs and Patent Act 1988

[30] nach dem Children and Young Persons Act 1933, s. 53 (as amended by subsequent Acts) wird ein wegen Mordes verurteilter Jugendlicher unter 18 Jahren nicht zu lebenslänglicher Freiheitsstrafe verurteilt

[31] abgeschafft durch den Criminal Justice Act 1967 (Part 2)

[32] zu den Entwicklungsbanken gehören: International Bank for Reconstruction and Development (World Bank), International Finance Corporation, Interamerican Development Bank, and African Development Bank

[33] nach dem Community Land Act 1975 kann der Grundbesitzer zum Verkauf seines Landes an die zuständige Behörde zum gegenwärtigen Werte gezwungen werden (s. 25 des Gesetzes)

[34] Town and Country Planning Act 1972, ss. 4–18

[35] Flächennutzungsplan (Bauleitplan einer Gemeinde) ist ein Begriff des deutschen Bundesbaugesetzes

[36] der Nord-Süd-Dialog ist für die Europäische Gemeinschaft von großer Bedeutung, da sie in ihrer Rohstoff- und Energieversorgung weitgehend vom Ausland abhängig ist

[37] über Rangklassen der Diplomaten vgl. heads of →missions

[38] vgl. Wiener Übereinkommen über diplomatische Beziehungen – BGBl 1964 II S. 957

[39] BGBl 1956 II S. 2024, 2033

[39a] Companies Act 1986, s. 329

[40] der Begriff „Invalidenversicherung" wurde in der Bundesrepublik 1957 durch „Arbeiterrentenversicherung" ersetzt.

Am die Gesetzesänderungen von 1956, 1958 und 1960 brachten schrittweise eine disability insurance für alle von der Alters- und Hinterbliebenenversicherung erfaßten Versicherten und deren Angehörige

Aus OASI wurde OASDI (→Old Age, Survivors and Disability Insurance)

[41] *Br* Disabled Persons (Employment) Act, 1968

[42] vgl. Art. 2 VIII des Abkommens über die Errichtung einer Weltorganisation für geistiges Eigentum (→WIPO)

[43] Übereinkommen der Internationalen Arbeitsorganisation über die Diskriminierung in Beschäftigung und Beruf – BGBl 1961 II S. 98; 1985 II S. 648; 1988 II S. 109

[43a] BGBl 1985 II S. 648

[44] z. B. Art. 7 EWG-Vertrag

[45] so Werner-König in „Glossare zur Arbeitsmarkt- und Berufsforschung" 1974, S.20

[46] *Br* Insolvency Act 1986

[46a] BGBl 1977 II S. 862

[47] die Übersetzung Pfändung für distraint/distress bzw. pfänden für to distrain/distress ist ungenau, da es sich nicht um eine staatliche Beschlagnahme handelt

[47a] Art. III s. 2 der Federal Constitution

[47b] §§ 241–6 Internal Revenue Code

[48] Trennen der Ja- von den Nein-Stimmen

[49] z. B. bill of lading, insurance policy, insurance certificate, commercial invoice, customs invoice, consular invoice and certificate of origin

[50] Publikation Nr. 400 der Internationalen Handelskammer (englisch und deutsch) – Revision 1983

[51] vgl. Broschüre 192 der IHK (→ICC) (cf. commercial paper)

[52] BGBl 1953 II S. 307; 1961 II S. 464

[52a] BGBl 1986 I S. 122

[53] Doppelbesteuerungsabkommen Großbritannien-Bundesrepublik – BGBl 1955 S. 612;

1966 II S. 359. Doppelbesteuerungsabkommen USA-Bundesrepublik – BGBl 1954 S. 1118; 1965 II S. 1611; S. 1966 II S. 746; 1982 II S. 846

[54] nach neuerer Gesetzgebung kann ein dower nicht nur der Ehefrau sondern auch dem Ehemann zustehen

[55] das neue amerikanische Recht (UCC) benützt anstelle von bill of exchange nur noch draft

[55a] BGBl 1985 II S. 897

[56] Road Traffic Act 1972, s. 5 (2), s. 6 (1)

[57] *Br* Entscheidungen können nur unter Beachtung der regulären Prozeßformen gefällt werden. *Am* Amendment V und XIV der Federal Constitution besagen, daß niemandem Leben, Freiheit od. Eigentum ohne gehöriges Rechtsverfahren entzogen werden darf

[58] *Br* Nullity of Marriage Act 1971, s. 2

[59] Legal Aid Act 1974, s. 15; 1982 s. 1

Zu E

[1] IRC, s. 911

[2] Social Security Pensions Act 1975

[3] BGBl 1983 II S. 88

[4] Federal Reserve Act, para 25 (a)

[5] IRC, s. 864 (c)

[6] Art. VI (7) des Deutsch-Amerikanischen Doppelbesteuerungsabkommens

[7] British Nationality Act, s. 8

[8] *Am* INA, s. 311

[9] Art. 2 (3) des Übereinkommens über ein Internationales Energieprogramm – BGBl 1975 II S. 705

[10] *Br* Employment Protection Act 1980; Employment Protection (Consolidation) Act 1978

[10a] Feind eines Unterzeichnerstaates der UN-Charta (Art. 53 und 107)

[11] Agreement on an International Energy Program Übereinkommen über ein Internationales Energieprogramm – BGBl 1975 II S. 701

[12] Deutsch-Britisches Abkommen über die gegenseitige Anerkennung und Vollstreckung gerichtlicher Entscheidungen in Zivil- und Handelssachen – BGBl 1961 II S. 302

[13] Art. 208 des Labor Management Relations Act

[13a] BGBl 1983 II S. 125

[14] *Br* equitable estates sind durch equitable interests ersetzt (Law of Property Act 1925, sec. I (3))

[15] *Br* Judicature Acts 1873/75; s. 36 of the Judicature Act 1925

[16] *Am* Field Code 1848. In der Bundesgerichtsbarkeit sind law und equity vereinheitlicht (merged) durch die Federal Rules of Civil Procedure, in Kraft getreten 1938. (Ausnahme: Beibehaltung der jury in common law-Zivilsachen [7th Amendment to the Constitution])

[17] vgl. Wieacker, Zur rechtstheoretischen Präzisierung des § 242 BGB, Tübingen 1956, S. 41

[18] BGBl 1985 II S. 540

[19] die estate duty ist abgeschafft durch Part III des Finance Act, 1975. An ihre Stelle trat die →Capital Transfer Tax.Die estate duty gilt noch für Todesfälle bis 13. November 1974

[20] *Br* durch den Law Reform (Married Women and Tortfeasors) Act 1935, s. 2, ist die Fiktion des separate estate abgeschafft. Alles Vermögen einer verheirateten Frau gehört ihr jetzt so, als ob sie eine feme sole wäre

[21] Société Européenne pour le Financement de Matériel Ferroviaire (Abkommen über die Gründung der Eurofima; BGBl 1956 II S. 908)

[22] BGBl 1954 II S. 494; 1959 II S. 1455

[23] BGBl 1969 II S. 1489; 1985 II S. 605

[23a] BGBl 1985 II S. 59

[23b] BGBl 1985 II S. 890

[24] BGBl 1971 II S. 1262

[24a] BGBl 1972 II S. 630

[24b] BGBl 1988 II S. 988

[24c] BGBl 1983 II S. 246; 1985 II S. 53

[25] BGBl 1969 II S. 1940

[26] BGBl 1965 II S. 1235; 1967 II S. 1786; 1984 II S. 1015

[26a] BGBl 1977 II S. 1445

[27] BGBl 1972 II S. 553

[27a] BGBl 1962 II S. 841

[27b] BGBl 1978 II S. 1460; 1956 II S. 507, 531; 1985 II S. 311

[27c] BGBl 1977 II S. 986

[28] BGBl 1957 II S. 1014, 1678

[28a] BGBl 1975 II S. 873

[28b] BGBl 1987 II S. 66

[29] BGBl 1952 II S. 447

[30] BGBl 1970 II S. 910

[30a] BGBl 1975 II S. 626; 1980 II S. 1379

[30b] BGBl 1977 II S. 1277; 1978 II S. 390

[31] BGBl 1959 II S. 622

[31a] Conférence Européenne des Ministres de Transports; BGBl 1971 II S. 1291

[32] BGBl 1971 II S. 86

[32a] BGBl 1969 II S. 2057; 1977 II S. 211

[32b] BGBl 1980 II S. 1094

[33] BGBl 1965 II S. 282

[33a] BGBl 1980 II S. 954

[33b] BGBl 1964 II S. 406

[34] BGBl 1971 II S. 18

[34a] BGBl 1964 II S. 1289

[35] BGBl 1959 II S. 998

[36] BGBl 1964 II S. 1371

[37] BGBl 1974 II S. 938; 1987 II S. 60

[38] BGBl 1956 II S. 660, 810 (von der Bundesregierung gekündigt – BGBl 1975 II S. 299)

[39] BGBl 1964 II S. 425
[39a] BGBl 1972 II S. 774; 1983 II S. 802
[39b] BGBl 1964 II S. 1369, 1386; 1980 II S. 1334
[39c] BGBl 1981 II S. 550
[40] BGBl 1961 II S. 82, 1026
[41] BGBl 1973 II S. 721
[41a] BGBl 1978 II S. 113
[41b] BGBl 1983 II S. 771
[41c] BGBl 1974 II S. 1286
[41d] BGBl 1981 II S. 533, 535
[42] BGBl 1956 II S. 564; 1979 II S. 290; 1983 II S. 338
[42a] BGBl 1978 II S. 322
[42b] BGBl 1977 II S. 1445; 1979 II S. 212; 1980 II S. 1379
[43] BGBl 1955 II S. 1128
[43a] BGBl 1970 II S. 636
[44] BGBl 1957 II S. 766
[44a] EG-Verordnung vom 25. 7. 1985
[45] BGBl 1957 II S. 854, 964
[46] BGBl 1973 II S. 1006
[47] BGBl 1959 II S. 610; 1965 II S. 1335
[47a] BGBl 1987 II S. 257
[48] BGBl 1969 II S. 1197; 1971 II S. 201
[49] BGBl 1962 II S. 2273
[50] BGBl 1981 II S. 966
[51] Art. 2 der →European Patent Convention
[52] BGBl 1976 II S. 826 ff.; 1987 II S. 539; 1988 II S. 763
[53] Art. 10 ff. der →European Patent Convention
[54] Art. 4 ff. der →European Patent Convention
[54a] BGBl 1973 II S. 705
[54b] BGBl 1956 II S. 581; 1970 II S. 1013
[54c] Protokoll und Zusatzprotokoll über die Gründung Europäischer Schulen – BGBl 1969 II S. 1301; 1978 II S. 994
[55] BGBl 1964 II S. 1261
[56] Art. 123–128 des EWG-Vertrages
[57] in der European Space Agency sind ESRO (European Space Research Organization) und ELDO (European Launcher Development Organization) aufgegangen
[57a] BGBl 1976 II S. 1862
[57b] BGBl 1984 II S. 683
[57c] BGBl 1974 II S. 1138
[57d] BGBl 1989 II S. 255
[58] Abkommen Großbritannien-Bundesrepublik Deutschland zur Vermeidung der Doppelbesteuerung und zur Verhinderung der Steuerverkürzung (prevention of fiscal evasion) bei den Steuern vom Einkommen – BGBl 1955 II S. 612
[59] s. 36 of the Finance Act 1952
[59a] Value Added Tax Act 1983, s. 17 Schedule 6
[59b] Value Added Tax (General) Regulations 1985, ss. 29–37
[60] Resale Prices Act, s. 5
[61] British Nationality Act 1948, s. 19
[62] IRC s. 162
[62a] Export Administration Amendments Act (of 1985)
[63] Restrictive Trade Practices Act 1956, s. 31
[64] BGBl 1976 II S. 484
[65] vgl. die Vereinbarung zwischen der Bundesrepublik Deutschland und der Regierung des Vereinigten Königreichs Großbritannien und Nordirland über die Auslieferung flüchtiger Verbrecher – BGBl 1960 II S. 2192 – sowie den Auslieferungsvertrag zwischen der Bundesrepublik Deutschland und den Vereinigten Staaten von Amerika – BGBl 1980 II S. 647, 1300; 1988 II S. 1087
[66] BGBl 1975 II S. 1369

Zu F

[1] *Br* Defamation Act 1952, s. 6
[1a] 29 U.S.C. §§ 201 ff.
[2] *Br* Theft Act 1968, s. 17
[3] *Br* Servants' Characters Act 1792; Seamen's and Soldiers' False Characters Act 1906
[4] Perjury Act 1911, s. 2
[5] seit dem Administration of Justice Act 1970 (s. 1) übernahm die Family Division den größten Teil der Tätigkeit der Probate, Divorce and Admiralty Division
[6] *Am* featherbedding ist gemäß s. 8 (6) des NLRA rechtswidrig
[6a] 21 U.S.C. ss. 301–392
[7] vgl. DBA Großbritannien-Bundesrepublik Deutschland – BGBl 1955 II S. 612
[8] BGBl 1969 II S. 1897
[9] BGBl 1971 II S. 1064
[10] BGBl 1957 II S. 214
[11] BGBl 1973 II S. 17
[12] Sale of Goods Act 1979, s. 14 (1)
[13] ss. 396 (1) f, 410 (4) e CA 1985
[14] BGBl 1987 II S. 688
[15] Satzung BGBl 1971 II S. 1036
[16] BGBl 1974 II S. 566
[17] Export Administration Act, s. 6
[18] *Br* Law of Property Act 1925, S. 146
[19] *Br* berührt nicht die Rechte des betroffenen Aktieninhabers, der nach den Forged Transfer Acts schadensersatzberechtigt ist
[20] Friendly Societies Acts 1896 to 1958
[21] BGBl 1956 II S. 487
[22] Family Law Reform Act 1969, ss. 1, 2
[23] *Br* Law of Property Act 1925, s. 76 and Sched. 2

Zu G

[1] *Br* Gaming Act 1968
[2] *Br* Betting and Gaming Duties Act 1972
[3] BGBl 1954 II S. 730
[4] Das Recht e-s Schiffahrtsstaates, seine Flagge nach eigenem Ermessen verleihen zu dürfen, erlischt, wenn eine echte Verbindung zwischen ihm und dem Schiff fehlt (Art. 5 des Abkommens über die Hohe See, Genfer Seerechts-Konferenz 1958)
[5] Chapter XI of the Charter of the United Nations
[6] *Br* s. 14 of the Bills of Exchange Act 1882
[7] der Begriff greenmail(ing) setzt sich zusammen aus „green" – Farbe der Geldscheine – und „blackmail" – Erpressung

Zu H

[1] BGBl 1962 II S. 775; 1987 II S. 547
[1a] BGBl 1959 II S. 981
[2] BGBl 1971 II S. 219
[3] BGBl 1958 II S. 577, 939
[4] RGBl 1928 II S. 624; BGBl 1953 II S. 116; 1960 II S. 1519
[5] RGBl 1929 II S. 135
[6] BGBl 1956 II S. 488, 763
[7] BGBl 1977 II S. 1453; 1971 II S. 219
[8] BGBl 1977 II S. 1472; 1979 II S. 780
[9] BGBl 1973 II S. 885
[10] Theft Act 1968, s. 22
[11] vgl. Schaps-Abraham ,,Das deutsche Seerecht", Bd. 2, S. 675/76
[12] Health and Safety at Work etc. Act 1974
[13] Civil Evidence Act 1972, ss. 1, 2
[14] BGBl 1977 II S. 215
[15] BGBl 1972 II S. 1089
[16] *Br* Highjacking Act 1971, s. 1
[17] genaue Definition im Consumer Credit Act 1974, s. 189 (1)
[18] *Br* Art. 29 BEA; Am UCC s. 3–302
[19] *Br* Art. 27 BEA
[20] Agricultural Holdings Act 1948 (Pachtgesetz)
[21] Sexual Offences Act 1967
[22] *Br* Administration of Estates Act 1925, s. 57; Law of Property Act 1925, s. 157
[23] BGBl 1952 II S. 686, 953; 1956 II S. 1880; 1989 II S. 547
[24] BGBl 1969 II S. 417

Zu I

[1] gültig ab 1. 1. 1988 (Publikation Nr. 447 der Intern. Handelskammer)
[1a] Comité Maritime International
[1b] ICC und CMI haben gemeinsam Verfahrensvorschriften für die Seeschiedsbarkeit ausgearbeitet (Publikation Nr. 324 der Intern. Handelskammer)
[1c] s. International →Maritime Arbitration Organization
[1d] A Alfred, B Benjamin, C Charlie, D David, E Edward, F Frederick, G George, H Harry, I Isaac, J Jack, K King, L Lucy, M Mary, N Nelly, O Oliver, P Peter, Q Queenie, R Robert, S Sally, T Tommy, U Uncle, V Victor, W William, X Xmas, Y Yellow, Z Zebra
[2] *Br* der Begriff ,,idiot" für mentally deficient persons ist durch den Mental Health Act 1959 abgeschafft
[3] *Br* der Begriff ,,imbecile" für mentally deficient persons ist durch den Mental Health Act 1959 abgeschafft
[4] *Br* State Immunity Act 1978
[5] *Br* Sale of Goods Act 1979 ss. 12–15
[6] Methode zur Einfuhrbeschränkung, die 1968 eingeführt wurde
[7] *Br* The Law Reform (Frustrated Contracts) Act 1943
[8] im deutschen Recht ist anstelle der Gefängnisstrafe die Freiheitsstrafe getreten
[9] BGBl 1983 II S. 142
[10] IRC s. 871 (a)
[11] Publikation Nr. 350 der Intern. Handelskammer
[12] Intern. Gesundheitsvorschriften Art. 51 – BGBl 1971 II S. 889
[13] *Br* Indecency with Children Act 1960 (as amended)
[14] Industrial Tribunals (Labour Relations) Regulations 1974 (as amended)
[15] *Am* INA, s. 311
[16] 5th Amendment of the Federal Constitution
[17] Land Registration Act 1925, s. 57
[18] *Br* Hotel Proprietors Act 1956
[19] dieses Führungsgremium ist unter verschiedenen Bezeichnungen wie ,,executive committee", ,,management committee" etc bekannt
[20] abgedruckt in ,,Incoterms 1953" der Internationalen Handelskammer (Broschüre 166). Daneben bestehen British Institute Cargo Clau-

ses 1946 und American Institute Cargo Clauses 1949

[21] *Br* Insurance Companies Acts 1958, 1967

[21a] Agreement Establishing the Inter-American Development Bank Übereinkommen zur Errichtung der Interamerikanischen Entwicklungsbank – BGBl 1976 II S. 38; 1989 II S. 575

[21b] BGBl 1986 II S. 749

[22] verboten durch Section 7, Clayton Act

[23] Torts (Interference with Goods) Act 1977 s. 1

[23a] Bankruptcy Reform Act 1979 s. 701

[23b] BGBl 1985 II S. 838

[23c] RGBl 1921 II S. 6, 1929 II S. 407; BGBl 1959 II S. 333

[24] Convention Internationale concernant le transport des marchandises par chemin de fer – BGBl 1956 II S. 35

[25] Convention Internationale concernant le transport des voyageurs et des bagages par chemin de fer – BGBl 1956 II S. 277

[26] BGBl 1956 II S. 411, 442 mit Änd.

[26a] Art. vii of the Patent Cooperation Treaty; BGBl 1976 II S. 649, 664; 1984 II S. 799, 975

[27] BGBl 1957 II S. 1358 mit Änd.

[28] BGBl 1952 II S. 664 mit Änd.

[29] BGBl 1970 II S. 297, 315

[29a] BGBl 1961 II S. 1119; 1962 II S. 12; letzte Änderung BGBl 1980 II S. 721, 733

[29b] BGBl 1974 II S. 565ff.; 1988 II S. 866

[29c] BGBl 1969 II S. 372

[29d] BGBl 1970 II S. 459

[30] Publikation Nr. 400 der Intern. Handelskammer

[31] Publikation Nr. 350 der Intern. Handelskammer

[32] BGBl 1956 II S. 412

[32a] BGBl 1977 II S. 1301

[32b] BGBl 1985 II S. 718

[32c] BGBl 1980 II S. 1362

[33] BGBl 1984 II S. 810

[34] BGBl 1965 II S. 1244

[34a] BGBl 1977 II S. 42

[35] BGBl 1979 II S. 142; 1980 II S. 525; 1985 II S. 795

[36] RGBl 1939 II S. 1049; BGBl 1953 II S. 116; 1954 II S. 466

[36a] BGBl 1972 II S. 663

[36b] BGBl 1969 II S. 249; 1977 II S. 164

[36c] BGBl 1969 II S. 961

[36d] BGBl 1987 II S. 640

[36e] BGBl 1986 II S. 1068

[36f] BGBl 1962 II S. 2274

[36g] BGBl 1984 II S. 209

[36h] BGBl 1972 II S. 672; 1973 II S. 16f.

[36i] BGBl 1955 II S. 633

[37] Art. 92–96 der Satzung der Vereinten Nationen und Statut des Gerichtshofs

[37a] BGBl 1973 II S. 1533

[37b] BGBl 1973 II S. 1570

[38] BGBl 1956 II S. 749 mit Änd.

[38a] BGBl 1983 II S. 246; 1985 II S. 1024

[38b] BGBl 1975 II S. 701

[38c] BGBl 1975 II S. 320; 1988 II S. 840 (Neufassung)

[39] BGBl 1971 II S. 868

[39a] BGBl 1969 II S. 417

[39b] BGBl 1959 II S. 933

[39c] BGBl 1985 II S. 842

[40] BGBl 1952 II S. 607; 1957 II S. 318

[41] Anschrift: 3 Paper Buildings, The Temple, London E. C. 4

[41a] Publikation Nr. 324 der Intern. Handelskammer

[42] Übereinkommen über die internationale Seeschiffahrts-Organisation BGBl 1982 II S. 874, 956; 1985 II S. 563; 1986 II S. 424

[42a] BGBl 1984 II S. 596; 1989 II S. 511

[42b] BGBl 1967 II S. 2435; 1971 II S. 1377

[43] BGBl 1967 II S. 637

[43a] BGBl 1989 II S. 107

[43b] BGBl 1973 II S. 1309; 1978 II S. 1158

[43c] BGBl 1959 II S. 673; 1968 II S. 862

[43d] BGBl 1975 II S. 284

[44] BGBl 1973 II S. 1311

[44a] RGBl 1928 II S. 23; BGBl 1953 II S. 116

[44b] BGBl 1976 II S. 1017; 1983 II S. 304

[44c] BGBl 1955 II S. 1062

[44d] BGBl 1976 II S. 678

[45] BGBl 1968 II S. 931; 1976 II S. 1089; 1985 II S. 426

[46] BGBl 1973 II S. 250

[46a] BGBl 1984 II S. 15

[46b] BGBl 1986 II S. 172

[47] Union Internationale des Chemins de Fer

[47a] BGBl 1987 II S. 671

[48] BGBl 1976 II S. 1746

[49] *Br* R. S. C. 1965, Ord. 17

[50] Family Law Reform Act 1969, 1987

[51] *Br* Die gesetzliche Erbfolge ist im Administration Act 1925 geregelt, ergänzt durch Intestates' Estates Act 1952 und den Family Provision Act 1969. Beide erweiterten den Anteil des überlebenden Ehegatten. Durch den Family Law Reform Act 1969 wurde ab 1970 die gesetzliche Erbfolge auch zwischen nichtehelichen Kindern und ihren Eltern hergestellt. Family Law Reform Act 1987

[52] Art. 23 des Abkommens zwischen BRD und Großbritannien über Soziale Sicherheit – BGBl 1961 II S. 242

[53] *Br* Administration of Estates Act 1925, s. 25

[54] New Scotland Yard Broadway, London SW 1

[55] *Am* Investment Company Act 1940; Investment Company Amendments Act 1970

[56] BGBl 1969 II S. 372, 1191

Zu J

[1] Fifth Amendment of the Constitution of the United States: "... nor shall any person be subject for the same offense to be twice put in jeopardy of life or limb"

[1a] *Br* die Trennung zwischen jobber und broker ist aufgehoben

[2] BGBl 1957 II S. 1046

[3] BGBl 1959 II S. 586

[4] Courts Act 1971

[5] Administration of Justice Act 1970, s. 11

[6] BGBl 1961 II S. 302, 1025

[7] der Judicature Act von 1873/1875 schuf den Supreme Court of Judicature sowie die Verschmelzung von law und equity (equity 1.). Judicature Act 1925 (genaue Bezeichnung: Supreme Court of Judicature [Consolidation] Act)

[7a] 28 U.S.C. §§ 1ff.

[8] im deutschen Recht heißen jetzt die ehrenamtlichen Richter beim Schwurgericht „Schöffen"

[9] *Br* Administration of Justice (Miscellaneous Provisions) Act 1933; Law Reform (Miscellaneous Provisions) (Scotland) Act 1980; Coroners' Juries Act 1983

[10] Art. VII of the Constitution of the United States of America

Zu L

[1] *Br* durch den Criminal Justice Act 1948, s. 1., abgeschafft

[2] BGBl 1983 II S. 774

[3] Part V of the Land Registration Act 1925

[4] *Br* Land Charges Act 1925

[5] Law of Property Act 1925, s. 97

[6] Lincoln's Inn Fields, London, W. C. 2

[7] deutsche Übersetzung s. Erasmus, „Erfinder- und Warenzeichenschutz im In- und Ausland", Bd. IV/2

[8] BGBl 1966 II S. 788

[9] mit den in Kraft gebliebenen Bestimmungen des Married Women's Property Act *(von 1882)*

[10] für Liste der Law Reports und ihre Abkürzungen vgl. „Where to Look for your Law" (Sweet and Maxwell)

[11] Legal Aid Act 1974

[12] *Br* im anglo-amerikanischen Recht wird nicht zwischen Miete und Pacht im deutschen Sinne unterschieden

[13] *Br* Landlord and Tenant Act 1954

[13a] RGBl 1928 II S. 624; BGBl 1953 II S. 116

[13b] BGBl 1955 II S. 502

[14] *Br* Law of Property Act 1925, s. 1

[15] Convention abolishing the Requirement of Legalization for Foreign Public Documents Übereinkommen zur Befreiung ausländischer öffentlicher Urkunden von der Legalisierung – BGBl 1965 II S. 876

European Convention on the Abolition of Legalization of Documents executed by Diplomatic Agents or Consular Officers →European

[16] *Br* Legitimacy Acts 1926, 1959 and 1976; *Scot* Illegitimate Children (Scotland) Act 1930

[17] Matrimonial Causes Act 1950, s. 17

[18] RGBl 1928 II S. 624 in Verbindung mit BGBl 1953 II S. 116; *Br* R. S. C., Ord. 37 rr. 5, 6, 6 A or 6 B

[19] dazu ausführlich Bülow-Böckstiegel, Bd. I, 520. 1

[20] vgl. Rechtshilfeordnung für Zivilsachen (ZRHO) §§ 11ff.

[21] *Am* Model Penal Code, s. 251. 1

[22] Model Penal Code, s. 2.07

[23] Convention on the Liability of Hotel-Keepers concerning the Property of their Guests Übereinkommen (der Mitgliedstaaten des Europarats) über die Haftung der Gastwirte für die von ihren Gästen eingebrachten Sachen – BGBl 1966 II S. 270

[24] z. B. Art. 2 des Europäischen Übereinkommens betr. Auskünfte über ausländisches Recht (→European Convention on Information on Foreign Law)

[25] *Br* Defamation Act 1952, s. 1; „Wireless broadcasts are to be treated as a publication in permanent form"

[26] *Am* vgl. Fraenkel „Das amerikanische Regierungssystem", S. 90: „Stark vereinfachend könnte man sagen, daß das amerikanische Wort 'conservative' auf deutsch 'liberal' und das amerikanische Wort ‚liberal' auf deutsch ‚sozial-demokratisch' (mit einem Bindestrich!) bedeutet."

[27] Customs and Excise Act 1952

[28] Patents Act 1977 s. 46

[29] *Br* Vehicles (Excise) Act 1962

[30] *Br* Sales of Goods Act 1979, ss. 39 et seq.

[31] *Br* Land Charges Act 1972, s. 2

[32] *Br* Administration of Estates Act 1925; Intestates' Estate Act 1952

[33] *Br* durch den Rights of Light Act von 1959 auf 27 Jahre erweitert

[34] *Br* Road Transport Lighting Acts 1957 and 1958

[35] Companies Act 1985, ss. 1, 25

[36] Land Charges Act 1972, s. 2 (1)

[37] z. B. in a grant to A and his heirs sind die Worte „and his heirs" words of limitation

[38] *Br* Limitation Act 1939; Law Reform (Limitation of Actions, etc) Act 1954; Limitation Act 1963 and Limitation Act 1975

[39] Limitation Act 1939, s. 16
[40] cf. Foreign Marriage Act 1947
[40a] BGBl 1983 II S. 64
[41] *Br* vgl. Insolvency Act 1986
[42] preference for holding money instead of securities
[43] BGBl 1983 II S. 359
[44] genauer Titel: The Stock Exchange Daily Official List
[45] Berne Convention for the Protection of Literary and Artistic Works, Art. 2 VIII
[46] *Br* Livestock Industry Act 1937; Livestock (Licensing of Bulls) Act 1931; the Hill Farming and Livestock Rearing Acts 1946–1954
[47] BGBl 1969 II S. 250
[48] Local Government Act 1972, s. 270 (1)
[49] der Local Government Act 1972 schuf eine Neuregelung für England (mit Ausnahme von Greater London, dessen local government 1963 reorganisiert wurde) und Wales. Am 1. April 1974 wurden die county, county borough und county district councils abgeschafft
[50] Local Land Charges Act 1975
[51] *Br* Street Offences Act 1959, s. 1; *Am* Model Penal Code, sec. 250.6
[52] BGBl 1953 II S. 334
[53] The Sunday Observance Act 1677
[54] Appellate Jurisdiction Acts 1876–1947
[55] *Br* Marine Insurance Act 1906, ss. 55 et seq.
[56] *Br* Bills of Exchange Act 1882, ss. 69, 70
[57] UCC, s. 3–804
[58] *Br* Marine Insurance Act 1906, ss. 6 (1), 84 (3) (b)
[59] *Br* Betting, Gaming and Lottery Act 1963 (as amended by the Gaming Act 1968 and the Lotteries Act 1975)
[60] BGBl 1983 II S. 72
[61] *Br* der Mental Health Act 1959 hat die Bestimmungen der Lunacy and Mental Treatment Acts, 1890 to 1930, aufgehoben

Zu M

[1] BGBl 1961 II S. 273, 293; 1963 II S. 1076
[2] BGBl 1970 II S. 293
[3] BGBl 1962 II S. 126; 1966 II S. 1543
[4] BGBl 1970 II S. 293, 418
[5] das internationale Register ist in Genf 32, Chemin des Colombettes, Place des Nations
[6] Kapitel Nr. 29 der Magna Carta, nach dem kein ,,freeman" ohne Gerichtsurteil gefangengehalten oder auf andere Weise bestraft werden darf, ist in gewandelter Form heute noch geltendes Recht
[7] Inheritance (Provision for Family and Dependants) Act 1975
[8] BGBl 1959 II S. 150, 1377; 1971 II S. 105; das UN-Übereinkommen zwischen der Bundesrepublik Deutschland und 45 anderen Staaten (nicht die USA)
[9] Defamation Act 1952, s. 3. Immer stärker setzt sich aber im juristischen Sprachgebrauch injurious falsehood durch
[10] *Am* Investment Company Act 1940
[11] Judicature Act 1925, s. 45 (1)
[12] *Br* R. S. C., Ord. 50, 5. 6
[13] *Am* nach dem MPC (s. 210.3) ist eine Straftat gegen das Leben manslaughter, wenn a) sie leichtfertig (recklessly) begangen ist oder b) eine Tötung, die anderenfalls Mord wäre, unter dem Einfluß ungewöhnlicher geistiger oder seelischer Störung begangen ist (under the influence of extreme mental or emotional disturbance)
[14] Homicide Act 1957, s. 2
[15] BGBl 1977 II S. 169; 1986 II S. 999
[16] BGBl 1977 II S. 165, 180
[16a] Publikation Nr. 324 der Internationalen Handelskammer (in Englisch, Deutsch, Französisch)
[16b] BGBl 1986 II S. 787
[17] RGBl 1928 II S. 23 in Verb. mit BGBl 1953 II S. 116
[17a] BGBl 1982 II S. 486
[18] Lanham Act 1938, s. 4
[18a] Clayton Act, s. 7
[19] Marriage Act 1949, s. 5
[20] Marriage Act 1949, s. 26
[21] Marriage Acts 1949–1983; Marriage (Scotland) Act 1977; Law Reform (Miscellaneous Provisions) (Scotland) Act 1980
[22] *Br* Marriage Act 1949, s. 1; Marriage (Enabling) Act 1960; Marriage (Prohibited Degrees of Relationship) Act 1986
[23] *Br* Matrimonial Causes Act 1973, s. 1
[24] Wortlaut von s. 17; "In any question between husband and wife as to the title to or possession of property either party or any such bank, corporation ... in whose books and stocks, funds or share of either party are standing may apply by summons ... to any judge of the High Court ... or ... to the judge of the Country Court of the district ..."
[25] Judicature Act 1925, s. 6 (2), s. 11 (3), s. 13
[26] *Br* Fraudulent Mediums Act 1951
[27] *Br* Insolvency Act 1986
[28] Statute of Frauds 1677, s. 4; Law of Property Act 1925, s. 40
[29] Companies Act 1985, ss. 2, 3, 18
[30] BGBl 1984 II S. 517
[31] *Am* nach verschiedenen Gesetzen und einzelstaatl. strafrechtl. und sonstigen Definitionen haben diese Wörter verschiedene technische Bedeutung
[32] MPC, sec. 4.01
[33] *Br* Mental Health Act 1983, s. 1
[34] *Br* Factor's Act 1889, s. 1

[35] *Am* Merchant Marine Act 1920 (regelt u. a. Seeschiffahrtsversicherungen); Merchant Marine Act 1936 (regelt die staatliche Subvention der Handelsschiffahrt)
[36] *Br* Merchant Shipping Acts (M.S.A.) 1894–1970; cf. s. 101 of the Merchant Shipping Act 1970
[37] *Br* cf. Law of Property Act 1925, s. 116
[38] BGBl 1965 II S. 1454
[39] *Br* Fair Trading Act 1973, s. 137
[40] cf. UCC, s. 4–104
[41] *Br* Midwives Act 1951
[41a] BGBl 1989 II S. 59
[42] Übereinkommen Nr. 97 der Internationalen Arbeitsorganisation – BGBl 1959 II S. 87, 1960 II S. 2204; 1962 II S. 22
[42a] BGBl 1989 II S. 58
[43] in Großbritannien und USA gebraucht
[44] *Br* Reserve Forces Act 1966. *Am* cf. Art. I s. 8 der Bundesverfassung; der Begriff bezieht sich auf die → National Guard
[45] *Br* Mines and Quarries Act 1954; Mines (Working Facilities and Support) Acts 1923 and 1925; Mines (Working Facilities) Act 1934
[46] BGBl 1976 II S. 202
[47] Ministers of the Crown Act 1975
[48] 2. Rangklasse der →diplomatic agents
[49] 3. Rangklasse der →diplomatic agents; diese Rangklasse ist seit Ende des 2. Weltkrieges verschwunden
[50] Wills Act 1837, ss. 7, 11; Wills (Soldiers and Sailors) Act 1918, s. 1; Family Law Reform Act 1969, s. 36
[51] Land Registration Act 1925, s. 3 (XV)
[52] MPC, s. 220.3
[53] MPC, s. 1.06 (3) (6)
[54] Criminal Law Act 1967, s. 1
[55] MPC, s. 6.08
[56] MPC, s. 1.04 (4)
[57] Insolvency Act 1986, s. 212
[58] *Br* cf. RSC. 1965
[59] *Br* cf. RSC. 1965
[60] *Br* Misrepresentation Act 1967 („Seller Beware")
[61] material misrepresentation ist entwickelt worden, um die Leistungsfreiheit des Versicherers auf die Fälle unrichtiger Angaben über erhebliche Umstände zu beschränken
[61a] BGBl 1955 II S. 701, 706
[62] nach Art. 14 des Wiener Übereinkommens über diplomatische Beziehungen (Vienna Convention on Diplomatic Relations) – BGBl 1964 II S. 958 – sind die Missionschefs in folgende drei Klassen eingeteilt:
a) Botschafter oder Nuntien (die bei Staatsoberhäuptern beglaubigt sind) ambassadors or nuncios (accredited to Heads of State)
b) Gesandte, Minister und Internuntien (die bei Staatsoberhäuptern beglaubigt sind) envoys, ministers and internuncios (accredited to Heads of State)
c) Geschäftsträger (die bei Außenministern beglaubigt sind) chargés d'affaires (accredited to Ministers for Foreign Affairs)
[63] *Br* Mock Auction Act 1961
[64] cf. Federal Constitution, Art. I, sec. 8, clause 5
[65] *Br* Post Office Act 1953, ss. 20–24
[66] BGBl 1986 II S. 334
[67] zuletzt neu benannt und verfaßt im Fair Trading Act 1973
[68] Merchant Shipping Act 1894, s. 39
[69] Bemerkung zu equitable estate
[70] *Br* Merchant Shipping Act 1894, s. 57
[71] Law of Property Act 1925, ss. 51, 52; 85 subs. 1
[72] Merchant Shipping Act 1894, ss. 31–46
[73] Merchant Shipping Act 1894, s. 57
[74] Ship Mortgage Act 1920
[75] cf. Merchant Shipping Act 1894, s. 57
[76] *Br* das mortmain law ist durch den Charities Act 1960, s. 38, abgeschafft
[76a] Ministry of Transport
[77] Agreement concerning the Adoption of Uniform Conditions of Approval and Reciprocal Recognition of Approval for Motor Vehicle Equipment and Parts Übereinkommen über die Annahme einheitlicher Bedingungen für die Genehmigung der Ausrüstungsgegenstände und Teile von Kraftfahrzeugen (Motorfahrzeugen) und über gegenseitige Anerkennung der Genehmigung – BGBl 1965 II S. 858
[78] *Am* vgl. Fußnote zu personal →property
[78a] BGBl 1987 II S. 454; 1989 II S. 47
[79] *Br* Judicature Act 1925, s. 43
[80] cf. Art. 97 des EWG-Vertrages (→EEC)
[81] *Br* die Todesstrafe für Mord wurde endgültig durch den Murder (Abolition of Death Penalty) Act 1965 abgeschafft
[82] *Br* Offences against the Person Act 1861, ss. 1, 11, 14, 15
[83] *Br* Criminal Law Act 1967, s. 6
[84] *Br* Copyright, Design and Patents Act 1988
[85] ICA, s. 4 (3), 5 (a) (1)

Zu N

[1] Bezeichnung für Südwestafrika laut Beschluß der VN-Generalversammlung vom 12. 6. 1968
[1a] BGBl 1959 II S. 334
[2] BGBl 1977 II S. 111; 1975 II S. 2
[3] BNA, sec 1
[4] *Br* "God Save the Queen"; *Am* "the Star-Spangled Banner"

[5] Art. 2vi) des Patent Cooperation Treaty; BGBl 1976 II S. 670
[6] BGBl 1976 II S. 671
[7] Seit dem Social Security Act 1975 ist der Terminus „national insurance“ vom Gesetzgeber aufgegeben. „National insurance“ ist in „supplementary benefits“ umgewandelt, dieses jedoch durch den Ausdruck „income support“ ersetzt
[8] abgeändert und ergänzt durch den Labor-Management Relations Act 1947
[9] mit folgenden Zielen: "to promote the progress of science; to advance the national health, prosperity and welfare; to secure the national defense; and for other purposes"
[10] Export Administration Act 1979, s. 5
[11] National Service Act 1948
[12] National Trust Acts 1907 to 1953
[13] British Nationality Act (BNA), 1981
[14] INA, s. 349
[15] *Br* BNA 1948, sec. 10; *Am* INA Title III
[16] BGBl 1976 II S. 485
[17] *Br* Nationality Act 1948, s. 10 (1)
[18] *Am* INA, s. 311
[29] INA, s. 334
[20] *Am* MPC, s. 202 (2) d
[21] vgl. Kegel ,,IPR“[4], S. 307
[22] vgl. Ehrenzweig ,,Festschrift für Rabel“ I S. 682
[23] vgl. z.B. §§ 138, 9 (3), 218 (2) StGB
[24] MPC, s. 210.4
[25] *Br* Bills of Exchange Act 1882, ss. 31, 32; *Am* Uniform Commercial Code, s. 3–102
[26] Bills of Exchange Act 1882, s. 8 (1)
[27] UCC, s. 3–805
[28] UCC, s. 3–805
[29] to negotiate a bill of exchange (promissory note etc) = to transfer it for value by delivery (if payable to bearer) or endorsement (if payable to order); *Br* BEA 1882, Art. 31ff.; *Am* UCC, s. 3–202
[30] New Towns Act 1965, as amended by the Statutory Corporations (Financial Provisions) Act 1974 and the New Towns Act 1975
[31] *Br* R.S.C. Ord. 80, r. 2
[32] BGBl 1970 II S. 434. Zu den Ländern, die das Abkommen unterzeichneten, gehören auch Großbritannien und Nordirland und die Bundesrepublik Deutschland; BGBl 1981 II S. 358
[33] *Am* "No title of nobility shall be granted by the United States" (Art. I, section 9 (8) der Constitution of the United States)
[34] *Br* Control of Pollution Act 1974, Part III
[35] BGBl 1952 II S. 2; 1957 II S. 39; 1960 II S. 475; 1973 II S. 115
[36] *Br* Representation of the People Act 1948, and Local Government Act 1933
[37] *Br* nach s. 20 (5) des Exchange Control Act 1947, ist der Inhaber von Wertpapieren dann ein nominee, wenn er die in dem Wertpapier verbrieften Rechte nur nach den Weisungen e-r anderen Person ausüben darf.

Über Abweichungen des nominee nordamerikanischer Prägung von dem nominee des engl. Gesellschaftsrechts vgl. R. Serick ,,Die Rechtsfigur des nominee im anglo-amerikanischen Gesellschaftsrecht“ in ,,Vom Deutschen zum Europäischen Recht“ Bd. I S. 417
[38] *Br* Matrimonial Causes Act 1973, s. 48
[39] INA, cypher 15, s. 101
[40] *Br* R.S.C. Ord. 15, r. 6
[41] Begriff des Außenwirtschaftsgesetzes von 1961
[42] Kap. XI der Satzung der Vereinten Nationen – BGBl 1973 II S. 479
[43] BGBl 1955 II S. 289
[44] Art. 5 des Vertrages bestimmt, daß ein bewaffneter Angriff gegen einen od. mehrere Mitgliedstaaten als ein Angriff gegen alle angesehen wird
[45] BEA 1882, Art. 68 (4)
[46] The Solicitors, Public Notaries, etc Act, 1949
[47] *Br* BEA 1882, s. 85 (2)
[48] BEA 1882, s. 51
[49] *Br* BEA 1882, s. 48ff.; *Am* UCC, ss. 3–510
[49a] UCC § 3–414 (1)
[50] *Br* R.S.C. Ord. 8, r. 2
[51] Restrictive Practices Court Rules, s. 4
[52] *Br* R.S.C. Ord. 27, r. 5
[53] Consumer Credit Act 1974, ss. 87–89
[54] *Br* Law of Property Act 1925, s. 198
[54a] Employment Protection (Consolidation) Act 1978
[55] *Br* Employment Protection (Consolidation) Act 1978, s. 49
[56] vgl. ,,Internationale Atomhaftungskonventionen“. Textsammlung Institut für Völkerrecht der Universität Göttingen 1964
[57] BGBl 1959 II S. 586, 989
[58] BGBl 1965 II S. 1334
[59] vgl. ,,Internationale Atomhaftungskonventionen“. Textsammlung Institut für Völkerrecht der Universität Göttingen, 1964
[60] BGBl 1964 II S. 907; 1965 II S. 124, 855
[61] BGBl 1974 II S. 785
[62] BGBl 1972 II S. 326
[63] *Br* Nullity of Marriage Act 1971
[64] *Br* Matrimonial Causes Act 1973, ss. 11–16; Nullity of Marriage Act 1971

Zu O

[1] *Br* Oaths Act 1888, 1909
[2] Perjury Act 1911, s. 15
[3] Art. 39 des Statuts des Internationalen Gerichtshofs
[4] *Am* Bundesverfassung, Art. I, s. 10
[5] *Br* Obscene Publications Act 1959 (as amended by the Obscene Publications Act 1964 and the Criminal Justice Act 1967, s. 25)
[6] Post Office Act 1953, s. 11
[7] *Am* MPC, s. 251.4
[8] Police Act 1964, s. 51
[9] MPC, Art. 242
[10] *Am* MPC, Art. 250.7
[11] *Br* Theft Act 1968, s. 16
[12] *Br* Theft Act 1968, s. 15
[13] *Br* Occupiers' Liability Act 1984
[13a] BGBl 1978 II S. 909
[14] Licensing Act 1964
[15] MPC, Art. 250 (riot, disorderly conduct etc)
[16] MPC, s. 1.05
[17] z. B. blood boiler, fell monger, soap boiler, rag and bone dealer; cf. Public Health (London) Act 1936
[18] Defamation Act 1952, s. 4
[19] *Br* Companies Act 1948, s. 45
[20] *Am* MPC, Art. 243
[21] die Unterscheidung zwischen Beamten und Angestellten fehlt heutzutage weitgehend
[21a] Charities Act 1960, s. 3
[22] Bankruptcy Act 1914, ss. 70 to 75
[23] *Br* Official Secrets Acts 1911, 1920, 1939
[24] Judicature Act 1925, s. 129
[25] Abkommen zwischen der Bundesrepublik Deutschland und den Vereinigten Staaten von Amerika über Offshore-Beschaffungen – BGBl 1956 II S. 2080
[26] *Br* Insolvency Act 1986, ss. 178, 315
[27] Law of Property Act 1925 ss. 44, 45; Law of Property Act 1969, s. 23
[28] MPC, s. 223.9
[29] IRC s. 165, 172
[30] Transport Act 1968
[31] *Br* Patents Act 1977
[32] *Am* Lanham Act, s. 13
[33] MPC, s. 243.1
[34] Land Charges Act 1972, ss. 2 (4), 4 (6)
[35] BGBl 1961 II S. 1151, 1663; BGBl 1962 II S. 47, 810; 1965 II S. 829
[36] Organización de los Estados Americanos (OEA)
[37] Organización de los Estados Centro-Americanos (ODECA)
[38] vgl. Art. 1 (4) des Deutsch-Britischen Abkommens über die gegenseitige Anerkennung und Vollstreckung von gerichtl. Entscheidungen in Zivil- und Handelssachen – BGBl 1961 II S. 302
[39] R.S.C. Ord. 7 and 28
[40] *Br* Partnership Act 1890, s. 14 (1); *Am* UPA, s. 16
[40a] BGBl 1971 II S. 238
[40b] BGBl 1969 II S. 1969
[41] INA, s. 101 (29)
[42] IRC, s. 904
[43] *Br* Housing Act 1957, s. 77 (offence on the part of the occupier as well as the landlord)
[44] Bills of Exchange Act 1882, s. 36 (3)
[45] Land Registration Act 1925, s. 3 (XVI)
[46] Companies Act 1985, s. 744
[47] Finance Act 1957, Part IV
[48] *Br* Insolvency Act 1986, s. 283
[49] *Br* Larceny Act 1861, s. 26
[50] BGBl 1988 II S. 1015
[51] BGBl 1988 II S. 402ff.

Zu P

[1] cf. European Convention on Customs Treatment of Pallets Used in International Transport Europäisches Übereinkommen über die Zollbehandlung von Paletten, die im internationalen Verkehr verwendet werden BGBl 1964 II S. 407
[1a] BGBl 1988 II S. 299
[2] *Br* durch die Krone (auf Empfehlung des Innenministers auf Grund des an diesen gerichteten Gnadengesuchs); *Am (in Bundessachen)* durch den Präsidenten (Art. II, s. 2 subd. 1 der Bundesverfassung); *(einzelstaatl.)* durch den Governor
[2a] BGBl 1970 II S. 293, 391
[3] *Br* Sex Discrimination Act 1975
[4] Parliamentary Commissioner Act 1967
[5] Representation of the People Acts 1948 and 1949
[6] Local Government Act 1953, s. 53
[6a] Immigration Nationality Act, s. 212
[7] Criminal Justice Act 1967, ss. 59–64; 1972 sec. 35
[8] *Am* M.P.C., s. 305.6
[9] *Am* M.P.C., s. 402
[10] *Am* M.P.C., s. 404.3 (2)
[11] *Am* M.P.C., s. 305.1
[12] *Am* M.P.C., s. 305.15
[13] *Br* R.S.C., Ord. 18, r. 12
[14] *Br* Law of Property Act 1925, s. 28 (3)
[15] *Br* Partnership Act 1890, s. 14 (1); *Am* UPA, s. 16
[16] *Br* Partnership Act 1890; *Am* Uniform Partnership Act 1914 (UPA) *(Mustergesetzentwurf, der von vielen Einzelstaaten zum Gesetz erhoben wurde); Scot* Partnership Act 1980

[17] *Br* Partnership Act 1890, s. 32 (c)
[18] *Br* Partnership Act 1890, ss. 32–35
[19] *Br* Limited Partnership Act (L.P. Act) 1907; *Am* Uniform Limited Partnership Act (ULPA) 1916 *(Mustergesetzentwurf, der von vielen Staaten zum Gesetz erhoben wurde)*
[20] *Br* Law of Property Act 1925, s. 38
[21] *Br* die wichtigsten (im Unterhaus vertretenen) politischen Parteien sind: Conservative Party, Labour Party, Liberal Party; *Am* die wichtigsten (im Kongreß vertretenen) politischen Parteien sind: Republican Party, Democratic Party
[22] Merchant Shipping Act 1894, s. 341; Merchant Shipping Act 1906, s. 23
[23] *Br* Criminal Justice Act 1925, s. 36
[24] *Br* Patents Act 1949, ss. 88, 89
[25] BGBl 1975 II S. 284
[26] BGBl 1976 II S. 649, 664; 1984 II S. 800, 976; 1986 I S. 548
[27] BGBl 1976 II S. 658
[28] Anschrift: 25, Southampton Buildings, London W.C. 2
[29] Anschrift: Commissioner of Patents, Washington 25, D.C.
[30] *Am* bei dem Commissioner of Patents, Washington D.C. (der Antrag muß umfassen: petition, specification and claims, oath, drawing and a filing fee)
[30a] BGBl 1976 II S. 670
[30b] Patent Act 1977, S. 25
[31] Uniform Act on Blood Tests to Determine Paternity
[32] Mental Health Act 1983 s. 145
[33] Immigration Act 1971, s. 2
[33a] jetzt: Prozeßkostenhilfe
[34] *Br* Pawnbrokers' Act 1872, s. 5
[35] *Br* BEA Art. 65
[36] *Br* BEA Art. 68
[37] *Br* BEA Art. 59; Cheques Act 1957, Art. 1
[38] UCC, ss. 4–105
[38a] Art. 39 der UN-Charta
[39] Peers werden immer durch letters patent ernannt
[40] Peerage Act 1963
[41] Life Peerage Act 1958
[42] durch Criminal Justice Act 1948, s. 1 abgeschafft
[43] IRC, ss. 532, 543
[44] nach dem National Insurance Act 1946, ss. 20, 21
[44a] UCC §§ 9–302; *Br* Social Security Pensions Act 1975
[45] International Convention for the Protection of Performers, Producers of Phonograms and Broadcasting Organisations – BGBl 1965 II S. 1244
[46] *Br* Marine Insurance Act 1906, Sched. I, r. 7
[47] *Br* Limitation Act 1980
[48] Hemmung der Verjährung durch Minderjährigkeit od. *Br* Geisteskrankheit, *Am* Abwesenheit des Beklagten od. Angeklagten
[49] *Br* Perjury Act 1911; *Am* MPC, s. 241.1
[50] *Br* R.S.C., Ord. 39 r. 15; Ord. 77, r. 14
[51] *Br* The Perpetuities and Accumulations Act 1964
[52] MPC, Art. 303 (1) (c)
[53] MPC, Art. 210
[54] *Br* Administration of Estates Act 1925, s. 55
[55] *Br* Administration of Estates Act 1925, s. 55 (I) (xi); *Am* in den Einzelstaaten verschieden gesetzlich geregelt. Es gibt häufig Ausnahmen (z. B. keine Gläubiger, kleiner Nachlaß), in denen der Zwischenberechtigte kraft Gesetzes wegfällt.
[56] die ganze Erbschaft bildet eine Treuhand, wobei der personal representative Treuhänder, die Erben und Vermächtnisnehmer die Begünstigten und die Erbmasse das Treugut ist
[57] Administration of Estates Act 1925, s. 1 (3)
[58] *Br* False Personation Act 1874; Representation of the People Act 1949, ss. 47, 146; Theft Act 1968
[59] *Br* Insolvency Act 1986, ss. 267ff.
[60] Justices of the Peace Act 1949, s. 44 (1)
[61] der Philippiner heißt Filipino
[62] International Convention for the Protection of Performers, Producers of Phonograms and Broadcasting Organisations – BGBl 1965 II S. 1244; für den Schutz von Tonträgern vgl. auch Abkommen über die Errichtung einer Weltorganisation für geistiges Eigentum (World Intellectual Property Organization), Art. 2 VIII
[63] BGBl 1973 II S. 1670
[64] BGBl 1956 II S. 950, 961
[65] *Br* Trade Union and Labour Relations Act 1974, s. 15
[66] cf. Additional Regulation with respect to the sanitary control of pilgrim traffic – BGBl 1965 II S. 420
[67] *Br* Pilotage Act 1913
[68] *Br* Pipe-Lines Act 1952
[68a] US Bankruptcy Code, Chapter 11
[69] die Genehmigung muß eingeholt werden von der Local Planning Authority nach den Bestimmungen des Town and Country Planning Act 1971, as amended by the Town and Country Planning (Amendment) Act and the Local Government Act 1972, s. 182, Sched. 16
[69a] BGBl 1980 II S. 1362
[70] die pleas, die früher in den superior courts verwandt wurden, sind durch statement of defence ersetzt
[71] *Br* Consumer Credit Act 1974, ss. 114–122, 189
[72] *Br* Consumer Credit Act 1974, s. 115
[73] *Br* Night Poaching Acts 1828 and 1844; Poaching Prevention Act 1862; Game Laws (Amendment) Act 1960, s. 3
[74] *Br* Firearms Act 1968, s. 5
[75] *Br* Police Act 1964 (as amended); Police Act 1969; Local Government Act 1972, ss. 107, 196; Police Act 1976

[76] Criminal Justice Act 1948, s. 22

[77] eine Definition der public policy ist von mehreren amerikanischen Gerichten als unmöglich bezeichnet worden; sie ist abhängig von den sich wandelnden sittlichen und moralischen Anschauungen des (vernünftigen) Bürgers. Näheres bei Simitis ,,Gute Sitten und ordre public", 1960, S. 117 *(Br)* und S. 153 *(Am)*

[78] vgl. Art. 6 EGBGB

[79] *Br* der Marine Insurance Act 1906, s. 4 erklärt eine solche Police für nichtig

[80] *Br* Marine Insurance Act 1906, s. 25

[81] *Br* Marine Insurance Act 1906, ss. 27, 28

[82] MPC, s. 240.7

[83] *Br* Trade Union Act 1913, s. 3

[84] das englische und amerikanische Strafrecht kennen keine politischen Straftaten im Sinne des deutschen Rechts. Im Auslieferungsverfahren steht dem politischen Verbrecher ein Asylrecht gegenüber dem Auslieferungsverlangen zu (*Br* Extradition Act 1870, s. 3)

[85] *Br* Ballot Act 1872; Representation of the People Act 1949, s. 53

[86] BGBl 1985 II S. 596

[87] *Br* Clean Air Act 1956

[87a] *Br* Rivers (Prevention of Pollution) Act 1951

[87b] BGBl 1982 II S. 4; 1984 II S. 231; 1988 II S. 976

[88] BGBl 1975 II S. 305; 1980 II S. 724; 1988 II S. 707, 708

[89] BGBl 1975 II S. 320; 1988 II S. 840

[90] BGBl 1975 II S. 139

[91] BGBl 1964 II S. 751; 1965 II S. 381; 1978 II S. 1495; 1979 II S. 62

[92] *Am* MPC, s. 230.1 (2)

[93] BGBl 1982 II S. 984

[94] *Br* Population (Statistics) Act 1938

[95] BGBl 1982 II S. 586; 1983 II S. 693; 1989 II S. 411

[96] *Br* Copyright Act 1956, s. 4

[97] *Br* Limitation Act 1980, ss. 15ff.; Land Registration Act 1925, s. 4 (es kann in e-m→ Land Registry eingetragen werden)

[98] Post Office Act 1981

[99] *Br* Bills of Exchange Act 1882, s. 13 (2)

[100] *Br* Nationality Act 1948, s. 24

[101] vgl. Berner Übereinkunft zum Schutz von Werken der Literatur und Kunst (Berne →Convention) – BGBl 1965 II S. 1219; Art. 7 [5]; *Br* Copyright Act 1956, s. 2

[102] vgl. Constitution of the United States, Art. I, s. 8 (7)

[103] *Br* (civil trials) cf. R.S.C. 1883, Ord. 36, rr. 34; (criminal trials) cf. Criminal Procedure Act 1851, s. 27

[104] *Br* Powers of Attorney Act 1971

[105] Law of Property Act, ss. 101–106

[106] vgl. Internationale Gesundheitsvorschriften – BGBl 1971 II S. 869, 884, 1975 II S. 459

[107] *Br* Land Charges Act 1925, s. 10

[108] BGBl 1982 II S. 990

[109] Insolvency Act 1986, s. 386, Sched. 6

[110] Companies Act 1985, Sched. 4, Part I, s. A Rule 3 (2)

[111] R.S.C. Ord. 33/3; Ord. 18/11/2

[112] Rent Act 1968, ss. 85–92

[113] Administration of Justice (Miscellaneous Provisions) Acts 1938

[114] MPC, s. 6.02 (2)

[115] *Br* Public Order Act 1936, s. 3

[116] Bundesverfassung, Art. II s. 1–4

[117] *Am* Bundesverfassung, Art. II s. 1.12th Amendment, 22nd Amendment

[118] *Am* Bundesverfassung, 22nd Amendment

[118a] vgl. Art. 6 II der Menschenrechtskonvention

[119] *Br* nach Law of Property Act 1925, s. 184, wird vermutet, daß dann, wenn mehrere Personen (z. B. durch ein Schiffsunglück) umgekommen sind, der jüngste zuletzt starb. Hinsichtlich der Erbschaftssteuer wird vermutet, daß sie gleichzeitig gestorben sind (Finance Act 1958, s. 29)

[120] Fair Credit Reporting Act, § 619

[121] das übergangene Kind oder Enkelkind erhält das Erbteil, das es bekommen hätte, wenn der Erblasser ohne Hinterlassung e-s Testaments gestorben wäre

[122] abgeschafft durch Powers of Criminal Courts Act 1973, s. 28, 29 und ersetzt durch extended term of imprisonment (→*term 2.*)

[123] *Am (AntitrustR)* Diskriminierungsverbot durch section 2 des Clayton Act (abgeändert durch den Robinson-Patman Act)

[124] *Br* muß nach dem Restrictive Trade Practices Act 1956 in der Regel registriert werden

[125] 42 U.S.C., § 415a

[126] *Br* Criminal Law Act 1967, s. 1

[127] Law of Property (Amendment) Act 1926, s. 4

[128] *Am* MPC, s. 250.12

[129] War Damage Act 1943

[130] Fifth Amendment of the Federal Constitution

[130a] Bundesverfassung, Art IV, s. 2, Art. XIV, sec. 1

[130b] BGBl 1981 II S. 943

[131] *Br* z. B. Defamation Act 1952, s. 7

[132] MPC, s. 210 (6) (2)

[133] Lotteries and Amendments Act 1976, s. 14

[134] *Br* Judicature Act 1925, s. 27 (1)

[135] *Br* Powers of Criminal Courts Act 1973, ss. 2, 12, 13; *Am* MPC, Art. 301

[136] *Br* Powers of Criminal Courts Act 1973, s. 11

[137] *Br* enthalten in den Rules and Orders of the Supreme Court

[138] *Br* der process des Supreme Court of Justice zur Eröffnung e-s Verfahrens besteht aus writs, originating summonses, motions und petitions (Ord. 5)

[139] *Br* Bills of Exchange Act 1882, ss. 25, 26

[140] *Br* Sexual Offences Act 1956, ss. 22, 23
[141] *Am* Labor Management Relations Act, s. 2 (12)
[142] R. S. C., Ord. 59; Courts Act 1971, s. 10 (5)
[143] das Verbot bestand in USA von 1917–1933 (der 18. Zusatzartikel [amendment] zur Bundesverfassung, aufgehoben durch den 21. Zusatzartikel [amendment], hatte die gesetzl. Grundlage geschaffen)
[143a] BGBl 1974 II S. 785
[144] *Br* BEA 1882, s. 83 (1)
[145] *Am* Uniform Law on the International Sale of Goods, Art. 11
[146] MPC, s. 223–2 (2)
[147] World Intellectual Property Organization, Art. 2 VIII
[148] MPC, s. 220
[149] *Am* die Kennzeichnung als real oder personal property (und als immovables od. movables) ist im einzelstaatl. Recht der USA nicht einheitlich und oft insbes. nach ihrem Zweck (ErbR, zwischenstaatl. bzw. internationales Kollisionsrecht) verschieden.
[150] cf. R. S. C., Ord. 51, r. 1 A
[151] *Br* Registered Designs Act 1949, s. 2
[152] *Br* Trade Marks Act 1938, s. 1
[153] Trade Marks Act 1938, s. 63
[154] *Br* Companies Act 1985, ss. 56–71, 744; *Am* Securities Act 1933
[155] *Br* Sexual Offences Act 1956, s. 22, ss. 30–32; Street Offences Act 1959, ss. 1, 4; *Am* MPC, s. 251.2
[156] Adoption Act 1958, s. 37, und neuestens Adoption Act 1976
[157] the British Protectorates, Protected States and Protected Persons Orders in Council von 1949–1953 und the British Nationality Act 1948, s. 3 unterscheiden zwischen Protectorates (Protektorate) and Protected States (geschützte Staaten)
[158] *Br* Employment Protection Consolidation Act 1978
[159] *Am* Bundesverfassung, 14. Zusatzartikel (amendment)
[160] Trustee Act 1925, s. 33
[161] in England ist protest als Voraussetzung für den Regreß seit 1882 abgeschafft. Außerhalb Englands ist jedoch protest im allgemeinen notwendig, um Rückgriff nehmen zu können
[162] *Br* BEA, 1882, ss 21, 51. – *Am* "foreign" bedeutet hier out-of-state, nicht out-of the country
[163] BEA 1882, s. 55 (5)
[164] Homicide Act 1957, s. 3
[165] *Am* MPC, s. 250.6
[166] *Br* Companies Act 1985, s. 372
[167] *Br* für copyright in pseudonymous works s. Copyright Act 1956, ss. 11, 20 (6) Sched. II
[168] Übereinkommen über psychotrope Stoffe (Convention on psychotropic substances) – BGBl 1976 II S. 1478
[169] *Br* Public Health Acts 1875 to 1925, 1936, 1961
[170] *Am* MPC, s. 251
[171] American Institute of Public Opinion (AIPO), gegründet *(von Gallup)* 1935
[172] *Br* Public Order Acts 1936, 1963
[173] MPC, Art. 250
[174] Störnholm in ,,Das Veröffentlichungsrecht des Urhebers" (S. 14), schlägt als Übersetzung für "publication" vor: Verbreitung (wenn es sich um die Rechte des Urhebers handelt), Erscheinen (wenn publication als Ausgangspunkt für Rechtsfolgen [Zitatrecht etc] angewendet wird)
[175] Land Charges Act 1972, s. 2
[176] der technische Begriff im Strafprozeß ist to sentence
[176a] Universal Declaration of Human Rights, Art. 5
[176b] UCC §§ 9–302
[177] *Br* nach dem Law of Property Act 1925, s. 205 (i) (xxi) bedeutet purchaser = a purchaser in good faith for valuable consideration and includes a lessee, mortgagee, etc
[178] *Br* Affiliation Proceedings Act 1957
[179] *Br* Fair Trading Act 1973, ss. 118–123

Zu Q

[1] *Br* BEA 1882, s. 19
[2] *Br* BEA 1882, ss. 16 (1) and 35
[3] *Br* nach dem Land Registration Act 1925, s. 7 kann ein qualified title in das Grundbuch eingetragen werden
[4] *Br* jetzt: revenue support grant
[5] über den Quality Stabilization Bill vgl. WuW 1964 S. 394
[6] BGBl 1971 II S. 869
[7] *Br* Mines and Quarries Act 1954, s. 180
[8] cf. WuW 6 (1965) S. 467

Zu R

[1] *Br* Race Relations Act 1976
[1a] BGBl 1975 II S. 274
[1b] BGBl 1970 II S. 219
[2] *Br* Sexual Offences Act 1956, s. 1; *Am* MPC, s. 213.1
[3] ab 1. 4. 1990 ersetzt durch community charge capping
[4] ab 1. 4. 1990 ist dieser Begriff ersetzt durch revenue support grant
[5] General Rate Act 1967, s. 19
[6] strafbar nach dem Conspiracy and Protection of Property Act 1875, s. 7
[7] *Am* MPC, s. 1.13 (16)
[8] zur Ausführung der →European Convention of Information on Foreign Law
[9] MPC, s. 223.6
[10] *Br* Law of Property Act 1925, s. 101
[11] Mental Health Act 1959, s. 105
[12] Art. II, s. 2 (3) der Bundesverfassung
[13] MPC, s. 211.2
[14] *Am* MPC, s. 2. 02 (2) (c)
[15] Companies Act 1985, ss. 425–427, 582
[16] Privacy Act 1974, s. 3a (4)
[17] Courts Act 1971, s. 21
[18] Companies Act 1985, ss. 159 et seq.
[19] Companies Act 1985, ss. 135–141
[20] Employment Protection (Consolidation) Act 1978, ss. 81 et seq.
[21] *Br* BEA 1882, s. 57 (2)
[22] *Br* BEA 1882, s. 15
[23] BGBl 1959 II S. 934
[24] Agreement relating to Refugee Seamen Vereinbarung über Flüchtlingsseeleute – BGBl 1961 II S. 829
[25] BGBl 1961 II S. 140; 1966 II S. 1432
[26] von 1937 und 1943
[27] Companies Act 1985, ss. 396 (1) f, 410 (4) e
[28] Companies Act 1985, s. 325
[29] Companies Act 1985, ss. 191 (7), 352, 353, 361
[30] Die Rechtsverordnungen des Bundes von bleibender Bedeutung werden außerdem in den Code of Federal Regulations aufgenommen
[31] Trade Marks Act 1938, s. 28.
[32] Companies Act 1985, ss. 191 (7), 352, 353
[33] *Br* Aliens Order 1953
[34] *Br* Vehicles (Excise) Act 1962
[35] *Br* Merchant Shipping Act 1894, s. 2
[36] Consumer Credit Act 1974, s. 189
[37] *Br* Rehabilitation Act 1974
[38] MPC, s. 408
[38a] Customs Excise Management Act 1971
[39] Matrimonial Causes Act 1973, Part II
[40] Income and Corporation Taxes Act 1970, ss. 5–27, as amended
[41] *Am* Bundesverfassung, 1. Zusatzartikel
[42] *Br* seit 1925 können remainders nur als equitable interest geschaffen werden und berühren deshalb den Käufer des legal estate nicht (Law of Property Act 1925, s. 1 [1], [3]; Sched. I, Part I)
[43] ersetzt durch →community home – Children and Young Persons Act 1969, ss. 35–50, Sched. 6
[44] 1) durch die verletzte Partei (defen|ce[~se], recaption, distress, entry, abatement and seizure); 2) kraft Gesetzes (im Falle e-s →retainer und →remitter); 3) durch Vertrag (accord and satisfaction, arbitration)
[45] Judicature Act 1925, ss. 122, 135
[46] *Br* Art. 21 of the Bills of Exchange Act 1882
[47] *Br* County Courts Act 1959, ss. 43, 44
[48] 28 U. S. C. A., §§ 71–83
[49] *Br* von 1965 und 1974, abgeändert durch Rent Act 1977
[50] Rentcharges Act verbietet (mit einigen Ausnahmen) neue rentcharges und enthält Bestimmungen für die allmähliche Abschaffung der bestehenden rentcharges
[51] U. S. Bankruptcy Code Chapter 11, 11 U. S. C. §§ 1101–1174
[52] *Br* County Courts Act 1959, Part IV
[53] N. E. Northeastern, Atl. Atlantic, So. Southern, S. E. Southeastern, S. W. South Western, N. W. Northwestern, Pac. Pacific; F. Supp. Federal Supplement; Fed. Federal; S. C. Supreme Court
[54] *Br* Administration of Estates Act 1925, s. 47
[55] *Am* Bundesverfassung Art. IV, s. 4
[56] *Br* Army Act 1955, ss. 154, 165
[57] das Gesetz ersetzt ein gleichnamiges Gesetz von 1964
[58] *Br* Misrepresentation Act 1967
[59] BGBl 1971 II S. 238
[60] *Br* Sale of Goods Act 1893, s. 19
[61] Companies Act 1948, s. 60
[62] *Br* Companies Act 1948, Sched. VIII, para 27
[63] Bundesverfassung Art. I, s. 9, und Amendments I–XI
[64] BGBl 1963 II S. 247
[65] Begriff des Außenwirtschaftsgesetzes von 1961 (natürliche Person mit Wohnsitz im Wirtschaftsgebiet)
[66] *Br* Administration of Estates Act 1925, s. 33 (4)
[67] Police Act 1964, s. 51
[68] Companies Act 1985, s. 378
[69] *Am* MPC, Art. 4
[70] Homicide Act 1957, s. 2
[71] die bisher erschienenen Bände umfassen: contracts, agency, torts, conflict of laws, trusts, property, judgments, restitution, security
[72] *Br* Carriage of Goods by Sea Act 1924, Sched. Art. IV, 2
[73] "every contract, combination in the form

of trust or otherwise, or conspiracy, in restraint of trade or commerce among the several States, or with foreign nations"
[74] MPC, s. 212.2
[75] Land Registration Act 1925, s. 58
[76] das Gesetz ersetzt die gleichnamigen Gesetze von 1956 und 1968
[77] *Br* right of retainer abgeschafft durch Administration of Estates Act 1971, s. 10
[78] ICR s. 37
[79] Social Security Act 1975, s. 39
[80] Companies Act 1985, ss. 363–365 und Schedule 15
[81] IRC, ss. 1501 et seq.
[82] *Br* Income Tax Act 1952, s. 18
[83a] ab 1. 4. 1990 anstelle von rate support grant
[84] Law of Property Act 1925, s. 149 (3)
[84a] Art. 61 des Statuts des Internationalen Gerichtshofs – BGBl 1973 II S. 505
[84b] z. B. Art. 61 of the Statute of the International Court of Justice
[85] *Br* R. S. C. Order 76, s. 2 (3)
[86] *Br* Wills Act 1837, ss. 19, 20
[87] *Br* R. S. C. Ord. 15, r. 16
[88] *Br* Law of Property Act 1925, s. 4 (3)
[89] es sei denn, daß dieser sie gegen Entgelt und ohne Kenntnis von der Unzulässigkeit (for valuable consideration without notice) erworben hat
[90] Life Peerages Act 1958
[91] *Am* MPC, Art. 250.1
[92] § 465 IRC
[93] BGBl 1962 II S. 842
[93a] BGBl 1977 II S. 811
[94] *Br* Larceny Act 1916, s. 23; *Am* MPC, s. 222.1
[94a] die Bezeichnung beruht auf der Entscheidung Aluminium Industrie Vaasen v. Romalpa Aluminium Ltd. (1976)
[94b] BGBl 1981 II S. 482
[95] Agriculture Act 1947, s. 11; Agriculture Act 1955, s. 4
[96] Gültig seit 1. 1. 1988. Publikation Nr. 447 der Internationalen Handelskammer (in Englisch und Deutsch)

Zu S

[1] International Convention for the Safety of Life at Sea Internationales Übereinkommen zum Schutz des menschl. Lebens auf See (von 1960) – BGBl 1965 II S. 480; *Br* Merchant Shipping (Safety Convention) Act 1948
[2] das Gesetz ist in folgende Teile gegliedert:
I. Contracts to which Act applies (Verträge, auf die das Gesetz Anwendung findet)
II. Formation of a Contract (Vertragsabschluß)
III. Effects of the Contract (Vertragswirkungen)
IV. Performance of the Contract (Vertragserfüllung)
V. Rights of Unpaid Seller against the Goods (Rechte des unbezahlten Verkäufers bezüglich der Güter)
VI. Actions for Breach of the Contract (Klagen wegen Vertragsbruches)
VII. Supplementary (Ergänzungsbestimmungen)
[3] *Br* Sale of Goods Act 1979, s. 2
[4] *Br* the Law of Wreck and Salvage wird gemäß dem Civil Aviation Act 1949, s. 51 auch für Flugzeuge angewandt
[5] *Br* zuständig sind der Admiralty Court of the Queen's Bench Division und bestimmte County Courts
[6] *Br* Bills of Exchange Act 1882, s. 16
[7] Agreement Establishing Interim Arrangements for a Global Commercial Communications Satellite System Übereinkommen zur vorläufigen Regelung für ein weltweites kommerzielles Satelliten-Fernmeldesystem – BGBl 1965 II S. 1499
[8] Companies Act 1985, s. 403
[9] *Br* R. S. C., Ord. 18, r. 19
[10] Income and Corporation Taxes Act 1970
[11] Insolvency Act 1986, ss. 1, 253
[12] vgl. das Abkommen über die Errichtung einer Weltorganisation für geistiges Eigentum (→ WIPO), Art. 2 VIII
[13] abgeschafft durch den Crown Proceedings Act 1947
[14] BGBl 1965 II S. 742
[15] Companies Act 1985, ss. 36–41
[16] *Br* Land Charges Act 1972 s. 3
[17] Art. 15 des Patentzusammenarbeitsvertrages
[18] Art. 16 des Patentzusammenarbeitsvertrages – BGBl 1976 II S. 768
[19] der Begriff securities bedeutet in erster Linie shares, stocks und bonds. Wird er im Sinne von Sicherheit *(cf. security interest)* gebraucht, so umfaßt er auch diejenigen Rechte und Papiere, die als Sicherheit dienen können, etwa mortgages, bills of exchange, bills of lading
[20] Securities Acts Amendments 1964
[21] *Br* R. S. C., Ord. 23; Ord. 58, r. 9
[22] Kapitel V der Charter der Vereinten Nationen – BGBl 1973 II S. 449
[23] vgl. dazu Eckstein, Das englische Konkursrecht 1935, S. 170
[24] BGBl 1972 II S. 1506
[25] *Br* Offences against the Person Act 1861
[26] Art. 51 Satzung der Vereinten Nationen

[27] MPC, s. 3.04

[28] Sie regulieren nach dem Financial Services Act das Verhältnis zwischen den im Investitions- und Anlagengeschäft tätigen Firmen und ihren Kunden

[29] *Br* Sale of Goods Act 1979, s. 2 (5)

[30] Art. I, s. 3; Art. XVII der Bundesverfassung; cf. Fraenkel „Das amerikanische Regierungssystem", S. 129ff.

[31] *Br* Criminal Justice Act 1967

[32] *Br* Matrimonial Causes Act 1973, s. 17

[33] R. S. C. Ord. 45, r. 1; Ord. 46, r. 5

[34] *Br* civil servants and local government officers; *Am* (MPC s. 240.0 [7]): public servant means any officer or employee of government, including legislators and judges and any person participating as juror, advisor, consultant or otherwise in performing a governmental function

[35] Representation of the People Act 1949, ss. 12–15, 23–25

[36] R. S. C., Ord. 65, r. 5

[37] R. S. C., Ord. 65, r. 4

[38] im Rechtsverkehr zwischen Großbritannien und Nordirland und der Bundesrepublik Deutschland geregelt in Art. 2 des Deutsch-Brit. Abkommens über den Rechtsverkehr von 1928 (RGBl 1928 II S. 624; BGBl 1953 II S. 116)

[39] R. S. C., Ord. 10, r. 1

[40] R. S. C., Ord. 65, r. 4

[41] vgl. Strupp-Schlochauer, Bd. 3, S. 262

[42] *Br* BEA 1882, s. 71

[43] set-off im streng juristischen Sinne (legal set-off) ist ein Rechtsinstitut des Prozeßrechts, nicht – wie in Deutschland – des materiellen Rechts

[44] *Br* R. S. C. 1965, Ord. 13, r. 9; Ord. 19, r. 9; Ord. 35, r. 2

[45] Settled Land Act 1925, s. 1; Settled Land and Trustee Acts (Court's General Powers) Act 1943

[46] *Br* Sex Discrimination Act 1975

[47] *Br* Sexual Offences Act 1956; Children and Young Persons Act 1963, S. 27

[48] *Am* MPC, Art. 213

[49] Companies Act 1985, ss. 324, 741

[50] MerchShA 1894, s. 5 (i)

[51] Companies Act 1985, s. 186

[52] *Br* Companies Act 1985, s. 130

[53] the Prevention of Fraud (Investment) Act 1958 verbietet Handel mit Wertpapieren ohne Genehmigung des Board of Trade

[54] sie sind meist mit einem mehrfachen Stimmrecht ausgestattet. Der Zweck ist hauptsächlich, den Gründern bzw. der Verwaltung die Kontrolle der Gesellschaft zu erleichtern

[55] § 1 erklärt als ungesetzlich und strafbar „jede Vereinbarung, jeden Zusammenschluß in Form eines Trust od. in anderer Form sowie jedes verschwörerische Zusammenwirken zum Zwecke e-r Beschränkung des Wirtschaftsverkehrs zwischen den Einzelstaaten od. mit fremden Nationen" ("Every contract, combination in the form of trust or otherwise, or conspiracy, in restraint of trade or commerce among the several States, or with foreign nations . . .")

[56] § 2 verbietet „das Monopolisieren und den Versuch hierzu" ("every person who shall monopolize or attempt to monopolize . . .")

[57] *Br* Aircraft and Shipbuilding Industries Act 1977

[58] *Br* Merchant Shipping Act 1894, s. 502ff.

[59] die internationalen Schiffahrtslinien bezeichnen ihre Kartelle als „Conferences"

[60] die Linienschiffahrt ist in sog. Schiffahrtskonferenzen international zusammengeschlossen und durch Tarifvereinbarungen an feste Frachtraten gebunden

[61] *Br* Social Security Act 1975, s. 14

[62] *Br* Bills of Exchange Act 1882, s. 10

[63] *Br* Simony Act 1713, repealed by the Statute Law (Repeals) Act 1971

[64] *Am* Uniform Simultaneous Death Act

[65] cf. R. S. C., Ord. 64, r. 1

[66] *Br* Defamation Act 1952

[67] *Br* Defamation Act 1952, s. 3

[68] *Br* Defamation Act 1952, s. 2

[69] Zusatzabkommen (zum Genfer Anti-Sklaverei-Abkommen von 1926) über die Abschaffung der Sklaverei, des Sklavenhandels und sklavereiähnlicher Einrichtungen und Praktiken (Supplementary Convention on the Abolition of Slavery, the Slave Trade and Institutions and Practices Similar to Slavery) BGBl 1958 II S. 204ff.

[70] Marine Insurance Act 1906, ss. 21, 22

[71] R. S. C. Ord. 20, r. 11

[72] *Am* Definition des Small Business (Small Business Act 1953, S. 2 [3]): Unternehmen, das eigentumsmäßig unabhängig ist und unabhängig betrieben wird, und das auf seinem Tätigkeitsgebiet nicht beherrschend ist (one independently owned and operated and not dominant in its field of operation) (15 U. S. C. § 632 [1953])

[73] Small Business Investment Act (SBIA) Gesetz zur Kreditunterstützung für Klein- und Mittelbetriebe

[74] Agriculture Act 1972, ss. 37, 65 as amended by the Agriculture (Miscellaneous Provisions) Act 1972, ss. 9, 26, Sched. 6

[75] *Br* Customs and Excise Act 1952, ss. 301–305

[76] *Br* Social Security Acts 1975 to 1980; Social Security Benefits Act 1975, Supplementary Benefits Acts 1966 to 1975; Social Security Pensions Act 1975; Social Security and Housing Benefits Act 1982

[77] *Am* das laufend ergänzte Gesetz von 1935 richtet sich an Arbeitnehmer in der Privatwirtschaft

[78] BGBl 1976 II S. 1358
[79] BGBl 1970 II S. 909
[80] *Br* im weitesten Sinn umfaßt der Begriff „social services" auch Erziehungswesen, Wohnungswesen und Gesundheitswesen
[81] MPC 5.01 (2) (g)
[82] Solicitors' Act 1974
[82a] Insolvency Act 1986, sec. 89
[83] Kulturabkommen zwischen der Bundesrepublik Deutschland und der Republik Südafrika – BGBl 1964 II S. 14
[84] BGBl 1976 II S. 1545
[85] BGBl 1975 II S. 121
[86] BGBl 1963 II S. 1539; 1964 II S. 785; 1965 II S. 830
[87] voller Titel des Weltraumvertrags: Vertrag über die Grundsätze zur Regelung der Betätigung von Staaten bei der Erforschung und Nutzung des Weltraums einschließlich des Mondes und anderer Himmelskörper (Treaty on Principles Governing the Activities of States in the Exploration and Use of Outer Space, Including the Moon and Other Celestial Bodies) – BGBl 1969 II S. 1969
[88] BGBl 1963 II S. 1562; 1965 II S. 463; 1966 II S. 788
[89] Bundesverfassung Art. I, s. 2 (5)
[90] *Br* R. S. C., Ord. 33, r. 3; Ord. 73, r. 2
[91] *Br* R. S. C., Ord. 18, r. 12.
[91a] BGBl 1978 II S. 62
[92] Insolvency Act 1986, ss. 177, 370
Companies Act 1948, s. 263; Bankruptcy Act 1914, s. 10
[93] Administration of Estates Act 1925, ss. 22–24; Settled Land Act 1925, s. 7 (1)
[94] *Br* R. S. C., Ord. 18, rr. 8, 12
[95] Special Roads Act 1949
[96] 1. International Atomic Energy Agency (IAEA)
2. International Labour Organization (ILO)
3. Food and Agricultural Organization (FAO)
4. United Nations Educational, Scientific and Cultural Organization (UNESCO)
5. World Health Organization (WHO)
6. International Bank for Reconstruction and Development (World Bank)
7. International Finance Corporation (IFC)
8. International Monetary Fund (FUND)
9. International Civil Aviation Organization (ICAO)
10. International Telecommunication Union (ITU)
11. Universal Postal Union (UPU)
12. World Meteorological Organization (WMO)
13. Intergovernmental Maritime Consultative Organization (IMCO)
[97] *Br* Sale of Goods Act 1979, s. 61
[98] *Br* R. S. C., Ord. 18, r. 8, r. 12
[99] *Br* Customs and Excise Act 1952, s. 307
[100] *Br* verboten durch County Courts Act 1959, s. 69
[101] *Br* Criminal Act 1977, s. 6 to 13
[102] *Br* abgeschafft seit 1971
[103] ICR ss. 141–145
[104] vgl. Fraenkel „Das amerikanische Verfassungssystem", S. 182: „Im allgemeinen Sprachgebrauch wird das Wort ‚the state' lediglich auf die Gliederungen der USA angewandt, entspricht also dem deutschen ‚Land'. Nur in der wissenschaftl. Literatur findet man ‚the state' im Sinne von ‚der Staat'"
[105] BGBl 1976 II S. 484
[106] BGBl 1976 II S. 485
[107] BGBl 1976 II S. 474
[108] BGBl 1977 II S. 598
[109] Insolvency Act 1986, ss. 99, 131
[110] R. S. C., Ord. 18, rr. 1, 15
[111] Insolvency Act 1986, s. 288
[112] *Br* Annual Abstract of Statistics (vom Central Statistical Office herausgegebenes, umfassendes Verzeichnis aller amtl. statistischen Dienststellen und der von ihnen herausgegebenen Veröffentlichungen); *Am* Statistical Abstract of the United States (herausgegeben vom Bureau of the Census; enthält eine Liste amtlicher und privater Stellen, von denen statistisches Material zusammengestellt wird, sowie ein ausführliches Quellenverzeichnis)
[113] Perjury Act 1911, s. 5
[114] Statutory Instruments Act 1946
[115] Settled Land Act 1925, s. 117 (1)
[116] Employment Protection (Consolidation) Act 1978, s. 49
[116a] Satzung der OECD-Kernenergie-Agentur – BGBl 1978 II S. 809
[117] nach dem Finance Act 1870, s. 2 (9) fallen unter stock u. a. alle Anleihen, Schuldverschreibungen und Aktien ohne Rücksicht darauf, ob sie von öffentl. od. privaten Stellen ausgegeben wurden
[118] Companies Act 1985, s. 744
[119] *Am* die Bestimmungen über Aktienübertragungen sind geregelt im UCC, Art. 8
[120] Stock Transfer Act 1963
[121] Theft Acts 1968, s. 22
[122] zur Frage der Rechtmäßigkeit →Resale Prices Act 1976, s. 24
[123] R. S. C. Ord. 50, rr. 10–15
[124] *Br* Sale of Goods Act 1979, ss. 44, 46; *Am* UCC s. 2–705
[124a] BGBl 1975 II S. 284
[125] *Br* Trade Union Act 1984, s. 11 (11); Employment Act 1988, s. 1 (7)
[126] R. S. C., Ord. 18, r. 19
[126a] Federal Bankruptcy Reform Act
[127] Convention on Frontier Workers and Student Employees Übereinkommen (der Westeuropäischen Union) über Grenzarbeitnehmer und über Gastarbeitnehmer BGBl 1960 II S. 438, 1961 II S. 570

[128] *Br* Mental Health Act 1959, s. 4
[129] *Br* Perjury Act 1911, s. 7
[130] vor dem County Court heißt die Zeugenladung witness summons
[131] *Br* R. S. C., Ord. 32, r. 7
[132] *Br* Companies Act 1985, s. 736
[133] *Br* Agriculture (Silo Subsidies) Act 1956
[134] *Br* Housing (Financial Provisions) Act 1958
[135] cf. Federal Food and Drugs Act
[136] Law Reform Act 1969, s. 14
[137] Marine Insurance Act 1906, s. 78 (2)
[138] BGBl 1954 II S. 596 i. Verb. mit BGBl 1960 II S. 1282
[139] *Br* Suicide Act 1961
[140] MPC, s. 210.5
[141] gewöhnlich wird von action at law und suit in equity gesprochen; cf. Judicature Act 1925, s. 225
[142] R. S. C., Ord. 14
[143] Part III of Marriage Act 1949, s. 26 (b)
[144] Criminal Justice Act 1948, s. 22
[145] *Br* Law of Property Act 1925, s. 58
[146] z. B. Montanunion *(→ECSC)*, EWG *(→ECC)* und EAG *(→EAEC)*.
[147] *Br* BEA 1882, ss. 65–68; *Am* UCC, ss. 3-410, 3–603
[148] Bundesverfassung, Art. VI, s. 2
[149] *Br* R. S. C., Ord. 18, r. 19
[150] *Br* Law of Property Act 1925, s. 100
[151] 11 U. S. C. A., § 93, g
[152] Internationale Gesundheitsvorschriften – BGBl 1975 II S. 460
[153] *Am* ein syndicate im Sinne der Internal Revenue Acts ist eine partnership (26 U. S. C. A. 7701)

Zu T

[1] The Companies (Tables A to F) Regulations 1985
[2] *Br* die in den USA nie übernommene Doktrin ist – bis auf wenige Ausnahmen – abgeschafft worden durch Law of Property Act 1925, s. 94
[3] *Br* Companies Act 1985, ss. 428–430
[4] *Am* MPC, s. 224.4
[5] *Am* MPC, s. 241.6
[6] in den Jahren 1932–1935 auch in Deutschland gebräuchlich
[7] *Br* Income Tax Act, s. 347; *Am* IRC, ss. 901–943
[8] Internal Revenue Code 1954, ss. 531–537
[9] *Br* Gemäß dem Finance Act 1965, ss. 49 ff. tritt die corporation tax an Stelle der früheren profits tax und income tax on companies
[10] Federal Estate Tax, cf. Internal Revenue Code 1954, ss. 2001–2007
[11] Internal Revenue Code 1954, Title 26
[12] *Br* Income Tax Act 1952; *Am* Federal Income Tax ist geregelt im Internal Revenue Code 1954, ss. 2001–2007
[13] Oil Taxation Act 1975, amended by Finance Act 1976
[14] Bundesverfassung, Art. I, s. 8
[15] Publikation Nr. 307 der Internationalen Handelskammer
[16] *Br* Television Act, 1954
[17] Europäisches Abkommen zum Schutze der Fernsehsendungen (von 1960) – BGBl 1967 II S. 1786
[18] international übliche Abkürzung aus teleprinter (Fernschreiber) und exchange (Vermittlung)
[19] das anglo-amerikanische Recht kennt keinen Unterschied zwischen Miete und Pacht
[20] Settled Land Act 1925
[21] *Br* für tenant for life hinsichtl. →settled land cf. Settled Land Act 1925, ss. 4 (2), 19 (1)
[22] gesetzliche Regelung der gewohnheitsrechtlich gewachsenen Ansprüche zuerst in Agricultural Holdings Act 1948, ss. 63, 64, 101
[23] *Br* R. S. C., Ord. 22
[23a] UCC §§ 2–601
[24] *Br* R. S. C., Ord. 22, r. 3
[25] *Br* Bills of Exchange Act 1882, s. 88
[26] in den USA heute ohne Bedeutung, in Großbritannien nur historisch zu verstehen als Überbleibsel des Lehenssystems (feudal system). Der König war der oberste Herr allen Grundbesitzes, der seinen lords als Gegenleistung gegen bestimmte Dienste Land verlieh. Die Besitzer von Grundbesitz waren tenants, das Besitzverhältnis von lord zu tenant die tenure. Die einzigen tenures in land, die (mit unbedeutenden Ausnahmen) heute noch bestehen, sind socage (= freehold) und term of years absolute (= leasehold)
[26a] MPC, s. 7.06
[27] *Br* für →persistent offenders – Powers of Criminal Court Act 1973, ss. 28, 29; *Am* MPC, s. 6.07, 6.09
[28] MPC, s. 6.06, 6.08
[29] MPC, s. 6.05 (2)
[29a] Art. 13 der ICC Vergleichs- und Schiedsgerichtsordnung
[30] Auxiliary and Reserve Forces Act 1949
[31] Bundesverfassung, Art. IV, s. 3
[32] MPC, s. 211.3
[33] BGBl 1965 II S. 1145
[34] *Br* Guardianship of Infants Act 1925, s. 5
[35] *Br* Theft Acts 1968 and 1978; *Am* MPC, s. 223.0
[36] *Br* vgl. die folgende Fußn.

[37] Road Traffic Act 1972, ss. 143–158, 162, 166, 167; Road Traffic Act 1974, Sched. 6, para 20, Sched. 7

[38] *Br* R. S. C., Ord. 16; *Am* UCC, ss. 3–803

[39] Patent Acts 1949, s. 65 (entsprechend für eingetragene Muster: Registered Designs Act 1949, s. 26)

[40] *Br* Malicious Damage Act 1861, s. 50

[41] IRC ss. 665–668

[42] MPC, s. 1.06

[42a] BGBl 1984 II S. 15

[43] BGBl 1979 II S. 445; 1981 II S. 453; 1983 II S. 643; 1987 II S. 317

[44] title und ownership betonen das Recht im Gegensatz zum Rechtsobjekt, während property beides umfaßt

[45] Companies Act 1985, ss. 185, 186

[46] Law of Property Act 1925, s. 76, and Sched. II

[47] Law of Property Act 1969, s. 23

[48] International tonnage certificate Internationaler Schiffsmeßbrief – BGBl 1967 II S. 2158, 2219

[49] Convention for a Uniform System of Tonnage Measurement of Ships Übereinkommen über ein einheitl. System der Schiffsvermessung – BGBl 1957 II S. 1471; 1967 II S. 2161

[50] Parlamentspartei des 17./18. Jahrhunderts

[51] BGBl 1976 II S. 24

[52] Town and Country Planning Act 1971

[53] BGBl 1983 II S. 133

[54] IRC s. 162

[55] *Br* Restrictive Trade Practices Act 1976, s. 43 (1)

[56] *Br* Trade Descriptions Acts 1968

[57] *Br* Trade Union and Labour Relations Act 1974, s. 29; Employment Act 1980, 1982, 1988; Trade Union Act 1984; Dock Work Act 1989

[58] *Br* Trade Marks Act 1938, s. 37

[58a] Vertragstext abgedruckt bei Zweigert/Kropholer, Quellen des internationalen Einheitsrechts, Bd. III-A

[59] Trade Marks Act 1938, s. 23 (1)

[60] *Br* Trade Marks Act 1938, s. 37

[61] cf. the Arrangement of →Madrid concerning the International Registration of Trade Marks

[61a] Federal Trade Commission Act, sec. 18

[62] *Br* Employment Acts 1980, 1982; Trade Union Acts 1984, 1988. Die größten britischen Gewerkschaften sind: the Transport and General Workers Union; the Amalgamated Engineering Union; the General Municipal, Boilermakers and Allied Trades Union; the National and Local Government Officers' Association; Manufacturing, Science and Finance; the National Union of Public Employees

[63] Insolvency Act 1986, ss. 238, 339

[64] IRC s. 267

[65] Law of Property Act 1925, s. 52

[65a] Uniform Fraudulent Conveyance Act § 101 (40)

[66] *Br* Judicature Act 1925, s. 59; R. S. C. Ord. 4

[67] Companies Act 1985, ss. 182 et seq.

[68] Companies Act 1985, ss. 182 et seq.

[69] Customs and Excise Act 1952, s. 59

[70] Art. 2 (2) des Europäischen Übereinkommens betr. Auskünfte über ausländisches Recht

[71] the 1981 Transport Act deals with activities of British Railway Board, road safety etc

[72] *Am* Bundesverfassung, Art. III

[73] Treason Felony Act 1848

[74] Representation of the People Act 1949, s. 100

[75] In Großbritannien werden Staatsverträge durch die Krone, d. h. das Ministerium, abgeschlossen, in den USA durch den Präsidenten, vorbehaltlich der Genehmigung des Senats (Bundesverfassung, Art. II, s. 2, subs. 2)

[75a] wichtig für Visum-Bestimmungen (E-2 Visa)

[76] steht dem Präsidenten nur mit Zustimmung einer ⅔ Mehrheit des Senats zu – Bundesverfassung Art. II, s. 2, subs. 2

[76a] wichtig für Visum-Bestimmungen (E-1 Visa)

[77] es gibt zahlreiche verschiedene Klagen mit meist historisch bedingten lateinischen Bezeichnungen

[78] MPC, s. 221.2 (2)

[79] durch den Tribunals and Inquiries Act 1958, wurde ein Council on Tribunals ernannt, der die Errichtung und Arbeit der in Sched. Ib des Gesetzes aufgeführten Tribunale überwacht – Tribunals and Inquiries Act 1971 (Consolidating the Tribunals and Inquiries Acts 1958 and 1966)

[79a] BGBl 1989 II S. 122

[80] BGBl 1956 II S. 2012, 2021

[81] von 1831, 1887, 1896, 1940 – durch Wages Act, 1986 aufgehoben

[82] UCC, Art. 9

[83] cf. Rule of Republic Trustee (Custodian Trustee) Rules 1926; Law of Property (Amendment) Act 1926, s. 3; Settled Land Act 1925, s. 117 (I) (30)

[84] by rules made under s. 4 (3) of the Public Trustee Act 1906 (cf. Public Trustee [Custodian Trustee] Rules 1926)

[85] Law of Property Act 1925, s. 205 (1) (29)

[86] Trust Indenture Act 1939

[87] Settled Land Act 1925, ss. 4, 117 (1) (31)

[88] Administration of Estates Act 1947, s. 47, as amended by Intestates' Estate Act 1952; Family Law Reform Act 1969

[89] *Br* Trustee Act 1925; Administration of Estates Act 1925, s. 1; Limitation Act 1939, s. 19

[90] Insolvency Act 1986, ss. 292 et seq.

[91] Trustee Investments Act 1961

[92] *Br* Judicial Trustees Act 1896 (heute ist der

judicial trustee oft ersetzt durch den public trustee)

[93] *Br* Trustee Act 1906. – Während des letzten Krieges hat der Public Trustee das feindliche Vermögen verwaltet

[94] cf. Art. 78ff. der Satzung der Vereinten Nationen

[95] Kapitel III der Satzung der Vereinten Nationen

[96] Kapitel XII der Satzung der Vereinten Nationen

[97] § 304 (6) 2 Bankruptcy Code

[98] verboten durch Clayton Act, s. 3 und Sherman Act, s. 1

[99] BGBl 1981 II S. 384

Zu U

[1] cf. Model Business Corporation Act, s. 6 und die entsprechenden einzelstaatl. Regelungen

[2] European Communities Act 1972, s. 9 (1)

[3] *Br* Arbitration Act 1950, s. 8

[4] *Br* Disposal of Uncollected Goods Act 1952

[5] *Br* Bankruptcy Act 1914, s. 47

[6] Law of Property Act 1925, ss. 1 (3), 34 (4), 205; Settled Land Act 1925, s. 36

[7] *Br* Representation of the People Act 1949, s. 101

[8] Social Security Act 1975, s. 58

[9] Social Security Act 1975, ss. 14–20; Social Security Pensions Act 1975

[10] Abkommen über Arbeitslosenversicherung zwischen der Bundesrepublik Deutschland und dem Vereinigten Königreich von Großbritannien und Nordirland – BGBl 1961 II S. 586

[11] vgl. Strupp-Schlochauer, Bd. 3, S. 471

[12] *Br* cf. Industrial Tribunals

[13] *Br* Food and Drugs Act 1955, ss. 8–11

[14] IRC § 210 2 (c)

[15] Sitz Paris (Union des Foires Internationales; UFI)

[16] BGBl 1965 II S. 1225 (Art. 21)

[17] Finance Act 1946, ss. 53–57; Prevention of Fraud (Investments) Act 1958, s. 12

[18] BGBl 1973 II S. 439

[19] Näheres vgl. Strupp-Schlochauer, Bd. 3, S. 579

[20] UNICEF wurde 1965 mit dem Friedens-Nobelpreis ausgezeichnet

[21] BGBl 1989 II S. 588

[22] BGBl 1971 II S. 472ff.

[23] BGBl 1955 II S. 101; 1973 II S. 1111; 1981 II S. 674

[24] BGBl 1973 II S. 1111

[25] das heute gültige Wehrgesetz, welches auch die Dienstpflicht von Ausländern regelt, heißt Universal Military Training and Service Act (1948)

[26] Weltpostvertrag in Deutsch und Französisch BGBl 1986 II S. 223

[27] Satzung des Weltpostvereins in Deutsch und Französisch BGBl 1965 II S. 1634; 1971 II S. 245; 1975 II S. 1513; 1981 II S. 674

[28] *Br* Sexual Offences Act 1956, s. 12, Sched. II und Sexual Offences Act 1967

[29] Companies Act 1948, s. 399

[30] *Br* Merchant Shipping Act 1894, s. 4

[31] *Br* Unsolicited Goods and Services Act 1971

[32] Town and Country Planning Act 1972

[33] Trade Marks Act 1938, s. 28

Zu V

[1] BGBl 1965 II S. 1423

[2] *Br* zu den vagrants gehören: idle and disorderly persons (unlicensed pedlars, beggars etc), rogues and vagabonds, incorrigible rogues

[3] vgl. von den vielen Gesetzen nur den General Rate Act 1975

[4] im deutschen Recht heißen die ehrenamtlichen Richter beim Schwurgericht jetzt „Schöffen"

[5] Bundesverfassung Art. II, s. 1

[6] Settled Land Act 1925, s. 117 (1) (31)

[7] Trustee Act 1925, ss. 44 et seq.

[8] Bundesverfassung, Art. I, s. 7, subs. 2

[9] *Br* R. S. C. Ord. 18, r. 19; Judicature Act 1925, s. 51; Judicature (Amendment) Act, 1959, s. 1 (1)

[10] Bundesverfassung, Art. II, s. 1, subs. 1

[11] BGBl 1969 II S. 1585

[11a] BGBl 1969 II S. 1585; 1971 II S. 1285; 1973 II S. 166, 1755

[11b] BGBl 1985 II S. 927

[11c] Company Act 1985, s. 228

[12] *Am* nach MPC sec. 1.04 (5) ist violation eine mit Geldstrafe od. Geldstrafe in Verbindung mit Einziehung od. einer anderen zivilrechtl. Strafe (fine and forfeiture or other civil penalty) bedrohte strafbare Handlung. Eine Verurteilung wegen violation hat (im Ggs. zu crime) keinen Rechtsverlust zur Folge

[13] *Br* der Domestic Violence and Matrimonial Proceedings Act 1976 erweitert u. a. die Befugnis der Gerichte, gewalttätige Personen zum Schutz bes. von Ehegatten und Kindern durch →injunction aus dem Haushalt zu entfernen

[14] *Br* Mental Health Act 1983, s. 102
[14a] Insolvency Act 1986, ss. 1, 253
[15] *Br* Law of Property Act 1925, s. 173; Bankruptcy Act 1914, s. 42
[16] Children and Young Persons Act 1933, ss. 92–95
[17] Education Act 1946, s. 15
[18] Monopolies and Restrictive Practices (Inquiry and Control) Act 1948, neu gefaßt durch den Restrictive Trade Practices Act 1976

Zu W

[1] Attachment of Earnings Act 1971
[2] Employment Protection Act 1975, s. 90
[3] *Am* in vielen Einzelstaaten gibt es gesetzl. Regelungen, die die Höhe des im voraus abzutretenden Lohns zum Schutze des Beschäftigten begrenzen
[4] *Br* Marine Insurance Act 1906, s. 4; Marine Insurance (Gambling Policies) Act 1906
[5] War Charities Act 1940, s. 11
[6] *Br* War Damage Acts 1964 and 1965
[7] *Br* Marine and Aviation Insurance (War Risks) Act 1952; the War Risks Insurance Act 1939
[8] *Br* Law Reform (Miscellaneous Provisions) Act 1949, s. 9
[9] *Br* Local Government Act 1933, ss. 36 et seq.
[10] *Am* Uniform Warehouse Receipt Act (→Uniform Commercial Code)
[11] *Br* Customs and Excise Act 1952, s. 80
[12] UCC, s. 2-315
[13] UCC, s. 2-314
[14] Sale of Goods Act 1893, ss. 53, 62 (1)
[15] UCC, s. 2-711
[16] UCC, s. 1-313
[17] *Br* Sale of Goods Act 1893, s. 12; Supply of Goods (Implied Terms) Act 1973, s. 1
[18] BGBl 1958 II S. 312, 1964 II S. 1295
[19] BGBl 1963 II S. 1159
[20] Albanien, dessen Mitgliedschaft seit 1962 ruhte, ist im Sept. 1968 auch formell aus dem Warschauer Pakt ausgetreten
[21] Salmon and Freshwater Fisheries Act 1923, ss. 66 ff.
[22] *Br* nach dem National Parks and Access to the Countryside Act 1949, s. 114 bedeutet waterway auch "a lake, river, canal etc suitable for sailing, boating, bathing or fishing"
[22a] BGBl 1983 II S. 133
[23] *Am* MPC, s. 210 (4)
[24] *Br* Weights and Measures Act 1963, as amended
[25] BGBl 1955 II S. 256, 630; 1962 II S. 803
[26] BGBl 1976 II S. 1266
[27] *Br* Whaling Industry (Regulation) Act 1934, as amended by the Sea Fish Industry Act 1938
[27a] BGBl 1982 II S. 559
[28] Customs and Excise Act 1952, s. 14
[29] *Br* Merchant Shipping Act 1894, s. 492
[30] BGBl 1987 II S. 673
[31] Social Security Act 1975, ss. 12, 24–26; Social Security Pensions Act 1975
[32] BGBl 1975 II S. 773
[33] *Br* Partnership Act 1890, s. 32 (c)
[34] Wills Act 1837, Wills Act Amendment Act 1852; Wills Act 1963, Wills Act 1968; Inheritance (Provision for Family and Dependants) Act 1975
[35] *Br* Wills Act 1837, s. 9
[36] *Br* the Wills (Soldiers and Sailors) Act 1918; the Navy and Marines (Wills) Acts 1930, 1939, and 1953
[37] Insolvency Act 1986
[38] Insolvency Act 1986, ss. 117 et seq.
[39] Companies Act 1985, s. 735; Insolvency Act 1986, ss. 73 et seq.
[40] Insolvency Act 1986, ss. 84 et seq.
[41] Insolvency Act 1986, ss. 97 et seq.
[41a] Insolvency Act 1986, ss. 90, 91
[42] IRC ss. 1441, 1442
[43] IRC s. 1462
[44] bei Ablehnung der Eidesleistung wegen religiöser Bedenken tritt an Stelle des Eides die (solemn) →affirmation
[45] *Br* Criminal Procedure Act 1865, r. 3
[46] Friendly Societies Act 1896, s. 8 (4)
[47] BGBl 1974 II S. 43, 1229; 1975 II S. 1103; 1977 II S. 339
[48] BGBl 1970 II S. 295
[49] BGBl 1967 II S. 1217
[50] BGBl 1967 II S. 1215; 1970 II S. 18
[51] BGBl 1976 II S. 24
[52] Merchant Shipping Act 1894, s. 510
[53] Merchant Shipping Act 1894, s. 477
[54] *(historisch:)* Klageschrift mit besonderen Formalitäten je nach der Natur des Klageanspruchs
[55] in welchen Fällen certiorari als Rechtsmittel zur Verfügung steht, bestimmt sich nach dem einzelstaatl. Prozeßrecht. In der Zuständigkeit des US-Supreme Court bezeichnet certiorari eine nach Ermessen des Gerichts gewährte Revision (im Ggs. zu dem verbindlich geregelten appeal)
[56] *Br* R. S. C., Ord. 6
[57] Insolvency Act 1986, ss. 214, 215

Zu Y

[1] *Br* Weights and Measures Act 1878, s. 10
[2] Income Tax Act 1962, s. 3
[3] durch den National Labor Relations Act von 1935 für illegal erklärt
[4] 1890, 1924 und 1950 (heute maßgebliche Fassung)
[5] Children and Young Persons Act 1933, s. 107; Children and Young Persons Act 1963
[6] Criminal Justice Act 1982, ss. 6, 7

Zu Z

[1] Vertrag zwischen der Bundesrepublik Deutschland und der Republik Sambia über die Förderung und den gegenseitigen Schutz von Kapitalanlagen – BGBl 1968 II S. 34
[2] Value Added Tax Act 1983, Schedule 5, s. 16